A DICTIONARY OF
HYMNOLOGY

A DICTIONARY OF

HYMNOLOGY

Setting forth the Origin and History of
Christian Hymns of all Ages and Nations

Edited by

JOHN JULIAN, D.D.

VOLUME I   A to O

JOHN MURRAY

FIFTY ALBEMARLE STREET

LONDON

First Edition .... January, 1892

Second Revised Edition with New Supplement........June, 1907

This new Dover Edition first published in 1957, is an unabridged and unaltered republication of the Second and last Revised Edition. The original work appeared as one volume but is now bound as two. It is published through special arrangement with John Murray.

TABLE OF CONTENTS.

PREFACE TO THE SECOND EDITION.

SINCE the publication of this *Dictionary of Hymnology* in 1892, hymnological studies have made great strides in many directions, and interest therein has led to the issue of many works on hymns and hymn-writers. Some of these productions are of an elementary character, others are of striking value, and all bear witness to the catholicity and importance of this branch of sacred study.

2. In addition numerous Hymn Books of an official, quasi-official, and un-denominational character have been published in various countries, especially in Great Britain and America. These collections contain matter hitherto unknown to the general public, the authorship, origin, and history of which are regarded as of supreme importance by the hymnological student, and of general interest to the Christian Church in all lands.

3. Fifteen years have also made great inroads in the ranks of Authors and Translators, and brought into prominence many hymn-writers and others whose work is of a valuable and enduring character.

4. When, therefore, the original edition of this *Dictionary* was exhausted in 1904, it was decided that, instead of issuing a reprint from the stereotyped plates as a second edition, advantage should be taken of the opportunity to revise the whole work, and to bring it up to date.

5. Although the book was stereotyped after the printing of the first Edition, yet the few errors in names and dates which were discovered in the text have been corrected and a certain amount of new matter has been added.

6. The most valuable and important part of the new Edition, however, is the *New Supplement*, in which are embodied many new features. In this the contents of the principal hymnals which have been issued during the past fifteen years are annotated; biographical notices of Authors and Translators are given; the history of National and Denominational hymnody has been extended to the present time; and new Indices have been included. The subject-matter contained herein has been arranged to secure the greatest amount of information in the least possible space. To insure success in the use of this work the student should refer, in the first instance, to pp. 1–1306; 1525–1597; and 1599–1729, and consult them in alphabetical order. Failing to find what he requires he must pass on to the *Cross Reference Indices*: for *First Lines*, to pp. 1307–1504; and 1730–1760: and for *Authors and Translators*, to pp. 1505–1521; and 1761–1768.

7. The task of amassing the information necessary for fulness of detail and accuracy has been great, but it has been lightened considerably by the aid given, willingly and cheerfully, by a large body of correspondents, to whom personal acknowledgment has been made for their generous assistance.

8. It is again a privilege and a duty to record with gratitude the co-operation of the Contributors whose signatures are appended to their respective articles, amongst whom the Rev. JAMES MEARNS, M.A., the Assistant Editor, is the most important. His minute and careful research in all departments of hymnological literature has greatly enriched the *New Supplement*, and contributed much towards its general accuracy and fulness of detail.

JOHN JULIAN.

TOPCLIFFE VICARAGE,
July, 1907.

PREFACE TO THE FIRST EDITION.

THE first pages of this "Dictionary of Hymnology, Setting forth the Origin and History of Christian Hymns of all Ages and Nations, with special reference to those contained in the Hymn Books of English speaking Countries," were completed more than ten years ago. Since that time, there has been a constant and rapid production of official and quasi-official hymn books of great importance in all English-speaking countries. To meet this emergency, and to make this work both trustworthy and exhaustive, constant revisions and additions were imperatively called for, which have considerably enlarged the work and delayed its publication.

2. Hymnological works, both historical and critical, and in several languages, have also been published during the same period. A careful study of these works—many of which are by distinguished scholars and experts in the various languages and departments—and a laborious and critical testing of their contents, have consumed a vast amount of time, with the result of great practical advantage to the Dictionary as a whole.

3. The APPENDIX (Parts I. and II.) also became a necessity; and, together with the "Cross Reference Index to First Lines" (pp. 1307–1504), the "Index of Authors, &c." (pp. 1505–1521), and the "Supplemental Index" to each (pp. 1598–1616), must be carefully consulted by the hymnological student.

4. Where it could possibly be avoided, nothing has been taken at second-hand. Minute technical accuracy has been aimed at, and, after great labour and inevitable delay, has, it is hoped, in most instances, been attained. The pursuit of this aim has very frequently demanded, for the production of one page only, as much time and attention as is usually expended on one hundred pages of ordinary history or criticism.

5. The MSS. used in this work number nearly ten thousand, and include (1) those in the great public libraries of Europe and America; (2) those in private hands; (3) those in the possession of the Assistant Editor; and (4) those of the Editor.

6. The Books, Magazines, Newspapers, Broadsheets, &c., collated and examined, have been too numerous to count. The Editor's collection of MSS., Books, Pamphlets, &c., will, on the publication of this work, become the property of the Church House, where they will be available for consultation.

7. The total number of Christian hymns in the 200 or more languages and dialects in which they have been written or translated is not less than 400,000. When classified into languages the greatest number are found to be in German, English, Latin, and Greek, in the order named. Other languages are also strongly represented, but fall far short of these in extent and importance. The leading articles on National and Denominational hymnody given in this work furnish a clear outline of the rise and develop-

ment of this mass of hymn writing. Arranged chronologically they set forth the periods when hymn-writing began in various languages, and the subjects which engaged the attention of the writers. It will be found that whilst the earliest hymns, as the *Magnificat*, the quotations in the Pastoral Epistles, &c., are in Greek, it required less than 170 years for the addition of Syriac to be made to the roll of languages. Latin followed in another 200 years. In another 50 years, the first notes in Early English were heard. German was added in the 9th cent.; Italian in the 13th cent.; Bohemian in the 15th cent., and others later, until the roll numbers over 200 languages and dialects. Careful attention to the chronology of the subject will also bring out the facts, that whilst Clement of Alexandria (p. 238) was singing in Greek, Bardesanes (p. 1109) was inspiring his followers in Syriac. Later on we find that the finest of the early poets were writing contemporaneously —Gregory of Nazianzus (p. 468) and Synesius (p. 1108) in Greek; St. Ambrose (p. 56), Prudentius (p. 914), and St. Hilary (p. 522) in Latin; and Ephraem the Syrian (p. 1109) in Syriac. Still later, as the roll of languages is increased, the grouping of names, countries and languages within given periods, will yield rich materials for the use of the historian and the divine.

8. In the following pages are set forth the countries where, the periods when, the languages in which, and in many instances, the men by whom the doctrines and ritual teachings and practices of Christianity were first enshrined in song; and by whom and in what languages and countries the greatest developments have taken place.

9. English readers especially will find that one of the leading features of this Dictionary is the effort made to bring this mass of historical, biographical, doctrinal, devotional, and ritual matter as fully as possible within the grasp of those who are acquainted with no other language but their own. Linguistically the English language is the key-note of this work, and the hymns contained in the hymn-books of English-speaking countries, and now in Common Use, are its basis.

10. Personal acknowledgment has been made with deep gratitude to more than one thousand correspondents for valuable assistance rendered by them in the production of this work. In addition to the Contributors whose signatures are appended to their respective articles, special reference has to be made to the assistance of MISS STEVENSON in compiling the " Indices of Authors, Translators, &c."; to the invaluable services of MR. W. T. BROOKE, whose acquaintance with early English hymnody is unrivalled; to MAJOR G. A. CRAWFORD, the compiler of the elaborate and complete " Indices of Cross Reference to First Lines, &c.," whose aid in revision from the first, and whose technical acquaintance with and accuracy in correcting the Press have been of eminent value; and to the REV. JAMES MEARNS, whose assistance has been so extensive, varied, and prolonged, as to earn the unsolicited and unexpected, but well deserved and cheerfully accorded position of ASSISTANT EDITOR of this work.

JOHN JULIAN.

WINCOBANK VICARAGE,
December, 1891.

LIST OF CONTRIBUTORS.

W. H. M. H. A.   Rev. W. H. M. H. AITKEN, M.A., General Superintendent of the Church Parochial Mission Society, and Canon Residentiary of Norwich.

H. L. B.   Rev. H. LEIGH BENNETT, M.A., Prebendary of Lincoln Cathedral, and sometime Rector of Thrybergh, Yorkshire.

L. F. B.   Rev. L. F. BENSON, D.D., Editor of the authorised *Hymnals*, &c., of the General Assembly of the Presbyterian Church in the United States, and other works.

J. T. B.   Rev. J. T. BINGLEY, L.R.A.M., F.G.O., sometime Precentor of Worksop Abbey Church.

F. M. B.   Rev. F. M. BIRD, M.A., Professor of Rhetoric and Christian Evidences, Lehigh University, United States of America.

W. J. B.   W. J. BIRKBECK, M.A., of Magdalen College, Oxford.

J. B.   Rev. JAMES BONAR, M.A., Greenock, Joint Editor of the Scottish *Free Church Hymn Book* and of the *Home and School Hymnal*.

W. T. B.   WILLIAM T. BROOKE, Walthamstow, London.

J. B.   Rev. JOHN BROWNLIE, Minister of the Presbyterian United Free Church, Portpatrick, and Author of *Hymns of the Greek Church, Translated, with Introduction and Notes*, and other works.

D. B.   Rev. DAWSON BURNS, D.D., Secretary of the United Kingdom Alliance.

J. D. C.   J. D. CHAMBERS, M.A., F.S.A. (Late), Recorder of New Sarum; Editor and Translator; *The Psalter, or Seven Ordinary Hours . . . of Sarum*; and *The Hymns*, &c.; *Lauda Syon*, &c.

Wm. C.   Rev. WILLIAM COOKE, M.A., F.S.A. (Late), Hon. Canon of Chester Cathedral; Joint Editor of *The Church Hymnal* and of *The Hymnary*.

G. A. C.   GEORGE ARTHUR CRAWFORD, M.A. (Late).

T. G. C.   Rev. T. G. CRIPPEN, Librarian at the Congregational Hall, Farringdon Street, London, and Author of *Ancient Hymns and Poems Translated from the Latin*, and other works.

| J. D. | Rev. JAMES DAVIDSON, B.A., Vicar of St. Paul's, Bristol; Author of *Proper Psalms for Certain Days*, &c. |

J. D.   Rev. JAMES DAVIDSON, B.A., Vicar of St. Paul's, Bristol; Author of *Proper Psalms for Certain Days*, &c.

J. L. D.   Rev. J. LEWIS DAVIES, Rector of Llaneigrad, N. Wales.

V. D. D.   Rev. VALENTINE D. DAVIS, B.A., sometime Minister of the Ancient Chapel of Toxteth, Liverpool; Editor of the *Inquirer*.

J. C. E.   J. C. EARLE, B.A., Oxford (Late).

F. J. F.   Rev. F. J. FALDING, D.D. (Late), Principal of the Congregational United College, Bradford.

E. C. S. G.   The Right Rev. EDGAR C. S. GIBSON, D.D., Lord Bishop of Gloucester.

A. E. G.   Rev. A. E. GREGORY, D.D., Principal of the Wesleyan Children's Home and Orphanage; Author of the *Fernley Lecture; The Hymn-Book of the Modern Church*, &c.; and Editor of *The Preacher's Magazine*.

A. B. G.   Rev. A. B. GROSART, D.D., LL.D. (Late), Editor of *The Fuller Worthies' Library*; *The Chertsey Worthies Library*; *The Works of Spenser*, &c., and Author of *Three Centuries of Hymns*, &c.

M. C. H.   M. C. HAZARD, Ph.D., Editor of the Congregational Publication Society, Boston, U.S.A.

J. A. H.   Rev. J. ALEXANDER HEWITT, D.C.L., Rector of Worcester, South Africa, and Author of *The Dutch Hymnal for Use in the Province of South Africa*, &c.

T. H.   Rev. THOMAS HELMORE, M.A. (Late), Priest in Ordinary of H.M. Chapels Royal; Musical Editor of the *Hymnal Noted*.

W. G. H.   Rev. W. GARRETT HORDER, Editor of *Congregational Hymns*; *The Poets' Bible*, &c.; and Author of *The Hymn Lover*, &c.

J. J.   Rev. JOHN JULIAN, D.D., the Editor.

J. M.   Rev. JAMES MEARNS, M.A., Vicar of Rushden, Buntingford, Assistant Editor.

J. T. M.   Rev. J. T. MUELLER, Diaconus and Historiographer of the Brethren's Unity, Herrnhut, Germany.

W. R. M.   Rev. W. RIGBY MURRAY, M.A., Manchester, Editor of *Church Praise*; *School Praise*; and *The Revised Psalter*.

C. L. N.   Rev. C. L. NOYES, D.D., Joint Editor of *The Pilgrim Hymnal*, Boston, U.S.A., &c.

J. H. O.	Rev. J. H. OVERTON, D.D. (Late), Prebendary of Lincoln Cathedral, and Rector of Epworth ; Author of *The English Church in the Eighteenth Century; Christopher Wordsworth, Bishop of Lincoln*, &c.
P. S.	Rev. PHILIP SCHAFF, D.D. (Late), New York.
W. A. S.	Rev. W. A. SHOULTS, B.D. (Late), of St. John's College, Cambridge.
W. S.	Rev. WILLIAM SMITH, Rector of Catwick, Hull.
G. J. S.	GEORGE JOHN STEVENSON, M.A. (Late), Author of *The Methodist Hymn Book, illustrated with Biography, History*, &c.; *Hymns and Hymn Writers of every Age and Nation.*
W. R. S.	Rev. W. R. STEVENSON, M.A. (Late), Editor of *The Baptist Hymnal; The School Hymnal*, &c.
W. G. T.	Rev. W. GLANFFRWD THOMAS (Late), Vicar of St. Asaph; sometime Vicar Choral of St. Asaph's Cathedral.
R. T.	The Ven. ROBINSON THORNTON, D.D., F.R.Hist.S. (Late), Vicar of St. John's, Notting Hill, London, and Archdeacon of Middlesex ; Boyle Lecturer, &c.
F. E. W.	Rev. F. E. WARREN, B.D., F.S.A., Rector of Bardwell, Bury St. Edmunds ; Author of *The Liturgy and Ritual of the Celtic Church* ; and Editor of *The Leofric Missal*.
S. W.	SUSANNAH WINKWORTH (Late), Translator of *Theologia Germanica*.
John Sarum.	The Right Rev. JOHN WORDSWORTH, D.D., Lord Bishop of Salisbury.
D. S. W.	Rev. DIGBY S. WRANGHAM, M.A. (Late), Vicar of Darrington, Yorkshire ; Editor and Translator of *The Liturgical Poetry of Adam of St. Victor*; and Author of *Lyra Regis*, &c.
C. H. H. W.	Rev. CHARLES H. H. WRIGHT, D.D., Ph.D., Bampton Lecturer, Oxford, 1878 ; Donnellan Lecturer, Dublin, 1880–81 ; and Examiner in Hebrew, in the University of London.
V., Y.	THE EDITOR, assisted by Various Contributors.

LIST OF MANUSCRIPTS.

The MSS. used in the preparation of this work include the following :—

I. Latin MSS.

I. The Bodleian.

i. Ashmole.
1285.		292, i.
1291.		1082, ii.
1398.	xiii.	H. pt. ii.
1523.		551, i.
1525.		551, i.

ii. Barlow.
5.	1042, ii.
41.	292, i.

iii. Bodley.
113.	886, i.
579.	1041, ii.
775.	1042, ii

iv. Canonici.
Bibl. 1.	xiii.	H. pt. ii.
„ 30.	xiii.	H. pt. ii.
„ 40	xiii	H. pt. ii.
Lat. 112.	1325.	H. pt. ii.
„ 273.	xv.	H. pt. ii.
Misc. 95.	xiii-xiv.	H. pt. ii.
„ 100.	xv.	H. pt. ii.
„ 266.	xii.	H. pt. ii.
„ 528.	xv.	H. pt. ii.
Script. 89.	xv.	H. pt. ii.
„ 131.	xiii.	H. pt. ii.
„ 223.	xv.	H. pt. ii.

v. Digby.
2.	xiii.	H. pt. ii.
19.	xiv.	H. pt. ii.
53.	xii.	H. pt. ii.
65.		533, ii.
86.	xiii.	H. pt. ii.
100.	xiv.	H. pt. ii.
166.	xiii-xiv.	H. pt. ii.

vi. Douce.
127.	1122, i.
222.	1042, ii.
296.	1122, i.

vii. Junius.
25.	1127, i.
74.	1127, i.
110.	1127, i.
121.	1043, i.

viii. Laud.
Lat. 5.	988, i.
„ 95.	988, i.

Lat. 96.		1122, i.
Misc. 4.		1139, i.
„ 216.	xi.	H. pt. ii.
„ 240.	xii.	H. pt. ii.
„ 269.	xiii.	H. pt. ii.
„ 352.	xiv.	H. pt. ii.
„ 363.	xv.	II. pt. ii.
„ 384.		652, ii.
„ 468.		1207, i.
„ 524.		1186, ii.
„ 668.		585, ii.
„ 748.	xv.	H. pt. ii.

ix. Liturg. Misc.
27.	1043, i.
104.	991, ii.
163.	295, i.
202.	1092, ii.
251.	1082, ii.
297.	1092, ii.
320.	375, ii.
338.	006, i.
340.	1043, i.
341.	1043, i.
354.	662, ii.
359.	1206, ii.
366.	272, ii.
370.	986, i.
372.	608, i.

x. Rawlinson.
A. 420.	xiii-xiv.	H. pt. ii.
B. 214.	xv.	H. pt. ii.
C. 73.		320, ii.
C. 90.		1186, i.
C. 108.	xv.	H. pt. ii.
C. 510.		586, i.
C. 553.	xv.	H. pt. ii.
C. 938.	xiii.	H. pt. ii.

xi. University College.
Hereford Missal	1042, ii.
York Missal	1043, i.

II. British Museum.

i. Additional.
8902.		1186, ii.
10546.		1220, ii.
11414.		1213, i.
11669.		1042, ii.
12194.		1043, i.
16905.		1042, ii.
17280.	xv.	H. pt. ii.
18192.		1082, ii.
18301.		551, i.
18302.		1215, ii.
18304.		967, ii.
18318.		586, ii.
19768.		1042, ii.
21170.	ni.	H. pt. ii.
21927.		1201, i.
22604.	xiii.	H. pt. ii.
23935.		1042, ii.
24193.		1219, ii.
24680.		1213, i.
26788.	xii.	1051.
30014.		584, ii.
30058.		1042, ii.
30846.		880, i.
30848.		576, i.
30849.		720, ii.
30850.		1206, ii.
30851.		547, i.
30935.		1201, ii.
31031.		007, ii.
31385.	xiv.	H. pt. ii.

ii. Arundel.
60.		1122, ii.
155.		1220, i.
156.		1043, i.
201.	xiii.	H. pt. ii.
214.		1082, ii.
340.		551, ii.

iii. Cotton.
Caligula A. xiv.		1042, ii.
Claudius A. iii.		1130, ii.
Cleopatra A. ii.		
„	xi.	H. pt. ii.
„ C. vi.		
„	ix.	H. pt. ii.
Julius A. vi.		546, ii.
Nero A. ii.	xi.	H. pt. ii.
„ E. i.	xi.	H. pt. ii.
Titus D. xxvii.		1206, ii.
Vespasian A. i.		291, i.
„ D. xii.		546, ii.
Vitellius E. xviii.		1220, ii.

iv. Harley.
524.	xv.	H. pt. ii.
863.		1122, ii.
2882.		1201, i.
2891.		705, i.
2928.		547, i.
2942.		1049, i.
2951.		886, i.
2961.		546, ii.
3072.	x.	H. pt. ii.
4664.		551, i.
4951.		426, ii.

v. Lansdowne.
387.	xv.	1051.
432.		608, i.

vi. Royal.
2 A. x.	99, ii.
2 A. xiv.	51, ii.
2 A. xx.	4, i.
2 B. iv.	1042, ii.
2 B. v.	1220, ii.
7 A. vi.	1201, ii.
7 E. ix.	967, ii.
8 B. i.	1201, ii.
8 C. xiii.	1042, ii.

III. Cambridge.

i. Corpus Christi College.
146.		1209, i.
190.	xi.	H. pt. ii.
371.	xii.	H. pt. ii.
390.	xiii.	II. pt. ii.
391.		547, i.
473.		1042, ii.

ii. St. John's College.
C. 15.	1122, i.

iii. University Library.
Gg. i. 32.	xv.	H. pt. ii.
Gg. v. 35.	xii.	H. pt. ii.
Ll. i. 10.	1122, i. & 1213, i.	
Nn. iv. 11.		551, i.

IV. Dublin.
Trinity College E. 4, 2.	1120.
Franciscan Convent.	1120.

V. Durham.
A. iv. 19.	1219, ii.
B. iii. 32.	546, ii.

VI. Lambeth.
427.	1128, i.
558.	91.

The MSS. in the above list include only the Latin MSS. found in British Libraries, and cited at pp. 1–1306 of this Dictionary. Many other MSS. have been examined at the British Museum, the Bodleian, Cambridge, Durham, Lambeth, Lincoln, York, &c., which are not included in this list because they are mostly later than 1200, and did not give results of sufficient importance to be referred to in the notes on the individual hymns. The references to *H. pt. ii.* mean that the MSS. so marked are only mentioned in *Pt. ii.* of the article **Hymnarium**, and in these cases the approximate dates of the MSS. are also given. In other cases the references in this work indicate the pages where concise descriptions of the various MSS. will be found.

In regard to the Latin MSS. it must be noted that the earliest and best only are cited in the body of the Dictionary, so that if *e.g.* a hymn is found in a MS. of the 11th cent., later MSS., unless of special importance, are not mentioned. References to a large number of MSS. in Continental Libraries will also be found in the notes on the individual Latin hymns, and at p. 813. These MSS. are mostly in the *Bibliothèque Nationale* and the *Arsenal* at Paris the *Stiftsbibliothek* at St. Gall, the *Vatican Library* at Rome, the *Ambrosian* at Milan, the *Royal Libraries* at Berlin and Munich, and the *Libraries* at Wolfenbüttel, Darmstadt, Einsiedeln, Zürich, &c. Besides these, various MSS. found in other libraries are cited through the works of *Daniel, Mone* and *Dreves*.

II. *English MSS.*

The English MSS. which have been largely used in this work, and especially by the Editor in the unsigned articles and those with his signature appended thereto, include the following groups :—

1. *C. MSS.*   *R. Campbell's MSS.*   Property of Mrs. E. Campbell.
2. *D. MSS.*   *P. Doddridge's MSS.*   Property of the Rooker family.
3. *E. MSS.*   *The Editor's MSS.*   Property of the Church House.
4. *G. MSS.*   *T. H. Gill's MSS.*   Property of the Church House.
5. *H. MSS.*   *W. J. Hall's MSS.*   Property of the Hall family.
6. *Hav. MSS.*   *The Havergal MSS.*   Property of the Havergal family.
7. *Mid. MSS.*   *A. Midlane's MSS.*   Property of the Church House.
8. *M. MSS.*   *J. Montgomery's MSS.*   Property of J. H. Brammall, Esq.
9. *R. MSS.*   *T. Raffles's MSS.*   Property of the Raffles family.
10. *S. MSS.*   *D. Sedgwick's MSS.*   Property of the Church House, Westminster.
11. *Sc. MSS.*   *Elizabeth Scott's MSS.*   Property of Yale University, U.S.A.

ABBREVIATIONS.

IN this Dictionary nearly eight hundred abbreviations have been used. Of these a large proportion are self-evident, and others, being in common use, are not repeated here. In this Table, therefore, those only are given which are for the most part peculiar to this work.

In several instances *pages* are given instead of *explanations*. This has been done because the details given on the pages indicated are not only too full for repetition, but are also of great value to the Reader. See also Supplemental List on p. xviii.

A. B. C. See p. 738, ii.
A. B. M. See p. 738, ii.
A. H. (Wetzel's). See p. 1226, ii.
A. M. E. See p. 738, ii.
A. P. M. See p. 738, ii.
A. V. Authorized Version.
A. & M. Ancient and Modern.
Add. Additional.
Aest. Aestiva.
Alford. See p. 39, ii.
Allg. Deutsche Biog. See p. xviii. 1.
Allg. G. B. See pp. 193, i. ; 512, ii.
Amer. Ger. American German.
Anth. Graec. Carm. Christ. See p. 456, ii.
Appx. Appendix.
Aug. Augustine.
Aut. Autumnalis.

B. M. British Museum.
B. M. S. See p. 738, ii.
B. MSS. Brooke MSS., p. 184, i.
B. V. M. Blessed Virgin Mary.
Bap. H. Bk. Baptist Hymn Book.
Bap. Hyl. Baptist Hymnal.
Barry. See p. 340, ii.
Bässler. See p. 656, i. 4.
Bäumker. See p. xviii. 2.
Bibl. Nat. Bibliothèque Nationale.
Bode. See p. 1565, ii.
Brev. Breviary.
Brit. Mag. British Magazine.
Brüder G. B. See p. 768, ii.
Burrage. See p. 1526, i.

C. B. Chorale Book.
C. M. S. See p. 738, ii.
C. MSS. Campbell MSS. See pp. xvi. ; 202, i.
C. P. & H. Bk. See *Mercer.*
C. Q. R. Church Quarterly Review.
C. U. Common Use.
Calig. Caligula.
Cassander. See p. 655, i.
Cathem Hynn. See p. 914, ii. (¹).
Ch. & Home. Church and Home.
Ch. Hys. Church Hymns.
Chope. See p. 223, ii.
Claud. Claudius.
Clichtovaeus. See p. 648, ii.
Coll. Collection.
Cong. H. Bk. Congregational Hymn Book.

D. C. District of Columbia.

D. MSS. Doddridge MSS. See pp. xvi. ; 305, ii. ; 1560, i.
Dan. Thes. Hymn. See *Daniel.*
Daniel. See p. 275, i.
Dreves. See p. xviii. 3.
Duffield. See p. 1526, i.

E. MSS. The Editor's MSS. See p. xvi.
E. U. Evangelical Union.
Ev. L. S. See p. 627, ii.
Evang. Hyl. Evangelical Hymnal.
Evang. Mag. Evangelical Magazine.
Evang. U. Evangelical Union.

F. C. Free Church.
F. C. S. See p. 738, ii.
Fabricius. See p. 586, ii.
Fasc. Fasciculus.
Fischer. See p. 377, i.

G. B. Gesang-Buch.
G. E. L. German Evangelical Lutheran.
G. L. S. See p. 626, ii.
G. MSS. Gill MSS. See pp. xvi. ; 421, i.
Goedeke's Grundriss. See p. 1565, i.
Gospel Mag. Gospel Magazine.

H. A. and M. Hymns Ancient and Modern.
H. B. S. Henry Bradshaw Society.
H. Bk. Hymn Book.
H. E. C. Hymns of the Eastern Church.
H. H. Bk. Home Hymn Book.
H. L. L. See p. 163, ii.
H. MSS. Hall MSS. See pp. xvi. ; 481, ii.
H. Noted. Hymnal Noted.
Harl. Harley.
Harland. See p. 491, i.
Hatfield. See p. 1526, i.
Hav. MSS. Havergal MSS. See pp. xvi. ; 496, ii. ; 498, i.
Heb. Hebrew.
Heerwagen. See p. xii. 4.
Hoffmann. See p. 418, ii.
Horae Ger. See p. 736, i.
Hy. Angl. Hymnarium Anglicanum.
Hy. Comp. Hymnal Companion.
Hymn. Sarisb. Hymnarium Sarisburiense.

Jul. Julius.

K. S. M. See p. 738, ii.
Kehrein. See p. 1042, i.

FULLER TITLES OF CERTAIN WORKS REFERRED TO ABOVE.

1. *Allgemeine Deutsche Biographie* (Leipzig, 1875, &c.) of the Munich Academy of Sciences.
2. *Das Katholische deutsche Kirchenlied in seinen Singweizen.* By W. Bäumker, vol. i., Freiburg in Baden, 1886; ii., 1883.
3. *Analecta Hymnica Medii Aevi.* Edited by G. M. Dreves, S.J.
4. *Litteraturgeschichte der evangelischen Kirchenlieder.* By F. F. T. Heerwagen, vol. i., Schweinfurth, 1792; ii., 1797.
5. *Geistliche Lieder im neunzehnten Jahrhundert.* By Otto Kraus. Gütersloh, 1879.
6. *Geistliche Lieder der evangelischen Kirche aus dem siebzehnten und der ersten Hälfte des achtzehnten Jahrhunderts.* By Dr. J. Mützell. Brunswick, 1858.
7. *J. M. Thomasii S. R. E. Cardinalis Opera Omnia,* vol. ii., Rome, 1747, contains a *Hymnarium.*
8. *Unverfälschter Liedersegen.* Berlin, 1851. Edited by G. C. H. Stip.

A DICTIONARY OF
HYMNOLOGY

DICTIONARY OF HYMNOLOGY.

A

A. In Bristol Bapt. *Coll.* by Ash & Evans. 1st ed. 1769 ; i.e. Joseph Addison.

A. in Collyer's *Coll.* 1812, this is the initial of Ann Gilbert, *née* Taylor.

A. C. C. in the *Hymnary.* "A Chester Canon ;" i.e. Canon William Cooke.

A. K. B. G. in the *Divine Hymnal*, 1860 ; i.e. A. K. B. Granville.

A. L. P. a *nom de plume* of Dr. Littledale's in the *People's H.* ; i.e. "A London Priest."

A. L. W. in various Collections ; i.e. Anna L. Waring.

A. M. G., i.e. *Anna Maria Glennie.* [Smith, née Glennie] in Thrupp's *Ps. & Hys.*, 1853.

A. R. Initials adopted by George Burder in the *Gospel Magazine.*

A. R. C. in *The Service of Praise*, by J. H. Wilson ; i.e. *Anne Ross Cousin, née Cundell.*

A. R. T. in the American Dutch Reformed *Hys. of the Church*, 1869 ; i.e. the Rev. Alexander Ramsay Thompson, D.D.

A. R. W. in the Amer. *Bapt. Praise Book*, 1871 ; i.e. A. R. Wolfe.

A. T., i.e. *Adelaide Thrupp*, in Thrupp's *Ps. & Hymns*, 1853.

A. T. R. in *Ps. & Hymns*, by the Rev. A. T. Russell, 1851, are the initials of the Editor.

A——y. in the *Gospel Magazine*, is the *nom de plume* of Job Hupton. It stands for Ashby, the parish in which he lived.

A beautiful land by faith I see. [*Heaven.*] Given *Anon.* in the Amer. *Shining Star*, N. Y. 1862, No. 74 in 4 st. of 4 l. and chorus, and entitled, "The beautiful land." It is in extensive use in America, and is found also in a few English S. S. collections. In S. Booth's *S. S. H. Bk.*, Brooklyn, U.S., 1863, it is credited to "J. Hall."

A car of fire is on the air. *W. W. Hull.* [*Death and Burial.*] Contributed to his *Coll. of Hys. for Gen. Use*, commonly known as *A Churchman's Hymns*, 1833. No. 2, in 3 st. of 6 l. In 1863 it was reprinted without alteration, in *Kennedy*, No. 1176.

A charge to keep I have. *C. Wesley.* [*Personal Responsibility.*] 1st pub. in his *Short Hymns on Select Passages of Holy Scripture*, 1762, vol. i., No. 188, in 2 st. of 8 l. and based on Lev. viii. 35. It was omitted from the 2nd ed. of the *Short Hymns, &c.*, 1794, but included in the *Wes. H. Bk.* 1780, and in the *P. Works of J. & C. Wesley*, 1868-72, vol. ix., pp. 60, 61. Its use has been most extensive both in G. Brit. and America, and usually it is given in an unaltered form, as in the *Wes. H. Bk.* No. 318 ; and the *Evang. Hymnal*, N. York, No. 320. The line, "From youth to hoary age," in the Amer. *Prot. Episcop. Hyl.*, No. 474, is from the Amer. *P. Bk. Coll.*, 1826.

A children's temple here we build. *J. Montgomery.* [*The Erection of a Sunday School.*] This hymn was written for the opening of the first Sunday School building in Wincobank, Sheffield. The ms.—which is in the Wincobank Hall Collection of mss.—is dated "December 18, 1840," and signed "J. M." The building was opened on the 13th of April, 1841, the hymn being printed on a fly-leaf for the occasion. In 1853, Montgomery included it in his *Original Hymns*, No. 313, in 6 st. of 4 l. and entitled it "The erection of a Sunday School." In the *Meth. S. S. H. Bk.* 1879, No. 512, st. iv. is omitted, and slight changes are also introduced. Orig. text in *Orig. Hys.*, 1853, p. 333. The hymn by Mrs. Gilbert, née Ann Taylor, "We thank the Lord of heaven and earth," was also written for, and sung on, the same occasion. This hymn has not come into C. U.

A day, a day of glory. *J. M. Neale.* [*Christmas.*] A carol written expressly for E. Sedding's *Antient Christmas Carols*, 1860. It is No. 6 of the "Christmas Carols," in 4 st. of 8 l. In 1867 it was reprinted in the *People's H.*, No. 29.

A debtor to mercy alone. *A. M. Toplady.* [*Assurance of Faith.*] Contributed to the *Gospel Magazine*, May, 1771, in 3 st. of 8 l., and included in Toplady's *Ps. & Hys*, 1776, No. 313, with the alteration, st. i., l. 4, of "offering" to "offerings." In 1860 the 1771 text was included in Sedgwick's reprint of Toplady's *Hymns*, &c., p. 140. In the older collections it was in most extensive use, both in the Ch. of England and with many of the Nonconformist bodies, but it is now very generally omitted from modern collections in G. Brit., although in America it still holds a prominent position.

A few more years shall roll. *H. Bonar.* [*O. and N. Year.*] Written about the year 1842, and first printed on a fly-leaf for use by the members of his congregation on a New Year's Day. In 1844 it was pub. in No. 2 of his *Songs for the Wilderness*, again in the 1st series of *Hys. of Faith and Hope*, 1857, p. 101; and later eds. It is in 6 st. of 8 l., s.m., and entitled, "A Pilgrim's Song." Its use in all English-speaking countries, either in its full, or in an abbreviated form, is very extensive. In some cases its exquisite refrain, with its delicate changes:—

> " Then, O my Lord, prepare
> My soul for that *great* day;
> O wash me in Thy precious blood,
> And take my sins away,"

is omitted, and it is thereby robbed of one of its most beautiful and striking features.

A form of words though e'er so sound. *J. Hart.* [*Kingdom of God in Power.*] 1st pub. in his *Hymns composed on Various Subjects*, 1759, No. 90, in 8 st. of 4 l. and based on i. Cor. iv. 20. "For the kingdom of God is not in word, but in power." In 1780, with slight alterations and the omission of st. vi. and vii. and the transposition of iv. and v. it was given in the *Lady H. Coll.* No. 95, and from thence has passed into a limited number of ultra-Calvinistic hymnals.

A fountain of Life and of Grace. *C. Wesley.* [*Living Water.*] 1st pub. in his *Short Hymns*, 1762, vol. ii., No. 866, in 2 st. of 8 l., and based on Rev. xxii. 17. In 1780 it was included in the *Wes. H. Bk.*, No. 77, and has been repeated in later eds. *P. Works*, 1868–72, vol. xiii. p. 240. It has also passed into most of the collections of the Methodist bodies, and is also found in other hymnals in G. Brit. and America.

A Friend there is ; your voices join. *J. Swain.* [*Jesus the Friend.*] Appeared as one of two hymns in his *Experimental Essays on Divine Subjects*, Lond. 1791, pp. 85–87, with the note "The two following pieces were occasioned by the death of an only son.' The second piece is:—" When Jesus, both of God and Man." In 1792 he included the former in his *Walworth Hys.*, in 10 st. of 4 l., and from thence it has passed into several collections, mainly those of the Baptists, but including also other Nonconforming bodies and a limited number in the Ch. of England. In America it is almost unknown. Orig. text, *Lyra Brit.*, 1867, pp. 537–8.

A fulness resides in Jesus our Head. *J. Fawcett* [*Fulness of Christ*], 1st pub. in his *Hymns adapted to the Circumstances of Pub. Worship and Priv. Devotion*, 1782, No. 96, in 5 st. of 8 l. This was reprinted in Rippon's

Sel., 1787, No. 150, and from thence passed into various collections in G. Brit. and America. Orig. text in Bap. *Ps. & Hys.*, 1858–80.

A glance from heaven, with sweet effect. *J. Newton.* [*Lightning.*] This hymn, dealing with the moral and spiritual thoughts suggested by " Lightning in the night," appeared in the *Gospel Magazine*, April, 1775, in the *Olney Hymns*, 1779, Bk. ii., No. 84, in 7 st. of 4 l., and later eds. It is No. 301 of Martineau's *Hys.*, &c., 1840–1851, and 429 in J. H. Thom's *Hymns*, 1858.

A glory in the word we find. [*Holy Scriptures.*] A cento given in J. Campbell's *Comprehensive H. Bk.*, Lond., 1837, No. 837, in 4 st. of 4 l., from whence it has passed, unaltered, into a few American hymnals. A part of this cento is from W. Hurn's *Coll.*, 3rd ed., 1833, No. 435. It is not in C. U. in G. Brit.   [W. T. B.]

A good High Priest is come. *J. Cennick.* [*Priesthood of Christ.*] 1st pub. in Pt. iii. of his *Sacred Hymns for the Use of Religious Societies*, Lon., 1744, No. cxxi. in 9 st. of 6 l., pp. 196–198. In 1753 G. Whitefield included st. i. iv. v. vi. and ix. in his *Coll. of Hys.*, No. xliv., and it was retained in subsequent eds. This arrangement, with slight alterations, was repub. in Rippon's *Sel.* 1787, No. 190, and later eds., and from thence has passed into other collections in G. Brit. and America. In some works it is still further abbreviated. Orig. text in *Lyra Brit.*, 1867, p. 134.

A helm upon my brow I wear. *S. J. Stone.* [*Christian Armour.*] Contributed to his poems, *The Knight of Intercession*, &c., 1872, in 4 st. of 4 l., from whence it passed into P. J. Richardson's *Lent Manual for Busy People*, &c., 1884, p. 64. Also repeated in the author's *Carmina Consecrata*, 1884.

A little child the Saviour came. *W. Robertson.* [*Holy Baptism.*] Contributed to the Scot. Estab. Ch. *Hymns for Pub. Worship*, 1861, and repub. in their *Scottish Hymnal*, 1870, No. 181, in 5 st. of 4 l. In the American collections it has attained to a more extensive use than in those in G. Brit., but in every case, as in Hatfield's *Ch. H. Bk.*, 1872, the *Hys. & Songs of Praise*, 1874, the *Pres. Hymnal*, Phil., 1874, and others, it is attributed in error to the elder W. Robertson, who was associated with the Scottish *Trs. and Par.* of 1745.

A little flock ! So calls He thee. *H. Bonar.* [*Church of Christ.*] A poem, in 13 st. of 4 l. on the Church as " The Little Flock." It appeared in the 1st series of his *Hymns of Faith and Hope*, 1857; and later eds. In *Kennedy*, 1863, No. 1404, it is re-arranged in three parts : (1) " Church of the everlasting God "; (2) " A little flock ! So calls He thee "; (3) " A little flock ! 'Tis well, 'tis well." In the American *Manual of Praise*, 1880, there is a cento beginning with the 1st stanza, and in the *College* and other hymn-books a second, as " Church of the Everliving God."

A little lamb went straying. *A. Midlane.* [*Children's Hymn.*] Written in Jan.,

1859, and first printed in the March No. of the *Good News Magazine*, 1860, 5 st. of 8 l. In 1864 it passed into the *H. Bk. for Youth*, No. 13, and subsequently into other collections, but mainly those for children.

A little ship was on the sea. *Dorothy A. Thrupp.* [*Peace.*] Contributed to Mrs. H. Mayo's *Sel. of Hymns*, &c., 2nd ed., 1840, in 9 st. of 4 l., entitled "The Little Ship on the Waves," and signed "D. A. T." As a hymn for children it is most popular, and is found in numerous collections both in G. Brit. and America.

A little while and every fear. *R. K. Greville.* [*Private Use.*] 1st printed in *The Amethyst*, Edin. Oliphant, 1834, and again in *The Church of Eng. H. Bk.*, &c., 1838, No. 592, in 3 st. of 8 l., and entitled "The Believer waiting for the Lord." In 1863 it was included with alterations in *Kennedy*, No. 783; but its use is not extensive, outside the collections of the Plymouth Brethren.

A little while—our Lord shall come. *J. G. Deck.* [*Advent.*] Appeared in the *Appendix* to *Hys. for the Poor of the Flock*, 1841, in 4 st. of 6 l., and later collections of the Plym. Brethren. It passed into Dr. Walker's *Cheltenham Coll.*, 1855; Snepp's *Songs of G. & G.*, 1872, and others. Orig. text in *Snepp*, with st. i. l. 4, "hath gone" for "has gone."

A look to Jesus saves the soul. *A. Midlane.* [*Jesus only.*] Written in March, 1862, and 1st pub. in his *Gospel Echoes*, 1865. No. 101, in 5 st. of 4 l. from whence it passed into Lord A. Cecil's Canadian *Hymn Book for Gospel Meetings*, Ottawa, 1871, No. 17, Broom's *Good News H. Bk.*, 1883, and others of a similar kind.

A mighty mystery we set forth. *G. Rawson.* [*Holy Baptism.*] Written in 1857, and 1st pub. in the Bapt. *Ps. & Hys.*, 1858–80, No. 695, in 4 st. of 4 l. It is based on Rom. vi 3, "Baptized into His death," &c. Its use is limited.

A mourning class, a vacant seat. [*Death of a Scholar.*] Appeared anonymously in the Amer. *Union Hymns*, Phil. S. S. U., 1835, No. 285, in 5 st. of 4 l., and headed "Death of a Scholar." It has been repeated in later editions of the *Union Hys.*, and is in extensive use in America. In G. Brit. it has been adopted by a few S. S. hymn-books only. Orig. text, *Meth. F. C. S. S. H. Bk.*, 1869, No. 358, with *the* for *his* in st. ii. l. 2.
[W. T. B.]

A nation God delights to bless. *C. Wesley.* [*National Peace.*] The second of two hymns on Job xxxiv. 29, 1st pub. in his *Short Hymns*, &c., 1762, vol. i., No. 771, in 2 st. of 6 l., in 2nd ed., 1794, and in *P. Works*, 1868–72, vol. ix. p. 268. It was included in the *Wes. H. Bk.*, 1780, No. 454, and retained in new ed. 1875, No. 466.

A Patre Unigenitus. *Anon.* [*Epiphany.*] *Daniel*, in vol. i., 1841, and later ed.

No. 210, gives only the first four lines of this hymn as belonging to a hymn for the Feast of the Epiphany, of uncertain authorship, date between the 10th and 13th centuries. In the ancient MSS. in the *British Museum*, however, this hymn is found in three of the 11th cent. (Harl. 2961, f. 230; Jul. A. vi. f. 36b; Vesp. D. xii. f. 43b). In the *Latin Hys. of the Anglo-Saxon Church* (Surtees Society), 1851, p. 53, it is reprinted in full from a Durham MS. of the 11th cent.

In 1853, *Mone* gave the full text in vol. i., No. 59, in 6 st. of 4 l., heading it, "In Epiphania ad nocturnum," and added an extended note on the text, with references to a 15th cent. MS. at Stuttgart; and to *Thomasius*, &c. This text, with the notes and an addition or two including a reference to a MS. of the monastery of Rheinau, of the 11th cent. was repeated by *Daniel*, vol. iv. (1855), p. 151. It is also in the *Hymn. Sarisb.* Lond., 1851, p. 26, as a hymn at Lauds in the Epiphany, and through the octave; where are also given the variations of *York* (used at Matins during the same period); of *Evesham*; *Worcester*, &c. It is also in *Wackernagel*, i., No. 173; in Card. Newman's *Hymni Eccl.*, 1838–65, and others. It may be noticed that the original is an acrostic from A to T inclusively. The *Gloria*, of course, does not follow this arrangement.
[W. A. S.]

Translations in C. U. :—

1. From God, to visit Earth forlorn. By J. D. Chambers in his *Lauda Syon*, Pt. 1, 1857, p. 109, in 6 st. of 4 l. This is given in an altered form as: "From God *the Father comes to earth*," in the *Appendix* to the *Hymnal N.*, No. 131.

2. God's Sole-Begotten came. By R. F. Littledale, made for, and 1st pub. in the *People's H.*, 1867, No. 44, and signed "A. L. P."

3. Sent down by God to this world's frame. By J. M. Neale: probably originally made for the *Hymnal N.*, 1852, as the first line in Latin appears in the original prospectus. Another Epiphany hymn was, however, given, and this *tr.* seems not to have been printed till the *St. Margaret's Hymnal*, 1875, whence it passed through the *Antiphoner and Grail*, 1880, into the *Hymner*, 1882, No. 20.   [J. J.]

A pilgrim through this lonely world. *Sir E. Denny.* [*Passiontide.*] 1st pub. in his *Sel. of Hymns*, &c., 1839, No. 11, in 8 st. of 4 l., and in his *Hymns and Poems*, 1848. It was also repub. in various collections of the Plymouth Brethren—including *Hys. for the Poor of the Flock*, 1841, and *Ps. and Hys.*, Lond. Walther, 1842, Pt. ii., No. 32. It is adopted also by Dr. Walker, in his *Cheltenham Coll.*, 1855; the *Hy. Comp.*, 1870, No. 162, and Snepp's *S. of G. & G.*, No. 220, and a few others amongst the Ch. of England hymnals. Its principal use, however, is in America, where it is found in numerous collections, mostly in an abbreviated form, and in many instances attributed in error to Dr. Bonar. Orig. text in *Lyra Brit.*, 1867, p. 183. It is well adapted for Holy Week, and for special services dwelling on the Sacrifice of Christ.

A sinful man am I. *H. Bonar.* [*Invitation.*] With the title, "Come unto Me," this hymn appeared in his *Hymns of Faith and Hope*, 3rd Series, 1867, in 7 st. of 4 l., s.m. In Kemble's *New Church H. Bk.*, 1873, it is given without alteration, but its use, both in G. Brit. and America, is very limited.

A solis ortûs cardine.   Ad usque. *Coelius Sedulius.* [*Christmas.*] This hymn, which opens with the same first stanza as the next annotated herein, with the exception of *Et* for "Ad" in line 2, may be distinguished therefrom by the second stanza, which reads:—

"Beatus auctor saeculi
  Servile corpus induit,
  Ut carne carnem liberans
  Ne perderet quos condidit."

It is a poem, dating from the first half of the 5th cent., in 23 st. of 4 l., entitled *Paean Alphabeticus de Christo* ("A triumphal song concerning Christ, arranged according to the letters of the alphabet.") The subject is a devout description of the Life of Christ in verse. The full text is found in an 8th cent. ms. in the *British Museum* (mss. Reg. 2 A. xx. f. 50), and is also given in the numerous editions of Sedulius's *Works* (that of Faustus Arevalus, Rome, 1794, especially); in the works of *Thomasius* from Vatican mss. of the 8th and 9th cents.; in *Wackernagel*, i., No. 48, and others. For ecclesiastical purposes it has been broken up into two hymns, the first known as *A solis ortûs cardine*, and the second, *Hostis Herodes impie*, with the *Rom. Brev.* form of the same, *Crudelis Herodes, Deum.* Following the order of this arrangement, the details are:—

i. *A solis ortûs cardine.* The text of this portion of the poem comprises 28 lines of the original (stanzas *a* to *g*, inclusive), and may be found in *Daniel*, i. No. 119, the old text and revised *Rom. Brev.* version being given in parallel columns, followed by various readings, &c. It is given in the *Rom. Brev.*, (text in Card. Newman's *Hymni Ecclesiae*, 1838) as the hymn at Lauds on Christmas Day; on the 30th of December, the only day in the Octave not occupied by a Festival; on the Octave itself; the Feast of the Circumcision; and on the Vigil of the Epiphany. The doxologies in the *Roman* and *Sarum* Uses are no part of the original hymn.

This hymn is met with in most old Breviaries. Also in two mss. of the 11th cent. in the *British Museum* (Harl. 2961, f. 226; and Jul. A. vi. f. 39b), &c. In the *Latin Hys. of the Anglo-Saxon Church*, 1851, p. 50, it is printed from a Durham ms. of the 11th cent. In the *Hymn. Sarisb.*, Lond., 1851, pp. 15, 16, it is given for Lauds on Christmas Day, with variations from the uses of *York*, *St. Alban's*, *Evesham*, *Worcester*, *Anglo-Saxon* mss. (Surtees Society, 1851) various Collections, &c. *York* assigns it to Lauds and Vespers on Christmas Day, and Lauds on the Vigil of the Epiphany. So *Worcester* and *Evesham*, with an extension to the Feast of the Purification. Its use is thus seen to have been very extensive in England. *Daniel*, iv. 144-5, gives further references of importance. The hymn, with the strophe *h* in addition, is given for Vespers on the Feast of the Annunciation, Dec. 18 (see *Coelestis ales nuntiat*), in the *Mozarabic Brev.* (Migne's *Patrol.*, tom. 86, col. 1291).

[W. A. S.]

Of this part of the poem (omitting the Mozarabic form) the following *trs.* have been made:—

Translations in C. U. :—

1. **From the far-blazing gate of morn.** By E. Caswall from the *Rom. Brev.*, 1st pub. in his *Lyra Catholica*, 1849, in 8 st. of 4 l., 49–51, and again in his *Hys. & Poems*, 1873, p. 27. This was given in the *Hymnary*, 1872, No. 126, as:— "From lands that see the sun arise," the first line being borrowed from Dr. Neale's l.m. version as under.

2. **From lands that see the sun arise, To earth's, &c.** By J. M. Neale, from the old text, 1st pub. in the *Hymnal N.*, 1852, in 8 st. of 4 l., and again in later editions of the same, and in other hymnals.

3. **From where the sunshine hath its birth.** By R. F. Littledale, made from the old text for, and 1st pub. in the *People's H.*, 1867, No. 26, in 8 st. of 4 l., and signed "A. L. P."

4. **From east to west, from shore to shore.** By J. Ellerton. This is a cento of 5 st., four of which are from this hymn (st. i., ii., vi., vii.), and the last is original, written in 1870) and 1st pub. in *Church Hys.*, 1871, No. 78. It is the most acceptable form of the hymn for congregational use.

Translations not in C. U. :—

1. From every part o'er which the sun. *Primer*, 1706.
2. From the faint dayspring's, &c. *Mant*, 1837.
3. From far sunrise at early morn. *Copeland*, 1848.
4. From the first dayspring's, &c. *Blew*, 1852.
5. From climes which see, &c. *Chambers*, 1857.
6. Now from the rising of the sun. *Wallace*, 1874.
7. From where the rising sun, &c. *F. Trappes*, 1865.

Other *trs.* of this hymn have been made into English through the German, thus noted by Mr. Mearns:—

Christum wir sollen loben schon. A full and faithful *tr.* by Martin Luther, 1st pub. in *Eyn Enchiridion*, Erfurt, 1524, and thence in Wackernagel's *D. Kirchenlied*, iii. p. 13, in 8 sts. of 4 l. Included in Schircks's ed. of Luther's *Geistliche Lieder*, 1854, p. 7, and as No. 25 in the *Unv. L. S.*, 1851.

Of this the *trs.* in C. U. are:—(1) *Christ, whom the Virgin Mary bore*, omitting sts. iii.-v. by C. Kinchen (J. Swertner?), as No. 42 in the *Moravian H. Bk.*, 1789, and continued, altered, in later eds. Included as No. 83 in Pratt's *Coll.*, 1829. (2) *Now praise we Christ, the Holy One*, from R. Massie's *M. Luther's Spirit. Songs*, 1854, p. 9, as No. 30 in the Ohio Luth. *Hyl.* 1880.

Other trs. are :—

(1) "To Christ be now our homage paid," as No. 154 in pt. iii. of the *Moravian H. Bk.*, 1748, No. 212 in pt. i., 1754. (2) "Soon shall our voices praise," by Miss Fry, 1845. (3) "Let now all honour due be done," by Dr. J. Hunt, 1853, p. 34. (4) "There should to Christ be praises sung," by Miss Manington, 1864, p. 23. (5) "Jesus we now must laud and sing," by Dr. G. Macdonald, in the *Sunday Magazine*, 1867, p. 151; and thence, altered, in his *Exotics*, 1876, p. 42.   [J. J.]

ii. The second portion of this poem is the Epiphany hymn *Hostis Herodes impie*, found in many Breviaries, and consisting of lines 29–36, 41–44, and 49–52, or in other words, the strophes commencing with *h, i, l, n, s.* The text is given in *Daniel*, i. No. 120, together with references to various Breviaries, &c.

In the *Hymn. Sarisb.*, Lond., 1851, it is given as the Hymn at first and second vespers on the Feast of the Epiphany, and daily through the Octave at Matins and Vespers; with various readings from the uses of *York* (which assigns it to first and second vespers and Lauds on the Epiphany, and daily through the Octave), of *Evesham* and *Worcester* (through the Epiphany at Vespers), *St. Alban's* (Vespers and Lauds), *St. Andrew de Bromholm*, Norfolk (Lauds). *Daniel*, iv. 148, 370, cites it as in a Rheinau MS. of the 9th cent., and a Bern MS. of the 9th cent. In the *British Museum* it is also found in a 11th cent. MS. (Jul. A. vi. f. 36) and others; and in the *Latin Hys. of the Anglo-Saxon Church*, 1851, p. 51, it is printed from a Durham MS. of the 11th cent. The strophe *Katerva matrum* (*the troop of mothers*) occurs in a MS. of the Harleian Library, of the 11th cent. (2961, f. 229b), as a hymn for the Holy Innocents. In the *Mozarabic Brev. Hostis Herodes impie* is the Hymn at Lauds for the Epiphany, the strophes *h, i, l, n, q, r, s, t, v, x, y, z* of the original being used, with doxology. Strophes *k, m, o, p,* with two additional, and a doxology, are used in this rite on the Feast of the Holy Innocents at Lauds; or "*In Allisione Infantium, sive Sanctorum Innocentium*," "On the dashing to pieces of the Infants, or Holy Innocents." (See Psalm cxxxvi., v. 9, English version; Ps. cxxxvii., v. 9, in the Latin; for the idea.) In Migne's *Patrol.* the hymns will be found in col. 184, 185, and 135, 136 of tom. 86 respectively.

[W. A. S.]

Translations in C. U. :—

1. How vain was impious Herod's dread. By A. T. Russell, in his *Ps. and Hys.*, 1851, No. 71, and with alterations, into *Kennedy*, 1863, No. 226.

2. Why, impious Herod, vainly fear. By J. M. Neale, in the 1st ed. of the *Hymnal N.*, 1852, No. 17, from whence it passed into later editions of the same, the *People's H.*, 1867, the *Hymner*, 1882, and others. In *H. A. and M.*, 1861, it is given in an altered form, as :—"Why *doth that impious Herod* fear?" but in the enlarged and revised ed. 1875, the opening line is again altered to, "*How vain the cruel Herod's fear.*" Another form is that of the *Hymnary*, 1872, where it reads :—"*The star proclaims the King is here.*" It was thus altered by the Editors of that Col.

Translations not in C. U. :—
1. Herod, grim foe, whence this dismay. *Blew*, 1852.
2. Why, Herod, impious tyrant, fear. *Chambers*, 1857.
3. Impious Herod, wherefore tremble. *Macgill*, 1876.

Various *trs.* of this have been made into German. The *trs.* from one of these are thus noted by Mr. Mearns:—

Was fürchtst du Feind Herodes sehr. A full and faithful *tr.* by Martin Luther, written Dec. 12, 1541, and 1st pub. in Klug's *Geistliche Lieder*, Wittenberg, 1544. Thence in *Wackernagel*, iii., p. 25, in 5 st. of 4 l. Included in Schircks's ed. of Luther's *Geistliche Lieder*, 1854, p. 18, and as No. 81 in the *Unv. L. S.*, 1851.

Of this the only *tr.* in C. U. is, "Why, Herod, unrelenting foe!" in full in R. Massie's *M. L.'s Spir. Songs*, 1854, p. 13, and thence in Dr. Bacon, 1884, and, altered, as No. 53, in the Ohio Luth. *Hymnal*, 1880.

Other trs. are :—
(1) "What dost thou fear, oh, enemy?" by Miss Fry, 1845, p. 23. (2) "Fiend Herod, why those frantic fears," by J. Anderson, 1846, p. 11 (ed. 1847, p. 36). (3) "Fiend Herod! why with fears art torn," by Dr. J. Hunt, 1853, p. 38. (4) "Herod, why dreadest thou a foe," by Dr. G. Macdonald in the *Sunday Magazine*, 1867, p. 331; and thence, altered, in his *Exotics*, 1876.

[J. J.]

iii. The *Rom. Brev.* form of *Hostis Herodes* is *Crudelis Herodes Deum*. The alterations in the text are st. i., l. 1-2, and the doxology only. In the *Rom. Brev.* it is appointed for the 1st & 2nd Vespers of the Feast of the Epiphany. The text is in *Daniel*, i. No. 120; Card. Newman's *Hymni Ecclesiae*, 1838–65, and other collections. [W. A. S]

Translations in C. U. :—

1. Why, Herod, why the Godhead fear ? By Bp. R. Mant, in his *Ancient Hymns*, 1837, p. 43; and in Chope's *Hymnal*, 1864, and others as :— "*In vain doth Herod rage and fear.*"

2. Why, ruthless king, this frantic fear ? By W. J. Copeland, in his *Hymns for the Week*, 1848, p. 70. In 1868 it was given as, "Why *doth the wicked Herod* fear?" in the *Sarum H.*, No. 66.

3. O cruel Herod ! why thus fear ? By E. Caswall. 1st pub. in his *Lyra Catholica*, 1849, p. 53, and his *Hymns and Poems*, 1873, p. 30. This is the *tr.* in C. U. in Roman Catholic collections for Schools and Missions.

4. Why, cruel Herod, why in fear ? By J. A. Johnston, in the *English H.*, 1852, and later editions. This is based upon older *trs.*

5. Why, cruel Herod, dost thou fear ? By R. C. Singleton, made for and 1st pub. in his *Anglican H. Bk.*, 1868, No. 58. In the 2nd ed., 1871, No. 73, it was altered to, "Why should the cruel Herod fear?"

6. Why doth that cruel Herod fear ? This, which is No. 120 in the *St. John's Hymnal*, Aberdeen, 1865 and 1870, is a cento from *Copeland* (st. ii.) and *Neale*, with alterations in the text of each.

Translations not in C. U. :—
1. Why, Herod, dost thou fear in vain. *Primer*, 1706.
2. Cruel Herod, wherefore fearest thou? *Hope*, 1844.
3. Why, Herod, shakes thy soul with fears. *F. Trappes*, 1865.
4. Why, cruel Herod, dost thou fear. *J. Wallace*, 1874.

[J. J.]

A solis ortûs cardine Et usque terrae limitem. [*Christmas.*] This hymn, which is of very complex authorship, departs from the foregoing in the second stanza, which begins :—

"Gaudete quicquid gentium,
Judaea, Roma et Graecia," &c.

The opening lines of the hymn, 1-4, we shall hardly be wrong in ascribing to *Sedulius*. The succeeding lines, 5-12, form the conclusion of the hymn for the Epiphany, "Quicunque Christum quaeritis," by Prudentius (*Cathem. Hymn.* xii.). The lines 13–24, commencing with "Fit porta Christi pervia," are received by the Benedictine editors of St. Ambrose as a genuine work of that Father (No. 13 among his hymns) on the authority of a treatise ascribed to St. Ildephonsus, "De perpetuâ Virginitate Beatae Mariae, et de ejus Parturitione;" certainly old, and most probably the work of Paschasius Radbertus (died A.D. 851). See the *Spicilegium* of Dacherius. The note in the Benedictine edition runs thus :—

"The knowledge of the twelfth hymn we owe to St. Ildephonsus, who more than once quotes the first strophe in his treatise *De Parturitione et Purificatione B. Mariae Virginis*, as having been written by St. Ambrose, whence it has been transferred to the later editions of the works of that holy Doctor. But the second and third strophes (i.e. verses 17–24) we have copied from the book of George Cassander, *De Hymnis Ecclesiasticis*, where this hymn is given without the author's name. And although there occasionally occurs in it a fault against the rules of prosody, yet we do not on that account judge it unworthy of St. Ambrose, since errors of this kind occur in the hymns not doubted to be his, though not frequently."

We may mention, however, that this portion ascribed to St. Ambrose, mainly coincides with a hymn found in the works of St. Rabanus Maurus. (See the edition of his writings by Geo. Colvenerius, *Col. Agrip.* 1627 ; or in Migne's *Patrol.*, tom. 112, the 6th vol. of the works of that writer; hymn No. 13, headed " In solemnitate Sanctae Mariae.") The authorship of the remaining lines is uncertain. *Daniel*, i. (No. 15), gives the text from, the collection of *Thomasius*, remarking the partial coincidence with Sedulius; but in iv. pp. 58, &c., he decides that this hymn is made up from different compositions; giving as his opinion that the groundwork was a poem in which the first letters of every four lines taken together make up the alphabet. The portion ascribed to St. Ambrose, " Fit porta," is found in an 11th cent. MS. in the *British Museum* (Harl. 2961, f. 225b). In the *Latin Hys. of the Anglo-Saxon Church*, 1851, p. 112, it is printed from a Durham MS. of the 11th cent.

As to the ritual use—it is the hymn at Lauds on the Feast of the Annunciation in the *Mozarabic Brev.* (Toledo, 1502, f. 361), while in Ximene's ed., 1517, " A solis ortûs cardine *ad* usque" is said at Vespers to line 21, when the Ambrosian strophes come in, with a Doxology. The Ambrosian portion, " Fit porta Christi pervia," &c., is the hymn in the *Constanz Brev.* (A.D. 1516) and some others, at Matins, on the Feast of the Annunciation of the B. V. M., and on the Festivals in her honour. It has been *tr.* as " From where the rising sun goes forth," by W. J. Copeland, in his *Hymns for the Week*, &c., 1848, and again in Schaff's *Christ in Song*, 1869. [W. A. S.]

A sure and tried foundation stone. *J. Montgomery.* [*Laying Foundation Stone.*] Written Sept. 4, 1822, for the laying of the Foundation Stone of St. Philip's Church, Sheffield, and printed for use at that ceremony. [M.MSS.] It was given in Montgomery's *Original Hymns*, 1853, No. 296, in 5 st. of 4 l., entitled " On Laying the Foundation Stone of a Place of Worship." Its use has been very limited, mainly owing to the superior excellence of his hymn, " This stone to Thee in faith we lay," which was written during the following month, and was included in his *Christian Psalmist*, 1825, whilst this hymn was omitted from all his earlier works.

A thousand oracles divine. *C. Wesley.* [*Holy Trinity.*] In his *Hymns on the Trinity*, 1767, this hymn is given as No. xvii. in the division of " Hymns and Prayers to the Trinity," in 4 st. of 8 l., p. 100. It was repeated in the *Wes. H. Bk.* 1780, and later eds. with the simple alteration of " His hosts " to " *the* hosts " in st. i. l. 6. From that collection it has passed into all the principal hymnals of the Methodist bodies in most English-speaking

countries, but is seldom found elsewhere. Few hymns are more dogmatic on the doctrine of the Trinity. The lines, " The Friend of earth-born man," and " For heaven's superior praise," are borrowed from Young's *Night Thoughts*. Night iv. ll. 603. 440. Orig. text as above, and *P. Works of J. & C. Wesley*, 1868–1872, vol. vii. pp. 312–13.

A time to watch, a time to pray. *J. M. Neale.* [*Good Friday.*] Appeared in his *Hymns for Children*, 1842, in 6 st. of 4 l., the last st. being Bp. Ken's doxology. It is given in Mrs. Brock's *Children's H. Bk.* with the omission of the doxology, and st. iii. l. 1, " *this* day," for " *to*-day," otherwise unaltered.

A voice comes from Ramah. *W. Knox.* [*Bereavement.*] Pub. in his *Songs of Israel*, 1824, in 3 st. of 8 l. and again in his *Poems*, 1847, pp. 117–8. It is based on Jer. xxxi. 15, 16, and entitled " Rachel Weeping." In *Kennedy*, 1863, No. 197, it is slightly altered.

A voice upon the midnight air. [*Passiontide.*] Dr. Martineau informs us that this hymn was contributed to his *Hys. for the Christian Church & Home*, 1840. It is No. 218, in 6 st. of 4 l., and is given as " Anonymous." It has since appeared in many Unitarian collections in G. Britain and America.

A widow poor, forlorn, oppressed. *C. Wesley.* [*Prayer.*] From the MS. of his *Hymns on the Four Gospels*, dated 1765, first pub. in the *P. Works of J. and C. Wesley*, 1868–72, vol. xi. p. 255, and again, without alteration, in the *Wes. H. Bk.* 1875, No. 827.

A widowed mother lost her son. *Dorothy A. Thrupp.* [*Compassion.*] Contributed to the 2nd ed. of Mrs. H. Mayo's *Sel. of Hymns, &c.*, 1840, in 4 st. of 4 l., entitled " The Widow and her Son," and signed " D. A. T." It is found in a few collections, including the *Ch. S. S. H. Bk.* 1879, No. 45.

Abash'd be all the boast of Age. *Bp. R. Heber.* [*Epiphany.*] Appeared in his posthumous *Hymns, &c.*, 1827, pp. 27–8, in 5 st. of 4 l. as the first of two hymns for the First Sunday after Epiphany. In its original form it is not in common use, but st. ii.–v. as—" O Wisdom, whose unfading power "—is given in *Kennedy*, 1863, No. 229 (with alterations), and the *Meth. S. S. H. Bk.* 1879, No. 77, also slightly altered.

Abba Father! we approach Thee. *J. G. Deck.* [*Sons of God.*] 1st pub. in the *Appendix* to the *Hymns for the Poor of the Flock*, 1841, No. 27, in 4 st. of 8 l.; again with the omission of st. iii. in *Ps. & Hys.*, Lond., Walther, 1842; Walker's *Cheltenham Coll.* 1855 ; Snepp's *S. of G. & G.* 1872, No. 21, and other collections. It is a plain evangelical hymn of no special merit. In America it is found in the Bapt. *Hy. & Tune Bk.* Phil. 1871, No. 792.

Abba Father, while we sing. *E. Osler* [*Providence*], written for and first pub. in Hall's *Mitre Hymn Book*, 1836, No. 187, in 3 st. of 6 l., and entitled " The Blessedness of God's Children"; and again in Osler's *Church & King*, June, 1837, where it is appended to an article on the Tenth Sunday after Trinity. It is found in several hymnals, including P. Maurice's *Choral Hy. Bk.*, 1861, No. 403, *Kennedy*, 1863, No. 1462, but usually with slight alterations.

Abba, gentle Jesus prayed. *J. S. B. Monsell.* [*To the Father.*] Appeared in the 2nd and enlarged ed. of his *Hys. of Love & Praise*, 1866, and thence, unaltered, into Snepp's *S. of G. & G.*, 1872.   [W. T. B.]

Abelard, Peter, b. at Pailais, in Brittany, 1079. Designed for the military profession, he followed those of philosophy and theology. His life was one of strange chances and changes, brought about mainly through his love for Heloïse, the niece of one Fulbert, a Canon of the Cathedral of Paris, and by his rationalistic views. Although a priest, he married Heloïse privately. He was condemned for heresy by the Council of Soissons, 1121, and again by that of Sens, 1140; d. at St. Marcel, near Châlons-sur-Saône, April 21, 1142. For a long time, although his poetry had been referred to both by himself and by Heloïse, little of any moment was known except the Advent hymn, *Mittit ad Virginem* (q.v.). In 1838 Greith pub. in his *Spicilegium Vaticanum*, pp. 123–131, six poems which had been discovered in the Vatican. Later on, ninety-seven hymns were found in the Royal Library at Brussels, and pub. in the complete ed. of Abelard's works, by Cousin, *Petri Abælardi Opp.*, Paris, 1849. In that work is one of his best-known hymns, *Tuba Domini, Paule, maxima* (q.v.). Trench in his *Sac. Lat. Poetry*, 1864, gives his *Ornarunt terram germina* (one of a series of poems on the successive days' work of the Creation), from Du Méril's *Poésies Popul. Lat. du Moyen Age*, 1847, p. 444.

       [J. J.]

Abide in me, and I in you. *Bp. E. H. Bickersteth.* [*Abide in Christ.*] Written in 1849, and first pub. in *Water from the Well Spring*, 1852. It was subsequently repub. in his *Ps. and Hys.* 1858, No. 79, and again in *The Two Brothers*, 1871, p. 230.

Abide with me, fast falls the eventide. *H. F. Lyte.* [*Evening.*] The history of this hymn to the date of its first publication, is given in the prefatory Memoir to his *Remains* by his daughter, Anna Maria Maxwell Hogg, Lond., Rivington, 1850, pp. ii., iii., as follows:—

"The summer was passing away, and the month of September (that month in which he was once more to quit his native land) arrived, and each day seemed to have a special value as being one day nearer his departure. His family were surprised and almost alarmed at his announcing his intention of preaching once more to his people. His weakness, and the possible danger attending the effort, were urged to prevent it, but in vain. 'It was better,' as he used often playfully to say, when in comparative health, 'to *wear* out than to rust out.' He felt that he should be enabled to fulfil his wish, and feared not for the result. His expectation was well founded. He did preach, and amid the breathless attention of his hearers gave them the sermon on the Holy Communion, which is inserted last in this volume [i.e. the *Remains*]. He afterwards assisted at the administration of the Holy Eucharist, and though necessarily much exhausted by the exertion and excite-

ment of this effort, yet his friends had no reason to believe it had been hurtful to him. In the evening of the same day he placed in the hands of a near and dear relative the little hymn, 'Abide with me,' with an air of his own composing, adapted to the words."

A note to the sermon referred to in this extract says, "Preached at Lower Brixham, Sept. 4, 1847." He died at Nice on the 20th of the November following [Lyte, **H. F.**]

The text of this hymn, which is usually regarded as the original, is that contained in his *Remains*, pub. in 1850. There are, however, several readings of the text. These readings are given in :—

1. *A fac-simile* of the original MS. in the autograph of the author, published by the Vicar of Lower Brixham, on behalf of the restoration of the church.
2. A leaflet on which it was first printed at Berryhead in September, 1847.
3. *Remains*, &c., 1850.
4. *Miscellaneous Poems*, 1868.

The variations of text are :—

st. i. l. 2. No. 1.   The darkness *thickens*, Lord, &c.
         Nos. 2 and 3.   The darkness *deepens*, Lord, &c.
st. iv. l. 4. No. 1.   Come, Friend of sinners, and *then* abide, &c.
         No. 2.   Come, Friend of sinners, and *thus* abide.
         No. 3.   Come, Friend of Sinners, and *thus 'bide.*
st. viii. l. 1. No. 1.   Hold *then* thy cross, &c.
         No. 2.   Hold *then* thy cross, &c.
         No. 3.   Hold *there* thy cross, &c.
         No. 4.   Hold *Thou* thy cross, &c.

In addition to these the hymn has also been pub. by J. Wright and Co., Thomas Street, Bristol, 1863, with Lyte's original music; and it has been translated into many languages, including Latin renderings in the *Guardian* (Nov. 1879 and Dec. 1881), *Church Times*, *Memorials of T. G. Godfrey-Faussett* (1878), *Hymno. Christ. Latina* (1871), &c.

The important position which this hymn has attained in many lands and tongues will justify an extract from Mr. Ellerton's note to the same in *Church Hymns* (folio ed. 1881). In that collection it is given with the "General Hymns." Mr. Ellerton says :—

"It is sometimes [nearly always] classed among evening hymns, apparently on the ground of the first two lines, and their similarity in sound to two lines in Keble's 'Sun of my soul.' This is a curious instance of the misapprehension of the true meaning of a hymn by those among whom it is popular; for a very little consideration will suffice to shew that there is not throughout the hymn the slightest allusion to the close of the *natural* day: the words of St. Luke xxiv. 29 are obviously used in a sense wholly metaphorical. It is far better adapted to be sung at funerals, as it was beside the grave of Professor Maurice; but it is almost too intense and personal for ordinary congregational use."

The use of this hymn is very extensive in all English-speaking countries. It is found in almost every collection published in G. Brit. during the past thirty years.   [J. J.]

Above, below, where'er I gaze. [*Creation.*] Contributed to *Christian Poetry*, Edinb., 1827, in 5 st. of 6 l., entitled, "Omnipresence of God," and signed Ιακωβ. Its authorship has not been determined. It came into C. U. in a few Unitarian collections at an early date, and is at present in use to a limited extent in G. Brit. and America, e. g: Amer. *Plymouth Coll.*, No. 86, and *Kennedy*, No. 1275.   [W. T. B.]

Above the clear blue sky, In heaven's, &c. *J. Chandler.* [*Children's Hymn.*]

Under date of Putney, March 20, 1875, the author wrote, " With the exception of ' Above the clear blue sky,' I have composed no hymns since those published in 1837, which are translations [*Hy. of the Primitive Church*]. I believe 1841 may have been the date of the publication of my smaller book [*Hys. of the Church, mostly Primitive*], but I have been an invalid for the last four years, away from my home, and have nothing to refer to here. 'Above the clear blue sky' appeared first in some Irish Collection of hymns some years ago; but that is all I can remember about it." (s. MSS.)

The Irish Collection referred to is probably *Hys. for Pub. Worship*, Dub., 1856, in which it is found. It had appeared however in the author's *Hymns of the Church, mostly Primitive*, in 1841, in 4 st. of 4 l., No. 83. Its use is somewhat extensive.

Abraham, when severely tried. *C. Wesley.* [*Faith.*] From *Hymns and Sacred Poems*, 1740, p. 12, and entitled " The Life of Faith Exemplified," being a paraphrase of Heb. xi. in 80 st. In 1780, 7 st. were included in the *Wes. H. Bk.*, No. 277, from whence it has passed into most of the collections of the Methodist bodies. Orig. text in *P. Works of J. & C. Wesley*, 1868–72, vol. i., p. 214.

Absent from flesh, O blissful thought. *I. Watts.* [*Death.*] This hymn is part of a poem on " Death and Heaven," in five Lyric Odes, of which it is No. 2 :—" The Departing Moment; or Absent from the Body," and is in 4 st. of 4 l. These Odes appeared in Dr. Watts's *Reliquiae Juveniles*, 1734. This ode is not in extensive use, although found in a few collections in G. Brit. and America. It is given, in a slightly altered form, in the *New Cong.*, No. 723. The orig. text is not found in modern collections.   [W. T. B.]

Abyssinian Hymnody. Till about the year 1864, when the Rev. J. M. Rodwell printed two articles in the *Journal of Sacred Literature*, nothing whatever was known in England of Abyssinian Hymnody, and it is only to these articles that reference can even now be made.

The selections from the *Degua*, or *Hymnal of Jared*, an Abyssinian saint who is believed to have lived in the 5th cent., and is traditionally said to have been caught up into heaven, (see Dillman's Cat. MSS. Æth. *Brit. Mus.*, p. 32, *n.*), are of striking originality and are translated by Mr. Rodwell into a kind of metrical prose. From them we give as a specimen the " Hymn of the Light."

Praise to the Saviour, the glory of the saints,
The light which hath come into the world;
His clothing was as light upon the mount,
But He is the true light in Himself.

He came from a world of light,
And that light hath come to us;
He will lead us back into that light
From whence He descended in love and pity.

He has come whom Moses announced—
The Crown of martyrs, the Founder of the Church,
The Light of light, who giveth light to the just.

Oh send out Thy light and truth,
That they may bring me to Thy holy hill;
Send forth Thy hand from on high to save.

God is a God who knoweth all things,
Clad in righteousness, robed in light;
A light announced Him, shining in the heavens,
And He is come, the Pilot of the souls of the just.

The Church's Bridegroom is the light of the world.
Let us therefore be clad in light,
And put away the works of darkness,
And walk as the children of the day.

He reigns over the treasures of light,
Who existed ere the worlds were made.
He will manifest that light ;
He will give comfort in our sorrows;
He will disperse the clouds and thick darkness,
And lead us to our rest above.
Halleluiah, O Thou firstborn of Zion !

O Adonai, Thou art the bearer of glad tidings:
Marvellous is the brightness of Thy beauty.
Halleluiah.   To Thee be glory.   Amen.

The MS. from which these hymns were translated is in the library of the B. & F. Bible Society, and is probably of the 14th century. Only two other copies appear to have found their way to Europe. From the invocation of saints, in the hymns for their festivals, one can hardly doubt that the hymns are of the 5th or 6th cent. In this they present an exceedingly strong family likeness to the hymns of St. Ephrem Syrus.

The first published *metrical* translation was a version of *The Vigil of the Four Beasts*, by Mr. W. C. Dix, and appeared in the *Churchman's Shilling Magazine* for May, 1867. In October of the same year an article on " Abyssinian Hymns," containing three metrical versions by Mr. Dix, was issued in the same magazine. Another article headed *Devotions of the Abyssinian Church* appeared in the *Monthly Packet* for July, 1868, and two hymns were added. None of these are in C. U., but one is given in Jellicoe's *Songs of the Church*, 1867. *The Song of the Saints*, the only other version of an Abyssinian hymn, originally published in Rev. L. C. Biggs's *Songs of Other Churches* in the *Monthly Packet* for Nov. 1871, and reprinted in the *Churchman's Manual of Public and Private Devotion*, 1882, completed the use of the translations of Mr. Rodwell by English hymn-writers, except, that in the columns of the *Church Times*, an additional translation or two, by Mr. Dix, may be found. It is earnestly to be wished that attention may be seriously drawn to the hymns of the whole Eastern Church. The profound ignorance of our leading hymnological scholars on subjects of this class is lamentable. The field Dr. Neale worked so well has lain comparatively fallow since his early death. The position which some of his *Hymns of the Eastern Church* have taken in our hymnals excites the wish that Abyssinia and Ethiopia may render us some service. These unwrought fields, though not equal to the rich treasury of Greek and Latin hymnody, are still worthy of the attention of English compilers.   [W. T. B.]

Accept, O Lord, Thy servant's thanks. *Bp. R. Mant.* [*Holy Scripture.*] This is one of the Original Hymns added by Bp. Mant to his *Ancient Hymns from the Roman Breviary*, 1837–71, in 4 st. of 8 l., and entitled " Hymn of Thanksgiving for Holy Scripture." Dr. Kennedy, in adopting it in his *Hymno. Christ.*, 1863, No. 1195, has given the original text, with the change of st. iii. l. 7, from " And He, Who gave the word, may

He" to "And O, may He Who gave the Word." The hymn is a plain poetical reflex of the sixth Article, and of the Collect for the Second Sunday in Advent. This hymn is also sometimes found in American collections, as the Pennsylvania Luth. Church Bk., 1868, and others.

Accept our thanks, O Lord, we pray. W. C. Dix. [St. Bede.] Contributed to the People's H. 1867, No. 252.

Accepted, Perfect, and Complete. Frances R. Havergal. [Complete in Christ.] Written at Hastings, Sept. 3, 1870, in 5 st. of 3 l., and based upon the three passages of Holy Scripture : Eph. 1. 6, "Accepted in the beloved "; Col. i. 28, "Perfect in Christ Jesus"; and Col. ii. 10, "Complete in Him." It was first pub. as a leaflet by J. and R. Parlane, Paisley, 1871 ; then, with the tune "Tryphena" (also by Miss Havergal), in Snepp's S. of G. & G., 1872, mus. ed. 1875 ; again in her work Under the Surface, 1874 ; and her Life Mosaic, 1879. [" HAV. MSS."]

Accepting, Lord, Thy gracious call. C. N. Hall. [Following Jesus.] This hymn was printed in the author's tract, Follow Jesus, and, again, from thence in his Hymns, composed at Bolton Abbey, and Other Rhymes, 1858, pp. 45–47, in 11 st. of 4 l. In Major's Bk. of Praise and the Meth. S. S. H. Bk. It is given in an abbreviated form. In the author's Ch. Ch. Hymnal, 1876, No. 257, it is included as "Lord! we obey Thy kind command," in 8 st. of 4 l. various stanzas of the original being rewritten to attain this end.

According to Thy gracious word. J. Montgomery. [Holy Communion.] No copy of this hymn is preserved in the "Montgomery MSS." Its first publication was in the author's Christian Psalmist, 1825, p. 405, in 6 st. of 4 l. with the motto "This do in remembrance of Me." From its first appearance it has been one of the most popular of hymns for "Holy Communion," and is found in most modern collections of a moderate type. Usually, how-ever, st. ii. l. 2, which reads : "Thy testa-mental cup I take," is altered to "The cup, Thy precious Blood, I take," as in Thring's Coll., No. 524, or, " I'll take," as in the Salisbury H. Bk., 1857, and Kennedy, 1863, No. 650. In 1853 it was republished by Montgomery in his Original Hymns, No. 129. In common with Montgomery's hymns it has no doxology. That usually found with it,

" To Thee, O Jesus, Light of Light,
　　All praise and glory be," &c.,

is from the Salisbury H. Bk., 1857. In Hedge & Huntington's Unitarian Hys. of the Church, Boston, U. S. A., 1853, No. 388, " Gethsemane, can I forget ? " is composed of st. iii., ii., iv., v. of this hymn.

According to Thy mercy, Lord. [Supplication.] This cento appeared in 3 st. of 4 l. as No. 720 in the Moravian H. Bk., 1789, and was repeated in later eds. (1849, No. 723). In Mr. Eberle's notes in the Moravian Mes-senger, March, 1870, it is marked as : i. Schneesing, tr. J. Swertner, ii. N. L. von Zin-zendorf, tr. F. W. Foster, iii. N. L. von Zinzen-

dorf, tr. J. Swertner. St. i. seems to be from st. iii. of Schneesing's hymn, " Allein zu dir, Herr Jesu Christ;" while st. ii., iii. seem based on Zinzendorf's " Ach mein verwundter Fürste." The cento is included as No. 132 in Dr. Pagenstecher's Coll., 1864. [J. M.]

Ach Gott vom Himmel, sieh darein. Martin Luther [Ps. xii.]. This free rendering of Ps. xii., adapted to the times, which Bunsen (Versuch, 1833, p. 854) calls "a cry for help from the Church founded on the Word of God for protection against its contemners and cor-rupters," was probably written in 1523 and 1st pub. in the Etlich cristlich lider, Witten-berg, 1524, in 6 st. of 7 l. The seventh st., a dox., was added in Eyn Enchiridion, Erfurt, 1524, but has not been tr. into English. In-cluded in Wackernagel, iii. p. 6, in Schircks's ed. of Luther's Geistliche Lieder, 1854, p. 76, and as No. 209 in the Unv. L. S. 1851. It is a companion to Luther's " Nun freut euch lieben Christengmein," and like it greatly furthered the cause of the Reformation.

Laux̄mann, in Koch, viii. 521–526, relates that Dr. Sprütze, or Sprengel, of Magdeburg Cathe-dral, had gone by request of the Romish autho-rities to preach at Brunswick three sermons which were to uproot the Lutheran heresies. On the 22nd Sun. after Trinity, 1527, he preached on the parable of the Unmerciful Servant (St. Matt. xviii. 23–35) and declared salvation by good works. At the end of his sermon, a citizen began to sing this hymn, and as the whole con-gregation joined in, the discomfited priest at once left the pulpit, and never again preached in Brunswick. Again, on the 2nd Sun. in Advent, 1529, a preacher in St. Jacob's, Lübeck, exhorted to prayers for the dead, when two boys began this hymn, and the congregation following, sang the whole. Lauxmann adds that st. iv. comforted P. J. Spener when he heard it sung on his entering the church at Frankfurt-am-Main, at a time when days looked dark for the Church of Christ ; that, when summoned to Dresden to occupy the responsible post of Court preacher, he was cheered by being saluted with it in the first Saxon village he entered ; and that in Dresden it was often, at his request, sung by the scholars before his door.

Translations in C. U. :—

1. **Oh Lord our God, from heaven look down,** in Miss Fry's H. of the Reformation, 1845, p. 30. In 1860 her trs. of st. v. vi. rewritten to 5 st. C.M., beginning, " Almighty God, Thy truth shall stand," were included in J. Whittemore's Supp. to all H. Bks., No. 44.

2. **O God ! look down from heav'n, we pray,** a free tr. condensing sts. ii., iii., as ii., by W. M. Reynolds, in the Evangelical Review, Gettysburg, July 1849, and as No. 965 in the General Synod's Luth. H. Bk., 1850.

3. **Ah God, look down from heaven and see,** by R. Massie in his tr. of Luther's Spiritual Songs, 1854, p. 32. In 1880 it was given in the Ohio Luth. Hymnal, 147, as :—" O God, look down from heaven and see."

4. **Ah God, from heav'n look down, and see,** omitting st. iii., by Miss Winkworth, as No. 101, in her C. B. for England, 1863.

Other trs. are :—

(1) "Helpe now, O Lorde, and loke on us," by *Bp. Coverdale*, 1539 (*Remains*, 1846, p. 567). (2) "Saif us, gude Lord, and succour send," in the *Gude and Godly Ballates* (ed. 1568, folio 45, ed. 1868, p. 76). (3) "O Lord in Mercy cast an Eye," by *J. C. Jacobi*, 1722, p. 93 (1732, p. 165). (4) "Look down, O Lord, from heaven behold," by *Miss Cox*, 1841, p. 207, and thence in Dr. Bacon, 1884, p. 6. (5) "Ah, God! from heaven high look down," by *J. Anderson*, 1846, p. 31 (1847, p. 51). (6) "Ah! Lord, from heaven Thy people see," by *Dr. J. Hunt*, 1853, p. 60. (7) "On us, O Lord, in mercy look," by *Dr. H. Mills*, 1856, p. 119. (8) Ah! God in heaven, look down anew," by *Dr. G. Macdonald*, in the *Sunday Magazine*, 1867, p. 449 ; and in his *Exotics*, 1876, p. 62, as "Ah God, from heaven look down and view." (9) "O God, from heaven our troubles view," by *F. W. Young*, in the *Family Treasury*, 1877, p. 653.   [J. M.]

Ach Gott, wie manches Herzeleid.

Martin Moller ? [*Cross and Consolation.*] First appeared in the 2nd ed., Görlitz, 1587, of Moller's *Meditationes Sanctorum Patrum*, entitled "A consoling prayer wherewith a troubled soul, amid all the crosses and tribulations of these last troublous times, can sweetly comfort itself and longingly delight itself in the Sweet Name of Jesus Christ. From the ancient hymn 'Jesu dulcis memoria.' " It is a very free paraphrase of the *Rhythm* in 12 st. of 6 l. Lauxmann, in *Koch*, viii. 466–468, says st. i., iv., v., x. have been special favourites in Germany, and inclines to ascribe the hymn to Moller. Wackernagel, in giving the text in his *D. Kirchenlied*, v. p. 84, says that Moller, in his 1596 *Manuale de Praeparatione ad Mortem*, gives it among those "composed by other spiritual persons" [perhaps as being based on the Latin], and that Conrad Hojer [or *Cunrad Höier*, Sub-prior at Möllenbeck, near Rinteln on the Weser] in his *Die fünff Heupt Stücke Christlicher Lehre*, Stadthagen, 1614, claims it as his own. He thus gives it under Hojer's name, but says that Hojer probably only altered it, and reduced it to more regular form. Included in many subsequent hymn-books, and recently as No. 734 in the *Unv. L. S.*, 1851.

Translations in C. U. :—

1. Jesus, my all, my highest good, a very free *tr.* in 7 st. of 4 l. (based on the version in 14 st. of 4 l., beginning with st. ix., "Jesu! du edler Bräutgam werth," included as No. 871 in the *Brüder G. B.* 1778;) as No. 454 in the *Moravian H. Bk.*, 1789, and continued, altered, in later eds. From this, 5 sts., based in order of sts. ix., ii., vii., iv., xii. of the original, were given as No. 718, in Bickersteth's *Christ. Psalmody*, 1832. In C. Wilson's *Genl. Psalmody*, 1842, No. 893, the order of sts. is ix., ii., iv., v.

2. O God, what manifold distress, a good *tr.* of st. i., ii., iv., xi., by *A. T. Russell*, as No. 222, in his *Ps. & Hymns*, 1851. Part ii. begins, "Jesu, my Lord and God, Thou art."

3. Ah God, my days are dark indeed, a very good *tr.*, omitting st. iii., v., in the 2nd Ser. 1858, of Miss Winkworth's *Lyra Ger.* p. 185, and repeated, as No. 136, in her *C. B. for England*, 1863. In the Ohio Luth. *Hymnal*, 1880, st. i., ii., iv., vii., ix., xii., are given as No. 416. Her *tr.* of st. iv., vi., vii., ix.-xi., beginning, "Jesus, my only God and Lord," were included as No. 215, in the *Meth. N. Con. H. Bk.* 1863, and the same, omit-

ting st. vi., as No. 300 in *Holy Song*, 1869. Her *trs.* of st. vii., viii., xi., xii., slightly altered and beginning "Jesu, my boast, my light, my joy," were given as No. 507, in *Kennedy*, 1863.

Other trs. are :—

(1) "O Lord! how many miseries," by *J. C. Jacobi*, 1720, p. 21 (1722, p. 76, 1732, p. 125). (2) "O God, how many an anxious hour," as No. 235 in pt. i. of the *Moravian H. Bk.*, 1754.

In Bunsen's *Versuch*, 1833, a greatly altered form of st. iii.-v., beginning, "Mein Herzenstrost ist Jesus Christ," was included as No. 465, without name of adapter. Of this form the *trs.* are :—

(1) "Christ to my heart true joy can give," good and full, in Miss Cox's *Sac. H. from the German*, 1841, p. 185. Thence, unaltered, as No. 77 in Alford's *Ps. & Hys.*, 1844, and as No. 206 in Hook's *Ch. School H. Bk.*, 1850. (2) "Jesus! I place my trust in Thee." by *Lady Eleanor Fortescue*, 1843 (1847, p. 73).   [J. M.]

Ach, Jesu, dein Sterben.

Anon., xviii. cent. [*Passion-tide.*] Included as No. 281 in the *Vollkommenes Schlesisches Kirchen G. B.*, Breslau, 1727 (Preface, Oct. 1, 1703), and repeated as No. 451 in Burg's *Breslau G. B.*, 1746, in 3 st. of 4 l., entitled "Dying to Sin through the Death of Jesus," and repeated as No. 83 in the *Unv. L. S.*, 1851. The *tr.* "Ah Jesus, the merit," by Miss Winkworth, appeared in the 2nd Ser., 1858, of her *Lyra Ger.* p. 32, and thence, as No. 50, in her *C. B. for England*, 1863.   [J. M.]

Ach! lehre mich ein Kindlein sein.

[*Children.*] Included as No. 41 in the *Evangelisches Kinder G. B.*, Basel, 1867, in 7 st. of 4 l., as by Emma Neustetel. The only *tr.* is, "O that I were a little child," in full, in Mrs. Bevan's *Songs of Praise*, 1859, p. 145, and thence, as No. 44, in J. E. Clarke's *Children's H. H. Bk.* c. 1860.   [J. M.]

Ach! treuer Gott, barmherzigs Herz.

P. Gerhardt. [*Cross and Consolation.*] Founded on a prayer "for patience under great trial," No. xxv. in Class iii. of J. Arndt's *Paradiesgärtlein*, 1612. Appeared in Crüger's *Praxis pietatis melica*, Frankfurt, 1656, No. 381, in 16 st. of 7 l., and included in many subsequent hymn-books, as recently in the *Unv. L. S.*, 1851, No. 693 ; also in Wackernagel's ed. of his *Geistliche Lieder*, No. 57 ; Bachmann's ed., No. 80.

Translations in C. U. :—

1. O God most true, most merciful !—A good *tr.* of st. i., iv., v., x., by A. T. Russell, as No. 224, in his *Ps. and Hys.* 1851, and thence altered and beginning, "O God of mercy full and free," as No. 665, in *Kennedy*, 1863.

2. O faithful God! O pitying heart, a good *tr.*, omitting st. iii., ix., xi., xiii., xv., in the 2nd Ser. 1858, of Miss Winkworth's *Lyra Ger.* p. 182, and thence, in the Gilman-Schaff, *Lib. of R. P.* ed. 1883, p. 837. The *trs.* of st. x., xii., xiv., xvi., beginning "O Thou, who diedst to give us life," appear as No. 327, in *Ch. Praise*, 1883.

3. Ah! faithful God, compassionate heart, by *J. Kelly*, 1867, p. 169.   [J. M.]

Ach, uns wird das Herz so leer.

C. J. P. Spitta. [*Longing for Heaven.*] 1st

pub. in the First Series, 1833, of his *Psalter und Harfe*, p. 134, in 6 st. of 4 l., entitled "Homesickness." *Tr.* as:—

Ah! this heart is void and chill.—A good *tr.*, omitting st. v., by Mrs. Findlater in the 2nd Ser., 1855, of the *H. L. L.* (ed. 1862, p. 110, 1884, p. 86). Included, slightly altered, and omitting st. ii., as No. 455, in the Pennsylvania *Luth. Ch. Bk.*, 1868. In W. B. Bradbury's *Golden Shower*, N. Y. 1860 (ed. 1870, p. 158) the *trs.* of st. ii., vi., are rewritten, and a chorus added. St. i., ii., iv. of this form, with the chorus, were included as No. 1279, in Robinson's *S. for the Sanctuary*, 1865, and, as No. 1048, in the *Bapt. Praise Bk.* 1871.

Other trs. are.—
(1) "Hungering, thirsting as we go," by *Miss Fry*, 1859, p. 17.　(2) "Ah! how empty is the heart," by *R. Massie*, 1860, p. 132.　　　　　[J. M.]

Acquaint thee, O mortal. *W. Knox.*

[*Invitation.*] The opening lines of this hymn are:—

"Acquaint thee, O mortal!
　Acquaint thee with God,
And joy, like the sunshine,
　Shall beam on thy road.
And peace, like the dew-drops,
　Shall fall on thy head;
And visions, like angels,
　Shall visit thy bed."

As a hymn on "Heavenly Wisdom," and based on Job xxii. 21, 27-28, it appeared in his *Harp of Zion*, 1825, in 3 st. of 8 l. It was also repeated in his *Poems*, 1847, p. 162, where it is said to have been "written for Mr. Pettet." The use of this hymn in G. Britain is very limited. In *Kennedy*, 1863, No. 1140, it is given as, "Acquaint thee, *my child*, acquaint thee," &c. In America, as in Robinson's *S. for the Sanctuary*, 1865, 2nd ed., 1872, No. 504, and others, it is: —"Acquaint *thyself quickly, O Sinner*," &c., and, in common with nearly every collection, the second stanza of the original is omitted. This stanza reads:—

"Acquaint thee, O mortal!
　Acquaint thee with God,
And the prayer of thy spirit
　Shall reach His abode;
And the wish of thy bosom
　Shall rise not in vain;
And His favour shall nourish
　Thy heart like the rain."

This hymn is also sometimes in C. U. as:— "Acquaint thee, *O Spirit*, acquaint thee with God," as in Longfellow and Johnson's *Bk. of Hymns*, Boston, 1846, and later eds. [J. J.]

Ad celebres, Rex coelice, laudes cuncta. [*St. Michael and All Angels.*]

A Notkerian Sequence for the Feast of St. Michael. *Daniel*, ii., p. 24, gives only the first five words, referring to MSS. formerly belonging to the monastery of St. Emmeram at Ratisbon. These MSS., which are now at Munich, belong to the 11th and 12th centuries. The full text is in a 12th cent. MS. in the *British Museum* (Add. 11669, f. 53); in *Daniel*, v. pp. 93, 94, in *Kehrein*, p. 135, and in *Mone*, i. p. 454. Also in the Missals of *Sarum*, *York* and *Hereford* as a seq. on that festival. In vol. ii. of the reprint of the *York Missal*, pub. by the Surtees Society, 1872, will be found, p. 316, the

variations of a MS. of Proses and Sequences in the Bodleian Library, No. 775, written in the reign of Ethelred, sometime between the years A.D. 994 and 1017. This last is the oldest form in which it is found. *Mone*, i., p. 455, gives the full text and a great variety of readings from MSS. at Munich and Stuttgart, of the 11th cent., &c., together with short notes on portions of the text. *Daniel*, v. p. 93, repeats *Mone's* references. They are also repeated with additions in *Kehrein*, No. 168.

[W. A. S.]

Translations in C.U. :—

1. To celebrate Thy praise, O King of heaven, by C. B. Pearson, in the *Sarum Missal in English*, 1000, p. 447. After revision it was reprinted in his *Sarum Sequences*, 1871, p. 119, as "To give Thee glory, Heavenly King."

2. To give Thee glory, Heavenly King.—No. 374, in the *Hymnary*, is a cento from Mr. Pearson's *tr.*, with alterations made by the editors with the translator's permission.

Ad coenam Agni providi. [*Easter.*]

This hymn is sometimes ascribed to *St. Ambrose*, but is not inserted among his undoubted compositions, by the Benedictine editors (see Migne's *Patrol.*, tom. 17; the fourth of the works of *St. Ambrose*). The original text, with that revised for use in the *Rom. Brev.*, "Ad regias agni dapes," is given in *Daniel*, i., No. 81; with various readings from the Collections of *Cassander*, and other authorities. It is headed "Hymnus Paschalis" ("A hymn for Easter-tide"). In *Mone*, it is No. 161 from MSS. at Lichtenthal of the 13th and 14th centuries, and from others of later date. He gives a long note embracing various readings, references, and criticism. Much of this is repeated in *Daniel*, iv. 73, who also gives readings from Rheinau MSS. of the 10th and 11th cent., and at iv. p. 353, readings from a MS. of the 9th cent., at Bern. It is also found in a 11th cent. MS. in the *British Museum* (Jul. A. vi., f. 48.), and is printed from a Durham MS. of the 11th cent., in the *Latin Hys. of the Anglo-Saxon Church*, 1851, p. 82. In the *Junius* MS. of the 8th and 9th cents. it is No. xxi. The *Sarum Brev.* text is in the *Hymn. Sarisb.*, Lond., 1851, p. 99, and various readings are added from English Monastic Uses, including those of *Worcester*, *St. Alban's*, *Canterbury*, &c., and in Biggs's *Annotated ed. of H. A. & M.*, 1867.)

Concerning its use we would add that from Low Sunday [1st after Easter] till the Vigil of the Ascension it was the proper Vesper hymn in the *Sarum* and *York* uses, and is also so found in other English breviaries, Saturdays excepted (when "Chorus novae Hierusalem" was sung) whenever no feast of Apostle or patron Saint interrupted the ordinary course of the Easter season. There is no doxology, for according to *Sarum* and *York* the last 2 verses of "Jesu Salvator Saeculi" were directed to be sung at the end of all hymns of that metre [Saturdays excepted].

Passing from its history, text, and use, to the hymn itself, its design, and teaching are well brought out by the following writers:—

In a curious work which gives interpretations of hymns, mystical and otherwise, entitled "*Expositio Himnorum cum notabili commento. Coloniae apud Henricum Quentell*, 1492 " (many other editions in the 15th and early part of the 16th centuries; one without a date may be older than the above. See *Daniel*, i. p. xvi., and No. 81. The writer's name was Hilarius), we find concerning this composition:

"The matter of this hymn is that the author calls us to the banquet of that Lamb Who taketh away the sins of the world; that is, to receive the Body and Blood of the Lord, of Whom it is written that he who receiveth the Body of Christ unworthily eateth and drinketh damnation to himself; but he who doth so worthily hath eternal life: but we are placed *'ad coenam Agni providi'* (at the banquet of the Lamb as those who are prepared)."

The allusion is to those who were solemnly baptized and clothed in white garments on Easter Eve, and admitted to Holy Communion on the following day.

Dr. Neale works out this allusion to the newly baptized and their white garments in his *Short Commentary on the Hymnal N.*, 1853, part i., pp. 26–27, where he says:—

"In order to understand this hymn, we must know for whom it was written. It was the custom of the early Church that Baptism should be solemnly administered to many *catechumens*, that is, persons who had been under instruction and preparation for it, on Easter Eve. This hymn then refers in the first place to them . . . *The Lamb's high banquet we await.* These newly baptized persons were now for the first time about to receive the Holy Communion, and therefore truly *waiting* for that *high banquet*, '*In snow-white robes*' [the 'Et stolis albis candidi' of the original], because, at Baptism, a white garment was given to the persons baptized, with words like these: 'Take this white vesture for a token of the innocence which, by God's grace, in this holy Sacrament of Baptism, is given unto thee and for a sign whereby thou art admonished, so long as thou livest, to give thyself to innocency of living, that after this transitory life thou mayest be partaker of life everlasting.'"

The chrisom-robes were worn from Easter Eve till Low Sunday (all the week-days of the octave are marked *in Albis* in the *Sacramentary* of S. Gregory). for which the ancient name was 'Dominica in albis depositis,' as in the *Ambrosian Missal*, or, shortly, 'Dominica in Albis,' because on this day the newly baptized first appeared without the chrisoms, or white robes, which they had worn every day since their baptism on Easter Eve.   [V.]

Translations in C. U. :—

1. At the Great Supper of the Lamb. From the *Sarum Brev.* by W. J. Blew. 1st printed on a fly-sheet for use in his church, cir. 1850, and then pub. in his *Hy. and Tune Bk.*, 1852, with music, in 4 st. of 4 l. This was repeated in Mr. Rice's *Sel.*, from that work, 1870, No. 52.

2. The Lamb's high banquet stands displayed, [we await]. By J. M. Neale. The first reading "*stands displayed*" was given in the original prospectus of the *Hymnal N.*, Feb., 1851. In the *Ecclesiologist* of April, 1851, the *tr.* reading "The Lamb's high banquet *we await*," appeared in full, and in 1852 it was repeated in the *Hymnal N.*, No. 29, with st. i. l. 2, "*royal*" for "*festal* state :" and st. ii. l. 3 "tasting *of*" for "tasting *there*." From the *Hymnal N.* it passed into the *People's H.*, 1867, No. 117, unaltered; with the omission of st. iii. into Skinner's *Daily Service H.*, 1864, No. 131, and again into other collections.

3. The Lamb's high banquet called to share. This *tr.* is well known through *H. A. and M.* It is Dr. Neale's *tr.* altered by the compilers. Referring to the use made by the editors of

various hymnals of his numerous *trs.*, Dr. Neale wrote in the *Preface* to his *Med. Hys.*, 2nd ed., 1863, p. vi., with a special reference to this *tr.* and the *H. A. and M.* alterations:—

"In some instances I thankfully acknowledge them [the alterations] to be improvements; in some, I think that, had the reproducers studied the Commentaries of *Clichtoveus* and *Nebrissensis*, they would have left the original as it was. I will give an example or two: In the glorious *Ad Coenam Agni providi*, the last word of the first line is undoubtedly the nominative case plural—

'The Lamb's high banquet *we await*,'

as it is in the *Hymnal Noted*. But in most reproductions that line is altered, I suppose from the editors either not seeing or not believing that the adjective applies to ourselves, not to the LAMB. Again, in the same hymn, 'Cruore ejus roseo,' is translated by:—

'And tasting of His *roseate* Blood.'

"The epithet is everywhere altered to *crimson*, because the editors did not see its force. The poet would tell us that, though one drop of our Lord's Blood was sufficient to redeem the world,

('Cujus una stilla salvum facere
Totum mundum quit ab omni scelere,'

as S. Thomas says,) yet out of the greatness of His love to us He would shed all. As everyone knows, the last drainings of life-blood are not crimson, but are of a far paler hue: strictly speaking, *roseate*. Change the word, and you eliminate the whole idea."

In his *Short Commentary on the Hymnal N.*, Dr. Neale gives the fact that Christ is the *True Rose* as a second reason for the word *roseate*. In the revised ed. of *H. A. and M.*, 1875, this latter alteration is amended, and the line reads:

"And tasting of His *precious* blood ; "

a new departure, which, we doubt not, Dr. Neale would have been slow to accept.

4. The Lamb's high banquet called to share. No. 277 in the *Hymnary* is a cento, mainly from E. Caswall's rendering of "Ad regias Agni dapes ; " but there are a few lines from *Dr. Neale* as above in st. i., ii. and iv.

5. The Supper of the Lamb to share. By Mrs. Charles, from the old text in *Daniel*, i. 87, appeared in her *Voice of Christian Life in Song*, 1858, p. 103, in 7 st. of 4 l. This was included in *Mercer, Ox. ed.*, 1864, with the omission of st. ii., and the addition of a doxology, and in Schaff's *Christ in Song*, 1870, p. 186, unaltered.

Translations not in C. U. :—
1. At supper of the Lamb prepared. *Primer*, 1599.
2. At this High Feast the Lamb hath made. *Chambers*, i. 189.
3. The Paschal Feast, not girt with night. *Kynaston*, 1862.   [J. J.]

This hymn has also been rendered into German, and again from the German into English thus :—

Kommt, seid gefasst zum Lammesmahl, a *tr.* in 8 sts. of 4 l., by Christian Knorr von Rosenroth, 1st pub. in his *Neuer Helicon*, Nürnberg, 1684, p. 129, and included as No. 118 in *Freylinghausen's G. B.*, 1704. The only *tr.* is "Come now to the Lamb's Feast," as No. 190 in the *Appendix* of 1743 to the *Moravian H. Bk.*, 1742 (1754, pt. i., No. 226).   [J. M.]

Ad laudes Salvatoris. [*Fest. Com. of Bp. & Conf.*] Text in *Wackernagel*, i. No. 255, from the Lübeck Missal, c. 1480, and others. Neale's *Sequentiæ ex Missalibus*, p. 231, from the Missals of Utrecht, 1513, and Salzburg, 1515, where it occurs as a Seq. for the Feast of a *Bishop & Confessor*, as may be seen from various passages in the hymn; though Neale styles it a Seq. for the *Common of a Confessor not a Bishop. Daniel*, v. p. 149, quotes the text from *Neale*. In *Kehrein* it is No. 465.

[W. A. S.]

Translation in C. U. :—

O ye who fear, yet fearing long, was made for and 1st pub. in the *People's H.*, 1867. No. 218 as a hymn "Common for Priests." It is by "S. M." i.e. *Sister Miriam*.

Ad perennis vitae fontem mens sitivit arida. *Card. Peter Damiani*. [*The Heavenly City.*]

1. The earliest form of this great poem on the "Glory of Paradise," is found in the *Liber Meditationum*, usually ascribed to St. Augustine, and because of its presence therein, it is often given as his. The Benedictine editors of St. Augustine's *Works*, however, included it under protest; and Archbishop Trench disposes of these claims in the following emphatic manner:—

"This poem has been often attributed to Augustine, finding place as it does in the *Meditationes*, long ascribed to him. These *Meditationes*, however, are plainly a cento from Anselm, Gregory the Great, and many others besides Augustine; from whom they are rightly adjudged away in the Benedictine ed., as indeed in earlier as well. The hymn is Damiani's, and quite the noblest he has left us." *Sac. Lat. Poetry*, 1849, p. 296, 2nd ed, 1864, p. 135.

2. Following the Benedictine editors, and anticipating Archbishop Trench, Cajetan included the poem in vol. iii. of his ed. of Damiani's Works, with the title "Petri Damiani, Cardinalis Ostrensis, ex dictis beati Augustini, Hymnus de Gloria Paradisi." (*Petri Damiani Opera*, pars iii., 915–918, *ed. Domini Constantini Cajetani.*) [Rome, 1606–1615, vol. iv. in 1640; Lyons, 1623; Paris, 1642 and 1643.]

3. *Daniel*, 1841–1856, gives the full text in vol. i. pp. 114–117, as from certain editions of the works of St. Augustine; at Strasburg, 1489; Venice, 1729; and adds that it is also found in Fabricius, Rambach, and others. Notes on the text are also added. He supplies corrections and additions in vol. ii. p. 382; iii. p. 281, and iv. pp. 203–4.

4. It is also given, in every case with notes and various readings, in *Du Méril*, 1843, p. 131. *Mone*, i. p. 422. *Trench*, 1849, p. 296. *Migne's Patrol.*, tom. 145, col. 861–864, and many others. One of the most interesting reprints is Dr. Kynaston's, *The Glory of Paradise. A Rhythmical Hymn, by Peter Damiani, ed. with translation.* Lond., F. Fellowes, Ludgate Street, 1857.

Translations in C. U. :—

1. On the fount of life eternal -By E. Caswall, 1st pub. in his *Masque of Mary*, 1858, and again in his *Hymns & Poems*, 1873, pp. 214–218, in 20 st. of 6 l. From this two centos have been compiled (1) beginning with the opening st. in the *Hymnary*, No. 614, and consisting of st. i., iii., v., viii, ix., xv., xvii., xix., and xx., with slight alterations. (2) "Who can paint that lovely city," in the R. C. *Hys. for the Year*, No. 51. This is composed of st. iii., v., vi., vii., and xix., also slightly altered.

2. For the Fount of life eternal, Is my thirsting,

&c.—No. 484, in the *People's H.*, is a cento arranged by Dr. Littledale for that collection, 1867, from *trs.* by Wackerbarth, 1846; Neale, *Joys and Glories of Paradise*, 1865, with additions from his own translation in *Lyra Mystica*, 1865.

3. For the Fount of life eternal, thirstily, &c.— By the Rev. J. Dayman, 1st pub. in the *Sarum H.*, 1868, No. 320, in 13 st. of 6 l.

Translations not in C. U. :—

1. My thirsty soul desires her drought. *Anon.* pub. in *The Song of Mary the Mother of Christ*, &c., 1601; reprinted in part by the Parker Soc. in *Sel. P. of the reign of Q. Elizabeth;* and in Dr. Bonar's *New Jerusalem*, 1852, from a MS. in the Brit. Mus.
2. My heart as hart for water thirsts. *Sylvester*, 1621.
3. Unto the spring of purest life. In the *Meditations, Soliloquia, and Manual of the Glorious Doctor, S. Augustin. Paris*, 1630.
4. For life eternal's living spring. *S. Augustin's Confessions*, 1679, given in some copies as translated by Abraham Woodhead.
5. For life's Eternal, &c. *Wackerbarth*, 1846.
6. Yearningly my fond heart thirsteth, &c.; *J. Banks*, in his *Nugae*, 1854; and previously in the *Churchman's Companion*, 1849.
7. For the Fount of living waters panting. *Kynaston*, 1857.
8. In the Fount of life, &c. *Mrs. Charles*, 1858.
9. For the Fount of living waters. *Kynaston*, 1862.
10. For the Fount of life eternal. *Neale* as above, 1865.
11. For the Fount of life eternal. *Littledale*, 1865.
12. For life's Eternal spring. *Morgan*, 1871.
13. The mind athirst pants for the fount, *R. B. Boswell's Ps. & Hys.*, 1838.   [J. J.]

Ad regias Agni dapes.

The Roman Breviary version of the Ambrosian *Ad coenam Agni providi*, above. It is the hymn at Vespers, "Sabbato in Albis," i.e. on Saturday in Easter-week, and afterwards on Sundays and week-days, when no Festival occurs and the Ferial Office is said, till the first Vespers of the Ascension. In addition to the ordinary editions of the *Rom. Brev.* the text is given in several modern Roman Catholic hymnals, Card. Newman's *Hymni Eccl.*, 1838–65; Biggs's *Annotated ed. of H. A. & M.*, 1867; *Daniel*, i. No 81, &c.   [W. A. S.]

Translations in C. U. :—

1. In garments dight of virgin white. By W. J. Copeland. 1st pub. in his *Hys. for the Week*, 1848, p. 81. In its original form it is not in C. U.; except in *Hys. and Introits*, 1852, No. 70, but as "*Now at the Lamb's high royal feast*," it was given in Murray's *Hymnal*, 1852, No. 57, and later collections. The opening line was borrowed from E. Caswall's *tr.* as under.

2. Now at the Lamb's high royal feast. By E. Caswall, in his *Lyra Catholica*, 1849, p. 94, and again in his *Hys. and Poems*, 1873, p. 53, in 7 st. of 4 l. This is the *tr.* usually found in Roman Catholic hymn-books. An altered form of this in 4 st. is No. 52 in the Irvingite *Hys. for the Use of the Churches*, 1864, beginning "*Guests at the banquet of the Lamb.*"

3. At the Lamb's High Feast we sing. By R. Campbell, written in 1849 [c. MSS.], and 1st printed in his collection commonly known as the *St. Andrew's Hymnal*, 1850, in 4 st. of 8 l. In the original MSS. the first two lines are added as a refrain to each verse, but are omitted in the printed text. Cooke and Denton's *Hymnal* was the first to bring it into prominent notice, although in an altered form which has been copied by many compilers. Its use exceeds that of all other *trs.* of the "Ad Regias Agni" put together; being found in a more or less correct form, in the most important collections of the Ch. of England. Many of the alterations in *H. A. and M.*, *Church Hys.*, *Thring*, and others date from Cooke and Denton's *Hymnal*, 1853, the *Salisbury H. Bk.*, 1857, and others. Another arrangement of Campbell's text is, "*To the* Lamb's High Feast we *press*," given in Rev. Francis Pott's *Coll.*, 1861, No. 90.

4. At the Lamb's right royal feast. By J. A. Johnston. 1st pub. in the 2nd ed. of his *English Hymnal*, 1856, No. 117, and repeated in the 3rd ed., 1861. It is an imitation, in the same metre, of R. Campbell's *tr.*, and takes the place of Johnston's *tr.* "Now at the banquet of the Lamb," in L.M., which appeared in the 1st ed. of the *English Hymnal*, 1852, No. 110.

5. The Banquet of the Lamb is laid. By R. C. Singleton, made for and first pub. in his *Anglican H. Bk.*, 1868, No. 119.

6. We keep the Festival. By A. R. Thompson, contributed to Schaff's *Christ in Song*, 1869.

7. Come, join the Kingly Banquet free. By F. Trappes, in his *Liturgical Hys.*, n. d., (1865), in 8 st. of 4 l. In 1871 st. i.–v. and viii. were given as a hymn in 3 st. of 8 l. in *Hys. and Carols*, Church Sisters' Home, St. John's Wood, 1871.

Translations not in C. U.:—
1. At the Lamb's regal banquet where. *Manual of Prayers and Litanies*, 1686.
2. From purple seas and land of toil. *Primer*, 1706.
3. Now at the Lamb's imperial Feast. *Bp. Mant*, 1837.
4. Passed the Red and angry sea. *Bp. Williams*, 1845.
5. The Red Sea now is passed. *Beste*, 1849.
6. In garments bright of saintly white. *Rorison*, 1851.
7. Come to the Lamb's right royal feast. *Wallace*, 1874.
8. Sing, for the dark Red Sea is past. *H. N. Oxenham*, 1867.   [J. J.]

Ad templa nos rursus vocat. *Charles Coffin.* [*Sunday Morning.*] In his *Hymni Sacri*, p. 8, ed. Paris, 1736, under the heading *Die Dominicâ ad Laudes Matutinas*. In the revised *Paris Brev.* of the Abp. Charles de Vintimille, 1736, it is the hymn for Sunday at Lauds; as also in the *Lyons* and other modern French Brevs. Text as above, and in Card. Newman's *Hymni Eccl.* 1838, p. 2. [W. A. S.]

Translations in C. U.:—
1. Morning lifts her dewy veil, by I. Williams, 1st pub. in the *British Mag.* 1834, vol. v. p. 28, in 9 st. of 4 l., and again in his *Hymns tr. from the Paris Brev.*, 1839, p. 3, and later editions. The following:—
2. Now morning lifts her dewy veil, is by J. Chandler, who, in his Preface to his *Hymns of the Prim. Church*, 1837, in which it appeared, thus alludes thereto:—

"I have ventured to take the greatest part of the 2nd hymn from the translation in the 'British Magazine,' which, notwithstanding the alterations I have made in it, still shines forth as the work of an evidently superior hand." p. ix.

This *tr.* has attained to a more extensive use than any other. It is given in *Mercer*, ed. 1864, No. 136, and *Sarum*, 1868, No. 293, in its full form. The most popular arrangement is that

of *Chope*, 1864, No. 111, Thring's *Coll.*, 1882, No. 9, and others, with omission of st. vii., viii., and some alterations.

3. Again the Sunday morn, by E. Caswall, appeared in his *Lyra Catholica*, 1849, p. 293, and again in his *Hymns and Poems*, 1873, p. 223. In its original form its use is very limited, but as:—

4. Again the holy morn, it is given in several collections, including the *Hymnary*, 1872, No. 7, *Hys. & Carols*, n. d., No. 15, the Roman Catholic *Hys. for the Year*, n. d., No. 83, and many others. Another form based upon Caswall's *tr.* is:—

5. When first the world sprang forth, in *Kennedy*, 1863, No. 701. It is probably by the editor, and is not found elsewhere.

6. Again the dawn gives warning meet. By Dr. Rorison, 1st pub. in his *Hys. and Anthems*, 1851, p. 10, in 4 st. of 8 l. and 1 st. of 4 l. It is repeated in later editions.

Translation not in C. U.:—
Once more the beams of orient light. *Chambers*, 1857.
            [J. J.]

Adam descended from above. *C. Wesley.* [*Lent.*] 1st pub. in his *Short Hymns*, &c., 1762, vol. i., No. 1044, but omitted from the 2nd ed., 1794. It was included in the *Wes. H. Bk.*, 1780, and is retained in the revised ed. of 1875, No. 129 (*P. Works*, 1868–72, vol. ix. p. 415). Another hymn by C. Wesley, beginning:—"Adam, descended from above, Thou only canst," &c., was pub. from his *MSS. Hymns on the Four Gospels*, in *P. Works of J. and C. Wesley*, 1868–72, vol. xi. p. 341, but it is not in common use.

Adam, our father and our head. *I. Watts.* [*The Fall.*] Appeared in his *Horæ Lyricæ*, 1706, in 13 st. of 4 l., and entitled "Jesus the only Saviour." Its use as a complete hymn is unknown. A cento therefrom of 5 st. was given in Rippon's *Bapt. Sel.*, 1787, No. 38, composed of st. i., ii., iv., v., and vii. This has passed into common use to a very limited extent.

Adam of St. Victor. Of the life of this, the most prominent and prolific of the Latin hymnists of the Middle Ages, very little is known. It is even uncertain whether he was an Englishman or a Frenchman by birth. He is described by the writers nearest to his own epoch, as *Brito*, which may indicate a native of either *Britain*, or *Brittany*. All that is certainly known concerning him is, that about A.D. 1130, after having been educated at Paris, he became, as quite a young man, a monk in the Abbey of St. Victor, then in the suburbs, but afterwards through the growth of that city, included within the walls of Paris itself. In this abbey, which, especially at that period, was celebrated as a school of theology, he passed the whole of the rest of his life, and in it he died, somewhere between the years 1172 and 1192 A.D. Possessed of "the pen of a ready writer," he seems to have occupied his life in study and authorship. Numerous as are the hymns and sequences satisfactorily proved to have been written by him, which have come down to us, there would seem to be little doubt that many more may have perished altogether, or are extant without his name attaching to them; while he was probably the author of several prose works as well. His Sequences remained in MS. in the care and custody of the monks of their author's Abbey, until the dissolution of that religious foundation at the Revolution; but some 37 of them, having found their way by degrees into more general circulation, were pub. by *Clichtoveus*, a Roman Catholic theologian of the first half of the 16th cent. in his *Elucidatorium Ecclesiasticum*, which passed through several editions from 1516 to 1556, at Paris, Basel and Geneva. Of the rest of the 106 Hymns and Sequences that we possess of Adam's, the largest part—some 47 remaining unpublished—were removed to the National Library in the Louvre at Paris, on the destruction of the Abbey. There they were discovered by M. Léon Gautier, the editor of the first *complete* edition of them, Paris, 1858.

The subjects treated of in Adam's Hymns and Sequences may be divided thus :—

Christmas 7; Circumcision, 1; Easter, 6; Ascension, 1; Pentecost, 5; Trinity, 2; the Dedication of a Church, 4, B. V. M., 17; Festivals of Saints, 53; The Invention of the Cross, 1; The Exaltation of the Cross, 1; On the Apostles, 3; Evangelists, 2; Transfiguration, 2.

Although all Adam of St. Victor's Sequences were evidently written for use in the services of his church, and were, doubtless, so used in his own Abbey, it is quite uncertain how many, if any, of them were used *generally* in the Latin Church.

To the lover of Latin hymns the works of this author should not be unknown, and probably are not; but they are far less generally known than the writings should be of one whom such an authority as Archbishop Trench describes as " the foremost among the sacred Latin poets of the Middle Ages." His principal merits may be described as comprising terseness and felicity of expression ; deep and accurate knowledge of Scripture, especially its typology; smoothness of versification; richness of rhyme, accumulating gradually as he nears the conclusion of a Sequence ; and a spirit of devotion breathing throughout his work, that assures the reader that his work is " a labour of love." An occasional excess of alliteration, which however at other times he uses with great effect, and a disposition to overmuch "playing upon words," amounting sometimes to "punning," together with a delight in heaping up types one upon another, till, at times, he succeeds in obscuring his meaning, are the chief defects to be set against the many merits of his style. Amongst the most beautiful of his productions may be mentioned, perhaps, his *Jucundare plebs fidelis; Verbi vere substantivi ; Potestate non natura; Stola regni laureatus ; Heri mundus exultavit; Laudes crucis attollamus* (Neale considers this " perhaps, his masterpiece "); *Ave, Virgo singularis ; Salve, Mater Salvatoris ; Animemur ad agonem;* and *Vox sonora nostri chori.* Where almost all are beautiful, it is difficult, and almost invidious, to make a selection. Of his Hymns and Sequences the following

editions, extracts, and translations have been published :—

i. *Original with Translations :*

(1) *Œuvres Poétiques d'Adam de S.-Victor. Par L. Gautier, Paris,* 1858. It is in two vols. duodecimo, and contains, besides a memoir of Adam of St. Victor, and an exhaustive essay upon his writings, a 15th cent. *tr.* into French of some 46 of the seqs., and full notes upon the whole series of them. (2) *The Liturgical Poetry of Adam of St. Victor, from the text of Gautier, with trs. into English in the original metres, and short explanatory notes by Digby S. Wrangham, M.A., St. John's Coll., Oxford, Vicar of Darrington, Yorkshire,* 3 vols. Lond., *Kegan Paul,* 1881. (3) In addition to these complete eds., numerous specimens from the originals are found in *Daniel, Mone, Königsfeld, Trench,* Loftie's *Latin Year,* Dom. Gueranger's *Année Liturgique, &c.*

ii. *Translations :—*

(1) As stated before, 46 of the Sequences are given by Gautier in a French *tr.* of the 15th cent. (2) In English we have *trs.* of the whole series by Digby S. Wrangham in his work as above ; 11 by Dr. Neale in *Med. Hymns:* 15, more freely, by D. T. Morgan in his *Hys. and other Poetry of the Latin Church ;* and one or more by Mrs. Charles, Mrs. Chester, C. S. Calverley, and the Revs. C. B. Pearson, E. A. Dayman, E. Caswall, R. F. Littledale, and Dean Plumptre. Prose *trs.* are also given in the Rev. Dom Laurence Shepherd's *tr.* into English of Dom Gueranger's works.

iii. *English Use:—*

From the general character of their metrical construction, it has not been possible to any great extent to utilise these very beautiful compositions in the services of the Anglican Church. The following, however, are from Adam of St. Victor, and are fully annotated in this work :—(1) in *H. A. & M.,* Nos. 64 and 434 (partly) ; (2) in the *Hymnary,* Nos. 270, 273, 324, 320, 382, 403, 418 ; (3) in the *People's H.,* 215, 277, 304 ; and (4) in *Skinner's Daily Service H.,* 236.   [D. S. W.]

Adami, Johann Christian, b. Jan. 13, 1662, at Luckau, Brandenburg, graduated M.A., at the University of Wittenberg, 1681, became diaconus, 1684, and pastor, 1691, at Luckau; from 1711 pastor primarius at Lübben, where he d. May 12, 1715.

His 25 hymns appeared in the *Evangelisches Zion, oder vollständiges G. B.,* Leipzig and Lübben, 1720, ed. by his son, for use in the Niederlausitz (*Bode,* p. 33; Wetzel's *A. H.,* vol. i., pt. i., p. 44; Jöcher's *Gelehrten Lexicon,* 1750, vol. i., col. 86). One has been *tr.,* viz. :—

Was klagst du mein Gemüthe. [*Cross and Consolation.*] Included as No. 1811 in the Berlin *G. L. S.,* 1832, and as No. 2396 in Knapp's *Ev. L. S.,* 1837 (1865, No. 2125). Dr. Jacobs, of Wernigerode, informs me that it appeared 1720 as above, p. 685, in 7 st. of 8 l. This is *tr.* as :—

"My soul, why this complaining," by Miss Burlingham, in the *British Herald,* 1866, p. 200, repeated as No. 337 in Reid's *Praise Bk.,* 1872.   [J. M.]

Adams, John, b. at Northampton, 1751; d. there, May 15, 1835. He was for several years a member of the Baptist denomination, but being expelled, on the ground of doctrine, from the chapel which he attended, he opened a place of worship on his own account and constituted himself the minister. On retiring from business in 1811, he removed to London, then to Olney, and finally returned to Northampton. Several of his hymns were printed in the *Gospel Magazine* in 1776. Very few, however, have come into general use.

Adams, John Greenleaf. Co-editor with Dr. E. H. Chapin of the Universalist *Hymns for Christian Devotion,* 1846 ; and, alone, of the *Gospel Psalmist,* 1861. He was b. in Portsmouth, New Hampshire, 1810. The collections named contain in each case 16 hymns by him. They are not, however, received outside his sect. The best are :—

1. **Heaven is here, its hymns of gladness.** [*Peace.*] Contributed to the *Hymns for Christian Devotion*, 1846, No. 419, in 4 st. of 4 l.

2. **God's angels ! not only on high do they sing.** [*Ministry of Angels.*] No. 830 in his *Gospel Psalmist*, 1861, and No. 240 in Longfellow and Johnson's *Hys. of the Spirit*, Boston. 1864.

[F. M. B.]

Adams, John Quincy. b. at Braintree (afterwards called "Quincy'"), Mass., 1767, was a son of President Adams. After graduating at Harvard College he was, from 1794 to 1801, minister to the Netherlands, to England, and to Prussia. In 1806 he was appointed Professor of Rhetoric in Harvard College ; in 1809 minister to Russia ; 1817 Secretary of State ; and, from 1824 to 1829, President of the United States. In 1831 he was elected a Member of the House of Representatives. Died suddenly, Feb. 21, 1848. His high position and principle are well known, as also the incidents of his political life. He was a member of the Unitarian body. His *Memoir*, by the Hon. Josiah Quincy, was published soon after his death, and also his *Poems of Religion and Society*, N. Y., 1848 (4th ed., 1854). He wrote, but never printed, an entire *Version of the Psalms*, seventeen of which, with five hymns, were inserted by his pastor, Dr. Lunt, in the *Christian Psalmist*, 1841. Of these the following are still in use :—

1. **Sure to the mansions of the blest.** [*Burial.*] This is part of a piece of 20 stanzas, which appeared in the *Monthly Anthology and Boston Review*, Jan., 1807. It is entitled "Lines addressed to a mother on the death of two infants, 19th Sept. 1803, and 19th Decr., 1806."

2. **Alas ! how swift the moments fly.** [*Time.*] Sometimes given as "How swift, alas, the moments fly," was written for the 200th anniversary of the First Congregational Church, Quincy, Sept. 29, 1839.

3. **Hark ! 'tis the holy temple bell.** [*Sunday.*] Of these Nos. 2 and 3 are found in *Lyra Sac. Amer.* and 2 in Putnam's *Singers and Songs of the Liberal Faith*, 1875.   [F. M. B.]

Adams, Nehemiah. b. at Salem, Mass., Feb. 19, 1806, and graduated at Harvard, 1826, and Andover, 1829. He was Congregational pastor at Cambridge, 1829–1834, and of Essex St. Church, Boston, 1834–1870. He d. 1878. In 1854 he published *South-side View of Slavery*, and in 1864 he edited *Church Pastorals*. His hymns are :—

1. **Come, take His offers now.** [*Invitation.*] An adaptation from C. Wesley, given in his *Church Pastorals*, 1864, and repeated in the *Hymns and S. of Praise*, N. Y., 1874.

2. **Saints in glory, we together.** [*Praise.*] This is also in *Ch. Pastorals* 1864, and the *Hys. & S. of Praise*, 1874, where it is said to be by "*S. E. Mahmied.*" This name, which has led compilers astray for some time, is purely fictitious.

[F. M. B.]

Adams, Sarah, née Flower. b. at Harlow, Essex, Feb. 22nd, 1805 ; d. in London, Aug. 14, 1848, and was buried at Harlow, Aug. 21, 1848. She was the younger daughter of Mr. Benjamin Flower, editor and proprietor of *The Cambridge Intelligencer ;* and was married, in 1834, to William B. Adams, a civil engineer. In 1841 she pub. *Vivia Perpetua*, a dramatic poem dealing with the conflict of heathenism and Christianity, in which Vivia Perpetua suffered martyrdom ; and in 1845, *The Flock at the Fountain ;* a catechism and hymns for children. As a member of the congregation of the Rev. W. J. Fox, an Unitarian minister in London, she contributed 13 hymns to the *Hys. and Anthems*, pub. by C. Fox, Lond., in 1841, for use in his chapel. Of these hymns the most widely known are— " Nearer, my God, to Thee," and "He sendeth sun, He sendeth shower." The remaining eleven, most of which have come into common use, more especially in America, are :—

1. Creator Spirit ! Thou the first. *Holy Spirit.*
2. Darkness shrouded Calvary. *Good Friday.*
3. Gently fall the dews of eve. *Evening.*
4. Go, and watch the Autumn leaves. *Autumn.*
5. O hallowed memories of the past. *Memories.*
6. O human heart ! thou hast a song. *Praise.*
7. O I would sing a song of praise. *Praise.*
8. O Love ! thou makest all things even. *Love.*
9. Part in Peace ! is day before us ? *Close of Service.*
10. Sing to the Lord ! for His mercies are sure. *Praise.*
11. The mourners came at break of day. *Easter.*

Mrs. Adams also contributed to Novello's musical edition of *Songs for the Months*, n. d. Nearly all of the above hymns are found in the Unitarian collections of G. Brit. and America. In Martineau's *Hymns of P. and P.*, 1873, No. 389, there is a rendering by her from Fénelon : —"Living or dying, Lord, I would be Thine." It appeared in the *Hys. and Anthems*, 1841.

Addiscott, Henry, b. at Devonport, 1806 ; educated for the Congregational Ministry ; ministered to charges at Torquay, 1837, Maidenhead, 1838–1843 ; and Taunton 1843–1860, and died suddenly in Liverpool, Oct. 2, 1860. He published no volume of poems or hymns, and is known to hymnology through his "And is there, Lord, a cross for me," a pleasing production on the words "Take up the cross and follow Me," which he contributed to the *New Cong.*, 1859, No. 650.

Addison, Joseph. b. at Milston, near Amesbury, Wiltshire, May 1, 1672, was the son of the Rev. Lancelot Addison, sometime Dean of Lichfield, and author of *Devotional Poems*, &c., 1699. Addison was educated at the Charterhouse, and at Magdalen Coll., Oxford, graduating B.A. 1691 and M.A. 1693. Although intended for the Church, he gave himself to the study of law and politics, and soon attained, through powerful influence, to some important posts. He was successively a Commissioner of Appeals, an Under Secretary of State, Secretary to the Lord Lieutenant of Ireland, and Chief Secretary for Ireland. He married, in 1716, the Dowager Countess of Warwick, and d. at Holland House, Kensington, June 17, 1719. Addison is most widely known through his contributions to *The Spectator, The Tatler, The Guardian*, and *The Freeholder*. To the first of these he contributed his hymns. His *Cato*, a tragedy, is well known and highly esteemed.

Addison's claims to the authorship of the hymns usually ascribed to him, or to certain of them, have been called in question on two occasions. The first was the publication, by Captain Thompson, of certain of those hymns in his ed. of the *Works of Andrew Marvell*, 1776, as the undoubted compositions of Marvell; and the second, a claim in the *Athenæum*, July 10th, 1880, on behalf of the Rev. Richard Richmond. Fully to elucidate the subject it will be necessary, therefore, to give a chronological history of the hymns as they appeared in the *Spectator* from time to time.

i. *The History of the Hymns in The Spectator.* —This, as furnished in successive numbers of the *Spectator*, is :—

1, The first of these hymns appeared in the *Spectator* of Saturday, July 20, 1719, No. 441, in 4 st. of 6 l. The article in which it appeared was on *Divine Providence*, signed " C." The hymn itself, " The Lord my pasture shall prepare," was introduced with these words :—

"David has very beautifully represented this steady reliance on God Almighty in his twenty-third psalm, which is a kind of pastoral hymn, and filled with those allusions which are usual in that kind of writing As the poetry is very exquisite, I shall present my readers with the following translation of it." (*Orig. Broadsheet, Brit. Mus.*)

2. The second hymn appeared in the *Spectator* on Saturday, Aug. 9, 1712, No. 453, in 13 st. of 4 l., and forms the conclusion of an essay on "Gratitude." It is also signed " C.," and is thus introduced :—

"I have already obliged the public with some pieces of divine poetry which have fallen into my hands, and as they have met with the reception which they deserve, I shall, from time to time, communicate any work of the same nature which has not appeared in print, and may be acceptable to my readers." (*Orig. Broadsheet, Brit. Mus.*)

Then follows the hymn :—" When all Thy mercies, O my God."

3. The number of the *Spectator* for *Tuesday*, Aug. 19, 1712, No. 461, is composed of three parts. The first is an introductory paragraph by Addison, the second, an unsigned letter from Isaac Watts, together with a rendering by him of Ps. 114th ; and the third, a letter from Steele. It is with the first two we have to deal. The opening paragraph by Addison is :—

" For want of time to substitute something else in the Room of them, I am at present obliged to publish Compliments above my Desert in the following Letters. It is no small Satisfaction, to have given Occasion to ingenious Men to employ their Thoughts upon sacred Subjects from the Approbation of such Pieces of Poetry as they have seen in my *Saturday's* papers. I shall never publish Verse on that Day but what is written by the same Hand ; yet shall I not accompany those Writings with *Eulogiums*, but leave them to speak for themselves." (*Orig. Broadsheet, Brit. Mus.*)

In his letter Dr. Watts, after some compliments to " Mr. Spectator," says :—

" Upon reading the hymns that you have published in some late papers, I had a mind to try yesterday whether I could write one. The 114th Psalm appears to me an admirable ode, and I began to turn it into our language"...and more to the same effect, finishing with: " If the following essay be not too incorrigible, bestow upon it a few brightenings from your genius, that I may learn how to write better, or write no more."

The hymn which follows is—" When Israel, freed from Pharaoh's hand," in 6 st. of 4 l. Although this rendering of Ps. 114 is unsigned in the *Spectator*, its authorship is determined by its republication in Dr. Watts's *Psalms of David*, 1719.

4. According to the promise thus given the remaining hymns in the *Spectator* appeared *in every case, on a Saturday.* The first was :— " The spacious firmament on high," which appeared on Saturday, Aug. 23rd, 1712, No. 465, that is, four days after the promise made in the note to Dr. Watts's letter and hymn. It is in 3 st. of 8 l. signed " C.," and is introduced at the close of an essay on the proper means of strengthening and confirming faith in the mind of man. The quotation, " The heavens declare the glory of God," Ps. xix. 1, &c., is followed by these words :—

" As such a bold and sublime manner of Thinking furnished out very noble Matter for an Ode, the Reader may see it wrought into the following one." (*Orig. Broadsheet, Brit. Mus.*)

5. The next hymn was given in the *Spectator* on Saturday, Sep. 20th, 1712, No. 489, in 10 st. of 4 l., and signed " O." It begins :—" How are Thy servants blest, O Lord," and closes an essay on " Greatness " as a source of pleasure to the imagination with special reference to the ocean. It is thus introduced :—

" Great painters do not only give us Landskips of Gardens, Groves, and Meadows, but very often employ their Pencils upon Sea-Pieces. I could wish you would follow their example If this small Sketch may deserve a Place among your Works, I shall accompany it with a Divine Ode, made by a Gentleman upon the Conclusion of his Travels." (*Orig. Broadsheet, Brit. Mus.*)

The " Travels " alluded to are evidently those of Addison on the Continent from 1699 to 1702. Referring to an incident in his return voyage, Lord Macaulay, in his essay on Addison in the *Edinburgh Review* of July, 1843, says :—

" In December, 1700, he embarked at Marseilles. As he glided along the Ligurian coast, he was delighted by the sight of myrtles and olive trees, which retained their verdure under the winter solstice. Soon, however, he encountered one of the black storms of the Mediterranean. The captain of the ship gave up all for lost, and confessed himself to a capuchin who happened to be on board. The English heretic, in the meantime, fortified himself against the terrors of death with devotions of a very different kind. How strong an impression this perilous voyage made on him, appears from the Ode, ' How are Thy servants blest, O Lord !' which was long after published in the *Spectator*."

6. The last hymn of this series was :—" When rising from the bed of death." It appeared in the *Spectator* on Saturday, Oct. 18th, 1712, No. 513, in 6 st. of 4 l. and signed " O." It is appended to a letter purporting to have been written by an " excellent man in Holy Orders whom I have mentioned more than once as one of that society who assist me in my speculations." The subject is " Sickness," and the concluding words are :—

" It is this Series of Thoughts that I have endeavoured to express in the following Hymn, which I have composed during this my Sickness."

7. The whole of these hymns, including that by Watts, have been in common use during most of the past, and during the whole of the present century ; and although lacking the popularity which they once possessed, they are still found in the front rank in all English-speaking countries. They have also been translated into various languages, including, " The Lord my pasture," &c. ; " When all Thy mercies," &c. ; " The spacious firmament," &c., into Latin in the Rev. R. Bingham's *Hymnologia Christiana Latina*, 1871,

ii. *Addison's Claims.*—The claims of Addison to the authorship of five of these six hymns (omitting that by Dr. Watts) are not of a character to be removed or explained away. 1. First we find them included in essays which are acknowledged to be his and bear his recognised signatures " C." and " O." 2. They are clearly by the same writer as the prose of the essays, and are the natural outcome and reproduction, in metre, of their turns of thought and modes of expression. 3. They are all *Saturday* hymns, and are declared by Addison himself to be in every case " by the same hand." That the hand was the hand of Addison is evident from a curious side-light which is thrown upon the subject by comparing the passage with which he introduced the hymn " When all Thy mercies," &c., on Saturday, Aug. 9, 1712, as given in the original Broadsheet of that day, and the same passage as rewritten, and published in the *first edition in book form* of the *Spectator*, late in the same year. The first (although already quoted we give it again for readiness of comparison) is :

" I have already obliged the public with some pieces of divine poetry which have fallen into my hands, and as they have met with the reception which they deserve, I shall, from time to time, communicate any work of the same nature which has not appeared in print, and may be acceptable to my readers." (*Orig. Broadsheet, Brit. Mus.*)

This passage reads thus in the *first ed.* of the *Spectator*, in book form, 1712 :—

" I have already communicated to the public some pieces of Divine Poetry, and as they have met with a very favourable reception, I shall from time to time publish any work of the same nature which has not yet appeared in print, and may be acceptable to my readers." (*Spectator*, 1st ed. *King's Copy, Brit. Mus.*)

This last reading is repeated in all subsequent editions of the *Spectator*, and was evidently rewritten to remove the somewhat unbecoming assertion that the hymns " have met with the reception *which they deserve ;* " to harmonize it with the paragraphs concerning hymns in later numbers of the *Spectator ;* and to render it and them uniformly consistent with the received impression that he was the author of those pieces of " Divine Poetry" which appeared in the *Saturday* numbers of the *Spectator*.

4. Addison died in 1719. In 1721 Thomas Tickell, one of the contributors to the *Spectator*, and to whom Addison left his papers with directions concerning their use, published the same in 4 vols., as *The Works of the Right Honourable Joseph Addison, Esqr.*, London, *Printed for Jacob Tonson, at Shakespear's Head, over against Katharine Street in the Strand, M.DCC.XXI.* In these vols. both the Essays and the Hymns are given. They are also repeated in *The Christian Poet. A Miscellany of Divine Poems all written by the late Mr. Secretary Addison, &c.*, London, *Printed for E. Curll, in the Strand. M.DCC.XX.VIII.* The positive evidence for Addison is thus complete.

iii. *Andrew Marvell.*—The first and only claim on behalf of Marvell was made by Captain Edward Thompson in *The Works of Andrew Marvell, Esqr. Poetical, Controversial, and Political, containing many original Letters, Poems and Tracts never before printed,* with a New Life of the Author. By Cap. Edward Thompson, in 3 vols. London, *Printed for the Editor, by Henry Baldwin. M.DCC.LXX.VI.* In his *Preface* to this work Thompson says :—

" Since the death of Mr. Thomas Hollis I have been favoured by his successor with many anecdotes, manuscripts, and scarce compositions of our author, such as I was unable to procure anywhere else ; and by the attention and friendship of Mr. Thomas Raikes, I have been put in possession of a volume of Mr. Marvell's poems, some written with his own hand, and the rest copied by his orders ; this valuable acquisition was many years in the care of Mr. Nettleton, which serves now (in his own words) to detect the theft and ignorance of some writers."

Thompson then proceeds in the same *Preface* to give extracts from this MS. but without naming, in any instance, the handwriting in which he found the quotations, thus leaving it an open question as to whether any given piece was in the handwriting of Marvell, or of some one else. The hymns in the *Spectator* which he claims for Marvell are :—" When Israel, freed from Pharaoh's hand" (Dr. Watts) ; " When all Thy mercies, O my God ; " and " The spacious firmament on high." The first of these he vehemently and coarsely accuses Tickell of stealing from Marvell ; the reason for attacking Tickell, instead of Addison, arising probably out of the fact that Steele's letter in the same number of the *Spectator* as the hymn, as noted above, is signed " T." This ignorance on his part of Steele's signature, is equalled by his further ignorance of the fact that the piece in question was given by Dr. Watts as his own in his *Psalms of David*, in 1719, and had thus been before the public as Watts's acknowledged work, for some 57 years!

The argument as against Addison for the two remaining hymns is summed up in the accusation of theft on Addison's part, and the statement :—

" How these came to Mr. Addison's hands I cannot explain ; but by his words [' I have already communicated,' &c., as above] they seem to be remitted by correspondents, and might perhaps come from the relations of Marvell."

To this we need only add that in no subsequent collection of Marvell's *Works* are these claims made, or the pieces reprinted : and that the able and learned editor of *The Complete Works in Verse and Prose of Andrew Marvell, M.P.*, the Rev A. B. Grosart (*Fuller Worthies Library*), maintains in his " Memorial Introduction," pp. lxii.-lxiv., that—

" The claim put in by Captain Thompson for Marvell having written the well-known Songs of Zion, called Paraphrases, commencing, ' The spacious firmament on high,' and ' When all Thy mercies, O my God,' and ' When Israel, freed from Pharaoh's hand,' and also the celebrated ballad of ' William and Margaret,' cannot be sustained. As matter of fact it went by default at the time the claim was originally made, seeing that, challenged to produce the MS. book alleged to contain these pieces, it *never was produced*, and seems to have been destroyed. I have no idea that Captain Thompson meant to impose ; but from his own account it is clear that while the MS. volume evidently contained many of Marvell's own poems—and for three of the greatest (one being the *Horatian Ode*) we are indebted to it—it is clear that subsequent, and long subsequent, to Marvell, some other scribe had turned the vacant leaves into an album or commonplace book."

The discussion of the claims on behalf of Marvell, which appeared in the *Gentleman's Magazine*, 1776, has not been overlooked. As, however, the writers argued from insufficient data, it would have produced confusion to have noticed that discussion in detail.

iv. *Richard Richmond.*—The latest claim to the authorship of the piece " When all Thy mercies, O my God," has been made on behalf of one Richard Richmond, sometime Rector of Walton-on-the-Ribble, Lancashire. This hymn is found in an *undated* letter in the MS. correspondence of John Ellis, one of Queen Anne's Under Secretaries of State. The writer of the letter begs for preferment at the hands of Ellis. The hymn is thus referred to therein :—

" Appropriate this most excellent hymn, suitable, sir, to your excellent virtues, and hope it may prove a motive for your honour's Christian benevolence to the author in adversity, to comfort the sorrows in life, shall be thankful to Heaven, and your worship's most gracious hand." (*Athenæum, July* 10, 1880.)

In addition to the arguments already set forth on behalf of Addison, we have, in this *undated* extract of bad English, a clear proof that the writer could never have penned those lines which appeared in the *Spectator* of Saturday, Aug. 9, 1712. The paragraph also, when rightly construed, shows that by the term *author* used therein, Richmond meant himself as the *writer* of the letter, and not as the *author* of the hymn. It is quite clear that he copied the hymn from the *Spectator*, and incorporated it, with slight alterations, in his letter, to give grace to his ill-worded appeal for preferment at the hands of Ellis.

From a literary, as distinct from a historical, point of view, there is abundant proof in the Essays and the Hymns that they were, in each case, the prose and poetic expressions of the same hand. This has already been indicated in the titles we find given to the Essays. One example will show how conclusively this argument may be wrought out. It is from No. 453, on " Gratitude " :—

" If gratitude is due from man to man, how much more from man to his Maker? The Supreme Being does not only confer upon us those bounties, which proceed more immediately from His hand, but even those benefits which are conveyed to us by others. Every blessing we enjoy, by what means so ever it may be derived upon us, is the gift of Him who is the great Author of good, and Father of mercies."

This thought is then illustrated by references to the examples set to Christian poets by Greek and Latin poets and Jewish writers, who all excel in their Odes of adoration and praise; and the essay closes with :—

" When all Thy mercies, O my God,
  My rising soul surveys;
Transported with the view, I'm lost
  In wonder, love, and praise."

In this the thought, style, and mode of expression, so far as prose and verse can agree, are the same, both in the Essay and in the Hymn. This evidence is also strengthened when we find that the *Hymns*, when compared with Addison's *Poems*, are strongly marked by the same individuality. We may add that Addison's signature varied in the *Spectator*, and embraced the letters " C," " L," " I," and " O "; and that the original text of each hymn is given in all good editions of that work.

[J. J.]

Addison, Lancelot, D.D., father of the above, b. at Crosby Ravensworth, Westmoreland. 1632, and educated at Queen's Coll.,

Oxford. Until the Restoration he spent part of his time at Oxford and part in retirement. He then became chaplain to the garrison at Dunkirk : and in 1663, to that at Tangier. In 1670 he was appointed Chaplain in Ordinary to the King, shortly after, Rector of Milston, Wilts, and Prebendary in the Cathedral of Salisbury. Finally, in 1683, he was preferred to the Deanery of Lichfield; d. 1703. In addition to some prose works, he published *Devotional Poems, Festival and practical, on some of the chief Christian Festivals, Fasts, Graces, and Virtues, &c.* Lond., Henry Bonwick, 1699.   [J. J.]

Ades Pater supreme. *Prudentius.* [*Evening.*] Given in all editions of his works, including *Aurelii Prudentii Clementis V. C., Opera Omnia,* vol. i. pp. 97–105, with notes (Lond., Valpy, 1824). It is No. vi. of the *Cathemerinon,* and extends to 152 lines. Of the complete hymn we have no *tr.* into English, but three centos therefrom have been *tr.* thus :

1. **Ades Pater supreme—Be present, Holy Father.** By J. M. Neale, in the enlarged ed. of the *Hymnal N.,* 1854, No. 10, being a rendering of ll. 1–12, 125–128, 141–152, and a doxology not in the original. This was repeated in the *People's H.* 1867, No. 436, and with alterations in the *Hymnary,* 1872, No. 17. In this last, two sts. (v. vi.) were added from ll. 129–132, and 137–140. This cento is usually given for Sunday evening.

2. **Fluxit labor diei—The toil of day is over.**— By J. A. Johnston, added to his *English Hymnal,* 1861, No. 256. It is a free rendering based upon st. iii.–vii. of Dr. Neale, as above.

3. **Cultor Dei memento—Servant of God, remember.** This portion of the hymn, given in *Daniel,* i., No. 110 ; Card. Newman's *Hy. Eccl.* 1838 and 1865 ; *Wackernagel* and others, is composed of ll. 125–152, with the addition of a doxology. It was used in the *Sarum Brev.* " At Compline on Passion Sunday, and Daily up to Maundy Thursday." Also in the *Mozarabic Brev.;* the *Mozarabic Hymnarium;* and in an 11th cent. MS. in the British Museum (Harl. 2961, f. 238). The *tr.* in C. U. is :—" Servant of God ! remember," by W. J. Blew. First printed with music on a broadsheet, and then in *The Ch. Hy. and Tune Bk.,* 1852 ; 2nd ed. 1855. It is from the *Sarum* text, and in 7 st. of 4 l. In 1870 it was included in Mr. Rice's *Hymns,* No. 105.

Translations not in C. U. :—

1. Remember, thou who lov'st the Lord. *Hy. Angl.* 1844.
2. Christian, ever keep in mind. *Copeland.* 1848.
3. Child of God ! remember thou. *Chambers.* 1857.
4. Come, Great Father, Mighty Lord,—*Francis Turner* (Bp. of Ely), in Dodd's *Christian's Magazine,* Sep., 1761.

[J. J.]

Adeste, Coelitum chori. *Nicholas le Tourneaux.* [*Easter.*] In the revised *Paris Breviary,* 1736, this hymn was for the Ferial Office at Matins (Sundays included) in Eastertide, beginning on Low Sunday and continuing to the Feast of the Ascension, and is marked with the initials " N. T." It is also used in like manner in the *Lyons* and other modern French Breviaries. The *Paris Brev.* text was reprinted in Card. Newman's *Hymni Ecclesiae,* 1838 and 1865, and J. Chandler's *Hys. of the Prim. Church,* 1837, No. 68. [W. A. S.]

Translations in C. U. :—

1. Angels, come on joyous pinion. By I. Williams, 1st pub. in his *Hys. tr. from the Paris Brev.*, 1839, p. 128, in 6 st. of 6 l. In 1851 it was given, somewhat altered, by Dr. Rorison in his *Hys. and Anthems*, No. 81. In the *Anglican H. Bk.*, 2nd ed., 1871, No. 152, it is altered to "Come, once more with songs descending."

2. Heavenly choirs with anthems sweet. By R. Campbell, written in 1849 [C. MSS.], and included in his collection commonly known as the *St. Andrew's Hymnal*, 1850, in 6 st. of 4 l. It is the most popular of the renderings of the "Adeste, Coelitum." In 1853 it was given, with alterations, and the omission of st. iii., in the Cooke and Denton *Hymnal*, No. 87. This was repeated by *Kennedy*, 1863, No. 697, with the addition of "Alleluia," as a refrain to each verse. In the *Appendix* to the *Hymnal N.*, enlarged ed., 1864, No. 38, st. iii. is restored; but the doxology is displaced in favour of a much weaker rendering. In Mr. Shipley's *Annus Sanctus*, 1884, the *tr.* is given from the Campbell MSS., and st. iii., vi., vii. are added by J. C. Earle.

3. Angels to our Jubilee. By W. J. Blew. 1st printed on a broadsheet for use in his church [E. MSS.], and then in his *Hy. and Tune Bk.*, 1852, in 8 st. of 4 l. This was repeated in the *People's H.*, 1867, No. 119, and *Rice's Sel.* from *Blew*, 1870, No. 50.

4. Come, ye heavenly Choirs descending. By Bp. J. R. Woodford, contributed to his *Hymns*, &c., 1852, No. 38, and republished in the *Parish H. Bk.*, 1863 and 1875 ; Chope's *Hymnal*, 1864, No. 100, and other collections. It is in 6 st. of 4 l., of which st. v. is from I. Williams as above.

Translations not in C. U. :—
1. Come, thou blest angelic throng. *Chandler*, 1837.
2. Descend from Heaven, ye Angel choirs. *Chambers*, 1857.   [J. J.]

Adeste fideles laeti triumphantes.

[*Christmas.*] As to the authorship and actual date of this hymn nothing positive is known. It has been ascribed to St. Bonaventura, but is found in no edition of his *Works*. Most probably it is a hymn of the 17th or 18th century, and of French or German authorship. The text appears in three forms. The first is in 8 st., the second, that in use in France, and the third the English use, both in Latin and English. The full text from *Thesaurus Animae Christianae*, Mechlin, N.D. (where it is given as a second sequence for Christmas and said to be "Ex Graduali Cisterciensi ") is :—

1.   Adeste, fideles,
     Laeti triumphantes;
Venite, venite in Bethlehem;
     Natum videte
     Regem Angelorum :
Venite adoremus Dominum.
	4. Stellâ duce, Magi
	     Christum adorantes,
	Aurum, thus, et myrrham,
	     dant munera.
	     Jesu infanti
	     Corda praebeamus :
	Venite adoremus Dominum.

2.   Deum de Deo ;
     Lumen de Lumine,
Gestant puellae viscera
     Deum Verum,
     Genitum non factum :
Venite adoremus Dominum.
	5. Aeterni Parentis
	     Splendorem Aeternum,
	Velatum sub carne videbimus,
	     Deum infantem,
	     Pannis involutum,
	Venite adoremus Dominum.

3.   En grege relicto,
     Humiles ad cunas,
Vocati pastores approperant.
     Et nos ovanti
     Gradu festinemus,
Venite adoremus Dominum.
	6. Pro nobis egenum
	     Et foeno cubantem
	Piis foveamus amplexibus ;
	     Sic nos amantem
	     Quis non redameret ?
	Venite adoremus Dominum.

7.   Cantet nunc hymnos,
     Chorus Angelorum :
Cantet nunc aula celestium,
     Gloria
     In excelsis Deo !
Venite adoremus Dominum.
	8. Ergo Qui natus
	     Die hodiernâ,
	Jesu Tibi sit gloria :
	     Patris Aeterni
	     Verbum Caro factum !
	Venite adoremus Dominum

In the English and French centos there are various readings; but we need only note three —st. v., l. 1, *Patris* for "Parentis"; st. vii., l. 1, *Io* for "hymnos"; and rarely, *exultans*, for "nunc hymnos"; st. viii., l. 2, *hodierno*, for "hodiernâ :" and of these the second is probably the original text. The English cento is composed of st. i., ii., vii. and viii., and the French, generally of st. i., iii., v., vi., and, very rarely, st. iv. also. Towards the close of the last century it was sung both in England and in France at Benediction during Christmastide. As early as 1797 the hymn was sung at the Chapel of the Portuguese Embassy, of which Vincent Novello was organist, and the tune (ascribed by Novello to John Reading, organist of Winchester Cathedral, 1675–1681, and of the College to 1692) at once became popular. The use of the French cento may be gathered from the following rubric from the *Nouveau Paroissien Nantais*, Nantes, 1837 :—

Aux Fêtes de Noël.

(*Response.*) Venite adoremus, venite adoremus, venite adoremus Dominum.

Les Chantres continuent : Adeste, fideles, etc.; et on répète à chaque strophe : Venite, etc.

The hymn was so familiar that it is not printed in full.

We find st. i., iii., v., and vi., in the *Office de St. Omer*, St. Omers, 1822, in the *Paroissien Complet du Diocèse d'Autun*, Autun, 1837, in the *Amiens Paroissien*, 1844, in the *Rouen Paroissien*, Rouen, 1873, and in the *Paroissien Romain*, Paris, N.D., but c. 1868, st. i., iii., iv., v. and vi., which are also in an undated Tours *Paroissien*. In the *Paroissien Complet*, Paris, of which the "Approbation" is dated July, 28th, 1827, the hymn is given in both the English and French forms. At p. 583 it occurs as, "Hymne Qui se chante, dans plusieurs églises de Paris pendant le temps de la Nativité;" this is the English form, with various readings, consisting of st. i., ii., vii., viii.; then follows, "Hymne pour le temps de Noël," the ordinary French version st. i., iii., v. and vi., and both also occur in *A Coll. of Ps., H., Anthems, &c.*, Washington, 1830.

                       [W. T. B.]

Translations in C. U. :—

1. Come, faithful all, rejoice and sing. Anon. in 4 st. of 5 l. in *Every Families Assistant at Compline, Benediction, &c.*, 1789. Somewhat altered it was republished in G. L. Haydock's *Coll. of Catholic Hys.*, 1823. In the *Vespers : or, Evening Office of the Church*, Dublin, 1808, it appeared as "Ye faithful souls, rejoice and sing." This is in use in a few Roman Catholic collections for Missions and Schools. In the *Crown of Jesus H. Bk.*, it reads, "Ye faithful, come, rejoice and sing."

2. Ye faithful, approach ye. By F. Oakeley. This is a *tr.* of the English form of the Latin text. It was written in 1841 for the use of the congregation of Margaret Street Chapel, London, of which he was then the Incumbent. It was never published by the translator, but came into notice by being sung in his chapel. The original text was included in the *People's H.*, 1867, No. 24, the *Wellington College H. Bk.*, 1863, &c., and has also been repeated in several Roman Catholic collections of recent date.

3. **O come all ye faithful, joyfully triumphant.** This form of Canon Oakeley's *tr.* is the most popular arrangement of the *Adeste fideles* we possess. It first appeared in Murray's *Hymnal*, 1852, and has passed from thence into a great number of collections both in G. Britain and other English-speaking countries, the second line sometimes reading "Joyful *and* triumphant," and again "*Rejoicing*, triumphant." The *Parish H. Bk.*, 1863–75, adopts this latter reading, and in addition it includes other alterations of importance.

4. **Be present, ye faithful.** In Chope's *Hymnal*, 1854, and later editions, is Canon Oakeley's *tr.* re-written.

5. **Approach, all ye faithful.** This *tr.* by " C." in the Irvingite *Hys. for the Use of the Churches*, 1864, dates from 1845. Another *tr.* beginning with the same first line, was included in the Cooke and Denton *Hymnal*, 1853. It can be distinguished easily from the Irvingite *tr.* by st. iv. This reads in Cooke and Denton, " The Son Everlasting," and in the Irvingite collections, " To Thee, who on this joyous day," &c.

6. **O come, all ye faithful, triumphantly sing.** By E. Caswall, 1st pub. in his *Lyra Catholica*, 1849, p. 250, and in his *Hys. and Poems*, 1873, p. 146. This *tr.* is in several collections, and sometimes slightly altered, as in the *New Mitre*, 1874, and others.

7. **Come hither, ye faithful.** This, as given in Schaff's *Christ in Song*, 1870, p. 37 ; and the Prot. Episco. *Hymnal*, 1872, is E. Caswall's *tr.* with alterations.

8. **O come, all ye faithful.** By W. Mercer. This *tr.* can be distinguished from others beginning with the same first line by the st. iii., which reads, " Raise, raise, choir of angels," &c. It was written for and first appeared in his *Ch. Psalter and H. Bk.*, 1854. In popularity it ranks next to the *tr.* by Canon Oakeley, being found in many collections throughout English-speaking countries.

9. **Be present, ye faithful.** By J. M. Neale. Pub. in the *Hymnal N.*, enlarged ed., 1858. Although opening with the same line it is a different *tr.* from that in Chope's *Hymnal*, noted above. The second stanza of *Chope* reads : " Very God of Very God," and this "God of God, eternal."

10. **O come, all ye faithful.** Two *trs.* by J. A. Johnston are given in his *English Hymnal*, the first (with st. ii., " He, God of God," &c.) in 1852, the second (st. ii., " Who God of God is ") in 2nd ed., 1856, and 3rd ed., 1861.

11. **Draw nigh, all ye faithful.** This is Dr. Neale's *tr.* re-written by J. Keble for the *Salisbury H. Bk.*, 1857. It was repeated in *Kennedy*, 1863, and, with slight changes, in the *Sarum H.*, 1868.

12. **O come, all ye faithful.** By J. Ellerton, written for, and first pub. in *Church Hys.*, 1871. It may be known by st. iv., which opens with

"Thou, who didst deign to be born for us this morning."

13. **Draw near, all ye faithful.** By R. C. Singleton, in the revised ed. of his *Anglican H. Bk.*, 1871.

14. **Assemble, ye faithful.** By T. Darling, in his *Hys. for the Ch. of England*, 1861.

15. **O come, all ye faithful.** This arrangement in the *Westminster Abbey H. Bk.*, 1884, is a cento compiled from the above *trs.*

16. **Hither, ye faithful, haste with songs of triumph.** In the American Presb. *Ps. & Hys.* Philadelphia, 1843, No. 174.

These *trs.* have as a rule much in common. The greatest variety is found in the rendering of the lines in st. ii., "Deum de Deo, Lumen de lumine." These are :—

God of God, light of light. *Oakeley.*
True God of God, true Light of Light. *Irvingite Coll.*
True Son of the Father. *E. Caswall.*
He God of God, Light of Light Eternal. *J. A. Johnston.*
God of God eternal, Light from Light proceeding. *J. M. Neale.*
True God of True God, True Light of True Light. *Cooke & Denton.*
Very God of Very God, Light of Light Eternal. *Chope's Hymnal.*
Though true God of true God, Light of Light Eternal. *W. Mercer.*
Who God of God is, Light of Light Eternal. *J. A. Johnston.*
God-head of God-head, True Light of the True Light. *Gainsburgh Coll.*
Godhead of Godhead, True light of True light. *Dr. Irons.*
God of God Almighty, Light of Light Eternal. *Sarum Hymnal.*
He, God of God, and Light of Light begotten. *J. Ellerton.*
True God of True God, Light of Light Eternal. *Thring's Coll.*
Though God of true God, Light of Light Eternal. Irish *Church Hymnal.*
For He, God of God, He, Light of Light eternal. *R. C. Singleton*, 1871.

These renderings show clearly that the majority of the translators had the *Nicene Creed* and not the *Adeste fideles* in their minds as they wrote. This is also the case with those *trs.* which are not in C. U.

Translations not in C. U. :—

1. Draw near, ye faithful Christians. *Evening Office of the Church*, 1760.
2. Ye faithful, come triumphant, come. *Orthodox Churchman's Magazine and Review*, Nov., 1805.
3. Raise we our voices to the Lord of Glory. *Ashbourne Coll.*, Uttoxeter, 1808.
4. Believers assemble, come with songs to Bethlem. Dr. Sutton's *Ps. & Hys.*, Sheffield, 1807.
5. Ye faithful, triumphant enter into Bethlehem. *Ps. & Hys.* Burnley, 1820.
6. O come, all ye faithful, joyful triumph raising. Basil Woodd. *Ps. & Hys.*, 1821.
7. With hearts truly grateful. *Ps. & Hys.* Washington, 1830.
8. O come, ye faithful, and your homage bring. *J. Chandler*, 1837.
9. O come, all ye faithful, raise the hymn of glory. F. C. Husenbeth's *Missal for Use of the Laity* (3rd ed.), 1840.
10. Ye faithful souls, approach and sing. J. Meade. *Selwood Wreath*, 1841.
11. Approach, ye faithful, come with exultation. Jane E. Leeson. *Christian Child's Bk.*, 1848.
12. Approach, ye faithful, and with glad accord. Jane E. Leeson. *Christian Child's Bk.*, 1848.
13. O hasten, ye faithful. J. R. Beste *Church Hys.*, 1849.

14. O come, all ye faithful. G. Rorison. *Hys. & Anthems*, 1851.

15. O come, all ye faithful. R. Campbell. *St. Andrew's Hymnal*, 1850.

16. Ye faithful, approach ye. W. J. Blew. *Church H. & Tune Bk.*, 1852.

17. O Christian people, come. I. Gregory Smith. *H. Bk. for the Service of the Church*, 1855.

18. Exulting triumphant, come from every nation. Anon. Guernsey, Reprinted in *Notes & Queries*, 5th Ser. xi. p. 418.

19. O hie, ye believers, raise the song of triumph. F. Trappes, 1865.

20. Come, all ye faithful, joyfully. *Anon.* in J. F. Thrupp's *Ps. & Hys.*, 1853.

21. In triumph, joy, and holy fear. J. C. Earle. Shipley's *Annus Sanctus*, 1884.

22. Come, O faithful, with sweet voice. C. Kent. Shipley's *Annus Sanctus*, 1884.   [J. J.]

Adesto sancta Trinitas. [*Holy Trinity*.]

The authorship of this short hymn on the Holy Trinity is unknown. Its earliest form is in a ms. of the 11th cent. in the *British Museum* (Vesp. D. xii. f. 115*b*) printed in the *Latin Hys. of the Anglo-Saxon Church*, 1851, p. 161. Amongst the English Breviaries it is in those of *York, Hereford,* and *Sarum;* on the Continent, those of *Mainz* and *Basel;* and also in those of the Orders of the *Carmelites, Dominicans,* and *Fratres Humiliati;* but with varying texts. In *Mone*, i. p. 10, the text is given together with references to mss., and notes on the text; the oldest ms. dating from the 14th cent. He also gives two refrains which are sometimes associated with the hymn. *Daniel*, i. No. 304, gives only the first four lines with a reference to *Cassander;* but in iv. p. 234, he gives the full text as in *Mone*, together with *Mone's* references. It is also in Neale's *Hymni Ecclesiae*, 1851, p. 157; *Hymn. Sarisb.* 1851, p. 115; the *Domin. H. Bk.*, &c. [W. A. S.]

Translations in C. U. :—

1. **Be present, Holy Trinity; Like Splendour, &c.** By J. M. Neale. Appeared in the *Hymnal N.* 1852, No. 35, in 5 st. of 4 l., and again in later editions. In 1867 it was repeated, unaltered, in the *People's H.*, No. 161, and in the *Hymnary*, 1872, No. 337.

2. **Be with us, Holy Trinity.** By J. A. Johnston, 1st pub. in 2nd ed. of his *English Hymnal*, 1856, No. 148, in 5 st. of 5 l. In *Kennedy*, 1863, No. 1122, it is slightly altered, specially in the doxology.

3. **Be present, Holy Trinity; Co-equal light, &c.** By J. D. Chambers, in his *Lauda Syon*, Pt. i., 1857, p. 215, in 5 st. of 4 l. In the *Salisbury H. Bk.* 1857, No. 123, and *Sarum*, 1868, No. 179, the *tr.* is an arrangement by J. Keble from Dr. Neale with lines 1, 2, of st. i. from this *tr.* by J. D. Chambers.

4. **O Holy Trinity! be present.** By F. Pott, in his *Hys. fitted to the Order of Com. Pr.*, 1861, No. 107, in 5 st. of 4 l., and in later editions.   [J. J.]

Adored for ever be the Lord. [*Ps. xxviii.*]

This cento in the Amer. *Episcopal Hymnal*, 1872, No. 421, is composed; st. i., of 4 lines, from *Tate and Brady's* version of Ps. 28, and st. ii.-iv. Anon.

Adoro Te devote, latens Deitas. *St. Thomas of Aquino.* [*Holy Communion*].

Of the actual date of the composition of this hymn we have no record. As in 1259 the author was engaged in Paris in writing on the Eucharist, and in 1263, in drawing up the existing office for the festival of *Corpus Christi,* at the request of Pope Urban IV., and for which he wrote the well-known hymns, *Pange lingua gloriosi Corporis mysterium; Lauda Sion; Sacris solemniis;* and *Verbum supernum* (q. v.), we may fix the date, somewhat indefinitely, as c. 1260. Although never incorporated in the public services of the Church, it was added at an early date to various Missals for private devotion.

In 1841 *Daniel* included it in vol. i. No. 242 with a short note. In 1853 he was followed by *Mone*, No. 209, with a slightly differing text, from a Reichenau ms. of the 13th or 14th cents., and extended notes, references, various readings and critical remarks; together with two refrains, one, which follows each stanza, (in Paar's *Nucl. Devot.* p. 232, and in *Hymnod. Sacra*, p. 330):—*Ave Jesu verum manhu, Christe Jesu adauge fidem omnium credentium:* and the second (ms.at Koblenz of the 17th cent.):—*Bone Jesu, pastor fidelium adauge fidem omnium in te sperantium.* These notes, &c., are repeated with additions, by *Daniel*, iv. p. 234. Dr. Neale's note, *Mediæval Hymns*, 1851 and 1867, &c., is :—

"The following hymn of S. Thomas Aquinas to the Holy Eucharist was never in public use in the Mediæval Church; but it has been appended, as a private devotion, to most Missals. It is worthy of notice how the Angelic Doctor, as if afraid to employ any pomp of words on approaching so tremendous a Mystery, has used the very simplest expressions throughout."

In addition to the foregoing, the text, slightly different from *Daniel* and *Mone*, specially in st. vi., is given in Card. Newman's *H. Eccl.* 1838 and 1865 (from a modern ed. of the *Paris Brev.* where it reads, "Adoro te supplex, latens Deitas"), and in *The Domin. H. Bk.* Lond., 1887. This last is also different, not only from *Daniel* and *Mone*, but from Card. *Newman* also. It has *Mone's* two refrains arranged as one in two lines.

Translations in C. U. :—

1. **O Godhead hid, devoutly I adore Thee.** By E. Caswall, 1st pub. in his *Lyra Catholica*, 1849, p. 247, in 7 st., and with the refrain as in *The Domin. H. Bk.* This was repeated in his *Hymns and Poems*, 1873, p. 161, with alterations. The *tr.* of 1849 is somewhat extensively used in R. C. Hymnals, sometimes with the omission of the refrain. It is given so also in Canon Oakeley's *tr.* of the *Paradise of the Christian Soul.*

2. **Humbly I adore Thee, hidden Deity.** By J. M. Neale, 1st pub. in his *Mediæval Hymns*, 1851 and 1867, &c., in 7 st. of 4 l. This was included with slight alterations in the *People's H.*, 1867, No. 178. It is also found in some works of private devotion.

3. **Thee we adore, O hidden Saviour, Thee.** By Bp. J. R. Woodford, written in 1850, and 1st pub. in his *Hys. arranged for the Sundays,* &c., of the *Ch. of England*, 1852, 2nd ed. 1855. Bp. Woodford adopted the reading as in Card. Newman's *H. Eccl.* (as above), with the omission of st. ii., iii., iv., thus reducing it to 4 st. of 4 l. In his st. iii. the lines 3, 4 are lines 3, 4 of Card. Newman's st. iv. A striking feature in this rendering is the change of the line, *Pie pellicane Jesu Domine* to *O fons puritatis, Jesu Domine,* adopted from the *Paris Brev.* by Card. Newman and Bp.

Woodford. In Bp. Woodford's rendering various changes have been made from time to time, two of which are worthy of notice, the first of st. i., and the second of st. iv. The first st. originally read:—

(1) " Thee we adore, O hidden Saviour, Thee,
    Who in Thy Supper with us deign'st to be ;
    Both flesh and spirit in Thy presence fail,
    Yet here Thy presence we devoutly hail."

This we find altered in *Hys. for Christian Seasons*, Gainsburgh, 2nd ed., 1854.

" Thee we adore, O hidden Saviour, Thee,
    Who in Thy *Sacrament dost deign* to be
    Both flesh and spirit *at* Thy presence fail," &c.

This was repeated in *H. A. & M.*, 1861 and 1875 ; *The Hymnary*, 1872, and others.

(2) Another reading of line 2 is:—" Who in Thy *Sacrament art pleased* to be." This was given in the *Sarum*, 1868, and repeated in the *New Mitre*, 1875.

(3) A third reading is:—

" Thee we adore, O hidden Saviour ! Thee,
    Who in Thy *Feast with us vouchsaf'st* to be,
    Both flesh and spirit *at* Thy Presence fail," &c.

This appeared in Chope's *Hymnal*, 1857.

(4) A fourth reading is :—

" Thee we adore, O *unseen* Saviour ! Thee,
    Who in Thy *Feast with us vouchsaf'st* to be,
    Both flesh and spirit *at* Thy Presence fail," &c.

This was given in Pott's *Hys. fitted to the Order of Com. Pr.*, 1861.

(5) The fifth reading is :—

" Thee we adore, O *unseen* Saviour ! Thee,
    Who in Thy *Feast art pleased with us* to be,
    Both flesh and spirit *at* Thy Presence fail," &c.

This appeared in the S.P.C.K. *Ch. Hymns*, 1871 ; and again in Thring's *Coll.*, 1882, and has the sanction of the translator.

(6) The sixth reading is in T. Darling's *Hys. for the Ch. of Eng.*, where l. 2 reads—" Who in *this mystery vouchsafest* to be." This is one of nine alterations by Mr. Darling. Mr. Darling's text is the most inaccurate of any with which we are acquainted.

The second change of importance is in st. iv., l. 3, which reads in the original—" To gaze on Thee unveiled, and see Thy face."

In the Gainsburgh *Hys. for Christian Seasons*, as above (2nd ed. 1854), this reads—" To gaze on Thee, *and see with unveiled face*," and was copied by *H. A. & M.*, 1861–75, *The Hymnary*, 1872, and others. Darling reads—" To gaze on Thee unveiled, and *face to face. For aye behold* Thy glory," &c. Minor changes are also given by various editors. These are of little moment, and appeared without the translator's sanction. Bp. Woodford's *authorised* text is in *Sarum*, 1868, No. 221. He has also sanctioned that adopted by *Church Hys.* and by Mr. Thring (E. MSS.).

4. Prostrate I adore Thee, Deity unseen. In the *App.* to *Hymnal N.*, No. 216, is based upon the *trs.* of *Pusey, Caswall*, and *Chambers*, with refrain.

5. I adore Thee truly, hidden Deity. By W. J. Irons, in his *Ps. & Hys. for the Church*, 1875.

Translations not in C. U. :—
1. Prostrate I adore Thee. Dr. Pusey. *Par. of the Christian Soul*, 1847.
2. Devoutly I adore Thee, unseen Deity. *J. D. Chambers*, 1857.

3. Devoutly I adore Thee, God in figures veil'd. *J. W. Hewett*, 1859.
4. O Dreadful unapproached Deity. *Isaac Williams*. H. *Paris Brev.*, 1839, p. 171. From the altered text, *Adoro te supplex, latens Deitas* in the *Paris Brev.*
5. I adore Thee devoutly, O Godhead concealed. *John Wallace*, 1874, *H. of the Church*, pp. 239–40.
6. Suppliant I adore Thee, latent Deity. *W. Palmer*. 1845. From the *Paris Brev.*
7. I adore the truth concealed. *C. H. Hoole*, in his *Poems and Trs.*, 1875.   [J. J.]

Adsis superne Spiritus, Pater benigne pauperum. [*Whitsuntide.*] An anonymous hymn in the *Paris Breviary*, 1736, for Whitsuntide at Compline. It is given in full in Card. Newman's *Hymni Ecclesiae*, 1838 and 1865.

Translations in C. U. :—

1. Haste hither, Heavenly Spirit. By W. J. Blew, printed on a broadsheet for use in his church, cir. 1850, and again, in his *Ch. H. & Tune Bk.*, 1852, in 5 st. of 4 l. In 1870 it was included in Mr. Rice's selection from that work.

2. O Holy Spirit, God most High. By Wm. Cooke, made for and 1st pub. in the *Hymnary*, 1872, No. 327, in 5 st. of 4 l.

Translations not in C. U. :—
1. Hail, Father of the poor. *I. Williams*, 1839.
2. Come, Thou heavenly Spirit pure. *J. F. Thrupp*, 1853.
3. Come, heavenly Spirit, come. *Horatius Bonar*, 1861.
4. Come, O Spirit, graciously. *E. L. Blenkinsopp*, 1864.   [J J.]

Adsunt tenebrae primae. [*Evening.*] An anonymous hymn in *Daniel*, i. 194, in 5 st. of 4 l., from the *Mozarabic Brev.* (Toledo, 1502, f. 304), *Thomasius*, Rome, 1747, ii. p. 425, and Migne's *Patrologia*, tom. 86, col 928. " Ymni de prima vigilia " ; also col. 965 See also *Daniel*, iv. 57, where may be found a severe criticism on one of the lines in the *Mozarabic Brev.*, which may be the correct reading, notwithstanding.   [W. A. S.]

Translation in C. U. :—

1. The night is closing o'er us. By W. J. Blew, 1st printed on a fly-leaf for use in his own church, and then pub. in his *Ch. H. & Tune Bk.*, 1852. Trin. to Adv., No. 41, in 5 st. of 4 l. In 1867 it was transferred to the *People's H.*, and in 1872 to the *Hymnary*, No. 622.

Advance, advance, the day is come. *G. Moultrie.* [*Processional.*] Written to the tune *Ein' feste Burg*, for the Wantage Sisterhood, and printed in the *Church Times*, June, 1874, in 5 st. of 9 l., and signed " G. M. June 6, 1874." A good hymn, and worthy of being better known.   [W. T. B.]

Adversa mundi tolera. *Thomas à Kempis.* [*Patience.*] This hymn is in his *Opera*, Nürnberg, 1494, f. 130b, in 29 lines arranged as 11, and entitled " Canticum de virtute patientiae." The full text is in *Wackernagel*, i. No. 377, and, omitting 12 lines, in *Daniel*, ii. p. 379, where it is headed *Carmen Thomae à Kempis de Patientiâ Christianâ*. Also in *Bässler*, No. 119, and *Königsfeld*, ii. 254.

Translations in C. U. :—

1. For Christ's dear sake with courage bear. By E. Caswall, in his *Masque of Mary*, 1858, p. 358, and again in his *Hymns and Poems*, 1873, in 5 st. of 4 l. with the heading "Hymn of Thomas à Kempis, on Christian Patience." In recent editions of the *Appendix* to the *Hymnal N.* it is given unaltered as No. 305. It also appears as :—

2. In Christ's dear Name with courage bear, in the Roman Catholic *Hys. for the Year*, No. 69.

Aemilie Juliane [Emilie].

Aeterna Christi munera, Et martyrum victorias. *Ambrosian.* This hymn, originally written for "Martyrs," has been adapted for "Apostles," and (in another form) for "Martyrs" in the *Rom. Brev.* Under these circumstances it will be necessary to notice the history and use of each.

i. *The original text.*

This hymn is received by the Benedictine editors of St. Ambrose as a genuine work of that Father, on the authority of the Ven. Bede; who, in his work, *De arte metricâ*, speaks of it as a "hymn for blessed martyrs, composed with most beautiful grace," "pulcherrimo est decore compositus hymnus beatorum martyrum." (See the Benedictine ed. of St. Ambrose, in Migne's *Patrol.*, tom. 16.) *Mone*, No. 733, in his note on the hymn, says, "*Vezzosi* remarks justly that the congregation of St. Maur [i.e. the Benedictine editors] ascribed this hymn on an obscure reference of Bede to St. Ambrose, whose it is not, though it is yet most likely of the 5th century."

Amongst the earliest mss. in which it is found are two of the 11th cent. in the *British Museum* (Harl. 2961, f. 248 ; Jul. A. vi. f. 64*b*), and another, perhaps of the 8th or 9th cent., formerly belonging to that eminent scholar in the Anglo-Saxon and cognate languages, Franciscus Junius. The latter was No. 110 among the mss. bequeathed to the Bodleian by Fr. Junius at his death in 1677, but "has been missing from the Library for more than 100 years." [F. Madan, Sub-Librarian, *Bodl. Lib.* Aug. 21, 1884.] It was, however, printed from a copy by Fr. Junius by Jacob Grimm, at Gottingen, in 1830, as, *Hymnorum veteris ecclesiae xxvi. Interpretatio Theotisca* [*Brit. Mus.*].

The text is given by *Daniel*, i. pp. 26–28 ; additional notes, ii. p. 381, iv. p. 87; *Mone*, No. 733; the ancient Breviaries of *Havelberg*; of the *Benedictines*, of the *Hermits* of the *Order of St. Augustin*, of York, of Milan, the *Mozarabic*, &c.; *Trench*, 1849 to 1864; *Lat. H. of Anglo-Saxon Ch.*, 1851, from a Durham MS. of the 11th cent.; *Simrock*, 1868; *Macgill*, 1876 and 1879. In some of these there are slight variations in the text.

It should be added that in some Monastic Breviaries this hymn has been adapted to Festivals of Confessors and Virgins. [W. A. S.]

Translations in C. U. :—

1. The eternal gifts of Christ the King, The Martyrs' glorious deeds we sing. By J. M. Neale, pub. in the enlarged ed. of the *Hymnal N.*, 1854, No. 80, in 5 st. of 4 l., and from thence into one or two collections, including the *Hymner*, 1882, No. 94. It is from the *York Brev.*, and consists of st. i., iii., iv., v. and viii. of the original.

2. The eternal gifts of Christ our King, The Martyrs' victories let us sing. By J. D. Chambers, from the *York Brev.*, 1st pub. in his *Lauda Syon*, Pt. ii., 1866, p. 15, in 5 st. of 4 l. In the *People's H.*, 1867, No. 211, it is given unaltered. In the *Hymnary*, 1872, No. 399, a mixed *tr.* from Neale, Chambers, and others, is given, and is wrongly ascribed, in the Index, to the *Hymnal N.*

Translations not in C. U. :—

1. The unfading crowns by Christ bestowed. *Copeland*, 1848.
2. The eternal gifts of Christ the King. *Blew*, 1852.
3. Sing to the Lord with joy and praise. *Macgill*, 1876 and 1879.

ii. *Form for Apostles.*

Aeterna Christi munera, Apostolorum gloriam. This form of the hymn is an adaptation for "Apostles" as distinct from "Martyrs." It is in numerous Breviaries, including the *Roman, York, Sarum* and others. The same text, however, is not strictly maintained. The lines of the original which are thus variously altered are 1–8 and 21–28, followed by a doxology not in the original and varying in the respective Breviaries in which the hymn is given.

The text from the *Durham MS.* of the 11th cent. is in *The Lat. Hys. of the Anglo-Saxon Ch.* (Surtees Society), 1851 ; the *Rom. Brev.*, Card. Newman's *Hymni Ecclesiae*, 1838 to 1865; and the *Sarum Hymnale*. (See *Usum Sarum*, 1850.) *Daniel* gives the *Rom. Brev.* text together with the original i. pp. 27–28; *Mone*, No. 662, gives the text from mss. of the 12th cent., &c., with extended notes. The hymn is also found in an 11th cent. ms. in the *British Museum* (Harl. 2961, f. 247).

Translations in C. U.:—

1. The Lord's eternal gifts. By E. Caswall, 1st pub. in his *Lyra Catholica*, 1849, p. 204, and in his. *Hys. & Poems*, 1873, p. 108. This is in use in a few Rom. Catholic hymnals for schools and mission services. Altered to "The *Eternal Spirit's* gifts," it is also No. 296 in Chope's *Hymnal*, 1864.

2. Eternal gifts of Christ the King. By W. J. Blew, was printed on a broadsheet for use in his church, cir. 1850 [E. MSS], and pub. in his *Ch. H. & Tune Bk.*, 1852. This is given in Rice's *Sel.* 1870, from that work as, " Th' eternal gifts of Christ the King," a borrowed line from Dr. Neale.

3. The eternal gifts of Christ the King. By J. M. Neale. It appeared in the *Hymnal N.*, 1852, No. 37, and later editions of the same work. Also unaltered (with the addition of Bp. Ken's doxology), in Skinner's *Daily Service H.*, 1864, and the *Hymner*, 1882, No. 86. In nearly every other case, however, where it has been adopted, various alterations have been introduced, as in Murray's *Hymnal*, 1852, the *Salisbury H. Bk.*, 1857, *H. A. & M.*, 1861–75 (repeated in *Kennedy*), the *Hymnary*, 1872, where it reads, "Christ *our* King," &c. In *Church Hys.*, 1871, No. 193, st. i.–iii., slightly altered (st. i., l. 3, 4), are from the *H. A. & M.*, arrangement of Dr. Neale, and not from J. D. Chambers as stated by Mr. Ellerton in his note thereon (*Ch. Hys.* folio ed. *Notes*, 193). The remaining st. iv., v., are from a MS. *tr.* by Mr. Ellerton.

4. The Eternal Spirit's gifts, The gifts of Christ the King. By G. Phillimore, given in the *Parish H. Bk.*, 1863 and 1875, and *Sarum*, 1868.

5. The eternal gifts of Christ the Lord. By R. F. Littledale, made for and 1st pub. in the *People's H.*, 1867, No. 197, and signed " F. R."

Translations not in C. U. :—

1. Lord, Who didst bless Thy chosen band. *Mant,* 1837.
2. The everlasting gifts of Christ. *Hope,* 1844.
3. The treasures of the King's abode. *Campbell,* 1850.
4. The eternal gifts of Christ our King. *Chambers,* 1866, p. 2.
5. With fitting voice and joy proclaim. *F. Trappes,* 1865.
6. O come with your canticles, come with your lays. *J. Wallace,* 1874.

iii. *Rom. Brev. form for Martyrs.*

Christo profusum sanguinem. This cento appeared in the *Rom. Brev*, 1632, for Festivals Common of Martyrs, and is thus composed: st. i., then new; st. ii.–iv. from " Aeterna Christi," lines 9–20, and st. v., lines 29–32, with the single alteration of l. 30 from " Ut ipsorum consortio " to " Ut *martyrum* consortio." In this form it is in all modern editions of the *Rom. Brev.* Text in *Daniel,* i. No. 26; Card. Newman's *Hymni Ecclesiae,* 1838 and 1865.

Translations in C. U. :—

1. Ye servants of a martyr'd God By R. Campbell, written in 1849 [E. MSS.], and given in the *St. Andrew's Hymnal,* 1850, p. 97, in 4 st. of 4 l.

2. **Ye servants of a martyred Lord.** No. 88 in Murray's *Hymnal,* 1852, is a cento of which st. i., ii., iii. and v. are Campbell's *tr.* as above, partly from Card. Newman's *tr.* of " Invicte martyr," iv., vi. and vii. are new, and original.

3. **Ye servants of our glorious King.** No. 272 in *H. A. & M.,* 1861, and 444 in 1875, is also a cento, thus compiled: st. i., compilers of *H. A. & M.;* ii., iii., *R. Campbell,* as above; iv., *Murray,* as above; v., *R. Campbell;* vi., another doxology for that in *Murray.*

Translations not in C. U. :—

1. Sing we the martyrs blest. *Caswall,* 1849.
2. Let us sing how martyrs bled. *J. Wallace.* 1874.

[J. J.]

Aeterna coeli gloria. [*Friday.*] This hymn is sometimes ascribed to St. Ambrose. Not being quoted, however, by early writers, it has not been received as certainly genuine by the Benedictine editors (Migne's *Patrol.* tom. xvii.). It dates from the 5th century, and if not by St. Ambrose, is purely Ambrosian. The text has often been reprinted, sometimes alone, and again with notes, references, and criticism. Of the latter the best are :—

1. *Daniel,* 1841, i. No. 46, where we have the old text in 5 st. of 4 l., with the revised version from the *Rom. Brev.* in parallel columns and headed "Hymnus ad Laudes" (" A hymn at Lauds "). It is the Hymn on Fridays in the Ferial Office at Lauds from the Octave of the Epiphany to the first Sunday in Lent, and from the Octave of Corpus Christi to Advent in the *Roman* and many other old Breviaries. *Daniel* gives the variations found in *Clichtoveus, Bebelius, Fabricius,* &c.

2. *Hymn. Sarisb.,* Lond., 1851, pp. 55, 56, for use at the periods mentioned above. In this work variations are given from the Use of *York;* from Monastic uses, as *Evesham, Worcester, St. Alban's, Canterbury,* &c.

3. In *Mone,* 1853, i., it is from an 8th cent. MS. at Trier ; and No. 159 is from a MS. of the 15th cent. at Stuttgart. He adds a long note on what he regarded as the acrostic character of the hymn.

4. *Daniel,* ii. p. 381, has a further reference, and in iv. p. 40, cites a Rheinau MS. of the 10th cent., and gives an extended note with special reference to *Mone's* conclusions respecting the acrostic character of the hymn. *Daniel* refuses to accept *Mone's* conclusions. The arrangement, however, is certainly alphabetical, with the exception that two lines begin with *c,* and one (the 9th) with *o* (*ortus*) instead of *h* (hortus). *Daniel's* text extends to *s,* and *Mone's* to *t.*

5. The old text is also found in two 11th cent. MSS. in the *British Museum* (Harl. 2961, f. 224 ; Jul. A. vi. f. 29) ; and in the *Latin Hys. of the Anglo-Saxon Church,* 1851, p. 27, it is printed from an 11th cent. MS. at Durham.

6. The text, old or revised, is also in Card. Newman's *Hymni Ecclesiae,* 1838 and 1865, and others, in addition to those works already noted. The variations in the text are very slight.

[W. A. S.]

Translations in C. U. :—

1. **Glory of the eternal heaven.** By Card. Newman from the *Rom. Brev.,* given in his *Verses,* 1853, and again in his *Verses on Various Occasions,* 1868. It is No. 30 in the *Hymnary,* 1872.

2. **Eternal glory of the heavens.** By E. Caswall. From the *Rom. Brev.,* 1st pub. in his *Lyra Catholica,* 1849, p. 31, and his *Hymns and Poems,* 1873, p. 19. It is given in many of the Roman Catholic hymnals for use in schools and missions, including the *Hys. for the Year,* N.D.

3. **Eternal glory of the sky, Blest hope, &c.** By J. M. Neale, from the *old text* in the enlarged ed. of the *Hymnal N.,* 1854, No. 25. It is given sometimes altered, in Skinner's *Daily Service H.,* 1864, No. 12 ; the *Hymner,* 1882, No. 40, and others.

4. **Eternal glory of the heaven.** By J. D. Chambers, from the *old text,* in his *Lauda Syon,* 1857, i. p. 29. From thence it has passed into the *People's H.,* 1867, No. 430.

Translations not in C. U. :—

1. O eternal praise of heaven. *Bp. Mant,* 1837.
2. Thou Glory of the eternal sky. *Hymn. Ang.* 1844.
3. Eternal glory of the sky, Hope, &c. *Bp. Williams,* 1845.
4. Glory of the heavens supernal. *Copeland,* 1848.
5. Christ, the glory of the sky. *Campbell,* 1850.

[J. J.]

Aeterna lux, Divinitas! [*Holy Trinity.*] An anonymous hymn for Trinity Sunday given in *Daniel,* 1843, ii. p. 369. It cannot be of an early date. *Daniel* does not indicate from whence he took his text. It is also in the *Corolla Hymnorum,* Cologne, 1806, p. 41, in 9 st. of 4 l. [W. A. S.]

Translations in C. U. :—

1. **O Thou immortal Light divine.** By E. Caswall, 1st pub. in his *Masque of Mary,* &c., 1858, p. 277, and his *Hymns and Poems,* 1873, p. 129. This text, in an abbreviated form, is given in a few Roman Catholic collections for Schools and Missions. It was also included, in an altered form, as, " O Light Eternal, God most High," in the *Hymnary,* 1872, No. 338.

2. Eternal Light, Divinity. By R. F. Littledale, made for, and 1st pub. in the *People's H.*, 1867, No. 163, and signed " L."   [J. J.]

Aeterne Rector siderum. *Card. Bellarmine.* [*Evening.*]

This hymn is in the *Roman Brev.*, 1632, as the Hymn at Lauds, on the Feast of the Holy Guardian Angels (Oct. 2nd). It was inserted in the *Breviary* by Pope Paul V., who when still Cardinal Camillo Borghese, in a conversation with Leonardo Donato, the Venetian ambassador, remarked, that if ever he became Pope he would not amuse himself like Clement VIII. in disputing with the Republic of Venice, but would proceed at once to excommunication. Donato, on his side, remarked that if ever he became Doge he would not set much value on the excommunication. One became Pope, the other Doge. The Doge employed the noted Fra Paolo Sarpi to write the history of the Council of Trent against the interests of the Papacy; the Pope opposed to him Cardinal Bellarmine. Possibly this respect for, and interest in the Cardinal may have led to the adoption of this hymn by the Pope. Text with note in *Daniel*, iv. p. 306. [See **Custodes hominum**.]   [W. A. S.]

Translations in C. U. :—

1. Almighty God, whose sceptre sways. By Bp. R. Mant, 1st pub. in his *Ancient Hymns, &c.*, 1837, p. 30, in 6 st. of 4 l., and included in Dr. Oldknow's *Hys. for the Ser. of the Ch.*, 1850.

2. Ruler of the dread immense. By E. Caswall, in his *Lyra Catholica*, 1849, p. 175; and his *Hys. and Poems*, 1873, p. 95. This is given in the *App.* to *Hymnal N.*, No. 183, for St. Michael and All Angels.

Translation not in C. U. :—

O'er the morning stars Who reignest. *Copeland*, 1848, p. 131.

Aeterne rerum conditor. *St. Ambrose.* [*Sunday Morning.*]

This hymn by St. Ambrose is received as genuine by the Benedictine editors. For this genuineness, the following evidence is complete :—

(1) St. Augustine, *Retract. Lib. I. C.* 21, writes : " In this book I have spoken in a certain place of the Apostle Peter, that the Church is founded on him as on a rock, which doctrine is sung also by the mouth of multitudes in the verses of the most Blessed Ambrose, when speaking of the cock he says :—

" Lo, e'en the very Church's Rock
Melts at the crowing of the cock."

(" Hoc ipsa petra ecclesiae
Canente, culpam diluit.")

(2) The Venerable Bede, *De arte metricâ*, followed by other writers, considers that the substance of this hymn is taken from the *Hexaemeron* of St. Ambrose (written about the year 389), Lib. V. c. 24. Or, as *Daniel* says, the hymn may have been written first, and then expanded into the prose version.

The use of this hymn has been most extensive. In the *Mozarabic Brev.* (1502, f. 2) it is the hymn at Matins on the 1st S. in Advent, and generally on Sundays in Advent, Lent, Palm Sunday, Whitsun Day, &c. ; in the *Sarum, York, Evesham, Hereford,* and *St. Alban's,* at Lauds on Sundays from the Octave of the Epiphany to Lent, and from the 1st Oct. to Advent; in the *Worcester* at Matins (so also some old Breviaries of the Benedictine Order (*Daniel*, i. p. 15); and in the *Roman,* for Sundays at Lauds, from the Octave of the Epiphany to the 1st. S. in Lent, and from the S. nearest to the 1st of Oct. to Advent.

The text of this hymn is found in the *Junius* MS. of the 8th cent., No. xxv., and in two 11th cent. MSS. in the *British Museum* (Harl. 2961, f. 218b; Jul. A. vi. f. 19). In the *Latin Hys. of the Anglo-Saxon Church*, 1851, it is printed from a Durham MS. of the 11th cent., and is given in the following works : *S. Ambrosii Opp.*, Paris, 1836, p. 200 ; *Daniel*, i. 15, iv. 3 ; *Trench*, 1864, 243 ; *Card. Newman's H. Eccl.*, 1838, &c. *Daniel* and *Trench* are specially rich in illustrative notes. The variations in the *Rom. Brev.* are also found in these works.   [W. A. S.]

Translations in C. U. :—

1. Maker of all, Eternal King. By W. J. Copeland from the *Rom. Brev.*, 1st pub. in his *Hymns for the Week, &c.*, 1848, in 9 st. of 4 l., and from thence it passed into the *People's H.*, 1867, &c.

2. Framer of the earth and sky. By Card. Newman. The earliest date to which we have traced this *tr.* is in R. Campbell's *St. Andrew's Hymnal*, 1850. In 1853 it was repeated in Card. Newman's *Verses*, and again in his *Verses on Various Occasions*, 1868. In this latter work this *tr.*, in common with others, is dated 1836-38. The text from Campbell is repeated with slight alterations in the *Hymnary*, 1872.

Translations not in C. U. :—

1. O God, Who by alternate sway. *Primer*, 1706.
2. Maker of all, enthroned above. *Mant*, 1837.
3. Eternal Maker, at Whose will. *I. Williams*, 1844.
4. Dread Ruler of the Universe. *Hymn. Angl.*, 1844.
5. Creator eternal of earth, &c. *Bp. Williams*, 1845.
6. Dread Framer of the earth, &c. *Caswall*, 1849.
7. O Thou Everlasting Maker. *J. Banks*, 1857.
8. Eternal Founder of the Worlds. *Chambers*, 1857.
9. Eternal Maker of the World. *Mrs. Charles*, 1858.
10. Maker of all, Eternal King. *Hewett*, 1859.
11. Eternal God, Thy word, &c. *Kynaston*, 1862.
12. Eternal God, Who built the sky. *Macgill*, 1876.
13. Eternal God, the primal cause. *Wallace*, 1874.
      [J. J.]

Aeterne Rex altissime, Redemptor. [*Ascension.*]

The text of this hymn has been so altered at various times that the true original and the origin of its various forms are most difficult to determine. The researches of the best hymnologists, when summarized, give the following results :

1. *Daniel*, vol. i. No. 162, gives the text in 7 st. of 4 l. and a doxology, from a 13th cent. MS. at Wurzburg ; interpolating therewith 6 st., which are only found in the *Mozarabic Brev.* He adds in parallel cols. the revised text of the *Rom. Brev.* 1632.

2. The *Rom. Brev.* form has continued down to and is in use at the present time, as the hymn at Matins for the Ascension-day, and from thence daily till the Festival of an Apostle or Evangelist interrupts the usual order. It is composed of st. i., iii., vi., vii., x., xi., xii. and xiii., of the old form, somewhat altered. This text is in all modern eds. of the *Rom. Brev.* and Card. Newman's *Hymni Eccl.*, 1838 and 1865.

3. We have next the *Hymn. Sarisb.*, Lond., 1851, pp. 101–2, where it is given as the Hymn at Vespers on the Vigil of the Ascension, and daily to Whitsuntide : also at Matins on the Feast of the Ascension itself. Variations are added from the *York Brev.*, which assigns it to the first and second Vespers of the Ascension, and throughout the Octave.—*St. Alban's*, "to the Ascension of the Lord at Vespers;"—*Worcester*, "the Ascension of the Lord at Matins," &c. Different readings are also given from a *Canterbury* MS. of the Anglo-Saxon times.

4. *Mone*, No. 171, gives st. i.–iv. of the old text from MSS. of the 14th and 15th cent. at Karlsruhe. This form he holds is by St. Ambrose. In addition he gives at No. 172, st. v.–vii. from MSS. of the 14th and 15th cent. at Karlsruhe, &c., and holds that they are not by St. Ambrose, and yet by a writer of the 5th cent. The *Mozarabic Brev.* sts. he considers to be the work of a Spanish imitator of Prudentius of the 5th cent.

5. It is also in the *Mozarabic Brev.* 1502, f. 195, in an 11th cent. MS. in the *British Museum* (Jul. A. vi. f. 51); and in another of the same cent. (Vesp. D. xii. f. 75*b*). In the *Latin Hys. of the Anglo-Saxon Church*, 1851, p. 90, it is printed from a Durham MS. of the 11th cent.

In 1855, *Daniel*, iv. pp. 79–83, gave an extensive note on this hymn, dealing with its complex authorship, &c. He entered fully and with much feeling into the verbal and metrical questions which led him to oppose some of the opinions of *Mone* on the authorship, &c., of the hymn. The note is too long for quotation, but may be consulted with advantage. The hymn "Tu Christe nostrum gaudium" is a portion of this hymn. It begins with line 17.   [W. A. S.]

Translations in C. U. :—

1. **Eternal King of heaven on high.** By Bp. R. Mant, from the *Rom. Brev.*, 1st pub. in his *Ancient Hymns*, 1837, p. 66, in 8 st. of 4 l. This is sometimes given in an abbreviated form, as in the Gainsburgh *Coll.* &c., 2nd ed. 1854.

2. **O Thou Eternal King most high.** By E. Caswall, from the *Rom. Brev.*, given in his *Lyra Catholica*, 1849, p. 101, and again in his *Hymns & Poems*, 1873, p. 57, in 8 st. of 4 l. (see orig. *tr.*) In 1858, 6 st. were included in the *Scot. Episc. Coll.*, No. 81, in Chope's *Hymnal*, 1864, and others, and in full with alterations in the *Hymnary*, 1872. Another altered form is, "O Thou most high! Eternal King," in the Irvingite *Hys. for the use of the Churches*, 1864. Some of these alterations are borrowed from Johnston's *tr.* of 1852. Caswall's *tr.* is extensively used in Roman Catholic hymnals for Schools and Missions.

3. **King Eternal, power unbounded.** By W. J. Copeland, from the *Rom. Brev.*, in his *Hymns for the Week*, &c., 1848, in 8 st. of 4 l. This was included in Stretton's *Church Hys.*, 1850, unaltered. In an altered form, "King Supreme! of power unbounded," it appeared in Rorison's *Hys. & Anthems*, 1851, and later editions.

4. **O King eternal, Lord most High.** By J. A. Johnston, in his *English Hymnal*, 1852, No. 118. It is also in later editions.

5. **Eternal Monarch, King most High.** By J. M. Neale, from the *Sarum Brev.*, pub. in the *Hymnal N.* 1852, No. 31. It is included in the *Hymner*, 1882, No. 67. After undergoing considerable alterations by the compilers of *H. A. & M.*, it came forth in the 1st ed. 1861, as "O Lord

most High, eternal King." This is repeated in the revised edition, 1875, and other collections.

6. **Christ above all glory seated.** By Bp. J. R. Woodford, made for and 1st pub. in his *Hys. arranged for the Sundays*, &c., 1852, in 6 st. of 4 l. (2nd ed. 1855.) In 1857 it was repeated in Chope's *Hymnal*; in 1863 and 1875, in the *Parish H. Bk.*, and also in *S. P. C. K. Ps. & Hys.*; *Sarum*; *Ch. Hys.*; Thring's *Coll.* and others. It is somewhat indebted to Copeland's *tr.*, two or three lines being verbatim therefrom. It is the most popular of all the versions of this hymn.

In Murray's *Hymnal*, 1852, an attempt was made to represent all the 8 st. of the *Rom. Brev.* by compiling a cento thus: st. i., ii., iii., Bp. Woodford; st. iv., v., vi., Copeland, slightly altered: st. vii., viii., Bp. Woodford; but it has gone almost, if not altogether, out of C. U.

7. **Most High and Everlasting King.** By R. F. Littledale, from the *Sarum Brev.*, made for and first pub. in the *People's H.*, 1867, No. 140, and signed in the Index "P. C. E."

8. **O King eternal, King most high.** By S. Eugene Tolet, from the *Rom. Brev.* in the *Wellington College H. Bk.*, 1860, and later eds.

Trs. not in C. U. :—

1. O Saviour Christ, O God most high. *Primer*, 1706.
2. O King eternal, God most High. *Blew*, 1852.
3. Eternal Monarch! Lord Supreme. *Chambers*, 1857, i. 192.
4. Most high and everlasting Lord. *P. Trappes*, 1865. [J. J.]

Aeterni Festi gaudia. *Adam of St. Victor.* [*St. Augustine.*] The earliest form of this sequence, which dates from the 12th cent. is in a Rheinau MS. of the 13th cent. cited by *Morel*, p. 203, where it reads *Interni festi gaudia*. This reading is followed by *Daniel*, ii. p. 250; *Kehrein*, No. 502; and others. L. Gautier, who printed from a 14th cent. MS. at Paris, gives the opening line as above— "*Aeterni festi gaudia*," the first word being the only change throughout the sequence. The full text, together with notes, is given in his *Œuvres Poétiques d'Adam de St.-Victor*, 1859, ii. pp. 156–160, and in D. S. Wrangham's reprint, *The Liturgical Poetry of Adam of St. Victor*, 1881, vol. ii. pp. 186–191. Dr. Neale says :—

"Gautier reads *Eterni*, but I understand the poet to mean that the external celebration of the Festival is only the outspoken expression of the internal joy of the heart." *Med. Hys.* 3rd ed. 1867, p. 133.

Clichtoveus, 1516, remarks that the author gives the

"title of *internal feast* to that interior joy and exultation in the Lord of the pious soul which it perceives to exist within itself when pervaded by the divine sweetness; and, feeling tranquillity and peace of conscience with God—separated and freed, too, from all the cares of the world—it gives itself up to God alone, and is continually intent on His praise and contemplation."
[W. A. S.]

The *trs.* of this sequence are, i. those which include the whole text, and ii. those in centos.

i. *The full text.* "*Interni festi gaudia.*"

1. **Our festal strains to-day reveal.** By J. M. Neale, in his *Med. Hys.*, 1862 and 1867, in 13 st. of 4 l. Not in C. U.

2. Our tuneful strains let us upraise. By D. S. Wrangham, from the text of *Gautier*, in his *tr.* of the *Liturgical Poetry of Adam of St. Victor*, 1881, vol. ii. pp. 187-191. Not in C. U.

ii. *Centos.* "*Interni, &c.;*" and "*Harum laudum, &c.*"

1. Our festal strains to-day reveal. By J. M. Neale. This is a cento composed of st. i.-v., viii., ix. of the original. It was given in the enlarged ed. of the *Hymnal N.*, 1854, &c.

2. The praises that the Blessed know. This is a second cento by Dr. Neale. It appeared in the *Hymnal N.*, with the foregoing, and is composed of st. x., xi., vii., vi. and xiii. in the order named; and begins with the Latin stanza "Harum laudum praeconia." It is repeated with st. xii. for vi. in the *People's H.*, 1867, No. 277.

3. Blessed souls in heaven rejoice. By Henrietta Mary Chester, written for the *Hymnary*, 1872, No. 380, and given therein under the signature of "H. M. C." This cento begins with "Harum laudum," &c., and consists of st. x., xi., v.,vi.–xiii. in the order named, and a doxology. [J. J.]

Aeterni Patris Unice. *Anon.* [*St. Mary Magdalene.*] This hymn has been ascribed to St. Odo of Cluny; and is found in a MS. of the 11th cent. in the *British Museum* (Vesp. D. xii. f. 153b) added to the "Lauda Mater ecclesia" (q. v.). Both hymns are apparently in a later handwriting than the first part of the MS. *Daniel*, i. No. 348, reprinted the text of Card. Newman, changing the opening word from "Eterne," to *Aeterni. Mone* (iii. p. 424), reprinted the text of a MS. of the 14th cent. and added thereto numerous references to MSS. and various readings; and *Daniel*, iv. 244, the revised text of the *Roman Brev.* **Summi parentis Unice.** The text of the *York Brev.* is given in Card. Newman's *Hymni Ecclesiae*, 1838, and the *Rom. Brev.* form in Biggs's *Annotated H. A. & M.* with st. ii. l. 2, "Reconditur aerario," for "Reconditur *est* aerario," in error. The older text sometimes reads, "Patris Aeterne Unice."
[W. A. S.]

Translations in C. U. :—
Translations of both forms are in C. U. :—

I. *Original Text.* "*Aeterni Patris Unice.*"

1. Son of the Eternal Sire on high. By J. D. Chambers. 1st pub. in his *Lauda Syon*, 1866, Pt. ii., p. 91. This was given in the *Appendix* to the *Hymnal N.*, 1862, as : "Thou Only Son of God on high."

2. Son of Eternal God most high. By R. F. Little-dale, written for the *People's H.*, 1867, and given therein as No. 265, under the initials "F. R."

Translation not in C. U. :—
Son of the Sire, the Eternal One. *Blew*, 1852.

II. *Rom. Brev.* "*Summi Parentis Unice.*"

1. Son of the Highest, deign to cast. By E. Caswall. Appeared in his *Lyra Catholica*, 1849, p. 164, and his *Hymns and Poems*, 1873, p. 89. In 1861 it was given with alterations in *H. A. and M.*, the same text being repeated in the revised ed., 1875. A less altered text is No. 75 in the *St. John's Hymnal*, Aberdeen, 1870.

2. O Jesu, Son of God, look down. This *tr.* is the above by E. Caswall, altered by the editors of the *Hymnary*, 1872, No. 576.   [J. J.]

Afflicted by a gracious God. *C. Wesley.* [*Affliction.*] From his *Short Hymns*, vol. ii. 1762, p. 375, and again in the *P. Works of J. & C. Wesley*, 1868–72, vol. xiii. p. 158, and based on Heb. x. 11. It was included, with slight alterations, in the revised ed. of the *Wes. H. Bk.* 1875, No. 331, replacing "Thou, Lord, hast blest my going out " (q. v.), which appeared in *Hys. & Sac. Poems*, 1740.

Afflicted soul, to Jesus dear. *J. Fawcett.* [*Support in Affliction.*] First pub. in his *Hymns adapted to the circumstances of Pub. and Priv. Devotion*, 1782, No. 13, in 7 st. of 4 l. In its original form it is rarely found in common use. An altered and abbreviated form, beginning "Afflicted Saint, to Christ draw near," was given by Rippon in his *Bapt. Sel.*, 1787, in 6 st., and later eds. This was repeated by Cotterill in his *Sel.* 1810, No. 50, and again in the 8th ed. 1819, No. 165, in 5 st., representing st. i., iii., v., vi. and vii. of the original. This is the arrangement which has come into C. U. in G. Brit. and America, sometimes as "Afflicted Saint, to God," &c. Orig. text in *Lyra Brit.* 1867, p. 225.

Affliction is a stormy deep. *Nathaniel Cotton.* [*Affliction.*] Part of his rendering of Ps. xlii., which appeared as "With fierce desire the hunted hart," in Dr. Dodd's *Christian's Magazine*, April, 1761, in 12 st. of 4 l., and signed "N." It was republished in his (posthumous) *Various Pieces in Verse and Prose*, 1791. In 1812 Collyer divided it into two hymns, Nos. 59-60, in his *Coll.*, the second beginning "Affliction is a stormy deep," in 5 st. These stanzas were transferred, with two slight alterations, to Stowell's *Sel.* 1831, and, sometimes with numerous alterations, to other hymnals, including Elliott's *Ps. & Hys.* 1835, and Bickersteth, *Christ. Psalmo.* 1833. Windle's text, in his *Met. Psalter*, Ps. 42, is from Stowell's *Sel.* 1831. Its modern use is not so extensive in G. Brit. as in America.

Again from calm and sweet repose. *Charles Philpot.* [*Morning.*] Pub. in Mary Anne Jevons's *Sacred Offering*, 1835, p. 141, in 5 st. of 4 l. and entitled "Morning Hymn." It is found in several American hymnals, including Hatfield's *Ch. H. Bk.* 1872, No. 15, but is unknown to the English collections. We have MS. date of 1822 for this hymn, but no direct evidence.   [W. T. B.]

Again our ears have heard the voice. *J. Montgomery.* [*Close of Service.*] This hymn of 2 st., for the close of Divine Service, was given in his *Christian Psalmist*, 1825, No 472, and again in his *Original Hymns*, 1853, No. 354. It was included in Bickersteth's *Christ. Psalmo.* 1833, but its use is very limited.

Again our earthly cares we leave. [*Divine Worship.*] Appeared in Cotterill's *Sel.* 1810, No. 98, in 4 st. of 4 l., and entitled, "For the blessing of God on Public Worship." It is based on J. Newton's "O Lord, our languid souls inspire," st. ii. being specially from Newton. The cento was most probably arranged and rewritten by Cotterill. Its use in G. Brit. is somewhat limited, but in America it is extensive, and is given in the collections of various denominations.

Again the Church's year hath run its round. *Godfrey Thring.* [*Advent.*] Written in 1865, and pub. in his *Hymns Congregational, and Others,* 1866, in 6 st. of 4 l. pp. 5 & 6 as an "Advent Hymn," and again in his *Hymns and Sacred Lyrics,* 1874, pp. 26–7, and in various hymnals. Authorized text in Thring's *Coll.* No. 102. It has been specially set to music by Henry Hugo Pierson, *Hymn Tunes,* 2nd Series, Simpkin & Marshall, 1872.

Again the day returns of holy rest. *W. Mason.* [*Sunday.*] 1st pub. in the *Protestant Magazine,* May 1796, as one of two hymns, this being for use "Before Morning Service," and the second : "Soon will [shall] the evening star with silent ray" for "Before Evening Service." The first hymn is in 5 st. of 4 l. and the second in 4 st. of 4 l., both being in the same measure, and each having the same chorus. Shortly after 1801 they were inserted in the form of a leaflet in the *Foundling Hospital Coll.,* and subsequently included in the enlarged edition of the same, in 1809. In 1811 both hymns were pub. in the author's *Works,* 4 vols, with the note appended to the second hymn,

"This and the foregoing hymn are adapted to an elegant movement of Pleyel, in his Opera 23rd. They have also been set to music by Dr. Burney and Mr. M. Camidge."

Both hymns have come into modern use through J. Kempthorne's *Ps. & Hys.* 1810, Cotterill's *Sel.,* 8th ed. 1819, and later collections. The morning hymn is the more popular of the two, and is in somewhat extensive use, but often as, "Again *returns the day* of holy rest"—as in Hall's *Mitre,* 1836, the *Leeds H. Bk.,* 1853, the *New Cong.,* and others. The American use of this hymn is very extensive.   [W. T. B.]

Again the Lord of life and light. *Anna L. Barbauld, née Aikin.* [*Easter.*] Contributed to Dr. W. Enfield's *Hymns for Public Worship,* &c., Warrington, 1772, No. LX., in 11 st. of 4 l. and appointed "For Easter Sunday." In the following year it was re-published in Mrs. Barbauld's (then Miss Aikin) *Poems,* Lond., J. Johnson, 1773, pp. 118–120, with alterations, and with the same title as in Dr. Enfield's *Hymns,* &c. In his *Coll.* of 1812 Dr. Collyer divided the hymn into two parts, Pt. i. being st. i.–iv., and Pt. ii. st. v.–ix., and xi., st. x. being omitted. This second part, as hymn 688, opened with :—"Jesus, the Friend of human kind." It has, however, fallen out of use. Of the centos which have been compiled from the original, there are in C. U :—

1. In *Mercer,* 1st ed. 1854, st. i., ii., vi., viii., iii., iv., from Cotterill's *Sel.,* 8th ed. 1819 ; Montgomery's *Christian Psalmist,* and other collections.

2. In *Hy. Comp.* and others : st. i., ii., vi., iii., and iv., from Bickersteth's *Christ. Psalmo.,* 1833 ; Gurney's Lutterworth *Coll.,* 1838, and Marylebone *Coll.,* 1851.

3. In S.P.C.K. *Ps. & Hys.,* 1852 and 1869, the same as No. 2, with the addition of a doxology.

4. In the Bapt. *Ps. & Hys.,* 1858 and 1880, st. i.–iv., Pt. i. from Dr. Collyer's *Coll.* as above.

5. In the Islington *Ps. & Hys.* 1830–62, *Kennedy,* 1863, as :—"This day be grateful homage paid," being st. iii., ii., iv., vi., viii., ix. The hymn in various forms is also in considerable use in America.

These facts will indicate the extent to which the original has been used, specially when it is remembered that these centos are repeated in many collections not indicated above. The full original text is given in *Lyra Brit.,* 1867, pp. 35–36, and Ld. Selborne's *Bk. of Praise,* 1862, pp. 61–62. The second cento has been rendered into Latin as :— *Ecce! iterum Dominus vitæ lucisque revelat,* by the Rev. R. Bingham, and included in his *Hymn. Christ. Lat.,* 1871, pp. 85–87. [J. J.]

Again the morn of gladness. *J. Ellerton.* [*Children's Hymn of Praise.*] Written at the request of the Vicar of Teddington, as a processional for Sunday School children on their way to church, 1874, and first pub. in *Children's Hys.,* *S.P.C.K.,* No. 16 ; and in J. Curwen's *New Child's O. H. Bk.,* No. 6.

Again we lift our voice. *C. Wesley.* [*Burial.*] Written on the death of one Samuel Hutchins, and included in *Hymns and Sacred Poems,* in 1749 (vol. ii.), "Samuel Hutchins was a Cornish smith, one of the first race of Methodist preachers, who died at an early age. An account of his life, written by his father, was published by J. Wesley in 1746." The hymn was embodied in the 1780 ed. of the *Wes. H. Bk.,* No. 51, and from thence it has passed into other hymnals. Orig. text, *P. Works of J. & C. Wesley,* 1868–72, vol. v. p. 214.

Ἄγε μοι, λίγεια φόρμιγξ. *Synesius, Bp. of Ptolemaïs.* Ode i. of the ten Odes which he composed at various periods of his life (375–430). The full Greek text is given in the *Anth. Græc. Carm. Christ.* 1871. No *tr.* is in C. U. Those which we have are :—

1. Come, sweet harp, resounding. By *I. Williams* in his *Thoughts in Past Years,* 1838.

2. Come, sweet-voiced lyre, to the soft Teian measure. By *A. Stevenson,* in his *Ten Hymns of Synesius, &c.,* 1865 ; and

3. Wake, wake, I pray thee, shrill-toned lyre ! By *A. W. Chatfield,* in his *Songs and Hymns of the E. Gr. Christian Poets,* 1876.

4. Partial *tr.* only, in H. S. Boyd's *Select Poems of Synesius, &c.,* 1814.

Of these *trs.* the only one from which a cento could be taken for C. U. is that of I. Williams.   [J. J.]

Ἄγε μοι ψυχὰ. *Synesius, Bp. of Ptolemaïs.* This is Ode iii. of the ten Odes, of which the above is the first. It was written to his "own beloved Libya," during a time of peace, and on his return from the court of Arcadius. It is the longest of the Odes, and is impassioned and patriotic. The full Greek text is given in the *Anth. Græc. Carm. Christ.,* 1871.

The *trs.* into English are :—(1) "Lift up thyself, my soul," by Mr. Chatfield, and pub. in his *Songs and*

Hymns, 1876, pp. 19–55, in 72 st. of 8 l. In explanation
of the metre which he has adopted in the translation,
Mr. Chatfield adds the following note :—
  " In the Greek, however short the metre and however long the ode, there is no weariness from monotony,
for the interchange of anapæst, dactyl, and spondee, in
the lines of from only four to six syllables each, makes
a constant and pleasing variety. But this being impossible in an English translation, I have adopted the
measure which Milton so beautifully employs in the
Hymn of the Nativity. For the convenience of those
who may wish to refer to the original, I mark the lines
at the head of each stanza."
  This *tr.* furnishes but few materials for the hymn-
book compiler, but for the musician some exquisite
sacred odes. (2) Another *tr.* is that of A. Stevenson:—
"Come, my soul, to sacred songs." This is unsuited
to public worship. It is given in his *Ten Hymns of
Synesius, &c.*, 1865. (3) There is also a partial *tr.* in
H. S. Boyd's *Select Poetry of Synesius*, 1814.

[J. J.]

Age after age has called her blessed.
Elizabeth Charles. [*B. V. M.*] 1st pub. as
No. 1 of the "Women of the Gospels," in her
Three Wakings, with Hys. and Songs, 1859.
It is headed " Mary the Mother of Jesus,"
and is based upon the words " All generations
shall call thee blessed." In Snepp's *Songs of
G. & G.*, 1872, it is unaltered.   [W. T. B.]

Ages, ages have departed. *J. Montgomery.* [*Anti-Slavery*.] Pub. in his *Poet's
Portfolio, &c.*, 1835, in 4 st. of 6 l. as No. 3 of
his " Songs on the Abolition of Negro Slavery
in the British Colonies, Aug. 1, 1834," and
entitled " Slavery that was."

Agnes, fair martyr. *Mary Dunlop
Moultrie.* [*St. Agnes.*] Written on her deathbed
in 1866, and first pub. in the *Church Times*,
Jan. 20, 1866, and again in her brother's
Hymns and Lyrics, 1867, entitled " The
Martyrdom of St. Agnes," Jan. 21, and consisting of 18 st. (pp. 168–71). In 1867, 11 st.
were given in the *People's H.* as No. 235, for
the Festival of " S. Agnes, V. M.," Jan. 21,
under the initials of " M. D. M."   These
stanzas were partly rewritten, specially the
first three, for the *People's H.*

Agnoscat omne saeculum. *V. Fortunatus.* [*Christmas.*] This hymn in 8 st.
dates from the latter part of the 6th cent.
Although wanting in the Vatican MSS., and
some other MSS. of Fortunatus's works, it was
given by *Fabricius*, in 1564, from a MS. of
the Benedictine Monastery of Morbach, and
has been repeated by *Thomasius*, and others,
including various editions of the author's
works (Migne's *Patrologia*, tom. 88, col. 264).
The full text is also in a MS. of the 11th
cent. in the *British Museum* (Harl. 2961, f.
226*b*). It is found in very few breviaries.
In those of *Constanz* and *York*, it is divided
into four hymns of two stanzas each with
the doxology, and appointed to be sung as
follows :—

Prime. " Agnoscat omne saeculum."
Terce. " Maria ventre concipit."
Sext. " Praesepe poni pertulit."
None. " Adam vetus quod polluit."

  The authorities for text and various readings are *Daniel*, i. No. 138; iv. 176; and *Hymn.
Sarisb.*, 1851, pp. 13–14. The *York Brev.*
text is also in Card. Newman's *Hymni Ecclesiae*,
1838 and 1865.

Translations in C. U. :—
  Dr. Neale, following the *York Brev.* arrange-
ment, gave, in the enlarged ed. of the *Hymnal
N.*, 1854, a *tr.* of each :—

Prime. " Let every age and nation own."
Terce. " The Virgin Mary hath conceived."
Sext. " He, by Whose hand the light was made."
None. " Now the old Adam's sinful stain."

and the same translations were repeated in all
subsequent editions of the *H. N.* From these
translations the editors of the *Hymnary*, 1872,
compiled No. 144, " Come, ye nations, thankful own," the metre being changed from the
L.M. of the *H. N.* to 7's.

Translations not in C. U. :—
  1. Let all the world confess from heaven. (" Agnoscat
omne.")   *Blew*, 1852.
  2. What the old Adam stained and soiled. (" Adam
vetus.")   *Blew*, 1852.
  3. Let thankful worlds confess from heaven.   *Chambers*, i. 77, embracing the whole hymn.   [J. J.]

Agnus Dei Qui tollis peccata mundi.
The use of this modified form of part of the
Gloria in Excelsis (q. v.), founded on John, i. 29,
seems to be referred to in the rubric for Easter
Eve in the *Sacramentary* of St. Gelasius, A.D.
492. In the time of Pope Sergius I. [687–
701] it was ordered by him to be sung at the
Communion of priest and people [" Statuit ut
tempore confractionis Dominici Corporis Agnus Dei, &c., a clero et populo decantaretur"].
Anastasius Bibliothecarius records this in
Historia de Vitis Romanorum Pontificum. It
is the opinion of Bona that Pope Sergius
ordered it to be sung thrice; Le Brun, on the
contrary, thinks it was only sung once. In the
11th century the last clause of its third repetition, " miserere nobis," began to appear as
" dona nobis pacem," and a little later in
Masses for the dead, the last clause, instead of
" dona nobis pacem," runs as a special prayer for
the departed, " dona eis requiem sempiter-
nam." This occurs also in the English Missals
of *Sarum, York* and *Hereford*, and is the universal custom of the Roman Church at the
present day, which also repeats the words, " Ecce
Agnus Dei, ecce Qui tollis peccata mundi," as
the priest turns to deliver the sacramental
wafer to the people.
  According to the *Sarum Use* the *Agnus Dei*
was incorporated in the Litany, but only to be
sung twice, and the third clause is placed
first. This was followed in the English
Litany of 1544 (as now in our own Litany),
and in the First Prayer Book of Edward VI.,
1549, was repeated in the Communion Office
with the following rubric :—

  " In the communion time the clerks shall sing : —
  " ' ii. O Lamb of God that takest away the sins of the
        world, have mercy upon us.
     ' O Lamb of God . . . grant us Thy peace.' "

This was omitted in 1552, and all subsequent revisions, though Bp. Cosin suggested
its restoration in 1662: but just as the *Adoro
Te* was used frequently as a private devotion,
so this translation of the *Agnus Dei* has continued in almost unbroken use in various
Eucharistic manuals of English divines; e.g. in
Bp. Cosin's *Coll. of Private Devotions*, 1627, and
the revised ed., 1664; Dean Lancelot Addison,
1699; Rev. Jas. King, 1726; and the very
popular *New Weeks' Preparation*, 1739.

Translations in C. U. :—

0 Lamb of God, that takest away, &c. By G. Moultrie. This metrical arrangement of the *Agnus Dei* was first pub. in the *Church Times*, July 23, 1864, and his *Hymns and Lyrics*, 1867, p. 118, in 3 st. of 5 l., and in 1872 was transferred to the *Hymnary*, with slight alterations in the last stanza. [V.]

The *Agnus Dei* has also come into English use through the German, in the following manner :—

(i.) **0 Lamm Gottes unschuldig.** By Nicolaus Decius, or Hovesch, first pub. in Low German in the *Coyctlyke leder*, Rostock, 1531, and in High German in V. Schumann's *G. B.*, Leipzig, 1539. Both forms are included in *Wackernagel*, iii. p. 568, in 3 st. of 7 l., as in the case of the Latin, st. i. only being printed in full. Included in almost all subsequent hymn-books as recently in the *Unv. L. S.*, 1851, No. 110. It has been much used in Germany at Holy Communion during the distribution of the elements; on Good Friday, at the close of sermon; and on other occasions. The *trs.* in C. U. are:—

1. **0 Lamb of God most holy.** By A. T. Russell as No. 26 in the Dalston German Hospital *Coll.*, 1848, in 2 st. of 7 l., repeated in his own *Ps. and Hys.*, 1851, No. 156, in 3 st. In both cases the sts. are identical, save in l. 7.

2. **0 Lamb of God, most stainless.** By Miss Winkworth, as No. 46 in her *C. B. for England*, 1863, in 3 st., identical, save in l. 7.

3. **0 Lamb of God, most Holy. Once for us sinners dying.** By Miss Borthwick, in full from *Knapp*, contributed as No. 66 to Dr. Pagenstecher's *Coll.*, 1864.

4. **Lamb of God, without blemish!** No. 75, in the Ohio Luth. *Hymnal*, 1880, in 3 st., identical, save l. 7.

Other trs. are :—
(1) "O Lamb of God, our Saviour," by J. C. Jacobi, 1722, p. 16 (1732, p. 31), and thence as No. 217 in pt. i. of the *Moravian H. Bk.*, 1754. (2) "O Lamb of God unspotted," as part of the Litanies at Baptism, p. xxiv. of the *Moravian H. Bk.*, 1801, and continued as a hymn in later eds. (3) "O Lamb of God, Who, bleeding," contributed by Prof. T. C. Porter to Schaff's *Christ in Song*, ed. 1879, p. 465. (4) "O Lamb of God, most holy, Upon the cross," from the version in Knapp's *Ev. L. S.*, 1837, No. 539 (ed. 1865, No. 506), sts. ii., iii. being from the Dresden *G. B.*, 1736 (*Fischer*, ii. 189), in the *British Herald*, Oct. 1866, p. 344, and repeated as No. 415 in Reid's *Praise Bk.*, 1872.

(ii.) **Christe du Lamm Gottes.** In the Reformation period this *tr.* of the *Agnus Dei*, in 3 st. of 3 l., was regarded as a prose antiphon rather to be included in the Liturgy than in the Hymn-book. Thus Erk, (*Choral Buch*, 1863, note to No. 38, p. 245,) quotes it as in Low German in the Brunswick *Kirchenordnung*, 1528, and in High German in that for Saxony, 1540. It is given as a hymn in the *Unv. L. S.*, 1851, No. 88. The *trs.* in C. U. are, (1) "Lamb of God, our Saviour," in full, by A. T. Russell as No. 20 in the Dalston German Hospital *Coll.*, 1848. (2) "Lamb of God, O Jesus! Thou who," &c., in full, as No. 68 in the Ohio Luth. *Hymnal*, 1880.

[J. M.]

Agricola, Johannes [Sneider], b. April 20, 1492, at Eisleben, where his father was a tailor. During his University course at Wittenberg, Luther took a great interest in him, entertained him at his own table, took him with him to Leipzig for the disputation, in 1519, with Dr. Eck, and in 1525 procured for him the position of Rector of St. Andrew's School at Eisleben, and preacher at St. Nicholas's Church there. He remained in Eisleben till 1536, working hand in hand with Luther ; but after his removal to Wittenberg, in 1536, as one of the lecturers in the University, he developed Antinomian views, and, in 1537, pub. a series of theses which Luther answered in six disputations, 1538–40. On his appointment as Court Preacher at Berlin, in 1540, he formally renounced these opinions, and professed adherence to Wittenberg orthodoxy. But after his subsequent appointment as General Superintendent of the Mark, he gradually not only sought the esteem of the great, but, in order to gain the favour of the Emperor, joined with two representatives of the Romish Church in drawing up a Formula of Union (THE INTERIM) which was presented to the Imperial Diet, held at Augsburg, and adopted by the Diet on May 15, 1548. By this action he disgusted the Lutherans, and procured for himself only discredit. He d. at Berlin, Sept. 22, 1566. He was one of the best preachers of his time, and compiled one of the earliest collections of German Proverbs, first pub. at Zwickau, 1529 [the *Brit. Mus.* copy was *printed* at Hagenau, 1529] (*Koch*, i. 278–281. *Allg. Deutsche Biog.*, i. 146–48).

Four hymns by him appeared in the early Lutheran hymn-books, two of which were retained by Luther in Babst's *Gesangbuch*, Leipzig, 1545.

1. **Ich ruf zu dir, Herr Jesu Christ.** [*Supplication.*] Wackernagel, iii. pp. 54–55, gives two forms of this, in 5 st. of 9 lines, the first from *Geistliche Lieder*, Erfurt, 1531, the second from an undated broadsheet before 1530, entitled, " A new hymn of supplication for Faith, Love, and Hope, and for a Holy Life ; composed by John of Eisleben, preacher to John Duke of Saxony." *Fischer*, i. 345, refers to the Nürnberg broadsheet, c. 1526, quoted in Wackernagel's *Bibliographie*, 1855, p. 89, and adds that in his opinion the disfavour into which Agricola fell after the outbreak of the Antinomian controversy caused the suppression of his name in the hymn-books. After appearing in Klug's *Geistliche Lieder*, 1529, the hymn was included in almost all subsequent hymn-books, and so recently as No. 379 in the *Unv. L. S.*, 1851.

It is sometimes erroneously ascribed to Paulus Speratus, an assumption originating with the *Riga G. B.* of 1664. It was a favourite hymn of Valerius Herberger, of P. J. Spener (who requested it to be sung at his deathbed), and of many others.

Translations in C. U. :—

1. **Lord Jesu Christ, I cry to Thee.** A good *tr.*, omitting st. iv., by A. T. Russell, as No. 200 in his *Ps. & Hs.*, 1851.

2. **Lord, hear the voice of my complaint.** A full and very good *tr.* as No. 116 by Miss Winkworth in her *C. B. for England*, 1863.

Other trs. are :—
(1) "I call on the, Lorde Jesu Christ," by *Bp. Coverdale*, 1539 (*Remains*, 1846, p. 560), repeated, slightly

altered, in the *Gude and Godly Ballates* (ed. 1568, folio 34), ed. 1868, p. 57. (2) " I cry to Thee, my dearest Lord," by *J. C. Jacobi*, 1722, p. 68 ; in his ed. 1732, p. 114, altered to " To Thee, O Lord, I send my cries," and thence as No. 310 in pt. i. of the *Moravian H. Bk.* 1754 ; omitted in 1789 and 1801 ; in the *Supplement* of 1808, st. i., iv. were included as No. 1082, and repeated in later eds. altered to " To Thee I send my fervent cries." (3) " I cry to Thee, O Christ our Lord ! " by N. L. Frothingham, 1870, p. 205.   [J. M.]

Ah, I shall soon be dying. *J. Ryland.* [*Death anticipated.*] Dr. Ryland's son says that this hymn was written by his father while walking through the streets of London, and dates it 1800, (s. mss.). This date is an error, as the hymn appeared in the *Evangelical Magazine*, Oct. 1798, in 8 st. of 4 l., as "Reflections," and with the note :—

"The following lines passed through the mind of a country minister as he was walking the streets of London, and considering how far several persons appeared now to be advanced in life whom he had known in their youth a very few years back, and how many others of his acquaintance had been already removed."

The hymn was repeated in the *Baptist Register*, 1800, p. 312, and in the 27th ed. of Rippon's *Sel.*, 1827–8, No. 550. pt. iii. From thence it has passed into collections both in G. Brit. and America. It is also included in Sedgwick's reprint of Dr. Ryland's *Hymns*, 1860.

Ah, Jesus, let me hear Thy voice. *A. Reed.* [*Desiring Christ.*] Contributed to his *Supplement to Dr. Watts*, 1817, No. 108, and also included in his *Hymn Book*, 1842, No. 335 in 5 st. of 4 l. under the title, "Desiring Christ." It was repub. in the *Wycliffe Chapel Sup.* 1872, No. 14. Its use in G. Brit. is very limited, but in America it is regarded with great favour. In his *Ch. H. Bk.* Dr. Hatfield omits st. 4. Orig. text in *Lyra Brit.* p. 476, and Schaff's *Christ in Song*, 1869.

Ah, Lord, with trembling I confess. *C. Wesley.* [*Backsliding.*] From his *Short Hymns*, &c., 1762, vol. ii., No. 30. It appeared in the *Wes. H. Bk.*, 1780 ; and is retained in the new ed., 1875, No. 317. It has also passed into various collections in G. Brit. and America, and is included in the *P. Works of J. & C. Wesley*, 1868–72, vol. x. p. 165.

Ah, lovely appearance of death. *C. Wesley.* [*Burial.*] 1st pub. in his *Funeral Hymns* (1st Ser.), 1746, No. v., and entitled "On the sight of a Corpse." The body is supposed to have been that of a young man who died at Cardiff, Aug. 1744 ; as, concerning him, C. Wesley wrote in his *Journal* of that date, "The Spirit, at its departure, had left marks of its happiness on the clay. No sight upon earth, in my eyes, is half so lovely." In 1780 it was included in the *Wes. H. Bk.*, but omitted in the revised ed. of 1875. Orig. text, *P. Works of J. & C. Wesley*, 1868–72, vol. vi. p. 193. The text of this hymn was revised by the author about 1782, and reduced to 5 st. Details of the ms. alterations are given in the *P. Works*, vol. vi. p. 212. Although omitted from the *Wes. H. Bk.*, 1875, it is still retained in many collections in G. Brit. and America.

Ah, mournful case, what can afford. *Ralph Erskine.* [*Longing for Heaven.*] 1st

pub. in his *Gospel Sonnets* (2nd ed., Edin., 1726) as section i. of pt. v., entitled "The deserted Believer longing for perfect Freedom from Sin," in 20 st. of 4 lines. St. xiv.-xx beginning—"O send me down a draught of love"—were included in the *Sacred Songs of Scotland*, 1860 (Edin., A. Elliott), p. 41, as No. 370 in Lord Selborne's *Bk. of Praise*, and adopted, as No. 230, in the Scottish *Pres. Hyml.*, 1876.   [J. M.]

Ah, my dear Lord, Whose changeless love. *C. Wesley.* [*In Temptation.*] 1st pub. in *Hymns and Sacred Poems* by J. & C. Wesley, 1739, in 14 st. of 4 l. In *Kennedy*, 1863, No. 1266, is composed of st. i., ii., iii., vii., x. and xii. In its original form it is unknown to modern hymnals, and the use of this cento is very limited. Stanzas xi.-xiv.—as "Fondly my foolish heart essays"—were given in the *Wes. H. Bk.* 1780, as No. 282. The same stanzas are No. 291 of the revised ed. 1875. Orig. text, *P. Works*, 1868–72, vol. i. p. 131.

Ah, my dear loving Lord. *C. Wesley.* [*Spiritual life within.*] This poem, of 15 double stanzas, in two parts, is the last of three entitled, "The Backslider," which appeared in *Hys. and Sacred Poems*, 1742. In 1780 the hymn "My gracious, loving Lord," was compiled therefrom, and included with alterations, in the *Wes. H. Bk.* from whence it has passed into many collections of the Methodist bodies. Orig. text, *P. Works*, 1868–72, vol. ii. p. 114.

Ah, what a wretch am I. *C. Wesley.* [*Watch-night.*] 1st pub. in *Hymns and Sacred Poems*, 1749, being No. 2 of "Hymns for the Watch-night," in 10 st. of 8 l. Of these, st. ix., x., beginning "Thou seest my feebleness," are found in some collections, including the *Leeds H. Bk.*, 1853, Bapt. *Ps. and Hys.*, 1858, and others. The cento "Gracious Redeemer, shake," in the *Wes. H. Bk.*, 1780 and 1875, and other collections, is also from this hymn. It begins with st. v. (Orig. text, *P. Works*, 1868–72, vol. v. p. 261). In the American *Bk. of Hys.*, 1848, and the *Hys. of the Spirit*, 1864, it reads, "Father, this slumber shake."

Ah, when shall I awake. *C. Wesley.* [*Prayer.*] From his *Hymns on God's Everlasting Love*, first pub. in 1741, in 11 st. of 8 l. (second series), No. vii. Of the original, 6 st. were included in the 1780 ed. of the *Wes. H. Bk.*, No. 294. Orig. text, *P. Works*, 1868–72, vol. iii. p. 61.

Ah, whither flee, or where abide. [*Retirement.*] Contributed by Miss Winkworth to *Lyra Mystica*, 1865, p. 263, in 7 st. of 8 l., as from the German. The original has not been traced.

Ah, whither should I go. *C. Wesley.* [*Lent.*] 1st pub. in his *Hymns on God's Everlasting Love*, 1741, No. 14, in 16 st. of 8 l. In 1780 st. i.-iv. were given in the *Wes. H. Bk.* as one hymn, and st. xiv.-xvi., "Lo in Thy hand," as a second, under the division "For mourners convinced of Sin." Although the latter was omitted from the revised ed., 1875, yet both hymns are found in a considerable number of collections, both in G. Brit. and America. Orig. text in *P. Works*, 1868–72, vol. iii. p. 89.

Ah, why am I left to complain. *C. Wesley.* [*Lent.*] From his *Short Hymns*, 1762; again 1794; and in *P. Works*, 1868–72, vol. x. p. 26. It was included in the *Wes. H. Bk.*, new ed., 1875, No. 777.

Ah, wretched souls who strive in vain. *Anne Steele.* [*Lent.*] A hymn on "The Christian's Noblest Resolution," which appeared in her *Poems on Subjects chiefly Devotional*, 1760, vol. i. p. 161, in 5 st. of 4 l., from whence it passed into the Bapt. *Coll. of Hys.* of Ash and Evans, 1769, No. 286, and signed "T."; into Rippon's Bapt. *Sel.*, 1787, No. 334, and others. It is also found in Sedgwick's reprint of Miss Steele's *Hymns*, 1863.

Ah, wretched, vile, ungrateful heart. *Anne Steele.* [*Lent.*] Under the title of "The Inconstant Heart," this hymn was pub. in her *Poems on Subjects chiefly Devotional*, 1760, vol. i. p. 119, in 5 st. of 4 l.; again in the next ed., 1780; and again in Sedgwick's reprint of her *Hymns*, 1863. Its use is unknown, or nearly so, in G. Brit., but in America it is given in several of the most important modern collections, including Hatfield's *Ch. H. Bk.*, 1872, No. 970, and others.

Αἰγύπτου φωστήρ. [*St. Mark.*] Three homoia (hymns of the same structure) from the office for St. Mark (Ap. 25) in the *Menaea*. The only *tr.* is that by Dr. Littledale—"Mark, shining light of Egypt"—which was made for and first published in the *People's H.*, 1867, No. 247, and signed "F. R." The doxology is not in the original.

Aikin, Anna L. [Barbauld, A. L.]

Ainger, Alfred, M.A., graduated Trin. Coll. Cambridge, B.A. 1860, M.A. 1864. In 1860 he became curate of Alrewas, Staffordshire; in 1864 Assistant Master of Sheffield Collegiate School, and in 1866 Reader at the Temple Church, London. Mr. Ainger's Harvest hymn "Another year is ended," was written for the Harvest Festival at Alrewas, 1862, in 5 st. of 8 l. On appearing in *Harland*, ed. 1864, No. 216, two stanzas were reduced to one, thus forming a hymn of 4 st. Its use is not extensive.

Ainsworth, Henry, was a leader of the Brownist party in England, and one of those nonconforming clergy who, in 1604, left this country for Amsterdam. He was a learned man and skilled in Hebrew. He became very poor in exile, living on the meanest fare, and acting as porter to a bookseller. He was of a warm temperament and apt to be quarrelsome; d. 1622 or 1623, suddenly, which gave rise to a suspicion of unfair play on the part of the Jewish community. His translations from the Hebrew Psalms were printed at Amsterdam and entitled *The Booke of Psalms: Englished both in Prose and Metre*, 1612. It contained a preface and had musical notes. There is a copy in the Bodleian Library.   [J. T. B.]

Aird, Marion Paul, b. at Glasgow, 1815, where she resided for some time, and then proceeded to Kilmarnock, where her *Home of the Heart and other Poems Moral and Religious* were pub. 1846–1863, her *Heart Histories*, *Violets from Greenwood, &c.*, in prose and verse, 1853, and *Sun and Shade*, 1860. Miss Aird is included in J. G. Wilson's *Poets and Poetry of Scotland*, 1876, vol. ii. p. 389. Very few of her hymns are in C. U., amongst these is "Had I the wings of a dove, I would fly."

Akerman, Lucy Evelina, née Metcalf. An American Unitarian writer, dau. of Thomas Metcalf, b. at Wrentham, Mass., Feb. 21, 1810, m. to Charles Akerman, of Portsmouth, N.H., resided at Providence, R.I., and d. there Feb. 21, 1874. Mrs. Akerman is known as a hymn writer through her :—

Nothing but leaves, the Spirit grieves, which was suggested by a sermon by M. D. Conway, and 1st pub. in the N. Y. *Christian Observer*, cir. 1858. In the Scottish *Family Treasury*, 1859, p. 136, it is given without name or signature, and was thus introduced into G. Brit. In America it is chiefly in use amongst the Baptists. Its popularity in Great Britain arose out of its incorporation by Mr. Sankey, in his *Sac. S. & Solos*, No. 34, and his rendering of it in the evangelistic services of Mr. Moody. The air to which it is sung is by an American composer, S. J. Vail.

Alanus de Insulis, or of Lille in Flanders, called also Alanus Anglicus, lived in the last half of the 12th and part of the 13th cent. There appears to be much doubt, which has resulted in much controversy, as to whether or not there were two individuals bearing the name of Alanus de Insulis, or whether Alanus the poet, known as "Doctor Universalis," was identical with Alanus the Bishop of Auxerre, the friend of St. Bernard. It is unnecessary to discuss the question here. There is no doubt that the poet is identical with the "Doctor Universalis." The principal works of this author were :—

1. *Parables*, a work described by Archbishop Trench in his *Sac. Lat. Poetry*, 3rd ed., 1874, as having been "in high favour before the revival of learning."
2. *Anti-Claudianus*, a moral poem of considerable length, divided into nine books, called "Distinctiones." It is upon this work that his fame chiefly rests.
3. *Liber de Planctu Naturae*, written partly in verse, and partly in prose.

Leyser (p. 1020) says of this author " Inter aevi sui poetas facile familiam duxit;" Oudin (*De Script. Eccles.*, ii. p. 1405) that the *Anti-Claudianus* is "singulari festivitate, lepore, et elegantia conscriptum;" Rambach (*Anthologie*, i. p. 329) speaks highly of his merits; while Archbishop Trench, though demurring somewhat to the full praises of the others, allows that in such passages as the one commencing, "Est locus ex nostro secretus climate" (which is the description of a natural paradise), "Ovidian both in their merits and defects, we must recognise the poet's hand," *Sac. Lat. Poetry*, 1849 and 1874.

Only one complete ed. of this poet's works is known, viz., *Alani Opera*, ed. C. de Visch, Antwerp, 1654; but his *Anti-Claudianus* and *Liber de Planctu Naturae* are given at length in T. Wright's *Anglo-Latin Satirical Poets, &c., of the 12th cent.*, Lon., 1872, vol. ii. Extracts from his works are also found in the authors above referred to, and others. One of his poems, "Omnis Mundi creatura," has been *tr.* into English. It is given in Worsley's *Poems and Translations*, 1863, p. 199. Latin text in *Trench* and *Königsfeld*. [D. S. W.]

Alard, Wilhelm, s. of Frans Alard, who was confessor of the Reformed Faith during the persecutions of the Duke of Alva, was b. at Wilster, Nov. 22, 1572. He was not only by birth a member of a noble Belgian family, but of one distinguished for three or four generations in classical and theological literature. Indeed, in 1721, a volume was published at Hamburg by one of the family entitled *Decas Alardorum scriptis Clarorum.* Wilhelm Alard, amongst other compositions, published three small volumes of Latin hymns :—

1. *Excubiarum Piarum Centuria,* Lipsiae, 1623.
2. *Excubiarum Piarum Centuria Secunda,* 1628.
3. *Excubiarum Piarum Centuria Tertia,* 1630.

These hymns were held in high esteem when they first appeared, the first volume passing through four editions during its author's lifetime. They are now almost forgotten. Archbishop Trench has given one short specimen from each of the first two centuries in his *Sac. Lat. Poetry,* 1849 and 1874, from the first, a hymn " Accessuri ad sacram Communionem Oratio ad Jesum Servatorem," p. 246; and from the second, " De angelo custode," p. 240. The latter very graceful composition, commencing, " Cum me tenent fallacia," is also in Loftie's *Latin Year,* and, *tr.* into English, in D. T. Morgan's *Hys., &c., of the Lat. Church,* 1880.

The poet during his latter years was pastor and superintendent at Krempe, in Holstein, where he d. May 9, 1645. [D. S. W.]

Alas! and did my Saviour bleed. *I. Watts.* [*Passiontide.*] 1st pub. in the 1st ed. of his *Hymns and Spiritual Songs,* 1707, and again in the enlarged ed. of the same 1709, Bk. ii., No. 9, in 6 st. of 4 l., and entitled " Godly sorrow arising from the Sufferings of Christ." At a very early date it passed into common use outside of the religious body with which Watts was associated. It is found in many modern collections in G. Brit., but its most extensive use is in America. Usually the second stanza, marked in the original to be left out in singing if desired, is omitted, both in the early and modern collections.

A slightly altered version of this hymn, with the omission of st. ii., was rendered into Latin by the Rev. R. Bingham, as "Anne fundens sanguinem," was included in his *Hymnol. Christ. Lat.,* 1871, pp. 245–247.

Alas! by nature how depraved. *J. Newton.* [*Lent.*] Appeared in the *Olney Hymns,* 1779, Bk. ii., No. 29, in 7 st. of 4 l., and based on the words, "How shall I put thee among the children?" Jer. iii. 19. As given in Snepp's *S. of G. & G.,* 1872, No. 450, and elsewhere, it is composed of st. i.–iv. of the original.

Alas! what hourly dangers rise. *Anne Steele.* [*Watchfulness.*] 1st pub. in her *Poems on Subjects chiefly Devotional,* 1760, vol. i. pp. 79–80, in 6 st. of 4 l., and entitled

" Watchfulness and Prayer," Matt. xxvi. 7 It was also reprinted in subsequent eds. of the *Poems,* and in Sedgwick's reprint of her *Hymns,* 1863. In Williams & Boden's *Coll.,* 1801, No. 362, it was abbreviated to 4 st., and this example has been mostly followed to the present day. Its use in G. Brit. is very limited; but in America it is somewhat extensive, and varies in length from 3 to 5 st., the *Sabb. H. Bk.,* 1858, No. 637, being an exception in favour of the complete text, with the single alteration of "*my*" to "*mine eyes*" in st. 1.

Alber, Erasmus, son of Tileman Alber, afterwards pastor at Engelroth, was b. at Sprendlingen c. 1500. After studying at Wittenberg under Luther and Melanchthon, he became, in 1525, schoolmaster at St. Ursel, near Frankfurt-am-Main, and in 1527 at Heldenbergen, in Hesse Darmstadt. In 1528 he was appointed by the Landgrave Philip of Hesse pastor at Sprendlingen and Götzenhain, where he devoted himself specially to the children of his charge. After 11 years' service he was appointed by the Elector Joachim of Brandenburg court preacher at Berlin, but proving too faithful for the court, was, in 1541, removed as chief pastor to Neu Brandenburg. In 1542 he became pastor at Stade, in Wetteravia, and while there received, in 1543, the degree of Doctor of Theology from the University of Wittenberg. He was then invited, in the beginning of 1545, by the Landgrave Philip IV. of Hanau Lichtenberg, to perfect the work of the Reformation in Babenhausen, but no sooner had he fairly entered upon it than, in the end of October, he received his dismissal. After a short stay at Sprendlingen and at Wittenberg, he became preacher at Magdeburg, where he strongly denounced the *Interim* (see *Agricola*). On the capitulation of Magdeburg, in 1551, after a 14 months' siege, he fled to Hamburg, and then went to Lübeck. Finally, in 1552, he was appointed by Duke Albrecht I. of Mecklenburg, General Superintendent of Mecklenburg, and preacher at St. Mary's Church in Neu Brandenburg. In addition to losing all his own and his wife's property by confiscation and necessary expenditure, he was there unable to obtain from the Town Council the payment of his stipend. On May 4, 1553, he applied for the payment of 60 florins to relieve his urgent necessities. The refusal broke his heart. He returned home to die, and fell asleep at 9 A.M. on May 5, 1553.

One of the best writers for children in his day, and an ardent controversialist and martyr of freedom of speech, he has been by some ranked, as a hymn-writer, next to Luther, in the Reformation period. His hymns, 20 in all, were first collected by Dr. Stromberger, and pub. at Halle, 1857. Being mostly long, and ungainly in style, not many of them have kept a place in the hymn-books, though they have been justly styled "powerful and living witnesses of a steadfast faith and a manly trust in God's Word" (*Koch,* i. 301–306; *Allg. Deutsche Biog.* i. 219–20; Dr. Stromberger's *Preface; Bode,* pp. 35–36—the last stating that his father was a schoolmaster at Sprendlingen.) Two have been *tr.* into English. One of these, beginning "Christe, du bist der helle Tag," is a *tr.,* and is noted under, "Christe qui lux es et dies."

The only original hymn by Alber *tr.* into English is—

1. Nun freut euch Gottes Kinder all. [*Ascension.*] 1st pub. on a broadsheet, N.P. N.D., c. 1549, and thence in Wackernagel, iii. p. 881, in 29 st. of 4 l. In a broadsheet at Nürnberg, c. 1555, it is entitled, "Of the Fruits of the Ascension of our Lord Christ and of the Gifts of the Holy Spirit," and begins—"Freut euch ihr Gottes Kinder all." This form is included in Dr. Stromberger's ed. of Alber's *Geistliche Lieder*, 1857, p. 5. In the hymn-books it is generally abridged, and so the Berlin *G. L. S.* ed. 1863, 339, gives 16 st. (i.–vi., ix.–xi., xiii., xviii., xxv.–xxix., of the first form). A *tr.*:—

O Children of your God rejoice, of st. i., ii., iv., xxvii. xxix., by A T Russell, is given as No. 122, in his *Ps. & Hys.* 1851. See also *Diterich, J. S. (Auf, Jesu Jünger).*   [J. M.]

Alberti, or **Albert, Heinrich,** s. of Johann Alberti, tax collector at Lobenstein, in Voigtland (Reuss), b. at Lobenstein, June 28, 1604. After some time spent in the study of law at Leipzig, he went to Dresden and studied music under his uncle Heinrich Schütz, the Court Capellmeister. He went to Königsberg in 1626, and was, in 1631, appointed organist of the Cathedral. In 1606 he was enrolled a member of the Poetical Union of Königsberg, along with Dach, Roberthin, and nine others. He d. at Königsberg, Oct. 6, 1651. His hymns, which exhibit him as of a pious, loving, true, and artistic nature, appeared, with those of the other members of the Union, in his *Arien etliche theils geistliche, theils weltliche zur Andacht, guten Sitten, Keuscher Liebe und Ehrenlust dienende Lieder*, pub. separately in 8 pts., 1638–1650, and in a collected form, Königsberg, 1652, including in all, 118 secular, and 74 sacred pieces. Of the 78 sacred melodies which he composed and pub. in these 8 pts., 7 came into German C. U. (*Koch*, iii. 191–197; *Allg. Deutsche Biog.*, i. 210–212, the latter dating his death, 1655 or 1656).

Two of his hymns have been *tr.* into English, viz.:—

i. Der rauhe Herbst kommt wieder. [*Autumn.*] 1st pub. as above in pt. viii., 1650, No. 9, in 9 st. of 6 l., entitled "On the happy departure, Sep. 2, 1648, of Anna Katherine, beloved little daughter of Herr Andreas Höllander," of Kneiphof. Included, as No. 731, in the *Unv. L. S.*, 1851, omitting st. iii., viii., ix.

The trs. are:—
(1) "The Autumn is returning," by Miss Manington, 1863, p. 175. (2) "Sad Autumn's moan returneth," in E. Massie's *Sacred Odes*, vol. ii. 1867, p. 1.

ii. Gott des Himmels und der Erden. [*Morning.*] First pub. as above in pt. v. 1643, No. 4, in 7 st. of 6 l., included as No. 459 in the *Unv. L. S.*, 1851.

Of this hymn Dr. Cosack, of Königsberg (quoted in *Koch*, viii. 186), says:—

"For two hundred years it is hardly likely that a single day has greeted the earth that has not, here and there, in German lands, been met with Alberti's hymn. Hardly another morning hymn can be compared with it, as far as popularity and intrinsic value are concerned, if simplicity and devotion, purity of doctrine and adaptation to all the circumstances of life are to decide."

Sts. ii., iii., v. have been special favourites in Germany, st. v. being adopted by children, by brides, by old and young, as a morning prayer.

The fine melody (in the Irish *Ch. Hymnal* called "Godesberg") is also by Alberti.

Translations in C. U. :—

1. God, the Lord of what's created, in full in J. C. Jacobi's *Div. Hys.* 1720. p. 35. In his 2nd ed. 1732, p. 169, altered to—"God, the Lord of the Creation"; and thence slightly altered as No. 478 in part i. of the *Moravian H. Bk.*, 1754, with a dox. as in the Magdeburg *G. B.*, 1696. In 1789, No. 743, altered to—"God, omnipotent Creator"; with st. ii., iv., vii., omitted; st. iii., viii. being also omitted in the 1801 and later ed. In 1868, st. iii.–v. were included as No. 511 in the Pennsylvania Luth. *Ch. Bk.*, with st. ii., vi., vii. from A. T. Russell.

2. God, Thou Lord of Earth and Heaven, in full, by H. J. Buckoll in his *H. from the German*, 1842, p. 22. His *trs.* of st. iv.–vi. beginning—"Now the morn new light is pouring," were included as No. 3 in the *Rugby School H. Bk.*, 1843 (ed. 1876, No. 4), and of st. v., vi., altered to "Jesus! Lord! on! our steps be guiding," as No. 130 in Dr. Pagenstecher's *Coll.*, 1864.

3. God, who heaven and earth upholdest. A good *tr.* omitting st. iv. and based on Jacobi, by A. T. Russell, as No. 64 in the Dalston Hospital *Coll.*, 1848. In his own *Ps. & Hys.*, 1851, No. 3, the *trs.* of st. vi., vii. were omitted, and this was repeated as No. 218, in the *New Zealand Hymnal*, 1872. The Pennsylvania Luth. *Ch. Bk.* takes st. i. partly from Miss Winkworth.

4. God who madest earth and heaven, Father, Son, and Holy Ghost. A good and full *tr.* by Miss Winkworth in her *Lyra Ger.*, 1st ser., 1855, p. 213 (later ed., p. 215, slightly altered). In full in R. M. Taylor's *Par. Ch. Hyml.*, 1872, No. 27. A cento from st. i., ll. 1–4; v., ll. 1–4; vi., ll. 1–4; with v., ll. 5, 6; and vii., ll. 5, 6, was included as No. 23 in the Irish *Ch. Hyml.* 1873. In 1868, included in L. Rehfuess's *Church at Sea*, p. 79, altered to—"Creator of earth and heaven." In 1863 it was altered in metre and given as No. 160 in the *C. B. for England*. From this Porter's *Church Hyml.*, 1876, No. 54, omits st. iii. Also in the Ohio Lutheran *Hymnal*, 1880, No. 293.

5. God who madest earth and heaven. A good *tr.* omitting st. vii., and with st. i., ll. 1–4, from Miss Winkworth, contributed by R. Massie, as No. 501, to the 1857 ed. of Mercer's *C. P. & H. Bk.* (Ox. ed. 1864, No. 7, omitting st. v.).

6. God of mercy and of might. A good *tr.* (omitting st. v., vi ,) by Dr. Kennedy, as No. 811, in his *Hymnol. Christ.*, 1863, repeated in Dr. Thomas's *Aug. H. Bk.* 1866, No. 510; and, omitting the *tr.* of st. vii., as No. 31, in *Holy Song*, 1869.   [J. M.]

Albertini, Johann Baptist, s. of Jakob Ulrich v. Albertini, a native of the Grisons, Switzerland, who had joined the Moravians, and settled among them at Neuwied, near Coblenz, b. at Neuwied Feb. 17, 1769. After passing through the Moravian school at Niesky, and their Theological Seminary at Barby, in both of · which he had Friedrich Schleiermacher as a fellow-student, he was, in 1788, appointed one of the masters in the Moravian school at Niesky, and in 1789 at Barby. In 1796, he was appointed tutor at the Theological Seminary at Niesky, and ordained as diaconus of the Moravian Church. Up to this time he had devoted himself chiefly to the study of the Oriental languages, and of botany, but now his studies of Holy Scripture for his theological lectures and for the pulpit, brought him to the feet of Christ, whose earnest and devoted disciple and witness he henceforth became. In 1804 he relinquished his tutorial work to devote himself entirely to ministerial labour in Niesky, where he was, in 1810, ordained presbyter. In Feb. 1814 he went to Gnadenberg, near Bunzlau, Silesia, as head of the Girls' School, and preacher; and while on a visit to Herrnhut, was, Aug. 24, 1814, constituted a bishop of the Moravian Church. By the synod of 1818, he was appointed to Gnadenfrei, near Reichenbach, Silesia, and after three years of faithful and successful labour, was chosen one of the heads of the Moravian Church (one of the *Unitäts-Aeltesten-Conferenz*), his special department being the oversight of their charitable and educational establishments; and in 1824 President of the Conference. In love and meekness he ruled and visited the churches till, in Nov. 1831, an illness seized him, which terminated fatally at Berthelsdorf, near Herrnhut, Dec. 6, 1831. (*Koch*, vii. 330–334; *Allg. Deutsche Biog.*, i. 216–217.) Distinguished as a preacher beyond the bounds of his church, he was, in the estimation of *Koch*, apart from *Novalis*, the most important hymn-writer of his time—spiritual, simple, and childlike. Yet it must be said that his brother Moravian, *C. B. Garve*, and *E. M. Arndt*, are more fully represented in hymnals since 1820. Albertini's hymns appeared to the number of 400, (many, however, being single verses,) in his *Geistliche Lieder für Mitglieder und Freunde der Brüdergemeine*, Bunzlau, 1821 (2nd ed. 1827). None of them have passed into English C. U., and the only three we have to note are :—

i. **Brenne hell, du Lampe meiner Seele.** [*Second Advent.*] On the Lamp of the Wise Virgin. 1st pub. 1821, as above, p. 130, in 3 st. of 8 l. The only *tr.* is, "Lamp within me! brightly burn and glow," by *Miss Winkworth*, 1869, p. 311.

ii. **Freund, komm in der Frühe.** [*Morning.*] 1st pub. 1821, as above, p. 273, in 5 st. of 10 l. *Tr.* as, "Come at the morning hour," by Miss Borthwick in *H. L. L.* 1862 (ed. 1862, p. 256; 1884, p. 190).

iii. **Längst suchtest du, mein Geist! ein nahes Wesen.** [*Christmas.*] 1st pub. 1821, as above, p. 9, in 5 st. of 6 l. *Tr.* as, "Long in the spirit world my soul had sought," by *Miss Winkworth*, 1855, p. 191 (later eds. p. 193), assigned to St. Thomas's Day.   [J. M.]

Alberus, Erasmus. [Alber.]

Albinus, Johann Georg, eldest s. of Zacharias Albinus, pastor at Unter-Nessa, near Weissenfels, Saxony, 1621–1633, and at Stuhlburgwerben, 1633–1635, was b. at Unter-Nessa, March 6, 1624. After his father's death, in 1635, he was, in 1638, adopted by his cousin, Lucas Pollio, diaconus at St. Nicholas's Church in Leipzig. After his cousin's death, in 1643, the Court preacher, Sebastian Mitternacht, of Naumburg, took an interest in him, and he remained at Naumburg

till he entered the University of Leipzig, in 1645. He studied for eight years at Leipzig, during which time he acted as house tutor to the Burgomaster, Dr. Friedrich Kühlwein, and was then, in 1653, appointed Rector of the Cathedral School at Naumburg. This post he resigned when, in 1657, he became pastor of St. Othmar's Church, in Naumburg. There he proved himself a zealous pastor, seeking ever "the glory of God, the edification of the Church, and the everlasting salvation, wellbeing, and happiness of his hearers." During his ministry he suffered greatly, not only from bodily infirmities, but from ecclesiastical encroachments and bickerings. The end came when, on Rogation Sunday, May 25, 1679, he quietly fell asleep in Jesus, at 2.30 P.M. On his tombstone his eldest son placed the inscription, "Cum viveret, moriebatur, et nunc cum mortuus vivit, quia sciebat, quod vita via sit mortis et mors vitae introitus." During his student days he was known as a poet, became, in 1654, a member of the Fruitbearing Society, and was also a member of Philipp v. Zesen's Patriotic Union. As a poet he was, says Koch, "distinguished by ease of style, force of expression, and liveliness of fancy, and his manner of thought was scriptural and pervaded by a deep religious spirit" (*Koch*, iii. 392–98; *Allg. Deutsche Biog.* i. 222–223). Of the many hymns he composed, and pub. in his various poetical works, only three have been *tr.* into English, viz. :—

i. **Alle Menschen müssen sterben.** [*For the Dying.*] This hymn, which *Koch*, iii. 397, calls "his best known hymn, and a pearl in the Evangelical Treasury of Song," was written for the funeral of Paul von Henssberg, a Leipzig merchant, and was thus sung, from broadsheets, June 1, 1652. It was given in Niedling's *Wasserquelle*, Altenburg, 1663, and gradually came into universal use, passing through Freylinghausen's *G. B.*, 1704, into most subsequent collections, as in the *Unv. L. S.*, 1851, No. 804, in 8 st. of 8 l. It was a great favourite of P. J. Spener, who sang it regularly on Sunday afternoons; of J. F. Hochstetter, Prelate of Murrhardt, and many others (*Koch*, viii. 628–631).

In the *Blätter für Hymnologie*, 1884, pp. 55-58, the text is quoted in full from the original broadsheet [Ducal Library, Gotha], the title of which ends "Mit seiner Poesie und Musick erweisen wollen Johannes Rosenmüller." Rosenmüller is not, however, known as a hymn-writer, and this statement is hardly sufficient to overthrow the traditional ascription to Albinus.

The *trs.* in C. U. are :—

1. **Death o'er all his sway maintaineth.** A good *tr.* of st. i., iii.-v., by *A. T. Russell*, as No. 260 in his *Ps. & Hys.*, 1851. Included, considerably altered and beginning, "Death in all this world prevaileth," as No. 745 in *Kennedy*, 1863.

2. **Hark! a voice saith, all are mortal.** A good *tr.*, omitting st. v., viii., as No. 196 by Miss Winkworth in her *C. B. for England*, 1863, and with a *tr.* of st. v. added as No. 429 in the Ohio Luth. *Hymnal*, 1880.

Other trs. are :—
(1) "All must die! there's no redemption," by *Dr. H. Mills*, 1856, p. 234, 1st pub. (reading "no *exception*") in the *Evang. Review*, Gettysburg, Oct. 1851. (2) "All that's human still must perish," by Dr. John Ker, in the *U. P. Juv. Miss. Mag.* July, 1859. (3) "'Tis God's decree that all shall die," by Dr. G. Walker, 1860, p. 107.

ii. Straf mich nicht in deinem Zorn. [*Ps.* vi.] Of the origin of this hymn, *J. C. Wetzel*, i. 46, and ii. 404, relates what seems rather an apocryphal story to this effect :—

Johann Rosenmüller, while music director at Leipzig, had been guilty of improper practices with some of his scholars. He was thrown into prison, but having made his escape, went to Hamburg. Thence he sent a petition for restoration to the Elector Johann Georg at Dresden, and to support his petition enclosed this hymn, which Albinus had written for him, along with the beautiful melody by himself (in the Irish *Ch. Hyml.*, 1876; called *Nassau*, in the Darmstadt *G. B.* 1698, p. 49).

This, if correct, would date it about 1655, and *Koch*, iii. 398, says it was printed separately in that year. The earliest hymn-book in which it is found is Luppius's *Andächtig Singender Christen Mund*, Wesel., 1692, p. 20. It is a beautiful hymn of Penitence (by *Miss Winkworth* assigned to Ash-Wednesday). Included as No. 273 in Freylinghausen's *G. B.*, 1704, and recently as No. 535 in the Berlin *G. L. S.*, ed. 1863, in 7 st. of 8 l. The *trs.* in C. U. are :—

1. O do not against me, Lord. A good *tr.* of st. i., iii., vi., vii., by A. T. Russell, as No. 79 in his *Ps. & Hys.*, 1851.

2. Not in anger, mighty God. A good *tr.* omitting st. ii., iv., as No. 41 in Miss Winkworth's *C. B. for England*, 1863, and thence as No. 205 in the *Temple H. Bk.* 1867, as No. 323 in the *Free Church H. Bk.* 1882, and omitting the *tr.* of st. vi., as No. 78 in the *Upp. & Sherb. School H. Bk.* 1874. In America as No. 398 in the *Evang. Hymnal*, New York, 1880, in full.

3. Not in anger, Lord, Thou wilt. A *tr.* of st. i., iii., vi., vii., signed " X. X." as No. 59 in Dr. Pagenstecher's *Coll.* 1864.

4. Cast me not in wrath away. A *tr.* of st. i.–iii., vii., by E. Cronenwett, as No. 235 in the Ohio Lutheran *Hymnal*, 1880.

Other trs. are :—
(1) " Lord! withdraw the dreadful storm," by *J. C. Jacobi*, 1720, p. 41 ; 1722, p. 63 ; in his second ed., 1732, p. 98, greatly altered, and beginning, " O my God, avert the storm." (2) " Not in anger smite us, Lord," by *Miss Winkworth*, 1855, p. 55. (3) " In Thine anger smite me not," by *N. L. Frothingham*, 1870, p. 159.

iii. Welt, Ade! ich bin dein müde. [*For the Dying.*] 1st printed on a broadsheet for the funeral of Johanne Magdalene, daughter of the Archidiaconus Abraham Teller, of St. Nicholas's Church, Leipzig, who died Feb. 27, 1649, and included in Albinus's *Geistlicher geharnischter Kriegesheld*, Leipzig, 1675. Also given in the Bayreuth *G. B.* of 1660, p. 542, and recently as No. 842 in the *Unv. L. S.* 1851, in 9 st. of 8 l. The *tr.* in C. U. is :—

World, farewell! Of thee I'm tired. A full and good *tr.* in the 2nd Ser., 1858, of Miss Winkworth's *Lyra Ger.*, p. 207. In her *C. B. for England*, 1863, No. 198, st. iii., iv., vi. were omitted. Her *trs.* of ll. 1–4, of st. viii., v., vi., iv., beginning. " Time, thou speedest on but slowly," were included as No. 1305 in Robinson's *Songs for the Sancty.*, 1865, as No. 1392 in the *H. & Songs of Praise*, New York, 1874, and *Ch. Praise Bk.*, 1882, No. 652. Another *tr.* is :— " World, farewell, my soul is weary," by *Miss Dunn*, 1857, p. 113. [J. M.]

Albrecht, s. of Casimir, Margrave of Brandenburg-Culmbach in Lower Franconia, b. at Ansbach, Mar. 28, 1522. After his father's death he was well and piously educated by his uncle and guardian, Georg of Brandenburg. Distinguished as a boy for daring, on attaining his majority he adopted the profession of arms, gaining for himself the title of the "German Alcibiades." He accompanied the Emperor Charles V. to his French war in 1544, and again, against the Schmalkald Evangelical Union, in 1546. But in 1552 he took his proper stand as an Evangelical prince against the Emperor, and set earnestly to work to break down the Imperial power. While ravaging Lüneburg he was met in battle, July 9, 1553, at Sievershausen, by his old friend Moritz, Elector of Saxony, and in the bloody conflict his forces were shattered, and Moritz mortally wounded. On Sept. 12 he was again defeated at Brunswick, and after being besieged at Schweinfurt, received his final overthrow at Eulenberg, June 13, 1554, escaping to France with only sixteen followers. In his troubles he acknowledged the hand of God on him, and repented of his former errors. By the intercession of his uncles he was permitted to appear at Regensburg to plead for the restoration of his lands. On his return he was seized with a fatal illness while visiting his brother-in-law, the Margrave Charles II. of Baden, at Pforzheim, and died there, repentant and firm in the faith, Jan. 8, 1557 (*Koch*, i. 339–343: *Allg. Deutsche Biog.*, i. 252–257, &c.). The only hymn ascribed to him is—

Was mein Gott will, das g'scheh allzeit. [*Trust in God.*] *Wackernagel*, iii. p. 1070–71, gives two forms of this hymn, the first from *Fünff Schöne Geistliche Lieder*, Dresden, 1556, the second from a broadsheet at Nürnberg, c. 1554. Both contain 4 st. of 10 l., but as st. iv. in 1556 is a doxology, the hymn may originally have had five st. or only three. *Bode*, pp. 324–5, quotes a broadsheet, Nürnberg, N.D., probably earlier than the above, where it has only 3 st. In the *Copenhagen G. B.*, 1571, it is entitled, "Des alten Churfürsten Markgraff Albrecht's Lied," which leads Wackernagel to remark, "Who wrote it for him, or who could have dedicated it to him, there is no proof." On the other hand, *Koch*, i. 341–343, *Lauxmann* in *Koch*, viii. 361–364, and *Fischer*, ii. 335–336, are inclined to ascribe it to him as author. Whoever was the author, the hymn is a very good one, and has always been a favourite hymn of consolation in sorrow, and at the hour of death, among the pious in Germany. The second form, which is that *tr.* into English, is included, as No. 641, in the *Unv. L. S.*, 1851.

The trs. are :—
(1) " God is my comfort and my tow'r," a *tr.* of st. ii. " Gott ist mein Trost, mein Zuversicht," as No. 329 in pt. i. of the *Moravian H. Bk.* 1754. (2) " The will of God is always best," by B. Latrobe, as No. 467 in the *Moravian H. Bk.* 1789, and repeated in later eds. (3) " God works His will, and best it is," by *Dr. G. Walker*, 1860, p. 45. (4) " Whate'er God will, let that be done," by *N. L. Frothingham*, 1870, p. 141, included in the Schaff-Gilman *Library of Rel. Poetry*, ed. 1883, p. 523. (5) " What my God wills, be done alway," in the *Family Treasury*, 1877, p. 111, without name of translator [J. M.]

Alderson, Eliza Sibbald, née **Dykes,** granddaughter of the Rev. Thomas Dykes, of Hull, and sister of the Rev. Dr. Dykes, b. in 1818, and married, in 1850, to the Rev. W. T. Alderson, some time chaplain to the West Riding Ho. of Correction, Wakefield. Mrs. Alderson is the author of the following hymns, the first of which is likely to attain a commanding position :—

1. **And now, beloved Lord, Thy soul resigning.** [*Passiontide.*] A hymn of more than usual merit, in 6 st. of 4 l., written in 1868 at the request of Dr. Dykes. In 1875, st. i., ii., v. and vi., were given in the revised ed. of *H. A. & M.,* No. 121, with a special tune *Commendatio* by Dr. Dykes. The full original text is restored in Thring's *Coll.,* 1882, No. 170.

2. **Lord of glory, Who hast bought us.** [*Almsgiving.*] Written in 1864, in 5 st. of 8 l., and pub. in the *App.* to *H. A. & M.,* 1868, No. 372, and repeated in the revised ed. 1875, No. 367, Mrs. Alderson says, " It was the very strong feeling that a tithe of our income was a solemn debt to God and His poor, which inspired it." Dr. Dykes's tune " *Charitas* " was composed for this hymn.

Aldridge, William, b. at Warminster, Wilts, 1737, for some years a minister in Lady Huntingdon's Connexion, and then of Jewry St. Chapel, London, d. Feb. 28th, 1797. A copy of his *Hymns,* 1776, is in the Cheshunt Coll. Library, and a second in the Brit. Mus. These *Hymns* reached the 5th ed. in 1789.

Ales diei nuntius. *A. C. Prudentius.* [*Tuesday Morning.*] This hymn is No. 1 in the *Cathemerinon* of Prudentius, and is in 25 st. of 4 l. The cento in use is composed of st. i., ii., xxi., xxv. of the poem, and will be found in *Daniel,* i., No. 103 ; additional notes, ii. p. 382 ; iv. p. 39. In the *Roman Brev.* it is the hymn for Tuesday at Lauds. Also in the *Hymn. Sarisb.,* Lond. 1851, pp. 47, 48 ; which contains, besides the *Sarum* text, variations from the *York Use ;* and among different readings from Monastic Uses, those of *St. Alban's, Evesham, Worcester, St. Andrew de Bromholm* (Norfolk). It is also in the *Aberdeen Breviary* and others.

The text of this cento is also found in three mss. of the 11th cent. in the *British Museum* (Harl. 2961, f. 222 ; Vesp. D. xii. f. 15 b ; Jul. A. vi. f. 25 b); in the *Latin Hys. of the Anglo-Saxon Church,* 1851, p. 18, it is printed from a Durham ms. of the 11th cent. ; in Macgill's *Songs of the Christian Creed and Life,* 1876 and 1879 ; and others. For the full text see *Prudentii Opera,* Deventer, c. 1490, London, 1824; *Wackernagel,* i., No. 27, and *Macgill,* as above, Nos. 84–86. [W. A. S.]

Translations in C. U. :—
1. **Hark! the bird of day sings clear.** By W. J. Blew. 1st pub. on a broadsheet, with music, c. 1850, and then in *The Ch. Hy. & Tune Bk.* 1852, in 4 st. of 6 l. It was repeated in Rice's *Hymns,* 1870, No. 107. This *tr.* is from the *Sarum Brev.* text.

2. **The winged herald of the day.** By J. M. Neale. 1st pub. in the enlarged ed. (1st ed. 1852) of the *Hymnal N.,* 1854, No. 19, and continued

in later editions. This *tr.* also from the *Sarum* text.

3. **Day's herald bird, with descant clear.** By J. D. Chambers, in his *Lauda Syon,* 1857, from the *Sarum* text, in 5 st. of 4 l. In 1867 it was rewritten as, " The herald bird of day proclaims," in the *People's H.,* No. 424.

4. **The bird, the harbinger of light.** A cento in the *Hymnary,* 1872, No. 23. It is compiled from all the above, together with Bp. Mant and Caswall.

Translations not in C. U. :—
1. The bird, the harbinger of light. *Mant,* 1837.
2. Now, while the herald bird of day. *Caswall,* 1849.
3. The cock's shrill horn proclaims the morn. *Copeland,* 1848.
4. The bird that hails the early morn. *Macgill,* 1876.
5. The bird that heralds in the light. *Macgill,* 1876.
The first of those by Dr. Macgill is a full *tr.* of Prudentius's text, and the second of the *Brev.* arrangement. Those by Bp. Mant and Caswall are *trs.* from the *Roman Brev.* The whole hymn is also translated in J. Banks's *Nugae,* 1854, pp. 157–161, as " The herald bird, the bird of morn."
6. The bird of day, messenger. In the 1545 *Primer,* and, as a reprint, in E. Burton's *Three Primers of Henry VIII.,* 1834. [J. J.]

Alexander, Cecil Frances, née **Humphreys,** second daughter of the late Major John Humphreys, Miltown House, co. Tyrone, Ireland, b. 1823, and m. in 1850 to the Rt. Rev. W. Alexander, D.D., Bishop of Derry and Raphoe. Mrs. Alexander's hymns and poems number nearly 400. They are mostly for children, and were published in her *Verses for Holy Seasons,* with Preface by Dr. Hook, 1846 ; *Poems on Subjects in the Old Testament,* pt. i. 1854, pt. ii. 1857 ; *Narrative Hymns for Village Schools,* 1853 ; *Hymns for Little Children,* 1848 ; *Hymns Descriptive and Devotional,* 1858 ; *The Legend of the Golden Prayers.* 1859 ; *Moral Songs,* N.D. ; *The Lord of the Forest and his Vassals,* an *Allegory,* &c.; or contributed to the *Lyra Anglicana,* the S.P.C.K. *Ps. and Hymns, Hymns A. & M.,* and other collections. Some of the narrative hymns are rather heavy, and not a few of the descriptive are dull, but a large number remain which have won their way to the hearts of the young, and found a home there. Such hymns as " In Nazareth in olden time," " All things bright and beautiful," " Once in Royal David's city," " There is a green hill far away," " Jesus calls us o'er the tumult," " The roseate hues of early dawn," and others that might be named, are deservedly popular and are in most extensive use. Mrs. Alexander has also written hymns of a more elaborate character ; but it is as a writer for children that she has excelled. [J. D.]

Alexander, James Waddell, D.D., s. of Archibald Alexander, D.D., b. at Hopewell, Louisa, county of Virginia, 13 Mar., 1804, graduated at Princeton, 1820, and was successively Professor of Rhetoric at Princeton, 1833 ; Pastor of Duane Street Presbyterian Church, New York, 1844 ; Professor of Church History, Princeton, 1849 ; and Pastor of 5th Avenue Presbyterian Church, New York, 1851 ; d. at Sweetsprings, Virginia, July 31, 1859. His works include *Gift to the Afflicted, Thoughts on Family Worship,* and others. His *Letters* were published by the Rev. Dr. Hall, in 2 vols., some time after his death, and his translations were collected and published at New York in 1861, under the title, *The Breaking Crucible and other Translations.* Of these translations the following are in use :—" O Sacred Head, now wounded," a *tr.* of " Salve Caput," through the German ; " Near the cross was Mary weeping," a *tr.* of "Stabat Mater"; and "Jesus, how sweet Thy memory is," a *tr.* of " Jesu dulcis memoria." The annotations of these *trs.* are given under their respective Latin first lines.   [F. M. B.]

Alexander, Joseph Addison, D.D., brother of Dr. J. W. Alexander, and a minister of the Presbyterian Church, b. in Philadelphia, April 24, 1809, graduated at Princeton, 1826, became Adjunct Professor of Latin, 1833, and Associate Professor of Biblical Literature, 1838, d. at Princeton, Jan. 28, 1860. Dr. Alexander was a great Hebraist, and published Commentaries on Isaiah, the Psalms, &c. His poem, *The Doomed Man,* was written for, and first published in, the *Sunday School Journal,* Phila., April 5, 1837. It has striking merit, but moves in one of those doctrinal circles which hymns generally avoid. Parts of it are found as hymns in a few Calvinistic collections, as, "There is a time, we know not when," in the New York *Ch. Praise Book,* 1881, No. 288. This is sometimes given with the second stanza, " There is a line, by us unseen," as in Nason's *Coll.,* and Robinson's *Songs for the Sanctuary,* 1865. Unknown to English collections.   [F. M. B.]

Alexander, Sir William, b. at Menstrie, the family estate, near Stirling, in 1580. In 1614 he was knighted by James I., and in 1633, created Earl of Stirling by Charles I., d. in London, Feb. 12, 1640, and was buried in the East Church, Stirling, April 12, 1640. He had the principal share in that version of the Psalms which, published as the work of King James, was sought to be forced upon the Scottish Church, 1634–37 [**Scottish Hymnody,** sect. ii. 3]. Bishop Williams, of Lincoln, in his funeral sermon for King James, says that James's " worke was staied in the one and thirty Psalme." A complete edition of Alexander's works, other than the Psalms, was published in 3 vols., 1870–72, as *The Poetical Works of Sir William Alexander, Earl of Stirling* (Glasgow, M. Ogle & Co.).

This is the usual account. Dr. Charles Rogers, however, in his *Memorials of the Earls of Stirling and the House of Alexander* (Edin., W. Paterson, 2 vols., 1877), conjecturally dates his birth 1567, says he was the only son of Alexander Alexander, describes him as Knight in 1609, and says his licence was for 21 (not 31) years.   [J. M.]

Alexander, William, D.D., Bishop of Derry, son of the Rev. Robert Alexander, Preb. of Aghadowey, Ireland, b. in Londonderry, April, 1824, and educated at Tunbridge School, and Exeter and Brasenose Colleges, Oxford. Entering holy orders, Bp. Alexander has held successively the Rectory of Camusjuxta-Morne, co. Tyrone, and the Deanery of Emly, 1864, and since 1867 has held the united Bishoprics of Derry and Raphoe. Bp. Alexander's sacred poetry is found in the *Dublin University Mag., The Spectator, Good Words, Lyra Brit.,* and *Lyra Anglicana,* together with his Oxford prize poems, *The Death of Jacob,* and *The Waters of Babylon,* and in his *Specimens Poetical and Critical,* privately printed, 1867. Little use, however, can be made of these compositions for hymnological purposes.

Alexander, William Lindsay, D.D., LL.D., of Pinkieburn, Musselburgh, s. of William Alexander, Esq., Leith, b. in the vicinity of Leith, August 24, 1808. After studying at the Universities of Edinburgh and St. Andrew's, he became, in 1828, Classical Tutor in what is now The Lancashire College. After studying for some time at Halle, he, in 1835, became minister of North College St. Congregational Church, Edinburgh, removing with his congregation in 1861 to a new church in George IV. Bridge, called the Augustine Church, and retired from the pastoral charge of the same in 1877. He d. at Pinkieburn, Dec. 20, 1884. He was, from 1854 to 1881, Professor in the Scottish Congregational Hall. In 1846 he received the degree of D.D. from the University of St. Andrew's, and in 1884 that of LL.D., from Edinburgh. He became a member of the O. T. Revision Company in 1870. He wrote and edited many valuable theological works. His *Sel. of Hys.* known as the *Augustine H. Bk.,* in which his original hymns and translations appeared, was first pub. in 1849. [**Scottish Hymnody,** § vi.]
       [J. M.]

Alford, Henry, D.D., son of the Rev. Henry Alford, Rector of Aston Sandford, b. at 25 Alfred Place, Bedford Row, London, Oct. 7, 1810, and educated at Trin. Coll., Cambridge, graduating in honours, in 1832. In 1833 he was ordained to the Curacy of Ampton. Subsequently he held the Vicarage of Wymeswold, 1835–1853 ; the Incumbency of Quebec Chapel, London, 1853–1857; and the Deanery of Canterbury, 1857 to his death, which took place at Canterbury, Jan. 12, 1871. In addition he held several important appointments, including that of a Fellow of Trinity, and the Hulsean Lectureship, 1841–2. His literary labours extended to every department of literature, but his noblest undertaking was his ed. of the Greek Testament, the result of 20 years' labour. His hymnological and poetical works, given below, were numerous, and included the compiling of collections, the composition of original hymns, and translations from other languages. As a hymnwriter he added little to his literary reputation. The rhythm of his hymns is musical, but the poetry is neither striking, nor the thought original. They are evangelical in their teaching, but somewhat cold and conventional. They vary greatly in merit, the most popular being " Come, ye thankful people, come," " In token that thou shalt not fear," and " Forward be our watchword." His collections, the *Psalms and Hymns of* 1844, and the *Year of Praise,* 1867, have not achieved a marked success. His poetical and hymnological works include—

(1) Hymns in the *Christian Observer* and the *Christian Guardian,* 1830. (2) *Poems and Poetical Fragments* (no name), Cambridge, J. J. Deighton, 1833.

(3) *The School of the Heart, and other Poems*, Cambridge, Pitt Press, 1835. (4) *Hymns for the Sundays and Festivals throughout the Year*, &c., Lond., Longman & Co., 1836. (5) *Psalms and Hymns, adapted for the Sundays and Holidays throughout the year*, &c., Lond., Rivington, 1844. (6) *Poetical Works*, 2 vols., Lond., Rivington, 1845. (7) *Select Poetical Works*, Lond., Rivington, 1851. (8) An American ed. of his *Poems*, Boston, Ticknor, Reed & Field, 1853. (9) *Passing away*, and *Life's Answer*, poems in *Macmillan's Magazine*, 1863. (10) *Evening Hexameters*, in *Good Words*, 1864. (11) On *Church Hymn Books*, in the *Contemporary Review*, 1866. (12) *Year of Praise*, Lond., A. Strahan, 1867. (13) *Poetical Works*, 1868. (14) *The Lord's Prayer*, 1869. (15) *Prose Hymns*, 1844. (16) *Abbot of Muchelnaye*, 1841. (17) *Hymns in British Magazine*, 1832. (18) A *tr.* of *Cantemus cuncti*, q.v. [J. D.]

Aliqua. The *nom de plume* of Mrs. Eliza O. Peirson, an American writer.

Aliquis. A volume of *Hys. for Villagers*, was pub. in 1821, under this *nom de plume*.

Alix. The *nom de plume* of J. H. Evans (q.v.) in the *Family Visitor*, 1827, &c.

All around us, fair with flowers. [*Life's Work.*] Given as *Anon.* in Longfellow and Johnson's *Bk. of Hymns*. 1846, No. 306, and their *Hymns of the Spirit*, Boston, U.S.A., 1864, No. 576, in 5 st. of 4 l.

All creation groans and travails. *J. M. Neale.* [*Cattle Plague.*] Written for the Fast Day for the Great Cattle Plague, 1866, and first published in the *Guardian.* Shortly afterwards it was issued by Novello, with suitable music. During the latter part of the same year it was included in Neale's original *Sequences, Hys., &c.*, pub. under the supervision of Dr. Littledale, Dr. Neale having died a few months before. It is entitled "Cattle Plague Hymn," and consists of 10 st. of 4 l. In 1872 it was reprinted in the *Hymnary.*

All from the sun's uprise. *G. Sandys.* [*Ps. c.*] This spirited and somewhat quaint rendering of Ps. c. appeared in his *Paraphrase upon the Psalms of David*, 1636, and 1640, pp. 120-21 : and again, as a part of his *Paraphrase upon the Divine Poems*, 1638 and 1640, in 3 st. of 8 l. It was also repeated in a beautiful edition of the *Paraphrase of the Psalmes*, 1648 [*Brit. Mus.*], and again in an edition by the Rev. Richard Hooper. As given in Martineau's earlier *Hymns*, &c., 1840, and in his later *Hys. of Praise and Prayer*, 1873, it is unaltered.

All glorious God, what hymns of praise. *P. Doddridge.* [*Praise.*] In the "D. MSS." this hymn is headed, "Of being prepared for the inheritance of the Saints in light. A song of praise for Col. i. 12," and is dated "Dec. 13, 1736," No. xxix. The same text was given in J. Orton's ed. of Doddridge's (posthumous) *Hymns*, &c., 1755, No. 298, in 5 st. of 4 l., and, with slight changes, in J. D. Humphreys's ed. of the same, 1839, No. 324. Although a hymn of praise of more than usual merit in many ways, it is rarely given in the English collections, and found in but a few of the American hymnals.

All glory and praise to Jesus our Lord. *C. Wesley.* [*Gift of the Holy Spirit.*]

Pub. from the *Wesley MSS.* in the Library of the Theological Institution, Richmond, in the *P. Works of J. & C. Wesley*, 1868-72, vol. xiii. p. 248, in 4 st. of 4 l. It previously appeared in the Amer. *Meth. Episc. H. Bk.*, 1849, No. 201. Beyond this it is but little known.

All glory to God in the sky. *C. Wesley.* [*Christmas.*] This is No. xviii. of his *Hymns for the Nativity of our Lord*, 1744, in 5 st. of 8 l. In 1780 it was given in full in the *Wes. H. Bk.*, No. 211, and has been repeated in all later editions. (*P. Works*, 1868-72, vol. iv. p. 125.) Its use amongst the Methodist bodies in all English-speaking countries is considerable ; but outside of Methodism it is but little known.

All glory to our gracious Lord. *C. Wesley.* [*Ps. cxviii.*] This paraphrase of Ps. cxviii. in 22 st. of 6 l., although pub. in the *Psalms and Hymns of J. & C. Wesley*, 1743, did not appear, in any form, in the *Wes. H. Bk.* until the revised ed. of 1875, when two centos were given as one hymn (No. 616), in two parts, the first being st. 1, 3, 10, 11, 12 and 15 ; and the second, "Jesus is lifted up on high," st. 17-22. Full original text in the *P. Works*, 1868-72, vol. viii. pp. 204-208.

All hail, dear Conqueror, all hail. *F. W. Faber.* [*Easter.*] Appeared in his *Jesus and Mary, or Catholic Hymns*, &c., 1849, No. xii. in 10 st. of 4 l. and entitled "Jesus Risen." It was repeated in later editions of the same work, and in his *Hymns*, 1862. It is usually given in modern collections in an abbreviated and sometimes altered form. Amongst the hymnals in which it is thus found are the *Appx.* to *Hymnal N.*, No. 155 ; *Hys. and Carols* (Ch. Sisters' Home), No. 40 ; and the Scottish Presb. *Ibrox Hyml.*, No. 3 ; whilst the *Holy Family Hys.* retain the full text.

All hail, Incarnate God. *Elizabeth Scott.* [*Glory of Christ's Kingdom.*] Contributed, under the signature of "S", to Ash and Evans's Bapt. *Coll. of Hys.*, 1769, No. 358, in 4 st. of 6 l., and headed "The increasing Glory and Perpetuity of the Messiah's Kingdom." In 1787, on its republication in Rippon's Bapt. *Sel.*, No. 430, to the st. ii. which reads :—

"To Thee the hoary head
Its silver honors pays ;
To Thee the blooming youth
Devotes his brightest days ;
And every age their tribute bring
And bow to Thee, all-conquering King"—

this note was added :—

"Composed on seeing an aged saint and a youth taken into church communion together."

In modern collections it is almost entirely confined to those of the Baptists and Congregationalists. It was introduced into the American hymnals through Staughton's ed. of *Rippon*, 1813. Orig. text in Bapt. *Ps. and Hys.*, 1858, No. 199. [W. T. B.]

All hail, mysterious King. *P. Doddridge.* [*Christ the King.*] This hymn on Rev. xxii. 16 is not in the "*D. MSS.*" It was 1st pub. (posthumously) in his *Hymns*, &c., 1755 No. 359, in 4 st. of 4 l., and entitled

"Christ the Root and Offspring of David, and the Morning Star." It is also repeated in later eds. of the same work, and in the corrected and enlarged ed. by J. D. Humphreys, 1839. Its use in Great Britain is limited, and confined almost exclusively to the older collections; but in America it is given in several hymnals.

All hail, Redeemer of mankind. *C. Wesley.* [*Holy Communion.*] One of the most pronounced and definite of C. Wesley's Sacramental Hymns. It appeared in the *Hymns on the Lord's Supper by J. & C. Wesley,* 1745, No. cxxiv, in 4 st. of 6 l., and was republished in the *P. Works of J. & C. Wesley,* 1868–72, vol. iii. pp. 308–9. Its use as a congregational hymn is of recent date. In Pott's *Hys. fitted to the Order of Com. Pr.* 1861, and Thring's *Coll.,* 1882, st. ii. is omitted. This is also done in the *Hymnary,* 1872; but in this last, verbal alterations are introduced into the text of the hymn, and an additional stanza, "Acceptance in His Holy Name," has been appended thereto. The most striking stanza in the original hymn is the third, in which the *daily celebration* of the Holy Communion is set forth:—

> "Yet may we celebrate below,
> And daily thus Thine offering show
>   Exposed before Thy Father's eyes;
> In this tremendous mystery
> Present Thee bleeding on a tree,
>   Our everlasting Sacrifice."

As a congregational hymn it is unknown outside the collections of the Ch. of England.

All hail the glorious morn. *John Peacock.* [*Res. and As. of Christ.*] 1st printed in his *Songs of Praise composed from the Holy Scriptures, in Two Parts,* Lond., Pasham, 1776. It is in 6 st. of 8 l., is No. 37, and is headed, "The Resurrection and Ascension of Christ." In 1806 it was included in Dobell's *Coll.* with slight alterations, and thence passed into a few American hymnals.   [W. T. B.]

All hail! the power of Jesus' Name. *E. Perronet.* [*On the Resurrection.*] In the Nov. number of the *Gospel Magazine,* 1779, the tune by Shrubsole, afterwards known as "Miles Lane," appeared with the following words:—

> "All hail! the pow'r of Jesu's Name;
> Let angels prostrate fall;
> Bring forth the Royal Diadem,
> To crown him Lord of all."

In the following April, 1780, the complete hymn, with the title, "On the Resurrection, the Lord is King," was given in the same magazine, the additional verses being:—

> "Let highborn seraphs tune the lyre,
>   And as they tune it, fall
> Before His face who tunes their choir,
>   And crown Him Lord of all.
>
> Crown Him ye morning stars of light,
>   Who fix'd this floating ball;
> Now hail the strength of Israel's might,
>   And crown Him Lord of all.
>
> Crown Him, ye martyrs of your God,
>   Who from His altar call;
> Extol the stem of Jesse's rod,
>   And crown Him Lord of all.

> Ye seed of Israel's chosen race,
>   Ye ransom'd of the fall,
> Hail Him Who saves you by His grace,
>   And crown Him Lord of all.
>
> Hail Him, ye heirs of David's line,
>   Whom David Lord did call;
> The God incarnate, man Divine,
>   And crown Him Lord of all.
>
> Sinners! whose love can ne'er forget
>   The wormwood and the gall,
> Go—spread your trophies at His feet,
>   And crown Him Lord of all.
>
> Let every tribe and every tongue
>   That bound creation's call,
> Now shout in universal song,
>   The crownèd Lord of all."

In 1785 it was included by the author in his *Occasional Verses, Moral and Sacred,* p. 99, and entitled, "On the Resurrection."

One of the earliest compilers to adapt the hymn was G. Burder, in the 2nd ed. of his *Coll.,* 1784, No. 190. It is headed "The Coronation Hymn," and consists of 4 stanzas, being st. i., vii., v., and viii. of the original, with the following alterations:—

> St. i., l. 4. "*And* crown."
> St. iii., l. 1. "*Ye souls redeem'd of Adam's race,*
>   Ye ransom'd *from.*"
> St. iv. "*Let en'ry tribe, and ev'ry tongue,*
>   *Throughout this earthly ball,*
>   *Unite in one harmonious song,*
>   *And crown him Lord of all.*"

It may be worth notice that this hymn is immediately followed by another written in imitation of it, and headed "The Prince of Peace" (adapted to the same tune). The 1st stanza is:—

> "Let saints on earth their anthems raise,
>   Who taste the Saviour's grace;
> Let saints in heav'n proclaim his praise,
>   And crown him "Prince of Peace."

This hymn is in 4 stanzas, and is signed "E." (i.e. Jonathan Evans). In the same year another and much altered form appeared in Dr. Rippon's *Sel. of Hys.,* 1787, No. 177. As this adaptation is the received text in G. Brit. and America, we give it (with the alterations and additions made by Dr. Rippon, in *italics*), together with the curious titles which were added to the stanzas:—

The Spiritual Coronation, Cant. iii. 11.

1. "ANGELS.

> All-hail, the power of Jesus' name!
>   Let angels prostrate fall:
> Bring forth the royal diadem,
>   *And* crown Him Lord of all.

2. MARTYRS.

> [Crown Him, ye martyrs of *our* God,
>   Who from His altar call;
> Extol the Stem of Jesse's rod,
>   And crown Him Lord of all.]

3. CONVERTED JEWS.

> [*Ye chosen seed of Israel's race,*
>   *A remnant weak and small;*
> Hail Him, who saves you by His grace,
>   And crown Him Lord of all.]

4. BELIEVING GENTILES.

> *Ye Gentile sinners,* ne'er forget
>   The wormwood and the gall;
> Go—spread your trophies at His feet,
>   And crown Him Lord of all.

5. SINNERS OF EVERY AGE.

> [*Babes, men, and sires, who know His love*
>   *Who feel your sin and thrall,*
> *Now joy with all the hosts above,*
>   *And crown Him Lord of all.*]

6. SINNERS OF EVERY NATION.
Let every *kindred, every tribe,*
    On this terrestrial ball,
    To Him all majesty ascribe,
    And crown Him Lord of all.

7. OURSELVES.
Oh that, with yonder sacred throng,
    We at His feet may fall;
    We'll join the everlasting song,
    And crown Him Lord of all."

By comparing this text with that of modern hymnals, it will be at once seen that this revised and rewritten form of the text is that upon which all modern forms of the hymn are based, and that the correct designation is " *E. Perronet*, 1779–80 ; *J. Rippon*, 1787." The first line has also been altered in some collections to (1) " All hail ! the great *Immanuel's* name " (sometimes " *Emmanuel* "). This was given in Wilks's edition of Whitefield's *Coll.*, 1798, and has been continued to modern hymnals. We have also : (2) " All hail ! the great *Redeemer's* name," in a very limited number of hymn-books.   [J. J.]

A claim to the authorship of this hymn has been made for the Rev. John Duncan, LL.D., who became in 1800 minister of the Scots church, Peter Street, Golden Square, London. The sole foundation, however, for this claim is the erroneous ascription of the hymn to Duncan in J. Dobell's *Sel.*, 1806. As Dobell's error took the form in later years of a persistent family tradition among Dr. Duncan's descendants, and as their claim on his behalf has received great attention, and is widely known, the following resumé of the facts is called for :—

Edward Perronet, after the rupture with Lady Huntingdon, continued to preach to a small congregation of dissenters at Canterbury, where he d. in 1792. He wrote many small poetical pieces of which a few were printed, but always anonymously. In 1779, Shrubsole, who had been a chorister in Canterbury Cathedral, and was then about 20 years of age, wrote for Perronet's hymn, then still in MS., the tune afterwards known as "Miles Lane." This tune, with the words of the first verse of the hymn annexed, was sent, doubtless by Shrubsole, to the *Gospel Mag.*, where it was published in Nov. 1779. Enquiry would then be naturally made for the remainder of the hymn, which accordingly was given complete in the magazine in April following. In 1785, *Occasional Verses* appeared, being a collection of Perronet's miscellaneous pieces, edited by one of his friends. His name is, as usual, not given, but that the volume consists of his works is unquestionable. One of the pieces is addressed to the memory of his father, the Rev. Vincent Perronet, and others, apparently, to various members of his family who are indicated by their initials only. In the "Address to the Reader" from "the Author," Perronet himself says—"The following miscellaneous productions were not originally intended for public view, as they are but the unpremeditated effusions of mere private amusement, and only occasionally shown by way of personal respect to a handful of the friends of the Author ; who having entrusted a copy of these, and many others, to a particular acquaintance, has been at length persuaded to admit of their being made public."

Not only is the hymn "All hail the power" in *Occasional Verses*, but it is immediately followed by another hymn, commencing "Hail, holy, holy, holy Lord !" written in the same metre, in the same manner, and clearly by the same hand. It may be added that the copy of *Occasional Verses* in the library of the *Brit. Mus.* has two tracts bound up with it. One of these, *Select Passages of the Old & New Testament versified*, 1756, is known to be by Perronet, and the *Brit. Mus.* copy contains his name in autograph with many MS. corrections of the text. The other tract, entitled *A Small Collection of Hymns*, &c., Canterbury, 1782, may also be ascribed to him with certainty. Ten years previously he had published another tract with a somewhat similar title :—*A Small Collection in Verse, Containing,* &c., 1772.

In 1787, Rippon published a recast of the hymn as above. In 1801, *Williams and Boden* reprinted *Rippon's* text (omitting one stanza), and gave the names of Perronet, as author of the hymn, and of Shrubsole, as composer of the tune.

Dr. Duncan settled in London about 1790, previous to which time he had preached in Hampshire and Dorsetshire, lastly in Wimborne, where he probably made the acquaintance of Dobell, who lived close by at Poole. When, many years afterwards, Dobell was compiling his *Selection*, Duncan appears to have been among those from whom he received advice or help, for Duncan's name is appended to one of the four "Recommendations" prefixed to the 1st ed. - It is more than probable therefore that it was from Duncan that Dobell obtained a copy of "All hail the power." The form in which the hymn is given by Dobell is neither Perronet's nor Rippon's, but a mixture of both, with two or three slight verbal alterations ; and if, as is highly probable, Dobell obtained the hymn from Duncan, and still more, if, as is possible, the arrangement sent to Dobell was really made by Duncan for the use of his own congregation, the ascription of the hymn to the latter is readily accounted for. The error is repeated in the 3rd ed. of Dobell's *Sel.*, London, N.D., showing either that Duncan omitted to notice it, or, as often happens, the correction was not attended to. Dobell also ascribes to Duncan another hymn, "Exalted high at God's right hand," which is first found in Rowland Hill's *Coll.* of *Ps. & Hys.*, 1783, and is always ascribed to him. Dobell's error in both cases probably arose from the same cause.

The mixed version of the hymn as given by Dobell is in 9 stanzas as follows :—Heading, *Coronation, Cant. iii. 11.* St. i. as *Rippon* i. ; st. ii. as *Perronet* ii. ; st. iii. as *Perronet* iii. ; st. iv. as *Rippon* ii. ; st. v. l. 1, as *Rippon*, l. 1 ; l. 2 as *Perronet*, v. l. 2, but changing of into *from* ; ll. 3, 4 as *Perronet* ; st. vi. as *Perronet* vi. ; st. vii. as *Perronet* vii. ; st. viii. as *Rippon* vi. ; st. ix. as *Rippon* vii.

In Isaac Nicholson's *Coll.*, 1807, the hymn is given with Rippon's text, omitting Rippon's st. v., but the editor, copying Dobell, has ascribed the authorship to Duncan.

In 1808, when Thomas Young, Perronet's successor at Canterbury, compiled his *Beauties of Dr. Watts*, &c., he used Dobell's *Sel.*, and, not knowing the author, repeated the ascription of "Exalted high" to Duncan, but correctly gives "All hail" to Perronet, from whose tract of 1756, and his *Occasional Verses*, he quotes some other pieces. In the 3rd ed. of the *Beauties of Dr. Watts*, &c., 1817, and in the 4th ed., 1826, Young, while retaining the *Perronet* ascription to "All hail," &c., omitted that of *Duncan* to "Exalted high," &c., thereby implying that he had discovered his error with regard to Duncan.

Shrubsole's tune appears to have become popular, especially among the dissenters, soon after its publication, and the name "Miles Lane" was in all probability given to it from its use by a congregation of Independents who met at a chapel in Miles Lane, London, till 1795, when they were succeeded by a body of Scotch Seceders. The name "Miles Lane" is found in Isaac Smith's *Collection of Psalm Tunes*, 4th ed.

[G. A. C.]

The use of this hymn in various forms and many languages is very extensive. In the number of hymn-books in which it is found in one form or another, it ranks with the first ten in the English language. A rendering in Latin, " Salve, nomen potestatis," is given in Bingham's *Hymnol. Christ. Latin.* 1871.

[J. J.]

All hail, Thou great Redeemer, hail.
Joseph Irons. [*Perseverance of the Saints.*] 1st pub. in his *Zion's Songs*, &c., 3rd ed., 1825, No. 157, thence into Snepp's *S. of G. & G.*, 1872, No. 412, unaltered.

All hail, Thou Resurrection. *W. H. Havergal.* [*Easter.*] Written in 1867, and first pub. in Snepp's *S. of G. & G.*, 1872, No. 253, in 3 st. of 8. l. It was also included in *Life Echoes*, 1883. (" HAV. MSS.")

All hail, triumphant Lord. [*Ascension.*] Appeared in the *Salisbury H. Bk.*,

1857, No. 100, in 3 st. of 6 l.; the *New Cong.*, 1859, Barry's *Ps. & Hys.*, 1868, the *N. Zealand Hymnal*, 1872, and others; but always without signature. It is evidently based upon C. Wesley's hymn for the Ascension, "God is gone up on high" (q.v.). Its authorship is unknown.

All hail, victorious Lord. *B. Woodd.* [*Ps. cx.*] This version of Ps. cx. in 4 st. of 6 l. appeared in the author's *Psalms of David and other Portions of the Sacred Scriptures*, &c., undated, but pub. about 1810. This work was revised and republished as *A New Metrical Version of the Psalms*, &c., in 1821. This paraphrase, as found in the Islington *Ps. & Hys.*, and the *New Cong.*, 1859, is composed of st. i. and iii. of the original. The full text is not found in any modern collection, and for collation must be consulted as above.

All hail, ye blessed band. [*Holy Baptism.*] This cento appears in *The Service of Song for Baptist Churches*, Boston, U.S.A., 1871, No. 815. Its construction is peculiar, as the following directions for its use at the public administration of Holy Baptism to adults will indicate:—

"Stanzas 3 to 8 inclusive of this hymn are designed to be sung during the intervals of a baptism; one verse as each candidate goes down into the water, or comes forth from it, according to choice. As it is generally found difficult for a congregation to sing unitedly and at the right time in the administration, it has been suggested that a choir sing these stanzas, the congregation uniting in the first two and the last two, as indicated."

To meet these requirements the cento has been thus composed:—

St. i., ii., "All hail, ye blessed band," to be sung by the congregation, are from Mrs. Lydia Sigourney's hymn, No. 515, in Winchell's *Additional Hymns*, U.S.A., 1832; st. iii., iv., "Saviour, Thy law we love," to be sung by the choir, are also by Mrs. Sigourney, and from the same source as st. i., ii. St. v., vi., "Here we behold the grave," to be sung by the choir, are by the Rev. C. H. Spurgeon, from *Our Own H. Bk.*, 1866, No. 934. St. vii., "Oh, what if we are Christ's," is by Sir H. W. Baker, from Murray's *Hymnal*, 1852, and, in common with st. viii., "Ashamed who now can be" (*Anon.*), has to be sung by the choir. The concluding stanzas, ix., x., "Come, sinners, wash away," are *Anon.* They are to be sung by the congregation. Taken together, it is the most dramatic hymn for Divine worship with which we are acquainted.

All hearts to Thee are open here. *J. Montgomery.* [*Divine Worship.*] Written for the special annual service of the Red Hill Sunday School, Sheffield, held May 12, 1837, and printed on a fly-leaf for the occasion. [M. MSS.] It was included in Montgomery's *Original Hymns*, 1853, No. 116, in 6 st. of 4 l. In J. H. Thom's *Hymns*, 1858, st. v. is omitted.

All heaven was hush'd, Our risen Lord. *G. Rawson.* [*Ps. cx.*] Contributed to the *Leeds H. Bk.* 1853, No. 149, in 8 st. of 4 l., from thence it has passed into a few collections, but its use is not extensive. In the author's *Hymns, Verses, & Chants*, 1876, pp. 23–24, it is given with slight variations. This is the authorized text of the hymn.

All is bright and gay around us. *J. M. Neale.* [*SS. Philip & James.*] This Saints' day hymn is in the 3rd series of the author's *Hymns for Children*, 1846, No. xviii.

in 4 st. of 8 l.; and again, without alteration, in later eds. of the same. In the S. P. C. K. *Ch. Hys.*, 1871, and some other collections, it is given as—"All is bright and *cheerful round us*"; but the alterations are very slight.

All is o'er;—the pain, the sorrow. *J. Moultrie.* [*Easter Eve.*] The original, entitled "Hymn for Easter Eve," is dated "April 2nd, 1836." It is in 20 st. of 6 l., and was pub. in his work, *My Brother's Grave and other Poems*, 1837 (3rd ed. 1852, p. 262). In the *Ps. & Hys. adapted to Pub. Worship*, Rugby, 1839, commonly known as *Buckoll's Coll.*, a cento, composed of st. i., ii., iii. and xx., unaltered, was given as No. 2. This was repeated in later editions of the same work, and has passed from thence into many collections, both in G. Brit. and in America. In the American hymnals it is usually altered, as in the *Hymnal of the Prot. Episcop. Ch.* 1872, No. 92; *Hys. & S. of Praise*, 1874; *Hys. of the Ch.* 1869, and others. In the last-named collection it is attributed to "J. E. L." (*i.e.* Jane E. Leeson) in error. The closing lines of st. i. read in the original:—

> "Yet once more to seal His doom,
> Christ must sleep within the tomb."

These lines have been omitted from Thring's *Coll.* 1882, No. 186, in favour of:—

> "Yet awhile, His own to save
> Christ must linger in the grave"—

by the Rev. J. Ellerton.

All knowing God! 'tis Thine to know. *T. Scott.* [*Charitable Judgment.*] This hymn is No. 115 in Enfield's Warrington *Sel.*, 1772, in 5 st. of 4 l., and is headed "Charitable Judgment." It is found in a few modern collections, principally amongst the Unitarians, but usually as—"All *seeing* God, 'tis Thine to know,"—and abbreviated, as in Martineau's *Hys.*, 1840, No. 496, and Courtauld's *Ps., Hys., and Anths.*, 1860, No. 328.   [W. T. B.]

All mortal vanities be gone. *I. Watts.* [*Vision of the Lamb.*] This is No. 25 of Bk. i. in his *Hymns and Spiritual Songs*, 1707, in 9 st. of 4 l., and based upon Rev. v. 6–9, "A vision of the Lamb." It is in use in G. Britain and America, although to a limited extent.

All people that on earth do dwell. [*Ps. c.*] The memories which have gathered round this rendering of the 100th Psalm, together with the uncertainty of its authorship, require us to trace its history, to note its true text, and to determine, if possible, its author.

I. HISTORY.—It appeared for the first time in the *Psalter*, pub. in London by John Daye, in 1560–1, and in the *Anglo-Genevan Psalter*, printed at Geneva, in 1561. In the full *English Psalter* of 1562 it is not found, but in an *Appendix* to the edition of 1564 (*Brit. Mus.*) it is given, and again in the body of the work in 1565 (*Brit. Mus.*). It was also included in the *Scottish Psalter* of 1564. From 1564 it reappeared in all editions of the *English* and *Scottish Psalters*, and is also found in most hymn-books published during the past 150 years.

II. Text.—The original text from the only copy of *Daye's Psalter*, 1560-1, known, and in which it is printed in the old black-letter text of the period, is as follows :—

" Psalme C.

Al people y^t on earth do dwel,
  sing to ye lord, with chereful voice
Him serve w^t fear, his praise forth tel,
  come ye before him and reioyce.

The Lord ye know is God in dede,
  with out our aide, he did us make :
We are his folck, he doth us fede,
  and for his Shepe, he doth us take.

Oh enter then his gates with prayse
  approche with ioye, his courtes unto :
Praise, laude, and blesse his name alwayes,
  for it is semely so to doe.

For why ? the Lord our God is good,
  his mercy is for euer sure :
His trueth at all tymes firmely stood
  and shall from age to age indure."
[*Orig. ed.* 1560-1, *London, J. Daye.*]

In what form this text reached Geneva, whether in ms. or in a copy of Daye's edition, cannot be determined. Within a few months, if not simultaneously, the same text, varying only in the spelling of some words (the *folck* of Daye's ed. being spelt *folke*, &c.), was given in the *Anglo-Genevan* ed. of 1561, and again in many later editions of the *English Psalter*. In the subsequent history of the text the following variations have crept in :—

St. i., l. 3. " Him serve with *fear*,"changed to "*mirth.*" This is found in the *Scottish Psalter* of 1650, and is taken from the c.m. version of Ps. c. given in the older English Psalters.

St. ii., l. 1. " The Lord ye know is," changed to " *Know that the Lord is*," &c., is also in the *Scottish Psalter* of 1650, and is from the same c.m. version as in st. i.

St. ii., l. 3. " Folck " changed to "*flock.*" This was possibly a printer's error to begin with, caused by transposing the *o* and *l*. It is found as early as the *Psalter* printed by " The Assignes of Richard Day, London, 1585," and has continued in the text from that date to Thring's *Coll.*, 1882. In that work Mr. Thring has reprinted the full text of 1560-1, and added thereto a doxology by Dr. Neale, based on Brady and Tate. This doxology is also found in *H. A. & M.*, and other collections.

III. Authorship.—This is somewhat difficult to determine. The evidence is this :—

1. Daye's Psalter, 1560-1.   No signature.
*2. Anglo-Genevan Psalter, 1561.   "*Tho. Ster.*"
*3. Britwell Psalter, 1561. " *W. Ke.*"
*4. Scottish Psalter, 1564. " *W. Ke.*"
5. Daye's Appendix, 1564.   No signature.
6. Daye's Psalter, 1565.   No signature.
7. Daye's Psalter, 1566.   No signature.
8. Crespin's Psalter (Geneva), 1569.   No signature.
9. Daye's Psalter, 1579.   No signature.
10. Daye's Psalter, 1587.   " *I. H.*"

These are all the Psalters known which have any value in determining the question. This evidence is certainly in favour of *W. Kethe*, and this is the more conclusive when we remember that the *Britwell Psalter*, 1561, and the *Scottish Psalter* of 1564, are reprints of the *Anglo-Genevan Psalter*, with

such corrections in spelling as an English work printed on the Continent would call for, and constitute together (*) a distinct family from the Daye Psalters. The metre is also in Kethe's favour, and decisive against both Sternhold and Hopkins. Its correct subscription is therefore " *W. Kethe*, 1560-1."

The historical account of the Psalters here named is given in the *English Psalters*, the *Scottish Hymnody*, and the *Old Version*, iii., v., in this work.

Although the history of tunes forms no part of our work, a few facts concerning " The Old Hundredth " may not be unacceptable. It first appeared in the enlarged edition of the French Genevan Psalter, published in 1551, as the tune to Ps. cxxxiv. The first half of the tune is a musical phrase which is found in various combinations both before and after that time ; but the latter part of the tune, and the form of the whole of it, is the work of Louis Bourgeois, who, and not Guillaume Franc, is now known to be the editor of this edition of the French Genevan Psalter. Kethe's version of Ps. c. was doubtless written for this tune.   [J. J.]

All powerful, self-existent God. [*God unchangeable.*] Pub. anonymously in B. Williams's *Coll. of H. for Pub. Worship on the Genl. Principles of Natural and Revealed Religion*, Salisb., 1778, No. 3, in 6 st. of 4 l. and headed " The Immortality of God." It is based on Ps. cii. v. 27. In 1781 it was also included in his *Bk. of Psalms*, Salisb., p. 286, as version vi. of Ps. cii. After passing through several Unitarian Collections, it appeared in Longfellow and Johnson's *Amer. Hys. of the Spirit*, 1864, No. 80, in 3 st., being st. i., iii., and vi. of the original in an altered form. Orig. text as above.   [W. T. B.]

All praise to Him who dwells in bliss. *C. Wesley.* [*Evening.*] 1st pub. in J. Wesley's *Coll. of Ps. & Hymns*, 1741, as " An Evening Hymn," in 5 st. of 4 l. In the *Poetical Works of J. & C. Wesley*, 1868-72, vol. ii. p. 27, it is repeated without alteration. Although in somewhat extensive use both in Great Britain and America, it has never found a place in the *Wes. H. Bk.* In the *Hymnary*, 1872, No. 75, a doxology has been added. Usually it is given in its original form.

All praise to our redeeming Lord. *C. Wesley.* [*Christian Fellowship.*] No. xxxii. of his *Hymns for those that seek and those that have Redemption in the Blood of Jesus Christ*, 1747, in 3 st. of 8 l. and entitled, " At Meeting of Friends." It was not included in the *Wes. H. Bk.* until after the death of J. Wesley, and was added in one of the editions of that collection during its partial revision in 1800-1. It has become a favourite hymn amongst the Methodist bodies in all English-speaking countries, but its use, otherwise than by the Methodists, is limited. Orig. text in *P. Works*, 1868-72, vol. iv. p. 252.

All praise to the Lamb! Accepted I am. *C. Wesley.* [*Assurance.*] Appeared in his *Hymns and Sacred Poems*, 1759, vol. i., No. 130, in 18 st. of 3 l. It is not in C. U. as a whole; but st. i., iii., v., and vi., slightly altered, are sometimes found as in the Amer. *H. Bk. of the Evang. Association.* Cleveland, Ohio, 1882, No. 326. Orig. text in *P. Works,* 1868–72, vol. v. p. 25. The well-known passage :—

> " Not a cloud doth arise
> To darken the skies,
> Or hide for a moment my Lord from my eyes : "

which reads in the original, " Not a *doubt,*" &c., is st. v. of this hymn.

All praise to Thee, who didst command. *Bp. R. Mant.* [*Common of Apostles.*] An original hymn given in his *Ancient Hymns,* &c., 1837, No. 07, in 6 st. of 4 l. and entitled, "Hymn of Thanksgiving for an Apostolic Ministry." In 1847 it was included in Fallow's *Sel. of Hys. for Pub. and Priv. Use,* No. 50; in 1853 in the Cooke & Denton *Hymnal,* No. 168, for "St. Matthias' Day ;" and in later collections. Orig. text in Rivington's ed. of the *Ancient Hymns,* 1871.

All-seeing God, Thy love sustains. *W. J. Irons.* [*Providence.*] A metrical form of the Collect for the 8th Sun. after Trinity, "O God, whose never failing mercy ordereth all things, both in heaven and earth, &c." given in his *Ps. & Hys. for the Church,* 1873, No. 167, in 4 st. of 7 l. and headed "Perceiving God's Providence." In 1882, it was included in Thring's *Coll., No.* 248, with " beneath *Thy sheltering* Wings," for "beneath the cherub's wings," st. ii., l. 6, but otherwise unaltered.

All thanks be to God. *C. Wesley.* [*Thanksgiving.*] One of the most celebrated open-air preaching places in Cornwall is the well-known Gwennap Pit, near Redruth. It is a circular hollow, covering an area of about 80 square yards, and sloping to a depth of some 50 feet. It has the appearance of a huge grass-covered funnel, with rings of seats formed out of the ground, and reaching from the bottom upwards. It seems to have had its origin in the running together of a mining shaft. In this amphitheatre the Wesleys frequently preached during their tours in Cornwall. In his journal C. Wesley notes under the date of Sunday, Aug. 10, 1746, that therein " for nearly two hours nine or ten thousand, by computation, listened with all eagerness" to him as he preached. The following day, being deeply impressed with the multitude, and the success of his work, he wrote the hymn: "All thanks be to God," &c. In the following year it was given as No. iii. of *Hymns for those that Seek and those that Have Redemption,* &c., 1747, in 8 st. of 8 l., and entitled, " Thanksgiving for the Success of the Gospel." When included by J. Wesley in the *Wes. H. Bk.* in 1780, st. iv. was omitted, and some alterations were also introduced into the text. That arrangement has been retained in later editions, and is repeated in other collections. Its use is somewhat extensive both in G. Brit. and America. Orig. text in *P. Works,* 1868–72, vol. iv. p. 210.

[J. J.]

All thanks to the Lamb, Who gives us to meet. *C. Wesley.* [*Christian Fellowship.*]

1st pub. in his *Hymns and Sacred Poems,* 1749, vol. ii., No. 238, in 7 st. of 4 l. ; from thence it passed into the *Wes. H. Bk.* in 1780, in full ; but in the revised ed., 1875, the last stanza is omitted. It is given in most of the collections of the Methodist bodies, but is rarely found in other hymn-books. Orig. text in *P. Works,* 1868–72, vol. v. p. 468.

All that I was, my sin, my guilt. *H. Bonar.* [*Pardon through Grace.*] 1st pub. in the *Bible Hymn Book,* of which Dr. Bonar was editor, 1845, No. 219, in 5 st. of 4 l. and based upon 1 Cor. xv. 10, " By the grace of God I am what I am." It was repeated in subsequent editions of the *Bible H. Bk.,* and again in the author's *Hymns of Faith and Hope,* 1st series, 1857, and later editions, with the title "Mine and Thine." Its use, both in G. Brit. and America, is somewhat extensive, and usually the text is unaltered, as in Stevenson's *Hys. for Church and H.,* 1873. The line, st. 4, l. 2, "Bade me in Christ believe," in Bapt. *Ps. & Hys.,* 1858 and 1880, and the *N. Cong.,* 1859, is from the former collection. The dox. as in *Kennedy,* 1863, is not in the original.

All that's good, and great, and true. *Godfrey Thring.* [*Praise and Thanksgiving.*] Written in 1863, and 1st pub. in his *Hymns Congregational and Others,* 1866, No. 24, in 7 st. of 4 l. and entitled " Nature's Harmony." It was repeated in his *Hymns and Lyrics,* 1874, pp. 108–9, and again in his *Ch. of E. H. Bk.,* 1882, where it is given most appropriately as a hymn for children.

All the night and nothing taken. *H. Alford.* [*Missions—S. S. Teachers.*] Contributed to his *Year of Praise,* 1867, No. 167, in 3 st. of 6 l., and appointed for the 5th Sun. after Trinity, being based on the Gospel of that day. It is repeated in Snepp's *S. of G. & G.,* 1872, No. 771.

All the night so dark and drear. *J. E. Bode.* [*Missions.*] From his *Hymns from the Gospel of the Day,* 1860, into the *App.* to the *S. P. C. K. Ps. & Hys.* 1869, No. 416. The special Gospel is that for the 5th Sun. after Trinity, St. Luke v. 1.

All the sacrifice is ended. *S. J. Stone.* [*Easter.*] Written for his *Lyra Fidelium* (on the article of the Creed, " He descended into Hell ; The third day He rose again from the dead "), and 1st pub. therein, 1866, No. v., in 6 st. of 6 l. It was repeated in *A Supplemental Hymnal,* Lond., Macintosh, 1873 ; in the author's *Ch. Service for Children,* 1884 ; and in his *Carmina Consecrata,* 1884.

All the world in sin was lying. *S. Baring-Gould.* [*Redemption.*] Printed in the *Church Times,* July 30th, 1864, and thence into the *People's H.,* 1867, No. 455, in 8 st. of 4 l.

All things are possible to him. *C. Wesley.* [*Concerning Holiness.*] No. 10 of his " Hymns for those that wait for full Redemption," which was given in the *Hymns & Sacred Poems,* 1749, vol. ii., in 8 st. of 6 l. (*P. Works,* 1868–72, vol. v. p. 300.) In the

Wes. H. Bk. of 1780, and later editions, and also in other collections in which it is found, st. iii. and vi. are omitted, the statement in the former,

> "I without sin on earth shall live,
> Even I, the chief of sinners I;"

and in the latter,

> "The unchangeable decree is past,
> The sure predestinating word,
> That I, who on the Lord am cast,
> I shall be like my sinless Lord:
> 'Twas fix'd from all eternity:
> All things are possible to me:"

being evidently unacceptable both to J. Wesley, and those who have reprinted the hymn from his collection. Its use as a congregational hymn outside the Methodist bodies is almost unknown.

All things are ready, Come. *A. Midlane.* [*Invitation.*] Written in July, 1860, and first pub. in *The Ambassador's Hymn Book*, 1861, No. 49, in 5 st. of 4 l. s.m., from whence it has passed into numerous collections both in G. Brit. and America. It ranks with the most popular of the author's productions. Orig. text, in Spurgeon's *O. O. H. Bk.* 1866, No. 504.

All things are ready! there's a place of rest. [*Holy Communion.*] This Eucharistic hymn, which is suited more to private devotion than public worship, we have failed to trace to its original source. It is known to us in three forms:—

1. All things are ready! Jesus waits to give. This is found in a collection of *Hymns*, pub. at *Chipping Norton*, 1859, in 3 st. of 4 l. and said to be *Anon.* showing that it had been copied from an earlier work.

2. All things are ready! there's a place of rest. This text in 4 st. is the same as the first four st. in Thring's *Coll.*, No. 526, which were taken by Mr. Thring from a collection now to him unknown. It consists of the first form of the hymn as above, and another stanza which is given as the first.

3. The cento in Thring. This is No. 2, with a fifth st. and a new line, st. iv., l. 4, by Mr. Thring.

All things bright and beautiful. *Cecil F. Alexander, née Humphreys.* [*God, our Maker.*] A successful and popular hymn for children, on the article of the Creed, "Maker of Heaven and Earth," which appeared in her *Hymns for Little Children*, 1848, in 7 st. of 4 l. It is usually given in an unaltered form, as in Thring's *Coll.*, 1882.

All things praise Thee, Lord most high. *G. W. Conder.* [*Praise.*] Pub. in 1874, in his *Appendix* to the *Leeds H. Bk.* of 1853, No. 6, in 6 st. of 6 l. It is given in many collections, its popularity arising to some extent from its remarkable word-painting. This is a distinguishing feature of the author's compositions both in prose and verse. The hymn is sometimes abbreviated by the omission of one or more stanzas. In Thring's *Coll.*, 1882, No. 249, st. iii. and iv. are thus omitted with advantage.

All we like wandering sheep have strayed. [*Passiontide.*] This Anon. hymn has not been traced beyond the Rev. T. M. Fallow's *Sel. of Hys. for Pub. and Priv. Use*, Lond., Masters, 1847, No. 58, in 4 st. of 4 l., where it is appointed for Good Friday. In 1852 it was repeated in the *English Hymnal*, No. 103, with the addition of a doxology; and in this form, with the change of the line, "Yet still He uncomplaining stands," to "Yet *uncomplaining still He* stands" in *Kennedy*, 1863, No. 600. [W. T. B.]

All wondering on the desert ground. *J. E. Bode.* [*Feeding the Multitude.*] One of the most popular and successful of his *Hymns from the Gospel of the Day*, 1860, in 5 st. of 4 l., the Gospel being the 25th Sun. after Trinity, St. John vi. 5. It has passed into various collections at home and abroad, including Alford's *Year of Praise*, 1867, the *New Zealand Hymnal*, 1872, and others. Orig. text in Lord Selborne's *Bk. of Praise*, 1862.

All ye Gentiles, praise the Lord. *J. Montgomery.* [*Ps. cxvii.*] 1st pub. in his *Songs of Zion*, 1822, in 3 st. of 4 l., and again in his *Original Hymns*, 1853, p. 91, where it is entitled, "Exhortation to Universal Praise and Thanksgiving." It is sometimes given as:—"All ye *nations*, praise the Lord," in both English and American hymnals. It was introduced into congregational use at an early date, and has attained to a fair position.

All ye that fear Him, praise the Lord. [*Ps. xxii.*] This hymn, as given in *Spurgeon's O. O. H. Bk.*, 1866, No. 22, pt. iii., is a cento thus composed:—St. i. from the *O. V.*, 1562, by *T. Sternhold*; st. ii., iii. from the *N. V.*, 1696, by *Tate & Brady*: st. iv., by the editor, based on the *O. V.*

All ye that [who] love the Lord, rejoice. *I. Watts.* [*Ps. cxlix.*] 1st pub. in his *Psalms of David, &c.*, 1719, in 8 st. of 4 l., and entitled, "Praise God, all His saints; or, The Saints judging the World." To it he appended a note in explanation of his rendering of verses 6–9, "Let the high praises of God be in their mouth," &c.

"This Psalm seems to be written to encourage the *Jews* in the wars against the *Heathen Princes of Canaan*, who were divinely sentenced to Destruction: But the four last Verses of it have been too much abused in later Ages to promote Sedition and Disturbance in the State; so that I chose to refer this *Honour*, that is here given to *all the Saints*, to the day of Judgment, according to those Expressions in the New Testament, Mat. xix. 28, *Ye shall sit on twelve Thrones, judging the Tribes, &c.*; i. Cor. vi. 3, *We shall judge Angels*; Rev. ii. 27 and iii. 21, *I will give him Power over the Nations, he shall rule them with a Rod of Iron*," &c.

Notwithstanding this defence, the unsuitability of these stanzas for congregational use is emphasised by their omission in most collections in G. Britain and America.

All ye that pass by. *C. Wesley.* [*Invitation.*] This "Invitation to Sinners" appeared in the *Hymns and Sacred Poems*, 1749, vol. i., No. xlii., in 7 st. of 6 l. In 1760 it was included, with the omission of st. iv., in M. Madan's *Ps. & Hys.*, No. xxi.; again in the collections of *De Courcy, R. Conyers*, and others in the Ch. of England; *Williams and Boden*, and others amongst the Congregationalists; and in the collections of various denominations: but not until the publication of the *Supp.* to the *Wes. H. Bk.* in 1830 was it added to that work, and thereby officially recognised by the Wesleyan Conference. It is retained in the revised ed. of the *Wes. H. Bk.*, 1875, and is in extensive use in G. Brit. and America. Orig. text in *P. Works*, 1868–72, vol. iv. p. 371.

All ye who faithful servants are. *Tate & Brady.* [*Holy Communion.*] This is Hymn ii. of the three hymns for Holy Communion which were given in the *Supp.* to the *N. V.*, 1699. It is based on Rev. xix., and is in 4 st. of 4 l. It is found in a few modern hymnals only, including *Kennedy*, 1863, No. 646, and the *Sarum*, 1868, No. 225, in both of which the changes in st. iv. of l. 1, "bless'd" to "*blest*," and l. 4, "Is call'd" to "*Is made* a welcome guest," are given. The text is otherwise correct.

All ye who seek a rest above. *Godfrey Thring.* [*Holy Communion.*] Written in 1863, and 1st pub. in his *Hymns Congregational and Others*, 1866, pp. 72–3, in 5 st. of 6 l. In 1874 it was republished in his *Hymns and Lyrics*, pp. 141–2; and again in his *Coll.*, 1st ed., 1880, but not in the 2nd ed., 1882.

All yesterday is gone. [*Invitation.*] This hymn, in 3 st. of 4 l., is found in a few English collections early in the present century, including Pratt's *Coll.*, 1829, through which it probably passed into the American collections. Its use in G. Brit. is very limited. In America it is found in several hymnals. It is an earnest and simple invitation to accept of present offers of salvation. Its authorship is unknown.

Alle Christen singen gerne. xviii. cent. [*Love to Christ.*] Included as No. 953 in J. J. Gottschaldt's *Universal G. B.*, Leipzig, 1737, in 11 st. of 12 l., and in the *Unv. L. S.*, 1851, No. 294. Repeated altered (reading *hören*) as No. 514 in the *Berlin G. B.*, 1829, in 4 st. of 8 l. The only *tr.* is, "All with Jesus are delighted," by Dr. H. Mills, 1845 (ed. 1856, p. 114).   [J. M.]

Alleluia = Hallelujah. Hymns beginning with this word are arranged in this work according to the mode of spelling adopted by the authors and translators.

Alleluia (Greek, 'Αλληλούια; Hebrew, הַלְלוּ־יָהּ). An ascription of praise derived from two Hebrew words meaning "Praise Jah," or "Praise the Lord." It occurs frequently in the Book of Psalms, from Ps. civ. onwards, both in the text and as a heading (Vulgate); once in the Book of Tobit (xiii. 18), and four times in the Revelation (xix. 1, 3, 4, 6).

It passed at an early date into frequent and general use among Christians. St. Jerome speaks of the Christian ploughman shouting it while at his work. [*Ep. xviii. ad Marcellam.*] Sidonius Apollinaris alludes to sailors using it as the "celeusma," or exclamation of

encouragement while plying the oar. [*Lib. ii. Ep.* 10.] Christian soldiers used it as a battle-cry, as when the Britons under the guidance of St. Germanus of Auxerre won the "Alleluia victory" over the Picts and Scots A.D. 429.

Tradition says that when the early Christians met on Easter morning, they saluted each other with the exclamation, "Alleluia, the Lord is risen."

The word passed early into liturgical use, and (untranslated, like other Hebrew words, "Amen," "Hósanna") assumed a fixed position in the services of the Church. Its uses are:—

i. In the Eastern Church it is closely connected with the *Great Entrance*. It occurs once at the close of the Cherubic Hymn in the Greek Liturgies of St. James (Hammond, C. E., *Lit. Eastern and Western*, p. 32), and of St. Mark (*Ibid.* p. 178), and three times in the same position in the Liturgy of Constantinople (*Ibid.* p. 101). It occurs frequently in the Greek *Offices for the Dead* (Goar, *Eucholog.* p. 526), and its use is not intermitted even in Lent (*Ibid.* p. 205). In the Greek *Menaea* it occurs thrice at the end of the Hexapsalmus at the Orthron; thrice after the Gloria Patri concluding the three opening Psalms of the first, the third, and the sixth Hours.

ii. Its liturgical use in the Western Church has been varied.

1. In the *Mozarabic* liturgy its normal and invariable position was after the Gospel, at the commencement and conclusion of the "Lauda," its use being continued even in Masses for the Dead, and even on such ferial occasions as the first day of Lent. It also occurs nearly as invariably in the "*Sacrificium*," or "*Offertorium.*" According to original usage the "Alleluia" was retained in the Spanish Church all the year round, but its omission in Lent was ordered by Can. xi. of the fourth Council of Toledo, and is witnessed to by Isidore of Seville (*De Eccles. Offic.* i. 13). Such omission only commences after the First Sunday in Lent, on which day additional "Alleluias" were inserted in the Introit.

2. *Gallican* usage is unknown, but in this, as in other points, it was probably identical with the Spanish rite.

3. In the *African* Church the use of "Alleluia" was confined to Sundays and to Easter and Ascension-tide (*Isidorus de Eccles. Offic.* i. 13).

4. In the *Roman Liturgy* it is used after the *Gradual*, before the Gospel. Originally its use was confined to Easter Day (Sozomen, *Hist. Eccl.* vii. 19), though some persons have supposed *Pascha* in this passage to mean Easter-tide. Afterwards it was used throughout the year except from Septuagesima Sunday to Holy Saturday, and according to present rule it is also omitted on ferial masses in Advent, on the Feast of Holy Innocents if it falls on a week-day, and on all Vigils except those of Easter and Pentecost, in Masses for the Dead, and on Ember Days.

5. In the *Roman Breviary* "Alleluia" is said after the opening "Gloria Patri" at all the Hours except from Septuagesima Sunday to Maundy-Thursday, when "Laus tibi, Domine, Rex aeternae gloriae" is substituted for it, and during Easter-tide it is added to all "Antiphons," of which at other seasons it would not form a part. It is also added during Easter-tide to the verses following the Antiphons to the Psalms, and to the Responsory after Lections before its following verse; and to the short Responsory after the chapter at Terce, Sext, and None, being said twice here, and twice after the first verse instead of part of the Responsory, and once after the second verse.

iii. Beyond this enumeration we need not go, as the labour involved in tracing out the use of "Alleluia" in the hundreds of local Breviaries which exist, would yield little return in practical utility. Dr. Neale's note on the use of Alleluia in his *Mediaeval Hymns*, 1851 and 1867, under "Alleluia dulce carmen," is very beautiful, but too long for quotation.

iv. We will close with a short list of Hymns, Sequences and Proses commenced with the word "Alleluia," or with the first two syllables of that word.

1. "Alle- cantabile sonet chorus cantorum et subjungat dulcibile -luya." A Sequence for the Feast of St. Bartholomew in the Tropary of Ethelred (994–1017, *Bodleian* MS. 775), printed in Surtees Society, vol. 60, p. 286. It consists of 17 lines, all but 7 of which end with the letter *a*, and in 3 out of the 7 exceptions the last vowel is *a*. The lines chiefly consist of 15 syllables, but are occasionally longer, varying from 18 to 23.

2. "Alle- coeleste necnon et perenne -luya." A *Prose* attached to the Paschal Sequence entitled "Mater Sequentiarum" [= Pangamus Creatoris, &c.], in the Tropary of Ethelred [Bodl. MS. 775, Surtees Soc. vol. 60, p. 291]. It occurs in the *Sarum*, *York*, and *Hereford Missals* as the Sequence for the Feast of the Nativity of the B. V. M. on Sept. 8. It consists of 84 short lines, all of which, with 9 exceptions, end with the letter *a*, and in 8 out of the 9 exceptional lines the last vowel is *a*. After the first line, containing 13 syllables, the remaining lines vary between 4 and 9 syllables.

3. Alleluia, Alleluia, Alleluia, O filii et filiae, &c. (q. v.).

4. "Alleluia Christo decantet omnis lingua." A Sequence for the festival of St. Erhardus (Jan. 8), a Bavarian Bishop of the 8th century, printed from an undated Ratisbon *Missal*, by Dr. Neale (*Sequentiae*, 1852, p. 91). It consists of 19 rugged lines, in length varying from 13 to 22 syllables, closing with 3 short lines of 9 syllables each.

5. "Alleluia, dulce carmen" (q. v.).

6. "Alleluia nunc decantet universalis ecclesia" (q.v.).

7. "Alleluia piis edite laudibus" (q. v.).

Two instances of striking merit of modern imitations of these ancient "Alleluias" are found in

8. "Alleluia, Alleluia, hearts to heaven and voices raise" (q. v.). An Easter hymn by Dr. Christopher Wordsworth, Bishop of Lincoln.

9. "Alleluia, sing to Jesus" (q. v.). An Eucharistic Hymn, by W. Chatterton Dix.   [F. E. W.]

Allelui(y)aticae Antiphonae. A name for the Easter Antiphons with their added Alleluias. *Sarum Breviary.* Cambridge reprint. Fasc. ii. 1882. Col. dccccxcvi.

[F. E. W.]

Alleluia, dulce carmen. [*Week before Septuagesima.*] The earliest form in which this hymn is found is in three MSS. of the 11th cent. in the *British Museum* (Harl. 2961, f. 235; Vesp. D. xii. f. 46 b; Jul. A. vi. f. 42 b). From a Durham MS. of the 11th cent., it was pub. in the *Latin Hys. of the Anglo-Saxon Ch.* (Surtees Society), 1851, p. 55. The text is in *Daniel*, i. No. 263, and with further readings in iv. p. 152; and in the *Hymn. Sarisb.* 1851, p. 59. In the latter readings are added from the *Worcester Brev.*, &c. Also in Biggs's *Annotated H. A. & M.*, p. 82.   [W. A. S.]

Translations in C. U. :—

1. **Alleluia! best and sweetest. Of the hymns of praise above.** By J. Chandler, 1st pub. in his *Hys. of the Primitive Church*, 1837, No. 59, in 4 st. of 6 l., as the first of two renderings of the hymn. This *tr.* is found in a great number of collections with the first two lines complete, but usually with a few alterations in the rest of the hymn. In the S. P. C. K. *Ps. & Hys.*, No. 37, it reads "Alleluia! peace instilling," and in the Bapt. *Ps. & Hys.*, 1858, No. 633, "Hallelujah! high and glorious."

2. **Alleluia! song of sweetness, Voice of everlasting glee.** By W. J. Blew, printed on a broadsheet for use in his church, cir. 1850 [E. MSS.], and then included in his *Ch. H. & Tune Bk.*, 1852, from whence it passed into Rice's *Sel.* from that work, 1870, No. 23.

3. **Alleluia! song of sweetness. Voice of joy, eternal lay.** By J. M. Neale. It appeared in the

1st ed. *Med. Hys.*, 1851, p. 130, in 4 st. of 6 l., and was "corrected for the *Hymnal N.*" (*Med. Hys.* 2nd ed. p. 184), where it was given in its new form, in 1852, No. 46, and again in the 2nd ed. of the *Med. Hys.*, 1863. This *tr.* equals in popularity that of Chandler, but it is more frequently and extensively altered. Without noticing minor instances, we find the following: "Alleluia, song of sweetness, Voice of joy *that cannot die*," in *H. A. & M.*, 1861 and 1875, and many others. "*Hallelujah!* song of gladness, Voice of joy *that cannot die*," in Thring's *Coll.*, 1882, &c. Of these altered forms of Neale's text, that of *H. A. & M.* is most frequently adopted.

4. **Alleluia! song of gladness, Utterance of perennial joy.** By J. A. Johnston, given in his *English Hymnal*, 1852, No. 75, and in later editions.

5. **Alleluia! song of gladness, Voice of everlasting joy.** This *tr.* appeared in Cooke and Denton's *Hymnal*, 1853, No. 44. It is based upon Chandler; but it has so much in it that is new, that practically it is ⁻ fresh *tr.* In 1857, it was included in the Winchester *Ch. H. Bk.*, No. 247, and subsequently in *Barry*, Snepp's *Songs of G. & G.*; *Hy. Comp.*; the *Stoke H. Bk.*, and others. It is also given, but somewhat altered, in the *Parish H. Bk.*; the R. T. S.'s. *Hys.*, No. 337; and the *New Cong.*, No. 714. In some of these it is ascribed to Dr. Neale in error.

6. **Alleluya! song of sweetness.** By J. D. Chambers, in his *Lauda Syon*, 1857, i. p. 120, and from thence, in an altered form, into the *Wellington College H. Bk.*, 1860, p. 65.

7. **Alleluia, sweetest anthem, Voice of joy that may not die.** By J. Keble. This *tr.* is based upon Dr. Neale's, and was contributed to the *Salisbury H. Bk.*, 1857, No. 63, and repeated, with alterations, in the *Sarum*, 1868. It was also included in Keble's *Misc. Poems*, 1869, p. 149.

8. **Alleluia! song of sweetness**, No. 61 in Pott's *Hymns*, &c., 1861, is the *H. A. & M.* text, slightly altered; and No. 102, *Ch. Hys.*, 1871, is st. i., ii. and iii., from Pott's *Hys.* and st. iv. from Neale direct.

9. **Alleluia, song of sweetness, Strain of everliving joy.** By R. C. Singleton, made for, and 1st pub. in his *Anglican H. Bk.* 1868. It was rewritten for the 2nd ed., 1871.

The close resemblance of these *trs.* to each other has made the annotations a task of some difficulty. By far the greater number of compilers have worked with second-hand materials, and these, when re-arranged, have produced complications in the text of the most embarrassing nature. *Ch. Hys.* No. 102, is an example. There we have Neale altered by the compilers of *H. A. & M.*, altered again by the Rev. F. Pott in his *Coll.*; again this arrangement, shorn of st. iv., by the editors of *Ch. Hys.* and the omission made good by adopting Neale's original *tr.* of that stanza. The text of *Thring* and others is equally complicated.

Translations not in C. U. :—

1. O, Glorious is the song. *J. Chandler* (2nd *tr.*), 1837.

2. Hallelujah! note of gladness. *W. L. Alexander*, 1849.

3. Alleluia, sweetest lay. *R. Campbell*, 1850.

4. Alleluia, song of sweetness. *Bonar*, 1856.
5. Alleluia, sweetest music. *Mrs. Charles*, 1858.
6. Alleluia, music sweetest. *Kynaston*, 1862.

[J. J.]

Alleluia nunc decantet. [*Common of Apostles.*] According to *Mone*, No. 667, this hymn is found in a Reichenau MS. of the 14th cent. among the Notkerian sequences, and marked as for SS. Philip & James. It is also in the *Sarum, York* and *Hereford Missals.* Dr. Neale included it in his *Seq. ex Miss.*, p. 214, as a "Seq. for the Com. of Apostles"; *Daniel*, v. 335, repeats the text, readings, and references of *Mone*, whose title is "De Apostolis" (troparium). It is also in *Kehrein*, No. 374. The sequence is in 27 lines of varying length. Of these 26 lines end in the letter "a." It will be noticed that in the hymn no reference is made to St. Paul; possibly, as suggested by *Mone*, because he was not an eye-witness of the life and sufferings of our Lord. The *tr.* in C. U. is :—

Let the Church sing Alleluia. By *R. F. Littledale.* Made for and first pub. in the *People's H.*, 1867, No. 198, and signed "*D. L.*"

Alleluia piis edito laudibus. This anonymous hymn, *Mone*, 1853, i. p. 87, assigns to the 5th cent., on the ground that it was included in the *Mozarabic Brev.*, in which no hymns were admitted which are of later date than the 8th cent., and that the shortened strophe indicated that date. He gives the text from a Munich MS. of the 10th cent., and adds numerous readings and a few notes. *Daniel*, 1855, vol. iv. pp. 63–65, repeats this text, with slight changes, together with *Mone's* various readings with additions.

It is the Hymn at Vespers in the *Mozarabic Brev.* (Toledo, 1502, f. 80) for the first Sunday in Lent, and the Saturday preceding. See Migne's *Patrol.*, tom. 86, col. 259, also col. 896; where it is described as the *Hymn on the occasion of leaving off flesh-meat, "Ymnus in Carnes tollendas."* The **Hymn** on Ash-Wednesday itself, however (*Feriâ quartâ in Capite Jejunii*: the head or beginning of the fast), is *Benignitatis fons Deus*, the same as at Lauds and Vespers on the three days' fast which precedes the Feast of the Epiphany in that rite (excepting the Vespers of the third day, or Eve of the Epiphany), *Patrol.*, col. 149.

The text is also in the *Hymn. Sarisb.*, Lon., 1851, pp. 60, 61, where it is given as the hymn at Matins on Septuagesima Sunday and through the week, and as from a MS. (date 1064), formerly belonging to Worcester Cathedral; which MS. professes to contain *Ambrosian Hymns for the different Hours, according to the Constitutions of our Father Benedict*, and to have St. Oswald as its compiler.

In the *Hymn. Sarisb.* various readings are also given from three old MSS. of the 10th or 11th centuries, which have interlinear Anglo-Saxon versions. The refrain of this hymn— "Alleluia perenne"—is an allusion to the fact that the Alleluias of heaven are continuous, whilst those of earth are broken.

In addition to the works noted above, the text is in Neale's *Hymni Ecclesiae*, 1851, p. 102; and the *Latin Hymns of the Anglo-Saxon Church* (Surtees Society), 1851, p. 57, from an 11th cent. MS. at Durham. In the

British Museum it is found in three MSS. of the 11th cent. (Harl. 2961, f. 235 b; Vesp. D. xii. f. 47; Jul. A. vi. f. 43.) For the *Use* of this and similar hymns, see **Alleluia.**

[W. A. S.]

Translations in C. U. :—

1. Alleluias sound ye, In strains of holy laud. By J. D. Chambers, 1st pub. in his *Lauda Syon*, 1857, in 9 st. of 6 l., including the refrain. In 1868, st. i., ii., iv., v., and viii. were included, with slight alterations, in *Sarum*, as No. 185.

2. Alleluia ! now be sung. By J. Skinner, made for and 1st pub. in his *Daily Service Hymnal*, 1864, No. 75, in two parts, part ii. being: "Bright and lovely morning star." This *tr.*, although somewhat elaborated, is suited to congregational use, and is worthy of being better known.

3. Sing Alleluia forth in duteous praise. By J. Ellerton. 1st pub., with an explanatory and historical note, in *The Churchman's Family Magazine*, 1865. In 1868 it was embodied in the Rev. R. Brown-Borthwick's *Suppl. Hymn and Tune Bk.*, and again, after revision by the translator, in the *App.* to *H. A. & M.* the same year. It was revised a second time for *Ch. Hys.*, 1871, and has also been printed elsewhere with the alteration of a word or two, but usually with the translator's consent. Orig. *tr.* as above; authorised *tr.* in *Ch. Hys.* Since its publication in *H. A. & M.*, 1868, it has been included in almost every hymnal of note in G. Britain, and most English-speaking countries. It is the most vigorous, musical, and popular rendering of the "Alleluia piis edite" which we possess.

Translation not in C. U. :—
Alleluia ! let the holy sounds of cheerful praises ring. *Crippen's Anc. Hys.*, 1868, p. 25. [J. J.]

Alleluia, sing to Jesus. *W. C. Dix.* [*Holy Communion.*] Written about the year 1866, the author's design being to assist in supplying a then acknowledged lack of Eucharistic hymns in Church of England hymnals. It was 1st pub. in his *Altar Songs*, 1867, No. vii., in 5 st. of 8 l., and appointed especially for Ascension-tide, with the title "Redemption by the Precious Blood." From *Altar Songs* it passed, unaltered, into the *App. to H. A. & M.*, 1868, No. 350, and subsequently into numerous collections both in G. Brit. and America, sometimes in a slightly altered and abbreviated form.

Alleluia ! With a diadem of beauty. *W. T. Brooke.* [*Saints' Days.*] This versification of Rev. J. M. Rodwell's prose translation of the Song of the Saints from the Abyssinian hymnal of *Jared* was 1st pub. in the *Monthly Packet*, Nov. 1871, in a series of articles on the "Songs of Other Churches," by the Rev. L. C. Biggs. In 1882 it was included in Mr. Brooke's *Churchman's Manual of Private and Family Devotion*, and is in 8 st. of 7 l. [W. T. B.]

Allen, Elizabeth-Lee. [Smith, E. L.]

Allen, Henry. [Alline, H.]

Allen, James, b. at Gayle, Wensleydale, Yorkshire, June 24, 1734, and educated with a view to taking Holy Orders, first with two clergymen at different times, and then for one year at St. John's Coll., Cambridge. Leaving the University in 1752 he became a follower of Benjamin Ingham, the founder of the sect of the Inghamites, but subsequently joined himself to the Sandemanians [see Scottish Hymnody]; and finally built a chapel on his estate at Gayle, and ministered therein to the time of his death; d. 31st Oct., 1804. He pub. a small volume, *Christian Songs*, containing 17 hymns, and was the editor and a principal contributor to the *Kendal Hymn Book*, 1757, and *Appendix* to the 2nd ed., 1761.

Allen, Jonathan. Concerning this hymn-writer, to whom is credited the hymn, " Sinners, will you scorn the message?" we can only say that this hymn appeared in *Hys. adapted to Pub. Worship, collected from various Authors*, Exeter, S. Woolmer, 1801, edited by Richard Pearsell Allen, Minister of Castle Street Meeting, Exeter; and that in D. Sedgwick's marked copy of John Dobell's *New Selection*, &c., 1806, it is attributed to Jonathan Allen. What authority Sedgwick had for this ascription we cannot determine. It is through him that it has gained currency. Allen's hymn, "Sinners, will you scorn, &c.," is sometimes given with st. i. and ii. transposed, as "Hear the heralds of the Gospel," as in the Amer. *Bap. Praise Bk.*, N. Y. 1871.

[W. T. B.]

Allen, Oswald, s. of John Allen, banker, of Kirkby Lonsdale, Westmoreland, and great-nephew of James Allen (q.v.); b. at Kirkby Lonsdale, 1816, and educated in that town. After residing for a time in Glasgow, he returned to Kirkby Lonsdale, and joined the staff of the local bank; d. October 2, 1878. In 1861 (Preface, Oct. 1861), he pub. *Hymns of the Christian Life*, Lond., Nisbet. It contains 148 hymns, a few of which are in C. U.

Allen, William, D.D., b. at Pittsfield, Mass., 1784, graduated at Harvard, 1802. He became Pastor of Pittsfield, 1810 ; President of Dartmouth University, 1817, and of Bowdoin College, 1820–1839. He d. at Northampton, 1868. He published the *American Biographical and Historical Dictionary*, 1809; *Psalms and Hymns*, 1835. The latter contains versions of all the Psalms, and 200 original hymns. Some of the hymns, especially those about slavery, are curious. Five are found in Campbell's *Comprehensive H. Bk.*, Lond., 1837 His compositions have almost entirely passed out of use. [F. M. B.]

Allendorf, Johann Ludwig Conrad, b. Feb. 9, 1693, at Josbach, near Marburg, Hesse, where his father was pastor. He entered the University of Giessen in 1711, but in 1713 passed on to Halle to study under Francke, and then, in 1717, became tutor in the family of Count Henkel of Odersberg. In 1723 he became tutor to the family of Count Erdmann v. Promnitz at Sorau, and in 1724 was appointed Lutheran Court preacher at Cöthen, when one of the Count's daughters was married to the Prince of Anhalt-Cöthen. After the death of his first wife the Prince married her younger sister, but the latter

dying in 1750, the need for a Lutheran Court preacher ceased, he being of the Reformed Confession. Allendorf was then summoned by Count Christian Ernst v. Stolberg to Wernigerode, where a sister of his former patronesses was the wife of the Count's eldest son. There he was assistant in two churches till 1755, when he was appointed pastor of the Liebfrau Church, and a member of the Consistory. In 1760 he became pastor of St. Ulrich's Church in Halle, and successfully laboured there till, on June 3, 1773, "As a Simeon of eighty years he received his peaceful summons home to rest in the arms of Jesus" (*Koch*, iv. 441–446; *Allg. Deutsche Biog.*, i. 349, &c.). His hymns, which are "hymns of love to Christ, the Lamb of God, and the Bridegroom of the believing soul," appeared principally in the *Einige gantz neue auserlesene Lieder*, Halle, N. D. (c. 1733), and the *Einige gantz neue Lieder zum Lobe des Dreyeinigen Gottes und zur gewünschten reichen Erbauung vieler Menschen*. The latter, known as the *Cöthnische Lieder*, contains hymns of the Pietists of the younger Halle School, such as Lehr, Allendorf, Woltersdorf, Kunth, &c.; and to its first ed., 1736, Allendorf contributed 45 hymns, while the 4th ed., 1744, contains in its second pt. 46, and the 5th ed., 1768, in its third pt. 41 additional hymns by him—in all 132.

Four of his hymns have been *tr.*, viz.:—

1. Das Brünnlein quillt, das Lebenswasser fliesset. [*H. Communion.*] Founded on Ps. lxv. 1st pub. in 1733, p. 14, and included, in 1736, as above, in 9 st. of 8 l., as a "Brunnenlied." Repeated as No. 1570 in the Berlin *G. L. S.* ed. 1863. The only *tr.* in C. U. is:—

The Fountain flows !—its waters—all are needing, omitting st. iv., vi., ix., by H. Mills in his *Horae Germanicae*, 1845 (ed. 1856, p. 43). The *tr.* of st. i.–iii., viii., altered to "The Fountain flows ! waters of life bestowing," were included, as No. 819, in the Luth. General Synod's *Coll.* 1850.

2. Die Seele ruht in Jesu Armen. [*Eternal Life.*] Founded on an anonymous hymn in 5 st. beginning, "Ich ruhe nun in Gottes Armen," included as No. 655, in pt. ii., 1714, of Freylinghausen's *G. B.*; but not in the *Einhundert ... Lieder*, Dresden, 1694 [Leipzig Town Library]. According to *Lauxmann* in *Koch*, viii. 689, Allendorf's hymn was first printed separately. In pt. ii. of the 4th ed., 1744, of the *Cöthnische Lieder*, as above, p. 264, in 13 st. of 10 l. entitled, "Of a soul blessed there with the beatific vision," Rev. xxii. 4. Written in the spirit of Canticles, it is included in full in the *Neue Sammlung*, Wernigerode, 1752, No. 92, but is generally abridged, Knapp, in his *Ev. L. S.*, 1850, No. 3059 (ed. 1865, No. 3123) altering it and omitting st. vi., ix., x. Lauxmann relates that Diaconus Schlipalius, of the Holy Cross Church in Dresden, told his wife on Jan. 1, 1764, while he was yet in perfect health, that he would die during the year. He comforted her apprehensions with st. vi.–xi. of this hymn, which consoled himself shortly before his death on April 6 of that year. The only *tr.* in C. U. is:—

Now rests her soul in Jesus' arms. A good *tr.* of st. i., ii., viii., xii., xiii., in the 1st Ser., 1855, of Miss Winkworth's *Lyra Ger.*, p. 250 (later eds. p. 252). Thence, omitting st. xii., as No. 362 in E. H. Bickersteth's *Ps. & Hys.*, 1858. Another *tr.* is, "In Jesus' arms her soul doth rest," by Mrs. Bevan, 1858, p. 42.

3. Jesus ist kommen, Grund ewiger Freude. [*Advent.*] First pub. in 1736 as above (ed. 1738, p. 102), in 23 st. of 6 l., as a hymn of triumph on the Coming of the Saviour to our world, St. John iii. 31. In the Speier *G. B.*, 1859, 11 st. are selected, and in the *Württemberg G. B.*, 1842, 6 st. are given as No. 84. The only *tr.* is, "Jesus is come, O joy heavenlighted," by Miss Warner, in her *H. of the Church Militant*, 1858 (ed. 1861, p. 433).

4. Unter Lilien jener Freuden. [*Longing for Heaven.*] A beautiful hymn on the Joys of Heaven, more suited for private than for Church use. It appeared as, "In den Auen jener Freuden," in the *Sammlung Geist- und lieblicher Lieder*, Herrnhut, 1731, No. 1004, in 8 st. of 6 l. When repeated in 1733, p. 67, and in 1736, in the *Cöthnische Lieder*, as above, Ps. lxxxiv. 3, was given as a motto, and the first line as *Unter Lilien.* Included in this form as No. 731 in the Berlin *G. L. S.* ed. 1863. Lauxmann, in *Koch*, viii. 687–689, relates that it was repeated on her death-bed by the first wife of Jung-Stilling, and that it was a favourite hymn of Wilhelm Hofacker, a well-known Württemberg clergyman. The only *tr.* is, "Glorious are the fields of heaven," by Mrs. Bevan, 1859, p. 131. [J. M.]

Alles ist an Gottes Segen. *Anon.* xvii. cent. [*Trust in God.*] This hymn on Christian faith and patience is mentioned by *Koch*, v. 605, as anonymous and as dating c. 1673. In the Nürnberg *G. B.* of 1676 it is No. 943 (ed. 1690, No. 949), in 6 st. of 6 l., marked "Anonymus." Included as No. 488 in the *Unv. L. S.*, 1851.

Translation in C. U.:—

All things hang on our possessing. Good and full in the 2nd Series, 1858, of Miss Winkworth's *Lyra Ger.*, p. 189, and thence, as No. 130, in her *C. B. for England*, 1863, and in full in the Ohio Luth. *Hymnal*, 1880, No. 326. [J. M.]

Alline, Henry [Allen], b. at Newport, R. I., June 14, 1748, was some time a minister at Falmouth, Nova Scotia, and d. at North Hill, N.S., Feb. 7, 1784. Alline, whose name is sometimes spelt *Allen*, is said to have founded a sect of "Allenites," who maintained that Adam and Eve before the fall had no corporeal bodies, and denied the resurrection of the body. These peculiar views may have a place in his prose works, but they cannot be traced in his 487 *Hymns and Spiritual Songs*, in five books, of which the 3rd ed., now rare, was pub. at Dover and Boston, U.S.A., 1797, and another at Stoningtonport, Conn., 1802. Of these hymns 37 are found in Smith and Jones's *Hymns for the Use of Christians*, 1805, and some in later books of that body. The best of these hymns, "Amazing sight, the Saviour stands," from the 1st ed. of *Hymns and Spiritual Songs* (1790?), is preserved in Hatfield's *Ch. H. Bk.*, 1872, No. 569, where it is given anonymously from Nettleton's *Village Hymns;*

also in the *Bapt. Praise Bk.*, and others. Alline's hymns are unknown to the English collections. [F. M. B.]

Allon, Henry, D.D., an Independent Minister, b. at Welton, near Hull, October 18, 1818, and educated at Cheshunt Coll., Herts. In 1844 he became co-pastor with the Rev. T. Lewis of the Union Chapel, Islington, and succeeded to the sole pastorate on the death of Mr. Lewis in 1852. In 1865 Dr. Allon became co-editor with Dr. Reynolds of the *British Quarterly Review*, and in 1877 the sole editor of that journal. His *Memoir of the Rev. J. Sherman*, pub. in 1863, and his Sermons on *The Vision of God*, 1876, are well known. As a composer of hymns he is represented by one hymn only, "Low in Thine agony," a good hymn for Passiontide, contributed to his *Suppl. Hymns*, 1868, No. 24. His services to Hymnody, especially in the musical department, have been of value. In addition to acting as co-editor of the *New Cong. H. Bk.* 1859, he pub. *Supplemental Hymns*, 1868, enlarged ed. 1875; *Children's Worship*, 1878; and *The Congregational Psalmist Hymnal*, 1886. His musical compilations are the *Congregational Psalmist*, London, 1858, in conjunction with Dr. Gauntlett, in which his Historical Preface and Biographical Notes display considerable research and accuracy (various eds. 1868, 1875, 1883, raising the original 330 to 650 tunes); *2nd sect.* of the same, *Chant Book*, 1860; *3rd sect.*, *Anthems for Congregational Use*, 1872; *4th sect.*, *Tunes for Children's Worship*, 1879. These musical works, together with his essay, "The Worship of the Church," contributed to Dr. Reynolds's *Ecclesia*, 1870; and his most valuable lectures delivered in connection with the Y. M. C. A. in Exeter Hall;—*Church Song in its Relation to Church Life*, 1861–2; and *Psalmody of the Reformation*, 1863–4,—have done much towards raising the musical portion of Nonconformist worship to a higher and more cultured position. [J. J.]

Allsop, Solomon S., b. 1824; resided in Jamaica, where his father laboured as a missionary, from 1827 to 1830, when he returned to England. Joining the Nonconformist ministry he has been successively Pastor at Whittlesea, Longford, March, and Burton-on-Trent. In 1879 he was President of the Baptist Annual Association. When at Longford, 1864–68, Mr. Allsop wrote several hymns for the local Anniversary. Of these, "Our hymn of thanks we sing to-day" was included in Stevenson's *Sch. Hymnal*, 1880, No. 323, in 5 st. of 6 l.

Alma Redemptoris Mater quae pervia coeli. [B. V. M.] One of four Antiphons to the B. V. M. used at the termination of the Offices, the remaining three being the *Ave Regina*, the *Regina coeli*, and the *Salve Regina*. It is ascribed to *Hermannus Contractus*, who d. 1054. In *Daniel*, ii. p. 318, the text is given in full, together with a note setting forth its use, with readings from a Munich MS. probably of the 13th cent. It is also in a 14th cent. *Sarum Breviary* in the *British Museum* (MSS. Reg. 2 A., xiv. f. 235 b);

in the *Roman Breviary*, Modena, 1480, f. 512; the *York Breviary*, 1493, (reprint, 1883, ii. 494), &c. Concerning its use we may add from *Daniel* and other authorities :—

That it is appointed to be said at the end of Compline from the Saturday before the first Sunday in Advent to the 2nd of February, inclusively, and that in the old Franciscan Breviary, dated 1497, it is to be sung till Quinquagesima Sunday. In the Breviaries of *Rome, Paris, Lyons,* &c., it is to be said at the end of Compline from the 1st Vespers of the 1st Sunday in Advent to the Feast of the Purification, inclusively; also after Lauds during this time, if the choir where the office is recited be left; if Prime, or other Hours, shall be said immediately after Lauds, then this Antiphon should be used at the end, once for all. Should the Feast of the Purification be transferred, on account of some privileged day (as Septuagesima Sunday) falling on the same time, yet the *Alma Redemptoris Mater* is not to be continued beyond Feb. 2, according to decrees of the Roman Congregation of Rites, 1681, 1693, 1705.

How well this Antiphon was known in England in the Middle Ages we may judge from the use which Chaucer made of it in his *Prioress's Tale*, where the whole story is associated therewith. In the tale it is introduced in the following lines :—

"This litel childe his litel book leming,
As he sate in the scole at his primere,
He *Alma Redemptoris* herde sing,
As children lered hir antiphonere:
And as he dorst, he drow him nere and nere,
And herkened ay the wordes and the note,
Til he the firste vers coude al by rote."

The Poet then explains the way in which the child mastered the Antiphon, together with the music to which it was set; and describes his singing it in the public streets, his murder by the Jews for so doing, and the subsequent results. This Antiphon is distinct from the Sequence, "Alma redemptoris Mater quam de coelis misit pater," given in *Daniel*, v. 113; *Mone*, ii. p. 200; Neale's *Seq. ex Missalibus*, p. 72, and others. The Sequence *Mone* quotes from a MS. of the 13th cent. Of this there is, so far as we are aware, no *tr.* into English. From the constant use of the Antiphon, both in public and private, by all Roman Catholics, translations, either in prose or verse, are in nearly all their devotional manuals. It is only necessary to specify the following :—

Translation in C. U. :—
Mother of Christ, hear thou thy people's cry. By E. Caswall, 1st pub. in his *Lyra Catholica*, 1849, p. 38, and in his *Hymns & Poems*, 1873, p. 22. Its use is confined to the Roman Catholic collections for schools and missions.

Translations not in C. U. :—
1. Kindly Mother of the Redeemer. Card. Newman, *Tracts for the Times*, No. 75, 1836.
2. Sweet Mother of our Saviour blest. *J. Wallace*, 1874. **[V.]**

Almighty Author of my frame. *Anne Steele.* [*Praise.*] The first hymn of her *Poems on Subjects chiefly Devotional*, 1760, vol. i. pp. 1–2, in 5 st. of 4 l., and entitled "Desiring to praise God.". It was repeated in the new ed. of the same, 1780, pp. 1–2, and again in Sedgwick's reprint of her *Hymns*, &c., 1863. It came into C. U. through the Bristol Bapt. *Coll. of Hys.* of Ash and Evans, 1769, No. 40. Its modern use, except in America, is very limited.

Almighty Father, bless the word. [*After Sermon.*] This hymn appeared anony-

mously in Dr. W. A. Muhlenberg's *Church Poetry.* Phila., 1823. It was repeated in the Amer. *Prayer Book Coll.*, 1826, as No. 39, in 2 st. It is found in several American collections, but is not in C. U. in Great Britain.

Almighty Father, God of grace. *T. Cotterill.* [*For Pardon.*] A metrical rendering of the Confession from the B. of C. Prayer given in his *Sel.* 1810, and continued in later eds. The ascription here to Cotterill is based on the authority of two marked copies of the 8th ed. of the *Sel.* 1819, in the *Brooke* and *Julian Libraries.* Orig. text in Snepp's *S. of G. & G.* 1872, No. 451.

Almighty Father, gracious Lord. *Anne Steele.* [*Providence and Grace.*] "Praise to God for the Blessings of Providence and Grace," is the title of this hymn in 16 st. of 4 l. in her *Poems*, &c., 1760, and 2nd edit. 1780. A cento therefrom in Dr. Alexander's *Augustine H. Bk.*, 1849–65, is composed of st. i., ii., vii.–ix., xv., and xvi. It is also found in some American collections. Another arrangement of stanzas beginning with the first st. was included in Cotterill's *Sel.*, 1810. Of this, st. iii., ll. 5–8, is altered from Cowper.

Almighty Father, heaven and earth. *E. A. Dayman.* [*Offertory.*] 1st pub. in the *Sarum Hymnal*, 1868, No. 292, and appointed as an "Offertory Hymn." Together with 2 st. as a "General Heading," and 2 st. as a "General Ending," it embodies two parts of 4 st. of 4 l., and a doxology. In the *Hymnary*, 1872, No. 522, it assumed the form of a single hymn, embracing the "General Heading," "Part i.," the 1st st. of the "General Ending," and the dox., thus omitting one stanza of the latter, and the whole of pt. 2. Some slight alterations are also introduced therein.

Almighty Father, let Thy love. *E. W. Eddis.* [*Matrimony.*] Written in 1863, and published in his Irvingite *Hys. for the use of the Churches*, in 1864, No. 114, and later editions.

Almighty Father of mankind. *M. Bruce.* [*Providence.*] We attribute this hymn to M. Bruce on grounds stated in his *Memoir* in this work. It was written probably about 1764, and 1st pub. in J. Logan's *Poems*, 1781, No. 3, in 3 st. of 4 l. Its use is not extensive in G. Brit., but it is found in many of the American hymnals. Text from Logan in Dr. Grosart's *Works of Michael Bruce*, 1865.

Almighty Father! robed with light. *E. T. Pilgrim.* [*Resignation.*] From his *Hymns written chiefly on the Divine Attributes of the Supreme Being*, 2nd ed., 1831, p. 8. It is Hymn iv. "On Resignation," in 3 st. of 4 l., and is based on the words, "Thy Will be done." It is in several collections.

Almighty Father, Thou hast many a blessing. [*Renunciation.*] Anon., in Longfellow and Johnson's Amer. *Book of Hys.*, 1846, No. 217; and their *Hymns of the Spirit*, 1864, No. 365, in 3 st. of 4 l.

Almighty God, be Thou our Guide. [*Security in God.*] Anon., in *Holy Song for all Seasons*, Lond., Bell & Daldy, 1869, No. 356, in 5 st. of 4 l.

Almighty God, Eternal Lord. [*Before a Sermon.*] A cento mainly from hymns by C. Wesley as given in the *Wes. H. Bk.* 1780. The 1st st. is from " Come, O Thou all victorious Lord," st. i., the 2nd, from "Thou Son of God, Whose flaming eyes," st. v., the 4th, from "Father of all in whom alone ; " and the 3rd and 5th, possibly by the compiler. As the cento has not been traced to an earlier date than Cotterill's *Sel.*, 1805, No. 71, it was probably compiled by Cotterill from the *Wes. H. Bk.* To modern collections in Great Britain it is almost entirely unknown, but its use in America is somewhat extensive. The concluding line, "And faith be lost in sight," anticipated Dr. Neale's " *Till hope* be lost in sight," in *H. A. & M.*, 1875, No. 226, st. iv., and other hymnals. The history of the hymns from which this cento is compiled may be found under their respective first lines.

Almighty God, in humble prayer. *J. Montgomery.* [*For Wisdom.*] This hymn is in the "M. MSS.," but undated. It was pub. in Montgomery's *Christian Psalmist*, 1825, No. 498, in 6 st. of 4 l. and entitled " Solomon's Prayer for Wisdom." It is repeated, without alteration, in his *Original Hymns*, 1853, No. 70. In modern collections it is usually given in an abbreviated form, as in Windle's *Metrical Psalter & Hymnal*, No. 11, Harland's *Ch. Psalter*, No. 199, the Amer. *Sabb. H. Bk.*, &c.

Almighty God of love. *C. Wesley.* [*Missions.*] A cento composed of Nos. 1157, 1158, and 1159 of his *Short Hymns, &c.*, 1762, vol. i. p. 391. In this form it was given in the *Wes. H. Bk.* 1780, and has been retained in all editions of that work. It has also passed into numerous collections, specially of the Methodist bodies, both in G. Brit. and America. Orig. text in *P. Works*, 1868–72, vol. ix. p. 469.

Almighty God, the pure and just. *E. Osler.* [*Lent.*] 1st pub. in the *Mitre H. Book*, 1836, No. 1, in 4 st. of 4 l. and again with slight variations in the Author's *Church and King*, July 1837. In *Kennedy*, 1863, No. 631, it is subject to further alterations which are repeated in detail from Cooke & Denton's *Hymnal*, 1853, No. 69, but with the omission of their doxology.

Almighty God, Thy Name I praise. *Dorothy A. Thrupp.* [*God the Father.*] Contributed to her *Hymns for the Young* (1st ed. N.D. c. 1830, 4th ed. Lond. 1836), No. 63, in 3 st. of 4 l. and entitled, " Praise to God for Mercies." From thence it passed into Mrs. Herbert Mayo's *Sel. of Hys. & Poetry, &c.*, Lond. E. Suter (1st ed. 1838, 4th ed. 1849), with the signature " D. A. T." It is found in several collections for children, including the *Ch. S. S. H. Bk.*, 1868, and others.   [W. T. B.]

Almighty God, Thy piercing eye. *I. Watts.* [*Omniscience.*] 1st pub. in his

Divine Songs, 1715, in 6 st. of 4 l., and entitled, " The All-seeing God," and again in all subsequent editions of the same work. It is given in various collections in Great Britain and America, principally in those for children, and sometimes in an abbreviated form. Orig. text in the *Meth. S. S. H. Bk.*, 1879, No. 298. In one or two American collections it is attributed to *Beddome* in error.

Almighty God, Thy sovereign power. *J. Julian.* [*Almsgiving.*] Written for and 1st pub. in *St. Mary's Ch. S. S. H. Bk.*, Preston, Lancashire, 1874, in 5 st. of 4 l.

Almighty God, Thy word is cast. *J. Cawood.* [*After Sermon.*] Written about 1815, and 1st pub. in Cotterill's *Sel.*, 8th ed. 1819, No. 268, in 5 st. of 4 l., and given for use "After a Sermon" [s. MSS.]. It was reprinted in Montgomery's *Christ. Psal.*, 1825, No. 252. From that date it grew in importance as a congregational hymn, until its use has become extensive in all English-speaking countries, in some cases with the omission of one or more stanzas, and in others, with the addition of a doxology. Two texts, purporting to be the original, are extant. The first is that of *Cotterill* as above, from which the hymn has been taken in a more or less correct form until 1862, when the second was given from the original MS. in Lord Selborne's *Bk. of Praise*, 1862, p. 470, and *Lyra Brit.*, 1867, p. 131. One of the best arrangements of the hymn is a slightly altered form of the latter in Thring's *Coll.*, 1882, No. 151.

Almighty God, to-night. *J. M. Neale.* [*Evening.*] A child's hymn at " Bedtime," pub. in his *Hymns for Children*, 1842, in 5 st. of 4 l., and again in later editions. In use in American *Songs of Christian Praise*, 1880.

Almighty God, whose only Son. *Sir H. W. Baker.* [*Missions.*] Contributed to the *App.* to *H. A. & M.*, 1868, No. 357, in 7 st. of 4 l., and repeated in the revised edition of 1875, and other collections.

Almighty King, whose wondrous hand. *W. Cowper.* [*Grace and Providence.*] No. 81, Bk. iii., of the *Olney Hymns*, 1779, in 5 st. of 4 l., and entitled " Grace and Providence." It has not attained to the position of many of Cowper's hymns, and is found in a few collections only, including Martineau's *Hymns, &c.*, 1840 and 1873.

Almighty Lord and King. [*God unchangeable.*] An anonymous hymn in Dr. Alexander's *Augustine H. Bk.*, 2nd ed. 1858.

Almighty Maker, God! *I. Watts.* [*Praise.*] 1st pub. in his *Horae Lyricae*, 1706, in 11 st. of 4 l., and entitled " Sincere Praise." In its complete form it is unknown to the collections, but centos differing in length and arrangement, but all opening with the first stanza, are found in numerous hymnals in G. Brit. and America.

Almighty Maker, Lord of all. [*Holiness.*] This hymn is given in J. H. Thom's Unitarian *Hys., Chants & Anthems*, 1858, No.

433, as from " *Rees's Col*," *i.e.* Kippis's *Coll.* of which Abraham Rees was one of the editors, 1795 : No. 206, where it is given as from " Select Collection of 1756."

Almighty Ruler of the skies. *I. Watts.* [*Ps. viii.*]

His L. M. paraph. of v. 1, 2, of Ps. viii., 1st pub. in his *Psalms of David*, 1719, in 5 st. of 4 l., and entitled " The Hosanna of the Children ; or, Infants praising God." His explanation of the opening stanzas is given in a note thus :—" These two first verses are here paraphrased and explained by the history of the Children crying *Hosanna* to Christ, Matt. xxi. 15, 16, where our Saviour cites and applies those words of the Psalmist."

Although not of the first importance, it might be utilized as a hymn for Palm Sunday. Its use is limited. The *New Cong.*, copying from the *Leeds H. Bk.*, 1853, omits st. iii. and v.

Almum flamen, vita mundi. [*Whitsuntide.*]

This hymn is of unknown origin and date. It is in the *Corolla Hymnorum*, Cologne, 1806, p. 40. *Daniel*, il p. 368, gives it in 7 st. of 9 l., without note or comment. It is not known to be in use in any liturgical work. [W. A. S.]

Translation in C. U. :—

Lord of Eternal Sanctity. By E. Caswall, 1st pub. in his *Masque of Mary and other Poems*, 1858, in 7 st. of 10 l., and again in his *Hymns and Poems*, 1873, p. 131. In this form it is not in C. U., but a cento, beginning with st. ii., " Come Thou, who dost the soul endue " (*Veni, Spiritus Creator*), was compiled for the *Hymnary*, 1872, No. 329, and received the sanction of Mr. Caswall, shortly before his death (E. MSS.). Another *tr.* not in C. U. is "Genial Spirit, earth's emotion," by Dr. Kynaston in his *Occasional Hymns*, 1862.

Alone ! to land alone upon that shore. *F. W. Faber.* [*Death.*]

Pub. in his *Hymns*, 1862, No. 148, in 10 st. of 6 l. From it two centos are in C. U., both beginning with the same first line as above, and altered throughout ; the first being No. 6 in the Scottish *Ibrox Hymnal*, 1871, and the second, No. 909, in the *Bapt. Hymnal*, 1879.

Altenburg, Johann Michael, b. at

Alach, near Erfurt, on Trinity Sunday, 1584. After completing his studies he was for some time teacher and precentor in Erfurt. In 1608 he was appointed pastor of Ilversgehofen and Marbach near Erfurt ; in 1611, of Trochtelborn ; and in 1621 of Gross-Sommern or Sömmerda near Erfurt. In the troublous war times he was forced, in 1631, to flee to Erfurt, and there, on the news of the victory of Leipzig, Sept. 17, 1631, he composed his best known hymn. He remained in Erfurt without a charge till, in 1637, he was appointed diaconus of the Augustine Church, and, in 1638, pastor of St. Andrew's Church. He d. at Erfurt February 12, 1640 (*Koch*, iii. 115–117 ; *Allg. Deutsche Biog.*, i. p. 363, and x. p. 766—the latter saying he did not go to Erfurt till 1637). He was a good musician, and seems to have been the composer of the melodies rather than of the words of some of the hymns ascribed to him. Two of his hymns have been *tr.* into English, viz. :—

1. Aus Jakob's Stamm ein Stern sehr klar. [*Christmas.*] Included as No. 3 of his *Christliche liebliche und andächtige newe Kirchen- und Hauss-Gesänge*, pt. i., Erfurt, 1620, in 3 st. of 5 l. According to Wetzel's *A. H.*, vol. i., pt. v. p. 41, it was first pub. in J. Förster's *Hohen Festtags-Schreinlein*, 1611. In the *Unv. L. S.*, 1851, No. 24. It has been *tr.* as "From Jacob's root, a star so clear," by Miss Manington, 1864, p. 13.

2. Verzage nicht du Häuflein klein. [*In Trouble.*] Concerning the authorship of this hymn there are three main theories—i. that it is by *Gustavus Adolphus* ; ii. that the ideas are his and the diction that of his chaplain, *Dr. Jacob Fabricius* ; and iii. that it is by *Altenburg*. In tracing out the hymn we find that :—

The oldest accessible form is in two pamphlets published shortly after the death of Gustavus Adolphus, viz., the *Epicedion*, Leipzig, N.D. but probably in the end of 1632 [Royal Library, Berlin] : and Arnold Mengering's *Blutige Siegs-Crone*, Leipzig, 1633 [Town Library, Hamburg]. In the *Epicedion* the hymn is entitled, " Königlicher Schwanengesang So ihre Majest. vor dem Lützenschen Treffen inniglichen zu Gott gesungen " ; and in the *Siegs-Crone*, p. 73, "Der S. Kön. Mayt. zu Schweden Lied, welches Sie vor der Schlacht gesungen." In both cases there are 3 sts. :—

     i. Verzage nicht, du Häuflein klein.
     ii. Tröste dich dess, dass deine Sach.
     iii. So wahr Gott Gott ist, und sein Wort.

The next form is that in J. Clauder's *Psalmodiae Novae Pars Tertia*, Leipzig, 1636, No. 17, in 5 st. of 6 lines, st. i.–iii. as above, and—

     iv. Ach Gott gieb in des deine Gnad
     v. Hilff dass wir auch nach deinem Wort.

No author's name is given. In the *Bayreuth G. B.*, 1668, p. 266, st. iv., v., are marked as an addition by Dr. Samuel Zehner ; and by J. C. Olearius in his *Lieder-Schatz*, 1705, p. 141, as written in 1638 (1633 ?), when the Croats had partially burnt Schleusingen, where Zehner was then superintendent.

The third form of importance is that given in Jeremias Weber's *Leipzig G. B.*, 1638, p. 651, where it is entitled " A soul-rejoicing hymn of Consolation upon the watchword—God with us—used by the Evangelical army in the battle of Leipzig, 7th Sept., 1631, composed by M. Johann Altenburg, pastor at Gross Sömmern in Düringen," [i.e. Sömmerda in Thuringia]. It is in 5 sts., of which sts. i.–iii. are the same as the 1633, and are marked as by *Altenburg*. St. iv., v., beginning—

     iv. Drümb sey getrost du kleines Heer
     v. Amen, das hilff Herr Jesu Christ,

are marked as "Additamentum Ignoti." This is the form in C. U. as in the Berlin *G. L. S.*, ed. 1863, No. 1242.

In favour of Altenburg there is the explicit declaration of the Leipzig *G. B.*, 1638, followed by most subsequent writers. The idea that the hymn was by *Gustavus Adolphus* seems to have no other foundation than that in many of the old hymn-books it was called *Gustavus Adolphus's Battle Hymn*. The theory that the ideas were communicated by the King to his chaplain, Dr. Fabricius, after the battle of Leipzig, and by Fabricius versified, is maintained by Mohnike in his *Hymnologische Forschungen*, 1832, pt. ii. pp. 55–98, but rests on very slender evidence. In *Koch*, viii. 138–141, there is the following striking word-picture :—

If, then, we must deny to the hymn Albert Knapp's characterisation of it as "a little feather from the eagle wing of Gustavus Adolphus," so much the more its original title as his "Swan Song" remains true. It was on the morning of the 1/16 Nov., 1632, that the Catholic army under Wallenstein and the Evangelical under Gustavus Adolphus stood over against each other at Lützen ready to strike. As the morning dawned Gustavus Adolphus summoned his Court preacher Fabricius, and commanded him, as also the army chaplains of all the other regiments, to hold a service of prayer. During this service the whole host sung the pious king's battle hymn—

     " Verzage nicht, du Häuflein klein."

He himself was on his knees and prayed fervently. Meantime a thick mist had descended, which hid the fatal field so that nothing could be distinguished. When the host had now been set in battle array he gave them as watchword for the fight the saying, "God with us," mounted his horse, drew his sword, and rode along the lines of the army to encourage the soldiers for the battle. First, however, he commanded the tunes *Ein feste Burg* and *Es wollt uns Gott genädig sein* to be played by the kettledrums and trumpets, and the soldiers joined as with one voice. The mist now began to disappear, and the sun shone through. Then, after a short prayer, he cried out : "Now will we set to, please God," and immediately after, very loud, "Jesu, Jesu, Jesu, help me to-day to fight for the honour of Thy Holy Name." Then he attacked the enemy at full speed, defended only by a leathern gorget. "God is my harness," he had said to the servant who wished to put on his armour. The conflict was hot and bloody. About 11 o'clock in the forenoon the fatal bullet struck him, and he sank, dying, from his horse, with the words, "My God, my God!" Till twilight came on the fight raged, and was doubtful. But at length the Evangelical host obtained the victory, as it had prophetically sung at dawn."

This hymn has ever been a favourite in Germany, was sung in the house of P. J. Spener every Sunday afternoon, and of late years has been greatly used at meetings of the Gustavus Adolphus Union—an association for the help of Protestant Churches in Roman Catholic countries. In translations it has passed into many English and American collections.

Translations in C. U. :—

1. **Fear not, O little flock, tho foe.** A good *tr.* from the text of 1638, omitting st. iv., by Miss Winkworth, in her *Lyra Ger.*, 1855, p. 17. Included, in England in *Kennedy*, 1863, Snepp's *S. of G. and G.*, 1871, *Free Church H. Bk.*, 1882, and others; and in America in the *Sabbath H. Bk.*, 1858, Pennsylvania *Luth. Ch. Bk.*, 1868, *Hys. of the Church*, 1869, *Bapt. H. Bk.*, 1871, *H. and Songs of Praise*, 1874, and many others.

2. **Be not dismay'd, thou little flock.** A good *tr.* of st. i.–iii. of the 1638 text in Mrs. Charles's *V. of Christian Life in Song*, 1858, p. 248. She *tr.* from the Swedish, which, in the *Swenska Psalm-Boken*, Carlstadt, N.D. (1866), is given as No. 378, "Förfäras ej, du lilla hop!" and marked Gustaf II. Adolf. Her version is No. 204 in Wilson's *Service of Praise*, 1865.

3. **Thou little flock, be not afraid.** A *tr.* of st. i.–iii. from the 1638 text, by M. Loy, in the Ohio Luth. *Hymnal*, 1880, No. 197.

Other trs. are all from the text of 1638.
(1.) "Be not dishearten'd, little flock," by Dr. H. Mills, 1856, p. 121. (2.) "Despond not, little band, although," by Dr. G. Walker, 1860, p. 41. (3.) "Be not dismay'd, thou little flock, Nor," by E. Massie, 1866, p. 143. (4.) "O little flock, be not afraid," in J. D. Burns's *Memoir and Remains*, 1869. p. 226.   [J. M.]

Altus Prosator, Vetustus. *St. Columba.*
This very curious hymn was first made known to modern scholars by the late Dr. J. H. Todd, in *Fasc.* ii. p. 205 of the *Liber Hymnorum* edited by him in 1869 for the Irish Archæological and Celtic Society, where it is given with a prose translation by the editor. A rhymed version of this by Dr. W. MacIlwaine is given in his *Lyra Hibernica Sacra*, Belfast, 1878, commencing, "The Father exalted, ancient of days, unbegotten," and the Latin text is reprinted in the *Appx.* thereto. In 1882 the Marquess of Bute issued a prose

version, together with the original text and valuable notes thereon as *The Altus of S. Columba, edited with Prose Paraphrase and Notes by John, Marquess of Bute*, Edinb., Blackwood, 1882.   [W. T. B.]

Alway in the Lord rejoice. *J. S. B. Monsell.* [*Joy in the Lord.*] Written in Italy and 1st pub. in his *Spiritual Songs*, 1857 and 1875, in 8 st. of 4 l. It is based on the Epistle for the 4th S. in Advent. It has not come into C. U. in G. Brit. In the Amer. *College Hyl.*, N. Y., 1876, No. 314, st. i.–iv. and vii. are given with slight alteration.

Am Grabe stehn wir stille. *C. J. P. Spitta.* [*Burial of the Dead.*] 1st pub. in Series i. of his *Psalter und Harfe*, Leipzig, 1833, p. 140 (ed. 1838, p. 155), in 6 st. of 4 l., entitled "At the Grave." Taken by his colleague, Pastor Borchers, as the text of his oration at Spitta's funeral, Sunday, Oct. 1, 1859 (Münkel's Spitta, 1861, pp. 283–284). Included as No. 2918 in Knapp's *Ev. L. S.* ed. 1850.

Translation in C. U. :—
The precious seed of weeping. An excellent *tr.*, as No. 98, by Miss Winkworth in her *C. B. for England*, 1863. Thence, unaltered, as No. 236 in Allon's *Supp. Hymns*, 1868, as No. 554 in the Pennsylvania Luth. *Ch.Bk.*, 1868, and as No. 1010 in the American Meth. Episco. *Hymnal*, 1878.

Other trs. are :—
(1.) "Now weeping at the grave we stand," by *Miss Winkworth*, 1858, p. 118. (2.) "Beside the dark grave standing," by *R. Massie*, 1860, p. 138.   [J. M.]

Am I a soldier of the Cross ? *I. Watts.* [*Holy Fortitude.*] Appended to his *Sermons*, pub. in 1721–24, in 3 vols., vol. iii., and intended to accompany a sermon on 1 Cor. xvi. 13. It is in 6 st. of 4 l., and entitled "Holy Fortitude." In Spurgeon's *O. O. H. Bk.*, No. 671, st. v. and vi. are omitted, but the rest are unaltered. Orig. full text in all editions of Watts's *Works*. In the *New Cong.*, No. 623, it is given in an abbreviated and slightly altered form as — "*Are we the soldiers* of the Cross ?" This is also found in Snepp's *Songs of G. & G.*, 1872, and other collections. It dates as early as the *Leeds H. Bk.*, 1853. The American use of this hymn is extensive.

Am I poor, do men despise me? [*Contentment.*] An anonymous hymn from the American S. S. Union Collection, given in the Meth. *F. C. S. S. H. Bk.*, No. 268.

Amazing grace, how sweet the sound. *J. Newton.* [*Grace.*] No. 41, Bk. i. of the *Olney Hymns*, 1779, in 6 st. of 4 l., entitled "Faith's Review and Expectation," and based upon i. Chron. xviii. 16, 17. In G. Brit. it is unknown to modern collections, but in America its use is extensive. It is far from being a good example of Newton's work.

Amazing love! transcendent grace. *Joseph Irons.* [*Predestination.*] 1st pub. in his *Zion's Songs, &c.*, 3rd ed. 1825, No. 146, and thence into Snepp's *S. of G. & G.*, 1872, No. 678, unaltered.

Ambrosius (St. Ambrose), second son and third child of Ambrosius, Prefect of the Gauls, was b. at Lyons, Arles, or Treves—probably the last—in 340 A.D. On the death of his father in 353 his mother removed to Rome with her three children. Ambrose went through the usual course of education, attaining considerable proficiency in Greek; and then entered the profession which his elder brother Satyrus had chosen, that of the law. In this he so distinguished himself that, after practising in the court of Probus, the Praetorian Prefect of Italy, he was, in 374, appointed Consular of Liguria and Aemilia. This office necessitated his residence in Milan. Not many months after, Auxentius, bishop of Milan, who had joined the Arian party, died; and much was felt to depend upon the person appointed as his successor. The church in which the election was held was so filled with excited people that the Consular found it necessary to take steps for preserving the peace, and himself exhorted them to peace and order: when a voice suddenly exclaimed, "Ambrose is Bishop," and the cry was taken up on all sides. He was compelled to accept the post, though still only a catechumen; was forthwith baptized, and in a week more consecrated Bishop, Dec. 7, 374. The death of the Emperor Valentinian I., in 375, brought him into collision with Justina, Valentinian's second wife, an adherent of the Arian party: Ambrose was supported by Gratian, the elder son of Valentinian, and by Theodosius, whom Gratian in 379 associated with himself in the empire. Gratian was assassinated in 383 by a partisan of Maximus, and Ambrose was sent to treat with the usurper, a piece of diplomacy in which he was fairly successful. He found himself, however, left to carry on the contest with the Arians and the Empress almost alone. He and the faithful gallantly defended the churches which the heretics attempted to seize. Justina was foiled: and the advance of Maximus on Milan led to her flight, and eventually to her death in 388. It was in this year, or more probably the year before (387), that Ambrose received into the Church by baptism his great scholar Augustine, once a Manichaean heretic. Theodosius was now virtually head of the Roman empire, his colleague Valentinian II., Justina's son, being a youth of only 17. In the early part of 390 the news of a riot at Thessalonica, brought to him at Milan, caused him to give a hasty order for a general massacre at that city, and his command was but too faithfully obeyed. On his presenting himself a few days after at the door of the principal church in Milan, he was met by Ambrose, who refused him entrance till he should have done penance for his crime. It was not till Christmas, eight months after, that the Emperor declared his penitence, and was received into communion again by the Bishop. Valentinian was murdered by Arbogastes, a Frank general, in 392; and the murderer and his puppet emperor Eugenius were defeated by Theodosius in 394. But the fatigues of the campaign told on the Emperor, and he died the following year. Ambrose preached his funeral sermon, as he had done that of Valentinian. The loss of these two friends and supporters was a severe blow to Ambrose: two unquiet years passed, and then, worn with labours and anxieties, he himself rested from his labours on Easter Eve, 397. It was the 4th of April, and on that day the great Bishop of Milan is remembered by the Western Church, but Rome commemorates his consecration only, Dec. 7th. Great he was indeed, as a scholar, an organiser, a statesman; still greater as a theologian, the earnest and brilliant defender of the Catholic faith against the Arians of the West, just as Athanasius (whose name, one cannot but remark, is the same as his in meaning) was its champion against those of the East. We are now mainly concerned with him as musician and poet, "the father of Church song" as he is called by Grimm. He introduced from the East the practice of antiphonal chanting, and began the task, which St. Gregory completed, of systematizing the music of the Church. As a writer of sacred poetry he is remarkable for depth and severity. He does not warm with his subject, like Adam of St. Victor, or St. Bernard. "We feel," says Abp. Trench, "as though there were a certain coldness in his hymns, an *aloofness* of the author from his subject."

A large number of hymns has been attributed to his pen; *Daniel* gives no fewer than 92 called Ambrosian. Of these the great majority (including one on himself) cannot possibly be his; there is more or less doubt about the rest. The authorities on the subject are the *Benedictine ed.* of his works, the *Psalterium,* or *Hymnary,* of Cardinal Thomasius, and the *Thesaurus Hymnologicus* of Daniel. The Benedictine editors give 12 hymns as assignable to him, as follows:—

1. Aeterna Christi munera.
2. Aeterne rerum Conditor.
3. Consors Paterni luminis.
4. Deus Creator omnium.
5. Fit porta Christi pervia.
6. Illuminans Altissimus.
7. Jam surgit hora tertia.
8. O Lux Beata Trinitas.
9. Orabo mente Dominum.
10. Somno refectis artubus.
11. Splendor Paternae gloriae.
12. Veni Redemptor gentium.

Histories of these hymns, together with details of *trs.* into English, are given in this work, and may be found under their respective first lines. The Bollandists and *Daniel* are inclined to attribute to St. Ambrose a hymn, *Grates tibi Jesu novas,* on the finding of the relics of SS. Gervasius and Protasius. These, we know, were discovered by him in 386, and it is by no means unlikely that the bishop should have commemorated in verse an event which he announces by letter to his sister Marcellina with so much satisfaction, not to say exultation.

A beautiful tradition makes the *Te Deum laudamus* to have been composed under inspiration, and recited alternately, by SS. Ambrose and Augustine immediately after the baptism of the latter in 387. But the story rests upon a passage which there is every reason to consider spurious, in the *Chronicon* of Dacius, Bp. of Milan in 550. There is no hint of such an occurrence in the *Confessions* of St. Augustine, nor in Paulinus's life of St. Ambrose, nor in any authentic writing of St. Ambrose himself. The hymn is essentially a compilation, and there is much reason to believe, with Merati, that it originated in the 5th cent. in the monastery of St. Honoratus at Lerins. [Te Deum.]   [R. T.]

Amen to all that God hath said.

C. Wesley. [*Divine Holiness, and Human Depravity.*] Appeared in *Hymns and Sacred Poems*, 1742, in 36 st. of 4 l., in three parts, and entitled "Unto the Angel of the Church of the Laodiceans." In 1780, J. Wesley compiled the following centos therefrom for the *Wes. H. Bk.*:—

1. **God of unspotted purity.** Composed of st. iii., iv., v., vi., viii.-xi. of Part i.

2. **O let us our own works forsake.** Composed of st. iii., viii., ix., x., of Part ii.

3. **Saviour of all, to Thee we bow.** Composed of st. i.-vi. of Part iii.

All these centos have passed into numerous hymnals in G. Brit. and America. Orig. text in *P. Works*, 1868-72, vol. ii. p. 358.

American Hymnody.

Psalmody rather than Hymnody was the usage of America prior to 1800. The famous *Bay Psalm Book*, or *New England Version* of 1640, published at Cambridge, New England, by Stephen Day, was the first volume printed in these Colonies; and from its rarity the few extant copies of the first edition are very highly valued. Isaiah Thomas, the founder of the American Antiquarian Society, supposed that "not less than seventy editions were printed in Boston, London, and Edinburgh." The revision of that version by Thomas Prince in 1757 met with less favour (and is scarcer) than the original, which about that time began to be superseded by the *Version of Tate & Brady*. Of *Tate & Brady's Version* many editions, with *Supplement of Hymns*, mostly by Watts, were printed at Boston between 1750 and 1800. Towards the end of the century numerous editions of Watts's *Psalms and Hymns* appeared, chiefly in New England, and continued to appear after the publication of the amended versions of Watts's *Psalms*, by Joel Barlow, in 1785, and Timothy Dwight, in 1800. Hymn-compiling began after the Revolution, and its course can best be followed under the headings of the several religious bodies.

I. *Protestant Episcopal Church.* — The Episcopal Church issued, in 1789, the Version of *Tate & Brady* with twenty-seven hymns, to which thirty more were added in 1808. These were superseded by an abridged version of the Psalms, mostly from *Tate & Brady*, in 1833, and a Collection of Hymns, numbering 212, published previously in 1827. The latter, entitled *H. of the Prot. Episc. Ch. set forth in General Convention* in the years 1789, 1808, and 1826, and commonly known as the *Prayer-Book Collection*, except for its originals, hardly deserved the repute it long enjoyed. It continued to be used exclusively in the Sunday services for 35 years, and was bound up with the Prayer Book till 1871.

After 1861, in some dioceses *Hymns Ancient and Modern*, or one or two *Selections* from it or other sources, were allowed. In 1866, sixty-six *Additional Hymns* were put forth; and in 1871 the present *Hymnal*. This, although a great advance upon the *Prayer Bk. Collection* of 1826, does not compare favourably with the leading Anglican books of to-day. It was slightly revised, and not materially improved, in 1874. The voluntary system of the English Church with regard to Hymnody has unfortunately not been permitted to her American daughter, who is in consequence far behind in hymnic knowledge, activity, and taste. Of private collections which might be used at week-night services, &c., we may mention Dr. C. W. Andrews's *Church Hymns*, of 1844 and 1857, and *Hymns for Church and Home*, 1859-60. The latter did much in preparing the way for the *Hymnal* of 1871-4.

II. *Presbyterians.*—This body, in common with the Congregationalists, for a long time used Watts chiefly. Their first official *Psalms and Hymns* appeared in 1828-29, and amended editions of it in 1830-1834, and in 1843. The *Church Psalmist* of 1843, with the *Supplement* of 1847, was long the chief manual of the New School body. Among prominent extant collections, the *Presbyterian Hymnal*, of 1874, is to be distinguished from the inferior *Hymnal of the Presbyterian Church* of 1867. Of books not put forth by authority, nor strictly denominational, and which have been used by Congregationalists and others as well as by Presbyterians, Leavitt's *Christian Lyre* of 1830-1 contained originals, and is of historic importance. The same is true of Thomas Hastings's *Spiritual Songs*, 1831, 2, 3, in which the hymns of the three leading American writers—Hastings, Ray Palmer, and S. F. Smith—first appeared. Dr. C. S. Robinson's *Songs for the Sanctuary*, 1865, and his *Spiritual Songs*, 1878, aim rather at popular usefulness than literary accuracy, and have won great success. On the other hand, *The Sacrifice of Praise*, 1869, was carefully edited with notes. The late Dr. E. F. Hatfield, one of the leading hymnological scholars of America, produced in *The Church Hymn Book*, 1872, a work exceptionally trustworthy for texts, dates, and ascriptions of authorship. No less valuable in these respects is *Hymns & Songs of Praise*, published in 1874 by Drs. Hitchcock, Eddy, and Schaff; these three eminent compilers having expended on it much care, skill, and taste. These two books, though not so widely circulated as some others, are essential to every hymnic library.

III. *Congregationalists.*—The first Congregational compilation which shewed thought and research was the *Hartford Selection* of 1799—by Nathan Strong and others—a work of unusual merit for its day. It contained many originals, as did also Nettleton's *Village Hymns*, 1824, which was long and widely used, and exerted an influence of considerable importance. Its Missionary Hymns, then a new feature, were numerous, and drawn largely from *Hymns for the Monthly Concert*, Andover, 1823, an important but almost unknown tract by L. Bacon (q. v.). Worcester's *Watts's, and Select Hymns*, 1823, long held a prominent place. So did Mason and Greene's *Church Psalmody*, 1831. Bacon's *Supplement to Dwight*, 1833, kept *Dwight's Watts* in use till the Connecticut Congregational *Psalms and Hymns* appeared in 1845. Abner Jones compiled *Melodies of the Church* in 1832, and his son Darius E. Jones, *Temple Melodies*, in 1851, and *Songs of the New Life*, 1869. Mr. H. W. Beecher's *Plymouth Collection*, 1855, represented the original mind of its editor, and has many points of interest. *The Sabbath Hymn Book*, 1858, prepared by Professors Park and Phelps of Andover, though careless in authorship and texts, was the most attractive and valuable of American hymnals to its date. Elias Nason's *Congregational Hymn Book*, 1857, and sundry others of lesser note, appeared in Boston. The year 1880 marks the reaction from the excessive bulk of 1200 to 1500 hymns to about 600 in the Oberlin (Ohio) *Manual of Praise*, Mr. C. H. Richards's *Songs of Christian Praise*, and Hall and Lasar's *Evangelical Hymnal*. The last named shows a new departure no less in its large use of recent material and following of English models, than in the admirable carefulness of its editing, and in a biographical index, covering thirty-three double columns, of authors, translators, and composers. The index is based upon that compiled by Major Crawford and the Rev. J. A. Eberle for the Irish *Ch. Hymnal*, 1876.

IV. *Baptists.*—The Baptists soon abandoned the exclusive use of Psalms, and commenced the compilation of independent collections of hymns. A *Philadelphia Collection* of theirs, published in 1790, cites one of Newport, Rhode Island, still earlier. Of Joshua Smith's *Divine Hymns*, a ninth edition bears date 1799. In New York, too, John Stanford issued a collection of 200, chiefly from Rippon, in 1792, and gave authors' names. The *Boston Collection*, 1808, *Parkinson's*, 1809–17, and *Maclay's*, 1816, were of note, and Winchell's *Arrangement of Watts, with Supplement*, 1817–32, had a great sale. The *Psalmist* by Baron Stow and S. F. Smith, published in 1843, was an exemplary work, and met with general acceptance throughout the north, as did Manly's *Baptist Psalmody*, 1850, in the south. *The Baptist Harp*, 1849, and *Devotional Hymnal* of 1864, are of some importance. A great many 32mos. and 48mos. of revivalistic character—the *Virginia Selection, Dover Selection, Mercer's Chester*, &c.— have been in use. Of more sober type is Linsley and Davis's *Select Hymns*, 1836. The leading books to-day are the *Baptist Hymn Book, Praise Book*, and the *Service of Song*, all of 1871. In addition to purely Baptist collections, editions of the chief Congregational Collections for the use of Baptists have had an extensive sale. These include the *Church Psalmody* of Mason and Greene, the *Plymouth Collection* of H. W. Beecher, and *The Sabbath Hymn Book* of Park and Phelps. Collections by FREE WILL BAPTISTS appeared in 1832 and 1858, and by THE OLD SCHOOL, or PRIMITIVE BAPTISTS in 1836 and 1858. The older of the two Baptist sects calling themselves CHRIS-

TIANS, made a large beginning in 1805 with the collection of Elias Smith and Abner Jones. Of their later collections the most noteworthy is the *Christian Hymn Book*, Boston, 1863. The other body of this name has its strength in the South and West. It has used a book compiled by its founder, Alexander Campbell, and another published at Dayton, Ohio.

V. *Methodists.*—American Methodists used at first a *Pocket Hymn Book* (a reprint of that by *Spence* which was attacked by J. Wesley), the 10th ed. of which appeared in 1790, and the 27th in 1802. In 1802 it was revised by Coke and Asbury. The latter issued a *Supplement* to it in 1810. In 1836 an official book, excluding all others for Sunday services, was issued, and another in 1849. These were displaced by the *Methodist Hymnal*, 1878. The *Southern Methodist Episcopal Hymns* of 1847 took less liberties with the texts, and adhered more closely to John Wesley's great collection than its Northern successor. The METHODIST PROTESTANT body has had three hymn-books, published respectively in 1837, 1859, and 1871. The WESLEYAN METHODISTS and the AFRICAN METHODISTS also use compilations of their own. Many books, Methodist in character if not in name, and adapted to camp-meetings and the like, came out about the beginning of the century and later, containing effusions, not a few of which had certain rude and fervid elements of poetic merit. Eminent among these was a Baltimore *Collection* of about 1800, several pieces from which are still in use. This type is now represented by the numerous *Gospel Songs*, &c., of America, and *Sacred Songs and Solos* (Sankey) in England, which are indeed spiritual songs, rather than hymns; having immense temporary popularity and influence, but are rather Jonah's gourds than plants of permanent standing in the song-garden. The splendid provision, both in quantity and quality, made by Charles Wesley, seems, here as in England, to have deterred those who followed his views and methods from attempting to produce serious hymns after his pattern in any considerable measure.

VI. *Universalists.*—The Universalists have been very active, and their activity began very early. In 1792 they issued two collections, that of *Richards* (q. v.) and *Lane*, in Boston, and one in Philadelphia. In 1808 appeared 415 *Hymns composed by different authors* (Hosea Ballou, Abner Kneeland, and four others) *at the request of the General Convention of Universalists*, an inferior work, as works produced under such circumstances usually are. Among later books are those of *Ballou and Turner*, 1821; *S. and R. Streeter*, 1829 ; *Hosea Ballou*, second collection, 1837; Adams & Chapin's *Hymns for Christian Devotion*, 1846 ; *J. G. Adams*, 1861 ; and *Prayers and Hymns*, 1868. All these contain originals.

VII. *Unitarians.*—The Unitarians have been still more prolific in compiling, and in composing nearly as much so, but not in the same perfunctory way, and with far greater success. Possessing a large share of the best blood and brain in the most cultivated section of

America, they exhibit a long array of respectable hymnists whose effusions have often won the acceptance of other bodies, and must be largely represented in these pages. Special service has been done at home by Dr. A. P. Putnam, of Brooklyn, whose admirable *Singers and Songs of the Liberal Faith* (1875), though a large volume, does not exhaust the subject, but is to be supplemented by another. Amongst their most notable collections, usually from Boston, are *Belknap's*, 1795; *Sewall's* (New York), 1820; *Greenwood's*, 1830–35; that of the *Cheshire Association* (Connt.), 1844; *Dr. J. F. Clarke's*, 1844–55; *Drs. Hedge & Huntington's*, 1853; S. Longfellow and S. Johnson's *Book of Hymns*, 1846–48, and *Hymns of the Spirit*, 1864; and the *Unitarian Hymn Book*, 1869. The last is the most widely used, but is by no means the one of most marked character, careful editing, or general literary merit.

VIII. *Roman Catholic.*—The Roman Catholic Church in the United States has done nothing worthy of mention, unless the reprint, with additions, of E. Caswall's *Lyra Catholica* of 1849 be regarded as a selection for congregational purposes.

IX. *Lutherans.*—Such Lutherans as in the latter part of the 18th cent. used the English tongue were supplied by the pious efforts of Dr. Kunze, 1795, of Strebeck, 1797, and of Williston, 1806; and later by the various collections of the Tennessee, Ohio, and General Synods; by those of the New York Ministerium, 1814–34; and by the Ministerium of Pennsylvania, 1865. The latter, prepared with unusual care, was revised in 1868 as the Church Book of the General Council.

X. *Reformed Dutch.*—The Reformed Dutch, now the "Reformed" body, had their own version of the Psalms as early as 1767, and issued successive collections of Psalms and Hymns, in 1789, 1814, 1831, and 1850. These were superseded and greatly improved upon by their *Hymns of the Church*, 1869.

XI. *German Reformed.*—This body, which in common with the Reformed Dutch has of late dropped from its title all that indicated its distinctive origin, has produced or included one or two hymnists, but no collection of note.

XII. The productions of several small denominations—*Adventists, United Brethren*, &c.—offer no special claim to notice beyond the fact that the collections of the Moravians are mainly based upon those of England, and that those of Mormondom might fill a chapter as literary curiosities, but cannot be considered here.

XIII. Comparatively few American hymnists have collected their verses in book form. Thus, in many cases, the only way, and that an insecure one, of indicating the original text of any hymn is by referring to the place of first publication so far as known. The number of such authors of hymns, and it may be added of compilations, is far greater than would be supposed by those who have not carefully studied the subject, and hitherto it has been inadequately treated. C. D. Cleveland's *Lyra Sacra Americana*, 1868, by no means covers the ground. This is the more to be regretted, as that work has become the

text book for the higher American hymnody of the hymnal compilers of Great Britain. Mr. Rider's *Lyra Americana* is but a meagre and random selection. In the present work it is designed to mention, though with inevitable baldness and brevity, all writers and hymns that have made any extended and lasting mark, including some lyrics, out of a number unduly large, that unfortunately are anonymous. The books chiefly, though by no means exclusively, taken as a basis for this survey, are the following; together with the total number of hymns in each, and the number embraced in each total of hymns of a purely American origin, the percentage being about one in seven.

Hymnals.	Total Hymns.	American Hymns.
Prayer Book Coll., 1826 . . .	212	21
Episcopal Hymnal, 1871. .	520	40
Methodist Episcopal H., 1849 .	1148	50
Methodist Hymnal, 1878 . .	1117	140
Baptist Psalmist, 1843 . .	1180	175
Baptist Hymn Bk., 1871 . .	1000	162
Baptist Praise Bk., 1871. .	1311	290
Baptist Service of Song, 1871 .	1129	100
Plymouth Collection, 1855 .	1071	256
Sabbath Hymn Bk., 1853 .	1290	180
Robinson's S. for Sanctuary, 1865 .	1344	245
Hatfield's Ch. Hymn Bk., 1872 .	1464	160
Hitchcock's Collection, 1874 .	1416	190
Presbyterian Hymnal, 1871 .	972	108
Reformed Hys. of the Ch., 1869 .	1007	146
Oberlin Manual, 1880 . .	595	110
C. H. Richards's Coll., 1880 .	660	140
Evang. Hymnal, 1880 . .	613	28

XIV. The English use of American hymns has been, until recent years, very limited, and mainly confined to the older collections of the English Nonconformists, and the Unitarian Hymnals. In the two hundred and fifty hymns of the higher order of merit in American hymnody, which are now in common use in Great Britain, are found choice selections from all the leading denominations in the States, and ranging from the earliest productions of President Davies to the latest of Dr. Ray Palmer and Bishop Coxe. The marked success which has attended the few translations from the Latin and German that have been embodied in English Hymnals attests their merit, and indicates a wealth of hymnic power in our midst which should be more fully developed and utilized. In Great Britain the noblest forms of American Hymnody are known to the few; whilst the *Gospel Songs* of our revivalistic schools are the mainstay of similar efforts in the mother country. Our review is materially increased by this extensive use of the more ephemeral form of our hymnody; success compelling attention where literary merit has failed to do so.

XV. The alphabetical arrangement required by a Dictionary precludes that grouping of the American work which would best set forth its nature and extent. In this Dictionary the hymns are annotated under their respective author's names. To assist, however, in ascertaining the full extent of American Hymnody, the subjoined synopsis, arranged in Denominational and Chronological order, has been compiled :—

SYNOPSIS OF AMERICAN HYMNODY.

1. Protestant Episcopal Church.

Alexander Viets Griswold, D.D.	1766–1843
Francis Scott Key	1779–1843
John De Wolf	1786–1862
Henry Ustic Onderdonk, D.D.	1789–1858
Sarah J. Hale	1795–1879
Wm. Augustus Muhlenberg, D.D.	1796–1879
James Wallis Eastburn	1797–1819
George Washington Doane, D.D.	1799–1859
William Croswell, D.D.	1804–1851
William R. Whittingham, D.D.	1805–1879
Roswell Park, D.D.	1807–1869
George Burgess, D.D.	1809–1866
Charles William Everest, M.A.	1814–1877
Harriett E. B. Stowe	1812
Christopher Christian Cox, M.D.	1816–1882
John Williams, D.D.	1817
Arthur Cleveland Coxe, D.D.	1818
Edward A. Washburn, D.D.	1819–1881
Frederick D. Huntington, D.D.	1819
Eliza Scudder	1821

Presbyterians.

Samson Occom	1723–1792
Samuel Davies	1723–1761
Thomas Hastings, Mus. Doc.	1784–1872
Josiah Hopkins, D.D.	1786–1862
Henry Mills, D.D.	1786–1867
Nathan S. S. Beman, D.D.	1786–1871
David Nelson, M.D.	1793–1844
Jane L. Gray	1796–1871
James W. Alexander, D.D.	1804–1859
Edwin F. Hatfield, D.D.	1807–1883
Joseph A. Alexander, D.D.	1809–1860
Alfred A. Woodhull, D.D.	1810–1836
Deodatus Dutton, Jun.	cir. 1810–1832
Thomas Mackellar	1812
George Duffield, Jun., D.D.	1816
Elizabeth Lee Smith	1817
Elizabeth Prentiss	1818–1878
Robert Morris, LL.D.	1818
Philip Schaff, D.D.	1819
Anson D. F. Randolph	1820
Aaron Robarts Wolfe	1821
Charles S. Robinson, D.D.	1829
Hervey Doddridge Ganse	1822
Catherine H. Johnson.	

3. Congregationalists.

Mather Byles, D.D.	1706–1788
Nathan Strong, D.D.	1748–1816
Timothy Dwight, D.D.	1752–1817
Joel Barlow	1755–1812
Phœbe Hinsdale Brown	1783–1861
Asahel Nettleton, D.D.	1783–1843
William Allen, D.D.	1784–1868
Charles Jenkins	1786
Thomas H. Gallaudet, LL.D.	1787–1851
Emma C. Williams	1787–1870
Leonard Withington, D.D.	1789
Eleazar T. Fitch, D.D.	1791–1871
Augustus L. Hillhouse	1792–1859
William Mitchell	1793–1867
William B. Tappan	1794–1849
John G. C. Brainerd	1796–1828
Joseph Steward	cir. 1799
Abby Bradley Hyde	1729–1872
Thomas C. Upham, D.D.	1799–1872
Jared B. Waterbury, D.D.	1799–1876
William Cutter	1801–1867
Leonard Bacon, D.D.	1802–1881
Nehemiah Adams	1806
George Barrell Cheever, D.D.	1807
Ray Palmer, D.D.	1808
Daniel C. Colesworthy	1810
Russell Sturgis Cook	1811–1864
Elias Nason	1811
George N. Allen	1812–1877
Samuel Wolcott, D.D.	1813–1886
Charles Beecher	1815
Zachary Eddy, D.D.	1815
Mary Torrey	1817–1869
James Henry Bancroft	1819–1844
Leonard Swain, D.D.	1821–1869
Henry Martyn Dexter, D.D.	1821
Jeremiah E. Rankin, D.D.	1828
Horatio R. Palmer, Mus. Doc.	1834

4. Baptists.

Philip Bliss	1838–1876
Caroline L. Smith	cir. 1852
Thomas Baldwin, D.D.	1753–1825
John Leland	1754–1841
Oliver Holden	1765–1844
Robert T. Daniel	1773–1840
Adoniram Judson, D.D.	1788–1850
Lydia Sigourney	1791–1865
Benjamin Cleveland	cir. 1792–
Joseph Belcher, D.D.	1794–1859
Nathaniel Colver, D.D.	1794–1870
James Davis Knowles	1798–1838
Sarah B. Judson	1803–1845
John Newton Brown, D.D.	1803–1868
George Barton Ide, D.D.	1806–1872
Samuel F. Smith, D.D.	1808
Lydia Baxter	1809–1874
Robert Turnbull, D.D.	1819–1877
Henry S. Washburn	1813
Sewell S. Cutting, D.D.	1813–1882
Sidney Dyer	1814
Jacob R. Scott	cir. 1815–1861
Edmund Turney, D.D.	1816–1872
Sylvanus D. Phelps, D.D.	1816
James N. Winchell	cir. 1819
Maria F. Anderson	1819
Basil Manly, Jun., D.D.	cir. 1820
William McDonald	1820
Edwin T. Winkler, D.D.	1823
Robert Lowry, D.D.	1826
Enoch W. Freeman	cir. 1829
Christopher R. Blackall, M.D.	1830
W. H. Doane	1831
Joseph Henry Gilmore	1834
Stephen P. Hill	cir. 1836
Gurdon Robins	1813–1883
H. C. Ayres	cir. 1849
Will. E. Witter	1854
Mary Ann Baker.	
S. A. Collins.	

5. Methodists.

Hannah Flagg Gould	1789–1865
George Perkins Morris	1802–1864
Thomas H. Stockton, D.D.	1808–1868
Samuel Y. Harmer	1809
William Hunter, D.D.	1811–1877
David Creamer	1812
Thomas O. Summers, D.D.	1812–1882
Elvina M. Hall	1818
Fanny J. Van Alstyne	1823
Robert A. West	cir. 1849
Harriett A. Phillips	1808

6. Universalists.

James Freeman, D.D.	1759–1835
George Richards	cir. 1755–1816
Hosea Ballou	1771–1852
Abner Kneeland	1774–1844
John Greenleaf Adams	1810
Edwin Hubbell Chapin, D.D.	1814–1880
J. H. Hanaford	

7. Unitarians.

John Quincey Adams	1767–1848
James Flint, D.D.	1779–1855
John Pierpont	1785–1866
Andrews Norton, D.D.	1786–1853
Eliza Lee Follen	1787–1860
Sarah White Livermore	1789–1874
Samuel Gilman, D.D.	1791–1858
Nathaniel L. Frothingham, D.D.	1793–1870
Henry Ware, Jun., D.D.	1794–1843
Caroline Gilman	1794
William Cullen Bryant	1794–1878
William B. O. Peabody, D.D.	1799–1847
William H. Furness, D.D.	1802
Ralph Waldo Emerson	1803–1882
Thomas Gray, Jun., M.D.	1803–1849
William P. Lunt, D.D.	cir. 1805–1857
Frederick H. Hedge, D.D.	1805
Henry W. Longfellow	1807–1883
Sarah E. Miles	1807
Stephen G. Bulfinch, D.D.	1809–1870
Oliver W. Holmes, M.D.	1809
Edmund H. Sears, D.D.	1810–1876
Sarah M. Marchesa Ossoli	1810–1850
Theodore Parker	1810–1860
Chandler Robbins, D.D.	1810–1882
James F. Clarke, D.D.	1810
Abiel Abbot Livermore	1811

Robert Cassie Waterston	.	1812
William H. Burl igh	. .	1812–1871
Jones Very	. .	1813–1880
Charles Timothy Brooks	.	1813
Lucy E. Akerman.	. .	1816–1874
Samuel Longfellow	. .	1819
James Russell Lowell	. .	1819
Samuel Johnson	. .	1822–1882
Octavius B. Frothingham	.	1822
Edward Everett Hale	.	1822
Thomas W. Higginson	.	1823
William H. Hulbert	. .	1827
William J. Loring.		
Joseph P. Bartrum.		

8. Reformed Dutch.

George W. Bethune, D.D.	.	1805–1862
Sarah E. York	. .	1819–1851
Alexander R. Thompson, D.D.		1822

9. German Reformed.

Edwin H. Nevin, D.D.	. .	1814
Henry Harbaugh, D.D.	.	1817–1867

10. Various.

Henry Alline	. .	1748–1784
Samuel J. Smith	. .	1771–1835
Lucius M. Sargent	. .	1786–1867
William Russell	. .	1798–1873
James Gilborne Lyons, LL.D.	c.	1800–1868
Erastus C. Benedict, LL.D.	.	1800–1880
Charles Dexter Cleveland, LL.D.	.	1802–1869
John Greenleaf Whittier	.	1807
Martha Cooke	. .	1807–1874
William G. Clark	.	1810–1841
Mary S. B. Shindler (Dana)	.	1810
Alice Cary	. .	1820–1871
Anna Warner	.	c. 1822
Phœbe Cary	. .	1824–1871
Robinson Porter Dunn, D.D.	.	1825–1867
Lucy Larcom	. .	1826
Grace Webster Hinsdale	.	1832
Emily Miller	. .	1833
Annie Hawks	. .	1835
Caroline W. Sewall [or Seward]	c. 1836
Margaret Elizabeth Winslow	.	1836
Isaac Beverley Woodbury	.	1819–1858
Emma Campbell	.	c. 1863
Frances Mace	.	1852
Harriet McEwan Kimball	.	c. 1866
Ellen E. Gates.		

To any one desirous of grasping the whole subject of American Hymnody, the foregoing synopsis will be of value. By reading the various articles in the chronological order given, the rise and growth of the hymnological literature of the various denominations may be determined, and the relative importance of each writer can be ascertained.

XVI. In conclusion I would add that nothing like an adequate survey of the field of American Hymnody has been attempted, within my knowledge, until now. I have aimed to mention every hymn of native origin which has come into at all extended use, and to give some account of the writer of each. The material has been gathered from all quarters, and, of course, under difficulties. I cannot hope to have attained absolute accuracy or completeness, though the effort in their direction has been strenuous. The limits assigned to the American portion of this Dictionary necessitated severe compression, and gave room for little beyond the dryest facts, names, dates, titles, and first lines. But these annotations when taken together can hardly have failed to notice any author or hymn whose merit has been generally or widely recognized; and they will make it apparent that the subject is larger than would be suspected by those by whom it has not been studied.

Acknowledgments are due to Dr. Ray Palmer, Bishop Coxe, and several more of the authors here mentioned, and to the representatives of some now deceased; to Dr. R. D. Hitchcock, President of the Union Theological Seminary, New York; to the late Dr. E. F. Hatfield, of New York; to Mr. Hubert P. Main, of the firm of Biglow and Main; to David Creamer, Esq., of Baltimore, the pioneer of hymnology in America; and to others, for help kindly given in the preparation of these Notes, and the Annotations on American hymns and hymn-writers throughout this Dictionary.

[F. M. B.]

Amidst the cheerful bloom of youth. [*Youth for God.*] An anonymous hymn in the American Presb. *Ps. & Hys.*, 1843, and the American Presb. *Ps. & Hys. for the Worship of God*, Richmond, 1867, in 5 st. of 4 l.

Amidst the mighty, where is he. *John Morison.* [*Cross and Consolation.*] 1st appeared as No. 29 in the Draft Scottish *Translations and Paraphrases*, 1781, as a version of Lam. iii. 37–40, in 4 st. of 4 lines. The only variation in the public worship edition issued in that year by the Ch. of Scotland and still in use is from *pine* to *clothes* in st. ii., l. 2. In the markings by the eldest daughter of *W. Cameron* (q.v.) ascribed to Morison. From the 1781 it has passed into a few modern hymnals, and is included as No. 286 in *Kennedy*, 1863, slightly altered. [J. M.]

Amidst Thy wrath, remember love. *I. Watts.* [*Ps. xxxviii.*] 1st pub. in his *Psalms of David*, 1719, in 10 st. of 4 l., with the title "Guilt of Conscience and Relief; or Repentance and Prayer for Pardon and Health." Various arrangements of stanzas are given in modern hymnals, no collection repeating it in its full form. In America it is generally known as "*Amid* Thy wrath," &c.

Amidst us our Beloved stands. *C. H. Spurgeon.* [*Holy Communion.*] Written for and 1st pub. in his *O. O. H. Bk.* 1866. It is in one or two American collections.

Ämilie Juliane. [Emilie Juliane.]

Among the deepest shades of night. *Ann Gilbert, née Taylor.* [*A Child's Hymn.*] Appeared in *Hymns for Infant Minds*, by J. and A. Taylor, 1810, in 5 st. of 4 l., and entitled "Thou God seest me." It is found in various collections for children. Orig. text in Stevenson's *H. for Ch. and Home*, with "*to* hell" for "*in* hell," st. iv., l. 1. It is sometimes given as "*Amongst* the deepest shades."

Amplest grace with Thee I find. *A. M. Toplady.* [*Christmas.*] 1st pub. in his *Poems on Sacred Subjects*, Dublin, 1759, pp. 73–4, in 8 st. of 4 l., and headed "On the Birth of Christ." Although not in C. U. in G. Britain, it has passed into a few American collections, and usually in an abbreviated form. Orig. text in Sedgwick's reprint of Toplady's *P. Works*, Lond., 1860.

[W. T. B.]

'Αναστάσεως ἡμέρα. This is the first of eight Odes which form the great hymn commonly known as "The Golden Canon, or The Queen of Canons," of *St. John of Damascus*. The Odes alternate with those of St. Cosmas in the Greek Office for Easter Day in the *Pentecostarion*, and each is sung in order in the service as appointed therein. The date of its composition was probably the middle of the eighth century, St. John having died about A.D. 780. The design of the series of Odes which constitute the Canon is to set forth the fact of the Resurrection, its fulfilment of ancient types and figures and prophecies, and the benefits which it has brought to mankind; out of which arises the call for praise and thanksgiving. This is accomplished in the following manner:—

Ode i. The fact of the Resurrection; a new Passover; therefore rejoice. iii. This is the New River from the Rock: and the New Light. iv. This is the Salvation seen by Habakkuk, the male that opens the womb, the yearling Lamb, the Antitype of the ark; therefore, rejoice. v. He is Risen, bring praises, not ointments; haste to meet the Bridegroom. vi. He has broken from Hades, and with it has brought freedom to man. vii. He came from the fiery furnace like the Holy Three, the Holy Women found Him, therefore keep the Festival. viii. Yea, on this morn of praise, taste the vine's new fruit, and keep the Festival. ix. Arise, shine ! praise Him, thou New Jerusalem, He is ours to the end; we therefore praise Thee, "O Christ, our Pascha."

Although a complete Greek Canon consists of *nine* Odes, only eight are given in this Canon for Easter, and in other Canons of the great Festivals. By a rigid rule the Odes must follow the order and keynote of nine Scripture Canticles, one, for example, being the *Benedicite*, and another Jonah's prayer. No. ii. Canticle is of a severe and threatening character, and is therefore omitted from Festival Canons. Hence the omission of an Ode based thereupon in this Canon for Easter; and why (as in the Canon for Christmas Day) Ode ii. is also missing. (See Greek Hymnody, § xvi. 11, and Χριστὸς γεννᾶται for the series of Canticles.)

The complete *Office*, as sung in the Greek Church every Easter Day, was included by Dr. Littledale in his *Offices from the Service Books of the Holy Eastern Church*, 1863, pp. 86–97, together with a literal *tr.*, pp. 209–224. The Canon is also found in the Abbé Migne's *Patrologia*, tom. xciv. p. 839. Dr. Neale introduces his *tr.* in his *Hys. of the Eastern Church* with the quotation of a most striking and eloquent description of an Easter morning in Athens, when, with great rejoicing, this Canon is sung:—

"As midnight approached, the Archbishop, with his priests, accompanied by the King and Queen, left the church, and stationed themselves on the platform, which was raised considerably from the ground, so that they were distinctly seen by the people. Everyone now remained in breathless expectation, holding their unlighted tapers in readiness when the glad moment should arrive, while the priests still continued murmuring their melancholy chant in a low half-whisper. Suddenly a single report of a cannon announced that twelve o'clock had struck, and that Easter day had begun; then the old Archbishop, elevating the cross, exclaimed in a loud exulting tone, 'Christos anesti, Christ is risen!' and instantly every single individual of all that host took up the cry, and the vast multitude broke through and dispelled for ever the intense and mournful silence which they had maintained so long, with one spontaneous shout of indescribable joy and triumph, 'Christ

is risen! Christ is risen!' At the same moment, the oppressive darkness was succeeded by a blaze of light from thousands of tapers, which, communicating one from another, seemed to send streams of fire in all directions, rendering the minutest objects distinctly visible, and casting the most vivid glow on the expressive faces, full of exultation, of the rejoicing crowd; bands of music struck up their gayest strains ; the roll of the drum through the town, and further on the pealing of the cannon announced far and near these 'glad tidings of great joy'; while from hill and plain, from the seashore and the far olive grove, rocket after rocket ascending to the clear sky, answered back with their mute eloquence, that Christ is risen indeed, and told of other tongues that were repeating those blessed words, and other hearts that leapt for joy ; everywhere men clasped each other's hands, and congratulated one another, and embraced with countenances beaming with delight, as though to each one separately some wonderful happiness had been proclaimed ;—and so in truth it was;—and all the while, rising above the mingling of many sounds, each one of which was a sound of gladness, the aged priests were distinctly heard chanting forth a glorious old hymn of victory in tones so loud and clear, that they seemed to have regained their youth and strength to tell the world how 'Christ is risen from the dead, having trampled death beneath His feet, and henceforth the entomb'd have everlasting life.'"

Mr. Hatherley, in his annotated and musical edition of the *Hys. of the Eastern Church*, 1882, has pointed out that this writer was wrong in regarding this Canon as the "glorious old hymn of victory." The glorious old hymn in one stanza is : Χριστὸς ἀνέστη ἐκ νεκρῶν (*Littledale*, p. 87), which Dr. Littledale has rendered :—

> "Christ has risen from the dead,
> Death by death down doth He tread,
> And on those within the tombs
> He bestoweth life." (p. 210.)

It is after this has been repeated several times, and certain ceremonies are performed, that the great Canon of St. John of Damascus is sung.

The eight Odes of this Canon, the first of which has taken a permanent position in the hymnals of most English-speaking countries, are :—

Ode i. 'Αναστάσεως ἡμέρα. **'Tis the day of Resurrection.** By *J. M. Neale* in *Hys. of the E. Church*, 1862, p. 42, in 3 st. of 8 l. (3rd ed. p. 38). It was first pub. as a hymn for congregational use in the *Parish Hymn Book*, 1863, No. 52, beginning, "The Day of Resurrection." From that date it grew in general esteem and has been extensively adopted, sometimes with the opening line as above, and again as by Dr. Neale. Orig. *tr.* in *H. E. Church*, p. 42. Blank verse *tr.* in Dr. Littledale's *Offices, &c.*, p. 211. The break in the refrain, st. iii., is copied from the original.

Ode iii. Δεῦτε πόμα πίωμεν. **Come and let us drink of that New River.** By J. M. Neale, from his *Hys. of the E. Ch.*, p. 44 ; also blank verse *tr.* in Dr. Littledale's *Offices, &c.*, of the *H. E. Ch.*, p. 212.

Ode iv. 'Επὶ τῆς θείας φυλακῆς. **Stand on thy watch-tower, Habakkuk the Seer.** By J. M. Neale, *Hys. of the E. Ch.*, p. 45 ; also blank verse *tr.* in Littledale's *Offices, &c.*, p. 213.

Ode v. 'Ορθρίσωμεν ὄρθρου βαθέος. **Let us rise in early morning.** By J. M. Neale, from *Hys. of the E. Ch.*, p. 46 ; also blank verse *tr.* in Littledale's *Offices*, p. 214. Of Dr. Neale's *tr.*, st. i.–iii. are given as No. 266 in Willing's *Bk. of Common Praise*, 1872.

Ode vi. Κατῆλθες ἐν τοῖς κατωτάτοις. **Into the dim earth's lowest parts descending.** By J.

M. Neale, *Hys. of the E. Ch.*, p. 47; also blank verse *tr.* in Littledale's *Offices, &c.*, p. 215.

Ode vii. Ὁ παῖδας ἐκ καμίνου. **Who from the fiery furnace saved the Three.** By J. M. Neale, in *Hys. of the E. C.*, p. 48; also in blank verse in Littledale's *Offices. &c.*, p. 217.

Ode viii. Αὕτη ἡ κλητή καὶ ἀγία ἡμέρα. **Thou hallowed chosen day! that first [morn of praise].** By J. M. Neale, in *Hys. of the E. Ch.*, p. 50. In 1867 it was given in the *People's H.*, and, in 1871, st. ii.-iv., beginning, "Come let us taste the wine's new fruit," as No. 28 in the Irvingite *H. for the Use of the Churches.* Dr. Littledale has also a *tr.* in blank verse in his *Offices, &c.*, p. 218.

Ode ix. Φωτίζου, φωτίζου, ἡ νέα Ἱεροουυαλήμ. **Thou new Jerusalem, arise and shine.** By J. M. Neale, in *Hys. of the E. Ch.*, p. 52, and also in blank verse in Dr. Littledale's *Offices, &c.*, p. 219.

We would add that Dr. Neale's translations have not the exultant freedom of the original; and that greater use of this Canon can be made than has been done hitherto. Dr. Littledale's fine blank verse translations might be turned into some of the more popular measures of modern hymnody with advantage and success. Mr. Chatterton Dix has supplied some good examples in *Lyra Messianica*, 1864. (See 4th ed. of *Hys. of the E. Ch.*, Lon., Hayes, 1882, for readings in former editions and literal translations of and music to each Ode.)   [J. J.]

Anatolius, one of the Greek hymn-writers. No details are known of him. From the fact that he celebrates martyrs who died in the 6th and early part of the 7th cent., it is certain that he is not to be identified (as by Neale) with the patriarch who succeeded Flavian in 449, and afterwards procured the enactment of the famous canon of the Council of Chalcedon, which raised Constantinople to the second place among the patriarchal sees (*Dict. of Ch. Biog.*, i. p. 110). A letter is said to exist showing that he was a pupil of Theodore of the Studium (759-826). More than a hundred hymns, all of them short ones, are found in the *Menæa* and *Octoechus.* Sometimes they are called ἀνατολικὰ στιχηρά. From this account, derived from *Anth. Graec. Curm. Christ.*, p. xli., it will be seen that his poems cannot be considered "the *spring*-promise" of the age of the Canons (*Neale*). A few of his hymns have been translated by Dr. Neale in his *Hys. of the E. Ch.*, and Dr. Littledale, in the *Offices of the H. E. Ch.*: see ζοφερᾶς τρικυμίας ("Fierce was the wild billow") and Τὴν ἡμέραν διελθών ("The day is past and over").   [H. L. B.]

Ancient of ages! humbly bent before Thee. *Sir J. Bowring. [Missions.]* A short hymn on behalf of missions, of more than usual merit. It appeared in his *Hymns*, 1825, in 2 st. of 7 l. In Miss Courtauld's Unitarian *Ps., Hys. and Anthems*, Lond., 1860, it is given as No. 16.

And am I born to die? *C. Wesley. [Death and Eternity.]* 1st pub. in his *Hymns for Children*, 1763, No. 59, in 6 st. of 8 l. J. Wesley included it in the 1780 ed. of the *Wes. H. Bk.* and it is retained in the revised ed. of

1875. From the *Wes. H. Bk.* it has passed into numerous hymnals both in G. Britain and America, and sometimes in an abbreviated form. Orig. text, *P. Works*, 1868-72, vol. vi. p. 426.

And am I only born to die? [*C. Wesley. [Death and Eternity.]* This hymn, similar in character to the above, appeared in the same work—*Hymns for Children*, 1763, in 6 st. of 6 l. In 1780 it was included in the *Wes. H. Bk.* and from thence it has passed into all the collections of the Methodist bodies, and several others, in G. Britain and America. Stevenson gives some interesting details of circumstances attending the singing of this hymn, in his *Meth. H. Bk. Notes*, 1860, p. 51. Orig. text in *P. Works of J. & C. Wesley*, 1868-72, vol. vi. p. 432.

And are our joys so quickly fled? *C. Wesley. [Christ walking on the sea.]* A long hymn of 14 st. of 6 l., on St. Matt. xiv. 23-33. (Christ and Peter.) 1st pub. in *Hymns and Sacred Poems*, 1749, under the heading "The Tempest." In its full form it is unknown to the collections; but a cento, "Oft when the waves of passion rise," was given in the *Leeds H. Bk.*, 1853, No. 291, and repeated in various hymnals, including Bapt. *Ps. & Hys.*, 1858; Sir J. Mason's Orphanage *H. Bk.*, and others. It is composed of st. iv., v., vii., viii., xiv., slightly altered. Orig. text in *P. Works*, 1868-72, vol. iv. p. 454.

And are we now brought near to God. *P. Doddridge. [Nearness to God.]* In the "D. MSS." this hymn is undated, and the text differs from that pub. by J. Orton in Doddridge's, *Hymns*, 1755, but whether the alterations were by Doddridge or Orton cannot be determined. The hymn is in 5 st. of 4 l., and entitled, "Nearness to God thro' Christ." In 1839, it was republished by J. Doddridge Humphreys, in *Scripture Hymns, by the Rev. Philip Doddridge, D.D., new and corrected ed.* The hymn in full is not in C. U.; but a cento, composed of st. i., ii. of the 1755 text, and two additional stanzas, based upon Doddridge's hymn, "High let us swell our tuneful notes" (q. v.), is in somewhat extensive use in America. It appeared in the *Amer. Prayer Bk. Coll.*, 1826, No. 95, and from thence passed into later hymnals, including the *Hymnal of the Prot. Episco. Church*, 1871.

And are we wretches yet alive? *I. Watts. [Lent.]* This somewhat uncommon and strongly worded hymn has passed out of use in G. Britain, but is still found in several modern American hymn-books of importance. It appeared in Watts's *Hys. and S. Songs*, 1707, Bk. ii., No. 105, in 5 st. of 4 l., and entitled, "Repentance flowing from the patience of God."

And are we yet alive? *C. Wesley. [Meeting of Friends.]* From his *Hymns and Sacred Poems*, 1749, vol. ii., No. 236, in 4 st. of 8 l., and entitled, "At Meeting of Friends." The 3rd st. is usually omitted, as in the 1780 ed. of the *Wes. H. Bk.*, and the revised ed., 1875. It is commonly used as the opening hymn of the Wesleyan Conference. In all English-speaking countries it is a favourite hymn with the Methodist bodies, and in America especially it is included in the collections of various denominations. Orig. text, *P. Works*, 1868–72, vol. v. p 466.

And art Thou, gracious Master, gone? *T. Kelly.* [*Reproach of the Cross.*] 1st pub. in the 1st ed. of his *Hymns, &c.*, 1804, p. 26, in 5 st. of 6 l., as the first of a series of hymns on the "Reproach of the Cross." It is also found in all subsequent eds. of the same work. In 1812, Dr. Collyer gave it in his *Sel.*; it was repeated by Montgomery in his *Christ. Psalmist*, 1825; and by Bickersteth in the *Christ. Psalmody*, 1833, thus coming into C. U. The hymn, "Shall I to gain the world's applause," is a cento therefrom, composed of ll. 1–4 of st. ii., iv. and iii., in the order named and slightly altered. This cento in L. M. appeared in Nettleton's (Amer.) *Village Hymns*, 1824, No. 411, and from thence has passed into a few American collections.

And art thou with us, gracious Lord? *P. Doddridge.* [*In trouble.*] Not in the "D. MSS." and 1st pub. in J. Orton's ed. of his *Hymns, &c.*, 1755, No. 98, in 5 st. of 4 l., with the heading, "The timorous Saint encouraged by the Assurance of the Divine Presence and Help. Is. xli. 10." The same text was repeated in J. D. Humphreys's ed. of Doddridge's *Hymns*, 1839. Its use is limited, and in Spurgeon's *O. O. H. Bk.*, st. ii. is omitted. In a few collections, including Lant Carpenter's Unitarian *H. Bk.*, Bristol, 1831, and others, a cento is given as, "Art thou still with us, gracious Lord?" It is composed of st. i., ii., and iv., slightly altered.

And can it be that I should gain. *C. Wesley.* [*Thanksgiving for Salvation.*] Written at Little Britain, in May, 1738, together with the hymn, "Where shall my wondering soul begin?" on the occasion of the great spiritual change which C. Wesley at that time underwent. His diary of that date gives minute details of the mental and spiritual struggles through which he passed, evidences of which, and the ultimate triumph, are clearly traceable in both hymns. It was 1st pub. in J. Wesley's *Ps. and Hymns*, 1738, and again in *Hymns and Sacred Poems*, 1739, p. 117, in 6 st. of 6 l. When included in the *Wes. H. Bk.*, 1780, st. v. was omitted, the same arrangement being retained in the revised ed. 1875, No. 201. It has passed from that hymnal into numerous collections in G. Britain and most English-speaking countries. Stevenson's note on this hymn, dealing with the spiritual benefits it has conferred on many, is full and interesting (*Meth. H. Bk. Notes*, p. 155). Orig. text in *P. Works*, 1868–72, vol. i. p. 105.

And can my heart aspire so high. *Anne Steele.* [*Submission.*] 1st pub. in her *Poems, &c.*, new ed., 1780, vol. iii. p. 132, in 4 st. of 4 l., headed, "Filial Submission," and based on Heb. xii. 7. It was included in Sedgwick's reprint of her *Hymns*, 1863, p. 147. Its use is mainly confined to American collections of various denominations.

And did the Holy and the Just. *Anne Steele.* [*Redemption.*] A more than usually successful hymn by this writer. It appeared in her *Poems, &c.*, 1760 and 1780, vol. i. p. 175, in 6 st. of 4 l., entitled, "The wonders of Redemption." It is based on 1 Pet. iii. 18. It was also included in Sedgwick's reprint of her *Hymns*, 1863, p. 108. It was first brought into C. U. by Ash and Evans in their Bapt. Bristol *Coll.*, 1769. Its use in G. Britain is limited, but in America it is found in many collections.

And did the Son of God appear. *J. Montgomery.* [*Christ our Pattern.*] This hymn was written for J. H. Gurney's *Coll. of Hys.*, Lutterworth, 1838, No. 7. Respecting it Gurney says in the Preface, "One hymn, No. 7, in this collection, written upon a subject suggested to him [Montgomery] by the Editor, has never before been published." This hymn was repeated in the Mary-le-bone *Ps. & Hys.*, 1851, and in Montgomery's *Original Hys.*, 1853, No. 126, in 6 st. of 4 l. The title is "Christ Jesus our Pattern in doing and suffering."

And dost Thou fast, and may I feast? *J. S. B. Monsell.* [*Holy Communion—Lent.*] 1st pub. in his *Hymns of Love and Praise*, 1863, in 9 st. of 4 l. It is appointed for the 1st Sun. in Lent, and based on the words, "Can God furnish a table in the wilderness?" Ps. lxxviii. 19. In Allon's *Supp. H.*, 1868 and 1875, st. i.–iv. and vii. are given as No. 158.

And have I, Christ, no love for Thee. *S. Stennett.* [*Holy Anxiety.*] Contributed to Rippon's Bapt. *Sel.*, 1787, No. 252, in 5 st. of 4 l. It has passed into several hymn-books. It is also found in his *Memoir* by W. Jones, 1824. Orig. text, Spurgeon's *O. O. H. Bk.*, 1866, No. 640.

And have I measured half my days? *C. Wesley.* [*Pleading for Pardon.*] Appeared in *Hymns & Sacred Poems*, 1749, vol. i., in 16 st. of 4 l., and again in the *P. Works*, 1868–72, vol. iv. p. 322. In 1780, J. Wesley included st. x.–xiii. and xvi. in the *Wes. H. Bk.* as :—" God is in this and every place." The same is retained in all subsequent editions of that work, and has passed into general use amongst the Methodist bodies, and also in a few American collections of other denominations.

And is it so? A little while. [*Death and Eternity.*] An anonymous hymn in the American Tract Soc. *Songs of Zion*, 1864, the Presb. *Ps. & Hys.*, Richmond, 1867, and others.

And is it true, as I am told? *Amelia M. Hull.* [*Child's Hymn.*] Contributed to Miss H. W. Soltau's *Pleasant Hymns for Boys and Girls*, N.D., but pub. in 1862. It consists of 6 st. of 6 l. It is usually found in an abbreviated form, and sometimes with alterations. The hymnals which number it amongst their contents include the *Hy. Comp.*, No. 421; Snepp's *Songs of G. & G.*, No. 923; Major's *Bk. of Praise*, &c.   [W. T. B.]

And is my soul with Jesus one?
Joseph Irons. [*Union with Christ.*] From his
Zion's Songs, &c., 3rd ed., 1825, No. 191, into
Snepp's *Songs of G. & G.*, 1872, unaltered
except in first line, which reads in the ori-
ginal, "And is my soul *and* Jesus one?"

And is salvation brought so near?
P. Doddridge. [*Salvation.*] Not found in
the "D. MSS." and 1st pub. by J. Orton in his
ed. of Doddridge's *Hymns*, &c., 1755, No. 262,
in 4 st. of 4 l. on Rom. x. 6-10, and repeated
in J. D. Humphreys's ed. of the same, 1839.

And is the gospel peace and love?
Anne Steele. [*Example of Christ.*] 1st pub.
in her *Poems on Subjects chiefly Devotional*,
1760-80, vol. i. pp. 122-123 : and repeated in
Sedgwick's reprint of her *Hymns*, &c., 1863,
pp. 75-76. It is in 7 st. of 4 l., and entitled,
"The Example of Christ." In 1787 it was
introduced into congregational use by Dr.
Rippon, in his *Bapt. Sel. of Hys*., No. 166.
This was followed by the *Bapt. New Sel.*,
1828, No. 121, and others to modern collections In Snepp's *Songs of G. & G.*, 1872,
No. 555, st. i., ii., iii., and vi. are given unaltered. It is also in American use.

And is the time approaching? *Jane
Borthwick.* [*Anticipation of Heaven.*] Appeared in her *Thoughtful Hours*, 1859, in 8 st.
of 4 l., and entitled "Anticipations." It is
not in C. U. in G. Britain, but is found in
several American hymnals.

**And is there in God's world so drear
a place?** *John Keble.* [*Repentance.*] 1st
pub. in his *Christian Year*, 1827, in 14 st. of
8 l. and appointed for the 2nd Sun. in Lent.
The heading is :—

"And when Esau heard the words of his father, he
cried with a great and exceeding bitter cry, and said
unto his father, Bless me, even me, O my father.
Genesis xxvii. 34. (Compare Hebrews xii. 17. 'He
found no place of repentance, though he sought it carefully with tears.') "

The poem is based upon these quotations
and is accompanied by the following note :—

"The author earnestly hopes, that nothing in these
stanzas will be understood to express any opinion as to
the general efficacy of what is called 'a death-bed repentance.' Such questions are best left in the merciful
obscurity with which Scripture has enveloped them.
Esau's probation, as far as his birthright was concerned,
was quite over when he uttered the cry in the text.
His despondency, therefore, is not parallel to anything
on this side of the grave."

This poem as a whole is not in C. U. A
cento therefrom composed of st. i., iii.-viii.,
was given in the Gainsburgh *Hys. for the
Christian Seasons* (1st ed., 1854), No. 116.

And is there, Lord, a cross for me?
H. Addiscott. [*Submission.*] 1st pub. in *The
New Cong. H. Bk.*, 1859, No. 650, and entitled
"Take up the Cross." It is appropriated
to the "Trials of the Christian Life."

And is this life prolonged to me?
I. Watts. [*Decision for Christ.*] Appended
to his *Sermons*, 1721-24, vol. iii., and later
eds., vol. ii., No. 39, in 6 st. of 4 l. It is based
on his Sermon 39 on 1 Cor. iii. 22, "Whether
Life or Death,—All are yours," to which he

gave the title, "The Right Improvement of
Life." The hymn is not in extensive use.
It is sometimes abbreviated. The text in the
New Cong. No. 488, is slightly altered.

And let our bodies part. *C. Wesley.*
[*Parting.*] From *Hymns & Sacred Poems*,
1749, vol. ii., No. 233, of 10 st. in two parts.
The first part, in 6 st., was included in the
Wes. H. Bk., 1780, and is retained in the
revised edition, 1875, No. 535. In some
collections a shorter version compiled from
this is given. Orig. text, *P. Works*, 1868-72,
vol. v. p. 462. From this hymn, and another,
a cento has been formed, " O let our heart and
mind," thus, st, i.,-iv., st. ii., iii. of the above,
st. v., vi., from st. viii. and v. of "Saviour of
sinful men " (q. v.) This is found in Bapt. *Ps.
& Hymns*, 1858 and 1880. The original hymn
is also found in a few American collections.
A second cento from this hymn alone was
given in Martineau's *Hymns*, &c., 1840, and
again in his *Hys. of Praise & Prayer*, 1873,
No. 694. It begins, "And what though now
we part," and is composed of st. i., l. 1-4, iii.,
iv., l. 4-8, and vi., l. 1-4, as in the *Wes. H. Bk.*
but somewhat altered.

And let this feeble body fail.
C. Wesley. [*Burial.*] From his *Funeral
Hymns*, 1759 (2nd Series), No. iii., in 9 st. of 8 l.
In 1830, 7 sts. were included in the *Supp. to
the Wes. H. Bk.* as hymn 734, and as hymn
948 are retained in the revised ed., 1875.
Orig. text, *P. Works*, 1868-72, vol. vi. p. 218.
In America it is used somewhat extensively,
and by various denominations.

And live I yet by power divine?
C. Wesley. [*Recovery from Sickness.*] This
hymn, in 17 st., on 2 Kings xx. 1-11, was
written in 1738 by C. Wesley during his
residence at Oxford, and as a thanksgiving
after a dangerous sickness. It was pub. in
Hymns and Sacred Poems, 1739. In 1780, the
hymn " God of my life, what just return " was
compiled therefrom, and included in the *Wes.
H. Bk.* as No. 149. It is also found in many
other collections, being held by the Methodist
bodies in much esteem. Orig. text in *P. Works*,
1868-72, vol. i. p. 74.

And may I hope that when no more.
Joseph Swain. [*Trust in God.*] Printed in
his *Walworth Hymns*, 1792, in 10 st. of 4 l.
In its full form it is not in C. U., but selec-
tions appear in Denham's *Saints' Melody*,
1837, &c., and also in the Amer. *Bapt. Praise
Book*. Orig. text in the 1869 reprint of
Swain's *Hymns*.   [W. T. B.]

And must I be to judgment brought?
C. Wesley. [*The Judgment.*] 1st pub. in his
Hymns for Children, 1763, No. 33, in 8 st. of
4 l., and headed " A thought on Judgment."
It is not in C. U. in G. Britain, but in
America st. i.-v. are given in the Amer. *Meth.
Episcop. Coll.*, 1849; the *H. Bk. of the Evan-
gelical Association*, Cleveland, Ohio, 1882, No.
839, and others. Full text in *P. Works*,
1868-72, vol. vi. p. 401.

And must I part with all I have?
B. Beddome. [*Self Denial.*] Given in Rip-

pon's *Sel.*, 1787, No. 281, in 4 st. of 4 l. It is almost unknown to modern collections in G. Brit., but in America it is found in several hymnals, including the *Bap. Hy. & Tune Bk.*, 1871; *Songs for the Sanctuary*, 1865; the Dutch Reformed *Hys. for the Church*, 1869; Hatfield's *Ch. H. Bk.*, 1872; and others. In all of these, the arrangement of the stanzas and the text varies, both from each other, and from the original. Orig. text in modern ed. of *Rippon*, and in R. Hall's ed. of Beddome's *Hymns*, 1817, No. 225, in 4 st. of 4 l.

And must this body die? *I. Watts.* [*Triumph over Death.*] 1st pub. in his *Hymns*, &c., 1707, in 6 st. of 4 l. and entitled "Triumph over Death in hope of the Resurrection" (Bk. ii, No. cx.). In an altered form it was given by J. Wesley in his *Ps. and Hys.* pub. at Charlestown, South Carolina, in 1736-7. It was not included in the *Wes. H. Bk.* in 1780, but added in the *Suppl.* of 1830; Wesley's text of 1736-7 being retained, with st. iii., l. 1, "And *ever*" for "And *often*" (the original reading of Watts) being omitted. In the revised ed. of 1875, this has again been abridged by the omission of the last stanza. The text of the *Wes. H. Bk.* is thus by Watts and J. Wesley. In other collections it is usually Watts unaltered. Its use in America is very extensive.

And now another day is gone, I'll sing, &c. *I. Watts.* [*Evening.*] "An Evening Song," in 4 st. of 4 l., from his *Divine Songs*, &c., 1715, into a few modern collections for children, including Major's *Bk. of Praise for Children*, No. 288, and others.

And now, 'mid myriad worlds enthroned. *Godfrey Thring.* [*Saturday.*] Written in 1868, and 1st pub. in his *Hymns & Sacred Lyrics*, 1874, pp. 19-20, and subsequently in various hymnals. Authorized text, Thring's *Coll.*, 1882, No. 79.

And now, my soul, another year. *S. Browne.* [*New Year.*] In his *Hymns & Spiritual Songs*, &c., 1720, Bk. i., pp. 44-5, in 8 st. of 4 l., and entitled "New Year's Day." Its use is very limited in G. Britain, but somewhat extensive in America. As given in modern hymn-books it is generally in an abbreviated form, as in Major's *Bk. of Praise*, No. 293, Snepp's *Songs of G. & G.*, No. 915.

And now the wants are told that brought. *W. Bright.* [*Close of Service.*] Written in 1865, and 1st pub. in his *Hymns and other Poems*, 1866, entitled "Hymn for the close of a Service," p. 36. In 1868 it was republished in the *Appendix* to *H. A. & M.*, with the addition of a doxology.

And will the Eternal King. *P. Doddridge.* [*Personal Dedication.*] Written according to the "D. MSS.," Jan. 3, 1736, and 1st pub. by J. Orton in his ed. of Doddridge's *Hymns*, 1755, in 3 st. of 4 l., and again in J. D. Humphreys's ed. of the same, 1839. Found in various collections. Orig. text in Bapt. *Ps. & Hys.*, 1858, No. 396,

And will the great Eternal God? *P. Doddridge.* [*Opening of a Place of Worship.*] Written for the opening of a new place of worship at Oakham. In the "D. MSS." it is undated. In 1755 it was included by J. Orton in his ed. of Doddridge's *Hymns*, &c., No. 49, in 6 st. of 4 l., and repeated in J. D. Humphreys's ed. of the same, 1839. In 1826 it was embodied in an altered form in the Amer. *Prayer Bk. Coll.* as, "And *wilt Thou, O Eternal God.*" This arrangement, in common with the original, is in extensive use in America. A cento from the original is also given in the *Wes. H. Bk.*, 1875, No. 994, as, "Great God, Thy watchful care we bless." It is composed of st. iii., iv., and vi., slightly altered.

And will the Judge descend? *P. Doddridge.* [*Judgment.*] This hymn is not in the "D. MSS" and was 1st pub. by J. Orton in Doddridge's *Hymns*, &c., 1755, No. 189, in 7 st. of 4 l. It is based upon St. Matt. xxv. 41, and headed "The final Sentence, and Misery of the Wicked." In its full form it is not usually given in the collections. The most popular arrangement is st. i., iv., v., vi. This is found in various collections in G. Britain. Its greatest use is in America, where it ranks in popularity with the best of Doddridge's hymns.

And will the Lord thus condescend? *Anne Steele.* [*The Love of Christ.*] 1st pub. in her *Poems*, 1760, vol. i. p. 67, in 6 st. of 4 l., based on Rev. iii. 20, and entitled "The Heavenly Guest." In 1769 it was included in the Bristol Bapt. *Coll.* of Ash and Evans, and came thus into C. U. It was also repeated in a new ed. of the *Poems*, 1780, and in Sedgwick's reprint of her *Hymns*, 1863, p. 42. At the present time its use is mainly confined to America.

And will the majesty of heaven? *P. Doddridge.* [*Condescension.*] This hymn on Ezek. xxxiv. 31, is in the "D. MSS." but undated. It was pub. by J. Orton in his ed. of Doddridge's *Hymns*, &c., 1755, No. 144, in 5 st. of 4 l., with slight differences from the MS. and with the MS. title of "God, the Shepherd of Men," expanded to "God's Condescension in becoming the Shepherd of Men." It was also republished in J. D. Humphreys's ed. of *Doddridge*, 1839.

And will ye go away? *S. Deacon.* [*Falling away from Christ.*] This is No. 273 of his *Barton Hymns*, 1797, in 6 st. of 4 l., and is headed "A Serious Question." It was probably in the 1st ed. of those hymns, 1785, but this we have not been able to ascertain. In 1804 it was repeated, without alteration, in John Deacon's *New and Large Coll. of Ps. and Hys.* No. 461. As known in a few modern collections, specially amongst the Baptists, it is rewritten and enlarged to 9 st. This form was given to it in Rippon's *Sel.*, 27th ed., 1827, No. 439, pt. ii., and retains only a few lines of S. Deacon's text. Its signature is "*Anon., Rippon's Sel., 27th ed. 1827, based on S. Deacon, 1797.*"

And wilt Thou now forsake me, Lord? [*Confidence.*] An anonymous hymn which appeared in vol. ii. (called Pts. iii. & iv.) of a *Sel.* by the Countess of Northesk, entitled *The Sheltering Vine*, 3rd thousand, 1853. A slightly different version is in the American *Sabbath H. Bk.*, N.Y., 1858, No. 761, and other American collections.

And wilt Thou yet be found? *C. Wesley.* [*Resignation.*] 1st pub. in *Hymns and Sacred Poems*, 1740, in 22 st. of 4 l., and entitled "Resignation." It was repeated in subsequent editions of the same, and in the *P. Works*, 1868–72, vol. i. p. 266. In its full form it is unknown to the collections, but a portion therefrom, consisting of st. ix.–xx., and beginning "When shall Thy love constrain," was given in the *Wes. H. Bk.* 1780, No. 133, and continued in all later editions. It has also passed from thence into other collections, and specially in those in use amongst the Methodist bodies. Another cento, beginning with st. x., "Ah! what avails my strife," is also in limited use; whilst a third, "And can I yet delay," opening with st. xv., is given in a large number of American hymnals.

Anderson, John, s. of Andrew Anderson, a miner, was b. near Yoker, Renfrewshire, in 1804, and educated at the University of Glasgow, and at the Divinity Hall of the Associate Burghers, at Perth. In 1827 he became the first minister of the Associate Burgher Church, at Helensburgh, Dumbartonshire. The congregation which he succeeded in gathering together passed with him into the communion of the Established Church of Scotland in 1839. In 1843, both minister and people made a second change, in joining the Free Church movement of that year. d. at Helensburgh, Jan. 10, 1867. In the ecclesiastical controversies of his day he took a prominent part, specially in the Voluntary controversy, the Free Church movement, and the Revival of 1858. His prose works were somewhat numerous, and included a *Life of Christ*, 1861. He also wrote some poetical pieces, and translations. He is known to hymnology as the first to publish a complete *tr.* of Luther's hymns as *Hymns from the German of Dr. Martin Luther*, 1846. In 1867, a short memoir, by John Oatt, together with extracts from his prose and poetical writings, appeared at Glasgow (T. Murray & Son) as *Notes of an Invalid*. [J. J.]

Anderson, John, b. in 1820 at Dumbarnie, Perthshire, of which parish his father, Dr. John Anderson, was some time minister, and educated at the University of St. Andrew's. In 1844 he was licensed as a Probationer in the Scotch Church, and subsequently was appointed to St. John's parish, Dundee; the East Church, Perth, 1845; and Kinnoul, 1853. He has pub. *The Pleasures of Home; The Legend of Glencoe; and Bible Incidents and their Lessons*, 1861.

Anderson, Maria Frances, b. in Paris, France, Jan. 30, 1819, and married to G. W. Anderson, Professor in the University of Lewisburg, Pennsylvania. Two of her hymns are given in the *Baptist Harp*, 1849. Of these.— "Our country's voice is pleading," has come into C. U. [F. M. B.]

Andreä, Johann Valentin, son of Johannes Andreä, afterwards Prelate of Königsbronn, b. Aug. 17, 1586, at Herrenberg in Württemberg. After completing his University studies, and acting for some time as a travelling tutor, he was, in 1614, appointed diaconus at Vaihingen, in 1620 Decan at Calw, in 1639 Court-preacher at Stuttgart, in 1650 Prelate of Bebenhausen, and in March, 1654, Prelate of Adelberg with his residence in Stuttgart : d. at Stuttgart, June 27, 1654. Distinguished as a man of high and deep piety, as a church reformer, as a philanthropist, and as a theological writer, poetry was not one of the serious employments of his life, though he was admitted in 1646 a member of the Fruit-bearing Society (*Koch*, iii. 151–167; *Allg. Deutsche Biog.*, i. 441–447). He wrote few hymns, and hardly any of these have kept a place in the German Hymn-Books. The only one translated into English is :—

Edele Lieb, wo bist so gar bei uns verstecket. [*Love forgotten*] First pub. in his *Geistliche Kurtzweil*, Strassburg, 1619, p. 133, in 10 st. of 6 l.—a poem rather than a hymn. *Tr.* as "Generous Love! why art thou hidden so on earth?" by Miss Winkworth, 1869, p. 235. [J. M.]

Andrew, St., of Jerusalem, *Abp. of Crete* (660–732). b. at Damascus; he embraced the monastic life at Jerusalem, whence his name, as above. He was deputed by Theodore, Patriarch of Jerusalem, to attend the 6th General Council at Constantinople (680). He was there ordained deacon, and became Warden of the Orphanage. "During the reign of Philippus Bardesanes (711–714) he was raised by that usurper to the Archiepiscopate of Crete; and shortly afterwards was one of the Pseudo-Synod of Constantinople, held under that Emperor's auspices in 712, which condemned the Sixth Œcumenical Council and restored the Monothelite heresy. At a later period, however, he returned to the faith of the Church and refuted the error into which he had fallen." (*Neale*). He died in the island of Hierissus, near Mitylene, about 732. Seventeen of his homilies are extant, the best, not unnaturally, being on Titus the bishop of Crete. He is the author of several *Canons, Triodia*, and *Idiomela;* the most celebrated being The Great Canon. [Greek Hymnody, § xvii. 1.] Whether he was the earliest composer of Canons is doubtful, but no earlier ones than his are extant. Those ascribed to him are :—1. On the Conception of St. Anne; 2. On the Nativity of the Mother of God; 3. The Great Penitential Canon. 4. On the Raising of Lazarus. 5, 6, 7, 8. On the First Days of Holy Week. 9. On the 25th Feast-day between Easter and Pentecost. Fuller biographical details in *Dict. Christ. Biog.*, vol. i. pp. 111–12. [H. L. B.]

Andrews, Lancelot. [Usher, James.]

Ἀνέστης τριήμερος. *St. Joseph the Hymnographer.* [*Ascension.*] This Canon for

Ascension Day is found in the *Pentecostarion*, and was written about the middle of the ninth century. It is commonly regarded as St. Joseph's greatest production, and places him high amongst the Greek sacred poets. Dr. Neale remarks that "This is the crowning glory of the poet Joseph; he has here with a happy boldness entered into the lists with St. John of Damascus, to whom, on this one occasion, he must be pronounced superior." (*H. of the E. C.*, 1st ed., p. 141.) The finest points of this Canon, such as the lower angels shouting to the higher as the Lord ascends (Ode iii.); the wonder at the Human Body of the Lord (Ode iv.); and the rejoicing of angels and of nature, have their origin in the earlier Canons; but their dramatic treatment by Joseph is of greater majesty. In common with all the festival Canons it consists of eight Odes only. [Greek **Hymnody**, § xvi. 10, and xviii. 3.] These Odes are as follows:—

Ode i. 'Ανέστης τριήμερος·
"After three days Thou didst rise."

Ode iii. 'Επάρατε πύλας·
"Exalt, exalt, the heavenly gates."

Ode iv. 'Ιησοῦς ὁ ζωοδότης·
"Jesus, Lord of·Life Eternal."

Ode v. Νεκρώσας τὸν θάνατον·
"Now that death by death hath found."

Ode vi. 'Ρανάτωσαν ἡμῖν ἄνωθεν·
"Rain down, ye heav'ns, eternal bliss."

Ode vii. Φωτεινή σε, φως·
"Wafting Him up on high."

Ode viii. Τὸν ἐν δυσί ταῖς οὐσίαις·
"Of twofold natures, Christ, the Giver."

Ode ix. ᾿Ω τῶν δωρεῶν.
"Holy gift, surpassing comprehension !"

The only *tr.* of this Canon into English is the above by Dr. Neale, which appeared in his *Hymns of the Eastern Church*, 1862. The acrostical arrangement of the original, derived probably from the alphabetical Psalms, and adopted to assist the memory, is reproduced by the translator. Odes v.–ix. have not come into C. U. Of the rest, i. and iii. are given in *Lyra Messianica*, 1864; iii. in Schaff's *Christ in Song*, 1870; iv. in the *People's*, 1867; and other collections. In the *Hymnary*, Ode iv. has an additional stanza by the Editors.

In Dr. Neale's *tr.* the Theotokion (address to the B. V. M.) is omitted. Mr. Hatherley, in the 4th ed. of the *Hymns of the Eastern Church*, 1882, gives the various readings of the several editions of the work, together with music for each Ode. He also draws attention to the fact that Ode viii. is not by St. Joseph, but by *John the Monk* [St. John of Damascus], whose Canon for the Ascension is also in the Office, and is sung together with that of St. Joseph.   [J. J.]

Angel of God, whate'er betide. *C. Wesley.* [*Personal Consecration.*] Pub. in *Hymns and Sacred Poems*, 1740, in 5 st. of 4 l., and entitled "At setting out to preach the Gospel." It is not given in the *Wes. H. Bk.*, but st. i., iv., ii. in the order named are in C. U. in America to a very limited extent, including

the *Hys. of the Spirit*, Boston, 1864, No. 418. Orig. text in *P. Works*, 1868–72, vol. i. p. 294.

Angel voices ever singing. *F. Pott.* [*Choir Festival.*] Appeared in his *Hymns fitted to the Order of Common Prayer*, 2nd ed., 1866, in 5 st. of 7 l., and from thence has passed into *Harland, Snepp, Thring, Church Hymns*, and others. It is one of the author's most successful and popular efforts. Its original title is "For the Dedication of an Organ, or for a Meeting of Choirs." Its use has extended to America, and other English-speaking countries.

Angel voices sweetly singing. *H. Bonar.* [*Heaven.*] 1st pub. in the 2nd Series of his *Hymns of F. and Hope*, 1861, in 12 st. of 4 l. As given in Snepp's *S. of G. and G.*, 1872, st. ii. and vii. are omitted. Otherwise it is unaltered.

Angelice Patrone, Beate Spiritus. [*Guardian Angels.*] This hymn, of unknown authorship and date, is in the *Corolla Hymnorum*, Cologne, 1806, p. 67. *Daniel* gives it without note or comment in ii. p. 376. It is also found in *Simrock*, p. 338; *Bässler*, No. 137, and others.   [W. A. S.]

Translation in C. U. :—

Sweet Angel of mercy. By E. Caswall. It appeared in his *Masque of Mary and Other Poems*, 1858, in 8 st. of 8 l., and in'his *H. and Poems*, 1873, p. 180. It is given in a few Rom. Catholic collections for Schools and Missions.

Angels, assist to sing. [*Ps. cxlviii.*] This version of Ps. 148 appeared in the *Christian Guardian*, 1808, with the signature "*Theophilus.*" From thence it passed into a few collections, including the *Leeds H. Bk.*, 1853, in 4 st.; Hatfield's *Amer. Church H. Bk.*, 1872, in 2 st. (i., ii.) and others; but its use is limited.   [W. T. B.]

Angels from the realms of glory. *J. Montgomery.* [*Christmas.*] This hymn, which ranks as one of the most popular of the author's compositions, first appeared in his *Iris* newspaper [Sheffield], Dec. 24, 1816, in 5 st. of 6 l., and entitled "Nativity." In the 8th ed. of Cotterill's *Sel.*, 1819, it was repeated without alteration, and again in the 9th ed., 1820. On its republication by Montgomery in his *Christian Psalmist*, 1825, No. 487, the title was, "Good tidings of great joy to all people," and the following changes were introduced :—

st. ii. l. 2, "flock" to "*flocks*."
st. iv. l. 2, "Waiting" to "*Watching*."
st. v. l. 3, "repeals" to "*revokes*."

These changes (together with the new title) were retained in his *Original Hymns*, 1853, No. 239; and must be regarded as the authorised text. By many compilers the closing stanza :—

"Sinners, wrung with true repentance,
Doom'd for guilt to endless pains," &c.

has been, in some instances, omitted, and in others a doxology has been substituted. That given in *A Hymn Book for the Services of the*

Church, &c., by the Rev. Isaac Gregory Smith, 1855, reads :—

> "Lord of heaven, we adore Thee,
> God the Father, God the Son,
> God the Spirit, One in glory,
> On the same eternal throne.
> Hallelujah!
> Lord of heaven, Three in One."

Another found in the *Salisbury Hymn Book*, 1857, and others, including the S. P. C. K. *Church Hymns* and Thring's *Coll.*, is :—

> "Saints and angels join in praising
> Thee; the Father, Spirit, Son!
> Evermore their voices raising
> To the eternal Three in One.
> Come ye, worship;
> Worship Christ, the new-born King."

Of the first four stanzas a rendering into Latin :—" Angeli, sancta regione lucis," by the Rev. R. Bingham, appeared in his *Hymno. Christ. Lat.*, 1871, pp. 79–81.

The use of this hymn in various forms in English-speaking countries is extensive, abbreviations being the rule. Amongst American Hymnals, the *Hymns of the Church*, 1869, and the *Bapt. Praise Bk.*, 1871, give the full revised and authorised text of 1825 and 1853. [J. J.]

Angels from your blissful stations.
W. H. Bathurst. [*The Second Advent.*] Printed in 1849 in his *Metrical Musings*, entitled "The Second Advent," pp. 34–35. It is in 5 st. of 6 l., and was included unaltered in Snepp's *S. of G. & G.*, 1872, where it is dated 1831 in error. [W. T. B.]

Angels roll the rock away. *T. Scott.*
[*Resurrection and Ascension.*] Contributed to Ash & Evans's Bristol Baptist *Col.*, 1769, as No. 106, where it is headed "The Resurrection and Ascension." It is in 6 st. of 4 l., each st. being followed by "Hallelujah," and is signed "G.," the signature of *Thomas Gibbons*; in the 2nd ed. it was signed "U." i.e. "unknown," but in later editions, the 3rd, 1778, the signature was *Dr. S.*, and the 5th 1786, *Dr. Sc—tt.* In this form it passed through Rippon's Bapt. *Sel.*, 1787, into C. U. both in G. Britain and America, and these sts., more or less altered, are still in extensive use. In 1773, T. Scott republished the hymn in his *Lyric Poems*, &c., as No. 14, with a new first verse,

> "Trembling earth gave awful sign,"

and the "Hallelujah" following each line of the 1st st., and with several alterations. *Hatfield* (Amer.) follows this 1773 text.

In 1775, Dr. Thomas Gibbons sent an altered version of the hymn to the *Gospel Mag.*, where it appeared in the Sept. number in 9 st. of 4 l. This with further alterations was included in 1784 in his *Hymns adapted to Divine Worship*, as No. 60, where he notes it as—" Altered and enlarged from an H. in Messrs. Ash & Evans's Col., p. 109." The confusion which has arisen respecting the authorship of this hymn is thus accounted for. Its use in one or another of its various forms is very extensive, and especially in America. An altered form of st. i., iv., and v. has been rendered into Latin — "Angeli,

rupem removete; magnam," by the Rev. R. Bingham, and pub. in his *Hymnol. Christ. Lat.*, 1871, p. 109. As Scott's original text is most difficult to acquire, we reprint it from the 1769 ed. of *Ash & Evans :*—

> "HYMN CVI. *Peculiar Measure.*"
> "*The Resurrection and Ascension.*"
> "Angels, roll the Rock away,
> Death, yield up thy mighty Prey.
> See! He rises from the Tomb,
> Glowing with immortal Bloom.
> "Hallelujah.
>
> "'Tis the Saviour. Angels, raise
> Fame's eternal Trump of Praise;
> Let the Earth's remotest Bound
> Hear the Joy-inspiring Sound.
> "Hallelujah.
>
> "Now ye Saints, lift up your Eyes
> Now to Glory see Him rise,
> In long Triumph up the Sky,
> Up to waiting worlds on high.
> "Hallelujah.
>
> "Heaven displays her Portals wide,
> Glorious Hero, through them ride;
> King of Glory, mount Thy Throne,
> Thy great Father's and Thy Own.
> "Hallelujah.
>
> "Praise Him all ye heavenly Choirs,
> Praise, and sweep your golden Lyres;
> Shout, O Earth, in rapturous Song,
> Let the Strains be sweet and strong.
> "Hallelujah.
>
> "Every Note with Wonder swell,
> Sin o'erthrown, and captiv'd Hell;
> Where is Hell's once dreaded King?
> Where, O Death, thy mortal Sting?
> "Hallelujah."

[W. T. B.]

Angels round the throne are praising.
Elizabeth Parson. [*Praise.*] A beautiful hymn of praise for children. It is No. xvii. of her *Willing-Class Hymns*, written in 1840–44, and afterwards printed for private circulation.

Angels that high in glory dwell.
I. Watts. [*Against Swearing, &c.*] 1st pub. in his *Divine Songs for Children*, 1715, in 6 st. of 4 l., and entitled "Against swearing and cursing, and taking God's name in vain." Its modern use is limited, and in the *Meth. F. C. S. S. H. Bk.*, No. 228, it is slightly altered.

Angels where'er we go attend.
C. Wesley. [*Ministry of Angels.*] Two centos beginning with this stanza are in C. U. as follows: (1) *Mercer, Ox. ed. App.* 1873, No. 532. This is compiled from the hymn "Which of the petty Kings of earth," by C. Wesley, which was included from his MSS. in Dr. Leifchild's *Orig. Hymns*, 1842, in 12 st. of 4 l., and again in the *P. Works of J. & C. Wesley*, 1868–72, vol. xiii. pp. 118–119, in 6 st. of 8 l., and based on Heb. i. 14. The arrangement in *Mercer* is—st. i. is Wesley iii., l. 1–4; ii. is Wesley i., l. 5–8; iii. and iv. are Wesley v.; and v. and vi. are Wesley vi. (2) The second cento is in the American Dutch Reformed *Hys. of the Church, N. Y.* 1869, thus: st. i. and ii., as in *Mercer*, slightly altered; iii. is Wesley i., l. 1–4; and iv. is lines 5–8 of st. vi. of Wesley's hymn, "Ye simple souls that stray." (q. v.) 1747.

Angelus Silesius. [Scheffler, Johann.]

Anima Christi sanctifica me. [*Holy Communion.*]

The author of this hymn is unknown, and the earliest date to which it has been assigned is the 14th cent. It is found in the very rare *Heures a Lusage de Lengres. Imprimé a Troyes chez Jean le Coq*, without year or pagination. It is also in the *Hortulus Animae*, Lyons, 1516; and 1519; *Rambach*, i. p. 360, and *Daniel*, i., No. 498.

In the last it is included among the hymns written by unknown authors, before the 16th cent., and not inserted by authority in the Offices of any Breviary or Missal. *Daniel* also gives an additional intercession from the *Lengres Hours*, which has been ascribed to Ignatius de Loyola. As he was born in 1491, and did not embrace a religious life until 1521, this ascription is certainly an error.

Translations in C. U. :—

1. Prose *trs.* of both forms as in *Daniel* are given in many Roman and Anglican books of devotion. Of the first form there is :—" Soul of Christ, sanctify me," in the *Treasury of Devotion*, 1869, p. 6; and of the second, with the same first line, in Shipley's *Divine Liturgy*, 4th ed., 1876, p. 1.

2. **Soul of Jesus, make me holy.** This is a metrical paraphrase and expansion of the original in 60 lines. It appeared anonymously in the *Old Porch*, April, 1855, and passed through the *Lyra Eucharistica*, 1863, p. 106, into a few Roman Catholic Collections for Schools and Missions, but usually in an abbreviated form. Given in the Irvingite *Hys. for the Use of the Churches*, 2nd ed., 1871, No. 301, as " Heart of Jesus, make me holy," and is there attributed to " J. W. Chadwick." Chadwick's, however, is the shorter form noted below. Another arrangement of this *tr.* is, " Blood of Jesus; stream of life." No. 85 of *Hys.* for use at St. Ethelburga's, Bishopsgate, London, 1875.

3. **Soul of Jesus, once for me.** By M. Bridges. This is also a paraphrase of the original. It was pub. in his *Hymns of the Heart*, 1849, in 8 st. of 6 l. It was included in Shipley's *Divine Liturgy*, 1862; *Lyra Eucharistica*, 1863, p. 171; and, reduced to 4 st., in the *People's H.*, 1867.

4. **Soul of Jesus, make me pure.** By J. W. Chadwick, pub. in the *People's H.*, 1867, No. 558, in 2 st. of 6 l.

5. **Soul of Christ, my soul make pure.** By E. A. Dayman, made for and 1st pub. in the *Hymnary*, 1872, No. 443, in 2 st. of 8 l. It is translated somewhat freely from the original.

6. **Soul of Christ, be my satisfaction.** Anon. in Card. Newman's *Hys. for the Use of the Birmingham Oratory*, 1875.

7. **Soul of my Saviour, sanctify my breast,** is in the *St. George's H. Bk.*, for use in St. George's Roman Catholic Cathedral, Southwark, 1882, No. 33, ed. by the Rev. Joseph Reeks.

8. **Sanctify me wholly, Soul of Christ adored.** By T. I. Ball. An imitation of the Latin, given in the 6th ed. of the *Appendix* to the *Hymnal N.*, 1877, No. 358, in 3 st. of 4 l. [V.]

This hymn has also been rendered into German, and thence again into English :—

Die Seele Christi heil'ge mich. A free *tr.*, in 5 st. of 4 l., by Johann Scheffler. No 53, in Bk. ii., 1657, of his *Heilige Seelenlust*, p. 169 (*Werke*, 1862, i. p. 106). Included as No. 80 in *Freylinghausen's G. B.*, 1704, and recently as No. 222 in the Berlin *G. L. S.*, ed. 1863. The only *tr.* in C. U. is, ."Thy Soul, O Jesus! hallow me," good and full, by M. Loy, as No. 231 in the Ohio Luth. *Hymnal*, 1880.

The other *trs.* have much in common. (1) "Thy Soul, my Jesu! hallow mine," in the *Supp.* to *German Psalmody*, ed. 1765, p. 25, and *Select H. from German Psalmody*, Tranquebar, 1754, p. 34. (2) "Jesu, Thy soul renew my own," in the Wesley *Ps. and Hys.*, 1741 (*P. W.* 1868-72, vol. ii. p. 15). (3) "The Soul of Christ me sanctify," as No. 136 in the *Moravian H. Bk.*, 1742. In 1789 altered to "Lord Jesus, sanctify Thou me," and repeated thus in later eds. [J. M.]

Anna Sophia,

dau. of the Landgrave Georg II. of Hesse-Darmstadt, was b. at Marburg, Dec. 17, 1638. Carefully educated, especially in Holy Scripture and the Christian Fathers, she was in 1657 elected Pröbstin of the Lutheran Fürsten-Töchter-Stift at Quedlinburg, where she became Abbess 1680, and died Dec. 13, 1683 (*Koch*, iii. 549-554; Stromberger's preface, &c.).

Her hymns, contemplations on the union of the soul with Christ, in the spirit of the Canticles, mostly appeared in her devotional work :—

Der Treue Seelen-Freund Christus Jesus mit nach denklichen Sinn-Gemählden, anmuthigen Lehr-Gedichten und neuen geistreichen Gesängen, abgedruckt und vorgestellet, Jena, 1658. The only one *tr.* into English is *Wohl dem der Jesum liebet* [Holy Scripture], her best hymn, 1658, *Appx.* p. 26. The *trs.* are: (1) "How happy they, who know and love," by Dr. G. Walker, 1860, p. 82. (2) "What joy to love the Saviour," in the *British Herald*, Nov. 1866, p. 363, repeated as No. 433 in Reid's *Praise Bk.*, 1872. [J. M.]

Anni peractis mensibus. [*Whitsuntide.*]

In the *Latin Hys. of the Anglo-Saxon Ch.* (Surtees Society), 1851, p. 95, it is quoted from the Durham MS. of the 11th cent. as a hymn for Pentecost, at Matins, in 5 st. of 4 l. It is also in an 11th cent. MS. in the *Brit. Mus.* (Vesp. D. xii. f. 81). *Tr.* by J. D. Chambers, in his *Lauda Syon*, 1857, in 5 st. of 4 l, as "A year's swift months have passed away." It was repeated in Skinner's *Daily Service Hymnal*, 1864, No. 146.

Annue Christe saeculorum Domine.

[*Common of Apostles.*] This hymn is of unknown authorship. Its full form consists of four general stanzas, and nine stanzas proper of saints.

It is found in three MSS. of the 11th cent. in the *British Museum* (Harl. 2961, f. 245, ff.; Jul. A. vi. 60, b, ff.; Vesp. D. xii. 98, b). In the Durham MS. of the 11th cent. (printed as *Latin Hys. of the Anglo-Saxon Church*, 1851, p. 124), the four general stanzas are added to "Jam bone pastor Petre " (pt. of " Aurea luce," q.v.). The full form is in *Mone*, No. 666, from a 15th cent. MS. beginning with the stanza to St. Andrew, "Andreas pie," followed by 8 sts. proper of the festivals of SS. James; James and John; Philip; Bartholomew; Thomas; Matthew; Simon and Thaddeus; and Matthias; and con cluding with 4 general stanzas. In the *York Brev.* the 4 general stanzas ("Annue Christe") are given as the hymn at Vespers at the Festival of an Apostle or Apostles, except in Eastertide. Also at Vespers and Matins occasionally, in the *Sarum Brev.* with the same exception. *Daniel*, i., No. 294, gives only four lines. The *Sarum Brev.* text is also in Card. Newman's *Hymni Ecclesiae*, 1838. [J. M.]

Translations in C. U. :—

1. O Christ, Thou Lord of worlds, Thine ear. By J. M. Neale. Pub. in the enlarged ed. of the *Hymnal N.*, 1854, No. 75, in 4 st. of 8 l., from whence it has passed into a few collections. In the *St. Raphael's Coll.*, 1860, special stanzas were introduced after the *Sarum* manner (these added stanzas are all original) for SS. Andrew, Thomas, John and James, Matthias, Peter, Bartholomew, Matthew, and Simon and Jude, and some of these were repeated in Skinner's *Daily Service Hymnal*, 1864, with additional verses for St. Barnabas and for SS. Philip and James, the latter altered from Bp. Wordsworth's hymn on that festival in his *Holy Year*, " Dlest be, O Lord, the grace of Love." It is altered in the *Hymnary*, 1872, to " O Christ, Thou Lord of *all*."

2. Ruler of the ages, Christ, we now implore Thee. By R. F. Littledale, made for and 1st pub. in the *People's H.*, 1867, No. 196, in 4 st. of 4 l., and signed " F. R."

3. Ruler of ages, Christ, vouchsafe to bow Thine ear. From the *Antiphoner and Grail*, 1880, and repeated in the *Hymner*, 1882. In the same books the varying verses of *Sarum* use are also translated.

Translations not in C. U. :—
1. Vouchsafe, O Christ, High Lord, &c. *Blew*, 1852.
2. O Christ, Thou Lord of worlds, Bestow, &c. *J. D. Chambers*, 1857.   **[V.]**

Ἄνωθεν, παρθένοι, βοῆς ἐγερσί-νεκρος ἦχος. *St. Methodius.* This hymn is found in *The Banquet of the Ten Virgins*, and is reprinted in the *Anth. Gr. Car. Christ.*, 1871. From the latter work it was translated by A. W. Chatfield, for his *Songs and Hymns*, &c., 1876, pp. 141–153, where it is given as " The Virgins' Song." No portion of this fine rendering has come into common use. A cento or two might be compiled therefrom with ease. Its structure, character, &c., are fully described in **Greek Hymnody**, § x. 2, q.v. The opening line of Mr. Chatfield's *tr.* is, " The Bridegroom cometh, overhead."

Another called, another brought, &c. *Frances R. Havergal.* [*Praise.*] " Written at Leamington, June 30, 1872. This hymn literally expresses F. R. H.'s thrill of praise, when her own prayers and conversations resulted in her friend (A. B.) enrolling ' on our Captain's side.' ' Another life to live for Thee, another witness won!'" (" HAV. MSS.") It was first printed in *The Christian*, July 11, 1872, and then pub. in her *Under the Surface*, 1874, and *Life Mosaic*, 1879, in 11 st. of 4 l.

Another day begun! *J. Ellerton.* [*Tuesday.*] Written Feb. 13, 1871. Appeared in the *Parish Magazine* for May, 1871, as one of three " Week Day Hymns," in 5 st. of 4 l., and appointed for Tuesday. During the same year it was included in *Church Hymns*, No. 56, with st. ii., l. 3, "sinful soil" changed to " guilty soil," and st. v. altered from the original, which read :—

" Another day of grace!
  To *bring* us on our way,
One step towards *our* resting-place,
  The *endless* Sabbath-day."

In 1882 the revised text was repeated in

Thring's *Coll.*, with st. ii. l. 3 re-written " And let not sin our conscience soil," by the editor. Authorised text in *Church Hymns*.

Another day has past along. *J. Edmeston.* [*Sunday Evening.*] In his *Cottage Minstrel*, 1821, a hymn of 4 st. appeared with the above first line, as No. 2, and headed " Lord, teach us to pray," while, as No. 10, " The Cottager's Reflections upon the Sabbath Evening," another hymn of 5 st., " Sweet is the light of Sabbath eve," was given. In Hatfield's *Amer. Church H. Bk.*, 1872, a cento from these was given as No. 48, consisting of st. i. of the first-named hymn, and st. i., ii., iii. and v. of the latter, with slight alterations.
                          [W. T. B.]

Another portion of the span. *Charlotte Elliott.* [*Saturday Eve.*] From her *Hymns for a Week*, 1839, in 9 st. of 6 l., into Snepp's *Songs of G. and G.*, 1872, No. 905.

Another six days' work is done. *J. Stennett.* [*Sunday.*] This poem " On the Sabbath " appeared as one of his " Miscellany Poems," in his *Works*, 1732, vol. iv. pp. 231–234, in 14 st, of 4 l. In its full form it is unknown to any hymnal : but centos therefrom are in modern collections, nearly all beginning with the first stanza as above :—

1. A cento in 6 st, in the Bristol Baptist *Coll.* of Ash and Evans, 1769, from whence it has passed through a series of Baptist Hymnals to the Bapt. *Ps. and Hymns*, 1858, No. 819, and other modern collections. It is composed of st. i., x., xi., xii., and xiii., with a stanza introduced as the second, " Come, bless the Lord, whose love assigns," &c., the authorship of which has not been traced. The cento, " Come, bless the Lord," &c., in Stowell's *Sel.*, 1831–77, is compiled from the Bapt. *Ps. & Hys.* text.
2. Another cento which was given in Williams and Boden's *Coll.*, 1801, No. 451, and thence through various collections to the *Leeds H. Bk.*, 1853, the *New Cong.*, No. 753, and others. It is the above cento with the omission of the original st. xii., " With joy," &c.
3. A third cento in Bickersteth's *Christian Psalmody*, 1833, No. 280, in 4 st., being i., x., and xiii. of the original, and the added stanza, " Come, bless the Lord," &c., as in No. i., is sometimes repeated in modern collections.
4. A fourth is given in Harland's *Ch. Psalter*, No. 22, Windle's *Metrical Psalter*, &c., No. 19, and others. It is composed of *Stennett's* st. i., x., xi., and xiii.
5. The last cento is repeated in the Islington *Ps. and Hys.*, 1862, No. 357, with the omission of st. xi. of the original.
6. A sixth cento, beginning, " Again our weekly labours end," and consisting of st. i., x., xi., and xiii. of *Stennett*, re-written for Cotterill's *Sel.*, 1810, No. 97, is given in several collections, old and new.
7. The seventh cento begins, " Another week its course has run." It is a slightly altered form of *Stennett's* st. i., x., xi., and xiii., and is included in the *Harrow School Coll.*

Most of these centos are in C. U. in America and other English-speaking countries.
                          [J. J.]

Another week begins. *T. Kelly.* [*Sunday.*] 1st pub. in his *Hymns*, 2nd ed., 1806, and again, 3rd ed., 1809. In 1812 it was transferred to his *Hymns adapted for Social Worship*. Subsequently, in common with the rest of the hymns therein, it was again embodied in the original work. It is in 8 st. of 4 l., and based upon Ps. cxviii. 24. In the American hymnals it is re-written, the change being from S.M. to C.M. It also varies considerably in the number of stanzas used from 3 in the *Church Praise Bk.*, N. Y., 1881, to

5 in Hatfield's *Ch. H. Bk.*, 1872. In the latter form it begins, "And now another week begins."

Another week for ever gone. [*Sunday.*] An anonymous hymn in Rippon's *Comprehensive Ps. and Hys.*, 1844, No. 345, pt. iv., in 3 st. of 4 l.

Another week has passed away. *W. H. Bathurst.* [*Sunday.*] 1st pub. in his *Ps. and Hymns*, &c., 1831, No. 129, in 5 st. of 4 l., and entitled "Saturday Evening." It is also in Bickersteth's *Christ. Psalmody*, 1833 and 1841, and others. As given in *Kennedy*, 1863, No. 865, slight alterations have been introduced. Orig. text as above. It has been rendered into Latin as, *Nobis nunc iterum præterit hebdomas,* by the Rev. R. Bingham, and included in his *Hymnol. Christ. Lat.* 1871.

Another year has now begun. *C. Wordsworth, Bp. of Lincoln.* [*New Year.*] 1st pub. in his *Holy Year*, 1st ed., 1862, No. 14, for "New Year's Day," and consists of 9 st. of 4 l. Orig. text in later editions. The cento in Snepp's *Songs of G. & G.* is composed of st. i., iii., v., viii., vii. and ix., and that in Barry's *Ps. & Hys*, 1867, of st. i.–iii., v., viii., ix.

Another year has passed away. [*O. and N. Year.*] An anonymous hymn in the *Meth. S. S. H. Bk.*, 1879, the *Meth. Free Ch. S. S. H. Bk.* and others. In some collections it is attributed to "Allen," and in others it is said to be "American." We have failed in securing authority for either statement.

Another year hath fled, renew. *A. T. Russell.* [*O. and N. Year.*] Written Nov. 20, 1850 (s. MSS.), and 1st pub. in his *Psalms and Hymns*, &c., 1851, No. 63, in 3 st. of 8 l. In 1863 it was republished in *Kennedy*, No. 140, in a slightly altered form, but in *Thring's Coll.*, 1882, No. 130, the original text is restored with the exception of st. i., l. 1, *has* for *hath*, and the repetition of the last line of each stanza which was repeated in the original to suit the tune to which the hymn was written. With the first line as "Another year *has* fled, renew," it is also in use in Canada, and other English-speaking countries.

Another year is dawning. *Frances R. Havergal.* [*New Year.*] Written in 1874 for the ornamental leaflets and cards pub. by Caswell, 1875. It was subsequently included in her work, *Under the Surface*, 1874, and *Life Chords*, 1880. It is in 6 st. of 4 l. [HAV. MSS.]

Anstice, Joseph, M.A., s. of William Anstice of Madeley, Shropshire, b. 1808, and educated at Enmore, near Bridgwater, Westminster, and Ch. Church, Oxford, where he gained two English prizes and graduated as a double-first. Subsequently, at the age of 22, he became Professor of Classical Literature at King's Coll., London; d. at Torquay, Feb. 29, 1836, aged 28. His works include *Richard Cœur de Lion*, a prize poem, 1828; *The Influence of the Roman Conquest upon Literature and the Arts in Rome* (Oxford prize Essay); *Selections from the Choice Poetry of the Greek*

Dramatic Writers, translated into English Verse, 1832, &c. His hymns were printed a few months after his death, as :—*Hymns by the late Joseph Anstice, M.A., formerly Student of Christ Church, Oxford, and Professor of Classical Literature, King's College, London,* Bridgwater, 1836, and thus introduced :—

"As none of the following Hymns had the advantage of being corrected and prepared for the press by their lamented Author, his family have not considered themselves at liberty to bring them before the public ; but, having reason to believe that a large circle of surviving friends will be gratified by possessing a memorial of the manner in which some of his leisure hours were employed, and of the subjects which chiefly occupied his thoughts, during the last few months of his life, they have consented to their being printed for private distribution.—Bridgwater, June, 1836."

This work contains 52 hymns on various subjects, together with a poem "To my Hymn Book." The circumstances under which they were written are thus detailed by Mrs. Anstice in a communication to the Rev. Josiah Miller, author of *Singers and Songs of the Church :—*

"The hymns were all dictated to his wife during the last few weeks of his life, and were composed just at the period of the day (the afternoon) when he felt the oppression of his illness—all his brighter morning hours being given to pupils up to the very day of his death." —*S. & S.*, p. 495.

A few of the hymns are of a joyful character, but the circumstances under which they were written account for the prevailing tone of sadness by which they are chiefly characterized. About one half of these hymns were included by Mrs. Yonge in her *Child's Christian Year*, 1841. Being thus brought before the public, many soon came into C. U. Those in most extensive use are: "Father, by Thy love and power;" "In all things like Thy brethren, Thou;" "Lord of the harvest, once again;" and, "O Lord, how happy should we be."   [J. J.]

Anthologia Davidica, or a Metrical Translation of the whole Book of Psalms, &c., by Presbyter Cicestrensis [*the Rev. Henry Latham*], Lond., Rivington, 1846. This work contains an excellent critical Preface, a long but imperfect list of Psalters and Partial Versions of the Psalms, and 159 extracts from 31 authors. The selection, although on the whole good, is weakened by numerous alterations. Some amends are made, however, by an appendix of original readings. A limited number of the older renderings of individual Psalms have passed into modern hymnals through this work.

Antiphon (Gr. Ἀντίφωνον; Lat. *Antifona.*). i. This word now ordinarily denotes a short versicle said at the beginning and close of a Psalm or Psalms in the Breviary Offices. But it has also borne the following meanings, which are not yet entirely obsolete :—

1. A Hymn or Psalm sung antiphonally—that is to say, alternately by two sides of a choir, instead of being recited by a single voice, or sung responsorially by the Priest and choir or congregation. Ignatius, third Bishop of Antioch in Syria, is said to have first introduced this mode of singing into the Church's services, after a vision in which he heard and saw angels so praising the Blessed Trinity (Amalarius,·*De Eccles. Offic.* iv. 7). The custom was transferred thence into Western Christendom by St. Ambrose, into his own diocese of Milan, whence it spread into more general use (Rabanus Maurus, *De Instit. Cleric.* ii. 50).

2. A sentence of Holy Scripture, or an original composition, sung by itself without reference to any Psalm. The sentence, "I heard a voice from heaven," &c., in the Anglican Burial Office, may be referred to as an instance of this, and similar examples occur in the Ambrosian and Mozarabic Offices for the Dead. (*Breviar. Goth.*, Migne's edit. p. 982.)

3. Certain portions of Psalms, or Sentences, generally but not always taken from Scripture, and introduced into the Liturgy. The old name for the Introit was "Antiphona ad Introitum," the last two words being frequently understood and not expressed. The "Offertorium" and "Communio" were likewise regarded as Antiphons. So were the short sentences introduced before the Gospel, as "Gloria in excelsis Deo, et in terra pax. Alleluia, Alleluia" before the Gospel on Christmas Day in the Milanese and some French Uses (Mart. *De Eccles. Rit. Lib. iv. cap. xii. § xxxii.*). Various Communion Sentences or Antiphons are provided in the *Gelasian Sacramentary* (Muratori, *Lit. Rom. Vol. p.* 698), *Stowe Missal* (*Lit. & Rit. of Celtic Church*, p. 242), and other ancient Service Books. Martene speaks of an "Antiphona ad Eucharistiam," commencing with the words "Venite populi," in the *Lyons Missal* (*ut supra*). In the Greek Liturgy of Constantinople the Introit consisted of three separate parts, each called an "Antiphonon," and consisting of partly variable, partly invariable elements (*Hammond*, *Lit. E. & W.* p. 92). An exact description of these Greek Antiphona will be found in Dr. Neale's Holy Eastern Church (*Introd. i.* 364).

4. A Sentence extracted or adapted from the Psalms or from some other source, and prefixed to each Psalm or group of Psalms, and repeated at the close. The rules regulating their use are very intricate, and have varied at different times and in different countries. The rules regulating their present use in the Latin Church may be found at the commencement of the *Roman Breviary*. There existed formerly great diocesan variety of wording, as well as of usage, of which Amalarius makes complaint at the commencement of his work, *De Ordine Antiphonarii.*

ii. In the 15th century we find the following varieties in the Antiphon to the Psalms at Terce, in the *Little Office of the B. V. M.* :—

> Maria virgo assumpta est (*Rome*).
> Quando natus es (*Sarum*).
> Dignare me laudare (*Paris*).
> Tota pulchra (*Sens*).
> Rubum quem viderat Moyses (*Limoges*).
> In odorem unguentorum (*Orleans*).
> Alma virgo Maria (*Cambrai*).

The list might be extended, and similar lists drawn up to almost any number. Antiphons were also prefixed to the prayers or suffrages of special memoriae (*Sarum Brev.* Reprint, pp. vii.–xi.).

iii. Among special Antiphons the following deserve separate mention :—

1. The 4 Antiphons of the B. V. M. appended to the Roman Compline. For these see "Alma Redemptoris"; "Ave Regina"; "Regina Coeli"; and "Salve Regina."

2. The 7 greater Antiphons, for use at Vespers in Advent, beginning on Dec. 17. They are all double— that is to say, sung entire both before and after the Magnificat. Their use is indicated by the words "O Sapientia" placed against Dec. 16 in the Book of Common Prayer. Their opening words are these :—
   1. O Sapientia, quae ex ore altissimi.
   2. O Adonay et dux domus Israel.
   3. O Radix Jesse qui stas in signum.
   4. O Clavis David et sceptrum domus.
   5. O Oriens, splendor lucis aeternae.
   6. O Rex gentium et desideratus.
   7. O Emanuel, rex et legifer.

To which Amalarius (*Lib. de Ord. Antiph.* cap. 13) adds an 8th, which is found in the Sarum and York and Hereford Breviaries :—
   8. O Virgo virginum quomodo fiet.

The Sarum Breviary also adds a 9th Antiphon :—
   9. O Thoma Didyme, per Christum quem.

The substance of 5 of the above Antiphons is expressed in irregular order in the Hymn, translated and arranged by Dr. Neale, "O come, O come, Emmanuel."

iv. The mystical meanings of Antiphons, and of their frequency, and of the mode of repeating them, are explained by Hugo à S.

Victor, *Speculum Ecclesiae*, cap. 3. Originally they were always sung whole before and after each Psalm, always having also certain versicles attached to them. Sometimes they were sung twice, and sometimes before each verse of a Psalm or Canticle. An instance of a Magnificat with an Antiphon intercalated between all the verses is printed by Martene (*De Antiq. Eccles. Rit. Lib. iv. cap. iv.*). Many minute points are discussed at length by the ritualists, e.g. why the "Alleluia" which closes the Antiphons to the Psalms in the third nocturn of Feasts of the Apostles is omitted on the Feast of St. John the Baptist, &c. (Amalarius, *Lib. de Ordine Antiphon,* c. 59).

v. Books, Services, and Seasons were sometimes named after the opening words of Antiphons. The *Gradual* was once known as the "*Ad te levavi*," from the first words of the Antiphona, "ad Introitum," for the First Sunday in Advent (*Leofric Missal*, p. xxii.). Vespers for the Dead were called *Placebo*, from the Antiphon of the first Psalm : and Matins for the Dead were called *Dirige*, from the corresponding Antiphon in that service. Sundays and other days were called after the opening words of their Introits, as the First Sunday in Lent *Invocavit me ;* the Second Sunday in Lent *Reminiscere*, and so forth. [F. E. W.]

The Antiphons which have been rendered into English for use in public worship are the above seven greater Antiphons for use at Vespers in Advent. These *tr.* are usually confined to the first seven, and are both in prose and metre. Taking the prose renderings first, we have the following :—

i. Prose Translations.

Of the Antiphons to the Magnificat in the *Roman Breviary*, prose versions into English exist in the Vesper Books and Primers of that communion ; and an adaptation of these has been issued for the use of English Churchmen.

Of the *Sarum* Antiphons, translations of those to the *Benedictus, Magnificat*, and *Nunc Dimittis*, will be found in the *Antiphoner and Grail*, parts i. and ii., 1880, and with the addition of those to the Psalms in J. D. Chambers's *Psalter ; or, Seven Hours of Prayer*, 1852 ; his *Order of Household Devotion*, 1854 ; and also in the *Day Hours of the Church of England*, and other books issued for the use of sisterhoods and other communities. Much information on the whole subject may be found in Dr. Neale's *Essays on Liturgiology*, 2nd edition, 1869, and in Neale and Littledale's *Commentary on the Psalms*, 1860–74, 4 vols.

Of the seven greater Antiphons, or the Os, the earliest *tr.* for Anglican use was made by Cardinal Newman for *Tracts for the Times*, No. 75, in 1836, but this is not in C. U. Another *tr.*, given in the St. Saviour's (Leeds) *Sacred Hymns and Anthems*, 1846, met with more favour, being repeated in R. Campbell's *St. Andrew's Hymnal*, 1850 ; Murray's *Hymnal*, 1852 ; in *H. and Introits* in the same year ; and with the alteration of a word or two, and the addition of No. viii., in the enlarged ed. of the *Hymnal Noted*, 1854. The seven as in *Murray* are retained in the *Introits* prefixed to some editions of *Hymns A. & M.*

ii. Metrical Translations.

1. An early metrical rendering of the separate Antiphons was made by Canon William Cooke, and appeared in the Cooke and Denton *Hymnal* of 1853. Canon Cooke's account of the same is: "Where it was possible, the translator and arranger (who was William Cooke), took the words of Mr. A. J. Beresford Hope's *tr.* of the hymn 'Veni, Veni, Emmanuel,' in the *Hymnal N.*; retaining the prayer of the Prose Anthem for the Advent of Christ." The opening line of each Antiphon is: i. "O Wisdom, who o'er earth below;" ii. "Ruler and Lord, draw nigh, draw nigh;" iii. "O Rod of Jesse's stem, arise;" iv. "Key of the House of David, come;" v. "O Morning Star, arise;" vi. "O Thou or Whom the Gentiles wait;" vii. "Draw nigh, draw nigh, Immanuel."

2. A second *tr.* by Earl Nelson appeared in the *Sarum Hymnal*, 1868, as "The Advent Anthems." The opening line of each is:—(1) "O Wisdom! spreading mightily;" (2) "Ruler of Israel, Lord of Might;" (3) "O Root of Jesse! Ensign Thou!" (4) "O Israel's sceptre! David's Key;" (5) "O Day Spring and Eternal Light;" (6) "O King! Desire of Nations! come;" (7) "O Law-giver! Emmanuel! King!" These were directed to be sung separately, or as one hymn, as desired.

3. These Antiphons were also *tr.* by W. J. Blew, and included in his *Church H. & Tune Bk.*, 1852.

4. Some time, Dr. Neale supposes about the 12th century, an unknown author took five of these Antiphons, and wove them into a hymn in the following order:—st. i. *O Emmanuel;* ii. *O Radix Jesse;* iii. *O Oriens;* iv. *O Clavis David;* v. *O Adonai.* This hymn began with the line:—

"Veni, veni, Emmanuel,"

and adding to each verse the refrain, which is not found in the original prose:—

"Gaude, gaude, Emmanuel
Nascetur pro te, Israel."

Daniel has given the full text in his *Thes. Hymn.* ii. 336 (1844). From Daniel's text *Dr. Neale* translated his:—

5. **Draw nigh, draw nigh, Emmanuel**, and pub. it in the 1st ed. of his *Mediaeval Hymns*, 1851, p. 119, in 5 st. of 6 l. That *tr.* he altered for the 1st ed. of the *Hymnal N.*, 1852, the same altered text being repeated in the enlarged ed. of 1854; and the 2nd and 3rd eds. of the *Mediaeval Hymns*, 1862 & 1863. The altered text is found in the *People's H.*, 1867, and also, with alterations by various hands, in the *Hymnary*, 1872, *H. Comp.*, 1876, Thring's *Coll.*, 1882, and others. It is from the original *tr.* of 1851 that parts ii.–v. and vii. of No. 74 in *Church Hys.* are taken, parts i. and vi. being from Canon Cooke's *tr.* from the original prose (see above). In the trial copy of *H. A. & M.* in 1859, an altered version of Neale's *tr.* was given beginning:—

6. **O come, O come, Emmanuel.** This was included in the 1st ed. of 1861, and again in the new ed. 1875; and is repeated in *Kennedy*, 1863; Allon's *Sup.* 1868; *Wes. H. Bk.*, 1875; and others. Another *tr.* is:—

7. **O come, Emmanuel, O come!** This is in the *Anglican H. Bk.*, and was made by the editor,

the *Rev. R. C. Singleton*, in 1867, and included therein in 1868. Dr. Macgill's *tr.*:—

8. **O Come, Immanuel, hear our call,** appeared in the Scottish *Presb. Hymnal*, 1876, No. 29, and was subsequently included in his *Songs of the Christian Creed and Life*, 1876 and 1879.

Translation not in C. U.:—
O come! come, Thou Emmanuel. *Chambers*, 1857.

A rendering through the German has been noted by Mr. Mearns as follows:—

Nun sende Herr, uns deinem Sohn, in the Trier *G. B.*, 1846, p. 9, in 8 st. of 4 l. In the harmonized ed. of 1847, it is said to be from the Munich *G. B.*, 1586. *Tr.* as "Send now Thy Son unto us, Lord," by Miss Huppus, as No. 310, in E. Paxton Hood's *Children's Choir*, 1870.

[J. J.]

Antiphonale = seq.

Antiphonarium. A book containing the Antiphons, Invitatories, Hymns, Responds, Verses, and in later times the Little Chapters. Originally the Antiphons and Responds were contained in separate volumes known as the *Antiphonarium* and *Responsoriale* (Amalarius, *Prol. ad Lib. de Ord. Antiphon.* Edit. Hittorp, p. 224). The arrangement of the volume is attributed to Gregory I., and its revision to Adrian I. The early *Antiphonaries* of various countries and dioceses exhibit great variety of text and usage.   [F. E. W.]

Anton Ulrich of Brunswick, b. Oct. 4, 1633, at Hitzacker, on the Elbe above Lauenburg, the portion as younger son of his father, Duke August, who three years afterwards succeeded to the Dukedom of Wolfenbüttel. He was the only child of the Duke's second marriage. In 1635 the Duke contracted a third marriage with Sophie Elisabethe of Mecklenburg. Father and stepmother alike were pious and fond of music and poetry, and their children were trained with a simple home life, in Lutheran orthodoxy; and, under J. G. Schottelius and Sigismund v. Birken, instructed in all the learning of the time. Under these influences, supplemented by a residence at the University of Helmstädt, 1650, Anton Ulrich grew up a lover of his mother tongue and of poetry—his first literary efforts being a number of hymns which he presented in MS. to his father as a New Year's gift, 1655. In 1659 he was admitted a member of the Fruitbearing Society. At the death of his father in 1666 the family circle was broken up, and, released from the healthful, if somewhat narrow, influences of his training and previous surroundings, he turned from hymn-writing to the affairs of the world. Henceforth the ruling passion, hitherto curbed, took the upper hand, and the desire for power and fame led him far astray.

In 1667 his elder brother appointed him Governor at Wolfenbüttel, and in 1685 made him Co-Regent of the Duchy of Brunswick. His desire for princely magnificence, fostered by a year's residence in France, led him into lavish expenditure, such as an imitation of the Palace of Versailles which he built at Salzdahlum, near Wolfenbüttel, and in Wolfenbüttel an Academy (opened 1687) for the education of young noblemen; a fine building for the Library, and a new opera house. Envious at the rapidly increasing power of the Hannover-Celle branch of the Wolfenbüttel line, he made alliance, in 1702, with France, against them, only to be deposed from the Co-Regency, although when his brother abdicated in 1704 he obtained full sway in Brunswick. By his secession to the Roman Catholic Church in 1709-10 (one of the results arising from the marriage of his granddaughter Elizabethe Christine to Charles of Spain, who was crowned Emperor in 1711), he lost the love of his subjects and the respect of his former princely friends, and attained neither temporal advantage, nor spiritual peace. When his fatal illness came on and he felt his end near, he summoned an Evangelical clergyman to prepare him for death, then received the Sacrament according to the Roman rite, and after giving his surviving children his blessing, d. at Salzdahlum, Mar. 27, 1714. His two sons succeeded each other, but as they died without male issue, the Dukedom passed to a son of his younger brother by Duke August's third marriage.

His hymns seem to have been mostly written before 1655, and were printed anonymously to the number of 44 as *Hocherleuchtete Geistliche Lieder, Einer hohen Personen*, N.P. 1665, and then enlarged to 60, and with melodies probably by his stepmother as :—*Christ Fürstliches Davids-Harpfen-Spiel zum Spiegel und Fürbild Himmel-flammender Andacht, &c.*, Nürnberg, 1667, with a preface on prayer, probably by J. G. Schottelius (reprinted with three hymns added, Wolfenbüttel, 1670). Of these 34 are included in the selections by H. Wendebourg from the Duke's *Geistliche Lieder*, pub. at Halle, 1856. Mostly composed before his 22nd year, many are in unusual metres and of the ·nature of experiments·in verse, showing him as allied with the Pegnitz Order, of which his former tutor and life-long friend Sigismund v. Birken (q. v.) was then President or Chief Shepherd. But although it may be said that the Duke's hymns are often too subjective and farfetched, and that his after life did not altogether fulfil the promise of his youth; yet there cannot be denied to them the expression in beautiful form of a deep sense of sin, an ardent longing for grace, and a heartfelt love to the Saviour. Their poetic worth, simplicity of diction, and practical usefulness gained them admission to the Leipzig *Vorrath*, 1673, the Nürnberg *G. B.*, 1676, and other hymn-books of the period, and to Bunsen's *Versuch*, 1833, and other recent collections (*Koch*, iii. 537–549; Wendebourg's *Preface; Allg. Deutsche Biog.*, i. 487–491; *Bode*, 37–38). Four have been *tr.* into English, two 1st pub. 1665, and two 1st pub. 1667; the references to the original eds. being kindly supplied from the copies in the Ducal Library at Wolfenbüttel by the Principal Librarian, Dr. O. v. Heinemann.

i. **Lass dich Gott.** [*Resignation.*] This beautiful hymn on Consolation in Trial appeared in 1667, p. 237, as above (ed. Wendebourg, 1856, p. 68), in 6 st. of 6 l., ll. 1, 6, of each st. being identical. Included as No. 468 in pt. ii., 1714, of

Freylinghausen's G. B., and as No. 787 in Bunsen's *Versuch*, 1833 (*Allg. G. B.*, 1846, No. 319). *Tr.* as :—

Leave all to God. A good *tr.* (omitting st. iv.) by Miss Winkworth in the 1st Series, 1855, of her *Lyra Ger.*, p. 159 (ed. 1876, p. 161), and thence as No. 155 in *Ps. & Hymns*, Bedford, 1859, as No. 302 in the *Free Church H. Bk.*, 1882, and in the Gilman-Schaff *Lib. of Rel. Poetry*, ed. 1883.

ii. **Nach dir, O Gott! verlanget mich.** [*Thirsting for God.*] One of his best hymns. Appeared in 1665, p. 21, 1667, p. 28, as above (ed. Wendebourg, 1856, p. 8), in 11 st. of 4 l. Included as No. 1129 in the Leipzig *Vorrath*, 1673, and as No. 1259 in Burg's *Breslau G B.*, 1746. *Tr.* as :—

O God, I long Thy Light to see. A good *tr.* by Miss Winkworth in the 1st Series, 1855, of her *Lyra Ger.*, p. 145, omitting st. ii., iii., vi. In the second ed. p. 146, *tr.* of st. ii., iii., were added. Repeated thus as No. 118 in her *C. B. for England*, 1863.

Other *trs.* are, all omitting st. ii., iii., vi., (1)"O Lord! I long Thy face to see," by Miss Cox, 1841, p. 97 (1864, p. 115); (2) "My soul is thirsting, Lord, for Thee," by Lady Eleanor Fortescue, 1843 (1847, p. 38); (3) "Call me, O God; I come; for I," by Dr. G. Walker, 1860, p. 77.

iii. **Nun tret ich wieder aus der Ruh.** [*Morning. For the Sick.*] Appeared in 1667, p. 2, as above (ed. Wendebourg, 1856, p. 1.), in 8 st. of 8 l. The *trs.* are, (1) "Once more from rest I rise again," by Miss Winkworth, 1855, p. 220 (1856, p. 222). (2) "From blest, unconscious sleep I wake again," by Miss Cox, 1864, p. 185.

iv. **Wer Geduld und Demuth liebet.** [*Patience and Humility.*] Appeared in 1665, p. 92, and 1667, p. 135, as above (ed. Wendebourg, 1856, p. 43), in 11 st. of 4 l. *Tr.* as *Patience and Humility*, by Miss Winkworth, 1869, p. 225.

[J. M.]

Apelles von Löwenstern. [Löwenstern.]

Ἄφραστον θαῦμα. *St. Cosmas.* From the Office for Easter Eve in the *Triodion*, i.e. the Lent volume which commences with the Sunday before Septuagesima, and goes down to Easter (see **Greek Hymnody,** xiv. 7). It is Ode 7 of the Canon, and is based on the Canticle, "The Song of the Three Children." Several Canons during Lent are composed of three Odes only; hence the name of the Len' volume "*Triodion.*" The *tr.* of this Ode, "Christ, Who set free the Children three," was made by Dr. Littledale for and first pub. in the *People's H.*, 1867, No. 110, signed "L.," and appointed for Easter Eve. The original dates from the early part of the eighth century, and is found in modern Greek Service Books. The hymn "The Sepulchre is holding" is a *tr.* by Dr. Littledale of Σήμερον συνέχει τάφος from the same *Office* as the above. The author of the original, and the date are unknown. Dr. Littledale's *tr.* was made for and first published in the *People's H.*, 1867, No. 111, signed "L.," and appointed, with the above, for Easter Eve. It is repeated in the Irvingite *Hymns for the Use of the Churches*, 2nd ed., 1871. [J. J.]

Apostle of our own dear home. *J. E. Millard.* [*St. Augustine.*] Written for the festival of St. Augustine, and 1st pub., with a second hymn for the festival of St. Mary Magdalene, in the *Ecclesiastic*, c. 1849, and again in *Lyra Sanctorum*, 1850, p. 92. From this later work it was transferred to the *People's H.*, 1867, and signed " J. E. M."

Apostles of the risen Christ, go forth. *H. Bonar.* [*Missions.*] Printed in the second series of his *Hymns of Faith & Hope*, 1863, pp. 142–3, where it is headed "The Great Message," and the motto is prefixed:—

> "Quo vos magistri gloria, quo salus
> Invitat orbis, sancta cohors Dei
> Portate verbum."   *Old Hymn.*

It is in 5 st. of 6 l. Its use is mainly confined to America.   [W. T. B.]

Apparebit repentina dies magna Domini. *Anon. cir. 7 cent.* [*Advent.*] The earliest reference which we have to this hymn is in Bede's *De Metris* (672–735). It is an acrostic, the first verse commencing with *A*, the third with *B*, the fifth with *C.*, &c. Dr. Neale speaks of it as a "rugged, but grand Judgment Hymn," dates it "as early as the 7th century," and declares that "it manifestly contains the germ of the *Dies Iræ*." The text is given in Cassander's *Hymni Ecclesiastici*, Col. 1556; *Thomasius*, vol. ii. p. 433; Rambach, *Anthologie*, i. p. 126; *Daniel*, 1841, vol. i. No. 161; Du Méril, *Poésies Populaires Latines*, 1843, p. 135; Trench's *S. Lat. Poetry*, 1849 and 1873, and others. [W. A. S.]

Translation in C. U.:—

1. That great day of wrath and terror. By J. M. Neale, in his *Med. Hymns*, 1851, p. 9. From this *tr.* a cento has been given in the *Cumbrae H. Bk.*, 1863, No. 235. Mrs. Charles has also rendered it as: "Suddenly to all appearing the great day of God shall come," in her *Voice of Christian Life in Song*, 1858, p. 142, but it is not in C. U.

Apparuit benignitas. [*Christmas.*] A beautiful poem on the Incarnation quoted by *Mone*, No. 51, from a 15th cent. MS. at Karlsruhe in 92 lines. There is no *tr.* of the whole poem, but a cento beginning with l. 5, **O amor quam exstaticus**, was *tr.* by the Rev. B. Webb, for the *Hymnal N.*, 1854, in 8 st. of 4 l., the doxology being an addition to the original text. This *tr.*, considerably altered in some instances, has passed into the *Salisbury H. Bk.*, 1857; *H. A. & M.*, 1861; *People's H.*, 1867; the S. P. C. K. *Church Hys.*, 1871; the *Hymnary*, 1872; Thring's *Coll.*, 1882, and others. It begins in each hymnal :—" O Love, how deep, how broad, how high !" The original lines *tr.* are given in L. C. Biggs's *Annotated H. A. & M.*, 1867, p. 177.

Appleton, Sarah [Miles].

Approach, my soul, the mercy seat. *J. Newton.* [*Lent.*] 1st pub. in the *Olney Hymns*, 1779, bk. iii., No. 12, in 6 st. of 4 l., and again in all later editions of the same work. It came into early use in the hymnals and has attained to a foremost position as one of the most popular of Newton's productions. In the *Olney Hymns* it is the second of two

hymns headed, "The Effort." The first hymn by Newton on this same subject begins :—"Cheer up, my soul, there is a mercy seat." No. 11, in 6 st. of 4 l. as above. Its similarity to "Approach, my soul," has led some to suppose it to have been re-written by an unknown compiler. In the American *College Hymnal*, N. Y. 1876, st. ii., iii. and iv. are given as No. 280, "Lord, I am come, Thy promise is my plea." The use of this hymn in any form is very limited.

Aquinas, St. Thomas. [Thomas of Aquino.]

Are there not in the labourer's day ? *C. Wesley.* [*Duty.*] 1st pub. in *Hymns & Sacred Poems*, 1749, vol. i. 124, in 5 st. of 6 l., and entitled, "The way of duty the way of safety." In 1780 it was embodied in the *Wes. H. Bk.*, and from thence has passed into most of the hymnals of the Methodist bodies in G. Britain and America. It was introduced into the collections of the Ch. of England by Toplady, through his *Ps. & Hys.*, 1776. Orig. text in *P. Works*, 1868–72, vol. v. p. 17.

Are we doing as we should do ? *T. Kelly.* [*Missions.*] Contributed to an ed. of his *Hymns*, &c., between 1838 and 1853, in 4 st. of 8 l. In the 1853 ed. (9th) it is given as No. 585, and headed "Questions for Conscience." Its use is limited.

Are we not sons and heirs of God ? *I. Watts.* [*Gravity and Decency.*] 1st pub. with his *Sermons on Various Subjects*, &c., 1721, and was composed on the subject of his sermon on Phil. iv. 8. It was also repeated in 6 st. of 4 l. in later eds. of the *Sermons*. In Rippon's *Sel.* 1787, it was given, No. 229, as :—"Behold the sons, the heirs of God." and as such is known to modern hymnals.

Are your souls the Saviour seeking ? [*Peace.*] This anonymous hymn was given by Mr. Denham Smith in his *Times of Refreshing*, 1860, in 4 st. of 8 l. It has passed into several collections, including *Com. Praise*, 1880; *Hys. for the Ch. Catholic*, 1882, &c.; but in all cases as "*Anon.*"

Arends, Wilhelm Erasmus, s. of E. F. Arnds, pastor at Langenstein, near Halberstadt, was b. at Langenstein, Feb. 5, 1677. He became, in 1707, pastor at Crottorf, near Halberstadt, and in 1718, pastor of the church of St. Peter and St. Paul in Halberstadt. He d. at the latter place, May 16, 1721 (*Koch*, iv. 389; *Allg. Deutsche Biog.*, i. 516; MS. from Pastor Spierling, Halberstadt, and Pastor Schafft, Langenstein). He is said to have contributed three hymns to pt. ii., 1714, of Freylinghausen's *G. B.* Of these Nos. 118, 303 are ascribed to him at p. 3 of the Grischow-Kirchner *Nachricht*, 1771, to Freylinghausen's *G. B.*, while the other is left anonymous. It is :—

Rüstet euch ihr Christenleute. [*Christian Warfare.*] First pub. as No. 360 in 1714 as above, in 4 st. of 11 l. Dr. Jacobs of Wernigerode informs me that Count Christian Ernst of Wernigerode (d. 1771), a well-known German hymnologist, ascribed it to Arends in a marked copy of the 1741 ed. of Freylinghausen's *G. B. Koch* styles it "a call to arms for spiritual conflict and victory." Included in many later hymn-books, and recently as No. 675 in the Berlin *G. L. S.,* ed. 1863.

Translation in C. U.:—

Christians, prayer may well employ you. A full and good *tr.* contributed by J. M. Sloan as No. 289 to Wilson's *Service of Praise*, 1865.   [J. M.]

Arglwydd arwain trwy'r anialwch. *W. Williams.* [*Strength to pass through the Wilderness.*] This was pub. in the 1st ed. of the author's *Alleluia,* Bristol, 1745, in 5 st. of 6 l., as follows:—

Nerth i fyned trwy'r Anialwch.

1. Arglwydd, arwain trwy'r anialwch
Fi bererin gwael ei wedd,
Nad oes ynof nerth na bywyd,
Fel yn gorwedd yn y bedd:
    Hollalluog
Ydyw'r un a'm cwyd i'r lan.

2. Colofn dân rho'r nos i'm harwain,
A rho'r golofn niwl y dydd;
Dal fi pan bwy'n teithio'r manau
Geirwon yn fy ffordd y sydd:
    Rho imi fanna,
Fel na bwyf yn llwfrhau.

3. Agor y ffynnonau melus
Sydd yn tarddu o'r Graig i maes;
'Rhyd yr anial mawr canlyned
Afon iachawdwriaeth grâs:
    Rho imi hyny;
Dim i mi ond dy fwynhau.

4. Pan bwy'n myned trwy'r Iorddonen—
Angeu creulon yn ei rym,
Ti est trwyddi gynt dy hunan,
P'am yr ofnaf bellach ddim?
    Buddugoliaeth,
Gwna imi waeddi yn y llif!

5. Ymddiriedaf yn dy allu,
Mawr yw'r gwaith a wnest erioed:
Ti gest angau, ti gest uffern,
Ti gest Satan dan dy droed:
    Pen Calfaria,
Nac aed hwnw byth o'm cof.

The first *tr.* of a part of this hymn into English was by Peter Williams, in his *Hymns on Various Subjects* (vii.), *Together with The Novice Instructed: Being an abstract of a letter written to a Friend. By the Rev. P. Williams, Carmarthen,* 1771, *Printed for the author;* and was as follows:—

"Hymn V.
Praying for Strength.
"Guide me, O Thou great Jehovah,
Pilgrim thro' this barren land,
I am weak, but Thou art mighty,
Hold me with Thy powerful hand:
    Bread of heaven,
Feed me 'till I want no more.

"Open Thou the pleasant fountains,
Where the living waters flow;
Let the river of salvation
Follow all the desert thro':
    May Thy presence
Always lead and comfort me.

"Lord, I trust Thy mighty power,
Wondrous are Thy works of old;
Thou deliver'st Thine from thraldom,
Who for nought themselves had sold:
    Thou didst conquer
Sin, and Satan and the grave."

These stanzas are a *tr.* of st. i., iii., v. W. Williams himself adopted the *tr.* of st. i., *tr.* st. iii. and iv. into English, added a fourth stanza, and printed them as a leaflet as follows:—

I.
"Guide me, O Thou great Jehovah,
   Pilgrim through this barren land;
I am weak, but Thou art mighty,
   Hold me with Thy pow'rful hand:
Bread of heaven, bread of heaven,
Feed me till I want no more.

II.
"Open now the chrystal fountain,
   Whence the healing stream doth flow;
Let the fire and cloudy pillar
   Lead me all my journey thro':
Strong Deliv'rer, strong Deliv'rer,
De Thou still my strength and shield.

III.
"When I tread the verge of Jordan,
   Bid my anxious fears subside;
Death of deaths, and hell's destruction,
   Land me safe on Canaan's side:
Songs of praises, songs of praises,
I will ever give to Thee.

IV.
"Musing on my habitation,
   Musing on my heav'nly home,
Fills my soul with holy longings:
   Come, my Jesus, quickly come;
Vanity is all I see;
Lord, I long to be with Thee!"

This leaflet was undated, but was c. 1772. During the same or the following year, it was included in the *Lady H. Coll.*, 5th ed., Bath, W. Gye, No. 94. Stanzas i.-iii. had previously appeared in *The Coll. of Hys. sung in the Countess of Huntingdon's Chapels in Sussex. Edinburgh: Printed by A. Donaldson, for William Balcombe, Angmoring, Sussex,* No. 202. This is undated; but Mr. Brooke's copy contains the autograph, "Elizabt. Featherstonehaugh, 1772," the writing and ink of which show it to be genuine. We can safely date it 1771. It was repeated in G. Whitefield's *Ps. & Hys.*, 1773; in *Conyers,* 1774, and others, until it has become one of the most extensively used hymns in the English language. There are diversities of text in use the origin of which in every case it is difficult to determine. The most widely known are:—

1. Where the 5th line in each stanza reads respectively, "Bread of heaven," "Strong deliverer," and "Songs of praises," the arrangement is from the *Lady H. Coll.,* 1771. This form is given in nineteen out of every twenty hymnals which adopt the hymn, including *H. A. & M.,* &c.

2. Where the 5th line reads respectively, "Lord of Glory," "Strong deliverer," "Lord and Saviour," the text is from Cotterill's *Sel.,* 1810 to 1819, where it is changed to the plural throughout.

3. Where the 5th line reads respectively, "Of Thy goodness," "Strong Deliverer," and "Grateful praises," the changes were made in Hall's *Mitre,* 1836.

4. The original, with the omission of lines 5 and 6 in each stanza, thereby reducing it to 8 7's, given in many American hymnals, appeared in the *Prayer Bk. Coll.,* 1826.

In addition to these there are altered texts, as follows:

5. *Guide us, O Thou great Redeemer.* In *Morrell & How,* 1854; Scottish *Episc. H. Bk.,* 1858, and others.

6. *Guide us, O Thou whose Name is Saviour.* By J. Keble, re-written for the *Salisbury H. Bk.,* 1857, and repeated in the *People's H.,* 1867, *Sarum,* 1868, the *Hymnary,* 1872, &c.

7. *Guide us, Jesu, Holy Saviour.* In the *Parish H Bk.,* 1863–75. This is Keble's alteration of Williams, again altered.

8. *Guide us, O Thou great Deliverer.* In the *English Hymnal,* by J. A. Johnston, 2nd ed., 1856, No. 167.

9. *O Thou Great Jehovah, lead us.* This form of the text is in *Kennedy,* 1863, No. 639.

10. *Guide us, O eternal Saviour.* In *The Calcutta H. Bk.,* 1862, No. 102.

This hymn in one form or another has been rendered into many languages, but invariably from the English. These *trs.* included the Rev. R. Bingham's rendering into Latin, "Magne tu, Jehova," of the 3 st. arrangement, given with the English text, in his *Hymno. Christ. Lat.*, 1871.   [J. J.]

Arise, and follow me. *H. Alford.* [*St. Matthew.*] This hymn is No. 261 of his *Year of Praise*, 1867. In his *Poetical Works*, 1868, p. 308, it is dated 1844; but it is not in his *Ps. & Hys.*, 1844, nor in his *School of the Heart*, &c., 1845. We have not traced it in a printed form beyond Johnston's *English Hymnal*, 1852, No. 205, where it is given with a doxology.

Arise and hail the happy [sacred] day. [*Christmas.*] Pub. anonymously in the *Liverpool Liturgy*, 1763, p. 155, in 5 st. of 6 l. In 1769 it was given in the Bristol Bapt. *Coll.* of Ash & Evans, No. 96, and subsequently in several of the older hymn-books. In modern collections it is sometimes found as, "Arise and hail the *sacred* day," as in Hall and Lasar's *Evangelical Hymnal*, N. Y., 1880. The chorus, "O then let heaven and earth rejoice," is not in the original. It appeared in some collections early in the present century. [See **Scott, Elizabeth.**]

Arise, in all Thy splendour, Lord. *Sarah Slinn.* [*Missions.*] In J. Dobell's *New Selection*, &c., 1806, No. 432, pt. 2, in 6 st. of 4 l., 5 st. of which are from No. 47 of J. *Griffin's Sel. of Missionary & Devotional Hys.*, Portsea, 1797. The hymn "Though now the nations sit beneath," was re-written for American use, by L. Bacon (q. v.) from *Dobell*.

Arise, my soul, arise, Shake off, &c. *C. Wesley.* [*Christ the Mediator.*] 1st pub. in *Hymns & Sacred Poems*, 1742, p. 264, in 5 st. of 6 l. and entitled "Behold the Man." (*P. Works*, 1868–72, vol. ii. p. 323.) In 1780 it was included in the *Wes. H. Bk.* as No. 194 in an unaltered form, and has been repeated in all subsequent editions (ed. 1875, No. 202). From the *Wes. H. Bk.* it has passed into all the collections of the Methodist bodies in all English-speaking countries, and also into many hymnals outside of Methodism both in G. Britain and America. It has also been rendered into various languages. One in Latin, by the Rev. R. Bingham :—" Surge, surge,Mens mea," is given in his*Hymnol.Christ. Lat.*, 1871. Mr. Stevenson has collected in his *Meth. H. Bk. Notes*, 1883, numerous illustrations of the direct value which this hymn has been to many.

Arise, my soul, arise, This earth, &c. *J. Gabb.* [*General.*] Contributed to the *English Sacred Songster*, 1873, together with his tune "*Heavenward*," No. 37, and re-published, unaltered, in his *Welburn Appendix*, 1875, No. 93, but set to another tune (*Leyden*) also by Mr. Gabb.

Arise, my soul, arise, Thy [The] Saviour's sacrifice, &c. *C. Wesley.* [*On the Titles of Christ.*] Appeared in *Hymns*

and Sacred Poems, 1739, in 15 st. of 6 l. In 1780, when included in the *Wes. H. Bk.*, it was given as one hymn in two parts (No. 187), but as early as 1809 the parts were numbered as separate hymns, and they are given thus in the revised ed., 1875, Nos. 194, 195; and in most collections of the Methodist bodies. The second part or hymn is, "High above every Name." In *Kennedy*, 1863, the second line of part 1, as above, begins, "*The* Saviour's sacrifice." Outside of the Methodist collections the use of both hymns is limited. (Orig. text, *P. Works*, 1868–72, vol. i. p. 146.)

Arise, my soul, in songs to own. *Joseph Irons.* [*Praise to God the Father.*] From his *Zion's Hymns*, &c., 3rd ed., 1825, No. 15, in 4 st. of 4 l., into Snepp's *Songs of G. & G.*, 1872, unaltered.

Arise, my soul, my joyful powers. *I. Watts.* [*Redemption.*] 1st pub. in his *Hymns and Spiritual Songs*, 1707, bk. ii., No. 82, in 6 st. of 4 l., and entitled "Redemption and Protection from Spiritual Enemies." Its use, generally in an abbreviated form, has been and still is limited, in G. Britain, but is somewhat extensive in America.

Arise, my soul, nor dream the hours. [*Redeeming the Time.*] An anonymous hymn in Longfellow and Johnson's *Amer. Hys. of the Spirit*, 1864, No. 568.

Arise, my tenderest thoughts, arise. *P. Doddridge.* [*Sorrow because of Sin.*] Written, June 10, 1739, on the text, Ps. cxix. 158 ["D. MSS."] and 1st pub. in J. Orton's ed. of Doddridge's *Hymns*, &c., 1755, unaltered, in 5 st. of 4 l. and headed, "Beholding Transgressors with Grief." Also repeated in J. D. Humphreys's ed. of *Doddridge*, 1839. It came into C. U. at an early date, both in the Ch. of England and amongst the Nonconformists, and is still retained in numerous collections in G. Britain and America. It is a powerful and strongly worded hymn of the older type, and is suited for use on behalf of missions.

Arise, ye people, and adore. *Harriet Auber.* [*Ps. xlvii.*] 1st pub. in her *Spirit of the Psalms*, 1829, in 4 st. of 4 l., "Hallelujah" being added to the last st. only. It is in many American Colls., and is more popular there than in England.   [W. T. B.]

Arise, ye saints, arise. *T. Kelly.* [*Christ the Leader.*] 1st pub. in the 3rd ed. of his *Hymns on V. P. of Scripture*, 1809, No. 77, in 7 st. of 4 l., and headed, "He teacheth my hands to war," Ps. xviii. 34. In 1812 it was taken out of the above, and included in Kelly's *Hymns adapted for Social Worship*, No. 88, but subsequently it was restored to the original work. Full text in *Hymns*, M. Moses, Dublin, 1853, No. 253. As in C. U. both in G. Brit. and America, it is in an abbreviated form, but the arrangement of stanzas differs in various collections.

Arise, your voices all unite. *Bp. R. Mant.* [*Praise.*] An original composition included in his *Ancient Hymns from the Rom.*

Brev., &c., 1837, No. 83, in 6 st. of 4 l. and entitled, "Hymn commemorative of the Object of Christian Worship," ed. 1871, No. 83.

Arm of the Lord, awake, awake. The terrors, &c. *C. Wesley.* [*Missions.*] A cento composed of stanzas from three of the *Hymns of Petition and Thanksgiving for the Promise of the Father*, pub. by J. & C. Wesley in 1746. Stanza 1, from hymn 18, st. 1; 2 from hymn 21, st. 2; 3 and 4 from hymn 22, st. 1 and 4. It was embodied in the *Supp.* to the *Wes. H. Bk.* in 1830, No. 696. In the revised ed. of that Coll., 1875, No. 443, the last stanza is omitted. Orig. text, *P. Works*, 1868-72, vol. iv. p. 186.

Arm of the Lord, awake, awake. Thine own, &c. *C. Wesley.* [*Missions.*] This hymn was included in the first three editions of *Hymns & Sacred Poems*, all of which were pub. in 1739 (p. 222), but omitted in the fourth and fifth editions. In 1749 it was included in another series of *Hymns & Sacred Poems*, as the second part of a paraphrase of the 51st of Isaiah in 10 st. of 4 l. In 1780, 6 st. were included in the *Wes. H. Bk.*, No. 375, and are retained in the revised ed. of 1875, No. 386. The same arrangement is also found in several collections both in G. Brit. and America. Orig. text, *P. Works*, 1868-72, vol. iv. p. 302. Another hymn opening with the same first line, and of a similar character, was pub. in C. Wesley's *Hymns written in the time of the Tumults, June* 1780, No. ix., Bristol, 1780. The Tumults referred to took place in London. It is not in C. U. Orig. text, *P. Works*, 1868-72, vol. viii. p. 273.

Armstrong, Florence Catherine, daughter of William Armstrong, M.D., of Collooney, Co. Sligo, Ireland, b. March 18, 1843. Her well-known hymn:—

O to be over yonder [*Longing for Heaven*] was written in 1862, and pub. without her consent in the *British Herald*, Feb. 1865, p. 24, and dated "Jany., 1865." It soon attained an extended circulation, and was given in several collections In 1875 Miss Armstrong acknowledged the authorship in her work, *The King in His Beauty and Other Poems.*

Arnds, W. E. [Arends, W. E.]

Arndt, Ernst Moritz, son of Ludwig Nicolaus Arndt, estate manager for Count Putbus, in the island of Rügen, was b. at Schoritz in Rügen, Dec. 26, 1769. After studying at the Universities of Greifswald and Jena, where he completed his theological course under Paulus, he preached for two years as a candidate, but in 1798 abandoned theology. After a pedestrian tour through South Germany, Hungary, Northern Italy, France, and Belgium, he became, at Easter 1800, lecturer at the University of Greifswald, and in 1805 professor of history there. But in 1806, lamenting over the tyranny of France, he wrote his fiery *Geist der Zeit* (pt. ii. 1809, iii. 1813, iv. 1818) which awakened the patriotism of his countrymen, but drew on

him the hatred of Napoleon, so that he had to flee to Sweden, and was not able to return to Greifswald till 1810. He again left Greifswald in 1812, and found a home with Baron v. Stein at St. Petersburg. After various wanderings, during which he wrote many pamphlets inciting his countrymen, as none else could, to deeds of valour, and composed his well-known songs (all of date 1813),

> " Der Gott, der Eisen wachsen liess.
> O du Deutschland, ich muss marschieren.
> Was blasen die Trompeten?
> Was ist des Deutschen Vaterland?"

which were said to have done more to inspire the troops than a victory won, he settled for some time at Cologne as editor of a patriotic newspaper. In 1818 he was appointed professor of history in the newly-founded University of Bonn. Being accused by the Conservative leaders then in power of teaching Republicanism, he was, in 1820, unjustly deposed (though his salary was continued to him), and was not restored till the accession of Friedrich Wilhelm IV. to the throne of Prussia in 1840. In token of respect he was elected Rector of the University 1840-1841, and lectured as professor till 1854. He continued his tranquil life at Bonn, varied by delusive hopes of better things from the Revolutionary periods of 1848 and 1859, till after having passed his ninety-first birthday (when he received some three hundred messages of congratulation which he personally answered) he departed to the Heavenly Fatherland, Jan. 29, 1860.

A man of learning, a true patriot, a distinguished poet, and a man greatly revered and beloved of the people, he was a worthy modern representative of the "old Arndt," author of the *True Christianity*; a man of deep religious feeling, and a true-hearted and earnest witness for the Evangelical Faith. By his well-known *Von dem Wort und von dem Kirchenliede*, Bonn, 1819, he was one of the prime movers in the reaction which has now rescued most of the German lands from the incubus of xviii. cent. Rationalistic hymn-books. To this pamphlet he annexed 33 hymns, his best known. Of the remaining 50 some 37 appeared in his *Geistliche Lieder*, Berlin, 1855, and the rest in the Frankfurt, 1818, and later editions of his *Gedichte*—the so-called complete edition of which, pub. at Berlin 1860, contains 427 secular and sacred pieces, ranging from 1787 to 1859, with a preface dated in Christmas week 1859. (*Koch*, vii. 140-148; *Allg. Deutsche Biog.*, i. 540-548.)

The following 14 hymns by him have been *tr.* into English :—

i. **Der heil'ge Christ ist kommen.** [*Christmas.*] 1st pub. in 1818, vol. i. p. 319, and *tr.* as "The blessed Christ is coming," by *C. T Astley*, 1860, p. 24, in 4 st. of 8 l.

ii. **Dich Geist der Wahrheit, Geist der Kraft.** [*Whitsuntide.*] A Prayer to the Holy Spirit. 1st pub. 1819 (No. 32), as above, in 8 st. of 4 l. *Tr.* by *J. Kelly*, 1885, p. 67, "O Spirit, Thou of love and might."

iii. **Die Welt thut ihre Augen zu.** [*Child's Evening Hymn.*] 1st pub. 1818 (vol. i. p. 265), as above, in 4 st. of 8 l. *Tr.* by *J. Kelly*, 1885, p. 109, "The busy world its eyes doth close."

iv. **Es lebt ein Geist, durch welchen alles lebt.** [*The Spirit of God.*] 1st pub. 1818 (vol. i. p. 281) as above in 5 st. of 4 l., and *tr.* as:— "There is a Spirit—universal Source," by *C. T. Astley*, 1860, p. 14.

v. Gegangen ist das Sonnenlicht. [*Evening.*] Written in 1813, and 1st pub. 1818 (vol. ii. p. 230) as above, in 5 st. of 8 l., entitled : " The traveller's evening hymn." *Tr.* as (1) "The sunlight has departed," by *Dr. Maguire,* 1883, p. 49 ; (2) "The fields and woods all silence keep," by *J. Kelly,* 1885, p. 112.

vi. Geht nun hin und grabt mein Grab. [*Burial of the Dead.*] Written in 1818, and 1st pub. 1819 (No. 19) as above in 9 st. of 6 l., and included in Bunsen's *Versuch,* 1833, and since in many other collections, e.g. *Unv. L. S.,* 1851, No. 815. It is the most popular of his hymns and was sung at his own funeral at Bonn, Feb. 1, 1860 (*Koch,* vii. 147). The *trs.* in C. U. are :—

(1) **Go and dig my grave to-day!** A good and full *tr.* in the 1st Series, 1855, of Miss Winkworth's *Lyra Ger.,* p. 241 (ed. 1856, p. 243), and repeated as No. 188 in her *C. B. for England,* 1863. In Schaff's *Christ in Song,* ed. 1879, p. 536.

(2) **Weary now of wandering here.** A *tr.* of st. i., iv., vi., ix., signed " F. C. C.," as No. 280, in Dr. Pagenstecher's *Coll.,* 1864.

Other *trs.* are : (1) " Go ! and let my grave be made," by Miss Cox, 1841, p. 83 (1864, p. 83) ; (2) "Prepare me now my narrow bed," by Lady Eleanor Fortescue, 1843 (1847, p. 26) ; (3) " Go now, my friends, and dig my grave," by Dr. G. Walker, 1860, p. 109 ; (4) " Now go forth and dig my grave," by A. M. Jeaffreson, in *Golden Hours,* 1873, p. 52.

vii. Gott, deine Kindlein treten. [*Children.*] 1st pub. 1818 (vol. i. p. 275) as above, in 5 st. of 4 l. It is *tr.* as "Oh, gracious God ! Thy children come before Thee," by C. T. Astley, 1860, p. 38.

viii. Ich weiss, woran ich glaube. [*The Rock of Salvation.*] Written in 1818, and 1st pub. 1819 (No. 28) as above in 6 st. of 8 l. In Knapp's *Ev. L. S.,* 1837, No. 1396 (ed. 1865, No. 1348), it begins "Ich weiss, an wen ich glaube." The *trs.* in C. U. are:—

(1) **I know in Whom I put my trust.** A good *tr.* of st. i., iv.–vi. of *Knapp's* text in the 2nd Series, 1858, of Miss Winkworth's *Lyra Ger.,* p. 162. Included as No. 1170 in *Kennedy,* 1863, and recently in Schaff's *Christ in Song,* ed. 1879, p. 426, and *Lib. of Rel. Poetry,* ed. 1883, p. 670.

(2) **I know Whom I believe in,** a *tr.* from *Knapp,* omitting st. ii., iii., as No. 288 in the Ohio Luth. *Hymnal,* 1880.

ix. Kann ich beten, Ist in Nöthen. [*The Power of Prayer.*] Written in 1818, and 1st pub. 1819 (No. 29) as above in 8 st. of 7 l., and *tr.* " When I can pray, Without delay," by *C. T. Astley,* 1860, p. 10.

x. Und klingst du immer Liebe wieder. [*The Love of Christ.*] 1st pub. 1855, as above, p. 57, in 5 st. of 6 l. *Tr.* by *J. Kelly,* 1885, p. 34, " And dost thou always love proclaim."

xi. Und willst du gar verzagen [*Trust in God.*] Written in 1854, and 1st pub. as above, 1855, p. 81, in 6 st. of 8 l. It is *tr.* as " And art thou nigh despairing," in the *Family Treasury,* 1877, p. 110.

xii. Was ist die Macht, was ist die Kraft. [*Holy Scripture.*] Written in 1818, and 1st pub. 1819 (No. 30) as above in 6 st. of 6 l., and included in Hofer's *Pilgerharfe,* Basel, 1863, No. 31. *Tr.* (1) " What is the Christian's power and might ? " by R. Massie, in the *British Herald,* April, 1865, p. 61. (2) " What is the Christian soldier's might, What is," by R. Massie in the *Day of Rest,* 1878, vol. viii. p. 335.

xiii. Wenn aus dem Dunkeln ich mich sehne. [*Hope in God.*] Written in 1818, and 1st pub. 1819 (No. 18) as above, in 7 st. of 6 l. Included, omitting st. ii., as No. 2401 in Knapp's *Ev. L. S.,* 1837 (ed. 1865, No. 2128). *Tr.* as " When in the depths of night I'm sighing," in the *British Herald,* Aug. 1866, p. 312, repeated as No. 410, in Reid's *Praise Bk.,* 1872.

xiv. Wer hat den Sand gezählt, welcher im Wasser haust. [*The Almighty God.*] 1st pub. 1818 (i. p. 297) and included in 1819 (No. 6) as above, in 4 st. of 8 l. *Tr.* as " Who can on the seashore," in Dr. Dulcken's *Golden Harp,* 1864, p. 32. There is also a free *tr.* in the Unitarian *Hys. for Children,* Glasgow, 1855, No. 28, beginning :—" Who has counted the leaves that fall ? "   [J. M.]

Arnold, Gottfried, son of Gottfried Arnold, sixth master of the Town School of Annaberg in the Saxon Harz, b. at Annaberg Sept. 5, 1666. His life was varied and eventful, and although much of it had little to do with hymnody from an English point of view, yet his position in German Hymnology is such as to necessitate an extended notice, which, through pressure of space, must be (typographically) compressed.

After passing through the Town School and the Gymnasium at Gera, he matriculated in 1685 at the University of Wittenberg—where he found the strictest Lutheran orthodoxy in doctrine combined with the loosest of living. Preserved by his enthusiasm for study from the grosser vices of his fellows, turning to contemplate the lives of the first Christians, he began those investigations in Church History on which his fame principally rests, and thought of preparing himself to become a lecturer and professor, the worldly spirit which pervaded the Church repelling him from seeking to become one of her ministers. Accepting in 1689 an appointment as family tutor at Dresden, he became a disciple of Spener, then Court Preacher. Seeing and testifying against the ill-living of those around him, he lost his appointment in 1693, but by Spener's recommendation obtained a similar post at Quedlinburg, the centre of a recent religious Revival, one of the leaders in which was the Senior Court diaconus, J. H. Sprögel. While at Quedlinburg he wrote and pub. his first work of importance : *The First Love, i.e., a true Picture of the First Christians in their Living Faith, and Holy Life,* 1696, a book glowing with faith and earnestness, which gained a rapid circulation (5th ed. 1727) and was very greatly valued by P. J. Spener. Being thus brought into notice he was in 1697 appointed by the Landgrave Ernst Ludwig of Hesse-Darmstadt as Professor of History at Giessen. Accepting the post in a hopeful spirit, he did not find himself at home in his surroundings, and, unable to work as he wished, was constrained to resign in 1698. Returning to Quedlinburg he found leisure in the house of his friend Sprögel to pursue the investigations for his *Unparteiische Kirchen- und Ketzer-Historie* (Frankfurt-am-Main, 1699–1700). This epoch-making work, the most important of all his publications, a monument of gigantic industry and based on the original sources, sought with impartiality to bring out clearly the most prominent and most beautiful features of the Church life of bygone ages, while the more important works that preceded it had been largely partisan. It was dedicated to the King of Prussia, who, Jan., 1702, named him Historiographer; it gained for him the King's help, but by the favourable views taken of the heretics, and the unfavourable light in which the action of the Church towards them was often regarded, a storm of indignation was raised against him throughout the Church. About this time he joined the " New Angel Brotherhood " (S. Matt. xxii. 30), of the followers of the mystic Jakob Böhme, wrote in 1700 his *Mystery of the Wisdom of God* (see below), in which Heavenly Wisdom was represented as a pure Virgin, union with whom would preclude any earthly marriage, and ceased to partake of Holy Communion in public. Thereupon the ecclesiastical authorities took action, and would have banished him from Quedlinburg had not the King of Prussia interfered and sent two commissions in 1700 and 1701 on Arnold's behalf.

Now came the turning point in his life. A thief who had broken into the house of the Sprögels was apprehended at Allstedt, about 40 miles south. To bring the thief to justice, Sprögel's wife and her youngest daughter, Anna Maria, went thither under Arnold's care. Preaching before the widowed Duchess of Sachsen-Eisenach, Arnold was summoned by her to become preacher at her Court at Allstedt, and before entering on his duties was, on Sept. 5, 1701, married in Church at Quedlinburg to Anna Maria Sprögel—a union productive of the happiest results, and which in great measure cured him of his Separatist tendencies, but which brought the ridicule of his enemies upon him, and caused his expulsion from the Angel Brotherhood. Entering upon his duties at Allstedt in 1702, he encountered much opposition, and thus, in 1705, gladly accepted from the King of Prussia an appointment as pastor and inspector of Werben in the Altmark (near the junction of the Elbe and Havel), as successor to his father-in-law, who had removed thence from Quedlinburg. As his persecutors gave him no rest, he accepted from the magistrates of Perleberg, a few miles farther north, the pastorate there, to which the King added the inspectorate of the district, beginning his labours on the 22nd Sunday after Trinity, 1707, by a sermon on St. Matt. xiii. 45. Unwearied in word and work, by preaching, by household visitation, and by the composition of devotional manuals (one of which, entitled *Paradiesischer Lustgarten*, 1709, reached a 7th ed. in 1746), he sought the good of his flock and won universal love and esteem. His excessive devotion to study (publishing no less than 58 works, some being folios, within 20 years) and his sedentary habits, brought on a severe attack of scurvy. On Whit-Sunday, 1714, when barely recovered from his illness, a recruiting party burst into the church and impressed some of the young men who were in the act of receiving Holy Communion. This outrage was his death-blow. On the next day, May 21, as pre-arranged, he preached a funeral sermon, but had to be supported by the sexton to enable him to finish it, "like a faithful soldier keeping his post till his last gasp." Three days he lay in an armchair, and was then removed to bed. In earnest exhortation to his friends to full renunciation of self and of the world and complete dedication to God, in peaceful communion with God not unmingled with the bitterness of an early end, the days passed, till on May 30, 1714, after he had raised himself in bed and exclaimed "Frisch auf, frisch auf! Die Wagen her und fort," his spirit peacefully passed away, his mortal body being consigned to the grave on June 1—accompanied by a weeping multitude comprising nearly all the inhabitants of the place.

As a poet Arnold holds a high place, though but few of his hymns (mostly written at Quedlinburg) are entirely fitted for use in public worship. Ehmann characterises his poems as full of originality, as pervaded with a deep zeal for sanctification and the fear of God, and with glowing devotion and intensity of love for Christ. All are tinged, some very deeply, with his mysticism, dealing largely in theosophic language with the marriage of the soul to God. They found admission into the hymn-books of the Separatists and the Pietists, and many of them in modern times are included in Knapp's *Ev. L. S.* They appeared in the following works :—

(1) *Göttliche Liebes-Funcken. Aus dem grossen Feuer der Liebe Gottes in Christo Jesu entsprungen.* Frankfurt am Main, 1698. Containing 145 pieces, including his best hymns. (2) *Anderer Theil der göttlichen Liebes-Funcken.* Frankfurt, 1701. 36 pieces. (3) *Das Geheimniss der göttlichen Sophia, der Weisheit, beschrieben und besungen.* Leipzig, 1700. The poetical portion of this work is in two parts :—i. *Poetische Lob- und Liebes-Sprüche* (100) ; ii. *Neue göttliche Liebes Funcken* (133). (4) *Das eheliche und unverehelichte Leben der ersten Christen*, &c. Frankfurt, 1702, with an appendix of 19 poems. (5) *Neuer Kern wahrer Weisheit*, &c. Leipzig, 1703, with a collection of hymns appended, entitled *Ein neuer Kern recht geistlicher lieblicher Lieder*—217 in all.

As these works contain a good many hymns by other authors, the task of discrimination is not easy, and thus it comes to pass that in the collected editions by *Albert Knapp* (Stuttgart, 1845) and by *K. C. E. Ehmann* (Stuttgart, 1856) a number of pieces are included which are not really by Arnold. Somewhat curiously, Miss Winkworth, in her *Christian Singers of Germany*, 1869, has selected three pieces, and only three, as favourable specimens of Arnold, and as it happens, not one is really by him. Knapp frequently abridges and alters, while Ehmann gives a valuable introduction, the unaltered text of 139 hymns, and, as an appendix, a selection from the poems not in regular form (*Koch*, vi. 138–159 ; *Ehmann's Introduction, Allg. Deutsche Biog.*, i. 587–588). The hymns here noted are arranged thus : I. Probably by Arnold ; II. Possibly by Arnold ; III. Not by Arnold, but not found earlier than in the works mentioned above. Of these the following have been rendered into English :—

I. *Hymns probably by Arnold*, 1–9.

1. Ew'ge Weisheit, Jesu Christ. [*Love to Christ.*] Founded on Canticles viii. 6, and 1st pub. 1700 as above, No. 68 (*Ehmann's* ed. 1856, p. 128), in 18 st. of 4 l., and included as No. 504 in *Freylinghausen's G. B.* 1704. *Tr.* as "Christ, thou'rt Wisdom unto me," No. 685 in pt. i. of the *Moravian H. Bk.* 1754.

2. Holdseligs Gottes-Lamm. [*Victory of Love.*] 1701 p. 61, as above (*Ehmann's* ed. 1856, p. 173), in 11 st. of 8 l., and thence as No 484 in *Freylinghausen's G. B.* 1704. *Tr.* as "Thou, God's beloved Lamb," as No. 629 in pt. i. of the *Moravian H. Bk.* 1754. In 1789 altered to "Thou, God's most holy Lamb," and in 1801 and later eds. to "Jehovah ! holy Lamb."

3. Ihr Sions-Töchter die ihr nicht. [*Love to Christ.*] Founded on Canticles iii. 11, and 1st pub. 1700 as above, No. 41 (*Ehmann's* ed. 1856, p. 107), in 13 st. of 4 l. Included as No. 716 in the *Herrnhut G. B.* 1735. *Tr.* as "Daughters of Zion, who're no more," No. 695 in pt. i. of the *Moravian H. Bk.* 1754.

4. Komm beug' dich tief, mein Herz und Sinn. [*Thanksgiving to Christ.*] 1st pub. 1702 as above, p. 549 (*Ehmann's* ed. 1856, p. 194), in 9 st. of 6 l. Included as No. 744 in *Freylinghausen's G. B.* 1705. *Tr.* as "Ourselves, dear Lord, we now resign," from st. vii., ix., as st. iii., iv. of No. 695 in the *Moravian H. Bk.* 1801, (ed. 1849, No. 826).

5. Mein König, schreib mir dein Gesetz. [*Brotherly Love.*] Founded on Ps. cxxxiii. and James ii. 8, and 1st pub. 1698, No. 125, as above (*Ehmann's* ed. 1856, p. 51, *Knapp*, 1845, p. 119), in 16 st. of 6 l. *Tr.* as No. 387 in *Freylinghausen's G. B.* 1704. *Tr.* as "Thy law, O Lord, be my delight," as No. 451 in the *Moravian H. Bk.* 1789, and repeated in later eds.

6. O Durchbrecher aller Bande (q.v.)

7. O stilles Lamm, ich such dein sanftes Wesen. [*Love to Christ.*] A poem 1st pub. 1698, No. 34, as above (*Ehmann's* ed. 1856, p. 270), in 21 lines, entitled "They are virgins. These are they which follow the Lamb," Rev. xiv. 4. In pt. ii. 1714, of *Freylinghausen's G. B.*, a recast beginning "O stilles Gottes-Lamm," in 5 st. of 8 l., was included as No. 429. The *trs.* are—from the second form : (1) "Meek, patient Lamb of God, to Thee," by *J. Wesley*, in *Ps. & Hymns*, 1741 (*P. Works*, 1868–72, vol. ii. p. 14), repeated as No. 545 in pt. i. of the *Moravian H. Bk.* 1754 ; (2) "Meek, patient Lamb of God, impart," as No. 434 in the *Moravian H. Bk.* 1789, and later eds.

8. So führst du doch recht selig, Herr, die Deinen. [*Trust in God.*] 1st pub. 1698, No. 138, as above (*Ehmann's* ed. 1856, p. 69), in 13 st. of 8 l., entitled "The best Guide." Included as No. 210 in *Freylinghausen's G. B.* 1704, and recently as No. 428 in the *Unv. L. S.* 1851. Dr. Schaff, in his *Deutsches G. B.*, 1860, says of it: "It was the favourite hymn of the philosopher Schelling. It is, however, more suited for private use than for Public Worship." It is a beautiful hymn, marked by profundity of thought and depth of Christian experience. The only *tr.* in C. U. is "How well, O Lord! art thou thy People leading," in full as No. 671 in pt. i. of the *Moravian H. Bk.* 1754, and repeated, abridged and altered to "Well art Thou leading, Guide supreme," in 1826 (1849, No. 195). The *trs.* of st. i., iii., xi. from the 1826 were included in J. A. Latrobe's *Collection,* 1841, No. 329. Another *tr.* is "How blest to all Thy followers, Lord, the road," by *Miss Winkworth,* 1855, p. 175 (ed. 1876, p. 177).

9. **Wie schön ist unsers Königs Braut.** [*Heaven.*] 1st pub. 1698, No. 139, as above (*Ehmann's* ed. 1856, p. 72, *Knapp,* 1845, p. 217), in 14 st. of 6 l. Included as No. 584 in *Freylinghausen's G. B.* 1704. The *trs.* are beginning with st. x. :—"Wie freuet sich mein ganzer Sinn," (1) "I'm glad, yea, sinner—likely bold," as No. 548 in pt. i. of the *Moravian H. Bk.* 1754. (2) "How doth my needy soul rejoice," as No. 882 in the *Moravian H. Bk.* 1789. In 1801 altered to "How greatly doth my soul rejoice," (1849, No. 1230).

II. *Hymns possibly by Arnold,* 10–11.

10. **Erschein, du Morgenstern.** [*Morning.*] 1st pub. 1703, p. 8 (*Ehmann's* ed. 1856, p. 196), in 4 st. of 8 l. Included as No. 751 in *Freylinghausen's G. B.* 1705, and No. 628 in *Porst's G. B.* ed. 1855. *Fischer,* i. 174, thinks A.'s authorship very doubtful. *Tr.* as "Thou Morning-Star appear," by *H. J. Buckoll,* 1842, p. 42.

11. **O der alles hätt' verloren.** [*The Heavenly Spirit.*] This beautiful hymn on Self-Renunciation appeared in 1703, p. 132 (ed. *Ehmann,* 1856, p. 210), in 8 st. of 4 l., but both *Koch,* vi. 159, and *Fischer,* ii. 138, regard A.'s authorship as very doubtful. Included as No. 719 in *Freylinghausen's G. B.* 1705, and recently as No. 614 in the *Unv. L. S.* 1851. In *Knapp's* ed. 1845, p. 8, beginning "O wer alles hätt' verloren," in 7 st. The only *tr.* in C. U. is, "Well for him who all things losing," a very good *tr.* omitting st. iii. by Miss Winkworth, in the 1st Series of her *Lyra Ger.*1855, p. 134 (ed. 1876, p. 135), and repeated in her *C. B. for England,* 1863, No. 132, omitting the *tr.* of st. vi. Included as No. 451 in the Pennsylvanian Luth. *Ch. Bk.* 1868, and, with the omission of st. vi.-vii., in the Amer. *Meth. Episcopal Hymnal,* 1878.

Other trs. are: (1) "O were all things perishable," as No. 682 in pt. i. of the *Moravian H. Bk.* 1754. (2) "Ah! the heart that has forsaken," by *Mrs. Findlater,* in the *Family Treasury,* 1859, pt. ii. p. 208, and thence (quoting the German as "Ach das Herz verlassend alles") in the 4th Series, 1862, of the *H. L. L.* (ed. 1862, p. 284, 1884, p. 209). (3) "O how blest who, all resigning," by *Mrs. L. C. Smith,* in the *Sunday Magazine,* 1865, p. 946.

III. *Hymns wrongly attributed to Arnold,* 12–14.

Seven hymns of this class have been *tr.* into English. Of these two are noted under *Lodenstein,* one under *Scheffler,* and one under *J. L. Faber.* The others are :—

12. **Es gehet mancher Weg und Bahn.** [*Life's Voyage.*] 1st pub. in *Der Weisheit Gartengewächs,* 1703, edited by Arnold. *Ehmann,* 1856, p. 245, includes it in 7 st. of 4 l., but says it is certainly not by Arnold. *Knapp,* 1845, p. 173, quotes it, beginning, "Gar mancher Weg, gar manche Bahn," as from a MS. dated 1734, and included it in his *Ev. L. S.* 1850, No. 1583 (ed. 1865, No. 1652). *Tr.* as "Full many a way, full many a path," by *Miss Winkworth,* 1869, p. 295.

13. **O du süsss Lust.** [*Communion with Christ.*] Appeared in 1698, No. 140, as above; but distinctly marked as "by another." In *Knapp,* 1845, p. 78. Included in 9 st. of 6 l., as No. 458, in *Freylinghausen's G. B* 1704, and as No. 398 in *Porst's G. B.,* ed. 1855. The *trs.* are: (1) "O thou Pleasure blest," as No. 690 in pt. i. of the *Moravian H. Bk.* 1754 ; (2) "Bliss beyond compare," founded on the 1754, as No. 283 in the *Moravian H. Bk.* 1789. In full as No. 68 in the *Bible H. Bk.* 1845, and as No. 672 in Reid's *Praise Bk.* 1872.

14. **Salb' uns mit deiner Liebe.** [*The Kingdom of God.*] 1st pub. 1702, p. 526, but distinctly marked as "by another." In *Knapp,* 1845, p. 19. Included as No. 746 in *Freylinghausen's G. B.* 1705, and recently, as No. 198, in Knapp's *Ev. L. S.* 1850 (ed. 1865, No. 209). *Tr.* as "Anoint us with Thy blessed love," by *Miss Winkworth,* 1869, p. 293.

Dr. Franz Dibelius in his elaborate biography (*Gottfried Arnold,* Berlin, 1873) at pp. 180–183, 246–248, quotes four hymns not included by Ehmann, which he thinks may' possibly be by Arnold. One of these is "Zum Leben führt ein schmaler Weg" (q. v.).

[J. M.]

Arnschwanger, Johann Christoph, son of Georg Arnschwanger, merchant in Nürnberg, was b. at Nürnberg Dec. 28, 1625. He entered the University of Altdorf in 1644, and that of Jena in 1647, where he graduated M.A. Aug. 9, 1647. After short periods of residence at Leipzig, Hamburg, and Helmstädt he returned to Nürnberg in 1650. There he was successively appointed Stadt-vicar in 1651, Diaconus of the St. Aegidien Church 1652, Morning Preacher in St. Walpurga's 1654, and Diaconus of the Church of St. Lorenz 1659, where he became Senior 1679, and Archidiaconus 1690. He d. at Nürnberg, Dec. 10, 1696. (*Koch,* iii. 517–520 ; *Allg. Deutsche Biog.,* i. 597.)

A lover of music and poesy, he was the correspondent of Anton Ulrich (q. v.) and a member of the Fruitbearing Society (1675). He did not join the Nürnberg Pegnitz Shepherd Order, seeking in his poetical work simplicity and fitness for popular use rather than their somewhat affected "learnedness." The best of his hymns, some 400 in all, the most important being those pub. in 1659, appeared in his :—

i. *Neue geistliche Lieder,* Nürnberg, 1659, in two books, each containing 20 hymns, set to music by the best organists and choir masters in Nürnberg.

ii. *Heilige Palmen und Christliche Psalmen,* Nürnberg, 1680, with 150 hymns in three divisions, with melodies by the musicians of Nürnberg.

Of these hymns the only one *tr.* into English is :—

Auf, ihr Christen, lasst uns singen. [*Easter.*] 1st pub. in 1659 as above, Bk. i., No. 13, in 12 st. of 11 l., entitled "On the Victorious Resurrection of Jesus Christ from the dead, in which our future Resurrection is also set forth." Included in the *Nürnberg G. B.,* 1676, No. 227, as No. 98 in pt. ii., 1714, of *Freylinghausen's G. B.,* and recently (reduced to st. i., ix.) as No. 213 in the *Berlin G. B.,* 1829. The only *tr.* in C. U. is, "Up, ye Christians, join in singing," from the Berlin *G. B.* in N. L. Frothingham's *Metrical Pieces,* Boston, U.S., 1870, p. 194, and thence altered and beginning, "Rise, ye Christians," as No. 644 in the *Swedenborgian Coll.,* Lond., 1880. [J. M.]

Around the throne of God, a band [in circling band]. *J. M. Neale.* [*Children's Hymn.*] This hymn appeared in Dr. Neale's *Hymns for Children,* 1st Series, No. xxxi., 1842, in 9 st. of 4 l. (with Bp. Ken's doxology), for Michaelmas Day. Two forms have been the outgrowth. The first, beginning with the same first line, is found, somewhat altered, in Harland's *Ch. Psalter,* &c., No. 248 ; Thring's *Coll.,* 1882, in 4 st., with "*Thine*" for "Thy," st. 3, l. 1, *H. A. & M.,* 1875, No. 335, and other hymnals, and the second, "Around the throne in circling band," in the *Sarum Hymnal,* 1868, No. 312, and others.

Around the throne of God in heaven Thousands of children. *Anne Shepherd.* [*Children's Hymn.*] Pub. in her *Hymns adapted to the Comprehension of Young Minds,* No. 29, in 6 st. of 5 l. The date of the 1st ed. of this work is undetermined. Dr. Moffatt *tr.* this hymn into the Bechuana language for his Kuruman *Coll.,* 1838. In 1853, 4 st.

were transferred to the *Leeds H. Bk.*, No. 877, and from thence passed into later collections. Orig. text in the *Meth. S. S. H. Bk.*, 1879, No. 448, with the change in st. v., l. 3, "that precious, purple flood" to "that *purple, precious* flood." It is in very extensive use in America and' other English-speaking countries. Orig. text in *Lyra Brit.*, 1867, p. 495.

Around the throne of grace we meet. *J. Montgomery.* [*Divine Worship.*] This hymn seems from its character and construction to have been written for one of the great Whitsuntide gatherings of S. School children in Sheffield, or for an occasion of a somewhat similar kind. No record, however, is found amongst the "M. MSS.," and we trace its first publication to his *Original Hymns*, 1853, No. 323, in 5 st. of 4 l., with the title, "Unity in Faith, Hope, and Feeling." Its use is limited.

Around Thy grave, Lord Jesus. *J. G. Deck.* [*Holy Baptism.*] 1st pub. in *Ps. & Hys.*, Lon., Walther, 1842, pt. i., No. 277, in 4 st. of 8 l. It is given in an unaltered form in Spurgeon's *O. O. H. Bk.*, 1866, No. 921 ; and in the Bapt. *Ps. & Hys.*, 1858, No. 699, with alterations made for that collection by Mr. George Rawson. The American collections, however, usually follow the original text.

Around Thy table, Holy Lord. *Mary Peters, née Bowly.* [*Holy Communion.*] 1st pub. in *Ps. and Hys.*, Lon., Walther, 1842, pt. i., No. 253, in 7 st. of 4 l. In 1847, it was included, with alterations by Mrs. Peters, in her *Hymns intended to help the Com. of Saints*, No. 39. The form in C. U., as in Dr. Walker's *Cheltenham Coll.* and others, is that of 1842. In the Amer. *Bapt. Praise Bk.*, N. Y., 1871, No. 795, the *Serv. of Song for Bapt. Churches*, Boston, 1871, No. 837, and others, there is a cento composed of the opening stanza of this hymn, together with st. v. and vi., from T. Cotterill's "Bless'd with the presence of their God," slightly altered.   [W. T. B.]

Around Thy table, Lord, we meet. [*Holy Communion.*] The hymn beginning with this first line in the 15th ed. of Stowell's *Sel.* (1877) is a cento the greater portion of which is an alteration and rearrangement of Mrs. Peters's hymn as above.

Arrayed in majesty divine, What power, &c. *J. Merrick.* [*Ps. civ.*] A cento from his paraphrase of Ps. civ. The original was pub. in his *Psalms, Translated or Paraphrased in English Verse*, 1765, in 140 lines beginning, "Awake, my soul, to hymns of praise," and repeated, with alterations and additions by the Rev. W. D. Tattersall, in his ed. of *Merrick*, 1797. The cento, as in Kippis's *Coll. of Hys.*, &c., 1795, and later editions, as also in one or two modern collections, is slightly altered from the original.

Arrayed in robes of virgin white. *G. Moultrie.* [*Martyrs.*] 1st pub. in the *Church Times*, June 10, 1865, under the signature "G. M.," and again in the Author's *Hymns & Lyrics*, 1867, in 6 st. of 6 l., with the heading, "Hymn for Festival of Martyrs,"

p. 157. In 1867 it was included in the *People's H.*, No. 210, with the substitution of the refrain for the last three lines of the original concluding stanza, thereby attaining uniformity throughout.

Art thou acquainted, O my soul? *C. Elliott.* [*Despondency.*] 1st printed in 1834, in the *Appendix* to the *Invalid's H. Bk.*, the entire *Appendix* being from Miss Elliott's pen. It is No. vi., is headed "Under Depression of Spirits," and based on Job xxii. 21. It is in 8 st. of 4 l., and is retained in subsequent editions.   [W. T. B.]

Art thou, Lord, rebuking nations. *W. H. Havergal.* [*In time of war.*] Written in September 1831, and printed for the Ch. Miss. Soc. Anniversary in Astley Church, Sept. 25, 1831, the text on that day being Amos viii. 11. It was in 5 st. of 6 l. Included in *Life Echoes*, 1883. [HAV. MSS.]

Art thou, sinner, sighing, weeping. *A. Midlane.* [*Invitation.*] Written on Dec. 4, 1879, and 1st pub. in the *Joyful Tidings H. Bk.*, 1880, No. 4, in 5 st. of 4 l. [E. MSS.], is in the metre of "Art Thou weary, &c.," and is frequently used in Mission services.

As birds their infant brood protect. *W. Cowper.* [*Divine Protection.*] Appeared in the *Olney Hymns*, 1779, Bk. i. No. 79, in 5 st. of 4 l. It is based on Ezek. xlviii. 35. It is found in several of the older hymnals, including *Cotterill's*, 1810 to 1819, *Bickersteth's*, 1833, and others, but its modern use is confined mainly to America.

As Christ our Saviour's gone before. *G. Thring.* [*Ascension.*] Written in 1863, and 1st pub. in his *Hymns Congregational and Others*, 1866, p. 42, and from thence has passed into the *Uppingham School H. Bk.*, the *Hy. Comp.*, Thring's *Coll.*, &c. It is based upon the Collect for Ascension Day.

As for Thy gifts we render praise. [*National Hymn.*] Licensed to Christopher Barker in 1578 and appended to the subsequent editions of the *Accession Service* in Q. Elizabeth's reign. It is headed "Anthem or Prayer for the preservation of the Church, the Queen's Majesty & the Realm, to be sung after evening prayer at all times." It has a chorus :—

" Save, Lord, and bless with good increase
Thy Church, our Queen and Realm, in peace."

After this chorus, which heads the Anthem, come 4 st. of 6 l. and the chorus added as above. The hymn has been reprinted in full in the Parker Society's edition of *Liturgies & Occasional Forms of Prayer in the reign of Queen Elizabeth*, Cambridge, 1847, p. 560, but the original spelling is not retained. In 1863 Dr. Kennedy gave in his *Hymnol. Christ.*, No. 736, a slightly varying form in the original spelling, but whether the variations are by him, or are due to differences in the early copies is unknown.   [W. T. B.]

As helpless as the [a] child who clings. *J. D. Burns.* [*Trust.*] 1st pub. in his little book of prayers and hymns, *The Evening Hymn*, 1857, No. 9, in 3 st. of 8 l., and headed "Childlike Trust." It is given in the *Appendix* to Dr. Walker's *Cheltenham Coll.*, the new ed. of Stowell's *Coll.* (1st ed., 1831), and others. It is a tender, childlike hymn, for private use, and is sometimes given as a hymn for children.

As high as the heavens, and as vast. *J. Conder.* [*Ps. xxxvi.*] The earliest date to which we have traced this version of Ps. xxxvi. is Conder's *Hymns of Praise, Prayer, &c.*, 1856, p. 13, in 5 st. of 4 l. In 1859 it was republished in the *New Cong.*, 1859, No. 49, in an unaltered form.

As many as in Adam die. *C. Wesley.* [*Holy Communion.*] This cento as in the *Meth. Free Ch. H. Bk.*, No. 711, is compiled from two of C. Wesley's *Short Hymns*, 1762, vol. ii., thus: st. i. from No. 248, on Matt. xxvi. 28; st. ii. from No. 88, on Matt. vii. 11. Full text in *P. Works*, 1868–72, vol. x. pp. 201 and 400.

As morn to night succeeds. *W. C. Dix.* [*Victory through Suffering.*] 1st pub. in the *People's H.*, 1867, No. 459, in 9 st. of 4 l.

As much have I of worldly good. *J. Conder.* [*Contentment.*] Appeared in his *Star in the East, and Other Poems*, 1824, pp. 60–61, in 4 st. of 6 l. and entitled "The Poor Man's Hymn, 'Hath not God chosen the poor of this world, rich in faith, and heirs of the kingdom,' James, ii. 5." In 1856 it was repeated in his *Hymns of Praise, Prayer, &c.*, p. 147, and headed with the text, "The disciple is not above his Master," Luke vi. 40. The congregational use of this hymn began with Bickersteth's *Christ. Psalmo.*, 1833, and Conder's *Cong. H. Bk.*, 1836, No. 433. It was repeated by the *N. Cong.*, 1859, No. 348, and Snepp's *Songs of G. & G.*, 1872, No. 740.

As nigh Babel's streams we sate. *G. Wither.* [*Ps. cxxxvii.*] A rendering of Ps. cxxxvii. in 6 st. of 6 l. from his *Version of the Psalms*, 1632, into the *Anthologia Davidica*, 1846, pp. 479–81. [**English Psalters,** § 10.]

As oft with worn and weary feet. *J. Edmeston.* [*Sympathy of Christ.*] This is No. iv. of his *Fifty Original Hymns*, Northampton, 1833, pp. 7–8. The hymn is founded on Heb. iv. 15, and is in 4 st. of 6 l. Orig. text, *Lyra Brit.*, 1867. Its use, which is somewhat extensive, is mainly confined to America. In the *Amer. Bapt. Praise Bk.*, N. Y., 1871, No. 984, it is attributed to "*Wilberforce*" in error.   [W. T. B.]

As panting, in the sultry beam. *John Bowdler.* [*Ps. xlii.*] A metrical rendering of Ps. xlii. from his *Select Pieces in Verse and Prose*, 1816, p. 60, in 2 parts, each containing 4 st. of 6 l. The first part is found in some of the older collections, including Elliott's *Ps. & Hys.*, 1835, and others, but has almost entirely fallen out of use in G. Brit.

It is still found in a limited number of American hymnals. Orig. text, *Lyra Brit.*, 1867, p. 83.

As pants the hart for cooling springs. *J. Merrick.* [*Ps. xlii.*] This metrical paraphrase of Ps. xlii. appeared in Merrick's *Psalms Tr. or Paraphrased in English Verse*, 1765, in 16 st. of 4 l. Various compilations have been made therefrom, as in Collyer's *Sel.* of 1812, the Islington *Coll.* of 1830, and others.

As pants the hart for cooling streams. *Tate and Brady.* [*Ps. xlii.*] Appeared in the *New Version of the Psalms*, 1696, in 6 double stanzas of 4 l. From it numerous compilations have been made extending from three stanzas to six, with T. & B.'s C. M. doxology sometimes added as in *H. A. & M.*, but usually without alterations, save in some special instances to be noted. A copy of the Book of Common Prayer with the *New Version* appended thereto being within the reach of all, full details of those arrangements from the original are uncalled for (see **Eng. Psalters,** § 13). The principal texts which have been altered are:—

1. That by the *Rev. H. F. Lyte*, which appeared in his *Spirit of the Psalms*, 1834, in 4 st. of 4 l., the third stanza being rewritten from *T. & B.* It is found in several collections both in G. Brit. and America, and may be recognized by comparing any given text with the *N. Cong.*, 57, or Snepp's *Songs of G. & G.*, 513.

2. Another version is found in Hall's *Mitre*, 1836. From Hall's MS. *Notes* in his private copy of the *Mitre*, we find the alterations were made by *E. Osler*, who assisted Hall in compiling that collection. This arrangement is limited in use.

As pants the hart for water-brooks. [*Ps. xlii.*] This L. M. version of Ps. xlii., of more than usual merit, is given anonymously in the *Presb. Hymnal*, Philadelphia, 1874.

As pants the wearied hart for cooling streams. *G. Gregory.* [*Ps. xlii.*] 1st pub. in 1787 in George Gregory's translation of Bp. Lowth's *Praelectiones Sacrae.* It is a *tr.* of the Bishop's Latin Version of Ps. xlii. It was given in an altered form in Cotterill's *Sel.*, 1819, p. 25, in 9 st. of 4 l., and repeated in Montgomery's *Christian Psalmist*, 1825, p. 58, with, in the latter case, the signature in the Index—"Bp. Lowth." It has come into C. U. in its altered form, both in G. Britain and America, but abbreviated. It is found in the Amer. *Prot. Epis. P. Bk. Coll.* as early as 1826.   [W. T. B.]

As showers on meadows newly mown. *T. Gibbons.* [*Divine Influence.*] Printed in 1784 as No. 28 in Bk. i. of his *Hymns adapted to Divine Worship*, in 6 st. of 4 l. It is founded on Ps. lxxii. 6, and headed "The Divine Influences resembled to Rain." In 1787 Dr. Rippon included it in his *Sel.*, No. 209. It was repeated in later editions, and from thence passed into many collections.

In America specially it has long been in C. U. in various forms, the most popular being st. iv., v., vi., as :—" As, in soft silence, vernal showers)"—sometimes altered to—" As *when in* silence, vernal showers."   [W. T. B.]

As some tall rock amidst the waves. *J. Newton.* [*St. Stephen.*] On "The Death of Stephen," in 6 st. of 4 l., and 1st pub. in the *Olney Hymns,* 1779, Bk. i., No. 120, and repeated, without alteration, in later eds. It was in C. U. as early as Cotterill's *Sel.,* 1810. It is seldom found in modern collections.

As the dew from heaven distilling. *T. Kelly.* [*Divine Worship*] This hymn is given in the collections in two forms :—(1.) The original, which was pub. by Kelly in the 1st ed. of his *Hymns, &c.,* 1804, p. 98, hy. xci., in 2 st. of 8 l., and based upon Deut. xxxii. 2. For some reason, not accounted for, Kelly omitted it from all subsequent editions of his *Hymns, &c.* The original text, however, is retained in the Bap. *Ps. & Hys.* 1858 and 1880, No. 812. In P. Maurice's *Choral H. Bk.,*1861, it is attributed to "Gwyther," in error. (2.) The second form is that given to it by J. Bulmer, in his *Hys. Orig. and Select,* 1835, Bk. iii., No. 176. It is found in modern editions of Rippon's *Sel.,* in Snepp's *S. of G. & G.,* and others, and can be detected at once by the third line of st. i., reading " *Richly unto all* fulfilling," for the orig. " And revives it, thus fulfilling." In this form the ascription is " *T. Kelly,* 1804, *J. Bulmer,* 1835."   [W. T. B.]

As the hart, with eager looks. *J. Montgomery.* [*Ps. xlii.*] 1st pub. in his *Songs of Zion,* 1822, in 4 st. of 6 l., and subsequently in various editions of his *Poetical Works.* It is only in limited use in G. Britain ; but is given in several American collections including *Songs for the Sanctuary,* 1865, and others. Also in Martineau's *Colls.,* 1840 and 1873.

As the sun's enlivening eye. *J. Newton.* [*Parting.*] Bull, in his life of Newton, p. 222, gives the following account of the origin of this hymn :—

" In November [1776] Mr. Newton underwent an operation for a tumour in his thigh. He was mercifully brought through it, and was very soon able to resume his ordinary duties. On this occasion he composed the 71st hymn, Bk. ii. in the *Olney Hymns.*"

As intimated, the hymn appeared in the *Olney Hymns,* 1779, in 7 st. of 4 l., and headed " Parting." It came into use in the older collections, and is still found in a few hymnals both in G. Britain and America. The hymn, " For a season called to part," which is given in the *New Cong.,* 1859, No. 848, and other collections, especially in America, is composed of st. iv., v., and vi. of this hymn.

As thy day thy strength shall be. *Frances R. Havergal.* [*Daily Strength.*] Written Jan. 1, 1859, and pub. in the *Sunday Magazine,* July 1867. It was also inscribed by the author in the Album of her sister (Miss M. V. G. Havergal), and from that has been lithographed in facsimile in Miss M. Havergal's *Memorials* of her. Miss Havergal's note on the hymn is :—

" The New Year's Bells were ringing in St. Nicholas' Church close to our Rectory (Worcester). I was sleeping with my sister Maria ; she roused me to hear them, and quoted the text, ' As thy days thy strength shall be,' as a New Year's Motto. I did not answer, but presently returned it to her in rhyme (the two first verses, I think). She was pleased, so I finished it the next day and gave it her. The last verse, with a slight alteration, was placed by my cousins on Aunt Izard's tomb, 1868, thus :—

" Now thy days on earth are past,
    Christ hath called thee home at last." [HAV. MSS.]

This hymn is not in C. U. in G. Brit., but it has been adopted by various American compilers, and is given in *Hys. and Songs of Praise,* N. Y., 1874, *Songs of Christian Praise,* N. Y., 1880, &c.

As to His earthly parents' home. *H. Alford.* [*Epiphany.*] Composed in 1865 for and 1st pub. in his *Year of Praise,* 1867, No. 36, in 4 st. of 4 l., and appointed for the " First Sunday after Epiphany." In 1879 it was transferred from thence to the *Meth. S. S. H. Bk.,* No. 144, in an unaltered form. It is also in other collections, including the Amer. *Hys. for the Church,* N. Y., 1869, No. 130.

As various as the moon. *T. Scott.* [*Changes in Life.*] Contributed to Dr. Enfield's *Hymns for Public Worship,* Warrington, 1772, No. 130, in 6 st. of 4 l., and headed, " The changes of human life appointed by God." In common with all the hymns in that collection it was unsigned. In 1795 it reappeared in the Unitarian hymn-book known as " Kippis's *Coll.* 1795," No. 379, with the signature " SCOTT." From the foregoing collections it has passed into various hymnals in G. Brit. and America, sometimes slightly altered, as " As changing as the moon." Orig. text as above. It is somewhat curious that Scott did not include this hymn in his *Lyric Poems and Hymns,* 1773.   [W. T. B.]

As when the deluge waves were gone. *Sir J. Bowring.* [*Joy after Sorrow.*] 1st pub. in the 3rd ed. of his *Matins and Vespers,* 1841, in 5 st. of 4 l., and entitled " Joy after Sorrow." In 1860 it was included unaltered in Miss E. Courtauld's *I's., Hys. and Anthems,* 1860, No. 370.

As when the weary traveller gains. *J. Newton.* [*Nearing Heaven.*] Included in the *Olney Hymns,* 1779, Bk. iii., No. 58, in 6 st. of 4 l. and entitled " Home in View," and continued in later editions of the same. It was given at an early date in the old collections, and is still in somewhat extensive use both in G. Britain and America, specially in the latter. In a great many cases the text is altered and abbreviated. The Bapt. *Ps. & Hys.* 1858, No. 576, is an exception in favour of the original. The Rev. R. Bingham has given a Latin rendering of the original with the omission of st. ii. in his *Hymnol. Christ. Lat.,* 1871, p. 67 :—" Ut quando fessus longâ regione viator."

As with gladness men of old. *W. C. Dix.* [*Epiphany.*] " Written about 1860 during an illness " (E. MSS.) and first printed in a small collection of hymns for private circulation, entitled *Hymns of Love and Joy,* and then in the trial copy of *H. A. & M.* In 1861 it was pub. in 5 st. of 6 l. almost simultaneously in the *St. Raphael's Hymnal*, Bristol, and in *H. A. & M.* From that date it has been incorporated in nearly every new hymnal and in new editions of the older collections in all English-speaking countries. Very slight variations in the text are sometimes found, as in the revised ed. of *H. A. & M.*, 1875. The author's authorized text is in *Ch. Hys.*, 1871, and Thring's *Coll.*, 1882. This hymn was brought into great prominence by Sir Roundell Palmer (Lord Selborne) in his paper on *English Church Hymnody*, at the Church Congress at York in 1866:—

"Of writers still living (the names of many, and of some very eminent, will at once occur to my hearers), I do not feel called upon to make myself, in this place, either the critic or the eulogist. But I may be permitted to say, that the most favourable hopes may be entertained of the future prospects of British Hymnody, when among its most recent fruits is a work so admirable in every respect as the Epiphany Hymn of Mr. Chatterton Dix ; than which there can be no more appropriate conclusion to this lecture, ' As with gladness men of old.' "

An anonymous hymn—"As in Eastern lands afar"—given in *Holy Song for all Seasons*, Lon., Bell and Daldy, 1869, in 4 st. of 8 l., is based upon, and is an imitation of "As with gladness men of old." We have not met with it elsewhere.   [J. J.]

Ascend Thy throne, Almighty King.
B. Beddome. [*Missions.*] A short hymn in 3 st. of 4 l. on behalf of Missions, which was given in Rippon's *Sel.*, 1787, No. 370, and repeated unaltered in all subsequent editions of the same. It was also included in R. Hall's ed. of Beddome's *Hymns*, 1817. The use of this hymn in G. Brit. has almost ceased, but in America it is given in a great number of collections, and is most popular.

Ascended Lord, accept our praise.
Bp. W. W. How. [*Thursday.*] Appeared in the *Parish Magazine*, as the first of three "Week-day Hymns," March, 1871, in 5 st. of 4 l. and appointed for Thursday. The same year it was included in *Ch. Hys.*, No. 58, with one change only, st. iii. l. 1, "*And* week " for " Yet, week," &c. This latter text, with the omission of st. ii., was also given in Thring's *Coll.*, 1882.

Aschenfeldt, Christoph Carl Julius, b. March 5, 1792, at Kiel. After studying at Göttingen he became, in 1819, pastor at Windbergen in Holstein. In 1824 he was appointed diaconus, and in 1829 chief pastor of St. Nicholas's Church in Flensburg ; as also, in 1850, Probst of the district of Flensburg, and in 1851 Superintendent of the German-speaking portion of the Duchy, when he resigned the last of these offices in 1854, being appointed oberconsistorialrath. He d. at Flensburg, Sept. 1, 1856. His 150 hymns, elegant in form, but marked with some of the eighteenth century coldness, were contributed to various works and appeared in collected forms as :—

(1) *Feierklänge. Geistliche Lieder und Gebete auf die Sonn- und Festtage*, Lübeck, 1823, containing 203 pieces,

of which 130 are by A. and the rest by his brother-in-law, Heinrich Schmidt, pastor in Eddelack, Holstein.
(2) *Geistliches Saitenspiel*, Schleswig, 1842, including 112 hymns, some of them altered versions of earlier pieces (*Koch*, vii. 156–159 ; *Allg. Deutsche Biog.*, i. 618).

Of his hymns the only one *tr.* into English is :—

Aus irdischem Getümmel. [*Following Christ.*] Founded on St. John xiv. 6, and contributed to Wehner's *Christosophisches G. B.*, Kiel, 1819, No. 40, in 3 sts. of 8 lines, entitled, " Jesus—the Way—the Truth—the Life," and being marked A—dt, has been erroneously ascribed to E. M. Arndt. Included in the *Feierklänge*, 1823, p. 269, and in various hymn-books, e.g. the Berlin *G. L. S.*, ed. 1863, No. 623. The *trs.* of this in C. U. are :—

1. **Amid life's wild commotion.** A full and good *tr.*, included as No. 226 in Bp. Ryle's *H. for the Church on Earth*, 1860, as No. 313 in *Kennedy*, 1863, and also in Schaff's *Christ in Song*, ed. 1869, p. 533, and *Lib. of Rel. Poetry*, ed. 1883, p. 601. The translator is unknown.

2. **Amid this world's commotion.** A good and full *tr.* by Mrs. Findlater in the 4th Series, 1862, of the *H. L. L.* (ed. 1862, p. 298 ; 1884, p. 218). Unaltered as No. 132 in Jellicoe's *Coll.*, 1867, and as No. 501 in Windle's *Coll.* [J. M.]

Ash, John, LL.D., b. at Stockland, Dorsetshire, cir. 1725, and studied for the Bap. Ministry under the Rev. Bernard Foskett, pastor of Broadmead, Bristol. He received a call from this congregation in 1748, removing to Pershore, on the death of Mr. Cooke, in 1751, d. at Pershore, Ap. 10, 1779. His works include an *English Dictionary ; Dialogues of Eumenes ;* and *Grammatical Institutes.* In conjunction with Dr. C. Evans, q. v., he edited the Bristol Bapt. *Collection of Hymns adapted to Public Worship.* Bristol, Pine, 1769, referred to in this Dictionary as the Bristol Bapt. *Coll. of Ash & Evans.* Dr. Ash was not a writer of hymns. [**Bapt. Hymnody.**]

Ask, and ye shall receive. *J. Montgomery.* [*Prayer.*] Written Sept. 16, 1832, and, according to notes by Montgomery on the original MS., sent in MS. to several persons at different times (M. MSS.). It was included by him in his *Original Hymns*, 1853, No. 67, in 5 st. of 4 l., and entitled, " Asking, Seeking, Finding." It is based upon Matt. vii. 7, 8. It is in C. U. both in G. Brit. and America, but in each case to a limited extent.

Ask, and ye surely shall receive. [*Prayer.*] A cento in the *Hys. for the Chapel of Harrow School*, 3rd ed. 1866, No. 243, in 5 st. of 4 l. The st. i.–v. we have been unable to trace, but st. vi. is from Montgomery's " Prayer is the soul's sincere desire," q. v.

Asleep in Jesus! blessed sleep. *Margaret Mackay.* [*Burial of the Dead.*] Appeared first in *The Amethyst ; or Christian's Annual for 1832* (Edin. W. Oliphant), edited by R. Huie, M.D., and R. K. Greville, LL.D., p. 258, in 6 st. of 4 l. It is thus introduced :—

"Sleeping in Jesus. By Mrs. Mackay, of Hedgefield. This simple but expressive sentence is inscribed on a tombstone in a rural burying ground in Devonshire, and gave rise to the following verses."

In reprinting it at p. 1 of her *Thoughts Redeemed*, 1854, Mrs. Mackay says the burying ground meant is that of Pennycross Chapel. She adds:—

"Distant only a few miles from a bustling and crowded seaport town, reached through a succession of those lovely green lanes for which Devonshire is so remarkable, the quiet aspect of Pennycross comes soothingly over the mind. 'Sleeping in Jesus' seems in keeping with all around."

From the *Amethyst* it has passed into numerous hymnals in G. Brit. and America, and was recently included, in full, and unaltered, as No. 241 in the Scottish *Presb. Hymnal*, 1876, and as No. 31 in the *Free Church H. Bk.*, 1882. In Thring's *Coll.*, 1882, No. 557, we have a cento composed of the first stanza of Mrs. Mackay's hymn, and st. ii.-vi. from Thring's "Asleep in Jesus, wondrous sleep," as noted below, but somewhat altered. This cento is unknown beyond Thring's *Coll.*   [J. M.]

Asleep in Jesus, wondrous sleep. *G. Thring*. [*Burial*.] Written in 1871, and 1st pub. in Preb. Hutton's *Lincoln Suppl.*, 1871; again, with music, in *Hymn Tunes*, 2nd series, by Henry Hugo Pierson, 1872; and in the author's *Hymns and Sacred Lyrics*, 1874, in 6 st. of 4 l. In 1880 it was included in the 1st ed. of Thring's *Coll.*, No. 235, but in the 2nd ed. it was superseded by the cento noted above.

Ἄσωμεν πάντες λαοί. *St. John of Damascus.* The Canon for St. Thomas's Sunday (i.e. Low Sunday), is based, in common with all the Greek Canons, upon the nine Canticles of the Greek service, with the omission of the second, as in the case of Christmas and Easter Days (see **Greek Hymnody, § xvii. 2,** and **Ἀναστάσεως ἡμέρα.**) It was written probably about the middle of the eighth century (St. John died about 780); and the Odes are found in the *Pentecostarion* in the service for St. Thomas's Sunday, commonly known in the Anglican Church as Low Sunday. The translations of the first four Odes are:—

Ode i. **Ἄσωμεν πάντες λαοί. Come, ye faithful, raise the strain..** This Ode is based upon the Canticle, "The Song of Moses," Ex. xv. The *tr.* is by J. M. Neale, and appeared in an article on "Greek Hymnology," in the *Christian Remembrancer*, April, 1859; and again in his *Hymns of the E. Church*, 1862, in 4 st. of 8 l. In 1868 it was included, with the substitution of a doxology for st. 4, in the *Appendix to H. A. & M.*, No. 291, and repeated in the revised edition of 1875. The *Hymnary* text, 1871–2, is, however, unaltered, but that of *Ch. Hys.* is both slightly altered and abbreviated. In all cases the translation is used as an Easter Hymn. In the original there is a refrain to every verse.

Ode iii. **Στερέωσόν με, Χριστέ. On the rock of Thy commandments.** This Ode is based upon the Canticle, "The Song of Hannah," 1 Sam. ii. *Tr.* by J. M. Neale as above. The tone of the *tr.* is graver than the original. Not in C. U.

Ode iv. **Μέγα τὸ μυστήριον. Christ, we turn our eyes to Thee,** is based on the Canticle, "The Song of Habakkuk," Hab. iii. *Tr.* by J. M. Neale as above, omitting st. iv. Not in C. U. as a congregational hymn, but is found in *Lyra Eucharistica*, 1863, p. 42.

Ode v. **Ἐκ νυκτὸς ὀρθρίζοντες. Thee, O Christ, we, very early rising,** is based on the Canticle, "The Song of Isaiah," Is. xxvi. 9–20. *Tr.* by J. M. Neale, ed. 1863, where the last two lines scarcely represent the original. Not in C. U. This Ode did not appear in the 1st ed. of Dr. Neale's *tr.* In Mr. Hatherley's annotated ed. the first line begins, "Reconciliation's plan devising."

The remaining Odes have not been rendered into English. Orig. Greek text, which dates from the middle of the 8th cent., is found in Modern Greek Service Books: and the various readings of Dr. Neale's *tr.* in 1st, 2nd, and 3rd ed. in Mr. Hatherley's annotated ed. of the same, 1882.   [J. J.]

Aspice, Infami Deus Ipse ligno. [*Passiontide*.] In the *Appendix* to the *Roman Breviary*, Bologna, 1827, it is the Hymn at Matins for the *Feast of the Passion of our Lord Jesus Christ*, to be observed on the Tuesday after Sexagesima Sunday. It is now adopted for use in England on the Friday after Sexagesima Sunday; by the Benedictine Order on Tuesday. See *Aspice ut Verbum Patris.*
          [W. A. S.]

Translations in C. U.:—

1. **See, where in shame the God of glory hangs.** By E. Caswall, 1st pub. in his *Lyra Catholica*, 1849, p. 65, in 5 st. of 4 l., and again in his *Hymns & Poems*, 1873, p. 56. This is given, with alterations in the *Hymnary*, 1872, No. 239, the *Catholic Hymnal*, No. 38, &c.

2. **Lo! on the inglorious tree.** By W. J. Blew. 1st printed for use in his church, and then pub. in his *Church Hy. & Tune Bk.*, 1852, Passiontide, No. 23, in 6 st. of 4 l., and from thence (much altered) into the *New Cong.*, 1859, No. 376, and the Rev. Howard Rice's *Sel.* of 1870, No. 40.

Aspice ut Verbum Patris a supernis. *Anon.* [*Passiontide*.] The only notice of this hymn in *Daniel* is in the Index at the end of vol. v., thus:—"Orat. Domini in monte Oliveti, Frib." In the *Appendix* to the *Roman Breviary* containing the offices said in particular districts and places, not universally, it is the hymn at first and second Vespers, and at Matins, on the Feast of the *Prayer of our Lord on Mount Olivet*, Tuesday after Septuagesima Sunday. This office has of late years been adopted in England (as well by religious orders as by seculars), and is appointed to be said on the Friday after Septuagesima Sunday (though the Benedictine Order observe it on the Tuesday). It is the first of a series of Friday services, which extend to Friday in Passion week, as follows:—

The Prayer in the Garden. The Commemoration of the Passion. The Crown of Thorns. The Spear and Nails. The Holy Winding Sheet. The Five Wounds. The Precious Blood. The Seven Dolours of the B. Virgin Mary.

As a general note on the hymns occurring in these offices we may remark that—

The festivals themselves were instituted at various times and in different localities: thus, that of the Holy Winding Sheet was granted, for observance on the 4th of May, to the Kingdom of Sardinia, by Pope Julius II. in 1506, in honour of this relic (or part of it) preserved at Turin; that of the Precious Blood to Mantua, because of a portion in the Collegiate Church of St. Andrew in that city; that of the Crown of Thorns to Paris and other places in France, to be observed on August the 11th, the anniversary of the day on which the relic was brought to Sens by Gauthier, Archbishop of that city, after having been obtained from the Venetians by the King St. Louis, afterwards deposited in the Sainte-Chapelle in Paris; that of the Five Wounds occurs in the modern Paris Breviary on the Friday after Ash-Wednesday. A relic of the Lance being preserved at Prague, Pope Innocent IV. (1243–1254) instituted the Office for observance in the German Empire, in the following terms: "Granted that the Lance and Nails, and other instruments used in the Lord's Passion for procuring our salvation, are everywhere to be venerated by the faithful in Christ; and year by year solemn offices are celebrated in the church, and take place, having respect to the Passion itself; nevertheless we consider it worthy and fitting if a solemn and special Feast should be celebrated and take place with reference to the special instruments of that Passion, and particularly in those regions in which the instruments are preserved." We see how the observance has extended. (See Guyet, *Heortolog.*, Lib. ii. &c., Cavalieri, *Comment. in Sacrae Rituum Congregationis Decreta*, Lib. i. *Cap.* iv. *Decret.* vii.).   [W. A. S.]

Translations in C. U. :—

1. See from on high, arrayed in truth and grace, by E. Caswall, first appeared in his *Lyra Catholica*, 1849, and again in his *Hymns & Poems*, 1873, p. 33, in 6 st. of 4 l., and entitled, "Prayer of Our Lord on Mount Olivet." The hymn :—

2. See from on high, the Source of saving Grace. in the *Hymnary*, 1872, No. 240, is an altered version of Caswall's translation.

Assembled at Thy great command

W. B. Collyer. [*Missions.*] 1st pub. in his *Hymns Partly Coll. and Partly Orig.*, 1812, No. 945, in 6 st. of 4 l., and entitled, "A Missionary Hymn for the Opening of the Service." It was repeated in later editions of the same collection, and also was adopted by several of the older compilers. It is rarely found in modern hymnals in G. Britain, but its use in America is extensive. Usually it is abbreviated to four or less stanzas.

Assembled in Thy house of prayer.

J. Montgomery. [*Divine Service.*] Written for the Sheffield S. S. Union, Whitsuntide gathering, 1840, and first printed on a fly-sheet for use at that time. The same year it was sent to Dr. Leifchild, and in 1842 it appeared as No. 31, in 6 st. of 4 l., in his collection of *Original Hymns*, and headed, "For a divine blessing on the ministry of the word." (M. MSS.) In Montgomery's *Original Hymns*, 1853, it reappeared with the same title as No. 98.

Astley, Charles Tamberlane, son of

John William Astley, of Dukinfield, Cheshire, born at Cwmllecoediog, near Mallwyd, North Wales, 12 May, 1825, and educated at Jesus Coll., Oxford (of which he was a Scholar), graduating B.A. 1847, M.A. 1849. Taking Holy Orders in 1849, he was Evening Lecturer, Bideford, 1849, Incumbent of Holwell, Oxford, 1850–54, Vicar of Margate, 1854–1864, and Rector of Brasted, 1864–78. Mr. Astley is the author of *Songs in the Night*, 1860. This work is composed partly of original hymns and partly of *trs.* from the German. The latter are noted in part under their first lines in German. Of the original hymns, "O Lord, I look to Thee," a

hymn for Private Use, in 10 st. of 4 l., is given in Stevenson's *H. for the Ch. and Home*, 1873, with the omission of st. viii. It was "written at Pisa, during illness, about December, 1858."

Astonished and distressed. B. Bed-

dome. [*Lent.*] Contributed to Rippon's *Sel.*, 1787, No. 40, in 4 st. of 4 l. and headed "The evil heart." From *Rippon* it has passed into several selections, and is found in use at the present time both in G. Britain and America, sometimes in an altered form. Orig. text as above. A revised version of the text was given in the posthumous ed. of Beddome's *Hymns*, edited by R. Hall, 1817, No. 469. This is not in C. U. In some collections this hymn is attributed to Toplady. This error arose out of the fact that Walter Row included it in his unsatisfactory ed. of Toplady's *Works*.   [W. T. B.]

At even ere the sun was set. H.

Twells. [*Evening.*] Written for and 1st pub. in the *Appendix* to *H. A. & M.*, 1868, in 7 st. of 4 l. It was originally in 8 st. The omitted st., No. iv., which has since been reinstated in *Church Hys.*, 1871, Thring's *Coll.*, 1882, and others, reads :—

> "And some are pressed with worldly care,
>   And some are tried with sinful doubt;
> And some such grievous passions tear,
>   That only Thou canst cast them out."

Since the first publication of the hymn in *H. A. & M.* in 1868, it has been included in almost every collection published from that date both in G. Britain and America. It ranks with the most popular of evening hymns. The text which has the widest acceptance is that of *H. A. & M.* Three changes, however, in the opening line are found in the collections. (1) "At even, ere 'the sun *did* set"; (2) "At even, *when* the sun was set"; and (3) "At even, *when* the sun *did* set." The last reading is adopted in Thring's *Coll.*, and, together with the second, is based upon the passage in St. Mark i. 32, "At even, *when the sun did set*, they brought unto Him all that were diseased," &c., in preference to the reading in St. Luke iv. 40, "Now, (revised, '*And*') *when the sun was setting.*" This preference has the support of the majority of commentators both ancient and modern, the ground taken being the acknowledged unlawfulness (with the Jews) of such a gathering of diseased persons until the sun had gone down, and the Sabbath was ended. The question was discussed by Mr. Twells and another in the *Literary Churchman*, June 9 and 23, 1882. The weight of evidence given therein was strongly in favour of the amended reading. Authorized text in *Church Hymns*.   [J. J.]

At evening time let there be light.

J. Montgomery. [*Evening.*] This hymn on Zech. xiv. 7, in 3 st. of 6 l. was written at Conway, N. Wales, in Sept. 1828, and is referred to by Holland in his *Memoirs* of Montgomery, vol. iv. p. 275. It was pub. in his *Poet's Portfolio*, 1835, pp. 181–2, and in his *Poetical Works*, 1841 and 1854. It is in extensive use in America. In 1858, the hymn "At evening time, when day is done," appeared in the Bap. *Ps. & Hys.* No. 996. This is repeated in later eds. of that collection, in the *Bapt. Hymnal*, 1879, and other hymnals. It is this hymn rearranged by George Rawson, and its right ascription is, "*J. Montgomery*, 1828, *rewritten by G. Rawson*, 1858."

At every motion of our breath.
J. Montgomery. [*Value of Time.*] Pub. in his *Christian Psalmist*, 1825, No. 512, in 5 st. of 4 l. and headed, "The Value of a Moment." In 1853 it was repeated in his *Original Hymns*, No. 224, but is not amongst the "*M. MSS.*" It is usually given in an abbreviated form. In J. H. Thom's *Hys.*, *Chants*, &c., 1858, it is in 9 st., and in the Scottish *Evang. Union Hymnal*, 1878, there are 4 sts.

At God's right hand in countless numbers. [*Anticipation of Heaven.*] This hymn, which is No. 1247 of the *Moravian H. Bk.* of 1849, and No. 403 of the Irish *Church Hymnal*, 1873, is thus composed : st. i. is a single verse written by Ignatius Montgomery as the opening of an "Ode" compiled for the funeral of the Rev. Christian Gottfried Clemens, who died at Bristol 14th Aug. 1815 ; st. ii. is a *tr.* of *Wenn schlägt die angenehme Stunde ;* and st. iii. a *tr.* of *O angenehme Augenblicke* (1766). These *trs.* are by *Bishop Molther* (cir. 1774), from the German of Christian Gregor. They appeared as single verses in the (*Moravian*) *Brethren's H. Bk.*, 1789, and were subsequently, in the edition of 1826, united by its editor, Bishop Foster, to the above stanza, "At God's right hand," &c, thus constituting the complete cento of 3 st. as in the Irish *Ch. Hymnal.* For these details we are indebted to Major Crawford's *Biog. Index* of that Hymnal.

At length the worst is o'er, and Thou art laid. *J. Keble.* [*Easter Eve.*] 1st pub. in his *Christian Year*, 1827, as the poem for Easter Eve, and continued in all subsequent editions of the same. It is in 8 st. of 8 l. In the Harrow School *Coll.* (var. dates), No. 115, the first stanza only is given.

At length this restless heart is still. *T. Davis.* [*Private Use.*] 1st pub. in his *Devotional Verse for a Month*, 1855, and from thence it passed into the Bapt. *Ps. & Hymns*, 1858, No. 966, in 5 st. of 4 l. To adapt it more fully for public worship the author re-wrote it for his *Hymns, Old & New*, &c., 1864, as, "Lord, I would count each moment Thine," No. 346. It was repeated in his *Annus Sanctus*, 1877, and is appointed for Nov. 16, and entitled "Walking at Liberty."

At the tomb where Christ hath been. *G. Moultrie.* [*Easter.*] Pub. in his *Hymns and Lyrics*, 1867, in 9 st. of 4 l., and entitled "Love is stronger than death." In the same year it was included in the *People's H.*, No. 120. In 1872 it was given in a revised form as "Near the tomb where Christ hath been," in the *Hymnary*, No. 294.

At Thy command, our dearest Lord. *I. Watts.* [*Holy Communion.*] This is No. xix. of his hymns "Prepared for the Holy

Ordinance of the Lord's Supper," in his *Hymns & S. Songs*, 1707, Bk. iii., in 4 st. of 4 l. It is headed "Glory in the Cross : or, Not ashamed of Christ crucified." In G. Britain its use is not equal to that to which it has attained in America.

At Thy feet, O Christ, we lay. *W. Bright.* [*Morning.*] 1st appeared in the *Monthly Packet* for October, 1867, and again in Canon Bright's *Hymns and Poems*, 2nd ed. 1874, in 5 st. of 6 l. In the revised ed. of *H. A. & M.*, 1875, it is given in full as No. 6, with the alteration in st. iii. l. 2 of "*on* Thy grace" to "*in* Thy grace."   [W. T. B.]

At Thy Feet, our God and Father. *J. D. Burns.* [*New Year.*] Printed in the Eng. Presb. *Ps. & Hys.*, 1867, No. 62, and in his *Remains* by Dr. J. Hamilton, 1869, pp. 224–5, in 6 st. of 4 l., and headed "New Year's Hymn," with the text, Ps. lxv. 2, prefixed. It has attained to a fair position in the hymnals of G. Britain, Canada, and America. The opening line sometimes reads, "At Thy feet, *O* God *our* Father."

At Thy transfiguration, Lord.   *C. Wordsworth, Bp. of Lincoln.* [*The Trans figuration.*] Appeared in his *Holy Year*, &c., 1862, No. 24, in 12 st. of 4 l., and again, with slight alterations, in later editions of the same, No. 26, but divided into two parts.

Atchinson, Jonathan Bush, b. at Wilson, New York, Feb. 17, 1840, and "licensed as a Methodist Preacher," Sept. 6, 1874. Of his hymns the following are the best known :—

1. **Behold the stone is rolled away.** [*Easter.*] This was Mr. Atchinson's first hymn. It appeared in the *S. School Times*, Dec. 1874. It is not in use in Great Britain.

2. **Fully persuaded, Lord, I believe.** [*Faith.*] Written in 1874 or 1875, and 1st pub. in *Gospel Hymns*, No. 1. It is given in I. D. Sankey's *Sac. S. & Solos*, No. 149, with music by W. F. Sherwin.

3. **I have read of a beautiful city.** [*Heaven.*] Written about the same time as the former, and pub. in *Gospel Hymns.* It is given in I. D. Sankey's *Sac. S. & Solos*, No. 403, with music by O. F. Presbrey.

4. **O crown of rejoicing that's waiting for me.** [*The Reward.*] This hymn is also in I. D. Sankey's *Sac. S. & Solos*, No. 174, where it is set to music by P. Bliss.   [F. M. B.]

Atkins, Lucy. [Wilson, L.]

Atkinson, John, D.D., b. at Deerfield, New Jersey, Sept. 6, 1835, and educated for the Ministry, which he now exercises in the American Methodist Episcopal Church. His very popular hymn, "We shall meet beyond the river," was written in Jan., 1867. It appeared in *Bright Jewels* (to music composed for it in Feb. 1867 by Hubert P. Main), in 1869, No. 43, in 4 st. of 8 l. From thence both words and music passed into I. D. Sankey's *Sac. S. & Solos*, No. 109.

Attend, and mark the solemn fast. *John Logan and John Morison.* [*True Fast-*

ing.] 1st appeared as No. 28 in the Draft Scottish *Translations and Paraphrases*, 1781, as a version of Isaiah lviii. 5–9, in 6 st. of 4 l. In the public worship ed. of that year issued by the Church of Scotland and still in use unaltered save st. vi., l. i. In the markings by the eldest daughter of W. Cameron (q. v.), given as the joint production of Logan and Morison. From the 1781 it has passed into a few modern hymnals, and is included as No. 65 in Rorison's *H. adapted to the Ch. Services*, 1860. In the Amer. *Sab. H. Bk.*, 1858, st. ii.-vi., beginning, "Do I delight in sorrow's dress," were included as No. 1148, while st. iii.-vi., beginning, "Let such as feel oppression's load," were included as No. 769 in Campbell's *Comp. H. Bk.*, 1837. [J. M.]

Attend, my ear, my heart rejoice. *P. Doddridge.* [*Reward of the Righteous.*] This hymn is not in the "D. MSS." It was pub. by J. Orton in Doddridge's *Hymns*, &c., 1755, No. 187, in 6 st. of 4 l., and headed, "The final Sentence, and Happiness of the Righteous." Its use is limited.

Attend, while God's exalted Son. *I. Watts.* [*New Creation.*] 1st pub. in his *Hymns & S. Songs*, 1709, Bk. ii., No. 130, in 6 st. of 4 l., and entitled, "The New Creation." It is in limited use in G. Britain and America. The hymn, "Mighty Redeemer, set me free," found in a few collections including the *New Cong.*, 1859, is composed of st. iv.-vi. of this hymn.

Attend, ye tribes that dwell remote. *John Morison.* [*The Hope of the Just.*] 1st appeared as No. 22 in the Draft Scottish *Translations and Paraphrases*, 1781, as a version of Isaiah xxxiii. 13–18, in 5 st. of 4 l. In the public worship ed. of that year, issued by the Church of Scotland and still in use, it is No. 21, with st. ii., ll. 2–4, and iii., ll. 3–4, rewritten. In the markings by the eldest daughter of *W. Cameron* (q. v.) ascribed to Morison. Included in a few modern hymnals as recently in Flett's *Coll.* Paisley, 1871, No. 296. Compare a recast of this beginning, "Attend, ye people, far and near," by Miss Leeson in her *Par. & Hys. for Cong. Singing*, 1853, No. 47.   [J. M.]

Attolle paullum lumina. [*Passiontide.*] The text of this hymn is in *Daniel* ii. p. 345; *Simrock*, p. 110; the *Corolla Hymnorum*, Cologne, 1806, p. 17, and is of unknown authorship and date. *Bäumker*, i. p. 495, cites it as in the *Sirenes Symphoniacae*, 1678. Dr. Neale dates it, in common with "Exite, Sion filiae, Videte, &c.," as being :—

"Clearly of the very latest date: certainly not earlier than the sixteenth, it may be the beginning of the seventeenth, century. Their intensely subjective character would be a sufficient proof of this: and their rhyme equally shows it. Feminine double rhymes, in almost all mediaeval hymns, are reserved for trochaic measures;—their use, as here, in iambics, gives a certain impression of irreverence which it is hard to get over. Notwithstanding the wide difference between these and mediaeval hymns, they possess, I think, considerable beauty, and perhaps will be more easily appreciated by modern readers." *Med. Hys.*, 3rd ed., 1867, p. 214.
                                              [W. A. S.]

Translations in C. U. :—

1. **Raise, raise thine eye a little way.** By J. M. Neale, appeared in the 1st ed. of his *Med. Hys.*, 1851, p. 148, in 7 st. of 7 l., being the first translation of this hymn into English. It is somewhat altered in the *Hymnary*, 1872, No. 248.

2. **O Sinner, lift the eye of faith**, is the above translation, in an altered form, made by the Compilers of *H. A. and M.*, and included in that collection in 1861. Concerning the alterations, Dr. Neale says in his 2nd ed. of the *Med. Hys.*, 1863, that "the alteration of the two trochaic into iambic lines" is "an improvement on the original metre." Although thus commended by Dr. Neale, the use of this form is almost exclusively confined to *H. A. and M.*

3. **O Sinners, lift your eyes and see.** By F. Pott, in his *Hymns*, &c., 1861, No. 189, in 6 st.
                                              [J. J.]

Atwood, Henry Adams Sergison, M.A., b. Jan. 13, 1800, educated at Queen's Coll., Oxford, graduating in 1822. He was successively Curate of Kenilworth, Chaplain to the Bishop of Lichfield, and Vicar, in 1839, of Ashleworth, Gloucestershire. In 1837 he published *Hymns for Private or Congregational Use, for every Sunday in the year.* He d. in 1877.

Auber, Harriet, daughter of Mr. James Auber, b. in London, Oct. 4, 1773. During the greater part of her quiet and secluded life she resided at Broxbourne and Hoddesdon, Herts, and died at the latter place on the 20th Jan., 1862. Miss Auber wrote devotional and other poetry, but only a portion of the former was published in her *Spirit of the Psalms*, in 1829. This collection is mainly her work, and from it some useful versions of the Psalms have been taken and included in modern hymn-books, about 20 appearing in Spurgeon's *O. O. H. Bk.*, 1866. Miss Auber's name is widely known, but it is principally through her exquisite lyric, "Our blest Redeemer, ere He breathed," and the Epiphany hymn, "Bright was the guiding star that led." (For criticism of her work, see **English Psalters, §. 17.**)

In addition to these and other hymns by Miss Auber, which are annotated under their respective first lines, the following are also in C. U., but principally in America :—

1. Arise, ye people, and adore. *Easter.*
2. As Thy chosen people, Lord. *Ps. lxviii.*
3. Can guilty man indeed believe? *Ps. xciv.*
4. Delightful is the task to sing. *Ps. cxlvii.*
5. Father of Spirits, Nature's God. *Ps. cxxxi.*
6. Hail, gracious Source of every good. *Ps. lxv.*
7. Hasten, Lord, the glorious time. *Ps. lxxii.*
8. Jehovah reigns, O earth, rejoice. *Ps. xcvii.*
9. Join, all ye servants of the Lord. *H. Scriptures.*
10. Jesus, Lord, to Thee we sing. *Ps. cx.*
11. O all ye lands, rejoice in God. *Ps. lxvi.*
12. O God our Strength, to Thee the song. *Ps. lxxxi.*
13. O praise our great and gracious Lord. *Ps. lxxxviii.*
14. On thy church, O power divine. *Ps. lxvii.*
15. Sweet is the work, O Lord. *Sunday.*
16. That Thou, O Lord, art ever nigh. *Ps. lxxv.*
17. The Lord, Who hath redeemed our souls. *Ps. xxxi.*
18. When all bespeaks a Father's love. *Ps. xi.*
19. When dangers press and fears invade. *Ps. lxii.*
20. When, O Lord, when life is o'er. *Ps. xv.*
21. Whom have we Lord, in heaven, but Thee. *Ps. lxxiii.*
22. Wide, ye heavenly gates, unfold. *Ascension.*

23. With hearts in love abounding. *Ps. xlv.*
24. With joy we hail the sacred day. *Sunday.*
25. Vainly through the night the ranger. *Ps. cxxvii.*

All these psalm-versions and hymns are from her *Spirit of the Psalms.* London, 1829.

[J. J.]

Auctor beate saeculi. [*Love of Jesus.*] This hymn is of unknown authorship and date. It is for the Feast of the Sacred Heart of Jesus; for which Feast in some eds. of the *Rom. Brev.* later than 1735 there are two distinct offices with different hymns; the day of observance being that following the Octave of Corpus Christi (viz. Friday before the 3rd Sunday after Whitsunday). *Auctor beate saeculi* is the hymn at second Vespers in the *first* office when the Feast is kept on its own day, and with the rank of a greater double; and at *both* Vespers when the Feast is transferred, or kept with the rank of a double of the first or second class, the reason being that in the former case the *first* Vespers are superseded by the second Vespers of the Octave of Corpus Christi. In England the *first* office is appointed to be said on the Sunday after the Octave of Corpus Christi, with the rank of a double of the second class; religious orders, as a rule, observing it on the Friday succeeding that Octave, thus the hymn occurs at both Vespers. In addition to modern eds. of the *Rom. Brev.* the full text is given in *Daniel*, iv. p. 311, but without note or comment. [W. A. S.]

Translations in C. U. :—

1. **Jesu, Creator of the world.** By E. Caswall. 1st pub. in his *Lyra Catholica*, 1849, p. 116, and in his *Hymns and Poems*, 1873, p. 66, in 6 st. of 4 l. This *tr.* is found in several collections, at times slightly altered, but generally as rendered by Caswall.

2. **O Thou, by Whom the worlds were framed.** This is based upon Caswall's *tr.* It is No. 347 in *Kennedy*, 1863; and, altered to "Thou blest Redeemer of the world," No. 82 in *Sarum*, 1868. In the latter it is appointed for "Sexagesima."

Audi, benigne Conditor. *St. Gregory the Great.* [*Lent.*] This hymn is given in St. Gregory's *Works* (see Migne's *Patrologia, tom.* 78, *col.* 849, 850.) In the *Roman Brev.* 1632 it occurs, almost unaltered, as the hymn at Vespers on the Saturday before the 1st Sun. in Lent, to the Saturday before Passion Sunday (the last exclusively), when the Ferial Office is said, Sundays included. In the *Hymn. Sarisb.* Lond., 1851, it is given as the hymn at Lauds on the 1st Sun. in Lent, and daily to the 3rd Sun. In *York* and *St. Alban's*, it is the hymn for the first four Saturdays in Lent and the following Sundays at Vespers. At *Canterbury* (from a MS. at Lambeth, No. 538, of the 15th cent. which states "these are the offices to the observance of which every monk of Christ Church, Canterbury, is held bound"), it is on Saturdays and Sundays, in Lent, at Vespers. At *Evesham*, 1st and 2nd Sun. at Vespers, and at *Worcester* and *St. Andrew-de-Bromholm (Norfolk)*, it is set down as a Vesper hymn in Lent. In the *British Museum* it is found in three MSS. of the 11th cent. (Harl. 2961, f. 236 b; Vesp. D. xii., f. 51; Jul. A. vi., f. 45). In the *Latin Hys. of the Anglo-Saxon Church*

1851, p. 62, it is from an 11th cent. MS. at Durham. The text is also in *Daniel*, i., No. 149, and with additional notes at iv. p. 121; in *Wackernagel*, i., No. 100; Card. Newman's *Hymni Eccl.*, 1838 and 1865, and others.

[W. A. S.]

Translations in C. U. :—

1. **Father of mercies, hear, Thy pardon, &c.** By Bp. G. W. Doane, 1st pub. in his *Songs by the Way*, 1824, from whence it passed into Hall's *Mitre*, 1836; Cooke & Denton's *Hymnal*, 1853; the *Sarum*, 1868; *New Mitre*, 1875; *Kennedy,* 1863, No. 394, and others. (Orig. *tr.* in *Songs by the Way*, ed. 1875.) This *tr.* is sometimes attributed, as in Miller's *Singers & Songs*, p. 12, to Dr. Neale, in error.

2. **Thou loving Maker of mankind.** By E. Caswall, from the *Rom. Brcv.* text. Appeared in his *Lyra Catholica*, 1849, p. 70, in 5 st. of 4 l., and again in his *Hymns & Poems*, 1873, p. 39. It is given in several Roman Catholic and other collections, and altered as, "O loving Maker of mankind," in the *Hymnary*, 1872, No. 211.

3. **Benign Creator, hear.** By W. J. Blew, from the *Paris Brcv.*, printed on broadsheet for use in his church, circ. 1850, and pub. in his *Church Hy. & Tune Bk.*, 1852, in 5 st. of 4 l.

4. **O Maker of the world, give ear.** By J. M. Neale. Appeared in the *Hymnal N.*, 1852, from whence it passed into Murray's *Hymnal*, 1852, and several later collections.

5. **Father of Mercies, hear, Before Thy throne, &c.** By J. A. Johnston. Contributed to his *English Hymnal*, 1852 to 1861, in 5 st. of 4 l.

6. **O Merciful Creator, hear, Regard our, &c.** By J. D. Chambers, in his *Lauda Syon*, 1857, i. p. 129, in 5 st. of 4 l. This has been repeated in the ed. of 1866; in Dr. Irons's *Hymns*, 1866; the *People's H.*, 1867, &c.

7. **O Merciful Creator, hear, To us in pity, &c.** This rendering in *H. A. & M.*, 1861 and 1875, Pott's *Hymns*, 1861, *Ch. Hys.*, 1871, &c., is a cento from the *trs.* of Neale, Chambers, and others. It is said in the Index to *H. A. & M.* to be by the "Rev. J. M. Neale, D.D., and Compilers: from the Latin." It seems from Mr. Ellerton's note in *Ch. Hymns*, that the Rev. F. Pott was one of those "Compilers," and that to him this arrangement is mainly due.

8. **O gracious Father, bend Thine ear.** Two hymns, beginning with this same stanza, are in C. U. (1) in the *Parish H. Bk.* 1863; and (2) in Chope's *Hymnal*, 1864. The latter is the *Parish H. Bk.* text, with another st. (ii.).

Translations not in C. U. :—
1. O Merciful Creator! hear our prayer. By *Drummond*, 1619, in Heber's *Hymns*, 1827.
2. Thou gracious Author of our days. *J. Chandler*, 1837.
3. Hear, our all-gracious Father, hear. *Mant*, 1837.
4. Merciful Maker, hear our call. *Williams*, 1839.
5. Gracious Creator, hear. *Copeland*, 1848.
6. Father of Mercies, pitying hear. *Rorison*, 1851.
7. O merciful Creator, heed. *Hewett*, 1859. [J. J.]

Audi nos, Rex Christe. *Anon.* [*Processional.*] 1st pub. from a MS. of the 11th cent. at Clermont, by Du Méril, in his *Poésies Populaires Latines du moyen âge*, Paris, 1847, pp. 56–58, together with an extensive note.

The text was repeated by *Daniel*, iv. p. 171, with reference to Du Méril. It is a Pilgrim's song, and as such it might be used as a Processional. Dr. Neale has printed Du Méril's text (without the various readings) in his *Hymni Ecclesiae*, 1851, p. 227; and Mr. Ellerton (with the readings) in his *Notes on Church Hymns*, 1881, No. 440, where he falls into the error of giving the date of the *first*, 1843, instead of the *second*, 1847, volume of Du Méril's work.

[W. A. S.]

Translations in C. U. :—

1. **O Christ, our King, give ear.** By J. M. Neale, 1st pub. in his *Med. Hymns*, 1851, in 8 st. of 3 l. including the chorus. The S. P. C. K. *Ch. Hymns*, 1871, No. 440, omits the chorus and st. ii.

2. **O blessed Trinity,** No. 299, in the *Hymnary*, is Dr. Neale's rendering expanded into 7 st. of 6 l. It was designed as a Processional for the Rogation Days.

Audimur: almo Spiritus. *C. Coffin.* [*Whitsuntide.*] From his *Hymni Sacri*, Paris, 1736, p. 57, as a Hymn for Whitsuntide. In the revised *Paris Breviary*, 1736, it is the Hymn for Lauds at Whitsuntide; as also in Lyons and other modern French Breviaries. Text in Card. Newman's *Hymni Ecclesiae*, 1838 and 1865. The *tr.* in C. U. is :—

Lo, the Father hears our prayer. By C. S. Calverley, made for and 1st pub. in the *Hymnary*, 1872, No. 321.

Translations not in C. U. :—

1. Our prayer is heard; the holy Dove. *J. Chandler*, 1837.

2. Now our prayers are heard on high. *I. Williams*, 1839.

3. We are heard: the gentle Spirit. *Blew*, 1852.

4. Our prayers are heard : the Spirit blest. *Chambers*, 1857.

Auf, auf, ihr Reichsgenossen. *Johann Rist.* [*Advent.*] 1st pub. in his *Sabbatische Seelenlust*, Lüneburg, 1651, p. 4, in 12 st. of 8 l., entitled, "On the Gospel of the First Sunday in Advent, which is written by the Holy Evangelist Matthew in his Gospel at the 21st Chapter." Included as No. 16 in the Leipzig *Vorrath*, 1673, and recently as No. 1 in the *Unv. L. S.*, 1851.

Translations in C. U. :—

1. **Arise, the Kingdom is at hand.** A *tr.* of st. i.–iii., ix., xii. by Miss Winkworth in the 2nd series, 1858, of her *Lyra Ger.*, p. 4, and repeated as No. 22 in her *C. B. for England*, 1863. Included in full as No. 438, in J. L. Porter's *Coll.*, 1876. The *trs.* of ll. 1–4 of st. i.–iii., xii. were included as No. 66 in Boardman's *Coll.*, Philadelphia, 1861, and an adaptation in 7 st. of C. M., as No. 115 in the Pennsylvania Luth. *Ch. Bk.*, 1868.

2. **Arise, ye heirs of glory.** A *tr.* of st. i, iii., xii., signed F. C. C. as No. 7 in Dr. Pagenstecher's *Coll.*, 1864.

3. **Awake! sons of the Kingdom, the King, &c.** A *tr.* of st. i.–iii., ix.–xii. based on Miss Winkworth's *tr.* of the same, as No. 16 in the Ohio Luth. *Hymnal*, 1880. [J. M.]

Auf, auf, weil der Tag erschienen. *J. A. Freylinghausen.* [*Advent.*] 1st pub. as

No. 1 in his *Neues geistreiches G. B.*, 1714, in 11 st. of 7 l., reprinted in Grote's ed. of his *Geistliche Lieder*, 1855, p. 1, and included as No. 129 in the Berlin *G. L. S.* ed. 1863.

Translations in C. U. :—

1. **Wake! the welcome day appeareth.** A good *tr.*, omitting st. vii., viii., by Miss Cox in her *Sac. H. from the German*, 1841, p. 3, and repeated with st. ix. slightly altered in her *H. from the German*, 1864, p. 23. Her *trs.* of st. i.–iv., xi., were included as No. 17 in Rorison's *Coll.* 1851 ; of st. i., iii., vi., x., as No. 233, in Hedge and Huntington's *Coll.*, 1853, and Robinson's *Songs for the Sanctuary*, 1865, No. 1176; and of st. i.–iv., xi., in J. L. Porter's *Coll.*, 1876, No. 404.

2. **Wake, oh wake, the day ariseth.** A *tr.* of st. i., iv., xi., by *A. T. Russell*, as No. 31 in his *Ps. & Hymns*, 1851. [J. M.]

Aufer immensam, Deus, aufer iram. [*National Fast.*] 1st pub. in *Vermanung an gantze Deutsche Nation*, Wittenberg, 1541, and included, altered, in *Hymni aliquot sacri, etc.*, *Collectore Georgio Thymo*, 1552, where it is marked as "author uncertain." Thence in *Wackernagel*, i. p. 271, in 8 st. of 4 l. It has been *tr.* into English through "Nimm von uns, Herr, du treuer Gott," a free *tr.*, in 7 st. of 6 l., by Martin Moller in his *Meditationes Sanctorum Patrum*, Görlitz, 1584, entitled "A beautiful daily prayer in all time of need." Thence in *Wackernagel*, v. p. 56, and as No. 579 in the *Unv. L. S.*, 1851.

The *trs.* are : (1) "Remove from us, O faithful God," by J. C. Jacobi, 1722, p. 123 (ed. 1732, p. 188, altered). (2) "Think on Thy Son's so bitter death," a *tr.* of st. vi. "Gedenk an dein Sohn's bittern Tod," as No. 398 in pt. ii., 1746, of the *Moravian H. Bk.* (ed. 1754, pt. i., No. 218). [J. M.]

Auferstehn, ja auferstehn wirst du. *F. G. Klopstock.* [*Burial of the Dead.*] This beautiful little poem, hardly to be called a hymn, on the Resurrection of the Body, was written after the death, on Nov. 28, 1758, of his first wife, Meta Moller, and 1st pub. in his *Geistliche Lieder*, vol. i., Copenhagen, 1758, p. 80, in 5 st. of 5 l. It was sung by the assembled thousands when, on March 22, 1803, he was laid to rest at Meta's side in the churchyard of Ottensen, near Altona. Commonly used also at Easter. Included as No. 1512 in the Berlin *G. L. S.* ed. 1863. The *tr.* in C. U. is :—

Thou my dust awaking from brief rest, by A. T. Russell, as No. 257 in his *Ps. & Hymns*, 1851, in 5 st. Rather based on the German than an exact translation. Included, beginning "Thou wilt raise our bodies from brief rest," as No. 744 in *Kennedy*, 1863.

Translations not in C. U. :—

(1) "Yes! soon away shall death's deep slumbers roll," by Sir J. Bowring in his *Hymns*, 1825, No. 99. (2) "Yes! thou wilt rise, wilt rise as Jesus rose," in W. Nind's *Odes of Klopstock*, 1848, p. 309. (3) "Arise, yes, yes, arise, O thou my dust," in Dr. A. Baskerville's *Poetry of Germany*, 1854 (ed. 1876, p. 25), and thence in the Gilman-Schaff *Lib. of Rel. Poetry*, ed. 1883, p. 774. (4) "Thou shalt rise! my dust thou shalt arise," by Miss Borthwick in *H. L. L.* 1855 (1862, p. 165, 1884, p. 128), and altered in Schaff's *Christ in Song*, 1869, p. 652 (ed. 1879, p. 520). (5) "Rise thou shalt, yes, rise," by J. S. Stallybrass, in the *Tonic Sol-fa Reporter*, July, 1857. (6) "Rise again! yes, thou shalt rise again, my dust,"

by Miss Fry, 1859, p. 172. (7) "Arise again, arise again," in C. S. Bere's *Garland of Songs*, 1861 (later eds. p. 29). (8) "Rise again! yes, rise again wilt thou," by Miss Winkworth, 1869, p. 333.   [J. M.]

Augusta, Johann, seems to have been born at Prag about the year 1500. He was consecrated Bishop of the Bohemian Brethren in 1532, became president of their "select council" in 1537, and d. at Jung-Bunzlau, Bohemia, Jan. 13, 1572. Two of his hymns, written in Bohemian, have passed into English through the German as follows :—

i. **Aj jak jsou milí tvoji přibytkové.** [*The Christian Church.*] Founded on Ps. lxxxiv. In the Bohemian Brethren's *H. Bk.*, 1559, f. 166, in 18 st. *Tr.* into German by J. Geletzky in the *Kirchengeseng*, Prag, 1566, and thence in *Wackernagel*, iv. p. 355, beginning "O wie sehr lieblich sind all dein Wohnung." *Tr.* from the German by J. Gambold as No. 269 in pt. i. of the *Moravian H. Bk.*, 1754 (1849, No. 763), beginning, "How amiable Thy habitations are."

ii. **Budiž veleben Pán Bůh náš pochválen.** [*The Christian Church.*] Founded on Ps. xlviii. In the Bohemian Brethren's *H. Bk.*, 1561. f. 168, in 8 st. *Tr.* into German by P. Herbert in the *Kirchengeseng*, 1566, and thence in *Wackernagel*, iv. p. 420, beginning, "Gott woll'n wir loben." The *trs.* from the German are (1) "Praise our God gracious," by J. Gambold, as No. 268 in pt. i. of the *Moravian H. Bk.*, 1754. (2) "Praise God for ever," as No. 491 in the *Moravian H. Bk.*, 1789 (1849, No. 761).   [J. M.]

Aurea luce et decore roseo. [*SS. Peter and Paul*]. This hymn is probably of the 6th cent. It has generally been ascribed to Elpis, wife of the philosopher Boethius; but *Mone*, on the ground that it is not in classical metre, thinks that this is improbable. *Mone's* text, No. 684, is from MSS. of the 14th and 15th cent. *Daniel*, i., No. 137, gives the text in 6 st., along with the *Roman Breviary* version; with further notes at iv. pp. 164, 371, including readings from a 9th cent. MS. at Bern. Among the *British Museum* MSS. it is found in two of the 11th cent. (Vesp. D., xii. f. 85 b.; Jul. A., vi. f. 55). The text of an 11th cent. MS. at Durham is given in the *Lat. Hys. of the Anglo-Saxon Ch.*, 1851, p. 105.

This hymn is found in many Breviaries, *e.g.*, the older *Roman*, the *York*, and the *Sarum*, assigned to the vigils of SS. Peter and Paul, &c. St. iii. for St. Peter, beginning, "Jam bone pastor Petre," was used separately for the festivals of St. Peter's Chair and St. Peter's Chains. St. iv. for St. Paul, beginning, "Doctor egregie, Paule," was also used separately for the festivals of his Conversion, &c.

In the revised *Roman Breviary*, 1632, it was considerably altered, st. i. beginning "Decora lux aeternitatis auream;" st. iii. beginning "Beate pastor Petre;" and st. iv. beginning "Egregie doctor Paule." This form is also in *Daniel*, i., No. 137.   [J. M.]

Translations :—

1. **Aurea luce et decore roseo.** This has been *tr.* by J. D. Chambers in his *Lauda Syon*, pt. ii., 1866, as "With golden splendour bright." This, in a form so altered as almost to constitute a new *tr.*, was given in the *Antiphoner & Grail*, 1880, and the *Hymner*, 1882, No. 116 : as "With golden splendour, and with roseate loveliness."

2. **Decora lux aeternitatis auream.** *Tr.* by E. Caswall in his *Lyra Catholica*, 1849, p. 159, and his *Hymns*, 1873, p. 87, as "Bathed in Eternity's all-beauteous beam;" and by F. W. Faber in his *Jesus & Mary*, &c., 1849, as "It

is no earthly summer's ray." This latter *tr.* is adopted by some Roman Catholic hymn-books for Missions and Schools, and is also in the Marquess of Bute's ed. of the *Rom. Brev.*, 1879.

3. **Beate pastor Petre clemens accipe.** *Tr.* by E. Caswall in his *Lyra Catholica*, 1849, p. 128, and his *Hymns*, 1873, p. 70. This *tr.* is adopted by the Marquess of Bute, *Rom. Brev.*, 1879, as "Peter, blest Shepherd, hearken to our cry."

4. **Egregie doctor Paule mores instrue.** *Tr.* by E. Caswall in his *Lyra Catholica*, 1849, p. 129, and *Hymns*, 1873, p. 71, as "Lead us, great teacher Paul, in wisdom's ways." Also adopted by the Marquess of Bute.   [J. J.]

Aurora jam spargit polum. [*Saturday Morning.*] This hymn is ascribed to St. Ambrose; but, not being quoted by early writers, it is not received as *certainly* genuine by the Benedictine editors; it may be his nevertheless. It is the Hymn at Lauds on Saturdays in the *Roman Brev.*, 1632, when the Ferial Office is said, from the Sunday after the Octave of the Epiphany to the first Sunday in Lent, and from the Octave of Corpus Christi to Advent. For the text in the *Rom. Brev.*, placed in juxtaposition with the original version, see *Daniel*, No. 47. See also the editions of St. Ambrose (Migne's *Patrol.*, tom. 17, the fourth and last of the works of that Father). Also in *Thomasius*, ii. p. 413, *Clichtoveus*, and others.

In the *Mozarabic Breviary*, ed. 1775, it is given among the hymns as "A hymn to be said on Saturdays in Lent at Matins." (*Migne's Patrol.*, tom. 86, col. 897.) In the *Hymnarium Sarisburiense*, Lond., 1851, p. 58, it is given as the hymn for Ferial Offices on Saturdays at Lauds from the Sunday after the Octave of the Epiphany to Lent, and from the Octave of Corpus Christi to Advent. *York, Hereford, Evesham*, &c., appear to have had the same use. (See p. 43, where the Sunday after the Octave of the Epiphany is called the Sunday *Domine, ne in irâ*, from the beginning of the responsory after the first Lesson at Matins : so the Sunday *Deus omnium* is named from a responsory at Matins on the Sunday after the Octave of Corpus Christi.) The variations of *York, Worcester, Evesham*, &c., are also given in that work. It is also in three MSS. of the 11th cent. in the *British Museum* (Harl. 2961, f. 225 ; Vesp. D. xii., f. 25 b ; Jul. A. vi., f. 30 b), and in the *Latin Hys. of the Anglo-Saxon Church*, 1851, from an 11th cent. MS. at Durham.

Mone, i. p. 372, cites it as in a MS. in the Town Library at Trier, probably of the 8th century; and *Daniel*, iv. p. 40, refers to a Rheinau MS. of the 10th cent. now at Zürich, in which it is also found.

The text of this hymn is also given in Card. Newman's *Hymni Ecclesiae*, 1838 and 1865; Macgill's *Songs of the Christian Creed and Life*, Lond., 1876; *Simrock*, p. 8; and by others.   [W. A. S.]

Translations in C. U. :—

1. **The morn has spread its crimson rays.** By R. Campbell, from the *Rom. Brev.*, made for and 1st pub. in his *St. Andrew's Hymnal*, Edin., 1850, p. 73, in 6 st. of 4 l., and given in later Scottish Episcopal collections,

2. Dawn sprinkles all the East with light. Contributed to the *Hymnal N.*, 1852, in 4 st. of 4 l. It is also No. 13 of Skinner's *Daily Service Hymnal*; and as "Dawn purples all the east with light," in the *Hymnal* of the American Protestant Episcopal Church, 1872. From the fact of its appearing in the *Hymnal N.* it has usually been attributed to Dr. Neale. On his own authority this is an error. ("s. mss.")

3. Now morn is o'er the zenith spread. By J. D. Chambers, from his *Lauda Syon*, 1857, p. 33, into the *People's H.*, 1867, No. 432, in 4 st. of 4 l.

Translations not in C. U. :—
1. With dawn's faint streaks the heaven, &c. *Mant*, 1837.
2. Forth from the glorious eye of morn. *Hymn. Anglic.* 1844.
3. Morn lights up earth's canopy. *Bp. Williams*, 1845.
4. The dawn is sprinkling in the east. *Caswall*, 1849.
5. The dawn is dappling o'er the sky. *Copeland*, 1848.
6. Now morning sprinkles all the sky. *Macgill*, 1876.

[J. J.]

Aurora lucis dum novae. *N. Le Tourneaux.* [*Easter.*] In the revised *Paris Breviary*, 1736, this hymn is appointed as the hymn at Lauds on the Sunday after Easter-day, and afterwards at Lauds in the Ferial Office from Easter to the Ascension. The text is given in Card. Newman's *Hymni Ecclesiae*, 1838 and 1865. It is *tr.* as :—

1. **Morn's roseate hues have decked the sky.** By Wm. Cooke, written for the *Hymnary*, and included therein, 1872, No. 267. From the *Hymnary* it passed into Thring's *Coll.*, 1882, No. 200. The refrain is not in the original.

2. **O come, and with the early morn.** By Bp. J. R. Woodford, in *Hys. for the Christian Seasons*, 2nd ed., 1855; the *Parish H. Bk.*, 1863, No. 55, &c.

Translations not in C. U. :—
1. The new morn hath risen. *I. Williams*, 1839.
2. The orient beams of Easter Morn. *J. D. Chambers*, 1857.

[J. J.]

Aurora lucis rutilat. [*Easter.*] This hymn is ascribed to St. Ambrose, but was not received among his undoubted works by the Benedictine editors. (See Migne's *Patrol.*, tom. 17; the 4th vol. of the works of St. Ambrose.) It *may* be his; but is not specially referred to as such by any early writer.

The text is in *Daniel*, i., No. 79 (the revised *Roman Breviary* version being given side by side with the original), who says it may be found *everywhere in old Breviaries, but for the most part mutilated.* It is No. 19 of the *Junius* ms. of the 8th cent., and *Mone*, No. 141, has it from a ms. of the Abbey of Reichenau of the beginning of the 9th cent., and from later mss. at Karlsruhe, &c. Amongst the *British Museum* mss. it is in two of the 11th cent. (Vesp. D. xii., f. 70; Jul. A. vi., f. 49); and in the *Latin Hys. of the Anglo-Saxon Ch.*, 1851, p. 84, it is printed from an 11th cent. ms. at Durham.

It will be found in the *Hymn. Saris.* Lond., 1851, pp. 94, 95; headed "Ad Matutinas, Quotidie usque ad Ascen. Dom.," "At Matins, daily, to the Ascension of the Lord" (i.e. commencing on Low Sunday, the Octave of Easter). This part ends at line 20. Then

follows, at Lauds, *Sermone blando Angelus* (to end). So the *York* use. At *Canterbury, St. Alban's, St. Andrew de Bromholm* (Norfolk), it would appear that *Aurora lucis* was said at Lauds entire. *Worcester* says "*Sermone blando Angelus* dicitur cum *Aurora :*" the two hymns are said one with the other : one, it may be, at Matins, the other at Lauds.

In the *Mozarabic Breviary* (Toledo, 1502, f. 297) it is given as the Hymn in the "Ordo Primi" in Easter-tide.

The revised version of this hymn, made for the *Roman Breviary*, 1632, begins **Aurora coelum purpurat** : and is therein divided as follows : (1) Lines 1–16 of the original became in a revised form the hymn for the Ferial Office at Lauds from Low Sunday to (exclusively) the Ascension; (2) Lines 17–32 of the entire hymn, *Tristes erant Apostoli* (with doxology of eight lines) are assigned to the *Common of Apostles and Evangelists in Easter-tide* (*Tempore Paschali*) at 1st and 2nd Vespers and at Matins; (3) Lines 32 to end, *Paschale mundo gaudium* (in the original *Claro Paschali gaudio*), to Lauds of the same *Common of Apostles and Evangelists.* This division of the latter part, for the *Common of Apostles and Evangelists*, was made by Pope Pius V. (Gavanti, *Thes. Sacrorum Rituum.*)

[W. A. S.]

In annotating the translations of this hymn, for the sake of unity and clearness, two divisions are given : (i.) *Trs.* of the *Original Text* (sometimes with variations), and (ii.) those *trs.* which are from the *Roman Breviary.*

I. The Original Text.

In rendering the hymn into English some translators have given the text in full, whilst others have taken a part only. Those in full, together with their use in modern hymnals, are :

1.—i. Aurora lucis rutilat. "Light's glittering morn bedecks the sky."

ii. Sermone blando Angelus. "With gentle voice the angel gave."

This *tr.* by Dr. Neale, in two parts, was published in the *Hymnal N.*, in 1852, and continued in later editions. Pt. i. consists of lines 1–20, and 4 lines, and a doxology not in the original, but in the *Sarum Brev.*, pt. ii. of lines 21–44, and the closing lines of pt. i. repeated.

In 1861, the Compilers of *H. A. & M.* gave this rendering in that collection with rather extensive alterations, and rearranged in three parts, thus :—

i. Aurora lucis rutilat. "Light's glittering morn bedecks the sky."

ii. Tristes erant Apostoli. "The Apostles' hearts were full of pain."

iii. Claro Paschali gaudio. "That Eastertide with joy was bright."

To these were added a stanza, and doxology as in the *Sarum Brev.*, to be sung at the end of each part :—

Quaesumus, Auctor omnium. "O Lord of all, with us abide."

Gloria Tibi Domine. "All praise be Thine, O risen Lord."

In the annotated edition of *H. A. & M.*, Mr. Biggs has given the Latin text from the *Sarum Breviary*. It is a reprint of the original with the addition of the last eight lines.

This *H. A. & M.* text was included, with omissions and further alterations, in *Kennedy*, 1863, No. 691, in two parts :—

i. **Aurora lucis, &c.**   "Light's glittering dawn."
ii. **Claro Paschali gaudio.**   "That Eastertide with joy was bright."

In 1864 Mr. Skinner gave Dr. Neale's rendering with omissions, but without alterations in the text, in his *Daily Service Hymnal*, No. 127.

i. **Aurora lucis, &c.**   "Light's glittering morn bedecks the sky."
ii. **Claro Paschali gaudio.**   "In this our bright and Paschal day."

Dr. Neale's rendering is also included in the *Hymnary*, 1872, altered by the editors, and divided into three parts :—

i. **Aurora lucis.**   "The glittering morn bedecks the sky."
ii. **Tristes erant Apostoli.**   "Deep sorrow on the Apostles came."
iii. **Claro Paschali gaudio.**   "Joy dawned again on Easter-day."

2. A second *tr.* of the full text was published by J. D. Chambers in his *Lauda Syon*, &c., 1857, pp. 182–185, in two parts :—

i. **Aurora lucis.**   "Light's very morn its beams displays."
ii. **Sermone blando.**   "In accents soft the Angel said."

This translation, as a whole, is not in congregational use, but portions are given in centos yet to be noted.

3. **Sermone blando.**   "With gentle voice the Angel gave." This rendering of lines 21–44, and the 8 lines from the *Sarum Brev.*, was given in the *Salisbury H. Bk.*, 1857, No. 103. It is mainly an alteration of Neale's *tr.*, and probably by J. Keble.

4. **Aurora lucis.**   "Now dawning glows the day of days," by Professor F. J. A. Hort, was written in 1858, for and pub. in the Rev. J. Ellerton's *Hymns for Schools & Bible Classes*, 1859, No. 34, in two parts :—

i. **Aurora lucis.**   "Now dawning glows the day of days."
ii. **Tristes erant.**   "Sad the eleven apostles sate."

With very slight alterations, pt. i. was included in *Church Hymns*, No. 130.

5. **Aurora lucis.**   "The dawn of light breaks o'er the sky." An altered form of Dr. Neale's *tr.* of lines 1–16 and the 8 concluding lines from the Sarum Brev. was included in *Hymns fitted to the Order of C. P.* by Rev. F. Pott, 1861, No. 89.

Translations not in C. U. :—
In addition to the foregoing there are also translations which have not come into common use. These include :—

(1) i. *Aurora lucis.* "The ruddy dawn is breaking."
ii. *Sermone blando.* "With gentle speech the Angel."
This rendering is by the Rev. W. J. Blew, and appeared in his *Church Hymn and Tune Book*, 1852. Each part is given as a separate hymn, and includes the 8 lines from the *Sarum Brev.*

(2) *Aurora lucis.* "The day-spring fair of light, &c.," by *Mr. A. J. B. Hope* in his *Hys. of the Ch.* 1844, comprising lines 1–20, and the *Sarum* ending as above.

(3) *Aurora lucis.* "Heaven with rosy morn, &c.," by *Bp. John Williams* (America), appeared in his *Ancient Hymns of Holy Church*. Hartford [America], 1845. It embraces the same lines as that of Mr. Hope.

II. *The Roman Breviary text.*

As the divisions of the text in the *Roman Breviary* have been strictly adhered to by translators, it will simplify our work by annotating those translations in the same order.

1. *Aurora coelum purpurat.*

1. **This holy morn, so fair and bright.** By J. Chandler, appeared in his *Hymns of the Primitive Church*, 1837, pp. 77–8, Latin text, pp. 197–8. In this form it is not in common use ; but altered in his *Hys. of the Church*, 1841, No. 44, to "Bright sunbeams deck the joyful sky," it was included in Dr. Hook's *Church School H. Bk.*, 1850, No. 84 ; the *Leeds H. Bk.*, 1853, No. 310 ; and the Bapt. *Ps. & Hys.* 1858 and 1880, No. 171. In the *Leeds H. Bk.* it is attributed to "Rose" in error.

2. **Morning spreads her crimson rays.** By Bp. Mant, in his *Ancient Hymns*, 1837, p. 55, and in the ed. 1871, p. 98. It was given as No. 43 in Stretton's *Church Hymns*, 1850.

3. **The dawn is purpling o'er the sky.** By W. J. Copeland, 1st pub. in his *Hymns for the Week*, 1848, p. 86, together with parts two and three.

4. **The dawn was purpling o'er the sky.** By E. Caswall, 1st pub. in his *Lyra Catholica*, 1849, pp. 98–9, and again in his *Hymns & Poems*, 1873, pp. 55–56. In 1860, it was included in the *Wellington College H. Bk.* ; in 1867, in the *People's Hymnal*, and also in other collections.

5. **With sparkling rays morn decks the sky.** By J. A. Johnston, in his *English Hymnal*, 1852, 1st ed., No. 107. It was replaced in the editions of 1856 and 1861 by : "Morn's glittering light bedecks the sky," No. 116, also by Mr Johnston.

6. **The morning purples all the sky.** By A. R. Thompson, of New York, contributed to Schaff's *Christ in Song*, 1870, p. 193. This is a free rendering, with an original refrain of four lines to each stanza.

Translation not in C. U. :—
Now morning purples all the skies. *Macgill*, 1876.

2. *Tristes erant apostoli.*

1. **Th' Apostles wept with hearts forlorn.** By W. J. Copeland, in his *Hymns for the Week*, &c., 1848, pp. 89–90. This was given in Stretton's *Church Hymns*, 1850, No. 46 ; in Murray's *Hymnal*, 1852, No. 59, and other collections.

2. **When Christ, by His own servants slain.** By E. Caswall, *Lyra Catholica*, 1849, pp. 205–6, and *Hymns & Poems*, 1873, p. 109.

3. **In sorrow steep'd, with hearts forlorn.** By J. A. Johnston, 1st pub. in his *English Hymnal*, 1852, No. 111., and again, rewritten, but with the same first line, in the 2nd ed., 1856, and the 3rd ed., 1861.

4. **As mourns a widowed bride.** By Archbishop Benson, written for and first published in the *Wellington College H. Bk.*, 2nd ed., 1863, where it is appointed for St. Philip and St. James's Day evening.

3. *Paschale mundo gaudium.*

1. **A fairer sun is risen on earth.** By W. J. Copeland, in his *Hymns for the Week*, 1848, pp. 91–92. It was included in Stretton's *Church Hymns*, 1850, No. 50 ; in Murray's *Hymnal*, 1852, No. 58, and other collections.

2. Now daily shines the sun more fair. By E. Caswall, in his *Lyra Catholica*, 1849, pp. 207–8, and *Hymns & Poems*, 1873, pp. 109–110. In 1863 it was given with alterations in the *Wellington College H. Bk.* and appointed for St. Mark's Day morning.

3. Now shines the sun with brighter ray. By J. A. Johnston, in his *English Hymnal*, 1852, No. 112. For the edition of 1856 it was re-written by the translator as, " Bright rose the sun that Easter-day." This latter rendering was repeated in the ed. of 1861.

III. Centos.

1. Hymns and Anthems, by G. Rorison, 1851. In this collection, No. 85, "The Apostles wept with hearts forlorn" is thus composed : st. i.–iii., Copeland as above (*Tristes erant*) altered ; st. iv.–vi. by Dr. Rorison.

2. The People's Hymnal, 1867. In this collection there are three centos from various translations: (1.) "In accents bland the Angel blest," No. 115. It is thus composed : st. i., ii., iii., v., vi., Chambers's *Lauda Syon*, altered ; st. iv. and viii., J. M. Neale, from *Hymnal Noted*; st. vii., Chope's *Hymnal*, 1857, No. 83 ; later editions, No. 211, altered. (2.) "The Apostles' hearts with grief were filled." St. i., editors ; st. ii.–v., Chambers, as above altered ; st. vi., Chope's *Hymnal*, as above, altered ; st. vii., J. M. Neale, as above. (3.) " In this our bright and Paschal day." St. i. and v., J. M. Neale, *H. Noted*; st. ii., iii., Chambers altered ; st. iv., J. A. Johnston, altered.   [J. J.]

Aurora vails her rosy face. *Ralph Erskine.* [*The Joys of Heaven.*] 1st pub. in his *Gospel Sonnets* (2nd ed., Edin., 1726), as section 6 of part v., entitled "The Song of Heaven desired by Saints on Earth," in 20 st. of 4 l. Of this 11 st., beginning with st. ii., "Happy the company that's gone," were included in the *Sac. Songs of Scotland*, 1860, (Edin., A. Elliott, p. 42). Re-written 1785 by John Berridge as No. 143 of his *Sion's Songs*, beginning "O happy saints, who dwell in light." (See Lord Selborne's *Bk. of Praise*, No. cxiii. and note thereto.)   [J. M.]

Aus Lieb' verwundter Jesu mein. xvi. cent. [*Holy Communion.*] This appears in the *Christ. Cathol. G. B., Nach der Paderbornischen Edition*, 1726, p. 263, in 16 st. of 4 l.; among the hymns for Corpus Christi, as "A Sigh of Love to Jesus." In the *Geistreiches G. B.*, Berlenburg, 1720, No. 90, it has 9 st. In the *Trier G. B.* (R. C.), 1846, p. 120, it is in 6 st. It has been *tr.* as :—

O Jesu, pierced for love of me. In full from the *Trier G. B.*, signed "Sister M.," in *Lyra Euch ristica*, 1863, p. 252 (ed. 1864, p. 298), and thence as No. 535 in the *People's H.*, 1867.   [J. M.]

Aus tiefer Noth schrei ich zu dir. *Martin Luther.* [*Ps. cxxx.*] This beautiful, though free, version of Ps. cxxx. was written in 1523. Ps. cxxx. was a great favourite with Luther, one of those he called Pauline Psalms —the others being Ps. xxxii., li., and cxliii. With its versification he took special pains, and the final result ranks with the finest of German Psalm versions. It first appeared

in 4 st. of 7 lines in *Etlich cristlich lider*, Wittenberg, 1524, and in *Eyn Enchiridion*, Erfurt, 1524. The form now in use considerably altered, and with st. ii. rewritten as ii., iii., appeared in the *Geystliche gesangk Buchleyn*, Wittenberg, 1524, in 5 st., was included as No. 1 in Luther's *Christliche Geseng zum Begrebnis*, Wittenberg, 1542, and since in almost all German hymn-books, as recently in the *Unv. L. S.*, 1851, No. 362. Both forms are included in Wackernagel's *D. Kirchenlied*, iii. pp. 7–8, and in Schircks's ed. of Luther's *Geist. Lieder*, 1854, pp. 66–68.

The fine melody (in the Irish *Ch. Hymnal* called *De profundis*; elsewhere, *Luther's* 130*th*, &c.) is possibly by Luther, and first appeared, with the 5 st. form, in 1524.

The hymn was sung, May 9, 1525, at the funeral of the Elector Friedrich the Wise in the Court church at Wittenberg ; by the weeping multitude at Halle when, on Feb. 20, 1546, Luther's body was being taken to its last resting-place at Wittenberg; and again as the last hymn in the Cathedral at Strasburg before the city was captured by the French in 1681. St. v. comforted the last hours of Christian, Elector of Saxony, 1591, of Johann Georg I., Elector of Saxony, 1656, and of King Friedrich I. of Prussia, 1723 (*Koch*, viii. 211–216).

Translations in C. U. :—

1. Out of the deep I cry to Thee, My. A free *tr.* of st. i.–iii. v., by B. Latrobe, as No. 231 in the *Moravian H. Bk.*, 1789 (1849, No. 287). In 1848, it was given, slightly altered from the edition of 1826, and beginning "Out of the depths I cry to Thee, Lord, look," as No. 4 in the Dalston Hospital *H. Bk.* The text of 1826, unaltered save st. ii., ll. 3–4, was included as No. 440 in the Irish *Ch. Hymnal*, 1873.

2. From deep distress to Thee I pray. In full by Dr. H. Mills in his *Horae Germanicae*, 1845 (1856, p. 71). Thence as No. 70 in the Luth. Gen. Synod's *Coll.* 1850–52, and as No. 464 in *Temple Melodies*, N. Y., 1851.

3. Out of the depths, O Lord. A paraphrase in 12 st. of 6 lines by Miss Fry in her *H. of the Reformation*, 1845, p. 141. The doxology is from the gloria to the version of Ps. i. by L. Oeler, 1525. This gloria is appended to Luther as No. 1558 in Burg's *Breslau G. B.*, 1746. Her st. viii., iii., ix., iv., v., in order beginning— "Lord, let Thy people be," were included as No. 100, and st. vi., vii., beginning—" Lord, Thou hast given Thy faithful word," as No. 97 in Whittemore's *Suppl. to All H. Bks.*, 1860.

4. Out of the deep I cry to Thee, O Lord God, &c. A good and full *tr.* by A. T. Russell as No. 74 in his *Ps. & Hys.*, 1851. Included in full in Dr. Bacon's ed. of *Luther's Hymns*, 1884, p. 10, and, omitting st. iv., as No. 85 in the *New Zealand Hymnal*, 1872.

5. From depths of woe I raise to Thee. Good and full by R. Massie in his *M. Luther's Spiritual Songs*, 1854, p. 73. Thence unaltered as No. 64 in the 1857 ed. of Mercer's *C. P. & H. Bk.* (Ox. ed., 1864, No. 150), and since in the *Scottish Hymnal*, 1870, the Scottish *Presb. Hymnal*, 1876 (omitting st. iv.), and the Canadian *Presb. H. Bk.*, 1880.

6. Out of the depths I cry to Thee, Lord God! oh hear my prayer. In full by Miss Winkworth in her *Lyra Ger.*, 1855, p. 65, and thence unaltered as No. 626 in the *Wes. H. Bk.*, 1875. The lines 1–4 of st. i., iii., v. form No. 548 in the Amer. Unitarian *Hy.* [*& Tune*] *Bk.*, Boston, 1868.

7. Out of the depths I cry to Thee, Lord God, O hear my wailing. A good but rather free *tr.*, as No. 215 in the *New Cong.*, 1859, and since as No. 501 in the *Meth. N. C.*, 1863, as No. 42 in Dr. Thomas's *Augustine H. Bk.*, 1866, and No. 119 in the Appendix of 1874 to the *Leeds H. Bk.* of 1853. Of this *tr.* st. ii.–v. are given in Dr. Dale's *English H. Bk.*, 1874, No. 483, as "Thy sovereign grace and boundless love."

8. Almighty God! I call to Thee. A good *tr.* omitting st. ii., included in the Amer. Episc. *H. for Ch. & Home*, 1860, No. 308, and repeated as No. 511 in the Amer. *Episc. Coll.*, 1871.

9. Out of the depths I cry to Thee, Lord hear me. Full and good, as No. 40 by Miss Winkworth in her *C. B. for England*, 1863, and repeated as No. 354 in the Lutheran General Council's *Ch. Bk.* 1868.

10. In deep distress I cry to Thee, O Lord, my God. A *tr.* of st. i., ii., v., signed F. C. C., as No. 184 in *Dr. Pagenstecher's Coll.*, 1864.

11. From lowest depths I cry to Thee. Full and good in E. Massie's *Sacred Odes*, vol. ii., 1867, p. 134, and thence as No. 251 in *J. L. Porter's Coll.*, 1876.

12. Out of the depths I cry to Thee, Lord, mark my lamentation, in full, based upon R. Massie as above, as No. 233 in the Ohio Luth. *Hymnal*, 1880.

Translations not in C.U. :—

(1) "Out of the depe cry I to the," by Bp. Coverdale, 1539 (ed. 1846, p. 577). (2) "Fra deip, O Lord, I call to the," in the *Gude and Godly Ballates* (ed. 1568, folio 57 ; ed. 1868, p. 98). (3) "Out of the deeps of long distress," by J. C. Jacobi, 1722, p. 61 (ed. 1732, p. 97, alt. and beginning "Out of the deeps of dark distress"). (4) "Guilty and vile, I call on Thee," by J. Anderson, 1846, p. 70 (1847, p. 84). (5) "From deep distress I cry to Thee, Oh," by Dr. J. Hunt, 1853, p. 10°. (6) "From trouble deep I cry to Thee," by Dr. G. Macdonald in the *Sunday Magazine*, 1867, p. 682, and repeated altered in his *Exotics*, 1876, p. 101. (7) "From lowest deeps I cry, O God," by N. L. Frothingham, 1870, p. 183. (8) "From deep distress I cry to Thee ; Lord listen," in the *Ch. of England Magazine*, 1872, p. 183. (9) "In deep distress I cry to Thee, Lord," in E. Walter's *Martin Luther*, 1884, p. 13. **[J. M.]**

Austin, John, born at Walpole, Norfolk, and educated at St. John's, Cambridge (cr. 1640). He became a Roman Catholic, entered Lincoln's Inn to study for the Bar : subsequently became a tutor, and finally devoted himself to literature. Died in London, 1669. (See Early English Hymnody, §. x.) His works include *The Christian Moderator, Reflections upon the Oaths of Supremacy*, and :—

Devotions in the Antient Way of Offices Containing Exercises for every day in the Week. 1668. This last work, through which Austin is associated with hymnody, attained a 2nd ed. in 1672, 3rd ed. 1684, and two 4th eds. 1685. (A second part, consisting of a *Harmony of the Gospels*, was also published, and is of excessive rarity. A third, according to Anthony à Wood, existed in MS.) It was a Roman Catholic Manual, and contained 43 hymns, 39 of which are in the first edition, and those added in the third edition are perhaps by the editor. A few of these were renderings from the Latin by R. Crashaw, altered and adapted by Austin. In 1686 it was adapted for members of the Church of England by Theophilus Dorrington, and again in 1687 by the Lady

Susanna Hopton under the editorship of George Hickes, afterwards a Nonjuring Bishop. Of the 5th ed., 1717, of the last adaptation, a reprint was published by Masters in 1856.   **[W. T. B.]**

Austin, William. A lawyer of Lincoln's Inn in the time of Charles I. His widow, Ann Austin, pub. in 1635, his

Devotionis Avgvstinianae Flamma. This contains 3 carols for Christmas Day, 3 poems for Good Friday, 1 for the Annunciation, and a poem by himself in anticipation of his own death. They are all of merit, and 4 may be found reprinted in *Days & Seasons*, 3rd ed., 1857, Lond. Mozley. In the Harleian MSS. Ralph Crane's *A Handful of Celestiall Flowers* contains other hymns, one of which, with Austin's initials, has been printed by Farr in his *Select Poetry of James I.* It begins, "What a gracious God have we," The popular carol—

> "All this night bright Angels sing,
> Never was such carolling."

No. xli. in Bramley and Stainer's *Christmas Carols, New & Old*, 2nd Series, is his—

> "All this Night shrill Chauntecleere
> Daye's proclaiming Trumpeter,"

the first of his "Carrols for Christmas-day."

Austin d. Jan. 16, 1633, and lies in the north transept of St. Saviour's, Southwark, where there is a stately monument representing him, his wife, and all his children, in the quaint fashion of those times.   **[W. T. B.]**

Αὔτη ἡ κλητή. [Ἀναστάσεως ἡμέρα.]

Author of all in earth and sky. *A. M. Toplady.* [*Lent.*] 1st appeared in his *Poems on Sacred Subjects*, 1759, in 22 st. of 4 l. and entitled "The Prayer of King Manasses Paraphrased." It was subsequently included in his *Hymns*, &c., 1856, p. 83, and in Sedgwick's reprint of the *Hymns*, 1860. The hymn, "Bowed with the sense of sin I faint," is composed of st. xv.–xix. and xxi. of the original.

Author of faith, Eternal Word. *C. Wesley.* [*Faith.*] This poem is a paraphrase of Heb. xi. It appeared in 88 st. of 4 l. in *Hymns & S. Poems*, 1740, with the title "The Life of Faith." In 1780 J. Wesley gave st. i.–vi. as No. 92 in the *Wes. H. Bk.* (ed. 1875, No. 95). From the *Wes. H. Bk.* it has passed into most of the collections of the Methodist denominations in G. Britain and America, and also into other hymnals. Full orig. text in *P. Works*, 1868–72, vol. i. pp. 209–221. The poem as a whole, is criticised in the *Wes. Magazine*, 1839, p. 381.

Author of faith, on me confer. *C. Wesley.* [*Faith.*] From his *Hymns on the Four Gospels*, MS. dated 1765, and 1st pub. in the *P. Works*, 1868–72, vol. x. p. 310, and from thence was transferred to the revised ed. of the *Wes. H. Bk.* 1875, No. 805, the third stanza being omitted. It is based on St. Matt. xvii. 20, "If ye have faith as a grain of mustard seed," &c.

Author of faith, to Thee I cry. *C. Wesley.* [*Lent.*] This hymn was first printed as the first of six hymns at the end of a tract entitled *A short View of the Differences between the Moravian Brethren in England, and J. & C. Wesley*, 1745. In 1749 it was reprinted in *Hymns & S. Poems*, vol. i. No. 10, in 5 st. of 6 l. in the *Wes. H. Bk.* 1780, No. 114

(ed. 1875), and in the *P. Works*, 1868–72, vol. iv. p. 324. It has also passed from the *Wes. H. Bk.* into various collections both in G. Britain and America, sometimes reading "Author of faith, to Thee *we* cry." A cento from this hymn, beginning, "Christ bids us knock and enter in," is given in the American *Church Pastorals*, Boston, 1864. It is composed of st. iv. and ii. slightly altered.

Author of faith, we seek Thy face. *C. Wesley.* [*Intercession.*] The original hymn appeared in 9 st. of 4 l. as No. 64, in vol. ii. of *Hymns & S. Poems*, 1749, and is repeated in the *P. Works*, 1868–72, vol. v. p. 233. The abbreviated form in C. U. was included by J. Wesley in the *Wes. H. Bk.*, 1780, No. 446 (rev. ed. 458). It consists of st. i.–v. and vii. It is found in various collections in G. Britain and America.

Author of friendship's sacred tie. *C. Wesley.* [*Friendship.*] 1st pub. in *Hymns and Sacred Poems*, 1749, vol. ii. p. 195, in 6 st. of 12 l. and again in the *P. Works*, 1868–72, vol. v. p. 408. In the *Wes. H. Bk.*, 1780, No. 510, a cento from this hymn was given, beginning, "Our friendship sanctify and guide." This has been repeated in various collections, and specially in those of the Methodist denominations both in G. Britain and abroad.

Author of life divine. [*Holy Communion.*] This hymn for the Holy Communion is from J. & C. Wesley's *Hymns on the Lord's Supper*, 1st pub. in 1745, No. 40, in 2 st. of 6 l. In 1875 it was included without alteration in the revised edition of *H. A. & M.*, and attributed to John Wesley. There is, however, no evidence that it was the composition of John as distinct from Charles, Wesley. In the absence of positive evidence either way the probabilities are in favour of Charles, rather than his elder brother. It is also in C. U. in America. Orig. text in *H. A. & M.* and *P. Works*, 1868–72, vol. iii. p. 244.

Author of life, with grateful heart. *S. Pearce.* [*Morning.*] Appeared at the end of his *Memoirs*, by Andrew Fuller, 1st ed., 1800, pp. 286–7, and again in the 2nd ed., 1801, in 5 st. of 4 l. and entitled "An Evening Song." The hymn beginning with this stanza in Major's *Book of Praise*, is a cento from S. Pearce, thus composed: st. i., the 1st st. as above; st. ii.–v. are st. iii.–vi. from Pearce's Morning Hymn in the same *Memoirs* as above, thus making a morning hymn. The text in *Major* is altered from the originals.

Author of our salvation, Thee. *C. Wesley.* [*Holy Communion.*] 1st pub. in *Hys. on the Lord's Supper*, 1745, No. 28, in 4 st. of 4 l., and based on the words, "As it is a sign and a means of Grace," being the first hymn on that division of the subject. It is not in use in G. Brit. In the *Hymnal of the Meth. Episco. Ch.*, N. Y., 1878, No. 851, it is given in an unaltered form. Also in the *P. Works*, 1868–72, vol. iii. p. 236.

Author of peace unknown. *C. Wesley.* [*Friendship.*] 1st pub. in his *Hymns and*

Sacred Poems, 1749, vol. ii., No. 236, in 4 st. of 6 l., and again in the *P. Works*, 1868–72, vol. v. pp. 426–7. It is one of several hymns composed by C. Wesley at the time of his marriage. In its original form it is not found in common use. In 1780, however, J. Wesley gave st. ii., iii., and iv. in the *Wes. H. Bk.* No. 498, as, "Centre of our hopes Thou art," and from that collection it has passed into several hymnals, specially those of the Methodist denomination.

Ave Christi Corpus verum. *Anon.* [*Holy Communion.*] The text of this hymn is given in *Mone*, No. 219, from a Reichenau MS. of the 14th cent., with the title "In elevatione sanguinis Christi," which shows it to be a devotion at the elevation of the Chalice in the Mass.

There are at least four hymns which commence with almost the same words, but must not be confounded. "*Ave Christi Corpus verum*"; "*Ave verum Corpus natum*"; "*Ave Christi Corpus carum*"; "*Ave verum Corpus Christi.*" [W. A. S.]

Translation in C. U. :—

Hail, O Flesh of Christ Divine. By R. F. Littledale, 1st pub. in the *Altar Manual*, 1863; the *Lyra Eucharistica* the same year; and the *People's H.*, 1867, No. 176.

Ave! Colenda Trinitas. [*Holy Trinity.*] This hymn, of unknown authorship, is given in the *Latin Hymns of the Anglo-Saxon Church*, Lon., 1851, p. 146, from a Durham MS. of the 11th cent. It is also in a MS. of the 11th cent. in the *British Museum* (Jul. A. vi. f. 71); and in Biggs's *Annotated H. A. and M.*, No. 132. It is *tr.* as:—

All hail, adored Trinity. By J. D. Chambers, in his *Lauda Syon*, pt. i., 1857, p. 218, in 4 st. of 4 l., and from thence into *H. A. and M.*, 1861; the *Hymnary*, 1872, Snepp's *S. of G. and G.*, 1872, and others, usually with slight alterations.

Ave Jesu! Ere we part. *C. H. Bateman.* [*Children's Evening Hymn.*] Appeared in the *Bible Class Magazine*, 1849, in 2 st. of 11 lines. In many collections, including Stevenson's *Hys. for Ch. & Home*, 1873, c. 13, a short hymn of 4 st. of 4 l., "Blessed Jesus, ere we part," has been compiled with alterations from this text.

Ave Jesu, Qui mactaris. *Anon.* [*Good Friday.*] Text in the *Paradisus animae Christianae* of J. M. Horst., sect. vi. "De vita et passione Domini," end of chap. iv. (ed. Cologne, 1630, p. 418). It is a *Hymn on the Seven Words uttered by Christ on the Cross.*

Translation in C. U. :—

Jesus, hail! Who, as Thou bleedest. By *E. B. Pusey.* Appeared in 1848 in vol. ii. of his *tr.* of the *Paradise of the Christian Soul*, and from thence it passed into the *Appendix* to the *Hymnal N.*, 2nd ed., 1864, No. 248.

Ave Maria, blessed Maid. *J. Keble.* [*B. V. M.*] From his Poem for "The Annunciation of the Blessed Virgin Mary," st. 7–10,

The original poem was written on the death of his mother, June 1, 1823. This fact supplies the key to the line of thought in the opening stanza :—

"Oh ! Thou Who deign'st to sympathize
 With all our frail and fleshly ties,
     Maker, yet Brother dear.
 Forgive the too presumptuous thought,
 If, calming wayward grief, I sought
     To gaze on Thee too near. "

The poem as originally written was too personal for publication in the *Christian Year*, and, in 1826 (dated Mar. 9, 1826), the four concluding stanzas were omitted, and those beginning in that work, " Ave Maria, blessed Maid," to the end, were substituted, and the poem in this its new form was first published therein in 1827. The original was included with a special note in his *Misc. Poems*, 1869, pp. 230–33, and the cento, as a hymn, in the *Appendix* to the *Hymnal N.*, 2nd ed., 1864, the *People's H.*, 1867, No. 192, and others.

Ave maris stella. *Anon.* [*B. V. M.*] This hymn, so well known as to its words, is of uncertain authorship. It has been wrongly ascribed to St. Bernard, as it is found in a St. Gall MS., No. 05, of the 9th cent., and to Venantius Fortunatus (by M. A. Luchi, 1789), but on insufficient authority. The text is given in *Daniel*, i., No. 171, with various readings. (Other notes are given in vol. iii. p. 286, and vol. iv. p. 136.) *Mone* gives five paraphrases of this hymn, Nos. 496–500; each line of the original being followed by versified explanations and simplifications, a certain testimony to the popularity of the original.

It has been treated with so much respect as hardly to have been altered in the *Roman Breviary*, 1632, and was retained in the revised Breviaries of French dioceses (Paris, Lyons, &c.), as one of the few exceptions of old hymns not supplanted. It is appointed for Vespers in the Little Office of the Blessed Virgin, *Officium parvum beatae Mariae*, Paris, Lyons, Le Mans, &c.; some, as Paris, Le Mans, &c., having it also in the Saturday Office of the Blessed Virgin, *Officium beatae Mariae in Sabbato*, and in Feasts which have no special or *proper* hymns.

In the *Roman Breviary* it is the Hymn for 1st and 2nd vespers in the Feasts of the Blessed Virgin Mary ; also in the Office of the B. V. M. on Saturdays, and in the Little Office, *Officium parvum Beatae Mariae Virginis*, at 1st vespers, there being no 2nd vespers in these two latter cases.

The hymn is found in three MSS. of the 11th cent. in the *British Museum* (Harl. 2961, f. 241; Vesp. D. xii. f. 63; Jul. A. vi. f. 56); and in the *Latin Hys. of the Anglo-Saxon Church*, 1851, p. 76, it is printed from an 11th cent. MS. at Durham. It is also given in *Bässler, Königsfeld, Simrock, Wackernagel*, i. No. 85, and various modern Roman Catholic collections.   [W. A. S.]

Translations in C. U. :—

1. **Hail, thou Star of Ocean.** By E. Caswall, 1st pub. in his *Lyra Catholica*, 1849, p. 197, where it began " Gentle Star of Ocean ;" and again, in an altered form, in his *Hymns & Poems*, 1873, p. 105, in 7 st. of 4 l. It is given in a

large number of Roman Catholic collections in G. Britain and America, often in an altered form, and sometimes beginning, " Hail, bright star of ocean."

2. **Hail, Sea Star, we bless thee.** This is by J. R. Beste in his *Church Hys.* (R. Cath.), 1849. Its use is not extensive.

3. **Hail, thou resplendent Star.** In *A Sel. of Catholic Hys.*, Glasgow, H. Margey, 1861, No. 41, the *St. Patrick's Catholic H. Bk.*, 1862, No. 60, and other collections this *tr.* is given without signature. It is based upon Caswall.

Translations not in C. U. :—

1. Hail, Ocean Star. *E. Caswall*, 1873.
2. The Star which o'er the sea. *J. W. Hewett*, 1859.
3. Hail ! Star of Ocean, Mary. *Chambers*, ii. 1866.
4. Hail ! Star of the sea, &c. (Prose). Mrs. Charles, 1858.   [J. J.]

Ave, plena gratiâ, cujus. *Anon.* [*The Purification.*] In the revised *Paris Missal* of 1736, this hymn is given as the Sequence for the Feast of the Purification. The text is in Card. Newman's *Hymni Ecclesiae*, 1838 and 1865.

Translations in C. U.:—

1. **Ave, Mary, full of grace.** By W. J. Copeland. 1st pub. in his *Hymns for the Week*, &c., 1848, p. 111, in 10 st. of 3 l., and repeated in Rorison's *Hymns and Anthems*, 1851, and later editions, in 5 st. of 6 l,

2. **Jesus, Son of Mary, hail,** No. 73 in Murray's *Hymnal*, 1852, and some later collections, is Copeland's *tr.* slightly altered.

3. **In His Mother's pure embrace.** No. 346 in the *Hymnary* is the same *tr.* altered by the editors of that selection.

4. **Hail, thou Mother, full of grace,** in the *Altar Hymnal*, 1884, is also Copeland's *tr.* altered by C. R.

Another *tr.* not in C. U. is, " Mary, hail to thee, we sing," in the *Monthly Packet*, Feb., 1868.   [J. J.]

Ave regina coelorum. [*B. V. M.*] One of the four Antiphons to the B. V. M. (see " Alma Redemptoris mater "). Among the MSS. in the *British Museum* it is found in the St. Alban's Book of the 12th cent. (MSS. Reg. 2 A. x. f. 62), and a *Sarum Breviary* of the 14th cent. (MSS. Reg. 2 A. xiv. f. 235 b). It is also in the *York Breviary*, 1493 (1883 reprint, ii. 493); in the *Roman Breviary*, Modena, 1480, f. 512, &c. The text in *Daniel*, ii. 319, is from a Munich MS. probably of the 13th cent., and other sources.   [J. M.]

Translation in C. U. :—

Hail, O Queen of Heaven enthroned ! By E. Caswall, in his *Lyra Catholica*, 1849, p. 39, in 8 lines; and again in his *Hys. & Poems*, 1873, p. 23. It is largely used in Roman Catholic collections for schools and missions. Another *tr.* is " Hail, thou mighty Queen of heaven," by J. R. Beste, in his *Church Hymns*, 1849, p. 66. It is not in C. U.

Ave verum corpus natum. *Anon.* [*Holy Communion.*] The text will be found in *Daniel*, ii. p. 327. Also as No. 213 in *Mone's* Collection ; with the heading, *In elevatione Corporis Christi*, and the statement that a Reichenau MS. of the 14th cent. says " Pope Innocent composed the following salutation " (" Salutationem sequentem composuit

Innocentius Papa"), and " this prayer has three years of indulgences granted by Pope Leo" (" haec oratio habet tres annos indulgentiarum a dom. Papa Leone "). Levis, *Anecdota sacra*, Turin, 1789, p. 107, gives the text with the variation *Esto nobis praestantior virtus in examine*, instead of *Esto nobis praegustatum mortis in examine*. It is in J. M. Horst's *Paradisus Animae* (ed. Cologne, 1644, p. 321), Sect. V., "De Sacram. Eucharistiae," as a private devotion at the elevation of the Host in the Mass (" sub elevatione "). It is also in *Kehrein*, No. 157. See *Ave Christi Corpus verum*, for a cognate hymn at the elevation of the Chalice.   [W. A. S.]

Translations in C.U. :—

1. **Hail to Thee ! true Body sprung.** By E. Caswall. 1st pub. in his *Lyra Catholica*, 1849, p. 249, in 10 lines ; and again, slightly altered, in his *Hymns & Poems*, 1873, p. 162. In the Roman Catholic hymnals the original *tr.* is generally used. In the *People's H.*, 1867, No. 177, we have a cento from this *tr.* of Caswall, that by J. R. Beste, and others.

2. **Hail, true Body, born of Mary,** No. 214 in the *Appendix* to *Hymnal N.*, 1864, is by H. N. Oxenham, from his *Sentence of Kaires and other Poems*, 1854 and 1867, somewhat altered.

3. **Hail, true Body Incarnated,** by W. J. Irons, is No. 67 of his *Ps. & Hys. for the Ch.*, 1873 and 1883. This rendering is specially adapted for Good Friday. 1st pub. in Dr. Irons's *Hymns*, 1866, No. 113.

4. **Hail, true Body! God of heaven.** By J. R. Beste, pub. with the Latin text in his *Ch. Hys.* (Rom. Cath.) Lond. 1849. It may be added that in most of the modern Roman Catholic collections the Latin text is also given, as in this case.

Translation not in C. U. :—

Hail, true Body, born of Mary. *E. B. Pusey*, 1848.
                                                      [J. J.]

Aveling, Thomas William Baxter, D.D., b. Castletown, Isle of Man, May 11, 1815, educated privately and at Highbury College for the Congregational Ministry, and ordained to the pastorate of Kingsland in 1838, d. at Reedham, July 3, 1884. In 1875 he received the degree of D.D. from the Howard University, United States. His published works include *The Irish Scholar, a Narrative*, 1841 ; *Naaman, or Life's Shadows and Sunshine*, 1853 ; *Voices of Many Waters, &c.*, 1855 ; *The Service of the Sanctuary, &c.*, 1859, &c., including contributions to periodicals. Dr. Aveling was sometime editor of *The Jewish Herald*. In 1834 he published a small volume of poems and hymns. Those of his hymns which have come into C. U. were mostly written from year to year to be sung when he preached his New Year's Sermon to the young. Some of them came to the public through the Magazines. We are not aware that they have been collected. The best known are :—"On ! towards Zion, on !" "Hail ! Thou God of grace and glory," and " Lord of the lofty and the low."   [J. J.]

Awake, again the Gospel trump is blown. *J. Keble.* [*Advent.*] Written on

Dec. 26, 1823, and first pub. in his *Christian Year*, 1827, in 13 st. of 6 l. for Advent Sunday, with the text from the Epistle of that day, " Now it is high time to awake out of sleep, for now is our salvation nearer than when we believed." Its use as a hymn for public worship is very limited. In *Kennedy*, 1863, No. 19, st. i., v., xii. and xiii., are given with the change in st. v., l. 1, of " E'en so," to " Behold the world."

Awake, and sing the song. *W. Hammond.* [*Praise.*] This hymn appeared with the heading, " Before Singing of Hymns, by Way of Introduction," in his *Psalms, Hymns, and Spiritual Songs*, 1745 (Lond., W. Strahan), pp. 84–86, in 14 st. of 4 l. In its complete form it is unknown to the hymnals. Centos therefrom are, however, in use in all English-speaking countries. The growth of these centos is somewhat complicated, and can be best set forth in detail thus :—

1. The first use of the hymn in an abbreviated form was by G. Whitefield. In his *Coll. of Hys. for Social Worship*, 1753, he included as No. 47, st. i., ii., xiii., and xiv., with alterations which we give with the original readings in brackets :

> " PRAISING CHRIST.
>
> 1. " Awake and sing the Song
>   Of Moses and the Lamb ;
>   [Tune] *Wake* ev'ry heart and ev'ry tongue
>   To praise the Saviour's Name.,
>
> 2. " Sing of His dying love,
>   Sing of His rising pow'r ;
>   Sing how He intercedes above
>   For [*all*] those whose sins He bore.
>
> 3. " Sing 'till [you] *we* feel [your] *our* hearts
>   Ascending with [your] *our* tongues,
>   Sing 'till the love of sin departs,
>   And grace inspires [your] *our* Songs.
>
> 4. " Sing 'till [you] *we* hear Christ say,
>   ' Your sins are all forgiv'n ' ;
>   [Go] *Sing* on rejoicing [all the way] *ev'ry day*,
>   [And sing your souls to heav'n.]
>   '*Till we all meet in heav'n.*"

2. The second form given to this cento was by M. Madan in his *Coll. of Ps. & Hys., &c.*, 1760, No. 35. In this we have st. i. and iii., as above, in Whitefield, and st. iv. expanded into two stanzas thus :—

> 4. " Sing on your heav'nly way,
>   Ye ransom'd sinners, sing,
>   Sing on, rejoicing, ev'ry day
>   In Christ, th' eternal King.
>
> 5. " Soon shall ye hear him say,
>   ' Ye blessed children, come ' ;
>   Soon will He call ye hence away,
>   And take His wand'rers home."

This cento was repeated by Dr. Conyers in his *Coll. & Hys.*, 1774, by De Courcy, in his *Coll.*, 1775, and thence through numerous hymnals into Mercer's and Thring's *Colls.*, Lord Selborne's *Bk. of Praise*, and others in the Ch. of England ; and through Lady Huntingdon's *Coll.*, 1764, into a limited number of Nonconformists' hymn-books. In many of these reprints the *ye* of st. v., l. 3, is changed to *you*. Amongst modern American collections in which this cento is given in full are :—Dutch Ref. *Hys. of the Ch.* N. Y., 1869 ; *Bap. Praise Bk.*, N. Y. & Chicago, 1871 ; Hatfield's *Ch. H. Bk.*, 1872, and the *Ch. Praise Bk.*, 1882 ; and, with the omission of st. iii., in the Episc. *Hys. for Ch. & Home*, Phil., 1860 ; Presb. *Ps. & Hys.* Richmond, 1867 ; *Ch.*

Pastorals, Boston, 1864 ; *Presb. Hymnal*, Phil., 1874 ; and the new *Episc. Hymnal*, 1871. The signature to this cento is " *W. Hammond*, 1745 ; *G. Whitefield*, 1753 ; *and M. Madan*, 1760."

3. The third cento appeared in Toplady's *Ps. & Hys.*, 1776, No. 118, in 6 st., the first five being *Madan's* text as above, with *us* for ye, in st. v. l. 3, and the addition of the following :—

> " There shall our raptur'd tongue
> His endless praise proclaim ;
> And sing, in sweetest notes, the song
> Of Moses and the Lamb."

This stanza is from Watts's *H. & S. Songs*, 1709, Bk. i., No. 49, st. vi. :—

> " Then will our love and joy be full,
> And feel a warmer flame ;
> And sweeter voices tune the song
> Of Moses and the Lamb."

This cento is the most widely adopted of any, both in G. Brit. and America. It is found in full in Snepp's *S. of G. & G.*, the *Meth. F. Ch. S. S. H. Bk.* and others ; and with the omission of st. iii., "Sing till we feel our hearts, &c.," in the *Hy. Comp.*, the *Bap. Hymnal*, &c. The collections are far too many to name, and any book can be tested by the text as above. The American modern hymn-books which adopt it in full include *Hys. & Songs of Praise*, N. Y., 1874, and the *Evang. Hymnal*, 1880, in full, with a slight alteration in st. vi. ; *Songs of Zion* (A. R. T. Soc.), 1864 ; *Sabbath H. Bk.*, N. Y. 1858 ; Bap. *Ser. of Song*, Boston, 1871, &c. ; and with omission of st. iii., in *Bap. Hy. & Tune Bk.*, Phil., 1871 ; *Manual of Praise*, Oberlin, O., 1880 ; *Evang. Hys.* Cleveland, O., 1882 ; and in Canada, the *Presb. H. Bk.*, Toronto, 1880. Its ascription is " *W. Hammond*, 1745 ; *G. Whitefield*, 1753 ; *M. Madan*, 1760 ; *A. M. Toplady* [*with Watts*], 1776."

4. The fourth form appeared in Hall's *Mitre H. Bk.*, 1836, No. 138. As a cento it has failed to gain a position ; but one stanza, No. iv. of cento 2, above rewritten, is retained in cento 5, below. It reads in *Hall* :—

> " Ye pilgrims on the road
> To Sion's city, sing ;
> Rejoicing in the Lamb of God,—
> In Christ, our heav'nly King."

5. In the American New School Presb. *Church Psalmist*, 1843, the arrangement of No. 3 above was given with the omission of st. iii., and the substitution of *Hall's* " Ye pilgrims," &c., with " Rejoice, ye," for st. iv. This text is second in popularity only to cento 3. It is given sometimes in 5 st. and again in 6, and is included, amongst other hymn-books, in the Bap. *Ps. & Hys.*, 1858 ; *New Cong.* 1859 ; *Windle* ; *Hys. for the Ch. Catholic*, 1882 ; late editions of Rippon's *Sel.*, and others in G. Brit.: and in America, in the *Meth. Episc. H. Bk.*, 1849 ; *Songs for the Sancty.*, N. Y., 1865, &c. The ascription to this is, " *W. Hammond*, 1745 ; *G. Whitefield*, 1753 ; *M. Madan*, 1760 ; *A. M. Toplady* [*with Watts*], 1776 ; Hall's *Mitre*, 1836."

6. In the *Parish H. Bk.*, 1863–1875, No. 105, we have st. i., ii., iv., v., vi., from *Toplady*, slightly altered, together with the addition of a doxology. This is " *W. Hammond*, 1745 ; *G. Whitefield*, 1753 ; *M. Madan*, 1760 ; *A. M. Toplady*, [*with Watts*], 1776 ; *Parish H. Bk.*, 1863."

7. The last arrangement we have to notice is

No. 335 of *Church Hys.*, 1871. This is *Toplady's* text, st. i., ii., iv., v., vi., with alterations in the 1 st. :—

> " Awake and sing the song
>   *Of glory to the Lamb,*"

which we meet for the first time, and st. v. :—

> " And sweeter voices swell the song
>   *Of glory to the Lamb,*"

of which the first line is *Watts's* (as above, No. 3) with *swell* for *tune*, and the second a fresh departure. It may be noted that this return to *Watts* was made by Cotterill in his *Sel.*, 1810. The signature to this cento is : " *W. Hammond*, 1745 ; *G. Whitefield*, 1753 ; *M. Madan*, 1760 ; *A. M. Toplady* [*with Watts*], 1776 ; *Ch. Hymns*, 1871."

In Bingham's *Hymno. Christ. Lat.*, 1871, there is a rendering into Latin of cento 5 in 5 st. slightly altered again, as :—" Jam cantilenam gratulantes tollite."

Beyond what we have here set forth in somewhat wearisome detail, other minute changes are to be found in collections of less importance than those noticed. These may be tested by the quotations given above, and a reference to the original text in *Lyra Brit.* 1867, pp. 263–5.   [J. J.]

Awake, awake, my sluggish soul.

O. Heginbothom. [*Watchfulness.*] 1st pub. in his *Hymns*, &c., 1794, in 6 st. of 4 l., and based upon St. Luke xii. 38–39. In 1812 it was transferred to Collyer's *Coll.*, No. 653, unaltered, and thus came into C. U. In some American collections, st. v. and vi. are omitted. In America it is also given as " Awake, awake, each drowsy soul," as in the *Bapt. Praise Bk.*, 1871, No. 558. In the Bap. *Ch. Praise Bk.*, N. Y., 1872, we have st. i., iii., and iv., and in *Ch. Pastorals*, Boston, 1864, st. i., iii., v. and vi.

Awake, awake, O Zion.

B. Gough. [*Second Advent.*] Appeared in his *Lyra Sabbatica*, &c., 1865, p. 151, in 6 st. of 8 l., and entitled, " The coming Millennium," with the quotation of Isa. lii. 1. From that work it passed into the *People's H.*, 1867 ; Allon's *Suppl. Hymns*, 1868, in 5 st., and in other collections both in G. Britain and America. It is also included as the opening hymn of Gough's *H. of Prayer and Praise*, 1875.

Awake, awake the sacred song.

Anne Steele. [*Christmas.*] 1st pub. in her *Poems on Subjects chiefly Devotional*, &c., 1760, vol. i. p. 85, in 6 st. of 4 l., and headed " The Incarnate Saviour." It was also included in the 1780 ed. of the *Poems*, and in D. Sedgwick's reprint of her *Hymns*, 1859. It came into C. U. by being adopted by Ash and Evans in their Bristol *Coll.*, 1769, No. 88, from whence it passed into a few hymnals. It is still in use in America, and is given in Hatfield's *Ch. H. Bk.*, 1872, the Bap. *Praise Bk.*, 1871, and *Songs for the Sanctuary*, 1865, the first omitting st. vi. and the remaining two st. iv.

Awake, glad soul, awake, awake.

J. S. B. Monsell. [*Easter.*] According to the Preface to his *Spiritual Songs*, this was one of his hymns " written amid the orange and olive groves of Italy, during a winter spent (for the sake of health) upon the shores of the Mediterranean Sea." It was pub. in his *Hymns of Love and Praise;* 1863, p. 90, in 5 st., and in his *Spiritual Songs,* 1875, in 8 st. of 8 l., the new stanzas being ii., iii. and iv. Three centos therefrom are in C. U. (1) in the *Hy. Comp.,* No. 178, consisting of st. i., vi., vii. and viii. (2) in the Scottish *Evang. U. Hymnal,* No. 40, of st. i., v., vii. and viii. (3) in the Amer. *College Hymnal, N. Y.,* 1876, No. 145, beginning, "The shade and gloom of life are fled." This is composed of st. vi. and viii. unaltered. Full text in Schaff's *Christ in Song,* 1869–70.

Awake, Jerusalem, awake. *C. Wesley.* [*Exhortation.*] A paraphrase of Isaiah lii., which appeared in the Wesley *Psalms and Hymns,* 1741, in 28 st. of 4 l., c. m., divided into three parts. Two centos from this are in C. U. in America. (1) The Amer. *Meth. Episc. Coll.,* N. Y., 1849, composed of st. i., iii. and iv. of Pt. i., and st. ii. of Pt. iii. (2) *H. Bk. of the Evang. Assoc.,* Cleveland, O., 1882; the same stanzas with the addition of st. iv., Pt. iii. The poem as given in the *P. Works of J. and C. Wesley,* 1868–72, vol. ii. pp. 168–173, has 4 st. in l. m. added to Pt. ii. These stanzas were first published in the 1st series of *Hymns on God's Everlasting Love,* 1741. Being a part of the same chapter in Isaiah they were omitted from the reprint of the *Hymns,* &c., and incorporated with this poem, in the *P. Works,* vol. ii., 1869.

Awake, my heart, arise my tongue. *I. Watts.* [*Spiritual Clothing.*] 1st pub. in his *Hymns and S. Songs,* 1707 (1709, Bk. i., No. 20), in 6 st. of 4 l., and again in later editions. It is based on Is. lxi. 10. It came into C. U. at an early date, and is still found in many collections in G. Brit. and America.

Awake, my love, awake, my joy. *J. Mason.* [*Morning.*] This is a cento adapted from Mason's Songs of Praise for Morning and Evening, and consists of st. i. from the Evening and ii.–iv. from the Morning Hymn. It was included in the Rev. T. Darling's *Hymns for the Ch. of England,* new ed., 1874, No. 198. The original text appeared in Mason's *Songs of Praise,* 1683, and in Sedgwick's reprint, 1859, pp. 16–18.

Awake, my soul, awake, my tongue. *Anne Steele.* [*Ps. ciii.*] This version of Ps. ciii. extends to 16 st. of 4 l. It appeared in her *Poems,* &c., 1760, vol. ii. p. 206, and new ed., 1780. The cento given in Martineau's *Hymns,* &c., 1840 and 1873; the Amer. Bap. *Service of Song,* Boston, 1872, and others, is composed of st. i., ii., xi. and xvi. slightly altered. Orig. text in Sedgwick's reprint of Miss Steele's *Hymns,* 1863.

Awake, my soul, in [to] joyful lays. *S. Medley.* [*Love of God.*] Appeared in J. H. Meyer's *Coll. of Hymns* for Lady Huntingdon's Chapel, Cumberland Street, Shoreditch, 1782, and again in Medley's *Hymns,* Bristol and Bradford, 1785, in 8 st. of 4 l. In 1787 it was included, with the omission of one stanza in Rippon's Bapt. *Sel.,* 1787, No. 13,

and again by the author in his *Hymns,* &c., 1800, with the addition of st. 4, and the transposing of st. v. and vi. The versions in common use are that of *Rippon,* 1787, in 7 st., and a selection therefrom, in 5 st. It is also in use in America. Orig. text in *Lyra Brit.,* 1867.

Awake, my soul, lift up thine eyes. *Anna L. Barbauld.* [*Watchfulness.*] Contributed to Dr. Enfield's *Hymns,* &c., Warrington, 1772, No. 126, in 6 st. of 4 l., and headed "The Conflict." In the following year it was repeated in her *Poems,* Lon., 1773, and again in her *Works,* &c., 1825, vol. i. p. 330. Its use has been and still is fairly extensive both in G. Brit. and America. Orig. text in *Lyra Brit.,* 1867, p. 34, and Lord Selborne's *Bk. of Praise,* 1862, p. 485. In the latter the date, 1773, is given in error.

Awake, my soul, stretch every nerve. *P. Doddridge.* [*Confirmation.*] This hymn is not given in the "D. MSS." It was 1st pub. by J. Orton in his ed. of Doddridge's *Hymns,* &c., 1755, No. 296, in 5 st. of 4 l., and entitled "Pressing on in the Christian Race." It was repeated in all subsequent editions of the *Hymns,* and also in Doddridge's *Scripture Hymns,* edited by J. Doddridge Humphreys, 1839. One of the earliest collections in which it is found is Ash and Evans's Bristol *Coll.,* 1769, No. 281, with the omission of st. iv. "That prize," &c. From that date it came into general use, sometimes in 4 st., and again in 5 st. until it became widely known both in Great Brit. and America. In modern collections it is held in greater favour by those of the Ch. of England than those of Nonconformists. Full orig. text in the *New Cong.,* No. 617, and the 4 st. form unaltered, in *Hy. Comp.,* No. 452. In the latter collection the editor suggests that in Confirmation it be sung after the benedictory prayer, "Defend, O Lord, this Thy servant," &c. This 4 st. arrangement has been rendered into Latin:— "Sursum, mens mea! Strenuè," by the Rev. R. Bingham, and given in his *Hymno. Christ. Lat.,* 1871, pp. 101–103. A slightly altered form of the hymn, as "*Awake, our souls, awake from sloth,*" is given in a few hymnals, including Walker's *Cheltenham Coll.,* 1855 and 1881. [J. J.]

Awake, my soul, to grateful praise. [*Morning.*] This hymn was given in J. H. Gurney's *Lutterworth Coll.,* 1838, No. 15, in 5 st. of 4 l., as by "Gardiner." It was repeated with the same ascription in the Marylebone *Ps. & Hys.,* 1851, and, without name or date, in *Kennedy,* 1863.

Awake, my soul, to meet the day. *P. Doddridge.* [*Morning.*] This hymn is in the "D. MSS." but undated. In 1755, it was pub. by J. Orton in Doddridge's *Hymns,* &c., No. 362, in 7 st. of 4 l. without alteration, the title being, "A morning hymn, to be used at awaking and rising." It was republished in J. D. Humphreys's ed. of the *Hymns,* 1839, No. 389. It is not in C. U. in G. Britain. In the American *Hymnal of the Meth. Episco. Ch.,* 1878, st. i., ii., vi., vii., are given, somewhat altered, as No. 96.

Awake, my zeal, awake, my love.
I. Watts. [*Personal call to duty.*] This may
be called a metrical paraphrase of his sermon
on i. Cor. iii. 22, "Whether Life or Death—
All are yours." It was appended with other
hymns, to his *Sermons*, 1721–4, in 6 st. of 8 l.,
and is repeated in later editions. Its use is
limited. In Hall's *Mitre*, 1836, it was given
as "Awake *our* zeal, awake *our* love," in 4
st. This also has almost passed out of use.

Awake, our drowsy souls. *Elizabeth
Scott.* [*Sunday.*] 1st pub. in the Baptist
Coll. of Ash and Evans, Bristol, 1769, No. 307,
in 5 st. of 6 l., and appointed as "A hymn for
Lord's Day Morning." From that collection
it passed into several later hymnals, including
Rippon, Dobell, and others; but it is almost
entirely unknown to modern hymn-books except in America, having been superseded by
"Awake, ye saints, awake, And hail," &c., a
recast of the same in 4 st. (st. iii. being the
original with "*and*" for "while," l. 3) made
by T. Cotterill, and given in the 1st ed. of
his *Selection*, 1810. This form of the hymn
is in somewhat extensive use both in Great
Britain and America, and is usually ascribed
correctly to "Elizabeth Scott and Thomas
Cotterill." In many of the modern American
hymnals, st. iv. is omitted; but the English
generally give the text from Cotterill as in
Bapt. *Ps. and Hys.*, 1858, in this case the
only alteration is "*blest*" for "bless'd" in st.
i., l. 5. Another form of the hymn is:—
"Servants of God, awake." It consists of
st. i.–iii. of Cotterill's recast, slightly altered.
It appeared in the Harrow School *H. Bk.*,
1855, and from thence passed into *Church
Hys.*, 1871, No. 39. In the *H. Bk. of the
Evang. Assoc.*, Cleveland, Ohio, 1881, No. 604,
st. i., ii. are given as "Children of God, awake";
and in the *Marlborough College Hys.*, 1869,
st. i.–iii. as "Come, sons of God, awake."
                           [W. T. B.]

**Awake, our souls, and bless His
name.** *P. Doddridge.* [*Christ the Door.*]
This hymn is not in the "D. MSS.," and was
1st pub. by J. Orton in his ed. of Doddridge's
Hymns, &c., 1755, in 4 st. of 4 l. It is based
on St. John x. 9. It is repeated in later
editions of the *Hymns*, and in J. D. Humphreys's ed. of the same, 1839. In *Kennedy*,
1863, No. 201, it is given as "Awake, my soul,
and bless His name."

Awake our souls, away our fears.
I. Watts. [*The Christian Race.*] 1st pub. in
his *Hymns and S. Songs*, 1707, Bk. i., No. 48,
in 5 st. of 4 l., and headed "The Christian
Race." It has been repeated in later editions
of the *Hymns*, and may be found in all editions of Watts's *Works*. Its use in the original,
and as altered, is as follows :—

1. The original was included in various hymn-books
at an early date, and is now in extensive use in all
English-speaking countries.

2. The original—with the single change of "*Thy
matchless*" for "Whose matchless power," in st. iii.
line 1—is interesting, from the fact that it was introduced
by *J. Wesley* in his *Ps. & Hys.*, pub. at Charlestown,
South Carolina, in 1736–7, and from thence has passed into
nearly all the Methodist hymn-books throughout the
world, in addition to many in the Ch. of England. In
the latter case the descent has been through M. Madan's
Ps. & Hys. 1760.

3. The readings in Windle's *Met. Psalter*, and one or
two others which have copied from him, are partly (st. ii.
ll. 3–4) from Rowland Hill's *Ps. & Hys.*, 2nd ed., 1787,
and partly (st. iii., iv.) by Mr. Windle.

4. In Hall's *Mitre*, 1836, the hymn is given as
"Awake, *my soul, dismiss thy* fears." At one time
this text was widely used, but is now almost unknown.

Other readings exist in minor collections,
and may be corrected by collating with the
orig. text as above.

Awake, sweet gratitude, and sing.
A. M. Toplady. [*Christ's Intercession.*] In
the *Gospel Magazine*, 1771, this hymn is given
in 10 st. of 6 l. From the *G. Magazine* it passed
at an early date into various collections, but
in an abbreviated form. These included Rippon's *Sel.*, 1787, to which possibly, more than
to any other hymnal, modern collections are
indebted for their text both in G. Brit. and
America. The full orig. text was included in
Sedgwick's reprint of Toplady's *Hymns*, 1860,
p. 150. It is curious to note that this hymn
was omitted from Toplady's *Ps. and Hys.*,
1776, and from an ed. of his *Hymns*, pub.
in 1856.

Awake, sweet harp of Judah, wake.
H. K. White. [*Heaven.*] In Southey's ed. of
H. K. White's *Remains*, 1807, this hymn is
given in 7 of 4 l., with the title "In heaven
we shall be purified, so as to be able to endure
the splendours of the Deity," and accompanied
with the following note :—

The last stanza of this hymn was added extempora-
neously by Henry one summer evening, when he was
with a few friends on the Trent, and singing it as he
was used to do on such occasions."

In the few modern collections in which this
hymn is found it is given in an abbreviated
form. The orig. text is in *Lyra Brit.*, 1867,
p. 628.   [W. T. B.]

**Awake, ye saints, and raise [lift]
your eyes.** *P. Doddridge.* [*Exhortation.*]
This hymn is not in the "D. MSS.," and was
1st pub. by J. Orton in his ed. of Doddridge's
Hymns, &c., 1755, No. 264, in 4 st. of 4 l., and
entitled "The near Approach of Salvation, an
Engagement to Diligence and Love. Rom.
xiii. 11." It was also repeated in J. D.
Humphreys's ed. of the same, 1839. It
came into C. U. at an early date, and is still
found in a few important collections in G.
Brit. and America. In R. Conyers's *Ps. and
Hys.*, 1774, it was altered to "Awake, ye
saints, and *lift* your eyes;" but this has
died out of use. Orig. text in *Lyra Brit.*,
1867, p. 191, and Lord Selborne's *Bk. of
Praise*, 1862, p. 296.

**Awake, ye saints, to praise your
King.** *I. Watts.* [*Ps. cxxxv.*] His C. M.
version of Ps. cxxxv., in 8 st. of 4 l., 1st pub.
in his *Ps. of David*, &c., 1719. In a note
thereto he says, "In the 5th stanza I have
borrowed a verse from Jer. xiv. 22, "*Are there
any among the vanities of the Gentiles that can
cause rain*." This st. begins "Which of the
stocks and stones they trust." As a whole
the paraphrase is not in general use. A cento
beginning "Great is the Lord, and works
unknown," is given in *N. Cong.*, No. 225. It
is composed of st. ii.–v. and viii.

Away, dark thoughts, awake, my joy. *J. Mason.* [*Christmas.*] This is Mason's "Song of Praise for the Birth of Christ," and appeared in his *Songs of Praise*, 1683, in 4 st. of 8 l., and in later editions including Sedgwick's reprint, 1859. Its use as a congregational hymn is limited. It is quaint, and on the whole unsuited to modern taste.

Away from every mortal care. *I. Watts.* [*Public Worship.*] 1st pub. in his *Hymns and S. Songs*, 1709, Bk. ii., No. 123, in 6 st. of 4 l., and entitled, "The benefit of Public Ordinances." It has been republished in all later editions of the *Hymns*, &c., and in *Watts's Works.* G. Whitefield included st. i., ii., iii., and vi., in his Coll., 1753. This arrangement is often repeated in modern hymnals. In Hatfield's Amer. *Church H. Bk.*, 1872, No. 122, the full text is given with *brings*, for "*bears* down," in st. iii., l. 3.

Away, my needless fears. *C. Wesley.* [*Submission.*] In *Hymns and Sacred Poems*, 1749, 55 hymns were given as "For Christian Friends," of which this was No. 35, in 10 st. of 8 l. From this two centos have come into C. U. as follows:—

1. In the *Supp.* to the *Wes. H. Bk.* 1830, st. i., vii., and ix. were given in 6 st. of 4 l., No. 675. This cento is also found in various collections of the Methodist bodies, and in the revised ed. of the *Wes. H. Bk.* 1875. No. 832.

2. In *A. M. Toplady's Ps. & Hys.* 1776, No. 75, and later editions, st. i.–v. and ix. were given with slight alterations, but this cento has almost entirely gone out of use. Orig. text in *P. Works*, 1868–72, vol. v. p. 448.

Away, my unbelieving fear. *C. Wesley.* [*Confidence.*] Hab. iii., 17, 18, 19, is the subject of this hymn. It appeared in *Hymns and Sacred Poems*, 1742, in 4 st. of 8 l., and again in the *P. Works*, 1868–72, vol. ii. p. 198. It did not form part of the *Wes. H. Bk.* until the revised ed. 1875, although, through having been given in M. Madan's *Ps. & Hys.*, 1760, it had been in C. U. in the Ch. of England and amongst Nonconformists for more than one hundred years. Its modern use is limited.

Away, thou dying saint, away. *T. Kelly.* [*Death.*] 1st pub. in the 3rd ed. of his *Hymns*, 1809, No. 134, in 5 st. of 4 l., and repeated in all subsequent editions. It is based on Eccles. xii. 7, "And the Spirit shall return to God who gave it." Orig. text in E. T. Prust's *Supp. H. Bk.*, 1869, No. 241.

Away with death, away. *H. K. White.* [*Death.*] This poem, entitled "Athanatos," was given by Southey in his ed. of H. K. White's *Remains*, 1807, and repeated in later editions, as also in the numerous reprints of H. K. White's *Poems.* It is unknown as a hymn, but 20 lines therefrom slightly altered and beginning, "Hail the heavenly scenes of peace," are in Martineau's *Hymns*, &c., 1840 and 1873.

Away with our fears, Our troubles and tears. *C. Wesley.* [*Whitsuntide.*] This is No. 32 of his "Hymns for Whitsunday," which were pub. at Bristol in 1746 as *Hymns of Petition and Thanksgiving for the Promise of the Father.* It is in 5 st. of 8 l. In 1776 four stanzas, somewhat altered, were given in A. M. Toplady's *Ps. & Hys.*, No. 236, and thus came into C. U. It did not form a part of the *Wes. H. Bk.* until the revised ed. of 1875. Orig. text in *P. Works*, 1868–72, vol. iv. p. 203.

Away with my [our] fears! The glad morning appears. *C. Wesley.* [*Thanksgiving.*] This hymn was written for use on the celebration of a Birthday, and in many respects it is eminently suited thereto. It was 1st pub. in *Hymns and Sacred Poems*, 1749, vol. ii., No. 190, in 14 st. of 6 l., and entitled "On his Birthday." Under the date "June 17, 1788," J. Wesley refers to this hymn in the following manner:—

"I this day enter on my eighty-fifth year; and what cause have I to praise God, as for a thousand spiritual blessings, so for bodily blessings also! How little have I suffered yet by the rush of numerous years! . . . Even now, though I find daily pain in my eye, or temple, or arm, yet it is never violent, and seldom lasts many minutes at a time. Whether or not this is sent to give me warning that I am shortly to quit this tabernacle, I do not know; but be it one way or the other, I have only to say:—

'My remnant of days I spend in His praise,
  Who died the whole world to redeem:
My days are His due, Be they many or few,
  And they all are devoted to Him.'"

When included in the *Wes. H. Bk.*, 1780, No. 221, st. ii. and xi. were omitted. This form is repeated in the new ed., 1875, and also in numerous hymnals of the Methodist bodies at home and abroad. Orig. text in *P. Works*, 1868–72, vol. v. p. 400.   [J. J.]

Away with our sorrow and fear. *C. Wesley.* [*Burial.*] No. viii. of his *Funeral Hymns*, 1746, in 5 st. of 8 l., and again in the *Wes. H. Bk.*, 1780, No. 71, and ed. 1875, No. 73. It is found in the hymnals of the various branches of the Methodist body in most English-speaking countries, and sometimes in other collections. In the Cooke & Denton *Hymnal*, 1853, No. 324, the first line reads, "Away with *all* sorrow and fear." Orig. text in *P. Works*, 1868–72, vol. vi. p. 197.

The hymn, with the same first stanza, in A. M. Toplady's *Ps. & Hys.*, 1776, No. 68, and later editions, together with others which have copied therefrom, is a cento, of which the 1st st. is st. i. of this hymn; st. iii. from Wesley's "Give glory to Jesus, our Head" (*Hys. & S. Poems*, 1749); and ii., iv., and v. from No. vii. of the above *Funeral Hys.* It is very little used, if at all, at the present time.

Awhile in spirit, Lord, to Thee. *J. F. Thrupp.* [*Lent.*] One of the best known and most popular of Mr. Thrupp's hymns. It was written for and 1st pub. in his *Ps. & Hys. for Pub. Worship*, 1853, No. 64, in 4 st. of 4 l. In 1861 the Rev. F. Pott included it in his *Hys.*, &c., No. 72, with st. iii. and iv. transposed, some minor alterations, and a doxology from the Latin. This form was repeated in *Ch. Hys.*, 1871, No. 103. Orig. text in Thring's *Coll.*, 1882, No. 154, with st. i., l. 2, "Into the desert would we flee," for "Would we unto the desert flee," an alteration from the Rev. F. Pott as above. The text of *Hys. & Songs of Praise: N. Y.*, 1874, is that of the Rev. F. Pott with a slight alteration, and the omission of the doxology.

Aylward, James Ambrose, b. in 1813, at Leeds, and educated at Hinckley, the Dominican Priory of St. Peter, to which a secular college was attached. Particulars touching the stages of his monastic life may be found in the *Obituary Notices of the Friar-Preachers, or Dominicans, of the English Province from the year of our Lord* 1650. He was ordained in 1836, and assisted in the school, taking the higher classical studies, in 1842. He became head of the school, and continued so till it was discontinued in 1852. At Woodchester he was made successively Lector of Philosophy and Theology and Prior. He died at Hinckley, and was buried in the cloister-yard of Woodchester. His sacred poems have become his principal monument, and of these he contributed very many to the first three volumes of the *Catholic Weekly Instructor*, and other periodicals. His essay on the *Mystical Element in Religion*, and on *Ancient and Modern Spiritism*, was not pub. till 1874. Referring to him, and to his MS. *tr.* of Latin hymns, a large number of which are incorporated by Mr. O. Shipley in *Annus Sanctus*, 1884, Mr. Shipley says: "The second collection of MSS. came from the pen of the late Very Rev. Father Aylward, of the Order of Preachers, a cultured and talented priest of varied powers and gifts, whose memory is held dear by all who knew and were influenced by him. He went to his reward in the year 1872, after nearly forty years' profession as a Dominican, and was buried in the picturesque cloistral-cemetery of Woodchester, of which model and peaceful religious house he was the first Prior."

[J. C. E.]

Ayres, H. C., b. about 1849, a member of the Baptist denomination, and a resident in Philadelphia, is the author of :—

1. **One there is who loves thee.** [*Love of Christ.*] A popular hymn and well known in G. Brit. through I. D. Sankey's *Sacred S. & Solos*, enlarged ed., No. 310. It was written during the Centennial Exhibition in Philadelphia, the theme having been suggested by the expression, "One there is Who loves and waits to bless," used by Mr. W. H. Doane (q. v.) in prayer at a meeting of friends at which Mr. Ayres was present. The MS. was presented to Mr. Doane a day or two afterwards. It was set to music by Mr. Doane, and pub. forthwith. The orig. text and music are in Mr. Sankey's *S. & Solos* as above. Mr. Ayres is also the author of :—

2. **No other Name.** [*The Name of Jesus.*] This hymn is unknown to the English collections. [J. J.]

B

B., in Ash and Evans's Bapt. *Coll.*, Bristol, 1st ed., 1769, i.e. Simon Browne.

B. in Nettleton's *Village Hymns* (American), 1824, i.e. Mrs. Phœbe Brown.

B. in *Hys. & Sac. Songs*, Manchester, Fletcher & Tubbs, 1855, i.e. Rev. G. B. Bubier.

B., in Horder's *Congregational Hymns*, 1884, i.e. the Rev. Stopford A. Brooke.

B. B., *Ash & Evans*, 1769, i.e. Benjamin Beddome.

B—d., in the same *Coll.*, later editions, i.e. Anna L. Barbauld.

B. S., in the same *Coll.*, 1769, i.e. Benjamin Seward.

B. T., in the *People's H.*, i.e. a *nom de plume* of the Rev. R. F. Littledale, and the initials of a former address.

Backward with humble shame we look. *I. Watts.* [*The Fall and the Redemption.*] 1st pub. in his *Hymns and Spiritual Songs*, 1707, bk. i., No. 57, in 8 st. of 4 l., and again in later eds. of the same. Its use, and that in an abbreviated form, is very limited.

Bacon, Francis, Lord Verulam, s. of Sir Nicholas Bacon, b. in London, 1561, d. 1626. He was educated at Trinity College, Cambridge, and there showed at an early age those remarkable powers which eventually gained him a world-wide and lasting renown. The story of his greatness and of his shame belongs more to the history of the nation than to hymnody, his contributions to the latter being confined to the metrical versions of seven (1, 12, 90, 104, 126, 137, 149) individual psalms, which were pub. in his *Certaine Psalmes*, Lond., Hannah Barrett and R. Whittaker, 1625; and reprinted in Dr. Grosart's *Fuller Worthies Miscellanies*, vol. i., 1870, and in various eds. of Bacon's collected *Works*.

Bacon, Leonard, D.D., was b. at Detroit (where his father was a missionary to the Indians), Feb. 19, 1802, and educated at Yale College, and at Andover. In 1825 he was ordained Pastor of the Centre Church, New Haven, and retained that charge till 1866, when he was appointed Professor of Theology in Yale Divinity School. This professorship he resigned in 1871; but till his death in 1881, he was Lecturer on Church Polity. He died Dec. 23, 1881. Dr. Bacon rendered important services to hymnology both as writer and compiler. While a student at Andover, he edited an important and now rare tract, entitled *Hymns and Sacred Songs for the Monthly Concert* [of Prayer for Missions], Andover, Sept. 1823. This contained the three hymns following, which are his :—

1. **Weep not for the saint that ascends.** *Death of a Missionary.*

2. **Land where the bones of our fathers are sleeping.** *Missions.* This was brought into notice in G. Britain through its insertion in the *Evangelical Magazine*, March, 1824.

3. **Wake the song of jubilee.** *Missions.*

Of these No. 1 is found in *Lyra Sac. Amer.*, p. 6, and No. 3 was adopted, with alterations, by Pratt in his *Ps. and Hys.* (Lond., Seeley & Co., 1829), from which it passed into Greene and Mason's *Church Psalmody*, 1831, and the *Church Psalmist* of the Evangelical Christians (N. Y.,

1845, 7th ed.). This altered text, with some further changes, was adopted by the author in his *Appendix* to T. Dwight's revised ed. of Watts's *Psalms*, 1833. This *Appendix* also contained three new hymns by him, viz. :—

4. Though now the nations sit beneath. *Missions.* This is based on a hymn by Sarah Slinn, " Arise in all Thy splendour, Lord " (q. v.), which Dr. Bacon had partly rewritten for his Andover Tract, above noted. In the *Appendix* to *Dwight* he substituted new verses for what remained of her's in the Tract, and then justly claimed the whole as his own.

5. O Thou Who hast died to redeem us from hell. *Holy Communion.*

6. God of our fathers, to Thy throne. *Thanksgiving.*

In 1845 Dr. Bacon was joint compiler with Dr. E. T. Fitch, and several others, of *Psalms & Hymns for Christian Use and Worship*, pub. " by the General Association of Connecticut."

To this collection he contributed the four hymns following :—

7. Here, Lord of life and light, to Thee. *Institution of a Minister.* This was written March 9, 1825, for his installation as pastor of the First Church, New Haven, and first pub. as above, No. 559, in 4 st. of 4 l., and headed " Ordination in an ancient New England Church."

8. O God, beneath Thy guiding hand. *American Anniversary Hymn.* This is a favourite American Anniversary hymn. It is abbreviated and altered from his hymn, " The Sabbath morn is as bright and calm," which he wrote for the Bicentenary of New Haven, 1833. In this revised form it was first pub. as above, No. 619, in 5 st. of 4 l., and appointed " For the twenty-second of December."

9. O God of Abraham, ever sure. *Prayer on behalf of the Young.* This was written as a substitute for Mrs. Hyde's " Dear Saviour, if these lambs should stray," the use of which was refused by the owners of the copyright of Nettleton's *Village Hymns* (1824). In the *Ps. & Hys.*, 1845, it is No. 635, in 4 st. of 4 l., and headed " Prayer for the children of the Church."

10. Hail, tranquil hour of closing day. *Evening.* This popular hymn was written under the same circumstances as the preceding, and as a substitute for Mrs. Brown's Twilight hymn, " I love to steal awhile away." It is No. 706 of the *Ps. & Hys.*, 1845, in 5 st. of 4 l., and entitled " Evening Twilight."

11. How sweet, thro' long remembered years. *Evening.* In the *Church Praise Bk.*, N. Y., 1882, No. 15, is composed of st. iii.–v. of No. 10.

[F. M. B.]

Bahnmaier, Jonathan Friedrich, s. of J. C. Bahnmaier, Town Preacher at Oberstenfeld, near Bottwar, Württemberg, was b. at Oberstenfeld, July 12, 1774. After completing his studies at Tübingen, his first appointment was, in 1798, as assistant to his father. He became Diaconus at Marbach on the Neckar in 1806, and at Ludwigsburg in 1810, where he was for a time the head of a young ladies' school. In 1815 he was appointed Professor of Education and Homiletics at Tübingen, but in the troublous times that

followed had to resign his post. He received in 1819 the appointment of Decan and Town Preacher at Kirchheim-unter-Teck, where he continued as a faithful, unwearied, and successful worker for 21 years. He was distinguished as a preacher, and greatly interested in the causes of education, of missions, and of Bible societies. He was also one of the principal members of the committee which compiled the Württemberg *G. B.* of 1842. He preached his last sermon at Kirchheim, on the 10th Sunday after Trinity, Aug. 15, 1841. Two days later he held a visitation at Owen. While inspecting the school at the adjacent village of Brucker, he was struck by paralysis, and being conveyed back to Owen, d. there, Aug. 18, 1841 (*Koch*, vii. 81–84; *Allg. Deutsche Biog.*, i. 766–767). Of his hymns two have been *tr.* into English :—

i. **Jesu als du wiederkehrtest.** [*Schools.*] 1st pub. in his *Christliche Blätter aus Tübingen*, pts. 9–12 for 1819, p. 85, in 2 st. of 8 l., entitled " Prayer after School ; " as one of 7 metrical prayers for Children, and for the School and House. Included as No. 2947 in Knapp's *Ev. L. S.*, 1837 (1865, No. 2614), and No. 513 in the Württemberg *G. B.*, 1842. The only *tr.* in C. U. is :—

Jesu, when Thou once returnest. In full by Miss Winkworth in her *C. B. for England*, 1863, No. 178.

ii. **Walte, fürder, nah und fern.** [*Missions.*] According to *Koch*, vii. 84, 1st printed separately 1827. Included as No. 97 in the *Kern des deutschen Liederschatzes*, Nürnberg, 1828, and as No. 260, beginning, " Walte, walte, nah und fern," in Bunsen's *Versuch.*, 1833, in 7 st. of 4 l., and since in the Württemberg *G. B.*, 1842, and other recent collections. One of the best and most useful of hymns for Foreign Missions. The *trs.* in C. U. are :—

1. **Far and near, Almighty Word.** A good and full *tr.* by Miss Cox in her *Sacred H. from the German*, 1841, p. 203, repeated, slightly altered, in her *H. from the German*, 1864, p. 223. Included in J. L. Porter's *Coll.*, 1876, and the *Bapt. Hymnal*, 1879. In Hedge and Huntington's *Hys*, Boston, U.S., 1853, and Dean Alford's *Year of Praise*, 1867, st. i. was omitted and the hymn thus began, " Word by God the Father sent."

2. **Spread thy triumph far and nigh,** by H. J. Buckoll. By omitting st. ii., iv. as No. 65 in the *Rugby School H. Bk.*, 1850 (in the *Rugby School H. Bk.*, 1870, No. 175, the *tr.* is complete). The *trs.* of st. iii., v.–vii. altered and beginning " Word of Him whose sovereign will," were included in the *Marylebone Coll.*, 1851, and Burgess and Money's *Ps. and Hys.*, 1857. The *Wellington College H. Bk.*, 1863, begins with the *tr.* of st. v., " Word of life, so pure and free."

3. **Spread, oh spread, thou mighty Word.** A full and very good *tr.* by Miss Winkworth in her *Lyra Ger.*, 2nd Series, 1858, p. 60, repeated in her *C. B. for England*, 1863, No. 176. Since included in *Kennedy*, 1863, *People's H.*, 1867, *Horder's Cong. Hys.*, 1884, and others ; and in America in the Pennsylvania *Luth. Ch. Bk.*, 1868, *Hys. and S. of Praise*, N. Y., 1874, *Evang. Hymnal*, 1880, and others. In Longfellow and Johnson's *Hys. of the Spirit*, Boston, 1864, it begins with st. v., " Word of life, most pure, most strong."

(1) "Go forth, thou mighty word of grace," by *Lady E. Fortescue*, 1843 (ed. 1847, p. 31). (2) "O Word of God, reign everywhere," by *Dr. G. Walker*, 1860, p. 85. (3) "Word of God! with glory crown'd," in L. Rehfuess's *Ch. at Sea*, 1868, p. 109.   [J. M.]

Bailey, Edward, a Wesleyan local preacher, and a representative of a London iron firm, was b. at Brentford, Middlesex, Aug. 16, 1846. At 12 years of age, through the death of his father, he was compelled to work for his own livelihood, and to support his widowed mother, who was paralysed. His heavy labours were relieved by literary efforts, the first to appear in print being in 1869. Mr. Bailey is known chiefly as the author of 25 tracts in prose and verse, which have been pub. by the Wesleyan, the Tract, and other Societies, and of several hymns. Some of the latter were written for Anniversary Services at various Sunday Schools with which he was associated, and others in times of personal affliction. Of these hymns the following are in the *Meth. S. S. H. Bk.*, 1879, and other collections :—

1. Gracious God! Almighty Father. *Missions.*
2. Tried, trusted, crowned. *Perseverance.*
3. When our hearts are glad and light. *For Guidance.*

Bailey, Philip James, b. at Nottingham, April 22, 1816. His father, a man of great ability and local celebrity as a politician and author, was for some time proprietor and editor of the *Nottingham Mercury*, a weekly newspaper. In his 16th year P. J. Bailey became a student at Glasgow University. He did not graduate, but after a time went to London to study for the legal profession. In 1835 he was called to the bar by the Society of Lincoln's Inn. In the years that followed, whilst ostensibly engaged in legal matters, he was really absorbed in the study of literature and philosophy, and in the conception and elaboration of the remarkable poem in connexion with which his name is chiefly known. This was pub. in 1839, under the title of *Festus, a Poem, by Philip James Bailey. The Angel-World* (1850); *The Mystic and the Spiritual Legend* (1855); and *The Universal Hymn* (1868), may all be considered as episodes of his chief work, and are in fact in later editions in substance incorporated with it. Mr. Bailey is the author of two other works of a different class,—*The Age, a Satire*, 1858, and a brief political treatise on the *International Policy of the Great Powers.*

From 1864 to 1876 Mr. Bailey lived for the most part in Jersey. Of late years he has resided at a seaside village in North Devon.

Festus has passed through 10 editions in England, and 30 in America. One of the lyrics comprised in this poem—"Is Heaven a place where pearly streams"—appears as a Hymn in Dr. R. W. Dale's *English Hymn Bk.* Part-of another—"Call all who love Thee, Lord, to Thee" (ed. 1848, p. 100)—has been expanded into a Hymn by G. Rawson (*Bap. Hymnal*, No. 568). Both compositions are eminently beautiful, and make one wish that Mr. Bailey had given us more of the same kind.

[W. R. S.]

Baker, F. A. [Jerusalem, my happy home.]

Baker, Sir Henry Williams, Bart., eldest s. of Admiral Sir Henry Loraine Baker, b. in London, May 27, 1821, and educated at

Trinity Coll., Cambridge, where he graduated, B.A. 1844, M.A. 1847. Taking Holy Orders in 1844, he became, in 1851, Vicar of Monkland, Herefordshire. This benefice he held to his death, on Monday, Feb. 12, 1877. He succeeded to the Baronetcy in 1851. Sir Henry's name is intimately associated with hymnody. One of his earliest compositions was the very beautiful hymn, "Oh! what if we are Christ's," which he contributed to Murray's *Hymnal for the Use of the English Church*, 1852. His hymns, including metrical litanies and translations, number in the revised ed. of *H. A. & M.*, 33 in all. These were contributed at various times to Murray's *Hymnal; H. A. & M.*, and the *London Mission H. Bk.*, 1876-7. The last contains his three latest hymns. These are not included in *H. A. & M.* Of his hymns four only are in the highest strains of jubilation, another four are bright and cheerful, and the remainder are very tender, but exceedingly plaintive, sometimes even to sadness. Even those which at first seem bright and cheerful have an undertone of plaintiveness, and leave a dreamy sadness upon the spirit of the singer. Poetical figures, far-fetched illustrations, and difficult compound words, he entirely eschewed. In his simplicity of language, smoothness of rhythm, and earnestness of utterance, he reminds one forcibly of the saintly Lyte. In common with Lyte also, if a subject presented itself to his mind with striking contrasts of lights and shadows, he almost invariably sought shelter in the shadows. The last audible words which lingered on his dying lips were the third stanza of his exquisite rendering of the 23rd Psalm, "The King of Love, my Shepherd is" :—

"Perverse and foolish, oft I strayed,
    But yet in love He sought me,
And on His Shoulder gently laid,
    And home, rejoicing, brought me."

This tender sadness, brightened by a soft calm peace, was an epitome of his poetical life.

Sir Henry's labours as the Editor of *H. A. & M.* were very arduous. The trial copy was distributed amongst a few friends in 1859 ; 1st ed. pub. 1861, and the *Appendix*, in 1868 ; the trial copy of the revised ed. was issued in 1874, and the publication followed in 1875. In addition he edited *Hymns for the London Mission*, 1874, and *Hymns for Mission Services*, N.D., c. 1876-7. He also pub. *Daily Prayers for those who work hard ; a Daily Text Book*, &c. In *H. A. & M.* there are also four tunes (33, 211, 254, 472) the melodies of which are by Sir Henry, and the harmonies by Dr. Monk. He d. Feb. 12, 1877.   [J. J.]

Baker, Mary A. Miss Baker, who is a member of the Baptist denomination, and a resident in Chicago, Illinois, is an active worker in the temperance cause, and the author of various hymns and temperance songs. Her most popular hymn :—

1. **Master, the tempest is raging**, *Peace*, was written in 1874 at the request of Dr. H. R. Palmer, who desired of her several songs on the subjects of a series of Sunday School Lessons for that year. Its theme is "Christ stilling the tempest." During the same year it was set to

music by Dr. Palmer, and pub. in his *Songs of Love for the Bible School*, 1874. It is found in other collections, including I. D. Sankey's *Sac. S. and Solos*, Lond., 1881. Its home popularity was increased by its republication and frequent use during the illness of Pres. Garfield. It was sung at several of the funeral services held in his honour throughout the States.

2. Why perish with cold and with hunger? *Invitation.* This is another of her hymns set to music by I. D. Sankey, and included in his *Sacred S. and Solos*, Lond., 1881.   [J. J.]

Bakewell, John, b. at Brailsford, Derbyshire, 1721. At about the age of eighteen his mind was turned towards religious truths by reading Boston's *Fourfold State.* From that date he became an ardent evangelist, and in 1744 (the year of the first Methodist Conference) he began to preach. Removing to London some short time after, he became acquainted with the Wesleys, M. Madan, A. M. Toplady, J. Fletcher, and other earnest evangelical men. After conducting for some years the Greenwich Royal Park Academy, he resigned in favour of his son-in-law, Dr. James Egan, and employed much of his time in preaching at various places for the Wesleyans. He d. at Lewisham, near Greenwich, March 18, 1819, aged 98, and was buried in the Wesleyan burying ground connected with the City Road Chapel, London. Mr. Bakewell was the author of a few hymns, the best known being, "Hail Thou once despised Jesus," the abbreviations of the same, "Paschal Lamb, by God appointed," and "Jesus, hail, enthroned in glory." A short memoir of him was pub. by Mr. Stelfox, Belfast, 1864.   [J. J.]

Bald zieh ich mit dem Sterbekleid. *Anon.* [*Eternal Life.*] Included as No. 3508 in Knapp's *Ev. L. S.*, 1837, in 2 st. of 4 l., with the note "Found in the hymn-book of my deceased wife." The only *tr.* in C. U. is :—

Soon in the grave my flesh shall rest. By Dr. H. Mills, in full, with 2 original st. added in his *Horae Ger.*, 1845 (1856, p. 250), and thence, as No. 983, in the Lutheran General Synod's *Hymns,* &c., 1852.

Another *tr.* is, "Soon all my sorrows I shall lay," by Dr. R. Menzies, in F. A. G. Tholuck's *Hours of Christian Devotion*, Edin., 1870, p. 541.   [J. M.]

Balde, Jacob. He was b. at Ensisheim, in Alsace, in 1603, and d. in 1668, at the age of 65. In the year 1624 he entered the order of the Jesuits, but it is rather as a patriot, deeply mourning over the miseries caused by the "Thirty Years' War," than as a priest, that he comes before us in his works. His reputation amongst his compatriots as a writer of Latin poetry could hardly have been greater than it is. With an exaggeration which, however pardonable, can scarcely be allowed to pass altogether unchallenged, he is extolled by such writers as *Herder*, and even more markedly by *A. W. von Schlegel*, as though he were unapproached by any other modern Latin poet. There is, however, no doubt that his acquaintance and sympathy with the misfortunes of his country result in a realism, and at times an earnestness, founded

upon deep religious feeling, in what he wrote, which is too often sought in vain in the works of other writers of the same class. He takes high rank, if not the first place, amongst such.

He was a prolific writer. His *Odes* and *Solatium Podagricorum* (the best known of his works) scarcely fall within the scope of a *Dictionary of Hymnology*; but, especially as it has been admitted by Archbishop Trench into his *Sacred Latin Poetry*, reference may be made here to his "Chorea Mortualis sive Iessus de sortis et mortis in humanas res imperio," a dirge upon the death of the Empress Leopoldina, wife of Ferdinand III., in her first childbirth, in 1649, and chanted in her funeral procession, and commencing "Eheu, quid homines sumus?" (Trench, *Sac. Lat. P.*, 2nd ed., 1864, pp. 270–274). It is a noble poem, in which the author allows himself, as he very rarely did, to forsake the classical metres in which he usually wrote. However difficult to translate, and Archbishop Trench says that it "almost defies translation," there is one translation into English, in the original metre, in the *Southern Magazine*, U.S., Jan. 1873; and D. T. Morgan has another, but not in the original metre, in his *Hymns & other Poetry of the Latin Church.* The original poem is given at length in *Trench*, as quoted from *Balde*, Coloniae, 1660, vol. iv. p. 424.

The merits of Balde's productions consist rather in the grandeur and solemnity of his utterances and the boldness of his imagery than in the perfection of his classical style. Success in the latter is hardly claimed for him by his most ardent admirers.   [D. S. W.]

Baldwin, Thomas, D.D., b. at Bozrah, or Norwich, Connecticut, 1753, was representative for some time of his native State in the Legislature. In 1783 he was ordained to the Baptist ministry, and from 1790 till his death, in 1825, he was Pastor of the Second Baptist Church, Boston. His best known hymns are :—

1. Almighty Saviour, here we stand. *Holy Baptism.* This hymn "For Immersion" was contributed to a *Coll. of Sacred and Devotional Hymns,* Boston, 1808, from whence it has passed into later Collections, including the *Baptist Praise Bk.*, N. Y., 1871, and others.

2. From whence does this union rise? *Communion of Saints.* First found in J. Asplund's *New Coll.*, Baltimore, 1793, beginning, "O whence does this union rise." Formerly very popular, and still in use as in the *Baptist Hy.* [*and Tune*] *Book*, Phila., 1871, No. 638. In the *Church Pastorals*, Boston, 1864, No. 981, it is altered to "From whence *doth* this union *arise.*"

3. Ye happy saints, the Lamb adore. *Holy Baptism.* For Immersion, first appeared in a *Coll. of Sacred and Devotional Hymns,* Boston, 1808, from whence it passed in an altered form as :—"Come, happy souls, adore the Lamb," into Winchell's *Supp. to Watts,* 1819. It is found in Spurgeon's *O. O. H. Bk.*, 1866, and many modern American Baptist collections.   [F. M. B.]

Balfern, William Poole, b. in 1818, at Hammersmith; entered the Baptist Ministry in 1848; and has laboured chiefly in the suburbs of London, and in Brighton. Mr. Balfern is the author of *Glimpses of Jesus* and other prose works of similar character, has been a frequent contributor to Religious Periodicals, and has pub. the following vols. of poetry :—

(1) *The Beauty of the Great King, and other Poems,* 1871, Lond., Passmore and Alabaster. (2) *Lyrics for the Heart,* 1876. (Same pubs.) (3) *Hymns of the Pas-*

sion, 1882, Lond., Nelson and Sons. (4) *Pilgrim Chimes for the Weeks of the Year*, 1881, is a selection from Mr. Balfern's poems made and pub. by Rev. Chas. Bullock.

Mr. Balfern's hymns have appeared in the *Bap. Hymnal*; *Ps. & Hys. for the Young*; the *Meth. S. S. H. Bk.*; *Songs of Gladness* (S. S. Union); *Bk. of Hymns for S. School*, Lond., Weeks & Co.; *Treasury of Sacred Song*, Kirkwall, W. Peace; and in a few collections of the Church of England. They include:—

1. Come unto Me, the Saviour speaks [said]. *Invitation.*
2. Hark, dear children, hear the angels. *Sunday.*
3. O gentle Teacher, ever near. *Divine Teacher.*
4. O Lamb of God, most lowly [holy]. *Holiness of Jesus.*
5. O morning star, whose distant ray. *Divine Guidance.*
6. O Thou Who art enthroned on high. *Praise.*
7. Shepherd of those sunlit mountains. *The Good Shepherd.*

All these hymns were contributed to the S. S. Union *Songs of Gladness*, 1871, and from thence have passed into other collections.

8. Say not, O wounded heart. *Love of Jesus.*

From his work, *The Beauty of the Great King*, 1871, into the *Bap. Hymnal*, 1879.

Whilst these hymns do not take a high rank as poetry, they are characterised by simplicity of expression, and by devout and earnest, often tender, Christian feeling. Balfern d. July 3, 1887.   [W. R. S.]

Ball, Thomas Isaac, b. 16 August, 1838. On taking Holy Orders in 1865, he successively became Curate of St. Salvador's, Dundee Mission; Incumbent of St. Mary's, The Cove, by Aberdeen; Domestic Chaplain to the Earl of Kinnoull; Curate of All Saints, Brougham Street, Edinburgh; Curate of St. Columba's, Edinburgh; Priest of St. Michael's Chapel, Edinburgh; and Examining Chaplain to the Bishop of Argyll and the Isles. Mr. Ball is the author of *The Orthodox Doctrine of the Church of England*, 1877, and of numerous tracts; and the compiler of *The English Catholic's Vade-mecum*, 1868. In 1863 he contributed various *trs.* from the Latin to the *Appendix* to the *H. Noted*, for use in St. Alban's, Holborn, London, of which he was co-editor with the Rev. H. A. Walker. He was also the sole editor of the *Supp.* thereto, 1882. These *trs.* are annotated under their respective original first lines.

Ball, William, a member of the Society of Friends, some time resident at Glen Rothsay, Rydal, Westmoreland, author of (1) *Nugae Sacrae, or Psalms, Hymns, and Spiritual Songs*, Lond., 1825. (2) *The Transcript and Other Poems*; (3) *Hymns, or Lyrics*, 1864; (4) *Verses composed since 1870*, &c., 1875; and other works. From the above the following hymns have come into C. U.:—

1. Praise to Jesus! Praise to God. *Praise.* This is given in the *Hymnary*, 1871, as "Praise to Jesus, Lord and God," and in the American *Hys. and Songs of Praise*, N. Y., 1874, as:—"*Hallelujah!* Praise to God." Orig. text in *Lyra. Brit.*, 1867, p. 645.
2. There is a pure and tranquil wave. *Hope.* From *Nugae Sacrae*, 1825, into Lord Selborne's *Bk. of Praise*, 1862; the *Lyra Brit.*, 1867, p. 646: and the *Westminster Abbey H. Bk.*, 1883, &c.

Ballou, Hosea, a celebrated leader of the sect of Universalists, was b. at Richmond, New Hampshire, April 30, 1771. He was entirely self-educated, and began to preach

when about 21. In 1807 he settled at Portsmouth, New Hampshire, passing to Salem, Mass., in 1815, and to Boston in 1817. He d. in 1852. To the Universalist *Hymns composed by different Authors*, pub. in 1808, he contributed 199 hymns. A few of these are still used by the Universalists, but one only, and that probably his best, has passed beyond their ranks. It is:—

When God descends with men to dwell. *The Second Advent.* Ballou also edited with Turner a second collection in 1821, and a third in his own name, 1837. [See American Hymnody, § VI.]

            [F. M. B.]

Bampfield, George Frederick Lewis, M.A., was b. at St. John's Wood in 1827, and was a posthumous child of Robert Westcote Bampfield, surgeon, in Covent Garden, London. In 1845 he entered Trinity College, Oxford, whence he migrated to Lincoln College as a scholar, and graduated in Arts in 1849. After being curate successively of Shoreham, and of St. Thomas's, Oxford, he was received into the Roman Catholic Church by the Rev. F. W. Faber, went through a noviciate of 18 months at the Oratory, was ordained priest in 1857 by Cardinal Wiseman in his private chapel, after which he visited Rome, and, returning to England, officiated as priest at Stratford and Waltham Cross, and took part in various missions. In 1868 the chief work of his life began. This was the opening of schools for children of the middle classes. He was assisted by priests and others who lived in community, under the title of "Institute of St. Andrew." Ten years later it was confirmed by authority. His hymn to "The Five Wounds" was contributed to Mr. Orby Shipley's *Annus Sanctus*, 1884. It begins "Ye priestly hands, which on the cruel cross."

            [J. C. E.]

Bancroft, Charitie Lees, née Smith, dr. of the Rev. Sidney Smith, D.D., Rector of Drumragh, County Tyrone, Ireland; was b. at Bloomfield, Merrion, in the county of Dublin, June 21, 1841; and married, in 1869, to Arthur E. Bancroft. Her hymns have appeared in periodicals, *Lyra Brit.*, Bishop Ryle's *Spiritual Songs*, and other collections, and also as leaflets. The following have come into C. U.:—

1. O for the [a] robes [robe] of whiteness. *Heaven desired.* This favourite children's hymn was 1st pub. as a leaflet in 1860. In 1867 it was included in *Lyra Brit.*, and thence has passed into several collections in G. Britain and America.
2. The King of glory standeth. *Christ the Saviour.* Contributed in 7 st. of 8 l. to the *Lyra Brit.*, 1867, and entitled "Mighty to save." In the *Hys. & Songs of Praise*, N. Y., 1874, No. 1196, it begins with st. iii., "He comes in bloodstained garments."
3. Before the throne of God above. *The Advocate.* Dated 1863, and given in Spurgeon's *O. O. H. Bk.*, 1866, *Laudes Domini*, N. Y., 1884.

In 1867 Mrs. Bancroft's hymns were collected and pub. as *Within the Veil, by C. L. S.*

Bancroft, James Henry, b. at Boston, 1819, graduated at Amherst College, 1839, and Andover, 1842. Ill-health prevented his ordination as a Congregational minister. He d. in Boston, Aug. 25, 1844. His hymn—

Brother, though from yonder sky [*Burial*], was written in 1842, for the funeral of Dudley Leavitt, a classmate at Andover, who died there suddenly Jan., 7, 1842. It was given in *The Psalmist: a New Coll. of Hys. for the Use of Baptist Churches*, Boston, 1843, No. 1098, and has won considerable acceptance in America, but is unknown in England.   [F. M. B.]

Bannerman, David Douglas, M.A., eldest s. of the late Rev. Professor James Bannerman, D.D., of the New College, Edinburgh, was b. at Ormiston, Haddingtonshire, January 29, 1842. After studying at the University of Edinburgh, where he graduated M.A. in 1861, he became, in 1869, collegiate minister of the Free Church, Dalkeith, and in 1879 minister of St. Leonard's Free Church, Perth. He contributed to the *Free Church H. Bk.* of 1882 a *tr.* of *Je te salue, mon certain Redempteur* (q. v.).   [J. M.]

Baptized into the name. *Thomas Davis.* [*Holy Baptism.*] From his *Hymns, Old and New*, &c., 1864, No. 414, in 2 st. of 8 l., into the *Church S. S. H. Bk.*, 1868, No. 325, unaltered. It was originally written for Adult Baptism, but is also appropriate for Confirmation. It is given also in the American *Bapt. H.* [*& Tune*] *Bk.*, Phila., 1871, No. 744.

Baptist Hymnody, American. [**American Hymnody, § IV.**]

Baptist Hymnody, English. In this article it is proposed to give a brief account of the practices of the Baptists in England in regard to psalmody during the last 250 years, a list of their principal hymn-writers, and a notice of the hymn-books chiefly used amongst them at the present time.

For the better understanding of some statements which will follow, it should be noted that, from the first quarter of the 17th century up to the present, Baptists in this country have been divided into two main sections, i.e. *General* and *Particular* Baptists, the former favouring the Arminian view of the Christian Atonement and human free-agency, or *General* Redemption; the latter inclining more to the doctrines usually associated with the name of Calvin, or *Particular* Redemption. This distinction is now fast disappearing. Both sections are represented in "The Baptist Union," and the names *General* and *Particular* are falling into disuse. Nevertheless, the historical traditions of the two are different, and their principal institutions and societies continue distinct.

I. *The Seventeenth Century.*

(1) Throughout the 17th century the *General Baptists*, with but few exceptions, disapproved of psalmody in an ordinary mixed congregation. This was owing partly to their wish to avoid anything which seemed to ignore the difference between the "Church" and the "World," and partly to their dread of formalism. In the year 1678 the devout and learned Thomas Grantham, a man of immense influence among the *General Baptists* of that time, pub. his *Christianismus Primitivus*, wherein, speaking of the duty of Thanks-

giving, he sets forth a number of reasons against "musical singing with a multitude of voices in rhyme and metre." He urges that Psalms and Hymns are to be sung by such only as God has fitted thereto by the help of His Spirit; that by *congregational* singing instruction is prevented, for "when all speak, none can hear"; that singing other men's words "opens a gap for forms of prayer"; that "once permit the singing by art pleasant tunes, and you will bring music and even instruments back again into public worship, and then, farewell to all solemnity." Eleven years later, in the *General Baptist Assembly* of 1689, the question of "promiscuous singing" was considered, when the persons holding the affirmative were desired to show "what Psalms they made use of for the *matter*, and what rules they did settle upon for the *manner*." Thereupon was produced, not the version of Sternhold and Hopkins, but "a book of metres composed by one Mr. Barton, and the rules for singing these Psalms *secundum artem*, viz., as the musicians do sing according to their gamut, *sol, fa, la, my, ray*, &c.; all which appeared so strangely foreign to the evangelical worship that it was not conceived anywise safe for the churches to admit such carnal formalities." And this opinion was endorsed with the general approbation of the Assembly.

(2) In the Calvinistic, or *Particular Baptist*, section of the denomination, congregational singing seems to have been regarded with more favour. In the records of the Broadmead Church, in Bristol, references to this part of worship are frequent. Thus, in the year 1671, it was a complaint made against them by "old Mr. Wright that had been Sheriff," that he could hear them sing Psalms from their meeting-place at his house in Hallier's Lane. There was a second Baptist community in Bristol, known as "Mr. Gifford's people," who, though willing to sing Psalms with others besides the church, scrupled to "sing in metre," and pleaded for permission to keep their hats on during this part of the service, or to "go forth." John Bunyan, who belonged to this section of the Baptists, not only in his famous Allegory frequently represents his pilgrims as singing, but also in his *Solomon's Temple Spiritualised* (A.D. 1688) speaks of this part of worship as belonging by God's appointment to the Church of the new covenant. But it is members of the church only—"Sion's sons"—that are to sing. He says:—

"To sing to God is the highest worship we are capable of performing in heaven; and it is much if sinners on earth, without grace, should be capable of performing it according to His institution acceptably. I pray God that it be done by all those that nowadays get into churches with spirit and with understanding."

Only a few months after Bunyan wrote these words a violent controversy broke out among the *Particular Baptists* of London concerning the lawfulness of congregational singing. In the year 1680 Hercules Collins, pastor of the Baptist Church in Wapping, in his *Orthodox Catechism*, had broached the assertion that singing was a public duty. Benjamin Keach, pastor of Horsley Down [see

Early English Hymnody, § XII. 1], in his *Tropes & Figures* (1682) and his *Treatise on Baptism* (1689), had followed in the same strain. But in 1690 one Isaac Marlow, an influential lay member of the church in Mile End Green, in a *Discourse concerning Singing*, entered the lists on the other side. Keach replied in his *Breach Repaired*, and presently others joined in the fray. As stated (l. c.), the General Assembly of *Particular Baptists* intervened in the interests of peace, and a truce followed; but the practice of congregational singing more and more prevailed.

These Baptists of the 17th century sang the *Psalms* in their ordinary worship. At length, however, the custom was introduced (by Keach, in 1673), in supposed imitation of the example of Christ and His Apostles, of singing a hymn at the close of the Lord's Supper. Next, hymns were sung on Thanksgiving Days, at Baptisms, and on other special occasions. These appear to have been composed either by the minister himself or some gifted friend. Thus, in connection with the controversy above named, it is stated that on one occasion, at Mr. Keach's place, when a brother minister was officiating, "a hymn was given up to him which he read and sang, and the people with him." For use at these times were prepared both the earlier hymns of Benj. Keach, and the Sacramental Hymns of Joseph Stennett, the elder. Joseph Boyse, a Presbyterian minister in Dublin, who appears to have been a Baptist in principle, pub. eighteen *Sacramental Hymns*, to which he appended a hymn on Baptism, and another on the ministry (Dublin, and again Lond., 1693).

[For further details see Ivimey's *History of the English Baptists*, vol. i.; *Byepaths in Baptist History*, by J. Jackson Goadby; and an article in the *British Quarterly Review*, vol. lxxi., on " Early Nonconformist Psalmody," by J. Spencer Curwen.]

II. *The Eighteenth Century.*

(1) During the first half of the 18th century the *General Baptists* for the most part retained their prejudices against congregational singing. Thus, in 1733, a case was presented from Northamptonshire to the General Assembly of *General Baptists* complaining that some churches in that district had "fallen into the way of singing the Psalms of David, or other men's composures, with tunable notes, and a mixed multitude." It is, however, an indication of a change of feeling, that this Assembly, unlike the one in 1689, whilst admitting the fact of the innovation, decided to leave the matter an open question. About the middle of the century, partly as a result of the great Methodist movement, many new congregations of *General Baptists* sprang up in the midland counties and the West Riding of Yorkshire, and these all, like their Methodist neighbours, believed in Christian Song. In the year 1770, the *New Connexion of General Baptists* was formed, and soon afterwards a *Collection of Hymns* was prepared for their use. In 1785 Samuel Deacon (q.v.), of Barton, near Market Bosworth, in Leicestershire, pub. a volume of original hymns known as *Barton Hymns*. These hymns are homely in style, but full of gos-

pel fervour. They had for a time considerable local popularity and reached a second edition in 1797. In 1791 the *General Baptist Association* sanctioned the preparation of a new *Collection of Hymns*, the former being very imperfect and nearly out of print. Accordingly in 1793 appeared a *Selection* edited by John Deacon, of Leicester, and another entitled *Hymns and Spiritual Songs selected from various authors*, the latter vol. being known by the name of *Dan Taylor's Hymns*. Nevertheless, in some of the older *General Baptist* churches the prejudice against congregational singing still survived, and, in 1785–7, a rather warm controversy was waged between Gilbert Boyce, a much-respected Lincolnshire minister, who in two pamphlets condemned the practice, and Dan Taylor, then of London, who defended it. A gentleman now living (1886) tells how he has heard from his mother of the songless worship of the *General Baptists*, at Morcott, in Rutland, and of the gladness expressed when one day, through the influence of the younger part of the congregation, the old custom was broken through, and a hymn heartily sung. By the close of the 18th century, however, singing, as a part of public worship, had become universal among the *General Baptists*.

(2) Returning to the *Particular Baptist* section of the denomination, and going back to the beginning of the century, we recall the name of Joseph Stennett, the elder. He may be regarded as the connecting link in *Baptist Hymnody* between the 17th and 18th centuries. His *Hymns for the Lord's Supper* belong to the former period (1697), those on *Believers' Baptism* to the latter (1712). He deservedly holds a front place among Baptist hymn-writers, not only as being among the first in order of time, but also from the sterling quality of some of his compositions. One of these, " Another six days' work is done," is a favourite Sunday-morning hymn in many Nonconformist congregations to this day. After his death, in 1713, it was long before a worthy successor appeared. Indeed, until nearly the middle of the century, the only Baptist hymn-writer of whom we know anything is Anne Dutton (1734), wife of the Baptist minister at Great Gransden, Huntingdonshire. J. A. Jones, who, in 1833, republished her hymns, styles her " the justly celebrated." Mrs. Dutton's compositions, however, are now (except by antiquaries) wholly forgotten. In 1747 appeared *Divine Songs, Hymns, and other Poems*, by Daniel Turner, M.A., of Abingdon; and in 1750, *Evangelical Hymns and Songs*, by Benjamin Wallin, pastor of Maze Pond. The hymns of neither of these writers possess any great merit, though of the two those of Turner have the more melody and true " poetic fire." To their names must be added that of John Needham, author of the well-known harvest hymn, " To praise the ever-bounteous Lord." His *Hymns Devotional & Moral* were printed at Bristol in 1768. Here, too, may be mentioned Edmund Jones, pastor at Exeter, who died in 1765, at a comparatively early age, the author of a hymn very popular for many years, " Come, humble sinner, in whose breast." But by far the most gifted Baptist

hymn-writer of this period was Anne Steele, the accomplished daughter of the Rev. Wm. Steele, Baptist minister, at Broughton, in Hampshire. Adopting the signature T.—in full *Theodosia*—she wrote a large number of hymns which were not only introduced into the Bristol hymn-book of Ash & Evans in 1769, and Dr. Rippon's *Sel.* in 1787, but are in common use at the present time. We have indeed now entered upon the palmy days of Baptist Hymnody, the thirty years or so which followed the first publication of Miss Steele's hymns. To this period belong Benjamin Beddome, a most prolific hymn-writer; Dr. Samuel Stennett (grandson of the Joseph Stennett already named), who contributed largely to Rippon's *Sel.*; Benjamin Francis, a native of Wales, but pastor for many years of a Baptist church in Gloucestershire; Robert Robinson; and John Fawcett, D.D., who (in 1772) on deciding to remain with his attached people at Wainsgate in Yorkshire, wrote, "Blest be the tie that binds," and in the course of the next few years composed several other hymns still in frequent use. Less known writers of this date are Wm. Tucker, of Chard, a Baptist layman, who in 1772 began to publish in the *Gospel Magazine* hymns strongly Calvinistic in sentiment; and James Newton, Classical Tutor to the Bristol Education Society, who about the same time wrote a few useful hymns, especially one for baptismal occasions. A much greater name is that of Dr. John Ryland, of Northampton, who at the age of 20, in 1773, wrote the first of a series of 100 hymns, most of which were composed to be sung in connexion with his sermons. John Adams, originally one of Ryland's members, about this time printed in the *Gospel Magazine* a few hymns now almost forgotten. John Fellows, most of whose works date from Birmingham, pub. hymns in 1773 and 1776, the former collection relating chiefly to the subject of Baptism. Richard Burnham, minister of Grafton Street Chapel, Soho, put forth in 1783 *New Hymns on divers subjects*, a volume which passed through several editions. Samuel Medley, the popular and useful minister of Byrom Street, Liverpool, began in 1786 to print hymns on broadsides as they were composed, and afterwards pub. them in two small volumes. In the following year (1787) John Dracup, of Steep Lane, in Yorkshire, pub. his *Hymns & Spiritual Songs*, and, in 1789, Charles Cole, of Whitchurch, put forth his *Threefold Alphabet of New Hymns*. In 1792 Joseph Swain, a young minister whose short and bright career at Walworth closed in four years afterwards, printed a collection of original hymns, several of which have a place in the principal Baptist hymn-books of the present day; and Samuel Pearce, of Birmingham, whose ministerial course both in brevity and fair promise greatly resembled Swain's, wrote a few hymns which were published with his life by Andrew Fuller in 1800. These were introduced into the later editions of Rippon's *Sel.* The history of the century closes not unfitly with the name of Job Hupton, minister at Claxton, in Norfolk, author of a fine hymn beginning "Come ye saints and

raise an anthem," altered by Dr. J. Mason Neale into a form more familiar to modern ears, "Come ye faithful, raise the anthem." In regard to the hymn-books used by the *Particular Baptists* during the 18th century, they were undoubtedly at first simply collections for special occasions, such as those of Boyse, Joseph Stennett, and Wallin, and were used as supplementary to the Psalms in one or other of the metrical versions. But in 1769 a volume was brought out popularly known as the *Bristol Hymn Book*, compiled by the Rev. John Ash, LL.D., of Pershore, and the Rev. Caleb Evans, D.D., of Bristol. This contained 412 hymns by various writers. An 8th ed. of this collection, valuable for its preface and list of authors, was pub. by Isaac James, at Bristol, 1801; and a 10th ed. with a small supplement, Norwich, 1827. In 1787 Dr. J. Rippon, of Carter Lane, and afterwards of New Park Street, London, pub. a *Selection of Hymns from the best authors, intended to be an Appendix to Dr. Watts's Psalms & Hymns*. It soon became the popular Baptist Hymn Book, was enlarged from time to time, and passed through more than 30 editions. It was intended, as indicated in the title, to be supplementary to Dr. Watts's *Psalms and Hymns*. Therefore the only hymns contained in it from Watts are from his *Lyric Poems, Sermons*, and *Miscellanies*. All editions contain the names of most of the authors. Prominent among these are those of Steele, Beddome, S Stennett, Doddridge, Fawcett, Needham, and D Turner. A few hymns are taken from J. Stennett, B. Francis, J. Ryland, Gibbons, and others. The 10th ed., 1800, and the 27th, 1827, were enlarged. No further change was made by Dr. Rippon, but on the expiration of the copyright of the 1st ed. in 1844, rival editions appeared with additions and alterations.

III. *The Nineteenth Century.*

But few hymn-writers of eminence have appeared among the Baptists of either section during the present century; though there are many who have written one or two hymns of merit. The first name that presents itself is that of John Burton, of Nottingham and Leicester, who wrote chiefly for Sunday Schools. Then comes the name of Mrs. Alice Flowerdew, a member of the old General Baptist Church in Worship St., London, and author of a well-known hymn on the seasons, pub. in 1811. John Mann, a bookseller, and member of the G. B. Church in the Commercial Road, London, in 1828 published a volume of *Hymns and Poems*. The Rev John Howard Hinton, M.A.—a minister of great influence in his day—composed a large number of hymns on the subjects of his sermons, and in 1833 published a collection therefrom. The Rev. John Eustace Giles, formerly of Leeds, wrote several missionary hymns, and in 1830 one of great excellence on the subject of Baptism. Mrs. Saffery, wife of a Baptist minister at Salisbury, wrote many hymns for special occasions, and in 1834 published a volume of *Poems on Sacred Subjects*. The Rev. James Harrington Evans, M.A., of John Street Chapel, Gray's Inn Lane, in 1818 prepared a selection of 179 hymns for use in his own place of worship and introduced therein a few of his own composition. This collection reached the 5th ed. in 1838 with 451 hymns. The Hon. and Rev. Baptist W. Noel, M.A., about the same time pub. a selection of hymns which passed through several editions. Of these a few were originals. About the year 1834 Dr. Amos Sutton, a distinguished General Baptist missionary, on the occasion of a visit to England, composed a hymn which has ever since been very popular at "Farewell Services," "Hail, sweetest, dearest tie that binds." Miss Leslie, of Calcutta, the accomplished daughter of another Indian missionary, is the author of a volume of poems and of the beautiful hymn, "They are gathering homeward from every land." Edward Mote, a Baptist layman of the strongly Calvinistic school, published, in 1836, "Hymns of Praise." David Denham, in 1837, published a Selection, including many of his own compositions. Later hymn-writers include the Revs. Cornelius Elven, Charles Haddon Spurgeon, F. W. Goadby, M.A., Thomas Goadby, B.A., Edward Hall Jackson, Dawson Burns, D.D., W. P. Balfern, T. Vincent Tymms, J. T. Wigner, Walter J. Mathams, Charles Clark, J. M. Wigner, W. H. Parker, B. Provis, and others.

It remains to mention the principal hymn-books in use in Baptist congregations from A.D. 1800 to the present time. Many have been prepared for the service of particular congregations. These, as being of little more than local and temporary interest, we pass over, confining ourselves to hymn-books which have been adopted by a large number of churches.

(1) Toward the end of the last century (1793) John Deacon pub. a hymn-book for the use of General Baptist Churches, of which a 2nd ed., with a large Appendix, the whole including 746 hymns, was pub. in 1804. At that date it is said to have been "pretty generally in use in General Baptist Connections." In 1830 this book, having been revised by a committee appointed by the Annual Association, was formally adopted as the General Baptist Hymn-book. In 1851, another book was substituted, entitled "The New Hymn Book." The compilers were two brothers, the Revs. J. B. Pike and J. Carey Pike. It, also, before formal adoption, was revised by a committee. In course of time an Appendix was prepared containing about 80 modern hymns. But in 1877 it was deemed expedient by the Association that another book should be compiled to include a large number of the best hymns of the present day. This book was pub. in 1879, under the title of the "Baptist Hymnal." The Rev. W. R. Stevenson, M.A., of Nottingham, was editor, nine other General Baptist ministers co-operating. It contains 920 hymns. The word General was omitted from the title, partly from the fact stated at the commencement of this article, that the two sections of the Denomination are now almost identical in Christian doctrine and practice, and partly from the expectation, which has in fact been realised, that a certain number of congregations in what has been known as the Particular Baptist section would adopt the new Hymnal. In 1880, by direction of the General Baptist Association, the School Hymnal, containing 343 hymns for the young, was prepared for the use of Sunday Schools and Families by the Rev. W. R. Stevenson, assisted by a committee.

(2) We have seen that at the close of the 18th century the hymn-books chiefly in use among the Particular Baptists were the Collections of Dr. Rippon and of Drs. Ash and Evans. In 1828 a book was prepared by Mr. John Haddon, sen., and revised by Doctors Murch, Price and Steane, with other ministers, to which was given the name of The New Selection. This was revised and enlarged in 1838 and again in 1871 by the addition of a Supplement, called Praise Waiteth, and in both forms it has had a considerable circulation. Originally prepared by Mr. John Haddon, jun., the collection entitled Psalms and Hymns, which has been extensively used by important churches for 26 years past, was first pub. in 1858. The principal compilers were Drs. S. G. Green and N. Haycroft and the Revs. W. F. Burchell and J. T. Wigner. It contained, until 1880, just 1000 hymns; but in that year a Supplement was added, under the editorship of the Rev. J. T. Wigner, containing 271 additional hymns, chiefly modern. In 1882 a companion book was put forth under the same editorship, entitled Psalms and Hymns for the Young, intended chiefly for use in Sunday Schools. In 1866, the Rev. C. H. Spurgeon published a collection of hymns prepared under his direction and entitled Our Own Hymn Book. It contains 1129 psalms and hymns, and is used not only at the Metropolitan Tabernacle, but also in many other congregations presided over by ministers who were once students under Mr. Spurgeon.

Three other collections of hymns, used exclusively by the more highly Calvinistic of the Particular Baptist churches, are: (1) Mr. Wm. Gadsby's Sel. of Hymns, pub. in 1814. A new ed. with a Supplement appeared in 1838. Successive alterations and additions have been made from time to time (most of J. Hart's hymns having been incorporated), until it now contains 1130 hymns. (2) The Selection, 1837, of David Denham, formerly of Unicorn Yard Chapel, Tooley Street, London, containing nearly 1200 hymns, and said to be used by upwards of 100 churches in Great Britain. (3) The Selection of John Stevens, formerly of Meard's Court Chapel, London Enlarged and rearranged by J. S. Anderson, of New Cross Road, S.E., it now contains 970 hymns.   [W. R. S.]

Baptist Hymnody, Scottish. [Scottish, § VI. 5.]

Baptist Hymnody, Welsh. [Welsh Hymnody, § IV.]

Barbauld, Anna Laetitia, née Aikin, daughter of the Rev. John Aikin, D.D., a dissenting minister, was b. at Kibworth-Harcourt, Leicestershire, June 20, 1743. In 1753 Dr. Aikin became classical tutor at a dissenting academy at Warrington. During her residence there she contributed five hymns to Dr. W. Enfield's Hymns for Public Worship, &c., Warrington, 1772. In the following year these were included in her Poems, Lond., J. Johnson, 1773. In May, 1774, Miss Aikin was married to the Rev. Rochemont Barbauld, a descendant of a French Protestant family, and a dissenting minister. For some years Mr. Barbauld conducted, in addition to his pastoral work, a boarding school at Palgrave, Suffolk. From this he retired in 1785. In 1786 he undertook the charge of a small congregation at Hampstead, and from thence he passed to the dissenting chapel (formerly Dr. Price's) at Newington Green, in 1802. He d. Nov. 11, 1808. Mrs. Barbauld continued to reside in the neighbourhood until her death, March 9, 1825. In the latter part of the same year her niece pub. *The Works of Anna Laetitia Barbauld, with Memoir, by Lucy Aikin*, 2 vols., Lond., Longman, 1825. As a writer of hymns Mrs. Barbauld was eminently successful. Their use, however, with the exception of five contributed to Dr. W. Enfield's collection, is almost exclusively confined to the Unitarian hymnals of Great Britain and America. Including these hymnals, the whole of her hymns are still in common use. These hymns appeared thus:—

i. *In Dr. W. Enfield's Hymns, &c.*, 1772.
1. Again the Lord of life and light. *Easter.*
2. Awake, my soul, lift up thine eyes. *Conflict.*
3. Behold, where breathing love divine. *Christian Charity.*
4. Jehovah reigns, let every nation hear. *God's Dominion.* A part of this was given in Collyer's *Sel.*, 1812, No. 586, as:—
5. This earthly globe, the creature of a day.
6. Praise to God, Immortal praise. *Harvest.*

ii. *Poems*, 1773 (*Preface dated Dec.* 1, 1772).
The whole of the above, and also:—
7. God of my life and author of my days. *To God the Father.* This is an "Address to the Deity," in 80 l. It is given in Martineau's *Colls.*, 1840 and 1873. From it the following centos were given in Collyer's *Sel.*, 1812:—
8. God, our kind Master, merciful as just.
9. If friendless in the vale of tears I stray.

iii. *Poems revised* 1792.
10. Come, said [says] Jesus' sacred voice. *Invitation.*
11. How blest the sacred tie that binds. *Christian Fellowship.*
12. Lo where a crowd of pilgrims toil. *Pilgrimage of Life.* From this is taken:—
13. Our country is Immanuel's ground [land].

iv. *Leisure Hour Improved* (*Ironbridge*), 1809.
14. Sweet is the scene when virtue dies. *Death.*

v. *Supplement to the Unitarian Coll. of Kippis, Rees, and others*, 1807.
15. When as returns the solemn day. *Sunday.*
16. Sleep, sleep to day, tormenting cares. *Sunday.*
17. How may earth and heaven unite. *Worship.*

vi. *Works, with Memoir*, 1825.
In vol. i. most of the above are reprinted, and the following are added:—
18. Joy to the followers of the Lord. *Joy.* (c. 1820.)
19. Pure spirit, O where art thou now. *Bereavement.* This is dated 1808.
20. Salt of the earth, ye virtuous few. *Salt of the Earth.*
21. When life as opening buds is sweet. *Death.* This is dated "November, 1814."

The more important of these hymns are annotated in this Dictionary under their first lines. Mrs. Barbauld's *Hymns in Prose for Children*, originally pub. in 1781, were long popular and have been translated into French, Italian, Spanish, and other languages. [J. J.]

Barclay, John. [Scottish Hymnody, § VIII. 10.]

Baring-Gould, Sabine, M.A., eldest s. of Mr. Edward Baring-Gould, of Lew Trenchard, Devon, b. at Exeter, Jan. 28, 1834, and educated at Clare College, Cam-

bridge, B.A. 1857, M.A. 1860. Taking Holy Orders in 1864, he held the curacy of Horbury, near Wakefield, until 1867, when he was preferred to the incumbency of Dalton, Yorks. In 1871 he became rector of East Mersea, Essex, and in 1881 rector of Lew Trenchard, Devon. His works are numerous, the most important of which are, *Lives of the Saints*, 15 vols., 1872–77; *Curious Myths of the Middle Ages*, 2 series, 1866–68; *The Origin and Development of Religious Belief*, 2 vols., 1869–1870; and various volumes of sermons. His hymns, original and translated, appeared in the *Church Times; H. A. & M.*, 1868 and 1875; *The People's Hymnal*, 1867, and other collections, the most popular being "Onward, Christian soldiers," "Daily, daily sing the praises," the *tr.* "Through the night of doubt and sorrow," and the exquisite Easter hymn, "On the Resurrection Morning." His latest effort in hymnology is the publication of original *Church Songs*, 1884, of which two series have been already issued. In the *Sacristy* for Nov. 1871, he also contributed nine carols to an article on "The Noels and Carols of French Flanders." These have been partially transferred to Chope's and Staniforth's Carol Books, and also to his *Church Songs*. [J. J.]

Barlow, Joel, b. at Reading, Connecticut, 1755, graduated at Yale 1778, and d. near Cracow, Poland, 1812. He was well known as an author and politician during and after the American Revolution. His publications include *Hasty Pudding; Columbia*, &c. In 1785, at the request of the (Congregational) General Association of Connecticut, he corrected and enlarged Dr. Watts's *Psalms*, supplying those omitted by Watts, and adapting the whole to American thought and circumstances. This work, pub. in 1786, went through various editions, and, although officially superseded by *Dwight* in 1800, it continued to be issued for many years after. Its title is somewhat curious as setting forth its design. It reads:—*Psalms carefully suited to the Christian Worship in the United States of America, being Dr. Watts's Imitation of the Psalms of David, as improved by Mr. Barlow.* Of his renderings of the Psalms, there are still in C. U.:—

1. Awake, my soul, to sound His praise. *Ps. cviii.* This is No. 233 in Hatfield's *Ch. H. Bk.*, 1872, and other collections.

2. Lord, Thou hast scourged our guilty land. *Ps. lx.* Altered from Watts. Also in Hatfield's *Ch. H. Bk.*, No. 1312.

3. Our land, O Lord, with songs of praise. *Ps. xxxi.* In the Phila. *Presb. Hymnal*, 1874.

4. In Thee, great God, with songs of praise. *National Hymn.* This is No. 3 in a slightly different form. It is No. 962 in N. Adams's *Church Pastorals*, Boston, 1864. [F. M. B.]

Barnaby, Sir Nathaniel, C.B., Director of Naval Construction in Her Majesty's Service, b. at Chatham in 1829, has been for many years interested in Christian education, and is Superintendent of the Bap. S. School at Lee, in Kent. He is the author of several hymns composed for use in the school at Lee. Of these, one beginning "To Jesus, our Captain, to Jesus, our King," and another,

"The soldier keeps his wakeful Watch," composed to the German tune, "The Rhine-Watch," are in W. R. Stevenson's *School Hymnal*, Lond., 1881. His hymns are spirited and popular.　　　　　　　　　　[W. R. S.]

Barnard, Edward William, M.A., of Trinity College, Cambridge, third s. of H. B. Barnard, of Cave Castle, Yorkshire, was b. March 15, 1791. He was Vicar of South Cave, Yorkshire, from 1816 to his premature death in 1828. His pub. works are:—

(1) *Trifles, in Imitation of the chaster style of Meleager*, 1818; (2) The *Protestant Beadsman*, Rivingtons, 1822; (3) *Flowers*, a series of short poems, original and translated. Privately printed at Martin's, Lond. 1827; (4) *Fifty Select Poems of Marc Antonio Flaminio, Imitated*. Chester, Fletcher, 1829. This posthumous vol. was pub. by his father-in-law, Archdeacon Wrangham. This vol. contains some few of Mr. Barnard's lyrical poetry, but by far the largest part of these compositions remain in MS. Miss Mitford, in her work, *My Literary Life*, 1850, speaks of Mr. Barnard as being eminent for scholarship, and of his poetry as "remarkable, not only for grace and beauty, but for a vigour of thought, a fulness, a body, very unusual in occasional verses." His *Protestant Beadsman* consists of a short account of each of the saints whom the Church of England commemorates in her services during the course of the ecclesiastical year, with original hymns for each Festival. These hymns number 22 in all, are marked with much sweetness and genuine devotional feeling, and are worthy of attention.　　　　　　　　　　[D. S. W.]

Barnard, John. [Scottish Hymnody, § VIII. 8.]

Barnes, Barnaby, fourth s. of Dr. Barnes, Bishop of Durham, b. about 1569, in Yorkshire. At the age of seventeen he entered Brasenose Coll., Oxford, but never obtained his degree. In 1591 he is said to have joined a military expedition to Normandy, in which country he remained until 1594. He wrote *A Divine Centurie of Spiritual Sonnets*, which was printed in 1595. He was buried in the church of St. Mary-le-Bow, Durham, in December, 1609.

He was the author of three plays, one pub. in 1607, as *The Devil's Charter*, and two in MS. not now to be traced, and of a volume of amatory poems, *Parthenophil & Parthenophe*, 1593, which was privately reprinted from the only known copy, in 1875, together with all Barnes's other poems. It is also included in Mr. Arber's recent *English Garner*. His prose work, *Fovre Bookes of Offices Enabling Privat persons for the speciall service of all good Princes & Policies*, 1606, has not been reprinted.　　　　　　　　　　[W. T. B.]

Barrows, Elijah Porter, S.T.D., b. at Mansfield, Connecticut, Jan. 5, 1805, and graduated at Yale, 1826. Ordained in 1832, he was Pastor of First Free Presbyterian Church, N. Y., 1835-7; Professor of Sacred Literature in Western Reserve College, 1837-52; of Hebrew Language and Literature at Andover, 1853-66; and of the same at Oberlin, Ohio, 1872. His publications include *Memoir of E. Judson*, 1852; *Companion to the Bible*, 1869; *Sacred Geography and Antiquities*, 1872, &c. His hymn:—

Hallelujah, Christ is mine [*Peace in Christ*] was written at Hudson, Ohio, in 1846, in 6 st. of 6 l. It was taken by Mr. Trowbridge (a Missionary of the American Board) to Constantinople, and there *tr*. into two or three languages. Its first publication in English was in the Oberlin *Manual of Praise*, 1880, No. 270. In this form, st. iii. and iv. are omitted. Dr. Barrows has also written several other hymns and versions of Psalms; but these have not come into C. U.

Barry, Alfred, D.D., second s. of Sir C. Barry, b. Jan. 15, 1826, and educated at King's Coll., Lond., and Trinity College, Cambridge, graduating in classical and mathematical honours in 1848 and obtaining a Fellowship the same year. Taking Holy Orders in 1850, he has held many important appointments, including the Sub-Wardenship of Trinity College, Glenalmond, and the Headmastership of Leeds Gr. Sch. In 1862 he passed from Leeds to Cheltenham as Principal of the College: thence in 1868 to King's College, London, as Principal; and in 1884 to Australia as the Bishop of Sydney and Metropolitan of Australia. In addition to these appointments, Dr. Barry was Boyle Lecturer 1875, Chaplain to the Bp. of Bath and Wells, and Chaplain in Ordinary to the Queen. His pub. works include *Introduction to the Old Testament; Notes on the Gospels; Notes on the Catechism; Life of Sir C. Barry; The Teacher's Prayer Book*; and various volumes of *Sermons*. Also a contributor to *Smith's Dict. of the Bible*. His hymns are few, and include that for *Sunday*, "As Thou didst rest, O Father," given in the Rugby School *H. Bk.*, 1876; and Thring's *Coll.*, 1882, &c. [J. J.]

Barth, Christian Gottlob, s. of C. F. Barth, house painter in Stuttgart, was b. at Stuttgart, July 31, 1799. He studied at Tübingen, where he was the principal founder of the Missionary Society, and was only restrained by his mother's entreaties from offering himself as a missionary. He became, in 1821, assistant at Neckarweihingen and Dornham, and, in 1822, curate in charge of Effringen and Schönbrunn, near Nagold. In 1824 he was appointed pastor of Möttlingen, near Calw, but resigned his charge in 1838, and settled in Calw, receiving in the same year the degree of D.D. from the University of Greifswald. He d. at Calw of apoplexy, Nov. 12, 1862. At Calw he devoted himself as a writer and preacher to children, as a preacher and writer in the cause of missions to the heathen and to the Jews, and as the founder and director of the Tract Society of Calw. One of his books, the *Bible History*, reached its 160th edition in 1872, and had then been translated into 24 European, 18 Asiatic, 7 African, and 3 South Sea languages. He frequently attended the meetings of the Religious Tract Society of London, and was a member of the Evangelical Alliance (*Koch*, vii. 199-210; *Allg. Deutsche Biog.*, ii. 94-95). Of his hymns there have been *tr*. into English:—

i. Auf einem Berg ein Bäumlein stand. [*Holy Scripture.*] Included in his *Lieder und Gedichte für Christenkinder*, Calw, 1842, p. 83, in 4 st. Previously in J. Köbner's *Christl. Harfentöne*, Hamburg, 1840, p. 115. The *trs.* are:—
(1) "Upon a hill there stands a tree," by *Dr. H. Mills*, 1845 (1856, p. 25), and thence in P. Stow's *Ocean Melodies*, Boston, U.S., 1849. (2) "A tree grows on a mountain," by *Mrs. Bevan*, 1859, p. 138. (3) "A tree stood on a mountain," in Dr. H. W. Dulcken's *Golden Harp*, 1864, p. 22. (4) "On a hill stands a beautiful tree," in W. B. Bradbury's *Fresh Laurels*, N. Y., 1867, p. 15, signed "L. W." (5) "Lo, on a mount a tree doth stand," by Mrs. H. R. Spaeth, as No. 60 in the Pennsylvania Lutheran *Little Children's Bk.*, Philadelphia, 1885.

ii. Erhebe dich, du Volk des Herrn. [*Missions.*] Written for the Basel Mission Festival, June 12, 1833, In his *Christliche Gedichte*, Stuttgart, 1836, p. 48, in 8 st. *Tr.* as "Ye people of the Lord, arise!" by *Dr. H. Mills*, 1856, p. 202.

iii. Hüter, ist die Nacht verschwunden. [*Missions.*] Written for the 20th anniversary, June 27, 1835, of the Basel Missionary Society, and 1st pub. in the *Mission*

Magazine for that year. In his *Christliche Gedichte*, Stuttgart, 1836, p. 54, in 8 st. The *trs.* are:—
(1) "Ho! watchman, is the night away," by *Dr. G. Walker*, 1860, p. 84. (2) "Watchman! Hath the night departed," in L. Rehfuess's *Church at Sea*, 1868, p. 107. [J. M.]

Bartholomew, William, is favourably known through the English libretti of Mendelssohn's *Elijah, Athalie, Antigone, Lauda Sion,* &c.; and Costa's *Eli,* and *Naaman,* &c. He was b. in London, Sept. 6, 1793. For some years he was engaged in writing English words for foreign music. In 1841 he attracted the attention of Mendelssohn, and from that day to Mendelssohn's death, in 1847, he was associated with him, adapting for him the words of the above-named oratorios. He subsequently assisted Sir M. Costa in like manner with *Eli* and *Naaman.* He d. Aug. 18, 1867. His hymns are generally taken from the above works, the finest and best known being "Praise Jehovah, bow before Him" (q.v.).

Barton, Bernard, commonly known as the "Quaker Poet," was b. in London Jan. 31, 1784, and educated at a Quaker school at Ipswich. In 1798 he was apprenticed to Mr. S. Jesup, a shopkeeper at Halstead, Essex, with whom he remained until 1806, when he removed to Woodbridge, Suffolk, and entered into business with his brother, as a coal and corn merchant. On the death of his wife at the end of the first year of their married life, he proceeded to Liverpool, where he acted as a private tutor for a short time. He returned to Woodbridge in 1810, where he secured an engagement in the local bank of the Messrs. Alexander. This appointment he held for 40 years. He d. at Woodbridge, Feb. 19, 1849. During the same year his daughter pub. his *Poems and Letters,* with a Memoir. His poetical works were numerous, including:—
(1) *Metrical Effusions,* 1812; (2) *Poems by an Amateur,* 1818; (3) *Poems,* 1820; (4) *Napoleon, and other Poems,* 1822; (5) *Poetic Vigils,* 1824; (6) *Devotional Verses founded on Select Texts of Scripture,* 1826; (7) *A Widow's Tale,* 1827; (8) *New Year's Eve,* 1829; (9) *The Reliquary,* 1836; (10) *Household Verses,* 1845. A complete list of his works is given in Joseph Smith's *Descriptive Catalogue of Friends' Books,* Lond., J. Smith, 1867, vol. i. pp. 196–200.

From these works about 20 pieces have come into C. U. as hymns. These are found principally in the Scottish *Evangelical Union Hymnal,* on the one hand, and various American Unitarian collections on the other. The best known are, "Lamp of our feet, whereby we trace," and "Walk in the light, so shalt thou know." From his *Devotional Verses,* &c., 1826, the following have passed into the Scottish *Evang. Union Hymnal,* 1878:—

1. **Fear not, Zion's sons and daughters.** *Gracious Promises.* This is part of a poem on Isaiah xliii. 1, "Fear not, Jacob, tribulated."

2. **Hath the invitation ended?** *Invitation.*

3. **See we not beyond the portal?** *Present vision Imperfect.* This is part of the poem on 1 Cor. xiii. 12, "Dim and dark our present vision."

4. **Those who live in love shall know.** *Peace.*

5. **Would'st thou share this benediction?** *Poor in Spirit.*

In addition, there are also in various collections:—

6. **Around Bethesda's healing wave.** *Consolation.* This is on pp. 182–185, in his *Napoleon, and other Poems,* 1822, in 10 st. of 6 l. A cento therefrom is given in a few American hymnals, including Mr. Beecher's *Ply-*

mouth *Coll.,* No. 746, as, "The waters of Bethesda's pool."

7. **There is a life more dear.** *Spiritual Life.* From the *Devotional Verses,* 1826, p. 96, into *Kennedy,* 1863, No. 1177, with the omission of st. v.

8. **Say not the law divine.** *Spiritual Law.* Also from the *Devotional Verses,* 1826, p. 34, into various American hymnals, generally Unitarian, as the *Hymn and Tune Bk.,* Boston, 1868, No. 342, &c., where, however, it is rewritten from an irregular metre to s.m. This had previously appeared in Hedge and Huntington's *Hys. for the Ch. of Christ,* Boston, U.S., 1853.

Other hymns, given in great part in American Unitarian collections, are annotated under their respective first lines.   [J. J.]

Barton Gray. [Sass, G. H.]

Barton, William, b. cir. 1603, and for some time Minister of St. Martin's, Leicester. d. May 14, 1678. He was the author of one of the earliest collections of hymns, as distinct from Versions of the Psalms, in the English language. He was a friend of Richard Baxter, and it was at Baxter's request that he made four metrical renderings of the *Te Deum* (q. v.). His Hymns and Versions of the Psalms were numerous [see **Early English Hymnody,** §§ v., vi., and **Psalters, English,** § xi.], and were pub. as follows:—
(1) *The Book of Psalms in Metre,* 1644, 2nd ed. 1645, 3rd ed. 1646, 4th ed. 1654. (2) *Psalms & Hymns composed for the Public Thanksgiving, Oct.* 24, 1651. This consists of versions of Ps. 48, 76, 46 and 135. A copy of this is in the Bodleian. (3) *A Century of Select Hymns,* known as the *Chapter Hymns,* 1659, 100 in all. (4) *Four Centuries of Select Hymns,* an imperfect edition, published, he said, against his will. It contains the 1659 *Century,* a new *Century of Chapter Hymns,* and two *Centuries of Psalm Hymns,* 1668. (5) A new and revised ed. of the *Chapter Hymns,* 1670. (6) A new and revised ed. of the *Psalm Hymns,* 1672. (7) Last revise of the *Psalm Hymns,* containing the *Third Century,* 1682. (8) The foregoing *Centuries* collected, a *Third Century of Chapter Hymns* added thereto, 20 additional hymns, the Catechism, Book of Canticles, the Catalogue of Virtuous Women (all in metre), were pub., with an Introduction by his son, Edward Barton, "Minister of Welford, in Northamptonshire," in 1688. This is Barton's work which is known as the *Six Centuries of Select Hymns and Spiritual Songs, collected out of the Bible,* &c., Lond., 1688. Of these works Nos. 1, 2, and 4 differ widely in text from each other; and together with the rest are again altered in the final revision published after his death, 1682, and several times reprinted. The last ed. was pub. by Robert Robinson of Cambridge in 1768. These versions deserve more attention from compilers than they have hitherto received. It must be noted, however, that the *Book of Psalms,* and the *Psalm Hymns,* are distinct works. (9) Barton also printed a 4to vol. in 1655, as, *A View of Many Errors and some gross Absurdities in the Old Translation of the Psalms in English Metre, as also in some other Translations lately published.* This work contains specimens of his own translations and epigrams, and commendatory verses by his friends.   [J. J.]

Bartrum, Joseph P. Of this American author nothing certain is known, save that he pub. *The Psalms newly Paraphrased for the Service of the Sanctuary,* at Boston, U.S.A., in 1833, and that he is supposed to have been an Unitarian. From *The Psalms,* &c., the version of Ps. cvi.:—"O from these visions, dark and drear," is given in several Unitarian collections in G. Britain and America. His version of Ps. lxxxvii., "Amid the heaven of heavens," is given in Holland's *Psalmists of Britain,* 1843, vol. ii. p. 339, together with a critical note on his work.   [F. M. B.]

Bateman, Christian Henry, s. of John Bateman, was b. Aug. 9, 1813, at Wyke, near Halifax. After studying in the Moravian Church and exercising his ministry there for a time, he became, in 1843, minister of Richmond

Place Congregational Church, Edinburgh. After 1846 he was successively Congregational minister at Hopton, in Yorkshire, and Reading, in Berkshire. On taking Holy Orders in the Church of England he became, 1869–71, curate of St. Luke's, Jersey, and Chaplain to the Forces; 1871–75, Vicar of All Saints, Childshill, Middlesex; 1877–84, curate of St. John's, Penymynydd, Hawarden. His hymns appeared mainly in :—

(1) *The Sacred Song Book* (Edin., Gall & Inglis, subsequently pub. as *Sacred Melodies for Children*; and as 200 *Sacred Melodies for Sunday Schools and Families*, was ed. by himself, with the Rev. James Gall, and latterly with Mr. Robert Inglis, the publisher. 1st pub. 1040 no 25; enlarged by a second part, 1846, to 60; revised and enlarged, 1854, to 80; 1862, to 130; and 1872, to 200; it reached a circulation of a million and a half before 1862, four millions before 1872, and above six millions before 1881. It was for many years the hymn-book for Sabbath School use in Scotland. (2) *The Children's Hymnal and Christian Year* (Lond., J. Hodges, 1872), including 11 original hymns, with others from many sources. His best known hymn is : "Come, children, join to sing" (q. v.).   [J. M.]

Bateman, Henry, a popular writer of hymns for children, was descended from the De Voeux, a Huguenot family. Born on March 0, 1002, in Bunhill Row, Finsbury, he was educated for commercial pursuits, and followed the trade of a timber merchant. He d. in 1872. During the greater part of his life he was addicted to the writing of poetry, but his hymns were mostly written between 1856 and 1864. His pub. works are :—

(1) *Belgium and Up and Down the Rhine*, 1858; (2) *Sunday Sunshine: New Hymns and Poems for the Young*, 1858; (3) *Home Musings: Metrical Lay Sermons*, 1862; (4) *Heart Melodies: Being 365 New Hymns and Psalms*, 1862; (5) *Fret Not, and Other Poems*, including Hymns with music, 1869.

From his *Sunday Sunshine* (Lond., Nisbet & Co., 1858) the following hymns have come into C. U. :—

1. A holy and a happy youth. *Youthful Piety.*
2. A noble river, wide and deep. *Finding of Moses.*
3. A sparrow with its plain brown coat. *Providence.*
4. A thought is but a little thing. *Little Things.*
5. A tranquil heart and pleasant thought. *Peace.*
6. A pebble in the water. *Little Things.*
7. Always by day, always by night. *Omniscience.*
8. And is it true that Jesus came? *Good Shepherd.*
9. At Jordan John baptizing taught. *Whitsuntide.*
10. Cross purposes, how sad they are. *Duty.*
11. Daniel was right as right could be. *Duty.*
12. From grassy nest on fluttering wing. *Providence.*
13. God does not judge as we must do. *Charity.*
14. God made the sea, the wide, deep sea. *Providence.*
15. Good night, good night, the day is done. *Evening.*
16. Great God, the world is full of Thee. *Omnipresence.*
17. How joyously amongst the flowers. *Cain & Abel.*
18. I always love those friends the best. *Jesus the Truth.*
19. If anything seems too hard to do. *Perseverance.*
20. In Eden's garden, fair and bright. *Holiness.*
21. In my soft bed when quite alone. *Omniscience.*
22. In the wild desert, far from home. *Providence.*
23. It is but little that I know. *Faith.*
24. May I touch His garment's hem. *Faith.*
25. No tears in heaven! ah, then I know. *Heaven.*
26. O lead me not, O lead me not. *The Lord's Prayer.*
27. On the green grass five thousand men. *Providence.*
28. Over the fields in hedgerows green. *Duty.*
29. Sometimes I do not like to feel. *Solitude.*
30. There is one thing quite sure to make. *Good Temper.*
31. Thou blessed Jesus, pity me, *Jesus the Guide.*
32. Through all the way, the little way. *Providence.*
33. 'Tis very wonderful, I'm sure. *Trust.*
34. Tramp, tramp upon their unknown way. *The Red Sea.*
35. When God bade Abraham sacrifice. *Resignation.*
36. When Jairus's daughter was so ill. *Power of Christ.*

37. When morning, fresh and bright and new. *Morning.*
38. The good old book! with histories. *Holy Scriptures.*
39. Year after year, with patient love. *A Parent's Love.*

In addition to the foregoing the following from his *Heart Melodies*, &c. (Lond., Snow, 1862), are also in C. U., and have attained to some popularity :—

40. Gracious Saviour, gentle Shepherd [thus before Thee]. *Evening.*
41. Let us pray, the Lord is willing. *Prayer.*
42. Was it for me, dear Lord, for me? *Good Friday.*

As will be gathered from the above list of hymns in C. U., the *Sunday Sunshine* has been the most successful of Mr. Bateman's works. This success is due mainly to the fact that the hymns deal with subjects easily treated of in hymns for children. His hymns are hearty and natural in tone. Some of the best of those pub. in the *Sunday Sunshine* were given in the *Book of Praise for Children*, 1875, edited by W. Garrett Horder, and from thence have passed into many collections for children. His best hymn is "Light of the world! Whose kind and gentle care" (q. v.). It is a prayer of more than usual merit for Divine guidance.   [W. G. H.]

Bathurst, William Hiley, M.A., s. of the Rt. Hon. Charles Bragge (afterwards Bathurst) some time M.P. for Bristol, b. at Clevedale, near Bristol, Aug. 28, 1796, and educated at Winchester, and Christ Church, Oxford, graduating B.A. in 1818. From 1820 to 1852 he held the Rectory of Barwick-in-Elmet, near Leeds. Resigning the Rectory in the latter year, through his inability to reconcile his doctrinal views with the Book of Common Prayer, he retired into private life, and d. at Lydney Park, Gloucestershire, Nov. 25, 1877. His works include, *The Georgics of Virgil: Translated by W. H. B.*, 1849; *Metrical Musings; or, Thoughts on Sacred Subjects in Verse*, 1849; and *Psalms and Hymns for Public and Private Use*, 1831 (2nd ed. 1842). This last contains 141 versions of Psalms, and 206 hymns. All the latter, and many of the former are original. Of his hymns, those in most extensive use are, "Hark! the distant isles proclaim," "Holy Spirit from on high," "Jesus, Thy Church with longing eyes," "Eternal Spirit, by whose power," "O for a faith that will not shrink," and "O Saviour, may we never rest." In addition to these and a few others (all of which are annotated under their first lines), the following are in C. U., but mainly in America :—

1. Before Thy cross, my dying Lord. *Faith.*
2. Before Thy mercy-seat, O Lord. *Holy Scriptures.*
3. Behold what unspeakable love. *Heaven.*
4. Does the Lord of Glory speak? *H. Scripture.*
5. Ere the world with light invested. *H. Spirit.*
6. Except the Lord our labours bless. *Ps. cxxvii.*
7. Full of weakness and of sin. *The Creator Spirit desired.*
8. Glory to the Almighty Father. *Praise.*
9. Holy Lord, our hearts prepare. *Preparation for Prayer.*
10. Holy Spirit from on high. *H. Spirit's direction implored.*
11. How blest are they who feel the weight. *Repentance.*
12. How strange that souls whom Jesus feeds. *Conflict.*
13. How sweet it is in early youth. *Youthful Piety.*
14. How sweet the hour of closing day. *Death.*
15. Led by a Father's gentle hand. *Communion of Saints.*

16. Lord, a better heart bestow. *Lent.*
17. Lord, bid the light arise. *To the Holy Spirit.*
18. Lord, shed Thy glory as of old. *Whitsuntide.*
19. Lord, what blessed consolation. *Safety of the Church.*
20. Lord, when our offerings we present. *Offertory.*
21. O for a beam of heavenly light. *Lent.*
22. O for that flame of living fire. *H. Spirit.*
23. O give thanks unto the Lord. *Ps. cv.*
24. Shepherd of Israel, from above. *On behalf of Children.*
25. This day the Lord hath called His own. *Sunday.*
26. When the world my heart is rending. *Heaven.*
27. Why search ye in the narrow tomb? *Ascension.*
28. Ye servants of the living God. *Praise.*

All these hymns were given in his *Psalms & Hymns,* &c., 1831 (Preface dated November 15th, 1830), and repeated, without alteration, in the 2nd ed., 1842. They are characterized by simplicity of language, and directness of aim; but do not in any instance rise above the ordinary level of passable hymnwriting. In some American collections Bathurst's name is contracted to "Bath," and this is regarded either as a complete surname or as a *Bath Coll.* The contraction was given by Bickersteth in his *Christ. Psalmody,* 1833. [J. J.]

Batman, Stephen (sometimes given as Bateman), was b. at Bruton, Somersetshire, and d. in 1584. Beyond the fact that he was a professor of divinity and the author of several works, nothing has been ascertained concerning him. E. Farr, in his *Select Poetry,* &c., *of the reign of Q. Elizabeth,* 1845, has given eight stanzas on "Life" from his work, *The travayled Pylgrime, bringing newes from all partes of the worlde, such like scarce hearde of before,* Lond. 1569.

His works have often quaint titles. They include, in addition to the above—(1) *Batman uppon Bartholome, his Booke, De Proprietatibus Rerum. Newly corrected, enlarged, and amended,* Lond., East, fol., 1582 (a work of Shaksperian interest). (2) *Christall Glasse of Christian Reformation,* Lond., 1569. (3) *Golden Booke of the Leaden Goddes,* Lond., 1577. (4) *Doome warning all men to the Judgment,* Lond., 1581, &c.

Batty, Christopher, b. at Newby Cote, near Settle, Yorkshire, 1715, d. April 19, 1797. He was a member of the "Inghamites," a religious denomination located principally in the northern parts of the counties of Lancashire and Yorkshire. He assisted James Allen (q. v.) in the production of the *Kendal Hymn Book,* 1757, to which he contributed 31 hymns. Very few of these are in C. U. at the present time. His "Captain of Thine enlisted host" (*Missions*), from the *Kendal H. Bk.,* 1757, is found in Kemble's *Coll.,* 1853, No. 475, and in Spurgeon's *O. O. H. Bk.,* No. 968. He completed his brother's poem, *Messiah's Kingdom,* which was printed in 1792. [See **Inghamite Hymnody.**]

Batty, William, brother of the above, also an "Inghamite," and the contributor of 15 hymns to the *Kendal H. Bk.,* 1757. Of these, "Content and glad I'll ever be" (*Salvation by Grace*) and, "From Salem's gate advancing slow" (*Passiontide*), are in C. U. outside of the Inghamite Society, and are given in Snepp's *Songs of G. & G.,* 1872. W. Batty died in 1788. [See **Inghamite Hymnody.**]

Baxter, Lydia, an American Baptist, was b. at Petersburg, N. York, Sep. 2, 1809, married to Mr. Baxter, and d. in N. Y. June 22, 1874. In addition to her *Gems by the*

Wayside, 1855, Mrs. Baxter contributed many hymns to collections for Sunday Schools, and Evangelistic Services. Of these, the following are the best known:—

1. **Cast thy net again, my brother.** *Patient toil.* Given in the *Royal Diadem,* N. Y., 1873.

2. **Go, work in my vineyard.** *Duty.* Also given in the *Royal Diadem,* 1873, and Mr. Sankey's *S. & Solos,* No. 4.

3. **I'm kneeling, Lord, at mercy's gate.** *Lent.* In *Coronation Hymns,* &c., N. Y., 1879.

4. **I'm weary, I'm fainting, my day's work is done.** *Longing for rest.* *Royal Diadem.* 1873.

5. **In the fadeless spring-time.** *Heavenly Reunion.* In the *Royal Diadem,* 1873, I. D. Sankey's *S. S. & Solos,* No. 256, and others. It was written for Mr. H. P. Main in 1872.

6. **One by one we cross the river.** *Death.* In *Songs of Salvation,* N. Y., 1870, I. D. Sankey's *S. S. & Solos,* No. 357, &c. It dates *cir.* 1866.

7. **Take the name of Jesus with you.** *Name of Jesus.* Written late in 1870, or early in 1871, for W. H. Doane, and pub. in *Pure Gold,* 1871. It is No. 148 of I. D. Sankey's *S. S. & Solos.*

8. **The Master is coming.** *Invitation.* In *Songs of Salvation,* 1870, No. 38.

9. **There is a gate that stands ajar.** *Mercy.* In *New Hallowed Songs,* and also the *Gospel Songs* of P. Bliss, 1874. It was written for S. J. Vail about 1872. It has attained to some popularity. It is given in Mr. Sankey's *S. & Solos,* No. 2.

[J. J.]

Baxter, Richard. Only s. of Richard Baxter, yeoman, Eaton Constantine, Shropshire, b. at Rowton, Shropshire, Nov. 12, 1615. He was educated at Wroxeter School, and for a time held the Mastership of the Dudley Grammar School. On taking Holy Orders, he became, in 1640, Curate of Kidderminster. Subsequently he was for some time chaplain to one of Cromwell's regiments. Through weakness he had to take an enforced rest, during which he wrote his *Saints' Everlasting Rest.* On regaining his health he returned to Kidderminster, where he remained until 1660, when he removed to London. At the Restoration he became chaplain to Charles II., and was offered the bishopric of Hereford, which he refused. On the passing of the Act of Uniformity, he retired from active duty as a Minister of the Church of England. In or about 1673 he took out a licence as a Nonconformist Minister and commenced lecturing in London. He d. Dec. 8, 1691. His prose works are very numerous. His poetical are:—

(1) *Poetical Fragments: Heart Imployment with God and Itself; The Concordant Discord of a Broken-healed Heart,* London, *Printed by T. Snowdon for B. Simmons, at the 3 Golden Cocks,* &c., 1681 (2nd ed. 1689; 3rd ed. 1699). It consists of accounts of his religious experiences in verse, and is dated "London, at the Door of Eternity; Rich. Baxter, Aug. 7, 1681." (2) *Additions to the Poetical Fragments of Rich. Baxter, written for himself, and Communicated to such as are more for serious Verse than smooth, London, Printed for B. Simmons at the Three Golden Cocks at the West-end of St. Paul's,* 1683. (3) *A Paraphrase on the Psalms, With other Hymns Left fitted for the Press,* pub. the year following his death (1692). [Early English Hymnody, § x., and English Psalters, § xii.] The *Poetical Fragments* were republished by Pickering, Lond., 1821. From this work his well-known hymn, "Now [Lord] it belongs not to my care," is taken (see "My whole, though broken, heart, O Lord.")

[J. J.]

Bay Psalter, The. Printed by Stephen Daye, at Cambridge, in New England, in 1640, but there is neither place nor printer's name on the title of this excessively rare volume, the first published in North America. It contains the Psalms only, but to the 2nd ed., pub. in 1647, are added a few spiritual songs. The 3rd, revised and amended by President Dunster, had a large addition of Scripture songs and hymns, written by Mr. Lyon. The translations were chiefly by the Rev. Richard Mather, the Rev. Mr. Weld, and the Rev. John Eliot. Francis Quarles, however, contributed several psalms. Originally known as the *Bay Psalm Book*, it afterwards was called *The New England Version of the Psalms*. (See Cotton's *List of Editions of the Bible & Parts thereof in English*, p. 117.) A copy is in the Bodleian, and two others have recently been acquired for America. [See **Eng. Psalters**, § XI., and **American Hymnody**.]   [W. T. B.]

Bayly, Charles. This writer is included by Dr. C. Rogers in his *Lyra Britannica*, 1867; but his hymns have not come into general use. In 1841 he edited *The Selwood Wreath*, Lond. (Preface dated "Frome, Sept. 28, 1840.") The contributors to this volume include John Sheppard, Francis Skurray, and James Joyce. Mr. Bayly's *Descriptive and Other Poems* were pub. in 1860. Dr. Rogers gives "Jesus, to Thee I trembling fly," and "Jesus Christ enthroned on high," as specimens of his hymn-writing, and states that he was born at Frome-Selwood, Somersetshire, and was a member of the legal profession.

Baynes, Robert Hall, M.A., s. of the Rev. Joseph Baynes, b. at Wellington, Somerset, Mar. 10, 1831, and educated at St. Edmund Hall, Oxford, graduating B.A. 1856, and M.A. 1859. Ordained in 1855, he held successively the Curacy of Christ Church, Blackfriars, the P. Curacy of St. Paul's, Whitechapel; of Holy Trinity, Maidstone, and of St. Michael's, Coventry. In 1870 he was Bp. designate of Madagascar; but resigned in 1871. In 1873 he was appointed Hon. Canon of Worcester Cathedral, and in 1880 Vicar of Holy Trinity, Folkestone. Canon Baynes is more widely known as the compiler of some most successful books of sacred poetry than as an original hymn-writer, although some of his hymns are of considerable merit, and are in extensive use. Of these the best known are "Jesu, to Thy table led," and "Holy Spirit, Lord of glory." He was editor of *Lyra Anglicana*, 1862; *English Lyrics*, 1865; *The Canterbury Hymnal*, 1864; and the *Supp. Hymnal*, 1869 (all pub. Lond., Houlston & Wright); *The Illustrated Book of Sacred Poems*, Lond., Cassell & Co., and is the author of original *Autumn Memories and other Verses*, Lond., Houlston & Wright, 1869. His hymns appeared in *The Canterbury Hymnal*, the *Autumn Memories*, and in the *Churchman's Shilling Magazine*, of which he was sometime editor. His *Home Songs for Quiet Hours* were pub. in 1878, and *Hymns for Home Mission Services in the Church of England*, 1879. To his eucharistic manual, *At the Communion Time*, a series of hymns for Holy Communion are added. D. March 12, 1895.   [J. J.]

Bazlee, John. Little is known of this writer beyond the facts that he was a minister of Lady Huntingdon's Connection, and had a chapel in Cumberland Street, Shoreditch. For use primarily of that congregation he pub., in 1768, *A Select Coll. of Psalms and Hymns, Extracted from Several Authors, and Published for the general use of the Church of Christ in her Militant State*, containing 252 hymns. This was re-issued in 1770, with a *Supplement* of 29 hymns; and a 3rd ed. appeared in 1775, with an *Appendix* of 51 hymns. This last was under the editorship of the Rev. Lawrence Coughlan. Two years later, on Coughlan's leaving Shoreditch, an anonymous *Collection* appeared; and again, in 1782, under the pastorate of John Henry Meyer, a *Selection* containing 442 hymns. As Bazlee's name is omitted from the edition published by Coughlan, some little confusion has arisen with regard to their respective claims.   [W. T. B.]

Be joyful in God, all ye lands of the earth. *J. Montgomery.* [*Ps. c.*] Pub. in his *Songs of Zion*, 1822, in 4 st. of 4 l., and in his *Poetical Works*, 1828 and 1846; but omitted from his *Original Hymns*, 1853. It is not in G. U. in G. Britain; but in America, from its appearance in the *Prayer Bk. Coll.*, 1826, to the present, it has been included in numerous hymnals throughout the States. Orig. text in the American *Baptist Praise Bk.*, N. Y., 1871, No. 255.

Be known to us in breaking bread. *J. Montgomery.* [*Holy Communion.*] 1st pub. in his *Christian Psalmist*, 1825, No. 528, in 2 st. of 4 l., and entitled "The Family Table." It was subsequently republished in his *Original Hymns*, 1853, No. 207, with the same title. Its use is limited in its original form, but as a part of the cento "Shepherd of souls, refresh and bless" (q.v.), it is widely known in America.

Be love, delightful theme. *B. Beddome.* [*Preciousness of Christ.*] From his posthumous *Hymns*, &c., 1817, No. 74, in 6 st. of 4 l., into a limited number of hymnals. In Maurice's *Choral H. Bk.*, 1861, it is attributed to J. Montgomery in error.

Be merciful, O God, to me. *C. Wesley.* [*Psalm lvii.*] Appeared in *Ps. & Hys.*, 1743, in 9 st. of 6 l. (*P. Works*, 1868–72, vol. viii. p. 127.) The hymn "My heart is fixed, O God, my heart," in the *Suppl.* to the *Wes. H. Bk.* 1830, and the revised ed., 1875, is composed of st. vii., viii., ix.

Be Thou, O God, by night, by day. [*Morning.*] This anonymous hymn, which is given in many American collections, has not been traced beyond Cheever's *American Commonplace Book of Poetry*, N. Y. 1831. It is in the *Plymouth Coll.*, 1855; Longfellow and Johnson's *Hys. of the Spirit*, 1864; and others, in 3 st. of 4 l., but always as "Anon." [W. T. B.]

Be Thou our [my] Guardian and our [my] Guide. *I. Williams.* [*Divine Guidance sought.*] Appeared in his *Hymns on the Catechism*, 1842, in 4 st. of 4 l. It is based on the petition in the Lord's Prayer, "And lead us not into temptation." In some collections it is changed from the plural to the singular throughout, as in *H. A. & M.*, revised ed., 1875, No. 282, &c. It is given in several collections in G. Britain and America.

Be thou ready, fellow-mortal. [*Readiness for Duty.*] Appeared anonymously in the Unitarian *Hys. for the Sanctuary*, Boston, 1849, No. 609. These *Hys.*, &c., were edited by the Rev. C. A. Bartol and others, and are known as *Bartol's Coll.* This hymn passed from that *Coll.* into the *Supplement* to Hedge & Huntington's *Hys. of the Church of Christ*, Boston, 1853, and again into other hymn-books.

Beadon, Hyde Wyndham, M.A., b. in 1812, and educated at Eton and at St. John's Coll., Cambridge, B.A., 1835, M.A., 1839. Taking Holy Orders in 1836, he became, in 1837, Vicar of Haselbury Plucknett, near Crewkerne, and, in 1838, Vicar of Latton, Wilts. He is also Hon. Canon of Bristol, and Rural Dean. His hymns were pub. in *The Parish Hymn Book*, 1863 and 1875, of which he was co-editor with the Rev. G. Phillimore, and Bp. Woodford. To that collection, in 1863, he contributed the following hymns:—

1. Fierce was the storm of wind. *Epiphany.*
2. Glory to thee, O Lord, Who by," &c. *Epiphany.*
This is usually given as, " All praise to Thee, O Lord, Who by," &c., and is found in several hymnals.
3. O God, Thy soldiers' crown. A *tr.* of "Deus tuorum militum" (q.v.).
This is sometimes given as, " O *Christ*," &c.
4. The Son of Man shall come. *Epiphany.*
The peculiarity of these hymns is that they are all in s.m. Their use is somewhat limited, with the exception of Nos. 1 and 2.   [J. J.]

Beale, Mary, née Craddock, dau. of Mr. Craddock, Minister of Walton-on-Thames, b. 1632, d. in Pall-Mall, 1697. She was distinguished in painting, and her house was the resort of men of letters and eminence in various professions. Her versions of Ps. xiii., lii., lxx., and cxxx. were included in Samuel Woodford's *Paraphrase in English Verse, upon the Books of the Psalms*, 1667. The Version of Ps. lxx. is given in Holland's *Psalmists of Britain*, 1843, vol. ii. p. 76.

Beata nobis gaudia Anni reduxit orbita. [*Whitsuntide.*] This hymn is sometimes ascribed to St. Hilary of Poitiers; but as in the case of others, upon insufficient evidence. [See **Hilary.**]

The full text, in 6 st. of 4 l., is given in *Daniel*, i., No. 7, together with the *Roman Brev.* version, and a few references, and notes. *Mone*, No. 183, gives the text from MSS. of the 13th and 14th centuries, supplies readings therefrom and closes with a note. *Daniel*, iv. pp. 160–161, quotes *Mone* almost verbatim, and adds readings from a Rheinau MS. of th 11th cent. The text is also found in two MSS. of the 11th cent. in the *British Museum* (Jul. A. vi. f. 53 b., Vesp. D. xii. f. 78); the *Latin Hys. of the Anglo-Saxon Church*, 1851, p. 93, where it is printed from an 11th cent. MS. at Durham; in the *Hymn. Sar.*, Lond. 1851, pp. 113, 114; in Card. Newman's *Hymni Ecclesiae*, 1838 and 1865; in *Simrock*, 1868; and other collections.

As to the use of this hymn, we may remark that in the *Mozarabic Brev.* it is the hymn at Lauds on Whitsunday, and daily to Trinity Sunday; in the *Sarum* for Second Vespers on Whitsunday, and daily at Vespers during the week; *York* adds First Vespers as well; *Canterbury* directs its use at Vespers; so also *St. Albans*, but with the addition of two stanzas from the hymn at

First Vespers on Whitsunday—" Jam Christus astra." In the *Rom. Brev.* it is the hymn at Lauds on Whitsunday, and through the octave to Trinity Sunday exclusively. Other Breviaries of less importance also vary in their use.

The *Rom. Brev.* text differs from the older form only in the two instances: st. i., l. 4, " Effulsit in discipulos," is changed to " *Illapsus est apostolis,*" and st. iv., l. 3, "Sacro dierum numero," to " Sacro dierum *circulo.*" *Daniel* draws attention to a curious question with regard to the word, *paraclitus*, or *paracletus*, in st. i., l. 3, of this hymn. The last syllable but one, the penultimate, should have a long vowel. Here, however, it is short, as in Prudentius, *Cathem.* V., v.·160. On this point *Daniel* refers to Gavantus (*Thes. S. R.* tom. iii. p. 263), and to a treatise by Jean Baptiste Thiers (1636–1703).

This hymn must not be confounded with " Beata nobis gaudia dant militum solemnia," given in *Mone*, No. 736, of which there are no *trs.* into English.   [W. A. S.]

Translations in C. U. :—

1. **Again the circling seasons tell.** By W. J. Copeland, appeared in his *Hymns for the Week*, &c., 1848, p. 102, in 7 st. of 4 l. In 1850 it was reprinted in Stretton's *Church Hys.*, and, in a re-written form, as "Again the circling year brings round," in the *English Hymnal*, 1852 and 1861, being a change from C.M. to L.M. In this arrangement Caswall's *tr.* of 1849 was also used somewhat freely.

2. **Hail the joyful day's return.** By R. Campbell, was written for his *St. Andrew's Hymnal*, and pub. therein in 1850, in 3 st. of 8 l., and from thence passed into the Scottish Episcopal *Coll.*, 1858; and with the single change of *the* to *this* st. i. l. 1 in Shipley's *Annus Sanctus*, 1884.

3. **Blest joys for mighty wonders wrought.** By J. M. Neale, appeared in the 1st ed. of *Hymnal N.*, 1852, No. 33. It has failed to win a position in the more important collections.

4. **Round roll the weeks our hearts to greet.** By W. J. Blew, written cir. 1850, first printed on a broadsheet, and then in his *Hymn and Tune Book*, 1st ed., 1852, 2nd, 1855, in 4 st. of 8 l. It was also included in the *People's H.*, 1867.

5. **Joy! because the circling year.** By J. Ellerton and F. J. A. Hort, made for and 1st pub. in *Church Hys.*, 1871. In 1875 it was also included in *H. A. & M.*, No. 153, with the omission of the last four lines. Mr. Ellerton in his note on this hymn (*Ch. Hys.*, folio ed., p. xliv.) attributes st. ii., " Like to quivering tongues of flame," to Bp. Mant's *Ancient Hymns*, 1837, in error. Mant has no *tr.* of the hymn. The stanza is from Campbell's *tr.* as above.

Translations not in C. U. :—
1. The rolling year pursues its way. *Primer*, 1706 (possibly by J. Dryden). This is given in O. Shipley's *Annus Sanctus*, 1884, p. 163.
2. The rowling year hath now brought back. A. J. B. Hope's *Hymns*, &c., 1844.
3. Blest is our joy! The time hath come once more. Bp. J. Williams, *Ancient Hymns*, 1845.
4. Again the slowly circling year. *E. Caswall*, 1849.
5. Blest season! which with gladness fraught. *J. D. Chambers*, 1857.
6. The circling year again, &c. *Wallace*, 1874.
7. Again amid the circling year. *F. Trappes*, 1865.
      [J. J.]

Beaumont, Sir John, elder brother of Francis Beaumont, the dramatic writer, b. in 1582, and educated at Oxford. In 1626 he was created a baronet by King Charles I., d. in 1628. His writings include, *The Crown of Thorns*, a poem in 8 books (not now known to exist); *Bosworth Field and other Poems*, 1629; and Poems on religious and political subjects. He is known to modern hymnals through one or two pieces only. His Poems have been reprinted by Dr. Grosart in his *Fuller Worthies Library.*

Beaumont, Joseph, eldest s. of Sir John Beaumont, was b. March 3, 1615, educated at Westminster, and Peter House, Cambridge, and d. Sept. 3, 1652. His *Original Poems in English and Latin* were pub. posthumously in 1749. In this work there is a fine poem on " Home " (p. 8). This has been condensed into a hymn, beginning " As earth's pageant passes by." (*Consecration to God.*) His *Psyche* (1st pub, 1647), together with selections from his *Original Poems,* &c., were reprinted in Dr. Grosart's *Chertsey Worthies,* 1877–80, in 2 volumes.

Beck, Thomas. Concerning this writer and compiler we have failed in gathering anything beyond the information contained in the title-pages of his works, and that he contributed to the *Gospel* and *Evangelical Magazines* under the signature of " T. B." His works include :—

(1) *Causes of the Dumb pleaded,* 1791, 2nd ed.; (2) *The Missionary, a Poem,* 1795; (3) *The Mission, a Poem,* 1796; (4) *Poetic Amusements,* 1809 ; (5) *Elegy on the Princess Charlotte,* 1817; (6) *Hymns calculated for the Purposes of Public, Social, and Private Worship, collected, composed, and arranged under their proper heads by Thos. Beck, Minister of the Gospel at Gravesend.* Printed for the Author by T. Fisher, Rochester, MDCCLXXXII.

From the last work the hymn, " Jesus, I [we] lift my [our] soul to Thee " (*H. Baptism*), is taken. It is given in the *H. Comp.* new ed., 1876, but previously appeared in Bickersteth's *Christ. Psalmody,* 1833.   [W. T. B.]

Becker, Cornelius, s. of Adrian Becker, merchant of Leipzig, was b. at Leipzig, Oct. 24, 1561. After studying at the University, where he graduated 1584, he kept a private school till his appointment, in the beginning of 1588, as one of the masters of the St. Thomas School, a post he vacated in Sept., 1588, on being appointed diaconus at Rochlitz. In 1592 he became diaconus, and in 1594, pastor of the church of St. Nicholas, Leipzig; and subsequently Professor of Theology in the University, from which, in 1599, he received the degree of D.D. On account of false accusations he was deprived of his charge on June 5, 1601, but was vindicated and restored on Nov. 29 following. He d. suddenly at Leipzig, May 25, 1604 (*Koch,* ii. 219–223 ; *Allg. Deutsche Biog.,* ii. 221). He wrote a few hymns, but his principal work was his version of the *Psalter,* 1602. (See **Psalters, German.**) The only version tr. into English is :—

Der Herr ist mein getreuer Hirt, Dem ich mich ganz vertraue. [*Ps. xxiii.*] Appeared in S. Calvisius's *Harmonia Cantionum Ecclesiasticarum,* Leipzig, 1598, and then in Becker's *Der Psalter Dauids Gesangweis,* Leipzig, 1602. Thence in *Wackernagel,* v., p. 369, in 3 st. of 7 l., entitled "The Good Shepherd." In Bunsen's *Allg. G. B.,* 1846, No. 2. It is tr. as "My Shepherd is the Saviour dear," by *Miss Dunn,* 1857, p. 19.   [J. M.]

Becon, Thomas. [Old Version, § ix. 9.]

Beddome, Benjamin, M.A. This prolific hymn-writer was b. at Henley-in-Arden, Warwickshire, Jan. 23, 1717, where his father, the Rev. John Beddome, was at that time Baptist Minister. He was apprenticed to a surgeon in Bristol, but removing to London, he joined, in 1739, the Baptist church in Prescott St. At the call of this church he devoted himself to the work of the Christian ministry, and in 1740 began to preach at Bourton-on-the-Water, in Gloucestershire. Declining invitations to remove to London or elsewhere, he continued pastor at Bourton until his death, on Sep. 3, 1795, at the age of 78. Mr. Beddome was for many years one of the most respected Baptist ministers in the West of England. He was a man of some literary culture. In 1770 he received the degree of M.A. from Providence College, Rhode Island. He was the author of an *Exposition of the Baptist Catechism,* 1752, in great repute at the time, and reprinted by Dr. C. Evans in 1772. It was his practice to prepare a hymn every week to be sung after his Sunday morning sermon. Though not originally intended for publication, he allowed thirteen of these to appear in the Bristol Bapt. *Coll.* of Ash & Evans (1769), and thirty-six in Dr. Rippon's Bapt. *Sel.* (1787), whence a number of them found their way into the General Bapt. *H. Bk.* of 1793 and other collections. In 1817, a posthumous collection of his hymns was pub., containing 830 pieces, with an introduction by the Rev. Robert Hall, and entitled " *Hymns adapted to Public Worship or Family Devotion, now first published from the Manuscripts of the late Rev. B. Beddome, M.A.*"

Preface dated "Leicester, Nov. 10, 1817." Some of the early copies bear the same date on the titlepage. Copies bearing both the 1817 and 1818 dates are in the *Brit. Mus.* The date usually given is 1818. Some hymns are also appended to his *Sermons,* seven vols. of which were pub. 1805–1819 ; and over twenty are given in the *Baptist Register* of various dates.

Beddome's hymns were commended by Montgomery as embodying one central idea, "always important, often striking, and sometimes ingeniously brought out." Robert Hall's opinion is just, when in his " Recommendatory Preface " to the *Hymns,* &c., he says, p. vii. :—

"The man of taste will be gratified with the beauty and original turns of thought which many of them exhibit, while the experimental Christian will often perceive the most secret movements of his soul strikingly delineated, and sentiments pourtrayed which will find their echo in every heart."

With the exception of a few composed for Baptisms and other special occasions, their present use in G. Britain is limited, but in America somewhat extensive. One of the best is the Ordination Hymn, "Father of Mercies, bow Thine ear." Another favourite is " My times of sorrow and of joy," composed, by a singular coincidence, to be sung on Sunday, Jan. 14, 1778, the day on which his son died, most unexpectedly, in Edinburgh. " Let party names no more," is very popular both in G. Brit. and America. " Faith, 'tis a precious gift," " Witness, ye men and angels, now," and the hymn for Holy Baptism, " Buried beneath the yielding wave," are also found in many collections. Beddome's popularity is, however, now mainly in America.   [W. R. S.]

In addition to about 40 of Beddome's hymns in C. U. which are annotated in this Dictionary under their respective first lines, there are also the following 69, all of which are in C. U. either in G. Brit. or America, in the former to a limited extent, and in the latter somewhat extensively.

1. All glory be to Him Who came. *Holy Baptism.* From his posthumous *Hymns*, &c., 1817, No. 598, in 4 st. of 4 l. into late eds. of *Rippon.*

2. Almighty God, we cry to Thee. *Prayer for guidance.* No. 336 of his *Hymns*, &c., 1817, in 4 st. of 4 l.

3. And shall I [we] sit alone? *Hope reviving.* No. 186 of his *Hymns*, &c., 1817, in 4 st. of 4 l., and No. 508 in the Amer. Ger. Reformed *Hys. of the Church*, N. Y., 1869. It is also in several other hymnals.

4. Arise, Thou Bright and Morning Star. *Christ, the Morning Star.* No. 106, in 3 st. of 4 l., in his *Hymns*, &c., 1817.

5. Awake, awake, my heart and tongue. *Passiontide.* This is No. 271, in his *Hymns*, &c., 1817, in 4 st. of 3 l. Stanzas ii.–iv. had, however, previously appeared in the 10th ed. of Rippon's *Sel.*, 1800, as No. 383, pt. ii., beginning, "To Him, Who on the fatal tree."

6. Awake, awake Thou mighty arm. *Missions.* This was pub. in the 10th ed. of Rippon's *Sel.*, 1800, No. 420. pt. iv. in 3 st. of 4 l., and again in Beddome's *Hymns*, &c., 1817, No. 698. In Spurgeon's *O. O. H. Bk.* it is No. 963.

7. Behold the day is come. *Judgment: Second Advent.* Pub. in his *Hymns*, &c., 1817, No. 798, in 4 st. of 4 l. In America it is given in the *Baptist Praise Bk.*, N. Y., 1871; *Songs for the Sanctuary*, 1865, &c. Not in use in G. Britain.

8. Behold the Eunuch, when baptized. *Holy Baptism.* Pub. in the 1st ed. of Rippon's *Sel.*, 1787, No. 471, in 7 st. of 4 l., as "The holy Eunuch, when baptized," but in Beddome's *Hymns*, &c., 1817, No. 625, it is given as "Behold the Eunuch," &c. It is known, however, to the hymnals as in Rippon's *Sel.*, "The holy Eunuch, when baptized."

9. Burden'd with guilt and pale with fear. *Lent.* Pub. in the Bristol *Coll.* of Ash and Evans, 1769, No. 216, in 3 st. of 4 l., and again in Beddome's *Hymns*, &c., 1817, No. 132.

10. Can sinners hope for heaven? *The Unbelievers.* Pub. in his *Hymns*, &c., 1817, No. 400, in 4 st. of 4 l., with the heading, "The Unrighteous excluded from heaven." It is in several American collections, including *Laudes Domini*, N. Y., 1884, No. 558.

11. Come, Holy Spirit, come; With energy, &c. *Whitsuntide.* Appeared in the 10th ed. of Rippon's *Sel.*, 1800, No. 211, pt. ii., in 4 st. of 4 l. Also in Beddome's *Hymns*, &c., 1817, No. 132.

12. Come, Jesus, heavenly Teacher, come. *Christ the Teacher.* Given as No. 128 in his *Hymns*, &c., 1817, in 3 st. of 4 l., and from thence into the Amer. Presb. *Ps. & Hys.*, Richmond, 1867.

13. Come, Thou Eternal Spirit, come. *Whitsuntide.* No. 142 of his *Hymns*, &c., 1817, in 3 st. of 4 l., and the Amer. *Bap. Praise Bk.*, N. Y., 1871, No. 511.

14. Come, ye humble, contrite souls. *Holy Baptism.* Adult Baptism is contemplated in this hymn, and "Candidates" are encouraged therein to proceed to the Holy Rite. Pub. in his *Hymns*, &c., 1817, No. 613, in 4 st. of 6 l. It is given in late editions of Rippon's *Sel.*

15. Death 'tis [is] an awful word. *Death.* On

the "Death of a Sinner," in his *Hymns*, &c., 1817, No. 780, in 5 st. of 4 l., and from thence into the 27th ed. of Rippon's *Sel.*, 1827, No. 580.

16. Did Christ o'er sinners weep? *Before Sermon.* Given in the 1st ed. of Rippon's *Sel.*, 1787, No. 367, in 3 st. of 4 l., and again in Beddome's *Hymns*, &c., 1817, No. 587. It is in extensive use in America.

17. Dost Thou my profit seek? *Chastisement.* This short hymn in 3 st. of 4 l., entitled, "Submission under Affliction." was included in Rippon's *Sel.*, 1st ed., 1787, No. 540, and signed, "Beddome." It is not found, however, in this form in Beddome's *Hymns*, &c., 1817, but No. 223, "Does the Lord my profit seek," in 2 st. of 8 l., is either the original of that in *Rippon*, or is based thereupon.

18. Each other we have owned. *Parting.* From his *Hymns*, &c., 1817, No. 665, in 5 st. of 4 l., into a few collections.

19. Eternal Source of every good. *Opening of a Place of Worship.* Dr. Hatfield, in his Amer. *Church H. Bk.*, N.Y., 1872, dates this hymn 1790. This may possibly arise from its appearance in a work with which we are unacquainted. It was included in Beddome's *Hymns*, &c., 1817, No. 732. It is in a few hymnals.

20. Father of Mercies, bow Thine ear, Attentive to, &c. *For Missions.* Given in the 1st ed. of Rippon's *Sel.*, 1787, No. 426, in 6 st. of 4 l., and again in Beddome's *Hymns*, &c., 1817, No. 700.

21. Father of Mercies, God of Love, Send down, &c. *Holy Spirit.* In his *Hymns*, &c., 1817, No. 141, on the "In-dwelling of the Spirit," in 4 st. of 4 l. It is found in a few Church of England collections.

22. Fountain of blessing, ever blest. *For Daily Bread.* 1st pub. in the Bristol *Coll.* of Ash & Evans, 1769, No. 42, in 4 st. of 4 l., and again in Beddome's *Hymns*, &c., 1817, No. 341, from whence it has passed into later collections.

23. From Thy dear pierced side. *Passiontide.* Included in his *Hymns*, &c., 1817, No. 94, in 3 st. of 6 l., on the "Fountain opened." It is found in several American collections, as the Amer. Meth. Episc. *Hymns*, 1849, the *Service of Song for Bap. Churches*, Boston, 1871, &c.

24. Go forth, ye saints, behold your King [Lord]. *Missions or Second Advent.* Appeared in the 10th ed. of Rippon's *Sel.*, 1800, No. 421, pt. iv., in 4 st. of 4 l. and headed, "Saints longing to see their King with His many crowns." It was repeated in Beddome's *Hymns*, &c., 1817, No. 702. It is given in a limited number of collections; and in Spurgeon's *O. O. H. Bk.* it is dated 1818 in error.

25. Great God, 'tis from Thy sovereign grace. *Grace.* This hymn on 1 Cor. xv. 8, was given in the 10th ed. of Rippon's *Sel.*, 1800, in 4 st. of 4 l.; and in Beddome's *Hymns*, &c., 1817, No. 10.

26. Great God, to Thee I'll make. *Hope.* No. 231, pt. ii., in the 10th ed. of Rippon's *Sel.*, 1800; and in Beddome's *Hymns*, 1817, No. 478.

27. Great God of Providence, Thy ways. *Providence.* Included in the 1st ed. of Rippon's *Sel.*, 1787, No. 35, in 4 st. of 4 l. It passed from thence into a few of the earlier collections, and was repub. in Beddome's *Hymns*, &c., 1817, No. 40.

28. Great God, my Maker and my King. *Justice and Goodness of God.* Also in the 1st ed. of

Rippon's *Sel.*, 1787, No. 18, in 4 st. of 4 l., and in Beddome's *Hymns*, &c., 1817, No. 11.

29. How free and boundless is the grace. *Freeness of the Gospel.* In Rippon's *Sel.*, 1st ed., 1787, No. 362, in 4 st. of 4 l., and again in Beddome's *Hymns*, &c., 1817, No. 373, with an additional st. "Come, without money, without price."

30. How great, how solemn is the work. *Adult Baptism.* 1st in Rippon's *Sel.*, 1st ed., 1787, No. 453, in 6 st. of 4 l., and appointed for use on the "Morning before Baptism ; or, at the waterside." It was repeated in Beddome's *Hymns*, &c., 1817, No. 619.

31. How many doubts and fears prevail. *Lent.* Given in the Bristol *Coll.* of Ash & Evans, 1769, No. 219, in 3 st. of 4 l., and again in Beddome's *Hymns*, &c., 1817, No. 435.

32. If secret fraud should dwell. *Sincerity.* No. 283, in the 1st ed. of Rippon's *Sel.*, 1787, in 3 st. of 4 l., and No. 232, in Beddome's *Hymns*, &c., 1817.

33. In all my ways, O God. *Family Altar.* From his *Hymns*, &c., 1817, No. 568, in 3 st. of 4 l., into modern eds. of Rippon's *Sel.*, No. 514.

34. In duties and in sufferings too. *Christ, the Example.* From his *Hymns*, &c., 1817, No. 92, in 3 st. of 4 l., into the Amer. Unitarian *Hy.* [& *Tune*] *Bk.*, Boston, 1868, No. 409.

35. Jesus, delightful, charming Name. *Name of Jesus.* An imitation of Newton's "How sweet the Name of Jesus sounds," given in the *Hymns*, &c., 1817, No. 108, in 5 st. of 4 l. It is found in several American collections, including the *Bap. Praise Bk.*, N. Y., 1871, No. 459.

36. Jesus, my love, my chief delight. *Christ, the Gift of God.* This is No. 171 in the 1st ed. of Rippon's *Sel.*, 1787, in 5 st. of 4 l., and No. 96 in Beddome's *Hymns*, &c., 1817.

37. Jesus, my Saviour, bind me fast. *Union with Christ.* From his *Hymns*, &c., 1817, No. 557, in 4 st. of 4 l., into the Amer. Presb. *Ps. & Hys.*, Richmond, 1867, No. 243, and several other American collections.

38. Jesus, my Saviour, let me be. *Conformity to Christ.* Also from his *Hymns*, &c., 1817, No. 199, in 4 st. of 4 l., into the same *Ps. & Hys.*, Richmond, 1867, No. 79.

39. Jesus, when faith with fixed eyes. *Passiontide.* Appeared in a *Coll. of Hys. for the Use of Christians of all Denominations*, 1782 ; again in Rippon's *Sel.*, 1st ed. 1787, No. 477, in 5 st. of 4 l. ; and again, as "A view of Christ's sufferings," in Beddome's *Hymns*, &c., 1817, No. 60. It is a good example of the author's powers. In Spurgeon's *O. O. H. Bk.*, No. 819, it is dated 1818 in error.

40. Lord, incline my wandering heart. *Fear of the Lord.* From the *Hymns*, &c., 1817, No. 167, in 3 st. of 6 l., into modern editions of Rippon's *Sel.*, No. 226, pt. iii.

41. Lord, though bitter is the cup. *Patience.* This hymn is in two forms. The first was given by Dr. Rippon in his *Sel.*, 1787, No. 264, in 3 st. of 4 l., as "Dear Lord, though bitter is the cup ;" and the second is No. 206 in Beddome's *Hymns*, as "Lord, though bitter," &c. In Rippon's *Sel.* it is in L. M., and in the *Hymns*, &c., in 7's.

42. Lord, with a grieved and aching heart. *Lent: the Publican.* Given in the 1st ed. of Rippon's *Sel.*,

1787, No. 236, in 3 st. of 4 l., and in the *Hymns*, &c., 1817, No. 477. It is in C. U. in America, as in *The Service of Song for Bapt. Churches*, Boston, 1871.

43. Love is the fountain whence. *Love to God.* From his *Hymns*, &c., 1817, No. 192, in 4 st. of 4 l., into the Amer. *Bap. Praise Bk.*, N.Y., 1871.

44. My few revolving years. *New Year.* From his *Hymns*, &c., 1817, No. 711, in 3 st. of 4 l., into the American *Sabbath H. Bk.*, N. Y., 1858, No. 1160. It is also given as "*Our* few revolving years," in several American hymnals.

45. My rising soul with strong desires. *Communion with God.* 1st pub. in the Bristol *Coll.* by Ash & Evans, 1769, No. 265, in 3 st. of 4 l. From thence it passed into Rippon's *Sel.*, 1787, No 97. It was also included in Beddome's *Hymns*, &c., 1817, No. 561.

46. O blest society. *Unity.* From his *Hymns*, &c., 1817, No. 637, in 4 st. of 4 l., into modern editions of Rippon's *Sel.*, No. 258, pt. iii.

47. O Lord, Thou art my Lord. *Joining the Church.* This hymn, for the use of a person about to be admitted into Church fellowship, is from Beddome's *Hymns*, &c., 1817, No. 646, in 5 st. of 4 l. It is found in a few collections both in G. Britain and America.

48. O Lord, Thy perfect word. *Holy Scriptures.* In his *Church Hymn Bk.*, N. Y., 1872, Dr. Hatfield dates this hymn 1760. This date may possibly be from a magazine. We trace the hymn only to Beddome's *Hymns*, &c., 1817, No. 686, in 3 st. of 4 l.

49. On Britain, long a favoured isle. *Prayer for National Peace.* 1st pub. as No. 17 in the *Supp.* added to the 3rd ed. of the Bristol *Coll.* of Ash & Evans, 1778. It was repeated in Rippon's *Sel.*, 1787, and other collections, and in Beddome's *Hymns*, &c., 1817, No. 747, in 5 st. of 4 l.

50. On wings of love the Christian flies. *Heavenward.* Appeared in the 1st ed. of the Bristol *Coll.* of Ash & Evans, 1769, No. 282, in 4 st. of 4 l., and repeated in Beddome's *Hymns*, &c., 1817, No. 545.

51. Shout, for the blessed Jesus reigns. *Missions.* 1st pub. in the 1st ed. of the Bristol *Coll.* of Ash & Evans, 1769, No. 373, in 6 st. of 4 l., then in Rippon's *Sel.*, 1787, No. 429, and others among the older collections, and thence to modern hymnals. It is No. 706 of Beddome's *Hymns*, &c., 1817.

52. So fair a face bedewed with tears. *Compassion of Christ.* This, at one time a favourite hymn, was given in Rippon's *Sel.*, 1787, No. 484, in 4 st. of 4 l., and in Beddome's *Hymns*, &c., 1817, No. 70. It is still in C. U.

53. Sprinkled with reconciling blood. *Access to God.* No. 357, in 4 st. of 4 l., in Rippon's *Sel.*, 1787 ; and No. 403, in Beddome's *Hymns*, &c., 1817.

54. Strait the gate, the way is narrow. *The Strait Gate.* From the *Hymns*, &c., 1817, No. 348, in 4 st. of 6 l. into the 27th ed. of Rippon's *Sel.*, 1827, with the omission of st. iv.

55. The mighty God will not despise. *The Prodigal.* 1st pub. in the Bristol *Coll.* of Ash & Evans, 1769, No. 226, in 4 st. of 4 l., then in Rippon's *Sel.*, 1787, No. 273, and again in Beddome's *Hymns*, &c., 1817, No. 349.

56. The wandering star, the fleeting wind. *In-*

consistency. This 1st appeared in Rippon's *Sel.*, 1787, No. 310, in 5 st. of 4 l., then in Beddome's *Hymns*, &c., 1817, No. 515, and is now in C. U. In America it is given in the Unitarian *Hy. & Tune Bk.*, Boston, 1868, No. 563.

57. There is a world of perfect bliss. *Heaven.* From his *Hymns*, &c., 1817, No. 822, in 7 st. of 4 l. into the Amer. *Bap. Praise Bk.*, 1871, No. 1072, with the omission of st. ii., iii., and vii.

58. This world's a dreary wilderness. *Christ, the Refuge.* Included in his *Hymns*, &c., 1817, No. 100, in 5 st. of 4 l. In the Amer. *Bap. Hy.* [& Tune] *Bk.*, Phila., 1871, No. 515. st. i. and v., with the addition of another stanza as No. ii., are given as "This world would be a wilderness."

59. Wait, O my soul, thy Maker's will. *Wisdom of God.* Given in the 1st ed. of Rippon's *Sel.*, 1787, No. 11, in 4 st. of 4 l., and in Beddome's *Hymns*, &c., 1817, No. 18, and headed in each instance, "The Wisdom of God." In the American collections it is usually abbreviated by the omission of st. iv., as in the *Bap. Praise Bk.*, N. Y., 1871, No. 153, or st. iii. and iv., and slightly altered, as in Longfellow and Johnson's *Hys. of the Spirit*, Boston, 1864, No. 454.

60. When Adam sinned, through all his race. *The Fall.* From his *Hymns*, &c., 1817, No. 260, in 6 st. of 4 l., into the American *Church Pastorals*, Boston, 1864, No. 750, with the omission of st. ii. and iv.

61. When by the tempter's wiles betrayed. *The Fall.* No. 122 in Rippon's *Sel.*, 1787, and No. 261 in Beddome's *Hymns*, &c., 1817, in 5 st. of 4 l.

62. When Israel through the desert passed. *Light shining in darkness.* Contributed to the Bristol *Coll.* of Ash & Evans, 1769, No. 80, in 5 st. of 4 l. and headed, "The Excellency of the Divine Word." It was repeated in Rippon's *Sel.*, 1787, No. 44, and in Beddome's *Hymns*, &c., 1817, No. 679.

63. When storms hang o'er the Christian's head. *God our Refuge.* Also in the Bristol *Coll.*, 1769, No. 406, in 4 st. of 4 l., and in Beddome's *Hymns*, 1817, No. 323. This hymn is sometimes given as "When storms hang o'er *my* head"; and as "When storms hang o'er the *children's* heads."

64. Where'er the blustering north-wind blows. *Missions.* Given in the 10th ed. of Rippon's *Sel.*, 1800, No. 420, pt. ii., in 3 st. of 4 l., and in Beddome's *Hymns*, &c., 1817, No. 701. In Rippon's *Sel.*, st. iii. is altered from Beddome's MS.

65. Why, O my soul, why weepest thou? *The Spiritual Mourner.* Contributed to the Bristol *Coll.* of Ash & Evans, 1769, No. 221, in 3 st. of 4 l., and repeated in Rippon's *Sel.*, 1787, No. 274, and in Beddome's *Hymns*, &c., 1817, No. 520.

66. Witness, ye men and angels now. *Joining the Church.* From his *Hymns*, &c., 1817, No. 647, in 4 st. of 4 l., into the Bap. *Ps. & Hymns*, 1858, No. 710, unaltered.

67. Ye trembling souls, dismiss your fears. *Trust.* Pub. in Rippon's *Sel.*, 1787, No. 288, in 6 st. of 4 l., and in Beddome's *Hymns*, &c., 1817, No. 549, with the omission of st. vi. The omission of that stanza would seem to indicate that it was added to the original hymn by Dr. Rippon. In Windle's *Coll.*, No. 443, Rippon's text is repeated, with the omission of st. ii.

68. Ye worlds of light that roll so near. *Christ, the Morning Star.* Contributed to the Bristol

Coll. of Ash & Evans, 1769, No. 112, in 5 st. of 4 l., and in Rippon's *Sel.*, 1787, No. 160, in each case with st. iv. bracketed for omission. In Beddome's *Hymns*, &c., 1817, No. 107, this stanza, which is specially adapted to the Epiphany, is omitted.

69. Your work, ye saints, is not comprised. *Adult Holy Baptism.* From his *Hymns*, &c., 1817, No. 632, in 6 st. of 4 l. into the 27th ed. of Rippon's *Sel.*, 1827, No. 470, pt. ii., and thence to later collections.

Beddome is thus seen to be in C. U. to the extent of about 100 hymns. In this respect he exceeds every other Baptist hymn-writer; Miss Steele ranking second.

The authorities for Beddome's hymns are : (1) *A Coll. of Hymns adapted to Public Worship*, Bristol, W. Pine, 1769, the *Coll.* of Ash & Evans; (2) Dr. Rippon's *Sel.* 1787, and later editions; (3) *Sermons printed from the Manuscripts of the late Rev. Benjamin Beddome, M.A.*, …*with brief Memoir of the Author*, Dunstable & Lond., 1805-1819 ; (4) Dr. Rippon's *Baptist Register*, 1795, &c.; (5) The *Beddome* MSS. in the Baptist College, Bristol ; (6) and *Hymns adapted to Public Worship, or Family Devotion, now first published, from Manuscripts of the late Rev. B. Beddome, A.M. With a Recommendatory Preface by the Rev. R. Hall, A.M.* Lond., 1817. In his Preface, Mr. Hall gives this account of the Beddome MSS.:— "The present Editor was entrusted several years ago with the MSS., both in prose and verse, with permission from the late Messrs. S. & B. Beddome, sons of the Author, to publish such parts of them as he might deem proper. He is also indebted to a descendant of the Rev. W. Christian, formerly pastor of the Baptist Church at Sheepshead, Leicestershire, for some of the Author's valuable hymns, which had been carefully preserved in the family. From both these sources, as well as others of less consequence, the present interesting volume has been derived."   [J. J.]

Bede, Beda, or Baeda, the Venerable. This eminent and early scholar, grammarian, philosopher, poet, biographer, historian, and divine, was b. in 673, near the place where, shortly afterwards, Benedict Biscop founded the sister monasteries of Wearmouth and Jarrow, on an estate conferred upon him by Ecgfrith, or Ecgfrid, king of Northumbria, possibly, as the Rev. S. Baring-Gould, *Lives of the Saints* (May), p. 399, suggests, "in the parish of Monkton, which appears to have been one of the earliest endowments of the monastery." His education was carried on at one or other of the monasteries under the care of Benedict Biscop until his death, and then of Ceolfrith, Benedict's successor, to such effect that at the early age of nineteen he was deemed worthy, for his learning and piety's sake, to be ordained deacon by St. John of Beverley, who was then bishop of Hexham, in 691 or 692. From the same prelate he received priest's orders ten years afterwards, in or about 702. The whole of his after-life he spent in study, dividing his time between the two monasteries, which were the only home he was ever to know, and in one of which (that of Jarrow) he died on May 26th, 735, and where his remains reposed until the 11th century, when they were removed to Durham, and re-interred in the same coffin as those of St. Cuthbert, where they were discovered in 1104.

It is unnecessary here to enter at further length into the details of Bede's quiet if laborious life, as the reader will find an exhaustive account of them by Bishop Stubbs of Chester, in Smith and Wace's *Dict. of Christian Biog.*, vol. i. pp. 300-304. It would be still more out of place in a work of this kind to discuss his writings generally. He was a voluminous author upon almost every subject, and as an historian his contribution to English history in the shape of his *Historia Ecclesiastica* is invaluable. But it is with him as a hymnist that we have to do here.

I. In the list of his works, which Bede gives at the end of his *Ecclesiastical History*, he enumerates a *Liber Hymnorum*, containing hymns in "several sorts of metre or rhyme." The extant editions of this work are :—

(1) Edited by *Cassander*, and published at Cologne, 1556 ; (2) in Wernsdorf's *Poetae Lat. Min.*, vol. ii. pp.239-244.

II. Bede's contributions to the stores of hymnology were not large, consisting principally of 11 or at most 12 hymns ; his authorship of some of these even is questioned by many good authorities, such as *Koch*, vol. i., p. 79. *Daniel*, however, in vol. i. pp. 201-203, claims the following as having been written by Bede, on the authority of *Cassander, Ellinger, Thomasius, Rambach,* and others.

1. "Hymnum canamus Gloriae" (*Ascension*). This fine hymn is found in the *York Hymnal*, and was therefore in use in the services of the Church. 2. "Adeste Christi vocibus" (*Nativity of B. V. M.*). 3. "Apostolorum gloriae" (*SS. Peter and Paul*). 4. "Illuxit Christi Spiritus" (*Pentecost*). 5. "Hymnum canentes martyrum" (*The Holy Innocents*). 6. "Il luxit alma saeculis" (*St. Agnes*). 7. "Nunc Andreae solemnia" (*St. Andrew*). 8. "Praecessor almus gratiae" (*Beheading of St. John Baptist*). 9. "Praecursor altus luminis" (*St. John the Baptist*). 10. "Primo Deus coeli globum" (*Hymn on the Creation*), a long hymn of 116 lines. 11. "Salve, tropaeum gloriae" (*St. Andrew's Address to his Cross*). To these *Mone,* vol. i. p. 284, adds, 12. "Ave sacer Christi sanguis" (*On the Elevation of the Chalice*), as claimed for Bede, but disallows the claim, and assigns a very late date to it. Of these Nos. 1 to 10 are referred to in *Daniel,* i., clxxii.-clxxxii. ; No. 5 in *Königsfeld,* with *tr.* into German; and No. 11, with words of marked commendation, in *Trench,* 3rd. ed. p. 219. Details of the *trs.* of Nos. 1, 5, 9, 10 are given under their respective first Latin lines.

While we cannot look for the refined and mellifluous beauty of later Latin hymnists in the works of one who, like the Venerable Bede, lived in the infancy of ecclesiastical poetry ; and while we must acknowledge the loss that such poetry sustains by the absence of rhyme from so many of the hymns, and the presence in some of what Dr. Neale calls such "frigid conceits" as the *epanalepsis* (as grammarians term it) where the first line of each stanza, as in "Hymnum canentes Martyrum," is repeated as the last ; still the hymns with which we are dealing are not without their peculiar attractions. They are full of Scripture, and Bede was very fond of introducing the actual words of Scripture as part of his own composition, and often with great effect. *Neale* notes two instances :—

(1) In "Hymnum canentes Martyrum"—

"Qui seminant in lacrymis,
  Longo metent in gaudio."

and (2) in "Hymnum canamus gloriae —

"Mirata adhuc coelestium
  Rogavit aula civium,
Quis, inquit, est Rex Gloriae?
  Rex iste tam laudabilis."

That Bede was not free from the superstition of his time is certain, not only from his prose writings, but from such poems as his elegiac "Hymn on Virginity," written in praise and honour of Queen Etheldrida, the wife of King Ecgfrith, and inserted in his *Ecclesiastical History*, bk. iv., cap. xx. [D. S. W.]

Beecher, Charles, s. of the well-known Dr. Lyman Beecher, whose autobiography he chiefly edited, and brother of Henry Ward Beecher, was b. at Litchfield, Connecticut, 1815. Mr. Beecher was for some time a Congregational pastor at Georgetown, Mass. He has pub. *Review of Spiritual Manifestations,* 1853 ; *Pen Pictures of the Bible,* 1855, &c. His hymns were contributed to his brother's *Plymouth Collection,* 1855, and include :—

1. There's rest in the grave. *Heaven.*

2. We are on our journey home. *Heaven.*

The latter is in the more extensive use, but both are unknown to the English collections. [F. M. B.]

Befiehl du deine Wege. *P. Gerhardt.* [*Trust in God.*] This hymn, which Lauxmann in *Koch*, viii. 392, calls "The most comforting of all the hymns that have resounded on Paulus Gerhardt's golden lyre, sweeter to many souls than honey and the honey-comb," appeared as No. 333 in the Frankfurt ed., 1656, of Crüger's *Praxis pietatis melica.* Thence in Wackernagel's ed. of his *Geistliche Lieder,* No. 66, and Bachmann's ed., No. 72, in 12 st. of 8 lines, and included as No. 620 in the *Unv. L. S.,* 1851. It is an acrostic on Luther's version of Ps. xxxvii. 5, "Befiehl dem Herren deine Wege und hoffe auf ihn, er wirds wohl machen," formed by the initial words of the stanzas, those in Wackernagel's ed. being printed in blacker type. This acrostic form has been preserved by *Jacobi* and *Stallybrass.*

According to tradition it was written in a Saxon village to console his wife after being compelled to leave Berlin. But, as already stated, the hymn was pub. in 1656, and though Gerhardt had to leave his office in 1666, he did not leave Berlin till his appointment to Lübben in 1669, while his wife died in Berlin in 1668. The hymn soon spread over Germany, found its way into all the hymn-books, and ranks as one of the finest hymns of its class. *Lauxmann* relates that it was sung when the foundation stone of the first Lutheran church at Philadelphia was laid, May 2, 1743, and again on Oct. 20, when the Father of the American Lutheran Church, Heinrich Melchior Muhlenberg, held the opening service. He also relates that Queen Luise of Prussia, during the time when Germany was downtrodden by Napoleon I., came to Ortelsburg in East Prussia, and there, on Dec. 5, 1806, wrote in her diary the verses of Goethe (*Wilhelm Meister,* Bk. ii, Chap. XIII.), thus rendered by Thomas Carlyle :—

Who never ate his bread in sorrow,
 Who never spent the darksome hours
Weeping and watching for the morrow,
 He knows ye not, ye gloomy Powers.

To earth, this weary earth, ye bring us,
 To guilt ye let us heedless go,
Then leave repentance fierce to wring us :
 A moment's guilt, an age of woe !

But drying her tears she went to the harpsichord, and from Goethe turned to Gerhardt, and played and sang this hymn. In his note, extending from p. 392 to p. 405, *Lauxmann* gives many other instances of its consoling effects, and says of it, "Truly a hymn which, as Luther's 'Ein feste Burg,' is surrounded by a cloud of witnesses."

Translations in C. U. :—

Commit thou all thy griefs. A noble but free *tr.*, omitting st. v., ix.-xi., by J. Wesley in *H. and Sacred Poems,* 1739 (*P. Works,* 1868-72, vol. i. p. 125), in 8 st. of 8 l. Though free, it has in far greater measure than any other caught the ring and spirit of Gerhardt. Included as No. 37 in the *H. and Spir. Songs,* 1753, and as Nos. 103-104 in the *Pocket H. Bk.,* 1785, but not included in the *Wes. H. Bk.,* till as Nos. 673,

674 in the *Supplement* of 1830 (st. iii., ll. 4–8, being omitted), and thence as No. 831 in the ed. of 1875. This *tr.* has come into very extended use, but generally abridged; Mercer, in the 1857 ed. of his *C. P. and H. Bk.*, giving it in full, but abridging it to 8 st. in his Ox. ed., 1864. Among recent collections it is found under its original first line in the Bapt. *Ps. and Hys.*, 1858, *Sarum H.*, 1868, Irish *Ch. Hymnal*, 1873, Scottish *Presb. Hymnal*, 1876, Horder's *Cong. Hys.*, 1884, and others; and in America in the *Plymouth Coll.*, 1855, *Sabbath H. Bk.*, 1858, *H. and Songs of Praise*, N. Y., 1874, *Evang. Hymnal*, N. Y., 1880, and many others. In the *United Presb. H. Bk.*, 1852, it began, "To God commit thy griefs." It is also found as follows :—

1. "Thou on the Lord rely " (Wesley's iii.), in Knight's *Coll.*, Dundee, 1871–74.
2. "Thy everlasting truth" (Wesley's v.), in Adams's *Ch. Pastorals*, Boston, U.S., 1864.
3. "Give to the winds thy fears" (Wesley's ix.), in *Kennedy*, 1863, and many English and American Colls.
4. "O cast away thy fears" (Wesley's ix. altered), in *United Presb. H. Bk.*, 1852.
5. "Through waves and clouds and storms " (Wesley's x.), in Davies and Baxter's *Coll.*, 1835.
6. "Leave to His sovereign sway" (Wesley's xiii.), in Adams's *Ch. Pastorals*, Boston, U.S., 1864.
7. "Thou seest our weakness, Lord " (Wesley's xv.), in Amer. Methodist Episcopal *Hymns*, 1849.
8. "Put thou thy trust in God," a greatly altered cento of which st. i. is based on iii., ll. 1–4; ii. on i., ll. 1–4; iii. on iii., ll. 1–4; and iv. on v., ll. 5–8; appeared as No. 77 in the *Mitre H. Bk.*, 1836, and since in various hymnals, e.g. S.P.C.K. *Ps. and Hys.*, 1853, *Kennedy*, 1863.

2. **Commit thy way, confiding.** In full by Dr. H. Mills in the *Evang. Review*, Gettysburg, July, 1849, and his *Horae Ger.*, 1856, p. 172. His st. i., ii., vi., xii. were included in the Lutheran General Synod's *Hymns*, 1852, and i., ii., v., vi., xi., xii. in the *Ohio Luth. Hymnal*, 1880.

3. **Thy way and all thy sorrows.** In full by A. T. Russell as No. 233 in his *Ps. and Hys.*, 1851, in 3 pts. Pt. ii. begins "In vain the powers of darkness " (st. v.), and pt. iii. with "Awhile His consolation " (st. ix.).

4. **Commit thy way to God.** A good *tr.*, omitting st. ix., x., xii., by Mrs. Charles in her *Voice of Christian Life in Song*, 1858, p. 239. Her *trs.* of st. i., ii., vi., viii., xi. form No. 138 in Jellicoe's *Coll.*, 1867, and i., vi.–viii., xi., No. 283 in Bp. Ryle's *Coll.*, 1860.

5. **Commit thy way, O weeper.** A free paraphrase, in 6 st. of 4 l., by J. S. Stallybrass for the *Tonic-Solfa Reporter*, July, 1857, repeated in Curwen's *Child's Own H. Bk.*, 1862, and new *Child's Own H. Bk.*, 1874.

6. **Commit thou every sorrow, And care.** *Tr.* of st. i.–iii., xii. by Miss Borthwick, as No. 240 in Dr. Pagenstecher's *Coll.*, 1864.

Translations not in C. U. :—

(1) "Commit thy Ways and Goings," by *J. C. Jacobi*, 1720, p. 15 (1722, p. 38, 1732, p. 63). (2) "Commit thou thy each grievance," No. 472, in pt. i. of the *Moravian H. Bk.* 1754 (1849, No. 191). (3) "Commit thy ways, thy sorrows," by Mrs. Stanley Carr in her *tr.* of *Wildenhahn's Paul Gerhardt*, 1845 (ed. 1856. p, 207). (4) "Commit thy secret grief," by *Miss Dunn*, 1857, p. 89. (5) "Commend thy way, O mortal," in Madame de Pontes's *Poets and Poetry of Germany*, 1858, vol. i., p. 424. (6) "Commit thou all thy ways, and all," by *Mrs. Bevan*, 1859, p. 124. (7) "Commit thy way unto the Lord, thy heavy," by Dr. R. P. Dunn in *Sacred Lyrics from the German*, Phil. 1859, p. 85. (8) "To God thy way commending," by *Miss Cox*, 1864, p. 161, and the Gilman-Schaff, *Lib. of Rel. Poetry*, ed. 1883, p. 510. (9) "Commit whatever grieves thee," by *J. Kelly*, 1867, p. 225. (10) "Commit thy way. O weeping," by Dr. J. Guthrie in his *Sacred Lyrics*, 1869, p. 92. (11) "Commit the way before thee," by *N. L. Frothing-*

ham, 1870, p. 164. (12) "Commit thy course and keeping," by *Dr. John Cairns*, c. 1850, but 1st pub. Edin. 1881, as an eight-page tract.   [J. M.]

Begin, my tongue [soul], some heavenly theme. *I. Watts.* [*Faithfulness of God.*] 1st pub. in his *Hys. and S. Songs*, 1707 (2nd ed., 1709, Bk. ii., No. 169), in 9 st. of 4 l., and entitled "The faithfulness of God in His promises." In 1776, Toplady included it, in an altered and abbreviated form, in his *Ps. and Hymns*, No. 388, as "Begin, my soul, some heavenly theme." This form of the hymn has been repeated in many collections, sometimes verbatim from Toplady, and again, with further alterations, as in the *Wes. H. Bk.*, 1830, and revised ed., 1875. Its use in America, usually abbreviated, is much more extensive than in G. Britain.

Behm, Martin, s. of Hans Behm [*Böhme, Boehm, Behemb, Behem, Böheim, Bohemus* or *Bohemius*], town-overseer of Lauban in Silesia, was b. at Lauban, Sept. 16, 1557. During a protracted famine, 1574, Dr. Paul Fabricius, royal physician at Vienna, a distant kinsman, took him to Vienna, where he acted as a private tutor for two years, and then went to Strassburg, where, from Johann Sturm, Rector of the newly founded University, he received much kindness. Returning home at his mother's request after his father's death, May, 1580, he was, at Easter, 1581, appointed assistant in the Town School, and on Sept. 20, ordained diaconus of the Holy Trinity Church. After his senior had been promoted to Breslau the Town Council kept the post nominally vacant for two years, and then, in June, 1586, appointed Behm chief pastor. For 36 years he held this post, renowned as a preacher, as a faithful pastor in times of trouble (famine 1590, pestilence 1613, war 1619), and as a prolific author. After preaching on the tenth Sunday after Trinity, 1621, he was seized with illness, and after he had lain for twenty-four weeks on a sick bed, there was ministered to him, on Feb. 5, 1622, the abundant entrance of which he sings in his hymn, "O Jesu Christ, meins Lebenslicht " (*Koch*, ii. 227–234; *Allg. Deutsche Biog.*, ii. 282).

He was one of the best hymn-writers of his time. His hymns are true and deep in feeling, dwelling specially on the Passion of Our Lord. They speedily passed into the hymn-books, and long held their place therein. Of about 480 hymns which he composed, the most important appeared in his :—

(1) *Centuria precationum rhythmicarum*, Wittenberg, 1606 (2nd ed., 1611).
(2) *Centuria secunda precationum rhythmicarum*, Wittenberg, 1608 (2nd ed., 1611).
(3) *Centuria precationum rhythmicarum*, Wittenberg, 1615 (complete ed. of the Three Centuries, Jena and Breslau, 1658). A selection of 79 Hymns, ed., with an introduction, by W. Nöldeke, appeared at Halle in 1857.

Four of his hymns have been *tr.* into English, three being in English C. U. :—

i. **O Heilige Dreifaltigkeit.** [*Morning.*] 1st pub. in his *Kriegesman*, Leipzig, 1593, in 7 st. of unequal length, repeated in 1608, as above, in 8 st. of 4 l. Both forms are in *Wackernagel*, v. p. 197; and the second in *Nöldeke*, 1857, p. 53; and, omitting st. vi.–viii., as No. 1126 in the Berlin *G. L. S.*, ed 1863. In 1593 it was entitled "The ancient Sancta Trinitas et adoranda Unitas in German ; " but it is rather a versification of the Prayer for Wednesday evening in

J. Habermann's *Gebet Buch* (Wittenberg, 1567).
The *trs.* in C. U., both of the second form, are:—

1. O Thou most Holy Trinity. A very good *tr.*
of st. i., iii.–v., by A. T. Russell, as No. 2 in his
Ps. and Hys., 1851, and thence in *Kennedy*, 1863,
and Dr. Thomas's *Augustine H. Bk.*, 1866.

2. O holy, blessed Trinity, Divine. A good *tr.* of
st. i.–v. by Dr. C. H. L. Schuette, as No. 295 in
the *Ohio Luth. Hymnal*, 1880.

3. O holy, holy, holy Three, by *H. J. Buckoll*,
1842, p. 21.

ii. **O Jesu Christ, meins Lebens Licht.** [*For the
Dying.*] His finest hymn. 1st pub. in a collection
entitled *Christliche Gebet*, 1610, and then in his
Zehen Sterbegebet, appended to his *Centuria secunda*, 1611 (see above), in 14 st. of 4 l., entitled
" Prayer for a happy journey home, founded upon
the sufferings of Christ." Thence in *Wackernagel*, v. p. 235, *Nöldeke*, 1857, p. 79, and the
Unv. L. S., 1851, No. 835. The *trs.* in C. U.
are:—

1. Lord Jesus Christ, my Life, my Light. A very
good *tr.* by Miss Winkworth in her *Lyra Ger.*,
2nd Series, 1858, p. 213, st. v., x. being omitted
and viii., ix. combined as one st. In her *C. B.
for England*, 1863, No. 190, she omitted her st
v., vi., and united her st. iv., vii. as iv. This *tr.*
is included more or less abridged in Wilson's
Service of Praise, 1865, and in America in the
Bapt. H. Bk., Phil., 1871, the Meth. Epis. *Hymnal*,
1878, and the *Ohio Luth. Hymnal*, 1880, &c.

2. Lord Jesus Christ, my soul's desire. A good
and full *tr.* by Dr. John Ker in the *Juv. Miss.
Mag.* of the U. P. Church, May, 1858, p. 25.
St. i., iii, v., vii. form No. 49 in the *Ibrox
Hymnal*, 1871.

Other *trs.* are:—
(1) " Lord Jesu, fountain of my life," by *J. C. Jacobi*,
1725, p. 52 (1732, p. 195), and repeated in the Moravian
hymn-books combined in 1826 with J. Cennick's
"Though I'm in body full of pain." (2) " Jesu, my
light and sure defence," as No. 54 in the *Moravian H.
Bk.*, 1742. (3) " O Jesu, life-light of my way," by
Miss Warner, 1858 (ed. 1861, p. 176).

iii. **O König aller Ehren.** [*Epiphany.*] Founded
on St. Matthew ii., and 1st pub. 1606 as above,
in 6 st. of 8 l. Thence in *Wackernagel*, v. p. 210,
Nöldeke, 1857, p. 31, and the *Unv. L. S.*, 1851,
No. 79. The *trs.* in C. U. are:—

1. O King of Glory, David's Son. A double
C. M. version of st. i., ii., v., vi. by Miss Winkworth in her *Lyra Ger.*, 2nd Series, 1858, p. 20,
and thence in Dr. Pagenstecher's *Coll.*, 1864,
No. 33. Her 2nd *tr.* :—

2. O Jesu, King of Glory, No. 37 in her *C. B.
for England*, 1863, is the above version rewritten
to the original metre. In the *Ohio Luth. Hyl.*,
1880, No. 54, with *trs.* of st. iii., iv. added.

iv. **Das walt Gott Vater und Gott Sohn.** [*Morning
Prayer.*] 1st pub. 1608 as above, in 11 st., and
thence in *Wackernagel*, v. p. 215, in *Nöldeke*,
1857, p. 51. *Tr.* as "O God Almighty, Father,
Son," by *H. J. Buckoll*, 1842, p. 15. [J. M.]

Behme, David, b. April 2, 1605, at
Bernstadt, in Silesia, became, 1630, Court
preacher to Duke Heinrich Wenzel of Münsterberg, and pastor of Vielguth near Bernstadt. In 1638 became pastor of his native
town, preacher to the court of Oels, and a
member of the Consistory. There he remained
as a faithful and exemplary pastor till his
death, Feb. 9, 1657 (*Koch*, iii. 56–57; *Allg.*

Deutsche Biog., ii. 284). *Mützell*, 1858, includes six hymns under his name, Nos. 300-
305. One has been *tr.* into English.

Herr nun lass in Friede. [*For the Dying.*] Founded
on the *Nunc Dimittis*. 1st appeared in the 5th ed., Breslau, c. 1663, of the *Vollständige Kirchen und Haus
Music*, p. 962, in 10 st. In *Mützell*, 1858, No. 301 as
a hymn on the Festival of the Purification of the Virgin
Mary. It is *tr.* as, " Lord, now let Thy servant," by
Miss Winkworth, 1858, p. 216.   [J. M.]

Behold, a stranger at the door. *J.
Grigg.* [*Expostulation.*] This is one of *Four
Hymns on Divine Subjects*, &c., 1765, in 11 st.
of 4 l., a second being the well-known " Jesus,
and shall it ever be ?" (q. v.). It came into
congregational use at an early date, but usually
in an abbreviated form. Both in G. Britain,
and in America, various arrangements of the
text are given in collections in C. U. The full
original text was reprinted in D. Sedgwick's
ed. of Grigg's *Hymns*, &c., 1861. It is also
found in Lord Selborne's *Bk. of Praise*, 1862,
and in *Lyra Brit.*, 1867, p. 254.

Behold! how glorious is yon sky.
[*Eternal Life.*] This hymn, in 2 st., is No. 749
in the *N. Cong.*, 1859, and No. 611 in Dr. Allon's
Cong Psalmist Hyl., 1886. It has evidently
been written for or adapted to the fine
German chorale, " Wie schön leuchtet der
Morgenstern " (see **Nicolai, P.**). But not one
single line can be said to be *tr.* either from
the hymn of Nicolai, or from the recast of
Nicolai's hymn made by J. A. Schlegel (q.v.);
and it must rank as an anonymous English
hymn.

**Behold, how good a thing it is, And
how,** &c. [*P. cxxxiii.*] From the *Scottish
Psalter*, 1650, into Spurgeon's *O. O. H. Bk.*,
1866, No. 133. In the American *Presb. Hymnal*, Phila., 1874, No. 593, it is altered to
" Behold, how good and pleasant," &c. In
this form it is also in other American collections.

Behold my Servant! see Him rise.
[*Christ the Ambassador.*] This Paraphrase,
the author of which is unknown, first appeared in the Draft Scottish *Translations and
Paraphrases*, in 1745, as No. v., on Is. xlii.
1–13, in 13 st. of 4 l. The opening sts. are:—

  1. "Behold my Servant ! see him rise
      exalted in my Might :
     Him have I chosen, and in him
     I place supreme Delight."
  2. "In rich Effusion, on his Soul,
      my Spirit's Powers shall flow :
     He'll to the Gentiles, and the Isles,
     my Truths and Judgments show.'

The paraphrase extended in this strain to
13 st., some of which are exceedingly good,
but the whole is too extensive to quote.

ii. In 1781 John Logan published a volume
of *Poems*, p. 108, No. 6, in which were several
hymns and paraphrases, including one based
upon the above, in 16 st., and opening thus:—

  " Behold ! the Ambassador divine,
    Descending from above,
    To publish to mankind the law
     Of everlasting love !
  " On Him in rich effusion pour'd
    The heavenly dew descends ;
    And truth divine He shall reveal
    To earth's remotest ends."

We have given reasons elsewhere for holding that this rewritten version of the 1745

paraphrase is the work of M. Bruce (q. v.). The full text is in Dr. Grosart's *Works of Michael Bruce*, 1865, pp. 140–144.

iii. During the same year that Logan published his *Poems*, i.e. 1781, the new and revised edition of the Scottish *Translations and Paraphrases* was also published. Of this edition J. Logan was one of the revising and editing committee. In this work this hymn is included in a *third* form, in which we have 15 st. of 4 l. Of these 60 lines, 22 full lines and 7, partly so, are from the 1745 *Trans. & Par.*; 16 full lines, and 5 partly so, from Bruce of 1781, the rest being new. The hymn thus presents one of the most peculiar pieces of patchwork with which we are acquainted. As an illustration of the way in which a man can build up for himself a reputation out of the works of others, and live on that reputation, as J. Logan has done for nearly a century, we give this cento in full, printing the 1745 text in SMALL CAPITALS; Bruce's text of 1764, as printed in Logan's *Poems*, in *Italics;* and the new matter in *ordinary Roman type.*

" xxiii. Isaiah xlii. 1-13.
1. BEHOLD MY SERVANT ! SEE HIM RISE
EXALTED IN MY MIGHT !
HIM HAVE I CHOSEN, AND IN HIM
I PLACE SUPREME DELIGHT.

2. *On him, in rich effusion pour'd,*
MY SPIRIT shall descend ;
My truths and judgments he shall show
to earth's remotest end.

3. Gentle and still SHALL BE HIS VOICE,
No THREATS FROM HIM PROCEED,
THE SMOKING FLAX HE SHALL NOT QUENCH,
NOR BREAK THE BRUISED REED.

4. THE FEEBLE SPARK TO FLAMES HE'LL RAISE ;
THE WEAK will NOT DESPISE ;
JUDGMENT HE SHALL BRING FORTH TO TRUTH,
AND MAKE THE FALLEN RISE.

5. The *progress of his zeal* and power
shall never know decline,
Till foreign lands and distant isles
receive the law divine.

6. HE WHO erected heav'n's bright arch
and bade the planets roll,
Who peopled all the climes of *earth,*
and form'd the human soul.

7. THUS saith THE LORD ; THEE HAVE I RAIS'D,
MY PROPHET THEE INSTALL;
IN RIGHT I'VE rais'd THEE, AND IN STRENGTH
I'LL SUCCOUR WHOM I CALL.

8. I will establish with THE LANDS
a covenant in thee,
To give the Gentile nations light,
AND SET THE PRIS'NERS FREE :

9. Asunder burst the gates of brass ;
the iron fetters fall ;
And gladsome light and liberty
are straight restor'd to all.

10. I AM THE LORD, AND BY MY NAME
OF GREAT JEHOVAH KNOWN ;
No idol shall usurp my praise,
NOR MOUNT INTO MY THRONE.

11. LO ! FORMER SCENES, PREDICTED ONCE,
CONSPICUOUS RISE TO VIEW ;
AND FUTURE scenes, PREDICTED NOW,
SHALL BE ACCOMPLISH'D TOO.

12. SING TO THE LORD in joyful strains !
LET EARTH HIS PRAISE RESOUND,
YE WHO UPON THE OCEAN DWELL,
AND FILL THE ISLES AROUND !

13. *O city of the Lord !* begin
the universal song ;
And let the SCATTER'D *villages*
THE cheerful NOTES PROLONG.

14. Let KEDAR's *wilderness afar*
lift up its lonely voice
And let the tenants of the rock
with accents rude rejoice.

15. Till 'midst *the streams of distant lands*
the islands sound his praise ;
And ALL COMBIN'D, WITH ONE ACCORD,
JEHOVAH'S GLORIES RAISE ! "

iv. William Cameron (q. v.), a member of the Committee with Logan, in his list of authors and revisers of the 1781 *Translations and Paraphrases,* a copy of which has been preserved, gives to Logan the credit of compiling this cento. It has been in authorized use in the Church of Scotland for 100 years, but is rarely found elsewhere. It must be designated, " *Scottish Tr. & Par.* 1745: *M. Bruce,* 1764, *printed in J. Logan's Poems,* 1781: *J. Logan,* 1781."

v. A cento, partly from the *Tr. & Par.* text above of 1781, and partly from that of 1764, was given in Bickersteth's *Christian Psalmody* in 1833, No. 238, and Miss Leeson's *Par. and Hymns,* 1853, No. 50, Pt. ii., beginning, " Sing to the Lord, in joyful strains," but has now gone almost altogether out of use. Another arrangement direct from the above 1781 text, st. xii.–xv., " Sing to the Lord," &c., was given in Kemble's *Psalms & Hymns,* 1853, and has been repeated in several collections.

vi. Another arrangement is : " Behold my servant, saith the Lord." It is composed of st. i.–iv, with alterations by Miss J. E. Leeson, and was included in her *Par. and Hymns,* 1853, No. 50, Pt. i. Its use is limited.

vii. In American hymnals, in addition to a reprint of most of the foregoing arrangements, we have, " Thus saith the Lord, who built the heavens," in Belknap's *Sacred Poetry ; or, Ps. & Hys.,* 1795, " O city of the Lord, begin." in the Presb. *Church Psalmist,* &c., N. Y., 1847, and others.   [J. J.]

Behold the amazing sight. *P. Doddridge.* [*Passiontide.*] In the D. MSS. this hymn is dated " May 8, 1737," and headed " The soul attached to a Crucified Saviour, from John xii. 32." In 1755, Job Orton included it in his ed. of Doddridge's (posthumous) *Hymns,* &c., No. 233, in 6 st. of 6 l. It is repeated in J. D. Humphreys's ed. of the same, 1839. It is in C. U. both in G. Brit. and America.

Behold the angel flies. *J. Bull.* [*Missions.*] This is given in P. Maurice's *Choral H. Bk.,* 1861, as " J. B. C.—Christ Guard." This we find, from a MS. memorandum by Dr. Maurice, to be the Rev. John Bull, Curate of Clipston. The hymn appeared in J. Bull's *Devotional Hys.,* Lond., 1827, and thence probably passed into the *Christian Guardian.*

Behold the glories of the Lamb. *I. Watts.* [*Praise.*] 1st pub. in his *Hymns,* &c., 1707 (2nd ed., 1709. Bk. i., No. 1), in 8 st. of 4 l., and entitled, " A New Song to the Lamb that was slain." It is a paraphrase of a part of Rev. v. Watts's biographers state that this was his first hymn, and was written in 1696 in answer to a challenge that he could not produce better hymns than those by W. Barton (q. v.) which were sung in the Chapel in Southampton which he attended, and against which he had laid a complaint. In the *Hymns,* &c., st. iv. and v. are bracketed for omission if desired, and in the Bap. *Ps. & Hys.,* 1858, and others, this is done. In Darling's *Hys.,* 1886, it is given as " *How great the glory of the Lamb.*" The use of the hymn is extensive, both in G. Britain and America. [See Early English Hymnody, § VI. 2.]

In the Draft Scottish *Translations and Para-phrases* of 1745, a somewhat peculiar cento is given as No. ix. in 12 st. of 4 l. It opens with this first stanza, and is thus composed : st. i., ii., iii., iv. corresponding stanzas from this hymn; st. v. Watts; st. vi. new; st. vii. Watts. From this point st. viii. to xii. are Watts's " Come let us join our cheerful songs " (q. v.) slightly altered. In the authorized issue of the *Trans-lations and Paraphrases*, in 1781, there is an-other cento, opening again with the same stanza, but differing from the last. It is thus composed : st. i., ii., iii., iv. Watts, as above, with new alterations; st. v. Watts, " Come let us, &c.," as altered in 1745; st. vi. Watts; vii. Watts altered ; st. viii. Watts, as above; st. ix. from 1745 ; st. x., xi. Watts, " Come let us, &c.," slightly altered. This complicated arrangement was made by *W. Cameron* (q. v.) for the 1781 issue of the *Trs.*, &c., and has been in use in the Church of Scotland for 100 years. It is also found in a few modern hymnals. It was given in the *Salisbury H. Bk.*, 1857, No. 171, with slight alterations. Full recast text in modern copies of the Scottish *Psalms*, &c. This, in common with the original, is in use in America. From this arrangement in the *Trs. & Paraphs.* a cento is given in Stevenson's *H. for the Church and H.*, 1873, No. 92, as " Hark, how the adoring hosts." In this st. i.-iv. and x. are omitted. In Miss J. E. Leeson's *Par. and Hymns*, &c., 1853, this arrangement of the hymn is given with extensive alterations and additions, as No. 110 in 12 st. of 4 l. Its use is limited, although st. ix.-xii. are very fine.   [J. J.]

Behold the Lamb [of God.] *M. Bridges.* [*Passiontide.*] 1st pub. in his *Hymns of the Heart*, &c., 1848, in 7 st. of 7 l., and entitled " Ecce Agnus Dei." It is found in many modern collections both in G. Britain and in America, but never in a full and correct form. Scarcely two texts can be found alike, whether they begin with the original first line, or as—" Behold the Lamb of God," as in *H. A. & M.*, *Thring*, and others. The original is also difficult to procure. We give it in full.

" Behold the Lamb !
Oh ! Thou for sinners slain,—
Let it not be in vain,
That Thou hast died :
Thee for my Saviour let me take,—
Thee,—Thee alone my re-fuge make,—
Thy pierced side !
" Behold the Lamb !
Into the sacred flood,—
Of Thy most precious blood
My soul I cast :—
Wash me and make me pure and clean,
Uphold me thro' life's changeful scene,
Till all be past !
" Behold the Lamb !
Archangels, — fold your wings,—
Seraphs, — hush all the strings
Of million lyres :
The Victim, veil'd on earth, in love,—
Unveil'd, — enthron'd, — ador'd above,
All heaven admires !

" Behold the Lamb !
Drop down, ye glorious skies,—
He dies,— He dies, — He dies,—
For man once lost !
Yet lo ! He lives, — He lives,—He lives,—
And to His church Him-self He gives,—
Incarnate Host !
" Behold the Lamb !
All hail,—Eternal Word !
Thou Universal Lord,—
Purge out our leaven :
Clothe us with godliness and good,
Feed us with Thy celestial food,—
Manna from heaven !
" Behold the Lamb !
Saints, wrapt in blissful rest,—
Souls, — waiting to be blest,—
Oh ! Lord,—how long !
Thou Church on earth, o'er-whelm'd with fears,
Still in this vale of woe and tears
Swell the full song.

" Behold the Lamb !
Worthy is He alone,—
Upon the iris throne
Of God above !

One with the Ancient of all days,—
One with the Paraclete in praise,—
All light,—all love ! "

A comparison of this text with that in any collection will show how far alterations may have been introduced. In addition to being altered, it is usually abbreviated as well. In some American collections, including Dr. Hatfield's *Church H. Bk.*, 1872, No. 500, a hymn is given as—" Archangels ! fold your wings," and attributed to " Samuel Egerton Brydges, 1820, a," which is really a portion of this hymn rewritten, beginning with line 2 of st. iii. as above.   [J. J.]

Behold the Lamb of God, who bore thy burdens, &c. *T. Haweis.* [*Passion-tide.*] From his *Carmina Christo*, &c., 1792. No. 5 in 4 st. of 4 l., and based on John i. 29. It is found in a few collections, and is worthy of more extended use. The text of *H. Comp.*, although claiming to be correct, is altered in st. i. and iv. and is from Bickersteth's *Christian Psalmody* of 1833.

Behold the lofty sky. *I. Watts.* [*Ps. xix.*] 1st pub. in his *Psalms of David*, &c., 1719, being a paraphrase of the first part of Ps. xix., and headed " The Book of Nature and Scripture. For a Lord's-Day Morning." It is in 8 st. of 4 l. ; and was given with the omission of st. vi. in J. Wesley's *Ps. & Hys.*, Charlestown, South Carolina, 1736-7, p. 58. The paraphrase, " Behold the morning sun," deals in 8 st. of 4 l. with another aspect of the same Psalm, and is given next after the above in the *Psalms*, &c., 1719. Both para-phrases, usually abbreviated, are in C. U., the latter specially in America. In Martineau's *Hymns*, 1840 and 1873, the hymn " Behold the lofty sky," No. 247, is a cento from these two paraphrases, st. i., ii. being from the first, and iii.-vi. from the second.

Behold, the Master passeth by ! [*St. Matthew's Day.*] This is a cento by *Bp. W. W. How*, based upon Bp. Ken's hymn for the same day, and first pub. in *Church Hymns*, 1871, No. 183, in 6 st. of 4 l., and Thring's *Coll.*, 1882, No. 510. It is thus composed :—
St. i.-iii. Original by Bp. How.
St. iv.-vi. By Bp. How from Bp. Ken, whose original stanzas are :—

Ken. st. xii.   " From worldly clogs, bless'd Matthew loose,
Devoted all to sacred use,
That, Follow Me, his ear
Seem'd every day to hear,
His utmost zeal he strove to bend,
Towards Jesus' likeness, to ascend.

„ st. xx.   " God sweetly calls us every day,
Why should we then our bliss delay
He calls to endless light,
Why should we love the night ?
Should we one call but duly heed,
It would to joys eternal lead.

st. xxiv.   " Praise, Lord, to Thee, for Matthew's call,
At which he left his wealthy all ;
At Thy next call may I
Myself and world deny ;
Thou, Lord, even now art calling me,
I'll now leave all, and follow Thee."

Bishop Ken's hymn appeared in his *Hymns for all the Festivals of the Year*, 1721 (ten years after his death) : and again in the same work, repub. as *Bishop Ken's Christian Year*, by Pickering, in 1868.

Behold the path that [which] mortals tread. *P. Doddridge.* [*Journey of Life.*] In the D. MSS., this hymn is No. 44, but is undated. It was pub. as No. 27 in J. Orton's ed. of Doddridge's (posthumous) *Hymns*, &c., 1755, and again in J. D. Humphreys's ed. of the same, 1839. It is in 7 st. of 4 l., and entitled "The Great Journey. Job xvi. 22." Its use is chiefly confined to America.

Behold the Prince of Peace. *J. Needham.* [*Meekness and Tenderness of Jesus.*] 1st pub. in his *Hymns*, &c., 1768, No. 87, in 7 st. of 4 l. The form, however, in which the hymn beginning with this first line is known is a cento, thus composed:—st. i.–iii. as above; st. iv., v., "Jesus! Thou light of men," &c.; from Needham's "Long had the nations sat," st. v., vi. In this form it is found in Sir Josiah Mason's *Orphanage H. Bk.* Birmingham, 1882, and others.

Behold the Redeemer of man. [*Passiontide.*] This hymn, in 5 st. of 4 l., is in Rowland Hill's *Coll. of Hys. for Children*, &c., Lond., 1808. It is not in the previous editions of 1790 or 1794, and may possibly be by R. Hill. As, however, no authors' names are given in the collection, and no further evidence is forthcoming, its authorship cannot be determined. It is found in several modern hymnals for Sunday Schools, as in the *Leeds S. S. H. Bk.*, 1832 to 1878, No. 49, and others.   [W. T. B.]

Behold the Saviour of mankind. *Samuel Wesley, sen.* [*Good Friday.*] Written previous to the fire at his Rectory of Epworth, which was burnt down in 1709. At this fire John Wesley was saved from death by being rescued through the bed-room window by some of the parishioners. During the fire the MS. of this hymn was blown into the Rectory garden, where it was subsequently found. It was 1st pub. in J. Wesley's *Ps. & Hys.*, Charlestown, South Carolina, 1736–7, p. 46; also in the Wesley *Hymns and Sac. Poems*, 1739, in 4 st. of 4 l.; and again in the *Wes. H. Bk.* in 1780, revised ed., 1875, No. 22. From that collection it has passed into various hymnals both in G. Britain and America. The original contains 6 st. of 4 l. St. ii. and v. are usually omitted.

Behold the Saviour on the cross. *Cento*, 1781. [*Passiontide.*] 1st appeared as No. 44 in the Draft Scottish *Translations and Paraphrases*, 1781, as a version of John xix. 30, in 6 st. of C. M. It is thus made up: st. i. is altered from st. i. and iv., and st. ii. is exactly st. v. of Joseph Stennett's "Behold the Saviour of the world" in his *H. on the Lord's Supper*, 1705 (ed. 1709, p. 57). Another hymn in that collection (ed. 1709, p. 66), "'Tis finished, the Redeemer cries," furnishes, in its st. i., the ground of st. iii., in its st. iii. of st. v., and in its st. v. of st. vi. The remaining st. (st. iv.) is a cento from Charles Wesley's "'Tis finish'd, the Messias dies" (q. v.). Thus though the hymn has generally been ascribed to "Blair" (see **Blair, Hugh**), as in the markings by the eldest daughter of W. Cameron (q. v.), he cannot be regarded as having done more than make the cento and rewrite the whole to C. M. In the public worship ed. of that year issued by the Church of Scotland and still in use, it is unaltered. From the 1781 it has passed

into a few modern hymnals, as in England, in Morrell and How's *Coll.*, 1854, and the Irvingite *Coll.*, 1864; and in America in the *Evang. Luth. H. Bk.*, 1834, Presbyterian *Ps. and Hys.*, 1843, and Adams and Chapin's *Coll.*, 1846. In Miss Leeson's *Paraphrases and Hymns for Cong. Singing*, 1853, No. 74, omitting st. v., vi. In the English Presb. *Ps. and Hys.*, 1867, No. 484, and *Church Praise*, 1883, No. 80, st. iii.–vi. beginning "'Tis finished! was his latest voice" were selected; and 'the same altered and beginning "'Tis finished—the Messiah cried" in the *Free Church H. Bk.*, 1873, No. 16.
                                    [J. M.]

Behold the servant of the Lord. *C. Wesley.* [*Submission.*] 1st pub. by J. Wesley in Pt. i. of his *Further Appeal to Men of Reason and Religion*, Dec. 22, 1744, and subsequently, by C. Wesley, in his *Hymns and Sacred Poems*, 1749, where it is entitled "An Act of Devotion" (vol. i. p. 120). It was embodied in the *Wes. H. Bk.*, 1780, No. 417, and thence has passed into various hymnals in G. Britain and America. Orig. text, *P. Works*, 1868–72, vol. v. p. 10.

Behold the sun that seemed but now. *G. Wither.* [*Afternoon.*] 1st printed in his *Hallelujah, or Britain's Second Remembrancer*, Lond., 1641, where it is No. 14 of his first part "Hymns Occasional." It is headed "At Sunsetting," and prefaced by the following note, "The singing or meditating to such purposes as are intimated in this Hymn, when we see the sun declining may perhaps expel unprofitable musings, and arm against the terrors of approaching darkness."

It is in 3 st. of 8 l., and its use is by no means equal to its merits. It was included in Farr's reprint of the *Hallelujah*, 1857; and thence, passing through Lord Selborne's *Book of Praise*, 1862, was given in Thring's *Coll.*, No. 20, with two slight alterations, *Thring* reading st. i., l. 4, "The" for "This"; and in st. ii., l. 5, "our" for "those." It is also in the *Westminster Abbey H. Bk.*, 1883. [Early English Hy., § VIII.]   [W. T. B.]

Behold the throne of grace. *J. Newton.* [*The Throne of Grace.*] Appeared in the *Olney Hymns*, 1779, Bk. i., No. 33, in 8 st. of 4 l., and based on 1 Kings iii. 5. Although extensively used both in G. Britain and in America, it is generally in an abridged, and sometimes altered form. In 1781 J. Wesley published the last four stanzas of the original as a hymn in the *Arminian Magazine*, p. 285, beginning "Since 'tis the Lord's command," but it failed to attract attention, and in that form is unknown to modern hymn-books.

Behold the wretch whose lust and wine. *I. Watts.* [*The Prodigal.*] This paraphrase of St. Luke xv. 13, &c., was 1st pub. in his *Hymns*, &c., 1709, Bk. i., No. 123, in 7 st. of 4 l. The peculiarity of its opening line has made against its adoption in its original form in modern hymnals.

In the draft Scottish *Translations and Paraphrases*, 1745, it was given unaltered as No. xxv., save st. vi., which was rewritten thus:—

"Bring forth the fairest Robe for him,
      the joyful Father said;
To him each Mark of Grace be shown,
      and every honour paid."

On the adoption of the hymn in the authorized issue of the *Translations and Paraphrases*, 1781, No. xl., it was given as "The wretched prodigal behold." This recast is composed as follows:—st. i.–v. recast from original by Watts, st. vi. new; st. vii. from 1745; st. viii. Watts; st. ix. new. This recast, which may be found in full in modern editions of the Scottish *Psalms*, &c., has been in common use in the Church of Scotland for 100 years.

In Miss J. E. Leeson's *Par. and Hymns*, &c., 1853, No. lxx., two hymns on the above passage, St. Luke xv. 13–25, are given; the first, "Nigh unto death with famine pined," being by Miss Leeson; and the second, "The prodigal's returning steps." This last is thus composed: st. i., ii. Miss Leeson, based on the *Scottish Par.*; iii., iv., *S. Par.* altered; v., vi., Miss Leeson.   [J. J.]

Behold we come, dear [good] Lord, to Thee. *J. Austin.* [*Sunday.*] This is the first hymn, in 7 st. of 4 l., in his *Devotions in the Antient Way of Offices*, 1668, and is appointed for Sunday at Matins. After passing through the various reprints of that work, and of the revised editions of Dorrington, and of Hickes (see **Austin, J.**), it was included, with slight alterations, in the *Salisbury H. Bk.*, 1857; Pott's *Coll.*, 1861; the *New Zealand Hymnal*, 1872, and others. It had, however, previously appeared in J. Wesley's *Ps. & Hys.*, Charlestown, South Carolina, 1736–7, No. 24, in 6 st.   [W. T. B.]

Behold what condescending love. J. *Peacock.* [*Christ blessing Children.*] 1st pub. in his *Songs of Praise, compiled from the Holy Scriptures*, 1776, p. 50, in 5 st. of 4 l. In the Amer. Meth. Epis. *Hymns*, 1849, No. 261; the Meth. Episc. *Hymnal*, 1878, No. 828; and Dr. Hatfield's *Church H. Bk.*, 1872, No. 1142 (dated 1806 in error), is a cento thus composed:—st. i., ii., iii., Peacock as above; st. iv., Doddridge from his "See Israel's gentle Shepherd stand," st. iii.; but in both cases slightly altered. The cento has its origin in that which was given in Toplady's *Ps. and Hys.*, 1776, No. 120, in 6 st. of which (with alterations) st. i.–iv. are taken.   [W. T. B.]

Behold what witnesses unseen. [*Cross and Consolation.*] 1st appeared as No. 12 in the Draft Scottish *Translations and Paraphrases*, 1745, as a version of Hebrews xii. 1–13, in 12 st. of 4 l. The author is unknown. In the revised ed., issued in 1751, a new stanza was added as iii., and slight alterations were made in other sts. In the *Draft* of 1781, the 1751 was repeated with various alterations, as No. 59; and with further alterations of 16 lines, in the public worship ed. issued in that year by the Church of Scotland, and still in use. In the markings by the eldest daughter of *W. Cameron* (q.v.), the alterations of 1781 are ascribed to Logan and Cameron. The text of 1781 has passed, in abridged forms, into a few modern hymnals, as Maurice's *Choral H. Bk.*, 1861, No. 209, omitting st. ix.; and the Eng. Presb. *Ps. & Hys.*, 1867; and *Church Praise*, 1883, reduced to 6 sts. In the American *Prayer Bk. Coll.*, 1826, No. 212 (ed. 1871, No. 183), and others it began, "Lo! what a cloud of witnesses;"

while in Rorison's *H. adapted to the Church Services*, 1860, it is, "A witness-host, by us unseen." In Anderson's *Coll.*, Edinburgh, 1818, No. 359 begins with st. vi. altered to, "Like Christ, have ye, to blood or death," and No. 360, with st. x., "A father's voice, with reverence, we." It is included, considerably altered, as No. 85 in Miss Leeson's *Paraphrases & Hymns*, 1853, in three parts, pt. ii. beginning, "Lo! for the joy before Him set," and pt. iii., "Through all the hard experience led."   [J. M.]

Behold what wondrous grace. *I. Watts.* [*Adoption.*] 1st pub. in his *Hymns, &c.*, 1707 (2nd ed. 1709, Bk. i., No. lxiv.), in 6 st. of 4 l., and entitled "Adoption." In J. Wesley's *Ps. & Hys.*, Charlestown, South Carolina, 1736–7, p. 19, it was given with alterations and the omission of st. ii. Its modern use is limited in G. Britain, but extensive in America.

In the Draft Scottish *Translations and Paraphrases*, 1745, this text was given, as No. xxx., in 5 st., in a recast form. As this text, and not that of Watts, has been followed in the authorized issue of the *Translations*, &c., of 1781, and as the *Translations*, &c., of 1745 are difficult to consult, we subjoin the original of Watts, and the text of 1745.

Watts.	*Translations, &c., 1745.*
Behold what wondrous grace The Father hath bestow'd On sinners of a mortal race, To call them Sons of God!	Behold th' amazing Height of Love the Father hath bestow'd On us, the sinful Sons of Men, To call us Sons of God!
'Tis no surprising thing, That we should be un known; The Jewish world knew not their King, God's Everlasting Son.	Conceal'd as yet this Honour lyes, by this dark World unknown; So the World knew not, when he came, God's everlasting Son.
Nor doth it yet appear How great we must be made; But when we see our Saviour here, We shall be like our Head.	High is the Character we bear; but higher we shall rise: Tho' what we'll be in future worlds is hid from mortal Eyes.
A hope so much divine May trials well endure, May purge our souls from sense and sin As Christ the Lord is pure.	But this we know, our Souls shall then their God and Saviour see; Unveil'd behold him, and transform'd unto his Likeness be.
If in my Father's love I share a filial part, Send down Thy Spirit like a dove, To rest upon my heart.	A Hope so great, and so divine, may Trials well endure; Refine the Soul from Sense and Sin, as Christ himself is pure.
We would no longer lie Like slaves beneath the throne; My faith shall Abba, Father, cry, And Thou the kindred own.	

A comparison of this text with that authorized in the *Translations*, &c., of 1781, No. lxiii., and which may be found in any modern copy of the Scottish *Psalms*, &c., will shew at once how much the latter is indebted to the former; and how far both differ from Watts. By whom the 1745 recast was made is not known, but that of 1781, which has been in use in the Ch. of Scotland for 100 years, is claimed by *W. Cameron* (q.v.) as his. [J. J.]

Behold where breathing love divine.
Anna L. Barbauld, née Aikin. [*Charity.*] Contributed to Dr. W. Enfield's *Hymns for Public Worship*, &c., Warrington, 1772, No. 117, in 8 st. of 4 l. In the following year it was republished in Mrs. Barbauld's (then Miss Aikin) *Poems*, Lon., J. Johnson, 1773, pp. 121–123. In this form it is not in extensive use, although included in Dr. Collyer's *Collection*, 1812, and repeated in Dr. Martineau's *Hymns*, 1840 & 1873. A cento from this hymn is given in the *Church S. S. H. Bk.*, 1868, No. 364, and other collections, beginning, "Blest is the man whose softening heart." It is composed of st. iii., iv., vii., viii., somewhat altered, and appeared in the 9th ed. of Cotterill's *Sel.*, 1820, No. 123. From thence it passed into various collections both in G. Britain and America. In *Kennedy*, 1863, No. 126, it begins, "Blest is the man whose *tender* heart." The full original text is given in *Lyra Brit.*, 1867, pp. 32–33.

Behold, where in a mortal form [the Friend of Man]. *W. Enfield.* [*Christ our Example.*] Appeared in the 3rd ed. of his *Hymns for Public Worship*, &c., 1797, in 8 st. of 4 l. It passed from thence into Bickersteth's *Christian Psalmody*, 1833, Reed's *Hymn-Book*, 1842, and others. In the Bapt. *New Selection*, 1828, No. 120, it was given as, "Behold, where in *the Friend of Man*," with the omission of st. ii., and in this form it is found in the Bap. *Ps. & Hymns*, 1858. The hymn is also in C. U. in America. The first form, abbreviated, is in *Songs for the Sanctuary*, N. Y., 1865, and the second is in *Hys. & Songs of Praise*, N. Y., 1874, and others.

Behold with pleasing extacy. — *P. Doddridge.* [*Missions.*] This hymn is No. 48 in the D. MSS., and dated "Oct. 30, 1737." It was pub. in Job Orton's ed. of Doddridge's (posthumous) *Hymns*, 1755, No. 121, in 7 st. of 4 l., in a slightly different form, and entitled "A Nation born in a day; or the rapid progress of the Gospel desired," Is. lxvi. 8, and again in J. D. Humphreys's ed. of the same, 1839. In its original form it has not come into common use: but st. iv. and v., beginning, "Awake, all conquering arm, awake," very slightly altered, were given in the American Bap. *Psalmist*, 1843, No. 857. Also in Spurgeon's *O. O. H. Bk.*, 1866, No. 962.

Behold yon new-born Infant grieved. *J. Merrick.* [*Ignorance of Man.*] 1st pub. in his *Poems on Sacred Subjects*, Oxford, Clarendon Press, 4to., 1763, pp. 25–27, in 8 st. of 4 l. It was also included in full by Montgomery in his *Christian Psalmist*, 1825, No. 333. In its full form it has not come into C. U.; but centos therefrom are given in numerous collections both in G. Britain and America. These are:—

1. "Author of good, to thee I turn [come]." This cento is composed of st. v.-viii., somewhat altered in Bickersteth's *Christ. Psalmody*, 1833, No. 157, and from thence has passed into several modern collections. In Dr. Kennedy's *Hymno. Christ.*, 1863, No. 1410, these stanzas are repeated as "Author of good, to Thee *we* turn," and thereto 8 lines have been added, probably by Dr. Kennedy.

2. "Author of good, we rest on Thee." This is a slightly altered form of the former cento, which is found in several American Unitarian collections.

3. "Eternal God, we look to Thee." This is an altered form of st. v., vi., and viii. It was included in the *Leeds H. Bk.*, 1853, No. 580, and is repeated in the *N. Cong.*, 1859, and other collections.

Taken in its various forms, very few of Merrick's compositions have attained to an equal position in popular favour. [J. J.]

Bei dir Jesu, will ich bleiben. *C. J. Spitta.* [*Confirmation.*] Founded on Ps. lxxiii. 23, and 1st pub. in the 1st Series of his *Psalter und Harfe*, 1833, p. 58, in 6 st. of 8 l., entitled, "I remain continually with Thee." In the Württemberg *G. B.*, 1842, No. 383, Knapp's *Ev. L. S.*, 1837, No. 1709 (1865, No. 890). The *trs.* in C. U. are:—

1. **In Thy service will I ever.** A full and good *tr.* by R. Massie in his *Lyra Dom.* 1860, p. 59, and thence in Schaff's *Christ in Song*, ed. 1879, p. 452. Altered and transposed as Nos. 542, 543 in Adams's American *Ch. Pastorals*, 1864. No. 543 begins with st. v., "Let Thy light on me be shining," and incorporates, as st. ii., a cento from st. i., ii. of Massie's *tr.* of Spitta's "Meine Stund ist noch nicht kommen" (q. v.). In Horder's *Cong. Hys.*, 1884, No. 267, st. iv., ll. 5–8, and v., ll. 5–8, are omitted.

2. **By Thee, Jesus, will I stay.** A *tr.* of st. i., v., vi. as No. 35 in Snepp's *S. of G. and G.*, 1876, marked as by "J. B. Walter, 1868."

Other trs. are:—
(1) "So will I abide for ever," by J. D. Burns in his *Memoir & Remains*, 1869, p. 236. (2) "Jesus, with Thee I would abide," by *Lady Durand*, 1873, p. 48.
[J. M.]

Beim frühen Morgenlicht. [*Morning.*] We have found this hymn in two forms, each differing somewhat from the other, and both differing from the text Caswall seems to have used for his translation. The earlier is in the *Katholisches G. B.*, Würzburg, 1828 [University Library, Würzburg], ed. by Canon S. Pörtner, for use in the Diocese of Würzburg; where it occurs as No. 88, at p. 183, in 14 st. of 4 l., and double refrain, entitled "The Christian Greeting." No author's name is given, but it is probably of Franconian origin, and does not seem older than the present century. The second is in F. W. von Ditfurth's *Fränkische Volkslieder*, Leipzig, 1855, pt. i., p. 12, in 13 st. of 4 l., with double refrain, entitled "Gelobt sey Jesus Christus." Eight stanzas of the first form are in the *Kath. Gesangbüchlein*, 7th ed., Aschaffenburg, 1860, and the second form is given in full in the *Evang. Kinder G. B.*, Basel, 1867, No. 59. The last four stanzas of the Würzburg *G. B.*, 1828, are here quoted for comparison.

xi. Die Finsterniss wird Licht,
　　Wenn fromm die Zunge spricht :
　　　Gelobt sey Jesus Christus !
　　Die Macht der Hölle flieht
　　Vor diesem süssen Lied :
　　　Gelobt sey Jesus Christus !

xii. Im Himmel selbst erschallt,
　　Mit heiligem Gewalt ! Gelobt, &c.
　　Des Vaters ewigem Wort,
　　Ertönet ewig dort : Gelobt, &c.

xiii. Ihr Menschenkinder all'
　　Singt laut im Jubelschall : Gelobt, &c.
　　Rings um den Erdenkreis,
　　Ertöne Gott zum Preis : Gelobt,. &c.

xiv. Singt Himmel, Erd' und Meer,
　　Und aller Engel Heer : Gelobt, &c.
　　Es schalle weit und breit,
　　In Zeit und Ewigkeit : Gelobt, &c,

The only tr. in C. U. is—
When morning gilds the skies, by E. Caswall, 1st pub. in H. Formby's *Catholic Hymns*, Lond., N. D., 1854 [approbation May 3, 1853], p. 44, in 6 st. of 4 l. and double refrain. In Caswall's *Masque of Mary*, 1858, 8 st. were added, and thus in his *Hymns & Poems*, 1873, p. 155, in 28 st. of 2 l. and refrain, entitled "The Praises of Jesus," the first line being given as "Gelobt sey Jesus Christ," which, as will be seen above, is the original refrain. The full text is given unaltered as No. 269 in the *Appendix* to the *H. Noted*, 3rd ed., 1867.

This hymn has attained considerable popularity, and is found in varying centos, as in *H. A. & M.*, 1868–75; *Hymnary*, 1872; *Bap. Hymnal*, 1879; *Scottish Free Church H. Bk.* 1882; Horder's *Coll.*, 1884; and in America in the *Bap. Praise Bk.*, 1871; *Evang. Hymnal*, N. Y., 1880; *Laudes Domini*, 1884, and others. Generally it appears under its original first line, but in the *People's H.*, 1867, it is divided into two parts, No. 446 beginning "The night becomes as day," which is st. xi. of the 1828, and st. xx. of the text of 1873. [J. M.]

Being of Beings, God of Love. *C. Wesley.* [*Believers one with Christ.*] A "Grace after Meat," given in *Hys. & Sac. Poems*, 1739, in 5 st. of 4 l. (*P. Works*, 1868–72, vol. i. p. 31). In the Drummond & Greville *Ch. of England H. Bk.*, 1838, No. 101, st. i., ii., v. were given as, "Eternal Father, God of Love." This was repeated in the American *Sabbath H. Bk.*, 1858.

Belcher, Joseph, D.D., a Baptist Minister, b. in Birmingham, England, April 5, 1794, took up his residence in America, 1844; and d. at Philadelphia, July 10, 1859. He pub. nearly 200 works, amongst them, *The Baptist Pulpit*, 1850; *History of Religious Denominations*, 1855; and *Historical Sketches of Hymns, their Writers, and their Influence*, 1859, reprinted at Albany, 1873. This last is extremely scrappy, sketchy, gossipy, and by no means trustworthy, but it contains some facts and recollections of value, and was for years the nearest approach to a general treatise on the subject in print.   [F. M. B]

Bell, Charles Christopher, the author of a few hymns in the *Meth. S. S. H. Bk.* 1879, was b. at Hickling, Notts, Dec. 10, 1845. Mr. Bell is a chemist by trade, and a member of the Church of England. His hymns are:—

1. Eternal Father, hear, we pray. *Evening.*
2. In thankful songs our hearts we lift. *Thanksgiving.*
3. Jesus, Who callest little ones to Thee. *Early Piety.*
4. O Thou, Whose love throughout this day. *Evening.*
5. Praise the Lord, for still He reigneth. *Praise to Christ.*

Of these hymns Nos. 4 and 5 are marked "Unknown," in the *Meth. S. S. H. Bk.* Mr. Bell's compositions are worthy of more extensive use than is now accorded to them.

Bell, Charles Dent, D.D., s. of Henry Humphrey Bell, b. at Warwick Lodge, Magherafelt, Ireland, on 10th February, 1818, and educated at the Royal Academy, Edinburgh, and the Royal School, Dungannon, and Trinity Coll., Dublin, graduating B.A., 1842, M.A., 1852, and D.D., 1878. Having taken Holy Orders, he was successively Curate of Hampton in Arden, and St. Mary's Chapel, Reading, and of St. Mary-in-the-Castle, Hastings, 1846; Incumbent of St. John's Chapel, Hampstead, 1854; Vicar of Ambleside, 1861; with Rydal, 1872; and Rector of Cheltenham, 1872. In 1869 he was also appointed Hon. Canon of Carlisle Cathedral. Dr. Bell's works include *Night Scenes from the Bible*, 1861; *Hills that bring Peace*, 1872; *The Saintly Calling*, 1873; *Voices from the Lakes*, 1877; *Songs in the Twilight*, 1881; *Hymns for the Church and the Chamber*, 1882; *Songs in Many Keys*, 1884; and for the Religious Tract Society, *Angelic Beings, and their Nature and Ministry*. He has also edited an *Appendix* to Dr. Walker's Cheltenham *Psalms and Hymns*, in 1873 (5th ed. 1878). To this *Appendix* were contributed :—

1. Another Sabbath closes. *Sunday Evening.*
2. Be near us, Triune God, we pray. *Matrimony.*
3. Be with us, gracious Lord, to-day. *Consecration of a Church.*
4. Christ ascends with songs exultant. *Ascension.*
5. Christ has risen! let the tidings. *Easter.*
6. Come, gracious Saviour, manifest Thy glory. *Advent.*
7. From the four winds, O living breath. *Missions.*
8. Good Lord, the valleys laugh and sing. *Harvest.*
9. Lord, at Thy mercy-seat we bow. *Foundation Stone of Church.*
10. O fill me with Thy Spirit, gracious Lord. *Whitsuntide.*
11. O Jesu, our salvation. Our Prophet, &c. *General Praise.*
12. On the sad night He was betrayed. *Passiontide.*
13. "Redeem the time," God only knows. *Time.*
14. The shadows lengthen, night will soon be here, *Evening.*
15. To God the Lord, I lift mine eyes. *General.*
16. With grateful heart and voice we raise. *Grace after Meat.*

These hymns being of recent date are not found, save in one or two instances, in any other collection than Dr. Bell's *Appendix* to Dr. Walker's *Ps. & Hymns*, and his *Appendix* to the *Hy. Comp.* noted below. With the exception of Nos. 14 and 16, the above were republished in Dr. Bell's *Hymns for Church and Chamber*, Lond., J. Nisbet & Co., 1882. This work also contains other hymns of merit, and should be consulted in preparing a Collection for congregational or private use. In 1884, Dr. Bell added an *Appendix Selected for the Use of Cheltenham Churches* to the *Hy. Comp.*, in which he embodied the hymns given in his former *Appendix*, and added thereto the following hymns from his *Hys. for the Church & Chamber*:—

17. Great God, Thy people's dwelling-place. *The New Year.*
18. He giveth His beloved sleep. *Safety during Sleep.*
19. O Lamb of God, Who died our souls to win. *Peace with God desired.*
20. O Saviour Christ, enthroned at God's right hand. *Christ the Anointed One.*
21. Rest in the Lord. Oh, words of love. *Exhortation to trust in God.*

In addition to these there were also given :—

22. For Erin plead we, God of love. *Hymn for Ireland.*
23. Jesu, our bright & Morning Star. *Epiphany.*
                                                        [J. J.]

Bell, Jane Cross. [Simpson, J. C.]

Beman, Nathan Sidney Smith, D.D., was b. at Canaan, Columbia Co., N. Y., Nov. 27, 1785; and graduated at Middleburg College, Vermont, 1807. He was a Congregational Pastor at Portland, Maine, 1810–12; Minister in Georgia, 1812–22; and Pastor of the First Presbyterian Church, Troy, N. Y., 1823–63. He d. at Carbondale, Illinois, Aug. 8, 1871. He edited *Sacred Lyrics*, Troy, 1832, and an enlarged collection under the same title, 1841. The latter was adopted by the

New School Presbyterian General Assembly as the *Church Psalmist*, 1847. Dr. Beman is known in hymnody mainly through his three hymns which are in common use :—

1. **Jesus, we bow before Thy throne.** *Missions.* This appeared in Dr. Hastings's *Spiritual Songs*, 1831, No. 174, in 4 st. of 4 l.

2. **Jesus, I come to Thee.** *Submission to Christ.*

3. **Hark, the judgment trumpet sounding.** *Judgment.* The last two were first pub. in his *Sacred Lyrics*, 1832, and all are given in Dr. Hatfield's *Church H. Bk.*, 1872. Dr. Beman's hymns are unknown to English collections. [F. M. B.]

Benedicite. This canticle is given in the *Septuagint* version of Holy Scriptures, and is therein a part [verse 35 to middle of v. 66] of the prayer of Azarias in the furnace, which occurs between vv. 23 and 24 of Dan. iii. It is not in the Hebrew version of the Holy Scriptures, and on this ground, amongst others, it is omitted from the Authorised Version. Its use in the Church, as a Canticle, dates from a very early period. It is in the *Greek, Ambrosian, Mozarabic, Roman, Sarum*, and other Office-books, usually at Lauds for Sundays and Festivals, but varying in form and length, full details of which are given in Dr. Smith's *Dict. of Christian Antiquities*, Art. *Benedicite*. In addition to the renderings into Latin for the use of the Western Church, the following are versions in English, the first of which, after that in Latin as noted above, is the version in the *Bk. of Common Prayer* :—

1. **O all ye works of the Lord.** By whom this rendering from the Latin was made is not known.

2. **O all ye works of God the Lord.** Anon. in Playford's musical ed. of the *Old Version*, 1677, and thence into the *Supp.* to the *New Version*, ed. 1708.

3. **Ye works of God, on Him alone.** By James Merrick, from his *Hys. & Poems on Sacred Subjects*, 1763.

4. **Angels holy, high and lowly.** By J. S. Blackie. This rendering of the *Benedicite* appeared in Dr. Bonar's *Bible H. Bk.*, 1845, No. 90, in 12 st. of 6 l., and again in Dr. Blackie's *Lays and Legends of Ancient Greece*, 1857, p. 163, in 7 st. of 4 l., and headed "Benedicite." Professor Blackie, in a note thereto, says :—

"This hymn was composed by me for the very beautiful Burschen melody, *Alles Schweige*, the music and words of which will be found in the collection of *Burschen Melodies*, published by me in *Tait's Magazine* for 1840, vol. vii. p. 259. Many of these melodies, though used on convivial occasions, have a solemnity about them, in virtue of which they are well fitted for the service of the Sanctuary" (p. 359). This rendering of the *Benedicite* is gaining in popular favour, and is found in several hymnals.

5. **O all ye works of God most high.** This paraphrase was given in various numbers of *The Sunday at Home*, in 1885. It is by the Rev. Richard Wilton.

Strictly speaking, Nos. 2, 3, and 5 are not in C. U. In addition to the above renderings there are also :—

(1) *Song of the Three Children Paraphrased, &c. By Lady Chudleigh. London*, 1703. This is reprinted in her *Poems*, 1709. (2) *Song of the Three Children in English Verse. By M. Le Pla. London. Printed by J. Morphew.* [Cir. 1720.] This was edited by S. Wesley, jun. (3) *Divine Hymns, or a Paraphrase upon the Te Deum & Benedicite.* Cambridge, T. Walker, 1691.

[J. J.]

Benedict, Erastus Cornelius, LL.D., b. at Branford, Connecticut, March 19, 1800, and educated at Williams College, graduating in 1821. In 1824 he was called to the Bar; and from 1850–54 was President of the New York Board of Education. He was also Regent of New York University, and filled other important posts of honour. He d. in New York, Oct. 22, 1880. He published several works, including the *Hymn of St. Hildebert*, N. Y., 1867. In 1868, he contributed "Jesus, I love Thee evermore," a *tr.* of "O Deus, ego amo Te" (q. v.), and "With terror thou dost strike me now," a *tr.* of "Gravi me terrore pulsas" (q. v.), to Dr. Schaff's *Christ in Song*. [F. M. B.]

Benedicta sit beata Trinitas. [*Holy Trinity.*] An anonymous sequence, the text of which is included in the *Sarum, York*, and *Hereford Missals* as the sequence for Trinity Sunday. In the reprint of the *York Missal* (Surtees Society, vol. 60) it is noted that it is No. 24, among the Proses and Sequences from the *Bodleian* MS., 775 (written in the reign of Ethelred, sometime between 994–1017). In this MS. it is headed "In pretiosa solemnitate Pentecostes." It is also in an 11th cent. Winchester collection of Sequences, now in Corpus Christi College, Cambridge, No. 473. *Tr.* as, "All blessing to the Blessed Three," by C. S. Calverley, made for and 1st pub. in the *Hymnary*, 1870–72, No. 336, in 9 st. of 4 l. [W. A. S.]

Benedictus. Translations into English of this Song of Zacharias (St. Luke i., 68–79) are given in the various versions of the Holy Scripture, those best known being the *P. Bk.* version in the Morning Prayer, the *A. V.* 1611, and the *Revised V.* of 1881. In addition there are metrical renderings in the form of hymns in the *O. V.* of Sternhold and Hopkins; the *N. V.* of Tate and Brady, and the following :—

(1) Drayton's *Harmony of the Church*, 1591; (2) G. Wither's *Hys. and Songs of the Church*, 1623–31; (3) G. Sandys's *Paraph. on the Psalms*, 1636; (4) Simon Ford's *Ps. of David*, 1688; (5) Bp. Patrick's *Ps. of David in Metre*, 2nd ed., 1695. [W. T. B.]

Bengel, Johann Albrecht, s. of Albrecht Bengel, diaconus at Winnenden, near Waiblingen, Württemberg, was b. at Winnenden, June 24, 1687. After the completion of his theological studies at Tübingen (M.A. 1704, D.D. 1751), he became assistant at Metzingen, near Urach, in 1707, Repetent at Tübingen in 1708, and assistant (general preacher) at Stuttgart in 1711. In 1713 he was appointed Preceptor and preacher at the Cloister School of Denkendorf, near Esslingen. His pupils were mostly preparing for the Church, and during his tenure of office some 300 passed through his hands. In 1741 he was appointed Prelate of Herbrechtingen; and in 1749 Prelate of Alpirsbach (the highest post in the Church of Württemberg) and member of the Consistory. He d. at Stuttgart, Nov. 2, 1752 (*Koch*, v. 89–99, *Allg. Deutsche Biog.*, ii. 331–333; *Bode*, 43–44). As a theologian and ecclesiastic Bengel exercised a great and abiding influence in Württemberg. As a hymn-writer he was not prolific, and few of his hymns are still in use. One has been *tr.* into English, viz. :—

Ich gedenk an deine Wunden. [*Cross and Consolation.*] 1st pub. as a companion to Meditation v. in S. Urlsperger's *Der Krancken Gesundheit und der Sterbenden Leben*, Stuttgart, 1723, p. 423, in 8 st. of 8 l., entitled "On believing and patient suffering." Included as No. 867 in the Hannover *G. B.*, 1740. Sometimes erroneously ascribed to *Urlsperger*. The only *tr.* in C. U. is, "I'll think upon the woes," omitting st. ii., iv., v., as No. 579, in the American Bap. *Psalmist*, 1843.   [J. M.]

Benigna-Maria, daughter of Count Heinrich xxviii. of Reuss-Ebersdorf, was b. at Ebersdorf, Dec. 15, 1695. Under the tuition of Ulrich Bogislaus v. Bonin, she attained a high culture, and became conversant with Latin, Greek, and Hebrew. After the death of her parents she retired to a manorhouse, near Pottiga, in the district of Lobenstein, and d. there July 31, 1751.

She was during all her life an invalid, but bore her afflictions with a meek and quiet spirit, and was ever humble in heart, fervent in prayer, and loving to all whom she thought to be of the truth, rich and poor alike. She regarded her brother-in-law, Count N. L. von Zinzendorf, as a schismatic, yet her hymns breathe the Herrnhut spirit, and were mostly published in the Moravian hymn-books (*Koch*, iv. 486–489). Of her hymns those tr. into English are:—

Komm Segen aus der Höh. [*Before Work.*] 1st pub. as No. 522 in the *Sammlung Geist- und lieblicher Lieder*, Leipzig und Görlitz, 1725, in 4 st. of 8 l. In the *Württemberg G. B.*, 1842, No. 516, altered and omitting st. ii. This is *tr.* as:—

Attend, O Lord, my daily toil. A good *tr.* from the Württ. *G. B.*, contributed by Dr. R. P. Dunn to *Sacred Lyrics from the German*, Philadelphia, 1859, p. 155, and thence, as No. 393, in Boardman's *Sel.*, Philadelphia, 1861. Another *tr.* is:— "God's blessing from on high descend," by Dr. G. Walker, 1860, p. 49.

ii. **Das ist mir lieb, dass meine Stimm und Flehen.** [*Ps. cxvi.*] 1725, as above, No. 14, in 11 st. The *trs.* are:—(1) "This yields me joy," No. 584, in the *Moravian H. Bk.*, 1801 (1849, No. 710). (2) "The time will come," of st. v. as st. ii., of No. 984, in the *Moravian H. Bk.*, 1801 (1849, No. 1235).   [J. M.]

Bennett, Henry, b. at Lyme Regis, April 18, 1813, and d. at Islington, Nov. 12, 1868. His hymns, written at various dates, were collected and pub. as follows:—

(1) *Hymns by H. B.*, Lond.: Printed for the Author, 1867. This contained 25 pieces. (2) *Hymns by the late Henry Bennett*, 2nd ed., 1869. This was pub. by request, with additional hymns (32 in all, and 6 unfinished).

From these editions of his *Hymns*, "Cling to the Mighty One," and "I have a home above," are in extensive use. The following are also in C. U.:—

1. Jesus, my [the] Holy One. *Jesus for Men.*
2. Lord Jesus, hide Thy people. *Jesus All in All.*

Bennett, M. E., née Dampier, dau. of W. J. Dampier, M.A., Vicar of Coggeshall, Essex, and wife of the Rev. J. W. Bennett, Vicar of St. Paul's, South Hampstead, pub. in 1882:—

Hymns for Children of the English Church: being Simple Verses for every Sunday and Holy Day in the Christian Year, Lond., W. Poole [1882].

From this work the following hymns were given in *The Universal Hymn Book* (1885):—

1. As by the wondrous working of the blessed holy Dove. *Christmas.*
2. Christ is our Great High Priest. *Epistle 5th S. in Lent.*
3. The infant Saviour, very soon. *Circumcision.*

These hymns, in common with many others in Mrs. Bennett's work, were written in 1881.

Bernstein, Christian Andreas, was b. at Domnitz, near Halle, where his father, Daniel Bernstein, was pastor. After completing his studies at Halle, he was appointed, in 1695, by A. H. Francke, a tutor in the Pädagogium there; was then ordained as assistant to his father (probably at the end of 1696); and d. at Domnitz, Oct. 18, 1699 (*Koch*, iv. 365, *Allg. Deutsche Biog.* ii. 484).

From extracts from the *Kirchenbuch* of Domnitz, kindly sent by Pastor Tauer, it appears that Bernstein was baptized there, July 12, 1672, and thus was probably b. July 9. He signed the book as assistant to his father on March 5, 1697. The funeral sermon, Oct. 20, 1699, was preached at his request by Francke, from Isaiah lxi. The statement by his father (who survived till Feb. 27, 1712), that Christian d. at the age of 27 years, 3 months, and 2 days, and in the 3rd month and 3rd day of his age, and 3rd year, 14th week of his ministry, seems hardly reconcilable with the other facts.

In Freylinghausen's *G. B.*, 1704–5, six of his hymns were included, four of which have been *tr.* into English:—

1. **Ihr Kinder des Höchsten! wie steht's um die Liebe.** [*Brotherly Love.*] 1704, as above, No. 386, in 0 st. Previously in G. Arnold's *Göttliche Sophia*, Leipzig, 1700, pt. ii. p. 309, as No. i. of the "Some hitherto unknown hymns." *Tr.* as:—"We in one covenant are joined," of st. v. by J. Swertner, as No. 384 in the *Moravian H. Bk.*, 1789.

ii. **Mein Vater! zeuge mich, dein Kind, nach deinem Bilde.** [*Names and Offices of Christ.*] 1704, as above, No. 62, in 14 st. The *trs.* are:— (1) "My Father! form Thy Child according to Thine Image," by *J. C. Jacobi*, 1722, p. 125 (1732, p. 12). (2) "Father, make me Thy child," No. 546 in pt. i. of the *Moravian H. Bk.*, 1754.

iii. **Schönster aller Schönen.** [*Love to Christ.*] 1st pub. in the *Geistreiches G. B.*, Halle, 1697, p. 246, in 8 st. *Tr.* as:—"Fairest of all beauties," No. 681 in pt. i. of the *Moravian H. Bk.*, 1154.

iv. **Zuletzt gehts wohl dem der gerecht auf Erden.** [*Cross & Consolation.*] 1704, as above, No. 440, in 7 st. The *trs.* are:—

(1) "At last he's well, who thro' the Blood of Jesus," No. 693, in pt. i. of the *Moravian H. Bk.*, 1754. Altered 1789, and changed in metre, 1801, beginning "At last he's blest." (2) "At last all shall be well with those, His own," by Miss Borthwick, in *H. L. L.*, 1858 (1862, p. 225; 1884, p. 172).   [J. M.]

Benson, Edward White, D.D., Archbishop of Canterbury, s. of Edward White Benson, of York, was born at Birmingham, 14th July, 1829, and educated at King Edward's School in that town, and Trinity Coll., Cambridge. At Birmingham his contemporaries under the head mastership of Dr. Prince Lee, subsequently first Bishop of Manchester, included Dr. Westcott, and Dr. Lightfoot, Bishop of Durham. At Cambridge he took the high position of Sen. Opt. and 1st cl. Classical Tripos, winning also the distinction of Senior Chancellor's Classical Medallist. He subsequently became a Fellow of his College. In 1852 he passed from Cambridge to Rugby as assistant master; in 1859 from Rugby to Wellington College, of which he was Head Master for fourteen years; in 1872 from Wellington College to Lincoln, as Chancellor of the Cathedral; in 1877 from Lincoln to Truro, as the first Bishop of that Diocese; and in 1883 from Truro to Canterbury, as the Primate of All England. In addition to these appointments he was also Prebendary of Lincoln and Chaplain to the Queen. The sterling value of Dr. Benson's work at Wellington College, at Lincoln, and at Truro, is strongly emphasised by his appointment to Canterbury. His literary labours have not been very extensive; but as a contributor to the *Dictionary of Christian Biography*, and the author of *Work, Friendship, Worship* (University Sermons at Cambridge), 1871; *Boy Life; Sundays in Wellington College*, 1874, and *Singleheart*, 1877, he is well and favourably known. His hymnological work embraces the co-editorship of the 1856 edition of the *Rugby School Hymn-book;* the editorship of the *Wellington College Chapel Hymn Book*, 1860, 1863, 1873, the translation of various Latin and Greek hymns, including *Angulare Fundamentum; Tristes erant Apostoli; Dies Irae; O Luce Qui mortalibus; Te lucis ante terminum; Φῶς ἱλαρὸν ἁγίας δόξης* (q. v.), and a limited number of original hymns. Of the latter the best is the Rogation Hymn, "O throned, O crowned with all renown" (q. v.).   [J. J.]

Benson, Richard Meux, M.A., educated at Christ Church, Oxford; B.A., in honours, 1847, M.A., 1849. On taking Holy Orders, he became curate of St. Mark's, Surbiton, 1849; and Vicar of Cowley, Oxford, 1850. He is also Student of Christ Church, Oxford. His works include *The Wisdom of the Son of David; Redemption*, 1861; *The Divine Rule of Prayer,* and others. His hymns, " O Thou whose all redeeming might," a *tr.* of " Jesu, Redemptor omnium," q. v., and " Praise to God Who reigns above," were contributed to *H. A. & M.*, 1861.

Bernard of Clairvaux, saint, abbot, and doctor, fills one of the most conspicuous positions in the history of the middle ages. His father, Tecelin, or Tesselin, a knight of great bravery, was the friend and vassal of the Duke of Burgundy. Bernard was born at his father's castle on the eminence of Les Fontaines, near Dijon, in Burgundy, in 1091. He was educated at Chatillon, where he was distinguished for his studious and meditative habits. The world, it would be thought, would have had overpowering attractions for a youth who, like Bernard, had all the advantages that high birth, great personal beauty, graceful manners, and irresistible influence could give, but, strengthened in the resolve by night visions of his mother (who had died in 1105), he chose a life of asceticism, and became a monk. In company with an uncle and two of his brothers, who had been won over by his entreaties, he entered the monastery of Citeaux, the first Cistercian foundation, in 1113. Two years later he was sent forth, at the head of twelve monks, from the rapidly increasing and overcrowded abbey, to found a daughter institution, which in spite of difficulties and privations which would have daunted less determined men, they succeeded in doing, in the Valley of Wormwood, about four miles from the Abbey of La Ferté—itself an earlier swarm from the same parent hive—on the Aube. On the death of Pope Honorius II., in 1130, the Sacred College was rent by factions, one

of which elected Gregory of St. Angelo, who took the title of Innocent II., while another elected Peter Leonis, under that of Anacletus II. Innocent fled to France, and the question as to whom the allegiance of the King, Louis VI., and the French bishops was due was left by them for Bernard to decide. At a council held at Etampes, Bernard gave judgment in favour of Innocent. Throwing himself into the question with all the ardour of a vehement partisan, he won over both Henry I., the English king, and Lothair, the German emperor, to support the same cause, and then, in 1133, accompanied Innocent II., who was supported by Lothair and his army, to Italy and to Rome. When Lothair withdrew, Innocent retired to Pisa, and Bernard for awhile to his abbey of Clairvaux. It was not until after the death of Anacletus, the antipope, in January, 1138, and the resignation of his successor, the cardinal-priest Gregory, Victor II., that Innocent II., who had returned to Rome with Bernard, was universally acknowledged Pope, a result to which no one had so greatly contributed as the Abbot of Clairvaux. The influence of the latter now became paramount in the Church, as was proved at the Lateran Council of 1139, the largest council ever collected together, where the decrees in every line displayed the work of his master-hand. After having devoted four years to the service of the Pope, Bernard, early in 1135, returned to Clairvaux. In 1137 he was again at Rome, impetuous and determined as ever, denouncing the election of a Cluniac instead of a Clairvaux monk to the see of Langres in France, and in high controversy in consequence with Peter, the gentle Abbot of Cluny, and the Archbishop of Lyons. The question was settled by the deposition by the Pope of the Cluniac and the elevation of a Clairvaux monk (Godfrey, a kinsman of St. Bernard) into his place. In 1143, Bernard raised an almost similar question as to the election of St. William to the see of York, which was settled much after the same fashion, the deposition, after a time, if only for a time, of William, and the intrusion of another Clairvaux monk, Henry Murdac, or Murduch, into the archiepiscopal see. Meantime between these two dates—in 1140—the condemnation of Peter Abelard and his tenets, in which matter Bernard appeared personally as prosecutor, took place at a council held at Sens. Abelard, condemned at Sens, appealed to Rome, and, resting awhile on his way thither, at Cluny, where Peter still presided as Abbot, died there in 1142. St. Bernard was next called upon to exercise his unrivalled powers of persuasion in a very different cause. Controversy over, he preached a crusade. The summer of 1146 was spent by him in traversing France to rouse the people to engage in the second crusade; the autumn with a like object in Germany. In both countries the effect of his appearance and eloquence was marvellous, almost miraculous. The population seemed to rise *en masse*, and take up the cross. In 1147 the expedition started, a vast horde, of which probably not a tenth ever reached Palestine. It proved a complete failure, and a miserable remnant shared the flight of their leaders, the Emperor Conrad, and Louis, King of France, and returned home, defeated and disgraced. The blame was thrown upon Bernard, and his apology for his part in the matter is extant. He was not, however, for long to bear up against reproach; he died in the 63rd year of his age, in 1153, weary of the world and glad to be at rest.

With the works of St. Bernard, the best ed. of which was pub. by *Mabillon* at Paris in the early part of the 18th cent. (1719), we are not concerned here, except as regards his contributions, few and far between as they are, to the stores of Latin hymnology. There has been so much doubt thrown upon the authorship of the hymns which usually go by his name,—notably by his editor, *Mabillon* himself,—that it is impossible to claim any of them as having been certainly written by him; but Archbishop Trench, than whom we have no greater modern authority on such a point, is satisfied that the attribution of them all, except the "Cur mundus militat," to St. Bernard is correct. "If he did not write," the Archbishop says, "it is not easy to guess who could have written them; and indeed they bear profoundly the stamp of his mind, being only inferior in beauty to his prose."

The hymns by which St. Bernard is best known as a writer of sacred poetry are: (1.) "Jesu dulcis memoria," a long poem on the "Name of Jesus"—known as the "Jubilus of St. Bernard," and among mediæval writers as the "Rosy Hymn." It is, perhaps, the best specimen of what *Neale* describes as the "subjective loveliness" of its author's compositions. (2.) "Salve mundi Salutare," an address to the various limbs of Christ on the cross. It consists of 350 lines, 50 lines being addressed to each. (3.) "Laetabundus, exultet fidelis chorus: Alleluia." This sequence was in use all over Europe. (4.) "Cum sit omnis homo foenum." (5.) "Ut jucundas cervus undas." A poem of 68 lines, and well known, is claimed for St. Bernard by *Hommey* in his *Supplementum Patrum*, Paris, 1686, p. 165, but on what Archbishop Trench, who quotes it at length, (*Sac. Lat. Poetry*, p. 242,) deems "grounds entirely insufficient." (6.) "Eheu, Eheu, mundi vita," or "Heu, Heu, mala mundi vita." A poem of nearly 400 lines, is sometimes claimed for St. Bernard, but according to *Trench*, "on no authority whatever." (7.) "O miranda vanitas." This is included in Mabillon's ed. of St. Bernard's *Works*. It is also attributed to him by *Rambach*, vol. i. p. 279. Many other hymns and sequences are attributed to St. Bernard. *Trench* speaks of a "general ascription to him of any poems of merit belonging to that period whereof the authorship was uncertain." Hymns, translated from, or founded on, St. Bernard's, will be found in almost every hymnal of the day, details of which, together with many others not in common use, will be found under the foregoing Latin first lines.   **[D. S. W.]**

Bernard of Morlaix, or of **Cluny,** for he is equally well known by both titles, was an Englishman by extraction, both his parents being natives of this country. He was b., however, in France very early in the 12th cent., at Morlaix, Bretagne. Little or nothing is known of his life, beyond the fact that he entered the Abbey of Cluny, of which at that time Peter the Venerable, who filled the post from 1122 to 1156, was the head. There, so far as we know, he spent his whole after-life, and there he probably died, though the exact date of his death, as well as of his birth is unrecorded. The Abbey of Cluny was at that period at the zenith of its wealth and fame. Its buildings, especially its church (which was unequalled by any in France); the services therein, renowned for the elaborate order of their ritual; and its community, the most numerous of any like institution, gave it a position and an influence, such as no other monastery, perhaps, ever reached. Everything about it was splendid, almost luxurious. It was amid such surroundings that Bernard of Cluny spent his leisure hours in composing that wondrous satire against the vices and follies of his age, which has supplied—and it

is the only satire that ever did so—some of the most widely known and admired hymns to the Church of to-day. His poem *De Contemptu Mundi* remains as an imperishable monument of an author of whom we know little besides except his name, and that a name overshadowed in his own day and in ours by his more illustrious contemporary and namesake, the saintly Abbot of Clairvaux.

The poem itself consists of about 3000 lines in a metre which is technically known as *Leonini Cristati Trilices Dactylici*, or more familiarly—to use Dr. Neale's description in his *Mediaeval Hymns*, p. 69—"it is a dactylic hexameter, divided into three parts, between which a caesura is inadmissible. The hexameter has a tailed rhyme, and feminine leonine rhyme between the two first clauses, thus:—

> "Tunc nova gloria, pectora sobria, clarificabit
> Solvit enigmata, veraque sabbata, continuabit,
> Patria luminis, inscia turbinis, inscia litis
> Cive replebitur, amplificabitur Israelitis."

The difficulty of writing at all, much more of writing a poem of such length in a metre of this description, will be as apparent to all readers of it, as it was to the writer himself, who attributes his successful accomplishment of his task entirely to the direct inspiration of the Spirit of God. "Non ego arroganter," he says in his preface, "sed omnino humiliter, et ob id audenter affirmaverim, quia nisi spiritus sapientiae et intellectus mihi affuisset et affluxisset, tam difficili metro tam longum opus contexere non sustinuissem."

As to the character of the metre, on the other hand, opinions have widely differed, for while Dr. Neale, in his *Mediaeval Hymns*, speaks of its "majestic sweetness," and in his preface to the *Rhythm of Bernard de Morlaix on the Celestial Country*, says that it seems to him "one of the loveliest of mediaeval measures;" Archbishop Trench in his *Sac. Lat. Poetry*, 1873. p. 311, says "it must be confessed that" these dactylic hexameters "present as unattractive a garb for poetry to wear as can well be imagined;" and, a few lines further on, notes "the awkwardness and repulsiveness of the metre." The truth perhaps lies between these two very opposite criticisms. Without seeking to claim for the metre all that Dr. Neale is willing to attribute to it, it may be fairly said to be admirably adapted for the purpose to which it has been applied by Bernard, whose awe-stricken self-abasement as he contemplates in the spirit of the publican, "who would not so much as lift up his eyes unto heaven," the joys and the glory of the celestial country, or sorrowfully reviews the vices of his age, or solemnly denounces God's judgments on the reprobate, it eloquently pourtrays. So much is this the case, that the prevailing *sentiment* of the poem, that, viz., of an awful apprehension of the joys of heaven, the enormity of sin, and the terrors of hell, seems almost wholly lost in such translations as that of Dr. Neale. Beautiful as they are as hymns, "Brief life is here our portion," "Jerusalem the Golden," and their companion extracts from this great work, are far too jubilant to give any idea of the prevailing tone of the original. (See **Hora Novissima.**)

In the original poem of Bernard it should be noted that the same fault has been remarked by Archbishop Trench, Dean Stanley, and Dr. Neale, which may be given in the Archbishop's words as excusing at the same time both the want, which still exists, of a very close translation of any part, and of a complete and continuous rendering of the whole poem. "The poet," observes Archbishop Trench, "instead of advancing, eddies round and round his object, recurring again and again to that which he seemed thoroughly to have discussed and dismissed." *Sac. Lat. Poetry*, 1873. p. 311. On other grounds also, more especially the character of the vices which the author lashes, it is alike impossible to expect, and undesirable to obtain, a literal translation of the whole. We may well be content with what we already owe to it as additions to our stores of church-hymns.

       [D. S. W.]

Berridge, John, b. at Kingston, Notts, March 1, 1716, and educated at Clare Hall, Cambridge. In 1749 he was ordained as curate to the parish of Stapleford, near Cambridge, and in 1755 he was preferred to the Vicarage of Everton, where he d., Jan. 22, 1793. His epitaph, written by himself for his own tombstone (with date of death filled in), is an epitome of his life. It reads:—

"Here lies the remains of John Berridge, late Vicar of Everton, and an itinerate servant of Jesus Christ, who loved his Master and His work; and after running on His errands for many years, was caught up to wait on Him above. Reader! art thou born again? (No salvation without a new birth.) I was born in sin, February, 1716; remained ignorant of my fallen state till 1730; lived proudly on faith and works for salvation till 1754; was admitted to Everton Vicarage, 1755; fled to Jesus for refuge, 1755; fell asleep in Jesus, January 22, 1793."

The first collection of Berridge's hymns was pub. as *A Collection of Divine Songs,* 1760. This was subsequently suppressed. In 1785 his *Sion's Songs; or, Hymns composed for the use of them that love and follow the Lord Jesus Christ in Sincerity* were pub. The work contains 342 hymns, some of which had previously appeared in the *Gospel Magazine* (from 1775 to 1777, 20 in all), under the signature of "Old Everton" and others were adapted from C. Wesley. The most popular of these in modern collections are, "Jesus, cast a look on me;" "O happy saints who dwell in light;" and "Since Jesus freely did appear." Concerning his hymns pub. in 1785, he says in his *Preface:*—

"Twelve years ago these hymns were composed in a six months' illness, and have since laid neglected by me, often threatened with the fire, but have escaped that martyrdom."   [J. J.]

Bertram, Robert Aitken, s. of Rev. J. M. Bertram, D.D., of St. Helena, b. at Hanley, 1836, and educated at Owen's College, Manchester, and as a Congregational minister has laboured in St. Helena, Manchester, Barnstaple, Nottingham and Llanelly. Mr. Bertram is author of several works, including *A Dictionary of Poetical Illustrations,* 1877; *A Homiletic Encyclopaedia of Illustrations in Theology and Morals,* 1880 and was also one of the editors of *The Cavendish Hymnal,* prepared in 1864 for the use of the congregation of Rev. Joseph Parker, D.D., at that time minister of Cavendish Chapel, Manchester. To that collection he contributed, under the initials "R. A. B.," the following hymns, several of which have passed into other hymn-books:—

1. As kings and priests we hope to shine. *Cross and Crown.*
2. Behold Thy servant, Lord. *Induction of a Minister.*
3. Father of Jesus, Lord of Love. *Love to God desired.*
4. Jesus, hail, Thou Lord of glory. *Ascension.*
5. Look down, O Lord, in love on these. *Reception into Church Membership.*
6. Lord of glory, throned on high. *Children's Hymn for New Year.*
7. Met to remember Thee, O Lord. *Holy Communion.*
8. O Christ, with all Thy members one. *Oneness with Christ.*
9. Our hearts still joy in Thee. *Sunday.*
10. Saviour, still the same Thou art. *Holy Baptism*
11. Seeking, Lord, Thy word to heed. *S. S. Teacher's Hymn.*
12. Sing loud for joy, ye saints of God. *Reception into Church Membership.*
13. Spirit of life, and power and light. *Whitsuntide.*
14. Swiftly fly, our changeful days. *Sunday.*

15. Ten thousand thousand are Thy hosts. *Communion of Saints.*
16. Thanks to Thy Name for every pile. *Opening of a Place of Worship.*
17. Thou Prince of Life, our praises hear. *Passiontide.*
18. With vision purged by Thine own grace. *Heaven.*

The hymn on "Hope," "Bending before Thy throne on high," in the *Cavendish Hymnal,* 1864, was contributed thereto by Mrs. Mary Ann Bertram, wife of our author, b. 1841, and d. 1864.   [W. R. S.]

Beset with snares on every hand. *P. Doddridge.* [*Mary's choice.*] This hymn is not in the D. MSS. It was 1st pub. by J. Orton in the posthumous ed. of Doddridge's *Hymns,* 1755. No. 207, in 4 st. of 4 l., and headed "Mary's Choice of the Better Part;" and again in J. D. Humphreys's ed. of the same, 1839. Although used but sparingly in the hymnals of G. Britain, in America it is found in many of the leading collections, and especially in those belonging to the Unitarians. The *tr.*—"In vitae dubio tramite transeo," in Bingham's *Hymno. Christ. Lat.,* 1871, p. 109—is made from an altered text in Bickersteth's *Christian Psalmody,* 1833.

Besnault, Abbé, a Priest of St. Maurice, Sens, in 1726, and one of the contributors to the *Cluniac Breviary,* 1686, and the *Paris Breviary,* 1736.

Bestow, dear Lord, upon our youth. *W. Cowper.* [*For the Young.*] This hymn is the second of three "Hymns before Annual Sermons to Young People, on New Year's Evenings" (the 1st and 3rd being by J. Newton), which were pub. in the *Olney Hymns,* 1779, Bk. ii., No. 8, in 6 st. of 4 l. and signed "C." In Cotterill's *Sel.,* 1810, No. 93, it was given as—"Bestow, *O* Lord, upon our youth." Both this form and the original are in C. U. The original, with the omission of st. iv., is in the *Meth. Free Ch. S. S. H. Bk.,* No. 155; in full, in the Amer. Presb. *Ps. & Hys. for the Worship of God,* Richmond, 1867, and others. Cotterill's text, with the omission of st. iv., is in Stowell's *Sel.,* 1831 and 1877.

Bethune, George Washington, D.D. A very eminent divine of the Reformed Dutch body, born in New York, 1805, graduated at Dickinson Coll., Carlisle, Phila., 1822, and studied theology at Princeton. In 1827 he was appointed Pastor of the Reformed Dutch Church, Rinebeck, New York. In 1830 passed to Utica, in 1834 to Philadelphia, and in 1850 to the Brooklyn Heights, New York. In 1861 he visited Florence, Italy, for his health, and died in that city, almost suddenly after preaching, April 27, 1862. His *Life and Letters* were edited by A. R. Van Nest, 1867. He was offered the Chancellorship of New York University, and the Provostship of the University of Pennsylvania, both of which he declined. His works include *The Fruits of the Spirit,* 1839; *Sermons,* 1847; *Lays of Love & Faith,* 1847; *The British Female Poets,* 1848, and others. Of his hymns, some of which have attained to some repute, we have:—

1. Tossed upon life's raging billow. *Sailor's Hymn.* Appeared in the *Christian Lyre,* 1830; in the *Seamen's Devotional Assistant* the same year, and in Dr. Bethune's *Lays,* 1847, p. 168,

in 3 st. of 8 l. It "is said to have been the Author's first and favourite hymn, having been written when he was on a voyage to the West Indies, for the benefit of his health, in the year 1825" (*Lyra Sac. Amer.* p. 297). It is a "Sailor's Hymn;" as such it was given in *Lyra Sac. Amer.*, and thence passed into *The Hymnary*, 1872, and other English collections.

2. O for the happy hour. *Whitsuntide.* "A Prayer for the Spirit," contributed to the *Parish Hymns*, Phila., 1843, and republished in the *Lays*, &c., 1847, p. 158, in 6 st. of 4 l. It is found in many modern collections.

3. It is not death to die. A translation of Cæsar Malan's "Non, ce n'est pas mourir," (q.v.) from his *Lays*, 1847, p 141, in 5 st. of 4 l. As stated above, Dr. Bethune died at Florence. His remains were taken to New York, and buried in Greenwood Cemetery. This hymn, in compliance with a request made by him before his death, was sung at his funeral. It is found in several English hymnals.

4. Light of the Immortal Father's glory. *Evening.* A *tr.* of the Greek hymn Φῶς ἱλαρόν (q.v.). It appeared in his *Lays*, &c., 1847, p. 137, in 2 st. of 8 l., and is in C. U.

5. Farewell to thee, brother *Parting.* "The departing Missionary," pub. in his *Lays*, &c., 1847, p. 170, in 5 st. of 4 l., and included in *Lyra Sac. Amer.*, 1868, and thence into English collections. It is not in C. U. in America.

6. O Jesus, when I think of Thee. *Easter.* This is said to bear the date of 1847. It was 1st pub. in his *Life*, &c., 1867. Included in *Lyra Sac. Amer.* (where it is stated to have been found in MS. amongst the author's papers), and from the *Lyra* into English collections. It is an Easter hymn of no special merit.

7. Come, let us sing of Jesus. *S. Schools.* Pub. in 1850, suited to Sunday schools, and is found in Snepp's *S. of G. & G.* and others.

8. O Thou Who in Jordan didst bow Thy meek head. *Adult Baptism.* Written for and much used by the Baptists. It is dated 1857.

9. There is no Name so sweet on earth. *Name of Jesus.* Said by Mr. H. P. Main to be by Dr. Bethune. It has been wrongly ascribed to E. Roberts, a musician.

10. When time seems short and death is near. *Death anticipated.* This was found in the author's portfolio, and was written on Saturday, April 27th, 1862, the day before his death at Florence (*Life*, &c., p. 409). It was included in the *Lyra Sac. Amer.*, 1868, and from thence passed into one or two English hymnals.

In his *Lays*, &c., 1847, Dr. Bethune included the following "Christmas Carols for Sunday School Children":

1. The Almighty Spirit to a poor, &c.
2. Joy and gladness, joy and gladness.
3. Full many a year has sped.
4. We come, we come, with loud acclaim.

In the same work there are also metrical renderings of Psalms ix., xix., xxiii., cxxvi., and cxxvii. In the *Lyra Sacra Americana*, 14 pieces by Dr. Bethune are given, including many of the above. [F. M. B.]

Betts, Henry John, was b. 1825, at Great Yarmouth, where his father was a Baptist minister. He entered the Baptist ministry in 1847, and laboured successively in London,

Edinburgh, Bradford (Yorks.), Manchester, Darlington, and Newcastle-upon-Tyne. Mr. Betts has pub. a small volume of hymns and poetical translations, entitled *Early Blossoms*, 1842; two vols. of sermons on *Scripture Localities and their Associations,"* 1853; *Lectures on Elijah*, 1856; and at different times single sermons and lectures. For some years he was editor of the *Primitive Church Magazine.* His *Children's Hosannah* appeared in 1864. From it the following hymns are in C. U.:—

1. Beautiful Star, whose heavenly light. *Christ the Star.*
2. Jesus, Thou art meek and lowly. *Jesus desired.*
3. Our Father God, Who art in heaven. *The Lord's Prayer.*
4. There is a lamp whose steady light. *Holy Scripture.*

These are found in Major's *Bk. of Praise*, and some other collections. [W. R. S.]

Bevan, Emma Frances, née Shuttleworth, dau. of the Rev. Philip Nicholas Shuttleworth, Warden of New Coll., Oxford, afterwards Bp. of Chichester, was b. at Oxford, Sept. 25, 1827, and was married to Mr. R. C. L. Bevan, of the Lombard Street banking firm, in 1856.

Mrs. Bevan pub. in 1858 a series of *trs.* from the the German as *Songs of Eternal Life* (Lond., Hamilton, Adams, & Co.), in a volume which, from its unusual size and comparative costliness, has received less attention than it deserves, for the *trs.* are decidedly above the average in merit. A number have come into C. U., but almost always without her name, the best known being those noted under "O Gott, O Geist, O Licht des Lebens," and "Jedes Herz will etwas li ben." Most of these are annotated throughout this Dictionary under their authors' names, or German first lines. That at p. 630, "O past are the fast-days,—the Feast-day, the Feast-day is come," is a *tr.* through the German from the Persian of Dschellaleddin Rumi 1207–1273. Mrs. Bevan also pub. *Songs of Praise for Christian Pilgrims* (Lond., Hamilton, Adams, 1859), the *trs.* in which are also annotated throughout this Dictionary as far as possible. [J. M.]

Beyond, beyond the [that] boundless sea. *J. Conder.* [*Omnipresence of the H. Spirit.*] Appeared in his *Star in the East with Other Poems*, 1824, pp. 74, 75, in 5 st. of 6 l., headed, "A Thought on the Sea Shore, 'Though He be not far from every one of us,' Acts xvii. 27;" and dated, "Happisburgh, June, 1822." In 1856 it was repeated in his *Hymns of Praise, Prayer*, &c., p. 53, with slight changes in st. iv. and v. The congregational use of this hymn began with Curtis's *Union Coll.*, 1827, No. 21, and extended to Conder's *Cong. H. Bk.*, 1836; the *Leeds H. Bk.*, 1853; the Bap. *Psalms & Hymns*, 1858; the *New Cong.*, 1859, and others. Its use is fairly extensive, both in G. Britain and in America. In Martineau's *Hymns*, 1840, and *Hys. of Praise and Prayer*, 1873, it reads— "O God, beyond that boundless sea," and st. iii. is also omitted.

Beyond the glittering, starry globes. *J. Fanch.* [*Ascension.*] This hymn appeared in the *Gospel Magazine*, June, 1776. It was signed "F.," i.e. *Fanch*, and is as follows:—

Christ seen of Angels: 1 Tim. iii., 16.

1. "Beyond the glitt'ring starry globes,
 Far as th' eternal hills,
 There, in the boundless worlds of light,
 Our great Redeemer dwells.

2. "Legions of angels, strong and fair,
 In countless armys shine,
 At his right hand, with golden harps
 To offer songs divine.

3. "'Hail, Prince!' (they cry) 'for ever hail!
    Whose unexampled love,
    Mov'd Thee to quit these glorious realms,
    And royaltys above.'

4. "Whilst He did condescend, on earth,
    To suffer rude disdain;
    They threw their honors at His feet,
    And waited in His train.

5. "Thro' all His travels here below
    They did His steps attend:
    Oft gaz'd; and wonder'd where, at last,
    This scene of love would end.

6. "They saw His heart transfixed with wounds,
    His crimson sweat and gore:
    They saw Him break the bars of death,
    Which none e'er before before.

7. "They brought His chariot from above
    To bear Him to His throne;
    Clapt their triumphant wings, and cry'd
    'The glorious work is done!'"

Of this text the following arrangements
have come into C. U.:—

1. The original, slightly altered, in Toplady's *Ps. &
Hys.*, 1776 (but omitted from the 2nd ed., 1787); De
Courcy's *Collection*, 4th ed., 1793, No. 254; Joseph
Middleton's *Hymns*, 1793, No. 277; and others.

2. "Beyond, beyond the starry skies," in Kempthorne's *Ps. & Hys.*, 1810, No. 85; and later works.

3. "Beyond this glittering starry sky." In Cotterill's
Sel., 1810, No. 29, with omission of st. iii. and iv., and
the addition of st. vi. In the 8th ed., 1819, this was
altered by the restoration of the original arrangement
of stanzas, st. iii. being also restored. It is found in later
collections.

4. "Beyond the glittering starry skies." In Elliott's
Ps. and Hys., 1835. This is the orig. text very slightly
altered. It is repeated in the *N. Cong.*, 1859, but attributed to *Gregg* in error.

The most popular forms of this hymn are
centos from it in its enlarged form in 28
stanzas. This expansion by the addition of
21 stanzas was made by *D. Turner* (q. v.)
and pub. in his *Poems* in 1794. Of these
21 st., 19 are given in Lord Selborne's *Bk. of
Praise*, 1862, together with the first four by
Fanch slightly altered. The centos from
the *Fanch-Turner* text are most confusing.
Opening with "Beyond the glittering, starry
skies," we have these groups amongst others:—

(1) Smith and Stow's Bap. *Psalmist*, Boston, U.S.,
1843, and others. (2) Bap. *Service of Song*, Boston,
U.S., 1871, &c. (3) Spurgeon's *O. O. H. Bk.*, 1866;
Snepp's *S. of G. and G.*, 1872; *Hys. & Songs of Praise*,
N.Y., 1874, and others. (4) Bap. *Ps. and Hys.*, 1858.
(5) *Bap. Hymnal*, 1879. These by no means exhaust
the list; but they are sufficient to show that no
arrangement nor text, other than the original, can be
depended upon where accuracy is required.

Another arrangement which is somewhat popular in
America is the S.M. hymn, "Beyond the starry skies."
It is rewritten from the Fanch-Turner text, and amongst
modern hymnals is found in the *Plymouth*, 1855; *Hys.
for Ch. and Home*, Phila., 1860; *Songs for the Sanctuary*,
N.Y., 1865–72; *Laudes Domini*, N.Y., 1884, and others.

In the American *Church Pastorals*, Boston, 1864, No.
168, is a cento from Turner's addition to Fanch's hymn.
It begins, "Blest angels who adoring wait."

In the *Baptist Register* of March, 1791, the
following note concerning the Fanch-Turner
text is given. It is addressed to Dr. Rippon
by D. Turner, and dated Feb. 22, 1791.

"As to your enquiry concerning the hymn 'Jesus
seen of Angels' [this hymn], it is true, as you were told
by our good brother Medley that one part of it was made
by my dear friend the Rev. James Fanch, of Rumsey,
and the other part by me."   [J. J.]

**Beyond the smiling and the weep-
ing.** *H. Bonar.* [*Heaven anticipated.*]
Pub. in his *Hys. of Faith and Hope*, 1st series,
1857, in 6 st. of 8 l., the last three lines being
a refrain. In G. Britain it is found in one or
two collections only, but in America its use
is somewhat extensive, but usually with abbre-

viations and the change in the refrain of
"Sweet hope!" to "Sweet *home!*" This
last change has destroyed the loving tenderness of the refrain, and could never have been
made by a poet. The refrain reads in the
original:

    "Love, rest, and home!
      Sweet hope!
    Lord, tarry not, but come."

Beyond the wicked [holy] city walls.
Cecil F. Alexander. [*Good Friday.*] 1st pub.
in her *Narrative Hymns for Village Schools*,
1859, No. 17, in 6 st. of 4 l. and headed,
"Where they crucified Him." It is sometimes
given as, "Beyond the *holy* city walls." This
alteration destroys all the point and meaning
of the hymn.

Bèze, Théodore de, b. at Vezelay, in
Burgundy, 1519; d. 1605. Beza's father
was of noble birth. He occupied the post of
bailiff at Vezelay. Beza received a first-rate
classical education under Melchior Wolmar.
Before he was 20 he wrote some poetry in
imitation of Catullus and Ovid, the licentiousness of which he mourned and condemned in
after years. A brilliant prospect of Church
emoluments turned his attention from the
distasteful study of law. The income of the
Priory of Longjumeau made him rich, and he
became a prominent member of the literary
world at Paris. But his entrance into
Orders was barred by a secret marriage with
Claudine Denosse. Subsequently, when the
offer of the abbey of Froidmont by his uncle
made it necessary for him to decide between
avowing his marriage and renouncing the
prospect, or repudiating his wife, he decided,
under the solemn conviction produced by a
dangerous illness, to abandon the Roman
Church, and break with his whole past life.
He left for Geneva (1548), and there publicly
married. His first scheme for a living was to
join his old comrade Jean Crespin, then at
Geneva, in printing; but his appointment to
the Professorship of Greek at Lausanne (1549),
left the printing office in the hands of Crespin.
Before his departure from Geneva he had
been on intimate terms with Calvin; and the
discovery of a metrical rendering of Ps. 16
on Beza's table at Geneva led Calvin to
suggest to him the completion of Marot's
Psalms. At Lausanne he became a friend of
Viret. He stayed there ten years, during
which he wrote a tragi-comedy, and 40 of
his metrical Psalms (36 pub. in 1551, 6
more in 1554). He had whilst at Lausanne a
narrow escape from death by the plague. In
1557 he went with Farel and Budæus to ask
for the intercession of the German Protestant
Princes in behalf of the persecuted Huguenots, and had interviews with Melanchthon.
In 1559 he was appointed pastor at Geneva,
Assistant Professor of Theology to Calvin, and
the first Rector of the newly founded College
of Geneva. With Peter Martyr and others
he represented the Huguenots in the conference with the Queen-Mother and Cardinal
Lorraine, at Poissy (1561), and remained at
Paris nearly two years afterwards. His
French metrical *Psalter*, in continuation of
Marot, was completed in 1562. Calvin's
death, 1564, left Beza the foremost figure at
Geneva. In 1571, at the summons of the

King of Navarre, he presided at the Synod of the Reformed Churches at Rochelle; and again (1572) at Nismes. His wife died in 1588, and he married again soon afterwards. His public life, as a theologian, a preacher, and administrator, ceased about 1598, though he preached again for the last time in 1600. He was honoured till his death; only three years before which the Landgrave of Hesse visited him, when passing through Geneva. The works of Beza are very numerous. As a controversialist, a commentator, an investigator of the text of the New Testament, he occupied a high place in his time. Among his chief works are: *Annotationes in N. T.*, 1556; *Novum Testamentum*, 1556; *Psalms, with paraphrase in Latin*, 1579; *Life of Calvin*, 1563. See French Psalters for an account of his continuation of Marot's Metrical Psalter.

[H. L. B.]

Bianco da Siena, b. at Anciolina, in the Val d'Arno, date unknown. In 1367 he entered the Order of Jesuates, consisting of unordained men who followed the rule of St. Augustine. This order was instituted in that year by one John Colombinus of Siena, and suppressed by Pope Clement IX. in 1668. Little is known of Bianco beyond the fact that he is said to have lived in Venice for some years, and d. there in 1434. His hymns were pub. at Lucca, in 1851, and edited by T. Bini, under the title, *Laudi spirituali del Bianco da Siena*. This work contains 92 pieces. Of these the following have been translated into English, and have come into C. U.:—

1. **Discendi, Amor santo.** *The Holy Spirit desired.* This is No. 35 in the above work and is in 8 st. Of these, Dr. Littledale gave 4 in the *People's H.*, 1867, No. 473, as, "Come down, O Love Divine."

2. **Gesù Christo amoroso.** *Missions.* This is No. 79 of the above work. It has been rendered into English by Dr. Littledale, and was pub. in the *People's H.*, 1867, No. 400, as, "O Jesu Christ, the loving."

3. **Vergine santa, sposa dell' Agnello.** *St. Lucy. V. M.* This is also from the foregoing work, No. 74, in 15 st. of 3 l. Dr. Littledale's *tr.* in the *People's H.*, 1867, No. 226, is in 7 st. of 4 l., and begins, "O Virgin Spouse of Christ the Lamb."

4. **Ama Jesu el tuo sposo diletto.** *Love for Jesus.* This is No. 45 in the above work, in 33 st. In 1866 Dr. Littledale contributed a cento therefrom to R. Brett's *Office of the Most Holy Name*. This was transferred to Brooke's *Churchman's Manual of Priv. & Family Devotion*, 1882. It begins, "Love Jesus, Who hath sought thee so."

Although the *trs.* Nos. 1–3 have not gone any further than the *People's H.*, Nos. 1 and 2 are worthy of more extended use.   [J. J.]

Biarowsky, Wilhelm Eduard Immanuel von, s. of F. M. F. von Biarowsky, a member of the Bavarian Government, was b. at Munich Oct. 8, 1814. After studying at Munich and Erlangen, he became, in 1840, German minister at Rolle, on the Lake of Geneva, and thereafter for some time assistant in Munich. He became, in 1845, pastor at Waitzenbach, Lower Franconia, but resigned in 1857, and after a year spent in Munich, was appointed

first pastor of the Neustadt Erlangen, and in 1860 decan of Erlangen. He d. at Erlangen, June 2, 1882 (*Koch*, vii. 309–310; *MS.*, &c., from his widow).

He took an interest in the preparation of the Bavarian *G. B.*, 1854, and strove for the retention of hymns in their original forms. His hymns (which are mostly translations from the Latin) appeared principally in his *Gedichte*, Stuttgart, 1854, and his *Glockenklänge*, Erlangen, 1869. One has been *tr.* into English, viz.:—

Mein Herr, vergiss mein nicht. [*Supplication.*] 1st pub. in Knapp's *Christoterpe*, 1844, p. 183, in 6 st. of 8 l., repeated in 1854 as above. Included as No. 1658 in Knapp's *Ev. L. S.*, 1850 (1865, No. 1727). *Tr.* as:— "My God, forget me not," by Miss Jane Borthwick in *H. L. L.*, 1862.   [J. M.]

Bickersteth, Edward, son of Henry Bickersteth, surgeon, of Kirkby-Lonsdale, Westmoreland, and brother of John Bickersteth, b. at Kirkby-Lonsdale, Mar. 19, 1786. In 1801, he received an appointment in the General Post Office, but relinquished it in 1806 for the study of law. Subsequently, in 1815, he took Holy Orders, and proceeded to visit the stations of the Church Miss. Society in West Africa. On his return he became the resident Secretary of the Society till 1830, when he was preferred to the Rectory of Watton, Herts, where he d. Feb. 28, 1850. His works, which are numerous, were pub., in 16 vols., in 1853. His *Christian Psalmody*, pub. 1833, enlarged ed. 1841, has had a most powerful and lasting influence upon the hymnody of the Church of England. Of the hymns contained therein a large proportion are still in C. U., and in many instances in the form in which they were given in that collection in 1833 and 1841. His hymns, contributed to the 1st ed. of his collection, are:—

1. Light of the world, shine on our Souls. *H. Scriptures.*
2. Lord of the harvest, hear us now. *During ministerial vacancy.*
3. Lord, shed Thy grace on every heart. *Social meeting.*
4. O for a single heart for God. *Single heart desired.*
5. O if we know the joyful sound. *Book Societies.*
6. Our Saviour Christ will quickly come. *Advent.*
7. The day of birth, my soul, improve. *Birthday.*
8. Walk with thy God—A sinner walk. *Enoch walked with God.*   [J. J.]

Bickersteth, Edward Henry, D.D., s. of the above, b. at Islington, Jan. 1825, and educated at Trinity College, Cambridge (B.A. with honours, 1847; M.A., 1850). On taking Holy Orders in 1848, he became curate of Banningham, Norfolk, and then of Christ Church, Tunbridge Wells. His preferment to the Rectory of Hinton-Martell, in 1852, was followed by that of the Vicarage of Christ Church, Hampstead, 1855. In 1885 he became Dean of Gloucester, and the same year Bishop of Exeter. Bishop Bickersteth's works, chiefly poetical, are:—

(1) *Poems*, 1849; (2) *Water from the Well-spring*, 1852; (3) *The Rock of Ages*, 1858; (4) *Commentary on the New Testament*, 1864; (5) *Yesterday, To-day, and For Ever*, 1867; (6) *The Spirit of Life*, 1868; (7) *The Two Brothers and other Poems*, 1871; (8) *The Master's Home Call*, 1872; (9) *The Shadowed Home and the Light Beyond*, 1874; (10) *The Reef and other Parables*, 1873; (11) *Songs in the House of Pilgrimage*, N.D.; (12) *From Year to Year*, 1883.

As an editor of hymnals, Bp. Bickersteth has also been most successful. His collections are:—

(1) *Psalms & Hymns*, 1858, based on his father's *Christian Psalmody*, which passed through several editions; (2) *The Hymnal Companion*, 1870; (3) *The Hymnal Com-*

panion revised and enlarged, 1876. Nos. 2 and 3, which are two editions of the same collection, have attained to an extensive circulation. [**Ch. of England Hymnody.**]

About 30 of Bp. Bickersteth's hymns are in C. U. Of these the best and most widely known are:—"Almighty Father, hear our cry "; "Come ye yourselves apart and rest awhile"; "Father of heaven above"; "My God, my Father, dost Thou call"; "O Jesu, Saviour of the lost"; " Peace, perfect peace"; "Rest in the Lord"; "Stand, Soldier of the Cross"; " Thine, Thine, for ever"; and " Till He come."

As a poet Bp. Bickersteth is well known. His reputation as a hymn-writer has also extended far and wide. Joined with a strong grasp of his subject, true poetic feeling, a pure rhythm, there is a soothing plaintiveness and individuality in his hymns which give them a distinct character of their own. His thoughts are usually with the individual, and not with the mass: with the single soul and his God, and not with a vast multitude bowed in adoration before the Almighty. Hence, although many of his hymns are eminently suited to congregational purposes, and have attained to a wide popularity, yet his finest productions are those which are best suited for private use.

[J. J.]

Bickersteth, John, M.A., s. of Henry Bickersteth, surgeon, b. at Kirkby-Lonsdale, June, 19, 1781, and educated at the Grammar School of that town, and Trinity College, Cambridge, where he graduated in honours. Taking Holy Orders, he became Vicar of Acton, Suffolk, and subsequently Rector of Sapcote, Leicestershire. He d. Oct. 2, 1855. The Dean of Lichfield is his second, and the late Bp. of Ripon his fourth son. In 1819 he pub. *Psalms and Hymns, selected and revised for Public, Social, Family, or Secret Devotion,* in which his hymns were included. A fourth ed., much enlarged, appeared in 1832. Of his hymns contributed to his *Coll.* in 1819, the following were transferred to his brother's *Christian Psalmody,* 1833 :—

1. Great God, let children to Thy throne. *S. Schools.*
2. Hast Thou, holy Lord, Redeemer. *H. Communion.*
3. Israel's Shepherd, guide me, feed me. *H. Communion.*

and were thus brought into wider notice than through his own work. No. 3 is sometimes given as " *Heavenly* Shepherd, guide *us,* feed *us,*" as in the Amer. Unitarian *Hys. of the Spirit,* Boston, 1864.   [J. J.]

Bienemann, Caspar, s. of Conrad Bienemann, a burgess of Nürnberg, was b. at Nürnberg, Jan. 3, 1540. After the completion of his studies at Jena and Tübingen, he was sent by the Emperor Maximilian II. with an embassy to Greece as interpreter. In Greece he assumed the name of *Melissander* (a *tr.* into Greek of his German name), by which he is frequently known. After his return he was appointed Professor at Lauingen, Bavaria, and then Abt at Bahr (Lahr ?), and General Superintendent of Pfalz Neuburg; but on the outbreak of the Synergistic Controversy he had to resign his post. In 1571 he received from the University of Jena the degree of D.D., and in the same year was appointed, by Duke Johann Wilhelm, of Sachsen Weimar, tutor to the Crown Prince Friedrich Wilhelm. But

when on the death of the Duke, in 1573, the Elector August, of Saxony, assumed the Regency, the Calvinistic court party gained the ascendancy, and succeeded in displacing Bienemann and other Lutheran pastors in the Duchy. Finally, in 1578, he was appointed pastor and General Superintendent at Altenburg, and d. there Sept. 12, 1591 (*Koch,* ii. 248–252; *Allg. Deutsche Biog.,* ii. 626). One of his hymns has passed into English.

Herr wie du willt, so schicks mit mir. [*Resignation.*] Written in 1574, while he was tutor to the children of Duke Johann Wilhelm of Sachsen Weimar, in expectation of a coming pestilence. He taught it as a prayer to his pupil the Princess Maria, then three years old, the initial letters of the three stanzas (H. Z. S.) forming an acrostic on her title, *Hertzogin zu Sachsen.* The Princess afterwards adopted as her motto the words " Herr wie du willt," and this motto forms the refrain of " Jesus, Jesus, nichts als Jesus," the best known hymn of the Countess Ludämilia Elizabeth of Schwarzburg-Rudolstadt (q. v.), (see *Koch,* viii. 370–371). This hymn " Herr wie " was 1st pub. in B.'s *Betbüchlein,* Leipzig, 1582, in 3 st. of 7 l., marked as C. Meliss D. 1574, with the title, " Motto and daily prayer of the illustrious and noble Princess and Lady, Lady Maria, by birth, Duchess of Saxony, Landgravine of Thuringia and Margravine of Meissen." Thence in *Wackernagel,* iv. p. 714. Included in the Greifswald *G. B.* 1597, and others, and in the *Unv. L. S.,* 1851, No. 578. The *trs.* in C. U. are:—

1. **Lord, as Thou wilt, whilst Thou my heart,** good and full, by A. T. Russell, as No. 195 in his *Ps. & Hys.,* 1851.

2. **Lord, as Thou wilt, deal Thou with me,** in full, by E. Cronenwett, as No. 409 in the Ohio *Luth. Hymnal,* 1880. Another *tr.* is:—

"Lord, as Thou wilt, so do with me," by *Dr. G. Walker,* 1860, p. 53.   [J. M.]

Biggs, Louis Coutier, M.A., the well-known writer on Hymns A. & M. and kindred subjects, graduated at Oxford B.A. 1863. On taking Holy Orders he was successively Curate of Grendon, Northants; Asst. Master in Ipswich School; Rector of Parracombe, Devon; and of Chickerell, near Weymouth, and Chaplain at Malacca, Singapore, and other stations, including Penang in 1875, 1877, and 1885. Mr. Biggs has pub. :—

(1) *Hymns Ancient and Modern with Annotations and Translations,* 1867; (2) *Supp. Hymns for use with H. A. & M.;* (3) *English Hymnology* (a reprint of articles from the *Monthly Packet*), 1873; *Songs of Other Churches* (pub. in the *Monthly Packet,* 1871–2); and one or two smaller hymnological works. A few of the renderings of English hymns into Latin given in his *Annotated H. A. & M.* are by him.

Bilby, Thomas, s. of John Bilby, b. at Southampton, April 18, 1794. In 1809 he joined the army, remaining eight years. Subsequently he studied the Infant School System under Buchanan, whose school at Brewer's Green, Westminster, is said to have been the first Infants' School opened in England. In 1825 he obtained the charge of a Training School at Chelsea, where some 500 teachers were instructed in his system. In 1832 he proceeded to the West Indies, where he introduced his system of teaching. On returning to England, he became the parish clerk of

St. Mary's, Islington. He d. Sept. 24, 1872. He was one of the founders of "The Home and Colonial Infant School Society." Jointly with Mr. R. B. Ridgway he published *The Nursery Book, The Infant Teacher's Assistant*, 1831–32; and the *Book of Quadrupeds*, 1838. His hymns appeared in *The Infant Teacher's Assistant*, the best known of which is, "Here we suffer grief and pain."

Binney, Thomas, D.D., b. at Newcastle-on-Tyne, in 1798, and educated at Wymondley College, Hertfordshire. Entering the ministry, he was successively pastor of a congregation at Bedford, an Independent Chapel at Newport, Isle of Wight, and of the King's Weigh House Chapel, London, 1829. The University of Aberdeen conferred upon him the LL.D. degree. He d. Feb. 23, 1874. His works, exceeding 50 in number, include *Life of the Rev. Stephen Morell*, 1826; *Money*, 1864; *St. Paul, his Life and Ministry*, &c. He wrote a few hymns, including "Eternal Light! Eternal Light," and "Holy Father, Whom we praise." (*Close of Service*.)

Bird, Frederic Mayer, b. at Philadelphia, U.S., June 28, 1838, and graduated at the University of Pennsylvania, 1857. In 1860 he became Lutheran pastor at Rhinebeck, N.Y.; in 1866 at Valatie, N.Y., where he remained until 1868. In 1868 he joined the American Protestant Episcopal Church (deacon 1868, priest 1869), and became Rector at Spotswood, New Jersey, 1870–74, and elsewhere to 1881, when he became Chaplain and Professor of Psychology, Christian Evidences, and Rhetoric in the Lehigh University, South Bethlehem, Pennsylvania.

Professor Bird compiled with Dr. B. M. Schmucker, (1) Pennsylvania *Hys. for the use of the Evang. Lutheran Church*, 1865, revised (and now used) as the Lutheran General Council's *Church Book*, 1868; (2) and with Bp. Odenheimer *Songs of the Spirit*, N. Y., 1871–2; and pub. (3) *Charles Wesley seen in his Finer and less Familiar Poems*, N. Y., 1866–7. He also has conducted the department of "Hymn Notes," in the N. York *Independent* since 1880. His library of hymnological works is the largest in the United States.

Birken, Sigismund von, s. of Daniel Betulius or Birken, pastor at Wildstein, near Eger, in Bohemia, was b. at Wildstein, May 5, 1626. In 1629 his father, along with other Evangelical pastors, was forced to flee from Bohemia, and went to Nürnberg. After passing through the Egidien-Gymnasium at Nürnberg Sigismund entered the University of Jena, in 1643, and there studied both Law and Theology, the latter at his father's dying request. Before completing his course in either he returned to Nürnberg, in 1645, and on account of his poetical gifts was there admitted a member of the Pegnitz Shepherd and Flower Order. At the close of 1645 he was appointed tutor at Wolfenbüttel to the Princes of Brunswick-Lüneburg, but after a year (during which he was crowned as a poet), he resigned this post. After a tour, during which he was admitted by Philipp v. Zesen as a member of the German Society (or Patriotic Union), he returned to Nürnberg in 1648, and employed himself as a private tutor. In 1654 he was ennobled on account of his poetic gifts by the Emperor Ferdinand III., was admitted in 1658 as a member of the Fruitbearing Society,

and on the death of Harsdörffer, in 1662, became Chief Shepherd of the Pegnitz Order, to which from that time he imparted a distinctly religious cast. He d. at Nürnberg, June 12, 1681. (*Koch*, iii. 478–485; *Allg. Deutsche Biog.*, ii. 660; *Bode*, pp. 44–46; the first dating his death, July, and the last dating his birth, April 25). In his 52 hymns he was not able to shake off the artificial influences of the time, and not many of them have retained a place in German C. U. Three have been *tr.* into English :—

i. **Auf, auf, mein Herz und du mein ganzer Sinn,** Wirf alles heut. [*Sunday.*] 1st pub. (not in 1661, but) in Saubert's *G. B.*, Nürnberg, 1676, No. 329, in 10 st. *Tr.* as :—

(1) "Arouse thee up! my Heart, my Thought, my Mind," by *H. J. Buckoll*, 1842, p. 10. (2) "Awake! awake!—to holy thought aspire," by *Dr. H. Mills*, 1856.

ii. **Jesu, deine Passion.** [*Passiontide.*] His finest hymn, 1st pub. in Saubert's *G. B.* Nürnberg, 1676, No. 83, in 6 st. of 8 l., and included as No. 240 in the Berlin *G. L. S.* ed., 1863. It did not appear in 1653. *Tr.* as :—

Jesu! be Thy suffering love. A good *tr.* of st. i.–iv., by A. T. Russell, as No. 87 in his *Ps. and Hys.*, 1851. Another *tr.* is :—

"Jesus, on Thy dying love," by W. Reid, in the *British Herald*, March, 1865, p. 46, repeated in his *Praise Bk.*, 1872, No. 435.

iii. **Lasset uns mit Jesu ziehen.** [*Passiontide.*] 1st pub. in J. M. Dilherr's *Heilige Karwochen*, Nürnberg, 1653, p. 412, in 4 st. of 8 l. Included as No. 250 in the Berlin *G. L. S.*, ed. 1863. The only *tr.* in C. U. is :—

Let us hence, on high ascending. Good and full, by A. T. Russell, as No. 184 in his *Ps. & Hys.*, 1851. His *trs.* of st. iii., iv., were adopted and altered to "Let us now with Christ be dying," as No. 635 in *Kennedy*, 1863.   [J. M.]

Birks, Edward Bickersteth, M.A., s. of Professor T. R. Birks, b. at Kelshall, Herts, in 1849, and educated at Cholmeley School, Highgate, and Trinity College, Cambridge (B.A. 1870, M.A. 1873, and also a Fellowship 1870). On taking Holy Orders, he became, in 1878, Curate of St. Mary's, Nottingham, and, after six months at Greenwich, in 1880, Vicar of Trumpington in 1881, and Vicar of St. Michael's, Cambridge, in 1884. Mr. Birks is the author of the metrical Litany, "Light that from the dark abyss," in the *H. Comp.*, 1876. It first appeared in *Evening Hours* in 1871 (having been composed in 1869 or 1870). Others of his pieces are to be found in *Leaves from the Christian Remembrancer*.

Birks, Thomas Rawson, M.A., b. Sept. 1810, and educated at Trinity College, Cambridge (B.A. 1834, M.A. 1837), of which he subsequently became a Fellow. Having taken Holy Orders in 1837, he became Rector of Kelshall, Herts, 1844; Vicar of Holy Trinity, Cambridge, 1866; Hon. Canon of Ely Cathedral, 1871; and Professor of Moral Philosophy, Cambridge, 1872. He d. at Cambridge, July 21, 1883. His works, to the number of 25, include Biblical, Astronomical, Scientific, Prophetic, and other subjects. He also wrote the *Memoirs of the Rev. E. Bickersteth* (his father-in-law), 2 vols., 1851. His hymns appeared in Bickersteth's *Christian Psalmody*, 1833; and, together with Versions of the Psalms, in his *Companion Psalter*, 1874. They number upwards of 100. [**Eng. Psalters, § xx.**] Very few are in C. U. in G. Britain, but in America their use is extending. They include:—

1. Except the Lord do build the house. *Ps. cxxvii.*
2. O come, let us sing to the Lord. *Ps. xcv.*
3. O King of Mercy, from Thy throne on high. *Ps. lxxx.*
4. O taste and see that He is good. *Ps. xxxiv.*
5. O when from all the ends of earth. *Ps. xiv.*
6. The heavens declare Thy glory. *Ps. xix.*
7. The Lord Himself my Portion is. *Ps. liii.*
8. The mighty God, the Lord hath spoken. *Ps. l.*
9. Thou art gone up on high, O Christ, &c. *Ps. xlvii.*
10. Whom have I [we] Lord in heaven, but Thee. *Ps. lxxiii.*

Of these versions of the Psalms, all of which date from 1874, the most popular is No. 3. Mr. Birks's compositions are worthy of greater attention than they have hitherto received.

[J. J.]

Bis ternas horas explicans. [*For the Sixth Hour.*] This hymn is in *Daniel*, i., No. 16, with a further note at iv. p. 13. *Daniel*, on the authority of Cassiodorus's commentary on Ps. cxix. 164, gives it as by St. Ambrose. *Daniel's* text is in 32 lines, of which he says, ll. 23–28, beginning "Orabo mente Dominum," are given by the Benedictine editors as a complete hymn of St. Ambrose. He cites it as in the *Hymnary* of Thomasius, and as in an 8th cent. ms. in the Vatican. *Tr.* as "Now twice three hours the sun hath told," by W. J. Copeland, in his *Hys. for the Week*, &c., 1848, p. 148. [J. M.]

Blackall, Christopher Ruby, M.D., b. in New York State, 1830, and educated for the medical profession. For 15 years he followed his profession, including service in the army during the civil war. Subsequently he managed, for 14 years, a branch of the Baptist Publication Society, taking at the same time great interest in S. School work. He edited the *Advanced Bible Lesson Quarterly*, for 3 years, and also *Our Little Ones*.

1. **The prize is set before us.** *Heaven anticipated.* This is one of Dr. Blackall's most popular hymns for children. It was written in 1874 for the Sunday School of 2nd Baptist Church, Chicago, Illinois, and set to music by H. R. Palmer. It 1st appeared in Palmer's *Songs of Love for the Bible School*, 1874, from whence it has passed into numerous collections, including I. D. Sankey's *S. S. and Solos*, Lond., 1881.

2. **Follow the paths of Jesus.** *Following Jesus.* This is included in the *Bap. Hy.* [*& Tune*] *Bk.*, Phila., 1871, No. 701.

3. **Do the right, never fear.** *Duty.* In W. R. Stevenson's *School Hymnal*, Lond., 1880, No. 269.

[J. J.]

Blackie, John Stuart, LL.D., b. at Glasgow, July, 1809, and educated at Marischal College, Aberdeen, and at the University of Edinburgh. After a residence on the Continent for educational purposes, he was called to the Bar in 1834. In 1841, he was appointed Professor of Latin in Marischal College, Aberdeen, and in 1850 Professor of Greek in the University of Edinburgh. On the death of Dr. Guthrie he was for some time the Editor of the *Sunday Magazine*. His published works include:—*A Metrical Translation of Æschylus*,

1850; *Pronunciation of Greek*, 1852; *Lyrical Poems*, 1860; *Homer and the Iliad*, 4 vols., 1869, &c.; *Lays and Legends of Ancient Greece*, &c., 1857; and *Songs of Religion and Life*, 1876. To the hymnological student he is known by his rendering of a portion of the *Benedicite* (q. v.), "Angels, holy, high and lowly," which is found in several hymnals.

Blacklock, Thomas, D.D., b. at Annan, Dumfriesshire, November 10, 1721. He studied at the University of Edinburgh, and was, in 1759, licensed to preach. In 1762 he was ordained parish minister of Kirkcudbright, but, on account of his blindness, had to resign and retire on an annuity. He went to Edinburgh and there received as boarders University students and boys attending school. In 1767 he received the degree of D.D. from the University of Aberdeen (Marischal College). He was one of the earliest and most helpful literary friends of Robert Burns. He d. at Edinburgh, July 7, 1791. His *Poems* were often printed —in 1756 at London, with a *Memoir* by the Rev. Joseph Spence, Professor of Poetry at Oxford; in 1793, at Edinburgh, with a *Memoir* by Henry Mackenzie, &c. They include 2 Psalm Versions, and 4 Hymns. "Hail, source of pleasures ever new," is altered from the Hymn to Benevolence, and " Father of all, omniscient mind," is from his version of Psalm 139. No. 16 in the *Trans. and Par.* of 1781, "In life's gay morn," &c., is also ascribed to him. [J. M.]

Blackmore, Sir Richard, was appointed a Physician in Ordinary to William of Orange in 1697, receiving knighthood at the same time in recognition of his services at the Revolution. His works embraced theology, medicine, and poetry, and a *Version of the Book of Psalms*. [**Eng. Psalters, § xvi.**] Whilst Dryden and Pope sneered at his poetical works, Addison (*Spectator*, 339), and Johnson (*Lives of the Poets*) gave them a good word, and specially his poem on the *Creation*. He d. October 9, 1729.

His version of the *Psalms* was the last issued in England with royal license for use in Churches; but notwithstanding this it never obtained any circulation, and except as to a few psalms in Collyer's *Sel.*, 1812, and one or two others, and various Unitarian collections in the early part of this century, it has remained utterly neglected by editors of all schools of thought.

Blair, Hugh, D.D., eldest s. of John Blair, merchant, Edinburgh, was b. at Edinburgh, April 7, 1718. In 1730 he entered the University of Edinburgh, where he graduated M.A. in 1739. In 1742 he was ordained parish minister of Collessie, in Fife, became, in 1743, second minister of the Canongate, Edinburgh, in 1754 minister of Lady Yester's, and in 1758 joint minister of the High Church (now styled St. Giles's Cathedral). In 1762, while still retaining his pastoral charge, he was appointed the first Professor of Rhetoric in the University of Edinburgh—a chair founded for him. He received the degree of D.D. from the University of St. Andrews, in 1757. He d. in Edinburgh, Dec. 27, 1800.

In 1744 Dr. Blair was appointed a member of the Committee of Assembly which compiled the *Trs. and Pars.* of 1745, and in 1775 of that which revised and enlarged them. To him are ascribed by the Rev. W. Thomson and the Rev. Dr. Hew Scott (*Scottish Hymnody*, Appendix) Nos. 4, 33, 34, 44, of the 1781 collection. He is also credited with the alterations made on Paraphrases 32 and 57, in 1745–51, and on Paraphrase 20, in 1781. The Rev. J. W. Macmeeken (Scottish Hymnody, Appendix) would ascribe these 4 Paraphrases to his second cousin, the *Rev. Robert Blair*, author of *The Grave* [eldest s. of the Rev. David Blair, b. in Edinburgh, 1699, ordained Parish minister of Athelstaneford, East Lothian, in 1731, appointed, in 1742, a member of the Committee which compiled the 1745 collection, d. at Athelstaneford, Feb. 4, 1746]. Dr. C. Rogers, in his *Lyra Brit.* (pp. 66 & 664, ed. 1867) holds that, though Dr. Hugh Blair may have altered Paraphrases 44 and 57, neither he, nor Robert Blair, wrote *any original* hymns. While the weight of opinion and of probability is in favour of Dr. Hugh Blair, no very definite evidence is presented on either side, though the records of the Presbytery of Edinburgh in 1748 show Dr. Hugh Blair as selected to revise Nos. 18 (7 in 1781), 21 (46 in 1781), and probably others [Scottish Paraphrases, W. Cameron, and notes on the individual hymns].   [J. M.]

Blair, Robert. [Blair, Hugh.]

Blair, William, D.D., b. at Clunie, Kinglassie, Fife, Jan. 13, 1830, and educated at Path-head School and St. Andrew's University, where he graduated M.A. in 1850, D.D. 1879. In 1856 he was ordained at Dunblane, as the United Presbyterian Minister in that town. Dr. Blair has pub. several prose works, including *Chronicles of Aberbrothoc*, and *Selections from Abp. Leighton with Memoir and Notes*, 1883. His hymn, "Jesu, Saviour, Shepherd bringing" (*The Good Shepherd*), and its accompanying tune, "Leighton," were contributed to the Scottish *Presb. Hymnal for the Young*, 1882. He is also the author of several New Year's hymns.

Blatchford, Ambrose Nichols, B.A., b. at Plymouth, 1842, and educated for the Unitarian Ministry at Manchester New College, London. He also graduated at the London University as B.A. In 1866 he became junior colleague to the late Rev. William James, Minister of Lewin's Mead Meeting, Bristol, and on the death of Mr. James, in 1876, the sole pastor. Mr. Blatchford's hymns were written for the S. School anniversary services at Lewin's Mead Meeting, on the dates given below, and were adapted to existing melodies. They were first printed as fly-leaves and include :—

1. A gladsome hymn of praise we sing. *Praise.* 1876.
2. Awake to the duty, prepare for the strife. *Duty.* 1878.
3. Lord, without Thy constant blessing. *Divine Help.* 1875.
4. Night clouds around us silently are stealing. *Evening.* 1878.
5. O Lord of Life, for all Thy care. *Praise.* 1875.
6. O'er the wide and restless ocean. *Life & Hope.* 1878.
7. Once more the shadows fall. *Evening.* 1880.
8. Softly the silent night. *Evening.* 1875.

Nos. 1, 2, 4, 5, and 6 were 1st pub. in W. R. Stevenson's *School Hymnal*, 1880, and Nos. 3, 7. and 8 in the *Sunday School H. Bk.* of the S. S. Association, Lond., 1881.   [J. J.]

Blaurer, Ambrosius, s. of Augustine Blaurer, Councillor of Constanz, was b. at Constanz, April 4, 1492. In 1513 he graduated at Tübingen and entered the convent of Alpirsbach, in the Black Forest, where he was chosen Prior. After studying Holy Scripture and the writings of Luther, he became dissatisfied with his position and left the convent in 1522, and went to Constanz. In 1523 he openly espoused the cause of the Reformation, and began to preach in 1525. In 1529 he commenced his work as Reformer of Swabia, in which, after the restoration of Duke Ulrich,

1534, he received his help and countenance till 1538, when the growing opposition of the Lutheran party led him to withdraw from Württemberg. He returned to Constanz, where he remained till 1548, when by the operation of the Interim [Agricola] and the seizure of the town by the Emperor, he was forced to flee to Griessenberg, in Thurgau, and in the end of 1549, to Winterthur. He became pastor at Biel, in the Jura, 1551, but returned to Winterthur, 1559, and d. there, Dec. 6, 1564 (*Koch*, ii. 62–76; *Allg. Deutsche Biog.*, ii. 691–693). *Koch* characterises him as the most important of the hymn-writers of the Reformed Church at the time of the Reformation. Some thirty in all of his hymns are preserved in MS. at Zürich and Winterthur. The only one *tr.* into English is :—

Wie's Gott gefällt, so gfällts mirs auch. [*Trust in God.*] *Wackernagel*, iii. p. 548, quotes it in 8 st. of 10 l. from a MS. of 1562 at Zürich, "Etlich geistliche gsang und lieder vor jahren geschriben durch meister Ambrosium Blaurern," and thinks it was probably written about 1526. In his *Bibliographie*, 1855, p. 220, he had cited a broadsheet, c. 1548, where it appears as one of "Zwey schöne Newe Lieder dess frommen Johansen Friderichen von Sachsen, welche Er in seiner Gefängkniss gedichtet hat" [i. e. 1547–52, after the battle of Mühlberg, 1547]; but this ascription *Wackernagel* thinks is as little justified by the personality as by the circumstances of the Elector. Though the authorship of the hymn be somewhat doubtful, its value is undeniable, and since its reception into the *Bergkreyen*, Nürnberg, 1551, it has appeared in most subsequent collections, and in No. 726 in the *Unv. L. S.*, 1851. The *trs.* are :—(1) "God's will is mine: I dare not stray," by *Dr. G. Walker*, 1860, p. 91. (2) "What pleaseth God, that pleaseth me," by *Miss Winkworth*, 1869, p. 124.   [J. M.]

Bleak winter is subdued at length. *J. Newton.* [*Spring.*] 1st pub. in the *Olney Hymns*. 1779, Bk. ii., No. 32, in 9 st. of 4 l. In its full form it is not in C. U., but an unaltered version of st. ii.–v. and ix. is given as: "Behold! long-wished for spring is come," in Rippon's *Sel.*, 1787, and later editions.

Bleibt bei dem, der euretwillen. *C. J. P. Spitta.* [*Following Christ.*] Founded on 1 John, ii. 28, and 1st pub. in the 1st Series, 1833, of his *Psalter und Harfe*, p. 113, in 4 st. of 8 l., entitled "Abide in Jesus." In the Württemberg *G. B.*, 1842, No. 382, and other collections. The *trs.* in C. U. are :—

1. **O abide, abide in Jesus.** A full and good *tr.* by R. Massie in his *Lyra Dom.*, 1860, p. 108, and thence in Bp. Ryle's *Coll.*, 1860; Adams's American *Ch. Pastorals*, 1864, No. 891, and Schaff's *Christ in Song*, ed. 1879, p. 495. Omitting st. ii. in the *Meth. N. Con. H. Bk.*, 1863, and J. L. Porter's *Coll.*, 1876. St. ii.–iv., beginning, "All is dying! hearts are breaking," are included in Robinson's *Songs for the Sanctuary*, N. Y., 1865; *H. and Songs of Praise*, N. Y., 1874; *Bap. Praise Bk.*, 1871, and others.

2. **O abide in Him, Who for us.** A full *tr.* by J. D. Burns, in his *Memoir and Remains*, 1869, p. 259; and repeated as No. 747 in Dale's *English H. Bk.*, 1874.

Other *trs.* are :—
(1) "Stay by One Who for your comfort," by *Miss Manington*, 1863, p. 53. (2) "Dwell in Christ, who once descended," by J. Kelly, 1885, p 37.   [J. M.]

Blenkinsopp, E. C. L. [Leaton-Blenkinsopp.]

Bless God, my soul: Thou, Lord

alone. *N. Tate.* [*Ps. civ.*] This version of Ps. civ. is found in Tate's *Miscellanea Sacra*, 1696, and in the same year in the *New Version.* Its appearance in the former work determines its authorship as distinct from Brady. [See **Eng. Psalters**, § XIII. 3.] From its ornate character some have concluded that most, if not all the renderings in the *New Version* which partake of that character, are by him. This conclusion is plausible and possible, but by no means certain. It was introduced into use in America early in the present century, and is still given in a few collections.

Bless, O my soul, the living God. *I. Watts.* [*Ps. ciii.*] This is Pt. i. of his L. M. version of Ps. ciii., 1st pub. in his *Psalms of David*, &c., 1719, Pt. ii. being, "The Lord, how wondrous are His ways." Both parts are in C. U. both in G. Britain and America. Pt. i. is in 8 st., and Pt. ii. in 9 st. of 4 l. In addition there are abbreviations of Pt. i., and a cento from Pts. i. and ii. in C. U. The most popular arrangement in modern American hymnals is that in *Songs for the Sanctuary*, N. Y., 1865, *Laudes Domini*, N. Y., 1884, and many others. It is composed of st. i., ii., iii., and viii., slightly altered. Other arrangements are also found both in G. Britain and America. A cento from Pts. i. and ii. appeared in Bickersteth's *Christian Psalmody*, 1833, and is made up of Pt. i. st. i.–iii., Pt. ii. st. iv. and v., and an additional stanza from another source.

Bless'd, Blessed, Blest. The arbitrary, and, in many instances, unreasonable, way in which editors of hymnals, both old and new, have changed about these words, without any regard to the form originally used by the author, has rendered it necessary to follow the author's reading in every instance. When, therefore, a hymn cannot be found in one form, it must be sought for in the other.

Bless'd are the humble souls that see. *I. Watts.* [*The Beatitudes.*] This metrical paraphrase of the Beatitudes (St. Matt. v. 3–12) appeared in the enlarged ed. of his *Hymns & S. Songs*, 1709, Bk. i., No. 102, in 8 st. of 4 l. It held a prominent position in the older collections, but of late it has fallen very much out of favour. As "Bless'd are," "Blessed are," or "Blest are," it is still found in a few collections both in G. Britain and America.

Bless'd are the pure in heart. *J. Keble.* [*Purification.*] This poem, in 17 st. of 4 l., is dated "Oct. 10, 1819." It was 1st pub. in his *Christian Year*, 1827. As a whole it is not in C. U. The following centos, some of which are found in numerous collections, have been compiled therefrom :—

1. In J. Bickersteth's *Ps. & Hys.*, 1832, No. 449, we have st. i. and xvii. This was repeated in Elliott's *Ps. & Hys.*, 1835, No. 258, as "*Blest* are the pure," &c. Although it has fallen out of use in G. Britain, it is still given in a few American collections, as the Amer. Meth. Epis. *Hymns*, 1849; *The Evang. Hymnal*, N. Y., 1880.

2. In his *Mitre H. Bk.*, 1836, W. J. Hall pub. a cento, as No. 249, which was composed of two stanzas from this poem, and two that were new. By whom this cento was arranged, by Hall, or his collaborator, E. Osler, is not known, as the H. MSS. simply say "Keble." As this is the most popular cento, and its whole contents are usually attributed to Keble, we give the full text, with the alterations and additions in the *Mitre* in italics :—

"*Blest* are the pure in heart,
For they shall see *their* God :
The secret of the Lord is theirs ;
Their soul is Christ's abode.

*The Lord, who left the sky,
Our life and peace to bring,
And dwelt in lowliness with men,
Their pattern, and their King ;*

Still to the lowly soul
He doth Himself im**part**,
And for His dwelling, and His throne,
Chooseth the pure in heart.

*Lord, we Thy presence seek ;
Ours may this blessing be!
O give the pure and lowly heart
A temple meet for Thee.*"

In Murray's *Hymnal*, 1852, No. 122, this cento was repeated with slight alterations, and the addition of a doxology. This text, sometimes with, and again without a doxology, has been adopted by most of the leading hymnals in G. Britain, and a few in America, including *H. A. & M.*; the *Hymnary*; *Church Hymns*; the *H. Comp.*; *Thring*; the *Bap. Hymnal*; the American *Sabbath H. Bk.*, N. Y., 1858, and others. In a note to this cento, No. 141, in the 1st ed. of *H. A. & M.*, Mr. Biggs, in his *Annotated H. A. & M.*, quotes these words from Keble: "Hymn No. 141 is materially altered ; not, however, without asking the writer's leave, *Rev. J. Keble.*" Whether this *leave* was given to Hall, in the first instance, in 1836, or to Mr. Murray on adopting Hall's text in 1852, cannot now be determined.

3. In several American collections, Hall's cento is repeated with the omission of st. ii. These include *Songs for the Sanctuary*, N. Y., 1865.

4. In the *Hys. for Christian Seasons*, Gainsburgh, 2nd ed., 1854, the cento is, st. i.–iv. are Keble's st. i., xii., xiv. and xvii. very much altered, and v. Hall, st. iv.

5. In Alford's *Year of Praise*, 1867, No. 251, the cento is Keble, st. i., ii., iii., xv., and xvii.

6. In Nicholson's *Appendix Hymnal*, 1866, st. iv., viii.–x. are given as No. 19, beginning, "Give ear, ye kings, bow down."

In addition to these, other arrangements are sometimes found, but are not of sufficient importance to be enumerated.   [J. J.]

Bless'd be the everlasting God. *I. Watts.* [*Easter.*] 1st pub. in his *Hymns*, &c., 1707, Bk. i., No. 26, in 5 st. of 4 l., and entitled "Hope of Heaven by the Resurrection of Christ." Its use sometimes as "Blessed," and again as "Blest," &c., is not extensive. Orig. text in Spurgeon's *O. O. H. Bk.*, No. 841.

In the Draft Scottish *Trans. & Paraphs.*, 1745, it is given as No. xl. in an unaltered form. In the authorized issue of the *Trans.*, &c., in 1781, No. lxi. st. iii. was omitted, the third stanza in this arrangement being altered from the original, which reads in Watts :—

"There's an inheritance divine,
Reserv'd against that day ;

'Tis uncorrupted, undefil'd,
And cannot fade away."

The recast text of 1781, which has been in use in the Church of Scotland for 100 years, is claimed by *W. Cameron* (q. v.), in his list of authors and revisers of that issue, as his own. Full text in modern copies of the Scottish *Psalms*, &c.   [J. J.]

Bless'd morning! whose young, dawning rays. *I. Watts.* [*Sunday— Easter.*] Appeared in his *Hymns*, &c., 1707 (1709, Bk. ii., No. 72), in 5 st. of 4 l., and entitled, "The Lord's Day : or, The Resurrection of Christ." The arrangements of this hymn in C. U. are :—

(1.) The original. Very limited.

(2.) "Blessed morning," &c., as in Dr. Hatfield's Amer. *Church H. Bk.*, N. Y., 1872, with the change in st. i., l. 4, of "last abode," to "*dark* abode."

(3.) "Blest morning," &c. This opening, sometimes followed by two or three slight alterations and the omission of st. v., is the most popular form of the text both in G. Britain and America.

(4.) "Blest morning," &c., in the *Hymnary*, 1872, No. 13. This is very considerably altered.

In addition to these, in 1781, this hymn was added with alterations, as "Hymn IV.," to the Scottish *Trans. & Paraphs.* It opens "Blest morning! Whose *first* dawning rays." The author of this recast is unknown.

Bless'd with the presence of their God. *T. Cotterill.* [*Holy Communion.*] 1st pub. in the *Uttoxeter Sel.* 1805, No. 31, in 6 st. of 4 l., and headed "For the Sacrament." It was repeated in Cotterill's *Sel.* 1810, No. 43, and continued in subsequent editions till the 9th, 1820, when it was omitted. St. iv., "The vile, the lost, He calls to them." is st. iii. of W. Cowper's hymn· "This is the feast of heavenly wine," from the *Olney Hymns*, 1779, Bk. ii., No. 53. The use of this hymn is not extensive, although found in a few modern collections. It is curious that Cotterill gives it as "*Blest* with," &c., in his index, but "*Bless'd* with," &c., in the body of the book. A cento from this hymn beginning, "In memory of the Saviour's love," appeared in R. Whittingham's *Coll.*, 1st ed., Potton, 1835; from thence it passed into Lord Selborne's *Bk. of Praise*, 1862, Stevenson's *Hys. for Ch. & Home*, 1873, and others. It is composed of st. iii., v., and vi. of the above very slightly altered.

Blessed are the sons of God. *J. Humphreys.* [*Christian Privileges.*] This is the first of six hymns added by J. Cennick to Pt. ii. of his *Sacred Hymns for the Use of Religious Societies*, Bristol, F. Farley, 1743, No. 72, p. 95. It is in 8 st. of 4 l., and is headed, "The Priviledges of God's Children." Concerning these six hymns J. Cennick says, "These were done by Mr. Joseph Humphreys." In Whitefield's *Coll.*, 1753, it was given as No. 14 in that part of the collection devoted to "Hymns for Society, and Persons meeting in Christian-Fellowship." As shortly after this date it fell out of use in its original form, and the text is somewhat difficult to find, we give the same in full:—

"Blessed are the Sons of God.	"They are Lights upon the Earth,
They are bought with Christ's own Blood,	Children of a heav'nly Birth;
They are ransomed from the Grave,	Born of God, they hate all Sin,
Life eternal they shall have.	God's pure Seed remains within.
"God did love them in his Son,	"They have Fellowship with God,
Long before the World begun;	Thro' the Mediator's Blood;
They the seal of this receive	One with God, with Jesus one,
When on Jesus they believe.	Glory is in them begun.
"They are justified by Grace,	"Tho' they suffer much on Earth,
They enjoy a solid Peace;	Strangers quite to this World's Birth,
All their Sins are wash'd away;	Yet they have an inward joy,
They shall stand in God's great Day.	Pleasure which can never cloy.
"They produce the Fruits of Grace,	"They alone are truly blest,
In the Works of Righteousness!	Heirs of God, joint Heirs with Christ;
They are harmless, meek, and mild,	With them number'd may I.be,
Holy, humble, undefil'd.	Here and in Eternity!"

The Rev. R. Conyers pub. in his *Coll.*

of *Ps. & Hys.*, 1st ed., 1767, as No. 84, the above hymn in a new form. Dealing with the hymn as an unbroken poem of 32 lines, he took the first 6 lines, added thereto the last lines of the hymn as altered by Whitefield ("With them," &c.) as a refrain, and constituted them as st. i.; the next 6 lines, with the same refrain as st. ii., and so on to the end, thus producing a hymn of 5 st. of 8 l. Toplady, in his *Ps. & Hys.*, 1776, No. 116, adopted Conyers's idea of using the last two lines of the hymn as a refrain, by adding them to Humphreys's st. i.-iv., vi., and v., in the order named, and thereby producing a hymn of 6 st. of 6 l. It is to this arrangement of the text that most modern editors both in G. Britain and America are indebted for their centos. Portions of the hymn in centos of varying lengths, are in extensive use.   [J. J.]

Blessed are they whose hearts are pure. *H. Alford.* [*St. Bartholomew.*] In Alford's *Poems*, 1868, this hymn is dated 1844. It is not in his *Ps. & Hymns* of that year. It is found in T. M. Fallow's *Sel.*, 1847. In 1852 it was repeated in *The English Hymnal*, in 1867 in Alford's *Year of Praise*, and again in other collections. In the Cooke and Denton *Hymnal*, 1853, it appears in the Index as "Blessed," &c.; but in the body of the book, No. 175, it begins, "How bless'd are they," &c. In some hymnals, both in G. Britain and America, it is attributed to "J. Conder."

                     [W. T. B.]

Blessed be Thy Name. *J. Montgomery.* [*Journeying.*] In the "M. MSS," this hymn is dated "January 13th, 1835," and is there stated to have been sent in MS. to several persons at different dates. In 1853 it was given in Montgomery's *Original Hymns*, No. 194, in 5 st. of 6 l. and headed, "Prayers on Pilgrimage.—'Lord, help me.' Matt. xv. 25." Adopted by several collections.

Blessed night, when first that plain. *H. Bonar.* [*Christmas.*] Pub. in his *Hys. of Faith & Hope*, 1st series, 1857, in 34 st. of 3 l., and headed, "The Shepherds' Plain." In the Irish *Church Hymnal*, 1873, two centos are given from this poem, (1) "Blessed night, when first that plain," and (2) "Mighty King of Righteousness"; and in Mrs. Brock's *Children's H. Bk.*, 1881, No. 72, a cento is given as "Blessed night, when *Bethlehem's* plain," with "Alleluia" as a refrain. No. 73, in the same *Coll.*, and in the same metre, "Hark, what music fills the sky," is attributed to Dr Bonar in error. It forms a good companion hymn to "Blessed night, when first that plain."

Blessed Redeemer, how divine. *I. Watts.* [*Divine Equity.*] A hymn on his sermon on St. Matt. vii. 12. It was pub. in an ed. after 1723, of his *Sermons on Various Subjects*, &c., 1721–3, in 6 st. of 4 l., and headed "The Universal law of Equity." In the older collections it is frequently found, especially the American, but in modern hymn-books it is seldom given, and then in an altered and abridged form.

Blessed Saviour, who hast taught me. *J. M. Neale.* [*Confirmation.*] Appeared in his *Hymns for the Young*, 1842 (new ed., 1860), in 6 st. of 8 l. In this form it is seldom if ever used. An abbreviated and altered text, as "Holy Father, Thou hast taught me," is found in some collections for children. It is compiled from st. i., iv., and v. and vi.

Blessing, honour, thanks, and praise. *C. Wesley.* [*Burial.*] 1st pub. in *Hymns and Sacred Poems*, 1742, in 5 st. of 8 l., as one of a number of "Funeral Hymns." In 1780 it was embodied in the *Wes. H. Bk.*, No. 49, from whence it has passed into numerous collections in G. Britain and America. Orig. text in the *Wes. H. Bk.*, 1875, No. 50, and in *P. Works*, 1868–72, vol. ii. p. 188. In the *Hymnary*, 1872, a cento, with the same first line, was given as No. 508, in 4 st. and was repeated in the S. P. C. K. *Church Hymns*, 1871. It is thus composed: st. i., ii. from the above, slightly altered; st. iii., iv. from the hymn, "Hark! a voice divides the sky," which follows the above, in the *Hymns and Sacred Poems*, 1742, the *Wes. H. Bk.*, and in the *P. Works*, vol. ii. p. 189. These stanzas are also altered from the original.

Blest are the souls that [who] hear and know. *I. Watts.* [*Ps. lxxxix.*] Pt. iii. of his C. M. rendering of Ps. 89, in 3 st. of 4 l., which appeared in his *Psalms of David*, &c., 1719, with the heading "The Blessed Gospel." Whitefield included it in his *Coll.* in 1753, No. 72; and Toplady in his *Ps. & Hys.*, 1776, No. 32. It thus came into general use, and is still found in numerous collections in G. Britain and America.

Blest be the dear uniting love. *C. Wesley.* [*Parting.*] Pub. in *Hys. & Sac. Poems*, 1742, p. 159, in 8 st. of 4 l., and again *P. Works*, 1868–72, vol. ii. p. 221. It was given in the *Wes. H. Bk.*, 1780, No. 520, with alterations, and the omission of st. v. and vi. This form of the hymn is in the revised ed., 1875, No. 534, and in most collections of the Methodist body. From Whitefield's *Coll.*, 1753, to the present it has also been in use amongst various denominations in one form or another, ranging from 5 stanzas in *White-field* to 3 stanzas as in several American collections. This hymn has been ascribed to J. Cennick in error.

Blest be the Lord, our Strength and Shield. *Anne Steele.* [*Ps. cxliv.*] Given in her *Poems*, &c., 1760, vol. ii. p. 240, in 14 st. of 4 l. (2nd ed., 1780), and in D. Sedgwick's ed. of her *Hymns*, 1859, p. 200. In 1836 a cento therefrom, based on st. i., x., xiii., and xiv. (very much altered), was included in Hall's *Mitre H. Bk.* The same cento is given in the Islington *Ps. & Hys.* with the omission of st. iii. as in the *Mitre*.

Blest be [is] the tie that binds. *J. Fawcett.* [*Brotherly Love.*] Miller, in his *Singers and Songs of the Church*, 1869, p. 273, says :—

"This favourite hymn is said to have been written in 1772, to commemorate the determination of its author to remain with his attached people at Wainsgate. The farewell sermon was preached, the waggons were loaded, when love and tears prevailed, and Dr. Fawcett sacrificed the attractions of a London pulpit to the affection of his poor but devoted flock."

Three sources of information on the matter are, however, silent on the subject—his *Life and Letters*, 1818; his *Misc. Writings*, 1826;

and his *Funeral Sermon*. Failing direct evidence, the most that can be said is that internal evidence in the hymn itself lends countenance to the statement that it was composed under the circumstances given above. Its *certain* history begins with its publication in Fawcett's *Hymns*, &c., 1782, No. 104, where it is given in 6 st. of 4 l. From an early date it has been in C. U., especially with the Nonconformists, and at the present time it is found in a greater number of collections in G. Britain and America than almost any other hymn by Fawcett. It is usually given as "Blest *is* the tie," &c., and in an abridged form. Orig. text in Spurgeon's *O. O. H. Bk.*, 1866, No. 892, and *Songs for the Sanctuary*, N. Y., 1865, No. 847.   [J. J.]

Blest day of God, most calm, most bright. *J. Mason.* [*Sunday.*] 1st pub. in his *Songs of Praise*, 1683, as the second of two hymns entitled "A Song of Praise for the Lord's Day," in 6 st. of 8 l. and 1 st. of 4 l. Early in the present century centos from this "Song" of various lengths began to be introduced into the hymn-books of the Church of England, and later, into Nonconformists' hymnals also; but in scarcely a single instance do we find the same arrangement in any three collections. In modern hymn-books both in G. Britain and America, the same diversity prevails, no editor having yet succeeded in compiling a cento which others could approve and adopt. No collection can be trusted either for text or original sequence of lines. The full orig. text, however, is easily attainable in Sedgwick's reprint of the *S. of Praise*, 1859. The opening line sometimes reads :—"Blest day of God, *how* calm, *how* bright," as in Mrs. Brock's *Children's H. Bk.*, 1881, No. 40, but the use of this form of the text is limited. Taking the centos together, their use is extensive.   [J. J.]

Blest hour when mortal man retires. *T. Raffles.* [*Hour of Prayer.*] Printed in the *Amulet* for 1829, pp. 304–5, in 6 st. of 4 l. One of the first to adapt it to congregational use was the Rev. J. Bickersteth, who included 4 stanzas in his *Ps. and Hys.*, 1832, as No. 242. Its modern use in any form in G. Britain is almost unknown, but in America it is one of the most popular of Dr. Raffles's hymns, and is given in many of the leading collections. The full text is No. 883 in Dr. Hatfield's *Church H. Bk.*, N. Y., 1872. Dr. Hatfield dates the hymn 1828, probably because contributions to the *Amulet* of 1829 would be sent to the editor in 1828.

Blest is the faith, divine and strong. *F. W. Faber.* [*The Christian Life.*] Appeared in his *Oratory Hymns*, 1854, in 6 st. of 4 l., and the chorus, "O Sion's songs are sweet to sing." In the 1855 ed. of the Cooke & Denton *Hymnal*, it was given with alterations to adapt it for use in the Church of England. In this form it is in a limited number of collections, the original being retained in the Roman Catholic hymnals.

Blest is the man, for ever bless'd. *I. Watts.* [*Ps. xxxii.*] His L. M. rendering of Ps. xxxii., pub. in his *Psalms of David*, &c., 1719, in 4 st. of 4 l. Dr. Watts's note thereupon explains the liberty taken with the Psalm as follows :—

"These two first verses of this Psalm being cited by the Apostle in the 4th chapter of Romans, to shew the freedom of our pardon and justification by grace without works, I have, in this version of it, enlarged the sense, by mention of the Blood of Christ, and faith and Repentance; and because the Psalmist adds. *A spirit in which is no guile*, I have inserted that sincere obedience, which is scriptural evidence of our faith and justification."

As a hymn in C. U. in G. Britain it has almost died out; but in America it still survives in a few collections.

Blest is the man, supremely blest. *C. Wesley.* [*Ps. xxxii.*] 1st pub. in the Wesley *Psalms & Hymns*, 1743, as a version of Ps. xxxii. in 9 st. of 8 l. In 1875 it was rearranged and included in the revised ed. of the *Wes. H. Bk.* as hymn 561 in two parts, Pt. ii. being, "Thou art my hiding place, In Thee" (*P. Works*, 1868–72, vol. viii. p. 65).

Blest is the man who feels. *W. H. Bathurst.* [*Ps. xciv.*] Appeared in his *Ps. and Hys.*, 1831, in 4 st. of 6 l., and begins with the 12th verse of the Psalm. By whom the effort was made to add thereto the former part of the Psalm, we cannot say; but the result is the following paraphrase :—"O Lord, with vengeance clad," found in the *Wes. H. Bk.*, 1875, No. 602, in which st. i. is almost entirely new, and the rest is from this hymn.

Blest is the man whose bowels move. *I. Watts.* [*Ps. xli.*] This L. M. version of Ps. xlii., st. 1–3, which was pub. in his *Psalms of David, &c.*, 1719, in 4 st. of 4 l., appears in some collections as "Blest is the man whose *mercies* move;" and in others, "Blest is the man whose *heart doth* move," the object being to get rid of the to, some, objectionable expression in the first line. These changes are adopted both in G. Britain and in America.

Blest is the man whose heart expands. *J. Straphan.* [*For Sunday Schools.*] 1st pub. in Rippon's *Sel.*, 1787, No. 523, in 6 st. of 4 l. The form in which it usually appears in 4 stanzas was included by Cotterill in his *Sel.*, 1819, No. 248, where it is appointed to be sung "At a Sermon for Charity Schools." A cento from this hymn, "Blest work, the youthful mind to win," is composed of st. v., iv., iii., and vi. considerably altered. It is found in this form in Baldwin's Preston *Sel. of Ps. & Hys.*, 1831, No. 21, and has been frequently repeated in later collections. A second cento, beginning with an alteration of st. iii., as "Blest is the work in wisdom's ways," has also come into use. In these varying forms this hymn, has attained to an extensive circulation.

Blest Jesus, Source of grace divine. *P. Doddridge.* [*The Water of Life.*] This hymn is No. 88 in the D. MSS., where it is undated. In J. Orton's ed. of Doddridge's (posthumous) *Hymns, &c.*, 1755, No. 221, it is given in 4 st. of 4 l., with a text slightly differing from the D. MSS. It is also in J. D. Humphreys's ed. of the same, 1839. Its most popular form is that given to it early in the century in some American Unitarian collections :—"Blest *Spirit*, Source of grace divine." In this form it is in the Unitarian *Hy.* [*and T.*] *Bk.*, Boston, 1868, and other hymnals.

Blest Saviour, when the fearful storms. [*Lent.*] This appeared under the signature of "M. H. W.," in Emma Parr's *Thoughts of Peace*, Lond., 1839, in 3 st. of 8 l. In 1863 it was included in *Kennedy*, as No. 427, in the slightly altered form of "O Saviour, when the fearful storms."

Blest season when our risen Lord. [*Whitsuntide.*] This hymn is No. 59 of J. H. Stewart's *Sel. of Ps. & Hys. for the Use of Percy Chapel*, Lond., 1813, in 5 st. of 4 l., where it is appointed for Monday in Whitsun-week. In common with all the hymns in the collection it is unsigned. In 1829 Josiah Pratt included st. i., ii., and iv., with slight alterations, in his *Ps. and Hys.*, No. 66. This was repeated in some American collections, and is known to modern hymnals as " Blest day when our ascended Lord," as in the *Songs for the Sanctuary*, N. Y., 1865, No. 412. [W. T. B.]

Blest truth, my soul and Christ are one. *J. Irons.* [*Final Perseverance.*] 1st pub. in the 3rd ed. of his *Zion's Hymns*, 1825, p. 173, in 5 st. of 4 l. In the later editions of that work he altered the opening line to :—"Blest truth, *the Church* and Christ are one." In this form, with slight alterations it is given in Snepp's *S. of G. & G.*, 1872, No 419, and one or two collections besides.

Blest voice of love! O Word Divine. *W. J. Irons.* [*Confirmation.*] Written at Brompton on the occasion of the confirmation of one of the writer's children, and pub. in *Hymns for the Christian Seasons*, Gainsburgh, 1st ed., 1854, No. 184, in 4 st. of 6 l. In 1861 it was also given in Dr. Irons's *App. to the Brompton Metrical Psalter* ; his *Hymns*, 1866 ; and in a revised form in his *Ps. & Hys.* 1873. In Thring's *Coll.*, 1882, the revised text of 1873 is adopted.

Blew, William John, M.A., s. of William Blew, b. April 13, 1808, and educated at Great Ealing School, and Wadham Coll., Oxford, where he graduated B.A. in 1830, and M.A., 1832. On taking Holy Orders, Mr. Blew was Curate of Nuthurst and Cocking, and St. Anne's, Westminster, and for a time Incumbent of St. John's next Gravesend. Besides *trs.* from Homer (*Iliad*, bks. i., ii., &c.) and Æschylus (*Agamemnon the King*), and works on the Book of Common Prayer, including a paraphrase on a *tr.* of the same in Latin, he edited the *Breviarium Aberdonense*, 1854; and pub. a pamphlet on *Hymns and Hymn Books*, 1858 ; and (with Dr. H. J. Gauntlett) *The Church Hymn and Tune Book*, 1852, 2nd ed., 1855. The hymns in this last work are chiefly translations by Mr. Blew of Latin hymns. They were written from 1845 to 1852, and printed on fly-sheets for the use of his congregation. Many of these *trs.* have come into C. U. The following original hymns were also contributed by him to the same work :—

1. Christ in the Father's glory bright. *Morning.*
2. God's ark is in the field. *Evening.* The second stanza of this hymn is from Bp. Cosin's *Hours*, in his *Coll. of Private Devotions*, 1627.
3. Hark, through the dewy morning. *Morning.*
4. Lord of the golden day. *Evening.*
5. O Lord, Thy wing outspread. *Whitsuntide.*
6. O Thou, Who on Thy sainted quire. *Whitsuntide.*
7. Sleeper, awake, arise. *Epiphany.*
8. Sweet Babe, that wrapt in twilight. *Epiphany.*

9. Ye crowned kings, approach ye. *Epiphany.* This is written to the tune, " Adeste fideles," and might easily be mistaken as a free *tr.* of the " Adeste."

Mr. Blew has also translated *The Altar Service of the Church of England, in the year* 1548, into English. His *trs.* are terse, vigorous, musical, and of great merit. They have been strangely overlooked by the compilers of recent hymn-books. He d. Dec. 27, 1894.   [J. J.]

Blick aus diesem Erdenthale. *Albert Knapp.* [*Ascension.*] Written 1851, and included in his *Herbstblüthen*, Stuttgart, 1859, p. 152, in 8 st. of 8 l., repeated in his *Ev. L. S.*, 1865, No. 657. It has been *tr.* as :—

Looking from this vale of sadness. A good but free *tr.* by Miss Burlingham in the *British Herald*, Sept. 1865, p. 142, and repeated, as No. 377, in Reid's *Praise Bk.*, 1872. Stanzas vii., viii., beginning " Prince of Peace ! how rich our treasure !" also form No. 303 in the Eng. Presb. *Ps. & Hys.*, 1867.   [J. M.]

Bliss, Philip, b. at Clearfield County, Pennsylvania, July 9, 1838. In 1864 he went to Chicago in the employ of Dr. George F. Root, the musician, where he was engaged in conducting musical Institutes, and in compos-ing Sunday School melodies. Originally a Methodist, he became, about 1871, a choirman of the First Congregational Church, Chicago, and the Superintendent of its Sunday Schools. In 1874 he joined D. W. Whittle in evangelical work. To this cause he gave (although a poor man) the royalty of his *Gospel Songs*, which was worth some thirty thousand dollars. His death was sudden. It occurred in the railway disaster at Ashtabula, Ohio, Dec. 30, 1876. He had escaped from the car, but lost his life in trying to save his wife. His hymns are numerous. Some of his verses have obtained wide popularity in most English-speaking countries. The more widely known, and specially those which are found in collec-tions in use in G. Britain, are in the follow-ing American works :—

i. *The Prize*, 1870.

1. I should like to die. *Death anticipated.* This is one of his earliest compositions, and is unworthy of the position it holds.

2. Through the valley of the shadow I must go. *Death anticipated.*

3. Whosoever heareth, shout, shout the sound. *Jesus the Way.* Written during the winter of 1869–70 after hearing Mr. H. Moorhouse (from England) preach on St. John iii. 16.

ii. *The Charm*, 1871.

4. Almost persuaded now to believe. *Procrastina-tion.* This was suggested by the following passage in a sermon by the Rev. Mr. Brundage, Bliss being present at its delivery :—" He who is almost persuaded is almost saved, but to be almost saved is to be entirely lost."

5. Ho ! my comrades ! see the signal. *Faithfulness.*

6. O ! Jerusalem, the golden city, bright, &c. *Heaven.*

7. On what Foundation do [did] you build ! *Christ the Foundation.*

iii. *The Song Tree*, 1872.

8. Light in the darkness, sailor, day is at hand. *Safety.* This hymn. "The Life-Boat," has attained to great popularity. The incident upon which it is based, that of the rescue of a ship's crew by a life-boat, is given in detail by Mr. Sankey in his *Sacred Songs*, &c., No. 99 (large ed.). It is sometimes known by its re-frain, " Pull for the shore," &c.

iv. *The Joy*, 1873.

9. In me ye may have peace. *Peace.*

10. To die is gain. *Death anticipated.*

v. *Sunshine*, 1873.

11. Down life's dark vale we wander. *Death anti-cipated.*

12. More holiness give me. *For Holiness.*

13. Only an armour-bearer. *Soldiers of the Cross.*

14. Standing by a purpose true. *Faithfulness.*

15. This loving Saviour stands patiently. *Invi-tation.*

vi. *Gospel Songs*, 1874.

16. A long time I wandered. *Peace and Joy.*

17. Brightly beams our Father's mercy. *Mercy.*

18. Come, brethren, as we march along. *Praise.*

19. Free from the law, O happy condition. *Redemption.*

20. Have you on the Lord believed ! *Fulness of Grace.* This hymn arose out of the following circum-stances :—" A vast fortune was left in the hands of a minister for one of his poor parishioners. Fearing that it might be squandered if suddenly bestowed upon him, the wise minister sent him a little at a time, with a note saying, ' *This is thine ; use it wisely ; there is more to follow.*' Hence also the refrain ' More to fol-low,' by which the hymn is known."

21. How much owest thou ! *Divine Claims.*

22. I know not the hour when my Lord will come. *Death anticipated.* Suggested by reading the book, *The Gates Ajar.*

23. See the gentle Shepherd standing. *The Good Shepherd.*

24. Though the way be sometimes dreary. *Divine Leading.*

25. Will you meet me at the fountain ! *Fountain of Living Water.* The incident out of which this hymn arose is thus stated in *The Christian*, No. 365, " At the Industrial Exposition at Chicago it was an every-day appointment to meet at the Central Fountain. Mr. P. P. Bliss, whose mind seemed always set on things above, caught up the words, and wrote this hymn, ' Meet me at the Fountain.' "

vii. *Gospel Hymns, No.* 1, 1875.

26. One offer of salvation. *The Name of Jesus.*

27. Wandering afar from the dwellings of men. *The Lepers.*

viii. *The International Lessons Monthly*, 1875.

28. Weary gleaner, whence comest thou ! *Duty.*

29. The whole world was lost in the darkness of Sin. *Light of the world.*

30. Man of sorrows ! what a name. *Redemption.*

31. The Spirit, O sinner, in mercy doth move. *Holy Spirit.*

ix. *Gospel Hymns, No.* 2, 1876.

32. At the feet of Jesus. *The good choice.*

33. Come, sing the Gospel's joyful sound. *Salvation.*

34. Cut it down, cut it down. *Justice and Mercy.*

35. Do you see the Hebrew captive ! *Prayer.*

36. Hallelujah, He is risen. *Easter.* Written in the spring of 1876 and first sung by Bliss on Easter after-noon, 1876, in the Court House Square, Augusta, Georgia, to 5900 people.

37. In Zion's rock abiding. *Safety.*

38. Repeat the story o'er and o'er. *Grace and Peace.*

39. Tenderly the Shepherd. *The Good Shepherd.*

x. *Gospel Hymns, No.* 3, 1878.

40. Hear ye the glad good news from heaven. *Faith and Salvation.*

41. I will sing of my Redeemer. *Praise.*

xi. *Gospel Hymns, No.* 4, 1881.

42. 'Tis known on earth and heaven too. *More about Jesus.*

xii. *Various.*

43. Sing over again to me. *Words of Life.* This appeared in a paper entitled *Words of Life*, 1874, The following are undated :—

44. March to the battle-field. *Duty and Victory.*

45. There is sin in the camp. *Hinderances.*

46. 'Tis the promise of God. *Praise.*

47. While the silvery moon-beams. fall. *New Birth.*

48. God is always near me. *Omnipresence.*

Two hymns, " I am so glad that our Father in heaven," and " Sowing the seed by the daylight [dawnlight] fair," (sometimes given as " Sowing *our* seed *in the morning* fair ") are usually attributed to Mr. Bliss. In his *Gospel Songs*, Cincinnati, 1874, however, he lays claim to the music only. Mr. Sankey attributes this last to " E. A. Oakey." With the exception of No. 48, these hymns are given in Mr. Sankey's *Sacred Songs & Solos,* l'ts. i. and ii. Their popularity is far beyond their literary merits, and is mainly due to the simple melodies to which they are wedded. As a writer of hymns of this class Mr. Bliss is second only to Mrs. Van Alstyne. Many anecdotes concerning hymns of this class are given in *American Evangelists ; an Account of their work in England and America, by the Rev. Elias Nason,* Boston, U.S., Lathrop & Co., 1877.

Mr. Bliss is usually known as " P. P. Bliss." This is found on the title-pages of his collections. On his own authority, however, we are enabled to say that his name originally stood thus : *"Philipp Bliss."* Early in life he separated the final *p* from his christian name, constituted it a capital P, and thus produced " P. P. Bliss." (For this article we are mainly indebted to Professor F. M. Bird, and Mr. H. P. Main.)　　　　　　　　　　　　　**[J. J.]**

Blomfield, Charles James, D.D., was b. at Bury St. Edmunds, 1786, and graduated at Trinity College, Cambridge. On taking Holy Orders he held positions of importance in the Church, including the Rectory of St. Botolph, Bishopsgate, London ; the Bishopric of Chester, 1824 ; and the Bishopric of London, 1828. He d. in 1857. It was under his patronage that Hall pub. his *Mitre H. Bk.,* in 1836, and to it he contributed two hymns for school anniversaries :—

1. In hymns of joy your voices raise.
2. O Thou, Who from the infant's tongue.

These hymns are unknown to modern collections [H. MSS.]

Blow ye the trumpet, blow. *C. Wesley.* [*Year of Jubilee, or the New Year.*] This is No. iii. of his seven *Hymns for New Year's Day,* 1750, in 6 st. of 6 l. It is based upon Lev. xxv. In 1772, and again in 1774, R. Conyers included st. i., iii., iv. and vi. in his *Coll.* This arrangement, however, gave way to one by A. M. Toplady which appeared in his *Ps. & Hys.,* 1776, No. 318, where st. ii. is given as vi., st. iv. as v., and a slight but significant alteration is introduced in st. iii. Originally lines 1-2 read :—

> Extol the Lamb of God,
> The all-atoning Lamb.

This was changed to :—

> Extol the Lamb of God,
> The *sin*-atoning Lamb.

The heated controversy between the Wesleys and Toplady on the questions, vital to them, of Arminianism and Calvinism gave point and meaning to this change. From Toplady's *Ps. & Hys.,* the text and arrangement of stanzas were taken by other compilers until the hymn acquired universal reputation as his composition. In 1830, it was included with three alterations in the *Supp.* to the *Wes. H. Bk.,* No. 645, and the error of authorship was rectified. In the revised ed. of the *Wes. H. Bk.,* 1875, two of the alterations are repeated : st. iv., l. 3, "*blest,*" for " bless'd " ; and st. v., "*Receive* it," for "Shall have it," &c. In varying forms, sometimes, as in *Toplady,* then

as in the *Wes. H. Bk.,* and again in some other shape, this hymn is in very extensive use in all English-speaking countries. Orig. text in *P. Works,* 1868-72, vol. vi. p. 12.　　**[J. J.]**

Blunt, Abel Gerald Wilson, M.A., some time Travelling Fellow of Cambridge University, was born in 1827, and graduated at Pembroke College, Cambridge, B.A., 1850 ; M.A., 1860. Taking Holy Orders in 1851, he was from 1856 to 1860 Incumbent of Crew Green, Cheshire. In 1860 he was preferred to the Rectory of St. Luke's, Chelsea. Mr. Blunt's hymns, written for festival occasions at St. Luke's, are :—

1. Evening comes, may we, O Lord. *Evening.*

2. From meadows bright with blossom. *Flower Services.* This is dated June, 1882.

3. Here, Lord, we offer Thee all that is fairest. *Flower Services.* This is the best known and most popular of Mr. Blunt's hymns. From its composition in 1879, when it was first sung at the Flower Service at St. Luke's, it has attracted attention until it is deemed essential to the completeness of most collections of importance.

4. Here, on this our festal day. *St. Luke.* Written in 1882 for St. Luke's, Chelsea. All these hymns are printed in a small *Supplement* in use at St. Luke's.

Boardman, Sarah B. [Judson, S. B.]

Bode, John Ernest, M.A., s. of Mr. William Bode, late of the General Post Office, b. 1816, and educated at Eton, the Charter House, and at Christ Church, Oxford, graduating B.A. 1837, and M.A. in due course. Taking Holy Orders in 1841, he became Rector of Westwell, Oxfordshire, 1847 ; and then of Castle Camps, Cambridgeshire, 1860. He was also for a time Tutor of his College, and Classical Examiner. His Bampton Lectures were delivered in 1855. He d. at Castle Camps, Oct. 6, 1874. In addition to his *Bampton Lectures,* and *Ballads from Herodotus,* he pub. *Hymns from the Gospel of the Day for each Sunday and Festivals of our Lord,* 1860 ; and *Short Occasional Poems,* Lond., Longmans, 1858. In addition to his well-known hymn, " O Jesu, I have promised " (q. v.), the following from his *Hys. from the Gospel* are also in C. U. :—

1. God of heaven, enthroned in might. *H. Trinity.*
2. Spirit of Truth, indwelling Light. *Whitsuntide.*

Boden, James, was b. April 13, 1757, in the house at Chester long occupied by Matthew Henry, and educated for the Congregational Ministry at Homerton College. In 1784 he became the pastor of the Independent Chapel, Hanley ; and, in 1796, of the Queen's Street Chapel, Sheffield. This last charge he held for nearly 43 years. He died at Chesterfield, June 4, 1841. In 1801 he assisted Dr. Williams, of the Masborough Theological College, near Sheffield, in compiling *A Coll. of above Six Hundred Hymns designed as a New Supp. to Dr. Watts's Ps. & Hys., &c.,* Doncaster, 1801. This collection is known as *Williams and Boden,* and to it is traced the anonymous modern version of " Jerusalem, my happy home " (q. v.). To this collection Boden contributed, under the signature " Boden," the following hymns :—

1. Bright source of everlasting love. *Charity Sermon.*
2. Come, all ye saints of God. *Passiontide.*
3. Come death, released from dread. *Death.*
4. Our great High Priest we sing. *Christ the H. Priest.*
5. Shall sin, that cruel foe ? *Lent.*
6. Triumphant sing ye favoured [ransom'd] saints. *Jesus, all in all.*

7. We come, dear Jesus, to Thy throne. *Prayer Meeting.*

Of these hymns, No. 1 appeared in the *Evangelical Mag.* Aug., 1798. Most of them are still in C. U., but chiefly in America. They are of no special merit.

In the *Gospel Mag.*, 1777, there are a few hymns under the signature " J——s B——n, Chester." Of these, one only (8), " Ye dying sons of men " (*Invitation*), was given in the Williams and Boden *Coll.*, and then, not with the full signature of " *Boden*," but as by " B——." On this evidence mainly the hymn has been ascribed to James Boden. It appeared in the *Gospel Mag.* twice in 1777, in Feb. and in Aug. It may be by our author; but seeing that it alone of the eight hymns above noted is signed " *B——*," and was given in the *Gospel Mag.* in 1777, and that the rest are signed " *Boden*," and did not appear in the *Gospel Mag.* in 1777, or in any other year, we regard the evidence as somewhat inconclusive. It has been suggested that possibly the " J——s B——n, Chester," was his father. The signatures appended to the hymns in the 1st ed. of *Williams & Boden*, 1801, were omitted from the 2nd ed., 1803, and portions of the Preface were rewritten.   [J. J.]

Body, George, D.D., born in 1840, and educated at St. John's College, Cambridge, where he graduated B.A. 1862, M.A. 1876. On taking Holy Orders he was successively Curate of St. James's, Wednesbury, 1863–65 ; Sedgley, 1865–67 ; Curate in charge of Christ Church, Wolverhampton, 1867–70 ; Rector of Kirkby-Misperton, 1870–84 ; and Canon of Durham, and Missioner of the Diocese, 1883. He was also Proctor for the Archdeaconry of Cleveland, 1880–1885 ; and received an Hon. D.D. from Durham University in 1885. His publications include *Life of Justification ; Life of Temptation*, &c. In 1874 he revised and added a Preface to the Rev. E. Husband's *Mission Hymnal ;* and in 1885 he did the same for *The Durham Mission H. Bk.* In these *Hymnals* appeared his :—

1. Father, Who dost Thy children feed. *Holy Communion.*

2. Jesus, speak to me in love. *Prayer for Peace.*

Βοηθὸς καὶ σκεπαστὴς ἐγένετό μοι εἰς σωτηρίαν. *St. Andrew of Crete.* This is known in the Greek Church as the Κανὼν ὁ μέγας—the Great Canon of Mid-Lent week. It was written probably about the end of the eighth century. Dr. Neale sums up its peculiarities and excellences thus :—

" It is a collection of Scriptural examples, turned to the purpose of penitential confession. It is impossible to deny the beauty of many stanzas, and the ingenuity of some tropological applications. But the immense length of the Canon, for it exceeds three hundred stanzas, and its necessary tautology, must render it wearisome, unless devotionally used under the peculiar circumstances for which it is appointed."—*Hymns of the E. C.*, 1862, p. 24.

The complete Canon is found in the *Triodion* of the Greek Church, and a selection is in the *Anth. Graec. Carm.* p. 199, and in *Daniel*, iii. pp. 52–4. Dr. Neale's *tr.* in his *Hys. of the Eastern Church*, 1862, p. 24, begins with *Daniel's* second stanza, Πόθεν ἄρξομαι θρηνεῖν, which he renders, " Whence shall my tears begin ?" and consists of 10 st. of 6 l. It is taken from the earlier portion of the Canon. In 1871–2, st. i., ii., vii., viii., and x. appeared in an altered form in the *Hymnary*, No. 218 ; also, in 1871, st. i., iv., vii., viii., and x. in *Church Hymns*, No. 112, and other arrangements in later collections, sometimes as, " Whence shall *our* tears begin ?" [See Greek Hymnody, § XVII., 1.] The whole Canon is given in a prose *tr.* in *The Orthodox Catholic Review*, 1875, vol. iv. pp. 35–72.   [J. J.]

Bogatzky, Carl Heinrich von. He was b. Sept. 7, 1690, on his father's estate of Jankowe, near Militsch, in Silesia. His father, J. A. v. Bogatzky, was descended from a noble Hungarian family, and entering the Austrian service attained the rank of Lieutenant-Colonel. Bogatzky's early education was picked up at various places as family arrangements permitted. He was for some time page at the Ducal Court of Weissenfels. From Weissenfels his father removed him to Breslau, to prepare for entering the army. During a long illness at Breslau he became convinced that God had other work for him to do. Receiving an offer of assistance from Count Heinrich XXIV., of Reuss-Köstriz, towards the expenses of an University course, he entered the University of Jena in 1713 ; but removed at Easter, 1715, to the University of Halle, still as a student of law. Before Christmas he received notice that his mother had died in Silesia, and that he must return. During the week that elapsed before setting out, while attending divine service, he received what he regarded as his first true views of Justification by Faith. Disowned by his father for objecting to enter the army, he returned from Silesia to Halle and enrolled himself, at Easter, 1716, as a student of theology. At Halle he began for his own edification his best known work, *The Golden Treasury*, 1st pub. at Breslau in 1718. During 1718 his health failed, and his voice became so seriously affected that he was unable to take any parochial charge. From thenceforth he devoted himself to religious authorship, and speaking in private gatherings. He left Silesia in 1740, and for five years resided at Saalfeld, where he wrote many works, including that on *True Conversion*, 1741. In 1746 he removed to Halle, where G. A. Francke gave him a free room in the orphanage. The rest of his life was spent mainly in that town. The most important of his publications at this time was his *Meditations and Prayers on the New Testament*, 7 vols., 1755–61. He d. at Halle, June 15, 1774. (*Koch*, iv. 468–478 ; *Allg. Deutsche Biog.*, iii. 37–39 ; *Autobiography tr.* by Samuel Jackson, Lond., 1856—the second dating his death, possibly through a misprint, as at Glaucha, near Halle, 1754.)

Bogatzky seems to have begun hymn-writing about 1718, and in all composed 411 hymns, some of which appeared in part, in his devotional works, 3 in the *Cöthnische Lieder*, 1733–36, 6 in the *Wernigerode G. B.*, 1735, and in a collected form at Halle, 1750, as *Die Uebung der Gottseligkeit in allerley Geistlichen Liedern*, with 362 hymns (2nd ed. Halle, 1755, with 396 ; 3rd ed., 1771, with 411, reprinted unaltered at Berlin, 1844). With this the Dowager Queen of Denmark was so much pleased that, as the 1st ed. was in very small type, she offered to contribute to an ed. in larger type, and when that was issued in 1750 (with 376 hymns), bought 300 copies, all of which she distributed.

His hymns have little poetic fire or glow of imagination ; but in his better productions there is stimulating zeal, warmth of religious feeling, and simplicity of religious faith, linking him rather with the earlier Halle School, than with the spiritual sensuousness of some of his fellow-contributors to the *Cöthnische Lieder*.

(1) The hymns by him in English C. U. are :

i. **Wach auf du Geist der ersten Zeugen.** [*Missions.*] 1st pub. 1750, as above, No. 133, in 14 st. of 6 l., entitled, " For faithful labourers in the Harvest of the Lord, for the blessed spread of the Word to all the world." Included in the *Berlin G. L. S.*, ed. 1863, No. 1383. *Tr.* as :—

Awake, Thou Spirit, Who of old. A good *tr.* of st. i.-iii., v.-viii. by Miss Winkworth, in her *Lyra Ger.*, 1st series, 1855, p. 41, and thence, omitting st. ii., altered in metre, and beginning, " Awake, Thou Spirit, Who didst fire," as No. 290 in the Pennsylvania Luth. *Ch. Bk.*, 1868. In Miss Winkworth's *C. B. for England*, 1863, No. 87, it is altered in metre to " Wake, Spirit, Who in times now olden," st. vii. being omitted, and this form is No. 190 in the Ohio *Luth. Hymnal*, 1880.

Another *tr.* is " O spirit of the early martyrs, wake," in the *British Herald*, Oct. 1865, p. 151. Not in C. U.

ii. Ich bin erlöst durch meines Mittler's Blut. [*Passiontide.*] 1750, as above, No. 330, in 10 st. of 9 l., entitled, " The believer's consolation in death." J. C. Wagner in his *Neues Hildburg-häusisches G. B.*, 1807 (1808, No. 231), included a greatly altered form beginning, " Ich bin erlöst ! Es floss des Mittler's Blut." The text *tr.* is that in Knapp's *Ev. L. S.*, 1837, No. 503, based on st. i., iii., v.-vii. of the original. The only *tr.* in C. U. is:—

I am redeem'd ! the purchase of that blood, from *Knapp*, by Dr. H. Mills in his *Horae Ger.*, 1845 (1856, p. 64) ; repeated, omitting st. ii., as No. 125 in Stryker's *Christian Chorals*, 1885.

(2) Hymns not in English C. U. :—

iii. Du Hüter Israel. [*Morning.*] 1750, as above, No. 7, in 15 st. *Tr.* as " Guardian of Israel, Thou," by H. J. Buckoll, 1842, p. 53.

iv. Einer bleibt König, wenn alles erlieget. [*Christ as King.*] 1st in the large type ed., 1750, No. 367, in 10 st. *Tr.* as " One reigneth still, though all else may be failing," by Miss Burlingham, in the *British Herald*, Dec. 1865, p. 185, and repeated, as No. 394, in Reid's *Praise Bk.*, 1872.

v. Heut ist dein Tag vorhanden. [*Sunday Morning.*] 1750, as above, No. 106, in 5 st. *Tr.* as " This is Thy day so glorious," by H. J. Buckoll, 1842, p. 8.

vi. Hirt und Hüter deiner Schaafe. [*Spiritual Watchfulness.*] 1750, as above, No. 279, in 16 st. *Tr.* as " Great Shepherd of the sheep, No longer," in S. Jackson's *tr.* of Bogatzky's *Life*, 1856, p. 187.

vii. Jehovah, hoher Gott von Macht und Stärke. [*The Almighty God.*] At Schreibersdorf in the Riesengebirge in 1720, standing on an eminence, he viewed the distant mountains which at first he thought were clouds, and deeply impressed by the majesty, glory, and omnipotence of God, he wrote this hymn after returning to the house (*Life*, 1856, p. 51). Included, as No. 558, in the *Sammlung Geist- und lieblicher Lieder*, Leipzig and Görlitz, 1725, and repeated, 1750, as above, No. 268, in 12 st. *Tr.* as " Jehovah, God of boundless strength and might," by Miss Winkworth, 1869, p. 274.

viii. O stilles Lamm, du hast für mich gelitten. [*Cross and Consolation.*] 1750, as above, No. 305, in 7 st. *Tr.* as " O silent Lamb ! for me Thou hast endured," by Mrs. Findlater, in *H. L. L.*, 1858 (p. 64, 1884, p. 122).

[J. M.]

Bohemian Brethren's Hymnody.

In the following article it is proposed to give, I. An outline of the history of the Brethren up to A.D. 1621 ; II. An account of their Bohemian and German hymn-books ; and III. Tables showing the extent to which German hymns are derived from the Bohemian.

I. History of the Brethren to 1621.

The history of the Bohemian Brethren seems at first sight to be out of place in an article on the Bohemian Brethren's Hymnology. The hymnody, however, together with the personal histories of the writers of their hymns and the compilers of their hymn-books, are so interwoven with the general history of the body, that the former can only be made clear with the aid of the latter. Thus has arisen the necessity for the resumé which we now present. Especially at its commencement, this history is enveloped in a certain cloudiness, which we, with the facts now at command, are unable to pierce. The best results attainable we now give, but more as a summary than in detail.

§ i. *Introduction.*—1. Through the Compact [Holy Communion in both kinds, and liberty of preaching] granted by the Council of Basel, 1431, the Roman Catholics had attained their desired ends, for one section of the Hussites, confiding in the promises of the Church, had accepted that concession ; the other, better acquainted with the tactics of the holy Fathers, had rejected it. Thus the schism between the two parties was completed ; and the Roman Catholics could complacently look on at the mutual extermination of the Hussites.

2. After the battle of Lipan, 1434, the Taborites had ceased to exist as a political party ; but the numerous and divergent religious doctrines, and tendencies comprehended under the name of the Taborites, did not cease, for numerous priests wandered through the land, and employed themselves in spreading strange doctrines, the result of which was that new sects sprang up on every hand. The best elements of this religious movement united themselves into small, free, congregations, the members of which remained within the pale of the Church, although having but little real connection with it, and grouped themselves around some one more considerable man from their midst, and acknowledged him as their leader.

§ ii. *First Period of the Unity.* 1. One of these congregations, or brotherhoods, existed at Chelčic, a village near Wodnan, learning and putting in practice the theories of a certain Peter, named Chelčicky, after his residence. Without the advantages of a theological, or even classical training ; having but an insufficient knowledge of the Latin language ; a simple layman, and, perhaps, small landowner ; " he watched, with a keen eye, the events that were passing around him ; investigated, with an independent mind, and a fearless criticism, the great questions of his age ; acknowledged no authority but the Bible ; and displayed an originality of thought, and power of diction, that made him, in spite of the obscureness of his position, a master among the learned, and a teacher among the unlettered."

2. At the head of another congregation at Prague, stood Gregory, who, in his turn, was a follower of Rokycana. The latter, however, being a Reformer only so far as was convenient for his own purposes, sent Gregory and his " Brethren " to Peter, when urged by them to go further. At last, in order to get rid of them, Rokycana, in 1457, induced King George to assign the domain of Senftenberg as a settlement to Gregory and his friends, and these were most likely joined by the Brethren from Chelčic. Senftenberg, lying in the midst of lonely hills to the south of the Erlitz mountains, was but scantily peopled, and still suffering from the devastations of the Hussite war. Kunwald, a small village on this barony, was designated as the place for the settlement. In the following years they organised their community, chose some Elders as its leading representatives, drew up certain principles of doctrine and practice, and chose as their name *Fratres Legis Christi*. The persecutions raised against them by King George (who feared a new organization of the Taborites) caused the Brethren to wander through Bohemia, where they became acquainted with similar small congregations, and increased in numbers to such an extent that they resolved on an entire separation from the Utraquist Church.

3. In the year 1467, the Elders convoked delegates of all congregations connected with them to a synod held at Lhotka, a hamlet, or rather farm, near Reichenau. The assembled deputies, about 60 (besides some " German Waldenses "), from nearly all parts of Bohemia and Moravia, resolved first on their final separation from the Church. They then chose, by lot, three from their number, as bishops ; viz., Matthias, Thomas, and Elias, who were then consecrated by prayer and the laying on of hands, by a Waldensian and by a Roman Catholic priest. But either at the same synod, or at any rate within the year 1467, scruples seem to have entered the minds of some of the Brethren as to whether such consecration would suffice. They therefore sent the Roman Catholic priest who had assisted in the consecration (Michael Bradacius), with a companion (whose name is unknown), to the Waldensian bishop Stefan (who lived in Austria, and was later burned at Vienna), in order to beg of him the episcopal consecration. Michael, having been consecrated a bishop by Stefan, on his return first

ordained the three originally chosen (Matthias, Thomas, and Elias) to the priesthood, and then consecrated them as bishops. Shortly after, he laid down, not only his episcopate received *ad hoc*, but also his Roman priesthood, and was newly ordained to the priesthood by one of the three new bishops whom he himself had consecrated. In this peculiar manner, so far as we can trace the history of the proceedings, the first consecration of bishops among the Brethren was effected.

4. The first tendency of the Brethren was plainly antagonistic to the course of this world. Their refusal to take the oath, and to join the military service; their contempt of learning; their refusal to permit their members to hold any office in the State; and other peculiarities, they inherited from Peter Chelčický, who thought to renew the world and human society by a strict observance of Christ's command to love one another, and maintained that all other commands and ordinances in the political and social life of men would cease spontaneously if that one command were but followed by all.

5. When, however, the members who joined the Unity without any acquaintance with Peter's first principles began rapidly to increase; when the Brethren perceived the need of learning to defend their convictions against their adversaries; when it seemed desirable not to refuse persons of high position who wished to join their congregations; then the number of those among them who rejected the old strict antagonism to the world displayed by Peter, rapidly augmented, and at the end of about twenty years there was a numerous party who might have been named the "Liberals" of the Unity. The principal leaders of this party were Lucas (named *Pragensis*) and Lawrence Krasonicky his friend, two men as learned as pious. The old strict party resisted all the proposed changes, and for a time prevailed; but at the synod of 1494 the liberal party obtained the victory; and the "small party" or *Amosites* (after their leader Amos), not being disposed to submit, separated themselves from the Unity. Some efforts made to put an end to this schism failed, and the Amosites lingered on as a small sect for about fifty or sixty years.

6. If the Amosites claimed to be the true Unity, they were right so far as they retained the ideas of Peter Chelčický. The new Brethren under Lucas, in the synod of 1495, resolved that the writings of Chelčiký, Gregory, and other founders of the Unity should be received only so far as they were found to agree with the Bible, thus warranting the possibility of progress in doctrine and practice.

§ iii. *Second Period of the Unity.*—1. The first period of the Brethren's history is clearly distinguished from the second period under Lucas, by opinions, doctrines, and even by terms and expressions. Lucas has every right to be named the "second founder" of the Unity. Through the more liberal principles of admission to the Unity its numbers increased to such a degree that about the year 1500 it consisted of three to four hundred congregations, and there was hardly a town or village in Bohemia or Moravia where some of its members were not to be found.

2. From 1467 (§ ii. 3) to 1500 there had been three bishops, and one of these, Matthias, had held the most commanding position, but without responsibility. On the death of Matthias in 1500, the highest position was given to a Select Council, the members of which were chosen by the synod, for life; and the four new co-ordinate bishops who superintended distinct dioceses, were made responsible to the Select Council. Then, for the first time, the doctrines of the Unity were worked out by Lucas in 63 works, in a learned and systematic form. The sources of his theology, which on the whole remained the theology of the Unity as long as it lasted, were not the writings of Peter Chelčický, with whom he contended whenever occasion offered, but the writings of Hus and Wyclif; the latter especially with regard to the doctrine of the Lord's Supper. Lucas published the first hymn-book of the Brethren (II. 1); a catechism or "interrogations" for teaching the children; and a volume of ample instructions for the priests. He also reorganised the Church services, varying and enriching them. The Unity flourished under Lucas, and gained the summit of its independence, although, externally, the Brethren suffered, not only from the aggressions of Dominican preachers, but also from cruel and bloody persecutions, dating from the year 1503, when King Vladislav issued a mandate strictly forbidding any Brethren's services to be held in Bohemia.

3. Lucas was already beginning to fear for the internal independence and continued existence of the Unity, when Luther appeared in Germany. Luther soon obtained friends and followers amongst the members of the Unity, but Lucas was not one of these. Misunderstanding Luther's doctrines of Free Grace and of Christian Liberty, he reproached Luther with want of moral strict-

ness, and with accommodation to many Roman Catholic dogmas. In the year 1523 he published an answer to Luther's *Vom Anbeten des Sakraments des heiligen Leichnams Jesu Christi*. In this he gave Luther clearly to understand that he did not wish for any nearer relations with him, on the ground that he himself held the Brethren to be nearer the truth. But many of the Brethren, and those the best and most important, dissented from the policy of Lucas; and these gained and exerted a great influence upon the whole Unity after his death.

§ iv. *Third Period of the Unity.*—1. After the death of Lucas, in 1528, we see the beginning of a third period in the Brethren's history, in which the Unity, sometimes giving itself up to strange influences, sometimes resisting and refusing them, lost more and more of its independent doctrines and existence. About the same time a heavy blow was struck at the external existence of the Unity.

2. At first, until 1546, the new tendency prevailed in the Unity, which (represented by John Horn, and, more especially, by John Augusta, the most important new members of the Select Council), aimed at giving publicity to the Brethren, and at forming alliance with the German Reformers. The connection with Luther, which had been broken off by Lucas, was renewed; and new connections were formed with Calvin and the Reformers of Strassburg. At the same time several Bohemian lords and noblemen (who until then had protected the Brethren who resided on their estates, but had never thought of joining the Unity) applied for admission, after having seen that German Electors and Princes were not ashamed to take Luther's part. In short, the despised and persecuted "sect of shoemakers and weavers" was now esteemed an interesting ancient Evangelical Church, and a body of sufficient political weight to command the attention of its adversaries.

3. All this was mainly due to John Augusta, in whom a severe and inflexible character was united with far-reaching designs, and an insuperable love of power. But on the other hand the consequence of this emergency of the Brethren from their retired position was that they became involved in the Bohemian insurrection of 1547; or if that cannot be absolutely proved, at any rate their adversaries used this turn of affairs in order to aim at the destruction of the Unity. Therefore, once more, as before in 1503, the Brethren were forbidden to conduct any divine service; and the Unity was commanded to dissolve itself. This time the edict was more strictly carried out than formerly, because the estates on which the Brethren had their principal settlements (where they lived under the protection of lords who were themselves members of the Unity) were confiscated to the Crown. Augusta himself, after having been indefatigable in encouraging and consoling the affrighted and persecuted Brethren, partly by letters and partly by nightly visits, while during the day he was obliged to conceal himself in the woods, was finally caught by treachery, and kept in close imprisonment in the castle of Pürglitz, a few miles west of Prague, for sixteen years. The Brethren were thus compelled to emigrate from Bohemia, in 1548. In two large companies, they with their wives and children crossed the mountains which bound Bohemia on the north, in order to seek for some place where they might serve God as their fathers had done. From that time we may distinguish three branches of the Unity: the *Bohemian*, which, after the death of Ferdinand I., flourished anew; the *Moravian* [see **Moravian Hymnody**], which has since become the principal branch of the Unity; and the *Polish*. The remarks which follow deal exclusively with the *first* of these three branches of the Unity.

4. While Augusta was kept in his long imprisonment, John Blahoslav stood at the head of the Unity; a master spirit, developed by a many-sided, polished, and classical education. The splendid large hymn-book published by him, or at his instigation (II. 6), and his theoretical work on music, testify to his musical attainments. Through his large collection of documents on the history of the ancient Brethren, and by his own writings on that subject, he became the founder of the Brethren's history; and at the same time the classical example for Bohemian prose style, the theory of which he gave in his Bohemian grammar. He proved himself also to have been an able diplomatist in his negotiations with the Court of Vienna. In their doctrine the Brethren, under Horn and Augusta, inclined to Luther until about 1546; under Blahoslav, who himself was not an original theologian, they tried to return to Lucas, but in fact they approached to Calvin. In ecclesiastical politics, also, Blahoslav had an object in view different from that of Augusta. Blahoslav, who wished to preserve the independence of the Unity, aimed at forming a confederation of the Brethren with the so-called New Utraquists, or Lutherans, in Bohemia; so

that each of the two Churches should retain its own confession, constitution, form of service, &c. ; but should be united by friendship and work in common, in a manner similar to that realised in Poland by the Consensus Sendomiriensis between the Brethren, the Reformed, and the Lutherans. Augusta aimed at a union of the said Churches, with a common confession, common constitution, &c. ; in short, at a uniform Evangelical Bohemian National Church ; and, after his liberation from imprisonment in 1564, he entered into negotiations with the Lutherans for attaining this object. Surely, however, Blahoslav's design was more adequate to religious conviction, and guaranteed more religious liberty than Augusta's. But, after the deaths of Blahoslav, in 1571, and of Augusta, in 1572, a common confession was composed in 1575, by the Lutherans and the Brethren, as the basis of a Bohemian Evangelical Church ; and thus Augusta's designs were attained. It is characteristic that the confession was not composed by clergymen at a synod, but by the states of the country at a diet at Prague. The idea of such a union of Churches was apparently taken from a political agreement between belligerent parties.

§ v. *Fourth Period of the Unity.*—1. With this year and this fact begins the last period of the Brethren's history : the disorganisation of the Unity. Though the aristocratic element among the Brethren still absolutely obeyed the commands of the Senior Kalef, in the transactions regarding the Confession of 1575, and on other occasions willingly subordinated itself to the discipline of the Church, yet its influence increased more and more. An illustrious product of the munificence of the Baron de Zerotin, and of the learning of the Brethren's ministers, is the Bible of Kralitz (1579–98), in 6 folio volumes, with commentary. The text of this (still published and circulated by the British and Foreign Bible Society) is as classical in the Bohemian language, as Luther's in the German.

2. But another result of the influence of the nobility was that the Unity, being deficient in Seniors of importance, became more and more implicated in the political aims of the nobility. The leaders in the combat of the Bohemians for religious liberty were members of the Unity, the most important being Wenzel Budovec de Budova. The first part of the struggle against the Emperor Rudolph II. met with a great success in securing the charter of 1609, by which, among others, the Bohemian Protestants were allowed an independent consistory in Prague. But in consequence of this the union between the Brethren and the Lutherans was made still closer, so that the Brethren lost this their old name, and accepted the common name chosen for all the Evangelical Bohemians, viz., *Utraquist Christians.* The second part of the struggle, the fatal insurrection of 1618, resulted in the disastrous battle of the White Mountain, near Prague, Nov. 8, 1620 (when the Imperial troops under Maximilian of Bavaria and Tilly, defeated the Evangelicals under the Winter-King, the Calvinistic Friedrich V. Count Palatine) ; in the bloody execution of the Bohemian Evangelical nobility (including Wenzel) at Prague, June 21, 1621 ; and *in the entire destruction of the Brethren's Unity.*

[Sources of the Brethren's History : (1) A. Gindely, *Geschichte der böhm. Brüder,* Prag, 1857. (2) B. Czerwenka, *Geschichte der evang. Kirche in Böhmen,* Bielefeld, 1869. (3) Goll, *Quellen und Untersuchungen zur Geschichte der böhm. Brüder,* Prag, 1878–82. (4) John Holmes, *History of the Protestant Church of the United Brethren,* London, 1825. (5) Edmund de Schweinitz, *The History of the Church known as the Unitas Fratrum,* Bethlehem, Pa., 1885, with a full account of the sources of the history.]

II. *The Bohemian and German Hymn-books of the Unity.*

§ i. *The Bohemian Hymn-books.*—1. The earliest known hymn-book is that extant in the Bohemian Museum at Prague. The title-page, the first leaf of the calendar, the last leaf of the alphabetical index and a leaf of the text, are missing. Judging from the type it seemed to have been printed at Prague, by Severin, who had printed a Bohemian Bible in 1488. On the last page is a colophon which may be thus *tr. :* " These hymns were finished on Wednesday in the Octave of the Baptism of God ; in the year of God One Thousand Five Hundred and One," i. e. Jan. 13, 1501. The book contains 89 hymns, of which 21 are by Konvaldský, Táborský, and Lucas (II. 8) ; of the rest, two (No. 32, 45) are from the hymn-book of the Taborites. This first hymn-book, it may be noted, is never mentioned among the works of the Brethren.

2. Bp. Blahoslav, in his *History of the Brethren* [MS. in the University Library of Prague, fol. 112], says, referring to the year 1505, "The Brethren for the first time had a large sized Kancional of sacred hymns printed." It seems to have contained some 400 hymns, but no copy is now known to exist.

3. Blahoslav (l. c. fol. 119) says further, "In the year 1519 the Brethren published a book of sacred songs and hymns for the use of the pious and faithful people, and that in a 2nd ed." This was printed by Paul Olivetsky, at Leitomishl, but no copy seems to have survived.

4. In the preface to the hymn-book of 1561 the Brethren's Seniors explain that Lucas of Prague, who had edited the book of 1519 (I. § iii. 2) was commissioned to rearrange and correct it. But as he d. in 1528 they set themselves to a comprehensive revision. On account of the length of time required they in the meantime published some new hymns, in 1531, at Jung Bunzlau. If this remark does not refer to the German book of 1531 (see below), neither a copy nor other trace of this edition is extant.

5. In 1541 the hymn-book which had been so long in preparation was printed by Paul Severin at Prague, and edited by Bp. John Horn. No copy is now known to exist, but its title is preserved in a polemical treatise by the Jesuit, D. W. Sturm, in his *Comparison of the Doctrine of the Brethren,* pub. at Prague in 1584. The title begins :—

" Písně chval božských. Písně duchovní evangelitské," &c., or, in English, "Hymns in praise of God. Evangelical Hymns, newly revised, corrected and collected, and with many newly written on the principal doctrines of the Holy Scripture. In honour and in praise of the one, sole, and eternal God in the blessed Trinity. Also for the help, use, and consolation of those, who love the Bohemian nation and language with true Christian devotion. John Horn, with his fellow labourers. 1541. Prague." The colophon on the last page may be rendered thus :—" In the year 1541 after the birth of the Son of God this Cancional was printed and finished on Saturday after St. Martin's Day [Nov. 12] in the Altstadt of Prague, by me, Paul Severin of Kuttenberg, citizen of this illustrious town."

According to Blahoslav [*Grammatika česká,* 1571, new ed., Vienna, 1857, p. 40] it was reprinted at Leitomishl in 1541. Tucher [Schatz des evang. Kirchengesangs, Leipzig. 1848, ii. p. 321], who seems to have had in his hands a copy of this edition, says it contains 484 hymns. I could discover no copy either of this edition, or that which the printer Vanek Austsky, or Austin, of Jung Bunzlau, was authorised to print in 1547.

6. In 1555 John Černý, John Blahoslav, and Adam Sturm, were commissioned by the synod of the Unity to publish a new hymn-book to include the compositions of John Augusta (I. § iv. 2), and others of the younger Brethren. It was ready for the press in 1560, and the printing was finished June 7, 1561. Of this fine folio, which contains 744 hymns (including 60 from the hymn-book of 1501), a copy is preserved in the Archives at Herrnhut. The title is almost identical with that of 1541. The colophon may be thus *tr. :*—

"This Cancional was printed and finished by Alexander of Aujezd [or of Pilsen], at Samter [Poland], at the castle of his Grace Lucas, Count of Gorka, Waywode of Lančic, Starost of Bus."

Later editions, differing very little as to their contents, appeared in folio at Eibenschütz, 1564, and Kralitz, 1576 and 1581; and in 4to, at Kralitz in 1583, 1594, 1598.

7. Among the later hymn-books may be mentioned (1) a folio pub. at Kralic (Moravia) in 1615, which contains 644 hymns besides a metrical psalter, and was probably ed. by the four Seniors whose crests are found on p. 529. Copies of this ed. and of the quarto reprint of 1618 are to be found in the University Library, Prague. (2) A 12mo, pub. at Amsterdam in 1659, and ed. by J. A. Comenius. This contains, besides a metrical psalter, 430 hymns with an appendix of 25; and is to be found in the Archives at Herrnhut.

8. The principal contributors to the hymn-books of 1501 and 1561 are the following:—

(1) **Matthias Konvaldský** [b. 1442 at Kunwald, near Lititz; Bp. of the Unity; d. Jan. 23, 1500, at Leipnik], contributed 4 (Nos. 31, 33, 35, 48) to the *H. Bk.* of 1501, and 5 others to the ed. of 1561.

(2) **John Táborský**, or John Vilimek [a Roman Catholic priest; afterwards member of the Select Council; d. Apr. 28, 1495, at Leitomishl], contributed 6 (Nos. 6, 7, 10, 25, 46, 51) to the *H. Bk.* of 1501.

(3) **Lucas Pragensis** (q. v.) contributed 11 (Nos 1, 12, 14, 28 (?), 42 (?), 46, 47, 81, 82, 86, 92) to the *H. Bk.* of 1501; and 106 others to that of 1561. Included are 11 *trs.* from the Latin, and 4 revisions of older Bohemian hymns.

(4) **John Augusta** (q. v.) contributed 141 to the *H. Bk.* of 1561.

(5) **John Blahoslav** [b. Feb. 20, 1523, at Prerau, Moravia; Bp. 1557; Secretary of the Unity, 1558; d. Nov. 24, 1571, at Kromau, Moravia] has 65 in the 1561 *H. Bk.*, 17 being revisions of older Bohemian hymns.

(6) **Adam Sturm** [from Moravia; ordained priest 1555; d. Oct. 5, 1565] has 38 in the *H. Bk.* of 1561.

(7) **Martin Michalec** [b. 1504 at Leitmeritz; Bp. 1537; d. Jan. 24, 1547, at Prossnitz] has 31 in the 1561 *H. Bk.*

(8) **Gallus Dřevinek** [B.A. of Prague, 1524; member of the Select Council, 1553; d. Nov. 22, 1563, at Prossnitz] has 18 in the 1561 *H. Bk.*

(9) **John Wolf** [ord. priest 1529; member of Select Council; d. Oct. 26, 1548, at Prerau] has 13 in the 1561 *H. Bk.*

(10) **John Paustenik** [ord. priest 1529; d. 1543, at Jung Bunzlau] has 10 in the 1561 *H. Bk.*

(11) **George Styrsa** [of Wildenschwert; manager of the Brethren's printing office at Jung Bunzlau, 1520-31] has 9 in the 1561 *H. Bk.*

(12) Among the other authors whose names appear in the 1561, may be mentioned *Wenzel Solin* (5 hymns); *Nicholas of Turnau* (4); *Matthias Červenka* (q. v.) (5); *George Ciklovsky* (3); *John Jelecký* (q. v.) (3); *John Hus* (q. v.) (2); *Rokycan* (1); *John Horn* (q. v.) (1); *Urban* (1). Of the 193 hymns whose authorship is unknown many appear in the Utraquist hymn-books of 1522, 1531, and 1559.

§ ii. *The Bohemian Brethren's German Hymn-books.* These are the following:—

1. *Ein New Geseng buchlen* MDXXXI. &c. [Nürnberg]. At the end is, "Printed at Jungen Buntzel, in Bohemia. By George Wylmschwerer in the year 1531. Finished on the 12th day of March." The book is in small quarto; and the printer is George Styrsa of Wildenschwert (see No. 11 above). The preface, addressed to the German congregations at Landskron and Fulnek, in Bohemia, is signed "Michael Weisse, Ewer Diener." All the hymns (155 in number) according to the preface seem to have been composed or translated by M. Weisse himself, and this was evidently the opinion of the editors of the 1639 (see below). Two are indeed in the Anabaptist *Aussbund* of 1583, ascribed to Anabaptist writers; but on

what grounds is not known. Of the 155 hymns, as it will be seen from the table given below, we have only been able to find 12 which are translated from the Bohemian or the Latin. Almost all came more or less into use in the German Lutheran hymn-books of the century.

In the same year, 1531, an edition of this hymn-book is said to have appeared at Ulm, under the title of *Piccartisches Gesang Buch* (Piccarts or Piccardites, first an opprobrious name for the Brethren used by their foes; then by their friends, but never by themselves). Wackernagel, in his *Bibliographie*, 1855, Nos. 329, 375, 376, 377, 437, quotes reprints at Strassburg, 1534, and at Ulm in 1538, 1539, and 1541.

2. *Ein Gesangbuch der Brüder inn Behemen und Merherrn. Die man auss hass und neyd, Pickharden, Waldenses,* &c. *nennet,* &c. [Wernigerode]. At the end is "Printed at Nürnberg by Johann Günther, 1544. This hymn-book is in 8vo, and contains 181 hymns; 149 being from the 1531 (6 being eliminated), and 32 being new. Many reprints appeared in Germany, e.g. by Johann Berg and Ulric Neuber, at Nürnberg, 1564, 1576, 1585, 1590. The preface, by John Horn, informs us that the alterations were caused by the fact that some of the doctrines of the Brethren were not correctly represented in the former book, especially as regards the Lord's Supper. During the period since 1531 (I. § iv. 1), the Brethren, influenced by Luther, had somewhat changed their views, and Horn was himself a principal representative of the leaning towards Lutheranism. If what Jireček (*Hymnologia Bohemica*, p. 94) says be true, that the 1st ed. of this hymn-book appeared in 1535 (Weisse d. 1534), the passages in the preface regarding Weisse are of course less repugnant. Wackernagel, 1855, pp. 579-580, reprints Horn's preface in full.

3. *Kirchengeseng darinnen die Heubtartickel des Christlichen glaubens kurtz gefasset und ausgeleget sind; jtzt vom newen durchsehen, gemehret, und Der Rö. Kei. Maiestat, in unterthenigsten demut zugeschrieben.* Anno Domini 1566 [Berlin]. According to Blahoslav's account, this hymn-book was sent in MS. to the Emperor Maximilian, in 1564, and was first printed in 1566, at Eibenschütz, in Moravia, after the death of Ferdinand, his father. It is in 4to, and contains 343 hymns; being the hymns of the edition of 1544, with the exception of 15 which are omitted, and 177 which are new. An *Appendix* is added with 106 hymns by Lutheran authors. The preface (addressed to the "Reformed Evangelical Christian Churches of the German nation") is signed by Michael Tham, John Jelecky, and Peter Herbert. This book was reprinted, unaltered, at Nürnberg, in 1580.

4. Later editions of the Brethren's German hymn-book appeared in 1606 at Kralitz, in Moravia, edited by Martin Polykarp; in 1639 at Lissa in Poland, edited by Daniel Vetter; and in 1661 at Amsterdam, edited by J. A. Comenius. In the edition of 1639 [Berlin] the names of the authors are given in the index of first lines. There is also a biographical list (reprinted by *Wackernagel*, i. p. 726) "Of those persons who translated the Bohemian hymns into German verse, and also prepared this hymn-book." All the hymns in the 1639, which are taken from the collections of Weisse and Horn, are said to be composed by these authors.

5. The principal contributors to the editions of 1566-1639, are the following:—

(1) **Peter Herbert** (q. v.), 94 hymns.

(2) **John Jelecky** (q. v.), 22 hymns.

(3) **Michael Tham** [ordained priest, 1534; ministered at Fulnek and d. there Aug. 27, 1571], 28 hymns. Three are *tr.* in the *Moravian H. Bk.*, 1754, pt. i., Nos. 275, 282, 296.

(4) **John Girk or Jirek** [b. at Strehlen in Silesia; ordained priest 1549; d. at Neidenburg in East Prussia, March 1, 1562], 5 hymns.

(5) **George Vetter or Strey** [b. 1536, at Zabřeh in Moravia; ordained priest 1567; d. Jan. 25, 1599, at Selovitz in Bohemia], 6 hymns, one of which is *tr.* as No. 283 in pt. i. of the *Moravian H. Bk.*, 1754.

(6) **Martin Polycarp** [Hradecenus, i. e. of Königgrätz in Bohemia; d. soon after 1606, at Trebitz in Moravia], 9 hymns.

(7) **John Korytansky** [minister at Landskron in Bohemia, and Posen in Poland; d. 1582], 2 hymns, one of which is *tr.* as No. 254 in pt. i. of the *Moravian H. Bk.*, 1754.

(8) **Paulus Klantendorfer** (q. v.), 1 hymn.

(9) The other authors are, (1) *Centurio Sirutschko* (4 hymns); (2) *Valentine Schultz* (3); (3) *Lucas Libanus* of Löbau (1); *Martin Cornelius* of Zittau (2).

III. *A comparison of the German Hymn-books with the Bohemian.*

i. The hymn-book of Weisse, 1531. To only 12 of the German hymns in this collection have I been able to find corresponding Bohemian hymns, which having been published before 1531 may have been the originals of Weisse's hymns. But many of them are adapted from older Latin hymns (usually in such cases being headed by the first lines of the Latin); so it is very difficult, almost impossible, to decide whether Weisse translated from the Latin directly or through the Bohemian; more especially as his *trs.* are very free.

	German First Line.	Bohemian First Line.	Author, Source, &c.
1	Christus der uns selig macht .	Maudrost Boha otce prawda .	See "Patris Sapientia."
2	Der Tag vertreibt die finstre Nacht.	Jižt zaře vzchodí z temnosti .	From the *Habrowan H. Bk.*, 1530. The Boh. h. has 1 st. more than the German.
3	Frouen wir uns all in ein .	Radujme se vždy společně .	See "Freuen wir uns all in ein."
4	Gelobt sei Gott im höchsten Thron	Radujme se všickni nynie .	This is noted under Weisse, M.
5	Gelobt sei Gott von Ewigkeit .	Křest'ané chvalmež Boha .	1st pub. in the H. Bk. of 1501. "Lauda Sion Salvatorem" is the tune.
6	Glaubige Seel, schau dein Herr und König	Věrna duše, radostně máš .	The German has 9 st. The Bohemian (from the *Utraquist H. Bk.*, 1530) has 8.
7	Komm heiliger Geist, wahrer Gott	Ó svatý přijdiž duše, napln srdce	Noted under *Weisse, M.*
8	Nun lasst uns den Leib begraben	Rozžehnejmež se stím tělem	Noted under *Weisse, M.*
9	O Gott wir loben dich. . .	Té Boha chválíme, pánem .	From the "Te Deum laudamus." Bohemian, 1st in the *H. Bk.* of 1501.
10	O Vater der Barmherzigkeit, Brunn	Hospodine, studnice dobroty	"Kyrie fons bonitatis." From the Latin by *Lucas.* Boh., 1st pub. in 1501.
11	O wie fröhlich ist die Zeit .	Nastal jest nám všem čas .	The Boh., 13 st., 1st pub. in 1501.
12	Singen wir fröhlich allesamt	Nuž velikonoční chválu .	"Victimae paschali laudes," from the Latin. Boh., 1st pub. in 1501.

ii. *The hymn-book by John Horn, of 1544.* To 7 of the hymns J. Horn added to the Brethren's hymn-book correspond the following Bohemian hymns.

1	Der König der Ehren Christus .	Již pán nad pány Kristus .	"Cum rex gloriae Christus." The Boh. h. by M. Michalec has 3 st. more.
2	Heiliger Geist, Herre Gott .	Navštěv nás, Duše svatý .	"Veni sancte spiritus et emitte coelitus," a pretty exact *tr.* Boh., 1st pub. in 1501.
3	Nu loben wir heut allesamt .	Svrchovaného krále pochvalmež .	"Summi triumphum regis," *tr.* from the Latin by *Lucas.*
4	Nun lasst uns zu dieser Frist .	Všickni věrné Křest'ané .	"Gaudeamus pariter omnes." The Boh. h. by M. Michalec is a pretty exact *tr.* from the German.
5	O liebster Herre Jesu Christ .	Pane Ježíši Kriste ty's .	The Boh. h. by J. Augusta.
6	O Mensch thu heut hören die Klag	Poslauchejte žaloby nebeského otce	The Boh. in the *Utraquists' H. Bk.*, 1522; in Lucas, 1519 (?).
7	O freu dich Jerusalem . .	Těš se dcerko sionská .	By *M. Michalec.* The Boh. has 3 st. more than the German.

iii. *The hymn-book of 1566.* We find 97 hymns, which correspond to Bohemian hymns in the Boh. *H. Bk.* of 1561. The same remarks, which we have made respecting Weisse's hymns and their original Bohemian, apply to many of these.

The German hymns.	The authors of the Germ. hymns according to the H. Bk. of 1639	The Bohemian hymns.	The authors of the Bohemian hymns, superscriptions and other notes.
1. Als Christus hie auf Erden war	J. Girk .	Pán Kristus, syn boží věčný, přišel	A. Sturm. "Jesu quadragenariae."
2. Aus dem Abgrund der Höllen Schlund	C. Sirutschko .	Zhlubokosti své úzkosti tebet' vzývám	J. Blahoslav. Ps. 130. "De profundis clamavi" (partial tr.).
3. Barmherziger Herre Zebaoth	J. Jelecky .	Ó stvořiteli všemohaucí, otče Bože	Lucas, tr. from "Kyrie Angelorum Domine."
4. Barmherziger Vater, allmächtiger	J. Jelecky .	Milosrdný otče, všemohaucí tvorče	M. Michalec. "Concentu parili."
5. Christi Auffahrt und Erhöhung	M. Polykarp .	Krista pána na vstaupení slavmež	"Festum nunc celebre magnaque gaudia."
6. Christo deinem Heiland sei heut Lob	Missing in the H. Bk. of 1639	Ke cti Krista krále prozpěvujž vesele	J. Augusta. "Psallat ecclesia mater illibata."
7. Christus der wahre Gottes Sohn gesandt	P. Herbert .	Ježíš Kristus jsa Bůh pravý	J. Augusta. "Audi benigne conditor."
8. Danksagung sei, Lob und Ehr	M. Polykarp .	Bud' chvála Bohu otci i synu	From the H. Bk. of 1501. "Congaudent angelorum."
9. Das ewige wahre Licht	Missing in the H. Bk. of 1639	Světlo nejtajnější z stolice vyšlo	Lucas, tr. from "Area virga primae matris."

	The German hymns.	The authors of the Germ. hymns according to the H. Bk. of 1639.	The Bohemian hymns.	The authors of the Bohemian hymns, superscriptions, and other notes.
10	Das ewige Wort, der wahre Gott	P. Herbert .	Slovo syn Boží jediný, bez počátku	J. Blahoslav. " Verbum caro factum est."
11	Das Leben Christi unsers Herrn	M. Tham .	Život Kristů zvelebujme, slávu jeho	J. Augusta. "Adsunt festa iubilea."
12	Das wahre Licht von Gottes Thron	Is missing in the H. Bk. of 1639	Světlo zastkvělo se předivné nad námi	J. Blahoslav. Introitus.
13	Der eingeborne Gottes Sohn .	P. Herbert .	Věčný syn jednorozený, Bůh pravý	M. Michalec. " En trinitatis speculum."
14	Der ewig gütige Gott hat seine Gůt	J. Girk .	Buoh dobrý, dobroty své v sobě nemoha	J. Táborský (from the H. Bk. of 1501). Tune: "Area virga primae matris."
15	Der Herr und Heiland Jesus Christ	P. Herbert .	Aj nynít' Pán Bůh přichází zborův	J. Jelecky. "The seven letters from the Revelation of St. John, ii., iii."
16	Der Herzog unsrer Seligkeit ist heut	P. Herbert .	Aj prvorozený ctí a slavau ozdobený	J. Blahoslav. "Viri Gallilaei quid aspicitis."
17	Der höchste Gott hat in seinem Rat	Missing in the H. Bk. of 1639	Tajné rady uložení nevzalo jest	Lucas. "Verbum bonum et suave."
18	Dies ist der Tag den Gott der Herr selbst	P. Herbert .	Den přítomný vší vzácnosti jest hodný	" Haec est dies quam fecit Dominus."
19	Ei lasst uns jetzt allesamt .	M. Polykarp .	Narození Páně v tento čas pamatujme	
20	Ein freudenreicher Tag ist entstanden	J. Jelecky .	Nastal nám den přeutěšený .	A. Sturm.
21	Ein neue Bahn wir alle han .	J. Korytansky .	Cesta k nebi nová živá od Boha	J. Augusta. Measure and tune of the German and the Bohemian are different.
22	Ein wunderbar schön Licht scheinet	Missing in the H. Bk. of 1639	Světlo zastkvělo se jest dnešní den	J. Blahoslav. "Lux fulgebit hodie," Introit, at the morning service.
23	Erbarm dich unser o lieber Herre Gott	M. Polykarp .	Lítost měj nad námi, náš Pane	Gallus Dřevinek. "Miserere nostri Domine."
24	Erhör uns heut o unser lieber Vater	M. Polykarp .	Uslyšiž nás, Hospodine, nebot'	G. Dřevinek. "Exaudi nos Domine."
25	Freud und Wollust dieser Welt	M. Cornelius .	Rozkoš i utěšenie tohoto světa	1st pub. in the Utraquists' H. Bk., 1522.
26	Frohlocke heut christgläubige Seel	P. Herbert .	Veseliž se srdce každého věrného	A. Sturm. "Exultet jam angelica."
27	Frohlockt und rühmt mit Herz und Mund	P. Herbert .	Radujme se v našem srdci z dobrých	M. Konvaldsky.
28	Gott der heilig Geist vom Himmel	P. Herbert .	Svatý duch s nebe přišlý, naplnil	J. Blahoslav. "Spiritus Domini replevit."
29	Gott der Vater sprach zu Christo	P. Herbert .	Pán Bůh otec nebeský synu svému	M. Michalec. Ps. 110
30	Gottes Sohn vom höchsten Thron	M. Tham .	S vysosti na tento svět otec .	The priest Miřinský (Utraquist); 1st pub. in the Utraquists' H. Bk., 1522.
31	Gott ist zwar gütig alle zeit .	J. Jelecky .	Dobrotivýt' jest Pán Bůh náš,	J. Augusta.
32	Gott unserm Herrn sei ewig Lob und	P. Herbert .	Stvořiteli věčnému bud' chvála od	A. Sturm.
33	Gott wolln wir loben, der mit edlen Gaben	P. Herbert .	Budiž veleben Pán Bůh náš, pochválen	J. Augusta.
34	Hallelujah singt all mit grosser Freud	P. Herbert .	Hallelujah zpívejme s radostí	A. Sturm. "Invitatorium."
35	Hallelujah singt all mit Freuden	P. Herbert .	Hallelujah Duchsvatý přišel.	J. Augusta.
36	Hallelujah singt und seid froh	Missing in the H. Bk. of 1639	Hallelujah sláva narozenému pánu	" Alleluia, dies sanctificatus illuxit."
37	Heilig und zart ist Christi Menschheit	P. Herbert .	Ó ušlechtilé přirození . .	J. Blahoslav. The Boh. h. has 1 st. more than the German.
38	Heiliger Geist du bist ein Gott	P. Herbert .	Duše svatý, jenž 's pán a Bůh všemohaucí	M. Michalec.
39	Herr Christ des Lebens Quell	P. Herbert .	Ó Kriste vzkříšený, král ' nad králi	" Vita Sanctorum, decus Angelorum."
40	Herr Gott schick uns zu deinen Geist	G. Vetter .	Bože náš myt' prosíme dej at' právě	Lucas, from the Latin. "Patrem natum Paracletum."
41	Herr Gott, Schöpfer heiliger gütiger	M. Tham .	Bože věčný všemohaucí otče svatý	
42	Herr Gott send deinen Geist der lieben	P. Herbert .	Sešliž Hospodine svatého ducha svého	J. Blahoslav.
43	Herr Gott Vater der du bist gütig	P. Herbert .	Bože otče jenž 's milostivý a dobrotivý	
44	Hoch gelobt seist du Jesu Christ	P. Herbert .	Vítej, Jezukriste, s nebeské vysosti	J. Augusta.
45	Hör Mensch ein traurig Geschicht	M. Tham .	Chtějmež my poslauchati, také	J. Paustenik.
46	Jauchzt zu Ehren Christo .	M. Polykarp .	Plesej Bohu, vzdávej mu chválu	J. Augusta. "Ps. 66."
47	Ich fahr auf, spricht Christus der Herr	P. Herbert .	Ját' vstupuji, dí Pán, vnebe k otci	J. Augusta. "Ascendo ad patrem meum."
48	Ich werd erfreut überaus, wenn ich	J. Jelecky .	Ját' sem v tom rozveselen .	M. Michalec. "Ps. 122. Laetatus sum in his," tune and measure of the Germ. and the Boh. hymns are different.

	The German hymns.	The authors of the Germ. hymns according to the H. Bk. of 1639.	The Bohemian hymns.	The authors of the Bohemian hymns, superscriptions, and other notes.
49	Jesu Gottes Lämmlein, der du bist des	P. Herbert	Ó beránku boží, jenž jsi obětován	A. Sturm.
50	Jesu Kreuz Leiden und Pein	P. Herbert	Umučenie našeho pána milostného	1st pub. in the Utraquists' H. Bk., 1522.
51	Jesus Christus unser Herr	Missing in the H. Bk. of 1639	Když syn boží v neděli vstal jest	Lucas. "Mane prima sabbati."
52	Jesus ward bald nach seiner Tauf	P. Herbert	Pán Ježíš po svém pokřtění puzen na	Lucas. "Ex more docti mystico."
53	Ihr Gottesboten rühmt allezeit	Missing in the H. Bk. of 1639	Vypravujtež, nebeští, slávu slova	Lucas. "Coeli enarrant gloriam Dei," tr. from the Latin.
54	Jubiliert heut alle Gemeinen (= Hallelu'ah freu dich Christenschar)	P. Herbert	Slavtež jméno jeho (= Hallelujah prozpěvuj)	M. Michalec. Easter Invitatory.
55	Komm Schöpfer heiliger Geist	P. Herbert	Přijdiž těšiteli duše svatý, a věrných	"Veni Creator Spiritus," from the Latin.
56	Lasst uns ansehn die Sterblichkeit	P. Herbert	Vizmež příklad smrtedlnosti, mrtvého	Lucas. "Rogamus te Domine Deus," tr. from the Latin.
57	Lasst uns Christi Sieg und Auffahrt	P. Herbert	Z vítěžství Ježíše, pána převelmi sl.	J. Blahoslav.
58	Lasst uns heut loben unsern König	Missing in the H. Bk. of 1639	Nejvyššího krále všech, Boha, chvalme	"Summi regis archangele Michael."
59	Lasst uns hören die Stimm und herzliche	P. Herbert	Prorockýslyšme žádosti plný hlas	J. Blahoslav. "Introitus, which the old Bohemians named 'Rorate' and used to sing on Advent Sunday before morning service."
60	Lasst uns hören die Stimm (see Hallelujah singt all mit grosser Freud, 34)			
61	Lasst uns loben Gott den Herrn	J. Girk	Ej nuž chválu vděčnau vzdávejmež	N. Turnovský. "Eja recolamus laudibus piis."
62	Lasst uns mit herzlicher Begier	P. Herbert	Nábožnými srdci nyní prosby čiňme	Lucas.
63	Lobsingt heut zu Ehren Christo Jesu	P. Herbert	Chválu vzdávejte Pánu Bohu mocnému	A. Sturm, corrected by Horn, "Laudem dicite Deo nostro."
64	Menschenkind was brüst du dich	M. Cornelius	Proč se pneš, ó člověče, k nebi pýchau	J. Wolf.
65	Nehmt wahr das Licht, welchs erleucht	P. Herbert	Aj světlo světa k osvěcování	J. Blahoslav. "Lumen ad revelationem."
66	Nehmt wahr der Weisen aus dem	M. Polykarp	Aj mudrci od východu obětovali dary	J. Augusta. "Invitatorium."
67	Nun lasst uns heut all einträchtiglich	P. Herbert	Prozpěvujmež všickni vesele a slavmež	J. Augusta. "Ecce concipies et paries filium."
68	Nun seht und merket lieben Leut	J. Jelecky.	Neděstež se všickni toho	J. Rokyta.
69	O du allmächtiger König und Herr	P. Herbert	Ó králi a pánc Bože Abrahamů	"Domine Rex, Deus Abraham."
70	O du unerforschlicher, allmächtiger	M. Polykarp	Bože nepostihlý a všemohaucí Kriste	
71	O Gott erbarm dich mein, wasch	P. Herbert	Smiluj se nade mnau, Bože shlad'	J. Augusta. "Ps. 51."
72	O Gott warum verlässest du	Missing in the H. Bk. of 1639	Hospodine proč odmítáš lid znající	J. Avgusta. "Ps. 10."
73	O heiliger Geist sei heut und allezeit	P. Herbert	Ducha svatého milost rač býti s námi	"Sancti Spiritus adsit nobis gratia," from the Latin.
74	O Hirt und Heiland Israel, der du	J. Jelecky	Ó pastýři izraelský, synu Boha živého	J. Augusta. "Ps. 80."
75	O Mensch schau an Christi Leben	C. Sirutschko	Přeblahoslavený člověk, jehož by byl	J. Blahoslav. Ps. 1. "Beatus vir qui non abiit."
76	O Vater aller Barmherzigkeit	M. Tham	Vzbud' nás, Pane, at' povstaneme	Lucas.
77	O welch eine wunderbare und unerhörte	Missing in the H. Bk. of 1639	Ó předivné a neslýchané navštívení	J. Blahoslav. "O admirabile commercium" (adapted from an old Boh. hymn).
78	O wie sehr lieblich sind all deine Wohnung	J. Jelecky.	Aj jak jsou milí tvoji příbytkové	J. Augusta. "s. 84." The first time in the Utraquists' H. Bk. of 1559.
79	O wie süss ist dein Gedächtnis	P. Herbert	Ježíši tvat' jest památka sladší nad	Tune: "Jesu dulcis memoria" (B. de Clairvaux).*
80	Preiset mit Freuden von ganzem Gemüte	P. Herbert	Chvály radostné nebeskému otci	J. Blahoslav. "Ut queant laxis resonare fibris."
81	Preis und Ehr sei Gott in der Höh	Missing in the H. Bk. of 1639	Sláva na výsostech Bohu a na zemi	"Gloria in excelsis deo," from the ecclesiastical Gradual, 1st pub. in the H. Bk., 1501.
82	Schau wie lieblich und gut ists	P. Herbert	Aj jak jest to milé a utěšené.	M. Cervenka. "Ps. 133."
83	Sei gelobet Herr Jesu Christ du König	M. Tham	Zdráv bud' králi nebeský zemský	Lucas. "Salve rex coeli et terrae," tr. from the Latin.

* The Brethren's hymn is not a translation of Bernard's Latin hymn, but of a communion-hymn by the famous follower of Hus: *Mag. Jacobellus*, "Jesu tui memoria," first published by *Collinus* (Prague, 1574) under the title, "Antiqua et constans confessio." The Bohemian translation was first printed in the *Utraquists'* H. Bk. of 1522.

The German hymns.	The authors of the Germ. hymns according to the H. Bk. of 1639.	The Bohemian hymns.	The authors of the Bohemian hymns, superscriptions, and other notes.
84	Selig sind zu loben Gottes Märtyrer	Missing in the H. Bk. of 1639	Ó přeblahoslavené blahoslavených	Lucas. "O beata beatorum martyrum."
85	Singet mit Freuden lobet und preist	P. Herbert .	Pokřikněmež všickni k chvále Pána	M. Michalec, though some say that Br. A. Sturm composed it. (Blahoslav, De cantionali).
86	Singt all zu Ehren . .	M. Polykarp .	Dejmež chválu Pánu a Bohu všemoh	"Festa Christi omnis christianitas."
87	Singt fröhlich und seid wohlgemut	M. Tham .	Hod radostný pamatujme syna božího	M. Michalec.
88	Steh auf Herr Gott o stehe auf	M. Tham .	Povstan', Pane, ó povstan', navštěviž	Lucas.
89	Uns ist heut allen ein seligs Kind	P. Herbert .	Dítě překrásné naro dilo se nám	J. Blahoslav. "Puer natus est nobis," he "adapted it from an old one and cast it into a new form."
90	Wach auf Christenmensch und betracht	M. Tham .	Probud' se již, duše věrná, přišlat'	Lucas. 1st pub. in the Utraquists' H. Bk., 1530.
91	Wach auf Jerusalem sei froh	M. Tham .	Probudiž se. ó Jeruzaléme, neb aj	J. Blahoslav. "Introitus."
92	Wacht fröhlich auf ihr Gerechten	Missing in the H. Bk. of 1639	Prábud'te se spravedliví, bydlitelé Siona	J. Blahoslav.
93	Weil dieser Tag vergangen ist	P. Klantendorffer	Práci denní vykonavše a k noci se	J. Blahoslav.
94	Weil wir vom Herren mancherlei guts	Missing in the H. Bk. of 1639	Aj ponevadž my dobré věci zdejší	Lucas. "Si bona suscepimus," tr. from the Latin.
95	Wer in guter Hoffnung will von hinnen	P. Herbert .	Kdož chce v dobré naději smrti své	Donát (a member of a noble family, one of whom was chamberlain to the emperor Charles IV.).
96	Wohlan ihr lieben Kinder, die wir sind	J. Jelecky .	Ej nuž my dítky, spolu křtem	George Ciklovský.
97	Wohlauf die ihr hungrig seid	P. Herbert .	Ej nuž lační žízniví, sytosti božské	J. Augusta.

The sources of the Bohemian Brethren's hymnology (besides the original hymn-books) are on the German hymn-books, *Wackernagel*, Leipz., 1867–77; Tucher, Schatz des evang. Kirchengesangs, Leipz., 1848; and on the Bohemian hymn-books, Jireček, *Hymnologia bohemica, dějiny církevního básnictví českého až do xuiii. století*, in the *Abhandlungen der königl. böhmischen Gesellschaft der Wissenschaften* vi. 9, Prague, 1878.   [J. T. M.]

Böhm, David [Behme].

Böhm, Martin [Behm].

Böhmer, Just Henning, s. of Valentin Böhmer, advocate of Hannover, b. at Hannover, Jan. 29, 1674. After studying Law at the Universities at Jena, Rinteln, and Halle, he graduated at Halle in 1698, and began to lecture in 1699. In 1701 he was appointed Professor extraordinary, in 1702 Doctor, and and in 1711 ordinary Professor of Law, at Halle. He subsequently received many honours, being appointed in 1731 Director of the University of Halle, in 1743 Chancellor of the Duchy of Magdeburg, &c., and was reckoned a very high authority especially in ecclesiastical law. While lecturing to his students, Aug. 8, 1749, he suddenly became ill, and after a stroke of palsy, d. Aug. 23, 1749. (Koch, iv. 373–375; Allg. Deutsche Biog., iii. 79–81, the latter dating his death Aug. 29.) Of his 21 hymns, 3 appeared in Freylinghausen's Geistreiches G. B. 1704–5. Two have been tr. into English, viz.:—

i. **Brich durch, mein angefochtnes Herz.** [*Passiontide.*] 1st pub. 1704, as above, No. 646, in 14 st. of 5 l., repeated as No. 218 in the Berlin G. L. S., ed. 1863. Tr. as:—

Courage, my sorely tempted heart! A good tr. by Miss Winkworth of st. i.–iii., vi., ix., xii.–xiv. in the 2nd Series of her Lyra Ger. 1858, p. 143, repeated as No. 126 in her C. B. for England, 1863. In Schaff's Christ in Song, ed. 1879, p. 356.

ii. **O auferstandner Siegesfürst.** [*Easter.*] 1704,

as above, No. 650, in 14 st. of 8 l., included as No. 314 in the Berlin G. L. S., ed. 1863. Tr. as:—

O risen Lord! O conquering King! A good tr. by Miss Winkworth of st. i., iv.–vi., xiii., xiv., in the 2nd Series of her Lyra Ger., 1858, p. 41. In full in Schaff's Christ in Song, ed. 1879, p. 208, and, with alterations and the omission of st. iv., in Allon's Supp. Hys., No. 325; N. Cong., No. 1041; and J. L. Porter's Coll., 1876, No. 757. In her C. B. for England, 1863, No. 62, altered, with the trs. of st. iv., xiv. omitted. [J. M.]

Böhmer, Maria Magdalena, sister of J. H. Böhmer (see above), was born at Hannover, where she died, unmarried, in 1743 or 1744 (Koch, iv. 373; Bode, p. 47). She contributed two hymns (Nos. 655, 660) to Freylinghausen's G. B., 1704; while one (No. 430) in his Neues Geistreiches G. B., 1714, and four (Nos. 188, 193, 194, 582) in the Neue Sammlung, Wernigerode, 1752, are also ascribed to her. The only hymn by her tr. into English is—

Eins Christen Herz. [*Longing for Heaven.*] 1st pub. as No. 655 in Freylinghausen's G. B., 1704, in 6 st. of 6 l., repeated as No. 701 in the Berlin G. L. S., ed. 1863. It is tr. as:—

Regardless now of things below. A very free tr. by J. Wesley in H. & Sacred Poems, 1740 (P. Works, 1868–72, vol. i. p. 222), in 4 st. Included, as No. 6, in the Wesley H. & Spiritual Songs, 1753; in the Supp. of 1830 to the Wes. H. Bk.; and in the Wes. H. Bk., 1875. [J. M.]

Boie, Nicolaus. [Boye.]

Bonar, Horatius, D.D. Dr. Bonar's family has had representatives among the clergy of the Church of Scotland during two centuries and more. His father, James Bonar, second Solicitor of Excise in Edinburgh, was a man of intellectual power, varied learning, and deep piety.

Horatius Bonar was b. in Edinburgh, Dec. 19th, 1808; and educated at the High School and the University of Edinburgh. After completing his studies, he was "licensed" to preach, and became assistant to the Rev. John Lewis, minister of St. James's, Leith. He was ordained minister of the North Parish, Kelso, on the 30th November, 1837, but left the Established Church at the "Disruption," in May, 1843, remaining in Kelso as a minister of the Free Church of Scotland. The University of Aberdeen conferred on him the doctorate of divinity in 1853. In 1866 he was translated to the Chalmers Memorial Church, the Grange, Edinburgh; and in 1883 he was chosen Moderator of the General Assembly of of the Free Church of Scotland.

Dr. Bonar's hymns and poems were, he tells us, composed amid a great variety of circumstances; in many cases he cannot himself recall these circumstances; they also appeared in several publications, but nearly all have been published or republished in the following:— (1) *Songs for the Wilderness*, 1843-4. (2) *The Bible Hymn Book*, 1845. (3) *Hymns, Original and Selected*, 1846. (4) *Hymns of Faith and Hope*, First Series, 1857; Second Series, 1861; Third Series, 1866. (5) *The Song of the New Creation*, 1872. (6) *My Old Letters*, a long poem, 1877. (7) *Hymns of the Nativity*, 1879. (8) *Communion Hymns*, 1881. In addition to numerous prose works, he has also edited *The New Jerusalem; a Hymn of the Olden Time*, 1852, &c.

Dr. Bonar's poems—including many beautiful lyrics, several psalm versions, and translations from the Greek and Latin, a large number of hymns, and a long meditative poem—are very numerous, too numerous, perhaps, for their permanent fame as a whole.

Dr. Bonar's scholarship is thorough and extensive; and his poems display the grace of style and wealth of allusion which are the fruit of ripe culture. Affected very slightly by current literary moods, still less by the influence of other religious poetry, they reveal extreme susceptibility to the emotional power which the phases of natural and of spiritual life exercise; the phases of natural life being recognised chiefly as conveying and fashioning spiritual life, used chiefly for depicting spiritual life, and handled for this purpose with greater delicacy of touch than in the *Olney Hymns*, and with less conscious purpose than in the *Christian Year*. As a result of this susceptibility, and from habitual contemplation of the Second Advent as the era of this world's true bliss, his hymns and poems are distinguished by a tone of pensive reflection, which some might call pessimism. But they are more than the record of emotion; another element is supplied by his intellectual and personal grasp of Divine truth, these truths particularly:—The gift of a Substitute, our Blessed Saviour; Divine grace, righteous, yet free and universal in offer; the duty of immediate reliance upon the privilege of immediate assurance through that grace; communion with God, especially in the Lord's Supper, respecting which he insists on the privilege of cherishing the highest conceptions which Scripture warrants; and finally, the Second Advent of our Lord: by his vigorous celebration of these and other truths as the source and strength of spiritual life, his hymns are protected from the blight of unhealthy, sentimental introspection.

To sum up: Dr. Bonar's hymns satisfy the fastidious by their instinctive good taste; they mirror the life of Christ in the soul, partially, perhaps, but with vivid accuracy; they win the heart by their tone of tender sympathy; they sing the truth of God in ringing notes; and although, when taken as a whole, they are not perfect; although, in reading them, we meet with feeble stanzas, halting rhythm, defective rhyme, meaningless iteration; yet a singularly large number have been stamped with approval, both in literary circles and by the Church.

In G. Britain and America nearly 100 of Dr. Bonar's hymns are in C. U. They are found in almost all modern hymnals from four in *H. A. & M.* to more than twenty in the American *Songs for the Sanctuary*, N. Y., 1865-72. The most widely known are, "A few more years shall roll;" "Come, Lord, and tarry not;" "Here, O my Lord, I see Thee face to face;" "I heard the Voice of Jesus say;" "The Church has waited long;" and "Thy way, not mine, O Lord."

In addition to these and others which are annotated under their respective first lines, the following are also in C. U.:—

i From *Songs for the Wilderness*, No. 1, 1843.
1. For Thee we long and pray. *Sunday Morning.*
2. Holy Father, hear my cry. *A Child's Prayer.*
3. I thought upon my sins and I was sad. *Christ our Peace.*
4. Peace to the world, our Lord is come. *A Millennial Song.*
5. Spirit of everlasting grace. *The Vision of Dry Bones.*

ii. From *Songs for the Wilderness*, No. 2, 1844.
6. Ho, ye thirsty, parched and fainting. *Invitation.*
7. O 'tis not what we fancied it. *The world renounced.*
8. Sing them, my children, sing them still. *Children exhorted to Praise.*
9. Time's sun is fast setting. *Advent.*
10. Weep, pilgrim, weep, yet 'tis not for the sorrow. *Faith.*
11. Yes, for me, for me He careth. *Christ the Elder Brother.*

iii. From *The Bible Hymn Book*, 1845.
12. Jesus, my sorrow lies too deep. *Jesus, the Great High Priest.*
13. There is a Morning Star, my soul. *The Morning Star.*
14. This is not my place of resting. *Pressing towards heaven.*

iv. From *Hymns, Original and Selected*, 1846.
15. Let there be light, Jehovah said. *Creation.*

v. From *Hymns of Faith and Hope*, 1st series, 1857.
16. Be brave, my brother. *The Fight of Faith.*
17. Blessed be God, our God. *Good Friday.*
18. Everlasting praises. *Doxology.*
19. Go up, go up, my heart. *Heavenly aspirations desired.*
20. I close my heavy eye. *Evening.* Sometimes given as "*We close our heavy eyes.*"
21. I see the crowd in Pilate's hall. *Good Friday.*
22. Jesus, while this rough desert soil. *Strength by the Way.*
23. Jesus, Whom angel-hosts adore. *The Word made Flesh.* From "The Son of God, in mighty love."
24. Make haste, O man, to live. *Exhortation to lay hold of Life.*
25. No seas again shall sever. *Heaven.*
26. Oppressed with noonday's scorching heat. *Shadow of the Cross.*
27. Rest for the toiling hand. *Burial.* From "Lie down, frail body, here."
28. Shall this life of mine be wasted? *Exhortation to Duty.*
29. These are the crowns that we shall wear. *Heaven.*
30. Thy works, not mine, O Christ [Lord]. *The Sin-bearer.*
31. Where the faded flower shall freshen. *Heaven.*

vi. From *Hymns of Faith and Hope.* 2nd series, 1861.
32. Be still, my soul, Jehovah loveth Thee. *Rest in the Love of God.*
33. Christ has done the mighty work. *Good Friday.*
34. Come, mighty Spirit, penetrate. *Whitsuntide.*
35. Deep down beneath the unresting surge. *Burial at Sea.*
36. Fear not the foe, thou flock of God [thou little flock]. *Battle-Song of the Church.*
37. For lack of love I languish. *Lent.*
38. From this bleak hill of storms. *Eternal Rest desired.*
39. He liveth long who liveth well. *The True Life.*
40. Here shall death's triumph end: the rock-barred door. *Easter.* From "The tomb is empty: wouldst thou have it full."

41. Jesus, Sun and Shield art Thou. *Jesus the First and Last.*
42. Jesus, the Christ of God. *Praise to Christ.*
43. Light of the world, for ever, ever shining. *Christ the Light of the World.* From "Why walk in darkness? Has the dear light vanished?"
44. Make use of me, my God. *Duty desired.*
45. Not what I am, O Lord, but what Thou art. *The Love of God.*
46. O Light of Light, shine in. *Cry of the Weary.*
47. O love of God, how strong and true. *Love of God.*
48. O love that casts out fear. *Love of God.*
49. O strong to save and bless. *Lent.*
50. O this soul, how dark and blind. *Lent.*
51. Safe across the waters. *Thanksgiving at end of a journey.*
52. Silent, like men in solemn haste. *Pressing onwards.*
53. Speak, lips of mine. *Exhortation to Praise.*
54. The Bridegroom comes. *Advent.*

vii. From *Hymns of Faith and Hope.* 3rd series, 1866.

55. Bear Thou my burden, Thou Who bar'st my sin. *Lent or Passiontide.*
56. Done is the work that saves. *Easter.*
57. Father, our children keep. *Prayer on behalf of Children.*
58. Fill Thou my life, O Lord my God. *Life's Praise.*
59. Finish Thy work, the time is short. *Earnest labour to the end.*
60. From the Cross the blood is falling. *Good Friday.*
61. He called them, and they left. *Obedience.*
62. Help me, my [O] God to speak. *Truth desired.*
63. Holy Father, Mighty God. *Holy Trinity.*
64. How are my troubles multiplied. *Ps. iii.*
65. How sweetly doth He show His face. *Flower Service.*
66. Light hath arisen, we walk in its brightness. *Sustaining power of Faith.*
67. Lo, God, our God has come. *Christmas.*
68. Lord, give me light to do Thy work. *Divine guidance desired.*
69. No, not despairingly. *Lent.*
70. Not to ourselves again. *Life in Christ, or, Living unto God.*
71. Now in parting, Father, bless us. *Post Communion.*
72. Sounds the trumpet from afar. *Battle-Song of the Church.*
73. Thee in the loving bloom of morn. *God in all.*
74. Through good report and evil, Lord. *Faithfulness.*
75. To Jehovah, God of might. *Praise to the Father.*
76. To the name of God on high. *Doxology.*
77. Upward, where the stars are burning. *Heavenward Aspirations.*
78. We take the peace which He hath won. *The Gift of Peace.*
79. When the weary, seeking rest. *Intercession for all Conditions of Men.*

viii. From *The Song of the New Creation,* 1872.

80. For the Bread and for the Wine. *H. Communion.*
81. Light of life so softly shining. *Light of Life.*
82. Yet there is room. The Lamb's bright hall of song. *Home Missions.*

ix. From *Hymns of the Nativity,* 1879.

83. Great Ruler of the land and sea. *Sailors' Liturgy.*

x. From *Communion Hymns,* 1881.

84. Beloved, let us love. *Brotherly Love.*

In several instances these hymns are given in an abbreviated form, and sometimes alterations are also introduced. In this latter respect however Dr. Bonar has suffered less than most modern hymn-writers.   [J. B.]

Bonar, Jane Catharine, née Lundie, daughter of the Rev. Robert Lundie, some time minister of the parish of Kelso, b. at Kelso Manse, December, 1821, married, in 1843, to Dr. H. Bonar, and d. in Edinburgh, Dec. 3, 1884. Her hymns appeared in Dr. Bonar's *Songs for the Wilderness,* 1843–4, and his *Bible H. Bk.,* 1845. Their use is very limited. Mrs. Bonar is chiefly known through her hymn :—

Pass away, earthly joy. *Jesus, all in all,* which appeared in the *Songs for the Wilderness,* 2nd Series,

1844, and again in the *Bible H. Bk.* 1845, No. 108, in 4 st. of 8 l., including the refrain, "Jesus is mine!" The original text is given in Dr. Hatfield's *Church H. Bk.* 1872, No. 661. Sometimes this is altered to "Fade, fade, each earthly joy," as in the American *Songs for the Sanctuary,* 1865, No. 774, and others. The last stanza of this hymn is also st. iv. of the cento, "Now I have found a friend," &c. (q. v.)

Bonaventura, Saint and Cardinal, commonly called "Doctor Seraphicus," was b. of pious and well-to-do parents at Bagnera, in Tuscany, 1221. His father's name was John, of Fidenza, and he was baptized in his father's name of John. It is said that his mother, when her boy of four years old was "sick unto death," made a vow that, if he recovered, he should become a member of the Order of St. Francis, and that, his recovery taking place immediately thereupon, she exclaimed, "O Bonaventura!" ("O what good luck"), the name adopted by the son when he entered the Franciscan Order in 1242.

He was sent by his Order as a student to the University of Paris probably in or about A.D. 1242, and became a Professor of Theology there in 1245. In 1256, at the age of thirty-five years, and thirteen years after his profession as a monk, he was, in his absence, unanimously elected General of his Order by a Chapter held at Rome in the presence of the then Pope, Alexander IV. His election proved a happy one for the Franciscans, whose Order was in a critical condition, threatened with a schism, and tainted with heresy. In 1267 he was offered the Archbishopric of York by Pope Clement IV., but declined it, on the ground that any further addition to the long list of Italian dignitaries, who were being forced upon the Church of England at that time against its will, would cause fresh strife, and end in his expulsion. Upon the death of Clement in the following year, it is said (with what amount of truth authorities differ) that he declined the Papacy itself, though strongly urged to accept it, in order to put an end to the dissension between the French and Italian Cardinals, which kept the chair of St. Peter vacant for more than two years. When at last the College of Cardinals had delegated to six of their number the power of filling up the vacancy, and these delegates, possibly by Bonaventura's advice, had elected Theobald, Archdeacon of Liège, under the title of Gregory X., the new Pope very soon after his election made Bonaventura a Cardinal, so sorely against the will of the latter, that he fled to Paris in order to escape from the fresh responsibilities that such a position involved, and was only induced to return for investiture by the positive orders of the Pope to that effect. When he reached Rome, having received his cardinal's hat on the way, he was (1273) consecrated Bishop of Alba, one of the six suffragans of Rome.

He did not long enjoy his new honours. In 1274 Gregory X. assembled a great Œcumenical Council at Lyons, at which 500 bishops, 70 abbots, and at least 1000 dignified clergy were present. The two leading churchmen of the age, Thomas Aquinas and Bonaventura, were summoned to attend, the former to die on his road thither, the latter before its proceedings closed, in which he had taken part. Bonaventura was taken ill on July 6th, and d. on July 14th, 1274. He was buried in the Con-

vent of the Minorites at Lyons in the presence
of the Pope and all the Council.

When we turn from the facts of Bonaventura's life
to discuss his literary qualities and achievements, the
same remark forces itself upon us, that has to be made
about so many of the great mediaeval writers, whose
compositions consist both of prose and poetry, viz.,
that the former very far outweigh the latter in quantity,
as well as in importance. His contributions to Latin
hymnology are few and far between; and, though generally
good, are scarcely, with one exception, in the front rank
of such compositions. Of his style, as a hymn-writer,
Archbishop Trench, who is not given to exaggerated
praise, says, "His Latin poetry is good, but does not call
for any especial criticism" (*Sacred Lat. Poetry*, p. 145);
while Dean Milman places his "Hymn to the Cross" as
only inferior in melody to the "Stabat Mater" of
Jacopone da Todi, and the "Dies Irae" of Thomas of
Celano. But, indeed, beyond the beautiful "Recordare
sanctae crucis," it is more than doubtful what hymns
can be certainly attributed to Bonaventura. *Trench*
gives us in his *Sac. Lat. Poetry* two others, very beautiful in their very different styles, "Quam despectus,
quam dejectus," and "Quantum hamum caritas tibi
praesentavit," both of which he extracts from what is
the best edition of our author's collected works, *Bonaventurae Opp.*, Lugduni, 1668. It is, however, by no
means certain that either was really his own. *Daniel*
gives us only the "Recordare Sanctae Crucis" as certainly written by Bonaventura, besides a hymn to the
Virgin, founded on the "Te Deum," ii. 293, commencing "Te Matrem Dei Laudamus." *Mone* attributes
to him also the "In passione Domini, qua datur salus
homini" (q.v.), and gives a "Planctus Bonaventurae
de Christo," beginning "O Crux, frutex salvificus,"
which, however, he says is not included in the poems
of Bonaventura as given in his collected works (i. 152);
a version of a hymn by him on the "Crown of Mary"
(ii. 172), an "Officium Compassionis" on the Blessed
Virgin (ll. 139), and a long "Psalter of the Virgin" (ii.
233), which, however, *Trench* doubts his having written.
An edition published by a Dominican editor in the 15th
century, of St. Bernard's "Oratio ad Christum in
crucem pendentem," according to *Mone*, attributes part
of it, "Salve, salve, Jesu pie," to Bonaventura and not
to Bernard, and calls it "Orationes Bonaventurae," &c.
This "statement of the editor," *Mone* adds, "is not to
be overlooked." Several of his hymns were in use in
public worship, and the continual copying of them by
different hands, which this involved, has rendered it very
difficult, if not impossible, to ascertain always their correct texts. Very few have been translated into English.

[D. S. W.]

Bond, Alessie. [Faussett, A.]

Bonn, Hermann (or Gude), son of Arnold
Gude, Councillor at Quakenbrück near Osnabrück, was b. at Quakenbrück about 1504.
He matriculated at Wittenberg in 1523, and
after studying under Luther and Melanchthon,
he was for some time employed as a tutor.
In 1530 he was appointed Rector of the newly
founded St. Mary's School, in Lübeck; and in
1531, Superintendent of Lübeck. In 1543 at
the request of the burgesses of Osnabrück he
proceeded thither, and in the course of that
year as the result of his work the principality
was won to the cause of the Reformation. He
d. at Lübeck, Feb. 12, 1548 (*Koch*, i. 428–436;
Allg. Deutsche Biog., iii. 133).

As a hymn-writer his work consisted mainly of revisions of the older Latin hymns, and *trs*. of some of
them and of a few High German hymns into Low
German. His hymns appeared as *Etlike schöne Geistlike
gesenge* appended to the Magdeburg *G. B.*, 1542-43. The
only one *tr*. into English is:—

O wir armen Sünder [*Fall & Redemption*]. First
pub. 1542 as above in 6 st. of 4 l., and thence in *Wackernagel*, iii. p. 735. It begins "Och wy armen sünders!
unse missedadt," and first appeared in High German in
the Magdeburg *G. B.*, 1588. Based on the old Judas
hymn, c. 1400, "O du armer Judas." *Tr*. as "We
wratcheit sinnaris pure" in the *Gude and Godly Ballates*
(ed. 1567-68, folio 13), ed. 1868, p. 21. (2) "Twas our
great transgression," in the *Christian Examiner*, Boston, U.S., Sept. 1860   [J. M.]

Bornschürer, Johannes, b. Nov. 5,
1625, at Schmalkalden. After studying at the
Universities of Marburg, Jena, Erfurt, and
Strassburg he became, in 1650, pastor at Brot-
terode in Hesse Cassel, 1657 at Steinbach-
Hallenberg, 1661 diaconus at Schmalkalden,
and in 1670 decan in the town of Tann,
where he d. Dec. 5, 1677 (*Koch*, iii. 430; *Allg.
Deutsche Biog.*, iii. 176). To the hymn-book
which he edited for use in Tann, pub. as
*Geistliche Lieder zu Ubung christlicher Gott-
seligkeit*, at Meiningen, 1676, he contributed
five hymns, one of which is:—

Gott Vater, höre unser Bitt [*Holy Baptism*]. This
prayer to the Holy Trinity for a blessing on the child,
appeared as No. 6 of the Baptismal Hys. in 1676, as
above, p. 405, in 4 st. of 0 l. In the *Unv. L. S.*, 1851,
No. 260. The only *tr*. in C. U. is "O God the Father!
hear our prayer," a good and full *tr*. by A. T. Russell,
Nos. 154, 155, in his *Ps. & Hys*., 1851, No. 155 beginning
"O Thou most Holy Trinity," being a *tr*. of st. iv.

[J. M.]

Borthwick, Jane, daughter of James
Borthwick, manager of the North British
Insurance Office, Edinburgh, was b. April 9,
1813, at Edinburgh, where she still resides.
Along with her sister Sarah (b. Nov. 26, 1823;
wife of the Rev. Eric John Findlater, of Loch-
earnhead, Perthshire, who d. May 2, 1886) she
translated from the German *Hymns from the
Land of Luther*, 1st Series, 1854; 2nd, 1855;
3rd, 1858; 4th, 1862. A complete ed. was
pub. in 1862, by W. P. Kennedy, Edinburgh,
of which a reprint was issued by Nelson &
Sons, 1884.

These translations, which represent relatively a larger
proportion of hymns for the Christian Life, and a smaller
for the Christian Year than one finds in Miss Winkworth,
have attained a success as translations, and an acceptance
in hymnals only second to Miss Winkworth's. Since
Kennedy's *Hymno. Christ*., 1863, in England, and the
Andover *Sabbath H. Bk.*, 1858, in America, hardly a hymnal
selections therefrom, hardly a hymnal in England or
America has appeared without containing some of these
translations. Miss Borthwick has kindly enabled us
throughout this Dictionary to distinguish between the
61 translations by herself and the 53 by her sister. Among
the most popular of Miss Borthwick's may be named
"Jesus still lead on," and "How blessed from the bonds
of sin;" and of Mrs. Findlater's "God calling yet!" and
"Rejoice, all ye believers."

Under the signature of *H. L. L.* Miss
Borthwick has also written various prose
works, and has contributed many translations
and original poems to the *Family Treasury*,
a number of which were collected and pub. in
1857, as *Thoughts for Thoughtful Hours* (3rd
ed., enlarged, 1867). She also contributed
several *trs*. to Dr. Pagenstecher's *Coll*., 1864,
five of which are included in the new ed. of
the *H. L. L.*, 1884, pp. 256–264. Of her original hymns the best known are "Come, labour
on," and "Rest, weary soul." In 1875 she
pub. a selection of poems translated from Meta
Heusser-Schweizer, under the title of *Alpine
Lyrics*, which were incorporated in the 1884
ed. of the *H. L. L.* She d. in 1897. [J. M.]

Borthwick, Robert Brown. [Brown-
Borthwick, R.]

Borthwick, Sarah. [Borthwick, J.]

Böschenstein, Johann, s. of Heinrich
Böschenstein, a native of Stein on the Rhine,
was b. at Esslingen, Württemberg, in 1472.
After taking Holy Orders as a priest he be-
came, in 1505, tutor of Hebrew at Ingolstadt.
Leaving this in 1514 he went to Augsburg,

where, in the same year, he pub. a Hebrew Grammar, and in 1518, by the recommendation of Reuchlin, was invited as tutor of Greek and Hebrew to Wittenberg, where he had Melanchthon as a pupil. In 1519 he went to Nürnberg; 1521 to Heidelberg; and in 1522 to Antwerp. After a short stay in Zürich, where he taught Hebrew to Zwingli, he settled, in 1523, at Augsburg, where he became by royal license teacher of Hebrew, and where he d. 1539. (*Koch*, i. 219-221, ii. 469-471; *Allg. Deutsche Biog.*, iii. 184-186, the latter stating that he resided at Nürnberg in 1525, and then went to Nördlingen, and d. there in great poverty 1540.) *Koch* quotes 4 of his hymns, the best being:—

Da Jesus an dem Kreuze stund. [*Passiontide.*] *Wackernagel*, ii. p. 1091, gives two forms, the first in 9 st. of 5 l ("Do Ihesus an dem creütze stůund"), from an undated leaflet, c. 1515, the 2nd from M. Vehe's *G. B.* 1537. It has been, but *Wackernagel* thinks erroneously, called a *tr.* from the Latin of Peter Bolandus ("Stabat ad lignum crucis"). Kehrein, in his *Kirchen- und religiöse Lieder*, Paderborn, 1853, p. 198, quotes it from a paper MS., which he dates xvth cent. The first form is No. 73 in Porst's *G. B.*, ed. 1855. The later version of the Seven Words on the Cross, "Da Jesus an des Kreuzes Stamm" (q. v.), has superseded it in most modern hymn-books. *Tr.* as "When Jesus on the Cross was found," No. 385 in pt. ii. of the *Moravian H. Bk.*, 1746. In 1789 it was rewritten as, "When Jesus hung upon the Cross." [J. M.]

Boswell, Robert, b. 1746, in Ayrshire. He received a classical education, and was an excellent Hebrew scholar. For some time he was a writer to the Signet in Edinburgh. He joined the followers of John Glas, a dissenting minister from the Church of Scotland, and was chosen to be leading elder of the Glassite congregation at Edinburgh. Whilst highly appreciating the Scottish *Version of the Psalms*, he thought it to be susceptible of improvement, and pub. a revised version in 1784 as *The Psalms in Metre from the Original*. In 1786 a 2nd ed. appeared with the new title *The British Psalter*. [See **Scottish Hymnody, § VIII. 8**.] He d. suddenly whilst preaching in London, Sunday, April 1st, 1804.

Boswell, Robert Bruce, was grandson of the Robert Boswell above named. He was a clergyman of the Church of England, and was for some years Incumbent of St. James's Church, Calcutta. He was compiler and editor of a book of *Psalms & Hymns*, pub. anonymously, in 1838, and printed at the Church Mission Press, Calcutta. In this work were about 50 Psalm Versions of his own composition. These have fallen out of use.

Botham, Mary. [**Howitt, M.**]

Bottome, F., S.T.D., was b. in Derbyshire, England, May 26, 1823. In 1850, having removed to America, he entered the ministry of the Methodist Episcopalian Church; and in 1872 he received the degree of S.T.D. from Dickinson's College, Carlisle, Penn. In addition to assisting in the compilation of R. P. Smith's *Gospel Hymns*, London, 1872: *Centenary Singer*, 1869; *Round Lake*, 1872, he has written:—

1. **Come, Holy Ghost, all sacred fire.** *Invocation of the Holy Spirit.* Appeared in R. P. Smith's *Gospel Hymns*, 1872. It is in several collections, including the Ohio *H. Bk. of the Evang. Association*, 1881, No. 364.
2. **Full salvation, full salvation.** *Joy of full Salvation.* Written in 1871, and pub. in a collection by Dr. Cullis of Boston, 1873. Also in the Ohio *H. Bk.*, 1881, No. 384.

3. **Love of Jesus, all divine.** *Love of Jesus.* Written in 1872, and pub. in his *Round Lake*, 1872. It is in several collections.
4. **O bliss of the purified, bliss of the free.** *Sanctification.* Written in 1869, and pub. in the *Revivalist*, and numerous hymn-books in America, including the Ohio *H. Bk.* as above, 1881, No. 477, &c.

His hymns, "Sweet rest in Jesus"; and "Oneness in Jesus," are also found in several collections for evangelistic services. [J. J.]

Bound upon the accursed tree. *H. H. Milman.* [*Good Friday.*] This popular hymn appeared in Bp. Heber's posthumous *Hymns*, &c., 1827, p. 62, as the first of three hymns for Good Friday, in 4 st. of 10 l., but omitted, curiously enough, from Dr. Milman's own *Ps. & Hys.*, 1837. One of the first, if not the first, to bring it into regular congregational use was Elliott, who gave it in his *Ps. & Hys.*, 1835. From that date it gradually grew in popular favour until its use has become extensive, both in G. Britain and in America. In the *Meth. S. S. H. Bk.*, 1879, it is in 3 st. of 8 l. This was a special revision for that collection. Orig. text in *Lyra Brit.*, 1867, p. 404; and Schaff's *Christ in Song*, 1870, p. 163.

Bourdillon, Mary, née **Cotterill,** daughter of the Rev. Joseph Cotterill, some time Rector of Blakeney, Norfolk, b. at Ampton, Suffolk, Aug. 30, 1819, married to E. D. Bourdillon, and d. at Dresden, Feb. 19, 1870. Her principal poetical work was *A Mother's Hymns for her Children*, 1849, 2nd ed. 1852, containing 21 pieces. Of these the following are in C. U.:—

1. **Above the clear blue sky,** Beyond, &c. *Praise.*
2. **Blessed Jesus, wilt Thou hear us?** *Child's Prayer.*
3. **Gracious Saviour, from on high.** *Holy Baptism.*
4. **Jesus, we thank Thee for Thy day.** *Sunday.*
5. **Lamb of God, who came from heaven.** *Christ the Example.*
6. **There was a lovely Garden once.** *Eden.*

These hymns are characterized by great simplicity and directness of aim, and are most suitable for children.

Bourignon, Antoinette, was b. at Lisle in 1616. From a very early period she was under the influence of religion, which took, in course of time, a mystical turn. Undertaking the work of a religious reformer, she visited France, Holland, England, and Scotland; and published several works dealing with *The Testimony of Truth; The Renovation of the Gospel Spirit,* &c. Her enthusiasm, peculiarity of views, and disregard of all sects raised on the one hand zealous persecutors, and on the other warm adherents. At her death at Franeker, in Friesland, Oct. 30, 1680, she left a large number of followers, especially in Scotland and France. Her works were pub. in 19 vols. at Amsterdam, 1686. She is known to hymnology through her hymn, "Venez Jésus, mon salutaire" (q.v.).

Bourne, George Hugh, D.C.L., son of Rev. R. B. Bourne, born at St. Paul's Cray, Kent, 8th Nov. 1840, and educated at Eton, and C. C. C., Oxford, graduating B.A., 1863; B.C.L., 1866; and D.C.L. 1871. Taking Holy Orders in 1863, he became Curate of Sandford-on-Thames, 1863. He was afterwards Head Master of Chardstock Coll., and is now (1886) Warden of the same school, which has been transferred to St. Edmund's, Salisbury. Dr. Bourne has written the following hymns:—

1. Scarce discerning aught before us. *General.* Written in Switzerland in 1861, and pub. in *Lyra Messianica*, 1864, p. 17, in 10 st. of 4 l., and repeated in the *App.* to the S. P. C. K. *Ps. & Hys.*, 1869, in an abbreviated form.

2. O Christ, the king of human life. *H. Matrimony.* A hymn on Holy Matrimony, written in 1867 for the marriage of Dr. A. B. Webb, Bp. of Bloemfontein, and included in the S. P. C. K. *Appx.* to the *Ps. & Hys.*, 1869, and thence into *Church Hymns*, 1871.

3. Of the wondrous Body, O my tongue be telling. A translation of "Pange lingua gloriosi corporis," q.v., contributed to *Lyra Eucharistica*, 2nd ed., 1864. Dr. Bourne has also written seven Post-Communion hymns for use in the Chapel of St. Edmund's College, Salisbury. These hymns have not been published.   [J. J.]

Bourne, Hugh, the principal founder of the Primitive Methodist Society, and the editor of their first hymn-books, was b. at Fordhays, Stoke-on-Trent, April 3, 1772. His father, Joseph Bourne, a person in humble circumstances, was a member of the Church of England, whilst his mother belonged to the Wesleyan Society. His education, for his circumstances, was fairly good; and by earnest application to study he acquired some knowledge of Hebrew, Greek, and Latin. His mind was of a strongly devotional cast, and the Methodist movement of those days had such attractions for him that he joined himself thereto in 1799. The following year he went to reside near the Mow Cop Colliery, near Burslem, where he had secured an engagement. There, with two or three men of kindred spirit, he carried on a system of Prayer Meetings which culminated in a great Camp Meeting, after the American fashion, upon the Mow Cop Mountain, on Sunday, May 31st, 1807. Other camp meetings followed, but were condemned by the Wesleyan Conference later in the same year. Hugh Bourne, however, continued his evangelistic work in connection with the Wesleyan Society until June 27, 1808, when he was excommunicated, without notice or trial, by the Quarterly Meeting held at Burslem on that day. Subsequent acts of coolness and indifference on the part of the Wesleyan authorities, together with continued success in his evangelistic work, led him gradually to organize the Primitive Methodist Connexion. The decisive break occurred in 1810. From that date to his death, on the 11th Oct., 1852, Bourne gave himself to the work of extending and building up the Society of which he was practically the founder. He was the first editor of its magazine, and the first to compile a hymnal for its use.

Hugh Bourne's first effort in hymnology was the pub. of a very small *General Collection of Hymns and Spiritual Songs for Camp Meetings, Revivals, &c.*, 1809. This was enlarged and improved in 1819, 1820, 1821, 1822, and again in 1824. To these editions he contributed 10 hymns. In 1829 a second collection was added by him to the foregoing, to which he contributed another 20 hymns. This is the *Large Hymn Book, for the Use of the Primitive Methodists.* From the first collection one hymn only is still retained in C. U.:—"Camp-meetings with success are crown'd," altered to "Camp-meetings God has richly own'd," also rewritten by J. Flesher as, "This meeting with Thy presence crown," in the authorised hymnal of the Connexion; and from the second collection two hymns as follows:—

1. O Righteous Father, Lord of all. *Prayer for Children.*

2. We have a great High Priest. *H. P. of Christ.*

To the *Large Hymn Book* 146 hymns were also contributed which bore the signatures sometimes of " H. B. & W. S." and again " W. S. & H. B." In a note we are informed that the hymns with these ascriptions were by "Hugh Bourne and Wm. Sanders, jointly." Of these the following are at present in the authorized *Primitive Methodist Hymn Book*, 1853, and, in common with most of the hymns in that book, are greatly mutilated, and attributed now to Wm. Sanders and again to H. Bourne, without any apparent reason:—

1. A Pharisee unwisely stood. *Lent.*
2. Almighty God, of love divine. *Praise.*
3. Assist us, O Almighty Lord. *Missions.*
4. Come, let us lift our heart and voice. *Christmas*
5. Come, with your sore diseases. *Invitation.*
6. Encouraged by Thy gracious word. *Prayer.*
7. Great Jehovah, Sovereign Lord. *Prayer.*
8. Hark, the Gospel news is sounding. *Invitation.*
9. Jesus, my Lord, was crucified. *Passiontide.*
10. Jesus, Who spilt His precious blood. *The Advocate.*
11. Led by the God of truth and grace. *Seeking Heaven.*
12. Light of the Gentile race. *Missions.*
13. My brethren in the Lord. *Altered to—*
       Ye foll'wers of the Lord. *Faithfulness.*
14. My soul is now united, &c. *Altered to—*
       By faith I am united. *Union with Christ.*
15. Now, Lord, I on Thy truth depend. *Altered to—*
       O Lord, I on Thy truth depend. *Divine Aid*
16. Now, Lord, Thy blessing we implore. *D. Blessing.*
17. O, heavenly Zion, rise and shine. *Altered to—*
       Arise, O Zion, rise, &c. *Missions.*
18. See, in the mountain of the Lord. *Missions.*
19. Tho' in a world of sickness. *Altered to—*
       While in this world of sickness. *Confidence.*
20. To Thee, great Source of light. *Confidence.*
21. To Thee, O God of power divine. *Goodness of God*
22. We now are journeying [going] to the place. *Heavenward.*
23. We read in Thy most holy word. *H. Baptism.*
24. Ye sleeping souls, arise. *Exhortation.*

In addition to these, all of which are given in the official Collection of the Primitive Methodist Society, there is also:—

25. Welcome, O Saviour, to my heart. *Prayer—* which is well known to the American hymnals.

From a literary point of view these hymns are not worthy of the position which has been accorded to them for so many years. Their simplicity is their redeeming feature.   [J. J.]

Bourne, William St. Hill, b. in 1846, and educated at Merchant Taylors' School, and the London College of Divinity. Taking Holy Orders in 1869 he became successively Curate of Holy Trinity, Derby ; Harrow-on-the-Hill ; St. Paul's, St. Leonards-on-Sea ; Ashford, Kent ; in 1875, Vicar of Pinner, Middlesex ; and in 1880, Vicar of All Saints, Haggerstone. Author of *Poems* in various periodicals ; *Church Work and the Working Classes*, pub. in *Church Bells*, 1875, &c. In 1879 he became editor of *The Mission Field*, for the *S. P. G.* As a hymn-writer he is known through the following hymns:—

1. Children's voices strive not vainly. *Sunday School Anniversary.* Written in 1868.

2. Christ, Who once among us. *The Good Shepherd.* Written in 1868, and 1st pub. in the revised *H. A. & M.*, 1875.

3. Enter with thanksgiving. *Processional for Dedication Service.* Written in 1880 for the reopening of the Parish Church of Pinner, and pub., with music, by Skeffington & Son.

4. For the freshness of the morning. *Praise for all things.* Written in 1868, first printed on a broad-sheet, and then included in *The Universal H. Bk.*, 1885.

5. In the Name of God the Father, In Whose Image we are made. *Purity.* Written in 1885 for the Church Purity Society, printed in *The Vanguard*, Dec. 1885, and in the *White Cross Hymnal*, 1886.

6. The evening shadowy dimness. *Evening.* Written in 1868, printed on a broad-sheet, and again in *The Universal H. Bk.*, 1885.

7. The Sower went forth sowing. *Harvest or Burial.* Written in 1874 for Harvest Festival at Christ

Church, South Ashford, Kent; printed in *Church Bells* the same year, and included in *H. A. & M.*, 1875. It is sometimes used as a Funeral hymn.

8. Through the feeble twilight. *Easter hymn for Church Workers.* Written in 1884 for the Additional Curates Society's *Home Mission Field*, and printed therein, April 1884.

Mr. Bourne has also printed several hymns on fly-sheets for special occasions. Some of these are worthy of the attention of hymnal compilers.   [J. J.]

Bowdler, John, b. in London, Feb. 4, 1783, and educated at the Sevenoaks Grammar School, and Winchester. In 1807 he was called to the Bar, but ill-health necessitated his residence abroad for a short time. On his return he resumed the duties of his profession. His weakness, however, increased, and gradually sinking, he d. Feb. 1, 1815. He was a person of more than usual parts, and gained the friendship of Macaulay, Wilberforce, and other men of eminence. In 1816 his *Select Pieces in Verse and Prose*, were pub. by his father with a brief *Memoir*, Lond., G. Davidson. The two vols. contain essays, reviews, poetical pieces, versions of 4 Psalms, and 6 hymns. Of his hymns and Psalm versions nearly all are in C. U. The best of these are, "As panting in the sultry beam;" "Children of God, who pacing slow;" and "Lord, before Thy throne we bend." The rest include:—

1. Beyond the dark and stormy bound. *Heaven.* This is a part of his hymn on the Sabbath. The original begins "When God from dust created man," is in 10 st. of 6 l., and dated 1812.

2. Children of God, who pacing [faint and] slow. *Encouragement.*

3. Lord, before Thy throne we bend. *Ps. cxx. 3.*

4. O God, my heart within me faints. *Ps. xlii.*

5. Sing to the Lord with cheerful voice. *Praise.* Entitled "Thankfulness," and dated "Jan. 1814."

6. To heaven I lift mine eyes. *Ps. cxxi.*
                                          [J. J.]

Bowed with the guilt of sin, O God. *H. Alford.* [*Lent.*] Contributed to his *Year of Praise*, 1867, in 5 st. of 4 l., and appointed for the 7th Sun. after Trinity. It is more suitable to Lent. In the Musical ed. of the *Year of Praise* it is dated 1866.

Bowles, Caroline Ann. [Southey, C. A.]

Bowly, Mary. [Peters, M.]

Bowring, Sir John, LL.D., a distinguished man of letters, was b. at Exeter, Oct. 17, 1792. His studies extended to philology, poetry, politics, and other branches of learning, whilst as editor of the *Westminster Review* for some years (he received the appointment in 1825) he did considerable work as a reviewer. He held several official appointments under the Government as Commissioner to France on commercial matters (1834-5); British Consul at Hong-Kong (1849); and Governor of Hong-Kong (1854). He was twice Member of Parliament, and was knighted in 1854. He d. Nov. 23rd, 1872. His published works are very numerous, and display an astonishing acquaintance with various languages. Those specially bearing on poetry include:—

(1) *Russian Anthology, with Biographical and Critical notices of the Poets of Russia*, 1821; (2) *Specimens of the Russian Poets*, 1823; (3) *Ancient Poetry and Romance of Spain*, 1824; (4) *Batavian Anthology, or Specimens of Dutch Poets*, 1824; (5) *Servian Popular Poetry*, 1827; (6) *Specimens of Polish Poets*, 1827; (7) *Poetry of the Magyars*, 1830; (8) *History of the Poetical Literature of Bohemia*, 1832, &c.

In addition to these works, which are mainly translations, Sir John Bowring wrote original verse. This was pub. interspersed with a few translations, as follows:—

(1) *Matins and Vespers with Hymns and Occasional Devotional Pieces*, Lond., 1823; 2nd ed., enlarged, 1824; 3rd ed., again enlarged, 1841; and the 4th, still further enlarged, in 1851. (2) *Hymns*: as a Sequel to the Matins, 1825. In addition he contributed to a few Unitarian hymnals, especially that of the Rev. J. R. Beard of Manchester, 1837. In that *Coll.* many of the hymns added to the 3rd ed. of *Matins*, &c., 1841, were first pub. A selection from these, together with a biographical sketch, was pub. by Lady Bowring in 1873, as a *Memorial Volume of Sacred Poetry*. This work contains hymns from the *Matins and Vespers*, together with others from Periodicals, and from his MSS.

Of his hymns a very large percentage have come into C. U. A few have been adopted by almost all denominations, as, "God is love, His mercy brightens"; "How sweetly flow'd the gospel sound"; "In the Cross of Christ I glory"; "Watchman, tell us of the night"; and others, but the greater portion are confined to the Unitarian collections of G. Brit. and America, of which denomination he was a member. In addition to the more important, which are annotated under their first lines, there are also the following in C. U. :—

1. Clay to clay, and dust to dust. *Burial* From his *Hymns*, 1825, into the *H. & Tune Bk.*, Boston, U.S., 1868, &c.

2. Come the rich, and come the poor. *Divine Worship.* Contributed to Beard's *Coll.*, 1837, No. 290, and repeated in Bowring's *Matins*, &c., 3rd ed. 1841. It is in a few American collections.

3. Drop the limpid waters now. *Holy Baptism.* From *Matins and Vespers*, 3rd ed., 1841, into *Kennedy*, 1863.

4. Earth's transitory things decay. *The Memory of the Just.* From his *Hymns*, 1825, into *Beard*, 1837; the American *Plymouth Coll.*, 1855; and the *Songs for the Sanctuary*, N.Y., 1865, &c.

5. Father, glorify Thy name. *The Father glorified.* Also from *Hymns*, 1825, into *Beard*, 1837; the *Hys. of the Spirit*, Boston, U.S., 1864, &c.

6. Father and Friend, Thy light, Thy love. *Omnipresence.* From *Matins and Vespers*, 2nd ed., 1824, into several collections, and sometimes in an abbreviated form.

7. Father of Spirits, humbly bent before Thee. Also in *Hymns*, 1825, and Dr. Martineau's *H. of P. & Prayer*, 1873. In Longfellow and Johnson's *Hys. of the Spirit*, Boston, U.S., 1864, it is given as, "Father of Spirits, gathered now before Thee."

8. From all evil, all temptation. *Preservation implored.* Contributed to Beard's *Coll.*, 1837.

9. From the recesses of a lowly spirit. *Prayer of trust.* From *Matins and Vespers*, 1st ed., 1823, into several American collections.

10. Gather up, O earth, thy dead. Pub. in his *Matins & Vespers*, 3rd ed., 1841, in 3 st. of 8 l.; and repeated, slightly altered, in *Kennedy*, 1863, No. 753.

11. Gently the shades of night descend. *Evening.* A cento from his poem on "Sunday Evening," in the *Matins*, &c., 1st ed., 1823, p. 6. It is given in the Boston *Hys. of the Spirit*, 1864; the Boston *H. & Tune Bk.*, 1868, and other collections.

12. How dark, how desolate. *Hope.* 1st pub. in his *Matins,* &c., 1823, p. 246. In Dr. Martineau's *H. of P. & Prayer,* 1873, it is No. 515.

13. How shall we praise Thee, Lord of Light! *Evening.* A cento from the same poem as No. 7 above. It is given in the *Hys. of the Spirit,* 1864, and other American collections.

14. Lead us with Thy gentle sway. *Divine Guidance desired.* *Hymns,* 1825, into *Hys. of the Spirit,* 1864, and others.

15. Lord, in heaven, Thy dwelling-place. *Praise.* Contributed to Beard's *Coll.,* 1837, No. 70, repeated in the author's *Matins,* &c., 3rd ed. 1841, p. 235, and given in a few American collections. In the *Hys. of the Spirit,* 1864, it is altered to "Lord *of every time and place.*"

16. O let my [thy] trembling soul be still. *Resignation.* From the 1st ed. of the *Matins,* &c., 1823, p. 251, in 3 st. of 6 l., into Beard's *Coll.,* 1837; the *Hys. of the Spirit,* 1864, and others. It is sometimes given as, "O let *thy,*" &c.

17. O. sweet it is to feel and know. *Monday Morning.* A poem in 16 st. of 4 l., given in his *Matins,* &c., 1823, p. 60. In 1837 st. i.–iii. were given in Beard's *Coll.* as No. 448, and entitled "God near in sorrow." In the 3rd ed. of the *Matins,* &c., 1841, this cento was repeated (p. 245), with the same title, notwithstanding the full poem was in the same book.

18. On the dust I'm doomed to sleep. *Resurrection.* Appeared in his *Matins,* &c., 1st ed., 1823, p. 252, in 2 st. of 8 l. In the 2nd ed., 1824, p. 232, it was altered to "*In* the dust," &c. This was repeated in 1841. In some hymnals it reads :—

19. The heavenly spheres to Thee, O God. *Evening.* This "Hymn to the Deity" appeared in the 2nd ed. of his *Matins,* &c., 1824, pp. 235–6, in 4 st. of 4 double lines. It is also in the 3rd ed., 1841 ; the Boston *Hys. of the Spirit,* 1864 and other American collections.

20. When before Thy throne we kneel. *Divine Worship.* From his *Hymns,* 1825, into Beard's *Coll.,* 1837, No. 93; the Boston *H. & Tune Bk.,* 1868, No. 21, and others.

21. Where is thy sting, O death! *Death.* Also from the *Hymns,* 1825, into the same collections as No. 20 above.

It will be noted that Beard's *Coll.,* 1837, is frequently named above. The full title of that hymnal is—

A Collection of Hymns for Public and Private Worship. Compiled by John R. Beard, Lond., John Green, 1837.

The Rev. John Relly Beard was an Unitarian Minister in Manchester, and the collection is dedicated "To the Manchester Meeting of Ministers." It contained a large number of original hymns. Bowring contributed 82, of which 33 were published therein for the first time. Some of his hymns are of great merit, and most of them are characterised by great earnestness and deep devotion. [J. J.]

Boyce. Twenty-one hymns appeared under this signature in Williams and Boden's *Coll.* of above *Six Hundred Hymns,* &c., 1801. [Boden, J.] The writer is sometimes described as "Samuel Boyce"; but nothing definite is known to us concerning him. Of these hymns the following are in C. U. :—

1. All hail, redeeming Lord. *Christ the Day-Spring.*

2. Grace, how melodious is the sound. *Fulness of Grace.*

3. Great Sovereign Lord, what human eye. *Harvest.*

4. O the transcendent love. *Christ the Sinner's Friend.*

5. Ye trembling captives, hear. *The Gospel Trumpet.*

Boyd, Robert, M.A. [*Bodius, Robertus*], eldest s. of James Boyd, of Trochrig, Ayrshire, and Archbishop of Glasgow, was b. at Glasgow in 1578. He studied at the University of Edinburgh, graduating M.A. in 1595. In 1597 he went to France, and lived principally at Tours till 1599, when he became Professor of Philosophy at Montauban. In 1604 he became Pastor at Verteuil. In 1606 he went to Saumur as pastor, and in 1608, became Professor of Theology there. Leaving Saumur in 1614, in 1615 he became Principal and Professor of Theology in the University of Glasgow, but resigned his appointments in 1621, and retired to his estate at Trochrig. In 1622 he was elected Principal of the University of Edinburgh, but had to resign at once by the King's command. In 1626 he was for a few weeks minister of Paisley, but had again to resign. He d. at Edinburgh Jan. 5, 1627. He was more celebrated as a theologian than as a poet. His principal poem is in Latin, and entitled *Hecatombe Christiana.* [See **Christe sanctorum.**] [J. M.]

Boyd, Zachary, M.A., was b. near Kilmarnock in 1585. He entered the University of Glasgow in 1601, and two years later went to St. Andrews, where he graduated M.A. in 1607. He then went to Saumur in France, where he became Second Regent in 1611. Returning to Scotland in 1621, he became in 1623 minister of the Barony Parish, Glasgow. He was thrice elected Dean of Faculty, twice Vice Chancellor, and thrice Rector, of the University of Glasgow. In that University he took great interest, and to it he bequeathed, by his will, in 1652, almost all his property, including a large mass of poetical and other manuscripts. He d. at Glasgow in March or April, 1653.

The 3rd edition of his version of *The Psalmes of David in Meeter* (which according to his preface to the 1648 ed. was suggested to him by the General Assembly, in 1644) was pub. at Glasgow, in 1646, and was, with that of 1648, largely used by the Committee who compiled the *Scottish Psalter* of 1650. In 1644 he pub. at Glasgow, *The Garden of Zion,* in 2 vols. ; vol. i. containing metrical histories of the most important godly and wicked Scripture characters ; and vol. ii. metrical versions of the Books of Job, Proverbs, Ecclesiastes, and the Song of Songs. To these were added (with a separate titlepage, dated 1645, but paged consecutively) *The Holy Songs of the Old and New Testament,* 5 of which had been embodied in the text of the 1st volume. He revised these *Songs ;* added thereto "David's Lament over Saul and Jonathan," printed them at the end of the 3rd edition of his *Psalmes,* in 1646. As there given they include a new version of the Song of Songs, 12 Old Testament and 3 New Testament Songs. In 1647 he was requested by the General Assembly to prepare versions of the Scriptural Songs, and in accordance with that request he again revised his versions, and reprinted them, with the addition of a version of the Lamentations, George Buchanan's Latin morning hymn, and an original morning hymn to Christ (the finest verses he ever wrote) at the end of the 1648 edition of his *Psalmes.*

His other principal poetical works are *Zion's Flowers* (4 poems from which were pub. in 1855, by Gabriel Neil) and *The English Academie,* still in MS. in the Glasgow University Library. Boyd's versions are generally distinguished rather by faithfulness than elegance. His version of Job seems to have suggested Nos. 24

(No. 6 in 1781) and 39 (No. 4 in 1781) in the *Trans. and Paraphrases*, 1745. (See **Scottish Trans. and Paraphrases**, and the note on " How still and peaceful is the grave.")   [J. M.]

Boyden, Henry, B.A., is the author of *Songs for the Household, Sacred and Secular* (Birmingham, E. Child, 1866), and many excellent hymns, printed on fly-sheets, for the use of his congregation on anniversary occasions at St. David's, Birmingham, some of which have been set to music by Dr. Belcher, Lond., Novello & Co. Mr. Boyden was b. at Birmingham in 1832, and is a graduate of Trinity Coll., Dublin, B.A. 1867. Taking Holy Orders in 1856, he has been successively Curate of St. Mary's, Honley; St. Mary's, St. George's, and St. Luke's, Birmingham; and since 1866 Vicar of St. David's, Birmingham.

Boye, Nicolaus, was b. at Wesslensbürn, or Weslingburen, in Holstein, where he became an Evangelical Preacher, and where he d. 1542. (*Koch*, i. 418; ii. 478; *Allg. Deutsche Biog.*, iii. 85.) The only hymn known as his is:—

O Gott, wir danken deiner Güt. [*Grace after Meat.*] 1st pub. in Low German in the *Geystlike leder uñ Psalmen*, Magdeburg, 1541, and in High German in the Bonn *G. B.*, 1564. Both forms are in *Wackernagel*, iii. p. 902, in 3 st. of 7 l. It was translated as " We thank the God, of thy gudnes," in the *Gude and Godly Ballates* (ed. 1567–68, folio 11), ed. 1868, p. 18.   [J. M.]

Boyse, Joseph, was b. at Leeds in 1660, received a good education, and in 1683 became a Presbyterian minister in Dublin, a position he maintained with honour and usefulness until his death in 1728. His prose works, chiefly sermons and controversial treatises, were collected and published by himself in two large folios, London, 1728. He was the author of two collections of hymns. The first, printed in Dublin, in 1693 (small 8vo) with another title-page (London, 1693, Thomas Parkhurst, Cheapside), is entitled as follows:—

"*Sacramental Hymns collected chiefly out of such passages of the New Testament as contain the most suitable matter of Divine Praises in the celebration of the Lord's Supper. To which is added one hymn relating to Baptism and another to the Ministry. By J. Boyse, with some by other hands.*"

Those by " other hands " are 3 in number, viz. one by G. Herbert, and two by Patrick. Of the remaining 21 by Boyse himself, 18 are for use at the Lord's Supper. From the fact that in the hymn on *Baptism* immersion is the only mode recognized, it is pretty certain that the author was Baptist in sentiment, though Presbyterian in ecclesiastical position. The other collection by Boyse was printed at Dublin in 1691. It contains 76 hymns, in three parts, with music, and is entitled :—

Family Hymns for Morning and Evening Worship, with some for the Lord's days . . . All taken out of the Psalms of David. A copy is in the Antrim Presbytery Library at Queen's College, Belfast.

Boyse's hymns are interesting from their early date, but have no merit as poetry. The hymn " Come pay the worship God requires " (*Divine Worship*), in Martineau's *Hymns*, 1840, No. 42, is by this author.   [W. R. S.]

Brackenbury, Robert Carr, of an old Lincolnshire family, was b. at Panton House, in that county, in 1752. He entered into residence at St. Catherine's Hall, Cambridge.

but joining the Wesleys, he left without taking a degree, and became a minister of the Methodist denomination. In that capacity he visited Guernsey, Jersey and Holland. He retired from active work in 1789, and d. at his residence, Raithby Hall, near Spilsby, Aug. 11, 1818.

His works include :—(1) *Sacred Poems, in 3 parts*, Lond., 1797 ; (2) *Select Hymns, in 2 parts*, Lond., 1795 ; (3) *Sacred Poetry ; or Hymns on the Principal Histories of the Old and New Testaments and on all the Parables*, Lond., 1800, and some prose publications. He also edited and altered William Cruden's *Divine Hymns*, N.D. The hymn, " Come, children, 'tis Jesus' command," was given in J. Benson's *Hys. for Children*, 1806. It does not appear in any of Brackenbury's works. Mrs. Smith, daughter of Dr. Adam Clarke, has included several incidents in his life in her *Raithby Hall.*

Bradberry, David, a Congregational minister, b. at Reeth Richmond, Yorkshire, Nov. 12, 1735. At 23 he entered the Mile End Academy as a student for the Congregational Ministry, and subsequently became pastor of a congregation at Alnwick (1762); Wellingborough (1764); Ramsgate (1767); Manchester (1787); and Kennington, London (1797). He d. Jan. 13, 1803.

In 1794 he pub. *Tetelestai ; the Final Close*, a poem on the Judgment; and also contributed to *A Supp. to the Version of the Psalms and Hymns of Dr. Watts, partly collected, altered, or transformed, in proper, peculiar, or broken metres*, Manchester, C. Wheeler, 1787 (Preface dated, Feb. 27, 1787.) Of the 42 hymns in this *Supp.*, 11 are by Bradberry. He is best known by his hymn for children, " Now let each heart [our hearts] conspire to raise " (*Sunday Schools*) in the *Wes. Reform H. Bk.*, No. 787, and others. It is the third of four hymns for children at the end of the *Supp.* 1787. In its altered form of " Now let *our hearts* conspire to raise," it was given in Rippon's *Sel.* 1787, No. 522.

Bradford, John, B.A., b. 1750, and educated at Wadham College, Oxford. He was for some time " Minister of the Gospel in Birmingham." He removed to Grub Street Chapel, London, in 1797, where he continued to preach till his death on July 16, 1805.

In 1792 he pub. *A Collection of Hymns*, Lond., Mathews, and others. It contained 280 hymns, some of which were his own. This collection was avowedly *Antinomian*. Very few of these hymns are in C. U.

Brady, Nicholas. [Psalters, English, § XIII. 4.]

Brainard, John Gardiner Calkins, b. at New London, Connecticut, 1796, and d. at Hartford, in 1828. He was educated at Yale College, and for some time practised law at Middleton, Connecticut. He also edited a paper at Hartford. His *Poems* appeared in 1825, 1832, and 1842. The hymn by which he is best known :—" To Thee, O God, the Shepherd Kings," was pub. in the Congregational *Ps. and Hys. for Christian use and Worship, prepared, &c., by the General Association of Connecticut*, 1845, No. 645, in 6 st. of 4 l., and headed " An agricultural hymn."   [F. M. B.]

Brammall, John Holland, nephew of John Holland, the biographer of Montgomery and author of the *British Psalmists*, was b. at Sheffield, Dec. 21, 1831, and educated at the Collegiate School of that town. Although engaged in banking, he has found time for both hymn-writing and music. Most of his hymns and some of his tunes were written for the Sheffield Wesleyan Sunday School Union. Of the former, " Onward, children, onward, leave the paths of sin," is best known. It was written for the Wes. S. S. Union of Sheffield in 1870, and 1st printed on their Whitsuntide fly-sheet of that year. It has been frequently used at similar gatherings of children. In 1879 it was given anonymously in the *Meth. S. S. H. Bk.*, No. 283.

Brandenburg-Culmbach, Margrave of. [Albrecht.]

Brandenburg, Electress of. [Luise Henriette.]

Brawn, Mary Ann, dau. of the Rev. Samuel Brawn, for 51 years pastor of the Baptist Chapel, Loughton, Essex, was b. at the Meads, Loughton, Aug. 15, 1828. She was descended on the mother's side from the martyr Thomas Hawkes, who was burned at the stake in 1555, at Coggeshall, Essex. From 1848 to 1875 Miss Brawn was engaged in educational work. Her poetical pieces are few in number, and chiefly on devotional subjects. They were first printed on fly-sheets for use in her father's chapel and elsewhere. They include:—

1. **God of Glory, at Thy feet** *Children's Prayer*. Written, Jan. 30, 1867, and pub. in Congreve's *Gems of Song*, No. 183.

2. **O Father, we are very weak.** *Children's Prayer*. This is the best known of Miss Brawn's hymns It is in *Meth. S. S. H. Bk.*, 1879, and several other collections for children.

3. **O Thou Who art in every place.** *Lent*.

4. **O'er life's tempestuous sea.** *Divine Guidance*.

Of these, Nos. 3, 4, were given in *The Domestic Worshipper*, 1850, a volume of prayers and hymns edited by the Rev. Samuel Green. [J. J.]

Bread of Heaven, on Thee I [we] feed. *J. Conder.* [Holy Communion.] This hymn takes rank as the most popular and widely used of the author's productions. It appeared in his *Star of the East*, &c., 1824, p. 57, in the following form:—

"FOR THE EUCHARIST.

"I am the living bread which came down from heaven . . . Whoso eateth my flesh, and drinketh my blood, hath eternal life. . . . I am the true vine."—John vi. 51–4, xv. 1.

"Bread of Heav'n ! on Thee I feed,	"Vine of Heav'n ! thy blood supplies
For thy flesh is meat indeed.	This blest cup of sacrifice.
Ever may my soul be fed	'Tis thy wounds my healing give :
With this true and living bread;	To thy Cross I look, and live.
Day by day with strength supplied,	Thou my life ! oh, let me be
Through the life of Him who died.	Rooted, grafted, built on Thee."

This text was repeated in Conder's *Cong. H. Bk.*, 1836, and his *Hymns of Praise*, &c., 1856, p. 86. It is in several Nonconformist hymnals, but sometimes, as in the Bap. *Ps. and Hys.*, 1858, No. 725, with "The blest" for "This blest cup," in st. ii., l. 2. In Pratt's *Ps. & Hys.*, 1829, No. 69. it was broken up into 3 st. of 4 l., and given as "Bread of heaven, on Thee *we* feed"; and this was repeated in some later collections. The most popular and widely used form of the hymn is the following, which was given in in the Cooke and Denton *Church Hymnal*, 1853, No. 202, as follows :—

"Bread of heaven, on Thee we feed,	"Vine of heaven! Thy Blood supplies
For Thy Flesh is meat indeed ;	This blest cup of Sacrifice ;
Ever may *our souls* be fed	*Lord*, Thy Wounds *our* healing give ;
With this true and living Bread ;	To Thy Cross *we* look and live:
Day by day with strength supplied	*Jesu ! may we ever* be
Through the life of Him Who died.	*Grafted, rooted*, built *in* Thee. Amen."

Great popularity was given to this text by its adoption by *H. A. and M.* in 1861, and subsequently by other important Church of England collections. In Thring's *Coll.*, 1882, there is a slight return to the original. It will be noted that in the revised text there is no change of doctrine involved. Both in it, and in the original, the same truth is set forth ; but the revised text is the more congregational and musical of the two. The American hymnals, in common with those of G. Britain, have adopted both texts, the revised being mainly found in the Protestant Episcopal collections. A Latin rendering of the *H. A. and M.* text by the Rev. C. B. Pearson as : "Pasce nos, Divine Panis," was given in Biggs's *Annotated H. A. and M.*, 1867. [J. J.]

Bread of the world in mercy broken *Bp. R. Heber.* [Holy Communion.] 1st pub. in his posthumous *Hymns*, &c., 1827, p. 143, in 2 st. of 4 l., and headed "Before the Sacrament." Its use has become most extensive in all English-speaking countries. Orig. text in Thring's *Coll.*, No. 529. In the *Mitre H. Bk.*, 1836, the opening line was altered to "Bread of *our life* in mercy broken," but this reading has fallen out of use.

Breay, John George, b. in 1796, and d. Dec. 5, 1839. Ordained Deacon in 1819 and Priest in 1820, he became Vicar of Haddenham, 1827, and of Christ Church, Birmingham, 1832. He was also Prebendary of Lichfield. His *Sel. of Ps. & Hymns* was pub. at Birmingham, 1836. To it he contributed the following hymns:—

1. A small and feeble band. *Holy Baptism*.
2. Almighty God, apply. *Confirmation*.
3. Almighty Saviour, bow Thine ear. *Charity Schools*.
4. Come, gracious Saviour, from above. *Holy Baptism*.
5. O God, accept our early praise. *After Sermon*.
6. O God, the feeble sinner's friend. *Confirmation*.
7. Saviour, bless Thy word to all. *After Sermon*.
8. There is beyond this world of night. *Charity Schools*.

The best known of these is No. 4. His *Memoir* was pub. in 1841. [W. T. B.]

Breithaupt, Joachim Justus, s. of Christian Breithaupt, Superintendent of the district of Hohenstadt or Honstedt, Hannover, was b. at Nordheim, in Hannover, Feb., 1658. After a theological course at Helmstädt he became, in 1680, Conrector of the Gymnasium at Wolfenbüttel, but left in 1681, and, after being Professor of Homiletics in Kiel, was appointed, in 1685, Court preacher and member of the Consistory at Meiningen. In 1687 he became Pastor and Professor of Theology at Erfurt, receiving in the same year the degree of D.D. from the University of Kiel. Driven from Kiel by the Pietistic Controversy, he was appointed in 1691 pastor of the Cathedral Church, and dean of the Theological Faculty, at Halle ; and in 1705, in addition, General Superintendent of the Duchy of Magdeburg. In 1709 he became Abt of Kloster-Bergen and In-spector of the Saalkreis. He d. at Kloster-Bergen, March 16, 1732 (*Koch*, iv. 331-342; *Allg. Deutsche Biog.*, iii. 291-292 ; *Bode*, p. 49). Of his 4 (5 ?) hymns one has passed into English :—

Jesus Christus, Gottes Lamm. [*Passiontide.*] Founded on Romans viii. 8-11. 1st in the *Geistreiches G. B.*, Halle, 1697, p. 549, in 5 st. The *trs.* are—(1) "Christ, th' eternal Lamb of God," by J. C. Jacobi, 1725, p. 13 (1732, p. 58), repeated as No. 537 in pt. i. of the *Moravian H. Bk.*, 1754. (2) "Jesus Christ, the Lamb of God," in G. Moultrie's *H. and Lyrics*, 1867, p. 64.

[J. M.]

Brennende Lieb du süsse Flamm. [*Thanksgiving.*] Included in *Wackernagel*, iv. p. 1072, in 5 st. of 8 l., from a xvi. cent. ms. at Munich, in which it begins "Brünninde lieb, du süesser Flam." In the *Unv. L. S.*, 1851, it is No. 554. It is *tr.* as "Thou burning Love, thou holy Flame," by *Miss Winkworth*, 1869, p. 157.

[J. M.]

Brethren, let us join to bless. *J. Cennick.* [*Praise.*] This is one of this writer's most popular hymns. It appeared in his *Sacred Hys. for the Children of God*, &c., 1742, in 5 st. of 4 l. One of the first to use it as a congregational hymn was G. Whitefield. He included it in his *Coll.*, 1753, but with altera-tions. It was repeated by M. Madan, in his *Ps. and Hys.*, 1760, No. 109, and others. Gra-dually its use extended until it became known in all English-speaking countries ; sometimes as in *Whitefield*, and again in its original form. Whitefield's text can be distinguished by st. ii. which opens :—"*Master, see* to Thee we bow," whilst the original reads, "Son of God, to Thee we bow." Orig. text in *H. Comp.*, No. 512.

Breton, Nicholas, second s. of William Breton, of Red Cross Street, Cripplegate, Lon-don, probably b. about 1542-3. His father's will, proved in 1559, shows that at his death, his eldest son was still a boy, and that in the event of his death, Nicholas was not to inherit until he was 24. It appears that he resided for some time at Oriel College, Oxford. From 1577 to 1626 he issued pamphlet after pam-phlet in prose and verse. In 1876 these were collected as far as possible by the Rev. A. B. Grosart, and printed in two vols. in his *Chert-sey Worthies' Library.* He d. probably in 1626, being then about 83 years of age. As a sacred poet he is distinguished by melody and grace, and it has been only the want of a cheap edition of his works that has prevented his taking higher rank in public esteem. [See **Early Eng. Hymnody,** § VII.]

Brettell, Jacob, s. of an Unitarian Minis-ter, b. at Gainsborough, April 16, 1793. In 1814 he entered upon the pastorate of an Uni-tarian congregation at Cockey Moor (now Ainsworth), Bolton, Lancashire ; and in 1816 upon that of Rotherham, Yorkshire. The latter charge he held until 1859, when he re-tired from active work. He d. at Rotherham, Jan. 12, 1862. In addition to minor pieces contributed to various newspapers, &c., he pub. :—

(1) *The Country Minister ; A Poem in four Cantos, with other Poems,* Lond., 1821; (2) *Sketches in Verse from the Historical Books of the Old Testament,* Lond., 1823.

In 1837 Mr. Brettell contributed 16 hymns to Beard's *Coll.* With one or two exceptions,

these have fallen out of use. The best known, but by no means the best hymn; is " The last full wain is on the road," *Harvest*, given in Dr. Martineau's *Hys.*, 1873. Another is, " He lived, as none but He has lived " (*Life of Jesus*). In compiling a volume of sacred poems these hymns, from their poetic character, might be consulted with advantage.   [J. J.]

Breviaries. 1. The name *Breviary* is that by which the Office Book which contains the services of the Canonical Hours is known in the Western Church. A large number of such books have been in use from time to time, each differing from the other in various par-ticulars, but all known by the same name. This Office Book is probably called a *Breviarium*, either from being a compendium of separate volumes which in early days contained its various parts, or from the services in their present shape and length having been some-what abbreviated from their form in primitive times.

2. Prior to the compilation of Breviaries, various books were in use in the daily offices, and from these the *Roman* and other Bre-viaries have been compiled. They are (1) the *Psalter;* (2) the *Scriptures ;* (3) the *Sermologus* and the *Homiliary*, used respec-tively at the second and third nocturns on Sundays and certain other days; (4) the *Pas-sionary* or *Passional ;* (5) the *Antiphonary ;* (6) the *Hymnal ;* (7) the *Collectaneum*, or *Ora-tionale ;* and (8) the *Martyrology*.

3. From these materials an enormous variety of Breviaries has been built up ; some of them generically different from the *Roman*, such as the *Horologion* or Breviary of the Eastern Church ; the *Ambrosian Breviary* of the Church of Milan ; and the *Mozarabic Breviary* of the Church of Spain ; others being merely varia-tions or offshoots of the *Roman Breviary*. The religious orders had their separate Uses, fol-lowing the Benedictine or Monastic arrange-ment of the Psalms, as distinct from the Gregorian or secular arrangement. Separate Provinces, and single Dioceses, had their own Uses ; so that the Mediaeval Breviaries of Eng-land, France, Germany, and other countries may be counted up by hundreds.

4. As this work is *hymnological*, and not *liturgical*, and as the liturgical contents of various Breviaries, especially that of Rome, have been treated fully in another place [see *Dict. of Christian Antiquities*, arts. *Breviary ; Divine Office ; Psalmody*, &c.], it will only be necessary to name a few leading Brevia-ries, especially those which have had the greatest influence on the hymnody of modern times. These are :—

(1) **The Mozarabic Breviary.** This *Breviary* is known in four forms, (1) in ms. ; (2) as arranged and printed by Cardinal Ximenes ; (3) Archbishop Loren-zana's revised edition of No. 2 ; and (4) Migne's *Patrol. Lat.* tom. lxxxvi. Each of these has a special hymno-logical interest, and, combined, they shed great light upon the question as to what hymns are and what are not truly *Mozarabic*.

(1) Of the ancient *MS. Breviary* there are copies in the *British Museum* the press marks of which are " Add. MSS. 30847-9."

(2) Cardinal Ximenes' edition of this *Breviary* is known to us through an edition published at Toledo, 1502, that is, fifteen years before the Cardinal's death. It is entitled, *Breviarium secundum regulam beati hysidori. Impressum in regali ciuitate Toleti* MDII. In this edition there are about 214 hymns. Of these 116

were from the *Mozarabic MSS.* as noted below, and the rest were taken by Ximenes from the *Ambrosian*, the old *Roman*, and other sources.

(3) The copy of Archbishop Lorenzana's revised edition of the *Breviary*, which we have been able to consult, is: *Breviarium Gothicum secundum regulam beatissimi Isidori Archiepiscopi Hispalensis Jussu Cardinalis Francisci Ximenii de Cisneros prius editum: nunc operâ excmi D. Francisci Antonii Lorenzana Sanctae Ecclesiae Toletanae Hispaniarum Primatis Archiepiscopi recognitum ad usum sacelli Mozarabum. Matriti anno MDCCLXXV. Apud Joachimum Ibarra S. C. R. M. & Dignit. Archiep. Typog. Regio permissu.* In this edition of the *Breviary* folios 1-450, which constitute the *Breviary* proper, are a reprint of Cardinal Ximenes' edition of 1502. The *Aurora* hymns, and those for the *Feasts* throughout the year, and for *Sick* and *Dead*, are also the same in both. In this 1775 edition of the *Breviary* there is added what is known as the *Mozarabic Hymnarium*. This is a body of Mozarabic hymns compiled from ancient *Mozarabic MSS.*, and printed with the readings and spellings of the MSS. This was compiled after the publication of the Toledo edition, 1502, but if added to the *Breviary* before this edition of 1775 we cannot determine. This so-called *Hymnarium* (the collected hymns are headed *Incipiunt ymni de toto circulo anni*) contains 95 hymns printed in full, and 84 first lines of others which are given in full in their proper places in the Offices. These 179 hymns are the Old Mozarabic hymns, and of these 110 were in the Ximenes ed., 1502.

(4) In Migne's *Patrologia*, tom. 86, Lorenzana's ed. is reprinted in full.

We may add that the *Mozarabic Breviary* (the ancient Use of the Spanish Church) which, apart from legendary accounts of an Apostolic origin, may be referred to St. Isidore, Archbishop of Seville (†636) and his brother Leander, as its compilers, was abolished in favour of the *Roman Breviary*, by Gregory VII. (1073–85), but in deference to strong national feeling its continued use was allowed in seven churches of Toledo.

(2) **The Ambrosian.** The original construction of this Breviary is attributed to St. Ambrose, Bishop of Milan (†397).

The oldest copy of this *Breviary* which we have been able to consult is: *Breuiarium iuxta institutionem Scti Ambrosij Archiepiscopi inclyte ciuitatis Mediolani accuratissime castigatum: ac quamplurimis additionibus ordine nouo ac facili perfectissime resarcitum, Venetiis. Apud Hieronymum Scotum,* 1539. The hymns which are found in this edition are given in the following table as a^1. This *Breviary* was largely revised by St. Charles Borromeo (†1584). The copy of this which we have collated is: *Breuiarivm Ambrosianvm Caroli S. R. E. Cardinalis tit. S. Praxedis Archiepiscopi iussu recognitvm, atqve editvm . . . . . Mediolani. Apud Pontios. et Baesutios fratres, M.D.LXXXII.* The hymns added to this edition are marked in the following table as a^2. In later editions several hymns have been again added, but as these hymns are in no sense *Ambrosian*, they do not appear as such in the table. This *Breviary* is in use in the diocese of Milan at the present time. We may add that in the following table the hymns common to both these editions of the *Ambrosian Breviary* are marked *a*.

(3) **The Roman.** This Breviary was the growth of centuries. St. Jerome (ob. 420), Cassian (ob. 423), Leo I. (Pope 440–61), and o'hers, have been named as its compilers and composers. It was a work, how ver, of gradual formation, and cannot be assigned to any single person. The complex work now known as the *Roman Breviary* assumed its present shape, roughly speaking, under Gregory VII. (1073–1085). It has undergone four principal revisions. In so saying we exclude the reforming Breviary of Cardinal Quignon, the use of which was permitted for over thirty years in the sixteenth century, from the pontificate of Paul III. to that of Pius V., 1536–68. The *first* of these four revisions took place about 1525, being mainly conducted by Zacharias Ferrerius, under Clement VII. ; the *second* was issued under Pius V. in 1568 ; the *third* under Clement VIII. in 1602 ; the *fourth* in 1632, under Urban VIII. Since then fresh offices, with new hymns, have from time to time been added to the Breviary by decrees of the Congregation of Rites, and the incorporation in this way of new hymns into the Breviary is a process which will continue to go on. At present there are about 158 hymns in the *Roman Breviary*, of which about sixty have been added since the days of Urban VIII. The large majority are taken from ancient sources, and very many of them have been translated into English, and are in common use outside the Church of Rome.

Three *Roman Breviaries* of the sixteenth, seventeenth and nineteenth centuries have been selected for use in

drawing up the following list of first lines of hymns, marked r^1, r^2, r^3, respectively. The first of them is anterior to any of the above-mentioned reforms ; the last includes all the most recent additions to the Breviary. The 1515 edition is a 12mo totum, rubricated, with many woodcuts, and according to colophon on the last page, printed, " Venetiis. Per Jacobum pentium de Leucho." Then follows an *Appendix* from which four of the hymns marked (r^1) are taken ; viz., three for the Visitation of the B. V. M., one for St. Joseph. Besides these two offices, the *Appendix* contains further offices, without special hymns for the Conception of the B. V. M. ; Paul the first Hermit ; the Holy Trinity. The opening rubric of the *Appendix* runs thus, " Incipit officium imaculate conceptionis virginis marie editum per reuerendum patrem dominum leonardum nogarolum prothonotarium apostolicum tertium ac sacre theologie doctorem famosissimum."

(4) **The Sarum.** This Breviary was in general use in England before the Reformation. It was not, like the *York* and *Hereford* Breviaries, confined to the Diocese from which it took its name, but it won its way into so nearly general acceptance, that it may be regarded as a national rather than a diocesan Use. It was not only accepted, with the above-named and a few local exceptions, throughout England and Wales, but its use seems to have prevailed, probably with modifications, throughout Ireland, from the twelfth century onwards. In the same century it was introduced into Scotland, the Diocese of Glasgow receiving it c. 1164, and other Dioceses following suit in the twelfth and thirteenth centuries. The *Aberdeen Breviary* (q. v.) represents an attempt made just before the Reformation to supersede the *Sarum Breviary*; and Walter Chepman, the owner of the first printing press in Scotland, complained to the Privy Council that his craft was injured by the continued importation of *Sarum* Office Books, and obtained an order from the Privy Council forbidding their introduction into Scotland for the future, 1509–10.

The *Sarum Breviary* does not belong to a distinct family of Office Books from the *Roman*, but must be classified as an offshoot of the *Roman* stock. There are a large number of textual and verbal variations. The particular Antiphons, Benedictions, Lections, Responsories, Hymns, Chapters, Preces, Versicles, differ to a great extent especially at certain particular seasons. No two pages of the *Roman* and *Sarum* Breviaries are probably in these respects exactly alike. But over and beyond these variations, there is a lesser but still a considerable number of structural and therefore more important differences. We subjoin a few specimens. The Absolutions which are prefixed to the Lessons in the different Nocturns in the *Roman*, are absent from the *Sarum Breviary*. The *Roman Breviary* provides one invariable form of Compline, while there are no fewer than twenty-two varieties of Compline in the *Sarum* Books for the different seasons of the ecclesiastical year. The *Sarum* rule was to say the Athanasian Creed daily at Prime, the *Roman* rule is to say it at Prime on Sundays only. By the *Sarum* rule the fifty-first Psalm was used at all the Hours on week-days not in Eastertide, and excepting Nocturns. By the *Roman* rule it is said only at Lauds and Vespers in Lent and Advent, and on a few fasting days. In this case, as in some other instances, the *Sarum* rubrics, which have remained unrevised since the sixteenth century, represent the older and unreformed *Roman* arrangement. In the same way some thirty of the hymns which in the following list are marked as *s* and r^1, are to be accounted for. They were recast, partly rewritten, in 1629, under Urban VIII., and such an entry as, " Ad regias agni dapes," r^2, represents the revised first line of a hymn which previously commenced with these words, " Ad coenam Agni providi " (r^1. *s. z.*). The Paris ed. 1531 has been reprinted by the Cambridge University Press, Pt. i., June 1, 1879 ; Pt. ii. 1883 ; Pt. iii. 1887.

(5) **The York.** This is another pre-Reformation variation of the *Roman Breviary*, the use of which was confined chiefly, if not entirely, to the diocese of York. It contains many hymns in common with the *Sarum Breviary*, but yields a limited number not to be found in any of the previously named books. A Venice ed. of this *Brev.*, dated 1493, has been reprinted by the Surtees Society, vol. i. 1880 ; vol. ii. 1883.

(6) **The Aberdeen.** This Breviary is one of the very few surviving Service Books of the pre-Reformation period of the Church in Scotland. It is substantially a *Sarum Breviary*, with certain necessary changes of wording, with a considerable amount of independent variation of text, and with the addition of a large number of commemorations of local saints. The Lections, Hymns, &c., for these series form a most important con-

tribution to the ancient hagiography of Scotland. It was compiled and edited by William Elphinstone, Bishop of Aberdeen (1483–1514). It was printed at Edinburgh by Walter Chepman, the *Pars hyemalis*, in 1509; the *Pars estivalis*, in 1510. It is thus the second earliest known printed book in Scotland. The colophon at the end implies that it was Bishop Elphinstone's hope that this Breviary would become the accepted Use of the [whole of the] Scottish Church, but there is no evidence of its having been accepted and used outside the limits of the Diocese of Aberdeen. The offices of the Compassion of the B. V. M., and of the Crown of Jesus, are only found in the *Appendix* to the Glammes copy of this Breviary. They are printed at the close of D Laing's Preface to the whole Breviary, which was published in facsimile in London in 1854.

(7) **The Paris.** Revised by Abp. Charles de Vintimille in 1736. The hymns in this Breviary are mainly by the following writers:—Charles Coffin (1676–1749); Charles Guiet (cir. 1684); Guillaume du Plessis de Geste, Bp. of Saintes (—1702); Abbé Besnault (fl. 1726); Claude de Santeüil (1628–1684); Jean-Baptiste de Santeüil (1630–1697); Isaac Habert, Bp. of Vabres (—1668); Denys Petau (1583–1652); Nicolas le Tourneaux (1640–1686); Jean Commire (1625–1702); St. Ambrose (cir. 340–397); Gurd. Vic.; Bernard of Clairvaux (1091–1153); M. Ant Muret (1526–1585); Thomas of Aquino (1227–1274); Prudentius (348–cir. 413); Fortunatus (cir. 530–cir. 609). These hymns have been made known to English readers through the *trs.* of Isaac Williams, John Chandler, and others. The hymns added to this Breviary since 1736 are not noted in the following table.

(8) **The Hereford.** See § 11 of this article.

(9) **Monastic Breviaries.** See § 12 of this article.

5. It will be observed that we have selected for use the most important Breviaries of the Church. As the vast number of Breviaries which exist, especially on the Continent of Europe, rendered a collation of each a task beyond the limits of this work, the most important for hymnological purposes only are taken.

6. As all Breviaries have the arrangement of their parts much in common, a description of the *Roman Breviary* will serve, except for technical purposes, as an illustration of all.

It is sometimes printed as a single volume, sometimes in two, more frequently in four parts, for the Winter, Spring, Summer, and Autumn quarters. Each part contains (1) The Kalendar with Rubrics, and the Absolutions and Benedictions for use before the Lections. (2) The Psalter or Psalms arranged for use on each day of the week. (3) The Proper of the Season, containing the Chapters, Lessons, Hymns, Versicles, Responses, Antiphons, Collects, for the Sundays and movable Fasts and Festivals of the Church's year. (4) The Proper of Saints, containing the above Chapters, &c., for the immovable Feasts. (5) The Common of Saints, containing Psalms with Antiphons, Lections, &c., for feasts of particular classes, Apostles, Martyrs, Evangelists, &c. (6) Offices for the Dedication of a Church; for Festivals of the Blessed Virgin, with the Little Office for the same; the Office of the Dead; the Gradual and Penitential Psalms, with Litanies and various Collects, Benedictions, and other devotions. (7) A collection of special Offices which are not binding on the whole Church, but are only used in certain countries, &c., to which a special supplement is added of Offices belonging exclusively to certain dioceses or religious orders.

7. The arrangement of the *Psalms*, although interesting in itself, does not fall within the scope of this work. It has been fully treated in the *Dict. of Christian Antiquities*, art. *Psalmody* (q. v.).

8. The *Canticles* in use in the *Roman Breviary* (and this is illustrative of their use in some other Breviaries) are as follows:—

The Song of the Three Children. Ab from *Dan. iii.* 58–88 (*Sept. version*). with two verses added. Sunday at Lauds.

The Song of Isaiah. *Is. xii.* 1–6. Monday at Lauds.

The Song of Hezekiah. *Is. xxxviii.* 10–20. Tuesday at Lauds.

The Song of Hannah. 1 *Sam. ii.* 1–10. Wednesday at Lauds.

The Song of Moses. *Exod. xv.* 1–19. Thu. at Lauds.

The Song of Habakkuk. *Hab. iii* 1–20. Fri. at Lauds

The Song of Moses. *Deut. xxxii.* 1–43. Sat. at Lauds.

The Song of St. Mary. *St. Luke, i.* 46–55. Daily Vespers.

The Song of Zacharias. *St. Luke, i.* 68–79. Daily Lauds.

The Song of Symeon. *St. Luke, ii.* 29–32. Daily Compline.

The Song of SS. Ambrose and Augustine. [*Te Deum.*] At the end of Matins on certain Sundays and Feasts.

To the above list is generally added:

The Creed of St. Athanasius. Sunday at Prime (*r.*); Daily (*s. y.*).

Other Canticles are occasionally used in the French Breviaries. The Mozarabic Breviary is the most varied in its use of Canticles, containing no less than seventy-seven. (Migne, *Patrol. Lat.*, tom. lxxxvi. pp. 846–886.)

9. The *Hymns* in all the Breviaries are found in the various services. In some cases they are derived from a common source, in others they are associated with one Breviary only, this being specially so in the case of the ancient *Ambrosian* and *Mozarabic Breviaries*, and of the *Paris Breviary* of 1736. The following list of hymns from the most prominent Breviaries does not include *Proses* and *Sequences*. The history of many of the hymns named, together with such *trs.* as have been made into English, will be found in this work under their original first lines.

10. LIST OF HYMNS. This list has been compiled from the *Ambrosian, Mozarabic, Roman, Sarum, York, Aberdeen*, and *Paris Breviaries*. The editions used are:—

a[1]. *Old Ambrosian Breviary*, Venice, 1539, but not in the revised edition.

a[2]. *Revised Ambrosian Breviary*, Milan, 1582, but not in the 1539 edition.

a. Hymns common to both.

m*. *Old Mozarabic Hymns* [see § 4 (1) of this article] given in the *Hymnarium* printed with Lorenzana's ed. 1775 of the *Mozarabic Brev.*, but not found elsewhere in the *Breviary*.

m[1]. *Old Mozarabic Hymns* given in the *Hymnarium*, and also found in Ximenes' ed. of the *Mozarabic Brev.*, 1502.

m[2]. Hymns introduced into the *Mozarabic Brev.*, 1502, from *Ambrosian, Old Roman*, and other sources. [With few exceptions these hymns are in Migne's *Patrol.*, Paris, 1862, tom lxxxvi].

r[1]. *Roman Breviary*, before the first great revision of 1525. Edition, Venice, 1515.

r[2]. *Roman Breviary*, after the 4th revision, 1632. Edition, Venice, 1635.

r[3]. *Roman Breviary.* Modern. Edition, Tournay, 1879.

r. All the hymns which are found in all the above editions of the *Roman Brev.* are marked *r*.

s. *Sarum Breviary.* Reprint. Cambridge, 1879–87.

y. *York Breviary.* Surtees Soc., Durham, 1880–83.

z. *Aberdeen Breviary.* London 1854.

p. *Paris Breviary.* Revised Paris, 1736.

First line of Hymn.	Breviary.	Use.
A Deo missus Gabriel .	z.	Annun. B. V. M.
A Patre unigenite . .	m[2].	2nd Mon. in Adv.
A Patre unigenitus . .	s. y. z.	Epiphany.
A solis ortus cardine Ad usque	m*. r. s. y. z.	Christmas. Ann. B. V. M. (m).
A solis ortus cardine Et usque (st. ii. Beatus)	m[1].	
A solis ortus cardine Et usque (st. ii. Gaudete)	m[1].	
Ad brevem se mortis .	m*.	Sat. in Easter Wk.
Ad coenam Agni providi	r[1]. s. y. z.	Low Sunday.
Ad nuptias Agni Pater .	p.	C. of Holy Women.
Ad prima verba virginis	p.	Visit. of B V. M.
Ad regias Agni dapes .	r[2].	Low Sunday.
Ad sacrum cujus . .	z.	C. of Matrons.
Ad sanctos cineres .	p.	St. Dionysius.
Ad templa nos rursus .	p.	Sunday. Lauds.
Adam vetus quod . .	y.	Christmas.
Adest diei Christe . .	m*.	Consec. of Bp.
Adest dies laetitiae . .	z.	St. Ninian.
Adest dies sanctissima .	m[2].	St. Nicholas.
Adest miranda passio .	m[1].	St. Vincent.
Adeste coelitum chori .	p.	Eastertide.
Adeste sanctae conjuges	p.	C. of Holy Women
Adeste sancti plurimo .	p	Oct of All Saints

First line of Hymn.	Breviary.	Use.	First line of Hymn.	Breviary.	Use.
Adesto nostris precibus .	$m.^2$	Wed. after Oct. Ep. 1st Sun. in Lent.	Christe coelestis medicina Patris	$m^1.$	Th. after Oct. Ep. 1st S. in Lent. For the sick.
Adesto plebs fidissima .	$m.^2$	St. Agatha.	Christe cunctorum. dominator alme	$a. m^*.$	Ded. of Ecclesia major, 3rd Sun. in Oct. (a.)
Adesto sancta Trinitas .	$s. y. z.$	Trinity Sunday.			
Adsunt, O populi, festa .	$m^2.$	St. Hippolytus.			
Adsunt punicea floscula	$m^1.$	SS. Justa & Rufina			
Adsunt tenebrae primae	$m^1.$	First Watch.	Christe cunctorum praesulum	$z.$	St. Blaan.
Aestimavit Hortulanum	$s. z.$	St. Mary Magd.			
Aeterna Christi munera i.	$a^1. r. y.$	C. of an Apostle.	Christe decreto Patris .	$p.$	Com. of Bishops.
Aeterna Christi munera ii	$a^2.r^1. m^*. y.$	C. of Martyrs.	Christe, immense . .	$m^2.$	3rd S. in Lent.
Aeterna coeli gloria . .	$r. s. y. z.$	Friday. Lauds.	Christe, lumen per petuum	$m^2.$	Tu. after Oct. Ep.
Aeterne lucis conditor .	$m^2.$	Friday after 1st S. in Lent.			,, ,, 1st S. in Lent.
Aeterne rector siderum .	$r^3.$	Guardian Angels.	Christe, lux lucis vera .	$m^2.$	St. Dorothea.
Aeterne rerum conditor.	$a. m^1.r.s.z.$	Matins (a), 1st S. in Adv. (m), S. Lauds (r.s.z.)	Christe, lux mundi salus	$m^1.$	2nd Sun. after Oct. Ep.
Aeterne rex altissime .	$m^1.r.s.y.z.$	Ascension	Christe, pastorum caput	$p.$	Com. of Bishops.
Aeterni Patris ordine .	$s.$	Presentation of B. V. M.	Christe, precamur annue	$m^2.$	Friday after 1st Sun. in Lent.
Aeterni Patris unice. .	$y.$	St. Mary Magd.	Christe, prolapsi reparator	$p.$	Nat. St. John Baptist.
Aeterni proles Patris .	$m^2.$	St. Bartholomew.			
Aeterno regi gloriae . .	$z.$	Crown of Jesus.	Christe, qui lux es et .	$a. m^1. s. y. z.$	Lent Compline.
Agathae sacrae virginis .	$a.$	St. Agatha.	Christe, qui regis omnia	$m^2.$	Th. after 1st Sun. in Lent.
Agne sepulchrum est .	$m^1.$	St. Agnes.			
Agnes beatae virginis .	$a.$	St. Agnes.	Christe qui rex es . .	$z.$	St. Ninian.
Agni genitor Domine [Unigenite, 1502].	$m^1.$	Sun. before Epiph.	Christe qui sedes Olympo	$p.$	St. Michael.
			Christe redemptor (i) .	$r^1. m^2. s. y.$	All Saints.
			Christe redemptor (ii) .	$r^1. s. y. z.$	Christmas.
Agnoscat omne seculum	y	Christmas.	Christe, rex mundi . .	$m^2.$	Of the Dead.
Ales diei nuntius, , .	$r. s. y. z.$	Tuesday. Lauds.	Christe salvator omnium	$m^2.$	Mon. after Oct. Ep.
Alleluia piis edite . .	$m^1.$	1st S. in Lent	Christe sanctorum decus	$r. s. y. z.$	SS. Michael (r. s. y). Gabriel (r. s), Raphael (r).
Alma Redemptoris mater	$a^2. r^2. y. s. p.$	Ant. after Compline.			
Almi prophetae progenies	$a. m^2.$	Decoll. of St. John Baptist.	Christe, tu rerum . .	$m^*.$	St. Clement.
			Christe, verus rex . .	$m^1.$	St. Servandus, &c.
Altissimi verbum Patris	$m^1.$	1st S. after Oct. of Epiph. & Sat. Lent.	Christi caterva clamitet	$m^1.$	1st S. in Adv.
			Christi cruentae splendida	$p.$	Crown of Thorns.
Alto ex Olympi vertice	$r^2.$	Dedication of a Ch.			
Amore Christi nobilis .	$a.$	St. John Evang.	Christi martyribus debita	$p.$	C. of Martyrs.
Andrea pie sanctorum .	$s. y. z.$	St. Andrew.	Christi miles gloriosus .	$s.$	St. Vincent.
Angulare fundamentum	$r^1. s. y. p. z.$	Dedication of a Ch.	Christi miles pretiosus .	$y.$	St. Vincent.
Anni peracto circulo. .	$m^*.$	Birthday of a King	Christi perennes nuntii .	$p.$	C. of Evangelists.
Annue Christe saeculorum	$s. y. z.$	C. of Apostles.	Christo profusum sanguinem	$r^2.$	C. of Martyrs.
Antra deserti teneris .	$r. s. y. z.$	St. John Bapt.	Christus est virtus Patris	$m^1.$	St. Jerome.
Apollinaris martyris . .	$a.$	St. Apollinaris.	Christus est vita veniens	$m^1.$	St. Stephen.
Apostolorum passio . .	$a. m^1.$	SS. Peter & Paul.	Christus tenebris obsitam	$p.$	Epiphany.
Apostolorum supparem	$a.$	St. Lawrence.	Cibis resumptis congruis	$m^1.$	Before Compline in Lent.
Ardet Deo quae femina .	$p.$	C. of Holy Women.			
Aspice infami Deus . .	$r^3.$	The Passion.	Clamantis ecce vox . .	$p.$	Epiphany.
Aspice ut verbum Patris	$r^3.$	The Lord's Prayer.	Clange lyram Zacharias .	$m.$	(See "Pange linguam Zacharie.")
Athleta Christi nobilis .	$r^3.$	St. Venantius.			
Auctor beate saeculi. .	$r^3.$	The Sacred Heart.	Clara sanctorum una .	$m^1.$	St. James Ap.
Auctor luminis filius .	$m^2.$	2nd S. in Lent.	Claro paschali gaudio .	$r^1. s. z.$	C. of Apostles.
Auctor perennis gloriae.	$m^*.$	Seventh Hour.	Clarum decus jejunii. .	$s. y. z.$	3rd Sun. in Lent.
Audi benigne conditor .	$a^2. r. s. y. p. z.$	Lent.	Clausus aurium meatus .	$m^*.$	Th. in Easter Wk.
Audimur almo Spiritus.	$p.$	Whitsunday.	Clementis festum . .	$m^1.$	St. Clement.
Audit tyrannus anxius .	$r^2.$	Holy Innocents.	Cleri patrem et . . .	$z.$	St. Nicholas.
Aurea luce et decore. .	$r^1. s. y. z.$	Vig. of SS. Peter & Paul.	Coelestis agni nuptias .	$r^3.$	St. Juliana Falconieri.
Aures ad nostras . . .	$r^1.$	Sundays. Lent.	Coelestis ales nuntiat .	$p.$	Annunciation.
Aurora coelum purpurat	$r^2.$	Sunds. after Easter	Coelestis aula panditur .	$p.$	C. of Virgins.
Aurora jam spargit polum	$m^*. r. s. y. z.$	Saturday. Lauds (do. in Lent, m).	Coelestis aulae principes	$p.$	C. of Apostles.
			Coelestis formam gloriae	$s. z.$	Transfiguration.
Aurora lucis dum novae.	$p.$	Eastertide.	Coelestis urbs Jerusalem	$r^2.$	Dedication of Ch.
Aurora lucis rutilat . .	$r^1. m^2. y. s. z.$	Eastertide.	Coeli cives applaudite .	$a^1.$	Augustine, Ep. & Conf.
Aurora rutilat lucis . .	$z.$	St. Columba.			
Ave maris stella . . .	$r. s. y. p.$	Feasts of B. V. M.	Coeli Deus sanctissime .	$m^*. r. s. y. z.$	W. Vespers.
Ave mater Anna. . .	$s. z.$	St. Anne.	Coelitum consors . . .	$p.$	St. Genovefa.
Ave regina coelorum .	$a^2. r^2. s. p. y.$	Antiphon after Compline.	Coelitum Joseph decus .	$r^3.$	St. Joseph.
			Coelo datur quiescere .	$p.$	St. Barnabas.
Barchinon laeto Cucufate	$m^1.$	St. Cucufatus.			
Bartholomaee coeli sidus	$s. y. z.$	St. Bartholomew.	Coelo quos eadem gloria.	$p.$	All Saints.
Beata nobis gaudia . .	$m^1. r. s. y. z.$	Pentecost.	Coelo receptam. plaudite	$p.$	St. Genovefa.
Beate martyr, prospera	$a. m^2. z.$	St. Vincent.	Coelo redemptor praetulit	$r^3.$	Maternity B.V.M.
Beate pastor Petre . .	$r^2.$	SS. Peter & Paul.	Coelorum regi psallite .	$a.$	St. Mary Mag.
Beate Symon et Thadaee	$s. z.$	SS. Simon & Jude.	Collaudemus Magdalenae	$s. z.$	St. M. Magd.
Bellator armis inclytus .	$a.$	St. Martin.			Sat. before Adv. (a)
Benignitatis fons Deus .	$m^1.$	1st day Jan. Fast.	Concentu parili Justam .	$m^2.$	St. Justa.
Bina coelestis aulae . .	$s. y. z.$	St. John Apost.	Concinat nostra concio .	$z.$	St. Columba.
Bis novem noster populus	$m^*.$	St. Engratia.	Conditor alme siderum .	$a^2. r^1. s. y. z.$	1st S. in Adv.
			Congaudentes cum angelis	$m^2.$	St. Catharine.
Caeteri nunquam nisi .	$p.$	Visit. of B. V. M.	Consors paterni luminis.	$m^*. r. s. y. z.$	Tuesday. Matins.
Carnis spuans mundiciam	$r^1.$	St. Joseph.	Convexa solis orbita . .	$m^1.$	None in Lent.
Castae parentis viscera .	$s. z.$	Of B. V. M.	Cor arca legem . . .	$r^3.$	Sacred Heart.
Caterva matrum . . .	$m^1.$	Innocents.	Corde natus ex parentis .	$y.$	Vigil of Christmas
Catharina mirabilis . .	$m^2.$	St. Catharine.	Corpus domas jejuniis .	$r^3.$	St. John Cantius.
Certum tenentes ordinem	$m^1.$	Terce.	Creator alme siderum .	$r^2.$	Advent.
Chorus dei fidelium magno	$a^1.$	St. Peter Martyr.	Crudelis Herodes Deum .	$r^2.$	Epiphany.
Chorus novae Hierusalem	$s. y. z.$	Low Sunday.			

First line of Hymn.	Breviary.	Use.	First line of Hymn.	Breviary.	Use.
Crux alma salve crux .	p.	Susception of Cross	Felices nemorum pangi-	p.	C. of Abbots, &c.
Crux sola languorum Dei	p.	Invention of Cross	mus		
Crux fidelis	s. y. z.	Invention of Cross	Felix Anna prae . . .	s. z.	St. Anne.
Cultor Dei memento . .	m¹. s. y. z.	Passion Sun. (s.y).	Felix dies mortalibus .	p.	Oct. of Ascension.
		Compline (m).	Felix dies, quam proprio	p.	Circumcision.
Cunctarum rerum omni-	m².	1st Mon. in Adv.	Felix felici praesule . .	a¹.	Galdinus, Apb.
potens					Milan.
Cunctorum rex omnipo-	m².	1st Sun. in Adv.	Felix morte tua qui . .	p.	C. of Martyrs.
tens			Felix per omnes festum	y.	SS. Peter & Paul.
Cunctus mundus patule .	m².	St. Thomas.	Felix terra quae fruc-	m².	St. Fructuosus.
Custodes hominum psal-	r³. p.	Guardian Angels.	tuoso		
limus			Felix Tarraco Fructuoso	m*.	St. Fructuosus.
			Feno jacere pertulit . .	m*.	Christmas.
Davidis soboles, gloria .	p.	Sat. of B. V. M.	Festi laudes hodierni .	r¹.	Feast of Trinity.
Debilis cessent elementa	p.	Circumcision.	Festis laeta sonent . .	p.	C. of Virgins.
Debitam morti sobolem .	p.	Concept.of B.V.M.	Festivisresonent compita	r³.	Precious Blood.
Decora lux aeternitatis .	r².	SS. Peter & Paul.	Festum Christe rex per .	m¹.	St. Thomas.
Decus sacrati nominis .	m¹.	St. Andrew.	Festum Columbae celebre	z.	St. Columba.
Dei canamus gloriam .	p.	Monday. Matins.	Festum matris gloriosae	s. z.	Visitat. of B. V.M.
Deus aeterni luminis .	m².	Tu. after Oct. Ep.	Festum insigne prodiit	m¹.	St. Agatha.
Deus creator omnium,	a. m*.s. y. z.	Sat. V-prs. (s.y.z.	Fidelis plebs ecclesiae .	a¹.	St. Anna.
polique		m*) Vespers (a)	Fit porta Christi pervia .	m*.	B. V. M.
Deus creator omnium,	m²	2nd Sat. in Lent.	Flagrans amore, perditos	p.	Lazarus, &c., vi-
lucis					sited by Christ.
Deus, ignee fons anima-	m¹.	Office of the Dead.	Fletus longaevi rex . .	z.	Concept. B. V. M.
rum			Fons Deus vitae perennis	m*.	St. Felix.
Deus, immensa Trinitas	m*.	C. of a just man.			
Deus, immensa Trinitas	m¹.	C. of Confessor.	Fortem virili pectore .	r².	C. of non-Virgins.
Deus, Pater ingenite . .	m².	W. after Oct. Ep.	Fortes cadendo martyres	p.	C. of Martyrs.
Deus, qui certis legibus .	m².	2nd Sun. in Lent.	Forti tegente brachio .	p.	Eastertide.
Deus, sacrati nominis .	m¹.	St. Andrew.	Frenentur ergo corpo-	m².	Tuesday in Lent.
Deus, sanctorum psalli-	m².	The Innocents.	rum		
mus			Fulgentis auctor aetheris	m².	Monday after Oct.
Deus, tuorum militum .	a.m¹.r.s.y.z.	C. of a just man(m)			of Epiph.
		C. of Martyrs	Fulget clara festivitas .	z.	St. Kentigern.
		(a. r. s. y. z.)	Fulget hic honor sepul-	m¹.	St. Eulalia.
			chri		
Dicamus laudes Domino	m².	Sext Lent.	Fumant Sabaeis templa.	p.	Purif. of B. V. M.
Die dierum principe .	p.	Sunday. Matins.	Fundere preces tempus	m¹.	Ninth Hour.
Dignas quis O Deus tibi.	p.	Thursday. Lauds.			
Divine crescebas puer .	p.	Epiphany.	Gallicae custos Geno-	p.	St. Genovefa.
Doctor egregie Paule. .	r¹. s. y.	St. Paul.	vefa gentis		
Domare cordis impetus .	r³.	St. Elizabeth of	Gallo canente venimus.	m*.	At cock-crow.
		Portugal.	Part of "Noctis tem-		
Dum Christe confixus .	p.	Passiontide.	pus"		
Dum morte victor obruta	p.	SS. Philip & James	Gaude Mater Ecclesia .	m².	St. Barbara.
Dum nocte pulsa. . .	r³.	St. Venantius.	Gaude mater pietatis .	a. r¹.	Transfig.
Dum spargit aram . .	p.	Comp. of B. V. M.	Gaudeat cuncta pia . .	m².	St. James.
			Gaudet caterva nobilis .	m².	St. Faustus, &c.
Ecce jam noctis . . .	r. s. y. z.	Lauds.	Gaudete flores martyrum	m¹.	Sts.-days in Adv.
Ecce parentes virginis .	z.	Present. of B.V.M.			St. Acisclus.
Ecce quem vates vetustis	m*.	Easter Monday.	Gentis Polonae gloria .	r³.	St. John Cantius.
Ecce, saltantis pretium .	p.	Decoll. of St. John	Germine nobilis Eulalia.	m².	St. Eulalia.
		Baptist.	Gesta sanctorum marty-	a¹.	St. George.
Ecce salvator omnium .	m².	2nd Mon. in Adv.	rum		
Ecce sedes hic tonantis .	p.	Dedication of a Ch.	Gloriam sacrae celebre-	r³.	The Winding
Ecce te, Christe, tibi. .	m*.	Consecration of a	mus		Sheet.
		Church.	Grates peracto jam die .	p.	Compline. Feb. 2
Ecce tempus idoneum .	s. z.	3rd S. in Lent.			to Ash W.
Ecquis ardentes rapitur.	p.	St. Martin.	Grates tibi Jesu novas .	a. m².	SS. Protasius &
Egregie doctor Paule .	r².	Conv. of St. Paul.			Gervasius.
		SS. Peter & Paul.			
Emergit undis et Deo .	p.	Oct. of Epiph.	Hac nocte hora praeclus.	m*.	At cock-crow.
En castitatis lilium . .	z.	C. of Virgins.	Part of "Noctis tem-		
En, clara vox. . . .	r².	Advent.	pus"		
En Evangelistae adest .	m².	St. Luke.	Haec dies sacrae fidei .	a¹.	St. Hieronymus.
En festum prodiit . .	m².	St. Euphemia.	Haec est dies qua. . .	r³.	St. Theresa.
En futura Annae . . .	z.	Concept.of B.V.M.	Haec illa solemnis dies .	p.	Annunciation.
En martyris Laurentii .	m¹.	St. Lawrence.	Haec rite mundi . . .	y.	C. of a Matron.
En, ut superba . . .	r³.	Sacred Heart.	Haec vera Christi famula	a².	C. of Martyrs.
Enixa est puerpera . .	s. z.	B. V. M.	Herasme presul nobilis .	a¹.	St. Erasmus.
Eterne, &c. See Aeterne.			Hic duorum chara frat-	m².	SS. Emeterius and
Ex more docti . . .	a². r. s. y. z.	Sun. Matins, Lent.	rum		Celidonius.
		Sun. Vespers,Lent	Hic est dies verus Dei .	a. m².	Eastertide.
		(a.)	Hic Joannes mire natus.	m¹.	Decoll. of S. John
Ex quo salus mortalium.	p.	C. of Martyrs.			Baptist.
Exiit cunis pretiosus .	p.	Nat. St. J. Bapt.	Hinc functionis dies . .	m*.	Of the Dead.
Exite filiae Sion . . .	p.	Crown of Thorns.	Hoc jussa quondam . .	p.	Transfiguration.
Exite Sion filiae . . .	r³.	Crown of Thorns.	Hominis superne condi-	?².	Friday Vespers.
Extimum vestis sacratae	m*.	Easter Tuesday.	tor		
Exulta nimium turba .	m¹.	St. Tirsus.	Honorem [Honore] sanc-	m¹.	St. Eugenia.
Exultemus concrepantes	z.	St. Magnus.	tae Eugeniae		
Exultet aula coelica . .	m².	St. Nicholas.	Horis peractis undecim .	m*.	Eleventh Hour.
Exultet coelum laudibus	r¹. s. y. z.	C. of Apostles.	Horres superbos nec .	p.	Wed. Vespers.
Exultet cor praecordiis .	s. z.	Holy Name.	Hortator ille primus. .	m².	Sat. in Lent.
Exultet laudibus sacrata	r¹.	Transfig.	Hostis Herodes impie .	m¹. r¹.s.y.z.	Vigil of Ep. (s.y.z).
Exultet orbis gaudiis .	r².	C. of Apostles.			Ep. (r¹. m¹).
			Huc vos gratifice plebs .	m¹.	St. Vincent, &c.
Fac Christe, nostri gratia	p.	Epiphany.	Huc vos, O miseri . .	p.	Epiphany.
Fando quis audivit Dei .	p.	Passion Sunday.	Hujus obtentu Deus . .	r¹. s. z.	=seq.
Favens redemtis vota .	m*.	Mid-Lent.			

First line of Hymn.	Breviary.	Use.
Hujus oratu Deus . .	r^2.	C. of non-Virgins.
Hujus supplicium pestis	m^*.	None, in time of War.
Hymnis dum resonat .	p.	All Saints.
Hymnis predulcibus. .	z.	St. Magnus.
Hymnum canamus gloriae	y.	Ascension.
Hymnum dicamus domino	a.	Feria Vin coena domino
Hymnum Mariae Virginis	m^2.	Assumption of B. V. M.
Iisdem creati fluctibus	p.	Thurs. Matins.
Illaesa te puerpera . .	p.	Compassion of B. V. M.
Illuminans, Altissimus[e]	$a. m^1$.	Epiphany .
Imago lucis paternae .	z.	Image of our Lord.
Immense coeli conditor .	$m^*. r. s. y. z.$	Monday. Vespers.
Imperatrix clementiae .	z.	Compas.of B.V.M.
Impleta gaudent viscera.	$s. y. z.$	Pentecost.
Impleta sunt quae . .	z.	See Vexilla.
Impune vati non erit .	p.	Decoll. of St. John Baptist.
In Annae puerperio . .	$s. z.$	St. Anne.
In majestatis solio . .	r^1.	Feast of Trin.
In matutinis surgimus .	m^1.	Th. after Oct. Ep. At cock-crow.
In Ninivitas se coactus .	m^2.	Th. in Lent.
In noctis umbra desides	p.	Advent. Compline
In passione Domini . .	s.	Image of our Lord.
Inclite rex magne . .	m^*.	Coron. of a King.
Incliti festum pudoris .	m^1.	St. Cecilia.
Inconcussa tuo, summe	p.	St. Peter's Chair.
Ingrata gens Judeica .	z.	Compas.of B.V.M.
Insigne festum Juliani .	m^1.	St. Julian.
Insignem Christi Crispinum	m^1.	St. Crispin.
Insignem Christi martyrem	m^2.	C. of Martyrs.
Instantis adventum Dei.	p.	Advent.
Intende nostris precibus.	m^*.	Sunday.
Intende qui regis Israel.	a.	Christmas Day.
Inter sulphurei fulgura .	p.	Whitsunday.
Intrante Christo Bethanicam domum	p.	Lazarus, &c., visited by Christ.
Inventor rutilis dux bone	m^1.	1st Sun. after Oct, of Epiphany.
Invicte martyr unicum .	r^2.	C. of Martyrs.
Inviolata integra et casta	$a^2. p. y. z.$	Of B. V. M.
Ira justa conditoris . .	r^3.	Precious Blood.
Iram quam merito . .	m^*.	In War, at Sext.
Iste Confessor Domini .	$m^1. r. s. y. z.$	C. of Confessors.
Iste electus Johannes .	m^1.	St. John Evang.
Iste quem la ti . . .	r^3.	St. Joseph.
Itote populi psallite . .	m^2.	SS. Simon & Jude.
Jactamur heu quot . .	p.	Mon. at Vespers.
Jam bone pastor Petre .	$r^1. s. y. z.$	St. Peter's chair, chains, & Vig. of SS.Peter & Paul.
Jam Christe nomen . .	$\cdot p$.	St. Eleutherius.
Jam Christe sol . . .	$a^2. r^1. z.$	Lauds. Lent.
Jam Christus astra . .	$a. r. s. y. z.$	Pentecost.
Jam cursus horae sextae	m^1.	Sext.
Jam dena nos perceptio.	m^*.	Tenth Hour.
Jam desinant suspiria .	p.	Christmas Day.
Jam legis umbra clauditur.	m^1.	Wed. Vesp. in Holy Week.
Jam lucis orto sidere. .	$a. m^2. r. s. y. p. z.$	Prime.
Jam meta noctis transiit	m^2.	Aurora.
Jam nil Hebraeis . .	p.	SS. Peter & Paul.
Jam non te lacerant . .	p.	C. of Martyrs.
Jam nunc ad illum . .	m^2.	St. Sebastian.
Jam nunc paterna . .	y.	Sunday Matins.
Jam nunc quae numeras	p.	C. of Doctors.
Jam passionis inchoandae	m^2.	St. Julian.
Jam sanctius moves opus	p.	Friday Matins.
Jam sol recedit . . .	r^2.	Trinity Sunday. Sat. Vespers.
Jam solis excelsum jubar	p.	Sext.
Jam surgit hora tertia .	$a. m^2$.	Terce.
Jam ter quaternis . .	y.	3rd Sun. in Lent.
Jam toto subitus . .	r^3.	Seven Dolours.
Jerusalem gloriosa . .	m^1.	St. Adrian.
Jesu auctor clementiae .	$s. z.$	Holy Name.
Jesu, corona celsior . .	$a. r.$	C. of Confessors.
Jesu, corona Virginum	$a.m^1.r.s.y.z.$	C. of Virgins.
Jesu, decus angelicum .	r^3.	Holy Name.
Jesu defensor omnium .	m^*.	Midnight.
Jesu dulcedo cordium .	p.	Transfiguration.
Jesu, dulcis amor meus.	r^3.	The Winding-sheet
Jesu, dulcis memoria .	$r^3. s. z.$	Holy Name.
Jesu, nostra redemptio .	$r^1. s. y. z. p.$	Ascension, Compline(s.z), Lauds (y. p.). Vsprs. (r¹).
Jesu, quadragenariae .	$s. y. z.$	Lent.
Jesu, Redemptor omnium perpes corona	$r. s. y. z.$	C. of Confessors.
Jesu, Redemptor omnium qui morte	m^*.	Easter Week. Terce.
Jesu, Redemptor omnium quem lucis	r^2.	Christmas.
Jesu, Redemptor omnium, Summi parentis	p.	Christmas.
Jesu, Redemptor saeculi	p.	Eastertide.
Jesu, rex admirabilis .	r^3.	Holy Name.
Jesu rex salvator . .	z.	11,000 Virgins.
Jesu, sacerdotum decus.	p.	C. of Bishops.
Jesu, Salvator seculi (i)	$s. y. z.$	Easter. Compline.
Jesu, Salvator seculi (ii)	$r^1. m^2. s.$	All Saints.
Jesu solamen miseris .	z.	Image of our Lord.
Joannes hujus artis . .	m^2.	Thursday in Lent.
Jonam prophetam mitis	m^2.	Tuesday in Lent.
Jordanis oras praevia .	p.	Advent.
Joseph stirpis Davidicae	r^1.	St. Joseph.
Jubes, et in praeceps .	p.	Tuesday. Matins.
Jucundum nobis hunc .	m^*.	St. Virissimus, &c.
Juliani vita martyris .	m^2.	St. Julian.
Jussu tyranni pro fide .	p.	St. John at Lat. Gate.
Katharinae collaudemus	z.	St. Katharine.
Labente jam solis rota .	p.	None.
Laetare coelum plausibus	p.	C. of Apostles.
Laetis terra sonet plausibus	p.	Nat. & Concept. B. V. M.
Lauda fidelis concio . .	z.	Crown of Jesus.
Lauda mater ecclesia .	y.	St. Mary Magd.
Laudem beatae Eulaliae	m^1.	St. Eulalia.
Laudes sanctorum martyrum	m^1.	C. of Martyrs.
Legis figuris pingitur .	r^3.	Crown of Thorns.
Lignum crucis mirabile.	p.	Exalt. of Cross.
Linquunt tecta magi .	p.	Epiphany.
Luciae festum celebret sancta	a^1.	St. Lucia.
Lucis Auctor clemens .	m^1.	Sun. Lent.
Lucis Creator optime .	$m^*. r. s. y. z.$	Sunday Vespers.
Lucis hujus festa colat .	$m^2. r^1.$	St. Anne.
Lugete pacis angeli . .	p.	Friday. Vespers.
Lustra (is) sex qui jam .	$r. s. y. z.$	Passion Sunday.
Lux alma Jesu . . .	r^2.	Transfiguration.
Lux de luce Deus fons .	p.	Oct. of St. Denis.
Lux ecce surgit . . .	$r. s. y. z.$	Thursday. Lauds.
Lux Deus Christe pietas	m^1.	St. Augustine.
Lux vera lucis claritas .	m^*.	Sunday.
Maerentes oculi spargite	r^3.	C. of Passion.
Magna res nobis . . .	z.	Concept. B. V. M.
Magnae Deus potentiae .	$m^*. r. s. y. z.$	Thurs. Vespers.
Magni palmam certaminis	a^1.	St. Perpetua.
Magnum salutis gaudium	a^1.	Distribution of Palms.
Mane nobiscum, Domine	m^2.	2nd Wedn. in Adv.
Maria castis oculis . .	r^2.	St. Mary Magd.
Maria ventre concepit .	y.	Christmas.
Maria sacro saucia . .	p.	St. Mary Magd.
Martinae celebri plaudite	r^3.	St. Martina.
Martine confessor Dei .	m^1.	St. Martin.
Martyr Dei egregie . .	a^1.	St. Sebastian.
Martyr Dei qui unicum .	$m^*.r^1.s.y.z.$	C. of Martyrs.
Martyr Dei Venantius .	r^3.	St. Venantius.
Martyris festum rutilat	m^2.	St. Marcellus.
Martyris gesta[ns] Zoylique [Zoili]	m^1.	St. Zoylus.
Mathia juste duodeno .	$s. y. z.$	St. Matthias.
Matris intactae veneranda conjux	p.	St. Joseph.
Matthaee sancte bino .	$s. z.$	St. Matthew.
Memento de Deo Deus .	p.	Little Office, of B. V. M.
Memento rerum Conditor	r^2.	Office of B. V. M
Memento salutis auctor .	$a. s.$	Office of B. V. M
Mille quem stipant solio	p.	St. Michael.

First line of Hymn.	Breviary.	Use.	First line of Hymn.	Breviary.	Use.
Miracula primeva ymnorum	m.	Prologue to Hymns (1775).	O luce quae tuâ lates	p.	Holy Trinity.
Miraculum laudabile	a.	Ordn. of St. Ambrose.	O luce qui mortalibus	p.	Sunday. Vespers.
Miramur, O Deus, tuae	p.	Wed. Matins.	O lux beata Trinitas (i).	m¹. s. y. z.	2nd Sun. after Oct. Epiph. (m). Sat. Vsprs. (r¹. s. y. z)
Miratur hostis posse	m².	Tuesday in Lent.			
Miris modis repente	r².	St. Peter's Chains.			
Miris probat sese modis	p.	St. Stephen.	O lux beata Trinitas (ii)	r¹.	Feast of Trin.
Missum Redemptorem	p.	Christmas.	O magne rerum Christe	m².	St. Aemilian.
Molles in agnos ceu lupus	p.	Holy Innocents.	O Maria noli flere	s. z.	St. Mary Magd.
Montes, superbum verticem	p.	Visit. of B. V. M.	O nata lux de	s. z.	Transfiguration.
			O Nazarene, lux	m¹.	Monday in Lent.
Mortale, coelo tolle	p.	Nat. & Concep. of B. V. M.	O nimis felix	r. s. y. z.	St. John Bapt.
			O Pater sancte mitis	s. y. z.	Trinity Sunday.
			O Petre, petra ecclesiae	m¹.	St. Peter's Chair.
Mundi salus affutura	s. z.	Visit. of B. V. M.	O pulchras acies	p.	C. of Abbots, &c.
Mundi salus qui nasceris	p.	Compline, Christmas & Ephy.	O quam glorifica	s. y. p.	Assump. of B. V. M. (s. y), Sat. (p), Little Office (p)
Mysterium ecclesiae hymnus Christo	a.	(1) Pur.f. of B.V. M.; (2) Office of B. V. M.; (3) Visit of B.V.M.; (4) Annunc. of B. V. M.			
			O quam juvat fratres	p.	Tues. Vespers.
			O qui perpetuus nos	p.	C. of Doctors.
			O qui tuo, dux martyrum	p.	St. Stephen.
			O quot undis	r³.	Seven Dolours of B. V. M.
Mysteriorum signifer	a.	St. Michael Arch.	O rerum Domine conditor	m¹.	St. Genesius.
Mysterium mirabile	r³.	The Winding-sheet	O sacerdotum inclita	m¹.	St. Babylas.
Mysticum melos persolvat	m*.	St. Faustus, &c.	O salutaris fulgens	s.	Visitation of B.V. M.:
			O sator rerum	s. z.	Transfiguration.
Nardi Maria pistici	r¹.	St. Mary Magd.	O sol salutis	r².	Lauds. Lent.
Nardus Columbae floruit	m¹.	St. Columba.	O sola magnarum	r².	Epiphany.
Nativitatem pueri	m².	St. John Baptist.	O splendor aeterni Patris	p.	Lent. Compline.
Natus Parenti redditus	p.	SS. Philip & James	O stella Jacob	r³.	Purity of B. V. M.
Necnon et ipsos protegit	m².	St. Agnes.	O Thoma Christi	s. y. z.	St. Thomas.
Nil laudibus nostris eges	v.	Monday. Lauds.	O triplex honor	m¹.	St. Fructuosus, &c.
Nobis Olympo redditus	p.	Ascension.	O Virgo pectus cui	p.	C. of Virgins.
Nocte surgentes vigilemus	r. s. y. z.	Sunday. Matins.	O verum regimen	m*.	For an army.
Noctis tempus jam praeterit	m¹.	4th Sun. in Lent. At cock-crow.	U vos aetherei plaudite	p.	Assump.of B.V.M.
Noctis tetrae primordia	m¹.	First Watch.	O vos cum citharis	p.	St. Mary of Egypt.
Non abluunt lymphae	p.	Oct. of Epiph.	O vos unanimes Christiadum chori	p.	Oct. of All Saints.
Non illam crucians	r³.	St. Martina.	Obduxere polum nubila	m*.	In time of rain.
Non parta solo sanguine	p.	C. of just men.	Obsidiones obvias	m¹.	First Watch.
Non usitatis ortus hic	m².	Friday in Lent.	Octavus horae circulus	m*.	Eighth Hour.
Non vana dilectum	p.	C. of Virgins.	Omnes fideles plaudite	s.	Present. of B.V.M.
Nos imago Trinitatis	s.	Image of Christ.	Omnibus manat cruor ecce venis	p.	Decoll. of St. John Bapt.
Novum sidus emicuit	m².	St. Elizabeth of Hungary.	Omnipotenti Domino	m².	St. Andrew.
Novum sydus exoritur	r¹.	Transfig.	Opes decusque regium	r³.	St. Elizabeth of Portugal.
Nox atra rerum	r. s. y. z.	Thurs. Matins.	Opprobriis Jesu satur	p.	Passiontide.
Nox et tenebrae	r. s. y. z.	Wed. Lauds.	Optatus votis omnium	a.	Ascension.
Noxium Christus simul	p.	Circumcision.	Opus peregisti tuum	p.	Ascension.
Nullis te genitor	r³.	St. Herm' negild.	Orbe nunc toto celebrentur ambo	p.	SS. Peter & Paul.
Nullis bibendi nemo	m².	Sat. in Lent.	Orbis exultans celebret	m².	St. Anne.
Nunc aurora, novae	p.	Sat. B. V. M. Little Office.			
Nunc cunctorum vox jucunda	m².	St. Elizabeth of Hunga'y.	Panditur saxo tumulus	p.	Lazarus, &c., visited by Christ.
Nunc gestis ex veteribus	a¹.	St. Styrus.	Pange, lingua gloriosae	z.	St. Katharine.
Nunc sancte nobis	a.m¹.r.s.y.z	Terce.	Pange, lingua, gloriosi corporis	a². m². r¹. s.y p. z.	Corpus Christi.
Nunc suis tandem	p.	Nat. St. John Bap.	Pange, lingua, gloriosi lauream	r².	Passion and Palm Sunday & Invention of Cross.
O beata Jerusalem	m*.	Restoration of a Church.	Pange, lingua, gloriosi praelium	m¹. r¹.s.y.z.	Good Friday (m), Inv. of Cross (m). Pass. & Palm Sunday (r¹.s.y.z)
O beate mundi	m¹.	St. Christopher.			
O castitatis signifer et forti	a¹.	C. of Martyrs.			
O Christe palma martyrum	a¹.	St. Mauricius.	Pange, lingua, gloriosi praelium certaminis	s.	Image of Our Saviour.
O Christe qui noster	p.	Whitsun Eve.	Pange, lingua, gloriosi praesulis	z.	St. Nicholas.
O Christi martyr et	m².	St. Barbara.			
O coeli sydus lucide	z.	St. Maurice.	Pange, linguam, Zachariae. [Changed to "Clange lyram Zacharias" in 1775.]	m¹.	St. John Baptist.
O coelorum alme princeps	m.z.	St. Michael.			
O crux ave spes	s.	Passion Sunday.			
O decus sacrum virginum	m².	Sat. Office of B. V.M. & Assump.	Pange sanctae Catharine gloriosa	a¹.	St. Catharine.
O Dei perenne verbum	m¹.	SS. Justus & Pastor			
O Dei sapientia	s. z.	Presentation of B. V. M.	Parata cum te poscerent	p.	Assump.of B.V.M.
O Dei Verbum Patris	m¹.	St. James.	Paschale mundo gaudium	r².	C. of Apostles.
O fons amoris Spiritus	p.	Terce.	Pastore percusso minas	p.	Conv. of St. Paul.
O fortis O clemens Deus	p.	Thurs. Vespers.	Pater superni luminis	r².	St. Mary Magd.
O gloriosa domina	r¹. z.	Assump. of B. V. M. (r¹). Compass. of B. V. M. (z).	Patris aeterni soboles	p.	Ded. of Church.
			Perfecto trino numero	m².	None.
			Perfusa non sic amne	m².	Thursday in Lent.
O gloriosa femina	s.	Lady Day.	Perfusus ora lachrymis	p.	St. Martin.
O gloriosa virginum	r².	Sat. of B. V. M.	Petrum tyranne, quid	p.	St. Peter in Prison
O jam beata quae suo	p.	C. of Holy Women	Petrus beatus catenarum	r¹.	St. Peter's Chains

First line of Hymn.	Breviary.	Use.
Placare, Christe, servulis	r².	All Saints. St. Gabriel.
Placet frementem publicis	m².	Friday in Lent.
Plagis magistri saucia .	p.	St. Mary Magd.
Plasmator hominis Deus	m*.r¹.s.y.z.	Friday Vespers.
Plaudat turba fidelium .	z.	St. Ninian.
Plaude coelestis curia .	r¹.	St. Joseph.
Plebs Deo dicata . . .	m¹.	SS. Cosmas and Damian.
Post ˙Petrum primum principem	a.	St. Andrew Ap.
Post ut occasum resolvit	m*.	Ascension.
Praeclarum Christi militem	m².	St. Matthew.
Praeclara custos virginum	r³.	Immac. Concep & Purity of B.V.M.
Praedicta Christi mors .	p.	SS. Philip & Jas.
Praesepe poni pertulit .	y.	Christmas.
Primo die quo Trinitas .	r².	Sunday. Matins.
Primo dierum omnium .	m*.r¹.s.y.z.	Sunday. Matins.
Pro speciali linteo . .	m².	St. Mary Magd.
Procul maligni cedite .	p.	St. Mary Magd.
Prome vocem, mens canoram	p.	Five Wounds of Christ.
Prome commissas tibi	p.	St. Peter's Chair.
Promissa mundo gaudia .	p.	SS.Joachim&Anne
Promissa, tellus, concipe.	p.	Ascension.
Promittis et servas datam	p.	Wed. Lauds.
Prompta cuncta Catholicae	m².	SS. Michael and Gabriel,
Proni rogamus Philippe	y.	St. Philip.
Psallat altitudo coeli	m¹.	Low Sunday.
Puer hic sonat Iohannes.	m¹.	St. John Baptist.
Puer sanctus veneratur ,	z.	St. Maurice.
Pulsum supernis sedibus	p.	Annunciation.
Qua lapsu tacito stella .	p.	Epiphany.
Quae coelo nova nunc .	p.	Assump.ofB.V.M.
Quae gloriosum tanta .	p.	Conv. of St. Paul.
Quae longa tandem Virgo	p.	Assump.ofB.V.M.
Quae stella sole pulchrior	p.	Epiphany.
Quae te pro populi criminibus nova	p.	Lent.Five Wounds of Christ.
Quae turma nuptialibus .	p.	St. Ursula.
Quaenam lingua tibi .	r³.	Lance and Nails.
Qualis potestas, Petre .	p.	St. Peter's Chair.
Quam Christe signasti .	p.	C. of Martyrs.
Quam nos potenter allicis	p.	Transfiguration.
Quar o die jam foetidus .	m².	3rd Sun. in Lent.
Quem misit in terras .	p.	C. of Apostles.
Quem nox, quem tenebrae	p.	St. John Evang.
Quem terra pontus .	r. s. y. z.	Feast of B. V. M.
Qui amne nunc quadrifluo	m*.	Fourth Hour.
Qui Christiano gloriantur	p.	St. Peter in Prison.
Qui natus es de virgine .	p.	Doxology.
Qui nos creas solus . .	p.	Sundays Sept. to Lent.
Qui nube rupta, te . .	p.	Doxology.
Qui sacris hodie . .	p.	Purif. of B. V. M.
Qui te, Deus, sub intimo	p.	C. of just men.
Qui te revelas Gentibus .	p.	Doxology.
Qui toti libri per Moysen	m*.	Fifth Hour.
Quicumque Christum .	r².	Transfiguration.
Quid moras nectis ? .	p.	Nat. St. John Bap.
Quid obstinata pectora .	p.	St. Stephen.
Quid sacram, virgo .	p.	C. of Virgins.
Quid tu relictis urbibus .	p.	C. of Abbots, &c.
Quieti tempus adest . .	m¹.	First Watch.
Quis ille, sylvis .	p.	Decoll. of St. John Bap.
Quo forma cessit par D o	p.	Crown of Thorns.
Quo fugis praeceps? .	p.	St. Martin.
Quo sanctus ardor te. .	p.	Visit. of B. V. M.
Quo vos magistri gloria .	p.	Whitsunday.
Quod convolutis artubus.	m*.	Midnight.
Quod carne Christum .	p.	Assump.ofB.V.M.
Quod chorus vatum .	s. y. z.	Purif. of B. V. M.
Quod lex adumbravit .	p.	Lent. Matins.
Quodcumque in orbe .	r².	St. Peter's Chair.
Quodcumque vinclis .	r¹.	St. Peter's Chair.
Quodquod diem determinent	m*.	Twelfth Hour.
Quomodo fiet petiit . .	z.	Annun. B.V.M.
Quos in hostes, Saule .	p.	Conv. of St. Paul.
Quos junxit unus. . .	p.	SS. Peter & Paul.
Quos pompa saeculi quos opes	p.	St. Joseph. H. of B. V. M.
Quot fregit uno castitas ,	p.	St. Ursula.

First line of Hymn.	Breviary.	Use.
Rebus creatis nil egens .	p.	Sundays. Septuagesima to Lent.
Rector potens verax .	a.m¹.r.s.y.z.	Sext.
Rector, Redemptor et .	m*.	C. of Saints.
Redditum luci, Domino vocanti	p.	Lazarus, &c., visited by Christ.
Referre prisci stemma .	m².	Sat. in Lent.
Regale Davidis genus .	p.	SS.Joachim&Anna
Regali solio fortis . .	r³.	St. Hermenegild.
Regi polorum debitas .	a.	St. Dionysius.
Regina coeli, laetare. .	a². r². p.	Ant. Lauds and Compline.
Regis superni nuntia .	r³.	St. Teresa.
Regnis paternis debitus.	p.	SS. Philip &James.
Regnator orbis summus.	p.	Guardian angels.
Regum progenies, Isacidum decus	p.	St. Joseph.
Rerum Creator omnium.	p.	Saturday. Lauds.
Rerum Creator optime (1)	m*. r.s.y.z.	Wed. Matins.
Rerum Creator optime(2)	r³.	Holy Redeemer.
Rerum Deus fons .	m*.	Satur. Vespers.
Rerum Deus tenax .	a. m*. r. s.	None. (a.r.s.y.z).
	y. z.	Vespers (m).
Resonat ecclesia laudum	z.	11,000 Virgins.
Rex aeterne Deus fons .	m*.	In War.
Rex aeterne Domine. .	r¹.	Easter-tide.
Rex confessorum inclite.	z.	St. Kentigern.
Rex gloriose Martyrum .	m¹. r. s.y.z.	C. of Martyrs.
Rex gloriose Praesulum	r³.	C. of all Popes.
Rex sempiterne coelitum	r².	Sunday. Matins.
Rex summe regum . .	p.	St. Louis.
Romane Christi fortis	m¹.	St. Romanus.
Sacer octavarum dies .	m¹.	Circumcision.
Sacer puritatum dies .	m².	Purif. B. V. M.
Sacrae parentes Virginis	s.	Presentation of B. V. M.
Sacrae triumphum martyris	m².	St. Martiana.
Sacrata Christi tempora.	m².	S. after Ascension
Sacrate veni Spiritus .	m².	Pentecost.
Sacratum Christi antistitem (1)	m.	St. Augustine.
Sacratum Christi antistitem (2)	m¹.	St. Gerontius.
Sacri senatus, Petre . .	p.	St. Peter's Chair
Sacri triumphales tui .	a.	SS. Nazarius and Celsus.
Sacris solemniis juncta .	m².r.s.y.p.z.	Corpus Christi.
Sacrum tempus in calculo	m*.	SS. Cyriacus and Paula.
Saepe dum Christi . .	r³.	B. V. M. Help of Christians.
Saevo dolorum turbine .	r³.	C. of Passion.
Salutis aeternae dator .	r².	All Saints.
Salutis humanae sator (1)	r².	Ascension.
Salutis humanae sator (2)	r³.	B. V. M. Pure Heart.
Salvator mundi Domine .	s. y. z.	Christmas (s. z), Trin. (y).
Salve, regina, mater . .	r².	Ant. Lauds and Compline.
Salvete Christi vulnera .	r³.	Precious Blood.
Salvete clavi et lancea .	r³.	Lance and Nails.
Salvete flores martyrum	r². p.	Holy Innocents.
Sancta mater istud . .	r³.	Seven Dolours of B. V. M.
Sancte Dei pretiose . .	s. y. z.	St. Stephen.
Sanctissimae Leocadiae .	m¹.	St. Leocadia.
Sanctorum meritis inclita	m¹. r. s. y. z.	C. of Martyrs.
Sat Paule sat terris . .	p.	Conv. of St. Paul.
Scripta sunt coelo duorum	m¹.	SS. Emeterius and Celidonius.
Scripta sunt in coelo piorum	m¹.	
Sebastiani martyris sollemne	m*.	St. Sebastian.
Sed cur vetustae . .	m².	Monday in Lent.
Sed mox in auras. . .	m².	Wedn. in Lent.
Sensus quis horror . .	p.	Fifth day of Oct. Ascension.
Sermone blando angelus .	s. y. z.	Low Sunday.
Si quid virginitas . .	p.	St. Ursula.
Signum novi crux . .	p.	Invention of Cross
S nae sub alto vertice .	p.	C. of Evangelists.
Sit qui rite canat. . .	p.	St. John Evang.
Sol angelorum respice .	m¹.	Compline.
Solemne festum ples .	m².	St. Sebastian.
Solemne nos jejunii . .	p.	Lent. Lauds.
Solemne rutilat ac , ,	m².	St. Matthew.

First line of Hymn.	Breviary.	Use.
Solve vocem mens sonora	m*.	Friday in Easter Week.
Somno refectis artubus	m*. r. s. y. z.	Monday. Matins.
Sperati sancti martyris	m¹.	St. Speratus.
Splendor paternae gloriae	a.m¹.r.s.y.z.	Mon i. Lauds (a. r. s. y.z) Epiph.
Squalent arva soli	m*.	For rain.
Stabat mater dolorosa	r³.	Seven Dolours of B. V. M.
Statuta decreto Dei	p.	Advent.
Stephani primi martyris	a.	St. Stephen.
Stupete gentes; fit Deus.	p.	Purif. of B. V. M.
Sublime Numen ter	p.	Holy Trinity.
Sudore sat tuo fides	p.	Conv. of St. Paul.
Suetus antro bustualis	m*.	Wed. in Easter Week.
Summae Deus clementiae	r³.	Seven Dolours of B. V. M.
Summae Deus clementiae	m*.r¹.s.y.z.	Saturday. Matins.
Summae Parens clemen-tiae (i.)	r².	Saturday. Matins.
Summe Parens clemen-tiae (2)	r².	Trinity Sunday.
Summe Confessor sacer	m¹.	C. of Confessors.
Summe largitor (y=seq.)		
Summi largitor praemii	s. y. z.	1st Sun. in Lent.
Summi Parentis unice	r².	St. Mary Magd.
Summi pusillus grex	p.	C. of just men.
Summi vatis preconium	a.	St. Alexandus and St. Simplicianus
Supreme motor cord'um	p.	Saturday. Vespers.
Supreme quales, Arbiter	p.	C. of Apostles.
Supreme Rector coelitum	p.	Whitsun Eve.
Surgentes ad te Domine.	m*.	Midnight.
Tandem laborum,gloriosi	p.	SS. Peter & Paul.
Tandem peractis O Deus	p.	Saturday. Matins
Te centies mille	m¹.	Sat. after Easter.
Te decet hymnus in	m*.	St. Dorothea.
Te deprecante corporum	r³.	St. John Cantius.
Te Joseph celebrent	r³.	St. Joseph.
Te lue a, mundi Conditor	p.	Sat. before Septu-agesima.
Te lucis ante	a.m*.r.s.y.z.	Compline.
Te lucis auctor	m*.	Sun. Matins in Lent.
Te majestatis Domine	m¹.	Terce.
Te mater alma	r³.	Maternity of B. V. M.
Te principem summo	p.	Tuesday. Lauds.
Te Redemptoris	r³.	B. V. M. Help of Christians.
Te Sancte rursus	p.	St. Louis.
Te splendor et	r².	St. Michael.
Telluris alme Conditor	r².	Tuesday. Vespers.
Telluris ingens Conditor	m*.r¹.s.y.z.	Tues. Vespers.
Tellus tot annos quid	p.	Invention of Cross
Templa nunc fument	p.	St. Louis.
Templi sacratus pande	p.	Purif. of B. V. M.
Tempus sopori congruum	m*.	Sunday night.
Ter sancte, ter potens	p.	Holy Trinity.
Thure fumantes quis hic	p.	St. Martin.
Tibi Christe, splendor	r¹. s. y. z.	St. Michael.
Tinctam ergo Christi	r³.	Lance and Nails.
Transmissus raptim prae-dicans. [Transmissa raptim praeda, 1775].	m².	Wed. in Lent.
Trinitati altissime matri Christi	a¹.	All Saints.
Tristes erant Apostoli	r. s. z.	C. of Apostles.
Tu Christe nostrum	s. z.	Ascension.
Tu natale solum	r³.	St. Martina.
Tu quem prae reliquis	p.	St. John Evang.
Tu rex Redemptor	m*.	Saturday. Matins.
Tu Trinitatis unitas (1)	m*. r. s. y. z.	Fri.Matins(r.s.y.z)
Tu Trinitatis unitas (2)	r².	Trinity Sunday.
Tuba clarifica plebs	m.*	Of Marriage.
Tunc coelum horruit et	z.	Image of our Lord
Tunc ille Judas carnifex.	m*.	Maundy Thurs.
Part of "Hostis He-rodes."		
Turba refulsit coelica	z.	St. Blaan.
Ultricibus nos undique	p.	Friday. Lauds.
Ultrix ipsa suos saevit	p.	St. Mary of Egypt
Uncta crux Dei cruore	p.	Exalt. and Suscep-tion of Cross.
Uni sit et trino Deo	p.	Doxology.
Unus bonorum fons	p.	Nativity & Concpt. of B. V. M.

First line of Hymn.	Breviary.	Use.
Urbem Romuleam quis furor	p.	St. John at Lat. Gate.
Urbis magister Tasciae.	m¹.	St. Cyprian.
Urbis Romuleae jam toga	m¹.	St. Torquatus.
Urbs beata Hierusalem	r¹. s. y. z.	Dedication of a Ch.
Urbs Jerusalem beata	p.	" "
Ut queant laxis	r. y. s. z.	St. John Baptist
Veni Creator Spiritus	r. s. y. p. z.	(1) Pentecost (r¹. s.y.p.z); (2) At vesting for Mass (s).
Veni Redemptor gentium	m¹. s. y. z.	Christmas Day.
Veni Superne Spiritus	p.	Whitsunday.
Venit e coelo	r³.	Agony in the Gar-den.
Verbum Patris quod	m¹.	4th Sun. in Lent.
Verbum quod ante	p.	Epiphany.
Verbum supernum pro-diens A Patre.	m¹. r. s. y. z.	1st Sun. in Adv.
Verbum supernum pro-diens nec Patris.	a. m². r. s. y. p. z.	Corpus Christi.
Vere gratia plena es	a.	Office of B. V. M.
Verus Redemptor Christe	m*.	Cons. of a Bp.
Vexilla regis prodeunt	a².r.s.y.p.z.	Passion Sunday. Palm Sunday (a). Exalt. and Inven-tion of Cross(a.z)
Victis sibi cognomina	p.	Circumcision.
Victor, Nabor, Felix, pii	a.	St. Victor.
Virginis proles, opifex-que	m¹. r. s. y. z.	C. of Virgins.
Virginis sacrae trium-phum (1)	m¹.	St. Christina.
Virginis sacrae trium-phum (2)	m².	St. Justa.
Virginum robur, Deus	p.	C. of Virgins.
Virgo Dei genetrix	p.	Compline of B. V. M.
Virgo parens vixit	z.	Of B. V. M.
Virgo singularis	s.	Adv. Compline B. V. M.
Virgo virginum prae-clara	r³.	Seven Dolours of B. V. M.
Vocaris ad vitam, sacrum	m¹.	Palm Sunday.
Vocis auditae novitas	m¹.	St. Saturninus.
Vos ante Christi tempora	p.	Sundays. Septu. to Lent.
Vos O virginei cum	p.	C. of Virgins.
Vos sancti proceres vos	p.	All Saints.
Vos succensa Deo	p.	C. of Doctors.
Vox clara ecce	m¹.r¹.s.y.z.	1st Sun. in Adv. (r¹. s. y. z). Weekdays in Adv. (m).
Vox ecce vatum vivida.	m².	SS. Justus and Abundus.

11. In addition to the *Breviaries* named above, two incomplete copies of the *Hereford Breviary* are available for collation. Among the Hereford hymns are the following, all of which are additional to those contained in the above table, and so far as we can trace, peculiar to this Breviary:—

First line of Hymn.	Use.
Aeternam celi gratiam	St. Raphael.
Alma chorus Domini	Holy Name.
Christi mater celicola	Visit. of B. V. M.
Corde natus ... Ipse jussit	Christmas. Prime.
Corporis formam caduci	Christmas. Terce.
De sacro tabernaculo	Visit. of B. V. M.
Ecce quem vates	Christmas. Sext.
Excelsorum civium inclita	St. Raphael.
Exultet coelum gaudiis	St. Raphael.
Gaude mater ecclesia	St Thomas of Hereford.
Gaudet chorus fidelium	St. Anne.
In Mariam vitae viam	Visit. of B. V. M.
Juste judex mortuorum	Christmas. None.
O digna laudibus	St. Ethelbert.
Pretiosa splendet Anna	St. Anne.
Quos alloquentes	SS. Phil. & Jas. (Si post Ascensionem.)
Sanctorum meritis jungat	St. Ethelbert.
Veni Creator ... Memento	Matins of B. V. M.

12. *Monastic Breviaries.* — We append a further list of first lines of hymns drawn from Monastic Breviaries. We have omitted the first lines of all hymns common to both the secular and monastic Service Books, except in the case of a few rare hymns the wider use of which it seemed important to record. It will be observed that the following hymns are drawn almost exclusively from the Proprium Sanctorum. *Benedictine, Cistercian, Dominican, Franciscan,* and *Augustinian* Breviaries have been collated. The following editions have been made use of :—

(*a*) Breviarium Monasticum secundum ritum Monachorum Ordinis S. Benedicti de observantia Congregationis Casinensis, alias B. Iustinae de Padua. Venetiis MDCI.

(*b*) Breviarium sacri Ordinis Cisterciensis. Parisiis MDCXVII.

(*c*) Breviarium secundum ordinem S. Dominici. Nurembergae MCCCCLXXXV.

(*d.*) Officia Propria sanctorum Ordinis Minorum. Antverpiae MDCCXXII.

(*e*). Breviarium Cartusiani Ordinis. Lugduni MDCXLIII.

(*f*) Breviarium Augustinianum, ad usum fratrum et monialium Ordinis Eremitarum Sancti Augustini. Venetiis MDCCLXXXIX.

In four specified cases the hymns are drawn from a MS. source in the British Museum.

First line of Hymn.	Breviary.	Use.
Ad glorias ad laureas	*f.*	St. Thomas Villanov.
Ad panem medicum currite	*f.*	Benediction of bread.
Ad preces nostras, deitatis	*a.*	Sunday in Lent. Vespers.
Adest triumphus nobilis	*c.*	St. Peter Martyr.
Adesse sancti coelites	*f.*	Relics of All Saints
Adsunt festa jubilea	*b.*	Visit. B. V. M.
Aeterni Patris unice.	*c. e.*	St. Mary Magd.
Aeterno regi gloriae .	*c.*	Invent. of Cross.
Agathae sacrae virginis	*b.*	St. Agatha.
Agnes beatae virginis	*b.*	St. Agnes.
Almi prophetae progenies	*b.*	St. John Bapt.
Amor Jesu dulcissime	*e.*	Name of Jesus.
Amore Christi nobilis	*b.*	St. John Evang. Both Feasts.
[Anni recurso tempore]	*b.*	Pt. of "Jesu corona celsior"
Apostolorum passio	*b.*	SS. Peter & Paul.
Apostolorum supparem	*b.*	St. Laurence.
[Aras nefandi numinis]	*b.*	Pt.of "Agnes beatae."
[Ascendant nostrae protinus]	*b.*	Pt. of "Mysteriorum signifer."
[Assertor aequi non]	*b.*	Pt. of Almi prophetae
Bellator armis inclytus	*b.*	St. Martin.
Bernardus doctor inclytus	*b.*	St. Bernard.
Bernardus inclytis ortus	*b.*	St. Bernard.
Cantemus Domino grandia	*f. Add. MS.* 30014	St. Monica.
Christe cunctorum dominator	*b.*	Dedic. of a Church
Christum rogemus et	*b.*	All Saints.
Christus lux indeficiens	*b.*	Corpus Christi.
Clara diei gaudia .	*b.*	St. Anne.
[Clero clarens et]	*b.*	Part of "Malachiae solemnia."
Coelestis regni nuptias	*f.*	St. Juliana (Falcon).
Coeli cives applaudite	*c. f.*	St. Augustine.
Coeli fidus amabile .	*f.*	Commem. of St. Augustine.
Coelorum Domino dum	*f.*	St. Philip Neri.
Concinat plebs fidelium	*d.*	St. Clara.
Creator alme siderum	*f.*	Holiest Redeemer.
Crucis arma fulgentia	*d.*	Stigmata of St. Francis.
Crucis Christi mons .	*d.*	Stigmata of St. Francis.
Decus morum, dux minorum	*d.*	St. Francis.

First line of Hymn.	Breviary.	Use.
Dei fide qua .	*a.*	Lent. Terce.
[Denariorum numero] .	*b.*	Pt. of "Hymnum dicamus."
Deus manens primordium	*a.*	Transfig. Lauds.
Discede corpus inclytum	*f.*	Trans. of St. Augustine.
Diva mortalis generis	*f.*	St. Laurence Justinian.
Dive coelestis patriae	*f.*	St. John a S. Facundo.
Dum Christiano purpurata	*f.*	1st Trans. of St. Augustine.
Dum praedo Hesperias	*f.*	2nd Trans. of St. Augustine.
Ecclesiae flos germinans	*f.*	Commem. of St. Nicholas (Tol.).
En gratulemur hodie	*a.*	St. Anthony.
En noctis medium .	*d.*	St. Gabriel.
Excelse princeps omnium	*f. Add. MS.* 30014	St. Monica.
Exultet claro sidere .	*c.*	St. Peter Martyr.
Exultet coelum gaudiis	*f.*	Conv. of St. Paul.
Fallacis undas saeculi	*d.*	St. Didacus.
[Fallax ad patibulum]	*f.*	Pt. of "Post Petrum."
Flores, o populi, fundite	*d.*	St. Hippolytus.
Gaude felix Ungaria.	*c.*	St. Elizabeth of Hungary.
Gaude mater ecclesiam laetam	*c.*	Pt. Dominic.
Generat virgo filias	*d.*	St. Clara.
Haec tuae virgo monumenta	*c.*	St. Katharine.
Hic est dies verus	*b. c.*	Eastertide.
[Hic locus nempe]	*b.*	Pt. of "Christe cunctorum."
Huc reges opibus.	*f.*	Commem. of St. Thomas (Vill.).
Hymnum dicamus Domino	*b.*	Holy Cross. Crown of Thorns. Passiontide.
Hymnum festivae gloriae	*c.*	Visit. of B. V. M.
Hymnum novae laetitiae	*c.*	St. Dominic.
Illuminans altissime	*b.*	Epiph. Vespers and Lauds.
In coelesti collegio	*d.*	St. Francis.
In divinis operibus	*b.*	Corpus Christi.
[In principio erat]	*b.*	Pt. of "Amore Christi."
In profunda noctis	*f.*	St. John Nepomuc
Incliti patres Dominacque	*f.*	Seven Founders Ord. Serv.
Incola abruptae rigidus	*f.*	St. William (Feb. 10).
Inopem canamus Didacum	*d.*	St. Didacus.
Integrum vitae sceleris que	*f.*	Commem. of St. Thomas (Vill.).
Intende qui regis Israel	*b.*	Christmastide.
[In rat Cistercium cum]	*b.*	Pt. of "Bernardus inclytis."
Invictus hero numinis	*f.*	St.John Nepomuc.
Ite matris ossa nostrae	*f.*	Trans. of St. Monica.
Ite maerores animi	*f.*	St. Nicholas (Tolent.).
Jam dies longo revoluta	*a.*	St. Justina.
Jam fasces lictor ferat	*f.*	St.John Nepomuc.
Jam ferox miles tibi.	*c.*	St. Katharine.
Jam nimis terris facinus	*f.*	Seven Founders Ord. Serv.
Jam Regina discubuit	*b.*	St. Bernard.
Jam surgit hora .	*b.*	Holy Week. Terce
Jam toto subitus vesper	*f.*	Seven Dolours, B. V. M.
Jam lux vera mentium	*d.*	St. Anthony.
Katherinae collaudemus	*c.*	St. Katharine.
Laeta stupet Thuringia	*c.*	St. Elizabeth of Hungary.
Lauda fidelis concio .	*c.*	Crown of Jesus.
Lauda mater ecclesia	*c. e.*	St. Mary Magd.
Laudibus cives resonent	*a.*	St. Benedict.

First line of Hymn.	Breviary.	Use.
Laudibus summus cele-bremus	f.	St. Nicholas (To-lent.).
Laudibus virgo nimis .	c.	St. Katharine.
Laus regi plena gaudio .	d.	St. Anthony.
Lingua pangat et . .	c.	Visit. of B. V. M.
Lucis hujus festa . .	b. e.	St. Anne.
Lumen in terris . . .	c.	St. Vincent.
Magister orbis maxime .	f.	St. Augustine.
Magnae dies laetitiae (1)	c.	St. Peter Martyr.
Magnae dies laetitiae (2)	c.	Visit. of B. V. M.
Magne pater Augustine	c. f.	St. Augustine.
Magne Vincenti nova .	c.	St. Vincent.
Magni parentis plaudite	f.	2nd Trans. of St. Augustine.
Magnum salutis gau-dium (1)	b.	St. Mary Magd.
Magnum salutis gau-dium (2)	b.	Palm Sunday.
Malachiae solemnia votis	b.	St. Malachy.
Martine par Apostolis .	a.	St. Martin.
Martyris Christi colimus	a.	St. Laurence.
Mente jocunda jubilent .	c.	St. Vincent.
Mentibus laetis jubilemus	d.	St. Gabriel.
Mundi creator maxime .	f. Add. MS., 30014	St. Nicholas (To-lent.).
Mundi redemptor optime	d.	St. Didacus.
Mysterium ecclesiae .	b. c.	B. V. M.
[Mysterium mirabile] .	b.	Pt. of "Hic est dies."
Mysteriorum signifer .	b.	St. Michael.
Noctu dum Nerius . .	f.	St. Philip Neri.
[Non illam crucians]. .	f.	Pt. of "Martinae celebri."
Novum sidus in supernis	c.	St. Anne.
Novus athleta Domini .	c.	St. Dominic.
O Clara luce clarior . .	d.	St. Clara.
O decus coeli simul . .	f.	St. Laurence Jus-tinian.
O feminarum gloria . .	f.	St. Monica.
[O grande cunctis] . .	b. e.	Pt. of "Optatus votis."
O mater augustissima .	f.	Trans. of St. Mo-nica.
[O praeferenda gloria] .	b.	Pt. of "Stephani primi."
O sole, Jesu, clarior . .	f.	Name of Jesus.
O Trinitas laudabilis .	f. Add M.S., 30014.	Holy Trinity.
O vita, Jesu, cordium .	f.	Name of Jesus.
O vos unanimes . .	f.	Relics of All Saints
Optatus votis omnium .	b. c.	Ascension-tide.
Orbis exultans celebret	b.	St. Anne.
Originale crimen necans	c.	Invent. of Cross.
Pangamus Nerio debita .	f.	St. Philip Neri.
Pange lingua gloriosae(1)	c.	St. Katharine.
Pange lingua gloriosae (2)	f.	Lance & Nails.
Paschali jubilo sonent .	f.	Lance & Nails.
Pastorem canimus ; grex	f.	St. Thomas (Vill.)
Pauperum patrì super .	f.	St. Thomas (Vill.)
Pia mater et humilis. .	e.	Com. of non-Vir-gins.
Plaude festivo pia . .	f.	Appar. of Image of B. V. M.
Plaude lingua gloriosum.	f.	Commem. of St. Augustine.
Plaude turba paupercula	d.	St. Francis.
[Poenas cucurrit fortiter]	b.	Pt. of "Deus tuo-rum militum."
Post Petrum primum .	b.	St. Andrew.
Post triduum jussus . .	b.	Pt. of "Apostolo-rum supparem."
Praeclara septem lumina	f.	Seven Founders Ord. Serv.
Praesens dies expendatur	c.	St. Katharine.
Praesulis dignos meritis.	f.	St. Laurence (Jus-tin).
Praesulum fidus ruti-lansque	f.	St. Simplician
[Procedit e thalamo] .	b.	Pt. of "Intende qui."
Procul phalanges hosticae	f.	St. William (Feb. 10).
[Profana dum accende-ret]	b.	Pt. of "Bellator armis."
Proles de coelo prodiit ,	d.	St. Francis.

First line of Hymn.	Breviary.	Use.
Qua Christus hora . .	a.	Lent. Sext.
Quicquid antiqui . . .	a.	St. Benedict.
Quicumque certum quae-ritis	f.	Sacred Heart.
Quocunque pergis virgi-nes	b.	Pt. of "Jesu corona virginum."
[Ramos virentes sumpse-rat]	b.	Pt. of "Magnum salutis."
Rex Christe Martini . .	a.	St. Martin.
Rex sempiterne Domine.	a. e.	Easter.
Rusticum solo Benedicte	a.	St. Benedict.
[Sacri junguntur uteri] .	b.	Pt. of "Adsunt festa."
Salve crux sancta . .	c.	Invent. of Cross.
[Sisti jubet martyrem] .	b.	Pt. of "Agathae sacrae."
Solemnitas fid-lium . .	c.	St. Anne.
Spes orbis, o fidissima .	f.	Commem. of St. Nicholas (Tol.).
Stephani primi Martyris	b.	St. Stephen. Both feasts.
[Sterili ventre prius] .	b.	Pt. of "Orbis ex-ultans."
Summi parentis filio. .	f.	Sacred Heart.
Te canunt omnes Nicolae	f.	(1) Canonization of St. Nicholas(To-lent.). (2) Feast of ditto. (3) Benediction of Bread.
[Te Christe rex piissime]	b.	Pt. of "Jesu co-rona celsior."
Te ferant linguae cele-brentque	f.	St. Monica.
Ternis ter horis . . .	a.	Lent. None.
Tot lacrymarum filius .	f.	St. Monica.
[Traduntur igni mar-tyres]	b.	Pt. of "Aeterna Christi munera."
Urbs alma summo . .	f.	Canonization of St. Nicholas (To-lent.).
Venit redemptor gentium	e.	Christmas.
Verbum supernum pro-diens salvare.	f.	Lance and Nails.
[Vere gratia plena] . .	b. e.	Pt. of "Mysterium Ecclesiae."
[Verso crucis vestigio] .	b.	Pt. of "Apostolo-rum passio."
Virginem divus rapuit .	a.	St. Justina.
Virginis sacri redeunt .	a.	St. Justina.
Virtutis heros maxime .	f.	St. John a S. Fa-cundo.
Vix in sepulchro conditur	f.	St. John Nepomuc.

13. In the above list several hymns already given in the former list are repeated, as indicated above ; and *Proses* and *Sequences* are omitted, together with many hymns peculiar to local Breviaries or found in works of another kind, and those specially associated with the ancient *Hymnaries*, and with *Missals*. For these lists see *Hymnarium, Missals,* and *Sequences,* and the *Cross-Reference Index.* We may note that some of the hymns in the *Mozarabic Breviary* are of great length. That for St. Eulalia's Day (Dec. 10) consists of forty-five stanzas of five lines, and that for St. Vincent's Day (Jan. 22) of seventy-three stanzas of four lines each.

14. The great bulk of the above Hymns are unknown in English dress, or in the vernacular of the various countries where they are now or have been once in use. But in recent years English readers have become acquainted with many translations from the *Mozarabic, Ambrosian,* and *York Breviaries,* by various hands ; the *Roman* by Bp. Mant, W. J. Copeland, and E. Caswall ; the *Sarum* by J. M. Neale and J. D. Chambers ; and the *Paris* by I. Williams,

J. Chandler, and J. D. Chambers. These translators, however, have not in every instance restricted themselves to Breviaries only. In common with W. J. Blew, R. Campbell, R. F. Littledale, J. Ellerton, J. W. Hewett, A. M. Morgan, H. M. Macgill, and others, they have gathered their treasures from various and widely scattered sources.   [F. E. W.]

Brewer, Jehoiada, the "Sylvestris" of the *Gospel Magazine,* 1776, &c., was b. at Newport, Monmouthshire, in 1752. He was educated for commercial pursuits, but subsequently became a Congregational Minister, and as such was pastor at Rodborough, Gloucestershire ; at Sheffield, to which he went in 1783 ; at Carr's Lane Chapel, Birmingham (1798); and at the Livery Street Chapel, in the same town. He d. Aug. 24, 1817. A *Memoir* of him appeared in the *Evangelical Register,* 1835, p. 396. His best-known hymn is—"Hail, Sovereign Love, that first began" (q. v.).

Bride of the Lamb, awake, awake. *Sir E. Denny.* [*Advent.*] 1st appeared in *Hys. for the Poor of the Flock, cir.* 1837–8, No. 128, in 7 st. of 4 l.: again in his *Sel. of Hys,* 1839, No. 332; and again in his *Hys. and Poems,* 1848, p. 36. In the last work it is entitled, "The Church cheered with the hope of her Lord's return." In 1855 it was included in Dr. Walker's *Cheltenham Coll.,* No. 389, and in 1872 in Snepp's *S. of G. and G.* In *Kennedy,* 1863, it is given in 3 st. of 8 l. It is also found in a few American collections.

Bride of the Lamb, rejoice, rejoice. *Sir E. Denny.* [*Advent.*] This companion hymn to the foregoing, "Bride of the Lamb, awake, awake," was given in his *Hys. and Poems,* 1848, p. 38–9, in 6 st. of 4 l. From thence it passed into Dr. Walker's Cheltenham *Coll.,* 1855, and into Snepp's *S. of G. and G.,* 1872.

Bridgman, Isaac. In the year 1823, at which time he was Curate of Trinity Church, Forest of Dean, a pamphlet controversy arose as to his dismissal from the curacy. Subsequently he joined the Congregationalists, and became the Minister of St. John's Chapel, Walworth. For that congregation he pub. :—

Six Hundred Hymns; Sacred Canticles, selected and composed by Isaac Bridgman, Lond., 1836.

This collection contains 600 hymns. His "dying experience" was pub. in 1847, and a volume of *Miscellanies* in 1848. He was b. 1790, and d. July 5, 1846. In Snepp's *S. of G. and G.,* his hymn, "Behold the Saints of God," is dated 1830. It is No. 44 in the *Coll.* of 1836.   [W. T. B.]

Bridges, Matthew, youngest s. of John Bridges, Wallington House, Surrey, and brother of the Rev. Charles Bridges, author of *An Exposition of the cxix. Psalm,* b. at The Friars, Maldon, Essex, July 14, 1800, and educated in the Church of England, but subsequently conformed to the Church of Rome. His works include, *Babbicombe, or Visions of Memory, with other Poems,* 1842 ; *Hymns of the Heart,* 1848 (enlarged in 1852) ; and *The Passion of Jesus,* 1852, besides some prose productions. From the last two works his hymns found in common use are taken, the greater number being from *Hymns of the Heart.* Besides the hymns

in use in G. Britain, as, "Behold the Lamb;" "My God, accept my heart this day," and others, the following, all of which were pub. in 1848, are found in several American collections, to which they were introduced mainly through the Rev. H. W. Beecher's *Plymouth Coll.,* 1855 :—

1. Bright were the mornings first impearl'd. *At the grave of Lazarus.*
2. Head of the hosts in glory. *All Saints.* From this is derived "Armies of God ! in union," which is given in some American collections.
3. Lo, He comes with clouds descending (q. v.).
4. Rise, glorious Conqueror, rise. *Ascension.*
5. Soil not thy plumage, gentle dove. *Morning.*

Of late years Mr. Bridges has resided in the Province of Quebec, Canada.   [J. J.]

Brigg, Julius, b. at Leeds, 1840, is the youngest son of John Newsom Brigg, woollen merchant, of that town, and an earnest worker in Sunday Schools, in connection with which he wrote numerous hymns and poems. Mr. Julius Brigg entered the Wesleyan Ministry in 1864, since which time he has been engaged in full circuit work. His contributions to hymnody include the following hymns :—

1. **Father, from Thy throne in glory.** *Sunday S. Teachers.* Written in October, 1861, to be sung at the Annual Meeting of the Wes. S. S. Teachers of Leeds. It was pub. in the *Meth. S. S. H. Bk.,* 1879, *The Golden Harp S. S. H. Bk.,* and others.

2. **Lord of angels, pure and holy.** *Divine Worship.* A hymn for children written in March, 1871, and included in the *Meth. S. S. H. Bk.,* 1879.

3. **Friends of truth and liberty.** *Temperance.* Dated Sept., 1872, and given in the Wesleyan *Temperance H. and Songs,* 1877.

4. **The many are not always right.** *For Bands of Hope.* Written in June, 1876, and included in various Temperance hymnals, and in Stevenson's *Sch. Hy.* 1880.

5. **If every little sunbeam.** *Temperance.* Dated Oct., 1877, and pub. in the Wesleyan *Temperance H. and Songs* the same year.

6. **Again we meet in gladness.** *S. S. Anniversary.* Written in 1880, and 1st pub. in Stevenson's *School Hymnal,* the same year.

Outside of hymnody Mr. Brigg has written somewhat extensively for the Wesleyan Magazines. He d. April 18, 1893.   [J. J.]

Bright and joyful is the morn. *J. Montgomery.* [*Christmas.*] This popular hymn was contributed to the 8th ed. of Cotterill's *Sel.,* 1819, No. 213, in 4 st. of 4 l., and repeated in Montgomery's *Christian Psalmist,* 1825, No. 489, and his *Orig. Hymns,* 1853, No. 17. Its use is somewhat extensive, both in G. Britain and America. The original text is usually given; but sometimes st. iii., l. 2, reads, "Christ, th' Incarnate Deity," for "The Incarnate Deity." It is sometimes dated 1825, in error.

Bright as the sun's meridian blaze. *W. Shrubsole, jun.* [*Missions.*] Written for the first meeting of the London Missionary Society, and dated Aug. 10, 1795 (*Fathers and Founders of the L. M. Soc.,* 1844). It subsequently appeared in the *Evangelical Magazine,* Sept., 1795, in 6 st. of 4 l., entitled, "On the intended Mission," "O send out Thy light and Thy truth," Ps. xliii. 3, and signed "Junior." Although thus printed anonymously, it "was duly acknowledged by Mr. Shrubsole in his lifetime, and the original ms., with numerous corrections, is in the possession of his family, in his own autograph." (*Singers and Songs,* p. 326.) It was included in some of the older collections, and is still in C. U. in G. Brit. and America. Orig. text in *Lyra Brit.*, 1867, p. 504.

Bright Queen of heaven. *H. Vaughan.* [*B. V. Mary.*] A poem in 4 st. of 4 l., entitled "The Knot," which appeared in Pt. ii. of his *Silex Scintillans, or Sacred Poems*, &c., 2nd ed., 1655, and again in the Rev. H. F. Lyte's reprint of the same, Lond., Pickering 1847 and 1883. In its original form it is not in common use; but as "Bright Queen of *saints*" it is found in the *People's H.*, 1867, No. 193. Orig. text in the Aldine ed. of *Vaughan*, 1883.

Bright shadows of true rest. *H. Vaughan.* [*Sundays.*] From the 1st part of his *Silex Scintillans*, 1650, where it is headed "Son-Days." It is in 3 st. of 8 l., and has been reprinted in the modern editions of Vaughan's work, as also in various selections of sacred poetry. In Dr. Martineau's *Hys. of P. and Praise*, 1873, it is No. 785. Orig. text, Aldine ed. of *Vaughan*, London, 1883, p. 97.

Bright the vision that delighted. *Bp. R. Mant.* [*Holy Trinity.*] This original hymn, one of several, was given in his *Ancient Hymns*, &c., 1837, No. 100, in 4 st. of 8 l., and headed "Hymn commemorative of the 'Thrice Holy'" (ed. 1871, p. 216). It is rarely given in its full form, st. iii. being usually omitted, as in the *H. Comp.*, No. 34. The most striking arrangement of the hymn is that beginning with the second half of the first stanza, "Round the Lord in glory seated," with the first half of the second stanza as a refrain. This is given in Thring's *Coll.*, No. 413, and is a most beautiful cento. Another form, beginning with the same line, is in the Irish *Church Hymnal*, No. 224. It is composed of st. i., l. 5–8, ii., iii. l. 5–8, and iv. T. Darling, in his *Hymns for the Ch. of England*, 1874, No. 110, has a cento in 4 st. of 4 l., as "*Near* the Lord in glory seated." In the ed. 1886, No. 160, another cento is substituted, beginning with st. i.   [J. J.]

Bright was the guiding star that led. *Harriet Auber.* [*Epiphany.*] 1st pub. in her *Spirit of the Psalms*, 1829, p. 142, in 4 st. of 4 l. In America it has attained to a much greater popularity than in G. Britain, being found in many collections, sometimes attributed to the Rev. H. F. Lyte, and again to Miss C. Elliott. Orig. text in Lord Selborne's *Bk. of Praise*, 1862–7, p. 46, and Dr. Hatfield's *Church H. Bk.*, 1872, No. 363.

Bright, William, D.D., b. at Doncaster, Dec. 14, 1824, and educated at University College, Oxford, where he graduated B.A. (first class in *Lit. Hum.*) in 1846, M.A. in 1849. In 1847 he was Johnson's Theological Scholar: and in 1848 he also obtained the Ellerton Theological Essay prize. He was elected Fellow in 1847, and subsequently became Tutor of his College. Taking Holy Orders in 1848, he was for some time Tutor at Trinity College, Glenalmond; but in 1859 he returned to Oxford, and in 1868 became Regius Professor of Ecclesiastical History and Canon of Christ Church. His publications include:—

(1) *Ancient Collects, selected from various Rituals*, 1857, 2nd ed., 1862; (2) *History of the Church from the Edict of Milan to the Council of Chalcedon*, 1860; (3) *Sermons of St. Leo the Great on the Incarnation*, translated, with notes, 1862; (4) *Faith and Life*, 1864–66; (5) *Chapters of Early English Church History*, 1877; (6) *Private Prayers for a Week*; (7) *Family Prayers*

for a Week; (8) *Notes on the Canons of the First Four Councils.* He has also edited (9) *Eusebius' Ecclesiastical History*, 1872; (10) *St. Athanasius's Orations against the Arians*, &c., 1873; (11) *Socrates' Ecclesiastical Hist.*; (12) with the Rev. P. G. Medd, *Latin Version of the Prayer Book*, 1865–69. His poetical works are, (13) *Athanasius and other Poems, by a Fellow of a College*, 1858; and (14) *Hymns & Other Poems*, 1866; revised and enlarged, 1874.

The last two works contain original hymns and translations. To the hymn-books he is known through his original compositions, seven of which are given in the revised ed. of *H. A. and M.*, and some are found elsewhere. In addition to "And now the wants are told," and "At Thy feet, O Christ, we lay" (q.v.), there are:—

1. **And now, O Father, mindful of the love.** *Holy Communion.* Pub. in *H. A. & M.*, 1875. Part of a composition in his *Hymns*, &c.
2. **Behold us, Lord, before Thee met.** *Confirmation.* Printed in the *Monthly Packet*, Nov. 1867, and, in a revised form, in the *Appendix* to *H. A. & M.*, 1868.
3. **How oft, O Lord, Thy face hath shone.** *St. Thomas.* Pub. in *H. A. & M.*, 1875.
4. **Once, only once, and once for all.** *Holy Communion.* Written in 1865, and pub. in his *Hymns*, &c., 1866, in 6 st. of 4 l. It was given in the *Appendix* to *H. A. & M.*, 1868; the new ed., 1875, and several other collections.
5. **We know Thee, Who Thou art.** *Prayer after Pardon.* Written in 1865, and pub. in his *Hymns*, &c., 1866, in 5 st. of 4 l. It was included in the *Appendix* to *H. A. & M.*, 1868, &c.

Canon Bright's hymns merit greater attention than they have received at the hands of compilers. He d. March 6, 1901.   [J. J.]

Bright with all His crowns of glory. *Sir E. Denny, Bart.* [*Christ in Glory.*] Pub. in the *Hys. for the Poor of the Flock*, 1838, No. 143, and his *Sel. of Hys.*, 1839, No. 333, and again in his *Hys. and Poems*, 1848, p. 53, in 4 st. of 6 l., and entitled "The King on His throne." It is a spirited hymn and worthy of more extended use than is accorded to it. In 1867 it was re-written in 3 st. for the *People's H.*

Brightest and best of the sons of the morning. *Bp. R. Heber.* [*Epiphany.*] 1st pub. in the *Christian Observer*, Nov. 1811, p. 697, in 5 st. of 4 l. (the last being the first repeated); and again in his posthumous *Hymns*, &c., 1827, p. 25. Few hymns of merit have troubled compilers more than this. Some have held that its use involved the worshipping of a star, whilst others have been offended with its metre as being too suggestive of a solemn dance. Cotterill gave it in the 8th ed., 1819, of his *Sel.*, and omitted it from the 9th, 1820; and Elliott, following the example in detail, had it in his 1st ed. *Ps. and Hys.*, 1835, and dropped it from the 2nd, whilst others have done much the same. It has, however, survived these changes, and has become one of the most widely used of the Bishop's hymns. In the American Presbyterian *Ps. & Hys. for the Worship of God*, Richmond, 1867, No. 69, it is given in an altered form as "Hail the blest morn! see the Great Mediator," and attributed in the Index to *Tate and Brady.* The Rev. R. Bingham has given a Latin rendering in his *Hymno. Christ. Lat.*, 1871: "Stella, micans coelo nitido magis omnibus una."   [J. J.]

Brightly did the light divine. *H. Alford.* [*St. Barnabas.*] In Dean Alford's *Poetical Works*, 1868, this hymn is dated 1844, although it is not found in his *Ps. and Hys.* of that year. In the musical ed. of his *Year of*

Praise, it is given as 1845; but in the ed. of words only it is undated. In the revised ed. of *H. A. & M.*, 1875, it is in an unaltered form.

Brightly gleams our banner. *T. J. Potter*. [*Processional*.] This hymn, which has attained to great popularity, is found in various forms, the most widely used of which are :—

1. The original, which appeared, with music, in *The Holy Family Hymns*, 1860, No. 5, in 8 st. of 8 l., and a chorus of 4 l. This is distinctly Roman in every way, as will be gathered from st. iii. and v., which read:—

(iii.) Mary, Mother, Ave!	(v.) Jesus! Mary! Joseph!
Israel's lily hail !	Sweet and holy Three !
Comfort of thy children	List the praise we pay you
In this sinful vale.	On our bended knee.
'Mid life's surging ocean,	May we sing your glory
Whither shall we flee,	In glad realms above,
Save, O stainless Virgin,	Bound for ever to you,
Mother, unto thee ?	By the bonds of love."

This text is repeated in numerous Roman Catholic hymnals for schools and missions, and may be consulted without any difficulty.

2. The text as in the *People's H.*, 1867, No. 1, was given in Walker's *App.* to the *Hymnal N.*, 1863. This is the nearest approach to the original, but is not in extensive use.

3. The third and most popular text is that which appeared in the 1867 *App.* to *Morrell and How*, and was repeated in the *App.* to *H. A. and M.*, 1868. In this the only portions of the original which are retained are st. i. and ii. (with considerable alterations) and the chorus, which is simply the opening lines repeated.

4. In the *App.* to the S. P. C. K. *Ps. and Hys.*, 1869, No. 421, this text is distinguished by the third stanza, "Pattern of our childhood," &c. It was repeated in *Church Hys.*, 1871, Mrs. Brock's *Children's H. Bk.*, 1881, Thring's *Coll.*, 1882, and many others. It has less of the original than any other arrangement of the hymn, and ranks next in extensiveness of use to that in *H. A. and M.* Mr. Ellerton's note to this hymn in the folio ed. of *Church Hys.* is in error by transposing the stanzas which he quotes.

5. The American use of this hymn in any form is very limited. In Richards's *Songs of Christian Praise*, N.Y., 1880, No. 464, we have st. i., ii. and iv., and in Stryker and Main's *Church Praise Bk.*, N.Y., 1882, No. 560, st. i., iii., and v. from No. 4 as above.

Although in some hymnals slight changes of these varying texts may be found, yet they are the generally accepted forms of the hymn. Taken together its use is very extensive; the revised versions, however, far outnumbering the original in use.   [J. J.]

Bring the glossy branch, unfading. *T. Davis*. [*Christmas*.] Pub. in his *Devotional Verse for a Month*, 1855, in 5 st. of 8 l., and entitled "Christmas Day." In 1877 it was republished in his *Annus Sanctus*, but omitted from his *Hys. Old and New*, 1864. It has been set to music by W. H. Havergal. In 1870 Snepp gave, in his *Songs of G. and G.*, No. 198, st. ii., iii. and v. slightly altered, as :— "Jesus, from the skies descending."

Brontë, Anne, sister of Charlotte, and daughter of the Rev. Patrick Brontë, B.A., Vicar of Haworth, Yorkshire, b. at Thornton, near Bradford, 1819; d. May 28, 1849. Anne Brontë was joint author with her sisters of a small volume of *Poems*, 1846, and personally of *Agnes Grey*, 1847; and *The Tenant of Wildfell Hall*, 1847, her *nom de plume* being *Acton Bell*. In 1851 a new edition of *Wuthering Heights*, by Ellis [*Emily*] Bell; and *Agnes Grey*, by Acton [*Anne*] Bell, was edited, with biographical notes, and selections from their papers by their sister, Charlotte Brontë. These selections consisted of poems and hymns by the two sisters. From those of Anne the following have come into C. U. :—

1. **I hoped that with the brave and strong.** *Time of Sorrow*. A hymn of much plaintive beauty, wrung from the writer by disappointment and affliction. It is in several collections, as Horder's *Cong. Hys.*, 1884, &c.

2. **My God, O let me call Thee mine.** *Lent*. Also very plaintive, but not so extensively in use. It is No. 291 in the *Bap. Hymnal*, 1879.

3. **Oppressed with sin and woe.** *Confidence*. The most popular, although not the best of her hymns. It is in many collections, both in G. Britain and America.

4. **Spirit of truth, be Thou my Guide.** *Spirit of Truth*. In a few hymnals, including Dr. Martineau's *Hys. of P. & Prayer*, 1873.   [J. J.]

Brooke, Stopford Augustus, M.A., was b. at Letterkenny, Donegal, Nov. 14, 1832, and educated at Trinity College, Dublin, graduating B.A. 1856; M.A. 1858. He carried off the Downes prize and the Vice-Chancellor's prize for English verse. On taking Holy Orders he was successively Curate of St. Matthew's, Marylebone, 1857–59; of Kensington, 1860–63; Chaplain to the British Embassy at Berlin, 1863–65; Minister of St. James's Chapel, York Street, London, 1866–75; and of Bedford Chapel, 1876. He was also appointed Chaplain in Ordinary to the Queen, in 1872. In 1865 he published the *Life and Letters of the late F. W. Robertson*; in 1874, *Theology in the English Poets*; in 1876, *Primer of English Literature*, &c. On seceding from the Church of England in 1881, he pub. for the use of his congregation, *Christian Hymns*, a collection of 269 pieces. Of these he is the author of :—

1. **Immortal Love, within Whose righteous will.** *Resignation and Prayer for Guidance*. No. 183, in 4 st. of 6 l. It has a strong likeness to Card. Newman's "Lead, kindly light," is in the same metre, and might be called a companion hymn thereto. It was repeated in Horder's *Cong. Hys.*, 1884.

2. **It fell upon a summer day.** *Christ blessing little children*. No. 250, in 10 st. of 4 l.

3. **It is finished, all the pain.** *Good Friday*. No. 80, in 6 st. of 4 l.

4. **Let the whole creation cry.** *Invitation to Praise God*. An imitation of Ps. 148. It is No. 47, in 10 st. of 4 l., and is of special merit. In st. iv., ll. 3, 4 are from another source.

5. **Mysterious Spirit, unto Whom.** *Rest and Joy in God*. Based on a *tr.* by J. G. Whittier from Lamartine. It is No. 159, in 3 st. of 8 l. It was repeated in Horder's *Cong. Hys.*, 1884.

6. **Now that day its wings has furled.** *Evening*. No. 13, in 5 st. of 4 l.

7. **O God, Whose love is near.** *Divine protection desired*. No. 103, in 7 st. of 4 l. This is Toplady's "Your harps, ye trembling Saints" re-written, only st. i. and iv. being absolutely by Mr. Brooke.

8. **O that Thou would'st the heavens rend And comfort, &c.** *Peace desired*. No. 149, in 4. st. of 4 l. The first line is from C. Wesley; also st. ii., l. 4, but the rest of the hymn is original.

9. **O Who is this that on a tree.** *Good Friday*. No. 79, in 8 st. of 4 l.

10. **Oft as we run the weary way.** *Heavenly Witnesses of the struggles of Men*. No. 188, in 6 st. of 6 l.

11. **Still the night, holy the night.** *Christmas Carol*. No. 55, in 3 st. of 8 l. It is a *tr.* from the German, and is noticed under **Mohr, Joseph**.

12. **Through the starry midnight dim.** *Christmas*. No. 53, in 6 st. of 3 l., and the refrain "Hallelujah."

13. **When the Lord of Love was here.** *Life of Christ*. No. 66, in 6 st. of 4 l. It has passed into *The Norwood Hymnal*; and with the omission of st. vi. and the transposition of st. iv. and v. into Horder's *Cong. Hys.*, 1884. This is his finest hymn.

In addition, Mr. Brooke has made extensive alterations in the text of the hymns which he has adopted from other writers, and has also inserted in many instances additional stanzas into well-known lyrics, and thereby brought them, to some extent, into harmony with his theological views. His own compositions are marked by great freshness of thought and tenderness of expression.   [W. G. H.]

Brooke, William Thomas, b. Jan. 9, 1848, and educated at the City of London School. After entering commercial life he felt a warm interest in hymnology, and from his intimate acquaintance with Daniel Sedgwick he gradually learnt all that Sedgwick had to teach. His hymns and translations were contributed to religious newspapers and periodicals. Many are still unpublished, but hymns of his will be found in the *Monthly Packet*, 1872; the *Methodist S. S. Hymnal*, 1879; the *Methodist Hymns for Missions*, 1882; his own *Churchman's Manual of Priv. and Fam. Devotion*, 1882; and in the *Altar Hymnal*, 1884. Following in Sedgwick's steps, he has authenticated the texts and authorship for several compilations (e.g.) *Methodist S S. H. Bk.*, 1879; the *Cong. Bk. of Praise for Children*, 1881, and others. Originally a Baptist, he became in 1867 a member of the Church of England.

Brooks, Charles Timothy. An American Unitarian Minister, b. at Salem, Mass., June 20, 1813, and graduated at Harvard, 1832, and the Divinity School, Cambridge, U.S., 1835. In that year he began his ministry at Nahant, subsequently preaching at Bangor and Augusta (Maine), Windsor (Vermont). In 1837 he became pastor of Newport, Rhode Island, and retained the same charge until 1871, when he resigned through ill-health. For details concerning his hymn, "God bless our native land," see **God save the King**, and p. 1566 i.   [F. M. B.]

Brother, now thy toils are o'er. *G. Moultrie.* [*Burial.*] Written during the singing of a requiem in the Church of St. Nicholas, Boulogne, in the summer of 1863, and first pub. in the *Church Times*, Sept. 3rd, 1864, and in his ed. of the *Primer*, 1864. In 1867 it was embodied in the author's *Hymns and Lyrics*, pp. 413–15, in 11 st. of 4 l., with the refrain; and, in an abridged form, in the *People's H.*, 1867, No. 380. Upon this last the Rev. John Ellerton's hymn, "Now the labourer's task is o'er" (q.v.), is based, and st. iii., vi., and vii. are specially represented therein as st. iii., v., and vi. Mr. Moultrie's hymn was originally intended "To be sung as the body leaves the church;" and is a free paraphrase of detached portions of the Roman Office for the Dead. Orig. text as above. Authorized arrangement in *People's H.*

Brother, thou art gone before us. *H. H. Milman.* [*Burial.*] This hymn is introduced by Dean Milman in his *Martyr of Antioch, a Dramatic Poem*, 1822, pp. 33–5, as being sung at "The Place of Burial of the Christians." At the close of a funeral at night, *Fabius*, Bishop of Antioch, is represented as saying:—

"So, by the side of martyr'd Babylas,
Brother, thou slumberest; silent as yon stars,

And silent as the falling dews around thee,
We leave thy verdant grave. But oh! shall we,
When we put off the load of mortal life,
Depart like thee as in a deeper sleep,
With the sweet smile of life on the closed lips,
Or in an agony of mortal pain,
By the pitch'd stake, or den of raging lions?"

One of the first to extract it from the dramatic poem, and constitute it as a hymn for C. U. was Elliott, who included it in his *Ps. and Hys.*, 1835. It soon became popular, and is given in a great number of hymnals in G. Britain and America. Orig. text in *H. Comp.*, with "fear" changed to "*fears*" in st. ii., l. 5.

Brought to the Font with holy care. *E. Osler.* [*Holy Baptism—General.*] 1st pub. in Hall's *Mitre H. Bk.*, 1836, No. 222, in 4 st. of 4 l., and entitled "For a Blessing on our Christian Privileges;" and again, with alterations, in the July number of the author's *Church and King*, for 1837. No. 238 in *Kennedy*, 1863, is the original *Mitre* text. Although not strictly speaking a hymn for Holy Baptism, yet it is suitable to be sung during a service when that Sacrament has been administered.

Brown, Abner William, M.A., b. at Mount Tirot, Jamaica, Sept. 1, 1800, but was removed from Jamaica to Scotland in 1802. His early education was at the Edinburgh High School, and University, from whence he passed to Lincoln's Inn to read for the Bar. Ill-health caused him to suspend all studies for some time. Ultimately he entered the University of Cambridge, and took his degree in 1830. Ordained in 1831 to the curacy of Pytchley, Northamptonshire, in 1832 he became the Vicar of the same parish, from whence he removed to Gretton, in the same county, in 1851. He d. there Sept. 15, 1872. He was an Hon. Canon of Peterborough Cathedral from about 1851. Canon Brown's hymnological productions are:—

(1) *Introits and Collect Hymns*, 1845; (2) *Pytchley School Hymn-Book*, 1848; (3) *Home Lyrics* (privately printed, and containing hymns by a deceased daughter), 1859; (4) *A Selection of Psalms and Hymns for Public Worship*, Lond., Hamilton, Adams, and Co., 1865.

To each of these works Canon Brown contributed original hymns. Beyond his own *Sel.*, very few of these hymns are in C. U. The most popular is "O God for ever near." [J. J.]

Brown, James Baldwin, B.A., s. of Dr. J. B. Brown, b. at the Inner Temple, Aug. 19, 1820. He received his education at University College, London, graduating B.A. in 1839. For a short time he studied for the Bar, but soon passed from the Inner Temple to Highbury College to prepare for the Congregational Ministry. In 1843 he became pastor of the London Road Congregational Chapel, Derby; and in 1846 of the Claylands Independent Chapel, Clapham Road, London. In 1870 his congregation removed to their new chapel at Brixton. In 1878 he was Chairman of the Congregational Union. He d. at Brixton, 1884. His prose writings were numerous. He is known to hymnology chiefly through his popular hymn, "For increase of Faith"—'Thou Who our faithless hearts canst read.'"

Brown, James Baldwin, LL.D., barrister, of the Inner Temple, and father of the above J. B. Brown. In 1813 he joined Dr.

Raffles and J. H. Wiffen (the translator of *Tasso*) in publishing, anonymously, *Poems by Three Friends*. In the new ed., 1815, the authors' names were given. He also contributed a few hymns to Dr. Raffles's *Liverpool Coll.*, 1853. They have however died out of use. A specimen, " The manna to the fainting Jews" (*Christ the Bread of Life*), is given in *Lyra Brit.*, 1867, p. 90.

Brown, John Newton, D.D., was b. at New London, Connecticut, June 29, 1803, and graduated at Madison University, 1823. From 1838 to 1845 he was Professor of Theology at Now Hampton, New Hampshire, and from 1845–1849 pastor at Lexington, Virginia. He d. in 1868. Dr. Brown was some time editor of the Baptist Publication Society, the *Christian Chronicle*, and the *National Baptist*. His works include *Encyclopaedia of Religious Knowledge*, 1831 ; *Memorials of Baptist Martyrs*, 1834 ; *Poems*, 1840. His hymn :—

Go, spirit of the sainted dead, appeared in *The Psalmist* (Revs. B. Stow and S. F. Smith), 1843, No. 1100, and thence has passed into other Baptist collections.   [F. M. B.]

Brown, Phoebe, née Hinsdale. A member of the Congregational body, b. at Canaan, Columbia County, New York, May 1, 1783, she was left an orphan when two years old. At nine she fell into the hands of a relative who kept a county gaol. These, says her son, " were years of intense and cruel suffering. The tale of her early life which she has left her children is a narrative of such deprivations, cruel treatment, and toil, as it breaks my heart to read." Escaping from this bondage at 18, she was sought by kind people, and sent for three months to a common school at Claverack, N.Y., where she learned to write, and made profession of faith in Christ. In 1805 she was married to Timothy H. Brown, a painter, and subsequently lived at East Windsor and Ellington, Connecticut, Monison, Mass., and at Marshall, Henry County, Illinois. She d. at the last-named place, Oct 10, 1861. Most of her hymns were written at Monison, Mass. Through a life of poverty and trial she was "a most devoted mother, wife, and Christian." Her son, the Rev. S. R. Brown, D.D., became the first American Missionary to Japan, and two of her grandchildren are now in the same mission. In addition to her hymns, two or more volumes of prose by her have been published. Her *Autobiography* and *Poems* were being prepared for publication, when the editor died, and they are yet to appear. Despite all her disadvantages, Mrs. Brown's talents and work are superior to those of any other early female hymnist of America. It is hoped that her MSS. may some day be competently examined, and selected portions from them be published. Four of her hymns appeared in Nettleton's *Village Hys.*, 1824, with the signature " B."

1. As once the Saviour took His seat. *Penitence.*

2. Go, messenger of love, and bear. *Missions.*

3. I love to steal awhile away. *Retirement.*

4. Welcome, ye hopeful heirs of heaven. *Young Converts.*

Of these No. 2 is a Missionary hymn, written in 1817, but first pub. in the *Village Hys.*, 1824 ;

No. 3 was written in 1818, and few hymns have a more pathetic history. It is this:—

Mrs. Brown was living at Ellington with "four little children, in a small unfinished house, a sick sister in the only finished room, and not a place above or below where I could retire for devotion." Not far off stood the finest house in the neighbourhood, with a large garden. Towards this the poor woman used to bend her steps at dusk, loving, as she writes, "to smell the fragrance of fruits and flowers, though I could not see them," and commune with Nature and God. This she did, never dreaming that she was intruding, her habits watched, or her motives misconstrued, till one day the lady of the mansion turned rudely upon her with "Mrs. Brown, why do you come up at evening so near our house, and then go back without coming in ? If you want anything, why don't you come in and ask for it ?" Mrs. B. adds, "There was something in her manner more than her words, that grieved me, I went home, and that evening was left alone. After my children were all in bed, except my baby, I sat down in the kitchen with my child in my arms, when the grief of my heart burst forth in a flood of tears. I took pen and paper, and gave vent to my oppressed heart."
The Poem then written is headed "An Apology for my Twilight Rambles, addressed to a Lady, Aug., 1818." The original has nine stanzas, the second beg'nning, " I love to steal awhile away." Years after, when Nettleton was seeking original matter for his *Village Hymns* (1824), this piece was abridged and altered into the present familiar form, either by Mrs. Brown herself, her pastor (Mr. Hyde), or Nettleton. Its popularity was great from the first. In 1853 it was included in the *Leeds H. Bk.*, and thus became known to English collections. It is found in *Lyra Sac. Amer.*, p. 29.

In 1819 Mrs. Brown wrote two hymns which were strangely overlooked by Nettleton, and did not appear till 1831 in Hastings's *Spiritual Songs*. These are :—

5. How sweet the melting lay. *Morning.*

6. O Lord, Thy work revive. *For a Revival.*

Both are found in *Lyra Sac. Amer.*, pp. 28–30. No. 6 was altered by the author for Nason's *Cong. H. Bk.*, 1857. This, according to Nason, is her authorized text. It is widely used in America, and is also found in a few English collections, including Reed's *H. Bk.* and the *N. Cong.*, and sometimes is attributed in error to Hastings. Her later hymns are :—

7. Great God, we would to Thee make known. This appeared in the *Mother's H. Bk.*, 1834.

8. We come, O Lord, before Thy throne. *For Sailors.*

9. Grant the abundance of the sea. *For Sailors.*

Two hymns for sailors, which appeared in Linsley and Davis's *Select Hymns*, 1836.

10. Assembled at [round] Thine altar, Lord. *Holy Communion.* This also appeared in the *Select Hymns*, 1836, and was altered for Nason's *Cong. H. Bk.*, 1857. It is a good hymn, and deserves wider adoption.

11. Jesus, this mid-day hour. *Noon.* " Written by special request for the Fulton Street [Noon] Prayer Meeting," about 1857.

In addition to the foregoing there are four hymns by her in *Parish Hymns* (Phila.), 1843, to which they were contributed ; and there may be many others in various collections which are uncredited.   [F. M. B.]

Brown, William, author of the hymn " Welcome, sacred day of rest" (*Sunday*), which appeared in *A Collection of Hymns, designed as an Appendix to Dr. Watts's Ps. and Hys.*, by T. Russell, M.A., 17th ed., 1839, No. 560, in 2 st. of 8 l., is known only as the writer of this hymn, and of a poetical work, pub. in 1822. The hymn is in somewhat extensive use in G. Brit. and America.   Orig. text in the S. P. C. K. *Ps. and Hys.* No. 195; and Dr. Hatfield's (Amer.) *Church H. Bk.*,1872, No. 39; in each case with the orig. line, st. i., l 2, changed from "Time of leaving worldly care," to "*Sweet repose from* worldly care."

Brown-Borthwick, Robert, b. at Aberdeen, May 18, 1840, and educated at St. Mary Hall, Oxford. Taking Holy Orders in 1865, he has been Curate of Sudeley (and Chaplain of the Winchcombe Union), Gloucestershire, 1865–6, and Evesham, 1866–8; Assistant Minister of Quebec Chapel, London, 1868–9; and Incumbent of Holy Trinity, Grange, near Keswick, 1869. He is now (1886) Vicar of All Saints, Scarborough. His publications, in addition to his prose works, are :—*Supplemental Hymn and Tune Book*, 1867 (4th ed., 1871); *Sixteen Hymns for Church and Home*, 1870; *Select Hymns for Church and Home*, 1871 ; and various *Kyries, Hymn Tunes, Chants*, &c. In addition he has rendered good service as one of the four Editors of the S. P. C. K. *Church Hymns.* In this last work three of his best hymns are found: "Come, O Jesu, to Thy Table"; "O Holy Jesu, Prince of Peace"; "Let us raise our grateful voices." Canon Westcott in his *Paragraph Psalter* acknowledges Mr. Brown-Borthwick's assistance in preparing that work for the press as of great value thereto. He d. March 17, 1894.

Of Mr. Brown-Borthwick's hymns the following appeared in his *Sixteen Hymns*, &c., 1870 :—

1. **Come, O Jesus, to Thy Table.** *Holy Communion.*
2. **Lord, in the watches of the night.** *Midnight.*
3. **O Holy Jesu, Prince of Peace.** *Holy Communion.*
The author's note to this hymn is, "This is not a congregational hymn, but a meditation, to be read while non-communicants are retiring, or to be sung by the choir alone, anthem-wise, kneeling."

These hymns were repeated in his *Select Hymns*, &c., 1871–85. The following is also in that collection :—

4. **Let us raise our grateful [gladsome] voices.** *Flower Services, or Thanksgiving.* "Written in Borrowdale, on a summer morning in 1870," and pub. in the S. P. C. K. *Church Hys.*, 1871, &c.   [J. J.]

Browne, Felicia Dorothea. [Hemans, F. D.]

Browne, Charlotte Elizabeth. [Tonna, C. E.]

Browne, Jane Euphemia. [Saxby, J. E.]

Browne, Mary Ann. [Gray, M. A.]

Browne, Moses, was b. in humble circumstances in 1703, and was distinguished as a poet and miscellaneous writer. He was Vicar of Olney, Bucks, and for some time Chaplain of Morden College, Blackheath, Kent, where he d. Sept. 13, 1787. His poetical works were :—

(1) *Poems*, 1739 ; (2) *The Works, and Rest of the Creation,* in two parts. Pt. i. *An Essay on the Universe;* Pt. ii. *Sunday Thoughts,* &c., 1752 (6th ed., 1805). His hymns are contained in Pt. iv. of the *Sunday Thoughts,* together with versions of Ps. 130 and 139. He is known chiefly through his hymn "When with a mind devoutly pressed" (*Penitence*), which is "Night Song, No. viii.," in 5 st. of 4 l., of the *Sunday Thoughts,* having originally appeared in his *Poems*, 1739, p. 457. He complains in a note of editors of hymn-books printing this hymn "from an imperfect copy." It has been ascribed from time to time to various authors. (3) He also pub. in 1772, a *tr.* of J. L. Zimmerman's *Excellency of the knowledge of Jesus Christ,* 1732, from which the hymn,

"'Tis not too hard, too high an aim," is taken. It is annotated under "Es ist nicht schwert."

Browne, Simon. A contemporary of Dr. Watts, b. at Shepton Mallet, Somersetshire, cir. 1680, and d. in 1732. After studying for the Independent Ministry under the Rev. John Moore, of Bridgewater, he became pastor of an Independent charge in Portsmouth, and then, in 1716, of the Independent-Chapel in Old Jewry, London. His later years were clouded by a peculiar malady, under the influence of which "he imagined that God had in a gradual manner annihilated in him the thinking substance, and utterly divested him of consciousness." It is supposed that the death of a highwayman at his hands during a violent struggle, followed by that of his wife and son a short time after, had much to do in producing this sad result. Whilst thus contending that he had no power to think, he produced a work in defence of Christianity, another in defence of the Trinity, a third as an Exposition of the 1st Ep. to the Corinthians, and a fourth in the form of a Dictionary. His publications number over 20. Of these works, he is known to hymnology through his :—

Hymns and Spiritual Songs, in Three Books, designed as a Supplement to Dr. Watts, &c., 1720, 2nd ed. 1741, 3rd ed. 1760. It contains 166 hymns, 7 doxologies, and a Preface of some historical interest.

In the old collections Simon Browne's hymns (all of which are from the above collection) held a prominent position, but in modern hymnals they are fast passing out of use. The best known and most widely used are "Come, Holy [gracious] Spirit, Heavenly Dove," "O God, on Thee we all depend," and "Lord, at Thy feet we sinners lie." In addition the following are also in C. U. :—

1. Eternal God, Almighty Cause. *Unity of God.*
2. Eternal God, of beings First. *God all in all.*
3. Frequent the day of God returns. *Sunday.*
4. Great First of beings, Mighty Lord. *Creation.*
5. Great God, my joyful thanks to Thee. *Thanksgiving.*
6. Great God, Thy peerless excellence. *Imitation of God.*
7. Great Lord of earth and seas and skies. *Providence.*
8. Great Ruler of the earth and sky. *Providence.*
9. Hail, Holy Spirit, bright, immortal, Dove. *Whitsuntide.*
10. Hail, happy day, the [thou] day of holy rest. *Sunday.*
11. I cannot shun the stroke of death. *Death.*
12. Lord, Thou art good; all nature shows. *Divine Goodness.*
13. Lord, what a feeble frame is ours. *Frailty of Life.*
14. O God, on Thee we all depend. *Confidence in God.*   [J. J.]

Browne, Sir Thomas. b. in St. Michael's, Cheapside, London, Oct. 19, 1605, and educated at Winchester, and at the Hall now known as Pembroke College, Oxford, graduating B.A. in 1626. He practised as a physician in Oxfordshire, Shipden Hall, near Halifax, Yorkshire, and at Norwich. In 1671 he was knighted by Charles II. at Norwich, and died there, Oct. 10, 1682. He wrote numerous scientific, antiquarian, and other works, including *Religio Medici*, 1642, and others, republished in Bohn's Library. The *Religio Medici* has been edited in the *Golden Treasury* series, Macmillan, 1882, with great fulness of detail. He is known principally to hymnology through his fine hymn, "The night is come; like to the day."

Browne, Thomas Briarly, of Wellington, was the author of *The Oxford Divines not Members of the Church of England*, 1839; *Thoughts of the Times*, 1838; and the *National Bankruptcy and other Poems*, Lond., Pickering, 1844. From this last work a version of the 148th Ps. has come into somewhat extensive use in English-speaking countries. It is the well-known "Praise the Lord of heaven, praise Him in the height." Orig. text in Lord Selborne's *Bk. of Praise*, 1862, p. 25.

Browning, Elizabeth, née Barrett, daughter of Mr. Barrett, an English country gentleman, and wife of Robert Browning, the poet, was b. in London 1809, and d. at Florence in 1861. As a poetess she stands at the head of English female writers, and her secular works are well known. Sacred pieces from her works are in C. U. in America. They include:—

1. God, named Love, whose fount Thou art. *Love.*
2. How high Thou art! Our songs can own. *Divine Perfection.*
3. Of all the thoughts of God, that are. *Death.*
4. What would we give to our beloved? Pt. ii. of No. 3.
5. When Jesus' friend had ceased to be. *Friendship.* Based on the death of Lazarus.

These hymns are in Beecher's *Plymouth Coll.* 1855; Hedge and Huntington's *Hys. for the Ch. of Christ*, Boston, U.S., 1853, &c.

Bruce, Charles, b. Oct. 25, 1837, at Braintree, Essex. Mr. Bruce has been engaged in literary work, and chiefly as an amanuensis. He has written about 25 books, mostly for the young, and also contributed to various magazines. Of the few hymns which he has composed the following are in C. U.:—

1. Father, O hear me. *Prayer.*
2. When little hearts believe and love. *Trust.*

Both are in the *Bk. of Praise for Children*, 1875.

[W. G. H.]

Bruce, Michael, son of a Scottish weaver, was born at Kinnesswood, Portmoak, Kinross-shire, Scotland, March 27, 1746, and educated at the village school, Edinburgh University (where he first became acquainted with John Logan), and the Theological Hall of the Associate Synod, held at Kinross, under the Rev. John Swanston, intending ultimately to enter the ministry, a hope which was frustrated by his untimely death. To assist in procuring University fees and maintenance he for some time conducted a school, during the recess, at Gairney Bridge, and subsequently at Forrest Mill, near Tillicoultry. Whilst yet a student he died at Kinnesswood, July 5th, 1767.

Logan, John, son of a farmer, born at Fala, Midlothian, 1748, and educated at Edinburgh University, in due course entering the ministry of the Church of Scotland and becoming the minister of South Leith in 1770. During the time he held this charge he delivered a course of lectures on philosophy and history with much success. While he was thus engaged, the chair of Universal History in the University became vacant; but as a candidate he was unsuccessful. A tragedy, entitled *Runnamede*, followed. He offered it to the manager of Covent Garden Theatre, but it was interdicted by the Lord Chamberlain "upon suspicion of having a seditious tendency." It was subsequently acted in Edinburgh. In 1775 he formed one of the Committee by whom the *Translations and*

Paraphrases of the Church of Scotland was prepared. In 1782 he was compelled to resign his charge at Leith in order to prevent deposition, and finally, having passed on to London, he supported himself partly by his pen, and died there, Dec. 28, 1788.

The names of Bruce and Logan are brought together because of the painful controversy which has long prevailed concerning the authorship of certain *Hymns and Paraphrases* of Holy Scripture which are in extensive use in the Christian Church both at home and abroad. During the latter years of Bruce's short life he wrote various Poems, and also Hymns for a singing class at Kinnesswood, which were well known to his family and neighbours, and were eventually copied out by Bruce himself in a quarto MS. book, with the hope that some day he might see them in print. Immediately upon his death, in 1767, Logan called upon his father and requested the loan of this book that he might publish the contents for the benefit of the family. This was granted. Not till three years afterwards did a certain work, containing seventeen poems, and entitled *Poems on Several Occasions, by Michael Bruce*, 1770. appear, with a Preface in which it was stated that some of the Poems were by others than Bruce. Bruce's father immediately pointed out the absence from the volume of certain hymns which he called his son's "Gospel Sonnets," and members of the singing class at Kinnesswood also noted the absence of hymns with which they were familiar. Letters of remonstrance and demands for the return of the quarto MS. book of Bruce by the father remaining unanswered, led him eventually to see Logan in person. No book was forthcoming, a few scraps of MS. only were returned, and Logan accounted for the absence of the book by saying he feared "that the servants had singed fowls with it." For a time the matter rested here, only to be revived with renewed interest by the publication, in 1781 (14 years after the death of Bruce, and 11 after the *Poems*, &c., were issued), of *Poems. By the Rev. Mr. Logan, One of the Ministers of Leith*. In this volume, an "Ode to the Cuckoo," a poem of exquisite beauty, and other poetical pieces which appeared in the *Poems on Several Occasions, by Michael Bruce*, were repeated, and claimed as his own by Logan. In addition, certain *Hymns and Paraphrases* were included, most of which were of sterling merit, and poetical excellence. It has been shown, we think, most conclusively by Dr. Mackelvie in his *Life* of Bruce prefixed to the *Poems*, 1837 and by Dr. Grosart in his *Works of M. Bruce*, 1865, that the "Ode to the Cuckoo," "Lochleven," and other poetical pieces were taken from the MS. book of M. Bruce. The *Hymns and Paraphrases*, most of which were included in the *Translations and Paraphrases* during the same year, were also claimed for Bruce. With these we have to deal, and as the question has been of more than usual interest we give the respective claims made on behalf of Bruce and Logan in parallel columns as follows:—

M. BRUCE.	J. LOGAN.
1. Bruce known to have written hymns for a singing class in Kinnesswood as early as 1764.	1. Logan then 16 years of age, and not known to have written anything to that date.

2. Bruce died 1767, and his father handed his MSS. to Logan, at Logan's request, for publication.

2. Logan acknowledged this by publishing, in 1770, *Poems on Several Occasions, by M. Bruce,* containing 17 poems. Some of these (not distinctly marked as such) he said were by others.

other side save that the hymns were printed in a volume of poetry which Logan claimed as his own.

6. Failing to find any evidence other than this on behalf of Logan, we must give the following hymns to M. Bruce, although his claims lack the clear and definite character of the three given before :—

3. Bruce's father on receiving the volume, and not finding the "Gospel Sonnets," as he called his son's hymns, wrote to Logan for an explanation.

3. Logan did not reply.

4. "When Jesus by the Virgin brought."
Known as—"*Just and devout old Simeon liv'd.*"
5. "Almighty Father of Mankind."
6. "Behold th' Ambassador divine."
Known as—"*Behold my Servant, see Him rise.*"
7. "Messiah ! at Thy glad approach."
8. "Where high the heavenly temple stands."

4. The father visited Logan and demanded his son's MS. back..

4. Logan replied, first that he could not find it, and then that he feared "that the servants had singed fowls with it."

iii. A third series of hymns, the Bruce or Logan authorship of which has been a matter of much dispute, appeared for the *first time* in the *Translations and Paraphrases* of 1781, and are not found in Logan's *Poems* of the same year. These, in common with the other *Trs. and Pars.,* were given anonymously. Those which had previously appeared in Logan's *Poems,* and, in some cases, in another and better form, were at once recognised as the hymns of the singing class at Kinnesswood; but those which, in addition, are given in W. Cameron's list to Logan were not so claimed at the time by friend or enemy. The claim upon these hymns as the work of Bruce was only made when it was found that Logan had given them to the Committee of the 1781 *Translations and Paraphrases,* and this apparently on the ground that a man who had confessedly stolen so much must necessarily have stolen all. This we cannot allow. On the evidence, therefore, that no claim was made by Bruce's family and friends to the Bruce authorship of anything *outside* of Logan's *Poems;* that the following were first published in the *Trs. & Paraphs.* of 1781; that at first their authorship was unknown to the general public and unclaimed by any one; and that it was only when Logan's claims to the authorship was made known that the counter-claim for Bruce was set up : we hold that, until clearer evidence is brought forward on behalf of Bruce, the hymns, or paraphrases, following must be ascribed to J. Logan :—

5. Immediately on the publication of Logan's *Poems* the *three* hymns following were identified by educated personal friends of Bruce as his, such identification being by actual quotations of stanzas :
1. "Few are thy days and full of woe."
2. "O happy is the man who hears."
3. "Behold the mountain of the Lord."

5. About 11 years after, i.e. in 1781, Logan published his *Poems,* in which were given *eleven* hymns as his own.

6. In addition, these claims were corroborated by the members of the singing class at Kinnesswood, his family, and his neighbours, to whom they were familiar, before seen in print.

6. Logan knew his authorship was thus disputed, but took no pains to vindicate his honesty.

These three hymns we therefore assign without reservation to M. Bruce.

ii. A second series of hymns which are claimed, on the one hand for M. Bruce and on the other for J. Logan, have caused, from the somewhat indefinite character of the evidence brought forward on both sides, some angry comments on the part of editors and controversialists. The sum of the argument is this :—

1. Bruce is known to have written hymns, other than the three given above, for the singing class at Kinnesswood. •

1. This is not denied by Logan or his friends.

9. "Who can resist th' Almighty arm."
10. "In streets and op'nings of the gates."
11. "Thus speaks the heathen : How shall man."
12. "Take comfort, Christians, when your friends."
13. "The hour of my departure's come."

We feel some reluctance in giving the last of these hymns to Logan, but with the evidence before us we cannot do otherwise. Internal evidence is in favour of Bruce, and the sentiments are natural to one who knew he was about to die. Beyond this, for Bruce, there is no evidence; and to Logan, as the defendant, we must give the benefit of the doubt.

2. These, in common with all his Poetical Pieces, were written in the same MS. volume as the three above, and with them were handed to J. Logan for publication by Bruce's father.

2. This also is not denied.

iv. The following, which are found only in the *Translations and Paraphrases* of 1781, are claimed by W. Cameron for Logan, and have never been seriously disputed by the friends of Bruce, the second being original, the first a revise from the *Trs. & Paraphs.* of 1745; and the third a revise of Doddridge and Dr. Hugh Blair :—

3. In common with the three hymns they were omitted from the volume of Bruce's *Poetical Works,* but included with them by Logan in his *Poems,* 1781, as his own.

3. Admitted by Logan's friends.

14. "Let Christian faith and hope dispel."
15. "Thus speaks the high and lofty One."
16. "What though no flowers the fig-tree clothe."

In addition, we see no cause to deny to Logan the few changes, and new stanza, which are found in Doddridge's—

4. These on their publication were claimed by Bruce's brother James as hymns known to him for years as the lost hymns of his brother Michael, and this was supported by the common consent of the members of the Kinnesswood singing class, and many other intimate friends of M. Bruce.

4. Admitted ; but for Logan it must be pointed out that from the beginning of the controversy none of these witnesses are brought forward as giving one single line of any one of those hymns (as was done with the three before noted) as evidence that they had known the hymns before they were in print. The statements are thus general, and not particular, and consist more of personal impressions than of definite and positive statements of facts.

17. "O God of Bethel, by Whose hand."

v. Of the above hymns 5 are recasts of hymns in the Scottish *Tras. and Paraphs.* of 1745. Those are : "Behold the mountain of the Lord" (see "In latter days the mount of God "); "When Jesus by the Virgin brought" (see "Now let Thy servant die in peace "); "Behold the Ambassador divine" (see "Behold my Servant, see Him rise"); "Let Christian faith and hope dispel" (see " Now let our souls ascend above"); and "What though no flowers the fig-tree clothe" (see "So firm the saints' foundation stands").

The whole of these Bruce-Logan hymns and recasts are annotated in full under their respective first lines (q.v.) in the body of this work. As one outcome of these annotations it is curious to note that every hymn which we have ascribed to M. Bruce has come into more or less extensive use *outside* of the *Translations and Para-*

5. Notwithstanding this indefiniteness, there is no positive evidence on the

phrases, and that not one which we have ascribed to Logan, except "Let Christian faith and hope dispel," and "Take comfort, Christians," &c., is found beyond that work, unless we give to Logan the plaintive "The hour of my departure's come" (which Dr. Grosart claims for Bruce), and the recast "O God of Bethel, by Whose hand," whose success is due to Doddridge. This is the verdict of 100 years' use of those hymns, and shows conclusively the poetic strength of Bruce and the weakness of Logan.

Authorities :—Scottish *Translations and Paraphrases* of 1745, 1751, 1781; *Poems,* &c., by M. Bruce, 1770; *Poems,* by J. Logan, 1781; Dr. Anderson's *British Poets;* Chambers's *Dict. of Eminent Scotsmen;* The *Poetic Wreath,* 1836; Dr. Mackelvie's *Life of Bruce,* prefixed to *Lochleven,* &c., 1837; Dr. Grosart's *Works of Bruce,* 1865; *Enc. Brit.,* 9th ed., 1881-6; numerous *Magazine articles* and private MSS.; Macmeeken's *History of the Scottish Metrical Psalms,* &c.. 1872. [J. J.]

Bruce, William, D.D., eldest s. of the Rev. William Bruce, United Secession minister at South Shields (who after 1818, conducted the Ardoch Academy, Cardross, Dumbartonshire), was b. at South Shields, April 7, 1812. He studied at the University of Glasgow, which, in 1860, conferred on him the degree of D.D., and became, in 1838, minister of Infirmary Street U. P. Church, Edinburgh (then Cowgate). He was Moderator of Synod in 1869. In 1870 he was appointed a member of the Hymnal Committee of the U. P. Church, and contributed 2 hymns to their *Presbyterian Hymnal,* 1876. These he included, with 9 others, in his *Hebrew Odes and other Poems,* 1874 (Edinb.: D. S. Stewart). He also pub., in 1878, *Memories: a Tale; and other Poems.* He d. at Bridge of Allan, Nov. 15, 1882. The two hymns contributed to the *Presb. Hymnal* are :—

1. Holy Father, Thou hast given. *Holy Scripture.*
2. The seed we bury in the earth. *Resurrection.*

[J. M.]

Brunn alles Heils, dich ehren wir. *G. Tersteegen.* [*Trinity Sunday.*] Based on the blessing of Israel, Numb. vi. 24-27, and 1st pub. in the 4th ed., 1745, of Tersteegen's *Geistliches Blumengärtlein* (Bk. iii., No. 75), in 5 st. of 4 l., entitled, "A prayer of faith at morning, at evening, at table, after sermon, and at all times." In the *Unv. L. S.,* 1851, it is No. 214. *Trs.* in C. U. are :—

1. Salvation's healing Spring ! to Thee. Full and good by H. J. Buckoll in his *H. from the German,* 1842, p. 52. In the Irish *Church Hymnal,* 1869, following the example of the *Rugby School H. Bk.,* 1850, st. i. is omitted, the rest is slightly altered, and it begins : "O Lord, our Maker! ever near." This arrangement was made by Buckoll as joint editor of the Rugby School *H. Bk.*

2. Thee, Fount of blessing, we adore ! In full by Miss Winkworth in her *Lyra Ger.,* 2nd Series, 1858, p. 62, and repeated, slightly altered, in her *C. B. for England,* 1863, No. 16.

Other trs. are :—
(1) "Thou source of health and all our weal," by *Dr. G. Walker,* 1860, p. 39.
(2) "Fountain of all salvation, we adore Thee," by *Lady Durand,* 1873, p. 108.   [J. M.]

Brunnquell aller Güter. *J. Franck.* [*Whitsuntide.*] 1st pub. in the Crüger-Runge *G. B.,* Berlin, 1653, No. 158, in 8 st. of 8 l., entitled, "A hymn of praise to God the Holy Ghost." Repeated in Crüger's *Praxis pietatis*

melica, 1656, No. 199, and most subsequent hymnals as the *Unv. L. S.,* 1851, No. 163. In Franck's *Geistliches Sion,* 1674, p. 26 (ed. 1846, p. 27). The *tr.* in C. U. is :—

Source of good, whose power controls. A full and very good *tr.* by R. Massie in *M. Luther's Spir. Songs,* 1854, p. 89, repeated unaltered save iii. l. 7, and iv. l. 5 as No. 143 in the ed. of 1857, of Mercer's *C. P. and H. Bk.,* in two parts, the second beginning with st. v. "As the hart with longing looks" (Ox. ed., 1864, No. 20, retains only st. i., ii., vii., viii.). In full but slightly altered as No. 1052 in *Kennedy,* 1863, while st. i., ii., v. are given in Alford's *Year of Praise,* 1867, and st. i., v., vi. in Martineau's *Hys.,* 1873. In the *Meth. N. Connexion Hys.,* 1863, No. 311, beginning "Mighty Spirit ! by Whose aid," is made up of st. vi. ll. 1-4, ii. ll. 5-8, and iv.   [J. M.]

Bryant, William Cullen. First in order of time of the great American poets, Bryant was b. at Cummington, Mass., Nov. 3, 1794, and was educated at Williams College. In 1815 he was called to the Bar, and practised for a time at Great Barrington. In 1825 he retired from the Bar, settled at New York, and devoted himself to literary pursuits, founding the *New York Review,* and editing for a short time the *New York Evening Post.* He d. June 12, 1878. His poetical and other works are well known. His hymns were written at intervals during his long life. They were collected and privately printed in 1869, and number over 20. Those in C. U. are :—

1. Almighty, listen while we raise. *Praise.* This is given as "Almighty *hear us,*" &c., in the Unitarian *H. and Tune Bk.,* Boston, 1868. It was introduced into G. Britain through Beard's *Coll.,* 1837.

2. Deem not that they are blest alone. *Mourning.* In this form it is in Beard's *Coll.,* 1837. It is best known as "*O deem* not they are," &c., and in this form it is No. 964 in *Songs for the Sanctuary,* N. Y., 1865-72, No. 452, in Dr. Martineau's *Hys. of P. and Praise,* Lond., 1873, &c.

3. Father, to Thy kind love we owe. *God's Loving-kindness.* This is given in several modern collections, including the Unitarian *H. and Tune Bk.,* Boston, 1868, *Martineau,* 1873, &c.

4. O God, whose dread and dazzling brow. *Compassion desired.* Is No. 57 in the Boston *H. and Tune Bk.,* 1868, as above.

5. When he who from the scourge of wrong. *Hope of the Resurrection.* This is seldom found in modern hymnals. Text in *Lyra Sac. Amer.,* 1868.

The above hymns (1-5) appeared in Dr. H. D. Sewall's (Unitarian) *Ps. & Hys. for Social and Private Worship,* 1820, and were written at the instance of a Miss Sedgwick. Following as near as possible the chronological order of the hymns we have next :—

6. O Thou Whose own vast temple stands. *Opening of a Place of Worship.* Written in 1835 for the Dedication of a Chapel in Prince Street, N. Y. This is the most widely known of this author's hymns. It was introduced into G. Britain as early as 1837, when it was included in Beard's *Coll.,* No. 405. It is in 4 st. of 4 l. Orig. text in *Songs for the Sanctuary,* N. Y., 1865, No. 1017, and *Martineau,* 1873, No. 727. Another form of the hymn is "Thou, Whose unmeasured temple stands," This is No. 569 in the Amer.

Presb. *Is. and Hys.*, Richmond, 1867, Horder's *Cong. Hys.*, Lond. 1884, No. 747, and others.

7. All that in this wide world we see. *Omnipresence.* This is dated 1836. In his *Coll.* in 1837, No. 17, Beard gives it as an original contributed thereto, thus fixing its first publication.

8. Thou unrelenting past. *The Past.* Dates from 1836. Also in *Martineau*, 1873, No. 508.

9. Not in the solitude. *God in the City.* Dates from 1836, and is No. 26 in *Martineau*, 1873.

10. Whither, midst falling dew. *Divine Guidance.* This, in common with Nos. 8 and 9, is more a poem than hymn. It is addressed " To a Waterfowl," and dates from 1836. In *Martineau*, 1873.

11. Dear ties of mutual succour bind. *Charity Sermons.* No. 905 in the Amer. Methodist Episcopal *Hymnal*, 1878. It dates from about 1836.

12. O Thou whose love can ne'er forget. *Ordination.* Given (but not as an original contributed thereto) in Beard's *Coll.* (Eng.), 1837.

13. Mighty One, before Whose face. *Ordination.* This is dated 1840 (but is probably earlier), and is given in several collections, including Mr. Beecher's *Plymouth Coll.*, 1855, and others.

14. Look from Thy sphere of endless day. *Home Missions.* This hymn has also attained to considerable use both in G. Britain and America. It dates from 1840. It is in the *S. for the Sanctuary*, N. Y., 1865, Horder's *Cong. Hys.*, 1884, &c.

15. Lord, who ordainest for mankind. *Thanks for a Mother's love.* Written at Dr. Osgood's suggestion, and printed in his *Christian Worship*, 1862. It is repeated in *Martineau*, 1873.

16. All praise to Him of Nazareth. *Holy Communion.* Dr. Hatfield in his *Church H. Bk.*, 1872, No. 736, gives this in 3 st. of 4 l. In the *Songs for the Sanctuary* it is in its full form of 5 st. It dates from 1864.

17. As shadows cast by cloud and sun. *Epiphany.* In the Methodist Episcopal *Hymnal*, N. Y., 1878. It was contributed to that *Hymnal*, 1877, but was composed for the Semi-Centennial Celebration of the Church of the Messiah, Boston, March 19, 1875.

18. When doomed to death the Apostle lay. *On behalf of Drunkards.* Also in the Methodist Episcopal *Hymnal*, 1878.

In addition to the above the following hymns by Bryant are in limited use:—

19. All things that are on earth. *Love of God.* In Beard's *Coll.*, 1837.

20. Close softly, fondly, while ye weep. *Death.* In Mr. Beecher's *Plymouth Coll.*, 1855.

21. How shall I know thee in the sphere which keeps? *The Future Life.* In the *Suppl.* to the Boston *Hys. for the Church of Christ*, 1853.

22. Standing forth in life's rough way. *On behalf of Children.* In Dr. Allon's *Children's Worship*, 1878; Horder's *Cong. Hys.*, 1884, and others.

23. When this song of praise shall cease. *Death anticipated.* In his *Hymns*, 1869, and W. R. Stevenson's *School Hymnal*, 1880, No. 313.

24. When the blind suppliant in the way. *Opening the eyes of the blind.* In the Methodist Episcopal *Hymnal*, 1878, N. Y., No. 201. It dates from 1874.

25. Wild was the day, the wintry sea. *The Pilgrim Fathers.* In *Hys. of the Spirit*, by Longfellow and Johnson. Boston, 1864.

In 1869, *Hymns by W. C. Bryant*, 12mo, were privately printed. In this work the texts of many of the older hymns are altered. The dates of his hymns are difficult to determine, and many of those given above are approximate only. Bryant's genius was cool, meditative, and not distinguished by lyric fire.

His hymns are correct and solid, but none reach the highest rank.   [F. M. B.]

Bubier, George Burden, s. of the Rev. William Bubier, b. at Reading, Feb. 2, 1823. After serving for some time in a bank at Banbury, he prepared for the Congregational Ministry, at Homerton College. He was successively pastor of congregations at Orsett, Essex, 1844 ; Union Chapel, Brixton ; Cambridge ; and Hope Chapel, Salford, 1854. In 1864 he was appointed Professor of Theology and Philosophy at Spring Hill Congregational College, Birmingham. He d. at Acock's Green, near Birmingham, March 19, 1869. In 1855 he was joint editor with Dr. George Macdonald, and the brother of the latter, of *Hymns and Sacred Songs for Sunday Schools and Social Worship, in two parts*, &c., Manchester, Fletcher and Tubbs, 1855. A great many of the 318 hymns in this collection have been repeated in later hymnals.

To that work he contributed 11 hymns under the signature "B." These, increased from other sources to 21, together with 6 Psalm Versions, were given with dates and in some instances with notes also, in his *Hymns and Devotional Verses*, Birmingham, 1867. Amongst those of his hymns in C. U. are:—

1. A fitly spoken word. *Kind Words.* Dated " January, 1855," and pub. in the *Hymns*, &c., as above, No. 285, in 6 st. of 4 l. Also in *H. and D. Verses*, 1867, p. 14. Given in Horder's *Cong. Hys.*, 1884.

2. Blest be the God of love. *Sunday Evening.* Written in " June, 1855," and pub. in *Hymns*, &c., in 6 st. of 4 l. as above ; *H. and D. Verses*, 1867, Horder, 1884, and others.

3. Great is Thy mercy, Lord. *Chosen by Christ.* Dated " January, 1854," and pub. in the two works as above, in 5 st. of 4 l. In *Horder*, 1884.

4. I would commune with Thee, my God. *Longing for God.* This is the most popular of this author's hymns, and is given in several collections. It was written " February 2nd, 1854," in 4 st. of 4 l. It is in both the *Hymns*, &c., 1855, and the *H. and D. Verses*, 1867. Orig. text in *Bap. Hymnal*, 1879, No. 376.

5. My God, I love Thee for Thyself. *Love to God.* This is not in the *Hymns*, &c., 1855. It is dated " June 13th, 1857 " in his *H. and D. Verses*, 1867, p. 22. It is given in the *Bap. Hymnal*, 1879, Horder, 1884, and others.   [F. J. F.]

Buchanan, George, b. at Killearn, Stirlingshire, 1506. He was an eminent writer, and for some time was tutor to the Earl of Moray, the natural son of James V. Having embraced the doctrines of the Reformation he attacked the Franciscans in a satirical poem written by the command of James V. His life being in danger he fled to England, then to France and Portugal. In Portugal he was confined in a monastery on account of his free expression of opinions. During that confinement he rendered the Book of Psalms into Latin Verse, and subsequently pub. it in Paris, 1564. In 1551 he obtained his liberty, and some time after returned to Scotland and became tutor to James VI. He d. at Edinburgh in 1582. His version of the Psalms was rendered into English in 1754 by the Rev. T. Cradock. A few years later James Fanch paraphrased several individual Psalms. James Merrick also adapted the 122nd.

Buchfelder, Ernst Wilhelm, b. June 5, 1645, at Bentheim, East Friesland, Hannover. At first he studied law, but was so much impressed by a sermon he heard at Cassel, in 1672, from Theodor Under-Eyck, that he forthwith began the study of theology at the University of Utrecht, and at the close of his studies, attended for two years on the ministry of Under-Eyck, then pastor of St. Martin's Church, Bremen. In 1678 he became pastor at Glückstadt in Holstein; 1679, rector of the classical school at Emden, in East Friesland; in 1684 preacher and inspector at Büdingen, in Wetteravia; in 1687 preacher at Mühlheim on the Ruhr; and finally preacher at Emden, where he d. March 8, 1711 (*Koch*, vi. 14–16; *Allg. Deutsche Biog.*, iii. 478, the latter saying he d. May 8). *Koch* adds :—

"Only one hymn by him has appeared in print, but one of such importance that it may be reckoned a jewel of the Reformed hymnody. It bears the true impress of his inner life and was probably written in that year, 1672, so memorable in his history." It is :—

Erleucht mich Herr, mein Licht. [*True and False Christianity.*] Included in the *Geistreiches G. B.*, Halle, 1697, p. 53, and repeated in Freylinghausen's *G. B.*, 1704, No. 245, in 16 st. of 7 l. Also in the *Unv. L.S.*1851, No. 309. It is tr. as :—

O Lord! afford a sinner light. A recast of the 1789 Moravian *tr.* (see below) in 8 st. of C. M.—viii. being by T. Bird, 1826—as No. 290 in the *Moravian H. Bk.*, 1826, repeated, abridged, in J. A. Latrobe's *Coll.*, 1852, No 316.

Other trs. are :—
(1) "Enlighten me, my Light," in the *Suppl.* to *German Psalmody*, ed. 1765, p, 35, and *Select Hys. from Ger. Psalmody*, 1754, p. 63. (2) "O Lord! afford Thy Light," as No. 641 in pt. i. of the *Moravian H. Bk.*, 1754. In 1789 considerably altered, and in 1826 st. viii. and xvi., beginning "The language of true faith," alone retained. (3) "Impart, O Lord, Thy Light," by *Dr. H. Mills*, 1845 (ed. 1856, p. 39).   [J. M.]

Buckoll, Henry James, M.A., s. of the Rev. James Buckoll, Rector of Siddington, near Cirencester, Gloucester; b. at Siddington, Sept. 9, 1803. He was educated at Rugby and Queen's College, Oxford, graduating B.A. in 1826, and became Assistant Master at Rugby the same year. He took Holy Orders in 1827, and d. at Rugby June 6, 1871. He was probably the editor of the first edition of the Rugby School *Collection*. In 1839 he edited a *Collection of Hymns* for the Rugby Parish Church, and in 1850 compiled, with Dr. Goulburn, a new ed. of the *Collection* for the Rugby School Chapel. That collection contains 14 of his hymns, a few of which were trs. from the Latin and German. His *Hymns translated from the German* were pub. 1842. It contained 67 translations from Bunsen's *Versuch*, 1833, most of which are in the original metres, and are annotated in this work under their first lines in German. Buckoll's hymns and trs. are mostly found in the hymnbooks of the Public Schools.   [J. J.]

Buckworth, John, b. at Colsterworth, Lincolnshire, Jan. 16, 1779, and d. April 2, 1835. On taking Holy Orders he became Curate of Dewsbury, and subsequently Vicar of the same parish. He pub. *Hymns for Sunday Schools* (3rd ed. 1814, 10th ed. 1830). This collection of 100 hymns contained a few originals by Buckworth. Of those hymns,

most of which are from the 3rd ed. 1814, the following are still in C. U. :—

1. **Assembled in our school to-day.** *Opening of a S. School.* This hymn has long been regarded, both in G. Britain and America, as anonymous.

2. **Children of God, O blessed name.** *Adoption.* In several collections, including the *Leeds S. S. H. Bk.*, 1833 to 1865; *Common Praise*, 1879, and others.

3. **Children, think on [of] Jesus' love.** *The love of Jesus.* In *Common Praise*, 1879, &c.

4. **Christ is [was] merciful and mild.** *For Infants.* In W. R. Stevenson's *School Hymnal*, 1880, No. 9.

5. **Holy children, read and pray.** *For Infants.* In W. F. Stevenson's *Hys. for Ch. & Home*, 1872, No. 52, &c.

6. **Jesus little children blesses.** *Love of Jesus.* In various collections, including Major's *Bk. of Praise*, No. 48.

7. **Lord, look upon a little child.** *Seeking Jesus.* This is the most popular and widely used of Buckworth's hymns. It is worthy of greater attention than it has hitherto received.

Nos. 6 and 7 were added to Pt. ii. of the *Hys. for S. S.* between 1827 and 1830. As however this ed. of the *Hymns*, &c., was not pub. by Buckworth, there is some uncertainty as to the authorship of these hymns.

             [J. J.]

Budden, William, contributed a few hymns to the *Evangelical Magazine* in 1795, &c., under the signature of "W. B." Some of these hymns were reprinted by John Dobell, in his *New Selection*, 1806. One of these is still in C. U. :—

Come, let our voices join. *Sunday School Anniversary.* 1st printed in the *Evangelical Mag.*, Dec., 1795, in 6 st. of 6 l., signed "W. B.," and headed, "A Hymn composed for the use of the Congregation and Sunday School Children belonging to the Rev. Mr. Ashburner's Meeting, Poole, Dorset." In 1806 it was included in Dobell's *New Sel.*, in 1808, in R. Hill's *Coll. of Hys. for S. Schools*, and others. It is generally known to modern hymn-books as, "Come, let our voice ascend." This altered form was given by T. Cotterill in the *Appendix* to the 6th ed. of his *Sel.*, 1815.   [W. T. B.]

Bulfinch, Stephen Greenleaf, D.D. This Unitarian minister was b. at Boston, June 18, 1809, and removed to Washington in 1818, his father being the architect of the Capitol. He graduated at Columbian College and the Cambridge Theological School. In 1831 he was ordained at Charleston, S.C., as assistant to Dr. Gilman. Subsequently he was pastor at Pittsburg, Pennsylvania; Washington, 1838; Nashua, New Hampshire, 1845; Dorchester, Mass., 1852; and East Cambridge, Mass., 1865. He d. at the last place, Oct. 12, 1870. His works include :—

(1) *Contemplations of the Saviour; A Series of Extracts from the Gospel History, with Reflections and Original and Selected Hymns.* Boston, Carter and Hendee, 1832. This has been reprinted in England. (2) *Poems*, Charleston, S.C., 1834. (3) *Lays of the Gospel*, 1845. In addition to these works, which contain his original hymns, he also pub. (4) *The Harp and Cross*, a selection of hymns, in 1857.

Those of his hymns which have attained to the greatest popularity are :—

1. **Hail to the Sabbath day.** *Sunday.* In the *Contemplations*, &c., p. 45. It is appended to Sect. xii. on the "Walk through the cornfields," and is in 5 st. of 4 l. It is in extensive use both in G. Britain and America, and is the best known of this author's hymns. In many collections it begins with st. ii., "Lord, in Thy [this] sacred hour."

2. **Hath not thy heart within thee burned ?** *Presence of Christ.* In the *Contemplations*, &c., p. 148, as the accompanying hymn to the Reflections on Jesus appearing to His disciples on their way to Emmaus. It is in 5 st. of 4 l., and is given in

the Collections of *Beard, Martineau,* and others in G. Britain.

3. O suffering friend of human kind. *Passiontide.* The hymn in 4 st. of 4 l. appended to Sect. xxxv. on "Peter's confession of Christ," in the *Contemplations,* &c., p. 109. It ranks next in popularity to "Hail to the Sabbath day."

In addition to these hymns which best represent Dr. Bulfinch's powers as a sacred poet, the following are also in limited use:—

4. **Burden of shame and woe.** *Crucifixion.*
5. **Holy Son of God most high.** *Miracles of Christ.*
6. **How glorious is the hour.** *The New Life.*
7. **It is finished! Glorious word.** *Good Friday.*
8. **There is a strife we all must wage.** *Life's Duty.*
These are from his *Poems,* 1834. The next—
9. **What power unseen by mortal eye.** *Cure of Nobleman's Son.* From the *Contemplations,* &c., p. 56.
10. **In the Saviour's hour of death.** *Good Friday.* Also from the *Contemplations,* p. 142:

Dr. Bulfinch's hymns were made known to English readers through Beard's *Coll.,* 1837, in which 19 were given. His hymns throughout are noted for solid and tranquil piety, and deserve a wider circulation than has been accorded to them. They embrace some good hymns on the miracles of Christ. [F. M. B.]

Bullock, William, D.D., a Missionary of the S. P. G. for 32 years, and sometime Dean of Halifax, Nova Scotia, and d. March 16, 1874. He is known to hymnody principally through his popular hymn (in its revised form by Sir H. W. Baker), "We love the place, O God" (q. v.). This appeared with other hymns of merit in his:—

Songs of the Church, Halifax, printed for the Author, 1854. Other hymns from the same work are in C. U. All his hymns were "written amidst the various scenes of missionary life, and are intended for the private and domestic use of Christians in new countries deprived of all public worship," and are worthy of renewed attention. Dean Bullock also pub. *Practical Lectures upon the History of Joseph and his Brethren,* 1826.

Bulmer, Agnes, née Collinson, third daughter of Edward Collinson, b. in Lombard Street, London, Aug. 31, 1775, and married in 1793 to Mr. Joseph Bulmer. Her husband's death took place in 1828, and hers on the 30th Aug., 1837. She pub. in 1836, *Memoirs of Mrs. Mortimer;* in 1833, *Messiah's Kingdom,* a poem in 12 books; in addition to articles contributed to the *Youth's Instructor,* &c. Her *Scripture Histories* appeared posthumously in 1837-8, and her *Select Letters* were pub. in 1842, with an introduction and notes, by the Rev. W. M. Bunting; and her *Memoir* in 1837 by her sister. Mrs. Bulmer was a member of the Wesleyan Society. Her best known hymn, "Thou who hast in Zion laid," was written for the laying of the foundation stone of the Oxford Road Wesleyan Chapel, Manchester, July 11, 1825, and included in the *Supp.* to the *Wes. H. Bk.,* 1830, No. 737.

Bulmer, John, b. in Yorkshire in 1784, educated for the Congregational Ministry at the Rotherham (Masborough) Independent College, and successively pastor at Haverfordwest, Rugeley, Bristol, Newbury, and Langrove, near Ross. He d. in 1857. He composed a few hymns, and compiled:—

(1) *Hymns, Original and Select,* 1834; (2) *Hymns and Evangelical Songs for the use of Sunday Schools;* (3) *Original Hymns intended to be sung at the Public Meetings and other Services of Temperance Societies,* 1836; and (4) *Beauties of the Vicar of Llandovery: Light from the Welshman's Candle;* being trs. from

the Welsh of Poems by Rees Prichard (died 1644), (2nd ed., 1830). See **Welsh Hymnody.**

From his *Coll.* of 1834 the following are still in C. U.:—

1. **Lord of the vast creation.** *Lent.*
2. **To Thee in ages past.** *Public Worship.*
These hymns are in the *N. Cong. H. Bk.* and others.

Bunsen, Christian Carl Josias, Baron, Prussian Minister at Rome, 1823–1838; at Berne, 1839–1841; Ambassador to England, 1841–1854; was b. at Corbach in Waldeck, 25th August, 1791; d. at Bonn, November 28th, 1860. Having gained high honours in the Universities of Marburg and Göttingen, he began life as an assistant master in the Gymnasium of Göttingen, but soon quitted that post to prosecute the enquiries which he felt to be the true aim of his life, and for which he had already, at the age of 24, conceived the idea of a comprehensive plan of philological and historical research, culminating in a synthesis of philology, history and philosophy, with the application of that synthesis to religious and civil legislation. To the accomplishment of this youthful scheme it may truly be said that his whole life was dedicated; for though employed in the diplomatic service of his country for 37 years, he unremittingly carried on his labours as a scholar, and always regarded public questions under the aspect of their bearing on the moral and religious welfare of man, governing his publications by his convictions on these points. In the pursuit of the aims thus indicated, he studied successively the languages and antiquities of the Germanic, Indo-Persic, Semitic, and Egyptian peoples, the fruit of his investigations being embodied in his:—

(1) "*Description of Rome,*" 1819; (2) "*Egypt's Place in the World's History,*" 1848; (3) "*Hippolytus and his Age,*" 1852; (4) "*Outlines of a Philosophy of Universal History,*" 1854; (5) "*Signs of the Times,*" 1855; (6) "*God in History,*" 1857-58; and lastly his (8) "*Bibel-Werk,*" or Critical Text of the Bible, with commentaries, which he did not live to complete.

The titles of these writings will indicate the fact that the studies and employments which over came nearest to his heart lay in the direction of theology, believing as he did that the revivification of practical Christianity was the "essential condition of universal wellbeing"—of "the salvation of Church and State."

"It is my conviction," he says (1821, æt. 29), "that all communion essentially consists in a common belief in the facts of the redemption of the human race through Christ; but when . . . a congregation is to be thereby formed, three points must be considered: first, agreement by means of a theological expression of the points of faith; secondly, congregational discipline; thirdly, a common form of worship."

It was for the third of these that Bunsen felt himself especially called to labour; writing in 1821:—

"When I thought myself in my late illness on the brink of eternity . . . I enquired what I ought to make my calling if God should prolong my life . . . and upon my theological labours I rested as the quarter in which my calling was to be sought. My thoughts were bent principally on my liturgical enquiries."

In 1822 he composed the Liturgy still in use at the German Chapel on the Capitol, followed in 1833 by his *Versuch eines allgemeinen evangelischen Gesang- und Gebetbuchs,* containing 934 Hymns and 350 prayers. In Germany the tendency of the centuries that had elapsed since the great age of hymn-writers had been to adapt their language and modify their thoughts in accordance with modern taste till, as Bunsen says, "Almost everywhere do we find the admirable ancient hymns driven out of use by modern ones which are feeble and spiritless." Luther's asperities of diction and metre had to be softened down, in order to fit them to be sung in an age rejecting nearly all but iambic or trochaic verses, and moreover each government, sect, or school of opinion, thought themselves justified in remodelling the older National Hymnody according to their own ideas, till at length little remained of their pristine rugged glory, they were defaced past recognition.

Bunsen's object in his *Versuch* was to provide materials for a national hymn-book for the whole of Protestant Germany, irrespective of territorial, ecclesiastical or sectarian divisions. To this end he sought out the finest German hymns, and his selection includes a large proportion of the best hymns in the language with no limitations of party. The success of Bunsen's work in Germany at large was attested by the rapid sale of an enormous edition, but when a reprint was called for he published instead a smaller ed. of 440 hymns. The motive was his patriotic ambition to produce a handy volume like the English Book of Common Prayer, and he fondly hoped that when the volume was printed at the Rauhe Haus in 1846, it would speedily supplant the locally introduced *Gesangbücher* of the 18th and 19th centuries. This hymn-book has in fact been adopted for public worship by some individual congregations in Germany, and by many scattered throughout Australia, New Zealand, &c., but it never became a National Hymn-book. Bunsen was among the first to go back to the authors and their original texts, and the abridgments and alterations he made were done with tact and circumspection. Perhaps nothing, however, can better prove the high estimation in which Bunsen's first "epoch-making" work is held than the fact that his work of 1833 has been republished as:—

Allgemeines Evangelisches Gesang-und-Gebet-buch zum Kirchen-und-Hausgebrauch: In völlig neuer Bearbeitung von Albert Fischer. Gotha, F. A. Perthes, 1881.

and that this republication, or rather recast, was conducted by the first German hymnologist living. A parallel case of inability to command universal acceptance for public use on the one hand, and of renovating influence on national hymnody on the other, is that of Lord Selborne's *Book of Praise.* Before the date of its publication in 1862, little or no regard was paid to original texts. Since then, however, few collections have been published in Gt. Britain and America in which the principle laid down by him has not been followed with more or less fidelity.

But it is not Germany alone, or even perhaps most widely, that has profited by Bunsen's zeal for hymnology. Through the medium of translations such as those of Miss Catherine Winkworth, Mr. Massie, Miss Cox, and others, many German hymns are as familiar to English and American readers as to Germans. The *Lyra Germanica* (of which more than 30,000 copies have been sold in England and probably as many more in Ame-

rica) is a household book wherever English is spoken, and few, if any, collections of hymns that have appeared in England or America since its publication have been compiled without some hymns taken from the *Lyra.*

But no sketch of Bunsen would be complete without mentioning that he himself had no mean talent as a writer of sacred poems. Some of these pieces are given in his Biography, and one is noted under "O lux beata Trinitas." Perhaps the whole scope of Bunsen's life-work can scarcely be summed up better than in his own words written in 1817 [aet. 26].

"To study and then to set forth the consciousness of God in the mind of man, and that which, in and through that consciousness, he has accomplished, especially in language and religion."   [S. W.]

Bunting, William Maclardie, s. of Dr. Jabez Bunting, a well-known Wesleyan minister, was b. at Manchester, Nov. 23, 1805, and educated at the Wesleyan Schools at Woodhouse Grove, and Kingswood, and at St. Saviour's Grammar School, Southwark. In 1824 he entered the Wesleyan Ministry, and continued in active circuit work for twenty-five years. Failing health then compelled him to retire upon the Supernumerary list, when he took up his residence in London, and d. there on Nov. 13, 1866. In addition to editing the *Select Letters of Agnes Bulmer,* &c., 1842, and engaging in other literary labours, he contributed hymns to the *Methodist Magazine* (under the *nom de plume* of *Alec*) from time to time, and specially 43 to Dr. Leifchild's *Original Hymns,* 1842. Of these Dr. Leifchild rejected 8, and abbreviated 2. In 1842 these 10 hymns were pub. as *An Instrument of Ten Strings, strung in aid of the Wesleyan Missions, By Alec.* Other hymns by him were included in his *Memorials,* &c., pub. by the Rev. G. S. Rowe in 1870. Although a few of these hymns have come into C. U., they have failed as a whole to command public attention. Those in C. U. are :—

1. Blessed are the pure in heart, They have, &c. *Purity.*
2. Blest Spirit! from the Eternal Sire. *Holy Spirit.*
3. Dear is the day which God hath made. *Sunday.*
4. Father, our child we place. *Holy Baptism.*
5. Holy Spirit, pity me. *Lent.*
6. O blessed, blessed sounds of grace. *After Sermon.*
7. O crucified, triumphant Lord. *Holy Baptism.*
8. O God, how often hath Thine ear. *Renewing the Covenant.* Written in 1824, and given in the *Supp.* to the *Wes. H. Bk.,* 1830. This is the best known of his hymns.
9. Thou doest all things well. *God all in all.*

Most of these hymns are in the revised *Wes. H. Bk.,* 1875; Nos. 1-4 and 6 were in Dr. Leifchild's *Original Hymns,* 1842, and all are in the *Memorials,* 1870.   [J. J.]

Bunyan, John. This great allegorist cannot be included amongst hymn writers, except on the ground that the piece, "He that is down needs fear no fall," from pt. ii. of his *Pilgrim's Progress,* 1684, is given in a limited number of hymnals. The son of a mechanic, he was b. at Elstow, 1628 ; was a Baptist minister at Bedford ; and d. in London, Aug. 1688.

Bürde, Samuel Gottlieb, was b. Dec. 7, 1753, at Breslau, where his father was keeper of St. Barbara's Church. After studying law at the University of Halle, he was (1776-78) tutor and superintendent of a charity school at Breslau. He then became private secretary to the Cabinet minister' von Haugwitz, was for two years employed in the department of Forestry, and after being for some time secretary to the department of Finance at Breslau, was appointed member of the Aulic Council and Director of Chancery at Berlin, where he d. April 28, 1831 (*Koch*, vi. 319–322 ; *Allg. Deutsche Biog.*, iii. 581–82. *Fischer*, ii. 432, says he died at Breslau).

As a hymn-writer he was by some of his contemporaries reckoned nearly equal to Gellert, by others as superior. Of the some 100 hymns which he composed, the best appeared in his *Geistliche Poesieen*, Breslau, 1787, and his *Geistliche Gedichte*, Breslau, 1817. Five have been *tr.* into English. Those in C. U. are :—

i. Steil und dornicht ist der Pfad. [*Christian Warfare.*] 1st pub. 1787 as above, p. 24, in 5 st. of 6 l., entitled "The Lord's Warrior." Included, as No. 1908, in Knapp's *Ev. L. S.*, ed. 1865. *Tr.* as :—

1. Steep and thorny is the way To our home. A good and full *tr.* by Miss Cox in her *Sacred H. from the German*, 1841, p. 109. St. i.–iv., altered and adapted to St. Simon and St. Jude are No. 146 in Rorison's *Coll.*, 1851. Revised for *Lyra Eucharistica*, 1863, p. 207, and her *H. from the German*, 1864, p. 175.

2. Steep and thorny is the way Leading on. Good and full *tr.* contributed by Edward Jackson as No. 189 to Dr. Hook's *Church School H. Bk.*, 1850, and repeated as No. 319 in Mercer's *C. P. and H. Bk.*, 1855 (Ox. ed., No. 200), and in Robinson's *Parochial Psalter*, 1860 and 1869.

Other trs. are :—
(1) "Lo! steep and thorny is the road," by *Lady E. Fortescue*, 1843 (1847, p. 45). (2) "Steep and thorny is the way On to life," by *Dr. H. Mills*, 1845 (1856, p. 157).

ii. Wenn der Herr einst die Gefangnen. [*Consolation.*] Founded on Ps. cxxvi. 1787 as above, p. 61, entitled " Longing after the Liberty of the Children of God," in 3 st. of 8 l. In Knapp's *Ev. L. S.*, 1837, No. 2402 (1865, No. 2103). It is *tr.* as:—

When the Lord recalls the banish'd. A good and full *tr.* by Miss Winkworth in her *Lyra Ger.*, 2nd Series, 1858, p. 227, repeated in her *C. B. for England*, 1863, No. 199. Included in *Kennedy*, 1863, Flett's *Coll.*, Paisley, 1871, the *Ohio Luth. Hymnal*, 1880, and others.

His hymns not in English C. U. are :—
iii. Der Frühling ist erschienen. [*Spring.*] 1st pub. 1817 as above, p. 118, as No. 5 of the "Edifying Hymns for Country People," in 5 st. *Tr.* as " 'Tis Spring, the time of singing," by Miss Burlingham, in the *British Herald*, May, 1866, p. 264, repeated as No. 405 in Reid's *Praise Bk.*, 1872.
iv. Nicht mehr als meine Kräfte tragen. [*In Sickness.*] 1787 as above, p. 71, in 5 st. *Tr.* as "Not more than I have strength to bear," by *Miss Warner*, 1858 (1861, p. 478).
v. Wir wallen Pilger allzumal. [*Pilgrimage of Life.*] 1787 as above, p. 13, in 12 st. *Tr.* as "We are but pilgrims here below," by *Dr. H. Mills*, 1845 (1856, p. 162). [J. M.]

Burder, George, b. in London, June 5, 1752, and trained as an engraver. At the age of 24 he commenced preaching with the Calvinist Methodists, but subsequently joined the Congregationalists, and was pastor successively at Lancaster, Coventry, and Fetter Lane, London. He was one of the active founders of the Religious Tract, the London Missionary, and the British and Foreign Bible Societies,

and some time editor of the *Evangelical Magazine*. He d. May 29, 1832. His works include *Village Sermons*, 1794; *Sea Sermons*, 1821; *Cottage Sermons*, 1826, and others. He is known to hymnology by his *Collection of Hymns from various Authors, intended as a Supp. to Dr. Watts*, &c., 1784. (Preface dated Nov. 20, 1784.) It had attained to the 25th ed. in 1827. To this collection he contributed 4 hymns, the best known being, "Sweet the time, exceeding sweet" (q.v.), sometimes altered to "Great the joy when Christians meet." The remaining three, all from the 1st ed. 1784, are :—

1. Come, dear Desire of nations, come. *Missions.*
2. Come ye that know and fear the Lord. *Love of God.* In Dr. Hatfield's *Church H. Bk.*, N.Y., 1872, 5 st. out of 9 are given as No. 236.
3. Lord, solemnize our trifling minds. *Before Sermon.* Altered to "*Great God, impress* our trifling minds," in the *N. Cong.*, No. 786, &c.

Burder's *Coll.* is of importance in the history of Congregational hymnody. The 1st ed., 1784, contained 187 hymns; 2nd ed., 1784, 211 ; 9th ed., 1803, 257 hymns; 18th ed., 1820, 277; and the last, the 25th ed., 1827, 294. His son, Henry Foster Burder, pub. a *Coll. of Ps. & Hys.*, 1826; and another son, the Rev. John Burder, also compiled a *Coll.* pub. without date. To the 18th ed., 1820, of G. Burder's *Coll.*, the wife of his son H. F. Burder contributed "And will the God Who reigns on high" (*Sunday Schools*), under the signature "S. M. Burder" [Sophia Maria].   [J. J.]

Burgess, Daniel, s. of a clergyman, b. at Collingbourne-Ducis, Wiltshire, 1645 (some accounts say 1647), was educated at Oxford, where he became a Fellow. Eventually he married, and losing his Fellowship, was introduced to the Earl of Cork, who appointed him his chaplain and gave him an incumbency in Ireland. Owing to his undoubted talent and agreeable manner he appears to have met with much success, until, through entertaining some new and strangely wild notions, he lost both the favour of the Earl of Cork and the living. He returned to London, and being well received by certain Dissenting ministers, joined their communion, and made known his secession from the Church. However, the change in his conduct was more marked than ever, and ultimately he ceased to be a credit to himself or his profession ; d. 1713. In the year following appeared his

Psalms and Hymns and Spiritual Songs, by the late Rev. Mr. Daniel Burgess, Minister of the Gospel. This work was edited by John Billingsley, and for a time attracted some attention.   [J. T. B.]

Burgess, George, D.D. Bishop Burgess was b. at Providence, Rhode Island, Oct. 31, 1809, and graduated at Brown University, 1826, where he was for some time a tutor. After studying for two years in Germany, he took Holy Orders, and in 1834 became Rector of Christ Church, Hartford. In 1847 he was consecrated Bishop of Maine, and also entered upon the Rectory of Christ Church, Gardiner. He d. in Haiti, April 3, 1866. His *Life* was pub. by his brother in 1869. His works include *The Book of Psalms translated into English Verse*, 1839 ; *The American Metrical Psalter*, N. Y., 1864 ; and *Poems*, Hartford, 1868. His *Psalms and Hymns in use are :—*

1. Lord, in Thy Name we spread the sail. *Sailor's Hymn.* This hymn is included in his *Poems*, 1868, p. 268, but is of unknown date and origin. The hymn, "While o'er the deep Thy servants sail," is an altered form of this hymn to be sung on behalf of sailors. It was apparently rewritten for the Connecticut *Psalms and Hymns*, 1845.

2. The harvest dawn is near. *Ps. cxxvi.* From his version of Ps. cxxvi., *Book of Psalms*, &c., 1839, beginning with st. v. Also his *Amer. Met. Psalter*, p. 250. It is widely used.

3. The floods, O Lord, lift up their voice. From *Ps. xciii.* in his *Book of Psalms*, 1839, st. iii., found in his *Amer. Met. Psalter*, p. 179.

4. When forth from Egypt's trembling strand. *Ps. cxiv.* From his *Book of Psalms*, 1839, and *Psalter*, 1864. It has been included in Spurgeon's *O. O. H. Bk.*, 1866.

Of these hymns Nos. 1 and 2 are found in almost every recent American collection but that of the Protestant Episcopal Church.

[F. M. B.]

Burgess, Henry, LL.D., was b. Jan. 30, 1808, and educated at a Dissenting College at Stepney. After labouring as a Nonconformist Minister for several years, he was ordained, in 1850, by the Bp. of Manchester, and officiated for some time in that diocese. In 1861 he was preferred to Whittlesey Vicarage, Cambridgeshire, where he d. Feb. 10, 1886. He was LL.D. of the University of Glasgow, and PH.D. of the University of Göttingen. Of his numerous works that which is associated with hymnology is :—

Select Metrical Hymns and Homilies of Ephraem Syrus. Translated from the original Syriac, with an Introduction, and Historical and Philological Notes. London: R. B. Blackadder, 1853.

These *trs.*, although unsuited for congregational use, because of the rugged blank verse form given them by Dr. Burgess, may yet be adapted, and with success, for C. U.

Buried beneath the yielding wave. *B. Beddome.* [*Holy Baptism.*] Pub. from Beddome's MSS. in his posthumous *Hymns*, &c., 1817, No. 603, in 5 st. of 4 l., from whence it has passed into numerous collections in G. Britain and America. Orig. text in Spurgeon's *O. O. H. Bk.*, No. 925. In some American collections it is dated 1787 in error.

Buried in baptism with our Lord. [*Holy Baptism.*] Two centos beginning with this first line are in C. U. They are :—

1. Hymn No. 942 in the Moravian *Liturgy and Hymns*, 1849, in 2 st. of 4 l., of which st. i. is from J. Hart's *Supp. Hymns*, &c., 1762, No. 76, st. i. ; and st. ii. is from the *Moravian H. Bk.*, 1789, No. 544.
2. In the American *Service of Song for Baptist Churches*, Boston, 1871, No. 831 is thus composed :— st. i., ii. from Hart's hymn as above: st. iii., the second stanza of the Moravian cento, slightly altered.

Buried in shadows of the night. *I. Watts.* [*Christ our Wisdom.*] 1st pub. in his *Hymns & S. Songs*, 1709, Bk. i., No. 97, in 5 st. of 4 l., and headed, "Christ our Wisdom, Righteousness," &c., 1 Cor. i. 30. In J. Wesley's *Ps. & Hys.*, Charlestown, South Carolina, 1736-7, No. 36, it was given with the omission of st. iii. This form was repeated with alterations in Toplady's *Ps. & Hys.*, 1776, No. 306, and others. It is found in several modern collections both in G. Britain and America.

Burleigh, William Henry, an active reformer and member of the Unitarian body, was b. at Woodstock, Connecticut, Feb. 12, 1812, and brought up on a farm at Stainfield in the same state. In 1837 he went to Pittsburg, Pennsylvania, where, having been previously apprenticed to the printing trade, he pub. the *Christian Witness* and *Temperance Banner*. In 1843 he undertook the duties of editor of the *Christian Freeman*, at Hartford. From 1849 to 1855 he was agent of the New York State Temperance Society; and from 1855 to 1870 Harbour Master at New York. Died at Brooklyn, March 18, 1871. His poetical pieces and hymns were contributed to various periodicals and journals. Many of these were collected and published as *Poems*, Phila. in 1841. This volume was enlarged by additional pieces, and republished by his widow, in 1871. The dates of these hymns and poems are most difficult to determine. Where possible they are given in detail. It is somewhat curious that Burleigh's hymns are generally more extensively used in England than at home. The introduction of some of his best compositions into the English collections is due to the *Lyra Sac. Amer.*, whence they were mostly taken by the compilers. Those in use in G. Britain and America are :—

1. Fades from the west the farewell light. *Night.* This poem, entitled "A Psalm of Night," is given in his *Poems*, N. Y., 1871, pp. 275-6. Although not in the 1st ed. of his *Poems*, 1841, it was in C. U. as early as 1844. It is in 5 st. of 8 l. From it the following centos have come into C. U. :—
(1) "Day unto day uttereth speech." This is composed of st. iii.-v., and was given in the *Christian Hys.* of the Cheshire Pastoral Association (Amer. Unitarian), 1844, as an "Evening Hymn."
(2) "O Holy Father, mid the calm." This cento in Longfellow and Johnson's *Bk. of Hys.*, 1846, and their *Hys. of the Spirit*, 1864, &c., is composed of st. iv.-v.
(3) "Not only doth the voiceful day," No. 324 in Longfellow and Johnson's *Hys. of the Spirit*, 1864, is composed of st. ii.-iii. Another arrangement beginning with the same stanza is in the *Lyra Sac. Amer.*, p. 41.
(4) "The brightening dawn and voiceful day." In the *Hymnary* (Lond.), 1872, is altered from the *Lyra Sac. Amer.* as above, with the addition of a doxology.
In and through these various forms, the use of this hymn is very extensive.

2. Father, beneath Thy sheltering wing. *Trust and Peace.* Appeared in Longfellow and Johnson's *Hys. of the Spirit*, 1864, No. 471, in 4 st. of 4 l. It is given in many American collections, and in the *Bap. Hyl.*, 1879, Horder's *Cong. Hys.*, 1884, and others in G. Britain. Orig. text in *Lyra Sac. Amer.*, p. 39, with "*that*" for "which" in st. ii. l. 4.

3. For the dear love that kept us through the night. *Morning.* From *Poems*, 1871, into Horder's *Cong. Hymns*, 1884.

4. From profoundest depths of tribulation. *Lent.* This appeared in the *Supp.* to Hedge and Huntington's *Hymns*, &c. (Unitarian), 1853, No 843.

5. Lead us, O Father, in the paths of peace. *Divine Guidance.* No. 32 of the *Lyra Sac. Amer.*, in 4 st. of 4 l., being "A Prayer for Guidance." With English compilers this hymn ranks amongst Burleigh's productions next in popularity to No. 8, and is found in most of the collections there named.

6. Not in vain I poured my supplication. *Lent.* This is a continuation of the same thought as No. 4 preceding, and follows it in the same *Supp.*

7. O deem not that earth's crowning bliss. *Mourning.* This passed from the *Lyra Sacra Amer.*, 1868, into the Eng. *Bap. Hymnal*, 1879; Horder's *Cong. Hys.*, 1884, and others. It is in his *Poems*, 1871, p. 258. The hymn, "From lips divine, like healing balm," in the Methodist Episcopal *Hymnal*, N. Y., 1878, is a cento from this hymn.

8. Still will we trust though earth seems dark and dreary. *Faith.* Appeared in the *Lyra Sac. Amer.*, 1868, pp. 43–44, in 5 st. of 4 l. This is the most widely adopted of this author's hymns by the English compilers. It is given in some of the best collections, as the *N. Cong.*, *Thring, Horder*, the *Bap. Hymnal, Allon*, &c.

9. There is a beautiful land by the spoiler untrod. *Heaven.* Dr. Cleveland (*Lyra Sac. Amer.*, 1868, p. 298) says, "This piece was first published in the *Independent*, Jan. 18, 1866."

10. They who have kept their spirit's virgin whiteness. *Purity.* In *Lyra Sac. Amer.*, 1868, p. 46.

11. Thou Who look'st with pitying eye. *Lent.* In *Lyra Sac. Amer.*, 1868, p. 47.

12. Through the changes of the day. *Evening.* From his *Poems*, 1841. It is given in the *Lyra Sac. Amer.*, p. 50, the S. P. C. K. *Ps. and Hys.*, 1852, Thring's *Coll.*, and others.

13. We ask not that our path be always bright. *Trust in God.* From the *Lyra Sac. Amer.*, 1868, into Horder's *Cong. Hys.*, 1884.

14. When gladness gilds our prosperous day. *Good in all.* Also from *Lyra Sac. Amer.* into Horder's *Cong. Hys.*, 1884.

It has been already noted that Burleigh's hymns have a more extended use in G. Brit. than in his own country. The foregoing notes will also show that his productions are more widely known and used outside of his own denomination than by his own people. Concerning the hymns included in the *Lyra Sac. Amer.*, Dr. Cleveland, the editor, says, "Most of these beautiful hymns of Mr. Burleigh's were given to me in MS. by the author," but he does not indicate what was new and what was old.　　　　　　　　　　[J. J.]

Burmeister, Franz Joachim, was a native of Lüneburg. He was ordained at Celle, May 4, 1670, and instituted as diaconus of St. Michael's Church, Lüneburg, July 10, 1670. This post he held till his death at Lüneburg, April 21, 1672. He was a friend of Rist, who crowned him as a poet in 1659, and in 1660 received him into his order of Elbe Swans. (*Koch*, iii. 448–450: *Allg. Deutsche Biog.*, iii. 628; MS. from Seminarlehrer Bode, Lüneburg.) His hymns were mostly contributed to the musical works of J. R. Ahle of Mühlhausen, 14 being set to music and pub. by Ahle in 1662, at Mühlhausen, as *Neue geistliche auff die hohen Festtage durchs gantze Jahr gerichtete Andachten.* Those *tr.* into English are:—

i. **Du keusche Seele du.** [*Visitation to Elisabeth.*] 1st pub. 1662 as above, No. 13 in 6 st. of 8 l., entitled on the "Festival of Mary's Visitation. On her visitation journey." As the hymn is very rare, the first and last sts. are here quoted from a copy kindly sent from Mühlhausen:—

i.
Du keusche Seele du,
Der Weiber Licht und Sonne,
Und deines Joseph's Wonne
Gehst nach Elisabethen zu,

Deinen Glauben dort zu stärken
An des Allerhöchsten Werken.

vi.
Die Welt ist solch ein Ort,
Darin wir Gastfrist pflegen;
Bald muss mein Leib sich legen,
Dann geht der Geist von hinnen fort,
Jesus woll' im Tod' und Leben
Mir sich zum Gefährten geben.

The only *tr.* in C. U. is:—

Thou virgin soul! O thou. By Miss Wink·worth in her *C. B. for England*, 1863, No. 82.

ii. **Was soll ich, liebstes Kind.** [*Epiphany.*] 1st pub., 1662, as above, No. 4, in 4 st. of 4 l., entitled "On the Festival of the Holy Three Kings." In the Berlin *G. L. S.*, ed. 1863, No. 212. *Tr.* as:—

O Blessed Babe divine. A good and full *tr.* by Dr. Kennedy as No. 194, in his *Hymno. Christ.*, 1863.　　　　　　　　　　　　　　[J. M.]

Burnham, Richard, b. 1749, d. 1810, was for many years pastor of a Baptist Church in London, first in Little Chapel Street, and afterwards in Grafton Street, Soho. He is said to have been an excellent preacher. His hymns, 452 in all, were pub. as follows:—

New Hymns on Divers Subjects, Lond., Gilbert and Plummer, 1783. This contained 141 hymns. A 2nd ed. with 74 additional hymns as *New Hymns on Various Subjects* (same publishers), 1785. To this was added *New Hymns on Divine Love, chiefly designed for Love Feasts or Christian Societies* (25 hymns and 2 poetical pieces), Lond., W. Smith, but no date (cir. 1787). The 3rd ed. of the *Hymns*, &c., is dated 1794, the 4th 1796, and the 5th 1803. This last contains 452 hymns. In addition 3 hymns were printed at the end of a Sermon on *Believer's Baptism*, 1805, and many others on leaflets which have not been reprinted.

Burnham's hymns rank with the most intensely Calvinistic in the English language, and have been much used by congregations of Calvinistic sentiments. In the last edition of Gadsby's *Sel.* there are 20; in Denham's *Sel.* 82; and in Snepp's *Songs of G. & G.* 10. His best known hymns are, "Jesus! Thou art the sinner's Friend," and "O glorious God of grace." The following, from the editions of his *Hymns*, &c., indicated in brackets, are still in C. U.:—

1. *Free grace, melodious sound* [1794]. *Grace.*
2. *God in Three appears all glorious* [1796]. *H. Trinity.*
3. *Great Jehovah's love endureth* [1794]. *God unchangeable.*
4. *How truly glorious is the love* [1803]. *Love of God.* In Snepp's *S. of G. & G.*, 1872, this is altered by Miss Havergal.
5. *Jesus draws the chosen race* [1794]. *Election.*
6. *Love will I ever sing* [1796]. *Love of God.*
7. *Now I know the great Redeemer* [1794]. *The Advocate.*
8. *The goodness of our glorious God* [1794]. *Divine Goodness.*
9. *The people of the Lord were chosen*, &c. [1796]. *Election.*
10. *Who can e'er fathom God's rich love* [1803]. *Love of God.*　　　　　　　　　　　　　[W. R. S.]

Burns, Dawson, D.D., b. in 1828, in Southwark, London, is the second s. of Dr. Jabez Burns. He entered the ministry among the General Baptists in 1851, and for a number of years was his father's colleague at Church Street Chapel, Edgware Road. He is now without pastoral charge, and devotes himself chiefly to literary and public work in connection with the Temperance Reformation. He is the author of several important works on the Temperance question, and of numerous contributions to periodicals and public congresses. In 1884 he published *Rays of Sacred*

Song for the Church and Home. Besides Scripture Studies and other poems, it contains 39 hymns for Public Worship. One of these, "Gladsome we hail this day's return" (*Reunion*), appeared in 1879 in the *Bap. Hymnal*, and has been very frequently used on anniversary occasions. Others are of sufficient merit to ensure their adoption as they become known. In 1882 Dr. Burns received the honorary degree of D.D. from Bates College, Maine, U.S.　　　　　　　　　　[W. R. S.]

Burns, James Drummond, M.A., was b. at Edinburgh, February 18, 1823. He studied and graduated M.A. at the University of Edinburgh. In 1845 he became Free Church minister of Dunblane, but resigned through failing health, in 1848, and took charge of the Presbyterian Church at Funchal, Madeira. In 1855 he became minister of Hampstead Presbyterian Church, London. Died at Mentone, Nov. 27, 1864, and was buried in Highgate Cemetery, London. His hymns appeared in :—

(1) *The Vision of Prophecy : and other Poems* (Edin., Edmonston and Douglas). This was originally published in 1854, and enlarged in 1858. The Poems are distinguished by vivid colouring and poetic imagination, along with directness, delicacy of execution, pensive sweetness, and tenderness. They have never however become widely popular. Included are 29 "Hymns and Meditations," some of which rank among the very best of our modern hymns for beauty, simplicity of diction, and depth of religious feeling. (2) *The Evening Hymn* (Lond., T. Nelson & Sons), 1857. This consists of an original hymn and an original prayer for every evening in the month—31 in all. The Hymns and Prayers alike are characterised by reverence, beauty, simplicity, and pathos. Some of the hymns in this volume are now well known; e.g. "Still with Thee, O my God," "Hushed was the evening hymn," "As helpless as a child who clings." (3) *Memoir and Remains of the late Rev. James D. Burns, M.A., of Hampstead. By the late Rev. James Hamilton, D.D.* (Lond., J. Nisbet & Co.), 1869. Besides 13 Sermons and the Memoir, this work includes 40 "Hymns and Miscellaneous Pieces." A number of these had appeared in periodicals. Some of them are very good though not equal to those previously published. Also 39 Translations of German Hymns, which appeared in the *Family Treasury,* &c., are rendered exactly in the metres of the originals and many had not previously been translated. The translations are generally very good. (4) Burns also wrote the article *Hymn* in the 8th ed. of the *Ency. Brit.*　　　　　　　　　[J. M.]

Burns, Robert. This poet's life had little in common with hymnology, although some of his pieces, in common with a few of Byron's, have come into use in G. Britain and America. His life, from his birth in the parish of Alloway, near Ayr, Jan. 25, 1759, to his death, at Dumfries, July 21, 1796, was one of varying lights and shadows, and has been told elsewhere, frequently and eloquently. It remains for us only to name his sacred pieces, their origin, and their use. Those in C. U. are :—

1. **O Thou great Being! What Thou art.** *Lent.* Burns's account of this piece as entered in his Commonplace Book, under the date of "March, 1784," is :—"There was a certain period of my life that my spirit was broken by repeated losses and disasters, which threatened, and indeed effected, the utter ruin of my fortune. My body, too, was attacked by that most dreadful distemper a hypochondria, or confirmed melancholy. In this wretched state, the recollection of which makes me shudder, I hung my harp on the willow-trees, except in some lucid intervals, in one of which I composed the following, 'Oh, Thou Great Being! what Thou art, &c.' " Chambers says in his *Life and Works of Burns,* 1850 (Library ed., 1856), vol. i., p. 57, that financial and physical downfall was in 1781, when the poet was 23. At the same time he wrote, "Winter, a Dirge." From the latter the hymn :—

2. **Thou Power Supreme, Whose mighty scheme,** *Trust in God,* is taken. The second piece was pub. in his *Poems,* Kilmarnock, 1786, and the first in *Poems,* Edinburgh, 1787. Orig. text in Chambers's Life, vol. i. pp. 57–58. The title of the first is "A Prayer, written under the pressure of violent anguish."

3. **O Thou unknown, Almighty Cause.** *Death anticipated.* This was written at the age of 26, during an illness in the summer of 1784. In his Commonplace Book he calls it, "A Prayer when fainting fits and other alarming symptoms of a pleurisy, or some other dangerous disorder which still threatens me, first put nature on the alarm." Under the title "A Prayer in the prospect of death," it was included in his *Poems,* Kilmarnock, 1786.

4. **The [that] man in life wherever placed.** *Ps. i.*

5. **O Thou, the first, the greatest Friend.** *Ps. xix.* Chambers (*Life,* vol. i. pp. 86–87) has given these two Psalm versions to the same date as No. 3, and attributes them to the same cause. They were pub. in the Edinburgh ed. of his *Poems,* 1787. Orig. text in *Life, &c.,* vol. i. pp. 86–87.

These hymns were all included in Dr. Martineau's *Hymns,* &c., 1840, and are also found in other and later collections both in G. Brit. and America.　　　　　　　[J. J.]

Burton, John, b. 1773, in Nottingham, where he resided until 1813, when he removed to Leicester, at which town he died in 1822. He was a Baptist, a very earnest S. School teacher, and one of the compilers of the *Nottingham S. S. U. H. Bk.,* 1812. This book reached the 20th ed. in 1861. The 1st ed. contains 43 hymns which have his signature. He is known almost exclusively by one hymn, "Holy Bible, book divine" (q.v.). He was also author of *The Youth's Monitor in Verse,* a series of *Little Tales, Emblems, Poems and Songs* (1803); of the *Young Plantation, in verse; The Shrubbery,* and other similar productions for the young. Robert Hall wrote a recommendatory preface to one of his works.

[W. R. S.]

Burton, John, jun., a popular hymn-writer for children, was b. July 23, 1803, at Stratford in Essex, in which place he carried on business as a cooper for about 50 years. He d. in 1877. Mr. Burton was a member of the Congregational body, and a Deacon of the Chapel where he attended. His contributions to hymnody began in 1822, when he sent his first production to the *Evangelical Magazine.* He continued to contribute to that and other periodicals for many years, his signature in the former being "*Essex,* J. B.," and in the *Child's Companion* "J. B. *Essex.*" His publications are :—

(1) *One Hundred Original Hymns for the Young,* 1850; (2) *Hymns for Little Children,* 1851; (3) *The Child-Life of David ;* (4) *The Book of Psalms in English Verse,* 1871; (5) *Scripture Characters in Verse,* &c.

His *Hymns for Little Children,* containing 54 pieces, has been republished in Philadelphia, U.S.A., as *My Own Hymn Book.* He also contributed to the *Union H. Bk. for Scholars,* 1840. Some of his hymns have attained a measure of popularity, including "O Thou that hearest prayer," "Come, let us sing our Maker's praise," and many others. In addition, the following are also in C. U. :—

1. **Children who are gone to glory.** *Saints' days.*

2. **Children, you have gone astray.** *Invitation.* Pub. in the *Child's Companion,* April, 1834, and his *One Hundred Hymns,* 1850, &c.

3. **Come, let us sing our Maker's praise.** *For Orphans.* In his *One Hundred Hys.,* 1850, No. 86, in 6 st. of 4 l.

4. **Father of mercies, hear ; On us,** &c. *Living*

influence implored. In his *One Hundred Hys.*, 1850, No. 97, in 6 st. of 4 l.: and partly re-written in 2 st. of 8 l. in *Kennedy*, 1863, No. 1209, beginning: "Father of mercies, hear *The song Thy children raise.*

5. **God is love, delightful truth.** *Love of God.* Pub. in the *Child's Companion*, Aug., 1835, and again in his *One Hundred Hys.*, 1850, No. 20, in 5 st. of 4 l. It is given in the *Silver St. S. S. H. Bk.*, 1880.

6. **Happy would it be for me.** *Early Piety.*

7. **Hark! a still small voice is heard.** *Christ's love for Children.* This appeared in the *Child's Companion*, July, 1836, and the revised ed. of the *Union H. Bk. for Scholars*, 1840; and again in his *One Hundred Hys.*, &c., 1850, No. 14, in 4 st. of 6 l. It is in various collections, including the *Meth. S. S. H. Bk.*, 1879, and others.

8. **Heavenly Father, we draw near Thee.** *Sunday Schools.* Pub. in his *One Hundred Hys.*, 1850, &c.

9. **I often say my prayers.** *Prayer.* Also from the *Union H. Bk.*, 1840; into Major's *Bk. of Praise*, &c.

10. **None is like God, who reigns above.** *Omnipresence.* Dated 1849, and given in his *One Hundred Hys.*, No. 4, in 5 st. of 4 l. It is reprinted in several school collections, as Stevenson's *School Hymnal*, 1880, No. 139.

11. **Pilgrims we are and strangers.** *Life a Pilgrimage.* From the *Evangelical Mag.*, 1829, 5 st. of 8 l., commencing "Now let our praise be given," and headed "The Pilgrim's Song," into the Bap. *Ps. & Hys.*, 1858, No. 553, in 4 st. of 8 l., st. i. being omitted.

12. **Remember thy Creator now.** *Early Piety.* From the *Child's Companion*, Sept. 1833, into his *One Hundred Hys.*, 1850, and the *Meth. S. S. H. Bk.*, No. 243.

13. **Saviour, while my heart is tender.** *Early Piety.* Also from the *One Hundred Hys.* It is in the Bap. *Hymnal*, 1879; Horder's *Cong. Hys.*, 1884; and others.

14. **That kind eye which cannot sleep.** *Omniscience.* But little known.

15. **The Lord attends when children pray.** *Prayer.* 1st printed in the *Child's Companion*, July, 1835, and again in Dec. 1837, and in the revised ed. of the *Union H. Bk.*, 1840; and his *One Hundred Hys.*, 1850, No. 31, in 5 st. of 4 l. It is in several collections including Dr. Allon's *Children's Worship*, 1878, &c.

16. **Though we are young our sins are great.** *Lent.* In the revised ed. of the *Union H. Bk.*, 1840; and his *One Hundred Hys.*, 1850 (in the latter as "Though I am," &c.), No. 9, in 6 st. of 4 l. It is included in Major's *Bk. of Praise*, &c.

17. **We do not love Thee as we ought.** *Lent.* In the *Meth. S. S. H. Bk.*, 1879, No. 286.

18. **Why did Jesus come from heaven?** *Passiontide.* From his *One Hundred Hys.*, 1850, No. 61, in 4 st. of 6 l., into Major's *Bk. of Praise.*

19. **Why should we spend our youthful days?** *Youthful Piety.* Printed in the *Child's Companion*, May, 1835, in his *One Hundred Hys.*, 1850, and as No. 252 in the *Meth. S. S. H. Bk.*, 1879.   [J. J.]

Butcher, Edmund, b. at Colchester, Essex, in 1757, and brought up as a linen-draper. After undergoing a preliminary training for the Unitarian Ministry, he was appointed to the charge of Leather Lane Chapel, Holborn, in 1789. From thence he removed to Sidbury Vale, Sidmouth, in 1798. Died April 14, 1822. Memoir in the *Christian Moderator*, 1827. His works include *Picture of Sidmouth; Tour through various parts of England; Sermons, to which are added suitable Hymns*, 1798; and the *Substance of the Holy Scriptures Methodized*, 1801. His hymns were given in the two latter works, in the *Protestant Dissenters' Magazine* (of which he was some time editor); in Kippis's *Collection*, 1795; the *Christian Guardian*, 1802–1808; Aspland's *Sel.*, 1810; and from his MSS. in Howse's *Selection of Hymns and Psalms*, 1837. They number 116 in all; but few, however, have attained to any position in modern hymnals. These include the following:

1. **Blest is the man that [who] fears the Lord.** *Ps. cxii.* Pub. in the Exeter Unitarian *Coll.*, 1812, in 5 st. of 4 l. It is in C. U. in G. Britain and America.

2. **Father of all, where shall we find?** *D. Worship.* In Dr. Martineau's *Hys.*, 1840, &c.

3. **Great God, as seasons disappear.** *Harvest.* This is the most popular of his hymns. It is annotated under its first line.

4. **Hosanna! let us join to sing.** *Resurrection.* Contributed to Aspland's *Sel.*, 1810, No. 290; and repeated in Dr. Martineau's *Hys.*, 1840, &c.

5. **With deepest reverence at Thy throne.** *God's Unsearchableness.* This is in American C. U. as in *Laudes Domini*, 1884, No. 248. It was contributed to Aspland's *Sel.*, 1810, No. 146.   [J. J.]

Βυθὸς ἁμαρτημάτων. *St. Joseph of the Studium.* This is a portion from the *Triodion* of the Canon at Lauds for the Sunday of the Prodigal Son, answering to Septuagesima of the Anglican Church, and now in use in the Greek Church. The Canon was written about the middle of the ninth century. Dr. Neale's *tr.* of Odes vii. and viii., Trop. 2, 3, in his *Hymns of the E. C.*, is thus introduced:—

"The Sunday before Septuagesima, and Septuagesima itself, are, respectively, in the Greek Church, the Sunday of the Pharisee and Publican, and the Sunday of the Prodigal Son, those parables forming the gospel for the day, and serving for the keynote to the Offices."

Dr. Neale's translation, "The abyss of many a former sin," is in 5 st. of 6 l. The foregoing note shows the appropriateness of the Odes to the service, specially Dr. Neale's st. iv. (*H. E. C.*, 1862, p. 128). In 1872 this *tr.* was given in the *Hymnary*, No. 217, as, "The deep of many a former sin."   [J. J.]

Butterworth, Joseph Henry, M.A., of Exeter College, Oxford, graduated B.A. in 1836. On taking Holy Orders he was successively Curate and Vicar of Stapleton, near Bristol, 1846–69, and Incumbent of St. Paul's, Cannes, 1870. Mr. Butterworth's hymns were contributed to the 1st ed. of Chope's *Hymnal*, 1857. They include a few *trs.* and the following original hymns:—

1. **Spirit of Wisdom! guide Thine own.** *Confirmation.*

2. **Thou, Lord, Who know'st the hearts of men.** *St. Thomas.*   [J. J.]

By Christ redeemed, in Christ restored. *G. Rawson.* [*Holy Communion.*] Written in 1857 for, and 1st pub. in, the Bap. *Ps. and Hys.*, 1858, No. 741, in 6 st. of 4 l., and appointed for "The Lord's Supper." It is a hymn of more than usual excellence, and has attained to a greater position in modern hymnals than any other of the author's numerous compositions. The text was revised by the author for his *Hymns*, 1876, No. xxxv. Orig. text, Bap. *Ps. and Hys.*, 1858. In Thring's *Coll.*, 1882, st. iv., l. 3, is changed from "By one blest chain of loving rite," to "*The shame! the glory! by this Rite.*" The greatest alterations, however, are found in the S. P. C. K. *Church Hymns*, 1871, No. 205, where in addition to minor alterations, including the opening line to:—"By Christ redeemed, *to God* restored," we have the following lines:—

"His body broken in our stead,
 Is here, in this memorial bread;
 And so our feeble love is fed,
   Until He come!

"His fearful drops of agony,
 His life-blood shed for us we see:
 The wine shall tell the mystery,
   Until He come!"

transmuted into the weak stanza:

" His Body slain upon the tree,
 His Life-blood, shed for us, we see;
 Thus faith shall read the mystery,
  Until He come."

It is but just to add, however, that " They were compressed into one verse with considerable reluctance by the editors, with Mr. Rawson's kind permission, in deference to the judgment of others." (Notes on *Church Hymns*, folio ed., p. xlix.) The American use of this hymn in its original, or a slightly altered form, is very extensive. [J. J.]

By cool Siloam's shady fountain [rill]. *Bp. R. Heber*. [*Epiphany*.] In its original form as " By cool Siloam's shady *fountain*," this hymn was given in the April No. of the *Christian Observer*, 1812. It was subsequently rewritten in c. m. as " By cool Siloam's shady *rill*," and pub. in his posthumous *Hymns*, &c., 1827, in 6 st. of 4 l., for the 1st Sunday after the Epiphany. From the *Hymns*, it has passed into a great number of hymnals both in G. Britain and America, sometimes in full, and again with the omission of one or more stanzas, and is most popular as a children's hymn. Authorized text in Stevenson's *Hys. for Ch. & Home*, 1873. [J. J.]

By faith in Christ I walk with God. *J. Newton.* [*Faith.*] A second hymn on " Walking with God," Gen. v. 24 (the first being Cowper's " O for a closer walk with God "), given in the *Olney Hymns*, 1779, No. 4, in 7 st. of 6 l. It is found in a few collections both in G. Britain and America, including the *Westminster Abbey H. Bk.*, 1883 ; the Amer. Bap. *Service of Song*, 1871, &c.

By faith the upper choir we meet. *C. Wesley.* [*Praise to Christ.*] This hymn is No. 191 in the *Church Pastorals*, Boston, U. S. A., 1864, and is composed of st. iii., iv. of " A thousand oracles divine " (q.v.).

By the picture of Thy passion. [*Passiontide.*] *C. Wesley.* 1st pub. in the Wesley *Hymns on the Lord's Supper*, 1745, No. 87, in 8 st. of 3 l. In 1867 it was included in the *People's H.*, No. 471, with the alteration in st. iii. l. 3 of " Thy blood's appealing," to " Thy *Blood* appealing." In the *Hymnary*, 1872, it begins with st. ii., " Jesu, let Thy sufferings ease me," and is appointed for Fridays throughout the year. Orig. text, *P. Works*, 1868-72, vol. iii. p. 277.

By Thy victorious hand struck down. *S. Browne.* [*Lent.*] This cento, as given in Spurgeon's *O. O. H. Bk.*, 1866, No. 570, is composed of stanzas from various hymns in S. Browne's *Hymns and Spiritual Songs*, 1720, as follows:—st. i. from No. 10; ii. from No. 9; iii. from No. 13; iv. from No. 11; v. and vi. from No. 16. It is a most successful arrangement of the stanzas selected, and well adapted to its purpose.

Byles, Mather, D.D., b. 1706, educated at Harvard, 1725, d. 1788. He was an eminent Congregational Minister of Boston, and, for his time and place, an elegant scholar. He corresponded with, and was well thought of by the English wits and literati. His Toryism brought him into trouble at the Revolution, causing him, in his own words, to be " guarded, reguarded, and disregarded."

His *Sermons* were pub. at various dates from 1729 to 1771, and his *Poems* in 1727, 1736, and 1744. Of the *Appendix* to *Tate and Brady*, pub. by S. Kneeland in 1760, he edited hymns 77 to 100 inclusive, of which hymns 78, 79, and 80 seem to be his own. Part of No. 78, beginning with st. vii., " When wild confusion wrecks the air," is a Judgment hymn, and has been included in Belknap's *Selection*, 1795, and later in the *Plymouth Coll.*, 1855, No. 1111, the *Bap. Praise Book*, 1871, and others. His hymns are unknown to English collections. [F. M. B.]

Byrom, John, M.A., F.R.S., b. at Manchester, Feb. 29, 1691, baptized the same day, and educated at Merchant Taylors' School, and Trinity College, Cambridge, where he graduated B.A. 1711 ; M.A. 1715. He was elected a Fellow of his College in 1714. After studying medicine for a time at Montpellier, he returned to London, and earned his livelihood by teaching shorthand. Elected F.R.S. in 1724, and succeeded to the family estates about the same time. He d. Sept. 28, 1763. His *Poems* were first pub. in 1773, in two vols. In 1814 a more complete edition was issued by Nichols, of Leeds. From these *Poems* less than half a dozen hymns have come into common use. One of these, however, has a reputation which has extended to all English-speaking countries. We refer to his " Christians, awake ! " (q.v.). His hymn, " My spirit longeth for Thee," is also worthy of attention.
  [J. J.]

Byron, George Gordon Noel, Lord, b. in London, Jan. 22, 1788, d. at Missolonghi, April 19, 1824. Lord Byron's name is associated with hymnody through a few pieces from his *Hebrew Melodies*, 1815, being in use in a limited number of hymnals, and these mainly in America. These include :—

1. The Assyrian came down like the wolf on the fold.
2. The king was on his throne.
3. The wild gazelle o'er Judah's hills.

Lord Byron's *Works with Life and Letters*, by T. Moore, in 17 vols., was pub. by J. Murray, London, 1832. [J. J.]

C

C. in the Bristol Bap. *Coll.* of Ash & Evans, 1769, i.e. R. Cruttenden.

C. in Collyer's *Hymns, &c.,* 1812, i.c. J. Conder.

C. in *New Golden Shower*, N. Y., 1870, i.e. Frances J. Van Alstyne, *née* Crosby.

C. C. Y. in the *Leeds Hymn Book*, 1853, and others, i.e. *Child's Christian Year*.

C. E. in Elliott's *Ps. & Hys.*, 1835, i.e. Charlotte Elliott.

C. F. *Hys. by C. F.* Birmingham, 1861, i.e. Christina Forsyth.

C. F. H. *Verses for Holy Seasons*, 1846, i.c. Cecil F. Alexander, *née* Humphreys.

C. F. H., author of *The Child's Book of Praise*, Lond., 1873, i.e. Claudia Frances Hernaman, *née* Ibotson.

C. H. I. *Songs in Sorrow and Songs in Joy*, Edinburgh, Taylor, 1864, i.e. C. H. Inglis.

C. H. L. S. in the *Evang. Lutheran Hymnal*, Columbus, Ohio, 1880, i.e. C. H. L. Schnette.

C. L. S. *Within the Veil*, i.e. Charitie L. Bancroft, *née* Smith.

C. & J. W. in various old hymn-books, i.e. C. & J. Wesley.

C. W. in same, i.e. C. Wesley.

Cabot, Eliza Lee. [Follen, E. L.]

Caddell, Cecilia Mary. This writer has published:—

(1) *Flower and Fruit; or, the Use of Tears*, 1856; (2) *Blind Agnese; or, the Little Spouse of the Blessed Sacrament*, 1856; (3) *The Martyr Maidens*, a Tale in *Historical Tales & Legends*, 1858; (4) *Nellie Netterville*, 1867 ; (5) *Summer Talks about Lourdes*, 1874.

Her hymns include :—
1. **Behold the lilies of the field.** *Providence.* In *The Dominican H. Bk.*, 1881, and others.
2. **It is finished! He hath seen [wept].** *Good Friday.* In the *People's H.*, 1867, and others. From *Lyra Messianica*, 2nd ed., 1865.   [J. J.]

Call all who love Thee, Lord, to Thee. [*The Second Advent.*] This cento is composed thus:—the first four lines and the last line of the hymn are from P. J. Bailey's poem, *Festus*, 1839, and the rest are by G. Rawson. It was 1st pub. in the *Leeds H. Bk.*, 1853, No. 664, in 3 st. of 8 l., and is repeated in Mr. Rawson's *Hymns, &c.*, 1876, p. 120. It is in several modern collections, including the *Baptist Hyl.*, 1879 ; Horder's *Cong. Hymns*, 1884, and others.   [J. J.]

Call Jehovah thy salvation. *J. Montgomery.* [*Ps. xci.*] The MS. of this version of Ps. xci. is not preserved with the M. MSS. The paraphrase 1st appeared in Montgomery's *Songs of Zion*, 1822 ; in 5 st. of 8 l., and again in his *Original Hymns*, 1853, No. 145. As a hymn for congregational use it is generally given in an abbreviated form, both in the older and in modern collections, as in *Kennedy*, 1863; the *Wes. H. Bk.*, 1875 ; and others. Orig. text as above. [See **English Psalters**, § xvii.] In America it has attained to a good position, and is sometimes found as, " Call the *Lord*, thy *sure* salvation." From this hymn also, the hymn, " God shall charge His angel legions," is taken. It is composed of st. iv. and v., and was given in the American *Prayer Bk. Coll.*, 1826, and later hymn-books.   [J. J.]

Callaway, William Fleetwood. A successful writer of hymns for children, and a Congregational Minister at Birmingham, was the s. of the Rev. John Callaway, for some time a Wesleyan Missionary in Ceylon. Mr Callaway was b. at Stafford, March 17, 1834. On the death of his father in 1841, he was removed into Cornwall. From thence he passed, in 1853, to York, where, influenced by the preaching of the Rev. James Parsons, he took a decided religious course, and joined the Congregationalists. Following up his commercial pursuits he went from York to Wem, Shropshire; and from thence to Birmingham. Having been engaged for some time as a lay preacher, when the pastorate of the Highgate Chapel, Birmingham, fell vacant in 1861, he received an invitation to preach. This led to his settlement as the pastor of that congregation. He d. May 22, 1886. Mr. Callaway's

hymn-writing began with compositions for Sunday School Anniversaries. He proceeded to compose words for German tunes for men's voices only, and ultimately assisted the late J. Curwen, with hymns and songs, in his Tonic-sol-fa movement. Of his hymns the following have come into C. U. :—

1. Afar, while Jesus passeth by. *Healing the Lepers.*
2. Jesus watched the children playing. *Christ the Child.*
3. To Jacob's well the woman went. *Water of Life.*
4. Vainly o'er the weary oar. *Stilling the Tempest.*
These descriptive hymns were written for Curwen's *New Child's Own H. Bk.* during 1873–4, and were 1st pub. therein in 1874. In addition there are :—
5. God loves little children. *S. S. Anniversary.*
6. O Saviour, most gracious and loving. *S. S. Anniversary.*
These were written for his own S. School, and 1st pub. in Curwen's *New Child's O. H. Bk.* in 1874.
7. How oft, O Lord, young English hearts. *Child's Mission Hymn.* Written for an Anniversary of the London Miss. Soc. held in Birmingham in 1878.   [J. J.]

Calm me, my God, and keep me calm. *H. Bonar.* [*Peace.*] Appeared in his *Hymns of Faith and Hope*, 1st series, 1857, in 8 st. of 4 l., and entitled, " The Inner Calm." Its use in G. Brit. is fair, but in America it ranks in popularity with the finest of Dr. Bonar's hymns. In one or two hymnals the opening line is altered to " Calm me, *blest Spirit*, keep me calm," as in Nicholson's *Appendix Hymnal*, 1866, but this is not popular. [J. J.]

Calverley, Charles Stewart, M.A., s. of the Rev. Henry Blayds, some time Vicar of South Stoke, near Bath (who took the name of *Calverley* in 1852), was b. at Martley, Worcestershire, Dec. 22, 1831. He entered Harrow in 1846, from whence he passed to Oxford, but coming under the censure of the authorities, he migrated to Cambridge in 1852, where, after gaining some of the best classical prizes of that University, he graduated first class in Classical honours. In due course he was called to the Bar and followed the Northern circuit. He died at Folkestone, Feb. 17, 1884. He is known to hymnody through several *trs.* from the Latin, which he made for the *Hymnary* in 1871, and were pub. therein in 1872.   [J. J.]

Calvinistic Methodist Hymnody. [**Welsh Hymnody**, § ii.]

Cambridge, Ada. [Cross, Ada.]

Camerarius, Joachim. [Eber, P. iv.]

Cameron, William, M.A., seems to have been b. in 1751, at or near Pananich, a hamlet near Ballater, Aberdeenshire, his father, a son of Cameron of Glen Nevis, being apparently then a farmer in the parish of Glenmuick. He studied at the University of Aberdeen (Marischal College), where he graduated M.A. in 1770, was ordained parish minister of Kirknewton, Midlothian, in 1786, and d. at Kirknewton, Nov. 17, 1811. Though not a member of the Committee appointed by the General Assembly of 1775, to revise the Scottish *Translations and Paraphrases* of 1745-51, yet the burden of revision seems to have fallen upon him (probably through the influence of Dr. Hugh Blair), as to him are ascribed the changes made in 1775-1781 in no less than 34 of that collection, which in the 1781 are numbered thus:—Nos. 1, 3, 4, 6, 7, 22, 24, 26, 32, 34, 36, 39–43, 45–47, 49–52, 54–57, 59–61, 63, 65–67. He is also said to be the author of Nos. 14 and

17, in the 1781 collection, and to have altered Nos. 5, 12 of those first included there. His published works are :—

(1) *Poems on Various Subjects* (Edin., Gordon & Murray), 1780, containing 8 poems, 3 fables, and 20 lyric odes, two of which are called hymns. (2) *Poems on Several Occasions* (Edin., A. Constable & Co.), 1813 ; with 2 poems (1 from 1780), 2 fables (from 1780), and 23 lyric odes. Of the lyric odes 6 are so-called hymns (2 from 1780), and 5 are Psalm versions. Of the remaining twelve, 7 are from his 1780 volume, and 5— including a continuation of Dr. Beattie's *Minstrel*, in two books—printed for the first time. But neither volume contains any of the original hymns or recasts he is said to have contributed to the *Translations and Paraphrases* of 1781.

The ascriptions above are taken from the markings by Cameron's eldest daughter in a copy of the *Psalms* and *Paraphrases* kindly lent by her son, Mr. R. G. Sillar, of Bexley, Kent. Another son, Mr. W. C. Sillar, of Blackheath, London, possesses a MS. volume of poems by his grandfather, which, however, like the printed volumes, contains none of the *Paraphrases* of 1781. To Cameron, No. 12 of the 1781, and the changes made, in 1781, on Nos. 13, 15, and Hymn iv. have been sometimes ascribed, but they are not assigned to him in his daughter's markings. These markings thus apportion the remainder of the Scottish contributions :—to *Logan*, Nos. 8–11, 27, 31, 53, 58, and Hymn v., besides No. 48, which he merely altered, and No. 59, in which he probably had no share : to *Logan* and *Morison*, No. 28 ; to *Morison*, Nos. 19, 21, 29, 30, 35, besides No. 38, which more probably owes its form in 1781 to *Bruce* or *Logan* : to *Blair* Nos. 4, 33, 34, 44 (a cento) : to *Robertson*, Nos. 25, 26, 42, 43 : to *Blacklock*, No. 16 : to *Randall*, No. 49 : and to *Ogilvie*, No. 62. They also give Logan as alterer of Nos. 2, 18, 23, 25, from the 1745–51 ; and of No. 30 of those added in 1781. Bruce's name is never mentioned. Nos. 6, 12, 18, 23, 52, are ascribed to Watts—so far as we can see without shadow of proof—while the recast from Watts, No. 50 in 1781, is ascribed to *Randall*.

A list by the late Principal Lee of Edinburgh (now, as revised by the late Dr. David Laing, in the possession of Mr. William Bonar, Kensington, London), professedly based on a list in the possession of Cameron, differs in ascribing No. 12 of the 1781 to *Cameron*, and the alterations on Nos. 13, 15 ; while not ascribing to him the alterations on Nos. 5, 32, 56. It marks as anonymous from the 1745, Nos. 23, 26, 30 (!), 52, 59. The recast from the 1745, No. 38, it ascribes to *Logan*, and the recast No. 50, from Watts, is given as anonymous from the 1745. [See **Scottish Trans. and Paraphrases.**]　　[J. M.]

Campanus, Johann, was b. on June 24, c. 1565, at Wodnian in Bohemia. At the University of Prag (Prague), he graduated B.A. 1592, M.A. 1596. In 1592 he became master at Iglau, thereafter at Teplitz, and then professor at Königingratz. He was in 1596 appointed Rector of the St. Heinrich school, in the Neustadt, Prag, and in 1600 Rector at Kuttenberg. Ultimately he became Professor of Greek and Latin and of Bohemian History in the University of Prag, where he was some time Dean of the Philosophical Faculty, and in 1612 Rector of the University. He died at Prag, Dec. 13, 1622.

Brought up at Wodnian as a Hussite, he became a Lutheran ; then a Calvinist ; was in 1619 assessor of the Utraquist Consistory of the Teynkirche in the Altstadt, Prag ; and on Nov. 16, 1622, formally became a Roman Catholic. His Latin Version of the Psalms, pub. at Prag, 1611, and his Latin Odes, Prag, 1612, were introduced for the senior scholars to sing in church and school. A complete ed. of his sacred poems appeared as *Sacrarum Odarum Libri Duo. Quorum Prior Psalmos Davidicos, Posterior hymnos Dominicales et feriales continet. Accessere Cantica Canticorum in Odaria* liii. *nec non Melodiae pro omnibus Psalmis, Odis, & Canticorum Odariis, ejusdem Authoris.* Frankfurt-am-Main, 1618. [Wernigerode.] A full list of his poems is given in his *Biographie*, by G. J. Dlabcz, Prag, 1819.

Two of his poems have passed into English :

i. *Rorando coeli defluant. Advent.* 1st pub. in his *Odarum Sacrarum. Liber Posterior*, Prag, 1612 [Strahow, Prag.], p. 1, "Ode 1, De Adventu Domini," in 5 st. of 4 l., with the heading :—

"Sol Christus est, ros Christus est, hic quem rigat
Fovetque, frigus pellit, aestum mitigat."

It appears in a full and good German *tr.* in Johann Franck's *Geistliches Sion*, 1674, No. 2, (ed. 1846, p. 2), beginning :—

"Ihr Himmel tröpfelt Thau in Eil."

Franck's version was included in the 1688 (No. 317) and later eds. of Crüger's *Praxis pietatis melica*; in Bunsen's *Versuch*, 1833, No. 85, and his *Allg. G. B.*, 1846, No. 29. Bunsen, 1833, p. 878, calls it "One of the most profound hymns of that believing yearning, which recognises in the Incarnation of Christ the pledge of the union of God with the soul." The only *tr.* in C. U. from Franck is :—

Ye heavens, oh haste your dews to shed, in full in the 2nd Series, 1858, of Miss Winkworth's *Lyra Ger.*, p. 3. Thence as No. 20 in her *C. B. for England*, 1863, and as No. 15 in Bosworth's *Coll.*, 1865. St. ii.–v. beginning, "O living Sun, with joy break forth," are included as No. 121 in Dr. Thomas's *Augustine H. Bk.*, 1866.

Another *tr.* is "Descend, ye heavens, in gentle dews," by Dr. *G. Walker*, 1860, p. 25.

ii. **Veni Redemptor gentium.** *Advent.* Ode ii. of his *Liber Posterior* ed., 1612, p. 2 (1618, p. 276), in 7 st. of 4 l., headed "Ex hymno Ambrosii.

"Alvus tumescit virginis
　Quantum potest vis Numinis."

Two stanzas may be compared with the Ambrosian, viz. :—

i.

"Veni Redemptor gentium,
Pulchrum renide lilium
Splendore fulgens flammeo ;
Hic partus est dignus Deo !"

vii.

"Praesepe iam tuum micat,
Lumenque noctis emicat,
Quod nulla lux interpolet
Ut luceat plus quam solet."

A full and good German *tr.* by Johann Franck, beginning "Komm, Heiden-Heiland, Lösegeld," appears in C. Peter's *Geistliche Arien*, Guben, 1667, No. 1, repeated in his own *Geistliches Sion*, 1674, p. 1 (ed. 1846, p. 1) ; and included in many subsequent collections as the *Berlin G. L. S.*, ed. 1863, No. 1596. The form *tr.* into English is that in Bunsen's *Versuch*, 1833, No. 78 (1881, No. 11). Bunsen, doubtless not knowing that it was a direct *tr.* from Campanus, calls it at p. 878 "the only successful version from the Ambrosian hymn [Veni Redemptor], more profound and delightful than the Latin." Bunsen omits st. ii., iii., and alters i., iv. The *trs.* in C. U. are :—

1. **Redeemer of the nations, come.** By Miss Winkworth in full from *Bunsen* in the 1st series of her *Lyra Ger.*, 1855, p. 186, repeated in her *C. B. for England*, 1863, No. 23, and in Dr. Thomas's *Augustine H. Bk.*, 1866.

2. **Come, Ransom of our captive race.** From Bunsen, omitting his st. iii., as No. 3 in Dr. Pagenstecher's *Coll.*, 1864, signed "F. C. C."

3. **O Glory of Thy chosen race.** In full from Bunsen by Dr. F. J. A. Hort for *Church Hymns*, 1871, No. 70, with an added doxology. [J. M.]

Campbell, Etta, sometime a teacher in Morristown, New Jersey, is the author of :—

1. **Come, ye children, sweetly sing.** *Jesus the Children's Friend.* Appeared in E. P. Hammond's *Praises of Jesus*, 1864 ; his *New Praises of Jesus*, 1869 ; and in other collections, including several in G. Britain.

2. **What means this eager, anxious throng.** *Jesus passes by.* Written during a religious revival in Newark,

U.S., 1863, and pub. in *Song Victories*. It is found in several collections, and was rendered exceedingly popular in Great Britain by Mr. Sankey in his Evangelical tour with Mr. Moody, 1874–6.   [J. J.]

Campbell, Jane Montgomery, daughter of the Rev. A. Montgomery Campbell, b. in London, 1817, d. at Bovey Tracey, Nov. 15, 1878. Miss Campbell contributed in 1861, a number of *trs.* from the German to the Rev. C. S. Bere's *Garland of Songs; or, an English Liederkranz*, 1862; and also to his *Children's Choral Book*, 1869. The best known and most widely used of these *trs.* is a portion of "Im Anfang war's auf Erden," as the harvest hymn, "We plough the fields and scatter" [see **Claudius**]. Miss Campbell also pub. *A Handbook for Singers*, Lond., S. P. C. K. N.D. This small work contains the musical exercises which she taught in her father's parish school.
[J. J.]

Campbell, Margaret, Lady Cockburn, née Malcolm, eldest daughter of Sir John Malcolm, G.C.B., married, June 20, 1827, to Sir Alexander Thomas Cockburn-Campbell, Bart. (one of the founders of the Plymouth Brethren in England), and d. at Alphington, near Exeter, Feb. 6, 1841. Her hymns were printed in lithograph from her MS. for private circulation. In the Plymouth Brethren *Ps. & Hys.*, Lond., Walther, 1842, some of these hymns were given, and thus came into C. U. The best known is, " Praise ye Jehovah, praise the Lord most holy."   [J. J.]

Campbell, Robert. Advocate, of Sherrington, Scotland, was b. at Trochraig, Ayrshire, Dec. 19, 1814. When quite a boy he attended the University of Glasgow. Though showing from his earliest years a strong predilection for Theological studies, eventually he fixed upon the Scottish law as a profession. To this end he entered the Law Classes of the University of Edinburgh, and in due course entered upon the duties of an advocate. Originally a Presbyterian, at an early age he joined the Episcopal Church of Scotland. He became a zealous and devoted Churchman, directing his special attention to the education of the children of the poor. His classical attainments were good, and his general reading extensive. In 1848 he began a series of translations of Latin hymns. These he submitted to Dr. Neale, Dr. Mills of Ely, and other competent judges. In 1850, a selection therefrom, together with a few of his original hymns, and a limited number from other writers, was pub. as

Hymns and Anthems for Use in the Holy Services of the Church within the United Diocese of St. Andrews, Dunkeld, and Dunblane. Edinburgh, R. Lendrum & Co.

This collection, known as the *St. Andrews Hymnal*, received the special sanction of Bp. Torry, and was used throughout the Diocese for some years. Two years after its publication he joined the Roman Catholic Church. During the next sixteen years he devoted much time to the young and poor. He d. at Edinburgh, Dec. 29, 1868.

From his collection of 1850, four *trs.* were given in *H. A. & M.*, 1861, "At the Lamb's high feast we sing;" "Come, pure hearts, in sweetest measures;" "Ye Choirs of New Jerusalem;" "Ye servants of a martyr'd God" (*altered*). Attention was thereby directed to his *trs.* They are smooth, musical, and well sustained. A large number, not included in his 1850 collection, were left by him in MS. From these Mr. O.Shipley has printed several in his *Annus Sanctus*, 1884. (c. MSS.)   [J. J.]

Campbell, Thomas, the Poet, has little in common with hymnody. A few of his pieces, including, "When Jordan hushed its waters still," are found in a limited number of hymnals. His poetical works, *The Pleasures of Hope, Gertrude of Wyoming*, and others, have been reprinted several times. He was b. at Glasgow, 1777; d. at Boulogne, 1844, and was buried in Westminster Abbey.

Camphuysen, Dirk Rafelszoon, s. of Rafael Camphuysen, surgeon at Gorinchem or Gorkum, Holland, was b. at Gorkum, 1586. Up to his eighteenth year he was a pupil of the painter Diderik Govertze. At the University of Leyden he studied theology, and embraced the opinions of Arminius. After acting for some time as a private tutor, he was appointed master of the fourth form in the Latin School at Utrecht, and occasionally preached in the Cathedral Church. In 1615 he was appointed preacher at Vleuten, but after two years was accused of being a Remonstrant, and forbidden to preach. Thereafter he led a somewhat troubled life, principally as a bookseller, residing at Amsterdam, then at Norden, in East Friesland, and at Harlingen. After a nine months' stay on the island of Ameland, he obtained leave to settle at Dokkum, in Friesland, where he became a flax merchant, solacing himself in the intervals of business with the composition of poetry. He d. at Dokkum, July 9, 1627 (*Allg. Deutsche Biog.*, iii. 739–740; Kobus and Rivecourt's *Biog. Handwoordenboek*, Zutphen, 1854; A. J. van der Aa's *Biog. Woordenboek*, Haarlem, 1855, iii. pp. 84–88. The notices of the 1624 and 1628 eds. of the *Rymen* have been kindly supplied by Dr. H. C. Rogge, Amsterdam).

" His religious poetry," says Sir John Bowring, "is superior to any which preceded it [in Holland]. There is a pure and earnest feeling throughout, an intense conviction of truth and an elevated devotion." His poems are contained in his *Stichtelyke Rymen*, 1st pub. in two parts at Hoorn, 1624 [University Library, Amsterdam]; a third part being added in an ed. N. P. N. D., cir. 1628 [do.]; and a fourth in the 12th ed., Rotterdam, 1658 (18th ed. Amsterdam, 1686). One of the best-known is :—

Wat is de Meester wijs en goedt. *May-Song.* 1st pub. in pt. iii., ed. 1628, p. 621, in 15 st. of 4 l. In the ed. Amsterdam, 1647, p. 283, entitled "May Morning Hymn of Contemplation." Sir John Bowring speaks of this as "one of the most popular productions of the Dutch poets ; its harmonious versification and its simplicity have made it the common source of consolation in distress." It has passed into English direct through the *tr.* beginning, "What love, what wisdom, God displays," in Sir John Bowring's *Batavian Anthology*, Lond., 1824, p. 119. It has also been rendered into English through the German *tr.* by Robert Roberthin.

Der Meister ist ja lobenswerth. A somewhat free version, in 17 st., in H. Albert's *Arien*, pt. iv., Königsberg, 1641, No. 12, with the motto, "O curas hominum." Included as No. 730 in the *Unv. L. S.*, 1851. The only *tr.* is, "Worthy of praise, the Master-hand," by *Miss Winkworth*, 1869, p. 187.

Camphuysen also wrote a version of the Psalter in the metres of Marot and Beza, 1st pub. at Amsterdam, 1630 [Royal Library, The Hague], entitled *Uytbreyding over de Psalmen des Propheten Davids*. His Ps. 139 :—

Heeft yemand lust zijn oogen te vermeyden, in 10 st. of 6 l. (ed. 1630, p. 368, 1679, p. 301), is *tr.* by Sir John Bowring, 1824, p. 122, as "If there be one whose thoughts delight to wander."   [J. M.]

Can creatures to perfection find? *I. Watts.* [*God unsearchable.*] Pub. in his

Hymns, &c., 2nd ed., 1709, Bk. ii., No. 170, in 8 st. of 4 l., and entitled, "God Incomprehensible and Sovereign." It is found in a few modern collections, as *Spurgeon's O. O. H. Bk.,* but usually in an abbreviated form. In the *Church Pastorals,* Boston, U. S. A., 1864, st. iv., v., vii., viii., are given as, "God is a King, of power unknown," and in the American *Hys. for the Ch. of Christ* by Hedge & Huntington, 1853, No. 123, st. v., vi., viii. begin, "God wounds the heart, and He makes whole."

[J. J.]

Canitz, Friedrich Rudolph Ludwig, Freiherr von, s. of Ludwig v. Canitz, privy and legal counsellor at Berlin; was b. at Berlin, Nov. 27, 1654, a few months after his father's death. After studying at the Universities of Leyden and Leipzig, he made in 1675–77 a tour in Italy, France, England, and Holland. In 1677 he was chosen gentleman of the bedchamber by the Elector Friedrich Wilhelm, and accompanied him in his campaigns in Pomerania, &c. He was then, in 1680, appointed chief magistrate of the district of Zossen and Trebbin, in the Mittelmark, and in 1681 counsellor of the Court and Legation. After a successful embassy to Frankfurt, 1682, he was appointed in 1683 chief magistrate of Mühlenhoff and Mühlenbeck. He executed many important missions under Friedrich Wilhelm and his successor Friedrich III., was a privy counsellor, and received in 1698 the dignity of Baron from the Emperor Leopold I. He d. at Berlin, Aug. 11, 1699 (*Koch,* iv. 238–248; *Allg. Deutsche Biog.,* iii. 756, the latter dating his death Aug. 1). His hymns were 1st pub. posthumously, and without his name. They were edited by Dr. Joachim Lange, Rector of the Berlin Gymnasium, as *Nebenstunden unterschiedener Gedichte,* Berlin, 1700. Of the 24 religious poems, only 2 have continued in German C. U., viz.:—

i. **Gott, du lässest mich erreichen.** *Evening.* 1700, as above, p. 6, in 6 st. *Tr.* as: "Father! hear me humbly praying" (beginning with st. ii. "Neige dich zu meinen Bitten"), by *H. J. Buckoll,* 1842, p. 99.

ii. **Seele du musst munter werden.** *Morning.* This beautiful hymn, the mirror of his life, was 1st pub. 1700 as above, p. 3, in 14 st. of 6 l. Included as No. 795 in Freylinghausen's *Neues geistreiches G. B.,* 1714, and as No. 471 in the *Unv. L. S.,* 1851. The trs. in C. U. are:—

1. **Come, my soul, thou must be waking.** A very good *tr.* by H. J. Buckoll, omitting st. ii., iv., viii., given in a note at p. 456 of Dr. Arnold's *Christian Life: its Cause, its Hindrances, and its Helps.* London, 1841. The note is to a passage in Sermon vi., on Col. iii. 3, dated March, 1840, in which Dr. Arnold says:—

"Some may know the story of that German nobleman [v. Canitz] whose life had been distinguished alike by genius and worldly distinctions, and by Christian holiness; and who, in the last morning of his life, when the dawn broke into his sick chamber, prayed that he might be supported to the window, and might look once again upon the rising sun. After looking steadily at it for some time, he cried out, "Oh! if the appearance of this earthly and created thing is so beautiful and quickening, how much more shall I be enraptured at the sight of the unspeakable glory of the Creator Himself." That was the feeling of a man whose sense of earthly beauty had all the keenness of a poet's enthusiasm, but who, withal, had in his greatest health and vigour preserved

the consciousness that his life was hid with Christ in God; that the things seen, how beautiful soever, were as nothing to the things which are not seen (p. 61).

Of the *tr.* Dr. Arnold says, "For the greatest part I am indebted to the kindness of a friend," which means that portions (viz. st. i., ll. 1–3, and one or two expressions) are taken from the anonymous version of 1838 (see below). In 1842 Buckoll included it in his *H. from the German,* p. 36, altering st. iii. l. 3, xii. ll. 1–3, and xiii. It is the text in Dr. Arnold's sermons which has passed into C. U. in the following forms, the references being to the *tr.* of the German stanzas.

(1) St. i., v.–vii., ix.–xi., American Epis. *H. for Ch. and Home,* 1860, altered.

(2) St. i., vi., vii., ix.–xii., in the *Salisbury H. Bk.,* 1857, and *Kennedy,* 1863. The *Anglican H Bk.,* 1871, and the *Evang. Hymnal,* N. Y., 1880, omit st. xii.

(3) St. i., vi., vii., ix., xi., xii., considerably altered and with an added doxology in *Sarum,* 1868. This text in full, or abridged, is found in *Church Hys.,* 1871; *Hymnary,* 1872; Stevenson's *H. for Ch. and Home,* 1873; *Bap. Hymnal,* 1879, and others; and in America in the Epis. *Hymnal,* 1871; *Laudes Domini,* 1884.

(4) St. i., vi., vii., ix.–xii., xiv., in *Harrow School H. Bk.,* 1855, 1866; *Marlborough College,* 1869, &c.

(5) St. i., vii., ix., xi., with an added st. in *Bk. of Common Praise,* 1863; and in G. S. Jellicoe's *Coll.* 1867.

2. **Come, my soul, awake, 'tis morning.** A good *tr.,* omitting st. ii., iv., viii., by Miss Winkworth in her *Lyra Ger.,* 1855, 1st series, p. 216, and thence, retaining only the trs. of st. i., vi., vii., xi.–xiii., in her *C. B. for England,* 1863.

Another tr. is :—

"Come, my soul! thou must be waking," in the *British Magazine,* July, 1838, p. 21. From this, st. i., ll. 1–3, and one or two expressions were adopted by Buckoll (see above). [J. M.]

Canon. [Κανών.] [Greek Hymnody, § xvi. 11.]

Cantemus cuncti melodum nunc, Alleluia. [*Epiphany.*] This Sequence is given by Father Joachim Brander (a monk of the Abbey of St. Gall), in his MS. collection of *Hymns, Sequences,* &c., 1507. Brander gives the following description, "Alia de Epiphaniâ Christi Sequentia jocunda b. Notkeri, titulis *Puella turbata.* Canitur praecipue in Octavâ Epiphaniae," ("Another joyful Sequence of Blessed Notker's [died 912] for the Epiphany of Christ, with the title: *The troubled Virgin.* It is sung especially in the octave of the Epiphany.") The title *Puella turbata,* "The troubled (or disturbed) Virgin," has caused some difficulty as to what may be its meaning; but for its use we may refer to St. Matthew ii. 3, Jerusalem being termed the *Virgin* daughter of Sion; the *troubling* there mentioned occurring at the season of the Epiphany. The words of the hymn are modelled on those of the 148th Psalm.

The text is given in *Mone,* No. 67; *Daniel,* ii. p. 52; and *Kehrein,* No. 44, in each case with notes, and extensive readings from ancient MSS., the oldest being of the 11th cent., and referred to by *Daniel.* The most curious difference is in the conclusion. *Mone* reads "Laus Trinitati aeternae, All., All., All., All., All., All.;" whilst *Daniel* and *Kehrein* have "Laus Trinitati aeternae in baptismo domini quae clarificatur: Hinc canamus: Alleluia." In addition the text is also in an 11th cent. MS. in the *Brit. Mus.* (Harl. 2961, f. 234 b), and in three 11th cent. MSS. at St. Gall, Nos. 376, 380, 381.

In his *Med. Hys.*, 1863, p. 34, Dr. Neale says, "Next to St. Notker himself, the most famous writer of the Proses named from him was Godescalcus," and at p. 42 of this Sequence, "We shall have another occasion to speak of the 'Deposition of Alleluia' at Septuagesima, for which this famous Sequence was written by Godescalcus." *Brander, Daniel,* and *Kehrein* all declare that the Sequence is by St. Notker. For Dr. Neale's ascription to Godescalcus we find no evidence, and must thus assign the Sequence to St. Notker [see Alleluia].   [W. A. S.]

Translations in C. U. :—

1. **The strain upraise of joy and praise, Alleluia.** By J. M. Neale, appeared in the *Hymnal N.*, enlarged edition, 1854, and in his *Mediæval Hymns*, 2nd ed., 1863 ; it has passed into almost every hymnal published since that date. In the 2nd ed. of his *Mediæval Hymns*, 1863, Dr. Neale gives the history of its somewhat peculiar construction, and complains most bitterly of its being sung to Troyte's chant. He says :—

"There is only one thing with respect to the use of any of my hymns that has grieved me : the rejection of the noble melody of the Alleluiatic Sequence, and that for a third-rate chant. What would be said of chanting the *Dies irae?* And yet I really believe it would suffer less than does the *Cantemus cuncti* by such a substitution. Further be it noticed, every sentence, I had almost said every word, of the version was carefully fitted to the music, the length of the lines corresponds to the length of each *troparion* in the original; and these are now stretched on the Procrustean bed of the same meaningless melody. That the original music cannot be learnt in an hour or two is most certain ; but seeing that I have heard it thoroughly well sung, and most heartily enjoyed, by a school choir, varying in ages from fourteen to five, is it not unworthy of the great choral meetings, as at Ely,.Salisbury, Sherborne, and elsewhere, including the words in their programmes, so utterly to spoil them in their performance.? Let it be remembered that I have some little right to speak on the subject, having been the first to introduce the Sequence to English readers, and there being, even now, no other translation but my own." (*Preface*, p. ix.)

Notwithstanding this earnest protest of the translator, the original melody is practically unknown. It is included in the *Hymnal N.* with the accompanying Harmonies. The adaptation from Dr. Neale's *tr.* in the *Hymnary*, 1872, No. 189 : "In sweet consent let all the anthem sing, Alleluia," cannot be called a new rendering of the Sequence.

2. **Let us all in concert sing.** By H. Alford, 1st pub. in a festival service book, and then included in J. Barnby's *Original Tunes to Popular Hymns*, 1st series, 1869. It is also given in several American collections.

3. **Let us all in chorus sing.** By R. C. Singleton, written in 1870, and pub. in the 2nd ed. of his *Anglican H. Bk.*, 1871.   [J. J.]

Capitan, Herr Gott, Vater mein.
[*Christian Faith and Life.*] 1st pub. in the Erfurt *Enchiridion* of 1526, and thence in *Wackernagel*, iii. p. 116, in 9 st. of 11 l. Generally entitled "The Margrave Casimir's Hymn," the beginnings of the stanzas forming the words "Casimir Marggraf zu Brandenburg." The hymn may have been written for him by the author of the similar hymn (q.v.), "Genad mir, Herr, ewiger Gott." *Tr.* as :—"Divine Protector, Lord, and Sire," by Dr. G. *Walker*, 1860, p. 43.   [J. M.]

Capito, Wolfgang, s. of Hans Köpfel or Kopphel, farrier and counsellor at Hagenau,

in Alsace ; was b. at Hagenau in 1478. At Freiburg, in Breisgau, he studied medicine (M.D. in 1498) ; then law, and, after his father's death, theology. In 1512 he was appointed preacher at the Benedictine Collegiate Church of Bruchsal. He subsequently held important appointments at Basel, Mainz, and Strassburg. At Strassburg, under the influence of Zell and Bucer, he openly declared for the Reformation, became a freeman of Strassburg, July, 1523, and on Aug. 1, 1524, married the daughter of a Strassburg burgess. Working hand in hand with Bucer, he acted as mediator between the Zwinglians and the Lutherans, and after Zwingle's death he drew up for the Swiss churches a form of church government and worship. He d. at Strassburg during the pestilence in the beginning of Nov. 1541 (*Koch*, ii. 94–101 ; *Allg. Deutsche Biog.*, iii. 772–775, the latter dating his birth 1472).

He was a good musician and a lover of poetry. Three hymns are known as by him, two of which are based on the Latin. The only one *tr.* into English is noted under "Da pacem" (q.v.).   [J. M.]

Captain of Israel's host and Guide.
C. Wesley. [*The Divine Guide.*] 1st pub. in his *Short Hymns*, &c., 1762, vol. i., No. 133, in 2 st. of 6 l., and based on Ex. xiii. 21, "The Lord went before them by day in a Pillar of a Cloud, &c." In 1780 it was included, with alterations, in the *Wes. H. Bk.*, No. 317. It is found in a large number of hymnals, but in every case with alterations of st. ii., ll. 3–4. The original st. reads :—

> By Thine unerring Spirit led,
> We shall not in the desert stray,
> *The light of man's direction need,*
> *Or miss our providential way.*
> As far from danger as from fear,
> While Love, Almighty Love, is near.

The alterations which have been made in lines 3–4 are many. The most important are :—

1. By J. Wesley, in the *Wes. H. Bk.*, 1780–1875 :—

> "*We shall not full direction need,*
> *Nor* miss our providential way."

Dr. Osborn observes (*P. Works*, vol. ix. p. 43) : "In 1780, Wesley altered the line so as to assert assured confidence, without seeming to assert an independence of human help, 'We shall not full direction need.' " This reading is generally followed by the Methodist collections.

2. In Bickersteth's *Christian Psalmody*, 1833, these lines read :—

> *By Thee with heavenly manna fed,*
> *We shall not lack in all our way.*

3. In the *Mitre Hymnbook*, 1836, the S.P.C.K. *Ps. and Hys.*, 1852, and later editions, this was changed to :—

> By *Thy paternal bounty* fed,
> We shall not lack in all our way.

This has been repeated in a few collections, as in *Thring's*, 1882, No. 266. Mr. Thring has also added a doxology.

4. In Conder's *Cong. H. Bk.*, 1836, and several later hymnals, it is again altered :—

> "*Our table by Thy bounty spread,*
> *Our wants supplied from day to day.*"

5. We must be content with another change :—

> "*Nor* light of man's direction need,
> *While we pursue our heavenward way.*"

Full orig. text in *P. Works*, 1868–72, vol. ix. p. 43.   [J. J.]

Captain of our Salvation, take.
C. Wesley. [*Holy Baptism.*] 1st pub. in his *Hymns for Children*, 1763. No. xli., in 4 st. of 6 l. (*P. Works*, 1868–72, vol. vi. p. 408). In 1780 it was given in the *Wes. H. Bk.*, No. 462. It is also found in the collections of other branches of Methodism. In 1852, when given

in the S.P.C.K. *Ps. & Hys.* for "Baptism," st. iii. was omitted. This form has been repeated in other hymnals. In 1871 it was included in the S.P.C.K. *Church Hymns*, for "Theological Colleges," a few judicious and appropriate alterations having been made to adapt it to that purpose.   [J. J.]

Captain of Thine enlisted host. *C. Batty.* [*Missions.*] Appeared in the *Kendal H. Bk.*, 1757, in 8 st. of 4. 1., and from thence passed into one of the early editions of Lady Huntingdon's *Coll.* From that *Coll.* st. i.-iii. were taken by *Williams and Boden*, 1801. This form of the hymn has descended to several modern collections, including the *N. Cong*, 1859, No. 921, where, however, it is attributed to C. Wesley in error. Snepps's text, in his *S. of G. & G.*, 1872, is st. i., iii., and iv. altered.   [J. J.]

Carlton, Mrs. Leah, a *nom de plume* of Mrs. Van Alstyne, q.v.

Carlyle, Joseph Dacre, B.D., some time Professor of Arabic in the University of Cambridge, and afterwards Vicar of Newcastle-on-Tyne, was b. at Carlisle, June 4, 1758. In 1799 he accompanied the Earl of Elgin to Constantinople with the object of exploring the literary treasures of the public Library of that city. He extended his journey into Asia Minor, and the islands and shores of the Archipelago. He d. at Newcastle, April 12, 1804. Amongst his MSS. were *Poems, suggested chiefly by Scenes in Asia Minor, Syria, &c.* These were pub. under that title, in 1805, by Susanna Maria Carlyle. His hymns, which appeared in J. Fawcett's *Ps. & Hys.*, Carlisle, 1802, include, "Lord, when we bend before Thy throne"—his most popular production; a paraphrase of the Lord's Prayer, "Father of heaven, Whose gracious hand"; and "Lord, when we creation scan." His works include *Specimens of Arabian Poetry*, 1796.   [J. J.]

Carlyle, Thomas, the Essayist and Historian, is known to hymnody solely through his *tr.* of Luther's "Ein feste Burg," q.v. He was b. near Ecclefechan, Dumfriesshire, Dec. 4, 1795, and d. at Chelsea, Feb. 5, 1881.

Carols. A carol is a song of joy originally accompanying a dance. Its origin and history, together with such collateral information as space will permit, may be best arranged under the following heads: i. *Derivation;* ii. *Historical Use of the Term;* iii. *The Carol and the Dance;* iv. *Sacred and Secular Carols;* v. *The Sacred Carol;* vi. *The Mysteries and Miracle Plays;* vii. *The Reformation Period;* viii. *Carol Literature;* ix. *Conclusion.*

i. *Derivation.*—The word Carol is derived from the Italian *Carola*, a ring-dance, from *carolare*, to sing. The Italian is said to come from the old French *querole*, or *carole*. The musical term *carola* in Boccaccio is synonymous with *ballata;* which the Crusca dictionary defines "canzone, che si canta balando," i.e. a song which is sung and danced at the same time.

ii. *Historical use of the Term.*—The word *carol* has been in use in English for at least some six hundred years. In the 13th cent. Robert of Gloucester wrote:—

"After mete, as rygt was, the menstrales geode aboute, And knytes and sweynes in *carole* gret route."

Chaucer, in the 14th cent. In his " Knight's Tale," l. 2205, we read :—

"What ladies fayrest ben, or best dancing,
Or which of 'hem can *carole* best or sing,
. . . .
Of all this now I make no mention."

In many instances also he uses it in connection with dancing as, for instance, in " The Romaunt of the Rose " :—

"These folke of which I tell you so
Upon a *karole wentirn* tho,
A ladie *karoled* 'hem, that hight
Gladnesse the blissful and the light.
Well could she sing and lustily,
None half so well and semely—
And couthe enough for soche doing
As longith unto *karolling*
There mightest thou karollis sene
And folke daunce and merry ben
Ne code I never thennis go
Whiles that I saw 'hem dancing so."

Gower, about the same date, wrote :—

"And if so befalle amonge
That she *carolle* upon a songe,
When I it here, I am so fedde,
That I am fro myself so ledde
As though I were in Paradise."

In the 16th cent. *Spenser* writes in the " *Epithalamion*," l. 133 :—

"But most of all, the damzels doe delight,
When they their tymbrels smyte,
And thereupon do daunce and *carrol* sweet,
That all the sences they do ravish quite."

In the same poem he also writes :—

"Hark! how the cheerful birds do chant their lays,
And *carol* of love's praise."

Shakespeare uses the word in his *Midsummer Night's Dream*, act ii. sc. 2, l. 43 ; in his *As You Like It*, act v. sc. 3. *Milton*, in the 17th cent. has it in *Paradise Lost*, bk. xii. l. 367: and in *Comus*, l. 849 ; Dryden, too, in the latter part of the same century, not to mention innumerable authors of more recent date. Under the term *Carol*, we may thus include a large class of popular songs, the first of which were characterised by dance-measures, both of time and action.

iii. *The Carol and the Dance.*—Both song and dance were employed in the earliest ages of mankind in some acts of Divine worship, whether of the true God or of heathen deities. Man's offerings were plainly to be of the very best, the most excellent in kind, and such as afforded the greatest test of self-abnegation and surrender on the part of the worshipper. Hence arose amongst the heathen, by perversion of revealed truth, human sacrifices. With better reason was it judged fitting that the Divine worship should be celebrated with the highest results of mental and artistic culture. Grace and aesthetic beauty of every sort in architecture, in painting, in sculpture, and in poetry were esteemed (as they ought to be) amongst the best of those gifts which, coming from God, ought to be dedicated to God. And, in its way, not *music* alone, but *dancing*, or "the poetry of motion" also was put on an equality with those other fine arts.

Ancient dancing was gymnastic, or mimetic ; either for exercise of the body, or to express the feelings of the mind. Homer, Aristotle, Herodotus, Pindar, Athenæus, and others of a more recent date, have abundant allusions to dances. The song and the dance were, however, gradually debased in the superstitious, and too often licentious, ceremonial of idolatrous worship. At no time, moreover, after the very first, can we regard them as having been exclusively sacred. The *dance* indeed, apart from its religious use in heathen temples, has come to be generally regarded, in this country at least, as wholly secular, and unfit for employment in the ordinary solemnities of Christian worship.

Instances of *dancing* as a part of Divine worship abound in the Old Testament. The 149th Ps. contains a direct precept, "Let the children of Sion be joyful in their King. Let them praise His name in the *dance ;*" and in the 150th Ps. "Praise Him in the cymbals and *dances.*" We also read, "There is a time to weep, and a time to laugh, a time to mourn, and a time to *dance*" (Eccl. iii. 4). These precepts are strikingly illustrated in the history of the Jews. The sublime Song of Moses had its appropriate antiphon when "Miriam the prophetess, the sister of Aaron, took a timbrel in her hand; and all the women went out after her with timbrels and with dances," and answered back the chorus of the men, "Sing ye to the Lord, for He hath triumphed gloriously ; the horse and his rider hath He thrown into the sea" (Ex. xv. 20). The *dances* of the daughters of Shiloh are recorded as of ordinary occurrence in the Book of Judges (ch. xxi. 21); and Jephthah's daughter, ignorant of his rash vow, came out to meet him on his return from his victory over the Ammonites " with timbrels and with dances" (Judges xi. 34). Other instances might be named ; but perhaps the most striking, and certainly the most generally well known, instance of jubilant religious dancing recorded in holy Scripture is that of King David, on the occasion of his bringing up the sacred Ark of God from the house of Obed Edom into the city of David, when, laying aside his royal robes, he took part in the ritual of the sanctuary, and, vested simply in the humble linen ephod (or surplice) of ministerial service, he *danced* before the Lord. It has moreover been well suggested that Hebrew poetry actually owed its origin and special characteristics to the *choral dance ;* in fact it began in *carolling.* It is evident that the sacred hymns were sung by opposite choirs ; one usually performed the hymn itself, the other a particular distich. The movements of the *dance* suggested the parallelisms of the *verse.* In the New Testament social festivities with dances are alluded to with not a breath of disfavour by Our Lord Jesus Christ Himself, in the parable of the Prodigal Son, and in the simile of the children playing in the market-place.

The following extract from *Philo the Jew,* describing the meetings of the *Therapeutæ,* will show how in the early part of the first cent. something very like *carolling* in its strictest sense was practised by that ascetic branch of the sect of the Essenes, in their nocturnal religious worship.

"And after supper they celebrate their sacred vigil. And the vigil is conducted on this wise. They all stand up in a crowd, and in the midst of the symposium first of all two choirs are formed, one of men, and one of women, and for each, one most honoured and skilled in song is chosen as a leader and director. Then they sing hymns composed to the praise of God, in many metres, and to various melodies, in one singing together in unison, and in another with antiphonal harmonies, moving their hands in time and *dancing* [ἐπορχούμενοι] ; and being transported with divine enthusiasm, they perform one while lyric measures, and at another tragic plainsong, strophes and antistrophes, as need requires. Then when each chorus, the men separately, and the women separately, has partaken of food by itself, as in the feasts of Bacchus, and quaffed the pure God-loving wine, they mingle together and become one choir out of two—the mimetic representation of that of yore standing on the shore of the Red Sea on account of the miracles wrought there . . . To this [the singing of the Song of Moses] the chorus of the male and female *Therapeutæ* afforded a most perfect resemblance with its variant and concordant melodies ; and the sharp searching tone of the women together with the baritone sound of the men effected a harmony both symphonious and altogether musical. Perfectly beautiful are their motions, perfectly beautiful their discourse ; grave and solemn are these carollers [χορευταί, dancers and singers—members of a choir—from χορός, a band of singers and dancers : a ring-dance] ; and the final aim of their motions, their discourse, and their choral dancers [χορευτῶν] is piety." (Translated from Dr. Mangey's ed. of Philo's *Works*, from the original Greek, compared with the Editor's Latin translation, 1742, vol. ii. pp. 484–5, *On the Contemplative Life.*)

With regard to the subsequent practice of *dancing* with *singing* in Christian Churches, it is surely not altogether unreasonable to conjecture (in the absence of historical proof) that the traditional account of such *carolling* as that of these *Therapeutæ,* if not of a similar choralism among their Christian fellow-countrymen, may possibly have had some influence on the minds of the rulers of the Church, leading them not sternly and absolutely to deprive their heathen converts of their customary dances of their former religious ceremonies. It must, however, be admitted that there is no record of the use of the sacred dance in the Primitive Church, unless, indeed, these *Therapeutæ* were Christians, an opinion which is not generally received.

[Dr. Burney, in his History of Music, confounds these *Therapeutæ* with the Christians ; probably misled by Eusebius. In the Supp. to Collier's *Dictionary* they are also called Christians. See Riddle's *Christian Antiquities*, p. 181, *note:* Eusebius's *Hist. Eccles.* l. ii., c. 17 : Burton's *Lectures on the First Three Centuries,* x. : and *Mosheim,* bk. i., pt. i., ch. ii. § x.]

Later on, in some places, dances under due restraint were tolerated. The third Council of Toledo, 589, however, forbade dances in churches, through the vigils of saints' days. That of Auxerre, 590, forbade secular dances in churches. In 858, Gautier, Bp. of Orleans, condemned the rustic songs and women dancers in the Presbytery on festival days. In 1209 the Council of Avignon prohibited theatrical dances and secular songs in church. In 1212 processions danced round the churches of Paris, and women danced in the cemeteries. We are informed by Jaques de Henricourt (a writer of the 14th cent.) that, as a condition of the remission, by the Bp. of Liége in the 13th cent., of a tax previously paid by the merchants of Verviers, a deputation of certain magistrates and clergy of Verviers, headed by a cross, danced under the corona in the nave of the Cathedral of St. Lambert, at Liége, on Tuesday in Whitsuntide. This was continued until the Cathedral was burnt down by the French revolutionary soldiers, in 1794. In the 17th cent. the apprentices and servants of York were accustomed to dance in the nave of the Minster on Shrove Tuesday; and in Wiltshire the inhabitants of Wishford and Batford, by a curious tenure, went up in a dance annually to Salisbury Cathedral. To this day, a dancing procession, chanting a curious *carol* to the tune of "Adam hatte sieben Sohne," takes place at Echternach in Luxemburg on Whitsun Tuesday. Also in the Cathedral at Seville, ever since the 12th cent., on Shrove Tuesday, and on the feasts of Corpus Christi, and of the Immaculate Conception, twelve young choristers, dressed as pages in antique Spanish costume, sing a jubilant *carol* at the lectern in the choir before the high altar, accompanied by an orchestra, ending in a ringing pneume [a succession of notes sung on one vowel]. This is followed by a *dance* round the lectern, and concluded by the choristers ranging themselves in line and playing "a regular and most harmonious fantasia on castanets." A few more instances might be given of *carolling* in its strictly literal sense in the Christian Church. Thus the dance, though generally discontinued, has never entirely died out, and the musical phase of the *carol* remains as vigorous as ever.

iv. *Sacred and Secular Carols.*—Under the term *carol* we may include a large class of popular songs, the first of which were characterised by dance measures, both of time and action. It has come eventually to be used to designate a kind of lyrical poem, usually, but not exclusively, on sacred subjects, intended to be sung with or without musical accompaniment, but it sometimes departs widely from the jubilant subjects of its original use, becoming more of the nature of the hymn, as its secular counterpart, the ballad, also, in like manner, rises in some instances into the sentimental and romantic poem. The melodies both of the *carol* and of the *ballad* are usually completed in the first stanza or verse, and repeated for each of the others.

v. *The Sacred Carol.*—The special difference between hymns, strictly so-called, and carols, may perhaps be most accurately marked by quoting the definition of the former given by St. Augustine:—

"Do you know what a hymn is? It is *singing* with the praise of God. If you praise God and do not sing, you utter no hymn. If you sing, and praise not God, you utter no hymn. If you praise anything which does not pertain to the praise of God, though in singing you praise, you utter no hymn." (See *Primer of Plain Song.* Novello.)

There is doubtless a wide border-land on which many a religious song may not inaccurately be classed under the head both of *hymn* and of *carol.* The most ancient Latin sacred lyrics are sometimes entirely direct addresses of prayer or praise to God, i. e. hymns. But they sometimes deflect (as do the Psalms themselves) from direct addresses to God into historical references to His miraculous works and providential interpositions in behalf of His people; or into subjective, contemplative admiration of the Divine dealings with His faithful servants as individuals, thereby indirectly promoting His glory, but not directly ascribing glory to Him, and thus "praising Him." Such songs do not come strictly within St. Augustine's definition; and it may therefore be suggested that they partake more or less of the nature of religious *carols*. And

this applies equally to many modern compositions called *hymns*. It seems, then, not too much to assert that from the very beginning the Christian Church has been using sacred lyrics, which, whether we range them under the head of *Psalms, Hymns, Spiritual Songs, Odes, Canticles,* or simply *Songs,* had among them some at least, if not many, having the special characteristics of the *carol*. The first of these is undoubtedly the *Gloria in Excelsis,* which Bp. Jeremy Taylor calls a *carol* in his *Life of Christ.* To many of the *Sequences* (q. v.) of a later age the same designation might justly be applied. With the gradual disuse of the ancient languages and the birth of modern European tongues, and also coeval with the secular songs of the minstrels, troubadours, and minnesingers, religious songs—*carols* in fact—came to be composed in the languages then best understood by the common people. Of these, though many have perished in many cases through wanton destruction in the 16th and 17th centuries, yet a sufficient number remain to mark the character of the later mediaeval carols, and thus to link the past with the present.

vi. *Mysteries and Miracle Plays.*—The continuous chain of the history of carolling gains many a link from the records of the *Mysteries and Miracle Plays.* These plays extend from the 4th cent., when Gregory Nazianzen, Archbishop and Poet, and a Father of the Church, banished pagan plays from the stage at Constantinople, and introduced select stories from the Old and New Testament, to the celebrated Ober-Ammergau Passion Play of to-day. The songs introduced into these religious plays were essentially *carols*, and in no country were they popular earlier than in England. A proverb of French origin, current in the 14th and 15th cents., shows that the singing of ballads and carols was then very general in Britain. It reads,

"Galli cantant, Angli jubilant, Hispani plangunt, Germani ululant, Itali caprizant."

The translation at the same period was,

"The French *sing* or *pipe*, the English *carol*, the Spaniards *wail*, the Germans *howl*, the Italians *caper*."

The last allusion is rather to their unsteady holding of notes than to their facility in florid singing. (*Popular Music of the Olden Time,* by W. Chappell, i. intro. ix.)

vii. *The Reformation Period.*—This was a period of darkness and despair to the carol writers and the carol and ballad singers. "The reign of Queen Elizabeth gave the death-blow to the long sinking race of English minstrels" (Dr. Rimbault's *Little Book of Songs and Ballads*), by the edict which pronounced them all "rogues, vagabonds, and sturdy beggars" (*Dict. of Music,* &c., by Sir G. Grove). Musicians held ballads in contempt, and great poets rarely wrote in ballad metre. Notwithstanding the advance made in music of the highest artistic kind, both abroad and at home, in the 16th and 17th cent. ballads, carols, and other ditties gradually shared the obloquy of the minstrels. These were all but lost and forgotten by the close of the 17th cent., the teaching of music was discouraged, and even in Shakespeare's day he makes the clown in the "Winter's Tale" boast of the exceptional cast of his chorus at his father's sheep-shearing feasts :—

'What will this sister of mine do with rice? But my father hath made her mistress of the feast, and she lays it on. She hath made me four-and-twenty nosegays for the shearers : three-man song-men all [i. e. singers of three-part songs], and very good ones : but they are most of them means [tenors] and bases : but one Puritan amongst them, and he sings psalms to hornpipes" [i. e. dance tunes]. Act. iv. sc. ii.

In the literature of the 16th cent. we have instances of the hold which even the *term* "Carol" had upon the national mind. In 1562 were published *Crestenmas carroles auctoryshed by my Lorde of London* [Bp. Grindal]; in 1564 we have *Carols exhorting men to put their trust in Christ alone;* and in 1579, *Carols or godly hymns for Christmas.* Later on we have a few lyrics of this class in the works of R. Southwell, G. Wither, W. Austin, Ben Jonson, R. Herrick, Jeremy Taylor, N. Tate, and others. In the 18th cent. also a carol may be found here and there, such as C. Wesley's "Hark, how all the welkin rings," but the true revival of carols and carolling is found in the collection and publication of carols in the early, and the writing of original carols in the latter part of the present century, aided probably not a little by the Christmas Carol broadsheets and chap-books which were somewhat extensively sold from 1800 to 1830, and less extensively somewhat later.

viii. *Carol Literature.*—The carol literature at the command of the hymnologist and literary student may be thus classified ; (1) *MSS.* (2) *Printed Carols, Old and New;* (3) *Lullaby Carols;* and (4) *Secular Carols.*

(1) *MS. Carols.*—The great MS. store-house is the library of the British Museum. Its treasures have been examined by many students, and some of the results have been published by T. Wright, M.A., and others. One of the earliest pub. by Mr. Wright is from a MS. of the 10th cent. It records, in Latin, the conversion of England by the mission of St. Augustine in the 6th cent. from St. Gregory the Great, in which the softening influence of Christianity on the harshness of the ancient language is recorded.

" Ecce lingua Britanniae	Jam Alleluia personat
Frendens olim barbarie	Proventu Evangelicae
In Trinitate unica	Exhilarata vineae."

(" Lo ! the British tongue, e'erwhile harshly grating barbarously, now, in praise of the Trinal Unity, sounds forth Alleluia, joyously inspired by the arrival of the glad Evangelic vine.")

The *Liber Eliensis* preserves the well-known first stanza of a carol by Canute, of the 11th cent. :—

" Merry sang the monks of Ely,
As Kenute the king rowed thereby,
Row, knights, now near the land,
And hear we these monks sing."

Du Meril gives from the *Brit. Mus.* MS., 1139, in his *Poésies Populaires Latines Du Moyen Age,* 1847, p 43, a " Chant sur Nativité du Christ," the first of which reads :—

" Nunc clericorum concio	nam summi Patris filio
devota sit cum gaudio ;	datur excelebratio ;
in tanto natalitio	Gaudeat homo ! "

There is a singularly interesting MS. in the Brit. Mus. (*Sloane,* 2593) generally ascribed to the reign of Henry VI. (1422 to 1461), and very difficult to decipher. Fortunately there is a modern printed copy in *Songs and Carols,*

edited by T. Wright, M.A. From its historical references, the date of one at least of these songs is fixed between 1362 and 1369. It may be inferred that the songs in this MS. belong to a numerous class of popular literature, that they were handed orally from generation to generation by those who sung them, and that a few of them only were copied down by accident as in this and similar MS. collections. The particular song alluded to is No. lii., p. 73, in Mr. Wright's *Songs & Carols,* 1847. It is in 8 st., and begins :—

" Thynk man qwerof thou art wrout,
Powre and naked thou were heder browt,
Thynk how Cryst thi sowle hath bowt
And fond to servyn hym to pay."

The remaining verses tell of famine, pestilence, death, storm, lightning, thunder, the burning of the tolbooth at Lynne; and exhorts men to take to heart these warnings of Divine " merveylis " :—

" Lok man, how thou ledyst thi lyf
And how thou spendyst thi wyttes v
Go to cherch, and do the schryf,
And bryng thi sowle in redy way."

The following Christmas Carol, in which we have a curious blending of Latin and English, is from the same MS. It is No. vi. in Mr. Wright's work :—

" Eya, Ihesu hodie
Natus est de virgine.
" Blyssed be that mayde Mary,
I'orn he was of here body,
Goddis sone that sytht on hy,
Non ex virili semine.
" In a manjour of an as
Ihesu lay and lulled was
Harde peynis for to pas
Pro peccante homine.
" Kynges comyer fro dyvess londe
With grete gyftes in here honde,
In Bedlem the childe they fonde.
Stellae ducti lumine.
" Man and chylde bothe old and ying
Now in his blysful comyng,
To that chyld mon we syng
Gloria tibi Domine.
" Nowel, nowel in this halle
Make merye I pray you alle
Onto the chylde may we calle
Ullo sine crimine."

Another carol in this MS. is as follows :—

" Alleluiah, Al. Al. Al. Al. Alleluia
deo patri sit gloria.
" Salvator mundi domine,
Fader of hevene blessed thou be
Thou gretest a mayden with an ave,
Quae vocatur Maria.
" Adesto nunc propitius
Thou sendyst thy son swete Jesus
Man to become for love of us
deo patri sit gloria."

There are about 76 songs in this MS., a large proportion of them being carols, which, translated into modern English, with good tunes from equally old sources, might be utilised with advantage by competent editors for present use. There are unfortunately no musical notes in this rare and interesting MS.

Another 15th cent. MS. supplied materials for *Songs and Carols now first printed from a MS. of the XVth cent.,* edited by Thomas Wright, Esq., M.A., F.S.A., &c. Printed for the Percy Soc., 1847. From this MS. we quote the following carol as being of more than usual interest :—

[last] " This *endris* nyght
          I saw a syght
          A stare as bryght as day;
          And ever among
          A mayden song
          Lullay, by by, lullay.

" This lovely lady sat and song, and to hyr chyld sayd,
   My sone, my broder, my fader der, why lyest thou thus
[Winter] My swete byrd   [hayd.
          Thus it ys betyde
[true]   Thow thou be kyng *veray* ;
          But nevertheless
          I wyl not ses
            To syng, by by, lullay.
" The chylde than spak in hys talking and to his moder
   I *be kydde am* kyng in *crybbe* thar I be layd.   [sayd.
[am renowned as] [manger]
          For aungeils bryght
          Done to me lyght
[not to be denied] Thou knost it ys *no nay* ;
          And of that syght
[quick]   Thou mayst be *lyght*
            To syng, by by, lullay,   [in stall
" Now swet son syn thou art kyng, why art thou layd
   Why ne thou ordende thi beddyng in sum gret kyngs
          Me thynkyth it is ryght   [hall ?
          That kyng or knyght
[lie]   Shuld *ly* in good aray ;
          And than among
          It wer no wrong
            To syng, by by, lullay.
" Mary moder, I am thi chyld, thow I be layd in stall,
   Lordes and dukes shall woschyp me, and so shall
          Ye shall well see   [kyngs all.
          That kynges thre
          Shall come the XII day,
          For this behest
          Geve me thi brest,
            And syng, by by, lullay.   [and dere,
" Now tell me, swet son, I the pray, thou art my leve
   How shuld I kepe to thy *pay*, and make the glad of
[satisfaction]   [chere ?
          For all thi wyll
          I wold fulfyll
[knowest] [faith] Thou *wetyste* full well in *fay*,
          And for all thys
          I wyll the kys,
            And syng, by by, lullay.
" My der moder, when tym it be, thou take me upon loft,
   And set me upon thi kne, and handyll me full soft.
          And in thi arme
[cover]   Thou *hyl* me warme
          And kepe me nyght and day ;
          If I wepe
          And may not slepe
            Thou syng, by by, lullay.
" Now, swet son, syn it is so that all thyng is at thi wyll
   I pray the graunte me a bone [boon] yf it be both
          That chyld or man   [ryght and skyll.
          That wyl or kan
          Be mery upon my day,
          To blyse them bryng,
          And I shal syng
            Lullay, by by, lullay."

What sermon on the *mystery of mysteries*,—
" *God manifest in the flesh*,"—could more
eloquently set forth its paradox, than this
most poetical relic of the 15th century ? No
record, alas ! is forthcoming of its original
melody. It is however set (in modernised
English) to an old English air, and beautifully harmonised by Dr. Steggall, in *Christmas Carols, by the Rev. Henry Ramsden
Bramley, M.A., and John Stainer, Esq., M.A.,
Mus. D.*, No. 25.

Another unique manuscript, of great historical interest (*Brit. Mus. Addit. MSS.*, 5665),
made before, or certainly very early in, the
reign of Hen. VIII., must not be left without
mention here. It contains :—

A Collection of Church Services, Hymns, and Carols.
A Modern Index of its contents has been carefully made
and prefixed to the MS. itself ; it includes 104 items. On
fol. 66 b, at the bottom, is a marriage certificate ; and
on the next leaf, a power of attorney to receive rents,
dated at Pyworthy, Devon, April 30, in the 3rd y. of H.

VIII. In another place there is a receipt for £26, anl.
pension to Langetre Church, 2nd y. of the same reign.
It seems to have belonged to some choir, and contains
(besides these miscellaneous insertions) much well transcribed vocal music in three parts—plain-song and very
operose descant, not scored in a modern way—most
difficult of interpretation even by experienced musical
antiquarians. There are some fifteen pieces, headed " *In
die Nativitatis*"; various *Misereres, Kyries, Hymns for
Saints' Days, Te Deums and other Canticles, Masses*,
a great number of *sacred* and some *secular* songs.

The whole of this book is in a measure a
reflection of the unsettled state of Church
services, and the upheaving of the old order
of things at the dawn of the Reformation. It
does not appear that any interpreter has as
yet published an intelligible version of the
entire MS., or of any of the most interesting
parts of it. Both *Sandys*, No. VII., and the
Editor of *Christmas with the Poets*, p. 6, have
indeed quoted, from folio 5 b, one carol, the
former printing the old English, the latter
modernising it. The following is a literal
version of this carol from the MS. itself :—

In die Nativitatis [with musical notation]. [Solo.]
Tenor. Nowell ! Nowell ! Nowell ! Nowell !
     " Who ys there that syngeth so Nowell Nowell."
     " I am here Syre crists Masse "
[Plain-song] " Wellcome my lord Syr Christs Masse "
[Chorus] " Wellcome to all both more and less."
          Com ner Nowell
     Dieus wous garde byewe Srs tydings
     A mayde hath borne a chylde full yong
     The weche causeth yew for to syng. Nowell.
     Criste is now born of a pure mayde
     In an ox stall he is laid
     Wherefore sing we all atte abrayde.* Nowell.
     Beuvex bien par tutta la company
     Make gode chere and be ryght merry
     And synge with us now joyfully. Nowell.

With similar mixture of verse and chorus,
in harmony of the most " operose " kind, we
find on fol. 8 b the following, also headed,

In die Nativitatis.
†   c c a F C D E F.
     Joseph wonder how this may be
     That mary wex gret wheny and she
     ever have levyd in chastite.
     Iff she be wt chylde, ;
          hit ys not by me.
     mervel not joseph.
     The holy gost wt mercifull distence
     In here [= her] hathe entryd wtowte offence
     God and man conceyved by his presence
     In virgyne pure wtowte violence.
     What the angel of god to me dothe say
     Joseph muste and will umble obey.
     Albye prevely [privily] y [I] wolde have stole away
     But now will y fre her till that y say
     Mervel not Joseph.

The following is from the same source
[MS. 5665, fol. 406] :—

     Jhesu fili virginis
          miserere nobis.
     Angelis ther were mylde of mode
     Song to that swete fode,
     With joye and blisse.
          miserere nobis.
[crib or cradle] In a *crache* was that chylde layde,
     Both oxe and asse with hym playde,
     With joye and blisse.
          miserere nobis.
[who]   Then for us *ho* shadde his blode,
     And also ho dyedde pro vobis,
     And for us I wiss,
          miserere nobis.

─────────────

* *Abrayde*, to awaken (also neuter), to rouse oneself
(Nares's Glossary). Hence the line may mean *Sing we
all loudly, " lustily."*
† These are the notes of the plain-song in letters.
See the Primer of Plain-Song, p. 26, 1st note.

And then to helle he toke the way,
To ransom them that there lay
With joy and blisse,
    miserere nobis.

Another, for Epiphany, begins thus :—

There were three Persons, and one Lord.
The Son baptized with one accord,
The Father said the blessed word,
    Hic est filius meus.

[The spelling here is modernised.]

In addition to the MSS. from which we have
quoted, there are others which have been consulted, in which many carols may be found
and illustrated, e.g. :—

Brit. Mus. Harleian Coll., 541, fol. 44. Do. 2252,
fol. 153-400. Do. 5396, fol. 4 ro. Arundel MS., 248,
14, v, and the Harleian MS., 682. Nares's Glossary of
Old English may be consulted for the interpretation of
16th and 17th cent. words.

(2) Printed Carols.—Printed Carols, whether
in collections or scattered in various other
works, and, as it were, buried under a mass of
heterogeneous literature, next claim attention.
In Ames's Typographical Antiquities, we learn
that Wynkyn de Worde printed in 1521 a set
of Christmas carols, and that "these were
festival chansons for enlivening the Christmas
celebrity." (See also Warton's Eng. Poetry,
iii. sec. 26.) The following list, though by
no means complete, will indicate the nature
and character of some of the rarer and less
known works in which carols may be found.
Including books and broadsheets, we have the
following :—

1. Paradise of Dainty Devises. 1576. Francis Ken-
nelmersh.
2. Psalms, Sonnets and Songs of Sadness and Piety.
1587. William Byrd [?].
3. St. Peter's Complaint. 1593. Robert Southwell.
4. Hymns and Songs of the Church. 1623. And
Hallelujah. George Wither. 1641.
5. Devotions. 1635. William Austin.
6. Underwoods. 1640. Ben Jonson.
7. Noble Numbers. 1647. Robert Herrick.
8. The Golden Grove. 1655. Jeremy Taylor.
9. Paraphrase upon the Canticles. S. Woodford.
10. Supp. to Tate and Brady. 1700. N. Tate.
11. Poems Amorous, Moral and Divine. 1718. Anon.
12. Hymns on the Nativity. 1746. And Hymns for
Children. 1763. By C. Wesley.
13. Complete Psalmodist. 1749. John Arnold.
14. The Christmas Box; or New Year's Gift. R. T. S.
c. 1820-30, containing all the carols which the Society
had previously issued as separate tracts.
15. Christmas Carols. [Original.] 1837. Lond., 4to.
16. A Good Christmas Box, containing a choice collection of Christmas Carols. Dudley. 1847.
17. New Carol-book for Christmas. Bilston. c. 1830.
18. Christmas Hymns and Sacred Pieces. Bermond-
sey. c. 1818.
19. Christmas Carols; three series with music, by
Dr. Gauntlett.
20. Christmas and Christmas Carols. c. 1845-50. J.
F. R., with a valuable preface.
21. Divers Carols for Xmas and Sundry Tides of Holy
Church. 1864. A. H. Brown. This has an interesting Introduction on the whole subject.
22. The Sacristy. 1871. No. 4 specially for the Rev.
S. Baring-Gould's tr. of Noels and Carols of French
Flanders.
23. Carols, Hymns, and Songs. 1882. J. H. Hopkins,
New York.
24. The American Works of Bp. Coxe, Dr. Croswell,
and others.
25. A Garland of Christmas Carols, Ancient & Modern,
by Joshua Sylvester. Lond., 1861.
26. Carols and Poems from the 15th cent. to the
Present Time. Edited by A. H. Bullen. 1885.

We have by no means exhausted the list;
but these works, and those now to be more
fully described, will be sufficient to indicate
the wealth of carol literature which we
possess. In addition there are :—

(a) Songs and Carols edited by Thomas
Wright, M.A., 1847, already referred to as
printed from the Sloane MS. 2593.

(b) Christmas Tide, its History, Festivities
and Carols, by W. Sandys, 1852. He gives an
excellent historical account of the Christmas
Festival in its sacred and secular celebration ;
42 Ancient Carols; a Mock Christmas Play;
and 12 other Carols, with their melodies in
short score.

(c) Christmas with the Poets. Bell & Daldy.
This is a magnificent volume, embellished
with 35 illustrations by Birket Foster. It
contains poems and Christmas carols from the
Anglo-Norman period to the present time.
It is divided into five sections. An outline of
these will give a bird's-eye view of their
contents.

(1) The Anglo-Norman Period to the Reformation.
One extract from this will give a good idea of the rest.
It is the translation of an Anglo-Norman Carol of the
13th cent., beginning (in Sandys's Christmas Tide)
"Seignors, ore entendez à nus": "Lordlings, listen to
our lay." The opening stanza is :—

    "Lordlings, listen to our lay,
        We have come from far away
            To seek Christmas ;
        In this mansion we are told
        He His yearly feast doth hold :
            Tis to-day !
        May joy come from God above
        To all those who Christmas love."

The chorus is the most decidedly pious part of this
carol :—

    "Den doint a tuz icels joie d'amurs
    Qui à danz noël ferunt honors ! " i. e.

    "May joy come from God above,
    To all those who Christmas love."

(2) The Elizabethan Era (1558-1603). This period
furnished the following amongst others :—

1. "Was not Christ our Saviour
        Sent unto us from God above ? "
                                Thomas Tusser.
2. "Behold, a silly [simple] tender Babe
        In freezing winter night."
                                Robert Southwell, d. 1595.
3. "I sing the birth was born to-night,
        The Author both of life and light."
                                Ben Jonson, 1600.
4. "Immortal Babe, who this dear day
        Didst change Thine heav'n for our clay."
                                Bp. Hall, cir. 1597.
5. "Run, Shepherds, run where Bethlehem blest
        appears,
        We bring the best of news, be not dismayed."
                                W. Drummond.
6. "O than the fairest day, thrice fairer night,
        Night to best days in which a sun doth shine."
                                W. Drummond.
7. "All after pleasures as I rid one day,
        My horse and I, both tired, bodie and minde."
                                G. Herbert.
8. "Sweet music, sweeter far
        Than any song is sweet." Edmund Bolton.
9. "The wrathful winter proaching on apace
        With blushing blast, and all yebared the treen."
                                Thomas Sackville.
10. "Some say that ever 'gainst that season comes,
        Wherein our Saviour's birth is celebrated."
                                W. Shakespeare.

(3) Poems by Herrick (1591-1674). Of these the
following may be mentioned as truly religious and
poetical carols :—

    I. "In numbers, and but these few,
        I sing thy birth, O Jesu."

    2. "What sweeter music can we bring
        Than carol for to sing ? "

    3. "Tell us thou clear and heavenly tongue,
        Where is the Babe but lately sprung,
        Lies He the lily-banks among ? "

4. " Down with the rosemary and the bays,
      Down with the mistletoe ;
      Instead of holly, now upraise
      The greener box, for show."

Of these No. 3 is the "Star Song," and 4 is for Candlemas Eve.

(4) *The Civil Wars, the Commonwealth, and the Restoration.* George Wither is the leading singer of the earlier part of this period. His carols include:—

1. " As on the night before this happy morn."   1623.
2. " Lord, with what zeal did Thy first martyr." 1623.
3. " Teach us by his example, Lord."   1623.
4. " That rage whereof the Psalm doth say." 1623.
5. " That so thy blessed birth, O Christ." 1623.

Passing to others we have :—

6. " It was the winter wild." *J. Milton.*
7. " Come, we shepherds, whose blest sight,'
                                    R. Crashaw.
8. " The blessed Virgin travailed without pain."
                                    Bp. Jeremy Taylor.
9. " All you that in this house be here."
                                    New Carols. 1661.
10. " Now that the time is come wherein
       Our Saviour Christ was born."
                            Poor Robin's Almanack, 1700.

(5) *The Eighteenth Century.* The editor of *Christmas with the Poets* (the collection with which we are now dealing) says, " Few poems bearing reference to the Christmas Festival appear to have been produced during that era of the revival of English literature which has acquired the epithet of Augustan." He quotes from John Grey, John Bampfylde, and R. J. Thorn ; but their verses have not the true ring of carol minstrelsy, and are not likely to have been used as such. Singularly enough, he omits all reference to J. Byrom's "Christians, awake, salute the happy morn," and C. Wesley's " Hark, how all the welkin rings."

(6) *Nineteenth Century.* In this division we have extracts from 29 poets, including Sir Walter Scott, W. Wordsworth, Southey, Goodwyn Barmby, Barry Cornwall, J. Keble, Shelley, S. T. Coleridge, and Tennyson.

(d) In 1822 some *Ancient Christmas Carols* were edited by Davis Gilbert, F.R.S., F.A.S., &c., with the tunes to which he had been accustomed to hear them sung when he was a child, in churches and in private houses on Christmas Eve, throughout the West of England, up to the latter end of the 18th century. They used to be practised several weeks beforehand ; and on the night of Christmas Eve, and on the Festival of the Nativity itself, they were sung with great fervour *at home,* after the 8 P.M. drawing of the cakes hot from the oven, and the festive draughts of ale or cyder, and *at Church,* instead of the metrical Psalms, specially at the afternoon service; and, he informs us, " none of the sports or gambols, so frequently practised on subsequent days, ever mixed themselves with the religious observances of Christmas Eve." The characteristic of these popular carols is that they consist for the most part of simple narratives of Holy Scripture with a grateful admonition to corresponding Christian duty and gratitude. They are set to music of a solemn tonality and a sprightly movement, derived apparently from very early composers, and mostly in the Ancient Church Modes. There are only *eight* carols, the first lines of which are :—

1. " The Lord at first did Adam make." This deals with the *Fall,* is in 7 st. of 8 l., and a refrain of four lines, and is set to a tune in the Dorian mode and ¾ time.

2. " When God at first created man." The *Fall,* the *Annunciation,* and the *Nativity* are dealt with. The melody is in the Eolian mode, and in ⁶⁄₈ time.

3. " A Virgin most pure as the prophets do tell." This is also given in W. Sandys's *Christmas Tide,* No. 23, p. 313, with a different form of the melody. From these

two sources it was rearranged in 1860, by the late E. Sedding, in his 1st *Set of Ancient Christmas Carols,* arranged for four voices. The melody is in the 7th or Mixo-Lydian mode.

4. " When righteous Joseph wedded was."

5. " Hark ! hark ! what news the Angels bring ! " This is in 5 st. of 4 l. L.M., and has no chorus.

6. " While Shepherds watched their flocks by night." These well-known words, by N. Tate, are set to an ancient melody, reminding one of the tune of the Latin hymn, " O filii et filiae " (*Hymnal N.,* 81).

7. " God's dear Son without beginning." This carol in 9 st. of 8 l. is sweetly pious in sentiment, and somewhat above the ordinary level of poetic feeling.

8. " Let all that are to mirth inclined." This is in 16 st. of 4 l., with a chorus of 2 l. :—
        " For to redeem our souls from thrall,
          Christ is the Saviour of us all."

In this carol the whole story of Christmas and Epiphany Tide is told in plain and terse rhymes, well calculated to catch the ear and touch the hearts of simple and unsophisticated carollers. The tune is bold and effective, in the Dorian mode on A, and in ⁴⁄₄ time.

(e) Some years ago an extremely rare book was brought from Stockholm, and placed in the hands of the Editors of the *Hymnal Noted ;* and the *Carols for Christmas-Tide,* and *Easter-Tide,* subsequently published in 1853 and 1854, were the fruits of the Rev. J. M. Neale's study of the verse, and the Rev. T. Helmore's interpretation and harmonisation of the musical notation it contained. This small duodecimo volume is the :—

Piae Cantiones Ecclesiasticae et Scholasticae, veterum Episcoporum, in Inclyto Regno Sueciae passim usurpatae. (Printed at Greifswald.)

These "pious songs of ancient bishops, everywhere in vogue in Sweden," were revised and edited in the year 1582 by the Most Rev. *Theodore Peter Rhuta,* of Nyland ; they are stated, in the titlepage, to be most highly esteemed by the Church of God, and the School at Abo, in Finland. The Dedication to his Patron the "Illustrious and Noble Lord Christian Horn, Free Baron of Aminna," enforces the Apostolic teaching as to the use of Psalms, Hymns and Spiritual Songs, by the practice of the " Old Fathers," who always joined music with the Word of God, as also by that of the wise governors and pious Bishops of the Christian Church. This dedication is dated from Rostock, May 23, 1582.

Every canticle of the 75 contained in the 200 pages of this little book has the notes of a melody to which all the verses are to be sung, some being also furnished with a second part, others with three or four parts. A few are noted throughout, after the manner of sequences, with recurring strains, but not in exact regular verses, as in the usual tunes of carols and hymns. The first part of the little book (to p. 70) contains *Cantiones de Nativitate,* then follow others, *de Passione,* and *de Resurrectione;* at pages 104, 105, 106 and 107 there are the *Descantus, Altus, Tenor* and *Bassus,* of a setting of the Hymn " *Jesu dulcis memoriae,*" in the Dorian mode on G. Next a Phrygian melody to a carol, " *In Festo Pentecostes,*" at p. 109. Songs, De Trinitate ; at p. 115, De Eucharistia ; at p. 112, Cantiones precum, some of them *Hymns* in the strictest sense. Some songs follow, lamenting, and inveighing against crimes, wickedness, and general corruption of manners. At p. 158, to 176, are songs, *De vita Scholastica ;* and the collection closes with a couple of songs under each of the following headings, *De Concordia ; Historicae Cantiones,* and *De Tempore Vernali.*

" The *Piae Cantiones* were published for the use of the Lutheran communion in Sweden. Neither words nor music, however, were changed from earlier sources ; and they occur in the Libraries of Germany, England and France, with no other difference than traditionary repetition and popular variations would naturally introduce." (See the Prefaces in the folio ed. of *Helmore and Neale's Carols for Christmas-* and *Easter-Tide* for further information.)

(*f*) Soon after the publication of the 12 *Carols for Christmas-Tide*, and of the 12 *for Easter-Tide* before mentioned, Mr. Edmund Sedding, in 1860, published a set of nine *Antient Christmas Carols*, corresponding with the 18mo ed. of *Helmore and Neale's Carols* in size, type, and four-part vocal arrangement in compressed score, and a *separate book of words;* a 9th ed. appeared in 1863; and that same year a *second set* of seven more carols by the same energetic " Cantor of S. Raphael, Bristol," was published, and to the prefaces of each set the reader is referred for further information.

(*g*) Three original carols of the late Dr. Neale may also here be noticed :—

(1) *"Dives and Lazarus,"* arranged by Edmund Sedding—the melody is of the 15th cent.—*"Now bring in good cheer."* (2) *"Good Christians all, awake,"* for Christmas Morning; music by the Rev. Thomas Helmore. (3) Lines written expressly to a Danish air by E. Herneman, given by Dr. Neale in MS. to W. S. Lambert, who also received a pianoforte copy of the music from Mrs. Neale. Mr. Lambert arranged it for 4 voices, to which Mr. Manns added wind instrument accompaniments. As a grand march also, it has been performed both at the Crystal Palace and elsewhere. The words are, it is believed, now for the first time published, through Mr. Lambert's courtesy to the writer :—

A *Soldier's Carol*, by Rev. John Mason Neale, M.A. (D.D.); written to the Danish air " Der Tapfer Landsoldat " (by E. Herneman).

1.

God bless the brave and true,
God bless the brave and true,
God bless and bring them thro',
Yes, God bless and bring them thro',
　Whatever be the fight !
　God bless and save the right,
And send the happy morning
That shall end a gloomy night !
True men have all one hope, boys,
One faith, one strength, one aim ;
And though the battles differ,
The crown shall be the same.
And therefore God with us !
And we will be with Him.
　　Hurrah ! hurrah ! hurrah !

2.

With God to guard and guide,
With God to guard and guide,
We laugh at all beside !
Yes, we laugh at all beside !
Cheer up, brave hearts, and trust !
You can, you will, you must !
　And see the God of battle, lads,
And not the arm of dust !
The world and all its legions,
They band against the right ;
But if we have the truth, boys
　We also have the might.
And therefore God for us,
And we will be for Him.
　　Hurrah ! hurrah ! hurrah !

3.

So—close, and firm, and near !
So—close, and firm, and near !
" *Together, front and rear !* " *
Let him, poor wretch ! who may
The cause to gold betray !
For us—the sword is drawn—
Yes, and the scabbard flung away !
Strike in, strike in for justice !
Be spent, as well as spend :
And then—this life may go, boys,
The other cannot end.
And therefore God for us,
And we will be for Him.
　　Hurrah ! hurrah ! hurrah !

* The famous word passed along the lines, when the British soldiers led themselves at Fontenoy, 1745.

(*h*) Dr. Rimbault's *Little Book of Christmas Carols*, and Mr. Husk's excellent Collection of *Songs of the Nativity*, must not be omitted from the list of books included in the various and abundant sources of supply of original carols accessible to " *readers*," and to *singers*, of this popular Christian minstrelsy.

(*i*) *Carols for use in Church during Christmas and Epiphany, by the Rev. R. R. Chope,* 1875. The book has in all 112 carols. These include many old traditional ones, and many quite new, which (a reviewer in the *Literary Churchman* states) " are quite worthy, as a rule, of appearing with their time-honoured compeers." There is also a learned and most interesting Introduction, by the Rev. S. Baring-Gould ; and in it will be found much which appeared also in the fourth part of the *Sacristy*.

(*j*) *Christmas Carols, New and Old*, the words edited by the Rev. Henry Ramsden Bramley, M.A., with illustrations by the Brothers Dalziel, and music edited by Dr. Stainer, N.D., is a handsome addition to carol literature of the present times; excellent in the poetry, picturesque in the illustrations, correct and refined in the music and its arrangements. There is an excellent preface in a smaller ed. of this book, and an index giving the source of the music and of the words of each carol. (Novello & Co.) Of the 70 examples in this work there are some 29 from traditional sources, 19 of which are to be found in other collections; thus 11 of them are in *Sandys*, 3 in *Gilbert*, 3 in *Christmas with the Poets*, 2 in *Helmore and Neale*, and 12 in *Chope*. From this collection we select the following carols as being excellent for their sound doctrine, religious unction, and poetic fervour. But where almost all are, in their several kinds, very good, this notice of a few must not be taken as any disparagement of the rest.

1. " Come, ye lofty ; come, ye lowly." Rev. Archer Gurney.
2. " Come, tune your heart." *Tr.* by Frances E. Cox from the German.
3. " Jesu, hail ! " *Tr.* by the Rev. H. R. Bramley from " Ave Jesu Deus."
4. " Good Christian men, rejoice." Dr. Neale.
5. " On the birth-day of the Lord." *Tr.* by Dr. Littledale from the Latin.
6. " The great God of heaven is come down to earth," by H. R. Bramley.
7. " God's dear Son without beginning," already noticed.
8. " The Babe in Bethlehem's manger laid." This is traditional from Chappell's *Coll.*
9. " The Virgin stills the crying." *Tr.* by H. R. Bramley. The melody to this carol is by J. Barnby. It is a favourable example of the modern tunes and their arrangement, happily combining the simplicity of pure diatonic melody with slight touches of modern harmony.
10. " Once again, O blessed time," by the Rev. W. Bright, D.D.; high-toned faith and warm devotion, with most harmonious verse, characterise this most charming Christmas song.
11. " All this night, bright angels sing," by W. Austin, 1635, set to music by Sir A. Sullivan.
12. " Forth then she came to seek where He did roam." Among the carols of a legendary and imaginative cast perhaps the most striking in this collection is this by Dr. Stainer. It is an original conception, and not, as it might be thought, the elaboration of a most lovely legend. The carol is very beautiful, and closes with a lovely lesson :—

" Know then, dear brother, in these Christmas hours,
　Sorrow, like snow, will melt if He but smile ;
And if He clothe thy wintry path with flowers,
　Amidst thy mirth think on His thorns awhile."

13. " A Babe is born, all of a Maid." This is a

good specimen of the 15th cent. of a mixture of the vernacular with well-known lines of the Old Office hymns, as noted before. The first stanza reads :—

" A Babe is born, all of a Maid
To bring salvation with us ;
No more are we to sing afraid,
Veni, Creator Spiritus."

14. " Immortal Babe, who this dear day," by Bp. Hall, is already noted above. It was written for the choir of Exeter Cathedral.

Concerning No. 6 above, " The great God," &c., Dr. Stainer has supplied the following facts :—

He says he has every reason to believe that the melody was originally the same as that of " A Virgin unspotted, &c." The editors [of the *Christmas Carols, New and Old*] received several MS. copies of the tune taken orally, agreeing with that which they have printed : but from Gloucestershire a tune was obtained that was always sung to these words [" A Virgin unspotted, &c."] but differing widely from its more usual form. It was considered so beautiful that Dr. Stainer got his co-editor to arrange other words for it. Thus we are indebted to the happy accident of a variation in the melody for another carol on the Nativity, " The great God of heaven is come down to earth," equal to the former [" A Virgin unspotted "] in the clearness and interest of its narrative, and far surpassing it in depth of thought, and elegance of diction.

(*k*) An excellent collection of *Carols, Hymns and Noels for Christmastyde* was published by T. W. Staniforth, in 1883. It contains 20 lyrics. The editor has caught the spirit and adopted the true style of church harmony, both in the arrangements of the tunes generally, and in the six he has composed himself. The work deserves wide circulation, and a clearer typography than the engraved pages of the first issue.

(*l*) *Church Songs* by the Rev. S. Baring-Gould, with music edited by the Rev. H. F. Sheppard, 1884–86.

(*m*) *Carols and Poems from the 15th cent. to the Present Time*, by A. H. Bullen, 1885, is rich in words.

(*n*) *In Excelsis Gloria : Carols for Christmas-tide*, 1885. This is set to music by A. H. Brown, and contains both ancient and modern Carols not found in other modern collections.

(*o*) *Carols for Easter and other Tides.* By the Rev. R. R. Chope, 1887.

(3) *Lullaby Carols.* One of the most striking of these we have already given, p. 209. Of others a few specimens must suffice. From the *Latin* we have "Sleep, my Babe ! O sleep, the Mother," a *tr.* of " Dormi, Fili ! dormi, Mater," by Mary D. Moultrie, in the Rev. Gerard Moultrie's *Hymns and Lyrics*, 1867 ; from the *German* of J. C. Rube, " Sleep well, my dear, sleep safe and free," in Jacobi's *Psalmodia Germanica*, 1722 ; from *Old English*, " My sweet little Babie, what meanest thou for to cry," in *Byrd* as above, and Montgomery's *Christian Poet*, 1827 ; " Sweet baby, sleep, what ails my dear ?" G. Wither, 1641 as above ; and "Hush, my dear, lie still and slumber," by I. Watts.

(4) *Secular Carols.* Amongst the less sacred or wholly secular carols may be mentioned the famous Queen's College *Boar's Head Carol* commonly ushering in the Christmas banquet ; not only there, but at all grand tables of monarchs and nobles ; songs in praise of holly and ivy ; wassailing songs, and those of the waits, all so well described by Sandys. It is perhaps allowable to add a a brief account of at least one specimen of a

class, by no means uncommon in earlier days, legendary in their origin, and sometimes childish in their character.

At Coventry, in 1483, Richard III. witnessed the " *Ludus Corporis Christi* "; and so also did Henry VII. in 1485. This play opens at the sending forth of the decree of Augustus, and the consequent journey of S. Joseph and the B. V. Mary to Bethlehem. On the way she sees a tree, and asks what it is. S. Joseph replies, " For s\uthe Mary it is cleped a cherry tree ; In tyme of year, ye might feed you thereon your fill." They converse on the tree, he desiring to hasten on ; she to have some of the fruit. He deems it impossible to get at it, but implies that He by whom she is with child could grant her wish. She prays God that, if it be His will, she may have some of the cherries. The tree immediately bows down to her. Joseph fears he has offended the Blessed Trinity, and humbles himself. Hence the subject of the carol still sung, with various readings, in many parts of England, " *Joseph was an old man*." Sandys, at p. 241; Chope, No. 26 ; and Bramwell and Stainer, No. 28 ; give each a different version. In Chope the legend is eliminated, doubtless that the rest of the song may not be excluded from use in Church. Mr. Baring-Gould considers this story " is the lingering of a very curious mysterious tradition, common to the whole race of man, that the eating of the fruit in Eden was the cause of the descendant of Eve becoming the Mother of Him who was to wipe away that old transgression,"[*] and he refers to Finnish epic poetry, the mythology of the Mexicans, a romance that has lately appeared from the catacombs of Egypt, and other rare sources of information in support of this view.

iv *Conclusion.*—The revival of carol singing already alluded to has stimulated both poets and composers to add fresh stores to that abundance already transmitted to our age from earlier and more thoroughly believing times. The translations from the Latin writers in the Ages of Faith, when happily turned into true English idiom, and versification (as so many are, specially those of the late lamented Dr. John Mason Neale), are not only most worthy of use, but are the best patterns (and fortunately the most imitated) for the hymn and carol writers of the present day. Time, the certain arbiter of true excellence, has tried the *old* as it will eventually the *new*. " It is impossible at one stretch to produce a quantity of new carols, of which words and music shall alike be original. They must be the gradual accumulation of centuries; the offerings of different epochs, of different countries, of different minds, to the same treasury of the Church. None but an empiric would venture to make a set to order." (Neale, Preface to *Carols for Christmas-Tide*.) [T. H.]

Carpenter, Joseph Edwardes, PH.D., journalist, compiler of popular songs and ballads, dramatic writer and author of songs and hymns, was b. in London, Nov. 2, 1813, and d. in London, May 6, 1885. For a short time he was on the staff of some local journals in Leamington. His works, original and compiled, number nearly 20. These include his *Songs: Sacred and Devotional*, 1866, and from this volume his hymns are taken. Dean Alford included his " Lord and Father of creation " (*Holy Matrimony*) in *The Year of Praise*, 1867. [J. J.]

Carr, Thomas William, M.A., s. of Thomas William Carr, B.A., Incumbent of Southborough, b. June 15, 1830, and educated at Wadham College, Oxford, where he graduated (in honours), 1853. On taking Holy Orders in 1856, he became Curate of St. Peter's

[*] " In the Carol, and the Mystery Play, this tradition is strangely altered, but its presence cannot fail to be detected." Introduction to Chope's *Carols*, p. xxi.

with Holy Cross, Canterbury. In 1857 he was preferred to the Rectory of Beaudesert, and in the same year to the Rectory of Loddington, North Hants. He entered upon the Rectory of Barming, near Maidstone, in 1865. His hymn on "The Seven Words from the Cross," beginning "Draw near, thou lowly Christian," was written at Loddington in Holy Week, 1865, and pub. by Dalton; revised in 1885, and pub. by Wells Gardner, Darton & Co. The *People's H.*, 1867, has the original text. [J. J.]

Cary, Alice, the elder of two gifted sisters, was b. near Cincinnati, Ohio, 1820, removed to New York in 1852, and d. there Feb. 12, 1871. The story of the two sisters—of their courageous move from a rural, western home, their life in the metropolis, their mutual affection, and inability to live apart—has attracted much admiring and sympathetic interest. As poets they were of nearly equal merit. Besides some prose works, Alice pub. a vol. of *Poems* in 1850. Her hymns are:—

1. **Earth with its dark and dreadful ills.** *Death anticipated.* This fine lyric is given in *Hys. and Songs of Praise*, N. Y., 1874, and dated 1870.

2. **Along the mountain track of life.** *Lent.* The authorship of this hymn, although sometimes attributed to Alice Cary, is uncertain. It appeared anonymously in H. W. Beecher's *Plymouth Coll.*, 1855, No. 438. It would seem from its tone and the refrain, "Nearer to Thee," to have been suggested by Mrs. Adams's "Nearer, my God, to Thee," which appeared in 1841.

In addition to these there are the following hymns by her in the *Lyra Sac. Amer.*, 1868:—

3. Bow, angels, from your glorious state. *Peace desired.*
4. I cannot plainly see the way. *Providence.*
5. Leave me, dear ones, to my slumber. *Death anticipated.*
6. Light waits for us in heaven. *Heaven.*
7. A crown of glory bright. *The Fadeless Crown.* In the *Meth. S. S. H. Bk.* (Lond.), 1879.   [F. M. B.]

Cary, Phœbe, sister of the above, b. near Cincinnati, Ohio, Sept. 4, 1824, and d. within six months of the death of the same sister at Newport, July 31, 1871. Her works include *Poems and Parodies*, 1854; and *Poems of Faith, Hope and Love*, 1868. With Dr. Charles F. Deems she compiled *Hymns for all Christians*, 1869. Her hymns are:—

1. **One sweetly solemn thought.** *Anticipation of Heaven.* This piece was not intended for public use, nor is it a suitable metre for musical treatment, yet it has won universal acceptance and popularity. In some instances this has been attained by change of metre as in the *Suppl.* to the Bapt. *Ps. & Hys.* 1880, No. 1185. Johnson's *Encyclopædia* is in error in saying it was "written at the age of 17." *The Congregational Quarterly* for Oct., 1874, says, "it was written, she tells us, in the little back third story bedroom, one Sabbath morning in 1852, on her return from church." This statement shows that it was composed when she was 28, and not 17. The popularity of the hymn in G. Britain arose mainly through its use in the Evangelistic services of Messrs. Moody and Sankey. In the Protestant Episc. *Hys. for Ch. and Home*, Phila., 1860, No. 383, it is given as "*A* sweetly solemn thought."

The following additional pieces by this author are in the *Lyra Sac. Amer.*, 1868:—

2. Go and sow beside all waters. *Seed Sowing.*
3. Great waves of plenty rolling up. *Gratitude.*
4. I had drunk, with lips unsated. *Living Waters.*
[F. M. B.]

Cäsar, Heinrich, was b. at Greussen in Thuringia, c. 1597, and became diaconus at Labiau, East Prussia, in 1624. He was instituted Feb. 25, 1627, as pastor at Loewenhagen, near Königsberg (Löwenhagen or Leuenhagen), and d. there, in his 72nd year, Aug. 11, 1669 (MS. from Pastor Winkler of Loewenhagen). The hymn:

In dieser Abendstunde, erheb ich [*Evening*], appeared with his name in the *New Preussisches vollständiges G. B.*, Königsberg, 1650, p. 650, in 16 st., and J. Crüger's *Praxis*, 1648, No. 22. Sometimes erroneously ascribed to Conrad Huober, of Strassburg. It is *tr.* as, "In this the evening hour," by *H. J. Buckoll*, 1842, p. 79.   [J. M.]

Cast thy burden on the Lord. [*Strength in God.*] This hymn appeared anonymously (in common with all the hymns therein) in Rowland Hill's *Ps. and Hymns*, &c., 1st ed., 1783, No. 64, in 5 st. of 4 l., and entitled, "Encouragement for the Weak." In this form it passed into several collections to 1853, when it appeared in the *Leeds H. Bk.*, No. 571, rewritten by G. Rawson. As the hymn in both forms is in C. U., and the latter somewhat extensively, we append the two.

R. Hill's text, 1783.	*G. Rawson's text*, 1853.
Cast thy burden on the Lord,	Cast thy burden on the Lord,
Only lean upon His word;	Only lean upon His word;
Thou wilt soon have cause to bless	Thou shalt soon *find* cause to bless
His eternal faithfulness.	His eternal faithfulness.
He sustains thee by His hand;	Wouldst thou know thyself a child?
He enables thee to stand;	Is thy proud heart reconciled?
Those whom Jesus once hath lov'd,	Is it humbled to the dust,
From His grace are never mov'd.	Full of awe and full of trust?
Human counsels come to nought;	Dost thou not rejoice with fear?
That shall stand which God hath wrought;	Never be high-minded here;
His compassion, love and power	Heed not what the tempter saith,
Are the same for evermore.	Cling to Christ in lowly faith.
Heaven and earth may pass away,	Fear not, then, in every storm
God's free grace shall not decay;	There shall come the Master's form;
He hath promised to fulfil All the pleasure of His will.	Cheering voice and present aid— "It is I, be not afraid."
Jesus, Guardian of Thy flock,	*He will hold thee with His hand,*
Be Thyself our constant Rock;	*And enable thee to stand;*
Make us by Thy powerful hand	*His compassion, love, and power*
Strong as Sion's mountain stand.	*Are the same for evermore.*

By comparing the portions in italics in each of the above it will be seen, st. i. and v. of the 1853 text are from Rowland Hill, 1783; and st. ii., iii. and iv. are by G. Rawson. In some hymnals, specially in America, alterations are introduced into the 1853 text, as for instance in the *Hys. and Songs of Praise*, N. Y., 1874, and others. The extent of these and other alterations may be gathered by comparing any given text with those above.   [J. J.]

Caswall, Edward, M.A., s. of the Rev. R. C. Caswall, sometime Vicar of Yately,

Hampshire, b. at Yately, July 15, 1814, and educated at Brasenose College, Oxford. graduating in honours in 1836. Taking Holy Orders in 1838, he became in 1840 Incumbent of Stratford-sub-Castle, near Salisbury, and resigned the same in 1847. In 1850 (Mrs. Caswall having died in 1849) he was received into the Roman Catholic communion, and joined Dr. Newman at the Oratory, Edgbaston. His life thenceforth, although void of stirring incidents, was marked by earnest devotion to his clerical duties and a loving'interest in the poor, the sick, and in little children. His original poems and hymns were mostly written at the Oratory. He d. at Edgbaston, Jan. 2, 1878, and was buried on Jan. 7 at Redwall, near Bromsgrove, by his leader and friend Cardinal Newman. Caswall's translations of Latin hymns from the *Roman Breviary* and other sources have a wider circulation in modern hymnals than those of any other translator, Dr. Neale alone excepted. This is owing to his general faithfulness to the originals, and the purity of his rhythm, the latter feature specially adapting his hymns to music, and for congregational purposes. His original compositions, although marked by considerable poetical ability, are not extensive in their use, their doctrinal teaching being against their general adoption outside the Roman communion. His hymns appeared in :—

(1) *Lyra Catholica*, which contained 197 translations from the *Roman Breviary, Missal*, and other sources. 1st ed. Lon., James Burns, 1849. This was reprinted in New York in 1851, with several hymns from other sources added thereto. This edition is quoted in the indices to some American hymn-books as *Lyra Cath.*, as in Beecher's *Plymouth Coll.* 1855, and others.

(2) *Masque of Mary, and Other Poems*, having in addition to the opening poem and a few miscellaneous pieces, 53 translations, and 51 hymns. 1st ed. Lon., Burns and Lambert, 1858.

(3) *A May Pageant and Other Poems*, including 10 original hymns. Lon., Burns and Lambert, 1865.

(4) *Hymns and Poems*, being the three preceding volumes embodied in one, with many of the hymns rewritten or revised, together with elaborate indices. 1st ed. Lon., Burns, Oates & Co., 1873. Of his original hymns about 20 are given in the Roman Catholic *Crown of Jesus H. Bk.*, N.D.; there are also several in the *Hymns for the Year*, N.D., and other Roman Catholic collections.   [J. J.]

Cawood, John, M.A., b. at Matlock, Derbyshire, March 18, 1775. His parents being in humble circumstances, he received in childhood but a limited education, and at 18 was engaged in the service of the Rev. Mr. Cursham, Sutton-in-Ashfield, Notts. Three years' study, however, under careful direction, enabled him to enter St. Edmund Hall, Oxford, in 1797. Obtaining his degree in 1801, he took Holy Orders, and became successively Curate of Ribsford and Dowles, and Incumbent of St. Ann's Chapel of Ease, Bewdley, Worcestershire. He d. Nov. 7, 1852. His hymns, 17 in all, were never published by himself. Of these 9 were included in Cotterill's *Sel.*, 8th ed., 1819, Nos. 268–276. Most of these have passed into other collections. These are :—

1. Almighty God, Thy word is cast. *After a Sermon.*
2. Hark! what mean those holy voices? (1819.) *Christmas.*
3. Begin a joyful song. (1819.) *Christmas.*
4. Behold yon wondrous star. (1819.) *Epiphany.*
5. Trembling with tenderest alarms. (1816.) *Finding of Moses.*
6. In Israel's fane, by silent night. (1816.) *Samuel.*
7. King o'er all worlds the Saviour shone. (1819.) *Good Friday.*

8. Christians, the glorious hope ye know. (1819.) *Plea for Missions.*
9. Hark! what mean those lamentations. (1819.) *Missions.*

In addition, Dr. Rogers pub. in his *Lyra Brit.*, 1867, from the author's MSS. :—

10. A child of sin and wrath I'm born. (1820.) *Infant's Prayer.*
11. The Son of God, in worlds on high. (1822.) *Christ's Humility.*
12. Blessed Father, Great Creator. (1837.) *Holy Trinity.*

These details are from the s. MSS., amongst which there are 5 hymns yet unpublished.

[J. J.]

Cecil, Richard, M.A., b. in London, Nov. 8, 1748, and educated at Queen's Coll., Oxford. Ordained deacon in 1776, and priest in 1777. He became the Vicar of two churches near Lewes shortly after; chaplain of St. John's Chapel, Bedford Row, London, 1780; and Vicar of Chobham and Bisley, 1800. He died in 1810. His poem :—

Cease here longer to detain me. *Desiring Heaven.* In 9 st. of 4 l., is supposed to be addressed by a dying infant to his mother. It was written for his wife on the death of a child "only one month old, being removed at daybreak, whose countenance at the time of departure was most heavenly." It was 1st pub. in Mrs. Cecil's *Memoir* of him, prefixed to his *Remains*, 1811, and is headed "Let me go, for the day breaketh." In the American hymn-books it is usually abbreviated, as in the *Plymouth Coll.*, 1855, and others.   [W. T. B.]

Cedant justi signa luctus. [*Easter.*] The date and authorship of this Sequence are unknown. Dr. Neale (*Med. Hys.*, 1st ed., 1851) regarded it of French origin, and certainly not earlier than the 13th cent., as evidenced by its subjective character, and the occurrence of one or two terms which were scarcely known to mediaeval writers. *Daniel* gives it in vol. ii. pp. 362–3, and Dr. Neale in *Hymni Ecclesiae*, 1851, p. 148. It is also in the *Tochter Sion*, Cologne, 1741, p. 251.

[W. A. S.]

Translation in C. U. :—

Far be sorrow, tears and sighing, by J. M. Neale, pub. in the 1st ed. of his *Med. Hymns*, 1851, in 6 st. of 7 l. with the "Alleluia," but omitted from later editions. In 1872 it was given with alterations, and in 4 st. in the *Hymnary*, No. 275. This arrangement had previously appeared in *Kennedy*, 1863, No. 698. Dr. Neale's opening line is, "Hence with sorrow and with sighing." It is also *tr.* as, "Joy, O joy, ye broken hearted," by *Kynaston*, 1862. [J. J.]

Cennick, John, a prolific and successful hymn-writer, was descended from a family of Quakers, but brought up in the Church of England. He assisted J. Wesley and then G. Whitefield in their labours for a time, and then passed over to, and died as a minister of, the Moravian Church. Born at Reading, Dec. 12, 1718, he was for some time a land surveyor at Reading, but becoming acquainted with the Wesleys in 1739, he was appointed by J. Wesley as a teacher of a school for colliers' children at Kingswood in the following year. This was followed by his becoming a lay preacher, but in 1740 he parted from the Wesleys on doctrinal grounds. He assisted Whitefield until 1745, when he joined the Moravians, and was ordained deacon, in London, in 1749. His duties led him twice to Germany and also to the North of Ireland. He d. in London, July 4, 1755. In addition to a few prose works, and some sermons, he published:—

(1) *Sacred Hymns, for the Children of God in the Days of their Pilgrimage*, Lond., J. Lewis, N.D. (2nd ed. Lond., B. Milles, 1741), Pts. ii., iii., 1742 ; (2) *Sacred Hymns for the Use of Religious Societies*, &c., Bristol, F. Farley, 1743 ; (3) *A Collection of Sacred Hymns*, &c., Dublin, S. Powell, 3rd ed., 1749 ; (4) *Hymns to the honour of Jesus Christ, composed for such Little Children as desire to be saved.* Dublin, S. Powell, 1754. Additional hymns from his MSS. were pub. by his son-in-law, the Rev. J. Swertner, in the *Moravian H. Bk.*, 1789, of which he was the editor. There are also 16 of his hymns in his *Sermons*, 2 vols., 1753–4, some being old hymns rewritten, and others new.

Many of Cennick's hymns are widely known, as, "Lo, He cometh, countless trumpets;" "Brethren, let us join to bless;" "Jesus, my all, to heaven is gone;" "Children of the heavenly King;" "Ere I sleep, for every favour;" "We sing to Thee, Thou Son of God;" and the Graces: "Be present at our table, Lord;" and "We thank Thee, Lord;" &c. Some of the stanzas of his hymns are very fine, but the hymns taken as a whole are most unequal. Some excellent centos might be compiled from his various works. His religious experiences were given as a preface to his *Sacred Hymns*, 1741. In addition to the hymns named, and others annotated under their first lines, the following are in C. U. :—

1. Be with me [us] Lord, where'er I [we] go. *Divine Protection.* [1741.]
2. Cast thy burden on the Lord. *Submission.* [1743.]
3. Not unto us, but Thee alone. *Praise to Jesus.* [1743.]
4. Thou dear Redeemer, dying Lamb. *Priesthood of Christ.* [1743.]
5. We sing to Thee, Thou Son of God. *Praise to Jesus.* [1743.]
6. When, O dear Jesus, when shall I? *Sunday Evening.* [1743.]   [J. J.]

Cerne lapsum servulum. *J. W. Petersen.* [*Lent.*] 1st pub. in the *Geistreiches G. B.*, Halle, 1697, p. 33, in 12 st., entitled, "Hymnus animi luctantis et vincentis," and thence as No. 263 in Freylinghausen's *G. B.*, 1704. It is a dialogue between the Soul (i.–vi., xi., xii.) and Jesus (vii.–x.), in 12 st. of 8 l. Freylinghausen also included as No. 271 a full *tr.* contributed by L. A. Gotter, beginning "Siehe! ich gefallner Knecht." This is No. 273 in Porst's *G. B.*, ed. 1855. The *trs.* are:—

(1) "Look on me Thy servant fall'n," as No. 631 in pt. i. of the *Moravian H. Bk.*, 1754. (2) "Jesus cometh to fulfil," a *tr.* of st. vii., as st. ii. of No. 762, in the *Moravian H. Bk.*, 1801 (1886, No. 994). (3) "Lamb of God, all praise to Thee." A *tr.* of st. xii., as st. iii. of No. 362, in the *Moravian H. Bk.*, 1801 (1886, No. 409).   [J. M.]

Červenka, Matthias (*Erythraeus*), was b. at Čelakowitz, Bohemia, Feb. 21, 1521. He was consecrated bishop of the Bohemian Brethren in 1553, and was also secretary of the Unity. He d. at Prerau, Moravia, Dec. 12, 1569. One of his hymns, written in Bohemian, has passed into English as follows :—

Aj jak jest to milé a utěsěné. [*The Christian Church.*] Founded on Ps. cxxxiii. In the Bohemian Brethren's *H. Bk.*, 1561, folio 170 b., in 28 st. *Tr.* into German by P. Herbert in the *Kirchengeseng*, Prag, 1566, and thence in *Wackernagel*, iv. p. 428, beginning, "Schau, wie lieblich und gut ist's allen Brüdern." *Tr.* from the German as No. 385 in the *Moravian H. Bk.*, 1789 (1886, No. 465), beginning, "How good and pleasant is it to behold."   [J. M.]

Chadwick, John White, was b. at Marblehead, Mass., U.S., Oct. 19, 1840;

graduated at the Cambridge Divinity School, July 19, 1864, and ordained minister of the Second Unitarian Church, Brooklyn, N.Y., Dec. 21, 1864. A frequent contributor to the *Christian Examiner; The Radical; Old and New; Harper's Magazine;* and has published many poems in American periodicals. His hymn on *Unity*, "Eternal Ruler of the ceaseless round," was written for the graduating class of the Divinity School, Cambridge, June 19, 1864. It is in Horder's *Congregational Hymns*, 1884. It is a hymn of superior merit.   [W. G. H.]

Chamberlain, Thomas, M.A., was b. in 1810, and educated at Westminster, and Christ Church, Oxford (B.A. in honours, 1831). From 1837 to 1842 he was Vicar of Cowley, Oxford, and in 1842 he became Vicar of St. Thomas the Martyr, Oxford. He was Student of Christ Church, and Hon. Canon (1862). He was also from 1844 to 1850 Rural Dean of Oxford. His pub. works include *Theory of Christian Worship*, 2nd ed. 1855 ; *The Seven Ages of the Church*, 1858 ; and a *Commentary on the Epistle to the Romans*, 1870. He also edited :—

(1) *Hymns Used in the Church of St. Thomas the Martyr, Oxford.* Oxford, W. R. Bowden, 1861. This collection has been enlarged from time to time. (2) *Hymns chiefly for the Minor Festivals, Edited by the Rev. T. Chamberlain, M.A., Student of Christ Church, and Vicar of St. Thomas the Martyr, Oxford.* Lond., J. Masters, 1863. This contains 23 hymns.

To these collections Mr. Chamberlain contributed the following hymns :—

1. Among the saints of God. *Royal Saints.*
2. Another year is well nigh gone. *S. next before Advent.*
3. Apostle and Evangelist. *St. Matthew.* "To be inserted before the Doxology of any common metre hymn."
4. Before the throne of God. *Ember Days.*
5. Hark! what mean those gladsome voices. *Christmas.* Adapted from other hymns.
6. O Guardian of the Church divine. *Ordination.* Adapted from other hymns.
7. Of all the twelve Thou callest. *St. John the Evangelist.*
8. Saint Mark goes forth to Afric's strand. *St. Mark.*
9. Sweet it is to blend in union. *St. Edward the King; and St. Dunstan.*
10. The Church is one throughout the globe. *Unity of the Church.*
11. The ten commandments once for all. *For Monastic Saints.*
12. The thoughts that filled the mind of Luke. *St. Luke.*
13. 'Twas Thou, O Lord, Who gav'st the word. *St. Augustine of Canterbury.*
14. When once the Lord from Egypt. *St. Edward the King; and St. Dunstan.*

In addition to these hymns, No. 135, "And now the saint by whose dread pains," consists of stanzas adapted to SS. Andrew, Thomas, Matthias, Barnabas, Peter, James, Bartholomew, Simon and Jude, and designed to be introduced in the hymn "The eternal gifts of Christ the King." D. Jan. 20, 1892.   [J. J.]

Chambers, John David, M.A., F.S.A., S. of Captain Chambers of the R. N., was b. in London in 1805, and educated at Oriel College, Oxford, graduating with honours, in 1827 (M.A. 1831). He was called to the Bar by the Inner Temple in 1831. In 1842 he pub. an elaborate treatise on the Jurisdiction of the Court of Chancery over the persons and property of Infants, and was appointed Recorder of New Sarum the same year. At Salisbury his attention was specially attracted to the Liturgical and other Ecclesiastical lore appertaining to the Cathedral, and to St. Osmund, its Bishop, 1078. St. Osmund compiled from different sources a series of Divine Offices, and Rules for their celebration within his diocese. These Rules were in two parts, the *Ordinale*, and the *Consuetudinary*.

The use of these Rules became very extensive; and although in certain parts the Uses of *York*, *Hereford*, *Bangor*, and *Lincoln* varied, yet John Brompton, the Cistercian Abbot of Jervaulx, writing within a hundred years after St. Osmund's death, says that these Rules and Offices had been adopted throughout England, Wales, and Ireland.

About 1230 (after the opening of the New Cathedral at Salisbury) these Rules were collected and rewritten in a complete volume, entitled *Tractatus de Officiis Ecclesiasticus* (MS. in the Cathedral Library). In the mean time the *Ordinale* had become partly welded into this *Consuetudinary*, and partly (especially that portion therein omitted from Maundy Thursday to Easter Eve) incorporated in the *Breviary*, *Missal*, and *Processional*, which had assumed definite shapes. From these materials, together with the aid of several MSS. and early printed Breviaries, Mr. Chambers pub. a *tr.* of :—

The Psalter, or Seven Ordinary Hours of Sarum, with the Hymns for the Year, and the Variations of the York and Hereford Breviaries, Lond. 1852. This was accompanied with a Preface, notes, and illustrations, together with music from a MS. folio *Antiphonary* or *Breviary* of the early part of the 14th cent. (in the Salisbury Cath. Lib.) collated with a similar MS. folio (*Lansdowne*, 463), both of *Sarum Use*. The hymns with their melodies, and the Canticles, were also collated with a MS. of the 14th cent. (Harl. 2951).

Mr. Chambers's subsequent publications include :—

(1) *The Encheiridion ; or, Book of Daily Devotion of the Ancient English Church according to Sarum Use.* Lond. 1860. To this a number of the appropriate Hymns and Collects were added. (2) *A Companion for Holy Communion for Clergy or Laity ; with a Prefatory Office for Confession, from the Ancient English Offices of Sarum Use,* 3rd ed. 1855. This was accompanied with notes and authorities. (3) *Lauda Syon, Ancient Latin Hymns of the English and Other Churches, Translated into corresponding Metres,* Pt. i. 1857 ; Pt. ii. 1866. (4) *An Order of Household Devotion for a Week, with Variations for the Seasons and Festivals, from the Ancient English of Sarum Use.* Lond. 1854. (5) *A Complete & Particular, yet concise account of the mode of conducting Divine Worship in England in the 13th and 14th centuries, contrasted with and adapted to that in use at the Present Time.* Lond. 1877. (6) A *tr.* from the original Greek of the genuine works of *Hermes Trismegistus,* the Christian Neoplatonist (A.D. 60), with notes and quotations from the Fathers.

Mr. Chambers's publications and *trs.* have had no small part in stimulating the great change which has taken place in the mode of worship in the Church of England. His *trs.* of Latin hymns are close, clear and poetical; they have much strength and earnestness, and the rhythm is easy and musical. Those in C. U. are mainly from the *Lauda Syon.* Greater use, however, might be made of these translations than has been done. Their earnestness and dignity would raise the tone of many collections. D. Aug. 22, 1893. [J. J.]

Chandler, John, M.A., one of the earliest and most successful of modern translators of Latin hymns, s. of the Rev. John F. Chandler, was b. at Witley, Godalming, Surrey, June 16, 1806, and educated at Corpus Christi College, Oxford, where he graduated in 1827. He took Holy Orders in 1831, and became Vicar of Witley in 1837. He d. at Putney, July 1, 1876. Besides numerous *Sermons* and *Tracts,* his prose works include *Life of William of Wykeham,* 1842 ; and *Horae Sacrae ; Prayers and Meditations from the writings of the Divines of the Anglican Church, with an Introduction,* 1844. His translations, he says, arose out of his desire to see the ancient prayers of the Anglican Liturgy accompanied by hymns of a corresponding date of composition, and his inability to find these hymns until he says,

"My attention was a short time ago directed to some translations [by Isaac Williams] which appeared from time to time in the *British Magazine,* very beautifully executed, of some hymns extracted from the *Parisian Breviary,* with originals annexed. Some, indeed, of the Sapphic and Alcaic and other Horatian metres, seem to be of little value; but the rest, of the peculiar hymn-metre, *Dimeter Iambics,* appear ancient, simple, striking, and devotional—in a word in every way likely to answer our purpose. So I got a copy of the *Parisian Breviary* [1736], and one or two other old books of Latin Hymns, especially one compiled by Georgius Cassander, printed at Cologne, in the year 1556, and regularly applied myself to the work of selection and translation. The result is the collection I now lay before the public." Preface, *H. of the Prim. Ch.,* viii., ix.

This collection is :—

(1) *The Hymns of the Primitive Church, now first collected, Translated, and Arranged, by the Rev. J. Chandler.* London, John W. Parker, 1837. These trs. were accompanied by the Latin texts. The *trs.* rearranged, with additional *trs.,* original hymns by Chandler and a few taken from other sources, were republished as (2) *The Hymns of the Church, mostly Primitive, Collected, Translated, and Arranged for Public Use, by the Rev. J. Chandler, M.A.* London, John W. Parker, 1841.

From these works from 30 to 40 *trs.* have come gradually into C. U., some of which hold a foremost place in modern hymnals, "Alleluia, best and sweetest ;" "Christ is our Corner Stone;" "On Jordan's bank the Baptist's cry ;" "Jesus, our Hope, our hearts' Desire ; " "Now, my soul, thy voice upraising ;" "Once more the solemn season calls ; " and, "O Jesu, Lord of heavenly grace ;" being those which are most widely used. Although Chandler's *trs.* are somewhat free, and, in a few instances, doctrinal difficulties are either evaded or softened down, yet their popularity is unquestionably greater than the *trs.* of several others whose renderings are more massive in style and more literal in execution. [J. J.]

Chapin, Edwin Hubbell, D.D., was the most distinguished man of the Universalists in later years. In his early days he was eminent as a lecturer; and as a preacher until his death. He was b. in Union village, Washington, N. Y., Dec. 29, 1814, and educated at Bennington, Vermont. He was successively pastor at Richmond, Virginia, 1837; Charleston, Mass.; Boston, 1846; and from 1848, of the Church of the Divine Paternity, New York city. He d. Dec. 26, 1880. He pub. several works, and edited, with J. G. Adams, *Hymns for Christian Devotion,* Boston, 1846. This is perhaps the most prominent Universalist Collection in the States. To it Dr. Chapin contributed the following hymns :—

1. Amid surrounding gloom and waste. *During a Storm.*
2. Father, at this altar bending. *Installation of a Pastor.*
3. Father, lo, we consecrate. *Opening of a Place of Worship.*
4. Hark ! hark ! with harps of gold. *Christmas.*
5. O Thou who didst ordain the word. *Ordination.*

6. Our Father, God! not face to face. *Opening of a Place of Worship.*
7. When long the soul has slept in chains. *Charitable Institutions.*

Of these No. 6 is the most widely used. In addition Dr. Chapin is the author of:—

8. Now host with host assembling. *Temperance.* This was given in Longfellow and Johnson's *Book of Hymns* (Unitarian), 1848, and from thence has passed into other collections. It is entitled "Triumph of Temperance," and is well known.   [F. M. B.]

Chapman, Robert Cleaver, was b. Jan. 4, 1803, and has been for more than fifty years a "Minister of the Gospel" at Barnstaple. In 1837 he pub. :—

Hymns for the Use of the Church of Christ. By R. C. Chapman, Minister of the Gospel, Barnstaple. 1837. This was reprinted in 1852. Some copies of the 1852 edition have bound up with them *An Appendix selected from Various Sources. By John Chapman.*

Several of these hymns were repeated in the Plymouth Brethren *Hymns for the Poor of the Flock*, 1838; *A Few Hymns and Some Spiritual Songs, selected* 1856 *for the Little Flock;* and in other collections. These include :—

1. Go behold [and search] the tomb of Jesus. *Easter.*
2. God's tender mercies follow still. *Heaven.* Composed of st. xxi. of "The Lamb of God exalted reigns."
3. King of glory set on high. *Ascension.*
4. My soul, amid this stormy world. *Longing for heaven.*
5. No condemnation—O my soul. *Peace in Believing.*
6. O God, Whose wondrous Name is Love. *Resignation.*
7. The Prince of Life, once slain for us. *Advent.*

Mr. Chapman's hymns and poems number 162, and are mainly in use with the Plymouth Brethren, with whom he was a Minister. They are given in his *Hymns and Meditations*, Barnstaple, 1871. He d. June 12, 1902.   [J. J.]

Charged with the complicated load. [*Pardon.*] This cento in 3 st. of 4 l. appeared in A. M. Toplady's *Ps. and Hys.*, 1776, No. 323. Sts. i. and ii. are probably Toplady's, whilst st. iii. is from C. Wesley's "Of my transgressions numberless," from his *Short Hymns*, 1762, vol. ii. p. 78, slightly altered. In Spurgeon's *O. O. H. Bk.*, 1866, Toplady's part of the cento is altered, Wesley's remains unchanged as in Toplady, and another stanza is added. The original cento was omitted from the 2nd and later editions of *Toplady.*   [W. T. B.]

Χαριστήριον ᾠδήν. *St. Theodore of the Studium.* This Canon for "Orthodoxy Sunday" or "the First Sunday in Lent is kept in memory, primarily, of the final triumph of the Church over the Iconoclasts in 842, and incidentally, of her victory over all other heresies" (*Neale*). It is given in *Daniel*, iii. pp. 101–109, in 56 stanzas, together with a note thereon. Dr. Neale in his prefatory Note to the Canon says :—

"The following Canon is ascribed to St. Theodore of the Studium, though Baronius [*Baronii Annal. Eccles. ad ann.* 842, *Tom.* ix. *p.* 1053, 21, *p.* 1059, *seq.*] has thought that it cannot be his, because it implies that peace was restored to the Church, whereas that hymnographer died while the persecution still continued. Very possibly, however, it was written on the temporary victory of the Church, which did occur in the time of St. Theodore; and then, in 842, may have been lengthened and adapted to the then state of things, perhaps by Naucratius, the favourite disciple of St. Theodore."—*Hymns of the E. C.* (2nd ed. 1863, p. 113.)

Dr. Neale's *tr.* is of a portion only of the Canon, including Ode i. Tropar. i. 2 ; iii. 6 ; iv. 1, 2, 3 ; v. 1, 3, 4, 5 ; vi. 1 ; ix. 2, 3, 4, 5. It is "A song, a song of gladness!" *Hymns of the Eastern Church*, 1862, in 11 st. of 8 l. In 1866, st. vi.-viii., x., xi., were included as, "The Lord, the Lord hath triumphed," in H. J. Palmer's *Supplemental Hymnal;* and again, with slight alterations, in the *People's H.*, 1867.   [J. J.]

Charles, D., jun. [Welsh Hymnody, § ii. 2.]

Charles, Elizabeth, née Rundle, is the author of numerous and very popular works intended to popularize the history of early Christian life in Great Britain; of Luther and his times; of Wesley and his work; the struggles of English civil wars; and kindred subjects as embodied in the *Chronicles of the Schönberg-Cotta Family*, the *Diary of Kitty Trevelyan*, &c., was b. at Tavistock, Devonshire, Her father was John Rundle, M.P., and her husband, Andrew Paton Charles, Barristerat-Law. Mrs. Charles has made some valuable contributions to hymnology, including original hymns and translations from the Latin and German. These were given in her :—

(1) *The Voice of Christian Life in Song; or, Hymns and Hymn-writers of Many Lands and Ages*, 1858; (2) *The Three Wakings, and other Poems*, 1859 ; and (3) *The Chronicles of the Schönberg- Cotta Family;* (4) *Poems*, N. York, 1867. This has some additional pieces.

Her hymn on the *Annunciation*, "Age after age shall call thee [her] blessed," appeared in her *Three Wakings*, &c., 1859.   [J. J.]

Charles, Thomas. [Welsh Hymnody, § ii. 2.]

Charlesworth, Vernon J., was b. at Barking, Essex, on April 28, 1839, and educated at Homerton College. In 1864 he became co-pastor with the Rev. Newman Hall at the old Surrey Chapel, and in 1869 the Head Master of Mr. Spurgeon's Stockwell Orphanage. Mr. Charlesworth has pub. *The Life of Rowland Hill*, &c., 1876, and, in co-operation with Mr. J. Manton Smith, *Flowers and Fruits of Sacred Song and Evangelistic Hymns*. To this work he contributed :—

1. As you gather round the family board. *Plea for Orphans.*
2. Blessed Jesus, Lord and Master. *Conferences.*
3. Come, brethren, let us sing. *Praise to God.*
4. Come to Jesus, He invites you. *Invitation.*
5. Heart to heart by love united. *Holy Matrimony.*
6. How blest in Jesus' name to meet. *Praise to Jesus.*
7. Our lamps are gone out, and the daylight is past. *The Foolish Virgins.*
8. Sweetest fellowship we know. *Walking in the Light.*
9. The day of the Lord is at hand. *Advent.*
10. There is a land as yet unknown. *Heaven.*
11. 'Tis a blessed thing while we live to sing. *Praise.*
12. When far from Thee, and heirs of woe. *Grace.*
13. Ye servants of Jesus, go forth. *Missions.*

In addition to these hymns, Mr. Charlesworth contributed—

14. I've nothing to bring Thee, Jesus. *Lent.*

to Fullerton & Smith's *Evangelical Echoes*. 1884, and has printed a considerable number as leaflets. Two of the most recent, "As the eastern hills are glowing" (*Morning*), and "Length'ning shadows darkly falling" (*Evening*), should find their way into common use. Mr. Charlesworth's hymns are very spirited and of a popular character.   [J. J.]

Charlotte Elizabeth. [Tonna, C. E.]

Chatfield, Allen William, M.A., b. at Chatteris, Oct. 2nd, 1808, and educated at Charterhouse School and Trinity College, Cambridge, where he was Bell's Univ. Scholar and Members' Prizeman. He graduated in 1831, taking a first class in classical honours. Taking Holy Orders in 1832, he was from 1833 to 1847 Vicar of Stotfold, Bedfordshire; and since 1847 Vicar of Much-Marcle, Herefordshire. Mr. Chatfield has published various *Sermons* from time to time. His *Litany, &c.* [Prayer Book] in Greek verse is admirable, and has been commended by many eminent scholars. His *Songs and Hymns of Earliest Greek Christian Poets, Bishops, and others, translated into English Verse,* 1876, has not received the attention of hymnal compilers which it merits. One hymn therefrom, " Lord Jesu, think on me," is a specimen of others of equal merit, which might be adopted with advantage. He d. Jan. 10, 1896.　　[J. J.]

Cheever, George Barrell, D.D., eminent in reform, philanthropy, and literature, b. at Hallowell, Maine, April 17, 1807, and graduated at Bowdoin College, 1825. Dr. Cheever was a Congregational Pastor at Salem, Mass., 1833 ; New York, 1839 ; and the Church of the Puritans, N. Y., 1846-67. He has published several works, and one, *Deacon Giles' Distillery*, procured him a month's imprisonment, in 1835. In 1831 he edited the *American Common Place Book of Poetry*, and in 1851 *Christian Melodies*. The latter contains 19 hymns by him. One of these, " Thy lovingkindness, Lord, I sing," is still in C. U. It is adopted in an abbreviated form of 4 st. by Dr. Hitchcock, in *Hys. & Songs of Praise*, N. Y., 1874, where it is dated 1845.　　[F. M. B.]

Cherubic Hymn, The. [Greek Hymnody, § x. 9.]

Chester, Henrietta Mary, née Goff. Mrs. Mary Chester is the eldest daughter of Mr. George Goff, who d. in 1830, at Lausanne, where he had long resided. Mr. Goff's ancestors settled in Ireland in the time of Cromwell, but the main branch of the family has been long established in Hampshire. Miss Goff was married, in 1856, to Mr. Harry Chester, who was well known as an Assistant Secretary of the Committee of Council of Education, and as one of the foremost of the promoters of the extension of popular education, in connection with the National Society, the London Diocesan Board, and other institutions. Mrs. Chester, who was left a widow in 1868, is the author of a small volume of Stories, called *Meg's Primroses* and of *A History of Russia*, both written for and published by the S.P.C.K. Her translations of Latin and German Hymns made for *The Hymnary* (and marked " II. M. C.") are distinguished by the accurate reproduction of the original in language of simple poetic beauty, and have the genuine ring of an English Hymn. [Wm. C.]

Children of the heavenly King. *J. Cennick.* [*Encouragement to Praise.*] This is the most popular of this author's hymns, and, in an abbreviated form, it is found in a large proportion of the hymnals published in the English language for more than 100 years. It appeared in his *Sacred Hymns for the Chil-*

dren of God, &c., 1742, Pt. iii., in 12 st. of 4 l. In 1753, G. Whitefield gave 6 st. in his *Coll.* as No. 38 of Pt. ii. M. Madan repeated this in 1760, and thus the abbreviated form came into use. Departures from Whitefield's arrangement are found in several instances, but as the full text has been included by Dr. Rogers in *Lyra Brit.*, 1867, p. 666, and can be easily consulted, they are not tabulated. Whitefield's text consisted of st. i., ii., iv., v., vii. and viii. In Bingham's *Hymno. Christ. Latina*, 1871, p. 123, there is a Latin rendering of the text as given in Bickersteth's *Christian Psalmody*, 1833, " Filii Regis superni, cantatis."　　[J. J.]

Children of the pious dead. [*All Saints.*] An anonymous hymn in 1 st. of 8 l. given in Spenser Murch's *Sabbath Scholars' H. Bk.*, 1849. In the *Appledore S. S. H. Bk.*, 6th ed., 1853, there is a different text, where in the last stanza the " sires "—those who through faith did mighty work : Heb. xi.—are they who approve the " fight of faith " below, whilst in *Murch's* book the Almighty is represented as watching the conflict. The unity of thought in the *Appledore* book seems to point it out as the original. This text is repeated in the *Meth. S. S. H. Bk.*, 1879. The hymn probably first appeared in a magazine. [W. T. B.]

Children of Zion, know your King. *J. Montgomery.* [*Appeal to the Jews.*] In the Bap. *Ps. & Hys.*, 1858 80, No. 764, this hymn is dated 1822. It is in the M. MSS., but without date, and the earliest appearance it made in any of Montgomery's works, so far as we can trace, is his *Original Hymns*, 1853, where it is given as in the MS. in 6 st. of 4 l. It is entitled, " Invitation to the Jews to acknowledge Christ."　　[J. J.]

Children's Hymns. In giving a brief sketch of this subject we find ourselves at every step face to face with the difficulty of lack of materials, from the destruction, by the busy little fingers of earlier generations, of the hymn-books we would so gladly treasure. It was long before it dawned on the Church that special hymns for children were needed—indeed, the only ancient hymn for children, that of Clemens Alexandrinus (see Greek Hymnody, § iii.), is more fitted for a youth of fifteen than for the period of childhood. Nevertheless, plenty of proof exists of the share the children had in the worship of the Church, e.g. the st. of Prudentius :

Te senes, et Te juventus,	Simplices puellulae,
Parvulorum Te cohors,	Voce concordes pudicis
Turba matrum, virginum-	Perstrepant concentibus
que,	Saeculorum sacculis !

or the story of the seven boys singing the " Gloria, laus, et honor," before the Emperor Louis, and so obtaining St. Theodulph's liberation, will at once show that though no special provision for children's hymns was made, yet the young were by no means neglected. Probably, in a less enlightened period, the mental capacity of the less educated common people was about that of their children, and so the lack of special provision was not felt. The early vernacular carols and hymns do not appear to have been composed for children, though the children then, as now, sang them, and the history of juvenile hymnody commences with the Reformation so far as England is concerned. It easily divides itself into four periods, each with its own special characteristic. (i.) 1562–1715. The period from Sternhold to the issue of Watts's *Divine and Moral Songs.* (ii.) 1715–1780. The interval from Watts till the establishment of Sunday Schools. (iii.) 1780–1810. The history of the Evangelical Sunday School movement. (iv.) 1840–1884. The recognition by all parties and denominations of the importance of early religious training. We have but limited space to devote to each of these, and, merely pointing out the leading characteristics of each period and author, for fuller information we shall leave the student to consult the biographical notices of the writers in other parts of this Dictionary.

i. 1562–1715. Whether the *Primers* of Henry VIII., Edward VI., and Elizabeth were specially intended for youth, we can hardly say; at any rate, the hymns therein contained were merely translations of the old Latin hymns, but the *Precationes Piae* of 1564, with its Latin hymns of Ellinger, Flaminius, Buchanan and others, was evidently prepared for school use, and ancient hymns long lingered at the schools of Harrow, Eton, St. Paul's, and a few colleges; nor are they quite extinct at the present time.

Of vernacular hymns, the 1560 edition of Sternhold and Hopkins mentions on the title that the version is :—

" Very meet to be used of all sorts of people privatly, for their Godly solace and comfort: laiying aparte all ungodly songes and ballades, which tend only to the norishing of vice and *corrupting of youth.*"

This was retained in the complete edition of 1562, and on most subsequent titlepages. The long struggle that ensued between Puritanism and Anglicanism, culminating in the Commonwealth and the Restoration, left little time for the cultivation of sacred poetry, and none for poetry for children. A hymn or two in Wither's *Hallelujah*, 1641, a child's grace by Herrick, 1647, seem all worth naming till 1655, when Jeremy Taylor appended his "Festival Hymns" to the *Golden Grove.* These, he remarks, are "fitted to the fancy and devotion of the younger and pious persons Apt for memory and to be joined to their other prayers." The idea was still that of private use, not of public worship; and when about 1674 Bishop Ken issued his "Three hymns" for the boys of Winchester College it is still the same. A worthy Baptist, Abraham Cheere, had in 1672 issued a volume which contains many short hymns and acrostics for children whom he had known, and whose names are given. A little later, Benjamin Keach (q.v.) printed his :—

War with the Devil; or, the Young Man's Conflict with the Powers of Darkness, in a Dialogue Discovering the Corruption and Vanity of Youth, the horrible Nature of Sin and deplorable Condition of fallen Man."

This became very popular as a chapbook, and with its quaint woodcuts and strong Calvinism suited the prevailing taste. It contains a few hymns, and was often given as a present, the copies yet remaining sometimes containing the autographs of donor and recipient expressed in the kindly quaint Nonconformist phraseology of the time. The examples of Ken and Taylor, of Keach and Cheere, were now followed by others, and two little penny

books by Bunyan and Mason for childish use were issued, but no copies are known to exist at the present time. Matthew Henry, in his *Family Hymns,* 1695 (enlarged in 1702), and the compiler of *A Col. of Ps. H. and Spiritual Songs, Fitted for Morning and Evening Worship in a Private Family,* 1701, intended their books for the use of children and others, and one edition of Dorrington's reform of *Austin's Devotions* annexes tunes for the hymns. The nonjuring Bishop, George Hickes, in his translation of Fénelon's *Instructions for the Education of a Daughter,* 2nd ed., 1708, gives in the " Little Office for Two or more Young Ladies under the same Governess; to be used at any time," an earlier translation of " Jesu, dulcis memoria," revised by himself, and two poems at the close, one of exquisite freshness and beauty. It is in 9 st. of 6 l. We have but space to quote st. 1, 2, 5, 8 and 9.

"To THEODORA.

Wouldst be happy? little child,
Be thou innocent and mild,
Like the patient lamb and dove,
Full of sweetness, full of love.
Modestly thy looks compose,
Sweet and blushing like the rose.

When in gardens thou dost play,
In the pleasant flowry May,
And art driven by sudden showers:
From the fresh and fragrant flowers;
Think, how short that pleasure is
Which the world esteemeth bliss.

When the fruits are sour and green,
Come not near them, be not seen
Touching, tasting, till the Sun

His sweet ripening work hath done.
Think, how harsh thy nature is
Till Heaven ripen thee for bliss.

Or lest thou shouldst drop away,
Like the leaf that fell to-day;
Still be ready to depart,
Love thy God with all thy heart:
Then thou wilt ascend on high
From Time to Eternity.

Paradise is sweeter there
Than the flowers and roses here;
Here's a glimpse, and then away,
There 'twill be for ever day,
Where thou ever in Heaven's spring
Shalt with saints and angels sing."

The other stanzas are of equal merit, and the whole is worthy of Breton or Wither at their best. It is so Elizabethan in tone and colour that it excites suspicion whether Hickes had not met with it in MS., and was the publisher only, not the author. The other poem is not so good, though it contains a pleasing "Hymn." But a greater is at the door; these early attempts are but the first-fruits; for Isaac Watts, whose Psalms and Hymns revolutionized Nonconformist hymnody, is also justly entitled to be called the first writer of children's hymns.

ii. 1715–1780. The immediate cause of the publication in August, 1715, of Watts's *Divine and Moral Songs for Children* seems, from the quaint dedication,

" To
Mrs. Sarah,
Mrs. Mary, *and* } Abney.
Mrs. Elizabeth }
Daughters of Sir Thomas Abney, Knt., and Alderman of London,"

to have been the writer's gratitude for the kindness and attention shown him by the children's parents in the two preceding years during his long illness and convalescence; but from the preface, "To all that are concerned in the Education of Children," we learn :—

"The greatest part of this little book was composed several years ago, at the request of a friend, who has been long engaged in the work of catechising a very great number of children of all kinds, and with abundant skill and success. So that you will here find nothing that savours of a party. The children of high and low degree, of the Church of England or Dissenters, baptized in infancy or not, may all join together in these songs."

This would seem to indicate we owe Watts's efforts to a Church of England clergyman. Both dedication and preface are omitted from all but very early editions, and will well repay perusal. The high note of toleration struck by Watts has, we are happy to say, been recognised by most compilers since, and there is far less of party spirit and sectarianism in the hymn-books for the use of children than in collections for those "of a larger growth." The success of the *Divine and Moral Songs* was immediate and lasting; edition after edition was issued, and for more than a century editions printed in country towns as well as in centres of population testified to the need felt and met. Many attacks have recently been made on the theology of these hymns, especially with reference to future punishment, and to a certain extent, with justice, but Watts is mild compared with some contemporary theologians in description and assertion, and he evidently photographed the phase of religious thought then existing. Since this flaw was not discovered for a century, when the work of the *Divine and Moral Songs* was well nigh done, the objection seems uncalled for, and we can all recognise the sterling practical value of the *Divine Songs:*—"I thank the goodness and the grace;" "Almighty God, thy piercing eye;" "And now another day is gone;" "This is the day when Christ arose;" "Lord, how delightful 'tis to see;" while of the *Moral Songs* (enlarged in a later edition) "'Tis the voice of the sluggard," and "The Rose," are still remembered. The exquisite "Cradle Hymn," after the fine praise of F. T. Palgrave, himself a writer of children's hymns of high merit, needs no commendation from us.

The popularity of Watts prevented, to some extent, similar attempts in the same direction. A broadside, however, of the reign of George I., is in existence which shows that hymns were occasionally sung by the children at the charity sermons on behalf of particular schools, and in *Poems, Amorous, Moral and Divine*, 1718, we find "The Incarnation, A Carol, Sung by some children in Church." Such slender beginnings and rare exceptions are these that, except these two facts, we cannot point to any single mention of special hymns for children in public use in the Church of England, till the third period of our story.

A curious book by John Vowler, issued at Exeter in 1738, has a preface by Doddridge, but it can hardly be called a hymn-book. Doddridge, however, in 1744, rendered into metre "The Principles of the Christian Religion, expressed in plain and easy verse," and this is admirably done. It is in 24 portions, and some valuable hymns might be extracted therefrom, though as a whole it is unsuited for modern use. The xviiith portion, "On the Nature and Design of the Lord's Supper," gives an interesting glimpse of juvenile Nonconformist worship and illustrates Doddridge's

well-known "My God, and is Thy table spread?" (q. v.).

> The memory of Christ's death is sweet,
> When saints around the table meet;
> And break the bread, and pour the wine,
> Obedient to His word divine.
> While they the bread and wine receive,
> (If on their Saviour they believe,)
> They feast, as on His flesh and blood,
> Cordial divine, and heavenly food!
> Their covenant thus with God renew,
> And love to every Christian shew.
> Well may their souls rejoice and thrive;
> Oh! may the blessed hour arrive
> When, ripe in knowledge and in grace,
> I at that board shall find a place!
> And now what there His people do,
> I would at humble distance view;
> Would look to Christ with grateful heart,
> And in their pleasures take my part;
> Resolved while such a sight I see,
> To live to Him who died for me.

From this, the non-communicating attendance of children was evidently approved by the writer, and the chastened devotion of the lines is eminently calculated for the purpose intended. Stormier times in the religious world were at hand, and the calm of Watts and Doddridge would not satisfy C. Wesley or J. Cennick, and to each of these we must give some attention. Cennick having joined the Moravians, issued at Dublin, in 1754, his *Hymns for Children*, in 2 vols. The work is of excessive rarity, the copy in the Fulneck Library being probably unique. It has never been properly examined by hymnologists, but later Moravian collections, notably that of 1789, take many hymns from this source. The specimens we have seen are tender, simple, and very mystical, but with little poetical beauty, full of Moravian tenets and fancies, but, as Pope says of Beaumont, "a man who has the art of stealing wisely" would find Cennick suggestive and worthy of attention. The best in the *Moravian H. Bk.*, 1789, are:— No. 622, "O Thou before whose Father's face," a prayer for the ministry of Angels, and two funeral hymns, Nos. 623 and 624, "Happy the children who are gone," and "How sweet the child rests." The second, No. 623, was long popular, but has been murdered by alteration, as in Dr. Allon's *Children's Worship*, No. 453. When, in 1763, C. Wesley published his *Hymns for Children*, he had already written many for the young which were scattered through other works. A second ed. of those hymns appeared in 1767 with the words *And Others of Riper Years* added to the title. The work was never very popular, and with the exception of "Gentle Jesus, meek and mild," has hardly a hymn in it known to modern collections outside the Wesleyan body. John Wesley, in a Preface dated March 27th, 1790, gives the clue to this, and as his words well illustrate our subject, we quote them:—

"There are two ways of writing or speaking to children: the one is, to let ourselves down to them; the other, to lift them up to us. Dr. Watts has wrote in the former way, and has succeeded admirably well, speaking to children as children, and leaving them as he found them. The following hymns are written on the other plan; they contain strong and manly sense, yet expressed in such plain and easy language, as even children may understand. But when they do understand them, they will be children no longer, only in years and stature."

When these words were written the day had already dawned when collections, not separate books by one author, should contain hymns on both plans, and be issued with richer provision for the needs and wants of the rising generations.

iii. 1780–1840. The establishment of Sunday Schools in different parts of the country immediately resulted in people finding Watts hardly sufficient, and consequently collections were made and fresh hymns written. It being impossible to enumerate the whole of these collections and hymns, we must restrict ourselves to the more important. Robert Hawker the Commentator's *Psalms and Hymns Sung by the Children of the Sunday School, in the Parish Church of Charles, Plymouth, at the Sabbath Evening Lecture*, passed through 13 editions at least, and was probably issued after 1787, when the Charles Sunday School was established, as it borrows from Rippon, whose earliest date is 1787. Of the 104 hymns it contains, 44 are from *Watts*, and 35 from the *Olney Hymns*. 2 (one a revision from Hart) are apparently Dr. Hawker's, the rest by various authors. In 1790 Rowland Hill issued his *Divine Hymns attempted in easy language for Children*, which contained 44 hymns. This was revised by Cowper before publication, and was intended for the "Southwark Sunday School Society." In 1808, a collection by Rowland Hill of 298 hymns was issued, and enlarged in 1819. The preface says that the Southwark Sunday School Society, like the parent Society, adopted

"A truly catholic and enlarged plan, so that the children educated by them are conducted to such places of worship, always where Evangelical truths are preached, but passing an equal portion of their Sabbath day's attendance in such congregations, whether Church or Chapel, as use or omit the liturgy of the Established Church."

He did not, however, reprint all the hymns of his own book of 1790, omitting, *inter alia*, "a hymn for a child that has ungodly parents," which might have caused scandal. Nor should we omit to mention the great philanthropist Jonas Hanway's book. In his sumptuous folio, *Proposals for Establishing County Naval Free Schools*, 1783, are embedded 18 hymns and 21 psalms. In 1793 the Moravians issued a small collection chiefly from their 1789 book. In 1800 appeared *H. for the Use of the Sunday Schools in Manchester*. This is decidedly superior in fitness and taste to anything previous to that date. In the same year a small collection was issued at Chatham. To the *Nottingham Collection*, a few years later, John Burton, sen., contributed his hymns; and the *Bristol* book of 1812 was one of the earliest to give the names of the authors. Meanwhile the Methodists had not been idle. They had recognized the need of new hymns, and Robert Carr Brackenbury and Benjamin Rhodes wrote some pleasing hymns for young Wesleyans. Joseph Benson, the biographer of John Fletcher, issued, in 1806, a collection from these sources and others, and this became, until 1825, the standard Wesleyan book. The publication in 1810 of Ann and Jane Taylor's classic *Hymns for Infant Minds* rendered previous collections incomplete, and the *Original H. for Sunday Schools*, and other books by Mrs. Gilbert (Ann Taylor) also tended in the same direction.

Two new factors in our history now appear; the issue of magazines for children (*The Youth's Magazine* commenced in 1805) and the formation of the *Sunday School Union*. The one brought many fresh hymns as contributions to its pages; the other provided an authorised hymn-book for Sunday Schools, and so checked the supply. In general collections, too, the entry in the list of subjects "For the Young" now begins to appear; but from that day to this in all collections the proportion allotted to children is most inadequate. The 2nd ed. of the Sunday School Union *Hymn Book for Scholars* is dated 1816, the 3rd of that *for Teachers* 1821. These continued in use till 1840, when they were enlarged. Many hymns were issued for anniversary services on fly-sheets, notably those of Montgomery for the Sheffield Whitsuntide gathering, and some of Montgomery's highest successes have been won in this field.

To the *Child's Companion*, established in 1824, John Burton, jun., sent his hymns; to the *Children's Friend*, Dorothy Ann Thrupp, under the signature of *Iota*, and H. F. Lyte, contributed; while in the *Protestant Dissenter's Juvenile Magazine*, 1833, &c., appeared T. R. Taylor's too few and gem-like lyrics. J. Cawood wrote some for his own parish, specimens of which are in the *Lyra Britannica*, 1868, and in Dr. Rogers's *Child's Hymnal*, N.D., but some of the most beautiful of his productions, now before us in MS. remain unedited. The issue, in 1833, of John Peel Clapham's *Leeds S. S. U. Bk.* is noteworthy. It has been repeatedly revised, and contains good work.

iv. 1841–1884. More need now began to be felt among Churchmen and Nonconformists of something different from the narrow Calvinism of earlier days, and as the Tractarian movement gained ground, if Tractarian children were to sing hymns at all, new ones had to be written; for, to express the formulas of the new school, there were no English hymns to be had. The first noteworthy attempt was Mrs. F. M. Yonge's *Child's Christian Year*, 1841. Keble wrote the preface and contributed two new hymns, but the bulk of the book is from J. Anstice, Isaac Williams's *Paris Breviary Hymns*, and J. H. Newman from the *Lyra Apostolica*. It was several times reprinted, but is more fitted for the children of the educated classes than for the poor. I. Williams himself issued in 1842 his *Ancient Hymns for Children*, a selection from his book of 1839, slightly altered; and his *Hymns on the Catechism*, a valuable little work, must also be mentioned. But in the same year, and with more success, Dr. Neale pub. the 1st series of his *Hymns for Children*, a 2nd following in 1844, and a third in 1846. These became really popular, and some may be found in C. U., alike in England and America, at the present time. Still a need was felt for something more simple, and in 1848 Mrs. Cecil Frances Alexander pub. her *Hymns for Little Children*. Charmingly simple and tender, clear in dogma, and of poetical beauty, combining the plainness of Watts with the feeling for and with childhood of the Taylor sisters, and uniting with both the liturgical associations of the English Prayer Book, they remain unequalled and unapproachable. "Every morning the red sun,"

"Once in royal David's city," "There is a green hill far away," will at once occur as instances in point. They have reached nearly a hundred editions. Subsequent efforts by Mrs. Alexander have not been so successful, her *Narrative Hymns, Moral Songs, Poems on the Old Testament* (2 series), containing nothing worthy of note; but her "We are but little children weak," contributed to Dr. Hook's *Church School Hymn Book*, 1850, strikes a higher key, and in the S. P. C. K. *Ps. & Hys.*, 1852, "The roseate hues of early dawn;" "Jesus calls us, o'er the tumult," are very good, though not specially adapted for the young. Miss Wiglesworth's attempts in the same field are noticeable, and in Helen Taylor's *Sabbath Bells*, N.D., and *Missionary Hymns*, 1846, will be found good hymns, proving that not in one school of thought merely was the gift of combined simplicity and beauty to be found. To this same period belong Miss Leeson, Mrs. Herbert Mayo, and Miss D. A. Thrupp. To Mrs. Mayo's *Hymns & Poems*, 1849, Miss Thrupp contributed some of her best hymns. The enthusiasm of the Rev. John Curwen, and the introduction of the Tonic Sol-fa System in many Nonconformist schools, led to the production of his *Child's Own Hymn Book*, very deservedly popular. Originally issued in 1840, as *Sacred Songs*, another selection as *Hymns and Chaunts* appeared in 1844; two years later they were combined as *The Child's Own Hymn Book*. It was subsequently enlarged, and in 1865 contained 169 hymns; but in 1874 the entire book was recast under the title of *The New Child's Own Hymn Book*. Biographical notes on this have been pub. by the editor's son. From 1850 onwards a constant stream of collections has passed through the press, of which we can notice but the most important. The Church of England Sunday School Institute revised their earlier book in 1868 under the editorship of a Committee, the work falling chiefly on Mr. George Warington, but the book was abandoned in 1879 for one more modern in tone. A little book of *Children's Hymns and School Prayers* was issued by the S. P. C. K. Compilers of *Church Hymns*, and in 1881 Mrs. Carey Brock issued *The Children's Hymnbook*, which passed under the revision of Bishops How and Oxenden and the Rev. John Ellerton. It has at once taken the leading place among Church books, and contains not only the best hymns hitherto published, but new hymns, some of which are of equal value. Among other Church collections we may name the Rev. J. C. Miller's, N. D.; the *Hymns and Carols*, ed. by W. C. Dix, 1869; *Hymns and Carols for the Children of the Church*, 1876; and *H. for the Children of the Church*, 1878. The last contained new compositions by Mrs. C. F. Hernaman and Mrs. E. H. Mitchell, which will win their way. The Wesleyans in 1870 revised their preceding book of 1826–35, and with some success, but a new revision was called for in 1879, and the result was the *Methodist Sunday School Hymnbook*, containing 589 hymns. This, in our judgment, ranks first in merit of any collection for children yet made, and is approached only by Mrs. Carey Brock and the Rev. G. S. Barrett. Among the Congregationalists several books of im-

portance appeared from time to time. Bubier's *H. & Sacred Songs*, 1855; Major's *Book of Praise for Home & School*, 1869; Allon's *Children's Worship*, 1878; and the present authorised selection, the Rev. G. S. Barrett's *Book of Praise for Children*, 1881, an enlargement of the Rev. W. G. Horder's book under the same title, issued in 1875. Less has been done among the Baptists, the only book of high merit being the Rev. W. R. Stevenson's *School Hymnal*, 1880. The English Presbyterians have *Psalms & Hymns for Children's Worship*, in addition to 61 hymns for the young in their *Church Praise*, 1882. In Scotland, which has done little in the way of original compositions in this line, we may name Rev. James Bonar's *School Worship*, 1878, and the United Presbyterian *Hymnal for the Young*, 1883. Among the "Friends" the *School & Mission Hymn Book*, 1873, is well edited. The Roman Church has only one book worth naming in this connection, the Rev. Henry Formby's *Catholic Songs*. This, issued partially about 1853, has been revised, and is now issued in two parts as the *Junior School Song Book* and the *Senior School Song Book*. It is of higher calibre than we generally find in hymnals of the Roman Catholic communion.

It only remains to notice the miscellaneous books not yet mentioned. The Sunday School Union issued their *Songs of Gladness* in 1871, containing originals by Miss Doudney, W. P. Balfern, and others, and this has been subsequently enlarged. Their latest publication is *The Voice of Praise*, 1886. It contains 600 hymns, and is a meritorious work. The issue in America of hymns of a revival type has been followed by the reprint, on this side the Atlantic, of many of this school, but they can scarcely win a lasting popularity, and belong rather to American hymnody. Dr. Rogers issued his pictorial *Child's Hymnal*, N. D., which contains some hymns not elsewhere accessible. In closing this survey we specially name Dr. W. Fleming Stevenson's *H. for Ch. & Home*, 1873, containing 100 hymns for children. The biographical index and the notes to the hymns are the best attempt hitherto made to collect facts as to children's hymns, Mr. Curwen's *Biographical Notes* already alluded to being its only rival.   [W. T. B.]

Chope, Richard Robert, M.A., b. Sept. 21, 1830, educated at Exeter College, Oxford, B.A., 1855, and took Holy Orders as Curate of Stapleton, 1856. During his residence at Stapleton the necessities of the Choir led him to plan his *Congregational Hymn and Tune Book*, pub. in 1857. In 1858 he took the Curacy of Sherborne, Dorset; in the following year that of Upton Scudamore, where he undertook the training of the Chorus of the Warminster district for the first Choral Festival in Salisbury Cathedral; and in 1861 that of Brompton. The enlarged ed. of *The Congregational Hymn Book* was pub. 1862, and *The Canticles, Psalter, &c., of the Prayer Book, Noted and Pointed*, during the same year. In 1865 he was preferred to the parish of St. Augustine's, Queen's Gate, South Kensington, and subsequently pub. *Carols for Use in Church during Christmas and Epiphany*, 1875; *Carols for Easter and Other Tides*, 1887;

and other works. Mr. Chope has been one of the leaders in the revival and reform of Church Music as adapted to the Public Services. He was one of the originators of *The Choir and Musical Record*, and was for some time the proprietor and assistant editor of the *Literary Churchman*.		[J. J.]

Χορός 'Ισραήλ. *St. Cosmas.* [*Transfiguration.*] This Canon of the Ascension is found in the Greek Service Book Office for that Festival, Aug. 6, and in *Anth. Graeca*, p. 176. It dates from the early part of the 8th cent., and in common with all festival Canons it consists of 8 odes, the 2nd ode being omitted (see **Greek Hymnody**, § xvi. 10). The only *tr.* into English is a cento principally from the first four odes, beginning as above and rendered " The choirs of ransomed Israel " by Dr. Neale in his *Hys. of the Eastern Church*, 1862, p. 84. It is thus derived : st. i. from ode i.; st. ii., iii. from ode iii.; st. iv. from ode iv.; st. v. from ode v. St. vi. is Dr. Neale's own, is a reference to the heavenly glory, and quite in the modern manner. It is introduced as a climax, but is not in the original, as that does not feel this need. From this *tr.* the following centos have been taken : *People's H.*, st. i., ii., vi. ; S. P. C. K. *Ps. & Hys.*, st. i., iv.-vi.; Palmer's *Supp. Hymnal*, 1866, st. i., iii., iv., vi., and " In days of old on Sinai," being st. iv.-vi. in *H. A. & M.*, 1868 and 1875. [J. J.]

Chorus novae Hierusalem. *St. Fulbert of Chartres.* [*Easter.*] As St. Fulbert d. cir. 1029, this hymn dates from about the beginning of the 11th cent. It is found in an 11th cent. MS. in the *Brit. Mus.* (Vesp. D. xii. f. 72 b), and from this is printed in the *Latin Hys. of the Anglo-Saxon Church*, 1851, p. 159. It is also in an 11th cent. MS. at St. Gall (No. 387). Its English use was extensive. It is given in the *Sarum Brev.* as the hymn at first Vespers of the Octave of Easter, and so for all Sundays to the Feast of the Ascension (*Hymn. Sarisb.*, 1851, pp. 90, 91); in *York*, the same, with the addition, " When the Sunday Office is said "; in *St. Alban's* through Easter week at Terce. It is also in the *Aberdeen Brev.*

The text is also in the following works : *Daniel*, i., No. 191, iv. p. 180, with various readings ; *Mone*, No. 162; Card. Newman's *Hymni Eccl.*, 1838 and 1865. Biggs's *Annotated H. A. & M.*, 1867, p. 129, and others.

The second stanza, " Quo Christus invictus Leo " (in *H. A. & M.*, " For Judah's Lion bursts His chains "), is based upon a mediaeval belief, thus preserved in the words of Hugh of St. Victor, " Quum leaena parit, suos catulos mortuos parit, et ita custodit tribus diebus, donec veniens pater eorum exhalet ut vivificentur. Sic Omnipotens Pater Filium suum tertiâ die suscitavit a mortuis." [W. A. S.]

Translations in C. U.:—

1. **Ye choirs of New Jerusalem, Your sweetest notes employ.** By R. Campbell, from the *Sarum Brev.*, written for and 1st pub. in his *Hys. and Anthems*, &c. (St. Andrew's), 1850, pp. 75–6, in 6 st. of 4 l. In 1858 it was included, with a slight alteration in st. ii., l. 3, and the omission of st. vi. in the Scottish *Episco. Coll.*, No. 77. This was partly rewritten, and a doxology was

added thereto by the compilers of *H. A. & M.*, and given in their " trial copy," 1859, No. 78, and then in their 1st ed. 1861. This is the form of the hymn which is in most extensive use. In Mr. Shipley's *Annus Sanctus*, Campbell's text is given from his MS.

2. **Thou New Jerusalem on high.** By J. M. Neale, from the *Sarum Brev.*, given in his *Mediaeval Hys.*, 1851. In revising it for the *Hymnal N.*, 1854, Dr. Neale rendered it, " Ye choirs of New Jerusalem, To sweet new strains," &c. This was repeated in his *Mediaeval Hys.*, 2nd ed. 1863, with st. ii. rewritten, and is the form of the hymn in C. U.

3. **Wake, choir of our Jerusalem.** By J. A. Johnston, in the *English Hymnal*, 2nd ed. 1856, and repeated in the 3rd ed., 1861.

4. **O choir of New Jerusalem.** By R. F. Littledale, from the *Sarum Brev.*, written for and 1st pub. in the *People's H.*, 1867, and signed " D. L."

5. **Ye choirs of New Jerusalem, Your sweetest praises bring.** By R. C. Singleton, written in 1867, and pub. in his *Anglican H. Bk.*, 1868.

Translations not in C. U. :—

1. Ye choirs of New Jerusalem, Begin, &c. *J. D. Chambers*, i., 1857.
2. Quire of the New Jerusalem. *W. J. Blew*, 1852–55.
3. The choir of New Jerusalem. *J. Keble*, 1857–66.
4. Sing, New Jerusalem. *J. W. Hewett*, 1859.
5. Jerusalem, thy song be new. Lord Braye. In Mr. Shipley's *Annus Sanctus*, 1884. [J. J.]

Christ from the dead is raised. *Tate and Brady.* [*Easter.*] A rhymed version of 1 Cor. xv. 20, the 3rd anthem appointed for Easter Day in the *Book of Common Prayer*. It is found in the *Supp.* to the *New Version*, for details of which see **Eng. Psalters**, § xiii., and **New Version**.

Christ is risen! Christ is risen! He hath burst, &c. *A. T. Gurney.* [*Easter.*] 1st pub. in his collection *A Book of Praise*, &c., 1862, No. 119, in 3 st. of 12 l. It is in C. U. in *three* forms :—

1. The original, which is seldom found outside the author's *Coll.*
2. The text as in *Church Hymns*, 1871, No. 132. In the *Church Times* of Feb. 19, 1875, the author denounces this arrangement, whilst in the folio ed. of *Church Hymns*, 1881, Mr. Ellerton (one of the editors) allows that " The variations in this hymn amount to an almost complete recasting of it. The fine conception of the hymn was grievously marred by faulty execution, and sincere thanks are due to the author for permitting his original to be so daringly manipulated " (p. xlii.). This text has been introduced into American use through the *Church Praise Bk.*, N. Y., 1882.
3. The text as in *H. A. & M.*, 1875, No. 138. Against this also the author complains in the same letter to the *Church Times*. It also has been introduced into American C. U. It was given in *Laudes Domini*, N. Y., 1884. [J. J.]

Christ is risen, the Lord is come. *H. H. Milman* [*Easter.*] This Easter hymn was given in the author's *Sel. of Ps. and Hys.*, &c., 1837, No. 2, for Easter, in 3 st. of 8 l., in his *Poems*. 1839, vol. ii. p. 342; and again in the 11th ed. of *Heber's Hymns*, 1842, p. 115, divided into 6 st. of 4 l. Amongst modern hymnals it is found in *Kennedy*, 1863, No. 702, with slight alterations, and the addition of the refrain " Alleluia ! " It is also in the *Coll. for Harrow School Chapel*, and others. [J. J.]

Christ is the Foundation of the house we raise. *J. S. B. Monsell.* [*Foundation Stone of a Church.*] Written for the laying of the Foundation Stone of St. Mary

Magdalene, Paddington, in 1865, and pub.
with an account of the ceremony in the *Church
Times*. In 1863 it was included in Dr. Monsell's *Hys. of Love and Praise*, 2nd ed., pp.
139–40, in 12 st. of 8 l., and repeated in his
Litany Hymns, 1870, and his *Parish Hymnal*,
1873, No. 200. In *Church Hymns*, No. 307, it
is abbreviated from the original. Authorised
text, *Parish H.*   [J. J.]

**Christ ist erstanden, Von der Marter
alle.** [*Easter.*] One of the earliest of German hymns, this is found in various forms as
early as the 12th cent., and four of these are
given by *Wackernagel*, ii. pp. 43–44. It was
sometimes used alone, sometimes as part of
the liturgical services at Easter, as at the
lighting of the lamps, and sometimes woven
into the early Passion plays (compare its use
by Goethe in *Faust*, pt. i.). *Wackernagel*, ii.
pp. 726–732, gives also seventeen versions
from the 15th cent. The versions vary in
length from 5 l. to 11 st. of 4 l. (Cf. Hoffmann von Fallersleben's *Geschichte des Deutschen Kirchenliedes*, Hannover, 1861, pp. 63,
178, 181, 187, 202, &c.) Two have been *tr.*
into English.

1. *Wackernagel*, ii., No. 935, in 3 st., from the
Geistliche Lieder, Erfurt, 1531 (previously in
Klug's *G. B.*, Wittenberg, 1529), and thence in
V. Babst's *G. B.*, 1545, and most succeeding
hymn-books, and recently as No. 126 in the
Unv. L. S., 1851. This form Luther held in
such esteem that of it he said, " After a time one
tires of singing all other hymns, but the ' Christ
ist erstanden ' one can always sing again." The
only *tr.* in C. U. is :—

Now is Christ risen, by A. T. Russell, in his
Ps. & Hys., 1851, *Appendix*, No. 2.

Other trs. are :—
(1) "Christ is now rysen agayne," by Bp. Coverdale,
1539 (*Remains*, 1846, p. 563). (2) "The Lord is risen,
and gone before," by *Miss Fry*, 1845, p. 70.

ii. *Wackernagel*, ii., No. 39, from a Munich
MS. of the 15th cent. In 9 l. *Tr.* as :—
"Christ the Lord is risen, Out of," by *Miss Winkworth*,
1869, p. 37.   [J. M.]

Christ lag in Todesbanden. *M. Luther.*
[*Easter.*] 1st pub. in *Eyn Enchiridion*, Erfurt, 1524, entitled "The hymn, 'Christ ist
erstanden,' improved." Thence in *Wackernagel*,
iii. p. 12, in 7 st. of 7 l., and the same in
Schircks's ed. of Luther's *Geistl. Lieder*, 1854,
p. 20, and in the *Unv. L. S.*, 1851, No. 127.
Only slight traces of the "Christ ist erstanden" (q. v.) are retained in Luther's hymn.
Sts. iv., v., are based on the sequence "Victimae paschali laudes" (q. v.), and one or two
expressions may have been suggested by the
"Surrexit Christus hodie" (q. v.). These German and Latin hymns, with the Scriptural
notices of the Passover Lamb, furnished Luther
with the materials of this beautiful poem, but
the working out is entirely original, and the
result a hymn second only to his unequalled
"Ein' feste Burg" (q. v.)

Translations in C.U. :—

1. **Christ in the bands of death was laid**, a good
tr., omitting st. vii., by A. T. Russell, as No. 104
in his *Ps. & Hys.*, 1851.
2. **Christ lay awhile in Death's strong bands**, a
full and good *tr.* by R. Massie in his *M. Luther's*

Spir. Songs, 1854, p. 16. In full and unaltered as
No. 104 in the ed., 1857, of Mercer's *C. P. &
H. Bk.* (Ox. ed., 1864, No. 197). St. i., vi., vii.
unaltered, with st. iv. ll. 1–4, and iii. ll. 5–7,
united as st. ii., were included, as No. 129, in
Church Hys., 1871. St. i., iv., vi., vii., altered and
beginning "Christ Jesus lay in Death's strong
bands," appear as No. 192 in Thring's *Coll.*, 1882.

3. **In the bonds of death He lay, Who**, a full
and good *tr.*, but not in the original metre, by
Miss Winkworth in her *Lyra Ger.*, 1st Series,
1855, p. 87. Slightly altered, and omitting st.
ii., as No. 714 in the *Wes. H. Bk.*, 1875. In
full, but altered, in Schaff's *Christ in Song*, 1869,
p. 261. The version beginning "In death's
strong bands Christ Jesus lay," No. 749 in J. L.
Porter's *Coll.*, 1876, is st. i., iv., vi., vii., mainly
from the *Lyra Ger.*, but partly from the *C. B.
for England*, with two lines from Mr. Massie.

4. **Three days in Death's strong grasp He lay**, a
good *tr.* of st. i., iv.–vi., based on Mr. Massie,
as No. 87 in Pott's *Coll.*, 1861.

5. **In Death's strong grasp the Saviour lay, For
our**, a good *tr.*, omitting st. v., vi., by Miss Winkworth in her *C. B. for England*, 1863.

6. **Jesus in bonds of Death had lain**, a *tr.* of st.
i., iv., vi., by Miss Borthwick, contributed as No.
79 to Dr. Pagenstecher's *Coll.*, 1861, and included in her *H. L. L.*, ed. 1884, p. 259.

7. **In Death's strong grasp the Saviour lay, For
our offences.** Of No. 84 in the Ohio *Luth. Hymnal*,
1880, st. i., ii., iii., ll. 1–4 are from Miss Winkworth's *tr.*, and the rest are mainly from Mr.
Massie.

Trs. not in C. U. :—
(1) "Christ dyed and suffred great payne," by Bp.
Coverdale, 1539 (*Remains*, 1846, p. 563). (2) "Christ
was to Death abased," by *J. C. Jacobi*, 1722, p. 21 (1732,
p. 38, altered), repeated as No. 225, in pt. i. of the *Moravian H. Bk.*, 1754, and continued in later eds., altered,
1789, to "Christ Jesus was to death abas'd." (3) "Once
in the bands of death the Saviour lay," by *Miss Fry*,
1845, p. 65. (4) "The ransom of our souls to pay," by
J. Anderson, 1846, p. 14 (1847, p. 39). (5) "Jesus was
for sinners slain," by *Dr. J. Hunt*, 1853, p. 44. (6) "In
Death's dark prison Jesus lay," by *Dr. H. Mills*, 1856,
p. 211. (7) "Christ, the Lord, in death-bonds lay," by *Miss
Warner*, 1858 (1861, p. 432). (8) "Death held our Lord
in prison," by Dr. G. Macdonald in the *Sunday Magazine*, 1867, p. 331, and altered in his *Exotics*, 1876, p. 52.
(9) "In the bands of Death Jesus lay, Prisoner," &c., in
S. Garratt's *Hys. and Trs.*, 1867, p. 28. (10) "In the
bands of Death He lay, Christ," &c., in the *Ch. of Eng.
Magazine*, 1872, p. 183. (11) "Christ was laid in Death's
strong bands," in *Dr. Bacon*, 1884, p. 22, based on Mr.
Massie.   [J. M.]

Christ, my hidden life, appear. *C.
Wesley.* [*Christ the Prophet.*] 1st pub. in
Hys. and S. Poems, 1742, p. 206, in 6 st. of
8 l., as the second hymn on "Waiting for
Christ the Prophet" (*P. Works.* 1868–72, vol. ii.
p. 262). In 1780 J. Wesley compiled a cento
therefrom, consisting of st. ii.–vi., and included
it in the *Wes. H. Bk.*, No. 348, as :—" Open,
Lord, my inward ear." In *Kennedy*, 1863,
No. 1196, is the same cento, slightly altered,
as :—" Open, Lord, *mine* inward ear." [J. J.]

Christ, of all my hopes the ground.
R. Wardlaw. [*Christ All, and in all.*] This
hymn appeared in the *Supp.* which he appended
to the 5th ed. of his *Sel. of Hymns*, &c. (1st ed.,
1803), in 1817, No. 458, in two parts, the 2nd
part beginning, "When with wasting sickness
worn." Pt. i. is in 6 st., and Pt. ii. in 7 st. of
4 l. Both parts have been adopted in G.
Britain and America. In the latter, however,

the most popular form of the hymn is a cento
composed of st. i., vi., x.-xiii., as in Dr. Hatfield's *Church H. Bk.*, N.Y., 1872, No. 896 ; or
the same cento reduced to 4 st. of 4 l., as in
several collections.   [J. J.]

Christ our Passover for us. *C. Wesley.*
[*Holy Communion.*] Pub. in *Hymns on the
Lord's Supper*, 1745, No. 84, in 4 st. of 8 l. ;
and again in *P. Works*, 1868 – 72, vol. iii.
p. 275. In the *Wes. H. Bk.* of 1875, No. 905 :—
" Jesus, Master of the Feast," is composed of
st. iii., iv. of this hymn. It is curious to note
that these same stanzas were introduced into
the hymnals of the Church of England by Toplady through his *Ps. and Hys.* in 1776. [J. J.]

**Christ [our] the Lord, is risen to-
day, Sons of men, &c.** *C. Wesley.*
[*Easter.*] This is one of the most popular and
widely used of C. Wesley's hymns. It appeared in the *Hys. and S. Poems*, 1739, in
11 st. of 4 l., with the heading "Hymn for
Easter." In his *Ps. and Hys.*, 1760, No. 32,
M. Madan introduced some alterations, and
omitted st. vii.-ix., thereby forming a hymn of
8 st. It is from this form of the hymn that
all subsequent arrangements of the text have
been made. It is curious that although it
was in several collections of the Church of
England in 1780, yet J. Wesley omitted it
from the *Wes. H. Bk.*, which he compiled and
published during that year, and it was not
until the issue of the *Supp.* to that collection
in 1830, that it appeared therein in any form,
and then the alteration of st. iv., l. 3, "Dying
once, He all doth save," to " *Once He died our
souls to* save," was adopted from Madan. Its
use is extensive in all English-speaking countries. The reading, " Christ, *our* Lord," &c.,
dates from Cotterill's *Sel.*, 1810 (*P. Works*,
1868–72, vol. i. p. 185).   [J. J.]

Christ the true anointed Seer. *C.
Wesley.* [*Christ the Prophet.*] From his *Scripture Hymns*, which were left in MS. at his
death. In the *Arminian Magazine* for May,
1789, J. Wesley announced his intention of
publishing these hymns. That publication,
however, was restricted to a few which were
given in the magazine from time to time.
The MS. was embodied in the *P. Works of J.
and C. Wesley*, 1868–72, vol. x., "Hymns on
the Four Gospels," &c. This hymn was given
in the *Supp.* of the *Wes. H. Bk.*, 1830, and is
retained in revised ed. of 1875.   [J. J.]

**Christ, Whose glory fills the skies,
Christ the true, &c.** *C. Wesley.* [*Morning.*] 1st pub. in J. and C. Wesley's *Hys. and
S. Poems*, 1740, p. 61, in 3 st. of 6 l., and entitled "A Morning Hymn" (*P. Works*,1868–72,
vol. i. p. 224). In 1776, A. M. Toplady included it, unaltered, in his *Ps. and Hys.*, No.
296, and for many years it was quoted as his
production. Montgomery, however, corrected
the error in his *Christian Psalmist* in 1825.
Its extensive use in the Church of England,
and by Nonconformists, is due mainly to Toplady and Montgomery. The latter held it in
special esteem, and regarded it as "one of C.
Wesley's loveliest progeny." In its complete
form it was not included in the *Wes. H. Bk.*
until 1875. Its use is very extensive. The
hymn :— " Thou, Whose glory fills the skies,"

as found in the *People's H.*, 1867, No. 570, is
the same hymn with slight alterations. In
the S. P. C. K. *Church Hymns*, the doxology
is from the Cooke and Denton *Hymnal*, 1853 ;
st. ii. and iii. have also been used in the cento
" O disclose Thy lovely face," q. v. It has
been rendered into Latin by the Rev. R.
Bingham, in his *Hymno. Christ. Lat.*, 1871, as
" Christe, cujus gloriae." The American use
of the original is extensive.   ·[J. J.]

Christ unser Herr zum Jordan kam.
M. Luther. [*Holy Baptism.*] Probably
written 1541, and pub. as a broadsheet in
that year (Wackernagel's *Bibliographie*, 1855,
p. 172). In Low German it appeared in the
Magdeburg *G. B.*, 1542, and in High German
in the *Geistliche Lieder*, Wittenberg, 154¾. In
Wackernagel, iii. p. 25, in 7 st. of 9 l., and
the same in Schircks's ed. of Luther's *Geist.
Lieder*, 1854, p. 59, and as No. 258 in the
Unv. L. S., 1851. The original title is "A
hymn on our Holy Baptism, wherein is briefly
embraced What it is? Who instituted it? What
is its use?" It is a Catechetical hymn setting
forth the Lutheran doctrine of Baptism, and
is based on St. Matt. iii. 13–17, and St. Mark
xvi. The only *tr.* in C. U. is :—

To Jordan came our Lord the Christ To do.   *Tr.*
in full in R. Massie's *M. Luther's Spiritual Songs*,
1854, p. 69 ; repeated with st. vii. altered, as No.
210 in the Ohio *Luth. Hymnal*, 1880. Also in
Dr. Bacon, 1884, p. 68.

Trs. not in C. U. :—
(1) " Christ baptist was be Johne in Jordan flude," in
the *Gude and Godly Ballates* (ed. 1568, folio 8), ed. 1868,
p. 12. (2) " The eye sees water, nothing more," a *tr.*
of st. vii., by J. Gambold, as No. 231 in the *Appendix*
of 1743 to the *Moravian H. Bk.*, 1742, and repeated 1754-
1849. (3) " To Jordan came our Lord the Christ, His,"
&c., by *J. Anderson*, 1846, p. 66 (1847, p. 81). (4)
" Where Jordan's stream was rolling on," by *Dr. J.
Hunt*, 1853, p. 96. (5) " Jesus, our Lord, to Jordan
came," by *Dr. H. Mills*, 1856, p. 210. (6) " To Jordan
when our Lord had gone," by Dr. G. Macdonald, in the
Sunday Magazine, 1867, p. 682, altered, in his *Exotics*,
1876, p. 98.   [J. M.]

Χριστὲ ἄναξ, σὲ πρῶτον. *Gregory of
Nazianzus.* [*Easter.*] This hymn to Christ
on Easter Day dates from the 4th cent., and
is found in various editions of St. Gregory's
Works, in *Daniel*, iii. 6, and in the *Anth.
Graec. Car. Christ.*, 1871. A translation, " O
Christ the King ! since breath pent up," &c.,
by A. W. Chatfield, appeared in his *Songs and
Hymns*, &c., 1876. [See **Greek Hymnody**, § iv.]
                                        [J. J.]

Christe, coelestis medicina Patris.
[*In time of Pestilence.*] This hymn is in the
Mozarabic Breviary, Toledo, 1502, f. 311, as
the hymn at Vespers in the Office for one or
more sick persons, and again (f. 60) on the
Thursday after the Octave of the Epiphany,
called the "Vespers of the Sick." *Daniel*, i.,
No. 163, gives the text, with a note, and
classes it with hymns written not earlier than
the 6th, nor later than the 9th cent. *Tr.* as :—

Christ from the Father sent to bring us healing.
Written by R. F. Littledale for the *Priest's
Prayer Book*, enlarged ed. 1866, and from thence
transferred to the *People's H.*, 1867. [W. A. S.]

Christe cunctorum dominator alme.
[*Consecration of a Church.*] This hymn of
unknown date and authorship, is found in

three MSS. of the 11th cent. in the *Brit. Mus.* (Jul. A. vi. f. 68 b; Vesp. D. xii. f. 112 b; Harl. 2961, f. 250), in the *Latin Hys. of the Anglo-Saxon Ch.*, 1851, p. 141, and in an 11th cent. Mozarabic Brev. in the *Brit. Mus.* The oldest MS. in which it is now found is one of the 9th cent. in the Library at Bern. *Daniel*, i., No. 96, and iv. pp. 110 and 364, has the full text with various readings from the Bern MS., and other sources. *Tr.* as:—

O Christ, Thou Ruler of the Universe, by *J. D. Chambers*, in his *Lauda Syon*, Pt. i., 1857, p. 237. Two centos from this vigorous *tr.* have been adopted, the first beginning with st. i., in Thring's *Coll.* 1882, and the second with st. ii.:—"Behold, O God, how thankful in Thy praise," in T. Darling's *Hymns*, 1885. Also *tr.* as, "Only begotten Word of God eternal." Printed for the use of St. Barnabas, Pimlico, 1884. St. viii. and ix. are original.

It has also been rendered into English through the German as follows:—

Du, dem der Himmel und die Erd' sich beuget, by A. J. Rambach, in his *Anthologie*, i. p. 176, in 9 st. Thence altered and beginning "O Herr, vor dem sich Erd' und Himmel beuget," in Knapp's *Ev. L. S.*, 1837, No. 1120 (1865, No. 1286). The only *tr.* in C. U. is:—

Eternal Son of God, O Thou, a *tr.* in L. M. of st. i.-iv., vi., ix. as No. 131 in the Ohio *Luth. Hymnal*, 1880.   [J. M.]

Christe, fili Jesu summi. [*St. Benedict.*]

The oldest known text of this hymn is found in a MS. of the 11th cent., at Stuttgart. It is also in a 13th cent. MS. in the *Brit. Mus.* (Add. 18301, f. 118). *Mone* gives it as No. 838, and thinks it is of the 6th cent.; and *Daniel*, iv. p. 184, gives the text without note or comment. *Tr.* as:—

Jesus Christ, with God the Father Consubstantial, Only Son, by G. Moultrie, 1st pub. in the *Church Times*, July 9, 1864; again in his *Hys. & Lyrics*, 1867: and in the *People's H.*, 1867, No. 242.   [J. J.]

Christe hac hora tertia. [*For the Third Hour.*]

This hymn is found in an *Anglo-Saxon Hymnary* of the 11th cent. in the *British Museum* (Vesp. D. xii. f. 39). In the MS. it is given for the Nativity, at Terce; the hymn for Sext being "Sexta aetate virgine" (f. 39 b); and that for None being "Hora nona quae canimus (f. 39 b). The three parts are printed from this MS. in the *Lat. Hys. of the Anglo-Saxon Ch.*, 1851, pp. 151-152. *Tr.* as "O Christ, our Lord, in this third hour," by J. D. Chambers, in his *Lauda Syon*, i. 1857, and repeated in Skinner's *Daily Service Hyl.*, 1864.   [J. M.]

Christe, qui lux es et dies. [*Lent.*]

An Ambrosian hymn, quoted by Hincmar, Abp. of Rheims, in his treatise, *Contra Godeschalcum . . . De unâ et non Trinâ Deitate*, 857, thus fixing its date at an early period. Although the Benedictine editors have assigned some hymns to St. Ambrose on the strength of their being quoted in the same work, yet they have rejected this as the work of that Father. (*Migne*, tom. 16-17.) The text and uses of this hymn are:—

(1) In the *Mozarabic Brev.*, Toledo, 1502, f. 304, b., it is given as a hymn for compline on Sundays, with an additional stanza which reads.

     "Tetre noctis insidias
       Hujus timoris libera ;
       Tue lucis magnalia
       Totum chorum inlumina."

(2) Daniel, i., No. 23, gives the text from two 13th cent. MSS. at Würzburg, &c. He also gives an additional verse which reads :—

     "Ad te clamamus domine,
       Noli nos derelinquere,
       Festina, ne tardaveris, .
       Succurre nobis miseris."

(3) *Mone*, No. 70, gives the text from a MS. of the 8th cent., preserved at Darmstadt, with readings of later MSS. and printed Breviaries, and an extended note.

(4) *Daniel* follows in 1855 (iv. pp. 54-5), with references to his former note, and to *Mone*, and further readings from MSS. and printed Breviaries.

(5) It is found in a MS., c. 890, in the Bodleian (Junius, 25 f. 127 b); in three MSS. of the 11th cent. in the *British Mus.* (Jul. A. vi. f. 22 b; Vesp. D. xii. f. 11; Harl. 2961, f. 220 b), and in the *Latin Hys. of the Anglo-Saxon Church* is printed from an 11th cent. MS. at Durham (Surtees Soc., 1851, p. 12).

(6) It is also found in *Hymn. Sarisb.* (Lond. 1851), the *Sarum* and *York* Breviaries ; Card. Newman's *Hymni Ecclesiae*, 1838 and 1865; *Wackernagel*, 1841, No. 21; *Bässler; Simrock*; Biggs's annotated *H. & A. M.*, and others. In the various Breviaries its use differed, but it was mainly confined to Lent.   [W. A. S.]

Translations in C. U.—

1. O Christ, That art the Light and Day, by W. J. Copeland, 1st pub. in his *Hys. for the Week*, 1848, p. 156. This is repeated, without alteration, in the *Appendix* to the *Hymnal N.*, No. 116. There are also altered versions of the same *tr.*, as "O Christ, Who art the Light and Day," in *H. A. & M.*, 1875, and the Irish *Church H.*, 1873; and as "O Christ, Thou art the Light and Day," in the *Hymnary*, 1872.

2. Christ, Who art both our Light and Day, by Mrs. Charles, in her *Voice of Christian Life in Song*, 1858, p. 92. This is found in Newman Hall's *Coll.*, 1876, and one or two others.

3. O Christ, Who art both Light and Day, by W. Mercer, included in the Oxford ed. of his *Church Psalter*, &c., 1864, No. 6.

4. Christ, Thou Who art the Light and Day, by R. F. Littledale, made for and 1st pub. in the *People's H.*, 1867, No. 435.

Translations not in C. U. :—

1. Thou, Christ, art our Light. *Hymn. Anglic.*, 1844.
2. O Christ, Who art our Life and Day. *W. J. Blew*, 1852-55.
3. Ray of the Eternal Sire Divine. *W. J. Blew*, 1852-55.
4. O Christ, Thou art our Light, our Day. *J. D. Chambers*, 1857.
5. O Christ, Thy Light brings endless day. *H. M. Macgill*, 1875.   [J. J.]

This hymn has also been rendered into English, through the German, as follows :—

i. **Christe, der du bist Tag und Licht,** 1st pub. in the *Erfurt Enchiridion*, 1526, fol. 26. In J. Zwick's *G. B.*, 1540, and others, it is ascribed to Wolfgang Meusel, or Meusslin, and so by *Koch*, ii. p. 92, who says it was written while M. was still a monk in the cloister at Lixheim. *Wackernagel*, iii. p. 121, gives it as anonymous, and as erroneously ascribed to M., in 7 st. of 4 l. In the Berlin *G. L. S.*, ed. 1863, No. 1150.

The trs. are :—

(1) "O Christ, that art the lyght and daye,' by Bp. Coverdale, 1539 (*Remains*, 1846, p. 584). (2) 'Christ, thow art the licht, bot and the day," in the *Gude and Godly Ballates*" (ed. 1567-8, folio 73), ed. 1868, p. 126. (3) "Christ, everlasting source of light," by *J. C. Jacobi*, 1725, p. 60 (ed. 1732, p. 179), and thence, as No. 243, in pt. i. of the *Moravian H. Bk.*, 1754. (4) "O Jesus, Thou our brighter day," by *H. J. Buckoll*, 1842, p. 63.

ii. **Christe, du bist der helle Tag,** by Erasmus Alber. *Wackernagel*, iii. p. 884, quotes this from *Die Morgengesang für die Kinder*, Nürnberg, c.

1556, where it is in 7 st. of 4 l. Included in the *Hamburg Enchiridion*, 1558, and recently as No. 507 in the *Unv. L. S.*, 1851. In Nöldeke's *Alber*, 1857, p. 43. St. vi., vii., says Lauxmann, have formed a very favourite evening prayer for families in Württemberg from olden times till now. The only *tr.* is:—

"We are Thy heritage indeed," of st. v., vii., as No. 244, in pt. i. of the *Moravian H. Bk.*, 1754. [J. M.]

Christe, qui sedes Olympo. *Jean Baptiste de Santeüil.* [*St. Michael and All Angels.*]

Given in the *Cluniac Brev.*, 1686, p. 1086, and in his *Hymni Sacri et Novi*, 1689, p. 40; and in the ed. of 1698, p. 182, as "Christe, summi Rex Olympi," and in 7 st. of 6 l. In the revised *Paris Breviary*, 1736, st. ii. was omitted, and various alterations were introduced. Other French Uses vary both from *Paris Brev.* and the original. "Christe, qui sedes Olympo," is the *Paris* text from which all the *trs.* into English have been made. It is given in Chandler's *Hys. of the P. Church*, 1837, p. 224: and in Card. Newman's *Hymni Ecclesiae*, 1838 and 1865. The stanza omitted from the *Paris Brev.* is:—

"Quotquot adstant, sempiternum
Qui tribunal ambiunt,
Hi tot ardent imperantis
Ferre jussa praepetes:
Ire terris, et redire,
Sacra per commercia."—Ed. 1698, p. 182.
[W. A. S.]

Translation in C. U. :—

Christ in highest Heaven enthroned, by W. Palmer, in his *Short Poems and Hys.*, 1845, in 6 st. of 6 l. From thence it passed, unaltered, into the St. Saviour's (Leeds) *Sacred Hymns & Anthems*, 1846, and with slight alterations and a doxology given in *Hys & Introits*, 1852. It is also given in Murray's *Hymnal*, 1852, as, "Christ, to Whom, enthroned in Heaven"; in *H. A. & M.*, 1861, and the *Hymnary*, 1872, as "Christ, in highest heaven enthroned;" and (st. iv.–vi., from Murray's *Hymnal*), as "Blest are they o'er all creation," in *Kennedy*, 1863.

Translations not in C. U. :—
1. O Christ, Who in heaven. *J. Chandler.* 1837.
2. O Christ, Who sitt'st with God on high. *I. Williams.* 1839.
[W. T. B.]

Christe Redemptor omnium Conserva tuos famulos. [*All Saints.*]

The oldest form of this hymn is in three MSS. of the 11th cent. in the *Brit. Mus.* (Jul. A. vi. f. 60; Vesp. D. xii. f. 94 b; Harl. 2961, f. 244), and is printed from an 11th cent. MS. at Durham, in the *Latin Hys. of the Anglo-Saxon Church*, 1851, p. 119. *Daniel* also refers (iv. p. 143) to a Rheinau MS. of the 11th cent. *Mone*, No. 635, gives the text of a 12th cent. MS. belonging to the Benedictine Abbey of St. Peter, at Salzburg, and *Daniel*, i., No. 243, has it from later authorities. Card. Newman's text in his *Hymni Ecclesiae*, 1838 and 1865, is from the *Sarum Brev.* The *Roman Brev.* hymn, **Placare, Christe, servulis**, is this hymn in a revised form. [J. M.]

Both the original and the *Rom. Brev.* texts have been rendered into English as follows :—

i. *Original Text.*
Translations in C. U. :—

1. O Christ! the world's Redeemer dear, by J. D. Chambers. 1st pub. in Pt. ii., 1866, of his

Lauda Syon, p. 105, in 7 st. of 4 l. and repeated in the *Appendix* to the *Hymnal N.*

2. O Christ, Redeemer of mankind, by R. F. Littledale, written for and 1st pub. in the *People's H.*, 1867, No. 293, in 7 st. of 4 l. and signed "F. R."

ii. *Roman Breviary Text.*
Placare, Christe, servulis.

This text is found in all editions of the *Rom. Brev.* since 1632, and in *Daniel*, i., No. 243. It is *tr.* as:—

O Christ, Thy guilty people spare, by E. Caswall. 1st pub. in his *Lyra Catholica*, 1849, pp. 191–2, and again in his *Hymns*, &c., 1873, p. 103. This is the *tr.* commonly used in Roman Catholic collections for missions and schools. Another *tr.* is: "O be not angry, Lord, with those," by *Wallace*, 1874. [J. J.]

Christe Redemptor omnium [gentium] Ex [De] Patre. [*Christmas.*]

This Ambrosian hymn is sometimes ascribed to St. Ambrose, but is rejected as such by the Benedictine editors of his works. (Paris Ed. 1686–90, tom. iii; *Migne*, tom. 17.) It is known in three forms. These are, i. The Original; ii. The *Roman Breviary* text; iii. and the *Paris Breviary* text.

i. *Original Text.*
Christe Redemptor omnium Ex Patre Patris unice.

This is found in three MSS. of the 11th cent. in the *Brit. Mus.* (Jul. A. vi. f. 32 b; Vesp. D. xii. f. 31; Harl. 2961, f. 227 b), and in the *Latin Hys. of the Anglo-Saxon Church*, 1851, p. 119, printed from an 11th cent. MS. at Durham. The text in *Daniel*, i., No. 75, "Christe Redemptor gentium, De Patre," is from later authorities. In his vol. iv. p. 145, *Daniel* gives the earlier renderings from a Rheinau MS. of the 11th cent. The *Hymn. Sarisb.* 1851, p. 12, gives the text, with readings from various English Uses. [W. A. S.]

Translations in C. U. :—

1. Jesu, the Father's Only Son, by J. M. Neale, given in the *Hymnal N.*, 1st ed., 1852, No. 13, and continued in later editions. In 1884 it was transferred to the *Hymner*.

2. O Christ, Redeemer of our race, by Sir H. W. Baker, appeared in the trial copy of the *H. A. & M.*, 1859; 1st ed., 1861, and the revised ed., 1875.

3. O Christ, Redeemer of mankind, by R. F. Littledale, made for and 1st appeared in the *People's H.*, 1867, and signed "F. R."

Translations not in C. U. :—
1. O Christ, Redeemer of us all. *Primer.* 1604.
2. Christ, whose redemption all doth free. *Primer.* 1619.
3. Redeemer of the race of man. *W. J. Blew.* 1852.
4. O Christ, Redeemer of the world. *J. D. Chambers.* 1857. [J. J.]

ii. *Roman Breviary Text.*
Jesu Redemptor omnium, Quem lucis ante originem.

This form of the hymn was given in the revised *Roman Breviary*, 1632, for Vespers and Matins on Christmas Day. The text is in *Daniel*, i., No. 75: and in Card. Newman's *Hymni Ecclesiae*, 1838 and 1865. [W. A. S.]

Translations in C. U. :—

1. Jesu, Redeemer of the world, by E. Caswall, 1st pub. in his *Lyra Catholica*, 1849, p. 48, and

again in his *Hymns*, &c., 1873, p. 26. From this text, with alterations, No. 21 in Chope's *Hymnal*, 1864 ; and No. 127 in the *Hymnary*, are taken. It is also the *tr.* used in several Roman Catholic *H. Bks.* for schools and missions.

2. Jesus, Redeemer, from on high, by W. J. Copeland, in his *Hys. for the Week*, 1848, p. 58, and as " Jesu, whom nations all adore," in Rorison's *Hys. & Anthems*, 1851.

3. Lamb, Whose Blood for all men streamed, by R. Campbell, in his *Hys. & Anthems*, 1850 ; and in *Annus Sanctus*, 1884.

Translations not in C. U. :—
1. Jesu, the Ransomer of man. *Primer.* 1685.
2. O Christ, the world's redemption. *Primer.* 1706.
3. Jesu, the Ransomer of man. *Evening Office.* 1710. A cento from Nos. 1 and 2, but partly original, reprinted in O. Shipley's *Annus Sanctus*, 1884.
4. Redeemer, Jesus, Life of man. *Bp. Mant.* 1837.
5. Jesus, Redeemer ere the light. *Husenbeth.* 1840.
6. Jesu, Redeemer of us all. *J. R. Beste.* 1849.
7. Jesu, our souls' redeeming Lord. *T. J. Potter*, in the *Catholic Psalmist*, 1859 ; and *Annus Sanctus*, 1884.
8. Jesu, Redeemer of the earth. *Bp. Williams.* 1845.
9. O Jesu, ere all ages known. *F. Trappes.* 1865.
10. Jesus, Saviour of mankind. *J. Wallace.* 1874.

From this text is also taken the hymn in the " Little Office of the Blessed V. Mary," in the *Rom Brev.*, **Memento rerum Conditor.** This has been *tr.* by E. Caswall, in his *Lyra Catholica*, 1849, and *Hymns*, &c., 1873, as " Remember, O Creator, Lord."

iii. *Paris Breviary Text.*
Jesu, Redemptor omnium, Summi Parentis unice. This recast is by C. Coffin. It was given in his *Hymni Sacri*, Paris, 1736, and again in the same year in the revised *Paris Brev.* The text is in Chandler's *Hys. of the P. Church*, 1837, No. 43, and in Card. Newman's *Hymni Ecclesiae*, 1838 and 1865.

Translations in C. U. :-
1. **Christ, Redeemer of our race**, by W. Mercer, in his *Church Psalter*, &c., 1864.
2. **O Jesus, Life of ruined man**, by R. C. Singleton. Written in 1867, and pub. in his *Anglican H. Bk.*, 1868. In the 2nd ed., 1871, it was revised as, " O Jesu, Saviour of us all."

Translations not in C. U. :—
1. Jesus, Thou holy Son of God. *J. Chandler.* 1837.
2. Jesu, born the world to free. *I. Williams.* 1839.
[J. J.]

Christe Rex, mundi Creator. [*Burial.*] This hymn is in an 11th cent. *Mozarabic Hymnarium* in the Brit. Mus. (Add. 30851, f. 160 ; and also in the *Mozarabic Brev.*, Toledo 1502, f. 316 ; and *Migne*, tom. 86. col. 923. The text is repeated in *Daniel*, iv. p. 117, and Neale's *Hymni Ecclesiae*, 1851, p. 219. *Tr.* as :—

Christ the King, the world's Creator, by R. F. Littledale, made for and 1st pub. in the *People's H.*, 1867, thence into the *Altar Hymnal*, 1884.

Christe! Sanctorum caput atque custos. *Robert Boyd.* [*Praise to Christ.*] Written at Trochrig in 1625, in 100 st. of 5 lines, 1st pub. as *Hecatombe Christiana I Hymnus*, ἑκατονστρόφος *ad Christum Servatorem* (Edin., Thomas Finlason, 1627), included in the *Delitiae Poetarum Scotorum hujus aevi Illustrium* (vol. i. p. 208, Amsterdam, 1637), reprinted in the *Poetarum Scotorum Musae Sacrae* (vol. i. p. 198, Edin. 1739), and elsewhere.

A cento of 5 st., being st. 6, 10, 32, 39, 96; beginning, " Nuncius praepes mihi labra summo," was *tr.* by *Dr. H. M. Macgill* as " O let some swift-winged angel," and contributed to the 1874 Draft Hymnal of the *United Presb. Church.* When included as No. 95 in the *Presb. Hymnal*, 1876, it began, " Lord ! let Thy Spirit holy," but when Dr. Macgill reprinted it together with the Latin in his *Songs of the Christian Creed and Life*, 1876, No. 42, it began, " Lord ! let Thy swift-winged angel." This was again altered in the 1879 ed. to, " Lord, let some swift-winged angel." It is one of the best of his translations. Another *r.* is, " Christ, of Thy saints the Head, the King," in 50 st. of 8 lines, by Sir William Mure, pub. as *A spirituall Hymne of the sacrifice of a sinner to be offred upon the altar of a humbled heart to Christ our Redeemer*, &c. Edinburgh, John Wreittoun, 1628.   J. M.]

Christe, sanctorum decus angelorum. *St. Rabanus Maurus.* [*St. Michael.*] This hymn is in four forms, not counting slight variations of text, as follows:—

i. *Original Text.*
Christe sanctorum decus angelorum, Auctor humani generisque rector. It is in three MSS. of the 11th cent. in the *Brit. Mus.* (Vesp. D. xii. f. 92 ; Jul. A. vi. f. 58; Harl. 2961, f. 243), and is also printed from an 11th cent. MS. belonging to the Dean and Chapter of Durham in the *Latin Hys. of the Anglo-Saxon Church*, 1851, p. 116. Of this text there is no translation.

ii. *Textus Receptus.*
Christe sanctorum decus angelorum, Rector humani generis et auctor. This is given by *Daniel*, i., No. 188, with various readings, and by *Mone*, No. 311, also with notes. To these are added in *Daniel*, iv. p. 165, readings from a MS. of the 11th cent., belonging to the Abbey of Rheinau ; and at p. 371 he says, that the hymn is also found in a MS. of the 9th cent. in the Town Library of Bern. Translations of this text are :—
1. O Christ, the Glory of the holy angels. *W. J. Blew.* 1852.
2. Christ, the holy angels' Grace. *J. W. Hewett.* 1859.
3. Christ, who of holy angels, Honour art. *J. D. Chambers*, ii. 1866.

iii. *Roman Breviary Text.*
Christe sanctorum decus angelorum, Gentis humanae Sator et Redemptor, given in the *Rom. Brev.*, 1632, for the Feast of St. Michael, at Lauds. The text is also in *Daniel*, i., No. 188 ; Card. Newman's *Hymni Ecclesiae*, 1838 and 1865 ; *Königsfeld*, ii 134 ; *Bässler*, No. 71, &c. In this arrangement, st. v. :—

> " Hinc Dei nostri genitrix Maria
> Totus et nobis chorus angelorum
> Semper assistant, simul et beata
>   Concio tota."

is changed to—

> " Virgo dux pacis genetrixque lucis
> Et sacer nobis chorus angelorum
> Semper assistat, simul et micantis
>   Regia coeli."

In the translations the full force of this change has been evaded by all with the exception of Caswall.

Translations in C. U. :—
1. **Christ of Thy angel host the Grace**, by Bp. Mant, in his *Ancient Hymns*, 1837, p. 68 (1871, p. 119). Bp. Mant surmounts the difficulty of st. v. by omitting it altogether. In the *Appendix* to *Hymnal N.*, No. 184, st. ii. of Bp. Mant's *tr.*

is omitted, and a modified rendering of st. v. is added thereto.

2. Christ of the holy angels Light and Gladness, by W. J. Copeland, in his *Hymns for the Week*, 1848, p. 128. This is repeated in the *People's H.*, 1867, and others.

Translations not in C. U. :—
1. O Christ, the Beauty of the angel worlds. *E. Caswall.* 1849.
2. Of holy angels, Ch st, Thou art the Glory. *F. G. Lee*, 2nd ed. 1869.
3. O Christ, the angels' Joy and Crown. *J. Wallace.* 1874.

iv. Roman Breviary Appendix.

This is given for the Feast of St. Raphael, Oct. 24. It is composed of st. i., iii.-v. of the *Textus Receptus*, with a very slight variation in st. i. The hymn might be adapted to St. Gabriel with equal facility. It is *tr.* by *Caswall*, 1849, as, "O Christ, the glory of the angel choirs," and by *J. Wallace*, 1874, as "O Christ, the angels' Joy and Crown."

[W. A. S.—J. J.]

Christi Blut und Gerechtigkeit. *N. L. von Zinzendorf.* [*Redemption.*] This fine hymn was written in 1739, during his return journey from St. Thomas's in the West Indies, and 1st pub. 1739, in *Appendix* viii. to the Herrnhut *G. B.*, 1735, as No. 1258, in 33 st. of 4 l. In Knapp's ed. of Z.'s *Geistliche Lieder*, 1845, p. 135, it is marked as "On St. Eustachius," which has been interpreted to mean that it was written on the island of St. Eustatius, in the Dutch West Indies, but quite as probably means that it was written on St. Eustachius's day, viz. on March 29, 1739. In the *Brüder G. B.*, 1778, No. 399, reduced to 20 st., and thus as No. 1261 in the *Berlin G. L. S.*, ed. 1863. St. i. is taken from the hymn, "In Christi Wunden schlaf ich ein," ascribed to Paul Eber (q. v.).

Translations in C. U. :—
i. **Jesu, Thy blood and righteousness**, a spirited but rather free *tr.*, omitting st. 6, 11, 13, 22, 23, 25–28, by J. Wesley, in *H. and Sacred Poems*, 1740 (*P. Works*, 1868–72, vol. i. p. 346). Of these 24 st. 16 were adopted in the *H. and Spiritual Songs*, 1753, No. 68, and 11 (1, 2, 6–8, 12, 13, 21–24) in the *Wes. H. Bk.*, 1780, No. 183 (ed. 1875, No. 190). In most collections it is still further abridged. The most usual cento is that given by M. Madan, in the 2nd ed., 1763, of his *Ps.* and *Hys.*, No. 175, which is of Wesley's st. 1, 12, 2, 13, 15, 24. This is found in Bickersteth's *Christian Psal.*, 1833, and has been recently given, omitting st. xiii., in Snepp's *S. of G. and G.*, 1876 ; Irish *Ch. Hymnal*, 1873 ; Spurgeon's *O. O. H. Bk.*, 1866 ; Pennsylvania Luth. *Ch. Bk.*, 1868, and other collections. Among the various British and American hymnals which begin with Wesley's first line, the other sts. used for making centos are taken from the *Wes. H. Bk.*, 1780 (6–8, 21–23).

The hymn is also found under these first lines:
1. **Jesus, Thy robe of righteousness** (st. i.), in the *Cong. H. Bk.*, 1836 ; *Leeds H. Bk.*, 1853 ; *N. Cong.*, 1859 ; Bapt. *Ps. & Hys.*, 1858, &c.
2. **Jesus! Thy perfect righteousness** (st. i.), in Cotterill's *Sel.*, 1810–19.
3. **Jesus, Thy grace and righteousness** (st. i.), in *Meth. N. Connexion*, 1847.
4. **Lord, Thy imputed righteousness** (st. i.), in American Dutch Reformed *Coll.*, 1847.

5. The holy, meek, unspotted Lamb (st. vi.), in American *Sabbath H. Bk.*, 1858.
6. Lord, I believe Thy precious blood (st. vii.), in Pennsylvania *Luth. H. Bk.*, 1865.
7. Lord, I believe were sinners more (st. viii.), in *Evang. Union Hymnal*, 1878.
8. Jesus, be endless praise to Thee (st. xxi.), in H. L. Hastings's *Hymnal*, 1880.
9. Jesus, the Lord, my righteousness (st. i.), in *The Enlarged London H. Bk.*, 1879.

ii. **Christ's crimson blood and righteousness**, a *tr.* of st. i., xiv., xv., xxx., by E. Cronenwett, as No. 260 in the *Ohio Luth. Hymnal*, 1880.

Another tr. is :—
"The Saviour's Blood and Righteousness," by C. Kinchen as No. 131 in the *Moravian H. Bk.*, 1742, and repeated, abridged, in later eds. (1886, No. 318). [J. M.]

Christi caterva clamitet. [*Advent.*] A hymn of unknown authorship, in the *Mozarabic Brev.*, Toledo, 1502, f. 1. *Mone*, No. 31, gives the text from a ms. of the 8th or 9th cent., belonging to the Town Library of Trier. It is also in an 11th cent. *Mozarabic Hymnarium* in the *Brit. Mus.* (Add. 30851, f. 111 b). *Mone's* notes and readings are extensive. He considers it to be of the 5th cent. *Daniel*, iv. 120, quotes *Mone's* text, references, and part of his notes. It is *tr.* as—

Hark ! a glad exulting throng, by P. Onslow, in the *Lyra Messianica*, 1864, p. 6, in 8 st. of 4 l., and from thence into *Alford's Year of Praise*, 1867, No. 2. [J. M.]

Christi corpus ave. [*Holy Communion.*] Levis, in his *Anecdota Sacra*, 1790, pp. 32, 33, gives this as "A salutation to the Lord Jesus Christ, by St. Anselm of Canterbury." On this authority it is sometimes ascribed to St. Anselm ; but from the fact that the hymn is not in his works, and that *Daniel*, ii. p. 328, and *Mone*, No. 214, give the text, and are doubtful of his authorship, this assumption is uncertain. *Mone* quotes it from a Reichenau MS. of the 14th cent. It is *tr.* as :—

Hail, Body born of Mary, by R. F. Littledale, 1st pub. in the *Altar Manual*, 1863 ; again in *Lyra Eucharistica*, 1863, and in the *People's H.*, 1867. [J. J.]

Christi hodierna celebremus natalitia. [*Christmas.*] A sequence in the Mass of the sixth day after Christmas Day, whether it be a Sunday or not, in the *Sarum Missal*, and for the third Mass of Christmas Day, in the *Hereford* and *York Missals*. In the *Hereford M.* the first line reads, " Christi hodierna pangimini omnes una." With the exception of the second verse, the intercisions and endings of the verses are in the letter *a*. The *Sarum* text is given in the Burntisland ed., 1867, col. 74 ; the *York*, in the Surtees Soc. reprint, vol. 59, p. 19 ; and the *Hereford*, in the reprint, 1874, p. 16. In the St. Gall MS., No. 614 (of the 10th cent.), it begins as in the *Hereford M.* In the Bodleian MS., No. 775, f. 136 (written c. 1000), and in an 11th cent. Winchester MS. now in Corpus Christi College, Cambridge (MS. 473), it begins with st. ii. "Coelica resonent." *Tr.* as :—

O come, loud anthems let us sing, by E. H. Plumptre, written for and 1st pub. in the *Hymnary*, 1872, No. 135. Also given in Dean Plumptre's *Things New and Old*, 1884. Also *tr.* as :—
Let us celebrate this day, Christ the Lord's nativity. *C. B. Pearson.* 1868. [J. M.]

Christi miles gloriosus. [*St. Vincent.*] A hymn for the Festival of St. Vincent at Lauds is found in a 12th cent. MS. in the Bodleian (Laud. Latin, 95 f. 144 b) and in a 14th cent. *Sarum Brev.* in the *Brit. Mus.* (MSS. Reg. 2. A. xiv., f. 183 b). It is reprinted in Card. Newman's *Hymni Ecclesiae*, 1838 and 1865. *Tr.* as :—

1. **Glorious was the Christian warrior**, by J. D. Chambers, in pt. ii. p. 58, of his *Lauda Syon*, 1866, from whence it passed unaltered into the *People's H.*, 1867.

2. **For his Lord, a soldier glorious.** An anonymous *tr.* in the *Antiphoner and Grail*, 1880, and again in the *Hymner*, 1882. The doxology (st. iii.) is from *Chambers.*   [J. J.]

Christi perennes nuntii. *Jean Baptiste de Santeüil.* [*SS. Mark and Luke.*] Pub. in the *Cluniac Brev.*, 1686, p. viii., and in his *Hymni Sacri et Novi*, 1689, 197; and in the ed. 1698, p. 240, as a hymn for the Evangelists, in 6 st. of 4 l. In 1736 it was included, with alterations, in the revised *Paris Brev.* as the hymn for 1st and 2nd Vespers on the Feasts of SS. Mark and Luke. It is also appointed for the same Feasts in other French Breviaries. The *Paris Brev.* text is given in Card. Newman's *Hymni Ecclesiae*, 1838 and 1865.   [W. A. S.]

Translations in C. U. :—

1. **Heralds of Christ, to every age**, by J. Chandler, from the *Paris Brev.*, in his *Hymns of the Prim. Church*, 1837, No. 92 (with the Latin text), in 5 st. of 4 l. This was repeated in the Cooke and Denton *Hymnal*, 1853; Dr. Oldknow's *Hys. for the Services of the Ch.*, 1854, &c. In the *English Hyl.*, 2nd ed., 1856 (3rd, 1861), it is given as : "Eternal gifts of Christ our King "; and in the *Hys. for Christian Seasons.* Gainsburgh, 1st ed., 1854, as "Heralds of Christ, through whom go forth."

2. **Christ's everlasting messengers**, by I. Williams, is the most widely used of the *trs.* of this hymn. It appeared in the Feb. number of the *British Magazine*, 1837, and again in the translator's *Hys. tr. from the Paris Brev.*, 1839, p. 277, in 5 st. of 4 l. It is found in several collections, including the *People's H.*, 1867; Alford's *Year of Praise*, 1867, &c.

3. **Heralds of Jesus through all time**, by E. Caswall, 1st pub. in his *Masque of Mary*, &c., 1858, and again in his *Hymns*, &c., 1873. In the *Hymnary*, 1872, it is given with alterations by the compilers as "Behold Christ's heralds through all time."

4. **Behold the messengers of Christ**, by the compilers of *H. A. & M.*, is based upon I. Williams, as above. It was given in the 1st ed., 1861, and again in the revised ed., 1875.

Translation not in C. U. :—
Praise for Thy saints to Thee, O Lord. *Bp. Mant.* 1837.   [J. J.]

Christian children, hear me. *J. M. Neale.* [*All Saints.*] Is found in his *Original Sequences, Hymns and other Ecclesiastical Verses*, 1866, pp. 30–33. It is a "Children's Sequence," in 9 st. of 6 l., for All Saints Day, and is accompanied with the note :— "This is written to the very lovely melody of *Laus devotâ mente*, in the Sarum Gradual." In 1867 it was included in the *People's H.*

Christian children must be holy. *C. F. Alexander.* [*Circumcision.*] Appeared in her *Narrative Hymns for Village Schools*, 1853, No. ii. on "The Circumcision," in 5 st. of 4 l. Given without alteration in Mrs. Brock's *Children's H. Bk.*, 1881.

Christian, seek not yet repose. *Charlotte Elliott.* [*Watch and Pray.*] Appeared in her *Morning and Evening Hymns for a Week*, 1839, appointed for Wednesday Morning, and entitled "Watch and Pray that ye enter not into temptation." It is in 6 st. of 3 l. with the refrain "Watch and Pray." Although unrecognized for some time by hymnal compilers, in the later collections, beginning about 1860, it holds a very prominent position, and its use in all English-speaking countries has become very extensive.   [J. J.]

Christians awake, salute the happy morn. *J. Byrom.* [*Christmas.*] This hymn is compiled from a poem of 48 lines, in two parts of 32 and 16 lines respectively, which was pub. in his posthumous *Poems*, &c., 1773, p. 58; and again in his *Works*, 1814, vol. ii. p. 37. It is one of two poems for Christmas Day. The popular form in which it now appears as in *H. A. & M.* was given to it in Cotterill's *Sel.*, 1819, No. 212. This was repeated by Montgomery, in his *Christian Psalmist*, 1825. From these two works it has passed into most collections now in use in English-speaking countries. There are also other centos in C. U. An altered version, beginning :—"With songs of praise salute," &c., is found in T. Darling's *Hymns*, &c. Orig. text, with which all centos should be compared, in *Lyra Brit.*, 1867, p. 116. [J. J.]

Christians! brethren! ere we part. *H. K. White.* [*Dismission.*] Appeared in Dr. Collyer's *Coll.*, 1812, No. 868, in 3 st. of 4 l., and entitled, "Dismission; or, A Parting Hymn." It was somewhat extensively used for some fifty years or more, but of late it has rapidly declined in popularity. It is usually given as, "*Christian brethren!* ere we part." With this beginning it is in use in four forms, as in (1) Harland's *Ch. Psalter;* (2) *Windle, Barry*, &c.; (3) *Snepp;* (4) Islington *Ps. & Hys.;* and as (5) "Come, Christian brethren, ere we part," in Spurgeon's *O. O. H. Bk.*, 1866. It is also in use, but to a limited extent, in America.   [J. J.]

Χριστὸς γεννᾶται· δοξάσατε. *St. Cosmas.* This is the first of eight Odes or Hymns, which form St. Cosmas's Canon for Christmas Day. The Greek Office for Christmas Day is of great length and interspersed with hymns by St. Germanus of Constantinople, St. Anatolius, John the Monk, St. Romanus the Melodist, and Casia, in addition to the Canon of St. Cosmas. The latter was written early in the 8th century, St. Cosmas dying about 760, and has been reprinted in Greek in Migne's *Patrologiae*, tom. lxxxix., in *Anth. Graeca Christ.* p. 165, in *Daniel*, iii. pp. 55–60, and in Dr. Littledale's *Offices*, &c., *of the Holy Eastern Church*, 1863, pp. 55–85. The translations into English are those in rhymed measure by Dr. Neale, in his *Hys. of* *the Eastern Church*, 1862, pp. 69–83, and the blank verse versions by Dr. Littledale in the second part of his *Offices*, &c., 1863, pp. 173–208. Dr. Neale regarded the Canon as "perhaps the finest, on the whole, of the Canons of Cosmas, and may fairly be preferred to the rival composition of St. John Damascene," *H. E. Ch.*, p. 69. Little use, however, has been made of it by the editors of English hymnals and books of Sacred Poetry, Dr. Neale's translation of the first Ode being the only one in Common Use. Dr. Littledale's note on this Canon explains the absence of Ode ii. from this and other Festival Canons :—

" It will be observed that the second ode does not appear in its place, but that the third follows immediately after the first. The reason is as follows. The nine Odes are theologically based on the nine Canticles of Lauds. i. The Song of Moses, Exodus xv. ii. The Song of Moses, Deut. xxxii. iii. The Song of Hannah, 1 Sam. ii. iv. The Song of Habakkuk, Hab. iii. v. The Song of Isaiah, Is. xxv. 19–20. vi. The Song of Jonah, Jo. ii. vii. The Song of the Three Children, Pt. i, 3–34. viii. The Song of the Three Children, Pt. ii., *Benedicite*. ix. *Magnificat* and *Benedictus* said together. The second song of Moses, which is said by the Western Church at the Saturday Lauds, is used only in Lent by the Eastern, and consequently a Canon for a festival season has no second ode at all. It is easy to trace the idea of each canticle running through its corresponding ode, especially in 1, 6, and 7."—*Offices, &c., of the Holy E. Church*, 1863, pp. 231–2.

The eight Odes which are thus based on their corresponding Canticles are :—

Ode. i. Χριστὸς γεννᾶται · δοξάσατε.

Christ is born! Tell forth His fame! By *J. M. Neale*, from his *Hys. of the E. Church*, 1862, in 4 st. of 6 l. In 1868 it appeared as "Christ is born! exalt His name!" in the *Sarum Hymnal*, No. 45, and from thence has passed in the same form into other collections. The original text was restored in the *Hymnary* in 1872, No. 142. In Dr. Littledale's *Offices*, &c., it is *tr.* as "Christ is born, Him glorify."

The remaining Odes are not in C. U. :—

Ode iii. Τῷ πρὸ τῶν αἰώνων.
" Him, of the Father's very Essence." *J. M. Neale*.
" The Son, before the worlds." *R. F. Littledale*.

Ode. iv. Ῥάβδος ἐκ τῆς ῥίζης.
" Rod of the Root of Jesse." *J. M. Neale*.
" Rod of the Root of Jesse." *R. F. Littledale*.

Ode v. Θεὸς ὢν εἰρήνης.
" Father of Peace, and God of Consolation." *J. M. Neale*.
" God of Peace, Father of Compassion." *R. F. Littledale*.

Ode vi. Σπλάγχνων Ἰωνᾶν.
" As Jonah, issuing from his three days' tomb." *J. M. Neale*.
" As the sea-monster vomited." *R. F. Littledale*.

Ode vii. Οἱ παῖδες εὐσεβείᾳ.
" The Holy Children boldly stand." *J. M. Neale*.
" The Children reared in piety." *R. F. Littledale*.

Ode viii. Θαύματος ὑπερφυοῦς ἡ δροσοβόλος.
" The dewy freshness that the furnace flings." *J. M. Neale*.
" The furnace, shedding dew, portrayed." *R. F. Littledale*

Ode ix. Μυστήριον ξένον.
"O wondrous mystery, full of passing grace." *J. M. Neale*.
" A mystery strange and wondrous." *R. F. Littledale*.

The hymn Μέγα καὶ παράδοξον θαῦμα (q. v.) (" A great and mighty wonder ") is from the same Office for Christmas Day. [See **Greek Hymnody**, § xvii. 3.]   [J. J.]

Christ's own Martyrs, valiant cohort. *J. M. Neale*. [*All Saints.*] Appeared first in the *Church Times*, Oct. 29, 1864, signed J. M. N., and after revision, in his *Hymns chiefly Mediaeval, on the Joys and Glories of Paradise*, 1865, and is described by the author as " an attempt of my own; intended as a processional Hymn for All Saints." It is in 10 st. of 6 l., and entitled "Christ's own Martyrs," pp. 81–84. In 1866 it was republished in Neale's *Original Sequences, Hymns*, &c., pp. 57–60, with the following note on st. i. l. 2 :—

White-robed and palmiferous throng.

" This word [palmiferous] has been objected to as not English. It occurs, however, in Cudworth, from whom, as an English writer, there is (I take it) no appeal. It has been characterised by Archbishop Trench, who quotes from Cudworth, as ' beautiful.' "

The text of 1865, with the change of st. vii. l. 6. "stained " for "veined " was included in the *People's H.*, 1867, No. 291.   [J. J.]

Christum ducem, Qui per crucem. *St. Bonaventura*. [*Lent.*] This is ascribed to St. Bonaventura, as a hymn for a *Little Office of the Passion*, at Lauds, and as such it is given in the various editions of his *Works*. *Mone*, No. 85, gives the text from MSS. of the 14th cent. at Strassburg and Karlsruhe, and an extended note. *Daniel*, iv. p. 219, repeats the text, but not the notes in full. It is also given in various mediaeval books of devotion as the *Cursus Collecti* and the *Hortulus animae*.   [W. A. S.]

Translations in C. U. :—

1. **To Christ, whose Cross.** By F. Oakeley in his *Devotions commemorative of the Most Adorable Passion of our Lord and Saviour Jesus Christ*, 1842, in 5 st. of 6 l. In 1864 this was included, unaltered, in Skinner's *Daily Service Hymnal*.

2. **To Christ, whose Cross repaired our loss.** This hymn, which is No. 258 in the *Hymnary*, is a cento; st. i., ii., being i. and ii. from the above; st. iii. from Oakeley's *tr.* of " Qui pressura," and st. iv. and v. from his *tr.* of " Qui jacuisti " in the same work. The last two hymns named are distinct from the " Christum ducem," and are printed in *Mone* and *Daniel*, immediately after it.

Translations not in C. U. :—
1. Christ, our Leader and Redeemer. *J. D. Chambers*, 1857.
2. To Him who death endured hath. Dr. Edersheim, in his *Jubilee Rhythm of St. Bernard*, 1867. [W. T. B.]

Christus der ist mein Leben. [*For the Dying.*] The oldest accessible form of this hymn is in M. Vulpius's *Ein schön geistlich Gesangbuch*, Jena, 1609, No. 148, in 7 st. of 4 l. *Wackernagel*, v. p. 435, gives this and also a second form from a *Christliches Gesangbüchlein*, Hamburg, 1612, in 8 st. In the *Unv. L. S.*, 1851, No. 808, st. i.–vii. are as 1609, and st. viii. as 1612. According to a tradition, seemingly baseless, it was written by Anna, wife of Count Heinrich of Stolberg, about 1600. Some would ascribe it to Simon Graf, who was only 6 in 1603. It has been a favourite hymn in prospect of death, and was thus sung by his wife and children to Heinrich Möwes, just before his death, Oct. 14, 1834, and repeated to Queen Elizabeth of Prussia on the third day of Advent, 1873 (*Koch*, viii. 614). *Tr.* as:—

1. **My life is hid in Jesus**, a good *tr.* of st. i.–vii., by Miss Winkworth, in her *C. B. for England*, 1863, No. 186.

2. **To me to live is Jesus**, a *tr.* of st. i.–iv., vii., signed "F. C. C.," as No. 289 in Dr. Pagenstecher's *Coll.* 1864.

3. **For me to live is Jesus**, in full, by E. Cronenwett, as No. 433 in the Ohio *Luth. Hymnal*, 1880.

Other trs. are:—
(1) "Christ is my light and treasure," by *J. C. Jacobi*, 1725, p. 55 (ed. 1732, p. 198). (2) "In Christ my life is hidden," by *N. L. Frothingham*, 1870, p. 149.
The hymn, "In Christ my life abideth," in 5 st., contributed by A. T. Russell, in the Dalston Hospital *H. Bk.*, 1848, No. 106, and repeated in his own *Ps. & Hys.*, 1851, No. 252, while not a *tr.* is based on the German. [J. M.]

Christus, Lux indeficiens. [*Holy Communion.*] This hymn is given in *Mone*, No. 204, in 10 st. of 4 l., from two 14th cent. MSS., at Karlsruhe, one of which belonged to the Abbey of Reichenau. *Mone* adds readings and notes. *Tr.* as:—

1. **Christ, Light unfailing, with Thy Flesh**, by J. D. Chambers, 1st in his *Companion to the Holy Communion*, 1855, and his *Lauda Syon*, 1857, in 10 st. of 4 l. In the *St. John's* (Aberdeen) *Hymnal*, 1870, No. 235, st. 3–4, 7–9 are omitted.

2. **Christ the Light that knows no waning**, by R. F. Littledale, in the *Altar Manual*, 1863; *Lyra Eucharistica*, 1863, and the *People's H.*, 1867. [J. J.]

Christus tenebris obsitam. *Jean Baptiste de Santeüil.* [*Epiphany.*] Pub. in his *Hymni Sacri et Novi*, 1689, p. 15 (ed. 1698, p. 72), in 4 st. of 4 l. In the revised *Paris Brev.*, 1736, st. i.–iii. were given, with the addition of three stanzas from another source. The hymn is also found in other French Brevs. The *Paris Brev.* text is given in Card. Newman's *Hymni Ecclesiae*, 1838 and 1865, and is that adopted by the translators. [W. A. S.]

Translation in C. U.:—
Through Judah's land the Saviour walks, from the *Paris Brev.*, by J. Chandler, in his *Hys. of the Primitive Church*, 1837, in 6 st. of 4 l. This is given in an abbreviated form in *Kennedy*, 1863, No. 273, and altered to "Through Jewry's darkness Jesus walks," in the *Hymnary*, 1872, No. 176.

Translations not in C. U.:—
1. And now heav'n's growing light is manifest. *I. Williams*, 1839.
2. He dwells on earth, along His path. *R. Campbell*, 1850, and revised as "The bright and morning star arose," from the *Campbell MSS.*, in Mr. Shipley's *Annus Sanctus*, 1884.
3. O'er dark Judea's gloomy shores. *J. D. Chambers.* 1857. [J. J.]

Church of England Hymnody.
[England Hymnody, Church of.]

Churches of Christ, by God's right hand. *J. Conder.* [*Colonial Missions.*] Appeared in his *Cong. H. Bk.*, 1836, No. 500, in 4 st. of 6 l., and based upon the words, " Make

straight in the desert a highway for our God." It was repeated in *The Choir and The Oratory*, 1837, p. 261, and entitled, "The Claims of our Colonies." Also in his *Hys. of Praise, Prayer*, &c., 1856, p. 120. In the *New Cong.*, No. 905, it is given without alteration. It is one of the very few hymns which recognizes the claims of our colonies upon the prayers and assistance, in matters spiritual, of the mother country, and as such, although not a hymn of any great merit, it is yet deserving of more extended use. [J. J.]

Churchyard, Thomas. [Old Version, § ix. 12.]

Churton, Edward, D.D., s. of the Ven. Ralph Churton, sometime Archdeacon of St. David's and Rector of Middleton Cheney, Northampton, was b. in 1800, and educated at the Charterhouse and Christ Church, Oxford, where he graduated in honours, in 1821. He was for some time one of the Masters at Charterhouse. He took Holy Orders in 1826; was the first Head Master of the Hackney Church of England School, 1830; Rector of Crayke, 1835; Prebendary in York Cathedral, 1841; and Archdeacon of Cleveland, 1846. He d. July 4, 1874.

Archdeacon Churton's works include: (1) *The Early English Church*, 1840. (2) *Memoir of Bishop Pearson*, 1844. (3) *Lays of Faith and Royalty*, 1845. (4) *Memoir of Joshua Watson*, 1861. He also edited several works, including *Lays of Faith and Loyalty*, 1845, &c. He is known to hymnology through his work, *The Book of Psalms in English Verse*, 1854. This is commonly known as the *Cleveland Psalter*. The Preface is of more than usual interest and value. Of his renderings of the Psalms, some of which are of great excellence [see **Psalters, English,** § ix.], a few have come into C. U., the best known being, "God of grace, O let Thy light." The following, mainly in *Kennedy*, 1863, are from the *Cleveland Psalter*:—

1. Come, arise and let us go. *Ps. cxxxii.*
2. Earth with all thy thousand voices. *Ps. lxvi.*
3. For ever, Lord, Thy faithful word. *Ps. cxix.*
4. God of truth, all faithful Lord. *Ps. cxliii.*
5. God my hope, my strength, my King. *Ps. cxlv.*
6. God rules in realms of light. *Ps. xciii.*
7. How shall I render to my God. *Ps. cxvi.*
8. I lift mine heart to Thee. *Ps. xxv.*
9. If our God had not befriended. *Ps. cxxiv.*
10. In Thee, O Lord, I trust. *Ps. xxxi.*
11. Lord, hear me, grant my sorrows boon. *Ps. lv.*
12. Lord, hear my suppliant prayer. *Ps. cxxx.*
13. Lord, hear the voice of my complaint. *Ps. v.*
14. Lord, I have called on Thee; for Thou. *Ps. xvii.*
15. Lord, my heart is with the lowly. *Ps. cxxxi.*
16. Lord, my Rock, to Thee I cry. *Ps. xxviii.*
17. Lord, to my sad voice attending. *Ps. lxi.*
18. O happy state on earth to see. *Ps. cxxxiii.*
19. O praise the Lord, for He is love. *Ps. cxxxvi.*
20. O stand in awe, and fear to sin. *Ps. iv.*
21. Raise the psalm to God all glorious. *Ps. xcviii.*
22. 'Tis the day all days excelling. *Ps. cxviii.*
23. To Thee our guilty deeds. *Ps. xc.*
24. Whene'er to Thee I make my prayer. *Ps. lvi.*

Archdeacon Churton's *trs.* from the Latin, Spanish, and Anglo-Saxon, were included in his *Poetical Remains*, Lond., 1876. [J. J.]

Cives celestis patriae. *Bp. Marbodus.* [*The heavenly Jerusalem.*] This hymn is given in *Mone*, No. 637, from a MS. at Admont dated 1098, in 16 st. of 6 l. It deals with the mystical meaning of the precious stones in the foundation of the heavenly Jerusalem. Dr. Neale, by whom the *tr.* in C. U. was made, and pub. in his *Med. Hys.*, 1851, p. 38, introduces it with the following preface:—

"The ruggedness of the translation is merely a copy of that of the original in the following poem of Marbodus, successively Archdeacon of Angers and Bishop of

Rennes, who died 1125. Its title, a Prose, clearly proves it to have been intended, if not used, as a Sequence in the Mass of some high festival, probably a dedication. The mystical explanation of precious stones is the subject of the good Bishop's poem *de Gemmis*, which seems in its time to have obtained a high reputation. The Prose, which I here give, is certainly not without its beauty; and is a good key to mediaeval allusions of a similar kind."

Dr. Neale appends to his *tr.* an extensive note on the mystical meaning of the precious stones, in which he quotes largely from a commentary on the prose by Marbodus. The *tr.* is:—

Ye of the heavenly country, sing. It is in 16 st. of 6 l. A cento, composed of st. i., xv., xvi. was given in the Irvingite *Hys. for the Use of the Churches*, new ed. 1870. Beyond this the *tr.* is not in C. U.   [J. J.]

Clamantis ecce vox sonans. *Nicholas le Tourneaux*. [*Epiphany.*] This is a hymn at first Vespers, during the Octave of the Epiphany, and the Baptism of our Lord, in the revised *Paris Brev.* of 1736. It previously appeared in the *Cluniac Breviary*, 1686, p. 230. The text is in Card. Newman's *Hymni Ecclesiae*, 1838 and 1865.   [W. A. S.]

Translations in C. U.:—

1. **The voice of one that cries aloud.** This *tr.*, based on J. Chandler's, was given in J. A. Johnston's *English Hymnal*, 1852, No. 63. In the 1856 and 1861 editions it was altered to "A voice of one that loudly cries."

2. **The Herald's cry with thrilling sounds,** by J. D. Chambers, in his *Lauda Syon*, 1857, p. 114. On p. 115 of the same work is a *tr.* of the Nocturn hymn, "Non abluunt lymphae Deum." From these two *trs.* the hymn, No. 175, in the *Hymnary*, 1872, "The Baptist's cry with thrilling sounds," is composed, st. i., ii. being from the first, and st. iii.–vi. from the second.

Translations not in C. U.:—
1. The voice of him who cries aloud. *J. Chandler*. 1837.
2. Judea's desert heard a sound. *I. Williams*, in *Brit. Mag.*, 1835, and *Hys. from Par. Brev.*, 1839.
3. Hark, in the wilderness. *R. Campbell*, from the *Campbell MSS.*, in Mr. Shipley's *Annus Sanctus*, 1884.
4. Lo the voice of one that crieth. *W. J. Blew*. 1852.
                                        [J. J.]

Clapham, Emma, second daughter of John Peele Clapham, was b. in Hanover Square, Leeds, Oct. 18, 1830. Miss Clapham, who has given much time and attention to Sunday Schools and philanthropic work, contributed under the initials of "E. C." the following hymns to the *Leeds Sunday School H. Bk.*, ed. 1858, edited by her father :—
1. Guide of my steps along life's way. *Jesus the Guide*.
2. Lord, we meet to pray and praise. *Meeting of Church workers*.
3. Saviour, where dwellest Thou? *Meeting of S. School Teachers*.

Miss Clapham has also contributed several pieces to newspapers and the periodical press.
                                        [J. J.]

Clapham, John Peele, was b. at Leeds, July 7th, 1801, and educated privately, and at the Fulneck Moravian School, and the Protestant Free Church Grammar School, Manchester. He was a magistrate for the West Riding of Yorkshire, and Treasurer of the County Courts in Yorkshire. He was a member of the Congregational body, and

took a warm interest in their religious and philanthropic work. Burley, Harrowgate and Ilkley were specially benefited by his zeal and munificence. His interest in Sunday Schools commenced at an early age, and continued to his death, on Nov. 19, 1875. In 1833 he edited the *Leeds Sunday School Hymn Book*, and also the revised edition, 1862. To this work he contributed the following hymns under the signature of "J. P. C.":—

i. To *Hymns Sel. and Original*, 1833.
1. God of union, God of love. *S. S. Teachers' Meeting*.
2. Let us unite to bless the Lord. *Sunday*.
3. Our Father, and our heavenly King. *The Lord's Prayer*.
4. Shall we grieve the Holy Spirit? *The work of the Holy Spirit*.
5. Strengthen Thy stakes, extend Thy cords. *Foundation-stone of a School*.
6. Sweet is the work, O Lord, to raise. *New Year*.
7. Thou gracious Father of the poor. *The True Riches*.
8. We dare not God's own holy day. *Sunday*.
9. When Jesus at a wondrous feast. *Feeding the Five Thousand*.

ii. To the same *Collection*, ed. 1858.
10. A little pilgrim on life's way. *Looking unto Jesus*. "The little pilgrim was no fiction, but a bonnie, loving, and lovable lad of nearly ten years old, our youngest son. He died at school, after a week's illness, and the refrain of his father's lines—'Jesus, my Saviour,' were the last words we could catch before he finished his pilgrimage." *Curwen's Biog.*, *Notes*, p. 7.
11. Accept our glad thanksgiving, Lord. *Praise*.
12. Come away from the train. *Sunday*.
13. Far too often men are crying. *The Gifts of the Holy Spirit*.
14. Father in heaven, for Jesus' sake. *Grace before Meat*.
15. Heavenly Teacher, Light divine. *Imitating Christ*.
16. How good and how pleasant. *Praise to God the Father*.
17. Now in Christian love and union. *Grace before Meat*.
18. O make us truly wise. *Early Piety desired*.
19. Pure religion, Christian love. *Praise to God the Father*.
20. Tempt us not, ye sons of pleasure. *Sunday*.
21. We own Thy care, we love Thy word. *Praise*.
                                        [J. J.]

Clapp, Eliza Thayer, a resident at Dorchester, Massachusetts, U.S., and author of *Words in the Sunday School;* and *Studies in Religion*, 1845, contributed at the request of Ralph W. Emerson three hymns and two poems to *The Dial*, 1841. From one of the hymns, in 9 st. of 4 l., pub. in *The Dial*, July, 1841, and entitled "The future is better than the past," the hymn "All before us lies the way" (*Onward with Confidence*) is taken. It was given in Hedge & Huntington's Unitarian *Hys. for the Church of Christ*, 1853, and has been repeated in several collections. It is usually attributed to Emerson, but in error. (George Cooke, in *Journal of Speculative Philosophy*, 1885.)   [V. D. D.]

Clara diei gaudia. [*St. Anne.*] The dates given to this hymn are uncertain, and range from the 9th to the 13th cent. *Mone*, No. 791, gives the text from MSS. at Freiburg, and in the Library of the Lyceum at Constanz, of the 15th cent. He adds a few readings to the text. *Daniel*, i. 289, iv. 175, refers to several Breviaries of the 16th cent., but none earlier than 1500, and to a MS. of the 11th or 12th cent. belonging to the town Library of Hamburg.   [W. A. S.]

Translation in C. U. :—

Spotless Anna! Juda's glory, by E. Caswall, in his *Lyra Catholica*, 1849, p. 263, in 6 st. of 4 l. On republishing it in his *Hymns, &c.*, 1873, p. 188, he added an original refrain. This refrain is a special invocation of St. Anne. In the 2nd ed. of the *Appendix* to *Hymnal N.*, 1862, it was altered as, " Holy Anna, Juda's glory," and from thence it passed into the *People's H.*, 1867. In the Roman Catholic *Hys. for the Year*, N.D., it is given as " Blessed Anna, Juda's glory." In T. Chamberlain's *Hys. used at the Church of St. Thomas the Martyr*, Oxford, 1861, No. 149, st. i.–iii. are by Caswall, and st. iv., v. by T. Chamberlain. [J. J.]

Clark, Alexander, D.D., b. March 10, 1835, d. July 6, 1879. Dr. Clark was for many years a Minister of the American Methodist Episcopal Church, and the editor of the *Methodist Recorder*, pub. at Pittsburgh. Two of his hymns :—

1. Heavenly Father, bless me now. *Lent.*
2. Make room for Jesus. *Lent.*

are given in I. D. Sankey's *Sac. S. & Solos.*

Clark, Charles, b. in London, April 19, 1838, was educated for the ministry at the Baptist College, Nottingham, and in 1862 became minister at North Parade Chapel, Halifax. He was subsequently minister at Mazepond, London; Broadmead, Bristol; Albert Street, Melbourne, Australia; and is now (1885) pastor of the Baptist Church, Haven Green, Ealing. His hymn for children, " Jesus, holy Saviour, Shepherd of the sheep," was contributed to the *School Hymnal* (Lond., 1880). [W. R. S.]

Clark, John Haldenby, M.A., b. at Chesterfield, Derbyshire, Jan. 28, 1839, and educated at the Grammar School there, and at St. John's Coll., Cambridge, where he graduated in 1861. On taking Holy Orders, he became Curate of Barmby Moor and Fangfoss. After labouring in various parishes he became, in 1870, Vicar of West Dereham, Norfolk. Mr. Clark is known through his translation, "Soldiers, who are Christ's below." In 1880 he pub. *The Marriage of Cana, and Other Verses :* Lynn. It contains a few *trs.* from the Latin, in addition to original verse. He d. April 14, 1888. [J. J.]

Clark, Willis Gaylord, b. at Otisco, Onondaga County, New York, 1810, d. June 12, 1841. He was sometime editor of the *Philadelphia Gazette*, and contributed to the *Knickerbocker Magazine*. His poetical writings were published in 1846. His hymn :—

We have met in peace together, was written for the 8th Anniversary of the American Sunday School Union, 1832. It is unknown to the English collections. [F. M. B.]

Clarke, James Freeman, D.D., is a grandson of James Freeman (q. v.), from whom he was named. He was b. at Hanover, New Hampshire, April 4, 1810, and graduated at Harvard College, in Arts, in 1829, and in Divinity, 1833. Receiving ordination as a Unitarian Minister, he was Pastor at Louisville, Kentucky, from 1833 to 1840 ; of the Church of the Disciples, Boston, from 1841 to 1850 ; and also from 1853. Dr. Clarke

for some time edited, whilst at Louisville, *The Western Messenger*, and is the author of *Orthodoxy, its Truths and Errors*, 1866 ; *The Christian Doctrine of Forgiveness*, 1852 ; *The Christian Doctrine of Prayer*, 1854, and other works. In 1844 he published the *Hymn Book for the Church of the Disciples.* This he enlarged in 1852. To each edition he contributed five hymns. Of these ten hymns five are found in the *Lyra Sac. Amer.* The best known of Dr. Clarke's hymns are :—

1. **Father, to us Thy children, humbly kneeling.** [*Holy thoughts desired.*] Dr. Clarke says this was manufactured from :—

2. **Infinite Spirit, who art round us ever** [*Holy thoughts desired*], which " was written in Kentucky about 1833, and printed in the *Dial* soon after."

3. **Brother, hast thou wandered far?** [*The Prodigal Son.*] This appeared in his *Disciples' H. Bk.*, 1844, and is somewhat extensively used. It appeared in an abbreviated form as, " Hast thou wasted all the powers ? " beginning with st. ii., in *Hys. for the Church of Christ*, Boston, 1853 ; Beecher's *Plymouth Coll.*, 1855, and subsequently in others in G. Britain and America. The next three are also in one or two English collections.

4. **To Thee, O God, in heaven.** [*Holy Baptism.*] 1844.

5. **To Him who children blessed.** [*Holy Baptism.*] 1844.

6. **Dear Friend, whose presence in the house.** [*Christ's presence desired.*] 1855. The beauty and value of this last hymn have been partly, and deserve to be more fully, recognized. It is found in *Lyra Sac. Amer.*, which also has the following on " The Protestant Reformation " :—

7. **For all Thy gifts we praise Thee, Lord.** This hymn was sung at the collation given by the Unitarians of New York and Brooklyn to the Members of the Convention assembled in the former city, Oct. 22, 1845. As originally written it contained 8 st. ; the last two are omitted from both *Lyra Sac. Amer.* and Putnam's *Singers and Songs of the Liberal Faith*. [F. M. B.]

Clarke, Samuel Childs, M.A., b. Jan. 6, 1821, and educated at Queen's College and St. Mary Hall, Oxford, graduating B.A., 1844, and M.A. 1846. On taking Holy Orders he became successively Curate of Thorverton, and of Dawlish, Devon ; Vicar of St. Thomas by-Launceston, and Head Master of the Launceston Grammar School, and Vicar of Thorverton, 1875 ; and Hon. Sec. of the Exeter Board of Education. Mr. Clarke has pub. some educational works : *Thoughts in Verse from a Village Churchman's Note Book*, 1848, and *Services of Song* for Christmas, Passiontide, Ascension, Harvest (S. P. C. K. catalogue), Advent, Eastertide, Missionary, Flower, and Children's Services. These Services of Song have been sanctioned for use in churches by the Bishops of Exeter and Salisbury. Mr. Clarke's hymns include :—

1. **All hail, all hail to the natal day.** *Christmas.* Contributed to the *Parish Church Hymnal.*
2. **Framer of the light.** *Morning.* In the *Parish Ch. Hyl.*, and Mrs. Brock's *Children's H. Bk.*, 1881.
3. **Great Giver of all good, to Thee again.** *Harvest.* This is the best known of our author's hymns. It was first printed in the *Musical Times*, 1863, with music by Barnby. In 1868 it was included in the *Appendix* to

the S. P. C. K. *Ps. and Hys.*, in 1872 in the *Hymnary*, and again in many other collections.

4. In all Thou didst while here on earth. *St. Thomas.* In Mrs. Brock's *Children's H. Bk.*, 1881.

5. In humble adoration. *Laying of the Foundation-stone of a Church.* In Harland's *Suppl. to Ch. Psalter and Hymnal*, 1876.

6. Jesus, on this blessed morn. *Christmas.* In the *Parish Ch. Hyl.*

7. Lord, most holy, God most mighty. *For travellers and absent ones.* In the *Home H. Bk.*, 1885, by H. P. Hawkins.

8. Lord of the new creation. *Sunday Morning.* In the *Parish Ch. Hyl.*

9. Now a new year opens. *The New Year.* In Mrs. Brock's *Children's H. Bk.*, 1881, and one or two American collections.

10. O dark and dreary day. *Good Friday.* In *Suppl.* to Harland's *Ch. Hyl.*; Mrs. Brock's *Children's H. Bk.*

11. O Lord, it is a joyful thing. *Evening.* In the *Parish Ch. Hyl.*, &c.

12. O Thou who dwellest in eternity. *Festival.* In *Suppl.* to Harland's *Ch. Hyl.*, 1876.

13. Once more the sheaves are gathered. *Harvest.* In *Suppl.* to Harland's *Ch. Hyl.*, the author's *Harvest-tide* Service of Song, &c., 1876.

14. Thou who through shades of night. *Evening.* In the *Parish Ch. Hyl.*, &c.

In addition to these hymns, most of those given in Mr. Clarke's *Services of Song* are his composition, as are also the 19 in his *Services for Children.* Lond., Pitman, N.D. Some of these are initialled "S. C. C." Taken as a whole these hymns are a good addition to the common store for Special Occasions, and should be consulted by hymn-book compilers. He d. Feb. 22, 1903.   [J. J.]

Clarum decus jejunii. *St. Gregory the Great.* [*Lent.*] The oldest form of this hymn is in two MSS. of the 11th cent. in the *Brit. Mus.* (Vesp. D. xii. f. 52; Harl. 2961 f. 238 b), and from a MS. of the 11th cent. at Durham in the *Latin Hys. of the Anglo-Saxon Church*, 1851, p. 65. It is also given in various editions of St. Gregory's *Works;* in *Migne*, tom. 178, col. 849; *Daniel*, i., No. 148; *Mone*, No. 71; *Hymn. Sarisb.*, 1851; Card. Newman's *Hymni Ecclesiae*, 1838 and 1865, and others. The use of the hymn in England was extensive. It is found in the *Sarum, York, Canterbury, Worcester*, and other English Brevs.

Translations in C. U. :—

1. The shining glory of the fast, by R. F. Littledale, made for and 1st pub. in the *People's H.*, 1867, with the signature "P. C. E."

2. Good it is to keep the fast, by Sir H. W. Baker, written for *H. A. & M.*, 1875.

3. From heaven, in glorious beauty shown. In the *Antiphoner and Grail*, 1880, and from thence into the *Hymner*, 1882, No. 49.

Translations not in C. U. :—

1. Fast's honour bright from Heaven come down. *W. J. Copeland.* 1848.

2. High token of the fast of Lent. *W. J. Blew.* 1852–55.

3. What honour hath the fast of Lent. *J. D. Chambers.* 1857.

4. That fasting serves a holy end. *J. W. Hewett.* 1859.

5. Depths of love with power divine. *Morgan.* 1880.
                                                        .[J. J.]

Claudius, Mátthias, s. of Matthias Claudius, Lutheran pastor at Reinfeld in Holstein (near Lübeck), was b. at Reinfeld, Aug. 15, 1740. An ancestor, who died as a Lutheran pastor in 1586, had Latinized his name, Claus Paulsen, to *Claudius Pauli*, and his descendants had adopted Claudius as their surname. Claudius entered the University of Jena, in 1759, as a student of theology, but

being troubled with an affection of the chest, and finding little attraction in the Rationalism of Jena, he turned his attention to law and languages. After a short visit to Copenhagen, as private secretary to a Danish count, he joined in 1768 the staff of the Hamburg News Agency (*Adress-Comptoirnachrichten*). Removing to Wandsbeck, near Hamburg, he undertook in 1771 the editing of the literary portion of the *Wandsbecker Bote*, and contributed a number of his poems to the *Göttingen Musen-Almanach*. In 1776 he was appointed one of the Commissioners of Agriculture and Manufactures of Hesse-Darmstadt, and in 1777 editor of the official Hesse-Darmstadt newspaper, which he conducted in the same spirit as his *Wandsbeck Bote*. At Darmstadt he became acquainted with Goethe (then living near by at Frankfurt), and with a circle of freethinking philosophers. During a severe illness in 1777, he realised, however, the spiritual emptiness of the life at Darmstadt; the buried seeds sown in his youth sprang up; and he once more became in faith as a little child. Renouncing position and income, he returned to Wandsbeck to re-edit the *Bote*, which he conducted in a distinctively Christian spirit. In 1788 he was appointed by the Crown Prince of Denmark auditor of the Schleswig-Holstein Bank at Altona, but continued to reside at Wandsbeck till 1813, when he was forced by the war to flee, and was unable to return till May, 1814. The next year he removed to the house of his eldest daughter in Hamburg, and d. there Jan. 21, 1815 (*Koch*, vi. 417–429; *Allg. Deutsche Biog.*, iv. 279–281). His fugitive pieces appeared in two parts as *Asmus omnia sua secum portans; oder sämmtliche Werke des Wandsbecker Bothen*, Wandsbeck and Hamburg, 1774 (pt. iii. 1777, iv. 1782, v. 1789, vi. 1797, vii. 1802, viii. 1812). While much of his poetry was distinctively Christian in its spirit, and many of his pieces might rank as popular sacred songs, yet he wrote no hymns designed for use in Church. Three pieces have, however, passed into the German hymn-books, all of which have been *tr.* into English, viz. :—

i. **Das Grab ist leer, das Grab ist leer.** [*Easter.*] 1st pub. in pt. viii., 1812, as above, p. 121, in 10 st. *Tr.* as "The grave is empty now, its prey," by *Dr. H. Mills*, 1859, printed in Schaff's *Christ in Song*, 1870.

ii. **Der Mond ist aufgegangen.** [*Evening.*] His finest hymn, conceived in a child-like, popular spirit—a companion to the more famous hymn, "Nun ruhen alle Wälder" (q. v.). According to tradition it was composed during his residence at Darmstadt, 176$\frac{6}{7}$, while walking on the so-called Schnempelweg, a foot-path leading by the river-side up to the Odenwald. 1st pub. in J. H. Voss's *Musen-Almanach*, Hamburg, 1779, p. 184, and then in pt. iv., 1782, as above, p. 57, in 7 st. of 6 l. Included as No. 452 in the *Oldenburg G. B.*, 1791, as No. 570 in the *Württemberg G. B.*, 1842, and No. 509 in the *Unv. L. S.*, 1851. The only *tr.* in C. U. is:—

The silent moon is risen, good and full, as No. 322, in the Ohio *Luth. Hymnal*, 1880.

Other trs. are :—

(1) "The fair moon hath ascended," in the *British Magazine*, Nov. 1837, p. 518. (2) "The moon on high

is beaming,",by *H. J. Buckoll*, 1842, p. 105. (3) "The moon hath risen on high," by *Miss Winkworth*, 1855, p. 229 (1876, p. 231). (4) "The moon up heaven is going," by J. D. Burns, in *Family Treasury*, 1860, p. 92, repeated in his *Memoir*, 1869, p. 269. (5) "The moon is upwards climbing," by *Miss Manington*, 1863, p. 124. (6) "The moon is up in splendour," by E. Massie, 1866, p. 115. (7) "The moon hath risen clear," in Alice Lucas's *Trs. from German Poets*, 1876, p. 12. (8) "The moon is up and beaming," in Mrs. A. W. Johns's *Original Poems and Trs.*, 1882, p. 61.

iii. Im Anfang war's auf Erden. [*Harvest.*] 1st pub. in pt. iv., 1782, as above, p. 42, in 17 st. of 4 l., and chorus (see also G. W. Fink's *Musikalischer Hausschatz der Deutschen*, Altona, 1860, No. 77). It occurs in a sketch entitled, *Paul Erdmann's Fest*. The neighbours are represented as coming to Paul's house and there singing this so-called "Peasants' Song," the last four sts. of which specially relate to the occasion ; the stanzas being sung as a solo, and all joining in the chorus. It can hardly be called a hymn, though it has passed into a few German hymnals principally for use in school. Beginning, "Auf! lasset Gott uns loben," 10 sts. were included as No. 482 in the Oldenburg *G. B.*, 1791. In T. Fliedner's *Liederbuch*, Kaiserswerth, 1842, No. 95 begins with st. vii., "Was nah ist und was ferne." The form most popular is that beginning with st. iii., "Wir pflügen und wir streuen," as in Dr. Wichern's *Unsere Lieder*, Hamburg, 1844, No. 55, and other collections. The sts. of the original which most nearly answer to the English versions are :—

iii.	
Wir pflügen und wir streuen	Der Strohhalm und die Sterne,
Den Samen auf das Land ;	Der Sperling und das Meer.
Doch Wachsthum und Gedeyen	
Steht nicht in unsrer Hand.	**ix.**
Alle gute Gabe	Er, Er macht Sonnaufgehen,
Kömmt oben her, von Gott,	Er stellt des Mondes Lauf,
Vom schönen blauen Himmel herab.	Er lässt die Winde wehen,
	Er thut den Himmel auf.
v.	**x.**
Der sendet Thau und Regen,	Er schenkt uns Vieh und Freude.
Und Sonn- und Mondenschein ;	Er macht uns frisch und roth,
Der wickelt Gottes Seegen Gar zart und künstlich ein.	Er giebt den Kühen Weide, Und unsern Kindern Brodt.
vii.	**xiii.**
Was nah ist und was ferne,	Darum, so woll'n wir loben,
Von Gott kommt alles her !	Und loben immer dar
	Den grossen Geber oben.
	Er ists ! und er ists gar !

The popular if somewhat boisterous tune usually set to this hymn (as in *H. A. & M.*) is by J. A. P. Schulz. The melody given in 1782 is said there to be Italian, and is not suited to the chorus popular in England.

Translations in C. U. :—

1. **We plough the fields and scatter,** by Miss J. M. Campbell, contributed to the Rev. C. S. Bere's *Garland of Songs*, Lond., 1861, p. 61 (later eds. p. 27). A free rendering in 3 st. of 8 l., with chorus, entitled, "Thanksgiving for the Harvest." Since its reception into the Appendix to *H. A. & M.*, 1868 (No. 360, ed. 1875, No. 383), it has passed into numerous hymnals in G. Brit. and America. In Thring's *Coll.*, 1882, No. 609, st. iv., "Our souls, Blest Saviour, gather," is an original st. by Rev. H. Downton, added to supply some distinctly Christian expressions to the hymn, and 1st pub. in the *Record* newspaper in 1875.

2. **We plough the fertile meadows.** Of this *tr.* there are two forms greatly differing, both ascribed to Dr. S. F. Smith, but whether either form is really by him we have failed to ascertain. What seems to be the original form, in 6 st. of

4 l. and chorus, is found in the *Meth. Free Ch. S. S. Hys.* ; Curwen's *New Child's Own H. Bk.*, &c. The other form, in 3 st. of 8 l. and chorus, is in Allon's *Supp. Hys. ; N. Cong.*, &c.

3. **We plough the ground, we sow the seed,** in 4 st. of 8 l. with chorus, without name of *tr.*, is No. 215 in G. S. Jellicoe's *Coll.*, 1867. [J. M.]

Clausnitzer, Tobias,

b. at Thum, near Annaberg, in Saxony, probably on Feb. 5, 1619. After studying at various Universities, and finally at Leipzig (where he graduated M.A. in 1643), he was appointed, in 1644, chaplain to a Swedish regiment. In that capacity he preached the thanksgiving sermon in St. Thomas's Church, Leipzig, on "Reminiscere" Sunday, 1645 (II. Sunday in Lent) on the accession of Christina as Queen of Sweden ; as also the thanksgiving sermon at the field service held by command of General Wrangel, at Weiden, in the Upper Palatine, on January 1, 1649, after the conclusion of the Peace of Westphalia. In 1649 he was appointed first pastor at Weiden, and remained there (being also appointed later a member of the Consistory, and inspector of the district,) till his death, on May 7, 1684 (*Koch*, iii. 354, 355 ; *Allg. Deutsche Biog.*, iv. 297 ; *Bode*, p. 53 ; MS. from Pastor Klinkhardt, Thum). Three hymns by him are known as follows :—

i. Jesu dein betrübtes Leiden. [*Passiontide.*] 1st pub. in his *Passions-Blume*, Nürnberg, 1662, a volume containing 12 sermons on the Passion of our Lord. The hymn appears at p. 17, in 7 st. of 6 l. entitled, "Clausnicer's Passion-Hymn which may be sung with each Meditation." This form is No. 496 in Burg's *G. B.*, Breslau, 1746. This hymn has passed into English through a recast, probably by Gensch von Breitenau, beginning, "Herr Jesu, deine Angst und Pein," in 6 st. of 7 l. 1st pub. in the *Vollständiges G. B.*, Plöen, 1675, No. 41, repeated as No. 101 in the *Unv. L. S.*, 1851. The only *tr.* in C. U. is :—

Lord Jesu! may Thy grief and pain, a good *tr.* of st. i., iii., vi., by A. T. Russell, as No. 84 in his *Ps. and Hys.*, 1851.

ii. Liebster Jesu wir sind hier, Dich und Dein Wort anzuhören. [*Public Worship.*] 1st pub. in the *Altdorffisches Gesang-Büchlein*, 1663, No. 20, in 3 st. of 6 l., as a Sunday Hymn for use before Sermon. It appeared with Clausnitzer's name in the Nürnberg *G. B.*, 1676, No. 891, and has since come into universal use. In the Berlin *G. L. S.*, ed. 1863, No. 1062. *Tr.* as :—

1. **Gracious Jesu! in Thy name,** a good and full *tr.* by A. T. Russell, as No. 82 in the Dalston Hospital *H. Bk.*, 1848. Included as No. 454 in the ed., 1857, of Mercer's *C. P. & H. Bk.* (Ox. ed. 1864, No. 56, considerably altered with st. i. l. 4, iii. ll. 1–4, from Miss Winkworth, and a doxology added).

2. **Gracious Jesu! we are here,** a recast of his 1848 *tr.*, made by A. T. Russell for his *Ps. & Hys.*, 1851, No. 19.

3. **Saviour, in Thy house of prayer,** a good and full *tr.* as No. 13 in J. F. Thrupp's *Ps. & Hys.*, 1853, repeated in Maurice's *Coll.*, 1861, No. 634. In *Kennedy*, 1863, No. 1251, altered and beginning, "Saviour, to Thy house of prayer."

4. **Blessed Jesus, at Thy word,** a full and good *tr.* by Miss Winkworth in her *Lyra Ger.*, 2nd

Series, 1858, p. 68, repeated in her *C. B. for England*, 1863, No. 12. Included in the Eng. Presb. *Ps. & Hys.*, 1867, and others; and in America in the Pennsylvania *Luth. Ch. Bk.*, 1868; *Evang. Hymnal*, N. Y., 1880, and others.

5. **Dear Lord, to hear Thee and Thy word**, a good *tr.* by Mrs. L. C. Smith; included as No. 50 in Dr. Stevenson's *H. for Ch. & Home*, 1873.

Trs. not in C. U.:—
(1) "Dearest Jesu! we are here, Thee to hear," by *J. C. Jacobi* (1720, p. 32; 1722, p. 43; 1732, p. 72, alt.). In the *Moravian H. Bk.*, 1789, No. 12 (1849, No. 3), recast by C. J. Latrobe. (2) "Dearest Jesu, we are here, for to hear," as No. 432 in pt. i. of the *Moravian H. Bk.*, 1754. (3) "Here in Thy presence we appear," by J. Swertner, as No. 10 in the *Moravian H. Bk.*, 1789 (1886, No. 9). (4) "Blessed Jesus, we are here," by *Miss Manington*, 1863, p, 145. (5) "Precious Jesus! here are we," in the *British Herald*, Nov. 1866, p. 360, repeated in Reid's *Praise Bk.*, 1872, No. 419. (6) "Dear Redeemer, we are here," by *N. L. Frothingham*, 1870, p. 204..

iii. **Wir glauben all an einen Gott, Vater, Sohn und heilgen Geist.** [*Trinity Sunday.*] 1st appeared in the Culmbach-Bayreuth *G. B.*, 1668, p. 132, with the initials "C. A. D." With Clausnitzer's name it was included as No. 572 in the Nürnberg *G. B.*, 1676, in 3 st. of 6 l. In the Bavarian *G. B.*, 1854. *Tr.* as:—

1. **We all believe in One true God, Father, Son and Holy Ghost**, in full by Miss Winkworth in her *C. B. for England*, 1863, No. 75, and thence as No. 118 in the American *Meth. Epis. Hymnal*, 1878, and the *Evang. Assoc. H. Bk.*, 1882, No. 64.
2. **One true God we all confess**, by E. Cronenwett, as No. 209 in the Ohio *Luth. Hymnal*, 1880.
[J. M.]

Cleft are the rocks, the earth doth quake. [*Good Friday.*] This hymn is sometimes attributed to Bp. Heber, but in error. It appeared in his posthumous *Hymns*, &c., 1827, pp. 64-5, in 7 st. of 5 l., and as "*Anon.*" Two centos therefrom have come into C. U.:—

1. "Cleft are the rocks," &c., in Alford's *Ps. and Hys.*, 1844, and his *Year of Praise*, 1867. This is composed of st. i., ii., vii.
2. "Despised is the Man of grief," in Dr. Martineau's *Hymns*, &c., 1840; and his *Hys. of P. and Prayer*, 1873, being st. iii., v., and vi. considerably altered.

These centos are usually ascribed to "C. Dawson," but upon what authority we cannot determine. [J. J.]

Clemens, Titus Flavius (Clemens Alexandrinus), St. Clement of Alexandria, was b. possibly at Athens (although on this point there is no certain information) about A.D. 170. His full name, Titus Flavius Clemens, is given by Eusebius (*H. E.*, vi. 13) and Photius (*Cod.* 111), but of his parentage there is no record. Studious, and anxious to satisfy his mind on the highest subjects, he is said to have been a Stoic and Eclectic, and a seeker after truth amongst Greek, Assyrian, Egyptian, and Jewish teachers. He himself enumerates six teachers of eminence under whom he studied the "true tradition of the blessed doctrine of the holy apostles." At Alexandria he came under the teaching of Pantænus, and embraced Christianity, Pantænus being at the time the master of the Catechetical School in that city. On the retirement of Pantænus from the school for missionary work, Clement became its head, cir. 190, and retained the position to 203. His pupils were numerous, and some of them

of note, including Origen, and Alexander, afterwards Bp. of Jerusalem. Driven from Alexandria by the persecution under Severus (202-203), he wandered forth, it is not known whither. The last notice we have of him in history is in a letter of congratulation by his old pupil, Alexander, then Bp. of Cappadocia, to the Church of Antioch, on the appointment of Asclepiades to the bishopric of that city. This letter, dated 211, seems to have been conveyed to Antioch by Clement. Beyond this nothing is known, either concerning his subsequent life or death, although the latter is sometimes dated A.D. 220.

The works of Clement are ten in all. Of these, the only work with which we have to do is *The Tutor*, ὁ Παιδαγωγός, in three books. The first book describes the Tutor, who is the Word Himself, the children whom He trains (Christian men and women), and his method of instruction. The second book contains general instructions as to daily life in eating, drinking, furniture, sleep, &c.; and the third, after an inquiry into the nature of true beauty, goes on to condemn extravagance in dress, &c., both in men and women. Appended to this work, in the printed editions, are two poems; the first, "A Hymn of the Saviour" (Ὕμνος τοῦ Σωτῆρος Χριστοῦ), and the second, an address "To the Tutor" (Εἰς τὸν Παιδαγωγόν). The first, beginning, Στομίον πώλων ἀδαῶν, is attributed to Clement in those MSS. in which it is found; but it is supposed by some to be of an earlier date: the second is generally regarded as by a later hand (see **Greek Hymnody,** § iii. For list of MSS. in which "The Tutor" is given, and for fuller details of Clement see *Dict. of Christian Biog.*, pp. 559-587).

The "Hymn of the Saviour," the earliest known Christian hymn, has been *tr.* into English as follows:—

Στομίον πώλων ἀδαῶν. The earliest *tr.* is "Shepherd of tender youth." This is by Dr. H. M. Dexter (q. v.). It was written in 1846, first pub. in *The Congregationalist* [of which Dexter was editor], Dec. 21, 1849, and is in extensive use in the United States. In Gt. Britain it is also given in several collections, including the *N. Cong.*, 1859; Bap. *Ps. & Hys.*, 1858; the R. T. Society's *Coll.*, &c.

There are also *trs.* not in C. U., viz.: (1) "Bridle of colts untamed," by Dr. W. L. Alexander, in the *Ante-Nicene Christ. Lib.*, vol. iv. p. 343; see also p. 345. (2) "Bridle of colts untaught," by Dr. H. Bonar, in *Sunday at Home*, 1878, p. 11. (3) Another *tr.* is by the Rev. A. W. Chatfield, in his *Songs and Hys. of the Earliest Greek Christian Poets*, 1876. Mr. Chatfield, following the *Anth. Graeca Car. Christ.*, 1871, p. 37, begins with the eleventh line: βασιλεῦ ἁγίων, λόγε πανδαμάτωρ. "O Thou, the King of Saints, all-conquering Word." His *tr.* extends to 40 lines. [J. J.]

Clephane, Elizabeth Cecilia, third daughter of Andrew Clephane, Sheriff of Fife, was b. at Edinburgh, June 18, 1830. and d. at Bridgend House, near Melrose, Feb. 19, 1869. Her hymns appeared, almost all for the first time, in the *Family Treasury*, under the general title of *Breathings on the Border*. In publishing the first of these in the *Treasury*, the late Rev. W. Arnot, of Edinburgh, then editor, thus introduced them:—

"These lines express the experiences, the hopes, and the longings of a young Christian lately released. Written on the very edge of this life, with the better land fully. in the view of faith, they seem to us footsteps printed on the sands of Time, where these sands touch the ocean of Eternity. These footprints of one whom the Good Shepherd led through the wilderness into rest, may, with God's blessing, contribute to comfort and direct succeeding pilgrims."

The hymns, together with their dates, are:—
1. Beneath the cross of Jesus. *F. Tres.*, 1872, p. 398.
2. I'm eyes for ever closed. *F. Tres.*, 1872, p. 398.

3. Who climbeth up too nigh. *F. Tres.*, 1872, p. 552.
4. Into His summer garden. *F. Tres.*, 1873, p. 245.
5. From my dwelling midst the dead. *F. Tres.*, 1873, p. 365.
6. The day is drawing nearly done. *F. Tres.*, 1873, p. 389.
7. Life-light waneth to an end. *F. Tres.*, 1874, p. 595.
8. There were ninety and nine that safely lay. *F.Tres.*, 1874, p. 595.

Of these Nos. 1 and 8 are in C. U. 　　　[J. M.]

Cleveland, Benjamin. Probably a Baptist, but known only by his *Hymns on Different Spiritual Subjects, in Two Parts,* whereof the 4th ed. appeared in Norwich, Connecticut, 1792. He is the author of :—

O could I find from day to day. [*Longing for Christ.*] This was preserved from oblivion by the *Hartford Sel.*, 1799, and is now in general use as altered and abridged to 4 st. by Nettleton, in his *Village Hymns*, 1824, No. 145. What is supposed to be the original text of the first four stanzas is found in Dr. Hatfield's *Church H. Bk.*, 1872, No. 876. 　　　[F. M. B.]

Cleveland, Charles Dexter, LL.D., b. at Salem, Mass., Dec. 3, 1802, and graduated at Dartmouth, 1827. Professor of Latin and Greek in Dickinson Coll., Pennsylvania, 1830, and of Latin in the University of New York, 1832. In 1834 he opened a seminary for young ladies in Philadelphia. He d. Aug. 18, 1869.

In 1850 he published *A Compendium of English Literature*; in 1858, another of *American Literature*; and in 1861, a third of *Classical Literature*, in addition to other works. His *Lyra Sacra Americana*, 1868, widely known in England, and from which many hymns have been introduced into the English hymnals, is inadequate and wholly uncritical, but it is better than Rider's *Lyra Americana*, 1865 (which was reprinted in substance by the R. T. S., Lon., 1865), and the Biographical sketches appended to it have some value. 　　[F. M. B.]

Clifford, C. L., a *nom de plume* of *Mrs. Van Alstyne* (q. v.).

Cling to the Crucified. *H. Bonar.* [*Abiding in Christ.*] Contributed to his *Bible H. Bk.*, 1845, No. 268, in 2 st. of 12 l., and based upon i. John ii. 28, "Abide in Him." It was repeated in his *Hys. of Faith & Hope*, 1857, and in several hymn-books, including the *H. Comp.*, &c. In the *N. Cong.* and Allon's *Suppl. Hys.* it is altered to "Abide in Him, abide."

Cling to the Mighty One. *H. Bennett.* [*Trust in Jesus.*] This hymn is usually dated 1864. It was given as No. 3 in his *Hymns, by H. B.*, 1867, in 3 st. of 8 l. It is found in several collections in G. Britain and America, as in Snepp's *S. of G. & G.*, 1872; *Hys. & S. of Praise*, N. Y. 1874, and others.

Clothed in majesty sublime. *Joanna Baillie.* [*Ps. xciii.*] This appeared in her *Fugitive Verses*, 1840, in 5 st. of 4 l. as "Thoughts taken from the 93rd Psalm." In this form it is not in C. U., but as "Arrayed in majesty divine," it is sometimes found.

From the preface to her *Fugitive Verses*, we learn that she contributed to a proposed revision of the Scottish *Trs. and Paraphs.* three hymns which she has headed, "For the Scotch Kirk." This revision never took place. Joanna Baillie was the daughter of a Scotch minister; b. at Bothwell, 1762, and d. at Hampstead, 1851. Her poetical pieces, including *Plays*, &c., are well known. 　　　[W. T. B.]

Clyne, Norval, M.A., s. of the late Captain John Clyne, of the Royal Scots Regiment,

was b. at Ballycastle, Ireland, Feb. 21, 1817, studied and graduated M.A. at the University of Aberdeen (Marischal College), and in 1846 became a member of the Society of Advocates in Aberdeen. He is the author of *Ballads from Scottish History*, 1863, &c. He was appointed one of the Aberdeen members of the Committee which compiled the Draft *Hymnal for the Scottish Church*, 1857, and contributed to it two hymns, viz., "Chief Shepherd of the chosen fold," and "Jesu! Heaven's eternal King," which he afterwards included in the *Aberdeen Hymnal*, of which he was the compiler (see **Scottish Hymnody**, vi. 7). Thence they have passed into various collections. A Christmas carol by him, "The blasts of chill December sound," originally pub. in *The Scottish Witness*, has been included, as No. 64, in the Rev. R. R. Chope's *Carols for use in Church*, 1875. 　　　[J. M.]

Cobbe, Frances Power, daughter of Charles Cobbe, D.L., of Newbridge House, Co. Dublin, was b. Dec. 4, 1822. She has written extensively on various subjects. The most important of her publications are :—

(1) *Essay on Intuitive Morals*; (2) *Religious Duty*; (3) *Broken Lights*, 1864; (4) *Duties of Women*; and others. She also edited the *Works* of Theodore Parker, in 12 vols.

Miss Cobbe has written only a few poems. Two of these were included in her *Italics*; *Brief Notes on Politics, People, and Places in Italy in 1864* (1864), and a third in a Birthday Address to Lord Shaftesbury. Her hymn, "God draws a cloud over each gleaming morn" (*Rest in the Lord*), was written in 1859, in reply to some verses by an acquaintance, which were of a sad and despairing tendency. It has passed into several collections, including Horder's *Congregational Hys.*, 1884, and others. D. in April, 1904. 　[W. G. H.]

Cobbin, Ingram, M.A., b. Dec., 1777, and educated for the Congregational Ministry at Hoxton Coll. Entering the ministry in 1802, he was successively pastor of congregations at Banbury, at Holloway, at Putney, and at Crediton. He was also for some time Secretary of the Home Miss. Society. He d. at Camberwell, March 10, 1851. His publications were numerous, including *Scripture Parables in Verse*, 1818; *The Village Hymn Book*, 1820; and a *tr.* of Cæsar Malan's *Hymns* [see **French Hymnody**], 1825. He also contributed the following hymns to the Bap. *New Sel.*, 1828 :—

1. As blows the wind, and in its flight. *Regeneration.*
2. Before the Almighty power began. *Sovereign Grace.*
3. If 'tis sweet to mingle where. *Prayer Meeting.*
4. Lord! there is a throne of grace. *Prayer.*
5. Lord! to Thy bounteous care we owe. *Harvest.*

Of these hymns, Nos. 3 and 4 are in the most extensive use, and are given in several modern collections, specially amongst the Baptists. 　　　[J. J.]

Coeleste organum hodie sonuit in terrâ. [*Christmas.*] This Sequence is of unknown authorship and date. *Mone*, No. 388, quotes this hymn from a 12th cent. MS. at Graz, and holds that it is by a French writer. *Morel* quotes it from the MS. collection of Brander, 1507 (St. Gall MSS., No. 546), where it is called a sequence, "patris alicujus S. Galli conventus." It is found in two 14th cent. MSS. in the *Brit. Mus.* (Lansdown, 432, f. 12 b; Caligula A. xiv. f. 44 b), &c. Every line of the Sequence ends in *a*. In the English Uses a curious but not uncommon diversity prevails. These may be gathered from their reprints, the *Sarum Missal.*, Burntisland, 1861; the *York Missal*, Surtees Soc., 1872; and the *Hereford Missal*, 1874. *Tr.* as :—

Hark, the heavens' sweet melody, by E.H. Plumptre, written for and 1st pub. in the *Hymnary*, 1872, No. 134. It was republished in the translator's *Things New & Old*, 1884. Another *tr.* is, "This day celestial melody," by *Pearson*, 1868. [J. M.]

Coelestis ales nuntiat. *Jean Baptiste de Santeüil.* [*Annunciation.*]

1st pub. in his *Hymni Sacri et Novi*, 1689, p. 2, and again in the same, 1698, p. 87, in 5 st. of 4 l. In 1736 it was included in the revised *Paris Brev.* Also reprinted in Card. Newman's *Hymni Ecclesiae*, 1838 and 1865. *Tr.* as :—

1. The angel spake [spoke] the word, by E. Caswall—his quoted opening line being, "Supernus ales nuntiat,"—in his *Lyra Catholica*, 1849, p. 267; and again in his *Hymns, &c.*, 1873, p. 170. This is given in the *Appendix* to the *H. Noted*, and in the *St. John's Hymnal* (Aberdeen), &c.

2. Hail blessed morn, when forth from heaven, by W. Cooke, made for the *Hymnary*, 1872, and given with the signature "A. C. C."

Translations not in C. U. :—
1. The herald light from Heav'n on golden wing. *I. Williams.* 1839.
2. The swift-winged herald from on high. *J. D. Chambers,* ii. 1866. [J. J.]

Coelestis aula panditur. *Jean Baptiste de Santeüil.* [*Virgins.*]

Given in the *Cluniac Brev.*, 1686, p. lxv., and in his *Hymni Sacri et Novi*, 1689, p. 217, and 1698, p. 254, for "Sanctis Virginibus." In the revised *Paris Brev.*, 1736, it was appointed for Virgins, not being Martyrs. The text is also given in Card. Newman's *Hymni Ecclesiae*, 1838 and 1865. *Tr.* as :—

Open is the starry hall, by I. Williams, 1st in the *British Magazine*, 1835, vol. viii., p. 518, and again in his *Hys. from the Paris Brev.*, 1839, p. 321. It has passed into *Hys. & Introits*, 1852; *Kennedy*, 1863; the *Hymnary*, 1872; the *Altar Hymnal*, 1884, &c.

Translation not in C. U. :—
The palace gates of Heaven expand. *J. D. Chambers,* ii. 1866. [J. J.]

Coelestis aulae principes. *Jean Baptiste de Santeüil.* [*Apostles.*]

In the *Cluniac Brev.*, 1686, p. i., and in his *Hymni Sacri et Novi*, 1689, p. 189, and ed. 1698, p. 235, in 6 st. of 4 l. In 1736 it was given in the revised *Paris Brev.*, as the hymn for the "Common of Apostles at Lauds." It is also in the *Lyons* and other French Breviaries. Text in Card. Newman's *Hymni Ecclesiae*, 1838 and 1865, and Chandler's *Hys. of the Prim. Church*, 1837, No. 87. [W. A. S.]

Translations in C. U. :—
1. Ye captains of a heavenly host, by I. Williams, in his *Hys. tr. from the Paris Brev.*, 1839, p. 274, and thence into the *App.* to the *H. Noted*.
2. Captains of the saintly band, by Sir H. W. Baker, in *H. A. & M.*, 1861; and in *Kennedy*, 1863.

3. The leaders of the Church of Christ, by G. Phillimore, in the *Parish H. Bk.*, 1863, in 5 double stanzas of 4 l., the last two being original. This was repeated in the 2nd ed., 1874, and in the S. P. C. K. *Church Hys.*, 1871.

4. Ye princes of the courts on high, by J. D. Chambers, in pt. ii., p. 4, of his *Lauda Syon*, 1866. The hymn, "Princes of the court on high," was adapted from this *tr.* by the Editors of the *Hymnary*, 1872, No. 388.

Translation not in C. U. :—
Hail, princes of the host of heaven. *J. Chandler.* 1887. [J. J.]

Coelestis formam gloriae. [*Transfiguration.*]

This hymn, of unknown authorship, is in the *Sarum Brev.* (Venice, 1495, Estiva, pt. ii. f. 174), for the Transfiguration. *Mone*, No. 65, gives it from a MS. of the 15th cent., together with a few notes. *Daniel*, iv. p. 279, repeats this text without the notes. It is also in Card. Newman's *Hymni Ecclesiae*, 1838 and 1865, and Biggs's *Annotated H. A. & M.*, 1867, p. 245. *Tr.* as :—

1. A type of those bright rays on high, by J. M. Neale, in the enlarged ed. of the *H. Noted*, 1854. In 1861 this is altered to "O wondrous type, O vision fair," by the compilers of *H. A. & M.*, No. 202. This was repeated in full in *Kennedy*, 1863: and, abbreviated, in the Irvingite *Hys. for the Churches*, 1864, but omitted from the *H. A. & M.*, 1875. The original *tr.* was repeated in the *Hymner*, 1882.

2. The shadow of the glory which one day. By C. S. Calverley, written for and 1st pub. in the *Hymnary*, 1872, No. 367.

Translations not in C. U.:—
1. The shape for Whose bright vision. *W. J. Blew.* 1852.
2. O glorious scene, and passing fair. *J. D. Chambers.* 1857. [J. J.]

Coelestis O Jerusalem. [*All Saints.*]

This hymn is usually given as from the revised *Paris Brev.*, 1736. It is not in that edition, but was added, for the Vigil of All Saints Day at Lauds (together with "Pugnate, Christi milites," the hymn at Matins for the same festival), in later editions. It is also found in the *Meaux Brev.*, 1834, and is given in 6 st. of 4 l. in Card. Newman's *Hymni Ecclesiae*, 1838 and 1865, and in Biggs's *Annotated H. A. & M.*, 1867, p. 212. Its author is unknown. [W. A. S.]

Translations in C. U. :—
1. O heavenly Jerusalem, by I. Williams, pub. in his *Hys. tr. from the Paris Brev.*, 1839, p. 258. This *tr.*, with slight alterations, was given in Mozley's *Hymnal*, 1852; *H. A. & M.*, 1861–75; the *People's H.*, 1867; *Spurgeon's O. O. H. Bk.*; and (in two forms, each opening with the above first line) in the Roman Catholic *Hys. for the Year*, N.D., No. 50. In addition to these it is given in an altered form as, "O heavenly Queen, High Salem," in Blew's *Ch. H. & Tune Book*, 1852; as, "O heavenly Jerusalem, city," &c., in the *Salisbury H. Bk.*, 1857; and as, "Jerusalem the heavenly," in the *Hymnary*, 1872.

2. Jerusalem the holy, by W. E. Green. Written for and pub. in *A Book of Church Hys.*, Lond., 1864, No. 246.

Translation not in C. U. :—
Jerusalem, the city. *Anon.* in the *Shilling Magazine*, 1867. [J. J.]

Coeli Deus sanctissime. [*Wednesday.*] This hymn is sometimes ascribed to St. Ambrose, but on insufficient authority. It is found in two forms, the first what is usually received as the original, and the second the revised text in the *Roman Breviary*, 1632. Both texts are given in *Daniel*, i., No. 52; and the first in *Mone*, No. 277, who notes the oldest form of the hymn from a MS. of the 8th cent., in the Town Library at Trier. The first form is in the *Mozarabic, York, Sarum*, and many other Breviaries, both English and continental, but the Roman form is only in that Brev. It is found in three MSS. of the 11th cent. in the *Brit. Mus.* (Vesp. D. xii. f. 19; Jul. A. vi. f. 27; Harl. 2961, f. 223), in a MS. of the 9th cent. at St. Gall, No. 20; and also printed from an 11th cent. MS. at Durham in the *Latin Hys. of the Anglo-Saxon Church*, 1851. See also *Migne*, tom. xvii.; and *Wackernagel*, i., No. 93.   [W. A. S.]

In annotating the *trs.* it will be necessary to take the two forms of the hymn :—

i. *The Textus Receptus.*

Translation in C. U. :—

O God, Whose hand doth spread the sky, by J. M. Neale, in the enlarged ed. of the *Hymnal N.*, 1854, in 5 st. of 4 l., and the *Hymner*, 1882.

Translations not in C. U. :—

1. O Thou most Holy God of heaven. *Hope.* 1844.
2. Most Holy God, the Lord of heaven. *J. D. Chambers.* 1857.

ii. *The Roman Breviary Text.*

Translations in C. U. :—

1. **All Holy God on high,** by W. J. Copeland, in his *Hys. for the Week*, &c., 1848, p. 33, in 5 st. of 4 l. This text is repeated in St. John's *Hymnal* (Aberdeen), 1870, No. 99.

2. **Lord of eternal purity,** by E. Caswall, in his *Lyra Catholica*, 1849, p. 24, and again in his *Hymns*, &c., 1873, p. 15, in 5 st. of 4 l. This *tr.* is in several hymnals, including the *People's, Martineau*, and others. In the *Hymnary*, 1872, it is altered to, " Most Holy God, enthroned on high," and in the Roman Catholic *Hys. for the Year*, to " O Lord of perfect purity."

Translations not in C. U. :—

1. Thrice Holy Sovereign of the sky. *Bp. Mant.* 1837.
2. Holiest God, who reign'st on high. *Hymn. Anglica.* 1844.
3. All Holy Sovereign of the sky. *R. Campbell.* 1850.
4. O Lord, Who thron'd in the holy height. Card. Newman, in his *Verses*, &c., 1853–68. This is altered in W. J. Blew's *Church H. & Tune Book*, 1852–55, to " O Lord, most holy, and most high."
5. O God of heaven, most holy Thou. *J. Wallace.* 1874.   [J. J.]

Coelitum Joseph decus. [*St. Joseph.*] This hymn for the Feast of St. Joseph, the husband of the B. V. M., which has been added to the *Roman Breviary* since 1632, is of unknown authorship. In addition to being in that Office, *Daniel* has reprinted it, iv. p. 296. *Tr.* as :—

Joseph, our certain hope below, by E. Caswall, in his *Masque of Mary*, 1858, in 5 st. of 4 l., and thence into his *Hymns*, &c., 1873, p. 74. This *tr.* is in use in Roman Catholic hymnals for Schools and Missions.

Translation not in C. U. :—

O Joseph, glory of the heavenly choir. *J. Wallace.* 1874.   [J. J.]

Coelo datur quiescere. *Jean Baptiste de Santeüil.* [*St. Barnabas.*] Given in the *Cluniac Brev.*, 1686, p. 970; and in his *Hymni Sacri et Novi*, 1689, p. 53, and again in 1698, p. 103, in 6 st. of 4 l. In 1736 it was included in the revised *Paris Brev.*, and appointed as the hymn at Matins for the Feast of St. Barnabas. It is also in the *Lyons* and other French Breviaries. The text from the *Paris Brev.* as given in Card. Newman's *Hymni Ecclesiae*, 1838 and 1865, has st. vii. and viii. from another source. *Tr.* as :—

1. **Crowned with immortal jubilee,** by I. Williams, from the *Paris Brev.* text, 1st pub. in the *British Magazine*, June, 1836 (vol. ix. p. 627, with the Latin), and again in his *Hys. tr. from the Paris Brev.*, 1839, p. 205. In 1841 it was included in the *Child's Christian Year*.

2. **Thou, Barnabas, hast won repose,** by R. F. Littledale, from the *Paris Brev.*, written for and pub. in the *People's H.*, 1867.

3. **To Barnabas, Thy servant blest,** by Harriet M. Chester, from the *Paris Brev.*, contributed to the *Hymnary*, 1872, and signed " H. M. C."

Translation not in C. U. :—

To Thee, O Barnabas, is given. *J. D. Chambers.* 1866.   [J. J.]

Coelo quos eadem gloria consecrat. *Jean Baptiste de Santeüil.* [*All Saints.*] Given in the *Cluniac Brev.*, 1686, p. 1097, and in his *Hymni Sacri et Novi*, 1689, p. 161, and again, 1698, p. 212, in 7 st. of 4 l. In 1736 it was given, unaltered, in the revised *Paris Brev.* as the hymn for the 1st and 2nd Vespers of the Feast of all Saints. It is also in other French Breviaries, and in Card. Newman's *Hymni Ecclesiae*, 1838 and 1865. *Tr.* as :—

Saints whom in heaven one glory doth await, by F. Pott, and pub. in his *Hymns*, &c., 1861, and in the *Hymnary*, 1872.

Translation not in C. U. :—

Ye that are now in heavenly glory one. *I. Williams.* 1834–9.   [J. J.]

Coelos ascendit hodie. [*Ascension.*] This hymn, of unknown date and authorship, is given by Dr. Neale (*Med. Hymns.* 1851–67), as " apparently of the twelfth century." The text is in *Daniel*, i., No. 492, in 12 lines with " Alleluia " as a refrain to each. It has been *tr.* by Dr. Neale, in *Mediaeval Hys.*, 1851–63, as " To-day, above the sky He soared," and this is repeated in Dr. Schaff's *Christ in Song*, 1870. J. W. Hewett has also rendered it into English as " The King of glory, Christ most High," in his *Verses by a Country Curate*, 1859, and the *Lyra Messianica*, 1864. These *trs.* are not in C. U. It has also been rendered into English through the German, " Gen Himmel."

Gen Himmel aufgefahren ist. A *tr.* in 6 st. of 2 l., with Alleluia, appeared in B. Gesius's *Geistliche Deutsche Lieder*, Frankfurt a. Oder, 1601, folio 45, with the Latin. *Tr.* as " The King of glory, Christ the Lord," by E. Massie, 1867, p. 219.   [J. M.]

Coffin, Charles, b. at Buzancy (Ardennes) in 1676, d. 1749, was principal of the college at Beauvais, 1712 (succeeding the historian Rollin), and rector of the University of Paris, 1718. He pub. in 1727 some of his

Latin poems, for which he was already noted, and in 1736 the bulk of his hymns appeared in the *Paris Breviary* of that year. In the same year he published them as *Hymni Sacri Auctore Carolo Coffin*, and in 1755 a complete ed. of his *Works* was issued in 2 vols. To his *Hymni Sacri* is prefixed an interesting preface. The whole plan of his hymns, and of the *Paris Breviary* which he so largely influenced, comes out in his words.

" In his porro scribendis Hymnis non tam poetico indulgendum spiritui, quam nitore et pietate consulendum esse existimavi. Pleraque igitur, argumentis convenientia e purissimis Scripturae Sacrae fontibus deprompsi quae idoneis Ecclesiae cantui numeris alligarem."

His hymns are described by a French critic as having less brilliancy than those of Santeüil (q.v.), but more simplicity and unction. They number 100 in the edition of 1736. Translations into English by J. Chandler, I. Williams and others, are noted under their respective Latin first lines.   [W. T. B.]

Coffin, Robert Aston, D.D., b. at Brighton in 1819, and educated at Harrow, and at Christ Church, Oxford. In 1843 he became Vicar of St. Mary Magdalene's, Oxford; but in 1845 he resigned and joined the Church of Rome. In 1855 he became Rector of the R. C. Church of St. Mary's, Clapham; and in 1882 the R. C. Bishop of Southwark. He d. at Teignmouth, April 6, 1885. In 1863 he pub. :—

Hymns and Verses on' Spiritual Subjects; being The Sacred Poetry of St. Alphonso Maria Liguori . . . . . . Translated from the Italian, and edited by Robert A. Coffin, Priest of the Congregation of the Most Holy Redeemer. Lond., Burns & Lambert. One or two of these *trs.* previously appeared in a small collection which he edited: *Hymns for the Confraternity of the Holy Family, Jesus, Mary, and Joseph.* Lond., Imprimatur, Dec. 21, 1856.

Some of these *trs.* are in C. U. in Roman Catholic hymn-books for schools and missions.
[J. J.]

Cole, Charles, b. May 20, 1733, at Wellow, in Somersetshire, d. 1813. In early life was a clothweaver; joined the Baptist church at Bradford, Wilts, and in 1758 began to preach at Whitchurch, Hants. In the year following he became pastor of the Baptist church there, a position he maintained with honour and usefulness for fifty years. He d. Dec. 3, 1813.

He pub. "*A Three-fold Alphabet of New Hymns.* I. *On the Public Ministry of the Word.* II. *On Baptism.* III. *On the Lord's Supper. To which is added a Supplicatory Supplement,* Lon., 1792." The title, "Three-fold Alphabet," was given from the fact that the hymns in each of the first three sections are arranged alphabetically, every letter being represented with the exception of X. The total number of hymns, including the *Supplement,* is 104. These hymns are sober and scriptural in sentiment, but prosaic in style. Several are found in the older collections as *Denham, Gadsby,* and others; but they have almost died out of use.   [W. R. S.]

Coleridge, Hartley, eldest s. of S. T. Coleridge, b. 1796, d. 1849, is known to hymnody through some pieces published in his (posthumous) *Poems by Hartley Coleridge, with Memoir by his Brother,* Lond., 1851, including "Be not afraid to pray: to pray is right" (*Prayer*); and "In holy books we read how God hath spoken" (*Voice of God in Nature*).

Coleridge, Samuel Taylor, was b. at St. Mary Ottery, Devonshire, 1772, educated at Christ's Hospital, London, and Jesus College, Cambridge, and d. in 1834. His *Child's Prayer at Evening,* "Ere on my bed my limbs I lay," in Martineau's *Hymns,* 1840 and 1873, is dated 1808.

Coles, Vincent Stuckey Stratton, s. of Rev. James Stratton Coles, b. at Shepton Beauchamp, March 27, 1845, and educated at Balliol College, Oxford, graduating B.A. 1868, and M.A. 1872. On taking Holy Orders in 1869, he became Curate of Wantage. In 1872 he was preferred as Rector of Shepton-Beauchamp, Somerset, and in 1884 Librarian of the Pusey Library, Oxford. Mr. Coles has contributed the following hymns to *H. A. & M.,* and the S. P. C. K. *Church Hys.*

1. **Lord, in whose eternal counsels.** *For guidance and growth in holiness.* It was 1st printed as a leaflet, written for E. C. U. Festival, c. 1870; and then included, after revision, in S. P. C. K. *Church Hys.,* 1871.
2. **Most Holy Father, bending low.** *Lent.* No. 45 in the *Eucharistic Hymnal,* 1877.
3. **O Lamb of God, whose love divine.** *Martyrs* (*Virgins*). Given in the *Appendix* to *H. A. & M.,* 1868.
4. **O Shepherd of the sheep.** *Martyrs* (*Bishop*). Also given in the *Appendix* to *H. A. & M.,* 1868.
5. **We pray Thee, heavenly Father.** *Preparation for Holy Communion.* Originally written for a Communicants' class, it was included in S. P. C. K. *Church Hys.,* 1871, and in the revised *H. A. & M.,* 1875.
6. **Lord, I cannot seek Thee.** *Spiritual Communion.* Contributed to *Lyra Eucharistica,* 1863, and repeated in the *Churchman's Altar Manual,* 1882.   [J. J.]

Colesworthy, Daniel C., a printer, editor, and bookseller, was b. at Portland, Maine, in 1810, and is now (1885) resident in Boston. He has pub. several volumes of verse, including *Sabbath School Hymns,* 1833; *Opening Buds,* 1838; *The Year,* 1873; and *School is Out,* 1876. Of his hymns the following are the best known :—

1. **A little word in kindness spoken.** *Kindness.* This appeared in his paper, *The Portland Tribune,* Sept. 25, 1841.
2. **While we lowly bow before Thee.** *Close of Service.* Included in E. Nason's *Cong. H. Bk.,* 1857, and thence has passed into several collections of later date, including *Songs for the Sanctuary,* N. Y., 1865–72; *Laudes Domini,* N. Y., 1884, and others.

Mr. Colesworthy is a member of the Congregational body.   [F. M. B.]

Collaudemus Magdalenae. [*St. Mary Magdalene.*] This is a hymn of unknown authorship, and probably of English origin, 15 st. and a doxology. It is given in a 14th cent. *Sarum Brev.* in the *British Mus.* (MSS. Reg. 2, A. xiv., f. 214 ff.) for the Feast of St. Mary Magdalene, in three parts: viz. :—1. "Collaudemus Magdalenae," i.-v. and dox.: *Vespers.* 2. "Aestimavit ortolanum," vi.-x. and dox.: *Nocturns.* 3. "O Maria noli flere," xii.-xv. and dox.: *Lauds.* In *Daniel,* i., No. 439, it is given in full as one hymn from the *Sarum Brev.* (See also Card. Newman's *Hymni Ecclesiae,* 1838 and 1865), the text is repeated from the *Sarum Brev.* The first part of the hymn (i.-iv. and dox.) is found as " Pange lingua Magdalenae," in the *Works* of St. Bernardine of Siena (d. 1444, canonized 1450), *Sermon* 46. *Mone,* Nos. 1055,

56, 58, 59, gives the "Pange lingua" text, together with readings from MSS. of the 14th and 15th centuries. *Daniel*, iv. p. 245, compared *Mone's* text with his own, and adds readings from the *Aberdeen Brev.* [W. A. S.]

In tracing out the *trs.* of this hymn we follow the *Breviary* divisions, viz.:—

i. Ad Vesperas.

Collaudemus Magdalenae. A *tr.* of this part altered from a *tr.* by G. Moultrie from his *Espousals of S. Dorothea*, 1870, p. 78, was given in the *Antiphoner & Grail*, 1880; and again in the *Hymner*, 1882, No. 119, as "Sing we now the praise of Mary." Another *tr.* beginning, "Holy Magdalene praising," by J. D. Chambers, is in his *Lauda Syon*, pt. ii. 1866, p. 88, but this is not in C. U.

ii. Ad Nocturnum.

Aestimavit ortolanum. Dr. Neale's *tr.* of this part of the hymn, on its appearance in the 2nd ed. of his *Mediaeval Hys.*, 1863, was prefaced with these words:—

"The very elegant hymn, *Pange lingua Magdalene*, of English origin, is in the *Sarum Diruviary*, divided into three, for Vespers, Matins, and Lauds. I translated it for the *Hymnal Noted*, but it was thought too complex for popular use. The Lauds hymn was accidentally kept, the other translations lost. It is in the Clewer edition of *The Day Hours.*"

Dr. Neale's *tr.* is, "As the gardener, Him addressing," and is given in the *Hymner*, 1882, No. 120, and others.

iii. Ad Laudes.

O Maria noli flere. This is given in the *Antiphoner and Grail*, 1880, and the *Hymner*, 1882, No. 121, as "Weep not, Mary, weep no longer." It is altered from a *tr.* by G. Moultrie. In these two works a *tr.* of the complete hymn may be found.

Translations not in C. U.:—

1. Sing we now of Mary's trial, joy and sorrow let us tell. G. Moultrie, in his *Espousals of St. Dorothea.* 1870.

2. Sing we now with praiseful voices. D. T. Morgan. 1871–83. [J. J.]

Collects in Verse. [Prayer, Book of Common.]

Collett, William Lloyd, M.A., was b. at Little Ilford, Essex, and graduated at Queen's College, Oxford, in 1842. On taking Holy Orders he held several appointments until 1855, when he was preferred to the Vicarage of St. Stephen's, Hammersmith. Mr. Collett compiled the *Appendix* added to the Cooke and Denton *Hymnal*, for use in St. Stephen's Church, 1855, and contributed to that *Hymnal* in 1855 his Ascensiontide hymn, "Hail, triumphant King of Glory," No. 153, in 3 st. of 8 l. [J. J.]

Collins, Henry, M.A., educated at Oxford, where he graduated about 1854. He was ordained to the Ministry of the Church of England, but in Nov., 1857, he entered the Roman communion, becoming a member of the Cistercian Order in 1860. Author of *Life of the Rev. Father Gentili*, &c., 1861; *The Spirit and Mission of the Cistercian Order*, 1866,

&c. His hymns, were pub. by him before leaving the Church of England, in his *Hymns for Missions*, 1854, first pub. at Leeds, and then by Shrimpton of Oxford, and Masters of London. It contains 37 hymns, of which two only were by him:—"Jesu, meek and lowly" (*Passiontide*), and "Jesu, my Lord, my God, my all." (*Love of Jesus desired.*) These hymns are in extensive use. [J. J.]

Collins, S. A., the wife of an American Baptist Minister, is the author of several hymns and temperance songs, including "Jesus, gracious One, calleth now to thee" (*Invitation*), in I. D. Sankey's *Sac. S. & Solos*, No. 2, 1881.

Collyer, William Bengo, D.D., b. at Blackheath, April 14, 1782, educated at Homerton College, where, when 16 years old, he was enrolled as a student for the ministry. At 20 he began his ministry at Peckham; on Dec. 17, 1801 ordained pastor of a small church consisting of ten communicants. From 1814 to 1826 he was also pastor of a Church meeting in Salters' Hall. On June 17, 1817, a new chapel was opened for him at Peckham. There, from the time of his settlement in 1801, he laboured with great success and honour until Dec. 11, 1853, on which day he preached for the last time. He d. Jan. 8, 1854.

Dr. Collyer was eminent in his day as an eloquent Evangelical preacher, when formalism in worship, and Arianism in doctrine, prevailed. He was a man of amiable disposition, polished manners, and Christian courtesy; popular with rich and poor alike. He was the author of a series of lectures on Divine Revelation, in seven volumes: *Scripture Facts, Prophecies, Miracles, Parables, Doctrines, Duties, Comparisons.* Dr. Collyer compiled a hymn-book with the title, *Hymns partly collected and partly original, designed as a supplement to Dr. Watts's Psalms and Hymns*, 1812. It was intended at first for the use of his own congregation only, and was to include many hymns composed by himself, to be sung after sermons which he had preached to them, but he was led to alter the plan. It comprises 979 hymns, 6 choruses, and 4 doxologies, arranged in groups according to their authors, and not subjects. Of this number 57 were written by Dr. Collyer, and are for the most part short descriptive or didactic poems, religious or moral essays in verse, and not hymns addressed to the Creator and Redeemer. Some of them are devoid of Christian truth, and are poems of nature or of sentiment. Some of them were written during the hard and sorrowful times of the wars of Bonaparte, and relate to famine and national calamity. Several were prepared for the public meetings of missionary and benevolent societies, which had their origin in his time. He also pub. *Services suited to the Solemnization of Matrimony, Baptism*, &c., 1837, which contained 89 of his hymns, &c.; *Hymns for Israel, a Tribute of Love for God's Ancient People*, 1848 (41 hymns). In Dr. Leifchild's *Original Hymns*, 1843, there are also 39 of his compositions. Many of his pieces appeared in the *Evangelical Magazine*, and were also appended to his numerous published *Sermons*. A few of his hymns are still in C. U., including, "Another fleeting day is gone"; "Assembled at Thy great command"; "O Jesu, in this solemn hour"; "O Thou, the helpless orphan's hope"; "Return, O wanderer, return," and the fine cento, "Great God, what do I see and hear."

[F. J. F.]

Colver, Nathaniel, D.D., an eminent preacher and abolitionist, b. at Orwell, Vermont, 1794, and entered the Baptist Ministry in 1836, becoming successively Pastor at Boston, Detroit, Cincinnati, and Chicago. After the war, in 1865, he founded the Colver Institute at Richmond, Virginia. He d. Sept. 25, 1870. In 1848 he contributed 17 hymns to Banvard's *Christian Melodist*, Boston, U.S. Of these the best known are:—"Come, Lord, in mercy come again," *Lent;* and "Weep for the lost! thy Saviour wept" (*Sympathy*), as in the *Bap. Praise Bk.*, N.Y., 1871, &c. [F. M. B.]

Come, all ye chosen saints of God. *J. Hart.* [*Passion Week.*] The following account of the origin of this hymn is given in the author's "Experience," which accompanies his *Hymns :—*

"The week before Easter, 1757, I had such an amazing view of the agony of Christ in the garden, as I know not well how to describe. I was lost in wonder and adoration, and the impression it made was too deep, I believe, ever to be obliterated. I shall say no more of this, but only remark that notwithstanding all that is talked about the sufferings of Jesus, none can know anything of them but by the Holy Ghost ; and, I believe, he that knows most knows but very little. It was upon this I made the first part of hymn 1, 'On the Passion,' which, however, I afterwards mutilated and altered."

The hymn was pub. in his *Hys. composed on Various Subjects*, 1759, in 2 parts of 24 st. in all. As given in modern collections, as in Spurgeon's *O. O. H. Bk.*, it is a cento from the original with variations in the text. [J. J.]

Come, and hear the grand old story. *H. Bonar.* [*Life of Christ.*] This is the first of 9 lines which introduce a hymn of 17 st. of 4 l. beginning, "Christ the Father's Son Eternal," 1st pub. in his *Hys. of Faith and Hope*, 2nd series, 1861. The hymn, in an abbreviated form, is given in N. Hall's *Christ Church Hyl.*, 1876, and others. [J. J.]

Come, and let us sweetly join. *C. Wesley.* [*Church Gatherings.*] This poem of 22 double stanzas, divided into five parts, was given in Pt. ii. of J. & C. Wesley's *Hys. & S. Poems*, 1740, and headed "The Love Feast." The five parts were subsequently used as separate hymns, as follows :—

1. **Come, and let us sweetly join.** This was given in the *Wes. H. Bk.*, 1780, No. 505, and has been repeated in most collections of the Methodist body.

2. **Come, Thou High and Lofty One.** This was included in Toplady's *Ps. and Hys.*, 1776, and in the *Wes. H. Bk.*, 1780, No. 506 (ed. 1875, No. 520), and has passed into various collections. From it the centos (1) " Jesu, we the promise claim " ; sometimes, "Jesus, we *Thy* promise claim," was given in Bickersteth's *Christ. Psalmo.*, 1833 ; and is found in modern hymnals, including Snepp's *S. of G. & G.*, 1872 ; and (2) "In the midst do Thou appear," as in Dr. Martineau's *Hymns*, &c., 1840, and his *Hys. of P. & P.*, 1873.

3. **Let us join, 'tis God commands.** This is No. 507 in the *Wes. H. Bk.*, 1780, and No. 521 in the revised ed., 1875. It has also passed into other collections, as the *Bap. Hymnal*, 1879, &c.

4. **Partners of a glorious hope.** No. 508 in the *Wes. H. Bk.*, 1780, and 522 in the revised ed. 1875, and other collections.

5. **Father, hail, by all adored.** No. 509 in the *Wes. H. Bk.*, 1780, and 523, 1875.

In addition to the above there are *three* centos in C. U. all beginning, "Come, and let us sweetly join," and each being distinct in itself. These are (1) *Leeds H. Bk.*, 1853, No. 738; (2) *N. Cong. Suppl.*, 1869; and (3) *Kennedy*, 1863. The original texts of all these parts and centos are in the *Wes. H. Bk.* as above, and the *P. Works*, 1868-72, vol. i. p. 350. [J. J]

Come away to the skies. *C. Wesley.* [*Birthday.*] Written on the anniversary of the birth of his wife, Oct. 12, 1755, and 1st pub. in his *Hys. for Families*, 1767, No. 165, in 8 st. of 6 l. *P. Works*, 1868-72, vol. vii. p. 198. In 1780 it was included in the *Wes. H. Bk.* as No. 478, and has been retained in all subsequent editions of that collection. It is also given in other collections of the Methodist body, and in a few American Hymnals. [J. J.]

Come, blessed Spirit, Source of light. *B. Beddome.* [*Holy Spirit.*] This hymn is given in his *Sermons*, 1816, vol. iv., and in his (posthumous) *Hymns*, 1817, No. 136, in 4 st. of 4 l., and in each instance it is undated. It is found in extensive use in American hymn-books in two forms; 1st the original, as in Dr. Hatfield's *Church H. Bk.*, 1872 (where it is dated 1770); and 2nd changed from L.M. to S.M. in the Meth. Episco. *Hymns*, 1849, "Come, Spirit, source of light."
[W. T. B.]

Come, children, hail the Prince of Peace. [*Praise to Christ.*] An anonymous hymn in 5 st. of 4 l. not traced beyond the *S. S. H. Bk.*, Phila., 1820, i., No. 162, and the Silver St. *S. Scholar's Companion* (7th ed.), 1821. From the time of its insertion, in 1843, in Bateman's *Sacred Melodies for Children*, it has been growing in favour both in England and America. In the latter it is sometimes found, as in the Baltimore *S. S. H. Bk.*, 1843, as "Come, let us praise the Prince of Peace," the order of the sts. being changed and the hymn altered. It is an imitation of " All hail the power of Jesus' Name." [J. J.]

Come, children, join the angelic [heavenly] throng. [*Praise to Christ.*] An imitation by an unknown writer of " All hail the power of Jesus' name," given in the Leeds *S. S. H. Bk.*, 1862, and in the Leeds *S. S. U. H. Bk.*, 1864: and also as " Come, children, join the *heavenly* throng," in the Silver Street *S. S. Companion*, 1880, in 4 st. of 4 l. [J. J.]

Come, children, join to sing. *C. H. Bateman.* [*Praise to Christ.*] 1st pub. in his *Sacred Melodies for Children*, 1843, No. 4, in 5 st. of 5 l. and the refrain ; again in later editions, and in his *Children's Hymnal*, 1872. It is given in several collections in G. Britain and Canada, and is one of the most popular of the author's hymns. [J. J.]

Come, dearest Lord, descend and dwell. *I. Watts.* [*Whitsuntide.*] Given in the enlarged ed. of his *Hys. and S. Songs*, 1709, Bk. i., No. 135, in 3 st. of 4 l. In 1753 G. Whitefield included it in his *Coll.* This was followed by R. Conyers in his *Coll.*, 1774, and others, until its use has become extensive both in G. Britain and America. In many cases, especially in America, the term "dearest," so objectionable to many, is changed to, "Come, *gracious* Lord," &c. [J. J.]

Come, desire of nations, come; Hasten, Lord, &c. *C. Wesley.* [*Second Advent.*] Written as one of the *Hymns Occasioned by the Earthquake, March 8, 1750*, and 1st pub. in a tract bearing that title during the same year.

The unusual visitation of the earthquake created a great sensation in London and the neighbourhood, and the excitement of the people did much to set forth the calm faith, and to bring out the sterling worth of the Wesleys. The feelings of both were embodied in the hymns which C. Wesley wrote on the occasion. This particular hymn was included in J. Wesley's *Select Hymns with Tunes annext,* 1761, and other works, and in the *Wes. H. Bk.* as one of the " Additional Hymns," circ. 1800. It is retained in the new ed., 1875, and is found in several collections in G. Britain and America. Orig. text in *P. Works,* 1868–72, vol. vi. p. 18.   [J. J.]

Come, Divine Immanuel, come. *C. Wesley.* [*Missions.*] " Written at the Land's End," and pub. in *Hys. and S. Poems,* 1749, vol. ii., No. 208, in 6 st. of 4 l. (*P. Works,* 1868–72, vol. v. p. 133). In 1753, G. Whitefield included it in his *Coll.,* No. 37, but it failed to gain popularity and is seldom found in modern collections. In the Amer. *Hys. and Songs of Praise,* N. Y., 1874, it is given in an altered form.   [J. J.]

Come, every pious heart. *S. Stennett.* [*Praise to Christ.*] Appeared in *A Collection of Hys. for the Use of Christians of all Denominations,* Lond. 1782, and again in Rippon's *Selection,* 1787, No. 489, in 6 st. of 6 l., and entitled, " A Song of Praise to Christ." As given in modern collections it is usually composed of st. i., iii.–v., as in the Bap. *Ps. and Hys.,* 1858–80, No. 269, where, however, it is dated 1832 in error. Its use in America is very extensive. In the *Church S. S. H. Bk.,* 1879, it is given as, " Come, every youthful heart," and in a few collections as " Come, ye who love the Lord, And feel His," &c., including Dr. Walker's Cheltenham *Ps. & Hys.,* 1855, and others.   [J. J.]

Come, Father, Son, and Holy Ghost, Honour the means, &c. *C. Wesley.* [*Adult Baptism.*] 1st pub. in *Hys. & S. Poems,* 1749, vol. ii., No. 181, in 6 st. of 4 l. (*P. Works,* 1868–72, vol. v. p. 388). In 1780 it was given in the *Wes. H. Bk.,* No. 464, and the revised ed., 1875, No. 476. It is in several collections in G. Britain and America, as the *Sarum,* 1868; the Amer. Meth. Episco. *Hymnal,* 1878, &c. In some American hymn-books, as *Hys. & Songs of Praise,* N. Y. 1874, st. iii., vi., are given slightly altered as " Father, in these reveal Thy Son."   [J. J.]

Come, Father, Son, and Holy Ghost, One God, &c. *C. Wesley.* [*For Spiritual Peace.*] 1st pub. in his *Short Hymns,* &c., 1762. In the form in which it was given in the *Wes. H. Bk.* in 1780, No. 243, and continued in later editions, it embodied Nos. 200, 201 and 202 of the *Short Hymns,* these being based on Numb. vi. 24–26 (*P. Works,* 1868–1872, vol. ix. p. 65). From this cento, No. 661 in Snepp's *S. of G. & G.,* 1872, " Eternal Sun of Righteousness," is taken. It is composed of st. iii.–vi. slightly altered.   [J. J.]

Come, happy children, come and raise. *Dorothy A. Thrupp.* [*Child's Song of Praise.*] Appeared in her *Hymns for the Young,* c. 1830 (4th ed. 1836), in 6 st. of 4 l.

In 1848 it appeared again in Dr. Miller's *Ps. & Hys.,* 1848, and others, as, " Come, Christian children, come and raise." This text, with slight alterations, the omission of st. vi., and the passing on of st. ii. (rewritten) to the end as st. v. was repeated in *Church Hymns,* 1871, No. 567. In the Meth. Free Church *S. S. H. Bk.,* 1868, Miss Thrupp's text is again altered as " Come, let the young unite and raise." The original hymn is sometimes said to have appeared in Mrs. H. Mayo's *Sel. of Hys.,* &c., 1838, but this is an error.   [W. T. B.]

Come, heavenly love, inspire my song. *Anne Steele.* [*Redeeming Love.*] This poem of 39 st. of 4 l. appeared in her *Hys. on Subjects chiefly Devotional,* 1700, vol. i p. 7 (2nd ed., 1780, vol. i. p. 7), and in Sedgwick's reprint of her *Hymns,* 1863, p. 4. From the poem the following centos are in C. U. :—

1. **Come, heavenly love, inspire my song.** This was given in the Bristol *Coll.* of Ash and Evans, 1769, No. 129 ; repeated by R. Conyers, in his *Coll.,* 1772, and again by others to modern hymnals. It is composed of st. 1, 2, 3, 7, 8, 37 and 39.

2. **Come, Holy Ghost, inspire our songs.** This was given in the Uttoxeter *Sel.,* 1805; and repeated in Cotterill's *Sel.,* 1010 19, and from thence has passed into a few collections in G. Britain and America. It is composed of st. 1. 2, 3, 7, 8, slightly altered from the original, and an added stanza probably by Cotterill.

3. **Come, heavenly Dove, inspire my song.** This is in the Amer. *Evangelical Hyl.,* by Hall and Lasar, N. Y., 1880, st. 1, 2, 3, 8, 32, 33, 37, and 39 being included therein.

4. **Come, Holy Spirit, guide my song.** This is composed of st. i., ii., vii. and xxxvii. slightly altered. It is No. 63 in Windle's *Coll.*

5. **The Saviour, O what endless charms.** This cento in Snepp's *S. of G. & G.,* 1872, No. 174, is composed of st. 2, 3, 8, 37, and 39.   [J. J.]

Come, Holy Ghost, all quickening fire; Come, and my hallowed, &c. *C. Wesley.* [*Whitsuntide.*] A " Hymn to God the Sanctifier," 1st pub. in *Hys. & S. Poems,* 1740, p. 45, in 8 st. of 6 l., and again in the *Wes. H. Bk.,* 1780, No. 341 (*P. Works,* 1868–72, vol. i. p. 240). In the American Meth. Episco. *Hymns,* 1849, st. iv., v., vii., viii. are given as " Humble and teachable, and mild."   [J. J.]

Come, Holy Ghost, descend from high. [*Holy Baptism.*] This cento, in 2 st. of 4 l., appeared in A. M. Toplady's *Ps. & Hys.,* 1776, No. 99. It is composed of st. i. of C. Wesley's " Come Father, Son, and Holy Ghost, Honour the means," &c., as above, but slightly altered ; and st. ii. probably by Toplady. This was repeated in T. Beck's (q. v.) *Hymns,* &c., 1782. In Bickersteth's *Christian Psalmody,* 1833, it is given in error as of Beck's composing, and this error is repeated in later collections.   [J. J.]

Come, Holy Ghost, my soul inspire; Spirit of, &c. *R. Mant.* [*Whitsuntide.*] Appeared in his *Holydays of the Church,* &c., vol. i., 1828, pp. 317–318, in 6 st. of 4 l. at the close of a Meditation and Collect, which follows an account of the life and work of St. Barnabas. In 1837 it was transferred to his

Ancient Hys. from the Rom. Brev., &c., as one of his "Original Hymns," No. 105, without alteration, and entitled, "Hymn to the Comforter for Faith, Hope, and Charity." It is also included in Bp. Mant's *Ancient Hymns*, &c., 1871. In *Kennedy*, 1863, No. 1180, the hymn, "Holy Ghost, my soul inspire," is this hymn in a slightly altered form. Another arrangement is:—"Holy Spirit, in my [our] breast," which was given in the enlarged ed. of Morrell & How's *Ps. & Hymns*, 1864, No. 119. [J. J.]

Come, Holy Spirit, come, Let Thy bright beams, &c. *J. Hart.* [*Whitsuntide.*]

Contributed to his *Hys. composed on Various Subjects*, 1759, No. 4, in 9 st. of 4 l., and headed, "To the Holy Ghost." One of the earliest to adopt it was Toplady, in his *Ps. & Hys.*, 1776, No. 237, with alterations which have come down to modern collections. This text is that usually adopted in Ch. of England hymnals. It is easily recognized by st. i., ll. 3, 4, which read:—

"Dispel the *sorrow* from our minds,
The darkness from our eyes,"

instead of—

"Dispel the darkness from our minds,
And open all our eyes,"

as in the original. Most of the American collections follow Toplady's text with slight variations, and abbreviations as in the *Bap. Praise Bk.*, N. Y., 1871; *Songs for the Sanctuary*, N. Y., 1865–72, &c. The abbreviated texts in the *Irish Church Hymnal*, 1873; Dr. Hatfield's *Church H. Bk.*, 1872; Stowell's *Ps. & Hys.*, 1831 and 1877, and others, are from the original. No. 151, in the *Mitre*, 1836, is a cento, st. i., ii. being from this hymn, and iii., iv. from C. Wesley's "Spirit of faith, come down," in each case with alteration. Full orig. text in *Lyra Brit.* 1867, p. 273. [J. J.]

Come, Holy Spirit, Heavenly Dove, My sinful maladies remove. *S. Browne.* [*Whitsuntide.*]

Few hymns in the English language have been subjected to so many alterations and changes as this, which according to the author's title, concerns "The Soul giving itself up to the Conduct and Influence of the Holy Spirit." An enumeration of all these changes would tend to increase rather than to lessen the complications which surround the various texts in modern hymnals. The most that can be done will be to give the original text, and then to indicate the sources of the important changes in C. U.

1. The hymn appeared in S. Browne's *Hys. & Spiritual Songs*, 1720, Bk. i., No. 131, pp. 173, 174, in 7 st. of 4 l., as follows:—

"Come, Holy Spirit, heav'nly Dove,
My sinful maladies remove;
Be Thou my light, be Thou my guide,
O'er every thought and step preside.

"The light of truth to me display,
That I may know and chuse my way;
Plant holy fear within mine heart,
That I from God may ne'er depart.

"Conduct me safe, conduct me far
From every sin and hurtful snare;
Lead me to God, my final rest,
In His enjoyment to be blest.

"Lead me to Christ, the living way,
Nor let me from his pastures stray;
Lead me to heav'n, the seat of bliss,
Where pleasure in perfection is.

"Lead me to holiness, the road
That I must take to dwell with God;
Lead to Thy word, that rules must give,
And sure directions how to live.

"Lead me to means of grace, where I
May own my wants, and seek supply;
Lead to Thyself, the spring from whence
To fetch all quick'ning influence.

"Thus I, conducted still by Thee,
Of God a child beloved shall be;
Here to His family pertain,
Hereafter with Him ever reign."

2. In 1769 Ash and Evans pub. in their Bristol *Coll.*, as No. 161, the following version:

"Come, Holy Spirit, heavenly Dove,
With light and comfort from above;
Be Thou *our Guardian*, Thou *our* Guide,
O'er every Thought and Step preside.

"Conduct *us* safe, conduct *us* far
From every Sin and hurtful Snare;
Lead to Thy Word that Rules must give,
And teach us Lessons how to live.

"The Light of Truth to *us* display,
And make us know and choose *Thy* Way;
Plant holy Fear in *every* Heart,
That *we* from God may ne'er depart.

"Lead *us* to Holiness, the Road,
That *we* must take to dwell with God;
Lead *us* to Christ, the living Way,
Nor let *us* from His pastures stray.

"Lead *us* to God, *our* final Rest,
In His enjoyment to be bless'd;
Lead *us* to Heaven, the Seat of Bliss,
Where Pleasure in Perfection is. B."

3. This version was included in Toplady's *Ps. & Hys.*, 2nd ed., edited by Walter Row, 1787, No. 395, with the following alterations:

St. i., l. 1, "Come *gracious* Spirit, heavenly Dove,"
st. ii., l. 3, Lead to Thy word; *for that* must give.

This version was again repeated with minor changes, including "*precepts*" for "*pastures*," in Cotterill's *Sel.*, 1819, and others.

4. The next change of importance came with Hall's *Mitre*, 1836, No. 79, in which the last stanza reads:—

"Lead *us* to God, *our only* rest,
To be with Him for ever blest;
Lead *us* to heaven *that we may share*,
Fulness of joy for ever there."

5. In *Mercer*, 1864, this verse is transposed as:—

"Lead us to heaven, that we may share
Fulness of joy for ever there;
Lead us to God, our final rest,
To be with Him for ever blest."

6. On comparing the texts of modern collections with these details we find that (1) the original is represented in Lord Selborne's *Bk. of Praise Hymnal*, 1867; and Dr. Hatfield's *Church H. Bk.*, N. Y., 1872; (2) the Ash & Evans text as in the Bap. *Ps. & Hys.*, 1858–80, with "*gracious*" for "*holy*"; (3) the interwoven text of *Browne*, *Ash & Evans*, *Toplady*, and *Hall*, as in the *H. Comp.*, with "*final* rest" for "*only* rest;" (4) the *Browne*, *Ash & Evans*, *Toplady*, *Cotterill*, and *Mercer* text, Oxford ed. of *Mercer*, No. 228; and, through the same source, the *Hymnary*, 1872, and *H. A. & M.*, 1875, &c. The American collections follow in the same tracks, and are generally reproductions of the English text. Two centos remain to be noticed, that in Thring's *Coll.*, 1882, where st. vi. of the original is rewritten by the editor, and the arrangement, "Come gracious Spirit, gift of love," which is found in the *S. S. Union H. Bk.*, and other collections for children. [J. J.]

**Come, Holy Spirit, Heavenly Dove,
With all Thy, &c.** *I. Watts.* [*Whitsuntide.*] 1st pub. in his *Hys. & S. Songs,* 1707, (ed., 1709, Bk. ii., No. 34, in 5 st. of 4 l.), and entitled, "Breathing after the Holy Spirit; or, Fervency of Devotion desired." The changes which have been made in this hymn are very numerous. About twenty texts are now in C. U., each differing from the other in some detail, and all joining in rejecting certain expressions in the original. The original reads:

> "Come, Holy Spirit, Heav'nly Dove,
>   With all Thy quick'ning pow'rs,
> Kindle a flame of sacred love
>   In these cold hearts of ours.
>
> "Look how we grovel here below,
>   Fond of these trifling toys:
> Our souls can neither fly nor go
>   To reach eternal joys.
>
> "In vain we tune our formal songs,
>   In vain we strive to rise,
> Hosannas languish on our tongues,
>   And our devotion dies.
>
> "Dear Lord! and shall we ever live
>   At this poor dying rate,
> Our love so faint, so cold to Thee,
>   And Thine to us so great?
>
> "Come, Holy Spirit, Heav'nly Dove,
>   With all Thy quick'ning pow'rs,
> Come, shed abroad a Saviour's love,
>   And that shall kindle ours."

The changes which have been made in this text have been mainly directed against st. ii. and iv. J. Wesley met the difficulty in his *Coll. of Ps. and Hys.,* 1743, by omitting st. ii. and making st. iv., l. 1, to read, "*And shall we then for* ever live." This text was given in the *Supp.* to the *Wes. H. Bk.,* 1830; the revised ed., 1875, and others. The reading of st. ii., ll. 3, 4, which has been received with the greatest favour is:—

> "Our souls, *how heavily they go*
>   To reach eternal joys."

This was given in G. Whitefield's *Coll.,* 1753, No. 99, and repeated by *M. Madan,* 1760; *Toplady,* 1776; *Bickersteth,* 1833, and thus to modern collections, The most acceptable reading of st. iv., l. 1, 2,

> "Dear Lord! and shall we ever be
>   *In* this poor dying *state*,"

was given in Bickersteth's *Christ. Psalmody,* 1833. The numerous minor changes in the text of this hymn we cannot note. The re-written forms of the text, one by Cotterill, in his *Sel.,* 1819, and the second by Hall or Osler, in the *Mitre,* 1836, are both failures. The American collections vary in their readings in common with those of G. Britain. In its various forms the use of this hymn is extensive.   [J. J.]

Come, Immortal King of Glory. *T. Olivers.* [*Advent—Judgment.*] One form of this hymn, in 20 st. of 6 l. was pub. by the author as a pamphlet, and printed by Griffith Wright, at Leeds, but undated. A second form in 36 st., with parallel Scripture references, was printed at Bristol, and dated 1763. The two forms were reprinted by D. Sedgwick in his reprint of Olivers's *Hymns,* 1868. Two centos have been compiled from the *second* form of the hymn as follows:—

1. Come, Lord Jesus, O come quickly. This is No. 336 in Snepp's *Songs of G. & G.,* 1872, and is composed of st. 9, 20, 21, 29, 32 and 35.

2. Lo! He comes with clouds descending! Hark! the trump, &c. This was given in Lord Selborne's *Bk. of Praise,* 1862, and is composed of st. 4, 5, 7, 9, 20, 21, 23, 24, 27, 29, 32, 35.

These centos are usually dated 1757. This date is uncertain with regard to the first form of the hymn, and certainly wrong as applied to the second form, from which they are taken. [See Lo He comes, &c.]   [W. T. B.]

Come in, thou blessed of the Lord; Enter in Jesus, &c. *T. Kelly.* [*Reception of a Member.*] Appeared in Kelly's *Appx.* of original hymns, added to *A Coll. of Ps. & Hys.,* Dublin, 1802, No. 268, in 5 st. of 4 l., as "Come on, thou blessed," &c. In his *Hys., &c.,* 1804, and later eds., it is changed to "Come in," &c. Of the 5 stanzas, 4 were repeated by Montgomery in his *Christ. Psalmist,* 1825, as an anonymous hymn. It has failed to attain a position in G. Britain, but in America it is given in several hymnals, including *Songs for the Sanctuary,* 1865-72, and others. It is sometimes given as, "Come in, thou blessed of the Lord, O come," &c.   [J. J.]

Come in, thou blessed of the Lord; Stranger nor foe, &c. *J. Montgomery.* [*Reception of a Member.*] In the M. MSS. this hymn is dated "July 1, 1834." It was pub. in Conder's *Cong. H. Bk.,* 1836, No. 471, in 6 st. of 4 l., and again in Montgomery's *Original Hymns,* 1853, No. 150. Its popularity is greater in America than in G. Britain. [J. J.]

Come, kingdom of our God. *J. Johns.* [*Prayer for the increase of Spiritual Life.* Contributed to Beard's Manchester Unitarian *Coll.,* 1837, No. 203, in 5 st. of 4 l., and headed, "Prayer for the kingdom of God." In 1840 it was repeated in Dr. Martineau's *Hymns,* &c., and subsequently in numerous Unitarian and other collections in G. Britain and America. It is sometimes used on behalf of Missions. The fifth stanza, which is the finest in the hymn, is usually omitted in the American collections. Orig. text in Dr. Martineau's *Hymns,* &c., 1873, and the American *Hys. and Songs of Praise,* N. Y., 1874, with, in the latter, st. v., l. 2, "raise *the*," for "raise Thy glorious throne."   [J. J.]

Come, labour on! Who dares, &c. *Jane Borthwick.* [*Labour for Christ*] This hymn was given in Miss Borthwick's *Thoughts for Thoughtful Hours,* 1859, in 7 st. of 5 l., but in the new ed. of 1863, p. 48, it was re-arranged as 7 st. of 5 l., and in this form it has come into C. U. in many hymnals, including *Thring,* the *H. Comp., Snepp,* &c., and a few American collections.   [J. J.]

Come, let our voices join to raise. *I. Watts.* [*Ps. xcv.*] His L. M. version of the 95th Ps., given in his *Ps. of David,* &c., 1719, in 7 st. of 4 l., and headed, "Canaan lost thro' Unbelief; or, a Warning to delaying Sinners." Its use in G. Britain is limited. In America it is found in a large number of hymnals. Sometimes, as in the *Church Pastorals,* Boston, 1864, it begins with st. ii., "Come, let our souls address the Lord."   [J. J.]

Come, let us adore the Lord's gracious hand. *J. Cennick.* [*Morning.*] Appeared in his *Sacred Hymns,* &c., 1743, Pt. ii., No. 30, in 4 st. of 8 l. In 1753 it was given as No. 13, in G. Whitefield's *Coll.*, but in this form it is almost unknown to modern hymnals. In some American hymn-books, as Worcester's *Ps. and Hys.*, 1834, and *Hys. and Songs of Praise*, N. Y., 1874, st. ii.–iv. are given as "Our Saviour alone, the Lord let us bless." [J. J.]

Come, let us anew, Our journey pursue, Roll round, &c. *C. Wesley.* [*New Year.*] This popular hymn is much used by the Methodists at their Watchnight and Covenant Services, and is widely known in all English-speaking countries. It was 1st pub. as No. 5 of 7 hymns in a penny tract, entitled *Hys. for New Years Day*, MDCCL., and is in 3 st. of 8 l. (*P. Works*, 1868–72, vol. vi. p. 14). In 1760 it was adopted by *M. Madan*, in 1776, by *Toplady*, and later on by others in the Church of England; by J. Wesley in the *Wes. H. Bk.*, 1780, No. 45, and by Nonconformists generally. [J. J.]

Come, let us ascend, My companion and friend. *C. Wesley.* [*Christian Fellowship.*] This is No. 231, in vol. ii. of the *Hys. & S. Poems*, 1749, in 8 st. of 6 l. (*P. Works*, 1868–72, vol. v. p. 457). M. Madan gave 6 stanzas in his *Coll.*, 1760; Toplady repeated the same in his *Ps. & Hys*, 1776, and thus the hymn came into use in the Church of England. With the change in st. iv. l. 3, of "In the city" to "In the *palace*," it was included in full in the *Wes. H. Bk.*, 1780, No. 486, and is retained in the revised ed., 1875, No. 499. Both this text, and that of *Madan*, are in C. U. Interesting notes on the spiritual benefits conferred on persons by this hymn, are given in Stevenson's *Meth. H. Bk. Notes*, 1883. [J. J.]

Come, let us join our cheerful songs. *I. Watts.* [*Praise.*] This is one of the most widely known and highly esteemed of Watts's compositions. It has no special history beyond the fact that it appeared in his *Hys. & S. Songs*, 1707, and the enlarged ed. 1709, Bk. i., No. 62, in 5 st. of 4 l., and was headed "Christ Jesus the Lamb of God, worshipped by all the Creation, Rev. v. 11–13." The most popular form of the hymn is in 4 st., the st. "Let all that dwell above the sky (iv.) being omitted. This text was adopted by *Whitefield*, 1753; *Madan*, 1760; *De Courcy*, 1775; *Toplady*, 1776, and many others amongst the older compilers, and is retained by far the greater number of modern editors, both in G. Britain and America. The hymn, in whole, or in part, has been rendered into many languages, including one in Latin, "Venite, Sancti, nostra laeta carmina," in Bingham's *Hymno. Christ. Lat.* 1871. [J. J.]

Come, let us join our friends above. *C. Wesley.* [*Communion of Saints.*] 1st pub. in his *Funeral Hymns*, 2nd Series, 1759, No. 1, in 5 st. of 8 l., and entitled, "A Funeral Hymn." Although it was not included in the *Wes. H. Bk.* until the addition of the *Supp.* in 1830, it had been in C. U. outside of Methodism for many years before, and was well known, especially through st. ii.:—

> "One family we dwell in Him,
>   One church above, beneath,
> Though now divided by the stream,
>   The narrow stream of death;

> One army of the living God,
>   To His command we bow :
> Part of His host have crossed the flood,
>   And part are crossing now."

The use of the hymn, either in full or in an abbreviated form, has extended to all English-speaking countries. Orig. text in *P. Works* 1868–72, vol. vi. p. 215; and notes of some interest concerning spiritual benefits derived by many from the hymn, in Stevenson's *Meth. H. Bk. Notes*, 1883, p. 561.

In addition to the use of the original text in its full, or in an abridged form, there are also the following hymns which are derived therefrom :—

1. "**The saints on earth and those above.**" This appeared in the *Appendix* to the 6th ed. of Cotterill's *Sel.* 1815, No. 227 ; in Montgomery's *Christian Psalmist*, 1825; and in several modern hymn-books. It is composed as follows:—St. i. From I. Watts's *Hys. & S. Songs*, 1709, Bk. ii., No. 152, st. v., which reads:—

> "The saints on earth and all the dead
>   But one communion make;
> All join in Christ, their living head,
>   And of His grace partake."

This is altered to:—

> "The saints on earth and *those above*
>   But one communion make:
> *Joined to their Lord in bonds of love*,
>   *All* of His grace partake."

St. ii.–v. are st. ii., iii., ll. 1–4, and v., ll. 4–8, of "Come, let us join," &c., slightly altered. In the S.P.C.K. *Church Hys.* the last line of the cento is altered, and in Thring's *Coll.* 1882, the last three lines are by Prebendary Thring.

2. "**Let saints below join saints above.**" This appeared in Murray's *Hymnal*, 1852, No. 127, and is C. Wesley's text partly rewritten, and reduced to 6 st. of 4 l.

3. "**Let saints on earth in concert sing.**" This, as given in *H. A. & M.* in 1861 and 1875, is Murray's arrangement of Wesley's text as above with the omission of st. 1. This is altered in the Harrow School *Hymns*, 1857, to "Let all below in concert sing."

4. "**Come, let us join our friends above, whose glory is begun.**" This, in the *Marlborough College Hys.*, 1869, No. 104, is C. Wesley's text somewhat altered, and with many of the lines transposed.

The combined use of the original and these altered forms of the text is very extensive in all English-speaking countries. [J. J.]

Come, let us lift our joyful eyes. *I. Watts.* [*Christ the Mediator.*] This is No. 108, Bk. ii., of his *Hys. and S. Songs*, 1707, in 6 st. of 4 l., and is entitled, "Access to a throne of grace by a Mediator." In the older collections, as G. Whitefield's, 1753, and others, it was given in full, but in modern hymnals st. ii. and iii. are usually omitted, most editors both in G. Britain and America declining to maintain concerning the Throne of God :—

> "Once 'twas a seat of dreadful wrath,
>   And shot devouring flame ;
> Our God appeared consuming fire,
>   And Veng'ance was His name.

> "Rich were the drops of Jesus' blood,
>   That calm'd His frowning face,
> That sprinkled o'er the burning Throne,
>   And turned the wrath to grace."

This hymn is sometimes misdated 1719, the date of Watts's *Psalms*. [J. J.]

Come, let us search our [hearts] ways and try. *I. Watts.* [*Truthfulness.*] 1st pub. in his *Sermons*, 1721–24, vol. ii. in 6 st. of 4 l. In this form it is seldom found in any hymn-book, either old or new. It was rewritten as "Come, let us search our hearts and try" (i.–iii. Watts ; iv. original), by E. Osler for Hall's *Mitre H. Bk.*, 1836, No. 171. Osler made further alterations in the text for his

Church and King, June, 1837, p. 138, where it is appended to an essay on the Church Service for the 4th S. after Trinity. The *Church and King* text is usually followed. It is in Windle's *Coll.*, No. 67 (st. iii., l. 1, *speak* for *talk*), the Harrow School *Hymns*, 1855-57. [J. J.]

Come, let us sing the song of songs. J. Montgomery. [*Praise.*] According to the M. MSS. this hymn was written in 1841. It was pub. in his *Original Hymns*, 1853, No. 89, in 7 st. of 4 l. Although but little known in G. Britain, it is somewhat extensively used in America, As altered in the *People's H.*, 1867, it has passed into the *Churchman's Altar Manual*, 1882, and others. [J. J.]

Come, let us to the Lord our God. J. Morison. [*Lent.*] 1st appeared as No. 30 in the Draft Scottish *Trans. and Paraphrases*, 1781, as a version of Hosea, vi. 1-4, in 6 st. of 4 l. Here are the following variations from the public worship ed. issued in that year by the Church of Scotland, and still in use :—

St. iii., l. 4, Rejoicing in his sight.
St. iv., l. 1, Then shall we know His grace and love.
St. iv., l. 2, If him we make our choice.

In the markings by the eldest daughter of *W. Cameron* (q. v.), it is given as " Morison altered by Logan." It is one of the finest of the *Paraphrases*, and has recently come into extensive use, as in England in the *Hy. Comp.*, 1871-1877 ; the *Bap. Hymnal*, 1879, &c.; and in America in the Andover *Sabbath H. Bk.*, 1858, and others. Included in full, and unaltered, in Thring's *Coll.*, 1882, No. 274, and the *Free Church H. Bk.*, 1882, No. 48. In the Irvingite *Hymns for the use of the Churches*, 1864, st. iii.-vi. beginning, " Long hath the night of sorrow reigned," are included as No. 13 (ed. 1871, No. 48), and appointed for Advent ; and the same as No. 494 in the American *Dutch Reformed H. Bk.*, 1869. Included in two parts, pt. ii. beginning, " Our hearts, if God we seek to know," as No. 62 in Miss Leeson's *Paraphrases and Hys. for Congregational Singing*, 1853. [J. M.]

Come, let us use the grace divine. C. Wesley. [*Confirmation.*] 1st pub. in his *Short Hymns*, &c., 1762, vol. ii., No. 1242, in 3 st. of 8 l., and based upon Jer. l. 5 (*P. Works*, 1868-72, vol. x. p. 46). In 1780 it was included in the *Wes. H. Bk.*, No. 518, from whence it has passed into other collections of the Methodist bodies. It was also given by Montgomery in his *Christian Psalmist*, 1825, and is found in some Nonconformist collections. The form in which it is usually given in the Church of England hymnals appeared in Bickersteth's *Christ. Psalmody*, 1833, as, " Come, let us *seek the grace of God*," as in Snepp's *S. of G. and G.*, 1872. [J. J.]

Come, let us who in Christ believe. C. Wesley. [*Praise to Christ.*] Appeared in his *Hys. on God's Everlasting Love*, 2nd Series, Lond. 1741, No. 8, in 14 st. of 4 l. In the *Wes. H. Bk.*, 1780, st. i., xii., xiii., xiv. were given as No. 200. This cento has been repeated in various collections in G. Britain and America, and is the received form of the hymn. See *Wes. H. Bk.*, 1875, No. 208, and the Amer. Meth. Episco. *Hymnal*, 1878, No. 28 (*P. Works*, 1868-72, vol. iii. p. 64). [J. J.]

Come, little children, learn to praise. [*Praise to God.*] Appeared in R. Hill's *Coll. of Hys. for S. Schools*, 1808, in 6 st. of 4 l. In this form it is unknown to the modern hymnals, but as " Come, children, learn your God to praise," it is given in several, including the *S. S. U. Coll.* and others. Possibly the hymn is by R. Hill, but we have no evidence to that effect. [W. T. B.]

Come, Lord, and tarry not. H. Bonar. [*Second Advent desired.*] Printed in May, 1846, at the end of one of the *Kelso Tracts*, and again in his *Hys. of Faith and Hope*, 1857. It is in 14 st. of 4 l., with the heading " Come, Lord," and the motto from St. Augustine, " Senuit mundus." Centos, varying in length and construction, but all beginning with st. l., are in extensive use in America. In G. Britain it is less popular. A cento, beginning with st. ii., " Come, Lord ; Thy saints for Thee," is also given in *Kennedy*, 1863, No. 22. [J. J.]

Come, Lord, and warm each languid heart. Anne Steele. [*Joys of Heaven.*] 1st pub. in her *Poems, chiefly Devotional*, &c., 1760, vol. i. p. 34 (2nd ed., 1780, vol. i. p. 34) ; and in Sedgwick's reprint of her *Hymns*, 1863, p. 21. In the Ash & Evans Bristol *Coll.*, 1769, 8 sts. were given as No. 402, and were thus introduced into the Nonconformist hymnals. R. Conyers (*Ps. & Hys.*, 2nd ed., 1774, No. 360) and W. Row, through Toplady's *Ps. & Hys.*, 2nd ed., 1787, No. 411, gave other centos to the Church of England. Centos, all beginning with st. i., and usually compiled from one of those collections, are found in a great number of hymnals both in G. Britain and America. [J. J.]

Come, magnify the Saviour's love. E. Osler. [*Passiontide.*] 1st pub. in Hall's *Mitre*, 1836, No. 95, and again in the author's *Church and King*, March, 1837 (p. 84), where it is given after a prose meditation on " Christ exalted through humiliation and suffering," being the theme for the Sunday next before Easter. From the *Mitre* it has passed into several collections. The *Mitre* text, which differs somewhat from *Church and King*, is generally adopted. [J. J.]

Come, mild and holy Dove. J. Austin. [*Whitsuntide.*] 1st pub. in 10 st. of 4 l. in his *Devotions in the Ancient Way of Offices*, 1668 (for Lauds for the Holy Ghost) and in the adaptations of the same by Dorrington and Hickes. No. 140 in the *Anglican H. Bk.*, 1868, is a cento from this hymn in 4 st. [W. T. B.]

Come, my soul, thy suit prepare. J. Newton. [*Prayer.*] Appeared in the *Olney Hymns*, 1779, Book i., No. 31, in 7 st. of 4 l., and in later editions of the same. It was included in some of the older collections, and is still in extensive use in G. Britain and America, sometimes in full, and again in an abbreviated form. Orig. text as above, and in *Lyra Brit.*, 1867. [J. J.]

Come, O Thou all victorious Lord. C. Wesley. [*Lent.*] Written during a visit to Portland, June, 1746 (see the author's *Journal* and *Meth. Mag.*, May, 1869), where the occupation of the quarrymen suggested the line of thought and the appeal :—

" Strike with the hammer of Thy word
And break these hearts of stone."

It was 1st pub. in *Hys. & S. Poems*, 1749, in 7 st. of 4 l., and headed, "Written before preaching at Portland." In 1780 it was included, with two minor alterations, in the *Wes. H. Bk.*, No. 82, and has been retained in all subsequent editions. From that collection it has passed into many others, in G. Britain and America. Orig text, *P. Works*, 1868–72, vol. v. p. 124. In *Kennedy*, 1863, No. 354, it appears in a slightly altered form as, "All gracious, all victorious Lord," but its use as thus altered is not extensive. A cento composed of st. iii., v. and iv. slightly altered was also given in the American Unitarian *Hys. for the Ch. of Christ*, Boston, 1853, as, "Give us ourselves and Thee to know." [J. J.]

Come, O Thou Traveller unknown.

C. Wesley. [*Prayer.*] This poem was 1st pub. in *Hys. & S. Poems*, 1742, in 14 st. of 6 l., and entitled "Wrestling Jacob." It is based on the incident in Jacob's life as recorded in Gen. xxxii. 24–32. Although a poem of great power and finish, it is unsuited to Public Worship. It received the most unqualified praise from I. Watts, who, J. Wesley said, did not scruple to say, "that single poem, *Wrestling Jacob*, was worth all the verses he himself had written" (*Minutes of Conference*, 1788); and J. Montgomery wrote of it as:—

"Among C. Wesley's highest achievements may be recorded, "Come, O Thou Traveller unknown," &c., p. 43, in which, with consummate art, he has carried on the action of a lyrical drama ; each turn in the conflict with the mysterious Being against whom he wrestles all night, being marked with precision by the varying language of the speaker, accompanied by intense, increasing interest, till the rapturous moment of discovery, when he prevails, and exclaims, 'I know Thee, Saviour, Who Thou art.'" (*Christ. Psalmist*, 1825. xxiii.–iv.)

Notwithstanding this high commendation, and of it as a *poem* it is every way worthy, its unsuitability for congregational purposes is strikingly seen in the fact that it is seldom found in any hymnal, either old or new, except those of the Methodist denominations. In 1780 it was given, with the omission of st. v. and vii. in the *Wes. H. Bk.*, No. 136, in two parts, Pt. ii. being, "Yield to me now, for I am weak." These parts were subsequently (ed. 1797) numbered as separate hymns, and as such are Nos. 140 and 141 in the revised ed., 1875. In the *Hys. for the use of the Meth. Episco. Ch.*, N. Y. 1849, it is broken up into four parts, each being numbered as a separate hymn, as:—"Come, O Thou Traveller unknown"; "Wilt Thou not yet to me reveal"; "Yield to me now, for I am weak"; and "The Sun of Righteousness on me." In their new *Hymnal*, 1878, which has taken the place of the 1849 book, the division, "Wilt Thou," &c., is included in the first, "Come, Thou, &c." There is also a cento from this poem in the *N. Cong.*, No. 1063, beginning, "O Lord, my God, to me reveal." Orig. text in *P. Works*, 1868–72, vol. ii. p. 173. [J. J.]

Come on, companions of our way.

J. Montgomery. [*Life a Pilgrimage.*] Written for the Sheffield Red Hill S. S. Anniversary and printed on a broadsheet, March, 1829 [M.MSS.] in 4 st. of 6 l. In 1853 it was included in his *Original Hymns*, No. 153. It is the Scottish *Evang. Union Hyl.*, 1878. [J. J.]

Come on, my partners in distress.

C. Wesley. [*Heaven anticipated.*] This hymn has interwoven itself into the personal spiritual history of Methodists probably more completely than any other hymn by C. Wesley. The instances given in Stevenson's *Methodist H. Book Notes*, 1883, p. 235, and the Index, although numerous and interesting, but very inadequately represent the hold it has upon the Methodist mind and feeling. Its literary merits also place it high amongst the author's productions. Its history is simple. It appeared in the *Hys. and S. Poems*, 1749, in 8 st. of 6 l.; in M. Madan's *Coll.*, 1760, in 5 st.; and again in the *Wes. H. Bk.*, 1780, with the omission of st. iii., as No. 324. The last form of the text has passed into numerous hymnals in all English-speaking countries. Two centos from the hymn are also in C. U., both commencing with st. ii. :—"Beyond the bounds of time and space." The first is in the *Leeds H. Bk.*, 1853, No. 638, and others, and the second in *Mercer*, Oxford ed. 1864–72, No. 404. Orig. text, *P. Works*, 1868–72, vol. v. p. 168. [J. J.]

Come, our indulgent Saviour, come.

P. Doddridge. [*Easter.*] 1st pub. in J. Orton's ed. of Doddridge's *Hymns*, &c., 1755, No. 245, in 5 st. of 4 l., and entitled "The Disciples' Joy at Christ's appearance to them after the Resurrection." It was also given in J. D. Humphreys's ed. of the same, 1839. The form in which it is usually known is, "Come, condescending Saviour, come." This was given in the Bristol *Coll.* of Ash & Evans, 1769, No. 211. It was repeated in Bickersteth's *Christian Psalmody*, 1833, and other collections, and was thus handed down to the modern hymnals. In Dr. Alexander's *Augustine H. Bk.*, 1849–65, st. i., ii., and iv. are given as, "Come, great and gracious Saviour, come"; and in the *Bapt. Hymnal*, 1879, st. iv. and v. as, "Enter our hearts, Redeemer blest." [J. J.]

Come, pure hearts, in sweetest measures.

R. Campbell. [*Feasts of Evangelists.*] This is a *tr.* of a Latin cento. Campbell's original ms. is headed "Psallat chorus corde mundo." Paraphrase upon three stanzas of Adam of St. Victor's two hymns, "De SS. Evangelistis." The cento is thus composed:—

St. i. Psallat chorus corde mundo. "Come, pure hearts, in sweetest measures." This was taken from the text of *Clichtoveus*, as in Trench's *Sac. Lat. Poetry*, 1849, and not from the original, which reads, "Plausu chorus laetabundo."

St. ii. Paradisus his rigatur. "See the rivers four that gladden," is st. 8 of "Jucundare plebs fidelis," as in *Daniel*, ii. p. 84.

St. iii. Horum rivo debriatis. "Here our hearts inebriated," is st. 9 of "Jucundare," &c., as above.

This paraphrase was pub. in his St. Andrews *Hys. & Anthems*, 1850, p. 96. It was repeated with slight alterations in Rorison's *Hys. & Anthems*, 1851, and one or two others, but its use was limited until 1861, when the compilers of *Hys. A. & M.* adopted st. i., ii. from Campbell, and replaced st. iii. with one of their own. In the *Hymnary*, st. i.–iii. are from Campbell, slightly altered, and st. iv. is new. The text of *Laudes Domini*, N. Y., 1884, is from *Hys. A. & M.* Full Latin texts are

in *Gautier*, ii., 1859; *Wrangham*, iii., 1883
(with *tr.*); *Daniel*, ii. 84–88.   [J. J.]

**Come, see the place where Jesus
lay, For he hath left, &c.** *J. Montgomery.*
[*Easter.*] Written for "The Seventh Anniversary of the Sheffield and Attercliffe
Missionary Union in aid of the London Missionary Society," and first sung in public in
Howard Street Independent Chapel, Sheffield,
on Easter Sunday, April 2nd, 1820. It was
printed on a flyleaf for use at these services,
and signed "J. M." In 1825 it was included,
after careful revision, by Montgomery in his
Christ. Psalmist, No. 407, in 6 st. of 4 l., and
entitled, "The power of Christ's Resurrection," No. 495, and again in *Original Hys.*,
1853, No. 127. Its use is extensive, the
revised text of 1825–53 being that which is
usually followed   [J. J.]

**Come, sinners, to the gospel feast,
Let every soul, &c.** *C. Wesley.* [*Invitation.*] 1st pub. in his *Hys. for those who seek
and those who have Redemption*, &c., 1747, in
24 st. of 4 l., and entitled "The Great Supper" (*P. Works*, 1868–72, vol. iv. p. 274). Two
centos, both beginning with st. i., are in
C. U.:—(1) that which was included in
M. Madan's *Coll.*, 1760, No. 22, in 8 st., and
is the source of the text as given in the
Church of England hymnals; and (2) the
Wes. H. Bk. cento given in that *Sel.*, 1780,
and repeated in various Nonconformist collections. A cento for Holy Communion is also
in the earliest eds. of the Lady Huntingdon
Coll., beginning:—

"Come, sinners, to the gospel feast;
  Jesus invites you for His guest."

In late eds. of the same *Coll.* it begins "Come,
sinner," &c. It is compiled from st. i., xii.,
xxii., xxiii. A hymn beginning:—

"Come, sinners, to the gospel feast;
  O come without delay,"

is included in many American collections, as
Dr. Hatfield's *Church H. Bk.*, 1872; the *Bap.
Praise Bk.*, 1871, &c. It has been traced to
the Bap. *Psalmist* of Stow & Smith, 1843,
No. 418. In some of those collections it is
taken for granted that it is the same cento as
that in the Lady Huntingdon *Coll.* It has,
however, nothing in common with that cento,
nor with Wesley's original, except the first
line. In st. i., l. 3 reads, "For there is room
in Jesus' breast," and through the remaining
four stanzas the changes are rung on the
expression, "There's room," a style of composition altogether foreign to C. Wesley's usual
method. It is *Anon.*, 1843.   [J. J.]

**Come then, my God, the promise
seal.** *C. Wesley.* [*Prayer.*] This is the
second of two hymns on St. Mark, xi. 24,
"What things soever ye desire when ye pray,"
&c., which appeared in his *Short Hys.*, &c.,
1762, vol. ii., No. 314, in 3 st. of 8 l., and
again in the *P. Works*, 1868–72, vol. xi. p. 45.
In 1780 it was given in the *Wes. H. Bk.*, No.
405, as "Come, O my God, the promise seal,"
and in this form it has passed into various
collections in G. Britain and America. [J. J.]

Come, Thou Almighty King. [*Holy
Trinity.*] The earliest form in which this
hymn is found is in 5 st. of 7 l., with the

title, "An Hymn to the Trinity," on a tract
of four pages, together with st. 1, 2, 6, 10,
11, and 12, of C. Wesley's hymn on "The
Backslider," beginning "Jesus, let Thy
pitying eye," &c., thus making up a tract of
two hymns. The date of this tract is unknown. It is bound up with the British
Museum copy of the 6th ed. of G. Whitefield's
Coll., 1757, and again with the copies in the
same library of the 8th ed., 1759, and the 9th,
1760. In subsequent editions beginning with
the 10th, 1761, both hymns were incorporated
in the body of the book. M. Madan included
it in the *Appendix* to his *Coll.* in 1763, No.
cxcv., and through this channel, together with
the Whitefield *Coll.*, it has descended to
modern hymnals. The loss of the titlepage
(if any) of the above tract renders the question
of its authorship one of some doubt. The first
hymn in the tract is compiled, as indicated,
from C. Wesley's hymn, "Jesus, let Thy
pitying eye," which appeared in his *Hys. &
S. Poems*, 1749, some eight years before the
abridged form was given in G. Whitefield's
Coll. The hymn, "Come, Thou Almighty
King," however, cannot be found in any known
publication of C. Wesley, and the assigning
of the authorship to him is pure conjecture.
Seeing that it is given, together with another
hymn, at the end of some copies of the 6th,
8th and 9th ed. of Whitefield's *Coll.* (1757,
1759 and 1760), and was subsequently embodied in that *Coll.*, the most probable conclusion is that both hymns were printed by
Whitefield as additions to those editions of his
collection, and that, as in the one case, the
hymn is compiled from one by C. Wesley, so
in this we have probably the reprint of the
production of an author to us as yet unknown.

Much stress has been laid on the fact that
the late D. Sedgwick always maintained the
authorship of C. Wesley, and that from his
decision there was no appeal. The "s. mss."
show clearly that (1) Sedgwick's correspondence respecting this hymn was very extensive;
(2) that he knew nothing of the *British Mus.*
copies noted above; (3) that he had no
authority for his statement but his own private
opinion based on what he regarded as internal
evidence alone; (4) and that all the Wesleyan
authorities with whom he corresponded, both
in G. Britain and America, were against him.
His authority is, therefore, of no value. The
evidence to the present time will admit of no
individual signature. It is "*Anon.*"

The use of this hymn, both in G. Britain,
the Colonies, and America, is very extensive.
It has also been rendered into various languages. Orig. text, *Lyra Brit.*, 1867, p. 656;
Snepp's *Songs of G. & G.*, 1872.   [J. J.]

Come, Thou Celestial Spirit, come.
P. Doddridge. [*Whitsuntide.*] This hymn
is undated in the D. mss., where it begins,
"Oh come, celestial Spirit, come." It was
pub. in the altered form by J. Orton, in Doddridge's (posthumous) *Hymns*, &c., 1755, No.
285, in 4 st. of 4 l., and again in J. D.
Humphreys's ed. of the same, 1839. In the
Bap. Praise Bk., N. Y., 1871, st. iv. is omitted.

**Come, Thou Conqueror of the na-
tions.** *C. Wesley.* [*Whitsuntide.*] From his
Hys. on the Expected Invasion, 1759, when

it was feared that an attack on England would be made by the French. The tract was pub. in 1759, this hymn being No. 8, in 8 st. of 6 l. In 1830 it was included, with the omission of st. v., in the *Supp.* to the *Wes. H. Bk.*, and is retained in the ed. of 1875. It is also found in other collections, including *Kennedy*, 1863, No. 1077, where it is given as "Come, *great* Conqueror of the nations," in 5 st., the abbreviation being made by the omission of st. iii. and iv. Orig. text, *P. Works* 1868–72, vol. vi. p. 160.   [J. J.]

Come, Thou desire of all Thy saints.

Anne Steele. [*Public Worship.*] This hymn appeared with the heading, "Intreating the Presence of Christ in His Churches," in the author's *Poems on Subjects chiefly Devotional*, 1760, vol. i. p. 76 (2nd ed., 1780, vol. i. p. 76). In 1769 it was reprinted in the Bristol *Coll.* of Ash & Evans, and was thus brought into C. U. Its American use is much greater than that in G. Britain. It is usually abbreviated, and is sometimes given, as in the *Church Pastorals*, Boston, U. S., 1864, as "Come, O Thou King of all Thy saints." This cento is made of st. i., vi., vii. Orig. text in Sedgwick's reprint of Miss Steele's *Hymns*, 1863. [J. J.]

Come, Thou Fount of every blessing.

[*Whitsuntide.*] As various and conflicting statements concerning this hymn abound, it will be necessary to trace, 1st its *History*, so far as known; and 2nd, to discuss the question of its *Authorship*.

i. *Its History.* This in detail is :—

1. In a Church Book, kept by Robert Robinson (q.v.), of Cambridge, and in the possession of the Rev. William Robinson, of Cambridge, his biographer, there is an entry in Robert Robinson's handwriting which reads :— "Mr. Wheatley of Norwich published a hymn beginning "Come, Thou Fount of every blessing" (1758). This entry forms part of a ms. list of the works which R. Robinson had written and published. This gives us a definite date, 1758.

2. Nothing has yet been found which can be identified as being issued by "Mr. Wheatley of Norwich" in which this hymn can be found.

3. The earliest known text in print is in *A Collection of Hymns used by the Church of Christ in Angel-Alley, Bishopsgate*, 1759, now in the library of the Drew Theological College, Madison, New Jersey, U.S.A. It is No. i., and in 4 st., beginning respectively :—
   St. i. "Come, Thou Fount of every blessing."
   St. ii. "Here I raise my Eben-ezer."
   St. iii. "O, to grace how great a debtor."
   St. iv. "O, that day when free from sinning."

4. This text was repeated in the *Hearers of the Apostles Collection of Hymns*, Nottingham, 1777; and in a *Dublin Collection*, 1785. Shortly afterwards, however, it seems to have fallen out of use.

5. The second and well-known form of the hymn in the first three stanzas as given above is found in M. Madan's *Ps. & Hys.*, 1760; G. Whitefield's *Ps. & Hymns*, 14th ed., 1767; the Countess of Huntingdon's *Coll.*, 1764; and most of the hymn-books pub. during the latter part of the last century. The text, as in Madan's *Ps. & Hys.*, 1760, which is the 1759 text with the omission of st. iv., is that usually adopted by modern compilers, and is given in *Lyra Brit.*, 1867, p. 479.

ii. *Authorship.*

This has been claimed for *Robert Robinson*, on the one part, and for the *Countess of Huntingdon* on the other. The evidence in each case is :—

(1) *For Robert Robinson.*
1. The entry in his own handwriting in the Cambridge Church Book, in which he enumerates it with his various productions as noted above.
2. His name is added to it in the 3rd ed. of *A Collection of Hymns adapted to Public Worship*, 1778; and

has since been repeated in almost every collection in which authors' names are given from that date to the present.

3. Mr. Dyer, in his *Memoirs of the Life & Writings of R. Robinson*, 1796, states that amongst Robinson's papers there was a letter from Dr. Rippon, the compiler of the well-known Bapt. *Sel. of Hymns*, 1787, in which he acknowledges that one or two hymns in that *Sel.* were by Robinson, and names "Come, Thou Fount of every blessing" as one. Dr. Rippon gives it as No. 509, and for the "New Year." It is in 3 st., and signed *Robinson.*

4. It is included in Benjamin Flower's ed. of Robinson's *Miscellaneous Works*, Harlow, 1807, vol. iv. p. 346.

5. The Rev. W. Robinson, in *Select Works of the Rev. Robert Robinson*, 1861, claims it for him.

ii. *For the Countess of Huntingdon.*

1. Bound up with a copy of J. & C. Wesley's *Hymns & Sacred Poems*, Dublin, 1747, are 21 leaves of writing paper. On the first leaf is written a list of several of the poetical publications of the Wesleys. Following it are hymns copied from Cennick, Watts, &c.; one by "Mrs. D. B.," and this hymn. These fill 10 leaves of the 21, and the rest are blank. On the title-page of this book is written in the same handwriting "Diana Bindon, 1759." On the inside of the cover of the book is pasted a Wesleyan Methodist quarterly ticket containing a small engraving of Christ washing one of the disciples' feet. On this is written, "Nov. 6, Diana Vandeleur," but the year is not given. The Wesley publications named on the first leaf reach down to 1756.

2. Amongst the ms. hymns is "Come, Thou Fount of every blessing." It is headed, "Hymn by the Countess of Huntingdon." It is in 5 st., i.–iv. being the same, with slight differences in the text, as that noted above as being in the *Coll. of Hys. used by the Church of Christ in Angel Alley, *Bishopsgate*, 1759; and st. v. beginning, "If Thou ever didst discover," from C. Wesley's hymn "Jesu, help Thy fallen creatures," from his *Hys. & Sac. Poems*, 1749, vol. ii., No. 51.

3. Upon this evidence alone (we write with the *Diana Bindon MS.* and D. Sedgwick's ms. correspondence before us) Sedgwick carried on a long controversy in the *Notes and Queries*, and other periodicals, in 1858–9, contending throughout that "Diana Bindon" was a personal friend of Lady Huntingdon's, and that she had made her ms. copy direct from another ms. by the Countess. And this he did not only upon the worthless evidence here given, but also whilst receiving, privately, direct testimony to the contrary, together with a positive denial made to him by Lady Huntingdon's biographer. His mss. show that having committed himself, he held it to be beneath him, and damaging to his reputation, to acknowledge his error.

From the foregoing account very much that appeared in the correspondence and is found in the s. mss., is omitted, and the bare facts alone are given. These facts conclusively show that the author was Robert Robinson, and *not* Selina, Countess of Huntingdon.

The original text is probably that given in the *Angel Alley Coll.* (see above, i. 3), 1759, in 4 st., but the accepted text, and that which is in very extensive use in all English-speaking countries, is that given in 3 st. of 8 l. in Madan's *Ps. & Hys.*, 1760 (see above, i. 5). [J. J.]

Come, Thou long expected Jesus.

C. Wesley. [*Christmas.*] Appeared in *Hys. for the Nativity of Our Lord*, 1744, No. x., in 2 st. of 8 l. The tract in which it appeared formed the first of those called the "Festival Hymns," which were subsequently pub. by Lampe in 1746. It was not included in the *Wes. H. Bk.* until the revised edition of 1875, No. 688, although it was given by Whitefield in his *Coll.*, 1753, and later editions; by Madan, in his *Ps. & Hymns*, 1760; by Toplady, in his *Ps. & Hymns*, 1776; and by others. It is found in a great number of hymnals in G. Britain and America, specially those of the Church of England, and usually without alteration, as in *Hy. Comp.*, No. 96. A marked departure from this rule is, "Come,

O Saviour, long expected," which appeared in Hall's *Mitre*, 1836, in 4 st. of 4 l., and again in the *New Mitre*, 1875, in 6 st., the last two stanzas being Edward Osler's doxology, "Worship, honour, glory, blessing," from the older *Mitre*, 1836, No. 282. Other altered forms are, "Come, Thou Saviour, long expected," in *Kennedy*, 1863, No. 89, "Hail, Thou long expected Jesus," in the American *Prot. Episco. Hymnal*, 1871. Orig. text, *P. Works*, 1868-72, vol. iv. p. 116.   [J. J.]

Come, Thou soul - transforming Spirit. *J. Evans.* [*Before Sermon.*] This hymn was contributed to G. Burder's *Coll. of Hys. from Various Authors*, 1784, No. 13, in 2 st. of 6 l., and entitled, "Imploring the aid of the Spirit." In modern hymnals it is found in *three* forms as follows:—

1. The original. This was reprinted from Burder, by W. Jay, of Bath, in his *Sel.*, 1797, No. 220, but without signature. From Jay it passed into other hymnals, with the addition of "*Jay*" as the author, as in the American *Meth. Episco. H. Bk.*, 1849. The original text is also in Snepp's *S. of G. & G.*, 1872.

2. In the Williams and Boden *Coll.*, 1801, the hymn was given in an altered form, and with the addition of the stanza, "Then, whene'er the signal's given," from "Lord, dismiss us with Thy blessing." In Kemble's *New Church H. Bk.*, 1873, this is repeated with further alterations, and the omission of the added stanza.

3. In Bickersteth's *Christ. Psalmody*, 1833, No. 382, is the original with the addition of two stanzas from "Lord, dismiss us with Thy blessing." This cento has almost died out of use.

Although these three forms of the hymn exist, most modern editors are falling back upon the original, especially in America, where its popularity is greater than in G. Britain.   [J. J.]

Come to a desert place apart. *J. Anstice.* [*Church Guilds.*] 1st printed in his *Hymns*, 1836, No. 39, in 5 st. of 4 l., and based on St. Mark, vi. 31-46. In 1841 it was included unaltered in the *Child's Christian Year*, and appointed for the 25th Sun. after Trinity. It is sometimes altered, as in the S. P. C. K. *Church Hys.*, 1871.   [J. J.]

Come to our [dark] poor nature's night.] *G. Rawson.* [*Whitsuntide.*] Contributed to the *Leeds H. Bk.*, 1853, No. 397, in 9 st. of 4 l., and from thence it has passed into numerous collections. In 1876 the author included a revised text, in 8 st., in his *Hymns*, &c., No. 46. This, however, is not in general use. Orig. text, *N. Cong*, No. 438. The hymn, "Come to our dark nature's night," in the 1876 ed. of *H. Comp.* is a slightly altered version of the orig. text with the omission of st. vii. In the American *Hys. & Songs of Praise*, N. Y., 1874, it is given as "Holy Ghost, the Infinite." [J. J.]

Come to the morning prayer. *J. Montgomery.* [*Daily Prayer.*] This invitation to daily worship was printed in the *Evangelical Magazine* for Dec. 1842, where it is dated "Aug. 4, 1842," in 4 st. of 4. l. It was also included by Montgomery in his *Original Hys.*, 1853, No. 79, and entitled "Daily Prayer." It is given in *Hy. Comp.*, No. 10, in an unaltered form. It is also found in a few American collections. The most popular form of the hymn in America is "Come at the morning hour." This is found in several collections, as the *Songs for the Sanctuary*, 1865; the *Bap. Praise Book*, 1871, &c.   [J. J.]

Come to Thy temple, Lord. *H. Alford.* [*Advent.*] 1st pub. in his *Ps. & Hys.*, 1844, No. 2, in 4 st. of 4 l., again in his *Poetical Works*, 1865, and his *Year of Praise*, 1867. It has passed into several collections. In T. Darling's *Hymns*, &c., 1885, it begins, "Thy temple visit, Lord."   [J. J.]

Come unto Me, ye weary. [*W. C. Dix.* [*Invitation.*] This hymn, which ranks as one of the best of Mr. Dix's efforts, was pub. in 1867 in the *People's H.*; in 1869, in the *Appx.* to the S. P. C. K. *Ps. & Hys.*; in 1871, in *Church Hys.*; in 1875, in *H. A. & M.*, and in other collections. It has also been reprinted in *Laudes Domini*, N. Y., 1884.   [J. J.]

Come, we [ye] that [who] love the Lord. *I. Watts.* [*Joy and Praise.*] 1st pub. in his *Hys. & S. Songs*, 1707, and again, 2nd ed., 1709, Bk. ii., No. 30, in 10 st. of 4 l., and entitled "Heavenly Joy on Earth." In its original and full form it is rarely found in modern collections, the *N. Cong.*, 1859, No. 693, and the Bap. *Ps. & Hys.*, 1858-80, being exceptions with the alteration of st. iii., l. 3, of "fav'rites" to "*children.*" It has undergone many alterations and revisions. Of these the principal are:—

1. "Come ye that love the Lord." This was given by J. Wesley in his *Ps. & Hys.*, pub. at Charlestown, U. S., 1736-7, during his stay in Georgia. In this form sts. ii. and ix. are omitted, and the rest are considerably altered. After slight revision this text was repeated by Wesley in the *Wes. H. Bk.*, 1780, and is in the revised ed. 1875, and in most collections of the Methodist communion.

2. "Come ye *who* love the Lord." This reading of the first line was given by Cotterill in the 8th ed. of his *Sel.*, 1819, and is followed by *H. Comp.* and others.

The different arrangement of stanzas, and the variations in the text which have been adopted by the numerous editors who have used it in one form or another may be counted by the hundred. The example set by *Wesley* in 1736, was followed by *Whitefield*, 1753; *Madan*, 1760; *Conyers*, 1772; *Toplady*, 1776, and onwards to the latest modern collection. No text can, as a rule, be relied upon. The original is easy to obtain in modern editions of *Watts*. The hymn, as a whole, is regarded as a good specimen of Watts's powers. [See **English Hymnody, Early**, § XIII.]   [J. J.]

Come, weary souls, with sin distressed. *Anne Steele.* [*Invitation.*] 1st pub. in her *Poems on Subjects chiefly Devotional*, 1760, vol. i. p. 27, in 5 st. of 4 l., and entitled, "Weary souls invited to rest" (2nd ed., vol. i. p. 27); and in Sedgwick's reprint of her *Hymns*, 1863. It is in extensive use both in G. Britain and America, and sometimes with "*sins*" for "sin" in the opening line. It was introduced into the Nonconformist hymnals through the Bristol *Coll.*, 1769, of Ash & Evans, and into those of the Church of England by *Conyers*, 1772, and *Toplady*, 1776.   [J. J.]

Come, ye followers of the Lord. *C. Wesley.* [*Prayer.*] One of six hymns which were 1st pub. in 1745, at the end of a Tract entitled, *A Short View of the Difference between the Moravian Brethren lately in England, and the Rev. Mr. John & Charles Wesley.* It was also given in *Hys. & S. Poems*, 1749, vol. ii., No. 28, in 6 st. of 8 l. When included in the *Wes. H. Bk.*, 1780, No 286, the last stanza was omitted. In this form it is found in several collections. Orig. text in *P. Works*, 1868–72, vol. v. p. 177.   [J. J.]

Come, ye lofty, come ye lowly. *A. T. Gurney.* [*Christmas.*] 1st printed as a "Christmas Hymn" in 1852 in the *Penny Post*, vol. ii. p. 321, in 5 st. of 8 l. In 1856 it was included in the author's *Songs of Early Summer*, p. 178, and in 1862 in his work, *A Book of Praise.* It has also been given in the *Lyra Messianica*, 1864, in the carol collections of Chope, Stainer & Bramley, and others, and in several American hymn-books, including Dr. Hatfield's *Church H. Bk.*, 1872, and others.   [W. T. B.]

Come, ye saints, and raise an anthem. *Job Hupton.* [*Praise to Christ.*] This hymn was 1st pub. in the *Gospel Magazine*, Sept. 1805, in 13 st. of 6 l., and entitled, "An Hymn of Praise to the Redeemer." It is signed "Ebenezer," and dated "A–y, June 1, 1805." A reprint was pub. by D. Sedgwick in his ed. of Hupton's *Hys. & Spiritual Poems*, &c., 1861.

In the *Christian Remembrancer*, July 1863 (vol. xlvi. pp. 117–18), Dr. Neale gave, in an article on "Hymns and Hymnals," a revised version of st. 1, 2, 4, 5, 8, 9, 10, and 12, as an illustration of the possibility of producing a hymn of merit out of somewhat crude materials. The first stanza by Hupton, and by Neale, will illustrate the way in which the latter suggested this might be accomplished.

  1. *Stanza i., by Job Hupton :*—
    " Come, ye saints, and raise an anthem,
      Cleave the skies with shouts of praise,
      Sing to Him who found a ransom,
      Th' Ancient of eternal days,—
        In your nature,
      Born to suffer in your place."

  2. *Stanza i., by Dr. Neale :*—
    " Come, ye faithful, raise the anthem,
      Cleave the sky with shouts of praise ;
      Sing to Him who found a ransom,
      Ancient of eternal days :
      God Eternal, Word Incarnate,
      Whom the Heaven of heaven obeys."

Job Hupton's text is unknown to the hymnals, but Dr. Neale's has come into somewhat extensive use. The text of the latter is in the *People's H.*, 1867, No. 476, with the reading of st. iii. ll. 3–4 as :—

  " With the ceaseless alleluias
    Which they raise, the sons of light,"

and not as in the *Christ. Remb.* The liberties taken by Dr. Neale with Hupton's text have been followed by others in dealing with his, *Church Hys.* being specially prominent in this respect. In fact no text can be relied upon until verified by a reference to the *Christian Remembrancer*, or the *People's H.*, with the corrections noted above.   [J. J.]

Come, ye saints, look here and wonder. *T. Kelly.* [*Easter.*] 1st pub. in 3rd ed. of his *Hymns*, &c., 1809, No. xvii., in 3 st. of 6 l., and based upon Mark xvi. 6, "Behold the place where they laid Him." It was repeated in his *Hys. adapted for Social Worship*, Dublin, 1812, No. xxvii. For the 1812 work the text was slightly altered in each stanza, and these alterations, with

one exception, noted below, were subsequently adopted as the authorized text. It is given in Snepp's *Songs of G. & G.*, No. 256, with "*blessed* regions" for *happy* regions, in st. iii., l. 3 ; "*blessed* regions" is the original reading, and was restored to the text by the author. It is in somewhat extensive use. In Boardman's *Sel. of Hys.*, Philadelphia, 1860, it is given as "Come, ye saints, draw nigh and wonder ;" and in the *H. Bk. of the Evang. Association*, Cleveland, Ohio, 1882, as "Come, ye saints, behold and wonder."   [J. J.]

Come, ye sinners poor and wretched. *J. Hart.* [*Invitation.*] 1st pub. in his *Hys. Composed on Various Subjects*, 1759, No. 118, in 7 st. of 6 l., and headed "Come, and welcome, to Jesus Christ." One of the first to adopt it was R. Conyers in his *Coll.*, 1774, with various alterations, and the omission of st. iv. *Toplady*, followed in 1776 with further alterations. Both versions were repeated in some hymnals, and again altered in others, until the altered forms of the hymn number over twenty. *Conyers* and *Toplady* are answerable for most of the popular changes in the text. The alterations are too many to enumerate. Orig. text in *Lyra Brit.*, 1867, p. 275. In addition to changes in lines of the other than the first, that line has been altered to (1) "Come, ye sinners heavy laden," in the *Bap. Praise Bk.*, N. Y., 1871 ; (2) "Come, ye sinners sad and weary," in the *Canterbury Hymnal*, 1863 ; (3) "Come to Jesus, O my brothers," in Longfellow and Johnson's *Bk. of Hymns*, 1846 ; and (4) "Come ye weary, heavy laden," in Hatfield's *Church H. Bk.*, 1872, and others.   [J. J.]

Come, ye thankful people, come. *H. Alford.* [*Harvest.*] 1st pub. in his *Ps. and Hymns*, 1844, No. 116, and subsequently, after revision, in his *Poetical Works*, 1865, and his *Year of Praise*, 1867, in 7 st. of 8 l. In 1861 the compilers of *H. A. & M.* included an altered version in that Collection. This was repudiated by the author, but still retained by the compilers of *H. A. & M.*, with an explanatory note in the Preface in some of the subsequent editions. The revised text in Alford's *P. Works*, 1865, is the authorized text, and that usually given in modern hymnals. This hymn has attained a greater popularity and more extensive use, both in Great Britain and America, than any other of the author's hymns.   [J. J.]

Come, ye weary sinners, come. *C. Wesley.* [*Invitation.*] 1st pub. in his *Hys. for those that seek, and those that have Redemption*, &c., 1747, in 4 st. of 8 l. (*P. Works*, 1868–72, vol. iv. p. 220). With slight alterations, and the omission of st. iii., it was included in the *Wes. H. Bk.*, 1780, No. 28, and has been retained in all later editions. This is also the text usually given in other collections, both in G. Britain and America. In the Meth. Episco. *Hymns*, 1849, and the New *Hymnal* of the same body, 1878, the hymn "Come, weary sinners, come," is a cento from this hymn. It was made by the Committee of the 1849 book. The original 8 of 7 is turned into s. m.   [J. J.]

Come ye yourselves apart and rest awhile, Weary, I know it, &c. *Bp. E. H. Bickersteth.* [*Ordination.*] 1st printed in a small collection of the author's original hymns under the title of *Songs in the House of Pilgrimage*, N.D. [1872]; and also included, unaltered, in the author's *H. Comp.*, 1876.

Command Thy blessing from above. *J. Montgomery.* [*Divine Worship.*] Written for the Sheffield Sunday S. Union, Whitsuntide gathering, June 3, 1816, and printed for that occasion, and in the *Evang. Mag.*, Sept., 1816, p. 372. In 1819 it was included in *Cotterill's Sel.*, No. 13, in 5 st. of 4 l., and there entitled "For God's blessing on His assembled people." In 1825 it was republished, with alterations, by Montgomery, in his *Christ. Psalmist*, No. 470, and again with the same text in his *Original Hymns*, 1853, No. 99. The arrangement, however, in C. U. are various, some following *Cotterill's* text, as in *Hy. Comp.*, from Bickersteth's *Christ. Psalmody*, 1833, others the revised text of 1825 and 1853, and others, as in *N. Cong.*, a mixture of the two. The American use also varies in like manner. [J. J.]

Communio, a liturgical term for the antiphon which was originally sung during the communion of the people in the Roman Rite, but which now the priest says after the ablutions at the Epistle side of the altar. It usually consisted of a verse of Holy Scripture, but the following instances of metrical Communions in the shape of short hymns are found in the *Sarum Missal*. No. 3 occurs also in the *York* and *Hereford*, and No. 4 in the *York Missal*.

1. De cruce depositum
    Videns corpus Christi
Moesta mater lacrymas
    Atque vultu tristi
Dixit; O dulcissime
    Fili quid fecisti
Quod has poenas asperas
    Et mortem subiisti?
                Compassion of B. V. M.

2. O Gabriel, refove flebiles,
Aegros sana, conforta flebiles,
Fac nos mites semper et humiles,
Et in fide fortes et stabiles.   *St. Gabriel.*

3. Per lignum servi facti sumus
Et per sanctam crucem liberati sumus
Fructus arboris seduxit nos
Filius Dei redemit nos.   *Holy Cross.*

4. Vera fides Geniti purgavit crimina mundi,
Et tibi virginitas inviolata manet.
Nativity of B. V. M., and of B. V. M. in Easter Tide.
                          [F. E. W.]

Communion of my Saviour's blood. *J. Montgomery.* [*Holy Communion.*] Appeared in his *Christian Psalmist*, 1825, No. 511, in 6 st. of 4 l., and entitled, "The Lord's Supper," and again, without alteration, in his *Original Hymns*, 1853, No. 130. It is not in extensive use in its original form, but altered, and beginning with st. ii., as, "To feed on Christ, the living bread," it is given in *Kennedy*, 1863, in 2 st. of 8 l., the doxology which closes the 2nd st. not being in the original. [J.J.]

Compston, John, second s. of the Rev. Samuel Compston, was b. at Smallbridge, Rochdale, Jan. 9, 1828. He became minister of the Baptist Church, Inskip, near Pres-

ton, in 1852, was subsequently pastor of churches at Bramley, near Leeds; Barnsley; and York Road, Leeds. In 1878 he removed into Somersetshire, to become pastor of the united Baptist churches of Fivehead and Isle Abbots, near Taunton. In 1880 he organized and became Secretary to the Taunton District Psalmody Union.

Mr. Compston pub. (1) *Lancashire S. School Songs*, 1853 (14th thousand, 1857), afterwards incorporated in the larger school hymn-book, entitled (2) *Sacred Songs for Home and School*, 1860, of which Rev. J. Lees was co-editor; (3) *Popular Sacred Harmonies*, 1863. Mr. Compston, however, is best known in connection with Temperance hymnody. In 1870 he edited (4) The *National Temperance Harmonist*, and in 1881 the (5) *National Temperance Hymnal*, a new and greatly improved ed. of the former work. It contains nearly 500 temperance hymns and songs set to appropriate music. Twenty of these hymns are by Mr. Compston.

Mr. Compston is also the author of several pamphlets written in connection with the temperance and other philanthropic movements. [W. R. S.]

Concinat orbis cunctus, Alleluya. [*Easter.*] This Sequence of unknown authorship is in the Bodleian MS. 775, f. 185, b. (written between 994 and 1017) and is given in the *Hereford Missal* for Tuesday, and in the *York* and *Sarum Missals* for Wednesday, in Easter week, and may be found in the reprints of those works. *Tr.* as:—

1. **Let the whole world chant and sing,** by E. H. Plumptre, written for and 1st pub. in the *Hymnary*, 1872. It was reprinted in Dean Plumptre's *Things New and Old*, 1884.

2. **Alleluia, let the nations,** by C. S. Calverley, written for and 1st pub. in the *Hymnary*, 1872.

Translation not in C. U.:—
Let all the world with prayer and praise. C. B. Pearson in *Sarum Sequences*, 1871.   [J. J.]

Concionator. One of A. M. Toplady's signatures in the *Gospel Magazine*.

Conder, Eustace Rogers, M.A., D.D., s. of Josiah Conder, b. April 5, 1820, near St. Albans. He studied at Spring Hill College, Birmingham; took his M.A. degree, with gold medal, in Philosophy, in the University of London, in 1844, and settled at Poole, Dorset, as Pastor of the Congregational Church there. In 1861 he removed to Leeds, as Minister of East Parade Chapel. In 1882 he received the degree of D.D. from Edinburgh University. The following hymns by Dr. Conder are in the Leeds *S. S. H. Bk.*, 1862–1878:—

1. Oh, bright are the mansions. *The Home of the Children of God.*
2. Where is the Land of cloudless day? *Jesus the Way to Heaven.*

Dr. Conder's *Heart Chords* were printed for private circulation in 1874.   [J. J.]

Conder, George William, only s. of George Conder, was b. at Hitchin, Herts, Nov. 30, 1821. After studying at Highbury College, London, he became, in 1845, co-pastor, with Mr. Judson, of High Wycombe Congregational Church. In 1849 he succeeded the late Dr. Winter Hamilton as minister of Belgrave Chapel, Leeds, passing thence to Cheetham Hill, Manchester, in 1864; and Queen's Road, Forest Hill, London, 1870. He d. at Forest Hill, Nov. 8, 1874. Whilst at Leeds he assisted in compiling the *Leeds H. Bk.*, 1853. He also pub. in 1874 an *Appendix* to that selection to which he contributed "All things praise Thee, Lord most high," and "Lord Jesus, Shepherd of mankind." [J. M.]

Conder, Joan Elizabeth, née Thomas, the wife of Josiah Conder, was the daughter of Roger Thomas, and granddaughter of the sculptor, L. F. Roubiliac, b. April 6, 1785, d. Jan. 22, 1877. Mrs. Conder contributed poems to *The Associate Minstrels*, 1810, under the signature "E."; to her husband's work, *The Star in the East*, 1824, anonymously; to the *Cong. H. Bk.*, 1836, in her own name; and to *The Choir and Oratory*, 1837, with an asterisk. Of these, seven were given in Conder's *Hys. of Praise, Prayer and Devout Meditation*, 1856. Of these the following appeared in the *Cong. H. Bk.*, 1836, and through that work have come into C. U.:—

1. The hours of evening close. *Saturday Evening.*
2. When Mary to the Heavenly Guest. *Mary anointing the feet of Jesus.*
3. What blissful harmonies above. *The heavenly choir.*
4. Not Thy garment's hem alone. *Desiring Pardon.* This last is the most popular of her hymns. The tune *St. Faith's* was composed for it by Mr. Beale, and pub. in *The Psalmist*, 1842. [F. J. F.]

Conder, Josiah, fourth s. of Thomas Conder, engraver and bookseller, and grandson of the Rev. John Conder, D.D., first Theological Tutor of Homerton College, was b. in Falcon Street (City), London, Sept. 17, 1789, and d. Dec. 27, 1855. As author, editor and publisher he was widely known. For some years he was the proprietor and editor of the *Eclectic Review*, and also editor of the *Patriot* newspaper. His prose works were numerous, and include:—

The Modern Traveller, 1830; *Italy*, 1831; *Dictionary of Ancient and Modern Geography*, 1834; *Life of Bunyan*, 1835; *Protestant Nonconformity*, 1818–19; *The Law of the Sabbath*, 1830; *Epistle to the Hebrews* (a translation), 1834; *Literary History of the New Testament*, 1845, *Harmony of History with Prophecy*, 1849, and others.

His poetical works are :—

(1) *The Withered Oak*, 1805; this appeared in the *Athenæum.* (2) *The Reverie*, 1811. (3) *The Star in the East*, 1824. (4) *Sacred Poems, Domestic Poems, and Miscellaneous Poems*, 1824. (5) *The Choir and the Oratory; or, Praise and Prayer*, 1837. Preface dated Nov. 8, 1836. (6) *Hymns of Praise, Prayer, and Devout Meditation*, 1856. This last work was in the press at the time of his death, and was revised and published by his son, the Rev. E. R. Conder, M.A. He also contributed many pieces to the magazines and to the *Associated Minstrels*, 1810, under the signature of "C." In 1838, selections from *The Choir and Oratory* were published with music by Edgar Sanderson, as *Harmonia Sacra.* A second volume was added in 1839. To Dr. Collyer's (q.v.) *Hymns*, &c., he contributed 3 pieces signed "C."; and to Dr. Leifchild's *Original Hymns*, 1843, 8 hymns.

As a hymn-book editor he was also well known. In 1836 he edited *The Congregational Hymn Book: a Supplement to Dr. Watts's Psalms and Hymns* (2nd ed. 1844). To this collection he contributed fifty-six of his own hymns, some of which had previously appeared in *The Star in the East*, &c. He also published in 1851 a revised edition of Dr. Watts's *Psalms and Hymns*, and in the same year a special paper on Dr. Watts as *The*

Poet of the Sanctuary, which was read before the Congregational Union at Southampton. The value of his work as Editor of the *Congregational Hymn Book* is seen in the fact that eight out of every ten of the hymns in that collection are still in use either in G. Britain or America.

As a hymn writer Conder ranks with some of the best of the first half of the present century. His finest hymns are marked by much elevation of thought expressed in language combining both force and beauty. They generally excel in unity, and in some the gradual unfolding of the leading idea is masterly. The outcome of a deeply spiritual mind, they deal chiefly with the enduring elements of religion. Their variety in metre, in style, and in treatment saves them from the monotonous mannerism which mars the work of many hymn writers. Their theology, though decidedly Evangelical, is yet of a broad and liberal kind. Doubtless Conder's intercourse with many phases of theological thought as Editor of the *Eclectic Review* did much to produce this catholicity, which was strikingly shewn by his embodying many of the collects of the *Book of Common Prayer*, rendered into verse, in his *Choir and Oratory.* Of his versions of the Psalms the most popular are "How honoured, how dear" (84th), and "O be joyful in the Lord" (100th). His hymns in most extensive use are, "Bread of heaven, on Thee I feed;" "Beyond, beyond that boundless sea;" "The Lord is King, lift up thy voice" (this last is one of his best); "Day by day the manna fell;" "How shall I follow him I serve;" "Heavenly Father, to whose eye" (all good specimens of his subdued and pathetic style); and "O shew me not my Saviour dying." This last is full of lyric feeling, and expresses the too often forgotten fact that the Church has a living though once crucified Lord.

The popularity of Conder's hymns may be gathered from the fact that at the present time more of them are in C. U. in G. Britain and America than those of any other writer of the Congregational body, Watts and Doddridge alone excepted. [W. G. H.]

In addition to the hymns named above and others which are annotated under their respective first lines, the following, including two already named (4, 16), are also in C. U.:—

i. From Dr. Collyer's *Hymns*, &c., 1812.

1. When in the hours of lonely woe. *Lent.*

ii. From *The Star in the East*, &c., 1824.

2. Be merciful, O God of grace. *Ps. lxvii.*
3. For ever will I bless the Lord. *Ps. xxxiv.*
4. How honoured, how dear. *Ps. lxxxiv.*
5. Now with angels round the throne. *Doxology.*
6. O Thou God, Who hearest prayer. *Lent.* Dated Sept. 1820. Usually abbreviated.

iii. From *The Congregational Hymn Book*, 1836.

7. Blessed be God, He is not strict. *Longsuffering of God.*
8. Followers of Christ of every name. *Communion of Saints.*
9. Grant me, heavenly Lord, to feel. *Zeal in Missions desired.*
10. Grant, O Saviour, to our prayers. *Collect 5th S. after Trinity.*
11. Head of the Church, our risen Lord. *Church Meetings.*

12. Holy, holy, holy Lord, in the highest heaven, &c. *Praise to the Father.*

13. Jehovah's praise sublime. *Praise.*

14. Leave us not comfortless. *H. Communion.*

15. Lord, for Thy Name's sake ! such the plea. *In National Danger.*

16. O be joyful in the Lord. *Ps. c.*

17. O breathe upon this languid frame. *Baptism of Holy Spirit desired.*

18. O give thanks to Him Who made. *Thanksgiving for Daily Mercies.*

19. O God, Protector of the lowly. *New Year.*

20. O God, to whom the happy dead. *Burial.*

21. O God, Who didst an equal mate. *Holy Matrimony.*

22. O God, Who didst Thy will unfold. *Holy Scriptures.*

23. O God, Who dost Thy sovereign might. *Prayer Meetings.*

24. O how shall feeble flesh and blood, *Salvation through Christ.*

25. O how should those be clean who bear. *Purity desired for God's Ministers.*

26. O say not, think not in thy heart. *Pressing Onward.*

27. O Thou divine High Priest. *Holy Communion.*

28. O Thou Who givest all their food. *Harvest.*

29. O Thou Whose covenant is sure. *Holy Baptism.*

30. Praise on Thee, in Zion-gates. *Sunday.*

31. Praise the God of all creation. *Doxology.*

32. See the ransomed millions stand. *Praise to Christ.*

33. The heavens declare His glory. *Ps. xix.*

34. Thou art the Everlasting Word. *Praise to Christ.*

05. Thy hands have made and fashioned me. *Thanks for Daily Mercies.*

36. To all Thy faithful people, Lord. *For Pardon.*

37. To His own world He came. *Ascension.*

38. To our God loud praises give. *Ps. cxxxvi.*

39. Upon a world of guilt and night. *Purification of B. V. M.*

40. Welcome, welcome, sinner, hear. *Invitation to Christ.*

41. Wheresoever two or three. *Continued Presence of Christ desired.*

iv. From *The Choir and the Oratory*, 1837.

42. Baptised into our Saviour's death. *Holy Baptism.*

43. In the day of my [thy] distress. *Ps. xx.*

44. O comfort to the dreary. *Christ the Comforter.*

v. From Leifchild's *Original Hymns*, 1843.

45. I am Thy workmanship, O Lord. *God the Maker and Guardian.*

46. O Lord, hadst Thou been here ! But when. *The Resurrection of Lazarus.*

47. 'Tis not that I did choose Thee. *Chosen of God.* This is altered in the *Church Praise Bk.*, N. Y., 1882, to " Lord, 'tis not that I did choose Thee," thereby changing the metre from 7.6 to 8.5.

vi. From *Hymns of Praise, Prayer*, &c., 1856.

48. Comrades of the heavenly calling. *The Christian race.*

When to these 48 hymns those annotated under their respective first lines are added, Conder's hymns in C. U. number about 60 in all.   [J. J.]

Conditor [Creator] alme siderum.

[*Advent.*] This hymn is sometimes ascribed to St. Ambrose, but on insufficient evidence. It was rejected as such by the Benedictine editors; and with this the best authorities agree. It is known in various forms, the more important being the following :—

1. The text as in *Daniel*, i., No. 72, in 6 st. of 4 l., and the doxology. This text, when corrected by readings given in his vol. iv. p. 118, and 368, from a MS. of the 9th cent. at Bern ; another of the 10th cent. at Munich, and others of the 10th and 11th cent. respectively, which belonged to the Abbey of Rheinau, is the oldest known.

2. In *The Latin Hys. of the Anglo-Saxon Church*, pub. by the Surtees Soc., 1851, p. 34, from an 11th cent. MS. at Durham. It is also in three MSS. of the 11th cent. in the *Brit. Mus.* (Vesp. D. xii. f. 276 ; Harl. 2961, f. 225 ; Jul. A. vi. f. 31).

3. The *Sarum Brev.* text, in *Hymn. Sarisb.*, 1851, with readings from the *York, Canterbury, St. Albans, Worcester*, and other English Breviaries

4. The revised form of the hymn in the *Rom. Brev.*, 1632, in *Daniel*, i., No. 72 ; *Wackernagel*, 1841, p. 604 ; Card. Newman's *Hymni Ecclesiae*, 1838 and 1865, and other collections.

5. *Mone's* text, No. 34, is from the Cistercian Breviaries specially a MS. of the 14th cent., formerly belonging to the Cistercian Nunnery of Lichtenthal. This text *Mone* considers as the original. *Daniel*, in iv. pp. 118 and 369, gives a summary of the evidence respecting this question of original text, and shows, that no MS. earlier than the foundation of the Cistercian Order appears to contain this text ; whereas the ordinary version is found in a MS. at Bern of the 9th cent.

6. In the *Sarum Brev.* it is appointed as the Vesper hymn on the Saturday before the 1st Sun. in Advent, and throughout Advent on Sundays and week-days when no festival occurs. In the *Rom. Brev.* it is the Vesper hymn in Advent on Sundays, and whenever the Ferial Office is said ; beginning with the Saturday preceding the 1st Sunday in Advent.

7. A cento composed partly from the *Rom. Brev.* version of this hymn is given for first and second Vespers on the feast of the Most Holy Redeemer (3rd Sun. in July) in the *Appendix* to the *Rom. Brev.* It consists of lines 1–4, 9–16 ; then a special stanza of 4 l. followed by lines 17–20 and a doxology. The Office in which this cento is found was first authorized for use in the Venetian territories. The origin of the Festival for which it was compiled is as follows :—The people of the city of Venice, when suffering from the effects of a plague which swept off a great number of the inhabitants and caused great terror, made a vow that if God would grant relief a church should be built by public subscription, dedicated to the *Most Holy Redeemer*, and a yearly visit paid to it in state by the magistracy of the city In 1576 the plague ceased, and the church of *Il Santissimo Redemptore* was built ; the annual act of homage being fixed for the third Sunday in July. The Government of the Venetian Republic obtained permission (when the devotion had greatly extended itself after many years of perseverance), on the 25th of April, 1722, from the Sacred Congregation of Rites, at Rome, that the Office of the Most Holy Redeemer should be said by all the clergy of the city of Venice with the rank of a *Lesser Double* ; in 1724 this licence was extended to the whole Venetian territory ; in 1729 the Feast was made a *Greater Double* ; in 1731 a *Double of the Second Class* ; finally, in 1737, an Octave was added.   [W. A. S.]

Of the various forms of this hymn the translators have usually confined themselves either to the *Sarum* or the *Rom. Brev.* The results are as follows :—

Translations in C. U. :—

i. *The Sarum Brev. Text : Conditor alme siderum.*

1. **Creator of the stars of night**, by J. M. Neale, in the 1st ed. of the *Hymnal N.*, 1852, No. 10, in 6 st. of 4 l. This is repeated without alteration in later editions of the *Hymnal N.* ; in Skinner's *Daily Hymnal*, 1864 ; in the *Hymner*, 1882, and others. It is also given as " Creator of the starry height, Thy people's," &c., in *H. A. & M.*, 1861 (the alterations being by the compilers, who had printed another arrangement of the text in their trial copy of 1859), and Allon's *Supplemental Hys.*, 1868, &c. In *Mercer*, Oxford ed., 1864, it is rewritten by Mercer. Another rendering, slightly altered, from the *Hymnal N.* is, " Creator of the starry height, Of faithful hearts," &c., in the *Hymnary*, 1872.

2. **Creator of the starry height**, by F. Pott, in his *Hymns*, &c., 1861. This is based upon Dr. Neale, and the *H. A. & M.*, revised text as above. It is repeated in *Church Hys.*, 1871.

3. **Creator of the starry height, The faithful, &c.**, by R. F. Littledale, in the *People's H.*, 1867, and signed " F."

4. In addition to the foregoing, other arrangements are given in *Chope, Thring*, and others. That in *Thring* is the most complicated of all. In it *Dr. Neale, H. A. & M.*, the *Rev. F. Pott*, the *Hymnary, Chope, Mr. Thring*, and others, are represented. The result is good.

Translations not in C. U. :—

1. Thou, who didst plant in time gone by. *Hymnarium Anglicanum.* 1844.
2. Kind Framer of the firmament. *W. J. Blew.* 1851.
3. Thou Framer of the starry heaven (with the stanza bracketed by *Daniel* as probably an interpolation into the hymn). *J. D. Chambers.* 1857.
4. Lord, who the stars of night. *J. W. Hewett.* 1859.
5. Fair Framer of the stars so bright. Dr. Edersheim's *Jubilee Rhythm,* &c. 1867.
6. Thou, who didst build the starry sky. *H. M. Macgill.* 1876.
7. Thou Builder of the starry skies. *J. A. Aylward.*
8. O Thou the Maker of each star. *Lord Braye.*

Nos. 7 and 8 are in Mr. Shipley's *Annus Sanctus,* 1884.

ii. *Roman Brev. Text : Creator alme siderum.*

1. **Creator of the starry height, Of hearts believing, &c.,** by W. J. Copeland, in his *Hymns for the Week,* &c., 1848, p. 53, in 6 st. of 4 l. This was given, in an altered form, as "Creator of the starry poles," in the *English Hymnal,* 1852, again altered, but nearer to the original *tr.* in Murray's *Hymnal,* 1852 ; and in later eds. of the *English H.* It is also given, without alteration but with the omission of the doxology, in *Lyra Messianica,* 1864.

2. **Creator of the starry frame,** by *E. Caswall,* in his *Lyra Catholica,* 1849, p. 43. This is the *tr.* in C. U. in Roman Catholic collections for schools and missions. It is also given in the *St. John's Hymnal* (Aberdeen), 1870. In his *Hymns and Poems,* 1873, Caswall altered the first stanza to "Dear Maker of the starry skies," and thereby seriously weakened the hymn.

3. **Maker of the starry sphere,** by R. Campbell, in his *Hys. and Anthems,* 1850, p. 42. This was repeated in the Cooke & Denton *Hymnal,* 1853 ; the *Salisbury H. Bk.,* 1857 ; *Kennedy,* 1863 ; *Sarum,* 1868, and other collection.

4. **O blest Creator of the stars,** by E. W. Eddis, in his Irvingite *Hys. for the use of Churches,* 1864.

5. **Blest Framer of the starry height,** by R. C. Singleton, in his *Anglican H. Bk.,* 1868.

Translations not in C. U. :—

1. Creator of the starry frame. *Bp. Doane.* 1824.
2. Creator of yon circles bright. *Bp. Mant.* 1837.
3. O bright Creator of the skies. *J. R. Beste.* 1849.
4. O God, Who mad'st those orbs of light. *F. Trappes.* 1865.
5. O great Creator of the sky. *J. Wallace.* 1874.
6. Great Maker of the glittering stars. *T. J. Potter.*
7. Creator of the stars above. *F. C. Husenbeth.*
8. Creator of the starry pole. *Card. Newman.*
9. The *Primers* of 1604, 1619, 1685, and 1706.

Nos. 6, 7, and 8 are in Mr. Shipley's *Annus Sanctus,* 1884.

[J. J.]

Congregational Hymnody, American. [American Hymnody, § III.]

Congregational Hymnody, English.

1. Notwithstanding the controversy which prevailed in the 17th cent. in the Baptist and Independent denominations as to the lawfulness or otherwise of singing in Divine Worship, the Independents, taken as a whole, were in favour of the practice. The distinction, however, which they, possibly unconsciously, drew between prayer and praise when set forth in prose, or in verse, was clearly marked. A set form in *prose,* either of prayer, as in the prayers and collects of the Book of Common Prayer ; or of praise, as in the *Gloria in Excelsis* and other hymns in the same service book was regarded as an abomination ; but petitions, supplications, praises, and thanksgiving of precisely the same character when given in *verse* were received with pleasure, and used in both public and private worship by all but the most rigid and austere. The rejection of the one set form, that of *prose,* was complete and final ; the growth of the other, that of *verse,* was gradual and enduring.

2. The earlier stages of this growth are given in detail, from the *Psalms and Hymns* of W. Barton, 1644, to those of I. Watts, 1705-1723, in the article on **Early English Hymnody,** § VI.-XIII. By W. Barton, through his *Book of Psalmes in Metre,* 1644, his *Psalms and Hymns,* 1651, and his various *Centuries of Hymns,* culminating in *Six Centuries of Select Hymns,* &c., 1688 [*see* **Barton, W.**] ; by T. Shepherd, by his *Penitential Cries,* 1691 ; by Matthew Henry, by his *Family Hymns,* 1695 ; by *A Collection of Divine Hymns,* 1694, gathered from six different authors, including R. Baxter and J. Mason ; and by minor efforts on the part of others, the way was prepared for the advent and work of Isaac Watts.

3. The value and importance of the hymnological contributions of Isaac Watts to the Christian Church, from the dawn of the 18th century to the present time, cannot be estimated. No collection of hymns in the English language, compiled for general congregational use, save some two or three of an exceptional type, has been published since 1720, without extracts from one or more of his works being embodied therein. In universality of use, Watts is only equalled by C. Wesley. This great result has been attained by a combination of excellences in which poetic power, catholicity of spirit, and simplicity in embodying the vital truths of Christianity in song have stood pre-eminent. His strength—and it was great—and his weaknesses—and they were not few—are set forth in the articles on the **English Psalters,** § XV. ; and on **Early English Hymnody,** § XIII.

4. For some years after the publication of his *Psalms of David* in 1719, Watts's *Psalms and Hymns* (the latter being his *Hymns and Spiritual Songs,* 1707-1709) constituted the hymn-book of the Congregational body. The great wave of religious thought and feeling which swept over the nation as the result of the work of Whitefield and the Wesleys, together with the poetical contributions of the latter, created on the one hand a desire for greater variety in the songs of the Christian life, and on the other partially supplied that want. It was found that Watts, in common with all men, had not the power to produce a complete work ; a work which should be of high and uniform excellence, and should grasp in full the varied and shifting scenes of life. There were depths of passion, despair, and woe which he had not fathomed ; there were heights of ecstatic joy which he had not reached. The broad field of Christian Song he had made his own. To others was left the cultivation of smaller spaces where the concentrated efforts of gifted men would yield rich results.

5. The conviction that Watts could not sing for all men, and had not sung for all time, was not long in dawning upon the members of his own community. The form in which this conviction received practical expression was first given in *Supplements* to Watts, mainly by individual Ministers of the Congregational

body, followed by *Collections* compiled, some by individual editors, and others by Committees sometimes acting on their own responsibility, and at other times under the auspices of the Congregational Union.

6. One of the first to compile a *Supplement* to Watts was Dr. Thomas Gibbons. His work was published in 1769, and followed by a second collection in 1784. The 1st ed. of Rowland Hill's *Coll. of Psalms and Hymns* is dated 1783. It was designed as a complete hymnbook, and was the first in the Congregational body to break away from the *Psalms and Hymns* of Watts. It ran into many editions, but those of a later date are the first edition rearranged with additions. All the hymns are given without any indication of authorship. Hence has arisen the difficulty of identifying the editor's contributions. Rowland Hill's *Coll.* was superseded at Surrey Chapel, by James Sherman's *Coll.* in 1844; and Sherman's *Coll.* by C. Newman Hall's *Christ Church Hymnal*, 1876. George Burder's *Coll. of Hymns*, 1784, was a return to the *Supplement* series. His range was limited, and included, as he puts it, " the respectable names of Doddridge, Newton, Hart, Wesley, Cowper, Toplady, and Cennick." W. Jay of Bath could not break away from Watts, and so in 1797 he published for his own congregation *A Selection of Hymns of Peculiar Metre.* Another *Supplement* followed in 1801. It was edited by Dr. E. Williams and the Rev. James Boden, and published at Doncaster. The authors' names were given in the first edition, but omitted from the second, and subsequently restored. It had a very limited circulation, and is known chiefly through Boden's contributions, and the anonymous " Jerusalem, my happy home." Two years after Williams and Boden, Dr. Wardlaw followed the example set by Rowland Hill, and published his *Selection of Psalms and Hymns* at Glasgow, 1803. John Dobell's *New Selection of more than Seven Hundred Evangelical Hymns* dates from 1806. It was also a *Supplement* to Watts. Its chief value is in its record of authors. In this respect, although very faulty, it was the most complete up to that time. Dr. Collyer's *Hymns partly Collected and partly Original*, 1812, was peculiar and valuable. Its peculiarity lay in the grouping of all the hymns of a given author under his name, beginning with Dryden and ending with himself; and its value in the number of original hymns contributed by Conder, Montgomery, Ann and Jane Taylor, Raffles, McAll, and others; and from the MSS. of H. Kirke White. This *Supplement* was followed in 1813 by another *Collection of Hymns, designed as an Appendix to Dr. Watts*, &c., by Thomas Cloutt, afterwards known as Thomas Russell. It ran into more than twenty editions, but added little or nothing to the treasury of sacred song. Dr. Raffles's *Collection* of 1816, and Dr. A. Reed's, of 1817, contained original hymns by their respective editors. A new departure took place in 1822 by the publication of *A Selection of Hymns for the Use of the Protestant Dissenting Congregations of the Independent Order in Leeds*, and edited by a committee consisting of the Revs. E. Parsons, R. Winter Hamilton, and T.

Scales. As a *Supplement* to Watts it was an improvement on former works. Efforts by others were made, but were too unimportant to be enumerated. The last *Supplement* to Watts of any importance was, curiously enough, the first official hymn-book of the Congregationalists.

7. In accordance with a resolution passed by the Congregational Union in 1833, J. Conder compiled a collection in conjunction with a Committee appointed for the purpose ; and in 1836 this collection was published as *The Congregational Hymn Book.* This collection of 620 hymns was enriched by some original hymns by Montgomery, and although the editor suffered severely from the common weakness of all hymn-writing editors in overestimating the value of his own productions, yet the sterling worth of the book is realized in the fact that eight out of every ten of the hymns therein are still in use in G. Britain or America. In fairness to Conder it must be added that all his hymns were submitted to the Committee, and some as anonymous, and received their approval before incorporation in the book. Dr. J. Campbell's *Comprehensive Hymn Book*, 1841, was M. Wilks's 1798 edition of Whitefield's *Ps. & Hys.* enlarged to 1000 hymns It was a very heavy book, and failed to secure general adoption. Dr. A. Reed's third effort resulted in *The Hymn Book*, 1842, a weak production on the old lines. Dr. Leifchild's *Original Hymns*, 1843, contained 370 hymns, for the most part published for the first time. The Revs. W. M. Bunting, Dr. Collyer, Dr. R. W. Hamilton, Dr. Raffles, J. Montgomery, Mrs. Gilbert, and others, well known to hymnody, failed to impart to the collection either life or popularity. It was a disastrous failure. Ten years afterwards a second Committee at Leeds, consisting of the Revs. H. R. Reynolds, T. Hudswell, G. W. Conder, W. Guest, and W. Morgan, published the well-known *Leeds Hymn Book*, 1853, as *Psalms, Hymns, and Passages of Scripture for Christian Worship.* It followed the conventional lines of most Nonconformist collections. The educated taste displayed in the text, the extension of the area of selection to the hymnological treasures of the Church of England, the Churches in Germany, and the Church of Rome; and the tone of confidence and strength which pervaded the whole book gave to it a literary character before unknown to Congregational hymnody. Its influence was soon felt throughout the whole denomination. Although a private enterprise, it gradually assumed a more than private character, until, in 1859, *The New Congregational Hymn Book*—after gathering from it its choicest treasures, and adding thereto much that was new and valuable—was published with the official imprimatur of the Congregational Union. From that date the older collection rose in historical importance, as it declined in general use. *The New Congregational Hymn Book* is, from the standpoint of the denomination, a good and sound collection. It has more of Watts than any other modern work; but this element, natural to the denomination, is balanced by a good selection from all ages and nations. Its *Supplement*, published in 1874, is very inferior.

The mutilations in the texts, made without any reason on poetical, theological, or ecclesiastical grounds, are very numerous, and are distinguished by extreme poetical weakness and by lack of sympathy with the authors. Taken as a whole, the weakness of the collection is in its size. It is too large to be uniformly excellent. Dr. Parker's *Cavendish Hymnal*, 1864, was a heavy production on the old lines, and a failure. Dr. Allon's *Supplemental Hymns for Public Worship*, 1868–75, is designed to be used with any Congregational hymnbook which may be lacking in hymns by modern writers, and in translations from Greek, Latin, and German. As it presupposes the use at the same time of another book, in which all the well-known hymns of the older writers are found, it claims to be supplemental only to those books. As such it is good, well arranged, and carefully edited. Another work of this kind is the *Appendix to the Leeds Hymn Book of* 1853, by G. W. Conder, published in 1874. It contains 205 hymns as against 341 in Dr. Allon's collection. Through its selection of Psalms and portions of Holy Scripture, pointed for chanting, its Suffrages, Advent Antiphons, and Metrical Litanies, it comes nearer to the modern collections of the Church of England than any other Hymnal or Appendix amongst the Nonconformists.

8. The latest additions to Congregational hymn-books are *The English Hymn Book*, 1874, by R. W. Dale, D.D.; the *Congregational Hymns*, 1884, by W. G. Horder; *The Congregational Psalmist Hymnal*, 1886, by H. Allon, D.D.; and the *Congregational Church Hymnal*, 1887, edited by the Rev. G. S. Barrett, B.A., and published by the Congregational Union.

9. Dr. Dale's work, he tells us in his Preface, "is called *The English Hymn Book* because I have endeavoured, as far as possible, to insert only those hymns which seem to me to be in harmony with the characteristic type of English piety. The religious life of this country, in its healthiest forms, is distinguished by a certain manly simplicity very alien from the sensuous sentimentalism which has been encouraged by some recent hymn-writers; even the pathetic hymns of the Middle Ages, and the noble songs of German Protestantism, do not express very naturally the religious thought and emotion of ordinary Englishmen." A work compiled upon these lines naturally falls back upon the older writers for much of its material, and knows nothing of some of the most popular of modern compositions. Of its 1260 hymns 58 begin with A., and of these there are 26 hymns which are neither in *Horder*, *Allon*, nor the *Congregational Church Hymnal*. These are mainly from Watts, Wesley, Anne Steele, Beddome, Bruce, Deck, Elizabeth Scott, and others amongst the older, and Bonar and Bishop Wordsworth amongst modern writers. The names of these authors of the hymns peculiar to Dr. Dale's book indicate with tolerable clearness what he means by "the characteristic type of English piety"; and "the religious thought and emotion of ordinary Englishmen." The hymns which come under other letters of the alphabet, and which are peculiar to this collection as distinct from *Horder*, *Allon*, and the *Congregational

Church Hymnal*, are mostly by the same writers or others of the same type (T. H. Gill, who is largely represented, being somewhat exceptional), and impart to the collection a clearness like that of crystal, and an uniformity and rigidness almost as cold.

10. Mr. Horder's *Congregational Hymns, A Hymnal for the Free Churches*, has, in addition to 841 metrical hymns, in which about 350 authors and translators are represented, in most cases in an unaltered form, many of the Psalms, together with Passages of Holy Scripture and Ancient Hymns in English prose, pointed for chanting. Its range is beyond anything before attempted by Congregationalists, its contents having been gathered from all ages and nations that could furnish a Christian hymn of a moderate type, and in an English dress. The classification is that usually adopted in Congregational hymn-books, but in greater detail, includes hymns for children, and a special section entitled "The Home Sanctuary," for private use. Taking, as in the case of Dr. Dale, the hymns in A as representative of the whole, there are 41 hymns, of which 7 are peculiar to the book. These are by Bubier, McDonald, Emerson, Whittier, Newton, and one each from the Latin and Greek writers. These names show that, whilst the solid groundwork of recognized Congregational hymnody is the strength and stay of the book (as seen in the 34 hymns under A which are common to *Dale* and others), poetic warmth and cultured expression have been sought after and attained. The tone of the book is bright and buoyant, and its literary standard is exceptionally high.

11. Dr. Allon's *Congregational Psalmist Hymnal* contains 921 hymns arranged in the manner common with Nonconformist collections, and derived principally from the *New Congregational Hymn Book*, 1859; its *Supplement*, 1869; and his own *Supplemental Hymns*, 1868. Of the 49 hymns under A, 7 are peculiar to it as distinct from *Dale, Horder*, and the *Congregational Church Hymnal*. These are by Watts, Deck, Chandler, Hammond, Elizabeth Scott, and two from the German. It maintains more distinctly than any other collection the historical traditions of Congregational hymnody, and is, from the historical standpoint, the representative book of that body. The music by which it is accompanied is excellent.

12. The latest collection is that issued in 1887 by the Congregational Union as the *Congregational Church Hymnal*. It contains nearly 800 hymns, arranged in the usual manner, and edited with great care. Under A there are 41 hymns, of which 14 are peculiar to itself. These are by Robertson, Lynch, Ingelow, Gill, Rev. Francis Pott, Canon Bright, Dean Alford, Prebendary Thring, and others, and two are from the Greek. Whilst retaining all the great hymns which gave character and distinction to the *Leeds Book* of 1853, and the *New Congregational Hymn Book* of 1859, it has thus added thereto valuable contributions, and especially from the hymnody of the Church of England. Through this somewhat extensive admixture of Anglican Hymnody it stands out in marked contrast to *Dale*, with its theological coldness; to *Horder*, with its poetic

warmth and large importation of refined American hymns; and to *Allon*, with its old-fashioned Congregationalism, broadened out into wider sympathies, and rendered additionally attractive by its admirable musical setting. In hymnological accuracy it is equal to either of these collections; its earnest spirituality is very marked; and its musical setting is excellent.

13. The high position which the hymnody of the Congregationalists has taken is due to many causes. The greatest names are Watts, Doddridge, and Conder. A few in the second rank have produced lyrics of great beauty. The third class is very large, their productions are numerous, and their merits uniformly weak. The freedom which enables any one to publish a collection of hymns, and any congregation to adopt it or not, has had much to do in producing this result. For all who could write there were abundant opportunities for publication, and for the pastor who ventured to compile a collection, there was the certainty, except in instances the most rare, of its adoption by his own congregation, and the encouraging possibility that it might be acceptable unto others. Such elements of success, stimulating authors and compilers, from W. Barton, in 1644, to the *Congregational Church Hymnal*, in 1887, could not fail to produce much that is of permanent interest and value.   [J. J.]

Congregational Hymnody, Welsh.
[Welsh Hymnody, § III.]

Congreve, George Thomas, b. at Islington, 1821, and educated for the medical profession, has practised in London for many years. As a Deacon of the Baptist Church, Rye Lane, Peckham, and Superintendent of its Sunday School, he has done much to advance the interests of that body, and to popularise Sunday School work. In the interest of Sunday Schools he published, in 1869:—

Gems of Song for the Sunday School. A Hymn-book adapted for General Use in Schools and Families. Lond., Elliott Stock. To this was added *Gems of Song Music*, 1871.

Of this collection about one million copies have been sold. Mr. Congreve contributed thereto:—

1. Beyond the dark river a land I behold. *Heaven.*
2 For ever beautiful abide. *Heaven.*
3. Hark! what voice the silence breaks. *Invitation.*
4. How sweet [holy] is the Bible, how pure is the light. *Holy Scriptures.*
5. Look back! 'tis time I marked the road. *New Year.*
6. Look to Jesus! yes I may. *Looking to Jesus.*
7. Mark the lilies, frail and fair. *Flower Services.*
8. O Saviour, dear Saviour, remember me now. *Lent.*
9. Shepherd sweet, and fair, and holy. *Prayer to the Good Shepherd.*
10. Sweet Star of ·the morning. *Christ the Morning Star.*
11. There is a throne of matchless grace. *The Throne of Grace.*

Most of these hymns have been repeated in other collections for children. They are elevated in tone and simple and direct in expression; and are specially useful for children's services.   [J. J.]

Conrad of Queinfurt was priest at Steinkirch on the Queiss, near Lauban, Silesia, and d. 1382 at Löwenberg, Silesia. D. G. Corner (see below) says that his tombstone in the St. Francis Chapel of the Cloister

at Löwenberg, bore the epitaph composed by himself:—

"Christe, tuum mimum salvum facias et opimum,
Condidit hic odas has voce lyraque melodas."

After the building had been in use for some time as a military arsenal an examination in this century failed to find any traces of this monument. (See Hoffmann von Fallersleben's *Geschichte des deutschen Kirchenliedes*, Hannover, 1861, p. 78.) He is the author of a hymn or sacred poem, long popular in Silesia:—

Du lentze gut, des jares tiurste quarte. [*Easter.*]
In 5 st. of 17 l. In *Wackernagel*, ii. p. 388; *Hoffmann v. Fallersleben*, p. 78; Kehrein's *Katholische Kirchenlieder*, i., 1859, p. 521; from MSS. of the 15th cent., at Breslau and Leipzig, and from Corner's *Gross Catolisch G. B.*, Nürnberg, 1631. It is *tr.* as "Fair Spring, thou dearest season of the year," by *Miss Winkworth*, 1869, p. 88.   [J. M.]

Consors Paterni luminis. *St. Ambrose.* [*Early Morning.*] This is one of the twelve hymns which the Benedictine editors regarded as undoubtedly the work of St. Ambrose; and it is cited as by St. Ambrose by Hincmar in his treatise, *De unâ et non trinâ Deitate*, 857.

It is found in the *Roman, Sarum, York, Aberdeen, Paris* (1643), and other *Breviaries*. In the *Sarum* use it was the hymn on Tuesday at Matins from the Sunday after the Octave of the Epiphany up to the first Sunday in Lent. *Mone*, i. p. 372, cites it as an 8th cent. MS. at Trier, where it is assigned to Tuesday Nocturns, and this is the use of the *Roman Breviary*. The text, in 3 st. and a doxology, is given by *Daniel*, i., No. 19 (at iv. p. 37 he cites it as in a 10th cent. Rheinau MS.); *Thomasius*, ii. p. 407; Newman's *Hy. Eccl.*, 1838 and 1865, &c. It is also found in three MSS. of the 11th cent. in the British Museum (Vesp. D. xii. f. 15; Jul. A. vi. f. 25; Harl. 2961, f. 222); in two MSS. of the 11th cent. at St. Gall, Nos. 413, 414); in an 11th cent. MS. in Corpus Christi College, Cambridge, No. 391, p. 233; and in the *Lat. Hys. of the Anglo-Saxon Ch.*, Surtees Soc., 1851, p. 18, is printed from an 11th cent. MS. at Durham. [J. M.]

Translations in C. U. :—
1. **Consort of paternal light.** By Bp. Mant, in his *Ancient Hymns*, 1837, p. 8 (ed. 1871, p. 16). This was repeated in *Kennedy*, 1863, No. 1447.
2. **Thou Consort of Thy Father's throne.** By J. D. Chambers, in his *Lauda Syon*, 1857, p. 15. This is given in the *Hymner*, 1882, with alterations, as "O Light of Light, O Dayspring bright."

Translations not in C. U. :—
1. Brightness of the Father's glory. *Bp. Doane*, 1824.
2. O God from God, O Light from Light. *Card. Newman*, 1865.
3. Son from the Father's brightness bright. *Hymnarium Anglicanum*, 1844.
4. Co-equal in Thy Father's Light. *W. J. Copeland*, 1848.
5. Pure Light of Light, eternal day. *E. Caswall*, 1849.
6. One with the Eternal Light. *R. Campbell*, 1850.
7. O Partner of the Father's Light. *R. Thornton*, in his *St. Ambrose: His Life*, &c., 1879. [J. J.]

Constantius, the *nom de plume* of J. Cottle (q.v.).

Cook, Russell Sturgis, b. at New Marlborough, Mass., March 6, 1811, was educated for the Congregational Ministry, and married a daughter of Dr. Cæsar Malan, of Geneva. From 1839 to 1856 he was one of the Secretaries of the American Tract Society. He was the originator of its system of colportage. Subsequently he became Secretary of the New York Sabbath Committee. He also edited the *American Messenger*. He d. at Pleasant Valley, New York, Sept. 4, 1864. His hymn:—

Just as thou art, without one trace. *Invitation.* Was pub. in the *American Messenger*, March, 1850, in 6 st. of 4 l. It was written as a companion hymn to Miss Elliott's "Just as I am, without one plea," and was sent by the author to her. It was soon adopted by editors of American hymn-books, sometimes in an abbreviated form, beginning with st. iii. as, "Burdened with guilt, wouldst thou be blest?" as in the *Sabbath H. Bk.*, 1858. It became known in G. Britain through Lord Selborne's *Bk. of Praise*, 1862. In that collection it was reprinted from an anonymous tract, in which st. ii. and vi. are omitted. This form of the hymn is usually given in the English collections. Full orig. text in Schaff's *Christ in Song*, 1869-70.   [F. M. B.]

Cooke, William, M.A., was b. at Pendlebury, near Manchester, in 1821, and was educated in private schools. In 1839 he went up to Trinity Hall, Cambridge, and took his B.A. degree in 1843, and his M.A. in 1847. Ordained Deacon in 1844, and Priest in 1845, by the Bishop [Blomfield] of London, and having served the Assistant Curacies of Hillingdon, near Uxbridge, and of Myholt and Brantham in Suffolk, he was presented, in 1848, to the Incumbency of St. John's, Charlotte Street, London; in 1850, to the Vicarage of St. Stephen's, Shepherd's Bush; and in 1856, to the Vicarage of Gazeley, Suffolk. In 1850, he was a Select Preacher to the University of Cambridge; and from 1849 to 1857, Examining Chaplain to the Bishop [Graham] of Chester, by whom he was made Honorary Canon of Chester in 1854. In 1868 he was elected a Fellow of the Society of Antiquaries of London. He is the author of *The Power of the Priesthood in Absolution,* in 1863; *Of Ceremonies, Lights and Custom* (a Letter to the Rev. T. W. Perry), and various Sermons. In 1849, he issued a Book of Hymns for the use of the Congregation worshipping at St. John's, Charlotte Street, London; in 1853 was joint editor with the Rev. William Denton of *The Church Hymnal;* and in 1872 was associated with the Rev. Benjamin Webb, Prebendary of St. Paul's, in the editorship of *The Hymnary.* For that collection he translated and composed several hymns, his signature in some cases being "A. C. C.," i.e. "A Canon of Chester." [J. J.]

Cooper, Edward. [Staffordshire Hymnbooks.]

Copeland, William John, B.D., b. at Chigwell, Sept. 1, 1804, and educated at St. Paul's School, and Trinity College, Oxford, graduating B.A. 1829, M.A. 1831, and B.D. 1840. He was a Scholar of his College, and afterwards Fellow and Dean. Taking Holy Orders, he became Curate of Hackney, and of Littlemore, and in 1849 Rector of Farnham, Essex, and Rural Dean of Newport. He was also Chaplain to the Bishop of St. Albans. Died at Farnham, Aug. 25, 1885. Mr. Copeland has published:—

Hymns for the Week, and Hymns for the Seasons. Translated from the Latin. Lond., W. J. Cleaver, 1848. He was also the Editor of Card. Newman's *Sermons.*

These *trs.* are mostly from the Roman Breviary, and preceded those by E. Caswall, pub. in 1849. Although they are not extensively used in their original form, yet they had a marked effect on the text of some later translators, and have contributed much towards the compiling of centos as found in modern hymn-books. Each *tr.* is annotated in this Dictionary under its first Latin line. In 1884 Mr. Copeland printed translations of Bp. Ken's Morning, Evening, and Midnight Hymns, the first lines of each, reading, (1) "Surge anima solis aemula"; (2) "Jam nocte laudo Te Deus"; (3) "Somno Deus nunc excitum."   [J. J.]

Cor arca legem continens. [*Love of Jesus.*] In the *Supplement* to *Pars Aestiva* in the *Roman Breviary*, Bologna, 1827, this hymn (in 6 st. of 4 l.) is found at p. 221 and is assigned to Lauds on the festival of the Sacred Heart (see "Auctor beate saeculi"); the hymn for Vespers being, "En ut superba criminum." Both hymns are also in *Daniel*, ii. p. 360. *Tr.* by E. Caswall in his *Lyra Catholica*, 1849, p. 119, and his *Hys. & Poems*, 1873, as, "Ark of the Covenant! not that." In 1853, st. i., iii., v. were given in *Hys. for the Ch. of Christ*, Boston, No. 378. Other *trs.* are:—

1. Jesus, behind Thy Temple's Veil. *Anon.* in the Marquess of Bute's *Rom. Brev.* in English, 1879, vol. ii. p. 593.

2. O tender Heart, strong ark which doth enshrine. Rosa Mulholland, in Mr. Shipley's *Annus Sanctus*, 1884.   [J. M.]

Cor meum Tibi dedo, Jesu dulcissime. [*Gift of the heart to Jesus.*] The authorship and date of this hymn are unknown. The text, under the heading "Ad Jesum," and in 4 st. of 6 l., is in *Daniel*, vol. ii. p. 370; the *Hymnodia Sacra*, Münster, 1753, p. 152, and the *Psalteriolum cantionum Catholicarum*, Cologne, 1722, p. 50. *Tr.* as—

1. My heart to Thee I give for aye, by R. F. Littledale, contributed to the *Priest's Prayer Book*, 1864, and the *People's H.*, 1867.

2. I give my heart to Thee, by Ray Palmer. Concerning this *tr.*, Dr. Schaff says in his *Christ in Song*, 1869-70, that the Latin text was "freely and happily reproduced by the Rev. Dr. Ray Palmer, for this collection, Aug. 20, 1868. I know of no other English version." Dr. Littledale's *tr.*, however, was pub. some four years before. Dr. Palmer's *tr.* was repeated, with alterations, in the 1869 *Supp.* to the *New Cong.*

3. All my heart to Thee I give, by J. Ellerton. Written June 3, 1874, set to music by Dr. John Naylor, and pub. by him as a sacred song. Lond., Novello, 1874.   [J. J.]

Corpus ave clarum Domini. [*Holy Communion.*] This hymn is given by *Mone*, No. 221, from a MS. at Mainz of the 15th cent. It is in 18 lines, and headed "Oratio metrice composita in elevatione corporis Christi." It is *tr.* as:—

Hail, glorious Body of the Lord, by R. F. Littledale. It was 1st pub. in the *Lyra Eucharistica*, 1863; then in the *Altar Manual*, 1863; and finally, with alterations by Dr. Littledale, in the *People's H.*, 1867.   [J. J.]

Cosin, John, D.D., s. of Giles Cosin, of Norwich, b. at Norwich Nov. 30, 1594; educated at the Free School of that city and Caius College, Cambridge. Taking Holy Orders he became (besides holding minor appointments) Prebendary of Durham Cathedral; Rector of Brancepeth, 1626; Master of Peterhouse, Cambridge, 1634, and Vice-Chancellor of the University and Dean of Peterborough, 1640. He suffered much at the hands of the Puritans; but after the Restoration in 1660, he became Dean and then Bishop of Durham. Died at Westminster, Jan. 15, 1672. His *tr.* of the *Veni Creator Spiritus* (q. v.), "Come, Holy Ghost, our souls inspire," was included in his *Coll. of Private Devotions*, 1627.   [J. J.]

Cosmas, St., The Melodist. (Died circ. A.D. 760.) The second among the Greek ecclesiastical poets. He was adopted by the father of St. John of Damascus, and educated with him by a Sicilian monk also named Cosmas, who had been redeemed from slavery by his adopted father. The two foster-brothers retired together to St. Sabas, and there stimulated, assisted and vied with one another in the composition of hymns. It is not certain whether some of the *Canons*, *Triodia*, and *Idiomela* under the name of Cosmas may not be the work of the elder Cosmas. (For details of works and criticism see **Greek Hymnody**, § xvii. 3.) He was elected Bishop of Maiuma in A.D. 743, and is commemorated in the Greek Calendar on Oct. 14. The story of Cosmas the elder is beautifully told in Milman's *Lat. Christ.*, vol. ii. 364. *Daniel*, vol. iii., gives 12 pieces by him, and Dr. Neale has *tr.* in his *Hys. of the Eastern Church*, 1862, the Canon for Christmas Day, and a cento from that for the Transfiguration. To English readers he is known through the *tr.* of this cento, "The choirs of ransom'd Israel," and its abbreviated form, "In days of old on Sinai."   [H. L. B.]

Coster, George Thomas, was b. in 1835 at Chatham, Kent; studied for the Congregational Ministry at New College, London; ordained in 1859 at Newport, Essex, and has since held pastorates at Barnstaple, Hull, South Norwood, and Whitby. He has pub. (besides many sermons and tracts) *Pastors and People*, 1869; *Allegories*, 1878; *Lorrin and other Poems*, 1859; *The Rhyme of St. Peter's Fall*, 1871, and *Poems and Hymns*, 1882. He has also contributed several poems on Scripture characters (a line in which he excels) to *The Poet's Bible*, and edited, in 1869, *Temperance Melodies and Religious Hymns*. Of his hymns the following are in C. U. :—

1. Dost thou bow beneath the burthen. *Fellowship with God.* This is an imitation of Dr. Neale's "Art thou weary." It is No. 1112 in the 1880 *Supp.* to the Bap. *Ps. and Hys.*
2. From north and south and east and west. *Missions.*
3. Lord of the sea! afar from land. *Sabbath at Sea.*
Nos. 2 and 3 are in Horder's *Congregational Hymns*, 1884.   [W. G. H.]

Cotterill, Jane, née Boak, daughter of Rev. John Boak, and mother of the Right Rev. Henry Cotterill, Bp. of Edinburgh; b. in 1790, married 1811 to the Rev. Joseph Cotterill; died 1825. Mrs. Cotterill contributed to the *Appendix* to the 6th ed. of *Cotterill's Sel.*, 1815, the following hymns:—1. "O! from the world's vile slavery," (*For Holiness*). 2. "O Thou! Who hast at Thy command," (*For Resignation*). These hymns were repeated in Montgomery's *Christian Psalmist*, 1825,

and Mrs. Cotterill's name was appended thereto for the first time. Their use is not extensive. The first, "O ! from the world's," &c., is found in *Kennedy*, 1863, No. 521, as, "From this enslaving world's control," the alterations being by Dr. Kennedy.   [J. J.]

Cotterill, Thomas, M.A., was the son of a woolstapler at Cannock, Staffordshire, where he was b. Dec. 4, 1779. After attending the local boarding-school of the Rev. J. Lomax, he proceeded to the Free School, Birmingham. He graduated at St. John's College, Cambridge (B.A. 1801, M.A. 1805), of which he became a Fellow. Taking Holy Orders, he became Curate of Tutbury in June, 1803 (not 1806, as stated by Miller in *S. & Songs of the Church*). His subsequent charges were the Incumbency of Lane End, Staffordshire, 1808–17, and the Perpetual Curacy of St. Paul's Sheffield, 1817–23. He d. at Sheffield Dec. 29, 1823 (not Jan. 5, 1824, as in the *Gentleman's Magazine*), aged 44. His volume of *Family Prayers* attained to the sixth edition in 1824. As a hymn-writer, Cotterill is less known than as the compiler of a *Selection of Psalms and Hymns* which has had a most marked effect on modern hymnals. The 1st ed. of that *Selection* was pub. in 1810, and the 9th in 1820. All subsequent issues were reprints of the last. The most important ed. is the 8th, 1819. Its value and influence are noted elsewhere (see **England Hymnody, Church of**). To that *Selection* Cotterill contributed at various dates 25 original hymns and versions of individual psalms. These, in common with all the hymns in the *Selection*, are given without author's name. Through the aid, however, of marked copies [in the collections of Brooke and Julian] and of members of Cotterill's family, we are enabled to identify most, if not all, of his original productions. In addition to those which are annotated under their first lines, we have—

i. In his *Sel. of Ps. & Hys. for Public and Private Use, adapted to the Festivals of the Church of England, &c.*, 1st ed., 1810 :—

1. Awake, O sword, the Father cried. *Atonement.*
2. Before Thy throne of grace, O Lord. *Lent.*
3. From Sinai's mount, in might array'd. *The Law and the Gospel.*
4. From Thine all-seeing Spirit, Lord. *Ps.* 139.
5. In all the ways and works of God. *Ps.* 145.
6. Out of the deeps, O Lord, we call. *Ps.* 130.
7. The Lord, who once on Calvary. *The Intercessor.*
This is based on "Where high the heavenly temple stands," q. v.

ii. In the *Appendix* to the 6th ed. of the same *Selection*, Staffordshire, 1815 :—

8. Blessed are they who mourn for sin. *Lent.*
9. Father of mercies, let our songs [way, ways]. *Thanksgiving.*
10. I was alive without the law. *Lent.*
11. Lord of the Sabbath, 'tis Thy day. *Sunday.*

iii. In the 8th ed. of the same, 1819 :—

12. Help us, O Lord, Thy yoke to wear. *Charity Sermons.* This is sometimes given as "Lord, let us learn Thy yoke to wear," as in *Kennedy*, 1863, &c.
13. I love the Lord, for He hath heard. *Ps.* 116.
14. Lo in the East a star appears. *Epiphany.* This in an altered form begins in *Kennedy*, 1863, No. 188, with st. ii., "The ancient sages from afar."
15. Lord, cause Thy face on us to shine. *For Unity.*
16. When Christ, victorious from the grave. *Easter.*
The 9th ed. of the *Selection*, 1820, was practically a new work. It was compiled by Cotterill, but revised by Dr. Harcourt, the Archbishop of York, and was dedicated to him. It was the outcome of the compromise in

the legal proceedings over the 8th ed., 1819. The 8th ed. contained 367 hymns in addition to 128 versions of the Psalms and 6 Doxologies, the 9th only 152. Its full title was *A Selection of Ps. and Hys. for Public Worship*, Lond., T. Cadell, 1820. It may be noted that copies of the 8th ed., 1819, are found with two distinct title-pages. One of these, accompanied with the preface, was for the general public, the second, without the preface, for the use of the congregations of St. James's and St. Paul's, Sheffield.

Of Cotterill's hymns the most popular are, " O'er the realms of pagan darkness," " Let songs of praises fill the sky," and " Jesus exalted far on high," but these are not distinguished by any striking features of excellence. He was more happy in some of his alterations of older hymns, and in the compiling of centos. Many of the readings introduced into the great hymns of the Church first appeared in his *Selection*. The most notable amongst these are, " Rock of Ages," in 3 st., as in *H. A. & M.*, 1861, the *Wes. H. Bk.*, and other collections; " Lo ! He comes with clouds descending ; " and " Great God, what do I see and hear." Cotterill's connection with the Uttoxeter *Ps. & Hys.*, 1805, is given in detail in the article on **Staffordshire Hymn-books**, and his lawsuit over the 8th ed. of his *Sel.*, 1819, in the article on **England Hymnody, Church of.**   [J. J.]

Cottle, Joseph, b. 1770, d. 1853. A native of Bristol, and from 1791 to 1798 a bookseller and publisher. He is best known as the friend of Coleridge and Southey, of whom, in 1837, he pub. *Recollections*, and in 1847 *Reminiscences*. He was the author of numerous works in prose and verse. In 1801 he pub. a *New Version of the Psalms of David*, of which a 2nd edition (privately printed), appeared in 1805. In 1828 he pub. *Hymns and Sacred Lyrics. In Three Parts, by Constantius*. Only a few copies were printed with this title, the greater part of the issue reading " *by Joseph Cottle*," instead of " *by Constantius*." " These Hymns, Psalms and Sacred Lyrics," Cottle says, " are all originals, written progressively through a period of 20 years." Some of them found their way into a few collections, but have little poetic merit, and are now disused.   [W. R. S.]

Cotton, George Edward Lynch, D.D., b. at Chester, Oct. 29, 1813, was the s. of Captain Thomas Cotton, who was killed in action on Nov. 13 in the same year. He was educated at Westminster, and Trinity College, Cambridge, graduating B.A. in 1836. His first appointment was as an assistant master at Rugby. From Rugby he passed to Marlborough as Head Master in 1852. In 1858 he was consecrated Bishop of Calcutta, as successor to Dr. Daniel Wilson. He was drowned, on disembarking from a steamer at Koshtea, Oct. 6, 1866. His hymn, " We thank Thee, Lord, for this fair earth " (q.v.) is deservedly popular.   [W. T. B.]

Cotton, Nathaniel, M.D., born in 1707, and educated for the medical profession at Leyden. Giving his attention more especially to brain diseases, he first assisted a physician, who devoted his attention to the insane, at Dunstable ; and they erected a large Asylum at St. Albans. In 1763 the poet Cowper became one of his patients, and, on his recovery,

conceived a warm attachment for his medical friend. Dr. Cotton d. at St Albans, Aug. 2, 1788. Several of his hymns appeared from 1760 onwards in Dr. Dodd's *Christian's Magazine*, some signed " Dr. Cotton, St. Albans," some " N.," and some without signature. His poetical works were pub. posthumously :— *Various Pieces in Verse and Prose*, 2 vols., Lond., Dodsley, 1791 ; and *Visions in Verse*, &c., with *Memoir*, 1808. His hymns came into use through Collyer's *Coll.*, 1812. They are :—

1. Amid the various scenes of ill. *Affliction Sanctified.* From *Various Pieces*, &c., 1791.
2. Tell me, my soul, O tell me why. *Sin the cause of fear.* From *Various Pieces*, &c., 1791.
3. This is the day the Lord of Life. *Sunday.* From *Various Pieces*, &c., 1791.
4. While sorrow wrings my bleeding heart. *Suffering.* From his version of Ps. xiii., " Offended Majesty, how long ? " in the *Christian's Magazine*, Feb. 1761.
5. With fierce desire the hunted hart. *Ps.* 42.

Dr. Cotton's most widely known hymn is, " Affliction is a stormy deep," q. v. It is a part of No. 5.   [J. J.]

Countess of Huntingdon Connexion. [**Huntingdon Hymnody, Countess of.**]

Cousin, Anne Ross, née Cundell, is the only daughter of David Ross Cundell, M.D., Leith, and is the widow of the Rev. William Cousin, late Minister of the Free Church of Melrose. She has contributed many poems to various periodicals ; 7 hymns to *The Service of Praise*, 1865, edited by the Rev. J. H. Wilson, of Edinburgh ; and 1 to the *Ps. and Hys. for Divine Worship*, 1866, the Hymnal of the English Presbyterian Church. 4 of her hymns are included in the Scottish *Presb. Hymnal*, 1876. Her most popular hymn, " The sands of time are sinking," was first pub. in *The Christian Treasury* for 1857, and gives its title to the collected edition of her poems published in 1876, as *Immanuel's Land and other Pieces by A. R. C.* This is a collection of 107 hymns and poems, many of which are very beautiful. In general they are, however, rather meditations than hymns suited for public worship. Of these the following, in addition to those annotated under their first lines, are in C. U. :—

1. King Eternal, King Immortal. *Christmas.*
2. O Christ, what burdens bowed Thy head. *Good Friday.*
3. To Thee, and to Thy Christ, O God. *Praise.*
4. To thy father and thy mother. *Filial Duty.*

    [J. M.]

Coverdale, Miles, D.D., a celebrated English Divine and Reformer, b. in Yorkshire, 1487, and educated at Cambridge. He was for some time a Canon of the Order of St. Augustine. On embracing the reformed faith, he went abroad, 1528, and associated with Tyndale and various continental Reformers. His translation of the Bible was published in 1535, and the second version of the New Testament, 1538. Returning to England, in 1551 he was promoted to the see of Exeter. On the accession of Mary he went to Denmark, and then to Geneva. At the latter place he assisted his fellow refugees in producing the celebrated Geneva Bible. In 1560, on the accession of Elizabeth, he returned to England, but instead of resuming his see, he accepted the Rectory of St. Magnus, London Bridge. He d. in Feb. 1569, and was buried in St. Bartholomew's church, by the Exchange.

Feb. 19, 1569. For his *Goostly Psalmes*, one of the earliest metrical efforts in the English language, but mainly from the German, see **English Psalters**, § v., and **Goostly Psalms**. [J.J.]

Cowper, William, the poet. The leading events in the life of Cowper are: b. in his father's rectory, Berkhampstead, Nov. 26, 1731; educated at Westminster; called to the Bar, 1754; madness, 1763; residence at Huntingdon, 1765; removal to Olney, 1768; to Weston, 1786; to East Dereham, 1795; death there, April 25, 1800.

The simple life of Cowper, marked chiefly by its innocent recreations and tender friendships, was in reality a tragedy. His mother, whom he commemorated in the exquisite "Lines on her picture," a vivid delineation of his childhood, written in his 60th year, died when he was six years old. At his first school he was profoundly wretched, but happier at Westminster; excelling at cricket and football, and numbering Warren Hastings, Colman, and the future model of his versification, Churchill, among his contemporaries or friends. Destined for the Bar, he was articled to a solicitor, along with Thurlow. During this period he fell in love with his cousin, Theodora Cowper, sister to Lady Hesketh, and wrote love poems to her. The marriage was forbidden by her father, but she never forgot him, and in after years secretly aided his necessities. Fits of melancholy, from which he had suffered in school days, began to increase, as he entered on life, much straitened in means after his father's death. But on the whole, it is the playful, humorous side of him that is most prominent in the nine years after his call to the Bar; spent in the society of Colman, Bonnell Thornton, and Lloyd, and in writing satires for *The Connoisseur* and *St. James's Chronicle* and halfpenny ballads. Then came the awful calamity, which destroyed all hopes of distinction, and made him a sedentary invalid, dependent on his friends. He had been nominated to the Clerkship of the Journals of the House of Lords, but the dread of appearing before them to show his fitness for the appointment overthrew his reason. He attempted his life with "laudanum, knife and cord,"—in the third attempt nearly succeeding. The dark delusion of his life now first showed itself—a belief in his reprobation by God. But for the present, under the wise and Christian treatment of Dr. Cotton (q. v.) at St. Albans, it passed away; and the eight years that followed, of which the two first were spent at Huntingdon (where he formed his lifelong friendship with Mrs. Unwin), and the remainder at Olney in active piety among the poor, and enthusiastic devotions under the guidance of *John Newton* (q. v.), were full of the realisation of God's favour, and the happiest, most lucid period of his life. But the tension of long religious exercises, the nervous excitement of leading at prayer meetings, and the extreme despondence (far more than the Calvinism) of Newton, could scarcely have been a healthy atmosphere for a shy, sensitive spirit, that needed most of all the joyous sunlight of Christianity. A year after his brother's death, madness returned. Under the conviction that it was the command of God, he attempted suicide; and

he then settled down into a belief in stark contradiction to his Calvinistic creed, "that the Lord, *after having renewed him in holiness*, had doomed him to everlasting perdition" (*Southey*). In its darkest form his affliction lasted sixteen months, during which he chiefly resided in J. Newton's house, patiently tended by him and by his devoted nurse, Mrs. Unwin. Gradually he became interested in carpentering, gardening, glazing, and the tendance of some tame hares and other playmates. At the close of 1780, Mrs. Unwin suggested to him some serious poetical work; and the occupation proved so congenial, that his first volume was pub. in 1782. To a gay episode in 1783 (his fascination by the wit of Lady Austen) his greatest poem, *The Task*, and also *John Gilpin* were owing. His other principal work was his *Homer*, pub. in 1791. The dark cloud had greatly lifted from his life when Lady Hesketh's care accomplished his removal to Weston (1786): but the loss of his dear friend William Unwin lowered it again for some months. The five years' illness of Mrs. Unwin, during which his nurse of old became his tenderly-watched patient, deepened the darkness more and more. And her death (1796) brought "fixed despair," of which his last poem, *The Castaway*, is the terrible memorial. Perhaps no more beautiful sentence has been written of him, than the testimony of one, who saw him after death, that with the "composure and calmness" of the face there "mingled, as it were, a holy surprise." Cowper's poetry marks the dawn of the return from the conventionality of Pope to natural expression, and the study of quiet nature. His ambition was higher than this, to be the Bard of Christianity (*Benham*, p. xlvi.). His great poems show no trace of his monomania, and are full of healthy piety. His fame as a poet is less than as a letter-writer: the charm of his letters is unsurpassed. Though the most considerable poet, who has written hymns, he has contributed little to the development of their structure, adopting the traditional modes of his time and Newton's severe canons. The spiritual ideas of the hymns are identical with Newton's: their highest note is peace and thankful contemplation, rather than joy: more than half of them are full of trustful or re-assuring faith: ten of them are either submissive (44), self-reproachful (17, 42, 43), full of sad yearning (1, 34), questioning (9), or dark spiritual conflict (38–40). The specialty of Cowper's handling is a greater plaintiveness, tenderness, and refinement. A study of these hymns as they stood originally under the classified heads of the *Olney Hymns*, 1779, which in some cases probably indicate the aim of Cowper as well as the ultimate arrangement of the book by Newton, shows that one or two hymns were more the history of his conversion, than transcripts of present feelings; and the study of Newton's hymns in the same volume, full of heavy indictment against the sins of his own regenerate life, brings out the peculiar danger of his friendship to the poet: it tends also to modify considerably the conclusions of Southey as to the signs of incipient madness in Cowper's saddest hymns. Cowper's best hymns are given in *The Book of Praise* by Lord Selborne. Two may be selected from them; the exquisitely tender "Hark! my soul, it is the Lord " (q. v.), and "Oh ! for a closer walk with God" (q. v.). Anyone who knows Mrs. Browning's noble lines on Cowper's grave will find even a deeper beauty in the latter, which is a purely English hymn of perfect structure and streamlike cadence, by connecting its sadness and its aspiration not only with the " discord on the music " and the " darkness on the glory," but the rapture of his heavenly waking beneath the " pathetic eyes " of Christ.

Authorities. *Lives*, by Hayley ; Grimshaw ; Southey; Professor Goldwin Smith ; Mr. Benham (attached to *Globe Edition*) ; *Life of Newton*, by Rev. Josiah Bull; and the *Olney Hymns*. The numbers of the hymns quoted refer to the *Olney Hymns*.   [H. L. B.]

Cox, Christopher Christian, M.D., was a Maryland physician, and long prominent in the public service. Born at Baltimore, Aug. 28, 1816, and graduated at Yale College, 1835. He practised medicine in Baltimore, 1838, and in Talbot County, Maryland, 1843. In 1861 he became Brigade Surgeon U. S. A., and resided in Washington. He d. Nov. 25, 1882. He was a member of the Protestant Episcopal Church. His hymns in C. U. are :—

1. **Silently the shades of evening.** *Evening.* Written in 1840 or 1846, and pub. in *Woodworth's Cabinet*, 1847, with music. It is much used in American hymn-books.

2. **The burden of my sins, O Lord.** *Lent.* Appeared in the *Cantate Domino*, Boston, 1859, together with two additional originals and two translations. These hymns are unknown to English collections.   [F. M. B.]

Cox, D. [or R.]   Old Version, § ix. 8.

Cox, Frances Elizabeth, daughter of Mr. George V. Cox, b. at Oxford, is well known as a successful translator of hymns from the German. Her *trs.* were pub. as *Sacred Hymns from the German*, Lond., Pickering. The 1st ed., pub. 1841, contained 49 *trs.* printed with the original text, together with biographical notes on the German authors. In the 2nd ed., 1864, *Hymns from the German*, Lond., Rivingtons, the *trs.* were increased to 56, those of 1841 being revised, and with additional notes. The 56 *trs.* were composed of 27 from the 1st ed. (22 being omitted) and 29 which were new. The best known of her *trs.* are " Jesus lives ! no longer [thy terrors] now " ; and " Who are these like stars appearing ?" A few other *trs.* and original hymns have been contributed by Miss Cox to the magazines; but they have not been gathered together into a volume.   [J. J.]

Coxe, Arthur Cleveland, D.D., LL.D. One of the most distinguished of American prelates, and son of an eminent Presbyterian minister, the Rev. Samuel H. Cox, D.D., was b. at Mendham, New Jersey, May 10, 1818. Graduating at the University of New York in 1838, and taking Holy Orders in 1841, he became Rector of St. John's, Hartford, Connecticut, in the following year. In 1851 he visited England, and on his return was elected Rector of Grace Church, Baltimore, 1854, and Calvary, New York, 1863. His consecration as Bishop of the Western Diocese of New York took place in 1865. His residence is at Buffalo. Bishop Coxe is the author of numerous works. His poetical works were mostly written in early life, and include *Advent*, 1837 ; *Athanasion*, &c., 1842 ; *Christian Ballads*, 1840 (Preface to the English edition, April, 1848); *Hallowe'en and Other Poems*, 1844 ; *Saul, a Mystery*, 1845, &c. Some of Bishop Coxe's hymns are found in the collections of every religous body in America, except the official collections of his own. This is accounted for by his too scrupulous modesty. As a member of the Hymnal Committee, in 1869-71, he refused to permit the insertion of his own lyrics. As he has not preserved memoranda, and has no precise recollection of dates, several dates here given are somewhat uncertain.

1. **Behold an Israelite indeed.** *St. Bartholomew.* First appeared in " Poems," published with his *Christian Ballads*, 1840, and found in an altered form in the *People's H.* the *Hymnary*.

2. **Body of Jesus, O sweet Food.** *Holy Communion.* Written at St. James's College, Maryland (since broken up by the Civil War), Ascension Day, 1858. It was first printed for private use, and then pub. in the *Cantate Domino*, Boston, 1859, No. 53, and again in other American collections. It is also in Schaff's *Christ in Song*, 1869, and in *The Churchman's Altar Manual*, 2nd ed., 1883.

3. **Breath of the Lord, O Spirit blest.** *Whitsuntide.* Bishop Coxe considers this more worthy of being called a hymn than anything else from his pen. It was written long before it appeared in the New York *Independent*, Whitsuntide, 1878. It is in the Schaff-Gilman *Library of Religious Poetry*, 1881, and Brooke's *Churchman's Manual of Private and Family Devotion*, 1883.

4. **Christ is arisen.** *Easter.* This is suggested by, and partly *tr.* from, the famous Easter Chorus in Goethe's *Faust*, " Christ ist erstanden " (see **Goethe**), and appeared in *Hallowe'en*, 1844.

5. **He who for Christ hath left behind.** *St. Matthew.* From his *Christian Ballads*, &c., 1840.

6. **In the silent midnight watches.** *Christ knocking.* From his *Athanasion*, &c., 1842 ; an impressive moral poem rather than a hymn on Christ knocking at the door, extensively used in America, and sometimes in England. Orig. text, Schaff's *Christ in Song*, 1869.

7. **Lord, when Thou didst come from heaven.** A hymn for *Epiphany*, on behalf of Western Missions, appeared among the " Lays " appended to *Hallowe'en*, 1844, and again in later editions of the *Christian Ballads*. It is sometimes abbreviated, as in *Lyra Sac. Amer.*, " Westward, Lord, the world alluring."

8. **Now pray we for our country.** *National Hymn.* A stanza from *Chronicles*, or meditations on events in the history of England, called up by visiting her abbeys and cathedrals, and appeared in *Christian Ballads*, 1840. Originally it began, " Now pray we for our *mother*," and, with the succeeding stanza, was a call upon Americans to pray for their *mother* country. It is adopted by Dr. Martineau in his *Hys.*, 1873.

9. **O walk with God, and thou shalt find.** *Holiness.* Appeared in his *Hallowe'en*, &c., 1844, and is found in *Lyra Sac. Amer.*

10. **O where are kings and empires now ?** *Church of God.* The 6th st. of his ballad "Chelsea," which appeared in the *Churchman,* 1839, and again in his *Christian Ballads,* 1840.

11. **Saviour, sprinkle many nations.** *Missions.* "Begun on Good Friday, 1850, and completed 1851, in the grounds of Magdalen College, Oxford." 1st pub. in *Verses for 1851, in Commemoration of the third Jubilee of the Society for the Propagation of the Gospel,* edited by the Rev. Ernest Hawkins, 1851. It was subsequently appended to the English ed. of his *Christian Ballads.* It is regarded as Biship Coxe's best piece, and to many minds it is the loveliest of missionary hymns. Its use in England is very extensive. It is not found in the American Episcopal hymnal for the reason given above.

12. **Still as our day our strength shall be.** *Temptation.* Appeared in his *Hallowe'en, &c.,* 1844, and *Lyra Sac. Amer.*

13. **Soldier, to the contest pressing.** *Christian Conflict.* From his *Hallowe'en,* &c., 1844, and *Lyra Sac. Amer.* It was written in 1834.

14. **There is a land like Eden fair.** From *Hallowe'en,* &c., into a few collections.

15. **We are living, we are dwelling.** *Christian Soldiers.* An impressive moral poem rather than a hymn, but extensively used. It appeared in his *Athanasion,* &c., 1840, and *Lyra Sac. Amer.*

16. **Who is this, with garments gory.** *Passiontide.* From his "Lays" appended to *Hallowe'en,* 1844, and again in his *Christian Ballads.* It is found in the *Child's Christian Year,* 4th ed. N.D., the *People's Hy.,* and other collections. It is in 4 st. of 8 l. The last stanza is sometimes given as a separate hymn :—"Hail, all hail, Thou Lord of Glory."

17. **When o'er Judea's vales and hills.** Written cir. 1840, and pub. in his *Hallowe'en,* &c., 1844, and again, with the author's final corrections, made in 1869, in Schaff's *Christ in Song* (1870 ed. p. 112). Also in the English edition of his *Christian Ballads.* From this "Hymn to the Redeemer," two shorter hymns have been compiled :—(1) "How beauteous were the marks divine." This is in almost universal American and occasional English use. (2) "O who like Thee, so calm, so bright," in the *Hymnary,* 1872.

Bishop Coxe has also translated the *Pange lingua gloriosi corporis* (q. v.), and is the author of the beautiful Christmas Carol, "Carol, carol, Christians," given in his *Christian Ballads,* &c.   [F. M. B.]

Crabbe, George, LL.B., b. at Aldborough, Suffolk, Dec. 24, 1754, and educated for the medical profession, but after practising for a short time, he turned his attention to literature, and subsequently took Holy Orders. He was successively Curate of Aldborough and of Stathern, and Incumbent of Evershot, Mirston and Trowbridge. Died at Trowbridge, Feb. 3, 1832. He received his degree from the Archbishop of Canterbury. Although well known as a poet, his hymns are very few, and but little known. His works include *The Village ; The Parish Register,* 1807 ; and others. From *The Parish Register,* his hymn, "Pilgrim, burdened with thy sin" (q.v.) is taken. Crabbe's collected *Works* were pub., with a *Memoir,* by his son, in 1834. [J. J.]

Craig, John, was b. in 1512, educated at the University of St. Andrews, and became a Dominican monk. Being suspected of heresy, he went, in 1537, to England, then to France, and finally settled among the Dominicans in Bologna. There, on reading Calvin's *Institutes,* he embraced and taught his views. Being accused of heresy, he was sent to Rome and imprisoned. He was sentenced to be burnt, August 19, 1559, but escaped at the death of Paul IV., on Aug. 18. From Rome he went by Bologna and Milan to Vienna, where he preached before the Emperor Maximilian II., who gave him letters of safe conduct to England. Having returned to Scotland, he became minister of the Canongate (then Holyrood House), Edinburgh, in 1561, and in 1563 joint minister with John Knox of St. Giles's. In 1571 he became minister of Montrose, in 1573 Superintendent of Mar and Buchan, and in 1579 minister of Holyrood and domestic chaplain to James VI. He d. 12th December, 1600.

In the *Scottish Psalter* of 1564–65, there are 15 Psalm versions by him, viz. : Ps. 24, 56, 75, 102, 105, 108, 110, 117, 118, 132, 136, 140, 141, 143, 145; see the first lines under **Scottish Hymnody,** § ii. 2. They are mostly in P.M. and thus only three were repeated in the *Scottish Psalter,* of 1650, considerably altered, as the second versions of Ps. 136, 143, and 145. Craig's best known work is *A shorte summe of the whole Catechisme,* Edinburgh, 1581, reprinted at Edinburgh in 1883, with a careful biographical introduction by T. G. Law. [J. M.]

Cramer, Johann Andreas, b. Jan. 27, 1723, at Jöhstadt or Johann-Georgen-Stadt, in the Saxon Harz, where his father was pastor. After studying at the University of Leipzig, where he graduated M.A. in 1745, he was in 1748 appointed preacher at Crellwitz, near Lützen, and in 1750 Court Preacher and member of the Consistory at Quedlinburg. Four years later he became German Court Preacher to King Frederick V. of Denmark, at Copenhagen. There he obtained great fame as a preacher and teacher; and was appointed in 1765 Professor of Theology in the University. But after the accession of Charles VII., in 1766, the free-thinking party in the State gradually gained the ascendancy, and procured his removal ; whereupon he was appointed, in 1771, Superintendent in Lübeck. When the orthodox party regained power in 1774, he was recalled to Denmark, as Vice-Chancellor, and First Professor of Theology in the University of Kiel, and in 1784 Chancellor. He d. at Kiel on the night of June 11–12, 1788 (*Koch,* vi. 334–344 ; *Allg. Deutsche Biog.,* iv. 550–551 ; *Bode,* pp. 54–55—the last dating his birth, Jan. 29).

Cramer was rather a writer of religious lyrics than of hymns, though at least 80 of his compositions passed into the hymn-books of his times. His Psalm versions are noted under **Psalters, German,** § VI. Those that have been *tr.* into English are all included either in the *Allgemeines G. B.,* Altona, 1780, which he edited for use in Schleswig-Holstein, or in his *Sämmtliche Gedichte,* Leipzig, 1782-3. They are :—

i. **Die ihr des Lebens edle Zeit.** *The duty of the Scholar.* 1780, as above, No. 820, in 12 st., repeated 1782, vol. ii. p. 319. *Tr.* as, "O ye, who from your earliest youth," by *Miss Winkworth,* 1869, p. 321.

ii. **Erheb, erheb, O meine Seele.** *Ps. civ.* In his *Poetische Uebersetzung der Psalmen,* Leipzig, 1763, pt. iii., p. 65, in 16 st. Included, 1780, as above, No. 124. The form *tr.* is that in the *Württemberg G. B.,* 1791, No. 36 (1842, No. 59), beginning with st. ii., "Herr, dir ist niemand zu vergleichen." *Tr.* as, "Lord, none to Thee may be compared," by Miss Burlingham, in the *British Herald*, Jan. 1866, p. 200, repeated in Reid's *Praise Bk.*, 1872, No. 373.

iii. **Erwachet, Harf' und Psalter.** *Morning.* Founded on Ps. cviii. 1st pub. in Zollikofer's *G. B.*, Leipzig, 1766, No. 71, in 6 st. Repeated, 1780, as above, No. 2, and as No. 41 of the hymns appended to his *Evangelische Nachahmungen der Psalmen Davids*, Kopenhagen, 1769, p. 272. *Tr.* by *H. J. Buckoll*, 1842, p. 59, as :—"Wake, harp and psaltery sounding."

iv. **Schuf mich Gott für Augenblicke.** *Immortality of the Soul.* 1780, as above, No. 136, in 12 st., repeated, 1782, vol. i. p. 181. *Tr.* (beginning with st. vi., "Geist ! das ist mein hoher Name"), by *Dr. H. Mills*, 1845, as :—"Man were better nam'd a spirit."

v. **Sterbend für das Heil der Sünder.** *Ascension.* In the *Bayreuth G. B.*, 1779, No. 173, in 4 st. Included, 1780, as above, No. 319, and 1782, vol. ii. p. 33. *Tr.* by *Dr. H. Mills*, 1845, as :—"Dying a guilty world to save."

vi. **Unerforschlich sei mir immer.** *God's Wisdom.* 1st pub. in his *Andachten in Betrachtungen, Gebeten und Liedern*, &c., vol. ii., pt. ii., Schleswig and Leipzig, 1768, and thence in *Rambach*, v. 54. Included in 1769 (see No. iii.), p. 250, and 1780 as above, No. 78. *Tr.* (1) in *Sacred Poems* by S. R. Maxwell, 1857, p. 126, as :— "Though inscrutable may ever" ; (2) by *Dr. G. Walker*, 1860, p. 94, as :—"Inscrutable to me although."
[J. M.]

Crashaw, Richard, s. of the Rev. William Crashaw, was educated at the Charter House and Pembroke Hall, and Peterhouse, Cambridge. Of the latter college he became a Fellow, and distinguished himself both in Latin and English poetry. In common with many others he was ejected from his Fellowship for refusing the Covenant. Entering the Roman Communion he went to Paris, seeking preferment. Failing for a time, he was assisted by Cowley, the poet, in 1646, and by him recommended to Queen Henrietta Maria, who was then residing in Paris. Under her patronage he travelled in Italy, and subsequently became a Canon in the Church of Loreto. Died in 1650. Prior to his leaving England he wrote his *Steps to the Temple*, 1646, in which are given versions of two Psalms ; and subsequently *The Delights of the Muses. Carmen Deo Nostro* was pub. posthumously in 1652. It contained hymns both original and translated. His *Poems* were edited by Turnbull, 1856 ; and by Dr. Grosart in 1869. [**English Psalters,** § x.; **English Hymnody, Early,** § IX.]   [J. J.]

Crasselius, Bartholomäus, son of Johannes Crasselt, sheepmaster at Wernsdorf near Glauchau, Saxony ; was b. at Wernsdorf, Feb. 21,1667. After studying at Halle, under A. H. Francke, he became, in 1701, pastor at Nidda, in Wetteravia, Hesse. In 1708 he was appointed Lutheran pastor at Düsseldorf, where he d. Nov. 10, 1724, after a somewhat troubled pastorate, during which he felt called upon to testify strongly and somewhat bitterly against the shortcomings of the place and of the times (*Koch*, iv. 418–421 ; *Allg. Deutsche Biog.*, iv. 566–67 ; *Bode*, p. 55 ; MS. from Pastor Baltzer, Wernsdorf ; the second dating his call to Düsseldorf 1706). Of the 9 hymns by him which Freylinghausen included in his *Geistreiches G. B.*, 1704, two have been *tr.* :—

i. **Dir, dir, Jehovah, will ich singen.** *Prayer.* A hymn of supplication for the spirit of grace rightly to praise and worship God, founded on St. John, xvi. 23–28, the Gospel for Rogation Sunday. 1st pub. in the *Geistreiches G. B.*, Halle, 1697, p. 587, in 8 st. of 6 l. Repeated as No. 291 in Freylinghausen's *G. B.*, 1704, and since in almost all collections, as in the *Berlin G. L. S.*, ed. 1863, No. 936.

The well-known tune (known in England as *Winchester New* as reduced to L. M. in *H. A. & M.*, No. 50) which appeared with this hymn in *Freylinghausen*, 1704, is altered from a melody to " Wer nur den lieben Gott lässt walten," in the *Musicalisch Handbuch der Geistlichen Melodien*, Hamburg, 1690. See L. Erk's *Choralbuch*, 1863, No. 63, and p. 247 ; also No. 261. The common, but erroneous ascription of this tune to Crasselius arose from confusion between the authorship of the tune and the words. There is no evidence that Crasselius wrote any tunes.

Translations in C. U. :—

1. **Jehovah, let me now adore Thee,** a good and full *tr.* by Miss Winkworth, as No. 117, in her *C. B. for England*, 1863, set to the 1704 melody.

2. **To Thee, O Lord, will I sing praises,** in full, by Dr. M. Loy, in the *Evangelical Review*, Gettysburg, July 1861, and as No. 216 in the Ohio *Luth. Hymnal*, 1880.

Other trs. are :—
(1) " To Thee, Jehovah, I'll be singing," in the *Supp. to Ger. Psalmody*, ed. 1765, p. 41, and in *Select H. from Ger. Psal.*, Tranquebar, 1754, p. 72. (2) " Draw me, O Father, to the Son," a *tr.* of st. ii., by P. H. Molther, as No. 185 in the *Moravian H. Bk.*, 1789. In the ed. of 1886 it is enlarged to 3 st. by the addition of the *tr.* of st. i. and viii., and in this form it begins :—" To Thee, Jehovah, will I sing." (3) " To Thee, O Lord, I come with singing," by Miss Burlingham, in the *British Herald*, April, 1866, p. 248, repeated as No. 402 in Reid's *Praise Bk.*, 1872.

ii. **Erwach, O Mensch, erwache.** *Lent.* Appeared in Freylinghausen's *G. B.*, 1704, No. 266, in 4 st. of 9 l. Included in Bunsen's *Versuch*, 1833, No. 298, and *Allg. G. B.*, 1846, No. 13. *Tr.* as " Awake, O man, and from thee shake," by *Miss Winkworth*, 1855, p. 61.

The hymn, " Heiligster Jesu, Heiligungsquelle," ascribed to Crasselius, is noted under *J. v. Lodenstein*. See also " Hallelujah ! Lob, Preis und Ehr."   [J. M.]

Creamer, David, b. at Baltimore, Nov. 20, 1812. He was in business till 1858, and from 1862 to 1879 in Government employment. He was the earliest American student of hymnology, and collector of hymns. Before 1860 he had gathered a hymnological library of 800 vols., many of them very rare. It now belongs to the Drew Seminary, Madison, New Jersey. In 1848 he pub. *Methodist Hymnology*, New Jersey, 12mo, pp. 470, a book then without precedent, except Burgess's smaller vol. pub. in London. He was also one of the compilers of *Hymns for the Methodist Episcopal Church*, 1849.   [F. M. B.]

Creutzberg, Amadeus. [Sinold, P. B.]

Creutziger, Elisabethe. [Cruciger.]

Crewdson, Jane, née Fox, daughter of George Fox, of Perraw, Cornwall, was b. at Perraw, October, 1809 ; married to Thomas Crewdson, of Manchester, 1836 ; and d. at Summerlands, near Manchester, Sept. 14, 1863. During a long illness Mrs. Crewdson composed her works published as :—

(1) *Lays of the Reformation*, 1860. (2) *A Little While, and Other Poems* (posthumous), 1864. (3) *The Singer of Eisenach*, N.D. ; and (4) *Aunt Jane's Verses for Children*, 1851. 2nd ed. 1855, 3rd 1871.

From these works nearly a dozen of her hymns have come into C. U. The best known are, " O for the peace which floweth as a river," and " There is no sorrow, Lord, too light." In addition to these and others which are annotated under their respective first lines, there are the following in various collections :—

1. Give to the Lord thy heart. 1864. *Offertory.*
2. How tenderly Thy hand is laid. 1864. *Resignation.*
3. Looking unto Jesus. 1864. *Jesus All in All.*
4. Lord, we know that Thou art near us. 1864. *Resignation.*
5. O Saviour, I have naught to plead. 1864. *During Sickness.* These plaintive lines were written a short time before her death.
6. O Thou whose bounty fills my cup. 1860. *Peace.*
7. The followers of the Son of God. 1864. *The Daily Cross.*
8. Though gloom may veil our troubled skies. 1864. *Resignation.*   [J. J.]

Croly, George. LL.D., b. in Dublin, Aug. 17, 1780, and educated at the Dublin University (M.A. 1804, LL.D. 1831). After taking Holy Orders, he laboured in Ireland till about 1810, when he took up his residence in London, and devoted himself to literature. In 1835 he succeeded to the united benefices of St. Stephen's, Walbrook, and St. Benet Sherehog, retaining the same till his death, which occurred suddenly in the public street, Holborn, Nov. 24, 1860. His prose publications, in addition to contributions to *Blackwood's Magazine*, were numerous, and dealt with biographical, historical, and scriptural subjects. His hymns were given in his—

Psalms and Hymns for Public Worship. Written and compiled by the Rev. George Croly, LL.D. Lond, Kendrick, 1854.

This collection contained 25 psalms, 50 hymns, and 6 poems. Of these 10 psalms, 12 hymns, and the 6 poems bear Dr. Croly's initial. The following have come into C. U. mainly through Windle's *Coll.* :—

1. Be still, be still, impatient soul. *Patience.*
2. Behold me, Lord, and if thou find. *Lent.*
3. Lift up your heads, ye gates of light. *Ascension.*
4. Lord, who hast sought us out, unsought. *Public Worship.*
5. Teach us, O Lord, this day. *Sunday.*
6. Thou, Lord of mercy and of might. *Lent.*

All these date from 1854, with the exception of No. 6, which appeared in his *Scenes from Scripture and other Poems,* 1851. [J. J.]

Cronenwett, E., a Lutheran Pastor at Butler, Pennsylvania, U.S.A., contributed to the *Evangelical Lutheran Hymnal, Published by Order of the Ev. Lutheran Joint Synod of Ohio and other States,* 1880, in addition to 20 trs. from the German, the following original hymns, some of which rank with the best in the collection :—

1. A holy state is wedded life. *Domestic Worship.*
2. Faith is wisdom from on high. *Faith.*
3. Heavenly Father, Jesus taught us. *Prayer.*
4. Lord, Thine omniscience I adore. *Omniscience.*
5. O Triune God, Thy blessing great. *Domestic Worship.*
6. Of omniscient grace I sing. *Omniscience.*
7. Of Zion's honour angels sing. *Ordination.*
8. The precepts of the word are pure. *Holy Scripture.*
9. The Spirit's fruits are peace and love. *Fruits of the Spirit.*
10. 'Tis a marvel in our eyes. *Foundation Stone laying of a Church.*
11. To Thee, our fathers' God, we bow. *Domestic Worship.*
12. Unto Cæsar let us render. *National Thanksgiving.*
13. We have a sure, prophetic word. *H. Scripture.*
                    [J. J.]

Crosby, Fanny. [Van Alstyne, F. J.]

Cross, Ada, née Cambridge, daughter of Henry Cambridge, b. at St. Germains, Norfolk, Nov. 21, 1844, and married, in 1869, to George Frederick Cross, who, in 1870, took Holy Orders as a curate in Eng., and subsequently, after holding various curacies in Australia, became, in 1877, Incumbent of Coleraine, in the diocese of Ballarat. Her works include *Hymns on the Holy Communion,* 1866 ; *Hymns on the Litany,* 1865, &c. ; and she has also contributed to *Lays of the Pious Minstrels,* 1862 ; *English Lyrics,* &c. ; and published a prose story, " *The Two Surplices,*" 1865, and tales in various magazines. Her hymns have attained to some popularity, and are characterized by great sweetness and purity of rhythm, combined with naturalness and simplicity. The best known are :—

1. Humbly now with deep contrition. 1865. *Lent.*
2. Jesus, Great Redeemer. 1866. *Holy Communion.*
3. Light of the world, O shine on us. 1865. *Domestic Worship.*
4. Saviour, by [to] Thy sweet compassion. *Lent.*
5. The dawn of God's dear Sabbath, 1866. *Sunday Morning.*   [J. J.]

Crossman, Samuel, B.D. From A. Wood's *Athenae Oxonienses* (1720, vol. ii. p. 730) we gather all that is known of this hymn-writer. Wood says concerning him :—

" Samuel Crossman, Bachelor of Divinity of Cambridge, and Prebendary of Bristol, son of Samuel Crossman, of Bradfield Monachorum, in Suffolk. He hath written and published several things, as The Young Man's Monitor, &c, London, 1664, 8vo, and several sermons, among which are two sermons preached in the Cathedral of Bristol, 30th Jan., 1679, and 30th Jan., 1680, being the days of public humiliation for the execrable murder of King Charles I., printed at London, 1681, 4to ; also a sermon preached 23rd April, 1680, in the Cathedral Church of Bristol, before the Gentlemen of the Artillery Company newly raised in that City, printed at London, 1680, 4to ; and, An Humble Plea for the quiet rest of God's Ark, preached before Sir Joh. Moore, Lord Mayor of London, at St. Mildred's Church in the Poultrey, 5th February, 1681, London, 1682, 4to, &c. He died 4th February, 1683, aged 59 years, and was buried in the South Aisle of the Cathedral Church in Bristol" [of which he had been appointed Dean a few weeks before].

Crossman's contributions to hymnody were given in a small pamphlet entitled :—

The Young Man's Meditation, or some few Sacred Poems upon Select Subjects, and Scriptures. By Samuel Crossman, B.D. London, Printed by J. H., &c., 1664.

This pamphlet, which was reprinted by D. Sedgwick, Lond., 1863, contains 9 sacred poems. Of these the following are in C. U. :—

1. **My life's a shade, my days.** *Resurrection.* This is in 6 st. of 4 l., together with a chorus to each stanza of 4 l. It is sometimes given as " Life is a shade, my days," as in *Kennedy,* 1863.
2. **Sweet place, sweet place alone,** Pt. i. *Jerusalem on high,* Pt. ii. These two parts form one poem on *Heaven.* The most popular portion is Pt. ii. This is given in numerous collections in G. Britain and America. Part i. is not so extensively used. From the two parts the cento " Earth's but a sorry tent," in the Dutch Reformed *Hys. of the Church,* N. Y. 1869, is also taken. See **English Hymnody, Early,** § x.
3. **Farewell, poor world, I must be gone.** *Death anticipated.* This is given in the *Comprehensive Rippon,* 1844, and in a few of the older American hymn-books.
4. **My song is love unknown.** In the *Anglican H. Bk.,* 1868.   [J. J.]

Crosswell, William, D.D., was b. at Hudson, N.Y., Nov. 7, 1804; graduated at Yale College, 1822 ; entered for a time upon law studies, but eventually he entered Hartford College as a Theological Student, and then took Holy Orders in the Protestant

Episcopal Church in 1829. In 1829 he became Rector of Christ Church, Boston; in 1840, of St. Peter's, Auburn, New York; and in 1844, of the Church of the Advent, Boston. Died suddenly at Boston, Nov. 9, 1851. Whilst at Hartford he assisted, during 1827-28, in editing *The Watchman*, and contributed to it many of his poetical pieces. His *Memoir* was written by his father, the Rev. Dr. Crosswell, of New Haven; and his *Poems*, collected by his father, were edited, with a short *Memoir*, by Dr. (now Bishop) Coxe, and pub. at Boston in 1860. Of his hymns the following are in C. U. :—

1. **Lord, go with us, and we go.** *Journeying.* This in *Hymns for the Church and Home*, 1860, No. 212, is a portion of his "Traveller's Hymn," 1st pub. in 1833. Concerning it Dr. Coxe says, "When on a journey with him, I reminded him of his 'Traveller's Hymn,' which I had seen but could not remember; and he told me, if I recollect aright, that it was a sort of *Impromptu*, which bubbled up when he was going with Dr. Wainwright from Boston to New York to attend the General Convention" (*Memoir*, p. xlii.); and in his notes, p. 282, he indirectly fixes the date of composition as 1832. Orig. text in 2 st. of 8 l., in *Poems*, p. 255.

2. **Lord, lead the way the Saviour went.** *For Sisters of Mercy.* Written in 1831 for the Howard Benevolent Society of Boston. Dr. Coxe has entitled it "Hymn for Sisters of Mercy," and says he "ventured to give it a name suited to the present state of the Church, in which Deaconesses and Sisters of Mercy are among other realizations of the poet's ardent hopes. Perhaps we owe them to his faithful prayers." (*Notes* to the *Poems*, p. 283.) It is generally accepted as the best American hymn for benevolent occasions. Orig. text, *Poems*, p. 256.

3. **Now gird your patient loins again.** *Advent.* This hymn for Advent is in 3 st. of 4 l. *Poems*, p. 209; *Hys. for Ch. and Home*, No. 55.

4. **O Saviour, leave us not alone.** *Lent.* This is from his hymn for Lent beginning, "Thou who, for forty days and nights," in 4 st. of 4 double lines. In its abbreviated form it is found in *Hys. for Ch. and Home*, No. 85. Orig. in *Poems*, p. 219, in 4 st. of 4 double lines.

5. **We come not with a costly store.** *Epiphany.* For the Epiphany, from his *Poems*, p. 215, and based upon the Gospel of the day, in 2 st. of 8 l.

6. **And now the solemn rite is past.** *Ordination.* This is composed of st. vii., viii. of his poem, "The Ordinal," in *Poems*, pp. 69-71, slightly altered. "The Ordinal" was written in 1828, and describes minutely his own ordination at his father's church, at New Haven, and the feelings inspired, by the solemnity. It was printed in *The Watchman*, 1828. (*Poems*, Preface, p. xxvii.) The portion given as "And now the solemn rite is past" was included in Hall's *Mitre*, 1836.

Dr. Crosswell also *tr.* the "Veni, Creator Spiritus" as "Creator, Spirit, come and bless us." His hymns are mostly unknown to the English collections.   [F. M. B.]

Crowley, Robert. The date of this writer's birth is unknown. He was educated at Magdalen College, Oxford, where he was elected to a Fellowship in 1542. He acted as a printer under Edward VI. On the accession of Mary, he became one of the Frankfurt exiles. When Elizabeth ascended the throne, he returned, and was successively Vicar of the parishes of St. Giles, Cripplegate, 1556, and St. Lawrence Jewry, 1576. He also became a Prebendary of St. Paul's in 1563. He d. June 18, 1588, and was buried in St. Giles's Church, Cripplegate.

Crowley is known to students of early English as the first editor of *Piers Plowman's Visions*, of which he printed two editions in 1550. He rendered into verse the Psalter and Litany, and composed several hymns, 1549, and also pub., in 1558, his *School of Virtue and of Good Nature*, which was composed of *trs.* of Latin hymns. He is generally regarded as the first person who rendered the entire Psalter into English verse. Specimens of his version are given in Holland's *Psalmists of Britain*, and in *Cotton*. He was also the author of the *Voice of the Last Trumpet*, 1550, given in Corser's *Collectanea Anglo-Poetica*, Pt. iv., and of a very rare poem,

"Pleasure and Payne, Heaven and Hell,
Remember these foure and al shall be well."

[J. T. B.]

Crown Him with many crowns. [*Christ the King.*] Four hymns are found in common use, each of which opens with this stanza. They are:—

1. By *Matthew Bridges*, which appeared in his *Hymns of the Heart*, 2nd ed., 1851, p. 58, in 6 st. of 8 l., and headed, "In capite ejus diademata multa. Apoc. xix. 12." This was repeated in his *Passion of Jesus*, 1852, p. 62, where the title runs, "Third Sorrowful Mystery, Song of the Seraphs. Apoc. xix. 12." In treatment and expression it has a more than slight resemblance to Kelly's "Look, ye saints, the sight is glorious" (q. v.). With alterations, and sometimes abbreviations, it appeared for congregational use in the *People's H.*, 1867; *H. A. & M.*, 1868 and 1875; *Sarum*, 1868; *Hymnary*, 1872; *Hy. Comp.*, and others.

2. In the *Appendix* to the S. P. C. K. *Ps. and Hys.*, 1869, there are 10 st. of 4 l., of which 8 st. are from M. Bridges, and 2, *i.e.* st. vii. and viii., "Crown Him the Lord of Might," &c., are by another hand.

3. In S. P. C. K. *Church Hymns*, 1871, we have a cento based upon Bridges's text, and thus composed, i. Bridges; ii.-iii. Bridges altd.; iv. Rev. G. Thring; v. Bridges altd.; vi. from S. P. C. K. as above; vii. ll. 1-4, Rev. G. Thring; ll. 5-8, Bridges.

4. The hymn opening with the same stanza in Thring's *Coll.*, 1882, is practically new, the 1st st. and l. 1 of the 5th being all that have been adopted from M. Bridges. Its original form in which it first appeared was, "Crown Him with crowns of gold." (In the American *College Hymnal*, N.Y., 1876.) This was in Mr. Thring's *Hys. and Sacred Lyrics*, 1874, p. 75, that portion of it contained in the *Church Hys.*, as noted above, having previously appeared in that collection. In 1880, on being transferred to Mr. Thring's *Coll.*, M. Bridges's opening stanza was substituted for the original in order to retain those fine lines :—

"Hark ! how the heavenly anthem drowns
All music but its own."

A portion of the original hymn is sometimes given in American hymnals as, "Awake, my soul, and sing." It begins with line 5 of st. i., and is No. 272 in the *Bap. H. and Tune Bk.*, Philadelphia, 1871.   [J. J.]

Crowns of glory ever bright. *T. Kelly.* [*Jesus Crowned.*] 1st pub. in the 2nd ed. of his *Hymns on Various Passages*, &c., 1806, in 5 st. of 4 l., but in all subsequent editions, after 1806, with alterations and an additional stanza. In modern hymnals it is given in *Kennedy*, 1863, No. 705, and in Snepp's *S. of G. & G.*, 1872, in the authorized form; but in the *People's H.*, 1867, No. 479, it is abbreviated and altered. It is also in use in America.   [J. J.]

Cruciger, Elisabethe, née von Meseritz, was the daughter of a family belonging to the Polish nobility. Her parents, suffering from the persecutions of these times, had been forced to seek refuge at Wittenberg. There, in May or June, 1524, she was married to Caspar Cruciger, son of a Leipzig burgess, who had enrolled himself as a student at Wittenberg in 1522. Cruciger, who was treated by Luther as his own son and accounted his most hopeful pupil, became in 1525 Rector of St. John's School and preacher in St. Stephen's Church, Magdeburg; and in 1528 was called to become professor in the philosophical faculty at Wittenberg, but, by Luther's wish, was appointed one of the professors of Theology. Of his wife, who d. at Wittenberg, May, 1535, little is known save that she was a friend of Luther's wife, a lover of music, and an affectionate wife and mother (*Koch*, i. 281–285; *Caspar Cruciger*, by Dr. Pressel, Elberfeld, 1862, p. 76; *Allg. Deutsche Biog.* xviii. 148, &c.). The only hymn known as by her is :—

Herr Christ, der einig Gotts Sohn. *Christmas.* 1st pub. in *Eyn Enchiridion*, Erfurt, 1524. In the *Geistliche Lieder*, Wittenberg, 1531, it is given as "ein geistlich liedt von Christo, Elisabet Creutzigerin," and from the *Rostock G. B.*, 1531, it seems clear that in Klug's *G. B.*, Wittenberg, 1529, it bore the same title. *Wackernagel*, iii. pp. 46–47, gives four forms, all in 5 st. of 7 l. In the *Unv. L. S.*, 1851, No. 37.

Koch, i., 282, calls it "a sublime hymn fully embracing in itself the true power of the Gospel." It has been ascribed to Andreas Knöpken, but for this external evidence is entirely wanting, and in the *Riga Kirchenordnung*, 1537, in which his hymns appeared, this hymn is ascribed to E. Cruciger. That he as a theologian might fitly have written a hymn such as this, displaying power of theological expression (cf. st. v.) and knowledge of Latin (cf. st. i. with Prudentius's "Corde natus ex parentis") may be granted, but ladies learned in Latin and theology were not unknown in those days.

Translations in C. U. :—

1. **The only Son from heaven.** A good *tr.* of st. i.-iii., by A. T. Russell, as No. 41 in his *Ps. & Hys.*, 1851, repeated, with alterations, as No. 119 in *Kennedy*, 1863.

2. **O Thou, of God the Father.** A *tr.* of st. i., iii., iv., by Miss Winkworth, as No. 155 in her *C. B. for England*, 1863, and thence as No. 277 in the Ohio *Luth. Hymnal*, 1880.

Trs. not in C. U. :—

(1) "Christ is the only Sonne of God," by Bp. Coverdale, 1539, (*Remains*, 1846, p. 553). Almost identical with (2) "Christ is the onlie Son of God," in the *Gude and Godly Ballates* (ed. 1567–8, folio 74), ed. 1868, p. 127. (3) "Lord Christ th' eternal Father's," in the *Suppl. to German Psalmody*, ed. 1765, p. 3. (4) "Christ, that only begotten," as No. 335 in pt. i. of the *Moravian H. Bk.*, 1754. (5) "Thou Maker of each creature," No. 193 in the *Moravian H. Bk.*, 1789, is st. iii., iv. of the 1754, rewritten by P. H. Molther. In later eds. a *tr.* of st. vi. of "Herr Jesu, Gnadensonne" (see *L. A. Gotter*, No. i.) was added.   [J. M.]

Crucis Christi mons Alvernae. [*St. Francis of Assisi.*] This hymn is given in a *Franciscan Breviary*, printed at Venice in 1495, as the hymn at first Vespers on the Feast of the Stigmata of St. Francis, Sept. 17th (Paris, 1597, p. 43). It is given, but imperfectly, in *Daniel*, i., No. 452.

The traditional account of the conferring of the *Stigmata*, or *Marks of the Passion*, on St. Francis, on Mount Alverna, is given in his *Life*, by St. Bonaventura, chapter xiii. (see his *Works*). The Marks of the Passion are said to have been imprinted by a Seraph, and on the occasion of one of the yearly visits paid by St. Francis to Mount Alverna, which he was wont to make at the beginning of Lent in honour of St. Michael. St. Bonaventura's account is given in the *Rom. Brev.*, where it furnishes the lessons for the second Nocturn at Matins on the Festival of St. Francis.   [W. A. S.]

Translation in C. U. :—

Let Alverna's holy mountain, by E. Caswall, in his *Masque of Mary*, 1858, and again in his *Hys. and Poems*, 1873, p. 196, in 7 st. of 6 l. It is given in several Roman Catholic hymn-books for Schools and Missions, including the *Crown of Jesus ;* the *Hymns for the Year*, and others.

Crüger, Johann, was b. April 9, 1598, at Gross-Breese, near Guben, Brandenburg. After passing through the schools at Guben, Sorau and Breslau, the Jesuit College at Olmutz, and the Poets' school at Regensburg, he made a tour in Austria, and, in 1615, settled at Berlin. There, save for a short residence at the University of Wittenberg, in 1620, he employed himself as a private tutor till 1622. In 1622 he was appointed Cantor of St. Nicholas's Church at Berlin, and also one of the masters of the Greyfriars Gymnasium. He d. at Berlin Feb. 23, 1662. Crüger wrote no hymns, although in some American hymnals he appears as "Johann Krüger, 1640," as the author of the supposed original of C. Wesley's "Hearts of stone relent, relent" (q.v.). He was one of the most distinguished musicians of his time. Of his hymn tunes, which are generally noble and simple in style, some 20 are still in use, the best known probably being that to "Nun danket alle Gott" (q.v.), which is set to No. 379 in *H. A. & M.*, ed. 1875. His claim to notice in this work is as editor and contributor to several of the most important German hymnological works of the 16th cent., and these are most conveniently treated of under his name. (The principal authorities on his works are Dr. J. F. Bachmann's *Zur Geschichte der Berliner Gesangbücher*, 1857; his *Vortrag* on P. Gerhardt, 1863; and his edition of Gerhardt's *Geistliche Lieder*, 1866. Besides these there are the notices in *Bode*, and in R. Eitner's *Monatshefte für Musik-Geschichte*, 1873 and 1880). These works are :—

1. *Newes vollkömmliches Gesangbuch, Augspurgischer Confession*, &c., Berlin, 1640 [Library of St. Nicholas's Church, Berlin], with 248 hymns, very few being published for the first time.

2. *Praxis pietatis melica. Das ist : Ubung der Gottseligkeit in Christlichen und trostreichen Gesängen.* The history of this, the most important work of the century, is still obscure. The 1st ed. has been variously dated 1640 and 1644, while Crüger, in the preface to No. 3, says that the 3rd ed. appeared in 1648. A considerable correspondence with German collectors and librarians has failed to bring to light any of the editions which *Koch*, iv. 102, 103, quotes as 1644, 1647, 1649, 1650, 1651, 1652, 1653. The imperfect ed. noted below as probably that of 1648 is the earliest Berlin edition we have been able to find. The imperfect ed., probably ix.

of 1659, formerly in the hands of Dr. Schneider of Schleswig [see *Mützell*, 1858, No. 264] was inaccessible. The earliest perfect Berlin ed. we have found is 1653.

The ed. printed at Frankfurt in 1656 by Caspar Röteln was probably a reprint of a Berlin ed. c. 1655. The eds. printed at Frankfurt-am-Main by B. C. Wust (of which the 1666 is in the preface described as the 3rd) are in considerable measure independent works.

In the forty-five Berlin and over a dozen Frankfurt editions of this work many of the hymns of P. Gerhardt, J. Franck, P. J. Spener, and others, appear for the first time, and therein also appear many of the best melodies of the period. As these Berlin and Frankfurt editions are constantly referred to throughout this work, in the notes on German hymns, we subjoin a list of all the editions we have found (not noting duplicates), at present (1887) existing, as follows:—

i. Berlin Editions.

Edition.	Date.	Hymns.	Edition.	Date.	Hymns.
iii.	1648	387	xxviii.	1698	1163
x.	1661	550	xxix.	1702	786
xi.	1664	617	xxx.	1703	1194
xii.	1666	641	xxxii.	1709	1202
xiii.	1667	710	xxxiv.	1711	1202
xv.	1671	761	xxxv.	1712	1202
xvi.	1672	761	xxxvi.	1714	1222
xvii.	1674	764	xxxvii	1716	1222
xviii.	1675	803	xxxviii	1718	1300
xix.	1678	769	xxxix.	1721	1300
xx.	1679	1001	xl.	1724	1316
xxii.	1684	1001	xli.	1729	1316
xxiii.	1688	1114	xlii.	1732	1316
xxiv.	1690	1220	xliii.	1733	1316
xxv.	1690	769	xliv.	1736	1316
xxvii.	1693	1124	xlv.	1736?	1316

ii. Frankfurt Editions.

	Date.	Hymns.		Date.	Hymns
1	1656	503	7	1676	1100
2	1662	606	8	1678	1169
3	1666	731	9	1680	787
4	1668	888	10	1683	254
5	1674	787	11	1693	1246
6	1674	208	12	1700	1246

Of the above the Royal Library, Berlin, possesses eds. xii., xvi., xix., xxiv., xxv., xxvii., xxix., xxxvi., xl., xliii., xlv., and Nos. 3, 4, 7, 9, 11; while the Hamburg Town Library has eds. xi., xviii., xx., xxiii., and Nos. 1, 5, 8, 10. In addition there are in public libraries in Germany the following, viz., eds. xiii., xvii., and Nos. 2, 6, in the Ducal Library, Wolfenbüttel; xv. in Ducal Library, Gotha; iii., xxxv., xxxvii. in Ducal Library, Wernigerode; ed. xliv. in the Royal Library, Munich; and No. 12 in the Leipzig Town Library. Ed. xxx. is in the Library of the Consistory, Berlin, and xxxiv. in possession of the Church at Börnicke near Nauen. The British Museum has eds. xxiii., xxv., and Nos. 1, 2.

In private hands I find in addition that eds. x., xxviii., xxxix., xli., xlii., are with Professor J. Bachmann, D.D., of Rostock; xxii., xxxviii., Dr. Zahn of Altdorf; xxxii. in my own possession.

3. *Geistliche Kirchen-Melodien*, &c., Leipzig, 1649 [Library of St. Katherine's Church, Brandenburg]. This contains the first stanzas only of 161 hymns, with music in four vocal and two instrumental parts. It is the earliest source of the first stanzas of various hymns by Gerhardt, Franck, &c.

4. *D. M. Luther's und anderer vornehmen geistreichen und gelehrten Männer Geistliche Lieder und Psalmen*, &c., Berlin, 1653 [Hamburg Town Library], with 375 hymns. This was ed. by C. Runge, the publisher, and to it Crüger contributed some 37 melodies. It was prepared at the request of Luise Henriette (q.v.), as a book for the joint use of the Lutherans and the Reformed, and is the earliest source of the hymns ascribed to her, and of the complete versions of many hymns by Gerhardt and Franck.

5. *Psalmodia Sacra*, &c., Berlin, 1658 [Royal Library, Berlin]. The first section of this work is in an ed. of A. Lobwasser's *German Psalter*; the second, with a similar title to No. 4, and the date 1657, is practically a recast of No. 4, 146 of those in 1653 being omitted, and

the rest of the 319 hymns principally taken from the *Praxis* of 1656 and the hymn-books of the Bohemian Brethren. New eds. appeared in 1676, 1700, 1704, 1711, and 1736.   [J. M.]

Cruttenden, Robert, b. cir. 1691, d. cir. 1764. He was educated for the ministry among the Dissenters, and when a young man frequently preached for his uncle, the Rev. Mr. Bragg. But finding that he did not really believe in the Evangelical doctrines, he gave up the ministry, and betook himself to trade, in which for a number of years he was successful. In his 52nd year, having retired from business, he was living near to Whitefield's Tabernacle, when, his attention being excited by what he heard concerning the preaching there, a strong impulse seized him to go and hear for himself. The result was his conversion through the ministry of John Cennick. Twelve months later he joined a Congregational Church, of which he continued a member until his death, about 20 years subsequently. The narrative of his *Experience*, as read to this Church on his application for membership, was pub. in 1744, with a preface by Whitefield, and republished in 1790, with the addition of a letter from Mr. Cruttenden to Mr. Cennick. To this narrative his *Psalms & Hymns*, 17 in all, were appended. The full title of the *Experience* is too quaint to be omitted. It is:—

" Sovereign Efficacious Grace displayed in the awakening and converting a Rational, Learned, Aged sinner, exemplified in the *Experience of Robert Cruttenden*, Esq., as delivered by himself to the *Congregational Church*, then meeting in Lime Street, near Leadenhall Market, 1743, in order to be admitted into their society. Published, prefaced and recommended by the late *Rev. George Whitefield*, 1744, as an extraordinary effect of the Divine Spirit. To which is prefixed a *Letter from Mr. Cruttenden to Mr. Cennick*, 1742. Also *several Psalms, Hymns, &c., composed by him*. Now particularly addressed to all rational Christians for their perusal. London, printed and sold by T. Wilkins, Aldermanbury, MDCCXC."

From his *Psalms & Hymns* in the *Experience* the following are still in C. U.:—

1. And is it yet, dear Lord, a doubt? *Desiring to love God.*
2. Did Jesus die, but not for me? *Pardon through Jesus.*
3. I own my guilt, my sins confess. *Lent.*
4. Let others boast their ancient line. *Adoption.*
5. Rise, Sun of glory, shine reveal'd. *Happiness desired.*
6. 'Tis false, thou vile accuser, go. *Divine Mercy.*
7. What adverse powers we feel within. *Sin and Holiness.*
8. What jarring natures dwell within. *Sin and Holiness.* This is part of No. 7.

Cruttenden's hymns are full of Christian experience: some, as "Let others boast their ancient line," have a good deal of spirit, and the versification is usually smooth and flowing.   [W. R. S.]

Crux benedicta nitet, Dominus qua carne pependit. *Venantius Fortunatus.* [*Holy Cross.*] This hymn, dating from the latter half of the 6th cent., is found in a 11th cent. MS. in the Bodleian (*Liturg. Misc.* 366, f. 21), and is given in its full form in Fortunatus's *Opera Poetica*, ed. F. Leo, (Berlin, 1881) from a St. Petersburg MS. of the 8th cent. and others. The abbreviated form of the hymn in 18 l. is that which is generally known. It is given in *Daniel*, i., No. 141, with notes and various readings;

Neale's *Hymni Ecclesiae*, 1851; Trench's *Sac. Lat. Poetry*, 1849 and 1864; and other collections. *Daniel* gives in vol. iv. p. 152, additional readings from a Rheinau MS. of the 11th cent., and an additional strophe (the 10th in the MS.) which is not found, so far as is known, in any MS. of Fortunatus. It reads :—

"O tam magna Deo magnalia tanta parasti
   Quanta mira facit gloria magna Deo."

On the closing lines of this hymn :—

"Appensa est vitis inter tua brachia, de quâ
   Dulcia sanguineo vina rubore fluunt,"

rendered by Dr. Neale as :—

"Twining about thine arms is the Vine, from whom in
   its fulness
Floweth the blood-red juice, Wine that gives life to
   the soul."

Archbishop Trench has the following beautiful note (ed. 1864, p. 131) :—

"The cross as the tree to which the vine is clinging, and from which its tendrils and fruit depend, is a beautiful weaving in of the image of the true Vine with the fact of the Crucifixion. The blending of one image and another comes, perhaps, yet more beautifully out, though not without a certain incoherence in the images, in that which sometimes appears in ancient works of Christian art—namely, Christ set forth as the Lamb, round which the branches of a loaded vine are clustering and clinging."   [W. A. S.]

Translations in C. U. :—

1. That blest Cross is displayed where the Lord in the flesh was suspended, by J. M. Neale, in his essay on the "Ecclesiastical Latin Poetry of the Middle Ages," in the *Encyclopaedia Metropolitana*, 1852; and again in his *Commentary on the Psalms*, 1860, in 9 st. of 2 l. In 1875 it was given in the *St. Margaret's Hymnal* ; in 1880, in the *Antiphoner and Grail*, and as "Lo, the blest Cross is displayed," &c., in the *Hymner*, 1882.

2. The blessed Cross shines now to us where once the Saviour bled, by Mrs. Charles, in her work *The Voice of Christian Life in Song*, 1858, p. 130, in 9 st. of 2 l. This was repeated in the *Lyra Messianica*, 1864, and the *People's H.*, 1867. In the *Hymnary*, 1872, it is in 4 st. of 8 l. This text is altered, and the last four lines are original, and were added by the compilers. [W. T. B.]

Crux, mundi benedictio. *St. Peter Damiani.* [*Holy Cross.*] This hymn, which dates from the first half of the 11th cent., is given in various editions of the author's *Works*, e.g. that at Paris, 1642, vol. iv. p. 6. It is also in *Thomasius*, 1747 : and *Migne*, tom. 145, col. 930. *Daniel*, i., No. 197, only quotes 4 lines from the former. Respecting this hymn, Dr. Neale remarks :—

"St. Peter Damiani, in almost all his compositions, seems to have had his eye on some earlier hymn : in the present case he clearly follows the Vexilla Regis. The following does not seem to have been publicly used by the Church," *Med. Hys.*, 1851, p. 36.

It is *tr.* as :—

O Cross by whom the earth is blest, by J. M. Neale, pub. in his *Mediaeval Hymns*, 1851, p. 36, in 6 st. of 4 l. It was revised for the 2nd ed., 1863, as, "O Cross, whereby the earth is blest." As in C. U. it is known in its earlier form as in the *Appendix* to the *Hymnal N.*, 1863, and Skinner's *Daily Service Hymnal*, 1864.   [J. J.]

Cummins, James John, s. of a merchant in Cork, Ireland, was b. in Cork, May 5, 1795. In 1834 he removed to London, and was for many years a Director of the Union Bank of Australia. He d. at Wildecroft, Buckland, Surrey, Nov. 23, 1867. He devoted much time to the study of Hebrew and Theology. He prepared for the use of his children in their preparation for Confirmation, *Seals of the Covenant Opened in the Sacraments.* This work, including several hymns and poems, was pub. in 1839. The hymns and other poetical pieces were also pub. in 1839 as *Poetical Meditations and Hymns by the Author of The Seals of the Covenant Opened.* In 1849 this work was republished with additions as *Hymns, Meditations, and other Poems.* The title on the cover of this work is *Lyra Evangelica*, and by this title it is usually known. The hymns, "Jesus, Lord of life and glory," 1839, (*A Litany*); "Shall hymns of grateful love," 1839, (*The New Song*), and others are from this work.   [J. J.]

Cundell, Anne Ross. [Cousin, A. R.]

Cunningham, John William, M.A., was b. in London, Jan. 3, 1780, and educated at St. John's College, Cambridge, where he graduated in honours, and subsequently became a Fellow of his College. In 1802 he was ordained to the Curacy of Ripley, in Surrey. The following year he removed to Ockham, and later to Clapham, where he was curate to the Rev. John Venn, who was the original of *Berkeley* in *The Velvet Cushion.* In 1811 he was presented by his family to the Vicarage of Harrow, which he held for fifty years. He d. Sept. 30, 1861. He published, in addition to pamphlets on various subjects :—

(1) *World without Souls*, 1805 ; (2) *The Velvet Cushion*, 4th ed. 1814 ; (3) *De Rancé, a Poem*, 1815 ; (4) *Morning Thoughts on the Gospel of St. Matthew*, 1824 ; (5) *Morning Thoughts on the Gospel of St. Mark*, 1827. The two series of *Morning Thoughts* contained hymns which were given without any signature. As there is an acknowledgment that with the verse, in the first case he was assisted by "a friend," and in the second "by friends," it is impossible to distinguish his work from that of his "friends."

With his name and publications the following hymns are associated :—

1. As the sweet flower that scents the morn. *Death of an Infant.* This poem appeared in *The Velvet Cushion* (4th ed. 1814, p. 157), in 6 st. of 4 l. In 1826 it was given in a revised form as a hymn in 3 st. of 4 l. in the American Episc. *Ps. & Hys.*, No. 127. In the Unitarian *Hys. for the Ch. of Christ* (Hedge & Huntington), 1853, No. 762, it is increased to 4 st. It has been attributed to Allan Cunningham, but in error.

2. Dear is the hallowed morn to me. *Sunday Morning.* This was given in Oliphant & Sons' *Sacred Poetry*, 4th ed., 1822, in 8 st. of 4 l., and signed "Cuningham." In 1833 Bickersteth gave st. i.–iii., vi., as No. 639 in his *Christ. Psalmody*, beginning, "Dear is to me the Sabbath morn." This has been repeated in English and American collections.

3. From Calvary a cry was heard. *Good Friday.* Pub. in his *Morning Thoughts on St. Matthew*, 1824, p. 103, in 5 st. of 4 l. It is in somewhat extensive use in America, and sometimes in 4 stanzas as in Dr. Hatfield's *Church H. Bk.*, 1872, No. 460.

4. How cheering the thought that the spirits in bliss. *Ministering Angels.* Pub. in his *Morning Thoughts on St. Matthew*, 1824, p. 15, in 2 st. of 4 l. In Bateman's *Sacred Melodies*, the Scottish Presb. *Hymnal for the Young*, 1882, &c., and several American collections, it is given as "How [dear is] delightful the thought that the angels in bliss."

5. The God of Israel never sleeps. *Watchfulness.* Pub. in his *Morning Thoughts on St. Mark*, 1827, p. 103, in 3 st. of 6 l. As No. 548 in Kennedy it is in an altered form.   [W. T. B.]

Curtis, John, b. 1784, d. 1857, was a native of Bristol, in which city, engaged in business pursuits, he spent his life. He was connected for many years with the choir at Broadmead Baptist Chapel. His hymn-book,

The Union Collection of Hymns & Sacred Odes, additional to the Psalms and Hymns of Dr. Watts, adapted to the use of the Church and the Social Circle, the Family and the Closet. London, B. J. Holdsworth, 1827,"

was for some time in use at Broadmead. It was designed for Independents and Baptists, all hymns on Holy Baptism being omitted: but it failed in securing the goodwill of either.   [W. R. S.]

Curwen, John, s. of the Rev. S. Curwen, of an old Cumberland family, b. at Heckmondwike, Yorkshire, Nov. 14, 1816, and educated at Coward College, and University College, London. In 1838 he became assistant minister in the Independent Church, Basingstoke; co-pastor at Stowmarket in 1841, and pastor at Plaistow, Essex, in 1844. There he developed and promoted the *Tonic Sol-fa* method of teaching to sing, using it in his own schools and church, and lecturing upon it in various parts of the country. Resigning his ministry through ill health, in 1867, he established a printing and publishing business in order the better to create a *Tonic Sol-fa* literature. In 1853 he assisted in founding the Tonic Sol-fa Association, for the promotion of that method of singing, and in 1862 the Tonic Sol-fa College. He d. May 25, 1880. Besides a number of works explanatory of the Tonic Sol-fa system, Mr. Curwen was the compiler of *Sacred Songs*, 1840, and *Hys. & Chants*, 1844. In 1846 these were combined as *The Child's Own Hymn Book*. This was enlarged in 1865, and recast as *The New Child's Own Hymn Book* in 1874. As a Sunday-school hymn-book this collection has been exceedingly and deservedly popular. For it Mr. Curwen composed two hymns:—

1. **I'm a little Pilgrim.** *Pressing Heavenwards.* This was written in place of another with the same first line, whose author had refused permission for its use in Mr. Curwen's book. The tune and chorus usually sung with it are American.

2. **O what has Jesus done for me?** *Passiontide.* This was also written in place of another having the same line.

These are the only hymns known to be his. *The Sabbath Hymn Book*, Lond. 1859, was also edited by Mr. Curwen.   [W. R. S.]

Cushing, William Orcutt, b. at Hingham, Massachusetts, Dec. 31, 1823, is the author of the following hymns which appear in I. D. Sankey's *Sacred Songs and Solos:—*

1. Beautiful valley of Eden. *Heaven.*
2. Down in the valley with my Saviour I would go. *Trusting to Jesus.*
3. Fair is the morning land. *Heaven.*
4. I am resting so sweetly in Jesus now. *Rest and Peace in Jesus.*
5. I have heard of a land far away. *Heaven.*
6. O safe to the Rock that is higher than I. *The Rock of Ages.*
7. Ring the bells of heaven, there is joy to-day. *Heavenly Joy over repenting Sinners.*
8. We are watching, we are waiting. *Second Advent anticipated.*

Mr. Cushing has also several additional hymns in some American Sunday School collections, and collections of Sacred Songs.   [J. J.]

Custodes hominum psallimus Angelos. [*Guardian Angels.*] This hymn is ascribed to Card. Bellarmine. According to *Gavantus* it was added to the *Roman Brev.* in 1608, by command of Paul V. It was not formally incorporated in the *Brev.* until after 1632, and, in common with "Aeterne Rector siderum" (q.v.), is in the Venice ed., 1635, in an *Appendix* with independent · pagination and a separate title-page. It is for Vespers in the Office for "the Holy Guardian Angels. Double of the second class," Oct. 2. It is also one of the few hymns from the *Rom. Brev.* given in modern French Breviaries. In the latter, however, it has a different doxology, and the text varies. The *Rom. Brev.* text is in *Daniel*, ii. p. 375; and the *Paris Brev.* in Card. Newman's *Hymni Ecclesiae*, 1838 and 1865. Tr. as :—

And are there then celestial habitants? by I. Williams, in his *Hys. tr. from the Paris Brev.*, 1839, p. 254. This was repeated in the *Child's Christian Year*, 1841, and later editions, where it is appointed for "St. Michael and All Angels." It is also tr. as :—"Praise we those ministers celestial." *E. Caswall.* 1849.   [J. M.]

Cutter, William, b. at North Yarmouth, Maine, May 15, 1801, and was removed in childhood to Portland, and educated at Bowdoin College, graduating in 1821. He was subsequently engaged for some time in business in Portland, and again in Brooklyn, New York. Died Feb. 8, 1867. Mr. Cutter, who was a member of the Congregational body, was a deserving writer, who has hitherto missed his due meed of acknowledgment. To his friend Mr. Colesworthy we are indebted for the details of his life and hymnological work. His hymns include :—

1. **Thy neighbour? it is he whom thou.** *Christian Brotherhood.* This appeared in the *Christian Mirror* for May 30, 1828 (Mr. Colesworthy thinks that he set the types for it), and again in Cheever's *American Poetry*, 1831. An altered form of the hymn, "Who is thy neighbour? he whom thou," soon came into use, and was often printed before it was included anonymously in W. B. O. Peabody's Unitarian *Springfield Coll.*, 1835. From being found in that collection it has been attributed to Peabody in error.

2. **Hide not thy talent in the earth.** *Duty.* Appeared in the *Christian Mirror*, Oct. 10, 1828. In some collections it begins with st. ii., "What if the little rain should say."

3. **She loved her Saviour, and to Him.** *Thankfulness and Duty.* Was 1st pub. in the *Christian Mirror*, but the date is uncertain. It was reprinted by Cheever in his *American Poetry*, 1831. In addition to the above, Cutter wrote several hymns which appeared in the *Mirror*, and in the *Sunday School Instructor*, of which he and Mr. Colesworthy were joint editors. His hymns are unknown to the English collections.   [F. M. B.]

Cutting, Sewell Sylvester, D.D., a Baptist Minister, was b. at Windsor, Vermont, Jan. 19, 1813, graduated at the University of Vermont, 1835, and was ordained at Boylston, Massachusetts, 1836. He was pastor at Southbridge, Mass., from 1837 to 1845. Editor of the *New York Recorder* 1845–50, and 1853–55 ; and of the *Christian Review,* 1850–53, and 1855–68. In 1868 he was appointed Professor of Rhetoric and History at the University, Rochester, N. York, and Secretary of the American Baptist Educational Commission. He d. at Brooklyn, Feb. 7, 1882. His *Historical Vindication of the Baptists* was pub. in 1858. His hymns in C. U. include :—

1. **Father, we bless the gentle care.** *The love of God.* Appeared in *Hys. for the Vestry and Fireside,* Boston, 1841.

2. **Gracious Saviour, we adore Thee.** *H. Baptism.* Appeared in Winchell's *Additional Hys.,* 1832, No. 509 (the author being then but 19); again in the *Psalmist,* 1843, and others.

3. **Great God, Thy glories blaze.** *Praise to God the Father.* Appeared in Linsley and Davis's *Select Hys.,* 1836–41, No. 514. In the *Psalmist,* 1843, it was altered to "God of the world, Thy glories shine." This is repeated in several collections, including the *Bap. Praise Bk.,* 1871, in 4 st. of 4 l. In the Bap. *Service of Song,* 1871, it is given as "God of the world, near and afar," is expanded into 5 st., and is dated 1835.

4. **O Saviour, I am blind, Lead Thou my way.** *The True Guide.* This hymn, in I. D. Sankey's *Sacred S. and Solos,* is also by Dr. Cutting.

[F. M. B.]

Czerwenka, M. [Cervenka, M.]

D

D., in Bristol Bap. *Coll.,* by Ash & Evans. 1st ed., 1769, i.e. P. Doddridge.

D. A. T., i.e. Dorothy A. Thrupp.

D. H. W., i.e. Mrs. Van Alstyne.

D. L., in the *People's H.,* i.e. Dr. Littledale.

D. P., i.e. *Desiderius Pastor,* a *nom de plume* of the Rev. Gerard Moultrie, in the *People's H.*

Dr B., in *Ash & Evans,* 1st ed., 1769, i.e. Dr. John Byrom.

Dr. Sc*tt, in *Ash & Evans,* 1st ed., 1769, i.e. Thomas Scott.

D. T., in *Ash & Evans,* 1st ed., 1769, i.e. Daniel Turner.

Dw., in *Supp.* to *Ash & Evans,* 1800, &c., i.e. T. Dwight.

Da Jesus, an des Kreuzes Stamm. [*The Seven Words.*] 1st appeared in the *Hannover G. B.,* 1646, No. 45, in 10 st. of 5 l., repeated in Crüger's *Praxis pietatis melica,* 1656, and many later collections. It was evidently written to supersede the older hymn noted under *Böschenstein.* Frequently, as by Bunsen in his *Versuch,* 1833, No. 168, and the *Berlin G. L. S.,* ed. 1863, No. 220, it is ascribed to J. Zwick. But the version of the Seven Words on the Cross given by *Wackernagel,* iii. p. 612, as by Zwick, and 1st pub. 1545, is in 7 st. of 8 l., beginning, "Im Ersten wort der hoptgrund stat," and is entirely different. *Tr.* as :—

1. **Seven times our blessed Saviour spoke.** A good and full *tr.* by Miss Cox in her *Sacred H. from*

the German, 1841, p. 31 (*H. from the Ger.,* 1864, p. 57, slightly altered). In 1848, st. i.–viii. were included, unaltered, as No. 135 in the *Dalston Hospital H. Bk.* In full, but slightly altered, as No. 401 in the 1857 ed. of Mercer's *C. P. and H. Bk.* Omitting st. ix., it was included in Rorison's *H. and Anthems,* 1851, No. 70 ; and again in Darling's *H. for the Ch. of England,* 1874, altered as, "Seven words our blest Redeemer spoke."

2. **When on the cross the Saviour hung.** A full and good *tr.* by Miss Winkworth in her *C. B. for England,* 1863, No. 53, repeated as No. 74 in the *Ohio Luth. Hymnal,* 1880.

3. **My soul, thy great Redeemer see.** A *tr.* of st. i., ix., x., by Miss Borthwick, as No. 70 in Dr. Pagenstecher's *Coll.,* 1864.

Other trs. are :—
(1) "When Christ hung on the cursed tree," by J. C. *Jacobi,* 1722, p. 17 (1732, p. 32), repeated, altered, as No. 162 in pt. i. of the *Moravian H. Bk.,* 1754. (2) "Seven words from Jesus' lips did fall," in Dr. J. Guthrie's *Sacred Lyrics,* 1869, p. 75. [J. M.]

Da pacem, Domine. [*For peace.*] An antiphon of the 6th or 7th cent., founded on ii. Kings xx. 19 ; ii. Chron. xx. 12, 15; and Ps. cxxii. 6. By a Bull of Pope Nicholas III., 1279, it was ordered to be sung at every mass before the *Agnus Dei,* In the *Paris Breviary* of 1643 it is given along with a Collect for Peace, which occurs in the *Sacramentary* of Gelasius, A.D. 494, as a *Commemoratio de Pace per Annum. Ad Laudes et Vesperas,* thus :—

"Da pacem, Domine, in diebus nostris, quia non est alius qui pugnet pro nobis, nisi tu Deus noster. V. Fiat pax in virtute tua. R. Et abundantia in turribus tuis. *Oratio.* Deus, a quo sancta desideria, recta consilia, et justa sunt opera : da servis tuis illam, quam mundus dare non potest, pacem : ut et corda nostra mandatis tuis dedita, et hostium sublata formidine, tempora sint tua protectione tranquilla. Per Dominum," &c. (*Pars Hiemalis,* 1657, p. 159.)

The same text is given in the *Sarum Brev.* (Cambridge Press Reprint, 1882, of the Paris ed., 1531, col. 11), and in the *York Brev.* of 1493 (Surtees Society's Reprint, 1880, i. col. 942). A *tr.* in full is given in the Evening Service of the Church of England. In *The Prymer in English,* reprinted from a MS. cir. 1410, in Maskell's *Monumenta Ritualia Ecclesiae Anglicanae,* 1846, ii. p. 35, they read :—

"*Ant.* Da pacem. Lord ʒyue pees in our daies, for ther is noon othir that shal fyʒte for us, but thou lord oure god. *Vers.* Lord, pees be maad in thi vertu. *Resp.* And plenteousnesse in thi toures. Prei we. For the pees. Deus a quo : God, of whom ben hooli desiris, riʒt councels and iust werkis : ʒyue to thi seruauntis pees that the world may not ʒeue, that in oure hertis ʒouun to thi commaundementis, and the drede of enemyes putt awei, our tymes be pesible thurʒ thi defendyng : Bi our lord iesu crist, thi sone, that with thee lyueth and regneth in the unite of the hooli goost god, bi alle worldis of worldis. So be it."

The other *trs.* are from two German versions, the earlier being :—

1. **Verleih uns Frieden gnädiglich,** given to it by Martin Luther, first in prose in 1527 (*Koch,* viii. 159), and then in metrical form in Klug's *G. B.,* 1529. *Wackernagel,* iii. p. 21, quotes it from the *Geistliche Lieder,* Wittenberg, 1531 ; and also gives a form in 4 st. of 5 l., pub. at Augsburg in 1532, st. ii.–iv. being founded on the prose collect. In many districts of Germany, Luther's stanza was sung immediately after sermon, either separately or with the hymn, "Erhalt uns Herr bei deinem Wort,"

(q.v.). In Schircks's ed. of Luther's *Geistliche Lieder*, 1854, p. 43, a second st. in 5 l., founded on 1 Tim. ii. 1, 2, and on the latter part of the prose collect, beginning, " Gieb unserm Fürsten und aller Obrigkeit," is added ; 1st pub. in *Das Christlich Kinderlied Dr Martini Lutheri Erhalt uns Herr*, &c., Wittenberg, 1566, ed. by Johann Walther, and thence in *Mützell*, No. 556, and added to Luther's stanza, as No. 981, in the Berlin *G. L. S.*, ed. 1863.

The *trs.* from Luther are : (1) " Lord, in Thy mercy and Thy grace," by *Miss Fry*, 1845, p. 137 ; (2) " Lord ! in mercy grant us peace," by *J. Anderson*, 1846, p. 65 (1847, p. 79) ; (3) " We Thee beseech, with one accord," by *Dr. J. Hunt*, 1853, p. 93 ; (4) " In these our days so perilous," by *R. Massie*, 1854, p. 68, included in *Dr. Bacon*, 1884, p. 54 ; (5) " Jehovah, grant us peace through all," by *Dr. G. Walker*, 1860, p. 39 ; (6) " Peace in our time, Lord God, bestow." by Dr. G. Macdonald in the *Sunday Magazine*, 1867, p. 682, and thence in his *Exotics*, 1876, p. 97, altered to " Peace to us in Thy mercy grant."

2. Gieb Fried zu unser Zeit, O Herr. A very free version in 3 st. of 10 l., by Wolfgang Capito. *Wackernagel*, iii. p. 731, quotes it from the *Form und Ordnung Gaystlicher Gesang und Psalmen*, Augsburg, 1533 (where the order of stanzas is ii., i., iii.), and the Strassburg *G. B.*, 1533. *Mützell*, No. 153, quotes the text from the *Gros Kirchen G. B.*, Strassburg, 1560, where it is entitled " A hymn of supplication for peace and whole-hearted returning to God, with confession that we have justly merited our unrest by our sin and declension from God." It appeared in many of the German hymn-books up to the middle of the 18th cent., but since then has fallen out of use. The only *tr.* in C. U. is :—

Geue peace in these our dayes, O Lord. A full and close tr. in the 1560–61 *Psalmes of Dauid.* In Daye's *Psalter*, 1565, and many later eds. of the *Old Version*, it is signed **E. G.** These initials almost certainly denote Edmund Grindal, afterwards Abp. of Canterbury (1575–1583), who lived at Strassburg during the Marian Exile, and is known to have acquired a sufficient knowledge of German to have enabled him to take office in the German Church. It is included in a few hymnals of this cent., e.g. in J. Bickersteth's *Ps. and Hys.*, ed. 1832, No. 504, rewritten to 4 st. of L.M., and repeated in this form in E. Bickersteth's *Christian Psalmody*, 1833, Snepp's *Songs of G. and G.*, 1872, &c.   [J. M.]

Da puer plectrum, choreis ut canam fidelibus. *A. C. Prudentius.* [*Miracles of Christ.*] This poem, written at the beginning of the 5th cent., is given in all editions of Prudentius's *Works* (*Cathemerinon*, No. 9), including that pub. in Rome, 1789, London, Valpy, 1824, vol. i. p. 123. It is also in a MS. of the 5th cent. in the Bibliothèque Nationale, Paris (8084 f. 29 b.). From this poem the hymn, **Corde natus ex Parentis, ante mundi exordium** (the *trs.* of which are annotated below), is taken. It usually consists of lines 10–12, 19–27, and 109–111, with slight alterations. In the *York Brev.* it is given at Compline for the Vigil of Christmas, and from thence to the Octave of the Epiphany. In the *Hereford Brev.* it is given for Prime. *Daniel*, i., No. 106, gives the text, together with an extended note relating to various readings, &c. The " Corde natus " text is also in a MS. of the 11th cent. in the *British Museum* (Harl. 2961 f. 228) ; and in a MS. of

the 11th cent. at St. Gall. (No. 413) ; *Simrock*, p. 38 ; *Bässler*, No. 43 ; *Königsfeld*, i. p. 40 (with German *tr.*); Card. Newman's *Hymni Ecclesiae*, 1838 and 1865 ; and others. The hymn in the *Mozarabic Brev.* " Psallat altitudo coeli " (Toledo, 1502 f. 131) is also from this poem. In the *Hereford Brev.* there are also three other centos from this poem, viz. : (1) " Corporis formam " for Terce ; (2) " Ecce quem vates " for Sext ; and (3) " Juste Judex " for None.   [W. A. S.]

Translations in C. U. of *Corde natus :—*

1. Of the Father sole begotten. By J. M. Neale, in the enlarged ed. of the *Hymnal N.*, 1854, (1st ed. 1852), in 6 st. of 6 l. with the refrain, " Evermore, and evermore." This refrain and the doxology are not in the original. This *tr.* is repeated in later eds. of the *Hymnal N.*, the *People's H.*, 1867, the *Hymnary*, 1872, &c. It is to be noted that some of the lines in this *tr.* are from Beresford Hope's *tr.* of the same text in his *Hys. of the Church*, 1844. In the *Parish H. Bk.* it is given as " Of the Father's *self* begotten." In *Laudes Domini*, N.Y., 1884, begins with st. ii., " He is here, whom Seers in old time."

2. Born of God the Father's bosom. This *tr.* appeared in the *Salisbury H. Bk.*, 1857, and again in J. Keble's *Miscellaneous Poems*, 1869. It is an alteration of Dr. Neale's *tr.* made by Keble for the *Salisbury H. Bk.*

3. Of the Father's love begotten. This *tr.* was given in the trial ed. of *H. A. & M.*, 1859, as " Of the Father's *will* begotten," but in the 1st ed. of 1861 it was given in its well-known form in 9 st. of 6 l. with the refrain, the additional stanzas being supplied by the *Hereford Brev.* text. The *H. A. & M. tr.* by Dr. Neale and Sir H. W. Baker is thus composed.:—i. Neale altered ; ii., iii., Baker ; iv.–vi., Neale altered ; vii., Baker ; viii., Neale altered ; ix., Baker. This arrangement was repeated in the revised *H. A. & M.*, 1875, and is the most popular *tr.* of the hymn in C. U. Usually, however, compilers introduce changes and abbreviations cn their own account, and not always to the advantage of the hymn. These changes are easily found by collating any given text with *H. A. & M.*

Translations not in C. U. :—

1. Son Eternal of the Father. *Hope.* 1844.
2. Yea ! from the Almighty mind He sprung. (*Hereford Brev.* text.) *Hymn. Anglicanum.* 1844.
3. Offspring of The Eternal Father. *J. D. Chambers.* 1857.
4. Of the Father's heart begotten. *W. J. Blew.* 1852–55.   [J. J.]

Dach, Simon, s. of Simon Dach, interpreter to the Court of Justice at Memel, Prussia, was b. at Memel, July 29, 1605. He attended the Cathedral school at Königsberg, the Town school at Wittenberg, and the Gymnasium at Magdeburg. In 1626 he returned to Königsberg, where, after studying philosophy and theology at the University, he for some time acted as a private tutor. In 1633 he was appointed assistant in the Cathedral school, and in 1636 Conrector. He then, in 1639, became Professor of Poetry in the University, was five times Dean of the Philosophical Faculty, and in 1656–57 Rector of the University. He d. at Königsberg, April 15, 1659 (*Koch*, iii. 182–191 ; *Allg. Deutsche Biog.*, iv. 685–688, &c.).

Dach was much of an invalid, and nearly broke down under the hard labour and poor pay of his early tutorial work at Königsberg, but found a true friend and generous patron in R. Roberthin (q.v.). In his later years the effects of the Thirty Years' War made themselves visible in Königsberg by depression of trade, famine, &c. In 1648 he lost Roberthin by death, and in 1649 many of his fellow professors fell victims to the pestilence, while during the last year of his life he suffered from a lingering consumption. These facts explain the sombreness of much of his verse. In 1636 he joined in forming the Poetical Union of Königsberg [*see* **Alberti**], and was its poetic soul. He was the most important poet of the Königsberg School, and one of the first lyric poets of his time—happy in expression, pure in style, and true hearted. But of the mass of his poems (some 1360 in all, many of which were "occasional" pieces for the Electoral House of Brandenburg, and for private friends) very few retain popularity ; the best known being his *Aennchen von Tharaw.*

Dach's hymns, some 165 in all, appeared in broadsheet form, in H. Alberti's *Arien*, 1638–1650, and in the Königsberg Hymn-books, 1639–1690. They deservedly place him amongst the best hymn writers of his time, and win him the distinction of being one of the most lovable, most profound and most elegant of the more contemplative hymn writers. Their personal and subjective character, and the fact that so many are hymns of preparation for death, have prevented all but a few from finding a place in modern hymnals.

Five of Dach's hymns have passed into English, all of which are included in the complete edition of his *Werke* by Hermann Oesterley, pub. at Tübingen, 1876. They are :—

i. **Ich steh in Angst und Pein.** [*Second Advent.*] The Königsberg University Library possesses a broadsheet, printed at Elbing, 1642, as a *Christliches Trauer-Lied* to Christoph Behm, on the death, on Nov 22, 1633, of his son Christoph, a student of theology. It was included in pt. iv., Königsberg, 1641, of H. Alberti's *Arien*, No. 5, in 10 st. of 6 l., entitled "Supremi Judicis urnam non metuit fisus sanguine, Christe, tuo." Repeated in *Oesterley*, p. 91, as No. 1421 in the *Leipzig Vorrath*, 1673, and, omitting st. viii., in the *Wittenberg G. B.*, 1742–1866, No. 893. The only *tr.* in C. U. is :—

A dread hath come on me, a good *tr.*, omitting st. viii., as No. 28 in Miss Winkworth's *C. B. for England*, 1863.

ii. **Kein Christ soll ihm die Rechnung machen.** [*Cross and Consolation.*] 1st pub. in pt. ii., Königsberg, 1640, of H. Alberti's *Arien*, No. 1, in 7 st. of 6 l., entitled "Non caret adversis, qui pius esse velit." Included in *Oesterley*, p. 108, and as No. 631 in the *Unv. L. S.*, 1851. The form *tr.* into English is of st. ii., iii., vii., beginning, "Wer dort mit Christo hofft zu erben," which is No. 812 in Bunsen's *Versuch*, 1833. The only *tr.* in C. U. is :—

Wouldst thou inherit life with Christ on high ? A good *tr.* from Bunsen, by Miss Winkworth, in her *Lyra Ger.*, 1st Ser., 1855, p. 129, and thence unaltered as No. 170 in the *New Zealand Hyl.*, 1872. In *Sacred Lyrics from the German*, Philadelphia, 1859, p. 61, it begins "Couldst thou inherit."

iii. **O wie selig seid ihr doch, ihr Frommen.** [*Eternal Life.*] The original broadsheet, printed at Danzig, 1635, with music by J. Stobäus, as the *Musikalisches Ehrengedächtniss* of Hiob Lepner, Burgomaster of the Königsberg Altstadt, who d. May 9, 1635, is in the Königsberg University Library. Included in B. Derschau's *G. B.*, Königsberg, 1639, p. 73, in 6 st. of 4 l., repeated in *Oesterley*, p. 95 ; the *Leipzig Vorrath*, 1673, No. 1460 ; in Burg's *G. B.*, Breslau, 1746, No. 1086 ; and many others. It is a fine hymn, founded on Rev. xiv., 13–14. Laux-

mann, in *Koch*, viii. 673, relates that J. A. Hochstetter, Prelate of Bebenhausen, near Tübingen (d. 1720), in July, 1719, summoned his household to accompany him in visiting the family burial-place in the Church, and there pointed out his resting-place, spoke to them of eternal life, and ended by requesting them to sing this hymn, and also "Christus der ist mein Leben" (q.v.). The only *tr.* in C. U. is :—

O how blest are ye beyond our telling, a good and full *tr.*, as No. 197 in Miss Winkworth's *C. B. for England*, 1863.

Other trs. are, (1) "O, how blest are ye whose toils are ended," by H. W. Longfellow (1846 or earlier). *P. Works*, Routledge, 1879, p. 648. (2) "Oh! how blessed are ye, saints forgiven," by Miss Borthwick in *H. L. L.*, 1854, p. 32 (1884, p. 35). This is from the double form in the Berlin *G. B.*, 1711, No. 655, which has six stanzas to be sung alternately with Dach's stanzas by the choir as the answer of the Blessed Ones ; with two concluding st. to be sung by choir and congregation together. These eight additional st. are by Jacob Baumgarten (b. 1668; d. 1722), and begin : "Ja, höchst selig sind wir, lieben Brüder ; (3) "O how blessed, faithful souls are ye," by *Miss Winkworth*, 1855, p. 252 ; (4) "How bless'd the saints; who, dying here," by *Dr. G. Walker*, 1860, p. 114. It may be noted that the hymn beginning, "O how blest the throng who now adoring," by *A. T. Russell*, in 4 st. as No. 266 in his *Ps. & Hys.*, 1851, while not a *tr.*, is yet based on this hymn by Dach.

In addition the following hymns by Dach have been *tr.* into English :—

iv. **Nimm dich, o meine Seel' in Acht** [*Treasures in Heaven.*] 1st pub. as No. 5 in pt. vii. Königsberg, 1648, of H. Alberti's *Arien*, in 10 st. of 4 l., entitled "As the noble Rottger von Tieffenbrock, a native of Livonia, departed this world at Königsberg in Prussia the 31st May, 1648," with the motto—

"Das ewige Gut
Macht rechten Muth."

Included by *Oesterley*, p. 208, and as No. 1762 in Knapp's *Ev. L. S.*, 1837 (1865 No. 1668). The *trs.* are, (1) "My soul, let this your thoughts employ," by *Miss Cox*, 1841, p. 133 ; (2) "Think, O my soul, that whilst thou art," by *Lady E. Fortescue*, 1843 (1847, p. 62) ; (3) "Beware, O man, lest endless life," by *Dr. H. Mills*, 1845.

v. **Schöner Himmelssaal.** [*Heaven.*] A beautiful hymn of homesickness for the heavenly country. *Oesterley*, p. 222, gives it as "On the death of Ursula Vogt, wife of Pastor Jacob Bollius, Oct. 30, 1655." Its composition was requested on June 3, 1649." The original broadsheet, with music by H. Alberti, as her *Christliches Sterbelied*, is in the Königsberg University Library. It did not appear in the Königsberg *G. B.*, 1657, but in the ed. of 1675 [Berlin] it is No. 496 (ed. 1690, No. 500), in 9 st. of 6 l. In the *Unv. L. S.*, 1851, No. 637. It is *tr.* as "O ye Halls of Heaven," by *Miss Winkworth*, 1869, p. 185.   [J. M.]

Dachstein, Wolfgang, was, prior to the Reformation, a monk at Strassburg, and organist of the Cathedral. In 1524 he espoused the cause of the Reformation, and in 1525 was appointed organist and assistant preacher at St. Thomas's Church, which offices he held till at least 1530 (*Koch*, ii. 103–104).

Along with his friend M. Greitter (q.v.) he edited the first Strassburg Hymn-book, the *Kirchen ampt*, pub. in 1525. Two of his Psalm versions have been *tr.* into English, but he is best known as author of the melody which is set to the first of these.

i. **An Wasserflüssen Babylon.** [*Ps. cxxxvii.*] 1st pub. 1525, pt. iii, as above, and thence in *Wackernagel*, iii. p. 98, in 5 st. of 10 l. The *trs.*, almost identical, are : (1) "At the ryvers of Babilon," by Bp. Coverdale, 1539 (*Remains*, 1846, p. 571). (2) "At the Rivers of Babylon," in the *Gude and Godly Ballates* (ed. 1568, folio 58, ed. 1868, p. 99).

ii. **O Herr, wer würt sein Wohnung han.** [*Ps. xv.*] 1st pub. 1525 as above, and thence in *Wackernagel*, iii. p. 98, in 3 st. of 7 l. *Tr.* as "O Lord, quha sall in hevin dwell with the," in the *Gude and Godly Ballates* (ed. 1568, folio 46, ed. 1868, p. 78).   [J. M.]

Daily, daily sing the praises. *S. Baring-Gould.* [*Processional.*] This popular processional was written in 1865, and printed on a card for St. John's Mission, Horbury Bridge, Yorkshire. It was again printed in the *Church Times*, 1865, and subsequently included in the *People's H.*, 1867, and other collections. Its use has also extended to some of the American hymn-books. In connection with the Uganda mission a short time before the murder of Bishop Hannington, the following touching circumstance is recorded in the *Rock*, Sept. 18, 1885, as having taken place in January, 1885. Two native lads who had been kidnapped, but subsequently released, reported—

"That they had been taken with Kakumba and Ashe's boy, as also Serwanga, a tall, fine fellow, a baptised lad whom Majasi [the leader of the hostile party] had caught, and Duta's wife Sarah and her child, to a place outside the capital. That Serwanga, Kakumba, and Ashe's boy had been tortured by having their arms cut off, and were then bound alive to a scaffolding, under which a fire was made, and they were *slowly burnt to death.* Majasi and his men mocked them, and bade them pray now if Isa Masiya [Jesus Christ] would rescue them from his hands. The dear lads clung to their faith, and in the fire they sang, *Killa siku tunsifu* (the hymn, 'Daily, daily sing the praises.')." [J. J.]

Dale, Ella, Mrs. Van Alstyne, q. v.

Dale, Thomas, M.A., s. of Thomas Dale, a bookseller in London, b. at Pentonville, Aug. 22, 1797, and educated at Christ's Hospital, and Corpus Christi College, Cambridge, graduating B.A. 1822, M.A. 1825. On taking Holy Orders, he became, after holding several curacies, Vicar of St. Bride's, Fleet Street, London; Canon of St. Paul's, 1843; Vicar of St. Pancras, 1846; and Rector of Therfield, Herts, 1860. In 1870 he was nominated to the Deanery of Rochester, but died before induction, May 14, 1870. His poetical works are :—

(1) *The Widow of Nain,* 1819; (2) *The Outlaw of Tauris,* 1820; (3) *Irad and Adah, a tale of the Flood; and Specimens of a New Translation of the Psalms,* 1822. These *Poems* were collected and pub. in one vol. in 1836; 2nd ed. 1842. ;

From these works the following hymns have been taken :—

1. **Dear as thou wert [wast], and justly dear** (1819). *Burial.* In the *Leeds H. Bk.*, 1853, and several American collections. It is from the *Widow of Nain,* and is given as a dirge sung at the funeral by the Village Minstrel.

2. **O never, never can we know** (1822). *Good Friday.* In the Bap. *Ps. & Hys.*, 1858–80.

3. **Speak, O ye judges of the earth** (1822). *Ps. lviii.* In the *Mitre H. Bk.*, 1836, &c.

4. **The Lord Whose Name is love** (1836). *Children's Praises.* In the *Mitre H. Bk,* 1836.

5. **When the spark of life is waning** (1819). *A Dying request.* This is No. viii. of Poems, appended to *The Widow of Nain,* 1819, p. 69. In Stevenson's *Hys. for Ch. & Home,* 1873.

Other hymns of a similar character might be taken from these works with advantage.

[W. T. B.]

Damascene, St. John. [John of Damascus.]

Damiani, or Damian, Peter, Saint, Cardinal, Bishop, and Doctor of the Church, whom Dom Gueranger calls "The austere reformer of the 11th century," was b. at Ravenna, about 988. He was the youngest of many children. His mother abandoned him as a babe, and his life was only saved by

his being discovered by a faithful female servant, who took care of him until such time as his mother relented and received him back again. Both his parents dying while he was very young, he fell into the hands of a married brother, who, treating him with great harshness and regarding him rather as a slave than a near relation, sent him, "when he was grown up, into the fields to feed swine." In spite of this treatment, he early developed a virtuous and pious disposition, and another brother, Damian (after whom he is said to have been named), who was arch-priest of Ravenna, took pity on him, and had him educated. The progress he made in learning was the admiration of his teachers, and led very soon to his being employed as a teacher. He was very strict, even as a youth, as regards his mode of life, habituating himself to frequent watching, fasting, self-mortification and prayer. Struck with the self-denial of two Benedictine monks, who happened to call where he was living, he embraced their profession, and became a "religious" (in the monastery of Avellino, in the diocese of Gubbio) of the order of the monks of the Holy Cross of Fontavellana. Of that community he, in A.D. 1041, became the Superior, and so extended its usefulness that he was looked upon as the second founder, the first having been Ludolphus, a disciple of St. Romuald. He founded no less than five monasteries under the same rule, the Priors of which remained under his jurisdiction. After twelve years of eminent service to the Church, he was induced by Pope Stephen IX. to accept, in 1057, very much against his own wish, the position of Cardinal-Bishop of Ostia. This, after much difficulty, he was allowed to resign by Pope Alexander II., in 1062, but coupled with the reserve of a power to employ him in important Church matters, as he might at any time find needful. With his bishopric he also resigned his post as Superior of his old monastery, where he once more took up his abode. During his retirement (a retirement constantly broken in upon by calls from the Pontiff to proceed in a legatine capacity to settle various questions of importance to the Church in different parts of Europe), he lived a life of extraordinary asceticism and self-mortification. It was on his return journey from Ravenna, whither he had been sent as legate to inquire into the enormities charged against Henry, Archbishop of Ravenna, and otherwise adjust the affairs of the Church there, that he was called to his rest in his eighty-fourth year. He died of fever, at Faenza, in the monastery of Our Lady, on the 22nd or 23rd of March, 1072.

Damiani endeavoured by his literary labours to advance the cause of order and morality, and to add his quota, by no means an insignificant one, in worth or amount, to the church's store of Latin hymns. "He has left," as *Archbishop Trench* remarks, "a considerable body of Latin verse," but it is only with his hymns that we are concerned in these pages.

It is not surprising to find these hymns, the work of such a devoted servant of the Church of Rome, deeply tinged with the superstitions of that Church, and thereby to Protestant minds disfigured; but, notwithstanding this drawback, there are very few amongst the compositions of Latin hymn-writers to compare with some of our author's in vivid word-painting and richness of description. Such compositions as "Ad perennis vitae fontem," and "Gravi me terrore pulsas, vitae dies ultima," have very few equals in merit in the school of poetry to which they belong, while the difference between them in thought and treatment is most marked, and exhibits to great advantage the versatility of their composer. In addition to the two hymns named (see " Ad perennis," concerning its disputed authorship), *Daniel* gives in vol. i. the texts of four hymns in full, and the first stanzas of ten others. The best known in addition to the two named are, "Crux, mundi benedictio ;" and " Paule doctor egregie " (q.v.).   [D. S. W.]

Dana, Mary S. B. [Shindler, M. S. B.]

Daniel, Hermann Adalbert, was b. at Köthen, Nov. 18, 1812. He studied at the University of Halle, graduating Ph.D. in 1835. In 1834 he was appointed one of the masters in the Paedagogium at Halle, in 1847 assistant inspector, and in 1854 professor there. He resigned his offices in 1870, and retired to Dresden. On his return from a visit to Westphalia he d. at Leipzig, Sept. 13, 1871 (*Allg. Deutsche Biog.*, iv. 731–734).

Daniel was the author of various geographical, scholastic and liturgical works. In the department of German Hymnology he is known as the compiler of a very indifferent hymn-book, the *Evangelishes Kirchengesangbuch*, Halle, 1842 (the only fairly good portion of the work being the index of authors compiled by Diaconus Dryander, of Halle) ; and as the author of the article *Gesangbuch* in Ersch and Gruber's *Encyclopaedia*, Leipzig, 1850. In the department of Latin Hymnology he did good service by his *Thesaurus Hymnologicus, sive hymnorum, canticorum, sequentiarum, circa annum MD. usitatarum, collectio amplissima:* vol. i. consisting of Latin hymns, Halle, 1841 ; vol. ii. with Latin sequences, 1843 ; vol. iii. with Greek hymns edited by R. Vorbaum, and Syriac hymns edited by L. Splieth, 1846 ; vols. iv., v. as a supplement to vols. i., ii. in 1855. It may be characterised as, the work of a man who greatly loved his subject, but to whose mind the instinct of accuracy was in great measure wanting. In his first volume he worked with a very imperfect critical apparatus, but in his last two volumes (to which in many cases he transferred the texts and notes of *F. J. Mone* almost verbatim) he did much to improve his work. Yet even with the help of the index in vol. v., the work is most unsatisfactory. The index is bad, the arrangement of the work is confusing, and the references, which are very numerous and painfully contracted, have no table of abbreviations. Still, with all its defects it is an invaluable work. It contains the texts of many hymns not otherwise easily accessible, and information of much interest and value. It is worthy of exhaustive Indices, and in its own department has yet to be superseded. In this Dictionary it is quoted as *Daniel*.   [J. M.]

Daniel, Robert T., was b. June 10, 1773, in Middlesex Co., Virginia, and removed in boyhood to Orange Co., North Carolina. He was engaged for some time as a blacksmith and cabinet-maker. In 1803 he was ordained to the Baptist Ministry, and acted as a missioner in North and South Carolina, Virginia, Tennessee, and Mississippi. Besides being an agent for various Baptist Missionary and Education Societies, he was an eminent revivalist. He d. at Paris, Tennessee, 1840. His hymn for Immersion, "Lord, in humble, sweet submission," appeared in Broaddus's *Dover Sel.*, 1828–31, in 6 st. of 4 l. ; Winchell's *Additional Hymns*, 1832 ; and is given in Spurgeon's *O. O. H. Bk.*, 1866.   [F. M. B.]

Daniell, John Jeremiah, b. at Bath, Oct. 6, 1819. In 1848 he was ordained by the Bp. of Manchester. His subsequent charges included the curacies of Gerrans, Menheniot, Kington-Langley, and others, and the vicarages of Langley-Fitzurse, Winterborne-Stoke, and Berwick St. James, Wilts, and Langley-Burrell, having been preferred to the last in 1879. Mr. Daniell is the author of several prose works, as : *Life of Mrs. Godolphin ; The Geography of Cornwall,*

&c. ; and of a poetical work, *Lays of the English Cavaliers.* His hymns in C. U. are :—

1. **Alleluia, thanks and glory.** *Children praising Jesus.* Contributed to the S. P. C. K. *Children's Hys.*, No. 69.
2. **Come, sing with holy gladness.** *Praise of Christ.* Contributed to the *Appendix of H. A. & M.*, 1868, and since adopted by several collections in G. Britain and America.

Mr. Daniell has also written several hymns for local use : but these have not appeared in the larger and more widely used collections. He d. Nov. 1, 1898.   [J. J.]

Danish Hymnody. [Scandinavian Hymnody.]

Dank, Dank, sey dir für dein Erbarmen. [*Holy Communion.*] Appeared as No. 158 in the Hamburg *G. B.*, 1787, in 3 st. of 6 l. Repeated as No. 357 in the Berlin *G. B.*, 1829, and as No. 298 in the Hamburg *G. B.*, 1842. In Dr. A. J. Rambach's *Nachricht* to the latter it is given as probably by C. C. Sturm, and as first pub. in the 1787 *G. B.* It was probably suggested by the hymn " Nun habe Dank für deine Liebe," in 9 st. of 6 l., which is included as a Post-Communion hymn in J. G. Zollikofer's *G. B.*, Leipzig, 1766, and is ascribed to Z. himself. *Tr.* as :—

Thanks, thanks be to Thee for Thy pity. A full and good *tr.* in Miss Warner's *Wayfaring Hymns*, 1869 (ed. 1877, p. 49), and thence, omitting st. ii., as No. 442 in Stevenson's *H. for Ch. and Home*, 1873.   [J. M.]

Darby, John Nelson, M.A., youngest s. of John Darby of Leap, King's Co., Ireland, was b. at Westminster, Nov. 18, 1800 ; educated at Trinity College, Dublin, where he graduated in 1819 ; and in due course was called to the Bar. He subsequently took Holy Orders ; but in a short time allied himself with the *Plymouth Brethren.* In the exercise of his ministry amongst them he visited most parts of the world, and translated the Bible into English, French, and German. His published works, including a *Synopsis of the Books of the Bible ; Notes on Revelations,* &c., are numerous. He d. at Bournemouth, April 29, 1882. His hymns in C. U. are :—

1. **Hark, ten thousand voices crying.** *The Second Advent anticipated. Praise.* Appeared in *Hys. for the Poor of the Flock,* 1837, and repeated in *Ps. and Hys. and S. Songs,* Lond., Walther, 1842, and *A Few Hys.,* &c., 1856. It is also given in a few collections other than those for use amongst the "Brethren."
2. **O Lord, thy love's unbounded, So sweet, &c.** *God's unchanging Love.* Given in *A Few Hys.,* &c., 1856, No. 82, in 8 st. of 4 l. Another hymn in the same collection, No. 85, begins with the same first line : "O Lord, Thy love's unbounded ! So full, so vast, so free !" This is in 2 st. of 8 l., and is attributed in the "s. MSS." to J. N. Darby, in common with the first.
3. **Rest of the saints above.** *Heaven.* In *A Few Hys.,* &c., 1856, No. 79, in 14 st. of 4 l.
4. **Rise, my soul, thy God directs thee.** *Divine Guidance.* 1st pub. in *Hys. for the Poor of the Flock,* 1837 ; and again in *Ps. and Hys.,* 1842 (as above) ; and *A Few Hys.,* &c., 1856, in 10 st. of 4 l. It is also in Dr. Walker's Cheltenham *Ps. and Hys.,* 1855–1881.
5. **This world is a wilderness wide.** *Following Christ.* This is No. 139, in 8 st. of 4 l., in *A Few Hys.,* &c., 1856.
6. **Though faint, yet pursuing, we go on our way.** *Divine Strength and Defence.* This hymn was given anonymously in the Bap. *Ps. and Hys.,* 1858, No. 558, in 5 st. of 8 l. In the 1871 ed. of the same collection, it appeared as by " John N. Darby (?) 1861." Here we have a doubt and an error. The doubt is with respect to the authorship ; and the error is in the date. A hymn pub. in 1858 cannot be accurately dated "1861." The evidence for the J. N. Darby authorship is most unsatisfactory. We can simply name it "*Anon.*"

All these hymns were published anonymously; and the ascriptions of authorship of 1–5 are given from the " s. mss." The same mss. say that he edited the work above referred to : *A Few Hymns and some Spiritual Songs, Selected,* 1856, *for the Little Flock.* Lond. Groombridge & Sons.   [J. J.]

Dark was my soul, and dead in sin. *J. Fawcett.* [*Life a Journey.*] 1st pub. in his *Hymns,* &c., 1782. No. 3, in 12 st. of 4 l., and headed "Thou shalt remember all the way," &c. Deut. viii. 2. From it a cento has come into C. U. as in Snepp's *Songs of G. & G.,* 1872, beginning, "Thus far my God hath led me on." It is composed of st. vi.-viii., xi., xii.   [J. J.]

Darkly rose the guilty morning. *J. Anstice.* [*Good Friday.*] Appeared in *Hymns by J. Anstice., M.A.,* 1836, p. 24, in 4 st. of 6 l. In 1841 it was included in *The Child's Christian Year,* and repeated in the *Leeds H. Bk.,* 1853, the 1874 *Suppl.* to the *N. Cong.,* and others, with st. i. l. 6, "thorn-plaited," for "thorn-platted"; and st. ii., l. 6, "sad Gethsemane" for "green Gethsemane." In 1858 it was rewritten by the Rev. J. Ellerton, for a class of Sunday school children, and given in his *Hys. for S. Schools & Bible Classes,* Brighton, 1858, as, "Now returns the awful morning." This was again rewritten for *Church Hys.,* 1871. Of this arrangement st. ii. and iv. are by Mr. Anstice, and i., ii., v. are by Mr. Ellerton.   [J. J.]

Darling, Thomas, m.a., s. of George Darling, m.d., b. in London, 1816, educated at the Charterhouse, and St. John's College, Cambridge, graduating b.a. 1838, and m.a. 1841. In 1839 he took Holy Orders, and subsequently became Incumbent of Thanington, near Canterbury, and in 1848 Rector of St. Michael Royal with St. Martin-Vintry, City of London. Mr. Darling published in 1855 *Hymns for the Church of England* (Lond. Longmans), arranged according to the Order of the Book of Common Prayer. The last edition (1887) contains 336 hymns, of which about 20 are by the editor. These hymns, which appeared from time to time in the various editions of his collection, are :—

1. All saints of the Lord. (1855.) *Easter.* In the 1887 ed. of the *Hymns,* this reads, " Ye saints of the Lord."
2. As chief among ten thousand see. (1858.) *Easter.*
3. At early dawn the mountain bound. (1857). *For Private use.*
4. Behold, I come ; and with me bring. (1860.) *Sunday next before Advent.*
5. Behold, the vineyard of the Lord. (1857.) *The Church of Christ.*
6. Father of heaven, all nature upholding. (1858.) *Trinity.*
7. From cleft in Pyrenean rock. (1858.) *Healing Water.* For Private use.
8. Lift high a festal canticle. (1857.) *Christmas.*
9. Most gracious Lord, in all distress. (1855.) *Common Trouble.*
10. The everlasting hills declare. (1858.) *Ascension.* Written at Bagneres de Luchon in the Pyrenees, 1858.
11. There are who mount with eagle wings. (1858.) *St. John the Evangelist.*
12. There is a stream whose waters flow. (1858.) *Living Water.*
13. To God the glory, while we tell. (1860.) *St. Michael and All Angels.*
14. We now with one accord. (1855.) *Praise.* In the 1887 ed. of the *Hymns,* &c., this is given as, " Let all men praise the Lord."

15. What light is this whose silvery gleam. (1855.) *Epiphany.*
16. Who, when beneath affliction's rod. (1855.) *Resignation.*

In addition to these Mr. Darling has most successfully adapted hymns from other writers. These include, "Lord Jesus, taken from Thy servants' sight"; "Shepherd of the ransomed flock"; "The winds of God have changed their note" (all of which see); and "By faith, from day to day," and "Where dwells the glorious King?" from "The God of Abraham praise" (q. v.). Mr. Darling's original compositions and adaptations are more richly poetical than is usual with modern hymns. They are at the same time very devotional and of practical value.   [J. J.]

Darracott, Risdon, pupil of Dr. Doddridge, and some time Presbyterian minister at Wellington, Somerset. Born 1717, d. Mar. 14, 1759. See "O God of Bethel," &c.

Das ist meine Freude hier. [*Joy in God.*] No. 519 in Freylinghausen's *Neues Geistreiches G. B.,* 1714, in 9 st. of 7 l. *Tr.* as:—

Now I find a lasting joy, a *tr.* of st. i., vi., vii., by Miss Borthwick, as No. 156, in Dr. Pagenstecher's *Coll.,* 1864.   [J. M.]

Daughter of Zion, from the dust. *J. Montgomery.* [*For the Jews.*] Appeared in the Leeds *Sel. of Hymns,* 1822, No. 254, in 5 st. of 4 l., and based on Is. lii. 1. In 1825 it was included by Montgomery in his *Christian Psalmist,* No. 555, and again in his *Original Hymns,* 1853, No. 241. In *Common Praise,* 1879, it is given as "Arise, O Zion ! from the dust." Its American use in its original form is extensive.   [J. J.]

Daughters of Sion, come, behold. *I. Watts.* [*Coronation of Christ.*] Appeared in his *Hys. and S. Songs,* 1707, in 6 st. of 4 l., and entitled "The Coronation of Christ, and Espousals of the Church" (Bk. 1, No. 72). In its full form its use is limited. A popular arrangement, beginning with st. ii., "Jesus, Thou everlasting King," is found in numerous collections, as in the *Wes. H. Bk.,* 1830. [J. J.]

Davies, Samuel, m.a., b. near Summit Ridge, Newcastle, Delaware, America, Nov. 3, 1723, and educated under the Rev. Samuel Blair, of Chester County, Pennsylvania, through the pecuniary assistance of the Rev. William Robinson, a Presbyterian Minister of New Brunswick. In 1745 he was licensed by the Presbytery of Newcastle as a probationer for the Ministry, and undertook duty in Virginia, in 1747. After visiting England in 1753, on behalf of the New Jersey College, and having received the degree of m.a., he was appointed President of New Jersey Presbyterian College, Princeton, in succession to Jonathan Edwards. He d. Feb. 4, 1761, at the early age of 37. His mss. were entrusted to Dr. T. Gibbons, who pub. therefrom 5 vols. of *Sermons.* In 1851 the *Sermons* were republished in 3 vols., including a *Memoir* by the Rev. A. Barnes. His hymns, 16 in all, were given by Dr. Gibbons in his *Hymns adapted to Divine Worship,* 1769. As a hymn-writer he followed the lines laid down by Watts, and his verses are solid, but somewhat dry and heavy. Those of his hymns which are still retained in C. U. are:—

1. Eternal Spirit, Source of Light. *Influences of the H. Spirit implored.* From Dr. Gibbons's *Hymns*, &c., 1769, Bk. ii., No. 29, this passed into several of the older collections. In later works it is more frequently found in the American hymnals than those of G. Britain. It is in 4 st. of 6 l., as in Dr. Hatfield's *Church H. Bk.*, N. Y., 1872, and the *Leeds H. Bk.*, 1853.

2. Great God of wonders, all Thy ways. *The Pardoning God.* This is one of the most, if not the most, popular of the author's hymns both in G. Britain and America. It has appeared in more than one hundred hymn-books in England alone, sometimes in full (5 st. of 6 l.), and at other times abbreviated, as in Spurgeon's *O. O. H. Bk.*, 1866; the *Bap. Hymnal*, 1879, &c. Its 1st publication was in Dr. Gibbons's *Hymns*, &c., 1769, Bk. i., No. 59.

3. How great, how terrible that God. *The Judgment.* In *Gibbons*, No. 37 of Bk. i., in 7 st. of 4 l.

4. Jesus, how precious is Thy name. *Jesus the Prophet, Priest, and King.* Is No. 31 of Bk. ii. in *Gibbons*, in 6 st. of 6 l. It was very popular with the older compilers, as *Ash and Evans*, *Rippon*, *Bickersteth*, and others in G. Britain, and also in America; but in modern collections it is rarely found. It is worthy of notice.

5. Lord, I am Thine, entirely Thine. *Holy Communion.* In *Gibbons* this is No. 28 of Bk. ii., in 7 st. of 4 l. It is very popular in America, but unknown to most English hymnals. In all editions of Rippon's *Sel.*, 1787–1844, it is given in 2 st. as "Lord, am I Thine, entirely Thine?" The hymn, "While to Thy table I repair," in the Andover *Sabbath H. Bk.*, 1858, is compiled from this hymn.

6. What strange perplexities arise. *Self-Examination.* This hymn is equal to No. 5 in American popularity, and exceeds it in G. Britain. In Dr. Hatfield's *Church H. Bk.*, N. Y., 1872, it is abbreviated and slightly altered. Full text in 6 st. of 4 l. is in Spurgeon's *O. O. H. Bk.*, 1866. It was 1st pub. in Gibbons's *Hymns*, &c., 1769.

7. While o'er our guilty land, O Lord. *Fast Day.* This hymn, besides appearing in its original form in some collections, and with abbreviations in others, is also the source of "On Thee, our Guardian God, we call," st. iv. of the original given in a few American collections; and of the same arrangement of stanzas, "On Thee we call, O Lord, our God," in the Andover *Sabbath H. Bk.*, 1858, and others. The original in *Gibbons* is Bk. i., No. 56, in 8 st. of 4 l.

The remaining hymns by Davies have failed to attain a position in the hymn-books either of G. Britain or America. [F. M. B.]

Davis, Richard, b. 1658, d. 1714, was a native of Cardiganshire, received a liberal education, and in early manhood was for some years master of a grammar school in London. In 1690 he received an invitation to the pastorate from the Independent Church at Rothwell (or Rowell), in Northamptonshire, and with this church he spent the remaining 24 years of his life. He was a remarkable man, and, in connection with his Evangelistic labours in the region round about, anticipated Wesley's institution of lay-preachers. He pub. a volume of 168 hymns. The date of the 1st ed. is unknown. The title of the 2nd ed. is :—

"*Hymns Composed on Several Subjects, and on Divers Occasions; in Three Parts. With an Alphabetical*

Table. By R. Davis, minister of the gospel. The second edition. Some of the Hymns composed by other hands. London: Printed for W. Marshall, at the Bible, in Newgate Street; and H. Barnard, at the Bible in the Poultry, 1694." A 7th ed. was published in 1748, with a recommendatory preface by Dr. John Gill, who in his youth had received much spiritual stimulus and guidance from Mr. Davis. The 8th ed. by *J. A. Jones*, of Mitchell Street Chapel, London, appeared in 1833.

However acceptable these hymns may have been to the villagers of the midland counties of England 190 years ago, they are too defective in metre, and altogether too uncouth in style for use now, and are of interest only to the student of early English hymnody.

[W. R. S.]

Davis, Thomas, M.A., s. of Dr. R. F. Davis, Rector of All Saints, Worcester, and of Pendock, Worcestershire, was b. Feb. 15, 1804. He was educated for the law, and practised as a solicitor for two years. He then entered Queen's Coll., Oxford, and graduated B.A. in 1833, and M.A. in 1837. On taking Holy Orders he became Curate of All Saints, Worcester. In 1839 he was preferred as Incumbent of Roundhay, Leeds. Mr. Davis's works, in which his hymns appeared, are :—

(1) *Devotional Verse for a Month*, 1855 ; (2) *Songs for the Suffering*, 1859 ; (3) *The Family Hymnal*, 1860 ; (4) *Hymns, Old and New, for Church and Home, and for travel by Land or Sea; consisting of 223 selected, and 260 Original Hymns*, Lond., Longmans, 1864 ; and (5) *Annus Sanctus; or, Aids to Holiness in Verse for every day in the Year*, 1877. (6) *Help Homewards in Verse for Every Day in the Year*, 1883. The hymns given in the earlier of these works are generally repeated in the later.

Of Mr. Davis's hymns the best known are "O Paradise Eternal"; "Holiest, holiest, hearken in love"; "'Tis sweet on earth to wake at morn"; "Let every voice for praise awake"; and "Baptized into the Name." Many of Mr. Davis's hymns are of considerable merit, and his works should be consulted by all hymn-book compilers. The "selected" hymns in his *Hys. Old & New* are marked thus †, the rest are original. From his various works the following hymns are in C. U. outside of his *Hymns Old and New* in addition to those named and others, which are annotated under their respective first lines :—

i. From *Devotional Verse for a Month*, 1855.
1. Come, Holy Spirit, come, Mercies revealing. *Whitsuntide.*
2. Dear is the eye of earthly love. *The Loneliness of Jesus.*
3. Heavy and dark the clouds o'erhung. *Good Friday.*
4. I will not mourn my weakness, Lord. *Affliction.*

ii. From the *Family Hymnal*, 1860.
5. Shall I fear, O earth, thy bosom? *Easter.*
6. Sing, ye seraphs, in the sky. *Universal Praise.*

iii. From *Hymns Old and New*, 1864.
7. Day by day and year by year. *Old and New Year.*
8. Does one small voice within the soul? *Conscience.*
9. Faith alone breathes calm devotion. *The Calm of Faith.*
10. Father, vouchsafe us grace divine. *Morning.*
11. Great Father of our race. *God the Father.*
12. How kind our Father's voice. *Morning.*
13. I thank Thee, Lord, for every night. *Morning.*
14. In holy contemplation, Give me, &c. *After a Bad Harvest.*
15. Let every voice for praise awake. *God is Love.*
16. Lord, send Thy Spirit from above. *For an Increase of Charity.*
17. My Father kept me through the night. *Morning.*
18. Our God is love, O sweetly sing. *God is Love.*
19. The floods lift up their waves, O God. *For use at Sea.*

20. The Lord our God is King. *God the King Eternal.*
21. To all Thy servants who this day. *Holy Communion.*
22. To Thine own peaceful skies. *Ascension.*
23. What though fields of earth have yielded. *After a Bad Harvest.*

iv. From *Annus Sanctus*, 1877.

24. Christian, be thou content. *Quinquagesima Sunday.*
25. Keep Thou my heart that it may ne'er. *Slow to Wrath.*
26. More light, more life, more love. *Light, Life and Love desired.*
27. Unworthy though I be. *Divine Guidance desired.*
28. Why comes this fragrance on the summer breeze? *God is Love.* [J. J.]

Day after day I sought the Lord. *J. C. Hare.* [*Ps. xl.*]. This version of Ps. xl. in two parts; pt. ii. beginning, "Show forth Thy mercy, gracious Lord," appeared in his *Portions of the Psalms in English Verse, Selected for Public Worship* (Lond. J. W. Parker), 1839, pp. 56–7, each in 5 st. of 4 l. In 1875 both parts were included in an unaltered form in the *Wes. H. Bk.*, 566. [J. J.]

Day by day the manna fell. *J. Conder.* [*The Lord's Prayer.*] Appeared in his *Cong. H. Bk.*, 1836, No. 516, in 6 st. of 4 l., and based upon the text, "Give us day by day our daily bread." In the following year it was given as the fourth of six hymns on "The Lord's Prayer" in Conder's work *The Choir and the Oratory*, 1837, p. 33, and repeated in his *Hys. of Praise, Prayer*, &c., 1856, p. 137. It is given in a great many hymnals in G. Britain and America. In some American collections it begins with st. iii., " Lord, my [our] times are in Thy hand." [J. J.]

Day by day we magnify Thee. *J. Ellerton.* [*Praise—Children's Hymn.*] Written to be sung daily at the opening of a National School in Brighton, and pub., in 1858, in the author's *Hys. for Schools and Bible Classes*, from whence it passed into *Church Hys.*, 1871, Thring's *Coll.* (slightly altered), the *Methodist S. S. H. Bk.*, and other hymnals. In the *Church Praise Bk.*, N.Y., 1882, st. iv.-viii. are given anonymously as No. 93. Orig. text in *Church Hys.*, No. 568. [J. J.]

Day of Judgment, day of wonders. *J. Newton.* [*Advent.*] Written in 1774, and 1st pub. in the *Olney Hymns*, 1779, Bk. ii., No. 77, in 7 st. of 5 l., and headed "The Day of Judgment." In the Rev. J. Bull's work on Newton, this hymn is referred to under the date of 1775 as follows:—

" ' Sunday, 26th, spoke in the evening from a hymn on the day of judgment.' This hymn, he says previously, took him the most of two days to finish."

The quotation "Sunday, 26th," &c. [June 26th, 1775] is from Newton's Diary. Few of our author's hymns have attained to greater popularity than this both in G. Britain and America. It has been translated into several languages, including Latin (st. i.–iii., vi.): "Dies mirandorum! dies," in Bingham's *Hymno. Christ. Latina.*, 1871. Orig. text in *Lyra Brit.*, 1867, p. 440. [J. J.]

Day of loss and day of gain. *J. S. B. Monsell.* [*Good Friday.*] Pub. in his *Spiritual Songs*, 1857 (People's ed., 1875, p. 64), in 20 st. of 3 l., and headed "The Dark Day." In the Rev. F. Pott's *Hymns*, &c., 1861, No. 80,

there is a cento from this hymn, st. 1, 10, 12, 13, 17–20 being employed. In his *Hys. of Love & Praise*, 1863, p. 82, Dr. Monsell gave st. 13–20, beginning, " Jesus! Gentle Sufferer! say." This, with the addition of a doxology, was repeated in his *Parish Hymnal*, 1875.

Dayman, Edward Arthur, B.D., 3rd s. of John Dayman, of Mambury, N. Devon, b. at Padstow in Cornwall, 11th July, 1807, and educated at Blundell's School, Tiverton, Devon, and Exeter Coll. Oxon. 1st Class in Lit. Hum. 1829, B.A. 1830, M.A. 1831, B.D. 1841. He was for some time Fellow and Tutor of his College, and Pro-Proctor, 1835. Taking Holy Orders in 1835, he became successively examiner for Univ. Scholarship for Latin, 1838; in Lit. Hum., 1838–9, and 1841–2, Sen. Proctor of the University 1840, Rector of Shilling-Okeford or Shillingstone, Dorset, 1842; Rural Dean, 1849; Proctor in Convocation, 1852; and Hon. Canon of Bitton in Sarum Cathedral, 1862. His works include *Modern Infidelity*, 1861, and *Essay on Inspiration*, 1864. He was joint editor with Lord Nelson and Canon (afterwards Bishop) Woodford of the *Sarum Hymnal*, 1868; which contains *trs.* from the Latin, and original hymns by him; and with Canon Rich-Jones, of *Statuta et Consuetudines Ecclesiae Cathedralis Sarisburiensis*, 1883. He also contributed several *trs.* from the Latin to *The Hymnary*, 1872. He has been for many years engaged in compiling an English Dictionary of Mediaeval Latin founded on Du Cange. The original hymns contributed by him to the *Sarum Hyl.*, 1868, are, with the dates of their composition, as follows:—

1. Almighty Father, heaven and earth, q.v. (1867.) *Offertory.*
2. O Lord, be with us when we sail. (1865.) *For use at Sea.*
3. O Man of Sorrows, Thy prophetic eye. (1865.) *Tuesday before Easter.*
4. Sleep thy last sleep. (1868.) *Burial.*
5. Upon the solitary mountain's height. (1866.) *Transfiguration.*
6. When the messengers of wrath. (1867.) *During Pestilence and Famine.*
7. Who is this with garments dyed? (1866.) *Monday before Easter.* [J. J.]

Days and moments quickly flying. *E. Caswall.* [*Old and New Year.*] This hymn appeared in 4 st. of 4 l. with the title, "Swiftness of Time," in his *Masque of Mary and other Poems*, 1858. With it was also given, under the title of "A Warning," one stanza, beginning "As the tree falls, So must it lie," &c. From these, together with abbreviations, additions, or alterations the following centos have been made :—

1. In *Chope's Hymnal*, 1862, the two with alterations.
2. In *H. A. & M.*, 1868, the same without alterations.
3. In the *Appendix* to the S. P. C. K. *Ps. and Hys.*, 1869, the first hymn, 4 st. with two additional stanzas.
4. In *Hymnary*, 1870–2. The first hymn of 4 st. with alterations, and a fifth st. by the editors.
5. In *Church Hys.*, 1871, a new cento of which st. i., ii., iii., are from the first hymn, much varied; v., vi., from S. P. C. K. *Ps. and Hys.*, altered; and iv., vii., viii., by the compilers.
6. In *H. A. & M.*, 1875, the first hymn of 4 st. slightly altered, and a new stanza.
7. In Thring's *Coll.*, 1882, the same first hymn with alterations by the editor.

Other centos found in a few additional collections are in American use. Orig. texts in Caswall's *Hys. & Poems*, 1873, p. 250. [J. J.]

De Courcy, Richard, M.A., b. in Ireland in 1743, and educated at Trinity College, Dublin. Having received Deacon's Orders, he became, in 1767, Curate to the Rev. Walter Shirley ; but his theological views being obnoxious to Dr. Smythe, the Archbishop of Dublin, he was refused Priest's Orders and inhibited from preaching. These circumstances led to his being invited by Lady Huntingdon to England, and his joining her band of preachers. After some time, through Lady Huntingdon's influence, he obtained Priest's Orders from the Bishop of Lichfield. In 1770 he became Curate of Shawbury, Salop, and in 1774 Vicar of St. Alkmond's, Shrewsbury. The latter he retained to his death in 1803. His theological views, work, and other matters concerning him, are dwelt upon with some detail in the *Life and Times of the Countess of Huntingdon*, 1839. His published works include *Some Elegiac Lines on the Death of the Rev. G. Whitefield*, 1771 ; *Christ Crucified*, a reply to Dr. Priestley, in 2 vols., 1791 ; and various *Sermons*, &c. In 1775 he also published :—

A Collection of Psalms and Hymns Extracted from different Authors, with 'a Preface by Mr. De Courcy, Shrewsbury, 1775. (Preface dated "Shrewsbury, December 6, 1775.")

To the 2nd ed. of this *Coll.*, pub. in 1782, several hymns were added, amongst which the following are by common consent attributed to De Courcy :—

1. Angels who the throne surround. *Praise of Christ.*
2. Hark ! from heaven a voice I hear. *Burial.*
3. Jesus the Saint's perpetual theme. *Christ, the Rose of Sharon.*
4. Lord, I thank Thee for Thy grace. *Thanksgiving for Salvation.*
5. Mount, my soul, to things above. *Looking Heavenward.*

These hymns are attributed to De Courcy on the ground that they cannot be found in any collection or work published before his *Coll.*, and that they have never been claimed by or on behalf of any other hymn-writer. All the hymns in his *Coll.* were pub. anonymously. Other hymns, sometimes attributed to him, have been traced to earlier hymn-books, and are consequently omitted from the foregoing list.   [J. J.]

De profundis exclamantes. [*All Souls.*] This anonymous Sequence from the *Missal of Liége*, of 1502, is given in Neale's *Sequentiae*, 1852 ; *Daniel*, v., p. 320; and *Kehrein*, No. 880. *Tr.* as :—

Christ, enthroned in highest heaven. By R. F. Littledale, written for and 1st pub. in the *People's H.*, 1867, No. 300, and signed "A. L. P."

De Wolf, John. Born at Bristol, Rhode Island, 1786, and educated at Brown University. Subsequently he was Professor of Chemistry in that University, from 1817 to about 1838. He also lectured in medical schools at St. Louis, and in Vermont. His later life was spent at Bristol, R. I., where he d. in 1862. His version of Ps. 148, " Angel bands in strains sweet sounding," appeared in a Providence newspaper about 1815, and again in the *Journal* of that city in an obituary notice of the writer. It was but locally known till included in the Protestant Episc. *Hymnal*, 1871, by the author's relative, Bishop Howe, of Central Pennsylvania.   [F. M. B.]

Deacon, John, b. 1757, d. 1821, half brother to Samuel Deacon (q.v.), joined in early life the G. Baptist Church at Barton Fabis. At the expiration of his apprenticeship he studied for the ministry under the Rev. Dan Taylor, and in 1782 became pastor of the G. Bapt. Church, in Friar Lane, Leicester. In 1791 the G. Baptists of the new connection, desiring a new Hymn-book, requested J. Deacon to prepare a *Selection* for their use. This was pub. in 1800. But the book was not adopted by all the churches, chiefly in consequence of alterations in some of Dr. Watts's hymns, disapproved of on doctrinal grounds. With most, however, it found favour, and a 2nd and enlarged ed. was pub. in 1804, containing 746 hymns. In the *Appendix* to this vol. are 11 hymns by John Deacon, all prepared for use at S. School anniversaries. In 1829, Deacon's collection was revised by a committee appointed by the G. Bapt. Association, and, the expressions objected to being amended, it was formally adopted as the hymn-book of the G. B. Connection. This position it held until 1851 [see **Bapt. Hymnody,** III. 1]. Besides the 11 hymns mentioned above, J. Deacon composed 33 others, which were sung by his congregation on special occasions, and still exist in ms.   [W. R. S.]

Deacon, Samuel, b. 1746, at Ratby, in Leicestershire, d. 1816 at Barton, near Market Bosworth, in the same county. He was s. of Samuel Deacon, sen., one of the first preachers of the Leicestershire General Baptists ; and half brother to John Deacon (q.v.) of Leicester. In 1771, S. Deacon settled at Barton, a small agricultural village, where, however, he presently established a considerable business as clock and watchmaker, and became well known for his mechanical skill. In 1779 he was invited to assist his father in ministering to the cluster of village congregations of General Baptists, of which Barton was the centre. He was popular and useful as a preacher, and continued minister of this church 37 years, receiving no pecuniary remuneration, but himself contributing liberally to various religious enterprises. In 1785 he published a vol. entitled, *A New Composition of Hymns & Poems chiefly on Divine Subjects; designed for the Amusement and Edification of Christians of all Denominations, more particularly them of the Baptist persuasion. Leicester : printed for the author by George Ireland.*" It contained 63 hymns, and 20 meditations. Subsequent editions were considerably enlarged, and the collection became known as the *Barton Hymns*. S. Deacon's style is very homely, and of his numerous hymns, " O who can comprehend the rest " (*Heaven*), and "Ye heavy-laden souls " (*Invitation*), represent most, if not all, now in C. U. S. Deacon was also the author of several religious books, some very popular in their day, and most of them in metre, but they do not contain any of his hymns. [See **Baptist Hymnody,** II. 1.] [W. R. S.]

Dear Angel! ever at my side. *F. W. Faber.* [*The Guardian Angel.*] Appeared in his *Jesus and Mary,* &c., 1849, and his *Hymns*, 1862, in 13 st. of 4 l. It is in use in an abbreviated form in various Roman Catholic hymnals for Schools and Missions. In some collections st. i.-vi., somewhat altered, and with the addition of a doxology, are given as: "Dear *Jesus*, ever at Thy side." It is in the *Plymouth Coll.*, 1855, and other American hymn-books, in addition to the *New Cong.*, 1859, and other English hymnals. In the *Methodist S. Scholars' H. Bk.*, 1870, the opening line is "*Bless'd Jesus*, ever at my side ;" whilst in one or two collections it is again changed to "Dear *Saviour*, ever at my side." This last is almost confined to America. The object of these changes is to adapt a Roman Catholic hymn for Protestant use by substituting our Blessed Lord for "the Guardian Angel."   [J. J.]

Dear Lord, accept a sinful heart. *W. Cowper.* [*Self-acquaintance.*] 1st pub. in J. Newton's *Twenty-Six Letters on Religious Subjects, &c., by Omicron*, 1774, in 6 st. of 4 l., and again in R. Conyers's *Coll.* of the same year. In 1779 it was also included in the *Olney Hymns*, Bk. iii., No. 26. It is found in a few modern collections, including Dr. Dale's *English H. Bk.*, 1874.   [J. J.]

Dear Lord, on this Thy servant's day. *Cecil F. Alexander.* [*St. Matthew.*] 1st appeared in *H. A. & M.*, revised ed. 1875.

Dear Lord, Thy condescending love. *J. Fellows.* [*Holy Baptism.*] Appeared in his *Hys. on Believers' Baptism*, 1773, in 7 st. of 4 l. In this, its original form, it is unknown to modern hymnals. Abbreviated and altered, it was given as, "Dear Lord, *and will* Thy *pardoning love*," in 4 st. in Rippon's *Sel.*, 1787, No. 446, and from thence has passed into various collections in G. Britain and America. It is composed of st. i., iv., v., vi., as (with further slight alterations) in Spurgeon's *O. O. H. Bk.*, 1866, No. 927. [J. J.]

Dear Refuge of my [the] weary soul. *Anne Steele.* [*God the Refuge.*] 1st pub. in her *Poems on Subjects chiefly Devotional*, 1760, vol. i. p. 144, in 8 st. of 4 l., and headed, "God the only Refuge of the troubled mind" (2nd ed. 1780), and in D. Sedgwick's reprint of her *Hymns*, 1863, p. 89. It was given also in the Bristol Bapt. *Coll.* of Ash & Evans, 1769, and in Bickersteth's *Christ. Psalmody*, 1833, and was thus brought into congregational use. It is included in numerous hymnals, both in G. Britain and America. In some collections, as the S. P. C. K. *Ps. & Hys.*, 1853–69, it is given as, "*Thou* Refuge of *my* weary soul ;" and again, as in *Kennedy*, 1863, "*Thou* Refuge of *the* weary soul." [J. J.]

Dear Saviour, tell us where. *B. Beddome.* [*H. Baptism. Adult.*] Pub. in Robert Hall's (posthumous) ed. of Beddome's *Hymns, &c.*, 1817, No. 607, in 5 st. of 4 l., and headed "Following the Flock." In a few collections, including the American *Bapt. Praise Bk.*, 1871, st. iv., v., slightly altered, are given as: "Here, Saviour, we do come." [J. J.]

Dear Saviour, when my thoughts recall. *Anne Steele.* [*Lent.*] 1st pub. in *Miscellaneous Pieces*, which were added as vol. iii. to her *Poems on Subjects chiefly Devotional*, in 1780, pp. 79–80, and not in the *Poems* in 1760, as stated in Spurgeon's

O. O. H. Bk., No. 616, where it is given in an unaltered form. It was reprinted in D. Sedgwick's reprint of Miss Steele's *Hymns*, 1863, p. 137, the original title reading "Penitence and Hope." Its use in America is extensive.   [J. J.]

Dearest of all¦ the names above. *I. Watts.* [*Reconciliation through Christ.*] 1st pub. in the 2nd ed. of his *Hymns and S. Songs.* 1709, Bk. ii., No. 148, in 5 st. of 4 l., and entitled, "God reconciled in Christ." It was included in many of the older collections such as those of *Whitefield* and *Toplady*, and has continued to hold a prominent position in the hymn-books to the present. Its use, in America especially, is very extensive.   [J. J.]

Death cannot make our souls afraid. *I. Watts.* [*Death of Moses.*] Appeared in the 1st ed. of his *Hymns and S. Songs*, 1707, in 4 st. of 4 l. Although included in the older collections of *Toplady* and others, it has almost died out of use in G. Britain. In America it is found in a few modern hymnals, and sometimes as "Death cannot make *my soul* afraid," a reading which appeared in *Toplady*, 1776, No. 82.   [J. J.]

Death has been here, and borne away. *Jane Taylor.* [*Death.*] In the 4th ed. of *Original Hys. for Sunday Schools*, 1816, No. 16, in 7 st. of 4 l., this hymn takes the place of one on the same subject and in a similar strain, which appeared in the 2nd ed. of 1813, as "Now one of our number is dead." "Death has been here," &c., has been in C. U. for many years, and is found in several modern collections for children, but usually in an abbreviated form.   [J. J.]

Death is sin's tremendous wages. *T. Kelly.* [*Wages of Sin.*] 1st pub. in the 3rd ed. of his *Hymns, &c.*, 1809, No. 300, in 5 st. of 6 l., and based on Rom. vi. 25. In some collections, st. iii.-v. are given as "Come, behold a great expedient," as in the Scottish *Evang. Union Hymnal*, 1878, and the *Laudes Domini*, New York, 1884.   [J. J.]

Death may dissolve my body now. *I. Watts.* [*Assurance of Heaven.*] 1st pub. in his *Hymns and S. Songs, &c.*, 1707, Bk. i., No. 27, in 6 st. of 4 l., and entitled, "Assurance of Heaven ; or, A Saint prepared to die." Its use in its full form, except in America, is limited. In Spurgeon's *O. O. H. Bk.*, No. 857, "With heavenly weapons I have fought," is composed of st. ii.-iv., slightly altered. The original hymn, with slight alterations in st. v. only, was included in the draft of the Scottish *Translations and Paraphrases*, 1745, as No. xxxiii. In the authorized issue of the *Trans. and Pars.*, 1781, a recast of the original was given as No. lv., "My race is run, my warfare's o'er." The alterations were numerous (the first line dating from the *Draft* of 1751) ; and in the markings by the eldest daughter of W. Cameron (q.v.) are ascribed to him. It must be designated, *Watts*, 1707, *S. Tr. and Pars.* 1781, *W. Cameron.*   [J. J.]

Death steals upon us unawares. *T. Shepherd.* [*Death.*] In *Penitential Cries. Begun by the Author of the Songs of Praise* [John Mason]. *And carried on by another*

Hand, Licensed and entered Sept. 12, 1693, this hymn appears, as the second of two on the "Death of Saints." It is in 4 st. of 8 l., and 1 st. of 4 l., No. xxxvi. In Dr. Kennedy's *Hymno. Christ.*, 1863, No. 1478, the first half of st. iii. is omitted, and the rest of the hymn is somewhat extensively altered, and brought more in harmony with modern forms and modes of expression. The *Penitential Cries*, together with J. Mason's *Songs of Praise*, were reprinted by D. Sedgwick in 1859.   [J. J.]

Death! 'tis a melancholy day. *I. Watts.* [*Death of the Wicked.*] Appeared in the 1st ed. of his *Hymns and S. Songs*, 1707 (2nd ed. 1709, Bk. ii. No. 52), in 6 st. of 4 l. It is usually abbreviated as in Dr. Hatfield's *Church H. Bk.*, N. Y., 1872. In the Presb. *Ps. & Hys. for the Worship of God*, Richmond, U.S.A., 1867, No. 631: "He is a God of sovereign love," is from this hymn.   [J. J.]

Deathless principle, arise. *A. M. Toplady.* [*Death Anticipated.*] This hymn first appeared in

"*A Memoir of some Principal Circumstances in the Life and Death of the Rev. Augustus Montague Toplady,* late Vicar of Broad Hembury, Devon. To which is added, written by himself, the Dying Believer's Address to his soul, and his own last Will and Testament. London, Pr. for J. Matthews, 1778, pr. 6d."

On p. 24 of this *Memoir* we read:

" The following soliloquy, written some years ago by Mr. Toplady upon the death of a valued friend, has been thought so apposite to himself in his own dying hour that it is presented without any further apology."

After a sentence referring to the Emperor Hadrian, and his poem, " Animula, vagula, blandula," &c., and a note embodying Pope's translation of Hadrian's " Animula," &c., and of "Musculus' Versus," the poem, "Deathless principle, arise" follows, in st. of irregular length. It was subsequently shaped into 6 st. of 8 l., and in this form is given in D. Sedgwick's reprint of Toplady's *Hymns and Sacred Poems*, 1860, p. 165. In its full form it is found in many collections, both old and new, but usually for private use. In some American collections a cento is given beginning: "Deathless spirit, now arise," as in Dr. Hatfield's *Church H. Bk.*, N. Y., 1872, whilst in others, as Longfellow & Johnson's Unitarian *Hys. of the Spirit*, Boston, 1864, there is a second cento, " Burst thy shackles! drop thy clay ! "   [J. J.]

Debilis cessent elementa legis. *Abbé Besnault.* [*The Circumcision.*] In the revised *Paris Breviary*, 1736, it is the hymn for first Vespers on the Feast of the Circumcision. It is also in the *Lyons* and other modern French Breviaries, and Card. Newman's *Hymni Ecclesiae*, 1838 and 1865. *Tr.* as :—

1. The ancient law departs. By the compilers of *H. A. & M.*, 1st appeared in the trial copy of that collection, 1859, and again in the 1st ed., 1861. It has passed into a few hymnals in G. Britain and America, and is sometimes altered.

2. The Law's weak elements. By the Editors of the *Hymnary*, 1872. It is an arrangement of the *trs.* of I. Williams, 1839, and *H. A. & M.*

Translations not in C. U. :—

1. Ye legal elements. *I. Williams.* 1839.
2. Let the departing law's weak factions cease. *J. D. Chambers*, 1857,

3. Now ancient shadows flee. *R. Campbell*, in Shipley's *Annus Sanctus*, 1884, from the *Campbell MSS.*   [J. J.]

Decius, Nicolaus (Nicolaus a Curia or von Hofe, otherwise Hovesch), seems to have been a native of Hof, in Upper Franconia, Bavaria, and to have been originally called *Tech.* He became a monk, and was in 1519 Probst of the cloister at Steterburg, near Wolfenbüttel. Becoming favourable to the opinions of Luther, he left Steterburg in July, 1522, and went to Brunswick, where he was appointed a master in the St. Katherine and Egidien School. In 1523 he was invited by the burgesses of Stettin to labour there as an Evangelical preacher along with Paulus von Rhode. He became preacher at the Church of St. Nicholas; was probably instituted by the Town Council in 1526, when von Rhode was instituted to St. Jacob's; and at the visitation in 1535 was recognised as pastor of St. Nicholas's. He d. suddenly at Stettin, March 21, 1541, with some suspicion of being poisoned by his enemies of the Roman Catholic faction (*Koch*, i. 419–421, 471, 472 ; ii. 483; *Allg. Deutsche Biog.*, iii. 791–793).

He seems to have been a popular preacher and a good musician. Three hymns are ascribed to him. These are versions of the " Sanctus," the " Gloria in excelsis," and the " Agnus Dei." The second and third are noted under these Latin first lines. He is also said to have composed or adapted the melodies set to them. [J. M.]

Deck, James George, eldest s. of John Deck, of Bury St. Edmunds, was b. in 1802 and educated for the army, and became an officer in the Indian service. Retiring from the army, and having joined the Plymouth Brethren, he undertook, in 1843, the charge of a congregation of that body, at Wellington, Somerset. In 1852 he went abroad and settled in New Zealand. His hymns were published in *Hymns for the Poor of the Flock*, 1837–8 ; *Psalms and Hymns*, &c., Lond., Walther (containing those in the former collection), 1842 ; the *Wellington Hymn Book*, 1857 ; *Hymns and Spiritual Songs*, 1860. Of his hymns now in use outside his own denomination, the greater part appeared in the 1837–8 book, and are found in his brother-in-law's (Dr. Walker's) *Cheltenham Ps. & Hys.*, 1855. His compositions are marked by directness of aim, simplicity of language, and great earnestness. The rhythm is good, and an expressive tenderness pervades many of them. Although dealing mainly with the "Second Advent," there are several on other subjects which are of more than average merit. In a collected form they were published in his *Hymns and Sacred Poems*, Melbourne, H. Seelenmeyer, 1876. The more important of his hymns are annotated under their respective first lines. Of the rest we have :—

i. From *Hymns for the Poor of the Flock*, 1838.

1. Behold yon bright and countless throng. *All Saints.* Repeated in Maurice's *Choral H. Bk.*, 1861.
2. How long, O Lord our Saviour. *Second Advent desired.* In the *Parish H. Bk.*, 1863 and 1875, this is altered to "How long, O Lord, *Beloved.*"
3. Jesus, spotless Lamb of God. *Good Friday.*
4. Lord Jesus, are we [we are] one with Thee ? *One with Christ.* In Walker's *Ps. and Hys.*, 1855–80, and several American hymn-books.
5. Lord, we are Thine, our God Thou art. *One with Christ,* Originally in 4 st. of 8 l., it appeared, in a re-

written form in 3 st. in Walker's *Ps. and Hys.*, 1855, as "Lord, we are Thine, in Thee we live."

6. O happy day when first we felt. *The Day of Peace.*
7. O Jesus Christ, the Saviour. *Jesus All in All.* In Walker's *Ps. and Hys.* it begins: "O Jesus Christ, *our Saviour.*"
8. O Jesus, gracious Saviour." *The Advocate.*
9. O Lord, when we the path retrace. *Christ our Example.*
10. O Lord, who now art seated. *Christ in glory.*
11. Saviour, haste ; our souls are waiting. *Second Advent desired.* This is given in Walker's *Ps. and Hys.*, in a rewritten form as "Saviour, hasten Thine appearing."
12. Soon shall our Master come. *Waiting for Christ.*
13. There is a place of endless joy. *Heaven.*
14. We're not of the world that fadeth away. *Christ's Sheep.*
15. When along life's thorny road. *Passiontide.*

ii. From *Appendix* to the 1841 ed. of the *Hymns for the Poor of the Flock.*

16. Lamb of God, our souls adore Thee. *Praise to Christ.* Sometimes it begins with st. ii., "Lamb of God, Thy Father's bosom."
17. Lamb of God, Thou now art seated. 2nd Pt. of No. 16.

iii. From *Psalms and Hymns, in Two Parts*, Lond., D. Walther, 1842.

18. Again we meet in Jesus' name. *Divine Worship.*
19. Great Captain of Salvation. *Burial.* In the Irish *Church Hymnal*, and other collections.
20. Jesus, Thy name indeed is sweet. *Hope of the Resurrection.*
21. O blessed Jesus, Lamb of God. *Praise to Jesus.*
22. O Lamb of God, still keep me [us]. *Christ's Presence desired.* This hymn is somewhat popular in America.
23. O Lord, in nothing would I boast. *Christ All in All.*
24. Oft we, alas! forget the love. *Holy Communion.*
25. The veil is rent ! lo, Jesus stands [our souls draw near]. *The Intercessor.*
26. We bless our Saviour's name. *Thanksgiving for Forgiveness.*

iv. From *Psalms and Hymns for Public and Social Worship* (Dr. Walker's *Coll.*), 1855.

27. Father, to seek Thy face. *Public Worship.*
28. Jesus, [I] we rest in [on] Thee. *Joy in Forgiveness.*
29. O Lord, 'tis joy to look above. *Joy in the service of Christ.*
30. Thou hast stood here, Lord Jesus. *Burial.*
31. 'Twas Thy love, O God, that knew us. *Praise to God.*
32. When first o'erwhelmed with sin and shame. *Peace with God.*

All these hymns, except No. 1, are given in Dr. Walker's *Coll.*, 1855–80, and most of them are also found in other collections. [J. J.]

Deck, Mary Jane. [Walker, M. J.]

Dei canamus gloriam. *C. Coffin.* [*Monday.*] In the revised *Paris Brev.*, 1736, and again the same year in his *Hymni Sacri*, Paris, 1736, p. 11. It is for Mondays at Matins. It is also in the *Lyons* and other modern French Brevs. The text is also in Chandler, 1837, p. 145 ; Card. Newman's *Hymni Ecclesiae*, 1838–65 ; and Biggs's *Annotated H. A. & M.*, 1867. *Trs.* in C. U. :—

1. Come, let us praise the Name of God, **Who** spread the lofty skies. By J. Chandler in his *Hys. of the Primitive Ch.*, 1837. It was included in Dr. Oldknow's *Hymns*, &c., 1850, and others. In *H. A. & M.*, 1861, this was altered to "Come, let us praise the Name of God, Who on the second day," &c., and in this form was repeated in other collections. In the revised ed. of *H. A. & M.*, 1875, it was again altered to "Sing we the glory of our God."

2. Glory to God, **Who** when with light. By J. D. Chambers in Pt. 1 of his *Lauda Syon*, 1857, p. 12. This was repeated, with alterations, in *Kennedy*, 1863.

Translation not in C. U. :—

Glory to God on high, Upon this, &c. *I. Williams. British Mag.*, July, 1834, and *Hys. from Paris Brev.*, 1839. [J. J.]

Dei fide qua vivimus. [*Lent.*] In the 11th cent. Durham MS., printed in *Lat. Hys. of the Anglo-Saxon Ch.*, 1851, p. 59, this is given as a Daily Hymn for Sext in Lent, in 4 st. of 4 l. It is in a MS., c. 890, in the Bodleian (Junius, 25 f. 126 b). In the *British Museum* it is found in three MSS. of the 11th cent. (Harl. 2961 f. 236 ; Jul. A. vi. f. 44 ; Vesp. D. xii. f. 48 b). The text is also in *Daniel*, i., No. 65, and in his vol. iv. p. 353, readings are added from a 9th cent. MS. at Bern. It is *tr.* by J. D. Chambers in his *Lauda Syon*, 1857, as "The faith of God which we receive." [J. M.]

Deign this union to approve. *W. B. Collyer.* [*Holy Matrimony.*] Appeared in his *Services suited to the Solemnisation of Matrimony*, &c., 1837, No. 8, in 2 st. of 6 l. It is given, unaltered, in the *Bapt. Hymnal*, 1879. It is also found in a few American hymn-books, including the Prot. Episco. Ch. *Hymnal*, 1871.

Deiner Kinder Sammelplatz. *N. L. von Zinzendorf.* [*Burial of the Dead.*] 1st appeared as No. 242 in the "Zweyter Anhang bis 1754," to the *Kleine Brüder G B.*, London, 1754, thus :—

> Deiner Kinder Sammelplatz,
> Allgnugsamer lieber Schatz !
> Der hat, wie man hat vernomm'n,
> Wieder eines mehr bekomm'n.
>
> Eine Seele, die so da
> Zu den Füssen Josuah
> Weint' und bate um remiss
> Der vicissitudinis ;
>
> Die ist auf Vocation
> Ausgeraucht aus ihrem Thon,
> Von dem Seitenwundenblitz
> Eingeschmelzt in ihren Ritz.
>
> Herze ! weisst du, was ich mach,
> Was ich denke zu der Sach ?
> Hätte mich mein Herr gefragt ;
> Hätt ich vielleicht nein gesagt.
>
> Aber da du nun schon bist,
> Wo dein rechtes Plätzgen ist ;
> Ja da hab ich nichts zu thun,
> Als zu schweigen und zu ruhn.
>
> Lämmlein, dieses Mitglied da
> Geht uns freilich sehre nah :
> Aber bist du uns nicht mehr,
> Als das eigne Leben wär ?

This form is quite unsuited for public use. though Knapp, in his 1845 ed. of Zinzendorf's *Geistliche Lieder*, p. 174, has tried to recast it —without much success. It was probably written between 1749 and 1755. Lauxmann, in *Koch*, viii., 651, however says that it was written 1746, on the death and funeral of an only brother. In the *Brüder G. B.* of 1778 it was included as No. 1720, with st. ii., iii. omitted, and otherwise greatly altered and much improved by Christian Gregor. This text, which begins, "Aller Gläubgen Sammelplatz," is No. 1565 in the Berlin *G. L. S.* ed. 1863. It is the usual funeral hymn among the German-speaking Moravians, and through the Württemberg *G. B.* of 1842 (No. 630) has become a great favourite in South Germany. Thus *Koch*, vii. 207, relates of Dr. C. G. Barth of Calw :—

"On the 15th of November [1862], according to his own desire he was buried in the grave of Machtolf [his predecessor] at Möttlingen, where also his mother, who had died there in 1828, was at rest, to the strains of the hymn, an especial favourite of his, 'Aller Gläub'gen Sammelplatz.'"

An additional verse, translated by Miss Winkworth as st. iii., is founded on Zinzendorf's st. iv., and is thus given in Knapp's *Ev. L. S.*, ed. 1850, No. 2895 :—

> " Hätt' Er uns darob gefragt :
> Ach, was hätten wir gesagt ?
> Heiss mit Thränen bäten wir :
> ' Lass die theure Seele hier ! ' "

It has been *tr.* as :—

Christ will gather in His own, a fine *tr.* from the 1778 text and the st. above, by Miss Winkworth, in her *Lyra Ger.*, 2nd Series, 1858, p. 120, and in her *C. B. for England*, 1863, No. 199. It was adopted unaltered as No. 191 in *H. A. & M.*, 1861, and has since been included in *Kennedy*, 1863 ; *Church Hys.*, 1871 ; *Bapt. Hyl.*, 1879, and others ; and in America in the *College Hyl.*, 1876 ; *Bapt. Service of Song*, 1871 ; *Evanj. Hyl.*, 1880, and others. It is given, in a slightly altered form, in Putnam's *Singers and Songs of the Liberal Faith*, Boston, U. S., 1875, and marked as an original hymn by W. C. H. Dall.

Another *tr.*, from the text of 1778, is "All the saints will meet on high," in J. D. Burns's *Memoir and Remains*, 1869, p. 223.   [J. M.]

Denham, David, b. 1791, was the s. of Thos. Denham, a Baptist minister in the East of London. He began to preach when very young, and in 1810 became pastor of the Baptist Church at Horsell Common. In 1816 removed to Plymouth, in 1826 to Margate, and in 1834 to the Baptist Church in Unicorn Yard, Tooley Street, Southwark. Ill-health compelled him to resign his charge in London, and he sojourned for a time at Cheltenham and Oxford. He d. in 1848 at Yeovil, in Somerset, and was buried in Bunhill Fields Burial Ground, London. In 1837 he pub. a collection of hymns, as :—

The Saints' Melody. A New Selection of upwards of One Thousand Hymns, Founded upon the Doctrines of Distinguishing Grace, and adapted to every part of the Christian's experience and devotion in the Ordinances of Christ, &c., 1837. This edition contained 1026 hymns. This number was subsequently increased to 1145 hymns.

This *Selection* is still in C. U. in more than one hundred congregations in G. Britain and the colonies. Denham's hymns, all of which are signed "D. Denham," are numerous. There is also one, apparently by his wife, "Mrs. M. A. Denham." Outside of his own *Selection* his hymns are rarely found. The best known is "'Mid scenes of confusion and creature complaints."   [W. R. S.]

Denham, Sir John, only s. of Sir John Denham, Chief Baron of the Exchequer, and afterwards Chief Justice of the King's Bench, Ireland, b. in Dublin, 1615, and educated at Trinity College, Oxford. In 1641 he was made governor of Fareham Castle for Charles I., and subsequently attended Charles II. in his exile. At the Restoration he was rewarded for his devotion to the Crown, and created a Knight of the Bath. Died in London, 1668, and was buried in Westminster Abbey. His poem, *Cooper's Hill*, is well known. The manly energy and nervous force of his verse was much more popular with Pope and Johnson and the 18th century school, than it is at

the present time. His *Version of the Psalms* was written about 1668, but not pub. until 1714. [**Psalters, English,** § 12.]   [J. J.]

Denicke, David, s. of B. D. Denicke, Town Judge of Zittau, Saxony, was b. at Zittau, January 31, 1603. After studying philosophy and law at the Universities of Wittenberg and Jena, he was for a time tutor of law at Königsberg, and, 1624–28, travelled in Holland, England and France. In 1629 he became tutor to the sons of Duke Georg of Brunswick-Lüneburg, and under father and sons held various important offices, such as, 1639, the direction of the foundation of Bursfeld, and in 1642 a member of the Consistory at Hannover. He d. at Hannover, April 1, 1680 (*Koch*, iii. 287 ; *Bode*, p. 58). His hymns, which for that time were in good taste, and are simple, useful, warm, and flowing, appeared in the various Hannoverian hymn-books, 1646–1659, which he edited along with J. Gesenius (q.v.). All appeared there without his name. Those *tr.* are :—

i. **Wenn ich die heilgen zehn Gebot.** *Ten Commandments.* Contributed to the *Hannover G. B.*, 1652, No. 69, as a hymn on the Ten Commandments, in 22 st. of 4 l., st. i.–x. being a confession of sins against them, and st. xi.–xxii. a meditation and prayer for God's mercy. Included in Crüger's *Praxis pietatis melica*, 1661, in Freylinghausen's *G. B.*, 1714, and recently in a few colls., as Sarnighausen's *G. B.*, 1855, No. 164, and the Ohio *G. B.*, 1865, No. 182. It is *tr.* as **Almighty Lord of earth and heaven.** By C. H. L. Schnette, as No. 206 in t.ie *Ohio Luth. Hyl.*, 1880. St. i.–iv. are literal ; st. v.–vii. seem based on v., vii., xvi., xvii.

Hymns not in English C. U. :—

ii. **Ach treuer Gott ! ich ruf zu dir.** [*Christian Life.*] 1st pub. in the *Hannover G. B.*, 1652, No. 135, in 17 st. This is *tr.* as :—(1) "My God ! I call upon Thy name," by *Miss Cox*, 1841, p. 177. (2) "Most holy God ! to thee I cry," by *Lady E. Fortescue*, 1843 (1847, p. 69).

iii. **Kommt, lasst euch den Herren lehren.** [*The Beatitudes.*] 1st pub. in the *Hannover G. B.*, 1648, in 11 st., No. 133. It may have been suggested by J. Heermann's "Kommt ihr Christen, kommt und höret " (9 st. in his *Sontags- und Fest-Evangelia*, Leipzig, 1638 ; Mützell, 1858, No. 94), but has only 3 lines in common with it. In the *Nürnberg G. B.*, 1676, No. 962, and many later hymn-books, it begins : "kommt und lasst uns Jesum lehren." It is *tr.* as "Come and hear our blessed Saviour," by *J. C. Jacobi*, 1722, p. 46. In his 2nd ed., 1732, p. 75, altered and beginning "Come, and hear the sacred story," and thence in the *Moravian H. Bk.*, 1754, pt. i., No. 469 ; st. x., xi. beginning, "Jesus, grant me to inherit," being repeated in later eds. and as No. 428 in J. A. Latrobe's *Coll.*, 1841.

iv. **Was kann ich doch für Dank.** [*Praise and Thanksgiving.*] 1st pub. in the *Hannover G. B.*, 1648, in 8 st., No. 154. St. vii. is altered from "Herr Jesu, führe mich," by J. Heermann (*Devoti Musica Cordis*; Breslau, 1630 ; Mützell, 1858, No. 57. *Tr.* as "What thanks can I repay ?" by *J. C. Jacobi*, 1725, p. 46 (1732, p. 147).

v. **Wir Menschen sein zu dem, O Gott.** [*Holy Scripture.*] 1st pub. in the *Hannover G. B.*, 1659, No. 180, in 10 st. Founded on the Gospel for Sexagesima Sunday—St. Luke viii. 4, &c. *Tr.* as :—(1), "Give us Thy Spirit, Lord, that we," a *tr.* of st. iii. by J. Swertner, as No. 8. in the *Moravian H. Bk.*, 1789 (1886, No. 9). (2) "Let the splendour of Thy word," a *tr.* of st. ix. by J. Swertner, as No. 15, in the *Moravian H. Bk.*, 1789. (1886, No. 17).   [J. M.]

Denny, Sir Edward, Bart. Sir Edward Denny, s. of Sir E. Denny, 4th baronet, of Tralee Castle, County of Kerry, was b. 2 Oct., 1796, and succeeded his father in August, 1831. He is a member of the *Plymouth*

Brethren, and has contributed largely to their hymnody. His first publication, in which many of his hymns appeared, was *A Selection of Hymns,* Lond. Central Tract Depôt, 1839. This was followed by *Hymns & Poems,* Lond., 1848 (third ed., 1870). He has also published several prose works. Many of his hymns are popular, and are in extensive use as:—" A pilgrim through this lonely world"; " Bride of the Lamb, rejoice, rejoice"; " Bright with all His crowns of glory"; " Light of the lonely pilgrim's heart"; "Sweet feast of love divine," and several others. In addition to these, which are separately annotated, and those which are confined in their use to the congregations of the "Brethren," there are also nearly 20 in limited use in G. Britain and America. Of these the following appeared, first in his *Selection of Hymns,* 1839; then, in the *Appendix* to *Hymns for the Poor of the Flock,* 1841; and then in his *Hymns & Poems,* 1848-70:—

1. **Break forth, O earth, in praises.** *Praise for Redemption.* This is given in several collections in G. Britain and America.

2. **Children of God, in all your need.** *The Great High Priest.* In limited use.

3. **Children of light, arise and shine.** *Looking unto Jesus.* In numerous hymnals in G. Britain and America.

4. **Children of light, awake, awake.** *Advent.* This hymn is an application of the Parable of the Ten Virgins to the Second Coming of Christ.

5. **Dear Lord, amid the throng that pressed.** *The Holy Women at the Cross.* The use of this hymn in America is somewhat extensive.

6. **Hope of our hearts, O Lord, appear.** *The Second Advent desired.* In the *Hys. for the Poor of the Flock,* 1837; and the author's *Hys. & Poems,* 1848-70, and various collections in Great Britain and America.

7. **Joy to the ransomed earth.** *Jesus the King.* Its use is limited.

8. **Lo 'tis the heavenly army.** *The Second Advent.* The original of this hymn is in 4 st. of 10 l., and as such it is usually given: but in the *People's H.,* 1867, it is arranged in 4 st. of 8 l., and is also slightly altered.

9. **O grace divine! the Saviour shed.** *Good Friday.* In limited use.

10. **O what a bright and blessed world.** *The New Earth.* This hymn is based upon Gen. v. 29, as interpreted from a *Millennial* point of view. Christ is regarded as the Rest (*Noah-Rest*) of His people, and the remover of the curse from the earth.

11. **Sweet was the hour, O Lord, to Thee.** *Christ at the Well of Sychar.* Limited in use.

12. **Thou vain deceitful world, farewell.** *Forsaking the World for Christ.* In several collections.

13. **Through Israel's land the Lord of all.** *Mission to the Jews.* In addition to its use in its full form, it is also given as: "O Zion, when thy Saviour came," as in Dr. Walker's *Ps. & Hys.,* 1855-71; Snepp's *Songs of G. & G.,* and others. This opens with st. ii.

14. **'Tis finish'd all—our souls to win.** *Jesus the Guide and Friend.* In several collections.

15. **'Tis He, the Mighty Saviour comes.** *Missions.* Given in *Snepp,* and one or two others.

16. **'Tis night, but O the joyful morn.** *Hope.* In a few hymnals; also, beginning with st. ii., "Lord of our hearts, beloved of Thee," in Dr. Hatfield's *Church H. Bk.,* N. Y., 1872.

17. **To Calvary, Lord, in Spirit now.** *Good Friday.* This is given in several hymnals, including Spurgeon's *O. O. H. Bk.,* 1866, &c.

The next is in the *Selection* of 1839, and the *Hys. & Poems,* 1848-70 :—

18. **O Blessed Lord, Thy feeble Sheep.** *The Good Shepherd.* Its use is limited.

The three with which we close are from J. G. Deck's *Ps. & Hys.,* 1842, Pt. ii., and the *Hymns & Poems,* 1848-70 :—

19. **Hark to the trump! behold it breaks.** *The Resurrection.* The design of this hymn is thus described by the author: "These lines are supposed to be the utterance of the saints at the blessed moment when they are actually ascending to meet the Lord in the air, as described in 1 Cor. xv. 51-57 and 1 Thess. iv. 16-18. It is given in several collections."

20. **Isles of the deep, rejoice, rejoice.** *Missions.*

21. **Where, in this waste unlovely [and desert] world!** *Rest for the Weary.* Its use is limited.   [J. J.]

Dent, Caroline, great-granddaughter of John Collet Ryland, and grand-niece of John Ryland (q.v.), was b. Aug. 14th, 1815, at Milton, near Northampton, where she still resides [1887]. In 1854 Miss Dent pub. *Thoughts & Sketches in Verse.* Most of these pieces were of her own composition; and the rest were contributed by her sister, Mrs. Trestrail [Trestrail]. The hymn *Jesus, Saviour! Thou dost know (The Sympathy of Jesus)* is part of a piece of 13 st. by Miss Dent in this volume. It is in the Bap. *Ps. & Hys.,* 1858, and the *Baptist Hymnal,* 1879, &c.

In 1861 the sisters were joint authors of a small book of consolatory verses, entitled *Our Darling,* printed for private circulation; and in 1867 Miss Dent edited *The Letters of Miss Frances Rolleston.* She has also written *Sunshine in the Valley,* a Religious Tale (1858).

[W. R. S.]

Deny Thee! what, deny the way? [*Denial of Christ.*] This poem appeared in Emma Parr's *Thoughts of Peace,* 1839, in 4 parts, Nos. 361-364, and signed "H. H." Of these parts i.-iii. are combined and altered in *Kennedy,* 1863, No. 1353, making a hymn of 5 st. of 8 l. and 1 st. of 5 l. Other arrangements are given in the American *Sabb. H. Bk.,* 1858 (4 st. of 4 l.); the *Bapt. Praise Bk.,* N. Y., 1871 (2 st. of 4 l.).   [W. T. B.]

Depth of mercy, can there be. *C. Wesley.* [*Desiring Mercy and Pardon.*] 1st pub. in *Hys. & Sac. Poems,* 1740, and headed " After a Relapse into Sin," in 13 st. of 4 l., *P. Works,* 1868-72, vol. i. p. 271. When included in the *Wes. H. Bk.,* 1780, No. 162, st. iii. was omitted, and st. viii. was included in st. ii., the result being 6 st. of 8 l. This arrangement was continued in later editions, and has passed into other collections, both in G. Britain and America. In Stevenson's *Meth. H. Bk., and its Associations,* 1870-83, is an interesting and pathetic account of an actress and her change of life through the instrumentality of this hymn. The account has been repeated in many books and in various forms. It is of American origin, and first appeared, as far as can be traced, in Belcher's *Historical Notes on Hymns and Authors.* Although possibly true, it lacks authentication. No one has yet ventured to say whether the circumstance occurred in G. Britain or America, or whether it was in the last century or in this. Failing these details, we are not surprised that the names of the town and of the actress are both wanting. [J. J.]

Der Glaube bricht durch Stahl und Stein. *N. L. von Zinzendorf.* [*Following Christ.*] According to the *Nachricht* to the *Brüder G. B.,* 1778, this was written after the edict of Jan. 1, 1727, by which Zinzendorf was forbidden to hold religious meetings in Dresden. In his *Deutsche Gedichte,* 1735, p. 124, it is, however, dated 1726. It appeared as No. 5 in the "Andere Zugabe," c. 1730, to his 1725-8 *Sammlung geist- und lieblicher Lieder* (3rd ed., 1731, No. 1059), in 8 st, of 8 l,

In the *Brüder G. B.*, 1778, st. 1, 5, 7, 8, altered, appear as No. 920, and thence as No. 551 in the Berlin *G. L. S.*, ed. 1863. In Knapp's ed. of his *Geistliche Lieder*, 1845, p. 78, omitting st. 2-4. *Tr.* as :—

Glory to God, Whose witness train. This appeared as a hymn in 6 st. based on the 1778 as No. 1062, in the *Supplement* of 1809 to the *Moravian H. Bk.*, 1801 ; st. 5 being from " Sollt es gleich bisweilen scheinen " (q. v.), and was continued in later eds. In somewhat varying forms it appears in J. A. Latrobe's *Coll.*, 1852, No. 135; and in America in the *Book of Hys.*, Boston, 1848 ; Hedge & Huntington's *Coll.*, 1853 ; *Dutch Reformed*, 1869 ; *Songs for the Sanctuary*, N. Y., 1865, and *Laudes Domini*, 1884. [J. M.]

Der Tag ist hin, Mein Geist und Sinn. *J. A. Freylinghausen.* [*Evening.*] A fine hymn of longing for the Everlasting Light of that better country where there is no night. 1st pub. as No. 615 in his *Geistreiches G. B.*, 1704, in 14 st. of 5 l., and thence in Grote's ed., 1855, of his *Geistliche Lieder*, p. 102. It has passed into many German hymn-books, and is included as No. 1547 in the Berlin *G. L. S.*, ed. 1863.

Translations in C. U. :—

i. **The day expires ; My soul desires,** omitting st. iv., v., vii.-ix., xi., by Miss Winkworth, in her *Lyra Ger.*, 1st Series, 1855, p. 228. Her *trs.* of st. i.-iii., xii., are included in the *St. John's Hyl.*, Aberdeen, 1870, No. 200. She recast her *tr.* as No. 168 for her *C. B. for England*, 1863, where it begins, " The day is done, And, left alone."

ii. **The day is gone, And left alone,** a good *tr.*, omitting st. iv., v., vii.-ix., xi., contributed by R. Massie, as No. 504, to the 1857 ed. of Mercer's *C. P. & H. Bk.* (Ox. ed., No. 22), and in the translator's *Lyra Domestica*, 1864, p. 138. Included in R. Minton Taylor's *Parish Hyl.*, 1872, and in *Kennedy*, 1863. In Dr. J. Patterson's *Coll.*, Glasgow, 1867, No. 391 begins 'with the *tr.* of st. x., " When shall the day."

iii. **The day departs, My soul and heart,** a good *tr.* by Miss Borthwick, omitting st. ii., iv., v., vii., xi., in the *Family Treasury*, 1861, pt. ii., p. 298, and thence in the 4th Ser., 1862, of the *H. L. L.* p. 22. In Wilson's *Service of Praise*, 1865, the *tr.* of st. viii. and x., and in Jellicoe's *Coll.*, 1867, those of vi., viii., were omitted. In Thring's *Coll.*, 1882, her *tr.* of st. vi., viii., x. were omitted, and the rest slightly altered. The same text is in J. B. Whiting's *Coll.*, 1882.

Translations not in C. U. :—

These *trs.* all omit st. iv., v., vii., ix., xi., and are : (1) " Lo, Day is sped ! " by *H. J. Buckoll*, 1842, p. 94. (2) " The day is gone ; my soul looks on," by *Mrs. Bevan*, 1858, p. 48. (3) " The day is o'er, My soul longs sore," by *Miss Cox*, 1864, p. 19. [J. M.]

Der Tag vergeht, die müde Sonne sinket. [*Evening.*] Included as No. 2764 in Knapp's *Ev. L. S.*, 1837, in 6 st. of 4 l. *Tr.* as :—

The day is gone, the weary sun declining, in full in Dr. H. Mill's *Horae Ger.*, 1845 (ed. 1856, p. 22), repeated, omitting st. v., as No. 948 in the Amer. Luth. Gen. Synod's *Coll.*, 1850. [J. M.]

Des Morgens wenn ich früh aufsteh. [*Morning or Evening.*] *Wackernagel*, v. p. 42, gives two forms, the one from the *Geistliche*

Lieder und Psalmen, Leipzig, 1582, the other from the Dresden *G. B.*, 1593. The latter, in 5 st. of 4 l., is included as No. 448 in the *Unv. L. S.*, 1851.

In the *Moravian H. Bk.*, 1789, there are three hymns which all seem to be intended as *trs.* of st. i. These are: (1) " Lord Jesus Christ, my life and light," No. 748. (2) " Lord Jesus, may I constantly," No. 753. (3) " Lord, in the morning when we rise," No. 763. In the current ed., 1886, No. 1173 is Nos. 753 and 748 ; while No. 1174 is No. 763, with two original st. added, of which ii. was No. 747 in 1789, and iii. was st. iii. of No. 886 in 1801. [J. M.]

Descend from heaven, immortal Dove. *I. Watts.* [*Christ in Glory.*] 1st pub. in his *Hymns & S. Songs*, 1707 (2nd ed., 1709, Book ii., No. 23), in 6 st. of 4 l. In the older collections two arrangements are found, the first dating from Whitefield's *Coll.*, 1753, No. 79, and the second from Toplady's *Ps. & Hys.*, 1776, No. 387 (later eds. No. 367), the last stanza of the latter being altered from Watts, Bk. ii., No. 47, by Toplady. In modern hymnals these centos have given place to others. The full and original text is rarely found in the hymn-books. [J. J.]

Descend, immortal Dove. *P. Doddridge.* [*Whitsuntide.*] This hymn is No. xlvii. In the " D. MSS.," in 4 st. of 4 l. ; is dated " Sept. 11, 1737," and headed, " The love of God shed abroad in the heart by the Spirit. Rom. v. 5." It was included in J. Orton's posthumous ed. of Doddridge's *Hymns*, &c., 1755, No. 259, and again in J. D. Humphreys's ed. of the same, 1839, No. 284. [J. J.]

Descere jam, anima, lectulum soporis. *St. Anselm of Lucca.* [*Love to Christ.*] This is a long poem found in la Bigne's *Bibl. Patrum*, Lyons, 1677, vol. xxvii. p. 444, under the title of " The Meditations of St. Anselm on the works of our Lord Jesus Christ." This title is said to be taken from a MS. at Mantua, and the poem is said to have been first edited by Lucas Wadding. A fragment, in 28 l., is in Trench's *Sacred Latin Poetry*, ed. 1864, p. 134. This is *tr.* in Mrs. Charles's *Voice of Christian Life in Song*, 1858, p. 175, as " Rise, my soul, from slumber, leave the bed of death." Another *tr.*, beginning with st. iii. in Trench, **Jesu mi dulcissime, Domine coelorum,** by Dr. H. Kynaston, was given in his *Occasional Verses*, 1862, No. 41, in 5 st. of 8 l., and repeated in the *People's H.*, 1867, and the *Hymnary*, 1872. It begins, " Jesu, solace of the soul." [J. M.]

Dessler, Wolfgang Christoph, s. of Nicolaus Dessler, jeweller, at Nürnberg, was b. at Nürnberg, Feb. 11, 1660. His father wished him to become a goldsmith, but, as he was not physically suited for this, he was permitted to begin the study of theology at the University of Altdorf. His poverty and bodily weakness forced him to leave before completing his course, and, returning to Nürnberg, he supported himself there as a proof reader. Becoming acquainted with Erasmus Finx or Francisci, then residing in Nürnberg, he was employed by Finx as his amanuensis, and at his request translated many foreign religious works into German. In 1705 he was appointed Conrector of the School of the Holy Ghost at Nürnberg, where he laboured with zeal and acceptance till

1720, when, by a stroke of paralysis, he was forced to resign. Finally, after an illness which lasted about 35 weeks, he d. at Nürnberg, March 11, 1722. Of his hymns, in all over 100, the best appeared, many with melodies by himself, in his volume of meditations entitled :—

Gottgeheiligter Christen nützlich ergetzende Seelenlust unter den Blumen göttliches Worts, oder andächtige Betrachtungen und Gedanken über unterschiedliche erläuterte Schriftsprüche, &c. Nürnberg, 1692 [Berlin] (*Koch*, iii. 531–535, and iv. 566–567).

From this work (the references to which have been kindly supplied by Dr. Zahn of Altdorf, from his copy), five hymns have been *tr.* into English, viz. :—

Hymns in English C. U. :—

i. Ich lass dich nicht, du musst mein Jesus bleiben. [*Constancy to Christ.*] Founded on Genesis xxxii. 36. 1st pub. 1692, as above, p. 553, along with Meditation xviii., which is entitled "The striving love." *Wetzel* (A. H., vol. i., pt. iv., p. 20) says it was sung, at her request, Sept. 5, 1726, at the deathbed of Christiana Eberhardina, a pious Queen of Poland. In the Berlin *G. L. S.*, ed. 1863, No. 728, in 9 st. of 10 l. Translated as :—

I will not let Thee go, Thou Help in time of need! a fine *tr.*, beginning with st. iv. (" Ich lass dich nicht, du Hülf in allen Nöthen"), and adding *trs.* of st. v., ix., by Miss Winkworth, in the 1st ser., 1855, of her *Lyra Ger.*, p. 59. Thence as No. 851 in the *Wes. H. Bk.*, 1875; No. 205 in the Scottish *Presb. Hymnal*, 1876 ; No. 139 in the Canadian *Presb. H. Bk.*, 1880.

Another tr. is, "I leave Thee not, Thou art my Jesus ever," by Dr. J. W. Alexander, 1st pub. in Dr. Schaff's *Kirchenfreund*, 1851, p. 140 (reprinted in the *Christian Treasury*, Edin. 1851, p. 378), and included in his *The Breaking Crucible*, &c., N. Y., 1861, p. 19. In Schaff's *Christ in Song*, 1869, p. 555.

ii. Mein Jesu dem die Seraphinen. [*Ascension.*] Founded on Jeremiah x. 7. 1st pub. 1692, as above, p. 348, along with Meditation xii., which is entitled "Christ's kingly and unapproachable glory." Thence as No. 278 in Freylinghausen's *G. B.*, 1704, and recently as No. 422 in the *Unv. L. S.*, 1851, in 8 st. of 8 l. Translated as :—

1. Jesu, Whose glory's streaming rays, a spirited *tr.*, omitting st. vii., viii., by J. Wesley, in *Hys. & Sac. Poems*, 1739 (*P. Works*, 1868–72, vol. i. p. 89). In the *Wes. H. Bk.*, 1780, st. i.–iii. were included as No. 129 (ed. 1875, No. 133), and st. iv.–vi., beginning "Into Thy gracious hands I fall," as No. 188 (ed. 1875, No. 196). Recently the first part has been given in America as No. 64 in H. L. Hastings's *Hymnal*, 1880, and the second as No. 496 in the *Meth. Epis. H. Bk.*, 1849, and as No. 464 in the Pennsylvania Luth. *Ch. Bk.*, 1868.

2. O Jesu, Lord, enthroned in glory, a good *tr.* of st. i., ii., v., by A. T. Russell, as No. 199 in his *Ps. & Hys.*, 1851.

3. My Jesus, Whom the seraph host, a good and full *tr.* by R. Massie, for the 1857 ed. of Mercer's *C. P. & H. Bk.*, No. 135 (omitted in Ox. ed.), reprinted in the translator's *Lyra Domestica*, 1864, p. 129.

4. My Jesus, if the seraphim, a good and full *tr.* by Miss Winkworth in the 2nd series of her *Lyra Ger.*, 1858, p. 50; and thence, unaltered, in Schaff's *Christ in Song*, 1869, p. 342. In her *C. B. for England*, 1863, No. 67, st. iv., vii.,

were omitted, and the rest altered in metre ; and thence as No. 141 in J. L. Porter's *Coll.*, 1876.

Other trs. are : (1) "O Jesu! 'fore whose radiation," by J. Gambold, as No. 623 in pt. i. of the *Moravian H. Bk.*, 1754 (1886, No. 312). (2) "My Saviour, whom in heavenly places," in J. Sheppard's *Foreign Sacred Lyre*, 1857, p. 78.

iii. Wie wohl ist mir, O Freund der Seelen. [*The Love of Christ.*] Founded on Canticles viii. 5. 1st pub. 1692, as above, p. 154, along with Meditation vi., which is entitled "The penitential forsaking and embracing." Included as No. 451 in Freylinghausen's *G. B.*, 1704, and recently as No. 438 in the *Unv. L. S.*, 1851, in 6 st. of 10 l. Lauxmann, in *Koch*, viii., 243, says of it :—

"This hymn dates from the period when Dessler as a youth was residing in his native town of Nürnberg in ill health. He had given up the occupation of goldsmith and set himself to study at Altdorf, but lack of money and of health compelled him to abandon this also. He then maintained himself as a proof reader in his native town, became the spiritual son and scholar in poesy of Erasmus Francisci, in whose powerful faith he found nourishment in his sorrows. Through his linguistic attainments, as well as through his hymns, he furthered the edification of the Christian populace ; and what he here sung may have afforded stimulus to himself in the still greater troubles which he afterwards had to endure during his corectorship, and finally in his last thirty-five weeks illness."

Fischer (ii. 391) calls it—

"One of the finest hymns of Pietism, that has produced many blessed effects, and has been the model and incitement to many hymns of like character."

It is *tr.* as :—

1. How well am I, Thou my soul's lover, in full as No. 621 in pt. i. of the *Moravian H. Bk.*, 1754. Greatly altered, and omitting st. ii., v., as No. 295 in the *Moravian H. Bk.*, 1789, beginning, "How blest am I, most gracious Saviour," and continued thus in later eds. In 1840 Dr. Martineau included a hymn in 4 st. of 4 l., beginning, "What comforts, Lord, to those are given," as No. 294 in his *Hymns, &c.* (ed. 1873, No. 384). Of this st. i., ii. are based on st. i., st. iii. on st. ii., and st. iv. on st. iii. of the 1789.

2. O Lord, how happy is the time, a somewhat free *tr.* of st. i.–v., with st. i., slightly varied, repeated as st. vi., by Greville Matheson. Contributed to the *H. & Sacred Songs*, Manchester, 1855 (ed. 1856, No. 226), repeated in the *Sunday Magazine*, 1872, p. 741, and in Dr. G. Macdonald's *Threefold Cord*, 1883, p. 38. In the *H. for the Sick Room*, N. Y., 1859 (1861, p. 70), and *H. of the Ages*, 3rd Series, Boston, U.S., 1864, p. 233, it is considerably altered. This text is given in Schaff's *Christ in Song*, 1869, p. 491, further altered, and beginning "O Friend of souls! how blest the time"; Miss Winkworth's *tr.* of st. v., altered, being substituted for Mr. Matheson's. In the *Meth. Epis. Hymnal*, 1878, No. 613, is st. i., ii., v. of Schaff's text.

3. O Friend of Souls, how well is me, a good *tr.* omitting st. iii. by Miss Winkworth in her *Lyra Ger.*, 1st Series, 1855, p. 144 From this l. 1–4 of st. i., iii., v., altered, were taken as No. 513 in *H. of the Spirit*, Boston, U.S., 1864.

Another is : "'Tis well with me, O Friend unfailing," by Miss Burlingham in the *British Herald*, Dec. 1865, p. 185, repeated as No. 395 in Reid's *Praise Bk.*, 1872.

Hymns not in English C. U. :—

iv. Frisch, frisch hinnach, mein Geist und Herz. [*Cross and Consolation.*] Founded on Heb. x., 36. 1st pub. 1692 as above, p. 423, in 7 st. It is *tr.* as "Courage, my heart, press cheerly on," by Miss Winkworth, 1869, p. 277.

v. Oeffne mir die Perlenpforten. [*Longing for Heaven.*] Founded on Rev. xxii. 14. 1st pub. 1692 as above, p. 384, in 6 st. It is *tr.* as "Now the pearly gates unfold," by Miss Winkworth, 1858, p. 176.

[J. M.]

Deus Creator omnium Polique rector.

St. Ambrose. [*Saturday Evening.*] St. Augustine in his *Confessions*, Bk. ix., refers thus to this hymn :—

"And behold, the corpse [of his mother] was carried to the burial; we went and returned without tears . . . It seemed also good to me to go and bathe, having heard that the bath had its name (*balneum*) from the Greek Βαλανεῖον, for that it drives sadness from the mind. And this also I confess unto Thy mercy, Father of the fatherless, that I bathed, and was the same as before I bathed. For the bitterness of sorrow could not exude out of my heart. Then I slept, and woke up again, and found my grief not a little softened; and as I was alone in my bed, I remembered those true verses of Thy Ambrose. For Thou art the

   "Maker of all, the Lord,
     And Ruler of the height,
   Who, robing day in light, hast poured
     Soft slumbers o'er the night,
   That to our limbs the power
     Of toil may be renew'd,
   And hearts be rais'd that sink and cower
     And sorrow be subdu'd."

[*The Confessions of St. Augustine.* Oxford : J. Parker. New ed. 1871, p. 195.]

St. Augustine also speaks in his *De Musicâ*, Lib. vi. c. 9, of singing the verse "Deus Creator omnium." The authorship and date [340–397] of this hymn as thus authenticated, have never been disputed.

The popularity of this hymn is seen in the fact that it is found in all the greater Breviaries, the *Roman* 1632 and *Paris* of 1736 excepted, its English use being specially marked. Its general use is on Saturdays from that preceding the 1st Sun. after the Octave of the Epiphany, to the Saturday before Quadragesima Sunday, both inclusive; and from the Saturday preceding the 1st Sun. in August to Advent. Variations from this are found in the *Sarum*, *Mozarabic*, *York*, &c. It is in a ms., c. 700, in the *British Museum* (Vesp. A. 1, f. 152 b), and Thomasius, ii. 419, gives readings from two Vatican mss. of the 8th cent. It is also in three mss. of the 11th cent. in the *British Museum* (Jul. A. vi.; Vesp. D. xii.; Harl. 2961), and in the *Latin Hys. of the Anglo-Saxon Church*, 1851, is printed from an 11th cent. ms. at Durham. Text is in *Mone*, No. 281; *Daniel*, i. No. 12, with notes at ii. p. 381, and iv. p. 1; *Hymn. Sarisb.* text and readings; *Wackernagel* and *Macgill* text only. The text is also in *Migne*, tom. 86, c. 924, and the Benedictine ed. of St. Ambrose's *Works*.

[W. A. S.]

Translation in C. U. :—

Maker of all things, God most high. By J. D. Chambers. 1st pub. in his *Order for Household Devotion*, 1854, and again in his *Lauda Syon*, 1857, p. 55, in 8 st. of 4 l. In 1862 it was included in the *Appendix* to the *H. Noted*, No. 115; in 1867 in the *People's H.*; in Dr. Martineau's *Hys. of Praise & Prayer* (abbreviated), 1873; and in other hymn-books. In the *Hymnary*, 1872, it is altered to "O blest Creator, God Most High."

Translations not in C. U. :—

1. Creator of all! through Whose all-seeing Might. *Hymnarium Anglicanum.* 1844.
2. Creator of the starry pole, God of all worlds, &c. *W. J. Copeland.* 1848.
3. Lord of the far-encircling globe. *W. J. Blew.* 1852-55.
4. Maker of all, O Lord and God most High. *J. W. Hewett.* 1859.
5. O God, Who clothed, Creator wise. *Dr. H. Kynaston.* 1862.
6. Maker of all! Thou God of love. *Dr. H. M. Macgill.* 1876-9.

A portion of this hymn beginning with st. v., "Ut cum profunda clauserit," has been *tr.* by Dr. Kynaston in his *Occasional Hys.*, 1862, No. 81, as a separate hymn, beginning "With darkest clouds while daylight's dearth." [J. J.]

Deus ignee fons animarum.

A. C. Prudentius. [*Burial of the Dead.*] This beautiful poem, in 44 st. of 4 l., is No. x. in his *Cathemerinon*, and may be found in all editions of his works, *e.g.* Deventer, 1490, Lond., 1824, &c. It is also in a ms. of the 5th cent. in the Bibl. Nat. Paris (8084, f. 32b), and in a Mozarabic Office Book of 11th cent. in the British Museum (Add. 30851, f. 160). Its liturgical use has been limited, but in the *Mozarabic Breviary* (Toledo, 1502, f. 313b) it is given in the Office for the Dead. The full text is in *Wackernagel*, i., No. 40, and a part in *Daniel*, 1., No. 115, pt. ii.

The form which has been most used is a cento beginning : Jam moesta quiesce querela, and consisting of st. 31, 15, 10–12, 32–36. This is found in *Babst's G. B.*, Leipzig, 1545, and many later collections, *e.g.* Dr. Zahn's *Psalter und Harfe*, Gütersloh, 1886, No. 480, and in *Daniel*, i., No. 115, pt. i. It was for generations a favourite funeral hymn among the Lutherans, and was sung in Latin in some parts of Germany till very recent times. Abp. Trench, in giving st. 31–44 in his *Sac. Lat. Poetry*, speaks of them as the "crowning glory of the poetry of Prudentius." It has been *tr.* into English direct from the Latin, and also through the German as follows :—

i. *From the Latin :—*

1. **Why weep ye, living brotherhood.** By W. J. Blew, in *The Church Hy. & Tune Bk.*, 1852–55, in 5 st. of 6 l., and again in H. Rice's *Hymns*, &c., 1870.

2. **Cease, ye tearful mourners.** By E. Caswall, in his *Masque of Mary*, &c., 1858, in 13 st. of 4 l., and again in his *Hys. & Poems*, 1873. It was repeated in an abridged form in the 1862 *Appx.* to the *H. Noted;* and in the *Hymnary*, 1872.

3. **Be silent, O sad lamentation.** By R. F. Littledale in the *People's H.*, 1867, under the signature of "A. L. P."

Other trs. are :—
1. Ah! hush now your mournful complainings. *Mrs. Charles.* 1858.
2. Now your sorrowful plaints should be hush'd. *J. W. Hewett.* 1859.
3. Hush, Mother, too loud is thy weeping. *H. Kynaston.* 1862.
4. No more, ah, no more sad complaining. *E. A. Washburn*, N. York, 1865, revised for Schaff's *Christ in Song*, Oct., 1868, and pub. therein, 1869.
5. Each sorrowful mourner be silent. *J. M. Neale*, in the *St. Margaret's Hymnal*, 1875.

ii. *From the German :—*
Of the "Jam moesta quiesce querela" many *trs.* have been made into German. Two of these have passed into English :—

i. **Hört auf mit Trauern und Klagen.** A free *tr.* in 10 st. of 4 l. 1st pub. in J. Eichorn's *Geistliche Lieder*, Frankfurt a. Oder, 1561, and thence in *Wackernagel*, iv. p. 191. Repeated in many later collections, often erroneously ascribed to Nicolaus Hermann as in Bunsen's *Versuch*, 1833, No. 632. *Tr.* as :—

O weep not, mourn not o'er this bier. A good and full version by Miss Winkworth in the 1st ser. of her *Lyra Ger.*, 1855, p. 249. In her 2nd ed., 1856, p. 251, it is altered, and begins: "Now hush your cries, and shed no tear," and repeated thus in her *C. B. for England*, 1863, No. 97. Also in *Ps. & Hys.*, Bedford, 1859, No. 269, and the Rugby *School H. B.*, 1866, No. 208.

ii. **Nun lasst uns den Leib begraben.** This version has so little from the Latin that it is noted under its own first line (q. v.).   [J. M.]

Deus Pater piissime. [*Saturday Evening.*] This hymn occurs as a vesper hymn for the Saturday before the 3rd Sunday in Lent to Passion Sunday, in a MS. Breviary, written about the 14th century, formerly belonging to the Monastery of Evesham (*MS. Barlow*, No. 41, in the Bodleian Library at Oxford). It is also in a 12th cent. MS. in the *British Museum* (Harl. 2928, f. 115 b.), and in a Bodleian MS. of the 13th cent. (Ashmole 1285, f. 38). In 1851 it was given in the *Hymnarium Sarisburiense*, p. 73. *Tr.* as :—

O God, O Father kind and best. By J. D. Chambers, in his *Companion to the Holy Communion*, 1855, and his *Lauda Syon*, 1857, p. 139, in 6 st. of 4 l. It is repeated in the *Appendix* to the *Hymnal N.*, 1863, and in Skinner's *Daily Service Hymnal*, 1864.   [W. A. S.]

Deus tuorum militum. [*Feasts of Martyrs.*] This anonymous Ambrosian hymn is in two forms, one in 32 lines and the second in 16 lines. It dates probably from the 6th cent. The question as to what was the original form of the hymn has not been determined. *Daniel's* (i., No. 97) heading of the texts (both forms) is "De Communi unius Martyris," and he remarks that the hymns for the *Common of Saints* are nearly always of greater length in old and unaltered Breviaries than in those which are of more recent date, or which have been revised. The older hymns having reference to some particular saint, certain stanzas are afterwards cut out to make the hymn suitable for general use. If this view be taken of the present hymn, then the longer form is the original, and the shorter form given in the Breviaries is an abbreviation therefrom. Against this conclusion there are two facts, the first that the lines in the fuller form, which are not given in the Breviaries, do not apply to any special martyr, and second, that the oldest form in which we now have the hymn is (omitting the doxology) in 16 lines. This form, with slight variations in the text, is in the *Mozarabic Brev.* (Toledo, 1502, 317 b); in a 10th cent. MS. at Munich, where it is adapted for the Nativity of St. Laurence, quoted by *Mone*, No. 740; and in the *Latin Hys. of the Anglo-Saxon Church*, Surtees Soc., 1851, from an 11th cent. MS. at Durham. This would suggest that the shorter form of the hymn is the older of the two. As the translations into English are generally from the *Rom. Brev.*, it may be noted that this is the shorter form, with slight variations in lines 6, 7 and 11. This hymn is also found in four MSS. of the 11th cent. in the *British Museum* (Jul. A. vi. f. 66 ; Vesp. D. xii., f. 107 ; Harl. 2961, f. 248 b ; Add. 30851, f. 153 b.). For texts, readings, references, &c., see *Migne*,

Daniel, Mone ; Cardinal Newman's *Hymni Ecclesiae*, 1838 and 1865 ; *Wackernagel*, and the various Breviaries.   [W. A. S.]

Translations in C. U. :
1. **O Thou of all Thy warriors, Lord.** By E. Caswall, in his *Lyra Catholica*, 1849, in 5 st. of 4 l., and his *Hymns*, &c., 1873, p. 110. This was given with alterations in Murray's *Hymnal*, 1852, and later collections, and without alterations in several Roman Catholic hymn-books.
2. **O God, the Christian soldiers' Might.** By R. Campbell. 1st pub. in his *St. Andrews Hymnal*, 1850, p. 97. A part of this is also embodied in No. 397 of the *Hymnary*, 1872.
3. **O God, Thy soldiers' crown and Guard.** By J. M. Neale, in the *Hymnal N.*, 1852–54, and later editions. In *H. A. & M.*, 1861–75, it is altered to "O God, Thy soldiers' great Reward." This is repeated in other collections.
4. **Of all Thy warrior Saints, O Lord.** By J. D. Chambers, given in his *Lauda Syon*, Pt. ii., 1866, p. 12, and repeated in the *People's H.*, 1867.
5. **O God, Thy soldiers' Crown.** By H. W. Beadon. 1st pub. in the *Parish H. Bk.*, 1863, No. 193, in the same collection, 1875, and in the *Hymnary*, 1872, where it reads, "O Christ, Thy soldiers' Crown."
6. **O God, the Christian soldiers' Might.** This, as given in the *Hymnary*, 1872, No. 397, is a cento from *Campbell, Neale, and Chambers*, with alterations by the editors.
7. **O God, of all Thy Saintly host.** By W. J. Irons, in his *Ps. & Hys. for the Church*, 1875.
8. In addition to the above, Nos. 17 and 93 in the *Hymner*, 1882, are centos from *Chambers & Neale*, and the first two lines of No. 27 in Chope's *Hymnal* are the opening lines of *Neale's tr.*, the rest being from another source.

Translations not in C. U. :—
1. Of Thy true soldiers, mighty Lord. *W. J. Copeland.* 1848.
2. O God of Thy soldiers. *Card. Newman.* 1868.
3. O. God, Thy soldiers' crown. *W. J. Blew.* 1852–55.
4. God of Thy soldiers. *J. W. Hewett.* 1859.
    [J. J.]

Δεῦτε ἅπαντες πιστοί. *St. Theophanes.* From the *Triodion*—"Idiomela on Friday of Tyrophagus, that is, of Quinquagesima.'

"At this period of the year the weeks are named, not from the Sundays that precede, but from those that follow them. Quinquagesima is termed Tyrophagus, because up to that time, but not beyond, cheese is allowed. The Friday previous is appropriated to the Commemoration of All Holy Ascetes; in order, as the Synaxarion says, that, by the remembrance of their conflict, we may be invigorated for the race that is set before us." *Hys. of Eastern Ch.*, 1st ed., 1862, p. 95.

To the above explanation Dr. Neale adds the *tr.* "Hither, and with one accord." In this *tr.* the length of strophe, the variation of refrain, and the alert cheering call are as in the original, but it lacks the nervous style and ornate diction of St. Theophanes. [J. J.]

Δεῦτε πόμα πίωμεν. [Ἀναστάσεως ἡμέρα.]

Δεῦτε τελευταῖον ἄσπασμον δῶμεν. [*Burial.*] Dr. Neale prefaces his translation of "The Stichera of the Last Kiss," with the following note :—

"The following Stichera, which are generally, (though without any great cause,) attributed to St. John Damascene, form, perhaps, one of the most striking portions of the service of the Eastern Church. They are sung towards the conclusion of the Funeral Office, whilst the friends and relations are, in turn, kissing the corpse; the priest does so last of all. Immediately afterwards, it is borne to the grave; the priest casts the first earth on the coffin, with the words 'The earth is the Lord's, and all that therein is: the compass of the world, and they that dwell therein.'" *Hys. of the E. C.*, 1st ed., 1862, p. 60; 4th ed., 1882, p. 46.

The original is found in the Burial Office of the Greek Church, in the *Euchologion*, in 13 st. Of these Dr. Neale has omitted st. vi. (which is very similar to vii.), ix., x., and the Theotokion address to the B. V. M. The last stanza is supposed to be spoken by the dead, is of double length, as in Neale, and is sung to a different tone. Dr. Neale's *tr.* is, "Take the last kiss,—the last for ever!" and was pub., with the introductory note, in *The Ecclesiastic and Theologian*, Aug., 1853 (vol. xv. p. 346), and again in his *Hys. of the E. C.*, 1862. It is not in common use. (See **Greek Hymnody**, § xvii. 2, and *Daniel*, iii. p. 125.) The original is given in *Bässler*, No. 18, together with a *tr.* into German; and in the 4th ed. of Dr. Neale's *Hys. of the E. C.*, 1882, Mr Hatherly has given a prose *tr.* of the stanzas omitted by Dr. Neale.　　[J. J.]

Dexter, Henry Martyn, D.D., b. at Plympton, Mass., Aug. 13, 1821, and educated at Yale College, and Andover. In 1844 he was ordained Pastor of a Congregational Church at Manchester, New Haven. In 1849 he removed to the Berkeley Street Congregational Church, Boston, where he remained until his appointment as Editor of the *Congregationalist*, in 1867. Dr. Dexter is the translator of Στόμιον πώλων ("Shepherd of tender youth") [see **Clemens, Titus**], in C. U. in G. Britain and America.　　[F. M. B.]

Dich, Jesu, loben wir. *J. Scheffler.* [*The Praises of Jesus.*] Appeared as No. 118 in Bk. iii. of his *Heilige Seelenlust*, Breslau, 1657, p. 376 (*Werke*, 1862, i. p. 196), in 13 st. of 6 l., entitled, "She [the soul] sings Him a song of praise." Included as No. 687 in Freylinghausen's *G. B.*, 1705, and as No. 249 in Knapp's *Ev. L. S.*, 1850. *Tr.* as:—

Thou, Jesu, art our King. A fine and full rendering by J. Wesley, in *Ps. & Hys.*, 1738, and *H. & Sacred Poems*, 1739 (*P. Works*, 1868-72, vol. i. p. 155). Included as No. 142 in the *Moravian H. Bk.*, 1742 (1886, No. 651), omitting st. 10; seven st. of the 1826 text being included in J. A. Latrobe's *Coll.*, 1841, No. 42. It appeared in full as No. 45 in the Wesley *H. & Spiritual Songs*, 1753, but was not included in the *Wes. H. Bk.* till the new ed., 1875, No. 737, omitting st. x. Six st. appeared in M. Madan's *Coll.*, 1760; seven in the *Wesley Association H. Bk.*, 1838; three in Maurice's *Choral H. Bk.*, 1861; and five in the *Meth. N. Connexion H. Bk.*, 1863.　　[J. M.]

Dicimus grates tibi, summe rerum. *Philipp Melanchthon.* [*On the Angels.*] 1st appeared as No. 1 of *De Angelis Duo Hymni*, Wittenberg, 1543, in 10 st. of 4 l., and there dated Sept. 27, 1543. (*Blätter für Hymnologie*, 1886, p. 27); again in the *Psalterium Davidis*, Wittenberg, 1544; the *Corpus Reformatorum*, vol. x., col. 584, Halle, 1842, and *Wackernagel*, i. p. 268, in 11 st. This passed into English

through **Herr Gott, dich loben alle wir**, a free *tr.* by P. Eber, first printed separately at Nürnberg, c. 1554, as *Ein schön New Geistlich Lobgesang*, then in J. Eichorn's *G. B.*, Frankfurt a. Oder, 1561; in *Wackernagel*, iv. p. 3, in 13 st. In the *Unv. L. S.*, 1851, No. 204, the text of 1561 is given, omitting the doxology. The only *tr.* in C. U. is:—

Lord God, we all give praise to Thee, in full, by E. Cronenwett, as No. 122 in the *Ohio Luth. Hyl.*, 1880.

Other translations are: (1) "To God let all the human race," by *J. C. Jacobi*, 1722, p. 28, repeated in the *Moravian H. Bk.*, 1754, and continued, altered, in later eds. (2) "O Lord our God! to Thee we raise, One universal," by *Miss Fry*, 1845, p. 131　　[J. M.]

Dickinson, William, pub. in 1846:— *Hymns for Passion Week and the Forty Days, Adapted for Churches or for Private Worship*, Lond., J. Nisbet & Co., 1846. These hymns deal with such events in the history of Our Lord, as "The Alabaster Box"; "The Barren Fig Tree"; "The Cleansing of the Temple"; "The washing of the Disciples' feet," &c.; and with the Parables of "The Wedding garment"; "The Talents," &c., which are not commonly versified, and are worthy of attention. The following have come into C. U.:—

1. Calm'd each soul, and clos'd each door. *Easter-day at Even.* This is in the *Rugby School H. Bk.*, 1876; and as "Calm they sit with closed door," in *Kennedy*, 1863; and *Holy Song*, 1869.
2. Ere that solemn hour of doom. *The Ten Virgins—Advent.* In *Kennedy*, 1863; and the *Rugby School H. Bk.*, 1876.
3. Hallelujah, who shall part? *Perseverance of the Saints.* In several collections, including Spurgeon's *O. O. H. Bk.*, 1866, &c.　　[J. J.]

Dickson, David, the reputed author of "Jerusalem, my happy home," in the form of "O mother dear, Jerusalem," was a Scottish Presbyterian Minister born at Glasgow in 1583, and for some time Professor of Divinity at Glasgow (1640), and then (1650) in the University of Edinburgh. He was deprived of his office at the Restoration for refusing the Oath of Supremacy, and d. in 1663. His *Life* was pub. by Robert Wodrow in 1726. His connection with the *Jerusalem* hymn is given under **Jerusalem, my happy home**, q.v. [J. J.]

Dickson, William, eldest surviving son of the late James Dickson, Edinburgh, was b. at Edinburgh, July 24, 1817. After being educated at the High School and University of Edinburgh, he entered his father's business, which he still [1887] carries on. He is a prominent elder in the Free Church, has for many years taken a great interest in Sabbath School work, and has for more than 30 years edited *The Free Church Children's Record*. He has annually written a New Year's hymn since 1842. "Childhood's years are passing o'er us," his best known hymn, originally printed in 1841, as a leaflet for class use, was, in 1846, included in the 2nd part of the *Sacred Song Book* (see **Bateman**), and has since been included in many hymnals.　　[J. M.]

Die dierum principe. *C. Coffin.* [*Sunday Morning.*] Included in the revised *Paris Breviary*, 1736, as the hymn for Sunday at Matins, and republished in the same year

in the author's *Hymni Sacri*, p. 7, in 6 st. of
4 l. It is also in the Lyons and several modern
French Breviaries. The orig. text is given
in Chandler's *Hys. of the Prim. Ch.*, 1837, No.
1; Card. Newman's *Hymni Ecclesiae*, 1838–65,
No. 1; and Macgill's *Songs of the Christian
Creed and Life*, 1876-7, No. 12. [W. A. S.]

Translations in C. U. :—

1. **Morn of morn, and day of days.** By I. Williams. 1st pub. in the *British Mag.*, April,
1837, and again in his *Hys. tr. from the Parisian
Breviary*, 1839, p. 1, in 28 l. In 1861 the compilers of *H. A. & M.*, rearranged it into 7 st. of
4 l., introducing also many alterations. This
arrangement has passed into various collections,
with at times the omission of st. iv. It is the
most widely used *tr.* of this hymn.

2. **This is the day the light was made.** By J.
Chandler. 1st pub. in his *Hymns of the Church
mostly primitive*, 1841, as a distinct *tr.* from
"The first of days the light beheld," which was
given in his *Hymns of the Prim. Ch.*, 1837. In
1850 it was included in Dr. Hook's *Church S. S.
H. Bk.*, No. 19. Later hymnals, quoting from
Dr. Hook's *Coll.*, have in some instances attributed the *tr.* to him. It is found in *Kennedy,
The Hymnary*, Mrs. Brock's *Children's H. Bk.*,
and others.

3. **Morn of morns, the best and first.** By J.
Ellerton, based partly on I. Williams, as above,
written in 1870, and pub. in *Ch. Hymns*, 1871,
No. 36. Its use is limited.

4. **O Day of joy, when first the light.** By W.
Cooke, made for and 1st pub. in the *Hymnary*,
1871–2, No. 5.

Translations not in C. U. :—
1. The first of days the light beheld. *J. Chandler.*
1837.
⊷ 2. Day of days the prince, on thee. *W. J. Blew.*
1852–55.
3. O day of earthly days the chief. *J. D. Chambers.*
1857.
4. This day—the king of days, heaven-born. *H.
Macgill.* 1876-7. [J. J.]

Die güldne Sonne. *P. Gerhardt.*
[*Morning.*] Lauxmann, in *Koch*, viii. 185, calls
this "A splendid hymn of our poet, golden as
the sun going forth in his beauty, full of force
and of blessed peace in the Lord, full of
sparkling thoughts of God." It first appeared
as No. 25 in the *Dritte Dutzet*, Berlin,
1666, of Ebeling's ed. of his *Geistliche Andachten*, in 12 st. of 10 l., entitled "Morning
Blessing." In the eds. of his *Geistliche
Lieder*, by Wackernagel, No. 98, and by
Bachmann, No. 101. Included in J. Crüger's
Praxis pietatis melica, 1672, and later eds.,
and recently as No. 449 in the *Unv. L. S.*,
1851. The beautiful melody (in the *Irish Ch.
Hyl.*, called "Franconia") is by Ebeling, and
appeared with the hymn 1666, as above.

Translations in C. U. :—

1. **The golden sunbeams with their joyous
gleams.** A *tr.* of st. i.–iv., viii., ix., xii., by Miss
Winkworth in her *Lyra Ger.*, 1st Series, 1855,
p. 214, repeated, omitting the *trs.* of st. ii., viii.,
ix., as No. 814, in *Kennedy*, 1863.

2. **Evening and Morning.** A very good *tr.* beginning with st. iv. ("Abend und Morgen "), and
being st. iv., viii.–xii., contributed by R. Massie,
as No. 500, to the 1857 ed. of Mercer's *C. P.
& H. Bk.* This form is included, in whole or
part, in the *Irish Ch. Hyl.* 1873, No. 8; Allon's

Suppl. Hys., No. 218; *N. Cong.*, No. 1195; J.
L. Porter's *Coll.*, No. 100; Martineau's *Coll.*,
No. 425; Horder's *Cong. Hyl.*, No. 556, &c. Beginning with the *tr.* of st. ix. ("Gott, meine
Krone ") as "Father, O hear me," it is included
as No. 636 in *Kennedy*, 1863, and the same in
Mercer's *Ox. ed.*, 1864, No. 384. Mr. Massie
included it, prefixing *trs.* of st. i.–iii., which
begin, "Golden and glorious," in his *Lyra Domestica*, 1864, p. 106, and this full form is repeated as No. 379 in Reid's *Praise Bk.*, 1872.

Translations not in C. U. :—
(1) " The sun's golden beams," by *Miss Dunn*, 1857,
p. 21. (2) "Sunbeams all golden," by *Miss Cox*, 1864,
p. 13. (3) " What is our mortal race " (beginning with
st. vii.); by *E. Massie*, 1866, p. 87. (4) " See the sun's
glorious light," by *E. Massie*, 1867, p. 8. (5) " The
golden morning," by *J. Kelly*, 1867, p. 270. [J. M.]

Die parente temporum. [*Sunday Morn-
ing.*] This hymn is given in the *Breviary* of
the Diocese of *Le Mans*, 1748, *Pars Hiemalis*,
p. 4, as the hymn on Sunday at Nocturns from
Whitsuntide to Advent. Text in Dr. Neale's
Hymni Ecclesiae, 1851, p. 20. [W. A. S.]

Translations in C. U. :—

1. **On this day, the first of days.** By Sir H. W.
Baker. *Tr.* for and 1st pub. in *H. A. & M.*,
1861, in 7 st. of 4 l. It was, so far as is known,
the first *tr.* into English of this hymn. It is
given in several hymn-books. In the *Hys. and
Songs of Praise*, N. Y., 1874, st. v.–vii. are given
as: "Father, Who didst fashion me."

2. **To-day when time began its course.** By R. F.
Littledale, was given in the *People's H.*, for
which it was made, in 1867, No. 421, with the
signature "D. L."

3. **This primal day, the Spring of Time.** By
R. C. Singleton. *Tr.* for the *Anglican H. Bk.*,
1867, and pub. therein 1868, No. 22.

4. **This day the Father, Source of all.** By W.
Cooke. *Tr.* for the *Hymnary*, in which it 1st
appeared in 1872, No. 9. [J. J.]

Dies absoluti praetereunt. [*Septua-
gesima.*] This hymn is found in two MSS. of
the 11th cent. (Nos. 313, 314) at St. Gall;
and is quoted in full in *Monc*, No. 68, and in
Daniel, iv. p. 179, both with notes and references. *Mone* is inclined to believe it to be
the work of a French poet. It is specially
rich in allusions to Holy Scripture. *Tr.* as :—

The bygone days in Time's dark ocean sleep.
By E. A. Dayman, written for and 1st pub. in
the *Hymnary*, 1872, No. 200. [W. A. S.]

Dies est laetitiae, In ortu regali.
[*Christmas.*] This Christmas hymn or carol,
which Luther spoke of as a work of the Holy
Spirit, seems to be of German origin, and is
probably not earlier than the 14th cent.

G. Goeze, of Jena, in 1703, started the theory that this
hymn was written by Benno, created Cardinal in 1085
by the Anti-Pope Clement III. Other German writers
of the 18th cent., misunderstanding this statement, forthwith pronounced it the work of Benno, Bishop of Meissen, who d. 1107. See *Wetzel*, i. 108, and a wonderful
combination of the two theories in O. F. Hörner's *Nachrichten von Liederdichtern des Augspurgischen Gesang-
buchs*, Schwabach, 1775, p. 62. For neither supposition is there the slightest vestige of evidence. It exists
in various forms, and as will be seen below, the early
German versions give no help in determining what
number of sts. it originally possessed. *Mone*, No. 47,
quotes it from a MS. of the 15th cent. now at Trier, and
from other sources; with notes and various readings.
The stanzas of the *Trier MS.* are :—2 "Mater haec est
filia." 3. "Orto dei filio." 4. "Angelus pastoribus."

5. "Ut vitrum non laeditur." 6. "In obscure nasci-tur." 7. "Orbis dum describitur." · 8. "Christum na-tum dominum." 9. "Christe qui nos propriis." He describes it as "having been recast and expanded."

Wackernagel, 1841, No. 53, gives st. 1, 3, 5, 4 from Lucas Lossius's *Psalmodia*, Nürnberg, 1553; but in his new ed. i., No. 332, he quotes the text of *Mone* with a 10th st.:—10. "Ut stellam conspiciunt," added for use at Epiphany, which he takes from J. Spangenberg's *Alte und Neue Geistliche Lieder*. Erfurt, 1544. *Ram-bach*, i. pp. 330–335, has st. 1, 3, 5, 4 with a note on the authorship. *Daniel*, i. p. 330, quotes the text of *Ram-bach* and *Wackernagel*, and at iv. pp. 254–257 gives the various readings and additional st. from *Mone*; with notes from other sources. The text is also found, gene-rally in st. 1, 3, 5, 4 in *Simrock*, *Königsfeld*, *Bässler* (these with German *trs.*) and other collections. Hoff-mann von Fallersleben (*Geschichte des Deutschen Kir-chenliedes*, ed. 1861, pp. 295–301) refers to it as in a 15th cent. ms. now at Graz with st. 1, 3, 5, 2, 6, 4; as in a ms. of 1422 now at Munich with st. 1, 3, 2, 4, 6, 5 (both of these with German *trs.*); and as in another 15th cent, ms. at Munich with st. 1, 2, 6, 3, 4.

Translation in C. U.:—

Royal day that chasest gloom. By J. M. Neale, pub. in his *Mediaeval Hys.*, 1851, in 3 st. of 10 l. This is a paraphrase rather than a literal rendering of the shorter form of the hymn. In 1854 it was rewritten by Dr. Neale for his *Christmas Carols*, and in this form it passed into the *People's H.*, 1867, No. 34.

This hymn also passed into English through the German:—

Der Tag der ist so freudenreich. *Wackernagel*, ii., p. 520, gives this as a 15th cent. *tr.*, and re-prints 11 (really 12) versions, varying from 1 to 13 st. The form *tr.* into English is that in Klug's *G. B.*, 1529, in 4 st., repeated as No. 29 in the *Unv. L. S.*, 1851. The *tr.* in C. U. is:—

A wondrous child, the Virgin-born, by A. T. Russell as No. 49 in his *Ps. & Hys.*, 1851. It begins with st. ii. (" Ein Kindelein so löbelich "), and is of st. ii., i.

Other trs. are :—(1) "Hail to the day ! so rich in joy," by *Miss Fry*, 1845, p. 13. (2) "To us the promised child is born," a *tr.* of st. ii. by *Dr. H. Mills*, 1856, p. 274.   [J. M.]

Dies irae, dies illa. [*Burial. Advent.*] In dealing with this great Sequence of the Western Church we shall note in detail, i. *The Text*; ii. *Its Authorship*; iii. *Its Liturgical Use*; and iv. *Its General Acceptance*.

i. *The Text.* For the use of the general reader the most accessible work on this sub-ject is *Daniel*, ii. pp. 103–106.

1. The oldest form known to the present time is that contained in a ms. in the Bod-leian, Oxford (*Liturg. Misc.* 163 *f.* 179*b*). This is a Dominican Missal written at the end of the 14th cent. and apparently for use at Pisa. This text is as follows: —

"Sequentia pro defunctis.

" Dies irae, dies illa, Solvet saeclum in favilla ; Teste David cum Sibilla.	" Liber scriptus proferetur, In quo totum continetur, Unde mundus judicetur.
" Quantus tremor est fu-turus Quando judex est ven-turus Cuncta stricte discussu-rus.	" Judex ergo cum sedebit, Quicquid latet apparebit, Nil inultum remanebit.
	" Quid sum miser tunc dicturus ? Quem patronum roga-turus ? Cum vix justus sit secu-rus.
" Tuba mirum *spargit* so-num, Per sepulchra regionum, Coget omnes ante thro-num.	
	" Rex tremendae majesta-tis, Qui salvandos salvas gra-tis, Salva me fons pietatis.
" Mors stupebit et natura, *Dum* resurget creatura, Judicanti responsura.	

" Recordare Jesu pie Quod sum causatuae viae, Ne me perdas illa die.	" Preces meae non sunt dignae, Sed tu bonus fac benigne, Ne perenni cremer igne.
" Quaerens me sedisti las-sus, Redemisti crucem pas-sus, Tantus labor non sit cas-sus.	" Inter oves locum praesta Et ab hoedis me seques-tra, Statuens in parte dextra
" Juste judex ultionis, Donum fac remissionis, Ante diem rationis.	" Confutatis maledictis Flammis acribus addictis, Voca me cum benedictis.
" Ingemisco tanquam reus, Culpa rubet vultus meus, Supplicanti parce Deus.	" Oro supplex et acclinis, Cor contritum quasi cinis, Gere curam mei finis.
" Qui Mariam absolvisti Et latronem exaudisti, Mihi quoque spem de-disti.	" Lacrymosa dies illa Qua resurget ex favilla Judicandus homo reus, Huic ergo parce Deus.

" Pie Jesu Domine ;
Dona eis requiem."

This text is the same as that in the modern *Roman Missal*, with the exception of the two words given in italics :—st. iii. l. 1, *spargit* instead of *spargens*; and st. iv. l. 2, *Dum* in-stead of *Cum*. These are probably errors on the part of the scribe, and cannot be accepted as true readings.

2. Another form of the text is in a ms. found amongst mss. of Felix Haemmerlein, a priest of Zürich who d. cir. 1457. This ms. is now at Zürich. The text, in 22 st. of 3 l., is given in *Daniel*, ii. p. 103.

3. The third text known has an approxi-mate date only, that of the *Variorum in Europa Itinerum Deliciae* of Nathaniel Chy-traeus, 1st ed. 1594 (*Brit. Mus.*). It is also in Mohnike's *Kirchen- und litterarhistorische Stu-dien*, vol. i. pt. i., Stralsund, 1824. Chytraeus gives it simply as one of the inscriptions he found in Mantua, and as in the Church of St. Francis. In the *Königsberg G. B.*, 1650, p. 305, it is said to have been " found on a Crucifix (*bey einem Crucifix*), at Mantua, in the Church of St. Francis." By later writers it is said to have been engraved on the marble base of a Crucifix in that church. Concern-ing this church and marble slab, a writer in the *Dublin Review*, vol. ix. 1883, p. 375, says :—

"Father Narcisso Bonazzi, Maestro di Capella to the Bishop of Mantua, has upon application most obligingly written to this effect: that the Church and Convent of St. Francis were suppressed in 1797 (the year of the French occupation of Mantua); that in 1811 the church was desecrated and the convent was turned into a mili-tary arsenal ; and that no trace of the slab can now be found, neither in the churches to which the monuments of St. Francis were removed, nor in the royal or civic museums of the town."

The text according to Chytraeus, p. 186, has the following stanzas, which are given *before* the opening stanza of the older form of the hymn :—

" Quaeso anima fidelis, Ah quid respondere ve-lis, Christo venturo de coelis,	" Dies illa, dies irae Quam conemur Praeve-nire, Obviamque Deo ire
" Cum a te poscet ratio-nem, Ob boni omissionem, Et mali commissionem ?	" Seria contritione Gratiae apprehensione Vitae emendatione."

Following these there are 16 st. correspond-ing to i.-xvi. of the oldest known form given above ; and then, instead of st. xvii.-xix., the concluding st. :—

" Ut consors beatitatis,
Vivam cum justificatis,
In aevum aeternitatis."

Daniel gives in vol. ii. pp. 103–105 what he understood to be the *Mantua* text. This differs from *Chytraeus's* text in these particulars :—

Chytraeus	Daniel.
1. Quaeso anima . .	1. Cogita (Quaeso) anima
2. Cum a te poscet . . Et mali . .	2. Cum deposcet . . Ob mali . .
5. Teste David cum Sybilla.	5. Teste Petro cum . .
10. Nil inultum . .	10. Nil incultum . .
11. Cum nec justus . .	11. Quum nec justus . .
13. Quod sum causa . . (l. 2. " Ne me per-das ": l. 3. Quod sum causa.	13. Quod sim causa . . (These lines reversed, 2 being "Quod" and 3 " Ne ").
14. Quaerens me sedisti . . Tantus labor ne sit . .	14. Quaerens me venisti . . Tantus labor non . .
16. Ingemisco vere reus . .	16. Ingemisco tanquam reus.
19. Statuens me parte . .	19. Statuens in parte . .
21. Ut consors . .	21. Consors ut . .

5. In the French Missals, e.g. that of *Paris,* 1738 ; and that of *Metz,* 1778, the opening lines read :—

" Dies irae, dies illa,
Crucis expandens vexilla,
Solvet seclum in favillâ.

Concerning the variations in the text in the opening lines of this Sequence, (6) " Teste David, cum Sybilla," (2) " Teste Petro cum Sybilla," and (3) " Crucis expandens vexilla," Archbishop Trench writes :—

" An unwillingness to allow a Sibyl to appear as bearing witness to Christian truth, has caused that we sometimes find this third line ['Teste David cum Sybyllâ '] omitted, and in its stead ' Crucis expandens vexilla,' as the second of this triplet. It rests on Matt. xxiv. 30, and on the expectation that the apparition of a cross in the sky would be this " sign of the Son of man in heaven." It is, however, a late alteration of the text ; and the line as above [' Teste David '] is quite in the spirit of the early and medieval theology. In those uncritical ages the Sibylline verses were not seen to be that transparent forgery which indeed they are ; but were continually appealed to as only second to the sacred Scriptures in prophetic authority ; thus on this very matter of the destruction of the world, by Lactantius, *Inst. Div.* vii. 16–24 ; cf. Piper, *Method. d. Christl. Kunst,* p. 472–507 ; these, with other heathen testimonies of the same kind, being not so much subordinated to more legitimate prophecy, as co-ordinated with it, the two being regarded as parallel lines of prophecy, the Church's and the world's, and consenting witness to the same truths. Thus is it in a curious medieval mystery on the Nativity, published in the *Journal des Savans,* 1846, p. 88. It is of simplest construction. One after another patriarchs and prophets and kings of the Old Covenant advance and repeat their most remarkable word about Him that should come : but side by side with them a series of heathen witnesses, *Virgil,* on the ground of his fourth Eclogue, *Nebuchadnezzar* (Dan. iii. 25), and the *Sibyl* ; and that it was the writer's intention to parallelise the two series, and to show that Christ had the testimony of both is plain from some opening lines of the prologue :—

'O Judaei, Verbum Dei Qui negatis, hominem Vestrae legis, testem Regis Audite per ordinem.	Et vos, gentes, non credentes Peperisse virginem, Vestrae gentis documentis Pellite caliginem.'

" And such is the meaning here—' That such a day shall be has the witness of inspiration, of David,—and of mere natural religion, of the Sibyl—Jew and Gentile alike bear testimony to the truths which we Christians believe.' All this makes it certain that we ought to read *Teste David,* and not, *Teste Petro.* It is true that 2 Pet. iii. 7–11 is a more obvious prophecy of the destruction of the world by fire than any in the Psalms ; but there are passages enough in these (as Ps. xcvi. 13 ; xcvii. 3 ; xi. 6), to which the poet may allude ; and the very obviousness of that in St. Peter, makes the reading, which introduces his name, suspicious."— *Sac. Lat. Poetry,* 1874.

ii. *The Authorship.* With regard to the authorship it seems certainly to have been of

Italian origin, the Missals of other nations having adopted it at later dates. The author was probably Thomas of Celano, a Franciscan Friar of the 13th cent. This is the opinion of *Daniel, Mohnike, Rambach, Fink, Lisco, Trench,* and others who have written specially on the subject. The reasons for ascribing its origin to the Franciscan Order, and to Thomas of Celano, are :—

(1) The earliest known mention of this hymn is made by Brother Bartolomæo degli Albizzi, or Bartholomæus Pisanus, of the Order of St. Francis, who died about A.D. 1380, in his *Liber Conformitatum,* a treatise setting forth the points in which St. Francis sought to imitate his Divine Master. It was printed at Milan in 1510, again in 1513, also in later years.

(2) Sixtus Senensis, a very learned Dominican but (as in duty bound) very zealous for his order, in his *Bibliotheca Sancta,* Venet. 1566, calls it an " uncouth poem " (*inconditus rhythmus*). This points to a Franciscan origin ; the old rivalry between the Franciscans and Dominicans, as is well known, was very great. Hence this writer's hostility furnishes a substantial argument.

(3) A resolution was adopted by the Dominican Order at Salamanca in 1576, to the effect that this Sequence should not be used in Masses for the Dead ; as being contrary to the Rubrics. (See *Annotat. in Rubr. Ordinis Prædicatorum,* Venet. 1582.)

(4) The learned and painstaking Lucas Waddingus (Luke Wadding) in his *Scriptores Ordinis Minorum,* Romæ, 1650, ascribes it to Thomas of Celano ; mentioning that others assign the authorship to St. Bonaventura, or to Matthæus Aquaspartanus (d'Acquasparta).

On the other hand, the learned Pope Benedict XIV. in his work *De Sacrificio Missæ, Sectio Prima,* § cxxiii., ascribes it (but only as a matter of opinion) to Cardinal Latinus Ursinus, or Frangipani, of the Dominican Order. This was probably Napoléon Frangipani, by some writers called Orsini, of the Dominican Order, created Cardinal of the title of St. Adrian by Pope Nicholas IV. ; he died at Perugia in 1294. Further, Antonius Possevinus, a learned Jesuit, in his *Apparatus Sacer,* Venet. 1603, 1606, &c., says that some ascribe it to Augustinus Bugellensis Pedemontanus, of the Order of St. Augustine ; adding that his own opinion is that it was the work of Humbert, the fifth General of the Dominican Order, who was born near Valence, died at Lyons in 1276, and was buried in the Dominican Church of that city. There is, however, little authority for these opinions, unless the fact that the oldest known text is found in a *Dominican Missal* of the latter part of the 14th cent. as noted above, lends weight to these statements. Still less is there weight in the opinions of Arnoldus Wein, a Benedictine Monk, and a great, if somewhat eccentric writer (b. 1554). In his *Lignum Vitae, Ornamentum et Decus Ecclesiae,* Venet. 1595, lib. v. cap. 70, a work which contains an account of illustrious men of his Order, he says that some have ascribed the " Dies Irae " to St. Gregory the Great, and some to St. Bernard.

Taking all the arguments and ascertained facts into account, we may conclude that the " Dies irae" was written by Thomas of Celano, a Franciscan Friar of the 13th cent., and the friend and biographer of St. Francis of Assisi.

iii. *Liturgical Use.* This Sequence is regarded as having been originally an Advent hymn. Its ritual use, however, is as the Sequence in the Mass for the Dead. It is first found in Italian Missals, and especially in those of the Franciscan Order. Among the oldest Missals in which it is known to occur are those of *Lübeck,* c. 1480 ; *Schleswig,* 1486 ; *Arras,* 1491 ; the *Dominican Processional,* Venice, 1494 ; the *Dominican Missal,* Venice, 1496 ; *Tournay,* 1498, &c. It is not given, however, in many Missals of the 15th and 16th centuries, nor in the collections of *Clichtoveus,* 1516 ; of *Adelphus,* 1519 ; and of *Torrentinus,* 1513, although these all contain the Sequences then most frequently in use in France, Germany, &c. It is in the *Brander* collection of 1507. We may note also the following details:—

1. In the *Roman Missal* it is the Sequence on All Souls' Day; in Masses celebrated on the occasion of a death or burial; and also on the third, seventh, or thirtieth day after burial; and, optionally, in daily or ordinary Masses for the Dead.
2. In the *French Missals*, as quoted above, it appeared in the *Arras*, 1491; and the *Tournay*, 1498.
3. Its *English* use was limited. It is given in some editions of the *Sarum Missal* as a "Prosa pro defunctis qui voluerit," in the *Trigintale S. Gregorii*, an office subsequently suppressed. (Burntisland reprint of the *Sarum Missal:* Pars Secunda, 1867, col. 883*-885*.)

iv. *General Acceptance.* The hold which this Sequence has had upon the minds of men of various nations and creeds has been very great. Goethe uses it, as is well known, in his *Faust* with great effect. It also furnishes a grand climax to Canto vi. in Sir Walter Scott's *Lay of the Last Minstrel.* It has been translated into many languages, in some of which the renderings are very numerous, those in German numbering about ninety, and those in English about one hundred and sixty. In G. Britain and America no hymn-book of any note has appeared during the past hundred years without the "Dies Irae" being directly or indirectly represented therein. *Daniel*, writing from a German standpoint, says:—

"Even those to whom the hymns of the Latin Church are almost entirely unknown, certainly know this one: and if anyone can be found so alien from human nature that they have no appreciation of sacred poetry, yet, as a matter of certainty, even they would give their minds to this hymn, of which every word is weighty, yea, even a thunderclap."

From another standpoint, Archbishop Trench says:—

"Nor is it hard to account for its popularity. The metre so grandly devised, of which I remember no other example, fitted though it has here shown itself for bringing out some of the noblest powers of the Latin language—the solemn effect of the triple rhyme, which has been likened to blow following blow of the hammer on the anvil—the confidence of the poet in the universal interest of his theme, a confidence which has made him set out his matter with so majestic and unadorned a plainness as at once to be intelligible to all,—these merits, with many more, have given the *Dies Irae* a foremost place among the masterpieces of sacred song."—*Sac. Lat. Poetry*, 1874, p. 302.

The opening line of this Sequence is taken verbatim from Zeph. i. 15 (Vulgate version). *Daniel*, ii. pp. 103–131, has extensive notes on each strophe, and a general dissertation on the hymn. This he supplements in v. p. 110–117. It has also been treated of by several writers, and specially by Mohnike in his *Kirchen- und litterarhistorische Studium*, Stralsund, 1824, and his *Hymnologische Forschungen*, Stralsund, 1832; and Lisco in his *Dies Irae, Hymnus auf das Weltgericht*, Berlin, 1840.

Authorities: — *Mohnike, Lisco,* and *Daniel,* as above; Trench's *Sac. Lat. Poetry*, 1849–74; Dr. Schaff in *Hours at Home,* N. Y., 1868; *Dublin Review*, 1883; *Königsfeld,* 1847. [Y.]

v. Translations in C. U. :—

1. **The day of wrath, that dreadful day.** As the *trs.* of this Sequence are in many instances so much alike in the opening line, it will be necessary in some cases to give the opening stanza in a complete form. This, the oldest *tr.* in C. U. reads:—

> "The day of wrath, that dreadful day
> Shall the whole world in ashes lay,
> As David and the Sibyl say."

This rendering is from the *Roman Missal*, and its first publication, so far as yet traced, was in N. Tate's *Miscellanea Sacra*, 1696, where it is given as "By the E. of Roscommon." It is also in the posthumous *Poems* of Wentworth Dillon, Earl of Roscommon, 1721 (Preface dated 1717). It subsequently appeared in a *Divine Office for the Laity*, 1763. Mr. Orby Shipley, in the *Dublin Review*, January, 1883, suggests the possibility of the *tr.* being by J. Dryden rather than by Lord Roscommon, on the ground of its appearance in the *Primer*, 1706, to which Dryden is believed to have largely contributed. It never appeared, however, in any edition of Dryden's works, and is not characterized by any of the peculiarities which distinguish Dryden's style. In 1812, Dr. Collyer gave in his *Coll.* 14 st. in two parts, pt. i. beginning, "The last loud trumpet's wondrous sound;" and pt. ii., "Thou Who for me didst feel such pain." In 1819, a cento composed of st. i., iii., vi., x., xv. and xvii., considerably altered, was given in Cotterill's *Sel.*, No. 201. This was followed by another cento broken into two parts, which appeared in Bickersteth's *Christian Psalmody*, 1833, beginning, pt. i., "The last loud trumpet's wondrous sound"; pt. ii., "Forget not what my ransom cost." The same arrangement was repeated in the earlier editions of Mercer, and other collections. The cento in Hall's *Mitre*, 1836, and the *New Mitre Hyl.*, 1875, beginning, "The last loud trumpet's," &c., is another arrangement of stanzas.

2. **That day of wrath, that dreadful day.** By Sir Walter Scott. This is a condensed rendering of the *Dies Irae*, introduced by Scott at the close of *The Lay of the Last Minstrel*, 1805, in 3 st. of 4 l., as having been sung in Melrose Abbey, "noble Angus" having decided

> "That he a pilgrimage would take
> To Melrose Abbey, for the sake
> Of Michael's restless sprite."

The details of the pilgrimage are wrought out with grand effect, and conclude with this "hymn of intercession."

> "That day of wrath, that dreadful day
> When heaven and earth shall pass away!
> What power shall be the sinner's stay?
> How shall he meet that dreadful day?"

Soon after the publication of the *Lay*, &c., in 1805, this *tr.* was given as a hymn for public worship in various collections. Dr. Collyer included it in his *Sel.*, 1812; *Cotterill* followed in 1819, as "The day," &c., and others later on, until its use has extended to all English-speaking countries. Various attempts have been made to "improve" these noble lines; st. iii. l. 3 being specially selected with this result :—

"Be Thou, O Christ, the sinner's stay," in Elliott's *Ps. & Hys.*, 1835.
"Thou art, O Christ, Thy people's stay," in Drummond & Greville's *Church of England H. Bk.*, 1838.
"Jesus, be Thou the sinner's stay," in the Scottish United Presb. *H. Bk.*, 1852.
"Be Thou, O Christ, our steadfast stay," in Breay's Birmingham *Sel.*, 1855.

The first of these changes is still in extensive use, but another change in the opening line, "On that dread day, that wrathful day," given in Cotterill's *Sel.*, 1810, is now unknown.

This condensed rendering of the *Dies Irae* has not only taken a strong hold upon the general public, but it has also elicited the admiration of those who through their education and wide reading are best qualified to judge. One such has said :—

"I know nothing more sublime in the writings of Sir Walter Scott—certainly I know nothing so sublime in any portion of the sacred poetry of modern times, I mean of the present century—as the 'Hymn for the Dead,' extending only to twelve lines, which he embodied in *The Lay of the Last Minstrel.* (Right Hon. W. E. Gladstone. Speech at Hawarden, Feb. 3, 1866.)

Sir Walter Scott's admiration of the original is well known. His biographer, J. G. Lockhart, says concerning his last illness :—

"But commonly whatever we could follow him in was a fragment of the Bible (especially the Prophecies of Isaiah, and the Book of Job) or some petition in the Litany—or a verse of some psalm (in the old Scotch metrical Version)—or of some of the magnificent hymns of the Romish ritual, in which he always delighted, but which probably hung on his memory now in connection with the church services he had attended while in Italy. We very often heard distinctly the cadence of the *Dies Irae;* and I think the very last stanza that we could make out was the first of a still greater favourite, 'Stabat Mater dolorosa,'" &c. (*Memoirs,* 1838, vol. vii. p. 391.)

3. On that great, that awful day. By Lord Macaulay, a condensed rendering, contributed to the *Christian Observer,* Jan. 1826 (vol. 26), and embodied in the early editions of the *Rugby School Chapel H. Bk.,* and a few collections. It has almost altogether passed out of common use.

4. Day of wrath, thou day of thunder. By H. J. Buckoll, from the *Roman Missal,* 1st pub. in the *Rugby School Chapel H. Bk.,* and continued in later editions.

5. Day of wrath, that awful day. By I. Williams. The first st. of this rendering from the *Paris Missal* is :—

"Day of wrath !—that awful day
Shall the banner'd Cross display,
Earth in ashes melt away !"

This rendering appeared first in the *British Mag.* for Jan. 1834, and was repeated in the translator's *Thoughts in Past Years,* 1838, and his *Hys. tr. from the Parisian Brev.,* 1839. In full, or in part, this *tr.* has been included in the *Leeds H. Bk.,* 1853 ; *The Parish H. Bk.,* 1863-75 ; Mather's *Hys. for the Ch. of God,* 1864 ; Mercer (based on *I. Williams*), Oxford ed., 1864, and several others. The rendering in R. Campbell's *St. Andrew's Hys. and Anthems* is also this by I. Williams, with alterations by Campbell.

6. Day of anger, that dread day. By H. Alford, from the *Paris Missal.* The opening st. of this *tr.* is :—

"Day of anger, that dread day
Shall the sign in Heav'n display,
And the earth in ashes lay."

It appeared in his *Ps. & Hys.,* 1844, in two parts, the second beginning, "Thou didst toil my soul to gain " ; and was repeated in his *Year of Praise,* 1867. In Windle's *Hymnal,* No. 83, there is given a cento from this *tr.* into which many alterations are introduced, and a refrain is added to each stanza which is altogether new to the hymn. The cento in the *Marlborough School Coll.,* 1869, No. 49, beginning with the first line from I. Williams, is from this *tr.* but greatly altered. Dean Alford's *tr.* is also given in a few American hymn-books.

7. Day of wrath, O day of mourning. By W. J. Irons, from the *Paris Missal.* It is well known that the Revolution in Paris in 1848 led to many scenes of terror and shame. Foremost was the death of Monseigneur D. A. Affre, the Archbishop of Paris, who was shot on June 25 on the barricades on the Place de la Bastille whilst endeavouring to persuade the insurgents to cease firing, and was buried on July 7. As soon as it was safe to do so his funeral sermon was preached in Notre Dame, accompanied by a religious service of the most solemn and impressive kind. Throughout the service the Archbishop's heart was exposed in a glass case in the Choir, and at the appointed place the *Dies Irae* was sung by an immense body of priests. The terror of the times, the painful sense of bereavement which rested upon the minds of the people through the death of their Archbishop, the exposed heart in the Choir, the imposing ritual of the service, and the grand rendering of the *Dies Irae* by the priests, gave to the occasion an unusual degree of impressiveness. Dr. Irons was present, and deeply moved by what he saw and heard. On retiring from the Church he wrote out this *tr.* of the *Dies Irae.* The surrounding circumstances no doubt contributed greatly to produce this, which is one of the finest of modern renderings of the grandest of mediaeval hymns. It was first issued in the privately printed *Introits and Hymns for Advent,* issued, without date, for the use of Margaret Street Chapel, London, where it bears the initials " W. J. I." It was also published in 1849 (Lond., Masters), with historical notes by Dr. Irons, and with the music to which it was sung in Notre Dame, harmonized by Charles Child Spencer. Dr. Irons also included it in his *Appx.* to the *Brompton Met. Psalter,* in his *Hymns,* &c., Brompton, 1866, No. 82, and in the new and enlarged ed. of his *Ps. & Hys.,* 1873–1883, No. 60. In popularity and extensiveness of use this *tr.* of the *Dies Irae* is surpassed only by Sir Walter Scott's. A few important changes have come into use which must be noted. The opening stanza is :—

"Day of wrath, O day of mourning,
See once more the Cross returning—
Heav'n and earth in ashes burning !"

This is given in J. A. Johnston's *English Hyl.,* 1852, as "Day of wrath, O day *dismaying,*" &c. ; in Thrupp's *Ps. & Hys.,* 1853, as "Day of *Judgment,* day of mourning " ; and in *Kennedy,* 1863, as "Day of *anger, day* of mourning." The second line of st. i. has also undergone these changes :—in the *Salisbury H. Bk.,* 1857, the *Sarum,* 1868, and others, to "See! the Son's dread sign returning." In this there is a change in the wording of the line only, and not a change of thought. The thought, however, is changed in the *H. Comp.* and *Snepp,* where we read, "See the Crucified returning." In *H. A. & M.* the reading of the *Roman Missal* is adopted in spirit although not in word, " See fulfilled the prophet's warning," and this has been repeated in several hymn-books. The concluding lines which read :—

"Lord, who didst our souls redeem,
Grant a blessed Requiem !"

were changed in the *Hymns and Introits,* 1852, and the Cooke and Denton *Hymnal,* 1853, to the *tr.* by I. Williams :—

"Lord all-pitying, Jesu blest !
Grant them Thine eternal rest."

This, with " Grant *us,*" for "Grant them," has been repeated, sometimes with and sometimes without the change, in most hymn-books which have adopted Dr. Irons's *tr.* Thring's *Coll.* is an exception in favour of:—

> " Jesu, Saviour ever Blest,
> Grant us then eternal rest."

8. **Nigher still, and still more nigh.** By E. Caswall, from the *Roman Missal*, in his *Lyra Catholica*, 1849, p. 241; and his *Hys. & Poems*, 1873, p. 126. This is repeated in the Irvingite *Hys. for the Use of the Churches*, 1864–71.

9. **Day of vengeance, day of sorrow.** By W. J. Blew, from the *Roman Missal*, given in his *Church Hy. & Tune Bk.*, 1852. In Mr. Rice's *Sel.* from that work, No. 7 begins with st. 9 of this *tr.*, " Day of dread, in wrath awaking." This *tr.*, which ranks with, if it does not surpass, Dr. Irons's noted above, has been strangely over looked by hymn-book compilers. A writer in the *Dublin Review* says of it, " for originality, force of expression, dignity, and rhythm [it] is unsurpassed, at least by any other Protestant version." (*Fifty Versions of Dies Irae*, 1883, vol. ix. p. 390.)

10. **Day of wrath and tribulation.** A cento in Rorison's *Coll.*, 1851, based on I. Williams and Dr. Irons. In the 2nd and later editions it reads, " Day of wrath ! O day of mourning."

11. **Day of wrath ! that day dismaying.** By J. A. Johnston, given in the 2nd ed. of his *English Hyl.*, 1856, instead of the altered version of Dr. Irons, as in the 1st ed., 1852. This new rendering was repeated in the 3rd ed., 1861.

12. **Day of anger, all arresting.** By W. B. Robertson, from the *Roman Missal*, 1st pub. in *Hosannah* ; or, *Chants and Hymns for Children and Teachers*, Glasgow (Preface dated 1854). It was reprinted in 1868, in a programme of music sung by a choir at the meeting of the United Presbyterian Synod of that year. In the Draft of the *Presb. Hyl.*, 1874, it was reprinted for approval, and finally appeared in that collection in 1876, with st. ix.–xviii. considerably altered.

13. **Day of doom, the last, the greatest.** By Archbishop Benson. Written at Rugby, and 1st pub. in the *Wellington Coll. H. Bk.*, 1860, and repeated in subsequent editions. It is appointed to be sung before the Litany on the Sundays in Advent, and is from the *Roman Missal.*.

14. **Day of terror, day of doom.** By A. P. Stanley, from the *Roman Missal*, appeared in G. Redmond Portal's *Hys for Use of the Parish of Albury*, 1864, in 9 st. of 6 l. In 1868 it was given in *Macmillan's Magazine*, and in 1869 in the *Appendix* to *Hys. for Use in the Chapel of Marlborough Coll.* as, " Day of wrath, O dreadful day," with an additional stanza. The same was repeated in the *Westminster Abbey H. Bk.*, 1883. In the *Hymnary*, 1872, it is given, with the addition of 3 stanzas by the Editors (" Nought of Thee my prayers can claim " ; " Make me with Thy sheep to stand " ; and " Full of tears and full of dread "), and divided into three parts, pt. ii. being, " When, in that tremendous day," and pt. iii., " O just Judge, to whom belongs." The ten-stanza form is repeated in a few American hymn-books, including *Laudes Domini*, 1884, and others.

15. **O Day of wrath ! that awful day !** By R. C. Singleton, from the *Roman Missal*, written in 1867, and pub. in his *Anglican H. Bk.*, 1868, No. 36. In the 1871 ed. it reads : " Day of wrath ! that awful day, Earth in ashes," &c., and marked as *tr.* in 1870.

16. **Day of wrath ! the heart dismaying.** By " F. J. P." from the *Paris Missal ;* in Dr. Rawes's *Hys. for the Year*, N.D. (1860); the *Catholic Hymnal*, N.D., and other Roman Catholic collections for Missions and Schools. This *tr.* has often been attributed to F. W. Faber, but in error. (*Dublin Review*, 1883, vol. ix. p. 390.)

17. **Day of wrath ! That day of woe.** From the *Roman Missal*, in *The Crown of Jesus H. Bk.*, N.D. [c. 1862].

18. **Day of wrath, that day dismaying.** This cento in the *Hymnary* is thus composed : st. i.–viii. are st. i.–viii. of No. 16 above, by " F. J. P." re-written by Canon William Cooke. Canon Cooke changed the present tense of this *tr.* back to the future of the original, and thus made the whole hymn refer not to an actual realization, but a dread anticipation of the Judgment. He has also rendered the opening stanza according to the *Roman Missal*. These changes, and other alterations render these stanzas almost a new translation. The remainder of the hymn (st. ix.–xx.) is from Dr. Irons, No. 7, as above.

19. **In that dim and awful day.** By " E. O." in Dale's *English H. Bk.*, 1875, No. 836.

Translations not in C. U. :—

1. Dear, dear soul, awake, awake. Joshua Sylvester. *Divine Weekes of Du Bartas*, 1621.

2. Hearest thou, my soul, what serious things. Richard Crashaw. *Steps to the Temple*, 1646.

3. A day full of horror must. Patrick Carey. *Trivial Poems and Triolets* (Sir W. Scott's ed. 1820), 1651

4. Ah, silly soul, what wilt thou say. William Drummond. *Posthumous Poems*, 1656, and Bp. Sage's ed. 1711.

5. That day of wrath, that dreadful day. A. Crowther and T. V. Sadler. *The Rosarist's Daily Exercise.* Amsterdam, 1657.

6. Day of wrath, that dreadful day. James Dymock's *The Sacrifice of the New Law*, 1687. Also in an *Office of the B. V. M.* of the same year, and altered, in Brooke's *Churchman's Manual of Priv. and Family Devotion*, 1883.

7. A day of wrath, that dreadful day. Anon. *The Following of Christ*, 1694.

8. The day of wrath, that doom-deciding day. Anon. *Bona Mors*, 1754.

9. The day of wrath, that dreadful day. Anon. *The Office for the Dead*, N.D. cir. 1780.

10. The day of wrath, that great and awful day, " T. T. S.," in *Christian Observer*, May, 1819.

11. The dreadful day, the day of ire. F. C. Husenbeth. *Catholic Miscellany*, 1823, and *Missal for the Laity*, 1831.

12. O day of anger, awful day. " O," in the *Christian Remembrancer*, May, 1825.

13. Day of Judgment, day of ire. William Hay. *Bengal Annual*, 1831.

14. O day of wrath, that dreadful day. R. Parkinson. *Saturday Magazine*, Sept. 22, 1832, and reprinted in his *Poems*, 1832.

15. Day of judgment, day of wrath. Anon. *Spiritual Repository*, 1833.

16. O that day of wrath dismaying. J. Chandler. *Hys. of the Primitive Church*, 1837.

17. Wrath and righteous retribution. " C. F. R. of Fulneck." *Christian Observer*, Jan., 1837.

18. Day of anger, day of mourning. J. R. D. Beste. *Catholic Hours*, 1839.

19. The day of wrath, that last dread day. Anon. *Catholic Magazine*, 1839.

20. O day of wrath, and dread surprise. Daniel French. *Sel. of Catholic Hys.*, 1839.

21. The day of wrath, that dreadful day. William Young. *Catholic Choralist*, 1842.

22. O that day, that day of ire. R. C. Trench. T. V. Fosbery's *Hys. for the Sick and Suffering*, 1844.

23. Day of wrath, that awful day. E. B. Pusey in the *Paradise of the Christian Soul*, 1847.

24. That day of wrath, that dreadful day. W. R. Wingfield. *Prayers for the Dead*, 1845.

25. A day of wrath, a dreadful day. " E. S.," in Dr. Hook's *Holy Thoughts and Prayers.* Preface to 3rd ed., 1848.

26. That dread day of wrath and shame. James D.

Aylward. 1st printed in the *Dublin Review*, April, 1883, but written in 1846.

27. That day of wrath and grief and shame. James D. Aylward. Also printed in the *Dublin Review*, April, 1883, but written in 1846.

28. Day of wrath and doom of fire. Lord Lindsay. *History of Christian Art*, 1847.

29. Day of wrath, that dreadful day. Howel W. Lloyd. *Paradise of the Christian Soul*, 1877.

30. Day of doom, that day of ire. W. J. Copeland. Printed in *Dublin Review*, 1883, but written in 1847.

31. Awful doomsday, day of anger. Anon. *Spiritual Repository*, 1847.

32. Woe is the day of ire. Richard D. Williams (*Shamrock* of the "Nation"). *Manual of Sisters of Mercy*, 1848.

33. Day of the Lord's avenging ire. Dean Disney. *Irish Ecclesiastical Journal*, May, 1849.

34. Day of wrath, beneath whose thunder. Archdeacon Rowan. *Irish Ecclesiastical Journal*, June, 1849, but written before.

35. Day of wrath, that dreadful day. F. G. Lee. *Poems*, 1850.

36. Lo, that day of wrath awaketh. A. T. Russell. *Ps. & Hymns*, 1851.

37. Most surely at the appointed time (through the German). A. T. Russell. *Ps. & Hymns*, 1851.

38. Day of vengeance, day of burning. R. G. Loraine. *English words to Mozart's Requiem Mass*, 1854.

39. Lo the day of wrath, the day. Mrs. E. Charles, *The Voice of Christian Life in Song*, 1858.

40. Ah that day of wrath and woe. William Bright. *Athanasius and Other Poems*, 1858.

41. Day of anger, that great day. J. W. Hewett. *Verses by a Country Curate*, 1859.

42. Day of anger, day of wonder. Philip S. Worsley. *Blackwood's Mag.*, 1860, and his *Poems and Translations*, 1863.

43. There comes a day, a dreadful day. Dr. G. Walker's *Hys. from the German*, 1860.

44. Day of Judgment, day appalling. H. Kynaston. *Occasional Verses*, 1862.

45. The day comes of indignation. Charles B. Cayley. *Church Times*, 1864.

46. Lo the day, the day of dooming. Francis Trappes. *Liturgical Hymns*, N.D. cir. 1865.

47. Great day of wrath, of days the day. J. H. S[weet]. *The Beautiful Latin Hymn*, 1866.

48. Day of wrath upon whose dawning. J. H. S[weet]. *The Beautiful Hymn*, 1866.

49. Day of awful wrath, great day, when. J. H. S[weet]. *The Beautiful Hymn*, 1866.

50. Day of wrath, O day of days. W. H. Robinson. *South London Chronicle*, May 26, 1866.

51. Day of anger, dreadful day. J. W. Thomas. *Poems on Sacred . . . Subjects*, 1867.

52. Day of wrath and tribulation. John Henry Hoskyns-Abrahall. *Christian Remembrancer*, Jan., 1868.

53. The day of wrath, that haunting day. R. C. Hutton. *Spectator*, March 7, 1868.

54. The day of wrath, that awful day. Anon. *Friend's Magazine*.

55. O the day, that day of anguish. John Wallace. *Hymns of the Church*, 1874.

56. Day of fury when earth dying. Charles Kent. *The Month*, Nov., 1874.

57. Day of wrath, that day whose knelling. Mr. Justice John O'Hagan. *Irish Monthly*, March, 1874.

58. Dawns the day, the day of dread. Anon. *Messenger of the Sacred Heart*, Nov., 1875.

59. Day of anger, sinners dooming. H. Macgill. *Songs of Christian Creed and Life*, 1876.

60. Day of ire, woe worth that day. William MacIlwaine. *Lyra Hibernica Sacra*, 1878.

61. Lo the day of wrath, that day. Osmond Seager. *Oremus*, 1878.

62. A day of wrath that day shall glow. C. Warren, 1878.

63. That day a day of wrath shall glow. C. F. S. Warren, 1878.

64. Cometh that day, that day of ire. Orlando Dobbin, 1878.

65. The day of wrath, that dreadful day. D. T. Morgan. *Hymns of the Latin Church*, 1880. Printed for private circulation, 1871.

66. Day of anger, that dread day, When the earth. W. Cowan. *Poems*, 1879.

67. O day of wrath, the last great dreadful day. Anon. "F. G. M." in the *Messenger of the Sacred Heart*, Nov., 1880.

68. O that day, the day of vengeance. Henry A. Rawes. *Fly Sheet*, 1884.

69. Day of wrath on which earth's framing. W. Hilton. *Messenger of the Sacred Heart*, 1884.

70. That day of wrath, that dreadful day, An extension of Sir W. Scott's *tr.* by Father Police. *Parochial Hymn-book*, 1881.

71. O day of wrath, of days the day. J. H. Sweet. *The Day of Judgment*, 1873.

72. Day of wrath upon whose dawning. J. H. Sweet. *The Day of Judgment*, 1873.

In addition to the above, the following are by American Translators :—

1. O that day, that day of ire. Mrs. M. J. Preston, 1851.

2. Day of wrath, portentous morning. Charles P. Krauth. *Winchester Republican*, 1851.

3. Day of wrath, that day dismaying. Dr. William R. Williams. *Miscellanies*, 1851.

4. Day of wrath the sinner dooming. Dr. Henry Mills. *Horae Germanicae*, 1856.

5. The Sibyl's leaf, the Psalmist's lay . . . "Somniator." *Poems*, 1859.

6. Day of ire, that day impending. Epes Sargent. *The Press*, 1859.

7. Day of wrath, that day of hasting. Robert Davidson. *Poems*, 1860.

8. Day of wrath, that day of burning. Abraham Coles. *Dies Irae in 13 original versions*, 1860.

9. Day shall dawn that has no morrow. A. Coles, 1860.

10. Day of vengeance, and of wages. A Coles, 1860.

11. Day of prophecy, it flashes. A. Coles, 1860.

12. Day of vengeance, end of scorning. A. Coles, 1860.

13. Day of wrath and consternation. A. Coles, 1860.

14. Day of wrath, that day of days. A. Coles, 1860

15. O that dreadful day, my soul. A. Coles, 1860.

16. Day foretold, that day of ire. A. Coles, 1860.

17. Lo it comes with stealthy feet. A. Coles, 1860.

18. Day of wrath, that day of dole. A. Coles, 1860.

19. O day of wrath, O day of fate. A Coles, 1860.

20. That day, that awful day the last. A. Coles, 1860.

21. Day of wrath, that day of wonder. George A. Crooke. *Episcopal Recorder*, 1863.

22. O that day of wrath and woe. A. H. Rogers. *The Lutheran*, 1864.

23. That day of wrath, that day of doom. James Ross. *The New York Observer*, 1864.

24. Day of threatened wrath from heaven. Erastus C. Benedict. *Christian Intelligencer*, cir. 1864.

25. Day of wrath, that final day. E. C. Benedict, 1864.

26. Day of wrath with vengeance glowing. E. C. Benedict, 1864.

27. Day of wrath, that day of burning. M. H. Bright. *The Round Table*, 1865.

28. Day of vengeance, lo that morning. General J. A. Dix. *Seven Great Hymns of the Church*, 1865.

29. Day of wrath, dread day of wailing. Anon. *Round Table*, Feb. 23, 1867.

30. A day of wrath and woe, that day. Anon. *Round Table*, 1867.

31. O day of wrath in that dread day. Anon. *The Living Age*, Jan. 26, 1867.

32. Day of wrath, day long expected. Roger S. Tracy. *Evening Post*, Jan., 1868.

33. Day of wrath, that day foretold. Dr. Philip Schaff. *Hours at Home*, May, 1868 ; and *Christ in Song*, 1869-70.

34. Day of anger, day of sighing. Horace Castle. *The University*, April, 1869.

35. The day of anger, ah that day. Henry J. Macdonald, 1869.

36. The day of wrath, ah me, the day. Robert McCorkle. *Evening Post*, 1869.

37. Day of wrath, of days that day. Edward Slosson. *Seven Great Hymns of the Church*, 1865.

38. Day of wrath, that day appalling. Sylvanus Phelps. *Poems*, 1869.

39. Day of wrath, that day of mourning. A. C. Kendrick. *Our Poetical Favourites*, 1869.

40. Lo the day, that day of ire. Oliver Taylor, 1869.

41. Day of wrath, that day appalling. Anon. *Hours at Home*, July, 1869.

42. That day of wrath, upon that day. W. G. Dix. *Hours at Home*, 1869.

43. Day of wrath, O direful day. Charles Rockwell. *Hours at Home*, 1869.

44. That day of wrath, that direful day. Anon. *Catholic Manual*, 1869.

45. Day of doom, O day of terror. Anon. *Catholic World*, May, 1873.

46. Day of wrath whose vengeful fire. Charles H. A. Esling. *Catholic Record*, 1874.

47. Day of Judgment, day of "urning," C. L. Weiser, 1875.

48. Day of wrath, that day undying. John Anketell. *American Church Review*, July, 1876.

49. Day of wrath, that awful day. John Anketell. *American Church Review*, 1876.

50. Day of wrath, thine awful morning. Samuel W. Duffield. *Warp and Woof*, 1870.

51. Day of wrath, O day of blaming. Samuel J. Watson. *Belford's Magazine*, May, 1878.

52. Day of wrath the world illuming. William W. Nevin. *Weekly Press*, Jan. 18, 1878.

53. Day of wrath, that dreadful day. Joel Swartz. *Lutheran Observer*, Aug. 22, 1878.

54. O day of days of anger. Anon. R. W. L. *The Churchman*, April 3, 1880.

55. Day, the ireful day affrighting. Matthias Sheeleigh, 1881.

56. The day of wrath, that certain day. Thomas MacKellar. *Hymns and a Few Metrical Psalms*, 1000, written in 1882, and "based on a literal rendering by J. Addison Campbell."

57. Day of wrath, that day of burning. Franklin Johnson, 1884.

58. Day of vengeance, day of fire. George Davie. *Catholic World*, Nov., 1884.

59. That day of wrath, of God's dread ire. John Mason Brown. *Catholic World*, Nov., 1884.

60. The Judgment day, that day of dread. Joseph J. Marrin. *Catholic World*, April, 1882.

61. Day of wrath, Oh day of burning. H. L. Hastings, in his *Songs of Pilgrimage*, 1886.

This extensive list of 133 translations of the *Dies Irae*, not in C. U. (73 English and 60 American) has been compiled mainly by the Rev. O. F. S. Warren, and Mr. W. T. Brooke. To this list a few more *trs.* will probably be added. The total number of *trs.* into English of this magnificent Sequence is thus over 150, and of these 19 renderings are in C. U. in G. Britain and America. The nearest approach to this is the *Adeste fideles* with 16 *trs.* in C. U., and 22 not in C. U., or 38 in all; and *Ein feste Burg*, with 18 in C. U. and 45 not in C. U., or a total of 63. [J. J.]

Dies sind die heilgen zehn Gebot. M. Luther. [*Ten Commandments.*] After the 13th cent. the Ten Commandments began to be used in Germany at the confessional, and for the instruction of children, and in later times on pilgrimages and as an introduction to the Litany during Passiontide. Luther's catechetical, metrical setting 1st appeared in *Eyn Enchiridion*, Erfurt, 1524, and thence in *Wackernagel*, iii. p. 15, in 12 st. of 4 l., each st. ending with "*Kyriolys.*" Included in Schircks's ed. of Luther's *Geistl. Lieder*, 1854, p. 47, and as No. 364 in the *Unv. L. S.*, 1851. The only *tr.* in C. U. is—

That men a godly life might live, in R. Massie's *M. Luther's Spiritual Songs*, 1854, p. 55, and thence, as No. 204, in the *Ohio Luth. Hyl.*, 1880, and in *Dr. Bacon*, 1884, p. 28.

Other *trs.* are :—(1) "These are the holy commaundentes ten," by Bp. Coverdale, 1539 (*Remains*, 1846, p. 544). (2) "Moyses upon the Mont Sinay," in the *Gude & Godlie Ballates* (ed. 1568, folio 5), ed. 1868, p. 6. (3) "These are the holy ten Commands," as No. 433, in pt. i. of the *Moravian H. Bk.*, 1754. (4) "These are the holy commandments," by *J. Anderson*, 1846, p. 53 (1847, p. 69). (5.) "The Lord Himself from Sinai's hill," by *Dr. J. Hunt*, 1853, p. 83. (6) "These are the holy ten Commands," by *Dr. G. Macdonald* in the *Sunday Magazine*, 1867, p. 571, thence, altered, in his *Exotics*, 1876, p. 84.   [J. M.]

Dignare me, O Jesu, rogo Te. [*Security in Christ Jesus.*] This hymn is given by *Daniel*, ii. p. 371, but without any indication of the source of the text. It is found in the *Hymnodia Sacra*, Münster, 1753, p. 153,

and in the *Psalteriolum Cantionum Catholicarum*, Cologne, 1722, p. 318. It is *tr.* as—

1. **Jesu, grant me this, I pray.** By Sir H. W. Baker, written for and 1st pub. in *H. A. & M.*, 1861, and continued in 1875. Also in other collections.

2. **Jesu, grant me of Thy grace.** By R. F. Littledale, given in the *People's H.*, 1867, and signed "A. L. P."

3. **Jesu, Lord, to me impart.** By R. C. Singleton, written in 1867, and included, in 1868, in his *Anglican H. Bk.*   [J. J.]

Dilherr, Johann Michael, was b. at Themar in Meiningen, Oct. 14, 1604, and educated at the Universities of Leipzig, Altdorf and Jena. In 1646 he became first pastor of St. Sebald's Church, and Antistes of the Nürnberg clergy, and d. at Nürnberg, April 8, 1669. He was reckoned one of the most learned men and the greatest preacher of his time. He wrote some 60 hymns, which appeared in various devotional works, and in his *Bey 1000 Alte und Neue Geistliche Psalmen, Lieder und Gebete*, Nürnberg, 1654, &c. Only one has been *tr.* :—

Nun lasset Gottes Güte. [*God's Care.*] Appeared in his *Weg zu der Seligkeit*, Nürnberg, 1646, p. 491, in 16 st., entitled "Hymn of God's Goodness and against fretting Cares." The *tr.* is from the form in the *Brüder G. B.* 1778, No. 267, in 8 st., beginning, "Lasst uns mit süssen Weisen." It is *tr.* as "The prayers of the needy," No. 1111 in the *Suppl.* of 1808 to the *Moravian H. Bk.*, 1801 (1849, No. 708).   [J. M.]

Dir, Herr, dir will ich mich ergeben. [*For the Dying.*] This stanza has not been traced further than the German word book of Mendelssohn's oratorio of *St. Paul* (1836), where it is set to Neumark's well-known chorale, "Wer nur den lieben Gott lässt walten." It reads :—

> "Dir, Herr, dir will ich mich ergeben,
> Dir dessen Eigenthum ich bin,
> Du, nur allein du, bist mein Leben,
> Und Sterben wird mir dann Gewinn,
> Ich lebe dir, ich sterbe dir,
> Sey du nur mein so gnügt es mir."

It is *tr.* as :—

To Thee, O Lord, I yield my spirit, Who. By W. Ball, as part of his *tr.* of the word book of *St. Paul*, 1836. Included in the *Leeds H. Bk.*, 1853; *N. Cong.*, 1859; *Kennedy*, 1863; *Horder's Cong. Hyl.*, 1884, and others. It is sometimes erroneously ascribed to Neumark.   [G. A. C.]

Disown'd of Heaven, by man opprest. *J. Joyce.* [*On behalf of the Jews.* 1st appeared in the *Christian Observer* for Nov. 1809, in 5 st. of 6 l., entitled, "Hymn applicable to the Present Condition of the Jews," and signed "J. J." In 1833-5 two altered versions appeared almost together, both beginning, "O why should Israel's sons, once blest." One was included by Elliott in his *Ps. & Hymns*, 1835, No. 137, and the second in Bickersteth's *Christian Psalmody*, 1833, No. 408. In later hymnals Bickersteth's text has been almost exclusively adopted, as found in Windle's *Coll.*, No. 305. Hall's alterations in the *Mitre*, 1836, No. 106, have passed out of use, in common with those of Elliott and others.   [J. J.]

Diterich, Johann Samuel, eldest son of A. M. Diterich, pastor of St. Mary's Church,

Berlin, was b. at Berlin, Dec. 15, 1721. After studying at the Universities of Frankfurt a. Oder, and Halle, he was for some time a private tutor in Berlin. He was, in 1748, appointed diaconus of St. Mary's Church in Berlin, and regimental chaplain, becoming, in 1751, archidiaconus, and, in 1754, pastor of St. Mary's. In 1763 he was appointed private Chaplain to the Queen, and in 1770 a member of the Supreme Consistory. He d. at Berlin, Jan. 14, 1797 (*Koch*, vi. 228–231; *Allg. Deutsche Biog.*, v. 258–259). His hymns appeared in the following works:—

(1) *Lieder für den öffentlichen Gottesdienst.* Berlin, 1765, with 236 hymns, edited by himself and his colleagues in St. Mary's Church. Designed as a supplement to Porst's *G. B.* of 1713. (2) *Gesangbuch zum gottesdienstlichen Gebrauch in den Königlich-Preussischen Landen.* Berlin, 1780, with 447 hymns principally edited by himself. (3) *Gesangbuch für die häusliche Andacht.* Berlin, 1787, with 421 hymns, principally of recent date.

None of these books give names of authors. Diterich seems to have contributed about 100 hymns either original or entirely recast, besides rewriting portions of many others. He distinguished himself as a leader in the unhappy process of "modernising" and "improving" the older German hymns, by which they were reduced to 18th cent. "correctness," and had all the life polished out of them. His 1765 collection formed the model of many wretched hymn-books, and his influence is even seen in such recent collections as the Hamburg *G. B.*, 1842, the Nassau *G. B.*, 1844, and the *G. B. für die evang. Landeskirche im Grossherzogtum Sachsen*, Weimar, 1883.

A number of the recasts from the older hymns which appear under Diterich's name are noted in this Dictionary under the names of their original authors. The following may be regarded as practically original:—

i. **Schon ist der Tag von Gott bestimmt.** [*Second Advent.*] 1765, as above, No. 129, in 8 st. of 7 l. Included as No. 390 in the Nassau *G. B.*, 1844. The only *tr.* in C. U. is:—

The trumpet sounds! the day is come! A full and good *tr.* in Dr. H. Mills's *Horae Ger.*, 1845 (ed. 1856, p. 332). Dr. Hatfield included st. i., iv., vi., vii., altered, in his *Ch. H. Bk.*, 1872.

The following, although not in English C. U., are available for hymnological purposes:—

ii. **Auf Erden Wahrheit auszubreiten.** *Christ's Ministry.* 1787, as above, No. 79, in 10 st. *Tr.* by *Dr. H. Mills*, 1845 (ed. 1856, p. 283), as "That men to truth might not be strangers."

iii. **Auf! Jesu Jünger! freuet euch!** *Ascension.* 1765, as above, No. 79, in 12 st., and is based on E. Alber's hymn "Nun freut euch Gottes Kinder all" (q. v.). Two forms have been *tr.* (1) "Auf, Christen, auf und freuet euch," in the Berlin *G. B.* 1780, No. 114; *tr.* as "Rejoice, ye saints, your fears be gone," by *Dr. H. Mills*, 1845 (ed. 1856, p. 324); and (2) "Ihr Jünger Jesu, freuet euch," in the *Trier G. B.* (R. C.), 1846, p. 94. *Tr.* as "Rejoice, ye saints, in glad accord," by *Dr. R. F. Littledale*, in *Lyra Messianica*, 1864, p. 371.

iv. **Herr, meiner Seele grossen Werth.** *Greatness of the Soul.* 1765, as above, No. 195, in 9 st. *Tr.* by *Dr. H. Mills*, 1845 (ed. 1856, p. 30), as "Lord, on the soul's enduring worth."

v. **Mein Heiland lebt.** *Er hat die Macht.* *Resurrection of the Dead.* 1765, as above, No. 123, in 8 st. *Tr.* by *Miss Manington*, 1863, p. 75, "My Saviour lives, and He the might."

vi. **O Jesu, wahrer Frömmigkeit.** *Jesus our Example.* Seems to have been suggested by J. J. Rambach's "Du wesentliches Ebenbild" in his *Haus G. B.*, 1735, No. 84. 1st pub. 1780, as above, No. 59, in 8 st. *Tr.* by *Dr. H. Mills*, 1845 (ed. 1856, p. 285), as "Jesus, of what we should approve."   [J. M.]

Diu rose ist diu schoenste under alle blüete. [*The Beauty of the World.*] *Wackernagel*, ii. p. 147, quotes this 12th cent. hymn in

13 l., from a Jena MS., through F. H. von der Hagen's ed. of the *Minnesinger* (pts. i.-iv., Leipzig, 1838, pt. v., Berlin, 1856). *Tr.* as "O Rose! of the flowers, I ween, thou art fairest," by *Miss Winkworth*, 1869, p. 41.   [J. M.]

Divine crescebas Puer. *Jean Baptiste de Santeüil.* [*Epiphany.*] 1st pub. in his *Hymni Sacri et Novi*, 1689, p. 14, and 1698, p. 71, in 4 st. of 4 l. In the revised *Paris Breviary* of 1736 it was appointed as the hymn for the Sundays at Lauds, from the Feast of the Circumcision to the Presentation of the Lord, unless Septuagesima Sunday should occur before the latter. It is also in the *Lyons* and other modern French Breviaries. Text also in Chandler's *Hys. of the P. Church*, 1837, No. 51; Card. Newman's *Hymni Ecclesiae*, 1838–65, and Biggs's *H. A. & M., with Annotations*, 1867, No. 62. There is no doxology in the original.   [W. A. S.]

Translations in C. U.:—

1. **In stature grows the heavenly child.** By J. Chandler, in his *Hys. of the Prim. Church*, 1837, p. 57, with doxology from the *Paris Breviary*, and in the 1841 ed., No. 32. This *tr.* is in numerous hymn-books, and sometimes with slight alterations, as in Thring's *Coll.* and others.

2. **The heavenly Child in stature grows.** This *tr.* was given in *H. A. & M.*, in 1861, and is continued in the revised ed, 1875. It is J. Chandler's *tr.* as above, with alterations by J. Keble. Outside of *H. A. & M.* its use is limited.

Translations not in C. U.:—

1. And Thou art growing up, O Child divine! *I. Williams.* 1839.
2. Thou didst grow, O Babe divine. *W. J. Blew.* 1852–55.
3. In wisdom, stature, Heavenly grace. *J. D. Chambers.* 1857.   [J. J.]

Dix, William Chatterton, s. of John Dix, surgeon, of Bristol, author of the *Life of Chatterton*; *Local Legends*, &c., b. at Bristol, June 14, 1837, and educated at the Grammar School of that city. Mr. Chatterton Dix's contributions to modern hymnody are numerous and of value. His fine Epiphany hymn, "As with gladness men of old," and his plaintive "Come unto Me, ye weary," are examples of his compositions, many of which rank high amongst modern hymns. In his *Hymns of Love and Joy*, 1861, *Altar Songs, Verses on the Holy Eucharist*, 1867; *Vision of All Saints*, &c., 1871; and *Seekers of a City*, 1878, some of his compositions were first published. The greater part, however, were contributed to *H. A. & M.*; *St. Raphael's H. Bk.*, 1861; *Lyra Eucharistica*, 1863; *Lyra Messianica*, 1864; *Lyra Mystica*, 1865; *The People's H.*, 1867; *The Hymnary*, 1872; *Church Hymns*, 1871, and others. Many of his contributions are renderings in metrical form of Dr. Littledale's *tr.* from the Greek in his *Offices . . . of the Holy Eastern Church*, 1863; and of the Rev. J. M. Rodwell's *tr.* of hymns of the Abyssinian Church. These renderings of the "songs of other Churches" have not received the attention they deserve, and the sources from whence they come are practically unknown to most hymnal compilers. Mr. Dix has also written many Christmas and Easter carols, the most widely known of which is "The Manger Throne." In addition to detached pieces in prose and verse for various magazines, he has published two devotional works, *Light;* and *The Risen Life*, 1883 ; and a book of instructions for children entitled *The Pattern Life*, 1885. The last-named contains original hymns by Mr. Dix not given elsewhere In addition to the more important of Mr. Dix's hymns which are annotated under their respective first lines, the following are also in C. U. :—

1. **God cometh, let the heart prepare.** *Advent.* In his *Vision of All Saints,* &c., 1871.

2. **Holy, holy, holy, to Thee our vows we pay.** *Holy Communion.* Pub. in his *Altar Songs,* 1867, in 6 st. of 6 l., and headed " Eucharistic Processional for Dedication Feast." In the S. P. C. K. *Church Hys.,* 1871, and others in an abridged form.

3. **How long, O Lord, how long, we ask.** *Second Advent.* Appeared in the *Appendix* to the S. P. C. K. *Ps. & Hys.,* 1869, and repeated in several collections.

4. **In our work and in our play.** *Children's Hymn.* Pub. in his *Hys. and Carols for Children,* 1869. and is largely adopted in children's hymn-books, as Mrs. Brock's *Children's H. Bk.,* 1881, and others. Also in the S. P. C. K. *Church Hys.,* 1871.

5. **In the hollow of Thine hand.** *For Fair Weather.* Appeared in the *People's H.,* 1867, and repeated in several others.

6. **Joy fills our inmost heart to-day.** *Christmas.* Printed in the *Church Times,* and then on a Fly-sheet by C. J. Palmer, as the third of *Four Joyful Hys. sor Christmas, circa* 1865. It is in the S. P. C. K *Church Hys.,* 1871, and other hymnals. It is also one of Mr. Dix's *Christmas Customs & Christmas Carols,* N.D.

7. **Lift up your songs, ye thankful.** *St. Ambrose.* Contributed to the *People's H.,* 1867.

8. **Now in numbers softly flowing.** *St. Cecilia.* Contributed to the *People's H.,* 1867.

9. **Now, our Father, we adore Thee.** *Praise to the Father.* Appeared in the *Appendix* to the S. P. C. K. *Ps. & Hys.,* 1869.

10. **O Christ, Thou Son of Mary.** *St. Crispin.* First printed in the *Union Review,* Sept., 1866, and thence into the *People's H.,* 1867.

11. **O Cross which only canst allay.** *Glorying and Trusting in the Cross.* Pub. in the *People's H.,* 1867.

12. **O Thou the Eternal Son of God.** *Good Friday.* Appeared in *Lyra Messianica.,* 1864 ; the author's *Hys. and Carols for Children,* 1869 ; the S. P. C. K. *Church Hys.,* 1871, &c.

13. **On the waters dark and drear.** *For use at Sea.* Pub. in *Hys. for Pub. Worship,* &c. (St. Raphael's, Bristol), 1861 ; the S. P. C. K. *Church Hys.,* 1871, &c.

14. **Only one prayer to-day.** *Ash-Wednesday.* Contributed to the *People's H.,* 1867.

15. **Sitting at receipt of custom.** *St. Matthew.* Appeared in the *People's H.,* 1867.

16. **The Cross is on thy brow.** *Confirmation.* In the 1869 *Appendix* to the S. P. C. K. *Ps. & Hys.*

17. **The stars above our head.** *Work and Humility.* In the 1869 *Appendix* to the S. P. C. K. *Ps. & Hys.*

18. **When the shades of night are falling.** *Evening Hymn to the Good Shepherd.* In the author's *Seekers of a City,* &c. [1878].

Most of Mr. Dix's best-known hymns, and also some of those named above, are in C. U. in America and other English-speaking countries. In G. Britain and America from 30 to 40 are in C. U. He d. Sept. 9, 1898. [J. J.]

Do no sinful action. *C. F. Alexander, née Humphreys.* [*Children to be Christ-like.*] Appeared in her *Hys. for Little Children,* 1848, No. 5, on " The first promise. To renounce the devil and all his works," in 7 st. of 4 l. It is in Mrs. Brock's *Children's H. Bk.,* No. 232, *Common Praise,* and others.

Do not I love Thee, O my Lord ? *P. Doddridge.* [*St. Peter's love of Christ.*] This hymn is not in the D. MSS. It was 1st pub. in J. Orton's posthumous ed. of Doddridge's *Hymns,* &c., 1755, No. 246, in 7 st. of 4 l.. and headed, " Appeal to Christ for the sin-

cerity of Love to Him." It is based on St. Peter's answer to Christ, " Lord, Thou knowest all things, Thou knowest that I love Thee." In 1839 it was repeated in J. D. Humphreys's ed. of Doddridge's *Hymns,* &c. Its use in America is extensive [see **English Hymnody, Early,** § XIV.].   [J. J.]

Doane, George Washington, D.D. Bishop Doane was b. at Trenton, N. Jersey, May 27, 1799, and graduated at Union College, Schenectady, New York. Ordained in 1821, he was Assistant Minister at Trinity Church, New York, till 1824. In 1824 he became a Professor at Trinity College, Hartford, Conn.; in 1828 Rector of Trinity Church, Boston; and, in 1832, Bishop of New Jersey. He founded St. Mary's Hall, Burlington, 1837, and Burlington College, Burlington, 1846. Died April 27, 1859. Bishop Doane's exceptional talents, learning, and force of character, made him one of the great prelates of his time. His warmth of heart secured devoted friends, who still cherish his memory with revering affection. He passed through many and severe troubles, which left their mark upon his later verse. He was no mean poet, and a few of his lyrics are among our best. His *Works,* in 4 vols., with Memoir by his son, were published in 1860. He issued in 1824 *Songs by the Way,* a small volume of great merit and interest. This edition is now rare. A second edition, much enlarged, appeared after his death, in 1859, and a third, in small 4to, in 1875. These include much matter of a private nature, such as he would not himself have given to the world, and by no means equal to his graver and more careful lyrics, on which alone his poetic fame must rest.

The edition of 1824 contains several important hymns, some of which have often circulated without his name. Two of these are universally known as his, having been adopted by the American *Prayer Book Coll.,* 1826:—

1. **Softly now the light of day.** *Evening.* This, in addition to its use in American hymnals, is also found in the English Collections, including Snepp's *Songs of G. & C.* Written in 1824.

2. **Thou art the way, to Thee alone.** *Christ the Way.* This, in the judgment of many, is the first of American hymns, and one of the most admirable and useful in the English language. In the United States its use is most extensive, and since its introduction into the English Collections by *Bickersteth* in 1833, Hall in his *Mitre,* in 1836, and others, it has grown in favour until it ranks with the most popular of the great English hymns.

Near in merit to the foregoing stands a companion piece in the same work, which deserves to be better known :—

3. **Lord, should we leave Thy hallowed feet.**

The next three have been overlooked at home, but have obtained considerable circulation in English Collections.

4. **Father of mercies hear, Thy pardon we implore.** *Ash Wednesday or Lent.* A translation of " Audi, benigne Conditor " (q.v.), pub. in his *Songs by the Way,* 1824, together with several other translations, thus anticipating by twelve years the great English movement in that direction. Orig. *tr.* in his *Songs by the Way,* 1875.

Miller (*S. & S.*, p. 12) attributes this *tr.* to Dr. Neale in error.

5. **Return and come to God.** *Invitation.* In his *Songs*, &c., 1824. It is found in Hall's *Mitre*, 1836 ; the *Bap. Hymnal*, 1879, and several others.

6. **To thee, O Lord, with dawning light.** *Morning.* This hymn is attributed to Heber by Miller (*S. & S.*, p. 381) in error. It is included in the S. P. C. K. *Hymns*, 1852 ; in *Windle* and others. It is from the *Songs*, &c., 1824.

His later hymns, the dates of which are generally preserved in the last ed. of his *Songs by the Way*, include the following, which are more or less in use :—

7. **Beloved, it is well.** *All well in Christ.* This is entitled "To my wife"; is dated Mar. 12, 1833, and was written in a copy of Dr. Bedell's "It is well." It is given in *Kennedy*, 1863.

8. **Broken-hearted, weep no more.** *Assurance of Peace.* The date of this hymn is not preserved. It is found as early as 1829, when it appeared in the 2nd ed. of Cleland's (Baptist) *Hymns*.

9. **Fling out the banner, let it float.** *Missions, Home & Foreign.* This hymn, sometimes dated 1824 in error, was written at Riverside, 2nd Sun. in Advent, 1848, and is one of the author's latest effusions. It is in extensive use both in G. Britain and America.

10. **He came not with His heavenly crown.** *The two Advents.* In his *Songs by the Way*, ed. 1875, this poem is dated Dec. 1827. In Dale's *English H. Bk.*, 1879, it is given with the omission of st. iii., and in the American Protestant Episcopal *Hymnal*, 1871, it begins with st. iv., "Once more, O Lord, Thy sign shall be." Full text in *Lyra Sac. Amer.*, p. 92.

11. **Lift not thou the wailing voice.** *Burial.* A funeral hymn, adopted by the *Anglican Hy. Bk.*, but dated 1826 in error, for 1830.

12. **What is that, mother ? The lark, my child.** This is not a hymn, but a familiar and long popular song.

13. **When darkness erst [once] at God's command.** *Israel in Egypt.* In *Kennedy*, 1863, No. 722.

14. **Young and happy while thou art.** *Youth for Christ.* A favourite piece in many juvenile collections. It is dated Sept., 1827, and is given in *Songs by the Way*, 1875.

The *Lyra Sac. Amer.* also contains the following :—

15. **Brightness of the Father's glory.** *Morning.* A *tr.* of "Consors Paterni luminis" (q.v.). It is from the *Songs*, &c., 1824.

16. **Child that kneelest meekly there.** *Child at Prayer.* Suggested by a cast from a piece of sculpture by Greenough representing a child at prayer.

17. **Grant me, Lord, Thy graces three.** *Faith, Hope, and Charity desired.*

18. **Perfect through suffering may it be.** *Uses of suffering.* Dated in *Songs by the Way*, "The Breakers, June 1, 1853."

19. **Yes, it is a faithful saying.** *Redemption.* In his *Songs*, &c., 1824.   [F. M. B.]

Doane, W. H., b. in Preston, Connecticut, 1831, and educated for the musical profession by eminent American and German masters. He has had for years the superintendence of a large Baptist Sunday School in Cincinnati, Ohio, where he resides. Although not a hymn-

writer, the wonderful success which has attended his musical setting of numerous American hymns, and the number of his musical editions of hymn-books for Sunday Schools and Evangelistic purposes, bring him within the sphere of hymnological literature. Amongst his collections we have :—

(1) *Silver Spray*, 1868 ; (2) *Pure Gold*, 1877 ; (3) *Royal Diadem*, 1873 ; (4) *Welcome Tidings*, 1877; (5) *Brightest and Best*, 1875 ; (6) *Fountain of Song* ; (7) *Songs of Devotion*, 1870 ; (8) *Temple Anthems*, &c.

His most popular melodies include "Near the Cross," "Safe in the Arms of Jesus," "Pass me not," "More Love to Thee," "Rescue the perishing," "Tell me the old, old Story," &c.   [J. J.]

Dobell, John, b. 1757, d. May, 1840, was a port-gauger under the Board of Excise, at Poole, Dorset, and a person of some local note. In 1806 he published :—

A New Selection of Seven Hundred Evangelical Hymns for Private, Family, and Public Worship (Many Original) from more than two hundred of the best Authors in England, Scotland, Ireland, and America, Arranged in alphabetical order ; Intended as a Supplement to Dr. Watts's Psalms and Hymns. By John Dobell. Lond., Williams and Smith, 1806.

Subsequently this *Sel.* was increased to "*More than Eight Hundred*" hymns, and the wording of the title-page was changed in several instances. Dobell's account of this work is :—

"The hymns here presented to the public I have collected from more than two hundred authors ; many of them are taken from Manuscripts which I deemed too valuable to be suffered to remain in obscurity, and some have been supplied by friends. As this work has been the labour of years, and the choice of many thousand hymns, it will, I trust, give satisfaction to the Church of God." *Preface*, p. iii.

In addition to a work on *Baptism*, 1807, and another on *Humanity*, 1812, Dobell also published ;—

The Christian's Golden Treasure ; or, Gospel Comfort for Doubting Minds, 1823. This work was in two vols., the first of which contained 124 hymns, several of which were by Dobell.

Of this writer's hymns very few are found in modern hymn-books. We have from the 1806 book :—(1) "Come, dearest Lord, and bless this day" (*Sunday Morning*); (2) "Great Ruler of the earth and skies" (*In time of War*) ; (3) "Now is the accepted time," (*Invitation*) — in C. U. in G. Britain and America, out of twenty or more. It is not as a hymn-writer, but as a diligent and successful hymnologist, that J. Dobell is best known.   [J. J.]

Dober, Anna, née Schindler, was b. April 9, 1713, at Kunewald, near Fulnek, Moravia. She went to Herrnhut in 1725, and in 1730 joined her friend and townswoman, Anna Nitschmann (q.v.), in forming the "Jungfrauenbund" (i. Cor. vii. 32–34, Rev. xiv. 4) of the unmarried sisters at Herrnhut. On July 13, 1737, she became the wife of L. J. Dober (consecrated Bishop, 1742, d. at Herrnhut, 1766), then General Elder of the Moravian Church. After assisting him in his labours for the conversion of the Jews at Amsterdam, she d. at Marienborn, near Büdingen, Hesse-Darmstadt, Dec. 12, 1739 (*Koch*, vi. 324). A faithful and gifted servant of Christ, she was the author of numerous hymns, full of personal devotion to her Lord, and of deep trust in Him; which passed into the Moravian collections, that of 1778 containing 18 by her.

Of one written May 26, 1735, beginning "Süsser Heiland deiner Gnade" [No. 1023 in *Appendix* ii. to the *Herrnhut G. B.*, 1735, in 13 st. of 4 l., and *tr.* as "Far greater than one thought or could suppose," as No. 64 in pt. ii. of the *Moravian H. Bk.*, 1754; st. iv.-xiii. already as No. 25 in 1742], Koch says st. iv., v. have become almost a Confession of Faith among the Moravians.

The only one of her hymns which has passed into use outside the Moravian hymnbooks is:—

Du heiliges Kind. [*The Lamb of God.*] 1st pub. in *Appendix* iii. to the *Herrnhut G. B.*, 1735, No. 1046, in 10 st. of 5 l. In the *Brüder G. B.*, 1778, No. 368, st. viii. was omitted. The only *tr.* in C. U. is:—

Holy Lamb, who Thee receive, a free *tr.* in 8 st. of 4 l., by J. Wesley, in *H. and Sac. Poems*, 1740 (*P. Works*, 1868–72, vol. i. p. 280). Thence in full as No. 39 in the *Moravian H. Bk.*, 1742, but abridged and altered in later eds. In 1801, No. 274, is st. i.–iv. from the 1789, which begins, "Lamb of God, who Thee receive," and st. vi.-vii. rewritten from Wesley's st. v.–viii. (1886, No. 308). St. i.–iv. of this 1801 arrangement are in Montgomery's *Christian Psalmist*, 1825, and Elliott's *Ps. & Hys.*, 1835. The original form was given in full as No. 28 in *H. and Spiritual Songs*, 1753, and repeated as No. 340 in the *Wes. H. Bk.* 1780 (ed. 1875, No. 350). St. i., iii.–v., viii., slightly altered, were adopted as No. 78 in Mercer's *C. P. and H. Bk.*, 1855 (Ox. ed., 1864, No. 373). Other centos are found in the *N. Cong.*, 1859; *Psalmist*, 1878, and in America in the Meth. Epis. *Hymns*, 1849; the Baptist *Service of Song*, 1871; Hatfield's *Ch. H. Bk.*, 1872, &c. Other forms in C. U. are:—

1. Blessed Lord, who Thee receive, st. 1, 3, 4, 8, altered as in the *Rugby School H. Bk.*, 1850–1876; *Kennedy*, 1863, and others.

2. Father, they who Thee receive, st. 1, 3, 4, 8, in Hedge and Huntington's *Coll.*, Boston, U. S., 1853; and the *Plymouth Coll.*, 1855.

3. Holy Lord, who Thee receive, st. 1, 3, 4, 8, in the *Irish Ch. Hyl.*, 1869–73.

4. Lamb of God, who Thee receive, st. 1, 3, 4, of Wesley altered, and two st. based on Wesley's 5, 8, in Bickersteth's *Chr. Psalmody*, 1833.

Another tr. is, "Child born without sin," in full, as No. 189 in the *Appendix*, of 1743, to the *Moravian H. Bk.*, 1742.   [J. M.]

Doddridge, Philip, D.D., was b. in London, June 26, 1702. His grandfather was one of the ministers under the Commonwealth, who were ejected in 1662. His father was a London oilman. He was offered by the Duchess of Bedford an University training for ordination in the Ch. of England, but declined it. He entered Mr. Jennings's Nonconformist seminary at Kibworth instead; preached his first sermon (ætat 20) at Hinckley, to which Mr. Jennings had removed his academy. In 1723 he was chosen pastor at Kibworth. In 1725 he changed his residence to Market Harborough, still ministering at Kibworth. The settled work of his life as a preceptor and divine began in 1729, with his appointment to the Castle Hill Meeting at Northampton, and continued till in the last stage of consumption he sailed to Lisbon, in 1751, where he died October 26, the same

year. Two hundred pupils in all, gathered from England, Scotland and Holland, were prepared in his seminary, chiefly for the dissenting ministry, but partly for professions. The wide range of subjects, including daily readings in Hebrew and Greek, Algebra, Trigonometry, Watts's Logic, outline of Philosophy, and copious Divinity, is itself a proof of Doddridge's learning. He was presented with his D.D. degree by the University of Aberdeen. His fame as a divine, combined with his wide sympathies and gentle, unaffected goodness, won for him the friendship of Watts, Col. Gardiner and Hervey, and the esteem of Secker and Warburton. He welcomed the work of Wesley and Whitefield, and entertained the latter on his visit to Northampton. His *Rise and Progress of Religion in the Soul* and *The Family Expositor* both did good work in their day. For criticism of his hymns see English Hymnody, Early, § XIV.   [H. L. B.]

After Dr. Doddridge's death his hymns were pub. by his friend Job Orton, in 1755, as:—

"*Hymns founded on Various Texts in the Holy Scriptures. By the late Reverend Philip Doddridge, D.D. Published from the Author's Manuscript by Job Orton ... Salop.* Printed by J. Eddowes and J. Cotton, &c., MDCCLV."

Concerning the *text* of the hymns, Orton says in his Preface :—

"There may perhaps be some improprieties, owing to my not being able to read the Author's manuscript in particular places, and being obliged, without a poetical genius, to supply those deficiencies, whereby the beauty of the stanza may be greatly defaced, though the sense is preserved."

The 1st ed. contained 370 hymns; the 2nd, 1759, 374; and the 3rd, 1766, and later eds., 375. In 1839 Doddridge's great-grandson re-edited the hymns from the original MS., and pub. the same as:—

Scriptural Hymns by the Rev. Philip Doddridge, D.D. New and corrected edition containing many hymns never before printed. Edited from the Original Documents by the Author's great-grandson, John Doddridge Humphreys, Esq. Lond. Darton & Clark, 1839.

This work contains 22 additional hymns. The text differs in many instances from Orton's, but these changes have not come into C. U. In addition to the MS. used by Orton and J. D. Humphreys, another containing 100 hymns (five of which are not in any ed. of the *Hymns*), all in the author's handwriting, and most of them dated, is referred to in this Dictionary as the "D. MSS." It is the property of Mr. W. S. Rooker and family. A MS., not in Doddridge's handwriting, of 77 "Hymns by P. Doddridge, Mar. 16, 17$\frac{38}{39}$," is in the possession of Mr. W. T. Brooke. The existence of these MSS. is accounted for from the fact that Doddridge's hymns were freely circulated in MS. during his lifetime. It is from his correspondence with R. Blair (q.v.) that the few compositions traceable to him in the *Scottish Trans. & Paraphrases* were derived.

The hymns by Doddridge which have attained to the greatest popularity are:—, "Awake, my soul, stretch every nerve"; "Do not I love Thee, O my Lord?" "Grace 'tis a charming sound"; "Hark, the glad sound, the Saviour comes"; "My God, and is Thy table spread?" "O happy day, that fixed my choice"; "O God of Jacob [Bethel], by Whose hand"; "See Israel's gentle Shepherd stand"; "Ye servants of the Lord." These hymns, with many besides, are annotated under their respective first lines. Of the rest, taken from the *Hymns*, &c., 1755, the following are also in C. U. :—

1. Behold the gloomy vale. *Death anticipated.*
2. Behold the Great Physician stands. *Christ the Physician.*
3. Captives of Israel, hear. *Spiritual Deliverance.*
4. Eternal God, our wondering souls. *Enoch's Piety and Translation.*
5. Eternal Source of life and thought. *Subjection to the Father.*
6. Exalted Prince of Life, we own. *Christ the Prince and Saviour.*
7. Father Divine, the Saviour cried. *Christ's Submission to the Father.*
8. Father Divine, Thy piercing eye. *Secret Prayer.*
9. Father of mercies, send Thy grace. *Sympathy. The Good Samaritan.*
10. Go, saith the Lord, proclaim my grace. *Forgiveness.*
11. God of Eternity, from Thee. *Redeeming the Time.*
12. God of my life, through all its [my] days. *Praising God continually.*
13. God of salvation, we adore. *Praise to God for Redemption.*
14. Great Father of mankind. *Gentiles brought into the Church.*
15. Great God, we sing that mighty hand. *The New Year.*
16. Great Leader of Thine Israel's host. *During Persecution.*
17. Great Lord of angels, we adore. *Ordination.*
18. Great Spirit of immortal love. *Purity of Heart desired.*
19. Great Teacher of Thy Church, we own. *The Divine Precepts.*
20. Hail, everlasting Prince of Peace. *Sympathy.*
21. Hail to the Prince of life and peace. *Praise to Christ.*
22. Hear, gracious [Saviour] Sovereign, from Thy throne. *The Blessings of the H. Spirit desired.*
23. How gentle God's commands. *God's Care of His Own.*
24. How rich Thy favours, God of grace. *God and His Living Temple.*
25. How swift the torrent flows [rolls]. *Our Fathers, where are they?*
26. Jesus the Lord, our souls adore. *Christ the Forerunner.*
27. Jesus, we own Thy Sovereign hand. *Christ to be fully known hereafter.*
28. Loud let the tuneful trumpet sound. *Gospel Jubilee.*
29. My gracious Lord, I own Thy right. *Life in Jesus.*
30. My [Dear] Saviour, I am [we are] Thine. *Joined to Christ through the Spirit.*
31. My soul, with all thy waking powers. *The Choice of Moses.*
32. Now let our voices join. *Singing in the ways of God.*
33. O injured Majesty of heaven. *Lent.*
34. O Zion, tune thy voice. *Glory of the Church of Christ.*
35. Peace, 'tis the Lord Jehovah's hand. *Resignation.*
36. Praise the Lord of boundless might. *The Father of Lights.*
37. Praise to Thy Name, Eternal God. *Growth in Grace desired.*
38. Remark, my soul, the narrow bounds. *The New Year.*
39. Repent, the Voice celestial cries. *Lent.*
40. Return, my roving heart, return. *Heart communing.*
41. Salvation, O melodious sound. *God our Salvation.*
42. Saviour of men, and Lord of love. *Ministry and Death of Christ.*
43. Searcher of hearts, before Thy face. *Peter to Simon Magus.*
44. Shepherd of Israel, Thou dost keep. *Induction, or Settlement of a Minister.*
45. Shine forth, eternal Source of light. *Knowledge of God desired.*
46. Shine on our souls, eternal God. *Sunday.*
47. Sing, ye redeemed of the Lord. *Joy on the Homeward Way.*
48. Sovereign of life, before Thine eye. *Life and Death in God's hands.*
49. The darkened sky, how thick it lours. *Sorrow followed by Joy.*

50. The day approacheth, O my soul. *Judgment anticipated.*
51. The King of heaven His table spreads. *The Gospel Feast.*
52. The promises I sing. *The unchanging promises of God.*
53. The swift-declining day. *Walk in the Light.*
54. These mortal joys, how soon they fade. *Treasures, Perishable and Eternal.*
55. Thy judgments cry aloud. *Retributive Providence.*
56. Thy presence, Everlasting God. *Omnipresence of the Father.*
57. 'Tis mine, the covenant of His grace. *Death anticipated.*
58. To Thee, my. God; my days are known. *Life under the eye of God.*
59. To-morrow, Lord, is Thine. *Uncertainty of Life.*
60. Triumphant Lord, Thy goodness reigns. *The Divine Goodness.*
61. Triumphant Zion, lift thy head. *The Church Purified and Guarded.*
62. Unite my roving thoughts, unite. *Peace.*
63. What mysteries, Lord, in Thee combine. *Christ, the First and Last.*
64. While on the verge of life I stand. *Death anticipated with Joy.*
65. With extacy of Joy. *Christ the Living Stone.*
66. Ye golden lamps of heaven, farewell. *Heaven opening.*
67. Ye hearts with youthful vigour warm. *The Young encouraged.*
68. Ye humble souls, that seek the Lord. *Easter.*
69. Ye sons of men, with joy record. *Praise of the Works of God.*
70. Yes, the Redeemer rose. *Easter.*

In Dr. Hatfield's *Church H. Bk.*, N. Y., 1872, Nos. 9, 12, 14, 15, 21, 23, 25, 29, 30, 32, 34, 35, 39, 40, 44, 47, 51, 61, 64, 65, 67, 69, 70, as above, are dated 1740. What authority there may be for this date we cannot say, these hymns not being in any "D. MSS." with which we are acquainted, and no dates are given in the *Hymns*, &c., 1755. Some later American editors have copied this date from Dr. Hatfield.

Doddridge's hymns are largely used by Unitarians both in G. Britain and America. As might be expected, the Congregationalists also draw freely from his stores. The Baptists come next. In the hymnals of the Church of England the choicest only are in use. Taken together, over one-third of his hymns are in C. U. at the present time.   [J. J.]

Donne, John, D.D., b. in London, 1573, and educated as a Roman Catholic, but at the age of nineteen he embraced Anglicanism. He acted for some time as Secretary to Lord Chancellor Ellesmere. At the desire of King James he took Holy Orders, and rising to great fame as a preacher, had the offer of fourteen livings during the first year of his ministry. He was chosen, in 1617, preacher at Lincoln's Inn. In 1621 he became Dean of St. Paul's, and soon afterwards Vicar of St. Dunstan's in the West. Died 1631, and was buried in St. Paul's. His work as a Poet and Divine is set forth by I. Walton in his *Lives*. He was the author of the plaintive hymn, "Wilt Thou forgive," &c. (q. v.). [See **English Hymnody, Early**, § VII.]. Donne's *Poems* (1633) have been recently edited in an admirable manner by the Rev. Dr. Grosart in his *Fuller Worthies Library*, where for the first time is printed a full and complete edition of the *Poems*.   [J. J.]

Döring, Carl August, s. of B. L. Döring, chief-forester at Mark-Alvensleben, near Magdeburg, was b. at Mark-Alvensleben,

Jan. 22, 1783. After completing his studies at the University of Halle, he was for some time private tutor at Waldenburg, in Silesia. In 1808 he was appointed a master in the school at Kloster-Bergen, near Magdeburg; and after its dissolution by Napoleon in 1810, acted for some time as a private tutor at Helmsdorf, near Eisleben. He was, in 1814, appointed afternoon preacher at St. Peter's Church, Magdeburg; in 1815 Archidiaconus of St. Andrew's Church at Eisleben; and in 1816 Pastor of the Lutheran Church at Elberfeld. He d. at Elberfeld, Jan 17, 1844 (*Koch*, vii. 159–168; *Allg. Deutsche Biog.*, v. 348–349).

One of the most prolific of German hymn-writers, he produced some 1200 hymns, not a few of which have passed into use in Germany through the Berlin *G. B.*, 1829, the *Nassau G. B.*, 1844, and other collections. They appeared mostly in his *Christliches Hausgesang-buch.* Of this pt. i. was pub. at Elberfeld, 1821, with 515 hymns by himself, and 169 by others; the 2nd ed., Elberfeld, 1825, omitting those by other authors, and increasing his own to 630. Part ii. was pub. at Elberfeld, 1830, with 551 hymns. Three have been *tr.* :—

i. **Ich weiss, dass mein Erlöser lebt, Er ward ja schon mein Leben !** [*Easter.*] 1821, as above, No. 100, in 6 st., *tr.* as " I know that my Redeemer lives; He is my life already," by *N. L. Frothingham*, 1870, p. 157.

ii. **Vater, Sohn und heil'ger Geist,** [*Confirmation.*] 1821, as above (No. 546), as a hymn for Confirmation. It is in 15 st. of various metres, st. i.–iii. being marked as to be sung by the congregation on behalf of the children; st. viii.–xiii. as a hymn of supplication by the children; st. iv–vii, by the parents and teachers; and st. xiv.–xv, by the congregation as a general supplication. Two parts are in German C. U., viz. st. i.–iii. as 'in Bunsen's *Versuch*, 1833, No. 614, beginning, " Segne, Vater, Sohn und Geist," as in Döring's ed. 1825, No. 502; and st. viii.–xiii., beginning, " Wir flehn um deine Gnade," in *Bunsen*, No. 615, the *Hamburg G. B.*, 1842, No. 276, and many recent collections. The only *tr.* in C. U. is—

Father, Son and Holy Ghost, Bless the Young. A good *tr.* of st. i.–iii. by J. S. Stallybrass, in the *Tonic Sol-fa Reporter*, January, 1859, and thence, as No. 329, in the Scottish *Presb. Hyl.*, 1876.

iii. **Taufe mich mit deiner Taufe.** [*Whitsuntide.*] 1821, as above, No. 135, in 4 st. It is *tr.* as " With other baptism, Lord, baptise," by *Dr. G. Walker*, 1860, p. 66.   [J. M.]

Doudney, Sarah, daughter of Mr. George E. Doudney, of Cosham, Hants, was b. near Portsmouth, but removed into a remote village in Hampshire at an early age. Her first efforts in literature were made when she was quite young, her poem, " The Lessons of the Water-Mill," a popular song, especially in America, having been written when she was only fifteen. Known mainly to the reading public through her stories, *A Woman's Glory*, *Stepping Stones*, and others, and through her contributions to the *Sunday Magazine*, *Good Words*, and other serials, her works, including fiction, and sacred and secular poems, have been widely read and appreciated. Her sacred poems are the least numerous of her writings. Some of these, as, " The Master hath come, and He calls us to follow," and " Saviour, now the day is ending," for use at the close of Evening Service, and of more than usual merit, create the desire for more of a like kind. Greater use, however, may be made of what she has written than has been done. By being buried in magazine literature, her hymns are somewhat difficult to trace. Her *Psalms of Life* was pub. by Houlston in 1871. In the Sunday School Union *Songs of Gladness*, 1871, the following were given :—

1. He hath gone into His garden. *The Vineyard of the Lord.*
2. In Thy holy garden ground. *The Vineyard of the Lord.*
3. Land of peace, and love, and brightness. *Heaven.*
4. Saviour, now the day is ending. *Sunday Evening.*
5. The Master hath come, and He calls us to follow. *Jesus and Mary of Bethany.*
6. We praise our Lord to-day. *Sunday.*
7. We sing a loving Jesus. *Praise of Jesus.*

Of these, Nos. 1, 2, 3, are in her *Psalms of Life*, 1871, and all have passed from the *Songs of Gladness* into other collections. Her :—

8. Room for the wanderer, room. *Christ's Invitation.*

is in W. R. Stevenson's *School Hymnal*, 1880.   [J. J.]

Douglas, Ellen, i.e. Mrs. Van Alstyne, q. v.

Down from the mountain Jesus came. *C. Wordsworth, Bp. of Lincoln.* [*Epiphany.*] Appeared in his *Holy Year*, 1862, in 7 st. of 4 l., for the 3rd Sun. after the Epiphany, concerning " The Manifestation of the Godhead in Christ, as the Physician of Body and Soul : as seen in the Gospel of the Week." As a complete hymn it is not in common use, but st. iii.–vi., as : " O God, made manifest in flesh," is given in the *Supp. to the N. Cong.*, 1869, No. 1083.   [J. J.]

Downton, Henry, M.A., s. of Mr. John Downton, Sub-Librarian of Trinity College, Cambridge, was b. at Pulverbatch, Shropshire, Feb. 12, 1818, and educated at Trinity College, Cambridge, where he graduated B.A. 1840, and M.A. 1843. Taking Holy Orders in 1843, he became Curate of Bembridge, Isle of Wight, 1843, and of Holy Trinity, Cambridge, 1847. In 1849 he was preferred to the Incumbency of St. John's, Chatham. He went to Geneva as English Chaplain in 1857; and was appointed Rector of Hopton in 1873. He was also for some time Domestic Chaplain to the late Lord Monson. He d. at Hopton, June 8, 1885. Mr. Downton pub. a *tr.* of Professor Ernest Naville's *Lectures on Modern Atheism*, 1865; and *Holy Scripture and the Temperance Question*, 1878. His hymns were chiefly contributed to the *Ch. of England Magazine*; A. T. Russell's *Ps. & Hymns*, 1851; Barry's *Ps. & Hymns*, 1862; and the *Sunday Magazine*. In 1873 he collected these and pub. them as *Hymns and Verses*. His *trs.* from the French of Alexandre Vinet are also in the volume. [See **French Hymnody**, § viii.] His best known hymns are " Another year, another year" (given anonymously in the Harrow School *Hymns*, 1855); " For Thy mercy, and Thy grace"; and " Harp awake, tell out the story." These have attained to great popularity, and are in extensive use.   [J. J.]

Δόξα ἐν ὑψίστοις Θεῷ, ἐν Βηθλεέμ. By *John the Monk*, generally held to be the same as *St. John of Damascus* (q.v.). This is found in the Office of the Greek Church for Christmas Day, where it is sung at the service " At the first hour of the Night," when " Collected again in the Church, we begin Compline according to custom, and after the Glory be to God on high, we go out into the Narthex making the Procession, and chanting there Idiomelic stichera to the first tone" (Littledale's *Offices*, &c., p. 178), of which the

Δόξα ἐν ὑψίστοις Θεῷ is a portion. The only translation into English is Dr. Littledale's blank verse version in his *Offices, &c., of the Holy Eastern Church*, 1863, p. 180, and the same rendered into 8-7's measure by *W. Chatterton Dix*, for the *Lyra Messianica*, 1864, p. 111, in which it first appeared. The original Greek text, which dates from about the middle of the eighth century, is given in Dr. Littledale's *Offices, &c.*, 1863, p. 63. The *tr.* is, "To-day in Bethlehem I hear" (*Littledale*), "To-day in Bethlehem hear I" (*Dix*).
[J. J.]

Δόξα ἐν ὑψίστοις θεῷ, καὶ ἐπὶ γῆς εἰρήνη. This is the Greek form of the *Gloria in excelsis Deo*, and is an expansion of the Angels' Hymn in St. Luke, ii. 14. It is given in *Daniel*, ii. pp. 268–69, in two forms, and accompanied by very extensive notes. The first form is from the *Apostolic Constitutions*, and the second is found at the end of the Psalms and Canticles contained in the *Codex Alexandrinus*. This latter is also given in full in **Greek Hymnody**, § x. 4, and in **Anth. Graec.**, pp. 38–39. Of the *Codex Alex.* text Mr. Chatfield has given a literal *tr.* in his *Songs and Hymns, &c.*, 1876, p. 161, v. "Glory to God in the highest," &c. The *tr* in the Communion Office of the Book of Common Prayer, "Glory be to God on high," is from the Latin version of the hymn. [J. J.]

Doxologies. The term Doxology may be applied to the *Tersanctus*, *Alleluia*, or any form of ascription of praise to the Blessed Trinity; but it is specially confined to the *Gloria in excelsis*, technically known as the *Greater Doxology* [see **Greek Hymnody**, § x. 4], and to the *Gloria Patri*, similarly known as the *Lesser Doxology*. Under the general heading of *Doxologies*, we might include the various forms of ascriptions of praise with which most of the collects and prayers are concluded in both Eastern and Western Office Books. It must suffice to give as samples the last words of the (1) "Great Intercession," and of the (2) "Prayer of Humble Access" in the *Clementine Liturgy*:

(1) "because to Thee belong all glory, worship, and thanksgiving, honour and adoration, to Father, Son, and Holy Ghost, now and always and for unceasing and unending ages. Amen." (Hammond, *Liturgies E. & W.* p. 19.)
(2) "through Thy Christ, with Whom to Thee be glory, honour, praise, laud, thanksgiving, and to the Holy Ghost for ever. Amen." (*Ibid.*, p. 20.)

It has also been the custom from earliest times to conclude sermons or addresses in public worship with varying forms of doxology. The form regularly used by St. Chrysostom was this:—

"through Jesus Christ our Lord, with Whom, to the Father, together with the Holy Ghost, be glory, might, and honour, now, and always, and for ever. Amen."

The *Gloria Patri*; or, *Lesser Doxology*, is of great, possibly but not demonstrably, Apostolic antiquity. Its Trinitarian language is derived from our Lord's commission to baptize in Mat. xxviii. 19. St. Basil the Great, or whoever was the author of the letter "De Spiritu Sancto ad Amphilochium," asserts that the first part in its present form was in use in both East and West as early as the time of St. Clement of Rome. No doubt the second

half is later than the first half, and was added afterwards, but at a date which it is impossible to fix exactly. It must have been before A.D. 529, in which year the second Council of Vaison (can. 6) enjoins the use of the second half in France, as being already in general use throughout the whole East, Africa, and Italy, and as directed against heretics who denied the eternity of the Son of God. Various forms of the *Gloria Patri* have been and are in use, viz.:—

1. Early varieties of the *Greek* form were these, (1) Δόξα Πατρὶ ἐν Υἱῷ, καὶ διὰ Πνεύματος ἁγίῳ κ.τ.λ, and (2) Δόξα Πατρὶ διὰ Υἱῷ καὶ διὰ ἁγίῳ Πνεύματος κ.τ.λ., but both were discarded in favour of the following: (3) Δόξα Πατρὶ, καὶ Υἱῷ, καὶ ἁγίῳ Πνεύματι, καὶ νῦν, καὶ ἀεί, καὶ εἰς τοὺς αἰῶνας τῶν αἰώνων. Ἀμήν: which is still in current use in the Eastern Church, because the former were employed by Arius and his followers to prove a difference of inferiority between the second and first Persons of the Holy Trinity (Bingham, *Antiq. of Christ. Ch.*, Bk. xiv. cap. 2). Another ancient but long obsolete form of words was, (4) Δόξα Πατρὶ, καὶ Υἱῷ, σὺν ἁγίῳ Πνεύματι.
2. The ordinary *Latin* form is, "Gloria Patri et Filio et Spiritui Sancto: Sicut erat in principio, et nunc, et semper, et in saecula saeculorum. Amen."
3. The ordinary *Anglican* form, which is not a literal translation of the Latin text, is: "Glory be to the Father, and to the Son, and to the Holy Ghost. As it was in the beginning, is now, and ever shall be, world without end. Amen."
4. The *Mozarabic* form, as ordered by the 12th and 14th canons of the ivth Council of Toledo, A.D. 633, and as found in the Introit appointed in the *Mozarabic Missal* for Christmas Day, is: "Gloria et honor Patri, et Filio, et Spiritui Sancto in saecula saeculorum. Amen."

Concerning the use of the Doxology we may note that in the Eastern Offices it is used after each "Stasis," or subdivision consisting of two or more Psalms. By the Western Rule of St. Benedict (cap. 18) it was directed to be used after each Psalm, and it is still so used in the *Roman Breviary*, except in the case of Psalms 62, 148, 149. It is also used at the close of the third, sixth, and eighth or ninth Responsories, with repetition of part of the Responsory in lieu of its second half; and after the four opening versicles at Matins, a position retained in the English Book of Common Prayer. The variations common to the Greek and Latin Service books, by which sometimes the first clause of the doxology is used without the second, may perhaps retain some witness to the separate history of the clauses.

Metrical Doxologies are naturally the outcome of the practice of concluding the Psalms with the *Gloria Patri*, being transferred to Hymns, and arranged according to their varying metres. In some instances the wording of the *Gloria Patri* was as strictly adhered to as the structure of the verse would admit, but in others the only resemblance is the expression of equal praise to the Three Persons in the Blessed Trinity. The following is a specimen in Sapphics taken from the *Mozarabic Breviary*:—

"Gloriam Patri celebrant honore,
Gloriam Nato recinent perenni,
Cum quibus Sanctus sociatus extat
Spiritus unus. Amen."
(For Feast of St. Cucufatus. *Migne*, p. 1171.)

Sometimes a reference to the event which is commemorated on any particular festival is introduced into the doxology, as in the concluding verse of the acrostic Epiphany hymn, "A Patre unigenitus" (q.v.).

" Gloria tibi, Domine,
　Qui apparuisti hodie,
　Cum Patre et Sancto Spiritu
　In sempiterna saecula."

(*Mone*, i. p. 79. See also an Easter doxology, *Ibid*. p. 195.)

It is to the metrical Latin doxologies that we owe the various English forms which we possess, not necessarily the actual metres, but certainly the principles upon which they are based. It is thence that the early metrical doxology of the 1535 *Primer* comes:—

" Glory be to The Trinitie,
　The Father, Son, and Spirit living :
　Which are One God and Persons Three,
　To Whom be praise without ending."

This is attached to the translation of Latin hymns. The forms in the later *Primers* are more regular, and also both *trs*. of the " Veni Creator," in the Ordinal. The various metrical renderings of the Psalms, as the Old Version, the New Version, and others, supply one for each metre. The older hymn-writers in many instances gave special attention to the point. I. Watts closed his *Hys. and Spiritual Songs*, 1707–9, with twenty versions, and introduced them by saying :—

"I cannot persuade myself to put a full period to these Divine Hymns till I have addressed a special song of Glory to God the Father, the Son, and the Holy Spirit. Though the Latin name of it, *Gloria Patri*, be retained in our nation from the Roman Church ; and though there may be some excess of superstitious honour paid to the words of it, which may have wrought some unhappy prejudices in weaker Christians, yet I believe it still to be one of the parts of Christian worship."

Later writers followed these examples until almost every conceivable form of metrical doxology is provided for in the hymnody of the Church.　　　　　　　[F. E. W.]

1. The numerous Metrical Doxologies which are found in Latin and English especially are marked by a distinction of some importance. As intimated above, the Latin doxology is so worded as to emphasise the day or season for which it is appointed in addition to offering praise to the Three Persons of the Holy Trinity, whilst the English doxology is concerned with the latter only. The result is a richness in the Latin which is unattainable elsewhere. If space admitted, a complete set of Doxologies from the ancient *Hymnaries* and *Breviaries* could have been given, but we must confine ourselves to some of the more important. The following are from the *Paris Breviary*, 1736 :—

i. *In Adventu.*
" Qui liberator advenis,
　Fili, tibi laus maxima
　Cum Patre, cumque Spiritu,
　In sempiterna secula."

ii. *In Nativitate Domini.*
" Qui natus es de Virgine,
　Jesu, tibi sit gloria
　Cum Patre, cumque Spiritu,
　In sempiterna secula."

iii. *In Epiphania Domini.*
" Qui te revelas Gentibus,
　Jesu, tibi sit gloria
　Cum Patre, cumque Spiritu,
　In sempiterna secula."

iv. *In Tempore Paschali.*
" Da, Christe, nos tecum mori ;
　Tecum simul da surgere :
　Terrena da contemnere ;
　Amare da coelestia."

" Sit laus Patri ; laus Filio,
　Qui nos, triumphata nec·,
　Ad astra secum dux vocat :
　Compar tibi laus, Spiritus."

v. *In Ascensione Domini.*
" Da, Christe, nos tecum mori :
　Tecum simul da surgere :
　Terrena da contemnere ;
　Amare da coelestia."

" Qui victor ad coelum redis,
　Jesu, tibi sit gloria
　Cum Patre, cumque Spiritu,
　In sempiterna secula."

vi. *In Die Pentecostes.*
" Sit laus Patri ; laus Filio :
　Par sit tibi laus, Spiritus,
　Afflante quo mentes sacris
　Lucent et ardent ignibus."

vii. *In Annunciatione Domini.*
" Mundo redemptor qui venis,
　Fili, tibi laus maxima
　Cum Patre : nec tibi minor
　Laus, utriusque Spiritus."

viii. *Officio Dedic. Ecclesiae.*
" Sit laus Patri, laus Filio,
　Par sit tibi laus, Spiritus,
　Divina cujus unctio
　Nos templa Christo consecrat."

2. The *Roman Breviary* Metrical Doxologies follow this same rule, differing only in the wording of the same. As an instance, the following may be compared with No. v. above :—

In Ascensione Domini.
" Jesu, tibi sit gloria,
　Qui victor in coelum redis,
　Cum Patre et almo Spiritu,
　In sempiterna saecula."

3. Other Breviaries, both ancient and modern, follow the same rule and extend it also to all Festivals and Special Offices. A collection of 29 Doxologies from the *Paris Breviary*, 1736, including those for several minor Festivals, is given in Card. Newman's *Hymni Ecclesiae*, 1838 and 1865, and *trs*. of the more important from various Breviaries and ancient hymns are found in the works of J. Chandler, W. J. Copeland, E. Caswall, J. D. Chambers, W. J. Blew, Bp. Mant, J. M. Neale, I. Williams, and other translators of Latin hymns.

4. Original English Metrical Doxologies are very numerous, and are found in the early versions of the Psalms and in the most modern hymn-books. The more lengthy of these which are in C. U. have been dealt with as separate hymns, and are given in the general " Index of Subjects and Seasons." Those which are composed of one, or at most two stanzas, are too numerous, and too much alike, to be given in detail. We can only append a list of the most exhaustive collections which are available to the reader. These are :—

1. Old Versions of the Psalms.
2. The *Old* and *New Versions*.
3. I. Watts's *Hymns*, 1707, and *Psalms*, 1719.
4. Wesley's *Gloria Patri*, 1746, in the Wesley *P. Works*, 1868–72, vol. iii.
5. J. Newton in the *Olney Hymns*, 1779.
6. The older collections of *Whitefield, Madan, Toplady, Conyers, Lady Huntingdon, Rippon*, the later Baptist *Selections*, 1828 & 1836, the Congregational *Collections* and others to 1860.
7. Large selections are given in *Kennedy*, 1863; the *Hy. Comp.* 1876 ; Snepp's *Songs of G. & G.*, 1872 ; and W. Stone's *Supplemental Hymnal*, 1873. This last is the largest collection of doxologies extant. The metres are very varied, and the doxologies number 120. In the majority of modern hymn-books of the Church of England the doxologies are given with the hymns, and are not appended as a separate section of each book.
8. Modern Nonconformist collections generally adopt the practice of giving the doxologies with the hymns. Spurgeon's *O. O. H. Bk.*, 1866, is an exception, the doxologies being given as a separate section between the Psalms and the hymn.

9. In modern American collections doxologies are usually appended at the end of the book and represent all the metres contained therein, as in the Protestant Episcopal *Hymnal*, 1871; the Methodist Episcopal *Hymnal*, 1878; Hatfield's *Church Hymn-Book*, 1872; the Baptist *Service of Song*, 1872, and others.

5. The provision which has thus been made, not only for the holy Seasons of the Church, but also for general purposes, and for the great variety of metre found in modern hymnbooks, is very abundant. Where sameness and painful reiteration are unavoidable, it is useless to expect uniform excellence throughout. When, however, the wearisome commonplace is broken by Bp. Ken's "Praise God, from Whom all blessings flow"; Watts's "Give to the Father praise"; Osler's "Worship, honour, glory, blessing"; or by one of the finer translations from the Latin, we realize that a noble hymn need not be weakened by an ignoble doxology.   [J. J.]

Dracup, John, was b. in 1723, but the place of birth and circumstances of early life not known. In 1755 he became pastor of the Independent Church at Steep Lane, Sowerby, near Halifax; but in 1772, having apparently changed his views on Baptism, left Steep Lane, and became a minister among the Baptists, first at Rodhill-end, near Todmorden, and then at Rochdale. In 1784, the members of the Independent Church at Steep Lane, having in the interval followed his example and become Baptists, invited him to re-settle among them. This he did, and continued their pastor until his death, May 28, 1795.

In 1787, Mr. Dracup pub. a small volume of 63 hymns with the title, *Hymns and Spiritual Songs, by John Dracup, Minister of the Gospel at Sowerby. Bolton, printed by R. Jackson.* Two of these, beginning "Free Grace to every heaven-born soul," and "Thanks to Thy name, O Lord, that we," had previously appeared in Lady Huntingdon's *Collection*, undated ed. cir. 1772, and again in the revised ed. of 1780. Both are in Denham's *Sel.* (1837); the former is in *Gadsby* (1853) and in Stevens's *Sel.* (1881), and the latter in Reed's *H. Bk.*, 1842, &c. A third hymn of Dracup's, very touching both in sentiment and language, is found in a small Baptist supplementary *Sel.* It begins, "Once I could say, 'My God is mine.'" His other hymns have seldom had more than a local use.   [W. R. S.]

Draw near, ye weary, bowed and broken-hearted. [*Jesus weeping at the grave of Lazarus.*] This hymn was given in *Christian Lyrics*, R. T. S., N.D., in 4 st. of 6 l. In 1853, 3 st. were included in the *Leeds H. Bk.*, No. 296, as from the *Christian Lyre*. Whether this is a mistake for the R. T. S. *Christian Lyrics* we cannot say, but the hymn is not in the *Christian Lyre* of 1830–1. Dr. Dale gives the same stanzas in his *English H. Bk.*, 1874, but appends no signature.
                                          [W. T. B.]

Drayton, Michael, b. 1563, d. 1631, was very popular in his days, and his name is still regarded with respect. He was the author of the Poly-olbion and many other works. His hymns were pub. as:—

"*The Harmonie of the Church, containing, 'The spiritual songes and holy hymes of godly men, patriarkes, and prophets, all sweetly sounding to the praise and glory of the Highest*, 1591.'"

Of this but a single copy is known. It was reprinted by the *Percy Society*, and again in the Rev. Richard Hooper's edition of *Poly-olbion*, in Smith's *Library of Old Authors*.
                                          [J. T. B.]

Dread Jehovah! God of nations. [*In Time of Trouble—National.*] This hymn appeared in the *Christian Observer*, in April, 1804, in 4 st. of 8 l. At that time Bonaparte was First Consul, and meditating an immediate invasion of England. A day of humiliation and prayer was appointed. In anticipation of this day the following editorial note, together with the hymn as given below, appeared in the *Christian Observer*:—

"His Majesty has been graciously pleased to appoint Friday, the 25th of May next, to be observed throughout England and Ireland as a day of public humiliation and fasting. We earnestly hope it may be observed in a proper manner. We subjoin a hymn for the occasion, which has just reached us in time to obtain a place in this number.

Hymn for the Fast Day.
May 25, 1804.

"Dread Jehovah! God of Nations,
    From thy Temple in the Skies,
Hear thy People's Supplications,
    And for their Deliv'rance rise.
Lo! with deep Contrition turning,
    In thy Holy Place we bend;
Fasting, praying, weeping, mourning,
    Hear us, spare us, and defend.

"Foes, who've ravag'd peaceful Regions,
    Now for us the Yoke prepare;
And if thou forsake our Legions,
    We, like them, the Yoke must wear.
Shall Religion's Foes enslave us?
    Shall their Heathen Tongues exclaim,
'Where's your God?' O rise to save us,
    And assert Thy glorious Name.

"Though our Sins, each Heart confounding,
    Long and loud for vengeance call;
Thou hast Mercy as abounding,
    Thou hast Blood can cleanse them all.
Let that Mercy veil Transgression,
    Let that Blood our Guilt efface;
Save thy People from Oppression,
    Save from Spoil thy Holy Place.

"Hear, O God! the Vows we tender;
    With our Hosts to battle go;
Shield the Head of each Defender,
    And confound the impious Foe.
So when ceas'd the Battle's raging,
    Thine shall be the Victor's Praise;
And in thy holy Bonds engaging,
    We will serve thee all our Days.
                                          "C. F."

In 1805, in John Gresham's *Select Portions of Psalms and Hymns*, 3rd ed., it is given as Hymn xiv., and a note states it to have been "Written by a Clergyman," and to have been separately published with music by Haydn. In 1819, *Cotterill*, having slightly altered the text, and omitted st. ii., included the hymn in his *Sel.* in 3 st., No. 337. Bickersteth went further in reducing it to the first and third stanzas, with alterations, in his *Christian Psalmody*, 1833. Hall adopted the same stanzas in his *Mitre H. Bk.*, 1836, but introduced many alterations therein. These alterations are repeated in the *New Mitre Hymnal*, 1874, together with a doxology in 2 st. of 4 l. Nearly all the modern collections, including the S. P. C. K. *Ps. & Hymns*, 1852–69; *Barry*, 1862–67; *H. Comp.* 1872; *Snepp*, 1872; *Harland*; Stevenson's *Hys. for Ch. & Home*; and many others, have the altered text as given in Bickersteth's *Christian Psalmody*, 1833, and not the original. In *Church Hys.*, 1871, No. 260, the hymn, "Lord Almighty, God of nations," is also *Bickersteth's* text with the alteration of the first and last lines of the hymn only. The hymn is in one form or another in somewhat extensive use in G. Britain and America.   [J. J.]

Dread Sovereign, let my evening song. *I. Watts.* [*Evening.*] Appeared in the 1st ed. of his *H. & S. Songs*, 1707, Bk. ii., No. 7, in 6 st. of 4 l., and headed, "An Evening Song." The opening stanza, when compared with J. Mason's "Song of Praise for the Evening" (*Songs of Praise*, 1683, No. xi.), is evidently suggested by Mason's st. i. The two are:—

Mason, 1683.	Watts, 1709.
"Now from the altar of my heart	"Dread Sovereign, let my evening song
Let incense flames arise ;	Like holy incense rise :
Assist me, Lord, to offer up	Assist the offerings of my
Mine evening sacrifice."	tongue
	To reach the lofty skies."

The hymn in its original form is in C. U. both in G. Britain and America. There are also altered texts in C. U., as (1) "Blest Saviour, let our evening song"; this is in *Common Praise*, 1879; and (2) "O Holy Father, let my song," in Bapt. *Ps. & Hys.*, 1858-80, &c.   [J. J.]

Drei König führt die göttlich Hand. [*Epiphany.*] Appeared in the *Alte Catholische Geistliche Kirchengesäng*, Cologne, 1621, in 9 st. of 6 l., and thence, omitting st. ii. in F. Hommel's *Geistliche Volkslieder*, 1871, No. 51 ; and in full, but altered, in the *Trier G. B.* (R. C.), 1846, p. 34. Nearly the same text, but beginning, "Es führt drei König Gottes Hand," from the *Catholische Kirchen Gesäng*, Cologne, 1625, is included, omitting st. ii., ix. in *Wackernagel*, v. p. 1251, and in H. Bone's *Cantate*, 1846 (ed. 1879, No. 82). *Tr.* as :—

Three kings were led by God's own hand, a good *tr.* from the *Trier* text, omitting st. ii., iv., vii., by Dr. R. F. Littledale, as No. 54 in the *People's H.*, 1867, signed "A. L. P."   [J. M.]

Dreieinigkeit, der Gottheit wahrer Spiegel. *J. Franck.* [*Trinity Sunday Evening.*] 1st pub. in C. Peter's *Andachts-Zymbeln*, Freiberg, 1655, p. 276, in the section entitled, "On the Holy Trinity," in 8 st. of 4 l. In Franck's *Geistliches Sion*, 1674, p. 31 (ed. 1846, p. 55). St. 1, 2 are based on "O Lux beata Trinitas," and st. 3-7, on Romans xi. 33-36. St. 8 ("Dein Nam ist gross") is taken from his *Vaterunserharpfe*, Frankfurt-am-Main, 1652. It passed into J. Crüger's *Praxis pietatis melica*, 1661; Freylinghausen's *G. B.*, 1704, and other collections, and is No. 14 in the Berlin *G. L. S.*, ed.1863. *Tr.* as :—

True mirror of the Godhead! Perfect Light. A good *tr.* of st. 1-3, 7, 8, by Miss Winkworth in her *Lyra Ger.*, 2nd Series, 1858, p. 64. Her *tr.* of st. 2, 7, 8, altered and beginning, "We praise Thee, Lord, with earliest morning ray," appear as "A Morning Psalm of Praise" in the *H. of the Spirit*, Boston, U.S., 1864, No. 103. [J. M.]

Drennan, William, M.D., b. at Belfast, May 23, 1754, and educated at Glasgow, where he graduated M.A. in 1771, and M.D. 1778. He subsequently practised at Belfast. He d. Feb. 5, 1820. In 1815 he pub. *Fugitive Pieces in Prose and Verse*, Belfast, 1815 ; and his *Poems* were collected and pub. with a *Memoir* by his sons in 1859. Of his poems six are grouped under the heading of "Religious Poems." Seven hymns, including five of these "Religious Poems," were contributed to Aspland's Unitarian *Sel.*, 1810 ; but in the 1859 *Poems and Memoir* most of them are in a longer

form. As most of these are still in C. U. amongst the Unitarians in G. Britain and America, we subjoin the list of first lines :—

1. All nature feels attractive power. *Law of Love.*
2. Bless'd who with generous pity glows. *Charity.*
3. Humanity ! thou sent of God. *Faith, Hope, Charity.*
4. In this fair globe, with ocean bound. *Love of God.*
5. O sweeter than the fragrant flower. *Doing Good.*
6. The heaven of heavens cannot contain. *Divine Worship.*
7. The husbandman goes forth afield. *Fruits of Benevolence.*   [W. T. B.]

Drese, Adam, was b. in Dec. 1620, in Thuringia, probably at Weimar. He was at first musician at the court of Duke Wilhelm, of Sachse-Weimar; and after being sent by the Duke for further training under Marco Sacchi at Warsaw, was appointed his Kapellmeister in 1655. On the Duke's death in 1662, his son, Duke Bernhard, took Drese with him to Jena, appointed him his secretary, and, in 1672, Town Mayor. After Duke Bernhard's death, in 1678, Drese remained in Jena till 1683, when he was appointed Kapellmeister at Arnstadt to Prince Anton Günther, of Schwarzburg-Sondershausen. He d. at Arnstadt, Feb. 15, 1701 (*Koch*, iv. 270-274 ; *Allg. Deutsche Biog.*, v. 397 ; *Wetzel*, i. 193-4, and *A. H.*, vol. i., pt. iv., pp. 28-30).

In 1680, the reading of Spener's writings and of Luther on the Romans led to a change in his religious views, and henceforth under good and evil report he held prayer meetings in his house, which became a meeting-place for the Pietists of the district. "His hymns," says Wetzel, "of which he himself composed not only the melodies, but also, as I have certain information, the text also, were sung at the meetings of pious persons in his house, before they came into print."

One has been *tr.* into English, viz. :—

Seelenbräutigam, Jesus, Gottes Lamm, appeared in the *Geistreiches G. B.*, Halle, 1697, p. 147, in 15 st. of 6 l., repeated (with the well-known melody by himself added, which in the *Irish Ch. Hyl.* is called "Thuringia"), in the *Darmstadt G. B.*, 1698, p. 134, as No. 197 in Freylinghausen's *G. B.*, 1704, and recently as No. 119 in the Berlin *G. L. S.*, ed. 1863. In Wagner's *G. B.*, Leipzig, 1697, vol. iii. p. 420, it begins, "Jesu, Gottes Lamm." The *tr.* in C. U. is:—

Bridegroom, Thou art mine, a *tr.* of st. 1, 2, 4, 8, 13-15, by Dr. M. Loy, as No. 283 in the *Ohio Luth. Hyl.*, 1880.

Another tr. is, "God and man indeed," of st. iii. as st. i. of No. 463 in the *Moravian H. Bk.*, 1789 (1886, No. 224).   [J. M.]

Dreves, Johann Friedrich Ludwig, s. of F. C. Dreves, burgomaster of Horn, in the Principality of Lippe-Detmold, was b. at Horn, Nov. 17, 1762. After the completion of his studies at the University of Marburg he was for some time corrector of the school at Detmold. In 1790 he became third pastor of the Reformed Church at Detmold, and after being pastor at Hillentrup from June 28 to Oct. 25, 1795, returned to Detmold as second pastor. He remained in Detmold till 1820, when he again became pastor at Hillentrup, and d. there Nov. 30, 1834. (*MS. from Pastor A. Koppen, Detmold.*) His hymn :—

Hier lieg ich, Herr ! im Staube. *Trust in God.* Was written at Detmold after the death, on Nov. 14, and before the burial, Nov. 17, 1793, of his first wife Lischen (Elizabeth) née Ewald. It was 1st pub. as No. 91 of the hymns for the sick and sorrowing appended to his Easter Sermon pub. at Lemgo, 1813, entitled *Wiedersehen*. It is in 12 st. of 8 l., and when included as No. 601 in the Berlin *G. B.*, 1829, st. v.-vii., ix., xii., were omitted, and the rest altered. This form was repeated in Bunsen's *Versuch*, 1833, No. 914. *Tr.* as :—

1. **My God, lo, here before Thy face**, a D. C. M. version from *Bunsen*, by Miss Winkworth in her *Lyra Ger.*, 1st Series, 1855, p. 38. Her st. iii., v., are altered in later eds. In full in the Schaff-Gilman *Lib. of Rel. Poetry*, ed. 1883, p. 821. In the American hymn-books it appears in the following forms from the 1855 text :—

(1) "My Father, God, before Thy face," No. 226, in Boardman's *Sel.*, Philadelphia, 1861, is from her st. i., ll. 1-4 ; iv., ll. 1-4, and vi.

(2) "O Father, compass me about," No. 362, in the *H. of the Spirit*, Boston, 1864, is her st. iv., ll. 1-4 ; v., ll. 1-4 ; vi., ll. 1-4 ; vii., ll. 4-8.

(3) "I know Thy thoughts are peace towards me," No. 978, in the *Sabbath H. Bk.*, 1858, is her st. v., vi.

(4) "Father, Thy thoughts are peace towards me," No. 905, in Robinson's *Songs for the Sanctuary*, 1865, is her st. v., l. 1-4, and vi.

2. **My God, behold me lying.** A good *tr.* of *Bunsen's* st. i., ii., iv., v., vii., by Miss Winkworth in her *C. B. for England*, 1863, No. 108.   [J. M.]

Drop, drop, slow tears. *Phineas Fletcher.* [*Penitence.*] Appeared in his *Poetical Miscellanies*, 1633 ; recently republished by Dr. Grosart in 4 vols., 1869, in his *Fuller Worthies Library*. This tender poem is given in Thring's *Coll.*, 1882, and in others. [See **English Hymnody, Early,** § VII.]   [J. J.]

Drooping soul, shake off thy fears. *C. Wesley.* [*Lent. Resignation.*] 1st pub. in *Hys. & Sac. Poems*, 1742, in 6 st. of 8 l. (*P. Works*, 1868-72, vol. ii. p. 293). In 1780, J. Wesley included st. i.-iv. in the *Wes. H. Bk.*, No. 137. This arrangement has been repeated in later editions, and in other collections. The expression in st. ii., l. 2—

> Fainting soul, be bold, be strong ;
> Wait the leisure of thy Lord.

is from Coverdale's prose version of Ps. xxvii. 16, in the *Bk. of Common Prayer*.   [J. J.]

Drummond, David Thomas Kerr, B.A., youngest s. of James Rutherford Drummond, of Stragreath, Perthshire, was b. at Edinburgh, Aug. 25, 1805. After studying at the University of Edinburgh, he went to Oxford, where he graduated B.A. He was ordained Priest in 1831, and, after serving various cures, became, in 1838, joint minister of Trinity Episcopal Church, Dean Bridge, Edinburgh. He resigned his charge and severed his connection with the Scottish Episcopal Church in 1843, when he became the minister of a church built for him (St. Thomas's English Episcopal Church, Edinburgh), where he continued to minister to a large and influential congregation until his death. He d. at Pitlochry, Perthshire, June 9, 1877. His hymns appeared to the number of 10 in the *Church of England Hymnbook*, 1838, of which he was joint editor with Dr. Greville, a member of his own congregation. [**Scottish Hymnody,** § VII.]   [J. M.]

Drummond, William, M.A., eldest s. of Sir John Drummond, Kt., of Hawthornden, near Edinburgh, was b. at Hawthornden, Dec. 13, 1585. He studied at the University of Edinburgh, and graduated M.A. in 1605. Suc-

ceeding, by the death of his father, in 1610, to the estate of Hawthornden, he resided there till his death, on Dec. 4, 1649. He was one of the most eminent literary Scotsmen of his time, and a friend of Sir William Alexander and Ben Jonson. His *Flowers of Zion* were pub. in 1623, and his *Works* were collected and pub. in two vols. at London, 1655-56, and again at Edinburgh, in one vol., in 1711. His *Poems* were issued by the Maitland Club, in 1832, with additions from the Hawthornden MSS., originally pub. by Dr. David Laing in the Transactions of the Society of Antiquaries of Scotland. They have since been edited by Peter Cunningham in 1833, and, in 1856, by W. B. D. Turnbull (Lond., J. R. Smith). Among the *Posthumous Poems*, 1st pub. in 1656, is a *tr.* of the *Dies Irae*, and among those added in 1711 are *trs.* of 20 of the *Roman Breviary* hymns. These, which are interesting as being among the earliest attempts of the kind, are included in the edition of 1856. Professor Masson has recently issued an interesting work on him as *Drummond of Hawthornden: the Story of his Life and Writings* (Lond., Macmillan & Co., 1879).   [J. M.]

In an article in the *Dublin Review*, 1883, and again in the preface to his *Annus Sanctus*, 1884, Mr. Orby Shipley has questioned Drummond's right to the *trs.* from the *Roman Breviary* which were given in his posthumous *Works*, 1711. The history of these translations, so far as we can gather, is this. In 1619 *The Primer ; or, Office of the Blessed Virgin Mary*, was issued, with a revised translation [see **Primers**], and all the hymns therein but one were new. These were repeated in a reprint in 1632. This reprint contains an address to the reader, in which occurs the following passage :—

"The Hymnes most of which are used by the holy Church in her publick Office ; are a new translation done by one *most skilfull in English poetrie*, wherein the literall sense is preserued with the true straine of the verse."

In 1711 a complete edition of Drummond's *Works*, under the editorship of Bishop Sage and Thomas Ruddiman, appeared, and in it 18 hymns, identical with those in the 1615 *Primer*, were given as from the MSS. in the Edinburgh University Library. These MSS., however, are not now to be found, and Mr. Shipley's contention is that Drummond merely transcribed these translations, and that his 1711 editors, finding them in his autograph, concluded they were his. He strongly dwells (see his preface to *Annus Sanctus*, pp. 12-14) on the improbability of a Catholic publisher applying to a Scotch Protestant for translations, and really this is his main argument. Against this we must set the following considerations. (1) Drummond undoubtedly translated the *Dies Irae* pub. by Phillips, in 1656. His attention had therefore been drawn to Latin hymnody. (2) The express words of the address to the reader in the 1615 edition, "one most skilful in English poetry," certainly suit Drummond. (3) The fact that Sage and Ruddiman, with Drummond's MS. before them, had no doubt on the matter. (4) The books presented by him to the Edinburgh University show him to have had a taste for Roman and ascetic theology. (5) The similarity in style to his *Flowers of Zion* of 1623. Mr. Shipley's theory therefore seems to rest on no solid basis. His evidence is purely internal and problematical. It is quite possible that in his foreign tours, for some time at least, Drummond was a concealed Roman Catholic. But this is as purely conjectural as Mr. Shipley's theory. The matter rests solely on the authority of Drummond's editors, Sage and Ruddiman, and the express assertion in the address of 1615 (noted above), that the translations were "done by one most skilfull in English poetrie." According to Mr. Shipley's theory this writer, who was "most skilfull in English poetrie," must have been a Roman Catholic; and failing to find one such poet amongst the Roman Catholics of that day to whom he can give a habitation or a name, he further adds that he is "unknown." Until it can be shown that at that date, 1615 (the 1st ed. of the *Primer*), there was a known Roman Catholic writer "most skilfull in English poetrie," we must abide by Drummond. [W. T. B.]

Drummond, William Hamilton, D.D., s. of an Irish physician, was b. at Ballyclare, Antrim, Ireland, 1772, and d. at Dublin, Oct. 16, 1865. Educated for the ministry at the University of Glasgow, he became, in 1793, the pastor of the Second Presbyterian Church, Belfast, and in 1816, of the Strand Street Chapel, Dublin. His poetical works include:—

(1) *Juvenile Poems*, 1797; (2) *Trafalgar*, 1805; (3) *The Giant's Causeway*, 1811; (4) *Clontarf*, 1817; and (5) *Who are the Happy? a Poem on the Christian Beatitudes, with other Poems on Sacred Subjects*, 1818.

In 1818 *A Selection of Ps. & Hys. for the Use of the Presbytery of Antrim, and the Congregation of Strand Street, Dublin*, was pub. at Belfast. This *Sel.* was probably edited by Dr. Drummond. It contained several of his hymns. Five of these (Nos. 84, 190, 201, 236, 264) were contributed to that edition.

From *Who are the Happy?* the following hymns have come into C. U. :—

1. **A voice from the desert comes awful and shrill.** *Advent.* This is in extensive use in the Unitarian hymn-books of America.
2. **Come, let us sound her praise abroad.** *Charity.*
3. **Father, I may not ask for less.** *Charity.* This is st. ii.–v. of No. 2, with a new introductory stanza. In this form the hymn was given in the *Leeds H. Bk.*, 1853.
4. **Give thanks to God the Lord.** *Victory through Christ.* Limited in use, although a hymn of much spirit. It appeared in the Belfast *Ps. & Hys.*, 1818.
5. **O had I the wings of a dove.** *Retirement.* This hymn is not suited to congregational use. It appeared in the Belfast *Ps. & Hys.*, 1818.

The original texts of these hymns are in *Lyra Brit.*, 1867, from whence also most of the biographical facts have been taken. A few of Drummond's hymns, in addition to those named, are found in some American Unitarian collections. [J. J.]

Dryden, John. The name of this great English poet has recently assumed a new importance to the students of hymns, from a claim made on his behalf in regard to a considerable body of translations from the Latin published after his death (1701), in a *Primer* of 1706. The discussion of this point will preclude us from giving more than an outline of his life.

i. *Biography.*—John Dryden was the s. of Erasmus, the third son of Sir Erasmus Dryden,

and was b. at Aldwinkle, All Saints, Northants, Aug. 9, 1631. He was educated under Dr. Busby at Westminster, and entered Trin. Coll., Cambridge, in 1650. He took his B.A. in 1654, and resided nearly 7 years, though without a fellowship. He was of Puritan blood on both his father's and mother's side, and his training found expression in his first great poem, *Heroic Stanzas on the death of Oliver Cromwell*, 1658. In 1660, however, he turned, like the bulk of England, Royalist, and in his *Astraea Redux*, and in *A Panegyric on the Coronation* (1661), celebrated the Restoration. In 1663 he married Lady Elizabeth Howard. The marriage was apparently not a happy one; and there seems to be plain proof of Dryden's unfaithfulness. In 1670 he was made Poet Laureate and Historiographer Royal, and he retained these posts until the accession of William (1688). He had joined the Roman Church in 1685, and remained steadfast to it at the fall of James II. This change is of special significance, as will appear below, in regard to his translations from the Latin. It greatly straitened his means, and compelled him to great literary exertion in his closing years. He d. May 18, 1701, and was buried in Westminster Abbey.

The poems of Dryden show high excellence in fields widely different from another. He was for years the leader of the English stage, as a writer of tragedy, comedy, and tragi-comedy. The specialities of his plays were a large substitution of the heroic couplet for blank verse, in imitation of Corneille, plots full of exaggerated passion, intrigue, and rant, and a catch-word dialogue. These features were caricatured by Buckingham and others in the *Rehearsal* (acted 1671). The gross immorality of his dramas has long made them unreadable; but his influence on poetry has been enduring. No metre so long dominated style as his heroic couplet, which, though inferior to Pope's in polish and precision, excels it in resonance, freedom and audacity, "The long resounding march and energy divine." He was the first to make poetry a lucid vehicle for political and religious discussion, in the *Religio Laici* (1682), and *The Hind and Panther* (1687). The finest satires in English are *Absalom and Achitophel* (Part i., 1681; Part ii., 1682, to which he contributed only a portion, the rest being by Nahum Tate), *The Medal*, and *Mac Flecknoe* (1682). He gave a new energy and fulness of meaning to the work of translation through his classical reproductions, of which his *Virgil* is the finest specimen (pub. in 1697). *Alexander's Feast* remains one of the most brilliant English odes. His prefaces and dedications had a large influence on our prose style, and are the first material efforts in the province of poetical criticism. The salient points of his genius are a transcendent literary force continually exerting itself in fresh forms; and that narrowing of the work of poetry to matters of political, social, human interest, which ruled supreme in Pope and his followers. (See *Dryden:* by Mr. G. Saintsbury, *Men of Letters* Series.)

ii. *Hymn Translations.* — Until recently, Dryden's known contributions to hymnody consisted of only three pieces. The best known of these is the *tr.* of "Veni Creator," pub. in vol. iii. of his *Miscellanies*, in 1693. Sir Walter Scott, in his *Life of Dryden*, 1808, pub. a *tr.* of the "Te Deum" ("Thee Sovereign God our grateful accents praise"), and a *tr.* of "Ut queant laxis," the hymn at Evensong for St. John the Baptist's Day (Scott calls it "St. John's Eve") ("O sylvan Prophet").

Mr. W. T. Brooke has pointed out one or two facts that slightly shake Scott's attribution of these two pieces to Dryden. He has discovered the *tr.* of the "Te Deum" in Dodd's *Christian's Magazine*, 1760, contributed by J. Duncombe, and *attributed to Pope.* And Scott's account of the two pieces is confused. He received them from a Mrs. Jackson, who told him that they were mentioned in Butler's "Tour through Italy," and that after Butler's death they passed into the hands of the celebrated Dr. Alban, and so came to hers. They are not however mentioned in the published edition of Butler's *Tour*; and "Butler" and "Dr. Alban" are the same person—Dr. Alban Butler, author of *The Lives of the Saints*. Alban Butler's *Tour* was edited and published by Charles Butler, his nephew, who also wrote a *Life of Alban Butler*. The confusion cannot now be unravelled: but is not enough to discredit Scott's decision, which may have rested on the handwriting. The *tr.* of the "Te Deum" is not like Pope, and has a Drydenesque Alexandrine in it, and other marks of Dryden's manner. One great Roman Catholic poet was perhaps confused with the other.

These three pieces, however, with slight variation of text, have been discovered independently by Mr. Orby Shipley and Mr. W. T. Brooke, in *The Primer, or Office of the B. V. Mary, in English*, 1706; and the discovery has led them to a strong conviction that the bulk of the 120 *trs.* of Latin hymns in this book are also Dryden's. It is shown under *Primers*, that there are remarkable evidences of unity of hand in these *trs.* Is this hand Dryden's? The case for Dryden is a constructive one, and may be thus summarised :—

The *tr.* in Scott, "O sylvan Prophet," is in a metre unknown to previous editions of the *Primer*; and there are altogether 11 *trs.*, generally representing Latin Sapphics, in the book in this metre. Five of these *trs.* have a further internal link in having the same gloria; three in having another common *gloria*. The presumption is irresistible that they are all by the author of "O sylvan Prophet." Again, the *tr.* of the "Te Deum" (also in *Scott*) is one of 8 pieces in Dryden's great metre, which is also new to the *Primers'* heroic couplets. Though not linked by common glorias, the tone of all these is Drydenesque, especially the *tr.* of "Sacris Solemniis," which has these characteristic lines, "They eat the Lamb with legal rites and gave Their mother synagogue a decent grave," and closes with an Alexandrine. The *tr.* "Creator Spirit, by Whose aid" is followed by two others in the same metre, which have a variation (in a single word) of its gloria. The three known hymns of Dryden are thus heads of groups presumptively of the same parentage. Proceeding further in the book, the large group of 8-syllable hymns exhibits 35, which are curiously marked as by a single hand through their glorias (see **Primers**). They have several Drydenesque phrases (e.g. "noon of night,' "gleamy white," a technical use of "yielding," "liquid," "equal"), turns of expression and cadences, and a significant link with the *tr.* of the "Te Deum" in the term "vocal blood" (cf. "vocal tears" in 2 other *trs.*) found in the *tr.* of "Deus tuorum militum." This technical method of inquiry when applied still further to other groups linked by a single gloria certainly points in the same direction; Drydenisms, links with groups already named, an occasional appearance of layman freedom of expression, and in one case ("Audit tyrannus" *tr.*), an echo of the heroic plays, emerge. The least characteristic group is that containing *trs.* of "Ave maris stella" and "Jesu dulcis memoria," in C. M.; and the latter *tr.* ("Jesu, the only thought of Thee"), beautiful as it is, is in the main only the *tr.* from the *Primer* of 1685 recast in C. M. But the adoption of C. M.—a new metre in these *Primers*—would be natural in one previously long familiar with the metrical Psalms; the *tr.* of "Ave maris stella" has the recurrent use of "equal," which is a mannerism of Dryden: and the word "way" in the *tr.* of "Jesu dulcis memoria" is used similarly in that of "Immense coeli conditor."

The result of a minute investigation, purposely conducted on somewhat mechanical lines, is a presumption almost amounting to proof, that the bulk of these 120 *trs.* are not only by the same hand, but by the hand of Dryden. A measure of doubt must however attach to the least characteristic pieces, from the following considerations :—

(1) The *trs.* of "Stabat Mater" and "Dies Irae" are reprinted from the *Primer* of 1687. This fact is of course not decisive against their parentage by Dryden, as it may be argued, that the *Primer* of 1687 also contains Dryden translations. But (2) the *tr.* of

the "Dies Irae" seems to be, notwithstanding some Drydenesque phrases, by Lord Roscommon. It is found in a text considerably varied from that of 1706 in Tate's *Miscellanea Sacra* (1696 and 1698); and is there attributed to Lord Roscommon. It appears also, but in a text identical with that of 1706, in Tonson's *Poems by The Earl of Roscommon*, 1717, which professes to give only the "truly genuine" poems of the Earl. If this *tr.* is not Dryden's, others also may not be his. And (3) the *Primer* of B. V. M. in which these *trs.* are found did not appear till five years after Dryden's death; and may have been edited by some one else. Mr. W. T. Brooke has drawn attention to variations in the text of *Scott* from that of the *Primer*; which may be accounted for by editorial revision; and the editor may have had blanks to fill in which Dryden had left.

It would be most natural to suppose that the *Primer* would be edited by a priest; but the fact that it is difficult to say whether the text in *Scott* or in the *Primer* is the more characteristic of Dryden either points to the existence of two authentic texts of the poet, or a revision by some one thoroughly intimate with Dryden's manner, e.g. (as Mr. Brooke acutely conjectures), Charles Dryden, who may have taken his father's MSS. with him to Rome.

The argument in favour of Dryden is presented with great force and skill by Mr. Orby Shipley in the *Dublin Review*, October, 1884, and in the preface to his *Annus Sanctus*.

In corroboration of the evidence given above, Mr. Shipley has collected some Roman Catholic traditions, which ascribe to Dryden "a considerable number" of Latin *trs.* "Jesu dulcis memoria" and "Dies Irae" are said to have been translated as penances. These traditions are however very indefinite; in some cases they do not date earlier than the present century; and in some (see Preface to *Annus Sanctus*) they are mistaken. He seeks a further corroboration of the theory from the appearance of several of these *trs.* in editions of *The Manual of Prayers*, 1750, and *The Garden of the Soul*, 1737. But it is shown under *Primers* that these books afford no real evidence on this subject.   [H. L. B.]

Du ewiger Abgrund der seligen Liebe. *N. L. von Zinzendorf.* [*The Love of God.*] Written for the birthday, Sept. 21, 1726, of his friend Count Henkel of Oderberg. Appeared as No. 7 in the "Andere Zugabe," c. 1730, to his 1725-8 *Sammlung geist- und lieblicher Lieder* (3rd ed. 1731, No. 19), in 8 st. of 10 l., entitled "Ein Erweckungs Lied an Fest-Tagen," and repeated in the *Herrnhut G. B.*, 1735, No. 11; in the *Brüder G. B.*, 1778, No. 36, in 3 st.; also in Knapp's ed. of Zinzendorf's *Geistliche Lieder*, 1845, p. 72; and in his own *Ev. L. S.*, 1850, No. 1136. *Tr.* as :—

1. **Eternal depth of Love Divine**, a free *tr.* of st. 1, 2, 4, 7, by J. Wesley in *H. and S. Poems*, 1739 (*P. Works*, 1868-72, vol. i. p. 173). It was not included in the *Wes. H. Bk.* till in the *Suppl.* of 1830, No. 586, omitting Wesley's st. iii. ll. 5-8, and iv. ll. 1-4. This form is in the new ed. 1875, No. 655, and in the *Wesley Association* and *New Connexion Collections*. With the omission of the last 8 lines it is No. 94 in the Amer. Meth. Epis. *Hymns*, 1849. These omitted lines are given as No. 730 : "O King of Glory, Thy rich grace," in the same collection.

2. **Thou deep abyss of blessed Love**, a free *tr.* of st. 1, 4, 8, by Mrs. Charles in her *Voice of Christian Life in Song*, 1858, p. 243, and thence in *Holy Song*, 1869, No. 298.

Another *tr.* is :—

"Ye bottomless depths of God's infinite love," by J. Gambold. The *tr.* of st. 1 appears as No. 238 in the *Appendix* of 1743 to the *Moravian H. Bk.*, 1742, and the full form as No. 392 in pt. ii., 1746 (1886, No. 24). Of this 3 st. beginning " O bottomless depths " appear in the Schaff-Gilman *Lib. of Rel. Poetry*, ed. 1883. [J. M.]

Du himilisco trohtin. [*Supplication.*] Wackernagel, ii. p. 24, quotes this 12th cent. hymn in 2 st. of 4 l., entitled " The Prayer of Sigihard." Sigihard was the writer of the Freising MS. of Otfrid's works (now at Munich), and in a note at the end of this MS. says, " Ego sigihardus indignus presbyter scripsi. Unaldo episcopus istud evangelium fieri jussit." *Tr.* as " Thou Heavenly Lord of Light," by *Miss Winkworth*, 1869, p. 29. [J. M.]

Du schönstes Gotteskind. *G. Tersteegen.* [*Christmas.*] 1st pub. in the 2nd ed., 1735, of his *Geistliches Blumengärtlein*, as No. 46 in Bk. iii., in 11 st. of 8 l., entitled " The great Christmas gift." Included, omitting st. 4, 5, 10, 11, as No. 704 in Bunsen's *Versuch*, 1833 (*Allg. G. B.*, 1846, No. 48). The only *tr.* in C. U. is :—

Thou fairest Child Divine, a good *tr.* from Bunsen, by Miss Winkworth in her *Lyra Ger.*, 2nd Ser., 1858, p. 16. Included, omitting the *tr.* of st. 8, as No. 359 in *Ps. and Hys.*, Bedford, 1864. Two centos are found in American hymnals :—

(1) " I was a foe to God," beginning with st. 2, as No. 373 in the Episcopal *H. for Ch. & Home*, 1860.
(2) " Once blind with sin and self," beginning with st. 3 in the *Dutch Reformed H. Bk.*, 1869, the *Bapt. Praise Bk.*, 1871, *H. & Songs of Praise*, N. Y., 1874, &c. [J. M.]

Du unvergleichlich's Gut. *J. Scheffler.* [*Love to God.*] Appeared as No. 195 in Bk. v. of his *Heilige Seelenlust*, Breslau, 1668, p. 655 (*Werke*, 1862, i. p. 323), in 8 st. of 6 l., entitled " She [The Soul] contrasts the Majesty of God with her Nothingness." Included as No. 726 in Freylinghausen's *G. B.*, 1705, and recently, as No. 15, in Knapp's *Ev. L. S.* 1850 (1865, No. 15). The only *tr.* in C. U. is :—

O God, of good the unfathom'd sea, a vigorous and full rendering by J. Wesley in *H. and Sac. Poems*, 1739 (*P. Works*, 1868-72, vol. i. p. 141), and thence in full, as No. 36, in the *H. & Spiritual Songs*, 1753, and as No. 5 in the *Pocket H. Bk.*, 1785. It did not appear in the *Wes. H. Bk.*, 1780, but was added in an ed. between 1797 and 1809, and is No. 38 in the revised ed. 1875. Various forms beginning with st. i. appear in the *Leeds H. Bk.*, 1853 ; the *Meth. N. Connexion*, 1863 ; the *Irish Ch. Hyl.*, 1869-73 ; *Baptist Hyl.*, 1879 ; *Westminster Abbey H. Bk.*, 1883, &c. ; and in America in the *Meth. Epis. Coll.*, 1849 ; *Evang. Hyl.*, N. Y., 1880 ; *Canadian Presb. H. Bk.*, 1880, &c. In the *Meth. Epis. South H. Bk.* 1847, No. 24, begins with st. 5, " Fountain of good ! all blessing flows."

Another *tr.* is :—" O Good beyond compare," by *Miss Winkworth*, 1869, p. 249. [J. M.]

Duffield, George, jun., D.D., s. of the Rev. Dr. Duffield, a Presbyterian Minister, was b. at Carlisle, Pennsylvania, Sept. 12, 1818, and graduated at Yale College, and at the Union Theological Seminary, New York. From 1840 to 1847 he was a Presbyterian Pastor at Brooklyn ; 1847 to 1852, at Bloomfield, New Jersey ; 1852 to 1861, at Philadelphia ; 1861 to 1865, at Adrian, Michigan ; 1865 to 1869, at Galesburg, Illinois ; 1869, at Saginaw City, Michigan ; and from 1869 at Ann Arbor and Lansing, Michigan. His hymns include :—

1. **Blessed Saviour, Thee I love.** *Jesus only.* One of four hymns contributed by him to Darius E. Jones's *Temple Melodies*, 1851. It is in 6 st. of 6 l. In Dr. Hatfield's *Church H. Bk.* it is given in 3 st. The remaining three hymns of the same date are :—

2. **Parted for some anxious days.** *Family Hymn.*
3. **Praise to our heavenly Father, God.** *Family Union.*
4. **Slowly in sadness and in tears.** *Burial.*
5. **Stand up, stand up for Jesus.** *Soldiers of the Cross.* The origin of this hymn is given in *Lyra Sac. Americana*, 1868, p. 298, as follows :—

" I caught its inspiration from the dying words of that noble young clergyman, Rev. Dudley Atkins Tyng, rector of the Epiphany Church, Philadelphia, who died about 1854. His last words were, 'Tell them to stand up for Jesus: now let us sing a hymn.' As he had been much persecuted in those pro-slavery days for his persistent course in pleading the cause of the oppressed, it was thought that these words had a peculiar significance in his mind ; as if he had said, 'Stand up for Jesus in the person of the downtrodden slave.' (Luke v. 18.) "

Dr. Duffield gave it, in 1858, in MS. to his Sunday School Superintendent, who pub. it on a small handbill for the children. In 1858 it was included in *The Psalmist*, in 6 st. of 8 l. It was repeated in several collections and in *Lyra Sac. Amer.*, 1868, from whence it passed, sometimes in an abbreviated form, into many English collections. [F. M. B.]

Duffield, Samuel Augustus Willoughby, s. of G. Duffield, jun., was b. at Brooklyn, Sept. 24, 1843, and graduated at Yale College, 1863. In 1866 he was licensed, and in 1867 ordained as a Presbyterian Minister, and is now [1886] Pastor of Westminster Church, Bloomfield, New Jersey. He pub. in 1867 a *tr.* of Bernard's *Hora novissima* (q.v.) : *Warp and Woof ; a Book of Verse*, 1868 (copyright, 1870) ; and *The Burial of the Dead* (in conjunction with his father), 1882. In the *Laudes Domini*, N.Y., 1884, the following *trs.* and an original hymn are by him :—

1. **Holy Spirit, come and shine.** A *tr.* of "Veni Sancte Spiritus." 1883.
2. **O Christ, the Eternal Light.** A *tr.* of "Christe lumen perpetuum." 1883.
3. **O land, relieved from sorrow.** *On Heaven*, written in 1875.
4. **O what shall be, O when shall be.** A *tr.* of "O quanta qualia." 1883.
5. **To Thee, O Christ, we ever pray.** A *tr.* of "Christe precamur annue." 1883. [J. J.]

Dum, Christe, confixus cruci. *C. Coffin.* [*Passiontide.*] Appeared in the *Paris Brev.*, 1736, and again in his *Hymni Sacri.* of the same year. It is the Ferial hymn at Lauds in Passion week, and till Maundy Thursday. It is also in the *Lyons Brev.* and others. The text is given in J. Chandler's *Hys. of the Prim. Church*, 1837, No. 65, and in Card. Newman's *Hymni Ecclesiae*, 1838 and 1865. *Tr.* as :—

O Thou, Who in the pains of death. By W. Cooke, written in 1872 for the *Hymnary*, No. 238.

Translations not in C. U. :—
1. O Thou, that nail'd upon the bleeding tree. I. Williams, *British Mag.*, April, 1834, and *Trs. from Paris Brev.*, 1839.
2. Whilst in the agonies of death. *J. Chandler*, 1837.
3. While on the Cross, O Christ! in death. *J. D. Chambers*, 1857. [W. A. S.]

Dum morte victor obrutâ. *C. Coffin.* [*SS. Philip and James.*] This hymn is in the *Paris Brev.*, 1736, where it is given as the hymn for the first Vespers of SS. Philip and James. So also in the *Lyons* and modern French Breviaries. It was included in the author's *Hymni Sacri*, 1736, and is also in J. Chandler's *Hys. of the Prim. Church*, 1837, No. 94, and in Card. Newman's *Hymni Ecclesiae*, 1838 and 1865. *Tr.* as:—

The Lord hath burst the bonds of death. By J. Chandler, in his *Hys. of the Prim. Church*, 1837, p. 105, in 6 st. of 4 l. The hymn No. 358 in the *Hymnary*, 1872, although beginning with the same first line, and assigned to Chandler in the Index, is so altered as to be almost beyond recognition. The most that can be said of it is that it is based on Chandler's *tr.* Another *tr.* is:—

When from Death's chambers Christ triumphant rose.
I. Williams, 1839.   [W. A. S.]

Duncan, Mary, née Lundie, daughter of the Rev. Robert Lundie, Parish Minister of Kelso, was b. at Kelso, April 26, 1814. On July 11, 1836, she was married to the Rev. William Wallace Duncan, Parish Minister of Cleish, Kinross-shire. In the end of December, 1839, she took a chill, which resulted in a fever, terminating fatally on Jan. 5, 1840. Her gifts and graces were early consecrated to her Master's service. She was a devoted wife and mother, and a true helpmeet to her husband in his parochial work. Her hymns, mostly written for her children between July and December, 1839, appeared, in 1841, in her *Memoir*, by her mother, and were issued separately, in 1842, as *Rhymes for my Children*, to the number of 23. The best known are, " Jesus, tender Shepherd, hear me," and " My Saviour, be Thou near me."   [J. M.]

Dunlop, Thomas, seventh son of Mr. James Dunlop, of Kilmarnock, was born at Kilmarnock, May 10, 1839. After studying at the Universities of Glasgow and Edinburgh, he became, in 1867, minister of the U. P. Church, Balfron, Stirlingshire, and in 1871 joint minister of Bristo U. P. Church, Edinburgh. This charge he resigned in 1875, and in the same year became minister of Emmanuel Congregational Church, Bootle. In 1874 he was appointed a member of the Psalmody Committee of the U. P. Church, and contributed the hymn, " I cannot, no, I will not let Thee go," to their *Presbyterian Hymnal*, 1876. In the Draft *Hymnal*, 1874, it began, " Jesus, I cannot, will not let Thee go," and contained 8 st. This form is included in the *Evang. Union Hymnal*, 1878, No. 152. He has recently been a frequent contributor to the Poets' Corner of the *Christian Leader*, a religious paper, pub. in Glasgow. [J. M.]

Dunn, Catherine Hannah, dau. of a Nottingham bookseller and printer, was b. at Nottingham, Nov. 7, 1815, and d. May 18, 1863. In 1857 she pub. a little volume of 36 *Hymns from the German*. Of these the best known are noted under " Hilf, Herr Jesu, lass gelingen " and " Nun sich der Tag geendet hat." They deserve more notice than they have as yet received. That at p. 37 is from " Liebster Jesu in den Tagen " [Freylinghausen's *G. B.*, 1714, No. 249], that at p. 98 from " Bete nur! bete nur," by J. G. F. Köhler [Knapp's *Ev. L. S.*, 1850, No. 1623],

and that at p. 119 from " Esist vollbracht! Gottlob es ist vollbracht." [For this last see Gryphius, A.]   [J. J.]

Dunn, Robinson Porter, D.D., an American Baptist, b. in 1825; was for some time Professor in Brown University, Providence, Rhode Island; and d. Aug. 28, 1867. His hymns, mainly translated from the Latin and other sources, include, " No, no, it is not dying"; " Jesus, Jesus, visit me"; " Jesus, our fainting spirits cry"; " We sinners, Lord, with earnest heart" (part of " Jesus, our fainting spirits cry," q.v.). These *trs.* appeared in some of the American hymn-books, and are in C. U.   [J. J.]

Dutton, Anne, b. cir. 1698, d. 1765, was a native of Northampton, and at the age of 22 became wife of Benj. Dutton, Baptist minister of Great Gransden, Hunts. In 1743 her husband, on returning from a visit to America, was wrecked and lost near to the English coast. From that time to her death she devoted her time and much of her income to the service of religion. 13 vols. of her letters were published, some being translated into the Dutch language. She was the author of several theological treatises, and in 1734 published a poem entitled, *A narrative of the wonders of Grace, in six parts*, to which was added *A Poem on the special work of the Spirit in the hearts of the Elect*, also *Sixty-one hymns on several Subjects*. These poems and hymns were reprinted in 1833, with a *Memoir* of the author, by John Andrews Jones.

The hymns are prosaic in style, and may be described as short chapters of Calvinistic theology set to rhyme and metre. They have almost entirely passed out of use. One beginning " Faith is a precious grace," not improbably suggested Beddome's well-known hymn with the same first line. And another on " The Soul's joy in God as its Portion " so much resembles, both in thought and expression, Ryland's fine hymn, " O Lord, I would delight in Thee," that it seems almost certain that, when writing it, he had in his mind, perhaps unconsciously, memories of Mrs. Dutton's composition.

                                    [W. R. S.]

Dutton, Deodatus, jun., b. cir. 1810, was a native of Monson, Massachusetts, U.S. He was a Licentiate of the third Presbytery, New York, but died before ordination, about 1832. His hymns in C. U. are:—

1. **On Thibet's snow-capt mountain.** *Missions.* This appeared in pt. ii. of the *Christian Lyrics*, 1831, in 3 st. of 8 l. It is an imitation of Bp. Heber's " From Greenland's icy mountains."

2. **O where can the soul find relief from its foes?** *Heaven.* The date and first pub. of this hymn is uncertain. It is given, together with the above, in the *Plymouth Coll.*, 1855. [F. M. B.]

Dust and ashes, sin and guilt. *J. Montgomery.* [*Image of Christ desired.*] In the M. MSS., this hymn is dated " Jan. 23, 1833." It was pub. in Montgomery's *Original Hymns*, 1853, p. 168, in 3 st. of 6 l., and headed " Renewal in the Image of Christ." Its use is mainly confined to America.

Dwight, Timothy, D.D. This is the most important name in early American hymnology, as it is also one of the most illustrious in American literature and education. He was b. at Northampton, Massachusetts, May 14, 1752, and graduated at Yale College, 1769; was a tutor there from

1771 to 1777. He then became for a short time a chaplain in the United States Army, but passed on in 1783 to Fairfield, Connecticut, where he held a pastorate, and taught in an Academy, till his appointment, in 1795, as President of Yale College. His works are well known, and need no enumeration. He d. at New Haven, Jan. 11, 1817. In 1797 the General Association of Connecticut, being dissatisfied with Joel Barlow's 1785 revision of *Watts*, requested Dwight to do the work *de novo*. This he did liberally, furnishing in some instances several paraphrases of the same psalm, and adding a selection of Hymns, mainly from Watts. The book appeared as—

" *The Psalms of David, &c. . . . By I. Watts, D.D. A New Edition in which the Psalms omitted by Dr. Watts are versified, local passages are altered, and a number of Psalms are versified anew in proper metres. By Timothy Dwight, D.D., &c. . . . To the Psalms is added a Selection of Hymns,*" 1800.

Dwight's lyrics are all professedly psalms, but they are by no means literal versions. His original compositions number 33. Of these many are still in common use, the most important being :—

1. **Blest be the Lord, Who heard my prayer.** *Ps. xxviii.* This is the second part of Ps. xxviii., in 5 st. of 4 l. It is in the English *N. Conq.*, 1859.

2. **I love Thy kingdom, Lord.** *Ps. cxxxvii.* This is version three of Ps. 137, in 8 st. of 4 l., and is in extensive use at the present time throughout the States. It is also included in many English, Irish, and Scottish collections, sometimes in the original form, as in Alford's *Year of Praise*, 1867 ; again as, " I love Thy Church, O God," which opens with the second stanza, as in the Scottish *Evangelical Union Hymnal*, 1878, in 3 st., and " We love Thy kingdom, Lord," in the *Irish Church Hymnal*, 1873. In Cleveland's *Lyra Sac. Amer.* 6 st. only are given from the original.

Next to this in popularity are his 2nd and 3rd renderings of *Ps. lxxxviii.* :—

3. **Shall man, O God of life and light.** (*3rd st.*)

4. **While life prolongs its precious light.** (*2nd st.*) Both of which are in extensive use. From his 4th version of the same Ps. (88), the following hymns have been compiled, each opening with the stanza indicated :—

5. **Just o'er the grave I hung.** *Stanza ii.*

6. **I saw beyond the tomb.** *Stanza iv.*

7. **Ye sinners, fear the Lord.** *Stanza xii.* This last is found in Spurgeon's *O. O. H. Bk.* The original version consists of 13 stanzas.

8. **O Thou Whose sceptre earth and seas obey.** *Ps. lxxii.* This is his second version of this Psalm, and was given in the *Comprehensive Rippon*, 1844.

The following, most of which are of a more jubilant character, are well known :—

9. **How pleasing is Thy voice.** *Ps. lxv.*

10. **In Zion's sacred gates.** *Ps. cl.*

11. **Lord of all worlds, incline Thy gracious [bounteous] ear.** *Ps. liii.*

12. **Now to Thy sacred house.** *Ps. xliii.*, st. 3.

13. **Sing to the Lord most high.** *Ps. c.*

14. **In barren wilds shall living waters spring.** *Ps. liii.*

15. **Lord, in these dark and dismal days.** *Ps. cxxxvii.*

No. 9 is found in *Lyra Sac. Amer.*, pp. 101–2, the seven stanzas of the original being abbreviated to five.

In addition to the *Psalms*, Dr. Dwight pub-lished three poems, *The Conquest of Canaan* 1785 ; *Greenfield Hill*, 1794 ; *Triumph of Infidelity*, 1788.   [F. M. B.]

Dyer, Sidney, who served in the U. S. Army from 1831 to c. 1840, is a native of White Creek, Washington County, New York, where he was b. in 1814. On leaving the army he was ordained a Baptist Minister in 1842, and acted first as a Missionary to the Choctaws, then as Pastor in Indianapolis, Indiana (1852), and as Secretary to the Baptist Publication Society, Phila. (1859). He has pub. sundry works, and in the *Southwestern Psalmist*, 1851, 16 of his hymns are found. The following are later and undated :—

1. **Go, preach the blest salvation.** *Missions.* In the *Bapt. Praise Book*, 1871, and *The Bapt. Hy. & Tune Book*, 1871.

2. **Great Framer [Maker] of unnumbered worlds.** *National Humiliation.* In the Boston Unitarian. *Hymn [and Tune] Bk.*, 1868, and others.

3. **When faint and weary toiling.** *Work whilst it is day.* In the *Bapt. Praise Book*, 1871.

4. **Work, for the night is coming.** *Duty.* This hymn is in wider use than the foregoing, but though often ascribed to Dyer, is really by *Miss Anna L. Walker,* of Canada, who pub. a volume of *Poems,* 1868. S. Dyer, in 1851, wrote a hymn on the same subject for a Sunday-school in Indianapolis, and hence the confusion between the two. In 1882 a cento beginning with the same stanza was given in Whiting's (English) *Hys. for the Church Catholic*, No. 366. Of this cento, st. i., ii. are by Miss Walker ; and st. iii., iv. by Miss Whiting, daughter of the editor of that collection.   [F. M. B.]

E

E., a signature in *The Associate Minstrels*, 1810, i.e. Mrs. Joan E. Conder.

E. F. H., in *Freedom's Lyre*, N. Y., 1840, i.e. E. F. Hatfield.

E. G., in *Old Version.* See O. V., § ix. 6.

E. L. B., in the *People's H.*, 1867, i.e. E. C. Leaton-Blenkinsopp.

E. O. D., in Mrs. C. Brock's *Children's Hymn Book*, 1881, i.e. Henrietta O. Dobrée.

E.—Y. D. R., in the *Christian Observer,* i.e. Sir Robert Grant.

Each coming night, O Lord, we see. *J. D. Burns.* [*Evening.*] 1st pub. in his *Evening Hymn* (a small volume of hymns and prayers), 1857, No. 16, on " Daily Mercies," and in 7 st. of 4 l. In 1858 it was given in 6 st. in the Bap. *Ps. & Hys.*, No. 914, and has been repeated elsewhere. It is not in the author's *Poems*, 1865.

Early English Hymnody [English Hymnody, Early].

Earth below is teeming, heaven is bright above. *J. S. B. Monsell.* [*Harvest.*] In his *Hys. of Love and Praise, &c.*, 1863, this hymn is given in 4 st. of 8 l. and a chorus. It is based upon the words, " They joy before Thee, according to the joy in harvest." For his *Parish Hymnal*, 1873, No. 197, st. iii. and iv. were partly rewritten, and materially improved. In Snepp's *Songs of G. & G.*, 1872. No. 851, the *Meth. S, S. H. Bk.*, 1879, the

American *Laudes Domini*, 1884, the 1863 text is followed, Monsell's later text being apparently unknown to the compilers.   [J. J.]

Earth hath detain'd me prisoner long. *I. Watts.* [*Praise.*] This "Song of the Angels above" appeared in his *Horæ Lyricæ*, 1706, in 22 st. of 4 l. In Toplady's *Ps. & Hys.*, 1776, 12 st. were given as No. 175, beginning with st. ii. in an altered form as "Earth has engross'd my love too long." The centos in modern hymnals, as Spurgeon's *O. O. H. Bk.*, 1866; Hatfield's *Church H. Bk.*, N. Y., 1872, and others are taken from this arrangement.   [J. J.]

Earth is passed away and gone. *H. Alford.* [*Advent.*] Contributed to his *Ps. & Hys.*, 1844, No. 4, in 4 st. of 4 l., and repeated unaltered in his *Year of Praise*, 1867, but appointed for the 6th Sun. after Epiphany. It is found in several collections in G. Britain and America, including the *Harrow School H. Bk.* and *Songs for the Sanctuary*, N. Y.,1865.

Earth, rejoice, the Lord is King. *C. Wesley.* [*Confidence in God.*] Appeared in *Hys. & S. Poems*, 1740, p. 115, in 14 st. of 4 l., and headed "To be sung in a Tumult." (*P. Works*, 1868-72, vol. i. p. 296.) In the *Supp.* to the *Wes. H. Bk.*, 1830, 6 st. were given as "Earth, rejoice; *our* Lord is King," and this arrangement is repeated in the revised ed. of 1875. In some of the American hymn-books the original reading is retained.   [J. J.]

Earth to earth, and dust to dust. Lord, we own, &c. *J. H. Gurney.* [*The Resurrection.*] Contributed to his *Coll. of Hys.* (*Lutterworth Coll.*), 1838, No. 42, in 4 st. of 6 l., and repeated in his *Ps. & Hys.* (*Marylebone Coll.*), 1851, No. 36. It is given, and generally unaltered, in several of the best collections in G. Britain and America. It is a distinct hymn in every way from Dr. G. Croly's "Earth to earth, and dust to dust! Here the evil and the just" (*Lyra Brit.*, 1867, p. 170), and is very suitable for funerals. [J. J.]

East, John, sometime Curate of St. Michael's, Bath, and Rector of Croscombe, Somerset, pub. :—

(1) *Psalmody for the Churches: A Collection of Psalms and Hymns arranged for Public Worship in the Churches and Chapels throughout the Rectory of Bath*, &c., &c., 1838. (2) *The Sabbath Harp*, a collection of Sacred Poetry, N.D.; and (3) *My Saviour; or, Devotional Meditations in Prose and Verse*, 3rd ed., 1836.

The following hymns by this author have come into C. U. :—

1. **Come unto Me, ye weary, come.** *Invitation and Response.* In his *Sabbath Harp*, N.D., in 4 st. of 4 l., and signed "J. E."

2. **Lord of the Soul and its light.** *The Light of Life.* From the *Sabbath Harp* into a few American hymnals.

3. **There is a fold whence none can stray.** *Heaven.* In *My Saviour*, &c., 3rd ed.; 1836, *Meditation*, No. 44, in 6 st. of 4 l.

4. **Where is my faith if I survey?** *Increase of Faith.* desired. Sometimes ascribed to J. East, but not traced to his works.   [W. T. B.]

Eastburn, James Wallis, s. of a New York bookseller and brother of Dr. Eastburn, Bp. of Massachusetts, was b. in London, England, Sept. 26, 1797. The family removed to New York in 1803, and he was educated at Columbia College, New York, where he graduated in 1816. Taking Holy Orders in 1818, he subsequently became a

Rector at Accomac, Virginia, where his "abundant and successful labours" were cut short by an early death. He d. at Santa Cruz, Dec. 2, 1819. With Robert C. Sands, an intimate friend, he wrote a poem on the history of an Indian Chief, which was pub. as *Yamoyden*, in 1820. His hymns include :—

1. **O holy, holy, holy Lord, Bright in Thy deeds,** &c. [*Holy Trinity.*] This hymn is said by Dr. Hatfield to have been written in 1815. It was included in the *Prayer-Book Coll.*, 1826, and again in other collections. It is a "Ter Sanctus" of merit, and is widely used.

2. **Mountains of Israel.** This is found in some old collections, and in Griswold's *Sacred Poets*, 1848, p. 482.

3. **Strangers no more we wildly rove.** *The Spiritual Temple.* This is given in *Lyra Sac. Americana.*   [F. M. B.]

Ebenezer, a *nom de plume* of Job Hupton in the *Gospel Magazine.*

Eber, Paul, s. of Johannes Eber, master tailor at Kitzingen, Bavaria, was b. at Kitzingen, Nov. 8, 1511. He was sent in 1523 to the Gymnasium at Ansbach, but being forced by illness to return home, was on his way thrown from horseback and dragged more than a mile, remaining as a consequence deformed ever after. In 1525 he entered the St. Lorentz school at Nürnberg, under Joachim Camerarius, and in 1532 went to the University of Wittenberg, where he graduated 1536, and thereafter became tutor in the Philosophical Faculty. He was appointed Professor of Latin in 1544, then in 1557 Professor of Hebrew and Castle preacher, and in 1558 Town preacher and General Superintendent of the Electorate, receiving in 1559 the degree D.D. from the University. He d. at Wittenberg, Dec. 10, 1569 (*Koch*, i. 271-278; *Allg. Deutsche Biog.*, v. 529).

At Wittenberg he was a close friend of Melanchthon, was privy to all his plans, and conducted the greater part of his correspondence. After Melanchthon's death in 1560, he became leader of his party, and had to engage in various controversies with the Crypto-Calvinists, &c.; the seeds of his fatal illness being sown on his return journey from the fruitless conference held at Altenburg with the theologians of Jena, which lasted from Oct. 20, 1568, to March 9, 1569.

Eber was, next to Luther, the best poet of the Wittenberg school. His hymns, some of them written for his own children to sing to Luther's melodies, are distinguished for their child-like spirit and beautiful simplicity. 17 hymns have been attributed to him, 4 of which are certainly his, and probably 2 others. Of these 6, 5 have been *tr.* into English, one of which is noted under "Dicimus grates," and the others are:—

i. **Herr Jesu Christ, wahr Mensch und Gott.** *For the Dying.* The first hymn-book in which this simple and beautiful hymn has been found is the Low German *Enchiridion*, pub. at Hamburg, 1565, where it is in 8 st. of 6 l., entitled "A prayer to Christ for a happy departure from this troublous life," and marked as "D. Paulus Eberus Filiolis suis faciebat MDLVII." *Wackernagel*, iv. p. 4, gives this and a second form in High German from the *Psalmen, Geystliche Lieder und Gesänge*, Strassburg, 1569. In his *Bibliographie*, 1855, p. 233, Wackernagel describes an undated broadsheet, which he would date 1550, and at p. 279 says it forms the 1st of *Neun Schöne Geistliche Lieder*, Nürnberg N.D., c. 1556. G. Döring, in his *Choralkunde*, Danzig, 1865, p. 434, says it appeared as "Panie Jezu ty's czlowiek i Bog" in the *Polish Cantional*, ed. by Pastor Seklucyan, and pub. at Königsberg, 1559. Lauxmann, in *Koch*, viii. 591-594, adds that it comforted Eber himself while he lay a-dying, Dec. 10, 1569; was repeated by Hugo Grotius a few minutes before his death, Aug. 28, 1645; and was a favourite hymn of Prince Wolfgang of Anhalt (d. 1566), Christian I., Elector of Saxony (d. 1591), of the Margrave Georg Friedrich of Brandenburg-Kulmbach (d. 1603), &c. Included as No. 820 in the *Unv. L. S.*, 1851. The *trs.* in C. U. are:—

1. Lord Jesus Christ, true Man and God, Who borest. Good and full, by Miss·Winkworth in the 1st Ser. of her *Lyra Ger.*, 1855, p. 239. Of this st. i.-iv. appear in the *Ps. & Hys.*, Bedford, 1859; i., ii., viii. in the *Harrow School H. Bk.*, 1866; and i.-iii., v., viii. in the Pennsylvania Lutheran *Church Bk.*, 1868. A cento from st. ii., ll. 3-6, iii., ll. 1-4, vii., ll. 3-6, beginning, "When from my sight all fades away," is No. 1181 in the American *Sabbath H. Bk.*, 1858.

2. Lord Jesus Christ, true Man and God, ThouWho. A *tr.* by *E. Cronenwett*, in 9 st, of L.M., based on st. i., ii., iv.-viii., as No. 434, in the *Ohio Luth. Hyl.*, 1880.

Other trs. are, (1) "O God, support me, death is near," by *Dr. G. Walker*, 1860, p. 103. (2) "Lord Jesus Christ, true Man and God, who hast," by *E. Massie*, 1867, p. 10.

ii. Wenn wir in höchsten Nöthen sein. *In Trouble.* Founded on a hymn by Joachim Camerarius, his former master at Nürnberg [b. at Bamberg, April 12, 1500, d. as Professor of Greek and Latin at Leipzig, April 17, 1574], which in *Wackernagel*, i. p. 324, runs thus:—

"In tenebris nostrae et densa caligine mentis,
    Cum nihil est toto pectore consilii,
Turbati erigimus, Deus, ad Te lumina cordis
    Nostra, tuamque fides solius erat opem.
Tu rege consiliis actus, Pater optime, nostros,
    Nostrum opus ut laudi serviat omne Tuae."

These lines comforted Melanchthon in 1546; and Lauxmann, in *Koch*, viii. 161-165, thinks probably Eber also. He relates that on Ascension Day, 1547, after the battle of Mühlberg, the Wittenbergers having received a message from the captive Elector to deliver their city to the Emperor Charles V. assembled for prayer in church; and quotes a portion of the prayer by Bugenhagen which greatly resembles Eber's hymn. But that the hymn was written then we have no proof, and the earliest source quoted by *Wackernagel*, iv. p. 6, is the *Naw Betbüchlein*, Dresden 1566, in 7 st. of 4 l., though in his *Bibliographie*, 1855, p. 312, he describes a broadsheet printed at Nürnberg, N.D., c. 1560. In M. Moller's *Meditationes sanctorum Patrum*, Görlitz, 1584, it is entitled "A beautiful prayer of the venerable Dr. Paul Eber, which he composed on the beautiful words of King Jehoshaphat, 2 Chron. xx. 12." Included as No. 583 in the *Unv. L. S.*, 1851.

A "Cry from the depths," though not in despair but in trustful confidence in God, it is one of the finest and most widely used hymns of the Reformation period. *Lauzmann* relates how the singing of this hymn and the prayers of Martin Rinkart (q.v.), Archidiaconus of Eulenburg near Leipzig, prevailed to move the heart of the Swedish Lieutenant-Colonel, who on Feb. 21, 1635, had demanded from the inhabitants a ransom of £4500, but eventually accepted 2000 florins; says that in com memoration of a similar deliverance from the Swedish army in 1642 the hymn was long sung at the end of the Sunday afternoon service at Pegau, near Leipzig, and adds other incidents regarding its use.

The only *tr.* in C. U. is:—

When in the hour of utmost need. A full and very good *tr.* by Miss Winkworth in the 2nd Ser. of her *Lyra Ger.*, 1858, p. 180, and thence as No. 141 in her *C. B. for England*, 1863. Included in full in the Amer. *Presb. Hyl.*, 1874, and the *Ohio Luth. Hyl.*, 1880. In full, though slightly altered, as No. 233, in *H. A. & M.*, 1861, but omitted in the revised ed., 1875. In the *Hymnary*, 1871, *Psalmist*, 1878, J. L. Porter's *Coll.*, 1876, Thring's *Coll.*, 1882, and the *Evang. Hyl.*, N. Y., 1880, st. v. is omitted.

Other trs. are, (1) "When we are under great distress," by *J. C. Jacobi*, 1720, p. 19 (1722, p. 119; 1732, p. 184, altered, and thence as No. 140 in pt. i. of the *Moravian H. Bk.*, 1754). (2) "When neither help nor counsel's nigh," by *Dr. G. Walker*, 1860, p. 89. (3) "When all our way is hedged around," by *N. L. Frothingham*, 1870.

His hymns not in English C. U. are:—

iii. Helft mir Gottes Güte preisen. [*New Year.*] Written on the name Helena, borne both by his wife and his daughter, the initial letters of each st. composing it. *Wackernagel*, iv. p. 6, quotes it from Eichorn's *Geistliche Lieder*, Frankfurt a. Oder, c. 1580, in 6 st. of 8 l., entitled, "A Thanksgiving and Prayer for the New Year, in remembrance of God's goodness, for the Children." Older but less correct forms are noted by *Mützell*, p. 486, as in the Copenhagen *G. B.*, 1571, and the Stettin, 1576. Included as No. 68 in the *Unv. L. S.*, 1851. It is *tr.* as, "Ye Christians in this nation," by *J. C. Jacobi*, 1722, p. 11 (1732, p. 10, altered and beginning, "Come, let us all, with Fervour.")

iv. In Christi Wunden schlaf ich ein. [*For the Dying.*] Appears in Jeremias Weber's *G. B.*, Leipzig, 1638, p. 797, marked as "Another" (the hymn immediately preceding is ascribed to Eber), in 3 st. of 4 l. In the Berlin *G. L. S.*, ed. 1863, No. 1468, the text is slightly varied, and arranged in 2 st. of 6 l. It was first ascribed to Eber in the Nürnberg *G. B.*, 1676. Lauxmann, in *Koch*, viii. 595-601, says of it, "That the hymn is much older than the date of its appearance [i.e. than 1638] seems obvious; that it breathes the childlike spirit of Eber is certain. More than this we cannot say." St. i., ll. 3-6, "Ja Christi Blut und Gerechtigkeit," has been adopted by many pious Germans, young and old, as a prayer in life and death, and Lauxmann relates many interesting incidents regarding its use by A. G. Spangenberg, by Wilhelm Hey, and others. These last lines were adopted by N. L. von Zinzendorf, as the first st. of his well-known hymn, "Christi Blut und Gerechtigkeit" (q.v.). It is *tr.* as, "I fall asleep in Jesus' arms," by *Miss Winkworth*, 1869, p. 121.

[J. M.]

Ebert, Jacob, was b. Jan. 26, 1549, at Sprottau, in Silesia. In the University of Frankfurt a. Oder he was successively Professor of Hebrew, of Ethics, and of Theology, and d. there Feb. 5, 1614 (*Koch*, ii. 270-271; *Bode*, p. 62). One hymn by him has been *tr.*:—

Du Friedefürst, Herr Jesu Christ. [*For Peace.*] 1st pub. in B. Gesius's *Geistliche Deutsche Lieder*, Frankfurt a. Oder, 1601, *folio* 197, in 7 st. of 7 l., entitled "In Time of War, a prayer for peace, D. Jacobus Ebertus," the D denoting that he was also Doctor of Theology. Thence in *Wackernagel*, v. p. 413, and in the *Unv. L. S.*, 1851, No. 585. Sometimes erroneously ascribed to L. Helmbold. The only *tr.* in C. U. is:—

Lord Jesu Christ, the Prince of Peace. A good *tr.*, omitting st. iii., as No. 182, by Miss Winkworth in her *C. B. for England*, 1863. Her *trs.* of st. i., ii., iv. form No. 153 in the *Ohio Luth. Hyl.*, 1880.

Another tr. is: "Lord Jesu, blessed Prince of Peace," by *J. C. Jacobi*, 1722, p. 121 (1732, p. 186), and thence as No. 311 in pt. i. of the *Moravian H. Bk.*, 1754.

[J. M.]

Ebrard, Johann Heinrich August,
D.D., was b. Jan. 18, 1818, at Erlangen,
Bavaria, and is now [1885] honorary professor
and pastor of the French Reformed Church
there.

While chief pastor at Speyer he was principal compiler of the excellent hymn-book for Rhenish Bavaria
(Rhein-Pfalz), pub. at Speyer, 1859, which, like others
of his good works there, was thrown aside to please the
Radicals. He is the author of various theological works,
poems, &c. His partial version of the Psalms is noted
under **Psalters, German.** Two have been *tr.* "Du selbst,
o Herr, bist ja mein Hirt und Hüter," Ps. xxiii., and
"Wie schön und lieblich ist es anzusehen," Ps. cxxxiii.,
in his *Ausgewählte Psalmen Davids*, Erlangen, 1852, pp.
31 and 48. Ps. xxiii. is *tr.* by C. T. Astley, 1860, p. 8;
and Ps. cxxxiii. by J. Kelly, 1885, p. 91.   [J. M.]

Ecce jam noctis tenuatur umbra.
St. Gregory the Great. [*Early Morning.*] The
oldest known form of this hymn is in three
MSS. of the 11th cent. in the *British Museum*
(Jul. A. vi. f. 21; Vesp. D. xii. f. 7; Harl.
2961, f. 219 b), and in the *Latin Hys. of the
Anglo-Saxon Church*, published in 1851, from a
MS. of the 11th cent. at Durham (Surtees Soc.,
1851). It is also given, in common with other
hymns by St. Gregory, in the various editions
of his *Works*, in *Migne*, and in *Daniel*, i.,
No. 147, and others. The text was revised
for the *Roman Brev.*, 1632 (Sunday at
Lauds), and it is from this revised text, as
in *Daniel*, i., No. 147, that most *trs.* have
been made. *Tr.* as :—

1. **Paler have grown the shades of night.** By
Card. Newman. This appeared in *Tracts for the
Times*, 1836, No.75 in the *Roman Breviary*, p.
52, in 3 st. of 4 l., and is repeated in Lord Bute's
English ed. of the *Breviary*. In 1850 R. Campbell altered it to "Behold the shade of night
departs," and included it in his *Hys. and
Anthems*, p. 2. From that collection it passed
into the Scottish Episc. *Coll.*, 1858, &c.

2. **Lo, now the melting shades of night are
ending.** By W. J. Copeland, from the *Roman
Brev.*, in his *Hys. for the Week*, 1848, p. 10, in
3 st. of 4 l. This *tr.* is not in C. U., but it seems
to have suggested the cento, "Now when the
dusky shades of night retreating" (q.v.).

3. **Lo, the dim shadows of the night are waning.**
An anonymous *tr.* in the *Antiphoner & Grail*,
1880, p. 66, and the *Hymner*, 1882, No. 84.

Other trs. are :—
1. Behold! night's shadows fade. *Hymn. Anglicanum.*
1844.
2. Lo, fainter now lie spread the shades of night. *E.
Caswall.* 1849.
3. Now thinly falls the shade of night. By *W. J.
Blew.* 1852-55.
4. See! vanished are the paling shades of night. *J.
D. Chambers.* 1857.
5. Pale grow the shadows night hath spread around
us. *J. W. Hewett.* 1859.
6. Lo, now the shadowy clouds of night are flying.
T. G. Crippen. 1868.   [J. J.]

**Ecce pulchra canorum resonet voce
Alleluia.** This Sequence is found in a
Bodleian MS. [775, f. 163], written in the reign
of Ethelred, sometime between the years
A.D. 994-1017. It occurs in the Common
of many martyrs in the *Sarum Missal*, and
in the Common both of one and of many
martyrs in the *Hereford* and the *York Missals.*
The text is given in the reprints of these
Missals. It is also in an 11th cent. Winchester

book now in the Library of Corpus Christi
College, Cambridge, No. 473. *Tr.* as:—

Heaven with alleluias ringing. By Mrs. Chester,
contributed to the *Hymnary*, 1872, No. 401, and
signed "H. M. C."

Translations not in C. U. :—
1. Lo sweetly sounds the deep-toned Alleluia. C. B.
Pearson. *Sarum Missal in English*, 1868.
2. Alleluias softly sounding. C. B. Pearson. *Sequences
from the Sarum Missal*, 1871.   [J. J.]

Ecce sedes hic Tonantis. *Abbé Besnault.* [*Dedication of a Church.*] In the revised *Paris Brev.*, 1736, this is the hymn at
second Vespers on the Feast of the Dedication
of a Church. So in the *Lyons* and other modern
French Breviaries. The text is given in
Card. Newman's *Hymni Ecclesiae*, 1838 and
1865.   [W. A. S.]

Translations in C. U. :—
This is the abode where God doth dwell. By I.
Williams. 1st pub. in the *British Magazine*,
July, 1837, and again in his *Hys. Tr. from the
Parisian Brev.*, 1839, p. 338, in 5 st. of 6 l. It
was repeated in the *Child's Christian Year*, 1841,
and other collections.

This is the house where God doth dwell. This
is a slightly altered form of the above *tr.* by I.
Williams. It appeared in the *Hymnary* in 1872,
No. 429.   [J. J.]

Ecce sollemni hac die canamus festa.
[*Nativity of B. V. M.*] The earliest known
form of this sequence is given in a MS. of the
10th cent. at St. Gall, No. 340. It is also in
five St. Gall MSS. of the 11th cent. (Nos. 343,
376, 378, 380, 381), beginning: "Ecce solemnis
diei," and in an 11th cent. MS. in the *British
Museum* (Add. 19768, f. 59 b). *Mone* (No. 341)
and others regard it as a Notkerian Sequence.
The text is also in *Kehrein*, No. 191, *Daniel*, ii.
p. 54, &c. *Tr.* as:—

We keep the feast in gladness. By R. F. Littledale, made for and 1st pub. in the *People's H.*,
1867, No. 279, under the signature of "D. L."
    [J. M.]

Ecce tempus idoneum. [*Lent.*] This
hymn is sometimes ascribed to St. Gregory
the Great, but upon insufficient authority. It
is found in a Bodleian MS. of the 12th cent.
(Laud. Lat. 95, f. 140 b), and in the British
Museum MS. Vesp. D. xii. f. 122b, in a hand of
late 12th cent. It is also in the *Sarum Brev.*
(in a 13th cent. copy in the Bodleian, *Rawlinson C.*, 73, f. 63) as the hymn at Vespers from
the Saturday before the third Sunday in Lent,
daily in the Ferial Office to Passion Sunday.
(*Hymn. Sarisb.*, Lon., 1851, p. 72.) It is also
in the *Aberdeen Brev.*, 1509. *Daniel* gives the
text, vol. i., No. 152, in 5 st. of 4 l. The text
is also in Card. Newman's *Hymni Ecclesiae*,
1838 and 1865.   [J. M.]

Translations in C. U. :—
1. **Lo, now is our accepted day.** By J. M. Neale,
in the 1st ed. of the *Hymnal N.*, 1852, and later
editions. It is given with another doxology in
the *Hymner*, 1882, No. 47. Two altered forms
are also in C. U., one in *H. A. & M.*, 1861-75,
arranged by the Compilers; and the second in
the *Hymnary*, 1872, by the Editors.

2. **Behold now is th' accepted time.** By J. A.
Johnston, in the 2nd ed. of his *English Hymnal*,
1856, and later editions. It is an altered form

of Dr. Neale's *tr.* as above. In *Kennedy*, 1863, No. 401, further alterations are introduced.

3. Behold ! the accepted time appear. By J. D. Chambers, in his *Lauda Syon*, 1857, p. 135. It was repeated in the *People's H.*, 1867, No. 63.

Translations not in C. U. :—

1. Behold the appointed time to win. *R. Campbell.* 1850.
2. Lo ye, the fitting time is this. *W. J. Blew.* 1852-55.
3. Lo, now is come the fit, accepted time. *J. W. Hewett.* 1859.   [J. J.]

Ecking, Samuel, a Baptist, b. at Shrewsbury, Dec. 5, 1757, d. Jan. 16, 1785, contributed hymns to the *Gospel Magazine*, in 1778 and 1779, under the signature of "S. E—k—g." Of these the hymn, " Peace, peace, my soul," is in C. U. This hymn is also found in his *Essays on Grace, Faith, and Experience.*   [W. T. B.]

Eddis, Edward William, a member of the Catholic Apostolic Church, commonly known as the "Irvingites," compiled for the use of their congregations, and pub. in 1864, *Hys. for the Use of the Churches* (Lond., Bosworth & Harrison). It contained 205 hymns, of which 19 were his original compositions, and 2 translations. The 2nd ed., in a revised form with 320 hymns and 44 doxologies, was pub. in 1871 (Lond., J. Strangeways). To this he contributed 40 new hymns and 1 translation, thus making 62 hymns. All these are signed "E. W. Eddis." Very few are found in any other collection. The exceptions include "O brightness of the Immortal Father's Face" (*tr.* from the Greek); "In us the hope of glory" (*The Second Advent desired*); and "Thou standest at the altar" (*H. Communion*). There are other hymns in this collection signed "E.," "G. E.," and "E. E.," which seem to indicate members of his family, but about which we can gain no definite information. The last, "E. E.," is probably his wife, as her name was "Ellen Eddis."   [J. J.]

Eddy, Zachary, D.D., b. at Stockbridge, Vermont, Dec. 19, 1815, and ordained to the Cumberland Presbyterian Ministry, in 1835. After acting as a Missionary in Western New York and Wisconsin, he was a Congregational pastor at Warsaw, N.Y., 1850-55, and at Northampton, Mass., 1857 ; then Reformed Dutch pastor at Brooklyn, 1867 ; and again a Congregational Minister at Chelsea, Mass., 1871, and at Detroit, from 1873 to 1884. Dr. Eddy was the principal editor of the Reformed Dutch *Hymns of the Church*, 1869 ; and with Drs. Hitchcock and P. Schaff, of *Hymns and Songs of Praise*, 1874. His hymns include :—

1. **Break forth, ye heavens, in song.** *Praise to the Holy Trinity.* This is No. 43, in 3 st. of 7 l., in *The Manual of Praise*, Oberlin, Ohio, 1880. It is a spirited hymn.
2. **Floods swell around me, angry, appalling.** *Lent. Affliction.* No. 421 in the *Hys. of the Church*, 1869, in 4 st. of 4 l.
3. **I saw on a throne uplifted in light.** *Christ in Glory.* No. 209 in the *Hys. of the Church*, 1869, in 4 st. of 4 l.
4. **Jesus, enthroned and glorified.** *Whitsuntide.* A prayer for the gift of the Holy Spirit, No. 229, in the *Hys. of the Church*, 1869, in 4 st. of 6 l.   [F. M. B.]

Edeling, Christian Ludwig, s. of Ludwig Edeling, Superintendent at Löbejün, near Halle, on the Saale, was b. at Löbejün, July 31, 1679. After the completion of his theological studies under Spener and Francke, he became, in 1704, tutor to Nicolaus Ludwig von Zinzendorf, and in 1706 Rector of the school at Gröningen, near Halberstadt. In 1710 he was appointed assistant preacher at Schwanebeck, near Halberstadt, where he became chief preacher in 1723, and Superintendent in 1739, and d. there Sept. 18, 1742 (*Koch*, v. 219-220 ; *Bode*, pp. 62-63 ; MS. from Oberpfarrer Graue, Löbejün).

His *Poetischer Vorrath*, now extant at Wernigerode, in MS. contains 27 hymns. Of these he contributed 10 to Freylinghausen's *Neues geistreiches G. B.*, 1714, viz., Nos. 63, 71, 221, 313, 522, 572, 594, 651, 695, 710. Two of these have been *tr.*

i. **Christen erwarten in allerlei Fällen.** *Trust in God.* 1714, No. 522, in 9 st. *Tr.* by *N. L. Frothingham*, 1870, p. 236, as "Christians may find in each scene of commotion."

ii. **Der Tag bricht an, die Nacht ist hin.** *Morning.* 1714, No. 695, in 12 st. The *trs.* are from Bunsen's *Versuch*, 1833, No. 677, beginning with 8 st., "Verbinde mich, mein Heil, mit dir." (It is based on "Der Tag bricht an und zeiget sich," in David von Schweinitz's *Penta-Decas Fidium Cordialium*, Danzig, 1640 ; reprinted in *Mützell*, 1858, No. 183, in 21 st. of 6 l., and the Berlin *G. L. S.*, ed. 1863, No. 1090.) The *trs.* are, (1) "My Saviour, make me cleave to Thee," by *Miss Cox*, 1841, p. 53. (2) "Lift up my soul to Thee, O Lord," by *Lady E. Fortescue*, 1843 (1847, p. 12).   [J. M.]

Edmeston, James, b. Sept. 10, 1791. His maternal grandfather was the Rev. Samuel Brewer, who for 50 years was the pastor of an Independent congregation at Stepney. Educated as an architect and surveyor, in 1816 he entered upon his profession on his own account, and continued to practise it until his death on Jan. 7, 1867. The late Sir G. Gilbert Scott was his pupil. Although an Independent by descent he joined the Established Church at a comparatively early age, and subsequently held various offices, including that of churchwarden, in the Church of St. Barnabas, Homerton. His hymns number nearly 2000. The best known are "Lead us, Heavenly Father, lead us," and "Saviour, breathe an evening blessing." Many of his hymns were written for children, and from their simplicity are admirably adapted to the purpose. For many years he contributed hymns of various degrees of merit to the *Evangelical Magazine.* His published works are :—

(1) *The Search, and other Poems*, 1817. (2) *Sacred Lyrics*, 1820, a volume of 31 hymns and 1 poem. This was followed by a 2nd Series, 1821, with 35 ; and a 3rd Series, 1822, with 27 pieces respectively. (3) *The Cottage Minstrel ; or, Hymns for the Assistance of Cottagers in their Domestic Worship*, 1821. This was pub. at the suggestion of a member of the Home Missionary Society, and contains 50 hymns. (4) *One Hundred Hymns for Sunday Schools, and for Particular Occasions*, 1821. (5) *Missionary Hymns*, 1822. (6) *Patmos, a Fragment, and Other Poems*, 1824. (7) *The Woman of Shunam, and Other Poems*, 1829. (8) *Fifty Original Hymns*, 1833. (9) *Hymns for the Chamber of Sickness*, 1844. (10) *Closet Hymns and Poems*, 1844. (11) *Infant Breathings, being Hymns for the Young*, 1846. (12) *Sacred Poetry*, 1847.

In addition to those of his hymns which have attained to an extensive circulation, as those named above, and are annotated in this work under their respective first lines, there are also the following in C. U. in G. Britain and America :—

1. Along my earthly way. *Anxiety.* In his *Sacred Lyrics*, 3rd set, 1822, in 8 st. of 4 l. It is given in several collections, but usually in an abbreviated form, and generally somewhat altered.

2. Dark river of death that is [art] flowing. *Death Anticipated.* Given in his *Sacred Lyrics*, 3rd set, 1822, p. 39, in 9 st. of 4 l. It is usually given in an abbreviated form, and sometimes as, "Dark river of death that *art* flowing."

3. Come, sacred peace, delightful guest. *Peace.* Appeared in his *Closet Hymns*, &c., 1844, in 4 st. of 4 l.

4. Eternal God, before thy throne, **Three nations.** *National Fast.*

5. For Thee we pray and wait. *Second Advent.*

6. God intrusts to all. *Parable of the Talents.* This is No. 13 of his *Infant Breathings*, 1846, in 5 st. of 4 l. It is a simple application of the parable to the life of a child. It is widely used.

7. God is here; how sweet the sound. *Omnipresence.* Given as No. 9 in his *Sacred Lyrics*, 1st set, 1820, in 6 st. of 4 l. In the *Bapt. Hyl.*, 1879, No. 45. St. i.–iii. are from this text, and iv. and v. are from another source.

8. How sweet the light of Sabbath eve. *Sunday Evening.* No. 10 in *The Cottage Minstrel*, 1821, slightly altered.

9. Is there a time when moments flow. *Sunday Evening.* No. 5 of his *Sacred Lyrics*, 1st set, 1820, in 7 st. of 4 l.

10. Little travellers Zionward. *Burial of Children.* No. 25 of his *Infant Breathings*, &c., 1846, in 3 st. of 8 l. In the *Leeds H. Bk.*, 1853, it begins with st. ii., "Who are they whose little feet?"

11. May we, Lord, rejoicing say. *National Thanksgiving.* Dated 1849 by the author in Spurgeon's *O. O. H. Bk.*, No. 1008.

12. Music, bring thy sweetest treasures. *Holy Trinity.* Dated 1837 by the author in Spurgeon's *O. O. H. Bk.*, No. 167. It is in his *Sacred Poetry*, 1847.

13. Roll on, thou mighty ocean. *Departure of Missionaries.* In his *Missionary Hys.*, 1822, in 4 st. of 4 l. It is in C. U. in America.

14. Sweet is the light of Sabbath eve. *Sunday Evening.* In 5 st. of 4 l., from the *Cottage Minstrel*, 1821, where it is given as No. 10, and entitled "The Cottager's Reflections upon the Sabbath Evening."

15. The light of Sabbath eve. *Sunday Evening.* In 5 st. of 4 l., as No. 11 in the *Cottage Minstrel*, 1821, p. 14, and headed, "Solemn Questions for the Sabbath Evening."

16. Wake, harp of Zion, wake again. *Missions to the Jews.* Dated 1846 by the author in Spurgeon's *O. O. H. Bk.* It is in his *Sacred Poetry*, 1847.

17. When shall the voice of singing? In his *Missionary Hymns*, 1822. It is in a few American collections.

18. When the worn spirit wants repose. *Sunday.* No. 18, of his *Sacred Lyrics*, 1st set, 1820, in 4 st. of 4 l. It is somewhat popular, and is given in several collections in G. Britain and America, as the Bapt. *Ps. & Hys.*, 1858–80; the *Church Praise Bk.*, N. Y., 1881, &c.

19. Why should I, in vain repining? *Consolation.* No. 14 in the 1st set of his *Sacred Lyrics*, 1820, in 4 st. of 4 l.   [J. J.]

Εἰ καὶ ἐν τάφῳ κατῆλθες ἀθάνατε.

St. John of Damascus. [*Easter.*] This is a Contakion (κοντάκιον), or short hymn, dating from about the middle of the eighth century, found in the *Pentecostarion*, in the Office for Easter Day. The original is given in Dr. Littledale's *Offices, &c., of the Holy Eastern Church*, 1863, p. 91, and a *tr.* in blank verse, "If into the tomb ‖ Thou didst descend, Immortal One," p. 216. This latter has been rendered into 7s measure by W. Chatterton Dix, as, "If the dark and awful tomb," and as such is found in Schaff's *Christ in Song*, 1869, p. 241.   [J. J.]

Εἰ καὶ τὰ παρόντα.

St. Methodius II. [*Looking unto Jesus.*] From the *Paracletice*, the Sunday of the Fourth Tone. Dr. Neale's *tr.*, "Are thy toils and woes increasing?" was pub. in his *Hymns of the E. C.*, 1862, in 5 st. of 5 l. In 1871-2 it was given with alterations in the *Hymnary*, having previously

appeared in Palmer's *Supplementary Hymnal*, 1866. It is also found in other collections, and sometimes as, "Are *our* toils and woes increasing."   [J. J.]

Ei wie so selig schläfest du. [*Burial.*]

Included as No. 179 in the *Anmuthiger Blumenkrantz*, 1712, in 7 st. of 4 l. It is sometimes erroneously ascribed to N. L. von Zinzendorf.

In the *Herrnhut G. B.*, 1735, No. 535, it is altered, and st. iii.–v. omitted, while in the *Brüder G. B.*, 1778, No. 937, is st. i., ii., vii. of the 1712, considerably altered. The altered st. ii., "Sein Leiden hat dich frei gemacht," is in the *Württemberg G. B.*, 1842, No. 619, inserted as st. ii. of the hymn, "Ei, wie so sanft verschläfest du [see Neumann, G.]. The hymn was sung, probably in the form of 1735, at Zinzendorf's funeral, and also at that of his second wife, Anna Nitschmann, he having d. on the 9th, and she on the 21st May, 1760 (see *Koch*, v. 337, 271, 312). The *trs.* are, (1) "How sweet the dream of her that sleeps," as No. 47 in the *Moravian H. Bk.*, 1742 (1754, pt. ii. No. 119). Adopted as No. 105 in the *Bible H. Bk.*, 1845. (2) "How sweetly this our brother sleeps," by *J. W. Foster*, as No. 845 in the *Moravian H. Bk.*, 1789 (1886, No. 1256).   [J. M.]

Eia recolamus laudibus piis digna.

St. Notker. [*Christmas; or, Circumcision.*] The earliest form of the text known is in a 10th cent. ms. at St. Gall (No. 340). It is also in three St. Gall mss. of the 11th cent. (Nos. 343, 380, 381), in the last two being included amongst the Notkerian Sequences, and in an 11th cent. ms. in the Bodleian (Douce, 222 f. 90). In several Missals it is assigned to the second Mass on Christmas Day; and again in others to the first, or to the octave, of the same festival. In the *Sarum* and *Hereford* Missals it is the Sequence for the Feast of the Circumcision. In addition to *Daniel*, ii. p. 3, and the reprints of the *Sarum* and *Hereford Missals*, the text is also given in *Wackernagel*, i., No. 143; *Kehrein*, No. 10; *Bässler*, No. 74; and *Königsfeld*, i. 94.   [W. A. S.]

Translation in C. U. :—

0 come and let us tell with praise. By E. H. Plumptre, written for and 1st pub. in the *Hymnary*, 1872, No. 160.

Translations not in C. U. :—

1. Sing we the joyful day. C. B. Pearson. *The Sarum Missal in English.* 1868.
2. Let us devoutly pay. C. B. Pearson. *Sequences from Sarum Missal.* 1871.   [J. J.]

Eight days amid this world of woe.

J. Anstice. [*Circumcision.*] From his *Hymns*, &c., printed for private circulation by his widow, in 1836, No. 10, in 5 st. of 5 l. into the *Child's Christian Year*, 1841, and numerous collections in G. Britain and America. [J. J.]

Eighteen centuries have fled.

J. Conder. [*Holy Communion.*] Appeared in the *Congregational H. Bk.*, 1836., No. 442, in 4 st. of 6 l., and based upon 1 Cor. xi. 26, &c., "Ye do shew the Lord's death till He come." It was repeated in the *Leeds H. Bk.*, 1853, and other collections, and in Conder's *Hys. of Praise, Prayer and Devout Meditation*, 1856. In the New York *Church Praise Bk.*, 1882, it is given as "Many centuries have fled."   [J. J.]

Ein' feste Burg ist unser Gott.

Martin Luther. [*Ps. xlvi.*] The common account of the origin of this, the most famous hymn of

Luther, is thus forcibly expressed by Heinrich Heine :—

"A battle hymn was this defiant song, with which he and his comrades entered Worms [April 16, 1521]. The old cathedral trembled at these new notes, and the ravens were startled in their hidden nests in the towers. This hymn, the Marseillaise Hymn of the Reformation, has preserved its potent spell even to our days, and we may yet soon use again in similar conflicts the old mailèd words." (*Werke*, ed. 1876, v. iii. p. 36.)

It is, however, in the last degree unlikely that if the hymn had been composed in 1521, it should not have been pub. in 1524, along with Luther's earlier hymns. A second theory advanced by Dr. K. F. T. Schneider in 1856, that it was written Nov. 1, 1527, and partly suggested by the death of his friend Leonhard Kaiser (burnt at the stake, Aug. 16, 1527, at the instigation of the Bishop of Ulm), rests on hypotheses too elaborate to be examined here, but is not sustained by any foundation of fact (see *Blätter für Hymnologie*, 1883, pp. 75–79 ; 103–105, &c.). A third theory is that it was composed at the time of the Diet of Augsburg in 1530. Thus D'Aubigné says :—

"Luther, full of faith, revived the courage of his friends, by composing and singing with his fine voice that beautiful hymn, since become so famous, *Ein' feste Burg ist unser Gott*. Never did soul that knew its own weakness, but which, looking to God, despised every fear, find such noble accents. This hymn was sung during the Diet, not only at Augsburg, but in all the churches of Saxony, and its energetic strains often revived and inspirited the most dejected hearts." (*Hist. of Reformation*, ed. 1847, p. 543).

The hymn, however, belongs to the previous year, 1529, and was probably written for the Diet of Speyer (Spires), when on April 20, 1529, the German Princes made their formal Protest againt the revocation of their liberties and thus gained the name of Protestants. Then, says Lauxmann, in *Koch*, viii. 120, "Luther with this hymn entered a protest before all the German people against endeavouring to obstruct the Gospel." It was first pub. in Klug's *G. B.*, Wittenberg, 1529, entitled "Der xxxvi. Psalm. Deus noster refugium et virtus." The Psalm is used only as a motto, the imagery throughout being entirely original. We may, however, compare some of the phrases of his prose version, 1524 :—

"Eine Hülfe in den grossen Nöthen, die uns troffen haben" (i.). "Darum fürchten wir uns nicht" (ii.). "Gott ist bei ihr darinnen, darum wird sie wohl bleiben; Gott hilft mir [1545 ihr] frühe" (v.). "Der Herr Zebaoth ist mit uns, der Gott Jacob ist unser Schutz (vii.).

Wackernagel, iii. pp. 19–21, gives four forms, No. 32, from the *Form und Ordnung Gaystlicher Gesang und Psalmen*, Augsburg, 1529 ; No. 33, from the *Geistliche Lieder*, Wittenberg, 1531; No. 34, a double form from the Riga *Kirchenordnung*, 1530, and the Rostock *G. B.*, 1531 : Nos. 32 and 34 (both) being in Low German, No. 33 in High German. The earliest High German text now accessible, that of 1531, is as follows :—

i.
Ein feste burg ist unser Gott,
  ein gute wehr und waffen.
Er hilfft unns frey aus aller not
  die uns ytzt hat betroffen.
    Der alt böse feind
    mit ernst ers ytzt meint,
    gros macht und viel list
    sein grausam rüstung ist,
auf erd ist nicht seins gleichen.

ii.
Mit unser macht ist nichts gethan,
  wir sind gar bald verloren :
Es streit fur uns der rechte man,
  den Gott hat selbs erkoren.
    Fragstu, wer der ist?
    er heist Jhesu Christ,
    der Herr Zebaoth,
    und ist kein ander Gott,
das felt mus er behalten.

iii.
Und wenn die welt vol Teuffell wehr
  unnd wolt uns gar vorschlingen,
So fürchten wir unns nicht zu sehr,
  es sol uns doch gelingen.
    Der Fürst dieser welt,
    wie sawr er sich stellt.
    thut er unns doch nicht,
    das macht, er ist gericht,
ein wörtlin kan yhn fellen.

iv.
Das wort sie sollen lassen stahn
  und kein danck dazu haben,
Er ist bey unns wol auff dem plan
  mit seinem geist und gaben.
    Nemen sie den leib,
    gut, eher, kindt unnd weib
    las faren dahin,
    sie habens kein gewin,
das reich mus uns doch bleiben.

The same text, modernised in orthography, is given in Schircks's ed. of Luther's *Geistliche Lieder*, 1854, p. 35, and as No. 218 in the *Unv. L. S.*, 1851. In st. i we see our strong hold and its besiegers; in st. ii. our weakness, our Saviour's power and might ; in st. iii. the vanity of the Prince of this World ; in st. iv. whatever earthly goods we lose we have our true treasure in heaven.

The hymn speedily spread over all Germany, and Lauxmann, in *Koch*, viii. 123–131, relates many incidents regarding hymn and chorale—the true National Hymn of Germany. Luther, in 1530, sang it daily at Coburg. Melanchthon, Jonas, and Cruciger, in their banishment from Wittenberg in 1547, were greatly comforted by hearing it sung by a little maiden on their entrance into Weimar. Gustavus Adolphus caused it to be sung by his whole army before the battle of Leipzig, Sept. 17, 1631, and it was on Sept. 15, 1882, sung "as by one man" by the assembled thousands on the field of Lützen, at the service held in commemoration of the Jubilee of the Gustavus Adolphus Society, which seeks to aid Protestant Churches in Roman Catholic countries. It was adopted by the Salzburg Emigrants of 1732, as their travelling hymn. Sung at Hermannsburg at the farewell service when Ludwig Harms was sending forth his first band of missionaries. During the Luther Celebrations, Sept. 12–14, and Nov. 10–12, 1883, it was sung in the Castle Church at Wittenberg, Sept. 12; at Eisleben at the unveiling of the Luther memorial in the Market Place, Nov. 10 ; and at countless celebrations in Germany, G. Britain, and America, in the original, or in various English versions.

Since the above remarks were put in type an elaborate monograph by Dr. J. Linke, of Altenburg, has appeared under the title *Wann wurde das Lutherlied Ein' feste Burg ist unser Gott verfasst?* Leipzig, 1886. Dr. Linke discusses with abundant research and polemic the various theories already noted, and the more recent combinations and hypotheses. His opinion is that the hymn was written on or about Oct. 31, 1525 ; and he quotes many interesting parallels from Luther's contemporaneous writings, and especially from his lectures on Zechariah, written about the end of October, 1525. But that such a hymn could remain in ms. from that date till the publication of Klug's *G. B.* in 1529, seems very improbable ; and no trustworthy evidence is forthcoming that it appeared in print before 1529.

In Klug's *G. B.*, 1529, likewise appeared the magnificent chorale by Luther, evidently the product of the same mind and of the same inspiration. It has been strikingly, if somewhat inappropriately, used by Meyerbeer in *The Huguenots ;* more recently by Mendelssohn in the fifth movement of his *Reformation Symphony*, 1830 ; and by Wagner as a motive in his *Kaisersmarsch*, written to commemorate the return of the Emperor William in 1871, after the Franco-German war. It has now become well-known in England, and in its proper form is included in the C. B. for England, 1863 (see below).

An attempt has recently been made to show that this is a patchwork of snatches from various portions of the Roman Gradual, which Luther, while a monk, must often have sung. But even if this were clearly shown, to Luther would still be due the honour of smelting these scattered fragments and producing from them a glorious melody, now all of one piece. (See the *Blätter für Hymnologie*, 1884, pp. 82, 101, &c.)

Translations in C. U. :—

1. God is our Refuge in Distress, Our strong Defence. A full but free version in J. C. Jacobi's *Psal. Ger.*, 1722, p. 83 (1732, p. 138 altered), and repeated, greatly altered (by F. Okeley ?), as No. 319 in pt. i. of the *Moravian H. Bk.*, 1754. St. i.-iii., greatly altered, from the 1754, were included as No. 595 in the *Moravian H. Bk.*, 1886; and much the same text in J. A. Latrobe's *Coll.*, 1852, No. 256, with Carlyle's *trs.* of st. i. ll. 5–8, ii. ll. 5–8, substituted.

2. A safe stronghold our God is still. By T. Carlyle, in a characteristic essay on "Luther's Psalm," in *Fraser's Magazine* for 1831, reprinted in his *Miscellaneous Essays* (ed. 1872, vol. iii. p. 61). This is the most faithful (st. iv. excepted) and forcible of all the English versions. Included in full and unaltered in the *Wes. H. Bk.*, 1875; the Scottish *Presb. Hyl.*, 1876; *Church Praise*, 1883, &c. In some collections, as the *H. & Songs of Praise*, N. Y., 1874, it is slightly altered. A form greatly altered by W. M. Reynolds appeared as No. 964 in the American Luth. General Synod's *Coll.*, 1850. The version in the Canadian *Presb. H. Bk.*, 1880, No. 227, is altered mainly from Gaskell, Massie, and Hedge (see below).

3. God is the city of our strength, in Miss Fry's *H. of the Reformation*, 1845, p. 61, in full, with the doxology *tr.* by Mr. Thring, 1882 (see below). Her *trs.* of st. i.-iv., rewritten to 5 st. of 6 l., were included as No. 51 in J. Whittemore's *Suppl. to All H. Bks.*, 1860, and repeated as No. 498 in Maurice's *Choral H. Bk.*, 1861.

4. A tower of strength is our God's name, omitting st. iv., by A. T. Russell, as No. 98 in the *Dalston Hospital H. Bk.*, 1848. Thence, altered, as No. 136 in his own *Ps. & Hys.*, 1851, beginning, "A strong tower is our God's great name," and further altered as No. 501 in Maurice's *Choral H. Bk.*, 1861, beginning, "A tower of strength is God's great name."

5. A tower of strength our God doth stand, in full, by H. J. Buckoll, as No. 45 in the *Rugby School H. Bk.*, 1850 (ed. 1876, No. 285). Repeated, more or less altered and abridged, in the *Rugby Church H. Bk.*, 1863; *Kennedy*, 1863, No. 25 (altered mainly from Carlyle); *Wellington College H. Bk.*, 1864, and *Marlborough College H. Bk.*, 1869.

6. A strong tower is the Lord our God, To shelter. In full, as No. 334, in W. Hunter's *Select Melodies*, 1852, marked as by W. M. Bunting. Repeated in *Cantate Domino*, Boston, U. S., 1859, No. 307.

7. A mighty fortress is our God, A bulwark. A full and good *tr.* by Dr. F. H. Hedge, contributed to Dr. W. H. Furness's *Gems of German Verse*, 1852, and then as No. 852 to his own *Hys. for the Church of Christ*, Boston, U.S., 1853. Reprinted in full and unaltered in Putnam's *Singers*

and Songs of the Liberal Faith, Boston, U.S., 1875, p. 214, with the note that "It has been sung on many occasions, as at the recent laying of the commemoration stone of Memorial Hall, at Cambridge [U.S.]." Included in full in the Schaff-Gilman *Lib. of Rel. Poetry*, ed. 1883, p. 384, and as No. 1343 in the ed. 1872 of Robinson's *Songs for the Sanctuary*. In full or abridged it appears in many American hymnals, as *Hys. of the Spirit*, 1864, Unitarian *H. Bk.*, 1869, Dutch Reformed *Hys. of the Church*, 1869, and others; and in England in Dr. Martineau's *Coll.*, 1873.

8. A sure stronghold our God is He. Full and good, by W. Gaskell, contributed in 1855 to the 2nd ed. of the 1st Ser. of Miss Winkworth's *Lyra Ger.*, p. 175, her *tr.* in the 1st ed. (see below) not being considered satisfactory. Slightly altered in metre as No. 124 in the *C. B. for England*, 1863, but restored as in the *Lyra Ger.* in the *Christian Singers of Germany*, 1869, p. 110. In full as No. 213 in Dr. Pagenstecher's *Coll.*, 1864, and as No. 284 in the Suppl. of 1884 to the *Scottish Hyl.* St. i., ii., were included, slightly altered, as No. 161 in the *Irish Ch. Hyl.*, 1869 (ed. 1873, No. 441).

9. A fortress firm is God our Lord. In full, by Dr. W. L. Alexander, in the *Scottish Cong. Magazine*, Jan. 1859. Repeated, reduced to 5 st. of 4 l., in W. Elliott's *Evangelical Hys.*, Plymouth, 1864.

10. A mountain fastness is our God. In full, by Bp. W. R. Whittingham, as No. 248 in the Amer. Episco. *Hys. for Ch. & Home*, 1860; and thence, with an added doxology not from the German, as No. 397 in the Amer. *Episco. Hyl.*, 1871.

11. A tower of strength is God our Lord. A *tr.* of st. i., ii., by Dean Alford, as No. 228 in his *Year of Praise*, 1867, and thence in Flett's *Coll.*, Paisley, 1871, and Dr. Dale's *Eng. H. Bk.*, 1879.

12. Our God stands firm, a rock and tow'r. By R. C. Singleton, a *tr.* of st. i., ii., with an original st. as iii., as No. 267 in his *Anglican H. Bk.*, 1868 (ed. 1871, No. 310). Repeated in the *Hymnary*, 1871, and J. L. Porter's *Coll.*, 1876; and in America in the *Presb. Hyl.*, 1874; *Evang. Hyl.*, N. Y., 1880; and *Ch. Praise Bk.*, 1882.

13. A mighty fortress is our God, A trusty. A full and good *tr.*, as No. 274 in the Pennsylvania Luth. *Ch. Bk.*, 1868; compiled by the committee of publication principally from the Carlyle, 1831, and Reynolds (1863 see below) texts.

14. A fortress strong is God our God. A good and full *tr.* by E. Thring, as No. 253, in the Uppingham and Sherborne *School H. Bk.*, 1874.

15. A tower of strength our God is still, A mighty, &c. In full, as No. 144, in the *Ohio Luth. Hyl.*, 1880, and marked as a compilation.

16. A Fortress sure is God our King. By Godfrey Thring, as No. 245 in his *Ch. of England H. Bk.*, 1882, repeated in Horder's *Cong. Hyl.*, 1884, and Allon's *C. P. Hyl.*, 1886. This is decidedly the best version for popular use, as Carlyle's is the most faithful and forcible. Mr. Thring omits st. iii., and gives a doxology added about 1546 in *Etliche Lieder*, Nürnberg, as altered in the appendix to Lobwasser's *Psalmen des Königlichen Propheten Davids*, 1574. The text used by Mr. Thring reads thus :—

Lob, Ehr und Preis dem höchsten Gott
Dem Vater aller Gnaden,
Der uns aus Lieb geschenket hat
Sein Sohn für unsern Schaden ;

Sammt dem heilgen Geist,
Von Sünden er reisst
Zum Reiche uns heisst
Den Weg zum Leben weist,
Der helf uns fröhlich ! Amen.

from an ed. of Lobwasser pub. at St. Gall in 1761.

17. A stronghold sure our God remains. In full, by Dr. J. Troutbeck, as No. 49 in the *Westminster Abbey H. Bk.*, 1883.

18. A Tower of safety is our God. A goodly, &c. A *tr.* in full by M. W. Stryker in his *H. & Verses*, 1883, p. 72 ; repeated in his *Christian Chorals*, 1885, No. 45.

Translations not in C. U. :—
(1) "Oure God is a defence and towre," by Bp. Coverdale, 1539 (*Remains*, 1846, p. 569), ll. 1–4 being literally from Luther and the rest a version of Ps. xlvi. (2) "God is our refuge and strong fence," in *Lyra Davidica*, 1709, p. 75. 3) "Dy our own strength there's nothing done," a *tr.* of st. ii., as No. 14 in the *Moravian H. B.*, 1742, adopted as st. ii. of No. 319, in 1754. (4) "A tow'r of safety is our God, His sword," by *Dr. H. Mills*, 1845 (1856, p. 169). (5) "God to us a tower will be," by *J. Anderson*, 1846, p. 37 (1847, p. 55). (6) "Our God's a mighty panoply," in C. T. Brooks's *Schiller's Homage of the Arts*, &c., Boston, U.S., 1847, p. 114. (7) "A mighty castle is our God," by *Dr. J. Hunt*, 1853, p. 65. (8) "Our God's a tower and shield," a 2nd version by *Dr. Hunt*, p. 66. (9) "A castle is our God, a tower," by *R. Massie*, 1854, p. 38, repeated as No. 755 in Reid's *Praise Bk.*, 1872. (10) "God is our stronghold, firm and sure," by *Miss Winkworth*, 1855, p. 173. (11) "Our God, a tower of strength is He, A good defence," in Dr. H. W. Dulcken's *Book of German Songs*, 1856, p. 260. (12) "God is our Rock and Tower of strength," by *Miss Dunn*, 1857, p. 69. (13) "A sure stronghold our God is still," based on Carlyle, by J. S. Stallybrass, in the *Tonic Solfa Reporter*, July, 1857. (14) "The Lord, our God is a strong tower," by W. Sugden, in the *Wes. Meth. Magazine*, 1858, p. 79. (15) "A stronghold firm, a trusty shield When raging," by Dr. R. P. Dunn, in *Sacred Lyrics from the German*, Phil., U.S., 1859, p. 127. (16) "A sure defence, a fort, a tow'r," by *Dr. G. Walker*, 1860, p. 40. (17) "God, our own God, is a strong tower," in the *British Messenger*, August, 1860. (18) "A safe stronghold our God is still, A sure defence," a double version in slightly varied metre by W. M. Reynolds, in the *Evang. Review*, Gettysburg, July, 1863. (19) "A Fortress firm and steadfast Rock," by *Miss Cox*, 1864, p. 227. (20) "Our God He is a castle strong," by Dr. G. Macdonald, in the *Sunday Magazine*, 1867, p. 450, and altered in his *Exotics*, 1876, p. 66. (21) "Our God, He is a fortress tower," by N. L. Frothingham, in the *Monthly Religious Magazine*, Boston, U.S., vol. 37, 1867, repeated altered in his vol. of 1870, p. 269. (22) "God is our Refuge and our Rock," by Dr. J. Ker, in a programme for a Psalmody meeting at Edinburgh, 1868. (23) "A mighty fortress is our God, A panoply," in Dr. J. Guthrie's *H. & Sacred Lyrics*, 1869, p. 71. (24) "Our God a tower of Strength is He, A goodly wall," by H. W. Longfellow, in the Second Interlude, added in 1872, to his *Golden Legend*, 1851 (*P. Works*, Routledge, 1879, pp. 479–481). (25) "A tower of strength our God is still," in the *Church of England Magazine*, 1872, p. 182. (26) "God is our fortress firm and sure," as No. 687 in Reid's *Praise Bk.*, 1872. (27) "High Tower and Stronghold is our God," based on Bp. Whittingham, 1860, in J. H. Hopkins's *Carols, H. & Songs*, 1882, p. 152, dated 1862. (28) "God is our Refuge—city strong," a 2nd *tr.* by M. W. Stryker, in his *H. & Verses*, 1883, p. 74. (29) "Strong tower and refuge is our God, Right goodly," by *Dr. L. W. Bacon*, 1884, p. 53, based on the *Luth. Ch. Bk.*, 1868 (see under No. xiii.). (30) "Our God's a fastness sure indeed, A trusty," by R. McLintock in the *Academy*, July 26, 1884. (31) "So strong a fortress is our God," by E. Walter in his *Martin Luther*, 1884, p. 22. It may be also noted that the hymns, "God is our Refuge in distress, Our Shield," No. 66 in the *N. Cong.*, 1859 ; and "God is our refuge and defence, our Shield," No. 104 in J. Whittemore's *Suppl. to All H. Bks.*, 1860, are versions of Ps. xlvi., but are not taken from Luther.

The following list of additional American translations has been kindly furnished by the Rev. B. M. Schmucker, D.D., Pottstown, Pennsylvania :—

(32) "A Rock and Refuge is our God," by Dr. J. A. Seiss, in *The Lutheran*, July 6, 1860. (33) "A mighty Fortress is our God, A shield," by Dr. J. A. Seiss in his *Ecclesia Lutherana*, 1860, p. 87. (34) "A Tower and Stronghold is our God," by W. H. Walter in his *Chorals and Hymns*, 1862, p. 12. (35) "God is our tower of strength and grace," by Dr. H. Harbaugh in the *Guardian* (American Reformed), May, 1863, p. 138. (36) "A fast-set Bulwark is our God," by Dr. C. P. Krauth in his *Jubilee Service*, 1867, p. 22. (37) "A mighty stronghold is our God," by Dr. J. Schwartz, 1879, in a printed programme for Union of Lutheran Synods. Revised in *Lutheran Book of Worship*, 1880, and in *Augsburg Songs*, 1885, No. 203. (38) "Our God is a stronghold, indeed," by Dr. S. R. Fisher in the (German Reformed) *Messenger*, Sept. 15, 1880. (39) "A mighty fortress is our God, To shelter," by J. H. Kurzenknabe in *Peerless Praise. Hymns and Music for the Sunday School*, 1882, p. 58. (40) "A moveless Fastness is our God," by Dr. M. Sheeleigh in his *Luther. A Song Tribute*, 1883, p. 102. (41) "A firm defence our God is still," by Dr. S. W. Duffield in his *English Hymns and their Authors*, New York, 1886, p. 2, marked as *tr.* in 1873.

Dr. B. Peck gives in his *Dr. Martin Luther's Ein' feste Burg ist unser Gott, in 21 Sprachen*, Chicago, 1883, 28 English versions in full. Of these 11 are among those noted in C. U., viz., Nos. 1 and 2 (1831 and 1850), 4 (1851), 5–10, 13. Of those not in C. U. he has Nos. 4, 9, 10, 11, 15, 18, 19, 21, 24, 35–38. Besides these, he gives :—(42) "A fast, firm fortress is our God," marked as *Anon.*, 1857. (43) "Our God's a fortress all secure, marked as *Anon.*, 1879. (44) "Tower of defence is our God," marked as by J. W. Bright. (45) "A mighty bulwark is our God," no marking.   [J. M.]

Ein Kindelein so löbelich. [*Christmas.*] This is a cento which appeared in the *Zwickau Enchiridion*, 1528, and is there entitled "Ein Gesang von der Gepurt Christ, den man auff Weinachten singet, gebessert." Thence in *Wackernagel*, iii. p. 520, in 4 st. of 10 l.

St. i. is found as st. ii. of the hymn "Der Tag der ist so freudenreich," but was probably originally a single st., afterwards interpolated into that hymn ; and it bears a slight resemblance to st. iii. of "Dies est laetitiae, In ortu regali" (q.v.). St. ii. is st. i. of "Der Tag der ist so freudenreich," entirely rewritten. St. iii., iv. are new. The only *tr.* is, "To us is borne a barne of blis," in the *Gude and Godly Ballates* (ed. 1568, fol. 27), ed. 1868, p. 45.   [J. M.]

Ein Lämmlein geht und trägt die Schuld. *P. Gerhardt.* [*Passiontide.*] Appeared in the 3rd ed., 1648, of J. Crüger's *Praxis pietatis melica*, No. 118, in 10 st. of 10 l., included in Wackernagel's ed. of his *Geistliche Lieder*, No. 13, and Bachmann's ed., No. 7. Founded on St. John i. 29, and Is. liii. 4–7, it is styled by Lauxmann, in *Koch*, viii. 40, "the masterpiece of all Passion hymns." It has kept its place in Germany (*Unv. L. S.*, 1851, No. 95), but from its complexity and variety of figures has not come into extended English use :—

Translations in C. U. :—

1. A Lamb goes forth : the sins He bears. A *tr.* of st. i., ii., by A. T. Russell, as No. 93 in his *Ps. & Hys.*, 1851.

2. A Lamb goes uncomplaining forth. A good *tr.*, condensing st. ii., iii., as ii., in Mrs. Charles's *Voice of Christian Life in Song*, 1858, p. 232. The second pt. of this *tr.* beginning, "Gate of my heart, fly open wide" (st. vii.), is in Bp. Ryle's *Coll.*, 1860 ; Reid's *Praise Bk.*, 1872 ; and the *Christian Hys.*, Adelaide, 1872.

3. A Lamb bears all its guilt away. In full in J. Kelly's *P. Gerhardt's Spir. Songs*, 1867, p. 49. Reduced to 4 st. in the *Ohio Luth. Hyl.*, 1880.

Translations not in C. U. :—
(1) "A Lamb goes forth and bears the Guilt, of all the World together," by J. Gambold, as No. 241 in pt. iii., 1746, of the *Moravian H. Bk.* (1886, No. 100), altered in 1801 to "A Lamb went forth" ; sts. v., ix., x., of this version, beginning, "Jesus, I never can forget," are included

in E. P. Hood's *Our H. Bk.*, 1868. (2) "A Lamb goes forth, and bears the Guilt of Adam's Generations," in the *Suppl. to Ger. Psal.*, ed. 1765, p. 13, and *Select Hys. from Ger. Psal.*, Tranquebar, 1754, p. 24. (3) "See, bowed beneath a fearful weight," by *Miss Dunn*, 1857, p. 32. (4) "A Holy, Pure and Spotless Lamb," by Miss Cox in *Lyra Messianica*, 1864, p. 230, and her *H. from the German*, 1864, p. 107. (5) "Forth goes a dear devoted Lamb," in Dr. J. Guthrie's *Sacred Lyrics*, 1869, p. 82. (6) "Behold a Lamb! so tired and faint," by Mrs. E. J. Carr, in *Songs of the Inner Life*, 1871, and repeated as No. 905 in Reid's *Praise Bk.*, 1872 (1872 has *trs.* of i., iv., from 1871, and other *trs.* of ii., iii., v.). (7) "A Lamb goes forth—for all the dues," by Catherine Macrea, as No. 990 in Reid's *Praise Bk.*, 1872.

[J. M.]

Ein neues Lied wir heben an. *M. Luther.* [*Martyrs.*] This was Luther's first hymn, if hymn it can be called, and was written in 1523. On June 30, 1523, two young Augustinian monks, Heinrich Voes and Johann Esch, from Antwerp, had been, after examination by the Cologne Inquisitor, Jacob von Hogstraten, and at the instigation of the Louvain professors, condemned to death and burnt at the stake in Brussels. On receipt of the news of this first martyrdom for the Evangelical cause Luther's spirit was fired, and he wrote this spirited narrative, ending with the prophetic words:—

Summer is even at our door,
The winter now hath vanished,
The tender flowerets spring once more,
And He, Who winter banished,
Will send a happy Summer.
(*Tr.* by *R. Massie*, 1854, p. 44.)

It was the springtide, not only of the Evangelical Church, but of that wonderful growth of German religious poetry which yet lives and flourishes. The hymn first appeared in *Eyn Enchiridion*, Erfurt, 1524, st. ix., x. being added in the *Geystliche gesangk Buchleyn*, Wittenberg, 1524. Thence in *Wackernagel*, iii. p. 3, in 12 st. of 9 l., and in Schircks's ed. of Luther's *Geistl. Lieder*, 1854, p. 83. The original title of the hymn was, "A new song of the two Martyrs for Christ, burnt at Brussels by the Sophists of Louvain." It produced a deep impression at the Reformation times and appeared in many of the early Lutheran hymn-books, but being rather a historical ballad than a hymn, has not appeared in recent collections. The only *tr.* in C. U. is:—

Flung to the heedless winds. A paraphrase in 2 st. of 8 l. of st. ix. :—

Die Asche will nicht lassen ab,
Sie stäubt in allen Landen ;
Hier hilft kein Bach, Loch, Grub noch Grab ;
Sie macht den Feind zu schanden.
  Die er im Leben durch den Mord
Zu schweigen hat gedrungen,
Die muss er todt an allem Ort
Mit aller Stimm und Zungen
Gar fröhlich lassen singen.

This appeared in a *tr.* of D'Aubigné's *Hist. of the Reformation*, pub. at Philadelphia, 1843, and is there said to have been *tr.* for that work by John Alexander Messenger. Included in the American Bapt. *Psalmist*, 1843, and since in many American hymnals, as the *Cheshire Association*, 1844 ; *Bk. of Hys.*, 1846–48 ; *Meth. Epis.*, 1849, &c.

Other trs. are :—

(1) "A new song I design to sing," by *J. Anderson*, 1846, p. 39 (1847, p. 57). (2) "A new song to the Lord we'll raise," by *Dr. J. Hunt*, 1853, p. 68. (3) "By help of God I fain would tell," by *R. Massie*, 1854, p. 40, and in *Dr. Bacon*, 1884, p. 12. (4) "A new song now we raise and sing," by W. M. Reynolds, in the *Evang. Re-*

view, Gettysburg, Oct. 1855. (5) "A brave new song aloud we sing," in the *Christian Examiner*, Boston, U.S., Sept. 1860, p. 243. (6) "A new song here shall be begun," by Dr. G. Macdonald, in the *Sunday Magazine*, 1867, p. 256, and, altered, in his *Exotics*, 1876, p. 71. (7) "O come, a new song let us raise," in the *Family Treasury*, Len. 1878, p. 592. [J. M.]

Einen Kaufmann sieht man ohne Gleichen. [*The Parable of the Pearl of great price.*] Included in J. Köbner's *Christliche Harfentöne*, Hamburg, 1840, p. 221, in 13 st. of 4 l., marked as "From the Kirchenfreund,' and entitled, "The Pearl of the Kingdom of Heaven." *Tr.* as, "Once a merchant travelled far and wide," by Miss Borthwick, in *H. L. L.*, 1855, p. 34 ; (1884, p. 97).

[J. M.]

Einst fahren wir vom Vaterlande. *A. Knapp.* [*Missions.*] 1st pub. in his *Christliche Gedichte*, Basel, 1829, vol. ii. p. 97, in 6 st. of 8 l., entitled "Voyage with Jesus." Included in his *Ev. L. S.*, 1837, No. 1161 (1865, No. 1134). Originally written for the departure of missionaries, it is also appropriate for emigrants generally. The only *tr.* in C. U. is:—

Now we must leave our Fatherland. A good and full *tr.* by Miss Winkworth in the 2nd Ser., 1858, of her *Lyra Ger.*, p. 113. From this st. i., ii., ll. 5–8, iv. ll. 1–4, v. ll. 1–4, vi. ll. 1–4, were included, slightly altered, in *Church Hymns*, 1871, and repeated, omitting st. v., ll. 1–4, in the Appendix of 1884 to the *Scottish Hyl.*

Another tr. is :—
"Our leave of country now is taken," by *Dr. H. Mills*, 1856, p. 205. [J. M.]

Εἱρμός. [Greek Hymnody, § xvi. 10.]

Eja carissimi. [*St. Andrew.*] This anonymous hymn is found in a MS. of the 12th cent., belonging to the Abbey of St. Peter at Salzburg. *Mone*, No. 691, gives it in full in 36 lines, and says that the verse form is of the 6th or 7th cent. *Tr.* as :—

O hasten, beloved, your praises to sing. By R. F. Littledale, appeared first in the *Church Times*, Nov. 26, 1864, and again in the *People's H.*, 1867, No. 224, for the Feast of St. Andrew, and signed "D. L." [J. J.]

Ἐκ νυκτὸς ἔργων. [Ἔσωσε λαόν.]

Ἐκ νυκτὸς ὀρθρίζοντες. [Ἄσωμεν πάντες λαοί.]

El. Nathan, a *nom de plume* of D. W. Whittle.

Eliakim, a *nom de plume* of Job Hupton, in the *Gospel Magazine*.

Elijah's example declares. *J. Newton.* [*Providence.*] This hymn on Elijah being fed by ravens appeared in R. Conyers's *Coll.*, 3rd ed., 1774, No. 267: in the author's *Twenty-six Letters, &c., by Omicron,* 1774 ; the *Gospel Magazine*, April, 1774 ; and in the *Olney Hymns*, 1779, Bk. i., No. 35, in 5 st. of 8 l. In the *Meth. Free Ch. S. S. H. Bk.*, 1869, st. i., ii., and v. are given as No. 244. [J. J.]

Ellerton, John, M.A., s. of George Ellerton, was b. in London, Dec. 16, 1826, and educated at Trinity College, Cambridge (B.A. 1849 ; M.A. 1854). Taking Holy Orders he was successively Curate of Easebourne, Sussex,

1850; Brighton, and Lecturer of St. Peter's, Brighton, 1852; Vicar of Crewe Green, and Chaplain to Lord Crewe, 1860; Rector of Hinstock, 1872; of Barnes, 1876; and of White Roding, 1886. Mr. Ellerton's prose writings include *The Holiest Manhood*, 1882; *Our Infirmities*, 1883, &c. It is, however, as a hymnologist, editor, hymn-writer, and translator, that he is most widely known. As editor he published: *Hymns for Schools and Bible Classes*, Brighton, 1859. He was also co-editor with Bishop How and others of the S. P. C. K. *Church Hymns*, 1871. His *Notes and Illustrations* of *Church Hymns*, their authors and translators, were published in the folio edition of 1881. The notes on the hymns which are special to the collection, and many of which were contributed thereto, are full, accurate, and of special value. Those on the older hymns are too general for accuracy. They are written in a popular form, which necessarily precludes extended research, fulness, and exactness of detail. The result is acceptable to the general public, but disappointing to the hymnological expert. Mr. Ellerton's original hymns number about 50, and his *trs.* from the Latin 10, or more. Nearly every one of these are in C. U. and include:

1. **Before the day draws near its ending.** *Afternoon.* Written April 22, 1880, for a Festival of Choirs at Nantwich, and 1st pub. in the *Nantwich Festival Book*, 1880. In 1883 it passed into the *Westminster Abbey H. Bk.*

2. **Behold us, Lord, a little space.** *General for Weekdays.* Written in 1870 for a mid-day service in a City Church, and pub. in *Church Hys.* in 1871. It has passed into several collections.

3. **Come forth, O Christian brothers.** *Processional for Choral Festival.* Written for a Festival of Parochial Choirs held at Chester, May, 1870, and 1st printed in the Service-book of the same. In 1871 it passed into *Church Hys.*

4. **Father, Name of love and fear.** *Confirmation.* Written in 1871 for a Confirmation in the North of England, and pub. in *Church Hys.*, 1871, and other collections.

5. **God, Creator and Preserver.** *In Time of Scarcity.* Written for and 1st pub. in *The Hymnary*, 1870; and again in the revised ed., 1872, and other hymn-books.

6. **Hail to the Lord Who comes.** *Presentation of Christ in the Temple.* Written Oct. 6, 1880, for Mrs. Brock's *Children's H. Bk.*, and pub. therein, 1881.

7. **In the Name which earth and heaven.** *Foundation of a Church.* Written for and 1st pub. in *Church Hys.*, 1871, and repeated in several collections. The hymn sung at the re-opening of the Nave of Chester Cathedral, January 25, 1872, was compiled by Mr. Ellerton from this hymn, and his "Lift the strain of high thanksgiving."

8 **King Messiah, long expected.** *The Circumcision.* Written Jan. 14, 1871, and 1st pub. in *Church Hys.*, 1871. It has passed into other collections.

9. **King of Saints, to Whom the number.** *St. Bartholomew.* Written for and 1st pub. in *Church Hys.*, 1871. It is very popular, and has been repeated in many hymnals.

10. **Mary at the Master's feet.** *Catechizing.* Written for and 1st pub. in *Church Hys.*, 1871.

11. **O Father, all-creating.** *Holy Matrimony.* Written Jan. 29, 1876, at the request of the Duke of Westminster, for the marriage of his daughter to the Marquess of Ormonde. It was pub. in Thring's *Coll.*, 1880 and 1882.

12 **O! how fair the morning broke.** *Septuagesima.* Written March 13, 1880, for Mrs. Brock's *Children's H. Bk.*, and included therein, 1881.

13. **O Lord of life and death, we come.** *In Time of Pestilence.* Written for and 1st pub. in *Church Hys.* 1871.

14. **O shining city of our God.** *Concerning the Hereafter.* 1st pub. in the Rev. R. Brown-Borthwick's *Sixteen Hymns with Tunes*, &c., 1870; and again in *Church Hys.*, 1871.

15. **O Son of God, our Captain of Salvation.** *St. Barnabas.* Written April 5, 1871, and 1st pub. in

Church Hys., 1871; and again in *H. A. & M.*, 1875, Thring's *Coll.*, 1882, and others.

16. **O Thou in Whom Thy saints repose.** *Consecration of a Burial Ground.* Written for the Consecration of an addition to the Parish Churchyard of Tarporley, Cheshire, 1870, and pub. in *Church Hys.*, 1871.

17. **O Thou Whose bounty fills the earth.** *Flower Services.* Written for a Flower Service at St. Luke's Church, Chelsea, June 6, 1880, and pub. in Mrs. Brock's *Children's H. Bk.*, 1881.

18. **Praise to our God, Whose bounteous hand.** *National Thanksgiving.* Written in 1870 for *Church Hys.*, but 1st pub. in the Rev. R. Brown-Borthwick's *Select Hymns*, &c., 1871, and then in *Church Hys.* later the same year.

19. **The day Thou gavest, Lord, is ended.** *The darkness, &c. Evening.* Written in 1870 for *A Liturgy for Missionary Meetings* (Frome, Hodges), and revised for *Church Hys.*, 1871. The revised form has passed into other collections.

20. **The Lord be with us when we bend.** *Close of Afternoon Service.* Written [in 1870] at the request of a friend for use at the close of Service on Sunday afternoons when (as in summer) strictly Evening hymns would be unsuitable. It was pub. in *Church Hys.*, 1871, Thring's *Coll.*, 1882, and others.

21. **This day the Lord's disciples met.** *Whitsuntide.* "Originally written in 1855 for a class of children, as a hymn of 8 verses of 5 lines each, beginning, 'The Fiftieth day was come at last.' It was abridged, revised, and compressed into C.M. for Mrs. Brock's *Children's H. Bk.*, 1880," and pub. therein, 1881.

22. **Thou in Whose Name the two or three.** *Wednesday.* Appeared in the *Parish Magazine*, May, 1871, as a hymn for Wednesday. After revision it was included in *Church Hys.*, 1871, and repeated in other collections.

23. **Thou Who sentest Thine Apostles.** *SS. Simon and Jude.* Written in June, 1874, for the revised edition of *H. A. & M.*, and pub. in the same in 1875.

24. **We sing the glorious conquest.** *Conversion of St. Paul.* Written Feb. 28, 1871, for and pub. later the same year in *Church Hys.* It was repeated in *H. A. & M.*, 1875.

25. **When the day of toil is done.** *Eternal Rest.* Written in Jan., 1870, and 1st pub. in the Rev. R. Brown-Borthwick's *Sixteen Hys. with Tunes*, &c., 1870, *Church Hys.*, 1871, and subsequently in several Scottish hymn-books. The tune "Preston," in *Church Hys.*, was written for this hymn.

To these hymns must be added those which are annotated under their respective first lines, and the translations from the Latin. The grandest of his original compositions is, "Throned upon the awful tree," and the most beautiful and tender, "Saviour, again to Thy dear Name we raise"; and of his *trs.*, "Sing Alleluia forth in duteous praise," and "Welcome, happy morning, age to age shall say," are the most successful and popular. The subjects of Mr. Ellerton's hymns, and the circumstances under which they were written, had much to do with the concentration of thought and terseness of expression by which they are characterized. The words which he uses are usually short and simple; the thought is clear and well stated; the rhythm is good and stately. Ordinary facts in sacred history and in daily life are lifted above the commonplace rhymes with which they are usually associated, thereby rendering the hymns bearable to the cultured, and instructive to the devout. His antitheses are frequent and terse, almost too much so for devotional verse, and are in danger of interrupting the tranquil flow of devotion. His sympathy with nature, especially in her sadder moods, is great; he loves the fading light and the peace of eve, and lingers in the shadows. Unlike many writers who set forth their illustrations in detail, and then tie to them the moral which they are to teach, he weaves his moral into his metaphor, and pleases the imagination and refreshes the spirit together. Now and again he falls into the weakness of ringing changes on words; but taken as a whole his verse is elevated in tone, devotional in spirit, and elegant in diction. See p. 1561, ii.   [J. J.]

Elliott, Charlotte, daughter of Charles Elliott, of Clapham and Brighton, and grand-daughter of the Rev. H. Venn, of Hudders-field, was b. March 18, 1789. The first 32 years of her life were spent mostly at Clap-ham. In 1823 she removed to Brighton, and died there Sept. 22, 1871. To her acquaint-ance with Dr. C. Malan, of Geneva, is at-tributed much of the deep spiritual-minded-ness which is so prominent in her hymns. Though weak and feeble in body, she pos-sessed a strong imagination, and a well-cultured and intellectual mind. Her love of poetry and music was great, and is reflected in her verse. Her hymns number about 150, a large percentage of which are in C. U. The finest and most widely known of these are, "Just as I am," and "My God, my Father, while I stray." Her verse is characterized by tenderness of feeling, plaintive simplicity, deep devotion, and perfect rhythm. For those in sickness and sorrow she has sung as few others have done. Her hymns appeared in her brother's *Ps. & Hys.* and elsewhere as follows :—

(1) *Psalms and Hymns for Public, .Private, and Social Worship; selected by the Rev. H. V. Elliott,* &c., 1835–48. In this *Sel.* her signature is "C. E." (2) *The Christian Remembrancer Pocket Book.* This was ori-ginally edited by Miss Kiernan, of Dublin. Miss Elliott undertook the editorship in 1834. (3) *The Invalid's Hymn Book.* This was originally compiled by Miss Kiernan, but before publication was re-arranged by Miss Elliott, who also added 23 hymns in the 1st ed., 1834. These were increased in the following edition to the 6th in 1854, when her contributions amounted to 112. From that date no change was made in the work. (4) *Hours of Sorrow Cheered and Comforted; or, Thoughts in Verse,* 1836. (5) *Morning and Evening Hymns for a Week,* printed privately in 1839 for sale for a benevolent institution in Brighton, and pub. in 1842. (6) *Thoughts in Verse on Sacred Subjects,* 1869.

Miss Elliott's *Poems* were pub., with a *Memoir* by her sister, Mrs. Babington, in 1873, and an additional volume of *Leaves* from her unpublished *Journals and Poems,* also appeared in 1870.

In addition to her more important hymns, which are annotated under their respective first lines, there are in C. U. :—

i. From *The Invalid's Hymn-book,* 1834–1841 :—

1. Clouds and darkness round about thee. (1841.) *Resignation.*
2. Not willingly dost Thou afflict [reject]. (1841.) *Divine Chastisement.*
3. O God, may I look up to Thee. (1841.) *Teach us to Pray.*
4. This is enough ; although 'twere sweet. (1834.) *On being debarred from Divine Worship.*
5. With tearful eyes I look around. (1841.) *The Invitation " Come Unto Me."*

ii. From H. V. Elliott's *Psalms & Hymns,* 1835–1839 :—

6. Glorious was that primal light. *Christmas.*
7. Hail, holy day, most blest, most dear. *Easter.*
8. My only Saviour, when I feel. *Jesus His people's Rest.*
9. Now let our heavenly plants and flowers. *Monday Morning.*
10. The Sabbath-day has reached its close. *Sunday Evening.*

iii. From Miss Elliott's *Hours of Sorrow,* 1836 :—

11. Father, when Thy child is dying. *Prayer for a Departing Spirit.*
12. Leaning on Thee, my Guide, my Friend. *Death Anticipated.*
13. My God, is any hour so sweet? *The Hour of Prayer.*
14. O faint and feeble-hearted. *Resignation enforced.*
15. There is a holy sacrifice. *The Contrite Heart.*

iv. From her *Hymns for a Week,* 1839 :—

16. Guard well thy lips; none, none can know. *Thursday Morning.*
17. There is a spot of consecrated ground. Pt. i.
18. This is the mount where Christ's disciples see. Pt. ii. *Monday Evening.*
19. This is the day to tune with care. *Saturday Morning.*

v. From *Thoughts in Verse on Sacred Subjects,* 1869.

20. As the new moons of old were given. *On a Birthday.*
21. I need no other plea. Pt. i.
22. I need no prayers to saints. Pt. ii. *Christ, All in All.*
23. Jesus, my Saviour, look on me. *Christ, All in All.*

Several of the earlier of these hymns were repeated in the later works, and are thus sometimes attributed to the wrong work.

[J. D.]

Elliott, Ebenezer, commonly known as the "Corn Law Rhymer," was b. near Rother-ham, Yorkshire, 1781, and d. at Barnsley, in the same county, in 1849. The greater part of his life was spent in Sheffield, where he was engaged in the iron trade, and it was in a Sheffield newspaper that many of his poetical pieces first appeared. He pub. :—

(1) *Night, a Descriptive Poem,* 1818. (2) *The Village Patriarch,* 1829. (3) *Corn Law Rhymes,* 1831. (4) *Poems,* 1834 ; and (5) *More Prose and Verse,* 1850.

A piece or two from these works have been adapted as hymns in some Unitarian Collec-tions. They include "Another year is swal-lowed by the sea," for the old and new year.

[J. J.]

Elliott, Emily Elizabeth Steele, third daughter of the late Rev. E. B. Elliott, of Brighton, author of the *Horae Apocalypticae,* was b. at Brighton, and now [1887] lives in London. She has contributed hymns, some of which have obtained wide acceptance, to the choir manuals, and *Additional Hymns,* 1866 (Nos. 8, 34) for use in St. Mark's Church, Brighton ; to the *Church Missionary Juvenile Instructor,* which she edited for six years. Her *Chimes of Consecration,* a volume of 70 hymns and poems, was pub. in 1873, and her *Chimes for Daily Service* in 1880. The latter contains 71 hymns in two parts. The second part of 48 hymns is also pub. separately as *Under the Pillow,* for use as a cheap large type hymn-book (with corresponding tune-book) for hospitals and infirmaries and the sick generally. Her hymn, "Let us keep the feast" (*H. Communion*), was 1st pub. in *The Feast of Sacrifice and The Feast of Remem-brance,* 1865, in 5 st. of 5 l.   [J. M.]

Elliott, Henry Venn, M.A., s. of Charles Elliott, and brother of Charlotte Elliott, b. Jan. 17, 1792, and educated at Hammer-smith by the Rev. H. Jowett, and at Trinity College, Cambridge. He graduated in 1810, and was subsequently a Fellow of Trinity. Taking Holy Orders in 1823, he became, in 1826, Minister of St. Mary's, Brighton, and remained there to his death on Jan. 24,

1865. His *Life*, by Josiah Bateman, was pub. in 1868. He pub. in 1835, *Psalms and Hymns for Public, Private and Social Worship*, 1835. To this collection his wife and sister contributed many hymns, and to the (2nd or 3rd ed.), c. 1839 edition, he added the following :—

1. For faith, Thy gift, O Lord. *Faith desired.*
2. In the sweet time of early morn. *Prayer on behalf of Children.*
3. Lovest thou not ? alas ! in thee. *Love desired.*
4. Saviour, I see Thy mansions fair. *Faith.*

Mr. Elliott's hymns have not come into extensive use, but his collection, often reprinted, had a marked influence upon latter hymn-books. [England Hymnody, Church of.]

[J. J.]

Elliott, Julia Anne, née Marshall, daughter of Mr. John Marshall, of Hallsteads, Ullswater, was married to the Rev. H. V. Elliott (q.v.), in 1833, and d. Nov. 3, 1841. Her hymns were contributed to her husband's *Ps. & Hymns*, 1835, anonymously, but in the Index to the "3rd thousand," 1839, her initials were added. These hymns are eleven in all, and concerning them, Miller has justly said (*S. & Songs*, p. 482), they

" show a most refined poetical taste, and a special faculty for appreciating and expressing, appropriately, phases of thought and feeling that are beautiful, and that might have escaped common observation."

Of these hymns the best known are, " Hail, thou bright and sacred morn," " On the dewy breath of even," and " We love Thee, Lord, yet not alone " (q.v.). The rest are :—

1. Father, if that gracious name. *Intercession.*
2. Great Creator, who this day. *Sunday.*
3. I would believe ; but my weak heart. *Lent.*
4. My God, and can I linger still. *Lent.*
5. O not when o'er the trembling soul. *Lent.*
6. O Thou, who didst this rite reveal. *H. Communion.*
7. Soon, too soon, the sweet repose. *Sunday Evening.*
8. Welcome to me the darkest night. *Resignation.*

[J. J.]

Elpis, first wife of the celebrated philosopher Boethius, was the daughter of Festus, Consul at Rome, 472, and sister of the mother of St. Placidus, a disciple of St. Benedict. The hymn " Aurea luce et decore roseo " (q. v.) is usually, but somewhat uncertainly, attributed to her. Others also bear her name (see Index). She d. at an early age, at Padua.

Elven, Cornelius, pastor for fifty years of the Baptist Church at Bury St. Edmunds, Suffolk, was b. in 1797, and d. in 1873. His hymn, " With broken heart and contrite sigh " (*Lent*), is found in several collections in G. Britain and America. It was written in Jan., 1852 (Miller's *S. & Songs*, p. 449), for use at special services by his own congregation, and was included in the Bapt. *Ps. & Hys.*, 1858.

Emergit undis et Deo. *Nicholas Le Tourneaux.* [*Epiphany.*] Contributed to the *Cluniac Brev.*, 1686, p. 234, and signed " N. T. P. R." In the revised *Paris Brev.*, 1736, it is the hymn at Lauds and Second Vespers at the Octave of the Epiphany. In the *Lyons* and *Amiens Breviaries* it is for Second Vespers only. In the *Paris Brev.* it is signed " N. T." The text is also in Card. Newman's *Hymni Ecclesiae*, 1838 and 1865 : and J. Chandler's *Hys. of the Primitive Church*, 1837, No. 55. *Tr.* as :—

1. Now Jesus lifts His prayer on high. By J. Chandler, in his *Hys. of the Primitive Church*,

1837, p. 61, in 6 st. of 4 l. It was repeated in Oldknow's *Hymns*, &c., 1850 ; Murray's *Hymnal*, &c., 1852 ; the *People's H.*, 1867, and several later collections ; and also altered as, " And now emerging from the stream," in the *English Hyl.*, 1852, No. 64. Another arrangement, adapted successfully for Holy Baptism as " When Jesus raised His prayer on high," was given in the Scottish Episco. *Coll.*, 1858, No. 105.

2. From the stream emerging, lo. This was given in the *English Hyl.*, 2nd ed., 1856 ; and the 3rd ed., 1861, as " From the stream emerging now." It is J. Chandler's *tr.* much altered.

3. The Lord comes forth from Jordan's stream. This is No. 167 in the *Hymnary*, 1872, and although set forth in the Index as by J. Chandler, it is really a cento from *Chandler*, the *English Hyl.* (version of 1852), and others, the form given to it, and many of the lines being from the *English Hymnal*.

Translations not in C. U. :—

1. He rises from the wave, and now. I. Williams, *British Mag.*, 1835 ; and *Trs. from Paris Brev.*, 1839.
2. From the wave behold Him rise. By *W. J. Blew*, 1852-55.
3. Emerging, lo ! from Jordan's flood. *J. D. Chambers*, 1857, i. 115.

The hymn Castis fit, expers sordium, which is *tr.* by W. J. Blew in his *Church Hy. & Tune Book*, 1852-55, as " Dove of purity unstained," and repeated in Rice's *Sel.*, 1870, is from this hymn and begins with st. iv.   [J. J.]

Emerson, Ralph Waldo, s. of an Unitarian Minister, was b. at Boston, U.S., May 25, 1803. He was educated for the Unitarian Ministry, and acted, 1829-32, as one of their ministers. Ultimately he left the ministry, and devoted himself to lecturing and literature. As a philosopher, essayist, and poet he rose to a distinguished position. He d. at Concord, Massachusetts, April 27, 1882. His published works include *Poems*, 1846 ; *Orations, Lectures, and Addresses*, 1844 ; *Representative Men*, 1850 ; *English Traits*, 1856, &c. His hymns are not numerous. They include :—

1. Out from the heart of nature rolled. *The Everlasting Word.* This is part of his poem *The Problem*, pub. in the *Dial*, July, 1840 ; and then in the 1st ed. of his *Poems*, 1846. It was included in the *Hys. of the Spirit*, 1864, No. 636 ; and Martineau's *Hymns*, &c., 1873, No. 112.

2. We love the venerable house. *The House of God.* Written in 1833, for the Ordination of the Rev. Chandler Robbins, who succeeded Emerson as Minister of the Second (Unitarian) Church, Boston. It is in the *Hys. of the Spirit*, 1864, No. 224 ; and Martineau's *Hys. of Praise and Prayer*, 1873.   [J. J.]

Emilie Juliane was dau. of Count Albert Friedrich of Barby and Mühlingen (on the Elbe, near its junction with the Saale). During the Thirty Years' war her father and family had to seek refuge in the Heidecksburg, the castle of his uncle, Count Ludwig Günther of Schwarzburg Rudolstadt, and Emilie was b. at the Heidecksburg, Aug. 16, 1637. After the death of her father (1641) and mother (1642), she was adopted by her mother's sister (who was her god-mother, and had become the wife of Count Ludwig Günther), and was educated at Rudolstadt with her cousins, under the care of Dr. Ahasuerus

Fritsch, and other tutors. She became the wife of her cousin, Albert Anton, July 7, 1665, and d. at Rudolstadt, Dec. 3, 1706 (*Koch*, iv. 56–63 ; *Allg. Deutsche Biog.*, i. 127 ; *Pasig's Introduction ; Bode*, pp. 63–64, &c.).

She was the most productive of German female hymn-writers, some 600 being attributed to her. Her early education in music and in poetry, and the influence of the kindred spirits of her cousin Ludämilia Elizabeth and of Dr. Ahasuerus Fritsch, no doubt fostered and developed her gifts. Her hymns, which are full of deep and child-like love to the Lamb of God, the Bridegroom of the Soul, partake too largely of the character of revelations of her inner life, and of reflections in verse, "improving" the events of her daily life, to be suited for Church use. A considerable number did, however, pass into the hymn-books, and the first here noted is a hymn of the first rank. Of those pub. in her lifetime the most appeared in her devotional works. (1) *Geistliche Lieder und Gebete vor und nach Erlangung göttl. Ehesegens*, Rudolstadt, 1683. (2) *Kühlwasser in grosser Hitze des Creutzes*, Rudolstadt, 1685. (3) *Tägliches Morgen- Mittags- und Abend-Opffer*, Rudolstadt, 1685 (2nd ed., enlarged, 1699). Others appeared in the editions of the *Rudolstadt G. B.* 1682–1704. After her death they appeared, collected, under the title of *Der Freundin des Lammes Geistlicher Brautschmuck*, pt. i., 1714, and enlarged 1742 ; pt. ii. 1742 ; pt. iii. 1770 ; a number of hymns by other authors, which the editors had found transcribed in the Countess's handwriting, being included by mistake. A selection of 108 of her *Geistliche Lieder*, ed. with an introduction, biographical and critical, by Dr. Pasig, appeared at Halle, 1855.

Three have passed into English, viz. :—

i. **Wer weiss wie nahe mir mein Ende.** *For the Dying.* This beautiful hymn was in last century the subject of an unpleasant controversy. It 1st appeared in the *Appendix* of 1688 to the *Rudolstadt G. B.*, 1682 ; and, like all the other hymns in that collection, it was given without an author's name. It at once passed into other collections, generally as anonymous, but sometimes under the name of the Countess. In the *Schwartzburgische Denkmahl einer Christ-Gräflichen Lammes-Freundin*, 1707, she was expressly named as author. On this G. M. Pfefferkorn (q.v.) claimed it as his own. The resulting controversy is given in detail in *Wetzel*, i. 4–26, ii. 294–307 ; iii. 156–191, and his *A. H.* i. 9–10, ii. 115–117 ; in Fischer, ii. 365–369 ; in Pasig's *Introduction*, xxiii.-xxxi. ; and in *Koch*, viii. 637–639.

No evidence whatever save his bare word has been adduced for Pfefferkorn. On the other hand a copy of the hymn in the handwriting of the Countess dated Neuhaus, 17 Sept., 1686 (two days before the sudden death of Duke Johann Georg of Sachse-Eisenach, which Pfefferkorn said suggested to him the composition of it) is still preserved in the Church Library at Gera, to which it was presented in 1707 by Anna Dorothea Countess of Schwarzburg-Rudolstadt. In a copy of the *Rudolstadt G. B.*, 1704, in which Emilie had marked her own hymns, this hymn is initialed like the rest, "Æ. J.," and in a letter she wrote to the Countess Magdalena Sophia of Schönburg-Hartenstein, she expressly affirmed her authorship. In 1714 the editors of her *Brautschmuck* claimed for it on these grounds—1. That she declared she was the author. 2. That her husband affirmed the same. 3. That the whole Court knew of it. 4. That she had herself contributed it to the *Rudolstadt G. B.*, 1688. On internal grounds, too, its resemblance to other hymns of the Countess bespeaks her authorship.

It is one of the finest German hymns in preparation for death ; and Lauxmann, in *Koch*, viii. 640–646, relates many instances regarding its use, especially in presentiment of death. Thus Dr. J. U. Frommann, diaconus at Tübingen, caused it often to be sung in church before his sudden death in November, 1715, during evening service ; and J. A. Bengel (q.v.), when receiving Holy Communion for the last time with his wife and children, caused st. x., xi. to be sung at the close of the service. The hymn is in Dr. Pasig's ed. of her *Geistliche Lieder*, 1855, p. 164, in 12 st. of 4 l., and the refrain,

"Mein Gott, ich bitt' durch Christi Blut,
Machs nur mit meinem Ende gut ! "

It is No. 609 in the *Unv. L. S.*, 1851.

The *trs.* in C. U. are :—

1. **Who knows how near my life's expended**, omitting st. ix., x., in Dr. H. Mill's *Horae Ger.*, 1845 (1856, p. 245). His *trs.* of st. i., vi.-viii. are included as No. 982 in the American Luth. Gen. Synod's *H. Bk.*, 1850–52, and as No. 430 in the *Ohio Luth. Hyl.*, 1880.

2. **Who knows how near my end may be !** Time speeds away, a good and full *tr.* by Miss Winkworth, in the 2nd Ser. of her *Lyra Ger.*, 1858, p. 204, and then as No. 187 in her *C. B. for England*, 1863. In the Pennsylvania Lutheran *Ch. Bk.*, 1868, st. i., vi., xi., xii., were included as No. 546.

Other *trs.* are : (1) "Who knows how soon my end may be," by *Dr. G. Walker*, 1860, p. 97 ; (2) "Who knows how near my end may be ? Time," &c., by *E. Massie*, 1867, p. 155.

In addition the following have been *tr.*, but are not in English C. U. :—

ii. "Herr ! mein Gott ! lehre mich !" *Evening*, in No. iii., 1685, p. 30. iii. "Jesu Güte hat kein Ende." *Morning*, in No. ii., 1685, p. 228. Both *trs.* are by *H. J. Buckoll*, 1842, p. 104.   [J. M.]

Empty'd of earth I fain would be. *A. M. Toplady.* [*Holiness desired.*] 1st pub. in his *Poems on Sacred Subjects*, 1759, as No. 25 of the "Petitionary Hymns," and headed, "The Believer's Wish." In April, 1771, he included it in a revised form, in 10 st. of 4 l., in the *Gospel Magazine.* This revised text is repeated in Sedgwick's reprint of Toplady's *Hymns*, 1860, p. 30, and is that in use in G. Britain and America. The cento from this hymn, "At anchor laid remote from home" (st. ix. and viii.), appeared in Rippon's *Sel.*, 1787, and is still in C. U.   [W. T. B.]

En dies est Dominica. [*Sunday Morning.*] This long hymn of 116 lines is given by *Mone*, No. 247, from a MS. of the 15th cent. at Karlsruhe. He heads it "Dominicis diebus, hymnus." The same MS. contains the ancient melody. The lines 3, 4 :—

"Ob octavam dominicae,
Resurrectionis sacrae ;'

rendered in the *Hymnal N.* :—

"For on this day the eighth and first,
Our rising Lord death's fetters burst : "

receive illustration from a quotation from St. Augustine (354–430), and noted by *Mone* :—

"The souls truly of all the saints are indeed at rest before the resurrection of the body ; but they have not that power of action with which they flourish when the body is received again, which action the eighth day signifies." *St. Augustine, Epist. Class ii. Epist.* 55, c. 13–23.

From this hymn the following centos are taken :—"En dies est Dominica" ; "Christi nam resurrectio" ; and "Hac die surgens dominus."   [W. A. S.]

The translations of the centos from this hymn are :—

i. **En dies est Dominica.** Of this cento there are three arrangements :—

1. **The Sunday morn again is here.** A *tr.* of ll. 1–4, 13–28, 113–116, by J. M. Neale, in the *Hymnal N.*, 1854, in 6 st. of 4 l., and again in later editions.

2. **Again the Lord's own day is here.** This altered form of Neale's *tr.* with the omission of st. v. is by the Compilers of *H. A. & M.* It was included in the 1st ed., 1861, and continued in the revised ed., 1875.

3. This day which Jesus calls His own. By H. Trend, is a *tr.* of ll. 1–4, 9–28, 113–116, from the *Lyra Mystica*, 1865, into the *People's H.*, 1867, No. 419.

ii. Christi nam resurrectio. This cento is composed of ll. 13–16, 33–36, 49–52, 101–112. *Tr.* as:—

O'er death triumphant Christ arose. In the *People's H.*, 1867, No. 418, is by H. Trend, from the *Lyra Mystica*, 1865.

iii. Hac die surgens Dominus. This cento embraces ll. 28–36, 61–68, 96–108, 113–116. *Tr.* as:

Christ being raised from death of yore. By J. M. Neale, appeared in the *Hymnal N.*, 1854, and was continued in later editions.   [J. J.]

En tempus acceptabile. [*Lent.*] The use of this hymn, probably of the 18th cent., varies according to the Breviary in which it is found. In the *Coutances Brev.* it is at Lauds from the 3rd Sunday in Lent to Passion Sunday (the latter exclusively); and in the *Amiens Brev.* at Matins on Sundays and week-days, when the Ferial Office is said, from Ash Wednesday to Passion Sunday. The text is given in Dr. Neale's *Hymni Ecclesiae*, 1851, p. 95, from the *Cahors Brev.* of 1746. *Tr.* as :

Lo! steals apace the welcome tide. By R. C. Singleton, written in 1867, and included in his *Anglican H. Bk.*, 1868.   [W. A. S.]

Encompass'd with clouds of distress. *A. M. Toplady.* [*The struggles of Faith.*] No. 18 of Toplady's series of hymns in the *Gospel Magazine*, Feb., 1772, in 4 st. of 8 l. Although not included in his *Ps. & Hys.*, 1776, it is given in several modern hymn-books, as Spurgeon's *O. O. H. Bk.*, 1866, and others. Also in the Sedgwick reprint of Toplady's *Hymns*, 1860.   [W. T. B.]

Enfield, William, LL.D., b. at Sudbury, Suffolk, March 29, 1741, of poor parents. Through the assistance of Mr. Hextall, the local Dissenting Minister, at 17 he entered the Daventry Academy under Dr. Ashworth. His first pastorate was of the congregation at Benn's Garden, Liverpool, to which he ministered from 1763 to 1770. In conjunction with Rev. J. Brekell of Key St. chapel, he edited

A New Collection of Psalms proper for Christian Worship, in three parts. I. Psalms of David, &c. II. Psalms of Praise to God. III. Psalms on various Subjects. Liverpool. Printed in the year 1764. Known as the *Liverpool Old Coll.* Later eds., 1767, 1770, 1787. In this last, 60 more hymns are added to the 3rd part.

From 1770 to 1785 Enfield was at Warrington, as minister to the Old Presbyterian congregation, and as teacher of Belles-lettres and other subjects, in the Dissenting Academy founded there in 1757. He pub. in 1774, *The Speaker*; 1783, *Institutes of Natural Philosophy*, and other works, including :—

Hymns for Public Worship: selected from Various Authors, and intended as a supplement to Dr. Watt's's Psalms. Warrington. Printed for the Editor, 1772. 3rd ed. 1789. London. Printed for J. Johnson, St. Paul's Churchyard, and W. Eyres, Warrington. Contains 160 hymns, rather more than half being the same as in the *Liverpool Collection.* In this *Coll.* some of Mrs. Barbauld's hymns appeared for the first time.

From Warrington he proceeded to Norwich as pastor of the Octagon chapel, and d. there Nov. 3, 1797. In 1791 he pub. an abridgment of Brucker's *History of Philosophy*, and at the time of his death was engaged with Dr. J. Aikin,

son of his late colleague at the Warrington Academy, in bringing out a *General Biographical Dictionary*, vol. i. 1796. He also pub.

A Selection of Hymns for Social Worship. Norwich. Printed by J. March for J. Johnson, St. Paul's Churchyard, London, 1795. 2nd ed., 1797 ; 3rd ed., 1802. London, J. Johnson. Printed by W. Eyres, Horse Market, Warrington. Contains 232 hymns, more than half by Watts, and of the rest 93 were retained from the *Warrington Coll.*

In this *Coll.* Enfield's own hymns first appeared, " Behold where in a mortal form " (*Example of Christ*) ; "Wherefore should man, frail child of clay " (*Humility*); and " O Thou, through all thy works adored " (*God the Ruler of Nature*). They are characteristic of the " moral preacher" and the Unitarian, and in taste are unexceptionable. Dr. Enfield received his degree from Edinburgh University. On his death Johnson brought out 3 vols. of his *Sermons* " on Practical Subjects," with a *Memoir* by Dr. Aikin.   [V. D. D.]

English Hymnody. This subject, embracing as it does all hymns associated with the Church of England and Nonconformist bodies in England, from the beginning of English hymn-writing to the present, is too vast and complicated for one article. For the sake of accuracy, clearness, and simplicity, it has been divided into parts which have taken the form of separate articles, each article being complete in itself. The leading articles, and those from which the rest diverge, are **English Hymnody, Early,** and **Psalters, English** ; and a thorough grasp of any subdivision can only be attained by acquaintance with these articles. The subdivisions include :—

1. Baptist.	15. Invalids.
2. Carols.	16. Lady Huntingdon's
3. Children's Hymns.	Colls.
4. Collects in Verse.	17. Litanies, Metrical.
5. Congregational.	18. Methodist.
6. Doxologies.	19. Missions.
7. England, Church of.	20. New Version.
8. English Hymnody, Early.	21. Old Version.
9. Epistles, Hymns on the.	22. Presbyterian, English.
	23. Primers.
10. Graces, Metrical.	24. Psalters, English.
11. Gospels, Hymns on the.	25. Public Schools.
	26. Roman Catholic, English.
12. Hospitals.	27. Sailors and Soldiers.
13. Inghamites.	28. Temperance.
14. Irvingites.	29. Unitarians.

Any additional articles which may be given will be found either under their proper title or through the Cross Reference Index.   [J. J.]

England Hymnody, Church of. In the article on *Early English Hymnody*, and in that on *English Psalters*, the contributions made by the Church of England to English Hymnody to 1700, and, in the case of *Psalters*, to the present time, are fully set forth. To this article is left the task of carrying on the history to the latest hymn-books which have issued from the press.

The origin and development of hymn-book making in the Church of England have their well defined periods, each is the outcome of renewed activity and spiritual life, and all bear witness to robust health and vigour.

i. *First Period.* 1700–1800.

For the first thirty years and more of the eighteenth century nothing was done in the form of hymn-book compiling in the Church of England. A movement, however, in the right direction had taken place by the establishment of the Society for Promoting Christian Knowledge in 1698; and the Society for the Propagation of the Gospel in Foreign Parts, in 1701. The outlook was considerably enlarged by the establishment of these Societies, and, especially through the latter, interest was, to some extent, awakened in "Foreign Parts"; but mainly those which were British possessions. One of the first to catch the spirit of the new movement was John Wesley, who gave himself to mission work in Georgia; and the outcome of that mission was the first hymn-book compiled for use in the Church of England. Wesley went to Georgia in 1735, and returned to England in 1737. His visit to the Moravian settlement at Herrnhut, and his first field sermon on the 2nd of April, 1738, followed, and then came the actual foundation of Methodism, officially dated as 1739. Three years before this, and whilst in Georgia, he published,

Collection of Psalms and Hymns. Charles-town. Printed by Lewis Timothy, 1737.

One copy only of this collection is known to exist: but a facsimile reprint, with a preface by Dr. Osborne, was pub. by T. Woolmer, Castle Street, City Road, London, in 1882. In a letter quoted in Bliss's edition of Wood's *Athenae Oxonienses,* Wesley himself states that he published a *Collection of Psalms & Hymns* in 1736. This collection is the Charles-town book, which thus dates 1736-7. This collection is divided into three sections or parts. The first contains 40 "Psalms and Hymns for Sundays"; the second, 20 "Psalms and Hymns for Wednesdays or Fridays"; and the third, 10 "Psalms and Hymns for Saturday," or 70 hymns in all. Those for Sunday are mostly hymns of praise; those for Wednesday or Friday, humiliation, repentance and prayer; and those for Saturday adoration of God as the Creator of the Universe. There is no provision for Holy Baptism or Holy Communion. Of the 70 hymns more than one-third are by I. Watts, the rest being by various members of the Wesley family, including five *trs.* by J. Wesley from the German, and adaptations from J. Austin, G. Herbert, J. Addison, and others. John Wesley's expansion of this book, together with his various poetical collections and the publications of his brother Charles, were distinctly outside of the Church of England. [**Methodist Hymnody,** § i.]

Beyond this little work, narrow in design and limited in circulation, nothing was done until the great wave of religious awakening had reached the hearts of several of the clergy, and a few began to do within the Church what J. Wesley and others were doing in the fields without. The line of theological thought taken was, however, in most cases more in accordance with the Calvinism of G. Whitefield than the Arminianism of J. Wesley. When, therefore, M. Madan published in 1760 the second important hymn-book for use in the Church of England, he went to the collection published by G. Whitefield in 1753 for many of his hymns. These hymns were in most cases by Watts and Wesley, and altered by Whitefield. The alterations made in Whitefield's book suited Madan better than the originals (alterations so bitterly resented by Wesley in the preface to his hymn-book of 1780), and he

took them without hesitation and without leave. The title of this book is:—

A Collection of Psalms and Hymns, Extracted from Various Authors, and published by the Reverend Mr. Madan ... London.   Printed by Henry Cock; and Sold at the Lock Hospital, near Hyde Park, 1760.

It contained 170 hymns. An *Appendix* of 24 hymns was added in 1763. The arrangement of the collection is very crude. No order of subjects or seasons is observed, except that 27 "Sacramental Hymns" are grouped together at the end, and an alphabetical arrangement is ignored. Notwithstanding this, the selection, although from a limited number of writers only, is excellent. The literary standard is high, and the tone throughout is exceedingly bright and joyous. More than two-thirds of these hymns are still in use in the Church of England.

In 1767 the Rev. R. Conyers, Vicar of Hemsley, Yorkshire, and friend of W. Cowper the poet, pub. his hymn-book under the title of:—

A Collection of Psalms and Hymns from Various Authors: For the use of Serious and Devout Christians of every Denomination. London: Printed by T. and J. Pasham in Black Friars, 1767.

This work seems to have had a good circulation, as it reached to a fourth edition in 1780, but whether its use extended, as its compiler designed, to any of the nonconforming bodies is not known. Conyers followed very much in the same path as Madan. In addition to embodying two-thirds of Madan's book in his own, he gathered the rest principally from the same common stores. He included a few originals from Newton and Cowper, but so far as is known he added nothing thereto of his own. It was an advance upon Madan's book in arrangement, was supplied with an index of subjects, and gave greater prominence to the Christian seasons; but its influence on later collections was not of a special character.

The compilation of Richard De Courcy, published as:—

A Collection of Psalms and Hymns Extracted from Different Authors. With a Preface by the Reverend Mr. De Courcy ... Shrewsbury. Printed and sold by T. Wood ... 1775. (2nd ed. 1782.)

introduced, especially in the 2nd and later editions, a number of hymns from Doddridge, Anne Steele, Mrs. Barbauld, and other Nonconformists, into C. U. in the Church of England. To the 2nd ed. he added a few hymns of his own.

The widening of the area of selections by De Courcy was anticipated to a great extent, so far as his 2nd and later editions were concerned, by A. M. Toplady, who pub. in 1776 his:—

Psalms and Hymns for Public and Private Worship, &c. London, 1776.

The 1st ed., in common with the 2nd and others, was without order or system. Although the greater part of the book was compiled from John and Charles Wesley and Isaac Watts, yet many names new to the Church of England were represented. Most of these were Nonconformists, as J. Allen, J. Cennick, J. Hart, W. Hammond, B. Wallin, and others. The number of his own hymns were few when compared with the number which he wrote: but the alterations and additions which he made in those by other hands were numerous. The 2nd ed. of the collection was edited by the

Rev. Walter Row in 1787. Some hymns were omitted and others added, the total being 412. In later editions the number was further increased. In 1814 they numbered 455, and 6 doxologies.

From 1776-87, at which dates Toplady's two editions were pub., to 1800, various collections were compiled, amongst which the more important were :—

1. *A Choice Coll. of Spiritual and Divine Hymns, taken from various Authors, &c.* By C. H[ull]. Bristol, 1776.

2. *A Collection of Ps. & Hys. on Various Subjects for Public and Private Worship, &c.* By W. Taylor and H. Jones. London, 1777.

3. *Select Ps. & Hys.* Macclesfield (2nd ed. 1780; new ed. 1795). Edited by D. Simpson.

4. *Ps. & Hys. Collected by W. B. Cadogan.* London, 1785. 2nd, 1707, 3rd, 1793; 4th, 1803.

5. *Psalms & Hymns.* By John Venn. London, 1785.

6. *The Ps. of David and other Portions of the Sacred Scriptures, &c.* [Basil Woodd.] London, 1794.

7. *Ps. Hys. & Anthems sung in the Chapel of the Hospital for the Maintenance and Education of Exposed and Deserted Young Children.* [*Foundling Hospital Coll.*] London. Music, 1774, 1797, 1801. Words only, 1797 and 1801.

Although this list shows that there was increased activity in the Church, and a fresher life, yet the hymn-books named above brought little of value to the common store of hymnody, and added not a single name of importance to the list of Church of England hymn-writers. This period closes with a limited number of hymn-books for Church use, and these were Calvinistic in doctrine, were built up upon the lines of the Nonconformists' collections, and were indebted for their contents to Dissenters and the Wesleys, to the extent of some seven-eighths of the whole. Basil Woodd's *Coll.*, 1794, and the anonymous reviser of the *Foundling Hospital Coll.*, 1797, indicated, however, a tendency towards a change for the better which soon took place.

The *Olney Hymns* (q.v.), by J. Newton and W. Cowper, the poet, were pub. during this period in 1779. Although outside of the hymn-books proper, that work exercised a powerful influence on the collections of the next two periods; added two of the greatest names to the roll of hymn-writers; and enriched the hymnody of all time.

ii. *Period.* 1801-1820

The increased interest in the singing of hymns rather than the psalm-versions of *Tate and Brady* during this period, is seen in the number of hymn-books which were published during the twenty years which it embraces, and the places where they were issued. The following list, although not complete, will give a fair idea of the growth and expansion of this new departure in the order of divine worship in the Church of England.

1. *Scriptural Hys. Sel. for the Congregation of All Saints Church, Liverpool.* By Robert Banister. Liverpool, 1801.

2. *Ps. & Hys. for Pub. and Private Devotion.* Sheffield, 1802.

3. *A Coll. of Ps. & Hys. from Various Authors, chiefly designed for Public Worship.* Carlisle, B. Scott, 1802 (4th ed., 1811), Edited by the Rev. J. Fawcett. To this collection J. D. Carlyle's hymns were contributed.

4. *Portions of the Ps. of David, Together with a Sel. of Hys. accommodated to the Service of the Church of England.* By Thomas T. Biddulph. Bristol, 2nd ed., 1804; 5th ed., 1813.

5. *A Sel. of Ps. & Hys. for Pub. and Private Use.* Uttoxeter, 1805. Compiled by J. Stubbs, T. Cotterill, and T. Gisborne.

6. *Versions and Imitations of the Ps. of David Sel. from Various Authors, and adapted to the public worship of the Church of England.* By John Davies. London, 1805.

7. *Ps. of David, &c.* (1st. ed., 1785.) New edition, with an *Appendix* containing :—

8. *Hys. for the principal Festivals of the Church of England.* By R. Cecil. 1806.

9. *Sel. Portions of Ps. extracted from various Versions and adapted to Pub. Worship, With an Appendix containing Hys. for the principal Festivals of the Church of England.* By John Venn. London, 1806. New ed., 1824; 4th ed. revised, 1831.

10. *A Sel. of Ps. & Hys. suited to Pub., Social, & Family Worship.* By the Rev. Henry Gauntlett. Wellington, 1807.

11. *A Sel. of Ps. & Hys. . . . . St. Mary's Chapel, Birmingham, and St. James' Chapel, Ashted.* Birmingham, 1807.

12. *Select portions of Ps. from the New Version, Hys. and Anthems Sung at the Parish Church in Sheffield.* Sheffield, 1807. Edited by Dr. T. Sutton, Vicar of Sheffield. 2nd ed., 1816.

* 13. *Portions of Psalms . . . . With Occasional Hys.* Uttoxeter, 1808. Included for use in Ashbourne Church.

14. *A Sel. of Ps. & Hys. By T. S., Rector of Sandford, Bucks.* Buckingham, 1808. Edited by the Rev. T. Scott.

15. *A Sel. from the New Version of Ps.*, 2nd ed., to which are added in the Appendix several Ps. & Hys. for various occasions not contained in the former edition. By R. Omerod. London, 1809.

16. *Ps. & Hys. for Use of Ely Chapel.* By J. Willcox. London, 1809.

17. *Select Portions of Psalms and Hys. from Various Authors, &c.* By J. Kempthorne. London, 1810.

18. *A Sel. of Ps. & Hys. for Public and Private Use.* By T. Cotterill. Newcastle, Staffordshire, 1810-1815.

19. *A Sel. of Ps. & Hys., &c.* By W. Whitelock. Kendal, 1811.

20. *A Coll. of Ps. & Hys., chiefly designed for the use of Public Worship.* [John Scott ?] Hull, 3rd ed., 1811.

21. *A Coll. of Ps. & Hys. from Various Authors, chiefly designed for the Use of Public Worship.* [C. Simeon ?] Cambridge, 7th ed., 1811.

22. *A Coll. of Hys. for Wrenbury Church, Cheshire.* Chester, 1811. By G. Vaudrey.

23. *Ps. & Hys. for the Parish Church of Greenwich.* By J. L. B[icknell.] London, 1811.

24. *A Sel. of Ps. & Hys. adapted to the Services of the Church, &c.* By J. H. Stewart. Lond. 1813. [*Percy Chapel Coll.*] Very popular.

25. *A Sel. of Ps. & Hys. from the New Version of the Church of England and Others, &c.* By the Hon. Gerard T. Noel. London, 2nd ed., 1813; 3rd ed., 1820.

26. *Ps. & Hys.* By W. Hurn. Ipswich, 1813. 2nd ed., 1824.

27. *Select Ps. & Hys. for the Use of the Churches in Dudley, &c.* By "L. B." Dudley. 3rd ed. with *Supplement*, 1813.

28. *A Sel. of Ps. & Anthems.* By W. Morgan. Bradford, 1815. 2nd ed., 1822.

29. *Ps. & Hys.* New Brentford, 1815.

30. *Portions of Ps., together with Hys., &c.* By H. W. Wilkinson. Sudbury, 1816.

31. *Ps. of David, as sung in Penrith Church.* Penrith, 1816.

32. *Hys. & Anthems for the use of Ramsgate Chapel.* Ramsgate, 1817.

33. *Ps. & Hys. for Pub. Worship.* Wellington. 2nd ed., 1817.

34. *Ps. & Hys. Sung in St. John the Baptist Chapel. Dock.* Plymouth Dock, 3rd ed., 1818.

35. *Select Ps. & Hys. for the Use of the Parish Church of St. Botolph, Without Aldersgate, London.* London, 1818.

36. *A Sel. of Ps. & Hys. used in the Parish Church of Barton-under-Needwood, &c.* Burton-upon-Trent, 1818.

37. *A Sel. of Ps. & Hys. for Pub. & Private Use, &c.* By T. Cotterill. Sheffield. 8th ed. 1819. This is the enlarged and suppressed edition.

38. *A Coll. of Hys. adapted to the Fasts & Festivals of the Church of England.* By E. N. Goymer. Ipswich, 1819.

39. *Ps. & Hys. Selected & Revised for Public, Social, Family or Secret Devotion.* By J. Bickersteth. London, 1819. 2nd ed., 1824; 4th ed., 1832.

40. *A Sel. of Ps. & Hys. for Use in St. Alban's Abbey,* St. Alban's, 1820.

41. *A Coll. of Ps. & Hys. for Use in Burnley Church.* Burnley, Lancashire, 1820.

42. *Sel. of Ps. & Hys. for Public Worship.* Lond., T. Cadell, 1820. This is T. Cotterill's 9th ed., and is dedicated to the Archbishop of York.

The places where these collections were pub. are instructive, as showing that the movement was extending to every part of the country. Whilst Basil Woodd and others issued their compilations in London, Charles Simeon published his at Cambridge. Thomas Cotterill began in Staffordshire and finished in Sheffield. Birmingham, Bradford, Burnley, Cambridge, Carlisle, Dudley, Greenwich, Hull, Ipswich, Kendal, New Brentford, Penrith, Plymouth, Ramsgate, Sudbury, Wrenbury, and other towns had their representative books, each distinct in its way, and all testifying to the increased interest taken in the use of hymns. Outside of London, Yorkshire and Staffordshire were the greatest contributors.

The books of this period are marked by features unknown to the older collections. In the infancy of the movement such congregations as saw good to use the collection of Madan, or Toplady, or De Courcy, or any other, did so without any question as to the legality of the use of hymns in the services of the Church. With the growth of the movement came also opposition thereto on this point, thereby causing many compilers to vindicate their position and proceedings by elaborate prefaces; or to stamp their work with *quasi* authority by a quotation from Queen Elizabeth's Injunctions to the Clergy, 1559, or by a formal dedication to the bishop of the diocese in which the book was published. This opposition reached its climax in 1819. In that year the 8th ed. of Cotterill's *Selection*, a large book issued at a high price, called forth a storm of opposition on the part of his congregation at St. Paul's, Sheffield, upon whom he tried to force the book. This opposition was strengthened by outside feeling, until nothing was left but an appeal to the Diocesan Court at York for a legal decision. Before the trial came on, Archbishop Harcourt suggested a compromise to the effect that the *Selection* should be withdrawn, that another should be compiled, each hymn in which should be submitted for his approval, and that the work should be dedicated to him. This was done, and the result was *A Selection of Psalms and Hymns for Public Worship.* London. Printed for T. Cadell, in the Strand, 1820. ‹ For forty years this *Sel.* continued in use in numerous churches in the North of England. Cotterill's fame, however, as a compiler is associated with the suppressed book of 1819. It did more than any other collection in the Church of England to mould the hymn-books of the next period; and nearly nine-tenths of the hymns therein, and usually in the altered form given them by Cotterill, or James Montgomery who assisted him, are still in C. U. in G. Britain and America. A comparison of this edition with the seven editions which preceded it suggests that this honour is largely due to the assistance rendered by Montgomery.

Another feature which was new to the hymnbooks, was the recognition of the fact that the Church of England used a Book of Common Prayer, and that the hymn-book in use in the same Church should be a companion thereto. The three books which hold a prominent posi-

tion in this respect are those by Basil Woodd, J. H. Stewart, and J. Kempthorne. Holy Baptism, Confirmation, the Saints' Days, &c., are all provided for, and the hymns are systematically arranged under these respective headings. But by far the larger portion of the collections were on the old lines with a little more system in their arrangement. The best of these was Cotterill's suppressed edition of 1819. Basil Woodd's book was the *Hymnal Companion* of its day.

In the selection of *Psalms* during this period the renderings of J. Merrick and I. Watts were very much favoured, those by Tate and Brady, possibly because they were bound up with the Book of Common Prayer, being specially ignored. Contemporary writers of psalm versions shared the same fate, and no new names were added to the list of those whose productions were embodied in the preceding period, except those of Basil Woodd in his own collections. T. Cotterill, J. Cawood, J. D. Carlyle, Sir R. Grant, R. Heber, and W. Hurn, were the most notable of the hymn-writers of this period. With the exception of Grant and Heber these writers do not take high rank.

iii. *Third Period.* 1821–1850.

This period was one of the most prolific in hymn-book compiling of any in the history of the Church of England. During the twenty years an average of over two distinct collections came out every year. The highest number was reached in 1833, when about *ten* collections were published within the twelve months. As most of the hymn-books published during this period are referred to in the annotations of hymns throughout this Dictionary, we subjoin a list, which, although not complete, is yet sufficiently so for all practical purposes. From 1820–1830, we have :—

1. *A New Metrical Version of the Ps. of David with an Appendix of Select Ps. & Hys.* By Basil Woodd. Lond., 1821. Dedicated to the Lord Bishop of Durham.

2. *A Church of England Psalm-Book, or Portions of the Psalter adapted by Selections from the N. and O. Versions to the Service of the Established Church, &c.* By the Rev. Rann Kennedy, A.M., Minister of St. Paul's Chapel, Birmingham. London, 1821. 12th ed., 1848. This book has running comments on various expressions which occur in the psalms and hymns.

3. *Sixty Ps. & Hys. 1st set*, 1823. This contained many original hymns. Sets 2 & 3 were subsequently added. 4th ed., 1862. By E. G. Marsh.

4. *Psalms extracted, &c. . . . Hys. for the principal Festivals, &c.* (1st ed., 1806.) New ed. Clapham, 1824. [J. Venn.]

5. *Psalms Original & Selected for Pub. Worship.* George Mutter, 1825. Enlarged ed., 1841.

6. *A Churchman's Hymn Book, &c.* Derby, Mozley. 5th ed., 1826.

7. *Hymns, &c.* Bp. Heber, 1827 ; 4th ed., 1828 ; 11th ed., 1842 ; and later in England and India.

8. *Selection of Ps. & Hys., &c.* W. Nunn. Manchester, 1827. 3rd ed., 1835.

9. *Ps. & Hys. Sel. and arranged for Pub. Worship.* Charles Bradley. London, 1828.

10. *A Sel. of Ps. & Hys. for the Use of a Country Congregation, &c.*: by a Clergyman. Basingstoke, 1828.

11. *Church Psalmody.* Compiled by a Clergyman's Family. London, 1829. This book was of a distinctly liturgical type.

12. *A Sel. of Ps. & Hys. for St. Mary's, Bryanston Square.* London, 1829.

13. *A Manual of Parochial Psalmody.* T. Hartwell Horne. London, 1829. Dedicated to "William, Lord Archbishop of Canterbury." It has a long and interesting Preface, and most elaborate "Arrangements" of psalms and hymns.

14. *Three hundred and fifty portions of Psalms . . . with a Coll. of Six Hundred Hymns, &c.* Lond., 1829. [Josiah Pratt's Coll.]

15. *The Psalmist.* Henry and John Gwyther. Birmingham, 1830. This contains many original hymns, also others new to the collections. It was not reprinted, but had some influence on later works.

16. *Ps. & Hys. intended as a Supplement to the New Version.* Islington, 1830. Enlarged in 1841. By the Rev. Daniel Wilson. It was for many years the favourite Evangelical hymn-book in North London and district. Much of this popularity arose from the 1841 ed. borrowing extensively from Lyte.

17. *A Church H. Bk. Being a Collection of Ps. & Hys.* Derby, 1825. [By the Rev. Philip Gell.]

18. *A Coll. of Ps. & Hys. chiefly designed for Pub. Worship.* Belper, 1825. [By the Rev. John Wakefield.]

The most important of these was Pratt's *Coll.*, 1829, not for its own intrinsic merits, nor for any marked influence which it had upon later compilations in G. Britain: but because of the great number of hymns which it supplied to American hymn-books published during the next twenty years. In these books nearly all the hymns are of the old-fashioned type, and are arranged in the order of subjects with little or no provision for the minor festivals of the Church. Bp. Heber's *Hymns*, 1827, were an exception, not only in the value of the hymns supplied and their arrangement, but also in adding the name of H. H. Milman to the roll of hymn-writers, and increasing his own reputation as a sacred poet.

From 1831 to 1840 the list is augmented by the following:—

1. *Ps. & Hys. for Pub. & Private Use.* 1831. W. H. Bathurst. These are all original. The 1842 ed. is a reprint.

2. *Church and Home Psalmody, &c.* T. J. Judkin. Lond., 1831. All original compositions by Judkin. Enlarged ed., 1842. Dedicated to "Thomas, Lord Bishop of Salisbury."

3. *Ps. & Hys.* Hugh Stowell. Manchester, 1831. 15th ed., 1877, was edited by his son as *A Sel. of Hys.*, &c.

4. *A Sel. of Psalms for Festivals, &c.* Thomas Mortimer. London, 1831. This contains some original hymns for Saints' days. It ran through several editions.

5. *A Sel. of Ps. & Hys. for Pub. Worship.* Preston, 1831. 16th thousand, 1871. By Mr. Baldwin, Vicar of Leyland, Preston.

6. *A Companion to the Prayer Book.* London, 1832. This collection gives 4 hymns for each Sunday (On the Collect, with a second on the same for Evening; on the Epistle; and on the Gospel). Hymns for Saints' Days from Bp. Mant's *Biographical Notices of the Apostles*, &c., and from J. Keble's *Christian Year*, were brought into congregational use through this book. A *Selection* from this book was pub. the same year.

7. *Festival and Communion Hys., &c.* Greenwich, 1832. Compiled by the Rev. John Shepherd, Minister of the Dartmouth Row Chapel of Ease to Lewisham. It contains originals by the editor.

8. *A Sel. of Ps. & Hys. for Pub. Worship.* Samuel Wilberforce. Lond., 1832. Dedicated to "Charles Richard, Lord Bishop of Winchester."

9. *A Sel. of Anthems, Ps. & Hys., &c.* By the Rev. T. Underwood, jun. Ross, 1832.

10. *Christian Psalmody.* E. Bickersteth, 1833. Dedicated to "John, Lord Bishop of Lincoln."

11. *A Coll. of Hys. for General Use, &c.* Lond., 1833. The title on the back of this book is *A Churchman's Hymns.* Edited by W. W. Hull.

12. *Christian Psalmody, comprising the Book of Ps. . . . and Cong. Hys.* By J. C. Franks, Vicar of Huddersfield. Huddersfield, 1833.

13. *A Sel. of Ps. & Hys. intended for Pub. Worship, &c.* By the Rev. W. Barnes, Rector of Richmond (Yorks.). 1833. This selection gives a prose introduction to each Psalm, and has a section of "Hymns founded chiefly on the Collects, Epistles, and Gospels for each Sunday in the Year."

14. *A Sel. of Ps. & Hys. to be used in Belgrave Chapel.* Lond., 1833.

15. *A Sel. of Ps. & Hys. adapted to the Services of the Church of England.* Lond. & Leeds, 1833. This is divided on the principle of the Psalter. Three hymns are given for each day of the month. There are also additional hymns for Special Occasions and Private Use.

16. *A Coll. of Ps. & Hys. . . . [for]* High Wycombe, Bucks. By the Rev. J. C. Williams, High Wycombe. 2nd ed., 1833.

17. *Ps., Hys. & Spiritual Songs, &c.*, by Rev. E. D. Jackson, author of "The Crucifixion," and other Poems. Manchester, 1833.

18. *The Spirit of the Psalms.* H. F. Lyte. Lond., 1834.

19. *The Weston Hymn Book.* Lond., 1834. This was compiled by the Misses Harrison, of Weston, Sheffield. Weston House is now the Public Museum of Sheffield. J. Montgomery assisted in compiling, contributed to, and revised the proofs of this collection.

20. *Ps. & Hys. for Pub., Private & Social Worship.* H. V. Elliott. Lond., 1835. Dedicated to the "Lord Bishop of Chichester."

21. *Hys. for Sundays & Festivals.* H. Alford. Lond., 1835.

22. *A Sel. of Ps. & Hys. chiefly adapted for Pub. Worship according to the Services of the Church of England.* Edward Davies and John A Baxter. Lond., 3rd ed., 1835. Dedicated to "Henry, Lord Bishop of Lichfield and Coventry," and very extensively used.

23. *Ps. & Hys. Adapted to the Services of the Church of England.* London, 1836. W. J. Hall, and known as the "Mitre H. Bk." Dedicated to "Charles James, Lord Bishop of London."

24. *A Sel. of Ps. & Hymns extracted from Various Authors, &c.* Bungay, new and stereotyped edition, 1833.

25. *Christian Psalmody.* Liverpool, 1837. Compiled by several Clergymen of Liverpool, and reached to 13 editions.

26. *Ps. & Hymns for Divine Service, &c.* By the Rev. Roger Carus Wilson, Vicar of Preston, Lancashire, 1837. Dedicated to "John Bird, Lord Bishop of Chester."

27. *A Sel. of Ps. & Hys., adapted chiefly to Pub. Worship . . . of the Church of England.* John George Breay, B.A., Minister of Christ Church, Birmingham, and Prebendary of Lichfield. Birmingham, 1837.

28. *Ps. & Hys. Original and Selected.* J. Holt Simpson, 1837. From the *O.* and *N. V.*, together with *trs.* by Bp. Mant, J. Chandler, and I. Williams. Hymns from the *British Magazine* first came into C. U. through this collection.

29. *A Sel. of Ps. & Hys. adapted to the Use of the Church of St. Margaret, Westminster.* By. H. H. Milman. Lond., 1837.

30. *Psalmody for the Church: A Coll. of Ps. & Hys. arranged for Public Worship in the Churches and Chapels throughout the Rectory of Bath*, &c., 1838. This was edited by the Rev. John East.

31. *A Coll. of Hys. for Pub. Worship.* J. H. Gurney. Lutterworth, 1838.

32. *A Sel. of Ps. & Hys. for Pub. Worship.* Kirkby Lonsdale. [Carus Wilson family.] Dedicated to "John Bird, Lord Bishop of Chester," by "the Editors." The 12th ed. is dated 1838.

33. *A Book of General Psalmody.* William Carus Wilson. Kirkby Lonsdale, 1838, 2nd ed., 1842. This book contains much new matter taken in many instances from current magazines.

34. *A Sel. of Ps. & Hys.* Norwich, 1838. This was for some time the authorized book of the Diocese.

35. *The Church of England Hymn Book.* D. T. K. Drummond, and R. K. Greville. Edinburgh, 1838. Dedicated "To the Archbishops and Bishops of the Established Church of England and Ireland."

36. *Ps. & Hys. for Rugby Parish Church.* Rugby, 1839. Edited by the Rev. H. J. Buckoll.

37. *Ps. & Hys.* W. Vernon Harcourt. York, 1840. Dedicated to his father the Archbishop.

38. *Ps. & Hys. for the Use of the Church at Accrington.* By Rev. J. Hopwood, the Incumbent. Accrington, 1840.

39. *Ps. & Hys. Selected and adapted to the purposes of Pub. Worship.* By Rev. E. Scobell, Incumbent of St. Peter's, Vere Street; and Evening Lecturer of the Parochial Church, St. Mary-le-Bone. 4th ed., 1840.

40. *Ps. & Hys. adapted to the Services of the Church according to the use of the United Church of England & Ireland; and also Private Reading. Designed to incorporate those Metrical Versions of Psalms, and those Hymns (above 400) which have received Royal, Archiepiscopal, and Episcopal Sanction. By the Rev. Jeremiah Smith, M.A., Vicar of Long Buckby, Northamptonshire, and Prebendary of Lichfield.* London, c. 1840. 6th ed., 1851. The mode adopted in the compiling of this book anticipated to some extent that which guided Bishop Bickersteth in editing the *Hymnal Companion*, 1870. The first sought out "Royal, Archiepiscopal, and Episcopal" sanction; the second, the use made of hymns by former editors.

Of these collections the most noticeable were *Stowell's*, 1831; *Bathurst's* book, 1831; *Bickersteth's*, 1833; *Lyte's*, 1834; *Elliott's*, 1835;

and the *Mitre*, 1836. Stowell's book follows the order of Common Prayer in its broader features, but did not provide for the minor festivals. With additions by his son it is still in use. Bathurst's book was entirely his own composition, as was also the *Spirit of the Psalms*, by Lyte; and both were important, not as hymn-books, but as fresh stores of original compositions. Bickersteth's collection was a great success. It was very much an imitation of Cotterill's suppressed edition of 1819; but upon broader lines, and a somewhat different arrangement. His texts show, when altered from the originals, that he was largely indebted to Cotterill, Toplady, and the *Wes. H. Bk.* His researches in hymnody were beyond anything before attempted in a collection for congregational use in the Church of England, and, especially in the enlarged edition of 1841, partook in this respect largely of the character of the best modern hymn-books. His ascriptions of authorship given in the index are generally correct with regard to the leading writers; but with the more obscure he is often in the wrong. Notwithstanding that it lacked the rich productions of later writers, it was the best Evangelical hymn-book of the Church until "compiled anew," as *Psalms and Hymns based on the Christian Psalmody*, in 1858; and then entirely superseded by the *Hymnal Companion* of 1870-76, both works being by his son, Dr. Bickersteth, Bishop of Exeter. Elliott's collection, 1835, was another Evangelical book of some importance. Its chief historical interest lies in the fact that it was mainly the channel through which Martin Madan's altered text of Watts, Wesley, and others, came into modern hymnals; and that in it some of his sister Charlotte's finest productions were given to the Church. Hall's *Mitre* was a book of another kind, and contained a greater proportion of original hymns than any collection then in use, fifty being by E. Osler alone. It was the outcome of suggestions and complaints against existing collections made to him as Editor of the *Christian Remembrancer*. The Psalms were grouped together as in the older books; and the hymns were arranged in the order of the Book of Common Prayer, with the omission of all the Saints' Days, and Morning and Evening hymns. It had the repute of being "High Church"; a most unaccountable reputation in the face of these omissions. Its psalms and hymns, except in one or two instances, never exceeded four stanzas, and the texts, except in the new hymns, were the most mutilated in existence. With all these drawbacks it attained to a circulation of four million copies. Possibly its approval by and dedication to Dr. Blomfield, Bishop of London, had much to do with this success.

The number of hymn-books put forth during this period, together with the increase of writers and new compositions, testifies most emphatically and eloquently of the growth of religious life throughout the Church. Services were becoming brighter and more animated and cheerful, and a stronger and healthier life was manifesting itself on every hand. The lawsuit instituted against Cotterill in 1819, and the suppression of his book, had also pointed out a danger on the one hand to which com-

pilers had to give heed, whilst the dedication of his revised book of 1820, "To the Most Reverend Edward Lord Archbishop of York," indicated the remedy on the other. Omitting the Welsh dioceses, these dedications included the two Archbishops and most of the Bishops of the Provinces of Canterbury and York. The remedy was found in these episcopal imprimaturs. Under these circumstances it is not surprising to find the use of hymns spreading rapidly throughout the Church; but it is curious to read in the preface of the Bungay *Ps. & Hys.*, 1836, "The position of *sitting*, too common in our congregations, admits of no defence," and to find the statement followed by an argument in defence of *standing* during the singing of the hymns. This protest was repeated in various collections of this period, but is not found later on.

From 1840 to 1850 the hymn-books published included :—

1. *Sel. of Hys. including Versions of Psalms, &c.,* by John A. La Trobe. London, 1841.

2. *Hys. Sel. for the Use of the Weaver Churches.* Sandbach, 1841. 2nd ed., 1845. Dedicated to "John Bird, Lord Bishop of Chester."

3. *Hys. Sel. for the Parish of Sandbach.* By the Rev. J. Latham. Sandbach, 1841. Contains several of J. Chandler's *trs.* from the Latin, and also originals by the editor. This is the same book as the preceding, adapted by the Editor for use in his own parish.

4. *The Church Psalm Book. A Sel. from the Old, New,* and other *Versions, with Hys. for the principal Festivals, &c.* By the Rev. S. Rowe, M.A., Vicar of Crediton, Devon. Plymouth, 4th ed., 1842 (1st ed. cir. 1834).

5. *Ps. & Hys., adapted to the Sundays & Holydays throughout the Year, &c.* H. Alford. London, 1844.

6. *The Praise of God.* By T. Bagnall Baker. London, 1844. Many original hymns by the Editor.

7. *Introits and Collect Hys.* A. Brown. Lond., 1845.

8. *Original Ps. & Hys. for the Use of Churches.* By Nathaniel Meeres. 1846.

9. *Hys. for the Fasts & Festivals, Issued for the Use of St. Stephen's, Camden Town.* Camden Town, 1846. This book reproduced some of the Saints' Days hymns from G. Wither's *Hys. & Songs of the Church,* 1623.

10. *A Sel. of Hys. for Pub. and Private Use, &c.* T. M. Fallow. London, 1847.

11. *Ps. & Hys. Original & Selected, &c.* Richard Shutte. London, 1847.

12. *A Sel. of Ps. & Hys., with Supplement.* C. S. Bird. Gainsborough, 1848. The 15 hymns in the Supplement are by the Editor.

13. *Ps. & Hys. Sel. and revised for Pub. Worship, with several Originals.* By the Rev. James Kelly, M.A., Minister of St. Peter's Episcopal Chapel, Queen's Square, St. James' Park. London, 1849.

14. *Introits & Hys. for Use in Margaret St. Chapel,* N.D. [1849]. This developed into *Hys. & Introits.* 1852.

15. *Ps. & Hys. for the Sanctuary, Family Altar, and Closet.* By the Rev. John C. Miller, M.A., Rector of St. Martin's, Birmingham. Lond., 1848.

16. *Church Hymns, or Hys. for the Sundays, Festivals and other Seasons of the Ecclesiastical Year as observed in the Church of England.* Compiled with an Introduction by Henry Stretton, M.A., Oxon., Perpetual Curate of Hixon, Diocese of Lichfield. Lond., 1850. This collection has a long and good Introduction, and draws largely from J. Chandler's and I. Williams's *trs.* from the Latin.

17. *Hys. for the Services of the Church, arranged according to the Seasons and Holydays of the Christian Year.* London, 1850. This collection consists almost entirely of *trs.* from the Latin by J. Chandler, Bp. Mant, and I. Williams. It was compiled by the Rev. Joseph Oldknow, of Holy Trinity, Bordesley, Birmingham.

18. *A Hymn Book for the use of Churches & Chapels.* London, 1850. Contains Introits and *trs.* from the Latin, especially those by E. Caswall.

19. *The Book of Common Praise.* London, 1850.

20. *A Sel. of Ps. & Hys.* By the Rev. H. K. Cornish, Vicar of Bakewell, Derbyshire. London, 1850.

The only book in this group which had any influence of importance upon later collections was that by *Alford*, 1844, and this arose principally through his original compositions included therein.

These twenty years were not only fruitful in hymn-writers and hymn-books; but during the later half of this period a new departure in hymnody took place which has revolutionised the whole system of hymn-writing and hymn-book making. Keble's *Christian Year* was gradually raising the poetical standard, and awakening renewed interest in the Book of Common Prayer, and the Fasts and Festivals of the Church, when that interest was intensified by the *Tracts for the Times*, the controversies which arose therefrom, and, from a hymnological point of view, by the translations of Latin hymns from the *Roman Breviary* by Dr. (now Cardinal) Newman, Bp. Mant, W. J. Copeland, E. Caswall, and others; and from the *Paris Breviary*, by I. Williams and J. Chandler. These translations were a new revelation to the Church, which dazzled some and grieved others. Upon the hymn-books of this period they came too late to have more than a modified effect, in the next they moulded many and influenced all.

The leading Church writers and translators of this period were:—

H. Alford, J. Anstice, W. H. Bathurst, J. Chandler, W. J. Copeland, Miss Cox, J. Edmeston, C. Elliott and other members of her family, W. H. Havergal, Bishop Heber, J. Keble, H. F. Lyte, Bp. Mant, H. H. Milman, Dr. Newman (before he seceded), E. Osler, H. Stowell, I. Williams, J. H. Gurney, and others.

iv. *Fourth Period.* 1851–1860.

The collections published during these ten years were in many respects widely different in character to any that preceded them, or that came after. Although each book was distinct in itself, yet they may be grouped with comparative ease. The work of translating from the Latin, revived in the former period by Bp. Mant and others, already noticed, was carried on with great vigour and success, especially by W. J. Blew, J. M. Neale, J. D. Chambers, and others. The translations from the German by Miss Cox, 1841, and H. J. Buckoll, 1842, were greatly augmented by A. T. Russell, R. Massie, Miss Borthwick and her sister, Mrs. Findlater, and Miss Winkworth. In addition to purely English sources, valuable material was thus fast accumulating; material which on the one hand had the impress of ancient use, and on the other records of the storm of the Reformation, and the calm that followed. Gradually the Dissenting element, which up to this period constituted nearly two-thirds of the total contents of the hymn-books in use in the Church of England, gave place, in some cases altogether, and in all cases to a very great extent, to the Latin and German, and to new hymns of a higher and more definite Church tone. This work of reconstruction was aided materially by the Church periodical literature of the day, not the least important being the *Ecclesiologist*, and *The Parish Church Choir*. Taken chronologically the books issued during this period are:—

1. *Ps. & Hys. for Pub. Worship. Sel. for some of the Churches in Marylebone*, 1851. C. Baring, T. Garnier, and J. H. Gurney, commonly known as the *Marylebone Collection*.

2. *Choir Service at the Church of St. John the Baptist, Burley Ville.* Ringwood. 2nd ed., 1852.

3. *The Hymnal Noted*, 1852 and 1854.

4. *Ps. & Hys. for the use of Rugby Parish Church*, 1851. [J. Moultrie.] Contains several originals. It was based upon the collection made by H. J. Buckoll for the same Church in 1839.

5. *Ps. & Hys., partly Original, Partly Selected for the Use of the Church of England.* By A. T. Russell, &c., 1851. This collection is especially noticeable for its *trs.* from the German.

6. *A Hymnal for Use in the English Church*, 1852. [F. H. Murray.] This is sometimes known as *Mozley's Hymnal*, from the Publisher, and again as *Murray's Hymnal* from the Editor. It was withdrawn in 1861 in favour of *H. A. & M.*

7. *The Church Hymn & Tune Book.* By W. J. Blew, 1852. Principally *trs.* from the Latin.

8. *The English Hymnal, or a Hy. Bk. for the Use of the Church of England, &c.* Lond., Parker, 1852. 2nd ed., 1856; 3rd, 1861. This is James A. Johnston's *Hymnal*. Most of the *trs.* from the Latin are by the Editor. Those in the latter editions differ materially from the first.

9. *Hys. for the Sundays & Holy Days of the Church of England.* By J. R. Woodford (q. v.), 1852. 2nd ed., 1855.

10. *Hys. & Introits.* By G. C. White, 1852, 1853, 1861.

11. *Hys. S. P. C. K.*, 1852, enlarged as *Ps. & Hys.*, 1855; 1st *Appendix*, 1863; 2nd, 1869. Superseded by *Church Hymns*, 1871.

12. *The Church Hymnal.* Lond., J. Whitaker, 1852. It was "issued in the first instance in fasciculi, and used in the Churches of the Editors," the Rev. William Cooke, and the Rev. William Denton, "that the principle on which it was based, and the hymns it contained, might be tested by experience." It was pub. in 1853, 2nd ed. 1855, and had a large circulation. Special *Supplements* were added, in some instances by others, for local use. The altered texts, and they are not few, are mainly by Canon Cooke.

13. *A Sel. of Ps. & Hys. Arranged for the Public Services of the Church of England.* By the Rev. C. Kemble. Lond., 1853. This collection was used extensively for many years. In 1873 it was superseded by *The New Church H. Bk.* by the same Editor.

14. *Ps. & Hys. for Public Worship.* By the Rev. J. F. Thrupp, Cambridge, 1853: 2nd ed. undated and a reprint only. This work contains a great number of originals by the Editor.

15. *Hys. of the Catholic Church.* Stratford-on-Avon, 1853.

16. *Hys. for the Use of St. John the Baptist, Oxford*, 1854. This collection was issued as *The Merton H. Bk.* in 1866, and as *The Parochial H. Bk.*, 1866.

17. *The Church Psalter & H. Bk., &c.* By the Rev. W. Mercer. Lond., 1854, 1860; rearranged Oxford ed., 1864.

18. *Ps. & Hys. for the Use of the Church of England at Home and in the Colonies.* Rev. J. W. Colenso, 1854.

19. *Ps. & Hys., compiled by the Rev. T. B. Morrell and the Rev. W. W. How.* 1854; enlarged ed., 1864; Supplement, 1867.

20. *Symmetrical Psalmody; or, Portions of the Ps. and other Scriptures, translated into Metrical Stanzas with corresponding accents in corresponding Verses for Musical Use.* By the Rev. W. V. Harcourt. Lond., 1855. One of the most curious and eccentric books known to hymnody.

21. *A Church Psalter & Hymnal, &c.* By the Rev. E. Harland, 1855: *Supplement*, 1863; followed by an enlarged edition, undated, and a second *Supplement* in 1876.

22. *A Hymn Book for the Services of the Church and for Private Reading.* Oxford & Lond., 1855; 2nd ed., 1857; 4th, enlarged, 1867. This is the Rev. Isaac Gregory Smith's collection, and to it he contributed several originals.

23. *Hys. for Use in Church.* By the Rev. H. W. Burrows, 1855. Late Fellow of St. John's, Oxford.

24. *Ps. & Hys. for Pub. & Social Worship.* By the Rev. E. Walker, Vicar of Cheltenham, 1855. To this Dr. Walker added an Appendix; and the Rev. C. D. Bell a second *Appendix*, in 1878. This is known as the *Cheltenham Coll.* It contains a great number of hymns by Plymouth Brethren writers, including those of Dr. Walker's brother-in-law, J. G. Deck.

25. *Ps. & Hys, for the Sanctuary, Family-Altar, and Closet.* Sel. by the Rev. John C. Miller, D.D., Rector of St. Martin's, Birmingham, 1856. (Later ed. of No. 15 on p. 336, ii.)

26. *A Common Psalter*, 1856. Compiled by the Rev. William Harrison, B.A., Oxford, 1832. Sometime Rector of Birch, Colchester, and Hon. Canon of Rochester.

27. *The Winchester Church H. Bk.* Winchester and London, 1857.

28. *The Salisbury H. Bk.* Edited by Earl Nelson, 1857.

29. *Hys. for the Church of England.* Lond., 1857. This is the Rev. T. Darling's collection. It was enlarged and altered several times. The latest ed. is 1887.

30. *Words of the Congregational Hymn & Tune Book.* 1857. This was subsequently revised and issued as *The Hymnal. By the Rev. R. R. Chope,* 1862.

31. *Ps. & Hys. based on the Christian Psalmody, &c.* 1858. This is the Rev. E. H. Bickersteth's revision of his father's collection of 1833.

32. *Hys. for the Use of a Parish Church.* Honiton, 1859. By the Rev. J. F. Mackarness, Rector of Honiton, 1855–1869; Bp. of Oxford, 1870.

33. *Hys. for the Christian Seasons.* Gainsburgh, 1854. Edited by the Rev. R. T. Lowe, Lea, Lincolnshire.

34. *Ps. & Hys. Sel. for Pub. Worship in the Church of England.* Bedford, 1859.

35. *The Shilling H. Bk.,* 1859. By the Rev. W. Stone, Vicar of St. Paul's, Haggerston.

36. *Ps. & Hys. for Pub. Worship.* By the Rev. H. H. Wyatt, sometime Incumbent of Holy Trinity Chapel, Brighton, and in 1886 Rector of Conington, Peterborough.

37. *A Church Hymnal for Parochial Use.* 1859.

38. *The Divine Hymnal. A Coll. of Hys. of Direct Homage for the Use of the Church.* By A. K. B. G[ranville]. 1860.

39. *Hys. and Anthems for the Services of the Church.* 1860.

40. *Hys. for Pub. Worship.* By the Rev. A. Wolfe. 1860. Lady Margaret Preacher at Cambridge in that year, and in 1887 Rector of Fornham All-Saints, Bury St. Edmunds.

41. *Hys. for Pub. Worship and Private Devotion (in use at S. Raphael's Church, Bristol).* By A. H. W. [Arthur Hawkins Ward, of Pembroke College, Cambridge, B.A., 1855.] Bristol, 1860.

42. *Hys. for Pub. Worship, &c.* Cir. 1860. By Rev. W. Knight. Sometime Secretary of the Church Miss. Soc., and in 1887 Rector of Pitt Portion, Tiverton.

43. *Parochial Psalter and H. Book.* By J. Robinson, 1860.

This list shows that one or two editors, as *Kemble*, repeated the old order of things, whilst others, as in the case of Dr. Oldknow and the *Hymnal Noted*, went to the other extreme, the first in almost, and the second in entirely ignoring English hymns. The middle course adopted by the majority were of two types, the one where English and *trs.* from the Latin, with here and there a *tr.* from the German, were the rule, as in Murray's *Hymnal*, 1852, and the Cooke and Denton *Church Hymnal*, 1853; and the second, where the proportions of Latin and German were reversed, as in A. T. Russell's *Ps. & Hys.*, 1851, and Mercer's *Ch. Psalter and H. Bk.*, 1854. Of all these collections issued during this period, at its close, in popularity and extensiveness of use Mercer's took the lead. This period was also marked by a somewhat strict adherence in the arrangement of the hymns to the order of the Book of Common Prayer; by the introduction of the printing of the words and the music together; and by the almost entire discontinuance of dedications to the Bishops. The translators and original writers of this period include:

J. M. Neale, W. J. Blew, J. A Johnston, J. R. Woodford, W. Cooke, J. F. Thrupp, W. Mercer, W. W. How, E. Harland, I. G. Smith, T. Darling. E. H. Bickersteth, A. K. B. Granville, Earl Nelson, J. Keble, and others.

v. *Fifth Period. Hymns Ancient and Modern,* 1861.

The state of matters hymnological at the close of the last period was somewhat chaotic. Blew's admirable collection was a dead letter. The *Hymnal Noted* had an exceedingly limited circulation. Collections of the type of Mur-

ray's *Hymnal,* and the *Cooke & Denton* selection were too much alike to ensure success to either. *Mercer's* held on its way triumphantly: whilst *Kemble* with others of the same school, as *Cotterill, Bickersteth, Carus Wilson,* the *Ps. & Hys.* of E. H. Bickersteth, *Stowell,* the S. P. C. K. *Ps. & Hys.,* and a host of others (enumerated above) were in use in more than two-thirds of the chapels and churches of the Church of England. Outside of the hymn-books much hymnological work had also been done, notably by Dr. Neale, with the Latin; A. T. Russell, Miss Cox, R. Massie, Miss Borthwick, Miss Winkworth, and others with the German; and Alford, Keble, Churton, Mrs. Alexander, Mrs. Toke and others, too numerous to name, in original compositions. At the opening of this period those who favoured the *Hymnal Noted* line of hymnody were content to let their work alone. The other extreme, having the command of nearly three quarters of the parishes in the land, were also satisfied with what they had done. It was with the intermediate party of the *Murray, Hymns and Introits,* and *Cooke and Denton* school that the greatest difficulty was found. The difficulty, however, was the mother of a magnificent success. The leaders in this movement saw that a large mass of Churchmen were prepared, through the hymnological work of the former period, for something hymnological of a moderate, definite, and popular character, and on the new lines which circumstances had been shaping for some five and twenty years. On the understanding that several books then in use were to be withdrawn in favour of a new work, a syndicate of the holders of the copyrights of those hymn-books, and others interested in hymnology, was formed, and in 1859 the trial copy of the new adventure was distributed amongst its supporters. It bore the simple title *Hymns.* It consisted of 130 compositions, 121 of which were old and in other collections. Of the remaining 9, 5 were translations by the Compilers and 4 were new original hymns. The note which accompanied these *Hymns* indicated the object of the collection and its use, and explains the absence of all sacramental and most festival hymns :—

"These hymns are printed for temporary use, and as a specimen, still open to revision, of the Hymn Book now in course of preparation by a committee of Clergymen, the publication of which has been postponed to Advent, 1860. Some of these hymns, such as Bishop Ken's morning and evening hymns, will ultimately be given more fully; and of some only the first lines are now inserted for want of space. The book will probably contain about 300 hymns; ample provision being made for Baptism, Confirmation, Holy Communion, Saints' Days, Harvest Festivals, School Feasts, Funerals, Fast and Thanksgiving Days, Missions, &c. . . . Any suggestions will be gladly received by the Secretary of the Committee, the Rev. Sir Henry Williams Baker, Bart."

When the book was published in 1861 as *Hymns Ancient and Modern,* 18 of the 130 hymns in this trial copy were omitted, and others were more or less altered. The work (not counting parts) contained 273 hymns. Of these 132 were from the Latin, 10 from the German, 119 were English, and already in use, and 12 were new original hymns. Of the 132 from the Latin, 116 were altered, 33 being from Neale, 29 from Chandler, 17 from Caswall, 11 from I. Williams, and the rest from about a dozen translators. Sir H. W. Baker contributed 6 new translations, the Compilers 5, and 5 were given unaltered from others. The translations from the German were by Miss Winkworth, Miss Cox, and Sir H. W. Baker, 9 being old, and 1 new (by Sir Henry). Of the English hymns, 92 were old hymns altered, 26 old hymns not altered, 10 new hymns by Sir H. W. Baker, 1 new by Mr. Whiting (much altered), and 1, also new, by Mr. Chatterton Dix. The new element in the book was represented, therefore, by 11 translations from the Latin, 1 from the German, and 12 original hymns. The alterations of the translations were mainly by the Compilers; but those of the English hymns they inherited for the most part from former editors. Nothing in the arrangement of the book was new, and the doctrinal standpoint was below several of the hymn-books which preceded it and about which little or nothing had been said. That a collection of hymns, thus constituted, should have been so much lauded, is as astounding as that it should have been so much abused. Its success was unparalleled in the history of hymnology, *Watts* and the *Wes. H. Bk.* alone excepted. This success arose from many causes. The book was published simultaneously with the withdrawal of others which had been its forerunners, and it was immediately adopted by many of the clergy who were pledged thereto. Its title was also one of the most happy ever adopted for a book. A great wave of religious enthusiasm was passing over the Church, and things old and primitive were esteemed of great value. Men were beginning to long for something of the old way of thinking, and fragrant with the old flavour. To get, therefore, a collection of "Hymns *Ancient* and Modern," was to gratify this longing, in utter ignorance of the fact that everything therein that was *old* had been at the threshold of their houses years before. The one word *Ancient* in the title was a magician's wand. The music was also an element of success of no mean importance. The *title* of the book was repulsive to Dissenters, but the *music* was attractive; and in addition to a vast sale in the Church of England, it soon found its way into a large number of chapels in England and elsewhere as a tune book solely for use with other collections. In a dozen years from its publication not twenty hymns as given therein were sung in thousands of churches and chapels, where at the same time not twenty tunes therein were unsung in the same places of public worship. Another, and that not the least, important element of its success was the abuse which was heaped upon it. Apart altogether from the party spirit of those attacks, the hymnological ignorance of the critics was something astounding. But it helped the cause which they intended to hinder, and drew attention to a work, which but for them, would have remained unknown to a large multitude of people.

vi. *Sixth Period.* 1862–1887.

The hymnological works which followed the publication of *H. A. & M.* were, omitting reviews and pamphlets which were numerous: 1st, *Works on Hymnody;* 2nd, *Collections not for Congregational use;* 3rd, *New editions of old books and appendices,* and 4th, *Independent Collections.*

1. *Works on Hymnody.*—The contributions of Dr. Neale, Mrs. Charles, and others to hymnological history during the former period, and the spirit of inquiry created by the publication of *H. A. & M.*, were followed by numerous magazine articles, pamphlets, and works of various designs and degrees of excellence both within the Church and amongst Nonconformists, as Mr. Biggs's *Annotated H. A. & M.*, 1867; his *English Hymnody,* and his *Songs of other Churches;* Dr. Littledale's and Dr. Neale's *trs.* from the Greek with accompanying notes; the *Lyras* of Mr. Orby Shipley; translations from the German by Miss Winkworth, Miss Borthwick and others; original compositions by various persons; the hymnological researches of D. Sedgwick, Josiah Miller (*Singers and Songs of the Church*), and Major Crawford in England, and Dr. Hatfield, Professor Bird, and others in America; the later works on Latin hymns of *Daniel, Mone, Wackernagel,* &c., in Germany; and the reprints of the *Missals* of *Sarum, York, St. Andrews* and *Hereford,* &c., and the *Latin Hymns of the Anglo-Saxon Church;* these publications and many besides in Great Britain, Germany, and America, produced a wealth of material and an accuracy of text which were unknown to the Compilers of *H. A. & M.* in 1861, and became available to them and others in after years.

2. *Collections not for Congregational use.*—The leading works of this kind, and those which had the greatest influence upon the books published after *H. A. & M.* were:—

1. *Lyra Eucharistica: Hys. & Verses on the Holy Communion Ancient & Modern, with other Poems.* 1863. By the Rev. Orby Shipley, enlarged 1864.
2. *Lyra Messianica: Hys. & Verses on the Life of Christ, Ancient and Modern. With other Poems.* 1864. The same Editor.
3. *Lyra Mystica.* 1865. The same Editor.
4. *The Book of Praise, from the best English Hymn Writers, Sel. and Arranged by Roundell Palmer.* 1862. 3rd ed. enlarged, 1867.
5. *Lyra Britannica, A Collection of British Hymns printed from the Genuine Texts. With Biographical sketches of the Hymn-writers.* By the Rev. Charles Rogers, LL.D., 1867. This was not a Church of England work; but it assisted materially in restoring the original texts of Church of England hymns.

These works contribute much in many ways in furthering the interest of English Hymnody, the *Book of Praise,* especially, in drawing attention to the incomplete texts of most hymn-books, and supplying the original readings, and the *Lyras* in furnishing translations from various sources.

3. *Supplements, New Editions of Old Books,* &c. These supplements and reprints included the following:—

1. *An Appendix to the Hymnal Noted.* By T. I. Ball. 1st ed., 1862, 213 hymns and 2 litanies; 2nd ed., 1863, 343 hymns; 3rd ed., 1867, 357 hymns; 6th ed., 1877, 371 hymns. The later editions are entitled *The Hymnal Noted, With Appendix revised and greatly enlarged.* Mr. Ball issued an additional *Supplement* at Edinburgh in 1882, which increased the total to 588 hymns. It has also Introits, Graduals, Tracts, and Sequences "according to the Roman Use."
2. *Appendix to the S. P. C. K. Ps. & Hys.* 1863.
3. *The Supplemental H. Book.* By the Rev. R. H. Baynes. 1866.
4. *The Appendix Hymnal.* By the Rev. H. L. Nicholson. 1866.
5. *The Supplementary Hymnal.* By the Rev. H. J. Palmer. 1866.
6. *Hys. for the Special Services and Festivals* [in Chester Cathedral.] Two Parts. 1867.

7. *Supplemental Hymn & Tune Book.* 1867. By the Rev. R. Brown-Borthwick.

8. *Appendix to H. A. & M.* 1868. By the Compilers.

9. *A Supplemental H. Bk.* [to the S. P. C. K. *Ps. & Hys.*]. By Richard Harvey. 1868.

10. *Appendix to H. A. & M. for St. Philip's, Clerkenwell.* 1868. This collection contains several original hymns by Mr. Whiting.

11. *Appendix* to the S. P. C. K. *Ps. & Hys.* 1869.

12. *Appendix to The Hymnal* for West Hackney. 1869. This contains the Rev. T. Hugo's original hymns.

13. *Appendix to the Hymnal Companion for the Use of Christ Church, Everton.* By W. H. M. Aitken. 1872.

14. *A Supplemental Hymnal.* 1873. By the Rev. W. Stone. It contains many of the Rev. S. J. Stone's best hymns.

15. *Appendix to H. A. & M. For the Use of St. Michael's, Folkestone,* 1873. By the Rev. E. Husband. It contains several original hymns by the Rev. G. Moultrie, the Editor and others.

16. *Hys. for Use in the Church of St. Ethelburga, Bishopsgate.* 1873. This is a special *Appendix* to the *People's Hymnal.*

17. *Litany Appendix.* By the Rev. T. B. Pollock. 1873.

18. *The Additional H. Bk.* 1875. By the Rev. J. C. Ryle. This contains 300 hymns for Pub. Worship. Most of these are new to the collections.

19. *Supplement* to Harland's *Church Psalter and Hymnal* (1855). By Lady Victoria Wellesley. 1876.

20. *Supplemental Hymns & Tunes.* 1882. By the Rev. E. Husband. Contains originals by the Editor.

21. *Appendix* to the *Hymnal Companion.* 1884. For use in the Cheltenham Parish Church by Canon Bell, with originals by the Editor.

22. *The Hymnal.* 1862. By the Rev. R. R. Chope. An enlarged ed. of his *Words of the Cong. Hy. & Tune Bk.* 1857.

23. *Hys. Sel. from the Church Hy. & Tune Bk.* [J. W. Blew's, 1852.] By the Rev. Howard Rice, Vicar of Sutton Courtney, Berks. 1870.

24. *Church Psalter & H. Bk.* By the Rev. W. Mercer. Oxford ed., 1864.

25. *Ps. & Hys. for Pub. Worship. Sel. for the Use of the Parish Churches of Islington.* Enlarged ed., 1862.

26. *Songs of the Church. A Supplemental Hymnal.* 1867. By the Rev. G. S. Jellicoe, Vicar of St. Peter's, Chorley, Lancashire.

27. *A Sel. of Hys. suited to the Services of the Church of England. By the (late) Rev. Hugh Stowell,* M.A., &c. Manchester, 1877. This is the 15th ed. of Stowell's *Sel.*, and was edited by his son, the Rev. T. A. Stowell.

28. *Savoy Hymnary.* Chapel Royal, Savoy, N.D. Appendix to *The Hymnary.*

29. *Supplemental Hy. & Tune Bk.* 1874. By the Rev. A. E. Evans.

30. *Supplemental Hymnal to H. A. & M.,* 1875. Lincoln. By the Rev. A. W. Hutton.

These numerous *Appendices* and *Supplemental Hymn-books* not only pointed out the weaknesses of the collections which, when published, were supposed to have been complete, but also brought to the front hymn-writers of great promise and sterling merit whose services have been utilized to the full in the latest hymnals, not only of the Church of England, but of Nonconformists also.

4. *Independent Collections.* — These again are numerous :—

1. *Hys. Fitted to the Order of Common Prayer and Administration of the Sacraments, &c.* 1861. By the Rev. F. Pott.

2. *Hys. Used at the Church of St. Thomas the Martyr, Oxford.* 1861. Enlarged ed., 1870. By the Rev. T. Chamberlain.

3. *The Choral H. Bk., Ps. & Hys. for Pub. and Private Use, &c.* 1861. By the Rev. P. Maurice.

4. *Words of Hys. in the Appendix of the Brompton Metrical Psalter.* 1861. By the Rev. W. J. Irons.

5. *The Church & Home Metrical Psalter & Hymnal.* By the Rev. William Windle, M.A., Rector of St. Stephen's, Walbrook, and St. Benet's. London, 1862.

6. *A Hymnal for Use in The Services of the Church.* By the Rev. J. B. Trend, B.A., Fellow of St. Augustine's College, Canterbury. 1862. This contains several *trs.* from the Latin by Dr. Trend, the Father of the Editor.

7. *Hymns for the Church Services.* Lincoln, 1862.

Supplements, 1867 and 1871. Edited by Prebendary H. W. Hutton of Lincoln.

8. *Ps. & Hys. for the Church, School, and Home. By the Rev. D. T. Barry, B.A., Incumbent of St. Ann's, Birkenhead,* 1862 ; Rector of Fishley, Norfolk, 1880. This collection attained to extensive use. It was issued with a different arrangement in 1867, and an *Appendix* was added in 1871. In the latest edition the title is changed to *The Parish Hymn Book,* the title of the collection pub. by the Rev. H. W. Beadon and others in 1863.

9. *A Book of Praise ; or, Hys. for Divine Worship in the United Church of England & Ireland, &c.* 1862. By the Rev. A. Gurney.

10. *The Daily Service Hymnal.* 1863. By the Rev. James Skinner. The revised small type ed. of 1864 contained an article explanatory of Commemoration Days, and Introits and Anthems.

11. *The Parish H. Bk.* 1863. By the Revs. H. W. Beadon, Greville Phillimore, and J. R. Woodford, all of whom contributed original hymns. In 1875 it was enlarged from 197 to 274 hymns.

12. *Hymnologia Christiana: or, Ps. & Hys. selected & arranged in the order of the Christian Seasons.* By B. H. Kennedy. 1863.

13. *The Canterbury Hymnal.* By the Rev. R. H. Baynes. 1863.

14. *A Book of Common Praise.* 1863.

15. *Hys. Old and New.* 1864. By the Rev. T. Davis.

16. *Hys. for the Use of the Parish Church of Albury.* By the Rev. G. R. Portal, M.A., Rector of Albury. 1864.

17. *Hys. New and Old.* 1864. By Lord Rollo.

18. *Hys. of the Church of God.* By the Rev. F. V. Mather, Perpetual Curate of St. Paul's Church, Clifton ; Chaplain to the Bp. of Gloucester & Bristol. 2nd ed., 1864.

19. *A Book of Church Hys.* 1865. Compiled for the Use of St. Saviour's, Clapham. It was adopted by several churches in the neighbourhood. It is found with a change of title as *Hys. for St. Saviour's, Clapham ; Holy Trinity, Clapham ; St. Michael's, Mitcham, &c.*

20. *A Sel. of Ps. & Hys. for Pub. Worship.* 1865. By the Rev. Abner W. Brown.

21. *Hys. of Prayer and Praise for the Services of the Church and for Private Devotion.* Calne, 1865.

22. *Hys. for use in Church.* By the Rev. W. J. Irons. 1866. An enlargement of his *Appendix,* 1861.

23. *Church Song. A Compilation of Ps. & Hys. for Anglican Use.* 1866. By the Rev. W. J. Beaumont, Rector of Cole-Orton, Diocese of Peterborough.

24. *The People's Hymnal.* 1867. By the Rev. R. F. Littledale.

25. *The Book of Praise Hymnal.* 1867. By Lord Selborne.

26. *Hys. of Prayer and Praise.* 1867. By the Rev. S. F. Jones. Prepared for the Special Services in Westminster Abbey.

27. *The Year of Praise.* 1867. By the Rev. H. Alford.

28. *The Temple Church Hymn Book.* Lond., 1867.

29. *The Sarum Hymnal.* 1868. By Earl Nelson, and the Revs. J. R. Woodford and E. A. Dayman.

30. *The St. Michael's Hymnal.* Teignmouth, 1868.

31. *The Bonchurch H. Bk. for use in Pub. Worship, Devotional Meetings, and Schools.* By the Rev. J. G. Gregory, M.A., Rector. 1868. This has been superseded by *A Sel. of Hys. for use in Emmanuel Church, Hove, Brighton,* 1869, by the same Editor.

32. *The Anglican H. Bk.* 1868. By the Rev. R. C. Singleton. Revised and enlarged, 1871.

33. *Hymnal for the Church and Home.* By the Rev. B. A. Marshall, M.A., Incumbent of St. Cuthbert's, Carlisle. 1868.

34. *Holy Song for All Seasons.* 1869. A Selection of 631 hymns. Contains much not found in other collections.

35. *Selections from a Hymnal suited for the Services of the Church, with some Introits and Antiphons, and an Appendix.* Privately printed by W. Knott, Greville St., Brook St., Holborn, E.C., 1869. This has three *Appendices.*

36. *The Hymnal Companion.* 1870. By the Rev E. H. Bickersteth.

37. *The Hymnary.* 1870. By the Revs. W. Cooke and B. Webb. Revised, 1872.

38. *Select Hys. for Church & Home.* 1871. *Appendix* 1885. By the Rev. R. Brown-Borthwick.

39. *Songs of Grace & Glory for Private, Family, & Pub. Worship. Hymnal Treasures of the Church of Christ from the 6th to the 19th Century.* By Charles B. Snepp, LL.M., Vicar of Perry Barr. 1872. This collection is strongly Calvinistic in doctrine. It is very

rich in hymns of high merit, and not usually met with in modern hymn-books. Miss F. R. Havergal wrote for it and assisted in its compilation. It has a separate *Appendix*, which brings the number of hymns to 1094. The Indices are very full, and the ascriptions of Authors and dates are very accurate.

40. *Church Hymns*, S. P. C. K. 1871.

41. *Hymns for the Use of the University of Oxford in St. Mary's Church.* Oxford, 1872.

42. *A Book of Litanies.* Lond., Rivingtons. 1874.

43. *The Parish Hymnal, after the Order of the Book of Common Prayer.* 1873. By the Rev. J. S. B. Monsell.

44. *Ps. & Hys. for the Church.* 1873, 1875, 1884. By the Rev. W. J. Irons.

45. *The St. Margaret's Hymnal.* 1875. This collection, printed for St. Margaret's, East Grinstead, is noticeable as containing many hymns and *trs.* by Dr. Neale not in other hymn-books.

46. *An Improved Hymnal.* 1875. By Joshua W. Smith.

47. *A Book of Prayer & Praise.* 1875. By the Rev. T. W. Fowle, M.A., Rector of Islip, Oxford.

48. *The New Mitre.* 1875. By the Rev. W. J. Hall, M.A. A small book of 202 hymns, some originals by B. Gough and the Rev. S. Baring-Gould, and many from the *Mitre* of 1836.

49. *Hymns Ancient & Modern.* Revised edition, 1875.

50. *The Churchman's Hymnal. A Bk. of Hys. fitted to the Order and Teaching of the Bk. of Common Prayer.* 1876. New ed. 18, N.D. Edited by the Rev. J. L. Porter, Vicar of St. John's, Ladywood, Birmingham.

51. *Hymnal Companion.* Revised edition, 1876.

52. *The Eucharistic Hymnal.* 1877. Contains original hymns of the highest Anglican type.

53. *Common Praise: Ps., Hys. & Spiritual Songs for use in the Church of England.* 1879. The Church of England Book Society's collection.

54. *The Church of England H. Bk.* By the Rev. G. Thring. 1880. Revised ed., 1882.

55. *Hys., Anthems, &c., for Pub. Worship.* Edited by the Rev. T. E. Powell for the Parish Church of Bisham. Contains several originals by the Editor.

56. *Hys. for the Church Catholic.* 1882. Edited by the Rev. J. B. Whiting, Vicar of St. Luke's, Ramsgate.

57. *Hys. from the Ancient English Service Books, together with Sequences from various sources.* Reprinted from the *Antiphoner & Grail.* Privately printed, 1882. The title on the cover of this small book is *The Hymner.* The *trs.* are direct from the Latin without any modification whatever, the Invocation of Saints and other features of a like kind being retained. The *Antiphoner & Grail* appeared in two parts in 1880.

58. *The Westminster Abbey Hymn Book.* Edited by the Rev. J. Troutbeck. 1883.

59. *The Berwick Hymnal.* 1887. By the Rev. A. W. Oxford, Vicar of St. Luke, Berwick St., London.

60. *The Altar Hymnal. A Bk. of Song for use at the Celebration of the Holy Eucharist.* 1884. Edited by Mrs. C. F. Hernaman. It contains much original matter and several new *trs.* from the Latin by Dr. Littledale and others.

61. *The Universal Hymn Book*, &c. By the Rev. A. J. Soden. 1885.

62. *Hymn Book for the Church of England.* By the Rev. A. Gault. 1886.

63. *Hymns for the Church of England.* By T. Darling. 1889. This is the last version of his *Hymns*, &c., first pub. in 1857.

64. *Cantica Sanctorum, or Hymns for the Black Letter Saints' Days in the English and Scottish Calendars. To which are added A few Hymns for Special Occasions.* Edinburgh, 1880. Edited by the Rev. G. Moultrie.

The new names added to the roll of Church of England hymn-writers and translators during this period include :—

Mrs. Alderson, Sir H. W. Baker, S. Baring-Gould, A. Barry, H. W. Beadon, C. C. Bell, E. W. Benson, W. Bright, R. Brown-Borthwick, T. Chamberlain, R. R. Chope, J. S. Clarke, V. S. S. Coles, T. Davis, E. A. Dayman, W. C. Dix, H. Downton, J. Ellerton, A. E. Evans, F. W. Farrar, J. G. Gregory, Miss Havergal, E. Husband, W. J. Irons, B. H. Kennedy, R. F. Littledale, W. D. Maclagan, H. A. Martin, J. S. B. Monsell, G. Moultrie, F. T. Palgrave, G. Phillimore, E. H. Plumptre, T. B. Pollock, F. Pott, T. E. Powell, G. R. Prynne, A. P. Stanley, S. J. Stone, G. Thring, L. Tuttiett, H. Twells, B. Webb, W. Whiting, C. Wordsworth, and many others.

The hymn-books named above number over 250. They represent about two-thirds of the whole published since J. Wesley printed his little book at Charles-Town in 1736 If small local publications amounting to little more than pamphlets, and collections for the public schools, special institutions, soldiers and sailors, and for little children, are added, the total will be about 500. The authors and translators number 250 at the most. To these must be added the Foreign Mission work of the Church which has been productive of hymn-writing and translating in many languages, most stations being supplied with hymn-books in the vernacular, and suited to the people's needs.

An accurate classification of these books, many of which are still in use, is a matter of some difficulty. Of the oldest type of hymn-book, that of Madan and Toplady, there are three at the most, and of these the best in every way is Snepp's *Songs of Grace and Glory*, 1872. It is a large book, and from its standpoint, of exceptional merit. Of the more moderate Evangelical collections which inherit the traditions of *Cotterill, Elliott, Bickersteth, Stowell, Miller,* and others, there are about twenty. The books, which can be scarcely distinguished from *Hymns A. & M.,* except in their arrangements of hymns, the substitution of one translation for another, and the presence of a few original compositions, number about fifteen. *Church Hymns* and companion works are six at the most. Of the *People's Hymnal* type there are less than that; and the *Altar Hymnal* is almost alone. Although all the books published during this period are not included in the foregoing list, yet that list, and this somewhat rough outline of its distinctive features present a fair summary of the latest results of the hymnody of the Church of England.

Some of the books in this list are small in size, limited in design, and weak in execution. In others, although the size is enlarged, and the design is widened, the execution is still defective. Books of the highest merit are few. Taken as a whole the latest collections differ widely from the books of the former period. That distinct partiality for Latin hymnody on the one hand, and for German on the other, which was so marked in the last period, has given place to a broader basis of selection, which finds treasures in each, and valuable assistance from both. New translations and original hymns have also accumulated, the latter especially, and are of distinguished merit as a whole. Sermons in verse are passing out of the collections. Subjective hymns are much less popular than heretofore. The tone of those of praise and prayer is brighter, and more hopeful. The range of subjects and services has broadened out until few remain unrepresented in the best collections. A perfect book there is not, and cannot be. To attain the perfection of Holy Scriptures, Divine Inspiration is needed. To present a book to the Church which shall be *The* Book of *Common* Praise, in the same sense and with the same acceptableness as the Prayer Book is, as *The* Book of *Common* Prayer, requires a combination of circumstances and of men which does not exist. The rude beginning made by John Wesley in 1736 has developed in one hundred and fifty years into hymn-books of great merit and practical usefulness.

The best of these we have enumerated, and, concerning them as a whole, we have set down their distinctive features, and their suitability to the needs of the Church at the respective periods of their production. The needs of the Church of to-day differ widely from her needs one hundred and fifty years ago, and those needs are emphasized by the number of hymnals which are in common use. An united effort to blend the excellences of these works in one *Common Book of Praise* is much to be desired. The task would be a great one, probably too great to be accomplished with success, when the *known* difficulties are taken in hand, and the *unknown* are developed. Meanwhile the great schools of thought and work have their manuals of praise, and these are, as a whole, as distinct and definite in their utterances as they are hallowed in their devotion. Of these we can only name a few of the highest rank.

The most complete work for Daily Prayers, frequent Celebrations, and Occasional Services, with a careful provision for the time of the day and the season of the year, together with a high tone of Eucharistic teaching and devotion, is *The Hymnary* of 1872. It has more translations from the Latin, and especially from the old Anglican Use of *Sarum*, than any other collection. To those who hold that authors should speak in their own tongue, the extensive alterations in the texts of English hymns is a grievous error. The translations, and especially those from the Use of *Sarum*, are very massive, almost too massive, for ordinary congregational use. They lack the cadence and ,ring which hold the multitude, and the fire which stimulates and heightens the devotion of the ordinary worshipper. The book is a great work, the greatest on the lines in the high Anglican school of thought, but it is very cold, and almost passionless.

Midway between the first edition of *The Hymnary* in 1870, and the complete edition, in 1872, another book of great importance was published. Coming forth under the auspices, and with the imprimatur, of the Society for Promoting Christian Knowledge, and with the avowed object of meeting the common needs of the Church, and not the aspirations of a party, *Church Hymns* presents what is commonly known as the old-fashioned, non-Calvinistic doctrine of the old English divines, side by side with provision for the immense developments of modern Church work. Of the 114 hymns translated from other languages, 69 are from the Latin, 30 from the German, and 12 from the Greek; and of the Latin nearly one half date from the 17th and the 18th centuries. The known writers and translators number about 122, and the unknown possibly 25 more. The provision for extra Occasional Services is very full and well arranged. The literary standard is high, and the book as a whole is richer in poetic, as distinct from devotional, verse, than *The Hymnary*, the *Hymnal Companion*, or *Hys. A. and M.* Its great drawback is its mutilated texts. Some of these were inherited, but others, and they are many, were the gratuitous and, in most instances, the uncalled for offerings of the Editors.

The popular voice does by no means indicate at all times or in all places the truest doctrine, or the noblest work; but it does at all times and in all places mark that which is acceptable to the greatest number; and this it has done for *Hymns Ancient and Modern*. From a hymnological and historical point of view its first edition was a somewhat feeble work. Its text was the most mutilated in the Church; its literary standard was not the highest possible; and its range of subjects was very limited. The *Appendix* of 1868 was an advance in each direction; whilst the revised edition of 1875 corrects many, but not all, of its serious shortcomings and faults. Its sale, including the editions of 1861, 1868, and 1875, of over twenty-five million copies shows its use to be far beyond that of any hymn-book in the English language, whether old or new; its success has created a host of imitators; its firm and courageous Church arrangement and tone have raised the whole character and complexion of English hymnody; and the stimulus which it has given to hymnological study has produced a rich harvest to all parties and many creeds. If the dates of the original Hebrew of the Psalms, paraphrases of which are found therein, are allowed, then the contents will date from about 1500 B.C. to 1875 A.D., or a period of 3375 years. In this respect, however, it is not unique, as all the best modern hymn-books begin with the same date. Its contents are gathered from most branches of the Church of Christ, both old and new, the oldest portion being, however, not so prominent as is usually supposed. This is specially the case with the Latin hymns, about one-half of which are not as old as the Psalm Versions of *Sternhold and Hopkins*, and not much older than the hymns of John Mason and Isaac Watts. The original writers and translators who are known number about 195, and another 20, which are anonymous, will represent the total with which it may be credited. The additions thereto which are being compiled and arranged as an *Appendix*, supplying as they do a fuller and more accurate provision for Daily Services, several Special Festivals and Occasional Services, and for the Home Mission movement, will give it the completeness which it now lacks, and ensure for it renewed popularity.

Bishop Bickersteth's *Hymnal Companion*, the first edition of which was published in 1870, and the revised edition in 1876, was compiled upon a plan adopted once before in principle, but not in detail (see § iii. 40), and has resulted in a great success. Taking twenty-five hymn-books, dating from 1836 to 1870, and embracing the high Anglican *Hymnary* on the one hand, and the Ultra-Calvinistic *Songs of Grace and Glory* on the other, he constituted them his "friends in council," and with their aid he laid the foundations and built up much of the body of his book. Two attempts have been made to ascertain what hymns may be regarded as standard hymns in the Church of England. The first was published in *The Churchman's Shilling Magazine*, in 1874, when 28 Anglican hymn-books were used. This resulted in 216 hymns standing the test, and were regarded as being in the first rank, 65 in the second, and 31 in the third. Of these the whole of the first rank,

64 of the second, and 10 of the third, were in the first edition of the *Hymnal Companion.* These were retained in the revised edition of 1876, and several others were added from the third rank. The second attempt to ascertain what were held in the Church of England as Standard Hymns, was published by the Rev. James King, in his *Anglican Hymnology,* in 1885. This work is an expansion of the first attempt, by using 52 works instead of 28, but the results are rendered untrustworthy through 5 of the 52 books being Dissenting collections, and 1 a volume of Essays. Mr. King gives 105 hymns in the first rank, 110 in the second, and 110 in the third. Of these 103, 96, and 78, respectively, are in the *Hymnal Companion.* If Mr. King's Dissenting collections and the volume of Essays, which he unwisely used, are deducted from these books, the result will be equally favourable to the *Hymnal Companion* with the first. In *Anglican* representativeness, as thus wrought out, Bishop Bickersteth's work is at the head of all hymnals in the Church of England; and in keeping with this unique position, it has also the purest texts, being in this respect almost as faultless as Lord Selborne's *Book of Praise.* Notwithstanding this excellence, and the very full provision made from nearly 200 authors and translators for the Ordinary Services and the Occasional Offices, its prevailing *subjectiveness,* together with its *non-representativeness* of the *Catholic* as distinct from the *Anglican* Church of the past fifty years, are serious drawbacks to many. Half-a-dozen hymns from the Greek, less than a dozen from the German, and something like fifteen from the Latin, do not make an imposing total from those vast stores. The book is undoubtedly one of the first in the Church, but it is seriously narrowed by this exclusiveness.

The Church of England Hymn-book adapted to the Daily Services of the Church throughout the Year, by Prebendary Thring, is built up mainly on the lines of *Church Hymns,* and, like it, is designed for services of every kind and degree. Its Eucharistic standpoint is that of the first edition of *Hys. A. & M.* Its original writers and translators number 300, without counting anonymous authors, and their hymns represent eight distinct languages, being one more than *Hys. A. & M.* or *Church Hymns.* The usual and well-known hymns from the Greek are repeated; and there are also 85 from the Latin, and 29 from the German. The texts rank next to the *Hymnal Companion* in purity, and the arrangement of the hymns is very distinct and clear. Hymns of a morbid cast and unnatural tone are rigidly excluded, as are those which breathe passionate entreaties for death, that there may be an immediate attainment of glory. Its literary standard is the highest amongst modern hymn-books, and its poetical merits are great. When to these features of excellence are added a list of contributors one-third larger than *Hys. A. & M.* or the *Hymnal Companion,* and twice as large as those represented in *Church Hymns;* a sound theological groundwork; and a provision for divine worship exceeding any other collection in fullness, and in minuteness of detail, it must be conceded that for practical Church use from the doc-

trinal standpoint which it holds, it will be difficult to find its equal, and impossible to name its superior.

In addition to these five books there are others of much merit in the foregoing list, especially T. Darling's *Hymns for the Church of England; The People's Hymnal;* the *Universal Hymn Book,* and the special tribute to Dean Stanley's memory, *The Westminster Abbey Hymn Book.* But when we are required by the general public of all denominations and creeds to set before them the hymnody of the Church of England in its highest forms, and in its fullest development for practical Church purposes, we are compelled to affirm that *The Hymnary* of 1872; *Church Hymns* of 1871; *Hys. A. & M.* of 1875; *The Hymnal Companion* of 1876, and *The Church of England Hymn-book* of 1882, each great in itself, do embody, when combined, the highest and richest results of a century and a half of hymnological labour and research in the Church of England.   [J. J.]

English Hymnody, Early.—I. *Introduction.*—Lord Selborne has called Dr. Watts the father of English Hymnody: and, as having lifted English hymns out of obscurity into fame, the title is a just one. It will be seen however, that there are facts in the history of the metrical Psalters and obscure hymns, which conditioned and moulded the work of Watts; that several of our choicest hymns in present use are found in books of the 16th and 17th century; that there are signs that hymns might have become a recognized part of church worship, but for the Puritan reaction; and that hymns, as distinct from paraphrases of Scripture, had become an acknowledged part of public worship among the Baptists and Independents at the close of the 17th century. The causes of the long delay in their acknowledgment will appear in succeeding sections. Hatred of the Papacy may have helped to discredit the Latin hymns among the Reformers. The marvellous power of the English Bible excluded almost every thing but actual Scripture from the service of praise during the growing ascendancy of Puritanism. After the Restoration, all singing among the Nonconformists became dangerous under the Conventicle Act. Under the more merciful laws of William III., Nonconformist hymns began to appear freely, and in the hands of Watts and his followers became a power. But this very fact for a long period discredited them within the Church, which adhered rigidly to the *Old* and *New Versions* of the Psalms. The object of this article, which closes with Watts and Doddridge, is to trace this history; indicating at the same time the position of vernacular hymns and paraphrases previous to the Reformation, the gradual decay of the influence of Latin hymns, and the transient reflection in England of the hymns of Germany.

II. *Hymn-singing before the Reformation.*

There is every reason to believe that sacred songs would form part of the repertory of the old English gleemen. One of the plans of Bishop Aldhelm for the evangelisation of his countrymen was to stand on the bridge as a gleeman, and mix sacred and secular songs together. The account of Cædmon, the old English Milton, who embraced the monastic habit for the express object of devoting himself to religious poetry (see *Bede*, B. 4, c. 24) points in the same direction. Scarcely anything however remains to us. The earliest piece of Anglo-Saxon poetry is the hymn which Cædmon composed in his sleep while watching in the stable at night, and which led him to make poetry his vocation. It is given in Sharon Turner's *Hist. of the Anglo-Saxons* (Bk. 12, cap. 1). In Cuthbert's letter, recounting the death of Bede, there is a short hymn sung by him in his last illness. (*Trs.* in Sharon Turner, *ibid.*, Bk. 12, cap. 4, and Bede's *Eccl. Hist.*, p. xix., Bohn Series.) In the *Latin Hymns of the Anglo-Saxon Church* (Surtees Society), there are interlinear glosses of the Latin Hymns. Bp. Aldhelm's Psalter is mentioned elsewhere. [**Psalters, English**, § III.] In Grein's *Bibliothek der Angelsächsichen Poesie*, there are paraphrases of the Lord's Prayer and Gloria Patri, which are translated in Professor Rawson Lumby's *Be Domes Doege* (Early Eng. Text Society). These, however, are not hymns, but meditations on the separate clauses for purposes of instruction. It would extend the scope of this article too widely in this and succeeding paragraphs to attempt to indicate hymn material in religious and devotional poetry (e.g. Cædmon's *Paraphrase*).

No collection of mediæval English hymns has yet been published : but the number of ancient Carols, and Hymns to the B. V. Mary, indicates a practice, which must have been more widely exemplified. (See Preface to Chope's *Carols ;* and for hymns to B. V. M., *Our Lady's Dowry*, by Rev. T. E. Bridgett ; a hymn to her in Chaucer ; and an alliterative hymn in Warton's *History of English Poetry*.) Mr. Furnivall, in *Hymns to the Virgin and Christ* (circa 1430), has published some *Poems of Christ* of great sweetness, especially a " Prayer to Jesus " and " The Love of Jesus," from which centos might be made. In this volume are also metrical renderings of the Creed and Ten Commandments. In Myrc's *Instructions for Parish Priests*, and in Canon Simmons's *Lay-Folks Mass Book*, are similar renderings of Pater Noster and Creed. In the latter is also a metrical version of *Gloria in Excelsis ;* and there are metrical devotions that under other circumstances might well be used as hymns. The object of them as they stand is, however, silent devotion during the celebration of Mass. If the mediæval literature could be explored, and any considerable number of vernacular hymns brought together, they would throw additional light on the devotions of the laity of England in those days, to that revealed in these volumes.

III. *The Influence of the Latin Hymns.*

It is not easy to account for the entire omission by our Reformers of those Latin Hymns, which formed an integral part of the Offices which they reproduced in the Book of Common Prayer. They were freely used by Luther, to whom they were endeared in the monastery ; and Coverdale, following his precedent, has three pieces formed on " Veni

Creator," and another on " Christe, qui lux," in his *Goostly Psalmes and Spiritual Songs* (1539 ?). There is also a well-known letter of Cranmer to Henry VIII. (Oct. 7, 1544. *Works*, c. p. 412, Parker Society) in which he sends a translation of " Salve festa dies," which he has made in the same metre as the Latin, so that the Latin tune may be used to it : suggesting that the king should cause some other to undertake the task of translating " in more pleasant English " than his own. But for some reason nothing was done ; and the C.M. rendering of " Veni Creator " (1549), and the L.M. rendering by Cosin (see below) (1662), are the only traces of the Latin hymns in the successive editions of the Book of Common Prayer. The omission is the more singular, because they were admitted in the books of private devotion, as appears from the history of the Primers. The Primers antecedent to the Reformation contain rude translations of the Latin hymns : so also do the illicit ones of the Gospellers and those of Henry VIII. But in 1553, just at Edward VI.'s death, a new Primer was issued, based on the Book of Common Prayer. Both this book and its immediate predecessors must have passed through Cranmer's hands ; but here we seem to see the change of policy regarding the Latin hymns, perhaps the result of the influence of Calvin. This Primer has no hymns. They reappear, however, in Elizabeth's Primer (1559), which is a revision of Henry VIII.'s books, the original Latin being found in her Horarium (1560); some of the hymns, with the addition of " Christe, qui lux," appearing in her *Preces Privatae* (1564). Perhaps the permission to use a " hymn or such-like song " in the Injunctions (1559) contemplated the introduction of naturalised Latin hymns among other things. But the fashion of psalm-singing was mastering the people ; and in the Liturgical Forms put forth for special occasions as the reign went on *Sternhold and Hopkins* is almost an authorized psalm-book. Except in a few isolated instances among the high church party, and in the Roman books of devotion, the Latin hymns entirely cease to affect the history for the whole period of this article. A notable book in the Church of England of this sort is *A Collection of Private Devotions, called The Houres of Prayer*, &c., by Bp. Cosin (1627), founded on the *Horarium* of Queen Elizabeth. The hymns are new. Some are original : others are fresh translations from the Latin, including at time of Holy Communion part of " Lauda Sion." It is in this book that the L.M. " Veni Creator," afterwards (1662) inserted in the Ordinal, first appears. The translation of " Jam lucis " (" Now that the day-star doth arise ") was afterwards reprinted in Playford's musical edition of *Sternhold and Hopkins*. There is something of the feeling of Ken's great hymns in some of the phrases of the translations from the Matins and Vesper hymns. In Crashaw's *Poems* (circa 1646–52) will be found translations of hymns in the Office for the Holy Cross ; and of " Vexilla Regis." " Lauda Sion," " Dies Irae," and others. Whether these pieces were composed before or after his entrance into the Roman communion seems uncertain. Two of them are adopted by Austin in his *Devotions in the Way of Antient Offices*. Austin (§ x.) has in this same book a *tr.* of "Veni Sancte Spiritus." Mr. W. T. Brooke has also pointed out two *trs.* by Austin from "Summe Pater, O Creator," in Horst's *Paradise*, 2nd ed., 1698. In William Drummond's *Works* (*Lib. of Old Authors*, by W. B. Turnbull) there are twenty translations of Latin hymns (among others "Veni Creator," "Urbs beata," "Christe Redemptor," and "Stabat Mater"). These *trs.* had appeared in *The Primer or Office of B. V. M.* 1615. They were only published as Drummond's in 1711 by Bishop Sage and Thomas Ruddiman. A doubt has been raised about the ascription to Drummond. [See **Drummond, William.**] This Primer of B. V. M. is one of a very interesting series of Offices for B. V. M. in English (1615, 1619, 1684, 1685, 1706) containing successive new *trs.* of the Latin hymns. In that for 1706 is found Dryden's well-known *tr.* of the "Veni Creator" ("Creator Spirit, by Whose aid"), and two other pieces of his. (**Dryden, J.**) [The entire series of Primers, those of Sarum, those of the Reformation, of Mary, of Elizabeth, and the Roman Primers of the 17th century, are treated under **Primers.**]

IV. *German Influence at Reformation.*

The English hymn-singing at the Reformation was the echo of that which roused the enthusiasm of Germany under Luther. The most notable proof of this is found in Coverdale's *Goostly Psalmes and Spiritual Songs.* [See **Psalters, English,** § v.] Following Luther's large-hearted adoption of material from many sources, it contains Psalm versions, paraphrases of Latin hymns (see § III.), and fifteen other hymns. Mr. Mearns has pointed out that only two of these fifteen hymns have not as yet been found in German sources. One is suggested evidently by the *Veni Creator ;* the other is a controversial hymn of the time ("Let go the whore of Babilon"). Nearly all the rest of the book is a more or less close rendering from the German : and some of the finest hymns are Luther's. This same German influence appears again, after a reaction in Calvin's direction, in the final developments of *Sternhold and Hopkins.* The admission of hymns as an *Appendix* to the *Psalter* is a departure from Calvin's precedents. The hymn, "Preserve us, Lord, by Thy dear Word," which Warton ridiculed under the name of "Turk and Pope," is again originally Luther's, the translation alone being Wisdome's. The translation of the *Pater Noster* by D. Cox is also from Luther. This German influence unfortunately dies away with these pieces, until its revival in Wesley. The narrower canons of Calvin admitting nothing but paraphrases of Scripture, and even of Scripture little outside the Psalms, become the stern rule of our hymnody for the next century and a half.

V. *Liturgical Paraphrases.*

The origin of our hymns lies in the Paraphrases. Very few of our original hymns are of earlier date than the close of the 17th century. They arose out of a lengthened period of Paraphrases, derived partly from Liturgical sources, but mainly from Holy Scripture. In Coverdale's *Goostly Psalmes and Spiritual Songs* (1539) there are metrical renderings of the *Crede* (2), the *Pater Noster* (2), the *Magnificat, Nunc Dimittis,* and *Misereatur ;* and expansions of *Mediâ vitâ* and *Gloria in Excelsis.* These are evidently the suggestion of the Latin Offices. In Crowley's *Psalter* (1549) there are metrical Canticles. The English editions of *Sternhold and Hopkins* in Elizabeth's reign (1560-2) show an increasing effort to make the book a Companion to the Book of Common Prayer by means of paraphrases of Canticles, Creeds, the Decalogue, &c. [See **Sternhold and Hopkins,** § v.] Paraphrases of the Canticles and the *Quicunque* appear in Parker's *Psalter,* and are common in the long series of metrical Psalters. They appear in Wither's *Hymns and Songs of the Church.* Tate and Brady versified the Canticles, Creed, Ten Commandments, Lord's Prayer, and the Easter Anthem and *Gloria in Excelsis.* The Puritan Barton made four different versions of the *Te Deum* at the suggestion of Baxter. [**Barton, W.**]

These metrical Canticles however led to grave abuse. In Puritan churches they were substituted for those in the Prayer Book (*Heylin*). Whittingham had introduced the practice at Durham (*Warton*). Cosin's stand against this may have been the foundation of the charge made against him in the Long Parliament (a charge which he denied), "of forbidding the singing of the Psalms in metre." (May, *Hist. of Long Parliament.*) Wren had prohibited the substitution of them in the diocese of Norwich. The Lords' Committee (1641) recommended the legalization of the practice, and it lingered after the Restoration. Wheatley deprecated it in the 18th cent. (see his *Illustration of the Book of Common Prayer,* cap. 3, sect. 13).

VI. *Scripture Paraphrases.*

The real cradle of English hymns is the English Bible ; and its power on the mind of England is forcibly exhibited by their history. The new-found Bible seemed to the Reformers the divinely-given well-spring of praise : large portions of it were actual songs, or rapturous utterances of the saints ; and in the Bible words alone they deemed themselves secure from human error. The great illustration of this belief is found in the long series of metrical Psalters, which formed the staple of public praise for Churchman and Nonconformist till the close of the 17th century. [**Psalters, English.**] To these were generally attached in England renderings of the Canticles [§ v.] (The *Te Deum* is of course not considered here.) Somewhat less frequently, the Songs of Moses, of Deborah, of Hannah and Habakkuk (ch. iii.) were versified. Selections from Isaiah, the Lamentations of Jeremiah, the Book of Ecclesiastes and Book of Wisdom, certain chapters of the Proverbs (e.g. by *John Hall,* often wrongly attributed to Sternhold) were occasionally rendered. The book of the O. T. which was most frequently reproduced was the Song of Solomon (*inter alios* by Spenser, Dod, Wither, Sandys, John Mason and Watts). The most incongruous experiments, showing the belief in the universal capability of Scripture for musical expression at the outset of the Reformation, are a *Metrical Version of the Genealogies*, twelve chapters of the *Acts of the Apostles*, rendered by *Christopher Tye* and sung in Edward VI.'s chapel, *Hunnis's Hyve full of Hunnye, containing the Firste Booke of Moses* (14 chaps.) (1578); and John Merbecke's *History of King David* in the Books of Samuel. Paraphrases of N. T., especially of passages of St. Paul's Epp., received a great development in Barton's *Chapter Hymns* (1659–88). [Barton, W.] They are a part of certain volumes which he calls *Centuries*, published at intervals in his lifetime, and the last after his death, containing paraphrases of Scripture and renderings of Psalms not admitted into his Psalters. The strictness of paraphrase was then beginning to relax, and in his later editions (e.g. *Six Centuries*, 1688) he allows himself to combine and omit chapters and verses in the same book of Scripture. A number of N. T. paraphrases, treated with increasing freedom of combination and omission, appeared in the next thirty years, and afterwards. Watts's 1st book of *Hymns*, consisting entirely of paraphrases, has several: so have Doddridge and many others.

The *Influence of the Paraphrases* has been great. With the exception of some by Watts, especially those preserved in The Scottish Paraphrases, the long series· has indeed little direct interest now: but indirectly, as determining the character of the English hymn that sprang out of them, their interest is considerable. That grand note of our greatest hymns, impregnation with Scripture, is in great measure the heritage of the paraphrases. The limitation to Scripture had held its ground so long from dread of error. Hence if a hymn, not verbally derived from Scripture, was to be accepted, it had to give plain evidence of its ground in Holy Writ. There is a characteristic passage in the preface to Barton's *Four Centuries* (1668), in which he says that the absence of the check of Holy Scripture had led to "horrid blasphemy" in the Papist hymns. He calls also "The Complaint of a Sinner" (*O. V.*) "nonsensical," and stigmatizes the expression "Thy bloody wounds are yet to see," in "The Humble Sute," as erroneous, drawing as his inference, the danger of deserting the text of Scripture. Watts, in the Preface to his hymns, is careful to say that he "might have brought some Text .... and applied it to the margin of every verse."

In the *second* place, in the paraphrases we find the origin of the great divisions of our hymns, *objective* and *subjective*. The free and joyous praise of Watts and Mason, and the simpler, less introspective expressions of sorrow and penitence are a heritage from the Psalms. The delineation of the subtler emotions, motives, and moods of Christian experience, as well as of the appropriation of gospel truths, though flowing partly from the running stream of religious poetry, is even more the reflection of the N. T. paraphrases.

And *thirdly*, in the free grouping of N. T. texts, which characterized the later paraphrases, we see how unconsciously the type of hymn, which we shall find below in Watts, emerged. The habit of Sermon and Commentary made it an almost irresistible impulse to interweave the familiar parallel passages, to make one passage a theme for expansion by others, to omit and combine for the sake of unity; all the while, as they believed, keeping within the letter of Scripture. Then came the license of some connecting verse, as a piece of machinery. And only one step more converted the Scriptural Paraphrase into the Scriptural Hymn. In a volume of *Family Hymns* by Matthew Henry (1695), the precedent of sermons is put forth as an apology for his practice of combining texts of Scripture. The loose interpretation which Watts gave to the term paraphrase comes out clearly in his first book of hymns. His first hymn, which he is said to have produced in his 21st year, at his father's challenge, as something better than the hymns of the Southampton chapel, is a paraphrase of part of Rev. v. in the style of Barton, "Behold the glories of the Lamb:" but others are far more free. Very few probably would now consider "My God, how endless is Thy love" (Bk. i. 81), or "Come, let us join our cheerful songs" (Bk. i. 63), or "Join all the glorious names" (Bk. i. 150), and other noted hymns, as paraphrases, if Watts had not so classed them.

VII. *Original Hymns of the Elizabethan age.*

The Injunctions of Elizabeth (1559) gave free permission to use any "hymn or such like song to the praise of Almighty God," at the beginning and end of morning and evening prayer. [Psalters, English, § VIII.] But, from the causes we have indicated, hymns, as such, were proscribed in public worship until the close of the 17th century; and the hymns that precede that period are found only in books of religious poetry, or private devotion. Until the publication of Wither's *Hymns* (1623) such hymns are few, and chiefly the utterance of simple and unlettered piety. The specimens here designated are of course not an exhaustive list of the pieces that lie buried in the dead volumes of devotional verse. Those for the Elizabethan age will be found chiefly in *Select Poetry, chiefly devotional, of the reign of Queen Elizabeth,* edited by E. Farr, Parker Society, 1845. The earliest are by William Hunnis, a gentleman of the Chapel Royal under Edward VI., and Master of the Children under Elizabeth. There are seven of his hymns in the *Select Poetry,* all of a simple, fervent tone. Next in order are the six original hymns, which enjoyed the exceptional honour of being sung publicly, through their attachment to Sternhold and Hopkins's *Psalter* (1560–2). These are "The Lamentation of a Sinner," by Marckant; "The Lamentation," anonymous; "The Humble Sute of a Sinner"; "The Complaint of a Sinner"; "A Prayer unto the Holy Ghost," to be sung before the sermon and "A Thanksgiving after the receiving of the Lord's Supper." Of a similar character to those of Hunnis are two by Nicolas Breton (*Sel. Poetry,* pp. 180–1), whose works have been reprinted by Grosart; two, by Francis Kinwelmersh (*Sel.*

Poetry, pp. 291-2), one (*ibid.*, p. 316), by Walter Devereux, Earl of Essex, published in *The Paradise of Dainty Devises* (1576-80); one by Timothy Kendal (1576. *Sel. Poetry*, p. 384); nine in John Norden's *Progresse of Pietie* (1591, pub. by the Parker Society); and one by Abraham Fleming (1602. *Sel. Poetry*, p. 546). In the works of William Loe, pastor of the English Church at Hamburg (pub. by Grosart), are "*A Month's Minde—Nine Musings on Death, Seauen Dumps on the Seauen Words*" (on the Cross). There are also metaphrases of the Psalms, Song of Songs, and Paull's Prayers in the volume. All the pieces are written purposely in monosyllables; and it is a singular testimony to the power of our short words, that the strength and simplicity of the compositions is enhanced rather than diminished by the restriction. In Dr. Donne's *Poems* (1633) are one or two hymns, composed in his sickness. One of these, "Wilt Thou forgive that sin?" was often sung in his presence at Evensong in St. Paul's. They are touching pieces. George Herbert is known to have sung some of his hymns to his viol. Walton has a beautiful story of his calling for it on the Sunday before he died, and singing, "The Sundays of man's life," &c. The music set to them was apparently known after his death. Some of them might be adapted to our freer musical settings. One, "Let all the world in every corner sing," has been treated successfully by both Sir George Elvey (*Ch. Hy.* 411) and Mr. Reay. "Throw away Thy rod" is also adapted in the *People's H.* (573). But notwithstanding their pungency and quaint devotion, they are too abrupt and irregular for congregational use. An attempt was made to regularize them in C. M. in a book which was much used after its publication in 1697—*Select Hymns from Mr. Herbert's Temple*. In the community at Little Gidding, hymns were used in the devotions, composed by Nicholas Ferrar, Herbert's friend and executor; but they are apparently lost, save a few specimens in J. E. B. Major's *Lives* of Ferrar. *The Synagogue*, by Christopher Harvie (1640), is an exact following of *The Temple* of Herbert which suggested it, but even less capable of congregational adaptation. In *Phineas Fletcher*, (1633, Grosart's edition), there are two hymns; one of which, "Drop, drop, slow tears," is of exceeding beauty for private use. The range of our hymns has nothing fresher, clearer, tenderer than a MS. hymn of 26 stanzas (4 lines), by F. B. P., "Hierusalem, my happie home" (1601). For a critical discussion of the date and author see the article in this Dictionary — Jerusalem, my happy home; Dr. Bonar's *New Jerusalem Hymns;* and letters in *The Literary Churchman*, July 20 and Aug. 3, 1884, by Major Crawford. The resemblances to "Urbs beata Hierusalem" are obvious, but the English hymn ignores the conception of the Church as the real Jerusalem, which is at the base of the Latin hymn. There is another hymn in L. M. in the MS. volume at the British Museum, which contains the longest, and probably the most authentic text of "Jerusalem, my happy home" (undated but earlier than 1616). This hymn is almost parallel in matter and plan, though not in versification.

VIII. *The first Hymn Book. George Wither.*

A great interest attaches to *Hymns and Songs of the Church* (1623), by George Wither. It is the earliest attempt at an English hymn-book, and we might almost think that, but for the Puritan reaction that set in immediately afterwards, the development of original hymns might have begun in the time of the Stuarts, within the church, instead of being delayed a century, to originate among the Nonconformists. Wither obtained a patent from the King, that his book should be bound up with every copy of the Metrical Psalms, and he evidently hoped that it would be used concurrently with them after morning and evening prayer, though "not as part of the Church's Liturgy." But the history of the book proved just the same as that of his subsequent version of the Psalms (1632). [**Psalters, English.**] Instead of fame and profit, it brought him persecution and loss, notwithstanding the approbation of the book by many members of Convocation. The first part of this book consists of the usual paraphrases of Scripture, including the Song of Solomon; the second is a series of hymns for all the Festivals, Holy Days (St. George's Day among them), Public Deliverances, Holy Communion, Ember Weeks, Seasonable Weather, Plenty, Peace, Victory, Deliverance from Public Sickness, and the King. Some of the poems in it were set to music by Orlando Gibbons. In 1641, many of these hymns were republished, with a few alterations, in the *Hallelujah, Britain's Second Remembrancer*, which was dedicated to the Long Parliament. No music is attached, but tunes are indicated at the head of the pieces, where they diverge from the usual metres of the *Old Version*. It is a book of Hymns for all sorts of times, states, and seasons, embracing a great circle of incidents, some of a minute character (e.g. When washing; On a boat; Sheep-shearing; House-warming; For lovers, Tailors, Jailer, Prisoner, Member of Parliament). Signs of the time, when the balance of power between King and Parliament hung so even and the great struggle was opening, will be easily seen in many hints and allusions. It is the work of a waverer on the border of the two camps. The general tone of it is one of simple practical piety, the language is of studied simplicity, and often of melodious grace; but much of it is not above the doggrel level of the *Old Version*, especially in the hymns peculiar to the *Hallelujah* itself. A list of Wither's best pieces (*Hymns*: Encycl. Britan. 9th ed.) and some choice specimens (*Book of Praise*) are given by Lord Selborne. There is too great a preponderance of meditation and recitative for general use. The very tender and sweet "Rocking Hymn" is only a lullaby. *The Sunset Hymn* is found in Thring's *Coll.* (Hy. 21), "Behold the sun that seemed but now." Far the finest—a noble lyric—is "Come, oh come, with pious lays" (*Hallel.*, Bk. 1, Hy. 1). Wither suffered as a poet, first from his political misfortunes, and afterwards from his rustic simplicity. His place in poetry is like that of Cowper, a reaction from a fantastic and artificial style to that of natural expression, singing of the woodland, the country and the home. As such, it earned the contempt of Pope ("wretched Withers") and Swift (Wither and Dryden are "Bavius and Mævius ") and the sympathy of Southey and others. The first to do him justice was Percy. (See *Percy's Reliques*, "Shall I, wasting in despair ? ")   [Wither George.]

IX. *Hymns of Herrick, Henry Vaughan, Jeremy Taylor, &c.*

The attention of the Puritans was engrossed in the Metrical Psalms. The so-called Hymns of Milton do not come under the definition of this work. The few hymns that were composed are consequently for the most part from royalist pens. Crashaw's belong more to the hymns of Latin origin, and are useless in their present shape. Herrick's *Noble Numbers* (pub. 1647, see Grosart's edition of *Robert Herrick*) contain hymns or hymn material. The carols for Christmas, The New Year, and the Circumcision, and a Star Song—all sung before Charles at Whitehall—are examples. His "Litanie to the Holy Ghost"—"In the hour of my distress," several verses of which are found in some hymn books (e.g. *Ch. H.* 390)— is full of tenderness ; but the jocund humour of the man oddly intrudes on even his gravest thoughts in some of the stanzas (e.g. "When the artless doctor sees, No one hope but of his fees," &c. . . . . . "When his potion and his pill . . . . meet for nothing but to kill," &c.). In Henry Vaughan's *Silex Scintillans* (1650–55. See Grosart's edition) there are many stanzas which might be admitted among hymns for private use, and expressed by freer and higher music. Two are admitted by Mr. Thring in his *Coll.* : "Beyond the veil " is of ethereal beauty. Jeremy Taylor's *Festival and Penitential Hymns*, 1654–5 (see Grosart's edition), are praised by Heber, and are characteristic of his genius ; but it can scarcely be said that the poetic form adds anything to their eloquence, and they are odes rather than hymns, probably not intended for music. The Advent Hymn, "Lord, come away, Why dost Thou stay ? " and that on Charity, "Full of mercy, full of love," are however admitted in Heber's *Hymns*, 1827. The Hymn on The Purification is one of the most regular and the best, and might perhaps be remodelled without losing its crystal lustre.

[Persons in search of the grotesque may be amused by two or three hymns composed by *John Goodwin, William Barton*, and others. Barton paraphrased Deborah's Song as a Thanksgiving for the battle of Worcester, and gives the congregation the alternative of singing Fairfax or Cromwell instead of Barak, "gunners" instead of " archers," &c.]

X. *Hymns of Crossman, Austin, Ken, &c.*

The Restoration was not favourable to the production of Nonconformist hymns. The Quaker and the Baptist held even psalm-singing a carnal ordinance ; the raising of a tune among other congregations proscribed by the Conventicle Act was a signal to the constables. In 1664 was published a series of nine poems by Samuel Crossman, Prebendary and afterwards Dean of Bristol, entitled "The Young Man's Meditation " (reprinted by D. Sedgwick), which is worth attention.

The 5th poem is good, the 7th, on The Resurrection, "My life's a shade" (See *Bk. of Praise*, cliii.), is equally so. The most beautiful is the 8th, in two parts, called "Heaven," from which two well-known hymns, "Sweet place, sweet place alone," and "Jerusalem on high " (see *Ch. Hy.* 394, *Wes. H. Bk.* 942), have been taken. The vision of the Heavenly City and the delight and sadness which it inspires are pourtrayed with equal delicacy ; and the crisp rhythm, the longing refrain, and a trace of Puritan feeling add to its charm. In Henry More's *Divine Dialogues* (1667) are seven long hymns on the doctrines of the Great Festivals, all written on the same plan,—a narrative portion succeeded by a practical application. Wesley made subsequent use of them ; though not devoid of devotion, they are rather coldly didactic. In 1668 appeared *The Devotions in the Antient Way of Offices*, by that saintly son of the Roman Church, John Austin, which were afterwards edited for Anglican use by Hickes, Dorrington, and others. Besides one or two adaptations of Latin Hymns from Crashaw, they contain original hymns appended to the offices ; and few compositions leave such an impression of simple love to the Saviour, and sweet bird-like praise. The 6th Hymn, "Hark, my soul, how everything " (*Bk. of Praise*, 26), and the 32nd, "Lord, now the time returns " (5 sts. in *Bk. of Praise*, 189), are perhaps the choicest. But the rest in the *Book of Praise* are in the same gentle strain, and the selection could be enlarged. At least as early as 1674 were composed Bp. Ken's three unique hymns, which so perfectly represent his saintly personality. The pieced verses of our hymn-books give little conception of the originals. In the matter of form, the harmonious strength of familiar stanzas scarcely prepares us for the abruptness and even weakness of those omitted. As regards substance, "The Midnight Hymn," with its Light of God illumining the darkness (cento in Thring's *Coll.* 62) has scarcely a place in our books ; the extracts from "The Morning Hymn" mainly exhibit the manly piety, the inviolate conscience and energy of duty, which George Eliot accentuates in Adam Bede ; and those from "The Evening Hymn" the spirit of serene humility and trust : but in Ken all this is but the lower side of a realization, in which his praise is mingling with the heard anthems of heaven, and life is only life because overstreamed by the presence of God. It is the intensity of this spiritual imagination —and not the thoughts, which are found in many similar hymns, as the natural suggestion of the time, and even less the language, which is bare of imagery, and only distinguished by the restraint of rhyme from direct massive prose—that lifts these hymns to an angel level reached by no other English hymns. The four volumes of Ken's *Poetical Works* have many passages full of pathos, and breathe his habitual spirit of high devotion. The *Anodynes* and *Preparations for Death* are very touching, read with the context of the sufferings they solaced : and we turn eagerly in search of ore to *The Hymns for the Festivals*. But they are the poems of old age ; the natural force is abating ; the

was received and educated by an aunt. In 489, through the death of his aunt, he was again reduced to destitution : but soon retrieved his fortunes by marrying a lady of wealth. A recovery from a dangerous sickness led him to reflect on his somewhat dissolute character, and to change his whole life. His wife retired into a convent, and he was ordained Deacon by the Bishop of Pavia. Under Pope Hermisdas he was advanced to the see of Pavia about 514, and was employed on two important missions to the Emperor Anastasius in order to oppose the spread of the Eutychian heresy; but in both instances he was unsuccessful. He d. in 521, and was buried in the Church of St. Michael, Pavia, July 17, 521. His works, eleven in all, were pub. amongst the *Auctores Orthodoxographici,* Basle, 1591 ; again, by Andrew Schott, Tournai, 1611, and in *Migne,* tom. lxiii. Sixteen of his hymns, some consisting only of a few lines, were included in *Daniel,* i., cxxi.-cxxxvi. Of these the following have been *tr.* by the Rev. S. A. W. Duffield :—

1. **Christe lumen perpetuum.** *Trust in Christ. Tr.* as "O Christ, the eternal light," in *Laudes Domini,* N. Y., 1883.

2. **Christe precamur annue.** *Evening. Tr.* as "To Thee, O Christ, we ever pray," in *Laudes Domini,* N. Y., 1883.

For fuller details concerning Ennodius and his works, see *Dicty. of Christ. Biog.,* art. *Ennodius.* [J. J.]

Enquire, ye pilgrims, for the way. *P. Doddridge. [Invitation.]* This is No. 137 of his posthumous *Hymns,* &c., 1755, in 6 st. of 4 l., and No. 155 in J. D. Humphreys's ed. of the same, 1839. It is based on Jer. l. 5. In most American hymnals it is given as "Inquire, ye pilgrims," &c. In the *Church Pastorals,* Boston, U.S., 1864, st. iv., iii., v., vi. are given in the order named as "Come, let us join our souls to God," and appointed for the admission of Church members. [J. J.]

Enslaved to sense, to pleasure prone. *C. Wesley. [Lent.]* This hymn, although of a penitential character, was pub. as a "Grace before Meat" in *Hys. and Sac. Poems,* 1739, in 8 st. of 4 l. (*P. Works,* 1868-72, vol. i. p. 32.) In the *Wes. H. Bk.,* 1780, it was given as the first hymn of section ii., "For mourners convinced of sin" (No. 104), and as such it was retained in the revised ed. of 1875. It is also used as a penitential hymn in several other collections in G. Britain and America. The *Grace,* "Come then, our heavenly Adam, come," *Wes. H. Bk.,* No. 1009, is st. v. of this hymn. [J. J.]

Enthroned on high, Almighty Lord. *T. Haweis. [Whitsuntide.]* 1st pub. in his *Carmina Christo,* &c., 1792 (2nd ed., 1802.). No. 15 in 5 st. of 4 l., and entitled, "Day of Pentecost." It was included in several of the older collections of G. Britain, but its modern use is mainly confined to America, where it is given in a large number of collections. In some of these, as in H. A. Boardman's Presb. *Sel. of Hymns,* 1860, it is attributed to "Humphries." This error is as early as J. Conder's *Cong. H. Bk.,* 1836, if not earlier. Orig. text in *Lyra Brit.,* 1867, p. 286. [J. J.]

Ἐπάρατε πύλας. [Ἀνέστης τριήμερος.]

Ἐπέβη ὡς λεών. *St. John of Damascus.* [*St. Paul.*] This is the ivth Ode in the Canon of St. Paul in the Office of SS. Peter and Paul, June 30, in the *Menaea.* It is given in Pitra's *Hym. Grec.* p. 76. Dr. Littledale's *tr.,* "Against the Church of Jesus," is good, and close to the original with the omission of the Theotokion (address to the B.V. M.). The *tr.* was 1st pub. in the *People's H.,* 1867, No. 237, and signed "F." It is appointed for the "Conversion of St. Paul." [J. J.]

Ἐφέστηκεν ἡ ἡμέρα. [Τὴν ἡμέραν τὴν φρικτήν.]

Ephrem, the Syrian. [Syriac Hymnody.]

Ἐπὶ τῆς θείας φυλακῆς. [Ἀναστάσεως ἡμέρα.]

Epiphaniam Domino canamus gloriosam. [*Epiphany.*] This Sequence occurs in a ms. of Sequences (circa 1000) in the Bodleian Library, Oxford, No. 775, f. 140. It is also in a Winchester ms. of the 11th cent. now at Corpus Christi College, Cambridge, and an 11th cent. ms. in the British Museum (Harl. 2961, f. 251 *b*). In the *Sarum Missal* it is the Sequence for the Feast of the Epiphany only. In the *Hereford Missal* it is appointed for the Epiphany itself, its Octave, and the Sunday in the Octave. In the *York Missal* it is divided into three parts : (1) "Epiphaniam Domini," (2) "Balaam de quo vaticinans," and (3) "Magi sibi stella." The first is to be said on the Feast of the Epiphany, the second on the first day after; the third on the second day after, and so on, to the Octave, when the entire Sequence has to be sung. If however the 2nd or 3rd part should fall upon a Sunday, then it gave place to the proper Sequence for the "Translation of St. William the Archbishop," the Festival of that day. Text in reprints of the *Sarum, Hereford,* and *York Missals,* and *Kehrein,* No. 27. [W. A. S.]

Translations in C. U. :—

1. **Sing we in triumphal gladness.** By R. F. Littledale, written for and 1st pub. in the *People's H.,* 1867, No. 45, and signed "A. L. P." It is in 7 st. of 6 l.

2. **O come and praise with chant and song.** By E. H. Plumptre, contributed to the *Hymnary,* 1872, in 6 st. of 8 l., and appointed for use at the Holy Communion during the Epiphany.

Translations not in C. U. :—

1. All glory to the Lord's Epiphany. C. B. Pearson. *The Sarum Missal in English,* 1868.
2. Let us duly magnify. C. B. Pearson. *Sequences from the Sarum Missal,* 1871. [J. J.]

Epistles, Hymns on the. [Prayer, Book of Common.]

Ἐψευσάμην σε τὴν ἀλήθειαν, λόγε. *St. Gregory of Nazianzus.* "A hymn at night, after failure to keep vow," found in various editions of his *Works,* and in the *Anth. Graec. Car. Christ.,* p. 28, 1871. From this latter work Mr. Chatfield made his *tr.,* "O Thou, the Word of truth divine," and pub. the same in his *Songs and Hys.,* &c., 1876, p. 121, in 3 st. of 4 l. The original dates 324-389. [Greek Hymnody, § iv.] [J. J.]

Ere another Sabbath's close. [*Sunday*.] We have traced this popular hymn to the *Missionary Minstrel*, a little 48mo coll., edited by "O. P." and pub. by Nisbet, Lon., May, 1826, a much enlarged edition being issued a few years later. It reads :—

i. Ere another Sabbath's close,
Ere again we seek repose,
Lord, our song ascends to Thee,
At Thy feet we bow the knee.

ii. For the mercies of the day,
For this rest upon our way,
Thanks to Thee alone be given,
Lord of earth and King of heaven.

iii. Cold our services have been,
Mingled every prayer with sin ;
But Thou canst and wilt forgive,
By Thy grace alone we live.

iv. One there is at Thy right hand,
Angels bow at His command ;
Yet He suffered in our stead,
And His wounds our pardon plead.

v. By the merits of Thy Son,
By the victory He won,
Pardoning grace and peace bestow,
Whilst we journey here below.

vi. Whilst this thorny path we tread,
May Thy love our footsteps lead ;
When our journey here is past,
May we rest with Thee at last.

vii. Let these earthly Sabbaths prove
Sweet foretastes of joys above ;
While their steps Thy pilgrims bend
To that rest which knows no end.

It has the initials appended, "O. P.," in common with about half of the hymns in the volume. One of the first, if not the first, to adopt it for congregational use was *Baptist W. Noel*, who included it with the omission of st. iv. and v. in his *Selection*, in 1832 (sometimes dated 1833 in error). From this fact arose the mistake of attributing it, at one time, to *Baptist W. Noel*, and at another, to his brother, *Gerard T. Noel*. In 1833 the same stanzas were repeated in Bickersteth's *Christian Psalmody*, and subsequently in other collections. Its use in all English-speaking countries is most extensive. From this hymn a cento beginning with st. ii., "For the mercies of the day," has come into extensive use in America, and is sometimes ascribed to "J. Montgomery, 1853," as in Dr. Hatfield's *Church H. Bk.*, N. Y., 1872. Its correct designation is "O. P., *Missionary Minstrel*, 1826."

[W. T. B.]

Ere Christ ascended to His throne. *B. Beddome.* [*Adult Baptism.*] Pub. in his posthumous *Hymns*, &c., 1817–18, No. 596, in 5 st. of 4 l., and headed "The Commission." In addition to its limited use in its full form, it is also abbreviated in some American collections. In the *Psalmist*, 1843, *Bapt. Praise Bk.*, N. Y., 1871, st. iii.-v. are given as, "Blest Saviour, we Thy will obey"; and in the *Sabbath H.* [*& Tune*] *Bk.*, N. Y., 1858 (*Bapt.* edition), the same stanzas as "Dear Saviour, we Thy will obey." These arrangements are not in use in G. Britain.

[J. J.]

Ere God had built the mountains. *W. Cowper.* [*Divine Wisdom.*] Pub. in the *Olney Hymns*, 1779, Bk. i., No. 52, in 4 st. of 8 l. and based on Prov. viii. 22–31. It is found in several collections, both old and new, in G. Britain, and is also in use in America. A rendering into Latin, "Priusquam Deus altos montes," by R. Bingham, was given in his *Hymno. Christ. Lat.*, 1871, p. 251. [J. J.]

Ere I [we] sleep, for every favour *J. Cennick.* [*Evening.*] Pub. in his *Sacred Hys. for the Children of God*, &c., 1741, No. 14, in 7 st. of 4 l., as the second of two hymns for evening. It was repeated in later editions of the same work, in Whitefield's *Coll.*, 1754; in M. Madan's *Ps. & Hys.*, 1760; the early editions of Lady Huntingdon's *Coll.*, and others of the old collections, and is also well known to modern hymnals, but usually in an abbreviated form, and sometimes as "Ere *we* sleep," &c. Orig. text in Stevenson's *Hys. for the Ch. & Home*, 1873, with the omission of st. vii., which reads :—

"So whene'er in death I slumber,
Let me rise ‖ With the wise,
Counted in their number." [J. J.]

Ere mountains reared their forms sublime. *Harriet Auber.* [*God eternal—Man passing away.*] Appeared in her *Spirit of the Psalms*, 1829, in 4 st. of 4 l. In the American hymn-books it is given in its original L. M. form, as in Hedge and Huntington's *Hys. for the Ch. of Christ*, 1853, and several later Hymnals; and in a peculiar form to suit the music adopted in *Church Pastorals*, Boston, 1864. From Miss Auber and H. F. Lyte having both pub. works with the title *The Spirit of the Psalms*, this hymn has sometimes been attributed to Lyte in error. [J. J.]

Ere the blue heavens were stretch'd abroad. *I. Watts.* [*Divinity and Humanity of Christ.*] 1st pub. in his *H. & S. Songs*, 1707, Bk. i. No. 2, in 6 st. of 4 l. In addition to its somewhat extensive use in its original form in G. Britain and America, it is also given in an altered form as, "Before the heavens were spread abroad," in *Songs for the Sanctuary*, N. Y., 1865–72, and others. [J. J.]

Ere the words of peace and love. *Bp. E. H. Bickersteth.* [*Holy Matrimony.*] Written in 1869, and pub. in his *H. Companion*, 1870. It is also in his *The Two Brothers, and Other Poems*, 1871, and appointed to be sung after the blessing, "Almighty God, who at the beginning," &c. From Bp. Bickersteth's *Notes* to the *H. Comp.* we gather that it was written for that collection. [J. J.]

Erhalt uns, Herr, bei deinem Wort. *M. Luther.* [*Peace and Orthodoxy.*] This hymn was probably written 1541. In that year a service of prayer against the Turks was held at Wittenberg, for which Luther prepared a special office, in which most of the music was arranged for the boys of the choir. It was printed in broadsheet form at Wittenberg, 1542; appeared in Low German, in the *Magdeburg G. B.*, 1542; and then in High German in Klug's *Geistliche Lieder*, Wittenberg, 1543–4. In Klug it was entitled "A hymn for the children to sing against the two arch-enemies of Christ, and His Holy Church, the Pope and the Turks." Thence in *Wackernagel*, iii. p. 26, in 3 st. of 4 l., and Schircks's ed. of Luther's *Geist. Lieder*, 1854, p. 44. Additional stanzas from various sources have often been appended to this hymn, the most popular being those by Justus Jonas, probably written in 1545, against the Council of Trent. These are:—iv. "Ihr Anschläg, Herr, zu nichte mach"; v. "So werden wir erkennen doch," and appear, added to Luther's three, at the end of the *Radtschlag des aller-heyligsten Vaters Babsts Pauli des Dritten, mit dem Collegio Cardinalium gehalten, wie das angesatzte Concilium zu Trient fürzunehmen sey."* *Anno* M.D.XLV. (Wackernagel's *Bibliographie*, 1855, p. 204.) This text, in 5 st., is No. 723 in Burg's *Breslau G. B.*, 1746.

The hymn soon came into universal use, at morning and evening devotions, before sermon, &c. Lauxmann, in *Koch*, viii. 133–134, gives various instances of the resentment of the Romanists, especially against st. i., l. 2, "Und steur des Papst und Türken Mord," which in many recent hymn-books appears as "Und steure deiner Feinde Mord." It came into use in England through Wisdome's version (see below), of which Warton in his *Hist. of Eng. Poetry*, sect. xlv. (evidently not knowing that Wisdome was merely the translator) thus speaks :—He is chiefly memorable for his metrical prayer, intended to be sung in the church, against the Pope and the Turk, of whom he seems to have conceived the most alarming apprehensions. It is probable that he thought Popery and Mahometanism were equally dangerous to Christianity, at least the most powerful and sole enemies of our religion . . . Happily we have hitherto survived these two formidable evils ! " The Turk, however, had come nearer to Wittenberg than to London, having under the rule of Suleiman the Lawgiver (1520–1566) conquered the greater part of Hungary, and even besieged Vienna. Moreover we find that in England in 1565 a form of prayer was issued to excite all godly people to pray "for the delivery of these Christians that are now invaded by the Turk." One passage from Luther's *Table Talk* will sufficiently show his sentiments: " Antichrist is the Pope and the Turk together ; a beast full of life must have a body and soul ; the spirit or soul of Antichrist is the Pope, his flesh or body the Turk. The latter wastes and assails and persecutes God's Church corporally ; the former spiritually and corporally too, with hanging, burning, murdering, &c. But, as in the apostles' time, the Church had the victory over the Jews and Romans, so now will she keep the field firm and solid against the hypocrisy and idolatry of the Pope, and the tyranny and devastation of the Turk and her other enemies." *Bohn's ed.*, p. 193.

Translations in C. U. :—

1. **Preserve us Lorde by Thy deare Worde.** By R. Wisdome in *Daye's Psalter*, 1560–1. St. i., ii., are close, iii. free, and iv. an added doxology. It was repeated in 1562, 1565, and many of the later eds. of *Sternhold and Hopkins*, and is found in a few hymnals of this century, e.g. st. i.–iii., altered to "blest Word," were included as No. 501 in J. Bickersteth's *Ps. & Hys.*, 1832.

2. **Oh God ! uphold us by Thy word, And let.** A paraphrase of st. i.–v., in Miss Fry's *H. of the Reformation*, 1845, p. 73, and thence, reduced to 4 st. of 8 l., beginning, "Lord, send forth Thy mighty Word," as No. 205, in J. Whittemore's *Suppl. to All H. Bks.*, 1860.

3. **O Lord, uphold us by Thy Word, And break.** A *tr.* of st. i.–iii., v., by W. M. Reynolds, as No. 966 in the American Luth. Gen. Synod's *Hymns*, 1850–52.

4. **From all her foes Thy Church, O Lord.** A good *tr.* of st. i.–iii., by A. T. Russell, as No. 135 in his *Ps. & Hys.*, 1851, repeated as No. 129 in Dr. Pagenstecher's *Coll.*, 1864.

5. **Lord, by Thy Word deliverance work.** A *tr.* of st. i.–iii., in R. Massie's *M. Luther's Spir. Songs*, 1854, p. 37, repeated, altered, and with *trs.* of st. iv., v. added, as No. 148 in the *Ohio Luth. Hyl.*, 1880.

.6. **Lord, keep us steadfast in Thy word.** A *tr.* of st. i.–iii. (set to the melody which appeared in *Klug*, 1543–4), as No. 103 in Miss Winkworth's *C. B. for England*, 1863 ; repeated as No. 316 in the Pennsylvania *Luth. Ch. Bk.*, 1868.

Translations not in C. U. :—
(1) " Keep us, O Lord, by Thy pure word," as No. 318 in pt. i. of the *Moravian H. Bk.*, 1754. (2) "Oh God !

uphold us by Thy Word, And scatter," by *Miss Fry*, 1845, p. 145. (3) "Great God ! preserve us by Thy Word," by *J. Anderson*, 1846, p. 36 (1847, p. 54). (4) " Preserve us, Lord, and grant that we," by *Dr. J. Hunt*, 1853, p. 63. (5) " Thou Father-God, our souls sustain," by *Dr. H. Mills*, 1856, p. 145. (6) "God, hold us up by Thy strong word," by *E. Massie*, 1867, p. 208. (7) " Lord, keep us by Thy word in hope," by Dr. G. Macdonald, in the *Sunday Magazine*, 1867, p. 450 ; repeated, altered, in his *Exotics*, 1876, p. 69. (8) "Lord keep us in Thy word and work, Restrain," based on *Miss Winkworth*, in Dr. Bacon, 1884, p. 67.   [J. M.]

Erskine, Ralph, was s. of Henry Erskine, who was Rector of Cornhill, Northumberland, before the Act of Uniformity in 1662, and after the Revolution of 1688 was Parish minister of Chirnside, Berwickshire. He was b. at Money laws, Northumberland, March 15, 1685, his father being then in exile from Scotland for taking part in conventicles. He entered the University of Edinburgh in 1699, was licensed to preach in 1709, in 1711 ordained second minister of the Abbey Church, Dunfermline, and became first minister in 1716. Joining in 1737 with the "Four Brethren," who, protesting against the action of the General Assembly on Patronage, had been loosed from their charges by the Commission in 1733 and had formed themselves into a Presbytery at Gairney Bridge, near Kinross, Dec. 5, 1733, thus founding the Associate Church, he was with them and three others cited to, and deposed by, the General Assembly of 1740. In 1740 the majority of his congregation seceded with him and built him a church in Queen Anne Street, Dunfermline, in which he continued to minister till his death. He did not, however, cease to preach in his turn in the Abbey Church till after May, 1742. He d. at Dunfermline, Nov. 6, 1752. His published works are included in his

Sermons and other Practical Works (Glas. 1764–1765), the complete folio ed. in 2. vols. ed by John Newlands (his son-in-law), contains a short memoir, 141 sermons, and (1) *Gospel Sonnets: or, Spiritual Songs.* These *Gospel Sonnets*, of which the 2nd and complete ed. appeared in Edinburgh, 1726, and the 5th finally revised, in London, 1741, though homely, enjoyed great popularity, and did much good in Scotland in the last century. (2) *A Paraphrase upon the Song of Solomon.* In this, first pub. in Edinburgh, 1736, the "Song" is spiritualized at great length. (3) *Scripture Songs.* These are in 2 Books. The Old Testament Songs are (i.) 14 Songs from Genesis to Job ; (ii.) Job's Hymns, 100 ; (iii.) The Song of Solomon, complete ; (iv.) 21 Songs from Ecclesiastes, Isaiah, and Jeremiah ; (v.) Lamentations, complete ; (vi.) 6 Songs from the Minor Prophets. The New Testament Songs are (i.) 17 Songs from the Gospels ; (ii.) 24 Songs from the Epistles ; (iii.) 16 Songs from the Revelation. Of these parts the 2nd (Glas., 1753), the 3rd (Glas., 1752), and the 5th (Glas., 1750), the Old Testament, were the first pub. separately. The remainder, pub. at Glasgow, in 1754 as *Scripture Songs*, in 3 Books, were undertaken by request of the Associate Synod, in 1748, but not being pub. before Erskine's death never came into Church use. Many are altered from Watts, and some from the *Trans. and Paraph.* of 1745. (4) *Miscellaneous Poems.* These include 3 English and 2 Latin Elegies, a poem on the Civil Magistrate and Religion, and 7 Epitaphs. *Smoking Spiritualised* is given at the end of the *Gospel Sonnets* [see **Scottish Hymnody**, § VI.] A number of pieces by Erskine were included, more or less altered, in the Moravian hymnbooks. The only one found in a modern hymnal which is well known being annotated, " Ah ! mournful case, what can afford," and another not now in C. U. under: " Aurora veils her rosy face."   [J. M.]

Es giengen trew frewlach also frŭ. [*Easter.*] A 13th cent. Easter carol on the visit of the Holy Women to the Sepulchre on Easter morning. It is given by *Wackernagel*, ii. p. 360, in 10 st. of 4 l. with " Alleluia "

from a paper MS. of 1516 now at Heidelberg. Hoffmann von Fallersleben, 1861, p. 84, has a text reading " Es giengen drî fröulîn," and in 13 st. The only *tr.* is " There went three damsels ere break of day," by Miss *Winkworth*, 1869, p. 85.   [J. M.]

Es ist ein Ros (Reis) entsprungen.

[*Christmas.*] *Wackernagel*, ii. p. 925, gives two forms, the first in 23 st. of 7 l. from the *Speier G. B.* (R. C.), 1600 (*Baümker*, i. p. 156, cites it as in the ed. of 1599), the second in 6 st. from the *Andernach G. B.* (R. C.), 1608. In his *Kleines G. B.*, 1860, No. 8, he gives st. i.–v., xxiii., from the Speier, with the fine melody found there. He thinks it was originally a 15th or 16th cent. Christmas or Twelfth Night Carol in the diocese of Trier.

It is founded on St. Luke i., ii., and on Isaiah xi. 1, 2. It interprets Isaiah's " Shoot out of the stock of Jesse " not as our Lord Jesus Christ, but as the Virgin Mary. The only *tr.* is " A spotless Rose is blowing," a *tr.* of st. i., ii. of the *Speier*, by *Miss Winkworth*, 1869, p. 85.   [J. M.]

Es ist nicht schwer ein Christ zu sein. C. F. Richter. [*True Christianity.*]

1st appeared as No. 228 in Freylinghausen's *Neues geistreiches G. B.*, 1714, in 8 st. of 4 l. It is a companion to his earlier hymn, " Es kostet viel ein Christ zu sein " (1st pub. as No. 659 in Freylinghausen's *G. B.*, 1704 ; but not *tr.* into English), and with it was republished in his *Erbauliche Betrachtungen vom Ursprung und Adel der Seelen*, Halle, 1718, where the earlier is entitled " On the seriousness and difficulty of True Christianity," and the later " on the Easiness and Lovableness of True Christianity." They are given as companion hymns in the *Unv. L. S.*, 1851, Nos. 305, 306, both in 8 st. The only *tr.* in C. U. of " Es ist nicht schwer," is :—

'Tis not a [too] hard, too high an aim. By Moses Browne. Included in *The Excellency of the Knowledge of Jesus Christ*, &c., Lond., 1772. This work is a *tr.* of a treatise by J. L. Zimmermann (*Die überschwengliche Erkenntniss Jesu Christi*), pub. at Halle in 1732, in which the hymn is introduced with a Latin version by Zimmermann. Browne's *tr.* of this hymn is very free, and is in 8 st.; st. i., vi., vii. being of 12, ii.–v. of 8, and viii. of 4 l. It had previously been contributed to the *Christian's Magazine*, April, 1762, p. 182, where it is given as " Luther's Hymn, in eight practical rules," and begins " 'Tis not too arduous an essay." The text of 1762 was repeated, with variations, as No. 369, in *A Coll. of Ps. & Hys.*, York, R. Spence, 1780, and in the 6th ed., 1806, of Moses Browne's *Sunday Thoughts*. The text of 1772, however, is that which has come down, mainly in centos, to modern hymnals. It is given in full in Miss Warner's *H. for the Ch. Militant*, N. Y., 1858 (ed. 1861, p. 568), and in Collyer's *Coll.*, 1812, Nos. 853–855. Besides appearing under its original first line, it is also found as follows :—

1. The promis'd part in Christ to claim (st. i. altered), in J. Bickersteth's *Ps. and Hys.*, 1832, No. 490 ; E. Bickersteth's *Christ. Psal.*, 1833, and E. H. Bickersteth's *Ps. and Hys.*, 1858.
2. Be strong, my heart! be high thy aim (st. i. alt.) in Mozley's *Ch. H. Bk.*, 1826, No. 314.
3. Nature will raise up all her strife (i., l. 5.), in Nettleton's American *Village Hys.*, 1825, No. 395.
4. Act but the infant's gentle part (ii.), in Dr. Bonar's *Bible H. Bk.*, 1845, No. 83.

5. The sovereign Father, good and kind (iii.) in Collyer's *Coll.*, 1812, No. 854.
6. The gentle sire, the best of friends (vi., l. 5), in Collyer's *Coll.*, 1812, No. 855.
7. Thy gracious God, thy best of friends (st. vi., l. 5, alt.), in Mozley's *Ch. H. Bk.*, 1826, No. 316.
Other trs. are, (1) " To be a Christian is not hard." By R. Massie. 1864. (2) " Give me, my child, the Father saith, thy heart." This begins with st. iii. as No. 357, in the *Moravian H. Bk.*, 1886.   [J. M.]

Es kennt der Herr die Seinen. C. J. P. Spitta. [*The Lord's own.*]

In the 2nd Series, 1843, of his *Psalter und Harfe*, p. 75, in 6 st. of 8 l., founded on ii. Tim. ii. 19, and entitled, " The Lord Knoweth His Own." Included as No. 1496 in Knapp's *Ev. L. S.*, 1850 (1865, No. 1561). The *tr.* in C. U. is :—

He knoweth all His people. A good and full *tr.* by Mrs. Findlater, in the 4th Series, 1862, of the *H. L. L.*, p. 25 (1884, p. 196), entitled, " The Little Flock." It was given in full as No. 439, in the *New App.*, 1869, to the S. P. C. K. *Ps. & Hys.* Included in Jellicoe's *Coll.*, 1867, omitting st. v., and in the Uppingham and Sherborne *School H. Bk.*, 1874, omitting st. ii., iii. In Stevenson's *H. for Ch. and Home*, 1873, st. i., iv., v. form No. 75, slightly altered and beginning, " God knoweth all His people."

Another tr. is, "The Lord His people all," by *R. Massie*, 1864, p. 63.   [J. M.]

Es reden und träumen die Menschen viel. [*Hope.*] By Johann Christoph Friedrich von Schiller,

b. Nov. 10, 1759, at Marbach, Württemberg, d. May 9, 1805, at Weimar. This little poem, hardly to be called a hymn, is one of his " Gedichte der dritten Periode," is entitled *Hoffnung* and is included in his *Werke*, Cotta, 1874, vol. i., p. 22, in 3 st. of 6 l. The only *tr.* in C. U. is :—

The world may change from old to new, a free *tr.* in 3 st. of 8 l., included as No. 127 in W. J. Fox's *Hys. & Anthems*, 1841, marked as by " Sarah F. Adams," but in later eds. as paraphrased from Schiller. This is repeated in E. Courtauld's *Coll.*, 1860, G. Gilfillan's *Selection*, 1875, and in America, in the *Book of Hys.*, 1846–48, Hedge & Huntington's *Coll.*, 1853, &c.

Among the *trs.* not in C. U. we note (1) " We children of men, we speak and dream," in *Stray Leaves*, Lond., 1827, p. 57. (2) " We speak with the lips and we dream in the soul," in Lord Lytton's *Poems & Ballads of Schiller*, 1844, vol. i. p. 74. (3) " Of better and brighter days to come," in E. A. Bowring's *Poems of Schiller*, 1851, p. 232. (4) " Men speak much and dream of a better time," in W. Nind's *German Lyrist*, 1856, p. 32. (5) " All men to speak and to dream are prone," in Dr. H. W. Dulcken's *Book of German Songs*, 1856, p. 278. (6) " Man talks and dreams that Time will unroll," in *Specimens of Schiller's Minor Poems*, Lond., 1867. (7) " Men talk with their lips and dream with their soul," in Dr. G. Macdonald's *Exotics*, 1876, p. 122. (8) " Of brighter and happier days to come," by J. D. Morell, in *English Echoes of German Song*, 1877, p. 116.   [J. M.]

Es spricht der Unweisen Mund wohl. M. Luther. [*Ps. xiv.*]

1st pub. as No. 6 in the *Etlich cristlich lider*, Wittenberg, 1524, in 6 st. of 7 l., entitled " The Thirteenth Psalm." *Wackernagel*, iii. p. 6, quotes it from *Eyn Enchiridion*, Erfurt, 1524. In Schircks's ed. of Luther's *Geistl. Lieder*, 1854, p. 78, and in the *Unv. L. S.*, 1851, No. 221. The only *tr.* in C. U. is :—

The mouth of fools doth God confess. In full in R. Massie's *M. Luther's Spir. Songs*, 1854, p. 29, repeated as No. 146 in the *Ohio Luth. Hyl.*, 1880, and adopted by *Dr. Bacon*, 1884, p. 8.

Other trs. are :—

(1) "The foolish wicked men can saye," by Bp. Coverdale, 1539 (*Remains*, 1846, p. 581). (2) "Vain foolish men profanely boast," by *J. C. Jacobi*, 1725, p. 66 (ed. 1732, p. 84), repeated as No. 112, in pt. i. of the *Moravian H. Bk.*, 1754. (3) "Thus speak the foolish with their mouth," by *J. Anderson*, 1846, p. 28 (ed. 1847, p. 49, altered to, "Thus with their mouth the foolish say"). (4) "Though fools in words may boldly say," by W. M. Reynolds, in the *Evang. Review*, Gettysburg, Oct. 1849. (5) "Thus with their lips the foolish say," by *Dr. J. Hunt*, 1853, p. 58. (6) "Although the mouth say of the unwise," by Dr. G. Macdonald, in the *Sunday Magazine*, 1867, p. 450, altered in his *Exotics*, 1876, p. 64, to "Although the fools say with their mouth."

[J. M.]

Es wollt' uns Gott genädig sein.

M. Luther. [*Ps. lxvii.*] First printed at the end of Luther's *Ein weise christlich Mess zuhaltē*, Wittenberg, 1524, and then in *Eyn Enchiridion*, Erfurt, 1524. Thence in *Wackernagel*, iii. p. 8, in 3 st. of 9 l., in Schircks's ed. of Luther's *Geistliche Lieder*, 1854, p. 45, and as No. 222 in the *Unv. L. S.*, 1851.

It is the ancient Psalm rewritten as a New Testament missionary hymn. It was thus appropriately used at the opening service conducted by C. F. Schwartz, July 11, 1792, of the Mission Church at Trichinopoli in Southern India (*Koch*, viii. 114). It was sung by Gustavus Adolphus and his host just before the battle of Lützen (see *Altenburg*, No. ii.).

Translations in C.U. :—

1. **Lord to us be merciful**, a free *tr.* in 6 st. of 4 l. in J. Anderson's *H. from German of Dr. M. L.*, 1846, p 45 (1847, p. 64). St. i.-iv. were taken slightly altered, and a st. v. added, by G. Rawson for the *Leeds H. Bk.*, 1853, No 82.

2. **May God unto us gracious be**, a good and full *tr.* by A. T. Russell as No. 147 in his *Ps. & Hys.*, 1851; repeated in *Dr. Bacon*, 1884, p. 35.

Other trs. are—(1) "God be mercyfull unto us, And sende," by Bp. Coverdale, 1539 (*Remains*, 1846, p. 580), almost identical with (2) "O God, be mercyfull to us," in the *Gude and Godly Ballates* (ed. 1568, folio 69), ed. 1868, p. 119. (3) "God be mercyfull unto us, And grant," by R. Wisdome (probably based on Coverdale) in the 1560 *Psalmes of David*, but not repeated in the English *Psalter*, 1562, or the Scottish *Psalter*, 1564. Reprinted by Dr. Livingstone at p. 26 of his *Dissertations to The Scottish Metrical Psalter*, 1864. (4) "May God be gracious to us here," a *tr.* of st. 1 as No. 205 in the *Appendix* of 1743 to the *Moravian H. Bk.* 1742 (1754, pt. i., No. 123). (5) "May God His grace to us dispense," a *tr.* of st. i. as No. 1116 in the *Suppl.* of 1808 to the *Moravian H. Bk.*, 1801. In later eds. altered to, "Thy mercy, Lord, to us dispense" (1886, No. 902). (6) "Now may our God His mercy," by *Miss Fry*, 1845, p. 119. (7) "Father, let us Thy mercy see," by *Dr. J. Hunt*, 1853, p. 77. (8) "May God bestow on us His grace," by *It. Massie*, 1854, p. 45, repeated as No. 756 in Reid's *Praise Bk.*, 1872. (9) "To us, O God, impart Thy grace," by *Dr. H. Mills*, 1856, p. 201. (10) "God unto us right gracious be," by Dr. G. Macdonald in the *Sunday Magazine*, 1867, p. 570. In his *Exotics*, 1876, p. 77, altered to "Would that the Lord would grant us grace." (11) "May God reveal to us His grace," by *N. L. Frothingham*, 1870, p. 215. (12) "Ah God, in mercy send Thy grace," in the *Monthly Packet*, vol. xiv., 1872, p. 206. [J. M.]

Es zieht ein stiller Engel. C. J. P.

Spitta. [*Cross and Consolation.*] In the 1st Series, 1833, of his *Psalter und Harfe* (p. 116), in 5 st. of 8 l., entitled "Patience." This beautiful little poem appears in many recent collections of German Sacred Poetry, often entitled "The Angel of Patience," and is included in J. Sturm's *Hausandacht*, 1868, p. 465. The only *tr.* in C. U. is :—

To weary hearts, to mourning homes. By J. G. Whittier, in 4 st. of 6 l. Mr. Whittier informs us that it was written in 1845 and 1st pub. in his *Poems*, Boston, U.S., 1849, p. 262.

In his *Poetical Works*, Lond., Macmillan & Co., 1874, p. 121, it is correctly described as "A Free Paraphrase from the German." It has been included in full in *The South Place Coll.*, 1873, Dr. Martineau's *H. of Praise and Prayer*, 1873, and Horder's *Cong. Hyl.*, 1884; and in America, omitting st. ii., in Hedge & Huntington's *Coll.*, 1853, *Plymouth Coll.*, 1855, and *Bapt. Praise Bk.*, 1871.

Other trs. are—(1) "A gentle angel walketh," by Miss Borthwick in *H. L. L.*, 1855, p. 19 (1884, p. 84); repeated in the Schaff-Gilman *Lib. of Rel. Poetry*, ed. 1883, p. 836. (2) "Lo, passed through Heaven's portals," in *Sacred Poems* by the Hon. S. R. Maxwell, 1857, p. 123. (3) "There goes a noiseless angel," by Miss Fry, 1859, p. 159. (4) "A gentle angel wendeth," by *R. Massie*, 1860, p. 20. (5) "A stilly angel wanders," by *Miss Manington*, 1863, p. 47. (6) "On silent wings an angel," in Dr. H. W. Dulcken's *Golden Harp*, 1864, p. 68. (7) "Throughout this earth in stillness," by Miss May in *Christian Lyrics*, Norwich and London, 1860, p. 123. (8) "A silent angel wanders," by *S. A. Storrs*, 1857, p. 63. [J. M.]

Ἔσωσε λαὸν, θαυματουργῶν Δεσπότης.

John the Monk, commonly regarded as the same as St. John of Damascus (q.v.) Regarding it as a Canon by St. John it would date from about the middle of the 8th cent. It is a Canon for Christmas Day, and the Odes are sung in service alternatively with those of St. Cosmas's Χριστὸς γεννᾶται δοξάσατε ("Christ is born, Tell forth His fame," q.v). In common with all festival Canons, Ode ii. is omitted. [See **Greek Hymnody**, xvi. 11.] The remaining eight are :—

Ode i. Ἔσωσε λαὸν, θαυματουργῶν Δεσπότης. "The Wonder-working Master saved His race." This is a rendering in blank verse by *Dr. Littledale*, and was published in his *Offices of the H. E. Church*, 1863, pp. 188–9. W. Chatterton Dix's version in the *Lyra Messianica*, 1864, pp. 57–8, is Dr. Littledale's blank verse turned into 7-6 measure.

Ode iii. Νεῦσον πρὸς ὕμνους, οὐκετῶν εὐεργέτα. "Bend to our hymns, Redeemer of Thine own." Blank verse *tr.* Littledale's *Offices*, p. 190. W. Chatterton Dix, the same *tr.* in 7-6 measure, *Lyra Messianica*, pp. 74–5.

Ode iv. Γένους βροτείον τὴν ἀνάπλασιν πάλαι. "The Prophet Habakkuk in ancient song." Blank verse *tr.* Littledale's *Offices*, &c., p. 193. "Habakkuk in ancient song," the same *tr.* in 6 of 7 measure by W. Chatterton Dix, *Lyra Messianica*, pp. 93–4.

Ode v. Ἐκ νυκτὸς ἔργων ἐσκοτωσμένης πλάνης. "From the night toils of darkened wandering." Littledale's *Offices*, &c., pp. 194–5.

Ode vi. Ναίων Ἰωνᾶς ἐν μυχοῦς θαλαττίοις. "Jonah, abiding in the ocean depths." Littledale's *Offices*, &c., p. 196.

Ode vii. Τῷ παντάνακτος ἐξεφαύλισαν πόθῳ. "The Children, fascinated with the love." Littledale's *Offices*, &c., pp. 199–200.

Ode viii. Μήτραν ἀφλέκτως εἰκονίζουσι Κόρης. "The youths with fire circled, unconsumed." Littledale's *Offices*, &c., pp. 201–2.

Ode ix. Στέργειν μὲν ἡμᾶς ὡς ἀκίνδυνον φόβως. "Easy it is for us, as free from risk." Littledale's *Offices*, &c., pp. 204–5.

The original Greek text is given in *Anth. Græc. Car. Christ.*, p. 205, in *Daniel*, accompanied with a short note; and in Littledale's *Offices*, &c., pp. 53-85. This Canon,

with two others by the same author, are in Iambics. [See Greek Hymnody, § xvii. 2.] [J. J.]

Essex, J. B.   [Burton, John.]

Estlin, J. P.   [Unitarian Hymnody.]

Eta, in E. P. Hammond's *Praises of Jesus*, 1864, i.e. Etta Campbell.

Eternal and immortal King. *P. Doddridge.* [*Faith.*] 1st pub. in his posthumous *Hymns*, &c., 1755, No. 321, in 5 st. of 4 l., and again in J. D. Humphreys's ed. of the same, 1839, No. 347. It is based on Heb. xi. 17. In several American collections it is altered to: "Almighty and immortal King," and reduced to 3 st.   [J. J.]

Eternal Beam of Light Divine. *C. Wesley.* [*In Affliction.*] Appeared in *Hys. & Sac. Poems*, 1739, p. 144, in 6 st. of 4 l. (*P. Works*, 1868–72, vol. i. p. 128; and again in the *Wes. H. Bk.*, 1780, No. 328. It has passed into several collections in G. Britain, America, and other English-speaking countries. In the Boston (U.S.) Unitarian *Hy. & Tune Bk. for the Ch. & Home*, 1868, it is altered to "Eternal *God, Thou* Light Divine": and in *Songs of Christian Praise*, N.Y., 1880, and others, as :—"Eternal *Source* of Light Divine." It is a soothing and inspiriting hymn, and well adapted for use in affliction.   [J. J.]

Eternal Father, strong to save. *W. Whiting.* [*For those at Sea.*] Of this hymn the following texts are known :—

1. The original MS., 1860, a reprint of which is preserved in Biggs's *Annotated H. A. & M.*, 1867, pp. 270–271.
2. The revised text by the Compilers of *Hymns A. & M.*, 1861, No. 222. This is most widely used of any.
3. A revision by the author made for the *App.* to the S. P. C. K., *Ps. and Hymns*, 1869, and repeated in *Church Hys.*, 1871, No. 321.
4. A Latin version also by Whiting, in Biggs's *Annotated H. A. & M.*, 1867, pp. 270–71. This version is of the *H. A. & M.*, revised text of 1861, and not of the original MS.

The lack of hymns for those at sea, together with its merits as a hymn, rendered it exceedingly popular from its first publication, and its use has become most extensive in English-speaking countries. Hodges, of Frome, has published a short tale founded thereupon, and entitled "*Hymn 222.*" Orig. text as above, authorized text, *Church Hymns*, No. 321.

[J. J.]

Eternal God, Almighty Cause. *S. Browne.* [*Unity of God.*] Given in his *Hys. and Spiritual Songs*, &c., 1720 (3rd ed. 1760), Bk. i., No. 176, in 8 st. of 4 l., and entitled, "One God." In its original form it is not in C. U., and the centos from it differ in almost every hymn-book. Usually st. i., ii., iv., viii. are given, as in Dr. Hatfield's *Church H. Bk.*, 1872. The stanza which is given in some American Unitarian collections, "Worship to Thee alone belongs," is not in the original, but is based on st. vi.   [J. J.]

Eternal Light, eternal Light. *T. Binney.* [*Sunday.*] Mr. Binney's account of this hymn, supplied in 1866 to Miller's *Singers and Songs*, &c., p. 457, is, "It was written about 40 years ago, and was set to music and published by Power, of the Strand, on behalf of some charitable object to which the profits went. It was some little time since set to music also by Mr. Burnett, of Highgate. It

has appeared, I believe, in one or two books of sacred poetry, and in a mutilated state in a hymn-book in America." It was given in the Bapt. *Ps. & Hys.*, 1858, No. 103, and again in several others, in 5 st. of 5 l. The hymn— "O Thou Who art enrob'd in Light," in the Oberlin, U.S., *Manual of Praise*, 1880, No. 77, is an altered form of this hymn, with the omission of st. ii. Orig. text in *Lyra Brit.*, 1867, p. 63.   [J. J.]

Eternal Lord, from land to land. [*Missions.*] Appeared in *The Missionary Minstrel*, London, Nisbet, 1826, edited by "O. P." It is No. 78 in 8 st. of 4 l., and is signed by the Editor. It came early into congregational use, and is still found in several collections, especially in America, the text varying from 4 stanzas in some hymnals to 6 stanzas in others.   [J. J.]

Eternal Lord of earth and skies [sky]. *C. Wesley.* [*Missions.*] This cento was given in the *Supp.* to the *Wes. H. Bk.*, 1830, No.694, in 4 st. of 6 l., and repeated in the revised ed., 1875. It is composed of parts of Nos. 1059, 1060, 1043, respectively of his *Short Hymns*, &c., 1762, vol. ii. These hymns are given in full in *P. Works*, 1868–72, vol. ix., and are based on Isaiah xlii. 4; xlv. 21, &c.   [J. J.]

Eternal Power, Whose high abode. *I. Watts.* [*Praise to God.*] This hymn supplies what the author called "The Conclusion," to his *Horæ Lyricæ*, 1705. It is in 6 st. of 4 l., and is entitled "God exalted above all Praise." In 1743, J. Wesley included it, with the omission of st. ii., and the alteration of st. i., l. 3, of "length" to *lengths*, and of st. iii., l. 1, from "Thy dazzling beauties whilst he sings," to "*Thee, while the first archangel sings*" (a change necessitated by the omission) in *Ps. & Hymns*, 1743, p. 66. In 1780 this version of the text was given in the *Wes. H. Bk.*, No. 307, and from the *Wes. H. Bk.* has passed into numerous collections in all English-speaking countries. According to Methodist usage Dr. J. Beaumont read the lines,

> "Thee, while the first archangel sings,
> He hides his face behind his wings,"

to the congregation in Waltham Street Chapel, Hull, on Sunday, Jan. 23, 1855; and during the singing of the second line he fell dead in the pulpit. The incident is given in detail in Stevenson's *Meth. H. Bk. and its Associations*, 1883, p. 225.   [J. J.]

Eternal Source of every joy. *P. Doddridge.* [*New Year.*] Dated in the D. MSS Jan. 1, 1736, and 1st pub. by Job Orton in his posthumous ed. of Doddridge's *Hymns*, &c., 1755, No. 43, in 7 st. of 4 l., and in J. D. Humphreys's ed. of the same, 1839, No. 55. In the D. MSS. the title is, "God crowning the Year with His goodness"; and in the Hymns, "The Year crowned with the divine goodness." It is usually given in an abbreviated form, the number of stanzas varying in the various hymn-books. Its use in G. Britain is much less extensive than in America. The text usually adopted is from the 1755 book, as in *Lyra Brit.*, 1867, p. 193; that, however, in the *Methodist S. S. H. Bk.* is from the Brooke MS. of Doddridge's *Hymns*. [See English Hymnody, Early, § IX.]   [J. J.]

Eternal Spirit, by Whose power.
W. H. Bathurst. [*Whitsuntide.*] Appeared in his *Ps. & Hys. for Public & Private Use*, 1831 (2nd ed., 1842), Hy. 57, in 5 st. of 4 l., and entitled, "Offices of the Spirit." Since its introduction into the Bapt. *Ps. & Hys.*, 1858-80, it has attained to a good position in modern hymn-books in G. Britain. It is also in use in America. Dr. Hatfield gives in his *Church H. Bk.*, 1872, the original text, with the date of the Preface [Nov. 15], 1830, and not the date of the publication of the *Ps. & Hys.* [J. J.]

Eternal Spirit, come. *C. Wesley.* [*Whitsuntide.*] Appeared in *Hys. of Petition and Thanksgiving for the Promise of the Father*, 1746, as No. 3 of the "Hymns for Whitsunday," in 4 st. of 6 l. (*P. Works*, 1868-72, vol. iv. p. 167). It is in C. U. in two forms:—

1. The first form is in 5 st., the additional st. being from No. 16 of the "Hys. for Whitsunday" as above. This arrangement was given in Toplady's *Ps. & Hys.*, 1776, No. 246.
2. The second form is that in the *Wes. H. Bk.* revised ed., 1875, No. 762. It was included in the *Supp.* to the *Wes. H. Bk.*, 1830, in 3 st. The stanzas omitted in 1875 are st. iii., iv. [J. J.]

Eternal Spirit, gone up on high. *C. Wesley.* [*Holy Communion.*] Appeared in *Hymns on the Lord's Supper, by J. & C. Wesley*, 1745, No. cxii. in 3 st. of 8 l. (*P. Works*, 1868-72, vol. iii. p. 298). In this form it is not in common use. A cento therefrom:— "O Jesu, Lord, gone up on high," was given in the *Hymnary*, 1870-72, No. 438, in 5 st., in which the text was both altered and transposed. Its use is limited. [J. J.]

Eternal Spirit, Source of truth. *T. Cotterill.* [*Assurance of Salvation desired.*] Appeared in his *Sel. of Ps. & Hys.*, &c., 1810, No. 66, in 5 st. of 4 l., and entitled, "For a well grounded hope of Salvation," st. ii. being based on J. Hart's "Bless'd Spirit of truth, Eternal God" (1759), st. ii. It was repeated in all subsequent editions of his *Sel.* In modern hymn-books it usually reads, "Eternal Spirit, *God* of truth," as in Dr. Hatfield's *Church H. Bk.*, N. Y., 1872." In this form it is in extensive use in America. Its use in G. Britain is st. iv. of this hymn is st. iv. of the cento "Spirit of Truth, Thy grace impart," q.v. [J. J.]

Eternal Wisdom, Thee we praise. *I. Watts.* [*Praise to the Creator.*] 1st pub. in his *Horæ Lyricæ*, 1705, as "A Song to Creating Wisdom," in 18 st. of 4 l., divided into five parts, and repeated in later editions of the same, and in Watts's complete *Works*. Centos from this poem, all beginning with the first stanza, are numerous, specially in the American hymn-books. J. Wesley set the example by giving 12 stanzas in his *Ps. & Hys.*, 3rd ed., 1743. This arrangement was republished in the *Wes. H. Bk.*, 1780, No. 217 (revised ed. 1875, No. 226), and in several other collections. Usually, however, the centos are much shorter than this, from 4 to 6 stanzas being the rule. [J. J.]

Eternity! eternity! How vast, yet near eternity. *A. T. Russell.* [*Eternal Life contemplated.*] Appeared in his *Ps. &*

Hys., 1851, No. 259, in 5 st. of 7 l. In the index it is marked as original, but it is in the metre and set to the melody of "O Ewigkeit" (q.v.). It is suggested by the German but cannot be called a *tr.* of it. It is included (generally from the altered text in *Kennedy*, 1863, No. 163) in the *Ibrox Hyl.*, 1871, Snepp's *Songs of G. & G.*, 1872, No. 1021 (where the ascription to "Daniel Wülffer, 1660, (tr.) F. E. Cox, 1841," is an error), J. L. Porter's *Coll.*, 1876, &c.; and in America in the *Sabbath H. Bk.*, 1858, *College Hyl.*, 1876, &c. [J. M.]

Eternity, Eternity, That boundless, &c. *J. Montgomery.* [*Eternity.*] In the M. MSS. this hymn is dated. "The Mount, December 20, 1836" (the "Mount" was his Sheffield residence), but it did not appear in print, so far as has been traced, until his *Original Hymns*, 1853, where it is given as No. 238 in 4 st. of 4 l., and headed with a line of one of his most popular hymns, "For ever with the Lord." [J. J.]

Etheridge, Elizabeth Ayton. [Godwin, E. A.]

Euchologion, The. [Greek Hymnody, § xiv.]

Εὐφραινέσθωσαν οἱ οὐρανοί. John the Monk. [*Annunciation.*] From the Greek Office of the Annunciation of B. V. M., in the *Menæa*. It dates from the middle of the eighth century. The only *tr.* into English is Dr. Littledale's:—"Let heaven rejoice and earth be glad," which was 1st pub. in the *Church Times*, July 2, 1864, as a "Hymn for Lady-Day," and again in the *People's H.*, 1867, No. 244, signed "L," and appointed for the Annunciation of B. V. M. This is one of Dr. Littledale's best *trs.* from the Greek, and is very close to the original. [J. J.]

Evans, Albert Eubule, B.A., was educated at St. Mary Hall, Oxford (B.A. 1866), and took Holy Orders in 1864. He held successively the Curacies of Slough, New Windsor, and Walmer; was an Organising Secretary of the S. P. G., Secretary to the South American Missionary Society, and Assistant Examiner to the Civil Service Commissioners; and became Rector of Kirk-Hallam, Ilkston, in 1875. Mr. Evans pub. *Pietas Puerilis*, 1865; *The Fourfold Message of Advent*, 1870; and some tales. His hymns appeared in the Rev. R. Brown-Borthwick's *Sixteen Hys.*, &c., 1870; his *Select Hys. for Church & Home*, 1871; Dr. Martineau's *Hymns*, &c., 1873; and the S. P. C. K. *Church Hymns*, 1871. These collections include the following:

1. Lo! the voice of Jesus. *Voice of Jesus.*
2. Look up, look up, my soul, still higher. *Upwards and Onwards.*
3. Lord, to Thee alone we turn. *Lent.*
4. Many mansions, O what rapture. *Heaven.*
5. O render thanks unto the Lord. *Septuagesima.*
6. There is a road that all may tread. *Christian Life a Pilgrimage.*
7. Trust in God and God alone. *Trust.* [J. J.]

Evans, James Harrington, M.A., s. of the Rev. Dr. Evans, priest-vicar of Salisbury Cathedral, was b. April 15, 1785, and educated at Wadham College, Oxford, where he graduated in 1803, and became a Fellow in 1805. Taking Holy Orders in 1808 he remained in the Church of England until 1815, when he seceded, and became a Baptist Minister. He was the Minister of John Street Baptist Chapel, Gray's Inn Road, London, for many years. He d. at Stonehaven, Scotland, Dec. 1, 1849. His *Memoir and Remains* were pub. by his son in 1852. In addition to various prose works, *Dialogues on Important Subjects*, 1819; *Checks to Infidelity*, 1840; and others, he also pub. :—

Hymns, Selected Chiefly for Public Worship, London, printed by E. Justius, 1818. This ed. contained 179 hymns, several of which he wrote. This *Sel.* was enlarged from time to time; the 3rd ed., 1822, contained 211 hymns; and the last, 1843, 451 hymns. Of his hymns, "Change is our portion here," and "Faint not, Christian, though the road," are the best known. Mr. Evans contributed to Carus Wilson's *Friendly Visitor* of 1827, &c., under the signature of "Alix." [W. R. S.]

Evans, Evan. [*Glangeirionydd.*] Born at Trefriw in Caernarvonshire. He is considered the chief Welsh Hymn-writer of this century, as Williams was of the last century. He published two books of hymns and tunes between 1829 and 1841. He was Vicar of Rhyl, and d. in 1850. Although his hymn-books and tunes are not in use now, yet many of his hymns are found in every collection in Wales.   [W. G. T.]

Evans, Jonathan, b. at Coventry in 1748 or 1749. He was the son of a working man, and as a youth was employed in a ribbon manufactory. About 1778 he joined the congregation at Coventry, over which the Rev. G. Burder was pastor. He began preaching at Foleshill, near Coventry, in 1782, and in 1795 he began his stated ministry there, retaining the same to his death on Aug. 31, 1809. Two biographical notices of him appeared in the *Evangelical Magazine* (Oct. 1809, and March 1847), and also several of his hymns. Two of his hymns appeared in Burder's *Coll.*, 1784, and another in the 2nd ed. the same year. His best known hymns are, "Come, Thou soul-transforming Spirit," and "Hark! the voice of love and mercy," q.v. He published no poetical work or collection of hymns. [J. J.]

Ever fainting with desire. *C. Wesley.* [*Holiness desired.*] Appeared in *Hys. and Sac. Poems*, 1742, p. 219, in 10 st. of 8 l., and headed, "A Prayer for Holiness" (*P. Works*, 1868–72, vol. ii. p. 274). In 1780 it was included in the *Wes. H. Bk.*, No. 344, with the omission of st. iii.–vi., and in this form it has been repeated in several hymn-books. The omitted stanzas contain expressions concerning entire holiness, which gave rise to much controversy, and caused J. Wesley to mark them for omission in later editions of the *H. & Sac. Poems* (*Works*, vol. x. p. 397; and *P. Works*, vol. ii. p. 274).   [J. J.]

Ever patient, gentle [loving], meek. *Charlotte Elliott.* [*Resignation.*] Contributed to *The Invalid's H. Bk.*, 1834, No. 97, in 4 st. of 6 l., and headed, "Let this mind be in you which was also in Christ Jesus," Phil. ii. 5. It was repeated in subsequent editions of the same. In Longfellow and Johnson's *Book of Hys.*, Boston, U.S., 1846, it was given with the omission of st. ii., anonymously, and with the opening line as "Ever patient, *loving*, meek." The original text was restored in the Andover *Sabbath H. Bk.*, 1858. [J. J.]

Ever round Thy glorious throne. *J. S. B. Monsell.* [*St. Michael and All Angels.*] Appeared in his *Spiritual Songs*, &c., 1857 (People's ed., 1875, p. 189, in 33 st. of 4 l., and based upon the words "Are they not all ministering spirits, sent forth to minister for them who shall be heirs of salvation," Heb. i. 14. In 1861, the Rev. F. Pott included 14 stanzas in his *Hymns*, &c., No. 221, and divided them into three parts:—i. as above; ii. "From the world's remotest prime"; and iii. "Angels marked with wondering gaze." A very effective cento of 6 stanzas might be compiled from this poem.   [J. J.]

Everest, Charles William, M.A., b. at East Windsor, Connecticut, May 27, 1814, graduated at Trinity College, Hartford, 1838, and took Holy Orders in 1842. He was rector at Hamden, Connecticut, from 1842 to 1873, and also agent for the Society for the Increase of the Ministry. He d. at Waterbury, Connecticut, Jan. 11, 1877 (See *Poets of Connecticut*, 1843). In 1833 he pub. *Visions of Death, and Other Poems;* from this work his popular hymn is taken :—

Take up thy cross, the Saviour said. *Following Jesus.* The original text of this hymn differs very materially from that which is usually found in the hymn-books. The most widely known form of the text is that in *H. A. & M.*, where it appeared in 1861. It was copied by the Compilers from another collection, but by whom the alterations were made is unknown. The nearest approach to the original is in Horder's *Cong. Hys.*, 1884. Orig. text in Biggs's *English Hymnology*, 1873, p. 24.   [F. M. B.]

Everett, James, b. at Alnwick, Northumberland, May 16, 1784. His early education was of a very elementary character, and gave little promise of the literary position which he subsequently attained. In his 19th year he underwent a great spiritual change, which led him to become a member of the Wesleyan Society, and subsequently a local preacher and minister of that connection. His work in the ministry, his controversy with the Wesleyan Conference, his expulsion from their Society in 1849, and his part in founding the Wesleyan Reform Connection, which, by amalgamation with the Wesleyan Methodist Association in 1857, constitute the United Methodist Free Churches, were matters of Methodist history. Although deeply involved in Methodist polity and work, he found time to publish some forty works, chiefly biographical, but including some which were poetical and hymnological. He d. at Sunderland, May 10, 1872. His poetical works include :—

(1) *Edwin*, 1831; (2) *The Reign of Terror & other Poems*, 1832; (3) a Collection of *Hymns for Sunday Schools*, &c., 1831. Mr. Everett also edited the *Wesleyan Reform H. Bk.*, 1853 [See **Methodist Hymnody**, § v.], and with the Rev. M. Baxter, *Hymn Bk. of the United Methodist Free Churches*, 1860 [**Methodist Hymnody**, § v.]. His Life by Richard Chew was pub. in 1875, as *James Everett; A Biography.*

His hymns, which are republished in the *H. Bk. of the United Methodist Free Churches*, 1860, are :—

1. **Beneath the altar of the Lord.** *Divine Worship and the Altar.*
2. **Lo, Creation springs to birth.** *The Thorn and its historical and spiritual associations.* Pub. in his *Reign of Terror*, &c., 1832.

3. **More anxious than the Persian sage.** *S. S. Anniversary.* Printed in the *S. S. Magazine*, May 19, 1823.

During Mr. Everett's residence in Sheffield in 1820–21, he wrote several hymns for the Sheffield S. Schools, which are preserved in fly-sheet form but not incorporated in any collection. [J. J.]

Everlasting! changing never. *T. H. Gill.* [*Holiness desired.*] Written in 1845, and 1st pub. in G. Dawson's *Ps. & Hys.*, 1846, No. 117, in 8 st. of 6 l. In 1853 it was transferred to Hedge and Huntington's American *Hys. for the Ch. of Christ*, No. 837. In later American collections as the *Hys. of the Spirit*, Boston, 1864, No. 431, and others. St. ii., iii., vi., vii., are given with slight alterations from this text, as " We the weak ones, we the sinners." In the author's *Golden Chain*, &c., 1869, p. 81, the hymn is given in a revised form. Concerning this revision the author says :—

"It was the most popular of my early hymns, and exactly expressed that spirit of general aspiration so prominent with ardent youth in the fifth decade of the century. The alterations introduced in the *Golden Chain* improved and strengthened the diction, as well as Christianised the hymn. Still the original has a newness, liveliness and charm which the altered version hardly retains." [J. J.]

Every morning the red sun. *Cecil F. Alexander.* [*Heaven.*] This hymn, in 5 st. of 6 l., is based on the article of the Apostles Creed, "And the life everlasting." It appeared in Mrs. Alexander's *Hys. for Little Children*, 1848, No. 20, and is repeated in later editions. It is found in several collections in G. Britain and America. In the American *Church Praise Bk.*, N. Y., 1882, it is altered to, "Every morn the glowing sun"; but the advantage of the change is questionable. [J. J.]

Every morning they are new. *G. Phillimore.* [*Morning.*] Written for and 1st pub. in the *Parish H. Bk.*, 1863, in 4 st. of 6 l. On being transferred to the *Hymnary*, 1872, No. 57, it was altered to "Every morning mercies new." This altered text was repeated in Thring's *Coll.*, 1882, and several others. In the American *Evang. Hymnal*, 1880; and the *Laudes Domini*, 1884, it is attributed to Dr. H. Bonar in error. [J. J.]

Ex more docti mystico. [*Lent.*] This hymn is found in two mss. of the 11th cent. in the *British Museum* (Vesp. D. xii. f. 54; Harl. 2961, f. 237); and in the *Latin Hys. of the Anglo-Saxon Church*, printed from an 11th cent. ms. at Durham (B. iii. 32, f. 18 *b*), by the Surtees Society, in 1851. Mone's (No. 73) text from a 15 cent. ms. is slightly different from this; as is also that in *Daniel*, i., No. 86; and in the *Hymn. Sarisb.*, 1851. *Daniel* prints also the text of the *Roman Brev.*, 1632, and in iv. p. 121, he gives readings from a Rheinau ms. of the 10th cent. *Mone* holds that the hymn is by St. Gregory the Great. Concerning its use we may note :—

In the Uses of *Sarum* and *York* it is the hymn at Vespers of the 1st Sun. in Lent to the second Vespers of the 3rd Sunday. In the *Rom. Brev.* it is the hymn at Matins for the 1st Sun. in Lent to Passion Sunday exclusively. In the Uses of *Evesham, Canterbury, and St. Albans*, st. i.–iv. are to be said at Matins, and the rest at Lauds, from the 1st to the 3rd Sun. in Lent. Some continental Breviaries differ from each of these.

The hymn **Quod lex adumbravit vetus**, in the revised *Paris Brev.*, 1736, given as the hymn on Sundays and Ferial days at Matins from Ash Wednesday to Passion Sunday (as also in the *Lyons* and other modern French Breviaries) is a recast of this hymn made by Charles Coffin for the *Paris Brev.*, and also pub. in his *Hymni Sacri*, 1736, p. 102. This text is in Card. Newman's *Hymni Ecclesiae*, 1838–65; and J. Chandler's *Hys. of the Prim. Church*, 1837, No. 60. The old text is in the works noted above: *Wackernagel;* and (Roman) *Card. Newman*, 1838–65; and Biggs's *Annotated H. A. & M.*, 1867. [W. A. S.]

Translations in C. U. :—

i. **Ex more docti mystico.** Of this there are the following *trs.* in C. U. :—

1. **Now with the slow-revolving year.** By E. Caswall from the *Rom. Brev.* text, in his *Lyra Catholica*, 1849, p. 72, and his *Hymns*, &c., 1873, p. 40. In 1850 it was included in Dr. Oldknow's *Coll.*, No. 70, and later in *The Crown of Jesus H. Bk.*, and other Roman Catholic hymn-books for Schools and Missions. In the *Hymnary*, 1872, No. 212, this *tr.* is also given as, " By precepts taught in ages past, Again the fast," &c.

2. **In solemn course, as holy lore.** By J. D. Chambers (*Sarum* text), pub. in his *Order of Household Devotion*, 1854, and his *Lauda Syon*, 1857, p. 126. In the *People's H.*, 1867, No. 61, st. iv. is omitted.

3. **The fast as taught by holy lore.** By J. M. Neale, from the *Sarum* text. Appeared in the *Hymnal N.*, 1854 ; and repeated in the *Hymner*, 1882. In Skinner's *Daily Service Hymnal*, 1863, it begins with st. iv., " In prayer together let us fall." This form is also in some American collections.

4. **By precepts taught in ages past, Now let us, &c.** This is Dr. Neale's *tr.* rewritten by the Compilers of *H. A. & M.*, and given in their trial copy, 1859, and the 1st and later editions, 1861–75. It retains the greater portion of Dr. Neale's rendering, but is cast in a more popular form.

Translations not in C. U. :—

1. From heaven's own school's mysterious ways. *Primer.* 1706.
2. Of sacred usage old. *Bp. Mant.* 1837.
3. By rite religious bound. *W. J. Copeland.* 1848.
4. Let us, the scholars of Christ's school. *W. J. Blew.* 1851.
5. By mystic lessons wisely taught. *J. W. Hewett.* 1859.
6. Come, let us keep this solemn feast. *J. Wallace.* 1874.

ii. **Quod lex adumbravit vetus.** Of this text from the *Paris Breviary*, 1736, the following *trs.* are in C. U. :—

1. **The solemn fast the Fathers saw.** By J. Chandler, in his *Hys. of the Primitive Church*, 1837, p. 67, in 6 st. of 4 l. In *Kennedy*, 1863, it was given with the omission of st. ii. as " With fast and prayer for sinful man."

2. **It is the holy fast.** By I. Williams, in his *Hys. tr. from the Parisian Brev.*, 1839, p. 108. It was repeated, with the omission of st. iii. and viii., in *The Child's Christian Year*, 1841, and later editions, &c.

3. **Good it is to keep the fast.** By Sir H. W. Baker, written for and 1st pub. in *H. A. & M.*, revised ed., 1875, No. 89. [J. J.]

Ex quo, salus mortalium. [*Jean Baptiste de Santeüil.*] [*Martyrs.*] Pub. in the

Cluniac Breviary, 1686, and in his *Hymni Sacri et Novi*, 1689, p. 199 (ed. 1698, p. 242), in 6 st. of 4 l. In 1736 it was included in the revised ed. of the *Paris Brev.*, and appointed as the hymn at 1st and 2nd Vespers of the Common of One Martyr; and again in the *Lyons*, and other modern French Breviaries. *Paris Brev.* text in Card. Newman's *Hymni Ecclesiae*, 1838–65. [W. A. S.]

Translation in C. U. :—

Our Lord the path of suffering trod. By I. Williams. In his *Hys. tr. from the Parisian Brev.*, 1839, p. 281, in 7 st. of 4 l. In 1861, it was recast by the Compilers of *H. A. & M.*, and given in that collection as, "For man the Saviour shed." This is repeated in the revised ed., 1875.

Translation not in C. U. :—

Since Christ His precious life-blood gave. *J. D. Chambers*, 1866, ii. p. 8.

Exalted high at God's right hand. [*Saints in Glory.*] In *A Coll. of Ps. and Hys. chiefly intended for Public Worship*, pub. by Rowland Hill, in 1783, No. cxciii., this hymn appeared in 9 st. of 4 l., in the form of a dialogue, the opening stanzas being:—

" *Q.* Exalted high at God's right hand,
    Nearer the throne than cherubs stand.
    With glory crown'd in white array,
    My wondering soul says, Who are they?

" *A.* These are the saints belov'd of God,
    Wash'd are their robes in Jesus' blood
    More spotless than the purest white,
    They shine in uncreated light."

The hymn thus proceeds, following the order of thought in Rev. vii. 12–17 to the end. No name is given by which its authorship may be identified. It is usually attributed to Rowland Hill on the ground that it appeared first in his *Coll.*, and no one has been known to dispute his claims. Orig. text in *Lyra Brit.*, p. 309. The popular form of this hymn is that given to it by Cotterill in his *Selection*, 1810, No. 122, which reads:—" *Lo! round the throne* at God's right hand," &c., as in Mercer's *Ch. Psalter & H. Bk.*, Ox. ed., No. 429, with st. 4, l. 4, thus, " And thus the loud hosanna raise." It is sometimes included in hymnals with the first line, " Lo, *near* the throne at God's right hand," " Lo! round the throne a glorious band," and one or two minor alterations. The authorship of the Rowland Hill form of the text has been attributed to John Duncan, on the authority of John Dobell; but we regard this as an error [see p. 42]. It is rightly described in Thring's *Coll.*, 1880, as " From Cotterill's *Sel.*, 1810, based on Rowland Hill, 1783.'   [J. J.]

Ἐξαποστειλάριον. [Greek Hymnody, § xvi. 7.]

Excelsorum civium inclita gaudia. [*St. Michael and All Angels.*] This anonymous hymn is given in the *Hereford Breviary* of 1505 for " St. Raphael." In Dr. Neale's *Hymni Ecclesiae*, 1851, p. 212, it is given as Celsorum civium inclita gaudia, and the same is repeated in *Daniel*, iv. p. 287. *Tr.* as:—

The mighty host on high. By J. M. Neale, in the *H. Noted*, 1854, in 5 st. of 7 l., and repeated in the *Hymnary*, 1872. This is from the text in his *H. Ecclesiae*, 1851.

Another tr. is :—
The exalted heavenly choir. *J. D. Chambers*. 1866.
[J. J.]

Exite filiae Sion, Regis pudicae virgines. *Isaac Habert.* [*The Crown of Jesus.*] Contributed to the *Paris Brev.*, 1643, Aest. p. 604, for use at Vespers on the festival of The Crown of Thorns, Aug. 11, together with a second part for use at Lauds, beginning **Legis figuris pingitur**, at p. 610. Both parts were given in the *Paris Brev.*, 1713, and also in some of the recent editions of the *Roman Brev.*, as in the Tournay ed., 1879, where the first part begins **Exite Sion filiae** (see *Daniel*, ii. p. 360). In the *Paris Brev.*, 1736, Pt. i. as above only is given. The *trs.* are from the *Roman Brev.* :—

i. Exite Sion filiae.
Daughters of Sion! Royal Maids. By E. Caswall, in his *Lyra Catholica*, 1849, p. 68; and his *Hys. & Poems*, 1873, p. 38. It is repeated in the 1862 *Appendix* to the *H. Noted*, No. 242, and Shipley's *Annus Sanctus*, 1884, p. 63.

ii. Legis figuris pingitur.
Christ's peerless crown is pictured in. By E. Caswall, as above (1849), p. 69; 1872, p. 39) into the 1862 *Appendix* to the *H. Noted*, No. 243, and Shipley's *Annus Sanctus*, 1884, p. 64.
[J. M.]

Exultet coelum laudibus. [*Festival of Apostles.*] The oldest known form of this hymn is in four MSS. of the 11th cent. in the *British Museum* (Jul. A. vi. f. 63; Vesp. D. xii. f. 96 *b*; Harl. 2961, f. 246 *b*; Add. 30851, f. 153), and in the *Latin Hys. of the Anglo-Saxon Ch.*, printed from an 11th cent. MS. at Durham (B. iii. 32 f. 36 *a*). It is also in one or two of the older French Breviaries. In the *Roman Brev.*, 1632, it begins **Exultet orbis gaudiis.** *Daniel*, i., No. 232, gives both texts, together with notes and readings. *Mone*, No. 663, refers to five MSS. dating from the 12th to the 15th cent., and his text differs slightly from that of *Daniel*. In the *Parisian Brev.*, 1736, it was altered by C. Coffin to **Laetare coelum plausibus.** The *trs.* which we have are from :—

i. Exultet coelum laudibus. This is *tr.* as:—
1. Let heaven resound with praises. By W. J. Blew, in *The Church Hy. and Tune Bk.*, 1852–55; and again in Rice's *Hymns*, &c., selected from the same, 1870.

2. Ye heavens, exult with joyful praise. By J. D. Chambers, in his *Lauda Syon*, 1857, p. 92, in 6 st. of 4 l., and is repeated in the *Appendix* to the *Hymnal N.*, No. 188; and in the *Hymner*, 1882.

ii. Exultet orbis gaudiis. This is the text of the *Roman Brev.*, 1632, and is *tr.* as:—
1. Let the round world with songs rejoice. By Bp. R. Mant, in his *Ancient Hymns*, &c., 1837, p. 72. (New ed., 1871, p. 127.) This is given without alteration in the *People's H.*, 1867, but usually it is altered, as in the following instances :—

(1) Let all on earth with songs rejoice." This was given in Murray's *Hymnal*, 1852; the *Salisbury*, 1857; in the *New Mitre* (with slight alterations), 1875; and with an additional stanza (st. ii.) and alterations in the *Hymnary*, 1872.
(2) " Let earth be glad and joyful sing." This appeared in the *English Hyl.*, 1852–61.
(3) " Let all on earth their voices raise." In this arrangement in *Church Hys.*, 1871, the older form of the text, earth re-echoing the praise of heaven, instead of heaven repeating the songs of earth, as in the *Roman*

Brev., has been adopted. Otherwise the text is from Bp. Mant, but somewhat altered.

2. Now let the earth with joy resound. By E. Caswall, in his *Lyra Catholica*, 1849, p. 202, and his *Hys. & Poems*, 1873, p. 107. It is included in the Roman Catholic *Hys. for the Year*.

Translations not in C. U. :—
1. Exult, thou world, exult with praise. *J. R. Beste.* 1849.
2. Now let the world with joy abound. *J. Wallace.* 1874.

iii. **Laetare coelum plausibus.**
1. Let heaven with acclamations ring. *J. D. Chambers.* 1866.   [J. J.]

Exultet cor precordiis. [*Most Holy Name of Jesus.*] An anonymous hymn given at 1st Vespers on the "Feast of the Most Sweet Name of Jesus," Aug. 7, in the *Sarum Brev.*, Venice, 1495, *Estiv.* pt. ii. f. 178. *Tr.* as :—

1. Exult all hearts, right gladly. By W. J. Blew, in *The Church Hy. and Tune Bk.*, 1852–55; and again in Rice's *Hymns*, &c., selected from the same, 1870.

2. Let every heart exulting beat. By J. D. Chambers, in his *Lauda Syon*, 1857, p. 243, in 8 st. of 4 l. This is repeated in an abbreviated, and sometimes altered, form in *H. A. & M.*, 1861; the *Hymnary*, 1872; Allon's *Suppl. Hys.*, 1868–75, and others.

3. Exult, all hearts, with gladness. This rendering, which is given in the Roman Catholic *Hys. for the Year* (N. D.), and in Spurgeon's *O. O. H. Bk.*, 1866, is an arrangement of a part of J. D. Chambers's *tr.*, very much altered, and with the L. M. changed to 7-6.

4. O let the heart exulting beat. By R. F. Littledale, written for and 1st pub. in the *People's H.*, 1867, No. 272, and signed "F. R."

Translation not in C. U. :—
With joyous strains, by ev'ry tongue. *J. W. Hewett.* 1859.   [J. J.]

F

F., in the *Gospel Magazine*, 1776; i.e. James Fanch.

F., in Bristol Bap. *Coll.* of Ash & Evans, 1st ed., 1769; i.e. T. Flatman.

F—s, in the same; i.e. John Fellows.

F. J. C., in *Bright Jewels*, N.Y., 1869; i.e. Mrs. F. J. Van Alstyne.

F. R., initials of Dr. R. F. Littledale, reversed in the *People's Hymnal*; i.e. "Frederick Richard."

Faber, Frederick William, D.D., S. of Mr. T. H. Faber, was b. at Calverley Vicarage, Yorkshire, June 28, 1814, and educated at Balliol College, Oxford, graduating B.A. in 1836. He was for some time a Fellow of University College, in the same University. Taking Holy Orders in 1837, he became Rector of Elton, Huntingdonshire, in 1843, but in 1846 he seceded to the Church of Rome. After residing for some time at St. Wilfrid's, Staffordshire, he went to London in 1849, and established the London "Orato-

rians," or, "Priests of the Congregation of St. Philip Neri," in King William Street, Strand. In 1854 the Oratory was removed to Brompton. Dr. Faber d. Sept. 26, 1863. Before his secession he published several prose works, some of which were in defence of the Church of England; and afterwards several followed as *Spiritual Conferences*, *All for Jesus*, &c. Although he published his *Cherwell Waterlily and Other Poems*, 1840; *The Styrian Lake, and Other Poems*, 1842; *Sir Lancelot*, 1844; and *The Rosary and Other Poems*, 1845; and his *Lives of the Saints*, in verse, before he joined the Church of Rome, all his hymns were published after he joined that communion. They were included in his:—

(1) A small book of eleven *Hymns*, 1849, for the School at St. Wilfrid's, Staffordshire. (2) *Jesus and Mary: or, Catholic Hymns for Singing and Reading*, Lond. 1849. In 1852 the 2nd ed. was pub. with an addition of 20 new hymns. (3) *Oratory Hymns*, 1854; and (4) *Hymns*, 1862, being a collected ed. of what he had written and published from time to time.

Dr. Faber's account of the origin of his hymn-writing is given in his Preface to *Jesus & Mary*. After dwelling on the influence, respectively, of St. Theresa, of St. Ignatius, and of St. Philip Neri, on Catholicism; and of the last that "sanctity in the world, perfection at home, high attainments in common earthly callings ... was the principal end of his apostolate," he says :—

"It was natural then that an English son of St. Philip should feel the want of a collection of English Catholic hymns fitted for singing. The few in the *Garden of the Soul* were all that were at hand, and of course they were not numerous enough to furnish the requisite variety. As to translations they do not express Saxon thought and feelings, and consequently the poor do not seem to take to them. The domestic wants of the Oratory, too, keep alive the feeling that something of the sort was needed: though at the same time the Author's ignorance of music appeared in some measure to disqualify him for the work of supplying the defect. Eleven, however, of the hymns were written, most of them, for particular tunes and on particular occasions, and became very popular with a country congregation. They were afterwards printed for the Schools at St. Wilfrid's, and the very numerous applications to the printer for them seemed to show that, in spite of very glaring literary defects, such as careless grammar and slipshod metre, people were anxious to have Catholic hymns of any sort. The MS. of the present volume was submitted to a musical friend, who replied that certain verses of all or nearly all of the hymns would do for singing; and this encouragement has led to the publication of the volume."

In the same Preface he clearly points to the *Olney Hymns* and those of the Wesleys as being the models which for simplicity and intense fervour he would endeavour to emulate. From the small book of eleven hymns printed for the schools at St. Wilfrid's, his hymn-writing resulted in a total of 150 pieces, all of which are in his *Hymns*, 1862, and many of them in various Roman Catholic collections for missions and schools. Few hymns are more popular than his "My God, how wonderful Thou art," "O come and mourn with me awhile," and "Sweet Saviour, bless us ere we go." They excel in directness, simplicity, and pathos. "Hark, hark, my soul, angelic songs are swelling," and "O Paradise, O Paradise," are also widely known. These possess, however, an element of unreality which is against their permanent popularity. Many of Faber's hymns are annotated under their respective first lines; the rest in C. U. include :—

i. From his *Jesus and Mary*, 1849 and 1852.

1. Fountain of love, Thyself true God. *The Holy Ghost.*
2. How shalt thou bear the Cross, that now. *The Eternal Years.*
3. I come to Thee, once more, O God. *Returning to God.*
4. Joy, joy, the Mother comes. *The Purification.*
5. My soul, what hast thou done for God ? *Self-Examination.*
6. O how the thought of God attracts. *Holiness Desired.*
7. O soul of Jesus, sick to death. *Passiontide.* Sometimes this is divided into two parts, Pt. ii. beginning, "My God, my God, and can it be."

ii. From his *Oratory Hymns*, 1854.

8. Christians, to the war ! Gather from afar. *The Christian Warfare.*
9. O come to the merciful Saviour that calls you. *Divine Invitation.* In many collections.
10. O God, Thy power is wonderful. *Power and Eternity of God.*
11. O it is sweet to think, Of those that are departed. *Memory of the Dead.*
12. O what are the wages of sin ? *The Wages of Sin.*
13. O what is this splendour that beams on me now ? *Heaven.*
14. Saint of the Sacred Heart. *St. John the Evangelist.*

iii. From his *Hymns*, 1862.

15. Father, the sweetest, dearest Name. *The Eternal Father.*
16. Full of glory, full of wonders, Majesty Divine. *Holy Trinity.*
17. Hark ! the sound of the fight. *Processions.*
18. How pleasant are thy paths, O death. *Death Contemplated.*
19. O God, Whose thoughts are brightest light. *Thinking no Evil.*
20. O why art thou sorrowful, servant of God ? *Trust in God.*
21. Souls of men, why will ye scatter ? *The Divine Call.*
22. The land beyond the sea. *Heaven Contemplated.*
23. The thought of God, the thought of thee. *Thoughts of God.*
24. We come to Thee, sweet Saviour. *Jesus, our Rest.*

In addition to these there are also several hymns in C. U. in Roman Catholic hymn-books which are confined to those collections. In the *Hys. for the Year*, by Dr. Rawes, Nos. 77, 110, 112, 117, 120, 121, 122, 125, 127, 128, 131, 140, 152, 154, 169, 170, 174, 179, 180, 192, 222, 226, 230, 271, 272, are also by Faber, and relate principally to the Blessed Virgin Mary. Several of these are repeated in other Roman Catholic collections.   [J. J.]

Faber, Johann Ludwig, was b. at Nürnberg, 1635. He studied at the Universities of Altdorf, Tübingen and Heidelberg, became in 1657 conrector, and in 1664 rector of the school at Oettingen, in 1666 rector of the school at Hersbruck, and in 1670 became fifth master in the Egidien Gymnasium at Nürnberg. He d. at Nürnberg, Nov. 28, 1678.

He was crowned as a poet by Sigismund von Birken in 1669. In 1664 he was admitted a member of the Pegnitz Shepherd and Flower Order, and his hymns were contributed to the *Poetische Andachtsklang*, Nürnberg, 1673, — a collection of verses by various members of the Order founded on the meditations in Dr. Heinrich Müller's *Geistliche Erquickstunden*, Rostock, 1664-1666. One of these has passed into English, viz. :—

Ich lass ihn nicht, der sich gelassen [*Love to Christ*], 1673, as above, No 50, in 8 st., founded on No. 300 of Müller's meditations. Sometimes erroneously ascribed to Gottfried Arnold. *Tr.* as "I leave Him not, Who came to save," by *Miss Winkworth*, 1869, p. 296. [J. M.]

Fading, still fading, the last beam is shining. [*Evening*.] This anonymous hymn appeared in *Hys. for Vestry and Fireside*, Boston, U.S., 1841, where it is ascribed to the *Sacred Minstrel*, a book of tunes, dated 1830.

It has attained to great popularity in America, and is given in a great number of modern hymn-books, although unknown to those in G. Britain. It is in a peculiar metre and of exceptional merit. Orig. text in *Songs for the Sanctuary*, N. Y., 1865 and 1872.   [J. J.]

Fain would my thoughts fly up to Thee. *J. Austin.* [*Hope.*] From his *Devotions in the Antient Way of Offices*, 1668, into Lord Selborne's *Bk. of Praise*, 1862–1867, and T. Darling's *Hymns*, &c., 1855 and 1887.

Faint not, Christian, though the road. *J. H. Evans.* [*Patient Endurance.*] Appeared in the 4th ed. of his *Hys. Selected chiefly for Pub. Worship*, 1833, in 7 st. of 4 l., and in the Rev. Carus Wilson's *Friendly Visitor*, Aug., 1835, with the signature "Alix." It is based on Heb. xii. 3. The hymn, "*Fear not, children, though the road*," in the *Meth. Free Ch. S. S. H. Bk.*, 1860, No. 311, is composed of st. i.-iii., and vi. of this hymn, slightly altered, together with a chorus from another source. It is popular in America.   [J. J.]

Fair are the feet which bring the news. *J. Mason.* [*Missions.*] 1st pub. in his *Spiritual Songs ; or, Songs of Praise*, 1683, p. 36, as "A Song of Praise for a Gospel Ministry," in 5 st. of 8 l. (Sedgwick's reprint, 1859, p. 26). In its full form it is unknown to modern hymn-books. The following centos therefrom are in C. U. :—

1. **Fair are the feet which bring the news.** In Longfellow and Johnson's *Hys. of the Spirit*, Boston, U.S., 1864, No. 343 is compiled from st. i., iii. and iv., considerably altered.
2. **Bless'd are the feet which bring the news.** This was given in Bickersteth's *Christ. Psalmody*, 1833, No. 429, and is altered from st. i., iii.-v.
3. **How blest the feet which bring the news.** In Hall's *Mitre*, 1836, No. 117 is st. i., v. altered.
4. **How beautiful the feet that bring.** This altered form of st. i.-iii., v. is by the Rev. J. Keble. It was given in the *Salisbury H. Bk.*, 1857, No. 188, the *Sarum H.*, 1868, *Kennedy*, 1863, and others.   [J. J.]

Fair shines the morning star. *J. Montgomery.* [*Year of Jubilee.*] Appeared in his *Christian Psalmist*, 1825, No. 556, in 5 st. of 6 l., and in his *Original Hymns*, 1853, No. 263, the title in each case being "The Year of Jubilee." In 1836 J. Conder adopted it for the *Cong. H. Bk.*, and others have followed, both in G. Britain and America : but its use is not so extensive as many of Montgomery's hymns. In the N. Y. *Church Praise Bk.*, 1882, No. 227, is a cento beginning with st. i. of this hymn, and st. ii.-iv. from C. Wesley's "Blow ye the trumpet, blow" (q.v.).   [J. J.]

Fair waved the golden corn. *J. H. Gurney.* [*Dedication of First Fruits.*] This application of the "First Fruits" as a hymn of prayer and praise for Children appeared in the author's Marylebone *Ps. & Hys.*, 1851, No. 38, in 6 st. of 4 l., and not in his Lutterworth *Coll. of Hys.*, 1838, as sometimes stated. It has attained to great popularity, and is found, generally unaltered, in most of the leading modern hymn-books. Bingham, in his *Hymno. Christ. Lat.*, 1871, has rendered it into Latin as "Pulchrius in Judae campis crepitante susurro."   [J. J.]

Faith, hope, and charity, these three. *J. Montgomery.* [*Faith, Hope, and Charity.*]

In the M. MSS. this hymn is dated "Jan. 27, 1834." It was printed in his *Original Hymns*, 1853, No. 164, in 4 st. of 4 l., and entitled "The Christian Graces." It is given in a few hymn-books in G. Britain and America: as Dr. Martineau's *Hys. of Praise and Prayer*, 1873; the New York *Hys. & Songs of Praise*, 1874, and others.   [J. J.]

Faith of our fathers! living still. *F. W. Faber.* [*A Pledge of Faithfulness.*] This hymn appeared as the first of two hymns, one "Faith of our Fathers," for England; and the second the same for Ireland, in his *Jesus and Mary; or, Catholic Hys. for Singing and Reading*, 1849, in 4 st. of 6 l. It was repeated in his *Oratory Hymns*, and several Roman Catholic collections for missions and schools. Its use illustrates most forcibly how in hymnody, as in other things, "extremes meet." In the original st. iii., ll. 1, 2, read:—

"Faith of our Fathers! Mary's prayers
Shall win our country back to thee."

In 1853 Drs. Hedge & Huntington altered these lines to :—

"Faith of our Fathers! *Good men's* prayers
Shall win our country *all* to thee."

for their Unitarian *Hys. for the Church of Christ*, No. 455. With this alteration it has passed into several Nonconformist collections in G. Britain and America. With the alteration of these few words the hymn is regularly sung by Unitarians on the one hand, and by Roman Catholics on the other, as a metrical embodiment of their history and aspirations.   [J. J.]

Faith, 'tis a precious gift. *B. Beddome.* [*Faith described.*] Of this popular hymn various forms are in C. U. both in G. Britain and America as follows:—

1. The original, which was given in the Bristol Bap. *Coll.* of Ash & Evans, 1769, No. 232, in 4 st. of 4 l. This was repeated in Rippon's *Sel.*, 1787, and later editions, and several modern hymn-books.

2. The text as in R. Hall's posthumous ed. of Beddome's *Hymns*, 1817, No. 165, where after st. ii. alterations are introduced, and another stanza (iv.) is added. This text is given in the Bap. *Ps. & Hys.*, 1858.

3. "Faith is a precious gift." This is an altered form of the hymn, in Dr. Alexander's *Augustine H. Bk.*, 1849-65, partly from the 1769, and partly from the 1817 texts; and in the American *Bap. Praise Bk.*, 1871, from the 1769 text.

4. "Faith is the gift of God," in Snepp's *Songs of G. & G.*, 1872, is an alteration of the 1817 text in 5 st.

Taken in its various forms this hymn is very extensively used.   [J. J.]

Faithful, O Lord, Thy mercies are. *C. Wesley.* [*God's Faithfulness.*] In several American hymn-books two hymns are given with this opening line, as follows :—

(1) No. 306, in Longfellow and Johnson's *Hys. of the Spirit*, 1864, in 2 st. of 4 l. This is No. 171 of C. Wesley's *Short Hymns*, &c., 1762, vol. i., on Ex. xxxiv. 6.

(2) The second is in the Bap. *Praise Bk.*, 1871, No. 216, and is composed of portions of Nos. 169, 170, 171 of the *Short Hymns*, &c. (*P. Works*, 1868-72, vol. ix, p. 55).
          [J. J.]

Falckner, Justus, from his interest as the first Lutheran clergyman ordained in America, demands a somewhat fuller notice than would otherwise be given.

He was fourth s. of Daniel Falckner, Lutheran pastor at Langenreinsdorf, Crimmitschau, Zwickau, Saxony, and was b. there, Nov. 22, 1672. He entered the University of Halle, Jan. 20, 1693, as a student of theology under A. H. Francke; but on completing his course felt the responsibility of the ministerial office in the German

Church of that time too great for him to undertake. Along with his elder brother Daniel, who had shortly before returned from America, we find Justus accepting at Rotterdam, April 23, 1700, a power of attorney for the sale of Penn's lands in Pennsylvania. In 1701 ten thousand acres of Penn's lands were sold to Provost Andreas Rudman and other Swedes residing on the Manatawny. By intercourse with Rudman or otherwise Justus was led to reconsider his views on the ministry, and was on Nov. 24, 1703, ordained in the Swedish Church of Wicacoa, Philadelphia, by Rudman, T. E. Björck, and Anders Sandel, all Swedish Pastors. His first charge was the pastoral oversight of the Dutch settlers on the Manatawny, near New Hannover; but shortly afterwards he was sent by Rudman to take his place as pastor of the Lutheran Congregations at New York and Albany. There he proved himself an earnest, faithful and diligent worker, ministering also as occasion permitted, until their organization became consolidated, to three congregations in New Jersey (on the Hackensack, in Bergen County, and on the Raritan) and two in the State of New York (Loonenburg and Neuburg). In 1723 the pastorate at New York became vacant either by the death or removal of Falckner. Michael Knoll, who became pastor at New York in 1732, states that Falckner d. in 1723. The entries in Church registers which have been held to prove that when he felt the weight of years he retired to New Jersey as a smaller and easier field of labour, seem to be signed by a Daniel Falckner — whether brother, nephew, or son does not appear (MSS., &c., from Pastor Köhler, Langenreinsdorf; from Dr. B. M. Schmucker, Pottstown, Pennsylvania, &c. Details from these sources are given more fully in the *Blätter für Hymnologie*, 1885, pp. 3–6).

To his *Catechism*, the first known publication by a Lutheran minister in America (written in Dutch and pub. at New York, 1708, as *Grondlycke Onderricht*, &c.), three hymns are appended which seem to be *trs.* from the German. The only hymn by Falckner *tr.* into English is :—

Auf! ihr Christen, Christi Glieder. [*Christian Warfare.*] It seems to have been written while he was a student at Halle, and appears in the *Geistreiches G. B.*, Halle, 1697, p. 430, in 11 st. of 6 l., entitled "Encouragement to conflict in the spiritual warfare." It is a vigorous and stirring hymn, and after its reception into Freylinghausen's *G. B.*, 1704, came into extended use, and is still found in many collections as in the *Unv. L. S.* 1851. The only *tr.* in C. U. is :—

Rise, ye children of salvation, omitting st. 4 in Mrs. Bevan's *Songs of Eternal Life*, 1858, p. 10. Three centos have come into use—the *trs.* of st. 1, 3, 9 in Dr. Pagenstecher's *Coll.*, 1864; of st. 1, 5, 9, 11 in the Eng. Presb. *Ps. & Hys.*, 1867, and the *Temple H. Bk.*, 1867; and of st. 1, 5, 11 in *Laudes Domini*, N. Y., 1884.

Another *tr.* is : "If our all on Him we venture," a *tr.* of st. iii. as st. ii. of No. 1064 in the *Supplement* of 1808 to the *Moravian H. Bk.*, 1801 (1886, No. 509).
          [J. M.]

Falk, Johannes Daniel, was b. Oct. 28, 1768, at Danzig, where his father was a wigmaker. With a stipend from the Town Council of Danzig, he entered the University of Halle in 1791, where he studied the classics and theology, remaining as a private tutor for some time after completing his course. In 1798 he married and settled as a man of letters at Weimar, where he was welcomed by Herder, Goethe and Wieland, and where he gained some reputation as a writer of satirical works. During the Napoleonic wars, after the battle of Jena, 1806, Falk found his true vocation as a philanthropist, first in the field hospitals and then in the care of destitute children. With the court preacher Horn he founded the "Society of Friends in Need," and shortly thereafter began his Refuge for poor children; receiving them without restrictions as to age, birth, country or creed, and after giving them a godly industrial training sought to find the girls places as domestic servants and to apprentice the boys to trade. He lived to see the Refuge in permanent buildings (which in 1829 were made into a public training school for neglected children, under the name of *Falk's Institute*) and saw some 300 of his scholars fairly started in life. He d. at Weimar, Feb. 14, 1826 (*Kraus*, pp. 120–125; *Allg. Deutsche Biog.*, vi. 549–551). His hymns are few in number, but one has attained considerable popularity :—

O du fröhliche. [*For the Great Festivals.*] Written in 1816, and included in his *Auserlesene Werke*, Leipzig, 1819, vol. i. p. 357, in 3 st. of 6 l., entitled " Hymn for all the Three Festivals." St. i. is for Christmas, ii. for Easter, iii. for Whitsuntide. This form is No. 667 in the *Unv. L. S.*, 1851, but being easy of expansion we find in the Speier *G. B.*, 1859, No. 247, two other stanzas for each season added — in all 9 st. The only *tr.* in C. U. is :—

Hail, thou glorious, thou victorious. A free version by Dr. Kennedy of Falk's three sts., with original st. for Sunday and for the Second Advent, in his *Hymno. Christ.*, 1863. [J. M.]

Fanch, James, known as the joint author with Daniel Turner of the hymn " Beyond the glittering, starry skies " (q.v.), was b. in 1704, and d. Dec. 12, 1767. He was for many years a Baptist Minister at Romsey, and Lockerly, Hants. In addition to Sermons, &c., he pub. a

Paraphrase on a Select Number of the Psalms of David, done from the Latin of Buchanan, to which are added some Occasional Pieces, 1764.　　[J. J.]

Fannie. A *nom de plume* of Mrs. Van Alstyne (q.v.) in *Bright Jewels*, N. Y., 1869, *Royal Diadem*, N. Y., 1873, &c.

Far down the ages now. *H. Bonar.* [*The Church Militant.*] Pub. in his *Hys. of Faith and Hope*, 1st Series, 1857, in 14 st. of 4 l. The centos in C. U. all begin with st. i., but differ in the choice of stanzas, and range from five in the S. P. C. K. *Church Hys.*,1871, to eight in the New York *Hys. and Songs of Praise*, 1874. Although in extensive use in various forms, it is seldom that any two collections have the same arrangement. [J. J.]

Far from my [our] heavenly home. *H. F. Lyte.* [*Ps. cxxxvii.*] This s. m. version of Ps. 137 is the most complete example of the author's method in paraphrasing the Psalms that we have : and furnishes us with a beautiful illustration of his tenderness and melody. It appeared in his *Spirit of the Psalms*, 1834, in 5 st. of 4 l. Its use exceeds that of any other of his Psalm versions, and is extensive both in G. Britain and America. Sometimes it is changed to "Far from our heavenly home ; " and in other cases, as in *H. A. & M.*, st. ii., which reads :—

" Upon the willows long My harp has silent hung ;
　How should I sing a cheerful song Till Thou inspire
　my tongue ? "

is omitted. Full orig. text in *H. Comp.*, No. 135. [Psalters, English, § xvii.] [J. J.]

Far from my thoughts, vain world, begone. *I. Watts.* [*Holy Communion.*] This hymn was given in his *H. & Sa. Songs*,

1707 : and again in 1709 (Bk. ii., Nos. 15, 16), in two parts, each part consisting of 6 st. of 4 l., and the second beginning, " Lord, what a heav'n of saving grace." Pt. i. was given with alterations and the omission of st. iii., iv. in G. Whitefield's *Coll.*, 1753, No. 2, thereby rendering it a most suitable hymn for the opening of Divine Service. This use of the hymn is still followed, especially in America, as in Dr. Hatfield's *Church H. Bk.*, 1872, &c. In the American *Church Pastorals*, Boston, 1864, No. 710, st. v., vi. are given as "Blest Jesus ! what delicious fare ! " Pt. ii. is also somewhat extensively used in G. Britain and America. [J. J.]

Far from my thoughts, vain world, depart. *J. Conder.* [*Holy Communion.*] Appeared in his *Cong. H. Bk.*, 1836, No. 148, in 6 st. of 4 l., on the words, " He was known of them in breaking of bread." In this same form it was repeated in his work *The Choir and the Oratory*, 1837, p. 190 ; and again in his *Hys. of Praise, Prayer*, &c., 1856, p. 85. A rearrangement of this hymn, given in the *Leeds H. Bk.*, 1853, No. 727, is more popular than the original. It begins with st. iii., "Lord, in this blest and hallowed hour," and is composed of st. iii., ii. and iv. Another arrangement is st. iii., ii., iv.–vi. This is in the Bap. *Ps. & Hys.*, 1858. [J. J.]

Far from the world, O Lord, I flee. *W. Cowper.* [*Retirement.*] In 1765, when the poet had recovered his balance of mind and had to leave the charge of Dr. Cotton at St. Albans, under whose care he had been placed by his family, his friends

" Subscribed amongst themselves an annual allowance, such as made his own diminished means just sufficient to maintain him respectably, but frugally, in retirement, and left him to follow his own course. His resolution to withdraw from the business of the world, and from its society, occasioned those poems which, because of the circumstances that gave rise to them, belong properly to the personal history of an author.
　' Far from the world, O Lord, I flee,
　　From strife and tumult far ;
　　From scenes where Satan wages still
　　His most successful war.' "

Southey, from whose *Life and Works of William Cowper*, ed. 1853, vol. i. pp. 105–6, the above is taken, quotes the complete hymn, and then goes on to say :—

" After many unsuccessful attempts to procure lodgings nearer Cambridge, John Cowper wrote to say he had found some at Huntingdon, which he believed might suit him."

On Saturday, June 22, 1765, Cowper was taken to Huntingdon by his brother, and there left alone.

" No sooner," says Cowper, " had he left me, than finding myself surrounded by strangers, and in a strange place, my spirits began to sink, and I felt (such was the backsliding state of my heart) like a traveller in the midst of an inhospitable desert, without friend to comfort, or a guide to direct him. I walked forth, towards the close of the day, and in this melancholy frame of mind, and having wandered about a mile from the town, I found my heart, at length so powerfully drawn towards the Lord, that having a retired and secret nook in the corner of a field, I kneeled down under a bank and poured forth my complaints before him. It pleased my Saviour to hear me, so that this oppression was taken off, and I was enabled to trust in him that careth for the stranger, to roll my burden upon him, and to rest assured that wheresoever he might cast my lot, the God of all consolation would still be with me. But this was not all. He did for me more than either I had asked or thought."

The following day, Sunday, June 23, 1765, Cowper attended church for the first time after his recovery. He was specially impressed by the devotion of one of the worshippers, and with the reading of the Gospel of the day (1st S. after Trinity), which contained the parable of the Prodigal Son. He says:—

"I went immediately after church to the place where I had prayed the day before, and found the relief I had there received was but the earnest of a richer blessing. How shall I express what the Lord did for me, except by saying, that he made all his goodness to pass before me. I seemed to speak to him face to face, as a man conversing with his friend, except that my speech was only in tears of joy, and groanings which cannot be uttered. I could say indeed with Jacob, not 'how dreadful,' but how lovely, 'is this place! This is none other than the house of God.' "—*Southey*, i. pp. 108–9.

Although Southey does not say that this hymn was written on this special occasion, and although he quotes the hymn three pages before he gives these details, yet, when we read in st. ii.,

"The calm retreat, the silent shade,
    With prayer and praise agree ;
And seem, by Thy sweet bounty, made
    For those who follow Thee,"

we feel that these must have been the circumstances and this the birth-place of the hymn. If so, its date will be *June* 23, 1765.

The publication of this hymn we have not been able to trace beyond the *Olney Hymns*, 1779, Bk. iii., No. 45, in 6 st. of 4 l., and headed "Retirement." We have seen it stated that it appeared in the *Gospel Magazine* prior to this, but this is an error. Its use is extensive for a hymn of so personal a character. It is very beautiful, and its associations with the poet's personal history give it a position of historical importance.   [J. J.]

Far from these narrow scenes of night. *Anne Steele.* [*Heaven.*] This hymn ranks in popularity as one of the first of Miss Steele's hymns. It was first pub. in her *Poems on Subjects chiefly Devotional*, 1760, vol. i. p. 157, in 11 st. of 4 l., and entitled "The Promised Land." It was repeated in her *Poems*, &c., 1780, and in D. Sedgwick's ed. of her *Hymns*, 1863, p. 96. In modern hymn-books it is found in various forms, ranging from 4 st. in the American *Bap. Hy.* [*& Tune*] *Bk.*, 1871, to 8 st. in the *Westminster Abbey H. Bk.*, 1883. It was brought into use in an abbreviated form in the Church of England through R. Conyers's *Coll.*, 1767, and A. M. Toplady's *Ps. & Hys.*, 1776 ; and amongst Nonconformists by the Bristol Bap. *Coll.* of Ash & Evans, 1769. In most American Unitarian collections a selection of stanzas rearranged from c.m. to s.m. is given, sometimes in 7 st., as in Dabney's *Sel. of Hys. & Ps.*, Andover, 1821 ; and again, in 5 st., as in the *Hy.* [*& Tune*] *Bk. for the Ch. & Home*, &c., Boston, 1868.   [J. J.]

Farewell, poor world, I must be gone. *S. Crossman.* [*Death anticipated.*] This is his "Pilgrim's Farewell to the World," in 7 st. of 4 l., in his *Young Man's Meditation, or Some few Sacred Poems*, &c., 1664 (Sedgwick's reprint [1863], p. 7). The form in which it appeared in the "Sacred Melodies," appended to the *Comprehensive* ed. of Rippon's *Sel.*, 1844, is 4 st. of 4 l. and a chorus. Of these, st. ii. and the chorus are anonymous. In 1855 Mr. Beecher adopted this form of the hymn

for his *Plymouth Coll.*, No 1220. In this the first four lines are from *Crossman* and *Rippon*, but altered to "Farewell, *dear friends*, I must be gone !" The second four lines and the chorus are from *Rippon;* and st. iii., iv. are anonymous.   [J. J.]

Farewell, thou once a sinner. *C. Wesley.* [*Death.*] Appeared in his *Hys. & Sacred Poems*, 1749, vol. ii., No. 56, in 7 st. of 8 l., and headed "On the Death of a Friend " (*P. Works*, 1868–1872, vol. v. p. 216). In Dr. Martineau's *Hymns, &c.*, 1840, No. 402, beginning "Farewell, thou once a *mortal*," is a cento from this hymn. It was repeated in his *Hys. of Praise and Prayer*, 1873. [J. J.]

Farningham, Marianne. [**Hearn, M.**]

Farrar, Frederic William, D.D., s. of the Rev. Charles Penhorn Farrar, sometime a missionary in India, and late Rector of Sidcup, Kent. He was b. at Bombay, Aug. 7th, 1831 : and educated at King William's College, Isle of Man, and at King's College, London. In 1850 he obtained a classical exhibition, and in 1852 a scholarship at the University of London, whence, after taking the degree of B.A., he passed to Trinity College, Cambridge. There, in 1852, he took (with other prizes) the Chancellor's Prize in English verse, and graduated in first-class classical honours in 1854. In the same year he entered Holy Orders, and was subsequently for some time an assistant master at Harrow School. In 1871 he was appointed to the head mastership of Marlborough College, which he held until 1876, when he was nominated a Canon of Westminster Abbey and Rector of St. Margaret's, Westminster. He had previously been chosen Select Preacher before the University of Cambridge in 1868, and again in 1874, 1875, and Hulsean Lecturer in 1870. He was also appointed in 1869 a Chaplain to the Queen, and in 1883, Archdeacon of Westminster. Archdeacon Farrar has achieved a high reputation both as a writer and a preacher. He is the author of some volumes of fiction for the young which soon attained great popularity, as well as of several important works in the departments of philology and theology. Of the latter, his *Life of Christ* and *Life and Work of St. Paul* are the best known. As a preacher, Archdeacon Farrar stands in the first rank as a master of graceful eloquence. His contributions to hymnody include, "Father, before Thy throne of light," "God and Father, great and holy," and a beautiful carol, "In the fields with their flocks abiding."   [G. A. C.]

Father, abide with us ! the storm-clouds gather. [*The Divine Presence desired.*] Given anonymously as No. 60 in the Rev. E. Clay's *Appendix*, issued in Feb., 1869, to his *Ps. & Hys.*, *adapted for the Services of the Ch. of England* (1st ed., 1858). In Snepp's *Songs of G. & G.*, 1872, No. 708, it is repeated without alteration.   [J. J.]

Father, again in Jesus' Name we meet. *Lady Lucy E. G. Whitmore.* [*Lent Evening.*] 1st pub. in her *Family Prayers*, &c., 1824, in 4 st. of 4 l., as No. 8 of the 14 hymns appended thereto. It is based on St. Luke xv. 20. In 1833 Bickersteth gave it, with slight alteration, in his *Christ.*

Psalmody, No. 584. This was repeated by several editors as the original text. In the Rev. F. Pott's *Hymns*, &c., 1861; the S.P.C.K. *Church Hys.*, 1871, and others, st. ii. is omitted. It is a hymn of more than usual merit, and is in extensive use in G. Britain. In America it is also found in a few collections, including *Laudes Domini*, 1884. In Windle it is attributed in error to "White." Orig. text in *H. Comp.* No. 14.   [J. J.]

Father, and can it be? *C. Wesley.* [*Lent.*] Appeared in his *Hys. & Sac. Poems*, 1749, vol. i., No. 92, in 7 st. of 8 l. It is No. 5 of 7 hymns written "After a Recovery" (*P. Works*, 1868–1872, vol. iv. p. 447). The hymn, "O unexhausted Grace," which is given in most of the Methodist hymn-books, is composed of st. iv.–viii., and was included in the *Wes. H. Bk.*, 1780, as No. 165. [J. J.]

Father and Lord of our whole life. *J. Keble.* [*Easter Eve.*] Written at Llandudno, Aug. 14, 1856, and first pub. in the *Salisbury H. Bk.*, 1857, and again in the *Sarum Hymnal*, 1868, No. 135. The original contains 9 st. of 4 l, and is found in Keble's *Miscellaneous Poems*, 1869, pp. 116–118. In the *Hymnary*, No. 260, beginning "Jesu, the Author of our Life," is a slightly altered form of this hymn.   [J. J.]

Father, at Thy footstool see. *C. Wesley.* [*For Unity.*] In his *Hymns & Sac. Poems*, 1749, vol. ii., this is No. 3 of 55 hymns "For Christian Friends," in 6 st. of 4 l. (*P. Works*, 1868–1872, vol. v. p. 408). When given in the *Wes. H. Bk.*, 1780, No. 500, st. v., vi. were omitted. This is repeated in the revised ed., 1875, and several collections in G. Britain and America. The hymn in Dr. Martineau's *Hymns* of 1840, and of 1873, beginning with the same first line, is a cento, a few lines of which are from this hymn, but the rest we have been unable to trace. [J. J.]

Father, before Thy throne of light. *F. W. Farrar.* [*St. Michael and All Angels.*] Written for the Anniversary of the Dedication of Marlborough College Chapel, 1855, the author being at that time Assistant Master of the College under Dr. Cotton. In 1856 it was included in the *Marlborough College H. Book;* and again in the revised edition of the same collection in 1869, No. 106. From the latter it passed into the Savoy Chapel *Appendix* to the *Hymnary* (Chapel Royal), the S. P. C. K. *Church Hymns*, 1871, No. 184, the *H. Comp.*, 1876, and many other collections. It is admirably suited for daily use in public schools.   [J. J.]

Father, behold with gracious eyes. *C. Wesley.* [*Public Worship.*] In the *Hys. for those that Seek and those that Have Redemption*, &c., 1747 (*P. Works*, 1868–1872, vol. iv. p. 270), this hymn, in 6 st. of 4 l., is set forth for use "At the Hour of Retirement." A. M. Toplady, on including it in his *Ps. & Hys.*, 1776, No. 60, omitted st. iii., added st. vi., vii. from Wesley's "Father of Jesus Christ, my Lord" (in the same *Hymns*, &c., 1747), and appointed the same for "Public Worship." From this text, and not the original, No. 780 in the *New Cong.*, 1859–1874, is taken; Top-

lady's st. iv., v. being omitted, and the rest somewhat altered.   [J. J.]

Father, by Thy love and power. *J. Anstice.* [*Evening.*] Printed by his widow for private circulation in *Hymns by the late Joseph Anstice, M.A.*, &c., 1836, No. 3, in 4 st. of 10 l. In 1841 it was given in *The Child's Christian Year*, with one change only, that of st. i., l. 8, "Lull Thy children to repose," to "Lull Thy *creatures* to repose," which in the *H. Comp.* is again changed to "*Grant* Thy children *sweet* repose," and accompanied by a note (*Notes*, 31) which shows that Bp. Bickersteth used *The Child's Christian Year* text as the original, in error. In the numerous hymn-books in which this beautiful hymn is found, not this line, but st. iv., l. i.–iv., have been the source of difficulty. They read in the original:—

> "Blessed Trinity ! be near
> Through the hours of darkness drear ;
> When the help of man is far,
> Ye more clearly present are."

The attempts which have been made to overcome the weakness of these lines have been many. The most important of these are :—

1. "Blessed Trinity, be near,
   Through the hours of darkness drear ;
   Then, when shrinks the lonely heart,
   Thou more clearly present *art.*"
   S. P. C. K. *Appendix* to *Ps. & Hys.*, 1869, their *Church Hymns*, 1871, and many others.
2. "Blessed Trinity, be near
   Through the hours of darkness drear ;
   Oh, enfold us in Thine arm,
   Screen from danger, save from harm."
                              Hymnary, 1872.
3. "Blessed Trinity, be near
   Through the hour of darkness drear ;
   Then when shrinks the lonely heart,
   Thou, O God, most present art."
   Hymnal Companion, 1870–76 ; Thring's *Coll.*, 1882 ; *Laudes Domini*, N. Y. 1884, and others.

Other arrangements of these lines are also given in some of the collections, but these are the most important. In addition there is also a re-arrangement of the text in the Cooke & Denton *Church Hyl.*, enlarged ed., 1855, No. 338, in 4 st. of 8 l.; and in the Rev. F. Pott's *Hymns*, &c., 1861, No. 23, in 4 st. of 6 l. In its various forms the use of this hymn is extensive.   [J. J.]

Father, ere we hence depart. *J. Hart.* [*Dismission.*] 1st pub. in his *Supplement* to his *Hymns composed on Various Subjects*, 1762, No. 82, in 2 st. of 4 l. In 1767 it was given in R. Conyers's *Coll.* as "Father, *before* we hence depart." · This was repeated in Toplady's *Ps. & Hys.*, 1776, No. 159, and is the received text of modern hymn-books in G. Britain and America.   [J. J.]

Father, God, Who seest in me. *C. Wesley.* [*Pleading the Atonement.*] Four hymns beginning with the same stanza are known to hymnody as follows:—

1. The original in C. Wesley's *Hymns on the Lord's Supper*, 1745, No. 119, in 4 st. of 4 l. (*P. Works*, 1868–1872, vol. iii. p. 304) ; R. Conyers's *Coll.*, 1767, &c.
2. The same with the omission of st. iv. in *Hys. for the Chapel of Harrow School*, 1855–1866.
3. "Father, *Lord*, Who seest in me," in a few of the older collections, and in *Windle*.
4. "*Gracious* God, *Thou* seest me," in the Meth. New Connexion *H. Bk.*, 1847, No. 462, and later editions.
5. A curious cento, also associated with this hymn, and beginning with st. i., is in Rippon's Bapt. *Sel.*, 1787, and later editions. This remarkable patchwork is made up from C. Wesley's four hymns : (1) "Father, God, Who

seest in me;" (2) "Father, see the victim slain;" (3) "Depth of mercy can there be;" (4) "Rise, my soul, with ardour rise," as follows :—

St. i., ll. 1–4, from No. 1; st. i. ll. 5–6, from No. 2.
St. ii., ll. 1–2, from No. 4; st. ii., ll. 3–6, from No. 3.
St. iii., ll. 1–6, from No. 4; st. iv., ll. 1–4, from No. 1.
St. iv., ll. 5, 6, from No. 2; st. v., ll. 1–4, from No. 3.
St. v., ll. 5, 6, from No. 4; st. vi., ll. 1, 2, from No. 2.
St. vi., ll. 3–6, from No. 1.   [J. J.]

Father, hear our humble claim. *C. Wesley.* [*For Unity.*] In Longfellow & Johnson's *Hymns of the Spirit*, Boston, U.S., 1864, No. 227, and in the *Songs for the Sanctuary*, 1865–1872, No. 823. This cento is taken from two hymns by C. Wesley: (1) "Come, and let us sweetly join"; and (2) "Father, Son and Spirit, hear," both of which appeared in *Hymns & Sac. Poems*, 1740, and each of which has furnished several centos to the hymn-books. This cento is st. i. from No. 1, and st. ii.–v. from No. 2. (See *P. Works*, 1868–1872, vol. i. pp. 351, 356, 357.)   [J. J.]

Father, hear the blood of Jesus. *C. Wesley.* [*Holy Communion.*] In Toplady's *Ps. & Hys.*, 1776, and others of the older collections, this hymn is composed of two hymns by C. Wesley, 1st pub. in his *Hymns on the Lord's Supper*, 1745; "Father, hear the blood of Jesus," in 2 st. of 8 l., and "Dying Friend of Sinners, hear us," in 2 st. of 8 l. (*P. Works*, 1868–1872, vol. iii. pp. 225–226). In modern hymn-books the first of these hymns is given alone, as in the *Laudes Domini*, N. Y., 1884.   [J. J.]

Father, hear the prayer we offer. [*Prayer.*] Given anonymously in J. S. Adams's *Psalms of Life*, 1857, No. 285, in 5 st. of 4 l.; in Longfellow and Johnson's Unitarian *Hymns of the Spirit*, Boston, U.S., 1864, No. 558, in 4 st. of 4 l.; in the *Songs for the Sanctuary*, N. Y., 1865; *Laudes Domini*, 1884, and others; and, with an additional stanza, in W. G. Horder's *Cong. Hymns*, Lond., 1884.   [J. J.]

Father, hear Thy children's praises. *H. J. Buckoll.* [*Commemoration.*] Appeared in the *Ps. & Hys. for the Use of Rugby School Chapel*, 1850, No. 54, in 5 st. of 4 l., and appointed "For the Founder's Commemoration, October 20th." From the *Rugby* book it has passed into that of *Harrow*, and others of the public schools, and a few general collections.   [J. J.]

Father, how wide Thy glory shines. *I. Watts.* [*Glory of God and Salvation of Men.*] 1st pub. in his *Horæ Lyricæ*, 1705, in 9 st. of 4 l., and headed "God glorious and Sinners saved." As early as 1738–1741 J. Wesley included it in an abbreviated form in his *Ps. & Hymns*, and it was subsequently given about 1800, in the *Wes. H. Bk.* Its early use in the Church of England was furthered by R. Conyers, De Courcy, A. M. Toplady, and others. Its use, but usually in an abbreviated form, is extensive in G. Britain and America. Full original text in modern editions of the *Horæ Lyricæ*, and Watts's *Works*.   [J. J.]

Father, I dare believe. *C. Wesley.* [*Holiness desired.*] This hymn is composed as follows :—

i. from *Short Hymns*, &c., 1762, vol. i., No. 881, Ps. cxxx. 8.
ii. from *Short Hymns*, &c., 1762, vol. ii., No. 1178, Jer. iv. 1.

iii. from *Short Hymns*, &c., 1762, vol. ii., No. 1179, Jer. iv. 14.

In this form it was given in the *Wes. H. Bk.*, 1780, No. 398, and has been retained in subsequent editions of the same, and has also passed into other hymn-books. Orig. text, *P. Works*, 1868–72, vols. ix., x.   [J. J.]

Father, I know that all my life. *Anna L. Waring.* [*Resignation.*] 1st pub. in her *Hymns and Meditations*, 1850, No. 1, in 8 st. of 6 l., and headed, "My times are in Thy hand." (Enlarged ed. 1863–1871.) One of the first, if not the first, hymn-book to bring it into C. U., was the *Leeds H. Bk.*, 1853, No. 892. Since then it has passed into numerous collections in G. Britain and America. Although faulty, and awkward in rhythm, it has attained to a considerable circulation, its deep devotional spirit and intense personality being very attractive to many. Although best adapted for private reading, it is suitable, under special circumstances, for congregational use. In the American Unitarian *Hy. [& Tune] Bk. for the Church and the Home*, Boston, 1868, No. 224, st. v., vii., viii., are given in an altered form as :—"I ask Thee for the daily strength:" st. i.–iv. being given as No. 223.   [J. J.]

Father, I stretch my hands to Thee. *C. Wesley.* [*Faith desired.*] From *Psalms & Hymns*, 1741, ln 6 st. of 4 l., and entitled "A Prayer for Faith" (*P. Works*, 1868–72, vol. ii. p. 13). In 1760 M. Madan included 3 st. in his *Coll.*, and thus introduced it into the Church of England. The altered text in the *Wes. H. Bk.* was given in the *Supp.* of that hymnal in 1830. Our authority for ascribing this hymn to C. Wesley with an expression of doubt is the following note by Dr. Osborn in the *P. Works*, 1868–72, vol. ii. p. 8.

"The reader will observe that of the 160 hymns contained in this volume as originally published [Ps. & Hymns, 1741], more than 130 may be traced (by reference given above in brackets) to previous publications by other authors; and were merely selected, arranged, and more or less altered by Wesley. Only three of those which have been so treated have been reprinted here; viz. 'Resignation,' 'Submission,' and the first 'Hymn to Christ.' The second with that title, together with 'A Thought in Affliction,' 'A Prayer for the Light of Life,' 'A Prayer of Faith' [*the above hymn*], and 'God's Love and Power,' are also reprinted, because they have not been identified in other collections, and may possibly be Wesley's."

The hymn is in several modern collections both in G. Britain and America.   [J. J.]

Father, I want a thankful heart. *C. Wesley.* [*Desiring to know God.*] This cento in the Scottish *Evang. Union Hymnal*, 1878, No. 212, in 2 st. of 6 l. (where it is ascribed to A. M. Toplady in error), is composed of st. vi. of C. Wesley's "Father of Lights, from Whom proceeds": and st. v. of his "Jesu! my Great High Priest above." These two hymns appeared in the Wesley *Hys. & Sac. Poems*, 1739. (*P. Works*, 1868–1872, vol. i. pp. 77, 88.)   [J. J.]

Father, if Thou my Father art. *C. Wesley.* [*Prayer for the Witness of the Spirit.*] Pub. in *Hys. and Sacred Poems*, 1740, p. 131, in 6 st. of 6 l., and headed, "Groaning for the Spirit of Adoption" (*P. Works*, 1868–72, vol. i. p. 307). In the *Wes. H. Bk.*, 1780, No. 365, st. ii.–vi. were given as "I want the Spirit of power within." This form of the hymn has been repeated in several collections in G. Brit. and America.   [J. J.]

Father, in high heaven dwelling.
G. Rawson. [*Evening.*] 1st pub. in the *Leeds H. Bk.*, 1853, No. 762, in 4 st. of 6 l., and based on a portion of Our Lord's Prayer (St. Luke xi. 3, 4). It was repeated in the *Bapt. Ps. & Hys.*, 1858–80, and several other collections in Great Britain and America. Mr. Rawson revised the text for his *Hymns*, 1876. In *Kennedy*, 1863, it is given as, " Father, *who in* heaven *art* dwelling."   [J. J.]

Father, in Whom we live. *C. Wesley.* [*Holy Trinity.*] 1st pub. in his *Hymns for those that Seek, and those that Have Redemption*, &c., 1747, No. 34, in 4 st. of 8 l., and entitled " To the Trinity." In 1776 Toplady included it in his *Ps. & Hys.*, No. 349, and thus brought it into use in the Church of England. It was included unaltered in the *Wes. H. Bk.* in 1797, and retained in the revised ed. of 1875, No. 253. It is also in several American hymn-books. A portion of the cento " Father of all, to Thee; Let endless," &c. (q.v.) is taken from this hymn.
  [J. J.]

Father, let me dedicate. *L. Tuttiett.* [*New Year.*] A New Year's Hymn in 4 st. of 8 l., which appeared in his *Germs of Thought on the Sunday Special Services*, 1864. It passed into the S. P. C. K. *Ps. & Hys.*, 1869, *The Anglican H. Bk.* 1868, and other collections. It is one of the best known of the author's compositions. Orig. text in *H. A. & M.*, 1875, No. 74. An abbreviated form of this hymn, beginning with st. i., l. 2, altered " This new year to Thee," is found in some collections. In a few American hymn-books it begins, " Father, *here we* dedicate." This is also in some English collections, as W. G. Horder's *Cong. Hymns*, 1884, &c. [J. J.]

Father, Lord of earth and heaven, Spare or take, &c. *C. Wesley.* [*Resignation.*] Written at Bristol during the illness of one of his children, and 1st pub. in his *Funeral Hymns*, 2nd Series, 1759, in 10 st. of 4 l., and entitled " A Prayer for a dying Child." It was not given in the *Wes. H. Bk.* until the revised ed., 1875 (*P. Works*, 1868–72, vol. vi. p. 251).   [J. J.]

Father of all, from land and sea. *C. Wordsworth, Bp. of Lincoln.* [*For Unity.*] Written by request after the Nottingham Church Congress, 1871, and set to music by H. J. Gauntlett, Mus.D. It was added to the *Holy Year*, 6th ed., 1872, and to *H. A. & M.*, 1875. It is also in a few American books.

Father of all, in Whom we live. *C. Wordsworth, Bp. of Lincoln.* [*Confirmation.*] This hymn in three parts appeared in his *Holy Year*, 1862, pp. 207–210, with directions for their use as follows :—

i. **Father of all, in Whom.** " Referring to the whole Congregation," in 3 st. of 8 l.

ii. **O God, in whose all-searching eye.** " Referring to those who come to be confirmed : to be used before the laying on of hands," in 5 st. of 8 l.

iii. **Our hearts and voices let us raise.** " After the Laying on of the hands of the Bishop : to be sung specially by those who have been confirmed."

From pt. ii. the following hymns have been taken, and are in C. U. :—

1. **Arm these Thy soldiers, mighty Lord.**

2. **Come, ever blessed Spirit, come.** In Skinner's *Daily*

Service Hymnal, 1864 ; the *Hymnary*, 1872, and others and also several American collections.

3. **O Christ, Who didst at Pentecost.** In the *People's H.*, 1867.   [J. J.]

Father of all, my soul defend. *J. Merrick.* [*Ps. xvi.*] 1st pub. in his *Psalms Tr. and Paraphrased in English Verse*, 1765, p. 27, and again in W. D. Tattersall's rearranged edition of the same, 1797. In the 8th ed. of his *Sel.*, 1819, No. 16, Cotterill gave a cento from this version (st. i., viii.–xi.) beginning, " God of our life, our souls defend." This was repeated in later collections. In *The Calcutta H. Bk.*, 1862, No. 16, this cento is repeated with the omission of st. ii., and the alteration of the opening line to " God of my life, my soul defend." Another cento is given in *Ps. & Hys. Selected for Public Worship*, &c., Bedford, 1859–64. It is composed of Cotterill's first stanza as above, and three stanzas from I. Watts's version of Ps. xvii., in his *Psalms of David*, &c., 1719, " Lord, I am Thine ; but Thou wilt prove."   [J. J.]

Father of all, to Thee; With loving hearts we pray. *J. Julian.* [*Lent.*] Written in 1874, and pub. in Thring's *Coll.*, 1882, and again in others.

Father of all! we bow to Thee. *Hugh Blair ?* [*The Lord's Prayer.*] First appeared as No. 10 in the Draft Scottish *Translations and Paraphrases*, 1745, as a version of Matthew vi. 9–14, in 7 st. of 4 l. In the Draft of 1781 it is No. 33 slightly altered, and in the public worship ed. issued in that year by the Church of Scotland, and still in use, st. ii. and st. vi. l. 1, were rewritten. In the markings by the eldest daughter of *W. Cameron* (q.v.) ascribed to Blair. The revised text of 1781 has been included in the Eng. Presb. *Ps. & Hys.*, 1867, No. 133 ; in Worcester's *Select Hys.*, Boston, U.S., 1835, No. 133 ; the American Presb. *Ps. & Hys.*, 1843, No. 307, and a few other modern hymnals. A considerably altered form, reduced to 6 st., and beginning, " Father of all ! to Thee we bow," is No. 21 in Cotterill's *Sel.*, 1819. [J. M.]

Father of all, Whose powerful voice. *C. Wesley.* [*The Lord's Prayer.*] 1st pub. in *Hymns & Sac. Poems*, 1742, p. 275, in 9 st. of 8 l., as a Paraphrase of the Lord's Prayer (*P. Works*, 1868–1872, vol. ii. p. 335). In the *Wes. H. Bk.*, 1780, it was given in three parts :—Pt. i. " Father of all, Whose powerful voice " ; Pt. ii. " Son of Thy Sire's Eternal love " ; Pt. iii. " Eternal, spotless Lamb of God," and numbered respectively 225, 226, 227. In this form it has been repeated in later editions of the *Wes. H. Bk.*, and has passed into other collections. In addition the hymn, " Father, 'tis Thine each day to yield," in Hall's *Mitre*, 1836, No. 214, and E. Osler's *Church & King*, June, 1837, is composed of Wesley's st. vi. altered, and a new stanza by Osler. The popular doxology " Blessing and honour, praise and love," much used in America, is the closing stanza of Wesley's paraphrase. This hymn is sometimes ascribed to *John* Wesley, but upon what authority we have been unable to ascertain. [J. J.]

Father of earth and sky. *C. Wesley.* [*The Lord's Prayer.*] In his *Short Hymns,*

&c., 1762, vol. ii., seven short hymns were given on the seven clauses of the Lord's Prayer as in St. Matthew vi. 9-13, and numbered 60-66. In the *P. Works*, 1868-1872, vol. x. p. 178, these short hymns are massed together as one hymn of 7 st. This arrangement was made for the *Supplement* to the *Wes. H. Bk.*, 1830, and is repeated in the revised ed., 1875, No. 653. The version of the Lord's Prayer as in St. Luke xi. 2-4, begins, "Father of me and all mankind," q.v. [J. J.]

Father of eternal grace [love]. *J. Montgomery.* [*The Image of God desired.*] Written in 1807, at the request of Mr. Gardiner, of Leicester, and pub. by him in his *Sacred Melodies*, 1808, in 4 st. of 4 l. In 1812 it was included in Dr. Collyer's *Coll.*, No. 919; in 1825 in Montgomery's *Christian Psalmist*, No. 464; and in 1853 in his *Original Hymns*, No. 186. It is in C. U. both in G. Britain and America. The hymn, "Father of eternal *love*," in Dr. Martineau's *Hymns*, &c., 1840 and 1873, is the same with slight alterations and the omission of st. ii. [J. J.]

Father of eternal grace! Thou hast loved, &c. *J. Conder.* [*Missions.*] Appeared in his *Cong. H. Bk.*, 1836, No. 241, in 3 st. of 4 l., and again as the last three stanzas of the hymn, "Thou from Whom all being sprang," which was given as the third of six hymns on "The Lord's Prayer," in 8 st. of 4 l., in his work, *The Choir and the Oratory*, 1837, p. 31. In its original form of three stanzas it was repeated in the *Leeds H. Bk.*, 1853; the Bapt. *Ps. & Hys.*, 1858 and 1880; the *New Cong.*, 1859 and 1874, and other collections, and in Conder's *Hys. of Praise, Prayer*, &c., 1856, p. 48. [J. J.]

Father of heaven above. *Bp. E. H. Bickersteth.* [*Holy Trinity.*] Written in 1870, and 1st pub. in his *H. Comp.* in 1870, the following note being added in the Annotated edition:—

"This hymn by the Editor was written for this hymnal in imitation of No. 2 'Supplemental Hymns,' by the Rev. Henry Moule. It is in the same measure, and, with that author's kind permission, includes two or three of his lines."

It was also given in his work, *The Two Brothers*, 1871, p. 232, and has passed into American use. [J. J.]

Father of heaven, whose love profound. *E. Cooper.* [*Holy Trinity.*] This hymn, the authorship of which was for a long time uncertain, is now known (on the authority of his son, the Rev. Henry Gisborne Cooper) to be the production of the Rev. Edward Cooper. It was contributed by him to the *Uttoxeter Selection*, 1805 (see **Staffordshire Hymnbooks**, No. i.), whence it passed into the *Ashbourne Coll.*, 1808 (*Ib.* No. ii.); Cooper's own *Selection*, Lichfield, 1811 (*Ib.* iv.); Cotterill's *Selection*, 1810-1820; and subsequently into most hymnals throughout English-speaking countries. It is based on the Litany and consists of 4 st. of 4 l., the doxology as in *H. A. & M.*, being a subsequent addition. In st. 4, l. 4, some hymnals read "all" instead of "us," but the original text follows the Litany in confining the prayer to the suppliant who offers it. The opening line has also been altered as follows:—(1) "Father of *all*, whose

love *from heaven*," in the Rev. I. Gregory Smith's *Hymn Book*, &c., 1855; (2) "Father of *all*, Whose *wondrous grace*," in the Rev. F. H. Murray's *Hymnal*, 1852; (3) "Father of *all*, Whose *wondrous love*," in the Cooke and Denton *Church Hymnal*, 1853. It has also been adapted as a hymn of praise by Miss Harriett Auber, in her *Spirit of the Psalms*, 1829. This is accomplished by rewriting ll. 3, 4 of each stanza. The first stanza reads:—

"Father of heaven! Whose love profound
A ransom for our souls hath found,
To Thee, great God! the song we raise;
Thee for Thy pardoning love we praise."

This form of the hymn is No. 74 in Dr. Dale's *English H. Bk.*, 1874. Original text in *Hy. Comp.*, No. 254. [G. A. C.]

Father of Jesus Christ my Lord, I humbly seek Thy face. *C. Wesley.* [*Before Private Prayer.*] This hymn is No. 2 of six hymns given at the end of a tract entitled, *A Short View of the Differences between the Moravian Brethren in England and J. and C. Wesley*, 1745, in 7 st. of 4 l. It was also included in the *Hymns for those who Seek, and those who Have Redemption*, &c., 1747, No. 39 (*P. Works*, 1868-1872, vol. iv. p. 250). Sometime after J. Wesley's death in 1791, but before 1809, it was given, unaltered, in the *Wes. H. Bk.* It has passed into several collections, and is in C. U. in G. Britain and America. [J. J.]

Father of Jesus Christ my Lord, My Saviour, &c. *C. Wesley.* [*Faith in the Promises and Power of God.*] From a hymn of 10 st. in 4 l. on Rom. iv. 16, &c., in *Hymns & Sac. Poems*, 1742, p. 248, 11 st. were given in the *Wes. H. Bk.*, 1780, as No. 350. The same arrangement is in the revised ed., 1875, and other collections (*P. Works*, 1868-72, vol. ii. p. 309). A cento from the original beginning (st. ix.), "In hope against all human hope," was given in the American Meth. Episco. *Hymns*, 1849. [J. J.]

Father of light, and life, and love. *J. Montgomery.* [*Public Worship.*] Written on Nov. 24, 1842, for the Molyneux Hospital, Dublin (M. MSS.), but omitted from its *Coll.* of hymns, 1854. In 1853 it was included in Montgomery's *Original Hymns*, No. 287, in 6 st. of 4 l., and in 1873 in Dr. Martineau's *Hys. of Praise & Prayer*, No. 757. [J. J.]

Father of lights, from Whom proceeds. *C. Wesley.* 1st pub. in *Hys. & Sac. Poems*, 1739, in 8 st. of 6 l., and entitled "A Prayer under Convictions." The first five stanzas were given in the *Wes. H. Bk.*, 1780, as No. 96, and repeated in later editions, and in other collections. Another arrangement appeared in Toplady's *Ps. & Hys.*, 1776, No. 284, and subsequent editions. It is in 8 st. The first six are from the original as above, and the remaining two are the first and last stanzas of Ps. cxxxix. in the Wesley *Hys. & Sac. Poems*, 1739. This cento is sometimes found in Church of England hymnals. Orig. texts, *P. Works*, 1868-72, vol. i. 76, 87. [J. J.]

Father of lights, we sing Thy Name. *P. Doddridge.* [*Ps. lxxxiv.*] This hymn is No. xlvii. in the D. MSS. in 6 st. of 4 l., and entitled "Providential Bounties Surveyed and Improved, St. Matt. v. 45." A slightly different text was given by Job Orton in his posthumous ed. of Doddridge's *Hymns*, 1755, No. 176, and the text in J. D. Humphreys's ed. of the *Hymns*, &c., 1839, No. 197, differs in a few words from both. The 1755 text is that in C. U. sometimes in an altered form. The hymn is given in most of the American Unitarian collections.   [J. J.]

Father of love and power. *G. Rawson.* [*Evening.*] 1st pub. in the *Leeds H. Bk.*, 1853, No. 761, in 3 st. of 7 l., again in the Bapt. *Ps. and Hys.*, 1858-1880, No. 917, and cthers; and in his *Hymns*, &c., 1876, No. 51. In a MS. note to this hymn (in the editor's copy) in the last named work, the author, finding that he had unconsciously given three lines from Marriott's " Thou Whose Almighty Word," in st. iii., has substituted the following stanza:—

" Spirit of holiness,
  Gentle transforming Grace,
    Indwelling Light ;
  Soothe Thou each weary breast,
  Now let Thy peace possessed,
  Calm us to perfect rest.—
    Bless us to-night."

This, together with stanzas i. and ii. in his *Hymns*, &c., constitute the author's revised text. In Skinner's *Daily Service Hyl.*, 1864, No. 28, the text is considerably altered, a doxology is added, and the whole is attributed to "C.L.," i.e. *Christian Lyrics*, 1860. [J. J.]

Father of Love, our Guide and Friend. *W. J. Irons.* [*Confirmation.*] Written for a confirmation, held at Brompton in 1844, in 3 st. of 8 l. One of the earliest collections in which it is found is *The Hys. for the Christian Seasons*, by the Rev. R. T. Lowe, Gainsburgh, 1854, No. 185. In 1861 the author included it in his Words of the *Hys. in the App. of the Brompton Metrical Psalter*, No. 7 ; in 1866 in his *Hys. for use in Church*, No. 20 ; in 1873 in his *Hys. for the Church* ; and in 1875 in his *Ps. and Hys. for the Church*. In the last two it is divided into 6 st. of 4 l. as in the Gainsburgh book of 1854. Outside of Dr. Irons's collections it has attained to a somewhat extensive use in G. Britain and America, and is found in many of the best selections. Originally written for Confirmation, it is also adapted for " The New Year," or, in " Time of Trial." Original text in Thring's *Coll.*, 1882, No. 284. [J. J.]

Father of me and all mankind. *C. Wesley.* [*The Lord's Prayer.*] This paraphrase of The Lord's Prayer as in St. Luke xi. 2-4, was given in his *Short Hymns*, &c., 1762, vol. ii., in 8 separate hymns numbered 342-349 ; but in the *P. Works*, 1868-72, vol. xi. p. 200, these hymns are massed as one, No. 1366, in 10 st. of 8 l. The cento in C. U. appeared in the *Wes. H. Bk.*, 1780, No. 242, in 5 st. of 4 l., and is compiled from the original hymns, Nos. 342 and 343. It is found in several collections in G. Britain and America, and sometimes as " Father *and God* of all mankind," as in Longfellow and Johnson's *Bk. of Hymns*, Boston, 1846-8, &c. Wesley's version of the Lord's Prayer as in St. Matthew vi. 9-13, begins, " Father of earth and sky," q.v.   [J. J.]

Father of [man] men, Thy care we bless. *P. Doddridge.* [*Family Worship.*] Appeared in J. Orton's posthumous ed. of Doddridge's *Hymns*, &c., 1755, No. 2, in 4 st. of 4 l., and headed, " God's gracious approbation of a religious care of our families." In J. D. Humphreys's ed. of the *Hymns*, printed from the original MS. in 1839, a considerable difference is found in the hymns, showing that Orton took more than usual liberties with Doddridge's text. The first st. reads :—

" Father of men, Thy care we trace,
  That crowns *with love our infant race ;*
  From Thee they sprung, and by Thy *power*
  Are still sustain'd through every hour."

The text followed by the compilers of hymnbooks from Ash & Evans in their Bristol Bapt. *Coll.*, 1769, to the *New Cong.*, 1859-69, was that of Orton, 1755 : often altered as in Ash & Evans's *Coll.* to " Father of *all*, Thy care we bless." This latter is the more popular reading of the two. The Meth. New Connexion *Hymns*, &c., 1835-60, has it as " Father of *man*, Thy care we bless."   [J. J.]

Father of mercies, God of love; My [Our] Father and my [our] God. *O. Heginbothom.* [*Praise to and Adoration of the Father.*] Pub. in his (posthumous) *Hys. by the late Rev. Ottiwell Heginbothom, of Sudbury, Suffolk*, 1794 ; and in J. M. Ray's *Coll. of Hys.*, &c., 1799. It is in C. U. in G. Britain and America, and is sometimes attributed to T. Raffles in error. It is also in limited use as, " Father of mercies, God of love, *Our* Father, and *our* God."   [J. J.]

Father of mercies, God of love; O hear a suppliant's cry. *T. Raffles.* [*The Penitent's Prayer.*] Published in Dr. Collyer's *Hymns*, &c., 1812, No. 909, in 6 st. of 6 l., and headed " The Penitent's Prayer." It was repeated in several of the older collections, and at the present time it is in somewhat extensive use. In America it is often ascribed to O. Heginbothom in error. [J. J.]

Father of mercies, God of peace. [*Harvest.*] Appeared anonymously in the revised ed. of Longfellow and Johnson's Unitarian *Book of Hymns*, 1848 (1st ed. 1846), in 4 st. of 6 l., and entitled " Thanksgiving Hymn." It is in their *Hys. of the Spirit*, Boston, 1864, and in other American Unitarian hymn-books.   [J. J.]

Father of mercies, in Thine house. *P. Doddridge.* [*Ordination.*] 1st pub. in J. Orton's posthumous ed. of Doddridge's *Hymns*, &c., 1755, in 7 st. of 4 l., and headed, " The Institution of a Gospel Ministry from Christ, Eph. iv. 11, 12. For an Ordination." In 1839, it was pub. from the original MS. by J. D. Humphreys in his ed. of the *Hymns*, &c., No. 315, as " Father of mercies, in *Thy* house," and with several additional differences. It is curious that Orton retained the original first line in the index of the 1st ed. of the *Hymns*, &c., but altered it in the body of the book. Orton's text is followed by all compilers. In the *Supp.* to the *Wes. H. Bk.*, st. ii., iii., v.–vii., were given as " The Saviour, when to heaven He rose." This cento is retained in the revised ed., 1875.   [J. J.]

Father of mercies, in Thy word.
Anne Steele. [*Holy Scripture.*] 1st pub. in her *Poems on Subjects chiefly Devotional,* 1760, vol. i. p. 58, in 12 st. of 4 l., repeated in the enlarged ed., 1780, and in Sedgwick's reprint of her *Hymns,* 1863, p. 36. In 1769, Ash & Evans gave a selection of 6 stanzas in their Bristol Bapt. *Coll.,* No. 79, and from this arrangement mainly the well-known hymn is taken. It is in extensive use in G. Britain and America, and is one of the most popular of Miss Steele's hymns.   [J. J.]

Father of Peace and God of Love.
P. Doddridge. [*Holiness desired.*] This hymn, from its historical connection with the Scottish *Translations and Paraphrases* of 1745 and 1781, has more than usual interest. Its history in detail is this :—

i. In Doddridge's MS. in the "Rooker MSS." No. iii. (see **Doddridge**), the text in his own handwriting is as follows :—

"ii. The Christian Perfected by the Grace of God in Christ ; from Heb. xiii. 20, 21.

   " Father of Peace, and God of Love,
     We own thy pow'r to save ;
     That pow'r by which our Shepherd rose
     Victorious o'er the Grave.

   " We triumph in that Shepherd's name,
     Still watchful for our good ;
     Who brought th' eternal cov'nant down
     And seal'd it with his blood.

   " So may thy spirit seal my soul,
     And mould it to thy will ;
     That my fond heart no more may stray,
     But keep thy cov'nant still.

   " Still may we gain superior strength,
     And press with vigour on ;
     Till full perfection crown our hopes,
     And fix us near thy throne."

Another MS. of Doddridge's *Hymns* is in the possession of the writer, dated Mar. 16, 1739–40. This hymn is No. 2, and reads, st. i. l. 3, *Saviour* for *Shepherd ;* st. iii. l. 4, *that* for *thy ;* and st. iv. l. 7, *crowns* for *crown.*

ii. Through the kind offices of Robert Blair a copy of the hymn fell into the hands of the Committee appointed to compile the Scottish *Trans. and Paraphs.,* and by them was included therein as No. 34, in 1745, with st. ii. l. 1, "*Saviour's* name " for " *Shepherd's* name," and st. iii. " *our* souls " for " *my* soul," " *them* to " for " *it* to," and " *our weak* hearts " for " *my fond* heart."

iii. In the revised ed. of the same work, in 1751, it was altered thus : st. i. as above ; st. ii. :—

   " Him from the Dead thou brought'st again,
     When, by his sacred Blood,
     Confirm'd and seal'd for evermore
     th' eternal Cov'nant stood.

3. " O may thy Spirit seal our Souls,
     and mould them to thy Will ;
     That our weak Hearts no more may stray,
     but keep thy Precepts still.

4. " Work in us all thy holy Will
     to man by JESUS shown :
     Till we, thro' him, improving still,
     at last approach thy Throne."

iv. In 1755, Job Orton included the text as in the "Rooker MSS." in Doddridge's *Hymns,* No. 325, and the same text was included in the ed. pub. by J. D. Humphreys in 1839.

v. In 1781 the Scottish Committee included the form of the text now in common use in the *Trans. and Paraphs.,* No. LX. It is thus composed :—

St. 1. Original as in " Rooker MSS."

St. 2 and 3, corresponding stanzas from the revised ed. of *Trs. and Pars.,* 1751, as above.

St. 4, a new st. by *W. Cameron,* thus :—

   " That to perfection's sacred height
     we nearer still may rise,
     And all we think, and all we do,
     be pleasing in thine eyes."

This arrangement and last stanza are assigned to Cameron on the authority of his daughter (see **Cameron, W.**) This form of the hymn is in somewhat extensive use in all English-speaking countries. It should be designated, " *P. Doddridge, Scottish Tr. & Par.,* 1751, *and W. Cameron.*"   [J. J.]

Father of the human race. *W. B. Collyer.* [*Holy Matrimony.*] 1st pub. in his *Services Suited to the Solemnization of Matrimony, &c.,* 1837, No. 10, in 3 st. of 4 l., and thence unaltered into Spurgeon's *O. O. H. Bk.,* 1866, No. 1046, and others in G. Britain and America.   [J. J.]

Father, our hearts we lift. *C. Wesley.* [*Christmas.*] 1st pub. in his *Hymns for the Nativity of our Lord,* 1745, No. 9, in 5 st. of 8 l. (*P. Works,* 1868–72, vol. iv. p. 114). In its full form it is not in C. U., but a cento beginning with the first four lines, and completed with odd lines from the rest of the hymn, is in C. U. in America. See Dr. Hatfield's *Church H. Bk.,* 1872, No. 408.   [J. J.]

Father, see this living clod. *C. Wesley.* [*Holiness desired.*] This hymn is composed as follows :—

   i. From *Short Hymns, &c.,* 1762, vol. i., No. 8. Gen. ii. 7.

   ii. From *Short Hymns, &c.,* 1762, vol. i., No. 197. Lev. xxvi. 13.

   iii. From *Short Hymns, &c.,* 1762, vol. i., No. 55. Gen. xvii. 1.

   iv. From *Short Hymns, &c.,* 1762, vol. i., No. 5. Gen. i. 26.

In this form it was given in the *Wes. H. Bk.,* 1780, No. 357, and has been repeated in later editions, and has passed into other collections. (*P. Works,* 1868–72, vol. ix.)   [J. J.]

Father, Son, and Holy Ghost. In solemn power, &c. *C. Wesley.* [*Adult Holy Baptism.*] Written for the baptism of a female adult, and pub. in *Hymns and Sac. Poems,* 1749, vol. ii., No. 183, in 2 st. of 8 l. (*P. Works,* 1868–72, vol. v. p. 389). In 1868 it was included in the *Sarum Hymnal,* No. 233 ; the S. P. C. K. *Church Hymns,* 1871, and one or two American collections. By the change of " her " to " his," as circumstances require, it can be used for both sexes. This plan is adopted in some hymn-books.   [J. J.]

Father, Son, and Holy Ghost, One in Three, &c. *C. Wesley.* [*Personal dedication to God.*] 1st pub. in the *Hymns on the Lord's Supper,* 1745, No. 155, in 6 st. of 6 l., and included in the *Wes. H. Bk.,* 1780, No. 418. It has been repeated in subsequent editions, and is also found in other hymn-books in G. Britain and America (*P. Works,* 1868–72, vol. iii. p. 333), sometimes beginning with st. v., " Now, O God, Thine own I am." The stanza (iv.)

   " Take my soul and body's powers ;
     Take my memory, mind, and will,
   All my goods, and all my hours,
     All I know, and all I feel.
   All I think, or speak, or do,
     Take my heart ;—but make it new ! "

has been a favourite quotation in some religious bodies for more than a hundred years. Its spirit of self-surrender, and its deep fervour have suited both the strongly enthusiastic and the truly devout. Other parts of the hymn have also awakened more than usual interest. (See G. J. Stevenson's *Meth. H. Bk. Notes*, 1883, p. 290.) In the Ohio *Evan. Lutheran Hyl.*, 1880, this hymn is ascribed to *I. Watts* in error.   [J. J.]

Father, Son, and Spirit, hear. *C. Wesley.* [*Communion of Saints.*] This poem on "The Communion of Saints," in 39 st. (in six parts), was pub. in the *Hys. and S. Poems*, 1740, p. 188 (*P. Works*, 1868–72, i. p. 356). From it the following centos have come into C. U.:—

1. Father, Son, and Spirit, hear.
2. Other ground can no man lay.
3. Christ our head, gone up on high.
4. Christ from whom all blessings flow.

These were given in the *Wes. H. Bk.*, 1780, as one hymn in four parts and numbered 501–504. They are repeated in the same form in later editions, and also in other collections.

5. Father, Son, and Spirit, hear. A cento in 8 st. of 4 l. from the original poem, given in Toplady's *Ps. & Hys.*, 1776, No. 240.
6. Christ from whom all blessings flow. St. i., iii. and v., of Pt. iv. of the original in W. F. Stevenson's *Hys. for Ch. & Home*, 1873.
7. Lord from whom all blessings flow. St. i., iii. and iv., from Pt. iv. of the original in the Bapt. *Ps. & Hys.*, 1858, and others.
8. Happy souls, whose course is run. From Pt. vi. of the original in the *Altar Hymnal*, 1884, No. 105.
9. Jesus Christ, who stands between. From Pt. v. of the original st. iv., v. in the American Meth. Episco. *Hymns*, 1849.
10. Join us, in one spirit, join. St. ii., iii., ix. and x. from Pt. iv. of the original in the American Unitarian *Hys. for the Ch. of Christ*, 1853.   [J. J.]

Father, Thy paternal care. *Sir J. Bowring.* [*The Divine Father, the Giver of all good Gifts.*] This cento is taken from his poem for the third Tuesday evening in Autumn, in his *Matins and Vespers*, 1823, p. 120. It is in 3 st. of 8 l., and is admirably suited for *Flower Services*. Its use amongst the American Unitarians is extensive.   [J. J.]

Father, Thy Son hath died. *H. Bonar.* [*Jesus, the Name of Names.*] This hymn on the life, death, resurrection, ascension, and glory of Jesus, with the simple but beautiful petition at the close of each stanza,

'Put honour on that Name of names,
    By blessing me,"

appeared in the 1st series of his *Hys. of Faith and Hope*, 1857, in 7 st. of 9 l., the refrain being changed, as "blessing," to "pardoning," &c., throughout. Although in C. U. in a few collections, its use is not equal to its merits. Possibly its peculiar metre may account for this neglect.   [J. J.]

Father, Thy will, not mine, be done. *J. Montgomery.* [*Resignation.*] This hymn is said in the "M. MSS." to have been written at Ockbrook, Derbyshire (a Moravian settlement), in 1841. It was given in Montgomery's *Original Hymns*, 1853, in 2 st. of 6 l., and entitled "In Affliction." It is in several collections both in G. Britain and America.   [J. J.]

Father, to Thee my soul I lift. *C. Wesley.* [*God the Giver of every good Gift.*]

This is the first of three hymns on Phil. ii. 13. "It is God which worketh in you both to will and to do," first pub. in his *Hymns and Sac. Poems*, 1749, vol. ii., in 3 st. of 8 l. (*P. Works*, 1868–72, vol. v. p. 374). It was given in the *Wes. H. Bk.*, 1780, No. 423, and later editions, but divided into 6 st. of 4 l. In addition to this text, which is in C. U. in G. Britain and America, another was included in Toplady's *Ps. & Hys.*, 1776, No. 21, in 7 st. of 4 l., of which st. i.–v. are from this hymn, and st. vi., vii. are from the last of the three hymns named above. The use of this text is limited. No. 210 in the S. P. C. K. *Ps. & Hys.* is from the former somewhat altered.   [J. J.]

Father, to Thy sinful child. *J. Conder.* [*Lent.*] Appeared in his *Cong. H. Bk.*, 1836, No. 517, in 7 st. of 4 l., and based upon the words "Forgive us our debts, as we forgive our debtors." In the following year it was republished in his work *The Choir and The Oratory*, 1837, p. 35, as Pt. v. of "The Lord's Prayer in Six Parts," and again in his *Hymns of Praise, Prayer, &c.*, 1856, p. 138. In the *New Cong.*, 1859, No. 535, st. vi. is omitted, and slight changes are also introduced. In Martineau's *Hymns, &c.*, 1840 and 1873, a part of this hymn is given as, "Lord, forgive me day by day" (st. iii.)   [J. J.]

Father, we humbly pray. *Bp. C. Wordsworth.* [*Rogation Tide.*] 1st pub. in his *Holy Year*, 1st ed. 1862, p. 96, in 20 st. of 4 l. In the latest editions of the *Holy Year* the 20 st. are divided into four parts, as (1) "Father, we humbly pray"; (2) "With genial rains and dews"; (3) "Bless, Lord, Thy holy Church"; (4) "The widow desolate." In the S. P. C. K. *Church Hys.*, 1871, No. 140, and Dr. Dale's *English H. Bk.*, 1874, No. 1232, the full text is given with the omission of st. xii. Minor alterations are also introduced.   [J. J.]

Father, Who art in heaven. *C. Wesley.* [*The Lord's Prayer.*] This version of the Lord's Prayer was printed from the "Wesley MSS." of Richmond College, Surrey, in *P. Works of J. & C. Wesley*, 1868–72, vol. x. p. 179, in 20 st. of 8 l., and as one of his "Hymns on the Four Gospels." In 1875, a cento beginning, "From trials unexempted," was given in the *Wes. H. Bk.*, No. 818. It is composed of st. xiii., xiv., xvi., xvii. [J. J.]

Father, Who on high. [*Holy Trinity.*] This cento has a somewhat curious and complicated history, the details of which are:—

It appeared in J. A. Latrobe's *Ps. & Hys.*, 1841, No. 3, in 4 st. of 6 lines. It is based on an English hymn by L. T. Nyberg beginning, "Holy Trinity," No. 452, in pt. ii. of the *Moravian H. Bk.*, 1754, in 2 st., for the second of which one beginning, "Had we angels' tongues," was substituted in the ed. of 1769— this st. ii. in 1769 being Mr. Latrobe's st. iv. In the *Supplement* of 1808 a hymn was included as No. 1033, beginning, "O eternal Word," in 2 st., of which st. i. is in the *Moravian Messenger*, Sept. 1868, ascribed to C. Gregor, and dated 1791; and is st. i. ll. 3–6, and ii. ll. 1, 2, of Mr. Latrobe. The remaining lines and st. iii.— which seems based on st. iv. of "Allein Gott in der Höh' sei Ehr" (q. v.)—are added to make the hymn suitable for Trinity Sunday, and as such it was included by Mercer as No. 164 in his *C. P. & H. Bk.*, 1857 (Ox. ed. 1864, No. 240), beginning, "Father, throned on high," and this was repeated, further altered, in Allon's *Suppl. Hys.*; as No. 1007 in the *N. Cong.*; and No. 19 in the *Meth. S. S. H. Bk.*, 1883. In the Eng. Presb. *Ps. & Hys.*, 1867, No. 378 is Mr. Latrobe's text unaltered.

The form beginning "O eternal Word," No. 215 in Dr. Pagenstecher's *Coll.*, 1864, is st. i., iv. from Latrobe's version, st. ii., iii. being taken from the Moravian versions of "Seelenbräutigam," by A. Drese (st. iii.), beginning, "God and man indeed," and of st. v. of J. A. Freylinghausen's "Wer ist wohl wie du," beginning, "Highest King and Priest."   [J. M.]

Father, Whose everlasting love. Thy only Son, &c. *C. Wesley.* [*Praise for Redemption.*] Appeared in his tract *Hymns on God's Everlasting Love*, 1741, in 17 st. of 4 l., No. i. It was afterwards reprinted in the *Arminian Magazine*, 1778, p. 430. Sometime after J. Wesley's death, but before 1809, st. i.-iii., viii., xii., and xvii., were given in the *Wes. H. Bk.*, in a slightly altered form. The cento is also found in other collections. Orig. text in *P. Works*, vol. iii. p. 3. [J. J.]

Father, Whose path is in the Sea. *J. Julian.* [*Evening at Sea.*] Written in 1874, and 1st pub. in the *Churchman's Shilling Magazine*, Oct. 1874, in 4 st. of 4 l., and again in a few hymnals.

Faussett, Alessie, née Bond, daughter of the Rev. William Bond, Rector of Ballee, county of Down; b. at Ballee Rectory, Jan. 8, 1841, and married to the Rev. Henry Faussett, Incumbent of Edenderry, county of Tyrone, 1875. Her poetical works are (1) *Thoughts on Holy Words*, 1867, printed for private circulation; (2) *The Triumph of Faith*, 1870; (3) *The Cairns of Iona, and other Poems*, 1873. Her hymns in C. U. include:—

1. **Be with us all for evermore.** *For Divine Protection.* Written in 1867, and first printed for private circulation in her *Thoughts on Holy Words*, 1867.

2. **O Lamb of God, that tak'st away.** *Lent.* Written in 1865, and first pub. in *The Triumph of Faith*, 1870.

These hymns were given in the Irish *Church Hymnal*, 1873.   [G. A. C.]

Fawcett, John, D.D., was b. Jan. 6, 1739/1740, at Lidget Green, near Bradford, Yorks. Converted at the age of 16 under the ministry of G. Whitefield, he at first joined the Methodists, but 3 years later united with the Baptist Church at Bradford. Having begun to preach he was, in 1765, ordained Bap. minister at Wainsgate, near Hebden Bridge, Yorks. In 1772 he was invited to London, to succeed the celebrated Dr. J. Gill, as pastor of Carter's Lane; the invitation had been formally accepted, the farewell sermon at Wainsgate had been preached and the waggons loaded with his goods for removal, when the love and tears of his attached people prevailed and he decided to remain. In 1777 a new chapel was built for him at Hebden Bridge, and about the same time he opened a school at Brearley Hall, his place of residence. In 1793 he was invited to become President of the Baptist Academy at Bristol, but declined. In 1811 he received from America the degree of D.D., and died in 1817, at the age of 78. Dr. Fawcett was the author of a number of prose works on Practical Religion, several of which attained a large circulation. His poetical publications are:—

(1) *Poetic Essays*, 1767; (2) *The Christian's Humble Plea, a Poem, in answer to Dr. Priestley against the Divinity of our Lord Jesus Christ*, 1772; (3) Three hymns, in the *Gospel Magazine*, 1777; (4) *The Death of Eumenio, a Divine Poem*, 1779; (5) Another poem, suggested by the decease of a friend, *The Reign of Death*, 1780; and (6) *Hymns adapted to the circumstances of*

Public Worship and Private Devotion, Leeds, G. Wright & Son, 1782. They are 166 in number, and were mostly composed to be sung after Sermons by the author.

Whilst not attaining a high degree of excellence as poetry, they are "eminently spiritual and practical," and a number of them are found in all the Baptist and Congregational hymn-books that have appeared during the last 100 years. The best known of these are, "Infinite excellence is Thine"; "How precious is the Book divine"; "Thus far my God hath led me on"; "Religion is the chief concern"; "Blest be the tie that binds"; "I my Ebenezer raise"; and "Praise to Thee, Thou great Creator." These hymns, together with others by Fawcett, are annotated under their respective first lines.   [W. R. S.]

In addition the following hymns, also by Fawcett, but of less importance, are in C. U.:

1. **Behold the sin-atoning Lamb.** *Passiontide.* No. 60 of his *Hymns*, 1782, in 7 st. of 4 l. In several hymnals in G. Britain and America.

2. **I my Ebenezer raise.** *Birthday.* No. 102 of his *Hymns*, in 10 st. of 4 l. Usually given in an abbreviated form.

3. **Infinite excellence is Thine.** *Jesus the Desire of Nations.* No. 42 of his *Hymns*, in 12 st. of 4 l. In several hymn-books in G. Britain and America in an abridged form.

4. **Jesus, the heavenly Lover, gave.** *Redemption in Christ.* No. 10 of his *Hymns*, &c., 1782, in 7 st. of 4 l., and headed, "The marriage between Christ and the Soul." In Snepp's *Songs of G. & G.*, 1872, it reads, "Jesus, the heavenly *Bridegroom*, gave," and st. v. is omitted.

5. **Lord, hast Thou made me know Thy ways?** *Perseverance.* No. 122 of his *Hymns*, &c., 1782, in 8 st. of 4 l. In the *Baptist Hyl.*, 1879, No. 451, st. iv.-vii. are omitted.

6. **O God, my Helper, ever near.** *New Year.* No. 108 of his *Hymns*, &c., 1782, in 6 st. of 4 l. The *New Cong.*, 1859-69 omits st. vi.

7. **O, my soul, what means this sadness?** *Sorrow turned to Joy.* No. 111 of his *Hymns*, &c., 1782, in 5 st. of 6 l., and based upon the words, "Why art Thou cast down, O my soul?" &c. It is in C. U. in America, and usually with the omission of st. ii. as in Dr. Hatfield's *Church H. Bk.*, 1872.

8. **Sinners, the voice of God regard.** *Invitation to Repentance.* No. 63 of his *Hymns*, &c., 1782, in 7 st. of 4 l. on Is. lv. 7, "Let the wicked forsake his way," &c. It is in C. U. in America, but usually in an abbreviated form.

9. **Thy presence, gracious God, afford.** *Before Sermon.* No 155 in his *Hymns*, &c., in 4 st. of 4 l., and a chorus of two lines. In Dr. Hatfield's *Church H. Bk.*, 1872, No. 126, the chorus is omitted. Fawcett has another hymn on the same subject (No. 79) and beginning, "Thy *blessing*, gracious God, afford," but this is not in C. U.

10. **Thy way, O God, is in the sea.** *Imperfect Knowledge of God.* No. 66 in his *Hymns*, &c., 1782, in 7 st. of 4 l. on 1 Cor. xiii. 9, "We know in part," &c. It is in several American collections, usually abbreviated, and sometimes as, "Thy way, O *Lord*, is in the sea." In this form it is in *The Sabbath H. Bk.*, 1858, &c.

11. **With humble heart and tongue.** *Prayer for Guidance in Youth.* No. 86 in his *Hymns*, &c., 1782, in 7 st. of 4 l. on Ps. cxix. 9. "Wherewith shall a young man cleanse his way." It is No. 954 in the Bapt. *Ps. & Hys.*, 1858-80.

About 20 of Fawcett's hymns are thus still in C. U. Two hymns which have been ascribed to him from time to time, but concerning which there are some doubts, are fully annotated under their respective first lines. These are, "Humble souls that seek salvation," and "Lord, dismiss us with Thy blessing." [J. J.]

Fearless, calm, and strong in love. *T. Davis.* [*Ordination.*] Lord Selborne says in his notes to the enlarged ed. of his *Book of Praise*, 1866, concerning this hymn, "I am indebted for this to the author," and in the body of his book he dates it 1862. It is repeated in W. R. Stevenson's *School Hymnal*, 1880, but not in the author's *Annus Sanctus*, 1877. It is suitable for meetings of lay readers and Sunday-school teachers.   [J. J.]

Feeble in body and in mind. *C. Wesley.* [*In Perplexity.*] Mr. Stevenson, in his *Methodist H. Bk. Notes*, 1883, has dated this hymn 1749, but has omitted all authority for the statement. It was pub. in Dr. Leifchild's *Original Hymns*, 1843, No. 212, in 5 st. of 4 l. In the Wesley *P. Works*, 1868–1872, vol. xiii. p. 256, it was given in 6 st. This is repeated in the *Wes. H. Bk.*, 1875, in a slightly altered form.   [J. J.]

Felices nemorum pangimus incolas. *Jean Baptiste de Santeüil.* [*Abbots and Monks.*] Appeared in the *Cluniac Breviary*, 1686, p. *i.*; his *Hymni Sacri et Novi*, 1689, and again in 1698, p. 250, in 7 st. of 4 l. In the revised *Paris Breviary*, 1736, it was appointed for "Abbatum, Monachorum, et Anachoretarum," at first Vespers (see also Card. Newman's *Hymni Ecclesiae*, 1838 and 1865). The only *tr.* in C. U. is:—

Sing we those who dwell concealed. By T. I. Ball, made for and first pub. in the *Appendix* to the *Hymnal N.*, 1862, No. 363, in 4 st. of 7 l.

Other trs. are :—
1. Happy are they whom God's protecting love. *I. Williams. British Mag.*, 1835, and *Hys. tr. from the Parisian Brev.*, 1839.
2. Sing we of those, whom in the forest wild. *E. Caswall*, 1858.
3. We sing the blest and pure. *J. D. Chambers*, 1866, p. 31.   [J. J.]

Felix dies mortalibus. *Jean Baptiste de Santeüil.* [*Ascension.*] In the *Cluniac Brev.*, 1686, p. 497, and his *Hymni Sacri et Novi*, 1689, p. 21, and ed. 1698, p. 104, in 7 st. of 4 l. In 1736 it was given in the revised *Paris Brev.* as the hymn for the first and second vespers on the octave of the Ascension. It is also appointed for the same season in the *Lyons* and other modern French Breviaries. The text is in Card. Newman's *Hymni Ecclesiae*, 1838 and 1865; and J. Chandler's *Hys. of the Prim. Church*, 1837. *Tr.* as :

1. **O happy day for mortals.** By W. J. Blew, first printed on flyleaf 1850–1851, and then included in his *Ch. Hy. & Tune Bk.*, 1852, in 5 st. of 6 l. In 1870 it was given in Rice's *Sel.* from that work, No. 63.

2. **For aye shall mortals bless the day.** By C. S. Calverley, made for and first pub. in the *Hymnary*, 1872, No. 317.

Trs. not in C.U. :—
1. O 'twas a day, both bright and good. *J. Chandler*, 1837.
2. Blest day when doom'd to die no more. I. Williams, *British Mag.* 1834; and his *Hys. tr. from the Parisian Brev.*, 1839.
3. O day with holy gladness fraught. *J. D. Chambers*, 1857, p. 199.
4. O happy day, to mortals dear. *R. F. Littledale, in Lyra Messianica*, 1864.
5. O day so dear to man once lost. *R. Campbell*, from his MSS. in Shipley's *Annus Sanctus*, 1884. [J. J.]

Felix dies quam proprio. *Abbé Besnault.* [*Circumcision.*] Appeared in the revised *Paris Brev.*, 1736, as the hymn for the Feast of the Circumcision at Matins. As such it is also repeated in the *Lyons* and other modern French Breviaries. Text in Card.

Newman's *Hymni Ecclesiae*, 1838–65; J. Chandler's *Hys. of the Prim. Church*, 1837, and Biggs's *Annotated H. A. & M.*, 1867. *Tr.* as :—

1. **O happy day, when first was poured.** By J. Chandler, in his *Hys. of the Primitive Church*, 1837, No. 48, in 6 st. of 4 l. In 1852 five stanzas were given in the *English Hymnal*, No. 54; and subsequently in other collections, including the *Salisbury*, 1857; the *People's H.*, 1867, and others. The text in the *Hymnary*, 1872, although beginning with the same first line, differs materially in many parts. In *Kennedy*, 1863, it begins, "O *sacred* day when first was poured"; and in Snepp's *Songs of G. & G.*, 1872, as, "O *blessed* day, when first was poured." This last arrangement was given in Murray's *Hymnal*, 1852, and *H. A. & M.*, 1861; but in each case with slight differences in the text. It is also found in the *Appendix* to the *H. Noted*.

2. **Blest day when from the Saviour flowed.** By R. Campbell, 1st pub. in his *Hys. & Anthems, &c.*, 1850, in 4 st. of 4 l. This is repeated in the *Hymnal* for St. John's, Aberdeen, 1870, and others.

3. **Blest day on which the Saviour shed.** By R. C. Singleton, written in 1867, and 1st pub. in his *Anglican H. Bk.*, 1868.

Trs. not in C. U. :—
1. O happy day, when this our state. *I. Williams*, 1839.
2. O happy day of all the year. *W. J. Blew*, 1852.
3. O happy day, with joy arrayed. *J. D. Chambers*, 1857, i. 101.   [J. J.]

Felix morte tuâ, qui cruciatibus. *Jean Baptiste de Santeüil.* [*One Martyr.*] Appeared in the *Cluniac Breviary*, 1686, p. xiii., and in his *Hymni Sacri et Novi*, 1689 (ed. 1698, p. 243). It was included in the *Paris Brev.*, 1736, and is also in Card. Newman's *Hymni Ecclesiae*, 1838 and 1865. *Tr.* as :—

How happy the mortal. By I. Williams, in his *Hys. Tr. from the Parisian Breviary*, 1839, p. 283, in 9 st. of 4 l. This is repeated with the omission of st. ii. in the *H. Bk. for the Use of Wellington College*, 1863.

Another tr. is :—
O happy is thy death. *J. D. Chambers*, 1866, p. 10.   [J. J.]

Fellows, John. Date of b. unknown; d. 1785. He was the author of the following :—

(1) *Grace Triumphant, a Sacred Poem in nine books*, 1770 ; (2) *Bromsgrove Elegy, in blank verse, on the Death of Rev. G. Whitefield*, 1771 ; (3) *An Elegy on the Death of Dr. Gill*, 1771 ; (4) *Hymns on Believers' Baptism*, Birmingham, 1773 ; (5) *The Apostle Paul's Defence before Felix, in verse*, 1775 ; (6) *Hymns in a great variety of Metres, on the Perfection of the Word of God and the Gospel of Jesus Christ*, 1776 ; (7) *The History of the Holy Bible, attempted in easy verse*, 4 vols., 1777 ; (8) *Six Instructive Views of Believers' Baptism*, a tract pub. both separately and as an Introduction to the 2nd edition of his "Hymns on Believers' Baptism" 1777 ; (9) *A Fair and Impartial Enquiry into the Rise, &c., of the Church of Rome*, 1779 ; and also (10) "*A Protestant Catechism.*"

Considering how numerous were the writings of J. Fellows, it is remarkable how little is known of him. It is stated by Dr. Joseph Belcher, in *Historical Sketches of Hymns* (Philadelphia, 1859), that he was a poor shoemaker, a member of the Baptist denomination, and that he lived in Birmingham. The evidence for this is tolerably clear.

That Fellows was a Baptist and not a Methodist, as Watt & Allibone say, is clear from his baptismal hymns. That he lived in or near Birmingham is likely from the fact that most of his books date from Birmingham, and are said to be printed for the author, though sold by G. Keith, Gracechurch Street, London. Also, to the 2nd ed. of his *Hymns on Believers' Baptism* (1777) is prefixed a note of commendation, signed by eight Baptist ministers, who say they are personally acquainted with the author; and the first three names are those of the Baptist ministers at Birmingham, Coventry and Bromsgrove. From the records of the Baptist church formerly in Cannon Street, Birmingham, it appears that a John Fellows joined it early in 1780, and continued a member till his death on July 30, 1785. But one of J. Fellows's earlier pieces is entitled a *Bromsgrove* Elegy. Combining these facts we infer that Fellows first lived at Bromsgrove, and then, removing to Birmingham, joined the church in Cannon Street.

His hymns on Baptism are 55 in number. 6 are in Rippon's *Sel.*, 1787. Some of his hymns are in all Baptist hymn-books, from *Rippon* to modern collections. These include the disputed "Humble souls who seek salvation"; the hymn on behalf of children, "Great God, now condescend"; and others, all of which are annotated under their respective first lines. In addition the following are in limited use:—

1. **Dear Lord, and will Thy pardoning love Embrace, &c.** *Adult Baptism.* No. 28 of his *Hys. on Believers' Baptism*, 1773, in 7 st. of 4 l., and headed "The Believer constrained by the love of Christ to follow Him in His Ordinance." In Rippon's *Sel.*, 1787, it was reduced to 4 stanzas: and in the *Bapt. Hymnal*, 1879, to 6, st. vi. being omitted. It is also sometimes given as "O Lord, and will Thy pardoning love, &c."

2. **Descend, Celestial Dove.** *Invocation of the H. Spirit at Holy Baptism.* No. 55 of his *Hys. on Believers' Baptism*, 1773, in 6 st. of 8 l. In Rippon's *Sel.*, 1787, these were re-arranged in 4 stanzas, and again in the American *Bapt. Hy. & Tune Bk.*, 1871, to 3 stanzas.

3. **Go, teach the nations and baptize.** *Holy Baptism.* No. 454, in Rippon's *Sel.*, 1787, in 3 st. of 3 l. It is given in a few American collections.

4. **Great God, we in Thy courts appear.** *Holy Baptism.* No. 43 in his *Hys. on Believers' Baptism*, 1773, and Rippon's *Sel.*, 1787, No. 452, in 5 st. of 4 l. It sometimes begins with st. iii., "In Thy assembly here we stand."

5. **Jesus, Mighty King of [in] Zion.** *Holy Baptism; Christ the Guide.* No. 29 of his *Hys. on Believers' Baptism*, 1773, in 6 st. of 4 l. and headed, "Believers buried with Christ in Baptism." *Rippon*, 1787, reduced it to 3 stanzas, and these have been repeated in later collections as the American *Bapt. Hy. & Tune Bk.*, 1871, &c. [W. R. S.]

Feneberg, Johann Michael, was b. Feb. 9, 1751, at Oberdorf, Allgäu, Bavaria. He was for some time tutor in St. Paul's College, at Regensburg, and in 1785 was appointed professor in the Gymnasium at Dillingen. In 1793 he became parish priest of Seeg, in Allgäu, where he had as assistants Christoph Schmid, Martin Boos and Johannes Gossner; but in 1805, on account of his Evangelical teaching, was removed to Vöhringen, near Ulm, where he d. Oct. 12, 1812. The only hymn by him *tr.* into English is:—

Liebe und ein Kreuz dazu. [*Cross and Consolation.*] Of the origin of this beautiful hymn *Koch*, vi. 554, relates that it was "written at Seeg in 1794, as he, in the experience of the blessings of the cross after the amputation of his right foot, rendered necessary by an unfortunate fall on Oct. 21, 1793, had once more, on Easter Sunday [1794], renewed in body and soul, been able to ascend the pulpit as 'a wooden-legged man.'" It appeared in the *Sammlung erbaulicher Lieder zum Gebrauche in christlichen Häusern*, Kempten, 1812 (ed. 1817, No. 102), in 8 st. of 4 l. It is *tr.* as, "Love and a cross together blest," by Miss Borthwick in *H. L. L.*, 1862, p. 38; 1884, p. 205. [J. M.]

Ferguson, Fergus, D.D., second s. of the Rev. Fergus Ferguson, of Bellshill, near Glasgow, and afterwards of Aberdeen, was b. at Glasgow, September 6, 1824, and educated at the University of Glasgow, where he gra-

duated B.A. 1845 and M.A. 1858. In 1845 he became minister of Blackfriars Street E. U. Church, Glasgow (now Montrose St.). He received the degree of D.D. in 1876, from Cumberland University, U.S. His two hymns appeared in *The Daystar*, the magazine of the Evangelical Union, and were contributed to the *E. U. Hymn-book* of 1856, and the *E. U. Hymnal* of 1878, he having been a member of both committees of compilation. They are:—

1. **He loved me, and gave Himself for me.** *The Love of Jesus.* Appeared in *The Daystar*, 1850, and repeated in the *E. U. H. Bk.*, 1856, and the *E. U. Hymnal*, 1878.

2. **How sweet to the believer's soul.** *Private Prayer.* Given in the *Daystar*, 1846, and again in the *E. U. H. Bk.*, 1856, and the *E. U. Hymnal*, 1878. [J. M.]

Ferrar, Nicholas, s. of Nicholas Ferrar, a merchant in London, was b. in the parish of St. Mary Stayning, Mark Lane, London, Feb. 23, 1592, and educated at Clare Hall, Cambridge, graduating B.A. 1610, and M.A. 1612. From 1612 to 1618 he travelled on the continent, and visited some of the chief cities of Italy, Germany, and Spain. On his return, he became an M.P. in 1624. The same year he retired from public life and purchased the lordship of Little Gidding, Huntingdonshire. After putting the mansion in repair, and re storing the church, he took up his abode there with his relatives to the number of 40 persons. He was ordained Deacon, but would not proceed further. The mansion at Gidding was distributed into apartments, oratories, and school rooms, and a round of devotion was maintained both day and night. He d. Dec. 1, 1637. His devotional pieces were written for the use of the Gidding community, and specimens have appeared in the Rev. J. E. B. Mayor's ed. of the *Lives* of Ferrar. He also translated *Divine Considerations of those things most profitable in our Christian profession*, from the Spanish of Juan Valdes. His *Memoirs*, by Dr. P. Peckard of Cambridge, were pub. in 1790. This is the Nicholas Ferrar introduced by Mr. Shorthouse in his romance of *John Inglesant* (ch. iv.). His description of the Protestant Nunnery at Little Gidding is one of the most exquisite chapters in that work. Ferrar was the friend and executor of the saintly George Herbert. [English Hymnody, Early, § VII.] [J. J.]

Festiva saeclis colitur. [*All Saints.*] This hymn is found in the three following forms:—

i. **Festiva saeclis colitur.** This form in 7 st. of 4 l. is contained in three MSS. of the 11th cent. in the British Museum (Vesp. D. xii. f. 93 b.; Julius A. vi. f. 58 b.; Harl. 2961, f. 243 b.); and in the *Lat. Hys. of the Anglo-Saxon Ch.* (Surtees Society), 1851, p. 117, is printed from an 11th cent. MS., at Durham (B. iii. 32, f. 34 b), as a hymn at Vespers on All Saints' Day. This form of the text has not been translated.

ii. **Jesu, Salvator saeculi Redemptis ope subveni.** This form in 5 st. (viz. omitting st. i., ii. of the first form, is found in two MSS. of the 11th cent. in the Brit. Mus., (1) a *Mozarabic Brev.* (Add. 30,848, f. 207), and (2) a *Mozarabic Hymnarium* (Add. 30,851, f. 164 b), and in an 11th cent. MS. in the Bodleian (Liturg. Misc. 320, f. 62). It is also in the *Mozarabic* (Toledo, 1502); *Roman* (Venice, 1478); *Sarum*, and various German Breviaries; and is also given by *Thomasius*, ii. p. 397; *Daniel*, i., No. 396; *Wackernagel*, i., No. 181. *Tr.* as:—

1. **O Jesu, Saviour of the earth.** By R. F. Littledale. Pub. in the *People's H.*, 1867, and signed "A. L. P."

2. **Jesu, Who cam'st the world to save.** Appeared in the *Antiphoner & Grail*, 1880, and the *Hymner*, 1882.

iii. **Salutis aeternae dator.** This is a recast of No. ii., which was made for and appeared in the revised *Roman Breviary*, 1632, and repeated in later editions. It is also in *Daniel*, i., No. 396. *Tr.* as:—

1. **O Jesus, Source of sanctity.** By Bp. R. Mant, in his *Ancient Hys.*, &c., 1837, p. 78, in 7 st. of 4 l. (ed. 1871, p. 137). This is in several collections, including the Cooke and Denton *Hymnal*, 1853, No. 164, where it begins, "O Jesu, our redeeming Lord," and is appointed for St. Andrew's Day. This recast, to adapt it for St. Andrew's Day, was made by Canon W. Cooke.

2. **Giver of life, eternal Lord.** By E. Caswall. Appeared in his *Lyra Catholica*, 1849, p. 193, in 6 st. of 4 l.; and again in his *Hys. & Poems*, 1873, p. 104.　　　　　　　　[J. M.]

Festum matris gloriosae. [*Visitation of the B. V. M.*] This hymn for the Feast of the Visitation B. V. M. is given for that Festival in the *Sarum Brev.*, Venice, 1495, Estiva pt. ii., fol. 130, and dates probably from the 15th cent. The full text is given in *Daniel*, i. 436, and a few readings are added in iv. p. 276 from the *Aberdeen Brev.* The text is also in Card. Newman's *Hymni Ecclesiae*, 1838 and 1865.　　　　　　[W. A. S.]

Translations in C. U.:—

1. **Saints, the glorious Mother greeting.** By J. D. Chambers, in his *Lauda Syon*, Pt. ii., 1866, p. 83, in 6 st. of 6 l. In 1867 it was repeated in the *People's H.*, No. 261.

2. **Now the glorious Mother's feast-day.** Given in the *Antiphoner & Grail*, 1880, and repeated in the *Hymner*, 1882.　　　　　　[J. J.]

Fever and fret, and aimless stir. F. W. Faber. [*Despondency.*] Pub. in the 1852 ed. of his *Jesus and Mary*, &c., No. 63, in 13 st. of 4 l., and headed "Low Spirits." It was repeated in his *Hymns*, 1862. In Martineau's *Hymns*, &c., 1873, st. iv., vi., viii., xi. and vii., are given as "Voices are round me; smiles are near." This arrangement forms a beautiful hymn for private use.　　[J. J.]

Few are thy days and full of woe. M. Bruce. [*The Resurrection.*] From evidence elsewhere produced [see **Bruce, M.**] we believe the original of this hymn to have been written by M. Bruce about 1764; that the same was handed by Bruce's father to John Logan a short time after Bruce's death (in 1767), and that it was published by J. Logan in his *Poems*, 1781, p. 95, No. 2, as his own. The nearest approach to the original text now attainable is given in Dr. Mackelvie's ed. of Bruce's *Works with Life*, 1837, pp. 254–57; and Dr. Grosart's *Works of M. Bruce*, 1865, pp. 127–130. In the same year that Logan's *Poems* were published, the new and revised edition of the Scottish *Translations and Paraphrases* was issued, and therein, as No. viii., was given a paraphrase of Job xiv. 1–15, in which six of the fourteen stanzas are almost entirely from

this hymn, and the remaining eight are but the amplification of the thoughts which are found in the remaining stanzas of the original. This version, which has been in use in the Church of Scotland for more than 100 years, should therefore be designated "*Michael Bruce altered by John Logan.*"

In addition to abbreviations of the text which begin with st. i., the following centos are in C. U.:—

1. **All nature dies and lives again.** This cento in Dabney's *Ps. & Hys.*, 1821, and later editions and other collections, is composed of st. vi.–viii., xii.–xiv.

2. **The mighty flood that rolls.** Composed of st. x.–iv. altered to s.m. in the American Prayer Book *Ps. & Hys.*, 1826, and later editions, and others.

3. **The winter past, reviving flowers.** Composed of st. viii., ix. altered, with three additional stanzas from another source. This is No. 306 in the American German Reformed *Ps. & Hys.*, 1834, and later editions.
　　　　　　　　　　　　　　　　[J. J.]

Fierce passions discompose the mind. J. Newton. [*Contentment.*] Pub. in the *Olney Hymns*, 1779, Book i., No. 131, in 8 st. of 4 l., and based upon Philippians iv. 11. It is given in a limited number of collections, including Lord Selborne's *Book of Praise*, 1862–7, where it is attributed to "W. Cowper" in error. It does not bear Cowper's signature, "C." in the *Olney Hymns*.　　　[J. J.]

Fierce raged the tempest o'er the deep. G. Thring. [*Stilling the Sea.*] Written in 1861, and 1st pub. in Chope's *Hymnal*, 1862, No. 187, in 4 st. of 4 l. It was repeated in the author's *Hys. Congregational and others*, 1866, No. 6; in his *Hys. & Lyrics*, 1874, p. 94, and in his *Coll.*, 1882. It has passed into numerous collections in G. Britain and America, and ranks as one of the most popular of Prebendary Thring's hymns. It has been specially set to music by Dr. Dykes, in Chope's *Hymnal*, and by others.　[J. J.]

Fierce [raged] was the storm of wind. H. W. Beadon. [*Stilling the Sea.*] Contributed to the *Parish H. Bk.*, in 1863, No. 24, and continued in the enlarged ed., 1875, No. 24, in 7 st. of 4 l. When included in the *Sarum Hymnal*, 1868, No. 74, it was attributed to the late W. Beadon Heathcote in error. This was corrected in the *Hymnary*, 1870–2 (where the hymn is given with slight alterations as, "Fierce *raged* the storm of wind"), and in the Notes to *Church Hymns*, fol. ed., 1881. In the latter the original text is given, with the exception of the doxology. The hymn is based on the Gospel for the 3rd Sunday after the Epiphany.　　[J. J.]

Fight the good fight; lay hold. J. Montgomery. [*The Fight of Faith.*] Written Feb. 14, 1834 (M. MSS.), and given in Ferguson's *Sel. of Hys. for British Seamen*, 1838; and in the same year, with alterations, in Joshua Fawcett's *Temple Offerings.* It was also included in Montgomery's *Original Hys.*, 1853, No. 158, in 5 st. of 6 l., and headed, "Valiant for the Truth." It is in several collections in G. Britain and America, but usually in an abbreviated form.　　[J. J.]

Finita jam sunt praelia. [*Easter.*] This hymn is of unknown date and authorship. *Daniel*, ii. p. 363, gives it without note or reference of any kind, and the source from whence he obtained the text is unknown. It has not been traced earlier than the *Hymno-*

dia Sacra, Münster, 1753, p. 99. Dr. Neale repeats *Daniel's* text in his *Hymni Ecclesiae*, 1851, p. 147; and in his *Mediaeval Hymns*, 1851, p. 116, he groups it with 6 others as being "apparently of the twelfth century." The first stanza is :—

> "Alleluia ! Alleluia !
> Finita jam sunt praelia ;
> Est parta jam victoria ;
> Gaudeamus et canamus : Alleluia !"

It extends to 5 st., each of which begins and ends with " Alleluia." The text is also in Biggs's Annotated *H. A. & M.*, 1867. *Tr.* as :

1. **Finished is the battle now.** By J. M. Neale, in his *Mediaeval Hymns*, 1851. In the *Hymnary*, 1872, No. 182, the opening lines are transposed, and several alterations are made in the text. It begins, "The crown is on the victor's brow." In the *People's H.*, 1867, and a few others, the text is unaltered. This was the first rendering of the hymn into English.

2. **The strife is o'er, the battle done.** By F. Pott. Made about 1859, and 1st pub. in his *Hys. fitted to the Order of Com. Prayer*, 1861, No. 91. In the same year it was given with extensive alterations in *H. A. & M.*, No. 114. This altered text has failed to commend itself to later compilers both in G. Britain and America, and the original *tr.* is given in most of the numerous hymnals which have adopted the hymn, in both countries. In the revised ed. of *H. A. & M.* the text is again altered, and st. iv. is omitted.

3. **No more of strife, no more of pain.** Anonymous in the *Parish H. Bk.*, 1863, No. 56, and again in the *Sarum Hymnal*, 1868.

Translations not in C. U. :—
1. Alleluia, Alleluia, for the battle now is o'er. *J. W. Hewett*, 1859.
2. The battle now is done. *H. Bonar*, 1857. [J. J.]

Findlater, Sarah. [See **Borthwick, Jane.**]

Finx, Erasmus, was b. at Lübeck, Nov. 19, 1627. After studying law at various universities and acting for some time as travelling tutor, he settled at Nürnberg as writer and corrector for the press, remaining there till his death, Dec. (Oct.?) 20, 1694. Under the name of Francisci (from his father's Christian name of Francis) he published a large number of historical and religious works. Of his some 200 hymns, which mostly appeared interspersed in his devotional works, two have passed into English :—

i. **O Herr gieb Acht.** [*Christian Warfare.*] In his *Ruhestunden*, pt. iii. p. 1007, Leipzig, 1680, in 12 st. *Tr.* as, "Lord, watch each hour," as No. 689 in pt. i. of the *Moravian H. Bk.*, 1754.

ii. **O wie ist der Weg so schmal.** [*The Narrow Way.*] In his *Gold-Kammer*, pt. iii. p. 303, Nürnberg, 1668, in 8 st. *Tr.* as, "O how narrow is the way," by *Miss Warner*, 1858 (ed. 1861, p. 445). [J. M.]

Firm was my health, my day was bright. *I. Watts.* [*Ps. xxx.*] Appeared in his *Psalms of David*, 1719, in 6 st. of 4 l., as a paraphrase of a portion of the 30th Psalm. In the *Anglican H. Bk.*, 1868, it is altered to " *My health was firm, my day was bright.*" Its use in either form is not extensive. [J. J.]

Fischer, Albert Friedrich Wilhelm, D.D., was b. April 18, 1829, at Ziesar, Brandenburg, and studied at the University of Halle. Since 1877 he has been chief pastor and superintendent at Gross-Ottersleben near Magdeburg.

He claims notice here as author of the *Kirchenlieder-Lexicon*, pub. at Gotha, in 2 vols., 1878–1879. Arranged somewhat on the plan of the present *Dictionary of Hymnology*, it contains notes on some 4500 German hymns (together with notes on a few Greek and Latin hymns, which are the originals of some of the German texts); the plan of selection being to annotate hymns found in the best hymn-books that have been in use in the Prussian province of Saxony from the Reformation to the present time. It is the first work in German that has attempted, on any large scale, to give critical detailed notes on individual hymns, and may be pronounced indispensable to the student of German Hymnology. Wherever the data given in this *Dictionary* may be found to differ it is as the result of later investigations.

Dr. Fischer was also the founder (1883), and is at present joint-editor of the *Blätter für Hymnologie* (now appearing monthly at Altenburg, and frequently referred to in these pages), the first German magazine devoted entirely to Hymnology.

In recognition of his services to *Hymnology* the degree of D.D. was conferred on him by the University of Jena in 1884. [J. M.]

Fischer, Christoph. [**Vischer, C.**]

Fitch, Eleazar Thompson, D.D. Born at New Haven, Jan. 1, 1791, and graduated at Yale College, 1810. In 1817 he was appointed Professor of Divinity in Yale, and retained the Professorship to 1863. Died Jan. 31, 1871. His published works include *Sermons*, &c. With Dr. Bacon and others he compiled the Connecticut Congregational *Psalms & Hymns*, 1845, and contributed to it 3 psalm versions and 3 hymns. Of these the following are in use : (1) "Lord, at this closing hour." (*Close of Divine Service.*) This is extensively used in America, and is also found in the English Presb. *Ps. & Hys.*, 1867. (2) "The God of Peace, Who from the dead." (*Close of Divine Service.*) (3) "By vows of love together bound." (*Holy Matrimony.*) [F. M. B.]

Fixed firmly His [God's] foundations keep. *R. Mant, Bp.* [*Ps. lxxxvii.*] Appeared in his *Book of Psalms in an English Metrical Version*, &c., 1824, pp. 296–298, in 7 st. of 4 l., as a L.M. paraphrase of Ps. lxxxvii. In 1863, st. i., ii., v. and vii., slightly altered as : "Fixed firmly *God's* foundations keep," were given in *Kennedy*, No. 904. [J. J.]

Flagrans amore, perditos. [*Lazarus, Mary and Martha visited by Christ.*] This hymn is appointed for use at 1st Vespers on the Feast of St. Lazarus, &c., in the revised *Paris Brev.*, 1736; and also in the *Lyons* and other modern French Brevs. It previously appeared in the *Cluniac Brev.*, 1686, p. 1068. Full text in Card. Newman's *Hymni Ecclesiae*, 1838–1865. It has been *tr.* as :—

As Jesus sought His wandering sheep. By I. Williams. 1st pub. in the *British Magazine*, May, 1836 (vol. ix. p. 504); and again in his *Hys. tr. from the Parisian Brev.*, 1839, p. 241, in 5 st. of 4 l. In 1841 it was given in the *Child's Christian Year*, and later in a few collections in G. Britain and America. [J. J.]

Flatman, Thomas, poet and miniature painter, was b. in London, cir. 1633, and d. cir. 1688. He was a barrister of the Inner Temple, but gave most of his time to poetry and painting. He was the author of some Pindaric Odes on the deaths of Prince Rupert, and of Charles II.; and of a prose satire on Richard Cromwell. His *Poems & Songs* were pub. in 1674 (3rd ed. 1682), and from this volume the following hymns have been transferred to Dr. Martineau's *Hymns*, 1840, and his *Hymns of Praise and Prayer*, 1873:—"Awake, my soul, awake, mine eyes" (*Morning*); "Sweet slumbers, come and chase away" (*Evening*). The similarity of these hymns to the Morning and Evening hymns of Bp. Ken suggests the possibility that they may have inspired the latter. Flatman's "Thoughts on Death" also contains the germ of Pope's "Vital Spark," &c., q.v.   [J. J.]

Fleet, John George, was b. in London on the 8th of July, 1818. At 15 years of age he was removed from school to his father's counting-house, and at 17 he had to undertake, through his father's death, the sole control of the business, and from that time he followed commercial pursuits. At an early age he joined as teacher in a small Sunday School which his sister had begun in Lime Street, London. His interest in Sunday Schools which was thus awakened led him, with some young fellow-teachers, to found the Church Sunday School Institute in 1843. Of that Institute he was honorary Secretary for 20 years; and for 15 years he was Editor of the *Church Sunday School Quarterly*. To the hymn-book pub. by the Institute, *The Church Sunday School Hymn Book*, 1848, he contributed the following hymns by which he is known to hymnology:—

1. How faint and feeble is the praise: *Angels' Worship*.
2. Let children to their God draw near. *Children's Worship*.
3. O Lord, our God, Thy wondrous might. *Collect 7th S. after Trinity*.
4. Source of life, and light, and love. *A Teacher's Prayer*.
5. What mercies, Lord, Thou hast in store. *Collect for 6th S. after Trinity*.
6. Words are things of little cost. *Sins of the Tongue*.

In addition to these hymns, Mr. Fleet contributed several to *The Church S. S. Quarterly* in 1852-3-8, and 1861, and has pub. a small vol. of poems and hymns entitled *Lux in Tenebris*, 1873.   [J. J.]

Fleming, Abraham, was a classical scholar, translator, and miscellaneous writer of the 16th cent., the dates of whose birth and death are unknown. He was for some time Rector of St. Pancras. He edited many of the classics with notes, and published also some original works. Amongst the latter there are:—

A Memorial of the Charitable Almes Deedes of William Lambe, gentleman of the Chapel Royal under Henry VIII., and citizen of London, 8vo, 1580. *The Diamant of Devotion*, 12mo, 1586; and *The Condyt of Comfort*. A hymn of his which appeared in *The Diamant of Devotion*, 1586, was republished by E. Farr, in *Select Poetry, chiefly Devotional, of the Reign of Queen Elizabeth*, 1841, p. 545 (Parker Society). [English Hymnody, Early, § vii.]   [J. J.]

Flemming, Paul, s. of Abraham Flemming or Fleming, then schoolmaster at Hartenstein, near Zwickau, Saxony (afterwards pastor of Wechselburg, near Mittweida), was b. at Hartenstein, Oct. $\frac{5}{15}$, 1609. He entered the St. Thomas School, Leipzig, in 1623, and matriculated at the University of Leipzig at Michaelmas, 1626. At the University he devoted himself to the study of medicine and of poetry, being laureated as a poet in 1631, and graduating M.A. in 1632. In order to find refuge from the troubles of the Thirty Years' War

he went to Holstein in 1633. In the same year he joined an embassy which Duke Friedrich of Schleswig-Holstein was about to send to his brother-in-law, the Russian Czar, as gentleman in waiting and "taster." In this expedition he was engaged from Oct. 22, 1633, to April 6, 1635. He then took part in the embassy sent by the Duke to the Shah of Persia, with the object of opening up the way for trade and Christianity into Central Asia. They set sail from Travemünde, near Lübeck, Oct. 27, 1635, and returned to Gottorf, Aug. 1, 1639. The expedition proved fruitless, and the many dangers and great hardships encountered broke Flemming's health. To qualify himself for medical practice in Hamburg he went to the University of Leyden, where he graduated M.D. in 1640; but shortly after his return to Hamburg he d. there, March 25 (April 2), 1640 (*Koch*, iii. 73–82; *Allg. Deutsche Biog.*, vii. 115–117).

Flemming was of an energetic temperament, with an ardent patriotism, and a deep love for the Evangelical Cause. He was a gifted poet, of true and deep feeling, who could write charming descriptions of the beauties of nature, and sweet and tender love songs. His secular poems, however, as a whole have the faults of the Silesian school of Martin Opitz; and it is by his hymns, and especially by his classical "In allen meinen Thaten," that his name lives.

His poems were first collected by the father of his betrothed as *D. P. Fleming's Teutsche Poemata*, and appeared in 1642 in two editions nearly alike, one at Naumburg and Jena, the other at Lübeck. The most complete ed. is that by J. M. Lappenberg, 2 vols., Stuttgart, 1865–66. Of his 41 religious poems (12 hymns, 9 odes, 20 sonnets) three have passed into English.

i. **In allen meinen Thaten.** *Trust in God.* This beautiful hymn was written in Nov., 1633, just before he started with the embassy to Moscow (see above); and may often have cheered his own sinking spirit then and in the more trying adventures of the second embassy. It 1st appeared in his *Teutsche Poemata*, 1642 (Lübeck ed. p. 287; Lappenberg's ed., i. p. 236), as No. 4 in Book i. of the Odes, in 15 st. of 6 l. It was included in the *Stralsund G. B.*, 1665, Freylinghausen's *G. B.*, 1704, and almost all recent collections. Sometimes, as in the *Unv. L. S.*, 1851, No. 646, it is given in full, but more frequently the special stanzas appropriate for travellers (vi.–ix., xiii., xiv.) are omitted. It is characterised in *Koch*, viii. 379, as a "pilgrim song suited for the Christian journey which we must all in faith make through joy and sorrow to our Eternal Home." *Lauxmann* adds that it has often been used appropriately at weddings, was the favourite hymn of Friedrich Wilhelm III. of Prussia, and was sung at the service in the Cathedral of Berlin, July 19, 1870, on the opening of the North German Diet immediately before the Franco-Prussian War. *Tr.* as:—

I leave to His good pleasure, a *tr.* of st. i., ii., iv., by A. T. Russell, as No. 232 in his *Ps. & Hys.*, 1851.

Other trs. are : (1) "In all my plans, Thou Highest," by *Dr. H. Mills*, 1856, p. 167. (2) "Where'er I go, whate'er my task," by *Miss Winkworth*, 1858, p. 108, repeated in L. Rehfuess's *Ch. at Sea*, 1868, p. 9. (3) "In every deed and word," in Madame de Pontes's *Poets & Poetry of Germany*, 1858, vol. i. p. 416.

His hymns not in English C. U. are:—

ii. **Ist's möglich, dass der Hass auch kann geliebet**

sein. *The Love of God.* In the *Lübeck* edition, 1642, p. 555 (*Lappenberg's* ed., i. p. 450), as No. 16 in Bk. i. of the Sonnets. *Tr.* as, "Can it then be that hate should e'er be loved," by *Miss Winkworth*, 1869, p. 175.

iii. **Lass dich nur Nichts nicht tauren.** *Cross and Consolation.* Probably written in Persia during the second embassy. In the *Lübeck* edition, 1642, p. 283 (*Lappenberg's* ed., i. p. 244), as No. 1 in Bk. i. of the Odes, in 3 st. of 6 l. The *trs.* are : (1) "Only let nothing grieve thee," by *Madame de Pontes*, 1858, v. i. p. 415. (2) "Let nothing make thee sad or fretful," by *Miss Winkworth*, 1869, p. 175.   **[J. M.]**

Fletcher, Phineas, ·s. of Dr. Giles Fletcher and cousin of John Fletcher, the dramatic poet, b. 1582, and educated at Eton and King's College, Cambridge. In 1621 he took Holy Orders, and having obtained the living of Helgay, Norfolk, he retained the same nearly 29 years. He d. at Helgay, 1650. His best known poem is, *The Purple Island,* 1633, an allegorical description of man, in the style of Spenser. This was reprinted in 1783. His *Locustes or Apollyonists,* a satire against the Jesuits, suggested to Milton some ideas for his *Paradise Lost.* His 6 psalms, 1st pub. in his *Purple Island,* 1633, were reprinted by Dr. Grosart in his reprint of Fletcher's *Poetical Works.* [English Hymnody, Early, § VII.] **[J. J.]**

Fletcher, Samuel, b. at Compton, near Wolverhampton, in 1785, and educated at the Wolverhampton Grammar School. In 1805 he went to Manchester, and entering into business, he gradually rose to a position of wealth and influence. He d. at Manchester, Oct. 13, 1863. Although engaged in extensive mercantile pursuits he took an active interest in literature, and was one of the chief promoters of Owens College, Manchester. His hymns appeared in a small collection which he prepared during an illness, for use in his own family, and subsequently pub. as *Family Praise,* 1850. From this collection the following hymns have come into C. U. :—

1. **Father of light and life.** *Family Worship, Morning.*
2. **Lord, as a family we meet.** *Family Worship.*

These hymns were given in the *New Cong.,* 1859. Miller's note on Mr. Fletcher (*Singers and Songs,* &c.), and an article in *Good Words,* July, 1864, are well written and full of information.   **[J. J.]**

Flint, James, D.D., b. at Reading, Mass., 1779, and graduated at Harvard, 1802. In 1806 he became pastor of a Unitarian Church at East Bridgewater, Mass., from which he passed to East Church, Salem, 1821. Died in 1855. In 1820 he contributed one hymn to *Sewell's New York Coll.,* and in 1843 he also pub. *A Collection of Hymns,* to which he contributed from 10 to 12 originals. His best known hymns are :—

1. **Here to the High and Holy One.** This hymn, "On leaving an Ancient Church," appeared in the *Cambridge Selection* of 1828.
2. **In pleasant lands have fallen the lines.** *Remembrance of our Fathers.* Written for the bicentenary of Quincy, Mass., May 25, 1840, and pub. in his *Coll.,* 1843.
3. **Happy the unrepining poor.** Appeared in Sewell's *New York Collection,* 1820. Dr. Flint's hymns are unknown to the English Collections.   **[F. M. B.]**

Flitner, Johann, was b. Nov. 1, 1618, at Suhl, Saxony, where his father was an iron-

master. After studying theology at Wittenberg, Jena, Leipzig, and Rostock, he became in 1644 precentor, and in 1646 diaconus at Grimmen, near Greifswald. On the outbreak of the first Prusso-Swedish war he was forced to flee to Stralsund, but returned to Grimmen in May, 1660. At the death of his senior in 1664, he ought, according to custom, to have been appointed town preacher, but was passed over not only then but also in 1673 and 1676, when the post again became vacant. The outbreak of the second Prusso-Swedish war, immediately after this third disappointment, forced him again to flee to Stralsund, where he d. Jan. 7, 1678 (*Koch,* ii. 442–445; Mohnike's *Hymnol. Forschungen,* pt. ii., 1832, pp. 3 51). His hymns seem to have been written during his enforced leisure at Stralsund. They appeared, with melodies, entitled *Suscitabulum Musicum,* as pt v. of his *Himlisches Lust-Gärtlein.* Greifswald, 1661 (Hamburg Library). The only one *tr.* into English is :—

Ach was soll ich Sünder machen. [*Lent.*] The most popular of his hymns. Appeared 1661 as above, p. 462, in 7 st. of 6 l., each st. ending "Meinen Jesum lass ich nicht" (see note on *Keymann*) and with the motto "Omnia si perdam, Jesum servare studebo !" Included in the *Leipzig Vorrath,* 1673, No. 1089, and recently in the *Unv. L. S.* 1851, No. 357. The only *tr.* in C. U. is :—

What shall I a sinner do ? A good *tr.,* omitting st. vi., as No. 110 in Miss Winkworth's *C. B. for England,* 1863.

Another tr. is : "What to do in my condition," in the *Supplement to German Psalmody,* ed. 1765, p. 48.   **[J. M.]**

Floods of waters high in air. *T. Whytehead.* [*Monday.*] Appeared in his *Poems,* 1842, No. xxv., in 5 st. of 5 l., and entitled "The Firmament." Although not given in the *Poems* as a *tr.* of *Immense coeli Conditor* (q. v.), it is evidently based upon that ancient hymn. In its original form it is not in common use. The altered version, "Lo! the firmament doth bear," was given in the *Hymnary,* 1872, as the hymn for "Monday Evening." Its use is limited.   **[J. J.]**

Flowerdew, Alice, was b. in 1759, and married to Mr. Daniel Flowerdew, who for a few years held a Government appointment in Jamaica, and d. in 1801. After his decease Mrs. Flowerdew kept a Ladies' Boarding-school at Islington. During her residence at Islington she was a member of the General Baptist congregation, in Worship Street (now at Bethnal Green Road). Subsequently she removed to Bury St. Edmunds, and some years later to Ipswich, where she d. Sept. 23, 1830. In 1803 she pub. a small volume of *Poems on Moral and Religious Subjects.* This work reached a 3rd ed. in 1811, and in that ed. appeared her well-known harvest hymn, "Fountain of mercy, God of love," q.v. Mrs. Flowerdew's maiden name has not been ascertained.   **[W. R. S.]**

Foleshill, a *nom de plume* of Jonathan Evans, in *The Christian Magazine,* 1790–1793.

Folget mir, ruft uns das Leben. *J. Rist.* [*Following Christ.*] 1st pub. as No. 1 in the "Viertes Zehen" of his *Himlische Lieder,* Lüneburg, 1642, in 16 st. of 8 l., entitled, "A devout hymn to God for the following of Christ in true godliness and all good works." Included in Freylinghausen's *G. B.*, 1704, No. 393, omitting st. x., xi., and this form was repeated in most subsequent colls., and is No. 307 in the *Unv. L. S.*, 1851. The only *tr.* in C. U. is :—

Follow me, in me ye live. A good *tr.* of st. i.-iii., vi., vii., ix., xv., xvi., by Miss Winkworth in the 1st Series of *Lyra Ger.*, 1855, p. 188, entitled "St. Andrew's Day." Her st. i., v., vi. are included in *Kennedy*, 1863 ; and her st. vii., viii., with a st. from her ii., iv., v. beginning, "Saviour, meet it is indeed," in the Pennsylvania *Luth. H. Bk.*, 1865.   [J. M.]

Follen, Eliza Lee, née Cabot, a well-known Unitarian writer, daughter of Samuel Cabot, b. at Boston, August 15, 1787, and married, in 1828, to Professor Charles Follen, who perished on board the "Lexington," which was burnt on Long Island Sound, Jan. 13, 1840. Mrs. Follen d. at Brookline, Mass., 1860. She was a voluminous writer. Her *Poems* were first pub. at Boston (Crosby & Co.), 1839, and whilst she was in England she issued another volume for children's use, entitled *The Lark and the Linnet*, in 1854. Both volumes also contain some translations from the German, and versions of a few Psalms. Her best known hymns are :—

1. How sweet to be allowed to pray. *Resignation.* Appeared in the *Christian Disciple*, Sept., 1818, and in her *Poems*, 1839, p. 116, in 4 st. of 4 l., and entitled, "Thy will be done."

2. How sweet upon this sacred day. *Sunday.* In her *Poems*, 1839, pp. 113–114, in 6 st. of 4 l., and entitled "Sabbath Day." It previously appeared in *Sabbath Recreations*, 1829.

3. Lord, deliver, Thou canst save. *Prayer for the Slave.* Found in *Songs of the Free*, 1836 ; but is not given in her *Poems*, 1839. In Adams and Chapin's *Hys. for Christian Devotion*, Boston, U.S., 1846, it is No. 802, in 5 st. of 4 l. In common with No. 2 it has found acceptance outside Unitarian Collections.

4. God, Thou art good, each perfumed flower. This is the original of J. H. Gurney's hymn, "Yes, God is good," &c. (q.v.) There is some obscurity about the text. It is found in her *Hymns for Children*, Boston, 1825, beginning, "God is good, each perfumed flower," and this obvious misprint (which destroys the metre) was usually copied in later books. It is also given with the same first line as an original piece, never before published, and signed "E. L. C." (initials of Mrs. Follen's maiden name), in Emily Taylor's *Sabbath Recreations*, Wellington, Salop, 1826, p. 203. This suggests that it was printed in the American book after the MS. was posted to England. Mrs. Follen may have written at first "Yes, God is good," but this cannot now be determined. It begins, "God, Thou art good," &c., in her *Poems*, 1839, p. 119, and in her verses, *The Lark and the Linnet*, &c., 1854, and in each case is in 6 st. of 4 l., with the title, "God is Good."

5. Will God, Who made the earth and sea. *A Child's Prayer.* Given in her *Poems*, 1839, p. 164, in 7 st. of 4 l. In Dr. Allon's *Children's Worship*, 1878, No. 212, it is abbreviated to 4 st. (i.-iv.), and attributed to "*H. Bateman*" in error.   [F. M. B.]

For all Thy love and goodness, so bountiful and free. [*Spring.*] This hymn is based upon one written by Mrs. Frances Jane Douglas, *née* How, in 1848, and pub. in her *April Verses*. The original was rewritten by Mrs. Douglas's brother, Bp. W. W. How, for the S. P. C. K. *Church Hys.*, 1871. Its use has extended to several hymn-books notwithstanding its awkward metre and faulty rhythm.   [J. J.]

For all Thy Saints, a noble throng. *Cecil F. Alexander.* [*St. James.*] Contributed to *H. A. & M.*, revised ed., 1875, and repeated in Mrs. Brock's *Children's H. Bk.*, 1881.

For all Thy saints, O Lord [God]. *Bp. R. Mant.* [*All Saints.*] An original hymn given with his *trs.* in his *Ancient Hymns*, &c., 1837, p. 80 (ed. 1871, p. 139), in 6 st. of 4 l., and entitled, "Hymn on All Saints." The form in which it usually appears, in 4 st., was given in the S. P. C. K. *Hymns*, &c., 1852. In addition the following arrangements are also in C. U. :—

1. For Thy dear saint, O Lord. This was given in *H. A. & M.*, 1861, No. 273. It is composed of st. i.-iii., v., of Bp. Mant's hymn, but considerably altered, and the substitution of another doxology.

2. For Thy true servants, Lord. This text in the Toronto *Church H. Bk.*, 1862, is the *H. A. & M.* text slightly altered.

3. For this, Thy saint, O Lord. Another altered text in Skinner's *Daily Service Hyl.*, 1864.

Of these arrangements, the S. P. C. K. is most popular, both in G. Britain and America. It sometimes reads, "For all Thy saints, O God."   [J. J.]

For all Thy [the] saints who from their labours rest. *Bp. W. W. How.* [*Saints' Days.*] 1st pub. in *Hymn for Saints' Day, and Other Hymns. By a Layman* [Earl Nelson], 1864, in 11 st. of 3 l., and the refrain "Alleluia." It was republished in *Lyra Britannica*, 1867 ; in the *Sarum Hymnal*, 1868 ; in the 1869 *Appendix* to the S. P. C. K. *Ps. & Hys.*, and subsequently in nearly every hymnal of importance published in G. Britain. It is also found in the best collections of all English-speaking countries, and, with hymnal compilers, it is one of the most popular of the author's compositions. It is sometimes given in American hymnals (as it is in the S. P. C. K. *Church Hys.*), as "For all *the* saints," &c., this being Bishop How's revised reading. In the Protestant Episcopal *Hymnal*, 1872, st. iii.-v. are given as a separate hymn (No. 186), beginning, "For the Apostles' glorious company." Orig. text as above. Authorized text in S. P. C. K. *Church Hymns.*   [J. J.]

For ever blessed be the Lord. *I. Watts.* [*Ps. cxliv.*] In his *Psalms of David*, 1719, this version in 3 st. of 4 l. forms the first of three C.M. hymns on Ps. cxliv., and is accompanied with the following note :—

"The sense of a great part of this Psalm is found often repeated in the Book of Psalms. I have therefore only taken three small parts of it, and form'd three distinct hymns on very different subjects."

Although frequently found in the older collections its modern use is limited.   [J. J.]

For ever we would gaze on Thee. *A. W. Chatfield.* [*Transfiguration.*] Written in March, 1874, "whilst journeying to, and attending at the Assize Court at Shrewsbury." and 1st pub. in the revised ed. of *H. A. & M.*, 1875, No. 461.

For ever will I bless the Lord. *J. Conder.* [*Ps. xxxiv.*] 1st pub. in his *Star in the East with Other Poems*, 1824, pp. 34–37, in 8 st. of 6 l. In 1836 it was repeated in his *Cong. H. Bk.*, No. 402, with the change of st. iii. l. 5, "*Oh*," to "*Then* try," &c., and st. vi., l. 3, of "The wicked *sin*," to "The wicked *sink*," and in 1856 this corrected form was given in his *Hys. of Praise, Prayer*, &c., p. 11, as the authorised text. In modern hymnals two centos are given from this hymn : (1) That in the *New Cong.*, 1859, No. 402, composed of st. i., ii., iii., vi. and vii.; and (2) "For ever I will bless the Lord," in *Kennedy*, 1863, No. 1348, st. i., iii., iv. and vii.   [J. J.]

For ever with the Lord. *J. Montgomery.* [*Heaven anticipated.*] 1st pub. in *The Amethyst*, an annual, in 1835, and again in the author's *Poet's Portfolio*, in the same year, p. 233, in 22 st. of 4 l., unequally divided into two parts, and headed, "At Home in Heaven, 1 Thess. iv. 17." It was repeated in his *Poetical Works*, 1841, p. 267; and in his *Original Hymns*, 1853, p. 231. In this last the second stanza of pt. ii. is omitted. Numerous centos from this hymn are in C. U., all except four beginning with st. i., but varying in length and arrangement. In America especially these centos have attained great popularity. The cento "Beneath the star-lit arch," in Beecher's *Plymouth Coll.*, 1855, is composed of st. vii., xii., xiii. and xxi. slightly altered. In Martineau's *Hymns*, &c., 1840 and 1873, there are also two centos from this hymn : (1) "In darkness as in light"; and (2) "My Father's house on high," and in the Presbyterian *Ps. & Hys. for the Worship of God*, Richmond, U.S.A., 1867, a third, (3) "My thirsty spirit faints."   [J. J.]

For mercies countless as the sands. *J. Newton.* [*Praise.*] Appeared in the *Olney Hymns*, 1779, Bk. i., No. 50, in 5 st. of 4 l., and based upon Ps. cxvi. 12, 13. Its use both in the older, and in modern collections both in G. Britain and America, is extensive. Orig. text in *H. Comp.*, No. 501.

The authorship of this hymn is sometimes attributed to W. Cowper, the poet, but in error. It is not given in any of the collected works of Cowper, and his signature in the *Olney Hymns* "C." is not added to this hymn, in any edition with which we are acquainted, and certainly not in the first of 1779. We attribute it to *J. Newton* on the ground that all unsigned hymns in the *Olney* are claimed by him.   [J. J.]

For Sion's sake I will not cease. *C. Wesley.* [*Missions.*] A poem on Ps. lxii., in 29 st. of 4 l., which appeared in *Hymns and Sacred Poems*, 1749, vol. i. Sometime after J. Wesley's death, probably about 1800, a cento therefrom was given in the *Wes. H. Bk.*, No. 149, beginning, "Thus saith the Lord, 'tis God's command." It is composed of st. xxi., xxiii.–xxvii., somewhat altered. Orig. text, *P. Works*, 1868–72, vol. iv. p. 312–316. In the revised ed., 1875, this cento was omitted in favour of "Why not now, my God, my God," which was formerly No. 411. [J. J.]

For Thy mercy and Thy grace. *H. Downton.* [*Old and New Year.*] Written in

1841, and 1st pub. in the *Church of England Magazine*, in 1843. p. 15, in 7 st. of 4 l., and entitled, "A Hymn for the commencement of the Year." In 1851 it was republished with one alteration, and the omission of st. ii. and iii., in A. Tozer Russell's *Ps. & Hys.* This was reproduced, with further alterations, in *H. A. & M.*, 1861. Numerous versions exist in modern hympals, Russell's abridged text, as in the *Sarum Hymnal*, being most in favour. In 1873 the author included it in its original form, with two unimportant alterations, in his *Hymns and Verses*, &c., pp. 7, 8. Orig. text as above, authorised text in Thring's *Coll.*, 1882, and the *Westminster Abbey H. Bk.*, 1883. The doxology sometimes added thereto as in *Church Hymns*, 1071, is not in the original and is seldom adopted. The hymn, in its various forms and readings, is the most popular, and most widely used of Mr. Downton's productions.   [J. J.]

Ford, Charles Lawrence, B.A., s. of Mr. W. Ford, artist, of Bath, was b. at Bath in 1830. Mr. Ford is a graduate of the London University, and is engaged in scholastic work. In 1862 he contributed several poetical pieces to Canon Baynes's *Lyra Anglicana*, in 1865 to his *English Lyrics*, and also to the *Illustrated Book of Sacred Poetry*, N.D. Mr. Ford's hymns and poems were collected and pub. as *Lyra Christi*, 1874. From these works the following have come into C. U. :—

1. Father, for Thy kindest word. (1862.) *Strength in Weakness.*

2. Lord, from this time we cry to Thee. *Christ the Guide of Youth.*

3. O Thou, by Whom the balm is borne. *In Affliction.*

4. This is my Body which is given for you. *H. Communion.*   [J. J.]

Forgive, blest shade, the tributary tear. *Anne Steele.* [*Death and Burial.*] In 1760 Miss Steele pub. in her *Poems on Subjects Chiefly Devotional*, &c., vol. ii. p. 71, an ode "On the death of Mr. Hervey," in 9 st. of 4 l., and beginning, "O Hervey, honoured name, forgive the tear." From this ode st. i., ii. are taken, altered to "Forgive, blest shade, the tributary tear," and used as a hymn in a few collections, including Ellen Courtauld's *Ps., Hys.*, &c., 1853, and the American *Church Pastorals*, Boston, 1864.   [J. J.]

Forgive, O Lord, our frailties [wanderings] past. [*Before Holy Communion.*] This hymn 1st appeared as a leaflet, and was then included in the *Foundling Coll.*, 1796 (but without music), in the following form :—

"BEFORE THE SACRAMENT. Dr. Cook.

Solo.

"Forgive, O Lord, our frailties past,
    Henceforth we will obey thy call ;
Our sins far from us let us cast,
    And turn to thee, devoutly all.

Chorus.

"Then with archangels we shall sing,
    Praises to heav'n's eternal King.

Duet.

"Hear us, O Lord, in mercy hear,
    Our guilt with sorrow we deplore ;
Pity our anguish, calm our fear,
    And give us grace to sin no more.

Chorus.

"Then with archangels we shall sing,
    Praises to heav'n's eternal King.

Solo.
" While at yon altar's foot we kneel,
And of the holy rite partake,
Our pardon, Lord, vouchsafe to seal,
For Jesus, our Redeemer's sake.
Chorus.
" Then with archangels we shall sing,
Praises to heav'n's eternal King."

In the following year, 1797, it was retained in the *Foundling Coll.* in the same form. The last stanza, however, was omitted in the ed. of 1801, but restored again in 1809. In 1810 it was given in the Rev. J. Kempthorne's *Psalms and Hymns*, as, " Forgive, O Lord, our wanderings past," No. clxviii., and the alteration of st. ii. l. 2, to " *With sorrow we our guilt deplore.*" From Kempthorne's *Ps. & Hys.* it has passed into a few collections, but usually in an altered form as in the *Irish Church Hymnal*, 1873, and others. The scarcity of the *Foundling Coll.* musical eds. of 1796 and 1809, and of the book of words only, eds. of 1797 and 1801, led most writers into the error of concluding that it was first printed in 1809, and that, having been included in J. Kempthorne's *Ps. & Hys.*, 1810, and thence passed into other collections, it was an original hymn by Kempthorne. All the evidence which we possess is against Kempthorne's claims, and we must designate it as " *Anon. Foundling Coll.*, 1796." [W. T. B.]

Forgive them, O my Father. *Cecil F. Alexander.* [*Good Friday.*] Contributed to the revised ed. of *H. A. & M.*, 1875, in 6 st. of 4 l., and based on the words " Father, forgive them, for they know not what they do." In 1881 it was repeated in Mrs. Brock's *Children's H. Bk.*, and is also found in one or two American collections. [J. J.]

Forsaken once, and thrice denied. *Cecil F. Alexander.* [*St. Peter.*] Contributed to the revised ed. of *H. A. & M.*, 1875, No. 416, and repeated in Mrs. Brock's *Children's H. Bk.*, 1881.

Forsyth, Christina, daughter of Thomas Forsyth, and sister of W. Forsyth, Q.C., sometime member for Cambridge, was b. in Liverpool in 1825, and d. at Hastings, March 16, 1859. During a long and painful illness she composed several hymns and poems which were issued as leaflets. These were collected after her death, and pub. in 1861, as *Hymns by C. F.* (*Lyra Brit.*, 1867, p. 233). From this volume the following have passed into a few collections :—

1. *Himself hath done it all.* O how those words. *Resignation.*
2. *Jehovah Elohim! Creator great.* *Names of Jehovah.*
3. *O Holy Spirit, now descend on me.* *Presence of the Holy Spirit desired.*
4. *O what a happy lot is mine.* *Union with Christ.*
[J. J.]

Fortem virili pectore. *Card. Silvio Antoniano.* [*Holy Women.*] Included by Pope Clement VIII. in the *Roman Breviary*, Venice, 1603, f. 37 b., in the Common, as the hymn for 1st and 2nd Vespers, and at Lauds in the Office for the Common of Holy Women. It is also in other Breviaries ; *Daniel*, iv. p. 311, and Card. Newman's *Hymni Ecclesiae*, 1838–65. The author, Cardinal Silvio Antoniano, was b. at Rome in 1540. Through

the influence and patronage of Pope Pius IV. he became Professor of the Belles Lettres in the Collegio Romano, and subsequently rose to be the head of the college, and a cardinal. He d. in 1603. [W. A. S.]

Translations in C. U. :—
1. **High let us all our voices raise.** By E. Caswall. 1st pub. in his *Lyra Catholica*, 1849, p. 223, in 5 st. of 4 l. It has been included in the *Hys. for the Year*, and other Roman Catholic collections for Missions and Schools; and in the *People's H.*, 1867, and other Anglican hymnbooks. In Caswall's *Hys. & Poems*, 1873, p. 118, another *tr.* in S.M. is substituted for this. It begins, " Laud we the saints most sweet."
2. **This woman more than woman strong.** By J. R. Beste, in his *Church Hymns*. 1849, p. 59.
3. **O'er all the Church thy praise be told.** By R. Campbell, in his *Hys. & Anthems*, 1850, in 5 st. of 4 l. In connection with this *tr.* there are two centos which must be noted. The first is No. 87 in the *Hymnal for the use of St. John the Evangelist*, &c., Aberdeen, 1870. This is composed of st. i. this *tr.*, st. ii.–iv. from the *People's H.* as above. The second is No. 417, in the *Hymnary*, 1872, beginning, " To share the Lamb's high marriage rites." The first stanza of this cento is J. D. Chambers's *tr.* of " Ad nuptias Agni Pater " (*Lauda Syon*, pt. ii., 1866, p. 47), and the remaining stanzas are this *tr.* by R. Campbell, slightly altered.
4. **How blest the matron, who, endued.** By the Compilers of *H. A. & M.*, 1861. [J. J.]

Fortes cadendo Martyres. *Jean Baptiste de Santeüil.* [*Many Martyrs.*] Appeared in the *Cluniac Breviary*, 1686, p. xxvii., and in his *Hymni Sacri et Novi*, 1689 (ed. 1698, p. 245). It was given in the *Paris Breviary*, 1736, and is also in Card. Newman's *Hymni Ecclesiae*, 1838 and 1865. *Tr.* as :—
Of the martyrs we sing. By I. Williams in his *Hys. tr. from the Parisian Breviary*, 1839, p. 287, in 8 st. of 4 l. This, abbreviated to 6 st., and altered, is No. 201 in Skinner's *Daily Service Hymnal*, 1864
Another tr. is :—
The valiant martyr-host to praise. *J. D. Chambers*, 1866, p. 16. [J. J.]

Forth from the dark and stormy sky. *Bp. R. Heber.* [*Lent.*] Appeared in his *Hymns*, &c., 1827, in 2 st. of 6 l., and appointed for the 2nd Sun. after Trinity. It was also included in the 1842 ed. of the same. The use of this hymn has been very varied. In the *New Mitre*, and Thring's *Coll.*, it is appointed for " Holy Communion " (its claim thereto being evidently the second line of st. i., " Lord, to Thine altar's shade we flee," and the concluding line of each stanza, " Turn not, O Lord, Thy guests away "): whilst in *Kennedy* it is given for " Passion Week," and in other collections for different seasons. In most cases the text is unaltered, as in Thring's *Coll.*, 1882, No. 532. Its American use is extensive. [J. J.]

Forth in Thy Name, O Lord, I go. *C. Wesley.* [*Morning.*] 1st pub. in *Hymns and Sac. Poems*, 1749, vol. i. p. 246. " For Believers Before Work," No. 144, in 6 st. of 4 l. It was included in the *Wes. H. Bk.*, in 1780, with the omission of st. iii. It has come into most extensive use both in G. Britain and America. In common with many of the older hymns it has undergone alterations at various hands. The line which has given the greatest trouble to the compilers is, "And prove Thy acceptable will." This has undergone many changes, but that given in the *Leeds H. Bk.*, in 1853, "And prove Thy *good and perfect* will," has been received by common consent as the best and most musical reading. Orig. text, *P. Works*, 1868–72, vol. v. p. 50. The doxology in *H. A. & M.* and some other collections is not in the original. In 1767, R. Conyers gave it in his *Coll.* as "Forth in Thy *strength*, O Lord, *we go*," but this alteration has passed out of use.   [J. J.]

Forth to the land of promise bound. *H. Alford.* [*Life a Pilgrimage.*] Written at Apton in December, 1828 (*Life*, 1872, p. 39), and was given in his *Ps. & Hymns*, 1844, No. 68, in 4 st. of 4 l., and again in his *Year of Praise*, 1867, No. 181. It is also in several American collections. Its subject is the journey of the Children of Israel spiritualised. [J. J.]

Forti tegente brachio. *C. Coffin.* [*Easter.*] Included in the revised *Paris Breviary*, 1736, in 8 st. of 4 l., as the Vesper hymn in the Sunday and Ferial Offices, beginning with Low Sunday and extending to the Feast of the Ascension. It was also given in the author's *Hymni Sacri*, 1736, p. 104, and is repeated from the *Paris Brev.* in Card. Nowman's *Hymni Ecclesiae*, 1838–65. [W. A. S.]

Translations in C. U. :—

1. **Protected by the Almighty hand.** By J. Chandler, in his *Hys. of the Primitive Church*, &c., 1837, p. 30, in 6 st. of 4 l. It is given in a few collections, including the 1862 *Appendix* to the *H. Noted.*

2. **Bound by a holy charm.** By I. Williams, in the *British Magazine*, April, 1837 (vol. xi. p. 387, together with the Latin text) ; and again in his *Hys. tr. from the Parisian Breviary*, 1839, p. 132, in 8 st. of 4 l. In the *Child's Christian Year*, 1841–71, it begins with st. ii., "Let us His praise unfold"; and in the *Hymnary*, 1872, No. 279, it is altered to "Beneath a mighty arm."

3. **Fenced by a strong right arm.** By W. J. Blew. 1st printed on flyleaf for the use of his own congregation, 1849–51, and then pub. in his *Church Hy. and Tune Bk.*, 1852, in 2 st. of 8 l., and 1 st. of 10 l. In this form it was repeated in Rice's *Sel.* from that work, 1870.

4. **Led by a mighty arm.** By J. A. Johnston. In the 1st ed. of his *English Hyl.*, 1852, this *tr.* is given in S.M., but in the 2nd ed., 1856, it was changed to 6's, in 4 st of 6 l. This is continued in later editions.

Trs. not in C. U. :—

1. Helped by the Almighty's arm at last. *J. D. Chambers*, 1857, p. 179.
2. By God's strong arm stretched forth to save. *R. F. Littledale* in *Lyra Messianica*, 1864.

From this hymn, st. iv.–viii. have been taken as a separate hymn, beginning :—"Jam Pascha nostrum Christus est." In its Latin form it is not in use as a separate hymn. The following *trs.* are in C. U. :—

1. **Now Christ our Passover is slain.** By W. J. Blew, in his *Church H. and Tune Bk.*, 1852–55, and again in Rice's *Hymns* from the same, 1870.

2. **Christ is become our Paschal Lamb.** This *tr.* in Chope's *Hymnal*, 1862, and the *Parish H. Bk.*,

1863–75, is from I. Williams, as above, rewritten from 6's to C.M.   [J. J.]

Fortunatus, Venantius Honorius Clementianus, was b. at Ceneda, near Treviso, about 530. At an early age he was converted to Christianity at Aquileia. Whilst a student at Ravenna he became almost blind, and recovered his sight, as he believed miraculously, by anointing his eyes with some oil taken from a lamp that burned before the altar of St. Martin of Tours, in a church in that town. His recovery induced him to make a pilgrimage to the shrine of St. Martin, at Tours, in 565, and that pilgrimage resulted in his spending the rest of his life in Gaul. At Poitiers he formed a romantic, though purely platonic, attachment for Queen Rhadegunda, the daughter of Bertharius, king of the Thuringians, and the wife, though separated from him, of Lothair I., or Clotaire, king of Neustria. The reader is referred for further particulars of this part of the life of Fortunatus to Smith and Wace's *Dict. of Christian Biography*, vol. ii. p. 552. It is sufficient to say here that under the influence of Rhadegunda, who at that time lived at Poitiers, where she had founded the convent of St. Croix, Fortunatus was ordained, and ultimately, after the death of Rhadegunda in 597, became bishop of Poitiers shortly before his own death in 609.

The writings, chiefly poetical, of Fortunatus, which are still extant, are very numerous and various in kind; including the liveliest *Vers de Société* and the grandest hymns ; while much that he is known to have written, including a volume of *Hymns for all the Festivals of the Christian Year*, is lost. Of what remains may be mentioned, *The Life of St. Martin of Tours*, his Patron Saint, in four books, containing 2245 hexameter lines. A complete list of his works will be found in the article mentioned above.

His contributions to hymnology must have been very considerable, as the name of his lost volume implies, but what remains to us of that character, as being certainly his work, does not comprise at most more than 9 or 10 compositions, and of some of these even his authorship is more than doubtful. His best known hymn is the famous "Vexilla Regis prodeunt," so familiar to us in our Church Hymnals in some English form or other, especially, perhaps, in Dr. Neale's translation, "The Royal Banners forward go." The next most important composition claimed for him is "Pange, lingua, gloriosi praelium certaminis," but there would seem to be little doubt according to Sirmond (*Notis ad Epist. Sidon. Apollin. Lib.* iii., *Ep.* 4), that it was more probably written by Claudianus Mamertus. Besides these, which are on the Passion, there are four hymns by Fortunatus for Christmas, one of which is given by *Daniel*, "Agnoscat omne saeculum," one for Lent, and one for Easter. Of "Lustra sex qui jam peregit," of which an imitation in English by Bp. Mant, "See the destined day arise," is well-known, the authorship is by some attributed to Fortunatus, and by some to St. Ambrose.

The general character of the poetry of Venantius Fortunatus is by no means high, being distinguished neither for its classical, nor, with very rare exceptions, for its moral correctness. He represents the "last expiring effort of the Latin muse in Gaul," to retain something of the "old classical culture amid the advancing tide of barbarism." Whether we look at his style, or even his grammar and quantities, we find but too much that is open to criticism, whilst he often offends against good taste in the sentiments he enunciates. Occasionally, as we see in the "Vexilla Regis," he rises to a rugged grandeur in which he has few rivals, and some of his poems are by no means devoid of simplicity and pathos. But these are the exceptions and not the rule in his writings, and we know not how far he may have owed even these to the womanly instincts and gentler, purer influence of Rhadegunda. *Thierry*, in his *Récits des Temps Mérovingiens, Récit 5me*, gives a lively sketch of Fortunatus, as in Archbishop Trench's words (*Sac. Lat. Poetry*, 1874, p. 132), "A clever, frivolous, self-indulgent and vain character," an exaggerated character, probably, because one can hardly identify the author of "Vexilla Regis," in such a mere man of the world, or look at the writer of "Crux benedicta nitet, Dominus qua carne pependit" q.v., as being wholly devoid of the highest aspirations after things divine. A quarto edition of his *Works* was pub. in Rome in 1786. [D. S. W.]

Forty days and forty nights. *G. H. Smyttan.* [*Lent.*] 1st pub. in the *Penny Post*, March, 1856 (vol. vi. p. 60), in 9 st. of 4 l., headed "Poetry for Lent; As sorrowful, yet always rejoicing," and signed "G. H. S." In 1861, 6 st. were given with alterations in the Rev. F. Pott's *Hymns, &c.*, and repeated in *H. A. & M.*, 1861–75; Mrs. Brock's *Children's H. Bk.*, 1881, and others. Other slightly altered texts are given in the *Sarum Hyl.*, 1868; the S. P. C. K. *Church Hymns*, 1871, and others. This hymn has extended to a few American collections. [J. J.]

Forward! be our watchword. *H. Alford.* [*Processional.*] Was written for and first sung in public at the tenth Festival of Parochial Choirs of the Canterbury Diocesan Union, on the 6th June, 1871, and pub. with music, also by the Dean, in the Festival Book of that year. Both words and music were subsequently included in the author's *Life* by his widow, in 1872 (*Appendix B*), in 8 st of 12 l. It has since appeared in many hymnals both in G. Britain and America, including *The Hymnary*, 1872; *H. A. & M.*, 1875, Thring's *Coll.*, 1882, &c. In the American *Laudes Domini*, N. Y., 1884, it is divided into two parts, the second beginning, "Far o'er yon horizon." [J. J.]

Forward go in glad accord. *L. Tuttiett.* [*Choral Festivals.*] Written for the Coventry Choral Festival, 1867, and subsequently used on similar occasions at Peterborough, and elsewhere. Its first publication as distinct from printing in the foregoing festival books, was in Biden's *Processional Hymns with Tunes*, N. D. (Northampton). Authorized text in *Church Hymns*, 1871, No. 318. [J. J.]

Forward let the people go. *T. Kelly.* [*Press Onward.*] Appeared in his *Hymns . . . Not before Published*, 1815, No. 70, in 5 st. of 6 l. It was subsequently included in the various editions of his *Hymns on Various Passages of H. Scripture, &c.* The hymn, No. 1166, in the 1869 *Supp.* to the *New Cong.*, "Onward let My children go," is composed of st. i., iii., ii. and iv., in the order named but somewhat altered. Both the original, and the altered form of the hymn are in other collections. [J. J.]

Fountain, John, was b. in 1767. He was a member of the Baptist Church in Eagle Street, London, and in Jan., 1796, was recommended to the Baptist Missionary Society as "a person whose heart was engaged in the work of missions and whose character was

suitable to such an undertaking." He set sail for India in April of the same year. He soon became sufficiently master of the Bengáli language to preach to the people, and gave promise of great usefulness; but after a brief bright course, died at Dinagepore, Aug. 20th, 1800.

Mr. Fountain had musical gifts, and, as appears from Rippon's *Baptist Register* for 1798, was probably the first who wrote out a Hindoo tune in musical notes. In the same number of the *Register* is a hymn entitled *The Penitent's Prayer & Resolve*, composed in Bengáli by Dr. W. Carey, and translated into English by J. Fountain. A hymn by Mr. Fountain is in the *Evangelical Magazine* for 1798. Another, beginning "Sinners, you are now addressed," appeared in Rippon's *Sel.* (1800), and is in Spurgeon's *O. O. H. Bk.*, 1866.

[W. R. S.]

Fountain of comfort and of love. *P. Doddridge.* [*Prayer on behalf of Ministers.*] 1st pub. in J. Orton's posthumous ed. of Doddridge's *Hymns, &c.*, 1755, No. 271, in 6 st. of 4 l., and again in J. D. Humphreys's ed. of the same, 1839, No. 296. In both cases the heading is the same, "Ministers comforted that they may comfort others"; but in the latter the opening line reads, "Fountain of comfort, *source* of love," this being the only difference in the text. (See English Hymnody, Early, § XIV.) [J. J.]

Fountain of grace, rich, full, and free. *J. Edmeston.* [*All-sufficiency of Christ.*] Pub. in his *Hys. for the Chamber of Sickness,* N.D. [1844], p. 19, in 4 st. of 4 l. In 1855 it was given anonymously in H. W. Beecher's *Plymouth Coll.*, No. 531. From that date it gradually grew in favour until it has taken its place in most of the leading American hymnbooks. [J. J.]

Fountain of mercy, God of love. *Alice Flowerdew.* [*Harvest.*] 1st pub. in her *Poems on Moral and Religious Subjects*, 3rd ed., 1811, in 6 st. of 4 l., and entitled, "Harvest Hymn." It has been contended by some that it is taken from John Needham's hymn, No. lvi., in his *Hymns Devotional and Moral, &c.*, 1763, which opens :—

" To praise the ever bounteous Lord,
    My soul, wake all thy powers:
He calls, and at His voice come forth
    The smiling harvest hours."

Needham's hymn, however, is very inferior in design and composition, and has nothing in common with this, by Mrs. Flowerdew, save the subject of Harvest. Mrs. Flowerdew's hymn was brought into congregational use by Cotterill in his *Sel.*, 1819, where it was given in 5 st., the last being by himself or Montgomery. The latter repeated it in his *Christian Psalmist*, 1825. In the *Anglican H. Bk.*, 1868, it is given as "O Fount of mercy, God of love." Its use in its original and other forms is extensive in most English-speaking countries. Orig. text in *Hy. Comp.*, No. 50.

An altered version of this hymn is very popular. It was given in Murray's *Hymnal*, 1852, as:—

" Father of mercies, God of love,
    Whose gifts all creatures share ; "

and later in numerous collections in G. Britain and America, including *H. A. & M.*, 1861 (where a doxology is substituted for the last st.), and others. Another form of this hymn was given anonymously in Longfellow and Johnson's American Unitarian *Book of Hymns,*

1846; their *Hys. of the Spirit*, 1864; and in Mrs. E. Courtauld's *Ps., Hys. & Anthems*, Lond., 1860. It begins, "Fountain of *life, and* God of love." [J. J.]

Fouqué, Friedrich Heinrich Carl de la Motte, was b. Feb. 12, 1777, at Brandenburg on the Havel, where his father, of an ancient and noble Huguenot family, was a retired officer of dragoons. Educated under the training of the French Reformed Church, it was intended that he should enter the University of Halle as a student of law. By his own preference however he entered the army, and in 1794 was appointed cornet in the Duke of Weimar's regiment of cuirassiers. In 1803 he married and retired to Nennhausen near Rathenow, Brandenburg. When, in March, 1813, the King of Prussia invited his people to arm against France, Fouqué offered himself as a volunteer and served as a lieutenant of cavalry till he was disabled at the battle of Lützen, May 2, 1813, and with the rank of major retired once more to Nennhausen. After the death of his wife, in 1831, he resided for some time at Halle, where he gave lectures in the University on the history of poetry; and finally settled in Berlin, where, two days after a stroke of apoplexy, he d. Jan. 23, 1843 (*Koch*, vii. 6–20; *Allg. Deutsche Biog.*, vii. 198–201, &c.).

Fouqué is best known as one of the leaders of the "Romantic" school of German literature, and by his wonderfully successful efforts to make the best features of the knight and minstrel life of the 12th cent. live again in the pages of his romances as an example and incitement to his own times. His fame rests not on his poems, but on his romances, especially that of *Undine* (1st ed. Berlin, 1811, 17th ed. 1870—frequently *tr.* into English). His hymns, while affording a true and thoughtful reflex of his religious feelings, cannot be said to have either great depth of Christian experience or genuine churchly ring, and hardly any have come into Church use in Germany. He himself only published 15 Mission hymns at Leipzig, 1822, as *Geistliche Lieder, Erstes Bändchen*. From his papers his second wife issued two collections, the *Geistliche Gedichte*, Berlin, 1846, and *Christlicher Liederschatz*, Berlin, 1862; but they contain few compositions that can be called hymns, and of these hardly any are suitable for church use.

Of his hymns those *tr.* into English are:—

i. **Was du vor tausend Jahren.** *Christ our Light.* Founded on St. Mark x. 46–52, and included 1846, p. 1, in 6 st. of 8 l., entitled, "The Faithfulness of the Saviour." Previously in Bunsen's *Versuch*, 1833, No. 761. *Tr.* as:—

A thousand years have fleeted, a good and full *tr.* by Miss Cox in her *Sacred Hys. from the Ger.*, 1841, p. 105, repeated, omitting st. ii.–iv., as No. 567 in Hedge and Huntington's *Hys. for the Ch. of Christ*, Boston, U.S., 1853.

Other *trs.* are: (1) "Thy mercy, Lord, is still the same," by *Lady E. Fortescue*, 1843. (2) "My Saviour, what Thou didst of old," by *Miss Winkworth*, 1855, p. 53.

His hymns not in English C. U. are:—

ii. **In die Segel sanft und linde.** *Missions.* 1822, p. 13, in 4 st., entitled "Prosperous Voyage," i.e. to the mission field. *Tr.* as "In our sails all soft and sweetly," by *Miss Winkworth*, 1858, p. 115.

iii. **Wie schäumt so feierlich zu unsern Füssen.** *Missions.* For missionaries about to set out on their voyage. 1822, p. 11, in 6 st., entitled "At the Sea." The *trs.* are: (1) "Thou, solemn Ocean, rollest to the strand," by *Miss Winkworth*, 1858, p. 112. (2) "Dark, mighty Ocean, rolling to our feet," by *Miss Borthwick*, in *H. L. L.*, 1858, p. 26, repeated in L. Rehfuess's *Ch. at Sea*, 1868, p. 5. [J. M.]

Four streams through happy Eden flow'd. *J. M. Neale.* [*St. Mark's Day.*] 1st

pub. in the 3rd Series of his *Hymns for Children*, 1846, p. 21, in 7 st. of 4 l., the last being Bp. Ken's doxology. It is given in a few collections only. The idea upon which the hymn is based is that the four rivers of Eden were typical of the four Evangelists, and of these St. Mark was one. [J. J.]

Fox, Jane. [**Crewdson, Jane.**]

Fox, William Johnson, the son of a small farmer in Suffolk, was b. in 1786. As a boy he worked as a weaver, but subsequently spent six years in a bank. He was educated for the ministry under Dr. Pye Smith, at Homerton. His first settlement was with an Orthodox Independent congregation; but he very soon became a Unitarian. In 1817 he settled in London as minister of the Parliament Court Chapel. In 1824 he removed to a new chapel at South Place, Finsbury, where he remained until 1852. He was a prominent member of the Anti Corn-law League; joined in founding the *Westminster Review*, and from 1831 to 1836 was owner of the *Monthly Repository*. From 1847 to 1863 he sat in Parliament as member for Oldham. He d. in 1864. In 1841 he pub. *Hys. and Anthems*, London, *Charles Fox*. This collection contained 150 selections from various authors, including Mrs. Sarah Adams, who was a member of his congregation. He included 13 of his own hymns. A new and enlarged ed. of his *Hymns*, &c., was pub. in 1873. A memorial edition of his *Works* was pub. in 12 vols. in 1865. His hymns which have come into C. U. outside of his collection include:—

1. A little child in bulrush ark. *Moses.*
2. Call them from the dead. *The Spirits of the Past.*
3. Gracious Power, the world pervading. *Public Worship.*
4. In the plan divine. *Perfection of God's designs.*
5. Jews were wrought to cruel madness. *Good Friday. B. V. M. at the Cross.*
6. The sage his cup of hemlock quaffed. *Resignation.*
[V. D. D.]

Frances, Grace J., a *nom de plume* of Mrs. F. C. Van Alstyne.

Franch, James. [**Psalters, English.**]

Francis, Benjamin, M.A., was b. in Wales in 1734. He was baptized at the age of 15, and began to preach at 19. He studied at the Bristol Baptist College, and commenced his ministry at Sodbury. In 1757 he removed to Horsley (afterwards called Shortwood), in Gloucestershire. There he remained, through a happy and very successful ministry of 42 years, until his death in 1799. He was the author of many poetical compositions:—

(1) *Conflagration, a Poem in Four Parts* (1770); (2) *Elegies* on the Deaths of the Revs. *George Whitefield, Caleb Evans, Robt. Day*, and *Joshua Thomas*; (3) *The Association*, a Poem (1790); (4) a *Poetical Address to the Stockbridge Indians*; (5) two satirical pieces on the Baptismal controversy; *The Salopian Zealot*; and *The Oracle*, the former passing through several editions and being reprinted in America.

Francis was the author of 5 hymns in Rippon's *Sel.*, 1787, all of which are still in C. U.:—

1. **Before Thy throne, eternal King.** *Meetings of Ministers: or Church Conferences.*

2. **Glory to the eternal King.** *Majesty of God.* In Snepp's *Songs of G. & G.*, 1872.

3. **In sweet [loud] exalted strains.** *Opening of a Place of Worship.* This was given in *Rippon*, No. 338, in 6 st. of 6 l. with the note:—"Sung on opening the Meeting House at Horsley, Gloucestershire, [his Chapel,] Sep-

tember 18, 1774; and also at the opening of the New Meeting House, at Downend, near Bristol, October 4, 1786." This hymn is abbreviated in the *Bapt. Hymnal*, 1879, to 4 st., and begins with st. iii. which is altered to "Come, King of glory, come." No. 1020 in Spurgeon's *O. O. H. Bk.* is the same arrangement of stanzas altered by Mr. Spurgeon to "Great King of Zion, now." In several American hymnals it reads: "Great King of glory, come."

4. My gracious Redeemer, I love. *The love of Christ to Men.* In various collections.

5. Praise the Saviour, all ye nations. *Offertory.* In Snepp's *Songs of G. & G.*, 1872, No. 739, "With my substance I will honour," is a cento from this hymn.

6. Ye objects of sense and enjoyments of time. *Death.* A long hymn of 16 st. of 4 l. given in the new and improved ed. of *Rippon*, 1837, No. 553, Pt. ii. with the heading, "The dying Christian bidding adieu to the world." This hymn had previously appeared in the *Baptist Register*, 1795.

It was as a writer of Welsh hymns, however, that Francis excelled. In 1774 he pub. his *Alleluia, neu Hymnau perthynol i Addoliad Cyhoeddus* (*Hymns pertaining to Public Worship*). To this he contributed 103 hymns. A second volume appeared in 1786, to which he contributed 91 hymns, being a total of 194 in all [s. MSS.]. Of these many are still in C. U. in Wales, the most popular being :—

1. Clod i'r bendigedig Oen—a oddefodd.
2. Deffro 'nghalon, deffro 'nghân—i ddyrchafu.
3. Gwyn fyd y dyn a gred yn Nuw.
4. Arglwydd grasol, clyw fy nghri—a'm griddfanau.
5. Wele gadarn sylfaen Sion.   [W. R. S.]

Francisci, Erasmus. [Finx.]

Franck, Johann, s. of Johann Franck, advocate and councillor at Guben, Brandenburg, was b. at Guben, June 1, 1618. After his father's death, in 1620, his uncle by marriage, the Town Judge, Adam Tielckau, adopted him and sent him for his education to the schools at Guben, Cottbus, Stettin and Thorn. On June 28, 1638, he matriculated as a student of law at the University of Königsberg, the only German university left undisturbed by the Thirty Years' War. Here his religious spirit, his love of nature, and his friendship with such men as Simon Dach and Heinrich Held, preserved him from sharing in the excesses of his fellow-students. He returned to Guben at Easter, 1640, at the urgent request of his mother, who wished to have him near her in those times of war during which Guben frequently suffered from the presence of both Swedish and Saxon troops. After his return from Prag, May, 1645, he commenced practice as a lawyer. In 1648 he became a burgess and councillor, in 1661 burgomaster, and in 1671 was appointed the deputy from Guben to the Landtag (Diet) of Lower Lusatia. He d. at Guben, June 18, 1677; and on the bicentenary of his death, June 18, 1877, a monumental tablet to his memory was affixed to the outer wall of the Stadtkirche at Guben (*Koch*, iii. 378-385; *Allg. Deutsche Biog.*, vii. 211-212; the two works by Dr. Hugo Jentsch of Guben, *Johann Franck*, 1877, and *Die Abfassungszeit der geistlichen Lieder Johann Francks*, 1876).

Of Franck's secular poems those before 1649 are much the best; his later productions becoming more and more affected and artificial, long-winded and full of classical allusions, and much inferior to those of Dach or Opitz. As a hymn-writer he holds a high rank and is distinguished for unfeigned and firm faith, deep earnestness, finished form, and noble, pithy, simplicity of expression. In his hymns we miss the objectivity and congregational character of the older German hymns, and notice a more personal, individual tone; especially the longing for the inward and mystical union of Christ with the soul as in his "Jesus, meine Freude." He stands in close relationship with Gerhardt, sometimes more soaring and occasionally more profound, but neither on the whole so natural nor so suited for popular comprehension or Church use.

His hymns appeared mostly in the works of his friends Weichmann, Crüger and Peter. They were collected in his *Geistliches Sion*, Guben, 1674, to the number of 110; and of these the 57 hymns (the other 53 being psalm versions of no great merit) were reprinted with a biographical preface by Dr. J. L. Pasig as *Johann Franck's Geistliche Lieder*, Grimma, 1846. Two of those *tr.* into English are from the Latin of J. Campanus (q. v.). Four other hymns are annotated under their own first lines :—"Brunquell aller Güter"; "Dreieinigkeit der Gottheit wahrer Spiegel"; "Jesu, meine Freude"; "Schmücke dich, o liebe Seele." The rest are :—

i. Hymns in English C. U.

i. Erweitert eure Pforten. [*Advent.*] Founded on Ps. xxiv. 7-10. 1st pub. in C. Peter's *Andachts-Zymbeln*, Freiberg, 1655, p. 25, in 7 st. of 8 l.; repeated 1674, p. 3, and 1846, p. 3, as above. Included in the 1688 and later eds. of Crüger's *Praxis pietatis*, in Bollhagen's *G. B.*, 1736, &c. The only *tr.* in C. U. is:—

Unfold your gates and open, a *tr.* of st. 1, 3, 6, by A. T. Russell, as No. 30 in his *Ps. & Hys.*, 1851; repeated altered as No 30 in *Kennedy*, 1863, and thus as No. 102 in *Holy Song*, 1869.

ii. Herr Gott dich loben wir, Regier. *Thanksgiving for Peace.* Evidently written as a thanksgiving for the conclusion of the Thirty Years' War, by the Peace of Westphalia, Oct. 24, 1648. 1st pub. in the *Crüger-Runge G. B.*, Berlin, 1653, No. 306, in 9 st. of 8 l., as the first of the "Hymns of Thanksgiving for Peace attained"; and repeated 1674, p. 182, and 1846, p. 77, as above. Included in Crüger's *Praxis*, 1653, and many later collections and, as No. 591, in the *Unv. L. S.*, 1851. The only *tr.* in C. U. is:—

Lord God, we worship Thee, a very good version of st. 2, 3, 6, 8, by Miss Winkworth in her *C. B. for England*, 1863, No. 183. Repeated in full in the S. P. C. K. *Ch. Hys.*, 1871; the *Hymnary*, 1872; the *Psalmist*, 1878; and in America in the Pennsylvania Luth. *Ch. Bk.*, 1868. In the American *Prot. Epis. Coll.*, 1871; the *Hys. & Songs of Praise*, N. Y. 1874; and the Ohio Luth. *Hyl.*, 1880, the *tr.* of st. 8 is omitted.

iii. Herr ich habe missgehandelt. *Lent.* Of this fine hymn of penitence st. i. appeared as No. 19 in Crüger's *Geistliche Kirchenmelodien*, Leipzig, 1649. The full form in 8 st. of 6 l. is No. 41 in the *Crüger-Runge G. B.*, Berlin, 1653, entitled "For the forgiveness of sins," repeated 1674, p. 39, and 1846, p. 37, as above. Included in Crüger's *Praxis*, 1653, and others, and in the *Unv. L. S.* 1851. The only *tr.* in C. U. is:—

Lord, to Thee I make confession, a very good *tr.*, omitting st. 4, 5, 6, by Miss Winkworth in her *C. B. for England*, 1863, No. 44, repeated in the *Appendix* to the *Hyl. for St. John's*, Aberdeen, 1865-1870; and in the Pennsylvania Luth. *Ch. Bk.*, 1868; *Evang. Hyl.*, N. Y., 1880; Ohio Luth. *Hyl.*, 1880. Another *tr.* is: "Lord, how oft I have offended," by *N. L. Frothingham*, 1870, p. 177.

iv. Herr Jesu, Licht der Heiden. *Presentation in the Temple.* Founded on the account in St.

Luke ii., and probably the finest hymn on the subject. Dr. Jentsch, 1876, p. 9, thinks it was written before Dec. 8, 1669, as C. Peter, who d. then, left a melody for it. We have not found the full text earlier than 1674, as above, p. 10, in 6 st. of 8 l., entitled "On the Festival of the Purification of Mary" (1846, p. 10). Included in the 1688 and later eds. of Crüger's *Praxis*, and in the *Unv. L. S.*, 1851, No. 197. The *trs.* in C. U. are :—

1. **Light of the Gentile world**, a *tr.*, omitting st. 6, by Miss Winkworth in the 1st ser. of her *Lyra Ger.*, 1855, p. 193 (ed. 1876, p. 195), and thence as No. 147 in the Pennsylvania Luth. *H. Bk.*, 1865. This version is in S.M. Double.

2. **Light of the Gentile Nations**, a good *tr.*, omitting st. 6, by Miss Winkworth in her *C. B. for England*, 1863, No. 80. Repeated in Dr. Thomas's *Augustine H. Bk.*, 1866, and in America in the Pennsylvania Luth. *Ch. Bk.*, 1868, and the Ohio Luth. *Hyl.*, 1880.

ii. *Hymns not in English C. U.*

v. **Du geballtes Weltgebäude.** *Christ above all earthly things.* St. i. in Crüger's *Kirchenmelodien*, 1649, No. 116. The full text (beginning "Du o schönes) is No. 239 in the *Crüger-Runge G. B.*, 1653, in 8 st., entitled "Longing after Eternal Life." Repeated 1674, p. 194, and 1846 p. 60, as above. The *trs.* are : (1) "Let who will in thee rejoice," by *Miss Winkworth*, 1855, p. 180 (1876, p. 182). (2) "O beautiful abode of earth," by *Miss Warner*, 1858 (1861, p. 233). (3) "Thou, O fair Creation - building," by *N. L. Frothingham*, 1870, p. 232.

vi. **Unsre müden Augenlieder.** *Evening.* Probably written while a student at Königsberg. 1st pub. in J. Weichmann's *Sorgen-Lägerin*, Königsberg, 1648, Pt. iii., No. 4, in 7 st.; repeated 1674, p. 213, and 1846, p. 91, as above. The only *tr.* is by *H. J. Buckoll*, 1842, p. 79, beginning with st. vi., "Ever, Lord, on Thee relying."   [J. M.]

Franck, Michael, s. of Sebastian Franck, merchant at Schleusingen, was b. at Schleusingen, March 16, 1609. At the Gymnasium of his native town he made good progress, but at his father's death it was found possible only to give his brothers Sebastian and Peter a university education. Michael was accordingly apprenticed to a baker, and in 1628 became a master baker at Schleusingen. Reduced to poverty by the sufferings of war, he fled in 1640 to Coburg, was there kindly received by one of the master bakers, and in 1644, somewhat unexpectedly, was appointed master of the lower classes in the town school. He d. at Coburg Sept. 24, 1667 (*Koch*, iii. 435–441 ; *Allg. Deutsche Biog.*, vii. 259–260).

He was a friend of Dach and Neumark ; was in 1659 crowned by Rist as a poet, and afterwards received into his order of Elbe Swans. In his times of trial he found consolation in hymn-writing. While many of his pieces are crude in form and expression, some are yet popular in style, and are full of faith.

The best of his hymns probably is :—

Ach wie flüchtig ! ach wie nichtig. [*For the Dying.*] Appeared as the third of three hymns by Franck pub. with music in four parts at Coburg, 1652, entitled *Die Eitelkeit, Falschheit und Unbeständigkeit der Welt* [Wernigerode], in 13 st. In his *Geistliches Harpffen-Spiel*, Coburg, 1657 [Gotha], No. 24 with the motto

"Der Mensch und all sein Thun must mit der Zeit hergehn ;
Wer Gott und Gottesfurcht recht liebt, wird ewig stehn."

Repeated in Crüger's *Praxis*, 1661, No. 530, and many subsequent collections, as in the *Unv.*

L. S., 1851, No. 803. It is a powerful picture of the vanity and nothingness of this world and all its treasures. The only *tr.* in C. U. is :—

O how cheating, O how fleeting, Is, &c. In full by Sir J. Bowring in his *Hymns*, 1825, No. 35. The *trs.* of st. i., iii., iv., xiii. were included in Curtis's *Union Coll.*, 1827, and of st. i.-iv., xiii. in the *Plymouth Coll.*, 1855.

Another tr. is : "Ah how fleeting, ah how cheating," by *N. L. Frothingham*, 1870, p. 153.   [J. M.]

Franck, Salomo, s. of Jakob Franck, financial secretary at Weimar, was b. at Weimar, March 6, 1659. Little is known of his early history. He probably studied at Jena, and seems thereafter to have held some appointment at Zwickau. In 1689 he became secretary of the Schwarzburg ducal administration at Arnstadt ; and in 1697 of the Saxon administration and of the consistory at Jena. He was then, in 1702, appointed secretary of the consistory, librarian, and curator of the ducal collection of coins and medals at Weimar. He. d. at Weimar July 11, 1725 (*Koch*, v. 420–426 ; *Allg. Deutsche Biog.*, vii. 213–214 ; *Schauer's* introduction, &c.)

He was a member of the Fruitbearing Society, and the author of a considerable number of secular poems, which are almost all "occasional" pieces and now forgotten. A diligent worker and a man of true piety, he had severe family afflictions to bear, and an undercurrent of meditation on death is present in many of his hymns. As a hymn-writer he is distinguished for ease and correctness of style ; for adaptation to popular understanding and to congregational singing ; for his love of adding refrains to his hymns ; and for his happiness in word-painting and in setting forth contrasts.

Of his hymns (about 330 in all) which still continue in use in Germany, the most important appeared in his (1) *Geistliche Poesie*, Weimar, 1685, and in his (2) *Geist- und Weltliche Poesien*, vol. i., Jena, 1711 ; vol. ii., Jena, 1716. A selection of 46 of his *Geistliche Lieder* with a biographical and critical introduction by Dr. J. K. Schauer appeared at Halle, 1855. Eight of his hymns have passed into English, as follows :—

i. *Hymns in English C. U.*

i. **Ach Gott verlass mich nicht.** *Supplication.* A beautiful hymn of supplication for God's help founded on Ps. xxxviii. 22. It is No. 1 in the *Appendix* to the *Anderer Theil des Naumburgischen Gesang Buchs*. Naumburg, 1714, p. 106, in 5 st. of 8 l., marked "Salomon Francke" (ed. 1717, p. 487, marked "Gottgelassen Unverlassen, Salomon Francke.") The editor of this collection, J. M. Schamelius, who was one of the best hymnologists of the time, evidently thus believed that it was by Franck, but it has not yet been found in any work pub. by Franck himself. Each st. begins and ends with "Ach Gott verlass mich nicht." It is included in Schauer's introduction, and in many recent hymnals, as in the *Berlin G. B.*, 1829, the *Württemberg G. B.*, 1842, *Hannover G. B.*, 1883, &c. The *trs.* in C. U. are :—

1. **Forsake me not, my God.** A full and good but rather free *tr.* in the *Family Treasury* (Edinburgh : Nelson), 1859, pt. ii. p. 168, and thence, in Boardman's *Selection*, Phil., U.S., 1861, and in the Pennsylvania Luth. *Ch. Bk.*, 1868.

2. **O God, forsake me not !** Thine hand, by M. W. Stryker, in his *Hys. and Verses*, 1883, p. 32, and repeated in his *Christian Chorals*, 1885.

ii. **Ich weiss es wird mein Ende kommen.** *For*

2 C 2

the Dying. 1711, as above, p. 91, in 7 st. of 6 l., entitled "The author's daily dying thoughts." Included by Schauer, 1855, p. 79; in Burg's *G. B.*, Breslau, 1746, &c. The *trs.* in C. U. are :—

1. I know my end must surely come. A *tr.* of st. i., vii., in 2 st. of 6-8's, by Miss Winkworth, in the 2nd series of her *Lyra Ger.*, 1858, p. 203. Thence in the *Ps. & Hys.*, Bedford, 1859, and in America the Pennsylvania Luth. *Ch. Bk.*, 1868.

2. I know the doom that must befall me. This is the above *tr.*, rewritten by Miss Winkworth to the original metre, and given in her *C. B. for England*, 1863, No. 185. To this *trs.* of st. iii., iv., vi., were added, and the others altered and beginning, "I know full well death must befall me," included in the Ohio Luth. *Hyl.*, 1880.

iii. So ruhest du, o meine Ruh. *Easter Eve.* 1685, as above, p. 29, in 7 st. of 4 l., entitled "On the burial of Jesus." It is a beautiful hymn on the entombment of Christ, founded on Rist's "O Traurigkeit" (q. v.). Included in *Schauer*, 1855, p. 44, and in many German collections, as the *Unv. L. S.*, 1851, No. 118.

Frequently it appears in altered forms. Thus J. A. Schlegel, 1766, p. 86, altered it to "So schlummerst du in stiller Ruh," and the *Berlin G. B.*, 1780, No. 102, further alters it to "Zur Grabesruh entschliefest du."

The *trs.* in C. U., all from the original, are :—

1. Thou who hast blest my soul with rest, a good *tr.*, omitting st. ii., v., by A. T. Russell, as No. 103 in his *Ps. & Hys.*, 1851.

2. Thou restest in the tomb beneath, a good *tr.*, omitting st. ii., v., as No. 83 in J. F. Thrupp's *Ps. & Hys.*, 1853.

3. Rest of the weary! Thou, a somewhat expanded version, omitting st. iii. by Miss Winkworth in her *Lyra Ger.*, 1st series, 1855, p. 85, repeated in the Pennsylvania Luth. *Ch. Bk.*, 1868.

4. So rest, my Rest! a very good *tr.*, omitting st. iii., by R. Massie, as No. 93 in the ed., 1857, of Mercer's *C. P. & H. Bk.* (Ox. ed., 1864, No. 184). This has been included in Chope's *Hyl.*, 1862 ; *Kennedy*, 1863 ; the *Hymnary*, 1872 ; Thring's *Coll.*, 1880–82, &c. ; and in America in the *Evang. Hyl.*, N. Y., 1880, and *Laudes Domini*, 1884. The form in Allon's *Suppl. Hys.*, No 324, is a recast partly taken from Miss Winkworth's *tr.* of "Nun gingst auch du" (see **Strauss, V. F.**).

Other trs. are : (1) "Now to the tomb Thyself art come," from Schlegel, by *Dr. H. Mills*, 1845 (1856, p. 316). (2) "So dost Thou rest," in the *British Herald*, Dec., 1866, p. 376, repeated as No. 421 in Reid's *Praise Bk.*, 1872. (3) "So thou art resting, O my Rest," in the *British Herald*, April, 1869, p. 52.

ii. *Hymns not in English C. U.*

iv. Ach was ist doch unsre Zeit. *For the Dying.* 1685, as above, p. 64, in 6 st., and *Schauer*, p. 31, each st. ending "Mensch, bedenke doch, das Ende." *Tr.* as "Oh! what is human life below," by Miss Cox in *Lyra Messianica*, 1864, p. 47, repeated in her *H. from the German*, 1864, p. 135, in the original metre, beginning, "What is human life below." Also *tr.* by *Miss Dunn*, 1857, p. 52 ; and by *E. Massie*, 1867, p. 3.

v. Gott, du Licht, das ewig bleibet. *Morning.* 1716, as above, p. 160, in 5 st., entitled "Morning Devotion," and in *Schauer*, p. 4. *Tr.* by *H. J. Buckoll*, 1842, p. 12 ; and by *Miss Manington*, 1863, p. 120.

vi. Heil'ger Tisch! Den Jesus decket. *Holy Communion.* 1711, as above, p. 69, in 6 st., entitled "Another Communion Meditation." In *Schauer*, p. 67. *Tr.* as, "This holy feast, by Jesus spread," by Miss Cox, in *Lyra Eucharistica*, 1863, p. 173.

vii. Ich weiss, es kann mir nichts geschehen. *God's Guidance.* 1711, as above, p. 221, in 5 st. (ll. 5, 6 of each st. being a refrain), entitled "On the words of Ps. lxxiii. 23, 24." In *Schauer*, p. 21. *Tr.* by *Miss Manington*, 1863, p. 22.

viii. Mein Gott, wie bist du so verborgen. *Providence.* 1711, as above, p. 76, in 6 st. (ll. 5, 6 of each st. being a refrain), entitled "The wonderfully blessed leadings of God." In *Schauer*, p. 16. *Tr.* by *Miss Manington*, 1863, p. 7.   [J. M.]

Francke, August Hermann, s. of Johann Francke, a lawyer in Lübeck, was b. at Lübeck, March 22, 1663. He studied at the Universities of Erfurt, Kiel, and Leipzig, graduated M.A. at Leipzig, 1685, and thereafter lectured on Biblical subjects at Leipzig for some time. About Michaelmas, 1687, he went to Lüneburg to work under the pious superintendent C. H. Sandhagen ; and there while composing his first sermon (on St. John xx. 31) he underwent that change which made him call Lüneburg his spiritual birthplace. After spending the greater part of 1688 at Hamburg, he stayed two months with P. J. Spener, at Dresden, and then returned about Lent, 1689, to Leipzig, where he resumed his Biblical lectures until the old orthodox party procured an edict forbidding them in the beginning of 1690. On March 10, 1690, he received a call to become diaconus of the Augustine Church at Erfurt, and there, by his stirring exhortations to renewal of heart, living faith and holy life, he drew many, even Roman Catholics, around him, but by a combination of the old orthodox Lutherans with the Romanists he was expelled from Erfurt, Sept. 27, 1691. After a lengthened visit to P. J. Spener, then Probst of St Nicholas's Church, Berlin, he was appointed by the Elector of Brandenburg, Dec. 22, 1691, as professor of Greek and the Oriental languages, and in 1698 ordinary professor of Theology in the University of Halle ; being also appointed in 1691 preacher at St. George's Church in Glaucha (suburb of Halle), a post which he exchanged in 1715 for the pastorate of St. Ulrich's, Halle. After his left side was paralysed in Nov. 1726, he patiently endured much suffering till his death on June 8, 1727, at Halle (*Koch*, iv. 305–322 ; *Allg. Deutsche Biog.*, vii. 219–231).

Francke was the spiritual son of P. J. Spener, and became one of the leaders in the "Pietistic" movement which so powerfully influenced Germany, 1680–1750, raised the tone of the community after the depression of the Thirty Years' War, revived the educational system, began systematic provision for the poor, and refined and purified domestic life. Francke was the spiritual leader and teacher, and under him and the band of professors that gathered to Halle, Halle became the headquarters of Pietism. During his time Halle sent out some 6000 graduates in theology, men imbued with his spirit, good exegetes, and devoted pastors, who spread their doctrines all over Germany, and in the early decades of the 18th cent. occupied a majority of the pulpits.

The extensive buildings at Halle, which now bear the title of the "Francke Institutions," are a monument of his simple faith and philanthropic zeal. He began at Easter, 1695, by opening a room in his house for instructing the poor children of Glaucha, with a capital of about thirteen shillings. About Whitsuntide, 1695, were the beginnings of the Paedagogium, 1697 of the Latin School, 1698 of the bookselling and apothecary businesses, 1705 of the mission to the East Indies, 1710 of the Bible Society. On a place formerly occupied by beer and dancing gardens, the foundation stone of the great Orphanage was laid July 13, 1698, in a spirit of humble faith in God and fervent prayer, trusting to Him for the means to pay for the work as it progressed ; and week by week as they were needed the supplies came in from far and near. In this work, as in regard to his sermons and lectures, Francke had great opposition to meet, but the Commission of Enquiry which his enemies procured resulted in a cabinet order of 1702, which is the Charter of his Institutions. In 1727 there were 134 orphans in the orphanage ; and besides these 2207 scholars in the various training schools, of whom some 360, as well as 225 poor students, received daily rations ; while in 1863 the value of the buildings was about £45,000., and nearly 3500 scholars received instruction.

Distinguished as a professor, as a philanthropist, as a pastor, and as a preacher of gospel simplicity and soul-stirring earnestness, Francke was not prolific as a hymn-writer. Only three hymns are known by him, two of which are :—

i. **Gottlob ein Schritt zur Ewigkeit.** *New Year.* 1st pub. in his *Schrifftmässige Anweisung recht und Gott wolgefällig zu beten*, Halle, 1695, p. 534, in 12 st. of 7 l., as a " Morning and Evening " hymn, entitled " The Voice of the Bride ('When shall I come and appear before God ? '), which she raises as often as she completes a step of her mortal life , and may be used by an upright and believing soul instead of the [usual] morning and evening hymn, as also at other times."

Reprinted in the *Geistreiches G. B.*, Halle, 1697, p. 294, Freylinghausen's *G. B.*, 1704, &c., and is No. 623 in the *Unv. L. S.*, 1851.

According to *Koch*, viii. 176–179, it was written immediately after his expulsion from Erfurt, Sept 27, 1691, while on his way to his mother's house at Gotha, and "in the experience of the overflowing consolation of the Holy Spirit." In the spirit of his favourite motto, " Quocunque die ante aeternitatem uno stamus pede," and based on 2 Cor. v. 6 and Rev. xxii. 17–20, it is modelled by a hymn by J. V. Andrea, 1636.

" Gottlob ein Schritt zur Ewigkeit
Ist abermals vorbei."

Koch adds that in his lifetime Francke found cases where this hymn had been blessed, that two days before his death he caused the hymn to be read to him, and said, " My faithful Jesus, I have given myself to Thee, soul and body that is sure ; " and that on the day on which he died, June 8, 1727, this hymn was one of those sung at the choir meeting at Herrnhut.

The trs. in C. U. are :—

1. Thank God, that towards eternity, a full and good *tr.* by Miss Winkworth, in her *Lyra Ger.*, 2nd series, 1858, p. 9. In 1860, ll. 1–4 of st. i., iv., vi., viii., greatly altered, and beginning, " Bless God, that towards eternity," were included as No. 74 in the Amer. Epis. *Hys. for Ch. and Home.*

2. Oh wouldst Thou in Thy glory come, a *tr.* of st. iv., vii.-xi., founded by Miss Winkworth on her 1858 version, and given as No. 173 in her *C. B. for England*, 1863.

Other trs. are : (1) "Another step is made with God," in the *Suppl. to Ger. Psalmody*, ed. 1765, p. 50. Previously in *Select Hys. from Ger. Psal.*, Tranquebar, 1754, p. 79. (2) " Thank God ! towards Eternity," by J. Gambold, as No. 626 in pt. i. of the *Moravian H. Bk.*, 1754 (1886, No. 1232). (3) " Thank God ! another stage of time," by *Dr. H. Mills*, 1856, p. 227.

ii. **Was von aussen und von innen.** *Cross and Consolation.* A fine hymn of Trust in God, founded on Ps. lxii. 5–8. Written in memory of Eleonore, *née* Kubitz, wife of J. H. Michaelis, professor at Halle, and appended to the funeral sermon preached by Francke on Ps. lxii. 2, in St. George's Church, Glaucha, Nov. 1, 1711. Included as No. 500 in Freylinghausen's *Neues geistreiches G. B.*, 1714, in 9 st. of 8 l., and recently as No. 2250 in Knapp's *Ev. L. S.*, 1837 (1865, No. 1997).

Lauxmann, in *Koch*, viii. 508–512, speaks of this lady as one who suffered severe afflictions, but " what from without or from within pressed on her soul she bore in quiet waiting on the help of the Lord, of Whom she could at last gratefully say ' He hath done all things well.'" *Lauxmann* adds, " This hymn is also a beautiful clear mirror of Francke's own thought and conversation, heart and life experiences." In his *Segensvolle Fussstapfen*, 1709, he was able already to relate thirty instances in which the Lord had enabled him to receive,

exactly at the time when he needed it, pecuniary help" in answer to his prayers during the building and conducting of the great Orphanage at Halle.

Of this hymn (which should be read with the history of his great work at Halle) the only *tr.* in C. U. is :—

What within me and without, a good and full *tr.* by Miss Winkworth in the 1st ed. of her *Lyra Ger.*, 1855, p. 126 (st. iii. being added in the 2nd ed., 1856), and thence as No. 139 in her *C. B. for England*, 1863. With the altered first line, " Lord, Thou art my Rock of strength," three centos are in American C. U. :—

1. St. ii., iv., vii., ix. in Boardman's *Sel.*, Phil., 1861.
2. St. ii., vii., ix. in the Pennsylvania Luth. *Ch. Bk.*, 1868, Dutch Reformed *Hys. of the Church*, 1869, and Richards's *Coll.* 1881.
3. St. ii., iv., ix. in Robinson's *Songs for the Sanctuary*, 1865, and the *Hys. & Songs of Praise*, N. Y., 1874.

[J. M.]

Franklin, Jonathan (b. 1760, d. 1833), was originally minister of a Baptist church at Croydon, but in 1808 removed to Redcross Street Chapel, London, where he remained until death. His *Hys. & Spiritual Songs* were pub. in 1801, and reprinted in 1810 and 1812. As a hymn-writer he is known by three hymns only, of very moderate quality, which appear as the closing hymns of Pt. i. of later editions of W. Gadsby's *Sel.*, 1st ed., 1814.   [W. R. S.]

Free, yet in chains, the mountains stand. *J. Montgomery.* [*Christian Union.*] Written for the Sheffield Sunday School Union, Whitsuntide gathering, 1837, and printed on a flyleaf for that occasion. [M. MSS.] It was included in his *Original Hymns*, 1853, No. 154, in 6 st. of 4 l., and headed, " Christian Union symbolized by Natural Objects." In the Scottish *Evang. Union Hyl.*, 1878, it begins, " Free, though in chains, the mountains stand." This reading is found in some copies of the *Original Hymns*, but is not the original text.

[J. J.]

Freeman, Enoch W., was for some time Baptist Minister at Lowell, Maine, U.S. He edited a *Sel. of Hymns*, 1829–31, to which he contributed 7 of his own. Of these, "Hither we come, our dearest Lord," is still in C. U.

Freeman, James, D.D. Born at Charlestown, Mass., April 22, 1759, and graduated at Harvard, 1777. He was "the first avowed preacher of Unitarianism in the United States." In 1782 he was " Reader " in King's Chapel, and assisted or guided that historic parish in its change from Episcopacy to the then new ways in teaching and discipline. In 1787 he was " ordained," and retained the pastorate of the King's Chapel till 1826. He altered its Liturgy, and prepared for its use the King's Chapel *Coll. of Ps. & Hys.*, 1799. Died Nov. 14, 1835. His hymn, " Lord of the worlds below," is based on Thomson's "Hymn on the Seasons." It appeared in the *Ps. & Hys.*, 1799, and is found in various collections. Orig. text in Putnam's *Singers and Songs of the Liberal Faith*, 1875.   [F. M. B.]

French Hymnody. The great development of French hymns, alike in the Roman Church and the Reformed Church of France, began with the present century. It has not been practicable to obtain detailed information about the Roman Catholic hymns ; the few

FRENCH HYMNODY

details that are given are due to the kindness
of Rev. Louis Mijola, Priest of the Church of
Notre Dame des Victoires, London. The history of the hymns of the Reformed Church has
been investigated by M. Atger in *Histoire et
Rôle des Cantiques dans les églises réformées.*
The hymns of the 18th and earlier centuries
have been treated in a series of articles in the
Semeur, May-August, 1837, kindly presented
by the author, M. Henri Lutteroth, editor of
the *Chants Chrétiens.* Much has been derived
from these sources in the following pages.

i. *Latin Hymns.*

Translations of the Latin hymns have been
less general in France than in England. The
vernacular editions of The Hours of the
Virgin Mary often have only prose renderings.
So also have the modern "paroissiens," and
the splendid *L'Année Liturgique* by Dom
Guéranger. A *tr.* of *Hymnes Communs de
l'Année,* by Nicolas Mauroy, appeared in 1527.
Guy le Fevre de la Boderie pub. among other
pieces designed to supplant Marot's psalms,
several *trs.* (*Hymnes Ecclésiastiques,* 1578,
2nd ed. 1582), by the command of Henry III.
Lemaistre de Saci pub. *Hymnes de l'église
pour toute l'année* at the end of his *Heures
de Port-royal* (1650). Rival translations were
made by the Jesuits in consequence of the
success of this book (30 eds.). Racine *tr.*
hymns from the Breviary, which were pub. in
an edition of *The Breviary* by Nicolas Le
Tourneux, afterwards condemned by the Archbishop of Paris (1688). Corneille also *tr.* all
the Breviary hymns in *L'Office de la Sainte
Vierge* (1670), and Louis Chassain in his *Les
Hymnes et les Proses de l'Office Divin,* Lyons,
1695. Recently a number of the Latin hymns
have been *tr.* in *Recueil de Poésies Lyriques,*
1854, by M. J. M. Hainglaise.

ii. *Roman Catholic Hymns.*

1. Several of the carols still in use are said
to be of great antiquity, and these are probably only survivals of more general vernacular
hymns. They are found in several *patois,* as
well as in the general language. The earliest
hymns that we are able to specify in this
sketch are the *Cantiques Spirituels,* by Guy
le Fevre de la Boderie (1578), consisting of *trs.*
from Prudentius, Vidas and Petrarch, and
some paraphrases of Scripture songs, along
with the Latin *trs.* (§ i.). *La Philomèle
Séraphique,* by a Capuchin, Jean l'Evangéliste
(1632), dedicated to Louise de Lorraine, niece
of Henry III.'s queen, and set to secular tunes,
is a Jansenist book, with a mystic tone.

2. The great poet Jean Racine has left four
very free paraphrases of Holy Scripture, two
of which, "Doué du langage des anges" (1
Cor. xiii.), and "Mon Dieu, quelle guerre
cruelle" (Rom. vii. 18 sequ.), are still in use.
They were composed for the ladies of St. Cyr
(1689), and were favourites with Louis XIV.
and Mme. de Maintenon.

3. The poet Pierre Corneille versified the
Imitation of Christ, by Thomas à Kempis
(1656). Wherever the thought takes the form
of an address to God, the matter, frequently
expanded by Corneille, has been often used as
hymn material, from its devotional purity and
simple grace. "Parle, parle, Seigneur; ton
serviteur écoute" (*Lib.* 3, c. 2), "O Dieu de

vérité" (*Lib.* 1, c. 23), and "Source de tous
les biens" (*Lib.* 4, c. 16), are in most collections. Three or four others are widely known.
The third of these has been *tr.* by Miss Anna
Warner in *Hys. of the Church Militant,* New
York, 1858, "Source of all good to which I
aspire."

4. Fénelon composed some hymns in the
hope of replacing the licentious ballads of the
Court. One on the Passion is commended by
M. Lutteroth, editor of the *Chants Chrétiens.*
Fénelon repeated one of his own hymns on his
deathbed. They are the hymns of sober
Quietism.

5. In connection with Fénelon stand the
Cantiques Spirituels of Mme. Guyon, pub. in
her *Poésies* (1648-1717); which have a special
interest through Cowper's *trs.* They are of
considerable bulk, and comprise nearly 900
pieces, written for the most part to popular
ballad tunes. A large portion of them were
composed during her imprisonment in the
Château of Vincennes, often under circumstances of extreme suffering and privation.
That a spirit of real, though highly strained,
devotion animates them will be universally
allowed; but the limited range of spiritual
emotions which they repeat has so little in
common with the active side of universal
Christian life (being in some measure even
peculiar to herself among the Quietist writers),
and the literary expression is so poor, that
they have gained no entrance into the circle of
accepted French hymns.

6. The Abbé Pellegrin pub. several volumes
under the titles of *Cantiques Spirituels; Noëls;
Cantiques* (1706-15), under the patronage of
Mme. de Maintenon. They consist of carols,
Scripture narratives and hymns, on the Mysteries of the Faith and religious and moral
subjects, and are set to tunes of operas and
vaudevilles. Some are still in use.

7. In modern times the use of hymns in the
Roman Church has greatly increased. They
are used at missions, pilgrimages, and in the
churches. A collection was compiled as early
as 1765 for the Seminary of St. Sulpice by
Père de la Tour. A piece of Voltaire, "En-
tendons-nous toujours vanter," still remained
in the ed. of 1833. Among the most esteemed
hymns and recueils of the present day are the
productions of Ven. Grignon de Montfort,
R. P. Hermann, and Marie Eustelle; and the
hymnals of St. Sulpice, R. P. Garin, R. P.
Lambilotte, and R. P. Hermann. (See also
Dictionnaire de Noëls et de Cantiques, Paris,
1867, p. 740.)

iii. *Huguenot Hymns.*

1. In the 1st vol. of *Les Marguerites de la
Marguerite des Princesses,* by Marguerite de
Valois, afterwards Queen of Navarre (pub.
1547), there is a collection of six *Cantiques
Spirituels,* full of real and tender devotion—a
strange contrast to the licentiousness of her
Heptameron. Appended to her *Miroir d'une
âme pécheresse* (1533) there is *L'Instruction
et foy d'ung Chrestien* by Clément Marot,
containing the *Pater Noster, Ave Maria,
Credo, Benediction devant Mengier, Graces
pour ung enfant,* and *Dixain d'ung Chrestien
malade à son amy.* Beza, at the request of
the National Synod of Montauban, *tr.* the

Saincts Cantiques (16 pieces), of O. T. and N. T. (1595), which were sanctioned for private use by the Synod of Montpellier.

2. M. Henri Bordier has pub. (*Le Chansonnier Huguenot*, Paris, 1871, 4 books. Religious Chansons, Political Chansons, War Chansons, Chansons of Martyrdom) a selection from 9 small books of chansons, ranging from 1532 to 1597, with a valuable preface. Like kindred pieces in England and Germany, they naturally mingle satire and polemical invective with their religious elements.

Some of the religious pieces are paraphrases of Holy Scripture, others carols, others hymns, founded on passages of Holy Scripture. Sometimes they transform for sacred use existing popular ballads. The most eminent writers are Anthoine Saunier, a friend of Farel; Matthieu Malingre, and Eustorg de Beaulieu, friends of Marot. In one of the prefaces there is the strongest passage to be found dealing with that desire which Marot, Sternhold, Coverdale, and Fénelon express to supplant the low ballads ("pleines d'ordure et d'impiété) by religious songs. Though of small literary merit, M. Atger has culled out several verses and entire pieces, of simple fervour and freshness. The whole collection is of great interest.

3. Nicolas Denisot, who collected a volume of poems in honour of Marguerite de Valois, and who had been preceptor to Jane Seymour in England, pub. *Cantiques et Noëls and Cantiques du premier avènement de Jésus-Christ* (1553), marked by considerable freshness and beauty, under the anagram, *Conte d'Alsinois*.

4. Charles de Navières *tr.* the Scripture Canticles (1579). *Cantiques à l'imitation de Salomon et des Psalmes de David* by Etienne de Maizon Fleur (pub. posthumously 1580), were often reprinted in a curious volume entitled *Cantiques du Sieur de Valagres, et les Cantiques de Maizon Fleur*. It contains, besides the pieces by these two authors, which are full of allusion to the Huguenot sufferings (Valagres speaking of the glorification of the martyrs of St. Bartholomew), productions by Ives Rouspeau, a Calvinist of Geneva, and Antoine de la Rochechandieu "one of the founders of the Reformed Church at Paris" (Atger). But in order to secure circulation among the Catholics, they are preceded by some fine selections from poets of the day in the Roman Church, among which are a beautiful poem by Philippe des Portes, and Ronsard's eulogy of Charles IX. (!) Some touching pieces, more meditative devotions than hymns, written in prison by Odet de la Noue, were pub., posthumously, by his friend le Sieur de la Violette (1594). Among several other names in M. Lutteroth's account of the 17th cent., that of François Térond, who pub. (1721) with some Psalm versions 8 hymns, deserves special notice. Of these a morning hymn ("Une voix dans mon cœur s'éveille"), an evening hymn ("Seigneur, sous ta sûre conduite,"), and one on the Resurrection ("Jésus, par un suprême effort"), are in present use.

iv. *Reformed Church Hymnody.*

1. Until the early years of the 18th cent. Marot and Beza's Psalter alone was used in the public worship of the Reformed Church. After the conclusion of his revision of the Psalter [Psalters, French, iii. 3], Pictet, with his colleagues Calandrin and Turretini, suggested to the Venerable Company at Geneva that it would be a "happy innovation" to

add to it hymns, reproducing the words of the Gospel, after the precedent of the Lutheran Church. He was commissioned to make the attempt, and, in 1705, pub. anonymously *Cinquante Quatre Cantiques Sacrez pour les Principales Solemnitez* (title-page of 1708 ed.). Of these, 12, which are either paraphrases or close deductions from Holy Scripture, were authorized for public worship; and these, or a slightly increased number, became an appendix to the Psalter throughout the Reformed Church.

The hymns of Pictet are of three classes: Scripture narratives, Scripture paraphrases, and real hymns. The narratives, on the Nativity, Passion, Resurrection, and Day of Pentecost, written at great length, but broken into pauses for singing, have never had great circulation. But among the paraphrases, "Béni soit à jamais le grand Dieu d'Israel" (*Benedictus*), "Mon cœur rempli des biens que Dieu m'envoye" (*Magnificat*), "Sois attentif peuple fidèle" (*Beatitudes*), "A celui qui nous a sauvez" (*Rev.* i. 6, iv. 11), and "Grand Dieu, nous te louons" (*Te Deum*), are still current. And several of the hymns are classic pieces. "Faisons éclater notre joye," the Christmas hymn; "Faisons retentir dans ce jour," and "Entonnons dans ce jour un Cantique nouveau," for Easter; "Venez Chrétiens et contemplons," a dramatic hymn for the Ascension, and "Célébrons tous par nos louanges," for Pentecost, are the finest pieces of sustained praise among French Hymns. "Esprit, notre Créateur," which has resemblances to "Veni Creator; "Seigneur mon Dieu, ma conscience," a prayer for repentance; "De tous les biens source pure et féconde," for Pentecost; "Peuple Chrétien ton Sauveur charitable," and "Tes biens O Dieu sont infinis," for the Lord's Supper, are widely used for their pure devotion.

2. Not till the last quarter of the 18th cent. was any further addition of hymns authorized. Jean Dumas pub. at Leipzig (1774) a collection of 307 hymns, which M. Bovet and M. Atger commend to the attention of compilers. The Reformed Church at Frankfurt, on its emancipation from conformity to the Lutheran ritual, pub. in 1787 *Nouveau Recueil de Psaumes et Cantiques*, which was revised 30 years afterwards by the Pastors Jean Renaud and Manuel, and only in 1849 gave place to the good collection (289 pieces), drawn from modern sources, now in use. A collection was authorized at Berlin (1793), and replaced by a new one in 1829. The Walloon Collection (pub. 1803) contains 133 hymns (20 of Pictet, a few of Térond, 40 of Frankfurt, 1787, others from St. Gall, 1771, Berlin, &c.) appended to its complete Psalter. (These details are due to M. Bovet's kindness.)

v. *The Réveil.*

1. The greatest name in the history of French hymns is that of César Malan (q.v.) of Geneva. The general store of hymns has grown up almost entirely from a number of small contributions; Malan alone emulates the wealth of production exhibited by Watts or Wesley. Like Watts, he gave the first great impulse towards the general recognition of hymns in public worship; like Charles Wesley, he was the poet and interpreter of a great religious movement craving devotional expression. The first idea of composing hymns seems to have been suggested to him by a friend in 1821.

His first volume, intended only for family use, *Cantiques Chrétiens pour les dévotions domestiques*, containing 35 hymns, was pub. in 1823. Another ed., containing 100 hymns, appeared in 1824. In the harmonized edition of these hymns arranged by Wolff Hauloch, a music master of Geneva (the melodies being by Malan himself), the original title is altered to one which

Malan had given originally to a version of 50 psalms (1824), *Chants de Sion:* and this title became the permanent one in the subsequent editions (1828, 200 hymns; 1832, 234 hymns; 1836, 300 hymns). In 1837 he published a volume of hymns and religious pieces for children, *Soixante Chants et Chansons pieuses,* 35 being hymns and 25 songs and stories of religious tendency. The 4th ed. of these (1853), entitled *Premiers Chants,* is enlarged to the number of 126, of which 59 are "Hymnes et Cantiques," 37 "Chansons pieuses," and 30 "Récits pieux." The melodies in all these books are Malan's. Several other hymns of his exist in MSS. His biographer estimates his total of compositions at a thousand. The hymns of Malan are no longer the power that they were in the days of the Réveil. But a large number of them are still in use, and the entire hymnody of the Reformed Church has been coloured by the Réveil and its interpreter. Malan's hymns have been *tr.* into English, first, *Hymns by the Rev. Cæsar Malan . . . Translated into English Verse,* 1825, by Ingram Cobbin; and the second, *Lyra Evangelica,* by Miss Arnold, 1866.

2. Next to Malan may be mentioned the lesser poets of the religious movement at Geneva at that time. Among the members of the Bible Class of Robert Haldane, which was the cradle of the movement in 1817, Ami Bost, H. Empaytaz, Guers, Galland, and Merle d'Aubigné have contributed to the treasury of hymns. Henri Empaytaz compiled a hymn-book for the Church of Bourg de Four (1824). It was revised in 1836 by Guers, Rochat and Olivier for the use of the Église Evangélique of Geneva, and is still in use in the Églises Evangéliques of Geneva and Lyons. A rendering of the *Te Deum* by Empaytaz, "Grand Dieu nous te bénissons," is very widely used. The work of Bost was more that of a musician than a writer of hymns. His complete works were only pub. in 1866, under the title of *Chœurs et Cantiques Chrétiens.* M. Atger says that his hymns bear the mark of the Réveil that gave them birth. The plaintive tones of that time are equally discernible in the hymns of Galland in *Chants Chrétiens* (Nos. 56, 72, 83). Two hymns by Merle d'Aubigné, the great historian, are in the *Chants Chrétiens* (65, 115). The first of them, "L'Éternel est ma part," is in many collections. To this period also belong the hymns of the devoted pastor in the High Alps, who died young, Felix Neff (1798–1829). Among them, " C'est Golgotha, c'est le Calvaire," and " Ne te désole point, Sion," are in common use.

3. The next marked epoch after the work of Malan at Geneva was the publication at Paris of the *Chants Chrétiens* by M. Henri Lutteroth in 1834. It culled out the choice pieces of the past (Racine, Corneille, Pictet, Térond, &c.); it added a number of hymns, which have since passed into wide circulation; and the music to which the hymns were set was greatly admired. The book has undergone modifications in its many editions; but in its definitive shape, attained in 1855, it contains 200 pieces, among which are hymns by Clottu, Chavannes, Vinet, Adolphe Monod, Scherer, &c. Forty-four are by M. Lutteroth himself, of which the 165th, " Alleluia ! Gloire et louanges;" 20th, " C'est moi, c'est moi, qui vous console," 14th, " C'est un rempart que notre Dieu;" and 23rd, "Il vient, il vient, c'est notre Rédemption," are very widely used. The didactic character of others has probably rendered them less popular, though full of real piety. One of the 3 hymns

by Mme. Lutteroth, 23rd, " Je veux t'aimer toi, mon Dieu," is of great sweetness, and found in most hymnals. The *Chants Chrétiens* is still the most popular hymn-book of the Reformed Church, and subsequent books have added comparatively little to its selection.

4. The most striking pieces in the *Chants Chrétiens* are those of Alexander Vinet, the great Swiss theologian. They had appeared for the most part in the *Semeur* (to which he frequently contributed), a periodical edited by M. Lutteroth. As refined and sensitive expressions of devotional feeling, Vinet's hymns are of a very high order. But the fine touch, the personal, reflective mood, and the delicate poetical images, adapt them more to private than public use. Mr. Henry Downton has *tr.* 7 of Vinet's pieces among his graceful renderings of French hymns in *Hymns and Verses,* 1873.

Several of Vinet's hymns are in every collection. "Sous ton voile d'ignominie," "O Seigneur, O Sauveur," "Toi qui dans la nuit de la vie," "Oh ! pourquoi l'amitié gémirait," "Pourquoi reprendre O Père tendre " (written after his daughter's death), "Dans l'abîme des misères," and "Roi des anges, nos louanges," are well-known examples.

5. Among the large group of remaining writers, only a few names can be mentioned :—

Guillaume Clottu, of Neuchâtel (1800–30) has left a few hymns, of which "Oui, pour son peuple Jésus prie," is well known. Frédéric Chavannes, a disciple and friend of Vinet, pub. his *Poésies Chrétiennes et Cantiques,* in 1836. A full selection of his pieces is found in the *Recueil des Églises Nationales de Vaud, Neuchâtel et Genève,* and also in that of the *Église Libre de Vaud.* The most popular are : "Seigneur, mon Dieu, mon âme angoissée," "Encore cette journée, J'éléverai la voix," and "Dans le désert, où je poursuis ma route." The hymns of Chavannes are highly esteemed for fervour and unaffected simplicity. Juillerat, a pastor at Paris, pub. his *Devant la Croix,* in 1859, a volume of hymns and sacred poetry. His evening hymn, "À la fin de cette journee," is in general use. " Levons-nous, frères " is highly praised by M. Chatelanat and M. Atger. Professor Henri Roehrich has contributed several hymns of a tender, meditative and prayerful cast to the Strasburg *Coll.* (1878). " O cieux, unissez-vous aux transports de la terre " has been adopted by M. Bersier and the Methodist Collection. Others are good, such as " Je veux te suivre ici-bas;" "Grand Dieu, mon Seigneur, mon Père;" and " Éternel, tendre Père." Adolphe Monod (1812–56) has left a beautiful hymn, "Que ne puis-je, O mon Dieu, Dieu de ma délivrance ? " A hymn by M. Ed. Schérer, editor of *Le Temps,* "Je suis à Toi," is one of the best French hymns. They are both *tr.* in Mr. Henry Downton's *Hymns and Verses,* 1873.

vi. *Lutheran Church.*

1. The line taken by the Lutheran French Church in regard to the translation and treatment of the Psalter and the use of hymns has been from the first distinct from that of the Reformed Church; the Psalter has been used partially, and treated in its typical and Evangelical relation, and *trs.* of the great German hymns have been used conjointly with it. *Pseaumes, Hymnes et Cantiques . . . mis en rime français selon la rime et melodies allemandes, Francfort,* 1612, contains 63 hymns or paraphrases. It appears from the preface that this is the 3rd edition. M. Douen mentions also *Les Pseaumes de Dauid. Auec les hymnes de D. M. Luther et autres docteurs de l'Église mis en vers français selon la rime et composition allemande, Montbéliard,* 1618. The chaplain of the Swedish Legation at Paris, Balthazar Ritter, pub. at Frankfurt, his native town to which he owed his education for the ministry, in 1673, a book, generally known as *Heures*

Chrétiennes (2nd ed., *Les occupations saintes des ames fidelles* [*Lambeth Lib.*], 1683). Some of the editions were reprinted at Hamburg (1685, 1686) and Berlin. The first part of this book is *Les Cantiques et les Pseaumes de l'Eglise* (1st ed., 93 pieces ; 2nd ed., 139 pieces). Five editions were pub. in Ritter's lifetime. His successor Gueis pub. the 6th (1722). The 7th, containing 200 fresh *trs.* from the recent German hymns, pub. by Jean Daniel Claudi (1739), entitled *Heures Chrétiennes ou occupations saintes* (*Brit. Mus.*), has 381 pieces. They are to be considered, not so much compilations of the several pastors, as successive developments of the hymn-book, which grew gradually from the *Pseaumes, Hymnes et Cantiques* of 1612, A few pieces are *trs.* from the Latin, but far the larger quantity are distinctly stated to be *trs.* from the German, the heading of the original being given at the top of the piece. The *Cantiques Spirituels* of Strasbourg form another series. *Nouvelle Edition des Cantiques Spirituels accommodé aux airs et melodies des originaux allemands et de Pseaumes de David, Strasbourg,* 1747 (*Brit. Mus.*). Evidently not the 1st ed. Other editions, 1758–1709.

2. *Oberlin's Hymn-book.* There is a very interesting volume at the *British Museum,* which was given to Francis Cunningham in 1820 by Oberlin himself, 5 parts, viz :—

Part i. is *Cantiques Spirituels traduit la plupart de l'allemand à l'usage des Eglises Protestantes de la Confession d'Augsbourg. Nouvelle Edition revue et corrigée à Strasbourg, N. D.* (203 pieces, 42 of them Psalms). Pt. ii. is a Collection of Prayers. Pt. iii. is *Cantiques choisis pour l'exercice de jeunesse. Cinquième Edition. Strasbourg,* 1808 (28 pieces, chiefly Psalms). Pt. iv. is *Cantiques choisis dans un but local et particulier, rangés par ordre alphabétique. Strasbourg,* 1815. Part v. consists of music for the preceding parts. Of the three parts, Pt. i. is evidently an ed. of the *Cantiques Spirituels* of Strasbourg. The plan of the book is a natural development of the 1747 edition : a fourth of the pieces are the same. This may perhaps be the hymn-book which *Stöber,* Oberlin's predecessor, is known to have introduced at Waldbach. Pt. iii. is evidently a children's hymn-book which had passed through five editions. A book of the same kind, with a title somewhat varied, is attributed to Stöber (possibly an earlier edition of this). Part iv. may be the *Appendix* to Stöber's hymn-book, which Oberlin is said to have introduced at Waldbach. The 203 pieces of the *Cantiques Spirituels* are composed of 128 pieces *trs.* from the German, and 40 French pieces (37 Pss.). The German *trs.* are quite independent of the Frankfurt *trs.* The Psalms are in some cases from Marot and Beza. One 'of the French pieces is "Que chantez-vous, petits oiseaux ?" by Abbé Pellegrin. The 28 pieces of Pt. ii. are chiefly Psalms. Some are marked as *trs.* by their German headings ; some (e.g. " Mon âme, O Dieu, se prosterne à tes pieds," often quoted as by Oberlin) have tunes from the Moravian Psalmodie, and may possibly be derived from it. Among the 92 pieces of Pt. iv. " De quoi t'alarmes-tu, mon coeur ?" which is often ascribed to Oberlin, has the German heading, " Was Gott thut ist wohl gethan," but is very little like the German hymns having this initial line. (It has been *tr.* by Mr. Downton in *Hymns and Verses,* 1873, " Why art thou cast down, Ob, my soul ?")

On the whole this book points to the conclusion that Oberlin was more a translator and collector than a composer of French hymns.

3. At Paris, the Frankfurt hymn-books were originally used in the chapel of the Swedish Embassy. The first hymn-book for the Lutheran Church there was compiled from the Frankfurt and from Swiss books (printed at Strasbourg about 1750) by Charles Baer. Chrétien Charles Gambs, chaplain to the Swedish Embassy, pub. *Recueil de Cantiques à l'usage de la Chapelle Royale de la légation*

de Suède. Paris, 1800. It was drawn partly from the collections of Dumas, Henry, Engel and St. Gall (Douen). After the foundation of the first consistorial church, a new collection, drawn from Gambs, Engel, Dumas, Henry, Basel and St. Gall, Strasbourg, Frankfurt, Hamburg, and the Walloon collections, was pub., entitled, *Recueil de Cantiques à l'usage des Chrétiens évangéliques. Paris,* 1819. It was compiled by the pastors Boissard and Goepp (250 pieces). This collection has been finally replaced by the *Recueil de Cantiques à l'usage des Églises Évangéliques de France,* 1851 (363 pieces). The relation of this ed. to its predecessors has been thus characterized for this article by M. Chr. Pfender, a Lutheran pastor, who has made these hymns his study :—

" It would be difficult to find in it perceptible traces of the hymns of Ritter. The hymns have changed with the theology. The ed. of Gambs has somewhat of a rationalistic complexion. The ed. of 1851 is a reaction in the evangelical direction, drawing largely from the Moravian and the Swiss sources, especially the *Chants de Sion,* with a slight admixture of those of the Oberlin books." The music is principally German. The 5th ed. (1876) has a few modifications of slight importance.

4. Besides the Paris hymn-book, collections have been pub. at Montbéliard, Strasbourg and Nancy.

That of Montbéliard, *Nouveaux Choix de Psaumes et de Cantiques,* has passed through two editions (1847, 1856). It contains 292 pieces, of which a few are previously unpublished hymns of the country of Montbéliard, the rest being from the Paris Lutheran books, and the usual Reformed hymn-books and the Psalter. The Nancy Collection, *Hymnes et Cantiques à l'usage des Églises et des familles Chrétiennes,* 1874, contains 301 pieces. The pieces peculiar to it are several of a simple plaintive faith by E. M. The Strasbourg Collection, *Recueil de Cantiques,* 1878, contains 112 pieces, drawn from the Montbéliard Collection, the *Cantiques Spirituels* of Strasbourg, 1758, and the Paris Lutheran hymn-book. Its specialities are 17 hymns of a tender meditative character, addressed directly to God, and unfolding the feelings of the heart, by *M. H. Roehrich.*

vii. *Moravian Hymns.*

As the French Lutheran hymns of the 18th cent. were for the most part *trs.* of the German Lutheran, so the French Moravian are *trs.* of the German Moravian. The 1st ed., *Recueil de Cantiques, traduits de l'allemand,* 1743, was the work of Philip Henri Molther and Jeremie Rissler, natives of Alsace.

This book contains 75 pieces. A second part raised the total to 160 pieces ; a third (*Recueil de Cantiques,* Basle, 1757), to 220 pieces, with some metrical litanies. The ed. of 1785, *Psalmodie de l'Eglise des Frères, ou recueil de Cantiques Spirituels, la plupart traduits de l'allemand,* Basle, contains 576 pieces. Instead of the alphabetical arrangement of the early editions, it is classified on the model of the standard German Moravian hymn-book (1778). About 370 pieces are professedly *trs.* from the German : about 200 are said to be originally French. The 9th ed. (1880) contains 700 pieces, of which only about 180 are retained from 1785 (69 of these being French originals). About 540 pieces are *trs.* from the German Moravian editions of 1778 and 1806 (*Supplement*)—hymns by the Zinzendorfs, Christian Gregor, &c. Of the rest, a few are *trs.* from non-Moravian German hymns, a few are well-known pieces of Pictet, Malan, Vinet, &c., the rest are apparently French hymns peculiar to the Brotherhood. About 80 of the distinctive pieces have passed into general French hymn-books. Among the most popular are " Alleluia ! louange à Dieu" (*tr.* from " Hallelujah ! Lob, Preis und Ehr," q.v.) ; " Chef, couvert de blessures," 1757 (*tr.* of St. Bernard's "Salve caput cruentatum," through the German of Paul Gerhardt, " O Haupt voll Blut und Wunden," re-written by Count Zinzendorf) ; "Demeure dans ta grâce" (*tr.* from J. Stegmann's "Ach bleib mit deiner Gnade," q. v.) ; " Jamais Dieu ne délaisse " (*tr.* from " Keinen hat Gott verlassen," q.v., attributed probably wrongly to A. Kessler) ; "Brillante étoile du matin," 1757 (apparently *tr.* from "Brich an du schönes Morgenlicht"); and "Qu'ils sont beaux sur les montagnes' (apparently French). The general character of this book is well given in the Geneva, Neuchâtel and Vaud *Supplement.* "The distinctive traits of these hymns are simple expressions of love for the Saviour, and contemplations of His Death. Often incorrect in form . . . there are no French hymns, which so nearly approach the Psalms in originality of inspiration, power of faith, and richness of experience." Their general mood, it may be added, is strongly subjective and meditative; often marked by a childlike simplicity ("naïveté presque enfantine." *Bersier.*).

viii. *Methodist Collections.*

1. The earliest French hymn-book in connection with Methodism deserves loving remembrance b. both France and England. It was drawn up under the auspices of the Wesleyan Missionary Society for the use of the thousands of French prisoners in the Medway, at Plymouth, and Portsmouth. The earliest mention of the book is found July 10th, 1813. (See *Methodist Magazine* of that year. Interesting details of the mission are given in the vols. for 1811.) It may have been compiled by Rev. W. Toase, who was in charge of the mission. The 1815 edition, *Choix de Cantiques à l'usage des Prisonniers Français,* contains 123 pieces: some of them by Pictet; some of them *trs.* from Watts, Cowper, and other English pieces; some from the metrical Psalm Versions; some from the Moravian, and others from sources not identified. The *trs.* are not of much value: and scarcely any of the pieces are found in subsequent Methodist collections.

2. The next series of books are those of John de Queteville (commenced ministry at Guernsey, 1786, died 1843). Rev. M. Gallienne, a Methodist minister in Alderney, says that Queteville's earliest collections were from the Port-Royal hymns, from Pictet, Marot and Beza. Afterwards he translated several of Wesley's hymns. The date of his earliest edition was about 1791–1792. The book reached its definite shape (app.) in 1818. The ed. of 1828, entitled *Recueil de Cantiques à l'usage de la Société appelée Méthodisté,* is arranged on the plan of the *Wes. H. Bk.* It was pub. at the request of the Conference, and contains no less than 762 hymns. It was frequently reprinted for use in the Channel Islands, but the poorness of the verse led eventually to the compilation of a new collection.

3. The new ed., *Recueil de Cantiques à l'usage des Églises Méthodistes des Iles de la Manche,* was pub. in 1868. It was the work of a Commission appointed by the Channel Islands District under the presidency of the Rev. M. Gallienne. It contains 454 pieces. The arrangement of De Queteville's book is exchanged for one more independent of the English *Wes H. Bk.* About 115 of De Queteville's pieces are retained. The new pieces are drawn from the sources of which all the Protestant hymnals avail themselves. The hymns that are special to the book are a few by Revs. M. and J. W. Delièvre and W. J. Handcock (the Secretary of the Commission). The book was sanctioned by the Conference.

ix. *French Methodist Hymn Book.*

The collection of De Queteville was too poor in a literary point of view to be really satisfactory in France. In 1831, if not earlier, appeared *Cantiques Chrétiens à l'usage des*

Assemblées religieuses, Risler, Paris. It was compiled by M. Cook, then a minister at Congenies in the Department of Gard. The last ed. (14th) was pub. in 1881.

The ed. of 1833 contains 226 pieces. They are drawn from Pictet, Térond, and other sources of the 18th century, from the Moravian, and Malan, and other early books of this century. The 14th ed., *Cantiques Chrétiens, Paris,* 1881, edited by an eminent French Methodist pastor, M. J. P. Cook, son of the original editor (to whom this article is much indebted), contains 134 pieces from the 1833 edition. It has altogether 361 pieces, the new pieces being drawn from the *Chants Chrétiens,* the Moravian, the R. C. Collection of St. Sulpice, and the Psalter of the Reformed Churches, and from the various authors among Methodists and Protestants already mentioned. This ed. is one of the best, as it is one of the most recent, collections; and furnished with careful indices of the subjects and texts, the names of authors and composers.

x. *Translations from the English.*

The earliest *trs.* from the English are those in the French Prisoners Book and Methodist Collection of De Queteville (§ viii.). In recent years a considerable number of our English revival hymns have been *tr.* into French for the use of similar movements in France and Switzerland. They will be readily recognised in the

(1) *Cantiques du Réveil,* (2) *Cantiques imités de l'Anglais,* (3) *Hymnes et Cantiques à l'usage des Réunions Populaires,* and its *Supplement,* (4) *Hymnes du Croyant,* and (5) *Cantiques Populaires* with its *Supplément.* In this last book will be found upwards of 60 *trs.* chiefly by MM. Saillens and R. McAll (who have indicated the originals for this article) of English hymns in Sankey's *Songs & Solos* and older books.

xi. *Children's Hymns.*

Among the numerous selections, Mons. H. Roehrich of Vandœuvres signalises for this article.

(1) *Recueil de petits Cantiques et chants d'école avec un choix de psaumes et cantiques, pub. par les soins du Consistoire de l'Église Nationale de Genève,* 6me *édition, Genève,* 1871. (2) *Hosanna. Cantiques pour écoles du Dimanche et cultes de la jeunesse, pub. par les soins de l'Église Évangélique de Genève,* 1882. (3) *Cantiques du Messager de l'école du Dimanche, Lausanne,* 1878. (4) *Cantiques pour les enfants du catéchisme et des écoles du Dimanche, pub. par le Synode de l'Église Neuchâteloise,* 1881. (5) *Cantiques et chants d'école, pub. par la Mission intérieure protestante à Nîmes, Paris,* 1883.

xii. *Collections of Hymns.*

French hymnals are very numerous. Besides those already mentioned, the principal are as follows:—

1. **The Reformed Church.** (1) *Psaumes et Cantiques pour le culte de l'Église Réformée,* published by the Consistory of Lyons. 1st ed. 1847; last 1878. (2) *Recueil de Psaumes et Cantiques à l'usage des Églises Réformées. Paris* and *Strasbourg.* Drawn up by a Conference of Pastors at Paris, 1857. 1st ed. 1859. It is one of the leading hymnals. (3) *Recueil de Cantiques Chrétiens pour l'usage de culte public et particulier. Frankfort,* 1849. 289 pieces, derived from 15 preceding collections. (4) *Recueil des Églises Nationales de Vaud, Neuchâtel et Genève,* 1866. 63 Ps., 87 hymns. Drawn up by a committee of the National Church in the 3 cantons. A *Supplement* was pub. in 1870 by several of the members of the Committee. A choice selection from French, Moravian, and other German sources. (5) *Nouveau Livre de Cantiques. Paris,* 1879. 217 pieces. A new compilation from the common sources of hymns, with not more than 20 new pieces. The editor is M. Bersier, who has contributed a valuable preface (§ xiii.). The text of the hymns has been revised in the interests of theological exactness. This system of revision of the text, and the difference in the music to which the hymns are set (a point of greater importance than in England—every hymn-book having its music as an integral part of it), often consti-

tute the only very salient distinction between many of the French Collections, all of them being variations of the same general material.

2. **Free Churches.** (1) *Psaumes et Cantiques pour les Assemblées de culte et pour l'édification privée.* 1st ed. 1851. Revised ed. 1864. The Collection used in the "Église Libre de Vaud." (2) *Recueil de Cantiques à l'usage des Églises Évangéliques Belges,* 1856. (3) *Recueil de Cantiques pour les assemblées de culte et pour édification privée,* 1860. The Collection published by "Les Églises Évangéliques de Genève et de Lyon."

3. **English Collections.** (1) *Extraits des Psaulmes versifiés, suivis de quelques Cantiques sacrés . . .* pour *. . . l'Église Protestante Épiscopale Française de Londres,* 1846. (2) *Chants Religieux . . . pour l'Église Protestante Française de Londres: par le Rev. W. G. Daugars,* 1846. (3) *Recueil de Psaumes et de Cantiques à l'usage des Églises Anglicanes Françaises . . . par le Rév. W. B. Bouvérie,* 1876. 88 Pss., 156 Cantiques. The hymn-book used at the Savoy Church, Bloomsbury Street. (4) *Le Livre du Sanctuaire.* The Liturgy used in the crypt at Canterbury has a few cantiques in it.

xiii. *Conclusion.*

The French hymns are intensely subjective. "On regrette," says the able preface to the *Nouveau Livre de Cantiques,* Paris, 1879, "qu'il ne soit pas trouvé parmi nous plus de poëtes pour chanter le drame divin de la Rédemption, les grands faits de l'Évangile célébrés dans les fêtes de l'Église, et qui, bien plus que les expériences de l'âme individuelle, se prêteraient au chant des assemblées chrétiennes." In expressing sentiment, emotion, childlike repose in Jesus, they have a delicacy which we cannot reproduce. On the other hand, the broader, more solid portions of our English hymns find no echo in French. The fact is abundantly illustrated by the *trs.* from the English, which are taken scarcely with an exception from our hymns of subjective sentiment. There is consequently little scope for the introduction of French *trs.* among us; the store of our subjective hymns being already more than sufficient. The strictures of the *Nouveau Livre de Cantiques* are not untrue of England, though far truer of France. "La plus grande partie des cantiques publiés à notre époque expriment surtout les expériences du chrétien, et mettent trop l'homme en face de lui-même, au lieu de le porter avant tout à contempler les célestes réalités qui seules soutiennent l'âme et la fortifient." [H. L. B.]

French Psalters. [Psalters, French.]

Freu dich du werthe Christenheit. [*Easter.*] *Hoffmann von Fallersleben,* ed. 1861, p. 172, gives this in 3 st. of 7 l. from a Breslau MS. about 1478. *Wackernagel,* ii. pp. 738–741, gives 6 versions.

The only *tr.* is: "Rejoice, dear Christendom, to-day," by *Miss Winkworth,* 1869, p. 87. Her st. i.–iii. are from *Wackernagel's* No. 963(2), a version written in a copy of the Bohemian Brethren's *G. B.,* 1566: and st. iv., a doxology, is from *Wackernagel's* No. 964 quoted from *Ein edel Kleinat der Seelen,* Dillingen, 1568.   [J. M.]

Freu dich sehr, o meine Seele. [*For the Dying.*] Included as No. 115 in C. Demantius's *Threnodiae,* Freiberg, 1620, in 10 st. of 8 l., entitled "Spiritual joy after the Eternal Joy." Repeated in many later hymnbooks, as in the *Unv. L. S.,* 1851, No. 814. Erroneously ascribed to Caspar von Warnberg, to Simon Graff, to Valerius Herberger, and others. The only *tr.* in C. U. is:—

Cease, my soul, thy tribulation, a somewhat free version of st. 1, 6, 7, 10, by T. E. Brown, as No. 15 in the *Clifton College H. Bk.,* 1873.

Other *trs.* are: (1) "Rouse thyself, my Soul, endeavour," in *Lyra Davidica,* 1708, p. 69. (2) "Jesus at my dissolution," a *tr.* of st. vii. as st. vii. of No. 89 in the *Moravian H. Bk,* 1801 (1886, No. 1238). (3) "O my soul be glad and cheerful," a *tr.* of st. i. in Miss Winkworth's *C. B. for England,* 1863, *Appendix,* No. iii. (4) "Joy, my soul! oh, joy attend thee," by *N. L. Frothingham,* 1870, p. 147.   [J. M.]

Freudentheil, Wilhelm Nicolaus, was b. June 5, 1771, at Stade, in Hannover, and studied at the University of Göttingen, from which, in 1841, he received the degree of D.D. He became, in 1816, diaconus of St. Nicholas's Church, Hamburg, and subsequently archidiaconus. He d. at Hamburg, March 7, 1853. One of his hymns has been *tr.* :—

Der Vater kennt dich, kenn auch ihn. [*God's Omniscience.*] Appeared in Severin Vater's *Jahrbuch für häusliche Andacht.* Halle, 1829, p. 56, in 6 st. *Tr.* as, "The Father knows thee! Learn of Him," by Mrs. Findlater, in *H. L. L.,* 1862, p. 52 (1884, p. 216).   [J. M.]

Freuen wir uns all in ein. [*Prayer for Unity.*] This, the first hymn of the Bohemian Brethren, was composed in 1457 at Lhotka, in celebration of the foundation of the Unity. Bp. Blahoslav (De Cantionali, 1561) names as author Matthias Konvaldsky, and adds: "licet hanc cantilenam multi tribuunt alii cuidam bono viro, qui vocabatur Gabriel Komarovsky." Originally written in Bohemian, it began, "Radujme se vzdy spolecne," and was first pub. in the Bohemian Brethren's *H. Bk.,* 1501, in 13 st. The *tr.* into German (*Freuen wir,* &c.) is by M. Weisse, is a free version of 12 st., first appeared in the *New Geseng buchlen,* 1531, and is reprinted in *Wackernagel,* iii., No. 357. An English *tr.* from Weisse ("With unity of heart and voice") appears in Benham's *Notes on the Origin and Episcopate of the Bohemian Brethren,* London, 1867, p. 51 (see also Bohemian Brethren, II., i. 1; viii. 1).   [J. T. M.]

Freut euch ihr Christen. [*Christmas.*] This appears in the *Geistliche Lieder und Psalmen,* Magdeburg, 1540; and thence in *Wackernagel,* iii. p. 841, in 4 st. of 8 l. In the *Leipzig G. B.,* 1582, altered to "Freut euch ihr lieben Christen," and this text is mostly followed in later collections. Included as No. 394 in Knapp's *Ev. L. S.,* 1850 (1865, No. 402). The only *tr.* in C. U. is:—

Rejoice, rejoice, ye Christians. A good and full *tr.* as No. 32 in Miss Winkworth's *C. B. for England,* 1863, thence into the Pennsylvania Luth. *Ch. Bk.,* 1868, and the *Ohio Luth. Hyl.,* 1880.   [J. M.]

Freylinghausen, Johann Anastasius, s. of Dietrich Freylinghausen, merchant and burgomaster at Gandersheim, Brunswick, was b. at Gandersheim, Dec. 2, 1670. He entered the University of Jena at Easter, 1689. Attracted by the preaching of A. H. Francke and J. J. Breithaupt, he removed to Erfurt in 1691, and at Easter, 1692, followed them to Halle. About the end of 1693 he returned to Gandersheim, and employed himself as a private tutor. In 1695 he went to Glaucha as assistant to Francke; and when Francke became pastor of St. Ulrich's, in Halle, 1715, Freylinghausen became his colleague, and in the same year married his only daughter. In 1723 he became also sub-director of the Paedagogium and the

Orphanage; and after Francke's death in 1727, succeeded him as pastor of St. Ulrich's and director of the Francke Institutions. Under his fostering care these Institutions attained their highest development. From a stroke of paralysis in 1728, and a second in 1730, he recovered in great measure, but a third in 1737 crippled his right side, while the last, in Nov., 1738, left him almost helpless. He d. on Feb. 12, 1739, and was buried beside Francke (*Koch*, vi. 322–334; *Allg. Deutsche Biog.*, vii. 370–71; *Bode*, pp. 69–70; *Grote's Introduction*, &c.)

Almost all Freylinghausen's hymns appeared in his own hymn-book, which was the standard collection of the Halle school, uniting the best productions of Pietism with a good representation of the older "classical" hymns. This work, which greatly influenced later collections, and was the source from which many editors drew not only the hymns of Pietism, but also the current forms of the earlier hymns (as well as the new "Halle" melodies, a number of which are ascribed to Freylinghausen himself) appeared in two parts, viz.:—

i. *Geist-reiches Gesang-Buch, den Kern alter und neuer Lieder . . . in sich haltend*, &c., Halle. Gedruckt und verlegt im Waysen-Hause, 1704 [*Hamburg*], with 683 hymns and 173 melodies. To the 2nd ed., 1705 [*Rostock University*], an *Appendix* was added with Hys. 684–758, and 21 melodies. Editions 3–18 are practically the same so far as the hymns are concerned, save that in ed. 11, 1719 [*Berlin*], and later issues, four hymns, written by J. J. Rambach at Freylinghausen's request, replaced four of those in eds. 1–10.

ii. *Neues Geist-reiches Gesang-Buch*, &c., Halle . . . 1714 [*Berlin*], with 815 hymns and 154 melodies. In the 2nd ed., 1719 [*Rostock University*], Hys. 816–818, with one melody, were added.

In 1741 these two parts were combined by G. A. Francke, seven hymns being added, all but one taken from the 1st ed., 1718, of the so-called *Auszug*, which was compiled for congregational use mainly from the original two parts: and this reached a second, and last, ed. in 1771. So far as the melodies are concerned, the ed. of 1771 is the most complete, containing some 600 to 1582 hymns. (Further details of these editions in the *Blätter für Hymnologie*, 1883, pp. 44–46, 106–109; 1885, pp. 13–14.) A little volume of notes on the hymns and hymn-writers of the 1771 edition, compiled by J. H. Grischow and completed by J. G. Kirchner, and occasionally referred to in these pages, appeared as *Kurzgefasste Nachricht von ältern und neuern Liederverfassern* at Halle, 1771.

As a hymn-writer Freylinghausen ranks not only as the best of the Pietistic school, but as the first among his contemporaries. His finest productions are distinguished by a sound and robust piety, warmth of feeling depth of Christian experience, scripturalness, clearness and variety of style, which gained for them wide acceptance, and have kept them still in popular use. A complete ed. of his 44 hymns, with a biographical introduction by Ludwig Grote, appeared as his *Geistliche Lieder*, at Halle, 1855. A number of them, including No. v., are said to have been written during severe attacks of toothache. Two ("Auf, auf, weil der Tag erschienen"; "Der Tag ist hin") are noted under their own first lines.

i. *Hymns in English C. U.*

i. **Monarche aller Ding.** *God's Majesty.* 1714, as above, No. 139, in 11 st. of 6 l., repeated in *Grote*, 1855, p. 88, and as No. 38 in the Berlin *G. L. S.*, ed. 1863. A fine hymn of Praise, on the majesty and love of God. *Tr.* as:—

Monarch of all, with lowly fear, by J. Wesley, in *Hys. & Sac. Poems*, 1739 (*P. Works*, 1868–1872, vol. i. p. 104), in 8 st. of 4 l., from st. i., ii., v.–vii., ix.–xi. Repeated in full in the *Moravian H. Bk.*, 1754, pt. i., No. 456 (1886, No. 176); and in J. A. Latrobe's *Coll.*, 1841. The following forms of this *tr.* are also in C. U.:

(1) **To Thee, O Lord, with humble fear,** being

Wesley's st. i., iii.–v., vii., viii. altered as No. 156 in Dr. Martineau's *Hys. for Christian Ch. & Home*, 1840, and repeated in Miss Courtauld's *Ps., Hys. & Anthems*, 1860, and in America in the Cheshire Association Unitarian *Coll.*, 1844.

(2) **Thou, Lord, of all the parent art,** Wesley's, st. iii.–v., vii. altered in the *College Hyl.* N. Y., 1876.

(3) **Thou, Lord, art Light; Thy native ray,** Wesley's st. iv., v., vii., in *Hys. of the Spirit*, 1864.

ii. **O reines Wesen, lautre Quelle.** *Penitence.* Founded on Ps. li. 12, 1714, as above, No. 321, in 7 st. of 8 l., repeated in *Grote*, 1855, p. 41, and in Bunsen's *Versuch*, 1833, No. 777 (ed. 1881, No. 435). The only *tr.* in C. U. is:—

Pure Essence! Spotless Fount of Light. A good and full *tr.* by Miss Winkworth in the 1st series of her *Lyra Ger.*, 1855, p. 43, and in her *C. B. for England*, 1863, No. 113.

iii. **Wer ist wohl wie du.** *Names and offices of Christ.* One of his noblest and most beautiful hymns, a mirror of his inner life, and one of the finest of the German "Jesus Hymns." 1704, as above, No. 66, in 14 st. of 6 l., repeated in *Grote*, 1855, p. 33, and is No. 96 in the Berlin *G. L. S.*, ed. 1863. The *trs.* in C. U. are:—

1. **O Jesu, source of calm repose,** by J. Wesley, being a free *tr.* of st. i., iii.–v., viii., xiii. 1st pub. in his *Ps. & Hys.*, Charlestown, 1737 (*P. Works*, 1868–1872, vol. i. p. 161). Repeated in full as No. 462 in pt. i. of the *Moravian H. Bk.*, 1754. In the 1826 and later eds. (1886, No. 233) it begins, "Jesus, Thou source." The original form was included as No. 49 in the Wesley *Hys. & Spir. Songs*, 1753, and, as No. 343, in the *Wes. H. Bk.*, 1780 (1875, No. 353). Varying centos under the original first line are found in *Mercer's C. P. & H. Bk.*, 1855–1864; *Kennedy*, 1863; *Irish Ch. Hyl.*, 1869–1873; J. L. Porter's *Coll.*, 1876, &c. It has also furnished the following centos:—

(1) **Messiah! Lord! rejoicing still,** being Wesley's st. iv.–vi. altered in Dr. Martineau's *Coll.*, 1840.

(2) **Lord over all, sent to fulfil,** Wesley's st. iv., iii., v., vi. in the Amer. *Meth. Epis. H. Bk.*, 1849.

2. **Who is like Thee, Who?** a *tr.* of st. i., ii., v., vii., x., xiii., as No. 687, in pt. i. of the *Moravian H. Bk.*, 1754. *Trs.* of st. xi., xiv. were added in 1789, and the first line altered in 1801 (1886, No. 234), to "Jesus, who with Thee." The *trs.* of st. i., ii., x., xiv., from the 1801, altered and beginning, "Jesus, who can be," are included in America in the Dutch Ref. *Hys. of the Church*, 1869; *H. & Songs of Praise*, N. Y., 1874; and Richards's *Coll.*, N. Y., 1881.

3. **Who is there like Thee,** a good *tr.* of st. i., ii., viii., xiv., by J. S. Stallybrass, as No. 234 in Curwen's *Sabbath H. Bk.*, 1859, repeated in the *Irish Ch. Hyl.*, 1873, and in W. F. Stevenson's *H. for Ch. & Home*, 1873.

4. **Who is, Jesus blest,** a *tr.* of st. i., ii., v., vi., xii., xiv., by M. Loy, in the Ohio Luth. *Hyl.*, 1880.

5. **Who, as Thou, makes blest,** a good *tr.*, omitting st. vii., ix., x., contributed by Dr. F. W Gotch to the *Baptist Magazine*, 1857. Repeated in the 1880 *Suppl.* to the Bapt. *Ps. & Hys.*, 1858.

The *trs.* not in C. U. are:—
(1) "Whither shall we flee," by *Miss Dunn*, 1857, p. 55. (2) "Who has worth like Thine," in the U. P. *Juvenile Miss. Mag.*, 1857, p. 217. (3) "Thou art First and Best," by *Miss Winkworth*, 1869, p. 267.

ii. *Hymns tr. into English, but not in C. U.*

iv. **Herr und Gott der Tag und Nächte.** *Evening.* 1705, as above, No. 755, in 6 st., *Grote*, p. 105. *Tr.* by H. J. Buckoll, 1842, p. 106, beginning with st. ii.

v. Mein Herz, gieb dich zufrieden. *Cross and Consolation.* 1st in the *Halle Stadt G. B.*, 1711, No. 503, in 11 st.; repeated 1714, No. 450, and in *Grote*, p. 71. *Tr.* by *Dr. G. Walker*, 1860, p. 86.

vi. O Lamm, das keine Sünde je beflecket. *Passiontide.* 1714, No. 85, in 19 st., *Grote*, p. 14. *Tr.* as, (1) "Lamb, for Thy boundless love I praises offer," of st. xii. as st. i. of No. 1023 in the *Suppl.* of 1808 to the *Moravian H. Bk.*, 1801 (1849, No. 121). (2) "O Lamb, whom never spot of sin defiled," in the *British Magazine*, June, 1838, p. 625.

vii. O Lamm, das meine Sündenlast getragen. *Easter Eve.* 1714, No. 95, in 8 st.; *Grote*, p. 23. *Tr.* as "Christ Jesus is that precious grain," a *tr.* of st. v. by F. W. Foster, as No. 71 in the *Moravian H. Bk.*, 1789 (1886, No. 921).

viii. Zu dir, Herr Jesu, komme ich. *Penitence.* Founded on St. Matt. xi. 27-30. 1714, as above, No. 306, in 4 st.; *Grote*, p. 39. *Tr.* by *Dr. H. Mills*, 1845 (1856, p. 80). [J. M.]

Freystein, Johann Burchard, s. of A. S. Freystein, vice-chancellor of Duke August of Saxony and inspector of the Gymnasium at Weissenfels, was b. at Weissenfels, April 18, 1671. At the University of Leipzig he studied law, mathematics, philosophy and architecture. He resided for some time at Berlin and Halle and then went to Dresden as assistant to a lawyer. After graduating LL.D. at Jena in 1695, he began an independent legal practice at Dresden. In 1703 he became Rath at Gotha, but returned to Dresden in 1709 as Hof- und Justizrath, and was also, in 1713, appointed a member of the Board of Works. Enfeebled by his professional labours, he d. of dropsy at Dresden, April 1, 1718 (*Bode*, p. 70; *Blätter für Hymnologie*, 1884, pp. 22–24; *Koch*, iv. 222). Of the six hymns of this pious lawyer and disciple of Spener, five seem to have first appeared in the *Merseburg G. B.*, 1716. The other (which has been *tr.* into English) is:—

Mache dich, mein Geist, bereit. [*Watchfulness.*] This fine hymn, a stirring call to fight against the World, the Flesh, and the Devil, founded on St. Matt. xxvi. 41; first appeared in the *Geistreiches G. B.*, Halle, 1697, p. 393, in 10 st. of 8 l., entitled, "On the words Watch and Pray." It was repeated in Wagner's *G. B.*, Leipzig, 1697, vol. iv. p. 1280; in Freylinghausen's *G. B.*, 1704, and many later collections, and in the *Unv. L. S.*, 1851. The *trs.* in C. U. are:—

1. **Rise, my soul, to watch and pray,** omitting st. 2, 4, 8, 10, by Miss Winkworth in her *C. B. for England*, 1863, No. 125, repeated in J. Robinson's *Coll.*, 1869, No. 10.

2. **Up, my soul, gird thee with power,** omitting st. iv.–vi., by E. Cronenwett, as 396 in the *Ohio Luth. Hyl.*, 1880.

Other *trs.* are: (1) "O my soul, with prayers and cries," in *Lyra Davidica*, 1708, p. 53. (2) "Wake, my soul, wake up from sleep," by J. S. Stallybrass in the *Tonic Sol-fa Reporter*, January, 1859. (3) "Have thy armour on, my soul," by Miss Burlingham in the *British Herald*, Feb. 1865, p. 29.

The hymn "O my spirit, wake, prepare," by A. T. Russell, as No. 104 in the *Dalston Hospital H. Bk.*, 1848, and repeated as No. 196 in Dr. Pagenstecher's *Coll.*, 1864, while not a *tr.*, is based on st. iii., viii., ix. of the German. [J. M.]

Friend after friend departs. *J. Montgomery.* [*Death and the Hereafter.*] In Montgomery's *Poetical Works*, 1841, vol. iii. p. 182, he has dated this poem 1824. It was pub. in his *Pelican Island and Other Poems*, 1827;

and in his *Poetical Works*, 1828 and 1841, but was not given in the first copies of his *Original Hymns*, 1853. In later copies of the same year it replaced a cancelled hymn ("This shall be the children's cry"), but was omitted from the Index. It is in C. U. in G. Britain and America. Orig. text in Dr. Hatfield's *Church H. Bk.*, N. Y., 1872. [J. J.]

Friend of sinners, Lord of glory. *C. N. Hall.* [*Jesus, the Friend.*] "Composed for the author's father, the writer of the well-known tract The Sinner's Friend," Bolton Abbey, Sept., 1857, in 5 st. of 8 l., and 1st pub. in his *Hymns composed at Bolton Abbey*, 1858. It is usually given in an abbreviated form, as in the author's *Christ Ch. Hyl.*, 1876, or that in Spurgeon's *O. O. H. Bk.*, 1866. It is also in C. U. in America. [J. J.]

Friends of the poor, the young, the weak. *J. Montgomery.* [*Poor Children's Plea.*] This hymn is intended to be sung by children in Orphan Homes and Institutions of a like kind, at their yearly and other gatherings. It is a plea for sympathy and material help. It appeared in Montgomery's *Christian Psalmist*, 1825, No. 424, and in his *Original Hys.*, 1853, No. 312, in 6 st. of 4 l. [J. J.]

Fritsch, Ahasuerus. [Liebster Immanuel.]

Fröhlich soll mein Herze springen. *P. Gerhardt.* [*Christmas.*] Included as No. 104 in the Frankfurt ed. 1656, of Crüger's *Praxis pietatis melica* in 15 st. of 8 l., reprinted in Wackernagel's ed. of his *Geistliche Lieder*, No. 5, and Bachmann's ed., No. 44; and included as No. 35 in the *Unv. L. S.*, 1851. Lauxmann, in *Koch*, viii. 26, thus analyses it:

First a trumpet blast: Christ is born, God's Champion has appeared as a Bridegroom from his chamber (i., ii.). In the following 4 sts. the poet seeks to set forth the mighty value of the Incarnation: is it not love when God gives us the Son of His Love (iii.), the Kingdom of Joy (iv.), and His Fellowship (v.). Yes, it is indeed the Lamb of God who bears the sin of the world (vi.) Now he places himself as herald by the cradle of the Divine Child (vii.). He bids, as in Matt. xi. 28, all men (viii.), all they that labour (ix.), all the heavy laden (x.), and all the poor (xi.), to draw near. Then in conclusion he approaches in supplication as the shepherds and the Wise Men (xii.–xv.). He adores the Child as his source of life (xii.), his Lamb of God (xiii.), his Glory (xiv.), and promises to be ever true to Him (xv.). It is a glorious series of Christmas thoughts, laid as a garland on the manger at Bethlehem.

He adds that at the second day of the Christmas celebration, 1715, at Glaucha, near Halle, C. H. v. Bogatzky (q.v.), by the singing of st. xiii., xiv., was first clearly led to understand justification by faith in Jesus Christ.

Crüger gave an original melody in 1656 (as in L. Erk's *Choralbuch*, 1863, No. 86), but the melody generally used (in *Church Hymns* called Bonn) is that by J. G. Ebeling in the *Geistliche Andachten*, 1666, to "Warum sollt ich mich denn grämen." The hymn is a very beautiful one, but somewhat long, and thus generally abridged.

Translations in C. U.:—

1. **Let the voice of glad thanksgiving.** A good *tr.* of st. i.–iii., vi.–ix., by A. T. Russell, as No. 15 in the *Dalston Hospital H. Bk.*, 1848, and repeated, omitting the *trs.* of st. vi.–viii. as No. 56 in his own *Ps. & Hys.*, 1851.

2. All my heart this night rejoices. A beautiful but rather free *tr.*, omitting st. iii.–v., xiii., xiv. by Miss Winkworth in the 2nd series of her *Lyra Ger.*, 1858, p. 13, repeated in full in Brown-Borthwick's *Suppl. Hy. & Tune Bk.*, 1867, and omitting the *tr.* of st. vi. in J. L. Porter's *Coll.* 1876. In Miss Winkworth's *C. B. for England*, 1863, No 31, the *trs.* of st. ii., vi., xii. are omitted. The more important centos are the *trs.* of st. i., ii., vii., viii. in *Ch. Hys.*, 1871, Allon's *Suppl. Hys.*, &c.; and the *trs.* of i., vii.–ix., xii., xv. in the *Suppl.* of 1880 to the Bapt. *Ps. & Hys.*, 1858; and in America in the Dutch Reformed *Hys. of the Church*, 1869, the *Hys. and Songs of Praise*, N. Y., 1874, &c. Other centos are in the *New Zealand Hyl.*, 1872, the *Evang. Hyl.*, N. Y., 1880, the *Methodist S. S. H. Bk.*, 1883, and *Laudes Domini*, N. Y., 1884.

3. All my heart with joy is springing. A good but free *tr.* by Dr. Kennedy, as No. 100 in his *Hymno. Christ.*, 1863, omitting st. iii.–v., ix., xiii., xiv. His *trs.* of st. i., ii., vi., vii. were repeated in the *Anglican H. Bk.*, 1871.

4. Lightly bound my bosom, ringing. In full, by Dr. M. Loy, in the *Ohio Luth. Hyl.*, 1880.

Trs. not in C. U. :—
(1) "Now in His manger He so humbly lies," a *tr.* of st. v. as No. 435 in pt. i. of the *Moravian H. Bk.*, 1754. (2) "Up, my heart! rejoice with singing," as a broadsheet for Christmas, 1770. (3) "Rise, my soul, shake off all sadness," by P. H. Molther, as No. 38 in the *Moravian H. Bk.*, 1789 (1886, No. 36). (4) "Now with joy my heart is bounding," by *J. Kelly*, 1867, p. 18. (5) "Up! with gladness heavenward springing," by *E. Massie*, 1867, p. 24. (6) "Joyful be my spirit singing," by *N. L. Frothingham*, 1870, p. 260. (7) "Joyful shall my heart, upspringing," by *M. W. Stryker*, 1883, p. 30.   [J. M.]

From all that dwell below the skies.

I. Watts. [*Psalm cxvii.*] This paraphrase appeared in his *Psalms of David*, 1719, as follows:—

" PSALM CXVII.   Long Metre.
i.
" From all that dwell below the Skies
Let the Creator's Praise arise:
Let the Redeemer's Name be sung
Thro' every Land, by every Tongue.
ii.
" Eternal are thy Mercies, Lord ;
Eternal Truth attends thy Word ;
Thy Praise shall sound from Shore to Shore
Till suns shall rise and set no more."

In this its original form this hymn is in extensive use in all English-speaking countries. It has also been *tr.* into several languages, including Latin, by Bingham, in his *Hymno. Christ. Latina*, 1871 :—" Magna Creatoris cunctis cunctis altum aethera subter."

2. A second form of the hymn appeared about 1780, under the following circumstances. John Wesley, in the Preface to his *Pocket Hymn-book for the Use of Christians of All Denominations*, dated Nov. 15, 1786, says :—

"A few years ago I was desired by many of our preachers to prepare and publish a small Pocket Hymn-book, to be used in common in our Societies. This I promised to do, as soon as I had finished some other business, which was then on my hands. But before I could do this, a Bookseller stepped in, and without my consent or knowledge, extracted such a Hymn-book chiefly from our works, and spread several editions of it throughout the kingdom. Two years ago I published a Pocket Hymn-book according to my promise. But most of our people were supplied already with the other Hymns. And these are largely circulated still. To cut off all pretence from the Methodists for buying them, our Brethren in the late Conference at *Bristol* advised me to print the same Hymn-book which had been printed at *York*. This I have done in the present volume; only with this difference," &c.

The hymn-book here referred to is :—

A Pocket Hymn-book designed as a constant Companion for the pious, collected from Various Authors. York, R. Spence [c. 1780], 5th ed., 1786.

From this hymn-book J. Wesley reprinted in his *Pocket Hymn-book*, 1786, Watts's " From all that dwell below the skies," with these additional lines in one stanza :—

" Your lofty themes, ye mortals, bring,
In songs of praise divinely sing;
The great salvation loud proclaim,
And shout for joy the Saviour's name :
In ev'ry land begin the song;
To ev'ry land the strains belong ;
In cheerful sounds all voices raise,
And fill the world with loudest praise."

The original, together with these lines from the *York* book, passed into several collections as a hymn in 4 st. of 4 l. The cento in this form is in C. U. in G. Britain and America.

3. A third form of the text is also in C. U. It appeared in the 1830 *Supplement* to the *Wes. H. Bk.*, No. 699. It is composed of Watts's original, four lines from the *York Pocket Book* text, and Bp. Ken's doxology, " Praise God from whom all blessings flow," &c. This was omitted in the 1875 revised ed. of the *Wes. H. Bk.*, in favour of Watts's original text.   [J. J.]

From all Thy saints in warfare, for all Thy saints at rest.

Earl Nelson. [*Saints' Days, Special and General.*] This hymn was suggested to the author by the hymn, " Ye saints ! in blest communion," by Dr. Monsell, in his *Hys. of Love and Praise*, 1863, the design being the same, which is to furnish a general beginning and ending suitable for a hymn for any special Saint's Day, and to supply intermediate stanzas suitable for the persons specially to be commemorated. It was 1st pub. in a small volume entitled, *Hymn for Saints' Day, and other Hymns. By a Layman*, 1864. " Some verses were contributed by friends of the author ; and the whole was revised by himself for the *Sarum Hymnal*, 1868" (*Church Hys.* folio ed., *Notes*, p. xliv.). Usually this text is repeated in the hymn-books. The S. P. C. K. *Church Hys.* is an exception in favour of a few minor alterations, and the addition of a new stanza (xviii.) for " All Saints."   [J. J.]

From distant corners [places] of our land.

W. L. Alexander. Written in 1847 for the Annual Meeting of the Congregational Union of Scotland, and is usually printed on the programme of the Anniversary from year to year. It was pub. in Dr. Alexander's *Augustine H. Bk.*, 1849, in 7 st. of 4 l., and from thence has passed into various hymnals, in some cases reading " From distant *places* of our land."   [J. J.]

From Egypt lately come.

T. Kelly. [*Seeking a Better Country.*] 1st pub. in his *Coll. of Ps. & Hys. extracted from Various Authors, with an Appendix*, 1802, No. 250, in 7 st. of 6 l. It was repeated in the numerous editions of his *Hys. on Various Passages of Scripture*, &c., from the first, 1804, to the latest, 1853. It is rarely given in its original and full form. The version, " From Egypt's bondage come," appeared in Cotterill's *Sel.*, 8th ed., 1819, and was repeated in Montgomery's *Christian Psalmist*, 1825. It came into general use, and is a popular form of the hymn. Other altered texts are in Bickersteth's *Christian Psalmody*, 1833; Hall's *Mitre*, 1836; the S. P. C. K. *Church Hymns*, 1871, &c. These begin with the same first line as in Cotterill, but differ somewhat in the body of the text. The same differences are repeated in the American collections, but most of these are in error as to date. In a few hymn-books the hymn opens with st. ii., "To Canaan's sacred bound," as in the Marylebone *Ps. & Hys.*, 1851.   [J. J.]

From every stormy wind that blows. *H Stowell.* [*The mercy-seat.*] Appeared in *The Winter's Wreath, a Collection of original Contributions in Prose and Verse* (Lond. and Liverpool), 1828 (Preface dated 1827), p. 239, in 6 st. of 4 l. This collection was an illustrated annual, begun in 1828 and continued to 1832 inclusive. In 1831 this hymn was re-written and included in the 1st ed. of the author's *Ps. & Hys.*, No. 216. This revised text is that which has been adopted by all editors of modern collections. It is given in full in the revised ed. of the same *Sel. of Hys.*, 1877, p. 168, with a return to the original of "*cold* and still," instead of "*stiff* and still," in st. vi. as in the revised text of 1831. The hymn, often in 5 st., is in very extensive use in all English-speaking countries. [J. J.]

From fisher's net, from fig-tree's shade. *J. S. B. Monsell.* [*St. Matthew.*] Appeared in his *Spiritual Songs*, 1857, in 12 st. of 4 l., on St. Matthew, the Apostle, and entitled, "The man of Business." It is sometimes given in an abridged form, beginning with st. iii., "Out of the busiest haunts of life," as in Porter's *Churchman's Hymnal*, 1876.   [J. J.]

From foes that would the land devour. *Bp. R. Heber.* [*National Hymn.*] Appeared in his posthumous *Hymns*, &c. 1827, for the 23rd Sun. after Trinity, in 2 st. of 8 l. Although not usually used as such it is well adapted as a national hymn. Dr. Kennedy gives it in his *Hymno. Christ.*, 1863, No. 735, in an unaltered form, as one of a group of national hymns, under "Easter." Although but little used in G. Britain, it is given in several American hymnals.   [J. J.]

From glory unto glory. *Frances R. Havergal.* [*Personal Consecration — New Year.*] Written at Winterdyne, Dec. 24, 1873, first printed as a New Year's leaflet, Jan. 1st, 1874, and then pub. in her work *Under the Surface*, March, 1874, in 20 st. of 4 l. Concerning this hymn the author says that it was the reflection of "that flash of electric light, when I first saw clearly the blessedness of true consecration, Dec. 2, 1873. I could *not* have written the hymn before. It is a wonderful word from 'glory unto glory.' May we more and more claim and realize all that is folded up in it." The sequel to this hymn is, "Far more exceeding," written April, 1876, 1st printed in *Our Own Fireside*; and then pub. in *Under His Shadow*, Nov. 1879 (HAV. MSS.).   [J. J.]

From Greenland's icy mountains.

Bp. R. Heber. Mrs. Heber's account of the origin of this hymn for Missions is that,

"In the course of this year [1819] a royal letter was granted authorizing collections in every Church and Chapel of England in furtherance of the Eastern operations of the Society for Propagating the Gospel. Mr. Reginald Heber went to Wrexham to hear the Dean of S. Asaph [his father-in-law] preach on the day appointed, and at his request, he wrote the hymn commencing 'From Greenland's icy mountains,' which was first sung in that beautiful Church." (*Memoirs*, vol. i. p. 519.)

The original ms. was subsequently secured from the printer's file by Dr. Raffles, of Liverpool, and has been reproduced in facsimile by Hughes of Wrexham. On a flyleaf of the facsimile is an interesting account of its origin, by the late Thomas Edgworth, solicitor, Wrexham. Mr. Edgworth's account agrees with that given by Mrs. Heber in the *Memoirs*, but is more circumstantial:—

"On Whitsunday, 1819, the late Dr. Shipley, Dean of St. Asaph, and Vicar of Wrexham, preached a Sermon in Wrexham Church in aid of the Society for the Propagation of the Gospel in Foreign Parts. That day was also fixed upon for the commencement of the Sunday Evening Lectures intended to be established in the Church, and the late Bishop of Calcutta (Heber), then rector of Hodnet, the Dean's son-in-law, undertook to deliver the first lecture. In the course of the Saturday previous, the Dean and his son-in-law being together in the Vicarage, the former requested Heber to write 'something for them to sing in the morning;' and he retired for that purpose from the table where the Dean and a few friends were sitting, to a distant part of the room. In a short time the Dean enquired, 'What have you written?' Heber having then composed the three first verses, read them over. 'There, there, that will do very well,' said the Dean. 'No, no, the sense is not complete,' replied Heber. Accordingly he added the fourth verse, and the Dean being inexorable to his repeated request of 'Let me add another, O let me add another,' thus completed the hymn of which the annexed is a fac-simile, and which has since become so celebrated. It was sung the next morning in Wrexham Church, the first time. E."

The text of the facsimile shows that Heber originally wrote st. ii. l. 7, "The savage in his blindness," but altered it in the ms. to "The *heathen* in his blindness." In the ms., st. ii., l. 2, reads, "Blow soft o'er Ceylon's isle." This is altered in the *Hymns*, 1827, to "Blow soft o'er *Java's* isle," but for what reason is unknown.

During the latter part of 1822 Heber was offered the Bishopric of Calcutta. Early in the following year a correspondent, signing himself "J.," forwarded the hymn to the editor of the *Christian Observer*, with a note in which, after referring to Heber's recent appointment to the Bishopric, and to the beauty of his muse, he adds, "the hymn having appeared some time since in print with the name of Reginald Heber annexed, I can feel no scruple in annexing the name to it on the present occasion." This note, followed by the hymn, was published in that magazine in February, 1823, and Heber was consecrated in the June following. In 1827 it was republished by his widow in *Hymns written and adapted to the Weekly Church Service*, p. 139, entitled, "Before a Collection made for the Society for the Propagation of the Gospel," and signed "R. H.," in common with the rest of Heber's hymns. It was subsequently reprinted in Heber's *Works*, in 1842. Its use is very extensive in all English-speaking countries; and it has been rendered into various languages, including Latin, in *Arundines Cami*, p. 225; and German by Dr. C. G. Barth, in his *Christ-*

liche Gedichte, Stuttgart, 1836, p. 65, and repeated in Biggs's *Annotated H. A. & M.*, 1867. [J. J.]

From hidden source arising. *R. F. Littledale.* [*Common of Evangelists.*] Written for and 1st pub. in the *People's H.*, 1867, No. 204, in 8 st. of 4 l., and signed "L." In 1869, st. i.–v. were given in the *Appendix* to the S. P. C. K. *Ps. & Hys.*, No. 313, and a new stanza ("For this Thy fourfold Gospel") was added thereto. In this form it passed into the S. P. C. K. *Church Hymns*, 1871. The idea of the hymn is both old and beautiful, that of comparing the four Evangelists to the four great rivers which issued from Eden. It is worked out in another form in sculpture and painting, where the rivers give place to the "four living creatures" of Rev. iv. 7. Mrs. Alexander has also utilized Ez. i. 10, in her hymn, "From out the cloud of amber light," in the same direction. [J. J.]

From highest heaven the Eternal Son. *Sir H. W. Baker.* [*Praise for Redemption.*] 1st pub. in *H. A. & M.*, 1861, and repeated, with the alteration in st. ii., l. 1, of "Sing out," to "*Rejoice*," in the ed. of 1875.

From Jesus' eyes, beside the grave. *Bp. C. Wordsworth, of Lincoln.* [*Consecration of Burial Ground.*] 1st pub. in his *Holy Year*, 1862, p. 223, in 13 st. of 4 l. In the latest editions of the *Holy Year* it is divided into two parts, Pt. ii. beginning, "I heard a voice from heaven, The dead," &c. A portion of this hymn, beginning with st. iii.—"Faith, looking on this hallow'd ground," is No. 281 in Skinner's *Daily Service Hymnal*, 1864. [J. J.]

From out the cloud of amber light. *Cecil F. Alexander.* [*St. Mark.*] Contributed to the revised ed. of *H. A. & M.*, 1875.

From pole to pole let others roam. *J. Newton.* [*Security in Christ.*] Pub. in the *Olney Hymns*, 1779, Bk. i., No. 69, in 6 st. of 4 l., and headed, "The Lord is my Portion." It is found in a few collections in G. Britain and America. In the American *Songs for the Sanctuary*, N. Y., 1865, st. ii.–v. are given as, "Jesus, Who on His glorious throne." [J. J.]

From the courier [guiding] star that led. *Bp. E. H. Bickersteth.* [*Love.*] Written in 1875, and 1st printed in a small volume for private circulation, *Songs in the House of Pilgrimage* [1875], in 5 st. of 10 l., and based on St. John xxi. 15–17, "Lovest thou Me?" &c. In 1876 it was given in the *H. Comp.*, No. 298, as "From the *guiding* star," &c., this being the only change in the text.

From the Cross uplifted high. *T. Haweis.* [*Passiontide.*] 1st pub. in his *Carmina Christo*, &c., 1792, in 4 st. of 6 l., and based on St. John vii. 37. Its use in G. Britain is very limited, but in America it is given in many collections. In the Dutch Reformed *Hys of the Church*, N. Y., 1869, it is attributed to "Harvey," in error, and the text is slightly altered. Orig. text in *Hys. and Songs of Praise*, N. Y., 1874. [J. J.]

From the depths to Thee, O Lord. *W. Bartholomew.* [*Lent.*] Contributed from his MSS. by his widow to Hall and Lasar's *Evangelical Hymnal*, N. Y., 1880, No. 292, in 3 st. of 5 l. The tune *Nineveh*, which accompanies it, is by Mrs. Bartholomew.

From the heaven of heavens descending. *Bp. E. H. Bickersteth.* [*S. S. Teachers.*] "A Centenary Hymn for Teachers," written for the Centenary of Sunday Schools, 1880, and published in the *Church Sunday School Institute Magazine*, June, 1880, in 6 st. of 4 l.

From whence these dire portents around. *S. Wesley, jun.* [*Good Friday.*] 1st pub. in his *Poems on Several Occasions*, 1736, p. 136, in 7 st. of 4 l., and headed, "On the Passion of Our Saviour." In 1737, 6 st. were given in J. Wesley's Charles-Town (America) *Coll. of Ps. & Hys.*, as No. 6 of the "Ps. & Hys. for Wednesdays and Fridays." It was repeated in the Wesley *Ps. & Hys.*, 1741, and in the 1830 *Supp.* to the *Wes. H. Bk.*, but omitted from the revised ed. of 1875. It is found in several modern collections in G. Britain and America. In one or two of the latter it reads, "From whence these *direful omens round?*" [J. J.]

From year to year in love we meet. *J. Montgomery.* [*S. S. Anniversary.*] This hymn was evidently written for one of the great gatherings of Sunday School children at Whitsuntide, at Sheffield. It is No. 545 in his *Christian Psalmist*, 1825, in 6 st. of 4 l. It did not appear in the first copies of the 1st ed. of his *Original Hymns*, 1853, but took the place of a cancelled hymn ("Our hearts are glad to hear," No. 338) in later copies of the same issue, but was omitted from the Index. It is popular with modern compilers. [J. J.]

Frothingham, Nathaniel Langdon, D.D., b. at Boston July 23rd, 1793, and graduated at Harvard 1811, where he was also sometime Tutor. From 1815 to 1850 he was Pastor of the First Church (Unitarian), Boston, and subsequently attended as a worshipper the church where he had been 35 years minister till his sight and strength failed him. He d. April 4th, 1870. His *Metrical Pieces*, in 2 vols., were pub. in 1855 and 1870.

1. **O God, Whose presence glows in all.** *Ordination.* This was written in 1828 for the ordination of W. B. Lunt, New York.

2. **We meditate the day.** *Installation.* Written in 1835 for Mr. Lunt's installation at Quincy, Mass., as Co-pastor with Peter Whitney.

3. **O Lord of life and truth and grace.** *Ordination.* Also a special hymn. It was composed for the ordination of H. W. Bellowes, New York, 1839. It is found in common with Nos. 1 and 2 in Frothingham's *Metrical Pieces*, 1855. These *Metrical Pieces* are unknown to the English Collections. [F. M. B.]

Frothingham, Octavius Brooks, M.A., son of Dr. N. L. Frothingham, was b. at Boston, Nov. 26, 1822, and educated at Harvard, graduating in Arts, 1843, and in Theology, 1846. In 1847 he became Pastor at Salem, from whence he passed to Jersey City, 1855; and again to the 3rd Unitarian Society, New York, 1860. His works are numerous and well known. Mr. Frothingham is known as a leader of the Free Religious movement. His hymn, "Thou Lord of Hosts, Whose guiding hand" (*Soldiers of the Cross*), was written for the Graduating Exercise of the class of 1846 (see also "God of the earnest heart"), and pub. in the same year in Longfellow and Johnson's *Book of Hymns*, No. 425. It has been adopted by Dr. Martineau in his *Hys. of Praise & Prayer*, 1873.   [F. M. B.]

Frühlingsluft, um blaue Berge spielend. [*Ascension.*] On types of the Resurrection, suggested by St. John xiv. 19. Appeared in Knapp's *Christoterpe*, 1836, p. 149, in 5 st. of 4 l., entitled, "To my sister." *Tr.* as "Breezes of Spring, all earth to life awaking," by Miss Borthwick in the *Family Treasury*, 1862, pt. i. p. 289, and in *H. L. L.*, 1862, p. 95 (1884, p. 234).   [J. M.]

Frühmorgens da die Sonn aufgeht. J. *Heermann.* [*Easter.*] 1st pub. in his *Devoti musica cordis*, Breslau, 1630, p. 66, in 19 st. of 4 l., with alleluias, and entitled, "Easter Hymn. How that Christ has arisen, and what we thence derive for instruction and consolation." Included in *Mützell*, 1858, No. 31; in Wackernagel's ed. of his *Geistl. Lieder*, No. 19; and in the *Unv. L. S.*, 1851, No. 136.

The trs. in C. U. are :—

1. **Lo! with this morning's dawning ray.** A good *tr.* of st. i., viii., ix., xv. by A. T. Russell, as No. 114 in his *Ps. & Hys.*, 1851.

2. **Ere yet the dawn hath fill'd the skies.** A good *tr.* of st. i., xii., xv., xvi., xviii., xix. by Miss Winkworth in the 2nd Series of her *Lyra Ger.*, 1858, p. 38. Repeated as No. 57 in her *C. B. for England*, 1863, and as No. 82 in the *Ohio Luth. Hyl.*, 1880. In the *Ibrox Hyl.*, 1871, the *trs.* of st. xviii., xix. are omitted.

Other trs. are : (1) "Doth Jesus live? why am I sad," of st. xv. as No. 333 in pt. i. of the *Moravian H. Bk.*, 1754. (2) "In the grey of the morning when shades pass away," by *Miss Dunn*, 1857, p. 44.   [J. M.]

Fry, Caroline. [Wilson, C.]

Fuger, Caspar. Two Lutheran clergymen of this name, apparently father and son, seem to have lived in Dresden in the 16th cent. The elder seems to have been for some time at Torgau, and then court preacher at Dresden to Duke Heinrich and his widow, and to have d. at Dresden, 1592. Various works appeared under his name between 1564 and 1592. The younger was apparently b. at Dresden, where he became third master and then corrector in the Kreuzschule. He was subsequently ordained diaconus, and d. at Dresden, July 24, 1617 (*Koch*, ii. 215–216; *Wetzel*, i. 303; *Wackernagel*, as below, and i. pp. 459, 513, 569). The hymn,

Wir Christenleut haben jetzund Freud [*Christmas*], is quoted by *Wackernagel*, iv. p. 10, from *Drey schöne Newe Geistliche Gesenge*, 1592, and from the *Dresden G. B.*, 1593, in 5 st. of 6 l. *Wackernagel* thinks it was written about 1552. *Bode*, p. 417, cites it as in Georg Pondo's *Eine kurtze Comödien von der Geburt des Herren Christi* extant in a MS. copy, dated 1589, in the Royal Library at Berlin. It is probably by the elder Fuger, though Wetzel and others ascribe it to the younger. Included in many later hymn-books, and recently as No. 57 in the *Unv. L. S.*, 1851. The only *tr.* in C. U. is:—

We Christians may rejoice to-day, a good and full *tr.* by Miss Winkworth in her *C. B. for England*, 1863, No. 34.   [J. M.]

Fulbert of Chartres, Saint and Bishop (St. Fulbertus Carnotensis), flourished in the 11th century, having been consecrated Bishop of Chartres (probably) in 1007, and dying on April 10th, 1028. His collected works were pub. at Paris in 1608, but with the exception of one hymn, "Chorus novae Hierusalem" (q.v.), are very little known. That hymn in its original Latin form was included in the *Sarum Breviary*, and, in one English form or another, finds a place in most of our English Hymnals as "Ye choirs of New Jerusalem." [D. S. W.]

Fulgens praeclara rutilat. [*Easter.*] This is given in the *Sarum, Hereford*, and *York Missals* as the sequence for Easter Day. It was also of common use in France. *Morel*, 1868, No. 68, gives it in part from a 14th cent. MS. at Lucerne, and this is repeated in *Kehrein*, 1873, No. 95. *Daniel*, ii. 175, and v. 61, refers to it, but does not give the text. The oldest form known is in the Bodleian MS. 775, c. 1000 (f. 142); in an 11th cent. Winchester book now in Corpus Christi College, Cambridge (No. 473); and in an 11th cent. MS. in the British Museum (H rl. 2961, f. 253). It was *tr.* as—

Bright glows the morn this Easter-day. By Dean Plumptre for the *Hymnary*; and pub. therein, 1872. It is appointed to be sung at Holy Communion on Easter-day. Another *tr.* is, "This day the dawn glows bright above the sun," by C. B. Pearson, and given in his *Sequences from the Sarum Missal*, 1870. [J. M.]

Fuller - Maitland, Frances Sara. See pp. 774, i.; 1557, i.

Fuller, Margaret. [Ossoli, M. F. C. S.]

Fumant Sabaeis templa vaporibus. *Jean Baptiste de Santeüil.* [*Purification.*] Appeared in the *Cluniac Breviary*, 1686, p. 930, and in his *Hymni Sacri et Novi*, 1689 (ed. 1698, p. 66). It was given in the *Paris Breviary*, 1736, and is also in Card. Newman's *Hymni Ecclesiae*, 1838 and 1865. *Tr.* as :—

Sweet incense breathes around. In the *Preface* (q. v.) to his *Hys. tr. from the Parisian Breviary*, 1839, I. Williams says that this *tr.* was supplied to that work "by a friend." It is given at p. 185, in 6 st. of 6 l. It appears in Skinner's *Daily Service Hymnal*, 1864, and others altered, and abbreviated to 4 st.

Another tr. is :—

To the temple's heights. J. D. *Chambers*, 1866, p. 63.   [J. J.]

Funcke, Friedrich, was b. at Nossen in the Harz, where he was baptised March 27, 1642. After receiving a general and musical education at Freiberg and Dresden, he became cantor at Perleberg, and then, in 1664, Stadt Cantor at Lüneburg. He was, in 1694, appointed pastor at Römstedt, a few miles south of Lüneburg, and d. there Oct. 20, 1699. He revised the *Lüneburg G. B.*, 1686, and contributed to it 43 melodies and 7 hymns (*Blätter für Hymnologie*, 1884, pp. 115, 135, 146; 1885, p. 121). One has passed into English, viz. :—

Zeuch uns nach dir, so kommen wir. [*Ascensiontide.*] 1st pub. in the *Lüneburg Stadt G. B.*, 1686, No. 593, in 5 st. of 4 l., signed "F. F.," and founded on Canticles i. 4. Repeated in Freylinghausen's *G. B.*, 1705, No. 699, the *Berlin G. L. S.*, ed. 1863, No. 341, and many other collections. Often wrongly ascribed to

2 D

Ludämilia Elizabeth (q.v.), or to *Friedrich Fa-
bricius* (b. April 20, 1642, at Stettin, and d. there
Nov. 11,1703, as Pastor of St. Nicholas's Church).
The only *tr.* in C. U. is :—

Draw us to Thee, Lord Jesus. A somewhat
free *tr.* omitting st. ii. by Miss Winkworth in
her *C. B. for England*, 1863, No. 68. Repeated
in Dr. Thomas's *Augustine H. Bk.*, 1866, *Marlborough College H. Bk.*, 1869, and in America in
the Pennsylvania Luth. *Ch. Bk.*, 1868.

Other trs. are : (1) "Draw us, Saviour, then will we,"
by *Miss Dunn*, 1857, p. 102. (2) "Draw us to Thee,
So shall we flee," by *N. L. Frothingham*, 1870, p. 275.

The hymn beginning, "Draw us to Thee, in
mind and heart," by A. T. Russell, in 4 st., as
No. 269 in his *Ps. & Hys.*, 1851, while not a *tr.*
of, is based on this German hymn. Repeated
in Dr. Pagenstecher's *Coll.*, 1864, and in J. L.
Porter's *Coll.*, 1876.   [J. M.]

Funeri ne date planctum. [*Burial.*]
A Sequence at a Child's Funeral, in *Graduel
de Paris*, 1754, and the *Paris Missal*, 1764.
Its authorship is unknown.   *Tr.* as :—

1. Let no tears to-day be shed. A terse and pathetic *tr.* by R. F. Littledale. This appeared
first in the *Church Times*, Nov. 10, 1865, again
in W. C. Dix's *Hymns & Carols*, 1869, and in the
S. P. C. K. *Church Hymns*, 1871, "For the
Burial of a Child." In the Preface to the latter
collection it is attributed to W. C. Dix in error.
This is corrected in the *Notes* of the folio edition.

2. Weep not at our pomp funereal. By T. I.
Ball, in the 1873 ed. of the 1862 *Appendix* to
the *Hymnal N.*, No. 369.

3. Wail ye not, but requiems sing. By Jane E.
Leeson, in her *Hys. and Scenes of Childhood*,
1842, pt. ii. p. 205, and the *S. Margaret's
Hymnal* [East Grinstead], 1875.   [J. J.]

Funk, Gottfried Benedict, was b. Nov.
29, 1734, at Hartenstein, Saxony, and educated
at the Gymnasium of Freiberg and the University of Leipzig. In 1756 he became tutor
in the family of J. A. Cramer, then court
preacher at Copenhagen. He returned to Germany in 1769 as subrector of the Cathedral
School at Magdeburg, becoming rector in 1772;
and being also appointed a member of the
consistory in 1785 and Doctor of Theology in
1804. He d. at Magdeburg, June 18, 1814.

One of the best teachers of his time, he was also
one of its most successful hymn-writers. His hymns,
25 in all, appeared (1) in the *G. B. für S. Petri,*
Kopenhagen, 1760. (2) Zollikofer's *Neues G. B.,*
Leipzig, 1766. (3) the *Magdeburg G. B.*, 1805. (4)
in his *Schriften*, Berlin, 1820–21.

Four of his hymns have passed into English, viz. :—

i. *Der unsre Menschheit an sich nahm. Second
Advent.* 1760, No. 973, in 7 st. 1820, v. i. p. 60. *Tr.*
by *Dr. H. Mills*, 1845 (1856, p. 37).

ii. *Lob sey Gott, der den Frühling schafft.
Spring.* 1760, No. 794, in 9 st. 1820, v. i. p. 34
(Gelobt sey). *Tr.* by *Miss Fry*, 1859, p. 109.

iii. *Lob sey Gott, der den Morgen. Morning.*
1766, No. 70, in 7 st. 1820, v. i. p. 25. *Tr.* by *H. J.
Buckoll*, 1842, p. 58; and by *N. L. Frothingham*, 1870.

iv. *Wie ist mein Herz so fern von dir. Penitence.* 1805, No. 266, in 5 st. 1820, v. i. p. 9. *Tr.* by
Dr. H. Mills, 1845 (1856, p. 123).   [J. M.]

Für allen Freuden auf Erden. *M.
Luther.* [*Praise of Music.*] 1st pub. in *Lob
und preis der löblichen Kunst Musica*, Wittenberg, 1538; and then in the *Geistliche Lieder,*

Wittenberg, 1543, entitled "Preface to all
good hymn-books." In *Wackernagel*, iii. p.
29, in 40 lines.

The trs. are : (1) "Search ye the world—search all
around, by *Dr. J. Hunt*, 1853, p. 178. (2) "Of all the
joys earth possesses," by Dr. G. Macdonald, in the *Sunday Magazine*, 1867, and in his *Exotics*, 1876. (3) "Of
all the joys that are on earth," by *Miss Winkworth*, 1869,
p. 1, repeated in Dr. Bacon, 1884.   [J. M.]

Furness, William Henry, D.D., b. in
Boston, 1802, and graduated at Harvard in
Arts and Theology, 1820. From 1825 he has
been an Unitarian Pastor in Philadelphia.
He is an accomplished scholar, and has been
an active worker in reforms of various kinds.
His publications are numerous and include a
Manual of Domestic Worship, 1840, and a *tr.*
of Schiller's *Song of the Bell*. His hymns are
somewhat numerous, and several of them
have great merit. The best and most widely
used are :—

1. Father in heaven, to Thee my heart. *Resignation.* Appeared in *The Christian Disciple*,
1822. It was repeated in this form in some of
the older collections, and a few modern hymnals,
including the Boston Unitarian *Hy. [& Tune] Bk.*,
1868. In 1846 it was given in Longfellow and
Johnson's *Bk. of Hys.* as "Father in heaven, to
Whom our hearts ;" again in their *Hys. of the
Spirit*, 1864, and in Dr. Martineau's *Hys. of
Praise & Prayer*, 1873. This hymn is sometimes
ascribed to "H. Ware," but in error.

2. Feeble, helpless, how shall I ? *Jesus our
Leader.* 1st pub. in the Cheshire Unitarian
Christian Hys., 1844, No. 272, in 5 st. of 4 l.
It is in several modern collections, including
Lyra Sac. Americana, 1868: Thring's *Coll.*, 1882.

3. Have mercy, O Father. *Divine direction desired.* Contributed to Dr. Martineau's *Hys. of
Praise and Prayer*, 1873, in 2 st. of 6 l.

4. Here in a world of doubt. *Ps. xlii.* Contributed to the N. Y. Lutheran *Coll.*, 1834, and
repeated in his *Manual of Domestic Worship*,
1840, Martineau's *Hymns*, &c., 1873.

5. Here in the broken bread. *Holy Communion.*
Appeared in the *Appendix* to the Philadelphia Unitarian *Coll.*, 1828. It is in a few modern collections, including the Boston Unitarian *Hymn [and
Tune] Bk.*, 1868.

6. Holy Father, Gracious art Thou. *Purity &
Peace.* Contributed to Dr. Martineau's *Hymns*,
&c., 1873, in 1 st. of 12 l.

7. I feel within a want. *Likeness to Christ
desired.* Appeared in the Cheshire (U. S.) Unitarian *Christian Hys.*, 1844, No. 687, in 4 st. of
4 l. It is in a few collections both old and new.

8. In the morning I will raise [pray]. *Morning.*
Appeared in his *Manual of Domestic Worship*,
1840, in 6 st. of 4 l., and repeated in Dr. Martineau's *Hymns*, &c., 1873. In Longfellow and
Johnson's *Book of Hymns*, 1846, and the Boston
Unitarian *Hymn [& Tune] Bk.* it begins with st.
ii., "In the morning I will pray."

9. O for a prophet's fire. *Holy Communion.*
Pub. in the *Appendix* to the Philadelphia Unitarian *Coll.*, 1828, and repeated in the Cheshire
(U. S.) Unitarian *Christian Hymns*, 1844, and
later hymn-books.

10. Richly, O richly have I been. *The Prodigal
Son.* In his *Manual of Devotion*, 1840. In
Longfellow and Johnson's *Book of Hys.*, 1846,
and their *Hys. of the Spirit*, 1864, it is given as
"O richly, *Father*, have I been"; whilst in

Hedge & Huntington's *Hys. for the Ch. of Christ*, 1853, the Boston Unitarian *Hy. [and Tune] Bk.*, 1868, and others, it opens with st. ii., "Unworthy to be called Thy son."

11. Slowly by Thy [God's] hand unfurled. *Eternal Light.* Given in his *Manual of Domestic Worship*, 1840, and repeated in a few hymnals. In Drs. Hedge & Huntington's *Hys. for the Ch. of Christ*, 1853, the first line was changed to "Slowly by *God's* hand unfurled." This is the reading of the Boston Unitarian *Hymn [& Tune] Bk.*, 1868. Dr. Martineau retains the original reading in his *Hymns, &c.*, 1873.

12. Thou only Living, only True. *Ordination.* In Dr. Martineau's *Hymns, &c.*, 1873, where it is dated 1868.

13. To the High and Holy One. *Consecration of Church.* In *Lyra Sac. Amer.*, 1868. From this is taken "To the truth that makes us free" (st. ii.), in the Boston *Hys. of the Spirit*, 1864.

14. What is the world that it should share? *Invocation of the Spirit.* Given in *The Christian Disciple*, 1822, and Dr. Martineau's *Hymns, &c.*, 1873. It begins with st. ii. of his hymn "Here in Thy temple, Lord, we bow." In *Lyra Sac. Americana* it reads, "Oh, is there aught on earth to share."

15. What is this that stirs within? *The Soul.* Appeared in his *Manual of Domestic Worship*, 1840. In 1844 it passed into the Cheshire (U.S.) Unitarian *Christian Hymns*, No. 318, and later into numerous collections, both old and new. Furness d. in 1896.   [F. M. B.]

G

G. in Bristol Bap. *Coll.*, by Ash & Evans, 1st ed. 1769, and Rippon's *Sel.*, 1787; i.e. Thomas Gibbons.

G. I. W., in Dr. Leifchild's *Original Hymns*, 1842; i.e. Mrs. G. I. Whiting.

G. J. S. The initials of George John Stevenson, appended to a short biographical sketch of *Bishop Ken*, which accompanied D. Sedgwick's reprint of Ken's *Hymns*.

G. M., in the *Church Times;* i.e. the Rev. Gerard Moultrie.

G. R., in the *Leeds S. School H. Bk.*, editions 1858 and 1878; i.e. George Rawson.

Gabb, James, B.A., was b. at Ebley, Gloucestershire, Feb. 3, 1830, and educated at Gonville and Caius College, Cambridge, graduating in honours in 1854. On taking Holy Orders he was curate of Barton-le-Street, 1854–64; domestic chaplain to the Earls of Carlisle at Castle Howard, 1855–75; curate of Bulmer, 1864–7; and rector of Bulmer from 1867. In 1864 he pub.:—

(1) *Steps to the Throne; or Meditations and Prayers in Verse* (Lond., Nisbet & Co.) containing 218 original versions of Psalms & Hymns. In 1871 a second volume, including many of the hymns in the former work, was pub. as (2) *Hymns and Songs of Pilgrim Life; or Steps to the Throne.* (Lond., Nisbet & Co.) It contained 103 hymns & songs. *The English Sacred Songster* (London, Sunday School Union), 1873, included 14 hymns by Mr. Gabb, one only being new, and 11 tunes. In 1875 the hymns in the foregoing works were collected, revised and pub. as (3) *The Welburn Appendix of Original Hymns and Tunes.* It comprises 116 hymns, the best known being "Jesus, Thou wast once a child," and "Saints exalted high in glory" (q. v.)

The music of *The Welburn Appendix* was edited by Dr. S. S. Wesley, he contributing thereto 22 tunes, 10 of which were from his *European Psalmist.* Mr. Gabb also contributed 44 tunes. This *Appendix*, although limited in use, is worthy of attention, with regard both to hymns and tunes, by hymnal compilers and their musical editors. Many of Mr. Gabb's hymns have been rewritten by him from time to time. *The Welburn Appendix* contains the authorised text.   [J. J.]

Gadsby, William, was b. in 1773 at Attleborough, in Warwickshire. In 1793 he joined the Baptist church at Coventry, and in 1798 began to preach. In 1800 a chapel was built for him at Desford, in Leicestershire, and two years later another in the town of Hinckley. In 1805 he removed to Manchester, becoming minister of a chapel in Rochdale Road, where he continued until his death, in January, 1844. Gadsby was for many years exceedingly popular as a preacher of the High Calvinist faith, and visited in that capacity most parts of England. He pub. *The Nazarene's Songs, being a composition of Original Hymns*, Manchester, 1814; and *Hymns on the Death of the Princess Charlotte*, Manchester, 1817. In 1814 he also pub. *A Selection of Hymns for Public Worship*, appending thereto a large number of his own compositions [Baptist Hymnody, § III., 2]. The edition of 1882 pub. by his son J. Gadsby contains 1138 hymns, of which 157 are by William Gadsby, and form Pt. ii. of the *Sel.* From his point of view they are sound in doctrine, but have little poetic fervour, and the rhyme is faulty in a large number of instances. Four of these hymns are in Denham's *Sel.* and one in the *Sel.* of J. Stevens.   [W. R. S.]

Gall, James, one of the Superintendents of the Carrubber's Close Mission, Edinburgh, was b. in 1808, and has been associated with that mission since its commencement in 1858. Before that he had taken great interest in Sunday Schools and Church Music. About 1836, he invented a system of printing music without small musical type, a mode of printing which has been greatly improved by others. He pub. *Anthems and Sacred Songs* in 1843, including two of his hymns:—

1. O come, let us sing to the God of Salvation. *Praise for Salvation.*
2. Who hath believed? Who hath believed? *Praise to Jesus.*

He was also associated with *The Sacred Song Book*, 1843, which afterwards was named *Sacred Melodies for Children*, and in 1872 200 *Sacred Melodies for Sunday Schools and Families* (see **Bateman, C. H.**). In this collection appeared:—

3. Go sound the trump on India's Shore. *Missions.*

Another popular hymn is:—

4. O! sing the Song of boundless love. *Praise for the Love of Jesus.*

This was written for the Scholars of the Free New North Mission Sabbath School, in May, 1877.

Mr. Gall has pub. several prose works, including *Instant Salvation; The World for Christ; Interpreting Concordance of the New Testament;* and others.   [J. J.]

Gallaudet, Thomas Hopkins, LL.D., b. in Philadelphia, Dec. 10, 1787, and graduated at Yale, 1805; was a tutor there from 1808–1810, and proceeded to Andover in 1811, remaining as a student till 1814. Having established an Institute for deaf mutes at Hartford, he visited Europe in its interest in 1814–15. From 1817 to 1830 he was the superintendent of that institution, and from 1838 to 1851 chaplain of the Insane Asylum, Hartford. He d. 1851. He pub. sundry juvenile works. In 1845 he contributed to the Connecticut Congregational *Ps. & Hys.*, No. 409, "Jesus, in sickness and in pain" (*Looking to Jesus in time of trial*). It is in 5 st. of 4 l. [F. M. B.]

Gambold, John, M.A., was b. April 10, 1711, at Puncheston, Pembrokeshire, where his father was vicar. Educated at Christ Church, Oxford, where he graduated B.A. in 1730, M.A. in 1734. Taking Holy Orders, he became, about 1739, Vicar of Stanton Harcourt, Oxfordshire, but resigned his living in Oct. 1742, and joined the United Brethren [Moravians], by whom he was chosen one of their bishops in 1754. He d. at Haverfordwest, Sept. 13, 1771. He pub. an ed. of the Greek Testament; *Maxims and Theological Ideas; Sermons,* and a dramatic poem called *Ignatius.* About 26 translations and 18 original hymns in the *Moravian Hymn Books* are assigned to him. One or two of his hymns, which were pub. by the Wesleys, have been claimed for them, but the evidence is in favour of Gambold. A collected ed. of his works was pub. at Bath in 1789, and afterwards reprinted. [G. A. C.]

Ganse, Hervey Doddridge, was b. Feb. 27, 1822, near Fishkill, New York, and removed to New York city in 1825. Graduated at Columbia College, 1839, studied Theology at New Brunswick, New Jersey, and was ordained in 1843. From 1843 to 1856 he was a Reformed Dutch Pastor, at Freehold, New Jersey, and from 1856 to 1876, of the Northwest Reformed Dutch Church, New York. Since January 1, 1876, he has been the pastor of the First Presbyterian Church, St. Louis. His chief hymns are:—

1. **Lord, I know Thy grace is nigh me.** *Faith.* Was composed on a winter's night in his bedroom, in a farmhouse near Freehold, New Jersey, while on a visit of consolation to former parishioners. The first couplet came into his mind without forethought, and he adds, "I composed on my pillow in the darkness; completing the verses with no little feeling, before I slept." This hymn appeared in the Reformed Dutch *Hymns of the Church,* New York, 1869, and is somewhat widely used.

2. **Eternal Father, when to Thee.** *Holy Trinity.* Dated 1872, and included in *Hys. & Songs of Praise,* N. Y., 1874, No. 7.

3. **From the vast and veiled throng.** *Adoration of the Heavenly Hosts.* Dated 1872, and pub. in the *Hys. & S. of Praise,* N. Y. 1874, No. 13.

4. **Is this the Son of God?** *Surrender to God.* Dated 1872, also pub. in the *Hys. & S. of Praise,* 1874, No. 541.

5. **Jesus, one word from Thee.** *Confidence and Security in Christ.* Dated 1872, and given in the *Hys. & S. of Praise,* 1874, No. 697.

6. **Thou Who like the wind dost come.** *Prayer for the Holy Spirit.* No. 378 in the *Hys. & Songs of Praise,* 1874, and dated 1873.

These hymns are unknown to the English collections. He d. in 1891. [F. M. B.]

Garve, Carl Bernhard, was b. Jan. 24, 1763, at Jeinsen, near Hannover, where his father was a farmer. He was educated at the Moravian schools in Zeist, and Neuwied, at their Pädagogium at Niesky, and their Seminary at Barby. In 1784 he was appointed one of the tutors at Niesky, and in 1789 at Barby; but as his philosophical lectures were thought rather unsettling in their tendency, he was sent, in 1797, to arrange the documents of the archive at Zeist. After his ordination as diaconus of the Moravian church, he was appointed, in 1799, preacher at Amsterdam; in 1801 at Ebersdorf (where he was also inspector of the training school); in 1809 at Berlin; and in 1816 at Neusalza on the Oder. Feeling the burden of years and infirmities he resigned the active duties of the ministry in 1836, and retired to Herrnhut, where he d. June 21, 1841. (*Koch,* vii. 334–342; *Allg. Deutsche Biog.,* viii. 392–94, &c.)

Garve ranks as the most important of recent Moravian hymn-writers, Albertini being perhaps his superior in poetical gifts, but certainly not in adaptability to church use. His better productions are almost entirely free from typically Moravian features; and in them Holy Scripture is used in a sound and healthful spirit. They are distinguished by force and at the same time elegance of style, and are full of deep love and devotion to the Saviour. Many of them have passed into the German Evangelical hymn-books, no less than 36 being included in the Berlin *G. B.,* 1829; and of those noted below No. i. is to be found in almost all recent German collections. They appeared mostly in the two following collections, both of which are to be found in the Town Library, Hamburg: (1) *Christliche Gesänge,* Görlitz, 1825, with 303 hymns, a few being recasts from other authors. (2) *Brüdergesänge,* Gnadau, 1827, with 65 hymns intended principally for use in the Moravian Communion.

Garve's hymns in English C. U. are:—

i. **Dein Wort, O Herr, ist milder Thau.** *Holy Scripture.* Perhaps his finest hymn. 1825, as above, p. 51, in 7 st. of 8 l. Included, as No. 410, in the Berlin *G. L. S.,* ed. 1863, and in the German hymn-books for Hannover, 1883, for the kingdom of Saxony, 1883, for the province of Saxony, 1882, &c. *Tr.* as:—

1. **Thy Word, O Lord, like gentle dews.** A good *tr.* of st. i.–iii., by Miss Winkworth, in the 1st Ser., 1855, of her *Lyra Ger.* p. 36. In the Pennsylvania Luth. *Ch. Bk.,* 1868, it is No. 314 in full, but rewritten to D. C. M. In 1864 it was included, altered, and with ll. 5–8 of each st. omitted, as No. 681 in *Hys. of the Spirit,* Boston, U. S., and this has been repeated in Dr. Martineau's *Hys. of Praise & Prayer,* 1873, and Dr. Allon's *Children's Worship,* 1878.

2. **Thy Word, O Lord, is gentle dew.** A good *tr.* of st. i.–iii., based on the *Lyra Ger.,* by Miss Winkworth, as No. 102 in her *C. B. for England,* 1863, and thence, in the Ohio Luth. *Hyl.,* 1880.

ii. **Hallelujah, Christus lebt.** *Easter.* 1825, as above, p. 105, in 8 st. of 6 l. Included in Knapp's *Ev. L. S,* 1850, No. 565. *Tr.* as:—

Hallelujah! Jesus lives! A good *tr.* (omitting st. iv., vi.) by Miss Borthwick, in the 4th Ser., 1862, of the *H. L. L.,* p. 30 (1884, p. 201). In *Lyra Messianica,* 1864, p. 295, and in G. S. Jellicoe's *Coll.,* 1867, No. 103, it begins, "Alleluia! Jesus lives."

iii. **O Vater der Gemeine.** *Trinity Sunday.* 1825, as above, p. 18, in 3 st. of 7 l. Included as No. 107 in Knapp's *Ev. L. S.,* 1837. *Tr.* as:—

Father of all created. In full, as No. 159, in Dr. Pagenstecher's *Coll.*, 1864, signed " F. C. C."

Another tr. is, " O Father, we adore Thee," in the *British Herald*, Oct. 1866, p. 324, repeated as No. 416 in Reid's *Praise Bk.*, 1872.

Hymns not in English C.U. :—

iv. **Der Herr ist treu, Der Herr ist ewig treu.** *God's Faithfulness.* 1825, p. 5, in 6 st., repeated in the Berlin *G. B.*, 1829, No. 60, beginning " Gott ist treu." *Tr.* by *N. L. Frothingham*, 1870, p. 253.

v. **Geduld! Geduld! ob's stürmisch weht.** *Trust in God.* 1825, p. 180, in 3 st., repeated in the Berlin *G. B.* 1829, No. 593, beginning " Geduld ! wie sehr der Sturm auch weht." *Tr.* by *N. L. Frothingham*, 1870. p. 265.

vi. **Sagt was hat die weite Welt.** *Holy Scripture.* 1825, p 49, in 6 st. *Tr.* as " Tell me, can the world display," in the *British Herald*, Nov. 1866, p. 360, repeated as No. 420 in Reid's *Praise Bk.*, 1872.

vii. **Wer bin ich, Herr, in deinem Licht.** *Self-Examination.* 1825, p. 210, in 16 st. *Tr.* by *N. L. Frothingham*, 1870, p. 258.

viii. **Zur Arbeit winkt mir mein Beruf.** *Before Work.* 1825, p. 233, in 9 st. *Tr.* by *E. Massie*, 1867.

A hymn sometimes ascribed to Garve is noted under " Gib deinen Frieden uns."

[J. M.]

Gascoigne, George, s. and heir of Sir John Gascoigne. The date and place of his birth are unknown, but it is probable that he was b. about 1525, and from a statement in the Address to Queen Elizabeth prefixed to one of his works, he seems to have spent a part of his early life in Westmoreland. He was educated at Trinity College, Cambridge, from whence he entered the Middle Temple as a student of law before 1548 ; but neglecting his studies he led a life of reckless extravagance and dissipation, on account of which he was disinherited by his father. In 1555 he migrated to Gray's Inn, but seems to have left it also. In 1557–58 he represented Bedford in Parliament. In 1565 he returned to Gray's Inn, and there, in the following year, two plays by him were represented, *The Supposes,* translated from the Italian of Ariosto, and *Jocasta,* adapted from the Phoenissae of Euripides. To the latter Gascoigne contributed three acts. In 1572 he was returned to Parliament as member for the borough of Midhurst : but objections being made to his character he appears not to have taken his seat, and not long afterwards went to the Low Countries and took service with William of Orange, from whom he received a captain's commission. His gallant conduct in the field obtained the favourable notice of that Prince, but after some time he was taken prisoner by the Spaniards and sent back to England.

During Gascoigne's absence his first book, *A Hundredth sundrie Floures bound up in one small Poesie,* the MS. of which he had left in the hands of a friend, was printed in 157⅔ without his permission, and after his return from Holland, he published in 1575 a corrected and enlarged edition of his *Poesies.* Thenceforward he seems to have led a literary life, and is said to have been in some way attached to the court. On the occasion of Elizabeth's celebrated visit to Kenilworth in the summer of 1575, Gascoigne was commissioned by Leicester to devise the masques, &c., performed for the Queen's entertainment. He d. at Stamford, Lincolnshire, Oct. 7, 1577, and was probably buried by his friend George Whetstone in the family vault of the Whetstones at Barnack, but this is not certainly known. At some time

between 1558 and 1568 Gascoigne married Elizabeth Breton, mother, by her first husband, of the poet Nicholas Breton, and by her had a son. His widow survived until 1585. Gascoigne is noticeable as being one of the earliest English dramatists, the first English satirist, and the first English critic in poetry. In 1869 his poems were collected and edited for the Roxburghe Library by W. C. Hazlitt, and in 1868 his *Notes of Instruction in English Verse ; The Steele Glas ;* and *The Complaynt of Philomene* were included in English reprints edited by Edward Arber, together with Whetstone's metrical life of Gascoigne. To modern hymnody he is known by " We that have passed in slumber sweet," an altered version of his morning hymn, " Ye that have spent the silent night ; " and other religious poems.   [G. A. C.]

Gaskell, William, M.A., s. of Mr. William Gaskell, was b. at Latchford (a suburb of Warrington, on the Cheshire side of the Mersey), 24 July, 1805. He was educated at Manchester New College and at the University of Glasgow, where he graduated M.A. in 1825. In 1828 he became co-pastor with the Rev. J. G. Robberds at Cross Street Unitarian Chapel, Manchester, a position he held until his death. Mr. Gaskell was a man of cultivated mind and considerable literary ability. His publications include *Lectures on the Lancashire Dialect,* 1853, a small volume of *Temperance Rhymes,* 1839, and various theological works. In 1832 he married Elizabeth Cleghorn Stevenson, who afterwards attained celebrity as the authoress of *Mary Barton,* and of other popular tales. He d. June 11, 1884, and is buried at Knutsford. To the 2nd ed., 1856, of the 1st Series of *Lyra Germanica* Mr. Gaskell contributed " A sure Stronghold our God is He," a *tr.* of Luther's " Ein' feste Burg" (q.v.), replacing a version by Miss Winkworth in the 1st ed. He also contributed 79 hymns to Beard's *Unit. Coll. of Hys. for Pub. and Priv. Worship,* 1837.   [G. A. C.]

The following hymns by Gaskell still in C. U. are found chiefly in Unitarian hymnbooks, including Martineau's *Hymns,* &c., 1840, and *Hys. of Praise and Prayer,* 1873 ; Hedge & Huntington's *Hys. for the Church of Christ,* Boston, U.S.A., 1853 ; Longfellow & Johnson's *Book of Hys.,* Boston, 1848, and their *Hys. of the Spirit,* Boston, 1864 ; and the American Unitarian Association's *Hymn [& Tune] Bk.,* &c., Boston, 1868 :—

1. Dark, dark indeed the grave would be. *Death and Burial.*
2. Darkness o'er the world was brooding. *The Day-spring.*
3. Dark were the paths our Master trod. *Sympathy with Christ.*
4. Father, glory be to Thee. *Doxology.*
5. Forth went the heralds of the cross. *Power of Faith.*
6. How long, O Lord, his brother's blood ? *In time of War.* From this " O hush, great God, the sounds of war," is taken.
7. I am free, I am free, I have broken away. *The New Birth.*
8. In vain we thus recall to mind. *H. Communion.*
9. Mighty God, the first, the last. *Infinite Knowledge.*
10. No more, on earth no more. *Death and Heaven.*
11. Not in this simple rite alone. *H. Communion.*
12. Not on this day, O God, alone. *Sunday.*
13. O God, the darkness roll away. *Missions.*
14. O God, to Thee our hearts would pay. *Old Year.*

15. O God, who knowest how frail we are. *Seeking Strength.*
16. O not to crush with abject fear. *Christ's Work.*
17. Our Father, through the coming year. The original begins, "Father, throughout the coming year."
18. Press on, press on, ye sons of light. *Continuance in well doing.*
19. Sleep not, soldier of the cross. *Faithfulness.*
20. Thanks, thanks unto God! Who in mercy hath spoken. *Gratitude for the Gospel.*
21. Through all this life's eventful road. *Walking with God.*
22. To Thee, the Lord Almighty. *Doxology.*
23. Unto Thy temple, God of Love. *Divine Worship.*
24. We join to [crave] pray with wishes kind. *H. Matrimony.*
25. We would leave, O God, to Thee. Original : " We would cast, O God, on Thee." *Rest in God.*
26. When arise the thoughts of sin. *Looking to Jesus.*

These hymns all appeared in Beard's *Coll.*, 1837. In addition there are :—

27. Calmly, calmly lay him down.
28. O Father, [gladly] humbly we repose.
29. O hush, great God, the sounds of war. *For Peace.*

The dates of these hymns we have not been able to determine. No. 27 is in Hopps's *Hys., for Pub. Worship*, 1858 ; and Nos. 28 and 29 are in Hedge & Huntington's *Hys. for the Church of Christ*, 1853.   [J. J.]

Gaude, Mater Ecclesia. [*St. Edward the Confessor.*]

This hymn was reprinted in Dr. Neale's *Hymni Ecclesiae*, 1851, p. 233, in 6 st. of 4 l., from the *Senlis Brev.* (*Breviarium Sylvanectense*, 1521), where it was given, "In Festo S. Ludovici Regis." In 1867 a *tr.* by Dr. R. F. Littledale was included in the *People's H.*, No. 287, beginning, "O Mother Church, to-day thy voice," and signed "A. L. P." It was appointed for the Festival of St. Edward the Confessor, Oct. 13.   [J. J.]

Gedicke, Lampertus, s. of Christian

Gedicke, superintendent of Gardelegen in the Altmark, was b. at Gardelegen Jan. 6, 1683. After the completion of his theological studies at Halle under Francke, he was for some time tutor in the orphanage at Halle, and then in a family at Berlin. Becoming an army chaplain he was successively appointed chaplain to the Guards (1709), accompanying them on several expeditions ; chaplain to the Wartensleben regiment and garrison preacher at Berlin (1713) ; and Probst and inspector of all the garrison and regimental chaplains (1717). He d. at Berlin, Feb. 21, 1735 (*Koch*, iv. 414, 415 ; *Bode*, p. 72, &c.). He contributed two hymns to the *Neu-vermehrtes geistreiches G. B.*, Berlin, 1711. One of these is :—

Wie Gott mich führt, so will ich gehn. [*Trust in God.*] 1711, as above, No. 798, in 6 st. of 7 l., repeated in *Freylinghausen*, 1714, and as No. 918 in the Berlin *G. L. S.*, ed. 1863. Often used at weddings. The only *tr.* in C. U. is :—

Just as God leads me I would go, a good *tr.*, omitting st. ii., as No. 258, in H. L. Hastings's *Hyl.*, 1880.

Other trs. are : (1) "As God shall lead I'll take my way," by *Dr. H. Mills*, 1845 (1856, p. 176). (2) "As God leads me, will I go," by *Miss Warner*, 1858 (1861, p. 498). (3) "As God doth lead me will I go," by Miss Burlingham in the *British Herald*, June, 1866, p. 278, repeated as No. 407 in Reid's *Praise Bk.*, 1872. [J. M.]

Geh aus, mein Herz, und suche Freud. *P. Gerhardt.* [*Summer.*]

This beautiful poem of thanksgiving for God's goodness in the delights of summer, and of anticipation of the joys of Paradise, appeared in the Frankfurt ed., 1656, of Crüger's *Praxis pietalis*

melica, No. 412, in 15 st. of 6 l. Reprinted in Wackernagel's ed. of his *Geistliche Lieder*, No. 103, and Bachmann's ed., No. 85 ; and included, as No. 732, in the *Unv. L. S.*, 1851. It may be compared with the hymn, "Der trübe Winter ist vorbei," by Friedrich von Spee (q. v.). Lauxmann, in *Koch*, viii. 141, speaks of the tune (called *Lucerne* in the Irish *Church Hymnal*) as :—

A Swiss melody which has naturalised itself in Württemberg to the hymn "Geh aus, mein Herz," and of which Palmer [Professor at Tübingen] assures us that the children's faces are twice as happy as often as they are allowed to sing it. Although evidently originally a song tune [by J. Schmidlin, 1770], yet its ring gives the freshness which one desires in an out-door hymn.

The *trs.* of this hymn in C. U. are :—

1. **Go forth, my heart, and seek delight**, a good *tr.*, omitting st. xiv., by Miss Winkworth, in the 1st series of her *Lyra Ger.*, 1855, p. 136. Her *trs.* of st. viii.–xi., beginning "Thy mighty working, mighty God," were included in the American *Sabbath H. Bk.*, 1858, and repeated in Boardman's *Coll.*, Philadelphia, 1861.

2. **The golden corn now waxes strong**, a very good *tr.* beginning with st. vii., " Der Waizen wächset mit Gewalt," contributed by R. Massie to the 1857 ed. of Mercer's *C. P. and H. Bk.*, No. 463 (Ox. ed., 1864, No. 500, omitting the *tr.* of st. x.). In the *Appendix* to the 2nd series of *Lyra Domestica*, 1864, Mr. Massie reprinted his *tr.* at p. 102, and prefixed a version of st. i.–vi., beginning "Go forth, my heart, nor linger here." In this form it was included in full in Reid's *Praise Bk.*, 1872.

Other trs. are : (1) "Come forth, my heart, and seek delight," by *Miss Cox*, 1841, p. 169 (1864, p. 149). (2) "Go forth, my heart, and revel in joy's flow," and "And oft I think, if e'en earth's sin-stained ground," a *tr.* of st. i., ix., by Mrs. Stanley Carr in her *tr.* of Wildenhahn's *Paul Gerhardt*, 1845 (ed. 1856, p. 235). (3) "Go forth, my heart, and seek for praise," by Dr. J. W. Alexander, in Schaff's *Kirchenfreund*, 1849, p. 419 ; reprinted in his work *The Breaking Crucible*, N. Y., 1861, p. 15. (4) "Go out, my heart, and pleasure seek," by *Miss Manington*, 1863, p. 164. (5) "Go forth, my heart! the year's sweet prime," by *E. Massie*, 1866, p. 36. (6) "Go forth, my heart, and seek delight, In this summer," by *J. Kelly*, 1867, p. 289. (7) "Go forth, my heart, and seek the bliss," by Mrs. E. L. Follen, in her *Lark and Linnet*, 1854, p. 30.   [J. M.]

Geletzky, Johannes. [Jelecky, J.]

Gellert, Christian Fürchtegott, s. of

Christian Gellert, pastor at Hainichen in the Saxon Harz, near Freiberg, was b. at Hainichen, July 4, 1715. In 1734 he entered the University of Leipzig as a student of theology, and after completing his course acted for some time as assistant to his father. But then, as now, sermons preached from manuscript were not tolerated in the Lutheran Church, and as his memory was treacherous, he found himself compelled to try some other profession. In 1739 he became domestic tutor to the sons of Herr von Lüttichau, near Dresden, and in 1741 returned to Leipzig to superintend the studies of a nephew at the University. He also resumed his own studies. He graduated M.A. 1744 ; became in 1745 private tutor or lecturer in the philosophical faculty ; and was in 1751 appointed extraordinary professor of philosophy, lecturing on poetry and rhetoric, and then on moral philosophy. An ordinary professorship offered to him in 1761 he refused, as he did not feel strong enough to fulfil its duties, having been delicate from a child, and after 1752 suffering very greatly from hypochondria. He d. at Leipzig, Dec. 13, 1769 (*Koch*, vi. 263–277; *Allg. Deutsche Biog.*, viii. 544–549, &c.).

As a professor, Gellert was most popular, numbering Goethe and Lessing among his pupils, and won from his students extraordinary reverence and affection, due partly to the warm interest he took in their personal conduct and welfare. In his early life he was one of the contributors to the *Bremer Beiträge*; and was one of the leaders in the revolt against the domination of Gottsched and the writers of the French school. His *Fables* (1st Ser. 1746; 2nd 1748), by their charm of style, spirit, humour and point, may justly be characterised as epoch-making, won for him universal esteem and influence among his contemporaries of all classes, and still rank among the classics of German literature.

As a hymn-writer he also marks an epoch; and while in the revival of churchly feeling the hymns of the Rationalistic period of 1760 to 1820 have been ignored by many recent compilers, yet the greatest admirers of the old standard hymns have been fain to stretch their area of selection from Luther to Gellert. He prepared himself by prayer for their composition, and selected the moments when his mental horizon was most unclouded. He was distinguished by deep and sincere piety, blameless life, and regularity in attendance on the services of the Church. His hymns are the utterances of a sincere Christian morality, not very elevated or enthusiastic, but genuine expressions of his own feelings and experiences; and what in them he preached he also put in practice in his daily life. Many are too didactic in tone, reading like versifications of portions of his lectures on morals, and are only suited for private use. But in regard to his best hymns, it may unfaly be said that their rational piety and good taste, combined with a certain earnestness and pathos, entitle them to a place among the classics of German hymnody. They exactly met the requirements of the time, won universal admiration, and speedily passed into the hymn-books in use over all Germany, Roman Catholic as well as Lutheran.

Two of Gellert's hymns are noted under their own first lines, viz., "Jesus lebt, mit ihm auch ich," and "Wie gross ist des Allmächtgen Güte." The following have also passed into English, almost all being taken from his *Geistliche Oden und Lieder*, a collection of 54 hymns 1st pub. at Leipzig, 1757, and which has passed through very numerous editions:—

I. *Hymns in English C. U.*

i. **An dir allein, an dir hab ich gesündigt.** *Lent.* 1757, p. 102, in 6 st. of 4 l., entitled "Hymn of Penitence." In Zollikofer's *G. B.*, 1766, and the Berlin *G. L. S.*, ed. 1863, No. 499. *Tr.* as:—

Against Thee only have I sinn'd, I own it. A good and full version, by Miss Winkworth, as No. 42 in her *C. B. for England*, 1863.

Another tr. is:—"Against Thee, Lord, Thee only my transgression," by *N. L. Frothingham*, 1870, p. 241.

ii. **Dies ist der Tag, den Gott gemacht.** *Christmas.* One of his best and most popular hymns. 1757, p. 72, in 11 st. of 4 l., repeated in the Berlin *G. B.*, 1765, No. 55, and the Berlin *G. L. S.*, ed. 1863, No. 154. *Tr.* as:—

This is the day the Lord hath made, O'er all the earth. A *tr.* of st. i.–iii., x., by Miss Borthwick, as No. 22 in Dr. Pagenstecher's *Coll.*, 1864, and included in *H. L. L.*, 1884, p. 256.

Other trs. are:—(1) "This is the day which God ordains," by *Dr. G. Walker*, 1860, p. 27. (2) "This day shall yet by God's command," in the *Family Treasury*, 1871, p. 278.

iii. **Für alle Güte sei gepreist.** *Evening.* 1757, p. 85, in 4 st. of 6 l., included in Zollikofer's *G. B.*, 1766, No. 78, and the Berlin *G. L. S.*, ed. 1863, No. 1160. *Tr.* as:—

To Father, Son, and Spirit praise. A good and full *tr.* by A. T. Russell, as No. 7 in his *Ps. & Hys.*, 1851.

Another tr. is:—"For all Thy kindness laud I Thee," by *H. J. Buckoll*, 1842, p. 96.

iv. **Gott ist mein Lied.** *Praise. On God's Might and Providence.* 1757, p. 78, in 15 st. of 5 l. In the Berlin *G. L. S.*, ed. 1863, No. 24. *Tr.* as:—

God is my song, His praises I'll repeat. A free *tr.* of st. i.–v., as No. 94 in Sir John Bowring's *Hymns*, 1825. Repeated, omitting st. ii., as No. 114 in Dale's *Eng. H. Bk.*, 1875.

Other trs. are:—(1) "Of God I sing," by *Dr. H. Mills*, 1856, p. 11. (2) "God is my song, With sovereign," by *N. L. Frothingham*, 1870, p. 243.

v. **Wenn ich, o Schöpfer, deine Macht.** *Praise.* This fine hymn of Praise for Creation and Providence was 1st pub. 1757, p. 62, in 6 st. of 7 l. In the Berlin *G. B.*, 1765, No. 25, and Berlin *G. L. S.*, ed. 1863, No. 72. *Tr.* as:—

Thou Great First Cause! when of Thy skill. In full in Dr. H. Mills's *Horae Ger.*, 1845 (1856, p. 5). St. ii., iii., v., vi., altered and beginning, "The earth, where'er I turn mine eye," are in the American Luth. Gen. Synod's *Coll.*, 1852.

Other trs. are:—(1) "When, O my dearest Lord, I prove," by *Miss Dunn*, 1857, p. 80. (2) "Creator! when I see Thy might," in Madame de Pontes's *Poets and Poetry of Germany*, 1858, v. i. p. 472. (3) "When I, Creator, view Thy might," by *Miss Manington*, 1863.

vi. **Wer Gottes Wort nicht hält, und spricht.** *Faith in Works.* This didactic hymn on Faith proved by Works, was first pub. 1757, p. 49, in 5 st. of 6 l. In Zollikofer's *G. B.*, 1766, and the Berlin *G. L. S.*, ed. 1863, No. 72. *Tr.* as:—

Who keepeth not God's Word, yet saith. A good and full *tr.* by Miss Winkworth, in her *Lyra Ger.*, 2nd Ser., 1858, p. 161. A greatly altered version of st. ii.–v., beginning, "True faith in holy life will shine," was included as No. 418 in *Kennedy*, 1863, and repeated in the *Ibrox Hyl.*, 1871, J. L. Porter's *Coll.*, 1876, and others.

II. *Hymns not in English C. U.*

vii. **Auf Gott, und nicht auf meinen Rath.** *Trust in God's Providence.* 1757, p. 134, in 6 st. *Tr.* as: (1) "Rule Thou my portion, Lord, my skill," by *Dr. H. Mills*, 1845 (1856, p. 164). (2) "On God and on no earthly trust," by J. D. Burns, in his *Remains*, 1869.

viii. **Auf, schicke dich.** *Christmas.* 1757, p. 109, in 7 st. *Tr.* as, "Come, tune your heart," by *Miss Cox*, 1841, p. 17 (1864, p. 39).

ix. **Dein Heil, o Christ! nicht zu verscherzen.** *Prayer.* 1757, p. 6, in 14 st. of 8 l. In J. A. Schlegel's *Geistl. Gesänge*, 3rd Ser., 1772, p. 193, recast as "Zu deinem Gotte beten," in 5 st. of 12 l.; and this in the Kaiserwerth *Lieder-Buch für Kleinkinderschulen*, 1842, No. 208, appears "Zu Gott im Himmel beten," in 8 st. of 4 l. The 1842 was *tr.* as, "O how sweet it is to pray," by *Mrs. Bevan*, 1859, p. 148.

x. **Der Tag ist wieder hin, und diesen Theil des Lebens.** *Evening.* 1757, p. 13, in 10 st., as "Self-Examination at Eventide." *Tr.* as, "Another day is ended," by *Miss Warner*, 1869 (1871, p. 9).

xi. **Du klagst, und fühlest die Beschwerden.** *Contentment.* 1757, p. 91, in 8 st. *Tr.* as, "Thy wounded spirit feels its pain," by *Dr. R. Maguire*, 1883, p. 153.

xii. **Erinnre dich, mein Geist, erfreut.** *Easter.* 1757, p. 27, in 13 st. *Tr.* as, "Awake, my soul, and hail the day," in Dr. J. D. Lang's *Aurora Australis*, Sydney, 1826, p. 43.

xiii. **Er ruft der Sonn, und schafft den Mond.** *New Year.* 1757, p. 154, in 6 st. In the Berlin *G. B.*, 1765, No. 233, as "Gott ruft." *Tr.* as, "Lord, Thou that ever wast and art," in the *British Magazine*, Jan., 1839, p. 36.

xiv. **Gott, deine Güte reicht so weit.** *Supplication.* 1757, p. 1, in 4 st., founded on 1 Kings iii. 5–14. The *trs.* are: (1) "O God, Thy goodness doth extend, Far as," by *Dr. J. D. Lang*, 1826, p. 10. (2) "Behold! Thy goodness, oh my God," by *Miss Fry*, 1845, p. 78.

xv. **Gott ist mein Hort.** *Holy Scripture.* 1757, p. 70, in 8 st. *Tr.* as, "I trust the Lord, Upon His word," by *Dr. H. Mills*, 1845 (1856, p. 23).

xvi. **Herr, der du mir das Leben.** *Evening.* 1757,

p. 121, in 5 st. *Tr.* as, " By Thee, Thou Lord of Heaven," by *H. J. Buckoll*, 1842, p. 97.

xvii. Herr, stärke mich, dein Leiden zu bedenken. *Passiontide.* 1757, p. 123, in 22 st. *Tr.* as, "Clothe me, oh Lord, with strength ! that I may dwell," by *Miss Fry*, 1859, p. 153.

xviii. Ich hab in guten Stunden. *For the Sick.* 1757, p. 128, in 6 st. [See the *Story of a Hymn*, in the *Sunday at Home* for Sept., 1865.] *Tr.* as: (1) "I have had my days of blessing," by Mrs. Findlater, in *H. L. L.*, 1855, p. 60. (2) " Once, happy hours with blessings crowned," by *A. B. H.*, in the *Day of Rest*, 1877, p. 405.

xix. Ich komme, Herr, und suche dich. *Holy Communion.* 1757, p. 89, in 5 st. The *trs.* are : (1) " I come, O Lord, and seek for Thee," by *Miss Manington*, 1863, p. 14. (2) " Weary and laden with my load, I come," by *Dr. R. Maguire*, 1872, p. 178.

xx. Ich komme vor dein Angesicht. *Supplication.* 1757, p. 140, in 13 st. The *trs.* are : (1) " Great God, I bow before Thy face," by *Dr. J. D. Lang*, 1826, p. 23. (2) " Now in Thy presence I appear," by *Dr. H. Mills*, 1845 (1856, p. 137).

xxi. Mein erst Gefühl sei Preis und Dank. *Morning.* 1757, p. 55, in 12 st. *Tr.* as, " I bless Thee, Lord, Thou God of might," beginning with st. vi., by *H. J. Buckoll*, 1842, p. 56.

xxii. Nach einer Prüfung kurzer Tage. *Eternal Life.* 1757, p. 158, in 12 st., as " The Consolation of Eternal Life." Though hardly a hymn for congregational use and too individualised, it has been a very great favourite in Germany. In the Berlin *G. B.*, 1765, No. 132, and the Berlin *G. L. S.*, ed. 1863, No. 1483. The *trs.* are : (1) " A few short days of trial past," in Miss Knight's *Prayers & Hys. from the German*, 1812 (1832, p. 107). (2) " A few short hours of transient joy," by *Dr. J. D. Lang*, 1826, p. 123. (3) " When these brief trial-days are past," by *J. Sheppard*, 1857, p. 98. (4) " A few short days of trial here," by Miss Burlingham, in the *British Herald*, July 1865, p. 98. (5) " Our few short years of trial o'er," by *Dr. J. Guthrie*, 1869, d. 124. (6) " When these brief trial-days are spent," by *Miss Winkworth*, 1869, p. 318. (7) " A few more days, a few more years," by *Dr. R. Maguire*, 1883, p. 165.

xxiii. O Herr, mein Gott ! durch den ich bin und lebe. *Resignation to the will of God.* 1757, p. 152, in 7 st. *Tr.* as, " In Thee, my God, I live and move," by *Dr. R. Maguire*, 1883, p. 113.

xxiv. So hoff' ich denn mit festem Muth. *Assurance of the Grace of God.* 1757, p. 115, in 4 st. The *trs.* are : (1) " Firm is my hope of future good," by *Dr. H. Mills*, 1845 (1856, p. 188). (2) " In Thee, O Lord, my hope hath stood," by *Dr. R. Maguire*, 1872.

xxv. Was ists dass ich mich quäle. *Patience.* 1757, p. 17, in 7 st. The *trs.* are: (1) " O foolish heart, be still," by *Miss Warner*, 1858 (1861, p. 452), repeated in Bp. Ryle's *Coll.*, 1860, No. 181   (2) " What billows these that o'er thee roll," by *Dr. R. Maguire*, 1872.

xxvi. Wie sicher lebt der Mensch, der Staub. *For the Dying.* 1757, p. 149, in 14 st. *Tr.* as, " How heedless, how secure is man ! " by *Dr. H. Mills*, 1845 (1856, p. 238).

One or two recasts from *Gellert's Lehrgedichte und Erzählungen*, Leipzig, 1754, came into German C. U., and one has passed into English, viz. :—

xxvii. Mensch, der du Christus schmähst, was ist in ihrer Lehre. *Love to Mankind.* 1754, pp. 27–56, being a poem entitled " The Christian." A recast from portions of this made by J. S. Diterich, beginning " Gieb mir, O Gott, ein Herz," in 9 st., appears as No. 219 in the Berlin *G. B.*, 1765; and has been *tr.* as " Grant me, O God ! a tender heart," by *Miss Knight*, 1812 (1832, p. 97).   [J. M.]

Gelobet seist du Jesu Christ. [*Christmas.*] This hymn has been called a *tr.* of the following Latin sequence :—

1. " Grates nunc omnes reddamus Domino Deo, qui sua nativitate nos liberavit de diabolica potestate.

2. " Huic oportet ut canamus cum angelis semper : Gloria in excelsis."

The text of this sequence is in *Daniel*, ii. p. 5, apparently from a Munich MS. of the 11th cent., and is also found in a 12th cent. MS. in the *British Museum* (Add. 11,669, f. 49). It has been ascribed to St. Gregory the Great, and to Notker Balbulus ; but is probably by neither. The earliest form in which the

German hymn has been found is in a MS. c. 1370, probably written in the district of Celle, and now in the Royal library at Copenhagen. In the *Blätter für Hymnologie*, 1883, p. 47, it is quoted as occurring thus :—

" Hinc oportet ut canamus cum angelis septem gloria in excelsis :—

> Louet sistu ihū crist,
> dat du hute ghebaren bist
> van eyner maghet : Dat is war.
> Des vrow sik alde hemmelsche schar. Kyr."

The introductory words, it will be noted, are a corrupted form of pt. ii. of the sequence ; the four lines following can hardly be said to have any connection with the sequence. This German stanza came into extensive use ; and is almost the only instance of popular vernacular song used in the Church services before the Reformation. In the *Ordinarium inclitae ecclesiae Swerinensis*, Rostock, 1519, there is a rubric in the service for Christmas, " Populus vero Canticum vulgare : *Gelavet systu Jesu Christ*, tribus vicibus subjunget " (*Hoffmann von Fallersleben*, ed. 1861, p. 194). To this single pre-Reformation stanza Martin Luther added six original sts. (which contain slight reminiscences of Fortunatus's " Quem terra, pontus, aethera "), and published the 7 st. (each stanza ending with Kyrieleis) on a broadsheet at Wittenberg, and then in *Eyn Enchiridion*, Erfurt, 1524. Thence in *Wackernagel*, iii. p. 9, in Schircks's ed. of Luther's *Geistl. Lieder*, 1854, p. 9 ; in the *Unv. L. S.*, 1851, No. 36 ; and in almost all German hymnbooks from the Reformation to the present time. Schamelius described it as " The blessings of the birth of Christ celebrated in paradoxes." It is *tr.* as :—

1. Jesus ! all praise is due to Thee. A good *tr.* by C. Kinchen, omitting st. vi., as No. 52, in the *Moravian H. Bk.*, 1742. When repeated in the ed. 1754, pt. i., No. 213, Kinchen's *tr.* of st. i., ii., iii., vii. were retained, and st. iv.–vi. were given in a cento partly from Jacobi (see below). The 1754 text was repeated, with alterations, in subsequent eds. of the *Moravian H. Bk.* (1886, No. 34), and is found, as No. 209, in Lady Huntingdon's *Sel.*, 1780. Two centos may also be noted :—

(1) " He, who the earth's foundations laid." (st. ii.), Cotterill's *Sel.*, 1819, No. 216. (2) " The Son of God, who fram'd the skies" (st. ii. l. 3), in the *Bible H. Bk.*, 1845, No. 221.

2. O Jesu Christ ! all praise to Thee. By A. T. Russell, in his *Ps. & Hys.*, 1851, No. 42, omitting st. iii., vi. Slightly altered, in *Kennedy*, 1863.

3. All praise to Thee, eternal Lord. A free *tr.* in 5 st. of 4 l. as No. 263 in the American *Sabbath H. Bk.*, 1858, and repeated unaltered in Schaff's *Christ in Song*, 1869, p. 53 (1879, p. 42). It is included in full and generally unaltered in various American collections, as the *Bap. H. Bk.*, 1871, *Presb. Hyl.*, 1874, *Laudes Domini*, 1884, &c. ; and in England in Soden's *Universal H. Bk.*, 1885.

Translations not in C. U. :—

(1) " Now blessed be Thou, Christ Jesu," by Bp. Coverdale, 1539 (*Remains*, 1846, p. 562). (2) " Due praises to th' incarnate Love," by *J. C. Jacobi*, 1722, p. 6 (1732, p. 6). (3) " Oh, let Thy praise, Redeemer, God ! " by *Miss Fry*, 1845, p. 16. (4) " Glory to Christ, the virgin-born," by *J. Anderson*, 1846, p. 9 (1847, p. 32). (5) " Glory and praise to Jesus' name, by *Dr. J. Hunt*, 1853, p. 36. (6) " All praise to Jesus' hallowed name," by *R. Massie*, 1854, p. 11, repeated in *Dr. Bacon*, 1884,

p. 20. (7) "Praised be Thou, O Jesus Christ," by Dr. G. Macdonald in the *Sunday Magazine*, 1867, p. 151, altered in his *Exotics*, 1876, p. 43. (8) "All glory, Jesus Christ, to Thee," in the *Ch. of England Magazine*, 1872, p. 45.   **[J. M.]**

Genad mir, Herr, ewiger Gott. [*Duties of a Sovereign.*] 1st in Klug's *G. B.*, Wittenberg, 1529. *Wackernagel*, iii. p. 117, quotes it from the *Geistliche Lieder*, Erfurt, 1531, in 9 st., entitled "The Margrave George's Hymn." The beginnings of the st. form the name *Georg Marggraf zu Brandenburg*. It is a companion hymn to the "Capitan Herr Gott" (q.v.): and probably by the same author. Casimir was b. Sept. 27, 1481, and d. Sept. 21, 1527; while Georg was b. March 4, 1484, and d. Dec. 17, 1543. The *trs.* are:—

(1) "O God, be kind; let no distress," by *Dr. G. Walker*, 1860, p. 44. (2) "Grant me, Eternal God, such grace," by *Miss Winkworth*, 1869, p. 125. **[J. M.]**

Gentle Jesus, Lovely Lamb. *C. Wesley.* [*Jesus All in All.*] Pub. in *Hys. and Sacred Poems*, 1749, in 7 st. of 4 l. (*P. Works*, 1868–72, vol. v. p. 21). The following arrangements of the text have come into C. U.:

1. Gentle Jesus, heavenly Lamb. In *Holy Song for All Seasons*, 1869, and other collections.

2. Jesus, all-atoning Lamb. In the *Wes. H. Bk.*, 1799, No. 422 (ed. 1875, No. 434). G. J. Stevenson has several reminiscences of this hymn in his *Meth. H. Bk. Notes*, 1883, p. 291. This form of the hymn is in extensive use.

3. Jesus, let me cleave to Thee. In the Presb. *Ps. & Hys.*, Richmond, U.S.A., 1867, No. 357, in 2 st. (st. ii. and iv. altered.)   **[J. J.]**

Gentle Jesus, meek and mild. *C. Wesley.* [*A Child's Prayer.*] 1st pub. in *Hymns & Sacred Poems*, 1742; and again in *Hymns for Children*, 1763, in 7 st. of 4 l. Following it is another hymn, marked pt. ii., and beginning, "Lamb of God, I look to Thee," also in 7 st. of 4 l., thus accounting for the statement sometimes made that the original is in 14 stanzas. Centos from both parts are found in most collections for children in English-speaking countries, and are exceedingly popular with the young. The construction of each cento may be traced by a reference to the orig. text in *P. Works*, 1868–72, vol. vi. p. 441, No. 336. "Lamb of God," &c., in the *Methodist S. S. H. Bk.*, 1879, is entirely from pt. ii., whilst "Gentle Jesus, meek and mild," is compiled from both.

Other arrangements are:—

(1) "Loving Jesus, gentle Lamb," in the American *Meth. Episco. Hymns*, 1849; and (2) "Holy Jesus, Saviour mild," in the *Bonchurch H. Bk.*, 1868. **[J. J.]**

Gently, my [Father] Saviour, let me down. *R. Hill.* [*Death anticipated.*] In the *Life of the Rev. Rowland Hill, M.A.*, by the Rev. Edwin Sidney, 1834, Mr. Sidney says, in describing the death of Mr. Hill, "Sometimes he repeated the first verse of his own beautiful hymn, 'Gently, my Saviour, let me down'"; but he does not indicate where the full text could be found, nor the date of its composition. Dr. Hatfield in his American *Church H. Bk.*, 1872, No. 1357, in 5 st. of 4 l., dates it 1832, that is, the year before Mr. Hill's death. In the American *Church Praise Bk.*, N.Y., 1882, No. 655, it is dated 1796. This is certainly an error. The hymn is essentially an old man's hymn, and Dr. Hatfield's date is consistent with this fact. The hymn was

given in 3 st. of 4 l. in the American Universalists' *Hys. for Christian Devotion*, 1846, No. 536, as "Gently, my *Father*, let me down." (See **Various**.)   **[J. J.]**

Gerhardt, Paulus, s. of Christian Gerhardt, burgomaster of Gräfenhaynichen, near Wittenberg, was b. at Gräfenhaynichen, Mar. 12, 1607. On January 2, 1628, he matriculated at the University of Wittenberg. In the registers of St. Mary's church, Wittenberg, his name appears as a godfather, on July 13, 1641, described still as "studiosus," and he seems to have remained in Wittenberg till at least the end of April, 1642. He appears to have gone to Berlin in 1642 or 1643, and was there for some time (certainly after 1648) a tutor in the house of the advocate Andreas Barthold, whose daughter (Anna Maria, b. May 19, 1622, d. March 5, 1668) became his wife in 1655. During this period he seems to have frequently preached in Berlin. He was appointed in 1651, at the recommendation of the Berlin clergy, Lutheran Probst (chief pastor) at Mittenwalde, near Berlin, and ordained to this post Nov. 18, 1651. In July, 1657, he returned to Berlin as third diaconus of St. Nicholas's church; but becoming involved in the contest between the Elector Friedrich Wilhelm (who was of the Reformed Church) and the Lutheran clergy of Berlin, he was deposed from his office in February, 1666, though he still remained in Berlin. In Nov., 1668, he accepted the post of archidiaconus at Lübben, on the Spree, was installed in June, 1669, and remained there till his death on June 7, 1676 (*Koch*, iii. 297–326; *Allg. Deutsche Biog.*, viii. 774–783, &c.).

The outward circumstances of Gerhardt's life were for the most part gloomy. His earlier years were spent amid the horrors of the Thirty Years' War. He did not obtain a settled position in life till he was 44 years of age. He was unable to marry till four years later; and his wife, after a long illness, died during the time that he was without office in Berlin; while of the five children of the marriage only one passed the period of childhood. The sunniest period of his life was during the early years of his Berlin ministry (i.e. 1657–1663), when he enjoyed universal love and esteem; while his latter years at Lübben as a widower with one surviving child were passed among a rough and unsympathising people. The motto on his portrait at Lübben not unjustly styles him "Theologus in cribro Satanae versatus."

Gerhardt ranks, next to Luther, as the most gifted and popular hymn-writer of the Lutheran Church. Gervinus (ed. 1842, pt. iii. p. 366), the well-known historian of German literature, thus characterises him:—

"He went back to Luther's most genuine type of hymn in such manner as no one else had done, only so far modified as the requirements of his time demanded. In Luther's time the belief in Free Grace and the work of the Atonement, in Redemption and the bursting of the gates of Hell was the inspiration of his joyful confidence; with Gerhardt it is the belief in the Love of God. With Luther the old wrathful God of the Romanists assumed the heavenly aspect of grace and mercy; with Gerhardt the merciful Righteous One is a gentle loving Man. Like the old poets of the people he is sincerely and unconstrainedly pious, naïve, and hearty; the blissfulness of his faith makes him benign and amiable; in his way of writing he is as attractive, simple, and pleasing as in his way of thinking."

With a firm grasp of the objective realities of the Christian Faith, and a loyal adherence to the doctrinal standpoint of the Lutheran Church, Gerhardt is yet genuinely human; he takes a fresh, healthful view both of nature and of mankind. In his hymns we see the transition to the modern subjective tone of religious poetry. Sixteen of his hymns begin with, "I." Yet with Gerhardt it is not so much the individual soul that lays

bare its sometimes morbid moods, as it is the representative member of the Church speaking out the thoughts
and feelings he shares with his fellow members : while
in style Gerhardt is simple and graceful, with a considerable variety of verse form at his command, and often
of bell-like purity in tone.

From the first publication of Gerhardt's
hymns they at once came into favour among
all ranks and creeds ; and a large proportion
are among the hymns most cherished and most
widely used by German-speaking Christians
at the present day. They appeared principally in the various eds. of Crüger's *Praxis*,
and the *Crüger-Runge G. B.*, 1653 (see Crüger,
J.). The first collected ed. was prepared by
J. G. Ebeling, and pub. in separate "*Dozens*,"
1–4 in 1666, 5–10 in 1667, i.e. 120 in all. In
the ed. of J. H. Feustking, Zerbst, 1707, a
few st. were intercalated (from MSS. in the
possession of Gerhardt's surviving son), but
no new hymns were added.

Among modern eds. of Gerhardt's hymns (mostly fol-
lowing the text of Ebeling) may be mentioned those by
Langbecker, 1842 ; *Schultz*, 1842 ; *Wackernagel*, 1843 ;
Becker, 1851 ; *Goedeke*, 1877, and *Gerok*, 1878. The
Historico-Critical ed. of Dr. J. F. Bachmann, 1866, is
the most complete (with 11 additional pieces hardly
Church hymns), and reverts to the pre-Ebeling text.

The length of many of Gerhardt's hymns
("Ein Lämmlein" is 10 st. of 10 l. ; "Fröhlich soll," 15 st. of 8 l., &c.), and the somewhat intricate metres of others, have caused
his hymns to be less used in English than
otherwise might have been the case ; but a
considerable proportion have come in some
form or other into English hymn-books. A
large selection, translated with scrupulous
faithfulness but not retaining much of the
lyric grace of the originals, was pub. by the
Rev. John Kelly, in 1867, as *Paul Gerhardt's
Spiritual Songs;* while many individual hymns
have been *tr.* by John Wesley, Miss Winkworth, Miss Cox, Miss Borthwick, and many
others. His *trs.* from St. Bernard are noted
under "O Haupt voll Blut." There are
separate notes on 19 of his greater hymns.
(See *Index.*) Besides these the following
have passed into English :—

I. *Hymns in English C. U.*

i. **Auf den Nebel folgt die Sonn.** *Thanksgiving
after great sorrow and affliction.* In Crüger's
Praxis, 1656, No. 249, in 15 st. of 7 l. ; thence
in Wackernagel's ed. of his *Geistliche Lieder*,
No. 87, and Bachmann's ed., No. 64. In the
Unv. L. S., 1851, No. 402. *Tr.* as :—

Cometh sunshine after rain. A good *tr.*, omitting
st. iv.–vii., x., xi., by Miss Winkworth, in her
Lyra Ger., 1st Ser., 1855, p. 100 (*trs.* of x., xi.
added to 2nd ed., 1856). Repeated, omitting the
trs. of st. ii., x.–xii., as No. 4 in her *C. B. for
England*, 1863. In the *Christian H. Bk.*, Cincinnati, 1865, No. 799, begins with st. xiii.,
"Now as long as here I roam."

Another tr. is :— "After clouds we see the sun," by
J. Kelly, 1867, p. 261.

ii. **Die Zeit ist nunmehr nah.** *Day of Judgment—Second Advent.* Founded on Acts iii. 20.
In the *Crüger-Runge G. B.*, 1653, No. 367, in
18 st. of 6 l., and thence in Wackernagel's ed. of
his *Geistliche Lieder*, 1843, No. 119 (1874, No.
124), and Bachmann's ed., No. 40. In the Berlin
G. L. S., ed. 1863, No. 1517. *Tr.* as :—

O Christ! how good and fair. Being a *tr.* of
st. iii., iv., vi., vii., x.–xiii., xvii., by Mrs. Charles,
in her *Voice of Christian Life in Song*, 1858,

p. 242. Her *trs.* of st. iii., x., xii., are No. 150
in G. S. Jellicoe's *Coll.*, 1867.

Other trs. are :—(1) "May I when time is o'er," of st.
vii., viii. as part of No. 831 in the *Moravian H. Bk.*,
1789 ; in the 1801 and later eds. (1886, No. 1229), beginning, "I shall, when time is o'er." (2) "The time is
very near," by *J. Kelly*, 1867, p. 341.

iii. **Gottlob, nun ist erschollen.** *Peace.* Thanksgiving for the Proclamation of the Peace of
Westphalia, in 1648, after the Thirty Years'
War. In Crüger's *Praxis*, 1656, No. 409, in
6 st. of 12 l., and thence in Wackernagel's ed.
of his *Geistliche Lieder*, No. 64, and Bachmann's
ed., No. 84 ; and in the *Unv. L. S.*, 1851, No.
589. *Tr.* as :—

Thank God it hath resounded. A full and good
tr. by Miss Winkworth, in her *Lyra Ger.*, 2nd
Ser., 1858, p. 156, repeated, omitting st. ii., in
her *C. B. for England*, 1863. St. i., v., vi., form
No. 49 in M. W. Stryker's *Christian Chorals*, 1885.

Another tr. is :—"Praise God! for forth hath sounded,"
by *J. Kelly*, 1867, p. 251.

iv. **Ich, der ich oft in tiefes Leid.** *Ps. cxlv.*
1st pub. in J. G. Ebeling's ed. of his *Geistliche
Andachten Dritte Dutzet*, 1666, No. 27, in 18 st.
of 7 l. Thence in Wackernagel's ed., No. 95,
and Bachmann's ed., No. 103 ; also in the Berlin
G. L. S., ed. 1863, No. 1004. *Tr.* as :—

I who so oft in deep distress. A good *tr.*, omitting st. ii.–iv., by Miss Winkworth, in her *Lyra
Ger.*, 2nd Ser., 1858, p. 149. Her *trs.* of st. i.,
xiii.–xvi., xviii., were included as No. 224, and
of st vi., viii., ix., xi. altered, and beginning,
"O God! how many thankful songs," as No. 168,
in *Holy Song*, 1869.

Another tr. is :—"Who is so full of tenderness," of
st. viii. as st. iv. of No. 1075 in the *Suppl.* of 1808 to
the *Moravian H. Bk.*, 1801 (1886, No. 537).

v. **Ich steh an deiner Krippen hier.** *Christmas.*
Included in Crüger's *Praxis*, 1656, No. 105, in
15 st. of 7 l. Thence in Wackernagel's ed.,
No. 9, and Bachmann's ed., No. 45 ; and in the
Berlin *G. L. S.*, ed. 1863, No. 167. A beautiful
hymn, in which the poet puts himself in the
place of the shepherds and the wise men visiting
Bethlehem ; and in praise and adoration tenders
his devotion, his love and his all, to the Infant
Saviour in the manger. *Tr.* as :—

My faith Thy lowly bed beholds. A *tr.* of st. i.,
iv., vii., xv., by A. T. Russell, as No. 57 in his
Ps. & Hys., 1851.

Other trs. are :—(1) "I stand beside Thy manger-bed,"
by *Miss Manington*, 1864, p. 38. (2) "Now at the
manger here I stand," by *J. Kelly*, 1867, p. 32.

vi. **Ich weiss dass mein Erlöser lebt.** *Easter.*
Founded on Job xix. 25–27. 1st pub. in J. G.
Ebeling's ed. of his *Geistliche Andachten Zehende
Dutzet*, 1667, No. 119, in 9 st. of 7 l. ; repeated
in Wackernagel's ed., 1843, No. 118 (1874, No.
123) ; in Bachmann's ed., No. 119 ; and in the
Berlin *G. L. S.*, ed. 1863, No. 301. *Tr.* as :—

**I know that my Redeemer lives, In this my faith
is fast.** A full and spirited *tr.* by J. Oxenford,
in *Lays of the Sanctuary*, 1859, p. 122. His
trs. of st. i., iii., vii.–ix., were included, altered,
as No. 779 in *Kennedy*, 1863.

Another tr. is :—"I know that my Redeemer lives,
This hope," &c., by *Miss Manington*, 1863, p. 78.

vii. **Ich weiss, mein Gott, dass all mein Thun.**
Supplication. A prayer for success in all Christian works and purpose ; founded on Jeremiah
x. 23, and Acts v. 38, 39. Included in Crüger's
Praxis, 1656, No. 332, in 18 st. of 5 l. In

Wackernagel's ed., No. 40 ; Bachmann's ed., No. 71, and the Berlin *G. L. S.*, ed. 1863. *Tr.* as :—

I know, my God, and I rejoice. A good *tr.* of st. i.–iii., viii., xi., ix., by Miss Winkworth, as No. 121 in her *C. B. for England*, 1863.

Another tr. is :—"My God ! my works and all I do," by *J. Kelly*, 1867, p. 102.

viii. Kommt, und lasst uns Christum ehren. *Christmas.* Founded on St. Luke ii. 15. 1st pub. in J. G. Ebeling's ed. of his *Geistliche Andachten* Fünffte Dutzet, 1667, No. 56, in 8 st. of 4 l. Thence in Wackernagel's ed., No. 6 ; Bachmann's ed., No. 110 ; and the *Unv. L. S.*, 1851, No. 43. *Tr.* as :—

1. Come, unite in praise and singing. Omitting st. vi., vii., contributed by A. T. Russell to Maurice's *Choral H. Bk.*, 1861, No. 707.

2. Bring to Christ your best oblation. A full and good *tr.* by R. Massie in his *Lyra Domestica*, 1864, p. 96 ; repeated in Snepp's *Songs of G. & G.*, and Reid's *Praise Bk.*, 1872.

Other trs. are :—(1) "Come, and let us Christ revere now," by *Miss Manington*, 1864, p. 25. (2) "Come. and Christ the Lord be praising," by *J. Kelly*, 1867, p. 24.

ix. Lobet den Herren, alle die ihn fürchten. *Morning.* Included in the Crüger-Runge *G. B.*, 1653, No. 7, in 10 st. of 5 l. In Wackernagel's ed., No. 100, and Bachmann's ed., No. 21, and in the Berlin *G. L. S.*, ed. 1000, No. 1063. *Tr.* as :

Praise God! revere Him! all ye men that fear Him ! This is from the version in Bunsen's *Allg. G. B.*, 1846, No. 167, st. i. being from Gerhardt, and st. ii., iii., from "Lobet den Herren, denn er ist sehr freundlich " (q. v.) ; and appeared in the Dalston Hospital *H. Bk.*, 1848, No. 55, signed " A. G."

Other trs. are :—(1) " Our Lord be praising, All His glory raising," by *H. J. Buckoll*, 1842, p. 27. (2) "Praise ye Jehovah, all ye men who fear Him," by *J. Kelly*, 1867, p. 279.

x. Nicht so traurig, nicht so sehr. *Christian Contentment.* In the 3rd ed., 1648, of Crüger's *Praxis*, No. 251, in 15 st. of 6 l., repeated in Wackernagel's ed., No. 53 ; Bachmann's ed., No. 16, and the Berlin *G. L. S.*, ed. 1863, No. 851. It is founded on Ps. cxvi. 7 ; Ps. xlii. 6–12 ; 1 Tim. vi. 6. *Tr.* as :—

Ah! grieve not so, nor so lament. A free *tr.* by Mrs. Findlater, of st. i., ii., vii.–x., xiii., xv., in the 1st Ser., 1854, of the *H. L. L.*, p. 48 (1884, p. 50). Repeated, abridged, in *Holy Song*, 1869, and Dale's *English H. Bk.*, 1875.

Other trs. are :—(1) "Why this sad and mournful guise," by *Miss Dunn*, 1857, p. 85. (2) "Not so darkly, not so deep," by *Miss Warner*, 1858 (1861, p. 58). (3) "O my soul, why dost thou grieve," by *J. Kelly*, 1867.

xi. Nun lasst uns gehn und treten. *New Year.* Included in the Crüger-Runge *G. B.*, 1653, No. 106, in 15 st. of 4 l. Thence in Wackernagel's ed., No. 12 ; Bachmann's ed., No. 24, and the Berlin *G. L. S.*, ed. 1863, No. 200. Evidently written during the Thirty Years' War. *Tr.* as :—

In pray'r your voices raise ye. In full, by J. Kelly, 1867, p. 45. From this, 8 st. are included as No. 48 in the Ohio *Luth. Hyl.*, 1880.

Other trs. are :—(1) "Now let each humble Creature," in the *Suppl. to Ger. Psal.*, ed. 1765, p. 4, and *Select H. from Ger. Psal.*, Tranquebar, 1754, p. 7. In the *Moravian H. Bk.*, 1789, No. 507 (1849, No. 1106), greatly altered, and beginning, "Year after year commenceth." (2) "O come with prayer and singing," by R. Massie in the *British Herald*, Jan., 1865, p. 8. (3) "Christians all, with one accord," by *E. Massie*, 1867, p. 168. (4) "With notes of joy and songs of praise," by *Dr. R. Maguire*, 1883, p. 24.

xii. Schaut ! schaut ! was ist für Wunder dar !

Christmas. 1st pub. in J. G. Ebeling's ed. of his *Geistliche Andachten* Fünffte Dutzet, 1667, No. 55, in 18 st. of 4 l. Thence in Wackernagel's ed., No. 4 ; Bachmann's ed., No. 109. *Tr.* as :—

Behold ! behold ! what wonders here. In full, by J. Kelly, 1867, p. 14. From this, 12 st. were included in the Ohio *Luth. Hyl.*, 1880, as Nos. 25, 26 : No. 26 beginning with the *tr.* of st. xiii., "It is a time of joy to-day."

xiii. Warum willt du draussen stehen. *Advent.* Suggested by Gen. xxiv. 31. Appeared in the Crüger-Runge *G. B.*, 1653, No. 78, in 9 st. of 8 l. ; viz., st. i.–vii., xi., xii., of the full form ; st. viii.–x. being added in Ebeling's *Geistliche Andachten* Fünffte Dutzet, 1667, No. 50. The full text, in 12 st., is also in Wackernagel's ed., No. 2 ; Bachmann's ed., No. 23, and the *Unv. L. S.*, 1851, No. 20. *Tr.* as :—

Wherefore dost Thou longer tarry. A good *tr.*, omitting st. viii.–x., by Miss Winkworth, in her *Lyra Ger.*, 2nd Ser., 1858, p. 6. In her *C. B. for England*, 1863, No. 153, the *trs.* of st. iii., v., xi., are omitted.

Other trs. are :—(1) "Wherefore dost Thou, blest of God," by R. Massie, in *Lyra Domestica*, 1864, p. 90. (2) "Why, without, then, art Thou staying," by *J. Kelly*, 1867, p. 5.

xiv. Was alle Weisheit in der Welt. *Trinity Sunday.* In Crüger's *Praxis*, 1656, No. 212, in 8 st. of 9 l. Thence in Wackernagel's ed., No. 1, and Bachmann's ed., No. 59, and the Berlin *G. L. S.*, ed. 1863, No. 50. *Tr.* as :—

Scarce tongue can speak, ne'er human ken. In full, by J. Kelly, 1867, p. 1, repeated as No. 111 in the Ohio *Luth. Hyl.*, 1880.

Another tr. is :—"The mystery hidden from the eyes," by R. Massie, in *Lyra Domestica*, 1864, p. 87.

xv. Was Gott gefällt, mein frommes Kind. *Resignation.* This beautiful hymn, on resignation to " what pleases God," first appeared in the Crüger-Runge *G. B.*, 1653, No. 290, in 20 st. of 5 l. Thence in Wackernagel's ed., No. 60 ; Bachmann's ed., No. 37, and the *Unv. L. S.*, 1851, No. 723. *Tr.* as :—

What God decrees, child of His love. A good *tr.* of st. i., ii., v., vi., viii., xii., xv., xviii., xx., by Mrs. Findlater, in the 3rd Ser., 1858, of the *H. L. L.*, p. 49 (1884, p. 170). Included, in full, in Bp. Ryle's *Coll.*, 1860, No. 171 ; and abridged in *Christian Hys.*, Adelaide, 1872, and beginning, "What God decrees, take patiently," in *Kennedy*, 1863, No. 1344.

Other trs. are :—(1) "What pleaseth God with joy receive," by *Miss Dunn*, 1857, p. 94. (2) "What pleases God, O pious soul," by *Miss Winkworth*, 1858, p. 193, (3) What pleaseth God, my faithful child," by *J. Kelly*, 1867, p. 189.

xvi. Wie schön ists doch, Herr Jesu Christ. *For Married Persons.* Founded on Ps. cxxviii. 1st pub. in Ebeling's ed. of his *Geistliche Andachten* Vierte Dutzet, 1666, No. 38, in 8 st. of 12 l. Thence in Wackernagel's ed., 1843, No. 108 (1874, No. 109) ; Bachmann's ed., No. 105, and the *Unv. L. S.*, 1851, No. 680. *Tr.* as :—

Oh, Jesus Christ ! how bright and fair. In full, by J. Kelly, 1867, p. 307, repeated, altered, and omitting st. iii.–v., in the Ohio *Luth. Hyl.*, 1880, No. 339.

II. *Hymns not in English C. U.*

xvii. Also hat Gott die Welt geliebt. *Good Friday.* On St. John iii. 16. In Crüger's *Praxis*, 1661, No. 372, in 17 st. *Tr.* as, "Be of good cheer in all your wants," by P. H. Molther, of st. 16, as No. 181 in the *Moravian H. Bk.*, 1789 (1886, No. 217).

xviii. Auf, auf, mein Herz mit Freuden. *Easter.* In Crüger's *Praxis*, 1648, No. 141, in 9 st. The *trs.* are: (1) "Up! up! my heart with gladness, See," by *J. Kelly*, 1867, p. 71. (2) "Up, up, my heart, with gladness, Receive," by *N. L. Frothingham*, 1870, p. 228.

xix. Du bist zwar mein und bleibest mein. *For the Bereaved.* A beautiful hymn of consolation for parents on the loss of a son. Written on the death of Constantin Andreas, younger son of Johannes Berkov, pastor of St. Mary's Church, Berlin, and first printed as one of the " Dulcia amicorum solatia " at the end of the funeral sermon by Georg Lilius. Berlin, 1650. Included in Ebeling's ed. of Gerhardt's *Geistliche Andachten* Sechste Dutzet, Berlin, 1667, No. 72, in 12 st. The *trs.* are: (1) "Thou'rt mine, yes, still thou art mine own," by *Miss Winkworth*, 1858, p. 123. (2) "Yes, thou art mine, still mine, my son," by J. D. Burns, in the *Family Treasury*, 1861, p. 8, and his *Remains*, 1869, p. 249. (3) "Mine art thou still, and mine shalt be," by *J. Kelly*, 1867, p. 333. (4) "Thou art mine own, art still mine own," by *Dr. J. Guthrie*, 1869, p. 100.

xx. Du, meine Seele, singe. Ps. cxlvi. In the Crüger-Runge *G. B.*, Berlin, 1653, No. 183, in 10 st. *Tr.* as, "O come, my soul, with singing," by Miss Burlingham, in the *British Herald*, January, 1866, p. 207, and as No. 423 in Reid's *Praise Bk*, 1872.

xxi. Gieb dich zufrieden, und sei stille. *Cross and Consolation—Ps. xxxvii.* 7. In *Ebeling* Erstes Dutzet, 1666, No. 11, in 15 st. *Tr.* as: (1) "Be thou content: be still before," by *Miss Winkworth*, 1855, p. 156, and in Bp. Ryle's *Coll.*, 1860, No. 269. (2) "Be thou contented! aye relying," by *J. Kelly*, 1867, p. 202. (3) "Tranquilly lead thee, peace possessing," by *N. L. Frothingham*, 1870, p. 246.

xxii. Hör an! mein Herz, die sieben Wort. *Passiontide.* On the Seven Words from the Cross. Founded on the hymn noted under **Böschenstein, J.** (q.v.). In Crüger's *Praxis*, 1656, No. 137, in 15 st. *Tr.* as: (1) " Come now, my soul, thy thoughts engage," by *Dr. H. Mills*, 1845 (1856, p. 309). (2) "Seven times the Saviour spake—my heart," by R. Massie, in the *British Herald*, Sept., 1865, p. 133. (3) "My heart! the seven words hear now," by *J. Kelly*, 1867, p. 63.

xxiii. Ich hab in Gottes Herz und Sinn. *Resignation.* In Crüger's *Praxis*, 1648, No. 249, in 12 st. *Tr.* as: (1) "I into God's own heart and mind," by *J. Kelly*, 1867, p. 219. (2) "To God's all-gracious heart and mind," by *Miss Winkworth*, 1869, p. 213, repeated in Statham's *Coll.*, Edin. 1869 and 1870.

xxiv. O Jesu Christ! dein Kripplein ist. *Christmas. At the Manger of Bethlehem.* In Crüger's *Praxis*, 1656, No. 101, in 15 st. *Tr.* as: (1) "Be not dismay'd—in time of need" (st. xi.) in the *Moravian H. Bk.*, 1789, No. 236. (2) "O blessed Jesus! This," by *Miss Winkworth*, 1858, p. 18. (3) "O Jesus Christ! Thy cradle is," by *Miss Manington*, 1864, p. 41. (4) "Thy manger is my paradise," by *J. Kelly*, 1867, p. 26.

xxv. Voller Wunder, voller Kunst. *Holy Matrimony.* In *Ebeling* Vierte Dutzet, 1666, No. 40, in 17 st. Often used in Germany at marriages on the way to church. *Tr.* as: (1) "Full of wonder, full of skill," by *Dr. H. Mills*, 1845 (1856, p. 215). (2) "Full of wonder, full of skill," in Mrs. Stanley Carr's *tr.* of *Wildenhahn's Paul Gerhardt*, ed. 1856, p. 52. (3) "Full of wonder, full of art," by *J. Kelly*, 1867, p. 302. (4) "Full of wonder, full of art," by *Miss Winkworth*, 1869, p. 215.

xxvi. Warum machet solche Schmerzen. *New Year.* On St. Luke ii. 21. In Crüger's *Praxis*, 1648, No. 97, in 4 st. Bunsen, in his *Versuch*, 1833, No. 120, gives st. iii., iv. altered to "Freut euch, Sünder, allerwegen." *Tr.* as: (1) "Mortals, who have God offended," by *Miss Cox*, 1841, p. 21, from *Bunsen*. (2) "Why should they such pain e'er give Thee," by *J. Kelly*, 1867, p. 43.

xxvii. Weg, mein Herz, mit den Gedanken. *Lent.* On St. Luke xv. In Crüger's *Praxis*, 1648, No. 36, in 12 st. *Tr.* as: (1) "Let not such a thought e'er pain thee," by *J. Kelly*, 1867, p. 83. (2) "Hence, my heart, with such a thought," by *Miss Winkworth*, 1869, p. 210.

Besides the above, a considerable number of other hymns by Gerhardt have been *tr.* by Mr. Kelly, and a few by Dr. Mills, Miss Manington, and others. The limits of our space forbid detailed notes on these versions.   [J. M.]

German Hymnody. German hymnody surpasses all others in wealth. The church hymn in the strict sense of the term, as a *popular religious lyric in praise of God to be sung by the congregation in public worship*, was born with the German Reformation, and most extensively cultivated ever since by the evangelical church in Germany. The Latin hymns and sequences of Hilary, Ambrose, Fortunatus, Gregory the Great, Notker, St. Bernard, Thomas of Aquino, Adam of St. Victor, Thomas of Celano, and others, were indeed used in public worship long before, but only by the priests and choristers, not by the people, who could not understand them any more than the Latin psalms and the Latin mass. The Reformed (as the non-Lutheran Protestant churches are called on the Continent) were long satisfied with metrical translations of the Psalter, and did not feel the necessity of original hymns, and some did not approve of the use of them in public worship.

The number of German hymns cannot fall short of one hundred thousand. Dean Georg Ludwig von Hardenberg of Halberstadt, in the year 1786, prepared a hymnological catalogue of the first lines of 72,733 hymns (in 5 vols., preserved in the library of Halberstadt). This number was not complete at that time, and has considerably increased since. About ten thousand have become more or less popular, and passed into different hymn-books. Fischer gives a selection of about 5000 of the best, many of which were overlooked by Von Hardenberg. We may safely say that nearly one thousand of these hymns are classical and immortal. This is a larger number than can be found in any other language.

To this treasury of German song several hundred men and women of all ranks and conditions—theologians and pastors, princes and princesses, generals and statesmen, physicians and jurists, merchants and travellers, labourers and private persons—have made contributions, laying them on the common altar of devotion. Many of these hymns, and just those possessed of the greatest vigour and unction, full of the most exulting faith and the richest comfort, had their origin amid the conflicts and storms of the Reformation, or the fearful devastations and nameless miseries of the Thirty Years' War; others belong to the revival period of the Spenerian Pietism and the Moravian Brotherhood, and reflect its earnest struggle after holiness, the fire of the first love and the sweet enjoyment of the soul's intercourse with her Heavenly Bridegroom; and not a few of them sprang up even in the unbelieving age of "illumination" and rationalism, like flowers from dry ground, or Alpine roses on fields of snow; others again proclaim, in fresh and joyous tones, the dawn of reviving faith in the land where the Reformation had its birth. Thus these hymns constitute a most graphic book of confession for German evangelical Christianity, a sacred band which enriches its various periods, an abiding memorial of its victories, its sorrows and its joys, a clear mirror showing its deepest experiences, and an eloquent witness for the all-conquering and invincible life-power of the evangelical Christian faith.

The treasures of German hymnody have enriched churches of other tongues and passed into Swedish, Norwegian, Danish, and modern English and American hymn-books. John Wesley was one of the first English divines who appreciated its value; and while his brother Charles produced an immense number of original hymns, John freely reproduced several hymns of Paul Gerhardt, Tersteegen, and Zinzendorf. The English Moravian hymn-book consists mostly of translations from the German. In more recent times, several accomplished writers, male and female, have vied with each other in translations and transfusions of German hymns. Among the chief English translators are Frances Elizabeth Cox; Catherine Winkworth; H. L. L., i.e. Mrs. Findlater and her sister, Miss Jane Borthwick; Richard Massie; Arthur Tozer Russell; James W. Alexander; H. Mills; John Kelly; not to mention many others who have furnished admirable translations of one or more hymns for church hymn-books, or private hymnological collections (as e.g. for Schaff's *Christ in Song*, N. York and London, 1870).

The history of German hymnody may be divided into six periods:—i. *The Mediaeval Period*, from the 8th to the 16th century; feeble beginnings, mostly on the basis of Latin hymns. ii. *The Reformation Period*, to the Peace of Westphalia, 1520-1648. iii. *The Confessional Period*, from Paul Gerhardt to Spener, 1648-1680. iv. *The Pietistic and Moravian Period*, from Spener to Gellert, 1680-1757. v. *The Rationalistic Period*, from Gellert to Arndt, 1757-1817. vi. *The Modern Evangelical Period*, from 1817 to present date.

i. First Period.

The Christianisation of the barbarians in western and northern Europe by Bonifacius, Ansgarius, and other missionaries, was accompanied with the introduction of the Latin language in theology and in public worship. This was an efficient means for preserving the unity of the church and facilitating literary intercourse among scholars, but prevented for a long time the free and full development of a vernacular hymnody. Nevertheless the German love for poetry and song produced a large number of sacred lyrics for private devotion, and versified translations of the Psalter and Latin hymns. Wackernagel gives, in the second volume of his great collection, no less than 1448 German hymns and sequences, from Otfrid to Hans Sachs (inclusive), or from A.D. 868 to A.D. 1518.

1. The oldest German poet is the Benedictine monk Otfrid, of Weissenburg (a pupil of Rabanus Maurus at Fulda). He prepared, in the middle of the ninth century, a versified Gospel history in the Alemannian dialect, divided into stanzas; each stanza containing four rhymed verses, the whole consisting of 1500 lines. This was the first German Bible for the laity. (See his *Krist*, edited by Graff, 1831, and nineteen specimens in *Wackernagel*, ii. 3-21.)

2. The *Kyrie eleison* and *Christe eleison*, which passed from the Greek church into the Latin, as a response of the people, to be repeated over and over again, especially on the high festivals, was popularly enlarged, and these brief poems were called from the refrain *Kirleison* or *Leisen*, also *Leichen*. They were the first specimens of German hymns which were sung by the people. The oldest dates

from the end of the ninth century, and is called the *Leich vom heil. Petrus*. It has three stanzas, of which the first reads:—

" Unsar trohtin hat farsalt	zeimo dingenten man.
sancte Petre giwalt	Kyrie eleyson ! Christe
Daz er mag ginerjan	eleison !" *

One of the best of these *Kirleisen*, but of much later date, is the Easter hymn:—

" Christ ist erstanden,	des sul wir alle fro sein,
von der marter all,	Christ sol unser trost sein,
	Kyrie leyson." †

Some of the best Latin hymns, as the " Te Deum," the " Gloria in excelsis," the " Pange lingua gloriosi praelium certaminis," the " Veni Creator Spiritus," the " Lauda Sion salvatorem," St. Bernard's " Jesu dulcis memoria," and " Salve caput cruentatum," were repeatedly translated. Not unfrequently words of the original were mixed with the vernacular, as in the Christmas hymn:—

" *In dulci jubilo*	*Leyt in presepio*
Nu singet und seyt fro !	Und leuchtet *in gremio*.
Unsres Herzens Wonne	*Alpha es et O.*"

A Benedictine monk, John of Salzburg, prepared a number of translations from the Latin at the request of his archbishop, Pilgrim, in 1366, and was rewarded by him with a parish. Wackernagel (ii. 409 sqq.) gives 43 of his hymns from MSS. In the Imperial Library of Vienna.

3. The " Minnesänger " of the thirteenth century—among whom Gottfried of Strassburg and Walther von der Vogelweide are the most eminent—glorified earthly and heavenly, sexual and spiritual love, after the model of Solomon's Song, and the Virgin Mary as the type of pure womanhood. The mystic school of Tauler, in the fourteenth century, produced a few hymns full of glowing love to God. Tauler is the author of the Christmas poem, " Uns kommt ein Schiff geladen," and the hymn of love to God:—

> " Ich muss die Creaturen fliehen
> Und suchen Herzens Innigkeit,
> Soll ich den Geist zu Gotte ziehen,
> Auf dass er bleib in Reinigkeit."

4. The German hymnody of the Middle Ages, like the Latin, overflows with hagiolatry and Mariolatry. Mary is even clothed with divine attributes, and virtually put in the place of Christ as the fountain of all grace. " Through all the centuries from Otfrid to Luther" (says *Wackernagel*, ii. p. 13), " we meet with the idolatrous veneration of the Virgin Mary. There are hymns which teach that she pre-existed with God at the creation, that all things are created in her and for her, and that God rested in her on the seventh day." One of the favourite Mary hymns was " Dich Frau vom Himmel, ruf ich an." Hans Sachs afterwards changed it into " Christum vom Himmel ruf ich an."

This change is characteristic of the effect which the Reformation exerted upon the

---

* *I. e.* " Our Lord delivered power to St. Peter that he may preserve the man who hopes in him. Lord, have mercy upon us ! Christ, have mercy upon us !"
† Wackernagel, ii., 43 seq., gives several forms. They were afterwards much enlarged. In a Munich MS. of the 15th cent. a Latin verse is coupled with the German:

" Christus surrexit	et quos hic dilexit
mala nostra texit	hos ad coelum vexit
	Kyrie leyson,"

worship of Mary. It substituted for it the worship of Christ as the only Mediator and Saviour through Whom men attain unto eternal life. The mediaeval hymnody celebrates Mary as the "Ewig-Weibliche," which draws men irresistibly heavenward. It resembles the Sistine Madonna of Raphael, who painted Christ as a child, even in heaven, on the arms of the Queen of Heaven.

ii. *Second Period.*

The Reformation of the sixteenth century taught or revived the primitive idea of the general priesthood of believers, and introduced the language of the people into public worship. It substituted a vernacular sermon for the Latin Mass, and congregational singing for the chanting of priests and choirs. The results were great and far-reaching, and of the utmost benefit to the Church of Christ.

1. *The Lutheran Hymnody till about* 1570. —The leader of the Reformation was also the first evangelical hymnist. To Luther belongs the extraordinary merit of having given to the German people in their own tongue the Bible, the Catechism, and the hymn-book, so that God might speak *directly* to them in His word, and that they might *directly* answer Him in their songs. He was also a musician and composed tunes to his best hymns. Some of them are immortal, most of all that triumphant war-cry of the Reformation which has so often been reproduced in other languages (the best English translation is Carlyle's), and which resounds with mighty effects on great occasions: " Ein' feste Burg ist unser Gott." Luther was a great lover of poetry and song, and availed himself of all existing helps for the benefit of public worship and private devotion. He began to write hymns in 1523, soon after he had completed his translation of the New Testament, and wrote his last two in 1543, three years before his death. He is the author of thirty-seven hymns; most of them (21) date from the year 1524.

He drew inspiration from the 46th Psalm for his " Ein' feste Burg," composed in the year 1529 ; from the 130th Psalm for his " Aus tiefer Noth schrei ich zu dir " (1523) ; from the 12th Psalm for his " Ach Gott vom Himmel sieh darein " (1523). He reproduced some of the best Latin hymns in new or improved translations, as " Herr Gott, dich loben wir " (*Te Deum laudamus*); " Komm, Gott Schöpfer, heiliger Geist (*Veni Creator Spiritus*); " Nun komm der Heiden Heiland " (*Veni Redemptor gentium*); " Mitten wir im Leben sind " (*Mediâ vitâ in morte sumus*). He produced also strictly original hymns, as " Nun freut euch, lieben Christen g'mein " (1523) ; " Erhalt uns Herr bei deinem Wort " (against the Pope and the Turk, 1541) ; " Vom Himmel hoch da komm ich her " (for Christmas, 1535), and in an abridged form: " Vom Himmel kam der Engelschaar " (for Christmas, 1543), and the stirring song of the two evangelical martyrs at Brussels in 1523, " Ein neues Lied wir heben an."

Luther is the Ambrose of German hymnody. His hymns are characterised by simplicity and strength, and a popular churchly tone. They breathe the bold, confident, joyful spirit of justifying faith which was the beating heart of his theology and piety. He had an extraordinary faculty of expressing profound thought in the clearest language. In this gift he is not surpassed by any uninspired writer; and herein lies the secret of his power.

He never leaves the reader in doubt of his meaning. He brings the truth home to the heart of the common people, and always hits the nail on the head. His style is racy, forcible, and thoroughly idiomatic. He is the father of the modern High German language and literature. His translation of the Bible may be greatly improved, but will never lose its hold upon the German - speaking people. Luther's hymns passed at once into popular use, and accompanied the Reformation in its triumphant march through German lands. Next to the German Bible they proved to be the most effective missionaries of evangelical doctrines and piety. How highly his contemporaries thought of them may be inferred from Spangenberg, likewise a hymnist, who said, in his preface to the *Cithara Lutheri* (1545) :—

" The rhymes are easy and good, the words choice and proper, the meaning clear and intelligible, the melodies lovely and hearty, and, *in summâ*, all is so rare and majestic, so full of pith and power, so cheering and comforting that you will not find his equal, much less his master."

The first German evangelical hymn-book, the so-called *Achtliederbuch*, appeared in the year 1524 and contained eight hymns, four of them by Luther, three by Speratus, one by an unknown author. The *Erfurt Enchiridion*, of the same year, numbered twenty-five hymns, of which eighteen were from Luther. The hymn-book of Walther, also of 1524, contained thirty-two ; Klug's *Gesangbuch*, edited by Luther, Wittenberg, 1529, had fifty-four ; Babst's of 1545, eighty-nine ; and the fifth edition of 1553, one hundred and thirty-one hymns. (See *Koch*, i. 250 sqq.) This rapid increase of hymns and hymn-books continued after Luther's death.

We can only mention the names of the principal hymnists who were inspired by his example.

Justus Jonas, Luther's friend and colleague (1493–1555) wrote, " Wo Gott der Herr nicht bei uns hält " (*Ps.* 124). *Paul Eber*, the faithful assistant of Melanchthon and Professor of Hebrew in Wittenberg (1511–1569), is the author of " Wenn wir in höchsten Nöthen sein," and " Herr Jesu Christ, wahr'r Mensch und Gott." *Burkhard Waldis*, of Hesse (1485–1557), versified the Psalter. *Erasmus Alber* (d. in Mecklenburg, 1553), wrote twenty hymns which Herder and Gervinus thought almost equal to Luther's. His " Christe, du bist der helle Tag," is a *tr.* from the Latin " Christe qui lux." *Lazarus Spengler*, of Nürnberg (1479–1534) wrote, about 1522, a hymn on sin and redemption, which soon became very popular, " Durch Adam's Fall ist ganz verderbt." *Hans Sachs*, the shoemaker- poet of Nürnberg (1496–1576), was the most fruitful " Meister-sänger " of that period, and wrote also some spiritual hymns. *Veit Dietrich*, pastor of St. Sebaldus in Nürnberg (d. 1549), wrote " Bedenk, o Mensch, die grosse Gnad." Markgraf *Albrecht* of Brandenburg (d. 1557): " Was mein Gott will, geschehe allzeit." *Paul Speratus*, his court-chaplain at Königsberg (1484–1551), contributed three hymns to the first German hymn-book (1524), of which the best is " Es ist das Heil uns kommen her." *J. Schneesing* (d. 1567) pub. in 1548 a hymn still in use, " Allein zu dir, Herr Jesu Christ." *J. Mathesius*, the pupil and biographer of Luther, and pastor at Joachimsthal in Bohemia (1504–1565), wrote a few ; *Nicolaus Herman*, his cantor and friend (d. 1561), 176 hymns, especially for children, and composed popular tunes. *Nicolaus Decius*, first a monk, then an evangelical pastor at Stettin (d. 1541), reproduced the *Gloria in excelsis* in his well known " Allein Gott in der Höh sei Ehr " (1525), and the *Agnus Dei* in his eucharistic " O Lamm Gottes unschuldig " (1531).

The German hymnody of the Reformation period was enriched also by hymns of the *Bohemian Brethren*, which were freely translated by *Michael Weisse* (Weys), and *Johann Roh* (Horn) of Silesia. Weisse was a native

German, who had joined the *Bohemian Brethren*, edited in 1531 their first German hymn-book, and was sent by them as a delegate to Luther in 1522. Luther at first favoured them, but afterwards they showed their preference for the Reformed doctrine of the Sacraments.

2. *The Lutheran Hymnody from about* 1570 *to* 1648.—The productive period of the Lutheran church closed with the Formula of Concord in 1577, which gave final shape to its creed after the violent synergistic, antinomian, ubiquitarian, crypto-Calvinistic and adiaphoristic controversies. The hymns from this time to the close of the Thirty Years' War bear upon the whole the same character of objective churchly piety. But the untold misery which that fearful war entailed upon Germany stimulated the production of a more subjective and experimental type of sacred poetry, and multiplied the hymns of the Cross (*Kreuz- und Trostlieder*).

The following are the chief hymnists from the close of the 16th cent. and the first half of the 17th cent. :—

Nicolaus Selnecker (1530–1592), a pupil of Melanchthon and one of the framers of the *Formula Concordiae*, is the author of nearly 150 hymns. *Bartholomaeus Ringwaldt* (1530–1598), an equally fertile singer, is best known through his name being associated with the German *Dies irae*, "Es ist gewisslich an der Zeit." *Martin Moller* (1567–1606); *Martin Behm* (1557–1622); *Martin Schalling* (1532–1576), author of "Herzlich Lieb hab ich dich, O Herr," 1567; *Valerius Herberger* (1562 1627), author of " Valet will ich dir geben," 1613. *Philipp Nicolai*, Pastor at Unna in Westphalia, afterwards in Hamburg, where he died, 1608, was a violent polemic against the Calvinists, but two of his hymns, from the year 1598 or earlier, namely, "Wie schön leuchtet der Morgenstern" (based on Ps. 45), and "Wachet auf! ruft uns die Stimme" (Matt. 25), are truly classical and universal favourites in German churches, as well as the sublime chorales which be adapted to them. Although he belongs to the churchly school, he introduced, by the sweet and tender tone of his "Morning Star," the unique series of German Jesus-hymns, in which the sentiment of the love of the soul to the heavenly Bridegroom is expressed in glowing language.

To the period of the Thirty Years' War (1618–1648) belong the following poets :—

Martin Opitz (1597–1639), who founded the Silesian school of poets, reformed the art of poetry and introduced greater purity of language and metrical regularity. *Johann Heermann* (1585–1647), a great sufferer of bodily ills, contributed many hymns of permanent value, as "Herzliebster Jesu, was hast du verbrochen," "O Jesu, Jesu, Gottes Sohn," "O Jesu Christe, wahres Licht," "Zion klagt mit Angst und Schmerzen." *Matthäus Apelles von Löwenstern* (1594–1648) is the author of "Christe, du Beistand deiner Kreuzgemeinde," and "Jesu, meine Freud und Wonne." *Michael Altenburg* (1584–1640) wrote the first three stanzas of the famous battle hymn of Gustavus Adolphus, "Verzage nicht, du Häuflein klein," which that hero had sung by his army before the battle of Lützen (Nov. 19, 1632). *Joh. Matthaeus Meyfart* (1590–1642) is known by his New Jerusalem hymn, "Jerusalem, du hochgebaute Stadt." To *Paul Fleming* (1609–1640) we owe the pilgrim hymn, "In allen meinen Thaten." Mention must be made also of *Johann Hermann Schein* (1586–1630); *Heinrich Held* (d. c. 1650); *Georg Weissel* (1590–1635); *Simon Dach* (1605–1659); *Valentin Thilo* (1607–1662). *Martin Rinkart* (1586–1649), at the conclusion of that terrible war, 1648, gave classic expression to the grateful feeling of relief in the German "Te Deum," "Nun danket alle Gott."

3. *The German Reformed Hymnody during the Reformation period.* — The Reformed churches of Switzerland and Germany were far behind the Lutheran in original hymnody, but took the lead in psalmody. *Zwingli* and *Calvin*, the Swiss reformers, held the principle that the Word of God should have supreme dominion in public worship, and that no productions of man should be allowed to take its place.

This principle raised the Psalter to new dignity and power. Versified versions of the Psalms became the first hymn-books of the Reformed churches. Clément Marot, court poet to Francis I. of France, had between 1533 and 1538, translated several psalms into French metre. These circulated in MS. first at the court, and then among the Huguenots, from whose use of them they assumed a party character. When Calvin was expelled from Geneva in 1538, he settled at Strasburg, and published there in the following year a small collection of 18 psalm versions and 3 other pieces with melodies attached. Of the psalms 12 are by Marot, 5 by Calvin himself, and 1 in prose. The melodies are mostly of German origin. Calvin returned to Geneva in Sept., 1541, and soon after that time another Psalter appeared at Strasburg, containing, besides the former 12, the 18 other psalms which Marot had already versified. Calvin then published at Geneva, in 1542, a new psalm book, containing Marot's 30 psalms, his own 5, and some shorter pieces, such as the Song of Simeon, the Creed, and the Decalogue. When Marot fled to Geneva in 1542, he revised these psalms for Calvin, and wrote for him 19 others which were published in the edition of 1543. Soon afterwards Marot left Geneva and died in 1544. Some years then elapsed when Theodore de Bèze (or Beza) completed the Psalter at Calvin's request. The first instalment was published in 1551, and the entire work in 1562. The musical editor of the Genevan Psalter was up to 1557 Louis Bourgeois. The additional tunes of 1562 (40 in number) were added by an unknown hand. After the completion of the Psalter the tunes were harmonized in 1565 by the celebrated Claude Goudimel, who perished in 1572 in the massacre at Lyons which followed the "Bartholomew" at Paris. Hence the *melodies* have often, but erroneously, been attributed to Goudimel, who had not even joined the Huguenot party until most of the Genevan Psalter had been published, and had no correspondence at any time with Calvin. [See **Psalters, French**.] The example set by Calvin and Beza was followed by the German Reformed, as well as the Dutch, English and Scottish Reformed churches. The Psalter of Israel became the favorite Reformed hymn-book, and is used as such in some branches of Scottish and American Presbyterianism, even to the exclusion of "uninspired" hymns.

The first German Reformed hymn-book appeared at Zürich, 1540, edited by *Johann Zwick*, of Constance, *Ambrose Blaarer* (or Blaurer), and his brother *Thomas Blaarer*. It contained versified psalms and original hymns, with a preface in defence of congregational singing. But the most popular collection for a long time was the versified Psalter of Ambrosius Lobwasser, a professor of law at Königsberg (b. 1515, d. 1585). It is a rhymed translation of the French Psalter of Marot and Beza, written at first for private devotion, and pub. at Leipzig in 1573. The poetry is the poorest part of the translation, and is well characterised by the name of the author (*Praisewater*); but the pious contents made it a rich source of devotion for a hundred years. It is a parallel to Rous's English

version of the Psalter. [See Scottish Hymnody.]
It is another interesting coincidence that Lobwasser, who furnished the popular Psalter to
the German Reformed or Calvinistic churches,
was a Lutheran, and that Francis Rous, who
furnished the most popular Psalter to Scotland,
was an English Puritan, and spent his whole
life in the south of England. What gave to
both such an authority was the belief that the
Hebrew Psalter is a complete and the only
inspired manual of praise for public worship.

iii. *Third Period.*

The third period extends from the middle
to the end of the seventeenth century, or from
Paul Gerhardt to Spener (1648–1680). It is
the transition from the churchly and confessional to the pietistic and devotional hymns,
or, as the Germans say, from the *Bekenntniss-
lied* to the *Erbauungslied*. The poets were
mostly orthodox, but with a mystic vein, and
possessed fervent experimental piety. They
include :—

Paul Gerhardt (1607–1676), a Lutheran pastor in
Berlin, afterwards in Lübben, is the prince of German
hymnists of the seventeenth century, and yields in
popularity only to Luther, whom he greatly surpassed
in poetic fertility. His 123 hymns are among the noblest
pearls in the treasury of sacred poetry. More than
thirty of them are still in use, and some of them have
been naturalised in English dress by John Wesley, James
W. Alexander, Miss Winkworth, A. T. Russell, John
Kelly, and others. We mention "Befiehl du deine
Wege," "O Haupt voll Blut und Wunden," "Wie soll
ich dich empfangen." Next to him comes *Johann
Franck* (1618–1677), burgomaster of his native town,
Guben, in Lower Lausitz, not so popular and hearty, but
superior in art and pathos. He characterised poetry as
"the nurse of piety, the herald of immortality, the pro-
moter of cheerfulness, the conqueror of sadness, and a
foretaste of heavenly glory." He had a strong vein of
mysticism, and began the series of the sweet pietistic
Jesus-hymns. Among his best are, "Jesu, meine
Freude," and the eucharistic "Schmücke dich, o liebe
Seele." The three brothers Franck (Sebastian, Michael,
and Peter) occupy an inferior rank. *Johann Rist*
(1607–1667), much praised and much censured by his
contemporaries, crowned as poet laureate by the Emperor
Ferdinand III. (1644), was the most-fertile poet of his
age, and produced or manufactured 610 hymns, published in ten collections between 1641 and 1664. Some
are of a high order, but many only rhymed prose, and
nearly all too prolix. One of his best is, "O Ewigkeit
du Donnerwort" (16 stanzas, but greatly abridged in
hymn-books). *Georg Neumark* (1621–1681), librarian
at Weimar, is the author of the popular hymn of trust
in God, "Wer nur den lieben Gott lässt walten," which
grew out of a providential deliverance from great distress. *Michael Schirmer* (1606–1673) wrote one of the
best Pentecostal hymns, which, with its popular tune, is
found in all German hymn-books : "O heil'ger Geist
kehr bei uns ein."

The following have also more or less enriched German hymnody :—

Johann Georg Albinus (1624–1679); *Johann Olearius*
(1611–1684); *Christian Keymann* (1607–1662); *C. F.
Nachtenhöfer* (1624–1685); *Gottfried W. Sacer* (1635–
1699); *Hartmann Schenck* (1634–1681); *Sigismund
von Birken*, called *Betulius* (1626–1681); *Christoph
Tietze* (1641–1703); *Salomo Liscow* (1640–1689); *Christian Knorr von Rosenroth* (1638–1689); *Ludaemilia
Elizabeth*, Countess of Schwarzburg-Rudolstadt (1640–
1672); *Anna Sophia*, Countess of Hesse - Darmstadt
(1630–1683); *Emilia Juliana*, Countess of Schwarzburg-
Rudolstadt (1637–1706); *Louise Henriette*, of Brandenburg (1627–1667), a Reformed princess, and wife of the
great Elector, is credited with four hymns, one of which
is an universal favourite: "Jesus, meine Zuversicht."
Johann Scheffler, called *Angelus Silesius* (1624–1677), a
physician by profession, stands alone as to his ecclesiastical position, but is not behind any of his contemporaries
in poetic genius. He was constitutionally a mystic, and
became so disgusted with the intolerant Lutheran orthodoxy of his surroundings that he entered the Roman
Catholic Church at Breslau, 1653, and became involved
in a most bitter controversy. But his hymns, some of

which were written before his transition, outlived the
strife, and are still found in every good hymn-book, e.g.
"Ich will dich lieben meine Stärke," and "Liebe, die du
mich zum Bilde." His heart was almost pantheistically
absorbed in Christ, and his last words were, "Jesus and
Christ, God and man, bridegroom and brother, peace and
joy, sweetness and delight, refuge and redemption,
heaven and earth, eternity and time, love and all, have
mercy on my soul." F. W. Faber furnishes an interesting parallel, both as a poet and as a convert from
Protestantism to Romanism.

iv. *Fourth Period.*

The *Pietistic* and *Moravian* period, from
Spener to Gellert (1680 to 1757), produced a
large number of hymns which breathe the
spirit of a second Reformation or Revival in
Germany. The Pietism of Philip Jacob
Spener, and August Hermann Francke, was
a reaction against the dry scholasticism and
cold formalism of the Lutheran Church, and
emphasised the importance of practical, personal, experimental piety. It corresponds in
many respects to Puritanism, which preceded
it, and to Methodism, which succeeded it, in
England, but it remained within the state
church. The Moravian movement resulted
in a separate community, which Count Zinzendorf organised on the remnant of the
Bohemian and Moravian Brethren or Unitas
Fratrum. The Pietistic and Moravian hymns
give expression to the various stages and
shades of Christian experience, are fresh and
lively, full of devotional fervor, but sometimes
degenerate into a playful and irreverent sentimentalism.

It is a remarkable fact that some of the
greatest religious revivals in the church—as
the Reformation, Pietism, Moravianism, Methodism—were sung as well as preached and
written into the hearts of the people, and
that the leaders of those revivals—Luther,
Spener, Zinzendorf, Wesley—were themselves
hymnists.

From the Pietistic and Moravian hymnody
we must distinguish the hymnists of the
German Reformed Church, which began to
relax the exclusive use of the Psalms, and
produced not a few hymns equal to the best
in the Lutheran Church of this period. The
chief Pietistic hymnists are :—

Philipp Jacob Spener (1635–1705), an Alsatian by
birth, pastor of St. Nicolai in Berlin, was in word and
example the leader of the Pietistic revival, and one of
the best men in German church history, but he had no
poetic genius, and his few hymns derive their value
from his name and fame rather than from intrinsic merit.
August Hermann Francke (1663–1727), the second leader
of Pietism, a hero of faith in God, and founder of the
famous Orphan House in Halle, where he was professor
of theology and pastor of a church, wrote a few hymns,
one on New Year, "Gott Lob,' ein Schritt zur Ewigkeit."
Christian Friedrich Richter (1676–1711), a pious physician and co-worker of Francke in his institutions at
Halle, is the author of 33 hymns; the two best known
represent Christian life in its difficulty and its ease,
"Es kostet viel ein Christ zu sein," "Es ist nicht schwer
ein Christ zu sein ;" "Es glänzet der Christen inwendiges
Leben." *Johann Anastasius Freylinghausen* (1670–
1739), son-in-law and successor of Francke as director
of the Orphan House, wrote a number of good hymns,
and published the best hymn-book of the Pietistic
school at Halle, 1704 and 1714. *John Daniel Herrnschmidt* (1673–1723), professor of theology in Halle and
colleague of Francke in the management of the Orphan
House : "Gott will's'machen, Dass die Sachen," "Lobe
den Herren, o meine Seele" (1714). *Christian Scriver*
(1629–1693), pastor in Magdeburg, court chaplain at
Quedlinburg, author of the highly popular devotional
"Seelenschatz," wrote a few hymns, "Der lieben Sonne
Licht und Pracht," "Jesu, meiner Seele Leben."
Gottfried Arnold (1666–1714), the famous church histo-

rian, wrote several hymns of remarkable depth and devotion to Christ: "Herzog unsrer Seligkeiten," "So führst du doch recht selig, Herr, die Deinen." The last was the favourite of the philosopher Schelling. Knapp calls it "the richest hymn in thought and experience, and full of majestic wisdom." We may compare it to Cowper's hymn on Providence, "God moves in a mysterious way." *John Jacob Schütz* (1640–1690), a lawyer and syndic of his native city, Frankfurt-on-the-Main, "Sei Lob und Ehr dem höchsten Gut." *Adam Drese* (1620–1701), "Seelenbräutigam, Jesu, Gottes Lamm" (1697). *Johann Heinrich Schröder* (1666–1699), pastor near Magdeburg, "Eins ist noth, ach Herr, diess Eine" (1697), "Jesu, hilf siegen, du Fürste des Lebens" (1697). *Laurentius Laurenti* (1660–1722), musical director of the Cathedral at Bremen, "Ermuntert euch, ihr Frommen," "Du wesentliches Wort." *Johann Caspar Schade* (1666–1698), diaconus of St. Nicolai in Berlin: "Mein Gott, das Herz ich bringe Dir," "Ruhe ist das beste Gut." *Joachim Lange* (1670–1744), professor of theology in Halle, and friend of Francke, the morning hymn, "O Jesu, süsses Licht." *Ernst Lange* (1650–1747), magistrate at Danzig, "Unter denen grossen Gütern." *Ludwig Andreas Gotter* (1661–1735), of Gotha, a pious and fruitful hymnist, "Herr Jesu, Gnadensonne," "Womit soll ich dich wohl loben," "Schaffet, schaffet, Menschenkinder." *Wolfgang Christian Dessler* (1660–1722), of Nürnberg, "Ich lass dich nicht, du musst mein Jesus bleiben," "Hinweg ihr zweifelnden Gedanken." *Johann Friedrich Starck* (1680–1756), pastor in Frankfurt, a faithful follower of Spener, and author of a very popular book of daily devotion, wrote 939 pious hymns, but of no poetic value. *Johann Jacob Rambach* (1693–1735), professor of theology at Halle, afterwards at Giessen, the most churchly of the Pietistic hymnists: "Grosser Mittler, der zur Rechten," "Heiland, deine Menschenliebe," "Mein Jesu, der du vor dem Schelden." *Johann Ludwig Conrad Allendorf* (1693–1773), editor of the "Cöthnische Lieder," "Die Seele ruht in Jesu Armen," "Unter Lilien jener Freuden," "Wo ist ein solcher Gott wie Du." *Leopold Franz Friedrich Lehr* (1709–1744), diaconus in Cöthen: "Mein Heiland nimmt die Sünder an." *Karl Heinrich Bogatzky* (1690–1774), lived in the Orphan House at Halle and wrote numerous devotional works, especially the *Schätzkästlein*, which is still extensively used: "Wach auf, du Geist der ersten Zeugen," "Ich weiss von keinem andern Grunde," "Mein Heiland, du hast mich gezogen." *Ernst Gottlieb Woltersdorf* (1725–1761), pastor in Bunzlau, founder of an orphan asylum, and a man of glowing zeal for the kingdom of God, "Komm, mein Herz, in Jesu Leiden," "Wer ist der Braut des Lammes gleich," "Wie selig ist das Volk des Herrn." *Benjamin Schmolck* (1672–1737), pastor primarius in Schweidnitz, one of the most prolific and popular hymnists: "Abba, lieber Vater, höre," "Ach sagt mir nichts von eiteln Schätzen," "Der beste Freund ist in dem Himmel," "Himmelan geht unsre Bahn," "Je grösser Kreuz, je näher Himmel," "Mein Jesu, wie du willst." *Philipp Friedrich Hiller* (1699–1769) is the most prolific hymn-writer of Württemberg and author of popular books of devotion : "Mir ist Erbarmung widerfahren," "Herr von unendlichen Erbarmen," "Jesus Christus herrscht als König."

(2) *The Moravian Hymnists* include some well-known names :—

Nikolaus Ludwig Graf von Zinzendorf (1700–1760), one of the most distinguished lights in German church history (whose motto was, "1 have but one passion, and this is He, only He "), had with other gifts a true genius for sacred poetry, and often extemporised hymns in public worship, or after the sermon, some of rare beauty and some eccentric and trifling. Of his 2000 pieces, 205 were translated for the English hymn-book of the Moravians. Several have been reproduced by John Wesley, Miss Winkworth, and Miss Borthwick. In fertility and fervour he resembles Charles Wesley. "Aller Gläub'gen Sammelplatz," "Christi Blut und Gerechtigkeit," "Jesu, geh voran," "Herz und Herz vereint zusammen," "Die Christen gehn von Ort zu Ort," "Christum über alles lieben." *Christian Renatus Graf von Zinzendorf* (1727–1752), second son of the former and his assistant, composed, during his short life, a few choice hymns, which were published by his father (1754). "Marter Gottes (Christi), wer kann Dein vergessen." The closing stanza, "Die wir uns allhier beisammen finden," is very extensively used at the close of devotional meetings. *August Gottlieb Spangenberg* (1704–1792), bishop of the Moravians, long resident in America, and author of the Moravian confession of faith (*Idea Fidei Fratrum*, 1777), is the author of a

beautiful hymn on Christian simplicity: "Heil'ge Einfalt, Gnadenwunder," and of "Die Kirche Christi, die Er geweiht." *Christian Gregor* (1723–1801), Bishop at Berthelsdorf, edited with Spangenberg the Moravian Hymn-book of 1778, which is still in use, also a choralbook (1784), and wrote one of the sweetest Jesus-hymns, from the holy of holies of loving intercourse with the Saviour, "Ach mein Herr Jesu ! Dein Nahesein."

(3) *Hymnists of the German Reformed Church.*

Joachim Neander (1650–1680), pastor at St. Martin, in his native city of Bremen, a poet of overflowing praise of God, and hence called "the Psalmist of the New Covenant," wrote some of the very best and most popular hymns, especially "Lobe den Herren, den mächtigen König der Ehren," "Sieh, hier bin ich, Ehrenkönig," "Unser Herrscher, unser König." *Friedrich Adolf Lampe* (1683–1729), Professor of Theology at Utrecht, then pastor at St. Ansgari in Bremen, author of an elaborate Commentary on the Gospel of John, and of thirty hymns distinguished for depth and warmth. "Mein Fels hat überwunden," "Mein Leben ist ein Pilgrimstand," "O Liebesglut, die Erd und Himmel paaret." *Gerhard Tersteegen* (1697–1769), a ribbonweaver in Mühlheim on the Ruhr, separatist, ascetic, evangelist and mystic of profound piety, author of 111 hymns (*Geistliches Blumengärtlein*, 1729), several of which are of the first rank, and are *tr.* by John Wesley, Miss Winkworth and Miss Borthwick, "Gott ist gegenwärtig ! Lasset uns anbeten," "Gott rufet noch, sollt ich nicht endlich hören," "Allgenugsam Wesen," "Ich bete an die Macht der Liebe," "Jesu, der du bist alleine," "Kommt, Kinder lasst uns gehen," "Nun so will ich denn mein Leben," "O Gott, O Geist, O Licht des Lebens," "Siegesfürste, Ehrenkönig," "Wie bist du mir so innig gut."

v. *Fifth Period.*

The fifth period extends from 1757–1817, when Rationalism broke into the German churches and made sad havoc in the hymnbooks and liturgies. It is the period of hymnological revolution. It began with the well-meant zeal for improving old hymns in style and expression and adapting them to the taste of the age. This zeal had some foundation in the uncouth language, the irregular rhymes, the antiquated words, and the Latinisms which disfigure many hymns of the 16th and 17th centuries. But it did not stop there. Klopstock, himself a great poet, published in 1758, along with his own spiritual odes, twenty-nine of the old hymns in altered form. He was followed by a swarm of hymnological tinkers and poetasters who had no sympathy with the theology and poetry of the grand old hymns of faith ; weakened, diluted, mutilated and watered them, and introduced these misimprovements into the churches. The original hymns of rationalistic preachers, court chaplains and superintendents, now almost forgotten, were still worse, mostly prosy and tedious rhymes on moral duties. Conversion and Sanctification were changed into self-improvement, piety into virtue, heaven into the better world, Christ into Christianity, God into Providence, Providence into fate. Instead of hymns of faith and salvation, the congregations were obliged to sing hymned sermons on the existence of God, the immortality of the soul, the delights of reunion, the dignity of man, the duty of self improvement, the nurture of the body, and the care of animals and flowers.

And yet this was the classical period of German poetry and literature. But Goethe, Schiller, Wieland, Lessing, Herder, wrote no hymns, and had little or no sympathy with evangelical religion, except Herder, who knew how to appreciate the old hymns.

2 E

We pass by the would-be hymns of rationalistic compilers of hymn-books, which have mostly gone out of use again. But there were during this period of dearth a few genuine hymnists whose works will not be forgotten, though they were affected somewhat by the moralising tone of their age. These include :—

Christian Fürchtegott Gellert (1716-1769), professor of poetry, eloquence and moral philosophy in Leipzig, a noble, truly pious, and highly gifted man, wrote *Spiritual Odes and Hymns* (1757), which are didactic rather than lyrical and emotional, but scriptural, warm, edifying, and justly popular, especially in North Germany : " Auf Gott, und nicht auf meinen Rath," "Diess ist der Tag, den Gott gemacht," "Gott, deine Güte reicht so weit," "Jesus lebt, mit Ihm auch ich," "Mein erst Gefühl sei Preis und Dank," "Wie gross ist des Allmächtigen Güte." *Friedrich Gottlieb Klopstock* (1721-1803), the German Milton, the singer of the " Messiah," wrote also some hymns of high poetic merit, but lacking in popular simplicity. " Auferstehn, ja, auferstehn wirst du " (Resurrection hymn), " Hallelujah, Amen, Amen " (funeral hymn), " Selig sind des Himmels Erben " (funeral hymn). *Johann Caspar Lavater* (1741-1801), pastor at Zürich, once a friend of Goethe, and a noble Christian philanthropist, wrote, " O Jesus Christus, wachs' in mir," " Fortgekämpft und fortgerungen," "Jesu, Freund der Menschenkinder." *Matthias Jorissen* (1739-1823), pastor of the German Reformed church in the Hague, made one of the best poetic versions of the Psalms. *Matthias Claudius* (1740-1815), called "Asmus," or the "Wandsbecker Bote," a faithful witness to the truth in an age of unbelief, wrote a popular evening hymn, " Der Mond ist aufgegangen."

vi. *Sixth Period.*

This dates from about 1817, and is the period of the revival of evangelical theology, piety, and hymnody. It is rich in hymns which combine the old faith with classical elegance of form, sound doctrine with deep feeling. We have :—

Friedrich von Hardenberg (1772-1801), called *Novalis*, was a youthful forerunner of the new epoch, a poetic genius of high order and burning love to Christ, connected with the Moravians, and also with the Romantic school. His hymns are among the very best, though somewhat sentimental. " Wenn alle untreu werden," "Was wär' ich ohne Dich gewesen," " Wenn ich Ihn nur habe." *Ernst Moritz Arndt* (1769-1860), professor of history in Bonn, and a noble German patriot, revived an interest in the old German hymns, 1819, and himself wrote one, which found its way into most hymn-books. "Ich weiss, an wen ich glaube." *Friedrich Adolf Krummacher* (1768-1845), pastor of St. Ansgari at Bremen, and author of the popular "Parables": " Eine Heerde und Ein Hirt," " Dein König kommt, o Zion," " Mag auch die Liebe weinen." *Friedrich Wilhelm Krummacher* (d. 1868), son of the former, pastor in Elberfeld, afterwards court chaplain at Potsdam, a most eloquent pulpit orator (sermons on Elijah, Elisha, David, the Advent, the Passion, &c.): "Du Stern in allen Nächten," "Behalte mich in Deiner Pflege." *Johann Baptist von Albertini* (1769-1831), of a noble family of the Grisons, in Switzerland, Moravian bishop at Berthelsdorf, fellow-student and friend of Schleiermacher, and a man of genius and piety : " Mit Deiner Gluth entzünde mich," " Selig sind, die nicht sehen und doch lieben." *Karl Bernhard Garve* (1763-1841), likewise a Moravian minister, and a gifted hymnist ; he died at Herrnhut : " Deinen Frieden gib uns Herr," "Der ersten Unschuld reines Glück." *Friedrich Rückert* (1789-1866), one of the greatest masters of lyric poetry, wrote a beautiful Advent hymn : " Dein König kommt in niedern Hüllen." *Albert Knapp* (1798-1864), minister at Stuttgart, one of the most fruitful and gifted religious poets, and editor of the " Liederschatz." His best hymns are: "Eines wünsch ich mir vor allem andern," " Ich bin in Dir, und Du in mir," " Heil, Jesus Christus ist erstanden," " Nicht menschlicher Rath, noch Erdenverstand," "Schöpfer meines Lebens." *Christian Gottlob Barth* (1799-1862), a friend of Knapp, and likewise a Swabian, reflected his indefatigable zeal for foreign missions in his hymns : " Der Du in Todesnächten," " Hüter, ist die Nacht verschwunden." *Meta Heusser-Schweizer* (1797-1876), of Switzerland, called by Dr. Koch " the most eminent and noble among all the female poets of our whole Evangelical Church."

"Ich weiss, dass mein Erlöser lebet " : " Herz, du hast viel geweinet," " Theuer ist der Tod der Deinen," " Willkommen, lieber Ostertag." Miss Jane Borthwick has translated a number of her poems in *Alpine Lyrics*. *Carl Rudolph Hagenbach* (1801-1874), Professor of Church History in Basel, " Stille halten deinem Walten," " Wachet auf! Erhebt die Blicke." *Johann Peter Lange* (1802-1884), professor of theology in Bonn, a most fruitful author, editor of the well-known "*Bibelwerk*," and of a collection of hymns, wrote several little volumes of poetry: " Was kein Auge hat gesehen," " Der Herr ist auferstanden." *Karl Johann Philipp Spitta* (1801-1859), a Lutheran pastor and superintendent in the kingdom of Hannover, is upon the whole the most popular hymnist of the nineteenth century. His *Psaltery and Harp* pas-es through a new edition every year (the 50th appeared with illustrations in 1884). His hymns are characterised by deep evangelical piety and simplicity, and have found an excellent translator in Richard Massie. "Bei Dir, Jesu, will ich bleiben," " Kehre wieder, kehre wieder," " O selig Haus, wo man Dich aufgenommen," " O wie freun wir uns der Stunde," " Stimm an das Lied vom Sterben," " Unser Wandel ist im Himmel," " Wenn meine letzte Stunde schlägt." *Karl Gerok* (born Jan. 30, 1815), prelate and court chaplain in Stuttgart, the most fruitful and popular religious poet of Germany now living. His collections of poems bear the poetic names *Palmblätter, Pfingstrosen, Blumen und Sterne*: "Es ist in keinem andern Heil," " Sei willkommen, Tag des Herrn."

The works chiefly used in this sketch are the following :—

(1) *Geschichte des Kirchenlieds und Kirchengesangs der christlichen, insbesondere der deutschen evangelischen Kirche*. Von Eduard Emil Koch, Dekan, &c. 3rd ed. completed by Richard Lauxmann and Prof. Adolf Wilhelm Koch. Stuttgart, 1866-1876, in 8 vols. (The second ed. appeared 1852 and 1853 in 4 vols.) (2) *Geschichte des deutschen Kirchenliedes bis auf Luthers Zeit*. Von Hoffmann von Fallersleben, Breslau 1832, 3rd ed. Hannover, 1861. (3) *Das deutsche Kirchenlied von Martin Luther bis auf Nicolaus Herman und Ambrosius Blaurer*. Von Dr. K. E. P. Wackernagel, Stuttgart, 1841. (4) *Das Deutsche Kirchenlied von der ältesten Zeit bis zu Anfang des xvii. Jahrhunderts*. Von Philipp Wackernagel. Leipzig, 1864-77, in 5 vols. (completed by his two sons). A truly monumental work of the greatest value. We always quote this work, unless the other is expressly mentioned. (5) *Geistliche Lieder der evangelischen Kirche aus dem sechszehnten Jahrhundert nach den ältesten Drucken herausgegeben*. Von Dr. Julius Mützell. Berlin, 1855, in 3 vols. (6) *Denkmäler deutscher Poesie und Prosa aus dem 8ten bis 12ten Jahrh.* Von K. Müllenhoff und W. Scherer. Berlin, 1864. (7) *Christian Singers of Germany*. By Catherine Winkworth. London, 1869. (8) *Kirchenlieder-Lexicon, Hymnologisch-literarische Nachweisungen über ca. 4500 der wichtigsten und verbreitetsten Kirchenlieder aller Zeiten*, &c. Von Albert Friedrich Wilhelm Fischer. Gotha, 1878-79, 2 vols. (9) Also the older hymnological collections and discussions of *Rambach, Bunsen, Knapp, Daniel, J. P. Lange, Stier, Stip, Geffcken, Vilmar*, &c. (10) *Douen, Clément Marot et le Psautier Huguenot*, 1879-80, 2 vols.

[P. S.]

German Psalters [Psalters, German.]

Germanus, St. [634-734.] One of the Greek hymn-writers, and one of the grandest among the defenders of the Icons. He was born at Constantinople of a patrician family; was ordained there ; and became subsequently bishop of Cyzicus. He was present at the Synod of Constantinople in 712, which restored the Monothelite heresy; but in after years he condemned it. He was made patriarch of Constantinople in 715. In 730 he was driven from the see, not without blows, for refusing to yield to the Iconoclastic Emperor Leo the Isaurian. He died shortly afterwards, at the age of one hundred years. His hymns are few. Dr. Neale selects his canon on The Wonder-working Image of Edessa as his most poetical piece (see Neale's *Hys. of the Eastern Church*, 1862, and later editions). The earliest biographical account of Germanus is found in

Basil's *Menology,* under May 12. Later we have a Memoir by Henschew (*Boll. Acta S. S. Mai,* iii., 155). His hymns are given in *Migne* and *Daniel,* and have been translated to a small extent into English by Dr. Neale. (For further biographical details see *Dict. Christian Biog.,* pp. 658–659.)   [H. L. B.]

Gerok, Karl von, D.D., was b. January 30, 1815, at Stuttgart, and studied theology at the University of Tübingen. He was, from 1836 to 1840, assistant at his father's church in Stuttgart; 1840–43, lecturer (repetent) at Tübingen, and after 1844 diaconus at Böblingen, near Stuttgart. In 1849 he returned to preach at Stuttgart, where he now resides (1886), as chief court preacher and oberconsistorialrath (*O. Kraus,* 1879, p. 165: *MS.* from Dr. von Gerok, &c.).

Gerok is well known as an eloquent preacher, and has published various volumes of sermons. His fame principally rests on his sacred poetry. The best known of his poetical works is his *Palmblätter,* 1857, which has attained a wonderful circulation, and reached a 56th edition in 1886. A new series appeared in 1878 as *Palmblätter Neue Folge* (9th ed., 1885, under the title *Auf einsamen Gängen*). A series of poems on the Book of the Acts of the Apostles appeared in *Pfingstrosen,* 1864, (8th ed. 1886). His other poetical works are, *Die letzte Strauss,* 1885 (5th ed., 1886), *Blumen und Sterne,* 1867 (11th ed., 1886), and *Deutsche Ostern,* 1872 (6th ed., 1883). The *Palmblätter* is in four parts: pt. 1 consisting of poems on Holy Words, i.e. mostly founded on sayings of Holy Scripture; pt. ii. on "Holy Times" (Advent, &c.); pt. iii. on "Holy Mountains," and pt. iv. on "Holy Waters," i.e. on Mountains and Waters mentioned in Holy Scripture. From it a few centos have passed into some of the recent German hymn-books; and a version apparently including *trs.* of all the poems in the ed. of the German used appeared in English as *Palm Leaves by Karl Gerok. Translated from the German by J. E. A. Brown.* London: Strahan & Co., 1869. A large number of the individual poems have also been *tr.* by Miss Borthwick (who has also *tr.* a few from the *Pfingstrosen*), Miss Burlingham, the Revs. Dr. R. Maguire, E. Massie, J. Kelly, and various others. But as none of these versions have passed into English C. U., and as the originals are poems and not hymns, we must refer the reader to the works of these translators.   [J. M.]

Gersdorf, Henriette Catharine von, dau. of Baron Carl von Friesen, was b. at Sulzbach, near Amberg, Bavaria, Oct. 6, 1648. In 1672 she married Baron Nicolaus von Gersdorf, of Dresden; and after his death, in 1702, retired to her estate of Grosshennersdorf, near Herrnhut, Saxony, where she for some time superintended the education of her grandson, Count N. L. von Zinzendorf; and where she d. March 6, 1726.

Her hymns, which are among the best of the period, appeared principally in the *Löbau G. B.,* 1725, and her *Geistliche Singe-Stunden, Löbau,* N. D., 1725, and were collected in her *Geistreiche Lieder und poetische Betrachtungen,* Halle, 1729. Through J. J. Rambach's *Haus G. B.,* 1735, and the *Hannover G. B.,* 1740, some 30 have passed into German use. Two have been *tr.* into English:—

i. **Ein Jahr der Sterblichkeit.** *New Year.* In the *Löbau G. B.,* 1725, No. 536, in 11 st., repeated 1729, p. 21. *Tr.* as, "Another year of mortal life," by *Dr. G. Walker,* 1860, p. 63.

ii. **Was darfst du, blödes Herz.** *Lent.* 1729, p. 70, in 16 st., entitled, "On the Grace of Justification." *Tr.* as, "What meanest thou, my soul," by *Dr. H. Mills,* 1845 (1856, p. 56).   [J. M.]

Gesenius, Justus, D.D., s. of Joachim Gesenius, pastor at Esbeck, near Lauenstein, Hannover; was b. at Esbeck, July 6, 1601. He studied at the Universities of Helmstedt and Jena, graduating M.A. at Jena in 1628. In 1629 he became pastor of St. Magnus's Church, Brunswick; in 1636 court chaplain and preacher at the Cathedral in Hildesheim; and in 1642 chief court preacher, consistorialrath, and general superintendent at Hannover. He d. at Hannover, Sept. 18, 1673 (*Koch,* iii. 230–237; *Allg. Deutsche Biog.,* ix. 87–88; *Bode,* p. 76, &c.).

Gesenius was an accomplished and influential theologian, a famous preacher, and distinguished himself by his efforts to further the catechetical instruction of the children of his district. Along with **D. Denicke** (q.v.) he edited the Hannoverian hymn-books of 1646–1660. Both he and Denicke aimed at reducing the older German hymns to correctness of style according to the poetical canons of Martin Opitz; not so much interfering with the theology or making the authors speak a terminology foreign to them. Consequently their recasts, while setting a bad example, and while often destroying much of the force and freshness of the originals, were not by any means so objectionable as the recasts of the Rationalistic period, and moreover were soon widely accepted.

As no authors' names are given in the Hannoverian hymn-books, it is difficult to assign the authorship of the new hymns and recasts therein contained. The following is generally, and apparently with reason, ascribed to Gesenius:

Wenn meine Sünd' mich kränken. *Passiontide.* His finest hymn as regards depth, warmth, and finish. 1st pub. in the *Hannover G. B.,* 1646, No. 49, in 8 st. of 7 l. It has been called a recast of the hymn "Hilf Gott, dass mir gelinge," but bears not the slightest resemblance to it. Included in Crüger's *Praxis,* 1656, and many later collections, as the Berlin *G. L. S.,* ed. 1863, No. 277. By a not unjust retribution it was soon recast, and appeared in the *Lüneburg G. B.,* 1661, as "Wenn mich die Sünden kränken." *Tr.* as:—

1. **When guilt and shame are raising.** In full, by J. C. Jacobi, in pt. ii., 1725, of his *Psal. Ger.,* p. 4 (1732, p. 34). In the *Moravian H. Bk.* of 1789, No. 106, it is altered to "O Lord, when condemnation"; and in the ed. 1886, it begins with st. v., "Lord, let Thy bitter passion." A cento of st. ii., iii., v., from the *Moravian H. Bk.,* 1801, was adopted by Montgomery in his *Christian Psalmist,* 1825, beginning, "O wonder far exceeding," and this is in the *New Zealand Hyl.,* 1872.

2. **O Lord, when my sins grieve me.** A good *tr.* of st. i., ii., iv., v., by A. T. Russell, as No. 81 in his *Ps. & Hys.,* 1851.

3. **When sorrow and remorse.** In full, by Miss Winkworth in her *Lyra Ger.,* 1st Ser., 1855, p. 74. A cento consisting of ll. 1–4 of st. i., iv.–vi., and of stanza vii., rewritten to S.M., is in the Pennsylvanian Luth. *Church Bk.,* 1868.

4. **O Lord, when condemnation.** A full and good *tr.,* included as No. 84 in the 1857 ed. of Mercer's *C. P. & H. Bk.* Probably by Mr. Mercer, but mainly taken from the *Moravian H. Bk.,* 1789, and from Miss Winkworth. Repeated, abridged, in his Oxford ed., 1864, No. 149, and in the Toronto *H. Bk.,* 1862.

5. **When o'er my sins I sorrow.** A good *tr.* based on her 1855 version, and omitting st. ii.–iv., by Miss Winkworth, as No. 48 in her *C. B. for England,* 1863.   [J. M.]

Gib deinen Frieden uns, o Herr der Stärke. [*The Peace of God.*] Included as No. 1520 in Knapp's *Ev. L. S.,* 1837, in 6 st. of 4 l., without name of author; but in the 1850 ed., No. 1857, ascribed to *C. B. Garve.* We have failed to discover any authority for this ascription, and the hymn is certainly neither in Garve's *Christliche Gesänge*, Görlitz, 1825, nor in his *Brüdergesänge*, Gnadau, 1827. The only *tr.* is :—

Give us Thy blessed peace, God of all might! A full and good version by Mrs. Findlater in the 4th series, 1862, of the *H. L. L.*, p. 87 (1884, p. 248); repeated as No. 141 in Jellicoe's *Coll.*, 1867.   [J. M.]

Gib uns, o Jesu, Gnad. [*Love to Christ.*] Included as No. 175 in F. Hommel's *Geistliche Volkslieder*, Leipzig, 1871, in 5 st. of 4 l., as from the *Würzburg G. B.* (R. C.), 1630, and D. G. Corner's *Gross Catolisch G. B.*, Nürnberg, 1631. He entitles it "Against the Lust of the World." *Bäumker*, ii. p. 317, cites it as in the *Ausserlesene, Catholische Geistliche Kirchengesäng*, Cologne, 1623. The only *tr.* is, "Jesu be ne'er forgot," by *Miss Winkworth*, 1869, p. 254. She quotes the first line as, "Jesu, gieb uns deiu' Gnad."   [J. M.]

Gibbons, Thomas, was b. at Reak, near Newmarket, May 31, 1720; educated by Dr. Taylor, at Deptford; ordained in 1742, as assistant to the Rev. Mr. Bures, at Silver Street Chapel, London; and in 1743 became minister of the Independent Church, at Haberdashers' Hall, where he remained till his death, Feb. 22, 1785. In addition to his ministerial office he became, in 1754, tutor of the Dissenting Academy at Mile End, London; and, in 1759, Sunday evening lecturer at Monkwell Street. In 1760 the College at New Jersey, U.S., gave him the degree of M.A., and in 1764 that of Aberdeen the degree of D.D. His prose works were (1) *Calvinism and Nonconformity defended*, 1740; (2) *Sermons on various subjects* 1762; (3) *Rhetoric*, 1767; (4) *Female Worthies*, 2 vols., 1777. Three vols. of sermons were pub. after his death. His poetical works were :—

(1) *Juvenilia ; Poems on various subjects of Devotion and Virtue*, 1750, was published by subscription. Among the subscribers is found the name of the Rev. Mr. George Whitefield, B.A. It was dedicated to the Countess of Huntingdon, and bears her coat of arms. In this volume are included versions of six of the Psalms, and a few hymns. (2) *Hymns adapted to Divine worship in two books. Book I. Derived from select passages of Holy Scriptures. Book II., Written on sacred subjects and particular occasions, partly collected from various authors, but principally composed by Thomas Gibbons, D.D.*, 1769. (3) *Hymns adapted to Divine worship in two books. Book I. Derived from select passages of the Holy Scriptures. Book II. Written on sacred subjects and particular occasions by Thomas Gibbons, D.D.*, 1784. (4) The *Sermons*, pub. in 1762, included fifteen hymns, one being appended to each sermon. (5) *The Christian Minister in three poetical epistles to Philander*, 1772. This volume included (i.) Poetical versions of several parts of Scripture. (ii.) Translations of poems from Greek and Latin writers. (iii.) Original pieces on various occasions. (6) *An English version of the Latin Epitaphs on the Nonconformist's Memorial, with a poem to the memory of the 2000 ministers ejected in 1662.* 1775. (7) *Select Portions of Scripture, and Remarkable Occurrences, versified for the Instruction and entertainment of Youth of both Sexes*, 1781. Reprinted in America, 1805.

Dr. Gibbons may be called a disciple in hymn-writing of Dr. Watts, whose life he wrote. His hymns are not unlike those of the second rank of Watts. He lacked "the vision and faculty divine," which gives life to hymns and renders them of permanent value. Hence, although several are in C. U. in America, they are dying out of use in G. Britain. The most popular are, "Now let our souls on wings sublime"; "Great God, the nations of the earth";

"Thy goodness, Lord, our souls confess"; "To Thee, my God, whose presence fills."
        [W. G. H.]

The less important of Dr. Gibbons's hymns, which are still in C. U. are :—

1. **And be it so that till this hour.** *Hope.* This is No. 50 in Bk. ii. of his *Hys. adapted to Divine Worship*, &c., 1769, in 5 st. of 4 l., and headed, "Encouragement against Despair; or, Hope still set before us." Originally a Sacramental hymn, in Rippon's *Sel.*, 1787, No 230, it was altered to a general hymn, with special reference to "Hope."

2. **Assist us, Lord, Thy Name to praise.** *Life, a race.* In Rippon's Bap. *Sel.*, 1787, No. 326, in 4 st. of 4 l.

3. **Eternal life, how sweet the sound.** *Eternal Life.* This is one of three hymns on Titus iii. 7, in his *Hys. adapted to Divine Worship*, &c., 1784, Bk. i., No. 156, in 5 st. of 4 l. In the American Dutch Reformed *Hys. of the Church*, 1869, No. 843 begins with st. ii., "Eternal life, how will it reign?"

4. **Father, is not Thy promise pledged?** *Missions.* This is Pt. iii. of his hymn, "Great God, the nations of the earth" (q. v.)

5. **Forgiveness, 'tis a joyful sound.** *Pardon.* From his *Hys. adapted to Divine Worship*, &c., 1769. Bk. i., No. 69, in 5 st. of 4 l. into several modern collections in G. Britain and America. It is based on St. Luke, vii. 47.

6. **From winter's barren clods.** [*Spring.*] Appeared in his *Hymns*, &c., 1784, Bk. ii., No. 27, in 5 st. of 4 l., and headed, "The Return of the Spring celebrated in the Powerful and Gracious Work of God." In 1787 it was repeated anonymously in Rippon's Bap. *Sel.*, No. 499. The hymn, "Great God, at Thy command, Seasons in order rise," begins with st. iii. of this hymn.

7. **Happy the men in ancient days.** *Public Worship.* In his *Hys. adapted to Public Worship*, &c., 1784.

8. **On Zion, his most holy mount.** *Gospel Feast.* From his *Hys. adapted for Divine Worship*, &c., 1769, Bk. i., No. 35, in 6 st. of 4 l. It was originally a Sacramental hymn, but in its abbreviated form, as in use in America, that element is eliminated.

9. **Our Father, high enthroned above.** *Lord's Prayer.* Appeared in the Bristol Bapt. *Coll.* of Ash & Evans, 1769, No. 41, in 9 st. of 4 l. In 1772 it was reprinted in a revised form, and with an additional stanza, in Gibbons's *Christian Minister*, p. 74.

10. **Thy goodness, Lord, our souls confess.** *Providence and Grace.* Appeared in the *Gospel Magazine*, 1775, and in his *Hys. adapted to Divine Worship*, &c., 1784, Bk. ii., No. 11, in 7 st. of 4 l. In Dobell's *Sel.*, 1806, st. i.-iv., and vi. were given with alterations, which were not improvements, as No. 9. This arrangement is repeated in modern hymn-books, including the *Bap. Hymnal*, 1879, and others.

11. **When Jesus dwelt in mortal clay.** *Jesus our Example.* From his *Hys. adapted to Divine Worship*, &c., 1784, Bk. i., No. 128, in 9 st. of 4 l. into a few American collections, including the *Bap. Praise Bk.*, 1871.

The more important of Dr. Gibbons's hymns are annotated under their respective first lines.
        [W. T. B.]

Gilbert, Ann. [Taylor, A. & J.]

Giles, John Eustace, was born at Dartmouth in 1805, and educated for the ministry at the Baptist College, Bristol. After preaching for a short time at Haverfordwest, he became, in 1830, pastor of the church in Salter's Hall, London. Leaving Salter's Hall in 1836, he ministered successively at Leeds, Bristol, Sheffield, Rathmines (Dublin), and Clapham Common, London. He d. at Clapham Common, June 24, 1875. His prose works include *A Funeral Sermon on the Death of Robert Hall; Lectures on Socialism*, &c. From childhood he composed hymns and poetical pieces. In 1834, at the request of the Baptist Missionary Committee, he composed a hymn in celebration of negro emancipation, and Nos. 9, 16, & 24 in their *Jubilee Coll.*, 1842. The hymn by which he is best known is :—

Hast Thou said, exalted Jesus! *Holy Baptism* (*Adult*). It is a composition of special merit, and in English Baptist congregations is probably oftener sung on Baptismal occasions than any other hymn. It was written "during a serious illness, in 1830, and in anticipation of having to baptize several persons at Salter's Hall, London, on his recovery." (*Singers and Songs*, 1869, p. 482.) It was printed in 1830 in 6 st. of 6 l. In 1858 it was given in the Bapt. *Ps. & Hys.*, No. 705, with the omission of st. ii. The full original text is in the *Bapt. Hymnal*, 1879, No. 639. It is also in several other collections. [W. R. S.]

Gill, Thomas Hornblower, was b. at Bristol Road, Birmingham, Feb. 10th, 1819. His parents belonged to English Presbyterian families which, like many others, had become Unitarian in their doctrine. He was educated at King Edward's Grammar School under Dr. Jeune, afterwards Bishop of Peterborough. He left the school in 1838, and would have proceeded to the University of Oxford, but was prevented by his hereditary Unitarianism (long since given up), which forbade subscription to the Articles of the Church of England then necessary for entrance to the University. This constrained him to lead the life of an isolated student, in which he gave himself chiefly to historical and theological subjects. Hence his life has been singularly devoid of outward incident; and its interest gathers about his hymns, and the seasons of overmastering thought and feeling which gave them birth. The only events that can be chronicled are the publications of his books (see below). It is in the singular combination of influences which has formed his character and determined his thinking that the real interest of his life consists. Here is to be found the true key to the understanding of his hymns. To his Puritan ancestry may be traced their deep religiousness; to his Unitarian training their ethical earnestness; and to his poetical temperament their freeness from conventionality. Delight in the divine songs of Watts was his earliest intellectual enjoyment; and in after years the contrast between their native force and fulness and their dwindled presentation in Unitarian hymn-books began that estrangement from his hereditary faith which gradually became complete. These various influences mingled in his own hymns and have conspired to render him what Dr. Freeman Clarke calls him, "a more intellectual Charles Wesley." He belongs to the small company of really original hymnists. His hymns are marked by a remarkable absence of, and even opposition to all antiquarian and sacerdotal ideas of Christianity, a keen discernment of the spirit rather than the mere letter of the Gospel; and profound thought on Scripture themes, so that some of his hymns are too subtle for use in the ordinary worship of the Church. Their style is characterized by a certain quaintness of expression reminding one of George Wither or John Mason, but modified by the influence of Watts's warmth of feeling. They have great sweetness of melody, purity of diction, and happy adaptation of metre and of style to the subject of each hymn. They are almost exclusively used by Nonconformists. Dale's *English H. Bk.* contains 39; the *Baptist Hymnal*, 19; Horder's *Cong. Hymns*, 11; Mar-

tineau's *Hys. of Praise & Prayer*, 11; and the *Congregational Church Hymnal*, 14. The following are Mr. Gill's published works :—

(1) *The Fortunes of Faith*, 1841; (2) *The Anniversaries* (Poems in commemoration of great Men and great Events), 1858; (3) *The Papal Drama* (an historical essay), 1866; (4) *The Golden Chain of Praise Hymns by Thomas H. Gill*, 1869; (5) *Luther's Birthday* (Hymns), 1883; (6) *The Triumph of Christ* (Memorials of Franklin Howard), 1883.

Mr. Gill's hymns number nearly 200. Of these, over 80 are in C. U. in G. Britain and America. The most widely used of these :— "Everlasting, changing never"; "O mean may seem this house of clay"; "O wherefore, Lord, doth Thy dear praise"; "Our God, our God, Thou shinest here"; "The glory of the spring, how sweet"; and "Thou biddest, Lord, Thy sons be bold"; are annotated under their respective first lines, the rest are noted below. [W. G. H.]

The 75 hymns which follow are all annotated from the author's MS. notes, kindly supplied for use in this work :—

1. **Ah tremblers, fainting and forlorn.** *Eternal Youth*. Written in 1868, and 1st pub. in his *Golden Chain*, &c., 1869, p. 149, in 9 st. of 4 l. In 1873 Martineau gave st. iv.-ix. in his *Hymns*, &c., No. 256, as, "Young souls, so strong the race to run." These were repeated in the *Bapt. Hymnal*, 1879, as No. 862.

2. **Alas the outer emptiness** *Consecration of the Heart*. Contributed to G. Dawson's *Ps. & Hys.*, 1846, No. 121, in 7 st. of 4 l. It was introduced to the American Unitarian collections through Hedge & Huntington's *Hys. for the Church of Christ*, 1853, No. 619.

3. **Alas these pilgrims faint and worn.** *Whitsuntide*. Written in 1853, and 1st pub. in his *Anniversaries*, 1858, p. 73, in 11 st. of 4 l., then in G. Dawson's *Ps. & Hys.*, 1862, the *Golden Chain*, &c., 1869, p. 107, &c.

4. **Alone with Thee, with Thee alone.** *Worship in Solitude*. Written in 1856, and 1st pub. in his *Golden Chain*, &c., 1869, p. 26, in 8 st. of 4 l.

5. **And didst thou, Lord, our sorrows take!** *Passiontide*. Written in 1849, and pub. in his *Golden Chain*, &c., 1869, p. 45, in 6 st. of 4 l. It is in several English collections.

6. **Behold the everlasting Son.** *Ascension*. Written in 1862, and 1st printed in the *Hagley Magazine*, and then in G. Dawson's *Ps. & Hys.*, 1862, and the *Golden Chain*, 1869, p. 47, in 8 st. of 4 l.

7. **Break, new-born year, on glad eyes break.** *New Year*. Written in 1855, and 1st pub. in his *Golden Chain*, &c., 1869, p. 144, in 6 st. of 4 l. It is one of the most popular of the author's hymns, and is found in many collections.

8. **Bright Presence! may my soul have part.** *Witness of the Spirit*. Written in 1849, and 1st pub. in his *Golden Chain*, &c., 1869, p. 100, in 8 st. of 8 l. It is repeated in *The Songs of the Spirit*, N. Y., 1871.

9. **Bright Thy presence when it breaketh.** *Public Worship*. Written in 1856, and 1st pub. in his *Golden Chain*, &c., 1869, p. 27, in 6 st. of 6 l. In the *Bapt. Hymnal*, 1879, and in Dale's *English H. Bk.* it is in an abridged form.

10. **Day divine! when sudden streaming.** *Whit-Sunday*. Written on Whit-Sunday, 1850, and 1st pub. in G. Dawson's *Ps. & Hys.*, 1859, and again in the *Golden Chain*, &c., 1869, p. 97, in 3 st. of 8 l. In some American collections, as the Dutch Reformed *Hys. of the Church*, 1869, it is given as "Day divine, when *in the temple*."

11. **Dear Lord and Master mine.** *Resignation*. Written in 1868, and 1st pub. in his *Golden Chain*, 1869, p. 162, in 7 st. of 4 l. It is in somewhat extensive use both in G. Britain and America.

12. **Dear Lord, Thou art not sorry.** *Passiontide*. Written in 1866, and 1st pub. in his *Golden Chain*, &c., 1869, p. 58, in 5 st. of 8 l.

13. **Dear Lord, Thy light Thou dost not hide.** *Christian Labours*. No. 125 in the *Golden Chain*, &c., 1869, p. 178, in 8 st. of 4 l. on the text, "Let your light so shine before men," &c., and was written in 1855.

14. **Do we only give Thee heed.** *Jesus the*

Gladdener of Life. Written in 1849, and 1st pub. in G. Dawson's *Ps. & Hys.*, 1853; and again in the *Golden Chain*, &c., No. 145, in 6 st. of 6 l. In use in G. Britain and America.

15. **Embrace your full Salvation.** *Heaven.* Written in 1870, and 1st printed in *The Congregationalist*, 1873, in 9 st. of 8 l. On including it in his *English H. Bk.*, 1874, Dr. Dale transposed some of the stanzas.

16. **Farewell, delightful day.** *Sunday Evening.* Written in 1867, and pub. in his *Golden Chain*, &c., 1869, No. 19, in 9 st. of 4 l. In the *Church Praise Bk.*, N. Y., 1882, st. i., viii., ix., are given with the alteration of the opening line as, "*Holy*, delightful day." Dr. Hatfield, in his *Church H. Bk.*, N. Y., 1872, has the same opening, but he omits st. iv.–vi. of the original.

17. **Father, glorious with all splendour.** *Holy Trinity.* This hymn of great merit was written in 1860, and pub. in the *Golden Chain*, &c., in 1869, No. 4, in 7 st. of 8 l. In some American collections, including *Hys. & Songs of Praise*, N. Y., 1874, No. 17, st. iv., vi., vii., are given as "Father, Thine elect who lovest."

18. **Father, hast Thou not on me.** *Eternal Love.* A Trinitarian hymn on eternal love, composed in 1867, and pub. in his *Golden Chain*, &c., 1869, No. 139, in 7 st. of 8 l. In 1869, st. v.–vii. were given in the *Suppl.* to the *New Cong.*, as "Mighty Quickener, Spirit blest."

19. **Full many a smile, full many a song.** *Joy in God the Father.* Written in 1854, and 1st pub. in his *Golden Chain*, &c., 1869, No. 8, in 9 st. of 4 l. In Dale's *English H. Bk.*, 1874, No. 21, st. ii., which applied personally to the author alone, was omitted.

20. **How can I, Lord, abide with Thee?** *Prayer.* "Produced in 1856. Struck with the didactic character of Cowper's and Montgomery's hymns, 'What various hindrances we meet,' and 'Prayer is the soul's sincere desire,' I greatly wished to set forth the soul's view of prayer, simply, naturally, poetically, and achieved this hymn with much aspiration and satisfaction." Printed in the *Golden Chain*, &c., 1869, No. 119, in 8 st. of 4 l., and headed "Pray without ceasing."

21. **How, Lord, shall vows of ours be sweet?** *Public Worship.* The author's earliest hymn. It was written in 1845, and 1st pub. in G. Dawson's *Ps. & Hys.*, 1846, No. 114, in 6 st. of 4 l., and again in the *Golden Chain*, &c., 1869, No. 2. It is in several American hymn-books.

22. **Is earth too fair, is youth too bright?** *Consecration of Youth to God.* Written in 1848, and 1st pub. in his *Golden Chain*, &c., 1869, No. 102, in 13 st. of 4 l., and entitled "The Hymn of Youth."

23. **Is not my spirit filled with Thine.** *God glorious in His works.* "Written in the summer of 1846 among the hills and streams of Derbyshire," and 1st pub. in the *Golden Chain*, &c., 1869, No. 15, in 9 st. of 4 l., and entitled "God glorious in His works."

24. **Let bolder hearts the strife require.** *Prayer against Temptation.* No. 218 in Martineau's *Hys. of Praise and Prayer*, 1873. It was written in 1851, and 1st pub. in the *Golden Chain*, &c., 1869, in 7 st. of 4 l.

25. **Lift thy song among the nations.** *National Hymn.* Written in 1853, and 1st pub. in G. Dawson's *Ps. & Hys.*, 1853, in 4 st. of 8 l. When repeated in the *Golden Chain*, &c., 1869, No. 62, an additional stanza (iii.) was given, and it was entitled "England's Hymn." It is a spirited hymn and worthy of greater circulation than it now has. The 1869 text is given in Dale's *English H. Bk.*, 1874, No. 1239.

26. **Lord, am I precious in Thy sight.** *Grieve not the H. Spirit.* Composed in 1850, and 1st pub. in G. Dawson's *Ps. & Hys.*, 1853. In 1869 it was included in the *Golden Chain*, &c., No. 70, in 7 st. of 4 l. It is in C. U. in America. A cento is also in the *Suppl.* to the *New Cong.*, 1869, No. 1095. It is composed of st. iii., v., vi. much altered, and not improved, and begins, "O Holy Spirit, dost thou mourn?"

27. **Lord, comes this bidding strange to us?** *Invitation to Rejoice.* Written in 1849, and 1st pub. in his *Golden Chain*, &c., 1869, No. 144, in 11 st. of 4 l.

28. **Lord, dost Thou ne'er Thy servants bless?** *Free Grace.* Written in 1855, on the words of Oliver Cromwell as used by him in a letter to his "beloved cousin Mrs. St. John," dated "Ely, 13th October, 1638." "Truly no poor creature hath more cause to put himself forth in the cause of his God than I. *I have had plentiful wages beforehand; and I am sure I shall never earn the least mite.*" (Carlyle's *Oliver Cromwell's Letters and Speeches*, &c., Letter ii.) The hymn was 1st pub. in the *Golden Chain*, &c., 1869, in 9 st. of 4 l.

29. **Lord, from Thee, what grace and glory.** *National Hymn.* This cento in Vince's *Coll.*, 1870, No.

450, is from the poem, on St. George's Day, written in 1853, and pub. in the author's *Anniversaries*, 1858, p. 47.

30. **Lord, from these trembling souls of ours.** *Praise.* Composed in 1859, and 1st pub. in his *Golden Chain*, &c., 1869, No. 3, in 10 st. of 4 l.

31. **Lord God, by Whom all change is wrought.** *God Eternal.* Written in 1869, the keynote being the words of St. Augustine, "Immutabilis mutans omnia," and 1st printed in the *Songs of the Spirit*, N. Y., 1871. In 1874 it was included in Dale's *English H. Bk.*; and, in 4 st., in the *Bapt. Hymnal*, 1879.

32. **Lord God of old, who wentest.** *Public Worship.* Composed in 1868, and 1st pub. in his *Golden Chain*, &c., 1869, No. 30, in 5 st. of 8 l.

33. **Lord, if our dwelling place thou art.** *Communion of Saints.* Written in 1856, and 1st pub. in his *Golden Chain*, &c., 1869, No. 150, in 8 st. of 4 l. The hymn, "Death has no bidding to divide," in Dale's *English H. Bk.*, 1874, begins with st. ii., and omits st. i., iv. of this hymn.

34. **Lord, in this awful fight with sin.** *Victory through Christ.* Written in 1857, and 1st pub. in his *Golden Chain*, &c., 1869, No. 128, in 7 st. of 8 l.

35. **Lord, in Thy people Thou dost dwell.** *Unity of Christ and His people.* Written in 1864, and 1st pub. in his *Golden Chain*, &c., 1869, in 12 st. of 4 l.

36. **Lord, Thou hast been our dwelling place.** *National Hymn.* "Begun among the Waldenses, 1864," and 1st pub. in his *Golden Chain*, &c., 1869, No. 59, in 8 st. of 7 l., entitled, "The hymn of the Waldenses," and supplemented with the note, "This hymn as a whole belongs to the Waldenses only, among whom it was begun, but all the people of God have an interest in the first two and the last verses." Acting upon this suggestion of the author, these stanzas were given in the *Suppl.* to the *New Cong.*, 1869, as No. 1025.

37. **Lord, Thou wouldst have us like to Thee.** *Holiness desired.* Written in 1846, and 1st pub. in G. Dawson's *Ps. & Hys.*, 1846, No. 120, in 8 st. of 4 l. It is in several American collections.

38. **Lord, Thy gracious voice hath spoken.** *Christ our Cæsar.* Written in 1849, and 1st pub. in G. Dawson's *Ps. & Hys.*, 1853; and again in the *Golden Chain*, &c., 1869, in 3 st. of 8 l.

39. **Lord, when I all things would possess.** *Humility.* Written in 1850, and 1st pub. in his *Golden Chain*, &c., 1869, No. 111, in 8 st. of 4 l. In Martineau's *Hymns*, &c., 1873, No. 304, st. ii., iv., vii. are omitted. This hymn is also in C. U. in America.

40. **Lord, when we come at Thy dear call.** *The Holy Ghost, the Sanctifier.* No. 72 in his *Golden Chain*, 1869, in 7 st. of 4 l., was written in 1856, and is given in the *Songs of the Spirit*, N. Y., 1871.

41. **May we not, Father, meetly mourn?** *Burial.* No. 151 in his *Golden Chain*, &c., 1869, in 9 st. of 4 l., was written in 1855.

42. **Methought my soul had learned to love.** *Resignation.* "Composed in 1852 and first printed in *Golden Chain*, 1869. It came from the very depths of my own heart, was inspired by a suppressed trouble which turned out one of the greatest blessings of my life." In the *Golden Chain*, &c., No. 114, it is given in 7 st. of 4 l., and is headed, "Not my will but Thine be done."

43. **My God, I do not flee from Thee.** *Joy.* Written in 1849, and 1st pub. in his *Golden Chain*, &c., 1869, No. 10, in 7 st. of 4 l. The *New Cong.*, 1869, No. 1119, begins with st. ii., "Father, Redeemer, Quickener mine," and also omits st. iv.

44. **My God, my Majesty divine.** *Child of God.* Written in 1845, and 1st pub. in G. Dawson's *Psalms & Hys.*, 1846, No. 116, in 8 st. of 4 l., and again, after revision, in the *Golden Chain*, &c., 1869, No. 135. The original text is in C. U. in America.

45. **Not, Lord, Thine ancient works alone.** *Public Worship.* Written in 1874, and 1st printed in *The Congregationalist*, in 6 st. of 6 l., and entitled, "The Living God." In Dale's *English H. Bk.*, 1874, st. iii. is omitted.

46. **Not yet I love my Lord.** *Lent.* Written in 1868, and 1st pub. in his *Golden Chain*, &c., 1869, No. 86, in 9 st. of 4 l. It is in several collections, including Martineau's *Hymns*, &c., 1873, No. 199.

47. **Not yet, ye people of His grace.** *Here and Hereafter.* A hymn on the "The Vision Beatific," No. 165, in his *Golden Chain*, &c., 1869, in 11 st of 4 l. It was written in 1866, and is in American C. U.

48. **O height that doth all height excel.** Written in 1853, and "was born of the words of Augustine in

the outset of the Confessions, 'Secretissime et Praesentissime,' and was the first of several hymns inspired by his wonderful antitheses about God." It was 1st pub. in G. Dawson's *Ps. & Hys.*, 1853, and again in the *Golden Chain*, &c., 1869, No. 13, in 9 st. of 4 l. It is in English and American C. U.

49. O Holy Ghost, Who down dost come. *Whitsuntide.* "Written at Malvern on Whitsunday, 1863; a day of singular spiritual enjoyment, and outward loveliness." It was 1st pub. in the *Golden Chain*, &c., 1869, No. 74, in 7 st. of 4 l., and headed, "A Breathing after the Holy Spirit," and is in several collections. In Martineau's *Hymns*, &c., 1873, No. 251, it begins with st. ii., "Spirit of Truth, Who makest bright," st. i. and vi. being omitted.

50. O not alone in saddest plight. *Divine Guidance desired.* Composed in 1856, and 1st pub. in his *Golden Chain*, &c., 1869, No. 120, in 9 st. of 4 l.

51. O not to fill the mouth of fame. *A Servant of Christ.* "Composed in 1849, and printed first in a small collection of poems entitled, I think, *The Violet.*" In 1853 it was given in G. Dawson's *Ps. & Hys.*; and in 1869, in the *Golden Chain*, &c., No. 121, in 6 st. of 4 l. Its use is mainly confined to America.

52. O not upon our waiting eyes. *Divine Love.* Written in 1849, and 1st pub. in his *Golden Chain*, &c., 1869, No. 29, in 5 st. of 4 l.

53. O saints of old, not yours alone. *Seeking God.* Written in 1848, and 1st pub. in G. Dawson's *Ps. & Hys.*, 1853; and again, after revision, in the *Golden Chain*, &c., 1869, No. 126, in 10 st. of 4 l. The American hymn-books have usually the original text, but in Dale's *English H. Bk.*, 1875, and Horder's *Cong. H. Bk.*, 1884, the text is abridged from the *Golden Chain*.

54. O smitten soul that cares and conflicts wring. *Heaven desired.* Written in 1854, and 1st pub. in his *Golden Chain*, &c., 1869, No. 75, in 8 st. of 4 l.

55. O Spirit, sweet and pure. *Constant Presence of the Holy Spirit desired.* Written in 1868, and given in his *Golden Chain*, &c., 1869, as No. 127, in 7 st. of 8 l.

56. O time, ne'er resteth thy swift wing. *Worth of Time.* Written in 1855, and 1st pub. in his *Golden Chain*, &c., 1869, No. 98, in 9 st. of 4 l.

57. O wherefore hath my spirit leave? *Spiritual Changes.* "Composed with great ardour and stir of soul in 1847, and first printed in the *Golden Chain*, 1869," No. 85, in 7 st. of 4 l.

58. O'er fulness of grace, blest Britain rejoice. *National Hymn.* Composed in 1868, and 1st pub. in his *Golden Chain*, &c., 1869, No. 61, in 11 st. of 4 l., and entitled, "The Thanksgiving Song of Protestant Britain"; to which was added the words of Milton: "Let us all go, every true Protestant Briton, throughout the three kingdoms, and render thanks to God the Father of Light, and to His Son, Jesus Christ our Lord."

59. Saviour, needs the world no longer? *Christ All in All.* "Written in 1847 . . . it was inspired partly by my contemplation of Shelley's hapless, Christless life." It was 1st pub. in G. Dawson's *Ps. & Hys.*, 1853, and again in the *Golden Chain*, &c., 1869, No. 35, in 7 st. of 6 l., and headed, "Lord, to whom shall we go." Its use is limited, and far less than its merits deserve.

60. Saviour, Who from death didst take. *The Resurrection of Christ, a cause of Confidence.* Written in 1856, and 1st pub. in his *Golden Chain*, &c., 1869, No. 96, in 5 st. of 6 l.

61. Sweet Spirit, would Thy breath divine. *The Holy Ghost, the Purifier, desired.* Written in 1856, and given as No. 71 in his *Golden Chain*, &c., 1869, in 10 st. of 4 l.

62. The happy fields, the heavenly host. *Heaven.* Written in 1848, 1st pub. in G. Dawson's *Ps. & Hys.*, 1853, and again in the *Golden Chain*, &c., 1869, No. 157, in 10 st. of 4 l.

63. Thy happy ones a strain begin. *Joy in God.* Written in 1846, and pub. in G. Dawson's *Ps. & Hys.*, 1846, No. 118, in 5 st. of 4 l. In the *Golden Chain*, &c., 1869, No. 146, the text is slightly changed. The text in C. U. in G. Britain and America is from the original.

64. Too dearly, Lord, hast Thou redeemed. *Lent.* Written in 1855, and 1st pub. in his *Golden Chain*, &c., 1869, No. 97, in 9 st. of 4 l.

65. Unto thy rest return. *Lent.* Written in 1866, and 1st pub. in his *Golden Chain*, &c., 1869, No. 92, in 6 st. of 8 l.

66. We come unto our fathers' God. *God our Abode.* "The birthday of this hymn, November 22nd, 1868 (St. Cecilia's Day), was almost the most delightful day of my life. Its production employed the whole day and

was a prolonged rapture . . . . . It was produced while the *Golden Chain* was being printed, just in time to be a link therein, and was the latest, as 'How, Lord, shall vows of ours be sweet?' was the earliest song included therein." In the *Golden Chain*, &c., 1869, it is No. 129, in 7 st. of 7 l., and is entitled, "The People of God."

67. We triumph in the glorious grace. *Citizens of Heaven.* Written in 1855, and 1st pub. in his *Anniversaries*, 1858, and again in his *Golden Chain*, &c., 1869, No. 153, in 12 st. of 4 l.

68. What sweetness on Thine earth doth dwell. *Nature revealing God.* [*Summer.*] Written in 1850, and 1st pub. in his *Golden Chain*, &c., 1869, in 8 st. of 4 l.

69. When shall I, Lord, a journey take. *Lent.* Written in 1856, and 1st pub. in his *Golden Chain*, &c., 1869, No. 80, in 8 st. of 4 l. It is in C. U. in G. Britain and America.

70. Whence this flaming joy that maketh? *The Prodigal's Return.* "Written in 1853 just before the hymn beginning 'Thrice blessed soul, who still hath made,' with the text 'Son, thou art ever with me' (*Golden Chain*, No. 134), which is its completement; and 1st printed in the *Golden Chain*," 1869, No. 81, in 6 st. of 6 l.

71. Would the Spirit more completely? *The Gifts of the Spirit.* Written in 1849, and 1st pub. in G. Dawson's *Ps. & Hys.*, 1853; and again in the *Golden Chain*, &c., 1869, No. 67, in 3 st. of 8 l.

72. Ye children of the Father. *Spiritual Worship.* Written in 1867, and 1st pub. in his *Golden Chain.* &c., 1869, No. 23, in 6 st. of 8 l.

73. Ye of the Father loved. *Praise.* Written in 1862, and 1st pub. in the *Golden Chain*, &c., 1869, No. 5, in 8 st. of 8 l.

74. Ye people of the Lord, draw near. *Holy Communion.* Written in 1855, and 1st pub. in his *Golden Chain*, &c., 1869, No. 127, in 7 st. of 4 l.

75. Ye souls, the Father's very own. *Holy Diligence.* Composed in 1867, and 1st pub. in his *Golden Chain*, &c., 1869, No. 142, in 9 st. of 4 l.

These hymns are usually abridged in the hymn-books, the length of most of them being against their use in their full form. Although they are gradually growing in popular esteem, the extent of their use is much more limited than their merits deserve.   [J. J.]

Gilman, Caroline, née Howard, daughter of Samuel Howard, and wife of Dr. S. Gilman (q.v.), was b. at Boston, U. S., in 1794, and married to Dr. Gilman in 1819. After Dr. Gilman's death in 1858, she resided for a time at Cambridge, U. S., and subsequently at Tiverton, Long Island. Mrs. Gilman is the author of several tales, ballads, and poems, and of the following hymns:—

1. Is there a lone and dreary hour? *Providence.* Contributed to Sewall's Unitarian *Coll.*, N. York, 1820, in 4 st. of 4 l. In 1867 Mrs. Gilman added a stanza thereto for the Charlestown *Services & Hymns.* The original hymn is in extensive use amongst the Unitarians in G. Britain and America.

2. We bless Thee for this sacred day. *Sunday.* Also contributed to Sewall's *Coll.*, 1820, in 4 st. of 4 l., to which another was added by Mrs. Gilman, for the Charlestown *Services & Hymns*, 1867. In extensive use.   [F. M. B.]

Gilman, Samuel, D.D., was b. at Gloucester, Massachusetts, Feb. 16, 1791; graduated at Harvard, 1811, and was a tutor there from 1817 to 1819. In 1819 he became the pastor of a Unitarian congregation at Charlestown, South Carolina, and retained the same to his death. He d. at Kingston, Mass., Feb. 9, 1858. His hymns include:—

1. O God, accept the sacred hour. *Holy Communion.* Contributed to Dr. Harris's *Hys. for the Lord's Supper*, July, 1820, republished in

Sewall's Unitarian *Coll.*, N. York, 1820, and in later collections.

2. We sing Thy mercy, God of love. *Holy Communion.* Published as in the case of No. 1.

3. Yes, to the [that] last command. *Holy Communion.* Published as in the case of Nos. 1 & 2.

[F. M. B.]

Gilmore, Joseph Henry, M.A., Professor of Logic in Rochester University, New York, was b. at Boston, April 29, 1834, and graduated in Arts at Brown University, and in Theology at Newton Theological Institution. In the latter he was Professor of Hebrew in 1861-2. For some time he held a Baptist ministerial charge at Fisherville, New Hampshire, and at Rochester. He was appointed Professor at Rochester in 1868. His hymn, "He leadeth me, O blessed thought" (*Ps. xxiii.*), is somewhat widely known. It was written at the close of a lecture in the First Baptist Church, Philadelphia, and is dated 1859. It is in the *Bap. H. [and Tune] Bk.*, Philadelphia, 1871.

[F. M. B.]

Gisborne, Thomas. [Staffordshire Hymn-books.]

Give ear, O Lord, to hear. *W. Hunnis.* [*Lent.*] Appeared in his *Seven Sobs of a Sorrowful Soul for Sin*, 1585, in 3 st. of 8 l., and entitled, "An humble sute of a Repentant Sinner for Mercie." In 1845 it was reprinted in E. Farr's *Select Poetry, &c., of the Reign of Queen Elizabeth*, vol. i. p. 157. From that work it passed into *Kennedy*, 1863, No. 398, in an altered form as, "Attend, O Lord, and hear." [W. T. B.]

Give glory to the Lord. *J. Montgomery.* [*Praise.*] Written June 1st, 1836 ["M. MSS."], and pub. as a fly-sheet for the Whitsuntide gathering of the Sheffield S. S. Union, 1839, in 6 st. of 4 l. It is No. 91 in his *Original Hys.*, 1853. It is in limited use in America. [J. J.]

Give glory unto God on high. *B. Barton.* [*Praise to the Holy Trinity.*] Pub. in his *Poetic Vigils*, 1824, p. 189, in 5 st. of 10 l. In its full form it is unknown to the collections, but the following centos therefrom are in C. U.:—

1. All glory to the Father be, Who made the earth. &c. This is No. 154 in the S. P. C. K. *Church Hys.*, 1871.

2. Ascribe we to the Father praise. This is apparently based upon st. i.-iv. of this hymn, and is No. 1117 in *Kennedy*, 1863.

3. Give glory unto God on high. This, in 5 st. of 4 l., is No. 1288 in *Kennedy*, 1863.

4. The Father, God, we glorify. This is No. 109 in the Cooke and Denton *Hymnal*, 1853. [J. J.]

Give laud unto the Lord. *John Pullain.* [*Ps. cxlviii.*] This version of Ps. 148 appeared, possibly in the lost *Anglo-Genevan Psalter*, appended to *The Forme of Prayers, &c.*, 1558, and certainly in the *Anglo-Genevan Psalter*, 1561 ; thence into the Scottish *Psalter*, in 1565, where Psalm 136 ("O Lord, the Lord benign) is in the same metre. It is not in modern use ; but is of historical importance as the first instance in psalms or hymns of the metre, 6.6.6.6.4.4.4.4. subsequently so successfully employed by *Tate and Brady*, in "Ye boundless realms of joy"; by I. Watts in "Lord of the worlds above"; and in the hymns of many other writers. The best stanza

of this version we give as an example of both the metre and the rendering :—

2. " Praise Him both moon and sun,
    Which are so clear and bright ;
    The same of you be done,
    Ye glistring stars of light :
        And eke no less,
        Ye heavens fair,
        And clouds of th' air,
        His laud express."

The full text is difficult to find except in the Psalters appended to old editions of the Bible and Prayer Book. [Old Version, § IX.] [J. J.]

Give me the wings of faith to rise. *I. Watts.* [*Heaven: All Saints.*] 1st pub. in his *H. & Spiritual Songs*, 2nd ed., 1709, Bk. ii., No. 140, in 5 st. of 4 l., and entitled, "The Examples of Christ and the Saints." It is in extensive use in all English-speaking countries, and generally in its original form as in the *Hy. Comp.*, No. 357. In *Kennedy*, 1863, the opening line reads :—" Be mine the wings of faith to rise," No. 1379. There are also other slight alterations in the text. [J. J.]

Give thanks to God the Sovereign Lord, [King]. *I. Watts.* [*Ps. cxxxvi.*] This C. M. version of Ps. 136 was pub. in his *Ps. of David, &c.*, 1719, in 10 st. of 4 l., with the following note :—

" In every stanza of this Psalm I have endeavoured to imitate the *Chorus* or Burden of the Song, *For His mercy endureth for ever*, and yet to maintain a perpetual variety."

The systematic way in which this end is accomplished is sketched out in the title which he gave to his Paraphrase. It reads : "God's Wonders of Creation, Providence, Redemption of Israel, and Salvation of his People." The form in which it is found in most modern collections, as in *N. Cong.*, 1859, No. 226, and others, eliminates the reference to the "Redemption of Israel," thus reducing the hymn to 6 st. The first line sometimes reads : "Give thanks to God, the Sovereign *King*." [J. J.]

Give to our God immortal praise. *I. Watts.* [*Ps. cxxxvi.*] This L. M. version of Ps. 136 appeared in his *Ps. of David* in 1719, in 8 st. of 4 l. In modern collections we find it given thus :—

1. The original in the *N. Cong.*, No. 227 ; Spurgeon's *O. O. H. Bk.*, No. 136, and others ; and in the Bap. *Ps. & Hymns*, 1858–80, No. 8, with st. v., l. 1, " *Israel* " for " The Jews " of the original.

2. A cento composed of st. i., iv., vii. and viii. This was given in Cotterill's *Sel.*, 1810-19, and from thence has passed into numerous collections, including *Windle*, S. P. C. K. *Ps. & Hys.*, and Stevenson's *Hys. for Ch. & Home*, amongst modern hymnals, with slight variations in the refrain. This is the most popular form of the hymn.

3. A cento combining st. i.-iv. and vii., viii. This appeared in Conyers's *Coll.*, 1767, and amongst later hymnals the *Leeds H. Bk.*, 1853, the Islington *Ps. & Hys.*, Kemble's *New Church H. Bk.*, and other collections. This form is also in use in America. [See Psalters, English, § xv.] [J. J.]

Glad sight, the Holy Church. [*Holy Baptism.*] The Syriac original of this hymn is sometimes attributed to Ephrem the Syrian (d. 378), but without sufficient authority. It is found in the Office for Baptism of the Church at Jerusalem. Daniel, iii. 226, in the portion devoted to Syriac hymnody—*Carmina Ecclesiae Syriacae curavit Ludovicus Splieth*—gives the Syriac text, and a Latin *tr.* by Splieth, which reads :—

" Expande alas tuas sancta Ecclesia et simplicem

agnum suscipe, quem Spiritus Sanctus ex aquis Baptismi genuit. De hoc Baptismo vaticinatus est filius Zachariae ; ego inquit, in aquis baptizo ; at ille qui venturus est in Spiritu Sancto. Exercitus caelestium circumadstat baptisterio, ut ex aquis suscipiant filios Deo similes. Ex aquis viros sibi delegit Gideon, qui ad praelium prodirent ; ex aquis Baptismalis sibi Christus adoratores delegit."

In 1862 the Rev. F. Pott contributed an article on " Hymnology " to the *Quarterly Review* (April, 1862), and gave therein a paraphrase in metre of the above Latin rendering, beginning, "Glad sight ! the holy Church," in 9 st. of 4 l. Although previously included in his *Hymns*, &c., 1861, No. 236, in 7 st. of 4 l., this publication brought it into fuller notice, and it was soon added, in one form or another, to several hymn-books, including the *People's H.*, 1867 ; the *Appendix* to *H. A. & M.*, 1868, the S. P. C. K. *Church Hys.*, 1871 ; the *Hymnary*, 1872 ; and other collections in G. Britain and America. The greatest deviation from the original *tr.* is in the *Church Hymns*. The changes, however, were made with the translator's permission.   [J. J.]

Gladden, Washington. [Various.]

Glassite Hymns. [Scottish Hymnody.]

Gloria in Excelsis.
The simple and original form of this hymn is contained in the song of the angels as given by St. Luke ii. 14, "Glory to God in the highest, and on earth peace, goodwill toward men." This simple form came early into use, and is found in the *Liturgy of St. James*, where it is directed to be recited by the Priest when the gifts were "scaled."

2. From this simple beginning it soon expanded until it assumed the form of an elaborate hymn. The most complete text as it existed in the 5th century, is given at the end of the Psalms and Canticles in the *Codex Alexandrinus* in the Brit. Museum, which dates from the close of the 5th century. In the *Facsimile of the Codex Alexandrinus*, pub. by the authorities of the Brit. Museum, it is in vol. iii. folio 569, ii. This is given in Greek Hymnody, p. **459**, i., § x. 4, together with a translation into English (q. v.).

3. The form given in the *Apostolic Constitutions*, vii. 47 (*Daniel*, ii. p. 268), differs in some measure from this by variations and the addition of some phrases (see *Dict. of Christian Ant.* p. 736).

4. The Latin form of the text is in an 8th century MS. in the Brit. Museum (Reg. 2 A. xx.). As given in the *Roman Missal* it reads :

"Gloria in excelsis Deo. Et in terra pax hominibus bonæ voluntatis. Laudamus te. Benedicimus te. Adoramus te. Glorificamus te. Gratias agimus tibi propter magnam gloriam tuam. Domine Deus, Rex cælestis, Deus Pater omnipotens. Domine Fili unigenite Jesu Christe. Domine Deus, Agnus Dei, Filius Patris. Qui tollis peccata mundi, miserere nobis. Qui tollis peccata mundi, suscipe deprecationem nostram. Qui sedes ad dexteram Patris, miserere nobis. Quoniam tu solus sanctus. Tu solus Dominus. Tu solus altissimus, Jesu Christe. Cum sancto Spiritu, in gloria Dei Patris. Amen."

5. The translations into English which are in C. U. are in prose and verse. The prose translation most in use is that in the Office for Holy Communion in the *Book of Common Prayer*. It is translated from the Latin text as above. The translation of the hymn in the Office of the Scottish Prayer Book is from the Greek text as in the article Greek Hymnody,

p. **459**, i., § x. 4. The principal difference between the two is in the second clause. This in the *Greek* is, "Lord the only begotten Son, Jesus Christ, and Holy Spirit." This reads in the *Scottish Office*, "And to Thee, O God, the only begotten Son Jesu Christ, and to Thee, O God, the Holy Ghost." The corresponding passage in the *Roman Missal* is "Domine Fili unigenite Jesu Christe," and in the *English Prayer Book*, "O Lord the only-begotten Son Jesu Christ." The concluding clause, in the form given to it in the *Roman Missal*, "Cum Sancto Spiritu, in gloria Dei Patris," and in the *English Prayer Book*, "with the Holy Ghost art most high in the glory of God the Father," is of unknown and, comparatively modern, interpolation (see *Daniel*, ii. p. 267). The translations into English verse are all from the prose translation in the *Book of Common Prayer*. They include the following :—

1. All glory be to God on high and peace on earth likewise. *Old Version.* In *J. Playford*, 1677.

2. To God be glory, Peace on earth. Given in the *Supplement* to the *New Version*, 1700, and continued until the N.V. gave way to modern hymn-books. It is in several collections both in G. Britain and America.

3. Let glory be to God on high. Appeared in the American Andover *Sabbath H. Bk.*, 1858, No. 467. Its authorship is unknown.

4. Glory in the highest to God. By Dr. Bonar in the *Sunday at Home*, 1878, p. 92.

In addition Mr. Chatfield has rendered the Greek text as in the *Antho. Graeca Carmi. Christi*, 1871, into prose in his *Songs & Hys. of the Earliest Greek Christian Poets*, 1876, p. 161, as "Glory to God in the highest," &c. See also "Glory be to God," &c., p. **427**, ii.
                                                    [J. J.]

This hymn has also been rendered into *German*, and from the German into *English* as follows :—

Allein Gott in der Höh sey Ehr. A rendering in 4 st. of 7 l., by Nicolaus Decius. 1st appeared in Low German as " Alleine God jn der höge sy ëre," in the Rostock *G. B.*, 1525 [Rostock University Library]. *Wackernagel*, iii. pp. 565–67, quotes it from the Rostock *G. B.*, 1526, and, in High Germany, from V. Schumann's *G. B.*, Leipzig, 1539. The well-known melody set to it in 1539 (*H. A. & M.*, No. 104) is also ascribed to Decius, probably partly adapted from the Latin plainsong. Text and melody speedily became favourites in Germany ; were used on high festivals, at Holy Communion, &c. ; and to this day are everywhere in use. Lauxmann, in *Koch*, viii. 104–111, relates many edifying incidents regarding them. In the *Unv. L. S.*, 1851, No. 185. The *trs.* in C. U. through the German are :—

1. To God on high all glory be. In full, as No. 226, in the *Appendix* of 1743 to the *Moravian H. Bk.*, 1742, and repeated, altered, in later eds. (1886, No. 191). St. i., iii., iv. nearly from the text of 1826, were included as No. 216 in Dr. Pagenstecher's *Coll.*, 1864.

2. To God on high be thanks and praise, Who deigns, &c. Of st. 1, by W. Ball, as part of his *tr.* of the German book of words of Mendelssohn's *St. Paul*, 1846. Included in the *Leeds H. Bk.*, 1853, No. 225 ; *N. Cong.*, 1859 ; Horder's *Cong. Hys.*, 1884 ; and others.

3. All glory be to God on high, And. A good and full *tr.* signed A. G. in the Dalston Hospital *H. Bk.*, 1848, No. 39.

4. All glory be to God on high, Who. A full

and good *tr.*, as No. 1, in Miss Winkworth's *C. B. for England*, 1863. Repeated in the *Temple H. Bk.*, 1867, and in America in the Pennsylvania Luth. *Ch. Bk.*, 1868, Ohio *Luth. Hyl.*, 1880, and the New York *Evang. Hyl.*, 1880.

5. To God on high be thanks and praise, For. In full, by R. C. Singleton, as No. 268, in the *Anglican H. Bk.*, 1868 (1871, No. 311). Repeated in J. L. Porter's *Coll.*, 1876, and in Stryker & Main's *Church Praise Bk.*, New York, 1882.

6. To God alone on high be praise. By J. D. Burns, in his *Remains*, 1869, p. 238. This is No. 66 in Dale's *English H. Bk.*, 1874.

7. To God alone the song we raise. In full, by T. E. Brown, as No. 45, in the *Clifton College H. Bk.*, 1872.

8. Alone to God on high be praise. A *tr.* of st. i. as st. i. of No. 95 in the Swedenborgian *Coll.*, 1880.

Translations not in C. U. :—

(1) "To God the hyghest be glory alwaye," by Bp. Coverdale, 1539 (*Remains*, 1846, p. 564). (2) "Onlie to God on heich be gloir," in the *Gude and Godlie Ballates* (ed. 1568, folio 28, 1868, p. 47). (3) "To our Almighty Maker, God," by *J. C. Jacobi*, 1722, p. 26 (1732, p. 50, reading "gracious God"). (4) "To God alone in the highest heaven," by *Miss Fry*, 1845, p. 41. (5) "To God on high we'll praises sing," signed "P.J." in the *Sunday Mag.*, 1874, p. 384.   [J. M.]

Gloria laus et honor. *St. Theodulph of Orleans.* [*Palm Sunday.*] That this hymn was written by St. Theodulph seems beyond all reasonable doubt. That it was written by him while imprisoned in the cloister, at Angers, about 820 or 821, is highly probable. Regarding its origin Clichtoveus, in his *Elucidatorium*, 1516, f. 31 *b*, tells a pretty story to the following effect:—

On Palm Sunday, 821, Louis the Pious, King of France, was at Angers and took part in the usual procession of the clergy and laity. As the procession passed the place where St. Theodulph was incarcerated he stood at the open window of his cell, and amid the silence of the people, sung this hymn which he had newly composed. The king was so much delighted with the hymn that he at once ordered St. Theodulph to be set at liberty and restored to his see; and ordained that henceforth the hymn should always be used in processions on Palm Sunday.

The story is not, however, a contemporary one; and moreover it seems clear that Louis the Pious was never in Angers after 818. It is also almost certain that St. Theodulph was never really restored to his see, but that he d. at Angers in 821.

The ritual use of this hymn was always as a Processional on Palm Sunday. According to the *Sarum* use the first four stanzas were to be sung before leaving the church by seven boys "in loco eminentiori," near the south door. In the use of *York* the boys of the choir seem to have gone up to a temporary gallery over the door of the church and there sang the first four stanzas. After each of the first three stanzas the rest of the choir, kneeling below, sang st. i. as a refrain. At the end of st. iv. the boys began the refrain and the rest of the choir, standing up, sang it along with them. In the *Hereford* use the procession went to the gates of the town. These being shut seven boys of the choir went to the summit and there sang the hymn. In the uses of *Tours* and *Rouen* it was also sung at the gate of the city. According to the modern *Roman* use it is sung when the procession returns to the church; two or four singers entering the church, and when the door has been closed, facing it and singing the hymn while the rest outside repeat the chorus.

The hymn is founded on Ps. xxiv. 7-10; Ps. cxviii. 25, 26; St. Matt. xxi. 1-17; and St. Luke xix. 37, 38. E. L. Dümmler, in his *Poetae latini aevi Carolini*, Berlin, 1877 ff. vol. i. p. 558, gives the full text in 78 lines. In the liturgical books ll. 1-36 only are given

(so in the *Paris MS.*, 18557, of the 10th cent. cited by *Dümmler*; and in the British Museum ms. Add. 19768, f. 36 *b*, of the 11th cent); while in the Graduals and Missals the almost universal use was to give only ll. 1-12. This is the form in a St. Gall ms. (No. 899) of the 9th cent, cited by *Dümmler*, and it is the form in English C. U. as in *H. A. & M.* The text is also found in an 11th cent. ms. in the British Museum (Harl. 4951, f. 196 *b*); in two 11th cent. mss. in the Bodleian (Liturg. Misc. 320, f. 18 b.; Liturg. Misc. 366, f. 18); in *Daniel*, i. No. 186; with notes at iv. p. 153; in *Bässler*, No. 69; in Dr. J. Kayser's *Beiträge zur Geschichte und Erklärung der alten Kirchenhymnen*, vol. ii., 1886, pp. 313-322, &c.   [J. M.]

Translations in C. U. :—

1. Glory and praise to Thee, Redeemer blest. By E. Caswall. 1st pub. in his *Lyra Catholica*, 1849, p. 232, in 5 st., with the repetition of the first two lines of the hymn as a refrain. It was also repeated in his *Hys. & Poems*, 1873, p. 121. It is found in several collections, including *Kennedy*, 1863, where it is altered and begins, "All glory be to Thee, Redeemer blest." The *English Hymnal*, 1852 text, is also considerably altered, although the first line is retained.

2. King and Redeemer! to Thee be the glory. By G. Rorison. 1st pub. in his *Hys. & Anthems*, 1851.

3. Glory, and honour, and laud be to Thee, King Christ the Redeemer. By J. M. Neale. Appeared in his *Mediaeval Hys.*, 1851, p. 22.

4. Glory, and laud, and honour. By J. M. Neale. This is a second *tr.* by Dr. Neale, made for and pub. in the *H. Noted*, 1854, in 8 st. of 4 l., but supplied a little earlier to the *Salisbury H. Bk.*, 1857, in a slightly different form. In this form it is in a few collections, but as:—

5. All glory, laud, and honour, as altered by the compilers of *H. A. & M.* for their trial copy, 1859, No. 59, in 6 st. of 4 l., it is most widely known in all English-speaking countries. Dr. Neale approved of this arrangement, especially of the opening line, and adds in his note (*Med. Hys.*):—

"Another verse was usually sung, till the 17th century; at the pious quaintness of which we can scarcely avoid a smile:—

'Be Thou, O Lord, the Rider,
    And we the little ass;
That to God's holy city
    Together we may pass.'"

6. Glory, laud, and honour be, Our Redeemer Christ to Thee. By W. J. Blew, in *The Church Hy. & Tune Bk.*, 1852-5, in 7 st. of 4 l., and in Rice's *Sel.* therefrom, 1870, No. 46. In the Scottish Episco. *Coll. of Hys.*, &c., 1858, it was given in 4 st. as, "Glory, *praise*, and honour be."

7. To Thee be glory, honour, praise. Appeared in the Irvingite *Hys. for the Use of the Churches*, 1864, No. 35, as a "Tr. by C., 1861." It is repeated in the ed. of 1871, and in the American Dutch Reformed *Hys. of the Church*, N. Y., 1869.

8. Glory, praise, and honour be, Jesus, Lord, &c. Given anonymously in Dale's *English H. Bk.*, 1874, No. 255, in 4 st. of 4 l. It is a paraphrase, and not a *tr.* of the original.

Another tr. is:—

Glory, praise, and honour be, Christ, Redeemer, &c.
J. W. Hewett. 1859.   [J. J.]

Gloria Patri. [Doxologies.]

Gloriosi Salvatoris. [*Holy Name of Jesus.*] This anonymous hymn, possibly of the 15th cent., is given from the *Meissen Breviary,* cir. 1510, in *Daniel,* i. No. 449, in 6 st. of 3 double lines, and headed, "In festo S. Nominis Jesu." Dr. Neale's text, in 7 st. of 6 l., is given in his *Hymni Ecclesiae,* 1851, p. 165, from the *Liége Breviary.* In his *Mediaeval Hymns,* 1851, he claims for his *tr.* that it was the first rendering into English, and says concerning the original, "A German hymn on the Festival of the Holy Name of Jesus." All that can be said of its date is, that it is clearly posterior to the *Pange Lingua* of St. Thomas, which it imitates."   [W. A. S.]

Translations in C. U. :—

1. **To the Name that brings salvation.** By J. M. Neale. Appeared in his *Mediaeval Hys.,* 1st ed. 1851, p. 142, in 6 st. of 6 l., and again in later editions. It is included, sometimes abbreviated, in the Scottish *Epis. H. Bk.,* 1858; the *Parish H. Bk.,* 1863-75; the *People's H.,* 1867; the *Hymnary,* 1872, and others. In the American *Hys. & Songs of Praise,* New York, 1874, it is abridged to 4 st., and begins, "Jesus is the Name we treasure." Another arrangement, beginning, "Name of Jesus, Name of pleasure," is in the *Hys. for the Chapel of Harrow School,* 1857.

2. **To the Name of our salvation.** This *tr.,* which was given in *H. A. & M.,* 1861, is based upon the above *tr.* by Dr. Neale; but is so altered that only 10 lines of the 36 contained in the hymn remain unchanged. It was repeated in *Kennedy,* 1863; the S. P. C. K. *Appendix,* 1869; the *Irish Ch. Hyl.,* 1873; and others. In the *Sarum,* 1868, the *H. A. & M.* text is somewhat altered. The *H. Comp.* gives Dr. Neale's *tr.* with variations from several hymn-books.

3. **Name of our triumphant Saviour.** By R. C. Singleton, written in 1867, and pub. in his *Anglican H. Bk.,* 1868.

4. **To the Name that speaks salvation.** By J. Ellerton, and pub. in the S. P. C. K. *Church Hys.,* 1871.   [J. J.]

Another tr. is :—

The glories of the Saviour's Name. *D. T. Morgan.* 1830.

Glorious in Thy saints appear. [*Holiness desired.*] A cento in 2 st. of 4 l. which appeared in Hedge & Huntington's Unitarian *Hys. for the Ch. of Christ,* Boston, U.S., 1853, No. 64; H. W. Beecher's *Plymouth Coll.,* 1855, No. 95, &c. It is from an anonymous hymn beginning "Abba Father, God of love," in 6 st. of 4 l. in *Hys. for Pub. Worship on the General Principles of Natural and Revealed Religion,* Salisbury, 1778, and commences with st. iii. This collection is known to the American Unitarian collections as the *Salisbury Coll.*   [W. T. B.]

Glorious things of Thee are spoken. J. Newton. [*Church of Christ.*] 1st pub. in the *Olney Hymns,* 1779, Bk. i., No. 60, in 5 st. of 8 l., and entitled, "Zion, or the City of God," Is. xxxiii. 20, 21. It has attained to great popularity in all English-speaking countries, and ranks with the first hymns in the language. It is used, however, in various forms as follows :—

1. Orig. text in Snepp's *Songs of G. & G. People's H.*
2. A cento composed of st. i., ii. and v. This appeared

in Cotterill's *Selection,* 1819, from whence it has passed into a great number of collections. It is by far the most popular arrangement of the hymn in use, and may be found in fifty or more hymnals, as in *H. Comp.,* No. 284, and sometimes with *Cotterill's* slight alterations, as in the Rev. F. Pott's *Hymns,* &c., 1861-67.

3. A cento composed of st. i., iii. and v., given in S. P. C. K. *Hymns,* 1852, but not popular.

4. A cento, st. i., ii. and doxology in four lines, not by Newton, in the *Cooke and Denton Hymnal,* 1853.

5. A cento, in 4 st. of 4 l., beginning, "Glorious things of *old were* spoken," is given in Isaac G. Smith's *H. Bk.,* 1855-57. It is thus composed: st. i., Newton altered; ii., I. G. Smith; iii., Newton; iv., dox. from *Cooke & Denton.* This is the least successful of any arrangement.

6. The whole hymn revised by J. Keble for the *Salisbury H. Bk.,* 1857, and included therein, as No. 130, with the four-line doxology from *Denton.* This, with slight returns to the original in two places (st. i., v.), and the omission of the doxology, was repeated in the *Sarum Hymnal* (broken into two parts, pt. ii. beginning "Blessed city, holy nation), 1868; and a cento therefrom again altered, in 6 st. of 4 l. in T. Darling's *Hymns,* &c., ed. 1887. Another cento, also with alterations, is given in the *Hymnary,* from which it passed into the *New Mitre Hymnal,* 1875.

7. Cento of st. i., ii., iv., v., unaltered as in the *Bk. of Praise Hymnal,* Thring's *Coll.,* and others.

8. In the S. P. C. K. *Church Hymns,* st. i.-iv. with slight alterations in st. i., ii., and iii.

In the American collections the same diversity of use prevails as in G. Britain. Sometimes the hymn is broken into two parts, with pt. ii. beginning, "Blest inhabitants of Zion." In addition other arrangements of minor importance are given in collections of less importance; but in most cases the original text is maintained. Stanzas i., ii., v., have been rendered into Latin by the Rev. R. Bingham, and included in his *Hymno. Christ. Latina,* 1871, "Dicta de te sunt miranda."   [J. J.]

Glory and thanks to God we give. *C. Wesley.* [*Thanksgiving.*] The circumstances which gave rise to this hymn are related in C. Wesley's *Journal.* On his third visit to Leeds he met the Society on March 14, 1744,

"in an old upper room, which was densely packed, and crowds could not gain admission. He removed nearer the door that those without might hear, and drew the people towards him. Instantly the rafters broke off short, close to the main beam, the floor sank, and more than one hundred people fell, amid dust and ruins, into the room below." Several were severely injured, but none were killed. C. Wesley himself escaped with slight injuries. "I lifted up my head," he said, "and saw the people under me, heaps upon heaps. I cried out, 'Fear not, the Lord is with us; our lives are all safe,' and then gave out, 'Praise God from Whom all blessings flow'" (Stevenson's *Methodist H. Bk. Notes,* 1883, p. 68; and C. Wesley's *Journal*).

The hymn, in 12 st. of 4 l., was given in *Hys. & Sac. Poems,* 1749, vol. ii., No. 174, and headed, "After a deliverance from death by the fall of an house." In J. Wesley's corrected copy of the *Hys. & Sac. Poems,* he has changed "house" to *horse,* but Dr. Osborn (*P. Works,* 1868-72, vol. v. p. 381), adds that "on the whole, the reading of the first and second editions [*house*] seems preferable." In its original form it was unsuited for congregational use. In 1780, st. vi.-ix., xi., xii., were given in the *Wes. H. Bk.,* No. 56, as one of the hymns "Describing Judgment": "The great archangel's trump shall sound." It has passed into several collections in G. Britain and America. It forms a striking hymn for "Advent," and displays great power in word painting. [J. J.]

Glory be to God on high, God Whose glory fills the sky. *C. Wesley.* [*Holy Trinity.*] This is a paraphrase of the *Gloria in Excelsis* of the Book of Common

Prayer. The paraphrase is in J. & C. Wesley's *Hys. & Sac. Poems*, 1739, p. 128. In 1761 it was republished by J. Wesley in his *Coll. of 132 Select Hymns with Tunes Annext*, but was not added to the *Wes. H. Bk.* till sometime after his death, and probably in 1800–1, although it had long been in use in the collections of *Whitefield, Madan, Toplady*, and others. In 1820 Cotterill included an altered and abridged version of the text in his *Selection*. In this, st. i.–iii. are altered slightly, st. iv. greatly, and st. v. is new. This version, again altered, and abridged, is found in the S. P. C. K. *Ps. & Hys.*, and other collections. (Orig. text, *P. Works*, 1868–72, vol. i. p. 115.) Another hymn, beginning with the first stanza of this hymn, with the repetition of lines 1, 2, as a refrain, and the addition of 4 stanzas with the same refrain to each, was given in Beard's Manchester Unitarian *Coll.*, 1837, and repeated without the refrain in Hedge & Huntington's *Hys. for the Ch. of Christ*, Boston, U. S. A., 1853, No. 12, and also in other American collections. The additions to C. Wesley's opening stanza were by John Taylor of Norwich.   [J. J.]

Glory be to God on high! Peace on earth, &c. *J. S. B. Monsell.* [*Christmas.*] Appeared in his *Hys. of Love and Praise*, 1863, p. 23, as the second hymn for Christmas, in 4 st. of 8 l., and repeated in his *Parish Hyl.*, 1873, No. 74. It is also given in Porter's *Churchman's Hyl.*, 1876, and others. In Snepp's *Songs of G. & G.*, 1872, it begins with st. ii., "We were lost, but we are found."   [J. J.]

Glory be to God the Father. *H. Bonar.* [*Praise.*] Pub. in his *Hys. of Faith and Hope*, 3rd series, 1866, in 4 st. of 6 l., and entitled "Praise." It is included in several collections in G. Britain and America, in its original form. In the *Suppl.* to the *N. Cong.*, 1874, and that to the Bap. *Ps. & Hys.*, 1880, the stanzas are transposed, ii., iv., iii., i., and the hymn begins, "Glory be to Him Who loved us." The last stanza is sometimes used as a doxology distinct from the hymn itself.   [J. J.]

Glory to God, and praise and love. *C. Wesley.* [*Praise for Salvation.*] Written by C. Wesley on the first anniversary of the great spiritual change which he underwent on Sunday, May 21, 1738, details of which are given under that date in his *Journal*. In 1740 it was included in *Hys. and Sac. Poems*, in 18 st. of 4 l., and headed, "For the Anniversary Day of one's Conversion." (*P. Works*, 1868–72, vol. i. p. 299.) One of the first to make use of the hymn for congregational purposes was R. Conyers, who gave a cento therefrom in his *Ps. & Hys.*, 1767, beginning, "O for a thousand tongues to sing," and consisting of st. vii., ix.–xii. This was followed by other centos (all beginning with the same stanza), in the collections of *De Courcy*, 1775; *Toplady*, 1776; and many others. The most widely known cento is that by J. Wesley, in the *Wes. H. Bk.*, 1780, No. 1, in 10 st., "O for a thousand tongues to sing." This is not only the opening hymn of the *Wes. H. Bk.*, but also of most collections of the Methodist bodies in all English-speaking countries. To this cause much of its popularity may be traced. Stevenson's annotations thereon in his *Methodist H.*

Bk. Notes, 1883, are of more than usual interest. Another cento, "Look unto Christ, ye nations; own," is in the American Meth. Episco. *Hymns*, 1849.

The opening line of the cento, "O for a thousand tongues to sing," is supposed to have had its origin in an expression of Peter Böhler, the Moravian, who, when consulted by C. Wesley about praising Christ, replied, "Had I a thousand tongues, I would praise Him with them all." The well-known line, "He breaks the power of cancelled sin," has given offence to a few, from the Taylor and Jones *Ps. & Hys.*, Lond., 1777, where it read, "He breaks the power of *death and* sin," to the American *Manual of Praise*, Oberlin, Ohio, 1880, where it reads, "He breaks the power of *reigning* sin." These changes, however, are limited in their use, the original text being usually retained.   [J. J.]

Glory to God on high, Let praises fill, &c. *James Allen.* [*Praise to Jesus.*] In the *Appendix* to the *Kendal Hymn Book*, pub. with the 2nd ed., in 1761, and of which Allen was the principal editor, this hymn appeared as follows:—

> "*Worthy the Lamb.*"
> "Glory to God on high,
>   Let praises fill the sky!
>   Praise ye His name.
> Angels His name adore,
> Who all our sorrows bore,
> And saints cry evermore,
>   'Worthy the Lamb!'
>
> "All they around the throne
>   Cheerfully join in one,
>   Praising His name.
> We who have felt His blood,
> Sealing our peace with God,
> Spread His dear name abroad—
>   'Worthy the Lamb!'
>
> "To Him our hearts we raise—
>   None else shall have our praise;
>   Praise ye His name.
> Him our exalted Lord,
> By us below adored,
> We praise with one accord—
>   'Worthy the Lamb!'
>
> "If we should hold our peace,
>   Stones would cry out apace;
>   Praise ye His name!
> Love does our souls inspire
> With heavenly, pure desire,
> And sets us all on fire—
>   'Worthy the Lamb!'
>
> "Join all the human race,
>   Our Lord and God to bless;
>   Praise ye His name!
> In Him we will rejoice,
> Making a cheerful noise,
> And say with heart and voice,
>   'Worthy the Lamb!'
>
> "Though we must change our place,
>   Our souls shall never cease
>   Praising His name;
> To Him we'll tribute bring,
> Laud Him, our gracious King,
> And without ceasing sing,
>   'Worthy the Lamb.'"

The use of this hymn in various forms is very extensive in G. Britain and America. The forms of the text which are most popular, are:

1. The original in an abbreviated form, and sometimes with slight verbal alterations as in Dr. Hatfield's *Church H. Bk.*, N. Y. 1872, No. 267.
2. An altered form which appeared in Toplady's *Ps. & Hys.*, 1776, No. 186, as:—

> "Glory to God on high!
>   Let *heav'n* and earth reply,
>   'Praise ye his name!'
> Angels his *love* adore,
> Who all our sorrows bore;
> And saints cry evermore,
>   'Worthy the Lamb!'"

This text, in 4 st., was repeated in Burder's *Coll.*, 1784, No. 112; in *Williams & Boden*, 1801, where it is attributed to *Burder's Coll.*; in the Bapt. *Ps. & Hys.*, 1858–80, and many others.

3. Another version was given in Rippon's *Sel.*, 1787, No. 387, in 6 st., beginning:—

" Glory to God on high !
  Let *earth and skies reply*,
    Praise ye his name :
  His love and grace adore,
  Who all our sorrows bore ;
  Sing aloud evermore,
    Worthy the Lamb."

This version of the hymn is given in several modern collections, either abbreviated, or in full, as in Kemble's *New Church H. Bk.*, 1873, the *New Cong.*, 1859, &c.

4. In the Oxford ed. of Mercer's *Ch. Psalter & H. Bk.*, 1864, two hymns (Nos. 557–558) are given beginning respectively as :—

" Glory to God on high !
  Let earth to heaven reply
    Worthy the Lamb !
  Let mortal tongue awake," &c.

and

" Begin the glorious lay,
  The Lord is risen to-day ;
    Worthy the Lamb," &c.

These hymns are based upon J. Allen's ; the first is probably by Mercer, and the second is by E. Jackson (q.v.).

5. In the Cooke & Denton *Church Hymnal*, 1853, No. 88, it opens :—

" Jesu, our risen King,
  Glory to Thee we sing,
    Praising Thy Name :
  Thy love and grace adore,
  Which all our sorrows bore,
  Crying for evermore,
    Worthy the Lamb."

This is also based on Allen, and was repeated in *Kennedy*, 1863, in Thring's *Coll.*, 1882, as " Jesus," &c., and in others.

Other arrangements are found in modern hymn-books, but all are based on the altered texts of *Toplady* and *Rippon*. The original is ascribed to *James Allen* on the authority of his private and marked copy of the *Kendal H. Bk.*, in the possession of Mr. C. D. Hardcastle, sometime of Keighley, Yorkshire. In that copy his initials " J. A." are added in his own handwriting [s. mss.].   [J. J.]

Glory to God, the angel said. [*Christmas*.] Appeared anonymously in the 7th ed. of the Silver Street *Sunday Scholar's Companion*, 1821, No. 6, in 5 st. of 4 l. It was reprinted (without signature) in Miss D. A. Thrupp's *Hys. for the Young*, R. T. S., 4th ed., 1836, and on this ground it has been ascribed to her. Positive evidence that it was written by Miss Thrupp is wanting. It is in several modern collections for the young, including the *Church S. S. H. Bk.*, 1868. [W. T. B.]

Glory to God the Father be. *J. Mason*. [*Praise for Joy in the Holy Ghost.*] This cento as given in the *Songs for the Sanctuary*, N. Y., 1865, No. 396, is compiled from J. Mason's *Spiritual Songs ; or, Songs of Praise*, &c., 1683, and is thus composed :—St. i. and v. from Song xv., st. vi. St. ii.-iv. from Song xxiv., st. i. ii. Although comparatively unknown, it is an effect e " Song of Praise."   [J. J.]

Glory to God, Whose sovereign grace. *C. Wesley.* [*Thanksgiving for success in Special Work.*] Appeared in *Hys. & Sac. Poems*, 1740, p. 140, in 8 st. of 4 l., and Bp. Ken's Doxology ; and again in *Select Hys. with Tunes Annext*, 1761. It was written as a " Thanksgiving Hymn " for the conversion of numbers of the Kingswood colliers, and the consequent renovation of the whole neighbourhood. It was

included in the *Wes. H. Bk.*, 1780, No. 195 (*P. Works*, 1868–72, vol. i. p. 287). Its use is not extensive outside the Methodist collections.   [J. J.]

Glory to the Father give. *J. Montgomery.* [*Children praising God.*] Written for the Sheffield Sunday School Union, 1825, and first printed as a broad-sheet. In the same year it was published in his *Christian Psalmist*, No. 544, and again in his *Original Hymns*, 1853, No. 334. It was included in Bickersteth's *Christ. Psalmody*, 1833, and since then also in several collections in G. Britain and America.   [J. J.]

Glory to the glorious One. *Ephrem the Syrian.* [*Sunday.*] This hymn appeared in Dr. Bonar's *Hys. of Faith & Hope*, 2nd series, 1861, in 11 st. of 6 l., where it is given as a " Sabbath Hymn," imitated from Ephrem (the Syrian). In an altered and abbreviated form of 7 st. of 6 l., this rendering was given in the Hymnary, 1872, No. 18. A blank verse *tr.* of the original was also pub. by Dr. Burgess in his *Select Metrical Hys. & Homilies of Ephraem Syrus*, &c., 1853, p. 83. The original is in the *Parænetica* (or, " Exhortations to Penitence ") of Ephrem, xli. tom. vi. p. 499.   [J. J.]

Glory to Thee! O Lord, Who from this world of sin. *Emma Toke.* [*Holy Innocents.*] Written in 1851, and contributed anonymously to the S. P. C. K. *Hys. for Public Worship*, 1852, No. 119, in 6 st. of 4 l. Its use in G. Britain is extensive, but in America somewhat limited. Usually the text is given in full and unaltered. *H. A. & M.* is an exception in favour of 5 st., and the American *Prot. Ep. Church Hymnal*, 1872, of 4 st. A doxology is sometimes added, as in the *Salisbury H. Bk.*, 1857 ; *Chope's Hymnal*, 1864. An altered version beginning, " All praise to Thee, O Lord," was given in the *Hymnary*, 1870–2, but it has failed to gain any position. A second altered form as, " We give Thee praise, O Lord," appeared in T. Darling's *Hymns*, various editions, but this also is a failure. [J. J.]

Glory to Thee, Whose powerful word. *C. Wesley.* [*For use at sea.*] Appeared in *Hys & Sac. Poems*, 1740, in 6 st. of 4 l. and headed, " In a Storm " (*P. Works*, 1868–72, vol. i. p. 231). It is found in several American collections, both old and new, but its use in G. Britain is limited almost exclusively to *Mercer*, where it is given as " All praise to Thee, Whose powerful word."   [J. J.]

Gmelin, Sigmund Christian, was b. March 15, 1679, at Pfullingen in Württemberg. After studying at the University of Tübingen, where he graduated in 1697 and became lecturer in 1700, he was in 1705 appointed assistant pastor at Herrenberg. There he associated himself with the Separatists ; denounced the Church as worldly and as requiring a mere outward profession ; objected to infant baptism, and departed from the views of the Church on the intermediate state, on the millennial reign, and on the reconciliation of all things. For these teachings he was deposed in 1706. After living for a time at Dörtenbach, near Calw, he retired to Wittgenstein, and finally to Schwarzenau, near Berleberg. He d. Oct. 12, 1707, probably at Schwarzenau

(*Koch*, v. 5; *Allg. Deutsche Biog.*, ix. 274). The only hymn by him *tr.* into English is :—

Ach treib aus meiner Seel'. [*Watchfulness*.] Included as No. 21 in the *Anmuthiger Blumen Krantz*, 1712, in 21 st. of 6 lines, and repeated as No. 231 in the Herrnhut *G. B.*, 1735, omitting st. xx. In full as No. 1101 in Schöber's *Liedersegen*, 1769. The only *tr.* in C. U. is :—

O Thou who all things canst control, a *tr.* in L. M. of st. i.–vi., by J. Wesley, in *H. and Sac. Poems*, 1739 (*P. Works*, 1868–72, vol. i. p. 12). It was not included in the *Wes. H. Bk.*, 1780; but was given, as No. 130, in Wesley's *Pocket H. Bk.*, 1785. In England st. i., ii. were included as No. 323 in *Ps. & Hys.*, 1854 (Colonial Ch. & S. Society), and st. i., ii., v., vi., as No. 467, in Martineau's *H. of Praise & Prayer*, 1873. In America st. i., ii., iv., v., were included, as No. 146, in the *Christian Lyre*, 1830, and repeated in the Methodist Episcopal South *Coll.*, 1847; the Unitarian *Book of Hymns*, 1846; and Boardman's *Coll.*, 1861. Stanzas i.–v. were also included in the Meth. Epis. *Coll.*, 1849, and the Evang. Association *H. Bk.*, 1882: st. i., ii. in the American Unitarian *H. Bk.*, 1869: and st. i., ii., vi., with a st. from iii. 3, 4, and v. ll. 3, 4, in the Pennsylvania Luth. *Ch. Bk.*, 1868. [J. M.]

Go forward, Christian soldier. *L. Tuttiett.* [*Confirmation.*] 1st pub. in his *Counsels of a Godfather*, 1861, in 8 st. of 4 l., and based upon Exod. xiv. 15. In 1867 it was included in the *Appendix* to Morrell & How's *Ps. & Hys.*, and from that date it has gradually increased in popularity until it has become in G. Britain and in America the most widely used of the author's hymns. Orig. text in the S. P. C. K. *Church Hymns*, 1871. [J. J.]

Go forward in your course. *H. Alford.* [*St. Stephen.*] Written in 1835, and 1st pub. in his *Hys. for the Sundays and Festivals throughout the Year*, 1836, in 7 st. of 4 l. (see his *Life*). In 1844 it was included in his *Ps. & Hys.*, and in 1867, in his *Year of Praise*. In its full, or in an abbreviated form, it is given in numerous hymnals in G. Britain, New Zealand, and America. [J. J.]

Go, labour on, spend and be spent. *H. Bonar.* [*Missions.*] "Written in 1843, and printed at Kelso in a small booklet of three or four hymns." In 1843 it was included in Dr. Bonar's *Songs for the Wilderness*, in 8 st. of 4 l., and entitled "Labour for Christ." In 1857 it was repeated in his *Hys. of Faith & Hope*, 1st series, in 8 st. of 4 l., and entitled "The Useful Life," with the motto "Ψυχή μου ... μου ... Ἀνάστα, τί καθεύδεις," from *Daniel*, iii. p. 128. Previous to this, however, it had been brought into C. U. through the *Leeds H. Bk.*, 1853, No. 604. In the *Suppl.* to the *New Cong.*, 1869, No. 1157, it is divided into two parts, Pt. ii. being st. v.–viii., "Go, labour on while it is day." This arrangement is also found in other collections, sometimes as, "Go, labour on while yet *'tis* day." This second part is in somewhat extensive use in America as a separate hymn. In the American *Sabbath H. Bk.*, 1858, No. 879, st. iv., vi.–viii. are given as, "Go, labour on; *your hands are weak*"; and, in *Holy Song*, 1869, No. 535, st. i., ii., vii., and viii., very much altered, as, "Go

forth to toil; to spend, be spent." This last arrangement is too wretched to be associated with Dr. Bonar's name. [J. J.]

Go, messenger of peace and love. *A. Balfour.* [*Departure of a Missionary.*] This hymn appeared in the Bapt. *New Selection*, 1828, No. 361, in 10 st. of 4 l., with the signature of "Balfour." In the revised and enlarged ed., 1838, it retained the same signature, but in the Bapt. *Ps. & Hys.*, revised ed., 1871 and 1880, it was reduced to 6 st. and the signature was expanded into "Alexander Balfour, 1828." Beyond this no definite information has been obtained. Its use is limited. [J. J.]

Go not far from me, O my [God] Strength. *Anna L. Waring.* [*Resignation.*] Appeared in her *Hys. & Meditations*, 4th ed., 1854, in 14 st. of 6 l., and based upon Ps. xlii. 7, 8 (10th ed. 1871, No. 26). Various centos, mostly beginning with st. i., are in C. U. in G. Britain and America. The opening line in Martineau's *Hys. of Praise and Prayer*, 1873, is, "Go not far from me, O my *God*." In *Kennedy*, 1863, No. 294, the cento begins with st. vii., "How blessed are the eyes that see."
[J. J.]

Go to dark Gethsemane. *J. Montgomery.* [*Passiontide.*] Of this popular hymn there are two texts, differing widely from each other, and both by Montgomery. The *first* appeared in Cotterill's *Selection*, 1820, and subsequent editions. It reads thus :—

" The last sufferings of Christ.

1. "Go to dark Gethsemane,
 Ye that feel the tempter's power;
 Your Redeemer's conflict see;
  Watch with Him one bitter hour :
 Turn not from His griefs away;
 Learn from Him to watch and pray.

2. "See Him at the judgment-hall,
 Beaten, bound, reviled, arraign'd :
 See Him meekly bearing all!
  Love to man His soul sustain'd !
 Shun not suffering, shame or loss ;
 Learn of Christ to bear the cross.

3. "Calvary's mournful mountain view;
 There the Lord of Glory see,
 Made a sacrifice for you,
  Dying on the accursed tree :
 'It is finish'd,' hear Him cry :
 Trust in Christ, and learn to die.

4. "Early to the tomb repair,
 Where they laid his breathless clay ;
 Angels kept their vigils there:
  Who hath taken Him away ?
 'Christ is risen !' He seeks the skies ;
 Saviour ! teach us so to rise."

In 1825, Montgomery included this hymn in its *second* and revised form in his *Christian Psalmist*, No. 491, as follows :—

" Christ our example in suffering.

1. "Go to dark Gethsemane,
 Ye that feel the tempter's power
 Your Redeemer's conflict see,
  Watch with Him one bitter hour ;
 Turn not from his griefs away,
 Learn *of Jesus Christ* to pray.

2. "*Follow* to the judgment-hall,
 View the Lord of life arraign'd ;
 O the wormwood and the gall !
  O the pangs his soul sustain'd !
 Shun not suffering, shame, or loss,
 Learn *of Him* to bear the cross.

3. "Calvary's mournful mountain *climb ;*
 There adoring at his feet,
 Mark that miracle of Time,
  —God's own sacrifice complete :
 'It is finish'd ;'—hear *their* cry ;
 Learn *of Jesus Christ* to die.

4. "Early *hasten to the tomb*,
    Where they laid his breathless clay;
    All is solitude and gloom,
    —Who hath taken Him away?
    Christ is risen :—He *meets our eyes*;
    Saviour, teach us so to rise."

[In Montgomery's marked copy of the 1st ed., st. iii.,
l. 5, reads "hear their cry." In the margin he altered
it in MS. to "hear *Him* cry:" and this reading was given
in later editions. In his *Original Hymns*, 1853, it reads,
"hear *the* cry."]

From the year 1825 the original and this revised text have passed on, side by side, unto
the present date, one editor copying from Cotterill's *Selection*, and another from Montgomery's *Christian Psalmist*, until, of the
hymnals now in C. U., of those which have
adopted the hymn, about one-third have the
original text of 1820, and, with a few exceptions, yet to be noted, the remaining two-thirds
have the text of 1825. Amongst those adopting the original text are many of the Public
School collections, as *Rugby*, *Harrow*, *Marlborough*, &c., and also *Mercer*, *Kennedy*, *Pott*,
The Anglican H. Bk., *Barry*, *Church Hys.*, &c.,
sometimes with abbreviations and very slight
alterations. Those following the revised form
of 1825, include *H. A. & M.*, *Hy. Comp.*,
Thring's *Coll.*, *Snepp*, *Alford*, S. P. C. K. *Ps. &
Hys.*, and others, and also most of the collections of the Nonconformists. In America,
where it is in extensive use, the text usually
adopted is that of 1825. In many cases it
must be noted that st. iv., "Early hasten to
the tomb," is omitted. Another form in three
stanzas was given in Hall's *Mitre Hymn-book*,
1836. This is repeated in the *New Mitre
Hymnal*, 1875, but is seldom if ever found
elsewhere.

It will be seen from the foregoing that Mr.
Ellerton's somewhat elaborate note in the S. P.
C. K. *Church Hymns*, folio ed. p. lxvi., is based
on an error, in concluding that the text in
Church Hys. was altered by an unknown hand
from Montgomery's *Christian Psalmist*, 1825,
whereas it is Montgomery's text of 1820, with
two very slight alterations only. Orig. text
as above; author's revised and authorized text
in his *Original Hymns*, 1853.   [J. J.]

**Go to the grave in all thy glorious
pride [prime].** *J. Montgomery.* [*Burial.*]
Written in February, 1823, on the death of
the Rev. John Owen, for some years a Secretary of the British and Foreign Bible Society,
who died at the close of 1822. In the issue of
the Sheffield *Iris* for Dec. 21, 1824, it is given
with the following note :—

"These lines were written nearly two years ago, at
the request of a friend, and were not then designed for
general circulation. This month, however, they have
appeared in a popular periodical work by consent of the
author. The circumstance is only mentioned to account
for their late and perhaps unsuitable publication here."

The "popular periodical work" in which it
appeared was the *Christian Observer*, Dec.,
1824. In 1825 Montgomery included it, with
the alteration of "glorious pride" to "glorious
prime," in his *Christian Psalmist*, No. 533, in
6 st. of 4 l., with the heading, "On the death
of a Minister cut off in his usefulness." It was
repeated in his *Original Hys.*, 1853. On May
11, 1854, st. iii.-vi. (st. i., ii. being omitted as
unsuitable) were sung at Montgomery's funeral,
to the tune "Brading," by Dr. Callcott, "arranged by W. H. Callcott." One of the first

to bring this hymn into C. U. was Dr. Martineau, in his *Hymns*, &c., 1840. Its use in
America is more extensive than in G. Britain.
                                          [J. J.]

Goadby, Frederic William, M.A., s.
of the Rev. Joseph Goadby, General Baptist
Minister, was b. at Leicester, Aug. 10, 1845,
and educated for the Baptist Ministry at
Regent's Park College. He also graduated
M.A. at the London University in 1868. In
1868 he became pastor of the Baptist Church
at Bluntisham, Hunts, and, in 1876, of that at
Watford, where, after a brief ministry of great
promise, he d. Oct. 15, 1880. Besides contributing to periodical literature, Mr. Goadby
wrote the following hymns :—

1. A crowd fills the court of the temple. *Palm
Sunday.*
2. O Lord, the children come to Thee. *A Child's
Prayer.*
3. O Thou, Whose hand has brought us. *Opening
of a Place of Worship.*

Of these hymns Nos. 1, 2, are in a few
collections, including Stevenson's *School Hymnal*, 1880, and No. 3 in the *Baptist Hymnal*,
1879.   [W. R. S.]

Goadby, Thomas, an elder brother of
the preceding, was b. at Leicester, Dec. 23,
1829. He studied for the ministry at the
Baptist College, Leicester, and at Glasgow
University, where he graduated B.A. in 1856;
was successively pastor of Baptist churches
in Coventry, London, and Derby. In 1873 he
was appointed President of Chilwell College,
now the "Nottingham Baptist College." Mr.
Goadby has contributed many papers to newspapers, reviews, and other periodicals, and has
pub. several sermons and addresses delivered
on public occasions from 1860 to 1881. In
1884 he pub. *Revelation, its Nature and Record*,
translated from the German of Ewald. His
compositions in verse are a short poem,
entitled *The Day of Death*, 1863, and hymns,
chiefly prepared for anniversary occasions.
Nine of these are in Stevenson's *School Hymnal*,
London, 1880. The most widely known is
"When the day of life is dawning, come, come
to Me." No. 140 is a fine centenary hymn,
"O God, who art through all the years, for evermore." No. 311, "Forward, Gospel heralds,"
is a stirring missionary hymn, its refrain being
evidently suggested by Dean Alford's well-
known verses, "Forward be our watchword."
The 9 hymns and their subjects are :—

1. A band of maiden pilgrims. *S. S. Anniversary.*
2. Forward, gospel heralds. *Missions.*
3. God of the earth and sky. *Evening.*
4. Morn awakes, and woodlands sing. *Morning.*
5. O God, Who art through all the years. *Praise to
the Father.*
6. O Thou, Whose holy love. *Prayer for Guidance.*
7. Prince of life, enthroned in glory. *Praise to Jesus.*
8. Shepherd of Israel, Jesus our Saviour. *The Good
Shepherd.*
9. When the day of life is dawning. *Invitation by
Christ.*   [W. R. S.]

God and Father, great and holy. *F.
W. Farrar.* [*God is Love.*] Written in 1856,
and included in the *Savoy Hymnary* (Chapel
Royal), about 1869, in 3 st. of 8 l., from whence
it has passed into various collections, including
the *Westminster Abbey H. Bk.*, 1883, and
others. In the American Unitarian *Hys. of
the Spirit*, 1864, it begins, "*Lord* and Father,
great and holy."   [J. J]

God hath two families of love. *J. M. Neale.* [*Evening.*] 1st pub. as an "Evening Hymn" in his *Hys. for Children*, 1st series, 1842, No. xiv., in 7 st. of 4 l., the doxology being Bishop Ken's "Praise God from whom," &c. The form in which it appeared in the S. P. C. K. *Church Hys.* has been adopted for "the correction of the popular error that the faithful departed are now reigning in heaven" (Ellerton's Notes on *Ch. Hys.*, 1881). The alterations made on this account in the *Church Hys.* text are so many and important that practically, both in form and in doctrine, it is almost a new hymn. Most of these changes are due to the compilers of that collection. The original is also in C. U. in G. Britain and America. [J. J.]

God in heaven His glory hides. *J. Gabb.* [*Praise in heaven and earth.*] 1st pub. in his *Steps to the Throne*, &c., 1864, in 5 st. of 4 l., and entitled, "Grace and Glory." In its original form it is unknown to the hymnals in common use, but it has been rewritten by the author in two forms:—(1) "God His perfect glory hides," given in his *Hys. and Songs*, &c., 1871, p. 105, and repeated in the *English Sacred Songster*, 1873. (2) "God in heaven his glory hides," in his *Welburn Appendix*, 1875, No. 106, to the author's tune, "Trentham." [J. J.]

God in His temple let us meet. *J. Montgomery.* [*Ps. cxxxii.*] Appeared in Cotterill's *Selection*, 1819, p. 74, in 4 st. of 8 l. In the revised ed. of 1820, lines 1–12 were given instead of the full text of the previous ed., thus making a hymn in 3 st. of 4 l. This was repeated in Montgomery's *Songs of Zion*, 1822, as No. 1 of Ps. 132, and the rest of the Cotterill text of 1819 as No. 2, beginning, "Lord, for Thy servant David's sake." Pt. i. was also included in his *Original Hymns*, 1853, No. 101. Both parts are in C. U. as separate hymns, but the first is found in the greater number of hymn-books. [J. J.]

God, in the Gospel of His Son. *B. Beddome.* [*The Gospels.*] Appeared in Rippon's Bap. *Sel.*, 1787, No. 54, in 6 st. of 4 l., and headed, "The Gospel of Christ." It was also included in Robert Hall's posthumous edition of Beddome's *Hymns*, 1817. Its use, especially in America, is very extensive, but sometimes in an abbreviated form. [J. J.]

God is a [the] Name my soul adores. *I. Watts.* [*God the Creator.*] Appeared in his *Horæ Lyricæ*, 1706, in 8 st. of 4 l., and entitled, "The Creator and Creatures." It is also in Watts's *Works* of various dates. Two or three centos from this hymn are in C. U., all commencing with st. i., one of the earliest of which is that in Toplady's *Ps. & Hys.*, 1776, No. 170. Dr. Martineau's cento in his *Hymns*, &c., 1840, and *Hys. of Praise & Prayer*, 1873, is composed of st. i., iii., iv., vii., viii. In some of the American collections the opening line begins, "God is *the* Name," &c., as in the *Plymouth Coll.*, 1855, and others. [J. J.]

God is gone up with a merry noise. *Bp. R. Heber.* [*Ascension.*] Pub. in his posthumous *Hymns*, &c., 1827, in 4 st. of 4 l., as the second of three hymns for Easter Day, Its appropriateness to Ascension-tide, rather than Easter-day, has led to its adoption, in some cases, for the Ascension. It is one of the least known of Heber's hymns, and is only adopted by *Kennedy* and a few others. [J. J.]

God is in His holy temple, All the earth, &c. *J. Montgomery.* [*Public Worship.*] Dated "Sheffield, Dec. 24, 1833" [M. MSS.], and pub. in his *Original Hymns*, 1853, No. 107, in 4 st. of 6 l., and headed, "For the great Congregation." In Dr. Hatfield's *Church H. Bk.*, N. Y., 1872, it is reduced to 3 st., and in the *Songs for the Sanctuary*, N. Y., 1865-72, to 2 st. In Clapham's *Leeds S. S. H. Bk.*, 1858 and 1878, it is somewhat freely altered, and is signed "G. R.," i.e. *George Rawson*, in error. [J. J.]

God is King; the nations quiver. *J. Keble.* [*Ps. xcix.*] 1st pub. in his *Psalter; or Ps. of David*, &c., 1839, in 6 st. of 6 l., and repeated in later editions. Its use is mainly confined to the hymn-books of the English public schools, although it is a lyric of high rank. It is well suited as a Processional Hymn for choral festivals, the meetings of guilds, and other services of a like kind. [J. J.]

God is love, His mercy brightens. *Sir J. Bowring.* [*The Love of God.*] This hymn is sometimes attributed in error to his *Matins and Vespers*, 1823. It actually appeared in his *Hymns* in 1825, in 5 st. of 4 l., st. i. being repeated as st. v. In 1853 it was given without the repetition of the first stanza, in the *Leeds H. Bk.*, from whence it passed into numerous collections. Its use in English-speaking countries is very extensive, and it has become one of the most popular of the author's hymns. Orig. text, Thring's *Coll.*, No. 292, with "the mist," altered to "the gloom," and the omission of the repetition of st. v. This is the generally accepted form of the hymn. [J. J.]

God is love; that anthem olden. *J. S. B. Monsell.* [*God is Love.*] A poem for the 1st S. after Trinity, appeared in his *Spiritual Songs*, 1856 and 1857, in 6 st. of 6 l. A second form of the text in 4 st., beginning, "God is love: *the heavens tell it*," was included in the Rev. F. Pott's *Hymns*, &c., 1861, No. 209. These stanzas, with a return to the original text save "Our" for "Their" in st. iv., l. 5, are found in the S. P. C. K. *Church Hys.*, No. 372, Thring's *Coll.*, and several others. The complete text of 1856–57 was repeated by Dr. Monsell in his *Parish Hymnal*, 1873. During his last illness the hymn was revised by the author for the people's ed. of his *Spiritual Songs*. The opening lines read:—

"God is Love: by Him upholden,
Hang the glorious orbs of light."

This form of the hymn is in Horder's *Cong. Hymns*, 1884, and others. In the notes to *Ch. Hymns*, fol. ed., 1881, it is regarded as the original text in error. [J. J.]

God is our Refuge and our Strength. *H. Alford.* [*Ps. xlvi.*] 1st pub. in the *British Magazine*, Dec., 1832, in 7 st. of 4 l., and signed +. In 1833 it was reprinted in his anonymous *Poems and Poetical Fragments.* When given in his *Ps. & Hys.*, 1844, p. 75, st. iv.-vi. were omitted. The text of the *Hys.*

of the Spirit, Boston, U. S. A., 1864, No. 310, is from the original.   [W. T. B.]

God is our Refuge, ever near. *J. Conder.* [*Ps. xlvi.*] Appeared in his *Cong. H. Bk.*, 1836, No. 403, in 2 st. of 7 l. When repeated in his work, *The Choir and The Oratory,* in the following year (Preface, Nov. 8, 1836), 16 lines were added thereto, but in another metre. These lines were omitted in his *Hys. of Praise, Prayer,* &c., 1856, p. 14, and also from all modern hymnals. Orig. text in *New Cong.*, 1859, No. 64.   [J. J.]

God is the Refuge of His saints. *I. Watts.* [*Ps. xlvi.*] Appeared in his *Ps. of David,* &c., 1719, in 6 st. of 4 l. and headed, "The Church's Safety and Triumph among National Desolations." It has passed in full, or in an abbreviated form, into numerous collections in all English-speaking countries. In the Unitarian *Hymn* [*& Tune*] *Bk.*, Boston, U.S.A., 1868, st. v., vi., are given as No. 345, "There is a stream, whose gentle flow." [J. J.]

God made all His creatures free. *J. Montgomery.* [*Freedom.*] This hymn is No. iv. of his "Songs on the Abolition of Negro Slavery," in the British Colonies, Aug. 1, 1834." It is in 6 st. of 4 l., and entitled, "Slavery that is not." These "Songs" were pub. in his *Poet's Portfolio,* 1835. As given in Longfellow and Johnson's Unitarian *Bk. of Hymns,* 1848, and other American collections, it is composed of st. i., ii., v., vi., slightly altered. It is not in C. U. in G. Britain.   [J. J.]

God moves in a mysterious way. *W. Cowper.* [*Providence.*] The commonly accepted history of this hymn is that it was composed by Cowper in 1773, after an attempt to commit suicide by drowning in the Ouse at Olney. In the *Memoirs* of Cowper by Hayley, and by Southey, as also in that of J. Newton, by Bull, there are painful details of his insanity in 1773. In Southey there is a distinct statement to the effect that his mania was suicidal, and that he made an attempt upon his life in October, 1773. Southey says (1853, vol. i. p. 174):—

"In the new character which his delirium had assumed [that it was the will of God that he should put an end to his life] the same perfect spirit of submission was manifested. Mr. Newton says 'Even that attempt he made in October was a proof of it; for it was solely owing to the power the enemy had of impressing upon his disturbed imagination that it was the will of God he should, after the example of Abraham, perform an expensive act of obedience, and offer, not a son, but himself.'" (May 26, 1774.)

This is conclusive as to the intended suicide; but there is no indication in the *Memoirs* that after his attack he wrote anything whatever until about April, 1774. Of this period Southey says:—

"His mind, though possessed by its fatal delusion, had recovered in some degree its activity, and in some of his most melancholy moments he used to compose lines descriptive of his own unhappy state." (1853, vol. i. p. 177.)

To our mind it is evident that Cowper must have written this hymn, either early in 1773, before his insanity became so intense as to lead him to attempt suicide in the October of that year, or else in April of 1774, when "he used to compose lines descriptive of his own unhappy state." Of these dates the latter is the more probable of the two, but neither will

agree with the popular account of the origin of the hymn. Its publication agrees with this date, as it appeared in J. Newton's *Twenty-six Letters on Religious Subjects; to which are added Hymns, &c.,* by *Omicron,* London, 1774. The actual date is fixed by Newton. He says:—

"Thursday, July 6th [1774]. *Omicron's Letters* are now published. May the Lord accompany them with His blessing. In reading them I could not but observe how different I appear on paper from what I know myself to be," &c.

In *Omicron's Letters* it is in 6 st. of 4 l., is entitled "Light shining out of Darkness," and is unsigned. It also appeared in the July number of the *Gospel Magazine* for 1774 (p. 307), in the same form and with the same title; but in this instance it is signed "J. W." We find it also in R. Conyers's *Coll. of Ps. & Hymns* of the same year, in the same form and with the same title, but without signature. It appears again in the *Gospel Magazine,* Dec., 1777, p. 555, at the end of a letter "On Affliction." This letter is unsigned. At the close of the hymn these words are added:—

"By Miss Ussington, late of Islington, who died in May, 1776. Taken from the original."

In this case the st. ii. is omitted; the eight lines of st. iii. and iv. are rearranged; a slight change is made in st. vi., and the following is added:—

"When midnight shades are all withdrawn
The opening day shall rise,
Whose ever calm and cloudless morn
Shall know no low'ring skies."

This uncertainty about the authorship of the hymn was set at rest in 1779, when J. Newton gave the original text and title from *Omicron's Letters* in the *Olney Hymns,* Bk. iii., No. 15, and signed it "C." From the first it gradually grew in importance and interest, until it has become one of the most widely known hymns in English-speaking countries. It has also been translated into several languages, including Latin, by R. Bingham in his *Hymno. Christi. Lati.,* 1871, as "Secretis miranda viis opera numen"; and Dr. Macgill in his *Songs of the Christian Creed and Life,* 1876, as, "Deus mundum, en, molitur." Montgomery's estimate of this hymn is very high. He says of it, "It is a lyric of high tone and character, and rendered awfully interesting by the circumstances under which it was written — in the twilight of departing reason" (*The Christian Poet,* 1825, Preface). Montgomery evidently thought the hymn was composed *before* the sad breakdown of 1773.
    [J. J.]

God of all consolation, take. *C. Wesley.* [*Parting of Friends.*] This is the last of his *Hys. for those that Seek, and those that Have Redemption,* &c., 1747, No. lii., in 8 double st. of 4 l. (*P. Works,* 1868–72, vol. iv. p. 280). In 1780, a cento in 12 st. beginning with st. i. was given in the *Wes. H. Bk.,* as No. 523 (new ed. 1875, 537), and has been repeated in most of the Methodist collections. Several interesting "associations" of this hymn are given in Stevenson's *Meth. H. Bk. Notes,* 1883. In Cotterill's *Sel.,* 6th ed., 1815, and subsequent editions, the hymn:—

"Not unto us, but Thee, O Lord!
Be praise and glory given," &c.,

appeared in 4 st. of 4 l., and headed, "The Saints kept by the power of God." From

Cotterill's *Sel.*, it passed into Bp. Bickersteth's *Ps. & Hys.*, 1858; the Islington *Ps. & Hys.*; the *Hy. Comp.*, and others. In *Kennedy*, 1863, it begins, "Not unto us, *to* Thee, O Lord." This cento is usually ascribed to "*J. Cennick and T. Cotterill*"; as in Miller's *Singers and Songs*, &c., 1869, p. 362, and the *Hy. Comp.* Notes. This error has arisen out of the similarity of the first line to J. Cennick's hymn :—

"Not unto us but Thee *alone*,
Bless'd Lamb, be glory given," &c.

The cento is based upon st. i., vi.–viii. of C. Wesley's hymn. The alterations by Cotterill are so numerous as almost to constitute a new hymn. Its correct ascription is, "*C. Wesley*, 1747; *T. Cotterill*, 1815." [W. T. B.]

God of all power, and truth, and grace. *C. Wesley.* [*Holiness desired.*] Pub. in *Hys. & Sac. Poems*, 1742, in 28 st. of 4 l., based on Ezekiel xxxvi. 13, &c., and headed, "Pleading the Promise of Sanctification" (*P. Works*, 1868–72, vol. ii. p. 319). It was also appended to J. Wesley's Sermon No. 40, and to J. Fletcher's *Last Check to Antinomianism.* It deals with the doctrine of Sanctification from the Methodist point of view. From the 1742 text the following centos have come into C. U. :—

1. **God of all power, and truth, and grace.** In the *Wes. H. Bk.*, 1780, No. 330, and later editions, is composed of st. i., iii., vi.–ix. and xiv. This was given in Hall's *Mitre H. Bk.*, 1836, No. 211, in an abbreviated form, as "O Thou, Whose mercy, truth, and love." This arrangement was by E. Osler, and is a distinct hymn from Osler's "O God, Whose mercy, truth, and love," which appeared in his *Church and King*, March, 1837, although in the latter he has borrowed a line or two from the former. [HALL MSS.]

2. **Father, supply my every need.** In the *Wes. H. Bk.*, 1780, No. 380, Pt. ii. is composed of st. xix.–xxii. It is also in other collections.

3. **Holy, and true, and righteous Lord.** In the *Wes. H. Bk.*, 1780, No. 381 is composed of sts. xxiii., xxvi.–xxviii. This is also in other collections.

All of these centos are in C. U. in G. Britain and America. [J. J.]

God of all-redeeming grace. *C. Wesley.* [*Holy Communion.*] No. 139 of his *Hys. on the Lord's Supper*, 1745, in 4 st. of 4 l. In 1760 it was given in Madan's *Ps. & Hys.*, No. 162, and later in other collections of the Church of England. It was also in the *Wes. H. Bk.*, 1780, No. 415, and later editions, and in a few collections in G. Britain and America. In the original st. iii. it reads, "Just it is, and good, and right"; but in the *Wes. H. Bk.*, J. Wesley changed it to "*Meet* it is, and just and right," thereby bringing it into harmony with the *Bk. of Common Prayer*, "It is very *meet*, right, and our bounden duty," &c. [J. J.]

God of almighty love. *C. Wesley.* [*Consecration to God.*] Appeared in *Hys. & Sac. Poems*, 1749, vol. i., No. 149, in 3 st. of 8 l., and entitled, "An hourly act of Oblation." In 1780 it was given with alterations in the *Wes. H. Bk.* as No. 314, and repeated in several collections in G. Britain and America. The cento, "Father, my lifted eye," in *Hys. for the Church of Christ*, Boston, U.S.A., 1853, is compiled with alterations from st. ii., iii., of this hymn. [J. J.]

God of eternal love. *I. Watts.* [*Ps. cvi.; God's love to Israel.*] 1st pub. in his

Ps. of David, &c., 1719, in 6 st. of 4 l., and entitled, "Israel punish'd and pardon'd; or, God's unchanging love." In a note he says :—

"The chief design of this whole Psalm I have expressed in the Title, and abridged it in this form, having enlarged much more on this same subject in the 77th, 78th, and 105th Psalms.

"Though the Jews now seem to be cast off, yet the Apostle Paul assures us that 'God hath not cast away His people whom He foreknew,' Rom. xi. 2. Their unbelief and absence from God is but for a season, for they shall be recalled again; v. 25, 26."

The use of this hymn is not extensive. Original text in Spurgeon's *O. O. H. Bk.*, 1866. [J. J.]

God of eternal truth and grace. *C. Wesley.* [*Perfect Love.*] This cento is thus composed :—

St. i.–ii., *Short Hymns*, &c., vol. ii., No. 1376, Mich. vii. 20. St. iii.–iv., *Short Hymns*, &c., vol. ii., No. 174, Matt. xv. 28. St. v.–vi., *Short Hymns*, &c., vol. ii., No. 297, Mark ix. 23.

These *Short Hymns*, &c., were pub. at Bristol, 1762 (*P. Works*, 1868–72, vol. x.). This cento was included in the *Wes. H. Bk.*, 1780, No. 333, and is found in other collections. [J. J.]

God of glory, God of grace, Hear from heaven, &c. [*Holy Trinity.*] This popular and widely used hymn for children has been traced to Murch's *Sabbath Scholar's H. Bk.*, 1849, where it is given anonymously. It passed into Dr. Rule's *Methodist S. S. H. Bk.*, 1857, and numerous collections of later date, including the *Meth. S. S. H. Bk.*, 1879, No. 6, q.v. orig. text; the *Scottish Pres. Hymnal for the Young*, 1882, No. 2, and many others. [W. T. B.]

God of grace, O let Thy light. *E. Churton.* [*Ps. lxvii.*] Written in 1854, and pub. in the same year in his *Cleveland Psalter*, in 7 st. of 4 l. In 1861 it was given unaltered in *H. A. & M.*, and repeated in the revised ed. 1875. It is also in the *Hymnary*, 1872, and other English collections, and a few of the American hymn-books. It is a favourite specimen of the author's style (see **Psalters, English,** § xix.). [J. J.]

God of Israel's faithful three. *C. Wesley.* [*Three Hebrew Children.*] Appeared in the *Hys. & Sac. Poems*, 1742, p. 213, in 5 st. of 8 l., with the title, "The Three Children in the Fiery Furnace" (*P. Works*, 1868–72, vol. ii. p. 267). In 1780 it was given with slight alterations and the omission of st. ii. in the *Wes. H. Bk.*, No. 349, and this arrangement has been repeated in several Methodist collections. In the revised *Wes. H. Bk.*, 1875, No. 359, st. i.–iii. only are given, whilst the American Meth. Episco. *Hymnal*, 1878, No. 677, has st. i., iii. [J. J.]

God of life, and light, and motion. *F. Oakeley.* [*Holy Trinity.*] Pub. in his *Lyra Liturgica*, &c., 1865, p. 145, in 14 st. of 4 l. In the *Hymnary*, 1872, No. 340, it appears as a hymn of 4 st. of 12 l., and the same text is repeated in the *Altar Hymnal*, 1884, No. 47. This arrangement is attained by omitting st. iv.–vi., and adding one of 4 lines at the close. The text in Hall & Lasar's *Evang. Hymnal*, N. Y., 1880, in 2 st. of 12 l., is from the *Hymnary*. In one or two collections the latter part of the hymn is given, beginning with st. x. as, "God the Father, Son and Spirit." [J. J.]

God of love, that [Who] hear'st the prayer. *C. Wesley.* [*None but Jesus.*] Pub. in *Hys. for those that Seek, and those that Have Redemption,* &c., 1747, p. 19, in 6 st. of 8 l. (*P. Works,* 1868–72, vol. iv. p. 228). The form in which it is known in modern collections was given in the *Wes. H. Bk.,* 1780, No. 494, in 8 st. of 4 l. In the American hymn-books it begins, "God of love, *Who* hear'st the prayer."   [J. J.]

God of mercy, God of grace, Shew the brightness of Thy face. *H. F. Lyte.* [*Ps. lxvii.*] 1st pub. in his *Spirit of the Psalms,* 1834, in 3 st. of 6 l. as his 2nd version of Ps. lxvii., and again in later eds. of the same. It is in most extensive use in all English-speaking countries, and usually the original text is given unaltered as in Thring's *Coll.,* 1882.   [J. J.]

God of my life, through all its [my] days. *P. Doddridge.* [*Praise for unfailing mercies.*] This hymn is dated in the Bapt. *Ps. & Hys.,* revised ed. 1871 and 1880, "1751," the year of Doddridge's death, but upon what authority it is not stated. Miller (*Singers and Songs,* 1869, p. 172) evidently took this date as the foundation of his note which reads :—

"This hymn may be read autobiographically, especially verse 3, in reference to the peaceful thankfulness in his heart when the last wave of his life was ebbing out at Lisbon. The words are :—

'When death o'er nature shall prevail,
And all its powers of language fail,
Joy through my swimming eyes shall break,
And mean the thanks I cannot speak.'"

No evidence beyond these unauthorised statements is forthcoming to show that this was the author's death-bed hymn, as this date, and Miller's note would imply. It was pub. in Doddridge's (posthumous) *Hymns,* &c., by J. Orton, 1755, No. 71, in 6 st. of 4 l., and headed, "Praising God through the whole of our existence, Psalm cxlvi. 2." In 1839 it was reprinted by J. D. Humphreys in his ed. of Doddridge's *Hymns,* &c., and accompanied by the following note :—

"It is interesting to remember, that, when pressed down by the hand of disease and tottering on the brink of eternity, the pious author of this hymn realized the divine consolations its perusal may inspire," p. 61.

This note seems to imply that the hymn was written before the author's illness at Lisbon, in 1751, and probably the date of 1740, given to it by Dr. Hatfield in his *Church H. Bk.,* N. Y., 1872, No. 182, is correct. In a few collections it is given as "God of my life, through all *my* days." Its use in all English-speaking countries is extensive.   [J. J.]

God of my life, Thy boundless grace. *Charlotte Elliott.* [*Resignation.*] Contributed to the 2nd ed. of the *Invalid's H. Bk.,* 1841, in 4 st. of 4 l., and based upon Ps. xxxi. 5, "Into Thine hand I commit my spirit; Thou hast redeemed me, O Lord God of truth." In the American hymn-books the last line of each stanza is often altered to suit the hymn to various tunes. In the *Songs for the Sanctuary,* 1865, st. i. l. 4 is, "Father, I come, I come to Thee"; in *Laudes Domini,* 1884, "I come to Thee." The remaining stanzas undergo similar changes. Orig. text in the Stryker and Main *Church Praise Bk.,* N. Y., 1882, where the line reads, "Father! I come to Thee." [J. J.]

God of my life, Thy constant care.

P. Doddridge. [*New Year.*] 1st pub. in his (posthumous) *Hymns,* &c., 1755, No. 134, in 6 st. of 4 l., and headed, "The possibility of dying this Year, Jerem. xxviii. 16; For New Year's Day." In 1839 it was republished, with slight variations in the text, in J. D. Humphreys's ed. of the *Hymns,* &c., No. 152. In Dr. Dale's *English H. Bk.,* 1874, No. 1174, st. i., iv.–vi., and in *Common Praise,* 1879, No. 325, st. i., iii., v., are given in each case as "God of *our* life, Thy constant care." An arrangement of st. ii.–v. also appeared in Cotterill's *Sel.,* 1810, and later editions, as, "How many kindred souls are fled." This is repeated in a few modern collections. [J. J.]

God of my life, to Thee I call. *W. Cowper.* [*Divine aid implored.*] Pub. in the *Olney Hymns,* 1779, Bk. iii., No. 19, in 6 st. of 4 l., headed, "Looking upwards in a storm," and signed "C." In the American Presb. *Ps. and Hys. for the Worship of God,* Richmond, 1867, No. 373, st. ii.–iv., are given as, "Friend of the friendless and the faint"; but ascribed to "Newton," in error. In the *Church Praise Bk.,* N. Y., 1882, the same arrangement, with the addition of st. vi., is given as No. 467. The S. P. C. K. *Hymns,* 1852, "God of our life, to Thee we call," is composed of st. i., ii., of this hymn, somewhat altered, and a third stanza from another source. In the *Anglican H. Bk.,* 1868, this hymn is again altered to, "My God, my Life, to Thee I call." [J. J.]

God of my life, to Thee, My cheerful soul, &c. *C. Wesley.* [*Birthday Hymn.*] No. 10 of his "Hys. for Believers," given in *Hys. & Sac. Poems,* 1749, vol. i., No. 123, in 8 st. of 6 l., and again in the *Wes. H. Bk.,* 1780, No. 219, with the omission of st. v. In the revised ed. of 1875, No. 229, the original stanzas are given in this order, i., ii., iv., iii., vi., viii., thus making a hymn of 6 st. The last stanza contains the lines :—

"Like Moses to Thyself convey,
And kiss my raptured soul away."

These lines are based upon the Jewish tradition that God drew the soul of Moses from the body by a kiss. Watts has the same idea in his poem on the death of Moses :—

"Softly his fainting head he lay
Upon his Maker's breast;
His Maker kissed his soul away,
And laid his flesh to rest."

(See *Horæ Lyricæ,* 1706.) C. Wesley's orig. text is in *P. Works,* 1868–72, vol. v. p. 15.   [J. J.]

God of my life, Whose gracious power. *C. Wesley.* [*Lent—In Temptation.*] 1st pub. in *Hys. & Sac. Poems,* 1740, in 15 st. of 4 l., and headed, "At the Approach of Temptation" (*P. Works,* 1868–72, vol. i. p. 322). From it the following centos have come into C. U. :—

1. The *Wes. H. Bk.,* 1780, No. 280 (new ed. 1875, No. 289), which is composed of st. i., ii., v., vi., ix., xi., xiv., xv. This is in several Methodist collections.
2. The *New Cong.,* 1859, No. 665, consisting of st. i., ii., v., vi., ix.
3. *Kennedy,* 1863, No. 180, consisting of st. i., ii., v., ix., xi., xiv.
4. The *Leeds H. Bk.,* 1853, No. 241, consisting of st. i., ii., ix., xi., xiv. This is repeated in the *Hys. of the Spirit,* Boston, U.S.A., 1864; the Unitarian *Hy.* [*and Tune*] *Bk.,* Boston, 1868, and other American collections.

Of these four centos the last is the most widely used. In his *Meth. H. Bk. Notes,* 1883,

p. 218, Mr. Stevenson has an interesting anec-dotal note on the *Wes. H. Bk.* cento. [J. J.]

God of my salvation, hear. *C.Wesley.* [*Lent.*] Pub. in *Hys. & Sac. Poems*, 1742, in 8 st. of 8 l., and headed, "After a relapse into sin " (*P. Works*, 1868–72, vol. ii. p. 200). In its full form it is unknown to the collections, but the following centos are in C. U. :—

1. In *Madan's Ps. & Hys.*, 1760, st. i., iv. v., are given as No. 10. This is repeated with slight altera-tions in the S. P. C. K. *Hymns*, 1852, and other collec-tions. It was also in R. Conyers's *Coll.*, 1767, and several of the older hymn-books.
2. Toplady's cento in his *Ps. & Hys.*, 1776, No. 354, of which st. iii. and vii. are by Toplady, is not in modern use.
3. Bickersteth's *Christian Psalmody*, 1833, No. 160, is composed of st. i., ii., iv., vi., with slight alterations. This is repeated in the *Hy. Comp.* with a return to the original text.
4. Mercer's *Ch. Psalter & H. Bk.*, 1855, consists of st. i., ii., iv., vi., viii.
5. Dr. Hatfield's *Church H. Bk.*, N.Y., 1872, No. 639, embodies st. i., ii., iv.
6. The *Wes. H. Bk.*, 1780, No. 168 (new ed. 1875, No. 175), is composed of st. i., ii., iv., vi., viii. This cento has passed into several Methodist collections.

This somewhat large number of centos (and the most important only have been named) in-dicate the extensive use which has been made of the hymn from *Madan* to the present. Of these centos that in the *Wes. H. Bk.* is the best known. [J. J.]

God of our health, our Life and Light. *Bp. R. Mant.* [*Holy Baptism.*] One of the original hymns added to his *Ancient Hymns from the Roman Breviary*, 1837, p. 96, in 5 st. of 6 l. (ed. 1871, p. 163), and entitled, "Hymn of Thanksgiving for Holy Baptism." It was repeated in *Kennedy*, 1863 ; the S. P. C. K., *Ps. & Hys. Appx.*, &c. The hymn No. 498, in the *Hymnary*, 1872, for a "School Festival," "We thank Thee, Lord, our Life and Light," in L.M., is a cento from this hymn. [J. J.].

God of that glorious gift of grace. *J. S. B. Monsell.* [*Holy Baptism.*] 1st pub. in his *Hys. and Miscellaneous Poems*, Dublin, 1837, p. 44, in 5 st. of 4 l., and entitled, "Bap-tismal Hymn." It was repeated in his *Parish Musings*, 1850, but omitted, strangely enough, from his *Parish Hymnal*, 1873, although rank-ing in popularity with the best of his hymns. It is found in many of the best collections, including the S. P. C. K. *Church Hymns*, No. 222 ; *Hy. Comp.*, 398 ; the *Wes. H. Bk.*, No. 896, and others, and usually without altera-tion, as in Lord Selborne's *Bk. of Praise*, 1862 and 1867. Its use has also extended to most English-speaking countries. [J. J.]

God of the living, in Whose eyes. *J. Ellerton.* [*Burial.*] Written for and 1st pub. in his *Hymns for Schools and Bible Classes* (Brighton), 1858, in 3 st. of 4 l. On July 6, 1867, it was expanded by the author into 5 st. of 6 l., and in this form was pub. in the Brown-Borthwick *Words of the Suppl. H. and Tune Bk.*, N.D. : and the *Select Hys. for Church & Home*, 1871. Also in the S. P. C. K. *Church Hymns*, 1871, No. 245. It is in somewhat ex-tensive use, the longer form being that usually adopted. The two forms are in Dr. Marti-neau's *Hys. of Praise and Prayer*, 1873, as Nos. 511 and 797. [J. J.]

God of the morning, at [Thy] Whose voice. *I. Watts.* [*Morning.*] 1st pub. in his *Hys. & S. Songs*, 1709, Bk. i., No. 79, in 6 st. of 4 l., as "A Morning Hymn." It is sometimes used in an abbreviated form, and as "God of the morning, at *Thy* voice." Its use in its full, or in abridged form, is extensive in G. Britain and America. [J. J.]

God of the prophet's power. *J. Cen-nick.* [*After Sermon, or Missions.*] Pub. in his *Sacred Hys. for the Children of God*, &c., 1741, No. 10, in 5 st. of 8 l. In its original form it is not in C. U. The hymn in many American collections, especially those of the Unitarians, beginning with the same first line, is a cento from this hymn with alterations in the text. It came into use early in the present century, and is found in the *Hys. of the Spirit*, Boston, 1864 ; the *Songs for the Sanctuary*, N. Y., 1865, and many others. [J. J.]

God of the seas, Thy thundering voice. *I. Watts.* [*God's Dominion over the Sea.*] No. 70, Bk. ii., of his *Hys. & S. Songs*, 1707, in 9 st. of 4 l., and entitled "God's Do-minion over the Sea." In this form its use is very limited. A more popular form was given in the American *Prayer Bk. Coll.*, 1826, No. 118, in 3 st. beginning, "God of the sea, Thine awful voice." It is an alteration of st. i., iii. and vi., and is found in several American col-lections. [J. J.]

God of the universe, to Thee. [*Con-secration of a Church.*] Appeared in Beman's *Sacred Lyrics*, Troy, 1841, and signed "Miss Mary O—, 1841." It is in use in a few Ame-rican collections, as Hatfield's *Church H. Bk.*, 1872, No. 1290, in 4 st., and the *Songs for the Sanctuary*, 1865, No. 1031, in 5 st. [J. J.]

God of truth, and power, and grace. *C. Wesley.* [*Holy Communion.*] "Pub. as a tract of four pages, without name or date, but probably before 1745," and included in the *P. Works*, 1868–72, vol. viii. p. 441. It is in 10 st. of 4 l. Of these st. i.–vii., ix. and x., were given in the revised *Wes. H. Bk.*, 1875, No. 910. [J. J.]

God of unexampled grace. *C. Wesley.* [*Passiontide.*] 1st pub. in his *Hys. on the Lord's Supper*, 1745, No. 21, in 9 st. of 8 l. (*P. Works*, 1868–72, vol. iii. p. 229). From this the following centos have come into C. U. :

1. In M. Madan's *Ps. & Hys.*, 1760, No. 159 is com-posed of st. i.–iii. This was added to the *Supp.* to the *Wes. H. Bk.*, 1830, and is retained in the revised ed., 1875.
2. In A. M. Toplady's *Ps. & Hys.*, 1776, No. 299 is composed of st. i.–iv., vi., viii. ix., with alterations.
3. In the *Wes. H. Bk.*, 1800–1, st. iv.–ix., beginning "Jesus drinks the bitter cup." This is in a few Metho-dist collections, but is omitted from the revised ed. of the *Wes. H. Bk.*, 1875.

The use of portions of this hymn is thus somewhat extensive, especially amongst the Methodist bodies. In common with Milton ("Hymn for the Morning of Christ's Nati-vity") and others, Wesley has pressed heathen mythology into the service of Christianity in this hymn. The fifth stanza reads :—

" Dies the glorious cause of all
   The true eternal *Pan*,
Falls to raise us from the fall
   To ransom sinful man.
" Well may *Sol* withdraw his light,
   With the Sufferer sympathise,
Leave the world in sudden night,
   While his Creator dies." [J. J.]

God save the King. [*National Anthem.*] The origin and authorship of the English national anthem have given rise to much controversy, and many theories respecting them have been advanced, often demonstrating little save the writers' misapprehension of the points really at issue. To enter at length into these discussions would be foreign to the purpose of this work, and it will therefore be sufficient to notice briefly the theories above referred to, and then to state the results attained by a careful examination of the facts, so far as we know them at present.

i. *Theories respecting the Melody.*—1. The melody has been attributed to Dr. John Bull, and supposed to have been performed by him on the organ at the Merchant Taylors' Hall, July 10, 1607, when King James I. dined there with the Company. Of the book by Richard Clark, in which this theory is propounded, all that it is necessary to say here is that it is a tissue of errors from beginning to end. Curiously enough, however, Clark *afterwards* became possessed of a MS. volume of compositions by Dr. Bull, in which is found a sort of organ voluntary, entitled merely an "Ayre," identical in rhythm with "God save the King," and bearing considerable resemblance to it in the form of its melody.

2. An old Christmas Carol ("Remember, O thou man"), which is found in *Songs and Fancies*, Aberdeen, 1682, bears in several of its phrases some likeness to "God save the King," and has hence led some to claim a Scottish origin for the latter; but the rhythm is different, and the Carol had already appeared in Ravenscroft's *Melismata*, 1611, from which it passed into the Scottish collection.

3. A similar, but even slighter, resemblance to a passage in one of Purcell's sonatas, led others to associate the melody of "God save the King" with the name of that great composer.

4. Others, again, have referred its origin to an anthem or, more properly, hymn said to have been sung in the private chapel of James II. on the occasion of the apprehended invasion of England by the Prince of Orange.

5. Others have supposed it to be a Jacobite composition of later date.

6. Another story runs that it was composed by Lully in honour of a visit paid by Louis XIV. and Madame de Maintenon to the lately founded (1686) convent of St. Cyr. This myth is derived from the *Souvenirs de la Marquise de Créquy*, a clumsy and audacious forgery, the work, it is believed, of one Cousen de St. Malo, published in Paris in 1834. The words therein given as the original French :—

> " Grand Dieu, sauvez le Roy !
>   Grand Dieu, vengez le Roy !
>   Vive le Roy !
> Que toujours glorieux,
> Louis victorieux,
> Voye ses ennemis,
>   Toujours soumis.
> Grand Dieu, sauvez le Roy !
>   Vive le Roy."

are merely a poor translation of the English. The addition to this fiction that Handel subsequently obtained the composition from the Sisters of St. Cyr, and introduced it into England as his own, is too absurd for further notice.

ii. *History of the Anthem.*—1. Henry Carey is commonly accepted as the author both of the words and music, but the ascription to him of either is open to considerable doubt. The air is said to have been sung by him in 1740, at a dinner to celebrate the recent capture of Portobello. This statement rests chiefly on a letter signed "W.," which appeared in the *Gentleman's Magazine* for 1796 (54 years after Carey's death), in which the writer asserts that he was present on the occasion. The story may, however, be true. "God save the King" is not included in any collection of Carey's works, and is first found in print in *Harmonia Anglicana*, N.D., but probably published about 1743 or 1744, and is there anonymous. It is headed "For two voices," the air differs slightly from the modern version, and the words consist of two stanzas only :—

> " God save our Lord the King,
>   Long live our noble King,
>   God save the King !
> Send him victorious,
> Happy and glorious,
> Long to reign over us,
>   God save the King.

> " O Lord our God, arise,
>   Scatter his enemies
>   And make them fall !
> Confound their politicks,
> Frustrate their knavish tricks,
> On him our hopes are fix'd.
>   O save us all."

Harmonia Anglicana was soon afterwards republished under the title of *Thesaurus Musicus*, and a copy of the first edition, in the possession of Mr. Cummings, gives the melody and words without any alteration whatever.

2. At the end of 1743 or in 1744 a concert was given by John Travers, organist of the Chapel Royal, which concluded with "A Latin Chorus." The words of this chorus are quoted by Mr. W. H. Cummings, in a series of six able articles published in the *Musical Times* (March to August, 1878), from a unique copy of the book of the words in his possession :—

> " O Deus Optime !
>   Salvum nunc facito
>   Regem nostrum ;
>   Sit læta victoria,
>   Comes et gloria,
>   Salvum jam facito,
>   Tu Dominum.

> " Exurgat Dominus ;
>   Rebelles dissipet,
>   Et reprimat ;
>   Dolos confundito ;
>   Fraudes depellito ;
>   In te sit sita spes ;
>   O ! Salva Nos."

On the opposite page is an English version, but it is merely a literal translation of the Latin, and in prose. There is nothing to indicate any connection with the stanzas in *Harmonia Anglicana*. Mr. Cummings observes that :—

" the words of the Latin Chorus are so evidently intended for the tune of our National Anthem, that they seem to some extent to support the notion that the Anthem might have been sung during the reign of James II."

We are of opinion that Mr. Cummings might justly have spoken still more decidedly, and that his fortunate discovery of the Latin chorus has restored to us the original text of the hymn sung in 1688.

3. On the 28th Sept., 1745, twelve days after the proclamation of the Pretender at Edinburgh, "God save the King" was sung

at Drury Lane Theatre, with harmonies and accompaniments by Dr. Arne. The words of the first three lines appear thus in Arne's autograph score :—

"God bless our noble King,
God save great George our King,
God save the King."

and B. Victor in a letter to Garrick quotes the beginning of the 2nd verse thus :—

"O Lord our God arise!
Confound the enemies
Of George our King!"

The performance was received with tumultuous applause, and the example of Drury Lane was soon followed by Goodman's Fields and Covent Garden.

4. In Oct., 1745, the music and words were printed in the *Gentleman's Magazine* "as sung at both playhouses," with the addition of a 3rd verse :—

"Thy choicest gifts in store
On George be pleased to pour,
Long may he reign ;
May he defend our laws,
And ever give us cause,
To say with heart and voice
God save the King."

The 1st and 2nd verses are exactly as in *Harmonia Anglicana*, with the exception of v. 1, l. 1, which is changed to "God save great George our King"; and of v. 2, l. 6, where "we fix" is substituted for "are fixed." Still Carey's name was never mentioned in connection with either tune or words, and when Arne was subsequently questioned on the subject, he replied :—

"He had not the least knowledge, nor could he guess at all who was either the author or composer, but that it was a received opinion that it was written for the Catholic Chapel of James II."

About the same time, a new edition of *Thesaurus Musicus* was issued, with a second volume added. Here the heading is, "A Loyal Song, Sung at the Theatres Royal, for two Voices"; the melody appears in almost its present shape ; and the words are slightly changed as follows :—

St. i. l. 1, "God save *great George our King*,"

as in the *Gentleman's Magazine*.

St. ii. l. 2, Scatter our enemies.
St. ii. ll. 6, 7, On *thee* our hopes *we fix*,
God save us all.

Then follows the additional stanza as in the *Gentleman's Magazine*, but with the 6th line thus : —

"With Heart and Voice to sing."

This curious alteration is probably due to the engraver, but the examples given above show the manner in which the words were adapted to the circumstances of the time. It is also worthy of remark that while in the later edition of *Thesaurus Musicus* the words and melody were both revised, the index retains the first line as in *Harmonia Anglicana*, "God save our Lord the King."

The air now rapidly increased in popularity, and after a time took its present position as the National Anthem of England.

5. It was not until 1795 that the authorship was claimed for Carey by his youngest son, George Saville Carey, avowedly with the object of obtaining a pension as a reward for the public service rendered by his father in writing the "Loyal Song." George Carey, in his account of the matter in 1799, quotes "God save the King," in 4 stanzas, of which the 3rd is that given in the *Gentleman's Magazine*, and the 4th is :—

"Long grant that Marshal Wade
May by thy mighty aid,
Victory bring ;
May he sedition hush,
And like a torrent rush,
Rebellious Scots to crush :
God save the King."

It need hardly be added that neither this stanza nor the 3rd could have been by Carey, who was dead when the Scottish rebellion broke out. George Carey, who was an infant at the time of his father's death, could have had no personal knowledge of the matter, but he states that he had often heard Mr. Pearce Galliard, a friend of his father, assert that the latter was the author of "God save the King," and, what is more important, he quotes a letter from Dr. Harington to himself stating that Mr. J. C. Smith (Handel's well-known amanuensis) :—

"has often told me that your father came to him with the words and music, desiring him to correct the bass, which Mr. Smith told him was not proper, and at your father's request he wrote down another in correct harmony. Mr. Smith, to whom I read your letter again, this day repeated the same again."

The date of this letter is June 13, 1795, not long after which Smith died, aged 83. Dr. Harington adds :—

"My curiosity was often raised to enquire after the author before Mr. Smith related the above, and I was often misinformed. Mr. Smith says he understood your father intended this as part of a birthday Ode, or something of that kind."

Here Mr. Cummings's discovery of the "Latin Chorus" assumes a special importance. Either the two English stanzas of 1743-4 are translated from the Latin, or the Latin from them. The latter alternative is almost inconceivable. It is impossible to imagine that a Latin version was made for Travers's concert, or if it had been made, why the English stanzas, if then already published, were not printed on the opposite page instead of a prose translation. Travers, as organist of the Chapel Royal, was exactly in the position to become possessed of a ms. from the Chapel of James II. He might, perhaps, not have known its origin, but, if he had, he would assuredly have kept the knowledge to himself, when employing the Jacobite hymn as the concluding piece of his concert, immediately following his new Ode for the birthday (Nov. 19, 1743) of the Princess of Wales. If this be so, it is difficult to doubt that the "Latin Chorus" represents the occasional hymn of 1688, and thus justifies the opinion expressed by Dr. Arne, probably in accordance with a tradition to that effect. If some copies of the anthem were preserved, one was not unlikely to have descended to Travers, and another to have been seen by Carey, who translated the Latin words into English. If then, along with the words Carey obtained the melody only, he would have to put a bass to it, which agrees with the account given by J. C. Smith. Mr. Cummings remarks that the bass of the song in *Harmonia Anglicana* is not worthy of Smith, who was an excellent musician, but we have no means of knowing whose the bass printed in 1743 really is. It may indeed be that by Carey himself which he took to Smith for correction. If, then, Carey's share in the National

Anthem is confined to the English translation of the Latin, and that, perhaps, only partially, it is easy to see why he never claimed the song as his own, and why his name was never publicly connected with it until many years afterwards. As to the melody, Carey must in this case have obtained it with the Latin words, in the same form, or in one similar to it, as that printed in 1743, and its immediate authorship must once more be restored to the domain of speculation.

6. The likeness of the Anthem to such pieces as " Remember, O thou man," is of no critical importance. In the compositions of the 16th and early part of the 17th century, we find the same or similar stock phrases continually recurring. Ingenuity of harmony was at that time more thought of than originality of melody ; but, as Mr. Cummings points out, the similarity between "God save the King" and Bull's " Ayre" (composed *without a title and without words*) extends also to its peculiar rhythm, and could hardly have been accidental. The "Ayre," no doubt, is in the minor mode, but this is in no way inconsistent with its being the *basis* on which " God save the King" was constructed.

7. An argument adduced in support of the claim for the song to a *Jacobite* origin, is the former existence at Fingask Castle of an old drinking cup on which was inscribed the following stanzas :—

> " God save the King, I pray,
>   God bless the King, I pray,
>   God save the King.
>   Send him victorious,
>   Happy and glorious,
>   Soon to reign over us,
>   God save the King.
>
> " God bless the Prince of Wales,
>   The true-born Prince of Wales,
>   Sent us by Thee.
>   Grant us one favour more,
>   The King for to restore,
>   As Thou hast done before,
>   The Familie. Amen."

It is hardly necessary to point out that an inscription of this kind, undated and unauthenticated, is usually worthless as evidence, but in the present instance the references to the King's restoration and to the *true-born* Prince of Wales show that it must have been written before the death of James II. in 1701, after which there was no titular Prince of Wales until the birth of Charles Edward, in 1720. It has also been remarked that the somewhat peculiar expression "*Send* him victorious" is more applicable to the Stuart than to the Hanoverian family. These stanzas may then be considered as one of those adaptations of the original to special circumstances, of which many examples exist. It is to be observed that the verses in *Harmonia Anglicana* which otherwise conform closely to the "Latin Chorus," also contain the word "send," for which there is no correlative in the latter. This may be taken to show that Carey was acquainted with the old Jacobite paraphrase and borrowed from it part of the 1st stanza, with the word "soon" in l. 6, changed to "long." Another indication that the English stanzas are translated from the Latin, is found in st. ii., l. 6, where, while "In Te" is, in accordance with the circumstances of the case, rendered by "On him," the third person, in

which the verb "sita est" is written, is copied so literally as to involve an imperfect rhyme, "are fix'd," corrected in 1745 to " we fix."

Our want of knowledge of the exact date of the publication of *Harmonia Anglicana* leaves it uncertain whether "God save the King" appeared in it in Carey's lifetime or after his death, which occurred in Oct., 1743 ; but the apparent ignorance of the English words on the part of Travers may incline us to believe they had not been printed when his concert was given.

iii. *Conclusion.*—The view of the case, of which the above is a sketch, reconciles many discrepancies, and on the whole it now seems more than probable that the occasional hymn or anthem, of which some tradition reached Arne and others, was really produced in 1688 ; that the composer *may* have been acquainted with Bull's "Ayre," and founded his melody upon it ; that some copies of the anthem were current among the Jacobites, and that one imitation of it, at least, was made by them in English before the end of the 17th cent. ; that the anthem became known to Carey about 1740, when he translated it (making some use, however, of the old adaptation); that he sang it in public, but never claimed it as an original composition; that about the same time he showed it to J. C. Smith; that another copy of the so-called anthem fell into the hands of Travers; and that almost immediately afterwards, through its performance at the theatres, "God save the King" attained the popularity which it has maintained to the present day.

iv. *Imitations of the Anthem.*—About 1766 the melody of "God save the King" became known on the Continent. It was set in Denmark as a national air to the words "Heil dir dem liebenden," a song in 8 st., written for the birthday of Christian VII. (a brother-in-law of George III. of England), by Heinrich Harries, editor of the *Flensburger Wochenblatt*, where it was pub. Jan. 27, 1790. Passing into Berlin, the words, recast by Balthasar Gerhard Schumacher, and beginning "Heil Dir, im Siegerkrantz," appeared in the *Spenersche* Zeitung, Dec. 17, 1793, and, with the tune, were afterwards adopted as the national air, first of Prussia, then of Saxony, and some other North German States. [For fuller details see the papers by Mr. Cummings referred to above, to which the present article is much indebted ; to Grove's *Dict. of Music;* and to Chappell's *Popular Music.*]

2. A successful and popular imitation of the National Anthem is :—

> " God bless our native land !
>   Firm may she ever stand,
>   Through storm and night ; "

which is in use in America. Full details of the composition of this hymn are given at p. 1566, i.

3. In 1828 an imitation appeared in W. W. Hull's *Coll. of Prayers for Household Use, with a few Hys. and other Poems*, p. 124 :—

> " God save our King ! O shed
>   All blessings o'er his head !
>   Comfort his heart ! "

This was repeated in Hull's *Coll.*, 1833, and in 1863 it was given in *Kennedy* as :—

> " Lord God, to Thee we pray ;
>   Save our Queen ! bless her sway
>   Over our land."

4. In the Havergal *Life Echoes*, 1883, there is a version of the Anthem adapted for the Marriage of the Prince of Wales, March 10, 1863, the adaptation beginning with st. ii., "God save the Prince of Wales." It is entitled "A New National Bridal Hymn." Another arrangement of the Anthem is in the same work, p. 140.

5. Numerous imitations of the metre of this Anthem are found in the hymn-books both old and new, one of the oldest being :—

"Come, Thou Almighty King,
    Help us Thy praise to sing,
        Help us to praise!"

the somewhat complicated history of which will be found under its first line. J. Marriott's "Thou Whose Almighty word," is another successful instance of the adaptation of the metre to sacred purposes.

6. During the Jubilee year, 1887, numerous alterations of the National Anthem, and additions thereto, were made to adapt it for the occasion. These alterations and additions from their special character cannot become permanent parts of the Anthem. Several hymns in the same metre, and others in varying metres, were also published; but the interest of these is mainly historical. (See **Various.**)   [G. A. C.]

God that [Who] madest earth and heaven. [*Evening.*] This hymn is given in the collections in various forms as follows :—

1. The original in one stanza. This was 1st pub. in Bp. Heber's posthumous *Hymns*, &c., 1827, p. 147.
2. The same with the addition of the stanza, "Guard us waking, guard us sleeping." This stanza is by Archbishop Whately, and is a free rendering of the ancient Compline Antiphon, "Salva nos, Domine, vigilantes, custodi nos dormientes, ut vigilemus in Christo, et requiescamus in pace." It is found in T. Darling's *Hymns*, &c., 1855, No. 8, as st. ii. of the hymn, and was appended to the Archbishop's *Lectures on Prayer*, 1860. These two stanzas constitute the hymn in its most popular form, and are in use in all English speaking countries, sometimes as, "God *who* madest," &c., as in *H. A. & M.*, 1861-75. A rendering of these stanzas into Latin, as "Deus, terras qui polosque," is given in R. Bingham's *Hymno. Christ. Latina*, 1871, p. 175.
3. These two stanzas and a doxology by T. Darling in his *Hymns*, &c., 1855, No. 8. This was repeated with alterations in the doxology in the *Salisbury H. Bk.*, 1857; in the Rev. F. Pott's *Hymns*, &c., 1861, and other hymn-books.
4. In the Oxford ed. of Mercer's *Ch. Psalter & H. Bk.*, 1864, No. 18, there is the following arrangement: i. "God, that madest," &c. (*Heber*); ii. "And when morn again shall call us" (*Mercer*); iii. "Guard us waking," &c. (*Whately*); iv. "Holy Father, throned in heaven" (*Mercer*). This is repeated in Brown-Borthwick's *Select Hymns for Ch. & Home*, 1871-85, with a transposition of st. ii. and iii., much to the advantage of the hymn.
5. In Major's *Book of Praise*, 1868, No. 281, is Mercer's arrangement without the doxology.

All these centos are in C. U. in G. Britain, America, and the colonies. See p. 1595, i.   [J. J.]

God the all-terrible! King, Who ordainest. *H. F. Chorley.* [*In Time of War.*] Written for a Russian air, and printed, in 4 st. of 4 l., in Hullah's *Part Music*, 1842. It is given in several collections either in its original or in a slightly altered form, as in Thring's *Coll.*, 1882, &c. In the *Universal H. Bk.*, 1885, No. 392, st. i.-iii. of this text, somewhat altered, are given as, "God, Lord of Sabaoth! King Who ordainest." In Stryker's *Christian Chorals*, New York, 1885, it begins, "O God, all terrible," and in the American *Hys. of the Spirit*, Boston, 1864, No. 262, st.

ii.-iv. are given in an altered form as, "God, the Omnipotent! Mighty Avenger."

During the Franco-German war, on the 28th Aug., 1870, the Rev. J. Ellerton wrote an imitation of this hymn, beginning, "God the Almighty One, wisely ordaining." It was pub. in the Rev. R. Brown-Borthwick's *Select Hymns for Ch. & Home*, 1871, No. 84, in 4 st. of 4 l. In 1871 a cento from these two hymns was given in the S. P. C. K. *Church Hys.*, No. 262, of which st. i.-iii. are from Chorley's hymn, and st. iv.-vi. are st. ii.-iv. from that by Mr. Ellerton.   [J. J.]

God the Creator bless'd. *J. Montgomery.* [*Sunday.*] Written in May, 1838, and pub. in a small pamphlet entitled, *A Message from the Moon, and Other Poems.* [1838.] In 1839 it was also given in *Votive Offerings; or a Help to Stannington Church.* This was a small volume, and was sold for the benefit of the funds of Stannington Church, near Sheffield. In 1853 the hymn, somewhat altered (st. iii., l. 2, "Christian Day," for "Christian's Day," l. 3, "*where* (met . .)" for "when met . .," st. iv. l. 1, "The Church *below hath* bless'd," for "The Church hath ever bless'd ") was given in Montgomery's *Original Hymns*, No. 11, in 6 st. of 6 l., and entitled "The Sabbath." It is in several modern American hymn-books, but is almost unknown to the collections in G. Britain.   [J. J.]

God the Father, God the Son, Holy Spirit, Three in one. *G. Thring.* [*Close of Evening Service.*] Written in 1871 and 1st pub. in Preb. Hutton's *Supplement*, Lincoln, 1871, No. 273, in 4 st. of 8 l. In 1872 it was repeated in H. H. Pierson's *Hymn Tunes*, No. 23, with a special tune by Pierson. Subsequently it was included in the author's *Hys. and Sacred Lyrics*, 1874, p. 184; and in his *Coll.*, 1882, No. 94. It is also found in several other collections.   [J. J.]

God the Father, Whose creation. *J. M. Neale.* [*Harvest.*] Pub. in the *Appendix* to the *H. Noted*, 2nd ed., 1864; and again in the author's posthumous *Original Sequences, Hymns*, &c., 1866, p. 69, in 6 st. of 6 l. It has since appeared in the *Appendix* to *H. A. & M.*, 1868; *People's H.*, 1867; and several other collections.   [J. J.]

God the heavens aloud proclaim. *J. Merrick.* [*Ps. xix.*] 1st pub. in his *Psalms Tr. and Paraphrased in English Verse*, 1765, and repeated in W. D. Tattersall's rearranged ed. of the same, 1797. As a complete version of Ps. ix. it is not in C. U. A cento composed of st. xv., xvi., xviii., xix., from Tattersall's arrangement, is in several American collections, including *The Springfield Coll.*, 1835; the Unitarian *Hy.* [*& Tune*] *Bk.*, Boston, 1868, and several other hymn-books. It begins, "Blest Instructor, from Thy ways." This psalm version by Merrick as rewritten by Miss Auber in her *Spirit of the Psalms*, 1829, is given in Dale's *English H. Bk.*, 1874, as "Heavenly Teacher, from Thy ways."   [J. J.]

God the Lord a king remaineth. *J. Keble.* [*Ps. xciii.*] 1st pub. in his *Psalter; or, Psalms of David*, 1839, p. 241, in 5 st. of 6 l. It was given in the *Sarum Hyl.*, 1868, Kennedy, 1863, and in several Public School collections, but its use is not equal to its merits. It is one of Keble's finest renderings of the Psalms. [See **Psalters, English, § XVIII.**]

[J. J.]

God the Lord, in mercy bending. [*Holy Communion.*] This hymn is a *tr.* by Dr. R. F. Littledale of a cento from the Greek Liturgies of SS. James and Mark, made for and 1st pub. in the *People's H.*, 1867, No. 170, in 5 st. of 6 l. It is an "Invocation of the Holy Ghost, before the Consecration." The Greek begins, Ἐλέησον ἡμᾶς, ὁ Θεός. [J. J.]

God, the omnipresent God. *C. Wesley.* [*Ps. xlvi.*] 1st pub. in *Hymns occasioned by the Earthquake, March 8, 1750, London. Printed in the year MDCCL.* It is in 12 st. of 8 l. (*P. Works*, 1868–72, vol. viii. p. 100). In its full form it is unknown to the collections, but st. iv., v., are given in the Bapt. *Ps. & Hys.*, 1858, as No. 662; the Irvingite *Hys. for the Use of the Churches*, 2nd ed. 1871, No. 229, &c., as "From the throne of God there springs."

[J. J.]

God, Who didst so dearly buy. *C. Wesley.* [*Praise desired of Believers.*] There are two centos beginning with this first line as follows :—

i. In the 1st ed. of the *Wes. H. Bk.*, 1780, No. 406, and later editions to 1875; and also in other Methodist collections, the cento is compiled from C. Wesley's *Short Hymns*, &c., 1762, as follows: st. i., No. 554; st. ii., No. 823 ; st. iii., iv., No. 882.

2. The second cento is No. 411, in the revised ed., *Wes. H. Bk.*, 1875, and is thus composed : st. i., the st. i. as above ; st. ii. from C. Wesley's *Hys. for the Use of Families*, 1767, No. 28, st. i. (*P. Works*, 1868–72).

[J. J.]

God's holy law transgressed. *B. Beddome.* [*Hope in the Gospel.*] Appeared in R. Hall's ed. of Beddome's (posthumous) *Hymns*, &c., 1817, No. 362, in 4 st. of 4 l., and entitled, "Hope alone from the Gospel." Its use in G. Britain is limited, but in America it is extensive ; but in most cases either abbreviated or altered. Orig. text in the *Hymnal of the Meth. Episco. Church*, 1878, No. 314, with "*Convinced of* guilt," &c., for "Burdened with guilt," &c., in st. i. l. 3. [J. J.]

Goethe, Johann Wolfgang von, s. of Johann Caspar Goethe, a lawyer at Frankfurt-am-Main ; was b. at Frankfort Aug. 28, 1749, and d. at Weimar, March 22, 1832. The greatest German poet of his day, and one of the most famous literary men of his own or any age, his sympathies were Classical rather than distinctively Christian ; and as he himself said (Conversations with Eckermann, January 4, 1827), he wrote no poems suited for use in public worship.

A few pieces, principally from his well-known dramatic poem of *Faust* (pt. i. 1808 ; pt. ii. pub. posthumously, 1832), are found under his name in one or two Unitarian hymn-books. Good *trs.* of both parts of *Faust* have been pub. by Dr. John Anster, Bayard Taylor, Sir Theodore Martin, and others ; while a very large number of other persons have pub. *trs.* of the first part. No attempt has accordingly been made to notice any *trs.* except those in the hymn-books.

i. *From Faust, pt. i.*, 1808.

i. **Christ ist erstanden! Freude dem Sterblichen.** *Easter.* The chorus of angels on Easter Day. *Tr.* as "Christ has arisen! Joy to our buried Head," by Dr. F. H. Hedge, in his *Supp. to Hys. for the Ch. of Christ*, Boston, U.S., 1853, No. 836. A free version is also noted under A. C. Coxe, No. 4.

ii. **Die Sonne tönt nach alter Weise.** *Praise.* The Song of the three Archangels in the Prologue in Heaven. *Tr.* as "The sun is still for ever sounding," by Dr. F. H. Hedge, as above, 1853, No. 190.

iii. **Verlassen hab ich Feld und Auen.** *Evening.* Faust's Soliloquy on entering his study with the dog. *Tr.* as "O'er silent field and lonely lawn," as No. 21 in W. J. Fox's *H. & Anthems*, 1841, repeated in English and American Unitarian collections.

ii. *Miscellaneous.*

iv. **Des Maurers Wandeln.** Written for the Freemasons' Lodge at Weimar, of which he became a member in 1780, and included in his *Werke*, 1828, vol. iii. p. 61, entitled "Symbolum." *Tr.* as "The Mason's ways are A type of Existence," by T. Carlyle, in his *Past and Present*, 1843, p. 318. Included, beginning "The future hides in it " (st. ii.), as No. 854 in Dr. Hedge's *Coll.*, 1853, as above.

Two pieces are also found in collections under his name, viz. :—

1. **Without haste! without rest,** in *Hys. of the Ages*, Boston, U.S., 3rd Ser., 1865, p. 76, and repeated as "Without haste and without rest," in Stopford Brooke's *Christian Hys.*, 1881, &c. It is suggested by "Wie das Gestern, Ohne Hast, Aber Ohne Rast, Drehe sich jeder, Um die eigne Last," in Goethe's *Zahme Xenien*, 2nd Ser., 1823 (*Werke*, 1828, iii. p. 245).

2. **Rest is not quitting The busy career.** (*Rest.*) This is part of a piece beginning "Sweet is the pleasure Itself cannot spoil." No. 853 in Dr. Hedge's *Coll.*, 1853, as above, marked as by "J. S. Dwight." There does not appear to be any equivalent poem in Goethe's *Werke*.

[J. M.]

Goffe, Eliza Fanny. [**Morris, E. F.**]

Golden harps are sounding. *Frances R. Havergal.* [*Ascension.*] Written at Perry Barr, Dec., 1871, under the following circumstances :—

"When visiting at Perry Barr, F. R. H. walked to the boys' schoolroom, and being very tired she leaned against the play-ground wall, while Mr. Snepp [editor of S. of Grace & Glory, 1872] went in. Returning in ten minutes he found her scribbling on an old envelope. At his request she gave him the hymn just pencilled, 'Golden harps,' &c. Her popular tune *Hermas* was composed for this hymn. *Hermas* was the tune she sang, as 'the pearly gates opened' for her, June 3, 1879." [HAV. MSS.]

The use of this "Ascension Hymn for Children," in G. Britain is limited, but in America it has attained to great popularity. It was pub. in the *Day Spring Magazine*, and the *Day of Days*, May, 1872 ; in *Under the Surface*, 1874, and in *Life Mosaic*, 1879. [J. J.]

Good is the Lord [our] the heavenly King. *I. Watts.* [*Ps. lxv.—Spring.*] 1st pub. in his *Psalms of David*, &c., 1719, in 6 st. of 4 l. and entitled, "The Blessings of Spring ; or, God gives Rain." It is found in several modern hymn-books, and sometimes abbreviated as in the *New Cong.*, 1859. Another hymn beginning, "Good is the Lord, our heavenly King," appeared in Bickersteth's *Christian Psalmody*, 1833, No. 498, with the ascription to "Watts" in the Index. The first stanza is st. i. of this version of Ps. lxv., with *our* for *the ;* the remaining three, each beginning, "Good is the Lord," are by another hand.

[J. J.]

Goode, William, M.A., b. in Buckingham, April 2, 1762, and received his early education, first in that town, and then under the care of the Rev. T. Bull, a Dissenting minister, at Newport Pagnel. Having a strong inclination for Holy Orders, he left the business in which he was engaged with his father, and, in 1780, entered Magdalen Hall, Oxford, where he graduated B.A. in 1784, and M.A., 1787. On taking Holy Orders in 1786, he became curate of Abbots Langley, Herts; then of St. Ann's,

Blackfriars, and subsequently rector of the latter parish, adding thereto one or two lecture-ships. He d. April 15, 1816. Mr. Goode's interest in foreign mission work was very earnest, and took a practical turn in assisting to found the Church Missionary Society. His prose works include *Sermons*, 1812 ; and *Essays on all the Scriptural Names and Titles of Christ*, &c., which were reprinted from the *Christian Guardian*, 1813–1816. His *Works*, together with a *Memoir*, were pub. in 1822 (6 vols.), and edited by his son. His version of the Psalms was pub. as :—

An Entire New Version of the Book of Psalms, in which an attempt is made to accommodate them to the worship of the Christian Church, in a variety of measures now in general use, with original Preface and Notes, critical and explanatory, By the Rev. William Goode, M.A., Rector of St. Andrew, Wardrobe, and St. Ann, Blackfriars ; Lecturer of St. John of Wapping ; and Lady Camden's Tuesday Evening Lecturer at the Church of St. Lawrence, Jewry. In two volumes. London : Printed for the Author by W. Wilson . . . and sold by Rivingtons, &c., 1811. 2nd ed., 1813 ; 3rd ed., 1816.

Pratt, in 1829 ; *Bickersteth*, in 1833 ; and *Kemble* in 1853, made extensive use of this version of the Psalms, the latter including nearly fifty pieces in his Coll. Most of these have fallen out of use, one only being retained in Kemble's *New Church H. Bk.*, 1873. In modern hymnals in G. Britain and America about twenty of Goode's versions are still in C. U. These include, " Jesus, with Thy salvation blest " ; " Lord, I delight to find my place " ; " Thou gracious God and kind " ; " With songs of grateful praise," &c. [See **Psalters, English**, § XVI.] The following are still in C. U. :—

1. Crown His head with endless blessing. *Ps. cxviii.*
2. Far as the isles extend. *Ps. lxxii.*
3. How blest are they whose hearts sincere. *Ps. cxix.*
4. How blest the man with mercy crowned. *Ps. xxxii.*
5. If the Lord had not heard, may Israel now say. *Ps. cxxiv.*
6. Jesus, with Thy salvation blest. *Ps. xx.*
7. Let Thy grace, Lord, make me [us] lowly. *Ps. cxxxi.*
8. Lo in Gethsemane's dark shade. *Ps. lxxxviii.*
9. Lo, the mighty God appearing. *Ps. l.*
10. Lord, I delight to find my place. *Ps. xxvi.*
11. Lord of mercy, just and kind. *Ps. xiii.*
12. Lord, Thy Church hath seen Thee rise. *Ps. lxviii.*
13. Now let our songs arise. *Ps. xcvi.*
14. O my God, by Thee forsaken. *Ps. xli.*
15. Prepare a new song Jehovah to praise. *Ps. cxlix.*
16. Songs anew of honour framing. *Ps. xcviii.*
17. Thou gracious God and kind. *Ps. lxxix.*
18. Though sinners boldly join. *Ps. ii.*
19. With songs of grateful praise. *Ps. cvii.* [J. J.]

Goostly Psalmes and Spiritualle Songes, by *Miles Coverdale*.

Written by Bishop Coverdale, the great translator of the Bible. Of this work an unique copy is at Queen's Coll., Oxford. In the 2nd edition of Foxe's Acts and Monuments it is quoted among a list of books prohibited in 1539. In subsequent editions this list is withdrawn. Townsend's edition of Foxe restores it under the date of 1546, on the authority of Bonner's Register (*Academy*, June 28,. 1884, Letter of Dr. A. F. Mitchell). A reprint of the book, without the tunes, has been published in Coverdale's *Remains*, 1846 (Parker Soc.). The Preface, in describing the motives that produced it, echoes the commonplace so frequent among translators of the Psalms. " Would God . . . our carters and ploughmen (had none)

other thing to whistle upon save psalms . . . and if women . . . spinning at the wheels had none other songs . . . they should be better occupied than with hey nony nony, hey troly loly." The *Spiritual Songs* are paraphrases of the " Ten Commandments," " Creed," " Pater Noster," " Mediâ Vitâ," " Gloria in Excelsis," " Magnificat," " Nunc Dimittis," " Christe Qui Lux," " Veni Creator " (3), and twelve hymns. There are also fifteen renderings of psalms, two of them being duplicates. It is extremely probable that the whole book is translated from German originals. All the hymns and psalm-renderings save five have been identified by Mr. Mearns as German. It is thus a witness to the impression which the hymns and psalms of Germany made on the early Gospellers. [**Psalters, English**, § V.; **English Hymnody, Early**, IV.]   [H. L. B.]

The following is a list of contents, the first lines of the German being given where the hymn is a translation :—

1. " O Holy Spirite our comfortoure."
2. " Come, holy Spirite, most blessed Lorde."
   Komm heiliger Geist, Herre Gott !
3. " Thou holy Spirite, we pray to the."
   Nun bitten wir den heiligen Geist.
4. " God the Father, dwell us by."
   Gott der Vater wohn uns bei.
5. " These are the holy commaundements ten."
   Dies sind die heilgen zehn Gebot.
6. " Man, wylt thou lyve vertuously."
   Mensch willt du leben seliglich.
7. " We beleve all upon one God."
   Wir glauben all an einen Gott, Schöpfer.
8. " In God I trust, for so I must."
   In Gott gelaub ich das er hat.
9. " O Father ours celestiall."
   Ach Vater unser, der du bist.
10. " O oure Father celestiall."
    Vater unser, der du bist.
11. " Be glad now, all ye christen men."
    Nun freut euch lieben Christengemein.
12. " Now is oure health come from above."
    Es ist das Heil uns kommen her.
13. " Christ is the only Sonne of God."
    Herr Christ der einig Gottes Sohn.
14. " In the myddest of our lyvynge."
    Mitten wir im Leben sind.
15. " By Adam's fall was so forlorne."
    Durch Adam's Fall ist ganz verderbt.
16. " Wake up, wake up, in God's name."
    Wach auf in Gottes Name.
17. " I call on the, Lorde, Jesu Christ."
    Ich ruf zu dir Herr Jesu Christ.
18. " Now blessed be thou, Christ Jesu."
    Gelobet seist du Jesu Christ.
19. " Christe is now rysen agayne."
    Christ ist erstanden von der Marter alle.
20. " Christ dyed and suffred great payne."
    Christ lag in Todesbanden.
21. " To God the hyghest be glory alwaye."
    Allein Gott in der Höh sey Ehr.
22. " My soul doth magnyfie the Lorde."
    Mein Seel erhebt den Herren mein.
23. " With peace and with joyfull gladnesse.'
    Mit Fried und Freud ich fahr dahin.
24. " Helpe now, O Lorde, and loke on us."
    Ach Gott vom Himmel sieh darein.
25. " Werfore do the heithen now rage thus."
26. " Oure God is a defence and towre."
    Ein' feste Burg ist unser Gott (partly)
27. " Except the Lorde had bene with us."
    Wo der Herre nicht bei uns wär'.
28. " At the ryvers of Babilon."
    An Wasserflüssen Babylon.
29. " Blessed are all that feare the Lorde."
    Wohl dem, der in Gottes Furcht steht.
30. " Blessed are all that feare the Lorde."
    Wohl dem, der in Gottes Furcht steht.
31. " O Lorde God, have mercy on me."
    O Herre Gott begnade mich.
32. " O God, be mercyfull to me."
    Erbarm dich mein, O Herre Gott.
33. " Out of the depe crye I to the."
    Aus tiefer Noth schrei ich zu dir.

34. " I lyft my soule, Lorde, up to the."
    Von allen Menschen abgewandt.
35. " God be mercyfull unto us."
    Es wollt uns Gott genädig sein.
36. " The foolish wicked men can saye."
    Es spricht der Unweisen Mund wohl.
37. " Prayse thou the Lorde, Hierusalē."
38. " Behold and se, forget not this."
39. " O Christ, that art the lyght and daye."
    Christe, du bist Licht und der Tag.
40. " O hevenly Lorde, thy godly worde."
    O Herre Gott, dein göttlich Wort.
41. " Let go the whore of Babilon."

Notes on the whole of these German hymns will be found throughout this Dictionary either under their first lines or by references from these, save in the following cases, where notes will be found under authors' names, viz. :—No. 9, under *Moibanus;* Nos. 8, 12, under *Speratus;* No. 13, under *Cruciger;* No. 15, under *Spengler;* Nos. 16, 27, under *Sachs;* No. 17, under *Agricola;* No, 22, under *Pollio;* No. 28, under *Dachstein;* No. 31, under *Greitter;* No. 32, under *Heyenwalt;* No. 34, under *Knöpken.* No. 39 is from "Christe qui lux es et dies," as *tr.* in the *Riga G. B.*, 1530.

In an interesting letter to the *Academy* of June 28, 1884, on "*Coverdale's Spiritual Songs,*" Professor Mitchell, of St. Andrew's, gives a list of first lines of their German originals, agreeing for the most part with the identifications made by myself, many months before. The blanks he would thus fill up :—For No. 1 he suggests "Herr Gott, din triiw mit gnaden leist" (*Wackernagel,* iii. p. 604, as by Johannes Zwick); for No. 25, "Ir Haiden, was tobt jr umb sust" (*Wackernagel,* 1841, No. 605, as by Joachim Aberlin); for No. 37, "Hierusalem, des louen stadt" (*Wackernagel,* iii. p. 570, from a Low German G. B. 1526); for No. 38, "Nun sieh, wie fein und lieblich ist" (*Wackernagel,* iii. p. 944, as by Conrad Huober); and for No. 41, "Lobt Gott, jr Christen allen" (*Wackernagel,* 1841, p. 690, from a Nürnberg collection, 1544). But in all these cases the resemblances are very slight indeed, and the earliest dates to which Nos. 38 and 41 have been traced, are respectively, 1545 and 1544.   [J. M.]

Gospels, Hymns on the. [Prayer, Book of Common.]

Got thir eigenhaf ist. [*Supplication.*] Quoted by *Wackernagel,* ii. p. 24, from a Munich MS. of the 8th or 9th cent., in 2 st. of 4 l. It is a rhymed version of one of the collects in the *Liber Sacramentorum* of St. Gregory the Great (*Opera,* vol. ii., Paris, 1675, col. 1503), which begins "Deus, cui proprium est miserere semper et parcere," and of which a prose *tr.* is given (beginning "O God, whose nature and property is ever to have mercy and to forgive") among the "Prayers and Thanksgivings, upon several occasions," in the *Bk. of Com. Prayer.* The only *tr.* from the German is "God, it is Thy property," by *Miss Winkworth,* 1869, p. 29.   [J. M.]

Gott der Vater wohn uns bei. [*Holy Trinity.*] Old Litany revised by *M. Luther.* The original of this hymn is probably of the 15th cent. or earlier. *Wackernagel,* ii., No. 684, quotes a form dating 1422, in 15 l., beginning "Sanctus Petrus, won uns bey." In Michael Vehe's *Gesangbüchlein,* 1537 (ed. 1853, p. 57), it is entitled, "A Litany in the time of Processions upon St. Mark's Day and in Rogation Week"; and consists of 5 st. of 12 l., followed by a series of Invocations of Patriarchs, Prophets, &c. Luther adopted st. i. ll. 1–6, rewrote st. i. ll. 7–12, and cut off the invocations to Mary, the Angels, and the Saints. His version appeared in the *Geystliche gesangk Buchleyn,* Wittenberg, 1524, thus :—

    " Gott der vatter won uns bey
    Und las uns nicht verterben.
    Mach uns aller sunden frey
    Und helff uns selig sterben.
    Für dem teuffel uns bewar,
    Hallt uns bey festem glauben

    Und auff dich las uns bawen,
    Aus hertzem grund vertrawen,
    Dyr uns lassen gantz und gar,
    Mit allen rechten Christen
    Entfliehen teuffels listen,
    Mit waffen Gotts uns fristen.
    Amen, Amen, das sey war,
    So singen wyr Alleluia.
    2.
" Ihesus Christus won uns bey, &c.
    3.
" Heylig geyst won uns bey," &c.

In the Erfurt *Enchiridion,* 1526, it bears the title, "The hymn 'Godt der vatter won uns bey,' improved and evangelically corrected." In Luther's form it speedily became popular, and Lauxmann, in *Koch,* viii. 102–104, relates many instances of its use—at weddings, by the dying, in times of trouble, &c. It is given in *Wackernagel,* lii. p. 10, as quoted above; in Schircks's ed. of Luther's *Geistl. Lieder,* 1854, p. 40, and in the *Unv. L. S.,* 1851, No. 187. The *trs.* in C. U. are :—

1. **God the Father! with us be. Shield us, &c.** A free *tr.* in 5 st. of 4 l., in J. Anderson's *H. from the German of Dr. M. L.,* 1846, p. 24 (1847, p. 46). From this, st. i.–iii. unaltered, and st. iv. altered, were adopted as No. 450 in the *Leeds H. Bk.,* 1853, and repeated in *Kennedy,* 1863.

2. **God the Father, with us be, And, &c.** In full, by A. T. Russell, as No. 1 in the *App.* to his *Ps. & Hys.,* 1851.

3. **O God, the Father! draw Thou nigh.** In full, by Dr. M. Loy, in the Ohio *Luth Hyl.,* 1880.

Translations not in C. U. :—
(1) "God the Father, dwell us by," by Bp. Coverdale, 1539 (*Remains,* 1846, p. 543). (2) "God the Father, our Defence," by *J. C. Jacobi,* 1722, p. 27. (3) "God our Father! dwell within," as No. 186 in pt. i. of the *Moravian H. B.,* 1754. (4) "Our Father God! to Thee we pray," by *Miss Fry,* 1845, p. 91. (5) "Father, in us Thy dwelling be," by *Dr. J. Hunt,* 1853, p. 53. (6) "God the Father, be our stay," by *R. Massie,* 1854, p. 26. (7) "Our God, our Father, with us stay," by *Miss Warner,* 1858 (1861, p. 82). (8) "O God the Father, with us dwell," in S. Garratt's *Hys. & Trs.,* 1867, p. 26. (9) "God the Father, with us be, Let," by Dr. G. Macdonald in the *Sunday Mag.,* 1867, p. 388; altered in his *Exotics,* 1876, p. 60. (10) "God the Father, with us stay," in Dr. Bacon, 1884, p. 44.   [J. M.]

Gott ist gegenwärtig. *G. Tersteegen.* [*Public Worship.*] Appeared in his *Geistliches Blumengärtlein,* 1729, as No. 11, in Bk. iii., in 8 st. of 10 l., entitled, "Remembrance of the glorious and delightful presence of God." It passed into Zinzendorf's *Geist- und liebliche Lieder,* 1731, No. 1139, has attained a wider use than any other of Tersteegen's hymns, and is found in most recent collections, as in the *Unv. L. S.,* 1851, No. 559. It is a poetical reflex of his inner nature, a beautiful expression of the characteristics of his peculiar vein of mystical piety. *Lauxmann* in *Koch,* viii. 355, calls it "A hymn of deepest adoration of the All Holy God, and a profound introduction to blessed fellowship with Him." *Tr.* as :—

1. **Lo, God is here! Let us adore,** by J. Wesley, in *H. & Sacred Poems,* 1739 (*P. Works,* 1868–72, vol. i. p. 167), a *tr.* catching the spirit of the original, but rather free, in 6 st. of 8 l., and omitting st. vii., viii. Included in the *Wes. H. Bk.,* 1780, No. 481 (1875, No. 494). The full text is in Mercer's *C. P. & H. Bk.,* 1857 and 1864; but it is generally found in centos. The most important are :—

i. *In the original metre.*
(1) St. i., ii., iv., as in the *Mitre H. Bk.,* 1836; Bickersteth's *Christ. Psal.,* 1841; Amer. *Meth. Epis.,* 1878,

&c. In the *Swedenborgian Coll.*, 1824 and 1880, and others, this cento begins, " The Lord is here! Let us adore."

(2) St. i.-iv. as in the *Leeds H. Bk.*, 1853 ; Bapt. *Ps. & Hys.*, 1858 ; *Hyl. Comp.*, 1870 ; *H. & Songs of Praise*, N. Y., 1874 ; Horder's *Cong. Hyl.*, 1884, &c.

(3) " Lo! God is here! Him day and night," beginning with st. ii. in Elliott's *Ps. & Hys.*, 1835.

ii. *In Long Metre.*

(1) The most important form is of st. i., ii., iv., with ll. 5–6 omitted. This is found in the *Salisbury Coll.*, 1778 ; *Wilberforce*, 1832 ; *Martineau*, 1840 ; *Cooke-Denton*, 1853 ; the S. P. C. K. *Ch. Hys.*, 1871. It is also extensively used in America, as in the *Bk. of Hys.*, 1846–8 ; *Presb. Hyl.*, 1874 ; *Dutch Ref.*, 1869 ; Bapt. *Praise Bk.*, 1871 ; *H. & Songs of Praise*, 1874, &c.

(2) In *Kennedy*, 1863, No. 1252, ll. 1–12, are the above ; while ll. 13–24 seem to be added by Dr. Kennedy to adapt it for the Reopening of a Church or similar festivals.

2. The Lamb is slain, let us adore, by W. Delamotte, as No. 134 in the *Moravian H. Bk.*, 1742, and repeated in later eds. (1886, No. 656, reading "The Lamb *was* slain "). Mainly taken from Wesley's *tr.* Included in varying forms in J. A. Latrobe's *Coll.*, 1841 ; in Walker's *Cheltenham Coll.*, 1855 ; and Reid's *Praise Bk.*, 1872.

3. God reveals His presence, by F. W. Foster and J. Miller, as No. 813 in the *Moravian H. Bk.*, 1789 (1886, No. 649), being a good *tr.* of st. i., ii., iv., vii., viii. The form in C. U. is that given to it by W. Mercer, in his *C. P. & H. Bk.*, 1855, No. 297 (Ox. ed., No. 426). He retained 13 lines as in the original *tr.*, slightly altered 5, and rewrote the rest (with little regard to the German), omitting st. iv. altogether. This text is in J. L. Porter's *Coll.*, 1876 ; *Ch. Praise*, 1883 ; *Free Ch. H. Bk.*, 1882 ; Irish *Ch. Hyl.*, 1873 ; *New Zealand Hyl.*, 1870 ; *Laudes Domini*, N. Y., 1884 ; Canadian *Presb. H. Bk.*, 1880, &c.

Translation not in C. U. :—
"The Lord is here; then let us bow before Him," by *Miss Dunn*, 1857, p. 76.   [J. M.]

Gott ist und bleibt getreu. [*Trust in God.*] Founded on 1 Cor. x. '13. Included as No. 302 in J. H. Hävecker's *Kirchen-Echo*, Helmstädt and Magdeburg, 1695, in 6 st. of 8 l., without name of author; repeated as No. 25 in the Berlin *G. L. S.*, ed. 1863. It has been ascribed to Dr. Johann Christian Wilhelmi (sometime advocate under the Hessian administration and syndic at Giessen), but is not included among the hymns in the *Eisenach G. B.*, 1721, given as by him in *Wetzel*, iii. 428 ; and no trustworthy evidence of his authorship has been adduced. *Tr.* as :—

God is for ever true! His loving. A *tr.* of st. i.–iv., by M. W. Stryker, in his *Hys. & Verses*, 1883, p. 34, repeated as No. 167 in his *Christian Chorals*, 1885.   [J. M.]

Gott rufet noch, sollt ich nicht endlich hören. *G.* Tersteegen. [*Advent.*] A beautiful hymn on God's gracious call to turn to Him; and what our answer should be. Founded on Ps. xcv. 7. 1st pub. in the 2nd ed., 1735, of his *Geistliches Blumengärtlein*, Bk. iii., No. 52, in 8 st. of 4 l., entitled, "To-day if ye will hear His voice." Included as No. 629 in the Berlin *G. L. S.*, ed. 1863. *Tr.* as :—

God calling yet!—and shall I never hearken? A good *tr.* by Mrs. Findlater, omitting st. vii., viii., in the 2nd Ser., 1855, of the *H. L. L.* p. 58 (1884, p. 116); and repeated as No. 553 in *Holy Song*, 1869. In America it has been somewhat widely used in the form given to it in

the Andover *Sabbath H. Bk.*, 1858, No. 556. Here the *tr.* of st. v. was omitted and the rest reduced to L.M., beginning, "God calling yet !—shall I not hear." The text of 1858 has been adopted in full in the Dutch Ref. *Hys. of the Church*, 1869 ; Bapt. *H. Bk.*, 1871 ; Presb. *Hyl.*, 1874 ; *H. & Songs of Praise*, N. Y., 1874 ; *Meth. Epis. Coll.*, 1878 ; and others. Omitting st. iv. it appears in Hatfield's *Ch. H. Bk.*, 1872 ; Oberlin *Manual*, 1880 ; *Ch. Praise Bk.*, 1882, &c. In the Pennsylvania Luth. *Ch. Bk.*, 1868, the full text of 1858 is included, with the addition of a recast of st. v.   [J. M.]

Gott sei gelobet und gebenedeiet. *M.* Luther. [*Holy Communion.*] St. i. dates from pre-Reformation times, was used at processions, during Mass as a post communion, and according to Bunsen (*Versuch*, 1833, p. 853) was sung by the people after the Epistle on Corpus Christi Day. This form is given by *Wackernagel*, ii. p. 748, from Ludewig Trutebul's *Enchiridion*, 1524 ; and by *Bäumker*, i. p. 719, from the Crailsheim *Schulordnung*, 1480. Luther adopted this st., added two others, and pub. the hymn in *Eyn Enchiridion*, Erfurt, 1524 (thence in *Wackernagel*, iii. p. 10), in 3 st. of 8 l., with two Kyrieleysons. Included in Schircks's ed. of Luther's *Geistl. Lieder*, 1854, p. 74, and as No. 271 in the *Unv. L. S.*, 1851. The *trs.* in C. U. are :—

1. God be blessed, and God be praised. A paraphrase in 54 l., in Miss Fry's *Hys. of the Reformation*, 1845, p. 93. Included, rewritten to 6 st. of 6 l., beginning, " Thou, who didst Thine Israel lead," in J. Whittemore's *Suppl. to all H. Bks.*, 1860, and in Maurice's *Choral H. Bk.*, 1861.

2. May God be praised henceforth, and blest for ever! In full in R. Massie's *M. Luther's Spir. Songs*, 1854, p. 78, repeated in the Ohio *Luth. Hyl.*, 1880, No. 273, and in *Dr. Bacon*, 1884, p. 33.

Translations not in C. U. :—
(1) " May God be praised and ador'd," as No. 234 in pt. i. of the *Moravian H. Bk.*, 1754. (2) " For that amazing love and grace," based on the 1754, as No. 568 in the *Moravian H. Bk.*, 1789 (1849, No. 1005, beginning, "Lord, what amazing "). (3) " Now Christ be praised and glorified," by *J. Anderson*, 1846, p. 75 (1847, p. 87). (4) " Glory and praise to God we give," by *Dr. J. Hunt*, 1853, p. 108. (5) " Let God be praised, blessed and uplifted," by Dr. G. Macdonald in the *Sunday Mag.*, 1867, p. 847. In his *Exotics*, 1876, p. 105, it begins, " Let God be blest, be praised, and be thanked."
                    [J. M.]

Gott verlässt die Seinen nicht! [*Cross and Consolation.*] Included as No. 1254 in the Breslau *G. B.*, 1743, in 3 st. of 6 l.; repeated in the ed. 1746, No. 128 ; in both cases without name of author. *Tr.* as :—

God doth not leave His own. A full and good *tr.* by Miss Warner in her *H. of the Ch. Militant*, 1858 (1861, p. 480). Included in the *Christian H. Bk.*, Cincinnati, 1865, No. 802 ; in Prust's *Suppl. H. Bk.*, Lond., 1869, No. 11 ; and in Dale's *English H. Bk.*, 1874, No. 597. [J. M.]

Gotter, Ludwig Andreas, s. of Johann Christian Gotter, Court preacher and Superintendent at Gotha, was b. at Gotha, May 26, 1661. He was at first privy secretary and then Hofrath at Gotha, where he d. Sept. 19, 1735. He was a pious, spiritually-minded man, with tendencies towards Pietism; and one of the best hymn-writers of the period. Of his printed hymns the earliest appeared in the *Geistreiches G. B.*, Halle, 1697. Of the 23 included in Freylinghausen's *Geistreiches G.B.*, 1704, and *Neues geistreiches G. B.*, 1714, seven have been *tr.* into English, besides his version of J. W. Petersen's "Salve, crux beata, salve" (q. v.). J. C. Wetzel, who had become acquainted with him during a visit Gotter made to Römhild in 1733, mentions a complete version of the Psalter (now in MS. in the Ducal Library at Wernigerode) by him, and quotes from his MS. the first lines of 42 hymns still unprinted (Wetzel's *A. H.*, ii. 22–30; *Koch*, iv. 400–402; *Allg. Deutsche Biog.*, ix. 456). Of his hymns those *tr.* into English are :—

i. *In English C. U. :—*

i. Erquicke mich, du Heil der Sünder. [*The Great Physician.*] On tho Gospel for the 3rd S. in Advent (St. Matt. xi.), turning it into a prayer for cures of our moral nature similar to the miracles of physical healing there recorded. In *Freylinghausen*, 1714, No. 771, in 10 st. of 6 l., and in Knapp's *Ev. L. S.*, 1837, No. 196. The only *tr.* in. C. U. is :—

Saviour of sinners, now revive us, of st. i., ii., v., x., by Miss Borthwick, as No. 236, in Dr. Pagenstecher's *Coll.*, 1864.

ii. Treuer Vater, deine Liebe. [*True and False Christianity.*] 1697, as above, p. 608, in 23 st. of 6 l., repeated in *Freylinghausen*, 1704; and in Porst's *G. B.*, 1713 (1855, No. 324). The only *tr.* in C. U. is :—

Father, Thine eternal kindness, omitting st. x., in J. C. Jacobi's *Psal. Ger.*, 1720, p. 3. Considerably altered in his ed., 1722, p. 50, and 1732, p. 78; and from this 8 st. were included as No. 542 in pt. i. of the *Moravian H. Bk.*, 1754. The *trs.* of st. xii., xiii., altered from the 1732, and beginning, "Has temptation well nigh won me," were included in the Scottish *Evang. Union H. Bk.*, 1856, and in Dr. J. Paterson's *Coll.*, Glasgow, 1867.

iii. Womit soll ich dich wohl loben. [*Praise and Thanksgiving.*] A beautiful hymn of Thanksgiving (founded on Ps. xci.) for the wonderful ways by which God in His love and goodness has led us, and of trust in the continuance of His love to the end. 1697, as above, p. 577, in 14 st. of 6 l., and the refrain (altered from Homburg's "Jesus, meines Lebens Leben.")

"Tausend, tausend Mal sei dir,
Grosser König, Dank dafür."

Repeated in *Freylinghausen*, 1704, and as No. 1033, in the Berlin *G. L. S.*, ed. 1863.

Lauxmann, in *Koch*, viii. 348–9, relates that st. iv. was adopted as a thanksgiving by the German Missionaries in Abyssinia on their deliverance by the capture of Magdala in 1868, and st. xi., by C. H. Bogatzky, after a narrow escape on one of his journeys in Bohemia; and adds that as the hymn, with its Swabian melody, was a great favourite of the poet Uhland, it was accordingly played by the trumpeters from the tower of St. George's Church, on July 14, 1873, at the ceremony of the unveiling of the statue erected to his memory in Tübingen.

The only *tr.* in C. U. is :—

Lord of Hosts! how shall I render. A good and full *tr.* in Dr. J. Guthrie's *Sacred Lyrics*, 1869, p. 131; and from this st. i., ii., ix., xiii., xiv., were included as No. 50 in the *Ibrox Hyl.*, 1871.

Another *tr.* is. "With what fervour of devotion," by J. C. Jacobi, 1732, p. 157.

ii. *Hymns not in English C. U. :—*

iv. Herr Jesu, Gnadensonne. [*Sanctification.*] Perhaps his finest hymn. 1697, as above, p. 525, in 8 st. The *trs.* are : (1) "Lord Jesus! Sun of graces," in the *Suppl.* to *Ger. Psal.*, ed. 1765, p. 43. (2) "O

shed abroad, Lord Jesus," a *tr.* of st. vi., as No. 1086, in the *Suppl.* of 1808 to the *Moravian H. Bk.*, 1801.

v. O Jesu meine Zuversicht. [*Lent.*] 1714, as above, No. 772, in 14 st. *Tr.* by *N. L.* Frothingham, 1870, p. 213, beginning with st. vii.

vi. Sei hochgelobt, barmherz'ger Gott. [*Praise for Redemption.*] On Eph. i. 3. 1st in the *Geistreiches G. B.*, Darmstadt, 1698, p. 485, in 16 st. *Tr.* as, "High praise to Thee, all-gracious God," by J. Wesley, in *Hys. & Sac. Poems*, 1740 (*P. Works*, 1868–72, v. i. p. 339).

vii. Wachet auf, ihr faulen Christen. [*Spiritual Watchfulness.*] On St. Matt. xxvi. 41. 1697, as above, p. 425, in 7 st., each beginning and ending with the word, "Wachet." *Tr.* as, "Arise! ye lingering saints, arise!" by Mrs. Findlater, in *H. L. L.* 1854.

[J. M.]

Gough, Benjamin, was b. at Southborough, Kent, in 1805, and d. Nov. 28, 1877. He was engaged in mercantile pursuits in London for some years. After retiring from business he resided at Mountfield, Faversham. He was a member and lay preacher of the Wesleyan denomination. His poetical works include :—

(1) *Lyra Sabbatica*, Lon., 1865 ; (2) *Kentish Lyrics*, Lon., 1867 ; (3) *Hymns of Prayer and Praise*, Lon., 1875; and several minor publications, the most important being (4) *Protestant Hymns & Songs for the Million*, Lon., 1878 ; (5) *Songs from the Woodlands, and Other Poems*, Lon., 1872; and (6) *Christmas Carols and New Year's Songs*, Lon. (N.D.).

Of Mr. Gough's hymns, about 20 are in C. U. in G. Britain and America, and of these the most popular and widely used is "Awake, awake, O Zion," q.v. Although possessing many features of popularity, his hymns do not rank high as literary productions. His works are also marred by numerous and feeble imitations of the great lyrics of the Church. Many of his earlier hymns were rewritten for his *Hys. of Prayer & Praise*, very much to their disadvantage. In addition to those which are annotated under their first lines the following are in C. U. :—

1. **Be thou faithful unto death.** *Faithfulness.* Appeared in his *Lyra Sabbatica*, &c., 1865, p. 77, in 3 st. of 8 l., and entitled "Christian Fidelity." In 1867 it was transferred to the *People's H.*, and again, in 1875, to the *New Mitre-Hymnal*, No. 151.

2. **Blessed are the dead who die.** *Burial.* Appeared in his *Lyra Sabbatica*, 1865, p. 89, in 4 st. of 8 l. and headed "For the dead in Christ." In Hatfield's *Church H. Bk.*, N. Y., 1872, it is slightly altered.

3. **Christ is risen from the dead.** *Easter.* In *Lyra Sabbatica*, 1865, p. 96, in 6 st. of 8 l., as "An Easter Carol ;" but in his *Hys. of Prayer & Praise*, 1875, p. 49, this is changed to "An Easter Hymn." In the *New Mitre-Hymnal*, 1875, st. iv., v. are omitted.

4. **Come, children, and join with ardour divine.** *Missions.* In his *Lyra Sabbatica*, 1865, p. 159, in 9 st. of 3 l., and entitled, "Children's Missionary Hymn ;" and the *Hys. of Prayer & Praise*, 1875, No. 39, in 4 st. of 6 l. In the latter work it is rewritten, very much to its disadvantage. The 1865 text is followed in the *Meth. S. S. H. Bk.*, 1879, No. 562.

5. **Come to Bethlehem and see.** *Christmas.* Appeared in his *Christmas Carols*, &c., N.D., p. 21, in 5 st. of 8 l. In the *New Mitre-Hymnal*, 1875, No. 26, it is dated 1873.

6. **For all the [Thy] saints in heaven and earth.** *All Saints.* From his *Lyra Sabbatica*, 1865, p. 119, in 4 st. of 8 l. into Snepp's *S. of G. & G.*, 1872, No. 748.

7. **God the Father, full of grace.** *Holy Trinity*, or *Public Worship.* Appeared in his *Kentish Lyrics*, 1867, p. 97, in 4 st. of 6 l.; and rewritten in a far less acceptable form, in his *Hys. of Prayer & Praise*, 1875, p. 80, in 4 st. of 6 l. No. 8 in the *Meth. S. S. H. Bk.*, 1879, is from the 1867 text.

8. **Ho, every one that thirsteth.** *Invitation.* Pub. in his *Lyra Sabbatica*, 1865, p. 83, in 5 st. of 8 l. ; and, altered to its disadvantage, in his *Hys. of Prayer & Praise*, 1875, p. 33, in 5 st. of 8 l. No. 291 in the *Meth. S. S. H. Bk.*, 1879 is from the 1865 text.

9. How beauteous on the mountains. *Missions.* In *Lyra Sabbatica*, 1865, p. 23, in 5 st. of 8 l.; and his *Hys. of Prayer & Praise*, 1875, p. 20. In Hatfield's *Church H. Bk.*, N. Y., 1872, No. 1246, is composed of st. i.–iii.

10. In Thy temple we adore Thee, gentle, pure, and holy Child. *Christmas.* In his *Christmas Carols*, &c., N.D., p. 39, in 3 st. of 4 double lines. In the *New Mitre-Hymnal*, 1875, No. 30, it is dated 1873, and begins, "In Thy cradle we adore Thee."

11. Jesus, full of love divine. *Love of Jesus.* Written in 1874, and pub. in the *New Mitre-Hymnal*, 1875, No. 84.

12. Lift the gospel banner. *Missions.* This is attributed to B. Gough, on the authority of Mrs. Gough. It is not in his published works, and its first appearance is unknown. In the *Meth. S. S. H. Bk.*, 1879, No. 394, it is in 4 st. of 8 l.

13. O Jesus, behold the lambs of Thy fold. *Sunday.* From his *Lyra Sabbatica*, 1865, p. 103, in 9 st. of 3 l. into the *Meth. S. S. H. Bk.*, 1879, No. 511, with the omission of st. ii.

14. Quicken, Lord, Thy Church and me. *Whitsuntide.* Appeared in his *Lyra Sabbatica*, 1865, p. 16, in 6 st. of 6 l.; and in his *Hys. of Prayer & Praise*, 1875, p. 6; and headed "For another Pentecost." It is No. 363, in Snepp's *S. of G. & G.*, 1872.

15. Sing we merrily to God. *Praise.* Appeared in his *Lyra Sabbatica*, 1865, p. 65, in 5 st. of 8 l., and his *Hys. of Prayer & Praise*, 1875, p. 27. In the *New Mitre-Hymnal*, 1875, No. 138, st. iii. is omitted.

16. There is a land of rest. *Heaven.* From his *Lyra Sabbatica*, 1865, p. 105, in 4 st. of 8 l. into the *New Mitre-Hymnal*, 1875, No. 155, where it is appointed for St. Mark's Day.

17. There is no condemnation. *Peace.* In his *Lyra Sabbatica*, 1865, p. 25, and his *Hys. of Prayer & Praise*, 1875, p. 22, in 3 st. of 8 l., and headed "No Condemnation." In Snepp's *S. of G. & G.*, 1872, it is No. 682.

18. Uplift the blood-red banner. *Missions.* In his *Lyra Sabbatica*, 1865, p. 155, and his *Hys. of Prayer & Praise*, 1875, p. 37, in 4 st. of 8 l., and headed "For the Conversion of the World." It is No. 408 in the *People's H.*, 1867; No. 88 in the *New Mitre-Hymnal*, 1875, &c.

[J. J.]

Gould, Sabine Baring-. [Baring-Gould, Sabine.]

Grace, J. Frances, a *nom de plume* of Mrs. Van Alstyne (q. v.).

Grace, 'tis a charming sound. *P. Doddridge.* [*Salvation by Grace.*] 1st pub. in his (posthumous) *Hymns*, &c., by J. Orton, in 1755, in 4 st. of 4 l., as follows:—

"cclxxxvi. *Salvation by Grace. Eph.* ii. 5.

1. Grace! 'tis a charming Sound,
    Harmonious to my Ear!
Heav'n with the Echo shall resound,
    And all the earth shall hear.

2. Grace first contriv'd a Way
    To save rebellious Man,
And all the Steps that Grace display,
    Which drew the wond'rous Plan.

3. Grace taught my wand'ring Feet
    To tread the heav'nly Road,
And new Supplies each Hour I meet,
    While pressing on to God.

4. Grace all the Work shall crown
    Thro' everlasting Days;
It lays in Heav'n the topmost Stone,
    And well deserves the Praise."

This text was repeated in J. D. Humphreys's ed. of the *Hymns*, &c., 1839, with the change in st. i., l. 2, of "my ear," to "*mine* ear."

In his *Ps. & Hys.*, 1776, A. M. Toplady gave a cento as No. 134 which was thus composed:—

i. *Doddridge*, st. i., with l. 2, "*the* ear" for "*my* ear."
ii. *Doddridge*, st. ii.
iii. *Toplady*:—

"'Twas grace that wrote my name
    In Thy eternal book;
'Twas grace that gave me to the Lamb,
    Who all my sorrows took."

iv. *Doddridge*, st. iii., with, in l. 1, "*forc'd*" for "taught."
v. *Toplady*:—

"Grace taught my soul to pray,
    And made my eyes o'erflow.
'Twas grace which kept me to this day,
    And will not let me go."

vi. *Doddridge*, st. iv.
vii. *Toplady*:—

"O let Thy grace inspire
    My soul with strength divine!
May all my powers to Thee aspire,
    And all my days be Thine."

From the original, or from this cento, all modern versions of the hymn are derived, and their construction can be determined by collation with the texts as given above. The use of the hymn in various forms is very extensive in all English-speaking countries. It is sometimes given as "Grace! 'tis a *joyful* sound," as in Harland's *Church Psalter & Hymnal*, No. 282. Doddridge's text, slightly altered, is rendered into Latin as "Gratia, quàm dulcis vox nostris auribus illa!" in R. Bingham's *Hymno. Christ. Lat.*, 1871. [J. J.]

Graces, Metrical. The Jewish and Early Christian "blessings" and "giving thanks" at meal-times were in prose, the metrical forms in use at the present time being of later origin. Our Lord's custom was evidence alike of what was a common practice in Jewish families, and of His sanction of the same. When He fed the multitudes He "looked up to heaven and *blessed* and brake the loaves" (St. Matt. xiv. 19; St. Mark vi. 41; St. Luke ix. 16) "and gave thanks" (St. Matt. xv. 36; St. Mark viii. 6; St. John vi. 11). This practice was continued by the Apostles (see 1 Tim. iv. 3-6) and by their immediate successors. In the Apostolic Constitutions (c. 47) there is "A prayer at Dinner-time," which Mr. Chatfield has translated as:—

"Thou art blessed, O Lord, Who nourishest
    me from my youth,
Who givest food to all flesh.
Fill our hearts with joy and gladness,
That at all times having all sufficiency,
We may abound to every good work
In Christ Jesus our Lord:
With Whom to Thee (be) glory, honour, and
    might
For ever and ever. Amen."

2. The early Fathers, Clement of Alexandria, St. Cyprian, St. Basil, Tertullian, St. Chrysostom, and others, give evidence in their writings that the *Grace* was a common institution in the early Church. This fact is emphasised by the presence of short *Graces* in the Gelasian and Gallican Sacramentaries. In the "Additional Services," appended to the Modern *Roman Breviary*, the "Grace before and after Meat" has developed into a somewhat elaborate service, with special provision for certain days and seasons. This retention of the mediaeval practice is also maintained in a more or less complete form in several Colleges and Grammar Schools throughout the country. A list of School Prayers and Graces is given in the Rev. J. W. Hewett's *Bibliotheca Sacra Academica*, Lond. Rivingtons, Pt. ii. Prose Graces are given in the *A. B. C. Catechisme and Prayers*, in various editions from 1545 to 1779; and Prose and Metrical Graces in Latin by Melanchthon and others in the *Precationes Piae*, 1564.

3. *Metrical Graces*, somewhat in the form

of the modern *Grace*, does not seem to have come into general use until the Reformation. In Henry the Eighth's *Primer*, 1545, they come into prominence, and from that period they form part of every English *Primer*. Several of these are in Dr. Burton's *Three Primers of the Reign of Henry VIII.*, 1862; in Clay's *Liturgies of* 1549 *and* 1552, &c., 1844, and in his editions of the *Elizabethan Liturgical Services*, 1847; and *Private Prayers*, 1851 (Parker Society). As a specimen of these Graces we append two from some fragments in our possession of a lost edition of the Elizabethan *Primer*. The first is the "Grace after Dinner," and reads :—

"Now You have well refreshed your bodyes, remember the lamentable afflictions and miseries of ye thousandes of your neighboures and brethren in Christ visited by the hand of God, some with mortall Plagues and diseases, some with imprisonments, some with extreme pouertye, and necessitie, so that eyther they cannot or they have not to feede on as you have done, remember therefore how muche and how deepely ye presente are bound to the goodness of God for your healthe wealth libertye, and many other his benefittes geuen vnto you.

    "Take hede ye neuer abuse the same,
    Giue thankes to god for euerything ;
    And alwaie praise his holy name
    Who doth not so is sore to blame
    No euill ensample see that ye geue
    Thus do the God's worde teache ys to lyve."

[It will be noted that the whole grace is really hortatory, and this is characteristic of this edition of the Primer in which the daily confession and absolution are given for private use in the singular number, the penitent thus being self-absolved.]

The second, the "Grace before Supper," is unfortunately incomplete, but its rhymed portion, so far as preserved, runs thus :—

    "Geve thāks to god with one accord
    For that shalbe set on this borde
    And be not carefull what to eate
    To eche thing liuing the lorde sendes meate
    For foode he will not see you perishe
    But will you feede foster and cherishe
    Take wel in worth that he hath sent . . ."

4. The two *Metrical Graces* which have taken the greatest hold on the Church throughout all English-speaking countries are those by John Cennick which appeared in his *Sacred Hymns for the Children of God, In the Days of their Pilgrimage*, London, 1741, p. 198, as follows :—

    "HYMN CXXX.
    Before MEAT.
    Be present at our Table, LORD ;
    Be Here, and Ev'ry Where ador'd ;
    Thy Creatures bless, and grant that we
    May feast in PARADISE with Thee."

    "HYMN CXXXI.
    After MEAT.
    We bless Thee, LORD, for this our Food ;
    But more for Jesu's Flesh and Blood ;
    The *Manna* to our Spirits giv'n,
    The Living Bread sent down from Heav'n ;
    Praise shall our Grateful Lips employ,
    While Life and Plenty we enjoy ;
    Till worthy, we adore thy Name,
    While banqueting with CHRIST, the LAMB."

The modern form of the second·*Grace* dates from Bickersteth's *Christian Psalmody*, 1833 (possibly earlier), where it reads :—

    "We *thank* Thee, Lord, for this our food,
    But *bless Thee more for Jesu's blood* !
    May Manna to our *souls* be given,
    The *bread of life* sent down from heaven."

This form has undergone slight changes : but it is substantially the same as that now in C. U.

5. In William Hammond's (q.v.) *Ps., Hys., and Spiritual Songs*, 1745, p. 310, there is a *Grace* for use "At Meals," in 3 st. of 8 l., which might be utilized with advantage. The opening stanza is :—

    "Thee let us taste in all our food,
    And relish Thy free grace,
    Always confess that Thou art good,
    And always sing Thy praise.
    Jesus, Thou art the living Bread,
    That Bread which came from heaven ;
    For as Thy precious blood was shed,
    For us Thy life was given."

This *Grace* would furnish a cento of more than usual merits.

6. The *Wesleyan Graces* are many, and of some importance. It is to the Nonjuring and other influences on the Wesley brothers that the development of the English Metrical Graces are mainly due. John Wesley taught the duty of "saying Grace," and Charles Wesley provided somewhat extensively for its observance. As early as 1739 Graces were given in their *Hys. and Sacred Poems*. Others appeared in *Hys. and Sacred Poems*, 1742; the *Hys. for Children*, 1763; and the *Hys. for Families*, 1767. In addition a special tract of 26 Graces was published in 1746. The contents of this tract are :—

i. Grace before Meat.

1. Father, accept our sacrifice.
2. Father of earth and heaven.
3. Jesus, to Whom alone we live.
4. Jesu, we Thy promise plead.
5. Life of the world, come down.
6. Lord of all, Thy creatures see.
7. O Father of all, Who fillest with good.
8. O Thou, Whose bowels yearned to see.
9. O, how can a criminal feast ?
10. Perishing for hunger, I.
11. Waiting for the Comforter.

ii. At, or After Meat.

1. And can we forbear, In taking our food ?
2. And can we forget, In tasting our meat ?
3. Away with all our trouble.
4. Blessing to God, for ever blest.
5. Father, Friend of human race.
6. Father, through Thy Son receive.
7. Father, we render Thee Thine own.
8. Glory [laud], love, and praise, and honour.
9. Jesus, life-inspiring Saviour.
10. O God of all grace, Thy bounty we praise.
11. Praise Him Who by His word.
12. Thankful for our every blessing.
13. Thanks be to God, Whose truth we prove.
14. Thee, Father, Son, and Spirit, we.
15. When shall we see the day ?

Several of these are given in whole or in part in the *Wes. H. Bk.*, 1875. Other *Graces*, by C. Wesley, which have come into C. U. are :—

i. From Hys. & Sacred Poems, 1739.

1. Being of beings, God of love.
In the *Wes. H. Bk.*, 1875, this is given as a hymn (No. 654), and st. i. also as a Grace.
2. Come Thou, our heavenly Adam [Father], come.
This is st. v. of "Enslaved to sense, to pleasure prone" (p. 351, i.).

ii. From Hys. and Sacred Poems, 1742.

3. Father, 'tis Thine each day to yield.
This is st. vi. of "Father of all, Whose powerful voice" (p. 368, ii.).

iii. From Hys. for Children, 1763.

4. For my life, and clothes, and food.
This is st. ii. of " Thou, my God, art good and wise."
5. Give Him then, and ever give.
This is st. iii. of "Happy man whom God doth aid."

iv. From Hys. for Families, 1767.

6. Meet and right it is to praise.
This is st. i. of that hymn.

v. From the Poetical Works, 1868–72.

7. O'erwhelm'd with blessings from above.

These *Graces* are all included in the *Wes. H. Bk.*, 1875, and most of them are found in other collections.

7. There remain several *Graces* which are in C. U. which we group in alphabetical order :—

1. Be known to us in breaking bread. By *J. Montgomery* (p. 119, ii.).
2. Daily, O Lord, our prayer be said. By J. Anstice, from his "*Lord of the harvest, once again.*"
3. Food, raiment, dwelling, health and friends. By J. Montgomery, in his *Christian Psalmist*, 1825.
4. For mercies that we taste and see. *J. Skinner.*
5. For us Thou spread'st a table, Lord. Appeared in *Hys. & Sacred Songs.* Manchester, Fletcher & Tubbs, 1855.
6. Great God, Thou Giver of all good. *J. Skinner.*
7. Great God, we bless Thy care. By J. G. Gregory, in his *Bonchurch H. Bk.*, 1868.
8. Great God, we praise Thy gracious care. By W. Freeman Lloyd, in the R. T. S.'s *The Child's Book of Poetry*, N.D.
9. Heavenly Father, grant Thy blessing. By C. H. Spurgeon, in his *O. O. H. Bk.*, 1866.
10. How kind and good to give us food. By *Mrs. J. C. Westbrooke.*
11. Join to bless the bounteous Giver. By C. H. Spurgeon, in his *O. O. H. Bk.*, 1866.
12. O what shall we poor children give. By J. G. Gregory, in his *Bonchurch H. Bk.*, 1868.
13. Our Father, bless the bounteous store. By C. H. Spurgeon, in his *O. O. H. Bk.*, 1866.
14. Parent of good, Whose bounteous grace. In the *Methodist S. S. H. Bk.*, 1879.
15. Thy providence supplies our food. By W. Cowper, from his " Almighty King, Whose wondrous hand" (p. 53, ii.).
16. To God, Who gives our daily bread. Anon. in Mrs. Brock's *Children's H. Bk.*, 1881.
17. We praise Thee, Lord, for every good. Anon. in Bickersteth's *Christian Psalmody*, 1833.
18. We Thank Thee, Father, for Thy love. By C. H. Spurgeon, in his *O. O. H. Bk.*, 1866.
19. With grateful heart and voice we raise. By C. D. Bell, in his Cheltenham *Appendix* to the *H. Comp.*, 1884.

8. In addition to these *Graces*, the **Index of Subjects** should also be consulted ; and for some in two and three lines each see Dr. Monsell's *Parish Hymnal*, 1873.   [W. T. B.]

Gracious Lord, incline Thine ear. *W. Hammond.* [*Christ desired.*] 1st pub. in his *Ps. & Hys.*, 1745, p. 258, in 10 st. of 4 l., and headed " I am sick of love. Cant. ii. 5," the opening stanza reading :—

"Gracious LORD, incline Thine Ear,
 My Complaint vouchsafe to hear ;
 Faint and Sick of Love am I,
 Give me CHRIST, or else I die."

In 1787 Dr. Rippon on including the hymn in his Bapt. *Sel.*, No. 296, omitted st. ii., vii. and ix., and re-wrote st. i., thus :—

"Gracious Lord, incline Thine ear,
 My *request* vouchsafe to hear ;
 Hear my never-ceasing cry ;—
 Give me Christ, or else I die."

This form of the hymn is in use amongst the Baptists, both in England and America. Another form in 6 st. (omitting st. ii., vi., vii., ix.) was given in Bickersteth's *Christ. Psalmody*, 1833, No. 644, with st. i. as :—

"Gracious Lord, incline Thine ear,
 · My *request* vouchsafe to hear ;
 Burden'd with my sins I cry,
 Give me Christ, or else I die."

This form of the hymn is in limited use in the Church of England.   [J. J.]

Gracious Lord, our children see. *W. Cowper.* [*Prayer on behalf of Children.*] 1st pub. in the *Olney Hymns*, 1779, Bk. ii., No. 12, in 3 st. of 8 l., entitled, " A Prayer for Chil-

dren," and signed " C." Its use in G. Britain is somewhat limited, but in America it is found in numerous collections. The reading of st. i., " Gracious *God*, our children see," dates from Bickersteth's *Christ. Psalmody*, 1833. [J. J.]

Gracious Saviour, gentle [holy] Shepherd. [*The Good Shepherd.*] In Miss Jane E. Leeson's *Hys. & Scenes of Childhood*, pub. in 1842, three hymns appeared as follows :—
1. "Shepherd, in Thy bosom folded," as *No. v.*`
2. "Loving Shepherd of Thy sheep," as *No. xvii.*
3. "Infant sorrow, infant weakness," as *No. xl.*

Upon these hymns the cento, " Gracious Saviour, gentle Shepherd," is based. It was first pub. in the *Salisbury H. Bk.*, 1857, No. 183, in 5 st. of 6 l., and was appointed for Holy Baptism. It is thus composed :—

i. " Gracious Saviour, gentle *Shepherd*,
    Little Ones are dear to Thee ;
    Gathered with Thine arms and *carried*
    In Thy bosom *they may be*
    Sweetly, fondly, safely tended ;
    From all want and danger free."

Of this stanza ll. 1–4 are from st. iii. of No. xl., as above, and ll. 5, 6 of No. v. The words in italics in this and the remaining stanzas are by Miss Leeson ; the alterations and additions being by the Rev. J. Keble.

ii. " *Tender Shepherd*, never leave them
     From Thy fold to go astray ;
     By Thy *look of love directed*,
     May they walk the narrow way ;
     Thus direct them, and protect them,
     Lest they fall an easy prey."

This stanza is rewritten from No. xvii. as above, no single line of the original being retained. It is based on the whole hymn, and not on any single stanza.

iii. " *Cleanse* their hearts *from* sinful *folly*
     In the stream Thy *love supplied ;*
     Mingled streams of Blood and water
     Flowing from Thy wounded side :
     And to heavenly pastures lead them,
     Where Thine own still waters glide."

The lines in italics are from Miss Leeson's No. v., st. ii. ; whilst ll. 5, 6, by J. Keble, have nothing in common with the three hymns.

iv. " Let Thy holy word instruct them :
     Fill their minds with heavenly light ;
     Let Thy love and grace constrain them,
     To approve whate'er is right,
     Take Thine easy yoke and wear it,
     And to prove Thy burden light."

This is a new stanza by J. Keble, the keynote being Miss Leeson's No. v., st. iii., l. 1— " Ever and anon instruct me."

v. " Taught to lisp the holy praises
    Which on earth Thy children sing,—
    Both with lips and hearts unfeigned
    May they their thank-offerings bring ;
    Then with all the saints in glory
    Join to praise their Lord and King ! "

This stanza is Miss Leeson's No. v., st. iii., rewritten.

In 1860 this cento was repeated in Jonathan Whittemore's Bapt. *Supp. to all Hymn-Books*, Lond., J. F. Shaw, No. 140, and signed " W.," i.e. " *Whittemore*." This subscription has led the cento to be described as by " Miss Jane E. Leeson, and the Rev. Jonathan Whittemore, Baptist Minister, b. April 6, 1802 ; d. Oct. 31, 1860." Seeing, however, that Whittemore's text is a repetition of the *Salisbury H. Bk.* text, with the single alteration of st. iii., l. 6, from " Where Thine own still waters glide," to " Where *the peaceful* waters glide," this ascription must be set aside in favour of " *Miss*

Jane E. Leeson, 1842; *J. Keble*, 1857." [E. MSS. and S. MSS.]

The use of this cento in all English-speaking countries is very great. The opening line sometimes reads, "Gracious Saviour, *holy* Shepherd," but this form is not received with general favour. [J. J.]

Gracious soul, to whom are given. *C. Wesley.* [*Resignation.*] Appeared in the *Hys. & Sac. Poems*, 1740, in 11 st. of 6 l., and based on the words, "Blessed are they that mourn." (*P. Works*, 1868–72, vol. i. p. 330.) As given in the American Meth. Episco. *Hymnal*, 1878, No. 487, it is composed of st. i., ii., vii., iii., in the order named. The cento, "Human soul, to whom are given," in the American Unitarian *Hys. of the Spirit*, 1864, is also from this hymn. [J. J.]

Gracious Spirit, Dove divine. *J. Stocker.* [*Whitsuntide.*] This hymn 1st appeared in the *Gospel Magazine*, July 1777, in 6 st. of 4 l., and entitled, "To God the Holy Ghost," as follows :—

1. "Gracious Spirit, Dove divine,
   Let Thy Light within me shine:
   All my guilty fears remove;
   Fill me full of Heav'n and Love.

2. "Speak Thy pard'ning Grace to me,
   Set the burden'd Sinner free:
   Lead me to the Lamb of God;
   Wash me in his precious Blood.

3. "Life and Peace to me impart;
   Seal Salvation on my Heart:
   Breathe thyself into my Breast,
   Earnest of immortal Rest.

4. "Let me never from thee stray;
   Keep me in the narrow Way:
   Fill my soul with Joy divine,
   Keep me, Lord, for ever thine.

5. "Guard me round, on ev'ry Side;
   Save me from self-righteous pride:
   Me with Jesu's Mind inspire;
   Melt me with celestial Fire.

6. "Thou my Dross and Tin consume;
   Let thy inward Kingdom come:
   All my Prayer and Praise suggest;
   Dwell and reign within my breast."

This is also given in full in Sedgwick's reprint of Stocker's *Hys. & Spiritual Poems*, &c., 1861, p. 7. In Glazebrooke's *Coll.*, st. 1–4 were given as "Gracious Spirit, *love* divine." This was repeated as from "Glazebrooke's C." in the Williams & Boden *Coll.*, 1801, No. 143. This was again repeated in J. Dobell's *New Selection*, &c., 1806, and later collections, and has become the recognised form of the hymn, the only alteration of the original being that of "Dove" to "*love* divine," in the opening line. Various alterations of the text are also in C. U., both in G. Britain and America, one, as "Gracious Spirit, *power* divine," being No. 1040 in *Kennedy*, 1863, and a second, "Holy Spirit, *Love* divine," in Powell's *Hys. & Anthems*, &c., 1881. These alterations may be ascertained by a collation with the original, as above. The hymn in its various forms is very popular, and is in extensive use in all English-speaking countries. [J. J.]

Gracious Spirit, dwell with me. *T. T. Lynch.* [*Whitsuntide.*] 1st pub. in his work, *The Rivulet, a Contribution to Sacred Song*, 1855, p. 79, in 6 st. of 6 l. It was brought into congregational use through the *Bapt. Ps. & Hys.*, 1858. From that date it

has steadily increased in popularity in G. Britain and America, and is given in full or in part in numerous hymn-books, especially those in use by Nonconformists. [J. J.]

Gracious Spirit, Holy Ghost. *Bp. C. Wordsworth of Lincoln.* [*Quinquagesima.—Love.*] 1st pub. in his *Holy Year*, 1st ed., 1862, in 8 st. of 4 l., and appointed for Quinquagesima, being a metrical paraphrase of the Epistle for that day. It is found either in full or in an abbreviated form in several collections, including some of the Public Schools, and a few in American C. U. In Martineau's *Hymns*, 1873, it begins, "Mighty Spirit, Gracious Guide." [J. J.]

Gradual. An anthem sung between the Epistle and Gospel with certain variations in form and use in Lent and Eastertide, which need not be described here. It is called the *Gradual* because it used to be sung either from one of the altar steps, or from one of the lower steps of the ambo into which the Deacon ascended to read the gospel. It was usually taken, with its verses, from the Book of Psalms, but occasionally from some other source. We subjoin a specimen of a metrical *Gradual*, for the Votive Mass of St. Sebastian, taken from the *Sarum Missal*, London, 1504.

" O Sancte Sebastiane,
Christi athleta gloriosissime,
Qui pro Christo reliquisti
Terrenae militiae principatum,
Et suscepisti magnum supplicium,
Intercede pro nobis ad Dominum.

O Sancte Sebastiane,
Christi martyr egregie,
Cujus meritis tota Lombardia
Fuit liberata a peste mortifera,
Libera nos ab ipsa et a maligno hoste.
Alleluia.

O Sancte Sebastiane
Nos trementes
Ac flentes
Imploramus tuum clemens auxilium
Ut possimus obtinere
Per te pestis mortiferae
Apud Christum remedium."
Burntisland Edit., 1861, p. 894*.
[F. E. W.]

Grant, James, b. probably in Edinburgh, but date unknown, and d. there on Jan. 1st, 1785. An ironmonger by trade, he carried on his business in West Bow, Edinburgh. From 1746 to 1752 he held several offices of importance in the Town Council of Edinburgh. Amongst several works of benevolence which received his aid the Orphan Hospital in Edinburgh was specially favoured, and to it the profits of the 1st and 2nd ed. of his *Hymns*, &c., were given. Those hymns and poems were mainly written to popular Scottish melodies, and were pub. as :—

Original Hymns and Poems, written by a Private Christian for his own use, and Published at the earnest desire of Friends. Edinburgh, 1784. (2nd ed., 1820, 3rd a reprint by D. Sedgwick, Lond., 1862.)

Of the hymns the best known is "O Zion, afflicted with wave upon wave." (*God's Unchangeable Love.*) It appeared as Hymn xvi. in the *Original Hymns*, &c., 1784, in 7 st. of 4 l., and is found in several modern collections, including the *New Cong.*, 1859, No. 610, and others. [J. J.]

Grant, Sir Robert, second s. of Mr. Charles Grant, sometime M.P. for Inverness, and a Director of the East India Company, was b. in 1785, and educated at Cambridge, where he graduated in 1806. Called to the English Bar in 1807, he became M.P. for Inverness in 1826; a Privy Councillor in 1831; and Governor of Bombay, 1834. He d. at Dapoorie, in Western India, July 9, 1838. As a hymn-writer of great merit he is well and favourably known. His hymns, "O worship the King"; "Saviour, when in dust to Thee"; and "When gathering clouds around I view," are widely used in all English-speaking countries. Some of those which are less known are marked by the same graceful versification and deep and tender feeling. The best of his hymns were contributed to the *Christian Observer*, 1806-1815, under the signature of "E—y, D. R."; and to Elliott's *Psalms & Hymns*, Brighton, 1835. In the *Ps. & Hys.* those which were taken from the *Christian Observer* were rewritten by the author (see *Preface*). The year following his death his brother, Lord Glenelg, gathered 12 of his hymns and poems together, and pub. them as:—

Sacred Poems. By the late Right Hon. Sir Robert Grant. London, Saunders & Otley, Conduit Street, 1839. It was reprinted in 1844 and in 1868.

This volume is accompanied by a short "Notice," dated "London, June 18, 1839."

[J. J.]

Granted is the Saviour's prayer. *C. Wesley.* [*Whitsuntide.*] 1st pub. in the *Hys. and Sac. Poems*, 1739, in 10 st. of 4 l., as a "Hymn for Whitsunday." (*P. Works*, 1868-1872, vol. i. p. 188.) It was repeated by A. M. Toplady in his *Ps. & Hys.*, 1776, No. 351, and in a few modern collections, including the *Hymnary*, 1872, the *Wes. H. Bk.*, 1875, in an abridged form. The cento, "Come, divine and peaceful Guest," in the *Songs for the Sanctuary*, N. Y., 1865, and others, is from this hymn, and begins with st. vi. Another cento, beginning with st. iii., "God, the everlasting God," is No. 175 in *The College Hymnal*, N. Y., 1876. [J. J.]

Grateful notes and numbers bring. [*Thanksgiving.*] This hymn appeared in the *Christians Magazine*, Feb., 1766, as "A New Ode as sung by the Women at the Magdalen Chapel," in 7 st. of 4 l., without signature, and with many repetitions and choruses as the parts were divided between the "First and Second Galleries." The following, omitting repetitions, is the text:—

"Grateful notes and numbers bring,
While Jehovah's praise we sing:
Holy, holy, holy, Lord!
Be Thy glorious name adored.

"Men on earth, and saints above,
Sing the great Redeemer's love:
Lord, Thy mercies never fail:
Hail, celestial goodness, hail!

"Though unworthy, Lord, Thine ear,
Our humble hallelujahs hear;
Purer praise we hope to bring
When with saints we stand and sing.

"Lead us to that blissful state,
Where Thou reignest supremely great;
Look with pity from Thy throne,
And send Thy Holy Spirit down.

"While on earth ordained to stay,
Guide our footsteps in Thy way;
'Till we come to reign with Thee,
And all Thy glorious greatness see.

"Then with angels we'll again
Wake a louder, louder strain;
There, in joyful songs of praise,
We'll our grateful voices raise.

"There no tongue shall silent be:
There all shall join sweet harmony;
That through heaven's all spacious round,
Thy praise, O God, may ever sound!"

There is no signature to the hymn, but there is every reason to conclude that it was by the Rev. William Dodd, the editor of the Magazine. In the 3rd ed. of Dodd's *Account . . . of the Magdalen Charity*, 1766 (dedication of this ed. dated Feb., 1766, 1st ed., 1761), the hymn is reprinted as "An Ode for the Magdalen Chapel"; and follows an "Anthem, for the use of Magdalen Chapel," beginning, "Let the solemn organ blow," which, when printed in the *Christians Magazine*, March, 1765, was given as "By the Rev. W. Dodd, Chaplain to the King. Set to Music by Mr. Bach, Composer to Her Majesty." The hymn is in Dodd's favourite metre; and his version of the 100th Ps., and his hymn, "Glory be to God on high," bear strong internal evidence to identity of authorship. In modern hymn-books it is found as follows:—

1. **Grateful notes and numbers bring.** In the *Ps. & Hys. for the Use of the Magdalen Chapel*, 1804, it was given with slight alterations in the irregular lines to harmonize the metre. In Bickersteth's *Christ. Psalmody*, 1833, No. 209, it was repeated with the omission of st. ii. and vii., and through this channel came into modern use.

2. **Grateful hearts and voices bring.** This form of the text was given in Hall's *Mitre H. Bk.*, 1836, No. 24, in 4 st. This, with the addition of a doxology, was repeated in the Cooke & Denton *Hymnal*, 1853, No. 126, and other collections.

3. **Holy, holy, holy Lord! Be Thy glorious Name adored.** In 1778, Benjamin Williams gave 6 st. from the original in his Salisbury *Coll.*, beginning with ll. 3-4, of st. i., "Holy, holy, holy Lord." From this four stanzas were taken by A. Kippis and his co-editors, and included in their *Coll.*, 1795, No. 184, as from the "Salisbury Collection." This form was repeated in later collections, and is very popular with Unitarians in G. Brit. and America.

4. **Heavenly Father, Sovereign Lord, Be Thy glorious Name adored.** This is an alteration of st. i., ii., iii., v., vi. (st. i. being from st. i., ii.), in 4 st. This was given in the Meth. Episco. *Hymns*, N. Y., 1849, No. 41, and repeated in the *Hymnal* of the same body, 1878, No. 20. The hymn, "Heavenly Father, Sovereign Lord, ever faithful to Thy word" (q.v.), No. 333 in their revised *Coll.*, 1831, is by C. Wesley.

The use of this hymn in these various forms is extensive in G. Britain and America.

[W. T. B.]

Grates, peracto jam die. *C. Coffin.* [*Evening.*] Appeared in the *Paris Breviary*, 1736, as the hymn for the day after the Presentation to Ash Wednesday, at Compline on Sundays and Ferial days, except when the Office of the B. V. M. is said. Also under the same rule from Trinity to Advent. In Coffin's *Hymni Sacri*, 1736, p. 97, it is given with the heading, "Ad Completorium post Trinitatem." Text in Card. Newman's *Hymni Ecclesiae*, 1838 (ed. 1865, p. 7). [W. A. S.]

Translations in C. U.:—

1. **And now the day is past and gone. Holy God, &c.** By I. Williams, in his *Hymns tr. from the Parisian Brev.*, 1839, p. 11, in 5 st. of 4 l. In 1852 it was given, with alterations, in the *English Hymnal*, No. 16. In the editions of 1856 and 1861, the text is again altered. Another altered text was given as "*Another day is past and gone*; O God," &c., in *Kennedy*, 1863, No. 839, in 2 st. of 12 l. This text with the omission of st. i., ll. 10-12, and "*Where* golden harps," for "And golden harps," st. ii., l. 8, in the Irish *Church Hymnal*, 1873, No. 18.

2. The day is past and gone. By W. J. Blew, 1st printed about 1850 for use in his church, and then included in his *Church H. & Tune Bk.*, 1852, " From Trinity to Advent," No. 8, in 6 st. of 4 l. It is partly from I. Williams's *tr.* above. In the *Hymnary*, 1872, No. 88, it is given with alterations and the omission of st. iv. The full text is No. 97 in Rice's *Hymns*, &c., 1870. *Chope*, 1864, repeats the text of his 1st ed., 1857.

3. The day is past, and still we live. By R. Campbell. 1st pub. in his *Hys. & Anthems*, 1850, p. 33, in 5 st. of 4 l. This was given in the Scottish Episco. *Coll.*, 1858, as No. 13.

4. Our thanks for this completed day. By J. D. Chambers, in his *Lauda Syon*, 1857, p. 43, in 5 st. of 4 l.; in Martineau's *Hys. of Prayer & Praise*, 1873, No. 573 is this *tr.* with slight alterations, and the omission of the doxology.

Translation not in C. U. :—
And now the day is past and gone, We sing, &c. *J. Chandler*, 1837.   [J. J.]

Graumann, Johann, D.D. (Poliander), was b. July 5, 1487, at Neustadt in the Bavarian Palatinate. He studied at Leipzig (M.A. 1516, B.D. 1520), and was, in 1520, appointed rector of the St. Thomas School at Leipzig. He attended the Disputation in 1519 between Dr. Eck, Luther, and Carlstadt, as the amanuensis of Eck; with the ultimate result that he espoused the cause of the Reformation and left Leipzig in 1522. In 1523 he became Evangelical preacher at Würzburg, but left on the outbreak of the Peasants' War in 1525, and went to Nürnberg, where, about Lent, he was appointed preacher to the nunnery of St. Clara. He then, at the recommendation of Luther, received from the Margrave Albrecht of Brandenburg an invitation to assist in furthering the Reformation in Prussia, and began his work as pastor of the Altstadt Church in Königsberg, in Oct., 1525. Here he laboured with much zeal and success, interesting himself specially in organising the evangelical schools of the province, and in combating the errors of the Anabaptists and the followers of Schwenckfeldt. He d. at Königsberg, April 29, 1541 (*Koch*, i. 355–59: ii. 475; *Bode*, p. 78, &c.). The only hymn of importance by him which has kept its place in Germany is :—

Nun lob, mein Seel, den Herren. *Ps. ciii.* Appeared as a broadsheet at Nürnberg, c. 1540, and in J. Kugelmann's *News Gesang*, Augsburg, 1540. Both of these are given by *Wackernagel*, iii. pp. 821–23, in 4 st. of 12 l. This fine rendering has been repeated in most subsequent hymnbooks, and is No. 238 in the *Unv. L. S.*, 1851. A 5th st., " Sey Lob und Preis mit Ehren," appeared in a broadsheet reprint at Nürnberg, c. 1555, and is in Burg's *G. B.*, Breslau, 1746, and other books, added to the original stanzas.

Lauxmann, in *Koch*, viii. 316–320, quotes Martin Chemnitz, 1575, as stating that it was written in 1525 at the request of the Margrave Albrecht, as a version of his favourite Psalm, and as saying that himself (i.e. Chemnitz) heard the Margrave joyfully singing it on his death-bed. *Lauxmann* adds that it was used by Gustavus Adolphus on April 24, 1632, at the first restored Protestant service at Augsburg. It was also sung by the inhabitants of Osnabruck, in Westphalia, as a thanksgiving at the close of the Thirty Years' War on Oct. 25, 1648, &c.

It is *tr.* as:—

My soul, now praise thy Maker! A good and

full *tr.* by Miss Winkworth, as No. 7 in her *C. B. for England*, 1863.

Other trs. are :—(1) " My soul! exalt the Lord thy God," by *J. C. Jacobi*, 1722, p. 86 (1732, p. 145). Included in the *Moravian H. Bks.* of 1754 (Nos. 127 and 315) and 1789. (2) " Now to the Lord sing praises," by *Dr. H. Mills*, 1845 (1856, p. 192).   [J. M.]

Gravi me terrore pulsas vitae dies ultima. *Card. Peter Damiani.* [*Advent— Death.*] Dr. Neale introduces his *tr.* of this hymn in his *Mediaeval Hymns*, 1851, p. 33, with the following note :—

" This awful hymn, the *Dies irae* of the individual life, was written by S. Peter Damiani, Cardinal Bishop of Ostia, the great coadjutor of S. Gregory VII. in his reform of the Church. He lived from 1002 to 1072, and spent the last years of his life in devotion and retirement at his Abbey of S. Croce d'Avellano, having resigned his Cardinalate. His realization of the hour of death is shown, not only in this hymn, but by the Commendatory Prayer, used from time to time in the Roman Church which begins, 'To God I commend thee, beloved brother'; and to Him Whose creature thou art I commit thee': originally composed by S. Peter as a letter to a dying friend."

The original text is given in Cajetan's ed. of Damiani's works (*Petri Damiani Opera*, Paris, 1642, vol. iv. p. 26); in *Migne*, tom. 145, col. 977, 978; in *Daniel*, i., No. 193; in *Trench*, 1849 (ed. 1874, p. 283); in *Bässler*, No. 83; and others, *Königsfeld* gives it in 15 st. from a Processional of the Dominican Order, Venice, 1572. It is also in the Venice edition of 1494. The additional stanzas are repeated by *Daniel*, iv. p. 291, but have not been translated.   [W. A. S.]

Translation in C. U. :—
Day of death! in silence speeding. By E. Caswall. 1st pub. in his *Masque of Mary*, &c., 1858, in 9 st. of 6 l.; and again in his *Hymns*, &c., 1873, p. 224. In the Roman Catholic *Crown of Jesus H. Bk.*, N.D., No. 182, it is given in full: but in the *Hymnary*, 1872, No. 106, st. iii. & vii. are omitted.

Translations not in C. U. :—
1. O what terror in thy forethought. *Neale*, 1851.
2. With terror thou dost strike me now. *Erastus C. Benedict* of New York, contributed to Schaff's *Christ in Song*, 1869.   [J. J.]

Gray, Jane, née Lewers, daughter of Mr. William Lewers, was b. at Castle Blayney, county Monaghan, Ireland, Aug. 2, 1796; and married to the Rev. John Gray, D.D., a Presbyterian minister. In 1820 they proceeded to America, where, in 1822, Dr. Gray became Pastor at Eaton, Pennsylvania. Mrs. Gray resided at Eaton till her death in 1871. Of 8 hymns which are known to be by her 6 were contributed to the (Old School) Presbyterian *Devotional Hymns*, Phila., 1842, of which Dr. Gray was one of the compilers; and 2 to the *Parish Hymns*, Phila., 1843. Of these the following are still in C. U. :—

1. Am I called? and can it be? *God's Invitation accepted.* Appeared in the German Reformed *Ps. & Hys.*, 1834, No. 454, and in the *Devotional Hymns*, 1842, and is in Spurgeon's *O. O. H. Bk.*, 1866, No. 576.

2. Hark to the solemn bell. *Burial.* This also dates from 1842, but is unknown to the English collections.   [F. M. B.]

Gray, Thomas, jun., M.D., was b. at Jamaica Plain Roxbury, Massachusetts, Feb. 4, 1803, and educated at Harvard College, where he graduated in 1823. After visiting

England and the Continent he took his M.D. in 1827, and commenced the practice of medicine in Boston, U.S.A. He subsequently exchanged the practice of medicine for that of chemistry. He d. in Boston, March 6, 1849. His hymns were mainly written for children, and for occasional services. They are of more than ordinary merit, and are much used by the Unitarians, of which body Dr. Gray was a member. They include :—

1. **Good-night, good-night, our song is said.** *Evening.* Popular with children.

2. **Jehovah! at Thine awful throne.** *Ordination.* "Written for the Ordination of Mr. George Whitney as Pastor of the Second Church and Society in Roxbury, June 15, 1831."

3. **Our Father, here again we raise.** *Morning.* In Gray's *Sunday S. Coll.*, 1833.

4. **Suppliant, lo! Thy children bend.** *Prayer.* Also in Gray's *Sunday S. Coll.*, 1833.

5. **We come in childhood's innocence.** *Opening of a Sunday School.* Given in Gray's *Sunday School Coll.*, 1844.

6. **While round Thy throne, O God, we bend.** *Anniversary of Sunday School.* "Written for the Jubilee of the Boston Sunday School Society, at the Federal Street Church, Sept. 14, 1831." It was given in Gray's *Coll.*, 1833.

For these details we are indebted to Putnam's *Singers and Songs of the Liberal Faith,* 1874, pp. 171–176.   [J. J.]

Great and glorious Father, humbly we adore Thee. *Bp. W. W. How.* [*Holy Communion.*] The note to this hymn in the S. P. C. K. *Church Hys.*, folio ed., p. xlix., is :—

"Written in 1869 with a view of setting forth each of the various aspects of the Holy Communion.—Our unworthiness to draw near (1); the Memorial before God (2); the Memorial before Man (3); Christ pleading His Passion for us above, yet present in His Sacrament (4); the receiving of the Heavenly Food (5); the offering of ourselves (6); the Angelic worship (7); adoration of the glorified Saviour (8)."

In 1871 it was included in the *Church Hymns*, with the tune "Oswestry," composed for it by Dr. Dykes. Since 1871 it has passed into several hymn-books in G. Britain, and into one or two in America.   [J. J.]

Great Author of my being. *C. Wesley.* [*Death desired.*] 1st pub. in his *Hys. and Sac. Poems,* 1749, vol. ii., in 8 st. of 8 l., as the third hymn of several on "Desiring Death." (*P. Works,* 1868–72, vol. v. p. 202.) In 1825 J. Montgomery included a cento therefrom in his *Christian Psalmist,* No. 338, but this has not come into C. U. Another cento is No. 574 in the American *Sabbath H. Bk.*, 1858, and later editions. Both centos begin "Great Author," &c.   [J. J.]

Great Creator, Who this day. *Julia Anne Elliott.* [*Sunday.*] Contributed to her husband's *Ps. & Hys.*, 1835, in 3 st. of 6 l. In the 1st ed. it was given without signature, but in later editions her initials "I. A. E." were added. It is in C. U. in G. Britain and America. In *Kennedy,* 1863, the original is given with one slight change as No. 898; and also in a much altered form beginning, "Father, Who the light this day," as No. 1457.   [J. J.]

Great Father of each perfect gift. *P. Doddridge.* [*Whitsuntide.*] This hymn is No. 89 of the D. MSS., but is undated. It was 1st pub. in J. Orton's (posthumous) ed. of Doddridge's *Hymns,* &c., 1755, No. 251, in 5 st. of 4 l., and headed, "The descent of the

Spirit, or His influence desired," Acts x. 44. It was also repeated in J. D. Humphreys's ed. of the same, 1839, No. 276. There are slight differences in the text of each, but that of Orton is commonly received as the original. The hymn is in several important collections in G. Britain and America. In the American *Bapt. Praise Bk.*, 1871, No. 522, it begins, "Great Father of *our feeble race.*"   [J. J.]

Great First of beings, Mighty Lord. *S. Browne.* [*Creation.*] 1st pub. in his *Hys. and Spiritual Songs,* 1720, and repeated in later editions, as No. 39, in 8 st. of 4 l., and headed, "All things made for God." In the American *Prayer Bk. Coll.*, 1826, 6 st. were given as No. 3, and this arrangement (sometimes with further omissions) is also found in other American collections.   [J. J.]

Great Former of this various frame. *P. Doddridge.* [*N. Year.*] This is No. 69 of the D. MSS., is dated, "Jan. 1, 173$\frac{7}{8}$," and headed, "The mutability of Creation, and the immutability of God." It was 1st pub. by J. Orton in his (posthumous) ed. of Doddridge's *Hymns,* &c., No. 64, in 6 st. of 4 l., and with the same heading; and again, with slight variations, in the text, by J. D. Humphreys, in his ed. of the same, 1839, No. 67. Although in C. U. in G. Britain and America, it is not so popular as many of Doddridge's hymns.   [J. J.]

Great God, and wilt Thou condescend? *Ann Gilbert.* [*To God the Father.*] 1st appeared in A. & J. Taylor's *Hymns for Infant Minds,* 1810, No. 5, in 5 st. of 4 l. (ed. 1886, p. 10). It is entitled, "Our Father, which art in heaven." For many years it was received as the production of *Jane Taylor;* but now, on the authority of Mrs. Gilbert's *Memorials,* it is rightly assigned to the latter. It is of this hymn that her biographer writes :—

"It may not be too much to say that the manner of the Divine Teacher has been seldom more nearly approached. Such might have been the little child whom 'He set in the midst.' In such words might the most mature Christian address his Father in heaven." *Memorials,* 1874, vol. i. p. 224.

This is the most popular of Mrs. Gilbert's hymns, and is in extensive use in all English-speaking countries.   [J. J.]

Great God, as seasons disappear. *E. Butcher.* [*Harvest.*] This hymn is adapted to Sermon xvi., in 6 st. of 4 l., in his *Sermons to which are added suitable Hymns,* 1798. It is found in two forms, the *first* chiefly in the Nonconformist collections, including Bap. *Ps. and Hys.,* 1858; Spurgeon's *O. O. H. Bk.,* 1866, No. 1033, and others; and the *second* in several hymn-books in the Church of England. The text in the latter, as found in Bp. Bickersteth's *Ps. & Hys.,* 1858; Harland's *Ch. Psalter,* &c., is much altered, and dates from Bickersteth's *Christ. Psalmody,* 1833.   [J. J.]

Great God, indulge my humble claim. *I. Watts.* [*Ps. lxiii.*] 1st pub. in his *Psalms of David,* &c., 1719, in 8 st. of 4 l., and headed, "Longing after God; or, The Love of God better than life." In modern hymn-books it is given as follows :—

1. The original text in full in a limited number of collections.

2. The cento given in some of the Methodist hymn-

books. This is composed of st. i.-iii., vi., viii. These stanzas, much altered, were given in J. Wesley's *Ps. & Hys.*, 1741, and later editions. They were again altered, and in this last revised form were included in the *Suppl.* to the *Wes. H. Bk.*, 1830, as No. 597 (revised ed. 1875, No. 577).

3. Centos of various lengths from the original, all beginning with st. i.

4. The cento, No. 83, in the *New Cong.*, 1859 : "Great God, permit my humble claim."

In one or more of these various forms this hymn is in C. U. in all English-speaking countries.   [J. J.]

Great God, now condescend. *J. Fellows.* [*Holy Baptism.*] Appeared in his *Infants Devoted to God, but not Baptized*, 1773, No. 22, in 7 st. of 4 l. In 1787, 5 stanzas were given in Rippon's Bap. *Sel.*, as No. 336, and this has become the recognised form of the hymn. It is in extensive use, especially in America, and is one of the best known of Fellows's hymns.   [J. J.]

Great God! o'er heaven and earth supreme. *E. Osler.* [*Sunday S. Anniversary.*] 1st pub. in Hall's *Mitre H. Bk.*, 1836, No. 281, in 3 st. of 8 l., and entitled, "Men Stewards of God's Bounties." In the June number of Osler's *Church and King*, 1867, it was repeated for the 2nd S. after Trinity, with the change in st. ii., l. 3, of "We take," to "We hail." In the S. P. C. K. *Hymns*, 1852, No. 193, it was given as "Great God! *in* heaven and earth supreme," and repeated in later editions. The hymn No. 424, in the Irish *Church Hymnal*, 1873, and beginning with the same line, is a cento, in 4 st. of which st. i., l. 1., and st. ii. and iv. are from Osler altered, and the rest is from Doddridge's "Jesus, my Lord, how rich Thy grace" (q. v.), st. ii. and v.   [J. J.]

Great God of Abraham, hear our prayer. *T. Cotterill.* [*For the Conversion of the Jews.*] 1st pub. in the 8th ed. of his *Selection*, 1819, No. 242, in 5 st. of 4 l., and headed, "For the conversion of the Jews" (see Cotterill, T.). It was repeated in the 9th ed., 1820, and all subsequent reprints of that ed. It is in many modern hymn-books, although it is not so popular as of old ; and in several it is ascribed to "*Davies*," an error which appeared in Bickersteth's *Christian Psalmody*, 1833.   [J. J.]

Great God of heaven and nature, rise. *P. Doddridge.* [*National Fast.*] In the D. MSS., No. 83, this hymn is dated "An hymn for the Fast day, Jan. 9, 17$\frac{39}{40}$." The Fast day was that appointed at the opening of the war with Spain. The hymn was pub. in J. Orton's (posthumous) ed. of Doddridge's *Hymns*, &c., 1755, No. 368, in 6 st. of 4 l., and with the more general heading, "An Hymn for a Fast-day in Time of War" : and again, with slight variations, in J. D. Humphreys's ed. of the same, 1839, No. 395. In some collections, as *Mercer*, the *New Cong.*, and others, it is abridged, and begins, "Great God of heaven and *earth*, arise." It is found in both forms in several modern collections.   [J. J.]

Great God, our infant voices raise. [*Praise to the Father.*] Pub. anonymously in Rowland Hill's *Hys. for the Use of S. Schools*, 1808, in 4 st. of 6 l. The hymn was designed to be sung by children, the congregation taking st. iv. as a chorus. In the Bristol *S. S. H. Bk.*, 1812, that st. was omitted, and has not since been restored. In Stowell's Manchester *Sel.*, 1831, No. 156, the opening line of the hymn begins, "Great God, our *voice to Thee we* raise," and in one or two other hymn-books the first line is again altered to "Great God, our *youthful* voices raise."   [W. T. B.]

Great God, the nations of the earth. *T. Gibbons.* [*Missions.*] This poem was 1st pub. in his *Hys. adapted to Divine Worship*, &c., 1769, Bk. ii., No. 69, in 46 st. of 4 l., divided into 7 parts, and headed, "The universal diffusion of the Gospel promised by God and pleaded by His people." The 7 parts are :—

i. "Great God, the nations of the earth," in 6 st. of 4 l. ii. "O when shall Afric's sable sons ?" in 6 st. of 4 l. iii. "Father, is not Thy promise pledged ?" in 6 st. of 4 l. iv. "When Jesus shall ascend His throne," in 6 st. of 4 l. v. "When Christ assumes His throne, this song," in 8 st. of 4 l. vi. "When Christ is throned on Zion's hill," in 5 st. of 4 l. vii. "The seed in scanty handfuls sown," in 7 st. of 4 l.

From this poem the following hymns and centos have come into C. U. :—

1. **Great God, the nations of the earth.** This was given in Rippon's Bapt. *Sel.*, 1787, No. 420, in 7 st. In the edition of 1800 it was increased to 16 st., of which viii.-x. were not by Gibbons, and their presence is explained in a note which reads :—"Verses 8, 9, and 10 of this hymn, in substance, were written off *Margate*, by Mr. William Ward, one of the Baptist Missionaries, on their departure for India, May 28, 1799." It is the first part of this arrangement of the hymn which is usually in C. U.

2. **Great God, is not Thy promise pledged?** This is composed of st. i. and v. of Pt. iii. It is in C. U. in America.

3. **Lord, send Thy word, and let it fly.** This is compiled from Pts. ii., iv. and vii. (st. 13, 14, 24, 26, and 46 of Gibbons's numbering), with slight alterations, and is in American C. U., as Hatfield's *Church H. Bk.*, 1872, No. 1236.

4. **Father, is not Thy promise pledged?** Included in Rippon's *Sel.*, 1787, No. 419, and again in later editions, and in other collections.   [W. T. B.]

Great God, this [hallow'd] sacred day of Thine. *Anne Steele.* [*Sunday.*] It was included in her *Miscellaneous Poems*, which were added to her *Poems on Subjects chiefly Devotional* (1st ed., 1760), as a third volume in 1780, p. 138, in 4 st. of 6 l. 1st pub. in 1769 in the Bristol Bapt. *Coll.* of Ash and Evans, No. 308, and from that date it came into general and somewhat extensive use. In some collections it begins, "Great God, this *hallow'd* day of Thine." Its use in this form is limited. Orig. text in D. Sedgwick's reprint of Miss Steele's *Hy nns*, 1863, p. 151.   [J. J.]

Great God, to me the sight afford. *C. Wesley.* [*God on Sinai.*] The cento which is known by this opening line is compiled from C. Wesley's *Short Hymns*, &c., 1762, as follows :—

St. i., ii., *Short Hymns*, vol. i., No. 166. St. iii., iv., *Short Hymns*, vol. i., No. 167. St. v., vi., *Short Hymns*, vol. i., No. 168.

The hymn given as the second part of the same, "Thy ceaseless, unexhausted love," is composed of :—

St. i., ii., *Short Hymns*, vol. i., No. 169. St. iii., iv., *Short Hymns*, vol. i., No. 170. St. v., vi., *Short Hymns*, vol. i., No. 171.

These two centos were given in the *Wes. H. Bk.*, 1780, as Nos. 240, 241. They are repeated in several collections in G. Britain and America.   [J. J.]

Great God, to Thee our songs we raise. [*Resignation.*] Appeared anonymously in the *Foundling Coll.*, 1796, and subsequent editions, in 3 st. of 6 l. In 1810 it was transferred, with slight alterations, to the Rev. J. Kempthorne's *Select Portion of Ps. & Hys.*, No. 132, and from thence it has passed into a few modern collections. In the Irish *Church Hymnal*, 1873, the text is altered somewhat freely. In D. Sedgwick's marked copy of Kempthorne's *Ps. & Hys.*, 1810, the authorship is ascribed to Kempthorne, but without authority. In common with other hymns of high merit, which come to us from the *Foundling Coll.*, its authorship is unknown.
[W. T. B.]

Great God, we sing that [Thy] mighty hand. *P. Doddridge.* [*New Year.*] Pub. by J. Orton in the posthumous ed. of Doddridge's *Hymns, &c.*, 1755, No. 157, in 5 st. of 4 l., and again with variations in the text, by J. D. Humphreys's ed. of the same, 1839, No. 282, the general heading in both being, "Help obtained of God, *Acts xxvi.* 22. For the New Year." In some collections it begins, "Great God, we *praise* Thy mighty hand"; and in others, "Great God, we sing *Thy* mighty hand." Usually, however, the alterations, both in the English and American hymn-books, are very slight.   [J. J.]

Great God, what do I see and hear? [*Advent.*] It is sometimes stated that this hymn is based upon the *Dies Irae*. With that sequence, however, it has no connection except that the two hymns are on the same subject. The commonly accepted statement that the hymn is by Martin Luther is still more apocryphal. A rendering of the *Dies Irae* into German which appeared in 1565 (*Wackernagel*, iv. pp. 344-5) was revised by Bartholomäus Ringwaldt and pub. in his *Handbüchlin*, 1586, and this was *tr.* by J. C. Jacobi, 1722. It is said that Ringwaldt's version was again *tr.* by another hand, c. 1802; and finally adopted by Dr. Collyer in 1812. How far this is correct will be gathered from the following facts:—

1. The opening stanza of Ringwaldt's text, 1586, is:—

"Est ist gewisslich an der Zeit
    Dass Gottes Sohn wird kommen,
In seiner grossen Herrlichkeit,
    Zu richten Bös und Frommen;
Da wird das Lachen werden theur
Wenn alles wird vergehn im Feur
    Wie Petrus davon schreibet."

2. The *tr.* by J. C. Jacobi, given in his *Psalmodia Germanica, &c.*, 1722, p. 95, is:—

"'Tis sure that awful Time will come,
    When Christ the Lord of Glory
Shall from his Throne give Men their Doom
    And change what's Transitory;
Who then will venture to retire,
When all's to be consum'd by Fire
    As Peter has declared?"

3. The anonymous stanza pub. in *Ps. & Hys. for Pub. and Private Devotion*, Sheffield, 1802, is:—

"Great God! what do I see and hear!
    The end of things created!
The Judge of mankind doth appear
    On clouds of glory seated!
The trumpet sounds! the graves restore
The dead which they contain'd before!
    Prepare, my soul, to meet Him."

The only resemblance this stanza has to Jacobi's *tr.*, or to the German from which he *tr.*, is in the subject, and the metre common to them all. Strictly speaking, therefore, the history of "Great God, what do I see and hear!" begins with the anonymous stanza in the Sheffield *Ps. & Hys.* of 1802. This stanza was repeated in J. Kempthorne's *Sel. Portions of Ps. & Hys.*, 1810; R. Aspland's Unitarian *Sel. of Ps. & Hys.*, 1810, and others.

4. In 1812, Dr. Collyer gave this stanza in his *Hys. partly Collected and partly Original, &c.*, No. 856, with the following additional stanzas:—

2. "The dead in Christ are first to rise,
    And greet th' archangel's warning;
To meet the Saviour in the skies,
    On this auspicious morning:
No gloomy fears their souls dismay,
His presence sheds eternal day,
    On those prepar'd to meet Him.

3. "Far over space, to distant spheres,
    The lightnings are prevailing;
Th' ungodly rise, and all their tears
    And sighs are unavailing:
The day of grace is past and gone,
They shake before the Judgment throne,
    All unprepar'd to meet Him.

4. "Stay, fancy, stay, and close thy wings,
    Repress thy flight too daring;
One wondrous sight my comfort brings,
    The Judge my nature wearing:
Beneath His cross I view the day,
When heaven and earth shall pass away
    And thus prepare to meet Him!"

To the hymn as thus constituted, Dr. Collyer added the following note:—

"This hymn, which is adapted to Luther's celebrated tune, is universally ascribed to that great man. As I never saw more than this first verse, I was obliged to lengthen it for the completion of the subject, and am responsible for the verses which follow."

5. The next stage in the history of the hymn is supplied by T. Cotterill. In the 8th ed. of his *Sel.*, 1819, No. 199, the original stanza of 1802 was given unaltered; but in the 9th ed., 1820, No. 163, it was followed by the remaining stanzas being altered thus:—

2. "The dead in Christ *shall* first *arise*,
    At the last trumpet's sounding,
Caught up to meet Him, in the skies,
    With joy their Lord surrounding:
No gloomy fears their souls dismay;
His presence sheds eternal day
    On those prepared to meet Him.

3. "*But sinners, filled with guilty fears*,
    Behold His wrath prevailing;
For they shall rise, and find their tears
    And sighs are unavailing:
The day of grace is past and gone:
Trembling they stand before the throne,
    All unprepared to meet Him.

4. "*Great God! what do I see and hear!*
    The end of things created!
The Judge of mankind doth appear
    On clouds of glory seated:
Beneath His cross I view the day,
When heaven and earth shall pass away,
    And thus prepare to meet Him."

6. From 1820 onwards the work of alteration has been carried on, *Cotterill's* text being more strictly adhered to than any other. More than twenty versions are found in hymn-books in C. U. at the present time, the most important being H. A. & M., 1875, from *Cotterill*, through Murray's *Hymnal*, 1852; the S.P.C.K. *Church Hymns*, 1871, from *Cotterill* through Bickersteth's *Christ. Psalmody*, 1833; the *Hy. Comp.*, 1876, also through *Bickersteth*; Thring's *Coll.*, 1882, from *Cotterill*, with alterations by the editor; and the *Hymnary*,

1872, from *Cotterill*, with emendations by the compilers. In the *Hymnary* it begins, "O God, what do I see and hear!" and in T. Darling's *Hymns*, 1887, "Lord God, what do I see and hear." In the American *Church Praise Bk.*, 1882, st. i., ii. and iv. are from *Hys. A. & M.* (see above), and st. iii. is from Dr. Mills's *tr.* of "Schon ist der Tag von Gott bestimmt" (p. 302, i.). With regard to all the versions of this hymn, careful collation shows that the Sheffield *Ps. & Hys.* of 1802, and *Collyer*, in 1812, supplied the materials; *Cotterill* in 1820 shaped the edifice, and individual editors have since added, in some cases adornments, and in others disfigurements, thereto. Some forms of the text have been rendered into several languages, including that in the *Appendix* to the S. P. C. K. *Ps. & Hys.*, 1863, into Latin by R. Bingham, in his *Hymn. Christ. Latina*, 1871, as "Magne Deus, quæ videnda!" [J. J.]

Great God, where'er we pitch our tent. *B. Beddome.* [*Family Worship.*] This hymn on "Going to a new habitation," appeared in Rippon's *Sel.*, 1787, No. 333, in 2 st. of 4 l., and from thence it has passed into a few modern collections. In Beddome's (posthumous) *Hys. adapted to Public Worship*, 1817, it is given as stanzas iii. and iv. of the hymn, "Bless'd Lord, my wandering heart recal." The text in *Rippon* and in Beddome's *Hymns*, is slightly different. The former is that in C.U. [J. J.]

Great God, Whose universal sway. *I. Watts.* [*Ps. lxxii.*] 1st pub. in his *Psalms of David*, &c., 1719, as the 1st part of his version of Ps. lxxii., in 6 st. of 4 l., and entitled "The Kingdom of Christ." It is followed by pt. ii., "Jesus shall reign where'er the sun" (q.v.), in 8 st. of 4 l. Three hymns, all beginning with the same stanza, "Great God, Whose," &c., are in C. U. as follows:—

1. The original as above. This is in a few modern collections in G. Britain. In America it is very popular.
2. In E. W. Eddis's Irvingite *Hys. for the Use of the Churches*, 1864, No. 8 is composed of st. i. and vi. of this hymn, and st. iv. and v. of "Jesus shall reign," &c.
3. In the same collection, No. 143 is made up of st. i., as above, and st. vi.–viii., of "Jesus shall reign," &c. These centos are limited in their use. [J. J.]

Great is the Lord, of high renown. *J. Keble.* [*Ps. xlviii.*] This version of Ps. xlviii. appeared in two parts in his *Psalter, or Ps. of David in English verse*, 1839, pt. i., consisting of 5 st. of 4 l., and pt. ii. of 7 st. of 4 l. The latter began:—"Our ears have heard, and now our eyes," and in 1863 was given unaltered in *Kennedy*, as No. 1078, and with the addition of a doxology. [J. J.]

Great is the Lord our God. *I. Watts.* [*Ps. xlviii.*] 1st pub. in his *Psalms of David*, &c., 1719, in 7 st. of 4 l., and headed, "The Church is the honour and safety of a nation." The popular form of this hymn is composed of st. i., ii., vi., vii. This is in extensive use in G. Britain and America, and embodies the oft-quoted stanza :—

> "These temples of His grace,
> How beautiful they stand.
> The honours of our native place,
> The bulwarks of our land."

In a few cases the text is altered, and sometimes, as in the *New Mitre*, 1875, a doxology is added. [J. J.]

Great is their peace who love Thy law. *I. Watts.* [*Ps. cxix.*] This cento in the *Leeds H. Bk.*, 1853, No. 162, is compiled from Watts's C.M. version of Ps. cxix. as follows :

St. i. from pt. i. st. iii. ; st. ii. from pt. v. st. i. ; st. iii. from pt. ii. st. iv. ; st. iv. from pt. v. st. vi.

The original version of Ps. cxix. extends to 18 parts, and was 1st pub. in Watts's *Psalms of David*, &c., 1719. [J. J.]

Great King of nations, hear our prayer. *J. H. Gurney.* [*Public Fast.*] 1st pub. in his Lutterworth *Coll. of Hys. for Pub. Worship*, 1838, No. 76, in 3 st. of 4 double lines, and headed, "Fast Day ; or, Time of Public Calamity." It was repeated in the Marylebone *Ps. & Hys.*, 1851, No. 66, and is found in numerous modern collections, including *H. A. & M.*, the S. P. C. K. *Church Hys.*, the *Hy. Comp.*, &c. It ranks as one of the best hymns for the occasion of Public Fasting. [J. J.]

Great King of Saints, enthroned on high. [*On behalf of Church Officers.*] This hymn was given anonymously in W. Urwick's *Coll. of Hymns*, &c., Dublin, 1829, No. 292, in 5 st. of 4 l., and headed, "Praise and Prayer for the Office-bearers of the Church." In 1836 it was included in J. Conder's *Cong. Hy. Bk.*, No. 193, and in some copies it was signed "Conder," in the index. This, however, was subsequently omitted. The history of this hymn goes back to Rippon's *Bap. Sel.*, 1787, No. 417, "Fair Sion's King, we suppliant bow," which was given in the 4th ed. of J. Dobell's *New Selection* (1st ed. 1806), No. 209 (second part), as, "Great King of Sion, gracious God." This was again rewritten and given in Urwick's *Hymns* as above. Its authorship has not been determined. [J. J.]

Great Ruler of all nature's frame. *P. Doddridge.* [*Providence.*] In the "D. MSS." this hymn is No. 54, is headed "God's mercy in moderating the storms of affliction, from Is. xxvii. 8," and is dated "Dec. 10, 1737." The same text was given in the posthumous ed. of Doddridge's *Hymns*, &c., 1755, No. 92, in 4 st. of 4 l., and again in J. D. Humphreys's ed. of the same, 1839, No. 108. Its use in G. Britain is limited, but in America it is extensive. The hymn, "Maker of all things, mighty Lord," by E. Osler, in Hall's *Mitre H. Bk.*, 1836, No. 48, is composed of st. i., ii. from this hymn (altered), and the rest by Osler. [J. J.]

Great Ruler of the earth and skies. A word of Thy, &c. *Anne Steele.* [*National Thanksgiving for Peace.*] 1st pub. in her *Poems on Subjects chiefly Devotional*, 1760, vol. i. p. 38, in 6 st. of 4 l., and entitled, "Praise for National Peace." In 1787 it was given in Rippon's Bapt. *Sel.*, No. 531, and subsequently in a large number of hymn-books in G. Britain and America, including the Cooke & Denton *Hymnal*, 1853; Stowell's *Ps. & Hys.*, 1831 (15th ed., 1877), &c. Orig. text in D. Sedgwick's reprint of her *Hymns*, &c., 1863. [J. J.]

Great Ruler of the earth and sky, In boundless deeps, &c. *S. Browne.* [*Providence.*] In 1716 John Clarke, of London, pub. *The Error of them who devise Evil. A Sermon Preach'd in the Old Jewry, Nov. 5,*

1716, *By Simon Browne*, and appended thereto this hymn on " Mysterious Providence," in 9 st of 4 l. It was afterwards included, with the same title as No. 129, in Browne's *Hys. & Spiritual Songs*, 1720. It is in a few modern books.   [J. J.]

Great Saviour, Who didst conde-scend. [*Public Worship.*] This children's hymn for use in Public Worship was given anonymously in Rowland Hill's *Hys. for the Use of S. Schools*, 1808, No. 177, in 5 st. of 4 l. In 1812 it was repeated in a Bristol *S. S. H. Bk.*; in 1836 in the *Cong. H. Bk.*; and again in others to modern hymn-books in G. Britain and America, including the *Meth. S. S. H. Bk.*, 1879, &c.   [W. T. B.]

Great Shepherd of Thine Israel. *I. Watts.* [*Ps. lxxx.*] Appeared in his *Ps. of David*, &c., 1719, in 12 st. of 4 l., and entitled, "The Church's Prayer under Affliction; or, The Vineyard of God wasted." It is usually given in modern hymnals, both in G. Britain and America, in an abbreviated form, and sometimes as, "Great *Leader* of Thine Israel." In the Irvingite *Hys. for the Use of the Churches*, 1864, No. 68, st. v.–viii., slightly altered, are given as, "Lord, Thou hast planted with Thine hands." The opening lines of this ver-sion of Ps. lxxx. :—

"Great Shepherd of Thine Israel,
    Who didst between the cherubs dwell,"

are from Sir J. Denham's version of the same Psalm, 1714.   [J. J.]

Great Source of being and of love. *P. Doddridge.* [*River of Living Water.*] 1st pub. in his (posthumous) *Hymns*, &c., 1755, No. 147, in 6 st. of 4 l., and headed, "The waters of the Sanctuary healing the Dead Sea." To this is added, in order to explain the 5th stanza, "To the Dead Sea the waters flow," the note :—

"The Sea or Lake, where Sodom, Gomorrah, &c., had stood, which was putrid and poysonous; and ancient writers say that no Fish could Live in it."

The same text, but with the omission of the note, was repeated in J. D. Humphreys's edi-tion of the *Hymns*, &c., 1839, No. 165. In some modern hymn-books st. v. is omitted, as in Martineau's *Hymns*, &c., 1873.   [J. J.]

Great Source of life, our souls con-fess. *P. Doddridge.* [*Thanksgiving for Per-sonal Benefits.*] This hymn is No. 10 in the "D. MSS." but is undated. It is in 5 st. of 4 l., and entitled, "Of walking before the Lord in the land of the living," Ps. cxvi. 9. The same text was given in his (posthumous) *Hymns*, &c., 1755, No. 59, but the title was changed to, "Deliverance celebrated and good resolutions formed"; and again in J. D. Humphreys's ed. of the *Hymns*, &c., 1839, No. 72. In some modern collections st. ii. is omitted, as in Mer-cer's *Ch. Psalter & H. Bk.*, ed. 1864, No. 507. Usually, however, it is given in full. [J. J.]

Great Source of unexhausted good. [*Providence Acknowledged.*] Appeared in the Exeter Unitarian *Coll.*, 1812, No. 186, in 5 st. of 6 l.; headed, "Grateful acknowledgement of God's constant Goodness"; and marked in the Index with an asterisk denoting that it was first published therein. In modern Ame-rican Unitarian collections, as the Boston *Hy. & Tune Bk.*, 1868, No. 148, it is abbreviated to 3 st.   [W. T. B.]

Great was the day, the joy was great. *I. Watts.* [*Whitsuntide—Missions.*] From his *Hys. & S. Songs*, 1709, Bk. ii., No. 144, in 6 st. of 4 l., into a few modern collec-tions. In the Bapt. *Ps. & Hys.*, 1858, No. 287, the lines :—

"Go, and assert your Saviour's cause;
    Go, spread the mystery of His Cross,"

are changed to :—

"Go, and your Saviour's Cross proclaim:
    Go, teach all nations in my Name."

This change is not generally adopted. [J. J.]

Greding, Johann Ernst. [Rube, J. C., No. i.]

Greek Hymnody. § i. *Introduction.* The ancient Greek hymns range themselves under two radically distinct classes: those written in the decaying classical metres, with increasing disregard to the rules of quantity : and the far larger and more important class found in the Service Books of the Eastern Church, which is more oriental in character, with an affinity to the Hebrew modes; and which, issuing from the hymns of the Old Covenant and the Angelic hymn at Bethle-hem, developes itself into the elaborated canons of the eighth and ninth centuries.

A. Classical Metres.

§ ii. A copious selection of Christian hymns in classical measures, chiefly Ana-creontic, may be seen in Daniel's *Thesaurus*, vol. iii., in *Anthologia Graeca Carminum Christianorum*, by Christ and Paranikas, and in *Poetae Veteres Graeci*, by La Rovière. The latest of these includes hymns by Leo the Wise (886–912), and the Patriarch Photius (died 891). Some of the most important will be noted in the following sketch. Two remarks may be made on them of a general character. They afford constant evidence of that change which shows itself in Latin as well as Greek, an increasing disregard of the old laws of quantity. (Instances may be seen in *Anthologia Graec. Car. Christ.*, Prolego-mena, p. xxxvi. The interchange of *o* and *ω* as equivalent sounds is a common illustration of the fact.) And secondly, none of these classical measures, except in three Iambic canons of St. John of Damascus (see below, §§ xvi. 11, xvii. 2), were ever, so far as can be gathered, admitted into the public worship of the Church.

§ iii. *Clement of Alexandria.* The earliest of these hymns, and the oldest of all Christian hymns, Στόμιον πώλων ἀδαῶν (Bridle of steeds untamed), is attached to the παιδα-γωγός of *Clement of Alexandria* (170–220). It has been disputed whether it is really by Clement himself, or has been added by another hand, as an act of devotion founded on the book to which it is annexed. "Though its phraseology is adapted to the perfect Gnostic of Alexandria in the second century" (*Liddon*), there is nothing in its bright versi-cles—full of childlike trust in Christ, as the Shepherd, the Fisher of Souls, the Everlasting Word, the Eternal Light—that is not to be found in the pages of Holy Writ. It is written in

Dimeter Anapæstics. (See *Anth. Graec. Car. Christ.*, p. 37, and *Daniel*, iii. 3.) It has been translated by Dr. Bonar; by Mr. Chatfield in *Songs and Hymns of the Earliest Greek Christian Poets*, p. 155; and in *Ante-Nicene Christ. Lib.* i. 341, seq. The latter of these gives the best idea of the original structure.

§ iv. *Gregory of Nazianzus* (329–89). Among the religious poetry of Gregory of Nazianzus, written for the most part after his retirement from the Court at Constantinople to his cell at Nazianzus, there are hymns of a high order; rapt contemplations of the Triune Godhead, tinged with Platonic phrases to some extent, but far more vividly recalling the Creed of Constantinople. The finest perhaps are Ὦ πάντων ἐπέκεινα (" All-circling Infinite ") in Hexameters, and the Anacreontic Σὲ τὸν ἄφθιτον μονάρχην (" Thee, King Immortal "). But the warmer tone of adoration in the "Hymn to Christ after Silence" at Easter Χριστὲ, ἄναξ, σὲ πρῶτον) (" Thee first, O Christ the King") appeals more to the emotions. A full selection of these hymns will be found in *Anth. Graec. Car. Christ.*, all of which have been gracefully translated in Mr. Chatfield's *Songs and Hymns, &c.* The selection in *Daniel* iii. is slightly fuller. The author of *The Life of Ken by a Layman* [J. G. Anderdon] has drawn a parallel, suggested originally by Ken himself, between our own prelate and Gregory. The sudden fall from his brilliant eminence — as the eloquent preacher of the Anastasis, the Patriarch enthroned by the Emperor's own hand, and the president of the Œcumenical Council of Constantinople—to ignominious abdication and return to the cell of his humbler life; the employment of his remaining years in sacred poetry; and even the traits of heart and temper which the poems exhibit, have analogies in Ken. " The Address to his own Soul," Τί σοι θέλεις γενέσθαι (" What wouldst thou have") (see *Anth. Graec. Car. Christ.*, p. 26, and Mr. Chatfield's vigorous translation), a caustic, scornful soliloquy, recalls often the sudden turns of Herbert, and the contempt of life and earth which inspires "The Exit" of Baxter and "The Challenge" of Sir Walter Raleigh. The morning and evening hymns of Gregory cannot be named beside Ken's; but on the other hand nothing else of Ken equals the loftiness of Gregory. [Gregory of Nazianzus.]

§ v. *Synesius* (375–430). Ten hymns of this eloquent and philosophic bishop, not all written at the same period of his life, and yet considered by him as forming a single book (see the 10th hymn, Μνώεο Χριστέ) (" Remember, O Christ"), are beautiful examples of that speculative adoration of the Triune Godhead, which the Platonic philosophy inspired. The 8th hymn, Ὑπὸ δώριον ἁρμογάν, gives a tender portraiture of his love of his wife and children; and the 3rd, Ἄγε μοι Ψυχά, the longest of all, written in times of greater peace for his beloved Libya after his return from the court of Arcadius, shows the fervour of his patriotism. They are written in Anacreontic, Logœlic, Spondaic, and Anapæstic metres, and are printed in the *Anth. Graec. Carm. Christ.*, p. 20, seq., from whence they have been translated by Mr. Chatfield.

The 10th hymn, in Mr. Chatfield's representation of it (" Lord Jesu, think on me,") has been adopted in *H. A. & M.*, and by Mr. Thring, but the Western form and expansion are the translator's. Though of great spirit, reality and beauty, the hymns of Synesius lie confessedly on the borderland of Christianity and Neo-Platonism, and often it is the Platonic rather than the specially Christian thought that inspires his most refined passages. It has been doubted, but perhaps erroneously, whether he believed in the Resurrection. (See *Anth. Graec. Carm. Christ.*, p. ix., and Chatfield's *Introduction*, p. i. seq.)

§ vi. *Sophronius*, Patriarch of Jerusalem (629). The poems of this prelate illustrate the distinction between the hymns in classical metres and those of the ritual of the Church which are to be treated below. Two or three *Idiomela*, written in the accustomed style, are found in the *Menaea* and *Horologion*. (See *Anth. Graec. Carm. Christ.*, pp. liii. 96.) His Anacreontic hymns, on the other hand, are not to be found in the Greek Service-books. They have been published in Cardinal Mai's *Spicilegium Romanum*, 1840, vol. iv., from which full extracts have been made in *Daniel*, iii., and *Anth. Graec. Carm. Christ.*, pp. 44–6. They are all written in the same metre, Ionic dimetre; but at intervals of fifteen or twenty lines varied by a couplet of different metre, "technically known as κουκύλλιον," generally expressive of some comment or aspiration arising out of the narrative given in the rest. They are long narratives, on the Annunciation, the Nativity, the Visit of the Magi, the Baptism, the Triumphal Entry, the Last Supper, the Cross, the Ascension; on St. Paul, St. John, St. Stephen, and certain saints. The most interesting is on the Holy Places, giving an insight into the appearance of Jerusalem and the spots held sacred in his day. It is in stanzas of four lines, the initial letters of the stanzas being the letters of the alphabet in order. These hymns of Sophronius have not been rendered into English.

§ vii. *Elias Syncellus. St. John of Damascus.* Of the remaining pieces in the *Anthologia* and *Daniel* only two are of conspicuous merit: a solemn reflection on death and judgment, deeply earnest, by Elias Syncellus (*Anth. Graec. Carm. Christ.*, p. 47), and a Prayer to Christ in Anacreontics, of great personal fervour, by St. John of Damascus. It has been versified in Mr. Lupton's St. John of Damascus (*Fathers for English Readers*, q. v.). The three great canons of St. John of Damascus in trimeter Iambics are an apparent exception to the rule that classical metres are not found in the Greek Service Books. But they are in reality a link between the two classes of hymns, for while written in Iambic metre, they are also conformed to the rules of syllable, accent, and acrostic, to which the Church hymns are subjected. See § xvi.

B. *Hymns of the Greek Church.*

§ viii. *Hymns of the Old Testament.* Of more enduring importance is the distinctively Christian growth, which has its root in the poetry and worship of the Old Covenant, and culminates in the hymns of the Eastern Church. If we could recover a more exact notion of the strophes of Hebrew poetry, of the musical accents, the antiphonal singing, the liturgical use of detached versicles of the Psalms, and other characteristics of Hebrew hymnody, a strong light might be thrown on some of the obscure parallels presented by the Greek system. A few points may however be noted with tolerable certainty. It is scarcely worth stating that the songs of the Old Testament, together with other rhythmic passages, passed in their Greek forms into the Christian Services. The use of the *Alleluia* and the *Hosanna* are equally obvious examples. The *Ter Sanctus* had been partially in previous use in the Jewish ritual: the *Hosanna* which so constantly accompanies it was partly the echo of the Triumphal Entry, but partly also of the older refrain used at the Feast of Tabernacles (See *Dict. of the Bible*: *Hosanna*). Antiphonal singing, introduced among the Greeks by Ignatius at Antioch, seems clearly traceable to a Hebrew origin, exemplified by the practice of the Therapeutæ, as stated by Philo, and the far older practice of the Temple choirs (1 Chron. vi. 31, seq. and xxv.). (See *Dict. Christ. Ant.: Antiphon.*) The refrains and short ejaculations of praise which are such a marked feature of Greek hymns have analogies in the Psalms, and the Eighteen Prayers of the synagogue. The use of broken versicles of the Psalms (στιχολογία) and Christian versicles interwoven with them (ἀπόστιχα, στιχηρὰ ἀπὸ στίχου), as well as the longer form Antiphon are probably derived from the Hebrew use. The Acrostic, on which the strophes of the Canons are threaded, resembles the system of the Alphabetical Acrostic Psalms, and is occasionally itself alphabetical.

§ ix. *Hymns of the New Testament.* The inspired songs that ushered in the Nativity became probably at an early period canticles of the church: the Angels' Hymn at Bethlehem is the germ of the *Gloria in Excelsis* (see § x. 4.) There is no trace however of a similar use of the heavenly songs of the Book of Revelation, beyond the adoption of a few of the acclamations in the later Greek hymns. Beside these Scriptural hymns others must have soon arisen. That the holy enthusiasm of the new life of Christianity would express itself in some similar forms to those of the *Magnificat* and *Nunc Dimittis* seems in itself almost inevitable: and notwithstanding a measure of doubt attaching to both expressions, the terms 'hymn' and spiritual song' (Eph. v. 19, 20; Col. iii. 16, 17) seem plainly to assert their existence.

[The word ὕμνος is found only in these two passages of the N. T., but the derivative verb is used of the hymn sung at The Last Supper, which was probably the series of *Psalms* called the *Hallel* (Pss. cxiii.–cxviii.). St. Paul, however, plainly distinguishes "hymns" and "psalms." Watts and the early English writers of hymns thought the Canticles and other passages of Holy Scripture suitable for singing were denoted by "Spiritual Songs." But it is more probable that they were new utterances inspired by the Holy Spirit, like those in the Corinthian Church.]

The form and matter of these hymns may be suggested to us by the rhythmic passages in the epistles of St. Paul, St. James and St. Peter. A disposition has shown itself to find in some of the most remarkable of these, where they are separable from the context,

actual quotations of existing hymns (e.g. 1 Tim. vi. 15, 16; Titus iii. 4–7; James i. 17). The verse which bears the strongest evidence of being a fragment of a hymn, "on penitence," is Ἔγειραι ὁ καθεύδων, καὶ ἀνάστα ἐκ τῶν νεκρῶν, καὶ ἐπιφαύσει σοι ὁ Χριστός ("Awake thou that sleepest," &c.), Eph. v. 14. Two of "the faithful sayings" in the Pastoral Epistles, which are evidently household words of the Christians, have a rhythmic character. Χριστὸς Ἰησοῦς ἦλθεν εἰς τὸν κόσμον ἁμαρτωλοὺς σῶσαι ("Christ Jesus came into the world to save sinners") (1 Tim. i. 15) has been called part of a hymn "on redemption": Εἰ γὰρ συναπεθάνομεν, καὶ συζήσομεν· εἰ ὑπομένομεν, καὶ συμβασιλεύσομεν· κ.τ.λ. ("If we die with Him, we shall also live with Him," &c.) 2 Tim. ii. 11–13, a fragment "on the glories of martyrdom": and the short versicles resembling one of the strophes of the canons, ἐφανερώθη ἐν σαρκὶ, ἐδικαιώθη ἐν πνεύματι, ὤφθη ἀγγέλοις, ἐκηρύχθη ἐν ἔθνεσιν, ἐπιστεύθη ἐν κόσμῳ, ἀνελήφθη ἐν δόξῃ. ("Manifested in the flesh, justified in the spirit," &c.) 1 Tim. iii. 16, part of a hymn "on Our Lord's Incarnation and Triumph." (See Liddon's *Bampton Lectures*, p. 327, note.) It is not easy to decide whether such hymns were then used in the worship of the Church. Pliny's letter to Trajan seems to prove the use of hymns at the Eucharist at a very early period (*Carmen Christo quasi Deo dicere invicem secum*). On the other hand it will be shown below that there was a scruple against the adoption of anything but psalms in the public devotions (see § xi.); and the context, in which St. Paul mentions "hymns" and "spiritual songs," is giving directions not for worship, but common life and social intercourse. (See *Dict. Christ. Ant.: Hymns.*)

§ x. *Primitive Greek Hymns.* 1. The earliest hymn in this class is the *Thanksgiving* at lamp-lighting (ἐπιλύχνιος εὐχαριστία), as St. Basil calls it, which has been frequently translated both in prose and verse,—Φῶς ἱλαρὸν ἁγίας δόξης (q. v.) It was old in St. Basil's day (370): but it is a misinterpretation of his words (*De Spiritu Sancto*, c. 29) to attribute it to Athenogenes (169).

2. *Methodius* (died circa 311). A hymn found in "The Banquet of the Ten Virgins," beginning Ἄνωθεν, παρθένοι, βοῆς ἐγερσίνεκρος ἦχος ("Up, maidens, the sound of the cry that raiseth the dead"), by this early writer, though not found in the Greek Service Books, may be most fitly mentioned here on account of certain rhythmical features. Unlike all other extant early hymns, it is of great length—twenty-four strophes—and thus suggests the possibility that some of the longer anonymous *Idiomela* of the Greek Service Books may be of early date (see § x.). The initial letters of the strophes are, as in the Anacreontic hymn of Sophronius (see § vi.) on "The Holy Places," the letters of the alphabet in their order, thus supplying a link between the Hebrew Alphabetical Psalms and the acrostichs of Romanus and the canons (see §§ xii., xvi). Each strophe is followed by the same refrain (ὑπακοή) sung in chorus by The Ten Virgins, the strophes themselves being sung by Thekla alone. The rhythm is plainly Iambic, though loose and irregular. The piece is full of sustained spirit and elation, and Mr. Chatfield's translation of it, "The

Bridegroom cometh," is the best in his volume (p. 141). (See *Anth. Graec. Carm. Christ.*, p. 33, and another translation in *Ante - Nicene Library : Methodius*, p. 111.)

3. The *Ter Sanctus* in its earliest form, as derived from the hymn in Isaiah vi. 3, was used for liturgical purposes in the Jewish church. There is an apparent allusion to its use in Christian worship in the catechetical lectures of St. Cyril (circa 347). It appears in the Clementine Liturgy (*Apost. Const.* 8, 12) in this form, Ἅγιος Ἅγιος Ἅγιος Κύριος Σαβαώθ· πλήρης ὁ οὐρανος καὶ ἡ γῆ τῆς δόξης αὐτοῦ· εὐλογητὸς εἰς τοὺς αἰῶνας· ἀμήν. ("Holy, Holy, Holy I Lord of Sabaoth; heaven and earth are full of His Glory. Blessed art Thou for ever. Amen.") The form varies slightly from this in the liturgies of St. Mark, St. James, and St. Chrysostom; and in the two latter the *Hosanna* is attached, "Hosanna to the Son of David: blessed be he that cometh in the name of the Lord: Hosanna in the highest." This precedent of combination was followed in the First Prayer Book of Edward VI. The hymn always occurs in the same position in Eastern liturgies, following the Eucharistic Preface. (See Neale's *Holy Eastern Church*, p. 541, and *Dict. of Christ. Ant.* under *Preface.*)

4. The Greek form of the *Gloria in Excelsis* is of early date. The germ of it is of course the Angels' hymn at Bethlehem (Luke ii. 14); and so far it occurs in the Liturgy of St. James. But the extended form of it is found at the end of the psalms and canticles contained in the *Codex Alexandrinus* (end of 5th cent.), and reads :—

Δόξα ἐν ὑψίστοις θεῷ, καὶ ἐπὶ γῆς εἰρήνη, ἐν ἀνθρώποις εὐδοκία· Αἰνοῦμέν σε, εὐλογοῦμέν σε, εὐχαριστοῦμέν σοι, προσκυνοῦμέν σε, δοξολογοῦμέν σε διὰ τὴν μεγάλην σου δόξαν · Κύριε βασιλεῦ, ἐπουράνιε, θεὲ πατὴρ παντοκράτωρ, κύριε υἱὲ μονογενὲς, Ἰησοῦ Χριστὲ, καὶ ἅγιον πνεῦμα. Κύριε ὁ θεὸς, ὁ ἀμνὸς τοῦ θεοῦ, ὁ υἱὸς τοῦ πατρὸς, ὁ αἴρων τὰς ἁμαρτίας τοῦ κόσμου, ἐλέησον ἡμᾶς· ὁ αἴρων τὰς ἁμαρτίας τοῦ κόσμου, πρόσδεξαι τὴν δέησιν ἡμῶν· ὁ καθήμενος ἐν δεξιᾷ τοῦ πατρὸς, ἐλέησον ἡμᾶς· ὅτι σὺ εἶ μόνος ἅγιος, σὺ εἶ μόνος κύριος, Ἰησοῦς Χριστὸς εἰς δόξαν θεοῦ πατρός. Ἀμήν. ("Glory to God in the highest and on earth peace, goodwill among men. We praise Thee, we bless Thee, we give thanks to Thee, we worship Thee, we give thanks to Thee for Thy great Glory. O Lord, Heavenly King, God the Father Almighty, Lord the only-begotten Son, Jesus Christ, and Holy Spirit! O I Lord God, Lamb of God, Son of the Father, that takest away the sins of the world, have mercy on us: Thou that takest away the sins of the world, receive our prayer : Thou that sittest on the right hand of the Father, have mercy on us: For Thou only art Holy, Thou only art the Lord Jesus Christ to the Glory of God the Father.")

Another version of the hymn, substantially the same, yet with some additional phrases and variations, is found in the *Apost. Const.* 7, 47. In some late MSS. the chapter in which it is found is entitled προσευχῆς ἑωθινῆς. It is also found in a spurious treatise of St. Athanasius, *De Virginitate*, as a morning hymn. Its eucharistic use is Western; except the Nestorian, none of the Eastern Liturgies contain it. (See

Anth. Graec., p. xxii., and *Doxology* and *Gloria in Excelsis* in *Dict. Christ. Ant.*)

5. *Te Deum.* There can be little doubt that the *Te Deum*, or some elements of it are originally Greek, although only a few clauses have been actually discovered. The first twenty-one verses of the *Te Deum* in Latin are found without variation in early MSS.; but there are four known variations in the form of the last nine verses. Two of these variations differ from the one adopted in our Prayer-Book only in the omission of certain clauses. But the other two, besides omitting one or two clauses, insert, though each in a different place among the clauses, the words "*Benedictus es Domine Deus patrum nostrorum et laudabile nomen tuum in aeternum.*" If we add these words to the familiar phrases, "Day by day we magnify Thee," "Vouchsafe, O Lord, to keep us this day without sin," we obtain precisely the following short Greek hymn, which is found in the *Codex Alexandrinus* immediately after the Greek form of the *Gloria in Excelsis.* (See above, 4.)

Καθ᾽ ἑκάστην ἡμέραν εὐλογήσω σε καὶ αἰνέσω τὸ ὄνομά σου εἰς τὸν αἰῶνα καὶ εἰς τὸν αἰῶνα τοῦ αἰῶνος. Καταξίωσον, Κύριε καὶ τὴν ἡμέραν ταύτην ἀναμαρτήτους φυλαχθῆναι ἡμᾶς. Εὐλογητὸς εἶ Κύριε ὁ θεὸς τῶν πατέρων ἡμῶν καὶ αἰνετὸν καὶ δεδοξάσμενον τὸ ὄνομά σου εἰς τοὺς αἰῶνας. ἀμήν. ("Day by day I will bless Thee and praise Thy Name, for ever and ever and ever. Vouchsafe, Oh Lord, to keep us this day also without sin. Blessed art Thou, O God of our fathers, and praised and glorified is Thy Name for ever.") (See *Dict. Christ. Ant.* : "Te Deum;" *Anth. Graec. Carm. Christ.*, p. 39 ; *Daniel*, vol. iii.).

6. *Early Vesper Hymn* (*Te decet laus*). *Hymn before Meals.* In the 7th book of the *Apostolic Constitutions* (c. 47) the *Gloria in Excelsis* is followed by two other short hymns. They are printed in *Anth. Graec. Carm. Christ.*, p. 40, and translated by Mr. Chatfield. The first is an Evening Hymn. The latter part of it is simply the *Nunc Dimittis*, and the early part begins with a verse of the Psalms. It then repeats the phrase in the *Gloria in Excelsis*, αἰνοῦμέν σε, ὑμνοῦμέν σε, εὐλογοῦμέν σε διὰ τὴν μεγάλην σου δόξαν, and slightly varies the clause concerning "The Lamb, that taketh away the sin of the world." The next phrases are well known in their Latin form, "*Te decet laus.*" Σοὶ πρέπει αἶνος, σοὶ πρέπει ὕμνος, σοὶ δόξα πρέπει τῷ πατρὶ καὶ τῷ υἱῷ καὶ τῷ ἁγίῳ πνεύματι εἰς τοὺς αἰῶνας τῶν αἰώνων. ἀμήν. ("Thou art worthy to be praised, Thou art worthy to be hymned, Thou art worthy to be glorified, Father, Son, and Holy Ghost, for ever and ever. Amen.") The second hymn is what we should call a short grace before meals.

7. *Trisagion.* This name has of late been discontinued as an equivalent of *Ter Sanctus*, for good reasons. The Greek term τρισάγιον indicates a short invocation found in the Greek Liturgies, shortly after the Little Entrance, and sometimes accompanied by a prayer called "the prayer of the Trisagion." It is entirely distinct from the *Ter Sanctus* common to Greek and Latin Liturgies, and runs thus : Ἅγιος ὁ θεός, ἅγιος ἰσχυρός, ἅγιος ἀθάνατος, ἐλέησον ἡμᾶς. "Holy God, Holy and Mighty,

Holy and Immortal, have mercy upon us." The legend of its origin relates that it was preternaturally communicated to the terror-stricken population of Constantinople during an earthquake in the time of St. Proclus (434-7). (See *Nicephorus Callistus*, Lib. 14, cap. 46.) It is considered, however, by Neale and others to be probably far older. It is said to have been introduced into the Liturgy in the reign of the younger Theodosius (408-50). It is found in the *Roman Missal* in The Improperia used on Good Friday. The Greek words and the Latin are there sung in response to each other by the two sides of the choir. So also in the *Sarum* and *York* Uses. (See *Dict. Christ. Ant.: Trisagion.*)

8. The Greek form of the *Gloria Patri* was perhaps founded on the Baptismal formula (Matt. xxviii. 19). The three early varieties of it may be seen under **Doxologies.** They were old in St. Basil's days (370).

9. *The Cherubic Hymn.* This hymn, so-called from its references to the Cherubim, is found in the chief Eastern Liturgies, except the Clementine, before the Great Entrance. It is not found in the heretical liturgies except in the Armenian; and this fact is an argument against its antiquity. It is generally ascribed to the time of Justinian. Cedrenus says that Justinian first ordered it to be sung in churches. It runs thus: Οἱ τὰ χερουβὶμ μυστικῶς εἰκονίζοντες, καὶ τῇ ζωοποιῷ Τριάδι τὸν τρισάγιον ὕμνον ἄδοντες, πᾶσαν τὴν βιωτικὴν ἀποθώμεθα μέριμναν, ὡς τὸν Βασίλεα τῶν ὅλων ὑποδεξάμενοι, ταῖς ἀγγελικαῖς ἀοράτως δορυφορούμενον τάξεσιν. ἀλληλούϊα. "Let us who mystically represent the Cherubim and sing the holy hymn to the Quickening Trinity, lay by at this time all worldly cares; that we may receive the King of Glory, invisibly attended by the angelical orders. Alleluia, Alleluia, Alleluia." (See *Dict. Christ Ant.: Cherubic Hymn.*)

10. *Hymn of Justinian.* A short hymn is found in the Liturgies of St. Mark and St. James, which Neale declares from internal evidence to be later than the Council of Ephesus (431), and which is generally considered the composition of the emperor Justinian (527-65). It runs thus: Ὁ μονογενὴς υἱὸς καὶ λόγος τοῦ θεοῦ, ἀθάνατος ὑπάρχων, καὶ καταδεξάμενος διὰ τὴν ἡμετέραν σωτηρίαν σαρκωθῆναι ἐκ τῆς ἁγίας θεοτόκου καὶ ἀειπαρθένου Μαρίας, ἀτρέπτως ἐνανθρωπήσας, σταυρωθείς τε, Χριστὲ ὁ θεὸς, θανάτῳ θάνατον πατήσας, εἷς ὢν τῆς Ἁγίας Τριάδος, συνδοξαζόμενος τῷ Πατρὶ καὶ τῷ ἁγίῳ Πνεύματι, σῶσον ἡμᾶς. "Only-begotten Son and Word of God, Immortal, Who didst vouchsafe for our salvation to take flesh of the Holy Mother of God and Ever-Virgin Mary, and didst without mutation become man, and wast crucified, Christ our God, and by death didst overcome death, being One of the Holy Trinity, and glorified together with the Father and the Holy Ghost, Save us." (*Anth. Graec. Carm. Christ.*, p. 52.)

11. If the materials of the Greek Service-books could be critically distinguished, several of the *Anonymous* pieces among the shorter hymns would doubtless be added to these early compositions. It is generally believed, that the *Hirmoi*, on which so many of the later odes are modelled, belong to the earlier centuries. The versicles which are attached to the psalms, either as antiphons or στίχηρα ἀπόστιχα, are also probably among the earliest essays at hymns. Nor is there any reason why some of the anonymous *Idiomela*, which partake of the same natural spirited freshness as these should not be equally early. The elaborate canons of later times add very little original thought to these more artless pieces, and they are often inferior in force. Their prevailing type is a strophe asserting at the opening some Christian fact or doctrine; and then grounding on it an acclamation of praise or culminating in the utterance of some glorious title or consequence.

§ xi. *Liturgical use.* Between these short and simple hymns, largely built up of joyous ejaculations, and the elaborate Odes and Canons of the 8th and 9th centuries there is a wide interval: and as the history of the development is obscure, it will be convenient to throw together here some account of the gradual introduction of hymns into the public worship of the church. Notwithstanding the very early mention of hymns as part of the Liturgy in Pliny's letter and by Justin Martyr, as well as the evidence of the Liturgies for the use of some of those already noted, there was manifestly a certain reserve as to their general introduction; in some parts of the Church they were allowed earlier than in others. An extract from the Epistle of the Second Council of Antioch (269) against Paul of Samosata shows that they were then in use in the Church of Antioch (*Dict. Christ. Ant.: Hymns*). Yet as late as the 4th and 5th centuries there was a scruple against the use of anything but Psalms in the Eastern monasteries (*Pitra*, pp. 42, 43), and in Spain the Council of Braga (561) forbade the use of hymns. No doubt, they were originally of popular origin, and then from their own power of spiritual edification passed into the services. In three different centres of the life of the Church the use of hymns received a powerful impulse from their employment by heretics. The Gnostic hymns of Bardesanes and Harmonius led Ephrem the Syrian (circ. 360) to adopt their metres and rhythms in his hymns for the Syrian Church. The Arian hymns drew the attention of Athanasius at Alexandria (*Pitra*) and Chrysostom at Constantinople to the hold which hymns had on the masses. The use of processional hymns in the narthex, lighted by torches, may have originated in the processions with crosses and torches which Chrysostom organized at Constantinople (*Dict. Christ. Ant.: Hymns*). How far these movements developed the structure of the Greek hymns, it is impossible to say; the strophes of Ephrem, with their final invocation, or refrain, have great similarity to the *troparia* of the Greek odes. On the other hand the syllabic metres of Ephrem seem much more regular than the varied lengths of verse in the *troparia*, while the great number of tunes (275) in the Syrian Church contrasts strongly with the eight tones, to which the Greek hymns seem confined, and probably points to deep-seated differences. See for Ephrem Syrus, *Hymns and Homilies of E. S.*, translated by Dr. Burgess.

§ xii. *Middle Period.*—1. *Romanus.*—The

principal link between the early hymns and the odes and canons is found in a group of pieces discovered in two very rare Liturgical MSS. at Moscow and Rome, by Cardinal Pitra. (Published in his *Analecta Sacra Inedita*, Paris, 1876, quoted by Lord Selborne, art. " *Hymns*," *Encycl. Britan.*) Twenty-nine of these compositions are by Romanus; among the authors of others are found the names of Cosmas, Anastasius and others, who must not be confused with later poets of the same names : others are anonymous. As a specimen of their structure Cardinal Pitra describes (*Hymnographie Grecque*) the celebrated Christmas hymn of Romanus, which is composed of twenty-four strophes of considerable length, the initial letters of the strophes composing the words τοῦ ταπεινοῦ 'Ρωμανοῦ ὕμνος ; the strophes, with the exception of the first, all contain the same number of rhythmical phrases, though of very different lengths, and the corresponding phrases in each strophe are composed of the same *number* of syllables, though of varying quantity. The first strophe has only one feature in common with the rest : the last line, containing the central idea of the poem, is repeated again as the close of every succeeding strophe ; and the strophes are so managed as to lead naturally up to it. He gives at length a poem for the 30th of June on the Holy Apostles (reprinted from *Hymnographie Grecque* in *Anth. Graec.*), and an anonymous one with the acrostic Εἰς Πέτρον καὶ Παῦλον for the same day, both identical in structure with that for Christmas. The characteristic of all these pieces is a picturesque, almost dramatic treatment, which contrasts with the doctrinal cast of the Canons. Thus the Christmas hymn opens with a description of the cave at Bethlehem, the Infant Christ, the Virgin Mother, the angels, shepherds, Magi. The poem proceeds with a dialogue in which these personages take part. The title of these pieces (κοντάκιον) has thrown an incidental light on the short poems of the same name found in the present Greek Office Books. Cardinal Pitra has discovered that in several cases the κοντάκια and οἶκοι, intercalated between the 6th and 7th Odes of the Canons, are single strophes picked out of these original Contakia ; and he discerns other traces of longer poems formed on the acrostic, τοῦ ταπεινοῦ κ.τ.λ., which are now buried in the Canons of the later age, which superseded them. See § xvi. 2, and **Romanus**.

2. *Sergius* (610–41). There is some affinity to the hymns of Romanus in the celebrated ἀκάθιστος ὕμνος, composed by the patriarch Sergius as a thanksgiving to the Mother of God for her defence of Constantinople from the attack of Chaganes, King of Persia. There is the same repetition of the last line of the strophe, and the same vivid narrative ; and the opening strophe has a separate form. On the other hand there is no acrostic, the strophes are shorter, and the alternate ones are followed by a long series of invocations, managed with great brilliance and variety. There is also an occasional and unmistakable adoption of rhyme. The hymn was sung standing, in commemoration of the long watch of the Mother of God. Considered as a poem, the chief part of it is full of splendour ; but

the worship of the Virgin, which is its *raison d'être*, scarcely admits of its adaptation even partially in England.

§ xiii. *Period of the Odes and Canons.* A change largely connected with the Iconoclastic controversy was wrought in Greek Service Books during the 7th, 8th, and 9th centuries. The names of the defenders of the sacred *icons* fill a large space in the calendar; and their elaborate doctrinal hymns dispossessed the more animated and pictorial poems of Romanus. The new form which rises into view, and continues henceforward to be the highest mode of poetical expression, is the Canon, of which St. Andrew of Crete is the first known master.

Whether the Canon was a new invention at this time, or had been in existence previously, although no earlier specimens are extant, is uncertain. A quotation from Gerbert, given by Cardinal Pitra (*Hym. Grecque*, p. 43) seems to prove its existence in the 5th century. M. Christ, however (*Anth. Graec.*), considers the word an interpolation. At any rate it is not until the time of St. Andrew of Crete that the Canon takes its supreme place in the system.

§ xiv. *Sources and Translations of the later Greek Hymns.* — 1. *Sources.* — The hymns which follow are found in the Service Books of the Greek Church. These are:—

(1) *The Menaea*, twelve volumes, one for each month (μὴν), answering approximately to the Propria Sanctorum of the Western Breviary (*Dict. Christ. Ant.* s. v.).

(2) *The Paracleticè*, or *Greater Octoechus*, containing the Ferial office arranged on a system for eight weeks.

(3) The *Lesser Octoechus*, containing the Sunday Services of the preceding volume. The name is derived from the eight Tones (ἦχοι), to which the Services of the eight weeks are respectively set. These Tones are the same, except in name, as the Gregorian Tones. The arrangement of the *Octoechus* to them is said to have been the work of St. John of Damascus.

(4) *The Triodion*, containing the entire services for Lent, and those for the three preceding Sundays (Sunday of the Pharisee and the Publican; Sunday of Apocreos, after which no flesh is eaten ; Tyrophagus, after which even cheese is forbidden). The name *Triodion* originates in the prevalence of hymns of that name (three odes).

(5) *The Pentecostarion Charmosynon*, containing the office for the seasons of Easter and Pentecost.

(6) *The Euchologion*, containing the occasional offices.

(7) *The Horologion*, containing the Hours of prayer.

The number of hymns in these volumes which contain (*Neale*) 4000 closely-printed quarto pages at least, is very large. They are little known in England. The best selection from them is that published by M. Christ in *Anth. Graec.* There is a more meagre one in *Daniel.* Cardinal Pitra has published a group of hymns connected with St. Peter and St. Paul. The great offices for Christmas, Easter, and Pentecost are printed in Dr. Littledale's *Offices of the Holy Eastern Church.*

2. *Translations*, &c. The difficulties in the way of studying the original services are almost removed for English classical scholars since the publication of Neale's *Introduction to the History of the Holy Eastern Church*, and Dr. Littledale's valuable book on *The Offices of the Holy Eastern Church*. The earliest, most spirited, and popular poetical translations are *The Hymns of the Eastern Church* by Dr. Neale (1862). Mr. Chatterton Dix has turned a portion of the blank verse of Dr. Littledale's *Offices* into metre, and published the same, partly in the *Church Times*, and subsequently in the *Lyras* pub. by Mr. Shipley. A few hymns have been translated in metrical form by Dr. Littledale, and appeared in the *Church Times* (1864), the *People's Hymnal* (1867), and the *Priest's Prayer-book*. There are also *trs.* by Dr. Macgill in his *Songs of the Christian Creed and Life*. Lond.: Pickering, 1876–79.

§ xv. *Structure and Versification.* A Greek hymn, as printed in the Service Books looks like a paragraph, or a collection of paragraphs, in rhythmical prose. The rhythmical phrases of the paragraphs are divided by a system of commas, which are obviously unconnected with punctuation. If rearranged, so as to make each rhythmical phrase a line of poetry, the paragraph assumes a resemblance to a piece of a Greek chorus, and snatches of classic rhythm foster the delusion. But it has proved impossible to reduce it to any known metre, or to establish any consistency between the paragraphs of a hymn by rules of prosody. Cardinal Pitra, however, who has investigated this matter with great acuteness, discovered that in the odes (where we have hymns composed of several paragraphs), and in groups of hymns confessedly similar (ὅμοια) and modelled on the leading one (προσόμοιον), the number of rhythmical phrases in each paragraph, and the number of syllables in each rhythmical phrase (short syllables counting as equivalent to long ones), is identical. M. Christ, who has also written a masterly essay on the subject in the *Anthologia Graec.*, has further established the fact that a fixed proportion of the accents in the corresponding phrases is always uniform. The *rhythm* of the hymns probably depended on this uniformity of accent more than on the law of the syllables. "In the decline of the language accent was trampling down quantity" (*Neale*). This growing inattention to quantity has been pointed out elsewhere (see § ii.). The increasing importance of accent is familiar in Latin hymns and in modern Greek. The general rhythmical impression of Greek hymns is thus described by Card. Pitra: "The system has no lack of flexibility, variety, or precision. The strophes are grave or spirited in turn, at one time possessing the solemn march of hendecasyllables, at another precipitating themselves in a stream of impetuous versicles, and most frequently blending both measures easily together" (*Hym. Grecque*, p. 24).

§ xvi. 1. *Names and Varieties of Hymns.* The names of the minor Greek hymns are very numerous. The *Antiphons* (ἀντίφωνα) have the character familiar to us in the Latin Breviaries.

2. The ἀπολυτίκια derive their name not so much from their place near the close of the vesper office, as from the Song of Simeon then originally sung (*Anth. Graec. Carm. Christ.*, p. lxix.).

There is a group of hymns, which are most usually found as satellites of the Canons.

3. The κάθισμα, so called, apparently, because sung seated, an intercalation between the third and fourth, or the sixth and seventh odes.

4. The κοντάκιον, intercalated after the sixth ode, which, as found at present, is a long single stanza, but which in many cases has been discovered by Pitra to be a relic of the long poems of the school of Romanus, the inventor of κοντάκια. (See § xii. and **Romanus.**) This discovery makes the derivation of the term from κόντος, the roller around which a roll of manuscript is bound, far more likely than that from κόντος, little, or that from the Latin *Canticum.* (*Dict. Christ. Ant.*, s. v.)

5. The οἶκος, which always follows the κοντάκιον, and is often also a relic of the school of Romanus, and of the same character, except that it sometimes closes with a series of invocations (χαῖρε—χαῖρε, Neale). *Pitra* derives it from the position of the choir, *grouped* round the leader, during its performance. But Neale and M. Christ (*Anth. Graec.*) compare it with the Italian *Stanza*, the cell which enshrines the thought.

6. The καταβασία, which is very often a repetition of the Hirmos of the ode, sung by the choir after *coming down* into the narthex.

7. The ἐξαποστειλάριον, which follows the canon, a hymn first introduced by Constantine, son of Leo the Wise (Emperor 913–59). Eleven of them connected with the Resurrection from his pen are quoted in *Anth. Graec. Carm. Christ.* p. 110.

8. The ὑπακοή, which occurs instead of the κάθισμα after the third ode. The derivation is doubtful. In the Virgin's Song of Methodius the ὑπακοή is a refrain. (See § x. 2.) But not so in the Greek Service Books. Neither Coresi's explanation, "an echo of what goes before" (*Dict. Christ. Ant.*, s. v.), nor Goar's, that the Church listens, (ὑπακούει) to some recital of God's marvellous dealings (*Neale*), is satisfactory.

9. The *Idiomelon*, sung at great Festivals, at matins (*Dict. Christ. Ant.*, s. v.), but most of all during the quiet hours of the night in the narthex (western part of the church), "glowing with the processional torches" (*Neale*), is much of the same character as other short hymns. But when several of them are combined under the name of *Stichera* (verses) *Idiomela*, a hymn results, which exceeds in length many of the odes; and some of the freshest pieces in the Service Books are in this class. Cardinal Pitra, following Leo Allatius, seems to think that the name arises from the fact that they have their own *musical* treatment attached to the words (ἴδιον μέλος). More commonly, however, μέλος is taken to denote rhythm or metre. It is impossible to trace any uniformity of structure in successive Idiomela: each one seems a law to itself, or, as Neale expresses it, its own model. Thus Stichera Idiomela are, at any rate practically, *Irregular Verses.*

10. *The Ode.* The *Ode* (ὠδή) is composed of a variable number of short and vivid strophes, each of which has its highest expression of feeling thrown into its closing line. All the strophes are uniform in the number of syllables and lines and in certain leading accents (see above, § xv.). The model on which the strophes are formed is sometimes the first strophe of the Ode, which in that case is always printed with inverted commas; often it is an older strophe taken from the *Hirmologion,* and then only the few first words of it are printed, somewhat as we print the tune of a ballad, at the head of the *Ode.* The name of this strophe is *Hirmus* (εἱρμος), which is usually explained as denoting its *drawing* the other stanzas after it (*Neale*); but the derivation is doubtful (see *Anth. Graec. Carm. Christ.,* p. lx.). The other strophes are named *Troparia,* a term which is again explained as denoting the *turning* of these strophes to the *Hirmus* (*Neale*). But the derivation is denied by M. Christ, and the fact that the term *troparion* is found attached to single stanzas independent apparently of any *Hirmus* is against it. Pitra considers the *troparion* as a very ancient Greek form, specially used for the short verse, which follows the recitation of the Psalms in the nocturnal office. The *Odes* occur in groups: sometimes a pair is found (διώδιον), but most frequently there is a series of three (τριώδιον), or the full complement of eight, in the great Festival Canons, nine in others, which forms the *Canon.* The *Triodia* belong chiefly to the Lenten volume, named in consequence *Triodion.* The Odes are always connected with the Canticles of the Greek Service, and often cramped and distorted by the necessity of allusion to them.

11. *The Canons,* which are the highest effort of Greek hymnody, sung for the most part at Lauds, are founded principally on the Canticles then used, viz.: 1. Song of Moses, Exod. xv. (Monday); 2. Song of Moses, Deut. xxxii. (Tuesday); 3. Song of Hannah (Wednesday); 4. Song of Habakkuk (Thursday); 5. Isaiah xxvi. 9–20 (Friday); 6. Jonah's Prayer; and 7. the earlier portion of the Prayer of the Three Children. To these are added—8. the remainder of the Prayer of the Three Children (*Benedicite*); and 9. *The Magnificat* and *Benedictus.* In correspondence with these nine divisions the Canon theoretically consists of nine odes: but as from the severe and threatening character of the second Canticle the ode corresponding to it is only found in Lent, the majority of Canons consist of eight odes only. The Canon as a whole has no greater unity, or relation of parts than the group of Canticles, on which it is founded; but it is threaded on an acrostic written in iambics, or sometimes hexameters or elegiacs, at the commencement of the first ode; the letters of the acrostic opening the several troparia, and sometimes (e.g. in the Iambic Canons of St. John of Damascus. See also *Anth. Graec. Carm. Christ.,* p. 240; Pitra, *Hym. Grecque,* p. 20) the versicles of the *troparion* also. The three Iambic Canons of St. John of Damascus are a link with the classical metres. (See above, § vii.) Besides conforming to the laws of syllables and accents and acrostic in its strictest form, they are iambics in quantity. The English reader will gain a good idea of the appearance of a Greek Canon from the reproduction of one given in Neale's *Introduction to the History of the Holy Eastern Church,* vol. ii. p. 833. In the Service Books the Odes of two Canons are found interlaced with one another.

§ xvii. *General view of later Hymn-writers.* This splendid development of the Greek hymns may be considered as arising in the middle of the 7th century, reaching its zenith in the close of the 8th, and dying (with the exception of a few later pieces, extending even to the 16th century) in the beginning of the 10th century. Its beginning is associated with Jerusalem in the person of St. Andrew of Crete, 660–732 (see § xvii. 1). There also, in the Laura of St. Sabas, lived its two greatest poets, Cosmas and St. John of Damascus (ibid. 2, 3), (flourished circa 750); and the third great poet, Theophanes (§ xviii. 2), (circa 830). Another centre of hymnody was Sicily, and Italy. The elder Cosmas, tutor of St. John of Damascus, Joseph the Hymnographer (xviii. 3) (830), and Methodius (died 836), were of Sicily. There was a colony of Greek monks in the monastery of Grotta Ferrata, at Tusculum, which produced a school of hymn-writers in the 12th century, named after the great melodists of older days, the chief of them being St. Bartholomew of Grotta Ferrata. But the most lasting though less eminent home of hymnody was naturally Constantinople. Poets from St. Sabas, such as Theophanes, or Sicily, such as Joseph and Methodius the Patriarch of Constantinople, were drawn thither by the circumstances of their lives, and continued their works there. At an earlier period (715–34), Germanus, one of the grandest of the defenders of the Icons, was a hymn-writer during his patriarchate. The great monastery of the Studium was a home of hymnody (see § xviii.), and emperors, such as even the Iconoclast Theophilus and Leo the Wise, and Constantine Porphyrogenitus, wrote hymns. Some of the most celebrated writers will be noted in the following sections, the choice being greatly guided by the English translations in Neale which are the chief source of information to general readers.

1. *St. Andrew of Crete.* A considerable number of hymns by this early writer of Canons are contained in the Greek Service Books. The most celebrated is the Great Canon, of four parts, and of the prodigious length of 250 strophes. It is sung entire, "cum labore multo et pulmonum fatigatione," on Thursday in Mid-Lent (Combefis, quoted in *Dict. Christ. Biog.,* s. v.), as well as partially on other days of Lent. (Portions are published in *Daniel,* iii. 47–54, and in *Anth. Graec. Carm. Christ.,* 147–161. Translations by Neale in *Hy. E. C.,* p. 23.) The strophes of this Canon have not the point of those of St. John of Damascus, and make no use of refrains. The aim of it is penitential; a spirit of true penitence breathes through it; it has many beautiful passages, and is rich in allusion to the personages of the Bible, either as warnings or examples to the penitent; but its excellences are marred by repetition and pro-

lixity. See Βοηθὸς καὶ σκεπαστής. Besides
this, his Canon on Mid-Pentecost (portions of
which are given in *Daniel*, iii. 48–9), and
several spirited *Idiomela* in the *Triodion*
and *Pentacostarion*, and the *Triodia* in Holy
Week (see translations, "O! the mystery
passing wonder," "Jesus hastening for the
world to suffer," Neale's *Hy. E. C.*, pp. 19–22),
are specified by Neale as among his choicest
pieces. His *Idiomela* for Christmas, εὐφραί-
νεσθε δίκαιοι ("Rejoice, ye righteous") (see
Anth. Graec., 97–8; *Daniel*, iii. 47; Littledale's *Offices*, p. 83) are full of spirit, setting
forth in a few pointed verses the ideas of the
longer canons.

2. *St. John of Damascus.* The Laura of St.
Sabas, between Jerusalem and Bethlehem, was
famous in more ways than one. Its Typicon
(book of rubrics) was the most venerable and
elaborate of its class, and is now the prevalent
one in the East (*Pitra*). The native hymns of
Syria, in their own language, would be heard
there as well as those of the Greeks. It became
the centre of a school of hymn-writers, of whom
the two chief—and also the foremost in the roll
of the Greek ecclesiastical poets—were Cosmas
and St. John of Damascus. The impress of the
latter on the Greek Service Books is distinct
and deep. It affected the music as well as the
poetry. The arrangement of the *Octoechus*,
according to the Eight Tones (see § xiv.), is
attributed to St. John of Damascus. The epithet
"Melodist," which attached in earlier times
to Romanus, is often given to St. John of
Damascus, Theophanes, Theodore of the Studium, and especially Cosmas; and appears to
denote those who were not merely hymn-
writers (ὑμνόγραφοι), but musicians. The
structure of the Odes and Canons also now
began to exhibit certain features, which
it never afterwards lost. The *Troparia* have
a pointed brightness which contrasts not only
with the long strophes of Romanus, but with
the heaviness of St. Andrew of Crete. It
has been thought that certain rhythmical
characteristics may have been borrowed
from the Syrian hymns of St. Ephrem (see
§ xi.). One of these may be the constant
use of refrains; though it must be borne
in mind that the refrain and the management of the preceding lines, so as to lead
up to it, are part of the tradition of Romanus.
At the same time the pictorial style of Romanus gave way to that doctrinal expression,
animated by living devotion, which pervades
the great body of Greek hymnody. The appropriation of the last strophe of the Ode to
an invocation or praise of the B. V. M. (θεοτοκίον, or, if at the foot of the cross, σταυρο-
θεοτοκίον) dates also from this period. The
Canons of St. John of Damascus are found in
the *Octoechus*, the oldest MSS. of which contained no other Canons than his (see *Pitra*,
p. 59, *Anth. Graec.* p. xlvi.), in the *Menaea* and
Pentecostarion. The latter are the more celebrated. They celebrate the grand themes of
Christmas, the *Theophany* (Baptism of Christ),
Pentecost, Easter, St. Thomas's Sunday, and
the Ascension. The first three are the Iambic
Canons (see § xvi. 11), which, perhaps from the
metrical shackles which he has imposed on
himself, are often laboured, and somewhat
turgid in language. The Canon for St.

Thomas's Sunday is a fine one, full of suggestion in regard to the unbelief of the Apostle.
(See Ἄσωμεν πάντες λαοί, and *Anth. Graec.*, p.
221.) The Canon on the "Ascension" is very
striking from its triumphant gladness and
dramatic realization. The "Easter Canon,"
known as "The Golden Canon," or "King of
Canons," is the grandest piece in Greek sacred
poetry. Nowhere are the best characteristics
of the Greek Canon exhibited so splendidly.
The formal allusions to the Canticles on
which the several odes are founded (see § xvi.
11), and the introduction of types, which in
later poets become often monotonous and
irrelevant, are here in complete keeping, and
give a fitting and natural enrichment; and
the brilliant phrases, culminating in acclamation, the freedom of the thoughts, the
ringing, victorious joy, and the lofty presentation of the import of the Resurrection,
compose a series of magnificent efforts
of imaginative devotion. (See Ἀναστάσεως
ἡμέρα and *Anth. Graec.*, p. 218; Littledale's
Offices, p. 211.) To these Canons are probably
to be added others under the name of John
Arklas, and perhaps (though this is more
doubtful), John the Monk. There are also
numerous *Idiomela*, two of which Neale has
translated. One of these (τὰς ἑδρὰς τὰς
αἰωνίας, q. v.) is very popular ("Those eternal bowers," *Hy. E. C.*, p. 55). The other,
which is not a hymn in the English sense, is
one of the most beautiful pieces in Neale's
volume (" Take the last kiss," *Hy. E. C.*, p. 49),
representing some lines of intense emotion in
the Burial Office in the *Euchologion*. (See
Δεῦτε τελευταῖον ἄσπασμον, and *Daniel*, iii.
123.) From the Burial Office for Priests in
the same volume is taken the beautiful
translation of ποία τοῦ βίου τρύφη ("With
pain earth's joys are mingled ") in *The People's
Hy.* by Dr. Littledale.

3. *St. Cosmas* (died circa 760). The great
works of this poet are his Canons for the
Festivals. Often, as in those for the Nativity,
the *Theophany* (Baptism of Christ) and Pentecost, the Odes of the several Canons by himself and St. John of Damascus are interwoven,
brotherlike, with each other. He has Canons
on "The Purification," "Transfiguration," and
"Palm Sunday." His canon on his favourite
Father, Gregory of Nazianzus, is also mentioned by Neale. To these must be added a
series of pieces (one a Diodion, two Triodia,
and two Canons) dealing with the narrative in
Holy Week. The ancient fame of the poems
of Cosmas was great, and commentaries were
composed on them (*Anth. Graec. Carm. Christ.*
p. li.). He is generally spoken of as the equal
of St. John of Damascus. But it can only be
in a doctrinal point of view that he can be
deemed the rival of his foster-brother. Neale
styles him the most learned of the Greek
poets; and on account of his fondness for
types, boldness in their application, and love
of aggregating them, compares him with
Adam of St. Victor. He speaks also of the
"compressed fulness of meaning," and "unusual harshness and contraction of his phrases."
The only piece which poetically approaches
the best efforts of St. John of Damascus is the
Christmas Canon, Χριστὸς γεννᾶται · δοξάσατε
(q. v.). It is pronounced by Neale to be

superior to the Iambic Canon of St. John of Damascus, with which it interlaces. It is said to be suggested by a sermon of Gregory of Nazianzus, from whom the ring of gladness with which it opens is borrowed (*Anth. Graec. Carm. Christ.*, p. 1.; *Littledale*, p. 281). In the other pieces there is seldom anything that answers to the force, spontaneity, sustained exultation of St. John of Damascus. The joyousness is confined chiefly to the refrains, and the general treatment follows the narrative manner of Romanus ; but somewhat loaded by typology and doctrinal statement. (A full selection may be seen in *Daniel*, iii. pp. 36, seq., and *Anth. Graec. Carm. Christ.*, 161, seq. ; *trs.* of the Christmas Canon in Neale, *Hy. E. C.*, pp. 66 ; Littledale's *Offices*, p. 187, seq.)

§ xviii. *The Poets of the Studium.* In the peaceful interval commencing with the restoration of the *Icons* by the Second Council of Nicaea (A.D. 787), and ending in the renewal of persecution by Leo the Armenian (A.D. 813), the great monastery of the Studium at Constantinople became the home of hymnography. Neale says that this period is marked by the commencement of decline in vigour and freshness and increase of "Byzantine bombast."

1. *St. Theodore* (died A.D. 826) was Hegumen of the monastery ; a man of "rigid, unbending, unyielding character," in outward life, but revealed as penetrated with love and penitence in his Lent Canons in the *Triodion* (*Neale*). A triumphal Canon for the great festival that commemorates the victory of the *Icons*, Orthodoxy Sunday, is by him. (See *tr.* in Neale's *Hy. E. C.*, p. 113, "A song, a song of gladness.") His Canon on the Judgment is pronounced by Neale "the grandest judgment hymn of the Church," previous to the composition of the *Dies Irae*. (See τὴν ἡμέραν τὴν φρίκτην, and Neale, *Hy. E. C.*, p. 104, "That fearful day," &c.) Certain Canons in the *Triodion* and *Pentecostarion* are by his younger brother *Joseph*, afterwards Bp. of *Thessalonica*. There is a Canon of much tenderness—the "Supplicant Canon by Theoctistus "—at the end of the *Paracletice*, which has been re-cast by Neale. (See *Hy. E. Ch.*, p. 153, and Ἰησοῦ γλυκύτατε).

2. *St. Theophanes* (circa 800–50). By the Greeks this poet is named with St. John of Damascus and Cosmas as in the highest rank of their hymn-writers. Like them, too, he is associated with Jerusalem, and possibly with St. Sabas (see **Theophanes, St.**). He is the most prolific of the Greek hymn-writers, with the exception of St. Joseph (*Neale*). The great bulk of his *Canons* and *Idiomela* are found in the *Menaea*, and the subjects to which he devotes them are the Martyrs and Confessors of the Greek Calendar. Neale points out the inevitable sameness and tediousness which results from devoting a separate canon to each saint, when all that can be said is, that they died for Christ; commending at the same time the wiser Latin practice in which "not even the Apostles have separate hymns, but supply themselves from the Common." Neither Neale nor the authors of the *Anth. Graec.* present anything of remarkable merit from these compositions. (See Δεῦτε ἅπαντες πίστοι and ὁ πλάστης μοῦ Κύριος.)

3. *St. Joseph the Hymnographer* (circa 840).

This most voluminous of the Greek poets belonged by birth to the Sicilian school of hymnographers, but like Methodius of Syracuse, the circumstances of his life drew him to Constantinople. Neale's judgment of him is unfavourable. His canons in the *Menaea* are celebrations of saints and martyrs, of whom little is known ; and the result is tautology, "common-place decked out in tragic language," verbiage in which Scriptural simplicity is exchanged for Byzantine tawdriness. The best features however of this style he tries to reproduce in "Stars of the morning," in his *Hy. E. C.* The cento from the canon for SS. Timothy and Maura, "Let our choir new anthems raise," is one of Neale's best pieces, and it derives additional interest to us from Kingsley's beautiful poem *Santa Maura*. (See τῶν ἱερῶν ἀθλοφόρων.) But much of its excellence is Neale's. And in "O happy band of pilgrims," and "Safe home, safe home in port," Neale himself confesses how little is really due to the original. One piece of St. Joseph, however, the "Canon on the Ascension" (ἀνέστης τριήμερος), though anticipated by the Canon of St. John of Damascus, is in doctrinal force and dramatic presentation very majestic. It is probably the finest hymn extant on the Ascension.

§ xix. *Subsequent Hymn-Writers* (900–1400). These may be dismissed rapidly ; neither in the amount or merit of their contributions can they rank with their predecessors. The enormous bulk of the service books pointed to retrenchment, rather than introduction of much new matter, and such a retrenchment was carried out after the schism between East and West. (See details Pitra, *Hymn. Grecque*, p. 62.) Among the pieces of this later time Neale has chosen for translation a cento from one of the eight Canons of *Metrophanes* (died 910) in honour of the Trinity, "O Unity of Threefold Light." (See τριφεγγὴς Μονὰς θεαρχικὴ.) Another of them is published in *Anth. Graec. Carm. Christ.*, pp. 354–7. In the same volume, pp. 110–12, are the Exaposteilaria of Constantine Porphyrogenitus (913–959) on the Resurrection. *Daniel* has also two canons of John Mauropus (died 1060), one of which is very jubilant. They were not however incorporated in the Greek Service Books. One or two hymns however were admitted as late as Philotheus (1360), patriarch of Constantinople, and even in the 16th century. See *Anth. Graec. Carm. Christ.*, p. xxxviii.

§ xx. *Conclusion.* The most remarkable characteristic of Greek hymnody is its objectiveness, with which is closely connected its faculty of sustained praise. Whether the theme be the mystery of the Triune Godhead or the Incarnation, or the mighty periods of Christ's incarnate work in earth and heaven; or whether some life or narrative of Holy Writ, considered in its doctrinal or typical reference—the attitude of the poet is always one of self-forgetful, rapt, or ecstatic contemplation. While in the English hymn the Scripture fact or type or doctrine is the text or motto, and the body of the hymn consists of the human blessings, warnings or enlightenments that flow from it, the mind of the Greek poet rests and delights in the Revelation itself, and leaves the human references subordinated, hinted, or even unexpressed. Visible everywhere, this contrast is most marked in the absorbed rapture with which the Greek poet hymns the Divine Perfections and the Incarnation, when compared with our self-regarding mode of praise. This habit of thought has however its disadvantages. By its discouragement of the development of human emotion, aspiration, and benefit, the range of subjects and reflection is narrowed; and in the later poets the repetition of the same types, epithets, and metaphors issues in sameness, conventional diction, and fossil thought. It is impossible to avoid the conviction, that the great bulk of Greek hymns would have had a richer value, if it had sought for inspiration in the deep spiritual analysis of St. Paul, or the interpretation of the changing moods of the soul, which are of such preciousness in the Psalms. The English translations omit one of the prevalent features of the original, the excessive honour and power ascribed to the Blessed Virgin. The place assigned to her is as high as in the Roman theology; the closing strophe of every ode is usually devoted to her (see § xvii.); and there are numberless canons on her scriptural and legendary history: the result being to lower that celebration of the Incarnation, which is intended to be guarded and enhanced. The difficulty of naturalizing the Greek hymns here arises from their wide divergence from English form. The sparkling Greek freezes in our metres, and the unity, proportion of parts, compactness, and selection of allied ideas, which we demand, have no correlatives in the loose, wandering, disconnected strophes. This is illustrated by the extant translations. With one exception ("Come, ye faithful, raise the strain,") none of the successful translations in Neale are exact reproductions of the odes of a canon, but either centos from them selected with an eye to unity, or shorter, more pointed pieces, to which he has given his own individuality, either of construction or language. Three of the most popular ones ("Art thou weary," "O happy band of pilgrims," and "Safe home, safe home in port"), by Neale's confession, contain so little of the Greek, that they ought not to have been called translations. Dr. Littledale's renderings are more nervous and faithful, though less lyrical, than Neale's; but these, too, are taken from the shorter hymns. It seems probable that the most successful translations will be either centos from the long canons, or renderings of the shorter hymns, in which there is often greater freshness and sweetness, with a more terse expression of the ideas.

[AUTHORITIES.—(1) Daniel's *Thesaurus Hymnologicus*, 1841–1855. (2) *Anthologia Graeca Carminum Christianorum*, by M. Christ and M. Paranikas, 1871. (3) *Hymnographie Grecque*, by Cardinal Pitra, 1867. (4) *Journal des Savants*, 1876; article by *Miller*. (5) *Christian Remembrancer*, vol. 55. (6) *Encyclopædia Britannica*, 9th ed., "Hymns." (7) Neale's *Introduction to History of the Holy Eastern Church*, 1851. (8) Neale's *Hymns of the Eastern Church*, 1862. (9) Littledale's *Offices of the Eastern Church*, 1863. (10) Chatfield's *Songs and Hymns of the Earliest Greek Christian Poets*, 1870. (11) *Lyra Messianica*, 1864. (12) *Orthodox Catholic Review*, 1875. (13) Mrs. Browning, *Greek Christian Poets*, 1863. (14) I. Williams's *Thoughts in Past Years*, 1838. (15) H. M. Macgill's *Songs of the Christian Creed and Life*, 1876–9. (16) Rev. S. G. Hatherly's ed. of Dr. Neale's *Hys. of the Eastern Church*, 1882. (17) Dr.

Littledale's *Offices*, &c. This contains the most extensive and accurate Glossary of Greek Ecclesiastical terms available to the English reader. (18) *Vcteres Graeci Poetae*, by La Rovière, 1614.]   [H. L. B.]

Greenwell, Dorothy, commonly known as "Dora Greenwell," was b. at Greenwell Ford, Durham, in 1821; resided at Ovingham Rectory, Northumberland (1848); Golborne Rectory, Lancashire; Durham (1854), and Clifton, near Bristol, where she d. in 1882. Her works include *Poems*, 1848; *The Patience of Hope*, 1861; *The Life of Lacordaire*; *A Present Heaven*; *Two Friends*; *Songs of Salvation*, 1874, &c. Her *Life*, by W. Dorling, was pub. in 1885.   [J. J.]

Greenwood, John Brooke, b. at Huddersfield, Feb. 9, 1828, and educated at the Huddersfield College, is a merchant shipper of cotton yarn to the continental markets. In 1853 he pub. *Records-Memorial* of E. B. Cave. He has written many hymns, chiefly for Sunday-school anniversary services, and other special occasions. Of these the following, which appeared with others in an *Appendix* to the *Leeds S. School H. Bk.*, pub. for the use of the Cheetham Hill (Manchester) S. School, are in C. U. outside that collection :—

1. **Crown with Thy benediction.** *Holy Matrimony.*

2. **Finding no place of rest.** *Return of the Dove to the Ark.*

3. **How long, O Lord, how long?** Thy children sigh. 1st pub. in the *Manchester Cong. Magazine.*

4. **There is no fold so fair as Thine..** *The Church of Christ.*

5. **What shall we render, Lord, to Thee?** *Holy Baptism.*

The full text of No. 2 is 7 stanzas, i.–iv. forming the original, and v.–vii. being a subsequent addition. Through a Roman Catholic relative of the author st. i.–iv. were given in the *Catholic Progress* with her initial "S." From thence it was taken by Mr. Orby Shipley and included in his *Annus Sanctus*, 1884, Pt. ii., p. 81, with the same signature. The full text is in Horder's *The Poet's Bible.*

Mr. Greenwood's hymns possess great tenderness and refinement, and are worthy of greater attention than they have received.

[W. G. H.]

Greg, Samuel, was b. in Manchester, Sept. 6, 1804, and educated by Dr. Lant Carpenter, at Bristol, and at the Edinburgh University. He subsequently became a millowner at Bollington, near Macclesfield. He died, May 14, 1877. The addresses given by him at services which he conducted for his workmen at Bollington were pub. posthumously as *A Layman's Legacy*, 1877, with a prefatory note by Dean Stanley. He was also author of *Scenes from the Life of Jesus*, 1854, 2nd ed. 1869. Some of his short poems were appended to his *Layman's Legacy*. He is known to hymnody as the author of :—

1. **My soul in death was sleeping.** *New Life in Christ.* Appeared in his *Scenes from the Life of Jesus*, 1854, and included in the *Bapt. Hymnal*, 1879, No. 400.

2. **Slowly, slowly darkening.** *Old Age.* Written in the midst of affliction, Sept. 1868, and pub. in his *Layman's Legacy*, 1877, in 11 st. of 4 l., and entitled "The Mystery of Life." In 1884 it was given in W. G. Horder's *Cong. Hymns*, No. 837. In Martineau's *Hymns*, 1873, it reads, " Now, slowly, slowly, darkening." It is a hymn of great merit, and is well suited for Private Devotion.

3. **Stay, Master, stay upon this heavenly hill.** [*Transfiguration.*] 1st pub. in his *Scenes from the Life of Jesus*, 1854, at the close of a chapter on the Transfiguration. It was reprinted in *Macmillan's Magazine*,

1870, pp. 543-6, together with Dean Stanley's hymn, "Master, it is good to be," on the same subject. It was included in W. G. Horder's *Cong. Hymns*, 1884, No. 774.   [W. G. H.]

Gregor, Christian, s. of Georg Gregor, a peasant living in the Silesian village of Dirsdorf, near Peilau, was b. at Dirsdorf, Jan. 1, 1723. In 1742 he went to Herrnhut, where he was at first employed in tuition. He became leader of the music in the [Moravian] Brethren's congregation at Herrnhaag, in 1748, and in 1749 at Zeist; but in 1753 he returned to Herrnhut as cashier of the Brethren's Board of Direction. He was, in 1756, ordained diaconus, in 1767 presbyter, and in 1789 bishop of the Brethren's Church. On Nov. 6, 1801, he attended a meeting, held at Herrnhut, of the Board of Direction of which he had been a member from 1764. Just as he entered his house at Berthelsdorf, near Herrnhut, he was struck with paralysis, and d. that same day. (*Koch*, vi. 436; *Allg. Deutsche Biog.*, ix. 630.)

He was a man greatly beloved and respected, simple of heart, loving, earnest and hardworking; and was entrusted with many important missions and visitations. His hymns are characterised by childlike fervour of devotion to his crucified Lord. A number appeared in *Das kleinen Brüder-Gesangbuchs dritter Theil*, Barby, 1767; but they were mostly contributed to the *Gesangbuch zum Gebrauch der evangelischen Brüder Gemeinein*, Barby, 1778, of which he was the principal editor. He was also an excellent organist, and edited, in 1784, a collection of accompanying tunes for the hymn-book of 1778, contributing thereto various melodies by himself. A little volume entitled *Historische Nachricht vom Brüder-Gesangbuche des Jahres 1778, und von dessen Lieder-Verfassern*, Gnadau, 1835 (2nd ed., 1851), occasionally referred to in these pages, is based on materials collected by Gregor.

His hymns in English C. U. are :—

i. **Bis dereinst mein Stündlein schlägt.** [*Love to Christ.*] 1778, No. 640, in 5 st. of 4 l. *Tr.* as :—

Till permitted hence to go, of st. i., ii., iv., as No. 563 in the *Moravian H. Bk.*, 1801 (1886, No. 1228). In 1826 an original st. by T. Bird was added, beginning, "'Till the day when I shall tread." Repeated thus in 1886, No. 1228, and in J. A. Latrobe's *Coll.*, 1841, No. 484.

ii. **Die Gottes Cherubim.** [*The Angels.*] Appeared as No. 1877 in *Appendix* xii. c., 1746, to the Herrnhut *G. B.* of 1735, thus :—

" Die Gottes Cherubim
Erheben ihre Stimm,
(Funkelnd von Blitz und Strahl,)
Ihr Lied ist, wenn ichs sagen darf,
Dazu spielt mehr als eine Harf:
Ehre dem Seitenmaal ! "

In 1778 it is included as No. 1600, beginning, "Die Gottes Seraphim," and expanded to three stanzas ; i. of the Angels ; ii. of the Redeemed ; iii. of the Church on Earth. Here the song, "Ehre dem Seitenmaal," is given to the Church on Earth, and a paraphrase of Is. vi. 3, to the Angels. The only *tr.* in C. U. is :—

The Seraphim of God, in full from the 1778, by J. Miller and F. W. Foster, as No. 792 in the *Moravian H. Bk.*, 1789 (1886, No. 1220), repeated in J. A. Latrobe's *Coll.*, 1841, No. 424. Another *tr.* is "The Cherubims of God," from the original form, as No. 93 in pt. iii. of the *Moravian H. Bk.*, 1748.

iii. **Heiliger, heiliger, heiliger, Herr Zebaoth.** [*Public Worship.*] The introductory hymn in 1778, in 4 st. of 8 l., as on "The Word of God." The only *tr.* is :—

Holy Lord, Holy Lord, Holy and Almighty Lord,

by F. W. Foster, C. G. Clemens, and J. Swertner, as No. 1 in the *Moravian H. Bk.*, 1789 (1886, No. 1). Included from the text of 1801, as No. 217 in Dr. Pagenstecher's *Coll.*, 1864.

iv. **Nach tausendfachen Plagen.** [*Passiontide.*] 1778, No. 128, in 8 l. It is *tr.* as :—

Behold, my soul, Thy Saviour, by P. H. Molther, as No. 352 in the *Moravian H. Bk.*, 1789. See No. vi.

v. **O angenehme Augenblicke.** [*Eternal Life.*] Written in 1766. In 1778, No. 1749, in 2 st. of 8 l. The *trs.* are :—

1. What heavenly joy and consolation, by P. H. Molther, of st. i., as No. 886 in the *Moravian H. Bk.*, 1789 (1886, No. 1314, st. iii.). Included as st. iii. of No. 403 in the Irish *Church Hyl.*, 1873.

2. O what joy, O what joy awaiteth me, No. 988 in the *Moravian H. Bk.*, 1801. In the 1886 edition it is marked as a *tr.* of No. v. as above. It bears more resemblance, however, to "O wie wallt mein Herz," which is No. 268 in the 1806 *Appendix* to the *Brüder G. B.* of 1778.

vi. **O süsse Seelenweide.** [*Passiontide.*] 1778, No. 167, in 11 st. of 8 l. St. i., ii. are ascribed to Gregor; iii., iv., xi. to Johann Prätorius; and v.-x. to C. R. von Zinzendorf (taken from Nos. 40 and 41 of the collected ed. of his hymns, 1754). The tr. is :

How is my soul delighted, a *tr.* of st. i., ii., iv., v., vii., x. by F. W. Foster, and J. Miller, as No. 360 in the *Moravian H. Bk.*, 1789. In the 1801 and later eds. (1886, No. 407), Molther's *tr.* of No. iv. was prefixed as st. i., new *trs.* of st. viii., x. given, and the rest altered. In the *Book of Com. Praise*, ed. 1872, No. 86, is st. i., ii., ll. 5–8, and iii., by Gregor ; and iv., ll. 5–8, by Prätorius, beginning, " Behold, my soul, thy Saviour."

vii. **O Tage wahrer Seligkeit.** [*Joy of Forgiveness.*] 1778, No. 398, in 6 st. of 8 l., included in the Berlin *G. L. S.*, ed. 1863. *Tr.* as :—

O days of solid happiness, in full as No. 340 in the *Moravian H. Bk.*, 1801 (1886, No. 386). Two centos from the text of 1849 are in C. U. :—

1. " What days of solid happiness," st. i.-iv., as No. 433 in the ed. of 1857 of Mercer's *C. P. and H. Bk.*

2. " Whene'er we contemplate the grace," st. iv.-vi. as No. 396 in the Irish *Church Hyl.*, 1873.

viii. **Wenn schlägt die angenehme Stunde.** [*Ascension.*] Written for Aug. 17, 1765, and included as No. 113 in 1767, as above, in 8 l. *Tr.* as :—

When, O when shall I have the favour, by P. H. Molther, c. 1774, included as No. 839 in the *Moravian H. Bk.*, 1789, repeated as st. ii. of No. 403, in the Irish *Church Hyl.*, 1873. In the 1886 ed. of the *Moravian H. Bk.*, No. 1314, it begins, "O when shall I have that great favour."

ix. **Wie wird mir einst doch sein.** [*Eternal Life.*] 1778, No. 1743, in 10 st. of 6 l. In the *Historische Nachricht* thereto, st. i.–iii. are marked as by Gregor, and st. iv.-x. as by N. L. von Zinzendorf. St. iv.-x. are recast from a hymn beginning, " Die Bäume blühen ab," written in the autumn of 1721, and included as No. 1245 in the 3rd ed., 1731, of his *Sammlung geist-und lieblicher Lieder*, in 46 st. of 4 l., the st. of the original used being in order 39, 42, 34, 18, 22, 29, 45. The only *tr.* in C. U. is :—

What shall I feel, when I, in full from the 1778, by C. I. Latrobe, as No. 885 in the *Moravian H. Bk.*, 1789 (1886, No. 1301). Two centos are in use :—

1. "How shall the joy be told"; st. i.–iv., vi., viii. altered in J. A. Latrobe's *Coll.*, 1841, No. 498.

2. "I hear the enraptured song"; st. 2, 6, 9, 10, as No. 582 in the *App.* of 1873 to Mercer's *C. P. & H. Bk.*

ii. *Hymns not in English C. U.:*—

x. **Ach mein Herr Jesu! dein Nahesein.** *Communion with Christ.* 1767, as above, No. 432, in 10 st. In the Berlin *G. L. S.*, ed. 1863, No. 925. Justly characterised by Dr. Schaff in his *Christ in Song*, 1869, p. 496, as "One of the sweetest hymns from the holy of holies of the believer's personal communion with his Saviour, and very characteristic of Moravian piety in its best form." The *trs.* are (1) "What peace divine, what perfect happiness," by P. H. Molther, as No. 278 in the *Moravian H. Bk.*, 1789 (1849, No. 362). In the 1886 ed. of the *Moravian H. Bk.*, No. 359, it begins with the *tr.* of st. v., "Gracious Redeemer, grant to us while here." (2) "Jesus, our Lord, when Thou art near," by *Dr. H. Mills*, 1845 (1856, p. 122). (3) "Ah dearest Lord! to feel that Thou art near," by *Miss Winkworth*, 1858, p. 168. (4) "Ah, Jesus, Lord, Thou art near to me," in the *British Herald*, Dec., 1866, p. 372, and as No. 304 in Reid's *Praise Bk.*, 1872. (5) "Jesus, my Lord, Thy nearness does impart," by E. Reynolds for Schaff's *Christ in Song*, 1869, p. 496.

xi. **Hallelujah! der Heiland lebt.** *Easter.* 1778, No. 203, in 17 st. (st. xiv. being by Matthäus Stach, and 1st pub. as st. ii. of No. 109, in 1767). *Tr.* as "Sing Hallelujah, Christ doth live," as No. 131 in the *Moravian H. Bk.*, 1801 (1886, No. 142), repeated in Bp. Ryle's *Coll.*, 1860, No. 131. Beginning with the *tr.* of st. ix., "The God of Peace, to guilty man," 6 st. were included as No. 90 in Reid's *Praise Bk.*, 1872.   [J. M.]

Gregory, John George, M.A., was b. in 1827 and educated at Emmanuel College, Cambridge (B.A. 1853, M.A. 1856). In 1853 he took Holy Orders, and has held, besides various curacies, the Incumbency of Nechells, Birmingham; the Rectory of Bonchurch, Isle of Wight; and the Incumbency of Park Chapel, Chelsea. In 1878 he became Incumbent of Emmanuel Church, Hove, Brighton. Whilst at Bonchurch he pub. *The Bonchurch Hymn Book*, 1868. The 3rd ed. was pub. for the use of his congregation at Park Chapel, Chelsea, in 1873. It was finally rearranged as *A Sel. of Hymns for use in Emmanuel Church, Hove*, Brighton, in 1880. To the 1st ed. of this collection he contributed :—

1. Almighty-God, our King. *Providence.*
2. Bind us to Thee, Lord, we pray. *Holiness desired.*
3. Christ, our Lord, enthroned on high. *Christmas.*
4. Defer not, O our God. *Missions.*
5. Every hour is passing. *The onward journey.*
6. Father, we adore Thee. *Holy Trinity.*
7. Great God, we bless Thy care. *Graces.*
8. High above all the angels doth Jesus now reign. *Advent.*
9. Holy Saviour, Thou Who reignest. *Advent.*
10. In faith and hope we bring this child. *Holy Baptism.*
11. In memory of Thy love. *Holy Communion.*
12. Jesus, Whose love so full, so free. *Divine guidance desired.*
13. Kind and gracious Saviour, lead us. *Easter.*
14. Lead Thou, Lord, and bid us follow. *Whitsuntide.*
15. Lord, hear Thy people pray. *Holy Baptism.*
16. Lord, our God, Thy wondrous grace. *Close of Divine Worship.*
17. O God, we would raise. *Praise.*
18. O what shall we poor children give. *Graces.*
19. The land of Immanuel, our Saviour, is yonder. *Heaven.*
20. We owe to Thee, O Lord. *Called of God.*
21. Zion's streets were thronging. *Jerusalem desolate.*

In the rearranged edition of his collection for Emmanuel Church, Hove, Mr. Gregory omitted Nos. 7, 8, 15, 18, 19, and 21 of the above, and added the following :—

22. Exalted o'er angels doth Jesus now reign. *Advent.* No. 8 rewritten.
23. I would take me to the Cross. *Good Friday.*
24. Jesus, our Lord, we look to Thee. *Advent.*

25. Lord God of endless love. *Close of Divine Service.*
26. Lord, it is sweet to rest. *Close of Divine Service.*
27. Lord Jesus, by Thy precious blood. *Passiontide.*
28. O brethren, let us sing. *Morning.*
29. O cheer thee, thou Christian. *Morning.*
30. O Lord, our Father, God and King. *Praise to the Father.*
31. Our Holy Saviour soon shall come. *Advent.*
32. Pray, Christian, pray, thy Father God will heed thee. *Prayer.*   [J. J.]

Gregory of Nazianzus (St. Gregory Nazianzen), Bishop of Sasima and of Constantinople, s. of Gregory, Bishop of Nazianzus in Cappadocia, and Nonna, his wife, was b. at a village near that city where his father had an estate, and called Arizanzus. The date of his birth is unknown, but is generally given as A.D. 325. In early childhood he was taught to read the Scriptures by his mother. From his home he passed with his brother Caesarius to a school at Caesarea, the capital of Cappadocia, where he was instructed by one Carterius, supposed by some to be the same as the subsequent head of the monasteries of Antioch, and instructor of St. Chrysostom. At Caesarea he probably met with Basil, with whom he maintained a life-long friendship. From Caesarea Basil went to Constantinople, and Gregory and his brother to Caesarea in Palestine. In a short time his brother passed on to Alexandria, whilst he remained behind to study rhetoric, and then followed his brother to that city. From Alexandria he went to pursue his study at Athens. On his journey there the ship in which he sailed encountered a severe hurricane, so much so, that all despaired of life. The voyage, however, terminated safely, and Gregory felt his deliverance to be a fresh call upon him to devote himself to God. At Athens, Julian (the Emperor) was a fellow student, and there he also met Basil again, and rendered him much assistance. His studies at Athens extended over some ten years. About 356 he returned to Nazianzus, from whence, after great persuasion on the part of Basil he joined the latter at Pontus, and devoted himself for some two or three years to an ascetic life. On returning to his home the holy office of the priesthood was forced upon him by his father: but instead of exercising his office he fled to Pontus, only to return again in a few months. Ordained, probably at Christmas, he preached his first sermon in the Church at Nazianzus on the following Easter-day, A.D. 362. In 370, through Basil, who had become Metropolitan of Cappadocia and Exarch of Pontus, Gregory consented most unwillingly to be consecrated as Bishop of Sasima. Subsequently he became for a short time his father's coadjutor at Nazianzus. About Easter, A.D. 379, he was called by the oppressed orthodox Christians of Constantinople to that city. The people's wish was supported by the voice of many of the bishops. He arrived there, it is supposed, about Easter. He found the adherents of the Nicene Creed few, and crushed by the heretics, and without a church in which to worship. His work, and the opposition he met with in that city, we cannot detail here. Failing health, and a dispute respecting the validity of his position as Bp. of Constantinople, led him, in A.D. 381, to retire to Nazianzus. After administering the affairs of that diocese for a short time he retired to his birthplace at Arizanzus, and occuplied his remaining years—probably about six —in writing poems, &c. He d. cir. 390.

St. Gregory's extant writings were pub. in two folio volumes, the first in 1778 ; and the second in 1840. This is commonly known as the Benedictine edition and is entitled *Sancti Patris nostri Gregorii Theologi vulgo Nazianzeni Archiepiscopi Constantinopolitani, Opera omnia quae extant vel ejus nomine circumferuntur, ad MSS. codices Gallicanos, Vaticanos, Germanicos, Anglicos, nec non ad antiquiores editiones castigata,* &c., &c. Vol. i. contains 45 Sermons, and vol. ii. Letters on Various Subjects, and his poems. The latter are in two Books : Bk. i. (1) dogmatic, (2) moral ; Bk. ii. historical, (1) relating to himself, (2) relating to others, including epitaphs, &c. The dogmatic poems are 38 ; the moral 40 ; those relating to his own life 99, and miscellaneous over 60. Many of these are given in the *Anth. Graec. Car. Chris.*, and *Daniel*, iii. pp. 5, 16, and 8 are translated by Mr. Chatfield in his *Songs and Hymns of the Greek Christian Poets*, 1876. For fuller details of St. Gregory's Life and Writings, his works in MS. and book form and other matters relating thereto, see *Dict. of Christian Biog.*, vol. i. pp. 741–761, and for criticism of his poetry, **Greek Hymnody,** § iv.   [J. J.]

Gregory I., St., Pope. Surnamed **The Great.** Was b. at Rome about A.D. 540. His family was distinguished not only for its rank and social consideration, but for its piety and good works. His father, Gordianus, said to have been the grandson of Pope Felix II. or III, was a man of senatorial rank and great wealth ; whilst his mother, Silvia, and her sisters-in-law, Tarsilla and Aemiliana, attained the distinction of canonization. Gregory made the best use of his advantages in circumstances and surroundings, so far as his education went. "A saint among saints," he was considered second to none in Rome in grammar, rhetoric, and logic. In early life, before his father's death, he became a member of the Senate ; and soon after he was thirty years of age, praetor of the city. But, though extremely popular amongst his countrymen, he had no mind to live "lapped in luxury," and accordingly, when his father died, he devoted the whole of the large fortune that he inherited to religious uses. He founded no less than six monasteries in Sicily, as well as one on the site of his own house at Rome, to which latter he retired himself in the capacity of a Benedictine monk, in 575. In 577 the then Pope, Benedict I., made him one of the seven Cardinal Deacons who presided over the seven principal divisions of Rome. The following year Benedict's successor, Pelagius II., sent him on an embassy of congratulation to the new emperor Tiberius, at Constantinople. After six years' residence at Constantinople he returned to Rome. It was during this residence at Rome, before he was called upon to succeed Pelagius in the Papal chair, that his interest was excited in the evangelization of Britain by seeing some beautiful children, natives of that country, exposed for sale in the slave-market there ("non Angli, sed Angeli"). He volunteered to head a mission to convert the British, and, having obtained the Pope's sanction for the enterprise, had got three days' journey on his way to Britain when he was peremptorily recalled by Pelagius, at the earnest demand of the Roman people. In 590 he became Pope himself, and, as is well known, carried out his benevolent purpose towards Britain by the mission of St. Augustine, 596. His Papacy, upon which he entered with genuine reluctance, and only after he had taken every step in his power to be relieved from the office, lasted until 604, when he d. at the early age of fifty-five. His Pontificate was distinguished by his zeal, ability, and address in the administration of his temporal and spiritual kingdom alike, and his missionaries found their way into all parts of the known world. In Lombardy he destroyed Arianism ; in Africa he greatly weakened the Donatists ; in Spain he converted the monarch, Reccared ; while he made his influence felt even in the remote region of Ireland, where, till his day, the native Church had not acknowledged any allegiance to the See of Rome. He advised rather than dictated to other bishops, and strongly opposed the assumption of the title of "Universal Patriarch" by John the Faster of Constantinople, on the ground that the title had been declined by the Pope himself at the Council of Chalcedon, and declared his pride in being called the "Servant of God's Servants." He exhibited entire toleration for Jews and heretics, and his disapproval of slavery by manumitting all his own slaves. The one grave blot upon his otherwise upright and virtuous character was his gross flattery in congratulating Phocas on his accession to the throne as emperor in 601, a position the latter had secured with the assistance of the imperial army in which he was a centurion, by the murder of his predecessor Mauricius (whose six sons had been slaughtered before their father's eyes), and that of the empress Constantina and her three daughters.

Gregory's great learning won for him the distinction of being ranked as one of the four Latin doctors, and exhibited itself in many works of value, the most important of which are his *Moralium Libri xxxv.*, and his two books of homilies on *Ezekiel* and the *Gospels*. His influence was also great as a preacher and many of his sermons are still extant, and form indeed no inconsiderable portion of his works that have come down to us. But he is most famous, perhaps, for the services he rendered to the liturgy and music of the Church, whereby he gained for himself the title of *Magister Caeremoniarum*. His *Sacramentary*, in which he gave its definite form to the Sacrifice of the Mass, and his *Antiphonary*, a collection which he made of chants old and new, as well as a school called *Orphanotrophium*, which he established at Rome for the cultivation of church singing, prove his interest in such subjects, and his success in his efforts to render the public worship of his day worthy of Him to Whom it was addressed. The *Gregorian Tones*, or chants, with which we are still familiar after a lapse of twelve centuries, we owe to his anxiety to supersede the more melodious and flowing style of church music which is popularly attributed to St. Ambrose, by the severer and more solemn monotone which is their characteristic.

The contributions of St. Gregory to our stores of Latin hymns are not numerous, nor are the few generally attributed to him quite certainly proved to be his. But few as they are, and by whomsoever written, they are most of them still used in the services of the Church. In character they are well wedded to the grave and solemn music which St.

Gregory himself is supposed to have written for them.

The Benedictine editors credit St. Gregory with 8 hymns, viz. (1) "Primo dierum omnium"; (2) "Nocte surgentes vigilemus"; (3) "Ecce jam noctis tenuatur umbra"; (4) "Clarum decus jejunii"; (5) "Audi benigne conditor"; (6) "Magno salutis gaudio"; (7) "Rex Christe factor omnium"; (8) "Lucis Creator Optime." *Daniel* in his vol. i. assigns him three others. (9) "Ecce tempus idoneum"; (10) "Summi largitor praemii"; (11) "Noctis tempus jam praeterit." For *trs.* of these hymns see under their respective first lines. (For an elaborate account of St. Gregory, see Smith and Wace's *Dictionary of Christian Biography*.)

[D. S. W.]

Greitter, Matthäus, was a monk and chorister of Strassburg Cathedral, but in 1524 espoused the cause of the Reformation. In 1528 he was appointed assistant pastor of St. Martin's Church, and afterwards at St. Stephen's. When the Interim [**Agricola**] was forced on Strassburg, he was the only one of the Lutheran pastors that sought to further it, a course which he afterwards deeply regretted. His death is dated by *Wetzel*, i. 349, as Dec. 20, 1550; by the *Allg. Deutsche Biog.*, ix. 636, as Nov. 20, 1550; while *Koch*, ii. 104, says he d. of the pestilence in 1552.

Greitter was a distinguished musician, and with his friend Dachstein (q.v.) edited the *Strassburg Kirchenampt*, 1524–5. Four psalm tunes by Greitter, and one by Dachstein were inserted by Calvin in his first Hymnbook published at Strassburg, 1539. All these were transferred to the first ed. of the French-Genevan Psalter in 1542, and two of them, both by Greitter (the tunes to psalms 36 and 91), were retained in the final ed. of 1562. Of his 7 Psalm versions 4 have been *tr.* into English:—

i. **Ach Gott, wie lang vergissest mein.** *Ps. xiii.* 1524. *Wackernagel*, iii. p. 89, in 4 st. *Tr.* as, "O Lord, how lang forever wil thow foirget," in the *Gude and Godly Ballates*, ed. 1568, folio 46 (1868, p. 78).

ii. **Da Israel aus Egypten zog.** *Ps. cxiv.* In *Die Zwen Psalmen: In exitu Israel*, &c., Strassburg, 1527, thence in *Wackernagel*, iii. p. 93, in 2 st. *Tr.* as, "Quhen, fra Egypt departit Israell," in the *G. & G. Ballates*, ed. 1568, folio 56 (1868, p. 95).

iii. **Nicht uns, nicht uns, o ewiger Herr.** *Ps. cxv.* 1527, as ii., and *Wackernagel*, iii. p. 93, in 4 st. *Tr.* as, "Not unto us, not unto us, O Lord," in the *G. & G. Ballates*, ed. 1568, folio 56 (1868, p. 95).

iv. **O Herre Gott, begnade mich.** *Ps. li.* 1525. *Wackernagel*, iii. p. 90, in 5 st. *Tr.* as, "O Lorde God, have mercy on me," by Bp. Coverdale, 1539 (*Remains*, 1846, p. 574).

[J. M.]

Greville, Robert Kaye, LL.D., was eldest s. of Rev. Robert Greville, rector of Edlaston, Derbyshire, and was b. at Bishop Auckland in 1794. He studied medicine at Edinburgh and London, and finally settled, though he did not practise, in Edinburgh. He was a distinguished botanist, and a well-known philanthropist. He edited and contributed to a number of the current annuals from 1830 to 1850. He was a member of the congregation of the Rev. D. T. K. Drummond, and joint editor with him of *The Church of England Hymn-book*, 1838, contributing thereto 9 hymns. He d. at Murrayfield, Edinburgh, June 4, 1866 (Miller's *Singers & Songs*, p. 438). [See **Scottish Hymnody**, § VI.] His hymns, dating from the collection of 1838, are:—

1. A little while and every fear. *Death anticipated.*
2. A lost and sinful world to save. *Christmas.*
3. Before Thy throne in fetters bound. *Temperance.*
4. God of the world, we praise Thy name. *Temperance.*
5. O Ancient of eternal days. *Praise to the Father.*
6. O God, the Judge of nations, hear. *National Fast.*
7. O God, we come before Thee. *Happiness desired.*
8. While still Thy all-creative hand. *God's Faithfulness.*
9. Ye humble souls in sorrow bending. *Burial.*

In addition to these hymns, some of which are still in C. U. and all are worthy of attention, the following is also by Dr. Greville:—

10. O God, from Thee alone. *Missions.*

It appeared in *The Church of England Magazine*, Jan. 18, 1839, in 6 st. of 4 l. In 1852 it passed into the S. P. C. K. *Hymns*, No. 188, and was repeated in later editions and in other collections. [J. J.]

Griffiths, Ann, of Dolwar Fechan, Montgomeryshire, was b. in 1776, and d. in 1805. She composed many beautiful hymns, a collection of which was pub. (posthumously) in 1806, and also in 1808, under the title of "*Hymnau ofawl i Dduw ar Oen*" ("Hymns of Praise to God and the Lamb"). Several of her hymns rank with the best in the Welsh language.

[W. G. T.]

Grigg, Joseph, was b. in 1728, according to the "s. mss.," but this date seems to be some 6 or 8 years too late. He was the son of poor parents and was brought up to mechanical pursuits. In 1743 he forsook his trade and became assistant minister to the Rev. Thomas Bures, of the Presbyterian Church, Silver Street, London. On the death of Mr. Bures in 1747, he retired from the ministry, and, marrying a lady of property, took up his residence at St. Albans. He d. at Walthamstow, Essex, Oct. 29, 1768. As a hymn-writer Grigg is chiefly known by two of his hymns, "Behold a stranger at the door"; and "Jesus, and can it ever be?" His hymn-writing began, it is said, at 10 years of age. His published works of various kinds number over 40. Those in which his hymns are found are:—

(1) *Miscellanies on Moral and Religious Subjects*, &c., London, Elizabeth Harrison, 1756. (2) *The Voice of Danger, the Voice of God. A Sermon Preached at St. Albans, and at Box-Lane, Chiefly with a View to the apprehended Invasion. By J. Grigg. London, J. Buckland*, 1756. To this is appended his hymn, "Shake, Britain, like an aspen shake." (3) *Four Hymns on Divine Subjects wherein the Patience and Love of Our Divine Saviour is displayed*, London, 1765. (4) *Hymns by the late Rev. Joseph Grigg*, Stourbridge, 1806. (5) During 1765 and 1766 he also contributed 12 hymns to *The Christians Magazine*.

In 1861 D. Sedgwick collected his hymns and poems, and pub. them with a memoir as :

*Hymns on Divine Subjects, * * * * London, 1861.* This volume contains 40 "Hymns," and 17 "Serious Poems." In the "s. mss." Sedgwick notes that in 1861 he omitted 3 hymns by Grigg, which were then unknown to him, viz. :—(1) On "The National Fast," appended to a sermon preached at Northampton, Feb. 13, 1761, by W. Warburton, and pub. in London, 1761. (2) "A Harvest Hymn by the late Rev. Joseph Grigg," in 6 st. in the *Evangelical Magazine*, July, 1822; and (3) On the Parable of Dives and Lazarus, dated "Feb. 15, 1767." [J. J.]

Grinfield, Thomas, M.A., b. Sept. 27th, 1788, and educated at Paul's Cray, Kent, and Trinity College, Cambridge. Taking Holy Orders in 1813, he was preferred to the Rectory of Shirland, Derbyshire, in 1827 (*Lyra Brit.*, 1867, p. 256). He d. in 1870.

His published works include :—

(1) *Epistles and Miscellaneous Poems*, London, 1815 ; (2) *The Omnipresence of God, with Other Sacred Poems*, Bristol, 1824 ; and (3) *A Century of Original Sacred Songs composed for Favourite Airs*, London, 1836.

From Nos. 2 and 3 the following hymns have come into C. U. :—

1. And is there a land far away from sin and woe? *Heaven.* No. 84 *of his Century of O. S. Songs*, 1836, in 4 st. of 4 l., and headed "The Heavenly Land."

2. O how kindly hast Thou led me [us]. *The Divine Guide.* No. 88 of his *Century*, &c., 1836, in 2 st. of 8 l.,

and entitled "Remembrance of the Way." In 1838 it was given as No. 166 in J. H. Gurney's Lutterworth *Coll.*, 1838; in his Marylebone *Ps. & Hys.*, 1851, No. 165; Lord Selborne's *Bk. of Praise*, 1862, No. 208, and other collections.

3. **Then it burst, the glorious view.** *Heaven.* 1st pub. in his *Omnipresence of God*, &c., 1824, p. 181, in 3 st. of 8 l., and entitled "The New Jerusalem." It is given in Snepp's *Songs of G. & G.*, 1872, No. 1003.

4. **They talked of Jesus as they went.** *The walk to Emmaus.* 1st pub. in his *Century*, &c., 1836, No. 52, in 5 st. of 8 l., and headed "The Visit to Emmaus." It was given in Lord Selborne's *Bk. of Praise*, 1862, No. 297, and in *Lyra Eucharistica*, 1863.

5. **Though far from thy [your] country, unfriended, unknown.** *Departure of Missionaries.* Appeared in his *Century*, &c., 1836, No. 38, in 5 st. of 4 l., and headed "Departure of Missionaries." In Dale's *English H. Bk.*, 1874. No. 1031, it is somewhat altered, and st. iii. and iv. are omitted.

6. **'Tis come, the time so oft foretold.** *Christmas.* No. 68 in his *Century*, &c., 1836, in 10 st. of 6 l., and headed "Angels announcing to Shepherds the Birth of a Saviour. A Christmas Ode." In J. H. Gurney's Lutterworth *Coll.*, 1838, st. i., vi., ix., x. were given as No. 254. These were repeated in his Marylebone *Ps. & Hys.*, 1851, as No. 260; and in Lord Selborne's *Bk. of Praise*, 1862, as No. 32.

7. **'Tis not in circumstances.** *Faith.* In its original form this is not in C. U., except in *The Comprehensive Rippon*, 1844, but it appeared as No. 44 in his *Century*, &c., 1836, as "All may be outwardly," in 4 st. of 12 l. In Dr. Dale's *Eng. H. Bk.*, 1874, No. 592, st. iii.–iv. are given in a slightly altered form.

8. **When my heart beguiling.** *Presence of Christ desired.* Pt. ii. of Song 2 in his *Century*, &c., 1836, in 13 l., and headed "Remember me. The Christian's request of his Saviour." In Dale's *English H. Bk.*, 1874, No. 534, l. 7 is omitted.

9. **Why art thou grieving?** *Trust.* No. 17 of his *Century*, &c., 1836, in 2 st. of 12 l., and headed "Why art thou disquieted? Hope thou in God." In Dale's *English H. Bk.*, 1874, No. 599, it begins "Why *are* we grieving?" and is divided into 6 st. of 4 l.

In addition to these hymns there are in the *Lyra Brit.*, 1867, the following :—

10. **All may be outwardly.** *The Heart the seat of Peace or Pain.* No. 44, but see No. 7 for this.

11. **Grant me, Lord, to walk with Thee.** *Simplicity.*

12. **O could we pilgrims raise our eyes.** *Walking by Faith.*

Of these, No. 10 is in *Sacred Melodies* appended to some editions of the *Comprehensive Rippon*, together with the following :—

13. **Happy those who rest have found.** *Repose in Jesus.* No. 59.

14. **How still amidst commotion.** *Hope.*

15. **O do not forsake me, my Father, my Friend.** *God's continued presence desired.*

16. **Sweetly let's join our evening hymn.** *For use at Sea.*

17. **Sweetly ye blow, celestial gales.** *For use at Sea.*

18. **Wake, my voice, O wake once more.** *Farewell.*

These hymns all appeared in his *Century*, &c., 1836. 　　　　　　　　　　　　　　**[W. T. B.]**

Griswold, Alexander Viets, D.D., b. at Simsbury, Connecticut, in 1766. After being for some time rector at Bristol, Rhode Island, he was consecrated bishop of the "Eastern Diocese," in 1811. He was subsequently Bishop of Massachusetts. He d. in 1843, and his memoirs were pub. by Dr. J. S. Stone. His well-known hymn :—

Holy Father, great Creator. *Holy Trinity.* Was written probably in 1835. It appeared in that year in his *Family Prayers*, in 4 st. of 6 l. and entitled "Hymn to the God of Christians." With some alterations by Bp. Coxe, it was given in *Hys. for Church and Home*, &c., Phila., 1860, No. 153. It was repeated in the *Hymnal . . . . of the Protestant Episcopal Church*, 1871, No. 145. 　　　　　　　　　　　　　　**[F. M. B.]**

Grosart, Alexander Balloch, D.D., LL.D., was b. at Stirling, N.B., on 18th June, 1835, and educated at the Falkirk Parish

School, and privately; the University of Edinburgh, and the Theological Hall of the United Presbyterian Church. His own *alma mater* conferred on him the degree of LL.D., and St. Andrew's University, D.D. On 29th October, 1856, he was ordained as minister of the First United Presbyterian Church, Kinross during which pastorate he became well known as editor of the *Works and Biographies* of Dr. Richard Sibbes, Thomas Brooks, and many others, in Nichol's *Puritan Divines* and *Puritan Commentaries*, and as author of the *Life and Works of Michael Bruce*, and of *Jesus Mighty to Save, or Christ for all the World and all the World for Christ; Small Sins; Lambs all Safe, or Salvation of Children; Prince of Light and Prince of Darkness, or the Temptation of Jesus*, and various practical books. Perhaps in literature his name came most prominently forward as author of *Lord Bacon not the author of the Christian Paradoxes* (1865)—a discovery accepted at once by Spedding and Von Ranke, and universally, and so removing a shadow that had long lain on an illustrious name. This has since been followed up by a number of noticeable kindred discoveries, e.g. that Phineas Fletcher, not Edmund Spenser, was the author of *Brittain's Ida* (the name and family history of Spenser's wife, "Elizabeth"); the identification of the *Phœnix* as Q. Elizabeth and of the *Turtle Dove* as the Earl of Essex in *Sir Robert Chester's Love's Martyr or Rosalins Complaint* (1601)—the only known book to which Shakespeare contributed verses (*New Shakspeare Society*, 1878); and unpublished MSS. of George Herbert, Richard Crashaw, &c. From Kinross he was translated to Prince's Park United Presbyterian Church, Liverpool; and in 1868 to Blackburn, Lancashire, where he is at present the minister of St. George's (Presbyterian Church of England).

Throughout his professional lifetime, Dr. Grosart has been a voluminous author, biographer, editor, and traveller. The *Fuller Worthies' Library*, 39 vols.; *Chertsey Worthies' Library*, 14 vols.; *Occasional Issues of Unique and Very Rare Books*, 38 vols.; *The Huth Library*, 39 vols.; editions of the *Works of Spenser*, 10 vols.; *Samuel Daniel*, 5 vols.; *George Daniel*, 4 vols.; *Townley MSS.*, 2 vols.; *Sir John Eliot MSS.*, 6 vols.; *Lismore Papers*, 10 vols.; *Prose Works of Wordsworth*, 3 vols.; The Spring Lecture, *Representative Nonconformists* (1879)—are only some of the fruits of his critical, annotatory, and biographical labours on our Elizabethan and other early literature. As an editor his books have been abundantly helpful in our department, and not a few of his authors belong to it, *e.g.* Spenser, Sidney, More, Beaumonts, Bruce, &c. He was the first to print many poems of *George Herbert, Richard Crashaw*, and others, and to translate their Latin and Greek poems. Much of our richest, finest, and rarest early English literature is only obtainable in Dr. Grosart's editions. These were nearly all privately printed, and limited. They are to be found in all our own great libraries, and in those of Europe and America. He has also contributed largely to the various literary and theological periodicals, *Encyclopaedia Britannica, National Biography*, &c. In 1868, he printed for private circulation a small vol. of 15 hymns, two of which have been introduced into Dr. Charles Rogers's *Harp of the Christian Home* (1876), viz., "The Living Way," and "Holiness." He has also printed a number of New-year and Watch-night Hymns, which have had a large circulation in Watchword Cards and leaflets; also two leaflets that have had a still wider circulation, "The Tear-dimmed lamp" and "God bless our Church and School." In *Leisure Hour* and *Sunday at Home*, &c., a number of his hymns have also appeared. He has announced his intention of sooner or later collecting a *Century* or more of his gradually accumulated Hymns. 　　　　　　　　　　　　　　**[J. J.]**

Groser, Horace George, s. of Wm. H. Groser (q. v.), was b. in North London, Dec. 22nd, 1863. He is a member of the Congregational Denomination, and is wholly employed in literary work as editor and author. In 1886 he pub. a religious story entitled *Bertha Pemberthy,* but the greater part of his writings have been short poems contributed to the *Sunday Magazine, The Girls' Own Paper,* and other periodicals. He is the author of several hymns, a good specimen of which is in the *Voice of Praise,* 1886, " When my spirit pants for rest " (*Lord, remember me*). [W. R. S.]

Groser, William, s. of a Baptist Minister, was b. in London in 1791. In 1813 he became pastor of a small Baptist church at Princes Risborough, Bucks ; in 1820 he removed to Maidstone, and in 1839 to London, where he resided until his death, in 1856. For some years subsequently to 1839, he was editor of *The Baptist Magazine,* and for the last five years of his life Secretary of the Baptist Irish Society. Mr. Groser also did good service to hymnody as an editor of hymn-books. The Baptist *New Selection,* prepared by Dr. Murch and others [see **Baptist Hymnody**], was edited by him in 1828. At the request of the Baptist Missionary Society he also prepared and edited in 1852, *A Sel. of Hys. adapted to Pub. Worship, and designed chiefly for the use of Baptist Churches in Jamaica.* London, Haddon & Co. This selection was reprinted in 1860 with the addition of 57 hymns ; but is no longer in use, having been superseded by the Bap. *Ps. & Hys.,* 1858. As a hymn-writer Mr. Groser is known by one hymn only :—

Praise the Redeemer, almighty to save. *Death Conquered.* It was composed during his residence at Maidstone, to the metre and tune of "Sound the loud timbrel," and appeared in the enlarged *Sel. of Hymns for the use of Bapt. Congregations,* London, 1840 ; again in Spurgeon's *O. O. H. Bk.,* 1866, and in the 1880 *Suppl.* to Bapt. *Ps. & Hys.*   [W. R. S.]

Groser, William Howse, B.SC., s. of Mr. W. Groser (for many years Secretary of the London Sunday School Union, and a relative of the Rev. W. Groser, noticed above), was b. in 1834, and educated at University College, London, and graduated B.SC. at the London University, in 1862. Although engaged in mercantile pursuits Mr. Groser devotes considerable time to natural science, and Christian work, especially in connection with Sunday schools. He was for twelve years editor of the *Bible Class and Youth's Magazine ;* and subsequently of the *Sunday School Teacher,* and of the *Excelsior.* His publications, mainly of a Biblical and educational character, are numerous. In 1875, he edited :—

Songs by the Way. A Hymnal for Young Christians and Enquirers, Lond. S. S. U.

He also contributed hymns to the S. S. Union hymn-books :—

(1) *Sunday Scholars' Hymn Book,* N.D. (1861) ; (2) *Songs of Gladness ; A Hymn-book for the Young,* 1871, containing 200 hymns. It was subsequently enlarged to 266 ; and (3) *The Sunday School Teachers' Hymn-book* (1871).

His hymns published in these books include :

i. *Songs by the Way,* 1875.

1. The Lord is our Shepherd. *The Good Shepherd.*

ii. In *Sunday Scholars' H. Bk.,* 1861.

2. Blest Saviour, who in days of old. *S. S. Anniversary.*

3. Great Lord of earth and time. *S. S. Anniversary.*
4. Swift as an eagle's flight. *Flight of time.*
5. Sunny days of childhood. *Early Piety.*

iii. In *Songs of Gladness,* 1871.

6. Borne upon time's noiseless wing. *New Year.*
7. How bright the morning broke. *Year of Jubilee.*
8. O happy they who know the Lord. *Early Piety.*
9. O'er the waters, dark and drear. *Divine Guidance Desired.*

These hymns were all composed between 1860 and 1875. All are in C. U. in G. Britain, and many also in America. Those in the *S. S. Teachers' H. Bk.* are the least suitable.

[W. R. S.]

Gross, Johann. [Rutilius, M.]

Grüenwald, Georg, was an Anabaptist shoemaker, who suffered martyrdom for his principles, being in 1530 burnt at the stake at Kopffstain, or Kufstein, on the Inn below Innsbruck. To him is ascribed, in a MS. Anabaptist Chronicle now in the Town Library at Hamburg, the hymn :—

Kommt her zu mir, sagt Gottes Sohn. [*Christ's Yoke.*] Founded on St. Matt. xi. 28–30. Appeared as " Ain schöns newes Christlichs lyed," in 1530. *Wackernagel,* iii. pp. 128–133, gives this in 16 st. and later forms. The form in V. Babst's *G. B.,* Leipzig, 1545, is that in C. U., as in the *Unv. L. S.,* 1851, No. 421. It has been generally ascribed to Hans Witzstadt of Wertheim, but *Wackernagel* in a long note decides in favour of Grüenwald.

The *trs.* are (1) " Cum heir, sayis Goddis Sone to me," in the *Gude and Godly Ballates,* ed. 1568, folio 16 (1868, p. 25). (2) " Come hither ! saith our blessed Lord," by *J. C. Jacobi,* 1725, p. 35 (1732, p. 121), repeated as No. 151 in pt. i. of the *Moravian H. Bk.,* 1754. (3) " Come hither, says the Son of God," by *Dr. H. Mills,* 1856, p. 47. (4) " Come hither, says our blessed Lord," by *Dr. G. Walker,* 1860, p. 80. [J. M.]

Grünbeck, Esther, née Magdalene Augusta Naverofsky, was b. at Gotha, Oct. 21, 1717, of a Polish-Jewish family who had become Christians. In 1734 she married Michael Grünbeck, a sculptor in Gotha, and in 1738 with him became a Moravian ; entering the Widows' Choir after his death in 1742. Marrying in 1746 David Kirchhof, a baptized Jew, she engaged with him for some time in mission work among the Jews in Prussia and Poland. After his death she became leader of the Widows' Choir at Zeist, near Utrecht, and d. there Oct. 13, 1796.

In the *Historische Nachricht* to the *Brüder G. B.,* 1778 (ed. 1851, p. 205), 8 hymns and part of a ninth in that collection are ascribed to her. Those in English use outside the Moravian hymn-books are :—

i. **Dem blut'gen Lamme.** *Self-Dedication.* Founded on Rom. vi., 13. 1st pub. 1739, as No. 1365 in the *Supplement* to the 8th *Appendix* to the Herrnhut *G. B.,* 1735 ; in 10 st. of 6 l., repeated as No. 753 in the Berlin *G. L. S.,* ed. 1863. The only *tr* in C. U. is :—

To the Lamb stain'd with Blood, *tr.* in full by C. Kinchen as No. 155 in the *Moravian H. Bk.,* 1742. Four forms are in use :—

1. " Unto the Lamb of God," in the *Moravian H. Bk.,* 1789, No. 263 (1886, No. 335), altered and omitting st. viii., ix.
2. " To Christ the Lamb of God," st. i., iv., vii. altered in J. A. Latrobe's *Coll.,* 1841, No. 313.
3. " Lord ! bring me to resign," a cento from st. vii., viii., as No. 437 in Dr. Martineau's *Hymns,* 1840 (1873, No. 288), and as No. 668 in the American *Bapt. Psalmist,* 1843.
4. " To Thee I wholly give." A cento beginning with st. ii. in Lady Huntingdon's *Sel.,* 1780. It was subsequently changed to " To Thee, my Lord, I give."

ii. **Gnade ist ein schönes Wort.** *Forgiveness of Sins.* 1st pub. 1739 as No. 1293 in the 8th *Appendix* to the Herrnhut *G. B.*, 1735, in 8 st. of 8 l. The only *tr.* is "Grace! Grace! O that's a charming sound," in full, by C. Kinchen, as No. 32, in the *Moravian H. Bk.*, 1742, altered and abridged in later ed. (1886, No. 319). A cento in 8 st. of C.M. from st. ii., iii., v.–viii., and beginning "Grace, how exceeding sweet to those," was included in the 1780 ed. of Lady Huntingdon's *Sel.*, No. 85; and reduced to 5 st. in Campbell's *Comprehensive H. Bk.*, 1837, and to 3 st. in C. H. Bateman's *Cong. Psalmist*, 1846.
[J. M.]

Gryphius, Andreas, was b. Oct. 2, 1616, at Gross-Glogau, in Silesia. He was educated at the School at Fraustadt, Silesia, 1631–34, and the Gymnasium at Danzig, 1634–36. After being for some time family tutor in the house of Baron Georg von Schönborn, near Fraustadt (who crowned him as a poet in 1637), he was forced by the Counter Reformation in Silesia to find refuge in Holland. He matriculated as a student at Leyden in 1638, and was afterwards till 1643 University Lecturer. Thereafter he accompanied the son of a rich Stettin burgess and two Pomeranian noblemen in a tour through France, Italy, Holland, and South Germany, and then, in the end of 1647, settled in Fraustadt. In 1650 he was appointed syndicus of the principality of Glogau, and while attending one of the meetings of the diet at Glogau was struck by paralysis and d. in the assembly house, July 16, 1664.

Gryphius ranks as one of the principal poets of Silesia. The troublous events of his life, however, cast a gloom over most that he wrote, and his hymns especially are sombre in character. He was the first writer of German tragedies (*Leo the Armenian; The Murdered Majesty; or, Charles Stuart of Great Britain*, &c.) and one of the earliest writers of German comedy (*Herr Peter Squenz; Horribilicribrifax; Die geliebte Dornrose*, an excellent little comedy in *Silesian dialect*, &c.).

Gryphius had begun writing sonnets about 1637, and his *Son- und Feyrtage Sonnete* were pub. at Leyden, 1639 [Berlin]; followed by his *Sonnete, Erste Buch*, 1643 [Berlin]. The first (pirated) ed. of his collected poems appeared as his *Teutsche Reimgedichte*, Frankfurt am Main, 1650 [Berlin], and the first authorised ed. as his *Teutscher Gedichte, Erster Theil*, Breslau, 1657 [Berlin]. Those *tr.* into English are:—

i. **Als der betrübte Tag zu Ende kommen.** *Entombment of Christ.* No. 19 in Bk. iv. of his *Odes* (1657, p. 40), in 13 st. *Tr.* as, "When that so troublous day was now concluded," as No. 167 in pt. i. of the *Moravian H. Bk.*, 1754.

ii. **Die Herrlichkeit der Erden.** *For the Dying.* His best hymn. No. 9 in Bk. i. of his *Odes* (1650, p. 99; not in 1643), in 15 st., entitled "Vanitas! vanitatum vanitas." The *trs.* are: (1) "Earth's boasted joys and splendour," by *Dr. H. Mills*, 1845. (2) "All glories of this earth decay," by *Miss Winkworth*, 1869, p. 177.

iii. **In meiner ersten Blüth.** *God is near.* No. 36 in Bk. iv. of his *Sonnets* (1657, p. 116; not in 1643), entitled "Andreas Gryphius on his Sunday and Festival Sonnetts." *Tr.* as, "In life's fair Spring," by *Miss Winkworth*, 1869, p. 179.

iv. **Je mehr wir Jahre zählen.** *New Year.* No. 9 in Bk. iii. of his *Odes* (1657, p. 79), in 8 st. *Tr.* as, "So many years of living," by *N. L. Frothingham*, 1870, p. 181 (from the recast "Wie viel wir"), in the Berlin *G. B.*, 1829, No. 835.

Another hymn has been frequently ascribed to Andreas Gryphius, but we have failed to find it either in his works or in the works of Christian Gryphius. It is:—

v. **Es ist vollbracht! Gottlob es ist vollbracht.** *For the Dying.* In the *Vollständiges Hauss- und Kirchen G. B.*, 9th ed., Breslau, 1726, No. 304, in 7 st. The *trs.* are: (1) "It is finished! finished! yea," by *Miss Dunn*, 1857, p. 119. (2) "It is complete. My God, I thank Thy care," by G. Moultrie, in his *Espousals of Saint Dorothea*, 1870, p. 65.
[J. M.]

Guest, Benjamin, b. in 1788, was for some time the proprietor of a private school at Brighton, and subsequently vicar of a parish in Rutlandshire, and then rector of Pilton, Northants. He d. at Blackheath, Jan. 30, 1869. His hymn on *Holy Baptism*, "Heavenly Father, may Thy love," was contributed to H. V. Elliott's *Ps. & Hys.*, 1835, No. 324, in 4 st. of 4 l. It is also given in several collections of a later date, as the *N. Cong.*, 1859, &c. (Miller's *Singers and Songs of the Church*, 1869, p. 531).
[J. J.]

Guide Thou, O God, the guardian hands. *G. Phillimore.* [*Ember Days.*] Written for and 1st pub. in *The Parish Hymn Book*, 1863 (No. 185), and appointed for "Ember Days." It consists of 6 st. of 4 l. In *The Hymnary*, 1872, st. v. and vi. are slightly changed; whilst in the S. P. C. K. *Church Hymns*, the metre has been altered from 8.6.8.4. to C.M. both with the consent of the author. It is also in other collections.
[J. J.]

Guiet, Charles, a Jesuit, born at Tours in 1601. Taught classical literature and moral theology. He was also a preacher and experienced in the ceremonial of the Church. He wrote a work on the order of reciting the divine offices and d. at Tours, March 30, 1664. *Jöcher Gelehrten-Lexikon. Miller* places his death about 1684. Some of his hymns were given in the *Paris Breviary*, 1736. [G. A. C.]

Guion, Jeanne B. de la Mothe [Guyon, J. B. de M.]

Gunn, Henry Mayo, was b. March 25, 1817, at Chard, Somerset, and educated at Mill Hill School, and at University College. He held several pastorates, beginning with Basingstoke in 1841, and closing with Sevenoaks in 1881. He d. May 21, 1886. He pub. various works, chiefly descriptive of the Nonconformist Churches and their principles. Besides translating some of the earlier Greek and Latin hymns for the *Excelsior*, edited by the late Dr. James Hamilton, he wrote many hymns, including:—

1. **Higher, higher to the Cross.** *The Cross of Christ.* Appeared, in 6 st. of 4 l., in the 1866 *Supplement* to the collection used in the Redland Congregational Church, Bristol. It is also issued in sheet form.

2. **Our fathers were high-minded men.** *Fidelity to Principle.* This was suggested by the disruption of the Church of Scotland in 1843. It was pub. in the Alton Sunday School *Collection*, 1844, in 3 st. of 8 l. It is in several hymn-books, including the Congregational Union *Bk. of Praise for Children*, 1881.

3. **To realms beyond the sounding sea.** *Prayer on behalf of Colonists.* Appeared in the *New Cong.*, 1859, No. 903, in 4 st. of 4 l.

4. **We want no priest but Jesus.** *Priesthood of Christ.* Printed for the annual meeting of the Wilts Congregational Union, 1872. It is largely circulated as a broadsheet, and has been *tr.* into Italian for the use of the Evangelical Church of Italy. [W. G. H.]

Günther, Cyriacus, was b. Jan. 15, 1649, at Goldbach, near Gotha. After studying at the Gymnasium of Gotha, and the University of Jena, he became First-form master at Eisfeld, Sachse-Meiningen; and then Third-form master in the Gymnasium at

Gotha. He d. at Gotha in the beginning of Oct. 1704 (*Koch*, iv. 263–9; *Bode*, p. 81). His son, who was clerk of St. George's Church at Glaucha, possessed a MS. collection of some 30 hymns by his father; and from this he allowed Freylinghausen to select 10 for his *Neues geistreiches G. B.*, 1714. These are above the average in merit, and Scriptural and good in style. Two have passed into English :—

i. Bringt her dem Herren Lob und Ehr. *Praise and Thanksgiving.* 1714, No. 556, in 7 st. of 7 l., repeated as No. 993 in the Berlin *G. L. S.*, ed. 1863. The only *tr.* in C. U. is :—

With joyful heart your praises bring, a good *tr.* of st. i., iv.–vi., by A. T. Russell, as No. 202 in his *Ps. & Hys.*, 1851.

ii. Halt im Gedächtniss Jesum Christ. *Love to Christ.* Founded on 2 Tim. iii. 8. 1714, No. 765, in 6 st. of 7 l., repeated as No. 297 in the Berlin *G. L. S.*, ed. 1863. On thankful remembrance of Christ's Incarnation (i.); Death (ii.); Resurrection (iii.); Ascension (iv.); Promised Second Advent (v.); ending with a prayer for faith (vi.). The only *tr.* in C. U. is :—

O keep before thy thankful eyes. A good and full *tr.* by A. T. Russell, as No. 182 in his *Ps. & Hys.*, 1851.

Other trs. are : (1) " Remember Jesus, God's dear Son," by *Dr. H. Mills*, 1845 (1856, p. 125). (2) " Bear Jesus Christ the Lord in mind," by Miss Cox, in *Lyra Eucharistica*, 1863, p. 215 (1864, p. 259), and in her *H. from German*, 1864, p. 111.   [J. M.]

Gurney, Archer Thompson, was b. in 1820, and educated for the legal profession. He was called to the Bar at the Middle Temple, but in 1849 he entered Holy Orders. He held several appointments, including the Curacy of Buckingham, 1854–58; the Chaplaincy of the Court Church, Paris, 1858–71, and other charges. He d. at Bath, March 21, 1887. His pub. works include :—

Spring, 1853; *Songs of the Present*, 1854; *The Ode of Peace*, 1855 ; *Songs of Early Summer*, 1856; and *A Book of Praise*, 1862.

To the *Book of Praise* he contributed 147 hymns. Very few of these are known beyond his own collection. He is widely known through his Easter hymn, " Christ is risen, Christ is risen." His " Memory of the blest departed " (*SS. Philip and James*) is in the *People's H.*, 1867.   [J. J.]

Gurney, John Hampden, M.A., eldest s. of Sir John Gurney, a Baron of the Exchequer, was b. in Serjeants' Inn, London, Aug. 15, 1802, and educated at Trinity College, Cambridge, where he graduated in 1824. On taking Holy Orders he became Curate of Lutterworth (1827–1844), and subsequently Rector of St. Mary's, Marylebone, and Prebendary of St. Paul's Cathedral. He d. in London, March 8, 1862. The S. P. C. K. and other religious societies had his cordial sympathy, and received his active support. His publications include several small volumes in prose, and the following :—

(1) *Church Psalmody ; Hints for the improvement of a Collection of Hymns published by the Society for Promoting Christian Knowledge*, 1853 ; (2) *A Collection of Hymns for Public Worship.* Lutterworth, 1838. This contains 300 hymns, and is known as his *Lutterworth Collection*; (3) *Psalms and Hymns for Public Worship, selected for some of the Churches of Marylebone.* London, 1851. This collection of 300 hymns and psalm versions is known as his *Marylebone Collection.* The

Preface is signed by " Charles Baring," " Thomas Garnier," and " John Hampden Gurney," but the work was practically done by Gurney.

To the *Lutterworth Collection*, 1838, he contributed :—

1. Earth to earth, and dust to dust. *Burial.*
2. Great King of nations, hear our prayer. *Fast Day.*
3. Lord, as to Thy dear Cross we flee. *Lent.*
4. Lord, at Thy word the constant sun. *Harvest.*
5. Saviour, what wealth was Thine. *Passiontide.*
6. Soon to the dust we speed. *Heaven anticipated.*
7. Thou God of mercy and of might. *Good Friday.*
8. Thou plenteous source of light and love. *Advent.*
9. Thou Who of old didst raise. *Ascension.*
10. Through centuries of sin and woe. *For Peace.*
11. We praise Thee, everlasting God. *Te Deum.*

These hymns were all signed " J. H. G.," and Nos. 1, 2, 3, 7, 8, 9 and 11, were repeated in the *Marylebone Coll.*, 1851 ; and to these were added :—

12. Fair waved the golden corn. *Child's Hymn.*
13. How vast the debt we owe. *Offertory.*
14. Lord of the Harvest, Thee we hail. *Harvest.* This is No. 4 above rewritten.
15. Lord, we lift our eyes above. *Love of Christ.*

In addition to these we are specially indebted to Gurney for, " We saw Thee not when Thou didst come " (q.v.), and " Yes, God is good," &c. (q.v.). Several of the above-named hymns are in extensive use in G. Britain and America. The most popular are annotated under their respective first lines.   [J. J.]

Guter Hirte, willst du nicht. *J. Scheffler.* [*The Good Shepherd.*] Appeared as No. 70 in Bk. iii. of his *Heilige Seelenlust*, Breslau, 1657, p. 218 (*Werke*, 1862, i. p. 128), in 5 st. of 6 l., entitled, " She [the Soul] beseeches Him, that He, as a Good Shepherd, would bring her, His lamb, to His fold." Included in Freylinghausen's *G. B.*, 1705, No. 702, and recently in the Berlin *G. L. S.*, ed. 1863. It is a hymn full of tenderness and pathos, and has been well translated as :—

1. **Wilt Thou not, my Shepherd true,** a full and very good *tr.* in Miss Cox's *Sacred H. from German*, 1841, p. 101. Thence with st. iii., ll. 3, 4, altered in the 1857 edition of Mercer's *C. P. & H. Bk.*, in *Kennedy*, 1863, &c. Slightly altered by Miss Cox for *Lyra Eucharistica*, 1863, p. 191, and her *H. from German*, 1864, p. 169; and thence unaltered in the *People's Hyl.*, 1867.

2. **Loving Shepherd, kind and true,** a full and good *tr.* in the 1st Ser., 1855, of Miss Winkworth's *Lyra Ger.*, p. 98, repeated, slightly altered, in the *Hyl. for St. John's, Aberdeen*, 1865–70. Considerably altered for metrical reasons in her *C. B. for England*, 1863, No. 152.

3. **While on earth, dear Lord, I roam,** a good but free *tr.* in Miss Dunn's *H. from German*, 1857, p. 109, and thence, omitting st. iii., iv., as No. 244, in Dr. Pagenstecher's *Coll.*, 1864.

4. **Loving Shepherd ! Guardian true,** included in *Holy Song*, 1869, is a *tr.* of st. i., iii.–v., in 4 st. of 4 l., with the refrain, " Tender Shepherd ! Thine I am, Keep till death Thy little lamb."

Another tr. is, " O Faithful Shepherd ! now behold," by *Lady Eleanor Fortescue*, 1843 (1847, p. 43).   [J. M.]

Guthrie, John, D.D., s. of John Guthrie, Milnathort, Kinross-shire, was b. at Milnathort, May 30, 1814, and after studying at the University of Edinburgh, where he graduated M.A. in 1835, was in 1840 ordained minister of the United Secession Church in Kendal.

Sympathising with the views of Dr. James Morison, he was, in 1843, deposed, and joined with Dr. Morison in forming the Evangelical Union. He continued in Kendal till 1848, becoming then minister of Dundas St. E. U. Church, Glasgow. In 1851 he went to Greenock; thence, in 1862, to Tolmer's Square, London, returning in 1866 to Glasgow as minister of Howard St. E. U. Church. He d. in London, September 18, 1878, while on his way to New Zealand. From 1846 to 1861 he was Professor to the Evangelical Union, and was re-elected in 1875. He received the degree of D.D. from Coburg University, U.S.A., in 1875. He was Convener of the Committee which compiled the *E. U. Hymn-book* of 1856, and a member of that which compiled the *E. U. Hymnal* of 1878 (to which he contributed 4 hymns). His hymns appeared in *The Daystar, The Evangelical Magazine*, &c. In 1869 he pub. *Sacred Lyrics; Hymns, original and translated from the German, with versions of Psalms*, Lon., J. Nisbet & Co., 1869. This work consists of 28 hymns, 17 *trs.*, and 37 Psalm versions. Some of the hymns have much beauty and sweetness. The *trs.* from the German are accompanied by interesting notes, and, while not ranking with the best by Miss Winkworth, are yet very good. The Psalm versions are of average merit. His hymns in C. U. are:—

1. **Blood of sprinkling, healing tide.** [*Blood of Sprinkling.*] Appeared in *The Evangelical Union H. Bk.*, 1856, in 3 st. of 8 l., and again, unaltered, in *The Evangelical Union Hymnal*, 1878. Composed in 1844.

2. **How lovely are thy tents.** [*Public Worship.*] 1st pub. in *Hys. & Spiritual Songs, collected by James Morison*, Kilmarnock, Pt. ii., 1844, in 7 st. of 6 l. It was repeated, unaltered, in *The Evangelical Union H. Bk.*, 1856; and *The Evangelical Union Hymnal*, 1878.

3. **'Tis evening : over Salem's towers, &c.** [*Christ weeping over Jerusalem.*] Appeared in *The Evangelical Union H. Bk.*, 1856, in 4 st. of 8 double lines, and again, unaltered, in *The Evangelical Union Hyl.*, 1878, No. 62, where it is dated 1846.

4. **Ye ransomed of Jesus.** [*Praise to Jesus.*] 1st pub. in *Hys. & Spiritual Songs*, &c. (see No. 2), Pt. ii., 1844, in 7 st. of 6 l.; and again, unaltered, in *The Evangelical Union H. Bk.*, 1856; and *The Evangelical Union Hyl.*, 1878, No. 98. [J. M.]

Guyet, Charles. [Guiet, C.]

Guyon, Madame. (1648–1717.) Jeanne Marie Bouvières de la Mothe was the leader of the Quietist movement in France. The foundation of her Quietism was laid in her study of St. Francis de Sales, Madame de Chantal, and Thomas à Kempis, in the conventual establishments of her native place, Montargis (Dep. Loiret), where she was educated as a child. There also she first learned the sentiment of espousal with Christ, to which later years gave a very marked development. She was married at sixteen to M. Guyon, a wealthy man of weak health, twenty-two years her senior, and her life, until his death, in 1676, was, partly from disparity of years, partly from the tyranny of her mother-in-law, partly from her own quick temper, an unhappy one. Her public career as an evangelist of Quietism began soon after her widowhood. Her first labours were spent in the diocese of Geneva, at Annecy, Gex, and Thonon, and in Grenoble. In 1686 she came to Paris, where she was at first imprisoned for her opinions in the Convent of St. Marie in the Faubourg St. Antoine,

but released after eight months at the instance of Madame de Maintenon. She then rose to the zenith of her fame. Her life at all times greatly fascinated those around her; and the court, Madame de Maintenon, Fénelon (who ardently sympathised with her doctrine of pure and disinterested love of God), and Madame de Maintenon's College of Ladies at Cyr, came under the spell of her enthusiasm. But the affinity of her doctrines with those of Molinos, who was condemned in 1685, soon told against her. Her opinions were condemned by a commission, of which Bossuet was president. She then incurred Bossuet's displeasure by breaking the promises she had made to him to maintain a quiet attitude, and not return to Paris. She was imprisoned at Vincennes, Dec. 1695, and in the following year removed to Vaugirard, under a promise to avoid all receptions and correspondence, except by special permission. In 1698 she was immured in the Bastille, and not released until 1702. The Quietist controversy had meanwhile ruined the saintly Fénelon in the favour of Louis XIV., and obtained the condemnation by the Pope (1699) of his book (*Maximes des Saints*) written in defence of the doctrine of disinterested love. The remainder of Madame Guyon's life was spent in retirement with her daughter, the Marquise de Vaux, at Blois. She was visited there by numbers of persons of all ranks, some of them from foreign countries; and she had a considerable correspondence. She heard Mass daily, and died in full communion with the Roman Church. Madame Guyon's works fill 40 volumes. The principal ones are:—

(1) *Les Torrents* (1683), a description of God's dealings with souls, founded on her own spiritual history. (2) *Le Cantique des Cantiques interprété selon le sens mystique. Le Moyen Court de faire oraison* (1684). Her (3) *Autobiography.* (4) *Poésies et Cantiques Spirituels* (pub. 1722). The *Cantiques Spirituels* comprise nearly 900 pieces. The dates of composition are mainly to be gathered from internal evidence; some appear to have been written in the country; many were certainly written in her imprisonments at the Convent of St. Marie and Vincennes; many also apparently in her last sickness at Blois. They were composed to ballad tunes, and with an effortless facility, five or six hymns being often written in a day, while confined to her bed. She believed them to originate from the Divine impulse, more than from herself. The *Cantiques* are at once illustrated and interpreted by her *Autobiography* (which is one of the most remarkable books in the delineation of spiritual enthusiasm) and by her *Commentary on the Song of Solomon*, which applies its passionate love to the union of Christ with the soul. The leading ideas are, (1) the absorption of the soul, utterly emptied of self, into the Infinite Being of God: which is expressed at other times as the entire occupation of the soul, reduced to nothingness ("le néant, le rien"), and deprived of all independent will, by the Personality of God. The perfect state of the soul is one of complete passiveness; its energy is the energy of God directing and wielding the human powers; prayer becomes not the expression of desire, but rapt contemplation, wordless intercourse, and reception of the Divine Voice to the soul. (2) Pure and disinterested love of God, as Himself the Perfect Love, uninfluenced by any consideration of His favour and blessing either here or in eternity. If it be His will to cast the soul into hell itself, even this is to be accepted without fear or deprecation, if the Love of God remains as the joy of His creature. (3) The Love of God is consistent with terrible, often unintelligible or apparently capricious infliction of suffering and desertion on the soul He loves.

A selection of 37 pieces from these poems was *tr.* by the poet Cowper, in 1782 (pub. by his friend William Bull, in 1801). Bull had introduced the poems to him, and requested him to translate some of them. Whether Bull or Cowper selected the pieces for translation is uncertain. Their leading theme is that of Love unshaken, submissive, not asking for release, though under the extremity of desertion and suffering inflicted by God's Hand, which is heavy with anger and seems threatening destruction. Mixed with these awful seasons there are others, in which the manifestation of the Divine Love floods the soul with transport. The points of affinity with Cowper's thought are obvious; and Bull may have hoped that the spectacle of her unmoved belief in the hidden love of God might help to drive away the terrible delusion of his reprobation. The nervous style is very different from the flabby lines of the French: and Cowper designedly modified the amative metaphors, which, especially when they represent the dealings of Christ with her as His spouse, in language suggested by the caprice of Cupid or that of conjugal infidelity, are very painful and unconsciously irreverent. (See his letters to W. Unwin, 1782–3.) The most characteristic pieces are those beginning, "'Twas my purpose on a day," "I suffer fruitless anguish," "Long plunged in sorrow," and "Source of Love, my brighter Sun."

The *trs.* from Madame Guyon's hymns which are in C. U. are mainly in American hymn-books. They include :—

1. **Ah! régnez sur toute la terre.** *Triumph of heavenly love desired.* From her *Cantique des Cantiques*, vol. ii, No. 236. *Tr.* by W. Cowper in his posthumous *Poems Translated from the French of Madame de la Mothe Guion*, &c., 1801, p. 14, in 3 st. of 4 l., as, "Ah! reign, wherever man is found." It is in Spurgeon's *O. O. H. Bk.*, 1866.

2. **Amour que mon âme est contente.** *The soul that loves God finds Him everywhere.* From vol. ii., Cantique 108. *Tr.* by W. Cowper, 1801, p. 33, in 9 st. of 4 l., as "O Thou, by long experience tried." This has been abbreviated and altered to "My Lord, how full of sweet content," in Hatfield's *Church H. Bk.*, N. Y., 1872, and others, and as "O Lord, how full of sweet content," in the Andover *Sabbath H. Bk.*, 1858; the *Songs for the Sanctuary*, 1865, &c. It is also in use in its original form. Cowper's *tr.* is more nervous than the original, but not always close thereto.

3. **Divin objet, auquel nul objet n'est pareil.** *The Nativity.* From her works, vol. iv., *Poëmes Héroïques*, 1. W. Cowper's *tr.* of the poem (1801, p. 1) begins "'Tis folly all—let me no more be told." The cento in C. U. begins on p. 4 with "Infinite God, Thou great unrivall'd One," and is composed of 14 l., not consecutive in all cases, and with extraneous additions.

4. **Esprit Saint, viens dedans nos cœurs.** *Charity.* From vol. ii., Cant. 96, beginning with st. iii. *Tr.* by W. Cowper, 1801, p. 26, as "Spirit of charity dispense." This is in American C. U.

5. **Je n'aime plus d'un amour mien.** *Life in the love of God.* From vol. iv., sect. 2, cant. 80. An anonymous *tr.* of a part of this as "I love my God, but with no love of mine," appeared in the Andover *Sabbath H. Bk.*, 1858; the *Church Praise Bk*, N. Y., 1881, &c., in 2 st. of 6 l. Of this *tr.* st. i. is apparently an expansion of the four first lines of this short hymn; st. ii. may be only an expansion of the two remaining lines, or may have added to it some verse of a hymn not identified. *Guyon*, vol. iii., cant. 136, is somewhat similar, especially at its close, but is on a much larger scale.

6. **L'amour me tient asservie.** *Divine love.* From vol. ii., cant. 155. *Tr.* by W. Cowper, 1801, p. 38, in 8 st. of 4 l., as "Love is the Lord whom I obey." It is generally used in an abbreviated form.

7. **La fontaine dans sa source.** *Living Water.* From vol. iv., cant. 81. *Tr.* by W. Cowper, 1801, p. 23, in 2 st. of 4 l., as "The fountain in its source." In 1812 it was given in Collyer's *Sel.*, No. 322, with an additional stanza by *Collyer*. This is the form of the text in C. U. in G. Britain and America.

8. **Mon cœur depuis longtemps plongé.** *The Joy of the Cross.* From vol. iii., cant. 97. *Tr.* by W. Cowper, 1801, pp. 81–84, in 12 st. of 6 l., as "Long plung'd in sorrow, I resign." The following centos therefrom are in C. U. :—
1. "Long plunged in sorrow, I resign."
2. "O Lord, in sorrow I resign."
3. "Self-love no grace in sorrow sees."
Of these centos 1 is in Spurgeon's *O. O. H. Bk.*, 1866; and 2 and 3 in American collections.

9. **Nous portons un doux témoignage.** *God's Chosen.* Vol. ii., cant. 78. *Tr.* by W. Cowper, 1801, p. 35, as "How happy are the new-born race." This is usually altered to "O happy they, God's chosen race," as in *Mercer*, 1854, and others.

10. **Souffrons, puisqu'il le faut, souffrons toute la vie.** *The love of God the end of Life.* From vol. ii., cant. 165. *Tr.* by W. Cowper, 1801, p. 50, in 4 st. of 4 l., as "Since life in sorrow must be spent." In the *Songs for the*

Sanctuary, 1865, and other American collections it is altered to "If life in sorrow must be spent."

In addition to these there are also *trs.* of hymns in C. U., the originals of which are attributed to Madame Guyon. These we have not identified in her poetical works :—

11. **By suffering only can we know.** *Resignation.* This is part of a poem written at nineteen. In a letter written from Blois in 1717, Madame Guyon thus alludes to it: "I remember that when I was quite young, only nineteen years of age, I composed a little song in which I expressed my willingness to suffer for God. . . . A part of the verses to which I refer is as follows: 'By suffering only can we know.'" The *tr.* in the American *Hys. for the Church of Christ*, 1853, is anonymous.

12. **I would love Thee, God and Father.** This we cannot identify. It appeared in the Andover *Sabbath H. Bk.*, 1858, No. 649, in 5 st. of 4 l. It is in *Songs for the Sanctuary*, 1865, Hatfield's *Church H. Bk.*, 1872, and others.

13. **'Tis not by skill of human art.** *Love.* Not identified. The *tr.* appeared in the *Hys. for the Church of Christ*, 1853, No. 606.

[H. L. B.]

H

H., in the Bristol Bapt. *Coll.* by Ash and Evans, 1769, i.e. Hudson.

H., in H. L. Hastings's *Songs of Pilgrimage*, Boston, 1886, i.e. the Editor.

H. B., i.e. Henry Bennett (q. v.).

H. K. B. E., i.e. Miss Hannah K. Burlingham of Evesham.

H. L. L., i.e. *Hymns from the Land of Luther.* [See **Borthwick, Jane.**]

H. M. C., in the *Hymnary*, i.e. Harriet Mary Chester (q. v.).

H—t, in the Bristol *Coll.* by Ash and Evans, i.e. Joseph Hart (q. v.).

Habert, Isaac, was a native of Paris, where he became Doctor of the Sorbonne, Canon and Lecturer in Divinity to the Chapter of the Cathedral, and Preacher to the King. On Dec. 17, 1645, he was consecrated Bp. of Vabres (Aveyron), a post which he held with esteem for over twenty years. He d. of apoplexy while on a visit to Pont-de-Salars, near Rodez, Sept. 15, 1668, and was buried in the Cathedral at Vabres.

He is best known as a writer against Jansenism; and as the editor of the *Liber Pontificalis*, Paris, 1643, which contains the Greek service with a Latin version by himself. He contributed a number of Latin hymns to the *Paris Breviary* of 1643. Those which are repeated in the *Paris Breviary* of 1736 are marked there *H. Vabr. Ep.*, or *Hab. Vabr. Ep.*   [J. M.]

Had I ten thousand gifts beside. [*Completeness in Christ.*] Appeared anonymously in R. Conyers's *Coll.*, 1774, No. 254, in 2 st. of 6 l. In this form it is in use in America. In the *Bapt. H.* [*& Tune*] *Bk.*, Phila., 1871, No. 429, a third stanza has been added from "There is no path to heavenly bliss," st. i. of No. 202, in Rippon's *Bap. Sel.*, 1787. The usual modern form of the hymn in use in G. Britain is, "All other pleas we cast aside," as in Mercer's *Ch. Psalter & H. Bk.*, 1855, No. 111 (Ox. ed. 1864, No. 45). This is repeated in *Kennedy* with the addition of a doxology.   [J. J.]

Haddock, Grace Webster. [**Hinsdale, G. W.**]

Haec illa solemnis dies. *Jean Baptiste de Santeüil.* [*Annunciation.*] Appeared in the *Cluniac Breviary*, 1686, p. 942, in his *Hymni Sacri et Novi*, 1689, p. 17 (ed. 1698, p. 86): "De Incarnatione Christi seu Annunciatione Dominica," in 6 st. of 4 l. It was repeated in the revised *Paris Brev.*, 1736, as the Hymn for the 1st and 2nd Vespers of Feast of Annunciation. Also in Card. Newman's *Hymni Ecclesiae*, 1838 and 1865. *Tr.* as:—

O joyful was the morn. By R. Campbell in his *Hymns and Anthems*, &c., 1850, p. 88. This, in a rewritten form, is given in the *Hymnary*, 1872, as, "O joyful rose this sacred morn."

Other trs. are:—

1. This is the day, the solemn day. *J. Chandler.* 1837. Sometimes given as "O day of glad solemnity," as in Murray's *Hymnal*, 1852.
2. This is the festal light. *I. Williams.* 1839.
3. Hail, festal morn, whose sacred ray. *J. D. Chambers.* 1866.   [J. J.]

Hagenbach, Carl Rudolph, D.D., s. of C. F. Hagenbach, professor of medicine at Basel, was b. at Basel, March 4, 1801. He studied at the Universities of Basel, Bonn, and Berlin. He returned to Basel in 1823 as University lecturer on Church history, was appointed ordinary professor of Church history in 1829, and d. at Basel, June 7, 1874 (*Koch*, vii. 95, 96; *Allg. Deutsche Biog.*, x. 344, 315, &c.). His hymns appeared principally in his *Gedichte*, Basel, 1846. Two are *tr.*:—

i. **Du Quell, der alle Herzen tränket.** *Passiontide.* On Christ thirsting on the cross. 1846, as above, vol. i. p. 33, in 4 st. *Tr.* as "Thou fountain for the panting heart," by *J. Kelly*, 1885, p. 40.

ii. **Stille halten deinem Walten.** *Resignation.* On patient waiting on God, founded on Ps. lxii. 2. In his *Gedichte*, 1846, vol. i. p. 85, in 8 st. of 6 l.; and in Knapp's *Ev. L. S.*, 1850, No. 1947. *Tr.* as:—

Since thy Father's arm sustains thee, a free *tr.* of st. i.–v. in the *Family Treasury*, 1861, p. 293; and in the Gilman-Schaff *Lib. of Rel. Poetry*, ed. 1883, p. 525, marked as *tr.* by "H. A. P." Included as No. 884 in *Laudes Domini*, N. Y., 1884.   [J. M.]

Hail, all hail, the joyful morn. *Harriet Auber.* [*Christmas.*] 1st pub. in her *Spirit of the Psalms*, 1829, p. 139, in 4 st. of 4 l. In the Oberlin *Manual of Praise*, 1880, No. 164, st. ii., iii. are given as, "Angels bending from the sky." The full text is given in *Hymns & Songs of Praise*, N. Y., 1874, No. 172.   [J. J.]

Hail! Alpha and Omega, hail. *J. Cennick.* [*Faith desired.*] Pub. in his *Sac. Hys. for the Children of God*, &c., 1741, No. 82, in 5 st. of 4 l., and entitled, "A Prayer for Faith." In 1774 it was given in R. Conyers's *Coll.*; No. 78, st. 3 being omitted. This arrangement has generally been followed by later editors, as in the *Moravian H. Bk.*, 1849, and others. In *Kennedy*, 1863, it reads: "*Great* Alpha and Omega, hail." In the *Moravian H. Bk.*, 1886, it begins with st. ii., "Hail, First and Last," &c.   [J. J.]

Hail, everlasting Spring. *P. Doddridge.* [*The Living Fountain.*] This hymn, based on Zech. xiii. 1, is dated in the D. MSS. "Nov. 7, 1736." It was 1st pub. in J. Orton's ed. of Doddridge's (posthumous) *Hymns*, &c., 1755, No. 170, in 3 st. of 8 l., and again in J. D. Humphreys's ed. of the same, 1839,

No. 191, and in each case without alteration. In *Hys. & S. of Praise*, N. Y., 1874, No. 515, it is given unaltered and in full. Elliott, in his *Ps. & Hys.*, 1835, No. 83, attributes the hymn to "Dodd," and this has been quoted as the author's name. It is simply a contraction of "Doddridge."   [J. J.]

Hail, Father, Whose creating call. *S. Wesley, jun.* [*Adoration of God the Father.*] 1st pub. as No. 1 of his *Poems on Several Occasions*, 1736, in 6 st. of 4 l., and entitled, "A hymn to God the Father." It was repeated in the 2nd ed., 1743; and in Nicholls's reprint, 1862, p. 365. In the *Ps. & Hys.* pub. by J. Wesley at Charlestown, South Carolina, 1736-7, it is No. 11. It was not included in the *Wes. H. Bk.* until the *Suppl.* 1830, No. 561 (revised ed., 1875, No. 042); although as "Hail, Father, Whose *commanding call*," it was given in Toplady's *Ps. & Hys.*, 1776, No. 189.   [J. J.]

Hail, God the Son, in glory crowned. *S. Wesley, jun.* [*Adoration of God the Son.*] This companion hymn to the foregoing by the same author, was 1st pub. in his *Poems*, &c., 1736, and repeated in J. Wesley's *Ps. & Hys.*, Charlestown, South Carolina, 1736-7, No. 12, in 6 st. of 4 l., and headed, "Hymn to God the Son." It was repeated in the 2nd ed. of the author's *Poems*, &c., 1743, and in Nicholls's reprint, 1862. In 1830 it was included in the *Suppl.* to the *Wes. H. Bk.*, No. 601; and in the revised ed. 1875, No. 665. It is also in other collections in G. Britain and America. Although not recognized in the *Wes. H. Bk.* until 1830, it was brought into use in the Church of England by Toplady in his *Ps. & Hys.* in 1776, No. 190.   [J. J.]

Hail, happy day! the [thou] day of holy rest. *S. Browne.* [*Sunday.*] 1st pub. in his *Hys. & Spiritual Songs*, &c., 1720, Bk iii. No. 1, in 9 st. of 4 l., and headed, "For the Lord's Day." It is in several modern American collections, altered and abbreviated, as in the *Songs for the Sanctuary*, 1865, No. 71, where it reads, "Happy day! *thou* day of holy rest." The stanzas chosen are i., ii. and iv.   [J. J.]

Hail, Holy Ghost, Jehovah, Third. *S. Wesley, jun.* [*Adoration of the Holy Ghost.*] This companion hymn to the author's "Hail, Father," &c., and "Hail, God the Son," &c., was 1st pub. in his *Poems*, &c., 1736, and repeated in J. Wesley's *Ps. & Hys.*, Charlestown, South Carolina, 1736-7, No. 13, in 6 st. of 4 l., and entitled, "Hymn to God the Holy Ghost." It was repeated in the 2nd ed. of the author's *Poems*, &c., 1743; and in Nicholls's reprint, 1862. Although included in Toplady's *Ps. & Hys.*, 1776, No. 191, it was not given in the *Wes. H. Bk.* until the *Suppl.* of 1830, No. 649 (revised ed., 1875, No. 750).   [J. J.]

Hail, holy, holy, holy Lord, Let angels, &c. *E. Perronet.* [*Holy Trinity.*] Appeared in his *Occasional Verses*, &c., 1785, p. 23, in 9 st. of 4 l., and entitled, "The Lord is King." It is a companion hymn to the author's "All hail the power of Jesus' Name," and in common with it repeats the last line of st. i. in each stanza with the change in st iv.,

vi. and ix. of "And shout, The Lord is King," to "O shout," "High shout," and "Loud shout." In Hatfield's *Church H. Bk.*, N. Y., 1872, No. 295 is composed of st. i.-iii., v and ix.   [J. J.]

Hail, holy martyrs, glorious names.
C. Wesley. [*For Martyrs.*] 1st pub. in *Hys. & Sac. Poems*, 1740, in 12 st. of 4 l., and headed, "Written after walking over Smithfield." (*P. Works*, 1868-72, vol. i. p. 345.) A cento in the *Leeds H. Bk.*, 1853, No. 605, beginning with the same first line, is thus composed: st. i., ii., iv.-vi. are from this hymn, with alterations; and st. iii. and vii. are by another hand. From this cento another was taken for the Bapt. *Ps. & Hys.*, 1858. It begins, "Father, though storm on storm appear," and includes st. iii.-v. and vii. [J. J.]

Hail, Name of Jesus, glorious Name.
[*Ascension.*] This hymn is based upon E. Perronet's "All hail the power of Jesus' Name," and several lines are taken from that hymn. It appeared in Jane E. Leeson's *Paraphrases & Hys*, 1853, in 2 st. of 8 l., and was repeated in the Irvingite *Hys. for the Use of the Churches*, 1864. Its ascription is "*E. Perronet*, 1779; *Jane E. Leeson*, 1853." [J. J.]

Hail, sacred day of earthly rest.
G. Thring. [*Sunday.*] Written in 1863, and 1st pub. in his *Hys. Congregational and Others*, 1866, p. 82, in 13 st. of 4 l. In the *Appendix* to the S. P. C. K. *Ps. & Hys.*, 1869, No. 314, it was given in 9 st. with st. i. l. 3 changed from "Hail, quiet spirit ¦bringing peace," to "Hail, day of light, that bringest light," by Bp. W. W. How. This text was repeated in Thring's *Coll.*, 1882, No. 65, and is the authorised form of the hymn. In *Laudes Domini*, N. Y., 1884, No. 92, st. i.-iii. and xiii. are altered from the original 8, 6, 8, 4 to 8, 8, 8, 4 measure, very much to the injury of the hymn. Full authorised text in the author's *Hys. & Sac. Lyrics*, 1874, p. 21.   [J. J.]

Hail, sovereign love, that first began.
J. Brewer. [*Christ the Hiding Place.*] 1st appeared in the *Gospel Magazine*, Oct. 1776, in 9 st. of 4 l., and signed "Sylvestris." It was given in full in J. Middleton's *Hymns*, 1793, No. 279; in *Williams and Boden*, 1801, No. 226; in undated editions of the Lady Huntingdon *Coll.*, No. 328, and others. Rippon, in the 27th ed. of his *Sel.*, 1827, No. 172, Pt. ii., set the example of abbreviation, and this example has been followed in almost all modern collections in G. Britain and America. In addition to abbreviated text there are also three altered forms of the hymn :—

1. **Hail, sovereign love, that first began.** No. 645 in the 1st ed. of Bickersteth's *Christ. Psalmody*, 1833. This had undergone considerable alteration, and further changes were made in the enlarged ed., 1841.
2. **Hail, sovereign love, that form'd the plan.** This is in somewhat extensive use in America, including Beecher's *Plymouth Coll.*, 1855, No. 548; *Songs for the Sanctuary*, 1865, No. 450, and others.
3. **Hail, boundless love, that first began.** In the Meth. F. Ch. *S. S. Hys.*, 1860, No. 62.

Full original text in *Lyra Brit.*, 1867, p. 87.
[J. J.]

Hail the day that sees Him rise.
C. Wesley. [*Ascension.*] 1st pub. in *Hys. & Sac. Poems*, 1739, p. 211, in 10 st. of 4 l., and entitled, "Hymn for Ascension Day" (*P.*

Works, 1868-72, vol. i. p. 187). It has come into C. U. in various forms, of which the following are the most popular :—

1. *The original.* This was given in the *Suppl.* to the *Wes. H. Bk.*, 1830, No. 630; in the revised ed., 1875, No. 718; and several other collections. The first stanza reads :—

> "Hail the day that sees Him rise,
> Ravish'd from our wishful eyes!
> Christ, awhile to mortals given,
> Re-ascends His native heaven."

2. The full text, with slight alterations, appeared in Whitefield s *Coll.*, 1753, No. 43. This form of the hymn may be known by st. vi. ll. 1, 2, which read :—

> "Still for us *He intercedes*;
> Prevalent *His death He pleads*."

3. An abbreviated text, given in Madan's *Ps. & Hys.*, 1760, No. 23, in 4 st. of 8 l. In this st. ii. and v. are omitted, and the alterations as in Whitefield are adopted. This has been repeated in several collections, both old and new, including the Dutch Reformed *Hys. of the Church*, N. Y., 1869, No. 187. In this last case the original reading (altered in Whitefield) is restored.

4. The most popular form of the hymn dates from 1820. In that year it was given in the 9th ed. of Cotterill's *Sel.*, No. 106, as follows (the italics being Cotterill's alterations) :—

> 1. "Hail the day that sees Him rise,
>   *Glorious to His native skies!*
>   Christ awhile to mortals given,
>   *Enters now the highest* heaven.
> 2. "There the *glorious* triumph waits;
>   Lift your heads, eternal gates!
>   *Christ hath vanquish'd death and sin,*
>   Take the King of glory in.
> 3. "*See, the heaven its Lord* receives!
>   *Yet* He loves the earth He leaves;
>   Though returning to His throne,
>   Still He calls mankind His own.
> 4. "Still for us *He intercedes;*
>   *His prevailing death He pleads;*
>   Near Himself prepares our place,
>   Harbinger of human race.
> 5. "*O* though parted from our sight
>   *Far* above yon azure height,
>   Grant our hearts may thither rise,
>   *Seeking* Thee above the skies."

This text was repeated almost verbatim in Bickersteth's *Christ. Psalmody*, 1833; Elliott's *Ps. & Hys.*, 1835; and others down to 1852, when, in the Rev. G. C. White's *Introits and Hys.*, the "Hallelujah" refrain was added to each verse. This form of the text, with the addition in some cases, as in *H. A. & M.*, of st. v. of the original ("See! he lifts His hands above"), is very popular, and is found in the *Hymnary*, 1872; *H. A. & M.*, 1861 & 1875; Thring's *Coll.*, 1882; the *Universal H. Bk.*, 1885; and others. It is *By C. Wesley*, 1739; *G. Whitefield*, 1753; *T. Cotterill*, 1820; *and G. C. White*, 1852.

5. The text of the *H. Comp.*, 1870 and 1876, is from the original with the "Hallelujah" refrain, and the change in st. ii., l. 1, of "pompous" to "*glorious*" and st. vi., l. 1, "Grant" to "Lord."

6. In the *Salisbury H. Bk.*, 1857, No. 106. A cento from the original, the *Cotterill-White*, text, and others, together with a doxology, was given as "Hail the day that sees Him go." This was replaced by the original, in the *Sarum Hymnal*, 1868.

7. The S. P. C. K. *Church Hys.*, 1871, omits st. iii. and vi. of the original, and gives variations from *Cotterill* and others.

8. In the 1863 ed. of the S. P. C. K. *Ps. & Hys.*, No. 230, there is a cento of which st. i.-iv. are altered from Wesley, and v., vi. are new to the hymn. It begins, " Master, Lord, to Thee we cry."

9. The American collections usually follow those of G. Britain in its various forms, and the source of each text can be determined by the foregoing annotations. In the *Church Pastorals*, Boston, 1864, No. 76, as " Master, may we ever say," is composed of st. vii.-x.

10. Several hymn-books also present slight variations either from the original, or from one of the altered forms, but those are too minute and numerous to give in detail.

When all its various forms are taken into account, this hymn ranks as one of the three hymns by C. Wesley which of all his compositions have attained to the greatest popularity. The other two are, " Hark! the herald angels sing," and "Jesu, lover of my soul."

[J. J.]

Hail the sign, the sign of Jesus. *S. Baring-Gould.* [*Missions.*] Written in 1866, and 1st printed in the *Church Times*, 1866. In 1867 it was included in the *People's H.*, and subsequently in other collections.

Hail, thou bright and sacred morn. *Julia A. Elliott.* [*Sunday Morning.*] 1st pub. anonymously in her husband's *Ps. & Hys.*, 1st ed., 1835, No. 296, in 2 st. of 6 l., but acknowledged in the " Third Thousand," 1839, by the addition of her initials " J. A. E." in the Index. It is given in several modern collections in G. Britain and America, including Whiting's *Hys. for the Ch. Catholic*, 1882, and *Songs for the Sanctuary*, N. Y., 1865, &c. [J. J.]

Hail, Thou God of grace and glory. *T. W. Aveling.* [*Prosperity of the Church desired.*] "One of four hymns sung on the occasion of the jubilee of the Old Congregational Chapel, Kingsland, which was held on June 16, 1844." (Miller's *Singers & Songs*, 1869, p. 531.) It was given in the *New Cong.*, 1859, No. 816, in 3 st. of 8 l. It has passed into several American collections, including Hatfield's *Church H. Bk.*, 1872, No. 1201 ; the *Laudes Domini*, 1884, No. 947, for " Christian Union " ; and others. [J. J.]

Hail, Thou once despised Jesus. *J. Bakewell.* [*Ascension.*] In a volume of *Poetical Tracts*, 1757-74, in the Bodleian Library, Oxford [*Hymni G. Pamph.* 1276 (1)], there is, bound up with others, a small pamphlet of 72 pages with the following title :—

A Collection of Hymns addressed to The Holy, Holy, Holy, triune God, in the Person of Christ Jesus, our Mediator and Advocate. [*Ps. xlvii. 6, in Hebrew; and Cant. iv. 16, in English.*] *London : Printed by M. Lewis, in Paternoster-Row. MDCCLVII.*

At page 40 of this pamphlet the following hymn is found :—

" HYMN XLVI.

1.

" Hail, thou once-despised Jesus,
  Hail, thou *Galilean* King !
Who didst suffer to release us,
  Who didst free salvation bring !

Hail, thou universal Saviour,
  Who hast borne our sin and shame;
By whose merits we find favour,
  Life is given thro' thy name !

i. [ii.]

" Jesus, hail ! inthron'd in glory,
  There for ever to abide ;
All the heav'nly host adore thee,
  Seated at thy Father's side :
Worship, honour, pow'r, and blessing,
  Thou art worthy to receive—
Loudest praises without ceasing
  Meet it is for us to give ! "

In M. Madan's *Coll. of Ps. & Hys.*, 1760, this hymn reappeared in the following expanded form, the added portions being in *italics* :—

" HYMN CX.

" Praise to Christ.

i.

" Hail thou once despised Jesus .
  Hail thou Galilean King !
Who didst suffer to release us,
  Who didst free Salvation bring !
Hail thou universal Saviour,
  Who hast borne our Sin and Shame,
By whose Merits we find Favour,
  Life is giv'n thro' thy Name !

ii.

" *Paschal Lamb by God appointed,*
  All our Sins were on Thee laid !
By Almighty Love appointed,
  Thou hast full atonement made :
Ev'ry Sin may be forgiv'n
  Thro' the Virtue of thy Blood,
Open'd is the Gate of Heav'n,
  Peace is made 'twixt Man and God.

iii.

" Jesus Hail ! enthron'd in Glory,
  There for ever to abide !
All the heav'nly Hosts adore Thee
  Seated at thy Father's Side :
There for Sinners Thou art pleading
  ' Spare them yet another Year '—
Thou for Saints art interceding
  Till in Glory they appear.

iv.

" Worship, Honour, Pow'r, and Blessing,
  Christ is worthy to receive—
Loudest Praises without ceasing
  Meet it is for us to give !
Help, ye bright angelic Spirits,
  Bring your sweetest, noblest Lays,
Help to sing our Jesu's Merits,
  Help to chaunt Immanuel's Praise ! "

This text was repeated with slight alterations (specially in st. ii., l. 3, " love *anointed*," for " love appointed," in R. Conyers's *Coll. of Ps. & Hys.*, 1774, No. 70 ; in the Lady Huntingdon *Coll. of Hys.*, Edinburgh, c. 1771 ; and others. The next important change in the hymn was made by A. M. Toplady, with the object of making it subservient to his stern Calvinistic views. His text in his *Ps. & Hys.*, 1776, No. 113, is :—

i. " Hail, thou once despised Jesus !
  Hail, thou Galilean King !
Thou didst suffer to release us,
  Thou didst free salvation bring.
Hail, thou *agonizing* Saviour,
  Bearer of our sin and shame !
By *thy* merits we find favour,
  Life is given through thy name.

[" Paschal Lamb," &c., omitted on doctrinal grounds.]

ii. " Jesus, hail, enthroned in glory,
  There for ever to abide !
All the heav'nly host adore thee,
  Seated at thy Father's side.
There for sinners thou art pleading,
  There thou dost our place prepare,
Ever for us interceding
  Till in glory we appear.

" Worship, honour, pow'r, and blessing,
  Thou art worthy to receive ;
Loudest praises, without ceasing,
  Meet it is for us to give.

Help, ye bright angelic spirits!
Bring your sweetest, noblest lays;
Help to sing our Saviour's merits,
Help to chaunt Immanuel's praise."

In *A Coll. of Ps. & Hys. on various subjects for Pub. and Private Worship. Designed for the Congregation of Northampton Chapel.* By William Taylor and Herbert Jones. Lond., 1777, No. 162, there is a cento from Madan's text, to which is added what has long been regarded as the *fifth* stanza of "Hail, Thou once despised Jesus." It is from James Allen's *Coll. of Hys. for the Use of those that Seek and those that Have Redemption in the Blood of Christ*, 1757, No. 97, and reads:—

" Soon we shall with those in glory,
His transcendent grace relate;
Gladly sing th' amazing story
Of His dying love so great.
In that blessed contemplation,
We for evermore shall dwell;
Crown'd with bliss and consolation,
Such as none below can tell."

The sources of the various arrangements of "Hail, Thou once despised Jesus," found in modern hymn-books in all English-speaking countries, can be easily determined by reference to the above texts, which, in every case, are printed from the originals. In addition to the numerous centos in C. U. which begin with "Hail, Thou once," &c., there are also (1) "Paschal Lamb, by God appointed," and (2) "Jesus, hail, enthroned in glory."

J. Bakewell's share in the composition of this hymn in its full modern form of 5 st. of 8 l. seems thus to have been very limited. Unless it can be shewn that he re-wrote and enlarged it for M. Madan's *Ps. & Hys*, 1760, of the 40 lines so confidently attributed to him, only 16 are his. In the Bodleian Library Catalogue, the pamphlet in which Bakewell's two stanzas appeared, is said to be "Assigned by Mr. Daniel Sedgwick to William Jones, of Nayland." From Sedgwick's MSS. we find that this was a guess on his part. The compiler of the pamphlet is unknown.   [J. J.]

Hail, Thou source of every blessing. B. Woodd. [*Epiphany.*] Appeared in his *Ps. of David and other portions of the Sacred Scriptures*, &c., N.D. [cir. 1810–21], No. 177, in 3 st. of 8 l., and again in his *New Metrical Version of the Ps. of David*, &c., 1821, No. 177. In Bickersteth's *Christian Psalmody*, 1833, it was given as by *Robinson* (i.e. R. Robinson, q. v.), and this error has been repeated in several collections. It is in extensive use, many collections following *Bickersteth's* text of 1833. Orig. text in the *Hy. Comp.*, No. 95, with st. iii., l. 7, "*all-inviting* Saviour," for "*universal* Saviour;" l. 3, "temples" for "temple."   [J. J.]

Hail to the Lord's Anointed. J. Montgomery. [*Ps. lxxii. Missions.*] Written for and included in a Christmas Ode which was sung at one of the Moravian settlements in the United Kingdom, Christmas, 1821 (*Biog. Index to the Irish Ch. Hymnal*). This settlement is said by some to have been Fulneck, of which Montgomery was a member, but the authorities at Fulneck cannot substantiate the statement. Its subsequent history began with its being sent, on the 9th of January, 1822, in MS. to Mr. George Bennett then on a mission tour in the South Seas (*M.'s Memoirs*, vol. iii. p. 277). In April of the same year it was repeated by Montgomery himself at a missionary meeting in Pitt Street Chapel, Liverpool (*M.'s Memoirs*, vol. iii. p. 284), and in the following month was printed in the *Evangelical Magazine*, and entitled "Imitation of the 72nd Psalm (Tune Culmstock)." To it was appended a note alluding to Montgomery's forthcoming *Songs of Zion.* Later in the same year it was included in that work; again in Montgomery's *Poetical Works*, 1828, vol. iii. p. 59; and in 1841, vol. iii. p. 287; and finally in his *Original Hymns*, 1853, No. 267. It consists of 8 st. of 8 l. The text is slightly varied in each of Montgomery's works, the authorised being that in his *Original Hymns.*

Of all Montgomery's renderings and imitation of the Psalms this is the finest. It forms a rich and splendid Messianic hymn. Its success has been great, partly due at the first by the publicity given to it by Dr. Adam Clarke in his *Commentary on the Bible*, in which it appeared in 1822 with a special note. It is found in all modern hymnals of note, in all English-speaking countries, and has been translated into several languages. In common with most of Montgomery's hymns, it has undergone but little change at the hands of compilers. Two changes are given in *H. A. & M.*, in 1861, which are attributed to the Rev. J. Keble. They are: st. ii., l. 7-8:—

" *From hill to vale the fountains
Of righteousness o'erflow,*"

for Montgomery's :—

"And righteousness, in fountains,
From hill to valley flow;"

and st. iv., l. 8 :—

"His name shall stand for ever,
His changeless name of love."

This last line of the hymn appears as follows in Montgomery's works, and elsewhere :—

Original. "His Name—what is it? LOVE."
P. W., 1828. "That Name to us is Love."
Orig. Hys., 1853. "That Name to us is LOVE."

In addition to these alterations by Montgomery and Keble, we find also the following :—

Rorison's *Coll.*, 1851. "His holiest Name is Love."
Mercer's *Coll.*, 1855. "His great, best Name of Love."
Hymnary, 1872. "Jesus, sweet Name of Love."
Monsell's *Parish Hymnal*, 1873. "The one great Name of Love."

Of these changes Montgomery's revised text of 1828 is in the most extensive use; *Mercer's* text ranks next, and then that by *Keble;* very few, if any, reprints of the *Hymnary* or of *Monsell* being found. The *Hymnary* text throughout is very much altered. In Wilson's *Service of Praise*, 1865, it is divided into two parts, Pt. ii. being, "Kings shall fall down before Him." A cento beginning, "Receive Messiah gladly," is in Martineau's *Hymns*, 1840, and "Arabia's desert ranger," is found in a few collections. The opening line in the *Anglican H. Bk.*, 1868, is "*All* hail the Lord's Anointed;" and to the usual cento of 4 st. Harland has added in his *Ch. Psalter*, &c., a doxology. Orig. text, *Evang. Mag.*, May, 1822; authorised text, "M. MSS." and his *Orig. Hymns*, 1853. [**Psalters, Eng.**, § XVII.] [J. J.]

Hale, Edward Everett, M.A., b. at
Boston, 1822, and graduated at Harvard.
From 1846 to 1856 he was pastor of an Uni-
tarian Church at Worcester; and from 1856
he has had the charge of South Church, Boston.
He has pub. several prose works of merit.
His hymn, "O Father, take the new-built
shrine" (*Dedication of a Church*), is dated
1858. It was pub. in Longfellow & Johnson's
Hys. of the Spirit, 1864, No. 223, in 2 st. of
4 l.; and was repeated in Martineau's *Hys. of
P. & Prayer,* Lon., 1873, No. 725. [F. M. B.]

Hale, Mary Whitwell, daughter of
Eliphalet Hale of Boston, U.S.A., was b. at
Boston, Jan. 29, 1810. After receiving a
good education she devoted herself to educational work in Boston, Taunton, Keene, N. H.,
and elsewhere. She d. Nov. 17, 1862. Her
hymn-writing was brought into notice by two
hymns, one on "Home," and the second on
"Music," which were written for a juvenile
concert at the Unitarian Church in Taunton,
April 1834. Several of the hymns and poetical
pieces which she subsequently wrote were
contributed to the *Christian Register* under
the initials "Y. L. E.," the concluding letters
of her name. Her *Poems* were pub. at Boston
in 1840. A few of her hymns also appeared
in the Unitarian *Christian Hys. for Public
and Private Worship,* commonly known as
the *Cheshire Collection,* in 1844. [American
Hymnody, § VII.] Putnam (to whom we are
indebted for these details) gives the following
of her hymns, with others, in full in his
Singers and Songs of the Liberal Faith, 1874:

1. "Praise for the glorious light." *Temperance Anni-*
versary.
2. "This day let grateful praise ascend." *Sunday.*
3. "Whatever dims the sense of truth." *A Mother's*
Counsel.
4. "When in silence o'er the deep." *Christmas.*

These hymns were given in the *Cheshire
Coll.,* 1844. Nos. 2 and 3 were taken from
her *Poems.* Some of the other pieces given
by Putnam are worthy of attention. [J. J.]

Hale, Sarah Josepha, née Buell, b.
at Newport, New Hampshire, 1795, and married to David Hale, a lawyer, who died in
1822. Mrs. Hale edited *The Ladies' Magazine,*
Boston, from 1828; and Godey's *Ladies' Book,*
Phila., from 1837, besides publishing several
works. Her hymn, "Our Father in heaven,
we hallow Thy name" (*The Lord's Prayer*),
appeared in Mason & Greene's *Church Psalmody,* 1831, No. 553, in 2 st. of 8 l. Mrs. Hale,
who was a member of the Protestant Episcopal
Church, d. in 1879. [F. M. B.]

Hall, Christopher Newman, LL.B., s.
of J. Vine Hall, was b. at Maidstone, May 22,
1816, and educated at Totteridge School, and
Highbury College, London. In 1841 he graduated B.A. at the University of London, and
LL.B. in 1856. From 1842 to 1854 he was
minister of Albion Church, Hull; and from
1854 he has been in charge of Surrey Chapel,
and its continuation, Christ Church, Westminster. He was also chairman of the Congregational Union of England and Wales in
1876. In addition to several prose works,
and numerous tracts (one of which, "Come to
Jesus," has been translated into 30 languages

and has reached a circulation of two millions),
he published:—

(1) *Hymns composed at Bolton Abbey, and Other
Rhymes,* Lond., Nisbet, 1858; (2) *Cloud and Sunshine,*
Lond., Hamilton, Adams & Co., 1870; (3) *Christ Church
Hymnal, for the use of the Congregation of Christ
Church, Westminster Road,* Lond., Nisbet, 1876; (4)
Pilgrim Songs in Sunshine and Shade, Lond. 1870
(this is No. 1 with additional verses); (5) *Supplemental
Pilgrim Songs;* and (6) *Songs of Earth and Heaven,*
Lond., Hodder & Stoughton, 1886.

In the *Christ Church Hymnal,* 1876, there
are 82 original hymns by Mr. Hall, 10 of
which previously appeared in his *Hys. composed at Bolton Abbey,* &c., 1858. All the 82
hymns are signed "N. H." Of his hymns
the most popular are, "Accepting, Lord, Thy
gracious call"; "Friend of sinners, Lord of
glory"; and "Hallelujah, joyful raise" (q.v.).
In addition the following are also in C. U.
outside of his *Hymnal:—*

1. Come, Lord, to earth again (1876). *Advent.*
2. Day again is dawning (1872). *Morning.*
3. Friend of sinners, hear my cry (1844). *Lent.*
4. God bless our dear old England (1876). *National
Hymn.*
5. I know who makes the daisies. *Providence.*
6. Lord, we do not ask to know (1876). *Missions.*
7. O Jesus, Who to favoured friend (1876). *B. V. M.
given into the charge of St. John.* [W. G. H.]

Hall, William John, M.A., was b. in
London, Dec. 31, 1793, and graduated at
Corpus Christi College, Cambridge. Taking
Holy Orders, he held several important ap-
pointments, including a Minor Canonry in St.
Paul's Cathedral, London, 1826; Priest In
Ordinary of H.M. Chapel Royal, St. James's,
1829, and the Vicarage of Tottenham, Middle-
sex, 1851. He d. at Tottenham, Dec. 16, 1861.
He pub. various *Sermons,* a volume of *Prayers
for the Use of Families;* and a valuable treatise on *Purgatory and Prayers for the Dead.*
He is known to hymnology as the editor of
*Psalms and Hymns adapted to the Services
of the Church of England,* London, 1836,
commonly known as the *Mitre Hymn-book,*
from the impression of a Mitre on the cover.
He was assisted in this work by E. Osler (q.v.)
and others, who supplied original compositions.
Many of the hymns were previously printed
in the *Christian Remembrancer,* of which he
was sometime the editor, and then the editor
and sole proprietor. The *Mitre H. Bk.,* issued
in 1836, with a dedication to Bp. Blomfield,
attained to a circulation of four million copies.
It introduced numerous hymns to modern collections, and had a marked influence on the
hymnody of the Church of England. In this
Dictionary all notes on hymns specially connected with the *Mitre H. Bk.* are from Mr.
Hall's MSS., and distinguished as "H. MSS."
His son, the Rev. William John Hall, M.A.
(b. March 17, 1830, and educated at Merchant
Taylors School, and at Trinity College, Cambridge; Minor Canon in St. Paul's Cathedral,
London, and Rector of St. Clement's, East-
cheap, with St. Martin-Orgar, London), is the
editor of the *New Mitre Hymnal, Adapted to
the Services of the Church of England,* Lond.,
1875. (Preface, *Advent,* 1874.) [J. J.]

Hallelujah = Alleluia. Hymns beginning with this word are arranged in this work
according to the mode of spelling adopted by
the authors and translators.

Hallelujah! Hallelujah! Hearts to heaven and voices raise. *C. Wordsworth, Bp. of Lincoln.* [*Easter.*] 1st pub. in his *Holy Year,* &c., 1862, p. 81, as the first of two hymns for Easter-day, in 5 st. of 4 double lines. Its use in all English-speaking countries is most extensive, and it ranks with the best of the author's hymns.   [J. J.]

Hallelujah! He cometh with clouds and with light. *Bp. E. H. Bickersteth.* [*Advent.*] Written in 1850, and 1st printed in a magazine, in 4 st. of 4 l. In 1858 it was given in the author's *Ps. & Hys.,* &c., No. 411; and again in *The Two Brothers,* &c., 1871. Its use is limited.   [J. J.]

Hallelujah! joyful raise. *C. Newman Hall.* [*Doxology.*] Dated "Surrey Chapel, November 19, 1857," and pub. in the author's *Hys. composed at Bolton Abbey,* &c., 1858, in 2 st. of 4 l. It is in C. U. in G. Britain and America, and is one of the most popular of the author's hymns. In his *Christ Church Hymnal,* 1876, it is No. 158.   [J. J.]

Hallelujah! Lob, Preis und Ehr. [*Trinity Sunday.*] The earliest text known is in a broadsheet entitled *Gaudium Aeternum,* &c. [Ducal Library, Gotha], printed at Dresden, 1655, in memory of a Dresden lawyer called Johann Scheffer. The dedication is "at Dresden, M. Martinus von Döring," but no clear indication is given as to the authorship of the hymn. It is founded on Rev. xxi., xxii., and is in 31 st. of 8 l. A full notice of this broadsheet is given in the *Blätter für Hymnologie,* 1884, pp. 77-79. The form now in use is given at p. 482 in the *Geistreiches G. B.,* Darmstadt, 1698, in 4 st., entitled "The Marriage Hymn," and is based on st. i., xv., xxvi., xxxi., of the longer form. It passed through Freylinghausen's *G. B.,* 1704, into many later collections (Berlin *G. L. S.,* ed. 1863, No. 1000), and has been a special favourite in Germany as a "Swansong" for the dying. It is sometimes erroneously ascribed to B. Crasselius.

The trs. are, (1) "Hallelujah, Love, Thanks and Praise," in the *Suppl. to Ger. Psal.,* ed. 1765, p. 70, and *Select H. from Ger. Psal.,* Tranquebar, 1754, p. 98. (2) "Hallelujah, Might, Honour, Praise," as No. 674 in pt. i. of the *Moravian H. Bk.,* 1754. (3) "Sing Hallelujah, honour, praise," as No. 336 in the *Moravian H. Bk.,* 1789 (1886, No. 424).   [J. M.]

Hallelujah! Raise, O raise. *J. Conder.* [*Ps. cxiii.*] A vigorous and successful paraphrase of the 113th Psalm, given in the *Cong. H. Bk.,* 1836, No. 25, in 6 st. of 4 l.; in his work, *The Choir and the Oratory,* 1837, p. 168; and in his *Hys. of Praise, Prayer,* &c., 1856, p. 29. It is found in most of the leading Nonconformist collections, including the *Leeds H. Bk.,* 1853, No. 152; Bapt. *Ps. & Hys.,* 1858, No. 793; the *New Cong.,* 1859, No. 178, and others. It is also in somewhat extensive use in America. From this hymn the following centos have also been compiled:—

1. "All His servants join to bless." In the *Songs for the Sanctuary,* N. Y., 1865, No. 131.
2. "Blessed be for evermore." In the *Hys. of the Spirit,* Boston, 1864, No. 105.

Although in C. U. in these various forms, it has not received the attention which it merits. [Psalters, English, § xix.]   [J. J.]

Halt an, mein Herz, in deinem Glauben. *B. Schmolck.* [*Cross and Consolation.*] 1st pub. in his *Heilige Flammen der himmlisch gesinnten Seele,* and apparently in the 2nd ed. 1705 (ed. 1707, p. 64; Görlitz, 1709, p. 138), in 3 st. of 6 l., entitled "Steadfastness conquers." Included in Burg's *G. B.,* Breslau, 1746, No. 105, and other collections. *Tr.* as:—

Hold on, my heart, with faith relying. A good and full *tr.* by A. T. Russell, as No. 235 in his *Ps. & Hys.,* 1851, and repeated, omitting st. ii., in P. Maurice's *Choral H. Bk.,* 1861, No. 680.

Another tr. is, "Hold on, my heart, in thy believing," in the *Christian Examiner,* Boston, U.S., Sept. 1860, p. 252.   [J. M.]

Hamilton, James, D.D., F.L.S., eldest s. of the Rev. William Hamilton, D.D., parish minister of Strathblane, Stirlingshire, was b. at Lonend, Paisley, Nov. 27, 1814. After studying at the Universities of Glasgow and Edinburgh, he became, in 1839, assistant in the parish of Abernyte, Perthshire. On Jan. 21, 1841, he was ordained minister of Roxburgh Place Church, Edinburgh, and on July 25, 1841, he became minister of Regent Square Presbyterian Church, London, where he remained till his death. He d. in London, Nov. 24, 1867. He was a well-known preacher, and a popular and useful writer. He took great interest in hymnology, contributed several hymnological articles to the *British and Foreign Evangelical Review,* and was a leading member of the committee which compiled the English Presb. *Psalms & Hymns,* 1867. In his *Life,* by the late Rev. W. Arnot, mention is made of his having written some Communion hymns, in 1831, but the only verses given in the *Life* are a *tr.* of "Wohlauf, wohlan zum letzten Gang" (see Sachse).   [J. M.]

Hamilton, James, M.A., was b. at Glendollar, Scotland, April 18, 1819, and educated at Corpus Christi College, Cambridge. Taking Holy Orders in 1845, he held various charges until 1866, when he became Incumbent of St. Barnabas's, Bristol. In 1867 he was preferred to the Vicarage of Doulting, diocese of Bath and Wells. Mr. Hamilton is the author of a few hymns of great merit. Of these the following are in C. U.:—

1. Across the sky the shades of night. *New Year's Eve.* "Written to the old chorale introduced by Mendelssohn into his *St. Paul,* 'To God on High be thanks and praise.'" (*H. A. & M.,* tune to 104 by Decius. See p. 425, ii.) It is in Thring's *Coll.,* 1882, &c.
2. O Jesu! Lord most merciful. *Passiontide.* Contributed to the *People's H.,* 1867. In the *Hymnary,* 1872, it was altered to "O Jesu, our Salvation, Low at Thy Cross," &c. This was repeated in the *Parish H. Bk.,* 1875, Thring's *Coll.,* 1882, and others, and is the most popular form of the hymn. It was written to Hassler's Passion Chorale, as in *H. A. & M.,* 111.
3. Praise, O praise the Lord of harvest. *Harvest.* Appeared in Thring's *Coll.,* 1881 and 1882.   [J. J.]

Hamilton, Richard Winter, LL.D., D.D., b. in London, July 6, 1794, and educated at Mill Hill School, and Hoxton College. In 1815 he became the minister of the Albion Street Chapel, Leeds, and then of Belgrave in the same town in 1836. He remained pastor of that congregation to his death, on July 18, 1848. His prose works were numerous, and, at the time of their publication, exceedingly popular. He was joint editor of:

A Sel. of Hys., &c., 1822 [Congregational Hymnody, 6], and contributed hymns to Clapham's Leeds *S. S. Union H. Bk.*, 1833; Leifchild's *Original Hymns*, 1842 (six hymns); and the *Leeds H. Bk.*, 1853. His *Nugae Literariae*, 1841, contained several of his hymns, and 13 versions of Psalms. Of his hymns the following are still in C. U.:—

1. I was often told my need. 1833. *Lent.*
2. Now all chafing cares shall cease. 1842. *Saturday Evening.*
3. O where is the land of the blest? 1833. *Heaven.*
4. Though poor in lot and scorned in name. 1853. *All things in Christ.*   [J. J.]

Hammond, William, B.A., b. at Battle, Sussex, Jan. 6, 1719, and educated at St. John's College, Cambridge. In 1743 he joined the Calvinistic Methodists; and in 1745, the Moravian Brethren. He d. in London, Aug. 19, 1783, and was buried in the Moravian burial-ground, Sloane Street, Chelsea. He left an Autobiography in Greek, which remains unpublished. His original hymns, together with his *trs.* from the Latin, were pub. in his :—

Psalms, Hymns, and Spiritual Songs. To which is prefix'd A Preface, giving some Account of a Weak Faith, and a Full Assurance of Faith; and briefly stating the Doctrine of Sanctification; and shewing a Christian's Completeness, Perfection, and Happiness in Christ. By William Hammond, A.B., late of St. John's College, Cambridge. London: Printed by W. Strahan; and sold by J. Oswald, at the Rose and Crown in the Poultry, mdccxlv.

A few of his original hymns from scriptural fidelity and earnestness have attained to a foremost position amongst English hymns. These include, " Awake, and sing the song," and " Lord, we come before Thee now." His *trs.* of Latin hymns were amongst the earliest published after those contained in the *Primers* and other devotional works of 16th and 17th centuries. They are of merit, and worthy of attention. Greater use might also be made of his original compositions. In addition to those named above, the following are. also in C. U.:—

1. Brightness of the Father's Face. *God the Son.*
2. How great the Christian's portion is. *Possession of All in Christ.*
3. If Jesus is yours. *God's unchangeable Love.*
4. In Thine own appointed way. *Divine Worship.*
5. Jesus, Who died the [a] world to save. *Easter.*
6. Lord, if on earth the thought of Thee. *Heaven anticipated.*
7. Now with joint consent we sing. *Divine Worship.*
8. O Lord, how little do we know. *Quinquagesima.*
9. Would you win a soul to God? *The Gospel Message.*   [J. J.]

Hankey, Katherine, has published several hymns of great beauty and simplicity which are included in her :—

(1) *The Old, Old Story,* 1866; (2) *The Old, Old Story, and other Verses,* 1879; (3) *Heart to Heart,* 1870, enlarged in 1873 and 1876. In 1878 it was republished with music by the author.

Miss Hankey's hymns which have come into C. U. are:—

1. Advent tells us, Christ is near. *The Christian Seasons.* Written for the Sunday School of St. Peter's, Eaton Square, London, and printed on a card with music by the author.
2. I love to tell the story Of unseen things above. *The love of Jesus.* This is a cento from No. 3, and is given in Bliss's *Gospel Songs,* Cincinnati, 1874, and other American collections.
3. I saw Him leave His Father's throne. *Lovest thou Me?* Written in 1868. It is No. 33 of the *Old, Old Story, and other Verses,* 1879.

4. Tell me the old, old story. This Life of Jesus in verse was written in two parts. Pt. i., " The Story Wanted," Jan. 29; and Pt. ii., "The Story Told," Nov. 18, 1866. It has since been published in several forms, and sometimes with expressive music by the author, and has also been translated into various languages, including Welsh, German, Italian, Spanish, &c. The form in which it is usually known is that in I. D. Sankey's *Sacred S. & Solos.* This is Part i. slightly altered.

Miss Hankey's works contain many suitable hymns for Mission Services and Sunday Schools, and may be consulted both for words and music with advantage.   [J. J.]

Hankinson, Thomas Edwards, M.A., who was educated at Corpus Christi College, Cambridge, where he won the Seatonian prize several times, was b. in 1804, and d. Oct. 6, 1843. In 1827 he pub. a volume of *Sacred Poems.* These were republished in an enlarged form by his brothers as a *Memorial* volume in 1844 (5th ed. 1860). The 1844 ed. included the following hymns which have come into C. U.:—

1. Come, see the place where Jesus lies. *Easter Eve.*
2. Let Thy Spirit, Lord, descending. *For Sunday Schools.* Written May 8, 1843.
3. Mighty God, may we address Thee? 1841. *For Sunday Schools.*
4. Our Father, if indeed Thou art. *Holy Trinity.*
5. We are a young and happy crew. 1840. *Dialogue hymn for Sunday Schools.*
6. Who shall ascend the holy place? *For Sunday Schools.* This is the most popular of his hymns, and is found in several collections, including *Sarum*, 1868, &c.   [W. T. B.]

Happiness, thou lovely name. *A. M. Toplady.* [*Happiness.*] 1st printed in the *Gospel Magazine,* Oct., 1774, in 4 st. of 8 l. It was not given by Toplady in his *Ps. & Hys.,* 1776; but appeared in 1793 in *Hymns Compiled by Joseph Middleton,* London, No. 271. In Bickersteth's *Christ. Psalmody,* 1833, No. 147, st. i.–iii. were given as "Happiness! *delightful* name!" This form of the text is also in later collections. There are also " Man to happiness aspires," in *Kennedy,* 1863, and " Lord, it is not life to live;" but the most popular form of the hymn is st. ii., iii., as, " Object of my first desire." This is in extensive use in G. Britain and America. Full text in D. Sedgwick's reprint of Toplady's *Hymns & Sac. Poems,* &c., 1860, p. 158. [J. J.]

Happy day of union sweet. *C. Wesley.* [*Christian Unity desired.*] From his *Short Hymns,* &c., 1762, vol. i., No. 995, slightly altered into the *Wes. H. Bk.,* 1780, but omitted in the revised ed., 1875, in favour of " True and Faithful Witness, Thou." This latter is a cento thus composed:—

St. i., *Short Hymns,* 1762, vol. i., No. 988, on Is. xi. 5. St. ii., *Short Hymns,* 1762, vol. i., No. 995, being the second half of the former hymn, "Happy day," &c.

Orig. texts in *P. Works,* 1868–72, vol. ix. pp. 385 and 388.   [J. J.]

Happy is he that fears the Lord. *I. Watts.* [*Ps. cxii.*] Appeared in his *Ps. of David,* &c., 1719, in 5 st. of 4 l., and headed, " Liberality Rewarded." It is in C. U. in G. Britain and America; and sometimes as, " Happy *the man* that fears the Lord," as in the *New Cong.*, 1859, No. 174.   [J. J.]

Happy man [child] whom God doth aid. *C. Wesley.* [*Praise to God for care over Children.*] 1st pub. in his *Hys. for Children,* 1763, No. 18, in 3 st. of 8 l. (*P. Works,*

1868–72, vol. vi. p. 387.) In the *Meth. S. S. H. Bk.*, 1879, No. 61, it is changed to "Happy *child* whom God doth aid," as being more suitable for children. [J. J.]

Happy sons of Israel. *G. Sandys.* [*Ps. lxiv.*] 1st pub. in his *Paraphrase upon the Ps. of David*, 1636, in 60 lines; again in his *Paraphrase upon the Divine Poems* (with which the *Par. upon the Ps.* was incorporated), 1638; and again in R. Hooper's ed. of Sandys's *Poems* in Smith's *Library of Old Authors* A cento from this paraphrase, beginning, "Sing the great Jehovah's praise," is No. 91 in the *New Cong.*, 1859. [J. J.]

Happy [saint] soul that free from harms. *C. Wesley.* [*Prayer to the Good Shepherd.*] Appeared in *Hys. & Sac. Poems*, 1749, No. 106, in 10 st. of 4 l., as No. 4 of "Hymns for those that wait for full Redemption." (*P. Works*, 1868–70, vol. v. p. 293.) In the *Wes. H. Bk.*, 1780, it was given with the omission of st. ii., iii., and repeated in the revised ed., 1875, No. 13. In Mercer's *Ch. Psalter & H. Bk.*, 1856 and 1872, it reads, "Happy *saint* that free from harms"; and in the Bapt. *Ps. & Hys.*, 1858, No. 550, st. vi.–x. are given as, "Jesus, seek Thy wandering sheep." [J. J.]

Happy soul, thy days are ended [ending]. *C. Wesley.* [*For the Dying.*] Appeared in *Hys. & Sac. Poems*, 1749, in 2 st. of 8 l., and headed, "For one departing" (*P. Works*, 1868–70, vol. v. p. 216). In 1830 it was given in the *Suppl.* to the *Wes. H. Bk.*, No. 725, and repeated in the revised ed., 1875, No. 922. It is also given in several collections in G. Britain and America. In some of these the opening line reads: "Happy soul, thy days are *ending.*" [J. J.]

Happy the heart where graces reign. *I. Watts.* [*Love to God.*] 1st pub. in his *Hys. & S. Songs*, 1707 (2nd ed. 1709, Bk. ii., No. 38), in 5 st. of 4 l., and entitled, "Love to God." Of this hymn st. iv. and the idea embodied in st. v. had previously appeared in Watts's hymn, "'Tis pure delight without alloy," given in his *Horæ Lyricæ*, 1706, st. iii., iv. It is in extensive use in G. Britain and America. [J. J.]

Happy the man who [that] finds the grace. *C. Wesley.* [*Happiness in Forgiveness.*] Appeared in *Hys. for those that seek and those that have Redemption*, &c., 1747, No. 18, in 9 st. of 4 l., and based on Prov. iii. 13, &c. (*P. Works*, 1868–72, vol. iv. p. 234). In the *Wes. H. Bk.*, 1780, it was given with the omission of st. iv., v., viii., as "Happy the man *that* finds the grace." Most of the forms of this hymn in use in G. Britain and America are based upon this text of 1780. [J. J.]

Happy the souls that first believed. *C. Wesley.* [*Primitive Christianity.*] 1st pub. at the end of *An Earnest Appeal to Men of Reason and Religion*, by J. Wesley, M.A., 1743, in 30 st. of 4 l., divided into two parts; and again in *Hys. & Sac. Poems*, 1749, No. 246 (*P. Works*, 1868–72, vol. v. p. 479). In 1780 J. Wesley compiled two centos therefrom, and

included them in the *Wes. H. Bk.* as :—(1) "Happy the souls that first believed"; and (2) "Jesus, from Whom all blessings flow." These centos are repeated in the revised ed., 1875, Nos. 16, 17, and in several other collections. [J. J.]

Harbaugh, Henry, D.D., b. in Franklin Co., Pennsylvania, Oct. 24, 1817, was of Swiss descent. In early life he was a farmer, carpenter, and teacher; but in 1840 he entered Marshall College, Mercersburg. Entering the ministry of the German Reformed body, he became, in 1844, Pastor at Lewisburg, Lancaster and Lebanon, Pennsylvania, and in 1864 Professor in Theology at Mercersburg. He d. Dec. 27, 1867. He was Editor of the *Guardian* and the *Mercersburg Review*, in which he advocated what was called "Mercersburg Theology." His published works include sundry books about Heaven; *Poems*, Phila., 1860, and *Hys. & Chants for Sunday Schools*, Lebanon, 1861. This last includes his hymns. The best known and most widely used of his compositions are :—

1. **Jesus, I live to Thee.** [*Life consecrated to Jesus.*] This hymn is dated 1850. It is No. 391 in the *Hys. of the Church*, N. Y., 1869; No. 255 in Allon's *Suppl. Hys.*, Lond., 1868, and is also in other collections.

2. **God most mighty, sovereign Lord.** [*National Hymn.*] Appeared in his *Poems*, 1860, in 8 st. of 4 l., and headed, "A National Litany hymn." In some collections it is abridged, as in Hatfield's *Church H. Bk.*, N. Y., 1872, No. 1307; and in others part of it is altered to "Christ by heavenly hosts adored," as in the Reformed Dutch *Hys. of the Church*, 1869, No. 935, and others.

3. **Make the cross your meditation.** [*Passiontide.*] This *tr.* of "Recordare sanctae crucis" (q.v.) appeared in the *Mercersburg Review*, 1858, p. 481, and in his *Poems*, 1860. It is worthy of more attention than it has received. [F. M. B.]

Harbottle, Joseph, was b. at Tottlebank, near Ulverston, Sept. 25, 1798. In 1819 he joined the Baptist Church at Tottlebank (of which his father was the pastor), and shortly afterwards began to preach. In 1822 he went to reside with Dr. Steadman, President of the Baptist College at Horton, near Bradford, and for a time was teacher of classics in that institution. He subsequently became Pastor at Accrington, and in 1841 one of the Tutors of a small Baptist College in that town. At Accrington and Oswaldtwistle, in the neighbourhood, he continued to minister until his death, Jan. 19, 1864. Mr. Harbottle wrote several hymns. One appeared in the *Comprehensive Rippon* (1844), "See how the fruitless figtree stands" (*Invitation*). Another, "Farewell, my friends beloved" (*Departure of Friends*), is much sung at valedictory meetings among the Baptists in G. Britain and America. His other hymns are inferior in quality, and have not been included in any popular Collection. [W. R. S.]

Harcourt, William Vernon, M.A., s. of Archbishop Harcourt of York, was b. at Sudbury Hall, Derbyshire, in 1789, and edu-

cated at Oxford. Taking Holy Orders he became, in 1823, Rector of Kirkby-in-Cleveland, and Canon Residentiary of York; and in 1837, Rector of Bolton Percy. On the death of his elder brother in 1861, he succeeded to the family property, Nuneham Park, Oxfordshire. He d. in 1871. In 1840 he pub. a volume of *Psalms & Hymns*, and in 1855 his *Symmetrical Psalmody*. This latter work is one of the curiosities of hymnody. His version of Ps. cxxxvi., "Thank the Lord Who made the earth," is in *Lyra Brit.*, 1867; Martineau's *Hymns*, 1873, and others.   [J. J.]

Hardenberg, Georg Friedrich Philipp von, was s. of Baron Heinrich Ulrich Erasmus von Hardenberg, director of the Saxon Saltworks at Weissenfels. He was b. May 2, 1772, at his father's estate of Widerstedt or Ober-Wiederstäd, near Eisleben. In the autumn of 1790 he entered the University of Jena, then went to Leipzig, and finally to Wittenberg. After concluding his studies, he went, in the end of 1794, to Tennstädt, near Erfurt, in order to learn administrative business under Kreisamtmann Just. In the autumn of 1797 he entered the School of Mines at Freiberg in Saxony, and in the autumn of 1799 went to Artern, at the foot of the Kyffhäuser-Berg, to be employed in the saltworks there. Soon after he began to spit blood, and while on a visit to Dresden the news of the sudden death of a younger brother, in Nov. 1800, brought on a hemorrhage which destroyed all hopes of his recovery. In January, 1801, he was removed to the house of his parents at Weissenfels, and d. there March 25, 1801. (*Koch*, vii. 4–9; *Allg. Deutsche Biog.*, x. 562–570; *Blätter für Hymnologie*, 1884, 3–6, &c.)

Hardenberg's various writings appeared under the name of **Novalis** (apparently taken from the name of one of the family estates), which he first adopted in his *Blüthenstaub*, pub. in the *Athenæum*, Brunswick, 1798; and it is as *Novalis* that he is best known. He was one of the leaders of the Romantic School which arose in Germany in the last years of the 18th cent., and of which his friends F. and A. W. Schlegel, Fouqué and Tieck are the best known members. It is, however, by his hymns that he will probably best be remembered. They arose in the time of deep sorrow into which he was cast on the death of his betrothed Sophie von Kühn, when his thoughts turned to the faith of his childhood (his father and mother were Moravians, and his early education was imparted by a Moravian pastor); and when from the barren religiosity of the latter days of Illumination his soul found its strength and solace in loving surrender to the Person of our Blessed Lord. His hymns, 15 in all, are distinguished by beauty of rhythm and lyric grace. While some have been included in recent German hymn-books (e.g. Nos. ii.–iv. in the Berlin *G. B.*, 1829, through the influence of F. Schleiermacher), yet for Church use they are too subjective, and in some cases even too sentimental. They must be regarded as beautiful, and deeply spiritual poems, rather than as hymns suited for public worship. Some of them are not altogether free from Pantheistic tendencies. The *Marienlieder* (i.e. the hymns to the B. V. M.) were not intended by himself to be published among his hymns, but were meant to be inserted in his unfinished romance of *Heinrich von Ofterdingen*, as hymns of pilgrims to the shrine of the B. V. M. at Loretto in Italy. Seven of his hymns were sent, on Jan. 20, 1800, to F. Schlegel for publication in the *Athenæum*. They did not however appear till in the *Musenalmanach für das Jahr* 1802, pub. at Tübingen, 1802. The rest of his hymns were pub. in his *Schriften*, Berlin, 1802. A handy little ed. of his *Gedichte*, with a critical and biographical sketch by W. Beyschlag, appeared in 1869 (2nd ed. 1877). Since the publication of T. Carlyle's Essay on *Novalis* in 1829, numerous "Studies" have appeared in English and American reviews and maga-

zines; and some of these may contain translations not noted below.

Hardenberg's hymns, all of which have been rendered into English, are as follows:—

I. *Hymns in English C. U.*

i. Ich sag' es jedem, dass er lebt. *Easter.* In his *Schriften*, 1802, pt. ii. p. 143, in 8 st. of 4 l. Repeated in the Württemberg *G. B.*, 1842, No. 165. *Tr.* as:—

I say to all men, far and near, in full, by Miss Winkworth in her *Lyra Ger.*, 2nd Ser., 1858, p. 40. In full in *Kennedy*, 1863; and in varying centos in America in the Dutch Ref. *Hys. of the Church*, 1869; *Bapt. Praise Bk.*, 1871; *Hys. & Songs of Praise*, N. Y., 1874, &c.

Other trs. are: (1) "I say to every one, He lives," by Helen Lowe, in her *Zareefa*, 1844, p. 166. (2) "To every one I say," by Dr. J. F. Hurst, in his *tr.* of K. R. Hagenbach's *Hist. of the Church 18 and 19 centuries*, N. Y., 1869, vol. ii. p. 283. (3) "I say to each man that He lives," by M. E. Bramston, in the *Day of Rest*, 1875, p. 69. (4) "He lives! He's risen from the dead," by Dr. G. Macdonald, in his *Exotics*, 1876, p. 22. [The hymn "He lives! He lives! let joy again," by Sir John Bowring, in J. R. Beard's *Coll.*, 1837, No. 145, seems based on this German.]

ii. Was wär ich ohne dich gewesen. *The Love of Christ.* *Musenalmanach*, 1802, p. 189, and his *Schriften*, 1802, pt. ii. p. 123, in 10 st. of 8 l. Included in various German hymn-books, and is No. 1562 in the Berlin *G. L. S.*, ed. 1863.

It is said that shortly after the death of Novalis his father was present at a Moravian service at Herrnhut during which this hymn was sung. When he asked who was the author of this wonderfully beautiful hymn, he was greatly moved on receiving the reply, "Your son." And then in a moment it became clear to him that the Christ who had been the Crown and Star of his heart ever since his youth, was also his son's Saviour and Deliverer, though he had sought and found Him by a different way.

The *trs.* in C. U. are:—

1. What had I been if Thou wert not, a free *tr.* of st. i.–iii., viii., v., by Miss Winkworth, in her *Lyra Ger.*, 1st Ser., 1855, p. 96. Centos from this are:—

(1) **Lord! when Thou mak'st Thy presence felt** (st. iii.) in the Swedenborgian *Coll.*, 1880.

(2) **Thou strong and loving God in man** (st. iv.), in *Hys. of the Spirit*, Boston, U.S., 1864.

(3) **Thou strong and loving Son of Man** (st. iv.), in H. L. Hastings's *Hymnal*, Boston, U.S., 1880.

2. Without Thee, Lord, what had we been, a paraphrase or transfusion in 3 st. of 8 l., by Dr. W. L. Alexander, written about 1830, but first pub. in the 2nd ed., 1858, of his *Sel. of Hys.*, No. 323.

Other trs. are: (1) "What might I not have been without Thee," by Helen Lowe, in her *Prophecy of Balaam*, 1841, p. 216. (2) "What without Thee, would I have been," by *Dr. H. Mills*, 1845 (1856, p. 78). (3) "Without Thee, what were I worth being," by Dr. G. Macdonald, in *Good Words*, 1871, p. 846. Thence (as "Without Thee what were all my being"), in his *Exotics*, 1876, p. 3.

iii. Wenn alle untreu werden. *Love to Christ.* *Musenalmanach*, 1802, p. 200, and his *Schriften*, 1802, pt. ii. p. 136, in 4 st. of 8 l. Included in the Berlin *G. B.*, 1829; the Berlin *G. L. S.*, ed. 1863, No. 1563, &c. *Tr.* as:—

Though all the world forsake Thee, a free *tr.*, in 6 st. of 4 l., by J. S. Stallybrass, as No. 417 in Curwen's *Sabbath H. Bk.*, 1859.

Other trs. are: (1) "Tho' all men faith had banished," by Helen Lowe, in her *Prophecy of Balaam*, 1841, p. 222; and thence in *Lyra Eucharistica*, 1864, p. 100. (2) "Though all to Thee were faithless," by *Miss Winkworth*, 1855, p. 165. (3) "Though all were faithless to Thee," by M. E. Bramston, in the *Day of Rest*, 1875,

p. 68. (4) "My faith to Thee I break not," by Dr. G. Macdonald, in his *Exotics*, 1876, p. 15.

iv. **Wenn ich Ihn nur habe.** *Jesus only.* *Musenalmanach*, 1802, p. 199, and his *Schriften*, 1802, pt. ii. p. 134, in 5 st. of 6 l. In various recent German hymn-books, as the Württemberg *G. B.*, 1842, the Berlin *G. L. S.*, ed. 1863, No. 1564, &c. *Tr.* as :—

If I Him but have, by Dr. G. Macdonald, as No. 172 in the Manchester *S. S. H. Bk.*, 1855 (see **Bubier**), and in his own *Exotics*, 1876, p. 13.

Other trs. are : (1) "If I have only Him," by Helen Lowe, in her *Prophecy of Balaam*, 1841, p. 221, repeated in *Lyra Messianica*, 1864, p. 207. (2) "Oh! could my soul possess His love," by Miss Fry, 1845, p. 114. (3) "If I only have Thee," by Dr. G. W. Bethune, in his *Lays of Love and Faith*, 1847, p. 139. (4) "If only He is mine," by Miss Borthwick, in *H. L. L.*, 1855, p. 54. (5) "If I have Christ, and Christ be mine," by *Dr. G. Walker*, 1860, p. 52. (6) "If I trust in God alone," by Frederica M. Rowan, in her *Medit. on Death and Eternity*, 1862, p. 88.

II. *Hymns not in English C. U*

v. **Es giebt so bange Zeiten.** *The Unchanging.* *Schriften*, 1802, pt. ii. p. 145, in 7 st. The *trs.* are : (1) "How dark the seasons lour," by Helen Lowe, in her *Zareefa*, 1844, p. 164. (2) "There are dark hours of sadness," by Madame L. Davésiés de Pontès, in her *Poets and Poetry of Germany*, 1858, ii. p. 408. (3) "There be such dreary seasons," by M. E. Bramston, in the *Day of Rest*, 1875, p. 55. (4) "The times are all so wretched," by *Dr. G. Macdonald*, 1876, p. 24.

vi. **Fern im Osten wird es helle.** *Christmas.* *Musenalmanach*, 1802, p. 193, and his *Schriften*, 1802, pt. ii. p. 190, in 6 st. The *trs.* are : (1) "Afar the Eastern sky is glowing," by Helen Lowe, in her *Prophecy of Balaam*, 1841, p. 218, and *Lyra Messianica*, 1864, p. 87. (2) "Dawn, far Eastward on the mountain," by Dr. G. Macdonald, in *Good Words*, 1872, p. 216, and his *Exotics*, 1876, p. 7.

vii. **Ich sehe dich in tausend Bildern.** *B. V. M. Schriften*, 1802, pt. ii. p. 157, in 8 l. *Tr.* as : (1) "In many a form I see thee oft," by Helen Lowe, in her *Prophecy of Balaam*, 1841, p. 229. (2) "In countless pictures I behold thee," by *Dr. G. Macdonald*, 1876, p. 36.

viii. **Ich weiss nicht was ich suchen könnte.** *Desire for Christ.* *Schriften*, 1802, pt. ii. p. 147, in 12 st. The *trs.* are : (1) "I know not what I could desire," by Helen Lowe, in her *Prophecy of Balaam*, 1841, p. 223, and *Lyra Mystica*, 1864, p. 218. (2) "How could I wish a greater treasure," by *Dr. H. Mills*, 1845 (1856, p. 72). (3) "I know not one hope left to draw me," by *Dr. G. Macdonald*, 1876, p. 26. (4) "What better good could e'er befall me," by R. Massie, in the *Day of Rest*, 1878, p. 111. (5) "I know not what I more should long for," by F. W. Young, in the *Christian Monthly*, 1880, p. 559.

ix. **Unter tausend frohen Stunden.** *Communion with God.* *Musenalmanach*, 1802, p. 197, and his *Schriften*, 1802, pt. ii. p. 132, in 4 st. The *trs.* are : (1) "Of all the golden hours whose light," by Helen Lowe, in her *Prophecy of Balaam*, 1841, p. 220. (2) "All my world was struck with storm" (st. ii.), by M. E. Bramston, in the *Day of Rest*, 1875, p. 55. (3) "Of a thousand hours me meeting," by *Dr. G. Macdonald*, 1876, p. 11.

x. **Weinen muss ich, immer weinen.** *Passiontide.* *Schriften*, 1802, pt. ii. p. 141, in 7 st. *Tr.* as, "Weep I must—my heart runs over," by *Dr. G. Macdonald*, 1876, p. 20.

xi. **Wenige wissen das Geheimniss der Liebe.** *Holy Communion.* *Musenalmanach*, 1802, p. 202, and *Schriften*, 1802, pt. ii. p. 138, in 2 st. *Tr.* as, "Few understand the mystery of love," by *Dr. G. Macdonald*, 1876, p. 17.

xii. **Wenn in bangen, trüben Stunden.** *In sorrow.* *Schriften*, 1802, pt. ii. p. 153, in 2 st. The *trs.* are : (1) "When in hours of pain and anguish," by Madame L. Davésiés de Pontès, in her *Poets and Poetry of Germany*, 1858, ii. p. 407. (2) "When in dreary, mournful hours," by Lady John Manners, in her *Gems of German Poetry*, 1865, p. 14. (3) "When in hours of fear and failing," by *Dr. G. Macdonald*, 1876, p. 32.

xiii. **Wer einmal, Mutter dich erblickt.** *B. V. M. Schriften*, 1802, pt. ii. p. 154, in 8 st. *Tr.* as, "Who once hath seen thee, mother fair," by *Dr. G. Macdonald*, 1876, p. 33.

xiv. **Wer einsam sitzt in seiner Kammer.** *Christ the Consoler.* *Musenalmanach*, 1802, p. 195, and his *Schriften*, 1802, pt. ii. p. 130, in 9 st. *Tr.* as, "Who in his chamber sitteth lonely," by Dr. G. Macdonald, in *Good Words*, 1872, p. 234, and his *Exotics*, 1876, p. 9.

xv. **Wo bleibst du, Trost der ganzen Welt.** *Advent. Schriften*, 1802, pt. ii. p. 150, in 12 st. *Tr.* as, "Earth's Consolation, why so slow," by *Dr. G. Macdonald*, 1876, p. 29.

Besides the above he had previously pub. a series of poems entitled "Hymnen an die Nacht" in the *Athenæum*, a magazine edited by A. W. Schlegel and F. Schlegel, where they appear in vol. iii., pt. ii., pp. 188-204, Berlin, 1800. They are a wonderful picture of the "night" of sorrow into which he was plunged at the death of his betrothed on March 19, 1797. There are five poems in prose, with interspersed verse, the sixth being in verse. The longer poems in verse-form are :—

1. Das furchtbar zu den frohen Tischen trat.
2. Gehoben ist der Stein.
3. Hinüber wall' ich.
4. Hinunter in der Erde Schoos.

There is a complete *tr.* by Henry Morley in his *Dream of the Lilybell*, &c., London, 1845. No. 2 has also been *tr.* by Dr. G. Macdonald in his *Threefold Cord*, 1883, p. 256; and No. 4 by Helen Lowe in her *Prophecy of Balaam*, 1841, p. 226 (*Lyra Mystica*, 1864, p. 220).

[J. M.]

Hark, a voice divides the sky. *C. Wesley.* [*Burial.*] Pub. in *Hys. & S. Poems*, 1742, in 5 st. of 8 l. (*P. Works*, 1868-72, vol. ii. p. 189). In 1780 it was given with slight alterations in the *Wes. H. Bk.* as No. 50, and repeated in the revised ed. 1875, No. 51. This is the text which is usually followed in G. Britain and America. It is sometimes found in an abbreviated form, as in Martineau's *Hymns*, 1840 and 1873. [J. J.]

Hark, for 'tis God's own Son that calls. *P. Doddridge.* [*Freedom in Christ.*] 1st pub. by J. Orton in his posthumous ed. of Doddridge's *Hymns*, &c., 1755, No. 226, in 5 st. of 4 l., and headed, "True Liberty given by Christ Jesus, John viii. 36," and again, with slight alterations, in J. D. Humphreys's ed. of the same, 1839, No. 250. In C. U. st. ii. is usually omitted. In the *Leeds H. Bk.*, 1853, No. 613, it begins, "Hark, for *the Son of God now* calls," and is reduced to 3 stanzas.

[J. J.]

Hark, from the tombs a doleful [warning] sound. *I. Watts.* [*Burial.*] 1st pub. in his *Hys. & S. Songs*, 1707 (ed. 1709, Bk. ii., No. 63), in 4 st. of 4 l., and entitled, "A Funeral Thought." Its use is mainly confined to America, where it is sometimes given as, "Hark, from the tombs a *warning* sound," as in the *Bapt. Praise Bk.*, 1871.

[J. J.]

Hark, hark, my soul ; Angelic songs are swelling. *F. W. Faber.* [*Evening.*] Pub. in his *Oratory Hymns*, 1854, and again in his *Hymns*, 1862, p. 385, in 7 st. of 4 l., and entitled, "The Pilgrims of the Night." Five stanzas in an altered form were given in the *Append.* to *H. A. & M.*, 1868, No. 325. By this means the hymn was brought prominently before the public, and became exceedingly

popular for a time. Its unreality, however, has excluded it from many of the best modern collections. In the *Bk. of Prayer & Praise for use in Sir Josiah Mason's Orphanage*, Erdington, 1883, No. 293, beginning, " Hark, hark, my soul, thy Father's voice is calling," is an imitation of this hymn. It is also in Allon's *Children's Worship*, 1878, No. 234.   [J. J.]

Hark, hark, the organ loudly peals. *G. Thring.* [*Processional.*] Written in 1862, and 1st pub. in his *Hys. Congregational, and Others*, 1866, p. 45, in 5 st. of 9 l., and given for " Trinity Sunday." It has passed into several modern hymn-books in G. Britain and America, and is often used at Choral Festivals, for which it is admirably adapted. Authorised text in Mr. Thring's *Coll.*, 1882, No. 302.

[J. J.]

Hark, how all the welkin rings. *C. Wesley.* [*Christmas.*] 1st pub. in *Hys. & Sac. Poems*, 1739, and again, in a revised form, in a new ed. of the same, 1743, in 10 st. of 4 l., and headed, " Hymn for Christmas Day." The form in which it is known to modern hymn-books has a somewhat intricate history. In G. Whitefield's *Coll.*, 1753, No. 31, it was given with the omission of st. viii. and x. as :

> " Hark, the herald angels sing
> Glory to the new-born King."

This text, with additional changes, was repeated in M. Madan's *Ps. & Hys.*, 1760, No. 8, in 8 st.; R. Conyers's *Coll.*, 1774, No. 335, in 4 st. of 8 l.; in De Courcy's *Coll.*, 1775, No. 30, in 6 st.; in Rowland Hill's *Coll.*, 1783, No. 201, in 6 st.; and in *Hymns* added to the *New Version* (q.v.), in 3 st. of 8 l., with the first two lines added as a refrain to each stanza. As this is the popular form of the hymn and is in C. U. in all English-speaking countries, a comparison with C. Wesley's revised text of 1743 will be of value :—

C. Wesley, 1743.	Book of C. Prayer.
1. " Hark, how all the wel- kin rings 'Glory to the King of Kings, Peace on earth and mercy mild, God and sinners re- conciled.'	1. " Hark [1] *the herald an- gels sing,* Glory to the [1] *new-born King ;* Peace on earth and mercy mild, God and sinners re- conciled : Joyful all ye nations rise,
2. " Joyful, all ye nations, rise, Join the triumph of the skies ; Universal nature say 'Christ the Lord is born to-day.'	Join the triumph of the skies, [2] *With th' angelic host proclaim, Christ is born in Beth- lehem. * [3] *Hark the herald angels,"* &c.
3. " Christ, by highest heaven adored, Christ, the everlast- ing Lord, Late in time behold him come Offspring of a Vir- gin's womb.	2. " Christ by highest heav'n ador'd, Christ the everlasting Lord, Late in time behold Him come, Offspring of a Virgin's womb : Veil'd in flesh the God- head [3] *He,*
4. " Veil'd in flesh, the Godhead see, Hail the Incarnate Deity ! Pleased as man with men to appear Jesus! our *Immanuel* here !	Hail th' Incarnate Deity. Pleas'd as man with *man* appear, Jesus our Immanuel here. [3] *Hark the herald angels,"* &c.

5. " Hail the heavenly Prince of Peace ! Hail the Sun of Right- eousness, Light and life to all he brings, Risen with healing in His wings.	3. " Hail the [1] *heav'n-born* Prince of Peace ! Hail the Sun of Right- eousness ! Light and life to all He brings, Ris'n with healing in His wings : Mild He lays His glory by,
6. " Mild He lays His glory by, Born—that man no more may die. Born — to raise the sons of earth, Born — to give them second birth.	Born that man no more- may die ; Born to raise the sons of earth, Born to give them se- cond birth. [3] *Hark, the herald angels,"* &c.

From this point Wesley's hymn proceeds as follows :—

7. " Come, Desire of Na- tions, come, Fix in us Thy hum- ble home ; Rise, the woman's conquering Seed. Bruise in us the ser- pent's head.	9. " *Adam's* likeness, Lord, efface ; Stamp Thy image in its place ; Second *Adam* from above, Reinstate us in Thy love.
8. " Now display Thy saving power, Ruin'd nature now restore ; Now in mystic union join Thine to ours, and ours to Thine.	10. " Let us Thee, though lost, regain, Then the Life, the Inner Man ; O ! to all Thyself im- part, Form'd in each be- lieving heart."

The alterations indicated by the italics in the *Hymns* to the *New Version* text are—[1] *Whitefield*, 1753; [2] *Madan*, 1760; [3] *Hymns* added to the *New Version* [New Version, § ii.] This text has been repeated in numerous collections to the present time ; and, sometimes with, and at other times without the refrain, is the most popular form of the hymn. In *H. A. & M.*, 1861 and 1875; *The Hymnary*, 1872; *Thring*, 1882, and many others, st. ii., ll. 5–8, reads :—

> " Veiled in flesh the Godhead see !
> Hail the Incarnate Deity !
> Pleased as Man with man *to dwell*,
> Jesus, our Emmanuel " [here omitted].

These alterations, now generally accepted, were given in J. Kempthorne's *Select Portions of Psalms*, &c., 1810, No. 27, but they are possibly older than that collection.

Seventy years after the hymn was adopted by M. Madan, the Wesleyan Conference embodied it in the *Suppl.* to the *Wes. H. Bk.*, 1830, No. 602; and repeated it in the revised ed., 1875, No. 683. This is *Madan's* text with the omission of st. ii. of *Wesley's* original, which was also st. ii. of *Madan's* arrangement. Other forms of the hymn are in C. U., the character of which may be determined by a comparison with the original as above.

One of several attempts which have been made to improve upon Wesley, and have failed to gain general acceptance, was that of T. Cotterill, in the various editions of his *Sel.* from 1810 to 1820. The opening stanza reads :—

> " Hark ! *the herald angels sing,*
> Glory to the *new-born King ;*
> *Glory in the highest heaven,*
> *Peace on earth and man forgiven.*"

In this stanza, lines 1, 2 are *Whitefield's* alterations; and 3, 4 are by *Cotterill*. In a limited number of hymn-books st. vii.-ix. are given as a separate hymn, beginning, " Come,

Desire of Nations, come." In Bingham's *Hymno. Christ. Latina*, 1871, p. 160, the text as in *H. A. & M.*, but without the refrain, is rendered into Latin as: "Audite! tollunt carmina." The *tr.* in Biggs's *Annotated H. A. & M.*, 1867, p. 49, "Psallunt nascentis angeli," is by A. J. B. Beresford-Hope.

The use of this hymn in its various forms has extended to all English-speaking countries. It is found in a greater number of hymnbooks, both old and new, than any other of C. Wesley's compositions; and, amongst English hymns, it is equalled in popularity only by Toplady's "Rock of Ages" and Bp. Ken's Morning and Evening hymns, and is excelled by none. In literary merit it falls little, if anything, short of this honour.   [J. J.]

Hark, how the watchmen cry. *C. Wesley.* [*Old and New Year.*] This is No. 8 of 19 "Hymns for the Watchnight," pub. in *Hys. & Sacred Poems*, 1749, vol. ii., No. 91, in 12 st. of 8 l. (*P. Works*, 1868–72, vol. v. p. 271.) From this hymn the following centos are in C. U.:—

1. **Hark, how the watchmen cry.** This is composed of st. i., ii., iv., and vi., and was given in the *Wes. H. Bk*, 1780, No. 305 (ed. 1875, No. 314). It is found in several modern collections.
2. **Angels your march oppose.** This embodies st. vii.–x., and was given as the 2nd part of "Hark, how the watchmen cry," in the *Wes. H. Bk.*, 1780, No. 306 (ed. 1875, No. 315). It is in several modern collections.
3. **Angels our march oppose.** This, as given in a few American hymn-books in 2 st. of 8 l., or 4 st. of 4 l. It is compiled from st. vii., vi., viii., ix., in the order named.
4. **Our Captain leads us on.** In *Hys. and Songs of Praise*, N. Y., 1874.   [J. J.]

Hark, in the presence of our God. *A. Midlane.* [*Angels' joy over repenting Sinners.*] Written in September, 1842, and pub. in the *Youth's Magazine*, Nov. 1842, in 6 st. of 4 l., and entitled "The Returning Sinner." In 1865, it was included in the author's *Gospel Echoes*, No. 157, and is in a limited number of Mission hymn-books. It has the special interest of being the author's *first* printed hymn.   [J. J.]

Hark, my [dull] soul, how everything. *J. Austin.* [*Praise of Creation.*] Pub. in his *Devotions in the Antient Way of Offices*, &c., 1668, p. 83, No. vi., as the hymn for Monday at Lauds. [See reprint of the 5th ed., 1717, pub. by Masters in 1856.] It is in C. U. in three forms:—

1. **The original** in 7's metre in Horder's *Cong. Hymns*, 1884, No. 620; the American *Bapt. Praise Bk.*, 1871, No. 247, and others.
2. **Hark, my dull soul, how everything.** This was rewritten in L.M. probably by J. Wesley, and was given in his *Ps. & Hys.*, pub. at Charlestown, South Carolina, 1736–7, p. 69, in 7 st. of 4 l. It is seldom found in modern collections.
3. **Hark, dull soul, how everything.** This was given in the original metre, in G. Whitefield's *Coll.*, 1753, No. 83, in 4 st.; in M. Madan's *Ps. & Hys.*, 1760, No. 101, in 7 st., and in other old hymn-books. It is rarely met with in modern collections.   [J. J.]

Hark, my soul, it is the Lord. *W. Cowper.* [*Divine Love.*] Pub. in Maxfield's *New Appendix*, 1768, and again in the *Gospel Magazine*, August, 1771, in 6 st. of 4 l., and signed "Omega." In 1774 it was included in R. Conyers's *Coll.*, No. 53; and in 1779 in the *Olney Hymns*, Bk. i., No. 118. It rapidly attained great popularity with hymn-book compilers; and is found at the present time in

most of the high-class hymnals in all English-speaking countries. It is a lyric of great tenderness and beauty, and ranks as one of Cowper's best hymns. [See **Cowper, W.**] In *Kennedy*, 1863, No. 503, the opening line is mutilated into "*Hearken*, soul, it is the Lord." This is not repeated elsewhere. The original has been *tr.* into several languages, including Latin: "Audin'? 'Adest Dominus," by John W. Hales, in the *Academy*, Nov. 3rd, 1883; and Italian:—"Senti, senti, anima mea," by W. E. Gladstone, in the *Nineteenth Century*, 1883.   [J. J.]

Hark, round the God of love. *H. F. Lyte.* [*Worship of Children acceptable to God.*] Printed anonymously in W. Carus Wilson's Magazine, *The Children's Friend*, 1838, in 4 st. of 4 l. It was reprinted in the "Memoir" prefixed to Lyte's *Remains*, 1850, as a specimen of his Sunday School hymns. It is found in W. F. Stevenson's *Hys. for the Church & Home*, 1873, c. 45; Allon's *Children's Worship*, 1878, No. 29; the *Meth. S. S. H. Bk.*, 1879, No. 543 (orig. text), and others. Although peculiar in metre and defective in rhyme, it is admirably adapted to Sunday Schools.   [W. T. B.]

Hark, she bids all her friends adieu. *I. Watts.* [*Death and Heaven.*] Pub. in his *Horæ Lyricæ*, 1706, Bk. iii., in 8 st. of 4 l., and headed, "On the Sudden Death of Mrs. Mary Peacock. An Elegiac Song sent in a Letter of Condolence to Mr. N. P., Merchant at Amsterdam." In its full form it is not in C. U.; but, with the omission of st. i. and viii., it was included in H. W. Beecher's *Plymouth Coll.*, 1855, No. 1221, as "Farewell, bright soul, a short farewell."   [J. J.]

Hark, ten thousand harps and voices. *T. Kelly.* [*Praise to Jesus.*] 1st pub. in his *Hymns*, &c., 2nd ed., 1806, in 7 st. of 6 l., and headed with the text "Let all the angels of God worship Him." In 1812 it was included in his *Hys. adapted for Social Worship*, No. 7, but subsequently it was restored to the original work (ed. 1853, No. 42). Its use is mainly confined to America, where it is given in several collections, including *Songs for the Sanctuary*, 1865, &c. In most cases it is abbreviated.   [J. J.]

Hark, ten thousand voices cry. *T. Kelly.* [*Easter, or Ascensiontide.*] 1st pub. in the 2nd ed. of his *Hymns*, &c., 1806, in 1 st. of 4 l. in 7's metre; 4 st. of 4 l. in 87, 87 metre, and the chorus:—

> "Then haste, ye saints, your tribute bring,
>   And crown Him everlasting King."

(Ed. 1853, No. 27.) This peculiarity of construction was overlooked by Elliott, who gave it with the omission of the chorus in his *Ps. & Hys.*, 1835, as a complete hymn in 7's; and the Editors of the *Leeds H. Bk.*, 1853, as 87, 5. In the Irish *Church Hymnal*, 1873, No. 199, the first stanza is rewritten:—

> "Hark, ten thousand voices *sounding*
>   *Far and wide throughout the sky,*
> 'Tis the voice of joy abounding,
>   Jesus lives, no more to die."

and the irregularity of metre is thereby overcome. In some collections, including *Kennedy*, 1863, No. 964, it begins with st. ii.: "Jesus comes, His conflict over."   [J. J.]

Hark! the glad sound, the Saviour comes. *P. Doddridge.* [*Advent.*] Dr. Doddridge's original MS. of this hymn, now preserved in the Rooker "D. MSS.," gives the following as the text:—

> " xiv.   Christ's Message,
> from Luke iv. 18, 19.
>
> " Hark the glad Sound ! The Saviour comes
> The Saviour promised long
> Let ev'ry Heart prepare a Throne
> And ev'ry Voice a Song.
>
> " On him the Spirit largely poured
> Exerts its sacred Fire
> Wisdom and Might and Zeal and Love
> His holy Breast inspire.
>
> " He comes the Pris'ners to release
> In *Satan's* bondage held
> The Gates of Brass before him burst
> The Iron Fetters yield.
>
> " He comes from the thick Films of Vice
> To clear the mental Ray
> And on the Eye-Balls of the Blind
> To pour celestial Day.
>
> " He comes the broken Heart to bind
> The bleeding Soul to cure
> And with the Treasures of his Grace
> T' enrich the humble Poor.
>
> " His Silver Trumpets publish loud
> The *Jub'lee* of the LORD
> Our Debts are all remitted now
> Our Heritage restored.
>
> " Our glad *Hosannas*, Prince of Peace
> Thy Welcome shall proclaim
> And Heav'ns eternal Arches ring
> With thy beloved Name.
>   " Dec. 28, 1735."

From this point the hymn has a twofold history, the first *Scottish*, and the second *English*.

i. *Scottish History.*—1. A copy of this MS. passed through Robert Blair (q. v.) [see **Doddridge** in **Various**] into the possession of the Committee appointed to prepare the *Trans. and Paraphrases* of the Church of Scotland, and by them was included therein as No. iv., in 1745, or 10 years after its composition, as follows:—

St. i.   As above with l. 3 " Let every Heart *a Throne prepare.*"
St. ii. As above, with l. 1 " largely *shed,*" for " pour'd."
St. iii. As above, with l. 1 " to *relieve* " for " to release."
St. iv. As above, with l. 1 " thick *scales* " for " thick films."
St. v. As above, with l. 2 " *souls* " for " soul."
St. vi. As above.
St. vii. As above.

2. In 1781, the new *Trans. and Paraphrases* of the Church of Scotland were published, and, as No. xxxix., it appeared thus:—

St. i., ll. 1, 2.   As above.
   ll. 3, 4.   " Let ev'ry heart *exult with joy,*
         and ev'ry voice *be* song."
St. ii., iii. As above, in 1745.
St. iv.   " He comes ! from *dark'ning scales* of vice
      to clear the *inward sight ;*
      And on the eye-balls of the blind
      to pour celestial *light.*"
St. v.   As in 1745, with l. 1 " *hearts* " for " *heart.*"
St. vi.   " *The sacred year has now revolv'd,*
      accepted of the Lord,
      When Heav'n's high promise is fulfill'd,
      and Isr'el is restor'd."
St. vii. ll. 1, 2.   As above.
   ll. 3, 4.   " And heav'n's *exalted* arches ring
      with thy *most honour'd* name."

This form of the hymn received the official sanction of the Church of Scotland, and has been in common use in her communion for more than a hundred years. The alterations of 1781 were by W. Cameron. The text must be designated " *P. Doddridge, 1735, Scottish*

Trs. and Par. 1745, *and W. Cameron* " [see **Cameron, W.**]

ii. *English History.*—1. We have no record of the printing of this hymn in England until ten years after it appeared in Scotland, when Job Orton gave it in his 1st ed. of Doddridge's (posthumous) *Hymns,* &c., 1755, No. cciii., and with one change only from the original MS., st. iv., l. 1, reading, " He comes from *thickest* films of vice."

2. The text of J. D. Humphreys's ed. of the *Hymns,* &c., 1839, No. 226, differs from that of Orton only in st. vi., which reads:—

> " His silver trumpets publish loud
> The *Lord's high Jubilee ;*
> Our debts are all remitted now,
> Our heritage *is free.*"

3. From the Orton ed. of the *Hymns,* &c., 1755, the hymn has passed in a more or less complete form into almost every hymnal of note published since 1755, from *Conyers's,* 1774, to the *Westminster Abbey H. Bk.,* 1883, in the Church of England ; *Ash & Evans* of 1769 to the *Baptist Hymnal* of 1879, in the Baptist Communion ; and all the leading hymnals of other denominations with the unaccountable exception of the *Wes. H. Bk.* In addition it is in extensive use in America and other English speaking countries. In popular use it is the most widely known of Doddridge's hymns.

4. The most popular form of the text is st. i., iii., iv., v., vii., as in the S. P. C. K. *Church Hys.,* and the *Hy. Comp.* That in 4 st. in *H. A. & M.,* and *Thring,* is from the earliest editions of the Countess of Huntingdon's *Collection.* The reading " to *bless,*" for " *enrich* the humble poor," dates from the last century.

5. The merits of this hymn have been thus referred to by Sir R. Palmer (Lord Selborne) : " A more sweet, vigorous, and perfect composition is not to be found even in the whole body of ancient hymns," *York Church Congress Report,* 1866, p. 330. It must be pointed out, however, that st. iv., " He comes from the thick films of vice," is based on lines 39, 40 of Pope's *Messiah :*—

> " He from thick films shall purge the visual ray,
> And on the sightless eye-balls pour the day."

6. Translations of various forms of the hymn have been made into several languages, including Latin, in Bingham's *Hymno. Christ. Latina,* 1871, p. 55, " Laeta vox coeli resonant auras," and in Macgill's *Songs of the Christian Creed & Life,* 1876 and 1879, as " Laeta vox ! venit Salvator." [**English Hymnody, Early,** § XIV.]   [J. J.]

Hark, the loud triumphant strains. *T. Kelly.* [*Missions.*] 1st pub. in the 3rd ed. of his *Hymns,* &c., 1809, No. 164, in 3 st. of 6 l. (ed. 1853, p. 577). In Hatfield's *Church H. Bk.,* N. Y., 1872, No. 303 is based upon this hymn ; st. i., ll. 1-2, and st. iii., ll. 1-2, being slightly altered from Kelly, whilst the rest of the hymn embodies its train of thoughts in another form.   [J. J.]

Hark, the nightly church-bell numbers. *Bp. E. H. Bickersteth.* [*Evening.*] Written in 1853 and 1st pub. in a tract, *The Cottager's Handbook of Family Prayers,* 1854. It was repeated in his *Supplement* to his *Ps.*

& *Hys.*, based on the *Christian Psalmody*, 1858, No. 7, and again in his work, *The Two Brothers*, &c., 1871, p. 247, and entitled, "The Village Evening Hymn."   [J. J.]

Hark, the song of jubilee. *J. Montgomery.* [*Missions.*] Pub. in the *Evangelical Magazine*, July, 1818, in 3 st. of 8 l., in the author's *Greenland and other Poems*, 1819, p. 183; Cotterill's *Sel.*, 8th ed., 1819, No. 235; Montgomery's *Christian Psalmist*, 1825, No. 561; and his *Original Hys.*, 1853, No. 98. Almost from the first Montgomery had some difficulty with the second line of st. ii. His readings are :—

1. *Greenland*, &c. "From the abysse to the skies."
2. *Cotterill.* "From the depths unto the skies."
3. *Ch. Psal.* "From the centre to the skies."
4. *Same, altered in MS.* "From the depths unto the skies."
5. *Orig. Hys.* "From the depths unto the skies."

This last is Montgomery's authorized text, and is usually followed by modern compilers. The hymn is in extensive use in all English-speaking countries, and has been translated into several languages.   [J. J.]

Hark, the sound of holy voices, chanting at the crystal sea. *Bp. C. Wordsworth of Lincoln.* [*All Saints' Day.*] 1st pub. in his *Holy Year*, 1862, No. 106, in 6 st. of 4 double lines (5th ed. 1868, No. 109). In 1863 it was given in the *Parish H. Bk.*, No. 190, and subsequently in other collections, until it has become throughout all English-speaking countries one of the most widely known and popular of the Bishop's hymns. In some collections st. ii., l. 2 is given as in the original :—

"King, Apostle, Saint, and Martyr, Confessor, Evangelist,"

and in others :—

"King, Apostle, Saint, Confessor, Martyr, and Evangelist."

The reason for this change is twofold : first, because of the division of the original line into two, and second, possibly because the old distinction between *Cónfessor*—i.e. one who witnesses for the faith by a good confession short of actual martyrdom ; and *Conféssor*, i.e. one who receives confessions—was beyond the comprehension of ordinary congregations. One of the first, if not the first collection in which this change was made, was the *Appendix* to *H. A. & M.*, 1868.

In the S. P. C. K. *Church Hymns*, No. 199, st. v. is bracketed for omission in singing if desired. This stanza reads :—

"Now they reign in heavenly glory, now they walk in golden light,
Now they drink as from a river, holy bliss and infinite ;
Love and Peace they taste for ever ; and all truth and knowledge see
In the beatific vision of the Blessed Trinity."

The Rev. J. Ellerton's note on this hymn in his *Notes*, &c., on *Church Hymns*, folio ed. p. xlviii. explains this arrangement as follows :

"In the earlier editions of Church Hymns the fifth stanza of this hymn, 'Now they reign in heavenly glory,' &c., was omitted in deference to the judgment of one of the Episcopal Referees of the Society for Promoting Christian Knowledge, who held that the verse was liable to be misunderstood as countenancing the popular error that the Blessed are already in the full fruition of their future and everlasting glory — the 'Beatific Vision.' It is scarcely needful to say that so

accurate a theologian as the Bishop of Lincoln had no sympathy with this view. His Lordship, while pressing for the restoration of this verse, explained that the whole hymn, from beginning to end, was to be regarded as the utterance in triumphant song of a vision of the *final* gathering of the saints, not as an exposition of their *present* condition in the Intermediate State. The Tract Committee of the Society therefore desired that the verse should in subsequent editions be restored ; but should, in deference to those who might still think it liable to misconstruction, be bracketed for optional use."

In a MS. note on this hymn, and this special stanza, Bp. Wordsworth adds that :—

"The whole hymn from beginning to end is in harmony with the Epistle for the festival of the day (Rev. vii. 2, &c.), and like it is the utterance in triumphant song of a vision of the *final* gathering of the Saints." [E. MSS.]

It may be added that, with the exception of the alteration noted above, the original text of this hymn is usually given in an unaltered form.   [J. J.]

Hark, the voice of Jesus calling, Come ye laden, &c. *A. Midlane.* [*The Invitation of Jesus.*] Written in August, 1860, and 1st pub. in the *Ambassador's H. Bk.*, 1861, No. 45, in 4 st. of 6 l. It was repeated in Spurgeon's *O. O. H. Bk.*, 1866, No. 497 ; again in many collections for Evangelical Meetings and Home Mission Services ; and also in the author's *Gospel Echoes*, 1865, No. 41. It is also in C. U. in America and Canada. [J. J.]

Hark, the voice of love and mercy. [*Good Friday—Holy Communion.*] The authorship of this popular hymn has long been a matter of dispute. On the one hand it has been claimed for the Rev. *Jonathan Evans*, and on the other for the Rev. *Benjamin Francis.* The evidence on behalf of each is as follows :—

i. *For Jonathan Evans.*

1. In 1784 the hymn appeared in the Rev. G. Burder's *Coll. of Hys.*, &c., No. 126, in 5 st. of 6 l., but in the index of authors it had no signature.
2. Forty-three years later, viz. in the 25th ed. of his *Coll.*, 1827, Burder filled the blank in with the name of *J. Evans.*
3. Dr. J. Styles, who succeeded J. Evans as Pastor of the Foleshill congregation [see **Evans, J.**], published from Evans's MSS. several hymns in the *Evangelical Magazine* ; and in the same Magazine, in March, 1847, he claimed this hymn for his predecessor.

ii. *For Benjamin Francis.*

1. Francis contributed to Rippon's Bapt. *Sel.*, 1787, five hymns, each of which was signed "*B. Francis*" ; and one hymn altered from *Gregg* [see **Francis, B.**]. In the same *Sel.* there were two hymns which were signed "*F——.*" The first of these was, "Hark, the voice of love and mercy" ; and the second, "Lord, Thou hast made me know Thy ways."
2. During Dr. Rippon's lifetime there were no changes made in this signature. At his death in 1836, the copyright of the *Sel.* expired, and some interested persons published "A New Edition."
3. In this "New Edition" the "*F——*" was expanded into "*Francis*," in the case of "Hark, the voice of love and mercy" ; but the signature of "Lord, hast Thou made me know Thy ways," remained as before.
4. On these grounds it is claimed for *B. Francis.*

These claims are not so satisfactory as could be desired, either for *Evans* or for *Francis* ; and this is still more evident when we find that the second hymn with the signature "*F——*" in *Rippon* ("Lord, hast Thou made me know Thy ways") is a cento from Dr. John Fawcett's hymn in 6 st. pub. in his *Hymns*, &c., 1782, No. 123, and composed of st. i., v. and vi. The "*F——*" in *Rippon*, in this instance, is John Fawcett (q.v.) of Yorkshire. "Hark, the voice of love and mercy," however, is not found in Fawcett's *Hymns*, 1782, and cannot be claimed for him. The evidence is in favour of *Jonathan Evans;* and the fact that Burder gave J. Evans in full in his *Coll.* of 1827 gives it great weight.

In America this hymn is as extensively used as in G. Britain, and in common with the hymn-books of G. Britain it is attributed in the American collections, now to "*B. Francis,*" and again to "*J. Evans.*" The hymn in its original form was intended for general use if st. iv. were omitted, and for Holy Communion, when it was used. It reads:—

> "Happy souls, approach the table,
>   Taste the soul reviving food!
> Nothing half so sweet and pleasant
>   As the Saviour's flesh and blood.
>   ' It is finished'!
> Christ hath borne the heavy load."

The original text in Burder's *Coll.* was repeated in Rippon's *Sel.* with the single change in st. ii., l. 2, of "Do these precious words afford," to "Do these *charming* words afford." *Rippon's* full text is in the *Lyra Brit.*, 1867, p. 653, accompanied by two notes on its authenticity. The Editor, however, was unaware that the hymn appeared in Burder's *Coll.* three years before it was given in Rippon's *Sel.*, 1787, and falls into the error of attributing its first appearance to Rippon's *Sel.* The text, with the omission of st. iv., is *tr.* into Latin in R. Bingham's *Hymno. Christ. Latina*, 1871, p. 221, as "Audin'? clara vox amoris."   [J. J.]

Hark, through the courts of heaven. *H. Alford.* [*Joy in heaven over repenting Sinners.*] Contributed to his *Ps. & Hys.*, 1844, p. 68, in 4 st. of 4 l., and repeated in his *Year of Praise*, 1867, No. 156. It is in limited use in G. Britain and America.

    [J. J.]

Hark! what mean those holy voices. *J. Cawood.* [*Christmas.*] This popular hymn appeared in 1819 in the 8th ed. of Cotterill's *Sel.*, No. 269, in 6 st. of 4 l., with the refrain, "Hallelujah." In common with all the hymns in that *Sel.* it was unsigned; but when republished by J. Montgomery in his *Christian Psalmist*, 1825, it was attributed to "Cawood." In some works, and collections, it is dated 1816; but in J. Cawood's son's correspondence with D. Sedgwick, it is undated [s. MSS.], and failing further information, it must remain as 1819. Of all Cawood's hymns this is the most popular. It is in extensive use in G. Britain and America. Orig. text in Snepp's *S. of G. & G.*, 1872, No. 205, with "*glory* sing" for "praises sing" in st. iv., l. 2.   [J. J.]

Harland, Edward, M.A., was b. at Ashbourne, Derby, 1810, and educated at Wadham College, Oxford, where he graduated B.A., 1831; M.A., 1833. On taking Holy Orders he became Curate of Newborough, 1833–36; of Sandon, 1836–51; Vicar of Colwich, Staffordshire, 1851; and Prebendary in Lichfield Cathedral, 1873. In 1858 he pub. *Index Sermonum.* His *Church Psalter and Hymnal* was first pub. in 1855, and contained 209 hymns and 8 doxologies. In 1863 a *Supplement* was added: in "186- " [1865] it

was revised and enlarged as the "2nd edition," and in 1876 a *Supplement* of 184 hymns was added to the 2nd ed., making 584 hymns in all, most of the "Christmas Carols," &c., of the 2nd edition being omitted. To the various editions of this *Hymnal*, Prebendary Harland contributed the following hymns:—

1. **Behold a humble train.** (1863.) *Presentation of Christ.*
2. **Beloved disciple! Illustrious name.** (1863.) *St. John Evangelist.*
3. **Breathing slaughter 'gainst thy people.** (1863.) *Conversion of St. Paul.*
4. **Heirs of Thy salvation.** (1863.) *St. Michael and All Angels.*
5. **Here life is a shadow, and soon will be o'er.** (1863.) *O. and N. Year.* Written "Oct. 12, 1862, on Wolseley Bridge, with the Trent flowing below." Included in the *Hymnal*, 1863.
6. **Holy men, in olden time.** (1863.) *Common of Evangelists.*
7. **In the time of trial.** (1863.) *For Resignation.* An imitation of, and companion hymn to, Montgomery's "In the hour of trial."
8. **Jesus calls to us to-day.** (1867.) *S. School Anniversary.*
9. **Jesus is the sure foundation.** (1863.) *St. Peter.*
10. **Jesus, King of glory.** (1863.) *Faithfulness and its Reward.*
11. **Jesus, these lips can ne'er proclaim.** (1863.) *Praise to Jesus.*
12. **Jesus, when Thy cross I see.** (1863.) *Passiontide.*
13. **Lord, I never will deny Thee.** (1863.) *St. Peter.*
14. **Lord Jesus, when Thou wouldst appear.** (1863.) *The Annunciation.*
15. **Lord, Thine ancient people see.** (1855 (?).) *For the Jews.*
16. **Lord, we bend before Thy throne.** (1867.) *Unfavourable Harvest.*
17. **Lord, when earthly comforts flee.** (1855.) *Resignation.*
18. **My Lord, and my God, blessed word that declared.** (1863.) *St. Thomas.*
19. **Now, Lord, to every heart make known.** (1855.) *Passiontide.* "This hymn was written at the time of the author's Ordination as Deacon, in 1833. He chose for his first text 1 Cor. i. 23, 'We preach Christ crucified,' the sermon and the hymn being composed for the same occasion. He has preached from the same text, and this hymn has generally been used on the return of that day, for more than fifty years." It was included in his *Hymnal*, 1855.
20. **O come, all ye faithful, Come, see the place.** (1867.) *Easter.* Pt. i.
21. **O come, ye that labour.** (1867.) *Easter.* Pt. ii.
22. **O for a humbler walk with God.** (1855.) *Lent.*
23. **O Heavenly Jerusalem, Thou city of the Lord.** (1863.) *Heaven.* "This hymn was suggested to the author in a dream. In the night of Oct. 5, 1862, he dreamed that he saw the choirs of heaven ten thousand times ten thousand, in white robes, marching into a glorious Temple singing this hymn. He awoke, rose from bed, procured a light, and wrote down the words on the back of a letter as he had heard them in his dream, and then retired to rest again. The next morning he found the hymn on his dressing table." It was given in his *Supplement*, 1863.
24. **O Thou by Whom the healing art.** (1863.) *St. Luke.*
25. **Stephen, first of martyrs, we.** (1863.) *St. Stephen.*
26. **The chorus raise of highest praise.** (1863.) *Praise.*
27. **This day in this Thy holy place.** (1867.) *Friendly Societies.*

In addition to these the *Suppl.* of 1876 contained his "And now this Holy day," for *Sunday.* The majority of Prebendary Harland's hymns are for the minor festivals, and are worthy of more attention than they have received. He d. June 8, 1890.   [J. J.]

Harmer, Samuel Young, s. of Samuel Harmer, a member of the Society of Friends, was b. at Germantown, Pennsylvania, Dec. 9, 1809. In 1827 he joined the American Methodist Episcopalian Church, and was engaged for several years as a Sunday School teacher and superintendent. In 1842 he became a local preacher of that body, and, in 1847, was admitted into the ministry. He has held appointments in Philadelphia and Iowa. His well-known hymn "In the Christian's home in glory" (*Heaven*) was written in 1856 for a camp-meeting collection which the Rev. John Gladding was then compiling. It has been slightly altered, and set to music by the Rev. W. McDonald of Boston, Massachusetts. (For these details we are indebted to Dr. Hatfield's *Poets of the Church*, N. Y., 1884.)   [J. J.]

Harp and voice Thy praises telling. *J. D. Burns.* [*Spiritual Worship.*] 1st pub. in his little book of prayers and hymns, *The Evening Hymn*, 1857, in 3 st. of 8 l., and entitled "Spiritual Worship." It was repeated with slight alterations in W. F. Stevenson's *Hys. for Church & Home*, 1873, No. 341, and other collections.   [J. J.]

Harp, awake! tell out the story. *H. Downton.* [*New Year.*] Appeared in *Hys. for the London German Hospital*, Dalston, 1848, No. 91; A. T. Russell's *Ps. & Hys.*, 1851, No. 64, in 4 st. of 8 l.; and again in the author's *Hys. & Verses*, 1873, p. 9. It is in several collections, including the S. P. C. K. *Church Hymns*, 1871; the *Westminster Abbey H. Bk.*, 1883, and others. In *Kennedy*, 1863, No. 141, it begins with st. i., l. 5, "Sing we, brethren, faithful hearted." This in Dale's *English Hymnal*, 1874, is altered to "Join we, brethren, faithful hearted."   [J. J.]

Harris, John, D.D., was b. at Ugborough, Devon, March 8, 1802, and educated for the Congregational Ministry at Hoxton Academy. He was Minister of the Congregational Church, Epsom, 1825–38; President of the Countess of Huntingdon's College at Cheshunt, 1838–50; and Principal of New College, London, 1850, to his death, Dec. 21, 1856. He received the degree of D.D. from Brown University in 1838. His works were numerous, including *The Great Teacher*, 1835; *Union: or, the Divided Church made one*, 1837; *The Pre-Adamite Earth*, 1846; two prize essays; a volume of poems, *The Incarnate One*, &c. His hymn, "Light up this house with glory, Lord" (*Opening of a Place of Worship*), appeared in the *New Cong.*, 1859, No. 882. It has become widely known, and is of more than usual merit.   [W. G. H.]

Harsdörffer, Georg Philipp, was b. at Nürnberg apparently on Nov. 1, 1607. He studied law at the Universities of Altdorf and Strassburg; and after five years spent in travelling in France, Holland, England and Italy, returned to Nürnberg in 1630. In 1637 he was appointed assessor of the Lower Court, and in 1655 senator (Rathsherr). He d. at Nürnberg, Sept. 19 or 20, 1658. He was joint founder with J. Klaj of the Pegnitz Shepherd

and Flower Order in 1644, of which he became the President. His hymns appeared mostly in his *Hertzbewegliche Sonntagsandachten*, Nürnberg, 1649 [Wernigerode]; in his *Nathan und Jotham*, Nürnberg, 1650–1651 [2nd ed. 1651–59 in Berlin]; and in the works of his friend J. M. Dilherr. Few of his hymns are still in German use, and only two appear to have passed into English, viz.:—

i. **Der sich auf seine Schwachheit steurt.** *Lent. Confirmation.* In J. M. Dilherr's *Geistliche Liebesflamme*, Nürnberg, 1651, p. 446, in 6 st. of 8 l., entitled, "On religious completeness" (or "godly perfection"). The form *tr.* into English begins "*Wer sich*," and is found in the 8th ed., 1722, of Börner's Dresden *G. B.*, in 6 st. of 10 l., marked "D. B. W. M." These initials represent Dr. Bernhard Walther Marperger, court preacher at Dresden [b. May 14, 1682, at Hamburg; studied at the Universities of Altdorf and Halle; from 1704–1724 held various clerical appointments in Nürnberg; became, 1724, Oberconsistorialrath and court preacher at Dresden, and d. there March 28, 1746]; but in Marperger's own *G. B.*, Leipzig, 1725, No. 522, it does not bear his name. This may of course be because it is based on *Harsdörffer*. *Tr.* as: "Who seeks in weakness an excuse," by Miss Winkworth, 1855, p. 149.

ii. **Die Nacht ist nun vergangen.** *Morning.* Appeared in J. M. Dilherr's *Bei 1000 alte und neue geistliche Psalmen Lieder*, &c., Nürnberg, 1654, p. 512, in 6 st., marked "Another. Georg Phil. Harsdörffer." The *trs.* are: (1) "The night is now departed," by *H. J. Buckoll*, 1842, p. 41. (2) "Night from the earth is wending," by *Miss Manington*, 1863, p. 117.   [J. M.]

Hart, Joseph, was b. in London in 1712. His early life is involved in obscurity. His education was fairly good; and from the testimony of his brother-in-law, and successor in the ministry in Jewin Street, the Rev. John Hughes, "his civil calling was" for some time "that of a teacher of the learned languages." His early life, according to his own Experience which he prefaced to his Hymns, was a curious mixture of loose conduct, serious conviction of sin, and endeavours after amendment of life, and not until Whitsuntide, 1757, did he realize a permanent change, which was brought about mainly through his attending divine service at the Moravian Chapel, in Fetter Lane, London, and hearing a sermon on Rev. iii. 10. During the next two years many of his most earnest and impassioned hymns were written. These appeared as :—

Hymns composed on Various Subjects, with the Author's Experience, London, 1759. During this year he became the Minister of the Independent Chapel, Jewin Street, London. In 1762 he added a *Supplement* to his *Hymns*; and in 1765 an *Appendix*. In modern editions of his *Hymns* these three are embodied in one volume as :— *Hymns composed on Various Subjects: With the Author's Experience, The Supplement and Appendix. By the Rev. Joseph Hart, late Minister of the Gospel in Jewin Street*, London. *Allott & Co.* [no date].

Hart d. on May 24, 1768. At one time his hymns were widely used, especially by Calvinistic Nonconformists. Many of them are of merit, and are marked by great earnestness, and passionate love of the Redeemer. The best known are: "Come, Holy Spirit, come"; "Come, ye sinners, poor and wretched"; "This God is the God we adore"; and "Lord, look on all assembled here." Those which are more limited in their use include :—

i. From his *Hymns*, &c., 1759.

1. **Descend from heaven, celestial Dove.** *Whitsuntide.* No. 6, in 6 st. of 6 l. In Snepp's *Songs of G. & G.*, 1872, No. 374, st. iv., v. are omitted. It is in extensive use in America.

2. **Great High Priest, we view Thee stooping.** *High Priesthood of Christ.* No. 56, pt. ii., in 3 st. of 8 l. In Snepp's *Songs of G. & G.*, 1872, No. 236; Hatfield's *Church H. Bk.*, N. Y., 1872, No. 435, &c.

3. How wondrous are the works of God. *Redeeming Love.* No. 21, in 9 st. of 4 l. In the Scottish *Evang. Union Hyl.*, 1878, st. i.-iv. are given as No. 11.

4. If ever it could come to pass. *Final Perseverance.* No. 58, in 3 st. of 6 l. Repeated in Snepp's *Songs of G. & G.*, 1872, No. 729.

5. Jesus is our God and Saviour. *Faith and Repentance.* No. 54, in 7 st. of 8 l. In Snepp's *Songs of G. & G.*, 1872, No. 146, st. iv. is omitted. In the *London H. Bk.* (enlarged), 1879, st. iii. and v. are given as "Nothing but Thy blood, O Jesus."

6. Jesus, while He dwelt below. *Gethsemane.* No. 75, in 23 st. of 6 l. In Snepp's *Songs of G. & G.*, 1872, No. 230, sixteen stanzas are broken up into three parts : (i.) "Jesus, while He dwelt below"; (ii.) "Full of love to man's lost race"; (iii.) "There my God bore all my guilt." A cento is also given in Hatfield's *Church H. Bk.*, N. Y., 1872, No. 441, as "Many woes had Christ [He] endured." It is composed of st. viii., ix., xiii., xx., xxiii., slightly altered. In the Scottish *Evang. Union Hyl.*, 1870, No. 34, 6 st. are given in two parts : pt. i. as, "Jesus, while He dwelt below"; pt. ii. "Eden from each flowery bed."

7. Lamb of God, we fall before Thee. *Christ All in All.* No. 17 in 4 st. of 8 l. It is in various collections, and as altered in *Kennedy*, 1863, No. 1171, is much improved.

8. Let us all with grateful praises. *Christmas.* No. 14 in 7 st. of 8 l. In Spurgeon's *O. O. H. Bk.*, 1866, it is reduced to 4 st. of 4 l.

9. Lord, look on all assembled here. *For a Public Fast.* No. 96, in 8 st. of 4 l. It is in several of the older hymn-books.

10. Lord, we lie before Thy feet. *Lent.* No. 74, in 6 st. of 6 l., and based on 2 Chron. xx. 20. In Spurgeon's *O. O. H. Bk.*, 1866, st. i., iii., vi. are given as No. 585.

11. Mercy is welcome news indeed. *God's Mercy in pardoning Sin.* No. 51, in 6 st. of 4 l., on St. Luke vii. 42. In *Spurgeon*, 1866, No. 544.

12. Much we talk of Jesu's blood. *Passiontide.* No. 41, in 4 st. of 8 l., on Lam. i. 12. In *Spurgeon*, 1866, it is abridged to 4 st. of 4 l.

13. Now from the garden to the cross. *Good Friday.* No. 63, in 9 st. of 4 l., and entitled, "The Crucifixion." In *Spurgeon*, 1866, No. 274, st. ii.-v., vi.-ix. are given as "See how the patient Jesus stands."

14. The Fountain of Christ Assist me to sing. *The Fountain.* No. 86, in 8 st. of 8 l. on Zech. xiii. 1. In *Spurgeon*, 1866, st. i., v., vii., viii., are given as No. 375.

15. The moon and stars shall lose their light. *Advent.* No. 48, in 4 st. of 4 l., on St. Matt. xxiv. 35. In *Spurgeon*, 1866.

16. The sinner that truly believes. *Saving Faith.* No. 88, in 5 st. of 4 l., and entitled, "Saving Faith" In *Spurgeon*, 1866, No. 533, st. ii. is omitted, and the opening line is altered to "The moment a sinner believes."

ii. From his *Supplement*, 1762.

17. Behold what awful pomp. *Advent.* No. 52, in 8 st. of 4 l. It is usually abridged as in the American Meth. Episco. *Hymns*, 1849, No. 1107.

18. Christ is the Eternal Rock. *The Offices of Christ.* No. 27, in 6 st. of 8 l. In Windle's *Metrical Psalter & Hyl.*, 1862, st. i., ii., v. are given as No. 53.

19. Christians, dismiss your fear. *Easter.* No. 33, in 4 st. of 8 l. into Dr. Alexander's *Augustine H. Bk.*, 1849, No. 79, in 7 st. of 4 l.

20. Dismiss with Thy blessing, Lord. *Close of Service.* No. 78, in 2 st. of 4 l. In a few collections.

21. Gird thy loins up, Christian soldier. *The Christian Armour.* No. 29, in 5 st. of 8 l., on Eph. vi. 11. Found in several of the older, and a few of the modern collections.

22. Glory to God on high, Our peace, &c. *Holy Communion.* No. 3, in 6 st. of 4 l. In Hatfield's *Church H. Bk.*, 1872, No. 704, st. v., vi. are omitted.

23. Holy Ghost, inspire our praises. *On behalf of Ministers.* No. 77, in 5 st. of 8 l. In the Scottish *Evang. Union Hyl.*, 1878, No. 412, st. iii.-v. are given as, "Happy soul that hears and follows."

24. Jesus once for sinners slain. *Holy Communion.* No. 18, in 6 st. of 4 l. In American use.

25. Lord, help us on Thy word to feed. *Close of Service.* No. 80, in 2 st. of 4 l. In several modern hymn-books.

26. O for a glance of heavenly day. *Lent.* No. 64, in 5 st. of 4 l. In Hatfield's *Church H. Bk.*, 1872, and other American collections it is usually repeated in full. In Bickersteth's *Christian Psalmody*, 1833, it

was given as, "Lord, shed a beam of heavenly day," and this is repeated in modern hymn-books.

27. Once more before we part. *Close of Service.* No. 79, in 2 st. of 4 l. Popular in G. Britain and America.

28. Once more we come before our God. *Before a Sermon.* No. 21, in 6 st. of 4 l., into *Hatfield*, 1872, No. 111, and others.

29. Sons of God by bless'd adoption. *Burial.* No. 45, in 3 st. of 8 l., into Snepp's *Songs of G. & G.*, 1872, No. 981, as "Sons of God by *blest* adoption."

30. Suffering Saviour, Lamb of God. *Holy Communion.* No. 14, in 8 st. of 4 l. In W. F. Stevenson's *Hys. for Church & Home*, 1873, st. iii., vii. are omitted.

31. That doleful night before His death. *Holy Communion.* No. 17, in 2 st. of 8 l. In the Scottish *Evang. Union Hyl.*, 1878, st. i. ll. 4-8, and st. ii., are given as, "To keep Thy Feast, Lord, we are met."

iii. From his *Appendix*, 1765.

32. Christians, in your several stations. *Christian Duty.* No. 7, in 5 st. of 6 l. It is slightly altered in Snepp's *Songs of G. & G.*, 1872, No. 742, and dated 1759 in error.

33. Prayer was [is] appointed to convey. *Prayer.* No. 12 in 6 st. of 4 l. into Snepp's *Songs of G. & G.*, 1872, No. 542, with alterations and the omission of st. ii., v. In some American collections it begins, "Prayer is to God, the soul's sure way." [J. J.]

Hartmann von der Aue seems to have been b. about 1170, apparently of the baronial family Von Owe or Au or Niedernau, near Rottenburg on the Neckar. He took part in one of the Crusades, most likely that of 1197, and was still living in 1207, but had died before 1220 (*Allg. Deutsche Biog.*, i. 634-636 ; *Goedeke's Grundriss*, 1884, i., 89-93, &c.).

The facts of his life have been considerably contested. Some have sought to connect him with Aub or Ouwe, near Rothenburg, on the Tauber; others with Au, near Freiburg in Baden. In his *Arme Heinrich* he calls himself Ritter und Dienstmann zu Aue, and was certainly a Swabian. He was one of the most notable poets of his time. His works are mainly metrical romances. Two deal with legends of the Arthurian cycle, *Erec* (Geraint and Enid), written about 1190 ; and *Iwein* (the Knight with the Lion), written about 1204—both based on *Christian of Troyes*. A third, *Gregorius* (a setting of the legendary early life of St. Gregory the Great), was written about 1200 on the basis of a French version. A fourth, the *Arme Heinrich* (the story of which is employed by H. W. Longfellow in his well-known *Golden Legend*, 1851), was his latest work. The remainder of his poems are love songs and songs of the Crusades, and were probably written c. 1193-1199. Various eds. of his individual works have been pub. during the last 50 years, and a collected ed. in 3 vols. by Fedor Bech appeared at Leipzig, 1867-69.

The only piece which can be called a hymn and has been *tr.* into English is

Min fröide wart nie sorgelos. *Crusader's Hymn.* This is in Bech's ed., pt. ii., p. 17, in 2 st. of 12 l. ; also in *Wackernagel*, ii. p. 60. *Tr.* as "My joy was ne'er unmixed with care," by *Miss Winkworth*, 1869, p. 42. [J. M.]

Haste, traveller, haste! the night comes on. *W. B. Collyer.* [*Invitation.*] Appeared in Rippon's *Bap. Sel.* 27th ed. 1827, No. 581, Pt. ii., in 7 st. of 4 l., with the refrain "Haste, traveller, haste," to st. i.-vi., and "Haste to Him, haste," to st. vii. It is in use in G. Britain and America. Its original title is "Fleeing from the wrath to come by flying to Christ." [J. J.]

Hasten, [O] sinner, to be wise. *T. Scott.* [*Exhortation to Repentance.*] Pub. in his *Lyric Poems*, &c., 1773, No. 23, in 4 st. of 4 l., as "Hasten, sinner, to be wise." The L. M. version of this hymn, "Hasten, O sinner, to be wise," appeared in Rippon's *Sel.*, 1787, No. 116, st. ii. with the additional stanza "O Lord, do Thou the sinner turn." Both forms are in C. U. in G. Britain and America : the original is in Snepp's *Songs of G. & G.*, 1872, No. 479, with Rippon's additional stanza reduced to 7's metre; and Rippon's text is in the Bap. *Ps. & Hys.*, 1858, No. 373. In the Oberlin *Manual of Praise*, 1880, No. 219, 3 st. are given in 7's metre as "*Haste*, O Sinner, *now* be wise."   [W. T. B.]

Hastings, Horace Lorenzo, was b. at Blandford, Mass., Nov. 26, 1831; commenced writing hymns, and preaching, in his 17th year, and laboured as an evangelist in various parts of the U. S. In 1866 he established *The Christian*, a monthly paper, in which many of his hymns have appeared, and in 1865 the Scriptural Tract Repository in Boston. He pub. *Social Hymns, Original and Selected*, Boston, 1865; *Songs of Pilgrimage, a Hymnal for the Churches of Christ*, Part i., 1880; and in August, 1886, the same completed, to the extent of 1533 hymns, 450 of which are original and signed "H." The best known of these is "Shall we meet beyond the river," written in N. Y. city, 1858, and lately pub. as a leaflet in 14 st. of 8 l. The text in *Gospel Hymns* and elsewhere consists of the 1st half of st. i., iv., xi. and ix. The *Hastings Birthday Book*, extracts from his prose writings, appeared 1886.   [F. M. B.]

Hastings, Lady Flora, daughter of the Marquess of Hastings, was b. at Edinburgh, Feb. 11, 1806, and d. July 5, 1839. Her hymns appeared in her posthumous *Poems by the Lady Flora Hastings, Edited by her Sister* [the Marchioness of Bute], 1841. The best known of her hymns is "O Thou, Who for our fallen race." (*The humility and love of Christ.*) This is usually given in an abbreviated form, as in W. F. Stevenson's *Hymns for Church and Home*, 1873.   [J. J.]

Hastings, Thomas, MUS. DOC., s. of Dr. Seth Hastings, was b. at Washington, Lichfield County, Connecticut, October 15, 1784. In 1786, his father moved to Clinton, Oneida Co., N. Y. There, amid rough frontier life, his opportunities for education were small; but at an early age he developed a taste for music, and began teaching it in 1806. Seeking a wider field, he went, in 1817, to Troy, then to Albany, and in 1823 to Utica, where he conducted a religious journal, in which he advocated his special views on church music. In 1832 he was called to New York to assume the charge of several Church Choirs, and there his last forty years were spent in great and increasing usefulness and repute. He d. at New York, May 15, 1872. His aim was the greater glory of God through better musical worship; and to this end he was always training choirs, compiling works, and composing music. His hymn-work was a corollary to the proposition of his music-work; he wrote hymns for certain tunes; the one activity seemed to imply and necessitate the other. Although not a great poet, he yet attained considerable success. If we take the aggregate of American hymnals published during the last fifty years or for any portion of that time, more hymns by him are found in C. U. than by any other native writer. Not one of his hymns is of the highest merit, but many of them have become popular and useful. In addition to editing many books of tunes, Hastings also pub. the following hymn-books:—

(1) *Spiritual Songs for Social Worship: Adapted to the Use of Families and Private Circles in Seasons of Revival, to Missionary Meetings,* &c., Utica, 1831-2, in which he was assisted by Lowell Mason; (2) *The Mother's Hymn-book*, 1834; (3) *The Christian Psalmist; or, Watts's Psalms and Hymns, with copious Selections from other Sources,* &c., N. Y., 1836, in connection with William Patton; (4) *Church Melodies*, N. Y., 1858, assisted by his son, the Rev. T. S. Hastings; (5) *Devotional Hymns and Poems*, N. Y., 1850. The last contained many, but not all, of his original hymns. (6) *Mother's Hymn-book*, enlarged 1850.

The authorship of several of Hastings's hymns has been somewhat difficult to determine. All the hymns given in the *Spiritual Songs* were without signatures. In the *Christian Psalmist* some of his contributions were signed "Anon," others "M. S.," whilst others bore the names of the tune books in which they had previously appeared; and in the *Church Melodies* some were signed with his name, and others were left blank. His MSS., and *Devotional Hymns*, &c., enable us to fix the authorship of over 50 which are still in C. U. These, following the chronological order of his leading work, are:—

i. From the *Spiritual Songs*, 1831:—

1. **Before Thy footstool kneeling.** *In Sickness.* No. 358, in 3 st. of 8 l.
2. **Bleeding hearts defiled by sin.** *Fulness of Christ.* No. 261, in 5 st. of 4 l.
3. **Child of sin and sorrow, Filled with dismay.** *Lent.* No. 315, in 2 st. of 8 l. It is sometimes given as "Child of sin and sorrow, *Where wilt thou flee?*" It is in extensive use.
4. **Delay not, delay not, O sinner draw near.** *Exhortation to Repentance.* No. 145, in 5 st. of 4 l. Given in several important collections.
5. **Forgive us, Lord, to Thee we cry.** *Forgiveness desired.* No. 165, in 4 st. of 4 l.
6. **Gently, Lord, O gently lead us.** *Pilgrimage of Life.* No. 29, in 2 st, of 8 l. It is given in several collections. The first two lines are taken from a hymn which appeared in the *Christian Lyre*, 1830.
7. **Go forth on wings of fervent prayer.** *For a blessing on the distribution of Books and Tracts.* No. 250, in 4 st. of 5 l. It is sometimes given as "Go forth on wings of *faith and* prayer," as in the *Bapt. Praise Bk.*, N. Y., 1871, No. 1252; but the alterations are so great as almost to constitute it a new hymn.
8. **Hail to the brightness of Zion's glad morning.** *Missionary Success.* No. 239, in 4 st. of 4 l. In several hymn-books in G. Britain and America.
9. **How calm and beautiful the morn.** *Easter.* No. 291, in 5 st. of 6 l. Very popular.
10. **In this calm, impressive hour.** *Early Morning.* No. 235, pt. i. in 3 st. of 6 l. In several collections.
11. **Jesus, save my dying soul.** *Lent.* No. 398, in 4 st. of 4 l. A deeply penitential hymn.
12. **Now be the gospel banner.** *Missions.* No. 178, in 2 st. of 8 l. In several collections (see below).
13. **Now from labour, and from care.** *Evening.* No. 235. Pt. ii. in 3 st. of 6 l. This hymn, with No. 10 above, "In this calm," &c., constitute one hymn of 6 st. in the *Spiritual Songs*, but divided into two parts, one for Morning and the other for Evening. Both parts are popular as separate hymns.
14. **O God of Abraham, hear.** *Prayer on behalf of Children.* No. 288, in 5 st. of 4 l. In use in G. Britain.
15. **O tell me, Thou Life and delight of my soul.** *Following the Good Shepherd.* No. 151, in 5 st. of 4 l., on Cant. i. 7, 8.
16. **Return, O wanderer, to thy home.** *The Prodigal recalled.* No. 183, in 3 st. of 4 l., with the refrain, "Return, return" (see below).
17. **Soft and holy is the place.** *Public Worship.* No. 351, in 4 st. of 4 l. In Dr. Hatfield's *Church H. Bk.*, N. Y., 1872, and some other collections, the opening line is altered to "*Sweet* and holy is the place."

13. That warning voice, O sinner, hear. *Exhortation to Repentance.* No. 231, in 4 st. of 6 l.

19. To-day the Saviour calls. *Lent.* No. 176, in 4 st. of 4 l. Dr. Hastings says, in a communication to Dr. Stevenson (*Hys. for Church and Home*, 1873), this hymn "was offered me in a hasty sketch which I retouched." The sketch was by the Rev. S. F. Smith.

20. Why that look of sadness. *Consolation.* No. 268, in 3 st. of 8 l.

21. Zion, dreary and in anguish. *The Church Comforted.* No. 160, in 4 st. of 4 l.

Concerning the two hymns, No. 12, "Now be the gospel banner"; and No. 16, "Return, O wanderer, to thy home," Dr. Stevenson has the following note in his *Hys. for Church and Home*, Lond., 1873:—

"In a letter to the Editor, Dr. Hastings wrote, not more than a fortnight before his death, 'These two hymns of mine were earlier compositions, the former ["Now be," &c.] for a Utica Sunday School celebration, the latter ["Return, O wanderer," &c.] after hearing a stirring revival sermon on the Prodigal Son, by the Rev. Mr. Kint, at a large union meeting in the Presbyterian Church, where two hundred converts were present. The preacher at the close eloquently exclaimed with tender emphasis, "Sinner, come home! come home! come home!" It was easy afterwards to write, "Return, O wanderer." ' "

Several additional hymns in the *Spiritual Songs*, 1831, have been ascribed to Dr. Hastings, but without confirmation. The sum of what can be said on his behalf is that the hymns are in his style, and that they have not been claimed by others. They are:—

22. Drooping souls, no longer mourn. *Pardon promised.* No. 40, in 3 st. of 8 l., of which st. i., ii. are altered from J. J. Harrod's *Public, Parlour, and Cottage Hymns*, Baltimore, 1823, that is, 8 years before the *Spiritual Songs* were published.

23. Dying souls, fast bound in sin. *Pardon offered.* No. 41, in 5 st. of 8 l. It is usually given in an abridged form.

ii. From his *Mother's Hymn Book*, 1834:—

24. Forbid them not, the Saviour cried. *Holy Baptism.* No. 44.

25. God of mercy, hear our prayer. *On behalf of Children*, No. 48, in 5 st. of 4 l. It was included in J. Campbell's *Comprehensive H. Bk.*, Lond., 1837, and subsequently in several collections.

26. God of the nations, bow Thine ear. *Missions.* No. 115, in 4 st. of 6 l. In several collections.

27. How tender is Thy hand. *Affliction.* No. 99, in 5 st. of 4 l.

28. Jesus, while our hearts are bleeding. *Death. Resignation.* No. 95, in 5 st. of 4 l. This is in extensive use and is one of his best and most popular hymns.

29. Lord, I would come to Thee. *Self-dedication of a Child.* No. 72, in 4 st. of 4 l.

30. O Lord, behold us at Thy feet. *Lent.* No. 59, in 4 st. of 4 l. It is doubtful if this is by Hastings. It is sometimes signed "Mrs. T."

31. The rosy light is dawning. *Morning.* No. 11, in 3 st. of 8 l.

32. The Saviour bids us [thee] watch and pray. *Watch and Pray.* No. 119, in 4 st. of 4 l.

33. Thou God of sovereign grace. *On behalf of Children.* No. 66, in 6 st. of 4 l.

34. Wherever two or three may meet. *Divine Service.* No. 56.

35. Within these quiet walls, O Lord. *Mothers' Meetings.* No. 58, in 5 st. of 4 l. In Spurgeon's *O. O. H. Bk.*, 1866, No. 1010, it begins, "Within these *peaceful* walls." This reading is from J. Campbell's *Comprehensive H. Bk.*, Lond., 1837. It is very doubtful if this is by Hastings.

iii. From the *Christian Psalmist*, 1836:—

36. Children, hear the melting story. *On the life of Christ.* No. 430, in 3 st. of 6 l. It is given as from the *Union Minstrel*, and the statement that it is by Hastings is very doubtful, and evidence to that effect being in the possession of his family. Dr. Hatfield, in his *Church H. Bk.*, dates it 1830, and gives it as "Anon."

37. Go, tune thy voice to sacred song. *Praise.* No. 190, in 5 st. of 5 l., and given as from "MS."

38. He that goeth forth with weeping. *Missions.* No. 212, in 2 st. of 8 l., and given as from "MS." It is in several collections.

39. I love the Lord, Whose gracious ear. *Ps. cxvi.* Page 186, in 4 st. of 6 l., as from "MS."

40. Lord of the harvest, bend Thine ear. *For the Increase of the Ministry.* No. 407, in 6 st. of 4 l., as from "MS." This hymn Dr. Hastings altered for his *Devotional Hys. & Poems*, 1850, but it has failed to replace the original in the hymn-books.

iv. From the Reformed Dutch *Additional Hymns*, 1846:—

41. Child of sorrow, child of care [woe]. *Trust.* No. 168, in 2 st. of 8 l.; appeared in W. Hunter's *Minstrel of Zion*, 1845.

42. Heirs of an immortal crown. *Christian Warfare.* No. 136, in 2 st. of 8 l.

43. O Saviour, lend a listening ear. *Lent.* No. 175. St. vi., i., iv., v., altered.

44. The Lord Jehovah lives. *Ps. xviii.* No. 26, in 4 st. of 6 l.

These three hymns, together with many others, are given in the Dutch Reformed *Hys. of the Church*, N. Y., 1869. In the 1847 *Ps. & Hymns* there were, including these, 38 hymns by Hastings, and 2 which are doubtful.

v. From Dr. Hastings's *Devotional Hymns and Religious Poems*, 1850:—

45. In time of fear, when trouble's near. *Encouragement in Trial.* Page 95, in 3 st. of 4 l. In use in G. Britain.

vi. From *Church Melodies*, 1858:—

46. For those in bonds as bound with them. *Missions.* No. 416, in 5 st. of 4 l., on Heb. xiii. 3.

47. Forget thyself, Christ bids thee come. *Holy Communion.* No. 683, in 3 st. of 6 l.

48. Jesus, Merciful and Mild. *Leaning on Christ.* No. 585, in 4 st. of 8 l. In several collections.

49. Pilgrims in this vale of sorrow. *Self-denial.* No. 397, in 4 st. of 4 l.

50. Saviour, I look to Thee. *Lent. In time of Trouble.* No. 129, in 4 st. of 7 l.

51. Saviour of our ruined race. *Holy Communion.* No. 379, in 3 st. of 6 l.

52. Why that soul's commotion? *Lent.* No. 211, in 3 st. of 8 l. It is doubtful if this is by Hastings.

vii. In Robinson's *Songs of the Church*, 1862:

53. Be tranquil, O my soul. *Patience in Affliction.* No. 519, in 4 st. of 4 l. Altered in Robinson's *Songs for the Sanctuary*, 1865.

54. Peace, peace, I leave with you. *Peace, the benediction of Christ.* No. 386, in 3 st. of 7 l.

55. Saviour, Thy gentle voice. *Christ All in All.* No. 492, in 3 st. of 7 l.

viii. In Robinson's *Songs for the Sanctuary*, 1865:—

56. God of the morning ray. *Morning.* No. 53, in 2 st. of 7 l.

Of Hastings's hymns about 40 are in the Reformed Dutch *Ps. & Hys.*, 1847; 39 in Robinson's *Songs for the Sanctuary*, 1865; 15 in Hatfield's *Church H. Bk.*, 1872; and 13 in the *Lyra Sac. Americana*, 1868. They are also largely represented in other collections. Many other of his compositions are found in collections now or recently in C. U., but these are not of the highest merit.   [F. M. B.]

Hatfield, Edwin Francis, D.D., was b. at Elizabethtown, New Jersey, Jan. 9, 1807, and educated at Middlebury College, Vermont, and at Andover. From 1832 to 1835 he was pastor of the 2nd Presbyterian Church, St. Louis. In 1835 he removed to New York, where he was at first pastor of 7th Presbyterian Church, and then of the North Presbyterian Church (1856–63) in the same city; and in

1864 he was appointed special agent to the Union Theological Seminary, New York. He also held from 1846 the appointment of Stated Clerk of the Presbyterian General Assembly. He d. at Summit, New Jersey, Sept. 22, 1883. His hymnological knowledge was extensive. His publications include:—

(1) *Freedom's Lyre; or, Psalms, Hymns, and Sacred Songs, for the Slave and his Friends*, N. Y., 1840, to which he contributed 24 hymns under the signature of "E. F. H."; (2) *The Church Hymn Book for the Worship of God*, N. Y., 1872, in which are 10 of his hymns; and (3) *Chapel Hymns*, N. Y., 1873. (4) *The Poets of the Church. Biographical Sketches of Hymn Writers, with Notes on their Hymns*, New York, 1884. This was a posthumous publication, and is far from being accurate.

His hymns and psalm versions in C. U. include:—

1. **Come, bless Jehovah's name.** (1837.) *Ps.* 134.
2. **Come, let us gladly sing.** (1837.) *Ps.* 95.
3. **Hallelujah, praise the Lord.** (1837.) *Ps.* 150.
4. **How perfect is Thy law.** (1837.) *Ps.* 19.
5. **How sweetly breaks the Sabbath dawn.** (1840.) *Sunday.*
6. **My Shepherd's name is love.** (1837.) *Ps.* 23·
7. **O sing hallelujah, praise ye the Lord.** (1837.) *Ps.* 146.
8. **Thee, Thee, we praise, O God, and now.** (1871.) A paraphrase of the *Te Deum.*
9. **'Tis Thine alone, Almighty Name.** (1872.) *Temperance.*
10. **Why, O God, Thy people spurn!** (1837.) *Ps.* 60.
11. **To God the Father, Son.** *Doxology.* In *Freedom's Lyre*, 1840. It is widely used.

These hymns and psalm versions are all in his *Church H. Bk.*, 1872, and the dates appended above are from that collection. No. 10 was pub. in his *Freedom's Lyre*, 1840, No. 25.   [F. M. B.]

Have faith in truth. *H. Bonar.* [*Faithfulness to truth.*] Appeared in the 2nd series of his *Hys. of Faith and Hope*, 1861, in 10 st. of 4 l. In Dale's *English H. Bk.*, 1874, it begins with st. ii., "Make sure of truth," and st. ix. is also omitted. It is a beautiful hymn, and should be more widely known.   [J. J.]

Have mercy, Lord, on me. *Tate & Brady.* [*Ps. li.*] This S.M. rendering of Ps. 51 was given in the *New Version*, 1698 (q.v.), in 17 st. of 4 l., divided into two parts, and is a good example of the renderings therein in that metre. [*Psalters, English,* § 13, γ.] As found in modern hymn-books in G. Britain and America it is given in an abbreviated form of three or more stanzas, and often with a doxology also from the N. Version. Few collections agree, however, in their selection of stanzas. The arrangement of stanzas as in *H. A. & M.*, 1875, is in more extensive use than any other.   [J. J.]

Have mercy on us, God Most High. *F. W. Faber.* [*Holy Trinity.*] 1st pub. in his *Jesus and Mary*, &c., 1849, in 11 st. of 4 l. and entitled, "The Most Holy Trinity." In addition to its being given in an abbreviated form in Roman Catholic collections, it is also in *H. A. & M*, 1861 and 1875, and other hymn-books. The arrangement in most extensive use is that of *H. A. & M.*, which is composed of st. i.-iii., v., and xi. In Allon's *Supplemental Hymns*, 1868, No. 3, is a cento by G. Rawson, part of which is from this hymn (specially st. i.-iii.), and the rest is by him, some of the lines being from his hymn,

"Transcendent mystery unknown," subsequently pub. in his *Hymns*, &c., 1876, p. 39 (see note on p. 40). The cento in Horder's *Cong. Hys.*, 1884, and others, begins with st. ii. of the original, "Most ancient of all mysteries."   [J. J.]

Have you ever brought a penny to the missionary box? *Emily E. S. Elliott.* [*Children's Mission Hymn.*] 1st pub. 1855, in the *Church Missionary Juvenile Instructor.* Included, slightly altered, as No. 19 of the Children's Hymns in Wilson's *Service of Praise*, 1865, in 6 st. of 4 l. In 1873, Dr. W. F. Stevenson included st. iii.-vi., beginning, "O how joyous is the music of the missionary song," in his *H. for Church and Home;* and this was repeated in Wilson's *Songs of Zion*, 1878, and in Allon's *Children's Worship*, 1878. In the latter it begins, "O joyous is the music."   [J. M.]

Havergal, Frances Ridley, daughter of the Rev. W. H. Havergal, was b. at Astley, Worcestershire, Dec. 14, 1836. Five years later her father removed to the Rectory of St. Nicholas, Worcester. In August, 1850, she entered Mrs. Teed's school, whose influence over her was most beneficial. In the following year she says, "I committed my soul to the Saviour, and earth and heaven seemed brighter from that moment." A short sojourn in Germany followed, and on her return she was confirmed in Worcester Cathedral, July 17, 1853. In 1860 she left Worcester on her father resigning the Rectory of St. Nicholas, and resided at different periods in Leamington, and at Caswall Bay, Swansea, broken by visits to Switzerland, Scotland, and North Wales. She d. at Caswall Bay, Swansea, June 3, 1879.

Miss Havergal's scholastic acquirements were extensive, embracing several modern languages, together with Greek and Hebrew. She does not occupy, and did not claim for herself, a prominent place as a poet, but by her distinct individuality she carved out a niche which she alone could fill. Simply and sweetly she sang the love of God, and His way of salvation. To this end, and for this object, her whole life and all her powers were consecrated. She lives and speaks in every line of her poetry. Her poems are permeated with the fragrance of her passionate love of Jesus.

Her religious views and theological bias are distinctly set forth in her poems, and may be described as mildly Calvinistic, without the severe dogmatic tenet of reprobation. The burden of her writings is a free and full salvation, through the Redeemer's merits, for every sinner who will receive it, and her life was devoted to the proclamation of this truth by personal labours, literary efforts, and earnest interest in Foreign Missions.   [J. D.]

Miss Havergal's hymns were frequently printed by J. & R. Parlane as leaflets, and by Caswell & Co. as ornamental cards. They were gathered together from time to time and published in her works as follows:—

(1) *Ministry of Song*, 1869; (2) *Twelve Sacred Songs for Little Singers*, 1870; (3) *Under the Surface*, 1874; (4) *Loyal Responses*, 1878; (5) *Life Mosaic*, 1879; (6) *Life Chords*, 1880; (7) *Life Echoes*, 1883.

About 15 of the more important of Miss Havergal's hymns, including "Golden harps are sounding," "I gave my life for thee," "Jesus, Master, Whose I am," "Lord, speak to me," "O Master, at Thy feet," "Take my life and let it be," "Tell it out among the heathen," &c., are annotated under their respective first lines. The rest, which are in C. U., number nearly 50. These we give, together with dates and places of composition, from the *Havergal* MSS., and the works in which they were published. Those, and they are many, which were printed in *Parlane's Series of Leaflets* are distinguished as (*P.*, 1872, &c.), and those in *Caswell's* series (*C.*, 1873, &c.).

1. **A happy New Year! Even such may it be.** *New Year.* From *Under the Surface*, 1874.

2. **Certainly I will be with thee.** *Birthday.* Sept. 1871, at Perry Barr. (*P.* 1871.) Pub. in *Under the Surface*, 1874, and *Life Mosaic*, 1879.

3. **Church of God, beloved and chosen.** *Sanctified in Christ Jesus.* 1873. (*P.* 1873.) Pub. in *Under the Surface*, 1874, and *L. Mosaic*, 1879.

4. **God Almighty, King of nations.** *Sovereignty of God.* 1872. Pub. in *Under the Surface*, 1874, and *L. Mosaic*, 1870.

5. **God doth not bid thee wait.** *God faithful to His promises.* Oct. 22, 1868, at Oakhampton. (*P.* 1869.) Pub. in *Ministry of Song*, 1869, and *L. Mosaic*, 1879.

6. **God of heaven, hear our singing.** *A Child's hymn for Missions.* Oct. 22, 1869, at Leamington. Pub. in her *Twelve Sacred Songs for Little Singers*, 1870, and her *Life Chords*, 1880.

7. **God will take care of you, All through the day.** *The Good Shepherd.* In Mrs. Brock's *Children's H. Bk.*, 1881.

8. **God's reiterated all.** *New Year.* 1873, at Winterdyne. (*C.* 1873.) Pub. in *Loyal Responses*, 1878, and *L. Mosaic*, 1879.

9. **Have you not a word for Jesus?** *Boldness for the Truth.* Nov. 1871, at Perry Barr. (*P.* 1872.) Pub. in *Under the Surface*, 1874, and *L. Mosaic*, 1879.

10. **He hath spoken in the darkness.** *Voice of God in sorrow.* June 10, 1869, at Neuhausen. (*P.* 1870.) Pub. in *Under the Surface*, 1874, and in *L. Mosaic*, 1879.

11. **Hear the Father's ancient promise.** *Promise of the Holy Spirit.* Aug. 1870. Pub. in *Under the Surface*, 1874, and *L. Mosaic*, 1879.

12. **Holy and Infinite! Viewless, Eternal.** *Infinity of God.* 1872. Pub. in *Under the Surface*, 1874, and *L. Mosaic*, 1879.

13. **Holy brethren, called and chosen.** *Election a motive for Earnestness.* 1872. Pub. in Snepp's *Songs of G. & G.*, 1876.

14. **I am trusting Thee, Lord Jesus.** *Faith.* Sept. 1874, at Ormont Dessous. (*P.* 1874.) Pub. in *Loyal Responses*, 1878, and *Life Chords*, 1880. Miss Havergal's tune, *Urbane* (Snepp's *S. of G. & G.*, 1048), was composed for this hymn. The hymn was the author's "own favourite," and was found in her pocket Bible after her death.

15. **I bring my sins to Thee.** *Resting all on Jesus.* June, 1870. (*P.* 1870.) Printed in the *Sunday Magazine*, 1870, and *Home Words*, 1872. Pub. in *Under the Surface*, 1874, and *Life Chords*, 1880.

16. **I could not do without Thee.** *Jesus All in All.* May 7, 1873. (*P.* 1873.) Printed in *Home Words*, 1873, and pub. in *Under the Surface*, 1874, and *L. Mosaic*, 1879.

17. **In full and glad surrender.** *Confirmation.* Miss Havergal's sister says this hymn was "The epitome of her [Miss F. R. H.'s] life and the focus of its sunshine." It is a beautiful hymn of personal consecration to God at all times.

18. **In the evening there is weeping.** *Sorrow followed by Joy.* June 19, 1869, at the Hotel Jungfrau-blick, Interlaken. "It rained all day, except a very bright interval before dinner. Curious long soft white clouds went slowly creeping along the Scheinige Platte; I wrote 'Ev-ning Tears and Morning Songs.' (Marg. reading of Ps. xxx. 5.)" (*P.* 1870.) Pub. in *Under the Surface*, 1874.

19. **Increase our faith, beloved Lord.** *Increase of Faith desired.* In *Loyal Responses*, 1878, in 11 st. of 4 l., on St. Luke xvii. 5. It is usually given in an abridged form.

20. **Is it for me, dear Saviour?** *Heaven anticipated.* Nov. 1871, at Perry Barr. (*P.* 1872.) Pub. in *Under the Surface*, 1874, and *L. Mosaic*, 1879.

21. **Israel of God, awaken.** *Christ our Righteousness.* May, 1871, at Perry Barr. (*P.* 1872.) Pub. in *Under the Surface*, 1874, and *L. Mosaic*, 1879.

22. **Jehovah's covenant shall endure.** *The Divine Covenant.* 1872. Pub. in Snepp's *Songs of G. & G.*, 1876.

23. **Jesus, blessed Saviour.** *New Year.* Nov. 25,

1872, at Leamington. (*P.* 1873.) Printed in the *Day-spring Magazine*, Jan. 1873, and pub. in *Life Chords*, 1880.

24. **Jesus only! In the shadow.** *Jesus All in All.* Dec. 4, 1870, at Pyrmont Villa. (*P. & C.* 1871.) Pub. in *Under the Surface*, 1874, and in *L. Mosaic*, 1879.

25. **Joined to Christ by [in] mystic union.** *The Church the Body of Christ.* May, 1871, at Perry Barr. (*P.* 1872.) Pub. in *Under the Surface*, 1874, *L. Mosaic*, 1879.

26. **Just when Thou wilt, O Master, call.** *Resignation.* In *Loyal Responses*, 1878, in 5 st. of 4 l., and Whiting's *Hys. for the Church Catholic*, 1882.

27. **King Eternal and Immortal.** *God Eternal.* Written at Perry Villa, Perry Barr, Feb. 11, 1871, and pub. in Snepp's *Songs of G. & G.*, 1876; *Under the Surface*, 1874; and *Life Mosaic*, 1879.

28. **Light after darkness, Gain after loss.** *Peace in Jesus, and the Divine Reward.* In Sankey's *Sac. Songs and Solos*, from her *Life Mosaic*, 1879.

29. **Like a river glorious, Is God's perfect Peace.** *Peace.* In her *Loyal Responses*, 1878, in 3 st. of 8 l., with the chorus, "Stayed upon Jehovah." In several collections.

30. **Master, speak! Thy servant heareth.** *Fellowship with and Assistance from Christ desired.* Sunday evening, May 19, 1867, at Weston-super-Mare. Pub. in *Ministry of Song*, 1869, and *L. Mosaic*, 1879. It is very popular.

31. **New mercies, new blessings, new light on thy way.** *New Life in Christ.* 1874, at Winterdyne. (*C.* 1874.) Pub. in *Under His Shadow*, 1879, *Life Chords*, 1880.

32. **Not your own, but His ye are.** *Missions.* Jan. 21, 1867. (*C.* 1867.) Pub. in *Ministry of Song*, 1869; *L. Mosaic*, 1879; and the *Hyl. for Church Missions*, 1884.

33. **Now let us sing the angels' song.** *Christmas.* In her *Life Mosaic*, 1879; and W. R. Stevenson's *School Hymnal*, 1880.

34. **Now the daylight goes away.** *Evening.* Oct. 17, 1869, at Leamington. Pub. in *Songs for Little Singers*, 1870, and *Life Chords*, 1880. It originally read, "Now the light has gone away."

35. **Now the sowing and the weeping.** *Sorrow followed by Joy.* Jan. 4, 1870, at Leamington. Printed in *Sunday at Home*, 1870; and pub. in *Under the Surface*, 1874, and *L. Mosaic*, 1879.

36. **O Glorious God and King.** *Praise to the Father.* Feb. 1872. Pub. in *Under the Surface*, 1874, and *L. Mosaic*, 1879.

37. **O Saviour, precious [holy] Saviour.** *Christ worshipped by the Church.* Nov. 1870, at Leamington. (*P.* 1870.) Pub. in *Under the Surface*, 1874, and *L. Mosaic*, 1879.

38. **O thou chosen Church of Jesus.** *Election.* April 6, 1871. Pub. in *Under the Surface*, 1874, and *L. Mosaic*, 1879.

39. **O what everlasting blessings God outpoureth on His own.** *Salvation everlasting.* Aug. 12, 1871, at Perry Barr. (*P.* 1871.) Pub. in *Under the Surface*, 1874, and *L. Mosaic*, 1879.

40. **Our Father, our Father, Who dwellest in light.** *The blessing of the Father desired.* May 14, 1872. Pub. in *Under the Surface*, 1874, and *L. Mosaic*, 1879. Miss Havergal's tune, *Tertius*, was composed for this hymn.

41. **Our Saviour and our King.** *Presentation of the Church to the Father.* (Heb. ii. 13.) May, 1871, at Perry Barr. (*P.* 1871.) Pub. in *Under the Surface*, 1874, and *L. Mosaic*, 1879.

42. **Precious, precious blood of Jesus.** *The precious Blood.* Sept. 1874, at Ormont Dessous. (*C.*) Pub. in *Loyal Responses*, 1878, and *Life Chords*, 1880.

43. **Sing, O heavens, the Lord hath done it.** *Redemption.* In her *Life Mosaic*, 1879, and the *Universal H. Bk.*, 1885.

44. **Sit down beneath His shadow.** *Holy Communion.* Nov. 27, 1870, at Leamington. (*P.* 1870.) Pub. in *Under the Surface*, 1874, and *L. Mosaic*, 1879.

45. **Sovereign Lord and gracious Master.** *Grace consummated in Glory.* Oct. 22, 1871. (*P.* 1872.) Pub. in *Under the Surface*, 1874, and *L. Mosaic*, 1879.

46. **Standing at the portal of the opening year.** *New Year.* Jan. 4, 1873. Pub. in *Under the Surface*, 1874, and *Life Chords*, 1880.

47. **To Thee, O Comforter divine.** *Praise to the Holy Spirit.* Aug. 11, 1872, at Perry Barr. Pub. in *Under the Surface*, 1874, and *L. Mosaic*, 1879. Miss Havergal's tune, *Tryphosa*, was written for this hymn.

48. True-hearted, whole-hearted, faithful and loyal. *Faithfulness to the Saviour.* In her *Loyal Responses*, 1878, and the *Universal H. Bk.*, 1885.

49. What know we, Holy God, of Thee? *God's Spirituality*, 1872. Pub. in *Under the Surface*, 1874, and *Life Mosaic*, 1879.

50. Who is on the Lord's side? *Home Missions.* Oct. 13, 1877. Pub. in *Loyal Responses*, 1878, and *Life Chords*, 1880.

51. With quivering heart and trembling will. *Resignation.* July, 10, 1866, at Luccombe Rectory. (*P.* 1866.) Pub. in *Ministry of Song*, 1869, and *L. Mosaic*, 1879.

52. Will ye not come to Him for life? *The Gospel Invitation.* 1873. Pub. in Snepp's *Songs of G. & G.*, 1876.

53. Worthy of all adoration. *Praise to Jesus as the Lamb upon the throne.* Feb. 26, 1867, at Oakhampton. Pub. in *Ministry of Song*, 1869, and *L. Mosaic*, 1874. It is pt. iii. of the "Threefold Praise," and was suggested by the "*Worthy is the Lamb,*" the "*Hallelujah*" and "*Amen*" choruses in Handel's *Messiah*.

54. Ye who hear the blessed call. *The Invitation of the Spirit and the Bride.* March, 1869, at Leamington. (*P.* 1869.) Pub. in *Ministry of Song*, 1869, and *Life Mosaic*, 1879. Suggested by, and written for, the Young Men's Christian Association.

55. Yes, He knows the way is dreary. *Encouragement.* 1867. Pub. in *Ministry of Song*, 1869.

Most of these hymns are given in Snepp's *Songs of Grace and Glory*, 1872 and 1876, his *Appendix*, 1874, and the Musical ed., 1880, and many of them are also in several other hymn-books, including *H. A. & M., Thring, Church Hys., Hy. Comp.*, &c., and some of the leading American collections.   [J. J.]

Havergal, William Henry, M.A., s. of William Havergal, was b. at High Wycombe, Buckinghamshire, 1793, and was educated at St. Edmund's Hall, Oxford (B.A. 1815, M.A. 1819). On taking Holy Orders he became in 1829 Rector of Astley, Worcestershire; in 1842, Rector of St. Nicholas, Worcester; and in 1860, Rector of Shareshill, near Wolverhampton. He was also Hon. Canon in Worcester Cathedral from 1845. He d. April 18, 1870. His hymns, about 100 in all, were in many instances written for special services in his own church, and printed as leaflets. Several were included in W. Carus Wilson's *Bk. of General Psalmody*, 1840 (2nd ed., 1842); and in *Metrical Ps. & Hys. for Singing in Churches*, Worcester, Deighton, 1849, commonly known as the *Worcester Diocesan H. Bk.*, and of which he was the Editor. In *Life Echoes*, 1883, his hymns are given with those of Miss Havergal. Of those in C. U. the greater part are in *Mercer*, and Snepp's *Songs of G. & G.* Although his hymns are all good, and two or three are excellent, it is not as a hymn-writer but as a musician that Canon Havergal is best known. His musical works and compositions included, in addition to numerous individual hymn tunes and chants, the Gresham Prize Service, 1836; the Gresham Prize Anthem, 1845; *Old Church Psalmody*, 1849; *History of the Old 100th Psalm tune*, 1854, &c. He also reprinted *Ravenscroft's Psalter* of 1611. His hymns in C. U. include:—

1. Blessed Jesus, Lord and Brother. *School Festivals*, 1833. Pub. in *Life Echoes*, 1883.

2. Brighter than meridian splendour. *Christ the glory of His Church.* 1830. Pub. in W. C. Wilson's *Bk. of General Ps.*, 1840; the Worcester *Ps. & Hys.*, 1849, &c.

3. Christians, awake to joy and praise. *Christmas Carol.* c. 1860. Printed on broadsheet, with music by the author, and sold on behalf of the Lancashire Cotton Distress Fund.

4. Come, Shepherds, come, 'tis just a year. *Christmas Carol.* 1860. Pub. in Snepp's *Songs of G. & G.*, 1872.

5. For ever and for ever, Lord. *Missions*, 1866, for the Church Miss. Soc. Pub. in Snepp's *S. of G. & G.*, 1872, and the *Life Echoes*, 1883.

6. Hallelujah, Lord, our voices. *Sunday.* 1828. Pub. in W. C. Wilson's *Bk. of General Ps.*, 1840; the Worcester *Ps. & Hys.*, 1849; *Life Echoes*, 1883, &c.

7. Heralds of the Lord of glory. *Missions.* First sung in Astley Church, Sep. 23, 1827. Pub. in Miss Havergal's *Starlight through the Shadows*, 1880; Snepp's *S. of G. & G.*, 1872, &c.

8. Hosanna, raise the pealing hymn. *Praise to Christ*, 1833, and 1st sung in Astley Church, June 9, 1833. Pub. in W. C. Wilson's *Bk. of General Psalmody*, 1840; the Worcester *Ps. & Hys.*, 1849; *Life Echoes*, 1883, &c.

9. How vast the field of souls. *Missions.* 1858. Printed for Shareshill Church Miss. Anniversary, 1863, and pub. in Snepp's *S. of G. & G.*, 1872, and the *Life Echoes*, 1883.

10. In doubt and dread dismay. *Missions.* Written in 1837, and pub. in W. C. Wilson's *Bk. of General Psalmody*, 1840; the Worcester *Ps. & Hys.*, 1849, &c.

11. Jerusalem the golden, The home of saints shall be. *Heaven.* Pub. in *Life Echoes*, 1883.

12. My times are in Thy hand, Their best, &c. 1860. Pub. in Snepp's *S. of G. & G.*, 1872, the *Records of the author's life and work*, and *Life Echoes*, 1883. The editor of the *Records* says (p. 159) "this hymn has been much appreciated, and well illustrates the devotional and cheerful spirit of the writer."

13. No dawn of holy light. *Sunday.* 1825. Printed in 1831 on a leaflet, and pub. in W. C. Wilson's *Bk. of General Psalmody*, 1840; the Worcester *Ps. & Hys.*, 1849; *Life Echoes*, 1883, &c.

14. Our faithful God hath sent us. *Harvest.* Written at Shareshill in 1863, for a Harvest Festival. Pub. in Snepp's *S. of G. & G.*, 1872, and *Life Echoes*, 1883.

15. Shout, O earth! from silence waking. *Praise to Jesus for Redemption.* 1841. Pub. in the Worcester *Ps. & Hys.*, 1849; Snepp's *S. of G. & G.*, 1872, &c.

16. So happy all the day. *Christmas Carol.* c. 1834. Pub. in Snepp's *S. of G. & G.*, 1872.

17. Soon the trumpet of salvation. *Missions.* 1826. Pub. in Snepp's *S. of G. & G.*, 1872.

18. To praise our Shepherd's [Saviour's] care. *The Good Shepherd.* Written after witnessing the death of Elizabeth Edwards, aged 12, of St. Nicholas, Worcester, and printed as a leaflet. Pub. in W. C. Wilson's *Bk. of General Psalmody*, 1840; the Worcester *Ps. & Hys.*, 1849; *Life Echoes*, &c., 1883. The author also pub. a *Memoir* of the child.

19. Widely 'midst the slumbering nations. *Missions.* 1828. Pub. in the Worcester *Ps. & Hys.*, 1849; Snepp's *S. of G. & G.*, 1872, &c.

In addition to these hymns, his carols, "How grand, and how bright," "Our festal morn is come," and others are annotated under their respective first lines. Most of these carols and hymns were reprinted in *Christmas Carols & Sacred Songs, Chiefly by the Rev. W. H. Havergal*, Lond., Nisbet, 1869.   [J. J.]

Haweis, Thomas, LL.B., M.D., b. at Truro, Cornwall, 1732. After practising for a time as a Physician, he entered Christ's College, Cambridge, where he graduated. Taking Holy Orders, he became Assistant Preacher to M. Madan at the Lock Hospital, London, and subsequently Rector of All Saints, Aldwincle, Northamptonshire. He was also Chaplain to Lady Huntingdon, and for several years officiated at her Chapel in Bath. He d. at Bath, Feb. 11, 1820. He published several prose works, including *A History of the Church, A Translation of the New Testament,* and *A Commentary on the Holy Bible*. His hymns, a few of which are of more than ordinary merit, were pub. in his

Carmina Christo; or, Hymns to the Saviour. Designed for the Use and Comfort of Those who worship the Lamb that was slain. Bath, S. Hayward, 1792 (139

hymns), enlarged. London, 1808 (256 hymns). In 1794, or sometime after, but before the enlarged edition was pub., two hymns "For the Fast-day, Feb. 28, 1794," were added to the 1st ed. These were, "Big with events, another year," and "Still o'er the deep the cannon's roar."

The most popular and widely used of his hymns are, "Behold the Lamb of God, Who bore," &c.; "Enthroned on high, Almighty Lord"; and "O Thou from Whom all goodness flows." The rest, all being from *Carmina Christo*, 1st ed. 1792, are :—

1. Dark was the night and cold the ground. *Gethsemane.*
2. From the cross uplifted high. *Christ in Glory.*
3. Great Spirit, by Whose mighty power. *Whitsuntide.*
4. Submissive to Thy will, my God. *Resignation.*
5. The happy morn is come. *Easter.*
6. Thou Lamb of God, that on the tree, *Good Friday.* The hymn, "Thy Head, the crown of thorns that wears," in Stryker & Main's *Church Praise Bk.,* N. Y., 1882, begins with st. ii. of this hymn.
7. To Thee, my God and Saviour, My heart, &c. *Praise for Redemption.*　　　　　　　　[J. J.]

Hawker, Robert, M.D., was b. at Exeter in 1753, and educated for the medical profession. In 1778 he took Holy Orders, and in 1784 became Incumbent of Charles the Martyr Church in Plymouth, where he remained until his death, on April 6, 1827. Dr. Hawker was well known as a controversial and theological writer. His name is also associated with hymns, especially "Lord dismiss us with Thy blessing," and a few others. He pub. :—

Psalms and Hymns sung by the Children of the Sunday School, in the Parish Church of Charles, Plymouth, at the Sabbath Evening Lecture, N.D. [c. 1787].

This collection is noticeable as having been one of the first hymn-books published in connection with the Sunday School movement. It had some slight influence on later collections [Children's Hymns, § iii.]. He also pub. in pamphlet form :—

The Abba, Amen, and Corpus Christi Hymns. By Dr. Hawker, London : A. A. Paris, 1818.

These hymns, which are accompanied by passages of Holy Scripture, are :—

1. Abba, Father! Lord we call Thee. *God the Father.*
2. We bless Thee, O Thou great Amen! *Amen.*
3. When first at God's command. *The Church of Christ.*　　　　　　　　[J. J.]

Hawker, Robert Stephen, M.A., grandson of Dr. Robert Hawker, was b. at Plymouth, Dec. 3, 1804, and educated at Pembroke College, Oxford (B.A. 1828, M.A. 1836). On taking Holy Orders in 1829, he became Curate of Wellcombe, Devon, and in 1834 Vicar of Morwenstow, Cornwall. He d. at Morwenstow, Aug. 15, 1873, having been received into the Roman Catholic communion the previous evening. He pub. several poetical works, including *Ecclesia,* 1840, in which some of his hymns appeared. Hymns by him were also pub. in *Lyra Messianica,* 1864. His "Child Jesus, a Cornish Carol," beginning, "Welcome, that star in Judah's sky," appeared in both these works. Very few of his hymns are in C. U.　　　　　[J. J.]

Hawkesworth, John, LL.D. (b. 1715, and d. Nov. 1773), a writer in the *Gentleman's Magazine,* proprietor and editor of the *Adventurer,* and friend of Johnson, Warton, and other literary men of note, pub., in 1760, *Poems and Translations,* and was the author of the well-known *Morning hymn* "In sleep's

serene oblivion laid." This hymn was composed in 1773, "about a month before his death, in a wakeful hour of the night, and dictated to his wife on rising. It appeared in the *Universal Theological Magazine* for March, 1802." (Miller's *Singers & Songs,* &c., p. 210.) It was given in Collyer's *Sel.,* 1812; the *Leeds H. Bk.,* 1853; and others; and is in somewhat extensive use in America. It sometimes begins, as in the American Unitarian *Hys. for the Church of Christ,* 1853, with st. ii., "New born, I bless the waking hour." [J. J.]

Hawkins, Ernest, B.D., s. of Major Hawkins, b. Jan. 25, 1802, at Hitchin, and educated at Balliol College, Oxford (B.A. 1842). He was for sometime a Fellow of Exeter College. On taking Holy Orders he became Curate of Burwash, sub-librarian of the Bodleian Library, Curate of St. George's, Bloomsbury, Minister of Curzon Chapel, Mayfair, London, Prebendary of St. Paul's, and Canon of Westminster. From 1838 to his death, Oct. 5, 1866, he also acted as secretary to the S.P.G. Besides his prose works, which were not numerous, he pub. *Verses in commemoration of the Third Jubilee of the S.P.G.,* 1851-2. To this little collection his hymns were contributed. The most extensively used of these, "Lord, a Saviour's love displaying" (*Missions*), has been adopted by many collections.　　　　　　　　[J. J.]

Hawks, Annie Sherwood. Mrs. Hawks was b. in Horsick, N. Y., May 28, 1835, and has resided for many years at Brooklyn. Her hymns were contributed to *Bright Jewels, Pure Gold, Royal Diadem, Brightest and Best, Temple Anthems, Tidal Wave,* and other popular Sunday School hymn-books. They include "I need Thee every hour" (written April, 1872), "Thine, most gracious Lord," "Why weepest thou? Whom seekest thou?" and others of the same type. [J. J.]

Hayn, Henriette Luise von, dau. of Georg Heinrich von Hayn, master of the hounds to the Duke of Nassau, was b. at Idstein, Nassau, May 22, 1724. In 1746 she was formally received into the Moravian community at Herrnhaag. There, and, after the dissolution of this community, at Grosshennersdorf, and, after 1751 at Herrnhut, she was engaged as teacher in the Girls' School; and after 1766 in caring for the invalid sisters of the community. She d. at Herrnhut, Aug. 27, 1782. (*Koch,* vi. 443–447; *Allg. Deutsche Biog.,* xi. 158, &c.) She was a gifted hymn-writer. A fervent love to Christ pervades her productions; and they are remarkably free from the unpleasant sentimentalism and that dwelling on the physical details of our Lord's Passion which mars so many of the Moravian hymns of that period. Over 40 hymns or portions of hymns by her are included in the *Brüder G. B.* of 1778. Only one has come into English use outside the Moravian hymn-books, viz. :—

Weil ich Jesu Schäflein bin. *Children.* This beautiful hymn for children, regarded as Lambs of the Good Shepherd, first appeared in the *Brüder G. B.,* 1778, No. 1179, in 3 st. of 6 l. It has been included in many recent German collections, as the Berlin *G. L. S.,* ed. 1863, No. 120. *Tr.* as :—

1. Jesus makes my heart rejoice, in full, by F. W. Foster and J. Miller, as No. 576 in the *Moravian H. Bk.*, 1789 (1886, No. 1006). Included, from the ed. of 1826, in Dr. Pagenstecher's *Coll.*, 1864, and others.

2. Seeing I am Jesus' lamb, a good and full *tr.* by Miss Winkworth in her *Lyra Ger.*, 2nd Ser., 1858, p. 90. Repeated in the *People's E.*, 1867, *Bk. of Praise for Children*, 1881, and in America in the Pennsylvania Luth. *Ch. Bk.*, 1868, &c.

3. I am Jesus' little lamb, a good and full *tr.* by Dr. W. F. Stevenson for his *H. for Ch. & Home*, 1873, c. 58, dated 1871. Repeated in Allon's *Children's Worship*, 1878, the *Methodist S. S. H. Bk.*, 1883, and others.

Another tr. is : "Since I'm Jesus' sheep I am," by R. Massie, in the *Day of Rest*, 1880, p. 622.   [J. M.]

He cometh, on yon hallowed Board. *Cecil F. Alexander.* [*Holy Communion.*] Appeared in *Lyra Anglicana*, 1865, p. 149, in two parts, pt. i. beginning as above, and pt. ii. as "O Jesu, bruised and wounded more," the second part having previously appeared in Mrs. Alexander's *Legend of the Golden Prayers*, &c., 1859. Pt. i. is given in the 1874 *Appendix* to Snepp's *Songs of G. & G.*, No. 1088, as "He cometh as the Bridegroom comes."   [J. J.]

He dies! the Heavenly Lover dies. *I. Watts.* [*Passiontide.*] 1st pub. in his *Horæ Lyricæ*, 2nd ed., 1709, in 6 st. of 4 l., and headed, "Christ Dying, Rising, and Reigning." In 1753, J. Wesley reprinted it in full, and without alteration, in his *Select Hys. for the Use of Christians of all Denominations*, 1753 ; and it was also adopted by others. The popular form of the text is that given to it by M. Madan in his *Ps. & Hys.*, 1760, No. 114, which reads (the italics being Madan's alterations) :—

He dies ! *the Friend of Sinners* dies !
Lo ! Salem's daughters weep around !
A solemn darkness veils the skies ;
A sudden trembling shakes the ground ;
Come saints and drop a tear or two,
For Him who groan'd beneath your load ;
He shed a thousand drops for you,
A thousand drops of richer blood !

Here's love and grief beyond degree,
The Lord of glory dies for men !
But lo ! what sudden joys *we see* !
Jesus, the dead, revives again !
The rising God forsakes the tomb !
(*The tomb in vain forbids His rise!*)
Cherubic legions guard Him home,
And shout Him welcome to the skies !

Break off your tears ye saints, and tell
How high our great Deliverer reigns !
Sing how He spoil'd the hosts of hell,
And led the monster death in chains !
Say "Live for ever, wond'rous King !
Born to redeem ! and strong to save " !
Then ask the monster, " Where's thy sting,
And where's thy Victory, boasting grave."

This text was repeated, with slight variations, by A. M. Toplady, in his *Ps. & Hys.*, 1776, No. 185, and also by other and later editors, and is, with the change of a word here and there, the received text of the hymn in G. Britain and America.

Miller (*Singers & Songs of the Ch.*, 1869), Stevenson (*Methodist H. Bk. Notes*, 1883), and others state that the foregoing alterations were made by J. Wesley. Wesley, however, did not include the hymn in the *Wes. H. Bk.* in 1780 in any form whatever. It was added, as altered by M. Madan, to the *Wes. H. Bk.* by the Wesleyan Conference in 1800 (i.e. nine

years after Wesley's death), and must have been taken from Madan's *Ps. & Hys.* of 1760, or some other collections which had copied from Madan. Wesley made use of the original text in 1753 (as above) ; but there is no evidence to show that he ever countenanced Madan's alterations, much less claimed them as his own.

Another altered version of this hymn appeared as, " He dies ! the Man of, Sorrows dies," in Hall's *Mitre*, 1836, and is repeated in several modern collections.   [J. J.]

He filled the cup with wine, and said. *Bp. E. H. Bickersteth.* [*Holy Communion.*] Written in 1850, and pub. in his *Ps. & Hys.*, 1858, in 6 st. of 4 l. In 1863 it was given in *Kennedy*, and later in the *New Cong.* and other collections. In the author's *Two Brothers and other Poems*, 1872, p. 251, it appeared in a new form as, "The hour is come ; the feast is spread." This revision was made for the *H. Comp.*, 1870. In the annotated ed. of the same Bp. Bickersteth says :—

"This hymn for the Holy Communion, by the Editor, has been revised for this work. He ventures to include it, as touching on one aspect of the Lord's Supper, not usually alluded to in sacramental hymns, viz., Matt. xxvi. 29."   [J. J.]

He has come! the Christ of God. *H. Bonar.* [*Christmas.*] Appeared in the 1st series of his *Hys. of Faith and Hope*, 1857, in 6 st. of 4 l., and headed "A Bethlehem Hymn," with the motto "Mundum implens in praesepio jacens," *Augustine.* In its full, or in an abridged form, it is in several collections in G. Britain and America.   [J. J.]

He is coming, He is coming, Not as once, &c. *Cecil F. Alexander, née Humphreys.* [*Advent.*] 1st pub. in her *Hys. Descriptive and Devotional*, 1858, No. v., in 8 st. of 4 l. It has passed into several collections in G. Britain and America, and is increasing in popularity.   [J. J.]

He is gone—Beyond the skies. *A. P. Stanley.* [*Ascension.*] In a note to this hymn given in his *Christ in Song*, 1870, p. 261, Dr. Schaff says concerning it :—

"It is here given complete from a ms. copy kindly furnished by the author to the editor, on Ascension Day, May 6, 1869. The Dean informs me that this hymn ' was written about ten years ago (1859), at the request of a friend, whose children had complained to him that there was no suitable hymn for Ascension Day, and who were eagerly asking what had been the feelings of the disciples after that event.' "

It first appeared in *Macmillan's Magazine* for June, 1862 (vol. vi. p. 153), and was signed "A. P. S." In the *Westminster Abbey H. Bk.*, 1883, it is given in full in 7 st. of 8 l. It has also furnished the following centos which are in C. U. :—

1. **He is gone—A cloud of light.** In the Bap. *Ps. & Hys. Suppl.*, 1880.
2. **He is gone—A cloud of light.** This revised and abbreviated version was given with the author's consent, in the Chapel Royal, Savoy, *Hymnary Appx.*, 1870, and repeated in the S. P. C. K. *Church Hys.* and other collections.
3. **He is gone—and we remain.** In Alford's *Year of Praise*, 1867, and also several American hymn-books.
4. **He is gone—Towards their goal.** In the *Wellington Coll. Chapel Hys.*, 1880.
5. **He is gone—we heard Him say.** In the Oberlin *Manual of Praise*, 1880.

Taken in these various forms, the use of this hymn is extensive.   [J. J.]

He is risen! He is risen! Tell it with a joyful sound. *Cecil F. Alexander, née Humphreys.* [*Easter.*] 1st pub. in her *Verses for Holy Seasons*, 1846, in 5 st. of 6 l. It is given in several collections, and sometimes as "Christ is risen! Christ is risen!" &c., as in the *Hys. for the Church Catholic*, 1882.   [J. J.]

He lives! the great Redeemer lives. *Anne Steele.* [*Easter.*] 1st pub. in her *Poems on Subjects chiefly Devotional*, 1760, vol. i. p. 64, in 5 st. of 4 l. and entitled, "The Intercession of Christ," and in Sedgwick's reprint of her *Hymns*, 1863, p. 40. It passed into the Nonconformist collections through Rippon's *Sel.*, 1787; and into those of the Ch. of England through Toplady's *Ps. & Hys.*, 2nd ed. 1787. It is one of the most popular of the author's hymns, and is in extensive use, especially in America.   [J. J.]

He sendeth sun, He sendeth shower. *Sarah Adams, née Flower.* [*Resignation.*] Contributed to and 1st pub. in W. J. Fox's *Hys. and Anthems*, 1841, No. 101, in 3 st. of 6 l. It is in extensive use, especially in America. Sometimes it is given as "God sendeth sun, He sendeth shower," as in the *Leeds H. Bk.*, 1853, and other collections.
[J. J.]

He that is down needs fear no fall. *J. Bunyan.* [*Humility.*] This hymn was given in Bunyan's *Pilgrim's Progress*, 1684, Pt. ii., as the Shepherd Boy's song heard by Great-heart, Christiana, and the rest of the pilgrims in the Valley of Humiliation. It is thus introduced :—

"Now, as they were going along, and talking, they espied a boy feeding his father's sheep. The boy was in very mean clothes, but of a very fresh and well-favoured countenance; and as he sat by himself, he sang. Hark, said Mr. Great-heart, to what the shepherd's boy saith. So they hearkened, and he said:

'He that is down needs fear no fall;
   He that is low, no pride;
He that is humble, ever shall
   Have God to be his Guide.

'I am content with what I have,
   Little be it or much;
And, Lord, contentment still I crave,
   Because Thou savest such.

'Fullness to such a burden is,
   That go on pilgrimage;
Here little, and hereafter bliss,
   Is best from age to age.'

"Then said the Guide, Do you hear him? I will dare to say, that this boy lives a merrier life, and wears more of that herb called heart's ease in his bosom, than he that is clad in silk and velvet; but we will proceed in our discourse."

This hymn was frequently included in the older hymn-books, but it is seldom found in modern collections.   [J. J.]

He was there alone, when even. *Sir J. Bowring.* [*Retirement and Devotion.*] Appeared in his *Hymns*, 1825, in 4 st. of 4 l. In 1848 it was given in Longfellow and Johnson's *Book of Hys.*, Boston, in 3 st. In this form it has been repeated in a few modern Unitarian collections.   [J. J.]

He who walks in virtue's [God's true] way. *Sir J. Bowring.* [*Peace.*] 1st pub. in the 2nd ed. of his *Matins and Vespers*, &c., 1824, in 3 st. of 8 l., and again in the 3rd ed., 1841. In its original form it is not often found in C. U. An altered text is given in *Kennedy*, 1863, as "He who walks in *God's* true way."   [J. J.]

He wills that I should holy be. *C. Wesley.* [*Holiness.*] A cento from his *Short Hymns*, &c., 1762, thus :—

St. i., ii.   *Short Hymns.* Vol. ii., No. 631. 1 Thes. iv. 3.
St. iii., iv.   *Short Hymns.* Vol. i., No. 325. Deut. xxx. 6.
St. v., vi.   *Short Hymns.* Vol. i., No. 888. Ps. cxliii. 10.
St. vii., viii.   *Short Hymns.* Vol. ii., No. 171. St. Matt. xiv. 36.

In this form it was given in the *Wes. H. Bk.*, 1780, No. 396, is continued in the revised ed., 1875, and is found in many collections in G. Britain and America.   [J. J.]

Head of Thy [the] Church triumphant. *C. Wesley.* [*In time of Trouble.*] 1st pub. in his *Hys. for Times of Trouble for the Year* 1745, No. xv., in 4 st. of 10 l. (*P. Works*, 1868–72, vol. iv. p. 79). The special *Trouble* was the threatened attack on England by Charles Edward Stuart, the young Pretender, in consequence of which, together with foreign wars, a National Fast was proclaimed. This Wesley tract, composed on that occasion, contained 15 hymns. This hymn was included in Whitefield's *Coll.*, 1753; Madan's *Ps. & Hys.*, 1760; Toplady's *Ps. & Hys.*, 1776; the early editions of the Lady Huntingdon *Coll.*, and others of the older hymn-books. Gradually it became very popular, and its use extended to most English-speaking countries. Notwithstanding this success it was excluded from the *Wes. H. Bk.* until the revised ed., 1875. It has been and still is often attributed to *De Courcy*. The mistake began with Bickersteth in his *Christ. Psalmody*, 1833. He copied from De Courcy's *Coll.*, in which authors' names were not given, and was thus led into the error. In the last stanza of the hymn there is a reference to the death of *Stephen*, which has led in a few instances to the adoption of the hymn for St. Stephen's day.

In Archdeacon Robinson's *Last Days of Bishop Heber*, pp. 179–180, quoted in Heber's *Life*, 1830, vol. ii. pp. 435–6, the Archdeacon says, under date "Trichinopoly, April 2, 1826" (the day before the Bishop's sudden death at that place):—

"On returning from church in the morning, I was so ill as to be obliged to go to bed, and with his [the Bishop's] usual affectionate consideration, he came and sat the greater part of the afternoon with me. . . . Our conversation this afternoon turned chiefly on the blessedness of Heaven, and the best means of preparing for its enjoyment. He repeated several lines of an old hymn which he said, in spite of one or two expressions which familiar and injudicious use had tended to vulgarize, he admired as one of the most beautiful in our language, for rich and elevated tone of devotional feeling.

'Head of the Church triumphant!
We joyfully adore Thee,'" &c.

This is great praise. The hymn, however, lacks the refinement which is so marked a feature in the finest of C. Wesley's compositions. Its use is extensive.   [J. J.]

Headlam, Margaret Ann, daughter of Ven. John Headlam, Archdeacon of Richmond, b. Jan. 4, 1817, is the author of :—

1. *Holy is the seed-time, when the buried grain.* *Harvest.* Written, c. 1862, for a Harvest Festival in

the parish of Whorlton, Durham, and pub. in a (privately printed) *Suppl.* to Pott's *Hys.*, &c. It was also given in the S. P. C. K. *Church Hys.*, 1871. In his note thereon (*Ch. Hys.*, folio ed. p. lvi.) Mr. Ellerton gives these details, and adds an omitted stanza, and an original tune (*Whorlton*) composed for it by Dr. Dykes.

2. Thy courts, O Lord, are open. *Re-opening of a Church.* Written for the re-opening of St. Oswald's Church, Durham, Aug. 1, 1883, and printed as a leaflet.   [J. J.]

Heal us, Emmanuel, here we are. *W. Cowper.* [*Lent.*] 1st pub. in the *Olney Hymns*, 1779, Bk. i., No. 14, in 6 st. of 4 l., and headed, "Jehovah Rophi, — I am the Lord that healeth thee." It is often found in the older collections in its original form, and it still retains its place in a few modern hymnals. Taken in its original, and the following altered forms of the text, its use is somewhat extensive :—

1. **Heal us, Emmanuel! hear our prayer.** This was given in the *Salisbury H. Bk.*, 1857, and was repeated in the S. P. C. K. *Church Hys.*, 1871, and others.
2. **Heal us, Emmanuel, here we stand.** In the Amer. Tract Society's *Songs of Zion*, 1864, &c.
3. **Heal us, Immanuel, we are here.** In the *New Cong.*, 1859, and others.
4. **Divine Physician of the Soul.** In *Kennedy*, 1863.
5. **Healer Divine, O hear our prayer.** In a few American hymnals, including the Episcopal *Hys. for Ch. & Home.* Phila., 1860.

The references in this hymn to the father of the deaf and dumb child (*St. Mark ix.* 24), and to the woman healed of the issue of blood (*St. Mark v.* 34), render it most appropriate for use when those portions of Holy Scriptures are read in public worship, *e.g.* March 2, and 9.   [J. J.]

Hear, Lord, the songs of praise and prayer. *W. Cowper.* [*Sunday School Anniversary.*] This hymn was pub. in Rowland Hill's *Divine Hys. attempted in Easy Language for Children*, &c., 1790, p. 58, No. 37, in 6 st. of 4 l. and headed, "A hymn for Sunday School Children. 'Better is a poor and wise child than an old and foolish king.' Eccl. iv. 13." In his Preface, p. vii., Hill says, Hymns 24 ["How happy are those little ones"] and 37 were also added by the gentleman that corrected the publication. It was also given in the *Christian Observer*, Oct. 1808, with the following letter as an introduction :—

"The following hymn, composed by the poet Cowper for the anniversary of the establishment of the Sunday Schools at Olney, and, perhaps, not ill calculated for general use on such anniversaries in other parishes, has never, I believe, appeared in print. If you agree with me in thinking the publication of it desirable, it is very much at your service. Its tendency is, certainly, the same with that of other productions of his pen. And its internal evidence, as to authorship, is so strong, that it is perhaps unnecessary for me to say I transcribe a copy sent by Mrs. Unwin, in her own handwriting, to her daughter, Mrs. Powley ... E. Kilvington, Ossett, Aug. 16."

The hymn is in 6 st. of 4 l., the opening stanza being :—

"Hear, Lord, the songs of praise and prayer,
In heaven, Thy dwelling-place,
From children made the public care,
And taught to seek Thy face."

In the *Leeds S. S. H. Bk.*, 1833, it is abbreviated to 3 st., and in this form it is known to modern collections. One or two of the remaining stanzas might be added with advantage.   [J. J.]

Hear what God the Lord hath spoken. *W. Cowper.* [*The Church in Glory.*] 1st pub. in the *Olney Hymns*, 1779, Bk. i., No. 65, in 3 st. of 8 l., and headed, "The future peace and glory of the Church." It is in somewhat extensive use both in G. Britain and America.   [J. J.]

Hearken, ye children of your God. *P. Doddridge.* [*Spiritual growth enforced.*] 1st pub. in J. Orton's posthumous ed. of Doddridge's *Hymns*, &c., 1755, No. 300, in 5 st. of 4 l.; and again, with slight changes, in J. D. Humphreys's ed. of the same, 1839. In Rippon's *Sel.*, 1787, No. 470, it was altered to "Attend, ye children of your God." This is repeated in several collections in America. In the Bapt. *Ps. & Hys.*, 1858, st. ii., iii.-v., are given as "Baptised into our Saviour's death, Our souls," &c. This is also repeated in other collections.   [J. J.]

Hearn, Marianne, known to the public only by her *nom de plume* of *Marianne Farningham*, was b. at Farningham, in Kent, Dec. 17, 1834. She resided for short periods at Bristol and Gravesend, and since 1865 at Northampton. Miss Farningham is a member of the Baptist denomination. Her literary work has been done chiefly in connection with the *Christian World* newspaper, on the staff of which she has been from its first publication. She is also editor of the *Sunday School Times*. Most of her contributions to the *Christian World* have been republished in book form, and include :—

(1) *Lays and Lyrics of the Blessed Life*, 1861. (2) *Poems*, 1865. (3) *Morning and Evening Hymns for the Week*, 1870. (4) *Songs of Sunshine*, 1878.

From these works the following hymns have passed into C. U. :—

1. **Father Who givest us now the New Year.** *Old and New Year.* From her *Songs of Sunshine*, 1878.
2. **Hail the children's festal day.** *S. School Anniversaries.* Appeared in the *Sunday School Times*, 1875.
3. **Let the children come, Christ said.** *Christ's invitation of children.* In G. Barrett's *Book of Praise for Children*, 1881. It was written in 1877.
4. **When mysterious whispers are floating about.** *Death anticipated.* Appeared in the *Christian World*, in the Autumn of 1864 ; and again in her work, *Poems*, 1865. In I. D. Sankey's *Sac. Songs & Solos*, it is entitled "Waiting and Watching for me" (the refrain of each stanza), and is altered to "When my final farewell to the world I have said." This is the most popular of Miss Hearn's hymns.   [W. R. S.]

Heathcote, William Beadon, B.C.L., was educated at New College, Oxford (B.C.L. 1840). He was for some time Fellow and Tutor of his College; Precentor of Salisbury Cathedral; Chaplain to the Bp. of Salisbury; and Select Preacher at Oxford. He was author of *The Psalter pointed to the Gregorian Tones*, and of *Prayers for Children especially in Parochial Schools, with a Morning and Evening Hymn*, Oxford, 1846. The hymn is given in two forms, one for *Morning* and the second for *Evening*. It begins :—"O Father, Who didst all things make." Mr. Heathcote d. in Aug. 1862.   [J. J.]

Heavenly Father, Sovereign Lord, Ever faithful, &c. *C. Wesley.* [*Promised Happiness.*] Appeared in *Hys. & Sac. Poems*, 1740, as a paraphrase of Isaiah xxxv., in 20 st. of 4 l. (*P. Works*, 1868–72, vol. i. p. 290). The hymn, "Faint the earth, and parched

with drought," in Martineau's *Hymns*, &c., 1873, and a few American collections, is composed of st. xi., xii., iii., v. (in the order named), very much altered. In the *Wes. H. Bk.*, 1780, No. 339, the original hymn was given in two parts, Pt: ii. beginning:—"Where the ancient dragon lay." In this form it is retained in the revised ed., 1875, and is also found in other collections.   [J. J.]

Heavenly Father, to Whose eye. *J. Conder*. [*In Temptation*.] Pub. in the *Cong. H. Bk.*, 1836, No. 518, in 8 st. of 4 l., as a paraphrase of the clause, "And lead us not into temptation, but deliver us from evil," in the Lord's Prayer. In *The Choir and the Oratory*, 1837, it is repeated as one of a series of hymns on the Lord's Prayer, and again in his *Hys. of Prayer and Praise*, 1856. It is usually given in an abbreviated form, and sometimes with the addition of a doxology. The last three stanzas, beginning, "Lord, uphold me day by day," are often used as a separate hymn.   [J. J.]

Heber, Reginald, D.D. Born at Malpas, April 21, 1783, educated at Brasenose College, Oxford; Vicar of Hodnet, 1807; Bp. of Calcutta, 1823; d. at Trichinopoly, India, April 3, 1826. The gift of versification shewed itself in Heber's childhood; and his Newdigate prize poem *Palestine*, which was read to Scott at breakfast in his rooms at Brazenose, Oxford, and owed one of its most striking passages to Scott's suggestion, is almost the only prize poem that has won a permanent place in poetical literature. His sixteen years at Hodnet, where he held a half-way position between a parson and a squire, were marked not only by his devoted care of his people, as a parish priest, but by literary work. He was the friend of Milman, Gifford, Southey, and others, in the world of letters, endeared to them by his candour, gentleness, "salient playfulness," as well as learning and culture. He was on the original staff of *The Quarterly Review*; Bampton Lecturer (1815); and Preacher at Lincoln's Inn (1822). His edition of Jeremy Taylor is still the classic edition. During this portion of his life he had often had a lurking fondness for India, had traced on the map Indian journeys, and had been tempted to wish himself Bishop of Calcutta. When he was forty years old the literary life was closed by his call to the Episcopate. No memory of Indian annals is holier than that of the three years of ceaseless travel, splendid administration, and saintly enthusiasm, of his tenure of the see of Calcutta. He ordained the first Christian native —Christian David. His first visitation ranged through Bengal, Bombay, and Ceylon; and at Delhi and Lucknow he was prostrated with fever. His second visitation took him through the scenes of Schwartz's labours in Madras Presidency to Trichinopoly, where on April 3, 1826, he confirmed forty-two persons, and he was deeply moved by the impression of the struggling mission, so much so that "he showed no appearance of bodily exhaustion." On his return from the service

"He retired into his own room, and according to his invariable custom, wrote on the back of the address on Confirmation 'Trichinopoly, April 3, 1826.' This was

his last act, for immediately on taking off his clothes, he went into a large cold bath, where he had bathed the two preceding mornings, but which was now the destined agent of his removal to Paradise. Half an hour after, his servant, alarmed at his long absence, entered the room and found him a lifeless corpse." *Life*, &c., 1830, vol. ii. p. 437.

Heber's hymns were all written during the Hodnet period. Even the great missionary hymn, "From Greenland's icy mountains," notwithstanding the Indian allusions ("India's coral strand," "Ceylon's isle"), was written before he received the offer of Calcutta. The touching funeral hymn, "Thou art gone to the grave," was written on the loss of his first babe, which was a deep grief to him. Some of the hymns were published (1811–16) in the *Christian Observer*, the rest were not published till after his death. They formed part of a MS. collection made for Hodnet (but not published), which contained, besides a few hymns from older and special sources, contributions by Milman. The first idea of the collection appears in a letter in 1809 asking for a copy of the *Olney Hymns*, which he "admired very much." The plan was to compose hymns connected with the Epistles and Gospels, to be sung after the Nicene Creed. He was the first to publish sermons on the Sunday services (1822), and a writer in *The Guardian* has pointed out that these efforts of Heber were the germs of the now familiar practice, developed through the *Christian Year* (perhaps following Ken's *Hymns on the Festivals*), and by Augustus Hare, of welding together sermon, hymnal, and liturgy. Heber tried to obtain from Abp. Manners Sutton and the Bp. of London (1820) authorization of his MS. collection of hymns by the Church, enlarging on the "powerful engine" which hymns were among Dissenters, and the irregular use of them in the church, which it was impossible to suppress, and better to regulate. The authorization was not granted. The lyric spirit of Scott and Byron passed into our hymns in Heber's verse; imparting a fuller rhythm to the older measures, as illustrated by "Oh, Saviour, is Thy promise fled," or the martial hymn, "The Son of God goes forth to war;" pressing into sacred service the freer rhythms of contemporary poetry (e.g. "Brightest and best of the sons of the morning"; "God that madest earth and heaven"); and aiming at consistent grace of literary expression. Their beauties and faults spring from this modern spirit. They have not the scriptural strength of our best early hymns, nor the dogmatic force of the best Latin ones. They are too flowing and florid, and the conditions of hymn composition are not sufficiently understood. But as pure and graceful devotional poetry, always true and reverent, they are an unfailing pleasure. The finest of them is that majestic anthem, founded on the rhythm of the English Bible, "Holy, Holy, Holy, Lord God Almighty." The greatest evidence of Heber's popularity as a hymnwriter, and his refined taste as a compiler, is found in the fact that the total contents of his MS. collection which were given in his posthumous *Hymns written and adapted to the Weekly Church Service of the Year*. Lond., *J. Murray*, 1827; which included 57 hymns by Heber, 12 by Milman, and 29 by other

writers, are in C. U. in G. Britain and America at the present time.   [H. L. B.]

Of Bp. Heber's hymns, about one half are annotated under their respective first lines. Those given below were pub. in Heber's posthumous *Hymns*, &c., 1827. Some of them are in extensive use in G. Britain and America; but as they possess no special histories they are grouped together as from the *Hymns*, &c., 1827:—

1. Beneath our feet, and o'er our head. *Burial.*
2. Creator of the rolling flood. *St. Peter's Day, or, Gospel for 5th S. after Trinity.*
3. Lo, the lilies of the field. *Teachings of Nature: or, Gospel for 15th S. after Trinity.*
4. O God, by Whom the seed is given. *Sexagesima.*
5. O God, my sins are manifold. *Forgiveness, or, Gospel for 22nd S. after Trinity.*
6. O hand of bounty, largely spread. *Water into Wine, or, Gospel for 2nd S. after Epiphany.*
7. O King of earth, and air, and sea. *Feeding the Multitude: or, Gospel for 4th S. in Lent.*
8. O more than merciful, Whose bounty gave. *Good Friday.*
9. O most merciful! O most bountiful. *Introit H. Communion.*
10. O Thou, Whom neither time nor space. *God unsearchable, or, Gospel for 5th S. in Lent.*
11. O weep not o'er thy children's tomb. *Innocents Day.*
12. Room for the proud! Ye sons of clay. *Dives and Lazarus, or, Gospel for 1st S. after Trinity*
13. Sit thou on my right hand, my Son, saith the Lord. *Ascension.*
14. Spirit of truth, on this thy day. *Whit-Sunday.*
15. The feeble pulse, the gasping breath. *Burial, or, Gospel for 1st S. after Trinity.*
16. The God of glory walks His round. *Septuagesima, or, the Labourers in the Market-place.*
17. The sound of war in earth and air. *Wrestling against Principalities and Powers, or, Epistle for 21st S. after Trinity.*
18. The world is grown old, her pleasures are past. *Advent ; or, Epistle for 4th S. in Advent.*
19. There was joy in heaven. *The Lost Sheep ; or, Gospel for 3rd S. after Trinity.*
20. Though sorrows rise and dangers roll. *St. James's Day.*
21. To conquer and to save, the Son of God. *Christ the Conqueror.*
22. Virgin-born, we bow before Thee. *The V. M. Blessed amongst women, or, Gospel for 3rd S. in Lent.*
23. Wake not, O mother, sounds of lamentation. *Raising the Widow's Son, or, Gospel for 16th S. after Trinity.*
24. When on her Maker's bosom. *Holy Matrimony, or, Gospel for 2nd S. after Epiphany.*
25. When through the torn sail the wild tempest is streaming. *Stilling the Sea, or, Gospel for 4th S. after Epiphany.*
26. Who yonder on the desert heath. *The Good Samaritan, or, Gospel for 13th S. after Trinity.*

This list is a good index of the subjects treated in those of Heber's hymns which are given under their first lines, and shows that he used the *Gospels* far more than the *Epistles* in his work.   [J. J.]

Hedge, Frederick Henry, D.D., s. of Professor Hedge of Harvard College, was b. at Cambridge, Massachusetts, 1805, and educated in Germany and at Harvard. In 1829 he became pastor of the Unitarian Church, West Cambridge. In 1835 he removed to Bangor, Maine; in 1850 to Providence, and in 1856 to Brookline, Mass. He was appointed in 1857, Professor of Ecclesiastical History at Cambridge (U.S.), and in 1872, Professor of German Literature at Harvard. Dr. Hedge is one of the editors of the *Christian Examiner*, and the author of *The Prose Writers of Germany*, and other works. In 1853 he edited, with Dr. F. D. Huntington, the Unitarian *Hymns for the Church of Christ*, Boston Crosby,

Nichols & Co. To that collection and the supplement (1853) he contributed the following *trs.* from the German:—

1. A mighty fortress is our God. (*Ein feste Burg.*)
2. Christ hath arisen! joy to, &c. (Goethe's *Faust.*)
3. The sun is still for ever sounding. (Goethe's *Faust.*) For 2 and 3 see **Goethe.**

There is also in the Unitarian *Hymn [& Tune] Bk. for The Church & Home*, Boston, 1868, a *tr.* from the Latin.

4. Holy Spirit, Fire divine. (" Veni Sancte Spiritus.")

Dr. Hedge's original hymns, given in the *Hys. for the Church*, 1853, are :—

5. Beneath Thine hammer, Lord, I lie. *Resignation.*
6. Sovereign and transforming grace. *Ordination.* Written for the Ordination of H. D. Barlow at Lynn, Mass., Dec. 9, 1829. It is given in several collections.
7. 'Twas in the East, the mystic East. *Christmas.*
8. 'Twas the day when God's anointed. *Good Friday.* Written originally for a Confirmation at Bangor, Maine, held on Good Friday, 1843. The hymn "It is finished, Man of Sorrows! From Thy cross, &c.," in a few collections, including Martineau's *Hymns*, &c., 1873, is composed of st. iv.-vi. of this hymn.   [F. M. B]

Heermann, Johann, s. of Johannes Heermann, furrier at Raudten, near Wohlau, Silesia, was b. at Raudten, Oct. 11, 1585. He was the fifth but only surviving child of his parents, and during a severe illness in his childhood his mother vowed that if he recovered she would educate him for the ministry, even though she had to beg the necessary money. He passed through the schools at Wohlau; at Fraustadt (where he lived in the house of Valerius Herberger, q. v., who took a great interest in him) ; the St. Elizabeth gymnasium at Breslau; and the gymnasium at Brieg. At Easter, 1609, he accompanied two young noblemen (sons of Baron Wenzel von Rothkirch), to whom he had been tutor at Brieg, to the University of Strassburg ; but an affection of the eyes caused him to return to Raudten in 1610. At the recommendation of Baron Wenzel he was appointed diaconus of Köben, a small town on the Oder, not far from Raudten, and entered on his duties on Ascension Day, 1611, and on St. Martin's-Day, 1611, was promoted to the pastorate there. After 1623 he suffered much from an affection of the throat, which compelled him to cease preaching in 1634, his place being supplied by assistants. In October, 1638, he retired to Lissa in Posen, and d. there on Septuagesima Sunday (Feb. 17), 1647. (*Koch*, iii. 16–36 ; *Allg. Deutsche Biog.*, xi. 247–249, &c.)

Much of Heermann's manhood was spent amid the distressing scenes of the Thirty Years' War ; and by his own ill-health and his domestic trials he was led to write his beautiful hymns of "Cross and Consolation." Between 1629 and 1634, Köben was plundered four times by the Lichtenstein dragoons and the rough hordes under Wallenstein sent into Silesia by the King of Austria in order to bring about the Counter-Reformation and restore the Roman Catholic faith and practice ; while in 1616 the town was devastated by fire, and in 1631 by pestilence. In these troublous years Heermann several times lost all his moveables ; once he had to keep away from Köben for seventeen weeks ; twice he was nearly sabred ; and once, while crossing the Oder in a frail boat loaded almost to sinking, he heard the bullets of the pursuing soldiers whistle just over his head. He bore all with courage and patience, and he and his were wonderfully preserved from death and dishonour. He was thus well grounded in the school of affliction, and in his *House and Heart Music* some of his finest hymns are in the section entitled "Songs of Tears. In the time of the persecution and distress of pious Christians."

As a hymn-writer Heermann ranks with the best of his century, some indeed regarding him as second only to Gerhardt. He had begun writing Latin poems about 1605, and was crowned as a poet at Brieg on Oct. 8, 1608. He marks the transition from the objective standpoint of the hymn-writers of the Reformation period to the more subjective and experimental school that followed him. His hymns are distinguished by depth and tenderness of feeling; by firm faith and confidence in face of trial; by deep love to Christ, and humble submission to the will of God. Many of them became at once popular, passed into the hymn-books, and still hold their place among the classics of German hymnody. They appeared principally in—

(1) *Devoti Musica Cordis. Hauss- und Hertz-Musica* &c. Leipzig and Breslau, 1630, with 49 hymns (2nd ed. 1636, with 54; 3rd ed. 1644, with 59). The first section is entitled "Hymns of Penitence and Consolation from the words of the Ancient Fathers of the Church." Seven of these, however, have no mention in their individual titles of the sources from which they are derived; and the remainder are mostly based not on Latin hymns, but on the prose meditations in Martin Moller's *Meditationes sanctorum patrum*, or on the mediaeval compilations known as the *Meditationes* and the *Manuale* of St. Augustine. (2) *Sontags- und Fest-Evangelia.* Leipzig and Breslau, 1636, being hymns on the Gospels for Sundays and festivals. (3) *Poetische Erquickstunden*, Nürnberg, 1656; and its *Fernere Fortsetzung*, also Nürnberg, 1656 [both in Wernigerode], are poems rather than hymns. The hymns of the *Hauss- und Hertz-Musica*, with a representative selection from Heermann's other poetical works, were edited by C. E. P. Wackernagel, prefaced by a long biographical and critical introduction, and published at Stuttgart, 1855.

Six of the most important of Heermann's hymns are annotated under their respective first lines. The other hymns by Heermann which have passed into English are :—

I. Hymns in English C. U.

i. **O Jesu, du mein Bräutigam.** *Holy Communion.* In his *Devoti Musica Cordis*, Breslau, 1630, p. 78, in 12 st. of 4 l. Thence in *Mützell*, 1858, No. 34, in Wackernagel's ed. of his *Geistliche Lieder*, No. 22, and the *Unv. L. S.*, 1851, No. 283. Seems to be founded on Meditation xi. in the mediaeval compilation known as St. Augustine's *Manuale.* *Tr.* as :—

O Jesu, Lord, who once for me, a good *tr.* of st. i., ii., iv., v., viii., by A. T. Russell, as No. 158 in his *Ps. & Hys.*, 1851.

Other *trs.* are : (1) "O Jesu! Bridegroom of my Soul," by *J. C. Jacobi*, 1722, p. 44 (1732, p. 73). (2) "Dear Saviour, who for me hast borne," by *Miss Dunn*, 1857.

ii. **Rett, O Herr Jesu, rett dein Ehr.** *In Time of Trouble.* A prayer for deliverance and peace for the Church. In his *Devoti Musica Cordis*, 1630, p. 119, in 5 st. of 4 l., among the "Songs of Tears." Thence in *Mützell*, 1858, No. 48, in *Wackernagel's* ed., No. 36, and the *Unv. L. S.*, 1851, No. 245. *Tr.* as :—

Thine honour rescue, righteous Lord, in full, by Dr. M. Loy, in the Ohio *Luth. Hyl.*, 1880.

iii. **Treuer Wächter Israel.** *In Time of War.* 1630, p. 115, in 13 st. of 7 l., among the "Songs of Tears." In *Mützell*, 1858, No. 47 ; in *Wackernagel's* ed., No. 35, and the *Unv. L. S.*, 1851, No. 594. Lauxmann, in *Koch*, viii. 549, says of it :—

"It is a powerful hymn filled with that prevailing prayer that takes heaven by force," and relates of st. vii., ll. v–7, "Eine Mauer um uns bau," that on Jan. 5, 1814, the Allied Forces were about to enter Schleswig. A poor widow with her daughter and grandson lived in a little house near the entrance of the town. The grand-

son was reading in his hymn-book those in time of war, and when he came to this said, "It would be a good thing, grandmother, if our Lord God would build a wall around us." Next day all through the town cries of distress were heard, but all was still before their door. On the following morning they had courage to open the door, and lo a snowdrift concealed them from the view of the enemy. On this incident Clemens Brentano composed a beautiful poem "Draus vor Schleswig."

It is *tr.* as :—

Jesu! as a Saviour, aid. A good *tr.* of st. vii., viii., xiii., by A. T. Russell, as No. 138 in his *Ps. & Hys.*, 1851.

iv. **Zion klagt mit Angst und Schmerzen.** *Church of Christ.* 1st pub. in his *Devoti Musica Cordis*, 2nd ed., 1636 (1644, p. 196), in 6 st. of 8 l., entitled, "From the beautiful golden saying of Isaiah, Chapter xlix." In *Mützell*, 1858, No. 101, in *Wackernagel's* ed., No. 53, and the *Unv. L. S.*, 1851, No. 256. *Tr.* as :—

Sion bow'd with anguish weepeth. A good *tr.* of st. i., iii., v., by A. T. Russell, as No. 141 in his *Ps. & Hys.*, 1851.

Another *tr.* is : "Zion mourns in fear and anguish," by *Miss Winkworth*, 1869, p. 198.

II. Hymns not in English C. U.

v. **Ach Jesu! dessen Treu.** *Love to Christ.* 1630, p. 144, in 33 st. One of his finest hymns, full of deep love to Christ, but from its great length very little used in Germany. *Tr.* as, "Ah! Jesus! Lord! whose faithfulness," by Miss Burlingham, in the *British Herald*, May, 1867, p. 72.

vi. **Der Tod klopft bei mir an.** *For the Dying.* 1656, p. 22, in 12 l. *Tr.* as, "That Death is at my door," by *Miss Winkworth*, 1869, p. 201.

vii. **Du weinest für Jerusalem.** *Christ weeping over Jerusalem.* 1630, p. 81, in 6 st., entitled, "On the Tears of Christ." Founded on St. Luke xix. 41–44, part of the Gospel for the 10 S. after Trinity. The *trs.* are : (1) "With tears o'er lost Jerusalem," by *Miss Cox*, 1841, p. 159. (2) "Our Lord wept o'er Jerusalem," by *Dr. H. Mills*, 1845 (1856, p. 295). (3) "Thou weepest o'er Jerusalem," by *Miss Winkworth*, 1855, p. 70.

viii. **Herr Jesu Christe mein getreuer Hirte.** *Holy Communion.* 1630, p. 74, in 9 st., founded on M. Moller's *Med. sanct. patrum*, pt. i. c. 11, and pt. v. c. 2. The *trs.* are : (1) "Dear Saviour, Thou my faithful Shepherd, come," by *Miss Dunn*, 1857, p. 111. (2) "Lord Jesus Christ, my faithful Shepherd, hear," by *Miss Winkworth*, 1858, p. 93, repeated in *Lyra Eucharistica*, 1863–64.

ix. **Herr unser Gott, lass nicht zu Schanden werden.** *Christ's Church.* 1630, p. 114, as one of the "Songs of Tears," in 5 st. *Tr.* as, "Ah! Lord our God, let them not be confounded," by *Miss Winkworth*, 1869, p. 197.

x. **Hilf mir, mein Gott, hilf dass nach dir.** *Christian Conduct.* 1630, p. 32, in 7 st., entitled, "For a better life. From the words of Augustine." Founded on No. i. of the *Meditationes* current under the name of St. Augustine. This meditation is apparently by St. Anselm of Canterbury. *Tr.* as, "Lord, raise in me a constant Flame," by *J. C. Jacobi*, 1725, p. 27 (1732, p. 105).

xi. **Jesu, der du tausend Schmerzen.** *In Sickness.* 1656, in the *Fernere Fortsetzung*, p. 79, in 12 l., entitled, "In great bodily pain." *Tr.* as, "Jesu, who didst stoop to prove," by *Miss Winkworth*, 1869, p. 200.

xii. **Jesu Tilger meiner Sünden.** *Lent.* 1656, in the *Fernere Fortsetzung*, p. 1, in 10 l., entitled, "For Victory in Temptation." *Tr.* as, "Jesu, Victor over sin," by *Miss Winkworth*, 1869, p. 201.

xiii. **O Jesu, Jesu, Gottes Sohn.** *Love to Christ.* 1630, p. 83, in 7 st., entitled, "Of the Love, which a Christian heart bears to Christ, and will still bear." A beautiful expansion of his motto "Mihi omnia Jesus." The *trs.* are : (1) "What causes me to mourn is this," a *tr.* of st. ii. by P. H. Molther, as No. 371, in the *Moravian H. Bk.*, 1789 (1886, No. 461). (2) "O Jesus, Jesus, Son of God," by Miss Burlingham, in the *British Herald*, Oct. 1865, p. 153, and in Reid's *Praise Bk.*, 1872.

xiv. **Treuer Gott ich muss dir klagen.** *In Trouble.* 1630, p. 103, in 12 st., entitled, "Hymn of a sorrowful heart for increase of faith." *Tr.* as, "Faithful God! I lay before Thee," by *J. C. Jacobi*, 1720, p. 9 (1722, p. 70; 1732, p. 117), and as No. 538 in pt. i. of the *Moravian H. Bk.*, 1754.

xv. **Wollt ihr euch nicht, o ihr frommen Christen.** *Second Advent.* 1636, p. 210, in 9 st., entitled, "On the day of the Holy Bishop Nicolaus. Gospel of Luke, 12

Chapter." *Tr.* as : (1) "O dear Christians, as 'tis needful, wou'd ye," as No. 153 in pt. i. of the *Moravian H. Bk.*, 1754. (2) "Help us, O Christ, to watch and pray," a *tr.* of st. ix. as st. iii. of No. 868 in the *Moravian H. Bk.*, 1789 (1849, No. 1221).

xvi. **Wo soll ich fliehen hin.** *Lent.* 1630, p. 20, in 11 st., entitled, "A hymn of consolation in which a troubled heart lays all its sins in true faith upon Christ. From Tauler." Based on M. Moller's *Meditationes*, vol. i. pt. i., No. 10. *Tr.* as, "O whither shall I fly," as No. 447 in pt. i. of the *Moravian H. Bk.*, 1754. In 1886, No. 279, it begins with "O Jesus, source of Grace" (st. ii.).   [J. M.]

Hegenwalt, Erhart.

Of this writer very little is known. He appears to have studied and graduated M.A. at Wittenberg. On Jan. 29, 1523, he attended the disputation of Zwingli, by which Zürich was won to the Reformation; and pub. an account of it in the same year. This narrative is dedicated to his friend and patron J. J. Rusinger, Abbot of Pfäffers (Pfeffers), and dated Zürich, May 3, 1523. Whether he is the same as Erhart Hegenwalt, who was admitted M.D. at Wittenberg, 1526, and was afterwards in practice at Frankfurt-am-Main, c. 1540, is not clear. The only hymn ascribed to him is :—

Erbarm dich mein, o Herre Gott. *Ps. li.* 1st pub. on a broadsheet dated "Wittenberg freytag nach Epiphanie im 1524 Jar. Erhart Hegenwalt." Thence in *Eyn Enchiridion*, Erfurt, 1524, *Wackernagel*, iii. p. 48, the *Unv. L. S.*, 1851, No. 366, &c., in 5 st. of 8 l. *Tr.* as : (1) "O God, be mercyfull to me," by *Bp.* *Coverdale*, 1539 (*Remains*, 1846, p. 576). (2) "Shew pity, Lord! O Lord forgive," by *J. C. Jacobi*, 1722, p. 59 (1732, p. 95), and as No. 120 in pt. i. of the *Moravian H. Bk.*, 1754. Jacobi borrows a good many lines from Isaac Watts's version of Ps. li.   [J. M.]

Heginbothom, Ottiwell,

b. in 1744, and d. in 1768, was for a short time the Minister of a Nonconformist congregation at Sudbury, Suffolk. The political and religious disputes which agitated the congregation, in the origin of which he had no part, and which resulted in a secession and the erection of another chapel, so preyed upon his mind, and affected his health, that his pastorate terminated with his death within three years of his appointment. His earliest hymn, "When sickness shakes the languid corse [frame]," was printed in the *Christian Magazine*, Feb. 1763. In 1791 the Rev. John Mead Ray communicated several of Heginbothom's hymns to the *Protestant Magazine;* and in the same year, these and others to the number of 25, were published as :—

Hymns by the late Rev. Ottiwell Heginbothom of Sudbury, Suffolk. Sudbury, Printed by J. Burket, mdccxciv.

These 25 hymns were repeated in J. M. Ray's *Coll. of Hys. from various authors intended as a Supplement to Dr. Watts's Psalms and Hymns,* 1799, and 12 in Collyer's *Collection,* 1812. In modern collections in G. Britain and America the following are in C. U. in addition to those annotated under their respective first lines :—

1. **Blest Jesus, when my soaring thoughts.** *Jesus, most Precious.*
2. **Come, humble souls; ye mourners come.** *Good Hope through Grace.*
3. **Come saints and shout the Saviour's praise.** *The Second Advent.*
4. **Come, shout aloud the Father's grace.** *Praise to God the Father.*
5. **Father of mercies, God of love.** *God the Father.*
6. **God of our life! Thy various praise.** *New Year.*
7. **Great God, let all our [my] tuneful powers.** *New. Year.*

8. **Hark, the loud trumpet of our God.** *National Fast.*
9. **Hark, 'tis your heavenly Father's call.** *A Prayer to be used by the Young.*
10. **I ask not [honour] wealth, nor pomp, nor power.** *Wisdom and Knowledge desired.*
11. **Now let my soul, eternal King.** *Praise of the Gospel.* Sometimes given as "To Thee, my heart, eternal King."
12. **See, mighty God, before Thy throne.** *Fifth of November; a National Hymn.*
13. **Sweet peace of Conscience, heavenly guest.** *A good Conscience.*
14. **To Thee, my Shepherd, and my Lord.** *The Good Shepherd.*
15. **Unhappy city, hadst thou known.** *Christ weeping over Jerusalem.* From this the cento, "And can mine eyes without a tear ?" is taken.
16. **When sickness shakes the languid corse [frame].** *Resignation.* Printed in the *Christian's Magazine*, Feb. 1763, and again in *Hymns*, &c., 1794.
17. **Yes, I will bless Thee, O my God.** *Praise of the Father.* The text is often altered. The cento "My soul shall ‛praise Thee, O my God," in the Unitarian *Hymn [and Tune] Book,* &c., Boston, 1868, is from this hymn.

Most of these hymns are in Collyer's *Collection,* 1812. There are also 8 in Hatfield's *Church H. Bk.*, N.Y., 1872, and 7 in the *Songs for the Sanctuary,* N.Y., 1865.   [W. T. B.]

Hehl, Matthäus Gottfried,

was b. April 30, 1705, at Ebersbach, near Göppingen, Württemberg, and studied at the University of Tübingen (M.A. 1723). He was assistant clergyman in a village near Tübingen when Zinzendorf visited Tübingen in 1733. Thereafter he became a Moravian, was ordained in 1744 a presbyter, and in 1751 was consecrated in London as coadjutor bishop for America. He arrived at Bethlehem, Pennsylvania, Dec. 10, 1751, and in Nov., 1756, removed to Lititz. On account of advancing years he resigned his office in 1781, and d. at Lititz, Dec. 4, 1787 (*Koch*, v. 348–349). His hymns were written during his stay at Herrnhut, and appeared in the Herrnhut *G. B.*, 1735, and its Appendices. One has passed into English non-Moravian use, viz. :—

Geht, erhöht die Majestät. *Supplication.* This is No. 1054 in Appendix iii. to the Herrnhut *G. B.*, 1735, in 4 st. of 10 l. In the *Brüder G. B.*, 1778, it is No. 1069, and in the *Historische Nachricht* thereto st. i., ii. are ascribed to Hehl, and iii., iv. to N. L. von Zinzendorf [Zinzendorf sts. beginning "Lamm und Haupt, das selbst geglaubt," are included by Knapp in his ed., 1845, of Zinzendorf's *Geistliche Lieder*, p. 218, and dated 1733]. *Tr.* as :—

Rise, exalt the Majesty, in full, by P. H. Molther, as No. 116, in the *Moravian H. Bk.*, 1742, with an added st. iii. from "Lamm und Haupt! es sey geglaubt," by N. L. von Zinzendorf [No. 1089 in *Appendix* iv. to the Herrnhut *G. B.*, 1735, in 1 st. of 10 l., and by *Knapp*, 1845, p.｛121, dated May 26, 1736]. In the 1789 and later eds. of the *Moravian H. Bk.* (1886, No. 768), it is greatly altered, and begins, "Rise, exalt our Head and King." Included in Montgomery's *Christian Psalmist*, 1825, and J. A. Latrobe's *Coll.*, 1841.   [J. M.]

Heinrich Ernst,

eldest s. of Christian Ernst, Count of Stolberg Wernigerode, was b. at Wernigerode, Dec. 7, 1716. During the lifetime of his father (who was one of the best hymnologists of his day, and founder of the fine Library at Wernigerode), he was Canon of Halberstadt. He succeeded to the estates in 1771, and d. at Halberstadt, Oct. 24, 1778.

He contributed four hymns to the *Wernigerode G. B.*, 1735. A selection from his *Geistliche Gedichte* was pub. at Halle, 1748–52. The rest of his printed hymns appeared in his *Betrachtungen der Sonn- und Festtäglichen Evangelien in Liedern*, Wernigerode, 1750 (all original), and in the *Neue Sammlung geistlicher Lieder*, Wernigerode, 1752, which includes 818 hymns, of which some 370 are by himself. Two of these have passed into English, viz.:—

i. **Eile, eile, meine Seele.** *Christian Warfare.* 1735, as above, p. 829, in 17 st., entitled, "On the Conflict and Victory of Believers." *Tr.* as "Haste, haste, my soul, from ruin flee," by *Dr. G. Walker*, 1860, p. 83.

ii. **Morgen soll es besser werden.** *The Morning of Joy.* In the *Neue Sammlung*, 1752, No. 537, in 5 st. *Tr.* as "Yes! it shall be well at morning," by Mrs. Findlater, in *H. L. L.*, 1862, p. 63 (1884, p. 225), erroneously ascribed to C. B. Garve (q. v.).   **[J. M.]**

Heinrich of Laufenburg was a native of Laufenburg, Aargau, Switzerland. The earliest notice of him is that in 1434 he was decan of the Collegiate Church of St. Maurice at Zofingen in Aargau. He afterwards held a similar post at Freiburg, in Baden; but in 1445 became a monk in the monastery of the Knights of St John at Strassburg ("Zum grünen Werde"). He was living there in 1458, but probably died in that year or soon after (*Koch*, i. 213–214; *Allg. Deutsche Biog.*, xix. 810–813, &c.).

He was the most important and most prolific hymn-writer of the 15th cent., and a number of his productions are of sweetness and abiding worth. Most of them are in honour of the B. V. M. Many are in intricate metres, while others are written to song tunes, or are recasts of songs, or translations from the Latin. A large number are included by *Wackernagel* in his second volume, principally taken from a paper MS. of the 15th cent., which he found in the town library at Strassburg.

Two of the best of his original hymns are:—

i. **Ach lieber Herre Jesu Christ.** *Cradle Hymn.* This beautiful prayer of a mother for her infant child is given by *Wackernagel*, ii. p. 534, in 5 st. of 6 l., from the *Strassburg MS.*, where it is entitled "Benedictio puerily." In his *Kleines G. B.*, 1860, *Wackernagel* gives it as No. 114 (omitting st. ii.) with the original melody, dating both 1429. The text is also in *Hoffmann von Fallersleben*, ed. 1861, No. 125. *Tr.* as:—

Ah! Jesu Christ, my Lord most dear. A full and very good *tr.* by Miss Winkworth in her *Christian Singers*, &c., 1869, p. 93. The address to the B. V. M. in st. ii.,

"Maria, müter Jesu Christ,
Sit du dins Kints gewaltig bist,"

is translated as:—

"Since in Thy heavenly kingdom, Lord,
All things obey Thy lightest word."

Her *tr.* was adopted with alterations by the Rev. H. White in the *Savoy Hymnary* (Chapel Royal, Savoy), 1870, No. 35, beginning, "Lord Jesu Christ, our Lord most dear." Instead of taking the very good original melody, Mr. White altered the hymn to 6-8 metre, and omitted st. iv., v. This form has been repeated in the S. P. C. K. *Church Hys.*, 1871; Mrs. Brock's *Children's H. Bk.*, 1881, and others.

ii. **Ich wollt dass ich daheime wär.** *Eternal Life.* A beautiful hymn of spiritual Homesickness. *Wackernagel*, ii. p. 540, includes a version in 13 st. of 2 l. from the *Strassburg MS.*; and another in 9 st. of 2 l. from a 15th cent. MS. at Berlin. *Hoffmann von Fallersleben*, 1861, gives the Strassburg text as No. 54; and a form in 9 st. from a MS. at Inzkofen, near Sigmaringen, dating 1470–1480, as No. 55. In his *Kleines G.B.*, 1860, Wackernagel gives as No. 74 a slightly altered form of the Strassburg text, along with the original melody. *Tr.* as "I would I were at last at home," by Miss Winkworth, 1869, p. 92.   **[J. M.]**

Heinrich of Meissen, better known by his title of Frauenlob or Frouwenlop [some

have regarded Frauenlob as his surname], was b. at Meissen, in Saxony, c. 1250, and educated at the Cathedral school there. Of humbler origin than the early Minnesingers, he adopted the profession of wandering minstrel as a means of livelihood. After residing for longer or shorter periods at the courts of many South and North German princes, he settled at Mainz about 1311; where he, the most important of the later Minnesingers, is said to have founded the first school of the Mastersingers. He d. at Mainz, Nov. 29, 1318 (*Allg. Deutsche Biog.*, vii. 321–323, &c.). His poems (edited by Ludwig Ettmüller, at Quedlinburg, 1843, as his *Leiche, Sprüche, Streitgedichte und Lieder*) are voluminous, overburdened by a display of learning, and often in intricate and artificial metrical forms. Two of his religious poems have passed into English, viz.:—

i. **Min Vreude ist gar zegangen.** *For the Dying.* *Wackernagel*, ii. p. 254, in 3 st. from a MS. at Vienna. Ettmüller, p. 162. The *tr.* is, "My joy is wholly banished," by *Miss Winkworth*, 1869, p. 78.

ii. **Nu wil ich nimmer mer verzwiveln.** *Faith.* In *Wackernagel*, ii. p. 245, in 14 l., from a MS. at Vienna. Ettmüller, p. 234. *Tr.* as, "Now will I nevermore despair of heaven," by *Miss Winkworth*, 1869, p. 80.

  [J. M.]

Held, Heinrich, was s. of Valentin Held of Guhrau, Silesia. He studied at the Universities of Königsberg (c. 1637–40), Frankfurt a. Oder (1643), and Leyden. He was also in residence at Rostock in 1647. He became a licentiate of law, and settled as a lawyer in his native place, where he d. about 1659, or at least before Michaelmas, 1661 (*Koch*, iii. 55–56; *Allg. Deutsche Biog.*, xi. 680; *Bode*, p. 87, &c.).

One of the best Silesian hymn-writers, he was taught in the school of affliction, having many trials to suffer in those times of war. His only extant poetical work is his *Deutscher Gedichte Vortrab*, Frankfurt a. Oder, 1643. Only one hymn from that volume came into German use. Much more important are his other hymns, which are known to us through Crüger's *Praxis*, and other hymn-books of the period. *Mützell*, 1858, includes Nos. 254–272 under his name.

Two of his hymns have been *tr.* into English:—

i. **Gott sei Dank durch alle Welt.** *Advent.* *Mützell*, 1858, No. 263, quotes this in 9 st. of 4 l. from a defective ed. of Crüger's *Praxis*, c. 1659. In the ed. of 1661 it is No. 85, marked Henr. Helt. Since then it has appeared in almost all German hymn-books (as in the Berlin *G. L. S.*, ed. 1863, No. 132), and takes rank as one of the finest Advent Hymns. *Tr.* as:—

1. **All the World exalt the Lord,** omitting st. vi. in *Select H. from Ger. Psal.*, Tranquebar, 1754, p. 4, and the *Suppl. to Ger. Psal.*, ed. 1765, p. 1. In 1789, the *trs.* of st. i., ii., iv., vii., ix. (altered) were included as No. 34 in the *Moravian H. Bk.* In the ed. of 1801 it was altered to "All the world give praises due" (ed. 1886, No. 44), and this text has been repeated in Dr. Pagenstecher's *Coll.*, 1864, and Willing's *Bk. of Com. Praise*, 1872.

2. **Be our God with thanks adored.** A *tr.* of st. i.–iv. by A. T. Russell in his *Ps. & Hys.*, 1851.

3. **Let the earth now praise the Lord.** A good *tr.*, omitting st. vii., by Miss Winkworth in her *C. B. for England*, 1863. Repeated in full in Schaff's *Christ in Song*, 1869, and, abridged, in

the American Pennsylvania Luth. *Ch. Bk.*, 1868, and Bapt. *Service of Song*, 1871.

ii. **Komm, o Komm, du Geist des Lebens.** *Whitsuntide.* A fine hymn of Invocation to the Holy Spirit. *Mützell*, 1858, No. 267, quotes it in 9 st. of 6 l. from a defective ed. of Crüger's *Praxis* pub. at Stettin c. 1664. In J. Niedling's *Geistliche Wasserquelle*, Frankfurt a. Oder, 1667, it is at p. 372 marked " H. Held " (not in Niedling's ed. 1663). In Luppius's *Andächtig singender Christen Mund*, 1692, p. 71, it is entitled " Devout Prayer and Hymn to God the Holy Ghost." Repeated in Freylinghausen's *G. B.*, 1704, and many subsequent hymn-books, as in the Berlin *G. L. S.*, ed. 1863, No. 363. It is sometimes erroneously ascribed to Joachim Neander. The *trs.* in C. U. are :—

1. **Holy Spirit, once again.** A full and good *tr.* by Miss Winkworth in the 2nd Ser., 1858, of her *Lyra Ger.*, p. 53. Included in full in the *Cantate Domino*, Boston, U.S.A., 1859. In Miss Winkworth's *C. B. for England*, 1863, st. ii., vi., vii. are omitted. This form of the text is repeated in W. F. Stevenson's *H. for Ch. & Home*, 1873, Hatfield's *Church H. Bk.*, 1872, &c. In the *Hyl. for St. John's, Aberdeen*, 1865, it begins " Holy Spirit, in us reign."

2. **Come, oh come, Thou quickening Spirit, True,** &c. A *tr.* of st. i., ii., iv., vii., ix. in Dr. Pagenstecher's *Coll.*, 1864, No. 98, signed E. T. L.

3. **Come, O come, Thou quickening Spirit, Thou for ever.** A good *tr.*, omitting st. iv.–vi. in the Pennsylvania Luth. *Ch. Bk.*, 1868, and marked as *tr.* by " Charles William Schaeffer, 1866." [Lutheran Pastor at Germantown.]

4. **Come, O come, Thou quickening Spirit, God from all eternity,** omitting st. iii., by E. Cronenwett, in the Ohio Luth. *Hyl.*, 1880.

Another tr. is, " Come, Thou Spirit ever living," by R. Massie in the *British Herald*, Dec., 1865, p. 179.

[J. M.]

Helder, Bartholomäus, s. of Johann Helder, Superintendent in Gotha, became, in 1607, schoolmaster at Friemar, and in 1616, pastor of Remstädt, near Gotha, where he d. of the pestilence, Oct. 28, 1635 (*Koch*, iii. 114, 115, 248 ; *Allg. Deutsche Biog.*, xi. 684, 685, &c.).

Helder pub. two works (both in the Royal Library, Berlin). (1) *Cymbalum Genethliacum.* Erfurt, 1615 ; and (2) *Cymbalum Davidicum.* Erfurt, 1620. The first contains 15 Christmas and New Year Hymns, and the second 25, mostly Psalm versions. In the *Cantionale Sacrum*, Gotha, 1646–48, over 50 hymns are given with his name as composer of the music and without definite ascription as regards the words. Two of these have passed into English, viz. :—

i. **In meiner Noth ruf ich zu dir.** *Supplication.* A prayer for grace, which appeared in the *Cantionale Sacrum*, pt. ii., Gotha, 1648, No. 71, in 3 st. of 6 l. *Tr.* by Miss Manington, 1863, p. 1, as " From out my woe I cry to Thee."

ii. **O Lämmlein Gottes, Jesu Christ.** *St. John Baptist's Day.* Founded on St. John i. 29. Appeared as No. 103 in the *Cantionale Sacrum*, Gotha, 1646, in 4 st. of 4 l., entitled, " On St. John's Day." Included as No. 391 in the *Unv. L. S.* 1851. The only *tr.* in C. U. is " O Jesus, Lamb of God, who art," in full, by A. Crull, as No. 120 in the Ohio Luth. *Hymnal*, 1880.

[J. M.]

Helmbold, Ludwig, s. of Stephan Helmbold, woollen manufacturer at Mühlhausen, in Thuringia, was b. at Mühlhausen, Jan. 13, 1532, and educated at Leipzig and Erfurt (B.A. in 1550). After two years' headmastership of the St. Mary's School at Mühlhausen, he returned to Erfurt, and remained in the University (M.A. 1554) as lecturer till his appointment in 1561 as conrector of the St. Augustine Gymnasium at Erfurt. When the University was reconstituted in 1565, after the dreadful pestilence in 1563–64, he was appointed dean of the Philosophical Faculty, and in 1566 had the honour of being crowned as a poet by the Emperor Maximilian II., but on account of his determined Protestantism he had to resign in 1570. Returning to Mühlhausen, he was appointed, in 1571, diaconus of the St. Mary's Church, and 1586, pastor of St. Blasius's Church and Superintendent of Mühlhausen. He d. at Mühlhausen, April 8, 1598. (*Koch*, ii. 234–248 ; *Allg. Deutsche Biog.*, xi. 701–702 ; *Bode*, pp. 87–88, &c.)

Helmbold wrote many Latin hymns and odes, and numerous German hymns for school use, including a complete metrical version of the Augsburg Confession. His Hymns for church use are mostly clear and concise paraphrases of Scripture histories and doctrines, simple and earnest in style. Lists of the works in which his hymns appeared (to the number of some 400) are given by *Koch* and *Bode*.

His hymns *tr.* into English are :—

i. **Herr Gott, erhalt uns für und für.** *Children.* On the value of catechetical instruction as conveyed in Luther's *Catechism for Children.* 1st pub. in Helmbold's *Dreyssig geistliche Lieder auff die Fest durchs Jahr.* Mühlhausen, 1594 (preface to tenor, March 21, 1585), and thence in *Wackernagel*, iv. p. 677, and *Mützell*, No. 314, in 4 st. of 4 l. In Porst's *G. B.*, ed. 1855, No. 977. The only *tr.* in C. U. is :—

O God, may we e'er pure retain, in full, by Dr. M. Loy, in the Ohio Luth. *Hyl.*, 1880.

ii. **Nun lasst uns Gott dem Herren.** *Grace after Meat.* Included in his *Geistliche Lieder*, 1575, in 8 st. of 4 l., and thence in *Wackernagel*, iv. p. 647, and the *Unv. L. S.*, 1851, No. 500. The *trs.* are : (1) " To God the Lord be rendered," as No. 326 in pt. i. of the *Moravian H. Bk.*, 1754. (2) " Now let us praise with fervour," in the *Suppl.* to *Ger. Psalmody*, ed. 1765, p. 75. (3) " To God the Lord be praises," as No. 778 in the *Moravian H. Bk.*, 1789 (1849, No. 1153).

iii. **Von Gott will ich nicht lassen.** *Trust in God.* Lauxmann in *Koch*, viii. 365–370, thus relates the origin of this the best known hymn by Helmbold :—

In 1563, while Helmbold was conrector of the Gymnasium at Erfurt, a pestilence broke out, during which about 4000 of the inhabitants died. As all who could fled from the place, Dr. Pancratius Helbich, Rector of the University (with whom Helmbold had formed a special friendship, and whose wife was godmother of his eldest daughter), was about to do so, leaving behind him Helmbold and his family. Gloomy forebodings filled the hearts of the parting mothers. To console them and nerve them for parting Helmbold composed this hymn on Psalm lxxiii. v. 23.

The hymn seems to have been first printed as a broadsheet in 1563–64, and dedicated to Regine, wife of Dr. Helbich, and then in the *Hundert Christenliche Haussgesang*, Nürnberg, 1569, in 9 st. of 8 l. *Wackernagel*, iv. pp. 630–33, gives both these forms and a third in 7 st. from a MS. at Dresden. Included in most subsequent hymn-books, e.g. as No. 640 in the *Unv. L. S.*, 1851. The *trs.* in C. U. are :—

1. **From God the Lord my Saviour,** by J. C. Jacobi, in his *Psal. Ger.*, 1722, p. 139, omitting st. vii. (1732, p. 134), repeated slightly altered (and with st. vi., ll. 1–4 from vii., ll. 1–4 of the German) as No. 320 in pt. i. of the *Moravian*

H. Bk., 1754. St. i.–iii., v., rewritten and beginning "From God, my Lord and Saviour," were included in the Amer. Luth. Gen. Synod's *Coll.*, 1850–52, No. 341.

2. Ne'er be my God forsaken. A good *tr.* of st. i., ii., iv., by A. T. Russell in his *Ps. & Hys.*, 1851, No. 229.

3. From God shall nought divide me. A good *tr.*, omitting st. ii., vii. by Miss Winkworth in her *C. B. for England*, 1863, No. 140. Partly rewritten in her *Christian Singers*, 1869, p. 154.

Other *trs.* are: (1) "God to my soul benighted," by *Dr. H. Mills*, 1845 (1856, p. 179). (2) "From God I will not sever," by Dr. N. L. Frothingham, 1870, p. 202.   [J. M.]

Help, Lord, for men of virtue fail.
I. Watts. [*Ps. xii.*] Appeared in his *Ps. of David*, 1719, in 8 st. of 4 l. In addition to its use in its original form, st. v., viii. are used as a separate hymn in Spurgeon's *O. O. H. Bk.*, 1866, as "Lord, when iniquities abound."   [J. J.]

Help, Lord! the busy foe. *C. Wesley.* [*Prayer during business.*] Pub. in his *Hys. & Sac. Poems*, 1749, vol. i., in 3 st. of 8 l. (*P. Works*, 1868–72, vol. v. p. 51.) In the *Wes. H. Bk.*, 1780, No. 287, st. ii., iii. were given as "The praying Spirit breathe," but in the revised ed., 1875, the opening stanza was restored. It is in its abridged form that it is usually known.   [J. J.]

Hemans, Felicia Dorothea, née Browne, was b. in Liverpool, Sep. 25, 1793. In 1800, her father having suffered severe losses in business, removed with his family near to Abergele, N. Wales, where she died sometime after. In 1812 she was married to Captain Hemans, who, on retiring from the army sometime after, removed to Bronnylfa, near St. Asaph. Some years after he left his wife and children and proceeded to Italy, where he died. In 1828 Mrs. Hemans removed to Wavertree, near Liverpool, and in 1831 to Dublin, where she d. May 16, 1835, and was buried in St. Ann's Church, Dawson Street, in that city. From 1808, when at 15 she pub. *Poems*, to 1834, when her *Scenes & Hymns of Life* appeared, she produced a great number of poems and other works, including:

(1) *The Domestic Affections and Other Poems*, 1812; (2) *The Sceptic*, 1820; (3) *Dartmoor*, 1821; (4) *Vespers of Palermo*, 1823; (5) *The Siege of Valencia*, 1823; (6) *Voice of Spring*, 1823; (7) *Forest Sanctuary*, 1825; (8) *Hymns for Childhood*, 1827 (English edition, 1834; first pub. in America); (9) *Records of Woman and Miscellaneous Poems*, 1828; (10) *Songs of the Affections*, 1830; (11) *Scenes and Hymns of Life* (dedicated to the poet Wordsworth), 1834. Then followed (12) *The Works of Mrs. Hemans; with a Memoir of her Life by her Sister* [Mrs. Hughes]. Edinburgh, W. Blackwood & Sons, 1839, in 7 vols. Her *Poems* were collected and published by Blackwood in 1849, and again as one of the *Chandos Classics*, 1886.

Three distinct ideas pervade Mrs. Hemans's poetry, the Fatherhood of God, Heaven as our Home, and mutual recognition when there. The work of the Atonement has a very subordinate place; and the Holy Spirit is scarcely recognised. The rhythm, even in her most popular pieces, is often disappointing, and a deep tone of sadness pervades most of her work. The gloom of disappointment and the traces of shadowed memories run like black threads through the web and woof of her productions. As a writer of hymns she

holds a subordinate place. The best are "Answer me, burning stars of light," "Calm on the bosom of thy God," "Come to the land of peace," and "Fear was within the tossing bark."   [J. D.]

Mrs. Hemans's hymns which have come into C. U. include:—

1. Answer me, burning stars of light. *Trust in God.* Written after the death of a sister-in-law, and pub. in her *Records of Woman*, &c., 1828, p. 242, in 4 st. of 8 l. (*P. Works*, N.Y., 1828, vol. ii. pp. 144, 268).

2. Calm on the bosom of thy God. *Death and Burial.* This hymn appears in the closing scene of her dramatic poem, *The Siege of Valencia*, 1823, p. 235, in 2 st. of 4 l. (*Works*, vol. iii. p. 379). It is supposed to be sung over the bier of Ximena, daughter of Gonzalez, the Governor of Valencia, during the final struggle of the siege. Mrs. Hemans subsequently added a third stanza ("Lone are the paths, and sad the bowers"); and in this form it is published separately as "A Dirge" in her *Works*, vol. iv. p. 330. It is one of the best known of her hymns.

3. Child, amidst the flowers at play. *Hour of Prayer.* This is given in her *P. Works*, 1828, vol. ii. p. 85, amongst the "Miscellaneous Pieces," in 3 st. of 4 l., as a hymn for *The Hour of Prayer.* Dr. Martineau in his *Hymns*, &c., 1873, dates it 1825.

4. Come to me, dreams [thoughts] of heaven. *Aspiration.* Appeared in her *National Lyrics*, 1834, p. 251, and again in her *Works*, 1839, vol. vii. p. 88.

5. Come to the land of peace. *The Angel's Greeting.* Pub. in her *Works*, 1839, vol. vi. p. 186.

6. Earth! guard what here we lay in holy trust. *Burial.* Given in her *Works*, 1839, vol. iv. p. 327. This is a poem, and not a hymn.

7. Father! that in the olive shade. *Gethsemane.* Written at the death-bed of her mother, Jan., 1827, and pub. in her *Hymns for Childhood*, in 4 st. of 4 l., as a *Hymn by the sick-bed of a Mother.* (*Works*, 1839, vol. vi. p. 147.) Sometimes as "O Thou, Who in the olive shade."

8. Father, Who art on high. *Prayer.* This is part of her "Cathedral Hymn," pub. in her *Scenes and Hys. of Life.* (*Works*, 1839, vi. p. 142.)

9. Fear was within the tossing bark. *Stilling the Tempest.* This hymn appeared in her *Hymns for Childhood*, 1827; her *Poet. Works*, N. Y., 1828, ii. p. 124; and her *Works*, 1839, vol. iv. p. 325.

10. He knelt, the Saviour knelt and prayed. *Gethsemane.* This hymn appeared in *The Almut* (an annual) in 1825, and her *P. Works*, N.Y., 1828, ii. p. 125. It is also introduced in her dramatic poem, *The English Martyrs: a Scene of the days of Queen Mary*, pub. in her *Scenes and Hys. of Life*, 1834, p. 16. A betrothed couple are condemned to death: but are allowed a short intercourse before execution. This they employ in prayer and the singing of this hymn, which is based upon the sacred scene in *Gethsemane.* "The English Martyrs" is the opening piece of the *Scenes and Hys. of Life*, 1834. (*Works*, vii. p. 130.)

11. I hear thee speak of the better land. *Heaven.* Pub. in her *Poetical Works*, N. York, 1828, ii. p. 193, and her *Songs of the Affections*, 1830, p. 225, in 4 st. of 7 l., and headed "The Better Land." (*Works*, 1839, vi. p. 123.) Popular as a sacred song, but not much used as a hymn.

12. Leaves have their time to fall. *The Hour of Death.* Pub. in her *Poet. Works*, N. Y., 1828, ii. p. 114, and in her *Forest Sanctuary*, 2nd ed., 1829, p. 276, in 10 st. of 4 l. (*Works*, 1839, iv. p. 177.) It is usually given in an abbreviated form.

13. Lowly and solemn be Thy children's cry to Thee. *Burial.* This hymn, in 9 st. of 6 l., forms the closing portion of her poem on *The Funeral Day of Sir Walter Scott.* [He d. Sept. 21, 1832.] The poem was given in her *Scenes and Hys. of Life*, 1834, p. 99. (*Works*, vii. p. 178.) In an abbreviated form this Burial hymn is in extensive use in G. Britain and America, and is found in more hymn-books than all the rest of Mrs. Hemans's hymns put together.

14. No cloud obscures the summer's sky. *Ps. xix.* Appeared in her *Hymns for Childhood*, in 10 st. of 4 l., and entitled "The Stars." (*Works*, 1839, iv. p. 253.) It is usually given in an abbreviated form, beginning with st. ii., "Child of the earth, Oh lift thy glance."

15. Now autumn strews on every plain. *Harvest.* One of her juvenile pieces, pub. in her *Poems*, Liverpool, 1808, p. 94, as a "Harvest Hymn."

16. O lovely voices of the sky. *Christmas Carol.* Appeared in her *Hymns for Childhood*, 1827, in 3 st. of 8 l., and her *Poet. Works*, N. Y., 1828, ii. p. 123. (*Works*, v. p. 307.)

17. Praise ye the Lord on every height. *Ps. cxlviii.* Pub. in her *Hys. for Childhood*, in 7 st. of 4 l. (*Works*, 1839, iv. p. 264.)

18. Saviour, now receive him. *Burial. Scenes and Hys. of Life*, 1834, p. 70, is a hymn entitled, "The Funeral Hymn" in the *Burial of an Emigrant's Child in the Forest*. It begins "Where the long reeds quiver." This extract opens with st. ii. altered.

19. The breaking waves dashed high. *Landing of the Pilgrim Fathers.* Pub. in her *Records of Woman*, &c., 1828, p. 261, in 10 st. of 4 l., and in her *Works*, 1828, p. 261, "The Landing of the Pilgrim Fathers in New England." (*Works*, 1839, v. p. 280.) Popular as a sacred song, but not much used as a hymn.

20. The Church of our fathers so dear to our souls. *The Holy Church.* This hymn has not been traced to date. Snepp, in *S. of G. & G.*, says 1834.

21. The kings of old have shrine and tomb. *The Graves of Martyrs.* In *The Forest Sanctuary*, 2nd ed., 1829, p. 284, "The Graves of Martyrs" in 7 st. Also *Poet. Works*, N. Y., 1828, ii. p. 150.

22. Where is the tree the prophet threw? *Faith.* Appeared in her *Poet. Works*, N. Y., 1828, ii. p. 170, and headed "The Fountain of Marah." Also in her *Works*, 1839, vi. p. 176. [J. J.]

Hence, vain intruding world, depart. *Anne Steele.* [*Retirement and Reflection.*] 1st pub. in her *Poems on Subjects chiefly Devotional*, 1760, vol. i. p. 124, in 8 st. of 4 l., again in the new ed., 1780; and again in Sedgwick's reprint of her *Hymns*, 1863. In its full form it is not in C. U., but an abridged form beginning with st. iv., "Eternity is just at hand," appeared in the 2nd ed. of Toplady's *Ps. & Hys.*, 1787, No. 410, and is repeated in several modern collections; but mainly in America. [J. J.]

Henley, John, b. at Torquay, March 18, 1800; engaged for some years in circuit work as a Wesleyan minister; and d. at Weymouth, May 2, 1842. His well-known and popular children's hymn for *Palm Sunday*, "Children of Jerusalem," appeared in the *Wes. S. School Tune Bk.*, in J. Curwen's *Hys. & Chants*, 1844, and in many modern collections for children. Orig. text in the *Meth. S. S. H. Bk.*, 1879. [J. J.]

Henry, Matthew, an eminent Nonconformist divine and commentator, was b. in Flintshire, Oct. 18, 1662, and educated for the Bar. Leaving his legal studies he became a Dissenting minister at Chester, where he resided for many years, and subsequently removed to Hackney. He d. whilst travelling between Chester and London, June 22, 1714. His *Exposition of the Old and New Testament* is well known. His connection with Hymnology lay in his having published a volume of *Family Hymns* in 1695. (See **English Hymnody, Early, § VI. 2.**) [J. J.]

Hensel, Luise, dau. of J. J. L. Hensel, Lutheran pastor at Linum, near Fehrbellin, Brandenburg, was b. at Linum, March 30, 1798. Though confirmed as a Lutheran in her fifteenth year, she gradually approximated to Roman Catholicism, and was formally received into that Communion, Dec. 7, 1818. During the remaining years of her life, she devoted herself mainly to the education of the young and the care of the sick. In 1874 she entered the Union of Daughters of Christian Love at Paderborn, and d. at Paderborn, Dec. 18, 1876. (*O. Kraus*, 1879, pp. 204-211; *Allg. Deutsche Biog.*, xii. 1-3, &c.) Her best hymns were written before she was 23, and in proportion as she became an Ultramontane

the poetical value of her productions declined. Her finest productions are distinguished by childlike simplicity, humility, resignation, and deep Christian love. They have won wide acceptance in Germany. The first two of those noted may be regarded as nursery classics.

A number of her hymns came into Clemens Brentano's hands as early as 1819, and were by mistake included as his in his posthumous works. A few were printed in F. Förster's *Sängerfahrt*, 1818, and a good many more in M. Diepenbrock's *Geistlicher Blumenstrauss*, Sulzbach, 1829. A complete ed. of her hymns was pub. by Professor C. Schlüter of Münster as her *Lieder* at Paderborn, 1870 (4th ed., 1879).

i. *Hymns in English C. U.*

i. Immer muss ich wieder lesen. [*Holy Scripture.*] This beautiful children's hymn on the Life of Christ as narrated in the Gospels, appeared in *Diepenbrock*, 1829, p. 265, in 7 st. of 4 l. (entitled "On the reading of Holy Scripture"); and in her *Lieder*, 1870, is dated Berlin, 1815. It is repeated in Knapp's *Ev. L. S.*, 1837, the Württemberg *G. B.*, 1842, &c. *Tr.* as :—

Ever would I fain be reading. A good and full *tr.* by Miss Winkworth in her *Lyra Ger.*, 2nd Ser., 1858, p. 24. It has been included in full in *Ps. & Hys.*, Bedford, 1859; *Kennedy*, 1863; *Bk. of Praise for Children*, 1881; and in America in Hatfield's *Church H. Bk.*, 1872, and others. In some collections it is abridged; and in the Unitarian South Place *Collection*, Lond., 1873, it begins, "Ever find I joy in reading."

Other trs. are :—

(1) "O how sweet the wondrous story," by *Mrs. Bevan*, 1859, p. 142. (2) "In that book so old and holy," in Dr. H. W. Dulcken's *Golden Harp*, 1864, p. 25. (3) "Still I read, and weary never," by "A. M. A," in the *British Herald*, Feb. 1868, p. 211.

ii. Müde bin ich, geh' zur Ruh. [*Evening.*] This beautiful child's evening prayer, the most popular of all her hymns, appeared in *Diepenbrock*, 1829, p. 270, in 4 st. of 4 l. In her *Lieder*, 1870, p. 54, dated Berlin, Autumn, 1816. Included in the *Unv. L. S.*, 1851, No. 528. *Tr.* as :—

1. Now that o'er each weary head. A free *tr.* of st. i.–iii. as No. 22 in C. H. Bateman's *Children's Hyl.*, 1872.

2. Weary now I go to rest. A good *tr.* of st. i.–iii. by E. Cronenwett as No. 324 in the Ohio *Luth. Hyl.*, 1880.

Other trs. are :—

(1) "Now I close my tired eyes," by *Mrs. Bevan*, 1859, p. 147. (2) "I am tir'd, and so I seek," by *Miss Manington*, 1863, p. 126. (3) "Weary now I go to bed," in Dr. H. W. Dulcken's *Golden Harp*, 1864, p. 40. (4) "Now with weariness opprest," a second *tr.* by *Dr. Dulcken*, p. 72. (5) "Wearied now I seek repose," by *J. Kelly*, 1885, p. 111.

ii. *Hymns not in English C. U.*

iii. Ich liebe einen Königs Sohn. [*Love to Christ.*] In *Diepenbrock*, 1829, p. 304, in 9 st., and in her *Lieder*, 1870, p. 67, dated Berlin, 1817. *Tr.* as "I love a royal only Son," by *E. Massie*, 1867, p. 174.

iv. O Sonne, wenn von deinem Licht. [*Love to Christ.*] In *Diepenbrock*, 1829, p. 257, in 6 st., and in her *Lieder*, 1870, p. 128, dated Sondermühlen, 1823. *Tr.* as "O Sun, if from thy light a ray," in J. D. Burns's *Memoir and Remains*, 1869, p. 270.

v. O Sorge, die mich niederdrückt. [*Encouragement.*] In *Diepenbrock*, 1829, p. 271, in 6 st., and in her *Lieder*, 1870, p. 13, dated Berlin, 1815. The *trs.* are :—(1) "O anxious care that weighs me down," by Miss Burlingham, in the *British Herald*, Sept. 1865, p. 144. (2) "Begone, O load of care, begone," by *J. Kelly*, 1885, p. 80.

vi. Was verlangst du, warum bangst du. [*Cross and Consolation.*] In *Diepenbrock*, 1829, p. 261, in 6 st., entitled "Sürsum corda." In her *Lieder*, 1870, p. 43, it is dated Berlin, 1816. *Tr.* as "What seekest thou ! Why fearest thou," by *C. T. Astley*, 1860, p. 28.

vii. **Zu dir, zu dir, hinweg von mir.** [*Consecration to Christ.*] In *Diepenbrock*, 1829, p. 267, in 5 st. In her *Lieder*, 1870, p. 31, dated Berlin, 1816. *Tr.* as "To Thee, to Thee, away from self," by *J. Kelly*, 1885, p. 72.

[J. M.]

Hensley, Lewis, M.A., b. May, 1824, and educated at Trinity College, Cambridge, where in 1846 he graduated as Senior Wrangler, and first Smith's Prizeman. From 1846 to 1852 he was a Fellow and Assistant Tutor of Trinity College. Taking Holy Orders in 1851, he held successively the Curacy of Upton-with-Chalvey, Bucks; the Vicarage of Ippolyts-with-Great-Wymondly, Hertfordshire, and that of Hitchin, in the same county; Rural Dean, 1867. His works include *Household Devotions; Shorter Household Devotions*, &c. His hymns appeared in his *Hymns for the Sundays after Trinity*, Lon., Bell & Daldy, 1864; and *Hymns for the Minor Sundays from Advent to Whitsuntide*, Lond., Bell & Daldy, 1867. His Advent hymn, "Thy Kingdom come, O God," is from the latter of these works. [J. J.]

Herberger, Valerius, s. of Martin Herberger, furrier and poet at Fraustadt, Posen, was b. at Fraustadt, April 21, 1562. He studied theology at the Universities of Frankfurt a. Oder and Leipzig, and became in 1584 master of the lower classes in the school at Fraustadt. In 1590 he was appointed diaconus of St. Mary's Church, Fraustadt, and in 1599 chief pastor; but in 1604 he and his flock were ousted from the church by King Sigismund III., of Poland, for the sake of the few Roman Catholics in the place. Out of two houses near one of the gates of the town they made a meeting-place, to which, as the first service was held on Christmas Eve, the name of the "Kripplein Christi" was given. He d. at Fraustadt, May 18, 1627 (*Koch*, ii. 301–311; *Allg. Deutsche Biog.*, xii. 28–29, &c.).

Herberger pub. two sets of sermons, the *Evangelische Herzpostille* and the *Epistolische Herzpostille*. His famous work, the *Magnalia Dei, de Jesu Scripturae nucleo et medulla*, 8 vols., 1601–1610, was designed to show Christ all through the Old Testament, but in his exposition he only reached the book of Ruth. As a pastor he worked unweariedly for the good of his people, especially during the time of the great pestilence (1613 to 1630), and during the troubles of the early part of the Thirty Years' War.

Herberger wrote only a few hymns, and of these the best known is:—

Valet will ich dir geben. *For the Dying.* 1st pub. on a broadsheet entitled :—

"A devout prayer with which the Evangelical citizens of Frawenstadt in the autumn of the year 1613 moved the heart of God the Lord so that He mercifully laid down His sharp rod of wrath under which nearly two thousand fell on sleep. And also a hymn of consolation in which a pious heart bids farewell (Valet) to this world. Both composed by Valerius Herberger, preacher at the Kripplein Christi." Leipzig, 1614.

The hymn was pub. in *Mützell*, 1858, No. 6, in 5 st. of 8 l. The title of the hymn itself is:—

"The Farewell (Valet) of Valerius Herberger that he gave to this world in the autumn of the year 1613, when he every hour saw death before his eyes, but mercifully and also as wonderfully as the three men in the furnace at Babylon was nevertheless spared."

In this pestilence 2135 perished at Fraustadt, but Herberger manfully stuck to his post, and passed through all unhurt, comforting the sick and helping to bury the dead.

The hymn is an acrostic on his name formed by the beginnings of the stanzas—Vale (i.), r (ii.) i (iii.) u (iv.) s (v). It is one of the finest German hymns for the dying. It speedily passed into the hymn-books, and is still a favourite. In the Berlin *G. L. S.*, ed. 1863, No. 1502. Sometimes given beginning "Abschied will " or "Lebwohl will."

The beautiful melody which appeared with the hymn in 1614 is by Herberger's precentor, Melchior Teschner, and is now well known in England, being included, e.g. in *H. A. & M.*, as St. Theodulph.

The *trs.* in C. U. are :—

1. **O World so vain, I leave thee,** a good *tr.*, omitting st. iv., by A. T. Russell, as No. 248 in his *Ps. & Hys.*, 1851.

2. **Farewell I gladly bid thee,** a good and full *tr.* by Miss Winkworth, as No. 137 in her *C. B. for England*, 1863.

Other trs. are : (1) "Grant in the bottom of my heart," a *tr.* of st. iii. as No. 29 in the *Moravian H. Bk.*, 1742. (2) "Farewell henceforth for ever," by L. T. Nyberg, in the *Moravian H. Bk.*, 1754, pt. i., No. 451 (1886, No. 1227). (3) "Shelter our souls most graciously," by L. T. Nyberg, in the *Moravian H. Bk.*, pt. ii., 1746, p. 794 (1886, as pt. of No. 793). (4) "Vain world, forbear thy pleading," by *Dr. H. Mills*, 1856, p. 107. (5) "I bid adieu for ever," in the *British Herald*, Aug. 1866, p. 306, repeated in Reid's *Praise Bk.*, 1872, No. 336. (6) "My parting spirit biddeth," in the *Family Treasury*, 1878, p. 496. [J. M.]

Herbert, Daniel, for many years a Congregational Minister at Sudbury, Suffolk (b. circa 1751, d. Aug. 29, 1833), pub. :—

Hymns & Poems, Doctrinal and Sentimental, for the Citizens of Zion, who are longing to know their election of God, and who love Evangelical Truths. These were pub. in 3 vols. (i., 1801; ii., 1819; iii., 1827). Both hymns and poems are very indifferent in quality, and strongly Calvinistic in doctrine. (*Singers & Songs*, by J. Miller, 1869.) [J. J.]

Herbert, George, M.A., the fifth s. of Richard Herbert and Magdalen, the daughter of Sir Richard Newport, was b. at his father's seat, Montgomery Castle, April 3, 1593. He was educated at Westminster School, and at Trinity College, Cambridge, graduating B.A. in 1611. On March 15, 1615, he became Major Fellow of the College, M.A. the same year, and in 1619 Orator for the University. Favoured by James I., intimate with Lord Bacon, Bishop Andrewes, and other men of influence, and encouraged in other ways, his hopes of Court preferment were somewhat bright until they were dispelled by the deaths of the Duke of Richmond, the Marquis of Hamilton, and then of King James himself. Retiring into Kent, he formed the resolution of taking Holy Orders. He was appointed by the Bp. of Lincoln to the Prebend of Leighton Ecclesia and to the living of Leighton Bromswold, Hunts, July 15, 1626. He remained until 1629, when an attack of ague obliged him to remove to his brother's house at Woodford, Essex. Not improving in health at Woodford, he removed to Dantsey, in Wiltshire, and then as Rector to Bemerton, to which he was inducted, April 26, 1630, where he d. Feb. 1632. The entry in the register of Bemerton is "Mr. George Herbert, Esq., Parson of Foughleston and Bemerton, was buried 3 day of March 1632."

His life, by Izaak Walton, is well known ; another Memoir, by Barnabas Oley, is forgotten. Herbert's prose work, *Priest to the Temple*, appeared several years after his death : but *The Temple*, by which he is best known, he delivered to Nicholas Ferrar (q.v.), about three weeks before his death, and authorized him to publish it if he thought fit. This was done in 1633.

The work became popular, and the 13th ed. was issued in 1709. It is meditative rather than hymnic in character, and was never intended for use in public worship. In 1697 a selection from *The Temple* appeared under the title *Select Hymns Taken out of Mr. Herbert's Temple & turned into the Common Metre To Be Sung In The Tunes Ordinarily us'd in Churches.* London, Parkhurst, 1697. In 1739, J. & C. Wesley made a much more successful attempt to introduce his hymns into public worship by inserting over 40 in a much-altered form in their *Hymns & Sacred Poems.* As some few of these came into their collection of *Ps. & Hys.*, 1741, revised 1743, they were long sung by the Methodists, but do not now form part of the *Wes. H. Bk.* No further attempt seems to have been made to use the *Temple* poems as hymns until 1853, when some altered and revised by G. Rawson were given in the *Leeds H. Bk.* of that year. From that time onward more attention was paid to Herbert alike by Churchmen and Nonconformists, and some of his hymns are now widely accepted. Many editions of his works have been published, the most popular being that of the Rev. Robert Aris Wilmott, Lond., Geo. Routledge & Son, 1857; but Dr. Grosart's privately printed edition issued in his *Fuller Worthies Library* in 1874, in three volumes, is not only the most complete and correct, but included also his psalms not before reprinted, and several poems from a ms. in the Williams Library, and not before published. The *Temple* has also been published in facsimile by Elliott Stock, 1876, with preface by Dr. Grosart; and in ordinary type, 1882, by Wells Gardner, with preface by J. A. Shorthouse. [Eng. Hymnody, Early, § vii.]

The quaintness of Herbert's lyrics and the peculiarity of several of their metres have been against their adoption for congregational purposes. The best known are : " Let all the world in every corner sing"; "My stock lies dead, and no increase"; "Throw away Thy rod"; "Sweet day, so cool, so calm"; and "Teach me, my God, and King." [W. T. B.]

Herbert, Petrus, seems to have been a native of or resident at Fulnek in Moravia. He was ordained priest of the Brethren's Unity in 1562, became a member of the Select Council in 1567, and was latterly Consenior of the Unity. By the Unity he was entrusted with many important missions. He was sent as a deputy to confer with Calvin : and again in 1562 to arrange with Duke Christoph of Württemberg for the education at Tübingen of young men from the Bohemian Brethren. He was also one of the deputies sent to Vienna to present the revised form of the Brethren's Confession of Faith to the Emperor Maximilian II. in 1564, and in 1566 to present their new German Hymn Book. He d. at Eibenschütz in 1571 (*Koch*, ii. 414 ; *Allg. Deutsche Biog.*, xiii. 263–264, &c.). Herbert was one of the principal compilers of the enlarged ed. of the Brethren's German H. Bk. pub. in 1566 as their *Kirchengeseng*, and contributed to it some 90 hymns. In the ed. of 1639 there are 104 hymns marked as his. His hymns are distinguished by simplicity and beauty of style. A number are *trs.* from the Bohemian. [See **Bohemian Hymnody :**—Augusta, J., and Červenka, M.] His hymns *tr.* into English include :

i. **Die Nacht ist kommen drin wir ruhen sollen.** [*Evening.*] Written probably under the pressure of persecution and oppression. In the *G. B.*, 1566, as above, in 5 st. of 7 l. (the last st. being a versification of the Lord's Prayer), and thence in *Wackernagel*, iv. p. 442, and the *Unv. L. S.*, 1851, No. 515. In J. H. Schein's *Cantional*, 1627, it appears as No. 99, with an additional st. not by Herbert, which reads :—

" Denn wir kein besser Zuflucht können haben,
Als zu dir, O Herr, in dem Himmel droben,
Du verlest keinen, gibst Acht auff die deinen,
Die dich recht meynen,"

This st. is included as st. v. in the version in Bunsen's *Versuch*, 1833, No. 43. *Tr.* as :—

1. **The night is come, wherein at last we rest,** in full from Bunsen by Miss Winkworth in her *Lyra Ger.*, 2nd Ser., 1858, p. 77, repeated as No. 105 in R. Minton Taylor's *Coll.*, 1872.

2. **Now God be with us, for the night is closing,** a good *tr.* from Bunsen, in the original metre, by Miss Winkworth, as No. 170 in her *C. B. for England*, 1863, and repeated in her *Christian Singers of Germany*, 1869, p. 139. This version has been included in various recent collections, though generally abridged or altered, as in the *Hymnary*, 1872; Thring's *Coll.*, 1882; and in America in the *Evang. Hyl.*, N. Y., 1880, &c. In *Laudes Domini*, N.Y., 1884, it is in two parts (Nos. 209–210), the second beginning, "Father, Thy name be praised, Thy kingdom given." This is st. vi. with an added doxology, as in the *Hymnary*, 1872.

Other trs. are :—
(1) "The night comes apace," as No. 293 in pt. i. of the *Moravian H. Bk.*, 1754. (2) "Lo! evening's shades to sleep invite," by *H. J. Buckoll*, 1842, p. 64.

ii. **O Christenmensch, merk wie sichs hält.** [*Faith.*] 1566, as above, in 18 st. of 4 l., repeated in *Wackernagel*, iv. p. 433. In Bunsen's *Versuch*, 1833, No. 390 (*Allg. G. B.*, 1846, No. 130), the hymn begins with st. iii. altered to "Der Glaub' ist ein lebend'ge Kraft," and consists of st. iii., viii., xi., xii., xvi., xviii. Bunsen calls it "a noble confession of the true Christian faith." *Tr.* as :—

Faith is a living power from heaven. A good *tr.* from Bunsen by Miss Winkworth in her *Lyra Ger.*, 2nd ser., 1858, p. 160, and thence in her *C. B. for England*, 1863. It is repeated, more or less altered and abridged, in *Kennedy*, 1863; and in America in the *Presb. Hyl.*, 1874, Baptist *Service of Song*, 1871, &c.

ii. *Hymns not in English C. U. :—*

iii. **Des Herren Wort bleibt in Ewigkeit.** [*Holy Scripture.*] 1566, as above, in 25 st., and in *Wackernagel*, iv. p. 432. *Tr.* as "God's holy Word, which ne'er shall cease," by J. Swertner, as No. 3 in the *Moravian H. Bk.*, 1789 (1849, No. 2).

iv. **Fürchtet Gott, O lieben Leut.** [*Martyrs.*] 1566, as above, in 13 st., and in *Wackernagel*, iv. p. 429. The *trs.* are, (i.) "O love God, ye people dear," as No. 267 in pt. i. of the *Moravian H. Bk.*, 1754. (2) "O exalt and praise the Lord" (from the version in the *Brüder G. B.*, 1778, beginning "Liebet Gott"), as No. 871 in the *Moravian H. Bk.*, 1789 (1886, No. 1306).

v. **Lasst uns mit Lust und Freud aus Glauben singen.** [*Eternal Life.*] A fine hymn on the Joys of Heaven. 1566, as above, in 12 st., and in *Wackernagel*, iv. p. 447. *Tr* as "In faith we sing this song of thankfulness," by Mrs. *Bevan*, 1858, p. 34.

vi. **O höchster Trost, heiliger Geist.** [*Whitsuntide.*] 1566, as above, in 13 st., and *Wackernagel*, iv. p. 407. The *trs.* are, (1) "O highest comfort, Holy Ghost," as No. 262 in pt. i. of the *Moravian H. Bk.*, 1754. (2) "O Comforter, God Holy Ghost," as No. 203 in the *Moravian H. Bk.*, 1789 (1849, No. 265).

Besides the above a number of hymns by Herbert (all of which appeared in the *Kirchengeseng*, 1566, and are included in *Wackernagel's* vol. iv.) were *tr.* in pt. i. of the *Moravian H. Bk.*, 1754. The numbers in the 1754 are 166, 259, 263, 264, 265, 266, 274, 277, 281, 287, and 294. [J. M.]

Here at Thy Cross, my dying God. *I. Watts.* [*Salvation in the Cross.*] 1st pub. in his *Hys. & S. Songs*, 1707, Bk. ii., No. 4, in 5 st. of 4 l. It is in C. U. in its original form, and as: "Here at Thy Cross, my dying *Lord*"; "Here at Thy Cross, *incarnate* God"; and

"Here at Thy Cross, *my Saviour* God," in various American hymn-books, the aim of these alterations being to remove the objection that might be made to the clause *my dying God*, in the opening line.   [J. J.]

Here, O my Lord, I see Thee face to face. *H. Bonar.* [*Holy Communion.*] Dr. H. Bonar's elder brother, Dr. John James Bonar, St. Andrew's Free Church, Greenock, is wont after each Communion, to print a memorandum of the various services, and a suitable hymn. After the Communion on the first Sunday of October, 1855, he asked his brother, Dr. H. Bonar, to furnish a hymn, and in a day or two received this hymn (possibly composed before), and it was then printed, with the memorandum, for the first time. It was pub. in *Hys. of Faith and Hope*, 1st series, 1857, in 10 st. of 4 l., and headed, "This do in remembrance of me." In addition to being in extensive use in its original, or in an abridged but unaltered form, it is also given as :—

1. Here would I, Lord, behold Thee face to face, in *Ps. & Hys.*, Bedford, 1859, &c.
2. Here, Lord, by faith I see Thee face to face, in *Hatfield's Church H. Bk.*, N. Y., 1872, &c.
3. Here, O my Lord, I humbly seek Thy face, in T. Darling's *Hymns*, &c., 1887.
4. And now we rise, the symbols disappear. Composed of st. v. and x. in the American Bapt. *Service of Song*, Boston, 1871.
5. I have no help but Thine, nor do I need, in the Leeds *S. S. H. Bk.*, ed. 1858.

In literary merit, earnestness, pathos, and popularity, this hymn ranks with the best of Dr. Bonar's compositions.   [J. B.]

Here we suffer grief and pain. *T. Bilby.* [*Heaven anticipated.*] Pub. in *The Infant School Teachers' Assistant*, 1832, in 6 st. of 3 l., with the refrain, " O that will be joyful." Although suited in sentiment more to the aged than the young, yet mainly through the tune to which it is set and the refrain, it has become a very popular hymn with children, and is in extensive use in Sunday-schools. Authorised text from the author's ms. in *Lyra Brit.*, 1867, p. 62.   [J. J.]

Heri mundus exultavit. *Adam of St. Victor.* [*St. Stephen.*] This sequence is by some considered to be the masterpiece of the poet, and is by Abp. Trench termed "a sublime composition." The full text, in 78 lines, together with a French *tr.* of the 15th cent., and extended notes, is given by Gautier in his *Oeuvres Poétiques d'Adam de S. Victor*; Paris, 1858, pp. 211–222. Gautier, in his 2nd ed., 1881, p. 78, quotes it from the *Limoges Sequentiary* of the 12th or 13th cent. (Bibl. Nat., Paris, No. 1139), a *Gradual* of the Abbey of St. Victor written before 1239 (Bibl. Nat., Paris, No. 14452, and other mss.). It is also found in *Daniel*, ii. p. 64 ; *Kehrein*, No. 714 ; Trench's *Sac. Latin Poetry*, ed. 1864, p. 212 ; *The Liturgical Poetry of Adam of St. Victor*, &c., by D. S. Wrangham, 1881, and others. *Daniel* thinks lines 63–78 (omitted by *Trench*) are of doubtful authenticity. The legendary miracles there noted as worked by the relics of St. Stephen are however recorded by St. Augustine in Bk. xxii. c. 8, of his *De Civitate Dei*, a work probably well known to the author of this hymn, and the lines are in almost all the mss. *Tr.* as :—

1. Yesterday with exultation. By *J. M. Neale*, pub. in the 2nd ed. of his *Mediaeval Hymns*, 1863, in 7 st. of 6 l. and 1 st. of 8 l. This was repeated in the *Appendix* to *H. A. & M.*, 1868, with st. viii. reduced to 6 l. ; and in the *Appendix* to the *H. Noted*, 1862, and others in its original form.

2. Jesu, Word of God Incarnate. By *W. Cooke*, made for and first pub. in the *Hymnary*, 1872.

Translations not in C. U. :—
1. Yesterday the happy earth. *Mrs. Charles*, 1858.
2. Mingling with the shouts of earth. *H. Kynaston*, 1862.
3. Death shall be thy birthday morn. Pt. ii. of No. 2.
4. Yesterday the world elated. *D. S. Wrangham*, 1881.   [J. M.]

Herman, Nicolaus, is always associated with Joachimsthal in Bohemia, just over the mountains from Saxony. The town was not of importance till the mines began to be extensively worked about 1516. Whether Herman was a native of this place is not known, but he was apparently there in 1518, and was certainly in office there in 1524. For many years he held the post of Master in the Latin School, and Cantor or Organist and Choirmaster in the church. Towards the end of his life he suffered greatly from gout, and had to resign even his post as Cantor a number of years before his death. He d. at Joachimsthal, May 3, 1561. (*Koch*, i. 390–398 ; *Allg. Deutsche Biog.*, xii. 186–188, &c.)

He was a great friend and helper of J. Mathesius (q.v.) (who in 1532 became rector of the school, but in 1541 diaconus and in 1545 pastor of the church), and it was said that whenever Mathesius preached a specially good sermon Herman straightway embodied its leading ideas in a hymn. His hymns, however, were not primarily written for use in church, but were intended for the boys and girls in the schools, to supplant profane songs in the mouths of the young men and women, or for the daily life of the "house-fathers and house-mothers" in Joachimsthal, at home, and in their work in the mines. He is a poet of the people, homely, earnest, and picturesque in style ; by his naïveté reminding us of Hans Sachs. He was an ardent lover of music and a very good organist. The chorales which he published with his hymns are apparently all of his own composition, and are among the best of the Reformation period.

Many of Herman's hymns soon passed into Church use in Germany, and a number are found in almost all books in present use. About 190 in all, they appeared principally in :—

(1) *Die Sontags Evangelia uber des gantze Jar, in Gesenge verfasset, für die Kinder und christlichen Haussvetter*, &c., Wittenberg, 1560 (dedication by Herman dated Trinity Sunday, 1559), with 101 hymns and 17 melodies. The best are those interspersed specially meant for children and not directly founded on the Gospel for the day. (2) *Die Historien von der Sindfludt, Joseph, Mose, Helia, Elisa und der Susanna, sampt etlichen Historien aus den Evangelisten*, &c., Wittenberg, 1562 (preface by Herman dated St. Bartholomew's Day, 1560), with 73 hymns and 20 melodies. In this case also the general hymns are the best. A selection of 60 (really 61) of his hymns, with a memoir by K. F. Ledderhose, was pub. at Halle, 1855.

One of Herman's hymns is noted under "Wenn mein Stündlein vorhanden ist." The others which have passed into English are :—

i. **Bescher uns, Herr, das täglich Brod.** *Grace before Meat.* 1562, as above, and thence in *Wackernagel*, iii. p. 1228, in 6 st. of 4 l. ; in *Ledderhose*, p. 70 ; and in the Berlin *G. L. S.*, ed. 1863, No. 1133. *Tr.* as :—

1. Thou art our Father and our God. This, by P. H. Molther, a *tr.* of st. vi., as No. 180 in the *Moravian H. Bk.*, 1789 (1849, No. 220, st. v.).

2. As children we are owned by Thee, a *tr.* of st. vi., as st. iii. of No. 191 in the *Moravian H. Bk.*, 1801 (1849, No. 220, st. iii.).

ii. **Die helle Sonn leucht jetzt herfür.** *Morning.* 1560, as above, and thence in *Wackernagel*, iii. p. 1184, in 4 st. of 4 l. ; in *Ledderhose*, p. 87 ; and in the *Unv. L. S.*, 1851, No. 450. *Tr.* as :—

The morning beam revives our eyes, a good and full *tr.* by A. T. Russell, as No. 71 in the *Dalston Hospital H. Bk.*, 1848.

iii. **Erschienen ist der herrliche Tag.** *Easter.* 1560, as above, in 14 st. of 4 l., entitled, "A new Spiritual Song of the Joyful Resurrection of our Saviour Jesus Christ ; for the maidens of the girls' school in Joachimsthal"; and thence in *Wackernagel*, iii. p. 1175 ; in *Ledderhose*, p. 23, and the *Unv. L. S.*, 1851, No. 134. It has reminiscences of the "Erstanden ist der heil'ge Christ" (see **Surrexit Christus**). *Tr.* as :—

The day hath dawn'd—the day of days, a good *tr.* by A. T. Russell of st. i., ii., xiii., xiv., as No. 113 in his *Ps. & Hys.*, 1851.

Another *tr.* is, "At length appears the glorious day," by *Dr. G. Walker*, 1860, p. 28.

iv. **Hinunter ist der Sonnen Schein.** *Evening.* 1560, as above, and thence in *Wackernagel*, iii. p. 1184, in 4 st. of 4 l. ; in *Ledderhose*, p. 88 ; and in the *Unv. L. S.*, 1851, No. 523. Some of the phrases may have been suggested by the "Christe qui lux es et dies" (q. v.). *Tr.* as :—

1. Sunk is the sun's last beam of light, a full and good *tr.* by Miss Cox in her *Sacred H. from the German*, 1841, p. 57. Included in Alford's *Ps. & Hys.*, 1844, and *Year of Praise*, 1867 ; in Dale's *Eng. H. Bk.*, 1875 ; in the Pennsylvania Luth. *Ch. Bk.*, 1868, and others. It is also given considerably altered and beginning, "Sunk is the Sun ! the daylight gone," in W. J. Blew's *Church H. and Tune Bk.*, 1851–55.

2. The happy sunshine all is gone, in full, by Miss Winkworth in her *Lyra Ger.*, 1st Ser., 1855, p. 225 ; repeated in her *C. B. for England*, 1863, and the Ohio *Luth Hyl.*, 1880.

Other *trs.* are : (1) "Did I perhaps Thee somewhat grieve," a *tr.* of st. iii. in the *Moravian H. Bk.*, 1789, No. 756. In the 1801 and later eds. (1886, No. 1181, st. iii.), it begins, "Where'er I Thee this day did grieve." (2) "The sun's fair sheen is' past and gone," by *H. J. Buckoll*, 1842, p. 68. (3) "The sun hath run his daily race," by *Lady E. Fortescue*, 1843, p. 14.

v. **Lobt Gott, ihr Christen alle gleich.** *Christmas.* Written c. 1554, but first pub. 1560 as above, as the first of "Three Spiritual Christmas Songs of the new-born child Jesus, for the children in Joachimsthal." Thence in *Wackernagel*, iii. p. 1169, in 8 st. of 4 l. ; in *Ledderhose*, p. 1; and in the *Unv. L. S.*, 1851, No. 47. It is one of the most popular German Christmas hymns. The melody set to it in 1560 is also by Herman; in 1554 to his "Kommt her ihr liebsten Schwesterlein" [in the *Hymnal Comp.* called "St. George's (old)"]. *Tr.* as :—

1. Let all together praise our God, a good *tr.* of st. i., iii., vi., viii., by A. T. Russell, as No. 52 in his *Ps. & Hys.*, 1851. Repeated in *Kennedy*, 1863, adding a *tr.* of st. ii., and beginning, "Let all creation praise our God."

2. Praise ye the Lord, ye Christians ! yea, in full, by E. Cronenwett, as No. 31 in the Ohio *Luth. Hyl.*, 1880.

Other *trs.* are : (1) "A wondrous change He with us makes," a *tr.* of st. viii., ix. as No. 438 in pt. i. of the *Moravian H. Bk.*, 1754, repeated 1789–1826. (2) "Come, brethren, let the song arise," by *Dr. G. Walker*, 1860,

p. 26. (3) "Praise God, now Christians, all alike," by *Miss Mannington*, 1864, p. 9. (4) "Praise God, upon His throne on high," in the *Sunday Magazine*, 1874, p. 384, signed "P. J." The hymn "Shepherds rejoice, lift up your eyes," given by J. C. Jacobi in his *Psal. Ger.*, 1722, p. 8, to Herman's melody (which was 1st pub. 1554) is, as stated in his Preface, taken from Bk. i. of Isaac Watts's *Horæ Lyricæ.*

vi. **So wahr ich leb, spricht Gott der Herr.** *Absolution.* 1560, as above, in 11 st. of 4 l., entitled "A hymn on the power of the keys and the virtue of holy absolution ; for the children in Joachimsthal." Thence in *Wackernagel*, iii. p. 1183 ; in *Ledderhose*, p. 47 ; and the *Unv. L. S.*, 1851, No. 429. It probably suggested the better known hymn, "So wahr ich lebe,". q. v., by Johann Heermann. *Tr.* as :—

Yea, as I live, Jehovah saith, I do not wish the sinner's death, in full, by Dr. M. Loy, as No. 245, in the Ohio *Luth. Hyl.*, 1880.   [J. M.]

Hernaman, Claudia Frances, née Ibotson, dau. of W. H. Ibotson, sometime Vicar of Edwinstowe, Notts, was b. at Addlestone, Surrey, Oct. 19, 1838, and married Sept. 1858, to the Rev. J. W. D. Hernaman, one of H. M. Inspectors of Schools. Mrs. Hernaman has composed more than 150 hymns, a great proportion of which are for children, and also some *trs.* from the Latin. Her publications include :—

(1) *The Child's Book of Praise ; A Manual of Devotion in Simple Verse by C. F. H. Edited by the Rev. James Skinner, M.A.,* &c., 1873 ; (2) *The Story of the Resurrection,* 1879 ; (3) *Christmas Story,* 1881 ; (4) *Christmas Carols for Children,* 1st series, 1884 ; 2nd series, 1885 ; (5) *The Way of the Cross,* a Metrical Litany, 1885 ; (6) *Hymns for the Seven Words from the Cross,* 1885 ; (7) *The Crown of Life : A volume of Verses for the Seasons of the Church,* 1886.

In addition to these original publications Mrs. Hernaman contributed hymns to the *Church Times*, to various magazines, and to

(1) *Hymns for the Children of the Church* (22 hymns). 1878 ; (2) *Hymns for the Little Ones in Sunday Schools* (10 hymns), 1884 ; (3) The Rev. M. Woodward's (Folkestone) *Children's Service Book,* 1883 ; (4) Mrs. Brock's *Children's Hymn Book,* 1881 ; and (5) *The Altar Hymnal,* 1884. Mrs. Hernaman edited *The Altar Hymnal,* and contributed thereto a few *trs.* from the Latin in addition to original hymns.

Mrs. Hernaman's hymns in C. U. appeared as follows :—

i. In her *Child's Book of Praise,* 1873.

1. Behold, behold He cometh. *Advent.*
2. Holy Jesus, we adore Thee. *Circumcision.*
3. How can we serve Thee, Lord. *For Choristers.*
4. Jesus, in loving worship. *H. Communion.*
5. Jesus, Royal Jesus. *Palm Sunday.*
6. Lord, I have sinned, but pardon me. *Penitence.*
7. Lord, Who throughout these forty days. *Lent.*
8. Reverently we worship Thee. *H. Trinity.*

ii. In her *Appendix to The Child's Book of Praise,* 1874, and *Hymns for Little Ones,* 1884.

9. Hosannah, they were crying. *Advent.*

iii. In her *Christmas Carol,* 1875.

10. Angels singing, Church bells ringing. *Christmas Carol.*

iv. In *Hymns for the Children of the Church,* 1878.

11. As Saint Joseph lay asleep. *Flight into Egypt.*
12. Come, children, lift your voices. *Harvest.*
13. God bless the Church of England. *Prayer for the Church.*
14. Happy, happy Sunday. *Sunday.*
15. He led them unto Bethany. *Ascension.*
16. Jesu, we adore Thee. *H. Communion.*

v. In her *Story of the Resurrection,* 1879.

17. Early with the blush of dawn. *Easter.*
18. Now the six days' work is done. *Sunday.*

vi. In *The Altar Hymnal*, 1884.

19. Arm, arm, for the conflict, soldiers (1880). *Processional.*
20. Calling, calling, ever calling. *Home Mission.* Written in 1878, and printed in *New and Old.*
21. Gracious Father, we beseech Thee. *Holy Communion.*
22. Hail to Thee, O Jesu. *Holy Communion.*
23. Magnify the Lord to-day. *Christmas.*
24. O Lamb of God, Who dost abide. *Holy Communion.*
25. This healthful Mystery. *Holy Communion.*

vii. In Mrs. Brock's *Children's Hymn Bk.*, 1881.

26. It is a day of gladness. *Girls' Friendly Societies.*

Mrs. Hernaman's *trs.* in *The Altar Hymnal* are annotated under their Latin first lines. There is also her *Good Shepherd* hymn, in three parts. (1) "Faithful Shepherd of Thine own;" (2) "Faithful Shepherd, hear our cry;" (3) "Shepherd, who Thy life didst give," which appeared in *Hys. for the Children of the Church*, 1878, and in *The Altar Hymnal*, 1884. She d. Oct. 10, 1898.   [J. J.]

Herr, des Tages Mühen und Beschwerden. *C. J. P. Spitta.* [*Evening.*] 1st pub. in his *Psalter and Harfe.* 1st Ser. Pirna, 1833, p. 93, in 4 st. of 8 l. It is one of the finest German evening hymns, but of rather an unsingable metre. In the Leipzig *G. B.*, 1844, and the *G. B.* for the Grand Duchy of Saxony. 1883, it begins, "Herr, des langen Tags Beschwerden." *Tr.* as :—

O Lord, Who by Thy presence hast made light, a good and full *tr.* by R. Massie in his *Lyra Domestica*, 1860, p. 8. This has been repeated in varying centos in the *Wes. H. Bk.*, 1875; *Suppl.* of 1880 to the Bapt. *Ps. & Hys.*; Thring's *Coll.*; Horder's *Cong. Hyl.*, 1884, &c.; and in America in *Laudes Domini*, N.Y., 1884.

Other trs. are :—
(1) "Oh Lord! Thy presence through the day's distractions," by *Miss Fry*, 1859, p. 6. (2) "My work was pleasant, Lord, my burden light," in the *Family Treasury*, 1875, p. 587, signed "J. G." (3) "O Thou Who didst my burden share," by *Dr. R. Maguire*, 1883, p. 30.   [J. M.]

Herr, grosser Gott, dich loben wir. [*General Thanksgiving.*] Included in *Der heilige Gesang zum Gottesdienste in der römisch-katholischen Kirche*, Landshut, 1777, p. 105, in 5 st. of 8 l. with the refrain,

"Herr, grosser Gott! dich loben wir,
Bekennen dich, und danken dir."

and entitled, "Hymn for a Festival of Praise and Thanksgiving. On the model of the Ambrosian hymn of praise, Te Deum Laudamus." Repeated in the *Constanz G. B.* (R. C.), 1812 (1825, p. 595), the *Trier G. B.* (R. C.), 1846, p. 231, &c. The only *tr.* in C. U. is :—

O God the Lord, to Thee we raise. In full, by Dr. R. F. Littledale, in the *People's Hyl.*, 1867 (signed "A. L. P."), and Porter's *Churchman's Hyl.*, 1876; and omitting st. iv. in the *Hymnary*, 1872, and Dale's *English H. Bk.*, 1875.   [J. M.]

Herr, lasse unser Schifflein heute. *F. Winkelmann.* [*For those at Sea.*] Included as for use at Services on Shipboard in Knapp's *Ev. L. S.*, 1837, No. 3104 (1865, No. 2762) in 3 st. In his Index of Authors Knapp ascribes it to *Friedrich Winkelmann*, who was, he says, a physician in Brunswick, and d. there in 1807. *Tr.* as, "O Lord, be this our vessel now" (quoting the German first line

as "O Herr lass") by Miss Winkworth in her *Lyra Ger.*, 1858, p. 111.   [J. M.]

Herr Zebaoth dein heiligs Wort. [*Holy Scripture.*] Included in the *Singende und klingende Berge*, Mühlheim, 1698 (*Fischer*, ii. 487), and repeated in Freylinghausen's *Neues geistreiches G. B.*, 1714, No. 205, in 6 st. of 8 l., and the *Unv. L. S.*, 1851. It is sometimes erroneously ascribed to Christian Knorr von Rosenroth. The only *tr.* in C. U. is :—

O Lord of Hosts, Thy holy word. A good *tr.* of st. i., iv., v., by A. T. Russell, as No. 21 in his *Ps. & Hys.*, 1851.   [J. M.]

Herrick, Robert, s. of Nicholas Herrick, goldsmith in Cheapside, London, was b. in London in 1591, and educated at St. John's College, and Trinity Hall, Cambridge. Taking Holy Orders in 1629, he was presented to the living of Dean-Prior, Devon. During Cromwell's Government he was ejected, but was reinstated at the Restoration. He d. in 1674. His *Noble Numbers* was pub. in 1647; and his *Hesperides, or the Works bothe Humane and Divine, of Robert Herrick*, in 1648. Various editions have followed, including that by Dr. Grosart, in 3 vols., in his *Early English Poets*, 1869. A *Selection*, with Memoir by Dr. Nott, was also pub. at Bristol, 1810; and another *Selection*, by F. T. Palgrave, in the *Golden Treasury* Series, 1877. Herrick's *Hesperides* is also one of the *Universal Library Series*, edited by H. Morley, 1884. [English Hymnody, Early, § IX.]   [J. J.]

Herrmann, Johann Gottfried, D.D., s. of Gottfried Herrmann, pastor at Altjessnitz, near Bitterfeld, Saxony, was b. at Altjessnitz, Oct. 12, 1707. After studying at the University of Leipzig (M.A. in 1731), he was appointed in 1731 diaconus at Ranis, near Neustadt on the Orla; in 1734 diaconus at Pegau, near Leipzig; in 1738 superintendent at Plauen; and in 1746 chief Court preacher at Dresden, and oberconsistorialrath. He d. at Dresden, July 30, 1791 (*Koch*, v. 503–505). The only hymn by him *tr.* into English appeared in the *Privilegirte neue und vollständige Voigtländische Gesang Buch*, Plauen, 1742, which he edited while Superintendent at Plauen. It is :

Geht hin, ihr gläubigen Gedanken. *The Love of God.* A fine hymn, founded on Eph. i. 3–12, on Faith produced and nourished by the everlasting love of God. 1st pub. 1742 as above (ed. 1751, No. 843), in 14 st. of 6 l., entitled "On the Everlasting Love of God." Included as No. 413 in the *Unv. L. S.*, 1851. The only *tr.* in C. U. is :—

On wings of faith, ye thoughts, fly hence. A good *tr.*, omitting st. viii., by Miss Winkworth, in the 1st Ser. of her *Lyra Ger.*, 1855, p. 121. Her *trs.* of ll. 1–4 of st. v., xii., x., xi. beginning "Ah! happy hours! whene'er upsprings," with a 5th st. not from Herrmann, added to complete the hymn, were included as No. 646 in the Amer. *Sabbath H. Bk.*, 1858. Another arrangement, consisting of ll. 1–4 of st. ii.–iv., vii., xiii., appeared as No. 233 in the *Sabbath H. Bk.*, 1858, and is repeated in several American collections. It begins :—"Ere earth's foundations yet were laid."   [J. M.]

Herrnschmidt, Johann Daniel, was b. April 11, 1675, at Bopfingen, in Württemberg, where his father, G. A. Herrnschmidt, was from 1673–1702 diaconus, and 1702–1714 Town preacher. He entered the University of Altdorf in 1696 (M.A. 1698), and in the autumn of 1698 went to Halle. In the spring of 1702 he became assistant to his father, and in July, 1702, Helfer at the Town church. In 1712 he became superintendent, court preacher and consistorialrath at Idstein, and in the same year graduated D.D. at Halle. He was finally, in 1715, appointed Professor of Theology at Halle, and in 1716 also sub-director of the Orphanage and the Pädagogium there. He d. at Halle, Feb. 5, 1723 (Koch, iv. 349–354, 569, &c.). He was one of the best hymn-writers of the older Pietistic school. His hymns are Scriptural, and mirror his inner life, but do not possess much poetic force. They were almost all written during his first residence at Halle, 1698–1702, and appeared mostly in Freylinghausen's Geistreiches G. B., 1704. Three have passed into English, viz. :—

i. Gott wills machen, dass die Sachen. Trust in God. 1704, No. 417, in 17 st. of 6 l., repeated as No. 706 in the Unv. L. S., 1851. It is founded on the Gospel for the 4th S. after Epiphany (St. Matt. viii. 23–27); and is full of clear cut, almost proverbial sayings. Tr. as : (1) "God will make it, canst thou take it," in the Suppl. to Ger. Psalmody, ed. 1765, p. 63. (2) "Storms and winds may blow and batter," as No. 455 in the Moravian H. Bk., 1789. In the 1801 and later eds. (1886, No. 626), it begins, "Storms of trouble may assail us." (3) "God so guides us, what betides us," by N. L. Frothingham, 1870, p. 251.

The two remaining hymns (ii., iii.) are annotated under Various.   [J. M.]

Hertzog, Johann Friedrich, LL.D., s. of Johann Hertzog, diaconus of the Church of the Holy Cross, in Dresden, was b. at Dresden, June 6, 1647. After the completion of his legal studies at the University of Wittenberg, he was, from 1671 to 1674, tutor to the sons of General-Lieutenant von Arnim. In 1674 he returned to Dresden to practise as an advocate, where he d. March 21, 1699 (Koch, iii. 361–63; Allg. Deutsche Biographie, xii. 251). The only hymn by him which has been tr. into English is :—

Nun sich der Tag geendet hat, Und keine Sonn mehr scheint. [Evening.] Fischer, ii. 129, says that, according to the testimony of Hertzog's brother, this hymn was written one evening in 1670 while the author was still a student at Wittenberg. St. i. and the melody appear as No. 8 in the 1 Zehen of A. P. Krieger's Neue Arien. In 6 Zehen, Dresden, 1667 [Leipzig Town Library]. Hertzog seems to have adopted this st. and added 8 others, the form in 9 st. being found in Luppius's Andächtig Singender Christen-Mund, Wesel, 1692, p. 123, in 9 st. Included as No. 622 in Freylinghausen's Geistreiches G. B., 1704, with a 10th st., which, according to Fischer, first appeared in the Leipzig G. B., 1693. Also in the Unv. L. S., 1851, No. 530. It speedily became popular, was often imitated, and still holds its place as one of the best German evening hymns. The trs. in C. U. are :—

1. And now another day is gone. A good tr., omitting st. vii., by J. C. Jacobi in his Psal. Ger., 1722, p. 111 (ed. 1732, p. 174, altered). St. vii., "With cheerful heart I close my eyes," while parallel with the German is really st. iv. of Watts's "And now another day is gone," in his Divine and Moral Songs. The 1732 text, slightly altered, is No. 479 in pt. i. of the Mora-

vian H. Bk., 1754, and st. i.–iii., vii., ix. altered are No. 391 in J. A. Latrobe's Coll., 1841. The form principally used is a cento beginning, "In mercy, Lord, remember me"; and being st. iii., vii., ix., x. slightly altered as No. 760 in the Moravian H. Bk., 1789, and repeated, omitting st. x., in later eds. (1886, No. 1183). This cento has recently been included in Windle's C. P. & Hyl., 1862, in Dr. Thomas's Augustine H. Bk., 1866, Dr. Martineau's Hys. of Praise & Prayer, 1873 ; and in America in the Meth. Epis. H. Bk., 1849 ; Hys. for the Ch. of Christ, Boston, 1853, &c.

2. And now another day is past. A version of st. i.–iv., vii.–ix., based on Jacobi, is found as No. 494 in the Appendix to the American German Reformed Ps. & Hys., 1834, and also in the Amer. Luth. Gen. Synod's H. Bk., 1850.

3. The shades of night have banished day. A full and very good tr. by Miss Dunn in her Hys. from the German, 1857, p. 16. Included, slightly altered and omitting st. vi., viii., in the Uppingham & Sherborne School H. Bk, 1874, and thence in Thring's Coll., 1882.

4. Now that the sun doth shine no more. A good tr., omitting st. iv., vi., x., by Miss Winkworth in her C. B. for England, 1863.

5. The day is done, the sun is set. A tr. of st. i.–iii., vii., marked as by F. C. C., as No. 176 in Dr. Pagenstecher's Coll., 1864.

6. Since now the day hath reached its close. In full as No. 311 in the Ohio Luth. Hyl., 1880, marked as a compilation.

Other trs. are : (1) "The waning day hath reached its close," by H. J. Buckoll, 1842, p. 84. (2) "The day is gone, and now no more," by Dr. G. Walker, 1860, p. 61. (3) "Now that the day from earth hath crept," by Miss Manington, 1863, p. 136.   [J. M.]

Hervey, James, M.A., s. of the Rector of Weston-Favell and Collingtree, diocese of Peterborough, was b. at Hardingstone, near Northampton, Feb. 14, 1714, and educated at the Free Grammar School, Northampton, and Lincoln College, Oxford. At Oxford he had John Wesley, then a Fellow of Lincoln, as his tutor. Ordained in 1736, he assisted his father for a short time, and then became Curate of Dummer. At the end of a year he passed on to Devonshire, first as a guest of Mr. Orchard, at Stoke Abbey, and then as Curate of Bideford. In 1742 he left Bideford and rejoined his father, whom he succeeded as Rector of Weston-Favell and Collingtree in 1752. He d. Dec. 25, 1758. His controversial and religious writings were very popular at one time, but have fallen out of use. His Meditations among the Tombs (suggested by a visit paid to Kilkhampton Church, Cornwall), Reflections on a Flower Garden, and a Descant on Creation, were pub. in one volume in 1746; and his Contemplations on the Night, and The Starry Heavens, with A Winter Piece, were pub. as a second volume in 1746. A complete edition of his Meditations and Contemplations were pub. with a Memoir (Lond., W. Tegg) in 1860. From these the following hymns have come into C. U. :—

1. Make the extended skies your tomb. The True Life. This was given in the Meditations among the Tombs, 1746, in 4 st. of 4 l. as the conclusion of a meditation on "The only infallible way of immortalizing our characters" :—

"The only infallible way of immortalizing our characters, a way equally open to the meanest and most exalted fortune is, 'To make our calling and election sure,' to gain some sweet evidence that our *names are written in heaven."* . . . . .

" Make the extended skies your tomb ;
Let stars record your worth," &c.

Its use in modern hymn-books is limited.

2. Since all the downward tracts of time. *Providence.* This appeared in the *Reflections ;on a Flower. Garden,* 1746, in 3 st. of 4 l. It is given as a note to the following sentence: " Be still, then thou uneasy mortal : * know that God is unerringly wise ; and be assured that, amidst the greatest multiplicity of beings, he does not overlook thee." . . . . .

" * *Permittas ipsis expendere numinibus, quid Conveniat nobis, rebusque sit utile nostris. Nam pro* jucundis aptissima *quæque dabunt dii : Carior est illis homo, quam sibi.*—Juv.

" Since all the downward tracts of time
God's watchful eye surveys ;
O! Who so wise to choose our lot,
And regulate our ways?

" Since none can doubt His equal love,
Unmeasurably kind ;
To His unerring, gracious will
Be ev'ry wish resign'd.

" Good when He gives, supremely good
Nor less, when He denies:
E'en crosses, from His sovereign hand,
Are blessings in disguise."

In addition to this hymn being in C. U. in this its original form, it is often found in 5 st. and beginning, " Since all the downward *tracks* of time."   [J. J.]

Herz der göttlichen Natur. *N. L. von Zinzendorf. [Supplication for Grace.]*

Written in 1728, and included as No. 15 in the *Andere Zugabe* to the 2nd ed., 1728, of his *Sammlung geist- und lieblicher Lieder,* 1725, (ed. 1731, No. 1143), in 7 st. of 8 l. In the *Brüder G. B.,* 1778, No. 975, it is abridged, and begins, " Herzenslamm, Immanuel !" while in the Wesleyan *Zionsharfe,* Winnenden, 1863, No. 24, it begins, " Gott, aus dem quillt alles Leben." The full text is in Knapp's *Ev. L. S.,* 1850, No. 1153.   *Tr.* as :—

O God of God, in Whom combine, a somewhat free *tr.,* omitting st. vii., and in 6-line sts., by J. Wesley in *H. & Sacred Poems,* 1739 (*P. Works,* 1868-72, vol. i. p. 162). It was included as No. 122 in Wesley's *Pocket H. Bk.,* 1785, but not included in the larger *H. Bk.* till the *Supplement* of 1830, No. 610 (revised ed. 1875, No. 666). Repeated as No. 333 in the *Leeds H. Bk.,* 1853. In the *Meth. N. Con. H. Bk.,* 1863, No. 191, it begins " O God the Son," and in Dale's *Eng. H. Bk.,* 1875, No. 494, it begins " Almighty God, in Whom combine."   [J. M.]

Herz und Herz vereint zusammen. *N. L. von Zinzendorf. [Communion of Saints.]*

Written in 1725, and said to have been occasioned by strife in the Brethren's Unity, healed by common love to the Saviour. 1st pub. in his *Die letzten Reden unsers Herrn und Heylandes Jesu Christi vor seinem Creutzes-Tode,* Frankfurt and Leipzig, 1725.

This work contains a poetical rendering of our Lord's Farewell Discourse as recorded in St. John xiv.–xvii., each chapter forming a section of the poem, which thus contains respectively 43, 83, 81, and 113 st. of 8 l.—in all 320 st. From this st. 53–59 of section ii. were included as No. 1305 in the 3rd ed., 1731, of the *Sammlung geist- und lieblicher Lieder,* 1725, and repeated in the *Herrnhut G. B.,* 1735, in 8 st. In the *Brüder G. B.,* 1778, No. 713, st. 55 of section ii., 1725, was omitted, and three sts. inserted as vii., viii., x., which are taken from st. 78, 81, and 104 of section iv. of the 1725 ; while the text of all the stanzas is considerably altered. (See the various forms in the *Blätter für Hymnologie,* 1883, pp. 49–52.) The text of 1778 is No. 1040 in the Berlin *G. L. S.,* ed. 1863. The text in Bunsen's *Versuch,* 1833, No. 480, in 6 st., is greatly altered from the 1778.

The *tr.* in C. U. is :—

Heart and heart together bound, a good *tr.* of Bunsen's text by Miss Winkworth in her *Lyra Ger.,* 1st ser. 1855, p. 124, repeated as No. 105 in her *C. B. for England,* 1863. Her st. iv.–vi. altered, and omitting iv., ll. 5–8, and beginning " Jesus, truest Friend, unite," were included as No. 278 in the Pennsylvania Luth. *Ch. Bk.,* 1868.

Other trs. are :—
(1) " Flock of Jesus, be united " (st. ii.), by J. Miller and F. W. Foster, as No. 389 in the *Moravian H. Bk.,* 1789, (1849, No. 485). (2) " Grant, Lord, that with Thy direction," (st. ix.) as No. 1055, in the *Suppl.* of 1808 to the *Moravian H. Bk.,* 1801. In the 1886 ed. of the *Moravian H. Bk.,* Nos. 1 and 2 are rewritten, and a *tr.* of st. i. prefixed, beginning, " Christian hearts in love united." (3) " Heart to heart in love united," in the *Christian Examiner,* Boston, U.S., Sept. 1860, p. 255.   [J. M.]

Herzliebster Jesu, was hast du verbrochen. *J. Heermann. [Passiontide.]*

1st pub. in his *Devoti Musica Cordis,* Breslau, 1630, p. 63, in 15 st. of 4 l., entitled " The Cause of the bitter sufferings of Jesus Christ, and consolation from His love and grace. From Augustine."

The Latin meditation on which the hymn is based is No. vii. of the *Meditationes* of St. Augustine. This book, however, is not an original work of that Father, but a mediæval compilation, mainly from St. Anselm of Canterbury, but in part from St. Augustine, St. Gregory the Great, and others. Meditation vii. is by St. Anselm.

It is a beautiful and thoughtful hymn, and has been extensively used in Germany. It is given in *Mützell,* 1858, No. 30, in the *Unv. L. S.,* 1851, No. 102, &c. The fine melody (given in the *C. B. for England*) is by J. Crüger, appeared in his *Newes vollkömmliches G. B.,* Berlin,1640, and is employed by J. S. Bach in his St. Matthew and St. John Passion Music.   *Tr.* as :—

1. What laws, my blessed Saviour, hast Thou broken, a good and full *tr.* by Miss Cox in her *Sacred H. from the German,* 1841, p. 25 (ed. 1864, p. 51, slightly altered). In 1874 her *trs.* of st. i.–iv., vii., altered, and beginning, " What law, most blessed Jesus," were included in Darling's *H. for Ch. of England.*

2. What law, beloved Jesu, hast Thou broken, a good *tr.* of st. i., iii., iv., ix., by A. T. Russell as No. 91 in his *Ps. & Hys.,* 1851.

3. Alas, dear Lord, what law then hast Thou broken, a very good *tr.,* omitting st. v., by Miss Winkworth as No. 52 in her *C. B. for England,* 1863.

Other trs. are :—
(1) " What then, dear Jesus, hadst Thou done or said," No. 166 in the *Moravian H. Bk.,* 1742. (2) " Dear Jesu! wherein wert Thou to be blamed," No. 223 in pt. i. of the *Moravian H. Bk.,* 1754. In the ed. of 1849, No. 103, it begins " Dear Jesus! wherein art ; " and in the 1886 ed., No. 92, with st. iv., " O wondrous grace, all earthly love exceeding." (3) " Alas, dear Lord, what evil hast Thou done," by *Miss Winkworth,* 1855, p. 77. (4) " O precious Jesus, what hast Thou been doing," by Miss Burlingham in the *British Herald,* July, 1865, p. 101, repeated in Reid's *Praise Bk.,* 1872. (5) " What didst Thou, Jesus, dearest One," by *Dr. J. Guthrie,* 1869, p. 78. (6) " O dearest Saviour ! what law hadst Thou broken," by *N. L. Frothingham,* 1870, p. 208.   [J. M.]

He's gone! see where His body lay.

T. Kelly. [Easter.] Pub. in the 1st ed. of his *Hymns,* &c., 1804, in 6 st. of 6 l. (ed. 1853, No. 32), and is based on St. Matt. xxviii. 6. In addition to the original, two altered forms of the text are in C. U. :—

1. "O joyful sound! O glorious hour." This alteration of st. ii.–iv. appeared in Hall's *Mitre H. Bk.*, 1836.
Its use is limited.   2. "Come, see the place where Jesus
lay, And hear angelic voices say." This version of the
text was made by the compilers of *H. A. & M.*, 1861, and
is in extensive use.   [J. J.]

He's gone! the spotless soul is gone.

C. Wesley. [*Burial.*] Written "On the death
of the Rev. James Hervey, Dec. 25, 1758,"
and pub. in Wesley's *Funeral Hymns*, 1759,
No. 38, in 4 st. of 6 l. (*P. Works*, 1868–72,
vol. vi. p. 279). It is adapted for general use
in the Amer. Meth. Episcopal Ch. *Hymns*,
1849.   [J. J.]

Hesse, Johann, D.D., s. of Johann von
Hesse, a merchant of Nürnberg, was b. at
Nürnberg, Sept. 21 or 23, 1490. He attended
the Universities of Leipzig (1506), Wittenberg,
where he graduated M.A., 1511, and heard
lectures from Luther and Johann v. Staupitz;
Bologna and Ferrara (D.D. at Ferrara, 1519).
During his residence in Italy he gained an
insight into the corruptions of the Church in
that country, and on his return home in 1520
he sided more and more with the party of
Reform. He had been appointed Canon of
Neisse in Silesia in 1515, and was in 1520
ordained priest at Breslau. He acted for some
time as a Provost of the Church of St. Mary
and St. George, at Oels, and was then summoned to Breslau, in 1521, to preach as a
Canon of the Cathedral. He did not at first
declare himself openly for the Reformation;
but on a visit to Nürnberg in the spring of
1523, preached a sermon in St. Sebald's
Church, in which he proclaimed himself on
the side of the Reformers. On this he was
invited by the magistrates of Breslau to become Evangelical pastor of St. Mary Magdalene's Church there; and in spite of the
opposition of the Pope and of King Sigismund
of Poland, he was formally installed, Oct. 21,
1523, as the first Evangelical pastor elected
by the people in Silesia. He d. at Breslau,
Jan. 6, 1547. (*Koch*, i. 360–367; *Allg. Deutsche
Biog.*, xii. 283–284, &c.) Two hymns have
been ascribed to Hesse, one of which has
passed into English, viz.:—

O Welt, ich muss dich lassen. *For the Dying.* *Wackernagel*, iii. p. 952, gives this in 10 st. of 6 l. from a
broadsheet printed at Nürnberg, c. 1555, and from a
Nürnberg *G. B.* of 1569. It is also in the *Unv. L. S.*,
1851, No. 839. Lauxmann, in *Koch*, viii. 589, says that
according to tradition it was written as a dying song for
criminals on their way to execution, in whose welfare
Hesse had begun to interest himself as early as 1526. In
Jeremias Weber's *G. B.*, Leipzig, 1638, p. 770, it is
entitled, "A funeral hymn for a person who on account
of his misdeeds is lawfully and publicly brought from life
to death, whose departure is pitifully shown that everyone may take it to heart." Its popularity was greatly
aided by the beautiful melody to which it is set. This
is given in its original form by Miss Winkworth, and in
H. A. & M. (No. 86) is called *Innspruck*. It appears in
G. Förster's *Aussrug guter alter und newer Teutscher
liedlein,* Nürnberg, 1539, in a four-part setting by
Heinrich Isaak (b. c. 1440, Capellmeister to the Emperor
Maximilian I.) to the words of the travelling artisan's
song "Innsbruck, ich muss dich lassen." This hymn
is *tr.* as:—

O world, I now must leave thee, a good *tr.* of st. i.,
iv.–viii., by Miss Winkworth, as No. 189 in her *C. B.
for England*, 1863, repeated, omitting st. vi., in the Ohio
Luth. Hymnal, 1880. Another *tr.* is:—"O world, I
leave thee; far I go," by *Dr. G. Walker*, 1860, p. 161.

Another form of the hymn is that with the same first
line given in Heinrich Knaust's *Gassenhawer, Reuter
und Bergliedlin christlich, moraliter unnd sitilich ver-
endert,* Frankfurt-am-Main, 1571, where it is in 3 st.,
signed "D. H. K." (i.e. Dr. Heinrich Knaust), and en-

titled, "Issbruck ich muss dich lassen christianly and
morally altered." Thence in *Wackernagel*, iv. p. 781.
The only *tr.* of this form is, "O world, I must forsake
thee," by *Miss Winkworth*, 1869, p. 91.   [J. M.]

Hessenthaler, Magnus, was b. in Oct.,
1621, at Hochdorf, near Waiblingen, Württemberg, where his father was pastor. He
became, in 1656, professor of history, diplomacy, and rhetoric, in the so-called "Colle-
gium illustre," or academy for sons of noblemen, at Tübingen, and also lecturer on moral
philosophy in the University. In 1663 he was
appointed by Duke Eberhard III., of Württemberg, as historiographer of Württemberg,
and removed to Stuttgart, where he d. April 2,
1681 (*Allg. Deutsche Biog.*, xii. 271).

A very complete set of his works is preserved in the
University Library at Tübingen; but neither there nor
in Stuttgart, Amsterdam or elsewhere have we been
able to find the *Evangelische Jubelstimme* which he is said
to have pub. at Amsterdam 1668, and which *Koch*, 2nd
ed. ii. 314, says contained 13 original hymns. In the
Nürnberg *G. B.*, 1676, there are 9 hymns (Nos. 73, 84, 94,
212, 213, 313, 466, 470, 901) under his name; and in the
ed. of 1690 a 10th (No. 568, "Wenn jemand seinen
Lebenslauf"). One has passed into English, viz.:—

Mein Jesu, wie gross ist die Lieb. *Saints' Days.*
In the Nürnberg *G. B.*, 1676, No. 313, in 10 st. of 4 l.,
appointed for festivals of apostles and martyrs. *Tr.*
as:—

True Shepherd, who in love most deep, by Miss
Winkworth, as No. 79 in her *C. B. for England*, 1863, in
5 st. of 4 l. Miss W. seems to have *tr.* some altered
and abridged version; at least the 5 st. she gives borrow
more or less from all the 10 st. of the original.
                                               [J. M.]

Heu! Heu! mala mundi vita. [*Ad-*

vent.] This poem was 1st pub. at length by
E. Levis in his *Anecdota Sacra*, Turin, 1789,
p. 119, and ascribed to the Franciscan *Peter
Gonella,* of Tortona. A slightly fuller form in
384 lines, beginning, "Heu! Heu! mundi
vita," was pub. by E. du Méril in his *Poésies
Populaires Latines du Moyen Age,* Paris, 1847,
p. 108, from a MS. of the 12th cent. in the
National Library at Paris. In 1849 Archbishop Trench pub. a portion of the poem in
his *Sacred Latin Poetry,* beginning "Eheu!
Eheu! mundi vita," with the following note:—

"The MS. is of the twelfth century, and the poem
itself can scarcely be of an earlier date. Three or four
stanzas of it had already got abroad. Thus two are
quoted by Gerhard, *Loci Theoll.* xxix. 11, and see
Leyser, *Hist. Poem. Med. Aevi*, p. 423. The attribution
of these fragments of the poem, and thus implicitly of
the whole, to St. Bernard, rests on no authority whatever: it is merely a part of that general ascription to
him of any poems of merit belonging to that period,
whereof the authorship was uncertain."

Mone, Nos. 298, 299, included it in two parts.
(i. "Heu! Heu! mala mundi vita." ii. "Cum
revolvo toto corde"), and held that it was
made up of two poems, though possibly by the
same Italian author. The first part (ll. 1–200)
he gives from a Reichenau MS. of the 14th
cent., &c.; and the second part (ll. 201–384)
from a MS. of the 13th cent. at Trier, &c. His
notes and renderings are extensive. In *Daniel,*
iv. p. 194, the text of both parts is quoted from
Mone. It is also in a MS. of the 11th cent. at
Bern (No. 424).   [J. M.]

The full text of this poem has not been
rendered into English. The following are
centos therefrom:—

i. **Cum revolvo toto corde.** This is *tr.* by T. G.
Crippen in his *Ancient Hymns and Poems,* 1868,
p. 47, in five parts, as in *Mone* and *Daniel.* No
portion of this *tr.* is in C. U.

ii. Appropinquat enim dies. This cento begins with line 321 of *Du Méril's* text, and line 117 of *Mone* and *Daniel*. Dr. Littledale *tr.* it for the *People's H.*, 1867, as "Now the day is hasting on," No. 19, where it is signed "F. R." This was repeated in the Irvingite *Hys. for the Churches*, enlarged 1871, and in both instances it is given for Advent.

iii. Dies illa, dies vitae. This cento begins with line 325 of *Du Méril's* text, and line 121 of the text as in *Mone* and *Daniel*. This was *tr.* as "Lo the Day, the Day of Life" [*Advent*], by Mrs. Charles, in her *Voice of Christian Life in Song*, 1858, p. 190. It was repeated in Schaff's *Christ in Song*, 1869-70, and other collections; and as "Lo, the day of Christ's appearing," in the *Hymnary*, 1872. Dr. Kynaston has also a *tr.* in his *Occasional Hymns*, 1862, No. 7, in 2 st. of 8 l. ("Day of Life, all sorrow ending"), which he entitles "A Hymn of Judgment." It is not in C. U. although worthy of that honour. [J. J.]

Heunisch, Caspar, was b. July 17, 1620, at Schweinfurt, in Franconia. After graduating at Jena, he became, in 1645, pastor at Priesenshausen, near Schweinfurt; in 1646 at Oberndorf; and in 1647 diaconus at Schweinfurt. He d. as superintendent at Schweinfurt, Oct. 18, 1690 (*Wetzel*, iv. 237-238). One of his hymns has been *tr.* into English:—

O Ewigkeit! du Freudenwort. *Eternal Life.* Included as No. 490 in the *Schleusingen G. B.*, 1688 [Ducal Library, Wernigerode], in 9 st. of 8 l., signed M. C. H., i.e. Magister Caspar Heunisch. It is a companion hymn to "O Ewigkeit, du Donnerwort" (q.v.), by Rist.

The *trs.* are: (1) "Eternity! delightful sound," by *J.C. Jacobi*, 1722, p. 101 (1732, p. 209). (2) "Eternity! that word, that joyful word," by *Miss Fry*, 1845, p. 112. (3) "Eternity! O word of joy," by Miss Burlingham, in the *British Herald*, Sept. 1865, p. 142, repeated in Reid's *Praise Bk.*, 1872. [J. M.]

Heusser - Schweizer, Meta, dau. of Diethelm Schweizer, pastor of the Reformed Church at Hirzel near Zürich, was b. at Hirzel, April 6, 1797, and was married in 1821, to Johann Jakob Heusser, a physician at Hirzel. Dr. Heusser d. at Hirzel in 1859, and his widow continued to reside there till her death on January 2, 1876 (*Koch*, vii. 377-381; *Allg. Deutsche Biog.*, xii. 339, 340).

She was of a true poetic genius, and may fairly be regarded as the most important of modern German female sacred poets. The Holy Scriptures and the mountain scenery of her lonely home were the chief sources of her poetic inspiration. She was trained in the school of affliction, and her poems breathe the spirit of deep and sincere piety and childlike dependence, are free from all affectation, and speak from the heart to the heart. Her poems first appeared at intervals in Albert Knapp's *Christoterpe*. The first series of them were pub. at Leipzig in 1858 as *Lieder einer Verborgenen;* reprinted with her name as her *Gedichte* at Leipzig, 1863. A second series was pub. at Leipzig in 1867. A large number of her hymns are found in Knapp's *Ev. L. S.*, 1850 and 1865; and in the *Deutsches G. B.*, 1860, of her friend Dr. Schaff, afterwards adopted as the official book of the American Reformed Church. A full selection of her poems was translated by Miss Jane Borthwick, and was pub. by Nelson in 1875 as *Alpine Lyrics*, and included as part of the new ed. of *Hymns from the Land of Luther*, 1884. The dates of composition, unless otherwise stated, have been kindly supplied by her daughter, Fräulein Ega Heusser.

I. *Hymns in English C. U.*

i. Herz, du hast viel geweinet. *Consolation.* Written in 1837, on her return from Pfäfers (Pfeffers). 1st pub. in Knapp's *Christoterpe*, 1841, p. 336, in 9 st. of 4 l., beginning "Du hast, O Herz geweinet," as "A Floweret from Pfäfers." Repeated 1858, p. 90, and in Knapp's

Christenlieder, 1841, No. 190, and *Ev. L. S.*, 1850, No. 2060 (1865, No. 2120). *Tr.* as:—

Long hast thou wept and sorrowed, in full, by Miss Borthwick, in *H. L. L.*, 4th Ser., 1862, p. 33. The *trs.* of st. i., vii.-ix., were included in Wilson's *Service of Praise*, 1865, and the whole in Schaff's *Christ in Song*, 1870.

Another *tr.* is:—"Heart, thou hast long been weeping," in Reid's *Praise Bk.*, 1872.

ii. Schweige still. *Consolation.* Written Jan. 25, 1849, and 1st pub. in Knapp's *Christoterpe*, 1852, p. 128, in 6 st. of 5 l., entitled "Be still," and repeated 1858, p. 108. *Tr.* as:—

Heart be still! a good *tr.*, omitting st. iv., in the *Christian Treasury*, June, 1853, p. 142. Included in the *Shadow of the Rock*, N. Y., 1869, and thence in full in Horder's *Cong. Hymnal*, 1884, and, omitting st iii., iv., in W. F. Stevenson's *H. for Ch. & Home*, 1873.

Other *trs.* are:—
(1) "Peace, be still! In this night," in the *Christian Examiner*, Boston, U.S., Nov. 1860. (2) "Peace, be still, Through the night," by *Miss Borthwick*, 1875, p. 94.

II. *Hymns not in English C. U.*

iii. Danket um alles; ihr Kinder der göttlichen Liebe. *Thanksgiving.* On 1 Thess. v. 18. Written April 1, 1821. 1st pub. in her *Lieder*, 1858, p. 117, in 9 st. *Tr.* as "Give thanks for all things, children of your God," by *Miss Borthwick*, 1875.

iv. Der du trugst die Schmerzen aller. *Supplication.* Written 1833, 1st pub. in Knapp's *Christoterpe*, 1835, p. 276, in 12 st. *Tr.* as "Thou hast borne our sins and sorrows," by Miss Borthwick, 1875.

v. Dunkel ists! des Lebens laute Töne. *The Mother's Prayer.* Written 1827. 1st pub. in Knapp's *Christoterpe*, 1834, p. 45, in 14 st., entitled, "At midnight, by the children's bedside." *Tr.* as "Darkness reigns—the hum of life's commotion," by Miss Borthwick, in *H. L. L.*, 1854, p. 21.

vi. Endlich, endlich, wirst auch du. *Encouragement.* Written 1823. 1st pub. in Knapp's *Christoterpe*, 1834, p. 41, in 14 st. *Tr.* as "Doubt it not—thou too shalt come," by Miss Borthwick, 1875.

vii. Hör' ich euch wieder, ihr Töne des Frühlings erklingen. *Spring.* This noble hymn was written in March, 1833 (1831 ?), after many troublous days and nights, during a journey from the snow-clad heights of Hirzel to the neighbouring Lake of Zug, where Spring had already begun. (*Koch*, vii. 380.) 1st pub. in Knapp's *Christoterpe*, 1836, p. 238, in 21 st., entitled "Hymn of Praise. In early Spring amid the first songs of the birds." In the hymnals the second part, "Lamm, das gelitten, und Löwe, der siegreich gerungen" (st. x.), is given for Ascensiontide. The *trs.* are, (1) "Voices of Spring, with what gladness I hear you again," by Miss Borthwick, in *H. L. L.*, 1862, p. 8. (2) "Lamb, that hast suffered, and Lion of Judah victorious," by Dr. H. Harbaugh, in the German Reformed *Guardian*, July, 1865. (3) "Lamb, the once crucified! Lion, by triumph surrounded," *tr.* April, 1868, by T. C. Porter, for Schaff's *Christ in Song*, 1869.

viii. Ich weiss, dass mein Erlöser lebet. *Consolation.* Written March 20, 1859, on Job xix. 25, and included from her MS. in Dr. Schaff's *Deutsches G. B.*, 1860, in 5 st. (see his note there), and then in her *Gedichte*, 1863, p. 145. *Tr.* as "Yes! my Redeemer lives, to save us," by Dr. H. Mills, in Schaff's *Christ in Song*, 1870.

ix. Ich weiss was mich erfreuet. *Joy in Believing.* Written 1850, and 1st pub. in Knapp's *Christoterpe*, 1852, p. 132, in 8 st. *Tr.* as "I know what bringeth gladness," in the *British Herald*, July 1866, and in Reid's *Praise Bk.*, 1872.

x. Noch ein wenig Schweiss und Thränen. *Pilgrim Song.* Written 1835, and 1st pub. in Knapp's *Christoterpe*, 1836, p. 244, in 5 st. *Tr.* as "A few more conflicts, toils, and tears," by Miss Borthwick, 1875.

xi. O Jesus Christ, mein Leben. *Love to Christ.* 1st pub. as No. 185 in the *Zürich G. B.*, 1853., in 6 st. H. Weber, in his *Das Zürcher-Gesangbuch*, Zürich, 1872, p. 287, quotes from a letter of the authoress, by which it appears that about the year 1844 some of her friends wished a hymn to the fine old melody, "Es ist ein Ros entsprungen." She came upon No. 1527 in Knapp's *Ev. L. S.*, 1837, "Jesus, der ist mein Leben," recast it, and adapted it to the required metre. As the hymn is thus only partly original, she did not include it in her published works. *Tr.* as "O Christ, my Life, my Saviour," by Miss Borthwick, 1875, p. 69.

xii. **So zieh in Gottes Frieden denn.** *Farewell to a Foreign Missionary.* 1st pub. in Knapp's *Christoterpe,* 1852, p. 134, in 11 st. *Tr.* as "Now, in the peace of God," by Miss Borthwick, 1875, p. 66.

xiii. **Theuer ist der Tod der deinen.** *Death of the Righteous.* Written on the death of a friend in 1849. 1st pub. in Knapp's *Christoterpe,* 1852, p. 136, in 6 st. *Tr.* as "Dear to Thee, O Lord, and precious," by Miss Borthwick, 1875, p. 49.

xiv. **"Ueber ein Kleines," so sprach er in nächtlicher Stunde.** *Eternal Life.* Founded on St. John xvi. 16. Written 1841, and 1st pub. in Knapp's *Christoterpe,* 1846, p. 30, in 10 st. *Tr.* as "A little while! so spake our gracious Lord," by Miss Borthwick in *H. L. L.,* 1858, p. 22.

xv. **Willkommen, lieber, lieber Tag.** *Easter.* Written 1825. 1st pub. in Knapp's *Christoterpe,* 1834, p. 54, in 12 st. *Tr.* as "We welcome thee, dear Easter day," by Dr. H. Mills in 1859, printed in Schaff's *Christ in Song,* 1870 (1879, p. 225).

xvi. **Wir werden bei dem Herrn sein allezeit.** *Eternal Life.* Founded on 1 Thess. iv. 17. Written 1845, and 1st pub. in Knapp's *Christoterpe,* 1846, p. 32, in 7 st. The *trs.* are, (1) "O sweet home echo on the pilgrim's way," by Miss Borthwick, in *H. L. L.,* 1858, p. 62. (2) "O blessed Voice—that Voice from Home," by Dr. R. Maguire, 1883, p. 162.

xvii. **Zu deinen Füssen lass mich liegen.** *Cross and Consolation.* Written 1865. 1st pub. in her *Gedichte,* 1867, p. 126, in 11 st. *Tr.* as "Low at Thy feet my spirit lies," by Miss Borthwick, 1875, p. 83.

Besides the above, many pieces have been *tr.* by Miss Borthwick, Miss Burlingham, Rev. J. Kelly and others. Being poems rather than hymns, they are omitted from this list.   [J. M.]

Heut ist des Herren Ruhetag. [*Sunday.*] Included as No. 27 in the *New ordentlich Gesang Buch,* Hannover, 1646, in 17 st. of 4 l., repeated as No. 1059 in the Berlin *G. L. S.,* ed. 1863. Sometimes erroneously ascribed to Nicolaus Selnecker. The only *tr.* in C. U. is:

This is the day of holy rest. A good *tr.* of st. i., ii., vii., xi., by A. T. Russell, as No. 11 in his *Ps. & Hys.,* 1851, and thence as No. 257 in the *New Zealand Hyl.,* 1872.   [J. M.]

Heut ist gefahren Gottes Sohn. [*Ascension.*] *Bäumker,* i. pp. 87, 633, cites this hymn as in the *Catholische Kirchen Gesäng.,* Cologne, 1628; the *Würzburg G. B.* (R. C.), 1628, &c. In Hommel's *Geistliche Volkslieder,* Leipzig, 1871, No. 102, it is given in 14 st. of 2 l., from the *Würzburg G. B.* (R. C.), 1630, &c. In the *Trier G. B.* (R. C.), 1846, p. 93, altered and reduced to 7 st. *Tr.* as :—

To-day the Son of God hath gone. In full from the *Trier G. B.,* contributed by Dr. Littledale to *Lyra Messianica,* 1864, p. 369. An original 8th couplet,

"And we, amid the Angel throng,
Shall sing to Thee the glad new song,"

accidentally omitted in 1864, was added when the hymn was included in the *People's Hyl.,* 1867, No. 150.   [J. M.]

Hewett, John William, M.A., was b. in 1824, and educated at Trinity College, Cambridge (B.A. 1849, M.A. 1852). From 1849 to 1852 he was a Fellow of St. Nicolas College, Shoreham; and subsequently he was Head Master of Bloxham Grammar School (1853–56), and Senior Classical Master in the North London College School (1874–78). He has also held curacies in London and the neighbourhood. He edited *The Sealed Copy of the Prayer Book,* 1848, and other works, and is the author of *History and Description of*

Exeter Cathedral; and another of *Ely.* His original hymns and translations appeared in his *Verses by a Country Curate,* 1859. From this work the following hymns have come into C. U. :—

1. In the Name of God the Father. *H. Communion.* The 2nd stanza begins, "Lo in wondrous condescension," and the 3rd, "Here in figure represented."
2. Jesu, now Thy new-made soldier. *After Holy Baptism.*
3. What time the evening shadows fall. *SS. Simon & Jude.*
4. Withdraw from every human eye. *St. Bartholomew.*

There are also two *trs.* in *H. A. & M.,* "Jesu, our Lenten fast to Thee," and "O Thou Who dost to man accord," q.v. His *Verses* contain several good hymns in addition to those named. In addition he contributed a few hymns (all signed by him) to the *Lyra Messianica,* 1864; and "Jesus, Thy presence we adore" (*H. Communion*) to *The Eucharistic Hymnal,* 1877.   [J. J.]

Hey, Johann Wilhelm, s. of H. A. Hey, pastor at Leina, near Gotha, was b. at Leina, March 26, 1789. He studied at the Universities of Jena and Göttingen, became in 1811 licentiate in theology, and, after varied tutorial work, was appointed in 1818 pastor at Töttelstädt, near Gotha. In 1827 he became court preacher at Gotha, where his preaching attracted large audiences, but being regarded as a Pietist, was in 1832 appointed superintendent of Ichtershausen. He d. at Ichtershausen, May 19, 1854 (*Koch,* vii. 262–266; *Allg. Deutsche Biog.,* xii. 344–345; MS. from Pfarrer Ortlob of Leina).

Hey's poems are mostly written for children. The best known are his *Fabeln für Kinder,* with illustrations by Otto Speckter, of which the first 50 appeared at Hamburg, 1833, the second 50 in 1837. Since then they have passed through a large number of editions in German, and have been several times *tr.* into English. At the end of each series is a "Serious Appendix," containing religious and moral songs. The whole of these two *Appendices* have been *tr.* into English as *Hymns and Poems for Little Children. Translated from the German.* London, 1853. Also in the *Fifty Fables,* 1867, and *Other Fifty Fables,* 1869, *tr.* by Sophie Klingemann, and pub. by F. A. Perthes at Gotha.

Very few of Hey's hymns are suited for Church use. Those which we have to note are :—

I. *Hymns for Church Use.*

i. **Wenn auch vor deiner Thür einmal.** *Christian Charity.* 1st pub. in Knapp's *Christoterpe,* 1835, p. 68, in 9 st. of 4 l., as the 5th hymn of a series on the words "Behold I stand at the door and knock," Rev. iii. 20. In Knapp's *Ev. L. S.,* 1837, No. 2412 (1865, No. 2146), it was altered to "Christ! wenn die Armen manchesmal," and this form passed into the Württemberg *G. B.,* 1842, and other recent collections. The only *tr.* is, "Ah, Christian! if the needy poor," by Mrs. Findlater, in *H. L. L.,* 3rd Ser., 1858, p. 30 (1884, p. 152).

ii. **Wenn je du wieder zagst.** *Passiontide.* On Christ in the Garden of Gethsemane. 1st pub. in Severin Vater's *Jahrbuch für häusliche Andacht,* Gotha, 1824, p. 173, as No. 9 of the "Reminiscences of the sufferings of Jesus; for the Quiet Days of the week before Easter," in 9 st. of 8 l., with the motto "Not my will, but Thine be done." Included in Bunsen's *Versuch,* 1833; Knapp's *Ev. L. S.,* 1850 and 1865, &c. *Tr.* as :—

Whene'er again thou sinkest. A good and full *tr.* by Miss Winkworth in her *Lyra Ger.,* 2nd Ser., 1858, p. 26, and repeated, abridged, in *Ps. & Hys.,* Bedford, 1864, and in *Holy Song,* 1869.

II. *Hymns for Children.*

All those to be noted appeared in the *Appendix* to the 2nd Series of his *Fabeln für Kinder,* Hamburg, 1837.

iii. **Alle Jahre wieder, kommt das Christus Kind.**
Christmas. 1837, p. 31, in 3 st. The *trs.* are: (1) "The blessed feast of Christmas," in *H. & Poems*, 1853, p. 81. (2) "Every year that endeth," by *Sophie Klingemann*, 1869, p. 31. (3) "As each happy Christmas," by Mrs. H. R. Spaeth, as No. 33 in the *Little Children's Bk.*, Philadelphia, 1885.

iv. **Aus dem Himmel ferne.** *God our Father.* 1837, p. 7, in 4 st. The *trs.* are: (1) "From the glorious heav'n above," in *H. & Poems*, 1853, p. 49. (2) "From the glorious heaven," by *Mrs. Bevan*, 1859, p. 139. (3) "From the angels' dwelling," in Dr. F. Silcher's *Song Book for the Young*, Nelson, 1868, No. 1. (4) "From His heaven above," by *Sophie Klingemann*, 1869, p. 7. (5) "From the far blue heaven," as No. 676, in the *Tribute of Praise*, Boston, U.S., 1873.

v. **Glöcklein klingt, Vöglein singt.** *Thanksgiving.* 1837, p. 17 (in the ed. 1886, N.D., as part of *Sonnenschein, Sternelein*), in 5 st. The *trs.* are: (1) "The bells they ring, The birds they sing," in *H. & Poems*, 1853, p. 63. (2) "Bells do ring, birds do sing," in Silcher's *Song Book*, 1868, No. 9. (3) "Bells are ringing, Birds are singing," by *Sophie Klingemann*, 1869, p. 17. (4) "Church bells ring," by Mrs. H. R. Spaeth, in *Little Children's Bk.*, 1885, No. 72.

vi. **Weisst du wie viel Sternlein stehen.** *God's care of His creatures.* 1837, p. 20, in 3 st. The *trs.* are: (1) "Canst thou sum up each brilliant star." In *H. & Poems*, 1853, p. 67. (2) "How many stars are shining," by *Mrs. Bevan*, 1859, p. 144. (3) "Can you tell the countless number," by *Sophie Klingemann*, 1869, p. 20. (4) "Canst thou count the stars that twinkle," in the Rev. C. S. Bere's *Children's Choral Bk.*, 1869, p. 4, repeated as No. 425 in the *Universal H. Bk.*, 1885.

vii. **Wen Jesus liebt Der kann allein,** *Love of Christ.* 1837, p. 37, in 4 st. The *trs.* are: (1) "They who love Jesus alone can be gay," in *H. & Poems*, 1853, p. 90. (2) "The love of Christ makes ever glad," by *Sophie Klingemann*, 1869, p. 37. (3) "Whom Jesus loves," by Mrs. H. R. Spaeth, in *Service & Hys. for Sunday Schools* (Southern Lutheran), Philadelphia, 1883, p. 178. (4) "Whom Christ holds dear," by Prof. M. H. Richards, as No. 98 in the *Little Children's Bk.*, Philadelphia, 1885.   [J. M.]

Hic reparandum generator fons animarum. *St. Paulinus of Nola.* [*Holy Baptism.*] In the *Cluniac Breviary*, Paris, 1686, p. 235, this is given in 6 st. and a doxology as a hymn for the Octave of the Epiphany, at Vespers. See also under **Various.** *Tr.* as "Ever sparkling, ever mounting"; by E. Caswall, in his *Masque of Mary*, 1858, and his *Hymns*, 1873, p. 218. In 1862 it was added to the *Appendix* to the *H. Noted.*   [J. M.]

Hie to the mountain afar. *J. Montgomery.* [*Freedom of the Slave.*] This is No. v. of his *Songs on The Abolition of Negro Slavery in the British Colonies*, Aug. 1, 1834, in 4 st. of 8 l. It is headed, "The Negro's Vigil: on the Eve of the first of August, 1834; 'They that watch for the morning;' Ps. cxxx. 6." It was pub. in his *Poet's Portfolio*, 1835, p. 220. In 1846, st. i., iii., slightly altered, were given in Longfellow and Johnson's *Bk. of Hymns*, Boston, U.S.A., as "Climb we the mountain afar."   [J. J.]

Hier legt mein Sinn sich vor dir nieder. *C. F. Richter.* [*Hoping for Grace.*] 1st pub. in Freylinghausen's *G. B.*, 1704, No. 309, in 12 st. of 4 l., and included in Richter's *Erbauliche Betrachtungen*, 1718, p. 376, as a hymn on spiritual conflict and victory. Repeated as No. 313 in the *Unv. L. S.*, 1851. *Tr.* as :—

My soul before Thee prostrate lies, a good and full *tr.* by J. Wesley in *Ps. & Hys.*, Charlestown, 1737; repeated, omitting st. iv., in his *H. & Sacred Poems*, 1739 (*P. Works*, 1868–72, vol. i. p. 85). Though not adopted in the *Wes. H. Bk.*, 1780 or 1875, the hymn came into C. U., by

being included (omitting Wesley's st. viii., but greatly altered) in the *Moravian H. Bk.*, 1754, and later eds. (1886, No. 511). A cento partly from Wesley and partly from the *Moravian H. Bk.*, 1801, is to be found in Martineau's *Hymns*, 1840 and 1873. The sts. most frequently employed in making centos are Wesley's i.–v., viii., ix. Selections from these are found in Montgomery's *Christ. Psalmist*, 1825, &c., Mercer's *C. P. & H. Bk.*, 1857; and in America in the Meth. Epis. *H. Bk.* of 1849, and their *Hymnal* of 1878; the Andover *Sabbath H. Bk.*, 1858; Bapt. *Service of Song*, 1871, &c.   [J. M.]

Higginson, Thomas Wentworth, M.A., was b. at Cambridge, U.S.A., Dec. 22, 1823, and educated at Harvard. From 1847 to 1850 he was Pastor of an Unitarian Church at Newburyport, and from 1852 to 1858 at Worcester. In 1858 he retired from the Ministry, and devoted himself to literature. During the Rebellion he was colonel of the first negro regiment raised in South Carolina. In addition to being for some time a leading contributor to the *Atlantic Monthly*, he pub. *Outdoor Papers*, 1863; *Malbone*, 1869; and other works. During his residence at the Harvard Divinity School he contributed the following hymns to Longfellow and Johnson's *Bk. of Hymns*, 1846:—

1. No human eyes Thy face may see. *God known through love.*
2. The land our fathers left to us. *American Slavery.*
3. The past is dark with sin and shame. *Hope.*
4. To Thine eternal arms, O God. *Lent.*

In the *Bk. of Hymns* these hymns are all marked with an asterisk. They, together with others by Mr. Higginson, are given in Putnam's *Singers and Songs of the Liberal Faith*, 1875.   [F. M. B.]

High in yonder realms of light. *T. Raffles.* [*Heaven.*] 1st pub. in 6 st. of 8 l. in the *Supplement* to the *Evangelical Magazine* for Dec. 1808, with the signature "T. R." In 1812 it was included in Collyer's *Coll.*, and subsequently in numerous hymnals in G. Britain and America, including Raffles's *Suppl.* to Watts, 1853, and his *Hymns*, 1868. It is the most popular of his hymns both in G. Britain and America, and is in extensive use.   [J. J.]

High let us swell our tuneful notes. *P. Doddridge.* [*Christmas.*] This hymn is undated in the D. MSS. It was 1st pub. in Job Orton's posthumous ed. of Doddridge's *Hymns*, &c., 1755, No. 101, in 5 st. of 4 l., and again in J. D. Humphreys's ed. of the same, 1839, No. 224. It was included in the *Supplement* to Tate & Brady's *New Version* (q.v.), under the same circumstances as Doddridge's "My God, and is Thy table spread," and a few other hymns. It is in extensive use, the text adopted in most cases being that in the *Supplement* to Tate & Brady.   [J. J.]

High Priest for sinners, Jesus, Lord. *J. Montgomery.* [*Our Saviour's Prayers.*] This poem appeared in his *Original Hymns*, 1853, p. 75, with a preamble of 6 l., followed by pt. i. in 6 st. of 6 l., and pt. ii. of 7 st. of 6 l. It is a metrical setting of a running account of the prayers offered by our Blessed Lord as recorded in the Gospels. A cento beginning with st. ii. of pt. i.: "Early Christ rose, ere dawn of day"; and a second, "O Father! save me from this hour" (pt. i. st. vi.), were given in the Scottish *Evang. Union Hyl.*, 1878.   [J. J.]

Hilary. Hilarius Pictaviensis, Saint,

Bishop, and, according to *St. Augustine*, "the Illustrious Doctor of all the Churches," was b., of heathen parents of an illustrious family and great wealth, at Poictiers early in the 4th century. He received, as a heathen, an excellent classical education, so that *St. Jerome* says of him that he "was brought up in the pompous school of Gaul, yet had culled the flowers of Grecian science, and became the Rhone of Latin eloquence." Early in life he married, and had a daughter named Abra, Afra, or Apra. About 350 he renounced, in company with his wife and daughter, the Pagan religion of his family, and became a devout and devoted Christian. After his baptism he so gained the respect and love of his fellow Christians, that in 353, upon a vacancy occurring in the see of his native town, he was, although married and a layman, elected to fill it, and received ordination as Deacon and Priest, and consecration as Bishop, "by accumulation," no uncommon occurrence in those days. From that time he was virtually, though not formally, separated from his wife, and lived a very ascetic life. Soon after his consecration he received a visit from St. Martin of Tours (who became thenceforward his devoted disciple), and distinguished himself by his unsparing opposition to the Arian heresy, which had gained many powerful adherents in Gaul at that time, obtaining for himself thereby the title in after years of "Malleus Arianorum," *the hammer of the Arians.* In 356 he was sent by the Emperor Constantius to Phrygia in exile, in consequence of a report made against his moral character by the Arian Council held at Beziers in Languedoc, over which the Arian leader, Saturninus, Bp. of Arles, presided, whose excommunication for heresy Hilary had some time before secured. His exile lasted until 362, when he returned to Poictiers by the Emperor's direction, though without his sentence of banishment being formally annulled. In spite of his consequent want of permission to do so, he left Poictiers towards the end of the same year, and spent two years in Italy, whence he was again sent back to Gaul in 364 by the new Emperor Valentinian, in consequence of his denouncing Auxentius, the Bp. of Milan, where Hilary was at that time resident, as having been insincere in his acceptance of the creed of Nicaea. Hilary lived for some three years after his final return to Poictiers, and d. Jan. 13, 368, though his Saint's Day (which gives his name to the Hilary term in our Law Courts) is celebrated on the following day, in order, probably, not to trench upon the octave of the Epiphany.

St. Hilary's writings, of which a large number are still extant though many have been lost, travel over a vast field of exegetical, dogmatic, and controversial theology. His principal work in importance and elaboration is his "Libri xii. de Trinitate," directed against the Arian heresy, while in his "Commentarium in Matthaeum" we have the earliest commentary on that gospel. The best edition of his works is that of *Constant*, originally pub. by the Benedictines, at Paris, in 1693, and reprinted, with some additions, at Verona, in 2 vols., by Scipio Maffei, in 1730.

St. Hilary was a sacred poet as well as a theologian, though most of his writings of this character perished, probably, in his *Liber Hymnorum*, which is one of his books that has not come down to us. It seems to have consisted of hymns upon Apostles and Martyrs, and is highly spoken of by *Isidore* of *Seville* in his *De Officio Ecclesiastico*. All that we have remaining are some lines of considerable beauty on our Lord's childhood (Dom Pitra's *Spicilegium Solesmense*, Paris, 1862), which are attributed, probably with justice, to him, and about 8 hymns, the attribution of which to him is more or less certainly correct. *Daniel* gives 7, 4 of which:—"Lucis Largitor splendide"; "Deus Pater ingenite"; "In matutinis surgimus"; and "Jam meta noctis transiit"; are morning hymns; one, "Jesus refulsit omnium," for the Epiphany; one, "Jesu quadragenariae," for Lent; and one, "Beata nobis gaudia," for Whitsuntide. *Thomasius* gives another as Hilary's, "Hymnum dicat turba fratrum" (for fuller details see under their respective first lines). Written as these hymns were in the first infancy of Latin hymnody, and before the metres of the old heathen Latin poets had been wholly banished from the Christian service of song, or the rhyming metres, which afterwards became so general and so effective, had been introduced into such compositions, they can scarcely be expected to take very high rank. At the same time they are not without a certain rugged grandeur, well befitting the liturgical purposes they were intended to serve. Containing as they also do the first germs of Latin rhymes, they have great interest for all students of hymnody, as thus inaugurating that treatment of sacred subjects in a form which was to culminate presently in the beautiful Church poetry of the 12th cent.   [D. S. W.]

Hildebert, who sprang from a family of

no great position, was b. at Laverdin, near Montoire, in France, 1057. Brought up at the feet of Berengarius of Tours (a pupil of Erigena) he so profited by the opportunities thus afforded him of acquiring learning, as to become one of the most cultivated scholars of his age. Having for some years been a Professor of Theology at Mans, he became at the age of forty (1097) Bp. of that see. He was translated, in 1125, to the Archbishopric of Tours, and d. 1134.

Hildebert's character as an individual has been very differently drawn by different writers, for while *Trench* describes him as "a wise and gentle prelate, although not wanting in courage to dare and fortitude to endure, when the cause of truth required it," who "must ever be esteemed one of the fairest ornaments of the French Church," *Bayle*, in his *Hist. & Crit. Dict.*, represents him as having "led a very scandalous life," even after his promotion to an archdeaconry. As to his character as a writer of Latin verse, the evidence is clearer and less contradictory. He is said, by the Benedictine editors of his works, to have written more than ten thousand Latin lines (as various in merit as voluminous in amount), sometimes in rhyme, more generally in heroic or elegiac metre, and upon subjects ranging from "An Address to the Three Persons of the Holy Trinity," to a legendary "Life of Mahomet." The large majority of his verses are of little value, while some rise to such a height of energy and grandeur as to induce *Trench* to prefer him to a higher place in sacred Latin poetry than any other writer except Adam of St. Victor, and almost to allow him to "dispute the palm" even with the latter. The first *complete* collection of his writings was made by the Benedictines, who edited them in conjunction with those of Marbod, bishop of Rennes, his contemporary, and pub. them at Paris, in 1708 (for specimens of the best work of Hildebert see Trench's *Sac. Lat. Poetry*, 1849 and 1873). The most striking of his pieces will probably be allowed to be (1) The "noble vision," "Somnium de Lamentatione Pictavensis Ecclesiae," of which Trench says, "I know no nobler piece of versification, nor more skilful management of rhyme, in the whole circle of sacred Latin poetry;" and (2) the "Oratio Devotissima ad Tres Personas SS. Trinitatis," which is thus characterised by the same high authority: "A poem . . . which gradually rises in poetical animation until towards the end it equals the very best productions which Latin Christian poetry anywhere can boast." The following graceful lines of Hildebert's "De Nativitate Christi" form part of a longer poem, and exhibit, not unfairly, the beauties and faults alike of their author's style. For the attempted translation of them which follows the present writer is responsible.

> " Nectareum rorem terris distillat Olympus,
> 　Totam respergunt flumina mellis humum.
> Aurea sanctorum rosa de prato Paradisi
> 　Virginis in gremium lapsa quievit ibi.
> Intra virgineum decus, intra claustra pudoris,
> 　Colligit angelicam Virginis aula rosam.
> Flos roseus, flos angelicus, flos iste beatus
> 　Vertitur in foenum, fit caro nostra Deus.
> Vertitur in carnem Verbum Patris, at sine damno
> 　Vertitur in matrem virgo, sed absque viro.
> Lumine plena suo manet in nascente potestas,
> 　Virgineum florens in pariente decus,
> Sol tegitur nube, foeno flos, cortice granum,
> 　Mel cera, sacco purpura, carne Deus.
> Aetheris ac terrae sunt haec quasi fibula, sancto
> 　Foederis amplexu dissona regna ligans."

> " Dew-dropping nectar on earth pours down from the heights of Olympus,
> Rivers of honey are shed over the face of the ground ;
> Out of the Garden of Eden a bright golden Rose of the blessed
> Into a Virgin's breast falls and reposes in peace.
> Hid 'neath its virginal glory, behind maiden chastity's portal,
> Held in a Virgin's womb, lies an angelical Rose :
> Bloom of a Rose, of a Rose angelic, this bloom ever-blessèd
> Turns to a weed, and God puts on the flesh of a man.
> Turned into flesh is the Word of the Father, tho' shorn not of glory,
> And to a Mother a Maid, though she hath known not a man.
> In the new-born is His power still filled with the light of His Godhead,
> And in His Mother remains virginal honour undimmed.
> Clouds the sun veil, the bloomd ry leaves, and the ear the grain covers,
> Wax hides the honey, sackcloth purple, humanity God.
> These are the clasps that connect this earth with high heaven above it ;
> Blending in holiest league kingdoms so widely apart."
> 　　　　　　　　　　　　　　[D. S. W.]

Hildegard, St., Virgin and Abbess, was b. at Bockelheim, or Bockenheim, Frankfurt, 1098. Her father, Hildebert, was one of the Knights of Meginhard, Count of Spanheim. When eight years old she was committed to the care of a sister of the Count, Jutta, the Abbess of St. Disibod, a position in which she was succeeded by Hildegard in 1136. Under the rule of Hildegard the convent became so crowded that a new one was built at Rupertsberg, near Bingen, into which, in 1147, Hildegard removed with eighteen Sisters. Hildegard gained great notoriety in very early life on account of visions to which, it is said, she was subject from her 6th to her 15th year. In later life she filled a considerable place in the history of her times, not only as a writer who had the courage of her opinions, and spared neither high nor low in her vigorous denunciations of their shortcomings, political as well as moral, but as a prophetess and preacher. At the instigation of St. Bernard she took a most prominent part in stirring up the unfortunate crusade which he preached, and engaged in many controversies with the hierarchy of her Church. Though she never ceased to be the abbess of the convent she had founded, much of her time was spent in travelling about the Continent, preaching and prophesying. She d. in 1179, and was buried at Rupertsberg, but her remains were removed, on the destruction of that convent by the Swedes, to Eilingen, in 1622.

Though St. Hildegard was a voluminous writer her contributions to the hymnody of her day were neither numerous nor important. *Mone* gives three sequences which are attributed to her, viz., one on the Holy Spirit,

"O ignis Spiritus paracliti "; another on the B. V. M., "O Virga ac diadema purpurae Regis"; and a third on St. Disibod, "O praesul verae civitatis." **[D. S. W.]**

Hilf, Herr Jesu, lass gelingen. *J. Rist.* [*New Year.*] 1st pub. in the *Drittes Zehn* of his *Himlische Lieder*, Lüneburg, 1642, No. 1, in 16 st. of 6 l., entitled " Godly beginning of the New Year in, and with the most sweet name of Jesus." It is one of the best German New Year's Hymns, and became speedily popular (though often abridged). It is in the *Unv. L. S.*, 1851, No. 70. *Tr.* as :—

1. **Help, Lord Jesus, let Thy blessing**, by Miss Dunn in her *H. from the Ger.*, 1857, p. 71. The *tr.* is good but free, and represents st. i., iv., vii., viii., xiii.–xvi. of the original. Repeated, abridged, in Dr. Pagenstecher's *Coll.*, 1864 ; the *Bapt. Hyl.*, 1879, and others.

2. **Help us, O Lord, behold we enter**, a *tr.* of st. i., iv., viii., xiii., xv., xvi., by Miss Winkworth, in her *C. B. for England*, 1863, No. 172 ; repeated in the Ohio *Luth. Hyl.*, 1880. **[J. M.]**

Hill, Rowland, M.A., s. of Sir Rowland Hill, Bart., was b. at Hawkstone, near Shrewsbury, Aug. 23, 1744, and educated at Shrewsbury Grammar School, Eton, and St. John's College, Cambridge (B.A. 1769). Taking Holy Orders, he was for a time curate of Kingston, near Taunton. Leaving his curacy, but without renouncing his Orders or his connection with the Church of England, he itinerated for some twelve years, preaching mostly in Wilts, Gloucestershire, Somersetshire, and London. At Wotton-under-Edge he built a Chapel, where he often preached, and also opened the well-known Surrey Chapel, London, in 1783. At the latter place he ministered for nearly fifty years. He took great interest in Evangelical and Mission work, was one of the founders of the London Missionary Society, and a member of the first committee of the Religious Tract Society. He d. April 11, 1833. He was the author of several prose works ; he also compiled the following hymn-books :—

(1) *A Collection of Psalms and Hymns for the Use of the Poor*, 1774. (2) *A Collection of Psalms and Hymns, chiefly intended for Public Worship*, 1783. This was enlarged in 1787, and a *Supplement* was added in 1796. Other revisions followed, the last being in 1830. (3) *Divine Hymns attempted in easy language for the Use of Children*, 1790 (2nd ed. 1794 ; later eds. 1808 & 1819). The hymns in this work, he tells us, are, with the exception of Nos. 24 and 37, his own, revised and corrected by some one he is not permitted to name (*Preface iv.–viii.*). (4) *A Collection of Hymns for Children*, 1808. (5) *Hymns for Schools*, 1832.

In these collections no authors' names are given, and his own contributions, except in the case of the children's *Hymns*, 1790, are difficult to determine. By common consent the following, including some from the 1790 *Hymns*, are attributed to him :—

1. **Come, Holy Ghost, the Comforter.** *Whitsuntide.* No. 30 of his *Divine Hys. for Children*, 1790, in 5 st. of 4 l. and headed " A Child's Prayer to God the Holy Spirit." It was repeated in the later editions of the *Divine Hys.*, and is found in modern hymn-books.

2. **Dear Friend of friendless sinners, hear.** *A Prayer for Rest in God.* In his *Ps. & Hys.* &c., 1783, No. 89, in 4 st. of 6 l., and headed " A Prayer for the promised Rest." In modern hymn-books its use is limited.

3. **Happy the children who betimes.** *Godly Education.* No. 8 in his *Divine Hys.*, 1790, in 5 st. of 4 l., and headed " The Blessings of a godly Education." It was repeated in later editions, and, sometimes with the omission of st. v., in modern collections for children.

4. **Lord, we raise our feeble voices.** *Praise to Jesus.* Major, in his *Bk. of Praise for Home & School*, dates

this hymn 1800. It is found in several collections for children.

5. **My parents gave me, Lord.** *A Child's Dedication to God.* No. 13 in his *Divine Hys.*, 1790, in 6 st. of 6 l., and headed "A Child's Hymn on easy Dedication to God in Holy Baptism." It is in a few modern collections.

6. **We sing His love Who once was slain.** *The Resurrection.* Appeared in the 1796 *Supplement* to his *Ps. & Hys.* It is in American C. U.

7. **When Jesus first at heaven's command.** *The Kingdom of Christ exalted.* Composed for the London Missionary Society, and printed in the *Evangelical Magazine*, 1797, vol. v. p. 263. It is appended to the author's sermon to the volunteers preached at Surrey Chapel, 1803, and was also included in the 1810 ed. of his *Ps. & Hys.*, No. 302, in 6 st. of 4 l. with the chorus, "Hail Immanuel," &c.

8. **With heavenly power, O Lord defend.** *Departure of Ministers.* Pub. in his *Ps. & Hys.*, 1783, No. 234, in 4 st. of 4 l., and headed "For Ministers at their Departure." In modern hymn-books it is generally given in 2 st.

9. **Ye that in these [His] courts are found.** *Public Worship.* This is usually attributed to R. Hill. It appeared, however, in Lady Huntingdon's *H. Bk.*, 1765, p. 404 (ed. 1773, p. 256), and can scarcely be his. In his *Ps. & Hys.*, 1783. It is usually given as "Ye that in *His* courts," in modern collections.

The person referred to as having revised the *Divine Hys.*, 1790, was the poet Cowper. The best known of R. Hill's hymns, "Cast thy burden on the Lord," and "Gently, my Saviour, let me down," are annotated under their respective first lines. (See also Index to Authors.) His *Life*, by the Rev. E. Sidney, M.A., was pub. in 1834.   [J. J.]

Hill, Stephen P. An American Baptist Minister, who pub. *Christian Melodies*, Baltimore, 1836, in which there are 25 of his hymns signed "H." His hymn "Come, saints, adore your Saviour God" (*Holy Baptism*) is one of these. It is also found in the *Sabbath H. Bk.*, Baptist edition, 1859, and others.   [J. J.]

Hill, Thomas, D.D., LL.D., s. of English parents, was b. at New Brunswick, New Jersey, Jan. 7, 1818. At the age of 20 he left the apothecary's shop in which he was employed, and began the study of Latin and Greek. He graduated at Harvard, 1843, and at the Cambridge Divinity School, 1845. His first charge was as pastor of the Unitarian Church at Waltham, Massachusetts; his second, that of President of Antioch College, Ohio, 1859; his third that of President of Harvard College, and his fourth that of pastor of "the First Parish in Portland, Maine, May 18, 1873." Dr. Hill has published numerous sermons, addresses, reviews, &c., and also a work—*Geometry and Faith*, 1849. Putnam (to whose *Singers and Songs of the Liberal Faith* we are indebted for this notice) says that he has "written or translated several hundred hymns or poems of decided excellence." These were mainly contributed to American magazines, the first having been printed in the *Christian Register*, in 1838. One of these, "All holy, ever living One" (*God our Light*), is in C. U. Several others of decided merit are given in *Putnam*, 1875, pp. 411-19.   [J. J.]

Hiller, Friedrich Conrad, was b. at Unteröwisheim, near Bruchsal, in 1662. In 1680 he began the study of law at the University of Tübingen, where he became a licentiate in civil and canon law. He d. at Stuttgart, Jan. 23, 1726, where he had been

since 1685 advocate in chancery at the ducal court.

His hymns, which found favour in Hannover, and have kept their place in Württemberg, appeared in his *Denckmahl der Erkentniss, Liebe und Lob Gottes, in neuen geistlichen Liedern*, &c., Stuttgart, 1711, with melodies by J. G. C. Störl. The only one *tr.* into English is:—

O Jerusalem du schöne. *Heaven.* 1711, as above, p. 535, in 7 st. of 6 l., entitled *Longing after Eternal Life.* It has been a great favourite in Württemberg, and was included in the *Württemberg G. B.*, 1742, and again in that of 1842. The fine melody set to it in 1711 is found in the *Sarum Hyl.*, 1868, No. 252.

The *trs.* are: (1) "O Jerusalem the golden," by R. Massie, 1864, p. 140, repeated in Reid's *Praise Bk.*, 1872. (2) "O Jerusalem! fair dwelling," in J. D. Burns's *Memoir and Remains*, 1869, p. 256. [J. M.]

Hiller, Philipp Friedrich, s. of Johann Jakob Hiller, pastor at Mühlhausen on the the Enz, Württemberg, was b. at Mühlhausen, Jan. 6, 1699. He was educated at the clergy training schools at Denkendorf (under J. A. Bengel) and Maulbronn, and the University of Tübingen (M.A. 1720). His first clerical appointment was as assistant at Brettach, near Neckarsulm, 1724-27. He afterwards held similar posts at Hessigheim and elsewhere, and was also, from 1729-31, a private tutor at Nürnberg. He was then, on St Bartholomew's Day, 1732, instituted as pastor of Neckargröningen, on the Neckar, near Marbach. In 1736 he became pastor of his native place, and in 1748 pastor at Steinheim, near Heidenheim. In his third year of residence at Steinheim he lost his voice, and had to employ an assistant to preach. He d. at Steinheim, April 24, 1769. (*Koch*, v. 107-126; *Allg. Deutsche Biog.*, xii. 425-426, &c.) Of Hiller's hymns the best appeared in :—

(1) *Arndt's Paradiss-Gärtlein . . . . in teutsche Lieder*, Nürnberg, N.D. [the copy in Berlin has a frontispiece dated 1730]. This was written during the time he was tutor at Nürnberg. P. Gerhardt had founded the fine hymn "O Jesu Christ, mein schönstes Licht," (q.v.) on one of the prayers in the volume of devotions which Johann Arndt had pub., 1612, under the title of *Paradies-Gärtlein ;* and Gerhardt's example led Hiller to think of turning the whole of these prayers into hymns. The book is in four parts, and contains 301 hymns, 297 being founded on Arndt and four original. (2) *Geistliches Liederkästlein*, Stuttgart, 1762, and a second series, Stuttgart, 1767. Each series contains 366 short hymns, one for each day of the year. A complete reprint of these and the other hymns of Hiller (1075 in all) was ed. by C. C. E. Ehmann in 1844 (2nd ed. 1858).

Hiller is the most productive and most important of the earlier hymn-writers of Württemberg; and is the poetical exponent of the practical theology of his friend J. A. Bengel. The hymns of his *Paradiss-Gärtlein*, while clear and Scriptural, are decidedly spun out (see No. xii. below). His *Liederkästlein* contains the hymns of his riper years, and reveals a depth of spiritual wisdom, an almost proverbial conciseness, an adaptation to console and direct in the most diverse events of life, and the most varied experiences of the soul, a suitability as a manual for daily devotion, and a simple popularity of style that speedily endeared it to the pious in Southern Germany. It has passed through many editions in Germany, while colonists (especially from Württemberg) have carried it from thence wherever they went. It is said, e.g., that when a German colony in the Caucasus was attacked by a hostile Circassian tribe some fifty years ago the parents cut up their copies of the *Liederkästlein* and divided the leaves among their children as they were being torn from them into slavery.

The use of Hiller's hymns in Germany has principally been in the hymn-books of Württemberg, and, through J. J. Rambach's *Haus G. B.*, 1735, in Hannover. The following have passed into English :—

I. *Hymns in English C. U.*

i. **Herr über Leben und der Tod.** *Cross and*

Consolation. 1730, pt. iii. p. 332, founded on Arndt's Prayer, 26 (28) of Class iii. The part *tr.* is st. viii.–xiv., "Herr, meine Burg, Herr Zebaoth," which is founded on the fourth part of the third section of Arndt's Prayer. The text is in Ehmann's *Hiller*, Nos. 885, 886.   *Tr.* as :—

O God of Hosts ! O mighty Lord, a *tr.* of st. viii., xiii., xiv., signed " F. C. C.," as No. 162 in Dr. Pagenstecher's *Coll.*, 1864.

ii. **Mein Gott in deine Hände.** *For the Dying.* *Liederkästlein*, pt. ii., 1767, for Aug. 3, in 9 st. of 4 l., founded on Ps. xxxi. 6. In *Ehmann*, No. 986, and in Knapp's *Ev. L. S.*, 1837 and 1865.   *Tr.* as :—

My God, to Thee I now commend, a good *tr.* of st. i., iii., iv., vi., viii., ix., by Miss Winkworth, in her *Lyra Ger.*, 1st Ser., 1855, p. 245. In her 2nd ed., 1856, she substituted a *tr.* of st. vii. for that of st. vi. The text of 1856 is in her *C. B. for England*, 1863, No. 194, and in the Ohio *Evang. Luth. Hyl.*, 1880 ; and the text of 1855 in the Pennsylvania Luth. *Ch. Bk.*, 1868.

Another tr. is : " My God, within Thy hand," by *Miss Warner*, 1858, p. 480.

iii. **Mein Herz, du musst im Himmel sein.** *Eternal Life. Liederkästlein*, p. ii., 1767, for Jan. 26, in 4 st. of 7 l., founded on St. Matt. vi. 21. In *Ehmann*, No. 639, and Knapp's *Ev. L. S.*, 1837.   *Tr. as* :—

Aspire, my heart, on high to live, in full, by Dr. H. Mills, in his *Horae Ger.*, 1845 (1856, p. 86), repeated, omitting st. iv., as No. 220 in the Amer. Luth. Gen. *Synod's Coll.*, 1850–52.

iv. **Wir warten dein, o Gottes Sohn.** *Second Advent. Liederkästlein*, pt. ii., 1767, for Jan. 24, in 4 st. of 8 l., founded on 1 Thess. i. 9, 10. In *Ehmann*, No. 1041, and the Württemberg *G. B.*, 1842, No. 640.   *Tr.* as :—

We wait for Thee, all glorious One, a good and full *tr.* by J. D. Burns, in the *Family Treasury*, 1859, pt. ii. p. 111, and his *Remains*, 1869, p. 264. Included in the *Christian H. Bk.*, Cincinnati, 1865, and in H. L. Hastings's *Songs of Pilgrimage*, 1886.

Another tr. is : " We wait for Thee, O Son of God," in the *British Herald*, April, 1866, p. 252, and Reid's *Praise Bk.*, 1872. This follows the altered form in C. B. Garve's *Christliche Gesänge*, 1825.

II. *Hymns not in English C. U.*

v. **Abgrund wesentlicher Liebe.** *Love of God.* 1730, pt. ii. p. 25, founded on Prayer 4 in Class II. of Arndt, which is " Thanksgiving for the Love of God, and prayer for it." *Tr.* as, " Thou fathomless Abyss of Love," by *Miss Winkworth*, 1869, p. 281.

vi. **Angenehmes Krankenbette.** *For the Sick. Liederkästlein*, 1762, p. 338, for Dec. 3, in 3 st., founded on St. Luke v. 18. *Tr.* as, " Bed of Sickness ! thou art sweet," by *Miss Winkworth*, 1869, p. 283.

vii. **Betet an, verlorne Sünder.** *Lent. Liederkästlein*, 1762, p. 43, for Feb. 18, in 3 st., founded on St. Matt. xviii. 14. *Tr.* as, " Sinners, pray ! for mercy pleading," by *Dr. H. Mills*, 1856, p. 50.

viii. **Das Lamm, am Kreuzesstamme.** *For the Dying. Liederkästlein*, pt. ii., 1767, for Feb. 12, in 8 st., founded on Acts vii. 59. In the Württemberg *G. B.*, 1842, No. 609, altered to " Der Hirt, am Kreuz gestorben." This form is *tr.* as, " The Shepherd by His passion," by J. D. Burns, in the *Family Treasury*, 1859, pt. ii. p. 64, and his *Remains*, 1869, p. 266.

ix. **Die Liebe darf wohl weinen.** *Burial of the Dead. Liederkästlein*, 1762, p. 286, for Oct. 12, in 7 st., founded on 1 Thess. iv. 13. *Tr.* as, " Love over the departed," by J. D. Burns in his *Remains*, 1869, p. 253.

x. **Die Welt nimmt einst zusammen.** *Second Advent. Liederkästlein*, pt. ii., 1767, for Jan. 2, in 5 st., founded on 2 Cor. v. 10. *Tr.* as, " The world shall yet be cited," by J. D. Burns in the *Family Treasury*, 1859, pt. ii. p. 111, and his *Remains*, 1869, p. 263.

xi. **Herr, meine Leibeshütte.** *For the Dying. Liederkästlein*, pt. ii., 1767, for Feb. 18, in 8 st., founded on

2 Peter, i. 14. The *trs.* are : (1) " Lord, my house of clay," by *Miss Warner*, 1858, p. 605. (2) " My fleshly house is sinking now," by *Dr. G. Walker*, 1860, p. 102.

xii. **Mein Jesus sitzt zur rechten Hand.** *Ascensiontide.* 1730, pt. iii. p. 408, as st. 118–125 of the hymn on Arndt's prayer 27 (29) in Class III. This prayer is a long paraphrase of the Apostles' Creed. *Tr.* as, " Our Jesus now at God's right hand," by *Dr. H. Mills*, 1845 (1856, p. 330).

xiii. **Singet Gott, denn Gott ist Liebe.** *The Love of God. Liederkästlein*, 1762, p. 51, for Feb. 20, in 3 st., founded on 1 John iv. 16. The *trs.* are : (1) " God is love—then sing His praises," by *Dr. H. Mills*, 1845 (1856, p. 16). (2) " God is love, sing loud before Him," by J. D. Burns in his *Remains*, 1869, p. 231.

xiv. **Singt doch unserm König.** *Ascensiontide. Liederkästlein*, 1762, p. 328, for Nov. 23, in 3 st., founded on Ps. xcvi. 10. *Tr.* as, " Laud your King and Saviour," by J. Sheppard in his *Foreign Sacred Lyre*, 1857, p. 94.

xv. **Untheilbare Dreifaltigkeit.** *Trinity Sunday.* 1730, pt. ii. p. 226, founded on Arndt's prayer 25 in Class II., entitled " Thanksgiving for the revelation of the Holy Trinity." The *tr.* is from the recast of st. vi.–xii. made by J. S. Diterich for the Berlin *G. B.*, 1765, No. 51, and beginning " Lob, Ehre, Preis und Dank sei dir." *Tr.* as, " Love, honour, thanks, to Thee we raise," by *Dr. H. Mills*, 1845 (1856, p. 110).

xvi. **Was freut mich noch wenn du's nicht bist.** *Joy in God. Liederkästlein*, 1762, for June 20, in 2 st., founded on Ps. xliii. 4. *Tr.* as, " What earthly joy can fill my heart," by R. Massie in the *British Herald*, Nov. 1865, p. 175.

xvii. **Wer ausharrt bis ans Ende.** *Cross and Consolation. Liederkästlein*, pt. ii., 1767, for May 19, in 4 st., founded on St. Matt. xxiv. 13. *Tr.* as, " He who to death maintaineth," by J. D. Burns in his *Remains*, 1869, p. 261.

xviii. **Wer kann dein Thun begreifen.** *God's Power. Liederkästlein*, 1762, p. 18, for Jan. 18, in 3 st., founded on Is. xlv. 7. *Tr.* as, " Who, Lord, Thy deeds can measure," by *Dr. H. Mills*, 1845 (1856, p. 15). [J. M.]

Hillhouse, Augustus Lucas, younger brother of James Hillhouse (commonly known as the poet Hillhouse), was b. at New Haven, Connecticut, 1792, and educated at Yale, where he graduated in 1810. For some time he conducted a school in Paris ; and d. near that city, March 14, 1859. His hymn :—

Trembling before Thine awful throne (*Joy in the Forgiveness of Sins*) was written cir. 1816, and pub. in the *Christian Spectator*, New Haven, April, 1822. It is a good hymn, and is in extensive use, but usually in an abbreviated form. The hymn, " Earth has a joy unknown to heaven," found in a few American hymnbooks, begins with st. iii. of this hymn. Orig. text in *Christ in Song*, 1870.   [J. J.]

Himmel, Erde, Luft und Meer. *J. Neander.* [*Thanksgiving.*] A beautiful hymn of praise and thanksgiving for the wonders and delights of Creation and Providence, founded on Acts xiv., 17. 1st pub. in his *Glaub- und Liebes-übung : auffgemuntert durch einfältige Bundes-Lieder und Danck-Psalmen*, Bremen, 1680, p. 162, in 6 st. of 4 l., entitled " Rejoicing in God's Creation," and with the note at the end, " Is also a Traveller's Hymn by land and water." It passed through Freylinghausen's *G. B.*, 1704, into later books, and is No. 707 in the *Unv. L. S.*, 1851. *Tr.* as :—

1. Heaven and earth, and sea and air, God's eternal. A good and full *tr.* by Miss Cox in her *Sacred H. from the Ger.*, 1841, p. 195. In more or less altered forms it is found in Alford's *Ps. & Hys.*, 1844, and his *Year of Praise*, 1867 ; in the *Marylebone Coll.*, 1851, &c. ; and in America in the *H. for the Ch. of Christ*, Boston, 1853, &c.

2. Lo, heaven and earth, and sea and air, a full and good *tr.* in *L. M.* by Miss Winkworth in her *Lyra Ger.*, 2nd Ser., 1858, p. 148, repeated in

her *C. B. for England*, 1863, and in *Ps. & Hys.*,
Bedford, 1859.

**3. Heaven and earth, and sea and air, All
their.** This is a cento, and a good one, in the
Pennsylvania Luth. *Ch. Bk.*, 1868. It is mainly
from Miss Winkworth, but partly from Miss Cox,
and partly new, and in the original metre.

**4. Heaven and earth, and sea and air, Still
their.** A full and good *tr.* by J. D. Burns,
included in his *Memoir*, &c., 1869, p. 229. Repeated in Dale's *Eng. H. Bk.*, 1875, *Bapt. Hyl.*,
1879, Horder's *Cong. Hyl.*, &c., 1884.

Other trs. are :—
(1) "Heaven and ocean, earth and air," by *Lady
E. Fortescue*, 1843, p. 33. (2) "Heaven, earth, land and
sea," by *Miss Manington*, 1863, p. 105.   [J. M.]

Himmelan geht unsre Bahn. *B.
Schmolck.* [*Ascensiontide.*] 1st pub. as the
concluding hymn in his *Bochim und Elim.*
Breslau, 1731 (No. 105, p. 275), in 10 st. of
6 l., entitled "The sweet thought of heaven."
It is a beautiful hymn of looking forward to
the heavenly aim and the heavenly prize. It
is found in many recent German hymn-books
as in the Berlin *G. L. S.*, ed. 1863, No. 706
(omitting st. vii.). *Tr.* as :—

1. Heavenward still our pathway tends, a good
tr., omitting st. iii., iv., vii., by Miss Cox in her
Sacred H. from the Ger., 1841, p. 117, and thence
in the Pennsylvania Luth. *Ch. Bk.*, 1868. She
revised her *tr.* for *Lyra Eucharistica*, 1864,
p. 296, and her *H. from the Ger.*, 1864, p. 211.
This revised form is in the *Bapt. Hyl.*, 1879.

2. Heavenward doth our journey tend, a good *tr.*,
omitting st. iii., iv., vii., by Miss Winkworth in
her *Lyra Ger.*, 1st Ser., 1855, p. 108, and
repeated in Harland's *C. P. & Hyl.*, No. 452,
Bapt. Ps. & Hys., 1858, &c. In her *C. B. for
England*, 1863, No. 65, altered in metre, and
thence, omitting the *tr.* of st. viii., in the Ohio
Evang. Luth. Hyl., 1880.

3. Heavenward our path still goes, a *tr.* of st. i.,
ii., ix., x., based on Miss Cox, as No. 231, in Bp.
Ryle's *Coll.*, 1860; repeated in Dr. Pagenstecher's
Coll., 1864. Altered and beginning "Heavenward still our pathway goes," in *Kennedy*, 1863.

Other trs. are :—
(1) "Heavenward may our course begin," by *Lady
E. Fortescue*, 1843, p. 50. (2) "Heavenward our pathway lies," by *Miss Dunn*, 1857, p. 63. (3) "Heavenward our pathway lies, In this world," &c., by Dr.
F. W. Gotch, in the *Bapt. Magazine*, Jan. 1857. (4)
"Heavenward our road doth lie," by *Miss Warner*,
1858, p. 117.   [J. M.]

Hincks, Thomas, B.A., F.R.S., was b. at
Exeter in 1818, and educated at the Royal
Academical Institution, Belfast, and Manchester College, York. He has been pastor of
Unitarian congregations at Cork, 1839; Dublin, 1841; Warrington, 1844; Exeter, 1846;
Sheffield, 1852, and Mill Hill, Leeds, 1855–
1869. He is the author of several scientific
works and papers. His hymns were contributed to *Vespers according to the use of Mill
Hill Chapel, Leeds*, 1868, a *Supplement* to the
collection used by that congregation. They
are :—
1. Hark, the evening call to prayer. *Evening.*
2. Heavenly Father, by Whose care. *Evening.*
3. Lord, in the holy hour of even. *Evening.*
4. To the Cross, O Lord, we bear. *Holy Communion.*

The most popular of these hymns is No. 2.

They are all of more than average merit, and
are worthy of attention.   [W. G. H.]

Hinds, Samuel, D.D., s. of Abel Hinds, of
Barbadoes, was b. in Barbadoes in 1793, and
educated at Queen's College, Oxford (B.A.
1815, D.D. 1831). He was for some time Vice-
Principal of St. Alban's Hall, Oxford (1827),
and also Principal of Codrington College,
Barbadoes. He held subsequently several
appointments in England and Ireland, including the Deanery of Carlisle, 1848, and the
Bishopric of Norwich, 1849. Resigning his
Bishopric in 1857, he retired to London,
where he d. Feb. 7, 1872. He pub. several
prose works, and also *Sonnets and other Short
Poems*, 1834. From that work his popular
hymn, "Lord, shall Thy children come to
Thee," sometimes given as, "O Lord, Thy
children come to Thee" (*H. Communion*,) in
the *Hy. Comp.* and others, is taken. [J. J.]

**Hinsdale, Grace Webster, née Had-
dock,** a Congregationalist, dau. of Professor
C. B. Haddock; was b. at Hanover, New
Haven, May 17, 1833, and married to Theodore Hinsdale, a lawyer of New York, in 1850.
Mrs. Hinsdale is a contributor to the periodical press, and has pub. *Coming to the King,
a Book of Daily Devotion for Children*, 1865;
republished in England as *Daily Devotions
for Children*, 1867. Her hymns include :—

i. From *Coming to the King*, 1865.

1. A light streams downward from the sky. *Heaven.*
2. My soul complete in Jesus stands (1855). *Safety
in Jesus.*

ii. From Schaff's *Christ in Song*, N.Y., 1869.

3. Are there no wounds for me? *Passiontide.* Written April, 1868.
4. Jesus, the rays divine. *Jesus ever present.* Written July, 1868.
5. There was no angel 'midst the throng. *Jesus, the
Deliverer; or, Redemption.* Written April, 1868. The
hymn, "Jesus, Thou art my Lord, my God," in the
1874 *Supplement* to the *New Cong.*, is composed of st.
viii.-x., xv.-xvii., slightly altered, of this hymn.
6. Thou stand'st between the earth and heaven. *Virgin and Child.* This poem was "written after viewing
Raphael's Madonna di San Sisto, in the Royal Gallery of
Dresden, Aug., 1867." (*Christ in Song.*) It is not
suited for congregational use.   [J. J.]

Hinton, John Howard, M.A., s. of the
Rev. James Hinton, Baptist minister of Oxford,
was b. in that city, Mar. 24, 1791. He graduated at the University of Edinburgh, and
began his ministry at Haverfordwest (1816).
Thence, in 1820, he removed to Reading, and
in 1837, to London, where for many years he
was pastor of the Baptist Church in Devonshire Square, Bishopsgate. In his later years
he returned to Reading, but spent his closing
days at Bristol, where he d. Dec. 17, 1873.

For the greater part of his life Mr. Hinton was one of
the best known ministers of the Baptist denomination,
and a recognised leader in all their public affairs. With
him the logical faculty predominated, and he was a keen
controversialist. His prose publications were numerous,
being chiefly works of Theology and Practical Religion,
but including also a *History of the United States of
North America; Memoirs of William Knibb*, &c. In
1864-5 his theological writings were collected and republished in seven volumes. He wrote a large number
of hymns, usually composing one to suit his sermon
when he could not find one adapted thereto in the book
used at his chapel. A few are printed at the end of his
Theological Lectures, &c. Many are preserved in MS. in
the Library of the Baptist Union, at the Mission House
in Furnival Street. Three only are in C. U. and are as
follows :—

1. Father of all, before Thy throne. *A Parental Prayer.*
2. Once I was estranged from God. *A Grateful Retrospect.*
3. O Thou that hearest, let our prayer. *Prayer for a Revival.*

These were in the Bapt. *Selection,* enlarged, 1838. No. 1 had appeared in the 1828 ed. of that *Sel.,* and in *Hymns by a Minister,* 1833. It is in Spurgeon's *O. O. H. Bk.,* 1866, and Nos. 2 and 3 are in the Baptist *Ps. & Hys.,* 1858.

These hymns are fair in quality, but Mr. Hinton was greater as a public man and theologian than as a hymn-writer.

[W. R. S.]

Hippel, Theodor Gottlieb von, s. of Melchior Hippel, rector of the Latin school at Gerdauen, in East Prussia, was b. at Gerdauen Jan. 31, 1741. He entered the University of Königsberg in 1756 as a student of theology, where he became an ardent disciple of Kant, and then, in 1762, turned to the study of law. In 1765 he became an advocate in Königsberg; in 1772, Town Judge; 1780, Burgomaster and Director of Police; 1786, Geheim Kriegsrath and City President. He d. at Königsberg, April 23, 1796 (*Koch,* vi. 301–309; *Allg. Deutsche Biog.,* xii. 463–66).

In his writings Hippel's great aim was to popularise and apply the ideas of his master Kant. In his inner life he was a combination of contradictions; on one side of a wonderful fervour of devotion and communion with the unseen; and on the other ambitious, miserly and worldly. His hymns, written in the manner of Gellert, and almost all composed 1757–60, appeared mostly in his *Geistliche Lieder,* Berlin, 1772, and were reprinted with additions in vol. viii. of his collected works (14 vols., Berlin, 1827–37). Two have passed into English.

i. **Gott hab' ich mich ergeben.** *Resignation.* 1772, p. 44, in 7 st. of 6 l., entitled "Submission to the will of God"; thence in the Berlin *G. L. S.,* ed. 1863, No. 908. In the Berlin *G. B.,* 1829, No. 581, altered to "Dir hab ich mich ergeben." The only *tr.* in C. U. is:—

To Thee, O Lord, I yield my spirit. Thine. A free *tr.* of st. i., ii., v., vii., by R. C. Singleton, as No. 271, in the *Anglican H. Bk.,* 1868.

ii. **Jetzt leb' ich, ob ich Morgen lebe.** *Preparation for Death.* 1772, p. 39, in 6 st., entitled "In recollection of Death." In the hymn-books sometimes repeated as in the original, sometimes as *Noch leb ich,* or as *Heut leb ich.* *Tr.* as: (1) "Now I live; but if to night," by Miss Warner, 1858, p. 305. (2) "Though still I live, I know not when," by Dr. G. Walker, 1860, p. 96.

[J. M.]

His Master taken from his head. *W. Cowper.* [*Death of a Minister.*] 1st pub. in the *Olney Hymns,* Bk. ii., No. 73, in 4 st. of 4 l. It was more frequently found in the older collections than in modern hymn-books, but it is still in use in America.   [J. J.]

Ho, ye that thirst, approach the spring. [*Lent.*] 1st appeared as No. 27 in the Draft Scottish *Translations and Paraphrases,* 1745, as a version of Isaiah lv., in 14 st. of 4 l. In the revised ed. issued in 1751, st. ii. was rewritten, and st. iv., vi., xii., slightly altered. Considerable alterations were made when it was included as No. 26 in the Draft of 1781; and in the public worship ed. issued in that year by the Church of Scotland, and still in use, it was further altered, and st. iii.–vi., viii. rewritten. The markings by the eldest daughter of *W. Cameron* (q. v.) ascribe the alterations of 1781 to Cameron, and the original of 1745 to *William Robertson;* but this ascription to Robertson is not made by any other of the authorities, and is at least doubtful. The revised text of 1781 has passed into a few modern hymnals; st.

i.–vi. being included in Burgess & Money's *Ps. & Hys.,* 1857, Eng. Presb. *Ps. & Hys.,* 1867, and the *Free Church H. Bk.,* 1882. The following abridged or altered forms have also been in use:—

1. **Ye thirsty souls, approach the spring** (st. i. altered), in Belknap's *Sacred Poetry,* Boston, U.S., 3rd ed., 1801, No. 298.
2. **Behold, He comes! your Leader comes** (st. v.), Twickenham Chapel *Coll.,* 1845, as for the 3rd S. after Epiphany.
3. **Seek ye the Lord, while yet His ear** (st. vii.), Eng. Presb. *Ps. & Hys.,* 1867; *Free Ch. H. Bk.,* 1882.

A version founded on the 1781, in four parts, viz.:—i. "Ho, every one that thirsteth, come." ii. "Thus saith the Lord, 'Incline your ear.'" iii. "Seek ye the Lord, while yet His ear." iv. "As rain and snow, on earth bestow," is found as No. 55 in Miss Leeson's *Paraphrases and Hymns for Congregational Singing,* 1853.   [J. M.]

Hobson, John Philip, M.A., s. of John Hobson, M.A., sometime Consular Chaplain at Shanghai, was b. at Shanghai, China, Sept. 3, 1849, and educated at the Blackheath Proprietary School and Worcester College, Oxford (B.A. 1872). On taking Holy Orders he became Curate of Greenwich, 1873, and Vicar of Stanstead Abbotts, Herts, 1878. Mr. Hobson has pub.:—

(1) *Scenes in the Life of David: a Service of Song,* 1877; (2) *Scripture Echoes in our Church's Collects,* 1881; (3) *Twenty Hymns . . . with Tunes;* and others.

Mr. Hobson's hymns in C. U. are:—

1. **Hail, Son of Man! Hail, mighty Lord.** *Ascension.* Written for and 1st pub. in his *Scripture Echoes,* &c., 1881; in the *Twenty Hys.* and the *Universal H. Bk.,* 1885.
2. **It is an unknown way.** *New Year.* Written in 1877, and pub. in the *Twenty Hys.* and the *Universal H. Bk.,* 1885.
3. **O Lord, the bishop of our souls.** *Ember Days.* Written for a special Ember service held at Ware, 1878, and pub. in the *Twenty Hys.* and the *Universal H. Bk.,* 1885.
4. **Saviour Divine, Thou art my King.** *Jesus, the King.* Suggested by Miss Havergal's "My King," &c. Written in 1876, and 1st printed in the *Fireside Magazine,* 1876, and again in the *Twenty Hys.,* &c. It is the best known of the author's hymns.
5. **We thank Thee that the glorious sound.** *Missions.* Appeared in *Life and Work,* 1884.

In the *Twenty Hymns* (Novello) there are others of special merit, and worthy of the attention of compilers.   [J. J.]

Hochheilige Dreifaltigkeit. *J. Scheffler.* [*Trinity Sunday.*] Appeared as No. 191 in Bk. v. of his *Heilige Seelenlust,* Breslau, 1668, p. 643 (*Werke,* 1862, i. p. 318), in 5 st. of 8 l. It was included, slightly altered and beginning, "Hochheilige Dreieinigkeit," in Freylinghausen's *G. B.,* 1704, and this form was repeated in many later hymn-books, as in the Berlin *G. L. S.,* ed. 1863, No. 31. It is a fine hymn of supplication to the Holy Trinity and for the special graces afforded by Father, Son, and Holy Spirit. *Tr.* as:—

1. **Most high and holy Trinity, Thou God,** a full and excellent *tr.* by Miss Cox in her *Sacred H. from the Ger.,* 1841, p. 45. In full and unaltered in Mercer's *C. P. & H. Bk.,* 1855, No. 163 (Ox. ed., 1864, No. 247), and other collections.
2. **Most high and holy Trinity! Who of.** A good and complete *tr.* by Miss Winkworth in her *Lyra Ger.,* 1st Ser., 1855, p. 119, and thence in Boardman's *Selection,* Philadelphia, U.S., 1861.

In her *C. B. for England*, 1863, No. 76, it was altered to the original metre, and this form is in the *New Zealand Hyl.*, 1870.

3. O High and Holy Trinity, by Dr. R. F. Littledale for the *People's H.*, 1867, No, 165, signed "L." This is also a good and full version.

[J. M.]

Höchster Priester, der du dich. *J. Scheffler.* [*Self-Dedication.*] Appeared as No. 176 in Bk. v. of his *Heilige Seelenlust*, Breslau, 1668, p. 593 (*Werke*, 1862, i. p. 295), in 5 st. of 4 l. Included in Freylinghausen's *G. B.*, 1704, and recently as No. 687 in the Berlin *G. L. S.*, ed. 1863. The hymn is founded on Romans xii. 1, and carries out the figure somewhat in detail. To a number of the orthodox Lutherans of the 18th cent. st. iii., iv., gave great offence, and were accused of false mysticism, &c. *Tr.* as :—

Great High-Priest, who deigndst to be, a good and full *tr.* by Miss Winkworth in her *Lyra Ger.*, 1st Ser., 1855, p. 32, and her *C. B. for England*, 1863, No. 129. It is repeated in full in the *Hyl. for St. John's, Aberdeen*, 1865–70, and the *Evang. Hyl.*, N.Y., 1880 ; and abridged in the *Harrow School H. Bk.*, 1866 ; Eng. Presb. *Ps. & Hys.*, 1867, &c. A considerably altered version, beginning, " Jesus, who upon the tree," in which st. iv., v. are condensed as iv., was included in the American *Sabbath H. Bk.*, 1858, and repeated in the *Bapt. H. Bk.*, Philadelphia, 1871.

Other trs. are :—

(1) " Greatest High-priest, Saviour Christ," by *J. C. Jacobi*, 1725, p. 39 (1732, p. 130) ; repeated in the *Moravian H. Bk.*, 1754, pt. i., No. 459. (2) "Grant, most gracious Lamb of God," as No. 273 in the *Moravian H. Bk.*, 1789 (1886, No. 351). [J. M.]

Hodenberg, Bodo von, was b. April 3, 1604. After the conclusion of his university studies he entered the service of the Dukes of Lüneburg. He was for some time tutor to the sons of Duke Georg, and subsequently (1646) chief magistrate and director of the mines at Osterrode in the Harz, for the principality of Grubenhagen. He d. Sept. 20, 1650 (*Koch*, iii. 239 ; *Allg. Deutsche Biog.*, xii. 537 ; *Bode*, p. 91). The only hymn known by him is the beautiful

Vor deinen Thron tret ich hiemit. *Morning.* 1st pub. in the *New Ordentlich G. B.*, Hannover, 1646, No. 217 (beginning " *Für* deinen Thron "), in 15 st. of 4 l., introduced by the words, " In the morning, at midday, and in the evening one can sing." In the *Lüneburg G. B.*, 1669, it is ascribed to Justus Gesenius, who had probably altered it somewhat. Included as No. 1131 in the Berlin *G. L. S.*, ed. 1863. The only *tr.* of this form is " Before Thy Throne I now appear," by *J. C. Jacobi*, 1720, p. 37 (1722, p. 108 ; 1732, p. 171). Another form is that given by Bunsen in his *Versuch*, 1833, No. 49, in 10 st., beginning :—

Ich danke dir mit Herz und Mund. St. i. is altered from st. xi. ; st. ii.-x. are st. ii., v.-x., xiv., xv. The only *tr.* of this form is " With heart, and mind, and every power," by *H. J. Buckoll*, 1842, p. 71. [J. M.]

Höfel, Johann, was b. June 24, 1600, at Uffenheim, in Franconia, and studied at the Universities of Giessen, Jena, and Strassburg, becoming in 1628 Doctor of Law at Jena. In 1633 he settled in Schweinfurt as a consulting lawyer, and d. there Dec. 8, 1683 (*Wetzel*, i. 435–436, and *A. H.* ii., 285–291). One of his hymns has been *tr.* into English :—

O süsses Wort das Jesus spricht. *Cross and Consolation.* Founded on St. Luke vii. 13. Included as No. 451 in the Coburg *G. B.*, 1655 [Göttingen University Library],

in 11 st. of 4 l., entitled, " The sweet saying of Jesus, ' Weep not,' Luke vii." According to *Koch*, iii. 141, it had previously appeared in his *Musica Christiana*, 1634. *Tr.* as " Oh, sweetest words that Jesus could have sought," by Mrs. Findlater, in *H. L. L.*, 1855, p. 8 (1884, p. 75). [J. M.]

Hoffmann, Gottfried, s. of Caspar Hoffmann, brewer at Plagwitz, near Löwenberg, in Silesia, was b. at Plagwitz, Dec. 5, 1658. After studying at the University of Leipzig (M.A. 1688), he was appointed in 1688 Conrector, and in 1695 Rector of the Gymnasium at Lauban. In 1708 he became Rector of the Gymnasium at Zittau, where he d. after a stroke of paralysis, Oct. 1, 1712. (*Koch*, v. 437–442 ; *Allg. Deutsche Biog.*, xii. 591–592.) Of his hymns, about 60 in all, written mostly for his scholars, only one has passed into English, viz. :—

Zeuch hin, mein Kind. *Death of a Child.* According to *Koch*, v. 442, this beautiful hymn was written in 1693, on the death of his little daughter Magdalene Elisabethe, was printed in the same year in her funeral sermon on Job i. 21, and included by Hoffmann in his *Laubansche Leichengesänge*, 1704. It is in Schwedler's *Lieder Mose*, Budissin, 1720, No. 306, and repeated in the Berlin *G. L. S.*, ed. 1863, in 6 st. of 9 l. *Tr.* as :—

Depart, my child. A good *tr.*, omitting st. iv., by Miss Borthwick, in *H. L. L.*, 1st Ser., 1854, p. 25 (1884, p. 28). Repeated in *Kennedy*, 1863, omitting st. iii., and beginning " Farewell, my child." Other *trs.* are : (1) " So, go, my child," by *E. Massie*, 1866, p, 139. (2) " Go hence, my child," by *Dr. J. Guthrie*, 1869, p. 109.

[J. M.]

Hogg, James, second son of Robert Hogg, was born in Ettrick Forest, Selkirkshire, January 25, 1772, according to his own account, though the baptismal date is December 9, 1770. He is perhaps best known as the *Ettrick Shepherd*, and friend of Professor John Wilson and Sir Walter Scott. He d. November 21, 1835, on his farm of Altrive in Yarrow. An edition of his *Poetical Works* was published in 1822 in 4 vols. (Edin., A. Constable) including the best of his poems— *The Queen's Wake*, 1813 ; *The Pilgrims of the Sun*, 1815 ; *Mador of the Moor*, 1816, &c. The two hymns by him which have come into use are, " Blessed be Thy name for ever," and " O Thou that dwellest in the heavens high." A complete edition of his prose and verse was pub. in 2 vols., 1865 (Glas., W. G. Blackie).

1. Lauded be Thy Name for ever. *Morning.* This is " The Palmer's Morning Hymn " (in 32 lines), which forms a part of Canto iv. of his poem *Mador of the Moor*, 1816. It is sometimes given in this form, but more frequently as " Blessed be Thy Name for ever " (2 st. of 8 l.), as in the S. P. C. K. *Hymns*, 1852, and others. It is also altered as " Lord of life, the Guard and Giver," as in *Mercer*, &c.

2. O Thou that dwellest in the heavens high. *Midnight.* This was given together with music, as " A Cameronian's Midnight Hymn," in 8 st. of 4 l., in his tale of *The Brownie of Bodsbeck*, 1818. Although found in several collections its use is not so great as that of No. 1. [J. M.]

Hohlfeldt, Christoph Christian, was b. Aug. 9, 1776, at Dresden. He became, in 1819, Advocate for the Poor (Armen-Advocat) at the Court of Appeal at Dresden, and d. at Dresden, Aug. 7, 1849 (K. Goedeke's *Grundriss*, 1862 ff., iii. p. 183). His hymns appeared in his *Harfenklänge*, Dresden and Leipzig, 1823, 1830 and 1836. The only one *tr.* into English is :—

Verlass mich nicht ! O du, zu dem ich flehe. *Supplication.* In his *Harfenklänge*, 1836, p. 214, in 6 st. of 4 l., entitled " Prayer." *Tr.* as :—

Forsake me not! O Thou, my Lord, my Light, by Mrs. J. P. Morgan, in the *Christian Union*, 1883. It is a *tr.* of st. i., ii., v., and is given as No. 116 in *Laudes Domini*, New York, 1884.   [J. M.]

Hold up thy mirror to the sun. *J. Keble.* [*St. Bartholomew.*]

In the annotated edition of the *Christian Year*, this poem is dated 1821. It was pub. in that work in 1827 in 17 st. of 4 l., and is based on St. John i. 50. In its full form it is unknown to the hymnals. In *Kennedy*, 1863, No. 300, there is a cento therefrom, beginning, "Eye of God's Word! where'er we turn," composed of st. v., vi., xiii., xiv. and xv. slightly altered. The somewhat peculiar expression, "Eye of God's Word!" is thus explained in a note thereto in the *Christian Year*. It is a quotation from the Rev. John Miller's *Bampton Lectures*, for 1817, p. 128:—

"The position before us is, that we ourselves, and such as we, are the very persons whom Scripture speaks of, and to whom, as men, in every variety of persuasive form, it makes its condescending though celestial appeal. The point worthy of observation is, to note how a book of the description and the compass which we have represented Scripture to be, possesses this versatility of power; *this eye, like that of a portrait, uniformly fixed upon us, turn where we will.*"

The cento is of more than usual merit as a hymn on *Holy Scripture*, but its use is limited.   [J. J.]

Holden, Oliver,

one of the pioneers of American psalmody, was b. in 1765, and was brought up as a carpenter. Subsequently he became a teacher and music-seller. He d. at Charlestown, Massachusetts, 1844. His pub. works are *American Harmony*, 1793; the *Worcester Collection*, 1797; and other Tune books. One of his most popular tunes is "Coronation." It is thought that he edited a small hymn-book, pub. at Boston before 1808, in which are 21 of his hymns with the signature "H." A single copy only of this book is known, and that is without title-page. Of his hymns the following are in C. U. :—

1. **All those who seek a throne of grace.** [*God present where prayer is offered.*] Was given in Peabody's *Springfield Coll.*, 1835, No. 92, in a recast form as, "They who seek the throne of grace." This form is in extensive use in America, and is also in a few collections in G. Britain.

2. **With conscious guilt, and bleeding heart.** [*Lent.*] This, although one of the best of Holden's hymns, has passed out of use. It appeared, with two others, each bearing his signature, in the *Boston Collection* (Baptist), 1808.

3. **Within these doors assembled now.** [*Divine Worship.*]   [F. M. B.]

Holiest, Holiest, hearken in love. *T. Davis.* [*Divine Presence desired.*]

Appeared in his *Hys. Old and New*, 1864, No. 155, in 4 st. of 5 l.; and again in his *Annus Sanctus*, 1877, where it is appointed for March 24. It is one of the most popular of the author's hymns, and is worthy of more extensive use than has yet been made of it.   [J. J.]

Holland, John,

b. in Sheffield, Mar. 14, 1794, and d. there, Dec. 28, 1872. During his long life he pub. more than 40 volumes in prose and verse, the most important of which hymnologically were his *Life of James Montgomery*, 1859 (7 vols.), and *The Psalmists of Britain*, 1843 (2 vols.), both of which are standard works. His earliest pub. poems

appeared in *The Lady's Magazine*, 1814, with the initials "H." or " J. H."; and his first volume of poetry, *Sheffield Park*, in 1820. His hymns number several hundreds, and date from 1813 to his death in 1872. Four of these were contributed to the *Jubilee Hymn Book of the Sunday School Union*, 1853. They were, however, written so exclusively for local Sunday School anniversaries and children's services, and contain so many local allusions, as to render most of them unsuitable for general use. One in the Meth. Free Church *Sunday S. H. Bk.*, 1860, "Lord, why are thus our British youth?" (*S. S. Anniversary*) is a fair example of his hymn-writing. His *Life of the Rev. John Summerfield, M.A.*, attained to great popularity in America. He assisted Montgomery in preparing and publishing the latter's *Original Hymns*, 1853, and wrote the introduction to the American edition of the same. His *Life*, by W. Hudson, was pub. in 1874.   [J. J.]

Holland, Josiah Gilbert,

was b. at Belchertown, Massachusetts, July 24, 1819. He was for some time on the staff of the *Springfield Republican*, and became in 1870 the editor of *Scribner's Magazine*. He has written several successful books, and some poetical pieces. One of the latter, "For summer's bloom, and autumn's blight" (*Praise in and through all things*), was included, from *Bitter Sweet*, 1858, in the Boston Unitarian *Hymn [and Tune] Bk. for the Church & Home*, 1868. He d. Oct. 12, 1881.   [J. J.]

Holme, James, B.A.,

s. of T. Holme, Orton, Westmorland, was b. in 1801, and educated at Caius College, Cambridge (B.A. 1825). Ordained in 1825, he held successively the Incumbency of Low Harrowgate, the Vicarage of Kirkleatham, and the charge of Bolton, near Bradford. He d. in 1882. He pub. *Leisure Musings and Devotions, &c.*, 1835; *Mount Grace Abbey*, a poem, 1843, and with his brother, the Rev. T. Holme (q.v.), *Hymns & Sacred Poetry*, Christian Bk. Soc., 1861. From this last work, "All things are ours, how abundant the treasure" (*Praise in Sickness*), in Snepp's *S. of G. & G.*, 1872, is taken. "God my Father, hear me pray" (*Lent*), in the *Anglican H. Bk.*, 1868, is attributed to him, and dated 1861. It is, however, from his *Leisure Musings*, 1835, p. 117, in 4 st. of 6 l., but it is not in the *Hys. & Sac. Poetry*. His hymn, "Lord Jesus, God of grace and love" (*H. Communion*), is from the *Hys. & Sac. Poetry*, 1861. These works are worthy of the attention of compilers of children's hymn-books.   [J. J.]

Holme, Thomas,

brother of the above, was b. Aug. 8, 1793, and educated at Appleby Grammar School. Taking Holy Orders in 1817, he was for twenty years Head Master of Kirby Ravensworth Grammar School. Subsequently he was Vicar of East Cowton, Yorkshire, where he d. Jan. 20, 1872. From *Hymns & Sacred Poetry*, 1861 (the joint work of himself and his brother James), the following hymns are taken :—

1. **Behold the lilies of the field, How gracefully, &c.** *Flower Service.*

2. **Lord, in mine agony of pain.** *Resignation.*

3. The Christian's path shines more and more. *Growth in Holiness.* This hymn previously appeared in a local collection about 1850.   [J. J.]

Holmes, Elizabeth. [Reed, Elizabeth.]

Holmes, Oliver Wendell, M.D., LL.D., s. of the Rev. Abiel Holmes, D.D., of Cambridge, U.S.A., was b. at Cambridge, Aug. 29, 1809, and educated at Harvard, where he graduated in 1829. After practising for some time in Boston, he was elected in 1847 to the chair of Anatomy, in Harvard. His writings in prose and verse are well known and widely circulated. They excel in humour and pathos. Although not strictly speaking a hymn-writer, a few of his hymns are in extensive use, and include :—

1. **Father of mercies, heavenly Friend.** *Prayer during war.*

2. **Lord of all being, throned afar.** *God's Omnipresence.* This is a hymn of great merit. It is dated 1848.

3. **O Lord of hosts, Almighty King.** *Soldiers' Hymn.* Dated 1861.

4. **O Love divine that stoop'st to share.** *Trust.* 1859.

Of these Nos. 2 and 4 are in his *Professor at the Breakfast Table,* and are in C.U. in G. Britain, in Martineau's *Hymns,* 1873, and others. In 1886 the D.C.L. degree was conferred upon Professor Holmes by the University of Oxford. He was a member of the Unitarian body. He d. Oct 7, 1894.   [F. M. B.]

Hölty, Ludwig Heinrich Christoph, s. of P. E. Hölty, pastor at Mariensee on the Leine, near Hannover, was b. at Mariensee, Dec. 21, 1748. He entered the University of Göttingen, 1769; completed his course, Easter, 1772; and became a Candidate of Theology, but never obtained a charge. He d. at Hannover, Sept. 1, 1776. His complete *Gedichte,* edited by his friend J. H. Voss, were pub. at Hamburg, 1783 (2nd ed. 1804). The only piece which can be called a hymn and has been *tr.* into English is :—

Ueb' immer Treu und Redlichkeit. *Conduct of Life.* 1st pub. in J. H. Voss's *Musenalmanach,* Hamburg, 1779, p. 117, in 9 st. of 4 l., entitled "The old countryman to his son." Included in the Oldenburg *G. B.,* 1791, No. 480. The *trs.* are, (1) "Let truth and spotless faith be thine," in the *Harp of Zion,* ed. by Basil Woodd, 1833, p. 101; (2) "With honest heart go on your way," in G. Dawson's *Ps. & Hys.,* 1846, No. 172.   [J. M.]

Holy and reverend is [His] the Name. *J. Needham.* [*Holiness of God.*] In 1768 J. Needham pub. in his *Hys. Devotional and Moral,* No. 25, in 8 st. of 4 l., a hymn beginning as above. This was in C. U. for many years. In 1853 *George Rawson* rewrote st. i., iii., and viii., and added another (ii.), thus forming a hymn of 4 st. This was given in the Bap. *Ps. & Hys.,* 1858, and has passed into several collections, especially in America. In some collections it reads "Holy and reverend is *His* name." The ascription of the cento is *J. Needham,* 1768; *G. Rawson,* 1853.   [J. J.]

Holy Bible, book Divine. *J. Burton, sen.* [*Holy Scripture.*] This popular hymn first appeared in the author's *Youth's Monitor in Verse,* &c., 1803, and again in the *Evangelical Magazine,* June, 1805, in 4 st. of 4 l., where it is signed, "Nottingham—J. B."

In 1806 it was also given as No. 1 of pt. ii. of the author's *Hys. for Sunday Schools; or, Incentives to Early Piety.* As it is frequently altered in modern collections we add the original text.

" Holy Bible, book Divine,
 Precious treasure, thou art mine;
 Mine to tell me whence I came,
 Mine to teach me what I am.

" Mine to chide me when I rove,
 Mine to shew a Saviour's love;
 Mine art thou to guide my feet,
 Mine to judge, condemn, acquit.

" Mine to comfort in distress,
 If the Holy Spirit bless;
 Mine to shew by living faith
 Man can triumph over death.

" Mine to tell of joys to come,
 And the rebel sinner's doom;
 Holy Bible, book Divine,
 Precious treasure, thou art mine."

This hymn has gradually grown into favour, and now it is in C. U. in most English-speaking countries.   [J. J.]

Holy Ghost, come down upon Thy children. *F. W. Faber.* [*Whitsuntide.*] Appeared in his *Oratory Hymns,* 1854, and again in his *Hymns,* 1862, in 6 st. of 4 l., the opening stanza being repeated as a chorus. The metre is most awkward and unmusical, and fully justifies the alterations made in the *Altar Hymnal,* 1884, where it is rewritten in 8. 7. 8. 7. metre, beginning "Holy Ghost, come down upon us."   [J. J.]

Holy Ghost, Thou source of light. [*Whitsuntide.*] Appeared anonymously in the Andover *Sabbath H. Bk.,* 1858, No. 458, in 4 st. of 4 l., and subsequently in several other collections. In the *Bapt. Praise Bk.,* N. Y., 1871, it is altered to "Holy *Spirit,* Source of Light."   [J. J.]

Holy Ghost, Whose fire celestial. [*Whitsunday.*] Appeared in Hawtrey's *Coll.* 1815, and again in Miss Auber's *Spirit of the Psalms,* 1829, where it was given with a few "Hymns for the Principal Festivals," p. 149, in 2 st. of 8 l. In Snepp's *Songs of G. & G.,* 1870–72, No. 351, it is attributed to *T. Cotterill* in error.   [J. J.]

Holy, holy, holy Lord, Ever be Thy Name adored. [*Praise.*] This is a curious cento, in *Kennedy,* 1863, from two hymns by C. Wesley, in *Hymns & Sacred Poems,* 1739, the first of which is "Lord and God of heavenly powers," on the words from the Office for Holy Communion, and the second, "Glory be to God on high" (q.v.), on the Thanksgiving in the same office. The lines taken from these hymns are with slight alterations as follows : st. i., ii., ll. 1–4, iii., ll. 5–8, the rest of the cento being by Dr. Kennedy.   [J. J.]

Holy, holy, holy Lord God Almighty. *Bp. R. Heber.* [*Holy Trinity.*] 1st pub. in his posthumous *Hymns,* &c., 1827, p. 84, in 4 st. of 4 l., and appointed for Trinity Sunday. It was soon adopted by hymn-book compilers, and is the best known and most widely used of the author's hymns. It is a splendid metrical paraphrase of Rev. iv. 8–11. Line 2 of st. i., " Early in the morning our song shall rise to Thee," has been subjected to several changes to adapt the hymn to any hour of the day. Some of these alterations are:—

1. "*Gratefully adoring* our song," &c. *Leeds H. Bk.*, 1853.
2. "*Morning and evening* our song," &c. *Kennedy*, 1863.
3. "*Holy, holy, holy*, our song," &c. *Hymnary*, 1872.
4. "*Morning, noon, and night*, our song," &c.

The most popular change is the first of these. The majority of hymn-books, however, retain the original reading. Although a special hymn for Trinity Sunday, it is sometimes appointed as a morning hymn, as in the S. P. C. K. *Church Hys.*, 1871.   [J. J.]

Holy, holy, holy Lord, God of Hosts! When heaven and earth. *James Montgomery.* [*Holy Trinity.*] Written Sept. 10, 1832 (M. MSS.), and included in the *Cong. H. Bk.*, 1836, No. 63, in 3 st. of 8 l.; the *Leeds H. Bk.*, 1853, No. 442; the author's *Original Hymns*, 1853, No. i.; and numerous collections in most English-speaking countries, and usually without alteration. In Spurgeon's *O. O. H. Bk.*, 1866, st. ii., iii. are given as "Holy, holy, holy Thee," and appointed as a doxology.   [J. J.]

Holy Jesus, in Whose [Thy] Name. *Bp. R. Mant.* [*Prayer in the Name of Jesus.*] Appeared as one of his original hymns appended to his *Ancient Hymns*, &c., 1837, p. 109, in 5 st. of 6 l., as a "Hymn commemorative of Prayer in, and to Christ" (ed. 1871, p. 183). It is sometimes given as "Holy Jesus, in *Thy* Name." In the Cooke & Denton *Hymnal*, 1853, st. ii. is omitted, several alterations are made, and a doxology by the editors is added. This form, with further changes, is repeated in *Kennedy*, 1863.   [J. J.]

Holy Jesus, mighty Lord. *Bp. C. Wordsworth* of Lincoln. [*Holy Innocents.*] 1st pub. in his *Holy Year*, 1862, No. 11, in 5 st. of 8 l. It is in C. U., but usually in an abbreviated form. The hymn "At Thy birth, Incarnate Lord," in the *Sarum Hyl.*, 1868, the S. P. C. K. *Church Hys.*, 1871, and others, is a cento beginning with st. iii. of this hymn. Some six lines are from this hymn, and the rest are by Earl Nelson, by whom the cento was arranged.   [J. J.]

Holy Jesus, Saviour blest. *Bp. R. Mant.* [*Jesus the Way, Truth, & Life.*] 1st pub. in his *Ancient Hymns*, &c., as one of the originals appended thereto, 1837, p. 134, in 6 st. of four l., and headed, "Hymn commemorative of 'The Way, the Truth, and the Life'" (ed. 1871, p. 225). It is altered in several instances, as in the Cooke and Denton *Hymnal*, 1853; the *Appendix* to the *H. Noted*, 1862, "Holy Jesus, Saviour *bless'd*."   [J. J.]

Holy offerings, rich and rare [Lord we bear]. *J. S. B. Monsell.* [*Offertory.*] Written for the Offertory at the opening of St. Mary Magdalene Church, Paddington, 1867, and 1st printed for use on that occasion. It was included in 1873 in the author's *Parish Hymnal*, No. 201, having previously appeared in the 1869 *Appx.* to the S. P. C. K. *Ps. & Hys.* It is also in *Church Hymns*, 1871, Thring's *Coll.*, 1882, and many others. It is in 10 st. of 8 l., and is usually divided

into parts, and in several instances it is also abbreviated. "Holy offerings, *Lord, we bear,*" in Brown-Borthwick's *Select Hymns for Church and Home*, 1871, is an altered form of this hymn.   [J. J.]

Holy Spirit, Lord of glory. *R. H. Baynes.* [*Confirmation.*] Printed in the *Churchman's Shilling Magazine*, May, 1868; and again in the author's *Autumn Memories & Other Verses*, 1869, in 5 st. of 6 l. In 1871 it was included with slight alterations in the S. P. C. K. *Church Hys.*, and again in other hymnals.   [J. J.]

Homburg, Ernst Christoph, was b. in 1605, at Mihla, near Eisenach. He practised at Naumburg, in Saxony, as Clerk of the Assizes and Counsellor. In 1648 he was admitted a member of the Fruitbearing Society, and afterwards became a member of the Elbe Swan Order founded by Rist in 1660. He d. at Naumburg, June 2, 1681. (*Koch*, iii. 388, 392; *Allg. Deutsche Biog.*, xiii. 43, 44.)

By his contemporaries Homburg was regarded as a poet of the first rank. His earlier poems, 1638–1653, were secular, including many love and drinking songs. Domestic troubles arising from the illnesses of himself and of his wife, and other afflictions, led him to seek the Lord, and the deliverances he experienced from pestilence and from violence led him to place all his confidence on God. The collected edition of his hymns appeared in two parts at Jena and Naumburg, 1659, pt. i. as his *Geistlicher Lieder, Erster Theil*, with 100 hymns [engraved title, Naumburg, 1658]; and pt. ii. as the *Ander Theil* with 50 hymns. In the preface he speaks of them as his "Sunday labours," and says, "I was specially induced and compelled" to their composition "by the anxious and sore domestic afflictions by which God . . . . . has for some time laid me aside." They are distinguished for simplicity, firm faith, and liveliness, but often lack poetic vigour and are too sombre.

Two of his hymns have passed into English, viz.:—

i. **Ach wundergrosser Sieges-Held.** *Ascension.* 1659, pt. i. p. 400, in 6 st. of 11 l., entitled, "On the Ascension of Jesus Christ." In the Berlin *G. L. S.*, ed. 1863, No. 327.

The trs. are: (1) "O wondrous Conqueror and Great," by Miss Burlingham, in the *British Herald*, Oct. 1865, p. 153, and Reid's *Praise Bk.*, 1872, No. 445. (2) "O glorious Saviour, conquering King," by *N. L. Frothingham*, 1870, p. 272.

ii. **Jesu meines Lebens Leben.** *Passiontide.* 1659, pt. i. p. 318, in 8 st. of 8 l., entitled, "Hymn of Thanksgiving to his Redeemer and Saviour for His bitter Sufferings." This is his most popular hymn, and has passed into many recent collections, including the Berlin *G. L. S.*, ed. 1863. *Tr.* as:—

1. **Jesu! life! the life of heaven.** *Tr.* of st. i., ii., vi.-viii., by A. T. Russell, for his *Ps. & Hys.*, 1851, No. 88.

2. **Of my life the Life, O Jesus.** A good *tr.* of st. i., ii., v., vii., viii., contributed by R. Massie to the 1857 ed. of Mercer's *C. P. & H. Bk.*, No. 404 (Ox. ed. 1864, No. 185), repeated in the Meth. N. Conn. *H. Bk.*, 1863.

3. **Christ the Life of all the living.** A good *tr.* of st. i., ii., v., vii., viii., by Miss Winkworth, in her *C. B. for England*, 1863, No. 49. Repeated in full in Dr. Thomas's *Augustine H. Bk.*, 1866, and the Ohio *Luth. Hyl.*, 1880; and abridged in the Pennsylvania Luth. *Ch. Bk.*, 1868, the *Hymnary*, 1872, and others.

4. **Thou eternal life bestowest.** *Tr.* of st. i.-iii., viii., by Miss Borthwick, contributed to Dr.

Pagenstecher's *Coll.*, 1864, No. 73, and repeated in *H. L. L.*, ed. 1884, p. 257.

Other trs. are: (1) "Jesu, Source of my Salvation," by *J. C. Jacobi*, 1732, p. 29, repeated in the *Moravian H. Bk.*, 1754 (1886, No. 97). (2) "Jesus! Source of life eternal," by Miss Burlingham, in the *British Herald*, Aug. 1865, p. 120, and Reid's *Praise Bk.*, 1872, No. 389. (3) "Jesus, of my life the living," by *N. L. Frothingham*, 1870, p. 198. [J. M.]

Homo Dei creatura. [*Judgment to come.*] This poem is a picture of the woes of the lost, and an exhortation to timely repentance. *Mone*, i. pp. 419–421, gives 115 lines (with various breaks) from a *Reichenau MS.* of the 14th cent., and conjectures that it was written in Italy in the time of Dante. *Daniel*, iv. p. 250, repeats *Mone's* text and most of his notes; and at v., p. 382, ascribes it to Dionysius the Carthusian (b. at Rickel in the diocese of Liège, became a Carthusian Monk at Roermond, or Ruremonde on the Maas, 1424, and d. there, March 12, 1471). In J. M. Horst's *Paradisus Animae Christianae*, Cologne, 1630, the text which has passed into English is given at p. 206 (sect. iii.), entitled, "D. Dominici Carthusiani exhortatio ad poenitentiam," and in 168 lines. Up to *Mone's* l. 72, the texts nearly agree; but the rest of *Mone's* text continues in the same gloomy strain, whereas in Horst's text the strain speedily changes to relate the bliss of the saints, and then ends by the warning to repentance. It has been *tr.* by E. Caswall in his *Masque of Mary*, &c., 1858, in 21 st. of 10 l., as "Creature of God, immortal man" (*Hymns*, &c., 1873, p. 208); and by I. Williams in his *Thoughts in Past Years*, 1838, as "Mortal, who art God's creation." [J. M.]

Hood, Edwin Paxton, was b. in Half-moon Street, London, Oct. 24, 1820. He was self-educated. In 1852 he became the Independent Minister at Nibley, Gloucestershire, where he remained until 1857, when he removed to Offord Road, London. He held several charges (Brighton, Manchester, &c.), the last being Falcon Square, London. He d. in Paris, June 12, 1885.

Mr. Hood was a striking and suggestive preacher, and one of the most voluminous writers of the age. His published works, including *The Age and its Architects*, 1852; *Exposition of Swedenborg*, 1854; *Lamps of the Temple*, 1856; *Thomas Carlyle*, 1875; *Oliver Cromwell*, 1882, &c., are too numerous to give in detail. He also edited (and was the chief contributor to) *The Eclectic Review* for 8 years, and *The Preacher's Lantern* for 2 years.

As a hymn-writer he is best known as the author of hymns for children. These hymns have a freshness and simplicity which are attractive to children. Some of the best and most popular were written for Sunday School Anniversaries at Nibley, 1852–7. He also edited:—

(1) *Our Hymn Book* (a similar title, but a distinct work from Mr. Spurgeon's Collection). This was pub. specially for the use of his own congregations, and was enlarged from time to time. 1st ed. Brighton, 1862, enlarged 1868, 1873, and 1879. The last ed. contains 47 of his hymns. (2) *The Children's Choir*, 1870.

His hymns in C. U. outside of his own collections are :—

1. **Angel of God, thy wings expanded.** *Missions.* In his *O. H. Bk.*, 1862.
2. **Bride of the Lamb, sweet spices bring.** *Easter.* In his *O. H. Bk.*, 1862.
3. **Earth in beauty smiles again.** *Summer* (1852–57).
4. **God, Who hath made the daisies.** *Early Piety* (1852–57).

5. **Heart-broken and weary, where'er thou may'st be.** *Christ's Invitation.* 1st pub. at the end of the first sermon in his *Dark Sayings on a Harp*, 1865, and then in his *Our H. Bk.*, 1879.
6. **I hear a sweet voice ringing clear.** *Divine Protection* (1862).
7. **I love to think, though I am young.** *Jesus the Holy Child.*
8. **O Jesus, Saviour, we are young.** *Child's Prayer for Guidance* (1852–57).
9. **Rest remaineth, O how sweet.** *Heaven our Rest.* In his *O. H. Bk.*, 1862. A pathetic hymn sung at his funeral.
10. **Saviour and Master, these sayings of Thine.** *The Sand and the Rock.* Written at the Portland Breakwater, in the winter of 1858–59, and 1st pub. in his first volume of *Sermons*, 1860, at the close of that on "The Sand and the Rock." He says, "I walked the other day over the Great Breakwater at Portland, and there, whilst the rain descended and the floods came I thought and wrote out these verses." The hymn is in his *Our H. Bk.*, 1879, Horder's *Cong. Hyl.*, 1884, &c. It has also been printed on a fly-leaf for use in Portland Prison.
11. **Sing a hymn to Jesus when the heart is faint.** *Consecration of Self to Jesus.* Suggested by a tune heard at Vespers in Fontainbleau Church, and 1st pub. in *Bye Path Meadow*, 1870, and again in *Our H. Bk.*, 1879.
12. **Sweet hallelujahs! The birds and the blossoms.** *Universal Praise.* Written for the S. S. Anniversary, Offord Road Chapel, 1860, and pub. in *Our H. Bk.*
13. **Teach me, O Lord, where'er I move.** *God's Presence desired.* (1852–57.)
14. **There is a word I fain would speak.** *Redemption.* Written for S. S. Anniversary at Offord Road Chapel, 1858, and pub. in *Our H. Bk.*, 1862.
15. **There's a beautiful land where the rains never beat.** *Heaven.* (1852–57.) In his *Children's Choir*, 1870, &c.
16. **Unless the Lord the city keep.** *God the Pastor's Strength.* Written at the request of the Deacons of Offord Road Chapel, for the Recognition Service of the Rev. J. C. Jones. In his *O. H. Bk.*, No. 317.
17. **We love the good old Bible.** *Holy Scripture.* (1852–57.) Given in several collections.

The most popular of these hymns are Nos. 4 and 7. Nos. 3, 4, 5, 6, 7, 8, 11, 16, 17 are from the *Children's Choir*, 1870. These are in numerous collections.   [W. G. H.]

Hook, Walter Farquhar, D.D., s. of Dr. Hook, sometime Dean of Worcester, was b. in London, Mar. 13, 1798, and educated at Winchester, and Christ Church, Oxford (B.A. 1820, D.D. 1837). Taking Holy Orders in 1820, he was successively Vicar of Holy Trinity, Coventry; Vicar of Leeds, 1837–59; Dean of Chichester, 1859; Chaplain in Ordinary to the Queen, &c. He d. at Chichester Oct. 20, 1875. He was the author of numerous Sermons, Pamphlets, Tracts, &c., but is most widely known through his *Church Dictionary*, and his *Lives of the Archbishops*. In 1846 he edited—

Verses for Holy Seasons, with questions for Examination, by C. F. H., Lond., 1846.

This was a volume of verses by Cecil Frances Humphreys, afterwards Cecil F. Alexander (q.v.). He also pub. :—

A Church School Hymn-book, Edited by Walter Farquhar Hook, D.D., Leeds, 1850.

In this collection all the hymns were given anonymously. Hence has arisen the error of attributing some of them to the editor. Dr. Hook was not a writer of hymns. [J. J.]

Hooper, Emma. [Whitfield, Emma.]

Hooper, Mary Fawler. [Maude, M. F.]

Hopkins, John. [Old Version, § IX. 2, x.]

Hopkins, John Henry. [Various.]

Hopkins, Josiah, D.D., was b. at Pittsford, Vermont, April 18, 1786. From 1809 to

1830 he was pastor of a Congregational Church, at New Haven, Vermont; and from 1830 to 1848 of the First Presbyterian Church, Auburn, N. York. He died at Geneva, New York, July 27, 1862. He was the editor of *Conference Hymns*, Auburn, 1846, and contributed hymns to the *Christian Lyre*, N. Y., 1830. From the latter work his hymns in C. U. are taken:—

1. O turn ye, O turn ye, for why will ye die. *Expostulation.*
2. Why sleep we, my brethren. *Expostulation.*

[F. M. B.]

Hopper, Edward, D.D., was b. in 1818, and graduated at Union Theological Seminary, New York, 1842. He is pastor of the Church of Sea and Land, N. Y. He is the author of

1. Jesus, Saviour, pilot me [us]. *Jesus the Pilot.*
2. They pray the best who pray and watch. *Watching & Prayer.*
3. Wrecked and struggling in mid-ocean. *Wreck & Rescue.*

Of these No. 1 appeared in the *Baptist Praise Bk.*, 1871, and 2 & 3 in *Hys. & Songs of Praise*, N. Y., 1874.   [J. J.]

Hopps, John Page, was b. in London, Nov. 6, 1834, and educated at the G. Baptist College, Leicester. Commencing public work in 1856, after a brief ministry at Hugglescote and Ibstock, in Leicestershire, he became colleague with George Dawson at the Church of the Saviour, Birmingham. From 1860 to 1876 he ministered to Unitarian congregations at Sheffield, Dukinfield, and Glasgow. Since 1876 he has preached in Leicester. Mr. Hopps has published many books and pamphlets, chiefly volumes of Sermons and Lectures. Most of his smaller works are controversial. In 1863 he commenced a monthly periodical called *The Truthseeker*, which he still edits. He has compiled the following hymn-books for Congregational, Mission, or School purposes:—

(1) *Hymns for Public Worship and the Home*, 1858; (2) *Hymns of Faith and Progress*, c. 1865; (3) *Hymns for Public Worship*, 1873; (4) *One hundred Hymns for Sunday Schools*, 1873; (5) *Hymns, Chants and Anthems for Public Worship*, 1877; (6) *The Children's Hymn Book*, 1879; (7) *The Young People's Book of Hymns*, 1881; (8) and six different editions of *Hymns for Special Services* (for Sunday afternoon and evening gatherings in the Temperance Hall and Floral Hall, Leicester).

Mr. Hopps has himself written various hymns, some of considerable merit. Several have appeared in Congregational, Baptist, Unitarian and other collections. Among the best known are the following:—

1. Cold and cheerless, dark and drear. *Winter.*
2. Father, lead me day by day. *Child's Prayer for Divine Guidance.*
3. Father, let Thy kingdom come. *God's Kingdom desired.*
4. God bless the little children. *Prayer for Children.*
5. We praise Thee oft for hours of bliss. *The blessings of Sorrow.*

These hymns are from his *Hys., Chants, and Anthems*, &c., 1877, and the *Hys. for Special Services.* The most popular is No. 2.

[W. R. S.]

Hora novissima, tempora pessima sunt, vigilemus. *Bernard of Cluny.* [*The Heavenly Jerusalem.*] This magnificent poem, evidently inspired by the last two chapters of the Revelation of St. John, was composed in the Abbey of Cluny, about 1145, and ex-

tends to about 3000 lines. It is found in a 13th cent. MS. in the Bodleian (Digby 65, f. 42).

i. *Publication.* It was included by Flacius Illyricus, in his *Varia poemata de corrupto Ecclesiae statu*, Basel, 1556. Illyricus was an ardent and enthusiastic Reformer; and as the greater part of the poem "is a bitter satire on the fearful corruptions of the age," it answered his purpose to use it in this manner. It was subsequently reprinted at Bremen, 1597; at Rostock, 1610; at Leipzig, 1626; at Lüneburg, 1640; in Wachler's *New Theological Annals*, December, 1820; and in Mohnike's *Studien*, 1824. In Trench's *Sac. Latin Poetry*, 1849, 96 lines were given, beginning with "Hic breve vivitur" (from which Dr. Neale's first translation was made); and in Dr. Neale's *Rhythm of Bernard de Morlaix, Monk of Cluny, on the Celestial Country*, 1858, there are 218 lines. In *Daniel*, ii. 380; *Bässler*, No. 139; *Königsfeld*, ii. 262; *Simrock*, p. 286, there are also extracts from the poem. The original is dedicated to Peter the Venerable, the General of the Order to which St. Bernard belonged, and is entitled, "De contemptu mundi." (Dr. Schaff, in his *Lib. of Religious Poetry*, 1883, p. 981, says this poem was printed in Paris in 1483. We have not seen this edition.)

ii. *Design and Execution.* Bernard states his argument thus:—

"The *subject* of the author is the Advent of Christ to Judgment: the joys of the Saints, the pains of the reprobate. His *intention*, to persuade to the contempt of the world. The *use*, to despise the things of the world: to seek the things which be God's. He fortifies his exordium with the authority of the Apostle John, saying, 'Little children, it is the last time'; where he endeavours to secure aforehand the favour of his readers, by setting the words of the Apostle before his own. At the commencement he treats of the Advent of the Judge, to render them in earnest, and by the description of celestial joy, he makes them docile." (Neale's *Rhythm*, &c., Preface.)

The *execution* of the poem, written as it was in "a rhythm of intense difficulty," was attained, as the author believed, through special divine grace and inspiration. His words in his dedicatory epistle are:—

"Often and of long time I had heard the Bridegroom, but had not listened to Him, saying—'Thy voice is pleasant in Mine ears.' And again the Beloved cried out, 'Open to Me, My sister.' What then? I arose, that I might open to my Beloved. And I said, 'Lord, to the end that my heart may think, that my pen may write, and that my mouth may set forth Thy praise, pour both into my heart and pen and mouth Thy grace.' And the Lord said, 'Open thy mouth.' Which He straightway filled with the spirit of wisdom and understanding; that by one I might speak truly, by the other perspicuously. And I say it in nowise arrogantly, but with all humility, and therefore boldly: that unless that Spirit of Wisdom and Understanding had been with me, and flowed in upon so difficult a metre, I could not have composed so long a work. For that kind of metre, continuous dactylic (except the final trochee or spondee), preserving also, as it does, the Leonine sonorousness, had almost, not to say altogether, grown obsolete through its difficulty. For Hildebert of Laverdin, who from his immense learning was first raised to the Episcopate and to the Metropolitan dignity; and Vuichard, Canon of Lyons, excellent versifiers, how little they wrote in this metre, is manifest to all." (Neale's *Rhythm*, &c., Preface.)

The poem is written in dactylic hexameters, with the leonine (sometimes a trisyllable or dactylic), and tailed rhyme, each line being broken up into three parts thus:—

"Hóra novíssima || tempora péssima || sunt: vigilemus!
Ecce minaciter || imminet arbiter || ille supremus!
Imminet, imminet || ut mala terminet || aequa coronet
Recta remuneret || anxia liberet || aethera donet."

iii. *Merits.* The two great authorities on this matter are Archbishop Trench and Dr. Neale. Referring to the numerous editions of the poem, the former says:—

" This is not wonderful; for no one with a sense for the true passion of poetry, even when it manifests itself in forms the least to his liking, will deny the breath of a real inspiration to the author of these dactylic hexameters." (*Sac. Lat. Poetry*, ed. 1874, p. 310.)

Archbishop Trench, whilst thus highly commending the poems, condemns the metre, and points out " its want of progress " :—

" The poet, instead of advancing, eddies round and round his subject, recurring again and again to that which he seemed to have thoroughly treated and dismissed." (*Ibid.* p. 311.)

In a note on his lines 45–58, he also says :—

" In these lines [' Urbs Syon aurea '] the reader will recognise the original of that lovely hymn, which within the last few years has been added to those already possessed by the Church. A new hymn which has won such a place in the affections of Christian people as has ' Jerusalem the golden,' is so priceless an acquisition that I must needs rejoice to have been the first to recall from oblivion the poem which yielded it." (*Ibid.* p. 314.)

Dr. Neale says concerning the poem as a whole, and specially of that portion which he has translated :—

" The greater part is a bitter satire on the fearful corruptions of the age. But as a contrast to the misery and pollution of earth, the poem opens with a description of the peace and glory of heaven, of such rare beauty, as not easily to be matched by any mediaeval composition on the same subject." (*Med. Hys.*, 3rd ed., p. 68.)

iv. *Translations.* The first to translate any portion of the poem into English was Dr. Neale, and no translation but his is in C. U. at the present time. His first *tr.* was of the 96 lines in Trench's *Sac. Lat. Poetry*, beginning with " Hic breve vivitur " (" Brief life is here our portion"). This was pub. in his *Mediaeval Hymns*, 1851, p. 53. In 1858 he pub. *The Rhythm of Bernard de Morlaix, Monk of Cluny, on the Celestial Country*, in which he gave 218 lines from the original, beginning with the first (" Hora novissima "), a *tr.* of the same, and an interesting Preface. The *tr.* and the Preface (slightly altered) were repeated in the 2nd ed. of his *Mediaeval Hymns*, 1863. From one or the other of these two works the centos following have been taken :—

i. **Hora novissima, tempora pessima sunt, vigilemus** = The world is very evil. This is the opening of several centos, all compiled from the first portion of the *Rhythm*, but composed of varying stanzas. Taken together they are in extensive use.

ii. **Hic breve vivitur, hic breve plangitur, hic breve fletur** = Brief life is here our portion. This cento varies from five stanzas in the *Hymns and Introits*, 1853, to twelve stanzas in the 1869 *Appx.* to the S. P. C. K., *Ps. & Hys.* No common rule is adhered to as to the number of stanzas or the order in which they are arranged : but in its various forms it is found in upwards of an hundred collections in G. Britain and America.

iii. **O bona Patria, lumina sobria te speculantur** = (1) For thee, O dear, dear country. (2) For thee, sweet, heavenly country. (3) For thee, O heavenly country. In common with the foregoing, these centos vary both in length and arrangement of stanzas. These centos are in more extensive use than those under No. ii.

iv. **O sacra potio** = O happy, holy portion. In the 1862 *Appendix* to the *H. Noted*.

v. **Urbs Syon aurea, Patria lactea, cive decora** = Jerusalem the golden. The centos beginning with this stanza are not so numerous as those in Nos. ii. and iii., but their use in all English-speaking countries exceed every other portion of the poem.

vi. **Urbs Syon inclyta, gloria debita glorificandis** = Jerusalem the glorious. In comparison with the foregoing the centos which begin with this stanza are not in extensive use.

vii. **Urbs Syon unica, mansio mystica, condita coelo** = Jerusalem the onely. This is given in the *Appendix* to the *H. Noted*, 1862.

viii. **Urbs Syon inclyta, turris et edita littore tuto** = Jerusalem exulting. This is given in a few collections only.

Taken together these centos, compiled from one *tr.* of 218 Latin lines, present a result unique in hymnody. Without doubt the ballad measure adopted by Dr. Neale has had much to do with this popularity; but the *tr.* possesses features of excellence which have won the approval of those for whom the ballad measure has no attractions.

The changes made in the text by various compilers are somewhat numerous. The best are those in Thring's *Coll.*, 1882, including the re-translation by Prebendary Thring of the concluding eight lines of the original, as in Dr. Neale's *Rhythm;* and the worst, in Dr. Neale's judgment, those in the *Sarum Hymnal*, 1868.

The *trs.* not in C. U. are :—

1. The last of the hours iniquity towers. By *Dr. A. Coles*, Newark, New Jersey, 1866.
2. These are the latter times, these are not better times : Let us stand waiting. By *S. A. W. Duffield*, 1867.
3. Here we have many fears, this is the vale of tears, the land of sorrow. *G. Moultrie*, in the *Church Times; and Lyra Mystica*, 1865.
4. Earth very evil is ; time through the last of his journeys is hasting. *Tr.* of the whole poem. *Jackson Mason*, 1880.
5. Hail Zion, city of our God, &c. (" Urbs Syon Inclyta.") *D. T. Morgan*, 1880.

Although these *trs.* are very much nearer the original than Dr. Neale's, and, in the case of Duffield and Moultrie, follow the metre of Bernard, yet there is little if any prospect of any of these being adopted for use in public worship.   [J. J.]

Hordle, William, was b. in Dorsetshire in the year 1778, and in 1800 became Pastor of the Congregational Church in Harwich, Essex, where, after a useful ministry of half a century, he d. Dec., 1849. During part of this time he kept a school, and at his death left considerable property to religious purposes. In the year 1814 Mr. Hordle wrote the hymn, No. 840, in the Bap. *Psalms & Hys.* (1858), " This sacred day, Great God, we close " (*Sunday Evening*) ; but it is not known that he was the author of any other published composition.   [W. R. S.]

Hornblower, Jane. [Roscoe Family.]

Horne, George, D.D., b. at Otham, near Maidstone, Kent, Nov. 1, 1730. and educated at Maidstone, and University College, Oxford (B.A. 1749). He subsequently became a Fellow, and in 1768 Master of Magdalen College. He was also Vice-Chancellor of his University, 1776; Dean of Canterbury, 1781, and Bishop of Norwich, 1791. He d. Jan. 17, 1792. Bp. Horne is widely known through his *Commentary on the Book of Psalms.* His hymns were included in his *Memoirs* by the Rev. W. Jones, 1795: again, in his *Essays and Thoughts on Various Subjects with Hymns and Poems,* 1808: and again, in his *Works,* 1809. Of his Hymns the best known is :—

See the leaves around us falling [*Autumn*], which appeared in his *Memoirs,* 1795, pp. 223–4, in 10 st. of 4 l., and entitled "The Leaf. 'We all do fade as a leaf.' Isa. lxiv. 6." It is also found in his *Essays,* 1808, and *Works,* 1809. Collyer included it in an abbreviated form in his *Coll.,* 1812, from whence it passed into modern Nonconformist hymnals. It was brought into use in the Church of England by Cotterill through his *Sel.,* 8th ed., 1819.

Bishop Horne's translation of the Latin Grace, "Te Deum patrem colimus" (q v,) :— "Thee, Mighty Father, we adore," has been strangely overlooked by hymnal compilers.

[J. J.]

Horne, William Wales, b. in 1773 at Gissing, in Norfolk. In 1793 he became minister of a small Baptist Church at Tibenham, in the same county; thence removed, in 1797, to Yarmouth, thence to Leicester, and about 1806, to London. In London he preached first at the City Chapel, in Grub Street; then, for many years, at Trinity Hall, Aldersgate Street, and Hephzibah Chapel, Limehouse, taking services every Sunday at both places; finally (the two congregations having united) at Ebenezer Chapel, Commercial Road. Whilst pastor of this church he died, in 1826.

Whilst minister at Tibenham, Horne pub. a small vol. entitled *New Songs of Sion; or Short Hymns collected from the Scriptures of the Old Testament.* London, Mathews, 1794. In 1802, when at Leicester, he pub. *A Selection of Hymns for Public Worship, selected from the best authors, including also a great many original hymns.* This contained 310 hymns, 9 being his own composition. In 1806, when minister in Grub Street, London, he pub. *Sion's Harmony; or the United Praises of Ransomed Sinners; a complete Selection of Hymns for Public Worship.* This contained 513 hymns, 22 being by him. In 1812 an *Appendix* appeared, and in 1823 a new ed. of the entire book, as *Sion's Harmony of Praise; a Selection of Psalms, Hymns, and Spiritual Songs, for Public, Social, & Private Worship, from the best Hymn Writers; with a variety of original pieces,* by W. W. Horne. Lond. printed by W. Woodcock,1823. This Selection contains 752 hymns, 95 being by Horne. Horne's own compositions have but little merit. Being Calvinistic in sentiment a few have been introduced into hymn-books used by congregations holding that form of doctrine. Two are in Snepp's *Songs of G. & G.,* and others in Denham's & Gadsby's *Selections.* These include :—

1. Draw near, ye saints, with sweetest praise. *Praise to Jesus.*
2. Death is no more a frightful foe (1806). *Victory over death.*
3. Sing to the Lord, Whose matchless love. *The Father's Love.* [W. R. S.]

Horres superbos, nec tuam. *C. Coffin.* [*Wednesday.*] Pub. in the *Paris Breviary,* 1736, for Wednesdays at Vespers: and again in his *Hymni Sacri* the same year. The text is also in J. Chandler's *Hys. of the Primitive Church,* 1837, No. 25, and Card. Newman's *Hymni Ecclesiae,* 1838 and 1865. Tr. as :—

1. O God, the hateful pride of man. By J. Chandler in his *Hymns of the Prim. Church,* 1837, p. 22, in 5 st. of 4 l., and repeated in Dr. Oldknow's *Hys. for the Ser. of the Church,* 1850.
2. Thou dost, Lord, abhor the proud. By I. Williams in his *Hys. tr. from the Parisian*

Breviary, 1839, p. 26, in 5 st. of 4 l. This is No. 1160 in *Kennedy,* 1863.

Another tr. is :—
Thou dost, O, God, the proud o'erthrow. *J. D. Chambers,* 1857. [J. J.]

Horst; Horstius, J. M. [Merlo, J.]

Hosanna to the living Lord. *Bp. R. Heber.* [*Advent.*] This hymn is found in two forms and both by Heber. The first is unknown in modern hymnals, the second is in very extensive use in English-speaking countries. In 1811 Heber contributed several hymns to the *Christian Observer,* prefacing them with a letter in which he strongly condemned the familiarity assumed by hymnwriters with the Divine, and with divine things; and promised to remedy the defect so far as it lay in his power so to do. This letter appeared in Oct. 1811, together with four hymns, the first of which was this for Advent Sunday. The first stanza reads :—

"Hosanna to the living Lord!
Hosanna to the Incarnate Word!
Hosanna in the earth be said,
And in the heavens which he hath made.
Hosanna !"

In 1827, it appeared in Heber's posthumous *Hymns, &c.,* p. 1, in a new and much-improved form. From this revised text all existing forms of the hymn in collections for congregational use have been made. The first stanza of the revised text is :—

"Hosanna to the living Lord!
Hosanna to the Incarnate Word!
To Christ, Creator, Saviour, King,
Let earth, let heaven, Hosanna sing!
Hosanna ! Lord! Hosanna in the highest!"

The full revised text is in Lord Selborne's *Bk. of Praise,* 1862, No. 141. The doxology, which is given in *H. A. & M.* and other collections, was added to the hymn as early as Stretton's *Church Hymns,* 1850. The hymn "Hosanna, Lord, the angels cry," in Martineau's *Hymns, &c.,* 1840, and later collections, begins with st. ii. of this hymn. [J. J.]

Hosianna David's Sohn. *B. Schmolck.* [*Advent.*] 1st pub. in his *Lustige Sabbath in der Stille zu Zion,* Jauer, 1712, p. 3, in 8 st. of 6 l., entitled "Hosannah for the Heavenly Manna. On the First Sunday of Advent." It is also suitable for Palm Sunday. Included in the Berlin *G. L. S.,* ed. 1863. Tr. as :—

1. Hail, Hosanna! David's Son. A good tr. of st. i., iii., vi., as No. 6 in the Dalston Hospital *H. Bk.,* 1848, repeated in Dr. Pagenstecher's *Coll.,* 1864, No. 13.

2. Glad Hosanna! David's Son. In full in the Ohio *Luth. Hyl.,* 1880, No. 17.

Another tr. is: "Hosanna to the Son of David! Raise," by Miss *Winkworth,* 1855, p. 67. [J. M.]

Hoskins, Joseph, was b. in 1745, but at what place is unknown. He was a Congregational Minister, who for ten years laboured with great success at Castle Green Chapel, Bristol, and d. Sept. 28, 1788, aged 43. During the three years previous to his death he had written 384 hymns, which in the year following, after correction and revision, were pub. by Messrs. Moody & Bottomley, Congregational Ministers. The book is entitled, *Hymns on Select Texts of Scripture and Occa-*

sional Subjects (Bristol, 1789). From this work the following hymns are in C. U. :—

1. Alas! my [the] Lord my Life is gone. *Spiritual darkness and death.*
2. Great Light of life, Thou nature's Lord. *God, the True Light.*
3. In Thy great Name, O Lord, we come. *Divine Worship.*
4. O how the hearts of those revive. *Joy in Salvation.*
5. Prisoners of sin and Satan too. *Hope.*
6. Saviour of sinners, deign to shine. *Christ's light desired.*
7. The time is short, ere all that live. *Shortness of Time.*

Hoskins's hymns are said to have been greatly esteemed by his friends and hearers, but they have little poetic merit. [W. R. S.]

Hoste dum victo triumphans. [*Holy Communion.*] In the *Cluniac Breviary*, Paris, 1686, p. 557, this is given as a hymn for the Octave of Corpus Christi, at the Vigil, and consists of 5 st. and a doxology. *Tr.* by E. Caswall, and pub. in his *Masque of Mary, &c.*, 1858, p. 307; and in his *Hymns, &c.*, 1873, p. 159, as "When the Patriarch was returning." It was given in the *People's H.*, 1867, the *Appx.* to *H. Noted*, 1862, &c.   [J. M.]

Houlditch, Anne. [Shepherd, A.]

House of our God, with cheerful anthems ring. *P. Doddridge.* [*New Year.*] 1st pub. in Job Orton's posthumous ed. of Doddridge's *Hymns*, 1755, No. 67, in 6 st. of 6 l.; and again in J. D. Humphreys's ed. of the same, 1839, No. 81. In Brown-Borthwick's *Select Hys. for the Church & Home*, 1871, and in the S. P. C. K. *Church Hys.*, 1871, is a cento beginning "House of our God, with hymns of gladness ring," which is mainly from this hymn. It is by J. Ellerton. The lines chosen are greatly varied from Doddridge, and st. v. ll. 2-4 are by Mr. Ellerton.   [J. J.]

How blest the man who never trod. *J. Keble.* [*Ps. i.*] Pub. in his *Psalter*, 1839, in 6 st. of 4 l. In the *Rugby School H. Bk.*, 1876, No. 284, and the *Wellington College H. Bk.*, 1880, p. 119, it is given in an altered form, as "Blest is the man who walks with God," and in the latter with the addition of a doxology. The "Mr. Knight's Coll." referred to in the Rugby book, is the *Ps. & Hys.* by the Rev. W. Knight, St. Michael's, Bristol, 4th ed., 1867.   [J. J.]

How blest Thy creature is, O God. *W. Cowper.* [*The Blessedness of Peace with God.*] Southey in his *Memoirs and Correspondence of William Cowper*, 1854, vol. i. pp. 99-104, gives an account of Cowper's insanity, his residence at St. Albans under the care of Dr. Cotton, and his partial recovery. At the beginning of his attack Cowper wrote a most painful poem, the nature and burden of which will be gathered from the following (the third) stanza, which reads :—

"Man disavows, and Deity disowns me,
  Hell might afford my miseries a shelter;
  Therefore, hell keeps her ever-hungry mouths all
      Bolted against me."

In contrast to this despair Southey states that

"During this [the latter part of his stay with Dr. Cotton] part of his abode at St. Albans, he again poured out his feelings in verse, and the contrast is indeed

striking between what he called this specimen of his first Christian thoughts, and that song of despair [noted above] which cannot be perused without shuddering. He cast his thoughts in the form of a hymn, which he entitled 'The Happy Change,' and took for his text part of a verse in the Revelations, 'Behold, I make all things new.'"

The hymn composed under these circumstances, in July, 1765, is full of peace and hope, as evidenced in st. iv. :—

"The soul, a dreary province once
  Of Satan's dark domain,
Feels a new empire formed within,
  And owns a heavenly reign."

The publication of the hymn in 6 st. of 4 l. with Cowper's original title, "The Happy Change," was in the *Olney Hymns*, 1779, Bk. iii., No. 44. In full or in part it is given in several hymn-books, especially in America. Sometimes it begins :—"How blest is man, O God," as in the American Unitarian *Hys. for the Church of Christ*, Boston, 1853.   [J. J.]

How can a sinner know. *C. Wesley.* [*The Marks of Faith.*] Pub. in *Hys. and Sacred Poems*, 1749, vol. ii., No. 161. It consists of 8 st., and each stanza is composed of 4 l. of 6's metre, and 4 l. of short metre (*P. Works*, 1868-72, vol. v. p. 363). In the *Wes. H. Bk.*, 1780, No. 93, st. iv., v. were omitted, and the rest were rewritten in S.M. throughout. In this form the hymn is in C. U. in G. Britain and America.   [J. J.]

How few and evil are thy days. *J. Montgomery.* [*Shortness of Life.*] Pub. in Cotterill's *Sel.*, 1819, No. 175, in 3 st. of 8 l., and again in Montgomery's *Greenland & Other Poems*, 1819. On its reappearance in his *Christian Psalmist*, 1825, No. 516, it was altered to "Few, few and evil are thy days." This was repeated in his *Original Hymns*, 1853, and is the received form of the text.   [J. J.]

How few receive with cordial faith. *W. Robertson.* [*Passiontide.*] 1st appeared as No. 6 in the Draft Scottish *Translations & Paraphrases*, 1745, as a version of Is. liii. in 16 st. of 4 l. In the revised edition, 1751, st. viii., x., xii. were slightly altered. In the *Draft* of 1781, No. 25, it was considerably altered; and with further alterations this was repeated in the public worship ed. of that year which is still in C. U. in the Church of Scotland. In the markings its eldest daughter of W. Cameron (q.v.), the original is ascribed to W. Robertson, and the alterations in 1781 to John Logan. The revised text of 1781 is included in full in the Eng. Presb. *Ps. & Hys.*, 1867, as two hymns, No. 170 beginning as above, and 171 as "We all like sheep have gone astray." In addition the following centos are in C. U. :—

1. The Saviour comes [came], no outward pomp. In Murray's *Hymnal*, 1852; the Bap. *Ps. & Hys.*, 1858; *Kennedy*, 1863, and others in G. Britain and America.
2. Rejected and despised of men. In the Andover *Sabbath H. Bk.*, 1858, &c.
3. Fair as a beauteous, tender flower. In *Hys. from the Parish Choir*, 1854.

In addition, Miss Leeson pub. an altered form of the hymn in 9 st. in her *Paraphrases & Hys. for Cong. Singing*, 1853, as pt. i., "Who hath believed the Witness-Word?"; and pt. ii., "We counted as condemned of heaven." Compare also Watts's *Hymns*, 1709, Bk. i., Nos. 141-2.   [J. M.]

How firm a foundation, ye saints of the Lord. *Keen.* [*Perseverance of the Saints.*] This hymn appeared in Rippon's *Selection*, 1787, No. 128, in 7 st. of 4 l., and entitled, "Exceeding great and precious promises." In 1822 it was repeated in A. Fletcher's Bap. *Coll. of Hys.*, No. 296, in 4 st., the omitted stanzas being ii., iv. & v. Two arrangements of the text were thus handed down to modern hymnals. In the 1835 ed. of Fletcher's *Coll.*, the full original text is restored. This is repeated in Spurgeon's *O. O. H. Bk.*, 1866, No. 732, and other hymn-books.

The authorship of this hymn has been the subject of much enquiry. We have (1) in modern editions of *Rippon* the name of "*Kirkham*"; (2) in *Fletcher's* 1835 ed. as above, "*Keen*"; (3) and in Spurgeon's *O. O. H. Bk.*, "*George Keith.*"

1. *Rippon's* original signature was "K—." In modern editions, which are not published by Dr. Rippon's representatives, the "K—" is extended into "Kirkham," but on what authority we cannot say.
2. The ascription in Miller's *Singers and S.*, 1869, p. 349, we find from the *Sedgwick MSS.*, is based upon nothing but the statement of an old woman whom Sedgwick met in an almshouse.
3. In Fletcher's *Coll.*, 1822, the "K—" of Rippon is extended to "Kn," and in the ed. of 1835 this is still further extended to "Keen," and so it remains. That this is more likely to be correct than either of the other two is gathered from the fact that Dr. Fletcher was assisted in his work by Thomas Walker, the editor of Dr. Rippon's *Tune Book*, to whom he specially refers in these words:—"Great assistance has been obtained from Mr. Walker, Compiler of Dr. Rippon's *Tune Book*, and the Editor of the Companion to it, called *Walker's Companion;* and it is but justice to acknowledge that the principal choice of Hymns and the application of Tunes, has been effected by his extensive knowledge of sacred poetry, and long tried acquaintance with the science of sacred music." *Preface, Lon., Nov.* 1822.

In addition, in the Index of the "Names of such Authors of the Hymns as are known," the name "*Keen*," with the abbreviation "*Kn*," is also given. Taking Mr. Walker's acquaintance with Dr. Rippon's work into account, we are justified in concluding that the ascription to this hymn must be that of an unknown person of the name of KEEN.

The following hymns bear the same signature as the above in Dr. Rippon's *Sel.*, 1787.

1. In songs of sublime adoration and praise (*Distinguishing Grace*). This is given in Spurgeon's *O. O. H. Bk.*, on Sedgwick's authority, as "*George Keith, 1787.*"
2. The Bible is justly esteemed (*Holy Scriptures*).

From the fact that these two hymns have a common signature in *Rippon's Sel.*, 1787, with "How firm a foundation," &c., and that the three appeared there for the first time, we also ascribe them to KEEN. Miller, in his *Singers and Songs of the Church*, 1869, bases his note on *George Keith* on the unsupported word of D. Sedgwick as above.   [J. J.]

How grand and how bright That wonderful night. *W. H. Havergal.* [*Christmas Carol.*] The words and music were written at Astley Rectory, in 1827, and published in *Fireside Music*, 1858. It was also printed as a carol leaflet and sold by hawkers throughout Worcestershire, where it attained great popularity. It is now known as *The Worcestershire Carol.* The words were included in Snepp's *Songs of G. & G.*, 1872.   [J. J.]

How great the wisdom, power, and grace. *B. Beddome.* [*Wonders of Redemp-*

tion.] Appeared in his (posthumous) *Hymns,* &c., 1817, No. 284, in 6 st. of 4 l., and headed "Wonders of Redemption." It has passed into several hymn-books, and in late eds. of the Bapt. *Ps. & Hys.*, 1858, it is dated 1790; but upon what authority is not stated.   [J. J.]

How happy are those children who. *J. Cennick.* [*Heavenly Joys.*] Pub. in his *Hys. to the Honour of Jesus Christ, Composed for such Little Children as Desire to be Saved,* 1754, in 9 st. of 4 l. This hymn is known to modern collections in the following forms:—

1. "Happy the children who are gone." This was given in C.M. in 6 st. of 4 l. in the *Moravian H. Bk.*, 1789, No. 623 (ed. 1886, No. 1254).
2. In 1790 Rowland Hill adapted st. i., ii., iv., v. of the *Moravian H. Bk.* version to L.M., and included it in his *Divine Hys. in easy language for the use of Children,* No. 44. This is the popular form of the text, and is given in several modern collections for children as Allon's *Children's Worship,* 1878, No. 453, &c.

The first stanza of the *Original* is :—

"How happy are those children who
In peace to heaven are gone ;
Who, cloth'd in long white garments, now
Stand singing round the throne."

The *Moravian H. Bk.* text is :—

"Happy the children who are gone
To Jesus Christ in peace,
Who stand around His glorious throne
Clad in His righteousness."

The *Rowland Hill* text is :—

"Happy the children who are gone
To live with Jesus Christ in peace,
Who stand around His glorious throne
Clad in His spotless righteousness."

[W. T. B.]

How happy every child of grace. *C. Wesley.* [*The Hope of Heaven.*] Pub. in his *Funeral Hymns*, 2nd series, 1759, No. 2, in 8 st. of 8 l., and from thence into the *Supplement of the Wes. H. Bk.*, 1830. G. J. Stevenson has given interesting "Associations" in his *Methodist H. Bk. Notes*, 1883, setting forth the spiritual help this hymn has been to many. (Orig. text, *P. Works*, 1868-72, vol. vi. p. 216.) Its use with the Methodist bodies in all English-speaking countries is extensive. A cento from this hymn, beginning "A stranger in the world below," is given in H. W. Beecher's *Plymouth Coll.*, 1855, No. 1273. It is composed of st. ii. and iii. A second cento in the American *Hys. and Songs of Praise*, N. Y., 1874, is, "O what a blessed hope is ours" (sts. vii., viii.). [J. J.]

How happy is the pilgrim's lot. [*Desiring Heaven.*] Appeared in the Wesley *Hymns for those that Seek, and those that Have Redemption*, 1747, No. 51, in 9 st. of 6 l. When given in the *Wes. H. Bk.*, 1780-1875, the fourth stanza was omitted. (*P. Works*, 1868-72, vol. iv. p. 278.) Although somewhat unreal as a hymn for general use, it has long been most popular with the Methodist bodies. Stanza v., "No foot of land do I possess," and vii., "There is my house, and portion fair," have gathered around them reminiscences, in many instances of a tenderly sacred character, some of which are noted in detail in Stevenson's *Methodist H. Bk. Notes*, 1883, p. 77. In Stevenson's *Notes* this hymn is attributed to John Wesley, and in the Index to the same work to Charles Wesley. The former is also the almost universal ascription in America, the argument usually put forth being that the personal circumstances evidently referred to suited John Wesley rather than Charles. The editors of the *Wes. H. Bk.* are in doubt, and have left the authorship an open question. As there is no *direct* evidence either way, we must follow their example.   [J. J.]

How happy the pair whom Jesus unites. *C. Wesley.* [*Holy Matrimony.*] Written in 1749, in contemplation of his coming marriage which took place at Garth, in Wales, on the 8th of April of the same year, and pub. in *Hys. & Sacred Poems*, 1749, in 6 st. of 4 l., as one of several hymns which were written under the same circumstances. (*P. Works*, 1868–72, vol. v. p. 427.) In its original form it is not in C. U. The hymn, "Appointed by Thee, we meet in Thy name," given in the *Wes. H. Bk.*, 1780, No. 472, and repeated in later editions, and in several other hymnals, is the same hymn in an abbreviated form.   [J. J.]

How honourable is the place. *I. Watts.* [*Safety of the Church.*] This hymn, which is based on Is. xxvi. 1–6, has a two-fold history; the first English, and the second Scottish.

i. *English History.* It was first published in Watts's *Hymns*, &c., 1707 (1709, Bk. i., No. 8), in 7 st. of 4 l., and entitled "The Safety and Protection of the Church." In this form it came into extensive use with some of the Nonconformist bodies, and maintained its position until recently.

ii. *Scottish History.*—In 1745 it was included in the *Translations and Paraphrases*, No. xxix. (see **Scottish Trs. and Paraphs.**) with the single alteration of st. iv. l. 4 of "*trust in*" for "*ventur'd on*" his Grace." The principal changes were made in 1781, when in the *Draft* st. i., ii., and vii. were rewritten, and a word or two in the remaining stanzas altered. This text with, in st. vii. l. 2, "*brave*" for "prop," was given in the authorized *Trs. and Par.* of 1781, No. xx., as "How glorious Sion's courts appear." W. Cameron (q.v.) ascribes this recast of Watts in his list of authors and revisers of the *Trs. & Par.* to Dr. Hugh Blair. It has been in authorized use in the Church of Scotland for more than 100 years, and is also given in a few English and American collections. J. E. Leeson's *Par. and Hymns*, 1853, No. xlvi., "In Judah's land let Zion's sons," is a cento by Miss Leeson from the *Scottish Par.* with alterations and additions by herself. St. i., iii. Miss Leeson; st. ii., iv. as above. In the American Presbyterian *Ps. & Hys.*, Richmond, 1867, No. 560, "How glorious is the sacred place," is an altered form of Watts, 1709.   [J. J.]

How long shall dreams of creature [earthly] bliss? *P. Doddridge.* [*God the Salvation of His People.*] Written Aug. 15, 1736, D. MSS., and pub. in his (posthumous) *Hymns*, &c., 1755, No. 125, in 4 st. of 4 l.; and again in J. D. Humphreys's ed. of the same, 1839. In one or two American collections it begins, "How long shall dreams of *earthly* bliss?" as in the Unitarian *Hys. for the Church of Christ*, Boston, 1853. [J. J.]

How many pass the guilty night. *C. Wesley.* [*Watchnight.*] Appeared in *Hys.*

and *Sac. Poems*, 1742, p. 135, in 6 st. of 6 l. as the first of a series of "Hymns for the Watchnight." (*P. Works*, 1868–72, vol. ii. p. 193.) In 1830 it was given in the *Supp.* to the *Wes. H. Bk.* with alterations, and the omission of st. iv. This was repeated in the revised edition, 1875. The opening line has undergone several changes, as : "How many pass *this* guilty night"; "How many pass *this solemn* night"; and "How many *spend* the guilty night." The original reading has by far the most extensive use.   [J. J.]

How precious is the book divine. *J. Fawcett.* [*Holy Scriptures.*] Pub. in his *Hymns*, &c., 1782, No. 41, in 6 st. of 4 l., and based upon the words, "Thy Word is a lamp to my feet and a light to my path." Its use is extensive, especially in America, but usually in an abbreviated form. In the *New Cong.*, 1859, No. 466, st. iii. is by another hand. Orig. text in *Lyra Brit.*, 1867, p. 226.   [J. J.]

How rich Thy bounty, King of kings. *P. Doddridge.* [*Divine Treasure in Earthen Vessels.*] Written Sept. 23, 1739 (D. MSS.), and pub. in his (posthumous) *Hymns*, &c., 1755, No. 175, in 5 st. of 4 l., and based upon 2 Cor. iv. 7. In 1839 it was repeated in J. D. Humphreys's ed. of the same, No. 300.   [J. J.]

How sad our state by nature is. *I. Watts.* [*Salvation through Christ.*] 1st pub. in his *Hys. & S. Songs*, 1707 (ed. 1709, Bk. ii., No. 90), in 6 st. of 4 l., and headed "Faith in Christ for Pardon and Sanctification." In 1736–7 it was included by J. Wesley in his Charlestown *Ps. & Hys.* p. 52, with the change of st. v., l. 4, "With all his hellish crew," to "With his *infernal* crew." Wesley's alteration was repeated by G. Whitefield in his *Coll.* 1753 ; by M. Madan, in his *Ps. & Hys.* 1760, and others. In Conyers's *Coll.*, ed. 1774, the line reads, "And form our souls anew." In modern hymn-books the difficulty is overcome by the omission of the stanza. Several interesting "Associations" in connection with this hymn are given in G. J. Stevenson's *Methodist H. Bk. Notes*, 1883.   [J. J.]

How shall a contrite [sinner] spirit pray. *J. Montgomery.* [*Lent. Prayer.*] Written Sept. 15, 1840, "M. MSS.," and pub. in an undated ed. of T. Russell's *Sel. of Hys. for Congregational Worship*, enlarged ed. with *Appendix;* and again in Dr. Leifchild's *Original Hymns*, &c., 1842, No. 76. Subsequently it was included in the author's *Original Hymns*, 1853, No. 73. In *Common Praise*, 1879, it is given as "How shall a contrite *sinner* pray ? " Its use, especially in its original form, is extensive.   [J. J.]

How shall I follow Him I serve. *J. Conder.* [*Resignation and Suffering.*] This hymn, in 11 st. of 4 l., on the words, "If any man serve Me, let him follow Me," is in his *Star in the East*, &c., 1824, p. 62. In 1836 it was rewritten and divided into two hymns, the first in 7 st. beginning with same first line, and included as No. 341 in the *Cong. H. Bk.*, 1836 ; and the second in 3 st., as "Thou Who for Peter's faith didst pray !" No. 588 in the same collection. The modern arrangements of these hymns, as in the Bap.

Ps. & Hys., 1858 ; the *New Cong.*, 1859 ; *Kennedy*, 1863, and others are from this 1836 text. In Conder's *Hys. of Praise, Prayer*, &c., 1856, p. 80, the two hymns are given as one, as in the *Star in the East*, &c. [J. J.]

How should the sons of Adam's race. *I. Watts.* [*Divine Majesty*.] 1st pub. in his *Hymns*, &c., 1709, Bk. i., No. 86, as a paraphrase of Job. ix. 2–10, in 6 st. of 4 l., and entitled " God, Holy, Just, and Sovereign." Its use is limited.

In the Scottish Draft *Trans. & Paraphs.* of 1745, it was given as No. 18 in an unaltered form ; but in the revised issue of 1751 it appeared in a recast form by Dr. H. Blair. It appears, slightly altered, as No. 7 in the authorised issue of 1781, and as such has been in use in the Church of Scotland for more than 100 years. In her list of authors and revisers of the 1781 issue, W. Cameron's daughter claims these alterations of 1781 for W. Cameron (q.v.). It is given in full in all modern editions of the Scottish *Psalms*.

In the American *Prayer Bk. Coll.*, 1826, the Scottish version reappears as : " Ah, how shall fallen man," and this has been repeated in other hymnals, including the Prot. Episco. *Hymnal*, 1871. It was rewritten for the *P. Bk. Coll.* by Bp. Onderdonk (q.v.). [J. J.]

How still and peaceful is the grave. *Hugh Blair.* [*Burial of the Dead*.] 1st appeared as No. 39 in the Draft Scottish *Trans. and Paraphs.*, 1745, as a version of Job iii. 17–20, thus :—

" How still and peaceful is the Grave !
    that silent Bed how blest !
The Wicked there from Troubling cease,
    and there the Weary rest.
" There the freed Pris'ner groans no more
    beneath Life's galling Load :
Mute is th' Oppressor's cruel Voice ;
    and broke the Tyrant's Rod.
" There Slaves and Masters equal ly,
    and share the same Repose :
The Small and Great are there ; and Friends
    now mingle with their Foes."

In the draft of 1781 it appeared as No. 4, rewritten in 5 st. ; and again, with three lines altered, in the public worship ed. issued in that year by the Church of Scotland, and still in use. In the markings by the eldest daughter of *W. Cameron* (q.v.) the original is ascribed to Blair, and the alterations in 1781 to Cameron. It is given also in several modern hymnals in G. Britain and America. [J.M.]

How sweet and awful is the place. *I. Watts.* [*The Great Supper*.] 1st pub. in his *Hys. and S. Songs*, 1707 (ed. 1709, Bk. iii., No. 13), in 7 st. of 4 l., and based upon St. Luke xiv. 17, &c. It is given, sometimes in an abbreviated form, in several modern collections in G. Britain and America. In Dr. Alexander's *Augustine H. Bk.*, 1849, and later editions it is given as, " How *sweetly* awful is the place ;" and in the *Bap. Hymnal*, 1879, "How sweet and *sacred* is the place." [J. J.]

How sweet from crowded throngs. *J. Conder.* [*For open-air Service*.] " Written for the Centenary Commemoration of Whitefield's Open-air Ministry, on Stinchcombe Hill, July 30, 1839," and pub. in the *Evangelical Magazine* of October the same year.

In 1856 it was also included in Conder's *Hys. of Praise, Prayer*, &c., p. 162. Dr. Kennedy has given it in an unaltered form in his *Hymno. Christ.*, 1863, No. 1442. Although remarkably well adapted for open-air services, its use is limited. [J. J.]

How sweet the name of Jesus sounds. *J. Newton.* [*The Name—Jesus*.] 1st pub. in the *Olney Hymns*, 1779, No. 57, in 7 st. of 4 l., and entitled, " The Name of Jesus." J. Wesley brought it into notice by inserting it in the *Arminian Magazine* in 1781. Notwithstanding this, however, it did not appear in the *Wes. H. Bk.* until the revised ed. of 1875. It is found, mostly with the omission of st. iv., " By Thee my prayers acceptance gain," in nearly every hymnal of repute which has appeared in the present century. It is superior in pathos, although less jubilant than Newton's " Glorious things of thee are spoken," which is regarded by many as his finest production; and ranks with the first hymns in the English language. Its use is most extensive in all English-speaking countries, and it has been translated into several languages, including Latin, by R. Bingham, in his *Hymno. Christ. Lat.* 1871, " Quam dulce, quam mellifluum," and Macgill, in his *Songs of the Christian Creed and Life*, 1876, " Jesus ! O quam dulce nomen." Its uniform excellence is broken by st. iv., which is usually omitted, and the line, " Jesus ! my Shepherd, *Husband*, Friend," in st. v. It is urged, and not without weight, that " the Bride, the Lamb's Wife," is not the individual soul, but the collective Church ; and that the expression " *Husband* " is unsuited to congregational use, as in no sense can it be said that Jesus is the *Husband* of *Men*. Various efforts have been made to overcome this difficulty, and thereby retain one of the best stanzas of the hymn. The principal changes are :—

1. " Jesus ! our Leader, Shepherd, Friend." Hatchard's *Sel.*, 1833.
2. " Jesus ! my Shepherd, Surety, Friend." J. H. Gurney's *Coll. of Hys.*, &c., 1838.
3. " Jesus ! our Shepherd, Brother, Friend." J. A. Johnston's *English Hymnal*, 1852.
4. " Jesus ! my Shepherd, Guardian, Friend." *Leeds H. Bk.*, 1853.
5. " Jesu ! our Brother, Shepherd, Friend." Cooke & Denton *Church Hymnal*, 1853.
6. " Jesus ! my Saviour, Shepherd, Friend." Barry's *Ps. & Hys.*, 1867.

The origin of most of the readings found in modern hymn-books may be gathered from this list. In two or three instances unsuccessful rearrangements of the order of the stanzas in the original have been made. The most notable of these appeared in the *Salisbury H. Bk.*, 1857. Cotterill's attempt in his *Sel.* (8th ed.), 1819, to get rid of the word *sweet* in the opening line by substituting, " How *blest* the name of Jesus sounds," has also been a failure. In Kemble's *Ps. & Hys.*, 1853, st. v.–vii. were given as " Jesus, my Shepherd, Husband, Friend," but it was omitted from his *New Church H. Bk.*, 1873 ; and in the *Parish H. Bk.*, 1863 and 1875, st. iii., v., vii. altered, together with the addition of a stanza by the editors were given as :" Jesus, the Rock on which we build." [J. J.]

How sweetly flowed the Gospel's sound. *Sir J. Bowring.* [*Jesus the Teacher*.]

Pub. in his *Matins and Vespers*, &c., 2nd ed., 1824, p. 234, in 4 st. of 4 l., and headed, "Jesus teaching the people." In 1837 it was included in Beard's Unitarian *Coll.*, No. 121, and subsequently in a number of hymn-books, especially modern American collections. Orig. text in *Laudes Domini*, N. Y., 1884, with, in st. i., l. 4, "And joy and *gladness*" for "And joy and reverence."   [J. J.]

How truly do I love Thee, Lord. [*Ps. xviii.*] This paraphrase of the 18th Psalm in Kennedy's *Psalter*, 1860, is rewritten from T. Sternhold, in the *Old Version*. Kennedy's rendering is in 39 st. of 4 l. In his *Hymnologia Christiana*, 1863, a portion is given in two parts, as No. 676, Pt. ii. being, "The Lord Himself will light my lamp." Another arrangement in C. U. is, "My God, the Rock in whom I trust." It begins with st. ii. of the 1860 version.   [J. J.]

How vast the treasure we possess. I. *Watts*. [*All things in Christ.*] This hymn, as in Bickersteth's *Christ. Psalmody*, enlarged ed., 1841, the Bap. *Ps. & Hys.*, 1858, and others, in 5 st. of 4 l., is a cento from two hymns appended to Watts's *Sermons*, 1721–4, the first beginning, "How vast the treasure we possess"; and the second, "My soul, survey thy happiness." In the cento, st. i. is from the first, and st. ii.–v. are from the second of these two hymns.   [J. J.]

How welcome was the call. Sir H. W. Baker. [*Holy Matrimony.*] Appeared in H. A. & M., 1861, and the revised ed., 1875. It has attained to great popularity, especially in America, and is a favourite marriage hymn.

How, William Walsham, D.D., s. of William Wybergh How, Solicitor, Shrewsbury, was b. Dec. 13, 1823, at Shrewsbury, and educated at Shrewsbury School and Wadham College, Oxford (B.A. 1845). Taking Holy Orders in 1846, he became successively Curate of St. George's, Kidderminster, 1846; and of Holy Cross, Shrewsbury, 1848. In 1851 he was preferred to the Rectory of Whittington, Diocese of St. Asaph, becoming Rural Dean in 1853, and Hon. Canon of the Cathedral in 1860. In 1879 he was appointed Rector of St. Andrew's Undershaft, London, and was consecrated Suffragan Bishop for East London, under the title of the Bishop of Bedford, and in 1888 Bishop of Wakefield. Bishop How is the author of the S. P. C. K. *Commentary on the Four Gospels; Plain Words*, Four Series; *Plain Words for Children; Pastor in Parochiâ; Lectures on Pastoral Work; Three All Saints Summers, and Other Poems*, and numerous *Sermons*, &c. In 1854 was pub. *Psalms and Hymns, Compiled by the Rev. Thomas Baker Morrell*, M.A., . . . *and the Rev. William Walsham How, M.A.* This was re-published in an enlarged form in 1864, and to it was added a *Supplement* in 1867. To this collection Bishop How contributed several hymns, and also to the S. P. C. K. *Church Hymns*, of which he was joint editor, in 1871. The Bishop's hymns in C. U. amount in all to nearly sixty.

Combining pure rhythm with great directness and simplicity, Bishop How's compositions arrest attention more through a comprehensive grasp of the subject and the unexpected light thrown upon and warmth infused into facts and details usually shunned by the poet, than through glowing imagery and impassioned rhetoric. He has painted lovely images inwoven with tender thoughts, but these are few, and found in his least appreciated work. Those compositions which have laid the firmest hold upon the Church, are simple, unadorned, but enthusiastically practical hymns, the most popular of which, "O Jesu, Thou art standing"; "For all the Saints who from their labours rest," and "We give Thee but Thine own," have attained to a foremost rank. His adaptations from other writers, as in the case from Bishop Ken, "Behold, the Master passeth by," are good, and his Children's hymns are useful and popular. Without any claims to rank as a poet, in the sense in which Cowper and Montgomery were poets, he has sung us songs which will probably outlive all his other literary works.

The more important of Bp. How's hymns, including those already named, and "Lord, Thy children guide and keep"; "O Word of God Incarnate"; "This day at Thy creating word"; "Who is this so weak and helpless"; and others which have some special history or feature of interest, are annotated under their respective first lines. The following are also in C. U.:—

i. From *Psalms & Hymns*, 1854.

1. Before Thine awful presence, Lord. *Confirmation.*
2. Jesus, Name of wondrous love [priceless worth]. *Circumcision. The Name Jesus.*
3. Lord Jesus, when we stand afar. *Passiontide.*
4. O blessing rich, for sons of men. *Members of Christ.*
5. O Lord of Hosts, the earth is Thine. *In time of War.*
6. O Lord, Who in Thy wondrous love. *Advent.*

ii. From *Psalms & Hymns*, enlarged, 1864.

7. Lord, this day Thy children meet. *Sunday S. Anniversary.*

iii. From *Supplement* to the *Psalms & Hymns*, 1867.

8. Hope of hopes and joy of joys. *Resurrection.*
9. O daughters blest of Galilee. *For Associations of Women.*
10. O happy feet that tread. *Public Worship.*
11. With trembling awe the chosen three. *Transfiguration.*

iv. From *Parish Magazine*, 1871, and *Church Hymns*, 1871.

12. O Jesu, crucified for man. *Friday.*
13. Yesterday, with worship blest. *Monday.*

v. From the S. P. C. K. *Church Hymns*, 1871.

14. Bowed low in supplication. *For the Parish.*
15. Great Gabriel sped on wings of light. *Annunciation of the B. V. M.*
16. O blest was he, whose earlier skill. *St. Luke.*
17. O God, enshrined in dazzling light. *Omnipresence. Divine Worship.*
18. O heavenly Fount of Light and Love. *Whitsuntide.*
19. O Lord, it is a blessed thing. *Week-days.*
20. O One with God the Father. *Epiphany.*
21. O Thou through suffering perfect made. *Hospitals.*
22. Rejoice, ye sons of man. *Purification of the B. V. M.*
23. Summer suns are glowing. *Summer.*
24. The year is swiftly waning. *Autumn.*
25. Thou art the Christ, O Lord. *St. Peter.*
26. To Thee our God we fly. *National Hymn.*
27. Upon the holy Mount they stood. *Transfiguration and Church Guilds.*
28. We praise Thy grace, O Saviour. *St. Mark.*

vi. From the S. P. C. K. *Children's Hymns*, 1872.

29. Behold a little child. *Jesus the Child's Example.*
30. Come, praise your Lord and Saviour. *Children's Praises.*
31. It is a thing most wonderful. *Sunday S. Anniversary.*
32. On wings of living light. *Easter.*

Bishop How's hymns and sacred and secular pieces were collected and pub. as *Poems and Hymns*, 1886. The *Hymns*, 54 in all, are also published separately. He d. Aug. 10, 1897. [J. J.]

Howard, Caroline. [Gilman, C.]

Howitt, Mary, née Botham, second daughter of Samuel Botham, a member of the Society of Friends, was b. at Uttoxeter, Staffordshire, circa 1804, was married in 1823 to William Howitt, and d. Jan. 30, 1888. Her publications have little in common with hymnody. They include poems, novels, translations of Swedish and Danish works, and numerous contributions to magazines. In addition she was joint author with her husband of *Literature and Romance of Northern Europe*, 1852, &c. Her hymns include:—

1. **God might have made the earth bring forth.** *The Use of Flowers.* From her *Birds and Flowers, and Other Country Things*, Lond., N. D. (Preface, Sept. 28, 1837), p. 122, in 8 st. of 4 l.
2. **How goodly is the earth.** *Flower Services.* From her *Hymns and Fireside Verses*, Lond., 1839, p. 167.
3. **O spirit, freed from earth.** *Death and Burial.* Altered from her poem, "The Ascent of the Spirit," in her *Ballads and Other Poems*, 1847, p. 318. Dr. Martineau dates this poem 1834.

Mrs. Howitt also contributed "Let me suffer, let me drain" (*The Willing Disciple*), and "Clothe me with Thy saving grace" (*The Cry of the spirit*) to *Lyra Britannica*, 1867.
[J. J.]

Huc ad montem Calvariae. [*Passiontide.*] This hymn is found in the Mainz G. B. (R. C.), 1661, p. 287, in 7 st., and is probably not of much earlier date. It is also in *Daniel*, ii. p. 353; Neale's *Hymni Ecclesiae*, 1851, p. 124, and other sources. Tr. as :—

1. **Up to the hill of Calvary.** By J. M. Neale, in his *Mediaeval Hys.*, 1851, p. 154, in 7 st. of 8 l. When included in *Kennedy*, 1863, it was divided into two parts, the second beginning with st. iv., "Have wealth and honour spread their wing."
2. **To Calvary ascending.** By H. Kynaston, pub. in his *Occasional Hymns*, 1862, p. 70, in two parts, the second beginning with st. iv., "Divitiis exutus es" ("Art poor? in all thy toiling.") The two parts were given in *Lyra Messianica*, 1864, and as No. 108, in the *People's H.*, 1867. [J. M.]

Hues of the rich unfolding morn. J. Keble. [*Morning.*] Written Sept. 20, 1822, and 1st pub. in his *Christian Year*, 1827, as the opening poem, in 16 st. of 4 l. From it the following centos have come into C. U.:—

1. **Hues of the rich unfolding morn.** (st. i.) In a few collections.
2. **O! timely happy, timely wise.** (st. v.) This is in a large number of hymn-books.
3. **New every morning is the love.** (st. vi.) This cento of various lengths is in extensive use in Great Britain and America, and, as a hymn, it ranks as one of the most popular of Keble's compositions. This is tr. into Latin by R. Bingham, in his *Hymno. Christ. Latina*, 1871, as "Omni oriente die lecto quum surgimus, horas."
4. **If on our daily course our mind.** (st. viii.) In several collections.

5. **As for some dear familiar strain.** (st. x.) In limited use.

The whole poem was given in Dr. Martineau's *Hymns*, &c., 1840; and again in his *Hys. of Praise & Prayer*, 1873. [J. J.]

Hughes, Thomas, M.A., b. at Donington Priory, near Newbury, Berks, Oct. 20, 1823, and educated at Rugby, and at Oriel College, Oxford (B.A. 1845), and called to the Bar, 1848. From 1865 to 1868 he was M.P. for Lambeth, and from 1868 to 1874 for Frome. Appointed a Queen's Counsel in 1869. He has published several popular works, including *Tom Brown's School Days*, 1856; *The Scouring of the White Horse*, 1858; *Tom Brown at Oxford*, 1861, and others. His hymn:—

"**O God of Truth whose Living Word**," *Truth*, 9 st. of 4 l., was given to the Hon. Mrs. Norton for insertion in *Lays of the Sanctuary*, 1859, p. 98, a collection published for a charitable purpose. It is a hymn of great force, and seems to gather up and embody the distinctive thoughts and feelings which have animated his life. It was probably suggested by Maurice's sermon on "The Word of God conquering by Sacrifice," in *Doctrine of Sacrifice*. It is usually given in an abridged form, as in the S. P. C. K. *Church Hys.* 1871 (6 st.), or W. G. Horder's *Congregational Hys.*, 1884 (7 st.).
He d. in March, 1896. [W. G. H.]

Huie, Richard, M.D., was b. at Aberdeen, 1795, and educated at the High School, Edinburgh, and the University of Edinburgh. Entering upon the medical profession, he practised at Dundee for some time, and then removed to Edinburgh in 1822. He d. June 10, 1867. He pub. ;—

The Family Hymn-Book, being a Selection of Hymns from the best authors, interspersed with a few Originals, and arranged for the purposes of Domestic Worship. By Richard Huie, M.D., Edinburgh, 1825.

To this *Sel.* he contributed 29 hymns. Of these the following are given in *Lyra Brit.*, 1867.

1. **Ask, and ye shall get the blessing.** *The Mercy-Seat.*
2. **What is faith?** It is to see. *Faith, Hope, and Charity.*
3. **Ye worldly cares and themes, be gone.** *Saturday Evening.*

The following cento is also from the *Family H. Bk.*, 1825, No. 250 :—

4. **O ye who with the silent tear.** *Burial.* It is st. i., iii. slightly altered, and was given in Bickersteth's *Christ. Psalmody*, 1833, as by "Whitmore"; in the 1836 ed., as by "Huie"; and in his son's *Ps. & Hys.* based on the *Ch. Psal.*, 1858, as by "Huil," which is probably a misprint for "Huie." [J. J.]

Hujus diei gloria. [*St. James the Great.*] A hymn for the Festival of St. James the Great, July 25. The text, in 8 st. of 4 l., is given by *Mone*, No. 697, from a Rheinau MS. of the 11th cent., from an 11th cent. MS. at Stuttgart, and from later sources. It is also found in *Daniel*, i., No. 349, with a further note at iv. p. 176; in *Wackernagel*, i., No. 179, &c. St. v. l. 3 ("Juncto sibi Christophoro") has been interpreted as referring to St. John the Evangelist, who was χριστόφορος as borne on Jesus' bosom (St. John xiii. 23). But in the Breviaries of *Rome*, *Paris*, *Lyons*, &c., St. Christopher is commemorated along with St. James at Lauds on July 25; while in the *Mozarabic* rite only St. Christopher and his companions are noticed on that day. A tr. by Dr. Littledale, "May this bright day, O Christ the King," was pub. in the *Church Times*, July 16, 1864; and again in the *People's H.*, 1867. [W. A. S.]

Hull, Amelia Matilda, daughter of William Thomas Hull, was b. at Marpool Hall, Exmouth, *circa* 1825. Her publications include :—

(1) *Hymns by A. M. H.*, South Petherton, N.D. [1850]; (2) *Heart Melodies*, 1864 ; (3) *The Silver Trumpet Answered ;* (4) *Fruit from the Tree of Life ;* (5) *A Hymn-Book for Children ;* (6) *Royal Musings concerning the King and His Work*, N.D. [1884].

Miss Hull also contributed 22 hymns to Miss H. W. Soltau's *Pleasant Hymns for Boys and Girls*, N.D. [1860]. From this collection her two popular hymns are taken :—

1. And is it true as I am told. *The Good Shepherd.*
2. There is life for a look at the Crucified One. *Life in Christ.*   [J. J.]

Hull, William Winstanley, M.A., s. of John Hull, M.D., an eminent physician in Manchester, was b. at Blackburn, March 15, 1794, and educated at Macclesfield and Brazenose, Oxford, where he took a first-class *Lit. Hum.* in 1814, and subsequently became a Fellow. At Oxford he made lifelong friendships with some, and acquaintance with most of the foremost men of his time, including Arnold, Keble, Whately, Milman, Rickards, Card. Newman, Stanley, and others. He entered Lincoln's Inn and was called to the Chancery Bar. He took a prominent part in London and at Oxford in the religious movements of the day. On retiring from the Bar he resided first at Tickwood Hall, Much Wenlock, and then at Knowle, Hazelwood, Derby. He d. Aug. 28, 1873. He published several prose works, including *Church Inquiry*, 1828 ; *Reasons for continuing to Protestants the whole Legislature of Great Britain and Ireland*, 1829 ; *Disuse of the Athanasian Creed*, 1831 ; *Defence of Dr. Hampden*, 1836, &c. His hymns and poems, chiefly distinguished by their earnest piety, were :—

(1) *A Collection of Prayers for Household Use, with a few Hymns and Other Poems*, Oxford, J. Parker, 1828 ; (2) *Poems on Various Subjects*, 1832 ; (3) *A Collection of Hymns for General Use, Submitted to the Consideration of the Members of the United Church of England and Ireland*, Lond., Hatchard, 1833. This *Coll.* is also known as *A Churchman's Hymns*, this title being printed on the cover ; (4) A second edition of his 1828 *Coll. of Prayers*, &c., Lond., Seeleys, 1851. Of these Nos. 1 and 2 contained 89 of his original hymns and poems. No. 3 contained 209 hymns, of which 83 were original and signed " *O.*" In No. 4 the texts are altered in several instances, and additional hymns and poems are also given.

Very few of Hull's hymns were repeated in other collections until 1863, when Dr. Kennedy included the following in his *Hymno. Christiana.* The bracketed dates are those of publication. Several of the first lines are altered from the originals, and sometimes additions are also given:—

1. A car of fire is on the air. (1833.) *Death and Burial.*
2. Comfort ye, people of the Lord : for He. (1828.) *God merciful in Judgment.*
3. Eternal Spirit, God of all. (1833.) *Increase of Faith.*
4. Father of all, Who from Thy throne. (1833.) *God ever present.*
5. Hear, holy Father, God of heaven. (1851.) *Lent.*
6. Lord God, to Thee we pray. (1828.) *National Hymn.* Altered form of " God save the King."
7. Lord, let Thy work be done. (1833.) *Missions.*
8. Mercy triumphs, Christ is born. (1851.) *Christmas.*
9. O Thou, the woman's promised Seed. (1833.) *Christmas.*
10. Once He came, how meek and lowly. (1828.) *Advent.*

11. Our hearts worship Thee, Lord, our voices proclaim. (1833.) *Blessedness of God's People.*
12. Raise up some warning voice, O Lord. (1833.) *Lent.*
13. Son of God, we kneel before Thee. (1851.) *Christ's constraining Love.*
14. The day must come, the judgment day. (1833.) *Advent.*
15. The sinful earth was sunk in woe. (1828.) *Christmas.*
16. 'Tis darkness all, and dreariness. (1833.) *Lent.*
17. To the God of all creation, (1833.) *Divine Worship.*
18. We have a name to live. (1833.) *Life in Christ.*
19. We have heard the solemn story. (1833.) *Easter.*
20. We know the Spirit's will. (1833.) *The Holy Spirit, the Guide.*
21. When on the blazing mount the stone. (1833.) *Giving of the Commandments.*
22. Ye that would worship the Lord. (1833.) *Ps. c.*

These hymns and others by the author are worthy of the attention of hymn-book compilers.   [J. J.]

Humani generis cessent suspiria. [*Annunciation.*] Appeared in the revised *Paris Missal*, 1685, for the "Feast of the Annunciation, and the Incarnation of Our Lord" (March 25). The text is also in Card. Newman's *Hymni Ecclesiae*, 1838 and 1865, in 13 st. of 5 l. *Tr.* by Dr. Neale in the *H. Noted*, 1854, as "The sighs and the sorrows," and repeated in the *Hymnary*, altered to, "Now the sighs and the sorrows."   [W. A. S.]

Humble souls who seek salvation. J. Fawcett. [*Follow the Lamb.*] The earliest date to which we have traced this hymn (although probably it previously appeared in a magazine with which we are unacquainted) is in John Fellows's *Hys. on Believers' Baptism*, 1773, No. 25, in 3 st. of 8 l. It next appeared in John Fawcett's *Hymns, &c.*, 1782, No. 117, with the heading "Invitation to follow the Lamb, Matt. iii. 15," and the following note :—

" The Author lays claim to this hymn, tho' it has appear'd under another name : he hopes the insertion of it, and the following [" Ye saints, with one accord "] will give no offence to those of his friends who are differently minded, as to the subject to which they refer."

With this note before us, we have no hesitation in ascribing this hymn to *John Fawcett.* Its use is mainly confined to America. [J. J.]

Humbly, my God, with Thee I walk. J. Montgomery. [*The walk of Faith.*] Written "at Dinsdale Hotel, Sept. 14, 1835," and sent in MS. to several persons from time to time (M. MSS.). It was given in his *Original Hymns*, 1853, in 6 st. of 4 l., as No. 167, and is in C. U. through a few collections.   [J. J.]

Humphreys, Cecil Frances. [Alexander, C. F.]

Humphreys, Joseph, s. of Asher Humphreys, minister at Burford, Oxfordshire, was b. at Burford, Oct. 28, 1720, and educated at a grammar school at Fairford, and at an academy for the training of young men for the ministry in London. From the latter he was expelled, Dec. 25, 1739, because of his attachment to Whitefield. For a short time he associated with the Wesleys, but eventually joined G. Whitefield, and subsequently preached at Bristol, London, and Deptford. He d. in London (date unknown), and was buried in the Moravian Cemetery at Chelsea.

He was a contributor to Whitefield's *Christian History* (1741–1748), 1742, &c., and pub., 1742, An Account of Joseph Humphreys's Experiences, &c. As a hymn-writer he is not widely known. His hymns were contributed to J. Cennick's *Sacred Hymns for the Use of Religious Societies* (Bristol), 1743, pt. ii., and are thus introduced : "These were done by Mr. Joseph Humphreys." Of these hymns, two only are in C. U. :—

1. Blessed are the sons of God. *Adoption.*
2. Come, guilty souls, and flee away. *Invitation.*

These are given in Spurgeon's *O. O. H. Bk.*, 1866, and other collections. No. 1 is the more popular of the two. It is sometimes abbreviated, and has the concluding lines of st. viii. added as a refrain to each stanza.   [J. J.]

Hunter, William, D.D., s. of John Hunter, was b. near Ballymoney, County Antrim, Ireland, May 26, 1811. He removed to America in 1817, and entered Madison College in 1830. For some time he edited the *Conference Journal*, and the *Christian Advocate*. In 1855 he was appointed Professor of Hebrew in Alleghany College : and subsequently Minister of the Methodist Episcopal Church, at Alliance, Stark Country, Ohio. He d. in 1877. He edited *Minstrel of Zion*, 1845 ; *Select Melodies*, 1851 ; and *Songs of Devotion*, 1859. His hymns, over 125 in all, appeared in these works. Some of these have been translated into various Indian languages. The best known are :—

1. **A home in heaven ; what a joyful thought.** *Heaven a Home.* From his *Minstrel of Zion*, 1845, into the *Meth. S.Scholar's H Bk.*, Lond, 1870, &c.

2. **Joyfully, joyfully onward I [we] move.** *Pressing towards Heaven.* This hymn is usually dated 1843. It was given in his *Minstrel of Zion*, 1845, and *Select Melodies*, 1851, and his *Songs of Devotion*, 1859. It has attained to great popularity. Two forms of the hymn are current, the original, where the 2nd st. begins "Friends fondly cherished, have passed on before " ; and the altered form, where it reads : "*Teachers and Scholars* have passed on before." Both texts are given in W. F. Stevenson's *Hymns for Church & Home*, 1873, Nos. 79, 80, c.

3. **The [My] heavenly home is bright and fair.** *Pressing towards Heaven.* From his *Minstrel of Zion*, 1845, into the *Cottage Melodies*, New York, 1859, and later collections.

4. **The Great Physician now is near.** *Christ the Physician.* From his *Songs of Devotion*, 1859.

5. **Who shall forbid our grateful [chastened] woe ?** This hymn, written in 1843, was pub. in his *Minstrel of Zion*, 1845, and in his *Songs of Devotion*, 1859.   [F. M. B.]

Huntingdon's Hymn-Books, Countess of. The history of the hymn-books issued from time to time by the Connection with which Lady Huntingdon's name is associated is very involved and obscure. Apart from the rarity of the original editions, each edition differs widely in contents. There is no absolute proof that any edition before that of 1780 was collected by her ladyship, while her biographer states that her brother-in-law, W. W. Shirley (q.v.), assisted her in the compilation of that edition. If so, such co-operation dates from 1770, as in the Bath edition of that year Shirley's "Sweet the moments, rich in blessing," first appears. Whether before that date the work of compilation was entered upon by Lady Huntingdon is unknown. The Connection has never issued an edition of the authorised book with authors' names, and it is impossible to assign the parts Shirley and

Lady Huntingdon took in altering the hymns of others found therein. It remains therefore for us to give details of the various editions of the Connectional hymn-book, and to add thereto such facts of interest as have come to our knowledge. The various editions are :—

i. *A Collection of Hymns, London, Printed for William Lee at Lewes, in Sussex, MDCCLXIV.* This contains 108 " Society Hymns " and " Doxologies," and 1 which is unnumbered, and 69 " Congregational Hymns." This edition apparently contained no originals. It is much indebted to J. Allen's *Kendal H. Bk.* of 1757 [Inghamite Hymnody], and to the Moravian Hymn-books.

ii. *The Collection of Hymns sung in the Countess of Huntingdon's Chapel, Bristol. Printed by E. Farley in Small Street, for Thomas Mills, Clerk, and to be had at his House in King's Mead Square, Bath,* 1765. This contained the Preface, as in No. 1, and had 127 " Society Hymns " (1 unnumbered) and Doxologies, 13 " Children's Hymns," and 91 " Congregational Hymns " with the " Doxologies " numbered as 92. A 12mo edition was also issued the same year. Many of the Inghamite and Moravian hymns were withdrawn in favour of Watts and the Wesleys.

iii. In 1770 appeared the *third* edition, printed at Bath by *S. Hazard for Thomas Mills, Clerk, and sold at his Circulating Library, King's Mead Square* [Bath]. This contained 240 hymns, including several by W. W. Shirley for the first time [see Shirley, W. W.].

iv. *A Collection of Hymns sung in the Countess of Huntingdon's Chapels, Bath. Printed by W. Gye, for T. Mills, Bookseller, and sold at his shop in Wine Street, Bristol. . . . This Hymn Book is sold in Bath by W. Gye only.* In this edition the hymns are differently arranged to any of the former editions, and are given as " Hymns " 140, " Hys before Sermon " 20, " after Sermon " 11, " for Christmas Day " 11, " N. Year's Day " 3, " G. Friday " 7, " Easter " 6, " Spring " 3, " Ascension Day " 5, " Whitsunday " 6, " on the Trinity " 6, " for the Sacrament " 51, " Funeral " 5, " Morning " 1, " Evening " 3, " Short Hys." 9, " Dismissions " 12, and Doxologies and Choruses. To it is added with special pagination an Appendix of 8 hymns. This division shows the relative importance attached by the Connection at that date to various doctrines and ordinances of religion. The position assigned to " the Sacrament " is somewhat striking. The date of this edition is not certain, but it must be very near to if not absolutely 1774. It contains additional original hymns by W. W. Shirley (q. v.). Hymns by Cowper, Grigg, and W. Williams are introduced for the first time.

v. *A Collection of Hymns sung in the Countess of Huntingdon's Chapels in Sussex. Edinburgh : Printed for William Balcombe,* N.D. The arrangement of the hymns in this edition differs from the former editions. This seems to have been No. 1 revised and altered.

vi. *The Collection of Psalms and Hymns sung in the Countess of Huntingdon's Chapels in Lincolnshire. Gainsb'rough : Printed by J. Mozley,* 1778. This contains 399 hymns, and some doxologies. It is not of the usual small oblong shape of the Huntingdon hymn-books, has apparently nothing original, and was probably a collection independently of the usual book.

vii. These varying editions took the definite shape which has been since retained in *A Select Collection of Hymns to be universally sung in all the Countess of Huntingdon's Chapels, Collected by her Ladyship. London, MDCCLXXX.* This contained 289 hymns, several doxologies and the words of the Choruses in Handel's *Messiah.* To this *Supplements* were added in 1796 and 1808. In later editions the Choruses are omitted.

viii. Before the issue of the authorised book of 1780 the Countess allowed her Preachers to make their own collections if they so desired. Thomas Maxfield's *Collection*, containing hymns " never before published," appeared in 1766, 1768, and 1778 ; the *Collection* by Herbert Taylor and W. Jones (to which Cowper and Newton contributed) in 1777 ; and a *Collection* for Cumberland Street, Shoreditch, together with others which might be named.

ix. Since the issue of the authorised edition of 1780, various independent *Supplements* have been published as *The Beauties of Dr. Watts with popular Hymns from the best Authors, and Various Originals : intended as a Supplement to the Countess of Huntingdon's Hymn Book. Selected by Thomas Young, Minister in that Connexion* 1819, and *Psalms and Hymns Selected by the Rev. Joseph Sortain, A.B., of Trinity College, Dublin, Minister of the late Countess of Huntingdon's Chapel, Brighton* (and dedicated " To the Congregation "), 1842. T. Haweis's (q.v.) *Carmina Christo ; or, Hymns to the*

Saviour, 1792, is also sometimes found bound up with the authorised collection.

In compiling the authorised edition of 1780 the Countess was assisted by W. W. Shirley. How far either or both were responsible for the previous editions we cannot say. It seems to us likely that they were jointly responsible for Nos. ii., iii., and iv.; that possibly Nos. i., v., and vi. were the work of others, v. and vi. being largely influenced by ii., iii., and iv.; and that vii. was certainly their combined work, in which the Countess bore the responsibility.   [W. T. B.]

Huntingdon, Selina, née Shirley, Countess of, daughter of Washington, Earl Ferrers, was b. Aug. 24, 1707; married to Theophilus Hastings, 9th Earl of Huntingdon, June, 1728; and d. in London, June 17, 1791. At at early age she received serious religious impressions, which continued with her, and ruled her conduct through life. She was a member of the first Methodist Society, in Fetter Lane, London, and the first Methodist Conference was held at her house in June, 1744. Her sympathies, however, were with the Calvinism of G. Whitefield, and when the breach took place between Whitefield and Wesley she joined the former. Her money was freely expended in chapel building, in the founding of Trevecca College, South Wales (now Cheshunt), and in the support of her preachers. A short time before her death the Connection which is known by her name was founded; and at her death it numbered more than sixty chapels. For use in these chapels she compiled *A Select Collection of Hymns*, details of which and its various editions are given under **Huntingdon's Hymn-Books, Countess of.** Her own part in hymn-writing is most uncertain. The hymns, "Come, Thou Fount of every blessing," and "O when my righteous Judge shall come" (q.v.), have been specially claimed for her, but upon insufficient testimony. No mention of these hymns as being by her is made in her *Life and Times*, 1839. Miller says, "although the Countess was not much known as a hymn-writer, yet it is proved beyond doubt that she was the author of a few hymns of great excellence" (*Singers & Songs*, 1869, p. 183): but he neither names the hymns, nor submits the evidence. It is most uncertain that she ever wrote a hymn; and it is quite clear that upon reliable evidence not one has yet been ascertained to be of her composing. Her history and that of her Connexion are elaborately set forth in *The Life and Times of Selina, Countess of Huntingdon*, Lond., Painter, 1839.   [J. J.]

Huntington, Frederic Dan, D.D., was b. at Hadley, Massachusetts, in 1819, and graduated at Amherst College, 1839, and Cambridge Divinity School, 1842. From 1842 to 1855 he was an Unitarian Minister in Boston; and from 1855 Professor of Christian Morals, and University Preacher, at Harvard. In 1859 he received Episcopal Ordination. He was for some time a Rector in Boston; and in 1869 he was consecrated Bishop of Central New York. With Dr. F. D. Hedge he edited the Unitarian *Hymns for the Church of Christ*, Boston, 1853. This collection contains three of his hymns:—

1. O Love Divine, lay on me burdens if Thou wilt. *Supplication.*
2. O Thou, in Whose Eternal Name. *Ordination.*
3. O Thou that once on Horeb stood. *God in Nature.*

The cento, "Father, Whose heavenly kingdom lies," in the *Hys. of the Spirit*, Boston, 1864, is from No. 2. Dr. Huntington has also edited, with Dr. Hedge, *Elim: Hys. of Holy Refreshment*, a collection of Sacred Poetry. From this work his hymn for *Burial*, "So heaven is gathering one by one," is taken.   [F. M. B.]

Huntington, Emily.   [Miller, E.]

Huntley, Lydia.   [Sigourney, L.]

Hupton, Job, was b. in 1762, at a small village near Burton-on-Trent. He was brought up to work at a forge, but after his conversion through the preaching of the Rev. John Bradford, one of Lady Huntingdon's ministers, whom he heard at Walsall, he began to preach; and after a few months at Trevecca College, was himself employed by Lady Huntingdon for some years as one of her itinerating ministers. Having changed his views on the subject of Baptism, he became, in 1794, pastor of the Baptist church at Claxton, in Norfolk, where he laboured with much success for many years. He d. Oct. 19, 1849.

Hupton wrote much both in prose and verse, his compositions appearing in the *Gospel Magazine* under the signatures of "Ebenezer," "Eliakim," and "J. H—n." His prose writings were collected and pub. in 1843, under the title *The Truth as it is in Jesus*. In 1861, D. Sedgwick reprinted his *Hymns & Spiritual Poems*, with a brief memoir.

Of his 22 hymns three only are in C. U. :—
1. Come ye saints and raise an anthem. *Praise.*
2. Glorious, high, and lofty One. *The Dominion of God.* In *Gospel Magazine*, June, 1806.
3. Jesus, Omnipotent to save. *Lent.*

The first of these, "Come ye," &c. (q.v.), in its altered form by Dr. Neale, is in extensive use, the rest are in a few hymn-books only. Hupton had a bold and vigorous imagination and great command of language. If in early life he had enjoyed better educational advantages, he would probably have attained to eminence as a poet.   [W. R. S.]

Hurditch, Charles Russell, was b. in Exeter, Dec. 20, 1839. In 1854 he underwent a spiritual change which led him subsequently to undertake religious work in some of the villages of Devonshire, and afterwards to succeed the late Mr. Henry Hull as the Secretary of the Young Men's Christian Association, Stafford Street, London. In 1865 he published *The London H. Bk. for Prayer Meetings and Special Services*. This was revised in 1880. In 1873 he also published *The Enlarged London H. Bk., a Collection of Hymns for Public, Social, and Private Use.* Of the smaller work more than half a million copies have been sold; and of the enlarged book the 86th thousand was issued in 1881. To the first (1865) he contributed Nos. 10 and 11 given below: the rest were published in the second book (1873).

1. Arise, ye saints, arise and sing. *God is Light.*
2. Arm of the Lord, awake! Exalt the Saviour slain. *Home Missions.*
3. Come, join the hosts above. *Praise of Jesus.*
4. Farewell to the present, farewell. *Friends parting.*
5. He dies! He dies! The Son of God most holy. *Good Friday.*
6. Hear the gospel's joyful sound. *Invitation.*
7. Jesus, do Thou my vision fill. *Jesus All in All.*
8. Let us by faith draw nigh. *Holy Communion.*

9. Lord, grant Thy Spirit's mighty power. *Divine Worship.*

10. Lord Jesus, we pray. *Second Advent desired.*

11. O Christ, Thou heavenly Lamb. *Divine Power desired.*

12. O God of all love! Thy presence here prove. *Divine Worship.*

13. O sacred Name! O Name of power. *Name of Jesus.*

14. O sinner, wilt thou further go? *Appeal and Response.*

15. O Sovereign Lord of earth and heaven. *Holy Baptism.*

16. Only Jesus would I see. *Jesus Only.*

17. Rejoice, rejoice, ye saints, rejoice. *Rejoicing in the Lord.*

18. Salvation's song be given. *Praise to Jesus.*

19. Soon shall these eyes, my Saviour, see. *Praise to Jesus.*

20. Soon shall we find our journey o'er. *Nearing Heaven.*

21. Stop, thou heavy-laden stranger. *Christ's Compassion.*

22. The atoning blood is flowing. *Redemption.*

23. These supplications hear. *Lent.*

24. Till we meet Thee in glory. *Constancy desired.*

25. We bless Thy precious Name. *Name of Jesus.*

26. What wondrous grace in Christ we see. *Christ's Humility.*

27. Ye dying sons of men; Christ calls, &c. *Invitation.*

Of these hymns, No. 1 was written as a companion hymn to "Come, let us all unite and sing. God is love;" No. 2, "about 1859;" No. 11, when he received the invitation to proceed to London, as noted above; No. 15, for the baptism of his youngest son; and No. 25 for a Conference which was held in London. All Mr. Hurditch's hymns are characterised by great simplicity and earnestness. [J. J.]

Hurlburt, William Henry, was b. at Charlestown, South Carolina, July 23, 1827, and educated at Harvard. He also studied at Berlin, Paris, and Rome. In 1848 he contributed the following hymns to Longfellow and Johnson's Unitarian *Book of Hymns:*—

1. My God, in life's most doubtful hour. *Faith desired, or, the Power of Trust.*

2. We pray for truth and peace. *Faith desired.*

3. We will not weep, for God is standing by us. *The Might of Faith.* [F. M. B.]

Hurn, William, b. at Breccles Hall, Norfolk, Dec. 21, 1754. His education was superior, enabling him, in 1777 to take the post of classical tutor in the Free Grammar School, Dedham, Essex. In 1779 he entered the army, but resigning his commission in 1780, he was ordained by Bishop Young of Norwich, in 1781. After holding various curacies, including Beighton Broome, Stowmarket, &c., he was presented in 1790 to the Vicarage of Debenham, Suffolk. In October, 1822, he resigned his Vicarage, and in April, 1823, undertook the pastorate of the Congregational chapel at Woodbridge, in the same county. This he retained to his death, Oct. 9, 1829. His poetical works included:—

(1) *Health Hill,* a descriptive poem, 1777; (2) *Blessings of Peace, a Lyric Poem,* 1784; (3) *Laughter in Death,* appended to *Preparation for Death* (a Sermon), 1792; and (4) *Psalms & Hymns, the greater part original; and the selected compositions altered with a view to purity of Doctrine and General Usefulness. By W. Hurn,* Vicar of Debenham. Ipswich, J. Raw, 1813. This contained 417 hymns, and a doxology. Of these 264 were by Hurn. After seceding from the Church of England this collection was enlarged and pub. as *Hymns and Spiritual Songs, with Metrical Versions from the Psalms: designed to teach the Christian Doctrine according to the Analogy of Scripture, by combining Knowledge and Practice, or the Duties with the Principles of the Gospel.* Woodbridge, 1824. This contained 420 of his hymns.

From the first edition of Hurn's collection the following hymns are in C. U.:—

1. Angels rejoiced and sweetly sung. *Christmas.*

2. Rise, gracious God, and shine. *Missions.* Altered in the *Salisbury H. Bk.,* 1857, to " Arise, O Lord, and shine."

3. The God of truth His Church has blest. *God's love of the Church.*

A biographical notice of Hurn was given in the *Evangelical Magazine,* 1829, and his *Brief Memorials* were pub. in 1831. [J. J.]

Husband, Edward was educated at St. Aidan's College, Birkenhead. Taking Holy Orders in 1866, he was successively Curate of Atherstone and Folkestone; and in 1878 Vicar of St. Michael and All Angels, Folkestone. In 1874 Mr. Husband pub. *The Mission Hymnal,* in which appeared his hymns as follows:—

1. Alas! poor world, I loved thee long. *Rest in Jesus.*

2. And dost Thou ask me, dearest Lord. *Christ's Invitation, " Follow Me."*

3. I must have Jesus only. *Jesus only desired.*

4. Sweet Blood, dear ransom of our souls. *The Blood of Jesus.*

These hymns are very simple, earnest, and impassioned: and bear a great resemblance to Faber's compositions. [J. J.]

Hushed the storm that lately raved. *Archbishop E. W. Benson. [The Annunciation.]* Written for and 1st pub. in the *Wellington College H. Bk.,* 1860, and also included the same year in the Rev. J. Moultrie's *Rugby Parish Church Collection,* and subsequently in other collections. [J. J.]

Hushed was the evening hymn. *J. D. Burns. [The Child Samuel.]* Pub. in his *Evening Hymn* (a small book of Prayers and Hymns), 1857, in 5 st. of 6 l. It is one of the most popular of the author's hymns, is very tender, and worthy of the position to which it has attained. [J. J.]

Huss, John. [Various.]

Hutten, Ulrich von, was b. at his ancestral castle of Steckelburg near Schlüchtern, on the Kinzig (Hesse-Cassel), April 21, 1488, and d. on the Island of Ufnau, in the Lake of Zürich, about the end of August, 1523.

He is better known as a herald of the Reformation, as a free lance, and as a satirist (he was one of the authors of the famous *Epistolae obscurorum virorum*), than as a hymn-writer. His complete works, German and Latin, appeared in 7 vols. at Leipzig, 1859, ff. One piece is:— Ich habs gewagt mit Sinnen. *[Patriotism.]* This piece is an appeal to popular sympathy for his cause, and headed by his motto, " Ich habs gewagt " (I have ventured it), was 1st printed on a broadsheet in 1521 (thence in *Wackernagel,* iii. p. 386, in 7 st.), and soon became a favourite song of the early adherents of the Reformation. It has been *tr.* as (1) "I've ventured, knowing what I risk'd," in Madame de Pontes' *Poets and Poetry of Germany,* 1858, vol. i. p. 364. (2) " I've ventured it of purpose free," by *Miss Winkworth,* 1869, p. 99. [J. M.]

Hutton, James, s. of a clergyman and cousin to Sir Isaac Newton, was b. in London, Sept. 3, 1715, and followed for some years the trade of a bookseller. In 1739 he visited the Moravian settlement at Herrnhut, where he became acquainted with Count Zinzendorf. He retired from business in 1745, and was ordained a diaconus of the Moravian Church in 1749. He d. May 3, 1795. He contributed several hymns to the *Moravian H. Bk.,* 1754.

All his hymns were included in an Appendix to his *Memoirs*, pub. by Daniel Benham in 1856. In the English *Moravian H. Bk.*, 1886, the following hymns are by Hutton :—

1. Besprinkle with Thy blood my heart. *Holiness desired.* In the *Moravian H. Bk.*, 1742, No. 185, it begins " Stream thro' the bottom of my soul."
2. Brethren, what do you desire ? *Missions. Moravian H. Bk.*, 1742.
3. Come faithful Shepherd, bind me. *Self-Consecration.*
4. How shall a young man cleanse his way ? (1754) *Holy Scripture.*
5. Teach me yet more of Thy blest ways. *Good Friday.* Sometimes " O teach us more." (*M. H. Bk.*, 1742.)   **[J. J.]**

Hyde, Abby Bradley, was b. at Stockbridge, Massachusetts, Sept. 28, 1799, and married to the Rev. Lavius Hyde, of Salisbury, Mass., Sept. 28, 1818. She d. at Andover, April 7, 1872. Her first poem, an *Address to Mr. Wolfe*, the Jewish missionary, appeared in a New Haven paper in 1822 or 1823, and from it Dr. L. Bacon (q.v.) took two hymns for his *Hys. & Sac. Songs for the Monthly Concert*, Andover, 1823. These hymns have merit, but are not now in C. U. Asahel Nettleton included 9 pieces by her in his *Village Hymns*, 1824, and 34 more were given in the revised and enlarged ed. of the same, 1851. An additional hymn appeared in Nason's *Congregational H. Bk.*, 1857. Of those hymns the following are still in C. U. :—

1. **Ah, what can I a sinner do ?** *Lent.* From Nettleton's *Village Hys.*, 1824, in 5 st. of 4 l., into a few collections.

2. **And canst thou, sinner, slight ?** *Grieve not the Spirit.* From Nettleton's *Village Hys.*, 1824, in 4 st. of 4 l., into a great number of American collections, and a few in G. Britain.

3. **Behold the glorious dawning bright.** *Second Advent.* From Nettleton's *Village Hys.*, 1824, in 4 st. of 4 l. Limited in use.

4. **Dear Saviour, if these lambs should stray.** *Prayer on behalf of children.* In Nettleton's *Village Hys.*, 1824, in 4 st. of 4 l. A touching hymn, and widely used.

5. **Say, sinner, hath a voice within ?** *Exhortation to Repentance.* In a letter to Mr. Nason, dated July 10, 1857, Mrs. Hyde says that this hymn " was written down from my lips by a young sister, when I was not able to hold up my head from the pillow." It appeared in Nettleton's *Village Hys.*, 1824, in 6 st. of 4 l., and is in extensive use.

All Mrs. Hyde's pieces in the *Village Hys.* are signed " Hyde."   **[F. M. B.]**

Hymn of Justinian. [Greek **Hymnody,** § x. 10.]

Hymnarium. Before the complex office book known as the *Breviary* assumed its present general order and shape at the close of the 11th and beginning of the 12th centuries, its various contents were distributed in separate volumes. One of these volumes was the *Hymnarium, Hymnale,* or *Hymnal,* which contained the hymns proper to the various sacred Seasons and Festivals, or assigned to the several Hours of the day. We are using the word *Hymnarium* in this article in the ancient meaning, and without reference to the many collections of hymns in modern times to which we ordinarily attach now the title of *Hymnary.*

In the first part of this article we shall

enumerate, with a necessarily brief description of them, certain ancient and important MS. *Hymnaria* which have descended to us, together with two ancient Service Books, miscellaneous in character, but akin to *Hymnaria,* and then give a complete list of the first lines of all the Hymns. In the second part are added the first lines of such later hymns as did not become incorporated in the authorized Breviaries of after times, and are therefore not included in the first lines of hymns previously given under the article *Breviary.* This second list also includes a few more first lines of hymns drawn from mediæval sources other than *Hymnaria,* for which it would be difficult to find a place elsewhere. *In such cases a special reference is given to the press mark of the* MS..

Sometimes a *Hymnarium* or *Collection of Hymns* is found as an independent volume. It was frequently (see the MSS. described below) appended to a *Psalter;* and occasionally to an *Antiphonary.*

Part i.—In compiling the first list of first lines of hymns an exhaustive use has been made of . the following MS. *Hymnaria* and *Service-books :*—

(*a*) **The Durham Hymnary.** A Collection of Latin Hymns used in the Anglo-Saxon Church, with an interlinear Anglo-Saxon gloss. The MS. is of the 11th cent., and is now preserved in the Library of the Dean and Chapter of Durham, B. iii. 32. It was probably written in the diocese of Winchester, c. 1050. It was printed in 1851 by the Surtees Society, forming vol. xxiii. of its publications, and is referred to in the annotations in this *Dictionary* as the *Latin Hymns of the Anglo-Saxon Church,* 1851.

(*b*) **Cottonian MS.** [*Julius A. vi.*] An 11th century Latin *Hymnarium.* The text of each hymn is given in its metrical form, and is followed by a prose paraphrase with an interlinear Anglo-Saxon gloss. The Hymns extend to fol. 72, and are followed by Canticles. (This MS. is quoted in this *Dictionary* as *Jul. A. vi.*) A late 10th century *Kalendar* is bound up with and is prefixed to this *Hymnarium,* which has perhaps led to this *Hymnarium* itself being sometimes erroneously assigned to the 10th century. This MS. has also two hymns without glosses : *Adsunt, o socii,* at f. 17, in a hand of the 12th cent., and *O genetrix aeterni,* at f. 89, in a hand of the end of the 11th cent.

(*c*) **Cottonian MS.** [*Vespasian D. xii.*] An early 11th century Latin *Hymnarium.* Each hymn is followed by a prose version of the same, accompanied by an interlinear Anglo-Saxon translation. The *Hymnary* extends to fol. 124, and is followed by Canticles, which extend to the end of the volume, and which are duplicated in a similar way. At folios 155, 156 are two hymns (" Aeterni Patris " and " Lauda mater ") in a hand of the 12th cent., and one (" Rex Christe tu ") in a hand of the 14th or later. *Ecce tempus idoneum,* at f. 122 *b,* is in a hand of late 12th cent. (This MS. is quoted in this *Dictionary* as *Vesp. D. xii.*)

(*d*) **Harleian MS., 2961.** This is a *Collectarium* or inchoate *Breviary,* without the *Psalter.* It was written in the 11th century, and once belonged to Leofric, first Bishop of Exeter, 1050-72. The later history of this MS. is given in the *Introduction* to the *Leofric Missal,* 1883, p. xxviii. The Collectarium occupies the first part of the MS. (ff. 1-216), and is followed by the *Hymnarium* (ff. 218-256). The Sequences of this MS. are indexed under **Sequences.** (This MS. is quoted in this *Dictionary* as *Harl.* 2961.)

(*e*) **The Antiphonary of Bangor.** A 7th century MS. Irish Service Book, originally belonging to the Monastery of Bangor, County Down. It is proved from internal evidence to have been written 680-691, during the life-time of Abbot Cronan. It is now preserved in the Ambrosian Library at Milan. It has been printed in Muratori's *Anecdota Bibliothecæ Ambrosianæ,* vol. iv. pp. 121-159 ; and Migne's *Patrol. Curs. Lat.* lxxii. 582. It has no claim to the title of *Antiphonary,* but it is a collection of miscellaneous devotional pieces, including several hymns.

(*f*) **Book of Hymns**; or, *Liber Hymnorum.*
An Irish MS. collection of devotional pieces, including a few hymns. Two copies of this MS. are in existence, both now at Dublin, and both written about the 11th century. The Trinity College (Dublin) copy has been partly published by the *Irish Archæological and Celtic Society*, vol. xvii. It is being edited by Dr. J. H. Todd.

(*g*) **C.C.C. 391.** This is a *Psalter* written soon after A.D. 1064, and now at Corpus Christi College (CCC), Cambridge (MS. No. 391). It seems to have been written at Winchester, and thence to have passed to Worcester before it fell into Archbp. Parker's hands. The *Psalter* is followed by a complete *Hymnarium*, and that again by a complete *Collectarium*, or inchoate *Breviary*, with miscellaneous devotions at its close.

(*h*) **Add. 30851.** This MS. is of the 11th cent., and is now in the British Museum. It is a Service Book of the ancient Church of Spain (*Mozarabic*), and contains a *Psalter* followed by Scripture canticles; then a *Hymnarium*; and lastly, miscellaneous Offices with hymns.

Some leaves of the *Hymnarium* are missing, and so, e.g. "Psallat altitudo," begins imperfectly on f. 132; and "Hierusalem gloriosa" begins imperfectly on f. 135. The hymns found among the Offices at the end are marked in the following list as *h**.

(*i*) **Junius 25.** This is one of the MSS. bequeathed by Francis Junius to the Bodleian Library. It was probably written c. 890 A.D.; and contains 26 hymns with an interlinear Frisian gloss. Junius made several transcripts of these hymns (e.g. *Junius* 110). A good ed. by E. Sievers, from the original MS., was pub. as *Die Murbacher Hymnen*, at Halle, 1874.

(*k*) **Harl. 2928.** This MS., in the British Museum, is of the 12th cent., and contains a complete *Hymnarium*. Being of later date than the MSS. a–i, it is not cited in the case of hymns found in three or more of the earlier MSS.

In the following list of hymns the letters *a, b, c, d, e, f, g, h, i, k* indicate the MSS. named above in which they are found. The orthography has been modernized.

First line of Hymn.	MSS.	Use.
A Patre unigenitus	*a. b. c. d. g.*	Epiphany. Lauds.
A solis ortus cardine, Ad usque	*a. b. c. d. g. h.*	Christmas. Lauds.
Ad brevem se mortis usum	*h.*	Sat. in Easter Week. Pt. of "Da, puer."
Ad coenam Agni providi	*a. b. c. g. h. i.*	Low Sunday. Vespers.
Adest diei Christe consecratio	*h.*	Consecration of a Bishop.
Adest miranda passio	*h.*	St. Vincent.
Adesto sancta Trinitas	*c.*	Holy Trinity.
Adstantes pariter sexus.	*h.*	St. Eugenia.
Adsunt, O populi, festa celebria	*h.*	St. Hippolytus.
Ad[s]sunt, o socii, festa	*b.*	Victory of Heraclius.
Adsunt tenebrae primae	*h**	First Watch.
Aeterna Christi munera Apostolorum	*a. c. d. h.*	C. of Apostles.
Aeterna Christi munera, Et martyrum	*a. b. d. g. h. i.*	C. of Martyrs.
Aeterna coeli gloria	*a. b. c. d. g.*	Friday. Lauds.
Aeternae lucis conditor	*i.*	Matins.
Aeterne rerum conditor.	*a. b. c. d. g. i.*	Sunday. Lauds.
Aeterne rex altissime	*a. b. c. g*	Ascension.
Aeterni Patris Unice	*c.*	St. Mary Magdalene.
Agnes sepulchrum est	*h.*	St. Agnes.
Agnoscat omne saeculum	*d.*	Christmas.
Ales diei nuntius	*a. b. c. d. g.*	Tuesday. Lauds.
Alleluia dulce carmen	*a. b. c. d. g.*	Septuagesima.
Alleluia piis edite laudibus	*a. b. c. d. g. h.*	Septuagesima.
Alma Gregorii meritis praecipue	*a. d.*	St. Gregory.
Almi prophetae progenies pia	*h.*	Nativ. St. John Bapt.
Almum sidereae jam patriae	*a. c. d. g.*	Septuagesima.
Altus prosi[a]tor vetustus dierum	*f.*	By St. Columba.
Andreas pie sanctorum mitissime	*a. b. c. d. g.*	St. Andrew.
Angulare fundamentum	*c.*	Pt. of "Urbs beata Hierusalem."
Anni peractis mensibus.	*a. c.*	Pentecost.
Anni peracto circulo	*h.*	Birthday of a King.
Annue Christe saeculorum Domine	*b. c. d. g.*	C. of Apostles.
Antra deserti teneris sub annis	*b.*	St. John Bapt. Pt. of "Ut queant."
Apostolorum passio	*h.*	SS. Peter and Paul.
Arbor decora et fulgida	*b. c. d.*	Pt. of "Vexilla regis."
Auctor salutis unicus	*a. b. c. d., g.*	Passiontide.
Audi benigne conditor	*a. b. c. d. g.*	Lent.
Audi Redemptor gentium	*a. b. c. d. g.*	Christmas at Matins.
Audite bonum exemplum	*e.*	St. Caemhlach.
Audite omnes amantes Deum	*e. f.*	St. Patrick.
Aurea luce et decore roseo	*a. b. c. g.*	SS. Peter & Paul.
Aurora jam spargit polum	*a. b. c. d. g. h.*	Saturday. Lauds.
Aurora lucis rutilat	*a. b. c. g. i.*	Easter.
Ave colenda Trinitas	*a. b.*	Holy Trinity.
Ave Dunstane praesulum	*a. c.*	St. Dunstan.
Ave maris stella	*a b. c. d. g. h.*	B. V. M.
Aveto placidis Praesul amabilis	*a.*	St. Augustine.
Barchinon laeto Cucufate vernans	*h.*	St. Cucufatus.
Bartholomaee coeli sidus	*a. b. c. d. g.*	St. Bartholomew.
Beata nobis gaudia	*a. b. c. g.*	Pentecost.
Beate Simon et Taddee inclite	*a. b. c. d. g.*	SS. Simon & Jude.
Benchuir bona regula	*e.*	Monks of Bangor.
Bina coelestis aulae luminaria	*a. b. c. d. g.*	St. John Apostle.
Bis novem noster populus sub uno	*h.*	The 18 Martyrs.
Cantemus in omni die concinentes	*f.*	B. V. M.
Caterva matrum personat	*d. h.*	Holy Innocents. Pt. of "A solis."
Celebra Juda festa Christi gaudia	*f.*	Apostles, &c.
Certum tenentes ordinem	*i.*	Terce.
Chorus novae Hierusalem	*c.*	Easter.
Christe coeli Domine	*i.*	To Christ.
Christe coelorum habitator alme	*a.*	Dedication of a Church.

First line of Hymn.	MSS.	Use.
Christe cunctorum dominator alme . .	a. b. c. d. h.	Dedication of a Church.
Christe hac hora tertia . . .	c. .	Christmas, at Terce.
Christe qui lux es et dies . .	a. b. c. d. g. h*. i.	Compline.
Christe Redemptor omnium, Conserva .	a. b. c. d. g. h*	Christmas.
Christe Redemptor omnium, Ex Patre .	a. b. c. d. g.	All Saints.
Christe Rex mundi Creator . .	h.	For the Dead.
Christe sanctorum decus angelorum .	a. b. c. d. g.	St. Benedict.
Christe sanctorum decus atque virtus .	a. b. c. d. g.	St. Michael.
Christe splendor gloriae . .	c. d. g.	See " O Christe splendor."
Christe tu rerum opifexque operum .	h.	St. Clement.
Christi caterva clamitet . .	h.	1st S. in Advent.
Christus est virtus Patris sapientia .	h.	St. Jerome.
Christus est vita, veniens in orbem .	h.	St. Stephen.
Christus in nostra insula quae vocatur .	f.	St. Bridget.
Clara magnaque sanctorum praeparantur gaudia (in the 1775 this begins with st. ii. "Mysticum melos")	h.	SS. Faustus, Januarius and Martial.
Clara sanctorum una Hierusalem .	h.	St. James Apostle.
Clarum decus jejunii . .	a. b. c. d. g.	Lent.
Clausus aurium meatus . .	h.	Th. in Easter Week. Pt. of "Da, puer."
Clementis festum celebratur hodie .	h.	St. Clement.
Coelestis aulae nobilis . .	a.	St. Augustine.
Coeli Deus sanctissime . .	a. b. c. d. g.	Wednesday, at Vespers.
Coeli vernantem patriam . .	g.	St. Oswald.
Conditor alme siderum . .	a. b. c. d. g.	Advent, at Vespers.
Confessor hic probabilis . .	h.	C. of Confessors.
Consors paterni luminis . .	a. b. c. d. g. h*	Tuesday. Matins.
Corde natus ex parentis . .	d.	Christmas. Pt. of "Da, puer."
Cultor Dei memento . .	d.	Lent, at Compline. Pt. of " Ades, Pater."
De Patris ergo lumine . .	a. c.	Pentecost, at Sext. Pt. of "Jam Christus."
Decus sacrati nominis . .	h.	St. Andrew.
Dei fide qua vivimus . .	a. b. c. d. g. i.	Lent, at Terce.
Deus aeterni luminis . .	i.	Matins.
Deus creator omnium Polique Rector .	a. b. c. d. g.	Vespers.
Deus ignee fons animarum . .	h.	At burial.
Deus immensa Trinitas, Unitas .	h.	C. of a Just Man.
Deus Pater piissime . .	k.	Vespers.
Deus qui certis legibus . .	i.	Midnight.
Deus qui claro lumine . .	i.	Vespers.
Deus qui coeli lumen es . .	i.	Matins.
Deus tuorum militum . .	a. b. c. d. g. h.	C. of a Martyr.
Dicamus laudes Domino . .	i.	Sext.
Dicamus omnes cernui . .	c.	Pt. of " Ex more docti."
Diei luce reddita . .	i.	Matins.
Doctor egregie Paule mores instrue .	a. b. d.	St. Paul. Pt. of " Aurea luce."
Eadmundus martyr inclitus . .	c.	St. Edmund.
Ecce jam noctis tenuatur umbra .	a. b. c. d. g.	Sunday. Lauds.
Ecce micantia veluti sidera . .	h.	St. Euphemia.
Ecce quem vates vetustis . .	h.	Pt. of " Da, puer." Easter Monday.
Ecce te Christe tibi cara semper .	h.	Dedication of a Church.
Ecce tempus idoneum . .	c.	Lent.
En martyris Laurentii . .	h.	St. Lawrence.
En pater gloriae rutilum gaudiis cunctis	h.	St. Martin.
Enixa est puerpera . .	a. b. c. d.	Pt. of " A solis ortus."
Ex more docti mystico . .	a. c. d.	Lent.
Exaudi Christe nos pueris . .	h.	St. Bartholomew.
Eximum vestis sacratae . .	h.	Easter Tuesday. Pt. of " Da, puer."
Exultet aula coelica . .	k.	St. Nicholas.
Exultet coelum laudibus . .	a. b. c. d. g. h.	C. of Apostles.
Faeno jacere pertulit . .	h.	Pt. of " A solis." Christmas.
Favens redemptis vota abstinentiae .	h.	Mid Lent.
Felix per omnes festum mundi cardines .	c. g. k.	SS. Peter and Paul.
Festiva lux emicuit . .	k.	St. Martial.
Festiva saeclis colitur . .	a. b. c. d. g.	All Saints.
Festum Christe rex, per orbem .	h.	St. Thomas.
Festum colentes celebre . .	g.	St. Mary Magdalene.
Fit porta Christo pervia . .	a. c. d. h.	Assumption of B. V. M.
Fons Deus aeternae pacis . .	h.	SS. Fucundus and Primicabus.
Fons Deus vitae perennis . .	h.	St. Felix.
Fratres unanimes foedere nexili .	d.	St. Martin.
Fulgentis auctor aetheris . .	i.	Matins.
Gabriel Dei archangelus . .	a. c. d.	Assump. of B. V. M.
Gallo canente venimus . .	h*	Pt. of " Noctis tempus." Cockcrow.
Gaudete flores martyrum . .	h.	Saints' Days in Advent.
Gaude visceribus mater in intimis .	d.	Nativity of B. V. M.
Germine nobilis Eulalia. . .	h.	St. Eulalia.
Hac noctis hora praescius . .	h*	Pt. of " Noctis tempus." Cockcrow.
Hic duorum cara fratrum . .	h.	Pt. of " Scripta sunt." SS. Emeterius, and Chelidonius.

First line of Hymn.	MSS.	Use.
Hic est dies verus Dei	*i.*	Easter.
Hic Johannes mire natus	*h.*	Decoll. St. John Baptist.
Hic salus aegris medicina fessis	*a. b. c. d.*	Dedication of a Church. Pt. of "Christe cunctorum."
Hierusalem gloriosa	*h.*	St. Adrian.
Hinc functionis dies est	*h.*	Of the Dead.
Hora nona quae canimus	*c.*	None.
Hostis Herodes impie	*a. b. c. d. g. h.*	Epiphany. Pt. of "A solis."
Huc vos gratifice, plebs pia convocat	*h.*	SS. Vincent, Sabina and Chrysteta.
Hymnum canamus Domino Hymni novi	*a.*	Ascension.
Hymnum canamus gloriae Hymni novi	*b. c. g. k.*	Ascension.
Hymnum cantemus Domino Hymnum	*a. b. c. d. g.*	St. Stephen.
Hymnum dicat turba fratrum	*e.*	To Christ (by St. Hilary),
Ignis Creator igneus	*e.*	Benediction of Candles.
Immense coeli conditor	*a. b. c. d. g.*	Tuesday. Vespers.
In te Christe, credentium	*f.*	By St. Columba.
In Trinitate spes mea fixa	*f.*	St. Michael.
Inclite Pater super	*g.*	St. Oswald.
Inclite Rex magne regum	*h.*	Coronation of a King.
Incliti festum pudoris	*h.*	St. Cecilia.
Inclito regi polorum	*h.*	St. Primicius.
Infantum meritis inclita gaudia	*d.*	Holy Innocents. Pt. of "Sanctorum meritis."
Inventor rutili dux bone luminis	*c. h.*	Easter.
Iste confessor Domini sacratus	*a. b. c. d. g.*	Com. of a Confessor.
Jacobe juste, Jesu frater Domini	*a. b. c. d. g.*	St. James the Less.
Jam lucc pastor Petre	*a. b. .d.*	St. Peter. Pt. of "Aurea luce."
Jam, Christe, sol justitiae	*c. k.*	Easter.
Jam Christus astra ascenderat	*a h. c, g*	Pentecost.
Jam lucis orto sidere	*a. b. c. d. g.*	Prime.
Jam rutilat sacrata dies	*a. b. c. d. g.*	St. Stephen.
Jesu corona virginum	*a. b. c. d. g, h.*	Com. of Virgins.
Jesu defensor omnium	*h**	Midnight.
Jesu nostra redemptio	*a. b. c. g.*	Easter.
Jesu quadragenariae	*a. b. c. g.*	Lent.
Jesu redemptor omnium, Perpes corona	*a. b. c. d. g. h.*	C. of a Confessor.
Jesu redemptor saeculi, Verbum Patris	*d.*	Vespers.
Jesus refulsit omnium	*a. b. c. d. g.*	Epiphany.
Jesu Salvator saeculi, Redemptis ope	*h*. k.*	All Saints.
Jucundis pangat saecula	*k.*	St. Martial.
Jucundum nobis hunc diem	*h.*	SS. Maximus and Julia.
Judaea tunc incredula	*a. b. c.*	Pentecost. Pt. of "Jam Christus."
Laetus hoc festum colat universus	*g.*	St. Mary Magdalene.
Largitas Christi veniam	*g.*	St. Mary Magdalene.
Lauda mater ecclesia	*c.*	St. Mary Magdalene.
Laudem beatae Eulaliae	*h.*	St. Eulalia.
Laudem Christo plebs dicata	*h.*	Festival of a Bishop.
Laurea regni redimitus olim	*c.*	St. Edmund.
Laus et corona militum	*c.*	St. Edmund.
Lucis auctor clemens, lumen immensum	*h**	First Watch.
Lucis creator optime	*a. b. c. d. g.*	Vespers.
Lustra sex qui jam peracta	*c. k.*	Passiontide. Pt. of "Pange l. g. praelium.
Lux Deus Christe, pietas redundans	*h.*	St. Augustine.
Lux ecce surgit aurea	*a. b. c. d. g.*	Thursday. Matins.
Magnae Deus potentiae	*a. b. c. d. g.*	Thursday. Vespers.
Magno canentes annua	*a. b. c. d. g.*	St. Benedict.
Magnus miles mirabilis	*a. b. c. d. g.*	St. Cuthbert.
Maria coeli regina	*a. c. d.*	B. V. M. Pt. of "Gabriel Dei."
Maria mater Domini, Aeterni Patris	*a. c. d.*	Assumption of B. V. M.
Maria virgo virginum	*a. c. d.*	B. V. M. Pt. of "Gabriel Dei."
Martiali pontifici Aquitanorum principi	*k.*	St. Martial.
Martine confessor Dei	*a. h.*	St. Martin.
Martine te deprecor	*f.*	St. Martin.
Martinus magnus pontifex	*h.*	St. Martin.
Martyr Dei qui unicum	*a. b. c. d. g. h.*	Com. of a Martyr.
Martyris Christi colimus triumphum	*a. c.*	St. Lawrence.
Martyris ecce dies Agathae	*k.*	St. Agatha.
Matthaee sancte bino pollens munere	*a. b. c. d. g.*	St. Matthew.
Matthia juste duodeno solio	*a. b. c. d. g.*	St. Matthias.
Mediae noctis tempore	*e. i.*	Midnight.
Meridie orandum est	*a. b. c. d. g. i.*	Lent, at Sext.
Mysteriorum signifer	*a. b. c. d. g.*	St. Michael.
Nobis ecce dies ordine congruo	*a. c.*	St. Andrew.
Nocte surgentes vigilemus omnes	*a. b. c. d. g.*	Nocturns.
Noctis tempus jam praeterit	*h**	Cockcrow. 4th Sun. in Lent.
Noctis tetrae primordia	*h**	First Watch.
Noli, Pater, indulgere	*f.*	By St. Columba.
Nox atra rerum contegit	*a. b. c. d. g.*	Thursday. Nocturns.
Nox et tenebrae et nubila	*a. b. c. d. g.*	Wednesday. Lauds.

First line of Hymn.	MSS.	Use.
Nunc sancte nobis Spiritus . . .	*a. b. c. d. g.*	Terce.
Nunc tibi virgo virginum . . .	*c. d. g.*	B. V. M.
Nuntium vobis fero de supernis .	*k.* . .	Epiphany.
O beata Hierusalem, praedicanda civitas	*h.* . .	Restoration of a Church.
O beate mundi auctor . . .	*h.* . .	St. Christopher.
O Christe splendor gloriae . .	*a. b.* .	Of Confessors.
O coelorum alme princeps . . .	*h.* . .	St. Michael.
O Dei perenne verbum . . .	*h.* . .	SS. Justus and Pastor.
O Dei Verbum Patris ore proditum .	*h.* . .	St. James brother of St. John.
O genitrix aeterni virgo Maria verbi	*b.* . .	B. V. M.
O gloriosa domina	*k.* . .	Pt. of "Quem terra."
O gloriosa femina	*a. b. c. d.* .	Pt. of "Quem terra."
O lux beata Trinitas . . .	*a. c. d. g.* .	Holy Trinity.
O magne rerum Christe Rector inclite .	*h.* . .	St. Aemilian.
O Nazarene lux Bethlehem Verbum Patris	*d. h.* .	Lent, at Compline.
O Pater sancte mitis atque pie .	*a. b. c.* .	Holy Trinity.
O Petre, petra ecclesiae . . .	*h.* . .	St. Peter's Chair.
O quam glorifica luce coruscas .	*a. b. c. d. g.*	Assumption B. V. M.
O rerum Domine, conditor omnium .	*h.* . .	St. Genesius.
O sacerdotum inclita corona . .	*h.* . .	St. Babilas.
O Thoma Christi perlustrator lateris .	*a. b. c. d. g.*	St. Thomas.
O triplex honor, o triforme culmen .	*h.* . .	St. Fructuosus. Pt. of "Felix Tarraco."
O veneranda Trinitas laudanda .	*a. b.* .	Holy Trinity.
Obduxere polum nubila coeli . .	*h.* . .	In time of rain.
Obsidiones obvias	*h** . .	First Watch.
Omnium Christe pariter tuorum .	*a. b. c. d. g.*	All Saints.
Optatus votis omnium . . .	*a. b. c. g.* .	Ascension.
Pange lingua gloriosi ; Praelium certaminis	*c. d. k.* .	Passiontide.
Parce, Domine, parce populo tuo .	*f.* . .	By St. Mugint.
Perfecto trino numero . . .	*a. b. c. d. g. i.*	Lent, at None.
Plasmator hominis Deus . . .	*a. b. c. d. g.*	Friday, at Vespers.
Plaudat polorum laudibus . .	*k.* . .	St. Mary Magdalene.
Plebs Deo dicata pollens . .	*h.* . .	SS. Cosmas and Damian.
Poculum esto vitae sitientibus .	*h.* . .	Pt. of "Favens redemptis." Mid Lent.
Post matutinas laudes . . .	*i.* . .	Lauds.
Post ut occasum resolvit . .	*h.* . .	Pt. of "Da, puer." Sat. in Easter Week.
Praeco benigne et decus ecclesiae .	*a. c. d.* .	St. Barnabas.
Praenuntiatrix usie Eximia . .	*k.* . .	St. Mary Magdalene.
Precamur Patrem Regem . . .	*e.* . .	The Apostles.
Primo dierum omnium . . .	*a. b. c. d. g. h** .	Nocturns. Sunday.
Prompta cuncta Catholicae . .	*h.* . .	St. Michael.
Proni rogamus Philippe os lampadis .	*a. b. c. d. g.*	St. Philip.
Psallat altitudo coeli . . .	*h.* . .	Pt. of "Da, puer." Low Sunday.
Puer hic sonat Johannes . .	*h.* . .	St. John Baptist.
Qua Christus hora sitiit . . .	*c. k.* .	Lent, at Sext.
Quaesumus ergo, Deus ut sereno .	*a. b. c.* .	Dedic. of a Church. Pt. of "Christe cunctorum."
Quarta die jam foetidus . . .	*h.* . .	Pt. of "A solis." 3rd S. in Lent.
Quem terra pontus aethera . .	*a. b. c. d. g.*	Annun. B. V. M.
Quieti tempus adest . . .	*h.** .	First Watch.
Quod chorus vatum venerandus olim	*a. b. c. d. g.*	Purification B. V. M.
Quod, quod volutis (convolutis) artubus	*h.** .	Midnight.
Recordemur justitiae . . .	*e.* . .	St. Comgill.
Rector potens verax Deus . .	*a. b. c. d. g.*	Sext.
Rerum Creator optime . . .	*a. b. c. d. g. h** .	Nocturns.
Rerum Deus tenax vigor . .	*a. b. c. d. g.*	None.
Restant nunc ad Christi fidem .	*h.* . .	SS. Nunilo and Alodia.
Rex aeterne Domine Creator Rerum .	*a. i. k.* .	Saturday, at Matins.
Rex angelorum dominator orbis .	*g.* . .	St. Oswald.
Rex angelorum praepotens . .	*d.* . .	Passiontide.
Rex Christe factor omnium . .	*d.* . .	Passiontide.
Rex Christe Martini decus . .	*k.* . .	St. Martin.
Rex Christe tu mirificas . .	*c.* . .	St. Martin.
Rex gloriose martyrum . . .	*a. b. c. d. g. h*	C. of Martyrs.
Romane Christi fortis assertor Dei .	*h.* . .	St. Romanus.
Sacratissimi martyres . . .	*e.* . .	C. of Martyrs.
Salve crux sancta salve mundi gloria	*c.* . .	Holy Cross.
Salvator mundi Domine . . .	*k.* . .	Vespers.
Sancta sanctorum opera . . .	*e.* . .	Abbots of Bangor.
Sancte Dei pretiose protomartyr Stephane	*a. c. d.* .	St. Stephen.
Sancti venite Christi corpus sumite .	*e.* . .	Communion of Priests.
Sanctissimae Leocadiae . . .	*h.* . .	St. Leocadia.
Sanctorum meritis inclita gaudia .	*a. b. c. d. g. h.* .	C. of Martyrs.
Scripta sunt coelo duorum . .	*h.* . .	SS. Emeterius, Chelidonius.
Sed cur vetustae gentis exemplum .	*h.* . .	Pt. of "O Nazarene." Fridays in Lent.
Sexta aetate virgine . . .	*c.* . .	Christmas, at Sext.
Sic ter quaternis trahitur . .	*a. c. d. i.*	Lent. Vespers or None.
Solve vocem mens sonoram . .	*h.* . .	Pt. of "Da, puer." Friday in Easter Week.
Somno refectis artubus . . .	*a. b. c. d. g. h** .	Monday, at Matins.

First line of Hymn.	MSS.	Use.
Spiritus divinae lucis	*e.*	Sunday at Matins.
Splendor paternae gloriae	*a. b. c. d. g. i.*	Tuesday at Matins.
Squalent arva soli pulvere multo	*h.*	For Rain.
Suetus antro bustualis	*h.*	Wed. in Easter Week. Pt. of "Da, puer."
Summa Dei bonitas	*a.*	St. Augustine.
Summae Deus clementiae	*a. b. c. d. g. h**	Saturday. Nocturns.
Summe confessor, sacer et sacerdos	*h.*	C. of Confessors.
Summe largitor praemii	*a. c. d.*	Lent.
Summe Salvator omnium	*a.*	Lent.
Surgentes ad te, Domine	*a. c. h**	Christmas. Nocturns.
Te centies mille legionum angeli	*h.*	Saturday before Easter.
Te deprecamur Dominum	*h**	A prayer in stanzas for chanting.
Te lucis ante terminum.	*a. b. c. d. g.*	Compline.
Te lucis auctor personent	*c.*	Easter.
Telluris ingens conditor.	*a. b. c. d g.*	Tuesday, at Vespers.
Tellus ac aether jubilent	*a. c.*	Maundy-Thursday.
Tempus noctis surgentibus	*i.*	Matins.
Tempus sopori congruum	*h**	First Watch.
Ternis ter horis numerus	*c. k.*	(No heading or title).
Tibi, Christe, splendor Patris	*a. b. c. d. g.*	St. Michael.
Tu Rex Redemptor omnium	*h**	Saturday. Matins.
Tu Trinitas Unitas, Orbem	*a. b. c. d. g. h**	Friday, at Nocturns.
Tunc ille Judas carnifex	*h.*	Pt. of "A solis." Maundy-Thursday.
Urbis magister Tasciae	*h.*	St. Cyprian.
Urbs beata Hierusalem	*c. h. k.*	Anniv. of Dedication of a Church.
Ut queant laxis resonare fibris	*a. b. c. g.*	St. John Baptist.
Ut tuae vitae Benedicte laudes	*a. b. c. d. g.*	St. Benedict.
Veni Creator Spiritus, Mentes	*a. b. c. g.*	Pentecost.
Veni redemptor gentium	*a. b. c. d. g. h*	Christmas.
Verus Redemptor Christe lumen luminis	*h.*	Consec. of a Bishop.
Verbum supernum prodiens A Patre	*a. b. c. d. g. h.*	Advent, at Nocturns.
Vexilla regis prodeunt	*a. b. c. d. g.*	Passiontide.
Virginis proles opifexque matris	*a. b. c. d. g. h.*	C. of Virgins.
Vocis auditae novitas refulsit.	*h.*	St. Saturninus.
Votiva cunctis orbita	*k.*	St. Mary Magdalene.
Vox clara ecce intonat	*a. b. c. d. g. h.*	Advent, at Matins.

Part II.—In this second part are given the first lines of hymns which are not included in the list in the first part of this article; and which are not (with a few exceptions) in the lists given under the article *Breviary.* In compiling this second list the following MS. *Hymnaria* are principally cited :—

(*q*) **Ashmole MS., 1525.** This is in the Bodleian, and formerly belonged to the monks at Canterbury. It is of the 13th cent., and contains a Psalter, Litany, Collects and Canticles ; with a complete *Hymnarium* for the ecclesiastical year.

(*r*) **Ashmole MS., 1523.** Also in the Bodleian. A Cluniac Bromholm MS., and of a similar nature as (*q*), but of the early 14th cent.

(*s*) **Additional MS., 18,301.** A MS. in the British Museum. This includes a *Hymnarium* of the 12th cent.

(*t*) **Cambridge University Library, Nn. iv. 11.**

This is a paper *Hymnarium* of the beginning of the 16th cent.

(*u*) **Liturg. Misc., 370.** This is in the Bodleian. It is a Psalter with a *Hymnarium* of the 13th cent.; apparently written for use at Padua.

(*x*) **Harleian MS., 4664.** A MS. of the beginning of the 14th cent., now in the British Museum. It contains a *Hymnarium* apparently written for use at Durham.

(*y*) **Arundel, 340.** A MS. of the 14th cent., now in the British Museum, and containing a *Hymnarium.*

The following list also includes a number of first lines drawn from mediaeval sources other than *Hymnaria,* for which it would be difficult to find a place elsewhere. In such cases references are given to the press marks of the MSS. The MSS. marked *Cott., Harl., Arundel, Reg., Add.* are in the British Museum. Those marked *Laud, Rawlinson, Digby, Ashmole, Canon,* are in the Bodleian. Those marked *c.c.c.* are in the Library of Corpus Christi College, Cambridge.

First line of Hymn.	MS. used, and where found.	Use.
Ad preces nostras Deitatis	*Add.*, 30,014	Lent.
Adest dies sanctissima	*s.*	St. Nicholas.
Adesto nobis inclite confessor.	*x.*	St. Cuthbert.
Alma Christi quando fides	*s. y. Laud. Mis.*, 468	St. Maurice.
Alma lux siderum.	*s. y.*	St. Dionysius.
Alpha et Ω magne Deus	*Arundel*, 201. *Canon. Mis.*, 266	To God.
Amorem sensus erige	*y*	Lent.
Andrea Christi famule	*r.*	Trans. of St. Andrew, pt. of "Summi Regis."
Angelus ad Virginem	*Laud. Mis.*, 748.	B. V. M.
Anglorum populi plaudite cuncti	*x.*	St. Cuthbert.
Anna partu solvitur	*Rawlinson, C.* 510	St. Anne.
Assertor aequi non ope regia.	*s. y.*	Pt. of "Almi prophetae." Decoll. St. John Baptist.
Astra polorum superascendens	*s. y.*	Ascension.
Audi virgo mater Christi	*Canon. Scriptt.*, 181	B. V. M.
Audite fratres facta	*Cott. Cleop. A.*, ii.	St. Monenna.

First line of Hymn.	MS. used, and where found.	Use.
Audite sancta studia .	*Cott. Cleop. A., ii.*	St. Monenna.
Augustine lux doctorum	*Canon. Scriptt.*, 89 . . .	St. Augustine.
Aula superna poli . .	*Camb. Univ. Lib. Gg.*, v. 35 . .	All Saints.
Aurea lux patriae Wentana .	*Cott. Nero E.*, 1.	St. Swithin.
Aures ad nostras, Deitatis preces	*u.*	Lent.
Ave dies praefulgida .	*c.c.c.* 371	St. Edward.
Ave gemma pretiosa .	*Cott. Cleop. C. vi.* . . .	St. Etheldreda.
Ave gloriosa Agnes .	*t.*	St. Agnes.
Ave Katherina, Martyr et Regina	*y.*	St. Katharine.
Ave maris stella, vera mellis stilla	*Rawlinson, C.*, 510	B. V. M.
Ave mater salvatoris, Vas	*Canon. Mis.*, 95.	B. V. M.
Ave regina coelorum Pia	*Canon. Lat.*, 112	B. V. M.
Ave stella maris Virgo .	*Laud. Mis.*, 368. . . .	B. V. M.
Ave stella matutina .	*Rawlinson, C.*, 108 . . .	B. V. M.
Ave Sunamitis lux Maria	*Rawlinson, C.*, 510 . . .	B. V. M.
Ave verbum ens in principio .	*Laud. Mis.*, 368. . . .	To Christ.
Ave virgo generosa .	*Canon. Mis.*, 100 . . .	St. Barbara.
Ave virgo mater Christi .	*Digby*, 166	B. V. M.
Ave virgo speciosa .	*Digby*, 19	B. V. M.
Ave virgo stella maris .	*Canon. Mis.*, 95. . . .	B. V. M.
Beate martyr prospera .	*r.*	St. Pancras.
Bonum simplex et perfectum .	*Rawlinson, C.*, 510 . . .	Holy Trinity.
Cantemus Domino grandia munera	*Add.*, 30,014	St. Monica.
Cantemus socii Domino.	*Harl.* 3072 . . . . ,	To Christ.
Cara parens pare carens	*Digby*, 166	B. V. M.
Ceteri tantum cecinere vatum	*r. Canon. Bibl.*, 30 . .	Pt. of " Ut queant." St. John Bapt.
Chori plaudant alacriter .	*t.*	St. Anne.
Chorus noster plaudat odis .	*Laud. Mis.*, 240. . . .	B. V. M.
Christe fili Jesu summi .	*s. y.* . . . *i*	St. Benedict.
Christe praesul pretiose .	*Laud. Lat.*, 95 . . .	St. Richard.
Christe qui virtus sator et vocaris	*s. y.*	All Saints.
Christe Salvator, pietatis auctor	*y.*	St. Nicholas.
Christi fidelis armiger .	*x.*	St. Oswald.
Christo coelorum agmina	*s. y.*	St. Maurice.
Cives coelestis patriae .	*Camb. Univ. Lib. Gg.* v., 35	Of the 12 precious stones.
Clara coelorum celebret.	*Add.*, 26,788 . . .	St. Heribert.
Coelestem regem veneremur .	*Canon. Lat.*, 273 . .	St. Augustine.
Coeli cives applaudite .	*Laud. Lat.*, 5 . . .	St. Augustine.
Coeli gemma bona . .	*Digby*, 100 . . .	St . Katharine
Confiteor Dominum nunc	*Camb. Univ. Lib. Gg.* v., 35	Nicene Creed.
Conjubilando coeli . .	*Add.*, 26,788 . . .	St Heribert.
Conscendat usque sidera	*s. t. y. Laud. Mis.*, 468 . .	St. Lawrence.
De Patre Verbum prodiens	*y.*	St. John Evangelist.
De profundis criminum .	*Digby*, 166 . . .	Lament. of a Sinner.
De sacro tabernaculo .	*Canon. Scriptt.*, 223 . .	Visit. B. V. M.
Dei testis egregius .	*r.*	St. Pancras.
Denum ter annorum cyclis .	*y.*	Epiphany. Pt. of " Jesus refulsit."
Deus, deorum Domine .	*Laud. Mis.*, 468 . . .	Invent. of St. Stephen.
Deus, qui mundum crimine jacentem	*Canon. Bibl.*, 30 . . .	Annunc. B. V. M.
Diem sacrati hominis .	*s.*	St. Andrew.
Dies absoluti praetereunt .	*y.*	Septuagesima.
Dulcis Jesu memoria .	*Laud. Mis.*, 668 ; *Rawlinson, C.*, 510..	To Christ.
Dunstanus en coelestia .	*q.*	St. Dunstan.
Dux gregis egregie .	*Digby*, 166	St. Thomas à Becket.
Excelse princeps omnium	*Add.*, 30,014	St. Monica.
Festa praesentis celebret diei.	*q.*	St. Benedict.
Festum nunc celebre magnaque gaudia	*s. u. y. Canon. Bibl.*, 30 . .	Vigil of Assumption, B. V. M.
Fons totius bonitatis .	*Add.*, 22,604 . . .	B. V. M:
Fontem misericordiae .	*Canon. Bibl.*, 1 . . .	St. Mary Magdalene.
Gaude flore virginali .	*Rawlinson, C.*, 553 . . .	B. V. M.
Gaude Gabrielis ore salutata .	*Rawlinson, C.*, 510 . . .	B. V. M.
Gaude mundi gaudium .	*Digby*, 86 . . .	B. V. M.
Gaude quae cuncta transisti	*Digby*, 19 . . .	B. V. M.
Gaude virgo concipiens .	*Ashmole*, 1398 . . .	B. V. M.
Gaude virgo laudabilis .	*Laud. Mis.*, 269 . . .	B. V. M.
Gaude virgo mater Christi	*Cott. Cleop. A., ii.* . .	B. V. M.
Gaudens in verbo sed turbata.	*Canon. Bibl.*, 30 . . .	Annun. B. V. M. Pt. of " Deus qui mundum."
Gemma Dei speciosa .	*Canon. Bibl.*, 40 . . .	St. Katharine.

First line of Hymn.	MS. used, and where found.	Use.
Hic est verus Christicola	s. y. .	One Confessor.
Hoc in templo summe Deus	t.	Pt. of "Urbs beata."
Hora novissima tempora pessima	Digby, 65.	The New Jerusalem.
Hujus diei gloria	s. y.	St. James.
Hymnum Deo vox jucunda	t.	St. Elizabeth.
Imbuit post hinc homines beatos	r. x. .	Pt. of "Christe sanctorum." St. Benedict.
In te concipitur o virgo regia	Digby, 2	B. V. M.
Jesu Christe auctor vitae	s. y. .	St. Mary Magdalene.
Jesu ex Deo genitus	Camb. Univ. Lib., Gg. 1, 32	To Christ.
Jesu redemptor omnium	s.	St. Martin.
Jesu vera dulcedinis	Laud. Mis., 368	To Christ.
Juste judex Jesu Christe	Laud. Mis., 216 ; Arundel, 201	To Christ.
Katharinae collaudemus Virtutum insignia	u.	St. Katharine.
Laudes Christo cum canticis	r.	St. Mary Magdalene.
Laudibus summis, celebremus omnes	Add., 30,014	St. Nicholas (Tolent.).
Laus angelorum inclita	s. y.	St. Andrew.
Lavacra puri gurgitis	t.	Pt. of "A solis."
Lux Deus aeterna	Digby, 65	Holy Trinity.
Lux et decus ecclesiae	u.	St. Prosdocimus.
Lux maris gaude	y.	Purif. B. V. M.
Macte summe confessorum	y.	St. Rupert, Pt. of "Eja fratres, extollamus." (Mone, No. 1115)
Magne pater Augustine	Laud. Lat., 5	St. Augustine.
Magno salutis gaudio	r.	St. Mary Magdalene.
Magno salutis gaudio	t.	Passiontide.
Mare, fons, ostium atque terrarum	Laud. Mis., 468	St. Willibald.
Maria Mater Domini, Maria soror	u.	St. Mary Magdalene.
Maria stella maris	Digby, 86 ; Laud Mis., 368	B. V. M.
Mariae virginis fecundat	Add., 22,684	B. V. M.
Martine par apostolis	r. x.	St. Martin. Pt. of "Rex Christe Martini."
Martyr egregie, Deo dilecte	y.	St. Blasius.
Me similem cineri	Reg. 2, A. xx.	To God.
Mente canam Domino	Reg. 2, A. xx.	Holy Trinity.
Miserere mei Deus	Digby, 166	Lament. of a sinner.
Mundi creator maxime	Add., 30,014	St. Nicholas (Tolent.).
Mysterium ecclesiae	Add., 31,385	B. V. M.
Mysterium mirabile	Add., 31,385	Pt. of "Hic est dies." Easter.
Nate Rex summe	y.	Assump. B. V. M.
Novum sidus emicuit	t.	St. Elizabeth.
O beata Trinitas	Laud. Mis., 468	Holy Trinity.
O crucifer bone, lucisator	Harl., 3072	Passiontide.
O cunctis excelsior	t.	B. V. M.
O dee cunctipotens	Camb. Univ. Lib., Gg. 1 , 35	To God and Christ.
O grande cunctis gaudium	Add., 31,385	Pt. of "Optatus votis." Ascension.
O inclite confessor Christi	Cott. Nero., A. ii.	St. Dunstan.
O mira creatura	Laud. Mis., 368	B. V. M.
O Pater aeterne	Digby, 65	Holy Trinity.
O quam beata femina	Laud. Lat., 95	St. Mary Magdalene.
O redemptor sume carmen	ccc. 190, and 473	To Christ.
O sancta mundi domina	s. y.	Nativ. B. V. M.
O sepulchrum Jesu Christi	Canon. Mis., 528	Sepulchre of Christ.
O Trinitas laudabilis	t. Add., 30,014	Holy Trinity.
O vere digna hostia	t.	Pt. of "Ad coenam."
O virgo beatissima	y.	Assump. B. V. M.
Olivae binae pietatis unicae	t.	Pt. of "Aurea luce."
Omnes superni ordines	Laud. Mis., 468	All Saints.
Omnipotens solus regnas	Camb. Univ. Lib., Gg. c., 35	To God.
Optata saeclis gaudia	Add., 26,788	St. Heribert.
Ortum Modwennae dat Hibernia	Cott. Cleop., A. ii.	St. Monenna.
Panditur mundus simul omnis illi	q.	St. Benedict.
Pange lingua gloriosae virginis	t.	St. Agnes.
Pange lingua gloriosi praesulis	Laud. Lat., 95	St. Richard.
Pange lingua Magdalenae	Rawlinson, A., 420	St. Mary Magdalene.
Pastis visceribus ciboque sumpto	Harl., 3072	After food.

First line of Hymn.	MS. used, and where found.	Use.
Pater noster qui es in coelis	*Digby*, 166	A metrical version.
Peccatrix quaedam femina	*u.*	St. Mary Magdalene.
Per te nitescat Rex Deus	*q.*	St. Dunstan.
Petrus beatus catenarum	*s.*	Pt. of "Felix per omnes." St. Peter.
Phoebus astris cum omnibus phoebae	*u.*	St. Justina.
Pie colamus annua	*Laud. Lat.*, 95 ; *Laud. Lat.*, 5	St. Mary Magdalene
Praefulgens sidus anglicum	*Digby*, 166	St. Thomas à Becket.
Psallat haec concio sonora carmina	*Cott. Cleop.*, *C. vi.*	St. Nicholas.
Quasi thus ardens in igne	*Laud. Mis.*, 240	St. Thomas à Becket.
Rector aeterni metuende saecli	*Add.*, 21,170	St. Otmar.
Regalis ostro sanguinis	*x.*	St. Oswald.
Regina clementiae Maria	*Digby*, 86 ; *Harl.* 524	B. V. M.
Salamonici mysteria	*Rawlinson, C.*, 938	St. Edith.
Salve de qua Deo gratum	*Digby*, 19	B. V. M.
Salve festa dies felix octava	*Digby*, 53	Eastertide.
Salve festa dies qua Christus	*Digby*, 53	Ascension.
Salve festa dies quam	*Digby*, 53	Pentecost.
Salve mater misericordiae	*Camb. Univ. Lib., Gg. v.*, 35	B. V. M.
Salve per quam fit sodalis	*Digby*, 19	B. V. M.
Salve sancta dies celebri	*c.c.c.*, 371	St. Dunstan.
Salve sancta facies nostri	*Ashmole*, 1291	Face of Christ.
Salve sancta parens	*t.*	St. Anne.
Salve virgo gloriosa	*Canon. Bibl.*, 40	B. V. M.
Salve virgo virginum	*Digby*, 86	B. V. M.
Sancte Blasi plebi tuae subveni	*y.*	St. Blasius.
Sancte Pater summa	*Camb. Univ. Lib., Gg. v.*, 35	The Lord's Prayer.
Sancte sator, legis	*Camb. Univ. Lib., Gg. v.*, 35	To Christ.
Sidus solare revehit	*t.*	St. Mary Magdalene.
Signum crucis mirabile	*t. Add.*, 30,848	Holy Cross.
Sion devetae filiae	*t.*	St. Agnes.
Sollemnis dies advenit	*s. y.*	St. John Evang.
Spiritus alme Dei	*Digby*, 65	Holy Trinity.
Stella maris quae sola paris	*Digby*, 65	B. V. M.
Stephano primo martyri	*s. y.*	St. Stephen.
Summe summi tu Patris Unice	*Canon. Mis.*, 95	Holy Trinity.
Summi regis potentia	*r.*	Transl. of St. Andrew.
Te canunt omnes Nicolae gentes	*Add.*, 30,014	St. Nicholas (Tolent.).
Te ferant linguae celebrentque omnes	*Add.*, 30,014	St. Monica.
Te matrem laudamus	*Rawlinson, B.*, 214	B. V. M.
Te nunc laudamus	*Camb. Univ. Lib., Gg. v.*, 35	The Te Deum.
Te nunc sancte speculator	*c.c.c.*, 390	St. Hedda.
Tortoris risit verbera	*r.*	St. Pancras. Pt. of "Dei testis."
Ut fons fecundus	*Laud. Lat.*, 95	To Christ.
Venter puellaris expers tamen maris	*Digby*, 166	B. V. M.
Vera regni perfruens	*Arundel*, 201	St. Guthlac.
Vere gratia plena es	*Add.*, 31,385	Pt. of "Mysterium ecclesiae."
Virens ave virgula	*Laud. Mis.*, 240	B. V. M.
Virgo decus coeli	*Add.*, 17,281	B. V. M.
Virgo Templum Trinitatis	*Laud. Mis.*, 352	B. V. M.
Virgo vincens vernancia	*Laud. Mis.*, 368	B. V. M.
Vita sanctorum decus angelorum	*s.*	Easter.
Vita sanctorum via spes salusque	*s. y. Add.*, 21,170	St. Gall.

The hymns in the above lists are mostly of unknown authorship. They are of varying merit, many, especially those in the second list, hardly rising above the level of doggerel. Many of them have never been printed and hence have escaped observation, and are not to be found in the collections of *Daniel* and *Mone*. The index of first lines may be of use to persons who are interested in the obscurer Latin hymns of the later middle ages. An examination of other MSS. than those specified as made use of in this article would no doubt swell the list. Private libraries and the libraries of separate colleges at Oxford and Cambridge remain to be searched for such a purpose.   [F. E. W. and J. M.]

Hymnum canamus Domino [gloriae]. *Venerable Bede.* [*Ascension.*] This hymn, usually ascribed to Bede, is found in two MSS. of the 11th cent. in the British Museum (*Vesp.* D. xii. f. 72 b; *Jul.* A. vi. f. 50), and in the *Lat. Hys. of the Anglo-Saxon Church* (Surtees Society), 1851, is printed from an 11th cent. MS. at Durham, in 11 st. of 4 l. (B. iii., 32 f. 25 b). In an 11th cent. MS. in the British Museum (Add. 30848 f. 153 b.) it begins, "Hymnum canamus *gloriae*," and this reading is followed by *Thomasius*, ii. p. 372; by *Daniel*, i., No. 172; by Card. Newman in his *Hymni Ecclesiae*, 1838 and 1865; and others.   [J. M.]

Translations in C. U. :—

1. **The hymn of glory sing we.** By W. J. Blew, in his *Church Hy. and Tune Bk.*, 1852–5; and again in Rice's *Sel.* from the same 1870.

2. **Sing we triumphant hymns of praise.** By B. Webb, in the *H. Noted*, 1854, in 7 st. of 4 l., and again in the *Hymner*, 1882.

3. **A hymn of glory let us sing.** By Elizabeth Charles in her *Voice of Christian Life in Song*, &c., 1858, p. 141, in 6 st. of 4 l. It was repeated in the *People's H.*, 1867; Schaff's *Christ in Song*, 1869 and 1870; and the *Hymnary* (much altered), 1872.

Translation not in C. U. :—
Sing we triumphant hymns of praise. J. D. Chambers, 1857.

All these *trs.* are from the "Hymnum canamus gloriae" form of the text.   [J. J.]

Hymnum canentes martyrum. *Venerable Bede.* [*The Holy Innocents.*] Included, ascribed to Bede, in Cassander's *Hymni Ecclesiastici*, Cologne, 1556, and repeated by *Ellinger*, 1578, p. 256; *Bässler*, No. 63, and others. Also in Dr. Giles's ed. of Bede's *Opera*, vol. i., Lond., 1843, p. 81, in 8 st. of 8 l. *Daniel*, i., No. 176, quotes only st. i. The first and last lines of each stanza are identical, a device which here produces a somewhat unnatural effect, and rather spoils an otherwise fine hymn. [See **Bede**.]   [J. M.]

Translations in C.U. :—

1. **The hymn for conquering martyrs raise.** By J. M. Neale, in his *Mediaeval Hys.*, 1851, p. 15, in 6 st. of 8 l., with short critical and historical notes. It was repeated in the *People's H.*, 1867, and in an abridged form in the *Hymnary*, 1872.

2. **A hymn for martyrs sweetly sing.** This in *H. A. & M.*, 1861, is Dr. Neale's *tr.* altered by the compilers.

3. **A voice from Ramah was there sent.** In *Kennedy*, 1863, No. 198, begins with st. iii. of Dr. Neale's *tr.* as above.

Translation not in C. U. :—
A hymn of martyrs let us sing. Mrs. Charles, 1858. (Tr. of 8 lines only.)   [J. J.]

I

I., in Bristol Bap. *Coll.* of Ash & Evans, 1st ed., 1769, i.e. W. Jesse.

I. A. E., in H. V. Elliott's *Ps. & Hys.*, 1835, i.e. Julia A. Elliott.

I. D., in *Ash & Evans*, 1769, i.e. I. Dixon.

I. L., in Beard's *Coll.*, 1837, i.e. John Lagniel.

I. S., in *Ash & Evans*, i.e. J. Stennett.

I am not worthy, Holy Lord. *Sir H. W. Baker.* [*Holy Communion.*] Written for and first pub. in *H. A. & M.*, 1875. It is also in several other hymnals.

I am, saith Christ, your glorious Head. *J. Newton.* [*Easter.*] 1st pub. in the *Olney Hymns*, 1779, Bk. i., No. 116, in 7 st. of 4 l., and headed "The Resurrection and the Life." The most popular form of the hymn is that given to it by Cotterill in the 8th ed. of his *Sel.*, 1819, No. 18. This is composed of st. iv., ii., v.–vii. in the order named, and altered to, "Pour down Thy Spirit, gracious Lord." It is in extensive use, and sometimes as: "Pour *out* Thy Spirit," &c. Another form was given in Stowell's Manchester *Sel.*, 1831, p. 87, and is still in C. U. It begins, "Fulfil Thy promise, gracious Lord," and is composed of st. iv.–vi., and slightly altered.   [J. J.]

I am the man who long have known. *C. Wesley.* [*Temptation.*] Pub. in *Hys. & Sac. Poems*, 1740, p. 84, in 20 st. of 4 l., and headed, "Written in stress of Temptation." (*P. Works*, 1868–72, vol. i. p. 273.) In 1780, J. Wesley included a *cento* in 8 st. from this hymn in the *Wes. H. Bk.*, No. 151, as:—"My sufferings all to Thee are known." This has been repeated in several collections in G. Britain and America. Mr. G. J. Stevenson has given in his *Meth. H. Bk. Notes*, 1883, many pleasing associations of this hymn.   [J. J.]

I asked the Lord that I might grow. *J. Newton.* [*The Sinner's Prayer Answered.*] Pub. in his *Twenty-six Letters on Religious Subjects, &c.*, by Omicron, 1774, in 7 st. of 4 l., and headed "The Converted Sinner," again in R. Conyers's *Coll.*, 1774, No. 353, and again in the *Olney Hymns*, 1779, Bk. iii., No. 36, with the heading changed to "Prayer answered by Crosses." Although of a specially personal and subjective character, it has been somewhat extensively adopted for congregational use, both in Great Britain and America.   [J. J.]

I cannot call affliction sweet. *J. Montgomery.* [*Affliction.*] The origin of this hymn is thus given by Holland in his *Memoirs* of Montgomery:—

"On the 24th May [1832] the poet returned to Sheffield from Bristol, where he had been attending religious meetings. An album was immediately put into his hand from a lady in London who had long been an admirer of his poetry, and although now on her deathbed, could not repress an intense desire to see his handwriting in her book. He was affected by her appeal, and inscribed the lines beginning 'I cannot call affliction sweet.'" *Memoirs*, v. 43.

This hymn is amongst the M. MSS., but is undated. It was pub. in Montgomery's *Poet's Portfolio*, 1835, p. 252, in 4 st. of 4 l., and headed "An After-Thought." It was repeated in his *Original Hys.*, 1853, and is in several modern collections.   [J. J.]

I gave My life for thee. *Frances R. Havergal.* [*Christ desiring the entire devotion of His Servants.*] Miss M. V. G. Havergal's MS. account of this hymn is :—

"In F. R. H.'s MS. copy, she gives this title, 'I did this for thee; what hast thou done for Me?' Motto placed under a picture of our Saviour in the study of a German divine. On Jan. 10, 1858, she had come in weary, and sitting down she read the motto, and the lines of her hymn flashed upon her. She wrote them in pencil on a scrap of paper. Reading them over she thought them so poor that she tossed them on the fire, but they fell out untouched. Showing them some months after to her father, he encouraged her to preserve them, and wrote the tune *Baca* specially for them. The hymn was printed on a leaflet, 1859, and in *Good Words*, Feb., 1869. Pub. also in *The Ministry of Song*, 1869. Though

F. R. H. consented to the alterations in *Church Hymns,* she thought the original more strictly carried out the idea of the motto, 'I gave My life for thee, What hast thou done for Me?'" (H. MSS.).

Miss F. R. Havergal also refers to this hymn in a letter quoted in her *Memoirs,* p. 105:—

"I was so overwhelmed on Sunday at hearing three of my hymns touchingly sung in Perry Church, I never before realized the high privilege of writing for the 'great congregation,' especially when they sang 'I gave My life for thee' to my father's tune *Baca.*"

The recast of this hymn for the S. P. C. K. *Church Hymns,* 1871, referred to above, begins, "Thy life was given for me." The original appeal of Christ to the disciple is thus changed into an address by the disciple to Christ. This recast has not become popular. The original, as in Snepp's *Songs of G. & G.,* 1872, is in extensive use in Great Britain and America.   [J. J.]

I give immortal praise. *I. Watts.* [*Praise. A Doxology.*] Appeared in his *Hys. & Spiritual Songs,* 2nd ed., 1709, Bk. iii., No. 38, in 4 st. of 8 l., and entitled, "A Song of Praise to the Blessed Trinity." In its original form it is not often found; but as "We give immortal praise," it is in C. U. in all English-speaking countries. This slightly altered text was given in G. Whitefield's *Ps. & Hys.,* 1753; in M. Madan's *Ps. & Hys.,* 1760; in A. M. Toplady's *Ps. & Hys.,* 1776, and others to modern hymn-books. In Kennedy, it is recast as "To God the Father yield," but this form is in limited use. [J. J.]

I have a home above. *H. Bennett.* [*Heaven.*] Pub. in the Bap. *Ps & Hys.,* 1858, No. 598, in 5 st. of 8 l. (in later eds. it is dated 1851), and in the author's *Hymns by H. B.* in 1867, in 10 st. of 4 l., and headed, "The Christian's Home." It has come into extensive use in G. Britain and America. [J. J.]

I have renewed, O Lord, my vow. *J. M. Neale.* [*First Communion.*] Pub. in his *Hys. for the Young,* 1844, No. 9, in 11 st. of 4 l., and headed, "The First Holy Communion." In the S. P. C. K. *Church Hys.,* 1871, No. 202, "Behold Thy servant drawing near," is composed of st. iv., v., viii. and x., slightly altered from this hymn. [J. J.]

I hear a sound [voice] that comes from far. *T. Kelly.* [*The Voice of Mercy.*] Pub. in the 2nd ed. of his *Hymns on Various Passages of Scripture,* 1806, in 6 st. of 4 l. (ed. 1853, No. 327). It is usually given in an abbreviated form, and sometimes as, "I hear a *voice* that comes from far," as in Hatfield's *Church H. Bk.,* N. Y., 1872, &c. [J. J.]

I hear the words of love. *H. Bonar.* [*Good Friday—Holy Communion.*] Appended in the 2nd series of his *Hys. of Faith & Hope,* 1861, in 10 st. of 4 l., and headed, "He died and lives." Two centos from this hymn are in C. U., both beginning with st. i. The first, suitable for Passiontide, is in Nicholson's *Appendix Hymnal,* 1866; and the second, for Holy Communion, in *Laudes Domini,* N. Y., 1884. [J. J.]

I heard the voice of Jesus say. *H. Bonar.* [*Christ's Invitation.*] Written at Kelso, and pub. in his *Hys. Original and Selected,* 1846, and in the 1st series of his

Hymns of Faith & Hope, 1857, in 3 st. of 8 l., and headed, "The Voice from Galilee." It has come into extensive use, and is one of the most popular of the author's hymns. It is often used in Home Mission Services, and is suited thereto. It has been rendered into Latin by Dr. Macgill in his *Songs of the Christian Creed and Life,* 1876, as "Loquentem exaudivi." [J. J.]

I know not if the dark or bright. *H. Alford.* [*Resignation.*] Written in 1862, and printed in *Macmillan's Magazine,* 1863, in 7 st. of 4 l. In 1865 it was included in the author's *Poetical Works,* and in 1884 in Horder's *Cong. Hymns.* [J. J.]

I know that my Redeemer lives, And ever prays for me. *C. Wesley.* [*Rejoicing in hope.*] Pub. in *Hys. & Sac. Poems,* 1742, p. 180, in 23 st. of 4 l., and entitled, "Rejoicing in Hope." (*P. Works,* 1868–72, vol. ii. p. 242.) Two centos from this hymn, both beginning with st. i., are in C. U.:—

1. In Toplady's *Ps. & Hys.,* 1776, No. 290, in 8 st. This is in use in the Church of England.

2. In the *Wes. H. Bk.,* 1780, in 9 st., No. 373 (ed. 1875, No. 384). This is the arrangement commonly found in the Methodist hymn-books (but sometimes abbreviated) in G. Britain and America. Stevenson has an interesting note on this cento in his *Meth. H. Bk. Notes,* 1883, p. 265. [J. J.]

I know that my Redeemer lives, He lives, and on the earth. *C. Wesley.* [*Resurrection.*] Appeared in *Hys. & Sac. Poems,* 1742, in 4 st. of 8 l., and based on Job xix. 25. (*P. Works,* 1868–72, vol. ii. p. 182.) It was included in the 1830 suppl. to the *Wes. H. Bk.,* and retained in the 1875 ed. This hymn was included in Toplady's *Ps. & Hys.,* 1776, No. 64, with an additional stanza from Wesley's *Funeral Hys.,* 1st series, 1746, No. 9, st. xiii., "Ev'n now I taste that bliss divine." [J. J.]

I know that my Redeemer lives. What comfort this, &c. *S. Medley.* [*Easter.*] This hymn is found in the 21st ed. of G. Whitefield's *Ps. & Hys.,* 1775, in 9 st. of 4 l., and in the 4th ed. of De Courcy's *Coll.,* 1793, No. 258; but in each case without signature. Medley included it in the London ed. of his *Hymns,* 1800. It was also repeated in the Cambridge ed., 1839. In an abbreviated form it is in somewhat extensive use, and is easily known by the frequent repetition of the words "He lives!" The cento, "The Saviour lives, no more to die," is also popular; but that in the American *Bapt. Praise Book,* 1871, "He lives, my kind, wise, heavenly Friend," is limited in use. Both forms of the text are in C. U. in G. Britain and America. [J. J.]

I lay my sins on Jesus. *H. Bonar.* [*Jesus, the Substitute.*] 1st pub. in the 1st series of his *Songs in th? Wilderness,* 1843, in 4 st. of 8 l., and headed, "The Fulness of Jesus." It was repeated in his *Bible H. Bk.,* 1845, No. 122, and in the 1st series of his *Hys. of Faith & Hope,* 1857. In the *Hys.,* &c., it is entitled "The Substitute." In the American Bapt. H. [& Tune] Bk., 1871, it is given as two hymns, the second beginning "I rest my soul on Jesus." In various forms the hymn is very popular for Home Mission

Services, and is in extensive use in G. Britain and America. [J. J.]

I left the God of truth and light. *J. Montgomery.* [*Repentance.*] In 1795, Montgomery commenced in his paper, the *Sheffield Iris,* a series of essays under the title of " The Whisperer, or Hints and Speculations, by Gabriel Silvertongue Gent." These essays, which were afterwards republished in a volume, abounded in the irreverent use of Holy Scripture. The state of mind which prompted him thus to write continued, he says, " for the space of ten years." (*Memoirs,* vol. ii. p. 116.) On seeing clearly the wrong which he had done, he destroyed all the copies of the work which he could find, and penned this hymn, in 1807, in token of his true repentance. (*Memoirs,* vol. v. p. 364.) It was first pub. in the *Evangelical Magazine,* subsequently in Cotterill's *Selection,* 8th ed., 1819, No. 295; and then by Montgomery as the first of his hymns in his *Christian Psalmist,* 1825. It is also in his *Original Hys.*, 1853, No. 171. In the *Christian Psalmist,* st. ii., l. 3, reads : " Through all His *bonds* of love I broke." In all his other works we find "*bands*" for "*bonds.*" In his marked copy of the *Ch. Psalmist,* he has changed "*bonds*" to "*bands*" in the margin. This is the authorized reading. In the *Hys. & Songs of Praise,* N. Y., 1874, No. 479, " Heart-broken, friendless, poor, cast down," is composed of st. vii., viii. of this hymn. [J. J.]

I lift my soul to God. *I. Watts.* [*Ps. xxv.*] Part i. of his version of Ps. xxv. in his *Psalms of David,* &c., 1719, in 6 st. of 4 l., headed " Waiting for Pardon and Direction." In the *Church Pastorals,* Boston, 1864, and other American collections, st. iii.–vi. are given as, " From the first dawning light." A cento in the *Leeds H. Bk.*, 1853, No. 31, begins with the same stanza. It is composed of st. ii., iv. of Pt. i.; st. i., vii., viii. of Pt. iii. The American arrangement is the more popular of the two. [J. J.]

I love the sacred book of God. *T. Kelly.* [*Holy Scripture.*] This hymn is in two forms, and both by Kelly. The first form was pub. in the 1st ed. of his *Hys. on Various Passages of Scripture,* 1804, in 7 st. of 4 l.; and the second in the Dublin ed., 1836, No. 391. Both forms are in C. U.; the first in *Windle,* and the revised in Snepp's *Songs of G. & G.,* 1872. Various collections in G. Britain and America, some in the original, and others in the revised form. These can be tested by *Windle* and *Snepp.* [J. J.]

I need Thee, precious Jesus. *F. Whitfield.* [*Longing for Jesus.*] This hymn first appeared as a hymn-sheet in 1855, in 6 st. of 4 double lines. It was then included in the author's *Sacred Poems and Prose.* On the publication of this volume in 1861, the author found that his first stanza, which began,

" I need Thee, precious Jesus, for I am full of sin,"

was omitted without his sanction, and the hymn began with st. ii. :—

" I need Thee, precious Jesu, for I am very poor."

Although the author at once reprinted the full text in self-defence, the mutilated hymn

came into C. U., and was generally received as the original. Both it and the original (usually in 4 sts.) are in extensive use in all English-speaking countries. In a more or less complete form it has also been *tr.* into numerous languages, including French, Dutch, German, Arabic, &c. The author specially desires that his original text may be followed, as in Bp. Ryle's *Hys. for the Church,* 1860. [J. J.]

I once was a stranger to grace and to God. *R. M. McCheyne.* [*The Lord our Righteousness.*] Appeared in the *Scottish Christian Herald,* March, 1836, in 7 st. of 8 l., and entitled " Jehovah Tsidkenu," " The Lord our Righteousness—The watchword of the Reformation,' and signed " Larbert . . . R. McC." In 1844 it was included by A. Bonar in his *Memoir & Remains* of McCheyne, p. 582, and dated " November, 18, 1834." Its use, especially in America, is extensive. [J. J.]

I prais'd the earth in beauty seen. *Bp. R. Heber.* [*Flower Services.*] Pub. in his posthumous *Hymns,* &c., 1827, p. 92, in 3 st. of 6 l., and appointed for the 4th S. after Trinity. It is well suited for Flower Services, and is found in several modern collections. [J. J.]

I sing the Almighty [Mighty] power of God. *I. Watts.* [*Praise for Creation and Providence.*] Appeared in his *Divine Songs for Children,* 1715, in 8 st. of 4 l., and headed, " Praise for Creation and Providence." Although seldom used in its complete form, arrangements of the text, varying in the number of stanzas taken, are in C. U. in all English-speaking countries. It is sometimes given as " I sing the mighty power of God," but this reading is not popular. [J. J.]

I sojourn in a vale of tears. *J. Mason.* [*Hope.*] 1st pub. in his *Songs of Praise,* &c., 1683, No. 30, in 9 st. of 8 l., as the " Song of Praise for the Hope of Glory," and repeated in D. Sedgwick's reprint, 1859, p. 46. From it three centos are in C. U. :—

1. I sojourn in a vale of tears. In use in America specially.
2. And dost Thou come, O blessed Lord. In Bickersteth's *Christian Psalmist,* 1833, No. 535, and others.
3. My Saviour is gone up to heaven.
In *Bickersteth,* 1833, No. 536. and others.

The text of all these centos is slightly altered from the original. [J. J.]

I thank Thee, Lord, for using me. *H. Bonar.* [*Joy in the Service of God.*] Appeared in the 3rd series of his *Hys. of Faith and Hope,* 1866, in 15 st. of 4 l., and headed, " Forget not all His Benefits." In the *Cong. Church Hyl.,* 1887, 12 st. are given as one hymn in two parts, Pt. ii. beginning, " I thank Thee, gracious God, for all." Several arrangements from this hymn, all opening with st. i., are in C. U. Sometimes these are given as, "*We* thank Thee, Lord, for using *us.*" The use thus made of this hymn is somewhat extensive. [J. J.]

I that am drawn out of the depth. *J. Mason.* [*Deliverance from Spiritual Affliction.*] 1st pub. in his *Songs of Praise,* &c., 1683, No. 23, in 5 st. of 8 l. and 1 st. of 4 l., and entitled " A Song of Praise for Deliverance from Spiritual Troubles." It was repeated in D. Sedgwick's reprint, 1859, p. 43. From this hymn the cento, "God's furnace doth in Zion stand," in Alexander's *Augustine H. Bk.*, 1849 and 1865, Spurgeon's *O. O. H. Bk.*, 1866, and others, is taken. It begins with st. iv. The cento in the American Unitarian *Hy. [& Tune] Bk. for the Church and Home*, Boston, 1868, "The world can neither give nor take," is composed thus :—st. i. from Mason's "My God, my reconciled God"; and st. ii., iii. from this hymn.   [J. J.]

I thirst, but not as once I did. *W. Cowper.* [*Thirsting for God.*] Given in the *Olney Hymns*, 1779. Bk. iii., No. 61, in 5 st. of 4 l., and headed, "My soul thirsteth for God." It is found in several American collections, and in a few also in G. Britain.

I thirst, Thou wounded Lamb of God. [*Union with Christ.*] This hymn, by John Wesley, first appeared in *Hys. & Sacred Poems*, 1740 (*P. Works*, 1868-72, vol. i. p. 265), thus—

1. "I thirst, Thou wounded Lamb of God,
   To wash me in thy cleansing Blood,
   To dwell within thy Wounds; then Pain
   Is sweet, and Life or Death is Gain.

2. "Take this poor Heart, and let it be
   For ever clos'd to all but Thee!
   Seal Thou my Breast, and let me wear
   That Pledge of Love for ever there.

3. "How blest are they who still abide,
   Close shelter'd in thy bleeding Side!
   Who Life and Strength from thence derive,
   And by Thee move, and in Thee live.

4. "What are our Works, but Sin and Death,
   'Till Thou thy quick'ning Spirit breathe?
   Thou giv'st the Power thy Grace to move;
   O wondrous Grace! O boundless Love!

5. "How can it be, Thou heavenly King,
   That Thou should'st us to Glory bring;
   Make Slaves the Partners of thy Throne,
   Deck'd with a never-fading Crown?

6. "Hence our Hearts melt, our Eyes o'erflow,
   Our Words are lost; nor will we know,
   Nor will we think of ought beside
   My Lord, my Love is crucify'd!

7. "Ah! Lord, enlarge our scanty Thought,
   To know the Wonders Thou hast wrought;
   Unloose our stammering Tongues, to tell
   Thy Love immense, unsearchable.

8. "First-born of many Brethren, Thou!
   To Thee, lo! all our Souls we bow,
   To Thee our Hearts and Hands we give,
   Thine may we die, Thine may we live!"

This hymn is made up from four German hymns, all of which appeared in *Appendix* vii. to the *Herrnhut G. B.*, 1735. (See notes on their first lines.) Of Wesley's hymn st. i., ii., are based on st. i., iii. of *N. L. von Zinzendorf's*

1. "Ach! mein verwundter Fürste!
   Nach dessen Blut ich dürste,
   In dem mein Sehnen ruht,
   An dessen Liebesherze
   Mir wohl ist, und der Schmerze
   Selbst heilsam, gut und sanfte thut.

3. "Nimm mich mit Liebeserbarmen
   Beim Herz und bei den Armen,
   Und setz ein Siegel drauf;
   Lass mich verschlossen werden
   Von dem Geräusch der Erden,
   Dir aber mache selber auf."

Stanzas iii.-vi. are based on *J. Nitschmann's*

1. "Du blutiger Verstöhner!
   Der Kreuzgemeine Diener!
   Du unser Seelenmann!
   Wir fall'n zu deinen Füssen,
   Und wollen sie umschliessen,
   So gut ein Arm des Glaubens kann.

2. "Wir sind ja kleine Kinder,
   Erlöste arme Sünder,
   Die deinen Lebenssaft,
   Der aus der Seitenhöhle
   Geflossen auf die Seele,
   In sich gesaugt zur Gotteskraft.

3. "Das ist der Heil'gen Stärke,
   Dass gar nicht unsre Werke
   Das blutbefreundte Lamm,
   Uns Gnade zu erzeigen,
   Bewegen oder neigen;
   Die Liebe dringt es wundersam.

4. "Wir wissen nichts zu sagen,
   Als dich erstaunt zu fragen,
   Ists möglich? Königssohn!
   Dass du gebornen Sclaven
   Hilfst in den Freiheitshafen,
   Und sie bestimmst zu Kron und Thron.

5. "Das macht uns Liebesschmerzen,
   Wie Wachs sind unsre Herzen,
   Ja wie die Stäublein gar;
   Wir lassen Thränen fliessen,
   Und wollen sonst nichts wissen,
   Als dass ein Lamm geschlachtet war."

Stanza vii. is based on st. i., ii. of *Zinzendorf's*

1. "Der Gott von unserm Bunde,
   Der sein Lob in dem Munde,
   Der Säuglingen bereit,
   Der lass uns kräftig fühlen,
   Wie die Register spielen
   Der Gotteslieb in dieser Zeit.

2. "Er geb uns muntre Kehlen,
   Die Wunder zu erzählen,
   Die seine Treue thut:
   Ein an den Wunden trinken:
   Ein inniges Versinken,
   Und einen kindlich frohen Muth."

Stanza viii. is based on st. xiv. of a hymn by *Anna Nitschmann*, which begins "Mein König deine Liebe."

14. "Nun, erstgeborner Bruder!
    Nun Meister an dem Ruder
    Des Schiffleins der Gemein:
    Ich geb dir Herz und Hände
    Dass ich bis an mein Ende
    Will deine treue Seele seyn."

Wesley's *tr.* was first adopted for congregational use as No. 61 in the *Moravian H. Bk.*, 1742, in full and unaltered. In the 1789 and later eds. it is abridged and begins "We pray Thee, wounded Lamb of God." In 1753 Wesley's full text was given in his *H. & Spiritual Songs*, No. 14, and repeated in the *Wes. H. Bk.*, 1780. It is also in the *Leeds H. Bk.*, 1853, *People's Hyl.*, 1867, and others. It is found in the following abridged or altered forms :—

1. **Jesu, Thou wounded Lamb of God** (i. alt.). The *Hym. Companion*, and others.
2. **O come, Thou wounded Lamb of God** (i. alt.). Whitefield's *Hymns*, &c., 1753; Madan's *Ps. & Hys.*, 1760, and others.
3. **O come, Thou stricken Lamb of God** (i. alt.). Walker's *Ps. & Hys.*, 1855, &c.
4. **Jesus, Thou holy Lamb of God** (i. alt.). Rugby Church *H. Bk.*, 1839.
5. **We pray Thee, wounded Lamb of God** (i. alt.), in Robinson's *Songs for the Sanctuary*, N.Y., 1865, &c.
6. **Take my poor heart, and let it be** (ii. alt.), in Snepp's *Songs of G. & G.*, 1872.
7. **Lord! take my heart, and let it be** (ii. alt.). Amer. Presb. *Hyl.*, 1874, &c.
8. **How can it be, Thou heavenly King** (v.). American Meth. Epis. South *Coll.*, 1847, &c.   [J. M.]

I too, forewarned by Jesus' love. *C. Wesley.* [*Death Anticipated.*] The two closing hymns of the Official *Hymnal of the Meth. Episcopal Church*, N. Y., 1878, are, "I too, forewarned by Jesus' love," and "In age and feebleness extreme." They are introduced by the following special note :—

"The following hymns were composed by Charles Wesley in extreme old age. The second hymn was his

last utterance in verse, and was dictated on his death-bed."

With regard to "I too, forewarned by Jesus' love," it was pub. in C. Wesley's *Short Hymns*, &c., 1762, vol. ii. p. 397, No. 783, on 2 Peter i. 14, and in 2 st. of 4 l. (*P. Works*, 1868–72, vol. xiii. p. 191.) As C. Wesley was b. in 1707, and d. in 1788, this gives his age as 55 when the hymn was pub., that is 26 years before he died. The hymn therefore was not written by him "in extreme old age." The statement concerning "In age and feebleness extreme" (q.v.), however, is correct. [J. J.]

I travel all the irksome night. *J. Montgomery.* [*Journey of Life.*] In Montgomery's *Greenland, and other Poems*, 1819, this poem of 21 st. of 4 l. is given as :—

"A night in a stage-coach : being a Meditation on the way between London and Bristol, Sept. 23, 1815."

It was repeated in his *P. Works*, 1828, vol. iii. p. 189, and again in later editions. In the *Plymouth Coll.*, N. Y., 1855, st. i., xix.–xxi. are given as No. 1116. In the Boston Unitarian *Hys. of the Spirit*, 1864, the arrangement is, st. i. from this poem, and st. ii. and iii. from another source. [J. J.]

I want a Sabbath talk with Thee. *Jane Crewdson, née Fox.* [*Sunday.*] This plaintive hymn for private use rather than public worship, appeared in *A Little While and other Poems*, Manchester, Tubbs & Brook, 1864, p. 14, and entitled, "Sabbath Musings for a Sick Chamber." It is based on the words, "Jesus Himself drew near, and went with them," St. Luke xxiv. 15. It is given in Snepp's *Songs of G. & G.*, 1872, No. 823, without alteration. [J. J.]

I want that adorning divine. *Charlotte Elliott.* [*For Purity.*] This poem on "The Pilgrim's Wants" appeared in the *Christian Remembrancer* pocket book, 1848, and as one of J. Groom's leaflets, 1848, in 9 st. of 4 l. Each stanza is based upon a passage of H. Scripture.

i. Col. iii. 12–17 ; ii. Rom. viii. 11, 16 ; iii. 1 John iii. 2, 3 ; iv. Rev. ii. 17 ; v. John iv. 2, 5 ; vi. 1 John ii. 15 ; vii. Matt. vi. 19, 21 : viii. Heb. xiii. 5, 6 ; ix. Philip iii. 8, 9.

It is also given in *Leaves from the Christian Remembrancer*, 1871, and in *Leaves from Unpublished Journals, Letters and Poems of Charlotte Elliott*, Lond., N.D. (cir. 1870). In Snepp's *Songs of G. & G.*, 1872, it is given in two parts, Pt. ii. being, "I want Thine own hand to unbind." [W. T. B.]

I want to be an angel. *Sidney P. Gill.* [*For Purity.*] In the s. MSS. (W. 50) there is a letter from Mrs. Anna Reed Wilson, of Newark, New Jersey, to Mr. Randolph, of New York, respecting this hymn and its authorship. It is dated "Newark, N.J., Feb. 6th, /73," and in it Mrs. Reed says :—

"My sister's full name is Miss Sidney P. Gill. (An odd name for a woman, but coming down from a Welsh ancestress.) The hymn was written in Philadelphia when my sister, *then* a very young lady, taught the Infant Sunday School of Dr. Joel Parker's Church, of which she was a member. She had been teaching a lesson on *Angels* (I believe), when a lovely little girl exclaimed 'Oh I want to be an angel.' The child within a few days was attacked by a fatal disease and died ; and under the strong impression of the circumstance, the little hymn was written, and sung in the S. School. The first knowledge we had of its being *in print* was

finding it in a Dayton, Ohio, newspaper . . . . I cannot give you the exact date of its composition, but think it must have been about /54."

This hymn has become a great favourite with children. It is in use in all English-speaking countries, and has been translated into several languages. In some collections it is given as "I *would* be *like* an angel." This is especially the case in G. Britain. In the Presbyterian *Ps. & Hys. for the Worship of God*, Richmond, U. S. A., 1867, the opening line is again altered to "I want to be *with* Jesus," but this change is not so popular as the former. [J. J.]

I was a wandering sheep. *H. Bonar.* [*The Lost Sheep.*] Pub. in the 1st series of his *Songs in the Wilderness*, 1843, No. 1, in 5 st. of 8 l., and headed, "Lost but Found, 'Ye were as sheep going astray ; but are now returned unto the Shepherd and Bishop of your souls, 1 Pet. ii. 25.'" It was repeated in his *Bible H. Bk.*, 1845, No. 264, and in his *Hys. of Faith and Hope*, 1857. It ranks with the most popular of Dr. Bonar's hymns, and is in C. U. (usually in an unaltered form), in all English-speaking countries. [J. J.]

I was wandering and weary. *F. W. Faber.* [*The Lost Sheep.*] 1st pub. in his *Jesus and Mary*, &c., 1849, in 7 st. of 9 l., and entitled, "The True Shepherd. For the Ragged School." Also found in his *Hymns*, 1862. It is a hymn of great beauty and pathos, admirably suited for private use, but from its peculiar quaintness cannot be popular with the general public. It is sometimes given as, "I was weary and wandering," to the manifest injury of the hymn. [J. J.]

I weep, but do not yield. *H. Bonar.* [*Lent. Chastisement.*] Appeared in the 1st series of his *Hys. of Faith and Hope*, 1857, in 22 st. of 4 l., and entitled "The Rod." From this poem the following centos are in C. U. :—

1. I weep, but do not yield. The original text abridged.
2. Come nearer, nearer still. In Newman Hall's *Christ Church Hymnal*, 1876.
3. I did Thee wrong, my God. In several collections in G. Britain and America.
4. I said, my God, at length. In the 1874 *Suppl.* to the *New Cong. H. Bk.*
5. My sky was once noon-bright. In the American *Sabbath H. Bk.*, 1858.

Through these centos the poem has become well known and widely appreciated. [J. J.]

I will praise Thee every day. *W. Cowper.* [*Praise for Salvation.*] Pub. in the *Olney Hymns*, 1779, Bk. i., No. 58, in 5 st. of 4 l., and headed, "O Lord, I will praise Thee." It is found in a few modern collections, including the *Cong. Church Hyl.*, 1887. [J. J.]

I will take refuge in my God. *J. Conder.* [*Resignation.*] In his *Hys. of Praise, Prayer*, &c., 1856, p. 173, this is given in 3 st. of 8 l., and is based on Phil. i. 24, "To abide in the flesh is more needful." As a whole it is not in C. U., but st. ii. is in the American *Church Pastorals*, Boston, 1864, as, "And shall I shun the sacred fight." [J. J.]

I worship thee, sweet will of God. *F. W. Faber.* [*Will of God.*] 1st pub. in his *Jesus and Mary : or Catholic Hymns*, &c., 1849, in 14 st. of 4 l., entitled "The Will of

God," and repeated in his *Hymns*, 1862. In its full form it is not usually found in C. U.; but broken up into centos it is found as :—

1. **He always wins who sides with God.** In the American Unitarian *Hys. of the Spirit*, Boston, 1864.

2. **I worship Thee, sweet Will of God.** In several collections in G. Britain and America.

3. **I bow before Thy will, O God.** In Dr. Dale's *English H. Bk.*, 1874.

4. **I bow me to Thy will, O God.** In Spurgeon's *O. O. H. Bk.*, 1866, and others.

5. **I love to kiss each print where Thou.** In the *Church Praise Bk.*, N.Y., 1882.

6. **I worship Thee, O blessed God.** In one or two minor collections.

Through these centos the hymn is widely known in G. Britain and America.   [J. J.]

Ich armer Sünder bin auch heilig.

[*Sanctification.*] Included as No. 394 in the Ohio *G. B.*, 1870, in 9 st. of 6. l., without name of author. *Tr.* as, "Who knew no sin and no deceiving," by E. Cronenwett, as No. 402 in the Ohio *Luth. Hyl.*, 1880. [J. M.]

Ich bin ein Gast auf Erden.

P. Gerhardt. [*Eternal Life.*] A beautiful Pilgrim hymn of Homesickness for the Heavenly Fatherland; founded on Ps. cxix. 19, and Heb. xi. 13-16. First pub. in Ebeling's ed. of his *Geistliche Andachten* Berlin, 1666, *Ander Dutzet*, No. 17, in 14 l: of 8 l: reprinted in Wackernagel's ed. of his *Geistliche Lieder*, 1843, No. 112, and Bachmann's ed., No. 98; and included as No. 824 in the *Unv. L. S.*, 1851.

The hymn is an echo of the thoughts that sustained Gerhardt in the many trials of his earthly pilgrimage. *Lauzmann*, in *Koch*, viii. 556, relates that on the first Sunday of May, 1852, the retired and aged schoolmaster of Altburg, near Calw, in Württemberg, was requested by his successor to act as organist for the day. He consented with joy, and sang with the congregation the first stanza of this hymn; but in the middle of the second his head fell on the tune-book, and his spirit departed. With the strains of this hymn his body was laid to rest a few days after.

Translations in C. U. :—

1. **A pilgrim here I wander**, a good *tr.*, omitting st. iv.–viii., by Miss Winkworth, in her *Lyra Ger.*, 2nd ser., 1858, p. 173, and in her *C. B. for England*, 1863, No. 148. Included in varying centos in *Ps. & Hys.*, Bedford, 1859; *Kennedy*, 1863; *People's H.*, 1867. In *Holy Song*, 1869, it begins, " As pilgrims here we wander."

2. **A pilgrim and a stranger**, a free *tr.* in 7 st., by Miss Borthwick, in *H. L. L.*, 3rd series, 1858, p. 13 (1884, p. 139). Included in full in the Schaff-Gilman *Library of Rel. Poetry*, and in varying centos in the Pennsylvania Luth. *Ch. Bk.*, 1868, Hatfield's *Ch. H. Bk.*, 1872, &c.

Other trs. are, (1) " On earth I'm but a pilgrim," by G. Wade, in the *U. P. Juvenile Miss. Magazine*, 1859, p. 252; (2) " A rest here have I never," by *J. Kelly*, 1867, p. 316.   See also note on " In exile here we wander."
   [J. M.]

Ich bin getauft auf deinem Namen.

J. J. Rambach. [*Holy Baptism.*] 1st pub. as one of the 8 hymns which form pt. iii. of his *Erbauliches Handbüchlein für Kinder*, Giessen, 1734, in 7 st. of 6 l., entitled " Daily Renewal of the Baptismal Covenant " (*Bode*, p. 286). Included as No. 363 in his *Geistreiches Haus G. B.*, 1735, and recently as No. 457 in the Berlin *G. L. S.*, ed. 1863. It is one of the finest of his hymns.   The *trs.* in C. U. are :—

1. **I am baptized into Thy name.** In full, by Miss Winkworth, in her *Lyra Ger.*, 2nd series, 1858,

p. 91. Repeated more or less abridged in *Holy Song*, 1869, and in America in Boardman's *Selection*, 1861; Bapt. *Service of Song*, 1871; and Meth. Epis. *Hyl.*, 1878.

2. **Baptized into Thy name most holy.** A good *tr.*, omitting st. vi., by Miss Winkworth, as No. 92 in her *C. B. for England*, 1863. Repeated in full, and with a *tr.* of st. vi. added, in the Ohio *Luth. Hyl.*, 1880. With st. iv. omitted it is found in the 1880 *Suppl.* to the Bapt. *Ps. & Hys.*, and in Allon's *Cong. Psalmist Hyl.*, 1886.

3. **Father, Son, and Holy Spirit, I'm baptized in Thy dear Name.** A good *tr.*, omitting st. vi., as No. 323 in the Pennsylvania Luth. *Ch. Bk.*, 1868, marked as *tr.* by Charles William Schaeffer, D.D., 1860.   [J. M.]

Ich rühme mich einzig der blutigen Wunden.

[*Love to Christ.*] These words are given on the frontispiece of the *Herrnhut G. B.*, 1735, as the motto of that collection. They are not however by N. L. von Zinzendorf, but are taken from st. ii. of a hymn beginning "Ach alles was Himmel und Erde umschliesset," which is No. 847 in the *Vollständiges G. B.*, Hamburg and Ratzeburg, 1679, in 8 st. of 4 l., and repeated as No. 60 in Porst's *G. B.* ed., 1855.   *Tr.* as :—

" I glory in nothing, but in the Wounds bloody," as No. 632, in pt. i. of the *Moravian H. Bk.*, 1754. In the 1789 and later eds. (1886, No. 451) it begins, " I'll glory in nothing but only in Jesus."   [J. M.]

Ich singe dir mit Herz und Mund.

P. Gerhardt. [*Thanksgiving.*] 1st pub. in the *Crüger-Runge G. B.*, Berlin, 1653, No. 186, in 18 st. of 4 l. Thence in Wackernagel's ed. of his *Geistliche Lieder*, No. 85, and Bachmann's ed., No. 27. Included in Crüger's *Praxis*, 1656, and most later collections, as recently in the Berlin *G. L. S.*, ed. 1863.   *Tr.* as :—

O Lord ! I sing with mouth and heart. In full in J. Kelly's *P. G.'s Spir. Songs*, 1867, p. 255. A cento in 6 st. is found in the Ohio *Luth. Hyl.*, 1880, No. 364.

Other trs. are, (1) " He never yet has made mistakes," of st. xvii., xviii., as No. 475, in pt. i. of the *Moravian H. Bk.*, 1754. (2) " I sing to Thee with Heart and Tongue," in the *Suppl.* to *Ger. Psalmody*, ed. 1765, p. 65. Included in the *Moravian H. Bk.*, 1789, No. 802 (1886, No. 647), altered, and beginning, " I'll praise Thee with my heart and tongue." (3) " I sing to Thee with mouth and heart," by *Miss Cox*, 1864, p. 154. (4) " I'll sing to Thee with heart and mouth," by *Miss Manington*, 1863, p. 108. (5) " My heart's warm gush breaks forth in mirth," by *E. Massie*, 1867.   [J. M.]

Ich weiss mir ein Blümlein, ist hübsch und fein.

[*Holy Communion.*] This is No. 278 in the *Unv. L. S.*, 1851 (*mir* being omitted for metrical reasons), and is there (as also by Miss Winkworth) erroneously ascribed to Basilius Förtsch (b. at Rossla in Thuringia, d. as pastor of Gumperta, near Orlamünde, in 1619). *Wackernagel* gives it as anonymous, and at v. p. 10 includes four forms, the oldest being from "*Drey schöne geistliche Lieder*," printed separately in 1579. In his *Bibliographie*, p. 309, he had cited a broadsheet *Zwey schöne newe geistliche Lieder*, which he dated Nürnberg, c. 1560. The form *tr.* by Miss Winkworth is that in the Leipzig *G. B.*, 1586, in 8 st. *Tr.* as, " I know a flower so sweet and fair," by Miss Winkworth in *Lyra Eucharistica*, 1863, p. 197, repeated in the Schaff-Gilman *Lib. of Rel. Poetry*, ed. 1883.

Ich will dem Herren, meinem Gott, lobsingen. *Thanksgiving.* Included, as No. 564, in Freylinghausen's *Neues geistreiches G. B.*, 1714, in 14 st. of 2 l. *Tr.* as:—

(1) "I'll sing unto my God, the Lord of nature," as No. 679, in pt. i. of the *Moravian H. Bk.*, 1754. (2) "To Thee, the Lord of all, I'll humbly sing," as No. 1103 in the *Suppl.* of 1808 to the *Moravian H. Bk.*, 1801 (1886, No. 654). [J. M.]

Ich will dich lieben, meine Stärke. *J. Scheffler.* [*Love to Christ.*] One of the finest of his hymns, breathing a deep spirit of ardent devotion to the Saviour. 1st pub. as No. 10 in Bk. i., 1657, of his *Heilige Seelenlust* (*Werke*, 1862, i. p. 41), in 8 st. of 6 l., entitled, "She [the Soul] promises to love Him even unto death." It passed through Freylinghausen's *G. B.*, 1704, into many recent collections, and is No. 317 in the *Unv. L. S.*, 1851. *Tr.* as:—

1. Thee will I love, my strength, my tower, Thee will I love, my joy, my crown, a fine *tr.*, omitting st. ii., by J. Wesley, in *H. & Sacred Poems*, 1739 (*P. Works*, 1868–72, vol. i. p. 176), two lines, ("That all my powers," &c., being taken from Bp. Ken. Included in the Wesley *H. & Spir. Songs*, 1753; *Wes. H. Bk.*, 1780 and 1875; and recently in many English and American collections. The form beginning, "I thank Thee, uncreated Sun," in the Amer. Meth. Epis. *Hymns*, 1849, and the *Plymouth Coll.*, 1855, commences with Wesley's st. iv.

2. Thee will I love, my strength, my glory, a free *tr.* of st. i., by A. T. Russell, as No. 57 in the Dalston Hospital *H. Bk.*, 1848. In his own *Ps. & Hys.*, 1851, No. 186, he added free *trs.* of st. v., vi.

3. I will love Thee, all my treasure! by Mrs. Findlater, in the 2nd ser., 1855, of the *H. L. L.*, p. 13 (ed. 1884, p. 80), omitting st. ii. Included, more or less altered or abridged, in *Cantate Domino*, Boston, U.S., 1859, Andover *Sabbath H. Bk.*, 1858, &c.

4. Thee will I love, my strength, my tower, Thee will I love, my Hope, my Joy, a good *tr.*, omitting st. ii., vii., by Miss Winkworth, as No. 150 in her *C. B. for England*, 1863.

Other trs. are, (1) "Alas that I not earlier knew Thee" (beginning with st. iii.) in the *Christian Examiner*, Boston, U. S., Sept., 1860, p. 246. (2) "Thee will I love, my Strength, my Tower, Thee will I love, my Joy, my Peace," by R. Massie, in the *British Herald*, April, 1865, p. 56, repeated in Reid's *Praise Bk.*, 1872, No. 384. (3) "Thee will I love, my crown, my treasure," by R. Massie, in the *Day of Rest*, 1879, p. 277. [J. M.]

Ide, George Barton, D.D., Baptist Minister, was b. at Coventry, Vermont, in 1806; educated at Middlebury College, Vermont; was pastor successively at Boston, Philadelphia, and Springfield, Massachusetts, and d. in 1872. He edited the *Baptist Harp*, Philadelphia, 1849. To that work he contributed 9 hymns. Of these, "Son of God, our glorious Head (*On behalf of ministers*) is still in C. U. [J. J.]

Ide, Mary. [Torrey, Mary.]

Idiomela. [Greek Hymnody, § x. 11.]

Idiomelon. [Greek Hymnody, § xvi. 9.]

Ἰδοὺ ὁ Νύμφιος ἔρχεται. [*Midnight.*] This midnight hymn of the Eastern Church is taken from the Ferial Midnight Office of the Greek Church, where it is given

at the beginning of the Horologion. The *tr.* "Behold the Bridegroom cometh," by G. Moultrie, was pub. in *Lyra Messianica*, 1864, p. 50; and again in Moultrie's *Hys. & Lyrics*, 1867, p. 18. It was brought into congregational use through the *People's H.*, 1867. It is in extensive use in America. [J. J.]

Ἰησοῦ γλυκύτατε. [Theoctistus, St.]

Ἰησοῦς ὁ ζωοδότης. [Ἀνέστης τριήμερος.]

Ἰησοῦς ὑπὲρ τοῦ κόσμου. *St. Andrew of Crete.* [*Palm Sunday.*] This is a cento from a canon of three odes, sung at Compline on Palm Sunday. The canon dates cir. 660–732, and is found in the Greek Office for Palm Sunday, in the *Triodion.* (See *Daniel*, iii. p. 50.) The cento therefrom translated by Dr. Neale, "Jesus, hastening for the world to suffer," is composed of the 3rd and 6th Troparia of the first ode; the 4th of the second Ode, and the 6th and 7th of the third Ode. It was pub. in *The Ecclesiastic and Theologian*, 1853, p. 349, and in his *Hys. of the Eastern Church*, 1862 (ed. 1882, p. 16). [J. J.]

If God is mine, then present things. *B. Beddome.* [*Security in God.*] This hymn is in C. U. in two forms:—

1. If God is mine, then present things. This appeared in the 10th ed. of Rippon's *Sel.*, 1800, No. 287. pt. ii., in 6 st. of 4 l., and is in somewhat extensive use in America, but usually in an abridged form.

2. If Christ is mine, then all is mine. This was given from Beddome's mss. in his (posthumous) *Hymns*, &c., 1817, No. 564, in 6 st. of 4 l. This is also in C. U., and more especially in America. [J. J.]

If human kindness meets return. *G. T. Noel.* [*Gratitude. Holy Communion.*] Given as No. 45 in 4 st. of 4 l. in the 1st ed. of his *Ps. & Hys.*, 1810. In the 3rd ed., 1820, it is No. 61. It is also in the author's *Arvendel, or Sketches in Italy and Switzerland*, 1826. It is in extensive use in G. Britain and America, and usually unaltered, as in the *New Cong.*, 1859; and others. [J. J.]

If I must die, O let me die. *B. Beddome.* [*Death Anticipated.*] This hymn was pub. in Dr. Rippon's *Baptist Register*, 1794, p. 319, in 4 st. of 4 l., in an obituary notice of Beddome. It there began:—

> "If I must die, O let me die
> Trusting in Thee alone."

In the *Bapt. Register*, 1800, p. 312, it is given as:—

> "Lord, must I die? O let me die
> Trusting in Thee alone."

This text was repeated in the 10th ed. of Rippon's *Sel.*, 1800, No. 550 (pt. iii.), and is found in a few modern collections, with sometimes two additional stanzas (ii. and v.), which were added in the 27th ed. of *Rippon*, 1827. In Beddome's (posthumous) *Hymns*, &c., 1817, No. 778, it is given in 4 st. from Beddome's mss. as:—

> "'If I must die'—Oh let me die,
> Trusting in Jesus' blood."

The American *Sabbath H. Bk.*, 1858, and others are from this text. [W. T. B.]

If Paul in Cæsar's court must stand. *J. Newton.* [*St. Paul's Voyage.*] Given in the *Olney Hymns*, 1779, Bk. i., No. 125, in

8 st. of 4 l. It is not usually found in C. U. in its full form. A part of the hymn beginning with st. v., "Believers now are tossed about," was given in the Edinburgh *Hys. for the Tabernacles*, 1800, and in Dr. Alexander's *Augustine H. Bk.*, 1849 and 1865.   [J. J.]

If Solomon for wisdom prayed. *J. Newton.* [*Lent.*] 1st pub. in the *Olney Hymns*, 1779, Bk. i., No. 32, in 8 st. of 4 l., as the second hymn on 1 Kings iii. 5, "Ask what I shall give thee." In its original form it is unknown to the hymnals; but st. v.-viii., as "And dost Thou say, Ask what thou wilt," is well known, and in extensive use. It appeared in this form in the *Arminian Magazine*, 1781, p. 231. It is given in many modern collections in G. Britain and America, and usually with slight alterations, which vary in different hymnals. In the Presbyterian *Sel. of Hys.*, Philadelphia, 1861, it begins, "Lord, dost Thou say," &c.   [J. J.]

If the Lord [my] our Leader be. *J. Newton.* [*Jacob's Ladder.*] Josiah Bull, in his *John Newton of Olney and St. Mary Woolnoth*, 1868, says, under date of June, 1774 :—

"Writing about this time to his sister-in-law, Mrs. Cunningham, who had removed to Scotland, he sends her a copy of his hymn, entitled 'Jacob's Ladder,' saying, 'Your removal led my thoughts to the subject of the following hymn, and therefore you ought to have a copy.'" (2nd ed. p. 202.)

In 1779, the hymn was given in the *Olney Hymns*, Bk. i., No. 9, in 5 st. of 8 l., with the title "Jacob's Ladder." It is found in a few modern collections in America.   [J. J.]

If there be any special thing. *E. Caswall.* [*Ingratitude.*] 1st pub. in his *Masque of Mary*, &c., 1858, in 6 st. of 4 l., and again in his *Hymns & Poems*, 1873, p. 247. It is in C. U. in three forms, (1) the original in the 1862 *Suppl.* to the *H. Noted;* (2) as, "O Jesu Christ, if aught there be," in the *Appendix* to *H. A. & M.*, 1868, and the revised ed., 1875; and, (3) "O Jesu Christ, if sin there be." This last is in the *Hymnary*, 1872, and was made by the author's permission by the editors. It changes a meditative piece into a hymn and prayer to Our Blessed Lord.   [J. J.]

Iisdem creati fluctibus. *C. Coffin.* [*Thursday.*] Appeared in the *Paris Breviary*, 1736, at Matins on Thursdays, and again in his *Hymni Sacri*, p. 22, of the same year. The text is also in J. Chandler's *Hys. of the Prim. Church*, 1837, No. 26, and in Card. Newman's *Hymni Ecclesiae*, 1838 and 1865. Tr. as :—

1. **The deep a two-fold offspring bore.** By J. Chandler, in his *Hys. of the Prim. Church*, 1837, p. 23, in 6 st. of 4 l. This was repeated in the *Hymnal for the use of St. John the Ev., &c.*, Aberdeen, 1870.

2. **This day behold the waters bear.** By J. D. Chambers, in his *Lauda Syon*, 1857, p. 24.

3. **The fish in wave, the bird on wing.** This *tr.*, as given in *H. A. & M.*, 1861 and 1875; Allon's *Suppl. Hys.*, 1868; *Kennedy*, 1863 (altered), and others, is by the Compilers of *H. A. & M.*, based upon J. Chandler as above, and the opening line from I. Williams's *tr.*, 1839.

4. **O praise the Lord, the King of kings.** This in the *Hymnary*, 1872, is by the editors, based upon J. D. Chambers's *tr.* as above.

Another tr. is :—
The fish in wave, and bird on wing, From selfsame waters spring. I. Williams, in *Brit. Mag.*, 1834, and his *Hys. tr. from the Parisian Brev.*, 1839.   [J. J.]

I'll praise my Maker with my [while I've] breath. *I. Watts.* [*Ps. cxlvi.*] 1st pub. in his *Psalms of David*, &c., 1719, in 6 st. of 6 l., and headed, "Praise to God for His Goodness and Truth." It is sometimes given in this form: but the more popular arrangement, which is in extensive use in all English-speaking countries, is that by J. Wesley, beginning, "I'll praise my Maker *while I've* breath." This is composed of st. i., iii., iv. and vi. somewhat altered. It appeared in Wesley's *Ps. & Hys.*, Charlestown, South Carolina, 1736–7; was repeated in the Wesley *Ps. & Hys.*, 1743, and in the *Wes. H. Bk.*, 1780. Another arrangement is, "Happy the man whose hopes rely." This is composed of st. iii., iv., and vi. somewhat altered, and was given in Cotterill's *Sel.*, 1810. Neither the original nor the arrangements by Wesley and by Cotterill have the doxology which is found in some collections.   [J. J.]

I'm but a stranger here. *T. R. Taylor.* [*Heaven the Home.*] This hymn, written apparently during his last illness, was pub. in his *Memoirs and Select Remains*, by W. S. Matthews, 1836, in 4 st. of 8 l., and headed "Heaven is my home. Air—'Robin Adair.'" In 1853 it was included in the *Leeds H. Bk.;* and later in numerous collections in G. Britain and America, sometimes as "We are but *strangers* here." Orig. text in *Bap. Ps. & Hys.*, 1858 and 1880, with *tempest* for "tempests" in st. ii. l. 1.   [J. J.]

I'm kneeling at the threshold, aweary, faint, and sore. *W. L. Alexander.* [*Death Anticipated.*] "I wrote it," writes Dr. Alexander, "after an evening spent with my venerable father then near the end of his earthly pilgrimage, and when he spoke much of his longing to depart to and join those who had been the companions of his pilgrimage, but had preceded him into the better land." (E. MS.) In 1865 it was printed in the *Sunday Magazine* in 5 st. of 8 l. From that magazine it first passed into a few American hymnals, and then into the 1874 *Supp.* to the *New Cong.*; the *Hy. Comp.*, 1876, and others. It is the most popular of Dr. Alexander's hymns.   [J. J.]

I'm not ashamed to own my Lord. *I. Watts.* [*Not ashamed of the Gospel.*] Pub. in his *Hys. & S. Songs*, 1707, Bk. i., No. 103, in 4 st. of 4 l., and based on 1 Tim. i. 12. Two forms of the hymn are in C. U. The first is the original as in the *New Cong.*, 1859; and the second is that in the Scottish *Translations and Paraphrases*. In the Draft *Trs. and Paraphs.*, 1745, Watts's text was given with the alteration of st. i., ll. 3, 4, to

"Maintain the glory of his cross
And honour all his laws."

In the authorized issue of the *Trs. and Paraphs.*, 1781, this alteration was retained, and others were introduced by W. Cameron (q. v.). This recast has been in use in the Church of Scotland for more than 100 years, and is easily distinguished from the original by the alteration noted above.   [J. J.]

Immense coeli Conditor. *St. Gregory the Great?* [*Monday.*] This hymn, on the Second Day of the Creation, has been frequently ascribed to St. Ambrose, but the Benedictine editors do not acknowledge it as his, nor is it claimed for him by Luigi Biraghi in his *Inni sinceri e carmi de Sant Ambrogio*, Milan, 1862. *Mone* thinks it is by St. Gregory, but it is not included in the Benedictine edition of St. Gregory's *Opera*. It is found as a Vesper hymn in almost all old Breviaries and hymnaries, generally assigned to Monday, as in the *Roman*, *Sarum*, *York*, *Aberdeen*, *Mozarabic* and other *Breviaries*.

Mone, No. 273, gives the text from a MS. of the 9th cent. at Trier, &c., and says the first verse is in an 8th cent. MS. at Trier. *Daniel* gives it at i., No. 50, and iv. p 59, from a Rheinau MS. of the 10th cent., &c. It is in four MSS. of the 11th cent., in the *British Museum* (Vesp. D. xii. f. 14 *b.*; Jul. A. vi. f. 24*b*; Harl. 2961, f. 221 *b*; Add. 30,848, f. 72 *b*), and in the *Lat. Hys. of the Anglo-Saxon Ch.*, 1851, p. 17, is printed from an 11th cent. MS. (B. iii. 32, f. 6) at Durham. Among the St. Gall MSS. it is found in No. 20, of the 9th cent., and Nos. 387, 413 of the 11th cent. Also in Card. Newman's *Hymni Ecclesiae*, 1838 and 1865, &c.   [J. M.]

Translations in C. U. :—

1. **Floods of water, high in air.** By T. Whytehead, in his *Poems*, 1842, p. 72, in 5 st. of 5 l. This is a paraphrase rather than a *tr.* of "Immense coeli Conditor." In 1872 it was given in the *Hymnary* as "Lo! the firmament doth bear."

2. **Lord of immensity sublime.** By E. Caswall. 1st pub. in his *Lyra Catholica*, 1849, p. 17, in 5 st. of 4 l., and again in his *Hys. & Poems*, 1873, p. 11. It was repeated in the *People's H.*, 1867.

3. **O Great Creator of the sky.** By J. M. Neale. Appeared in the enlarged ed. of the *H. Noted*, 1854, in 5 st. of 4 l., and thence into the *Hymner*, 1882, &c.

Translations not in C. U. :—

1. All present Framer of the sky. *Bp. Mant*, 1837.
2. Almighty Maker of the heaven. *A. J. B. Hope*, 1844.
3. Maker of Heaven! Who spread'st yon proud. *Hymnarium Anglicanum*, 1844.
4. God of the boundless space. *W. J. Copeland*, 1848.
5. Thou Whose almighty Word, The firmament, &c. *R. Campbell*, 1850.
6. Lord of unbounded space. *W. J. Blew*, 1852–55.
7. Lord of unbounded space. Card. Newman, *Verses on Various Religious Subjects*, 1853, and the Marquess of Bute's *Rom. Brev. in English*, 1879.
8. Creator of the heavens, Whose arm. *J. D. Chambers*, 1857.
9. Great Creator of the sky. *J. Wallace*, 1874,
10. Creator, God immense and wise. *Primer*, 1736.
    [J. J.]

Immortal spirit! wake, arise. *Charlotte Elliott.* [*Morning.*] Printed in her *Hymns for a Week*, 1839, and pub. in the same 1842, in 10 st. of 4 l., and appointed for Tuesday Morning. It is based on Heb. xii. 1, "Let us run with patience the race that is set before us." In Whiting's *Hys. of the Ch. Catholic*, 1882, it is given in 6 st., and in the Presb. *Sel. of Hys.*, Philadelphia, 1861, No. 400, in 5 st. The latter begins, "Lord, I to Thee commit my way," that is, st. v. and vi. rewritten, while st. ii.–v. are the original st. vi.–x.   [J. J.]

In a land of strange delight. *J. Montgomery.* [*Midnight.*] Pub. in Collyer's *Coll.*, 1812, No. 920, in 4 st. of 4 l., and headed, "A Midnight Thought." In 1819 it was repeated in Cotterill's *Sel.*, No. 343, and Montgomery's *Greenland and Other Poems;*

in 1825, in his *Christian Psalmist;* and in 1853, in his *Original Hymns.* Various readings of st. iv., ll. 3, 4, are in C. U. These are all by Montgomery, and appeared as follows :—

1. In Collyer's *Coll.*, 1812 :—

> "When I wake to meet my doom,
> I will hide in His embrace."

2. In Cotterill's *Sel.*, 1819, and in the *Christian Psalmist*, 1825 :—

> "Fearless in the day of doom,
> May I see Him face to face."

3. In *Greenland*, &c., 1819 :—

> "Fearless in the day of doom,
> May I stand before His face."

4. In *Original Hymns*, 1853 :—

> "When I wake to meet my doom,
> May I see Him face to face."

Of these readings No. 2 is the finest, and is also the most popular.   [J. J.]

In age and feebleness extreme. *C. Wesley.* [*Trust in Jesus.*] This stanza of 6 l. was the last of the magnificent series of hymns and spiritual songs associated with the name of Charles Wesley. Dr. Whitehead, his physician, seems to have been the first to give the details to the public. This he did in his *Life* of John Wesley. In Jackson's Official *Memoirs of the Rev. Charles Wesley*, small ed., 1848, p. 455, the details are :—

"Hence it appears that Mr. John Wesley still entertained a hope of his brother's recovery. The decree, however, was gone forth, and no means could avail for the preservation of his life. While he remained in a state of extreme feebleness, having been silent and quiet for some time, he called Mrs. Wesley to him, and requested her to write the following lines at his dictation :—

> ' In age and feebleness extreme,
> Who shall a sinful worm redeem?
> Jesus, my only hope Thou art,
> Strength of my failing flesh and heart;
> O could I catch a smile from Thee,
> And drop into eternity.'

"For fifty years Christ as the Redeemer of men had been the subject of his effective ministry, and of his loftiest songs; and he may be said to have died with a hymn to Christ upon his lips. He lingered till the 29th of March, 1788, when he yielded up his spirit into the hands of his God and Saviour, at the advanced age of seventy-nine years and three months."

The stanza was included in the *Wes. H. Bk.* in 1875, but it had previously appeared elsewhere. It is not suited for congregational use. Its interest lies in its origin and its after associations. In G. J. Stevenson's *Meth. H. Bk. Notes*, 1883, pp. 522–30, these after associations are gathered together in a long and interesting note.   [J. J.]

In Christ I've all my soul's desire. [*Christ All in All.*] Appeared in the *Christian Magazine*, 1790, and signed "W. G. Bristol." In 1806, it was transferred, with alterations, to John Dobell's *New Selection*, No. 55, in 5 st. of 4 l. This, the recognized form of the text, is in C. U. in G. Britain and America, including Snepp's *Songs of G. & G.*, 1872, and the Dutch Reformed *Hys. for the Church*, N. Y., 1869.   [J. J.]

In domo Patris summae majestatis. [*Eternal Life.*] The text of this hymn is given by *Mone*, No. 302, from a 15th cent. MS. at Karlsruhe, and with the title "A hymn of the various mansions and rewards of the Elect in the Heavenly Jerusalem." The *tr.* by J. M. Neale, "My Father's home eternal," was pub. in his *Hys. chiefly Mediaeval* *on the Joys and Glories of Paradise*, 1865, p. 38, and repeated in the *People's H.*, 1867. Dr. Neale says of his *tr.* that it " is little more than an imitation and abbreviation of the Latin." Also *tr.* as " In my Father's house on high," in *Lyra Mystica*, 1865, by " H. R. B."   [W. A. S.]

In dulci ·jubilo singet und sit vro. [*Christmas.*] This hymn is a macaronic, partly Latin and partly German. It was a great favourite in Germany till comparatively recent times. It has been often ascribed to Peter of Dresden, who d. cir. 1440, but is certainly older. *Wackernagel*, ii. pp. 483–486, gives 8 versions, varying from 3 to 7 st. of 8 l. (See *Hoffmann von Fallersleben's* monograph *In dulci jubilo*, Hannover, 1861, p. 46.)

The *trs.* are, (1) " In dulci jubilo, now let us sing with mirth and jo," in 3 st. (as in the *Psaltes Ecclesiasticus*, Mainz, 1550), in the *Gude and Godly Ballates*, ed. 1568, f. 28 (1868, p. 47). (2) " Let Jubil trumpets blow, and hearts in rapture flow," in 4 st. (as in Klug's *G. B.*, Wittenberg, 1529), in *Lyra Davidica*, 1708, p. 7. (3) " In dulci jubilo—to the house of God we'll go" (as in *Klug*, 1529), by Sir J. Bowring, in his *Hymns*, 1825, No. 21. (4) " In dulci jubilo, sing and shout, all below," in 4 st. (as in a Breslau 15th cent. MS.), by *Miss Winkworth*, 1869, p. 94. (5) " In dulci jubilo, Let us our homage shew," by R. L. de Pearsall, first in the *Musical Times*, and then in Novello's *Part Song Book*, 2nd Series, vol. x., 1887, No. 296 (as in *Klug*, 1529).

It has also passed into English through a recast (from the text of *Klug*, 1529), entirely in German, which begins "Nun singet und seid froh." This is in 4 st., and was 1st pub. in the *Hannover G. B.*, 1646, p. 222, and has been repeated in many subsequent collections as in the Berlin *G. L. S.* ed., 1863, No. 174.

Tr. as "Now sing we, now rejoice," a good and full *tr.* by A. T. Russell, as No 48 in his *Ps. & Hys.*, 1851. Another *tr.* is, "We all indeed were perish'd," a *tr.* of st. iii., as No. 302 in pt. i. of the *Moravian H. Bk.*, 1754.

                   [J. M.]

In every object here I see. *J. Newton.* [*Nature lifting the soul to God.*] Printed in the *Gospel Magazine*, June, 1774, and included in the *Olney Hymns*, 1779, in 2 st. of 6 l., and headed, "A Thought on the Seashore." It was given in the Leeds *S. S. U. H. Bk.*, 1833 and 1879, as No. 128.   [J. J.]

In exile here we wander. *W. Cooke.* [*Septuagesima.*] This hymn, pub. in the *Hymnary*, 1872, under the signature "A. C. C." was suggested to Canon Cooke by P. Gerhardt's " Ich bin ein Gast auf Erden " (q. v.), but it is not a *tr.* of that hymn. It was written for the *Hymnary*. The alteration in Thring's *Coll.*, 1882, of st. iii., ll. 4–8, to

     " And we shall rise in that great day
        In bodies like to Thine,
     And with Thy saints, in bright array,
        Shall in Thy glory shine."

is the author's authorized text.   [J. J.]

In evil long I took delight. *J. Newton.* [*Looking at the Cross.*] Pub. in the *Olney Hymns*, 1779, Bk. ii., No. 57, in 7 st. of 4 l., and headed, " Looking at the Cross." Although not referred to by Josiah Bull in his account of Newton (*John Newton*, &c., 1868), it seems to be of special autobiographical interest as setting forth the great spiritual change which Newton underwent. In its full form it is rarely found in modern hymnbooks. Two arrangements are in C. U. (1) " In evil long I took delight," abridged, and

(2) " I saw one hanging on a tree." The latter is mainly in American use.   [J. J.]

In Gottes Namen fahren wir. [*Travellers' Hymn.*] This is found in varying forms from the 14th to 16th century, and was very much used by travellers on land and water, by the crusaders, at pilgrimages and processions, &c. *Wackernagel*, ii. pp. 515–517, gives 6 versions, and at iii. pp. 1229–33, gives 5 versions, varying from 2 to 29 st., the oldest being from a Munich MS. of 1422. (See also *Hoffmann von Fallersleben*, 1861, pp. 70–73, 212–215, &c.) The forms *tr.* into English are :—

i. *Wackernagel*, ii., No. 680, from the *Psaltes Ecclesiasticus*, Mainz, 1550, in 4 st. *Tr.* as, " Now in the name of God we go," by *Miss Winkworth*, 1869, p. 43.

ii. *Wackernagel*, ii., No. 682, from M. Vehe's *Gesangbüchlein*, Leipzig, 1537, in 12 st., and altered, in H. Bone's *Cantate*, 1847, No. 365. *Tr.* as, "Onward in God's name we wend," by R. F. Littledale, for the *People's Hyl.*, 1867, No. 137, omitting st. v., vi. It is appointed for Rogationtide, and signed " F. R." Repeated in Dale's *English H. Bk.*, 1875.

iii. *Wackernagel*, iii., No. 1437, in 3 st., from the *Bonn G. B.*, 1561; included as No. 1194 in the Berlin *G. L. S.*, ed. 1863. *Tr.* as, "In God's name, let us on our way," by Miss Winkworth, in her *Lyra Ger.*, 2nd ser., 1858, p. 107. Repeated as No. 180 in her *C. B. for England*, 1863, and in the Ohio *Luth. Hyl.*, 1880. Another *tr.* is, "In God's name we our way do go," as No. 323 in pt. i. of the *Moravian H. Bk.*, 1754.

In Knapp's *Ev. L. S.*, ed. 1865, No. 2744, this third form is ascribed to Johann Hiltstein, 1557. Hiltstein's hymn (*Wackernagel*, iii. p. 1140, and *Unv. L. S.*, 1851, No. 648) is essentially different.   [J. M.]

In grief and fear, to Thee, O Lord. *W. Bullock.* [*In time of Trouble.*] Appeared in his *Songs of the Church*, Halifax, N. Scotia, 1854, pp. 221–222, in 5 l. of 4 st., entitled, "The Church in Plague or Pestilence," and based upon the words, "God is our Refuge and Strength, a very present help in trouble." In 1861 it was given in *H. A. & M.*; in 1863 in Kennedy, and again in many other collections, and usually with the omission of st. iii., which reads :—

     " Our sins Thy dreadful anger raise,
        Our deeds Thy wrath deserve;
     But we repent, and from Thy ways
        We never more will swerve."

The *H. A. & M.* text, with st. i., l. 3, thus: "And while Thy judgments are abroad," and the stanza above quoted, will give the orig. text. Its use is somewhat extensive. [J. J.]

In humble faith, and holy love. *T. Rennell.* [*Holy Trinity.*] These stanzas by Dean Rennell form the words of the anthem known by the above first line, No. 304 of the *Musical Times* series, the music being by Dr. George M. Garrett. In its original form the hymn is not used as such in the collections, but rewritten by Dr. Kennedy as, " A triple light of glory shines," it was included in his *Hymno. Christ.*, 1863.   [J. J.]

In latter days, the mount of God. [*The Church the House of God.*] In the Scottish *Translations and Paraphrases* of 1745, this is given as No. xxviii. on Is. ii. 2–6, as follows :—

1.

" In latter Days, the Mount of God,
     his sacred House, shall rise
Above the Mountains and the Hills,
     and strike the wond'ring Eyes.

2.

" To this the joyful Nations round,
   all Tribes and Tongues shall flow ;
Up to the House of God, they'll say,
   to *Jacob's* God, we'll go.

3.

" To us he'll point the Ways of Truth :
   the sacred Path we'll tread :
From *Salem* and from *Zion*-Hill
   his Law shall then proceed.

4.

" Among the Nations and the Isles,
   as Judge supreme, he'll sit :
And, vested with unbounded Pow'r,
   will punish or acquit.

5.

" No Strife shall rage, nor angry Feuds,
   disturb these peaceful Years ;
To plow-shares then they'll beat their swords,
   to Pruning-hooks their Spears.

6.

" Then Nation shan't 'gainst Nation rise,
   and slaughter'd Hosts deplore .
They'll lay the useless Trumpet by,
   and study War no more.

7.

" O come ye, then, of *Jacob's* house,
   our Hearts now let us join :
And, walking in the Light of God,
   with holy beauties shine."

The author of this piece is unknown, and the piece itself has passed out of use. From it, however, there has grown a hymn concerning the authorship of which much discussion has arisen. The details of this controversy are given under **Bruce, M.** (q.v.). From evidence there adduced we hold that the revision of the above, known as, " Behold the mountain of the Lord," was written by M. Bruce about 1764; that after his death in 1767, the MS. was given to J. Logan for publication ; that in 1781 Logan published it in his *Poems* as his own ; and that the same year, as one of the revisers of the Scottish *Translations and Paraphrases,* he secured, after some alterations and the addition of a stanza, also altered from the original of 1745, its insertion therein.

2. The text as given in Logan's *Poems,* 1781, p. 106, No. 5, and which is the nearest approach to Bruce's original that can be attained, is as follows :—

1.

" Behold ! the mountain of the Lord
   In latter days shall rise,
Above the mountains and the hills,
   And draw the wondering eyes.

2.

" To this the joyful nations round
   All tribes and tongues shall flow ;
Up to the hill of God, they'll say,
   And to His house we'll go.

3.

" The beam that shines on Zion's Hill
   Shall lighten every land,
The King who reigns in Zion's towers
   Shall all the world command.

4.

" No strife shall vex Messiah's reign,
   Or mar the peaceful years ;
To ploughshares soon they beat their swords,
   To pruning-hooks their spears.

5.

" No longer hosts encountering hosts,
   Their millions slain deplore ;
They hang the trumpet in the hall
   And study war no more.

6.

" Come then—O come from every land,
   To worship at His shrine ;
And, walking in the light of God,
   With holy beauties shine."

3. As already indicated, this text with slight alterations, and the original st. iv. as above, altered to " Among the nations," &c., was

given in the Scottish *Translations and Paraphrases,* 1781, No. xviii., as follows :—

St. i., as above, 1781, with l. 3, " *On mountain tops, above,*" &c. St. ii., as above, 1781. St. iii., as above, 1781. St. iv., from 1745, st. iv. altered. St. v., " *No strife shall rage, nor hostile feuds disturb those* peaceful years," &c., 1781. St. vi., l. 1, as 1781 ; 2, " *Shall crowds of* slain deplore " ; ll. 3 and 4 as 1781. St. vii., " Come, then, *O house of Jacob ! come* " ; ll. 2, 3, 4 as 1781. Modern editions are somewhat different from this.

4. In this last form the hymn has been in authorized use in the Church of Scotland for more than 100 years, and is found in the hymnals of most English-speaking countries. It should be designated as *Scottish Trs. & Paraphs.,* 1745, *rewritten by M. Bruce, and altered by J. Logan.*

5. In Miss J. E. Leeson's *Par. and Hymns,* &c., 1853, this hymn is given as rewritten by her for that collection as, " The mountain of Jehovah's house." It is in 5 st. of 4 l. Another form, dating from Belknap's *Ps. & Hymns,* Boston, 1795, beginning " O'er mountain tops, the mount of God," is in C. U. in America.   [J. J.]

In life's gay dawn, when sprightly youth. *T. Blacklock.* [*Children.*] 1st appeared as No. 16 in the Draft Scottish *Translations and Paraphrases,* 1781, as a version of Eccles. xii. 1, in 4 st. of 4 lines. In the public worship ed. issued in that year by the Church of Scotland, and still in use, *dawn* in st. i., l. 1, was altered to *morn,* and 8 other lines rewritten. In the markings by the eldest daughter of *W. Cameron* (q. v.) ascribed to Blacklock. Included in *Paterson's Coll.,* Glasgow, 1867, and in America in the *Springfield Coll.,* 1835. In the American Prot. Episcopal *Coll.,* 1826, No. 92, it was altered to " O, in the morn of life, when youth." This was followed in America in the *Bap. Psalmist,* 1843 ; Cheshire Association *Christian Hymns,* 1844 ; and further altered to " In the glad morn of life, when youth," in *Adams & Chapin's Coll.,* 1846, or to " In the bright morn of life, when youth," as in the *Bap. Praise Bk.,* New York, 1871.   [J. M.]

In natali Domini. [*Christmas.*] This hymn probably is of the 14th or 15th cent. *Wackernagel,* i. pp. 202–203, gives five versions varying from 2 to 6 st., the oldest being from a 15th cent. MS. at Munich. The form *tr.* into English is his No. 323—which appeared with the German in 6 st. of 7 l. in the *Enchiridion geistliker leder,* Wittenberg, 1571. *Daniel,* i., No. 474, quotes it from *Wackernagel's* 1st ed. (1841). It has passed into English through the German " Do (Da) Christus gebaren war Fröwden sick der Engel schar," which appeared with the Latin, 1571, as above, and thence in *Wackernagel,* iv. p. 790, in 6 st. of 7 l., repeated as No. 26 in the *Unv. L. S.,* 1851. *Tr.* as :—

Hark ! the heavenly hosts proclaim. A good *tr.* of st. i., ii., iv., by A. T. Russell, as No. 50 in his *Ps. & Hys.,* 1851. Slightly altered and beginning " Hark, the angel choirs," as No. 101 in *Kennedy,* 1863. Another *tr.* is " On the birthday of the Lord." By Dr. Littledale in *Lyra Messianica,* 1864.   [J. M.]

In never ceasing songs of praise. *B. Beddome.* [*The overruling of all for Good.*] Pub. in his (posthumous) *Hymns,* &c., 1817, No. 34, in 5 st. of 6 l. In this form it is not in C. U. ; but the hymn " Temptations, trials, doubts and fears," included in the 1800 ed. of Rippon's *Sel.*, No. 286, pt. ii., has many lines in common. Whether Beddome's 1817 text is *Rippon's* 1800 text expanded from 3 st. of 4 l. to 5 st. of 6 l., or whether the 1800 text was abridged by Rippon from Beddome's MS., we cannot say.   [J. J.]

In noctis umbrâ desides. *C. Coffin.*

[*Advent.*] Appeared in the *Paris Breviary*, 1736, for Compline in Advent; and again in Coffin's *Hymni Sacri*, 1736, p. 93. The text is also in J. Chandler's *Hys. of the Primitive Church*, 1837, No. 12, and Card. Newman's *Hymni Ecclesiae*, 1838 and 1865. *Tr.* as:—

1. While we our weary eyelids close. By J. Chandler, in his *Hys. of the Prim. Ch.*, 1837, p. 10. It is repeated in a few collections.

2. When shades of night around us close. By the Compilers of *H. A. & M.* 1st printed in their trial copy, 1859, and then in the 1st ed., 1861.

3. When night has veiled the earth in shade. By the Editors of the *Hymnary*, 1872, principally from the *trs.* by J. Chandler and J. D. Chambers.

Translations not in C. U.:—
1. And now with shades of night opprest. *I. Williams.* 1839.
2. When clouds of darkness veil the sky. *R. Campbell.* 1850.
3. In Night's dim shadows lying. *W. J. Blew.* 1852–5.
4. In shadowy night, whilst drowsy sleep. *J. D. Chambers.* 1857.   [J. J.]

In passione Domini, qua datur salus homini. *St. Bonaventura.* [*Passiontide.*]

This is ascribed to St. Bonaventura, and is given in his *Opera*, Mainz, 1609, vol. vi. p. 417, as a hymn for a *Little Office of the Passion* at Matins. *Mone*, No. 84, gives the text from three MSS. of the 14th cent., one at Strassburg, and two (one of which belonged to the abbey of Reichenau) at Karlsruhe. He mentions another MS. at Karlsruhe as assigning it to Compline on the festival of the Crown of Thorns; and *Daniel*, iv. p. 219, in giving the text of *Mone*, cites it as a hymn at Matins on this festival in the *Constanz Breviary*, 1516.
                                       [W. A. S.]

Translations in C. U.:—
1. In the Lord's atoning grief. By F. Oakeley. Written in 1841 for use in Margaret Street Chapel, London, of which the translator was then the Incumbent, and pub. in his *Devotions Commemorative of the Passion of Our Lord*, &c., 1842. In 1852 it was included, with alterations, in *Hys. and Introits*, and thence, in 1861, into *H. A. & M.*, in 5 st. of 4 l. This text has been repeated in several collections, and sometimes abridged to 3 st. as in Thring's *Coll.*, 1882.

2. In our Lord's atoning grief. This arrangement of Canon Oakeley's *tr.* appeared in the Cooke & Denton *Hymnal*, 1853, No. 68, and was repeated in Chope's *Hymnal*, 1864. St. i., ii., iv. are from *Oakeley*, and iii. is new.

Translation not in C. U.:—
Thy wondrous passion life, O Lord. *J. D. Chambers.* 1857.   [J. J.]

In streets and openings of the gates.

J. Logan. [*Voice of Wisdom.*] 1st pub. in the Scottish *Translations and Paraphrases*, 1781, No. x., in 7 st. of 4 l. We have ascribed this paraphrase to J. Logan on evidence given in the memoir of M. Bruce in this work (q.v.). In Miss J. E. Leeson's *Paraphs. and Hys.*, 1853, No. 43, this hymn opens with the same first line; but it is a rewritten form of the hymn in 4 st. by Miss Leeson.   [J. J.]

In the beginning God said "Be!"

J. Montgomery. [*Creation.*] This hymn is dated in the original MS. "Written at Dinsdale, Sep. 22, 1835." In 1853 it was included in Montgomery's *Original Hymns*, No. 2, in 4 st. of 4 l., and entitled "The Creation and Dissolution of all Things." Its use is limited.   [J. J.]

In the Cross of Christ I [we] glory.

Sir J. Bowring. [*Glorying in the Cross.*] Pub. in his *Hymns*, 1825, in 5 st. of 4 l., and based upon Gal. vi. 14. It has passed into numerous collections in G. Britain and America, and is one of the most widely known of the author's hymns. It is sometimes given as "In the Cross of Christ *we* glory." [J. J.]

In the fields with their flocks abiding. *F. W. Farrar.* [*Christmas Carol.*]

Written in 1871 for one of the Harrow Concerts, and subsequently embodied by Mr. John Farmer in his Oratorio *Christ and his Soldiers*. From the Oratorio it was transferred, together with the original music, to Mrs. Brock's *Children's H. Bk.*, 1881. It is also in several other collections.   [J. J.]

In the hour of my distress. *R. Herrick.*

[*Litany to the Holy Spirit.*] This Litany was pub. in his *Noble Numbers*, &c., 1647, in 12 st. of 4 l.; and in Dr. Grosart's *Early English Poets*, 1869, vol. iii. p. 132. The form in which it is found in C. U. is that of a cento. The stanzas chosen vary in the hymnals, those usually omitted being too quaint for congregational use. In some collections it begins "In the *time* of my distress." It is also sometimes given as "In the hour of *deep* distress," with the refrain "Good Spirit, comfort me." This form of the text appeared in Cotterill's *Sel.*, 1819, where it was given as a sequel to "O Thou from Whom all goodness flows." It is in extensive use in G. Britain and America. Orig. text in *Lyra Brit.*, 1867, p. 306. [See English Hymnody, Early, § ix.]   [J. J.]

In the hour of trial. *J. Montgomery.*

[*In Trial and Temptation.*] Montgomery's original MS. of this hymn is dated "October 13, 1834;" and on it the names of twenty-two persons are written to whom he sent MS. copies, together with the dates on which they were sent [M. MSS.]. The text is the same as that given in Montgomery's *Original Hymns*, 1853, No. 193, in 4 st. of 8 l., with the exception of st. iii., l. 4, which reads, "O'er the sacrifice." Four forms of the text (besides minor alterations), are in C. U.:—

1. The authorized text of 1853. This was given in Mercer's *Ch. Ps. & H. Bk.*, 1854, and has become exceedingly popular in G. Britain and America. This text is that given in the *Hy. Comp.* with st. i., l. 2, *Jesu* for "Jesus," and Bp. Bickersteth's note in (1876) on his text: "This hymn, by J. Montgomery (1825) is given, as varied by F. A. Hutton (1861)," is in error both with regard to date and text.

2. An altered text by Mrs. Frances A. Hutton, given in Prebendary H. W. Hutton's (Lincoln) *Supplement and Litanies*, N.D. This text is easily recognised by

numbers and in merit, in the front rank of the Singers of the Church. [J. J.]

Irons, Joseph, s. of William Irons, of Ware, was b. at Ware, Nov. 1785, and was for some years the friend of John Newton when the latter was Rector of St. Mary, Woolnoth, and an attendant upon his ministry. On the death of Newton, Irons joined the Nonconformists, and was for some time Pastor of a Nonconformist Chapel at Sawston, and then of the Grove Chapel, Camberwell, London. He d. April 3, 1852.

J. Irons's reputation as a preacher amongst the Nonconformists was very great. His sermons were intensely Calvinistic and very powerful; and the perorations, not unfrequently in poetical blank verse, were most striking and effective. His hymns are powerful, and at times poetical, but from their strong Calvinistic teaching have failed to become popular. They were published for use by his own congregation, and until several were adopted by Spurgeon in his *O. O. H. Bk.*, 1866, and Snepp in his *Songs of G. & G.*, 1872, were seldom found in any other collection for congregational use.

J. Irons's poetical works, including those in which his hymns appeared, were:—

(1) *Zion's Hymns intended as a Supplement to Dr. Watts's Psalms and Hymns. Printed for the Author by G. Youngman, Saffron Walden*, 1816. This ed. contained 247 hymns. It was enlarged, 2nd ed., 1819,; 3rd ed., 1825; 5th ed., 1827 (611 hymns). The title was afterwards changed to *Zion's Hymns, for the use of Zion's Sons and Daughters.* (2) *Nymphas. Bride and Bridegroom communing. A Paraphrastic Exposition of The Song of Solomon, in Blank Verse*, 1840; (3) *Judah, The Book of Psalms Paraphrased in Spiritual Songs for Public Worship*, 1847; and (4) *Calvary. A Poem in Blank Verse.*

From his *Zion's Hymns*, the following hymns, in addition to a few annotated under their respective first lines, are in C. U.:—

i. *From the 1st edition*, 1816:—

1. Hark, 'tis the Shepherd's voice. *The Good Shepherd.*
2. Holy Spirit, heavenly Dove. *Before Sermon.*
3. Jehovah's love first chose His Saints. *The Father's Love.*
4. Precious Bible, what a store. *Holy Scriptures.*
5. See from Zion's fountain rises. *The Water of Life.*
6. Zion, beloved of God. *The Church the Bride of Christ.*

ii. *From the 2nd edition*, 1819:—

7. In yonder realms where Jesus reigns. *The heavenly Mansions.*
8. O the happiness arising. *Happiness in Christ.*
9. What boundless and unchanging love. *The Father's Love.*

iii. *From the 3rd edition*, 1825:—

10. Are the saints predestinated? *Predestination.*
11. Arise, my soul, with songs to own. *Praise for Covenanting grace.*
12. Aspire, my soul, to yonder throne. *The Father Infinite.*
13. Awake, awake, ye saints of God. *Holiness of the Church desired.*
14. Father, we glory in Thy choice. *Holy Trinity.*
15. For ever, O delightful word. *Praise of God everlasting.*
16. Hark, how the choir around the throne. *Triumphs of Grace.*
17. Hark, how the glorious hosts above. *The Church Triumphant.*
18. Holy Father, let Thy love. *Holy Trinity.*
19. How safe are all the chosen race. *Final Perseverance.*
20. I sing the gracious, fixed decree. *Predestination.*
21. Jesus saw His Church elected. *The Church the Bride of Christ.*
22. Let party names no more be known. *Unity desired.*
23. Now let Jehovah's covenant love. *Saints precious to Jesus.*
24. O my Lord, how great Thy wonders. *Praise for Redemption.*
25. Of Israel's covenant I boast. *Praise for Covenanting Grace.*

26. One with Christ, O blissful thought. *Union with Christ.*
27. Praying soul, dismiss thy fear. *Christ the Intercessor.*
28. Rising on the One Foundation. *The Church the Temple of the Holy Spirit.*
29. We sing the Father's Love. *Holy Trinity.*

His paraphrases of the Psalms given in his *Judah*, &c., 1847, are almost unknown to modern hymn-books. The following are in C. U.:—

30. My heart expands with good enditing. *Ps.* xlv. This is given in Spurgeon's *O. O. H. Bk.*, 1866, as "Warm with love my heart's inditing."
31. My soul lies grovelling low. *Ps. cxix.*
32. O give thanks unto the Lord. *Ps. cvii.*

Although the use of these hymns is mainly confined to *Spurgeon* and *Snepp*, a few are found in other collections both in G. Britain and America. [J. J.]

Irons, William Josiah, D.D., s. of Joseph Irons above, was b. at Hoddesdon, Herts, Sep. 12, 1812, and educated at Queen's College, Oxford (B.A. 1833, D.D. 1854), and took Holy Orders 1835. In 1837 he became Incumbent of St. Peter's, Walworth, and was subsequently Vicar of Barkway, Incumbent of Brompton, Rector of Wadingham; and in 1872, Rector of St. Mary-Woolnoth, formerly held by his father's friend, John Newton. He was also Bampton Lecturer in 1870, and Prebendary of St. Paul's Cathedral. He d. June 18, 1883. Dr. Irons took a somewhat prominent part in the ecclesiastical controversies of his day, and published extensively thereon in the form of Sermons, Letters, Pamphlets, &c. His important work, the Bampton Lectures, 1870, was on *Christianity as taught by St. Paul.* His hymnwriting and translating began during his Curacy at St. Mary, Newington, 1835–1837, and was continued to his death. Many were first printed as broadsheets, and subsequently included in the Rev. R. T. Lowe's (Rector of Lea, Lincolnshire) *Hys. for the Christian Seasons*, Gainsburgh, 1st ed., 1854, and in his own collections. Of these separate publications the most important were his *tr.* of the *Dies Irae*, and *Quicumque vult*, and a few special *Hymns* (Hayes) in 1867. His hymnological works, in addition to these, were:—

(1) *Metrical Psalter*, 1857; (2) *Appendix to the Brompton Metrical Psalter*, 1861 (22 hymns); (3) *Hymns for Use in Church*, 1866 (100 hymns). These contained hymns by Dr. Irons, and others. The next contains his Translations and Original Hymns only. (4) *Psalms and Hymns for the Church*, 1st ed., 1873 (126 h.); 2nd ed., 1875 (190 h.); 3rd ed., 1883 (308 h.). The principal object of this last work was to supply special hymns on the Collects, Epistles, and Gospels, and for Advent and Lent, together with special hymns for the Festivals; and this to a great extent Dr. Irons was enabled to accomplish. His versions of individual Psalms are directly from the Hebrew, line for line.

In addition to those of Dr. Irons's hymns and translations, which are annotated under their respective first lines, the following are in C. U. outside of his own collections, the details appended being from his MS. notes:—

1. Blest voice of love, O Word divine. *Confirmation.* Written for a Confirmation at Brompton, and pub. in Lowe's *Hys. for the Christian Seasons*, 1854, No. 184; in the *Appendix to the Brompton Metrical Psalter*, 1861; and the author's later collections.
2. Can earthly voices fitly sing. *Public Opening of a School.* Written at Brompton on the occasion of the opening of a School, and pub. in the 1861 *Appendix* as above, and in the author's later collections.
3. Children of earth, for heaven we seek. *Epi-*

phany. A meditation on the Collect for the 1st S. after the Epiphany, and pub. in his *Ps. & Hys.* 1875.

4. **Eternal Spirit, God of Grace.** *Whitsuntide.* Written in 1865, and pub. in his *Hys. for Use in Church,* 1866, and in a revised form in his *Ps. & Hys.,* 1873.

5. **Faithful Creator, Lord Divine.** *Consecration to God.* Pub. in his *Ps. & Hys.,* &c., 1873.

6. **Father of love, our Guide and Friend.** *Confirmation.* Written for a large Confirmation at Brompton, in 1844, and pub. in Lowe's *Hys. for the Christian Seasons,* 1854, No. 185, and in the 1861 *Appendix* as above, and the author's later collections.

7. **Hail, holy rest, calm herald of that day.** *Sunday.* Pub. in his *Ps. & Hys.,* &c., 1873.

8. **Is not this our King and Prophet?** *Palm Sunday.* Pub. in his *Ps. & Hys.,* &c., 1873.

9. **It is not finished, Lord of grace.** *Preparation for Heaven.* Written in 1850. It is No. 45 of his *Hymns,* 1866, in 6 st. of 5 l.

10. **Jesu, Who for us didst bear.** *Words from the Cross.* In his *Hymns,* 1866, No. 42.

11. **Joy of joys, He lives, He lives.** *Easter.* Written in 1873. In the *N. Mitre,* 1875; and the author's *Hymns,* 1875.

12. **Lord, hear my prayer, bow down Thine ear.** *Lent.* Pub. in his *Ps. & Hys.,* 1873.

13. **Lord, in Thy wrath Thou thinkest yet.** *Lent.* In his *Hymns,* 1866, No. 91.

14. **Lord, Thy voice hath spoken.** *The Beatitudes.* In *Hys. for use in the Church of Saint Ethelburga, Bishopsgate,* 1873, and Dr. Irons's *Ps. & Hys.,* 1875.

15. **No sorrow and no sighing.** *Heaven.* Pub. in his *Ps. & Hys.,* 1873, in 5 st. of 4 l. In Thring's *Coll.,* 1882, st. i.–iii. were given from the 1875 text, and a new stanza was added by Dr Irons at Prebendary Thring's request.

16. **O God with us, the Saviour.** *For use during a Retreat.* Given in his *Ps. & Hys.,* 1873.

17. **O how long, how long.** *Ps. xiii.* Appeared in his *Ps. & Hys.,* &c., 1873.

18. **O Saviour, now at God's right hand.** *Jesus the High Priest.* Pub. in the 1861 *Appendix* as above, and revised in the author's latter collections. In the *Ps. & Hys.,* 1873., st. i., ii., v. are from 1861, iv. from 1866; and iii. is new.

19. **O who are they so pure and bright?** *Holy Innocents..* Written on the death of Infants in the Epidemic of 1837, and pub. in Lowe's *Hys. for the Christian Seasons,* 1854, No. 20, and in the 1861 *Appendix* as above, in 3 st. of 8 l. In the 1866 *Hymns* it was divided into 6 st. of 4 l., and this arrangement was repeated in the 1873 *Ps. & Hys.*

20. **Sing with all the sons of men.** *Easter.* Given in his *Ps. & Hys.,* 1873.

21. **Thanks be to God for meet and right.** *Processional.* Pub. in his *Hymns,* &c., 1866, and again in his *Ps. & Hys.,* 1873.

22. **To whom but Thee, O God of Grace.** *Passiontide.* Appeared in his *Hymns,* &c., 1866; and in his *Ps. & Hys.,* 1873.

23. **Triumphant Lord, Thy work is done.** *Ascension.* Pub. in the 1861 *Appendix* as above, in 3 st. of 4 l. In the 1866 *Hymns* the st. (iii.) "O by Thy spotless, wondrous birth" was added; and in this enlarged form the hymn was repeated in the *Ps. & Hys.,* 1873.

24. **We praise Thee, O our God—to Thee.** *Children's Hymn of Praise to the Holy Trinity.* Written for the Schools at St. Mary's Newington, and pub. in the 1861 *Appendix* as above, and repeated in the *Hymns,* &c., 1866, and the *Ps. & Hys.* 1873.

25. **Who is this from Bethlehem coming?** *Purification of B. V. M.* Appeared in the *Ps. & Hymns,* 1873.

26. **Why art thou weary, O my soul?** *Ps. lxi.* Given in his *Hymns,* &c., 1866, and his *Ps. & Hys.,* 1873, in 6 st. of 7 l. In Thring's *Coll.,* 1882, st. iii. is omitted.

Amongst modern hymn-writers, Dr. Irons ranks with the first. His hymns have not been largely used outside of his own congregation; but their high excellence, variety of subjects and metres, intense earnestness, powerful grasp of the subject, and almost faultless rhythm must commend them to the notice of hymn-book compilers. Prebendary Thring has enriched his *Coll.* (1882) with most of those named above. They are of more than usual excellence, and others remain of equal merit.   [J. J.]

Irvingite Hymnody. This brief title, which has been given by hymnologists to the

hymnody of **The Catholic and Apostolic Church,** is adopted throughout this work. The origin of the first hymn-book of this denomination is thus set forth in its Preface:—

"In addition to the Divine Songs and Anthems, principally from Holy Scripture, which have been hitherto in use among these congregations, a desire has long existed for a larger selection of hymns, for use both in the public worship of the Church and in private devotional exercises. The object in preparing this book has been to provide such Hymns as may aid, and serve to express, our faith and hope. Of these Hymns, some are original, and appear now for the first time in print: some have long been in use in different sections of the Church."

This collection was compiled by a committee of which Mr. E. W. Eddis was the leading member, and was published in 1864, as *Hymns for the Use of the Churches.* It contained 205 hymns. In 1871 it was enlarged to 320 hymns and 44 doxologies. The 3rd edition is a reprint of that of 1871 with a few verbal alterations. The original hymns contributed to this book were by Mr. E. W. Eddis and other writers, who have appended their initials to their hymns, but decline to give their names to the public. Some of these hymns have passed into other collections. Several of those by Mr. Eddis are of great merit, especially those of Praise, and might be transferred to other collections with advantage. This is the Official (and only) hymn-book of "The Catholic and Apostolic Church." [J. J.]

Is heaven a place where pearly streams. *P. J. Bailey.* [*Heaven.*] Appeared in his poem *Festus,* 1839. In the *Leeds H. Bk.,* 1853, it was given as "Is heaven a clime where diamond dews?" and in Dale's *English H. Bk.,* 1874, as "Is heaven a place where diamond dews?" In one or another of these forms it is also found elsewhere.   [J. J.]

Is the [thy] cruse of comfort wasting. *Elizabeth Charles.* [*The Cruse of Oil.*] Appeared in her *Three Wakings,* 1859, and repeated in the *Hy. Comp.,* revised ed., 1876, and appointed for "Almsgiving." It is also in several other collections, and sometimes as "Is *thy* cruse," &c.   [J. J.]

Is there in heaven and earth, who can? *B. Beddome.* [*Salvation through Jesus.*] Appeared anonymously in the 10th ed. of Rippon's *Sel.,* 1800, No. 294, pt. ii., in 6 st. of 4 l., and thence into a few later hymnals. In Beddome's (posthumous) *Hys.,* &c., 1817, No. 696, it is given as "Is there a friend in earth or heaven?" and headed "The All-sufficient Saviour."   [J. J.]

Israel in ancient days. *W. Cowper.* [*The Gospel in the Old Testament.*] Pub. in the *Olney Hymns,* 1779, Bk. i., No. 132, in 6 st. of 6 l., and headed "Old Testament Gospel." It is a poetical summary of some of the principal types of the Jewish Dispensation and their fulfilment in Jesus Christ. It is found in several modern collections. [J. J.]

Israel's Shepherd, guide me, feed me. *J. Bickersteth.* [*The Good Shepherd.*] This hymn is found in a *Select Portion of Psalms & Hymns,* 4th ed., Lancaster, W. Minshall, printer, 1816, No. 78, in 4 st. of 8 l., and again, with slight alterations, in the author's own *Ps. & Hys.,* 1819. Thence it passed into

Cotterill's *Sel.*, 1819; E. Bickersteth's *Christian Psalmody*, 1833; and numerous other collections. In a few hymn-books it begins: "*Heavenly* Shepherd, guide *us*, feed *us*." (See p. 142, i.)   [J. J.]

Ist Gott für mich, so trete. *P. Gerhardt.* [*Trust in God.*] Included in the Frankfurt ed., 1656, of Crüger's *Praxis pietatis melica*, as No. 380, in 15 st. of 8 l., reprinted in Wackernagel's ed. of his *Geistliche Lieder*, No. 63, and Bachmann's ed., No. 79, and included as No. 418 in the *Unv. L. S.*, 1851. It is a magnificent hymn of Christian confidence, founded on Romans viii. It was probably suggested by the troublous experiences of his life, but the idea that st. xiii. refers to his conflict with the Elector is disproved by the fact that the hymn was pub. in 1656, while the contest did not begin till 1662. Lauxmann, in *Koch*, viii. 408, quotes Langbecker as saying, "This heroic hymn of Gerhardt's is worthy to be placed side by side with Luther's 'Ein feste Burg'"; and himself says of it:—

"The hymn bears the watchword of the Lutheran Church as Paul gives it, 'If God be for us, who can be against us?' One thinks of Philip Melanchthon's last words as he, worn out with the manifold conflicts after Luther's death and with many bitter and grievous trials, lay a-dying on April 19, 1560, he once more raised himself in bed and cried 'If God be for us, who can be against us?' When one asked him if he wished anything, he replied, 'Nothing, save Heaven!' and gave up his spirit. In the same spirit it has been entitled 'A Christian hymn of Consolation and of Joy,' and has spoken to the hearts of many troubled ones and strengthened them with new courage for the fight of Faith."

The 15th st., "Mein Herze geht in Sprüngen," has been a special favourite in Germany, and Lauxmann, in *Koch*, relates of it in regard to a well-known German theologian:—

While still young, Professor Auberlen of Basel departed from this life in 1864. This highly gifted and highly cultured witness for the Faith was by an early death compelled to give up his greatly blessed labours, many projects, and a happy family life. On the 2nd of May, a few hours before his death, a friend said to him, "Christ's disciples follow in His pathway, first Death and the Grave, then Resurrection and Ascension." To this he replied, "Of the fear of death, thank God, I know nothing, and can say with Paulus Gerhardt:

'Ist Gott für mich, so trete
  Gleich alles wider mich.'"

In the same night (his last upon earth) he repeated st. xv. of this hymn. Soon after, his light, as a taper, quietly went out.

Translations in C. U.:—

1. **If God be on my side.** A good *tr.*, omitting st. iv.-vi., by Miss Winkworth, in her *Lyra Ger.*, 1st Ser., 1855, p. 130. Included, abridged, in *Holy Song*, 1869, and the *Evang. Hyl.*, New York, 1880. Centos from this *tr.* are:—

(1) *If Jesus be my friend* (st. i., l. 5), in the Andover *Sabbath H. Bk.* 1858, Hatfield's *Church H. Bk.*, 1872, &c.

(2) *Since Jesus is my friend* (st. i., l. 5 altered), in Robinson's *Songs for the Sanctuary*, N. Y., 1865, *Laudes Domini*, 1884, &c.

(3) *Here I can firmly rest* (st. ii.), in the Andover *Sabbath H. Bk.*, 1858, Pennsylvanian Luth. *Ch. Bk.*, 1868, and other American collections.

2. **If God Himself be for me.** A good *tr.*, omitting st. iv.-vi., x., contributed by R. Massie to the ed., 1857, of Mercer's *C. P. & H. Bk.*, No. 161 (Ox. ed., No. 406, abridged), and included in his own *Lyra Domestica*, 1864, p. 110. Varying centos are found in the Pennsylvania Luth. *Ch. Bk.*, 1868, Eng. Presb. *Ps. & Hys.*,

1867, and the *Free Church H. Bk.*, 1882. In *Laudes Domini*, N. Y., 1884, No. 378 begins "I build on this foundation" (st. iii.).

3. **Is God for me? I fear not.** A spirited if rather free version, omitting st. v., xi., xii., by Mrs. Bevan in her *Songs of Eternal Life*, 1858, p. 39; repeated, abridged, in Snepp's *Songs of G. & G.* In Reid's *Praise Bk.*, 1872, it appears as three hymns: (1) as above; (2) No. 622, beginning "There is no condemnation" (st. vi.), and (3) No. 623, beginning "In heaven is mine inheritance" (st. x.).

4. **Is God for me? t'oppose me.** In full, by J. Kelly, in his *P. Gerhardt's Spir. Songs*, 1867, p. 208. His *trs.* of st. iii., xiv., xv., beginning "My Faith securely buildeth," are No. 414 in the Ohio *Luth. Hyl.*, 1880.

Other *trs.* are, (1) "Is God for me? what is it," by *J. C. Jacobi*, 1725, p. 41 (1732, p. 139). Included in the *Moravian H. Bk.*, 1754; and repeated, abridged, in the 1789 and later eds., beginning "Is God my strong salvation"; (2) "The world may rise against me round" and "The world may fall beneath my feet," *trs.* of st. i., xiii., by Mrs. Stanley Carr in her *tr.* of Wildenhahn's *Paul Gerhardt*, 1845 (1856, pp. 173, 174).

[J. M.]

Iste Confessor Domini sacratus [colentes]. [*Saints' Days.*] This hymn is found in the Common of Confessors in the *Sarum, York, Aberdeen, Mozarabic, Roman* and other Breviaries. In the *Roman Brev.* of 1632 (text in *Daniel*, i., No. 226) it is altered considerably, beginning "Iste confessor Domini *colentes.*"

Daniel, after giving the text at i., No. 226, notes at iv. p. 371, that it is contained in a 9th cent. MS. at Bern as a hymn on St. Germanus. It is in three MSS. of the 11th cent. in the *British Museum* (Vesp. D. xii. f. 108; Jul. A. vi. f. 66 b; Harl. 2961, f. 249), and in the *Lat. Hys. of the Anglo-Saxon Ch.*, 1851, p. 136, is printed from an 11th cent. MS. at Durham (B. iii. 32, f. 40). Also in three MSS. (Nos. 387, 413, 414) of the 11th cent. at St. Gall. Also in Card. Newman's *Hymni Ecclesiae*, 1838 and 1865. The text usually *tr.* is from the *Rom. Brev.* of 1632.   [J. M.]

Translations in C. U.:—

1. **The Confessor of Christ, from shore to shore.** By E. Caswall, in his *Lyra Catholica*, 1849, p. 216, and again in his *Hys. & Poems*, 1873, p. 114. This is also given in some Roman Catholic collections for Missions and Schools.

2. **He, the Confessor of the Lord, with triumph.** By J. M. Neale, in the *H. Noted*, 1852, No. 41.

3. **This is the day when Jesus' true Confessor.** By R. F. Littledale, made for and first pub. in the *People's H.*, 1867, and repeated, except the alternative first stanza and the third, in the Marquess of Bute's *Rom. Brev. in English*, 1879, i. p. 842.

4. **He, whom in all lands celebrate the faithful.** Appeared in the *Antiphoner & Grail*, 1880, and the *Hymner*, 1882, and appointed for St. Silvester.

Translations not in C. U.:—

1. *Unto Thine holy Confessor, our voices.* W. J. *Blew*, 1852.

2. *This Thy Confessor Lord! of fame sublime.* J. D. *Chambers* (from the older text), 1866.

3. *O'er all the world the faithful sing.* J. Wallace, 1874.   [J. J.]

It is my sweetest comfort, Lord. *E. Caswall.* [*Christ's Humanity.*] 1st pub. in his *Masque of Mary*, &c., 1858, p. 255, in 4 st. of 4 l., and headed "Christ's Humanity;" and again, in a revised form, in his *Hys. & Poems*, 1873, p. 276. It is given in several modern hymn-books.   [J. J.]

It is the Lord, behold His hand.
J. Montgomery. [*In Times of Distress.*]
Written Aug. 22, 1832, during the epidemic
of cholera in Sheffield, and for use in that
town (M. MSS.). It was pub. in Montgomery's *Original Hymns*, 1853, No. 290, in
6 st. of 4 l., and entitled "During the Cholera
—Confession and Supplication." In *Kennedy*,
1863, No. 457, it is abbreviated, and altered.
The companion hymn, also written on Aug.
22, 1832, and for the same purpose, was "Let
the land mourn through all its coasts." This
was pub. in the *Original Hys.*, 1853, No. 289,
in 6 st. of 4 l., and is in C. U. in G. Britain
and America. The hymns, "Sing Hallelujah,
sing," and "Walking on the winged wind,"
were written by Montgomery at the close of
the same year as a "Thanksgiving for Deliverance from the Cholera" (M. MSS.), and also
pub. in his *Original Hymns*, 1853.   [J. J.]

It is Thy hand, my God. J. G. Deck.
[*In Affliction.*] The origin of this hymn is
thus stated by the author in *Joy in Departing: a Memoir of the Conversion and Last
Days of Augustus James Clarke, who fell
asleep in Jesus, May 2nd,* 1845. By J. G.
Deck, London, 1847, p. 34 :—

"It was written originally to comfort a bereaved
mother and widow in her hour of sorrow, and the Lord
made it a comfort to the soul of this young disciple."

The date of its composition is unknown.
It was pub. in *Psalms & Hymns & Spiritual
Songs in two Parts*, Lond., D. Walther, 1842,
pt. ii., No. 70, in 6 st. of 4 l., and headed " In
Sorrow." It was repeated in numerous col-
lections, and is in C. U. in G. Britain and
America, and sometimes with the erroneous
signature of "J. N. Darby."   [J. J.]

Italian Hymnody. [Various.]

**I've found the Pearl of greatest
price.** J. Mason. [*Praise of Christ.*] 1st
pub. in his *Spiritual Songs, or Songs of Praise
to Almighty God, &c.,* 1683, No. 13, in 4 st.
of 8 l. and 1 st. of 4 l., and headed "A Song
of Praise for Christ;" and again in D. Sedgwick's reprint, 1859, p. 210. Various arrangements of the text are in C. U. in G. Britain
and America, including the alteration, " I've
found the precious Christ of God," in the
Enlarged London H. Bk., 1873, and others.
The alterations and transpositions in the text
are too numerous to enumerate. They can
easily be detected by reference to the Sedgwick reprint as above. The opening lines of
the original read:—

"I've found the Pearl of greatest Price,
    My heart doth sing for joy;
And sing I must; *a Christ I have;
    O what a Christ have I?*"

The words in italics Mason expanded into
a poem which was included in his *Poetical
Remains*, 1694. This poem was given in *A
Pocket Hymn-Book designed as a constant
Companion for the Pious, collected from Various
Authors*, York, R. Spence (5th ed., 1786, No.
113), the first stanza being:—

" A Christ I have, O what a Christ have I.
He built the globe, he spread the starry sky !
And yet for me, and Adam's sinful race,
He bled and dy'd to manifest his grace."

In 1786 this book was reprinted at the
request of the Conference held at Bristol that
year, with omissions and additions by J.

Wesley, as *A Pocket Hymn-Book for the Use
of Christians of All Denominations.* London,
1786. Wesley's Preface is exceedingly plain
and severe. This hymn and one by James
Allen were omitted, with others, in the reprint, and the omission is specially explained :

"But a friend tells me 'Some of these, specially those
two that are doggerel double distilled, namely, " The
despised Nazarene," and that which begins, " A Christ
I have, O what a Christ have I," are hugely admired,
and continually echoed from *Berwick-upon-Tweed* to
London.' If they are I am sorry for it : it will bring a
deep reproach on the judgment of the Methodists."

Usually these strictures are said to have
been applied by Wesley to "I've found the
Pearl of greatest price," in the 1st st. of which
the line " A Christ I have, &c.," is embedded.
This is not so. They apply to the hymn from
the *Poetical Remains* of 1694, in which the
first line of each stanza begins, " A Christ
I have, O what a Christ have I." It is to be
noted that the words, "doggerel double
distilled," are not J. Wesley's, but are given
by him as a quotation from " a friend." [J. J.]

J

J., in Collyer's *Sel.*, 1812, i.e. Jane Taylor.

J. A., in *Gospel Magazine*, 1776, i.e. John
Adams.

J. A. E., in Dale's *English Hymn Book*,
1874, i.e. Julia A. Elliott.

J. B., *Essex*, in *Child's Companion*, i.e. John
Burton.

J. C. and **T. C.**, in *English and Scottish
Psalters.* See Old Version.

J. C. W., in Bristol Bap. *Coll.* of Ash
and Evans, 1769, i.e. J. & C. Wesley.

J. E., in *The Christian's Magazine*, 1790-
1793, i.e. Jonathan Evans.

J. E., *Coventry*, in *The Gospel Magazine*,
1771-1778, i.e. Jonathan Evans.

J. E. L., in the Irvingite *Hymns for the
Use of the Churches*, 1864 and 1871, i.e. Jane
E. Leeson.

J. E. M., in the *People's Hymnal*, 1867, i.e.
J. E. Millard.

J. J., in *The Christian Observer*, 1809, i.e.
J. Joyce.

J. L., in Beard's Unitarian *Coll. of Hymns*,
1837, i.e. John Lagniel.

J. M., in *late* editions of Bristol Bap. *Coll.*
of Ash & Evans (1st ed., 1769), i.e. J. Montgomery.

J. M., in P. Maurice's *Choral Hymn Book*,
1861, i.e. Jane Maurice.

J. P., in *Fresh Laurels*, N. Y., 1867, i.e.
Josephine Pollard.

J. S., in the Bristol Bap. *Coll.* of Ash &
Evans, 1769, i.e. J. Stennett.

Jackson, Edward, M.A., was b. in 1812,
and took Holy Orders in 1845, and became
Clerk in Orders of Leeds Parish Church the
same year, Incumbent of St. James's, Leeds,
1846, and Hon. Canon of Ripon, 1875. He
received his M.A. from the Archbishop of
Canterbury, 1847. In 1875 Canon Jackson
pub. a *Supplement of Hymns for Use in Public*

Worship, Mission Services, and Schools, to which he contributed several original hymns, and a few adaptations from the German. Some of these have passed into other collections and include :—

1. And now we go away and leave this hallowed place. *Close of Service.*
2. Assembled in Thy temple, Lord. *Divine Worship.*
3. Begin the glorious lay. *Easter.*
4. Behold the sacred rite. *H. Communion.*
5. Come, little child, with me. *S. Schools.*
6. Gathered in this sacred place. *Divine Worship.*
7. Gathered in this upper room. *Mission Service.*
8. God is gone up on high, Bless ye, &c. *Ascension.*
9. Hail to the holy morn. *Christmas.*
10. Hear us, holy Jesus. *Lent.*
11. How blest in Jesus' steps to tread. *Imitation of Christ.*
12. Lord, once more we sing Thy praises. *School Festival.*
13. Met at this most solemn time. *Close of the Year.*
14. Most Holy Lord and God, Lo, in Thy courts. *Divine Worship.*
15. O no! it is not death to fly Above earth's, &c. *Death the entrance into Life.*
16. One more year is passed away. *Old & New Year.*
17. Spirit of Christ and God, Pt. i. *Whitsuntide.*
18. Spirit of cleansing grace, Pt. ii. *Whitsuntide.*
19. Spared by Thy goodness, gracious Lord. *Parish Festival.*
20. The power that rules the globe. *Christ's Power to Heal.*
21. To God all glory be. *Holy Trinity.*
22. To those who tread with duteous pace. *The Christian Seasons.* [J. J.]

Jackson, Edward Hall, s. of a civil engineer, was b. in Birmingham, April 19, 1838. In 1856 he joined a Baptist Church, and in 1859 became a Baptist minister. In that capacity he has laboured in Liverpool, Billesdon (Leicestershire), Castle Donington, Ripley, and Louth; and as an occasional lecturer he has been widely popular. His hymns have been composed chiefly for S. School Anniversaries. Three were introduced into the *Baptist Hymnal,* 1879, and seven into the *School Hymnal,* 1880. The following are found in several S. S. collections :—

1. A thousand blessings on the place. *The Sunday School.*
2. Brethren, we have found the Lord. *Invitation to Church Fellowship.*
3. Fearless, calm, and strong in love. *Teachers' Meeting.*
4. Hark for a voice to the children calling. *Invitation Heavenwards.*
5. How fair are the lilies, what fragrance they yield. *Flower Services.*
6. I have a work, O Lord. *Teachers' Prayer.*
7. Jesus, hear us for the young. *Teachers' Prayer.*
8. Little vessels on life's waters. *Prayer for the Young.*
9. Love each other, little children. *Love and Patience.*
10. Shall Jesus bid the children come? *Children invited to Christ.*
11. The golden land is shining. *Heaven.* [W. R. S.]

Jackson, Martha Evans. [Shelley, Martha E.]

Jacobi, John Christian, a native of Germany, was b. in 1670, and appointed Keeper of the Royal German Chapel, St. James's Palace, London, about 1708. He held that post for 42 years, and d. Dec. 14, 1750. He was buried in the Church of St. Paul's, Covent Garden. His publications included :—

(1) *A Collection of Divine Hymns, Translated from the High Dutch. Together with their Proper Tunes and Thorough Bass. London: Printed and Sold by J. Young, in 'St. Paul's Churchyard; . . .* 1720. This edition contains 15 hymns. Two years later this collection, with a few changes in the text and much enlarged, was republished as (2) *Psalmodia Germanica; or a Specimen of Divine Hymns. Translated from the High*

Dutch. Together with their Proper Tunes and Thorough Bass. London: J. Young . . . 1722. This edition contained 62 hymns, of which 3 (" He reigns, the Lord our Saviour reigns"; "Is God withdrawing"? "Shepherds rejoice ") and the first stanza of another (" Raise your devotion, mortal tongues," from "Hosannah to the Prince of Life ") were taken from I. Watts. A 2nd Part was added in 1725, and was incorporated with the former part in 1732. Lond., G. Smith. After Jacobi's death the *Psalmodia Germanica* was republished, in 1765, by John Haberkorn, with a *Supplement* of 32 pieces. [G. A. C.]

Jacobus de Benedictis, commonly known as **Jacopone,** was b. at Todi in Umbria, early in the 13th cent., his proper name being Jacopone di Benedetti. He was descended from a noble family, and for some time led a secular life. Some remarkable circumstances which attended the violent death of his wife, led him to withdraw himself from the world, and to enter the Order of St. Francis, in which he remained as a lay brother till his death, at an advanced age, in 1306. His zeal led him to attack the religious abuses of the day. This brought him into conflict with Pope Boniface VIII., the result being imprisonment for long periods. His poetical pieces were written, some in Italian, and some in Latin, the most famous of the latter being " Cur mundus militat sub vanâ gloriâ " (possibly by Walter Mapes), and the " Stabat Mater dolorosa." Archbishop Trench says of him :—

" An earnest humourist, he carried the being a fool for Christ into every-day life. The things which with this intent he did, some morally striking enough, others mere extravagances and pieces of gross spiritual buffoonery—wisdom and folly, such as we often find, side by side, in the saints of the Roman Calendar—are largely reported by Wadding, the historian of the Franciscan Order, and by Lisco, in a separate monograph on the *Stabat Mater,* Berlin, 1843, p. 23. These often leave one in doubt whether he was indeed perfectly sound in his mind, or only a Christian Brutus, feigning folly, that he might impress his wisdom the more deeply, and utter it with more freedom." *Sac. Latin Poetry,* 3rd ed., 1874, p. 268.

Sketches of the life and writings of Jacopone, drawn entirely from the original sources (*Trench*), have been pub. as follows :—

(1) By Mohnike, *Studien* Stralsund, 1825, vol. i. pp. 335–406 ; (2) by Ozanam, *Les Poëtes Franciscains en Italie au Treizième Siècle,* Paris. In addition there are articles in the *Biographie Universelle ; Macmillan's Magazine,* Aug., 1873 ; and the *Enc. Britannica,* 9th ed. [J. J.]

Jacque, George, s. of George Jacque, Douglas, Lanarkshire, was b. near Douglas, Jan. 18, 1804. After studying at the University of Glasgow, he became, in 1835, minister of the South U. P. Church, Auchterarder, Perthshire. He has pub. *The Clouds; a Poem,* 1866 ; and *Hope, its Lights and Shadows,* 1875. He was appointed a member of the Hymnal Committee of the U. P. Church in 1870, and contributed the following to their *Presb. Hymnal,* 1876 :—

1. Hark, how heaven is calling. *Divine Worship.*
2. O Thou in Whom are all our springs. *National Hymn.* [J. M.]

Jactamur heu quot fluctibus. *C. Coffin.* [*Evening.*] Pub. in the *Paris Breviary,* 1736, as the hymn for Mondays at Vespers, and in his *Hymni Sacri,* 1736, p. 13. It is also in the *Lyons* and other modern French Breviaries ; Chandler's *Hys. of the Primitive Church,* 1837, No. 19, and Card. Newman's *Hymni Ecclesiae,* 1838 and 1865. [W. A. S.]

Translation in C. U. :—

When storm and tempest o'er us roll. By J. Chandler in his *Hys. of the P. Church*, 1837, p. 16. This is repeated in a few collections. In the *Hymnary*, 1872, it is given as, " When earth's fierce tempest o'er us rolls."

Translations not in C. U. :—

1. Now us with winds and waves at war. *I. Williams.* 1839.
2. We lift our eyes oppressed with ills. *J. M. Neale.* In R. Campbell's *Hys. & Anthems.* 1850.
3. Tost on the ocean drift. *W. J. Blew.* 1852 and 1855.
4. Tost on the wave, by tempest driven. *J. D. Chambers.* 1857.   [J. J.]

Jahn, Martin. [**Janus, M.**]

Jam Christe sol justitiae. [*Lent.*] In this hymn Lent is regarded as a season of waiting and penitential preparation for the Second Creation at Easter. It does not seem to be earlier than the 6th cent. It is found in two mss. of the 11th cent. in the *British Museum*, viz. in a *Hymnarium* (Vesp. D. xii. f. 120), and in a *Mozarabic Breviary* (Add. 30848, f. 98). From the former of these it is printed in the *Lat. Hys. of the Anglo-Saxon Ch.*, 1851, p. 155. It is found in the older *Roman* (e. g. Venice, 1478) and *Aberdeen Breviaries.* Also in *Mone*, No. 69; *Daniel*, i., No. 214, &c. In the revised *Roman Breviary*, 1632, it begins **O sol salutis, intimis,** and this form is repeated in later eds. of that Breviary; in *Daniel*, i., No. 214; and in Card. Newman's *Hymni Ecclesiae*, 1838 and 1865.   [J. M.]

Both forms of this hymn have been *tr.* into English as follows :—

i. **Jam Christe sol justitiae.** This is *tr.* by J. D. Chambers, in his *Lauda Syon*, 1857, p. 129, as :—"O Christ ! Thou Sun of justice, come."

ii. **O sol salutis, intimis.** The *trs.* in C. U. are :

1. **The darkness fleets, and joyful earth.** By E. Caswall, in his *Lyra Catholica*, 1849, p. 74, and again in his *Hys. & Poems*, 1873, p. 41. It is in C. U. in its original translated form, and also (1) the same with slight alterations as in the *Hymnary*, 1872; (2) the same abbreviated ; (3) as "When darkness fleets, and joyful earth," as in the *People's H.*, 1867; and as (4) "Jesu, true Sun of human souls," in the 1862 *Appendix* to the *H. Noted.*

Translations not in C. U. :—

1. O sovereign Sun, diffuse Thy light. *Primer*, 1706, in Shipley's *Annus Sanctus*, 1884.
2. Salvation's Sun, the inward gloom. *Bp. Mant*, 1837.
3. Lord, Sun of salvation, pour. *A. J. B. Hope*, 1844.
4. O Jesu, Sun of health divine. *W. J. Copeland*, 1848.
5. O Jesu, Sun of Justice, shine. *J. Wallace*, 1874.
6. Jesu, Sun of our Salvation. *D. T. Morgan*, 1880.
    [J. J.]

Jam Christus astra ascenderat. *St. Ambrose?* [*Whitsuntide.*] This hymn is ascribed to St. Ambrose by *Thomasius, Mone* and others, but is not assigned to him by the Benedictine editors. It is a metrical setting of Acts ii. 1–16, without much beauty or point. *Thomasius*, ii. 374, cites it as in a Vatican ms. of the 8th cent. It is in three mss. of the 11th cent. in the British Museum; two of the English Church (Vesp. D. xii. f. 79; Jul. A. vi. f. 52), and one of the ancient Spanish Church (Add. 30848, f. 158) ; and in the *Latin Hys. of the Anglo-Saxon Church*, 1851, p, 95, is printed from an 11th cent. ms.

at Durham (B. iii. 32, f. 28). Also in an 11th cent. ms. at St. Gall, No. 387. In the *Sarum Breviary* it was the hymn at First Vespers on Whitsunday and daily to Trinity Sunday ; the second part, Impleta gaudent viscera, being assigned to Lauds. In the *York* and *Roman Breviaries* it was the hymn at Matins in Whitsuntide. In the Durham ms. "De Patris ergo lumine" (l. 13) is assigned to Sext, and "Judaea tunc incredula" (l. 25) to None in Whitsuntide. The printed text is also in *Mone*, No. 182; *Daniel*, i., No. 57, and iv. p. 83; and the Littlemore *Hymnale secundum Usum* . . . . *Eccl. Sarisburiensis*, 1850, p. 70.   [J. M.]

Both parts of this hymn have been *tr.* into English, and are in C. U. as follows :—

i. **Jam Christus astra ascenderat.** *Tr.* as :—

1. **Above the starry spheres.** By E. Caswall, in his *Lyra Catholica*, 1849, p. 104; and again in his *Hys. & Poems*, 1873, p. 59. It is usually slightly altered, as in *H. A. & M.*
2. **Now Christ ascending whence He came.** By J. M. Neale, in the *H. Noted*, 1854, the *Hymner*, 1882, &c. Sometimes as "Now Christ, gone up to whence He came," as in the *Salisbury Hy. Bk.* 1857.
3. **Now Christ unto the stars above.** By R. F. Littledale, in the *People's H.*, 1867, signed "L." ; and again, somewhat altered, in the Irvingite *Hys. for the Use of the Churches*, 1871.
4. **Christ had regained the sky.** By E. A. Dayman, in the *Sarum Hymnal*, 1868, in 9 st. of 6 l., and again in the *Hymnary*, 1872, in 6 st. of 6 l.

Translations not in C. U. :—

1. O our redemption, Jesu Christ. *Primer*, 1604.
2. O Jesu, Who our souls doth save. *Primer*, 1619.
3. Now Christ hath pierced the skies to claim. *Primer*, 1706.
4. Now Christ beyond the stars had gone. *W. J. Copeland*, 1848.
5. Now Christ had climbed the starry skies. *W. J. Blew*, 1852–55.
6. Now, Christ above the starry skies. *J. D. Chambers*, 1857.
7. Now far above the starry plain. J. D. Aylward, in Shipley's *Annus Sanctus*, 1884.
8. To former scenes of glorious light. By H. Trend, in *Lyra Messianica*, 1864.
9. Now Christ beyond the stars is gone. *J. Wallace*, 1874.

ii. **Impleta gaudent viscera.** *Tr.* as :—

1 **Breathed on by God the Holy Ghost.** By R. F. Littledale, in the *People's H.*, 1867, and signed "A. L. P."
2. **With joy the Apostles' breasts are fired.** Anonymous in the *Antiphoner & Grail*, 1880, and the *Hymner*, 1882.

In addition to these *trs.* Mr. Blew has a *tr.* beginning "To men from every nation call'd." This opens with st. ii. of "Impleta gaudent viscera," beginning "Notique cunctis gentibus."   [J. J.]

Jam desinant suspiria. *C. Coffin.* [*Christmas.*] The hymn for Matins of Christmas Day in the *Paris Breviary*, 1736; and again in his *Hymni Sacri*, 1736, p. 36. It is also in the *Lyons* and other French Brevs., J. Chandler's *Hys. of the Primitive Church*, 1837, No. 41, and Card. Newman's *Hymni Ecclesiae*, 1838 and 1865.   [W. A. S.]

Translations in C. U. :—

1. **Cease, weary mortals, cease to sigh.** By J. Chandler in his *Hys. of the P. Church*, 1837, p. 44. This was repeated in Johnston's *English*

Hymnal, 1852, and again, with alterations, in 1856 and 1861.

2. Away with sorrow's sigh. By I. Williams, in his *Hys. tr. from the Parisian Brev.*, 1839, p. 53. This is given in Lord Selborne's *Bk. of Praise*, 1862.

3. God from on high hath heard. By Bp. J. R. Woodford. Written about 1850, and 1st pub. in his *Hys. Arranged for Sundays*, &c., 1852 and 1855. It is found in numerous hymn-books, and in various forms, the principal of which are :—

(1) The original *tr.* in Chope's *Hymnal*, 1864.
(2) The text in S.M. as in *H. A. & M.* This was given in the trial copy of *H. A. & M.*, 1859, and in the eds. of 1861 and 1875. It is also in many other collections. It is an altered version of Bp. Woodford's *tr.*, was made without his knowledge, and was never accepted by him. [E. MSS.]
(3) The *Parish Hymn Book*, 1863 and 1875. This text is thus composed : st. i.–v. and viii. are from Bp. Woodford's *tr.*; and st. vi., vii. are by the Rev. G. Phillimore. [E. MSS.].
(4) The *Sarum Hymnal* text, 1868, No. 40. This is Bp. Woodford's revised and authorized text. [E. MSS.]. It is given, slightly altered, in the *Hymnary*, 1872.
(5) The S. P. C. K. *Church Hymns*, 1871. This text is thus composed : st. i.–iii., Bp. Woodford's original *tr.*; st. iv., v. the same but slightly altered; st. vi., from Bp. Woodford's revised text in the *Sarum*, 1868 ; st. vii., viii., by G. Phillimore, as in the *Parish H. Bk.*

It should be noted in connection with this *tr.* that the beautiful lines in the *Sarum* text,

" Adoring tremble still,
And trembling still adore,"

are from I. Williams's *tr.*, 1839, where they are given as one line.

4. Now suspend the wistful sigh. By G. Rorison, in his *Hys. & Anthems*, 1851, No. 23, and the 1862 *Appendix* to the *H. Noted*, No. 125.

5. Clear through the silent night. This *tr.* in T. Darling's *Hys. for the Ch. of England*, 1887, is a slightly altered form of the *H. A. & M.* text beginning with st. ii.

6. Calmed be our griefs, hushed every sigh. By J. D. Chambers in his *Lauda Syon*, 1857. This was repeated in the *Hymnal for the Use of St. John the Evangelist*, Aberdeen, 1870.

7. Hark ! on the midnight air. In Skinner's *Daily Service Hymnal*, 1864; and the *Altar Hymnal*, 1884. This text is as follows: sts. i.-iv. by Bp. Woodford in the *Parish H. Bk.* as above ; st. v. from G. Phillimore's addition to the same, altered ; and the rest by A. H. Ward.

8. Now let mournful sighing cease. By R. F. Littledale in the *People's H.*, 1867, and signed " A. L. P."

Translations not in C. U. :—
1. Ye people, cease from tears. *R. Campbell.* 1850.
2. Let sighing cease and woe. *W. J. Blew.* 1852.
3. Now signs of mourning disappear. *Lord Braye.* In O. Shipley's *Annus Sanctus*, 1884. [J. J.]

Jam lucis orto sidere. [*Morning.*] This hymn has frequently been ascribed to St. Ambrose, but it is not assigned to him by the Benedictine editors, or by Biraghi in his *Inni sinceri e carmi di Sant' Ambrogio*, 1862. It is certainly ancient, and may possibly be as old as the 5th cent. *Mone*, i. p. 372, cites it as in an 8th cent. MS. at Darmstadt, and in two MSS. of the 8th cent. at Trier; in each case appointed for Prime. It is found in three MSS. of the 11th cent. in the British Museum (Vesp. D. xii. f. 7 *b* ; Jul. A. vi. f. 21 ; Harl. 2961 f. 219 *b*). In the *Lat. Hys. of the Anglo-Saxon Church* (Surtees Society), 1851, p. 9, it is printed from an 11th cent. MS. at Durham (B. iii. 32 f. 4). It is also in an 11th cent. MS. at Corpus Christi College, Cambridge (391, p.

230) ; in the St. Gall MSS. 313, 314 of the 11th cent., &c. In almost all Mediaeval Breviaries, including the *Sarum, York, Aberdeen, Mozarabic* of 1502, *Roman* (Venice, 1478, and the revision of 1632) and *Paris* of 1643 ; uniformly as a hymn at Prime in the Daily Office. The text is also in *Daniel*, i., No. 48, with a reference at iv. p. 42 to it as in a Rheinau MS. of the 10th cent. ; in the *Hymnarium Sarisb.*, 1851, p. 38 ; in *Wackernagel*, i., No. 67 ; in Card. Newman's *Hymni Ecclesiae*, 1838 and 1865, &c. In the *Paris Brev.*, 1736, it is recast by Charles Coffin, and this text is in J. Chandler's *Hys. of the Primitive Church*, 1837, No. 3 ; Card. Newman's *Hymni Ecclesiae*, 1838 and 1865 ; Macgill's *Songs of the Christian Creed and Life*, 1876. [J. M.]

Both forms of this hymn have been *tr.* into English, and have come into extensive C. U. as follows :—

i. *The Original Text.*

1. Brightly shines the morning star. By Bp. R. Mant, in his *Ancient Hymns*, &c., 1837, p. 4 (ed. 1871, p. 8). In *Kennedy*, 1863.

2. Now hath arisen the star of day. By H. Alford, in his *Ps. & Hys.*, 1844, No. 106 ; and again in his *Year of Praise*, 1867.

3. Now doth the sun ascend the sky. By E. Caswall, in his *Lyra Catholica*, 1849, p. 9 ; and again in his *Hys. and Poems*, 1873, p. 6. This was repeated in Oldknow's *Hymns*, &c., 1850; with slight alterations in the *People's H.*, 1867 ; and also in other collections.

4. Now that the daylight fills the sky. By J. M. Neale, in the *Hymnal N.*, 1852, No. 4. This is given unaltered in several hymn-books. In *H. A. & M.*, 1861 and 1875, it begins with the same first line, but the text is very much altered by the compilers. This is repeated in *Kennedy*, 1863, No. 821. The text in Pott's *Hymns*, &c., 1861, is altered by the editor. In the S. P. C. K. *Church Hys.*, 1871, the text of *H. A. & M.* is taken with slight alterations. The text in Thring's *Coll.*, 1882, is Neale's altered by Thring. In addition to these it is altered in the *English Hymnal*, 1852 and 1861, to " Now that the day-star mounts the sky [on high] ; " in the *Sarum Hyl.*, 1868, " While now the daylight fills the sky ; " and the *Hymnary*, 1872, " Again the daylight fills the sky." When these arrangements of Neale's *tr.* of the hymn are all taken into account it is found that his *tr.* is the most widely used of any.

5. The star of light is rising bright. By W. J. Blew, in his *Church Hymn & Tune Bk.*, 1852-55, and again in Rice's *Sel.* from the same, 1870.

6. As mounts on high the orb of day. By R. C. Singleton, written in 1867, and pub. in his *Anglican H. Bk.*, 1868.

7. The star of light ascends the sky. By G. Moultrie, in his *Hys. and Lyrics*, 1867, and the Irvingite *Hys. for the Use of the Churches*, 1871.

Other translations are :—
1. Now that the day-star doth arise. Bp. Cosin, in his *Coll. of Private Devotions*, 1627. (Rivington's ed., 1838, p. 39).
2. The morning star has risen, and we. W. W. Hull, in his *Coll. of Hymns*, 1833.
3. The star of morn to night succeeds. Card. J. H. Newman, in *Tracts for the Times*, No. 75, p. 55.
4. Now that the star of light hath risen. *A. J. B. Hope.* 1844.
5. Yon herald star hath brought the morn. *Hymnarium Anglicanum*, 1844.

6. While now the sun his course begins. Bp. J. Williams, in his *Ancient Hys.*, Hartford, U. S. A., 1845.

7. Now day's bright star is risen afar. *W. J. Copeland.* 1848.

8. Now the day-star bright is born. *G. Rorison.* 1851.

9. The star of light hath risen, and now. *J. D. Chambers.* 1857.

10. Riseth now the star of day. H. Bonar, in his *Hys. of Faith & Hope*, 1857.

11. The star of day hath risen, and we. J. Keble, in his *Misc. Poems*, 1870.

12. The star of morn is in the skies. *H. M. Macgill.* 1876.

13. The day-star shows his radiant face. *J. Wallace.* 1874.

ii. The Paris Breviary Text.

1. Once more the sun is beaming bright. By J. Chandler, in his *Hys. of the Primitive Church*, 1837, p. 3 : into the *Wes. H. Bk.*, 1875, and others. In the Cooke and Denton *Church Hyl.*, 1853, it was altered to "Now whilst the sun is beaming bright;" and in Mercer's *Ch. Psalter & H. Bk.*, 1864, it is rewritten from c.m. to l.m. as "The star of morn now wakes from sleep."

2. Now that the day-star glimmers bright. By Card. J. H. Newman, in his *Verses on Religious Subjects*, 1853; and his *Verses on Various Occasions*, 1868, p. 234, where it is dated "Littlemore, February, 1842." In the American Unitarian *Hys. for the Church of Christ*, 1853, No. 365, it was given in 4 s⁴ as "Now that the sun is beaming bright." This was repeated in Spurgeon's *O. O. H. Bk.*, 1866 ; W. F. Stevenson's *Hys. for Church and Home*, 1873 ; Martineau's *Hymns*, &c., 1873, and others. In Beecher's *Plymouth Coll.*, 1855, and others, it reads, "Now that the sun is gleaming bright."

Other trs. are :—

1. Now morn's star hath woke from sleep. I. Williams, in the *British Magazine*, Jan. 1834; and his *Hys. tr. from the Parisian Breviary.* 1839, p. 5.

2. The star of light hath risen, and now (st. iii., "As wane the hours," &c.). *J. D. Chambers.* 1857.

3. The star of light has risen, O Lord, &c. By G. Phillimore in the *Parish H. Bk.*, 1863 and 1875.

4. The star of morn is in the skies. *H. M. Macgill.* 1876.   [J. J.]

Jam non te lacerant carnificum manus. *Jean Baptiste de Santeüil.* [*Common of One Martyr.*] Appeared in the *Cluniac Breviary*, 1686, p. xviii., and in his *Hymni Sacri et Novi*, 1689, p. 202, and again in edition 1698, p. 244, in 5 st. of 4 l. It was included in the *Paris Brev.*, 1736, and is also found in the *Lyons* and other modern French Brevs., and in Card. Newman's *Hymni Ecclesiae*, 1838 and 1865. *Tr.* as :—

Fear no more for the torturer's hand. By I. Williams, in his *Hys. tr. from the Parisian Brev.*, 1839, p. 285. This was repeated in the *Hymnal for the Use of St. John the Evangelist*, &c., *Aberdeen*, 1870; and as, "Fear no more the clanking chain," in *Kennedy*, 1863. In this st. i., ii. are reversed, st. iv. is rewritten, and the doxology is omitted.

Translation not in C. U. :—

No more thy limbs are rent. *J. D. Chambers.* 1866.
                                                       [J. J.]

Jam sanctius moves opus. *C. Coffin.* [*Friday.*] Appointed in the *Paris Breviary*, 1736, for Fridays at Matins after Whitsuntide. It was also included in the author's *Hymni Sacri*, 1736, p. 25, in 6 st. of 4 l., in J. Chandler's *Hys. of the Primitive Church*, 1837, No. 29, and in Card. Newman's *Hymni Ecclesiae*, 1838 and 1865.   [W. A. S.]

Translations in C. U. :—

1. And now, O God, Thy mind resolves. By J.

Chandler in his *Hys. of the Prim. Church*, 1837, p. 26.

2. To day, O Lord, a holier work. This *tr.* in *H. A. & M.*, 1861 and 1875, in *Kennedy*, 1863, and others, is Chandler's *tr.* altered by the compilers of *H. A. & M.*

3. To day, O God, Thy mind resolves. This *tr.* in the *Hymnal for the Use of St. John the Evangelist*, &c., *Aberdeen*, 1870, is Chandler's *tr.* altered by the editor.

4. To day, O Lord, Thy will resolves. This *tr.* in the *Hymnary*, 1872, is also Chandler's *tr.* but altered by the editors of the *Hymnary.*

Translations not in C. U. :—

1. Now a holier work, O Lord. *I. Williams.* 1839.

2. A greater, holier work this day. *J. D. Chambers.* 1857.   [J. J.]

Jam solis excelsum jubar. *C. Coffin.* [*Easter.*] Given in the *Paris Breviary*, 1736, as the hymn at Sext in Paschal-tide. In the author's *Hymni Sacri*, 1736, p. 92, it begins, "Nunc solis," &c. The *Paris Brev.* form is repeated in J. Chandler's *Hys. of the Primitive Church*, 1837, No. 6, and in Card. Newman's *Hymni Ecclesiae*, 1838 and 1865. [W. A. S.]

Translation in C. U. :—

Behold the radiant sun on high. By J. D. Chambers, in his *Lauda Syon*, 1857, p. 38, in 3 st. of 4 l. This was repeated, with alterations, in the *Hymnary*, 1872.

Translations not in C. U. :—

1. And now the sun's meridian beams. *J. Chandler.* 1837.

2. The sun is soaring high. *I. Williams.* In the *British Magazine*, Jan. 1834, and his *Hys. tr. from the Parisian Brev.*, 1839.

3. Fast climbs the sun heaven's crystal mount. *W. J. Blew.* 1852.   [J. J.]

Jam toto subitus vesper eat polo. [*B. V. M.*] The hymn at Matins in the office of the Seven Dolours of the B. V. M., commemorated on the 3rd S. in September. This office has been added to the *Roman Breviary* since 1736. It is bound up with the *Pars Autumnalis* of the British Museum copy of the Antwerp ed., 1757, and was authorized then for use in Germany by the "Fratres ordinis servorum B. M. V." In the Kempten ed., 1746, it is given among the offices not of universal obligation, and marked as to be used in all the hereditary possessions of the House of Austria. The text of this hymn is in recent editions of the Breviary, and also in *Daniel*, iv. p. 306. *Tr.* as :—

Come, darkness, spread o'er heaven thy pall. By E. Caswall, in his *Lyra Catholica*, 1849, p. 171, and again in his *Hys. & Poems*, 1873, p. 93. It has been repeated in a few hymn-books. Another *tr.* is, "Let darkness vanish from the heavens now," by *J. Wallace*, 1874.   [J. M.]

Janus, Martin, seems to have been a native of Silesia, and to have been born about 1620. After receiving his license in theology, he became Precentor of the two churches at Sorau, in Silesia, then, about 1653, was appointed Rector of the Evangelical School at Sagan, and Precentor at the church near the Eckersdorf gate. He became Pastor at Eckersdorf about 1664, but was expelled by the Imperial Edict of March 13, 1668, by which all Evangelical pastors and teachers were driven out of the principality. He is said to have become Precentor at Ohlau, in Silesia, and d.

there about 1682. The only hymn by him *tr.* into English is :—

Jesu meiner Seelen Wonne. *Love to Christ.* Included in the *Christlich Herzens Andacht*, Nürnberg, 1665 [Wolfenbüttel], No. 24, in 18 st., repeated with his name in the Nürnberg *G. B.*, 1676, &c., and in Porst's *G. B.*, ed. 1855, No. 715. Sometimes erroneously ascribed to J. Scheffler. The *tr.* is, "O! at last I did discover," beginning with st. v. as No. 464 in pt. i. of the *Moravian H. Bk.*, 1754. In the 1789 and later eds. (1886, No. 338) it begins "O! at last I've found my Saviour."   [J. M.]

Je Te salue, mon certain Rédempteur. *Jehan Calvin* (?). [*Praise to Christ.*]

This hymn, entitled "Salutation à Jésus-Christ," first appeared in the edition of the *French Psalter*, published at Strassburg in 1545, the Strassburg copy of which unfortunately perished in the destruction of the Town Library during the bombardment of Strassburg in the Franco-German war. It has been ascribed to Calvin, but F. Bovet, in his *Histoire du Psautier des Églises Réformées*, 1872, and Dr. E. Reuss, of Strassburg, who included it in 8 st. of 8 lines in the "Lesser Works of Calvin" (*Corpus Reformatorum*, 1867, vol. xxxiv.), both regard his authorship as very doubtful. O. Douen, in his *Clément Marot et le Psautier Huguenot*, 1878-79, thinks it probable that the author was *Jean Garnier*, then Minister of the French Congregation at Strassburg. Mr. Dannerman gives an interesting summary of the evidence as a preface to his translation (see below). It is *tr.* as

1. I greet Thee, who my sure Redeemer art. A good, full and close *tr.* in the original metre, made in 1868, by Elizabeth Lee Smith, wife of Prof. H. B. Smith, of New York, and contributed to Schaff's *Christ in Song* (ed. 1869, p. 678). Included in W. F. Stevenson's *Hys. for Church & Home*, 1873, omitting st. i., vi., vii., beginning with st. ii., "Thou art the King of mercy and of grace," and slightly altering st. iii. l. 8·(st. iv. of original).

2. I greet Thee, my Redeemer sure. A full, good and close *tr.* by D. D. Bannerman (q. v.), first pub. in *The Catholic Presbyterian*, Dec. 1879, p. 458. Included in full, and unaltered, in the Schaff-Gilman *Library of Religious Poetry* (ed. 1883, p. 610), and unaltered, but omitting st. ii., viii., as No. 119, in the *Free Church H. Bk.*, 1882.   [J. M.]

Jehovah ! 'tis a glorious Name. *P. Doddridge.* [*Trust in Jehovah.*]

In the D. MSS. this hymn is headed, "The Saint encouraging himself in the Lord his God," and is dated "Oct. 9, 1737." It was included in J. Orton's ed. of Doddridge's (posthumous) *Hymns*, &c., 1755, No. 20, in 3 st. of 4 l., and again in J. D. Humphreys's ed. of the same, 1839, No. 24. In the *Bapt. Hyl.*, 1879, it is slightly altered.   [J. J.]

Jelecky, Johannes,

better known in the Germanised form Geletzky, was ordained a priest of the Bohemian Brethren's Unity in 1555. He was some time President of the community at Fulnek, in Bohemia, and afterwards at Grödlitz, in Bohemia. He d. at Grödlitz, Dec. 28, 1568. He was sent by Bp. Blahoslav to negotiate with the Anabaptists of Austerlitz. To the *Kirchengeseng*, 1566, he contributed 22 hymns and translations. Two have passed into English, of which one is noted under Augusta, J. The other is

Dankt Gott dem Herren. *Children.* 1566, as above, in 7 st. In *Wackernagel*, iv. p. 364. *Tr.* as "In Faith, O teach us," beginning with st. v., as No. 279, in pt. i. of the *Moravian H. Bk.*, 1754.   [J. M.]

Jersey, Margaret Elizabeth Villiers, née Leigh, Countess of,

eldest daughter of

Lord Leigh, of Stoneleigh, in the county of Warwick, was b. Oct. 29, 1849, and in 1872 was married to the Earl of Jersey. In 1871 the Religious Tract Society published a small collection of her hymns and poems under the title of *Hymns and Poems for very Little Children.* A second series under the same title appeared in 1875. They "were mostly written by Lady Jersey before she married, for the use of a little sister, it being difficult to find hymns composed in language simple enough for a very young child." And certainly they are distinguished by a charming simplicity both of thought and language. Six of these hymns were included in W. R. Stevenson's *School Hymnal*, 1880. Some of these are repeated in the *Voice of Praise* (London S. S. Union) and other collections. Her hymns in C. U. are :—

1. Here am I, for thou didst call me. *Child Samuel.*
2. Holy Jesus, Who didst die. *A Child's Prayer.*
3. I am a little soldier. *A child of God.*
4. O let me praise my God and King, *Praise to God the Father.*
5. Speak the truth, for that is right. *Speaking the Truth.*
6. There are many lovely things below. *Heaven.*
                                                  [W. R. S.]

Jerusalem, Jerusalem, enthroned once on high. *Bp. R. Heber.* [*Christ Weeping over Jerusalem.*]

Pub. in his posthumous *Hymns*, &c., 1827, p. 102, in 5 st. of 4 l., and appointed for the 10th S. after Trinity, the account of Christ weeping over Jerusalem being the Gospel for that day. In T. Darling's *Hymns for the Ch. of England*, ed. 1861 1875, it is altered to "Thou city of Jerusalem." The original is in several collections. [J. J.]

Jerusalem luminosa. [*Eternal Life.*]

This hymn, in 100 lines, was 1st pub. by *Mone*, No. 304, from a 15th cent. MS. at Karlsruhe, in which it is entitled, "On the glory of the heavenly Jerusalem as concerning the endowments of the glorified body." Of this and the two cognate hymns of this MS. ("Quisquis valet" and "In domo Patris," q.v.) Dr. Neale says, "The language and general ideas prove the writer (unknown, but apparently of the 15th cent.] to have been subject to the influence of the school of Geert Groot and Thomas à Kempis" (*Hys. chiefly Mediæval on the Joys and Glories of Paradise*, 1865, p. 44). Lines 25 ff., "In te nunquam nubilata," may be compared with a passage in St. Cyprian's *De laude martyrii* :—

"All things there have nothing to do with either cold or heat; nor do the fields rest, as in autumn; nor again does the fertile earth bring forth fruit in the early spring; all things belong to one season, they bear the fruits of one summer : indeed, neither does the moon serve to mark the months, nor does the sun run through the spaces of the hours; nor does the day, put to flight, give way to night; joyful rest reigns over the people, a placid dwelling contains them."

Dr. Neale's rendering of the ll. 25-30 is :—

"There the everlasting spring-tide
    Sheds its dewy, green repose;
There the Summer, in its glory,
    Cloudless and eternal glows;
For that country never knoweth
    Autumn's storms nor winter's snows."
                                                  [W. A. S.]

Translation in C. U. :—

Light's abode, Celestial Salem. By J. M. Neale, pub. in the *H. Noted*, 1858, in 7 st. of 6 l., and again in his *Hys. chiefly Mediæval on the*

Joys and Glories of Paradise, 1865. In its full or in an abridged form it has been included in several hymn-books, including *H. A. & M.*, the *Hymnary*, &c. In the *Hyl. for the use of S. John, &c., Aberdeen, Appendix*, 1870, it is altered to "Seat of Light! Celestial Salem," and in the *St. Margaret's Hymnal* (East Grinstead), 1875, as "O how blessed, O how quickening." [J. J.]

Jerusalem, my happy home. [*The Heavenly Jerusalem.*] The importance of this poem, the varying forms in which it, or some portions of it, are found in modern hymn-books, and the doubt which attaches to its authorship, necessitate an exhaustive treatment of its text and history. The fact that two versions are known, both dating from the latter part of the 16th cent. (those of F. B. P. and W. Prid), points naturally to a common source from whence each was taken. After indicating this probable source of the poem, we will give the text and history in detail.

i. *Probable source of the Poem.* For some centuries the volume known to us as *The Meditations of St. Augustine* (*Liber Meditationum*) had been popular, and had widely influenced the thought of the Church. At the time of the Reformation, Roman Catholic and Protestant alike vied in translations of it, in whole or in part. In many editions Card. P. Damiani's hymn on *Paradise*, "Ad perennis vitae fontem," is given as a part of the *Manual*, and has thus become frequently ascribed to St. Augustine. In the *Liber Meditationum* [ed. *Divi Aurelii Augustini Hipponensis Episcopi Meditationes, Soliloquia et Manuale*, Venice, 1553, c. 25] the following passage is found :—

Mater Hierusalem, Civitas sancta Dei. . . . . Felix anima mea, semperque felix in saecula, si intueri meruero gloriam tuam, beatitudinem tuam, pulchritudinem tuam, portas et muros tuos, et plateas tuas, et mansiones tuas multas, nobilissimos cives tuos, et fortissimum Regem tuum Dominum nostrum in decore suo. Muri namque tui ex lapidibus preciosis, portae tuae ex margaritis optimis, Plateae tuae ex auro purissimo, in quibus jocundum Halleluia sine intermissione concinitur, Mansiones tuae multae, quadris lapidibus fundatae, sapphiris constructae, laterculis coopertae aureis, in quas nullus ingreditur nisi mundus, nullus habitat inquinatus. Speciosa facta es et suavis in deliciis tuis, mater Hierusalem. Nihil in te tale, quale hîc patimur, qualia in hac miserâ vitâ cernimus. Non sunt in te tenebrae, aut nox, aut quaelibet diversitas temporum. Non lucet in te lux lucernae, aut splendor lunae, vel jubar stellarum, sed Deus de Deo, Lux de Luce, Sol Justitiae semper illuminat te. Agnus candidus et immaculatus, lucidum et pulcherrimum est lumen tuum. Sol tuus et claritas tua et omne bonum tuum, hujus pulcherrimi Regis indeficiens contemplatio. Ipse Rex Regum in medio tui, et pueri ejus in circumitu ejus. Ibi hymnidici Angelorum chori. Ibi societas supernorum civium. Ibi dulcis solemnitas omnium ab hac tristi peregrinatione ad tua gaudia redeuntium. Ibi Prophetarum providus chorus. Ibi duodenus Apostolorum numerus. Ibi innumerabilium Martyrum victor exercitus. Ibi sanctorum Confessorum sacer conventus. Ibi veri et perfecti Monachi. Ibi sanctae Mulieres, quae voluptates seculi et sexûs infirmitatem vicerunt. Ibi Pueri et Puellae qui annos suos sanctis moribus transcenderunt. Ibi sunt oves et agni, qui jam hujus voluptatis laqueos evaserunt. Exultant omnes in propriis mansionibus, dispar est gloria singulorum, sed communis est laetitia omnium. Plena et perfecta ibi regnat Caritas quia Deus est ibi omnia in omnibus quem sine fine vident, et semper videndo in ejus amore ardent, amant et laudant, laudant et amant. Omne opus eorum laus Dei, sine fine, sine defectione, sine labore. Felix ego et vere in perpetuum felix, si post resolutionem hujus corpusculi audire meruero illa cantica coelestis melodiae, quae cantantur ad laudem Regis Aeterni, ab illis supernae Patriae civibus beatorumque spirituum agminibus. Fortunatus ego, nimiumque beatus, si et ego ipse meruero cantare ea, et assistere Regi meo, Deo

meo, et Duci meo, et cernere eum in gloriâ suâ, sicut ipse polliceri dignatus est, dicens : *Pater volo ut quos dedisti mihi sint mecum, ut videant claritatem meam, quam habui apud te ante constitutionem mundi.* Et alibi. *Qui mihi ministrat, me sequatur, et ubi ego sum, illic et minister meus erit.* Et iterum. *Qui diligit me diligetur à Patre meo, et ego diligam eum, et manifestabo ei meipsum.*

This passage, together with Card. P. Damiani's hymn, seems to have been the source of the hymn by **F. B. P.**, as it is certainly of that by W. Prid.

ii. *The Hymn by F. B. P.* This is in a MS. book in the *British Museum*, numbered *Add.* 15,225. The MS. is undated, but is of the latter part of the 16th or the beginning of the 17th cent. The full text is as follows :—

A SONG MAD BY F: B: P.
To the tune of Diana.

" 1 Hierusalem my happie home
    When shall I come to thee
When shall my sorrowes haue an end
    Thy ioyes when shall I see

" 2 O happie harbour of the saints
    O sweete and pleasant soyle
In thee noe sorrow may be founde
    Noe greefe, noe care, noe toyle

" 3 In thee noe sickenesse may be seene
    Noe hurt, noe ache, noe sore
There is noe death, nor uglie devill
    There is life for euermore

" 4 Noe dampishe mist is seene in thee
    Noe could, nor darksome night
There everie soule shines as the sunne
    There god himselfe giues light

" 5 There lust and lukar cannot dwell
    There envie beares noe sway
There is noe hunger heate nor coulde
    But pleasure everie way

" 6 Hierusalem : Hierusalem
    God grant I once may see
Thy endlesse ioyes and of the same
    Partaker aye to bee

" 7 Thy wales are made of precious stones
    Thy bulwarkes Diamondes square
Thy gates are of right orient pearle
    Exceedinge riche and rare

" 8 Thy terretties and thy pinacles
    With carbuncles doe shine
Thy verie streetes are paued with gould
    Surpassinge cleare and fine

" 9 Thy houses are of Ivorie
    Thy windoes cristale cleare
Thy tyles are mad of beaten gould
    O god that I were there

" 10 Within thy gates nothinge doeth come
    That is not passinge cleane
Noe spiders web, noe durt noe dust
    Noe filthe may there be seene

" 11 Ah my sweete home Hierusaleme
    Would god I were in thee
Would god my woes were at an end
    Thy ioyes that I might see

" 12. Thy saints are crownd with glorie great
    They see god face to face
They triumph still, they still reioyce
    Most happie is their case

" 13 Wee that are heere in banishment
    Continuallie doe mourne
We sighe and sobbe, we weepe and weale
    Perpetually we groane

" 14 Our sweete is mixt with bitter gaule
    Our pleasure is but paine
Our ioyes scarce last the lookeing on
    Our sorrowes still remaine

" 15 But there they liue jn such delight
    Such pleasure and such play
As that to them a thousand yeares
    Doth seeme as yeaster day

" 16 Thy viniardes and thy orchardes are
    Most beutifull and faire
Full furnished with trees and fruits
    Most wonderfull and rare

" 17 Thy gardens and thy gallant walkes
    Continually are greene
There groes such sweete and pleasant flowers
    As noe where eles are seene

" 18 There is nector and ambrosia made
  There is muske and civette sweete
  There manie a faire and daintie drugge
  Are troden under feete

" 19 There cinomon there sugar groes
  There narde and balme abound
  What tounge can tell or hart conceiue
  The ioyes that there are found

" 20 Quyt through the streetes with siluer sound
  The flood of life doe flowe
  Upon whose bankes on everie syde
  The wood of life doth growe

" 21 There trees for euermore beare fruite
  And evermore doe springe
  There euermore the Angels sit
  And evermore doe singe

" 22 There David standes with harpe in hand
  As maister of the Queere
  Tenne thousand times that man were blest
  That might this musicke hear

" 23 Our Ladie singes magnificat
  With tune surpassinge sweete
  And all the virgiuns beare their parts
  Sitinge aboue her feete

" 24 Te Deum doth Sant Ambrose singe
  Saint Augustine dothe the like
  Ould Simeon and Zacharie
  Haue not their songes to seeke

" 25 There Magdalene hath left her mone
  And cheerefullie doth singe
  With blessed Saints whose harmonie
  In everie streete doth ringe

" 26 Hierusalem my happie home
  Would god I were in thee
  Would god my woes were at an end
  Thy ioyes that I might see
    finis finis "

In 1601 this hymn, abbreviated to 19 stanzas,
was printed in *The Song of Mary the Mother of
Christ . . . . with the Description of Heavenly
Jerusalem. London · E. Allde*, 1601. This
text, being derived from the above, is very
corrupted and incomplete, and variations in
arrangement and in phrase are numerous.
These two versions, if the latter is not derived
from the former, must have had one common
source, and suggest the possibility of an earlier
and probably printed version of the hymn
now unknown being the source of both.

iii. *W. Prid's hymn on The New Jerusalem.*
This hymn is contained in :—

*The Glasse of vaine-glorie: Faithfully translated (out
of S. Avgvstine his booke, intituled Speculum peccatoris)
into English by W. P.[rid], Doctor of the Lawes. Printed
at London by John Windet dwelling at the signe of the
white Beare, nigh Baynard's Castle 1585 (2nd ed. 1593).*

From this hymn or song of 176 lines we
will quote those stanzas only which have to do
with the New Jerusalem hymn. It reads :—

   "PSALME OF ZION.

" 1 O Mother deare Hierusalem,
  Jehouas throne on hie :
  O Sacred Cittie, Queene and Wife,
  Of Christ eternally.

" 2 My hart doth long to see thy face,
  my soule doth still desire,
  Thy glorious beautie to behold,
  my mind is set on fire.

" 3 O comely Queene in glorie clad,
  in honour and degree :
  Al faire thou art exceeding bright
  no spot there is in thee.

" 4 O piereless dame and daughter faire
  of loue, without annoy :
  Triumph, for in thy beautie braue,
  the King doth greatly ioy.

" 5 Thy port, thy shape, thy stately grace,
  thy fauour faire in deede :
  Thy pleasant hew and countinance,
  all others doth exceede."

Stanzas 6–12, which follow, are an indifferent
paraphrase of passages from *The Song of
Solomon.* The writer returns to his subject in
st. 13–18 :—

" 13 O then thrise happie should my state
  in happinesse remaine :
  If I might once Thy glorious Seate,
  and princely place attaine.

" 14 And view thy gallant gates thy wals
  thy streetes and dwellinges wide,
  Thy noble troup of Citizens
  and mightie king beside.

" 15 Of stones full precious are thy towres
  thy gates of pearles are tolde,
  There is that Alleluia sung
  in streates of beaten gold,

" 16 Those stately buildings manifold,
  on squared stones do rise,
  With Saphyrs deckt, & lofty frames
  enclosed Castlewise.

" 17 Into the gates shall none approche,
  but honest, pure and cleane :
  No spot, no filth, no loathsome thing,
  Sball enter in (I meane).

" 18 O mother deare Jerusalem,
  the comfort of vs all,
  How swete thou art and dilicate,
  no thing shall thee befoll."

Stanzas 19–22 are much in common with
F. B. P.'s hymn. Stanzas 23–28 are :—

" 23 He is the king of kings beset,
  amidst his Seruants right :
  And they his happie houshold all,
  do serue him day and night.

" 24 There, there the quiers of Angels sing,
  there the supernall sort,
  Of citizens (that hence are rid
  from dangers deepe) do sport.

" 25 There be the prudent Prophets all,
  Thappostles six and six ;
  The glorious martirs on a row,
  and Confessors betwixt.

" 26 There doth the crew of righteous men,
  and matrons all consist ;
  Yong men & maids that here on earth
  their pleasures did resist.

" 27 The sheepe & lambs that hardly scaple,
  The snares of death and hell ;
  Triumph in ioy euerlastingly
  whereof no tongue can tell.

28 And though the glorie of ech one,
  doth differ in degree ;
  Yet is the ioy of all alike,
  and common (as we see)."

Stanzas 29–33 continue to borrow from the
Meditations of St. Augustine. At the close of
st. 34 the writer takes a fresh departure, and,
referring to our Blessed Lord, says :—

  " According to his promise made
   (Which here I enterlace) ; "

and st. 35–38 consist of "enterlaced" texts
accordingly. Stanzas 39, 40 are of no special
note; and the poem concludes with st. 41–44 :—

" 41 O blessed are the pure in heart,
  their Soueraigne they shall see ;
  And they most happie heauenly wights
  that of his houshold bee.

" 42 Wherefore, O Lord, dissolue my bonds,
  my giues and fetters strong :
  For I haue dwelt within the tents
  of Cedar ouer long.

" 43 And grant, O God, for Christ his sake,
  that once deuoide of strife ;
  I may thy holy hill attaine,
  to dwell in all my life.

" 44 With Cherubins and Seraphins,
  and holy soules of men :
  To sing thy praise O Lord of hostes,
  for euer and euer. Amen."

In his Preface to *The Glasse of Vaine Glory,*
Prid says this is a
"Song of Sion which I have here translated out of
S. Augustine's Booke of Prayers, Chap. 24, into Englishe
meeter . . . I have as neare as I could possibly, followed
the verie wordes of mine Authour."

To this point the history is clear. It is certain that W. Prid translated direct from the
work known to us as St. Augustine's *Meditations;* and it is highly probable that F. B. P.
derived his directly from the same source, or

indirectly through the translation of another. It now remains for us to show how later writers have availed themselves of these materials.

iv. *Additional forms of the Hymn.* From this point we have a great variety of texts, the more important of which are as follows :—

(i.) The most noted of these is a broadside of the 18th cent., which was reprinted by Dr. H. Bonar in his work *The New Jerusalem; a Hymn of the Olden Time,* 1852. Dr. Bonar attributes this text to David Dickson, a Scottish Presbyterian Minister (1583-1663). It is in 248 lines, all of which, with the exception of ll. 25-32, and 233-236, are altered either from F. B. P. or from W. Prid. From the following extract from Robert Wodrow's *Life of D. Dickson,* 1726, it is evident that Wodrow regarded the production as an original poem by Dickson :—

"Some short poems on pious and serious subjects, such as the 'Christian Sacrifice,' 'O Mother dear, Jerusalem,' and (on somewhat larger, octavo 1649), 'True Christian Love,' to be sung with the common tunes of the Psalms. . . . ." This is all of his I have seen in print.

The opening stanza of this combined version of F. B. P. and W. Prid, is :—

"O Mother dear, Jerusalem !
    When shall I come to thee ?
When shall my sorrows have an end,
    Thy joys, when shall I see ?
O happy harbour of God's saints !
    O sweet and pleasant soil !
In thee no sorrow may be found
    No grief, no care, no toil."

The full text is given in Dr. Bonar's work as above.

(ii.) Contemporary with this broadside in Scotland was another in England. It is in the *Rawlinson Collection,* 4to, 566, 167, and entitled "*The true description of the everlasting ioys of Heaven. To the Tune of, 'O man in desperation.'*" It is undated, but "Printed for F. Coles, T. Vere, and J. Wright," who are known to have issued many broadsides, ranging from 1650 to 1670. This broadside we date from internal evidence, circ. 1660, or a little later. The first six stanzas will be sufficient to show that it is merely F. B. P. more or less altered, and that it contains no trace whatever of W. Prid's version.

"1 Jerusalem, my happy home,
    When shall I come to thee ?
When shall my sorrows have an end ?
    thy joys when shall I see ?

"2 Where happy harbour is of Saint,
    with sweet and pleasant soyl :
In thee no sorrow ever found,
    no grief, no care, no toyl.

"3 In thee no dampish Mists are seen,
    nor cold, nor darksome night :
In thee all souls for ever sing
    there God always gives light.

"4 *Heaven is the Spring where waters flow
    to quench our heat of sin
There is the tree where truth doth grow
    to lead our lives therein.*

"5 *There Christ is judge that stints the strife
    when men's devises fail
There is the bread that feeds the life
    that death cannot assail*

"6 *The tidings of salvation dear
    comes to our ears from thence:
The fortress of our faith is there
    and shield of our defence.*"

The last three stanzas (which we have given in italics to mark them off from the rest) are the familiar lines prefixed in an altered form to several editions of the English Bible in the early part of the 17th cent. and beginning :—

"Here is the spring whence waters flow."

By a slight alteration in the opening line that and the eleven lines which follow are made to set forth the beauties and treasures of Holy Scripture instead of those of Heaven. (See p. 1530.) The concluding lines of the poem fix the date at or a short time after the Restoration of Charles II. (1660) :—

"God still preserve our Royal King,
    Our Queen likewise defend,
And many happy, joyful days
    good Lord, unto them send.

Thus to conclude I end my song
    wishing health, wealth, and peace :
And all that wish the Commons good,
    good Lord their wys increase."

(iii.) In 1693 William Burkitt, the Expositor, pub. an *Help and Guide to Christian Families.* This work is in three parts, together with the addition of 8 *Divine Hymns on several Occasions.* The last hymn is as follows :—

"*An* HYMN: *a longing for Glory.*

"1 *Jerusalem !* my happy Home,
    When shall I come to Thee ?
When shall my labours have an End ?
    Thy Joys when shall I see ?

"2 Thy Gates are richly set with Pearl,
    Most glorious to behold ;
Thy Walls are all of precious Stone,
    Thy Streets are pav'd with Gold.

"3 Thy Gardens and thy pleasant Fruits
    Continually are green ;
There are such sweet and pleasant Flow'rs
    As ne'er before was seen.

"4 If heaven be thus glorious
    Lord, why must I keep thence ?
What Folly is't that makes me loth
    To die, and go from hence ?

"5 Reach down, reach down thine Arm of Grace,
    And cause me to ascend
Where Congregations ne'er break up,
    And Sabbaths have no End.

"6 When wilt thou come to me, O Lord ?
    O come, my Lord, most dear ;
Come nearer, nearer, nearer still ;
    I'm well when thou art near.

"7 My dear Redeemer is Above,
    Him will I go to see,
And all my Friends in Christ below,
    Shall soon come after me.

"8 *Jerusalem !* my happy Home,
    O how I long for Thee !
Then shall my Labours have an End,
    Thy Joys when once I see.
                Amen, Hallelujah,
            Come, LORD JESUS."

This text is a cento and is thus composed. St. i., ii., iii., viii., are from F. B. P. somewhat altered. St. iv., v. are from Daniel Burgess's "Hymn on the Sabbath Day," beginning, "O God, Whose glorious majesty," where st. ii. and iii. read :—

"2 If Heaven be the land of peace,
    Lord, why must we keep thence ?
What folly is't that makes us loth
    To dye and to go hence."

"3 Reach down, Reach down thine arm of Grace,
    Lord, fit us to ascend
Where Congregations ne'er break up,
    And Sabbaths have no end."

Stanza vi. of Burkitt's text is from T. Shepherd's *Penitential Cries,* No. 25, st. iv., ll. 1-4, slightly altered. These *Cries,* as is well known, were begun by J. Mason and finished by T. Shepherd, and were pub. with J. Mason's *Spiritual Songs, or Songs of Praise,* 1693. Stanza vii. is from J. Mason's *Sp. Songs,* 1683, No. 30, st. viii., ll. 1-4, which read :—

"My dearest Friends, they dwell above,
    Them will I go to see ;
And all my Friends in Christ below
    Will soon come after me."

The text of Burkitt was repeated with slight alterations in *A Collection of Hymns and Sacred Poems.* Dublin : Printed by S.[Samuel] Powell, *in Crane Lane,* 1749, No. 84. In R. Hill's 1794 *Supp.* to his *Ps. & Hys.* six stanzas were given from *Burkitt* (iii. and vii. being omitted); and in 1798 five only, *Burkitt's* st. viii. being also omitted. In this form the cento has passed into modern collections.

In the American *Church Pastorals,* 1864, it is somewhat altered, and broken up, without any regard to the original sequence of the stanzas, into the following hymns :—(1) "Jerusalem, my happy home"; (2) "Jerusalem, Jerusalem, would God," &c.; (3) "Jerusalem, the happy seat"; (4) "Jehovah, Lord, now come, I pray"; (5) "O Lord, that I Jerusalem"; and (6) "O passing happy were my state."

(iv.) Another transformation of F. B. P.'s text appeared in *Psalms & Hymns . . . . by W. S.,* London, 1725. It is in 40 st. of 4 l. and is superior to many arrangements of the poem. The following lines are fair specimens of the rest :—

"There David sits with Harp in Hand
    As Master of the Choir :
Most happy they who understand,
    And may His Music hear."

(v.) In Williams & Boden's *Col. of above Six Hundred H. designed as a New Supplement to Dr. Watts's Psalms & Hymns, Doncaster*, 1801, the most popular form of the hymn is found as No, 193, and reads :—

> "*The Heavenly Jerusalem.*
>
> "1 Jerusalem ! my happy home,
>   Name ever dear to me !
> When shall my labours have an end
>   In joy, and peace, and thee ?
>
> "2 When shall these eyes thy heaven-built walls
>   And pearly gates behold ;
> Thy bulwarks with salvation strong,
>   And streets of shining gold !
>
> "3 O when, thou city of my God,
>   Shall I thy courts ascend ;
> Where congregations ne'er break up,
>   And Sabbaths have no end ?
>
> '4 There happier bow'rs than Eden's bloom,
>   Nor sin nor sorrow know ;
> Blest Seats ! thro' rude and stormy scenes
>   I onward press to you.
>
> "5 Why should I shrink at pain & woe,
>   Or feel, at death, dismay ?
> I've Canaan's goodly land in view,
>   And realms of endless day.
>
> "6 Apostles, martyrs, prophets there,
>   Around my Saviour stand ;
> And soon my friends in Christ below,
>   Will join the glorious band.
>
> '7 Jerusalem ! my happy home,
>   My soul still pants for thee ;
> Then shall my labours have an end,
>   When I thy joys shall see."

It is signed " Eckinton C." In *Ps. & Hys. for Pub. or Priv. Devotion, Sheffield Printed by James Montgomery At The Iris Office*, 1802, the text is repeated with the change in st. iv., l. 1, of *Eden for Eden's*. The " Eckinton C." text was repeated in J. Montgomery's *Christian Psalmist*, 1825, No. 129. It has gradually grown in popular favour, and is now in C. U. in a more or less accurate form in all English-speaking countries, [The association of James Montgomery's name with the " Eckinton C." text is peculiar and suggestive. From 1792 to 1794 Montgomery lived with and was an assistant to Joseph Gales, a printer, bookseller, and auctioneer at Sheffield. In 1794 Montgomery succeeded to the printing business, and continued his acquaintance with Gales and his family. Gales's parents and three sisters resided at Eckington (about six miles from Sheffield) at the time, and the father and daughters were members of the Parish Church Choir. Montgomery frequently visited the family at Eckington. Amongst the *Montgomery MSS.* there is a copy of Dickson's version of the New Jerusalem hymn which was sent in MS. to Montgomery by a Moravian friend with a request that he would rewrite it, or condense it into a suitable hymn for public worship. In the MS. certain stanzas corresponding to those in the " Eckinton C," are marked in pencil as stanzas which maintained a continuity of thought, and a few suggestions are penciled in the margin in shorthand. About this time (1796–1800) a small collection of hymns was printed by Montgomery for the use of the Eckington Parish Church Choir, and in this the text of " Jerusalem, my happy home," known as the " Eckinton C" version, was given. Mr. J. H. Brammall (q. v.) remembers this little pamphlet well, but has lost his copy. Under these circumstances it is almost, if not quite, safe to say that the *Eckinton C.* version of " Jerusalem, my happy home" is by Montgomery.] (See 1905 SUPPLEMENT.)

(vi.) This list of versions of the New Jerusalem hymn, although far from being exhaustive, yet contains all that is of value for ascertaining the origin and history of the various texts which are in modern hymn-books. We may note in addition an American form of the hymn, given in Dr. Bonar's work, *The New Jerusalem, &c.*, 1852, the opening of which is :—

> " O heavenly Jerusalem,
>   Thou City of my King ;"

and another in 3 st. in Card. Newman's *Hymns for the Use of the Birmingham Oratory*, Dublin, J. F. Fowler, 1857 :—

> " O fair, O fair Jerusalem."

v. *The Initials " F. B. P."* Various attempts have been made to explain these initials, the principal of which are :—

(1) Dr. Neale's suggestion in his *Hymns Chiefly Mediaeval on the Joys & Glories of Paradise*, 1865, p. 16, is : " It [the *Brit. Mus. MS.*] contains several other pieces of poetry, evidently by Roman Catholics ; one

headed—' Here followeth the song Mr. Thewlis wrote himself ;' and another, ' Here followeth the song of the death of Mr. Thewlis.' Now John Thewlis was a priest, barbarously executed at Manchester, March 18, 1617. It is probable therefore, that ' F. B. P.' was another sufferer (in all likelihood a priest) in the persecution either of Elizabeth, or of James I."

(2) Again, in the 2nd ed. of the same work, 1866, p. 19, Dr. Neale says, " I have since been informed by Mr. Daniel Sedgwick, whose knowledge of English Hymnology is as astounding as it is unrivalled, that the initials stand for Francis Baker Porter, a Secular Priest for some time imprisoned in the Tower, and the author of a few short devotional treatises."

(3) J. Miller, in his *Singers and Songs of the Church*, 1869, p. 85, says : " It has been suggested that the initials ' F. B. P.' stand for Francis Baker, ' Pater ' or priest."

From an intimate acquaintance with the late Daniel Sedgwick we are in a position to state that what he contributed to Dr. Neale was "Francis Baker, Pater," and that Dr. Neale misread " Pater " as " Porter." J Miller's suggested reading was also from Sedgwick. This reading by Sedgwick was a pure guess on his part, and cannot be received. The writer, probably a Roman Catholic, and possibly a priest, remains unknown. [W. T. B.]

Jerusalem, thy joys divine. [*The Heavenly Jerusalem.*] This poem, in 27 st. of 8 l. and headed by 1 st. of 4 l., appeared in *The Song of Mary the Mother of Christ; containing the story of his life and passion; the teares of Christ in the garden; with the description of the Heavenly Jerusalem*, 1601. (See " Jerusalem, my happy home.") This poem was partially reprinted in the Parker Society's *Select Poetry of the Reign of Queen Elizabeth*, 1845, p. 427. It is from this poem that *Kennedy*, 1863, " Jerusalem, thy joys divine," is compiled. [W. T. B.]

Jervis, Thomas, s. of a Presbyterian Minister of the same name, was b. at Ipswich in 1748, and educated for the Ministry at Hoxton. In 1770 he was appointed classical and mathematical tutor at the Exeter Academy. From 1772 to 1783 he was tutor to the sons of the Earl of Shelburne, at Bowood, where Dr. Priestley was librarian. In the latter year Jervis succeeded Dr. A. Rees at St. Thomas's Southwark, moving in 1796, after the death of Dr. Kippis, to the Princes' St. Chapel, Westminster. From 1808 to 1818 he was minister at the Mill Hill Chapel, Leeds. After his retirement he lived in the neighbourhood of London, and d. there in 1833. Jervis was one of the four editors of *A Coll. of Hys. & Ps. for Public & Private Worship*, London, 1795. [See Unitarian Hymnody.] He contributed 17 hymns to the 1st ed., and 4 to its *Supplement*, 1807. Of these several are found in later Unitarian collections in G. Britain and America, including :—

1. God to correct a guilty world. *Divine Providence.*
2. Great God, Thine attributes divine. *Confidence in God.*
3. Lord of the world's majestic frame. *Praise a Duty.*
4. Shall I forsake that heavenly Friend ? *Constancy desired.*
5. Sweet is the friendly voice which [that] speaks. *Peace to the Penitent.*
6. Thou, Lord, in mercy wilt regard. *Penitence.*
7. With sacred joy we lift our eyes. *Divine Worship.* This is given in *Laudes Domini*, N.Y., 1884, as : " With joy we lift our eyes."

These hymns all date from 1795, and the most popular are Nos. 4 and 6. [V. D. D.]

Jesaiä, dem Propheten, das geschah.
M. Luther. [*The Sanctus.*] This paraphrase of Isaiah vi. 1-4, was 1st pub. in Luther's *Deudsche Messe und ordnung Gottis Diensts*, Wittenberg, 1526, repeated in the Erfurt *G. B.*, 1527, the *Geistliche Lieder*, Wittenberg, 1529 and 1531, &c., in 16 l., entitled "The German Sanctus." Thence in *Wackernagel*, iii. p. 18. Also in Schircks's ed. of Luther's *Geistl. Lieder*, 1854, p. 58, the *Unv. L. S.*, 1851, No. 191, &c.

According to the ritual directions of the *Deudsche Messe*, in the Holy Communion the Bread was first consecrated and received by the communicants, and then this *Sanctus*, or else Luther's "Gott sei gelobet," or "Jesus Christus unser Heiland" (from Huss) was sung. The Wine was then consecrated and received (see *Blätter für Hymnologie*, 1883, p. 89).

Translation in C. U. :—
Unto the seer Isaiah it was given. By A. T. Russell, for his *Ps. & Hys.*, 1851, No. 13.·

Other trs. are, (1) "We read that to Isaiah it befel," by *Miss Fry*, 1845, p. 138. (2) "To Isaiah the ancient seer," by *J. Anderson*, 1846, p. 82. In his ed., 1847, p. 93, it begins, "Isaiah once, that prophet old." (3) "The rapt Isaiah saw the glorious One," by *Dr. J. Hunt*, 1853, p. 165. (4) "Isaiah, filled with deep prophetic awe," by Dr. W. M. Reynolds, in the *Evang. Review*, Gettysburg, Oct. 1853. (5) "These things the Seer Isaiah did befall," by *R. Massie*, 1854, p. 85, repeated in *Dr. Bacon*, 1884, p. 50. (6) "To Isaiah, the prophet, this was given," by Dr. G. Macdonald, in the *Sunday Magazine*, 1867, p. 841. In his *Exotics*, 1876, p. 111, it begins, "Unto the seer Isaiah it was given." [J. M.]

Jesu, accept the grateful songs.
C. Wesley. [*Jesus All in All.*] Pub. in *Hys. & Sac. Poems*, 1749, in 22 st. of 4 l., and headed "Afte. Preaching in Church" (*P. Works*, 1868-72, vol. v. 110). From this one of the most popular centos in use by the Methodist bodies was given in the *Wes. H. Bk.*, 1780, No. 36, as "Jesus the Name, high over all." It is composed of st. ix., x., xii., xiii., xviii. and xxii. This cento, with the omission of its st. i. and iv. was given as "Jesus, the Name to sinners dear," in Dr. Alexander's *Augustine H. Bk.*, 1849 and 1865. G. J. Stevenson's note on the *Wes. H. Bk.* cento in his *Meth. H. Bk. Notes*, 1883, p. 45, is long and interesting. The last stanza :—

> "Happy, if with my latest breath,
> I may but gasp His Name ;
> Preach Him to all, and cry in death,
> 'Behold, behold the Lamb,'"

has had a special charm for many Ministers of the Gospel. Several instances are given by Stevenson as above. [J. J.]

Jesu, at Whose supreme command.
C. Wesley. [*Holy Communion.*] Pub. in *Hys. & Sac. Poems*, 1742, and again in the *Hys. for the Lord's Supper*, 1745, No. 30, in 8 st. of 4 l. (*P. Works*, 1868-72, vol. iii. p. 237). With slight alterations it was included in the *Wes. H. Bk.*, as one of the "Additional Hymns," in 1800. It has passed into several collections in G. Britain and America. In addition two forms of the text are in C. U. :—

1. Blest Jesu, to Thy gracious Board. This form, opening with st. ii. slightly altered, was given in the *Salisbury H. Bk.*, 1857, and is repeated in other hymnals.
2. Jesu, by Thy supreme command. This text in the *Hymnary*, 1872, is Wesley's very much altered, together with the omission of st. iii., and the addition of a doxology. [J. J.]

Jesu Corona celsior. [*Common of Confessors.*] This hymn is cited by *Morel*, p. 179, as in a 14th cent. ms. at Einsiedeln. It is

---

also in a ms. of, at the latest, 1415, in the British Museum (Add. 30014 f. 167 *b*), in the St. Gall ms., No 526, of the 15th cent., in the *Roman Breviary* (Venice, 1478), the *Ambrosian Breviary*, 1539, &c. *Daniel*, i., No. 98, gives the older text and also the revised form in the *Roman Breviary* of 1632, "For Feasts of a Confessor not a Bishop." *Mone*, No. 747, gives only *Daniel's* st. iii.-viii., beginning "Anni recurso tempore," from a 15th cent. ms. at Karlsruhe. He thinks that its metrical form proves it to have been composed in France in the 11th cent. The *Roman Brev.* text, 1632, is in Card. Newman's *Hymni Ecclesiae*, 1838 and 1865. [J. M.]

Translation in C. U. :—
Jesus, eternal Truth sublime. By E. Caswall. Pub. in his *Lyra Catholica*, 1849, p. 219, in 8 st. of 4 l., and again in his *Hys. & Poems*, 1873, p. 115. It is found in a few collections, including Skinner's *Daily Service Hymnal*, 1864, &c., and the Marquess of Bute's *Roman Breviary in English*, 1879, vol. i. p. 861.

Translations not in C. U. :—
1. Jesu, than crown of Kings art Thou. *W. J. Blew*, 1852-5.
2. Jesus, surpassing happiness. *J. Wallace*, 1874.
[J. J.]

Jesu Corona Virginum. [*Common of Virgins.*] This beautiful hymn, founded on Canticles ii. 16, Isaiah xxviii. 5, and Rev. xiv. 4, has been ascribed to St. Ambrose, but is not adjudged to him by the Benedictine Editors. *Thomasius*, ii. 402, gives it from a Vatican ms. of the 8th cent. It is found in four hymnaries of the 11th cent. in the *British Museum* (Vesp. D. xii. f. 111 *b*; Jul. A. vi. f. 68; Harl. 2961, f. 250; Add. 30851, f. 155), and in the *Lat. Hys. of the Anglo-Saxon Ch.*, 1851, p. 140, is printed from an 11th cent. ms. at Durham. (B. iii. 32 f. 41.) It is also in 3 mss. of the 11th cent. at St. Gall (Nos. 387, 413, 414). Among Breviaries it is included in the *Roman* (Venice, 1478), *Ambrosian* of 1539, *Sarum*, *York*, *Aberdeen*, &c., the Sarum use being at Lauds and Second Vespers on festivals of Virgins and Martyrs. *Daniel*, i., No. 99, gives the text, and at iv. pp. 140, 368, cites it as in a 10th cent. Rheinau ms., and in a 9th cent. ms. at Bern. The *Roman Brev.* text is also in Card. Newman's *Hymni Ecclesiae*, 1838 and 1865. [J. M.]

Translations in C. U. :—
1. Thou Crown of all the Virgin choir. By E. Caswall. Pub. in his *Lyra Catholica*, 1849, p. 221 ; and again in his *Hys. & Poems*, 1873, p. 116, but altered to "*Dear* Crown of all the Virgin choir." The original *tr.* is given in Roman Catholic hymn-books for missions and schools. It is also in other collections.
2. Jesu, the Virgin's Crown, do Thou. By J. M. Neale in the 1854 ed. of the *H. Noted*. The most popular form of this *tr.* is its altered text by the compilers of *H. A. & M.*, 1861 and 1875. It begins with the same first line, and is in several collections.
3. O Jesu, Crown of Virgins, Whom. By R. F. Littledale. Made for and 1st pub. in the *People's H.*, 1867, and signed D. L.
4. O Jesu, Crown of Virgins, Thou. This in the *Hymnary*, 1872, is Dr. Neale's *tr.* as above, altered by the Editors of the *Hymnary*.

Translations not in C. U. :—

1. Jesus, receive our suppliant cry. *J. R. Beste*, 1849.
2. Jesu the Crown, and sweet Reward. *R. Campbell*, 1850.
3. Jesu, the Virgins' coronal. *W. J. Blew*, 1852-5.
4. Jesu, the Virgin's Crown. In love, &c. *J. W. Hewett*, 1859.
5. Jesu, the Crown of Virgins, Whom. *J. D. Chambers*, 1866.
6. Jesus, the Virgin's crown, their spouse. *J. Wallace*, 1874.   [J. J.]

Jesu deine tiefe Wunden. *J. Heermann.* [*Passiontide.*] 1st pub. in his *Devoti Musica Cordis*, Leipzig and Breslau, 1644, p. 174, in 6 st. of 8 l., entitled "Consolation from the wounds of Jesus in all manner of temptation. From the Manual of St. Augustine." The *Manuale* is a mediæval compilation from various sources, and meditation xxii., on which the hymn is based, is adapted from the work of St. Bernard of Clairvaux on Canticles. Included in *Mützell*, 1858, No. 106, in Wackernagel's ed. of his *Geistliche Lieder*, No. 59, and the *Unv. L. S.*, 1851.

It is one of the finest of Hermann's hymns, and is much used in Germany. Count N. L. von Zinzendorf said of it, "The crown of all our old hymns is in truth Augustine's 'Jesu deine tiefe Wunden,' in which is contained our whole doctrine and practice. *Lauxmann* says (in *Koch*, viii. 37), that st. i.–iii. were often used by young men and maidens as their daily prayer against this world's temptations. He also relates how the singing of this hymn comforted the well known Württemberg theologian Philipp David Burk in his last hours (March 22, 1770).

Translations in C. U. :—

1. **Lord! Thy death and passion give.** A good and full *tr.* by Miss Winkworth in her *Lyra Ger.*, 1st Ser., 1855, p. 72 ; repeated, omitting st. ii., iii., in the Pennsylvanian Luth. *Ch. Bk.*, 1868, No. 177. St. v., vi., beginning, "Lord, in Thee I place my trust." are included, altered, in the *Hys. of the Spirit*, Boston, U.S.A., 1864, and American Unitarian *Hymn Bk.*, 1869.

2. **Oh, what precious balm and healing.** A good and full *tr.* by R. Massie, contributed to the 1857 ed. of Mercer's *C. P. & H. Bk.*, No. 87 (Ox. ed., 1864, omitted), and reprinted in his own *Lyra Domestica*, 1864, p. 125.

Another *tr.* is, "Christ, thy holy Wounds and Passion" (from the altered text in the Hannover *G. B.*, 1657 [1659, No. 65, by Justus Gesenius ?], which begins "Jesu deine heilge Wunden"), by J. C. Jacobi, 1722, p. 14. In his ed. 1732, p. 27, it begins "Christ, thy sacred wounds," thence in the *Moravian H. Bk.*, and repeated in the 1789 and later eds. (1849, No. 107), altered and beginning, "Christ, Thy wounds and bitter passion." In the ed. of 1886, No. 1238, only the *tr.* of st. v. is retained, beginning, "All my hope and consolation."   [J. M.]

Jesu, dulcis amor meus. [*Passiontide.*] This hymn is almost entirely composed of separate lines transposed and in some instances altered from St. Bernard's "Salve mundi salutare" (q. v.). It is the hymn at Lauds in the Office of the "Most Holy Winding Sheet of our Lord Jesus Christ ; double of the First Class." This office has been added to the *Roman Breviary* since 1736, and is appointed for the Saturday after the 2nd S. in Lent. The text is found in the *Appendix* to the *Pars Verna* of the *Roman Breviary*, Bologna, 1827, p. cclxxviii., and is repeated in later eds. and in *Daniel*, iv. p. 323. *Tr.* as :—

Jesu, as though Thyself wert here. By E. Caswall. Pub. in his *Lyra Catholica*, 1849, p. 82 ; and again in his *Hys. & Poems*, 1873, p. 46. It is found in several hymn-books, and often with the omission of st. ii. Another *tr.* is

"Jesus, sweetest love of mine." *J. Wallace*, 1874.   [J. M.]

Jesu dulcis memoria. *St. Bernard.* [*The Holy Name of Jesus.*] This hymn has been generally (and there seems little reason to doubt correctly) ascribed to St. Bernard ; and there are many parallels to it in his genuine prose works, especially that on the Canticles. It has been variously dated 1130, 1140 or 1153 ; but as positive proof is lacking that it is unquestionably the work of St. Bernard it is manifestly impossible to fix a date for its composition. The years 1130 and 1140 were very stormy times indeed with him, and have nothing in common with the hymn. [See **Bernard of Clairvaux**, p. 136, i.] Possibly it was written shortly after the Second Crusade which he preached (1146), and for the disaster of which he was blamed. The most probable moment of his life would then be about 1150, when he was residing in retirement and was weary with the world. Dr. Schaff in his *Christ in Song* justly styles the hymn as "the sweetest and most evangelical ... hymn of the Middle Ages." It is the finest and most characteristic specimen of St. Bernard's "subjective loveliness," and in its honied sweetness vindicates his title of *Doctor mellifluus*. It is, however, open to the charge of eddying round its subject, so that Abp. Trench says of it : "With all the beauty of the stanzas in particular, the composition, as a whole, lies under the defect of a certain monotony and want of progress." It is best known as the *Joyful* (or *Jubilee*) *Rhythm* of St. Bernard on the Name of Jesus ; but sometimes by the title of *In commemorationem dominicae passionis.* The title *Cursus de aeterna sapientia* was probably suggested by Ecclesiasticus xxiv. (especially vv. 20, 21 ; see Dr. Edersheim in the *Speaker's Commentary* on the "Apocrypha ") ; the Eternal Wisdom being Our Lord Jesus Christ.

I. MS. forms of the Text.

The earliest form of the text now known (and it may be added the best, and most probably the original) is contained in a MS. of the end of the 12th cent., now in the Bodleian, Oxford *Laud Misc.* 668 f. 101), in 42 st. of 4 l. The first lines of these stanzas are :—

1. Dulcis Jesu memoria.	22. Bonum mihi diligere.
2. Nil canitur suavius.	23. Jesu mi dilectissime.
3. Jesus spes poenitentibus.	24. Quocunque loco fuero.
4. Jesu dulcedo cordium.	25. Tunc amplexus, tunc oscula.
5. Nec lingua potest dicere.	26. Jam quod quaesivi video.
6. Jesum quaeram in lectulo.	27. Hic amor ardet dulciter.
7. Cum Maria diluculo.	28. Hic amor missus coelicus.
8. Tumbam profundam fletibus.	29. O beatum incendium.
9. Jesu Rex admirabilis.	30. Jesus cum sic diligitur.
10. Mane nobiscum Domine.	31. Jesu flos matris virginis.
11. Amor Jesu dulcissimus	32. Jesu sole serenior.
12. Jesum Christum recognoscite.	33. Cujus amor sic afficit.
13. Jesu auctor clementiae	34. Tu mentis delectatio.
14. Cum digne loqui nequeam.	35. Mi dilecte revertere.
15. Tua Jesu dilectio.	36. Sequor quocumque ieris.
16. Qui te gustant, esuriunt.	37. Portas vestras attollite.
17. Quem tuus amor ebriat.	38. Rex virtutum, rex gloriae.
18. Jesu decus angelicum.	39. Te coeli chorus praedicat.
19. Desidero te millies.	40. Jesu in pace imperat.
20. Amor tuus continuus.	41. Jesus ad Patrem rediit.
21. Jesu summa benignitas	42. Jam prosequamur laudibus.

Practically the same form is found in a 13th cent. ms. in the Bodleian (*Rawlinson, C.*, 510 f. 3 *b*; also beginning *Dulcis Jesu*); and in a ms. of 1288 at Einsiedeln. The text of the Einsiedeln ms. is printed by *Morel*, No. 109, the only important difference being that this ms. does not contain stanza 39. The hymn is also found in a ms. of the 15th cent. in the Bibl. Nat., Paris (*Fonds italiens*, 559 f. 106. This ms. contains the poems of Jacobus de Benedictis, otherwise called Jacopone or Giacopone da Todi), in 43 st. From a collation kindly supplied by M. Leopold Delisle, the chief librarian, it appears that in this ms. stanza 27 is omitted and two stanzas added, viz. :

43. Jesu stringam vestigia. | 44. Veni, veni, Rex optime.

A ms. of the 15th cent. at Mainz (see *Mone*, i. p. 332) contains in all 50 st., viz. 1–42, 44 as above, and :—

45. Cor nostrum quando visitas.	47. Hic amantem diligite.
46. Hoc probat ejus passio.	48. Jesu mi bone, sentiam.
	49. Tu verae lumen patriae

together with the two following :—

50. Tuum dulcorem sitio, Quo solo me reficio, In me quia deficio, Ad te, Jesu, respicio.	51. Hic amor est suavitas Et pietas et castitas, Et sanctitas et puritas; Nam Deus est et charitas.

Among the St. Gall mss. the hymn is found in No. 1394, in a hand of 13th cent. ; in No. 519 cir. 1439, and No. 520 of 1436. Herr Idtenson, the librarian, has kindly informed me that these three mss. all contain st. 39 ; but that of the stanzas numbered 43–51 not one is found in No. 1394, and in Nos. 519, 520, only stanza 48. The variations of text are exceedingly numerous and very bewildering. The mss., moreover, not only disagree as to the order of the stanzas, but often as to the order of lines (and of words) in the individual stanzas. As in the four earliest mss. none of the stanzas 43–51 are to be found (one, viz. st. 48, is in *Mone's* Frankfurt ms. of the 14th cent. ; the rest have not been traced earlier than the 15th cent.) it is hardly likely that they are by St. Bernard ; and st. 44 has not the quadruple rhyme. These stanzas are quite unnecessary to the hymn and break its course ; though in themselves some of them are not at all unworthy of St. Bernard.

II. *Printed forms of the Text.*

A form in 48 stanzas (viz. 1–42, 44–49) is found in the Benedictine ed. of St. Bernard's *Opera*, Paris, 1719, and later editions. *Daniel*, i., No. 206, gives it in 48 st. (from Bernard's *Opera*, Paris, 1690, G. Fabricius's *Poetarum vet. eccles. opera Christiana*, Basel, 1564, and other sources), viz. st. 1–42, 44–49, adding in his notes st. 43 from *Fabricius*, and the readings of the *Roman Breviary*, 1722; while at iv. pp. 211–217 he gives further notes principally from *Mone*. [For order of stanzas see below. St. 37 here begins "Coeli cives occurrite" (l. 2), and st. 49 "Tu fons misericordiae" (l. 2).] The Laud ms. (see above) affords a much better text than that which *Daniel* gives, and it is hoped will not escape the notice of future editors of Latin hymns. *Mone*, No. 258, prints 24 st. with a doxology (" Aeterna sapientia," &c.) from a 14th cent. ms. at Frankfurt-am-Main (where the stanzas are in order 1, 2, 3, 9, 5, 20, 11, 18, 48, 15, 16, 19,

21–26, 32, 34, 13, 40, 39, 41); and also gives the readings of a 15th cent. ms. at Mainz (see above). *Wackernagel*, i., No. 183, gives 50 st. from Bernard's *Opera*, 1719, and *Fabricius*, 1564. The full text is also in J. M. Horst's *Paradisus animae Christianae*, 1644, and later editions. Centos will be found in Abp. Trench's *Sac. Lat. Poetry*, 1864 (15 st.) ; F. A. March's *Latin Hys.*, 1875 (24 st.); *Königsfeld*, 1847 (11 st.) ; *Bässler*, 1858 (11 st.), and others.

III. *Ritual use of the Rhythm.*

The length of the hymn and the fact that it was not specially appropriate for any of the usual offices of the Church made its use for some time limited. In the Frankfurt ms., employed by *Mone*, of the 24 st. selected three are apportioned to each of the eight canonical hours of the day ; and *Fabricius* arranges the 47 st. of his text according to a similar plan.

The text of *Mone* is the arrangement made by Heinrich Suso, otherwise called St. Amandus or Heinrich von Berg [b. at Constanz, March 21, 1300, became a Dominican 1318, d. in the Dominican convent at Ulm, Jan. 25, 1365], who was one of the Mediaeval Mystics, and a member of the society of The Friends of God, along with Tauler (q.v.) and others. In his youth he had taken the Everlasting Wisdom depicted in the Salomonic Books as the object of his love, and in his later years founded a Brotherhood of the Everlasting Wisdom. For this brotherhood he compiled his *Horologium sapientiae*, or *Horae de aeterna sapientia*. In a ms. of the 14th cent. written in Germany and now in the *Brit. Mus.* (*Add.* 18318, f. 141 *b*) it is marked as " Quicunque desiderat sapientiam aeternam familiarem sibi sponsam habere, debet ei has horas cottidie devote legere." In the printed ed. which the British Museum catalogue dates Venice, 1492, it is marked as " Incipit cursus seu officium de eterna sapientia compositum a beate Henricho Suso ordinis praedicatorum." Of this office (meant, as will be seen, for daily use by the Brotherhood) there is a *tr.* which the British Museum catalogues dates Douay, 1580, and which is entitled " Certayne sweete Prayers of the glorious name of Jesus, commonly called Jesus Mattens, with the flowers thereto belonging : written in Latin above two hundred yeres ago, by H. Susonne." This contains a series of *trs.* from St. Bernard which are poor but are very poor. The first begins, " O Jesu meeke, ye sweetest thought."

The form in 50 st. seems to have been used as a *Rosary*, being arranged in five decades and answering to the 50 *Ave Marias* of the Rosary. When a separate office of the Holy Name of Jesus came into general use, apparently about 1500, centos from this poem were embodied in it. Such an office appears to have been added to the *Sarum Breviary* about 1495 (certainly in the Paris ed. 1499), and contains two centos, (i.) " Jesu dulcis memoria," for Matins, and (ii.) " Jesu, auctor clementiae," for Lauds; and the same centos are in the *Hereford Brev.*, 1505 ; the *Aberdeen Brev.*, 1509–10; and the *York Brev.*, 1526 (not in the *York Brev.*, 1493). In the regular *Roman Breviary* the hymn does not appear in any form till the revision of 1568 ; and then only in the patchwork noted under " Lux alma, Jesu, mentium," and appointed for the festival of the Transfiguration. An office of the Holy Name seems to have been authorised for use in the Franciscan Order by Clement VII. (Pope 1523–34), but was not authorised for general use before 1721, and by decree of Dec. 20, 1722, was ranked as a double of the second class. It appears in the Antwerp, 1733, and later eds. of the *Roman Breviary*, and includes three centos, (i.) " Jesu dulcis memoria," for Vespers ; (ii.) " Jesu, Rex admirabilis," for Matins ; (iii.) " Jesu decus angelicum," for Lauds. In the

Paris Breviary of 1680, a cento beginning "Jesu dulcedo cordium" is appointed for Lauds on the festival of the Transfiguration.

[J. M.]

IV. *Translations into English.*

After giving an account of the full *trs.* of the poem, we purpose dealing only with those centos which have been *tr.* into English, and most of which are in C. U. at the present time. As in annotating the *trs.* we follow the text of *Daniel* (which is itself the Benedictine text), a comparative table is here given to serve as a chart. The columns headed D represent the stanzas in the order in which *Daniel* gives them; and the columns headed M the order in which the corresponding stanzas are given in Section I. of this article.

D.	M.	D.	M.	D.	M.	D.	M.
1.	i.	13.	xlvi.	25.	xxi.	37.	xxxii.
2.	ii.	14.	xii.	26.	xxii.	38.	xxxiii.
3.	iii.	15.	xlvii.	27.	xxiii.	39.	xxxiv.
4.	iv.	16.	xiii.	28.	xxiv.	40.	xxxv.
5.	v.	17.	xiv.	29.	xxv.	41.	xxxvi.
6.	vi.	18.	xlviii.	30.	xxvi.	42.	xxxvii.
7.	vii.	19.	xv.	31.	xxx.	43.	xxxviii.
8.	viii.	20.	xvi.	32.	xxvii.	44.	xlix.
9.	ix.	21.	xvii.	33.	xxviii.	45.	xxxix.
10.	x.	22.	xviii.	34.	xxix.	46.	xl.
11.	xlv.	23.	xlix.	35.	xxxi.	47.	xli.
12.	xi.	24.	xx.	36.	xliv.	40.	xlii.

V. *Translations of the Full Form.*

1. A full *tr.* was given by E. Caswall in his *Masque of Mary*, 1858, and again in his *Hys. & Poems*, 1873, p. 139. In this he repeated several stanzas of his earlier *tr.* from the *Roman Breviary* (see below), including four of the five stanzas which compose the Vesper hymn. This *tr.* has been broken up into the following centos:

(i.) **Jesu dulcis memoria = Jesu, the very thought of Thee.** Usually the *tr.* of the *Roman Brev.* text is followed here.

(ii.) **Jesu Rex admirabilis = O Jesu, King most wonderful.** This is generally given from the *tr.* of the *Roman Brev.* text (see below). It is distinguished from that by st. ii., "Stay with us, Lord; and with Thy light."

(iii.) **Amor Jesus dulcissimus = Jesu, Thy mercies are untold.** Composed of st. xii., xiii., xv., vii. in *H. A. & M.*, 1875.

(iv.) **Jesu decus angelicum = O Jesu, Thou the beauty art.** This is usually taken from the *Roman Brev.* text (see below). It is distinguished from this by st. ii., "For Thee I yearn, for Thee I sigh."

2. In the *tr.* of J. M. Horst's *Paradise of the Christian Soul*, edited by Dr. E. B. Pusey in 1847, *The Rhythm* is *tr.* in five decades of varying metre, thus:—

(i.) **Jesu, dulcis memoria = Jesu, who dost true joys impart.**

(ii.) **Mane nobiscum, Domine = Stay with us, Lord, and lift Thy gracious light.**

(iii.) **Qui Te gustant esuriunt = They who of Thee have tasted hunger more.**

(iv.) **Jam quod quæsivi video = Now what I sought do I behold.**

(v.) **Tu mentis delectatio = Thou art the mind's delight.**

This *tr.* is not in C. U. It is vigorous and musical, and from it some excellent centos might be compiled. The *tr.* used in the *tr.* of *The Paradise of the Christian Soul*, pub. by Burns,

1850, is E. Caswall's as above, divided into five decades.

3. **Jesu, how sweet those accents are.** By W. J. Copeland, in his *Hys. for the Week*, &c., 1848, p. 137, reduced to 30 st. of 4 l. In Darling's *Hymns*, &c., 1887, the following hymns are said to be based on this *tr.*; but they have so little in common either with Copeland's *tr.* or St. Bernard's original that Mr. Darling may claim them as his own. The most that can be said is that they were suggested by Copeland's *tr.*:—

(1.) Lord Jesus, since the faith of Thee.
(2.) To Thee, O Christ, our thoughts aspire.
(3.) What name so full of melody?

4. **Jesu, name of sweetest thought.** By Dr. Edersheim, in his *The Jubilee Rhythm of St. Bernard of Clairvaux*, &c., 1867. This is a very spirited and musical *tr.*, and from it some five or six centos of great excellence might be compiled. It has been strangely overlooked. It is in 48 st. of 4 l.

5. **Jesu, remembrance passing sweet.** By T. G. Crippen, in his *Ancient Hys. & Poems*, 1868, p. 163, in 48 st. of 4 l.

6. **O Jesus, Thy sweet memory.** By Mrs. Charles in her *Voice of Christian Life in Song*, 1858, in 19 st. of 4 l. This *tr.* is rarely quoted in the collections.

VI. *Translations from the Sarum Uses.*

In the *Sarum Breviary* there are *two* centos, and in the *Sarum Gradual* one, all of which have been rendered into English as follows:—

(i.) **Jesu dulcis memoria.** This is appointed for Matins on the Festival of the Holy Name in the *Sarum Brev.*, 1499, and is composed of the following stanzas: 1, 2, 3, 5, 9, 10, as above. This has been *tr.* as:—

1. **Jesu, the very thought is sweet.** By J. M. Neale, in the *H. Noted*, 1852, No. 18, with added doxology. This *tr.* may be distinguished from Neale's *tr.* from the *Sarum Gradual* (below) through st. iv., which reads here "No tongue of mortal can express." This *tr.* is found in a large number of hymn-books in G. Britain and America, the text, slightly altered, as in *H. A. & M.*, being the most popular. In the *Salisbury H. Bk.*, 1857, it begins "Jesu! memorial name so sweet;" and in the *Sarum H.*, 1868, "Jesu, sweet memories of Thy Name."

2. **Jesu, how sweet Thy memory Within my,** &c. By W. J. Blew, in his *Church Hy. and Tune Bk.*, 1852-55.

3. **Jesu, how sweet Thy memory is! To every heart,** &c. By J. D. Chambers, in his *Lauda Syon*, 1857, p. 244.

(ii.) **Jesus, auctor clementiae.** In the *Sarum Brev.*, 1499, this is the hymn for Lauds at the Festival of the Holy Name. It consists of st. 16, 22, 35, 37, 25, 43, 45, and an additional stanza. *Tr.* as:—

1. **Jesu, Well-spring of all mercy.** By W. J. Blew, in his *Church Hy. and Tune Bk.*, 1852-55, and again in Rice's *Sel.* from the same, 1870.

2. **Jesu, Thou Fount of mercy, hail.** By J. D. Chambers, in his *Lauda Syon*, 1857, p. 245, and again in the *Hymner*, 1882, somewhat freely altered as "Jesu, of mercy Source alone."

(iii.) **Jesu dulcis memoria.** This longer extract from the poem appears in the *Sarum Gradual*, 1532, as a Sequence (commonly called the *Rosy Sequence*) for the Festival of the Holy Name. It consists of st. 1-7, 47, 48. It is *tr.* as:—

Jesu, the very thought is sweet. By J. M. Neale, in the *H. Noted*, 1854, No. 72, and a few other collections, including the *People's H.*, 1867. It is distinguished from Neale s *tr.* above by st. iv., which begins "Jesu, Thou sweetness pure and blest," which is also the opening of No. 1474 in *Kennedy*, 1863, and others. In the *Sarum Hyl.*, 1868, No. 67, Pt. i. is composed of st. i.–v. from this *tr.*, and st. vi.–viii. from the *tr.* above, i. 1, also by Dr. Neale, and in both instances slightly altered; and Pt. ii. from this *tr.* being st. viii., vi., vii. and ix., also altered.

VII. *Translations from the Roman Use.*

In the *Roman Breviary*, 1722, three centos were given for the 2nd S. after the Epiphany, being the Festival of the Holy Name of Jesus, as follows :—

(i.) **Jesu dulcis memoria.** This is appointed for *Vespers*, and is composed of st. 1, 2, 3, 5, and an added st., "Sis Jesu nostrum gaudium." *Tr.* as :—

1. **Jesu, the very thought of Thee.** By E. Caswall, in his *Lyra Catholica*, 1849, p. 56 ; and again in his *Hys. & Poems*, 1873, p. 31. This *tr.* is the most widely used of any made from *The Rhythm*, and is usually given unaltered, except at times a slight change in st. iv. In *Kennedy*, 1863, it is slightly altered, and st. iii., ll. 5–8, are added from Caswall's *tr.* of "Jesu, Rex admirabilis."

2. **Sweet and with enjoyment fraught.** By Bp. Mant in his *Ancient Hys.*, &c., 1837, p. 50 (1871 ed., p. 90).

Other trs. are :—
1. Thy sweet remembrance, Lord, imparts. *R. Campbell.* 1850.
2. O'Jesu dear, how sweet Thou art. F. S. Pierpoint in 2nd ed. *Lyra Eucharistica*, 1864.
3. The memory sweet of Jesus' Name. J. D. Aylward in Shipley's *Annus Sanctus*, 1884, p. 45.

(ii.) **Jesu, Rex admirabilis.** This is appointed for *Matins* at the same Festival, and is composed of st. 9, 11, 4, 14, and the added stanza, "Te nostra Jesu vox sonet." *Tr.* as :—

1. **O Jesu, King most wonderful.** By E. Caswall, in his *Lyra Catholica*, 1849, p. 57 ; and his *Hys. & Poems*, 1873, p. 32. This *tr.* is widely used.

Other trs. are :—
1. O Jesu, King of Saints adored. *Bp. Mant.* 1837.
2. Jesu, King o'er all adored. *R. Campbell.* 1850.
3. Jesu, the King all wonderful. *W. J. Blew.* 1852–55.
4. O Jesu, Lord, most mighty King. J. D. Aylward, in Shipley's *Annus Sanctus*, 1884, p. 46.

(iii.) **Jesu, decus angelicum.** This is appointed for *Lauds* at the same Festival, and is composed of st. 22, 20, 27, 10, 35. *Tr.* as :—

1. **O Jesu, Thou the beauty art.** By E. Caswall, in his *Lyra Catholica*, 1849, p. 58 ; and his *Hys. & Poems*, 1873, p. 33. This also is in extensive use.

2. **Jesu, highest heaven's completeness.** By R. Campbell, in his *Hys. & Anthems*, 1850, p. 17, and in the *People's H.*, 1867.

3. **Crown of the angels, Thy sweet Name.** By J. D. Aylward, in O. Shipley's *Annus Sanctus*, 1884, p. 46.

VIII. *Translations from the Paris Use.*

In the *Paris Breviary*, 1736, the hymn for Lauds for the Festival of the *Transfiguration* is :—

Jesu dulcedo cordium. This is composed of st. 4, 10, 11, 18, 21, 44, of *The Rhythm*, and is *tr.* as :—

1. **Jesu, the heart's own Sweetness and true Light.** By I. Williams, in his *Hys. tr. from the Parisian Breviary*, 1839.

2. **Jesu, delight of every heart.** By J. D. Chambers, in his *Lauda Syon*, 1857.

IX. *Various Centos.*

The following hymns are translations of stanzas compiled from *The Rhythm.* They vary much in length and character. Some are in C. U. and others are worthy of that distinction :—

1. In Rorison's *Hys. & Anthems*, 1851, there are two centos arranged by Dr. Rorison from various *trs.*, with additions of his own, as :—
1. "Jesu, how sweet the memories are."
2. "Jesu, the angels' Light and song."

2. In J. A. Johnston's *English Hymnal*, 2nd ed., 1861, portions of E. Caswall's *tr.* of the full text, somewhat extensively altered, were given as two hymns, Nos. 65, 66, as :—
1. "O Jesu, King adorable."
2. "O Jesu, Thou the glory art."

3. In Dr. Kynaston's *Occasional Hymns*, 1862, there are two centos from *The Rhythm*, as :—
1. "Source of recollection sweet."
2. "Jesu, Bridegroom, Saviour, Friend."

4. The Rev. R. C. Singleton's *tr.* in the *Anglican H. Bk.*, 1868, No. 258, "Jesu, how sweet the thought of Thee," is from the *Roman Brev.*, with an additional stanza (v.) from *The Rhythm* (x.).

5. In the Roman Catholic *Hys. for the Year*, 12 st. are given from *The Rhythm*, divided into three parts :—
1. "Jesu, the very thought of Thee." The 2nd st. begins "No sound, no harmony so gay."
2. "Thee, then, I'll seek, retired apart."
3. "O King of love, Thy blessed fire."

6. The hymn given in the American *College Hyl.*, N. Y., 1876, as, "O Thou in Whom our love doth find," is from E. Caswall's full *tr.*, st. 41, 11, 16, 18, very slightly altered.

7. The hymn, "O Jesus, Lord of all below," in the American *Hys. for the Church of Christ*, Boston, 1853, is composed of E. Caswall's *tr.* of the *Roman Brev.* form of "Jesu, Rex admirabilis," st. iii.–v. slightly altered.

8. The most popular cento in C. U. is, "Jesus, Thou joy of loving hearts," by Dr. Ray Palmer. It is composed of the *tr.* of st. 4, 3, 20, 28, 10, of *Daniel's* text, and appeared in the American Andover *Sabbath H. Bk.*, 1858, No. 686. It is found in all the best English and American hymn-books now in C. U., and is usually given in an unaltered form. In the *Hymnary*, 1872, it is altered to "O Jesu, joy of loving hearts."

9. In the 1862 Appendix to the *Hymnal N.* there are two centos: (1) "Tu mentis delectatio," *tr.* by T. I. Ball as "Thou the spirit's pleasure," and (2) "Jesu, Tua dilectio " ("Tua, Jesu dilectio "), *tr.* as "Jesu ! the soul hath in Thy love."

10. Another cento, *tr.* by Dr. J. W. Alexander, was pub. in Schaff's *Kirchenfreund*, N. Y., April, 1859 ; and in Schaff's *Christ in Song*, 1869 and 1870. It begins, "Jesus, how sweet Thy memory is ! Thinking of Thee," &c.

11. In the Primers of 1684 and 1685, and in the Evening Office of 1725, there are the following centos :—
1. "Thou, Jesus, art the admired King."   (1684.)
2.   "Jesus the only thought of Thee
       Fills with delight my memory."   (1685.)
3. "If Jesus called to mind imparts."   (1725.)

These centos are printed in full in O. Shipley's *Annus Sanctus*, 1884; and the *Primers*, &c., are described in the Preface to the same [see also **Primers.**]

12. In R. Beste's *Church Hys.*, 1849, there are 14 st. of 4 l. from *The Rhythm*, as: " Jesus, how sweet the thought of Thee."

13. Dr. J. Wallace gave 14 st. in 4 l. in his *Hys. of the Church*, 1874, as " Jesus, to think of Thee." (See **Various.**)

This elaborate and extensive use of St. Bernard's *Rhythm* is almost if not entirely unique in hymnody. A few hymns exceed it in the number of their translations into English, as the " Adeste fideles," the " Dies Irae," and the " Ein' feste Burg," but no other poem in any language has furnished to English and American hymn-books so many hymns of sterling worth and well-deserved popularity.   [J. J.]

X. *Translations through the German.*

The hymn has been frequently *tr.* into German. Four of these versions have passed into English, viz. :—

i. **Ach Gott, wie manches Herzeleid** (q. v.).

ii. **O Jesu süss, wer dein gedenkt.** *Wackernagel*, v. p. 449, gives this in 18 st. of 4 l. from the 1612 ed. of Johann Arndt's *Paradiss-Gärtlein;* and also gives a version in 52 st. from the 1711 ed. of the *Paradiss-Gärtlein.* According to *Bäumker*, i. p. 385, the 18 st. of 1612 form part of a version in 48 st. in Conrad Vetter's *Paradiess-vogel*, 1613 ; Vetter in his preface stating that this version had been for some time in print. There does not appear to be any reason for assigning this *tr.* either to *Arndt*, or, as has sometimes been done, to *Martin Moller.* A selection of 16 st. is No. 773 in the *Unv. L. S.*, 1851. *Tr.* as :—

When memory brings my Jesus to my sense. A very free *tr.* in 41 st. of 4 10's. 1st pub. in A. W. Boehm's *tr.* of Arndt's *True Christianity*, vol. i., 1712, p. 597. This was revised by J. C. Jacobi, reduced to L.M., and included in his *Psalmodia Germanica*, 1720, p. 25 (1722, p. 130), beginning " When Thought brings Jesus to my sense." In *Jacobi's* ed., 1732, p. 17, it is altered to "Sweet Jesus! when I think on Thee." In the *Moravian H. Bk.*, 1754, pt. i., No. 236, is a cento of 17 st. from *Jacobi*, 1732 ; to which are added 3 st. from Isaac Watts (st. v. of his " Far from my thoughts, vain world, be gone ;" and st. iv., v. of his " 'Twas on that dark, that doleful night "), in all 20 st. Centos, beginning with st. i., from the text of 1754, are found in Montgomery's *Christian Psalmist*, 1825, Surrey Chapel *H. Bk.*, 1858, &c. Other more or less altered forms of *Jacobi* are :—

1. **Dear Jesus, when I think of Thee** (*Jacobi's* st. i. altered). *Moravian H. Bk.*, 1789 (1849, No. 465).

2. **Of Him Who did Salvation bring** (*Jacobi's* st. iii.) in Madan's *Ps. & Hys.*, 1760, and in varying centos in the Amer. Meth. *Epis. Hymns*, 1849, *Hys. & Songs of Praise*, N. Y., 1874, &c.

3. **Come all, and hear of Jesus' love** (*Jacobi's* st. xl. altered), in Dr. Hawker's *Coll.*, Plymouth, 1847.

iii. **An Jesum denken oft und viel.** By M. Rinkart, in his *Jesu Hertzbüchlein.* This work was completed in MS. 1630, and first printed 1636. Only the 2nd ed., Leipzig, 1663, is now extant [Royal Library, Hannover], and there the *tr.*, being broken up into sets of 3 st., begins at p. 31 and ends p. 121. The complete text, in 48 st., is in Dr. J. Linke's ed. of Rinkart's *Geistl. Lieder*, 1886, p. 352. In the Lüneburg Stadt *G. B.*, 1686, No. 246 consists of st. 1, 2, 4, 12, 15, 28, 39, and this form is in the Berlin *G. L. S.*, ed. 1863. *Tr.* as :—

Sweet meditation on the Lord. A *tr.* of st. 1, 2, 4, 12, 39, by H. L. Hastings, 1879, included in his *Hymnal*, 1880, and *Songs of Pilgrimage*, 1886.

iv. **Jesu, deiner zu gedenken.** A free *tr.*, in 48 st., by N. L. von Zinzendorf, included as No. 1148 in the 3rd ed., 1731, of his *Sammlung geist- und lieblicher Lieder. Tr.* as "Jesu! on Thee to be thinking," as No. 237 in pt. i. of the *Moravian H. Bk.*, 1754.   [J. M.]

Jesu dulcissime, e throno gloriae. [*Love to Christ.*] This is found in the *Psalteriolum cantionum Catholicarum*, Cologne 1722, p. 334 ; in the *Hymnodia Sacra*, Münster 1753, p. 161 ; in *Daniel*, ii. 371, &c. It is probably not earlier than 1650, and is in 4 st. of 4 l.   [J. M.]

Translations in C. U. :—

1. **Jesu, most loving One, Who from Thy glory's throne.** By R. F. Littledale, in the *People's H.*, 1867.

2. **O precious Saviour, from Thy throne.** By R. C. Singleton, written in 1867, and included in the *Anglican H. Bk.*, 1868.

3. **Jesu, most pitiful, Who from heaven's throne.** By J. Ellerton, in Brown-Borthwick's *Sixteen Hys. with Tunes*, 1870, and again in the Brown-Borthwick *Select Hys.*, 1871.

Another *tr.* is :—
O Jesu, most sweet! From Thy glorious throne. *J. W. Hewett*, 1859.   [J. J.]

Jesu, for the beacon-light. *Sir H. W. Baker.* [*Festival of Martyrs. •For a Doctor.*] Written for and first pub. in the *Appendix* to *H. A. & M.*, 1868, and repeated in the revised ed., 1875.   [J. J.]

Jesu geh' voran. *N. L. von Zinzendorf.* [*Following Christ.*] 1st appeared as No. 525 in the *Brüder G. B.*, 1778, in 4 st. of 6 l. It is a slightly altered centò (probably made by Christian Gregor) from two hymns by Zinzendorf, on both of which see notes. St. i. is st. x., iii. is st. iv., and iv. is st. xi. of " Seelenbraütigam, O du Gottes-Lamm " ; and st. ii. is st. xi. of " Glanz der Ewigkeit." In the text of 1778 it has passed into many German hymn books, e.g. the Berlin *G. L. S.*, ed. 1863, No. 634 ; and has become a great favourite, especially as a children's hymn. *Tr.* as :—

1 **Jesus, still lead on.** A very good but free *tr.* by Miss Borthwick, in the *Free Church Magazine*, 1846, p. 14, repeated, slightly altered, in *H. L. L.*, 1st Ser., 1854, p. 23 (1884, p. 26). From the *H. L. L.* it has passed into many recent hymnals, e.g. the *People's*, 1867 ; *Church Hys.*, 1871 ; Thring's *Coll.*, 1882 ; *Bapt. Hyl.*, 1879 ; *N. Cong. Hyl.*, 1887, &c. ; and in America in the *Sabbath H. Bk.*, 1858 ; *Presb. Hyl.*, 1874 ; *H. & Songs of Praise*, N. Y., 1874, &c., generally in full and unaltered.

2. **Jesu! guide our way.** A good and full *tr.* by A. T. Russell, written March 20, 1846, and pub. in his *Ps. & Hys.*, 1851, No. 61. This, generally omitting st. iii., has been repeated in the *Book of Praise Hyl.*, 1867 ; American *Presb. Hyl.*, 1874 ; *Evang. Hyl.*, N. Y., 1880, &c. The versions in the Eng. Presb. *Ps. & Hys.*, 1867, and John Robinson's [some time Chaplain of the Settle Union, Yorkshire, who d. Jan. 1886] *Coll.*, 1869, are partly from Mr. Russell and partly from Miss Borthwick.

3. **Jesu, day by day.** A full and close *tr.* by Miss Winkworth, as No. 174 in her *C. B. for England*, 1863 ; and in her *Christian Singers*, 1869. Repeated in J. L. Porter's *Coll.*, 1876, and M. W. Stryker's *Christian Chorals*, 1885.

4. **Jesu! be our Guide.** By L. Heyl, as No. 406 in the Ohio *Luth. Hyl.*, 1880.

Other *trs.* are, (1) " Jesus, lead the way," by J. D. Burns, in the *Family Treasury*, 1859, pt. i. p. 289, and his *Memoir & Remains*, 1869, p. 241. (2) " O Jesus, show the way," in Dr. J. F. Hurst's *tr.* of K. R. Hagenbach's *Hist. of the Church 18 and 19 centuries*, N. Y., 1869, vol. i. p. 433. (3) " Jesus, day by day," partly from Miss Winkworth, as No. 1014 in Reid's *Praise Bk.*, 1872. (4) " Jesus, day by day, Guide us on our way," as No. 485 in the *Moravian H. Bk.*, 1886.   [J. M.]

Jesu, if still Thou art to-day. *C. Wesley.* [*For Pardon.*] Pub. in *Hys. & Sac. Poems*, 1740, in 21 st. of 4 l., and headed,

" These things were written for our Instruction " (*P. Works*, 1868-72, vol. i. p. 262). It is a résumé of the miracles of our Lord, together with their spiritual teachings. In 1780 the poem was divided (with the omission of st. xiii.) into two parts, and included in the *Wes. H. Bk.* as two hymns (Nos. 131,132), the second part being, " While dead in trespasses and sins." Both parts have passed into other collections, Pt. i. sometimes being given as " Jesus, if Thou art still to-day," as in Spurgeon's *O. O. H. Bk.*, 1866. Sometimes Pt. i. is used as a special hymn for the 3rd S. after the Epiphany, for which it is most suitable. In the Reformed Dutch *Hys. of the Church*, N. Y., 1869, st. vii.-x. of Pt. ii. in the *Wes. H. Bk.* are given as, " O Lord, impart Thyself to me."   [J. J.]

Jesu, komm' doch selbst zu mir. *J. Scheffler.* [*Love to Christ.*] A fine hymn of longing for spiritual union with Christ, 1st pub. as No. 3 in Bk. i., 1657, of his *Heilige Seelenlust* (*Werke*, 1862, i. p. 29), in 9 st. of 4 l., entitled, " She [the Soul] longs after Jesus alone." It passed through Freylinghausen's *G. B.*, 1704, into many later German collections, and is No. 761 in the *Unv. L. S.*, 1851. The *trs.* in C. U. are :—

1. Jesus, Jesus, visit me. A good and full *tr.* by Dr. R. P. Dunn, contributed to *Sacred Lyrics from the German*, Philadelphia, 1859, p. 125. Repeated, generally omitting st. iv.-vi., in Hatfield's *Church H. Bk.*, 1872, Baptist *Service of Song*, 1871, Amer. Presb. *Hyl.*, 1874, *Laudes Domini*, N.Y., 1884, and others.

2. Jesus! Saviour! come to me. Let me, &c. A good and full *tr.* by Dr. M. Loy in the *Evang. Review*, Gettysburg, July, 1861 ; repeated as No. 279 in the Ohio *Luth. Hyl.*, 1880.

3. Jesu, Jesu, come to me. Longeth, &c. A good *tr.* from the greatly altered text (" Jesu, Jesu, komm zu mir ") of the *Trier G. B.* (R. C.), 1846, p. 121, in 7 st.; in *Lyra Eucharistica*, 1864, p. 29, signed " M." Repeated as No. 94 in the *Hyl. for St. Ethelburga's*, Lond., 1873.

Other trs. are: (1) " Dearest Jesus, come to me," as No. 465 in pt. i. of the *Moravian H. Bk.*, 1754 (1886, No. 453), repeated in some eds. of Lady Huntingdon's *Coll.* (2) " Jesus, come Thyself to me," by *Miss Manington*, 1864, p. 29. (3) " Jesus, Jesus, come to me ! How I long," &c., by Miss Burlingham, in the *British Herald*, July, 1865, p. 109. (4) " Jesus, Jesus, 'come to me! Oh how," &c., in the *British Herald*, April, 1867, p. 55, repeated as No. 243 in Reid's *Praise Bk.*, 1872. (5) " Jesus, Saviour, come to me, Lo, I thirst," &c., in the *Family Treasury*, 1877, p. 111.   [J. M.]

Jesu, Lord, we look to Thee. *C. Wesley.* [*Family Union desired.*] Appeared in *Hys. and Sac. Poems*, 1749, vol. i., No. 146, in 6 st. of 4 l., and again in the *Wes. H. Bk.*, 1780, No. 495. (*P. Works*, 1868-72, vol. v. p. 52.) The cento " Lord, we all look up to Thee," in T. Davis's *Hys. Old and New*, 1864, No. 231, and in Spurgeon's *O. O. H. Bk.*, 1866, was adapted by Mr. Davis from this hymn.
                                          [J. J.]

Jesu, Lover of my soul. *C. Wesley.* [*In time of Danger and Temptation.*] 1st pub. in the Wesley *Hys. and Sac. Poems*, 1740, in 5 st. of 8 l., and headed " In Temptation " (*P. Works*, 1868-72, vol. i. p. 259). In 1800 it was added to the *Wes. H. Bk.*, but before this it had been included in a few hymnbooks of the Church of England, amongst

which were M. Madan's *Ps. & Hys.*, 1760; R. Conyers's *Ps. & Hys.*, 1774; A. M. Toplady's *Ps. & Hys.*, 1776, and others. During the past hundred years few hymns have been so extensively used. Its popularity increases with its age, and few collections are now found from which it is excluded. It is given in the hymn-books of all English-speaking countries, and has been translated into many languages.

2. The opening stanza of this hymn has given rise to questions which have resulted in more than twenty different readings of the first four lines. The first difficulty is the term *Lover* as applied to our Lord. From an early date this tender expression was felt by many to be beneath the solemn dignity of a hymn addressed to the Divine Being. Attempts have been made to increase the reverence of the opening line by the sacrifice of its pathos and poetry, The result was " Jesu, *Refuge* of my soul," a reading which is still widely adopted ; " Jesus, *Saviour* of my soul," and " *Father, Refuge* of my soul." Wesley's reading, however, has high sanction. In the *Wisdom of Solomon*, xi. 26, we read : " But Thou sparest all, for they are Thine, O Lord, Thou *Lover* of souls."

The second difficulty was in ll. 3, 4 :

> " While the nearer waters roll,
> While the tempest still is high."

To a great number of hymn-book compilers, these words have been a stumbling-block and a rock of offence. Various attempts have been made to surmount the difficulty from the 1st ed. of Lady Huntingdon's *Coll.* of Hymns, 1764, to the S. P. C. K. *Church Hymns*, 1871. Wesley's opening lines are :—

> " Jesu, Lover of my soul,
> Let me to Thy bosom fly,
> While the nearer waters roll,
> While the tempest still is high."

Amongst the numerous attempts to improve these lines are the following :—

1.   " While the *billows near me* roll."
This is in Lady Huntingdon's *Coll.*, 1764, as above, and more than a hundred years later, in Harland's *Ch. Psalter & Hyl.*, 1876, besides several collections between the two dates.
2.   " While the *raging billows* roll."
This reading appeared in Rippon's Bap. *Sel.*, 1787; Bickersteth's *Christ. Psalmody*, 1833, and others, and is widely used.
3.   " While the *threat'ning* waters roll."
In Kempthorne's *Ps. & Hys.*, 1810, and a few modern hymn-books.
4.   " Jesus, *Refuge* of the soul,
      To Thy sheltering arms we fly."
This is in Cotterill's *Sel.*, 1815. In the 1819 ed. it was changed to,
5.   " *To Thy sheltering cross we* fly," and the entire hymn was omitted in 1820.
6.   " Jesus, *Saviour* of my soul,
      Let me to Thy *mercy* fly."
In Basil Woodd's *Ps. & Hys*, 1821.
7.   " Jesus, Lover of our souls,
      We to Thee for safety fly ;
      While the ocean round us rolls,
      While the tempest still is high."
This appeared in W. Urwick's *Collection*, Dublin, 1829, and has passed into a few collections.
8.   " Jesus, *Refuge* of the soul,
      We to Thee for safety fly ;
      While the *waters round us* roll,
      While the tempest still is high."
This is *Urwick's* reading altered, and was given in Frank's *Christ. Psalmody*, Huddersfield, 1833.
9.   " Let me to Thy *shelter* fly."
In Davies and Baxter's *Sel.*, Lond., 1835.
10.   " While the *gathering* waters roll."
In Murray's *Hymnal*, 1852; Pott's *Hymns*, &c., 1861; *H. A. & M.*, and others.
11. " *To Thy sheltering wings I* fly."

In Rowe's *Church Psalm Book*, cir. 1840.
12.   " *I will* to thy bosom fly."
In the *Covenant Hymns*, London, 1849.
13.   " *To Thy mercy we would* fly,
            While the *billows near us* roll."
In the Rugby School *Ps. & Hys.*, 1850.
14.   " While the *troubled* waters roll."
In the *Primitive Methodist H. Bk.*, 1853.
15.   " While the *waters near me* roll,
            While *temptation's wave mounts* high."
These changes, and a doxology of 4 l., were given in
the *Salisbury H. Bk.*, 1857.   The line, " While the
waters nearer roll," was repeated in *Church Hymns*.
16.   " While the *waves around me* roll."
In T. Davis's *Hys. Old & New*, 1864.
17.   " *O Thou* Lover of my soul."   In the American
Unitarian *Hys. of the Spirit*, 1864.

3. In addition to these individual changes,
there are others, and also several combinations,
as for instance :—

> " *Jesus, Refuge* of *the* soul,
>   To thy *sheltering arms we* fly ;
> While the *raging billows* roll,
>   While the *tempest's roar* is high,"

in *Kennedy*, 1863, in which there are *six*
alterations, each of which was made by a
different person and at a different date, the
last being by *Dr. Kennedy*, in 1863. These
numerous quotations do not exhaust the
changes and combinations of changes which
the ingenuity of compilers have forced upon
Wesley's lines. In the whole range of hymnody, we know of no stanza or portion of a
stanza which has undergone so many alterations. As an editorial curiosity those four
lines are in their transformations unique. In
the latest hymn-books, as Thring's *Coll.*, the
Westminster Abbey H. Bk., Horder's *Cong.
H. Bk.*, and others in G. Britain and also
America, it is pleasing to find that Wesley's
lines are unaltered. In this these collections
are at one with a large number of hymnals of
various dates whose uniform use is emphatically in favour of the original text. The
fact that in a wide expanse of waters a distant
part may be lashed into fury by a passing
storm whilst around a given ship there is
perfect calm; and that these circumstances
are often reversed, and the " nearer waters "
are those affected, and the distant waters are
sleeping in the silent air—seems to have escaped the notice of the two score or more
editors who have vainly striven to improve
Wesley's text. In life, as in nature, storms
are local. One ship may be dashed hither
and thither by the fury of " the nearer waters ;"
whilst another is sleeping in the far distance
on a throbless sea. Men cry for help, not
against dangers which are both distant and
undefined; but out of the depths of their immediate troubles. Their life is amid " the
nearer waters" of local surroundings and
passions and temptations, and to them the
Lover of souls is indispensable.

4. Many charming accounts of the origin of
this hymn are extant, but unfortunately, some
would add, they have no foundation in fact.
The most that we can say is that it was
written shortly after the great spiritual change
which the author underwent in 1738 ; and
that it was published within a few months of
the official date (1739) which is given as the
founding of Methodism. It had nothing
whatever to do with the struggles, and dangers
with lawless men, in after years. Nor with a
dove driven to Wesley's bosom by a hawk,
nor with a sea-bird driven to the same shelter

by a pitiless storm. These charming stories
must be laid aside until substantiated by direct
evidence from the Wesley books; or from
original MSS. or printed papers as yet unknown.

5. Mr. G. J. Stevenson's " associations"
of this hymn in his *Meth. H. Bk. Notes*, 1883,
are of more than usual interest and value.

6. This hymn has been *tr.* into several
languages, including Latin, by R Bingham in
his *Hymno. Christi. Latina*, 1871, as, " Meæ
animæ Amator ;" and H. M. Macgill in his
Songs of the Christian Creed & Life, 1876, as,
" Jesu ! Animae Amator."   [J. J.]

Jesu, meek and gentle. *G. R. Prynne.*
[*A Child's Prayer.*] Written in 1856, and
pub. in the author's *Hymnal Suited for the
Services of the Church*, &c., 1858, in 5 st. of
1 l. In 1861 it was given in *H. A. & M.*, and
subsequently in most collections published in
G. Britain and America. The author has
also republished it in his work *The Soldier's
Dying Visions, and Other Poems*, 1881, and
has added the following note :—

" This little hymn has found its way into most English Hymn-books. It is commonly thought to have
been written for children, and on this supposition I have
been asked to simplify the fourth verse. The hymn was
not, however, written specially for children. Where it
is used in collections of hymns for children, it might be
well to alter the last two lines in the fourth verse thus :—
  " Through earth's passing darkness,
      To heaven's endless day."

Usually the original text is given as in *H. A.
& M.*, 1875.   [J. J.]

Jesu meine Freude. *J. Franck.* [*Love
to Christ.*] This beautiful hymn appears in C.
Peter's *Andachts Zymbeln*, Freyberg, 1655, No.
211, in 6 st. of 10 l., followed by a seventh
stanza marked off * * "Vater aller Ehren,"
from Franck's *Vaterunserharfe* (i.e. one of his
metrical versions of the Lord's Prayer). It is
also in J. Crüger's *Praxis*, Frankfurt, 1656,
No. 385 (with the melody by Crüger still in
German use); in Franck's *Geistliches Sion*,
1674, No. 85 (1846, p. 58), and in most later
hymn-books generally in the original 6 st., as
in the *Unv. L. S.*, 1851, No 762.

It is modelled on a Song in H. Alberti's *Arien*, pt. iv.,
Königsberg, 1641, No. 24, which begins, " Flora meine
Freude; Meiner Seelenweide." When the hymn began
to be extensively used many of the older Lutherans
objected that its depth of spiritual experience unfitted
it for use in public worship; just as in our days Bp. C.
Wordsworth, in the preface to his *Holy Year*, objected
on similar grounds to the use of " Jesus, lover of my
soul," by an ordinary congregation. Lauxmann, in
Koch, viii. 279-286, relates many instances in which the
use of this hymn was blessed. He adds that it was *tr.*
into Esthonian in 1667 ; into Russian in 1724, by command of Peter the Great; and about the same time into
Latin.

Translations in C. U. :—

1. **Jesus, my chief pleasure.** A good *tr.*, omitting st. iii., contributed by R. Massie, as No.
436, to the 1857 ed. of Mercer's *C. P. & H. Bk.*
(Ox. ed., 1864, No. 339, omitting the *tr.* of st.
iv.). Mr. Massie included the *tr.* in his *Lyra
Domestica*, 1864, p. 132, and it is also in Reid's
Praise Bk., 1872 ; Schaff's *Christ in Song*, &c.

2. **Jesu, priceless treasure.** A good *tr.*, omitting
st. iii., by Miss Winkworth, as No. 151, in her
C. B. for England, 1863, repeated, adding a *tr.*
of st. iii., in her *Christian Singers*, 1869, p. 228.
Included in the Ohio *Luth. Hyl.*, 1880, No. 280,
with a *tr.* of st. iii. not by Miss Winkworth.

3. **Jesus, Thou art nearest.** A *tr.* of st. i., ii.,

v., vi., by M. W. Stryker, as No. 119 in his *Christian Chorals*, 1885.

Other trs. are, (1) "Jesu! Source of gladness," by J. *C. Jacobi*, 1722, p. 74. Slightly altered in his 2nd ed., 1732, p. 128, and repeated in the *Moravian H. Bk.*, 1754. In the *Moravian H. Bk.*, 1789, No. 453 (1849, No. 655), the three opening lines of this version and little else are from Jacobi. (2) "Jesus, my chief pleasure, Comfort," by *Dr. H. Mills*, 1845 (1856, p. 90). (3) "Jesu, my joy-giving," by *N. L. Frothingham*, 1870, p. 150. (4) "Jesu, Fount of Pleasure," by J. H. Hopkins, in his *Carols*, &c., 3rd ed., 1882.   [J. M.]

Jesu, my God and King. *C. Wesley.* [*Jesus The King.*] 1st pub. in *Hys. & Sac. Poems*, 1739, p. 171, in 11 st. of 6 l., and entitled "Hymn to Christ the King" (*P. Works*, 1868–72, vol. i. p. 152). In the 1830 *Supplement* to the *Wes. H. Bk.*, st. i.–vii. were included as No. 689. These are repeated as No. 727 in the revised ed., 1875. In *Kennedy*, 1863, st. iii.–v. and vii. are given as "Hail your dread Lord and ours."   [J. J.]

Jesu, my great High Priest above. *C. Wesley.* [*Lent.*] Pub. in *Hys. & Sac. Poems*, 1739, in 5 st. of 8 l., and headed Ps. 139, 23, "Try me, O God, and seek the ground of my heart" (P. Bk. version), and again in *P. Works*, 1868–72, vol. i. p. 87. When included in the *Wes. H. Bk.*, 1780, No. 97, it was reduced to 4 st., and began, "Jesu, my Advocate above." This arrangement, either in full or abbreviated, is given in several modern hymnals. The last stanza of the original is sometimes given as a short hymn beginning, "O sovereign Love [Lord], to Thee I cry."   [J. J.]

Jesu, my Master and my Lord. *C. Wesley.* [*Close of the Year — Temptation.*] Appeared in *Hys. & Sac. Poems*, 1749, vol. ii., in 4 st. of 8 l., as No. 6 of "Hymns for the Watch Night" (*P. Works*, 1868–72, vol. v. p. 268). In the *Wes. H. Bk.* 1780, st. ii.–iv. were given (No. 301) as "Into a world of ruffians sent"; but in the revised ed., 1875, the original first stanza was restored. In both forms the hymn is in C. U.   [J. J.]

Jesu, my Saviour, Brother, Friend. *C. Wesley.* [*Jesus All in All.*] 1st pub. in *Hys. & Sac. Poems*, 1742, p. 214, in 15 st. of 4 l., and headed "Watch in all things" (*P. Works*, 1868–72, vol. ii. p. 271). In 1780 J. Wesley divided st. i.–xi. into two hymns, and gave them in the *Wes. H. Bk.* as (1) "Jesu, my Saviour, Brother, Friend" (No. 303); and (2) "Pierce, fill me with an humble fear" (No. 304). This arrangement is repeated in the revised ed., 1875, and other collections. In several American Unitarian hymn-books the first part is altered to "Great God, my Father, and my friend"; and in some Presbyterian collections as "Great God, our Father, and our Friend"; but the use of these forms has not extended to G. Britain; neither has that in the American Meth. Episco. *Hymns*, 1849, No. 586, which is composed of st. vi. vii., and begins "Jesu, I fain would walk in Thee." In the American Meth. Episco. *Hymns*, 1849, Pt. ii. begins, "Lord, fill me with an humble fear."   [J. J.]

Jesu, my Strength, my Hope. *C. Wesley.* [*Self-Consecration.*] Appeared in *Hys. & Sac. Poems*, 1742, p. 146, in 7 st. of

8 l., and headed "A Poor Sinner" (*P. Works*, 1868–72, vol. ii. p. 208). In 1780 st. i.-vi. and ii. were given in the *Wes. H. Bk.* as No. 292 (ed. 1875, No. 301). This is repeated in several collections. There are also the following additional centos from this hymn in C. U. :—

1. **I rest upon Thy word.** In the American *Church Pastorals*, Boston, 1864.

2. **I want a heart to pray.** In the American Dutch Reformed *Hys. of the Church*, 1869, &c.

3. **Jesus, our strength, our hope.** In the Cooke and Denton *Hymnal*, 1853, &c.

4. **My God, my Strength, my Hope.** In several American collections.

5. **O God my Strength, my Hope.** In Martineau's *Hymns*, 1840; the Bap. *Ps. & Hys.*, 1858, and others.   [J. J.]

Jesu nostra redemptio, Amor et desiderium. [*Ascension.*] This fine hymn is probably of the 7th or 8th cent. It is found in three mss. of the 11th cent. in the British Museum, two of the English Church (Vesp. D. xii. f. 69; Jul. A. vi. f. 48 *b*.), and one of the ancient Spanish Church (Add. 30848, f. 153 *b*.); in the St. Gall ms. No. 387, of the 11th cent.; in a ms. cir. 1064, in Corpus Christi College, Cambridge (No. 391, page 247); and in the *Latin Hys. of the Anglo-Saxon Ch.*, 1851, p. 83, is printed from an 11th cent. ms. at Durham (B. iii. 32, f. 24 *b*). It is in the old *Roman* (Venice, 1478), *Sarum*, *York*, *Aberdeen*, and many other *Breviaries*. The printed text is also in *Daniel*, i., No. 56; *Mone*, No. 173; J. Chandler's *Hys. of the Prim. Church*, 1837; and Card. Newman's *Hymni Ecclesiae*, 1838 and 1865. The use of *Sarum* was at Compline from the vigil of the Ascension to Whitsuntide; that of *York* at Lauds; and the *Roman* at Vespers. In the revised *Roman Breviary* of 1632 it begins, *Salutis humanae Sator*. This is repeated in J. Chandler's *Hys. of the Prim. Church*, 1837, No. 71, and Card. Newman's *Hymni Ecclesiae*, 1838 and 1865.   [J. M.]

This hymn has been *tr.* in both its original and in the *Roman Breviary* forms, as follows :—

i. **Jesu nostra redemptio.** The *trs.* in C. U. are :—

1. **O Christ, our hope, our heart's desire.** By J. Chandler, in his *Hys. of the Prim. Church*, 1837, p. 83. This *tr.* is the most popular of any of this hymn. In addition to being in C. U. in the original *tr.* in some collections it was altered by the compilers of *H. A. & M.* in 1861 to "Jesu, our hope, our heart's desire" (again altered in ll. 2–4 of st. i. in 1875), and in the *Hymnary*, 1872, to "O Jesu, our Redemption, Love." The *Hymnary* text is rewritten in L.M., and is much altered throughout.

2. **O Jesu, our Redemption.** By E. Caswall in his *Lyra Catholica*, 1849, p. 290; and again in his *Hys. and Poems*, 1873, p. 146. This is repeated in several collections. In the *Hymnary* this is rewritten in L.M. as "O Jesu, our Redemption, Love."

3. **Jesu, Redemption, all divine.** By J. M. Neale, in the *H. Noted*, 1852, and one or two other hymn-books.

4. **Our Redemption, our Salvation.** By W. J. Blew, in his *Hymn and Tune Bk.*, 1852–55; and again in Rice's *Sel.* from the same, 1870.

5. **Jesu, our Redemption blest.** By R. F. Littledale, in the *People's H.*, 1867.

Translations not in C. U. :—

1. O our Redemption, Jesu Christ. *Primer*, 1604.
2. O Jesu, Who our souls dost save. *Primer*, 1619.
3. Jesu, Who our Redemption art, God, Maker of all things, &c. *I. Williams*, 1839.
4. Jesu, Who our Redemption art, Who in the deep love, &c. *Hymnarium Anglicanum*, 1844.
5. Jesu, Redeemer, Thou Who art. *J. D. Chambers*, 1857.
6. Jesu, our Redeemer, now. *Mrs. Charles*, 1858.
7. Jesu, Redemption dear. *J. W. Hewett*, 1859.
8. Jesu, Thou Redeemer dear. *Dr. Edersheim*, 1867.
9. Jesu, our Ransom from above. In Shipley's *Annus Sanctus*, 1884.

ii. **Salutis humanae Sator.** This *Roman Breviary* form of the text has been thus *tr.* :—

1. O Jesu, Lord of heavenly grace. By J. Chandler, in his *Hys. of the Prim. Church*, 1837, p. 81, into *Mercer* and others.
2. O Thou pure light of souls that love. By E. Caswall, in his *Lyra Catholica*, 1849, p. 100, and his *Hys. & Poems*, 1873, p. 56. This *tr.* is in several collections.

Translations not in C. U. :—

1. Jesus, Who man's Redeemer art. *Primer*, 1685 and 1710, in Shipley's *Annus Sanctus*, 1884.
2. O Christ, the Saviour of mankind. *Primer*, 1706.
3. Saviour of men, our joy supreme. *Bp. Mant*, 1837.
4. O Lord, Redeemer of the world. *A. J. B. Hope*, 1844.
5. Author of lost man's salvation. *W. J. Copeland*, 1848.
6. Saviour of men, Who dost impart. *F. C. Husenbeth*, 1840.
7. Jesu, slain for earth's release. *R. Campbell*, 1850.
8. Hail Thou, Who man's Redeemer art. *T. J. Potter*, in Shipley's *Annus Sanctus*, 1884.
9. Thou Who didst die for sinners' sake. *J. Wallace*, 1874.   [J. J.]

Jesu, now Thy new-made soldier. *J. W. Hewett.* [*After Baptism.*] Pub. in his *Verses by a Country Curate*, 1859, in 7 st. of 6 l. and entitled "A Hymn after Baptism." It is followed by a quotation from one of the author's sermons, and a dedication reads :—

"To Mr. and Mrs. T——, my faithful and consistent Church parishioners, for the baptism of whose grandson this Hymn was composed, I inscribe the same with affectionate regard.—The Country Curate. Whitsun Monday, 1859."

It was included in the S. P. C. K. *Appendix*, 1869; in the *Hymnary*, 1872; Thring's *Coll.*, 1882; and also in several others, but usually somewhat abridged.   [J. J.]

Jesu quadragenariae. [*Lent.*] This hymn has been ascribed to St. Hilary, but is certainly of later date. It is found in the *Sarum, York, Aberdeen*, and a number of German *Breviaries* (e.g. Halberstadt, 1500, and Havelberg, 1518), appointed for Lent at Vespers or Lauds; sometimes from the 1st to the 3rd S., or, as in the *Sarum* use, in the daily office at Lauds from the 3rd S. in Lent to Passion Sunday. The text is also in two MSS. of the 11th cent. in the *British Museum* (Vesp. D. xii. f. 53; Jul. A. vi. f. 46); and in the *Lat. Hys. of the Anglo-Saxon Ch.*, 1851, p. 64, is printed from an 11th cent. MS. at Durham. (B. iii. 32 f. 19.) It is also found in two MSS. of the 11th cent. at St. Gall (Nos. 413, 414); in *Daniel*, i., No. 6, the *Hymnarium Sarisburiense*, 1851, p. 77, and Card. Newman's *Hymni Ecclesiae*, 1838 and 1865.   [J. M.]

Translations in C. U. :—

1. Jesu, the Law and Pattern, whence. By J. M. Neale. Pub. in the *H. Noted*, 1852, No. 21, in 6 st. of 4 l. It has passed into several collections, including the *Hymner*, 1882.

2. Jesu, Who this our Lenten tide. By J. D. Chambers. Appeared in his *Lauda Syon*, 1857, p. 138, in 6 st. of 4 l., and repeated in the *People's H.*, 1867.
3. Jesu, our Lenten fast of Thee. By J. W. Hewett. Pub. in his *Verses by a Country Curate*, 1859, p. 39, in 6 st. of 4 l. In *H. A. & M.*, 1861 and 1875, it was given with alterations by the compilers.
4. In watch and prayer by Thee. By F. Pott. Made for and 1st pub. in his *Hys. fitted to the Order of Com. Prayer*, 1861, in 6 st. of 4 l. In 1871 it was revised by the Translator for the S. P. C. K. *Church Hys.*, and given therein as "In hunger, watch, and prayer."
5. Jesu, in fast for sinful man. This rendering in the *Hymnary*, 1872, is Dr. Neale's *tr.* as above, slightly altered by the Editors of the *Hymnary*.

Translation not in C. U. :—
Jesu, Whose holy life displays. *W. J. Blew*, 1852–5.
                                         [J. J.]

Jesu, Redeemer of mankind. *C. Wesley.* [*Lent. Holiness desired.*] Appeared in *Hys. and Sac. Poems*, 1742, p. 246, in 14 st. of 4 l., and based upon Titus ii. 14, "He gave Himself for us that He might redeem us from all iniquity" (*P. Works*, 1868–72, vol. ii. p. 303). Six stanzas, beginning with st. ix., were given in the *Wes. H. Bk.*, 1780, No. 394, as "What is our calling's glorious hope." This text has been repeated in several collections.   [J. J.]

Jesu Redemptor omnium, Perpes corona praesulum. [*Comm. of Confessors.*] This hymn is found in four hymnaries of the 11th cent. in the *British Museum*, viz. : three of the English Church (Vesp. D. xii. f. 109; Jul. A. vi. f. 67; Harl. 2961, f. 249b), and one of the Spanish Church (Add. 30,851, f. 154b). In the *Latin Hys. of the Anglo-Saxon Ch.*, 1851, p. 137, it is printed from an 11th cent. MS. at Durham. (B. iii. 32, f. 40 b.) It is also found in the *Roman* (Venice, 1478), *Sarum, York, Aberdeen*, and other *Breviaries*. In the *Sarum* use it was the hymn at Lauds and Second Vespers on the festival of a Confessor and Bishop. *Daniel*, i., No. 237, gives the text, and at iv. p. 369, cites it as in a 9th cent. MS. at Bern. The *Roman Brev.* text is in Card. Newman's *Hymni Ecclesiae*, 1838 and 1865. *Tr.* as :—

1. Redeemer blest of all who live. By E. Caswall. 1st pub. in his *Lyra Catholica*, 1849, p. 217, in 5 st. of 4 l.; and again in his *Hys. & Poems*, 1873, p. 115. It is repeated in some Roman Catholic collections for missions and schools, and also in other hymn-books.
2. Jesu, the world's Redeemer, hear. By J. D. Chambers. Pub. in the enlarged ed. of the *H. Noted*, 1854; and repeated in the *Hymnary*, 1872, &c.
3. O Thou, Whose all redeeming might. By R. M. Benson. Contributed to *H. A. & M.*, 1861, and repeated in the revised ed., 1875.
4. Jesu, Redeemer, the renown. By J. D. Chambers. This second rendering by Mr. Chambers appeared in his *Lauda Syon*, Pt. ii., 1866, and was repeated in the *People's H.*, 1867.

Translations not in C. U. :—
1. Jesu, Redeemer Thou of all. *W. J. Blew*, 1852–5.
2. Jesus, Redeemer of mankind. *J. Wallace*, 1874.

In the *York Breviary* of 1493, st. iii., iv., slightly altered and beginning **Haec rite mundi gaudia**, are given as the hymn for 1st Vespers and for Matins in the office of the Common of one Matron, usually called the *Common of ·Holy Women.* This form is found in the reprint of that Breviary by the Surtees Society, ii. 77 (1883). The *tr.* from this text is :—

The world and all its boasted good. This appeared in the enlarged edition of the *H. Noted,* 1854, in 3 st. of 4 l. It is usually ascribed to Dr. Neale, but in error.   [J. M.]

Jesu, Redemptor saeculi, Qui tertio post funera. *C. Coffin.* [*Easter.*] This hymn, as given in the *Paris Breviary,* 1736, for Compline during the Octave of Easter and up to the Ascension, began :—

" Jesu, Redemptor saeculi,
  Qui tertio post funera
  Redux ab inferis die,
  Mortem resurgendo necas."

The hymn was repeated in Coffin's *Hymni Sacri,* &c., 1736 ; in Card. Newman's *Hymni Ecclesiae,* 1838 and 1865, and in J. Chandler's *Hys. of the Primitive Church,* 1837. Although several *trs.* of this hymn have been made, none are in C. U. They are :—

1. O Thou Who wast for sinners slain. *J. Chandler.* 1837.
2. Thou, Who to save the world, &c. *I. Williams,* in the *British Mag.,* April, 1837 ; and again in his *Hys. tr. from the Parisian Brev.,* 1839.
3. Jesu, for all Thy blood was shed. *R. Campbell,* 1850.
4. Jesu, Redeemer, Thee we praise. *J. D. Chambers,* 1857.
5. Jesu, the earth's Redeemer Thou. Another rendering slightly different from the former, by R. Campbell, circ. 1850, printed from his MSS. in Mr. Shipley's *Annus Sanctus,* 1884.
6. Jesus, Who didst redeem mankind. *J. C. Earle* in *Annus Sanctus,* 1884.   [J. J.]

Jesu Redemptor saeculi, Verbum Patris altissimi. [*Easter.*] This is found in two MSS. of the 11th cent. in the *British Museum,* viz. in a hymnarium (Harl. 2961, f. 220*b*), and in a *Mozarabic Breviary* (Add. 30848, f. 66*b*). In the later Breviaries, as the *Sarum, York, Paris* (1643), &c., it begins, " Jesu Salvator saeculi." The text of the *Harleian MS.* (in 4 st. and a doxology) is printed in the *Lat. Hys. of the Anglo-Saxon Ch.,* 1851, p. 165. *Daniel,* i., No. 218, only gives st. i.; and *Mone,* No. 291, st. i.-iii., and a doxology differing from the *Harleian.* In the *Sarum* use (see the *Hymnarium Sarisb.,* 1851, p. 92) it is the hymn at Compline from the Saturday in Easter week to the Festival of the Ascension. It is also directed that st. v., vi. are to be said at the end of every hymn of the same metre, only excepting " Chorus novae Hierusalem," till the Ascension, p. 11, ii. In order the more accurately to distinguish this hymn from that by C. Coffin as above, we give the first stanza in full :—

" Jesu Redemptor saeculi,
  Verbum Patris altissimi,
  Lux lucis invisibilis,
  Custos tuorum pervigil."   [J. M.]

Translations in C. U. :—
1. **Jesu, the world's redeeming Lord, Of Sire most high,** &c. By W. J. Copeland, in his *Hys. for the Week,* 1848, p. 161.
2. **Jesu, Who broughtest redemption nigh.** By J. M. Neale, in the *Hymnal Noted,* 1852, No. 30.
3. **Jesu, the world's redeeming Lord, The Father's**

co-eternal Word. This appeared in the trial ed. of *H. A. & M.,* 1859, and the eds. of 1861 and 1875. It is an altered form of W. J. Copeland's *tr.* as above. In *Kennedy,* 1863, the *H. A. & M.* text is slightly changed to " O Thou, the world's redeeming Lord."

4. **Jesu, Redeemer of the earth.** By R. F. Littledale in the *People's H₄,* 1867, signed " F."
5. **Jesu, the world's redeeming Lord, Eternal Son, co-equal Word.** This *tr.* in the *Hymnary,* 1872, is Dr. Neale's *tr.* as above, altered, together with a little from *Copeland.*

Translations not in C. U. :—
1. Saviour Christ, Who all below. *Hymnarium Anglicanum.* 1844.
2. Jesu! to earth the Saviour given. *J. D. Chambers.* 1857.   [J. J.]

Jesu, sacerdotum decus. *Guillaume de la Brunetière.* [*Common of Bishops.*] Appeared in the *Cluniac Breviary,* 1686, xl., " Commune Doctorum," and again in the *Paris Breviary,* 1736, " Commune Pontificum," at Lauds. The text is also in J. Chandler's *Hys. of the Primitive Church,* 1837, No. 98, and Card. Newman's *Hymni Ecclesiae,* 1838 and 1865. *Tr.* as :—

Jesu, Thy priest's eternal prize. By E. Caswall, in his *Masque of Mary,* &c., 1858, and his *Hys. and Poems,* 1873. It is given in the 1862 *Appendix* to the *H. Noted,* and also in several Roman Catholic hymn-books for missions and schools.

Translations not in C. U. :—
1. Jesu, Who didst Thy pastor crown. I. Williams, in the *British Magazine,* Nov. 1837, and his *Hys. tr. from the Parisian Brev.,* 1839, p. 295.
2. O Christ, Who art our pastor's Lord. *J. Chandler,* 1837.
3. O Jesu, Honour of Thy priests. *J. D. Chambers,* 1866.   [J. J.]

Jesu, Saviour, Son of God, Bearer of the sinner's load. *H. Bonar.* [*Behold the Man.*] Appeared in his *Hys. of Faith and Hope,* 2nd series, 1861, in 36 lines, and headed, " Ecce Homo ! " In Dale's *English H. Bk.,* 1874, it is abridged to 6 st. of 4 l. It is a most suitable hymn for Passiontide. [J. J.]

Jesu, shall I never be ? *C. Wesley.* [*The Mind of Christ desired.*] Pub. in *Hys. & Sac. Poems,* 1742, p. 221, in 20 st. of 4 l., and headed, " Let this Mind be in you, which was also in Christ Jesus " (*P. Works,* 1868-72, vol. ii. p. 276). A hymn therefrom of 13 st., beginning with the first, was given in the *Wes. H. Bk.,* 1780, No. 345, and has been repeated in several other collections. There are also three additional centos in C. U.: (1) " Jesus, plant and root in me " ; (2) " Jesus, root and fix in me " ; and (3) " God of Jesus, hear me now." The last appeared in Martineau's *Hymns,* 1840.   [J. J.]

Jesu, Shepherd of the sheep, Thou Thy flock, &c. *W. Hammond.* [*The Good Shepherd.*] 1st pub. in his *Ps., Hys. & S. Songs,* 1745, p. 78, in 11 st. of 4 l., and entitled " Christ the Shepherd." In 1783 R. Hill gave 8 st. in his *Ps. & Hys.,* as No. 49, beginning :—

" Jesus, Shepherd of the sheep,
  Gracious is Thine arm to keep."

This was repeated in later collections. In Cotterill's *Ps. & Hys.,* 1810-1819, another arrangement from *Hammond* as :—

" Jesus, Shepherd of the sheep,
  Powerful is Thine arm to keep."

This is usually confounded with R. Hill's arrangement of Hammond's text. It is, however, a distinct cento.   [J. J.]

Jesu, soft harmonious Name. *C. Wesley.* [*Prayer for Unity.*] Given in *Hys. & Sac. Poems*, 1749, vol. ii. p. 243, in 4 st. of 8 l. (*P. Works*, 1868–72, vol. v. p. 475). It was included in the *Wes. H. Bk.*, 1780, No. 524, and has been repeated in several collections, and sometimes as "Jesus, *blest* harmonious Name," as in the *Leeds H. Bk.*, 1853. In Martineau's *Hymns*, 1840 and 1873, st. ii. is given as "Lord, subdue our selfish will." This forms a poetic gem of two stanzas.   [J. J.]

Jesu, the word of mercy give. *C. Wesley.* [*Ember Days. For Ministers.*] Compiled from his *Short Hys. on Select Passages of H. Scriptures*, 1762, as follows :—

St. i., ii., *Short Hys.*, vol. i., No. 638, on 2 Chron. vi. 41.
St. iii.–vi., *Short Hys*, vol. i., No. 397, on Judges v. 31.

In this form it was given in the *Wes. H. Bk.*, 1780, No. 434, and has passed into several later collections (Orig. text, *P. Works*, 1868–72, vol. ix.).   [J. J.]

Jesu, Thou art my Righteousness. *C. Wesley.* [*Christ our Righteousness.*] 1st pub. in *Hys. and Sac. Poems*, 1740, p. 96, in 6 st. of 4 l., and entitled "Christ our Righteousness." It was repeated in J. Wesley's *Select Hys. with Tunes*, 1761. The form, however, by which it is best known is that given to it by J. Wesley in the *Wes. H. Bk.* 1780, No. 337, beginning with st. iii., "For ever here my rest shall be." In this form it has become known in all English-speaking countries, and is in extensive use. It has also been translated for use on Mission Stations. The original hymn was included in M. Madan's *Ps. & Hys.*, 1760; A. M. Toplady's *Ps. & Hys.*, 1776, and others, and was thus brought into use in the Church of England. It is sometimes dated 1745 in error. Another arrangement is that of st. iv., v. in the Reformed Dutch *Hymns of the Church*, N. Y. 1869, as: "My dying Saviour and my God." Pleasing reminiscences of the *Wes. H. Bk.* form of the hymn and of its spiritual benefits to many persons are given in G. J. Stevenson's *Meth. H. Bk. Notes*, 1883, p. 249. Orig. text in *P. Works*, 1868–72, vol. i. p. 283.   [J. J.]

Jesu, to Thy table led. *R. H. Baynes.* [*Holy Communion.*] Pub. in his *Canterbury Hymnal*, 1864, No. 227, in 7 st. of 3 l., and headed with the text, "To know the love of Christ, which passeth knowledge." It has passed into numerous hymnals, both in G. Britain and America. It is the most widely used of Canon Baynes's hymns.   [J. J.]

Jesus, and didst Thou condescend? [*The Miracles of Christ.*] This hymn appeared in the Bristol Bapt. *Coll.* of Ash & Evans, 1769, No. 224, in 5 st. of 4 l., headed, "Imploring Mercy," and signed, "Am—a." In *The Union Collection of Hymns and Sacred Odes*, &c., by J. Curtis, of Bristol, 1827, No. 56, it was repeated in 4 st., and signed as in *Ash & Evans*. In this form it has passed into several collections, including the *New Cong.*, 1859; *Laudes Domini*, N. Y., 1884; and as "And didst Thou, Jesus, condescend?" in the American *Bapt. Hymn* [*and Tune*] *Bk.*, 1871.

As to the authorship, D. Sedgwick has given in his MSS., "Amelia Curtis, 1827," and on a fly-leaf of a copy of the 1827 ed. of *Ash and Evans*, "Amelia Wakeford." The *New Cong.* gives "Bradley," and *Laudes Domini* "Mrs. Amelia Wakeford." Possibly this last may be right, but we have no positive evidence either way (Sedgwick's contradiction of himself renders his evidence valueless), and must leave it as in *Ash & Evans*, "Am—a." [J. J.]

Jesus, and shall it ever be. *J. Grigg.* [*Glorying in Jesus.*] The somewhat complicated history of this hymn begins with its publication by J. Grigg in his *Four Hymns on Divine Subjects wherein the Patience and Love of Our Divine Saviour is displayed*, 1765, as follows :—

"Jesus! and shall it ever be!
A mortal man ashamed of Thee?
Scorn'd be the thought by rich and poor;
O may I scorn it more and more!

"Ashamed of Jesus! sooner far
Let evening blush to own a star.
Ashamed of Jesus! just as soon
Let midnight blush to think of noon.

"'Tis evening with my soul till He,
That Morning Star, bids darkness flee;
He sheds the beam of noon divine
O'er all this midnight soul of mine.

"Ashamed of Jesus! shall yon field
Blush when it thinks who bids it yield?
Yet blush I must, while I adore,
I blush to think I yield no more.

"Ashamed of Jesus! of that Friend
On Whom for heaven my hopes depend!
It must not be! be this my shame,
That I no more revere His name.

"Ashamed of Jesus! yes, I may,
When I've no crimes to wash away;
No tear to wipe, no joy to crave,
No fears to quell, no soul to save.

"Till then (nor is the boasting vain),
Till then I boast a Saviour slain :
And oh, may this my portion be,
That Saviour not ashamed of me!"

These crude verses were given in an unaltered form in a few of the older hymn-books. It was soon found, however, that they called for revision with the results following :—

1. In the April number of the *Gospel Magazine*, 1774, it was given with alterations and the omission of st. iii. and iv., with the heading, "Shame of Jesus conquer'd by Love. By a Youth of Ten Years." It was without signature, and began, "Jesus! and can it ever be." We believe that this was the *first* instance in which it was set forth that it was written at ten years of age; and we have failed to find any evidence other than this for the statement. In the *Meth. Free Church H. Bk.* 1860, it is altered to "Lord Jesus! can it ever be."

2. The second version of the text was given in Rippon's *Bap. Sel.*, 1787, No. 451, where it is stated to have been "Altered by B. Francis." The alterations are somewhat extensive, st. iv. is omitted, and a new stanza is added ("His institutions would I prize," &c.). This text may be distinguished by st. i. :—

"Jesus! and shall it ever be
A mortal man asham'd of Thee!
Asham'd of Thee, Whom angels praise,
Whose glories shine through endless days."

3. The *third* version which we have traced is in J. Kempthorne's *Select Portions of Ps. . . . and Hys.*, &c., 1810, p. 175, in 4 st., and beginning, "Asham'd of Jesus! Can it be?" This was taken from the *Gospel Magazine*, as above, with the omission of its st. ii., and slight alterations. It was repeated in Elliott's *Ps. & Hys.*, 1835, and later collections, sometimes with *can* changed to *shall.*

4. The *fourth* version begins :—

"Jesus! Redeemer! can it be
That sinners are ashamed of Thee?"

This was given in 4 st. in Cotterill's *Sel.*, 8th ed., 1819, No. 81. This text was altered from that in the *Gospel Magazine*, and was a failure.

5. The fifth version is a recast by Bp. W. W. How, and was printed in the S. P. C. K. *Hys. for Occasional Services,* No. 5, 1882, in 5 st. of 4 l. It is also in the S. P. C. K. sheet of *Hys. for Mission Services.* It begins :—

    " Ashamed of Thee ! O dearest Lord,
       I marvel how such wrong can be ;
    And yet how oft in deed and word
       Have I been found ashamed of Thee ! "

It is a good mission hymn, but it has little in common with that by Grigg.

Other and somewhat minute changes have been introduced into the text by various hymn-book compilers, but these are the most important, and practically cover the whole ground. [J. J.]

Jesus, arise with saving might. [*Missions.*] This hymn appeared in Kemble's *Ps. & Hys.*, 1853, No. 479, in 3 st. of 4 l., as a "Prayer for the Heathen," and ascribed to "Birks." It was repeated in later editions of the *Ps. & Hys.*, and in Kemble's *New Church H. Bk.*, 1873, with the same signature. It is not in Professor Birks's *Companion Psalter,* 1874, and was not received by him as his composition. If his, the fact had faded from his memory (E. MSS.). [J. J.]

Jesus, at Thy command. [*Life a Voyage—Christ the Pilot.*] This hymn is in an undated edition of Lady Huntingdon's *Coll. of Hymns,* pub. at Bath about 1774. It is No. 136, in 7 st. of 6 l. It is also given in Coughlan's 1775 *Appendix* to J. Bazlee's [q. v.] *Select Collection of Ps. & Hys.*, No. 311, where it is entitled, " The Believer's Pilot." In 1776 it reappeared in A. M. Toplady's *Ps. & Hys.*, No. 312, in De Courcy's *Coll.*, 2nd ed., 1782, and again in later hymn-books. In modern collections it is sometimes attributed to Toplady, and again to De Courcy (q. v.), but in error. It is associated with the Lady Huntingdon Connexion from the first, and is possibly by one of that denomination. A part of this hymn is given in the American *Church Pastorals,* Boston, 1864, as, " By faith, I see the land." It begins with st. v., and is taken from Toplady's *Ps. & Hys,* as above. [J. J.]

Jesus, behold the wise from far. [*Hymn to Christ.*] This hymn in its original form appeared in J. Austin's *Devotions in the Antient Way of Offices,* &c., 1668 ; again in Theophilus Dorrington's ed. of the same, 1686 ; and Lady Susanna Hopton's ed., 1687. The form by which it is known to modern hymn-books was given to it by J. Wesley, and appeared in his *Coll. of Ps. & Hys.* pub. at Charles-Town, 1736–7, No. 17, as a " Hymn to Christ," in 6 st. of 6 l. (*P. Works,* 1868–72, vol. i. p. 116). This form of the hymn is in C. U. in G. Britain and America, and sometimes in an abbreviated form. Its designation is " *J. Austin,* 1668 ; *J. Wesley,* 1736." [J. J.]

Jesus, bestow the power. *C. Wesley.* [*In Temptation.*] Pub. in *Hys. & Sac. Poems,* 1749, vol. ii., in 6 st. of 8 l., as No. 7 of " Hymns for the Watchnight " (*P. Works,* 1868–72, vol. v. p. 269). When included in the *Wes. H. Bk.,* 1780, No. 302 (ed. 1875, No. 311), st. i. was omitted, and some slight changes in the text were made. This text, which begins, " Bid me of men beware," is that in C. U. in G. Britain and America. In the American *Church Pastorals,* 1864, it reads, " Lord, let me calmly wait." [J. J.]

Jesus calls us ; [mid] o'er the tu-mult. *Cecil F. Alexander, née Humphreys.* [*St. Andrew.*] Contributed to the S. P. C. K. *Hymns,* &c., 1852, No. 116, in 5 st. of 4 l. Its use has become very extensive in most English-speaking countries. Usually the original text is followed, but here and there slight variations are introduced, as, for instance, in *H. A. & M.,* where st. iv. l. 4, reads, " That we love Him more than these," for " Christian, love Me more than these." In 1871 a mutilated text was given in the S. P. C. K. *Church Hymns.* This led to a revision of the original by Mrs. Alexander, which was given in the folio ed., 1881, and later editions of *Church Hys.,* as Mrs. Alexander's authorised text. It is easily recognised by the refrain of st. i.–iii., " Softly, clearly—' Follow Me.' " This text differs very materially from the original, and in comparison with it, will commend itself to very few. In the *Anglican H. Bk.,* 1868, the opening line reads, " Jesus call us, *mid* the tumult." Other alterations are also introduced very much to the injury of the hymn. [J. J.]

Jesus came ; the heavens adoring. *G. Thring.* [*Second Advent.*] Pub. in Chope's *Hymnal,* 1864, No. 155, in 5 st. of 6 l., and in the author's *Hys. Congregational and Others,* 1866, p. 9 ; his *Hys. and Sac. Lyrics,* 1874, p. 28 ; and his *Coll.,* 1882. It has passed into numerous hymn-books in Great Britain and America, and is one of the most widely used of Prebendary Thring's compositions. In the American *Bapt. Praise Bk.,* 1871, it is given in an abridged form, beginning with st. iii., " Jesus comes to souls rejoicing." The text is slightly modified throughout. [J. J.]

Jesus Christ from highest heaven. *S. Baring-Gould.* [*Second Advent.*] Written in 1865, and first printed in the *Church Times* of that year. In 1867 it was included in the *People's H.,* in 8 st. of 4 l., and classed with the General hymns. It has since passed into several collections. [J. J.]

Jesus Christ is risen to-day. *Easter.* This version of the anonymous Latin hymn, " Surrexit Christus hodie," is first found in a scarce collection entitled :—

Lyra Davidica, or a Collection of Divine Songs and Hymns, partly new composed, partly translated from the High German and Latin Hymns ; and set to easy and pleasant tunes. London : J. Walsh, 1708.

Of the history of this collection nothing is known, but the character of its contents may perhaps lead to the supposition that it was compiled by some Anglo-German of the pietist school of thought. The text in *Lyra Davidica,* 1708, p. 11, is as follows :—

    " Jesus Christ is risen to day, Halle-Halle-lujah.
      Our triumphant Holyday
      Who so lately on the Cross
      Suffer'd to redeem our loss.

    " Hast ye females from your fright
      Take to Galilee your flight
      To his sad disciples say
      Jesus Christ is risen to day.

    " In our Paschal joy and feast
      Let the Lord of life be blest
      Let the Holy Trine be prais'd
      And thankful hearts to heaven be rais'd."

We subjoin the original Latin for the purpose of comparison :—

De Resurrectione Domini.

1. " Surrexit Christus hodie
      Humano pro solamine.
                      Alleluia.
2. " Mortem qui passus corpore
      Miserrimo pro homine.   Al.
3. " Mulieres ad tumulum
      Dona ferunt aromatum.
4. [" Quærentes Jesum dominum,
      Qui est salvator hominum.]
5. " Album videntes angelum
      Annunciantem gaudium:
6. [" Mulieres o tremulæ,
      In Galilaeam pergite!]
7. " Discipulis hoc dicite,
      Quod surrexit rex gloriæ.
8. " [Petro dehinc et ceteris
      Apparuit apostolis.]
9. " Paschali pleno gaudio
      Benedicamus Domino.
10. [" Gloria tibi domine,
      Qui surrexisti a morte.]
11. [" Laudetur sancta Trinitas,
      Deo dicamus gratias."]

The oldest Latin text known is that given by *Mone*, No. 143, from a Munich MS. of the 14th cent. This MS. does not contain st. 4, 6, 8, 10, 11 (enclosed in brackets above). Of these st. 6, 11 are found in a Breslau MS., cir 1478; and st. 4, 8, 10 in the *Speier G. B.* (Roman Catholic), 1600. The Breslau MS. has the following readings:—ii, l. 1, *pridie* (not *corpore*); v. l. 1, *cernentes*; ix. l. 1, *In hoc paschali gaudio.* [See note on **Surrexit Christus hodie.**]

The modern form of the hymn appears first in Arnold's *Compleat Psalmodist,* 2nd ed., pt. iv., 1749, where the first stanza of 1708 is alone retained, and stanzas 2 and 3 are replaced by new ones written without any reference to the original Latin. This recast is as follows:—

" Jesus Christ is ris'n to-day. Hallelujah.
  Our triumphal holyday
  Who did once upon the Cross
  Suffer to redeem our Loss.

" *Hymns of praises let us sing*
  Unto Christ our heavenly King
  Who endur'd the Cross and Grave
  Sinners to redeem and save.

" *But the pain that he endured*
  Our Salvation has procured
  Now above the Sky he's King
  Where the Angels ever sing."

Variations of this form are found in several collections. The following is in Kempthorne's *Select Portions of Psalms,* &c., 1810:—

" HYMN LXXXII.

" Benefits of Christ's Resurrection to sinners.
          " Rom. iv. 25.
        " *For Easter Day.*

" Jesus Christ is ris'n to day;
  Now he gains triumphant sway;
  Who so lately on the cross
  Suffer'd to redeem our loss.
                      Hallelujah.

" Hymns of praises let us sing,
  Hymns to Christ our heav'nly King,
  Who endur'd both cross and grave,
  Sinners to redeem and save.
                      Hallelujah.

" But the pains, which he endur'd,
  Our salvation have procur'd;
  Now He reigns above the sky,
  Where the angels ever cry
                      Hallelujah."

The next form is that which was given to it in the *Supplement* to Tate & Brady. This was added to the *Supplement* about 1816. [See **New Version,** § ii.] This text is:—

" Jesus Christ is risen to-day,
  Our triumphant holy day;
  Who did once, upon the cross,
  Suffer to redeem our loss.
                      Hallelujah.

" Hymns of praise then let us sing
  Unto Christ our heavenly King:
  Who endur'd the cross and grave,
  Sinners to redeem and save.
                      Hallelujah.

" But the pains which He endur'd
  Our salvation hath procur'd:
  Now above the sky He's King,
  Where the angels ever sing.
                      Hallelujah."

To this has been added by an unknown hand the following doxology:—

" Now be God the Father prais'd,
  With the Son from death uprais'd,
  And the Spirit, ever blest;
  One true God, by all confest.
                      Hallelujah."

This doxology, from *Schaff's Christ in Song,* 1870, p. 198, is in the *H. Comp.* and one or two other collections.

Another doxology is sometimes given, as in Lord Selborne's *Book of Praise,* 1862, Thring's *Coll.,* 1882, and others, as follows:—

" Sing we to our God above—Hallelujah!
  Praise eternal as His love; Hallelujah!
  Praise Him all ye heavenly host, Hallelujah!
  Father, Son, and Holy Ghost. Hallelujah!"

This is by C. Wesley. It appeared in the Wesley *Hys. & Sac. Poems,* 1740, p. 100; again in *Gloria Patri, &c., or Hymns to the Trinity,* 1746, and again in the *P. Works,* 1868–72, vol. iii. p. 345.

The above text from Tate and Brady's *Suppl.,* cir. 1816, is that adopted by the leading hymn-books in all English-speaking countries, with in some cases the anonymous doxology, and in others with that by C. Wesley. It must be noted that this hymn sometimes begins:—

" Christ the Lord, is risen to day
  Our triumphant holy day."

This must be distinguished from:—

" Christ the Lord, is risen to-day,
  Sons of men and angels say,"

by C. Wesley (p. **226,** i.); and,

" Christ the Lord, is risen to-day,
  Christians, haste your vows to pay:"

a *tr.* of " Victimae Paschali " (q. v.), by Miss Leeson; and,

" Christ the Lord, is risen to-day,
  He is risen indeed:"

by Mrs. Van Alstyne (q. v.).

Another arrangement of " Jesus Christ is risen to-day " is given in T. Darling's *Hymns,* &c., 1887. This text is st. i., ii., *Tate & Brady Suppl.,* with a return in st. i. l. 3, to the older reading; and st. iii., iv. by Mr. Darling.

It may not be out of place to add, with reference to this hymn, that the tune to which it is set in *Arnold,* and to which it is still sung, is that published with it in *Lyra Davidica.* The tune is also anonymous, and was probably composed for the hymn. The ascription of it by some to *Henry Carey* is destitute of any foundation whatever, while *Dr. Worgan,* to whom it has been assigned by others, was not born until after the publication of *Lyra Davidica.*   [G. A. C.]

Jesus Christ, my Lord and Saviour. *Jane Taylor.* [*Christ, the Children's Example.*] Pub. in *Hys. for Infant Minds,* by Anne and

Jane Taylor, 1810, in 6 st. of 4 l., and headed, "The Example of Christ" (ed. 1886, p. 99). It has attained to great popularity, and is in extensive use in G. Britain and America. In some American hymnals, including Beecher's *Plymouth Coll.*, 1855, ll. 3, 4 of st. ii.—

> "But the Lord was meek and lowly,
> Pure and spotless, free from sin,"

is added as a refrain to each stanza, with line 4 as "And was never known to sin." This reading of this line is repeated in some English collections, including Mrs. Brock's *Children's H. Bk.*, 1881.   [J. J.]

Jesus Christus, nostra salus. *J. Hus?*

[*Holy Communion.*] This hymn has been ascribed to Hus, and is included in the *Monumentorum Joannis Hus altera pars*, Nürnberg, 1558, but his authorship is at least doubtful. *Wackernagel*, vol. i., gives three forms, No. 367, in 10 st. from a Munich ms. of the 15th cent.; No. 368 from the 1558, as above, in 9 st.; No. 369 from Leisentritt's *G. B.* (R. C.), 1584, in 7 st. The last text is also in *Daniel*, ii. 370. In his *Cantiones Bohemicae*, Leipzig, 1886, preface, pp. 22, 31, 43, &c., G. M. Dreves discusses the authorship, and cites it as in 10 st., in a ms. cir. 1410, belonging to the Abbey of Hohenfurth; in a *Gradual*, cir. 1420, in the Bohemian Museum at Prag, &c. The text of Leisentritt's *G. B.*, 1584, is *tr.* as :—

Jesus Christ our true salvation. By R. F. Littledale, in the 2nd ed. of *Lyra Eucharistica*, 1864, p. 354, and the *People's H.*, 1867.

This hymn has also passed into English through the German, viz. :—

Jesus 'Christus unser Heiland, Der von uns den Gottes Zorn wandt. This is by M. Luther, and 1st appeared in *Eyn Enchiridion*, Erfurt, 1524, in 10 st. of 4 l., entitled "The Hymn of St. John Hus improved." Thence in *Wackernagel*, iii. p. 9. Also in Schircks's ed. of Luther's *Geistl. Lieder*, 1854, p. 70; in the *Unv. L. S.*, 1851, No. 279, &c. Only st. i. is at all directly taken from the Latin, so that if Luther "improved" the hymn he did so by superseding it. *Tr.* as :—

Lord Jesus Christ! to Thee we pray, From us. In full, by W. M. Reynolds, in the *Evang. Review*, Gettysburg, Oct., 1849, repeated as No. 264 in the Ohio *Luth. Hyl.*, 1880.

Other trs. are, (1) "Our Saviour Christ, King of grace," in the *Gude and Godlie Ballates*, ed. 1568, f. 9 (1868, p. 15. (2) "Our Saviour Christ by His own death," as No. 276 in Pt. i. of the *Moravian H. Bk.*, 1754. (3) "To avert from men God's wrath," by C. I. Latrobe, as No. 557 in the *Moravian H. Bk.*, 1789 (1849, No. 959). In the ed. of 1886, No. 973, it begins, "That we never should forget" (st. ii.); (4) "Jesus Christ, our Saviour, Who," by *J. Anderson*, 1846, p. 72. In his ed. 1847, p. 85, altered to "Christ our Lord and Saviour"; (5) "Jesus the Christ—the Lamb of God," by *Dr. J. Hunt*, 1853, p. 106. (6) "Christ who freed our souls from danger," by *R. Massie*, 1854, p. 75, and in *Dr. Bacon*, 1884, p. 30. (7) "Christ Jesus, our Redeemer born," by *Dr. G. Macdonald* in the *Sunday Magazine*, 1867, p. 840, and his *Exotics*, 1876, p. 103.   [J. M.]

Jesus Christus, unser Heiland, Der den Tod überwand. *M. Luther.* [*Easter.*]

1st pub. in *Eyn Enchiridion*, Erfurt, 1524, in 3 st. of 4 l., each stanza ending with "Kyrieleyson." Thence in *Wackernagel*, iii. p. 11. Also in Schircks's ed. of Luther's *Geistl. Lieder*, 1854, p. 24, the *Unv. L. S.*, 1851, No. 139, &c. *Tr.* as :—

1. *Christ, our Lord, who died to save.* By J. Anderson, in his *H. from the German of M. Luther*,

1846, p. 13 (1847, p. 38), repeated, unaltered, in the *Leeds H. Bk.*, 1853, No. 315.

2. *Jesus Christ, our great Redeemer.* By A. T. Russell, as No. 105 in his *Ps. & Hys.*, 1851.

3. *Jesus Christ to-day is risen.* By R. Massie, in his *M. Luther's Spir. Songs*, 1854, p. 15, repeated in Reid's *Praise Bk.*, 1872, the Ohio *Luth. Hyl.*, 1880, &c.

Other trs. are, (1) "See! triumphant over death," by *Miss Fry*, 1845, p. 71. (2) "Christ the Lord to-day is risen," by *Dr. J. Hunt*, 1853, p. 43. (3) "Jesus Christ, our Saviour true," by *Dr. G. Macdonald* in the *Sunday Magazine*, 1867, p. 332, repeated, altered, in his *Exotics*, 1876, p. 54. (4) "Christ the Saviour, our Prince all-hailed," by *N. L. Frothingham*, 1870. (5) "Jesus Christ, who came to save," in *Dr. Bacon*, 1884.   [J. M.]

Jesus, exalted far on high. *T. Cotterill.*

[*Circumcision. The Holy Name, Jesus.*] Pub. in the *Uttoxeter Sel.*, 1805, and again in Cotterill's *Sel. of Ps. & Hys.*, 1st ed., 1810, in 5 st. of 4 l. It has attained to extensive use, and is usually given in an unaltered form, as in the Oxford ed. of Mercer's *Ch. Psalter & H. Bk.* In *Kennedy*, 1863, No. 605, "O Thou Who in the form of God," is an altered form of a part of this hymn, and begins with st. iii. [See Staffordshire Hymn-Books.] [J. J.]

Jesus, full of all compassion. *D. Turner.*

[*Lent.*] Appeared in the Bristol Bap. *Coll.* of Ash & Evans, 1769, No. 223, in 10 st. of 4 l., headed "The Supplication," and signed "D. T." It was repeated in full in Rippon's *Sel.*, 1787, No. 295; and again in later collections. It is in a large number of modern hymn-books in G. Britain and America, but usually in an abridged form. It is justly regarded as Turner's finest hymn.   [J. J.]

Jesus, gentlest [holy] Saviour, God of might, &c. *F. W. Faber.* [*Holy Communion.*]

This hymn of "Thanksgiving after Communion" was pub. in his *Oratory Hymns*, N.D. [1854], No. 20, in 12 st. of 4 l.; and again in his *Hymns*, 1862, No. 91. It is given in its full form in some Roman Catholic hymn-books for Missions and Schools, and altered and abbreviated in various collections, including (1) the S. P. C. K. *Church Hymns*, 1871, as "Jesu, Lord and Saviour"; (2) J. G. Gregory's *Bonchurch H. Bk.*, 1868, as "Jesus, holy Saviour"; (3) Mrs. Brock's *Children's H. Bk.*, 1881, as "Jesu, gentlest Saviour"; and (4) Martineau's *Hymns*, 1873, as "Father, gracious Father." In Nicholson's *Appendix Hyl.*, 1866, the hymn is divided into two parts, Pt. ii. beginning "Jesu, dear Redeemer." In these various forms its use is extensive.   [J. J.]

Jesus, I love Thy charming Name. *P. Doddridge.*

[*Jesus precious to the Believer.*] In the D. MSS. this hymn is No. 56, is entitled "Christ precious to the Believer," and is dated "Oct. 23, 1717." It was given by J. Orton in his ed. of Doddridge's (posthumous) *Hymns*, &c., 1755, No. 335, with the same title, and in 5 st. of 4 l., and was repeated in J. D. Humphreys's edition of the same, 1839, No. 361. At an early date exception was taken to the opening line, "Jesus, I love Thy *charming* Name"; and in modern hymn-books the result is seen in the text being changed to "Jesus, I love Thy *sacred* Name," and to "Jesus, I love Thy *saving* Name."

The former of these two is a successful alteration. [J. J.]

Jesus, I my cross have taken. *H. F. Lyte.* [*Hope.*] This hymn is found in a volume of *Sacred Poetry*, Edinburgh, Oliphant & Sons, 3rd ed., 1824, in 6 st. of 8 l., headed "Lo! we have left all, and followed Thee," and signed "G." In 1825, it appeared in Montgomery's *Christian Psalmist*, No. 94, with the same signature; in W. Carus Wilson's *Family Visitor*, May, 1826, without signature; in *Hys. for Private Devotion*, Lond., Hatchard, 1827, also without signature; and then in Lyte's *Poems Chiefly Religious*, 1833, p. 41, but in a slightly different form, and as given in Lord Selborne's *Bk. of Praise*, 1862, p. 402. In an abbreviated form it has passed into numerous collections in most English speaking countries. It is also altered and broken up as :—

1. "Church of God, by Christ's salvation,"
2. "Jesus, we our Cross have taken."
3. "Know, my soul, thy full salvation."
4. "Saviour, I my cross have taken."
5. "Take, my soul, thy full salvation."   [J. J.]

Jesus, I sing Thy matchless grace. *P. Doddridge.* [*Jesus, the Head of the Church.*] This hymn begins in the D. MS., "Jesus, I own Thy matchless grace." It is entitled "Christ our Head," and is undated. It was given with the first line as above in J. Orton's posthumous ed. of Doddridge's *Hymns*, 1755, No. 290, in 5 st. of 4 l., and the title changed to "Christ the Head of the Church," and again in J. D. Humphreys's ed. of the same, 1839. The 1755 text is that in C. U.   [J. J.]

Jesus, immortal King, arise. *A. C. H. Seymour.* [*Missions.*] This hymn appeared in the author's *Vital Christianity exhibited in a Series of Letters on the most Important Subjects of Religion, addressed to Young Persons*, 1810, in 7 st. of 4 l. In the *Coll. of Ps. & Hys.* by Henry Foster Burder (not George Burder (q.v.) as usually understood, but his son), st. i.–iii., and vii. were given anonymously as "Jesus, immortal King, arise." This was repeated in the *New Cong.*, 1859, as by "Burder." Several American collections copied from the *New Cong.*, and hence the association of Burder's name with the hymn. In Bickersteth's *Christian Psalmody*, 1833 (in 5 st.), and several other hymnbooks it is given without signature. It is sometimes attributed to "*Noel's Coll.*" and again to others. The 5-st. arrangement, as in *Bickersteth*, 1833, is in use in America.   [J. J.]

Jesus, immortal King, go on [display]. *T. Kelly.* [*Missions.*] Appeared in Kelly's *Coll. of Ps. & Hys.* &c., Dublin, 1802, No. 252 (the second hymn with the same number), in 5 st. of 4 l.; and again in his *Hymns*, &c., 1804 (ed. 1853, No. 532). Its use in this form is mainly confined to America. In Alford's *Ps. & Hys*, 1844, No. 41, and his *Year of Praise*, 1867, it was given as "Jesus, immortal King, display."   [J. J.]

Jesus is God, the solid earth. *F. W. Faber.* [*The Godhead of Jesus.*] This is given in his *Hymns*, 1862, p. 33, in 7 st. of 8 l., with the title "Jesus is God." In Nicholson's *Appendix Hyl.*, 1866, it is divided into two hymns,

the second being "Jesus is God; alas to think." Another arrangement is in American C. U., as in Hatfield's *Church H. Bk.*, 1872, and others. This begins with "Jesus is God! The glorious band Of golden angels sing."   [J. J.]

Jesus is our great salvation. *J. Adams.* [*Election.*] Pub. in the *Gospel Magazine*, May, 1776, in 6 st. of 6 l., and signed "J. A." In 1787 it was given in Rippon's *Bap. Sel.*, No. 108, in 5 st., and with the author's name. After J. Adams (q.v.) was expelled from the Baptist denomination, the hymn was continued in *Rippon*, but the author's name was withdrawn. The hymn is found in several modern hymn-books of a marked Calvinistic type, as Snepp's *Songs of G. & G.*, 1872, &c. This and other hymns by Adams were identified by his son, the Rev. S. Adams, sometime Vicar of Thornton, Leicestershire. (S. MSS.)   [J. J.]

Jesus, lead us with Thy power. *W. Williams.* [*In Temptation—Security in Jesus.*] Pub. in his *Gloria in Excelsis; or Hys. of Praise*, &c., 1772, No. 35, in 3 st. of 8 l. In modern hymn-books it is usually given as "Jesus, lead *me by* Thy power." Original text in Lord Selborne's *Bk. of Praise*, 1862.   [J. J.]

Jesus lebt, mit ihm auch ich. *C. F. Gellert.* [*Easter.*] 1st pub. in his *Geistliche Oden und Lieder*, Leipzig, 1757, p. 147, in 6 st. of 6 l., entitled "Easter Hymn." The keynote of this, one of Gellert's finest hymns, is St. John xiv. 19. It is in the metre and has reminiscences of "Jesus, meine Zuversicht" (see Luise Henriette), but has yet a genuine lyric character of its own. It passed into Berlin G. B., 1765, and almost all later German hymn-books, and is No. 304 in the Berlin G. L. S., ed. 1863. Since 1861 hardly a hymn-book of importance has appeared in English-speaking countries without containing some version of it.

Originally written and still generally used for Easter, it is very appropriate for use by the dying, or for the consecration of a grave-yard. It has often recently been sung at funeral services, e.g. at the Lord Mayor's funeral (G. S. Nottage), in St. Paul's, April 18, 1885; at that for Bishop McDougall of Labuan, in Winchester Cathedral, Nov. 19, 1886, &c.

Translations in C. U. :—

1. **Jesus lives, and so shall I.** A full and good *tr.* by Dr. J. D. Lang, in his *Aurora Australis*, Sydney, 1826, p. 57. This is found in full in America in the *Plymouth Coll.*, 1855, and *Cantate Domino*, 1859; and, abridged, in the Dutch Reformed *Hys. of the Church*, 1869, Bapt. *H. Bk.*, 1871, &c.

2. **Jesus lives! no longer now.** A full and very good *tr.* by Miss Cox, in her *Sacred H. from the German*, 1841, p. 35. She revised it for *Lyra Messianica*, 1864, p. 275, and still further for her *H. from the German*, 1864, p. 61. It has come into very general use in English-speaking countries in the following forms:—

(1) In the original metre. From the 1841 it passed, more or less altered and abridged, into the Dalston Hospital *H. Bk.*, 1848; *H. for the Ch. of Christ*, Boston, U. S., 1853; *Plymouth Coll.*, 1855 (in the last it begins "Jesus lives, thy terrors now"), &c. In later books the text of 1864 is generally followed, as in the Scottish Presb. *Hyl.*, 1876; *Cong. Hyl.*, 1887; Canadian Presb. *H. Bk.*, 1880, &c.

(2) In 7.8.7.8.4 metre. This, the most popular form of the hymn, was given in Rorison's *Hys. & Anthems*, 1851, and repeated in Murray's *Hymnal*, 1852. The two last lines of each stanza were omitted, "Alleluia" was added to each stanza, and the text was considerably altered. *Rorison* gives in order st. i., ii., iv.–vi., while the 1852 nearly follows his text, but gives in order st. i., vi., iv., v., ii., and adds a doxology. To follow out the variation of text and order in later books would be bewildering, the most usual form being that given in Murray's *Hymnal*, 1852, repeated (without the doxology) in *H. A. & M.*, 1861. The *H. A. & M.* text (with Dr. Gauntlett's beautiful tune St. Albinus) has passed into very many English, American, and other hymn-books.

The principal forms in the 7.8.7.8.4. metre which do not begin with the original first line are :—

(a) **Jesus lives! Thy terrors now Can no longer, Death, appal us**, in *Church Hys.*, 1871, &c. Otherwise this is the *H. A. & M.* text.

(b) **Jesus lives! thy terrors now Can, O Death, no more appal us**, in Thring's *Coll.*, 1880–82. Here st. i. l. 2, was altered with Miss Cox's consent in order to avoid an apparent denial of the resurrection of Jesus which some musical settings of the opening line might produce. Otherwise (st. iii. being omitted) the text and order of her 1864 version are nearly followed.

(c) **Jesus lives! henceforth is death** (st. ii.) in Alford's *Year of Praise*, 1867.

(d) **Jesus lives! to Him the throne** (st. v.), in Rorison's *Coll.*, ed. 1860.

3. **Jesus lives ; I live with Him.** A good and full *tr.* by Dr. J. Guthrie, in his *Sacred Lyrics*, 1869, p. 121, repeated in the *Ibrox Hyl.*, 1871.

The trs. not in C. U. are, (1) "My Saviour lives! I will rejoice," by *Lady E. Fortescue*, 1843 (1869, p. 18). (2) "Jesus lives! With Him shall I," by *Miss Warner*, 1869 (1877, p. 18). In Sir John Bowring's *Matins and Vespers*, 3rd ed., 1841, p. 231, there is a hymn in 3 st. of 8 l., beginning "Jesus lives, and we in Him," which is based on Gellert. This previously appeared as No. 150 in J. R. Beard's *Coll.*, 1837.   [J. M.]

Jesus, Lord of life and glory, Bend from, &c. *J. J. Cummins.* [*Lent.*] A sweet and musical Litany, which appeared in his *Poetical Meditations and Hymns*, 1839, in 7 st. of 4 l., with the refrain, "By Thy mercy, O deliver us, Good Lord." In 1849, it was reprinted in his *Hymns, Meditations, and Other Poems*, Lon., Royston & Brown, pp. 26–27. It is in C. U. as :—

(1) Orig. text. st. i., iii.–vii., with "our *Hope*," for "our Rock," in *H. A. & M.*, 1868 and 1875.

(2) "Jesu, Lord of life and glory." As in *H. A. & M.*, with change to *Jesu* only in the *Hymnary*, 1872.

(3) "Jesus, Lord, we kneel before Thee." In the *Salisbury H. Bk.*, 1857, No. 74, with the alteration of the first line, the omission of st. v. and the addition of st. vii. The same text was repeated in *Kennedy*, 1863, the *Anglican H. Bk.*, 1868, and in the 1869 *Appendix* to the S. P. C. K. *Ps. & Hys.*

(4) The same first line, but composed of st. i., iii., iv., vi., and vii., in *Chope's Hymnal*, 1864, and *Thring's Coll.*, 1882.

(5) The same text as *Salisbury H. Bk.*, with "*Jesu*" for "Jesus," in *The Parish H. Bk.*, 1863 and 1875, *Sarum*, 1868, &c.

The sub-title of the *Hymns*, &c., of 1849, and by which the book is generally known, is *Lyra Evangelica*. Orig. text therein.   [J. J.]

Jesus, Master, Whose I am. *Frances R. Havergal.* [*Servant of Christ.*] Written for her nephew, J. H. Shaw, in Dec., 1865, printed as a leaflet (Parlane's Series), and then pub. in her *Ministry of Song*, 1869, and the *Life Mosaic*, 1879. In the original MS. it is divided, st. i.–iii. being "Jesus, Master, Whose I am," and st. iv. vi., "Jesus, Master, Whom I serve." The hymn is suitable for Confirmation, or for personal Consecration to Christ.
    [J. J.]

Jesus, my all, to heaven is gone. *J. Cennick.* [*Jesus the Way.*] Appeared in his *Sac. Hys. for the Use of Religious Societies*, 1743, No. 64, in 9 st. of 4 l. In 1760, M. Madan included 8 stanzas in his *Ps. & Hys.*, No. 17. This text in a more or less correct form has been handed down to modern hymn-books, including *Common Praise*, 1879, and others. Orig. text in *Lyra Brit.*, 1867, p. 133.
    [J. J.]

Jesus, my kind and gracious Friend. *R. Burnham.* [*Jesus the Sinners' Friend.*] Appeared in the 4th ed. of his *Hys. Particularly designed for the Congregation meeting in Grafton Street, Soho*, 1796, No. 202, in 6 st. of 4 l., and headed "Praying for the Redeemer's mindfulness." In this form it is almost unknown, but as "Jesus, *Thou art the sinners'* Friend," it is the most popular of Burnham's hymns. Its use in America especially is very extensive. It is sometimes attributed to "Richard Parkinson" in error.
    [J. J.]

Jesus, my Lord, how rich Thy grace. *P. Doddridge.* [*Offertory.*] This hymn is No. 94 in the D. MSS., but is undated. The heading is, "On relieving Christ in the Poor." In 1755 it was pub. in Doddridge's (posthumous) *Hymns*, &c., No. 188, in 5 st. of 4 l. ; and again in J. D. Humphreys's ed. of the same, 1839, No. 209. It is in C. U. in its original form ; but the most popular forms are the following :—

1. **Fount of all good, to own Thy love.** This is Doddridge's text rewritten by E. Osler, for Hall's *Mitre H. Bk.*, 1836, No. 160, in 4 st. of 4 l. It has been included in several collections.

2. **Fountain of good, to own Thy love.** This is *Osler's* text with eight alterations, and the addition of a doxology from *Tate & Brady*. It was given in Stretton's *Church Hys.*, 1850, No. 64 (it is possibly older), Johnston's *English Hymnal*, 1852 and 1861 ; Thring's *Coll.*, 1882, and others. In *Mercer*, Alford's *Year of Praise*, 1867, the *Hy. Comp.*, and many others, the doxology is omitted. In addition there are other arrangements of *Osler's* text, as in *Stretton*, including that in Pott's *Hymns*, &c., 1861, where st. i.–iii., vi. are slightly altered from *Stretton*, and iv., v., vii., are new. This form of the text is repeated, with slight variations, in the S. P. C. K. *Church Hymns*, 1871.

3. **High on a throne of radiant light.** This begins with st. ii. of the original, and is found in a few collections.

4. **Jesus, our Lord, how rich Thy grace.** In the American *Songs for the Sanctuary*, N. Y., 1865.

All these arrangements from Doddridge's text, together with the original, are in C. U. in America and other English-speaking countries. The best arrangement is that in Thring, 1882, from *Stretton*, 1850.   [J. J.]

Jesus, my Lord, I cry to Thee. *C. Wesley.* [*For Sanctification.*] This cento is from his *Short Hys. on Select Passages of H. Scriptures*, 1762, as follows :—

St. i., ii., *Short Hys.*, &c., vol. ii., No. 299, on St. John ix. 25.

St. iii., iv., *Short Hys.*, &c., vol. i., No. 341, on Deut. xxxii. 39.

St. v., vi., *Short Hys.*, &c., vol. i., No. 1004, on Isaiah xxvii. 3.

In this form it appeared in the *Wes. H. Bk.*, 1780, No. 397, and has passed into several collections (Orig. text, *P. Works*, 1868–72, vols. ix. and xiii.).   [J. J.]

Jesus, my Lord, my God, my all! How can I love Thee, &c. *F. W. Faber.* [*Holy Communion.*] Appeared in his *Jesus* *and Mary*, &c., 1849, in 9 st. of 4 l., with the refrain,

> " Sweet Sacrament ! we Thee adore !
> O, make us love Thee more and more ! "

It is headed " Corpus Christi." In C. U. it is broken into parts, as : (1) " Jesus ! my Lord," &c. ; (2) " Ring joyously, ye solemn bells " ; and (3) " Sound, sound His praises higher still." Its use is mainly confined to Roman Catholic hymnals.   [J. J.]

Jesus, my Saviour, and my King.
S. Browne. [Prayer for Unity.] 1st pub. in his *Hys. and Spiritual Songs*, 1720, Bk. i., No. 147, in 4 st. of 8 l., and headed, " Prayer for brotherly love." In its original form it is not in C. U. The following centos are associated therewith :—

1. **O God, our Saviour, and our King.** This is No. 1186 in *Kennedy*, 1863, where st. i., ii. are from this hymn, and st. iii., iv. are from J .Wesley's *tr.* " O Thou to Whose all searching sight " (See " Seelenbräutigam "), st. iii. and iv. altered.

2. **O Lord, my Saviour, and my King.** No. 645 in the Bap. *Ps. & Hys.*, 1858, is from Browne's hymn, but somewhat altered.   [J. J.]

Jesus, my Saviour, bind me fast.
B. Beddome. [Divine Drawings implored.] Pub. in his (posthumous) *Hymns*, &c., 1817, No. 557, in 4 st. of 4 l., and headed " Draw me." In the 27th ed. of Rippon's Bap. *Sel.*, 1827, st. ii.-iv. were given, together with a new opening stanza, as " If Thou hast drawn a thousand times." This is repeated in Spurgeon's *O. O. H. Bk.*, 1866, No. 163, and others ; especially the American hymn-books.
                                        [J. J.]

Jesus, my Shepherd is. *J. Conder.* *[Ps. xxiii.]* Pub. in Collyer's *Coll.*, 1812, No. 897, in 6 st. of 6 l., headed, The Good Shepherd," and signed " C." In Conder's *Star in the East*, &c., 1824, it was pub. in a new form, and began " The Lord my Shepherd is." This was repeated in the *Cong. H. Bk.*, 1836, No. 401, and in Conder's (posthumous) *Hys. of Praise, Prayer*, &c., 1856, p. 8, and is the authorised form of the hymn.
                                        [J. J.]

Jesus, our Lord, who tempted wast.
H. Alford. [Lent.] 1st pub. in his *Ps. & Hys.*, &c., 1844, No. 29, in 7 st. of 4 l., and again in his *Year of Praise*, 1867, No. 73, in 5 st., the second and third stanzas being omitted. The original text is repeated in full, but with slight alterations, in several collections.   [J. J.]

Jesus, our souls' delightful choice.
P. Doddridge. [Spiritual Conflict.] This hymn is No. 1 of the D. MSS., is in 4 st. of 4 l., is headed " On the Struggle between Faith and Unbelief," and is dated " Sep. 7, 1735." J. Orton included it in his ed. of Doddridge's (posthumous) *Hymns*, &c., 1755, No. 197 ; and J. D. Humphreys in his ed. of the same, 1839, No. 220. It is in a few modern collections, including Spurgeon's *O. O. H. Bk.*, 1866.
                                        [J. J.]

Jesus setzt ein vor seinem End.
[Holy Communion.] Kehrein, in his *Katholische Kirchenlieder*, vol. i., 1859, p. 636, quotes this from D. G. Corner's *Gross Catholisch G. B.*, 1631, where it is in 12 st. of 2 l., entitled " A New Hymn for Corpus Christi." Repeated

---

in the Bamberg *G. B.*, 1670, p. 264 ; Münster *G. B.*, 1677, p. 247 ; and other Roman Catholic collections.   *Tr.* as :—

Before to His sad death He went, a *tr.* of st. i.-viii. as No. 203 in the Ohio *Luth. Hyl.* 1880.   [J. M.]

Jesus shall reign where'er the sun.
I. Watts. [Foreign Missions.]. This is one of the most popular hymns by Watts, and was given in his *Psalms of David*, 1719, as Pt. ii. of his version of Ps. lxxii., in 8 st. of 4 l. Although it has attained to a high position in modern hymnals, it is rarely found in the collections published before the present cent. It increased in popularity with the growth and development of Foreign Missions, and is now used most extensively in all English-speaking countries. One of the earliest to adopt it for congregational use was Rowland Hill. It is found in his *Ps. & Hymns*, 1st ed., 1783 ; but abbreviated to 6 st. This was followed by some compilers in the Church of England, including Cotterill in *Ps. & Hys.*, 1810-1820 ; Bickersteth, 1833, and others ; by the Wesleyans in their *Supplement*, 1830 ; the Baptists, and other denominations, until at the present day it is given in almost every English hymnbook of any standing or merit. As an example of the way in which *The Psalms of David* were *imitated in the language of the New Testament*, by Watts, it is unusually good. It is also in his best style. In modern collections it is generally given in an abbreviated form, ranging from 4 st., as in *H. A. & M.*, to 6 st., as in the *Wes. H. Bk.* Changes are also introduced in the text, but most of these date from the beginning of the present century. It has been rendered in full and in part in many languages, including " Omnibus in terris Dominus regnabit Iesus," by the Rev. R. Bingham, in his *Hymno. Christ. Lat.*, 1871, p. 103. In this rendering st. ii., iii., and vii. are omitted. [See **Psalters, Eng.,** § xv.] Mr. G. J. Stevenson gives, in his *Methodist H. Bk. Notes*, 1883, p. 351, an account of the striking and historical use which was made of this hymn when various islands in the South Seas officially renounced heathenism and embraced Christianity :—

" Perhaps one of the most interesting occasions on which this hymn was used was that on which King George, the sable, of the South Sea Islands, but of blessed memory, gave a new constitution to his people, exchanging a Heathen for a Christian form of government. Under the spreading branches of the banyan trees sat some thousand natives from Tonga, Fiji, and Samoa, on Whitsunday, 1862, assembled for divine worship. Foremost amongst them all sat King George himself. Around him were seated old chiefs and warriors who had shared with him the dangers and fortunes of many a battle ; men whose eyes were dim, and whose powerful frames were bowed down with the weight of years. But old and young alike rejoiced together in the joys of that day, their faces most of them radiant with Christian joy, love, and hope. It would be impossible to describe the deep feeling manifested when the solemn service began, by the entire audience singing Dr. Watts's hymn, " Jesus shall reign where'er the sun " . . . Who so much as they could realize the full meaning of the poet's words ? for they had been rescued from the darkness of heathenism and cannibalism, and they were that day met for the first time under a Christian constitution, under a Christian king, and with Christ Himself reigning in the hearts of most of those present. That was indeed Christ's kingdom set up in the earth."   [J. J.]

Jesus, tender Shepherd, hear me.
Mary Duncan, née Lundie. [Child's Evening Hymn.] This beautiful little hymn was composed for her children in 1839, and 1st pub. in

3 st. of 4 l. in her *Memoir*, 1841 (ed. 1843, p. 311). It is No. 3 in her *Rhymes for my Children*, 1842, entitled "An Evening Prayer." It has been included in England in the Baptist *Ps. & Hymns*, 1858, the *Hy. Comp.*, 1876, and others; in America, in the *Episcopal H. Bk.*, 1871, the *Evang. Hymnal*, N. Y., 1880, the *Songs of Christian Praise*, N. Y., 1881, and in other collections. [J. M.]

Jesus, the Christ of God. *H. Bonar.* [*Praise to Christ.*] Appeared in his *Hys. of Faith & Hope*, 2nd series, 1861, in 7 st. of 4 l., and entitled "Praise to Christ." It is found in numerous collections in G. Britain and America. In some hymn-books it begins with st. ii. :—

> "Jesus, the Lamb of God,
>   Who us from hell to raise;"

but this form of the text is not so popular as the original. [J. J.]

Jesus, the needy sinner's Friend. *C. Wesley.* [*Holy Communion.*] This cento is composed of Nos. 366, 367, and 368 of "Hys. on the Four Gospels," pub. from the Wesley mss. in the *P. Works of J. & C. Wesley*, 1868–72, vol. x. p. 282. It appeared as No. 875 in the revised edition of the *Wes. H. Bk.*, 1875, with the concluding lines changed from :—

> "We banquet on the heavenly Bread,
>   When Christ Himself imparts,
> By ministerial hands convey'd
>   To all believing hearts :"

to —

> "We banquet on the heavenly Bread,
>   When Christ Himself imparts,
> By *His disciples'* hands conveyed
>   To all believing hearts." [J. J.]

Jesus, Thou all-redeeming Lord, Thy blessing, &c. *C. Wesley.* [*General.*] Appeared in *Hys. & Sac. Poems*, 1749, vol. i. p. 316, in 18 st. of 4 l., and entitled "Before Preaching to the Colliers in Leicestershire" (*P. Works*, 1868–72, vol. v. p. 121). In 1780 two hymns compiled, with slight alterations, therefrom: (1) "Jesus, Thou all-redeeming Lord," being st. i., ii., iv., v., vi.–ix.; (2) "Lovers of pleasure more than God," being st. xi., xii., xvii., xviii., were included in the *Wes. H. Bk.*, Nos. 34, 35, and continued in subsequent editions. Also found in other collections. In addition to these, a cento beginning "Lover of souls, Thou well canst prize," is given in *Kennedy*, 1863, No. 627. It is compiled from the *Wes. H. Bk.*, pt. i., as above, st. iii.–viii., with slight alterations and a doxology. [J. J.]

Jesus, Thou needest me. *H. Bonar.* [*Oneness with Christ Explained and Desired.*] Pub. in his *Hys of Faith & Hope*, 2nd series, 1861, in 8 st. of 4 l., and headed "The Lord needeth Thee." It has passed into a few collections, including Dale's *English H. Bk.*, 1874, &c [J. J.]

Jesus, Thou Soul of all our joys. *C. Wesley.* [*Choral Festivals.*] Appeared in *Hys. & Sac. Poems*, 1749, vol. ii., No 90, in 8 st. of 6 l., as the second of two hymns on "The True Use of Music." In the *Wes. H. Bk.*, 1780, it was included as No. 196 (ed. 1875, No. 204). It has passed into several collections, sometimes abbreviated, as in *Mercer*; and again, in the altered form, "Jesus, in

Whom Thy saints rejoice," as in the Cooke and Denton *Hymnal*, enlarged ed., 1855. [J. J.]

Jesus, Thou wast once a child. *J. Gabb.* [*Holiness desired.*] This hymn is found in three forms :—

(1) It was first pub. in the author's *Steps to the Throne*, &c., 1864, in 5 st. of 4 l., and repeated in his *Hymns and Songs*, &c., 1871, with the title "Christ-Incarnate." In this form it is a prayer for Holiness.
(2) The above text was rewritten by the Rev. C. H. Spurgeon as a hymn for Mothers' Meetings, and included in his *O. O. H. Bk.*, 1866, No. 1012, from whence it passed into Snepp's *Songs of G. & G.*, 1872.
(3) In 1875 the same hymn was rewritten by the author in 6 st. of 4 l., and given, with his tune "Moorlands," in his *Welburn Appendix*, 1875, No. 49, as above.

Of these texts the first is by far the most beautiful and simple. [J. J.]

Jesus, Thy Church with longing eyes. *W. H. Bathurst.* [*Second Advent.*] 1st pub. in his *Ps. & Hys.*, 1831, No. 41, in 6 st. of 4 l., and headed "Second Coming of Christ." It has passed into a large number of hymn-books, both in G. Britain and America, and ranks as one of the most popular of Bathurst's hymns. It is a most suitable hymn on behalf of Foreign Missions. Orig. text in Thring's *Coll.*, 1882. [J. J.]

Jesus, Thy name I love. *J. G. Deck.* [*Jesus, All and in All.*] Appeared in *Ps., Hys. and Spiritual Songs*, London, D. Walther, 1842, Pt. ii., No. 6, in 4 st. of 8 l. In *A Few Hys. and some Spiritual Songs selected* 1856 *for The Little Flock*, No. 109, it is given in a rewritten form as "Jesus! that Name is love." Outside of the Plymouth Brethren hymnbooks the original text is given sometimes with slight alterations, as in Hatfield's *Church H. Bk.*, N. Y., 1872, No. 1005. [J. J.]

Jesus, when I fainting lie. *H. Alford.* [*Death anticipated.*] 1st pub. in his *Year of Praise*, 1867, No. 208, in 3 st. of 6 l., and appointed for the 16th S. after Trinity. It was one of two hymns which were sung at the author's funeral, the second being his "Ten thousand times ten thousand." [J. J.]

Jesus, where'er Thy people meet. *W. Cowper.* [*Opening of a Place of Worship.*] The Rev. J. Bull, in his *John Newton of Olney and St. Mary Woolnoth*, &c., gives the following account of this hymn :—

"1769. In a letter to Mr. Clunie, in April, Mr. Newton speaks of a journey to Kettering, and of his preaching there, and says : 'I have been pretty full-handed in preaching lately. I trust the Lord was graciously with us in most or all of our opportunities. We are going to remove our prayer-meeting to the great room in the Great House. It is a noble place, with a parlour behind it, and holds one hundred and thirty people conveniently. Pray for us, that the Lord may be in the midst of us there, and that as He has now given us a Rehoboth, and has made room for us, so that He may be pleased to add to our numbers, and make us fruitful in the land.'
"It was for this occasion that two of the hymns in the *Olney Selection* were composed, the 43rd and 44th of the second book. The first, beginning 'O Lord, our languid frames inspire,' by Mr. Newton; and the second, 'Jesus, where'er Thy people meet,' by Mr. Cowper."

In a note Mr. Bull adds :—

"Elsewhere the editor of this volume has erroneously stated that these hymns were written when the Great House was *first* used for religious services. This could not have been as Mr. Cowper was then unknown at Olney. The present more correct statement explains the reference in Mr. Cowper's hymn to the renewal of former mercies, and to a more enlarged space."

The first of these references is in st. iii., ll. 1, 2 :—

> " Dear Shepherd of Thy chosen few !
> Thy former mercies here renew :."

and the second to st. v., ll. 3, 4 :—

> " Come Thou and fill this wider space,
> And bless us with a large increase."

The hymn was pub. in the *Olney Hymns*, 1779, Bk. ii., No. 44, in 6 st. of 4 l. It is preceded, as stated above, by J. Newton's " O Lord, our languid souls inspire," which is headed " On opening a Place for Social Prayer," and is given as No. " XLIV. C. *Another*," meaning, another hymn on the same subject. It is given in modern hymn-books in its original form, and also as follows :—

1. The arrangement in the *Salisbury H. Bk.*, 1857, is thus :—St. i., ii., iv., v. and viii. are slightly altered from *Cowper* : st. iii., vi., vii. and ix. are by *J. Keble*, and the doxology is by *Bp. Ken*. This text was repeated, with the omission of the doxology, in the *Sarum Hymnal*, 1868. In the *Anglican H. Bk.*, 1868, five stanzas are taken from the *Salisbury H. Bk.*, and one from the original, and further altered as " O Jesu, where Thy people meet."
2. In *Kennedy*, 1863, the text is from the *Salisbury H. Bk.*, 1857.
3. In the S. P. C. K. *Church Hys.*, 1871, the arrangement is :—St. i., ii., *Cowper* ; st. iii., *Keble* ; st. iv., v., *Cowper* ; st. vi., ll. 1–2, *Cowper* ; ll. 3–4, *Keble*. In the stanzas from Cowper the text is as in the *Salisbury H.Bk.*
4. In Martineau's *Hymns*, &c., 1840 and 1873, Cowper's st. i., ll. and iv. are given as " O Lord, where'er Thy people meet."

The use of this hymn in its various forms is extensive in all English-speaking countries. It has also been translated into many languages, and is one of the most popular of Cowper's hymns. Orig. text in Lord Selborne's *Book of Praise*, 1862, p. 150.   [J. J.]

Jesus, while He dwelt below. *J. Hart*. [*Passiontide*.] A descriptive hymn of great power on The Passion of Our Lord. It was pub. in Hart's *Hymns*, &c., 1759, No. 75, in 23 st. of 6 l., and headed " Jesus ofttimes resorted thither with His disciples," John xviii. 2. The following centos have been compiled therefrom :—

1. " Jesus, whilst He dwelt below." Pt. i.
   " Full of love to man's lost race." Pt. ii.
   " There my God bore all my guilt." Pt. iii.
   These centos were given in Snepp's *Songs of G. & G.*, 1872, No. 230.
2. " Jesus, while He dwelt below." Pt. i.
   " Eden from each flowery bed." Pt. ii.
   These were given in the Scottish *Evang. Union Hymnal*, 1878, No. 34, and others.
3. " Comes once more the awful night."
   In the S. P. C. K. *Church Hys.*, 1871, this is very much altered from the original.
4. " Comes again the dreadful night."
   In Whiting's *Hys. for the Ch. Catholic*, 1882. Also altered from Hart.

Through these various centos great use is made of this hymn.   [J. J.]

Jesus, while [whilst] this rough desert soil. *H. Bonar*. [*Jesus' presence desired*.] Pub. in his *Hys. of Faith and Hope*, 1st series, 1857, in 5 st. of 4 l., and headed " Strength by the way." In *Kennedy*, 1863, it reads, " Jesus, *whilst* this rough desert soil."   [J. J.]

Jevons, Mary Ann, née Roscoe. [Roscoe Family.]

Jewitt, William Henry, nephew of Mr. Orlando Jewitt, the engraver, was b. at Headington, Oxford, March 17, 1842. Mr. Jewitt is an architect and artist. He has

written several hymns of more than usual merit. The earliest were pub. as *Hys. on the Te Deum*, Manchester, J. Anson, 1874. This little work contains 23 pieces. He also pub. in 1886 a vol. of tales in verse, entitled " The Romance of Love." His hymns in C. U. are :

1. Christ the Lion of royal Judah. *St. Mark*.
2. O Christ, the Father's mirrored Light. *All Saints*.
3. O, Father, mid the cherubim. *St. Michael and All Angels during the Offertory*.
4. O Father of the world supreme. *God the Creator, or Flower Services*.
5. O Lord of Life, and Light, and Love. *St. Michael and All Angels*.
6. O Son Eternal, uncreate. *The Eternal Sonship of Christ*.
7. We know that Thou shalt come. *Advent*.
8. We know Thee, Lord, the eternal Way. *SS. Philip and James*.

Of these hymns Nos. 4, 5, 6, 7, are from the *Hys. on the Te Deum*, 1874 ; No. 1 was contributed to the *Universal H. Bk.*, 1885 ; No. 2 appeared in the *Manchester Diocesan Magazine* ; No. 8 in the *Penny Post* ; and No. 3 in the *Altar Hymnal*, 1884. In addition to these Mr. Jewitt is the author of Nos. 21, 24, 38, 42, 44, 45, 46, 47, 87, 88, 95 and 96, in Chope's *Carols for Easter* and other Christian seasons (Lond., Novello), 1884.   [J. J.]

Jex-Blake, Thomas William, s. of Thomas Jex-Blake of Burnwell, was b. in 1832, and educated at Rugby, and University College, Oxford (D.A. in 1st class 1855 ; D.D. 1873). He was some time Fellow of Queen's College, Oxford ; from 1858 to 1868 Assistant Master at Rugby ; Principal of Cheltenham College, 1868 to 1874 ; Head Master of Rugby, 1874 to 1887 ; and Rector of Alvechurch, Redditch, 1887. Dr. Jex-Blake's well-known hymn, " Lord, we thank Thee for the pleasure " (*Thanksgiving*) was written at the request of Dr. Cotton (then Head Master of Marlborough), in September, 1855. It is in the *Rugby* and other Public Schools hymnbooks, and several general collections. Dr. Jex-Blake's published works do not contain any original poetical compositions.   [J. J.]

John Arklas. [Greek Hymnody, § xvii. 2, and John of Damascus.]

John of Damascus, St. The last but one of the Fathers of the Greek Church, and the greatest of her poets (*Neale*). He was of a good family in Damascus, and educated by the elder Cosmas in company with his foster-brother *Cosmas the Melodist* (q. v.). He held some office under the Caliph. He afterwards retired to the laura of St. Sabas, near Jerusalem, along with his foster-brother. There he composed his theological works and his hymns. He was ordained priest of the church of Jerusalem late in life. He lived to extreme old age, dying on the 4th Dec., the day on which he is commemorated in the Greek calendar, either in his 84th or 100th year (circa 780). He was called, for some unknown reason, *Mansur*, by his enemies. His fame as a theologian rests on the work πηγὴ γνώσεως, the first part of which consists of philosophical summaries, the second dealing with heresies, and the third giving an account of the orthodox faith. His three orations in favour of the *Icons*, from which he obtained the name of *Chrysorrhous* and *The Doctor of Christian Art*, are very celebrated. The immense impetus he gave to Greek hymnology is discussed in **Greek Hymnody**, § xvii. 2. The arrangement of the *Octoechus* in accordance with the Eight Tones was his work, and it originally contained no other Canons than his. His Canons on the great Festivals are his highest achievements. [See **Greek Hymnody**, §§ vii., xvii. 2, and ἐπέβη ὡς λέων.] In addition to his influence on the form and music, Cardinal Pitra attributes to him the doctrinal character of the later Greek hymnody. He says that the rhythm of the Canons may be often traced in the prose of the πηγὴ γνώσεως. He calls him the Thomas Aquinas of the East. The great subject round which his hymns are grouped is The Incarnation, developed in the whole earthly career of the Saviour. In the legendary life of the saint the B. V. M. is introduced as predicting this work: the hymns of John of Damascus should eclipse the Song of Moses, rival the cherubim, and range all the churches, as maidens beating their tambours, round their mother Jerusalem (Pitra, *Hymn. Grecque*, p. 33). The legend illustrates not only the dogmatic cast of the hymns, but the introduction of the *Theotokion* and *Staurotheotokion*, which becomes the prevalent close of the Odes from the days of St. John of Damascus: the Virgin Mother presides over all. The Canons found under the name of *John Arklas* (one of which is the Iambic Canon at Pentecost) are usually attributed to St. John of Damascus, and also those under the name of *John the Monk*. Some doubt, however, attaches to the latter, because they are founded on older rhythmical models (εἱρμοι), which is not the case with those bearing the name of the Damascene, and they are not mentioned in the ancient Greek commentaries on his hymns (see *Anth. Graec. Car. Christ.* p. xlvii.). One of these is the Iambic Canon for Christmas. [See **Greek Hymnody**, §§ vii. and xvii. 2.]

His numerous works, both in prose and verse, were published by *Le Quien*, 1712 ; and a reprint of the same with additions by *Migne*, Paris, 1864. Most of his poetical writings are contained in the latter, vol. iii. pp. 817–856, containing those under the title *Carmina* ; and vol. iii. pp. 1364–1408, the *Hymni*. His Canon of SS. Peter & Paul is in *Hymnographie Grecque*, by Cardinal Pitra, 1867. They are also found scattered throughout the Service Books of the Greek Church, and include Iambic Canons on the Birth of Christ, the Epiphany, and on Pentecost ; *Canons* on Easter, Ascension, the Transfiguration, the Annunciation, and SS. Peter & Paul : and numerous *Idiomela*. In addition, Cardinal Mai found a MS. in the Vatican and published the same in his *Spicilegium Romanum*, which contained six additional *Canons*, viz. : In St. Basilium ; In St. Chrysostomum ; In St. Nicolaum ; In St. Petrum ; In St. Georgium, and in St. Blasium. But M. Christ has urged grave objections to the ascription of these to St. John of Damascus (*Anth. Graec. Car. Christ.* p. xlvii.). Daniel's extracts in his *Thes. Hymn.*, vol. iii. pp. 80, 97, extend to six pieces. Dr. Neale's translations of portions of these works are well known, and fully detailed in this work. For fuller details of St. John, authorities, &c., see *Dict. of Christian Biog.*, vol. iii. pp. 409–422 ; and for a popular account of him and his works, Lupton's *St. John of Damascus*, in *The Fathers for English Readers*, 1882.   [H. L. B.]

John the Monk. [**Greek Hymnody**, § xvii. 2, and **St. John of Damascus**.]

Johns, John, b. at Plymouth, March 17, 1801, the son of an artist. Educated at the grammar school and by the Rev. I. Worsley, Unitarian minister at Plymouth, and after-

wards spent two years at Edinburgh. In 1820 became minister of the old Presbyterian chapel at Crediton, where he remained till his removal to Liverpool in 1836, as Minister to the Poor. He was a man of fine poetic temperament and retiring disposition, but his work among the people called out his great practical and organising ability. He died a sacrifice to the fever which raged in the district where he laboured, June 23, 1847. Besides his reports to the Liverpool Domestic Mission Society, and frequent contributions to the *Monthly Repository*, *Christian Reformer*, and *Christian Teacher*, he published three volumes of poetry, *Dews of Castalie ; a collection of Poems*, 1828 ; *The Valley of the Nymphs*, 1829 ; and *Georgics of Life*, 1846. There are 35 of his hymns in Dr. Beard's *Collection*, 1837, and several of them are in other Unitarian books. The best known of his hymns are :—

1. Come, Kingdom of our God. *Prayer for the Kingdom of God.*
2. Farewell, our blighted treasure. *Death of a Child.*
3. Great God, avert from us the thought. *Heaven.*
4. Hush the loud cannon's roar. *Common Brotherhood and Peace Universal.*
5. O know ye not that ye. *Purity.* This is altered from "What, know ye not that ye?"
6. Thanks to God for these who came. *Preachers of the Word.* Altered from "Welcome, welcome these who came."
7. Thou must be born again. *Necessity of the New Birth.*

These hymns were contributed to Beard's *Coll.*, 1837, and passed thence into other collections.   [V. D. D.]

Johnson, Samuel, M.A., was b. at Salem, Massachusetts, Oct. 10, 1822, and educated at Harvard, where he graduated in Arts in 1842, and in Theology in 1846. In 1853 he formed a Free Church in Lynn, Massachusetts, and remained its pastor to 1870. Although never directly connected with any religious denomination, he was mainly associated in the public mind with the Unitarians. He was joint editor with S. Longfellow (q. v.) of *A Book of Hymns for Public and Private Devotion*, Boston, 1846 ; the *Supplement* to the same, 1848 ; and *Hymns of the Spirit*, 1864. His contributions to these collections were less numerous than those by S. Longfellow, but not less meritorious. He d. at North Andover, Massachusetts, Feb. 19, 1882. His hymns were thus contributed :—

i. To *A Book of Hymns*, 1846.

1. Father [Saviour] in Thy mysterious presence kneeling. *Divine Worship.*
2. Go, preach the gospel in my name. *Ordination.*
3. Lord, once our faith in man no fear could move. *In Time of War.*
4. O God, Thy children gathered here. *Ordination.*
5. Onward, Christians, [onward] through the region. *Conflict.* In the *Hys. of the Spirit*, 1864, it was altered to "Onward, onward through the region."
6. Thy servants' sandals, Lord, are wet. *Ordination.*
7. When from Jordan's gleaming wave. *Holy Baptism.*

ii. To the *Supplement*, 1848.

8. God of the earnest heart. *Trust.*

iii. To the *Hymns of the Spirit*, 1864.

9. City of God, how broad, how far. *The Church the City of God.*
10. I bless Thee, Lord, for sorrows sent. *Affliction—Perfect through suffering.*
11. Life of Ages, richly poured. *Inspiration.*
12. Strong-souled Reformer, Whose far-seeing faith. *Power of Jesus.*

13. The Will Divine that woke a waiting time. *St. Paul.*

14. Thou Whose glad summer yields. *Prayer for the Church.*

15. To light that shines in stars and souls. *Dedication of a Place of Worship.*

Of these hymns No. 8 was "Written for the Graduating Exercises of the Class of 1846; in Cambridge Divinity Schools"; and No. 10 "Written at the request of Dorothea L. Dix for a collection made by her for the use of an asylum." It is undated. A few only of these hymns are in use in Great Britain. [F. M. B.]

Johnston, James Aitken, was ordained by the Bishop of Jamaica in 1834, and was preferred to the Perpetual Curacy of St. John's, Waterloo Road, London, in 1848. He d. in 1872. He was the editor of

The English Hymnal, or a Hymn-Book for the Use of the Church of England. With an Appendix containing Selections from Metrical Versions of the Psalms. London: Parker, 1852.

A new and thoroughly revised ed. was pub. in 1856. This was reprinted in 1861 as the 3rd ed. From a ms. supplied by Johnston to D. Sedgwick [S. MSS.] we find that he was the author or translator of 34 hymns in the 3rd ed., but this list does not include "O Jesu, Lord, the Way, the Truth" (SS. *Philip and James*), attributed to him in Thring's *Coll.*, 1882, In his *trs.* he is considerably indebted to others, and his original hymns display no special merit. [J. J.]

Join all the glorious Names. *I. Watts. [Names and Titles of Jesus Christ.]* Pub. in his *Hys. & Sac. Songs*, 1709, Bk. i., No. 150, in 12 st. of 8 l., as the second of two hymns on "The Offices of Christ, from several Scriptures." It has been freely altered, abbreviated, and divided from M. Madan's *Ps. and Hys.*, 1760, to the present time. The line which has caused most trouble to the editors has been st. x., l. 1, "My dear, Almighty Lord," the term "dear" being very objectionable to many. The line has undergone the following amongst other changes :—

1760.	*M. Madan.*	" *Thou* dear Almighty Lord."
1769.	*Ash & Evans.*	" My *great* Almighty Lord."
1830.	*Wes. H. Bk.*	" O Thou Almighty Lord."
1833.	*Bickersteth.*	" *Divine* Almighty Lord."
1835.	*H. V. Elliott.*	" *Almighty, Sovereign* Lord."
1851.	*J. H. Gurney.*	" *Almighty, gracious* Lord."
1858.	*Bap. Ps. & Hys.*	" My *Saviour and my* Lord."
1876.	*Presby. Hymnal.*	" *Jesus*, Almighty Lord."

To this list may be traced most of the changes found in modern hymn-books. There are others also of less importance. In addition to abbreviations which begin with the original first line, there are also the following centos :—

1. **Arrayed in mortal flesh.** This was given in R. Conyers's *Coll.*, 1774, in 5 st., and in other hymn-books.

2. **Great Prophet of my God.** In Alford's *Year of Praise*, 1867, &c.

3. **Jesus, my Great High Priest.** This, in Spurgeon's *O. O. H. Bk.*, 1866, is composed of st. viii., vi., and ix. of this hymn, and st. vi., "Immense compassion reigns," from No. 148 of Bk. i. of Watts's *Hymns*, " With cheerful voice I sing."

4. **My dear Almighty Lord.** In Spurgeon's *O. O. H. Bk.*, 1866, No. 372.

The original hymn is justly regarded as one of Watts's finest efforts. In its various forms its use is extensive in most English-speaking countries. It has been *tr.* in whole, or in part, into various languages, including Latin, in R. Bingham's *Hymno. Christ. Lat.*, 1870, as

"Pange nomen omne mirum." [See English Hymnody, Early, §§ vi., xiii.]   [J. J.]

Jonas, Justus (Jobst, Jost, Jodocus), s. of Jonas Koch, burgomaster of Nordhausen, in Thuringia, was b. at Nordhausen, June 5, 1493. He studied at Erfurt (M.A. 1510), and Wittenberg (LL.B.); returning to Erfurt in 1517, where, in 1518, he was appointed Canon of the St. Severus Church, Professor, and, in 1519, Rector of the University. In the fı stal ode on his rectorate (by his friend Eoban Hesse) he was called the *Just Jonas*, and henceforth he adopted *Jonas* as his surname, and it is as *Jonas* that he is known. In 1521 he was appointed Probst of the Schlosskirche (All Saints) at Wittenberg, D.D., and Professor of Church Law in the University. Here he worked for twenty years as a true and devoted friend and helper of Luther and Melanchthon, and was then, from 1541 to 1546, superintendent and chief pastor at Halle. After Luther's death he passed through various troubled experiences, but became in 1553 superintendent and chief pastor at Eisfeld on the Werra, where he d. Oct. 9, 1555. He added two stanzas to Luther's "Erhalt uns Herr, bei deinem Wort" (q.v.). The only original hymn by him which has passed into English is :—

Wo Gott der Herr nicht bei uns hält. *Ps. cxxiv.* 1st pub. in *Eyn Enchiridion*, Erfurt, 1524, and thence in *Wackernagel*, iii. p. 42, in 8 st. In the *Unv. L. S.*, 1851, No. 254. *Tr. as,* "If God were not upon our side, by Miss Winkworth, 1869, p. 117.   [J. M.]

Jones, Edmund, s. of the Rev. Philip Jones, Cheltenham, was b. in 1722, and attended for a time the Baptist College at Bristol. At the age of 19 he began to preach for the Baptist Congregation at Exeter, and two years afterwards he became its pastor. In 1760 he pub. a volume of *Sacred Poems.* After a very useful ministry he d. April 15, 1765. From an old MS. record of the Exeter Baptist Church, it appears that it was under his ministry in the year 1759, that singing was first introduced into that Church as a part of worship. As a hymn-writer he is known chiefly through :—

Come, humble sinner, in whose breast. This hymn appeared in Rippon's *Bap. Sel.*, 1787, No. 355, in 7 st. of 4 l., and headed, "The successful Resolve—'I will go in unto the King,' Esther iv. 16." It has undergone several changes, including :—

1. " Come, sinner, in whose guilty breast." In the *Meth. Free Ch. S. S. H. Bk.*, 1860.

2. " Come, trembling sinner, in whose breast." This is in a great number of American hymn-books.

3. " Come, weary sinner, in whose breast." Also in American use.

Miller, in his *Singers & Songs of the Church*, 1869, p. 333, attributes this hymn to a Welsh Baptist hymn-writer of Trevecca, and of the same name. *Rippon*, however, says in the 1st ed. of his *Sel.* that Edmund Jones, the author of No. 333, was pastor of the Baptist Church at Exon, Devon. This decides the matter.   [W. R. S.]

Jones, Griffith, of Llanddowror, was b. at Cilrhedyn, Carmarthenshire, of respectable parents, in 1683. He was ordained deacon by Bishop Bull in 1708. In 1711 he became Vicar of Llandeilo-Abercowyn, and Vicar of Llanddowror in 1716. In 1730, he first commenced his circulating schools in Wales, which proved of incalculable blessings to thousands. He d. April 8, 1761, at the house of Mrs. Beavan, who had helped him with his schools, and also bequeathed £10,000 towards their maintenance. He laboured in the parish of Llanddowror for 45 years. He published many books and some hymns, selected from the works of different authors. One of his books was called *Anogaeth i folianu Duw*, or " Admonition to praise God."   [W. G. T.]

Jones, Samuel Flood, M.A., s. of William Jones, for many years the Secretary of the Religious Tract Society, was b. in London in 1826, and educated at Pembroke College, Oxford (B.A. 1851). Taking Holy Orders he was Minister of St. Matthew's, Spring Gardens, London, 1854–76; Lecturer of Bow, London, 1858–76; Minor Canon, Westminster Abbey, 1859; Precentor, 1869; Vicar of St. Botolph, Aldersgate, London, 1876; and Priest in Ordinary to the Queen, 1869. In 1860 he pub. *Hymns of Prayer and Praise*, Lond., Dalton & Lucy. This book contained 100 hymns, of which the following were by Mr. Jones:—

1. Here all is strife and war. *The Present and the Future.*
2. Jesus, my Advocate in heaven. *Jesus the Advocate.* This is adapted from "Star of the Sea."
3. Lord of light, this day our Guardian be. *Morning.*
4. This is the day of light, When first the silv'ry dawn. *Sunday.* Written long before 1860.

Mr. Jones's most popular hymn is :—

5. Father of Life, confessing. *H. Matrimony.*

This was written about 1867, at the request of the late Dean Stanley for use at Marriages in Westminster Abbey. It has passed into several hymn-books. Mr. Jones's brother, William Henry Rich-Jones, M.A., Vicar of Bradford-on-Avon, and Canon of Salisbury (b. 1817, d. 1885), contributed :—

1. Haste, my soul, thy God adore. *God the Sustainer.*
2. Lord, Thy solemn Passion past. *Ascension.* (In W. J. Blew's *Coll.*, 1852–55, but not his).

to his *Hymns*, &c., as above; and his wife Catherine Flood Jones (b. 1828) also contributed :—

Pilgrim, bend thy footsteps on. *Onward.*

to the same work. He d. Feb. 26, 1895. [J. J.]

Jonson, Benjamin, commonly known as *Ben Jonson*, the s. of a clergyman, was b. at Westminster in 1573, and educated at Westminster School, and St. John's, Cambridge. He d. in London, Aug. 6, 1637. His history and dramatic abilities are well known to all students of English literature. He is known in association with hymnody mainly through his carol, "I sing the birth—was born to-night," which is still in use. It is given in his *Underwoods* in the 2nd vol. (folio) of his *Works*, 1640, and entitled "A Hymn on the Nativity of my Saviour." Two additional hymns therein, "The sinner's sacrifice" and "A Hymn to God the Father," have much merit, but are unsuited for congregational use. His Works have been edited by Gifford, and more recently by Lieut.-Col. Francis Cunningham. [See **English Hymnody, Early,** § v.; and for *Life, Enc. Brit.*, 9th ed.]   [J. J.]

Jordanis oras praevia. *C. Coffin.* [*Advent.*] Pub. in his *Hymni Sacri*, 1736, p. 34; and again in the *Paris Breviary* the same year as the hymn for Sundays and Ferial days in Advent at Lauds. It is also in the *Lyons* and other Modern French Breviaries; Card. Newman's *Hymni Ecclesiae*,

1838 and 1865; and J. Chandler's *Hys. of the Primitive Church*, 1837, No. 37. It is *tr.* as :—

1. **On Jordan's bank the Baptist's cry.** J. Chandler. 1st pub. in his *Hys. of the Prim. Church*, 1837, p. 40, in 6 st. of 4 l. It is one of the most popular of Chandler's translations, and is given in a large number of hymn-books, those which contain the original *tr.*, however, being in the minority, and include the *People's H.*, 1867, the *Westminster Abbey H. Bk.*, 1883, and the *Universal H. Bk.*, 1885. Of the numerous versions of the text, in most instances embodying slight alterations only, the best known are, Murray's *Hymnal*, 1852; the *Salisbury H. Bk.*, 1857; *Kennedy*, 1863; *Chope*, 1864, &c. The most popular arrangement is that by the Compilers of *H. A. & M.* It appeared in their trial copy, 1859; and with another doxology in the 1st ed., 1861; and the revised edition, 1875. A few of the altered lines are taken from Murray's *Hymnal*, 1852, and the Cooke and Denton *Hymnal*, 1853. The most marked alteration is st. iv. "To heal the sick, stretch forth Thy hand." The following, together with others, give the *H. A. & M.* text with further alterations: the S. P. C. K. *Church Hys.*, 1871; the *Hymnary*, 1872 : T. Darling's *Hymns*, &c., 1887, &c. The Rev. F. Pott's version in his *Hymns*, &c., 1861, and Prebendary Thring's in his *Coll.*, 1882, are specially good. In the *English Hymnal*, 1856, and 1861, *Chandler's* text is altered to "On Jordan's banks a herald-cry;" and in the *New Mitre Hymnal*, 1875, No. 158, is a cento, st. i.–iii. being from *Chandler's tr.*, and st. iv., v. are Dr. Watts's version (L. M.) of Ps. 117, pub. in his *Ps. of David*, 1719, and not from his *Hymns*, &c., 1709, as stated by the editor.

2. **Lo! the desert-depths are stirred.** By W. J. Blew. Printed for use in his Church, circ. 1850, and pub. in *The Church H. & Tune Book*, 1852 and 1855. It was repeated in Rice's *Hymns*, 1870.

3. **Lo! the great Herald's voice.** By Bp. J. R. Woodford. Contributed to the *Parish H. Bk.*, 1863; and repeated in the enlarged ed., 1875.

4. **Behold the Baptist's warning sounds.** By R. C. Singleton. Pub. in his *Anglican H. Bk.*, 1868, and again, after slight revision, in the 2nd ed. of the same, 1871.

Translations not in C. U. :—

1. Lo, the Baptist's herald cry. *I. Williams*, 1839.
2. Lo! the Prophet sent before. *G. Rorison*, 1851.
3. O, hark! through Jordan's echoing bounds. *J. D. Chambers*, 1857.
4. What sounds doth Jordan's streams appal. In O. Shipley's *Annus Sanctus*, 1884, by "W. M. A." [J. J.]

Joseph of the Studium. [Joseph of Thessalonica.]

Joseph of Thessalonica. This hymn-writer is known in Greek hymnody as Joseph of the Studium. He is not however the same person wrongly named by Dr. Neale in his *Hys. of the Eastern Church* as *Joseph of the Studium*, author of the great Canon for the Ascension. That Joseph is *St. Joseph the Hymnographer* (q.v.). Joseph of Thessalonica, younger brother of St. Theodore of the Studium, q.v. (see *Hys. of the Eastern Church*), was some time Bishop of Thessalonica, and died in prison, after great suffering inflicted by command of Theophilus. [Greek Hymnody, § xviii. 1.] He was probably the author of the Triodia in the Triodion, and certainly of five Canons in the Pentecostarion to which his name is prefixed. His pieces have not been *tr.* into English. [H. L. B.]

Joseph, St., the Hymnographer. A native of Sicily, and of the Sicilian school of poets is called by Dr. Neale (in his *Hys. of the Eastern Church*), *Joseph of the Studium*, in error. He left Sicily in 830 for a monastic life at Thessalonica. Thence he went to Constantinople; but left it, during the Iconoclastic persecution, for Rome. He was for many years a slave in Crete, having been captured by pirates. After regaining his liberty, he returned to Constantinople. He established there a monastery, in connection with the Church of St. John Chrysostom, which was filled with inmates by his eloquence. He was banished to the Chersonese for defence of the *Icons*, but was recalled by the empress Theodora, and made Sceuophylax (keeper of the sacred vessels) in the Great Church of Constantinople, through the favour of the patriarch Ignatius. He stood high also in the favour of Photius, the rival and successor of Ignatius, and accompanied him into banishment. He d. at an advanced age in 883. He is commemorated in the Calendars of the Greek Church on April 3rd. He is the most voluminous of the Greek hymn-writers. There are more than two hundred Canons under the acrostic of his name, in the *Menaea*. Cardinal Pitra says he is reported to have composed a thousand. There is some difficulty in distinguishing his works from those of the brother of Theodore of the Studium, *Joseph of Thessalonica*. This latter poet, and not the more celebrated *Joseph the Hymnographer*, was named *Joseph of the Studium.* [Greek Hymnody, § xviii. 1, 3.] [H. L. B.]

Josephson, Ludwig Carl Leopold, was b. January 28, 1809, at Unna, Westphalia, and studied at the University of Bonn. In 1832 he became Pastor at Iserlohn, Westphalia, and after other appointments became in 1863 Pastor and Superintendent at Barth, near Stralsund, in Western Pomerania. He d. at Barth, Jan. 22, 1877 (MS. from Superintendent Baudach, Barth, &c.) His hymns appeared in his *Stimmen aus Zion*, Iserlohn, 1841, and from this a number passed into Knapp's *Ev. L. S.*, 1850 and 1865. One has been *tr.* into English.

Es ruht die Nacht auf Erden. *For the Sick.* For use during a sleepless night. 1st pub. 1841 as above, p. 36, in 10 st. of 4 l., repeated in *Knapp*, 1850, No. 2485 (1865, No. 2738). *Tr.* as "Now darkness over all is spread," by *Miss Winkworth*, 1858, p. 83. [J. M.]

Joy to the followers of the Lord. *Anna L. Barbauld.* [*Joy.*] Written about 1820, and pub. by her sister in *The Works of Anna Lætitia Barbauld, with a Memoir.* 1825, vol. i. p. 339, in 6 st. of 4 l. In Dr. Martineau's *Hymns*, 1840, and again in 1873, it is given as "Joy to those that love the Lord." This is also in other collections. In Ellen Courtauld's *Ps., Hys. & Anthems*, 1860, it begins with st. iii., "'Tis a joy that, seated deep," altered to "Joy there is, that, seated deep." [J. J.]

Joy to the world, the Lord is come [nigh]. *I. Watts.* [*Ps. xcviii.*] 1st pub. in

his *Psalms of David*, &c., 1719, in 4 st. of 4 l., as the 2nd pt. of his version of Psalm 98. T. Cotterill gave, in the 1st ed. of his *Sel.*, 1810, a much altered version of text, which was repeated in the authorized ed. of 1820 with the repetition of st. i. as st. v. This arrangement is known by st. ii., which reads, "Ye saints, rejoice, the Saviour reigns," &c. Bickersteth's arrangement in his *Christian Psalmody*, 1833, is also in 5 st.; but the added stanza (iii.) is from *Watts's* version of the first part of the same Psalm. Both of these texts have been repeated in later collections. In addition there are also the following: (1) "The Lord is come; let heaven rejoice," in Hall's *Mitre H. Bk.*, 1836; and (2) "Joy to the world, the Lord is nigh," in the Irvingite *Hys. for the Use of the Churches*, 1864. In its various forms, but principally in the original, it is in use in most English-speaking countries. It has also been translated into several languages, including Latin, in R. Bingham's *Hymno. Christ. Lat.*, 1870, "Lætitia in mundo! Dominus nam venit Iësus!" [J. J.]

Joyce, James, M.A., was born at Frome, Somersetshire, Nov. 2, 1781, and was for some years Vicar of Dorking, and d. there Oct. 9, 1850. He pub. *A Treatise on Love to God,* &c., 1822; *The Lays of Truth, a Poem,* 1825; and *Hymns with Notes,* 1849, This last is a small work which he compiled for his parishioners. It is composed of passages of Holy Scripture, Meditations, and 20 Hymns. Of his hymns, the following are in C. U.:—

1. Disown'd of Heav'n, by man opprest. [*On behalf of the Jews.*] This appeared in the *Christian Observer*, Nov., 1809, in 5 st. of 4 l., headed, "Hymn applicable to the present condition of the Jews," and signed "J. J." The form in which it is known to modern collections is, "O why should Israel's sons, once bless'd." This appeared in Bickersteth's *Christian Psalmody*, 1833, and is widely used. The cento, "Lord, visit Thy forsaken race—vine," in use in America, as Bickersteth's (1833) somewhat altered.

2. High on the bending willows hung. [*On behalf of the Jews.*] This hymn was given in the December number of the *Christian Observer*, 1809, in 6 st. of 4 l., as "A second hymn applicable to the present condition of the Jews," and signed "J. J."

3. Israel bewails her freedom gone. [*On behalf of the Jews.*] This is his "Third Hymn applicable to the present condition of the Jews," and was given in the *Christian Observer*, Dec., 1809, with No. 2. It is in 6 st. of 4 l., and signed "J. J." [J. J.]

Jubes: et, in praeceps aquis. *C. Coffin.* [*Tuesday.*] Pub. in his *Hymni Sacri*, 1736, p. 15, and again in the *Paris Breviary* of the same year, for Tuesdays at Matins. It is also in the *Lyons* and other modern French Brevs.; in Card. Newman's *Hymni Ecclesiae*, 1838 and 1865; and in J. Chandler's *Hys. of the Primitive Church*, 1837. *Tr.* as:—

1. He speaks the word; the floods obey. By J. Chandler, in his *Hys of the Prim. Church*, 1837, p. 17. It was repeated in Dr. Oldknow's *Hymns*, &c., 1850; and as "God speaks the word; the floods obey," in the "Additional *Ps. & Hys.*" given in the Scottish Episco. *Coll.*, 1858.

2. The word is given, the waters flow. By I. Williams. Appeared in the *British Magazine*, July, 1834; and again in his *Hys. Tr. from the Parisian Brev.*, 1839, p. 18.

3. He spake! and gathering into one. By J. D. Chambers, in his *Lauda Syon*, 1857, p. 16; and the *Salisbury H. Bk.*, 1857.

4. Thou spakest, Lord, and into one. By the Compilers of *H. A. & M.*, 1861, based upon I. Williams's *tr.* above. This is repeated in other collections.

5. Thou spakst the word, the waters flow. This in the *Hymnal for the Use of St. John the Evangelist's, Aberdeen*, 1870, is I. Williams's *tr.* altered.

6. O Father, Who this earth hast given. This in the *Hymnary*, 1872, is I. Williams's *tr.* re-written in L. M. It is appointed for Septua-gesima.   [J. J.]

Jubilate. [Prayer, Book of Common.]

Jubilemus omnes una. [*Advent.*] This sequence for the 4th S. in Advent is found in a 12th cent. English *Gradual* in the British Museum (Reg. 2, B. iv. f. 65), and a *Sequentiary*, cir. 1199 (Calig. A. xiv. f. 44). Also in two 14th cent. French Missals in the *British Museum* [Add. 16,905 (of Paris), f. 18 *b*; and Add. 30,058 (of Sens), f. 16 *b*], 14th cent. *Sarum Missal* (Lansdown, 432, f. 11 *b*), &c. The printed text is in the reprints of the *Sarum, York, Hereford* and *Arbuthnott Missals;* in Neale's *Sequentiae*, 1852, p. 8; *Daniel*, v. p. 174 (from *Neale*); *Kehrein*, No. 5. *Tr.* as:—

Honour and glory, thanksgiving and praise. By E. A. Dayman, for the *Hymnary*, and pub. therein, 1872. It is repeated in the *Laudes Domini*, N.Y., 1884. Other *trs.* are:—

1. Let us all rejoice together. *J. D. Chambers*, 1866.
2. Before the all-creating Lord. C. B. Pearson, in *Sarum Missal in English*, 1868.   [J. M.]

Jubilemus pia mente. [*For the Dying. In Time of Pestilence.*] The only MS. form of this sequence we have been able to find is in a 15th cent. *Sarum Missal* in the Bodleian (*Liturg. Misc.*, 372, f. 261 *b*). It is also found in the eds. of the *Sarum Missal* printed at Venice, 1494; London, 1498, &c.; and in the Burntisland reprint is given at cols. 887*-889*.

This sequence occurs in a Mass, Pro mortalitate evitanda (for escaping death by pestilence), which is introduced by a notice which states that Pope Clement, with all the Cardinals in conclave, composed and arranged the Mass, and granted to all those who were truly penitent, and had made their confession, and had heard this Mass, 260 days of indulgence (i.e. remission of canonical penalties), and that all those who heard this Mass should carry in the hand a lighted candle while hearing Mass on the five days following; and should hold it in the hand, kneeling, throughout the whole Mass. And so sudden death could not hurt them. And this was certified and approved in Avignon and its neighbourhood. The Pope mentioned was Clement VI., elected Pope, May 7, 1342. The contagion alluded to was brought to Italy in 1347 by merchants from the Levant, and soon spread over Europe, causing a fearful amount of mortality. Clement, at Avignon, then the seat of the Papacy, distinguished himself by trying in various ways to alleviate and ter-minate this scourge, providing for the nursing and sup-port of the sick, the burial of the dead, &c.

Translation in C. U.:—
Holy Trinity, before Thee. By Harriet Mary Chester, made for and pub. in the *Hynnary*, 1872, in 7 st. of 6 l., and signed "H. M. C."

Another tr. is:—
With pious minds let us rejoice. C. B. Pearson, in the *Sarum Missal in English*, 1868.   [W. A. S.]

Jucundare plebs fidelis. *Adam of St. Victor?* [*Common of Evangelists.*] A fine sequence founded on Ezek. i. 4–28, x. 9–22, and Rev. iv. 6–8. The "living creatures" are made symbolical of the Evangelists, St. Matthew being represented by the man, St. Luke by the ox, St. Mark by the lion,

and St. John by the eagle. Then under another figure the Evangelists are compared to the four rivers which watered Paradise (by later writers St. Matthew is represented by Gihon, St. Mark by Tigris, St. Luke by Euphrates, and St. John by Pison). The sequence has generally been ascribed to Adam of St. Victor, and is included in L. Gautier's ed. of Adam's *Oeuvres poetiques*, vol. ii., 1858, p. 425; but in his ed. 1881, p. 223, Gautier says that the rhythm is unlike Adam, and as he thinks Adam's authorship is doubtful, he does not print the text, but merely refers to it in a *Gradual* of St. Victor before 1239 (Bibl. Nat., Paris, No. 14448), a Paris *Gradual* of the 13th cent. (B. N., No. 15615), and other sources. F. W. E. Roth, in his *Latei-nische Hymnen des Mittelalters*, 1887, No. 252, gives the readings of a *Gradual* of the end of the 12th cent. (now at Darmstadt), where it is given as a sequence for SS. Mark and Luke. It is in a *York Missal*, cir. 1390, now in the Bodleian, but belonging to University College, Oxford; in an early 14th cent. *Paris Missal* in the British Museum (Add. 16905, f. 298); in the *Magdeburg Missal* of 1480 and others. The printed text is also in *Daniel*, ii. p. 84; *Trench*, ed. 1864, p. 62; *Kehrein*, No. 427; Wrangham's *Liturgical Poetry of Adam of St. Victor*, 1881, vol. iii. p. 162. In the uses of *St. Victor*, of *Cluny*, and of *Paris* it was the sequence for the festival of St. Matthew. The full *trs.* of this hymn are, (1) "Faithful flock in whose pos-sessing," by J. M. Neale, in his *Med. Hys.*, 1851, p. 78; altered in later editions to "Children of a heavenly Father"; and (2) "O be joyful, faithful nation," by D. S. Wrangham, in his *Liturgical Poetry of Adam of St. Victor*, 1881, iii. p. 163. Portions of the hymn are also included in "Come, pure hearts in sweetest measure" (p. 250, ii.). (See also "Sing to God," in Various.)   [J. M.]

Judkin, Thomas James, M.A., s. of a London tradesman, was b. at London, July 25, 1788, and was educated at Caius College, Cam-bridge (B.A. 1815, M.A. 1818), mainly at the expense of Sir William Curtis, an alderman of the City of London. After taking Holy Orders in 1816, he held various curacies, until 1828, when he was preferred as minister of Somers Chapel, St. Pancras, London. He d. Sept. 11, 1871. He pub. *Twelve Signs of the Times; Popish Aggression;* and other works, including a volume of sonnets as *Bygone Moods.* His hymns were published mainly for the use of his own congregation and appeared as:—

(1) *Church and Home Psalmody; being a Collection of Psalms from the Old and New Versions, and Origi-nal Hymns, for Congregational and Domestic Purposes,* 1831. In 1834 this was enlarged and issued as (2) *Church and Home Melodies, being a New Version of the more devotional parts of the Psalms, together with a Version of the Collects, and Original Hymns; for Con-gregational and Domestic purposes.* This was divided into (1) "Spirit of the Psalms." (2) "Collects in Verse." (3) "Hymns on the Gospels," and (4) "Ori-ginal Hymns." (3) The 3rd ed. was pub. in 1837. At the end of the volume two title-pages were supplied, that the book, if so desired, might be divided into two, one as *The Spirit of the Psalter; The Collects in Verse;* to-gether with Hymns suggested by the Gospels for the day throughout the Year ; and the other, *Sacred Melodies; or Original Hymns for Congregational and Domestic Use.*

From the 1st ed. of his *Coll.* the following hymns are in C. U. :—

1. Enthroned is Jesus now. *Ascension.*
2. Holy Spirit, Fount of blessing. *Whitsuntide.*
3. How shall I pray, O Lord, to Thee. *Prayer.*
4. We are journeying to a place. *Heavenward.*
5. When in the dark and cloudy day. *Jesus, all in all.*

[J. J.]

Judson, Adoniram, D.D., b. at Maldon, Massachusetts, Aug. 9, 1788, where his father was Pastor of a Baptist Church. He graduated at Brown University, Providence, Rhode Island, 1807; and went in 1815, together with his first wife, as a Missionary to India. After encountering various hindrances from the East India Company, they began their mission in Burmah. On June 8, 1824, Rangoon having been taken by the British, Dr. Judson was imprisoned by the natives, and was kept in captivity until the Burmese capitulated to the British in 1826. His first wife dying on Oct. 24, 1826, he married the widow of his late colleague, G. D. Boardman (*neé* Hull, see below), April 10, 1834. He d. at sea, April 12, 1850, and was buried in the deep. He translated the Bible into Burmese, and wrote several tracts in that language. A Burmese-English Dictionary was compiled from his papers. His *Memoirs*, by Dr. Wayland, were pub. in 1853. His hymns include :—

1. **Our Father God, [Lord] Who art in heaven.** *The Lord's Prayer.* This hymn is dated "Prison, Ava, March 1825," and was written during his imprisonment above referred to. It was given in his *Memoirs*, 1853, vol. i. p. 308. It is in C. U. in G. Britain and America.

2. **Our Saviour bowed beneath the wave.** *Holy Baptism.* This dates from 1829, or earlier, and is in 7 st. It is said to have been "sung at the Baptism of several soldiers at Moulmein, British Pegu." St. i.-iii. usually form the hymn.

3. **Come, Holy Spirit, Dove divine.** *Holy Baptism.* This is composed of st. vii., v., vi. of No. 2, and is found in Winchell's *Coll.*, 1832.

[F. M. B.]

Judson, Sarah, née Hull, daughter of Ralph Hull, was b. at Alstead, New Haven, Nov. 4, 1803, and married first to the Rev. George D. Boardman, and afterwards to Dr. Judson (see above). She d. at St. Helena, Sept. 1, 1845. Her fine missionary hymn, "Proclaim the lofty praise," is in W. Urwick's *Dublin Coll.*, 1829, No. 142, in 4 st. of 8 l. Its appearance in America prior to this has not been traced.   [F. M. B.]

Jussu tyranni pro fide. *Nicolas le Tourneaux.* [*St. John at the Latin Gate.*] Appeared in the *Cluniac Breviary*, 1686, p. 188, and the *Paris Breviary*, 1736, as the hymn at Lauds for the Feast of St. John, Ante Portam Latinam. It is also in several modern French Breviaries; Card. Newman's *Hymni Ecclesiae*, 1838 and 1865; and J. Chandler's *Hys. of the Primitive Church*, 1837, No. 45. It is *tr.* as :—

1. **John, by a tyrant's stern command.** By I. Williams. Pub. in his *Hys. Tr. from the Parisian Breviary*, 1839, p. 203, in 5 st. of 4 l. It has been repeated in a few hymn-books, including the *English Hymnal*, 1852 and 1861, &c.

2. **An exile for the faith.** By E. Caswall. Pub. in his *Lyra Catholica*, 1849, p. 289, in 6 st. of 4 l., and again in his *Hys. & Poems*, 1873,

p. 195. In addition to its use in its original form in Roman Catholic hymn-books for missions and schools, and others, it is also given in part as follows :—

1. In *H. A. & M.*, 1861 and 1875, and others which have copied therefrom, st. i.-iii. are by E. Caswall, and iv., v. are by the compilers.

2. In the *Parish H. Bk.*, 1863 and 1875, st. i.-iv. are by E. Caswall, with st. iii. re-written, and v., vi. are by G. Phillimore. This was repeated in the S.P.C.K. *Church Hys.*, 1871, and others.

3. In the *Hymnary*, 1872, is the *Parish H. Bk.* text, slightly altered, with the addition of a doxology based on Caswall's *tr.*

3. **For Jesu's sake, to lonely lands.** By F. Pott, based upon *E. Caswall* as above, was given in his *Hymns*, &c., 1861.

Another tr. is :—

Beloved disciple of thy Lord. *J. Chandler*, 1837.

[J. J.]

Just as I am, without one plea. *Charlotte Elliott.* [*The Lamb of God.*] Written for and 1st pub. in the *Invalid's Hymn Book*, 1836, in 6 st. of 4 l., and headed with the text, "Him that cometh unto Me, I will in no wise cast out" (see Index to *Invalid's H. Bk.*). During the same year it also appeared in Miss Elliott's *Hours of Sorrow Cheered and Comforted*, with the additional stanza, "Just as I am, of that tree love," &c. From this last work the hymn has been transferred to almost every hymnal published in English-speaking countries during the past fifty years. It has been translated into almost every European language, and into the languages of many distant lands. The testimony of Miss Elliott's brother (the Rev. H. V. Elliott, editor of *Psalms and Hymns*, 1835) to the great results arising from this one hymn, is very touching. He says :—

"In the course of a long ministry, I hope I have been permitted to see some fruit of my labours; but I feel far more has been done by a single hymn of my sister's."

The text of this hymn is usually given in full, and without alteration, as in *Church Hymns*, 1871, No. 408. It ranks with the finest hymns in the English language. Its success has given rise to many imitations, the best of which is R. S. Cook's "Just as thou art, without one trace." A Latin rendering, "Ut ego sum! nec alia ratione utens," by R. Bingham, is given in his *Hymno. Christ. Lat.*, 1871, and a second by H. M. Macgill, in his *Songs of the Christian Creed and Life*, 1876, as, "Tibi, qualis sum, O Christe!" [J. J.]

Justinian's Hymn. [Greek Hymnody, § x. 10.]

K

"K——," in Dr. Rippon's Bap. *Selection.* [How firm a foundation, &c.]

Kn, in Dr. A. Fletcher's *Collection.* [How firm a foundation, &c.]

Kämpff, Johann, was a native of Staffelstein in Franconia. After studying at the Universities of Wittenberg and Jena, he was appointed in 1604 diaconus at St. Margaret's

Church, and subsequently at the Augustiner-kirche in Gotha. Along with his colleague at the Augustinerkirche, he fell a victim to the pestilence, and d. Oct. 30, 1625 (*Koch*, iii. 114; MS. from Dr. Otto Dreyer, Superintendent at Gotha). The only hymn by him which has passed into English is

Wenn ich in Todesnöthen bin. *For the Dying.* A beautiful prayer of faith, founded on St. John xix. 34. Appeared, with his name, as No. 2 in pt. iii. of the *Cantionale Sacrum*, Gotha, 1648, in 8 st. of 7 l. Included in Freylinghausen's *G. B.*, 1704, and in Porst's *G. B.*, ed. 1855, No. 885. *Tr.* as :—

When in the pains of death my heart. A good *tr.* of st. i., ii., vii., viii. by A. T. Russell, as No. 249 in his *Ps. & Hys.*, 1851.   [J. M.]

Κανών. [Greek Hymnody, § XVI. 11.]

Καταβασία. [Greek Hymnody, § XVI. 6.]

Κατῆλθες ἐν τοῖς κατωτάτοις. [Ἀναστάσεως ἡμέρα.]

Κάθισμα. [Greek Hymnody, § XVI. 3.]

Keach, Benjamin, was b. at Stoke-Hammond, Bucks, Feb. 29, 1640. Early in life he joined a Baptist Church, and at 18 began to preach. For the next 10 years he laboured as an evangelist in the towns and villages of his native county, suffering at times much persecution for his principles as a Baptist and Nonconformist. In 1664, he pub. a small book entitled *The Child's Instructor; or, a New and Easy Primer.* For this he was tried before Lord Chief Justice Hyde, and condemned to a fine, imprisonment and the pillory. In 1668 he removed to London, and became pastor of a Particular Baptist Church which met, first in private houses, and afterwards in Horselydown, Southwark. There a large congregation gathered round him, to which he ministered with great acceptance and usefulness until his death in 1704. Keach deserves special mention for the part he took in introducing singing into Baptist congregations, having been the first who did so. [Baptist Hymnody and English Hymnody, Early, § XII.] He wrote many hymns, the earliest appearing in his *War with the Powers of Darkness*, 4th ed., 1676. Nearly 300 by him were pub. in 1691 as *Spiritual Melody*, their subjects being the Metaphors of Holy Scripture. This subject had been previously expounded by him in his *Tropologia, a Key to open Scripture Metaphors.* 2 vols. folio, 1682. His *Distressed Sion Relieved, or The Garment of Praise for the Spirit of Heaviness*, was pub. in Lond., 1689. It is mainly in blank verse, is dedicated to William and Mary, and is written in praise of Protestantism against Romanism. In 1691 he also pub. *The Breach Repaired in God's Worship; or Singing of Psalms, Hymns & Spiritual Songs proved to be a Holy Ordinance of Jesus Christ*, &c. (London, J. Hancock): and also *Spiritual Melody* the same year. His latest poetical work appeared in 1696: *A Feast of Fat Things: containing several Scripture Songs and Hymns.* Keach was a voluminous writer, forty-two works being pub. by him, in addition to prefaces and introductions to the books of others. His hymns have passed out of C. U.   [W. R. S.]

Keble, John, M.A., was b. at Fairford, in Gloucestershire, on St. Mark's Day, 1792. His father was Vicar of Coln St. Aldwin's, about three miles distant, but lived at Fairford in a house of his own, where he educated entirely his two sons, John and Thomas, up to the time of their entrance at Oxford. In 1806 John Keble won a Scholarship at Corpus Christi College, and in 1810 a Double First Class, a distinction which up to that time had been gained by no one except Sir Robert Peel. In 1811 he was elected a Fellow of Oriel, a very great honour, especially for a boy under 19 years of age; and in 1811 he won the University Prizes both for the English and Latin Essays. It is somewhat remarkable that amid this brilliantly successful career, one competition in which the future poet was unsuccessful was that for English verse, in which he was defeated by Mr. Rolleston. After his election at Oriel, he resided in College, and engaged in private tuition. At the close of 1813 he was appointed Examining Master in the Schools, and was an exceedingly popular and efficient examiner. On Trinity Sunday, 1815, he was ordained Deacon, and in 1816 Priest, by the Bishop of Oxford, and became Curate of East Leach and Burthorpe, though he still continued to reside at Oxford. In 1818 he was appointed College Tutor at Oriel, which office he retained until 1823. On the death of his mother in the same year, he left Oxford, and returned to live with his father and two surviving sisters at Fairford. In addition to East Leach and Burthorpe, he also accepted the Curacy of Southrop, and the two brothers, John and Thomas, undertook the duties between them, at the same time helping their father at Coln. It should be added, as an apology for Keble thus becoming a sort of pluralist among "the inferior clergy," that the population of all his little cures did not exceed 1000, nor the income £100 a year. In 1824 came the only offer of a dignity in the Church, and that a very humble one, which he ever received. The newly-appointed Bishop of Barbadoes (Coleridge) wished Keble to go out with him as Archdeacon, and but for his father's delicate state of health, he would probably have accepted the offer. In 1825 he became Curate of Hursley, on the recommendation of his old pupil, Sir William Heathcote; but in 1826, on the death of his sister, Mary Ann, he returned to Fairford, feeling that he ought not to separate himself from his father and only surviving sister. He supplied his father's place at Coln entirely. 1827 was memorable for the publication of the *Christian Year*, and 1828 for the election to the Provost-ship of Oriel, which his friends, rather than himself, seem to have been anxious to secure for him. In 1829 the living of Hursley was offered to him by Sir William Heathcote, but declined on the ground that he could not leave his father. In 1830 he published his admirable edition of *Hooker's Works.* In 1831 the Bishop of Exeter (Dr. Philpotts) offered him the valuable living of Paignton, but it was declined for the same reason that Hursley had been declined. In the same year he was also elected to the Poetry Professorship at Oxford. His *Prælectiones* in that capacity were much admired. In 1833 he preached his famous

Assize Sermon at Oxford, which is said by Dr. Newman to have given the first start to the Oxford Movement. Very soon after the publication of this sermon the *Tracts for the Times* began to be issued. Of these *Tracts* Keble wrote Nos. 4, 13, 40, and 89. In 1835 his father died, and Keble and his sister retired from Fairford to Coln. In the same year he married Miss Clarke and the Vicarage of Hursley, again becoming vacant, was again offered to him by Sir W Heathcote, and as the reason for his previous refusal of it no longer existed, he accepted the offer, and in 1836 settled at Hursley for the remainder of his life. That life was simply the life of a devoted and indefatigable parish priest, varied by intellectual pursuits. In 1864 his health began to give way, and on March 29, 1866, he passed away, his dearly loved wife only surviving him six weeks. Both are buried, side by side, in Hursley churchyard.

In his country vicarage he was not idle with his pen. In 1839 he published his *Metrical Version of the Psalms.* The year before, he began to edit, in conjunction with Drs. Pusey and Newman, the *Library of the Fathers.* In 1846 he published the *Lyra Innocentium,* and in 1847 a volume of *Academical and Occasional Sermons.* His pen then seems to have rested for nearly ten years, when the agitation about the Divorce Bill called forth from him in 1857 an essay entitled, *An Argument for not proceeding immediately to repeal the Laws which treat the Nuptial Bond as Indissoluble;* and in the same year the decision of Archbishop Sumner in the Denison case elicited another essay, the full title of which is *The Worship of Our Lord and Saviour in the Sacrament of the Holy Communion,* but which is shortly entitled, *Eucharistical Adoration.* In 1863 he published his last work, *The Life of Bishop Wilson* (of Sodor and Man). This cost him more pains than anything he wrote, but it was essentially a labour of love.

In the popular sense of the word "hymn," Keble can scarcely be called a hymn-writer at all. Very many of his verses have found their way into popular collections of Hymns for Public Worship, but these are mostly centos. Often they are violently detached from their context in a way which seriously damages their significance. Two glaring instances of this occur in the Morning and Evening hymns. In the former the verse "Only, O Lord, in Thy dear love, Fit us for perfect rest above," loses half its meaning when the preceding verse, ending "The secret this of rest below," is excised, as it generally is in collections for public worship, and the same may be said of that most familiar of all Keble's lines, "Sun of my soul, thou Saviour dear," which has of course especial reference to the preceding verse, "'Tis gone, that bright and orbed blaze," &c. The *Lyra Innocentium* has furnished but few verses which have been adopted into hymn collections; the *Psalter* has been more fortunate, but the translations from the Latin are almost unknown.

Taking, however, the word "hymn" in the wider sense in which Dr. Johnson defines it, as "a song of adoration to some superior being," Keble stands in the very first rank of hymn-writers. His uneventful life was the very ideal life for such a poet as Keble was, but not the sort of life which would be best adapted to train a popular hymn-writer. *The Christian Year* and the *Lyra Innocentium* reflect in a remarkable degree the surroundings of the writer. They are essentially the works of a refined and cultured mind, and require a refined and cultured mind to enter into their

spirit. Keble, all his life long, and never more than in the earlier portion of it, before he wrote, and when he was writing *The Christian Year,* breathed an atmosphere of culture and refinement. He had imbibed neither the good nor the evil which the training of a public, or even of a private, school brings. It was not even the ordinary home education which he had received. He had been trained, up to the very time of his going to college, by his father, who was clearly a man of culture and refinement, and had been himself successively Scholar and Fellow of Corpus. When he went to Oxford, he can scarcely be said to have entered into the whirl of university life. The Corpus of those days has been admirably described by Keble's own biographer, Sir John Coleridge, and by Dean Stanley in his *Life of Dr Arnold*; and the impression which the two vivid pictures leave upon the mind is that of a home circle, on rather a large scale, composed of about twenty youths, all more or less scholarly and refined, and some of them clearly destined to become men of mark. When he removed across the road to Oriel, he found himself in the midst of a still more distinguished band. Whether at home or at college he had never come into contact with anything rude or coarse. And his poetry is just what one would expect from such a career. Exquisitely delicate and refined thoughts, expressed in the most delicate and refined language, are characteristic of it all. Even the occasional roughnesses of versification may not be altogether unconnected with the absence of a public school education, when public schools laid excessive stress upon the form of composition, especially in verse. *The Christian Year* again bears traces of the life which the writer led, in a clerical atmosphere, just at the eve of a great Church Revival, "cujus pars magna fuit." "You know," he writes to a friend, "the *C. Y.* (as far as I remember it) everywhere supposes the Church to be in a state of decay." Still more obviously is this the case in regard to the *Lyra Innocentium.* It was being composed during the time when the writer was stricken by what he always seems to have regarded as the great sorrow of his life. Not the death of his nearest relations—and he had several trials of this kind—not the greatest of his own personal troubles dealt to him so severe a blow as the secession of J. H. Newman to the Church of Rome. The whole circumstances of the fierce controversy connected with the *Tract* movement troubled and unsettled him; and one can well understand with what a sense of relief he turned to write, not *for,* but *about,* little children, a most important distinction, which has too often been unnoticed. If the *Lyra* had been written *for* children it would have been an almost ludicrous failure, for the obscurity which has been frequently complained of in *The Christian Year,* is still more conspicuous in the latter work. The title is somewhat misleading, and has caused it to be regarded as a suitable gift-book for the young, who are quite incapable of appreciating it. For the *Lyra* is written in a deeper tone, and expresses the more matured convictions of the author; and though it is a far less successful achievement as a whole, it rises in places to a higher strain of poetry than *The Christian Year* does.

Another marked feature of Keble's poetry is to a great extent traceable to his early life, viz. the wonderful accuracy and vividness of his descriptions of natural scenery. The ordinary school-boy or undergraduate cares little for natural scenery. The country is to him a mere playing-field. But Keble's training led him to love the country for its own sake. Hence, as Dean Stanley remarks, "Oxford, Bagley Wood, and the neighbourhood of Hursley might be traced through hundreds of lines, both in *The Christian Year* and the *Lyra Innocentium.*" The same writer testifies, with an authority which no other Englishman could claim, to "the exactness of the descriptions of Palestine, which he [Keble] had never visited." And may not this remarkable fact be also traced to some extent to his early training? Brought up under the immediate supervision of a pious father, whom he venerated and loved dearly, he had been encouraged to study intelligently his Bible in a way in which a boy differently educated was not likely to do. Hence, as Sir John Coleridge remarks,

"*The Christian Year* is so wonderfully scriptural. Keble's mind was, by long, patient and affectionate study of Scripture, so imbued with it that its language, its train of thought, its mode of reasoning, seems to flow out into his poetry, almost, one should think, unconsciously to himself."

To this may we not add that the same intimate knowledge of the Bible had rendered the memory of the Holy Land so familiar to him that he was able to describe it as accurately as if he had seen it? One other early influence of Keble's life upon his poetry must be noticed. Circumstances brought him into contact with the "Lake poets." The near relation of one of the greatest of them had been his college friend, and John Coleridge introduced him to the writings not only of his uncle, S. T. Coleridge, but also of Wordsworth, to whom he dedicated his *Prælectiones*, and whose poetry and personal character he admired enthusiastically. To the same college friend he was indebted for an introduction to Southey, whom he found to be "a noble and delightful character," and there is no doubt that the writings of these three great men, but especially Wordsworth, had very much to do with the formation of Keble's own mind as a poet. It has been remarked that in Keble's later life his poetical genius seemed to have, to a great extent, forsaken him; and that the *Miscellaneous Poems* do not show many traces of the spirit which animated *The Christian Year* and the *Lyra Innocentium.* Perhaps one reason for this change may be found in the increased interest which Keble took in public questions which were not conducive to the calm, introspective state of mind so necessary to the production of good poetry. The poet should live in a world of his own, not in a world perpetually wrangling about University Reform, about Courts of Final Appeal, about Marriage with Deceased Wife's Sister, and other like matters into which Keble, in his later years, threw himself—heart and soul.

It is not needful to say much about Keble's other poetical works. *The Psalter* was not a

success, and Keble did not expect it to be. "It was undertaken," he tells us, "in the first instance with a serious apprehension, which has since grown into a full conviction, that the thing attempted is, strictly speaking, *impossible.*" At the same time, if Keble did not achieve what he owned to be impossible, he produced a version which has the rare merit of never offending against good taste; one which in every line reflects the mind of the cultured and elegant scholar, who had been used to the work of translating from other languages into English. Hymnal compilers have hitherto strangely neglected this volume; but it is a volume worth the attention of the hymn-compiler of the future. There is scarcely a verse in it which would do discredit to any hymn-book; while there are parts which would be an acquisition to any collection. His translations from the Latin have not commended themselves to hymnal compilers. Some of his detached hymns have been more popular. But it is after all as writer of *The Christian Year* that Keble has established his claim to be reckoned among the immortals. It would be hardly too much to say that what the Prayer Book is in prose, *The Christian Year* is in poetry. They never pall upon one; they realise Keble's own exquisite simile:—

"As for some dear familiar strain
Untired we ask, and ask again;
Ever in its melodious store
Finding a spell unheard before."

And it would hardly be too bold to prophesy that *The Christian Year* will live as long as the Prayer Book, whose spirit Keble had so thoroughly imbibed, and whose "soothing influence" it was his especial object to illustrate and commend.   [J. H. O.]

Keble's hymns, poetical pieces, and translations appeared in the following works:—

(1.) *The Christian Year: Thoughts in Verse for the Sundays and Holydays Throughout the Year. Oxford: John Henry Parker*, 1827. Preface dated "May 30th, 1827." The last poem, that on the "Commination," is dated March 9, 1827. The poems on the "Forms of Prayer to be used at Sea," "Gunpowder Treason," "King Charles the Martyr," "The Restoration of the Royal Family," "The Accession," and "Ordination," were added to the 4th edition, 1828. The Messrs. Parker have pub. a large number of editions to date, including a *fac-simile* reprint of the first edition, and an edition with the addition of the dates of composition of each poem. A *fac-simile* of Keble's MS. as it existed in 1822 was also lithographed in 1882, by Eliot Stock, but its publication was suppressed by a legal injunction, and only a few copies came into the hands of the public. Since the expiration of the first copyright other publishers have issued the work in various forms.

(2.) Contributions to the *British Magazine*, which were included in *Lyra Apostolica*, 1836, with the signature of "γ."

(3.) *The Psalter or Psalms of David; In English Verse; By a Member of the University of Oxford. Adapted for the most part, to Tunes in Common Use; and dedicated by permission to the Lord Bishop of Oxford. . . . Oxford, John Henry Parker: J. G. & F. Rivington, London, MDCCCXXXIX.* Preface dated "Oxford, May 29, 1839."

(4.) *The Child's Christian Year: Hymns for every Sunday and Holy-Day. Compiled for the use of Parochial Schools. Oxford: John Henry Parker*, 1841. This was compiled by Mrs. Yonge. Keble wrote the Preface, dated "Hursley, Nov. 6, 1841," and signed it "J. K." To it he contributed the four poems noted below.

(5.) *Lyra Innocentium: Thoughts in Verse on Christian Children, their Ways and their Privileges . . . Oxford: John Henry Parker: F. & J. Rivington, London*, 1846. The Metrical Address (in place of Preface) "To all Friendly Readers," is dated "Feb. 8, 1846."

(6.) *Lays of the Sanctuary, and other Poems. Com-*

*piled and Edited by G. Stevenson de M. Rutherford...
London: Hamilton, Adams & Co.*, 1859. This was a
volume of poems published on behalf of Mrs. Elizabeth
Good. To it Keble contributed the three pieces noted
below.

(7.) *The Salisbury Hymn-Book*, 1857. Edited by Earl
Nelson. To this he contributed a few hymns, some
translations from the Latin, and some rewritten forms
of well-known hymns, as "Guide me, O Thou great
Jehovah," &c.

(8.) *Miscellaneous Poems by the Rev. J. Keble, M.A.,
Vicar of Hursley. Oxford and London: Parker & Co.*,
1869. The excellent Preface to this posthumous work is
dated "Chester, Feb. 22, 1869," and is signed "G. M.,"
i.e. by George Moberly, late Bp. of Salisbury. This
volume contains Keble's Ode written for the Installation
of the Duke of Wellington as Chancellor of the University of Oxford, in 1834, his poems from the *Lyra
Apostolica*, his hymns named above, his translations from
the Latin, and other pieces not published in his works.

The most important centos from *The Christian Year*, which are in C. U. as hymns, and
also the hymns contributed to the *Salisbury
H. Bk.*, 1857, are annotated in full under the
first lines of the original poems. The *trs.* from
the Latin and Greek are given under the
first lines of the originals. There are also
several of his more important pieces noted in
the body of this work. All these may be
found through the *Index of Authors and
Trs.* at the end of this *Dictionary*. Those that
remain (mainly centos) and have no special
history, are the following (the dates given being
those of the composition of each piece);—

i. From *The Christian Year*, 1827 and 1828.

1. Creator, Saviour, strengthening Guide. *Trinity
Sunday,* (March 3, 1826.)
2. Father, what treasures of sweet thought. *Church-
ing of Women.* (March 13, 1827.)
3. God is not in the earthquake: but behold. *9th S.
after Trinity. The still small voice.* (Aug. 13, 1822.)
4. In troublous days of anguish and rebuke. *9th S.
after Trinity. The still small voice.* (Aug. 13, 1822.)
5. Lessons sweet of spring returning. *1st S. after
Epiphany. Spring.* (May 17, 1824.)
6. My Saviour, can it ever be? *4th S. after Easter.
The promised Comforter.*
7. O Father of long suffering grace. *18th S. after
Trinity. God's longsuffering.* (Oct. 6, 1823.)
8. O God of mercy, God of might, How should, &c.
H. Communion. (Jan. 31, 1827.)
9. O Lord my God, do Thou Thy holy will. *Wednesday before Easter. Resignation.* (Aug. 13, 1821.)
10. O say not, dream [think] not, heavenly notes.
Catechism. (Feb. 16, 1827.)
11. O shame upon thee, listless heart. *SS. Philip &
James.* (Aug. 3, 1825.)
12. O who shall dare in this frail scene? *St. Mark's
Day.* (1820.)
13. Red o'er the forest peers the setting sun. *23rd
S. after Trinity. The Resurrection of the body.* (Nov.
12, 1825.)
14. Spirit of Christ, Thine earnest give. *Ordination.*
(March 28, 1828.)
15. Spirit of light and truth, to Thee. *Ordination.*
(March 28, 1828.)
16. Spirit of might and sweetness too. *Confirmation.*
(Feb. 21, 1827.)
17. Sweet nurslings of the vernal skies. *15th S. after
Trinity. Consider the lilies. Live for to-day.* (Feb.
3, 1826.)
18. The days of hope and prayer are past. *4th S. after
Easter. The promised Comforter.*
19. The live-long night we've toiled in vain. *5th S.
after Trinity. Miracle of the Fishes.* (1821.)
20. The midday sun with fiercest glare. *Conversion of
St. Paul.* (Mar. 2, 1822.)
21. The shadow of the Almighty's cloud. *Confirmation.* (Feb. 22, 1827.)
22. The silent joy that sinks so deep. *2nd S. after
Epiphany. Turning Water into Wine.*
23. Then, fainting soul, arise and sing. *4th S. after
Easter. The promised Comforter.*
24. When brothers part for manhood's race. *St.
Andrew's Day.* (Jan. 27, 1822.)
25. Who is God's chosen priest? *St. Matthias's Day.*
26. Why doth my Saviour weep? *10th S. after
Trinity. Christ weeping over Jerusalem.* (1819.)

27. Why should we faint and fear to live alone? *24th
S. after Trinity. God's goodness in veiling the future.*
(June 7, 1825.)
28. Wish not, dear friends, my pain away. *16th S.
after Trinity. Resignation.* (1824.)

ii. From *The Psalter*, 1839.

29. From deeps so wild and drear. *Ps. cxxx.*
30. God our Hope and Strength abiding. *Ps. xlvi.*
31. How pleasant, Lord of hosts, how dear. *Ps.
lxxxiv.*
32. Lord, be my Judge, for I have trod. *Ps. xxvi.*
33. Lord, Thy heart in love hath yearned. *Ps. lxxxv.*
34. Lord, Thou hast search'd me out and known. *Ps.
cxxxix.*
35. My God, my God, why hast Thou me? *Ps. xxii.*
36. My Shepherd is the living God. *Ps. xxiii.*
37. My Shepherd is the Lord; I know. *Ps. xxiii.*
38. Praise the Lord, for He is love. *Ps. cxxxvi.*
39. Praise ye the Lord from heaven. *Ps. cxlviii.*
40. Sing the song unheard before. *Ps. xcvi.*
41. Sound high Jehovah's Name. *Ps. cxxxv.*
42. The earth is all the Lord's, with all. *Ps. xxiv.*
43. The mercies of the Lord my God. *Ps. lxxxix.*
44. The seed of Jacob, one and all. *Ps. xxii.*

iii. From *The Child's Christian Year*, 1841, and later editions.

45. Bethlehem, above all cities blest. *Innocents' Day,*
46. Lo, from the Eastern hills the Lord. *10th S. after
Trinity. The Gospel.* (Late editions.)
47. Our God in glory sits on high. *1st S. after
Easter. The Epistle.*
48. When Christ to village comes or town. *16th S.
after Trinity. The Gospel.* (Late editions.)

iv. From *Lyra Innocentium*, 1846.

49. Christ before thy door is waiting. *Presence of
Christ in His poor; or Offertory.*
50. How [When] the new-born saints, assembling.
Offertory.
51. Once in His Name Who made thee. *Holy Baptism.*
52. Who for the like of me will care? *Naamans'
Servant-maid.*

v. From *Lays of the Sanctuary*, 1859.

53. Lord, lift my heart to Thee at morn. *Emigrant's
Midnight Hymn.*
54. O Love unseen, we know Thee nigh. Cento from
No. 53.
55. Slowly the gleaming stars retire. *Morning Hymn
for Emigrants at Sea.*
56. The twilight hour is sweet at home. *Evening
hymn for Emigrants at Sea.*

The editor of Keble's *Miscellaneous Poems*
says concerning Nos. 53, 55, and 56:—

"The three hymns for Emigrants, for use at Midnight, Morning, and Evening, were written at the request of his friend Sir Frederic Rogers, at that time
Emigration Commissioner. They were printed in the
first edition of the 'Prayers for Emigrants,' which he
had compiled, but were subsequently omitted, perhaps
as being thought not sufficiently simple for the class of
people for whose use the Book of Prayers was chiefly
intended." Preface, p. vi.

When, to the 56 centos and hymns given
above, are added those annotated elsewhere in
this Dictionary, it is found that nearly 100
hymns (counting centos as such) by Keble are
in C. U. at the present time, and of these some
rank with the finest and most popular in the
English language.   [J. J.]

Keimann, Christian, s. of Zacharias
Keimann, Lutheran pastor at Pankratz, in
Bohemia, and after 1616 at Ober-Ullersdorf,
was b. at Pankratz, Feb. 27, 1607. In the
autumn of 1627 he entered the University of
Wittenberg, where he graduated M.A., March
19, 1634; and in the next month was appointed by the Town Council of Zittau as
Conrector of their Gymnasium, of which
he became Rector in 1638. He d. at Zittau,
Jan. 13, 1662 (*Koch*, iii. 369; *Allg. Deutsche
Biog.*, xv. 535, &c.). Keimann was a distinguished teacher. He was the author of a

number of scholastic publications, of a few Scriptural plays, and of some 13 hymns. Almost all of his hymns came into church use. They take high rank among those of the 17th cent., being of genuine poetic ring, fresh, strong, full of faith under manifold and heavy trials, and deeply spiritual. Two have passed into English :—

i. **Freuet euch, ihr Christen alle.** *Christmas.* This beautiful hymn is included in 4 st. of 10 l. as No. 24 in pt. iv. of A. Hammerschmidt's *Musikalische Andachten*, pub. at Freiberg in Saxony, 1646 ; and is set to a tune by Hammerschmidt introduced by Hallelujah repeated twelve times. In the *Unv. L. S.*, 1851, No. 34. According to *Koch*, viii. 25, it was composed as part of a piece written by Keimann for his scholars to perform at Christmastide, 1645, and pub. as *Der neugeborne Jesus*, at Görlitz, 1646. Stanza iv. may refer to the truce of 1645 between Saxony and Sweden. *Tr.* as :—

O rejoice, ye Christians, loudly. A good and full *tr.* by Miss Winkworth, as No. 33 in her *C. B. for England*, 1863, where it is set to the original melody.

ii. **Meinen Jesum lass ich nicht ; Weil er sich für mich gegeben.** *Love to Christ.* 1st appeared in A. Hammerschmidt's *Fest- Bus- und Dancklieder*, Zittau and Leipzig, 1658 (engraved title, 1659), pt. iii., No. 4, in 6 st. of 6 l. It is an acrostic on the dying words uttered on Oct. 8, 1656, by the Elector Johann Georg I. of Saxony : Meinen (i.), Jesum (ii.), lass (iii.) ich (iv.) nicht (v.) ; st. vi. giving in the initial letters of lines 1–5 (J. G. C. Z. S.) the name, viz. Johann Georg Churfürst zu Sachsen, and then in line 6 the motto in full. Founded on the words of Jacob in Gen. xxxii. 26, it has comforted and strengthened many in life and at the hour of death ; and has served as the model of many later hymns. Included as No. 737 in the Berlin *G. L. S.*, ed. 1863. *Tr.* as :—

I will leave my Jesus never ! A good *tr.*, omitting st. iii., included as No. 448 in the Pennsylvania Luth. *Ch. Bk.*, 1868, marked as Unknown *tr.*, 1864.

Other *trs.* are :—(1) " Never will I part with Christ," by *J. C. Jacobi*, 1722, p. 80 (1732, p. 132), and thence in the *Moravian H. Bk.*, 1754 (1886 as pt. of No. 452 altered, and beginning, " Jesus will I never leave "). (2) " I will not let Jesus go," by J. S. Stallybrass in the *Tonic Solfa Reporter*, Dec. 1860. (3) " Jesus will I ne'er forsake," by *E. Massie*, 1867, p. 117. (4) " My Redeemer quit I not," by *N. L. Frothingham*, 1870, p. 185.   [J. M.]

Keinen hat Gott verlassen. [*Trust in God.*] *Wackernagel*, v. p. 275, gives this hymn from the *Geistliche Lieder*, Erfurt, 1611, and the *Christliches Gesangbüchlein*, Hamburg, 1612, in 8 st. of 8 l. Also in *Mützell*, 1855, No. 590, and the Berlin *G. L. S.*, ed. 1863, No. 847. In the 1612 it is entitled " A hymn on the name of the serene right honourable princess and lady, Lady Katharina, by birth and marriage Margravine and Electress of Brandenburg." As she d. Sept. 30, 1602, the hymn probably dates from the 16th cent. The initials of the 8 st. form the name *Katarina*. The common ascription to Andreas Kessler, who was only b. in 1595, is baseless. *Tr.* as :—

(1) "Haste, Lord, within my worthless heart." A *tr.* of st. vi. by C. Kinchen, as No. 33 in the *Moravian H. Bk.*, 1742. In 1789 and later eds. (1886, No. 444, ascribed without ground to Catharine Grossmann) it begins " O Lord, accept my worthless heart." (2) " Amen, this the conclusion," a *tr.* of st. viii., as No. 603, in the *Moravian H. Bk.*, 1801 (1886, No. 719).   [J. M.]

Keith, George. [How firm a foundation.]

Kelly, John, was b. at Newcastle-on-Tyne, educated at Glasgow University, studied theology at Bonn, New College, Edinburgh, and the Theological College of the English Presbyterian Church (to which body he belongs) in London. He has ministered to congregations at Hebburn-on-Tyne and Streatham, and is now (1887) Tract Editor of the Religious Tract Society. His translations of

Paul Gerhardt's *Spiritual Songs* were pub. in 1867. Every piece is given in full, and rendered in the metre of the originals. His *Hymns of the Present Century from the German* were pub. in 1886 by the R. T. S. In these *trs.* the metres of the originals have not always been followed, whilst some of the hymns have been abridged and others condensed. His translations lack poetic finish, but are faithful to the originals.   [W. G. H.]

Kelly, Thomas, B.A., s. of Thomas Kelly, a Judge of the Irish Court of Common Pleas, was b. in Dublin, July 13, 1769, and educated at Trinity College, Dublin. He was designed for the Bar, and entered the Temple, London, with that intention ; but having undergone a very marked spiritual change he took Holy Orders in 1792. His earnest evangelical preaching in Dublin led Archbishop Fowler to inhibit him and his companion preacher, Rowland Hill, from preaching in the city. For some time he preached in two unconsecrated buildings in Dublin, Plunket Street, and the Bethesda, and then, having seceded from the Established Church, he erected places of worship at Athy, Portarlington, Wexford, &c., in which he conducted divine worship and preached. He d. May 14, 1854. Miller, in his *Singers & Songs of the Church*, 1869, p. 338 (from which some of the foregoing details are taken), says :—

" Mr. Kelly was a man of great and varied learning, skilled in the Oriental tongues, and an excellent Bible critic. He was possessed also of musical talent, and composed and published a work that was received with favour, consisting of music adapted to every form of metre in his hymn-book. Naturally of an amiable disposition and thorough in his Christian piety, Mr. Kelly became the friend of good men, and the advocate of every worthy, benevolent, and religious cause. He was admired alike for his zeal and his humility ; and his liberality found ample scope in Ireland, especially during the year of famine."

Kelly's hymns, 765 in all, were composed and published over a period of 51 years, as follows :—

(1) *A Collection of Psalms and Hymns extracted from Various Authors, by Thomas Kelly, A.B., Dublin*, 1802. This work contains 247 hymns by various authors, and an Appendix of 33 original hymns by Kelly.

(2) *Hymns on Various Passages of Scripture, Dublin*, 1804. Of this work several editions were published : 1st, 1804 ; 2nd, 1806 ; 3rd, 1809 ; 4th, 1812. This last edition was published in two divisions, one as *Hymns on Various Passages of Scripture*, and the second as *Hymns adapted for Social Worship*. In 1815 Kelly issued *Hymns by Thomas Kelly, not before Published*. The 5th ed., 1820, included the two divisions of 1812, and the new hymns of 1815, as one work. To the later editions of 1820, 1826, 1836, 1840, 1846, and 1853, new hymns were added, until the last published by M. Moses, of Dublin, 1853, contained the total of 765.

As a hymn-writer Kelly was most successful. As a rule his strength appears in hymns of Praise and in metres not generally adopted by the older hymn-writers. His " Come, see the place where Jesus lay " (from " He's gone, see where His body lay "), " From Egypt lately come " ; " Look, ye saints, the sight is glorious " ; " On the mountain's top appearing " ; " The Head that once was crowned with thorns " ; " Through the day Thy love has spared us " ; and " We sing the praise of Him Who died," rank with the first hymns in the English language. Several of his hymns of great merit still remain unknown through so many modern editors being apparently adverse to original investigation. In addition to the hymns named and others, which are annotated under their respective first lines, the following are also in C. U. :—

i. From the *Psalms and Hymns*, 1802 :—

1. Grant us, Lord, Thy gracious presence. *Commencement of Divine Worship.*
2. Jesus, Immortal King, go on [display]. *Missions.*
3. Saviour, through the desert lead us. *Divine Guidance Desired.*
4. The day of rest once more [again] comes round. *Sunday.*
5. We've no abiding city here. *Seeking Heaven.*

ii. From the *Hymns on V. Passages of Scripture*, 1st ed., 1804 :—

6. Boundless glory, Lord, be thine. *Praise for the Gospel.*
7. By whom shall Jacob now arise? *Epiphany.*
8. Glory, glory to our King. *Praise to Christ as King.*
9. How pleasant is the sound of praise. *Praise for Redemption.*
10. How sweet to leave the world awhile. *In Retirement,* or *For a Retreat.*
11. In form I long had bowed the knee. *Jesus, the Saviour,* or *Praise for Salvation.*
12. It is finished! sinners, hear it. *Good Friday.*
13. Jesus, the Shepherd of the sheep. *The Good Shepherd.*
14. Let reason vainly boast her power. *Death.*
15. Poor and afflicted, Lord, are Thine. *Affliction.*
16. Praise we Him to Whose kind favour. *Close of Service.*
17. Spared a little longer. *Safety in God.*
18. Stricken, smitten, and afflicted. *Passiontide.*

iii. From the *Hymns, &c.*, 2nd ed., 1806 :—

19. Far from us be grief and sadness. *Joy of Believers.*
20. Give us room that we may dwell. *Missions.*
21. Glory, glory everlasting. *Praise of Jesus.*
22. God has turned my grief to gladness. *Joy after Sorrow.*
23. Happy they who trust in Jesus. *Peace in Jesus.*
24. Hark, the notes of angels singing. *Angels praising Jesus.*
25. Hark! 'tis a martial sound. *Christian Life a Warfare.*
26. I hear a sound [voice] that comes from far. *The Gospel Message.*
27. Jesus is gone up on high. *Divine Worship.*
28. Now [O] may the Gospel's conquering power. *Home Missions.* In the 1853 ed. of the *Hymns* it begins " O may the Gospel's conqu'ring force."
29. O Zion, when I think on thee. *Desiring Heaven.*
30. Praise the Saviour, ye who know Him. *Praise of Jesus.*
31. See from Zion's sacred mountain. *The Fountain of Life.*
32. The atoning work is done. *Jesus the High Priest.*
33. Zion is Jehovah's dwelling. *The Church of God.*
34. Zion stands by hills surrounded. *The Safety of the Church.*
35. Zion's King shall reign victorious. *Missions.*

iv. From the *Hymns, &c.*, 3rd ed., 1809 :—

36. Behold the Temple of the Lord. *The Church a Spiritual Temple.*
37. Blessed Fountain, full of grace. *Fountain for Sin.*
38. Brethren, come, our Saviour bids us. *Holy Communion.*
39. Fly, ye seasons, fly still faster. *Second Advent Desired.*
40. God of Israel, we adore Thee. *Evening.*
41. Gracious Lord, my heart is fixed. *Trust and Peace.*
42. Hark, a voice! it comes from heaven. *Death.*
43. Hark, that shout of rapt'rous joy. *Second Advent.*
44. If our warfare be laborious. *Labour and Rest.*
45. Lo, He comes, let all adore Him. *Missions.*
46. Nothing know we of the season. *Time of Second Advent uncertain.*
47. O had I the wings of a dove. *Holiness and Heaven desired.*
48. O where is now that glowing love. *Despondency.*
49. Our Father sits on yonder throne. *God the Father.*
50. Ours is a rich and royal Feast. *H. Communion.*
51. Shepherd of the chosen number. *Safety in the Good Shepherd.*
52. We're bound for yonder land. *Life, a Voyage.*
53. Welcome sight ! the Lord descending. *The Second Advent.*

54. What is life ? 'tis but a vapour. *Death anticipated.*
55. Who is this that comes from Edom ? *Ascension.*
56. Why those fears? Behold 'tis Jesus. *Stilling the Sea.*
57. Without blood is no remission. *Passiontide.*
58. Yes, we trust the day is breaking. *Missions.*

v. From *Hymns: Not before Published*, 1815 :—

59. Behold the Lamb with glory crowned. *Exaltation of Christ.*
60. God is love, His word has said it. *God is Love.*
61. God of our salvation, hear us. *Opening or Close of Divine Worship.*
62. In Thy Name, O Lord, assembling. *Commencement of Divine Worship.*
63. Keep us, Lord, O [and] keep us ever. *Divine Worship.*
64. Let sinners saved give thanks, and sing. *Praise for Salvation.*
65. Praise the Lord Who died to save us. *Passiontide.*
66. Salvation is of God alone. *God the Author of Salvation.*
67. Saviour, come, Thy [saints] friends await Thee [are waiting]. *Second Advent desired.*
68. Sweet were the sounds that reached our ears. *Divine Mercy.*
69. We'll sing of the Shepherd that died. *The Lost Sheep.*
70. When we cannot see our way. *Trust and Peace.*
71. Who is this that calms the ocean? *Stilling the Sea.*

vi. From the *Hymns on V. Passages of Scripture, &c.*, eds. 1820 and 1826 :—

72. Grace is the sweetest sound. *Divine Grace.*
73. Now let a great effectual door. *Missions,*
74. Now may the mighty arm awake. *Missions.*
75. Now may the Spirit from above. *Home Missions.*
76. Sing, sing His lofty praise. *Praise of Jesus.*
77. Sound, sound the truth abroad. *Missions.*
78. Speed Thy servants, Saviour, speed them. *Departure of Missionaries.*

vii. From the *Hymns on V. Passages, &c.*, 1836 :—

79. Come, O Lord, the heavens rending. *Prayer for Blessings.*
80. The night is far spent, the day is at hand. *The Second Advent.*

viii. From the *Hymns on V. Passages, &c.*, circa 1845 :—

81. Joyful be the hours to-day. *Sunday.*
82. Lord, behold us few and weak. *Opening of Divine Service.*
83. Meet Thy people, Saviour, meet us. *Meetings for Prayer.*
84. Saviour, send a blessing to us. *Prayer for Blessings.*
85. Sing of Jesus, sing for ever. *Praise of Jesus.*

ix. From the *Hymns on V. Passages, &c.*, 1853 :—

86. Precious volume, what thou doest. *H. Scripture.*
87. Unfold to us, O Lord, unfold. *Divine aid to reading H. Scripture.*

All these hymns, together with those annotated under their respective first lines are in the 1853 ed. of Kelly's *Hymns* pub. in Dublin by M. Moses, and in London by Simpkin, Marshall & Co. Kelly's musical editions are issued by the same publishers.   [J. J.]

Kempenfelt, Richard, of Swedish descent, was b. Oct., 1718. In Jan., 1741, he obtained a lieutenant's commission in the British Navy. He became captain in 1757, and admiral in 1780. He was drowned in the " Royal George," which sank in harbour at Portsmouth on Aug. 29, 1782. Admiral Kempenfelt was an admirer of Whitefield and the Wesleys, and interested himself much in evangelistic work. His hymns were pub. as *Original Hymns and Poems. By Philotheorus.* Exeter, printed by B. Thorn, 1777, and were dedicated " To the Rev. Mr. Fletcher, Vicar of

Madeley, in Shropshire." They were reprinted, with a Preface, by D. Sedgwick, in 1861. Although most of these hymns are given in the older collections, only a few remain in modern hymn-books, and, including centos, are :—

1. Bear me on Thy rapid wing. *Praise to Jesus in Heaven.*
2. Burst, ye emerald gates, and bring. *Praise to Jesus in Heaven.*
3. Gentle Spirit, waft me over. *Heaven desired.*
4. Hail, Thou eternal Logos, hail. *Adoration of Jesus.*
5. Hark, 'tis the trump of God. *The Last Day.*
6. O my Redeemer, come. *The Last Day.*

Of these Nos. 1 and 2 are from the same hymn; and Nos. 5 and 6 also from another. The original texts of Nos. 3, 5, and 6 are in *Lyra Brit.*, 1867, pp. 349–52.   [J. J.]

Kempff, Johann. [Kämpff, J.]

Kempis, Thomas à. [Thomas of Kempen.]

Kempthorne, John, B.D., s. of Admiral Kempthorne, was b. at Plymouth, June 24, 1775, and educated at St. John's, Cambridge (B.A. 1796, B.D. 1807), of which he subsequently became a Fellow. On taking Holy Orders, he became Vicar of Northleach, Gloucestershire, in 1816; Vicar of Wedmore, Somersetshire, 1827, and the same year Rector of St. Michael's and Chaplain of St. Mary de Grace, Gloucester. He was also a Prebendary in Lichfield Cathedral from 1826, and sometime Examining Chaplain to the Bishop of that diocese. He d. at Gloucester, Nov. 6, 1838. His hymnological work is :—

Select Portions of Psalms from Various Translations, and Hymns, from Various Authors. The whole Arranged according to the yearly Seasons of the Church of England, with attempts at corrections and improvements. By the Rev. John Kempthorne, B.D. . . . . London. Hatchard. 1810.

In this collection there are a few hymns of merit, as " Forgive, O Lord, our wanderings past," " Great God, to Thee our songs we raise," and " Praise the Lord, ye heavens adore Him," which are usually ascribed, on D. Sedgwick's authority, to J. Kempthorne. These hymns, however, are not by Kempthorne, but were taken by him for his collection from the Foundling Hospital *Ps. & Hys.*, 1796 and 1801–9; and there is no evidence whatever that he had anything to do with that hymn-book. As that book is frequently quoted by hymnologists, we append the title-page of the 1801 ed., which is a reprint of that of 1797 :—

Psalms, Hymns, and Anthems ; sung in the Chapel of the Hospital for the Maintenance and Education of Exposed and Deserted Young Children. London, Printed in the Year M.DCCC.I. At the end of some copies of this edition there is pasted in a four-paged sheet of hymns which include, with others, " Praise the Lord, ye heavens adore Him " (q.v.).

In the 1st ed. of his own *Select Portions of Psalms*, &c., 1810, Kempthorne did not in any way indicate his own hymns, but in the 2nd ed. of 1813 (which is a reprint of the 1st ed. with an *Appendix* of 11 hymns) he says in his Preface :—

" For Hymn 140 and Hymn, p. 267. *Appendix ;* for almost all of Ps. 42, p. 197 ; Ps. 51, p. 57 and 61 ; Ps. 84, p. 195 ; Ps. 86, p. 134 ; Ps. 115, p. 49 ; Hymn 127 ; and for a considerable part of Ps. 22, p. 64 ; Ps. 122, p. 103 ; Ps. 133, p. 141 ; Ps. 139, p. 38 ; Hymns 20, 43, 54, 81, 97, 101, 118, and several others, the Editor is responsible, and acknowledges his obligations to some kind friends."

Of these hymns and psalm versions, which Kempthorne claims as his own, only one or two are in C. U.   [J. J.]

Ken, Thomas, D.D. The bare details of Bp. Ken's life, when summarised, produce these results :—Born at Berkhampstead, July, 1637; Scholar of Winchester, 1651; Fellow of New College, Oxford, 1657; B.A., 1661; Rector of Little Easton, 1663 ; Fellow of Winchester, 1666; Rector of Brighstone, 1667; Rector of Woodhay and Prebendary of Winchester, 1669 ; Chaplain to the Princess Mary at the Hague, 1679 ; returns to Winchester, 1680 ; Bp. of Bath and Wells, 1685; imprisoned in the Tower, 1688; deprived, 1691 ; died at Longleat, March 19, 17$\frac{1}{10}$.

The parents of Ken both died during his childhood, and he grew up under the guardianship of Izaak Walton, who had married Ken's elder sister, Ann. The dominant Presbyterianism of Winchester and Oxford did not shake the firm attachment to the English Church, which such a home had instilled. His life until the renewal of his connection with Winchester, through his fellowship, his chaplaincy to Morley (Walton's staunch friend, then bishop of Winchester), and his prebend in the Cathedral, calls for no special remark here. But this second association with Winchester, there seems little doubt, originated his three well-known hymns. In 1674 he published *A Manual of Prayers for the Use of the Scholars of Winchester College*, and reference is made in this book to three hymns, for " Morning," " Midnight," and " Evening," the scholars being recommended to use them. It can scarcely be questioned that the Morning, Evening, and Midnight hymns, pub. in the 1695 edition of *The Manual*, are the ones referred to. He used to sing these hymns to the viol or spinet, but the tunes he used are unknown. He left Winchester for a short time to be chaplain to the Princess Mary at the Hague, but was dismissed for his faithful remonstrance against a case of immorality at the Court, and returned to Winchester. A similar act of faithfulness at Winchester singularly enough won him his bishopric. He stoutly refused Nell Gwynne the use of his house, when Charles II. came to Winchester, and the easy king, either from humour or respect for his honesty, gave him not long afterwards the bishopric of Bath and Wells. Among the many acts of piety and munificence that characterised his tenure of the see, his ministration to the prisoners and sufferers after the battle of Sedgmoor and the Bloody Assize are conspicuous. He interceded for them with the king, and retrenched his own state to assist them. He attended Monmouth on the scaffold. James II. pronounced him the most eloquent preacher among the Protestants of his time; the judgment of Charles II. appears from his pithy saying that he would go and hear Ken " tell him of his faults." Among the faithful words of the bishops at Charles's death-bed, none were so noble in their faithfulness as his. He was one of the Seven Bishops who refused to read the Declaration of Indulgence, and were imprisoned in the Tower by James for their refusal, but triumphantly acquitted on their trial. At the accession of William III. he refused, after some doubt on the subject, to take the oaths, and was at length (1691) deprived of his see. His charities had left him at this time only seven hundred pounds, and his library, as a means of subsistence; but he received hospitality for his remaining years with his friend Lord Weymouth, at Longleat. The see of Bath and Wells was again offered him, but in vain, at the death of his successor, Bp. Kidder. He survived all the deprived prelates. His attitude as a nonjuror was remarkable for its conciliatory spirit. The saintliness of Ken's character, its combination of boldness, gentleness, modesty and love, has been universally recognised. The verdict of Macaulay is that it approached "as near as human infirmity permits to the ideal perfection of Christian virtue." The principal work of Ken's that remains is that on the Catechism, entitled *The Practice of Divine Love.* His poetical works were published after his death, in 4 vols. Among the contents are, the *Hymns for the Festivals,* which are said to have suggested to Keble the idea of *The Christian Year;* the *Anodynes* against the acute physical sufferings of his closing years; and the *Preparatives for Death.* Although many passages in them are full of tender devotion, they cannot rank either in style or strength with the three great hymns written at Winchester. (See **English Hymnody, Early, § x.**) The best biograpies of Ken are *The Life of Ken by a Layman,* and, specially, his *Life,* by the Very Rev. E. H. Plumptre, Dean of Wells, 1888.

[H. L. B.]

Bishop Ken is known to hymnody as the author of the *Morning, Evening,* and *Midnight Hymns,* the first and second of which at least have found a place in almost every English collection for the last 150 years. The general history of these hymns, as we now know it, is as follows:—

1. In 1674 Ken pub. his Manual of Prayers for Winchester Scholars as

A Manual of Prayers For the Use of the Scholars of Winchester College [here arms of William of Wykeham within a border]. *London, Printed for John Martyn,* 1674, 12mo, pp. 69.

From a passage in this work it may fairly be inferred that the author had already composed hymns for the use of the scholars. He says:—

"Be sure to sing the Morning and Evening Hymn in your chamber devoutly, remembering that the Psalmist, upon happy experience, assures you that it is a good thing to tell of the loving kindness of the Lord early in the morning and of his truth in the night season."

Two hymns only seem to be here referred to, but the expression "night season" may include both the *Evening* and *Midnight* hymns, and the latter would be only used occasionally. The hymns are not given in the *Manual* of 1674, or succeeding editions, until that of 1695, when the three hymns are added as an *Appendix.* The title of this edition is:—

A Manual of Prayers For the Use of the Scholars of Winchester College. And all other Devout Christians. To which is added three Hymns for Morning, Evening, and Midnight; not in former Editions: By the Same Author. Newly Revised. London, Printed for Charles Brome at the Gvn, at the West end of St. Paul's Church, **1695.**

2. In 1704 Richard Smith, a London pub-

lisher, issued a book similar in appearance to the *Manual,* and entitled *A Conference between the Soul and Body concerning the Present and Future State.* This edition contained a strong recommendation by Dodwell, an intimate friend of Ken, but no hymns. To the 2nd ed., however (1705), were added two (*Morning* and *Evening*) hymns, with Ken's name appended, but containing two additional verses to the *Evening* hymn, and differing in several other respects from the text of the *Manual.* Thereupon Charles Brome, to whom the copyright of the latter belonged, issued a new edition with an *Advertisement* stating that Ken "absolutely disowned" the hymns appended to the *Conference,* "as being very false and uncorrect," and that the genuine text was that given in the *Manual* only. Brome's *Advertisement* reads:—

"Advertisement—Whereas at the end of a Book lately Publish'd call'd, 'A Conference between the Soul and Body,' there are some Hymns said to be writ by Bishop Ken, who absolutely disowns them, as being very false and uncorrect; but the Genuine ones are to be had only of Charles Brome, Bookseller, whose just Propriety the Original copy is."

3. In 1709, however, the spurious hymns were again pub. as Ken's in a book entitled

A New Year's Gift: in Two Parts: to which is added A Morning and Evening Hymn. By Thomas, late L. B. of Bath and Wells. The Third Edition with additions. London Printed by W. Onley. 1709.

Brome met this, as before, with a new edition of the *Manual,* in which the *Advertisement* of 1705 as above was repeated, but the text of the hymns considerably revised. This revised text was followed in all subsequent editions of the *Manual,* but as, until lately, it was thought to have appeared first in the edition of 1712, published soon after Ken's death, its genuineness was suspected by many. The question as it then stood was fully discussed in an able letter by Sir Roundell Palmer (Lord Selborne), prefixed to the reprint of Ken's *Hymns,* pub. by D. Sedgwick in 1864. Since that time the discovery in the Bodleian Library of a copy of the *Manual* of 1709 shows that the revision was made in that year, and confirms the conclusion at which Lord Selborne had previously arrived, that it was Ken's genuine revised text. The title of this edition is:—

A Manual of Prayers For the Use of the Scholars of Winchester College, And all other Devout Christians, To which is added three Hymns for Morning, Evening, and Midnight; By the same Author. Newly Revised. London: Printed for Charles Brome at the Gun, the West end of St. Paul's Church, 1709.

The *Advertisement* before referred to is at p. 130. The alterations of 1709 may therefore be accepted as being made by Ken himself, and it seems not improbable that the revision was suggested by the recent republication of the spurious text in spite of Brome's disclaimer in 1705, and possibly by adverse criticism of the original text. Lord Selborne pointed out in his *Letter* that Ken altered a passage in his *Practice of Divine Love* (1st ed., 1685) because "some Roman Catholic writer professed to discover the doctrine of Transubstantiation" therein. This alteration was made in the 2nd ed., 1686, and explained in the Preface to have been made "to prevent all misunderstanding for the future." A passage also in the *Manual*—"Help me, then, ye blessed Hosts of Heaven, to celebrate that unknown sorrow, &c." — was claimed in a Roman Catholic pamphlet as a passage which "taught the scholars of Winchester to invocate the whole Court of Heaven." This passage Ken altered " to prevent all future misinterpretations," and prefixed an *Advertisement* to the 1687 ed. of the *Manual* explaining why he had done so. In looking through the texts of the three hymns for 1695, and 1709, and especially at the doxologies, and at st. x. and xi. in the *Evening Hymn*, " You my Blest Guardian, whilst I sleep," &c. (1695); and " O may my Guardian while I sleep," &c. (1709), do we not see a good and sufficient reason to account for the revision of the hymns ?

4. With regard to the text given in the *Conference*, Lord Selborne observes that it is not improbable that alterations and various readings, originating with Ken himself, might have obtained private circulation among his friends, long before he had made up his own mind to give them to the public ; a suggestion which may possibly help to explain the fact, that a writer, patronised by Dodwell, was misled into believing (for such a writer ought not lightly to be accused of a wilful fraud) that the text, pub. in the *Conference* in Ken's name was really from his hand. That Ken occasionally altered passages in his writings when for any reason he considered it necessary, is certain ; and there can be little doubt that the text of the three Winchester hymns was more or less unsettled before 1695. At any rate, before their first appearance in that year in the *Manual* the *Evening* hymn had found its way into print. It was pub. in

" *Harmonia Sacra; or Divine Hymns and Dialogues . . . Composed by the Best Masters . . . The Words by several Learned and Pious Persons. The Second Book,*" London, Henry Playford, 1693.

The first volume of this work appeared in 1688, and was dedicated to Ken. It is not improbable therefore that Playford, when collecting materials for his second volume, obtained the words of the *Evening Hymn* directly from the author. The text is here subjoined :—

" AN EVENING HYMN.
" The words by Bishop Ken.
" Set by Mr. Jeremiah Clarke.

" All praise to Thee my God this night
For all the blessings of the light ;
Keep me, oh keep me, King of kings,
Under Thy own Almighty Wings.

" Forgive me, Lord, for Thy dear Son,
The ill that I this day have done,
That with the world, myself and Thee,
I, ere I sleep, at peace may be.

" Teach me to live, that I may dread
The Grave as little as my bed ;
Teach me to die, so that I may
Triumphing rise at the last day.

" Oh may my Soul on Thee repose,
And with sweet sleep mine eyelids close,
Sleep that may me more vig'rous make,
To praise my God when I awake.

" When in the night I sleepless lie,
My soul with heav'nly thoughts supply ;
Let no ill dreams disturb my rest,
No pow'rs of darkness me molest.

" My dearest Lord, how am I griev'd
To lye so long of Thee bereav'd !
Dull sleep of sence me to deprive,
I am but half my days alive.

" But though sleep o'er my weakness reigns,
Let it not hold me long in chains,
But now and then let loose my heart,
Till it an Hallelujah dart ;

" The faster sleep the sence does bind,
The more unfetter'd is the mind ;
Oh may my soul from matter free
The unveil'd Goodness waking see.

" Oh ! when shall I in endless day,
For ever chase dark sleep away,
And endless praise with th' heavenly choir,
Incessant sing and never tire ;

" You my best Guardians, whilst I sleep,
Close to my bed your vigils keep,
And in my stead all the night long
Sing to my God a grateful song.

" Praise God from whom all blessings flow,
Praise Him all creatures here below ;
Praise Him above, the angelick host,
Praise Father, Son, and Holy Ghost."

In comparing this text with that of 1695, the following differences are found :—

1693.	1695.
St. i., l. 1, All praise	*Glory.*
St. iii., l. 3, so that	*that so.*
St. iv., l. 4, praise	*serve.*
St. vi., ll. 1 and 2	rewritten.
„ ll. 3 and 4	transposed as 1 and 2.
St. vii., l. 1, weakness	*frailty.*
„ l. 3, But now	*And now.*
St. viii., l. 4, The	*Thy.*
St. x., l. 1, best Guardians	*blest Guardian.*

Stanza x. was also expanded in 1695 into two by the addition of new 3rd and 4th lines to st. x., and the construction of st. xi. out of two new lines followed by lines 3 and 4 of 1693.

The hymn was set by Clarke as a Cantata for a solo voice, with the Doxology as a chorus in four parts.

5. We now submit the texts of the *Morning, Evening,* and *Midnight* hymns, as they appear in the 1695 and the 1709 editions of the *Manual* respectively :—

Awake my soul and with the sun. [*Morning.*] The texts of 1695 and 1709 are subjoined in parallel columns for the purpose of comparison, the variations of 1709 being printed in italics.

1695.	1709.
" *A Morning Hymn.*	" *A Morning Hymn.*
" Awake my Soul, and with the Sun,	" Awake, my Soul, and with the Sun,
Thy daily stage of Duty run ;	Thy daily Stage of duty run ;
Shake off dull Sloth, and early rise,	Shake off dull Sloath, and *joyful* rise,
To pay Thy morning Sacrifice.	To pay thy Morning Sacrifice.
" Redeem thy mis-spent time that's past,	" *Thy precious time mis-pent, redeem,*
Live this day, as if 'twere thy last :	*Each present day thy last Esteem,*
T' improve thy Talent take due care,	Improve thy Talent *with* due Care,
'Gainst the great Day thy self prepare.	*For* the Great Day thy self prepare.
" As all thy Converse be sincere,	" *In Conversation* be sincere,
Thy Conscience as the Noon-day clear ;	*Keep* Conscience as the Noon-*tide* clear.
Think how All-seeing God thy ways,	Think how All-seeing God thy ways,
And all thy secret Thoughts surveys.	And all thy Secret Thoughts surveys.
" Influenc'd by the Light divine,	" *By influence of* the Light Divine,
Let thy own Light in good Works shine :	Let thy own Light *to others* Shine,
Reflect all Heaven's propitious ways,	Reflect all Heaven's propitious *Rays,*
In ardent love and chearful praise.	In ardent Love, and chearful Praise.
" Wake, and lift up thy self, my Heart,	" Wake, and lift up thy self, my Heart,
And with the Angels bear thy part,	And with the Angels bear thy part,
Who all night long unwearied sing,	Who all Night long unwearied Sing,
Glory to the Eternal King.	*High Praise* to the Eternal King.

"I wake, I wake, ye heavenly Choire,
May your Devotion me inspire,
That I like you my Age may spend,
Like you may on my God attend.

"May I like you in God delight,
Have all day long my God in sight,
Perform like you my Maker's Will,
O may I never more do ill.

"Had I your Wings, to Heaven I'd fly,
But God shall that defect supply,
And my Soul wing'd with warm desire,
Shall all day long to Heav'n aspire.

"Glory to Thee who safe hast kept,
And hast refresh't me whilst I slept.
Grant Lord, when I from death shall wake,
I may of endless Light partake.

"I would not wake, not rise again,
Ev'n Heav'n it self I would disdain ;
Wer't not Thou there to be enjoy'd,
And I in Hymns to be employ'd.

"Heav'n is, dear Lord, where e'er Thou art,
O never then from me depart ;
For to my Soul 'tis Hell to be,
But for one moment without Thee.

"Lord I my vows to Thee renew,
Scatter my Sins as Morning dew,
Guard my first springs of thought, and will,
And with thy self my Spirit fill.

"Direct, controul, suggest this day,
All I design, or do, or say ;
That all my Powers, with all their might,
In thy sole Glory may unite.

"Praise God, from whom all Blessings flow,
Praise him all creatures here below,
Praise Him above y' Angelick Host.
Praise Father, Son, and Holy Ghost."

"I wake, I wake, ye Heavenly Choir,
May your Devotion me inspire,
That I like you my Age may spend,
Like you may on my God attend.

"May I like you in God delight,
Have all day long my God in sight,
Perform like you my Maker's Will,
O may I never more do ill.

"Had I your Wings to Heaven I'd fly,
But God shall that Defect supply,
And my Soul wing'd with warm desire,
Shall all Day long to Heaven aspire.

"All Praise to Thee, who safe hast kept,
And hast refresh'd me whilst I slept.
Grant, Lord, when I from Death shall wake,
I may of endless Light partake.

"I would not wake, nor rise again,
And Heaven itself I would disdain,
Were't not Thou there to be enjoy'd,
And I in Hymns to be employ'd.

"Heav'n is, Dear Lord, where e'er thou art,
O never then from me depart :
For to my Soul, 'tis Hell to be,
But for one Moment void of Thee.

"Lord, I my Vows to Thee renew,
Disperse my Sins as Morning Dew,
Guard my first Springs of Thought and Will,
And with thy self my Spirit fill.

"Direct, controul, Suggest this Day,
All I design, or do, or say,
That all my Powers with all their Might,
In thy sole Glory may Unite.

"Praise God from whom all Blessings flow,
Praise him all Creatures here below,
Praise Him above, ye Heavenly Host.
Praise Father, Son, and Holy Ghost."

Among the alterations made in 1709, the word *joyful* instead of *early* in st. i. occurs in the *Conference* of 1705, thus seeming to confirm the suggestion of Lord Selborne, referred to above, that some at least of the readings in the *Conference* may have originated with Ken himself. The change in the order of two words in st. x., *Thou not* for *not Thou*, made in 1712, is also anticipated by the *Conference*. In st. vi. l. 1 of the hymn, some later editions of the *Manual* issued by C. Brome after 1712 give "Awake, awake," for "I wake, I wake." Lord Selborne inclines to the belief that the latter reading is possibly due to the printers,

but as it is found not only in every edition up to 1712, including the revision of 1709, but in the *Conference* of 1705, this seems improbable. Lord Selborne adds, "'I wake' in the sense of bodily waking from natural sleep, would be out of place, after five whole stanzas had been already spoken or sung," but is it not rather a response to the exhortation with which the 1st and 5th stanzas commence? After addressing in them his own Soul, the singer suddenly exclaims, "I wake," and then turns to the "Heavenly Choir" with an expression of hope to be enabled to follow their example of unceasing adoration of the Most High. If this be so, it is far more likely that the reading "Awake" is due to some later editor or printer who failed to catch the author's full meaning. The various *Morning Hymns* by Ken which have appeared in the *Appendix* to Tate and Brady's Version of the Psalms, and in most hymnals published during the past 150 years are compilations from this hymn, with, in many instances, slight alterations of the text either of 1695 or of that of 1709. In some modern hymnals the difficulty of the length of the hymn is overcome by dividing it into two or more parts.

All praise [Glory] to Thee, my God, this night. [*Evening.*] The texts of 1695 and of 1709 are as follows :—

1695. "An Evening Hymn.	1709. "An Evening Hymn.
"Glory to thee my God, this night, For all the Blessings of the Light ; Keep me, O keep me King of Kings, Under Thy own Almighty Wings.	"All Praise to Thee my God this Night, For all the Blessings of the Light,* Keep me, O keep me King of Kings, Beneath thy own Almighty Wings.
"Forgive me, Lord, for thy dear Son, The ill that I this day have done, That with the world, my self, and Thee, I, e're I sleep, at peace may be.	"Forgive me, Lord, for thy dear Son, The ill that I this Day have done ; That with the World, my self, and Thee, I, e're I sleep, at Peace may be.
"Teach me to live, that I may dread The Grave as little as my Bed ; Teach me to die, that so I may Triumphing rise at the last day.	"Teach me to live, that I may dread The Grave as little as my Bed ; To dye, that this vile Body may Rise Glorious at the awful day.
"O may my Soul on thee repose, And with sweet sleep mine Eye-lids close ; Sleep that may me more vig'rous make, To serve my God when I awake.	"O ! may my Soul on Thee repose, And with sweet Sleep mine Eye-lids close ; Sleep, that may me more Vig'rous make, To serve my God when I awake.
"When in the night I sleepless lye, My Soul with Heavenly thoughts supply, Let no ill dreams disturb my rest, No powers of darkness me molest.	"When in the Night I sleepless lie, My Soul with Heavenly Thoughts supply ; Let no ill dreams disturb my Rest, No Powers of darkness me molest.
"Dull sleep of sense me to deprive, I am but half my days alive ; Thy faithful lovers, Lord, are griev'd To lye so long of Thee bereav'd.	"Dull Sleep of Sense me to deprive, I am but half my time alive, Thy faithful Lovers, Lord, are griev'd, To lye so long of Thee bereav'd.

* In the original misprinted "Night."

"But though sleep o'r my
  frailty reigns,
Let it not hold me long
  in chains ;
And now and then let
  loose my heart,
Till it an Halleluiah
  dart.

"But tho' Sleep o'er my
  frailty Reigns,
Let it not hold me long
  in Chains ;
And now and then let
  lose my Heart,
Till it an Hallelujah
  dart.

"The faster sleep the sense
  does bind,
The more unfetter'd is
  the mind ;
O may my Soul from
  matter free,
Thy unvail'd Goodness
  waking see !

"The faster Sleep the
  Senses binds,
The more unfetter'd are
  our Minds,
O may my Soul from
  matter free,
Thy *loveliness uncloud-
  ed* see !

"O when shall I in endless
  day,
For ever chase dark sleep
  away,
And endless praise with
  th' Heavenly Choire,
Incessant sing, and never
  tire ?

"O when shall I in endless
  Day,
For ever chase dark Sleep
  away,
And *Hymns with the Su-
  pernal* Choir,
Incessant Sing, and never
  seat !

"You my Blest Guardian,
  whilst I sleep,
Close to my Bed your
  Vigills keep,
Divine Love into me in-
  still,
Stop all the avenues of
  Ill.

"*O may my* Guardian
  while I sleep,
Close to my Bed *his* Vi-
  gils keep,
His Love Angelical instill,
Stop all the Avenues of
  Ill.

"Thought to thought with
  my Soul converse,
Celestial joys to me re-
  hearse,
And in my stead all the
  night long,
Sing to my God a grate-
  ful Song.

"*May he Cœlestial Joys re-
  hearse,
And thought to thought
  with me converse,
Or in my stead all the
  Night long,
Sing to my God a Grate-
  ful Song.*

"Praise God from whom
  all blessings flow,
Praise him all Creatures
  here below,
Praise him above y' An-
  gelick Host,
Praise Father, Son, and
  Holy Ghost."

"Praise God from whom
  all Blessings flow,
Praise him all Creatures
  here below,
Praise him above *ye
  Heavenly* Host,
Praise Father, Son, and
  Holy Ghost."

You, ever wakeful near
  the Throne,
Prostrate, adore the
  Three in One.

*You Joyful Hymn the
  ever Bless'd,
Before the Throne and
  never rest.*

"I now awake do with you
  joyn,
To praise our God in
  Hymns divine :
With you in Heav'n I
  hope to dwell.
And bid the night and
  world farewell.

"*I with your Choir Cœles-
  tial joyn,
In offering up a Hymn
  Divine*
With you in Heaven I
  hope to dwell,
And bid the Night and
  World farewell ;

"My Soul when I shake
  off this dust,
Lord, in thy Arms I will
  entrust ;
O make me thy peculiar
  care,
Some heav'nly Mansion
  me prepare.

"My Soul, when I shake
  off the Dust,
Lord, in thy Arms I will
  intrust.
O make me Thy peculiar
  Care,
Some *Mansion for my
  Soul* prepare.

"Give me a place at thy
  Saints feet,
Or some fall'n Angel's
  vacant seat ;
I'll strive to sing as loud
  as they,
Who sit above in brighter
  day.

"Give me a place at thy
  Saints' Feet,
Or some fallen Angel's
  vacant Seat ;
I'll strive to sing as loud
  as they,
Who sit above in brighter
  Day.

"O may I always ready
  stand,
With my Lamp burning
  in my hand,
May I in sight of Heav'n
  rejoyce,
When e're I hear the
  Bridegroom's voice.

"O may I always ready
  stand,
With my Lamp burning
  in my Hand,
May I in sight of Heav'n
  Rejoyce,
When e'er I hear the
  Bridegroom's Voice.

"Glory to Thee in light
  array'd,
Who light thy dwelling
  place hast made,
An immense Ocean of
  bright beams,
From thy All-glorious
  Godhead streams.

"*All Praise* to thee in
  light array'd,
Who light thy dwelling
  place hast made.
A *boundless* Ocean of
  bright Beams,
From thy All-glorious
  God-head Streams.

"The Sun, in its Meridian
  height,
Is very darkness in thy
  sight :
My Soul, O lighten, and
  enflame,
With Thought and Love
  of thy great Name.

"The Sun in its Meridian
  height,
Is very darkness in Thy
  sight !
My Soul, O lighten and
  inflame,
With Thought and Love
  of thy Great Name.

"Blest Jesu, Thou on
  Heav'n intent,
Whole nights hast in
  Devotion spent,
But I, frail Creature,
  soon am tir'd,
And all my Zeal is soon
  expir'd.

"Bless'd Jesu, Thou on
  Heav'n intent,
Whole Nights hast in
  Devotion spent,
But I, frail Creature,
  soon am tir'd,
And all my Zeal is soon
  expir'd.

"My Soul, how canst Thou
  weary grow,
Of Antedating Heav'n
  below,
In sacred Hymns, and
  Divine Love,
Which will eternal be
  above ?

"My Soul how canst thou
  weary grow,
Of antedating *Bliss* be-
  low ;
In Sacred Hymns, and
  Heav'nly Love,
Which will Eternal be
  above.

"Shine on me Lord, new
  life impart,
Fresh ardours kindle in
  my heart ;
One ray of thy All-
  quickening light
Dispels the sloth and
  clouds of night.

"Shine on me, Lord, new
  Life impart,
Fresh Ardours kindle in
  my Heart ;
One Ray of thy All-
  quick'ning Light,
Dispells the sloth and
  clouds of Night.

"Lord, lest the tempter
  me surprize,
Watch over thine own
  Sacrifice,
All loose, all idle
  thoughts cast out,
And make my very
  dreams devout.

"Lord, lest the Tempter
  me surprize,
Watch over thine own
  Sacrifice ;
All loose, all idle
  thoughts cast out,
And make my very
  dreams devout.

"Praise God from whom
  all blessings flow,
Praise him all Creatures
  here below,

"Praise God, from whom
  all Blessings flow,
Praise him all Creatures
  here below ;

8. A reference to the text given in *Harmonia Sacra* shows that the change from "Glory" to "All praise" in l. 1. is only a restoration of the original reading ; and without being aware of this fact, Lord Selborne points out that the expression "All praise" is remarkably consistent with Ken's frequent use of it in other writings. The same alteration was made in 1709 in the *Morning Hymn*, st. 9, and in the *Midnight Hymn*, st. 7 ; while at the same time "Glory" in the *Morning Hymn*, st. v. l. 4, is changed to "High Praise."

As in the case of "Awake my soul," this hymn has been divided, subdivided, and rearranged in a great many ways during the last 150 years. In one form or another it will be found in most hymnals pub. during that period.

My God, now I from Sleep awake. [*Midnight.*]
The texts of 1695 and 1709 are subjoined :—

1695.

1709.

" *A Midnight Hymn.*

" *A Midnight Hymn.*

"Lord, now my Sleep does
  me forsake,
The sole possession of
  me take,
Let no vain fancy me
  illude,
No one impure desire
  intrude.

" *My God now I from sleep
  awake,*
The sole Possession of
  me take,
*From Midnight Terrors
  me secure,
And guard my Heart
  from Thoughts impure.*

"Blest Angels ! while we
  silent lye,
You Halleluiahs sing on
  high,

"Bless'd Angels ! while
  we silent lye,
You Hallelujahs Sing on
  high,

Praise him above y' An-   Praise him above ye
gelick Host,   Heavenly Host,
Praise Father, Son, and   Praise Father, Son, and
Holy Ghost."   Holy Ghost."

Like the *Morning* and *Evening Hymns*, this hymn has been divided and rearranged in various ways, and is found in one form or another in most hymnals published during the last 150 years.

6. The various centos from these hymns which are in C. U. in English-speaking countries are :—

i. From the *Morning Hymn.*

1. All praise to Thee Who safe hast kept.
2. Awake, my soul, and with the sun.
3. Glory to Thee Who safe hast kept.
4. I wake, I wake, ye heavenly choirs.
5. I would not wake nor rise again.
6. Wake, and lift up thyself, my heart.

ii. From the *Evening Hymn.*

1. All praise to Thee, my God, this night.
2. Glory to Thee, my God, this night.

iii. From the *Midnight Hymn.*

1. All praise to Thee in light array'd.
2. Glory to Thee in light array'd.
3. Lord, now my sleep doth me forsake.
4. My God, now [when] I from sleep awake.

The following list of editions of the *Manual* from 1674 to 1712 inclusive, and the libraries in which they are to be found, was kindly supplied by the late Mr. G. W. Napier :—

1674, B M (*British Museum*); 1675, *B. M.* and *Bodleian*; 1677, *B. M.*; 1679, *Bod.*; 1681, *B. M.*; 1681, *B. M.* (the first pub. with Bishop Ken's name); 1692, *B. M.* and *G. W. Napier*; 1695, *Bod.* (the first ed. containing the three hymns); 1697, *B. M.*; 1700, *B. M.*; 1703, *Nap.*; 1705, *Nap.*; 1709, *Bod.* and *Nap.*; 1712, *Nap.*

7. Bp. Ken has not escaped the not unusual charge of plagiarism, in connection with his celebrated hymns. Charges of this kind have been made from time to time, the nature and value of which we will endeavour to summarize. These are: (1) he borrowed from *Sir Thomas Browne;* (2) he did the same from *Thomas Flatman;* (3) he did neither, but *Paraphrased from the Latin.*

(1) *Sir Thomas Browne.* In 1643 Sir Thomas Browne pub. his *Religio Medici* (it was pub. surreptitiously in 1642), and therein (Pt. ii. § 12) gave the following hymn in a monologue on *Sleep* :—

"It is that death which Adam died before his mortality ; a death whereby we live a middle and moderating point between life and death. In fine, so like death, I dare not trust it without my prayers, and an half adieu unto the world, and take my farewell in a colloquy with God :—

" The night is come, like to the day
Depart not thou, great God, away.
Let not my sins, black as the night,
Eclipse the lustre of thy light.
Keep still in my horizon ; for to me
The sun makes not the day, but Thee.
Thou Whose nature cannot sleep,
On my temples sentry keep ;
Guard me 'gainst those watchful foes,
Whose eyes are open while mine close.
Let no dreams my head infest,
But such as Jacob's temples blest,
While I do rest, my soul advance :
Make my sleep a holy trance :
That I may, my rest being wrought,
Awake into some holy thought
And with as active vigour run
My course as doth the nimble sun.
Sleep is a death ;—O make me try
By sleeping, what it is to die !
And as gently lay my head
On my grave, as now my bed.
Howe'er I rest, great God, let me
Awake again at last with Thee.
And thus assur'd, behold I lie
Securely, or to wake or die.

These are my drowsy days ; in vain
I do not wake to sleep again :
O come that hour, when I shall never
Sleep again, but wake for ever !

"This is the dormitive I take to bedward ; I need no other *laudanum* than this to make me sleep ; after which I close mine eyes in security, content to take my leave of the sun and sleep unto the resurrection."

The poet James Montgomery drew attention to the striking similarity of thought and mode of expression between this hymn and the Evening Hymn by Ken, in his *Select Christian Authors*, 1827. This has also been done several times in *Notes and Queries*, during the past twenty years, and not always in the best spirit. That the similarity pointed out by Montgomery does exist is very clear : but to say that Ken deliberately *stole* Browne's work no one with any acquaintance with poets and profound thinkers would venture to affirm. Possibly *sect.* 3 below may do something towards solving the difficulty.

(2) *Thomas Flatman.* In his *Poems and Songs*, small 8vo, 1674, he has the following

"HYMN FOR THE MORNING.

" Awake my soul, awake mine eyes !
Awake my drowsy faculties !
Awake and see the newborn light
Spring from the darksome womb of night !
Look up and see the unwearied sun
Already has his race begun :
The pretty lark is mounted high,
And sings her matins in the sky.
Arise my soul ! and thou, my voice,
In songs of praise early rejoice.
O great Creator ! Heavenly King !
Thy praises let me ever sing !
Thy power has made, thy goodness kept
This fenceless body while I slept.
Yet one day more hast given me
From all the powers of darkness free ;
O keep my heart from sin secure,
My life unblameable and pure,
That when the last of all my days is come,
Cheerful and fearless I may wait my doom."

In *Notes and Queries*, 3rd S., x. 205, Mr. W. T. Brooke suggests that this is the origin of Ken's *Morning Hymn.* It is impossible to say that Ken never saw Flatman's hymn, but certainly if he had he made very little direct use of it. The subject is the same, and a few expressions are almost identical ; but the mode of treatment and the burden of the thought are essentially different. Such similarity as does exist in the two hymns suggests two men looking at and writing about the same thing in the same pious and thankful spirit, rather than one man copying from another.

(3) *Paraphrases from the Latin.* A writer in *Notes and Queries*, 3rd S., xii. 327, says :—" *Bishop Ken's Hymns.*—These are certainly not *original* compositions. They are paraphrases, and very beautiful ones, of three noble hymns in the *Roman Breviary.* " Awake, my soul," is "A solis ortus" ; "Glory to Thee " is "Te lucis ante terminum." The Midnight Hymn has a similar origin, but I forget the Latin. S. J." This idea of a Latin origin of the hymns is also set forth by Dr. Greenhill in his edition of Browne's *Religio Medici*, 1881, p. 289 : "Compare this [Browne's hymn] with the beautiful and well-known *Evening Hymn* of Bishop Ken ; and these again with several of the *Hymni Ecclesiae* [Card. Newman's 1838 and 1865], especially that beginning 'Salvator mundi, Domine,' with which Ken and Browne, both Wykehamists, must have been familiar." To our mind this suggestion is nearer the truth than any other ; but even from this point of view it is too much to call the three hymns *paraphrases.* The most that can be said of them is that the Latin hymns referred to may, and possibly did, suggest them, but only as a text of Holy Scripture suggests a sermon.

8. The title of Bp. Ken's hymns on the Festivals of the Church, published posthumously in 1721, is : *Hys. for all the Festivals of the Year.* They were republished by Pickering as : *Bishop Ken's Christian Year or Hymns and Poems for the Holy Days and Festivals of the Church*, Lond., 1868. From this work the following centos have come into C. U. :—

1. All human succours now are flown. *Visitation of the Sick.*
2. I had one only thing to do. *A New Creature.*
3. O purify my soul from stain. 10*th S. after Trinity*, or *A Prayer for Purity.*

4. O Lord, when near the appointed hour. *Holy Communion.*

5. Unction the Christian name implies. *Confirmation.*

See NEW APPENDIX.   [G. A. C.]

Kennedy, Benjamin Hall, D.D., s. of the Rev. Rann Kennedy, sometime Incumbent of St. Paul's, Birmingham, and editor of *A Church of England Psalm-Book,* &c., 1821 (12th ed. 1848), was b. at Summer Hill, near Birmingham, Nov. 6, 1804, and educated at King Edward's School, Birmingham; Shrewsbury School; and St. John's College, Cambridge. He graduated B.A. in 1827 (First Class Classical Tripos and First Chancellor's Medallist). He was Fellow of his College 1828–36; Head Master of Shrewsbury School, 1836–66; and Regius Professor of Greek in the University of Cambridge and Canon of Ely, 1867. Dr. Kennedy took Holy Orders in 1829, and was for some time Prebendary in Lichfield Cathedral and Rector of West Felton, Salop. He was elected Hon. Fellow of St. John's College, Cambridge, in 1880. Besides his *Public School Latin Grammar, Palaestra Latina, Palaestra Stili Latini,* &c., his editions of some of the Classics, and *University Sermons,* Dr. Kennedy pub. the following :—

(1) *The Psalter, or the Psalms of David, in English Verse. By a Member of the University of Cambridge,* 1860; (2) *Hymnologia Christiana, or Psalms & Hymns Selected and Arranged in the Order of the Christian Seasons* (quoted in this *Dictionary* as *Kennedy*), 1863.

i. From these two works many psalms and hymns have passed into other collections. The following versions of the Psalms first appeared in *The Psalter,* 1860, and again in the *Hymno. Christ.,* 1863. In many instances they have undergone considerable alteration in the latter work, and those of great length are broken into parts :—

1. All ye people, come and clap, &c. *Ps. xlvii.*
2. Arise, O Lord, with healing rod. *Ps. x.*
3. As pants the hind for cooling streams. *Ps. xlii.*
4. As Thy mercy lasts for ever. *Ps. cix.*
5. Be merciful to me, O God. *Ps. lvii.*
6. Be Thou my Judge, and I will strive. *Ps. xxvi.*
7. Bless ye the Lord, His solemn praise record. *Ps. cxxxiv.*
8. Bow down Thine ear, and hear my cry. *Ps. lxxxvi.*
9. Come, ye children, list to me. *Ps. xxxiv.*
10. Ever, O my God and King. *Ps. cxlv.*
11. Ever will I bless the Lord. *Ps. xxxiv.*
12. Every king shall bow before Him. *Ps. lxxii.*
13. Full oft my chafing thoughts, &c. *Ps. lxxiii.*
14. God, avert the deadly blow. *Ps. lix.*
15. God, in Judah's homes is known. *Ps. lxxvi.*
16. God of my righteousness. *Ps. iv.*
17. Hear Thou my prayer, O Lord. *Ps. cxliii.*
18. Help us, O Lord, the good decay. *Ps. xii.*
19. How blest are they who flee, &c. *Ps. cxix.*
20. How blest the man, who fears to stray. *Ps. i.*
21. How blest the man whose errors, &c. *Ps. xxxii.*
22. How good it is to praise the Lord. *Ps. xcii.*
23. How long art silent, Lord? how long. *Ps. xxxv.*
24. How long forgotten, Lord, by Thee. *Ps. xiii.*
25. How long wilt Thou conceal Thy face. *Ps. lxxxix.*
26. I lift mine eyes unto the hills. *Ps. cxxi.*
27. I love the Lord, for He is nigh. *Ps. cxvi.*
28. I muse upon Thine ancient praise. *Ps. lxxvii.*
29. I praise Thee, Lord, who o'er my foes. *Ps. xxx.*
30. I trod the path of life, my strength. *Ps. cii.*
31. In trouble to the Lord I prayed. *Ps. cxx.*
32. Jehovah reigns, arrayed in light. *Ps. xciii.*
33. Judge me, O God; maintain my cause. *Ps. xliii.*
34. Lord, hear my prayer, and let my cry. *Ps. cii.*
35. Lord, I am not lofty-minded. *Ps. cxxxi.*
36. Lord, I lift my soul to Thee. *Ps. xxv.*
37. Lord, my Rock. I cry to Thee. *Ps. xxviii.*
38. Lord, save me from the foeman's wrath. *Ps. cxl.*
39. Lord, Thou wilt guard with faithful love. *Ps. xxxvii.*
40. Lord, Thy love and truth I praise. *Ps. ci.*

41. My God, my God, to Thee I cry, Ah! why hast Thou, &c. *Ps. xxii.*
42. My heart is fain, O God, my heart. *Ps. cviii.*
43. My portion is the living Lord. *Ps. cxix.*
44. My Saviour is the living Lord. *Ps. xi.*
45. My Shepherd is the Lord, no care. *Ps. xxiii.*
46. My trust is in Thy holy Name. *Ps. lxxi.*
47. My voice to God ascends on high. *Ps. lxxvii.*
48. Not in envy, not in anger. *Ps. xxxvii.*
49. Not in Thy fury, Lord, reprove. *Ps. xxxviii.*
50. O grant us, God of love. *Ps. lxvii.*
51. O God, be merciful to me. *Ps. li.*
52. O God of hosts, a vine. *Ps. lxxx.*
53. O God, subdue the power of sin. *Ps. vii.*
54. O Lord, in Thine accepted day. *Ps. lxix.*
55. O Lord our King, how bright Thy fame. *Ps. viii.*
56. O Lord, the God of my salvation. *Ps. lxxxviii.*
57. O praise ye the Lord, Praise Him in His shrine. *Ps. cl.*
58. O rejoice, ye righteous, in the Lord. *Ps. xxxiii.*
59. Oft, as to scatter kings. *Ps. lxviii.*
60. Out of the depths to Thee I cry. *Ps. cxxx.*
61. Praise, O my soul, the Lord and all. *Ps. ciii.*
62. Praise, O my soul, the Lord; how great. *Ps. civ.*
63. Praise the Lord, for good is He. *Ps. cxxxvi.*
64. Praise the Lord, for it is wise. *Ps. cxlvii.*
65. Praise the Lord from heaven on high. *Ps. cxlviii.*
66. Praise the Lord, His people; raise. *Ps. cxlvi.*
67. Praise ye the Lord, all nations. *Ps. cxvii.*
68. Praise ye the Lord, for good is He. *Ps. cxviii.*
69. Praise ye the Lord, for very good. *Ps. cvii.*
70. Praised be the Lord, my Rock of might. *Ps. cxliv.*
71. Save me, O God, the dangerous, &c. *Ps. lxix.*
72. Save me through Thy name, O God. *Ps. liv.*
73. Seek we Jehovah's house, they said. *Ps. cxxii.*
74. Sing a new song unto the Lord. *Ps. xcvi.*
75. Sing the Lord, ye sons of heaven. *Ps. xxix.*
76. Sing unto the Lord with mirth. *Ps. c.*
77. Take note, O Lord, of all my fears. *Ps. lvi.*
78. The heavens declare Thy wondrous fame. *Ps. lxxxix.*
79. The heavens, O God, Thy glory tell. *Ps. xix.*
80. The king, O Lord, with hymns of praise. *Ps. xxi.*
81. The life of man is like the grass. *Ps. ciii.*
82. The Lord in thy distressful day. *Ps. xx.*
83. The Lord is King; glad earth, and ye. *Ps. xcvii.*
84. There is no God, so saith the fool. *Ps. xiv.*
85. Thou searchest all my secret ways. *Ps. cxxxix.*
86. To Thee I call, O Lord, be swift. *Ps. cxli.*
87. 'Twas dream-like, when the Lord's decree. *Ps. cxxvi.*
88. Unless the Lord with us had wrought. *Ps. cxxiv.*
89. Unto my feet a lantern shines Thy word. *Ps. cxix.*
90. Unto the Lord I make my moan. *Ps. cxlii.*
91. We sat and wept by Babel's stream. *Ps. cxxxvii.*
92. When Israel came from Egypt's strand. *Ps. cxiv.*
93. When through the dismal waste. *Ps. lxviii.*
94. Who rules his life by God's behest. *Ps. cxxviii.*
95. Whoe'er his secret home has made. *Ps. xci.*
96. With weary care brought low. *Ps. lxix.*
97. With my whole heart I will praise Thee. *Ps. cxxxviii.*
98. Within Thy tabernacle, Lord. *Ps. xv.*
99. Ye Judges of the earth, be still. *Ps. lxxxii.*

ii. The following also appeared in *The Psalter,* 1860, and again in *Hymno. Christ,* 1863, mostly altered, and based upon the corresponding *Psalms* by George Sandys (q.v.), pub. in his *Paraphrase upon the Psalms of David,* 1636 :—

100. Blest he whose timely mercies heed. *Ps. xli.*
101. Hide not, O Lord, Thy cheering face. *Ps. xl.*
102. I waited for a gentle word. *Ps. xl.*
103. Israel of God, be Christ your Guide. *Ps. cxv.*
104. Who in the Lord securely lay. *Ps. cxxv.*

iii. To the Rev. A. T. Russell's *Psalms & Hymns,* 1851, Dr. Kennedy was indebted to a limited extent in preparing his *Psalter,* 1860. In his Preface he says, p. viii., "Mr. Russell's metres, and occasionally his words, have been adopted in the following Psalms: 2, 24, 39, 45, 46, 50, 84, 85, 90, 110, 111, 113." Of these the following, sometimes with alterations of the 1860 text, were given in the *Hymno. Christ.,* 1863 :—

105. God is our sure defence, our aid. *Ps. xlvi.*
106. My heart is full, and I must sing. *Ps. xlv.*
107. Not vain, O Lord, Thy loving word. *Ps. lxxxv.*

108. O Lord of hosts, my soul cries out. *Ps. lxxxiv.*
109. O ye who on His service wait. *Ps. cxiii.*
110. Praise the Lord with exultation. *Ps. cxi.*
111. The earth and all that it contains. *Ps. xxiv.*
112. Unto my Lord Jehovah said. *Ps. cx.*
113. Why do the heathen rage. *Ps. ii.*

iv. Dr. Kennedy also contributed to his *Hymno. Christ.*, 1863, the following original hymns :—

114. Another week is past and I. *Saturday Evening.*
115. Eternal Source of life and light. *Trinity.*
116. For life and light, and wants supplied. *Evening.*
117. Lord in whom I live and move. *Evening.*
118. Lord, let the love in us abound. *Passion Week.*
119. Lord of all power and might. *Ascension.*
120. O Lord, ope Thou our lips. *General.*
121. One alone hath power to give. *Easter.*
122. Sin-laden, weary, lost, I flee. *Lent.*
123. To us this day is born a Child. *Christmas.*
124. We ask not of Thee worldly good. *Whitsuntide.*
125. Whilst the careless world is sleeping. *Advent.*

Also the following additional versions of Psalms :—

126. The Lord is King, He reigns on high. *Ps. xciii.*
127. When tempests round us gather. *Ps. cxxx.*

v. Besides the foregoing the *Hymno. Christ.* included numerous translations from the German, recasts of hymns by other writers, versions of individual Psalms, and additional original hymns, by Dr. Kennedy, many of which have passed into other collections, and all of which are annotated in this work under their respective first lines. Altogether his contributions to the *Hymno. Christ.* number about two hundred, and embrace two thirds, or more, of his *Psalter* of 1860. As a popular hymnal the *Hymno. Christ.* has been a failure : but as a storehouse to which compilers of hymn-books can resort, it is of great and permanent value. D. April 6, 1889.   [J. J.]

Kent, John, was b. at Bideford, Devonshire, Dec. 1766, and d. Nov. 15, 1843. As a working shipwright his opportunities for acquiring the education and polish necessary for the production of refined verse were naturally limited. His hymns are strongly worded, very earnest and simple, and intensely Calvinistic. A few were published in Samuel Reece's *Collection*, 1799. The 1st ed. of his *Collection of Original Gospel Hymns*, was pub. in 1803, and the 10th ed., with " The Author's Experience," in verse, 264 hymns, 15 longer pieces, and a *Life* by his Son in 1861. The Calvinistic teaching so prominent in his hymns has restricted their use to a limited number of collections. The greatest use made of them in modern hymn-books has been by Mr. Spurgeon (*O. O. H. Bk.*, 1866) and Mr. Snepp (*Songs of G. & G.*, 1872). In the following list the dates in brackets indicate the dates of publication :—

1. Before the Almighty began (1841). *Election.*
2. Betroth'd in love, ere time began (1803). *Election.*
3. Christ exalted is our song (1803). *Christ the sinner's Surety.*
4. Come saints, and sing in sweet accord (1803). *Stability of the Covenant.*
5. Hark, how the blood-bought host above (1803). *Election.*
6. How sweet the notes of yonder choir (1841). *Christmas.*
7. In types and shadows we are told (1803). *Pardon.*
8. Indulgent God, how kind (1803). *Electing Love.*
9. Let Zion in her songs record (1803). *Pardon—Grace exalted.*
10. Love was the great self-moving cause (1803). *Free Grace.*
11. Precious is the Name of Jesus (1841). *The Precious Name.*

12. Salvation by grace, how charming the song (1803). *Free Grace.*
13. Saved from the damning power of sin (1803). *Eternal Love.*
14. Sons of God, in tribulation (1803). *Affliction.*
15. Sons of peace, redeemed by blood (1803). *Good Friday.*
16. Sovereign grace o'er sin abounding (1827). *Perseverance of the faint.*
17. 'Tis the Church triumphant singing (1803). *Praise.*
18. 'Twas not to make Jehovah's love (1803). *Election.*
19. 'Twas with an everlasting love (1803). *Election.*
20. What cheering words are these (1803). *Safety in God.*
21. With David's Lord, and ours (1803). *The Divine Covenant.*   [J. J.]

Kern, Christian Gottlob, was b. Jan. 13, 1792, at Söhnstetten, near Heidenheim, Württemberg, where his father was pastor. After the completion of his theological studies at Tübingen he was for two years assistant clergyman at Plochingen. In 1817 he became Theological Tutor (repetent) at Tübingen, in 1820 Second Pastor (Helfer) at Besigheim, and, in 1824, Preacher and Professor at the Clergy School of Schönthal. He finally became, in 1829, Pastor of Dürrmenz-Mühlacker, near Pforzheim, and d. there Aug. 5, 1835 (*Koch*, vii. 210 ; *Allg. Deutsche Biog.*, xv. 632). His hymns appeared mostly in Knapp's *Christoterpe.* One has been *tr.*, viz. :—

Wie könnt ich sein vergessen. *Holy Communion.* This beautiful hymn was 1st pub. in Knapp's *Christoterpe*, 1837, p. 192, in 5 st. of 8 l., headed " At the Celebration of Holy Communion." Included in Knapp's *Ev. L. S.*, 1837, No. 966 (1865, No. 948), the Württemberg *G. B.*, 1842, and others. Dr. Schaff, in his *Deutsches G. B.*, 1874, No. 171, gives it from a MS. copy supplied by the daughter of the author, and says it was written in 1820. *Tr.* as :—

Oh how could I forget Him ! A full and very good *tr.* by Miss Winkworth, in her *Lyra Ger.*, 2nd Ser., 1858, p. 101 ; and thence in Schaff's *Christ in Song*, 1869, p. 622. Abridged in her *C. B. for England*, 1863 ; in *Holy Song*, 1869 ; in the *College Hymnal*, N. Y., 1876, and others. Another *tr.* is, " Will not my memory treasure," in J. D. Burns's *Memoir & Remains*, 1869, p. 271.   [J. M.]

Kethe, William, is said by Thomas Warton in his *Hist. of Eng. Poetry*, and by John Strype in his *Annals of the Reformation*, to have been a Scotsman. Where he was born, or whether he held any preferment in England in the time of Edward VI., we have been unable to discover. In the *Brieff discours off the troubles begonne at Franckford*, 1575, he is mentioned as in exile at Frankfurt in 1555, at Geneva in 1557 ; as being sent on a mission to the exiles in Basel, Strassburg, &c., in 1558 ; and as returning with their answers to Geneva in 1559. Whether he was one of those left behind in 1559 to " finishe the bible, and the psalmes bothe in meeter and prose," does not appear. The *Discours* further mentions him as being with the Earl of Warwick and the Queen's forces at Newhaven [Havre] in 1563, and in the north in 1569. John Hutchins in his County history of Dorset, 1774, vol. ii. p. 316, says that he was instituted in 1561 as Rector of Childe Okeford, near Blandford. But as there were two Rectors and only one church, leave of absence might easily be extended. His connection with Okeford seems to have ceased by death or otherwise about 1593.

The Rev. Sir Talbot H. B. Baker, Bart., of Ranston, Blandford, who very kindly made researches on the spot, has informed me that the Registers at Childe Okeford begin with 1652-53, that the copies kept in Blandford date only from 1732 (the earlier having probably perished in the great fire there in 1731), that no will can be found in the district Probate Court, and that no monument or tablet is now to be found at Childe Okeford.

By a communication to me from the Diocesan Registrar of Bristol, it appears that in a book professing to contain a list of Presentations deposited in the Consistory Court, Kethe is said to have been presented in 1565 by Henry Capel, the Patron of Childe Okeford *Inferior*. In the 1813 ed. of *Hutchins*, vol. iii. pp. 355-6, William Watkinson is said to have been presented to this moiety by Arthur Capel in 1593.

Twenty-five Psalm versions by Kethe are included in the *Anglo-Genevan Psalter* of 1561, viz. Ps. 27, 36, 47, 54, 58, 62, 70, 85, 88, 90, 91, 94, 100, 101, 104, 107, 111, 112, 113, 122, 125, 126, 134, 138, 142,—the whole of which were adopted in the *Scottish Psalter* of 1564-65. Only nine, viz. Ps. 104, 107, 111, 112, 113, 122, 125, 126, 134, were included in the *English Psalter* of 1562; Ps. 100 being however added in 1565 (see first lines of the rest under **Scottish Hymnody**, ii. § 2). Being mostly in peculiar metres, only one, Ps. 100, was transferred to the *Scottish Psalter* of 1650. The version of Ps. 104, "My soul, praise the Lord," is found, in a greatly altered form, in some modern hymnals.

Warton calls him "a Scotch divine, no unready rhymer," says he had seen a moralisation of some of Ovid by him, and also mentions verses by him prefixed to a pamphlet by Christopher Goodman, printed at Geneva in 1558; a version of Ps. 93 added to Knox's *Appellation* to the Scottish Bishops, also printed at Geneva in 1558; and an anti-papal ballad, "Tye the mare Tom-boy." A sermon he preached before the Sessions at Blandford on Jan. 17, 1571, was printed by John Daye in 1571 (preface dated Childe Okeford, Jan. 29, 157½), and dedicated to Ambrose Earl of Warwick. See **Sternhold & Hopkins**, §§ 9-11.   [J. M.]

Key, Francis Scott, was b. in Frederick County, Maryland, 1779, and educated at St. John's College, Annapolis. He practised as a lawyer in Washington, District of Columbia, and was the United States District Attorney there till his death on Jan. 11, 1843. His poetical pieces, which were printed in various works, were collected and pub. in N. Y. as *Poems* in 1857. His hymns in C. U. include:—

1. **Before the Lord we bow.** *National Thanksgiving.* This Thanksgiving hymn for the 4th July was pub. in 1832, and was probably written for the celebration of that year. It is in use in G. Britain and America.

2. **If life's pleasures charm [cheer] thee.** *The heart for God only.* Appeared in *The Christian Lyre*, 1830.

3. **Faith is the Christian's evidence.** *Faith.*

4. **Lord, with glowing heart I'll praise Thee.** *Praise for Pardon and Peace.* Pub. in Dr. Mühlenberg's *Church Poetry*, 1823, the *Prayer Bk. Coll.*, 1826, &c.; and altered as "Lord, with *fervor I would* praise Thee," in the Unitarian *Hys. for the Church of Christ*, Boston, 1853. In the Oberlin, Ohio, *Manual of Praise*, 1880, it begins with st. ii., "Praise, my soul, the God that sought thee."

Of these hymns Nos. 1, 2, and 4 are in the *Lyra Sac. Americana*, 1868, together with the following :—

5. Behold the grant the King of kings. *All things in Christ.*
6. My God, my Father, may I dare. *God, the Father.*
7. When troubles, wave on wave, assail'd. *Efficacy of Prayer.*

F. S. **Key** was also the author of "The Star Spangled Banner" (1814). For original text of his pieces see the *Poems*, 1857.   [F. M. B.]

Keymann, Christian. [Keimann, C.]

Kiel, Tobias, was b. Oct. 29, 1584, at Ballstädt near Gotha. After completing his theological studies at Jena, he became in 1606 Schoolmaster at Ballstädt, and in 1613 Pastor

at Eschenbergen. He was then, in 1627, appointed Pastor at Ballstädt, and d. there six days after his settlement. (*Brückner's Kirchen und Schulenstaat des Herzogthums Gotha*, 1753, ii., pt. xii. p. 13; iii., pt. viii. p. 12, &c.) In 1721 some 60 of his hymns were extant in ms. The only one *tr.* into English is

Herr Gott, nun schleuss den Himmel auf. *For the Dying.* In J. M. Altenburg's *Kirchen- und Hausgesänge.* Erfurt, 1620, No. 6, in 3 st., entitled "On the Festival of the Purification of Mary:" and in the *Unv. L. S.*, 1851, No. 818. *Tr.* as "Lord God, now open wide Thy heaven," by *Miss Winkworth*, 1858, p. 215.

[J. M.]

Killinghall, John. The date of his birth is unknown. He was admitted pastor of a congregation at Beccles, Suffolk, Oct. 13, 1697. Through some indiscretion of conduct he retired from the ministry for a time. Subsequently, about 1702, he became the pastor of the Congregational Church, Southwark, then meeting in Deadman's Place (the Church of the Pilgrim Fathers). He d. Jan. 1740. His memoir is included in the *Brief Records of the Independent Church at Beccles*, 1838, by S. W. Rix. (Miller's *Singers & Songs*, 1869, p. 156.) His hymn :—

In all my troubles, sharp and long (*Joy in Affliction*) appeared in the *Life of Faith exemplified and recommended in a Letter found in the Study of the Rev. Joseph Belcher, late of Dedham, in New England, since his Decease. An Answer to this question, " How to live in this World so as to live in Heaven ?" To which is added a few Verses by the late Rev. Killinghall, upon reading of it.* London. 1741. It is in 3 st. of 4 l., and is found in modern hymn-books in the following forms :—(1) "In all my troubles, sharp and strong," in Reed's *H. Bk.*, 1842, and others ; (2) "In every trouble, sharp and strong," in several collections, including the Enlarged *London H. Bk.*, 1873, &c.; and (3) "In every trying hour," in several American books, as *Songs for the Sanctuary*, N. Y., 1865, &c. In several of the older collections this hymn is attributed to "Coombes"—why we know not.   [J. J.]

Kimball, Harriet McEwan, a native and resident of Portsmouth, Newhaven, is the author of *Hymns*, Boston, 1866 ; *Swallow Flights of Song*, 1874, &c. Her hymns include :—

1. **At times on Tabor's height.** *Faith and Joy.*
2. **Dear Lord, to Thee alone.** *Lent.*
3. **It is an easy thing to say.** *Humble Service.*
4. **We have no tears Thou wilt not dry.** *Affliction.* Appeared in the *Poets of Portsmouth*, 1864, and the Unitarian *Hys. of the Spirit*, 1864, and others. In Miss Kimball's *Hymns*, 1866, this hymn begins with st. iii. of "Jesus the Ladder of my faith."

Several of Miss Kimball's poems were included in Baynes's *Illustrated Book of Sacred Poems*, 1867.   [F. M. B.]

Kindred in Christ, for His dear sake. *J. Newton.* [*Welcome to Christian Friends.*] Pub. in the *Olney Hymns*, 1779, Bk. ii., No. 70, in 6 st. of 4 l., and headed, "A Welcome to Christian Friends." It is in C. U. in its original form, and also as :' (1) "Kindred in Christ, to us 'tis given," adapted for *Union and Home Missionary Meetings*; and (2) "May He by Whose kind care we meet," also suitable for similar gatherings.   [J. J.]

King, Catherine. [Pennefather, C.]

King, Elizabeth. [Mills, Elizabeth.]

Kingsbury, William, was b. in 1744, educated at an Independent academy in London, and became Pastor of the ancient Congregational Church, Above Bar, in Southampton, where he d. in 1818, after an honourable and useful ministry of fifty-four years. He was the author of several published sermons and pamphlets, including :—(1) *A Sermon on the King's recovery,* 1780 ; (2) *The Manner in which Protestant Dissenters perform Public Worship represented and vindicated,* 1796 ; (3) *An Apology for Village Preachers,* 1799 ; (4) *A Funeral Sermon on the Death of the Rev. Mr. Towle,* 1807, &c. Kingsbury was one of the ministers under whose patronage Dobell pub. his *New Selection,* 1806, and to that book contributed two hymns :—" Great Lord of all thy churches, hear ! " No. 213 (*Divine Worship*), and " Let us awake our joys," No. 100 (*Jesus the King*). Both these hymns are in C. U., the second being specially popular in America.

[W. R. S.]

Kinner, Samuel, was a native of Breslau, and after he had graduated M.D. was for some time a physician there. He then entered the service of the Duke of Liegnitz-Brieg as Rath and Court Physician, and d. at Brieg, Aug. 10, 1668, at the age of 65 (J. H. Cunradus's *Silesia Togata,* Liegnitz, 1706, p 150). One hymn ascribed to him has been tr., viz. :—

Herr Jesu Christ, du hast bereit. *Holy Communion.* In Jeremias Weber's *G. B.,* Leipzig, 1638, p. 394, in 8 st. of 7 l., entitled " A beautiful hymn on the Supper of the Lord. Samuel Kinner." In Burg's *G. B.,* Breslau, 1746, No. 1665, entitled " For worthy reception, before Holy Communion." *Tr.* as :—

Lord Jesus, Thou art truly good. A full and good *tr.* by E. Cronenwett, as No. 265 in the Ohio *Lutheran Hymnal,* 1880. [J. M.]

Kippis, Andrew, D.D., was b. at Nottingham, March 28, 1725, and educated for the ministry under Dr. Doddridge at Northampton, 1741–46. After a short residence with congregations at Boston and Dorking, he settled in London in 1753, as minister of the Princes Street Chapel, Westminster. There he remained till his death in 1795, holding rank as the leading Presbyterian minister in the metropolis. For many years he was classical tutor at the Hoxton Academy, and afterwards at the Hackney College. He contributed largely to the *Gentleman's Magazine* and the *Monthly Review,* and edited five volumes of a new edition of the *Biographia Britannica,* a work commenced in 1778, and interrupted by his death on Oct. 8, 1795. His Life of Captain Cook was also pub. separately, and to his edition of Lardner's *Works* (1788) a *Memoir* was prefixed. His degree of D.D. was conferred by the University of Edinburgh in 1767.

He was joint editor of *A Collection of Hymns and Psalms for Public and Private Worship,* selected and prepared by Andrew Kippis, D.D., &c. ; Abraham Rees, D.D., &c. ; Rev. Thomas Jervis, and Rev. Thomas Morgan, LL.D., London, 1795. This collection, commonly known as *Kippis's,* but sometimes as *Rees's,* passed through many editions, a *Supplement* being added in 1807, and was very generally used during the early decades of this century by congregations of Presbyterians and others, then become Unitarian in London and throughout the country [Unitarian Hymnody, § 9]. It contained 690 hymns.

The aim of the editors in their selection was to avoid " everything of a doubtful or disputable kind," and they adopt the language of Dr. Watts in the preface to his Hymns, " The contentious and distinguishing words of

sects and parties are excluded." The alterations and omissions to adapt various hymns to the standard of the editors are considerable, though very little compared to what was done by others-before and after them. The tone of the collection is somewhat colourless, and it gradually gave place among Unitarians to others which contained fuller and more varied expression of distinctively Christian feeling.

Two hymns by Kippis appear in this *Collection.*

1. " **Great God, in vain man's narrow view,**" *The Incomprehensibility of God,* which was generally adopted in later Unitarian books, and appears in Martineau's *Hymns,* 1840 and 1873.

2. " **How rich thy gifts, Almighty King,**" *National Thanksgiving,* which is four stanzas of the hymn, "Say, should we search the globe around," written for the thanksgiving appointed Nov. 29, 1759, and appended to his Sermon on that occasion. It was given in full in Pope's *Coll.,* 1760 ; and the Liverpool Octagon *Coll.,* 1763. In Lindsey's *Coll.,* 1774, five stanzas are given; in other early books only four, as in *Kippis.* The last two stanzas, somewhat altered, appear anonymously as : " With grateful hearts, with joyful tongues," in the *Cong. H. Bk.,* 1836, and the *New Cong.,* 1859.

[V. D. D.]

Kirkham. [How firm a foundation, &c.]

Klantendorfer, Paulus, was a minister among the Bohemian Brethren, and d. in 1566. To their *Kirchengeseng,* 1566, he contributed one hymn, viz. :—

Weil dieser Tag ist vergangen. *Evening.* 1566, as above, and thence in *Wackernagel,* iv. p. 349, in 6 st. of 4 l. *Tr.* as, " Because this day is at an end," as No. 291 in pt. i. of the *Moravian H. Bk.,* 1754. In 1789 a tr. of st. vi. of " Herr Jesu! meines Lebens Heil " (see **Neumeister**) was added. In later eds. (1886, No. 1179) it begins, " Another day is at an end." [J. M.]

Klopstock, Friedrich Gottlieb, the eldest of the 17 children of Gottlob Heinrich Klopstock (then advocate and commissionsrath at Quedlinburg, and after 1735 amtmann at Friedeburg, on the Saale, near Halle), was b. at Quedlinburg, July 2, 1724. From 1739 to 1745 he attended the famous school at Schulpforte, near Naumburg (where he conceived the first idea of his *Messias*) ; then he entered the University of Jena, in the autumn of 1745, as a student of theology, and the University of Leipzig at Easter, 1746. At Leipzig he made acquaintance with J. A. Cramer (q.v.) ; and became one of the contributors to the *Bremer Beiträge,* in which the first three books of his *Messias* appeared. In 1748 he became tutor in the house of a merchant named Weiss at Langensalza ; and in 1750 accepted an invitation to visit Zürich (the literary capital of Switzerland), where his *Messias* had been received with great enthusiasm. He was then, in the spring of 1751, invited by the Danish prime minister, Count von Bernstorff, to take up his residence at the Court of King Frederick V., at Copenhagen, in order to be able to finish his *Messias* free from the cares of a profession ; and was, in 1763, appointed Legationsrath. After the Count ceased, in the end of 1770, to be prime minister, Klopstock retired to Hamburg, in 1771, on a pension. The rest of his life was passed mainly at Hamburg, except about a year spent at Carlsruhe, at the Court of the Margave Carl Friedrich of Baden, who appointed him Hofrath. He d. at Hamburg, March 14, 1803, and was buried with civic honours on the 22nd, under a lime-tree in the churchyard at Ottensen (*Koch,* vi. 322 ; *Allg. Deutsche Biog.,* xvi. 2°1, &c.).

Klopstock ranks among the classic poets of Germany. In his *Oden* (collected at Hamburg, 1771 ; enlarged, Leipzig, 1798 ; finally enlarged, Leipzig, 1804) he is seen at his best ; his earlier compositions of this class being the finest modern examples for perfection of form, lyric grace, majesty, and purity of rhythm. His most famous work is his *Messias*, which on its first appearance created an enthusiasm such as had not been awakened by any German work for centuries. It was suggested by Milton's *Paradise Lost*, but Milton's calm majesty, firmness of touch, and unity of action were all foreign to Klopstock's nature—his genius was lyric rather than epic. With all its defects of style and construction, it is still a noble work, and could only have been written by a true poet and a sincere Christian ; though to us its interest perhaps consists as much in its historical importance and results as in its intrinsic merits. (Books 1–3 written in prose at Jena, and then in hexameter verse at Leipzig, and 1st pub. in the *Neue Beyträge*, Bremen, 1748. Books 1–3 revised, and 4, 5 added at Halle, 1751 ; 6–10 added in the Copenhagen ed., 1755 ; 11–15, Copenhagen, 1768 ; 16–20, Halle, 1773. Finally revised ed. in 4 vols., Leipzig, 1800.)

In his hymns Klopstock is not seen at his best. He seems to have had little appreciation of the requirements which the writer of hymns for use in public worship has to meet. His hymns are emotional and subjective, little suited to congregational tunes, and not sufficiently simple in style. In his first collection (1) *Geistliche Lieder*, Copenhagen, 1758, he included a number of indifferent recasts of earlier German hymns ; his second collection (2) *Geistliche Lieder*, Copenhagen, 1769, consists entirely of original compositions. The only one of his hymns which is still much used in Germany is " Auferstehn, ja auferstehn, wirst du " (q.v.). The others which have passed into English C. U. are :—

i. **Deine heilige Geburt.** *Supplication.* In his *Geistliche Lieder*, 1758, p. 44, in 14 l., repeated in Knapp's *Ev. L. S.*, 1837, No. 468. *Tr.* as " Saviour ! by Thy holy birth," by Dr. W. L. Alexander, in 2 st. of 8 l. It was written about 1830, but 1st pub. in the 2nd ed., 1858, of his *Sel. of Hys.*, No. 339, entitled " Christ's aid invoked."

ii. **Herr, du wollst sie vollbereiten.** *Holy Communion.* In his *Geistliche Lieder*, 1758, p. 135, arranged for antiphonal singing by choir and congregation. The form *tr.* into English is " Herr, du wollst uns vorbereiten," being the first two stanzas for choir altered as No. 246 in the Württemberg *G. B.*, 1842, in 2 st. of 12 l. *Tr.* as " Grant us, Lord ! due preparation," by L. Heyl, in the Ohio *Luth. Hymnal*, 1880. Another *tr.* is, " O God, do Thou Thy folk prepare," by *Dr. G. Walker*, 1860, p. 64.

iii. **Nicht nur streiten, überwinden.** *Christian Warfare.* 1st pub. in the *G. B. für St. Petri Kopenhagen*, 1760, No. 639 ; repeated in his *Geistliche Lieder*, 1769, p. 23, in 5 st. of 8 l., entitled " The Victory of the Faithful." In the Berlin *G. L. S.*, ed. 1863. *Tr.* as " Labour ever, late and early," a full but rather free *tr.* by Dr. Kennedy, in his *Hymno. Christ.*, 1863.

iv. **Zeige dich uns ohne Hülle.** *Sunday.* In his *Geistliche Lieder*, 1769, p. 88, in 4 st. of 8 l., entitled " Preparation for Divine Service." Included in the Berlin *G. L. S.*, ed. 1863. It is the only hymn by Klopstock much used in English. *Tr.* as " Lord, remove the veil away," a good and full *tr.* by Miss Borthwick, in *H. L. L.*, 3rd Ser., 1858, p. 47 (1884, p. 168). Included in full in *Kennedy*, 1863 ; Eng. Presb. *Ps. & Hys.*, 1867 ; *Temple H. Bk.*, 1867 ; Dale's *Eng. H. Bk.*, 1875, and others. It is abridged in W. F. Stevenson's *Hys. for Ch. & Home*, 1873, *Laudes Domini*, N. Y., 1884, and others.

Hymns not in English C. U.

v. **Ach wie hat mein Herz gerungen.** *Strength in Weakness.* 1769, p. 101, in 10 st. *Tr.* as " Ah me, what woes this heart have wrung," by J. Sheppard, in his *Foreign Sacred Lyre*, 1857, p. 68.

vi. **Du wollst erhören Gott, ihr Flehn.** *For the Dying.* 1758, p. 73, in 11 st. The form *tr.* is the recast (probably by J. S. Diterich), as No. 120, in the Berlin *G. B.*, 1765, beginning " Dein sind wir Gott ! in Ewigkeit." *Tr.* as " We're Thine, O God, for evermore," by *Dr. H. Mills*, 1845 (1856, p. 241).

vii. **Selig sind des Himmels Erben.** *For the Dying ;*

or, *At Funerals.* 1758, p. 15, in 4 pts., arranged for choir and congregation, in all 10 st. Founded on Rev. xiv. 13. Sung at the funeral of J. C. Lavater, January 4, 1801. *Tr.* as " Blessed are the heirs of heaven," by G. Moultrie, in his *Hys. & Lyrics*, 1867, p. 337.

viii. **Stärke, die zu dieser Zeit.** *For the Dying.* 1758, p. 1, in 3 st. *Tr.* as " Strengthen, Lord, the weary soul," by G. Moultrie, in his *Hys. & Lyrics*, 1867, p. 355, marked as an " orison for the departing spirit."

ix. **Um Erden wandeln Monde.** *The Lord's Prayer.* In his *Oden*, vol. ii., Leipzig, 1798, p. 119, marked as written in 1789, and entitled " Psalm." It is an ode of 58 lines, embodying and amplifying the Lord's Prayer. Sung at his own funeral. *Tr.* as, (1) " Moons round their planets roll," by *J. Sheppard*, 1857, p. 46. (2) " Round their planets roll the moons," by *Miss Winkworth*, 1869, p. 332.

x. **Wenn ich einst von jenem Schlummer.** *Morning.* 1769, p. 57, in 3 st. In the Württemberg *G. B.*, 1842, No. 562. The *trs.* are, (1) " When I rise again to life," by W. Nind, in his *Odes of Klopstock*, 1848, p. 307. (2) " When I wake from out that slumber," in A. Baskerville's *Poetry of Germany*, 1854, p. 39, repeated in the Schaff-Gilman *Lib. of Rel. Poetry*, ed. 1883, p. 282. (3) " Father, let no day to come " (the text used begins with st. ii. altered to " Gieb dass keiner meiner Tage "), by *J. Sheppard*, 1857, p. 88. (4) " Since I one day from yonder sleeping," by *Miss Warner*, 1869, p. 40.

xi. **Zitternd freu ich mich.** *The Vision of God.* 1st pub. in the *Nordische Aufseher* ed. by J. A. Cramer, vol. ii. (Kopenhagen, 1760). In his *Oden*, Hamburg, 1771, p. 25, in 90 lines, and marked as written in 1759. *Tr.* as, (1) " With trembling I rejoice," by *W. Nind*, 1848, p. 130. (2) " I joy, but tremblingly," by *J. Sheppard*, 1857, p. 24. (3) " Trembling I rejoice," by *Miss Winkworth*, 1869, p. 329.

Besides the above a considerable number of Klopstock's *Oden* are *tr.* by J. Sheppard in his *Foreign Sacred Lyre*, 1857. A full selection from the *Oden* appeared as *Odes of Klopstock from 1747 to 1780. Translated from the German by William Nind*, London, W. Pickering, 1848. 　　　　　　　　　　[J. M.]

Knak, Gustav Friedrich Ludwig, s. of Christian F. L. Knak, Justiz Commissarius at Berlin, was b. at Berlin, July 12, 1806. He matriculated as a student of theology at the University of Berlin, Easter, 1826. In the autumn of 1829 he became tutor in a private school at Königs-Wusterhausen, near Berlin, where he worked manfully for the sick and dying during the cholera year 1831. He returned to Berlin in August, 1832, and acted as one of the editors of the well-known *Geistlicher Lieder Schatz* (referred to in this Dictionary as the Berlin *G. L. S.*), to which he contributed a number of hymns, and for which he wrote the preface dated Dec. 11, 1832. In the autumn of 1834 he was ordained pastor of Wusterwitz, near Dramburg, in Pomerania ; and in the end of 1849 was appointed Gossner's successor as Pastor of the Lutheran-Bohemian congregation (Bethlehemskirche) in Berlin. During a holiday visit to a married daughter at Dünnow, near Stolpemünde, he was taken suddenly ill, and d. there July 27, 1878 ; his body being removed to Berlin and laid to rest in the graveyard belonging to his church (*O. Kraus*, 1879, p. 266 ; *Allg. Deutsche Biog.*, xvi. 261, &c.).

Knak was a man of prayer, a faithful and successful preacher and pastor, and greatly interested in Missions at home and abroad, especially in the Lutheran missions to China and the Chinese Orphanage at Hong Kong. As a hymn-writer he is distinguished by elegance of style, harmony of rhythm, and deep love to the personal Christ. His hymns appeared in his *Simon Johanna, hast du mich lieb ?* Berlin, 1829 (enlarged editions pub. at Berlin 1840, and again in 1843 as his *Zionsharfe*; in the Berlin *G. L. S.*, ed. 1832; and in his *Liebe um Liebe . . . Nachtrag zu dessen Zionsharfe.* Werder, 2nd ed. 1849 (3rd ed. Berlin, 1850).

Those of Knak's hymns which have passed into English are:—

i. **Lasst mich geh'n, lasst mich geh'n.** *Longing for Heaven.* Of the origin of this favourite hymn, *O. Kraus*, 1879, p. 269, gives the following account:—

"Knak's earnest zeal in the cause of missions to the heathen had the natural result, that for many years he was summoned as festival preacher to the most distant Mission services. On the way to fulfil these engagements many of Knak's hymns had their origin. About 1845, one day the pastor of Wusterwitz [his cure] came to pastor Sondermann at Coprieben, and asked him to play the well-known popular melody 'Morgenroth, Morgenroth,' as he had just composed a hymn to that tune. As the desired melody rang out, the poet struck up for the first time that hymn since sung by hundreds of thousands, 'Lasst mich geh'n! Lasst mich geh'n.' Later, Knak's blind organist, Voigtländer, in Berlin, composed the pleasing melody, to which at the present time the hymn is generally sung."

This hymn appears to have been written on July 23, 1846, and is included in his *Liebe um Liebe*, 1849 (3rd ed., 1850, No. 48), in 5 st. of 5 l., entitled "Longing after Jerusalem." It soon attained wide popularity, and is given as No. 1597 in the Berlin *G. L. S.*, ed. 1863. *Tr.* as:—

1. **To the sky, to the sky.** A good and full *tr.* by J. M. Sloan, contributed to J. H. Wilson's *Service of Praise*, 1865, No. 165, and *Songs of Zion*, 1878, No. 94, in both cases set to Voigtländer's melody.

2. **Let me go, let me go, Jesus, face to face, to know.** In full, by Mrs. Edmund Ashley, in the *British Herald*, Sept., 1867, p. 139; repeated in Reid's *Praise Bk.*, 1872. In the *Christian Hys.*, Adelaide, 1872, No. 347 begins with st. ii. "Glorious light, glorious light."

Other trs. are, (1) "Let me close, let me close," as No. 12 in *Heart Melodies*, Lond., Morgan, N.D., signed "A. P. E. J." (2) "Let me flee, let me flee," by *E. Massie*, 1866. (3) "Let me go, let me go, Lord to me," by Mrs. H. R. Spaeth, in the *Southern Luth. Service & Hys. for S. Schools*, Philadelphia, 1883. (4) "Let me go! ah, let me go," by *J. Kelly*, 1885.

Other hymns by Knak which have been *tr.* into English are:—

ii. **Herr, du hast uns reich gesegnet.** *Close of Divine Service.* *Zionsharfe*, 1843, No. 92, in 2 st. *Tr.* as "Lord, we've tasted Thy rich blessing," in L. Rehfuess's *Church at Sea*, 1868.

iii. **Ich bin ein Pilger Gottes hier auf Erden.** *Pilgrimage of Life.* *Liebe um Liebe*, 3rd ed. 1850, No. 45, in 4 st. *Tr.* as "God's pilgrim am I here, on earth below," by *J. Kelly*, 1885.

iv. **Jesus sei mit dir auf allen Wegen.** *Birthday wish.* *Liebe um Liebe*, 3rd ed. 1850, No. 36, in 22 lines. *Tr.* as (1) "Jesus be with thee in thy ways, Jesus favour," in L. Rehfuess's *Church at Sea*, 1868. (2) "Jesu be with thee in all thy ways, Jesu crown," by *J. Kelly*, 1885.

v. **Mit der Sehnsucht heissen Blicken.** *Love to Christ.* *Zionsharfe*, 1840, p. 4, in 6 st. *Tr.* as "With the glow of ardent longing," by Miss Burlingham, in the *British Herald*, Sept. 1865, p. 141.

vi. **Sei getrost, o Seele.** *Cross and Consolation.* *Zionsharfe*, 1840, p. 2, in 3 st. *Tr.* as "O my soul, be comforted, Give not," by *J. Kelly*, 1885.

vii. **Wenn Seelen sich zusammenfinden.** *Communion of Saints.* Berlin *G. L. S.*, ed. 1832, No. 1857, in 5 st. *Tr.* as "When they may chance to meet together," by *Dr. H. Mills*, 1845 (1856, p. 186).

viii. **Zieht im Frieden eure Pfade.** *Farewell.* *Zionsharfe*, 1843, No. 86, in 11 lines. *Tr.* as "Now in peace go on your ways," in L. Rehfuess's *Church at Sea*, 1868.   [J. M.]

Knapp, Albert, was b. July 25, 1798, at Tübingen, where his father (1800, Oberamtmann at Alpirsbach in the Black Forest, and 1809, Oberamtmann at Rottweil) was then advocate at the Court of Appeal. In the autumn of 1814 he entered the Theological Seminary at Maulbronn, and in 1816 the Theological College at Tübingen, where he also graduated M.A. at the University. In November, 1820, he became assistant clergyman at Feuerbach, near Stuttgart; and in July, 1821, at Gaisburg, near Stuttgart. He was appointed, in Feb., 1825, diaconus (Helfer) at Sulz on the Neckar, and also pastor of the neighbouring village of Holzhausen; in June, 1831, archidiaconus at Kirchheim-unter-Teck, along with Bahnmaier (q.v.); in May, 1836, diaconus of the Hospitalkirche in Stuttgart; and in October, 1837, archidiaconus of the Stiftskirche. He was finally appointed, in December, 1845, Stadtpfarrer at St. Leonhard's Church in Stuttgart, where, after having been for some time partially disabled by paralysis, he preached his last sermon, Feb. 13, 1863. He d. at Stuttgart, June 18, 1864 (*Koch*, vii. 213; *Allg. Deutsche Biog.*, xvi. 263, &c.).

Knapp as a *Poet* possessed not merely very considerable talent, but also natural originality. He was pre-eminently a lyric poet; the best of his secular poems being those which celebrate the history and the scenery of his beloved Swabia. His poems are characterised by rich play of fancy, wealth of ideas and of figures, masterly word-painting, capacity of feeling, ease of expression, and sonorous and musical rhythm. Unfortunately the very flow of his imagination betrayed him, for the greatest fault of his poems is that they are at once too numerous and too long (and it must be added sometimes too rhetorical and too eager to point a moral); what was easy writing becomes hard reading.

As a *Hymn-writer*, among the recent hymn-writers of Germany, Knapp holds a high place, perhaps we might say the highest of all. To his hymn-writing he brought his powers as a poet, and the depth of his nature as an earnest and sincere disciple of Jesus Christ. In his hymns his aim was to make known the fulness of the grace of God, and to reveal the wealth and depth of Holy Scripture, and the love of God to all mankind. Their earnestness, their experimental Christianity, their Scripturalness and their beauty of form have gained for many of them a place in all recent German hymn-books. They have somewhat unaccountably been neglected by English translators. It is certainly surprising that in the *Hymns from the Land of Luther* not one version from Knapp finds a place. While all the hymns of Spitta's *Psalter und Harfe* have passed into English, and many of them in half a dozen different versions, comparatively few of Knapp's hymns have been translated, though they may rank much higher as poetry, and are more suited for Church use than those by Spitta.

As a *Hymnologist* Knapp did good service by his *Christoterpe* [complete set in Berlin], an annual which he edited from 1833 to 1853, in which many of his own pieces appeared, and also many of the best poems and hymns of Hey, Meta Heusser-Schweizer, and various others. He was also the compiler of the *Evangelischer Lieder-Schatz* (frequently referred to in this Dictionary as Knapp's *Ev. L. S.*), the most elaborate German hymnbook of recent times. Of this the 1st ed., with 3590 hymns, appeared at Stuttgart in 1837, and a Supplement entitled *Christenlieder*, 1841, added 250 more. In his 2nd ed., 1850 (3067 hymns) he omitted many of the third-rate hymns of his 1st ed., added many of a higher class, and gave the hymns more nearly (but by no means exactly) as the authors wrote them. The 3rd ed., 1865 (3130 hymns, concluded by his son), was further improved, and the notices of the authors of the hymns were revised and enlarged. As a comprehensive collection with a specially full representation of good modern hymns it has no rival in German. He was also one of the editors of the Württemberg *G. B.* of 1842. The editions which he prepared of the Hymns of Gottfried Arnold (1845) and N. L. von Zinzendorf (1845) are of interest, but he took most unwarrantable liberties with the originals; many pieces being not merely abridged but rewritten "to suit the requirements of the 19th century."

Knapp's original hymns appeared principally in his *Christoterpe* and *Evangelischer Lieder-Schatz*, as above; and also in his

(1) *Christliche Gedichte*, 2 vols., Basel, 1829.
(2) *Neuere Gedichte*, 2 vols., Basel, 1834, sometimes ranked as vols. iii., iv. of No. 1. (3) *Gedichte, Neueste Folge*, Stuttgart, 1843. (4) *Herbstblüthen*, Stuttgart, 1859. Those which have passed into English C. U. are:—

i. Aus deiner Eltern Armen. *Holy Baptism.* This and No. iv. seem to have been written for the baptism of his own children. 1st pub. in his *Christoterpe*, 1850, p. 222, in 3 st. of 8 l., entitled "Baptismal Hymn," and repeated in his *Ev. L. S.*, 1850, No. 846 (1865, No. 875). The *tr.* in C. U. is

Thy parent's arms now yield thee. In the original metre by Miss Winkworth in her *Lyra Ger.*, 2nd Ser., 1858, p. 89; and thence in *Kennedy*, 1863. Slightly altered for metrical reasons in her *C. B. for England*, 1863, No. 89.

ii. Blick aus diesem Erdenthale (p. 150 i.).
iii. Einst fahren wir vom Vaterlande (p. 326 ii.).
iv. O Vaterherz, das Erd' und Himmel schuf. *Holy Baptism.* A beautiful hymn of supplication to (i.) God the Creator; (ii.) God the Redeemer; (iii.) God the Sanctifier; on behalf of the child, ending with a prayer to the Holy Trinity for guidance and blessing throughout its life. 1st pub. in his *Christenlieder*, 1841, No. 89, in 4 st. of 9 l., repeated in his *Ev. L. S.*, 1850, No. 847 (1865, No. 876). The *tr.* in C. U. is:—

O Father-Heart, Who hast created all. A good and full *tr.* by Miss Winkworth in her *Lyra Ger.*, 2nd Ser., 1858, p. 87, repeated in the Schaff-Gilman *Lib. of Rel. Poetry*, ed. 1883, p. 437. In the hymnals it appears in the following forms, all beginning with st. i. :—

1. **O Father, Thou Who hast created all.** In *H. A. & M.*, 1861 and 1875, and others.
2. **Father! Who hast created all.** In Adams's *American Ch. Pastorals*, 1864, being the *H. A. & M.* version reduced to c.m.
3. **Father, Who hast created all.** In the Pennsylvania Luth. *Ch. Bk.*, 1868, in 8.6.8.6.8.8. metre.
4. **Father of heaven, Who hast created all.** In *Kennedy*, 1863; the S. P. C. K. *Church Hys.*, 1871; Thring's *Coll.*, 1882; and in America in M. W. Stryker's *Christian Chorals*, 1885.

Hymns not in English C. U :—

v. Abend ist es; Herr, die Stunde. *Evening.* Written at Sulz, June 19, 1828 (*Koch*, vii. 224). 1st pub. in his *Christliche Gedichte*, 1829, i. p. 9, in 10 st. *Tr.* as "It is evening, and the hour, Lord," by *Miss Manington*, 1863, p. 130.

vi. Eines wünsch ich mir vor allem Andern. *Love to Christ.* 1st pub. in his *Christliche Gedichte*, 1829, i. p. 151, in 4 st., entitled "My Wish." Lauxmann, in *Koch*, viii. 59, says it was written, April 23, 1823, while Knapp was at Gaisburg, for the use of a young girl at Stuttgart who was about to be confirmed. Dr. Schaff classes it as the finest and most popular church hymn of its author. *Tr.* as "More than all, one thing my heart is craving," by T. C. Porter, April 13, 1868, for Schaff's *Christ in Song*, 1869, p. 625.

vii. Geh hin! der Herr hat dich gerufen. *Burial of a child.* Written, 1844, on the death of his son Manuel. 1st pub. in his *Christoterpe*, 1849, p. 139, in 4 st. *Tr.* as "Go hence! the Lord hath called thee home," by Dr. J. Guthrie, in his *Sacred Lyrics*, 1869, p. 112.

viii. Geh zum Schlummer ohne Kummer. *Burial.* Written in memory of his first wife, who d. April 11, 1835. 1st pub. in his *Ev. L. S.*, 1837, No. 3432 (1865, No. 3006), in 5 st. *Tr.* as "Softly slumber, softly slumber," by R. Massie, in the *Day of Rest*, 1878.

ix. Geist des Lebens, heil'ge Gabe. *Whitsuntide.* Written at Sulz for Whitsuntide, 1828 (*Koch*, vii. 225). 1st pub. in his *Christliche Gedichte*, 1829, i. p. 86, in 13 st. *Tr.* as "Thou Spirit, Who dost life impart," by J. *Kelly*, 1885, p. 63.

x. Hättest du Licht und Heil. *The Blessings of Salvation.* In his *Christliche Gedichte*, 1829, i. p. 149, in 7 st. *Tr.* as "Ob, Jesus! had'st Thou not brought near," by *C. T. Astley*, 1860, p. 30.

xi. Heulend spielen Stürme mit den Schiffen. *For those at Sea.* 1st pub. in his *Christliche Gedichte*, 1829, ii. p. 26, in 10 st., entitled "The Walk on the Sea, Matthew xiv. 24–32." *Tr.* as "Howling storms are sporting with the vessel," in L. Rehfuess's *Church at Sea*, 1868, p. 38.

xii. Ihr Kinder lernt von Anfang gern. *Children.* Written 1839, and 1st pub. in his *Christenlieder*, 1841, No. 212, in 9 st., entitled "The Use of the Fourth (Fifth) Commandment." *Tr.* as "Betimes O learn, ye children, well," by *Dr. G. Walker*, 1860, p. 68.

xiii. Jesus, ew'ge Sonne. *The Glory of Christ.* In his *Neuere Gedichte*, 1834, ii. p. 50, in 7 st. *Tr.* as "Jesus, everlasting Sun," by *J. Kelly*, 1885, p. 35.

xiv. Schwellet sanft, ihr weissen Segel. *For those at Sea.* 1st pub. in his *Ev. L. S.*, 1837, No. 3109, in 5 st. *Tr.* as "Gently swell, ye white sails, driven," in L. Rehfuess's *Church at Sea*, 1868, p. 13.

xv. Sohn des Vaters, Herr der Ehren. *Waiting on God.* In his *Christliche Gedichte*, 1829, i. p. 162, in 3 st. *Tr.* as (1) "Son of the Father! mighty Lord, An answer," by *C. T. Astley*, 1860, p. 1. (2) "Lord of glory, God's dear Son, Let this thing," &c., by *R. Massie*, 1864, p. 124.

xvi. Streichet hin, ihr leisen Flügel. *The Fleetness of Time.* In his *Ev. L. S.*, 1837, No. 2903, in 3 st. *Tr.* as "O ye winds of time! still hieing," in L. Rehfuess's *Church at Sea*, 1868, p. 42.

xvii. Weh' mich vom sanften Mittag an. *The Waiting Soul.* The original of this hymn is J. Newton's "Breathe from the gentle South, O Lord " (*Olney Hys.*, 1779, Bk. iii., No. 10). Knapp's *tr.* is full and good, and is included in his *Christoterpe*, 1837, p. 294, and *Ev. L. S.*, 1837, No. 2251. The text *tr.* is that in S. Hofer's *Pilgerharfe*, Basel, 1863, No. 118, which begins with st. iii. altered to "O Herr, ich möchte stille sein." Mr. R. Massie was quite unconscious that he was reproducing a hymn of Newton's by a process of double translation. His versions are, (1) "O Lord, I gladly would be still," in the *British Herald*, June, 1865, p. 85. (2) "Lord, I would still and patient be," in the *Day of Rest*, 1877, vol. viii. p. 379.

xviii. Wenn ich in stiller Frühe. *Morning.* In his *Christliche Gedichte*, 1829, i. p. 25, in 3 st., entitled "The Morning Star." *Tr.* as, (1) "When in the cool, still morning," by R. Massie, in the *British Herald*, April, 1865, p. 56, and Reid's *Praise Bk.*, 1872. (2) "When from my sleep awaking," by R. Massie, in the *Day of Rest*, 1877, p. 375.

xix. Wie hold ist diese Stille. *Sunday Morning.* Written 1842. In his *Gedichte, Neueste Folge*, 1843, p. 3, in 7 st. In his *Ev. L. S.*, 1850, No 1176 (1865, No. 1217), it begins "Wie süss." *Tr.* as "O quiet, silent sweetness," in L. Rehfuess's *Church at Sea*, 1868, p. 27.

Five additional hymns by Knapp are *tr.* by Dr. H. Mills in his *Horae Germanicae*, 1845 and 1856. A version by Knapp from Cæsar Malan is noted under "Non, ce nest pas mourir."   [J. M.]

Knight, Joel Abel. In Dobell's *New Selection* of 700 *Evangelical Hymns*, 1806, is a hymn on the death of a child, commencing, "Alas! how changed that lovely flower," the name affixed being "Knight." It also appears with the same signature in Denham's *Selection*, 1837, and in some American hymnbooks. The writer was most probably the Rev. Joel Abel Knight, an Evangelical divine, who, in 1789, pub. a vol. of Sermons, and was the author of a small volume of *Sacred Poems.* Knight was a man of some note, and friend of J. Newton, Greathead, Rippon, and Ryland. He was also the author of "My Father's at the helm."   [W. R. S.]

Knoll, Christoph, was b. in 1563 at Bunzlau in Silesia, and entered the University of Frankfurt a. Oder in 1583. In 1586 he was appointed assistant (Signator) in the school at Sprottau in Silesia. He then became, in 1591, diaconus, and in 1620 archidiaconus, at Sprottau. On Nov. 23, 1628, he was expelled by the Lichtenstein dragoons, but was eventually allowed to become pastor at the neighbouring village of Wittgendorf, where he d. in 1650 (S. J. Ehrhardt's *Presbyterologie Schlesiens*, 1780–89, iii. pp. 386, 505, &c.). His well-known hymn,

Herzlich thut mich verlangen, *For the Dying*, is said to have been written during a pestilence in 1599, and was first printed at Görlitz in 1605 (see *Blätter für Hymnologie*, 1887, pp. 8, 56, &c.). In *Wackernagel*, v. p. 350 (from Buchwalder's *G. B.*, Görlitz, 1611, &c.), the *Unv. L. S.* 1851, No. 822, &c., in 11 st. of 8 l. *Tr.* as " My heart is filled with longing," by Miss Winkworth in her *C. B. for England*, 1863, Appx. No. iv. [J. M.]

Knollis, Francis Minden, D.D., s. of the Rev. James Knollis, Vicar of Penn, Bucks, was b. Nov. 14, 1815, and d. at Bournemouth, Aug. 25, 1863. He was educated at Magdalen, Oxford (B.A. 1837, D.D. 1851), and took Holy Orders in 1838. He was for sometime Fellow of his College, Chaplain to Lord Ribblesdale, and Incumbent of Fitzhead. His publications were somewhat numerous, including *A Wreath for the Altar; A Garland for the School, or Sacred Verses for Sunday Scholars*, 1854. His well-known hymn, "There is no night in heaven " (*Heaven and its blessedness*), appeared in Rutherford's *Lays of the Sanctuary and Other Poems*, 1859, p. 134, in 10 st. of 4 l. It is headed " The One Family. Thoughts for the Feast of St. Michael and All Angels." [J. J.]

Knöpken, Andreas (Cnophius), was b. at Küstrin (Cüstrin) about 1490. He was for some time assistant in the school at Treptow, in East Pomerania, under Bugenhagen. But as they both espoused the cause of the Reformation, they had to flee from Treptow in 1521, Bugenhagen to Wittenberg, and Knöpken to Riga. At Riga Knöpken conducted a successful disputation with the monks, and was appointed by the Council and burgesses evangelical archidiaconus of St. Peter's Church, where he began his work Oct. 23, 1522. He d. at Riga, Feb. 18, 1539.

Knöpken's hymns are almost all Psalm versions. Three appeared under the title of *Ethlike psalmen dorch Andream Knöpken vordütscht* as an *Appendix* to B. Waldis's *De parabell vam vorlorn Szohn*, Riga, 1527. The rest appeared in the *Riga Kirchenordnung*, 1530, 1537, &c. See the introduction to Dr. J. Geffcken's reprint (Hannover, 1862) of the various eds. of this *Kirchenordnung*.

Knöpken's hymns tr. into English are :—

i. **Hilff Gott, wie geht das immer zu.** *Ps. ii.* 1527, as above, and thence in *Wackernagel*, iii. pp. 99–103, in 8 st. of 7 l., beginning " Help Godt, wo geyt dat yümer to." The High German form is in the *Zwickau Enchiridion*, 1528. *Tr.* as " Quhat is the caus, O God omnipotent " in the *Gude and Godlie Ballates*, 1568, f. 44 (1868, p. 74).

ii. **Von allen Menschen abgewandt.** *Ps. xxv.* 1527, as above, and thence in *Wackernagel*, iii. pp. 105–109, in 12 st. of 7 l., beginning " Van allen Mynschen afgewandt." In High German in V. Schumann's *G. B.*, Leipzig, 1539. *Tr.* as " I lyft my soule, Lorde, up to the, My God," by Bp. Coverdale, 1539 (*Remains*, 1846, p. 578).

A hymn frequently, but erroneously, ascribed to Knöpken is noted under Cruciger, E. (p. 271 i.). [J. M.]

Knorr, Christian, Baron von Rosenroth, s. of Abraham Knorr von Rosenroth, pastor at Altrauden in Silesia, was b. at Altrauden, July 15, 1636. After studying at the Universities of Leipzig (where he graduated M.A. 1659, along with J. B. Carpzov, the famous Orientalist) and Wittenberg, he made an ex-

tended tour through France, England, and Holland. At Amsterdam he became acquainted with an Armenian prince, with the chief Rabbi, Meier Stern, from Frankfurt-am-Main, with Dr. John Lightfoot, Dr. Henry More, and others, and as the result of intercourse with them, devoted himself to the study of the Oriental languages, of chemistry, and of the cabalistic sciences. For his learning in these departments he was taken into the service of the like-minded Palsgrave Christian August of Sulzbach, who in 1668 appointed him Geheimrath and prime minister (Kanzlei-director). He was created Baron von Rosenroth by the Emperor Leopold I. in 1677, and d. at Sulzbach (near Amberg, Bavaria), May 8, 1689, it is said at the hour he had himself predicted. (*Wetzel*, ii. 43, and *A. H.*, ii. 411; Hörner's *Nachrichten von Liederdichtern*, Schwabach, 1775, p. 142, &c.)

Knorr edited various Rabbinical writings, published various cabalistic works (e.g. his *Kabbala denudata*, 2 vols., Sulzbach, 1677), and was one of the seekers after the philosopher's stone. His hymns appeared as *Neuer Helicon mit seiner Neun Musen, das ist : Geistliche Sitten-Lieder*, &c. Nürnberg, 1684 [Hamburg Library], a work containing 70 hymns mostly flowing in expression and metre. Of these 12 are poetic versions from Boethius's *De Consolatione Philosophiae*, 8 are from Latin hymns, and 8 are recasts of older German hymns. Sixteen of his hymns were included by Freylinghausen in his *G. B.*, 1704 and 1714. Koch speaks of them not unjustly as " truly pious and spiritual," as " of genuine poetical elevation and glowing desire after inner union with Christ," and as the fruits of a " noble and chastely earnest mysticism."

Two of Knorr's hymns have passed into English. One is a *tr.* of " Ad coenam Agni " (p. 12 ii.). The other is

Morgenglanz der Ewigkeit. *Morning.* This fine hymn appeared, 1684, as above, p. 159, in 7 st. of 6 l., entitled " Morning Prayer," and is included in the Berlin *G. L. S.*, ed. 1863, No. 1121. It is based on a hymn by M. Opitz (see Opitz, No. ii.), but is more happily expressed, and has attained much greater popularity. *Fischer*, ii. 94, speaks of it as " one of the freshest, most original, and spirited of Morning Hymns, as if born from the dew of the sunrise." In all the *trs.* in C. U. st. ii., v. are omitted. *Tr.* as :—

1. **Light of heaven's eternal day !** A good *tr.* by A. T. Russell, as No. 68 in the Dalston Hospital *H. Bk.*, 1848, repeated in his own *Ps. & Hys.*, 1851, and the Cheltenham *College H. Bk.*, 1866.

2. **Dayspring of Eternity ! Dawn on us this** morning-tide. A good *tr.* by Miss Winkworth in her *Lyra Ger.*, 1st Ser., 1855, p. 219. In full in the *Hyl. for St. John's, Aberdeen*, 1870, and E. Courtauld's *Ps., Hys. & Anthems*, 1860 ; and abridged in *Hys. of the Spirit*, Boston, U.S., 1864, Dr. Martineau's *Hymns*, 1873, and others.

3. **Jesus, Sun of Righteousness.** A good but rather free *tr.* by Miss Borthwick, in *H. L. L.*, 2nd Ser., 1855, p. 23 (1884, p. 88), included in the *Hy. Comp.*, 1876 ; *Evang. Union Hyl.*, 1878 ; *Ch. Praise*, 1883, &c. ; and in America in the *Sabbath H. Bk.*, 1858 ; *Pennsylvania Luth. Ch. Bk.*, 1868, and others. In E. T. Prust's *Suppl. H. Bk.*, 1869, *Baptist Hyl.*, 1879, and others, ll. 5, 6 of each st. are omitted. In Hatfield's *Church H. Bk.*, N. Y., 1872, *Hys. & Songs of Praise*, N. Y., 1874, and others, it is rewritten to 6 lines of 7's.

4. **Come, Thou bright and morning star.** A good

tr. contributed by R. Massie to the 1857 ed. of Mercer's *C. P. & H. Bk.*, No. 502 (Ox. ed. 1864, No. 1), and in his own *Lyra Domestica*, 1864, p. 136. Repeated in R. Minton Taylor's *Hymnal*, 1872, No. 42; Marlborough College *H. Bk.*, 1869; Rugby *School H. Bk.*, 1876, and others.

5. **Sun of heaven's eternal day.** A good *tr.* contributed by Dr. John Ker to the *United Presb. Juv. Miss. Mag.*, 1858, p. 73 ; repeated in the *Ibrox Hyl.*, 1871.

6. **Dayspring of Eternity, Light of uncreated Light.** By Dr. B. H. Kennedy, as No. 824 in his *Hymno. Christ.*, 1863.

7. **Dayspring of Eternity! Hide no more thy radiant dawning.** A good *tr.* by Miss Winkworth (based on her 1855 version), as No. 159 in her *C. B. for England*, 1863. Repeated in R. Minton Taylor's *Hymnal*, 1872, No. 43, and the *Bk. of Ch. Praise*, 1865 (Bosworth).

8. **Dayspring of Eternity, Brightness of the Father's glory.** A good but free *tr.* by J. H. Hopkins, 1st pub. in Dr. Walter's *Chorals & Hys.*, 1866, and then in his own *Carols, Hys. & Songs*, 1882, p. 145. Included in the *Hys. & Songs of Praise*, N. Y., 1874.

9. **Dayspring of Eternity, Brightness of the Light divine.** In Brown-Borthwick's *Select Hys.*, 1871, and *Ch. Hys.*, 1871, compiled mainly from the *trs.* by Miss Winkworth and Miss Borthwick, but partly from Dr. Kennedy and Mr. Russell. Thence in J. L. Porter's *Coll.*, 1876, and the *Psalmist*, 1878.

10. **Dayspring of eternal day.** A good *tr.* by Edward Thring, contributed to the *Uppingham and Sherborne School H. Bk.*, 1874, No. 5.

Other trs. are: (1) "Day-dawn of Eternity," by *H. J. Buckoll*, 1842, p. 35. (2) "Daystar from Eternity," in J. Slieppard's *Foreign Sacred Lyre*, 1857, p. 84. (3) "Morning glance of verity," by *Miss Manington*, 1863, p. 111. (4) "Brightness of Eternal Day," by Miss Burlingham, in the *British Herald*, May, 1866, p. 264, and Reid's *Praise Bk.*, 1872, No. 404.   [J. M.]

Knowles, James Davis, an American Baptist Minister, was b. at Providence, Rhode Island, 1798; educated at Columbian College; became pastor of the 2nd Baptist Church, Boston, 1825, and Professor at Newton Theological Institute, 1832. He d. in 1838. His hymn, "O God, through countless worlds of light" (*Dedication of a Place of Worship*), appeared in the Baptist *Psalmist*, 1843; the Meth. Episco. *Hymns*, 1849, &c.
[F. M. B.]

Knox, William, b. at Firth, Lilliesleaf, Roxburgh, Aug. 17, 1789, and educated at the parish school, and the grammar school at Musselburgh. For some time he was engaged in farming at Wrae, near Langholm, Dumfriesshire; but not succeeding to his satisfaction, he left Wrae in 1817, and finally settled in Edinburgh in 1820, where he subsequently obtained employment as a contributor to the public journals. He d. in Edinburgh, Nov. 12, 1825. His poetical works were, (1) *The Lonely Hearth*, North Shields, 1818; (2) *Songs of Israel*, 1824; (3) *The Harp of Zion*, 1825; and (4) these three works, together with a short Memoir, as his *Poems*, &c., Lond., J. Johnson, 1847. The *Songs* and *Harp* are mainly paraphrases of portions of Holy Scripture. A few have come into use as congregational hymns, as, "A voice comes from Ramah," "Acquaint thee, O mortal," "O

sweet as vernal dews that fall" (*Ps. cxxxiii.*), and others.   [J. J.]

Koch, Eduard Emil, was b. Jan. 30, 1809, at the Solitude, near Stuttgart. After the completion of his theological studies at Tübingen in 1830, he was for some time assistant clergyman at Ehningen, near Böblingen, and in 1837 became pastor at Gross-Aspach, near Marbach, on the Neckar. In 1847 he was appointed third pastor, then second, and in 1853 chief pastor and decan at Heilbronn. In 1864 he took an easier post as pastor at Erdmannhausen, near Marbach. He d. while on a visit to Stuttgart, April 27, 1871 (*Allg. Deutsche Biog.*, xvi. 373-375).

Koch claims notice here as the author of the *Geschichte des Kirchenlieds und Kirchengesangs der Christlichen, insbesondere der deutschen evangelischen Kirche.* The 1st ed. appeared at Stuttgart, 1847, in 2 vols., and the second at Stuttgart, in 4 vols., 1852-53. Of the 3rd ed. he only lived to complete vols. 1-6, 1866-1869, vol. 7 being edited from his MSS. by his son (recently Court chaplain to Prince Alexander of Bulgaria), and pub. 1872; with an 8th volume by R. Lauxmann (founded on vol. iv. of 1853), 1876, and finally a very incomplete index in 1877. All the references in this Dictionary are to the third ed., unless the contrary is stated, and the following notice refers exclusively to it. Regarded as the work of one man, and as covering the whole field of German Hymnody, it is a wonderful achievement, and worthy of the highest admiration. It was a great advance on anything previously attempted, and as a comprehensive survey will not soon be superseded. Regarded more in detail, it has two main sides, biographical and bibliographical. As a collection of biographies with historical connections it possesses great merit. The biographies are for the most part full, careful, and interesting, and have been taken as the basis of the biographical notices by the present writer, who has pleasure in directing attention to them as containing especially much fuller details of the spiritual life of the authors than he has been able to give. As a collection of notes upon individual hymns, and notices of the works of the authors brought under review it is impossible to speak by any means so highly. Had Koch been content to indicate in any way the information which he had himself gathered from the books he was able to consult, his work might not have appeared so complete, but would in reality have been much more valuable. As it is, the information given is very often confused and inexact, and what is much worse, it is often when definite totally wrong, plainly showing that the writer had never seen many of the books which he cites : so that no single statement (especially of the period 1600-1750) can be taken without verification. The practical result to the present writer was that he was compelled in 1885 to make a visit to Germany for the purpose of consulting the hymnological collections in various of the principal libraries. All the references by page or number to the works of German authors have been made either by himself or by others at his request specially for this Dictionary.   [J. M.]

Koitsch, Christian Jacob, was b. Sept. 13, 1671, at Meissen, where his father was a leathercutter. He entered the University of Leipzig in 1692, and then went as a student of theology to Halle, where, under the influence of Francke and Breithaupt, he became one of the first "awakened" students. After he had finished his course, Francke appointed him, in 1696, as one of the Masters, and in 1700 as Inspector, of the Paedagogium at Halle. In 1705 he became Professor and Rector of the Gymnasium at Elbing, and d. at Elbing, Aug. 21, 1734. (*Bode*, p. 99 ; *Allg. Deutsche Biog.*, xvi. 455, &c.) To Freylinghausen's *Geistreiches G. B.*, 1704, and its 2nd ed., 1705, he contributed 8 (or 9) hymns ; and two others to his *Neues geistreiches G. B.*, 1714. Of these the following have passed into English, viz. :—

i. **Du bist ja, Jesu, meine Freude.** *Christian War-*

fate. 1704, as above, No. 308, in 6 st. *Tr.* as "Thou, Jesu, art my Consolation," by Miss Burlingham, in the *British Herald*, March, 1866, p. 232, repeated in Reid's *Praise Bk.*, 1872.

ii. **Lasset uns den Herren preisen.** *Thanksgiving.* Founded on Ps. lxxii. 18, 19. 1704, as above, No. 488, in 7 st. *Tr.* as "Now unite to render praises," by W. Okely, as No. 800 in the *Moravian H. Bk.*, 1789 (1886, No. 648).

iii. **Mein Herze, wie wankest und fladderst du noch.** *Self-Renunciation.* 1705, as above, No. 718, in 8 st. *Tr.* as "O Saviour, the truest, the best of all friends" (st. vi.), as No. 429 in the *Moravian H. Bk.*, 1886.

iv. **O Ursprung des Lebens, o ewiges Licht.** *Love to Christ.* A fine hymn on Christ as the Fountain of Life. 1704, as above, No. 356, in 7 st. of 6 l.; and in the Berlin *G. L. S.*, ed. 1863, No. 825. The *tr.* in C. U. is "O Fountain eternal of life and of light." A good *tr.*, omitting st. iii., as No. 1100 in the *Suppl.* of 1808 to the *Moravian H. Bk.*, 1801. In the 1826 and later eds. (1886, No. 631), a *tr.* by J. Swertner of st. iii. was incorporated—this st. having appeared as No. 267 in the *Moravian H. Bk.*, 1801. Included, altered and abridged, in Mercer's *C. P. and H. Bk.*, 1855 and 1864, and the *Irish Ch. Hyl.*, 1873. Another *tr.* is "O everlasting source of life and light," by Miss Borthwick, in *H. L. L.*, 1862, p. 79 (1884, p. 241).   [J. M.]

Kolbe, Frederick William,

was b. Nov. 3, 1821, at Gütersloh, Westphalia, and having been trained at the Mission College of the Rhenish Society at Barmen, was sent, in 1844, as a missionary to the Cape of Good Hope. There he laboured in the district of Worcester till 1848, when he proceeded to Damaraland and joined the first missionaries to the Ovaherero. There he contributed 35 hymns and school songs to the first Herero hymnal, printed at Cape Town, in 1849. In 1853 he joined the London Missionary Society, and since then his sphere of work has again been in the Colony, first at George, and for nearly 20 years at the Paarl. There he prepared an enlarged edition of the Dutch hymn-book of the London Missionary Society, adding 100 hymns written by himself (some original, but) most of them translations of well-known English and German hymns. Many of these translations by Mr. Kolbe are now in extensive use among the Church of England, Congregational, and Dutch Reformed native congregations throughout South Africa. The Church of England Dutch *Hymnal*, compiled by Rev. J. A. Hewitt in 1877, comprising 201 hymns, has 37 of Mr. Kolbe's translations and four of his original hymns. Mr. Kolbe has recently prepared a new *Supplement* to the Dutch Hymn-book of the London Society, referred to above, containing translations of "Lead, kindly light," "Art thou weary," "Take my life," and other modern English hymns.   [W. R. S.]

Kolross, Johann (Rhodanthracius),

is said to have been a pastor at Basel, and to have died there in 1558. In his *Encheridion*, Nürnberg, 1529 (later ed., 1534. It is a manual of orthography), he calls himself teacher of German (*Teutsch Lehermayster*) at Basel; and so in his Scriptural play (*Ein schön spil von Fünfferley betrachtnussen den menschen zûr Büss reytzende.* It is on the motives of the Dance of Death at Basel), performed at Basel on the 1st S. after Easter, 1532, and printed at Basel, 1532 (Goedeke's *Grundriss*, 1886, ii. 181, 337, 343, &c.). The only hymn by him *tr.* into English is:—

Ich dank dir lieber Herre. *Morning.* 1st pub. separately at Nürnberg, c. 1535, and thence in *Wackernagel*, iii. p. 86, in 9 st. of 8 l. Included in V. Schu-

mann's *G. B.*, Leipzig, 1539, the Berlin *G. L. S.*, ed. 1863, No. 1111, &c. It has been characterised as containing "all the leading thoughts of the Reformation." The *trs.* are from the greatly altered form in 6 st., beginning "Das walten deine Wunden," given as No. 1800 in *Appx.* xii., c. 1744, to the *Herrnhut G. B.* 1735, and in the *Brüder G. B.*, 1778, No. 1509. They are, (1) "Thy Wounds, Lord, be my Safeguard," as No. 324 in pt. i. of the *Moravian H. Bk.*, 1754. In the ed. of 1849, 2 st. are repeated, st. v. beginning "Lord Christ I give Thee praises," as No. 1006, and st. iv. beginning "Amidst this world's profaneness," as No. 610.

To Kolross has also been ascribed (as in the *Zürich G. B.*, 1570) a version of *Ps. cxxvii.*, which 1st appeared in the *Zwickau Enchiridion*, 1525, and begins "So (Wo) Gott zum Haus nicht giebt sein Gunst." A rendering of *Ps. cxxvii.* is given under this first line in J. C. Jacobi's *Psalmodia Germanica*, 1722, p. 35 (1732, p. 60), but it is not from the German, and is simply the L.M. version of this Psalm by Isaac Watts. A hymn also ascribed to Kolross is noted under **Magdeburg, J.**   [J. M.]

Komm heiliger Geist, Herre Gott.

M. Luther. [*Whitsuntide.*] *Wackernagel*, ii. p. 748, gives as No. 986 a double form of st. i. from two MSS. of the 15th cent. at Munich; as No. 987 a form from the Basel *Plenarium*, 1514; and as No. 988 a form from the *Obsequiale*, Ingolstadt, 1570. This stanza is a *tr.* of an antiphon, not earlier than the 11th cent., which reads "Veni Sancte Spiritus: reple tuorum corda fidelium, et tui amoris in eis ignem accende: Qui per diversitatem linguarum cunctarum gentes in unitate fidei congregasti. Alleluia" (see *Daniel*, ii. p. 315). *Bäumker*, i. pp. 643, 644, says the Latin antiphon is still sung in many dioceses in Germany on Sundays before High Mass, and cites the German as in the *Crailsheim Schulordnung* of 1480. Martin Luther adopted this old German stanza with alterations, and adding two original stanzas, pub. the whole in *Eyn Enchiridion*, Erfurt, 1524. The complete form in 3 st. of 8 l., with "Alleluia," is in *Wackernagel*, iii. p. 14, in Schircks's ed. of Luther's *Geistl. Lieder*, 1854, p. 28, and the *Unv. L. S.*, 1851, No. 174. The hymn soon became popular in Germany. *Koch*, viii. 87, says that in the Peasants' War it was sung by Münzer and his forces immediately before the battle of Frankenhausen, May 25, 1525; that it was sung by Leonhard Kayser when at the stake at Passau, Aug. 16, 1527; and that st. ii. was the last pulpit utterance of J. M. Dilherr, in March, 1669. *Tr.* as:—

1. Come Holy Ghost! Come Lord our God! In full by J. C. Jacobi, in his *Psalmodia Germanica*, 1722, p. 25 (1732, p. 42). Included in the *Moravian H. Bk.*, 1754, slightly altered, but in the 1789 and later eds. (1886, No. 239) greatly altered, probably by J. Swertner. The text of 1789 is repeated in the Irish *Church Hyl.*, 1873. In 1846 W. J. Blew printed a recast for choir use, and included it in his *Ch. H. & Tune Bk.*, 1852–55, with an added doxology.

2. Holy Spirit, gracious Lord. By Miss Fry, in her *Hys. of the Reformation*, 1845, p. 108, in 40 lines. Her version of st. i., rewritten to 2 st. of 8 l., is No. 152 in Whittemore's *Suppl. to all H. Bks.*, 1860.

3. Blest Comforter! come;—Lord our God! In full by A. T. Russell, as No. 17 in his *Ps. & Hys.*, 1851; repeated by Dr. Bacon in his *Hys. of*

Martin Luther, 1884, p. 27, altered to "Come, Holy Spirit, Lord our God, And pour."

4. Come, Holy Ghost! Lord God, fulfil. A good and full *tr.* by R. Massie, in his *Martin Luther's Spir. Songs*, 1854, p. 19. Repeated in Mercer's *C. P. & H. Bk.*, 1857, unaltered save "full fill" in st. i. l. 1. (Ox. ed., 1864, No. 435, as 6 st. of 4 l.) ; and in the Ohio *Luth. Hyl.*, 1880, reading "and fill."

5. Come, Holy Spirit, God and Lord. In full by Miss Winkworth, in her *Lyra Ger.*, 1st Ser., 1855, p. 117 ; and her *C. B. for England*, 1863, No. 72. Repeated in Dr. Thomas's *Augustine H. Bk.*, 1866, and the Pennsylvania Luth. *Church Bk.*, 1868.

6. Come, Holy Spirit! gracious Lord! Help us. By M..E. Tupper, as No. 57 in Judd's *S. S. H. Bk.*, Halifax, 1870.

Other trs. are :—
(1) "Come, holy Spirite, most blessed Lorde," by Bp. Coverdale, 1539 (*Remains*, 1846, p. 542). (2) "Come holy holy Ghost, Lord our God," in *Lyra Davidica*, 1708, p. 51. (3) "Lord God, the Holy Spirit, come," by *J. Anderson*, 1846, p. 17 (1847, p. 41). (4) "Come, Holy Ghost! Come, Lord our God! Thy," by *J. Hunt*, 1853, p. 49. (5) "Come, Holy Ghost! rule Thou within," by *Dr. H. Mills*, 1856, p. 143. (6) "Come, Holy Ghost, come, mighty God," by *E. Massie*, 1867, p. 209. (7) "Come, Holy Spirit, Lord and God," by Dr. G. Macdonald in the *Sunday Mag.*, 1867, p. 388, and his *Exotics*, 1876, p. 57.   [J. M.]

Kommt, Kinder, lasst uns gehen.

G. Tersteegen. [*Christian Pilgrimage.*] 1st pub. in the 3rd ed., 1738, of his *Geistliches Blumengärtlein*, Bk. iii. No. 62, in 19 st. of 8 l., entitled "Hymn of Encouragement for Pilgrims." Repeated in full in the *Unv. L. S.*, 1851, No. 322 ; and, abridged, in many other German collections. Illustrating this hymn, Lauxmann, in *Koch*, viii. 564, says that Tersteegen

"once said to some of his friends, who visited him on his birthday : 'My friends, if I should die to-day I would only have three words to say to you as a last farewell: 1. Place your whole confidence on the grace of God in Christ Jesus ; 2. Love one another ; 3. Watch and pray !' This is the quintessence of this noble travelling song for Christian pilgrims and strangers here below (1 St. Peter ii. 11, 12), whose course is a march through the Desert to Canaan. The whole life of Tersteegen is proof of the genuineness and sincerity of the spirit that breathes throughout this hymn."

Translations in C. U. :—

1. Come, brothers, let us onward. A *tr.* of st. i., ii., v., x., xiv., xvii., xviii., by Mrs. Findlater, in *H. L. L.*, 1st Ser., 1854, p. 51 (1884, p. 52). The *trs.* of st. i., ii., xvii., xviii., were included in J. A. Johnston's *English Hyl.* (ed. 1861, No. 192).

2. Come, brethren, let us go. A good *tr.* of st. i., ii., vi. xi., xii., xiv.–xix., by Miss Winkworth, in her *Lyra Ger.*, 1st Ser., 1855, p. 161. A cento in 6 st. of 4 l., from the *trs.* of st. i., xi., xvi., xvii., is included in the *Parish H. Bk.*, 1863 and 1875. Centos beginning with the *tr.* of st. xi., "Come, children, let us go," are in the Eng. Presb. *Ps. & Hys.*, 1867, and the Cong. *School Hyl.*, 1881.

Other trs. are, (1) "Come, children! on ; this way," by *Miss Warner*, 1858, p. 224. (2) "Come, children, let's be going," in the *Christian Examiner*, Boston, U. S., Sept., 1860, p. 252. (3) "Come, brethren, let us hurry," in L. Rehfuess's *Church at Sea*, 1868, p. 99.   [J. M.]

Κοντάκιον. [Greek Hymnody, § XII. 1—XVI. 4.]

Κόπον τε καὶ κάματον. [*Rest in Jesus.*] In the 1st ed. of Dr. Neale's *Hys. of the Eastern Church* he gives this hymn as by "S. Stephen the Sabaite, A.D. 725—A.D. 794"; calls it "Idiomela in the Week of the First Oblique Tone," and adds, "These stanzas, which strike me as very sweet, are not in all the editions of the *Octoechus*. I copy from a dateless Constantinopolitan book." In subsequent editions of the *Hys. of the E. Church* the words "I copy from a dateless Constantinopolitan book" were omitted. This omission has caused numerous fruitless searches for the text in the authorized editions of the *Octoechus*. The Constantinopolitan book referred to by Dr. Neale cannot be found amongst Dr. Neale's books, nor has a copy corresponding thereto been as yet discovered.

The so-called translation of this Idiomela, "Art thou weary, art thou languid ?" was accompanied in the 3rd ed., 1866, of Dr. Neale's *Hys. of the E. Church*, with a note in the Preface to this effect :—

"The Hymns at page 206 ['O happy band of pilgrims'], 209 ['Safe home,' &c.], and 'Art thou weary,' contain so little that is from the Greek, that they ought not to have been included in this collection ; in any future Edition they shall appear as an Appendix."

In accordance with this expressed wish of Dr. Neale's these hymns were given as an *Appendix* to the 4th ed. of the *Hys. of the E. Church*, 1882, edited by the Very Rev. S. G. Hatherley. The most therefore that can be said of these three hymns is that they are based upon the few words quoted by Dr. Neale which he found in his extensive reading of the Greek Sacred Poets, and that those words have yet to be traced to their original source.

"Art thou weary, art thou languid," appeared in the 1st ed. of the *Hys. of the E. Church*, 1862, in 7 st. of 4 l. It was at once included in T. Darling's *Hys. for the Ch. of England*, 1862 ; and the *Parish H. Bk.*, 1863 ; and subsequently in almost every hymn-book published in G. Britain and America. It has been set to a great number of tunes, those in *H. A. & M.* being *Christus Consolator* by Dr. Dykes ; and *Stephanos* by Sir H. W. Baker, harmonized by W. H. Monk. Sir A. Sullivan's tune in *Church Hymns* is entitled *Rest*. In the *Contemporary Review* for Dec. 1875, there is a rendering of "Art thou weary," &c., into Latin by W. E. Gladstone. This, together with Dr. Neale's text and a short note, were given in the *Times* of Dec. 2, 1875. The Latin begins, "Scis te lassum? scis languentem ?"

Another rendering by H. M. Macgill in his *Songs of the Christian Creed & Life*, 1876, is "Sisne lassus, aerumnosus."

An expanded version of this hymn appeared in 1887 under the following circumstances:—

"Several years ago," says Dr. Boyd of St. Andrews, N.B., "an anonymous correspondent sent me 'Art thou weary,' in print with the added stanzas." Thinking that he had been favoured with Dr. Neale's original form of the hymn, and not having Dr. Neale's works at hand for correction, Dr. Boyd wrote a short notice of the hymn in this expanded form, and had it inserted in the May, 1887, number of *Life and Work. A Scottish Magazine*, &c., p. 73, as 'A Regrettable Omission in a Favourite Hymn.' The added stanzas are :—

" '5. Is this all He hath to give me
          In my life below ?
Joy unspeakable and glorious
     Thou shalt know.

" ' 6. All thy sins shall be forgiven—
    All things work for good :
    Thou shalt Bread of Life from Heaven
    Have for food.

" ' 7. From the fountains of Salvation
    Thou shalt Water draw :
    Sweet shall be thy meditation
    In God's Law.

" ' 9. Festal Palms, and Crowns of Glory,
    Robes in Blood wash'd white,
    God in Christ His People's Temple—
    There no night.' "

The hymn as thus expanded into 11 st. has been printed as a leaflet, with the heading "Complete Version of Hymn 163" [in the *Scottish Hymnal*, 1884]. That these additional stanzas are neither by Dr. Neale nor from a Greek hymn, is evident to any one acquainted with Dr. Neale's works and with the Service Books of the Greek Church.

In King's *Anglican Hymnology*, 1885, p. 194, there is a most striking account of Mr. King's visit to the Monastery at Mar Saba, where St. Stephen resided and wrote. It is one of the redeeming features of that most unsatisfactory and unreliable work. [J. J.]

Kosegarten, Ludwig Gotthard, was b. Feb. 1. 1758, at Grevismühlen, Mecklenburg, and studied at the University of Rostock-Bützow (PH. D. 1785, D.D. 1792). After being for some time Rector of the school at Wolgast, near Greifswald, he became, in 1792, pastor at Altenkirchen, on the island of Rügen. This post he held till the 21st S. after Trinity, 1815 (officiating during vacations), though he had in 1808 been also appointed Professor of History at Greifswald. In 1817 he became third Professor of Theology and pastor of St. James's Church at Greifswald, and d. there Oct. 26, 1818. His *Dichtungen* appeared at Greifswald, 1812–13, in 8 vols., and 1824–27 in 12 vols. Four additional hymns are given at the end of his *Akademische Reden*, ed. by G. C. F. Mohnike, and pub. at Stralsund, 1832. One is *tr.*, viz. :—

Jerusalem, du hochgebaute Stadt. *Eternal Life.* 1832, as above, p. 287, in 5 st. of 8 l., entitled "Homesickness." He wrote this, his last poem, with a foreboding of his approaching death, and recited it in the introduction to his last sermon on the 9th S. after Trinity 1818 (July 19). It is a beautiful poem, founded on the better-known hymn by Meyfart (q.v.), and on the Latin hymn "Urbs beata Hierusalem," q.v. Abp. Trench in his *Sac. Lat. Poetry*, 1864, p. 312, quotes ii.-iv. with approbation. *Tr.* as :—
Jerusalem, thou city built on high, **Would God I were in thee.** A full and good *tr.* by J. M. Neale in his *Hys. chiefly Mediaeval on the Joys and Glories of Paradise*, 1865, p. 97. Repeated in the *St. Margaret's Hyl.* (East Grinstead), 1875. [J. M.]

Krause, Jonathan, s. of Christian Wilhelm Krause, Master of the Clothworkers and Sexton at Hirschberg, in Silesia, was b. at Hirschberg, April 5, 1701. Entering the University of Leipzig in 1718, he went in 1723 to Wittenberg, where he graduated M.A. He was then for some time travelling tutor to a young Baron von Birken, and 1727–32 a tutor in the family of Baron von Nostitz, at Polgsen, near Wohlau. On Aug. 20, 1732, he was ordained as Diaconus of Probsthayn, near Liegnitz, and in 1739 became chief pastor of the Church of St. Peter and St. Paul at Liegnitz. In 1741 he was also appointed Superintendent and Assessor of the Consistory.

He d. at Liegnitz, Dec. 13, 1762 (S. J. Ehrhardt's *Presbyterologie Schlesiens*, 1780–89, iv. p. 280, &c.). He edited the Liegnitz *G. B.* of 1745. His hymns appeared in his

(1) *Die zum Lobe Gottes eröffnete Lippen der Gläubigen*, &c., Hamburg, 1732, and (2) *Gnade und Wahrheit Gottes in Christo Jesu, in heiligen Liedern über alle Sonn- und Fest-Tags Evangelien und Episteln*, Leipzig and Lauban, 1739. [Berlin Royal Library.]

The only hymn by Krause *tr.* into English is

Alleluja! schöner Morgen. *Sunday Morning.* This hymn, a great favourite in Southern Germany, 1st appeared 1739 as above, p. 487, in 9 st. of 6 l., entitled "Morning-Hymn on Sunday." Repeated thus in the Liegnitz *G. B.*, 1745, No. 1 ; but in recent colls., as the Württemberg *G. B.*, 1842, and the *Unv. L. S.*, 1851, No. 482, it begins "Hallelujah!" Sometimes erroneously ascribed to B. Schmolck. *Tr.* as :—

Hallelujah! Fairest morning. A good *tr.*, omitting st. v., vii., viii., by Miss Borthwick, in *H. L. L.*, 3rd Ser., 1858, p. 28 (1884, p. 150). Included in full in the *Appx.* of 1869 to the S. P. C. K. *Ps. & Hys.*, in *Holy Song*, 1869, and others. In the S. P. C. K. *Church Hys.*, 1871, the *trs.* of st. iii., iv. are omitted, and the rest slightly altered; and this form is followed in *Laudes Domini*, N. Y., 1884. In G. S. Jellicoe's *Coll.*, 1867, it begins "Alleluia."

Other trs. are, (1) "Hallelujah! beauteous morning," by *Miss Manington*, 1863. (2) "Hallelujah! day of gladness," by R. Massie, in the *Day of Rest*, 1876, p. 35. [J. M.]

Krewziger, Elisabethe. [Cruciger.]

Krishnu Pal, the first Hindoo who was baptized in Bengal, was b. about 1764, and baptized at Serampore by the celebrated Baptist missionary, William Carey, on Dec. 28, 1800. He became a useful Christian minister, and wrote several hymns in the Bengali language. One of these was *tr.* into English by Dr. Marshman in 1801 as "O thou, my soul, forget no more" (*Christ the Friend*). It was included in the 27th ed. of Rippon's *Bap. Sel.*, 1827, No. 170, Pt. 2, in 6 st. of 4 l., in Bickersteth's *Christian Psalmody*, 1833, in 5 st., and again in later collections, including the *Baptist Hymnal*, 1879, and others. Krishnu d. at Serampore, Aug. 22, 1822.
[W. R. S.]

Krummacher, Friedrich Adolf, was a native of Tecklenburg, Westphalia, where his father, Friedrich Jacob Krummacher was Burgomaster and Hoffiscal. He was baptized there, July 22, 1767, and apparently born July 13, 1767. In 1786 he entered the University of Lingen (since 1819 ranked as a Gymnasium), and in 1787 that of Halle. After concluding his theological studies in 1789, he was for some time tutor in the family of Senator Meyer in Bremen ; was then appointed, in 1790, Corrector of the Gymnasium at Hamm, and in 1793 Rector of the Gymnasium at Mörs (Meurs), near Düsseldorf. In the end of 1800 he became Professor of Theology and Eloquence at the Reformed University of Duisburg. When, after the battle of Jena (Oct. 14, 1806), Duisburg was taken from Prussia, the salaries of the professors ceased, but Krummacher lectured on till his audience consisted of one student. He was then, in the autumn of 1807, appointed pastor of Kettwig, on the Ruhr; in 1812 Chief Court Preacher and General Superintendent at Bernburg; and finally, in 1824, he became chief pastor of the St. Ansgarius Church at Bremen. By reason of growing infirmities he resigned his charge in June, 1843, and d. at Bremen, April 4, 1845 (*O. Kraus*, 1879, p. 310 ; *Blätter für Hymnologie*, 1886, p. 80, &c.).

Krummacher is best known as a preacher ; and as the author of the well-known *Parabeln*, first pub. 1805, which passed through many eds., and ranks as the standard German work of its class. His hymns are little suited for church use, being often allegorical and high-flown, and not for the most part sufficiently simple and direct, though in some cases he does write in a popular, natural style, and with a beauty of his own. His hymns mostly appeared in his *Festbüchlein*, a work consisting of allegorical narratives, conversations, &c., with interspersed hymns. Of this the 1st part, entitled *Der Sonntag*, was pub. 1808 (2nd ed. 1810 ; 3rd ed. 1813 ; 4th ed. 1819) ; pt. ii., entitled *Das Christfest*, in 1810 (2nd ed. 1814 ; 3rd ed. 1821) ; and pt. iii., entitled *Das Neujahrsfest*, in 1819.

Those of Krummacher's hymns *tr.* into English are :—

i. **Allgemach aus Dämmerung und Nacht.** *Advent.* In his *Festbüchlein*, pt. ii., 1810 (1814, p. 154), in 5 st. of 4 l., entitled "The Prophets of Nature " ; and given after the conversation on Zacharias, the father. of St. John the Baptist. Included as No. 34 in J. P. Lange's *Deutsches Kirchenliederbuch*, Zürich, 1843. The unity of idea is violated by the concluding lines of st. v.

" Wie die leisen Lispel den Propheten
    Einst auf Horeb's Felsenspitz' umwehten."

And thus in his preface, p. vii., Dr. Lange suggests that st. v. should read thus :—

" Allgemach und siegreich fort und fort
    Bricht durch unser Fleisch das ew'ge Wort ;
    Die Propheten grüsst es durch Gesichte,
    Dann wird's Mensch und himmlische Geschichte."

Tr. as :—

Slowly, slowly from the caves of· night. A full and good *tr.* from Lange by Dr. Kennedy, as No. 42 in his *Hymno. Christ.*, 1863.

ii. **Eine Heerde und ein Hirt.** *Missions.* 1st pub. in the 3rd. ed., 1821, of pt. ii. of his *Festbüchlein*, p. 163, in 6 st. of 6 l., at the close of the section on "Israel and the Strangers." In the Berlin *G. L. S.*, ed. 1863, No. 1365, and many other recent collections. The *trs.* are :—

1. **One, only One, shall be the fold.** By Miss Dunn, in her *Hys. from the German*, 1857, p. 49.

2. **One Shepherd and one fold to be.** In *Cantica Sanctorum*, 1880, No. 96.

iii. **Ja fürwahr! uns führt mit sanfter Hand.** *Ps. xxiii.* In his *Festbüchlein*, pt. i. (3rd ed. 1813, p. 118), in 5 st. of 4 l., with Hallelujahs. It is given in the story of the festal rededication of a village church destroyed in time of war, as a choral hymn sung by boys and girls after the Holy Communion. In the Württemberg *G. B.*, 1842, No. 72. *Tr.* as :—

1. **Yes! our Shepherd leads with gentle hand, Through.** A good and full *tr.* by Miss Borthwick, in *H. L. L.*, 1st Ser., 1854, p. 59 (1884, p. 60), repeated in *Kennedy*, 1863 ; Mrs. Brock's *Children's H. Bk.*, 1881 ; the *Christian H. Bk.*, Cincinnati, 1865, and others.

2. **Yea! our Shepherd leads, with gentle hand, Along.** In full by M. W. Stryker, as No. 164 in his *Christian Chorals*, 1885.

iv. **Mag auch die Liebe weinen.** *Love, Faith and Hope.* *Festbüchlein*, pt. i., 1808, p. 136, in 3 st. of 4 l., in the section entitled "The Setting Sun," for Sunday evening. It is appended to a story in which the father has been speaking of the Resurrection of Christ the Sun of Righteousness, as celebrated on that day, the hymn being introduced as sung by the family and neighbours, as he ceased to speak. Included in the Württemberg *G. B.*, 1842, No. 628. It is most suited to be sung at a choral funeral. *Koch*, 2nd ed., iv. p. 695, says it was sung at the author's funeral at Bremen, April 10, 1845, and that st. iii. is on the cross over his grave. He adds that st. i., iii. were sung July 17, 1850, at the funeral of Dr. August Neander, the church historian in Berlin ; ·followed by an address by Krummacher's son, Friedrich Wilhelm (author of the well-known *Elijah, Elisha*, and other works). *Tr.* as :—

Though Love may weep with breaking heart. A good and full *tr.* by Miss Winkworth in her *Lyra Ger.*, 2nd Ser., 1858, p. 121. Repeated in Flett's *Coll.*, Paisley, 1871, and in H. L. Hastings's *Songs of Pilgrimage*, 1887.

Other trs. are, (1) "Let love weep,—It cometh," by *Miss Warner*, 1858, p. 584. (2) "Yea, Love may weep when death prevails," by *Dr. G. Walker*, 1860, p. 57.

A number of other pieces by Krummacher are *tr.* in the *Sacred Lyrics from the German*, Philadelphia, 1859 ; by C. T. Brooks, 1847 ; by Mrs. Follen, 1851 ; and by Miss Fry, 1859. As they are poems rather than hymns they are not noted here.   [J. M.]

Kunth, Johann Sigismund, was b. Oct. 3, 1700, at Liegnitz, Silesia, and studied theology at the Universities of Jena, Wittenberg, and Leipzig. He was in 1730 appointed pastor at Pölzig and Bröckau, near Ronneburg, by Count Henkel von Donnersmark. In 1737 he became chief pastor at Löwen, Silesia, and in 1743 pastor and superintendent at Baruth, near Jüterbog, Brandenburg. He d. at Baruth, Sept. 7, 1779 (S. J. Ehrhardt's *Presbyterologie Schlesiens*, 1780–89, ii. p. 137, &c.). The only hymn by him *tr.* into English is

Es ist noch eine Ruh vorhanden. *Eternal Life.* This fine hymn (founded on Heb. iv. 9 ; St. Matt. xi. 28, 29 ; Job. vii. 1–3 ; Ps. cxxvi. 5, 6, and Rev. vii. 16, 17) appears in the *Einige geistreiche Lieder.* Cöthen, 1733, No. 22, in 7 st. of 7 l. In the Berlin *G. L. S.*, ed. 1863, No. 1535.

According to Richter (*Biog. Lexikon*, 1804, p. 183) it was written by Kunth while on a journey from Wittenberg to Silesia, i.e. c. 1725; and this agrees with the statement of Fischer (*Supplement*, 1886, pt. i. p. 48) that it appeared in the *Neu eingerichtetes geistreiches G. B.*, Leipzig, 1730. *Koch*, 2nd ed., vol. iv. p. 712, says it was written in 1731 or 1732, while Kunth was journeying with his patron, Count Erdmann Heinrich von Henkel, who was on his way to take possession of some property in Silesia. On the way the carriage broke down, and this delay gave the Count occasion to murmur at the ceaseless unrest of this life. Kunth, reminding him of the believer's everlasting rest, stepped aside a moment, and then returned with this hymn. *Koch* adds that it comforted the dying hours of Heinrich Möwes (q.v.), being read to him by his wife in his last moments on earth.

The translations are :—

(1) "Yes, there remaineth yet a rest," by *Miss Winkworth*, 1855, p. 195.   (2) "There is a day of rest before thee," by *Mrs. Bevan*, 1858, p. 3.   (3) "Yes, still for us a rest remaineth," by Miss Borthwick, contributed to H. E. Goldschmidt's *German Poetry*, 1869, p. 431.
    [J. M.]

Küster, Samuel Christian Gottfried, s. of S. C. K. Küster, inspector and chief pastor at Havelberg, Brandenburg, was b. at Havelberg, Aug. 18, 1762. After studying at the University of Berlin (D.D. 1835) he became third pastor of the Friedrich-Werder Church at Berlin, in 1786 ; in 1793 second pastor ; and in 1797 chief pastor and superintendent, on the death of his father (who had been called to this church in 1771). He d. at Eberswalde (Neustadt- E.), near Berlin, Aug. 22, 1838 (*Allg. Deutsche Biog.*, xvi. 439, &c.).

He was one of the editors of the Berlin *G. B.*, 1829. and contributed to it two hymns, Nos. 294 and 549 ; and in 1831 pub. a small volume of *Kurze lebensgeschichtliche Nachrichten* regarding the authors of the hymns therein contained.

One of Küster's hymns has passed into English, viz. :—

O Jesu, Freund der Seelen. *Love to Christ.* 1829, as above, No. 549, in 6 st. of 8 l. Suggested by the "Schatz über alle Schätze" [see Liscovius]. *Tr.* as :— O Jesus, Friend unfailing. A good and full *tr.* by Miss Burlingham, written June 13, 1865, and 1st pub. in the *British Herald*, July, 1865, p. 100. Repeated in full in Reid's *Praise Bk.*, 1872 ; W. F. Stevenson's *H. för Ch. & Home*, 1873 ; Dale's *English H. Bk.*, 1875, and others; and abridged in Newman Hall's *Christ Church Hyl.*, 1876 ; *Baptist Hyl.*, 1879 ; *Suppl.* of 1800 to Bapt. *Ps. & Hys.*, 1858, &c.   [J. M.]

Kynaston, Herbert, D.D., was b. Nov. 23, 1809, and educated at Westminster School, and Christ Church, Oxford (of which he was sometime Student), where he graduated in 1831 (1st class Lit. Hum.). Taking Holy Orders in 1834, he became Head Master of St. Paul's School, London, in 1838 ; Select Preacher of the University of Oxford, 1842-43; Rector of St. Nicholas-Cole-Abbey, with St. Nicholas Olave, 1850-60, and Prebendary of Holborn in St. Paul's Cathedral, 1853. He d. Oct. 1878. His *Miscellaneous Poems* were pub. in 1840, and his hymns as follows :—

(1) *Occasional Hymns* (original and translated), 1862. (2) *Occasional Hymns*, 2nd series, pt. i., 1864. (3) *Occasional Hymns*, 2nd series, pt. ii., chiefly on the Miracles, 1866.

These hymns and translations, which are of more than usual merit, have been either strangely overlooked or are unknown to most modern editors. A few were included in the *Hymnary*, 1872. Dr. Kynaston also contributed to the *Guardian* from time to time several renderings into Latin of his own hymns, and of hymns by others, but these have not been republished.   [J. J.]

Kyrie eleison. *M. Luther.* [*The Litany.*] This setting of the Litany was composed in the beginning of 1529, and first pub. in Klug's *G. B.*, Wittenberg, 1529, and thence in the *Riga G. B.*, 1530, and the *Rostock G. B.*, 1531. It is No. 959 in the Berlin *G. L. S.*, ed. 1863. *Tr.* as :—(1) "Good Lord ! us deliver," by *J. Anderson*, 1846, p. 62. In his ed., 1847, rewritten, beginning, "Lord save ! and keep us free." (2) "Have mercy on us, Lord, we pray," by *Dr. J. Hunt*, 1853, p. 90. (3) "Lord, have mercy," by *R. Massie*, 1854, p. 64.   [J. M.]

Kyrie! Gott Vater in Ewigkeit. [*Public Worship.*] A recast of the Kyrie summum ("Kyrie fons bonitatis"), sung in mediæval times on Festivals from Trinity to Christmas, and found in a 12th cent. MS. in the B. Museum (Reg. 2 B. iv. f. 12b.) It was printed apparently at Wittenberg, in 1541, and thence in *Wackernagel*, iii. p. 226, in 3 st. of unequal length ; repeated in the *Unv. L. S.*, 1851, No. 176. Two "Kyries" by Johann Spangenberg, somewhat resembling this, are given by *Wackernagel*, iii. p. 928. *Tr.* as :— "O Lord God the Father for evermore." A good and full version by A. T. Russell, as No. 14 in his *Ps. & Hys.*, 1851.   [J. M.]

L

L., in Bristol Bap. *Coll.* of Ash & Evans, 1769, i.e. Leach.

L., in the *People's Hymnal*, 1867, i.e. R. F. Littledale, q. v.

L. H. C., in *Ash & Evans* as above, i.e. Lady Huntingdon's *Collection.*

L. L., in *Ash & Evans*, as above, i.e. *Liverpool Liturgy*, 1763. [See Unitarian Hymnody, 7.]

La Trobe, Benjamin, was b. in Dublin, April 19, 1725, and educated at the University of Glasgow. He entered the Ministry of the Moravians, and subsequently became superintendent of that body in England. He d. Nov. 29, 1786. Several of his *trs.* of German hymns appeared in the *Moravian H. Bk.*, 1789.   [G. A. C.]

La Trobe, Christian Ignatius, eldest s. of the above Benjamin La Trobe, was b. at the Moravian Settlement, Fulneck, Leeds, Yorkshire, Feb. 12, 1758, and educated in England and at the Brethren's College, Niesky, Silesia. Taking orders in the Moravian Church, he became in 1784 Secretary to their Society for the Furtherance of the Gospel, and in 1795 Secretary to the Unity of the Brethren in England. He d. at Fairfield, near Liverpool, May 6, 1836. He is best known through his *Selection of Sacred Music*, in six volumes, which appeared in 1806-25. His hymnological contributions consist of a few translations from the German.   [G. A. C.]

La Trobe, John Antes, M.A., grandson of B. La Trobe, and s. of C. I. La Trobe, was b. in London in 1795, and educated at St. Edmund Hall, Oxford, graduating B.A. 1826, and M.A. 1829. Having taken Holy Orders in the Church of England, he was appointed Incumbent of St. Thomas, Kendal, in 1840, and retained the same to 1865. In 1858 he was nominated Hon. Canon of Carlisle Cathedral. He d. in 1879. His musical works include *The Music of the Church*, 1831, and his poetical, *Sacred Lays and Lyrics*, 1850. He also published a

Selection of Hymns, including Versions of Psalms, arranged under Subjects, so as to form A Small Body of Divinity, and suited for Private, Social, and Public Worship. Lond., Seeleys, 1841.

This selection contains many of his own hymns. In 1852 a 2nd ed. was pub. with authors' names. "How strange is heavenly love" (*The love of God*), "O bring to Jehovah [the Lord] your tribute of praise" (*Ps. l.*), are two of the very few of his hymns in C. U.   [G. A. C.]

Labente jam solis rotâ. *C. Coffin.* [*Afternoon, Sunday.*] Appeared in his *Hymni Sacri*, 1736, p. 93, as "Prono volutus impetu," and again in the *Paris Breviary* the same year, as "Labente jam solis rotâ." It is also in J. Chandler's *Hys. of the Primitive Church*, 1837, No. 8, and in Card. Newman's *Hymni Ecclesiae*, 1838 and 1865. *Tr.* as :—

1. **Now the day's declining wheel.** By I. Williams, in the *British Magazine*, Jan. 1834 ; and

again in his *Hys. Tr. from the Parisian Breviary*, 1839, p. 9, in 14 irregular lines. Rearranged as a hymn in 3 st. of 4 l., in 4 of L.M., it was given in the *English Hymnal*, 1852, No. 10, and repeated in 1856 and 1861.

2. As now the sun's declining rays. By J. Chandler, in his *Hys. of the Prim. Church*, 1837, p. 7. It was soon incorporated in several hymnbooks as an afternoon hymn, and gradually grew in favour until few modern hymn-books of the first rank are found without it. Usually the text is given without alteration as in the *People's H.*, 1867. The text of *H. A. & M.*, 1861 and 1875, is Chandler altered by the Compilers, the changes being in st. i. and the doxology. This text is repeated in Thring's *Coll.*, 1882, and others. In *Kennedy*, 1863, Chandler's *tr.* is revised by the Editor.

3. As now the sun's departing rays. By. R. C. Singleton, written in 1870, and given in his *Anglican H. Bk.*, 2nd ed., 1871.

Translations not in C. U. :—
1. And now the sinking orb of day. *J. Chandler*, L.M. version in his *Hymns*, &c., 1841.
2. Again the dawn gives warning meet. *G. Rorison*, in his *Hys. & Anthems*, 1851, based on W. Palmer's *tr.* in his *Short Poems & Hys.*, Oxford, 1845.
3. The day to night is calling. *W. J. Blew*, 1852–55.
4. The sun hath downward turned his way. *J. D. Chambers*, 1857.
5. Now with rapid wheel inclining. *D. T. Morgan*, given in his *Hys. and Other Poetry of the Latin Ch.*, 1880, under Coffin's original first line. [J. J.]

Laetabundus exultet fidelis chorus : Alleluia. Regem regum. *St. Bernard of Clairvaux.* [*Christmas.*] The earliest form known of this *Sequence* is in a *Gradual* apparently written in England during the 12th cent. and now in the British Museum (Reg. 2 B. iv. f. 177), and another ms. in the B. M. containing a collection of *Sequences*, apparently written c. 1199 (Calig. A. xiv. f. 50 *b*). It is in the St. Gall ms., No. 338, at p. 334, in a hand of the 13th cent. Among *Missals* it is found in an early 14th cent. *Paris*, and a 14th cent. *Sens* in the British Museum ; in a *Sarum*, c. 1370 ; a *Hereford*, c. 1370 ; and a *York*, c. 1390, all now in the Bodleian ; in the *St. Andrews*, *Magdeburg* of 1480, and many French and German *Missals*. It was also used as a hymn in the *Sarum Breviary*, e.g. in a ms. of the 14th cent. in the British Museum (Reg. 2 A. xiv. f. 187 *b*). The printed text is also in *Daniel*, ii. p. 61 ; *Kehrein*, No. 13, and others.

Of this poem Dr. Neale says " This *Sequence* or Hymn is of rare perfection in its kind, and perhaps as widely known as any hymn of the Church " (*Med. Hys.* 1851, p. 49). As will be seen by the note above, its use was specially general in England and in France. In the *Sarum Missal* it was used as the Sequence on the Fourth Day in the octave of the Assumption of the B. V. M. ; and in the *Sarum Breviary* as a hymn at the second Vespers of the Purification, and also of the Assumption of the B. V. M. In the *Hereford Missal* it is appointed for use within the octave of the Epiphany ; and in the *York Missal* in the Mass at Daybreak on Christmas day. [J. M.]

Translations in C.U. :—
1. Full of gladness, Let our faithful choir, &c. By J. M. Neale, in the *Hymnal N.*, 1854, in 6 st.
2. With hallowed mirth, sing all ye faithful choirs on earth. By J. D. Chambers, in his *Lauda Syon*, Pt. ii., 1866, p. 65. This was repeated with slight variations in the *People's H.*, 1867.
3. Come, ye faithful choirs on earth. This rendering in the *Hymnary*, 1872, is based upon the *Hymnal N.*, as above.

4. Faithful chorus, Loud exult, &c. In the *Hymner*, 1882, is based upon the *Hymnal N.*, as above.

Translations not in C. U. :—
1. Be the tidings. *J. M. Neale*, in 1st ed. of his *Mediæval Hys.* 1851 ; but afterwards omitted.
2. Full of joy, in sweet accord. *J. W. Hewett.* 1859.
3. With holy gladness full. *J. W. Hewett.* 1859. A second translation.
4. Now by Thy faithful choirs. *C. B. Pearson.* In the *Sarum Missal in English*, 1868, and his *Sequences from the Sarum Missal*, 1871. [J. J.]

Lamb of God for sinners slain, By Thy mercy born again. *Bp. J. R. Woodford.* [*Holy Baptism.*] Pub. in his *Hymns*, &c., 1852, No. 55, in 4 st. of 4 l., and repeated in the *Parish H. Bk.*, 1863 and 1875 ; the *Sarum*, 1868 ; the 1863 *Appendix* to the S. P. C. K. *Ps. & Hys.*, No. 291, and others. In Skinner's *Daily Service Hymnal*, 1864, it is adapted for Holy Baptism, and for Confirmation, and in each case Skinner has attributed it to C. Wesley in error. The *Sarum* is also in error in giving the date of its composition as 1860. [J. J.]

Lamb of God for sinners slain, To Thee I feebly pray. *C. Wesley.* [*Looking unto Jesus.*] Appeared in *Hys. & Sac. Poems*, 1742, p. 49, in 6 st. of 8 l. (*P. Works*, 1868–72, vol. ii. p. 98). In 1776, st. i.–iii, and vi. were included in Toplady's *Ps. & Hys.*, No. 279, and thus came into use in the Church of England. J. Wesley's cento for the *Wes. H. Bk.*, 1780, No. 161, was composed of st. i., iii., v., vi. This is retained in the ed. of 1875, and is in extensive use. [J. J.]

Lamb of God, that in the bosom. [*Advent.*] This cento appeared in Bayley's *Manchester Ps. & Hys.*, 1789, No. 4, and again in others, including Stowell's Manchester *Ps. & Hys.*, 1831, p. 95, in 8 st. of 4 l., st. i., iii., v., vii. being the " Air," and the alternate stanzas the " Chorus." Stanzas iii. and iv. are from C. Wesley's " Love divine, all loves excelling," q.v., and the rest are anonymous. This cento is in the 1877 ed. of Stowell's *Ps. & Hys.*, and several other collections. In Chope's *Hymnal*, 1864, No. 192, st. i. is the opening stanza of this cento, and the remaining 4 stanzas are from C. Wesley's " Love divine, all loves excelling." [J. J.]

Lamb of God, Whose bleeding love. *C. Wesley.* [*Holy Communion.*] This is No. 20 of the Wesley *Hys. on the Lord's Supper*, 1745, in 4 st. of 8 l. (*P. Works*, 1868–72, vol. iii. p. 228). It was given in the older hymn-books of the Church of England as Madan's *Ps. & Hys.*, 1760 ; Toplady's *Ps. & Hys.*, 1776, and others, and also in some Nonconformist collections, but was not included in the *Wes. H. Bk.* until the *Supplement* of 1830. An altered version of this hymn, beginning, " Lamb of God, Whose *dying* love," appeared in Hall's *Mitre H. Bk.*, 1836, No. 269, in 2 st. of 8 l. That arrangement was by E. Osler, and was repeated, with slight changes, in his *Church & King*, March, 1837. Another form of the hymn is, " *Blest* Lamb of God, whose *dying* love." It is found in the Rugby School *H. Bk.*, 1850 ; *Kennedy*, 1863, and others. [J. J.]

Lampe, Friedrich Adolf, D.D., s. of Heinrich Lampe, pastor of the Reformed church at Detmold, was b. at Detmold, apparently Feb. 18, and was certainly baptized there Feb. 19, 1683. He remained at Detmold till the death of his grandfather (General-Superintendent Zeller) in 1691, and then joined his widowed mother at Bremen. He entered the Lyceum (Academic Gymnasium) at Bremen, in 1698 ; and in 1702 went to the University of Franeker in Holland. After a short residence at the University of Utrecht he became, in 1703, pastor of the Reformed church at Weeze, near Cleve ; in 1706 at Duisburg ; and in 1709 second pastor of St. Stephen's Church in Bremen, where in 1719 he became pastor primarius. In 1720 he was appointed German preacher and professor of dogmatics at the University of Utrecht (the degree of D.D. being also conferred on him) ; and in 1726 professor of Church History and Rector of the University. After a severe illness in the winter of 1726–27 he resigned in June, 1727, and returned to Bremen as third pastor of St. Ansgar's Church and professor at the Lyceum. He d. at Bremen, Dec. 8, 1729. (*Allg. Deutsche Biog.*, xvii. 5t9 ; *F. A. Lampe Sein Leben und seine Theologie.* By Dr. Otto Thelemann, 1868, &c.)

Lampe was the most important theologian that had appeared in the German Reformed Church since the Reformation period. He was the great exponent of the Federal or Covenant theology in his *Geheimniss des Gnadenbundes*, 1712 ff. ; the author of a well-known commentary on St. John's Gospel, 1724–26 ; of various catechetical works, &c. As a hymn-writer Lampe is not so important ; but yet ranks as one of the best writers in the Reformed Church. His hymns are Scriptural, and characterised by glowing piety, deep spiritual insight, firm faith, and play of fancy ; but are often somewhat obscure and involved, and not seldom' very lengthy. Nine first appeared in his *Balsam aus Gilead*, Bremen, 1713, and the rest principally in his *Bündlein XXV. Gottseliger Gesänge*, Bremen, 1723 [Royal Library, Berlin], and later eds. The ed. of 1731 (*XXX. Geistliche Lieder*, &c.) contains also an appendix of 13 hymns from his MS.

Comparatively few of Lampe's hymns are in modern German C. U. Those which have passed into English are :—

i. **Mein Leben ist ein Pilgrimstand.** *For Travellers.* 1723, No. 10, p. 39, in 8 st., entitled "Travelling Thoughts." In the Berlin *G. L. S.*, ed. 1863. *Tr.* as, "My life is but a pilgrim-stand," by *Dr. H. Mills*, 1845 (1856, p. 150).

ii. **O Fels des Heils am Kreuzesstamm.** *Holy Communion.* 1723, No. 5, p. 21, in 12 st. of 5 l. entitled "Devotional Hymn at Holy Communion." In Dr. J. P. Lange's *Kirchenliederbuch*, 1843, st. xii. is omitted, and it begins "O Fels des Heils, O Gotteslamm." The *tr.* in C. U. is :—

O healing Rock, O Lamb of God. A *tr.* of st. i.–iii., v., xii., by Dr. R. Maguire, in his *Melodies of the Fatherland*, 1883, p. 107. Repeated, omitting st. iii., in R. Gault's *H. Bk. for Ch. of England*, 1886.

iii. **O Liebesgluth, wie soll ich dich.** *Love to Christ.* Founded on St. John iii. 16. 1723, No. 19, p. 50, in 6 st. Previously in his *Geheimniss des Gnadenbundes*, pt. iv., vol. ii., 2nd ed., Bremen, 1721, p. 1086. In Bunsen's *Versuch*, 1833, omitting st. ii., iv. *Tr.* as : (1) "O Fire of Love, what earthly words," by *Mrs. Bevan*, 1858, p. 61. (2) "O wondrous love of Christ ! how bright," by *Dr. G. Walker*, 1860, p. 75.

iv. **So ist von meiner kurzen Pilgrimschaft.** *New Year.* 1723, No. 24, p. 69, in 16 st. The form *tr.* is that in the Berlin *G. B.*, 1829, No. 424, altered, and beginning "Wie schnell verstrich, O Herr voll Mild' und Huld." *Tr.* as, "How swift, O Lord, most kind, most bountiful," by *N. L. Frothingham*, 1870, p. 255.

[J. M.]

Langbecker, Emanuel Christian Gottlieb, s. of Christian Gottlieb Langbecker, clothier in Berlin, was b. at Berlin, Aug. 31, 1792. After being for some time engaged in

his father's business, he entered the service of Prince Waldemar of Prussia in 1827, becoming his household secretary in 1840. He d. at Berlin, Oct. 24, 1843 (*Koch*, vii. 39–42 ; Registers of St. George's Church, Berlin, &c.).

His hymns appeared in the Berlin *Wochenblatt*, 1822, &c. ; in his *Gedichte*, Berlin, 1824, 2nd Series, 1829 ; and in the Berlin *G. L. S.*, of which he was the principal editor, and for which he compiled the biographical notices in the 1st ed., 1832. He also pub. various hymnological works, including his historical sketch *Das deutsch - evangelische Kirchenlied*, Berlin, 1830 ; the first critical ed. of P. Gerhardt's *Leben und Lieder*, Berlin, 1841 ; *Gesang-Blätter aus dem xvi. Jahrhundert*, Berlin, 1838, &c.

One of his hymns is in English C. U. :—

Wie wird mir sein, wann ich dich, Jesus, sehe. *Longing for Heaven.* Founded on 1 John iii. 2. In his *Gedichte, Zweite Sammlung*, Berlin, 1829, p. 65, in 5 st. of 6 l., entitled "In prospect of Eternity." It was a favourite hymn of C. H. Zeller (q.v.) Included in the Berlin *G. L. S*, 1832, No. 1922 (1863, No. 722). The *tr.* is :—

What shall I be ! my Lord, when I behold thee. A full and good *tr.* by Mrs. Findlater, in *H. L. L.*, 2nd Ser., 1855, p. 56 (1884, p. 114). Repeated, in full, in Bp. Ryle's *Coll.*, 1860 ; and, omitting st. iv., in the *Meth. N. Conn. H. Bk.*, 1863.

[J. M.]

Lange, Ernst, was b. at Danzig, Jan. 3, 1650, where his father, Matthias Lange, was in the service of the Senate. He was for some time secretary in Danzig, and thereafter in Warsaw. In 1691 he was appointed judge in the Altstadt of Danzig, and in 1694 senator. He d. at Danzig, Aug. 20, 1727 (*Bode*, p. 103 ; *Allg. Deutsche Biog.*, xvii. 623, &c.). After a visit to the Netherlands in 1698, Lange allied himself with the Mennonites and Pietists in Danzig, and came into conflict with the Lutheran clergy. His hymns were mostly written about the time when the pestilence visited Danzig, in 1710, and principally appeared in his *LXI. Gott geheiligte Stunden*, without place or date of pub., but probably at Danzig, 1711 (Preface dated " Danzig, Feb. 12, 1711 "). The idea of this work was as a thankoffering for preservation during this trying time ; and it embraced 61 hymns, viz., one for each year of his life. A number of additional hymns seem to have been contributed in MS. to Freylinghausen's *Neues geistreiches G. B.*, 1714. His Psalm versions are noted under **Psalters, German.** Lange's hymns which have passed into English are :—

i. **Im Abend blinkt der Morgenstern.** *Epiphany.* 1711, as above, p. 4, in 19 st. of 4 l., entitled, "The Saviour Who appeared at Bethlehem to the Wise men from the East, set forth ; from Matt. ii. 1–12." A new st. was added as xx. (probably from his MS.), when the hymn was included by *Freylinghausen*, 1714, No. 59. Repeated, abridged, in Knapp's *Ev. L. S.*, 1837, No. 435 (1865, No. 414). The *tr.* in C. U. is :—

The wondering sages trace from far. A *tr.* of st. i., ii., xx., by Miss Cox, in her *Sacred H. from the German*, 1841, p. 23 (1864, p. 43). Repeated in Hedge & Huntington's American *Hys. for the Ch. of Christ*, Boston, 1853 ; Schaff's *Christ in Song*, 1869 and 1870, &c.

Another tr. is : " At eve appears the Morning Star," by *Lady E. Fortescue*, 1843, p. 5.

ii. **O Gott, du Tiefe sonder Grund.** *God's Majesty.* 1st printed as No. 140, in *Freylinghausen*, 1714, in 10 st. of 14 l.; repeated in the Berlin *G. L. S.*, ed. 1863. F. Schleiermacher called it "A masterpiece of sacred poetry." The *tr.* in C. U. is :—

O God, Thou bottomless abyss. A spirited *tr.*, omitting st. vi., ix., and in 8 st. of 12 l., by J. Wesley, in his *Coll. of Ps. & Hys.*, Charlestown, 1737, No. 16, and the Wesley *Hys. and Sacred Poems*, 1739 (*P. Works*, 1868–72, vol. i. p. 143). The lines—

" Thy wakened wrath doth slowly move,
    Thy willing mercy flies apace "

are adapted from the *New Version* of Ps. ciii. 8. The hymn passed into the *Wes. H. Bk.*, 1780, in two parts, Nos. 231 and 232 (ed. 1875, Nos. 240, 241). In other hymn-books it has appeared in a variety of centos. As these are all from the text of the *Wes. H. Bk.*, more or less altered and transposed, it will suffice to give their first lines with references to the text of 1780. These centos include :—

(1) **While Thee, Unsearchable, I set** (i., l. 9 alt.). Martineau's *Hymns*, 1840.
(2) **Unchangeable, all-perfect Lord** (ii., l. 9). Longfellow & Johnson's *Bk. of Hys.*, Boston, U.S., 1848.
(3) **Thy parent-hand, Thy forming skill** (iii). Amer. Meth. Epis. South *Coll.*, 1847.
(4) **Thou, true and only God, lead'st forth** (v.). *Wes. H. Bk.*, 1780, No. 232.
(5) **Thine, Lord, is Wisdom, Thine alone** (vi.). Scottish *Evang. Uniom H. Bk.*, 1856.
(6) **Parent of good! Thy bounteous hand** (vii.). Martineau's *Hymns*, 1840.
(7) **Parent of good! Thy genial ray** (vii. alt.). Dr. Thomas's *Augustine H. Bk.*, 1866.

These details show the extensive use of this hymn in English-speaking countries.

Another *tr.* is, " O God, Thou bottomless Abyss! How shall I competently know Thee," as No. 673 in pt. i. of the *Moravian H. Bk.*, 1754. In the ed. 1886, No. 174, it begins, " O God, Thou fathomless abyss."

iii. **Unter denen grossen Gütern.** *Brotherly Love*, or, *Quinquagesima.* A free paraphrase of 1 Cor. xiii. 1st pub. 1711, as above, p. 37, in 5 st. of 10 l., entitled, " The preeminence of Love. From 1 Cor. xiii. 1, 2, 3, 13." When included as No. 423, in *Freylinghausen*, 1714, a new stanza was added as st. vi., and this form is No. 798 in the *Unv. L. S.*, 1851. *Tr.* as :—

Many a gift did Christ impart. A full and good *tr.* by Miss Winkworth, in her *Lyra Ger.*, 1855, p. 50; repeated, abridged, in *Kennedy*, 1863. In the American Unitarian *Hys. of the Spirit*, Boston, 1864, and in the *Laudes Domini*, N. Y. 1884, &c., it begins with the *tr.* of st. ii., l. 5, " Though I speak with angel tongues." [J. M.]

Lange, Joachim, D.D., s. of Mauritius Lange, senior councillor at Gardelegen in the Altmark, was b. at Gardelegen, Oct. 26, 1670. He entered the University of Leipzig in the autumn of 1689, where he shared rooms with A. H. Francke; and in 1690 followed Francke to Erfurt, and in 1692 to Halle. By the recommendation of J. C. Schade he was appointed, in 1693, tutor to the only son of F. R. L. von Canitz, at Berlin. Subsequently he became, in 1696, rector of the school at Cöslin in Pomerania; in 1698 rector of the Friedrichswerder Gymnasium at Berlin, and in 1699 pastor of the Friedrichstadt church; and in 1709, professor of theology at Halle (D.D. 1717), where he d. May 7, 1744 (*Koch*, iv. 343; *Allg. Deutsche Biog.*, xvii. 634, &c.). In his day Lange was best known as a commentator on the whole Bible (*Biblisches Licht und Recht*, &c., 7 folio vols., Halle, 1730–1738); as a defender of Pietism against the " Ortho-

dox " Lutheran controversialists of the early 18th cent.; and as the author of over 100 theological works. Only two hymns are known by him, one of which is :—

O Jesu, süsses Licht. *Morning.* 1st pub. in the *Geistreiches G. B.*, Halle, 1697, p. 4, in 8 st. of 8 l. Repeated in Freylinghausen's *G. B.*, 1704, No. 608, and recently, as No. 469, in the *Unv. L. S.*, 1851.

Jesu, Thy light again I view. A free *tr.*, in 7 st. of 6 l., by J. Wesley, in *Hys. & Sacred Poems*, 1739 (*P. Works*, 1868–72, vol. i. p. 159); repeated as No. 661 in pt. i. of the *Moravian H. Bk.*, 1754 (1886, No. 344, abridged). The form most used is that in the *Wes. H. Bk.*, 1780, No. 419, where st. i. is omitted; and it begins with st. ii., altered to " O God, what offering shall I give." This form is in *Mercer*, 1857 and 1864, *Kennedy*, 1863, and others; and in America, in the Meth. Epis. *Hymns*, 1849, *Evang. Association H. Bk.*, 1882, &c. In the American *Sabbath H. Bk.*, 1858, a cento from Wesley's st. iii., vi., vii., is given as No. 917, beginning, " Now, O my God, Thou hast my soul."

Other trs. are: (1) " O let me always think Thou'rt near," by J. Swertner, of st. vii., as No. 430 in the *Moravian H. Bk.*, 1789. In the 1801 and later eds. (1886, No. 567) it is altered, and begins, " O let us always think Thee near." (2) " O Jesu, welcome Light," by *H. J. Buckoll*, 1842, p. 47. (3) " O Jesu, Light most sweet." In the *Family Treasury*, 1879, p. 230. [J. M.]

Lange, Johann Christian, D.D., was b. at Leipzig, Dec. 25, 1669, and studied at the University of Leipzig (M.A. 1689). In 1697 he was appointed extraordinary professor of Philosophy, in 1698 professor of Morals, and in 1707 professor of Logic and Metaphysics at the University of Giessen. He then became, in 1716, superintendent and first court preacher at Idstein, near Wiesbaden, graduating D.D. in the same year; the districts of Saarbrück and Usingen being also put under his care respectively in 1722 and 1728. He d. at Idstein, Dec. 16, 1756 (*Koch*, iv. 398, &c.). His hymns, distinguished by fervent love to Christ, were written mostly during his residence at Lüneburg, 1691–94, as tutor in the house of J. W. Petersen (q.v.). Only one has passed into English, viz :—

Mein Herzens-Jesu, meine Lust. *Love to Christ.* On the Names and Offices of Christ. This is found, without his name, in J. H. Hävecker's *Kirchen Echo*, 1695, No. 64, in 18 st. of 7 l., repeated in the *Geistreiches G. B.*, Halle, 1697, p. 140, *Porst's G. B.*, ed. 1855, No. 64, &c. With this hymn Lange comforted himself on his death-bed. *Tr.* as: (1) " Sweet Jesus who my Wish fulfills." In *Lyra Davidica*, 1708, p. 44. (2) " Jesu! my Heart's most joyful Rest." In the *Suppl. to Ger. Psalmody*, ed. 1765, p. 7, and *Select Hys. from the Ger. Psal.*, Tranquebar, 1754, p. 9. (3) " Jesu, Thou my Heart's pleasing Feast." As No. 675 in the *Moravian H. Bk.*, 1754. (4) " Jesus, Thou art my heart's delight." As No. 274 in the *Moravian H. Bk.*, 1789 (1886, No. 358). [J. M.]

Lange, Johann Peter, D.D., s. of Peter Lang or Lange, farmer and carrier on the estate of Bies, near Sonnborn, Elberfeld, was b. at the Bies, April 10, 1802. In 1822 he entered the University of Bonn as a student of theology; and in the beginning of 1826 he became assistant to Pastor Emil Krummacher of Langenberg. In June 1826 he was appointed second pastor at Wald near Solingen; in 1828 second pastor of the Reformed church at Langenberg, and in 1832 second pastor at Duisburg. He was then appointed professor of Church History and Dogmatics at Zürich, as successor to D. F. Strauss, and entered on his duties at Easter, 1841; receiving shortly thereafter D.D. from Bonn. After Easter, 1854, he was professor of Systematic Theology at Bonn (also Consistorialrath after 1860), and continued to lecture up to five days before his death. He d. at Bonn, July 8, 1884 (*Koch*, vii. 361; *O. Kraus*, 1879, p. 324, &c.).

Lange is best known as a theologian, and by such works as his *Life of Christ*, 1844; his *Bibel-Werk*, 1857, ff., a commentary on the whole Bible which he edited in conjunction with various German scholars (English ed by Dr. P. Schaff and others), &c. During his tenure of office at Zürich, he began the fashion of giving University lectures on hymnology (1842), and pub. a large hymn-book (*Deutsches Kirchenliederbuch*, Zürich, 1843) with an elaborate introduction and a considerable body of notes. He is the most important modern hymn-writer of the German Reformed Church. He was, however, a thinker rather than a poet. His productions are primarily thoughtful, picturesque, imaginative, and deeply spiritual poems for private reading; and have little of the popular tone and style fitted for use in the services of the church. They appeared mostly in his (1) *Biblische Dichtungen*, vol. i., Elberfeld, 1832; vol. ii. Elberfeld, 1834; (2) *Gedichte*, Essen, 1843; (3) *Vom Oelberge*, Frankfurt-am-Main, 1852; 2nd ed. 1858.

Comparatively few of Lange's hymns are in German C.U. Those which have passed into English are :—

i. *Hymns in English C. U.*

i. **Der Herr ist auferstanden.** *Easter.* In his *Biblische Dichtungen*, vol. i., 1832, p. 155, in 17 st. of 7 l. In his *Vom Oelberge*, 1852, p. 28, only st. i., vii., xiv.-xvii., were retained, and this form is No. 517 in Dr. Schaff's *Deutsches G. B.*, 1874. *Tr.* as :—

The Lord of Life is risen. A good *tr.* of the 1852 text, by Dr. H. Harbaugh, in the German Reformed *Guardian*, April 1860, p. 106, repeated in *Hys. for the* [German] *Ref. Ch. in the United States*, Philad., 1874; also in Schaff's *Christ in Song*, 1869 and 1870.

ii. **Unsre Lieben sind geschieden.** *For Mourners.* In his *Biblische Dichtungen*, vol. ii., 1834, p. 172, in 10 st. of 6 l., entitled, "The Home Going." In F. Seinecke's *Evang. Liedersejen*, 1862, No. 412. *Tr.* as :—

Our beloved have departed. By Mrs. Findlater, omitting st. v., vii., ix., in *H. L. L.*, 2nd Ser., 1855, p. 28 (1884, p. 93). Repeated, in full, in *Holy Song*, 1869. The *trs.* of st. i., ii., viii., x., altered, and beginning, "Do we mourn for friends departed," are in J. A. Johnston's *English Hymnal*, 1856; and the same cento, varied, and beginning, "Weep we sore for friends departed," is in *Kennedy*, 1863.

iii. **Was kein Auge hat gesehen.** *Eternal Life.* A fine hymn, founded on 1 Cor. ii. 9. In his *Biblische Dichtungen*, vol. ii., 1834, p. 92, in 13 st. of 6 l. A form, in 7 st., is included in Dr. Schaff's *Deutsches G. B.*, 1874. *Tr.* as :—

What no human eye hath seen. A good *tr.*, by Miss Borthwick, omitting st. ii., viii., xi., xiii., in *H. L. L.*, 2nd Ser., 1855, p. 73 (1884, p. 130). Repeated, in full, in *Holy Song*, 1869, and *Kennedy*, 1863; and abridged in the *Meth. N. Conn. H. Bk.*, 1863, and Flett's *Coll.*, Paisley, 1871.

ii. *Hymns not in English C. U.*

iv. **Auf den dunklen Bergen.** *Passiontide.* 1832, p. 145, in 12 st. *Tr.* as : "Upon the mountain dark and drear," by *Dr. R. Maguire*, 1883, p. 68.

v. **Es ist noch nichts verbrochen.** *Encouragement.*

1834, p. 103, in 8 st. *Tr.* as : "Sure the Lord thy God hath spoken," by *Dr. R. Maguire*, 1883, p. 121.

vi. **Gott mit uns! mit uns auf Erden.** *Christmas.* A fine hymn, written in 1830 on "Immanuel—God with us." 1832, p. 71, in 6 st. *Tr.* as : "God with us! In flesh combining," by *C. T. Astley*, 1860, p. 27.

vii. **Hier und dort im wilden Meere.** *Christ at Bethany.* 1832, p. 138, in 9 st. *Tr.* as : "Mid the ocean deep and wide," by *Dr. R. Maguire*, 1883, p. 52.

viii. **Ich weiss ein stilles, liebes Land.** *The Churchyard.* 1834, p. 167, in 12 st. *Tr.* as : "I know a sweet and silent spot," by Mrs. Findlater, in *H. L. L.*, 1858, p. 54 (1884, p. 174).

ix. **Lass mich diese Welt verstehen.** *Cross and Consolation.* *Gedichte*, 1843, p. 61, in 5 st. *Tr.* as : "In the light, Lord, of Thy cross," by *J. Kelly*, 1885.

x. **Mein Vater ist der grosse Herr der Welt.** *Privileges of Christians.* Founded on 1 Cor. iii. 21. 1834, p. 106, in 8 st. *Tr.* as :—"My Father is the mighty Lord, Whose arm," by Mrs. Findlater, in *H. L. L.*, 1854, p. 54 (1884, p. 55).

xi. **Schöne Sonne, kommst du endlich wieder.** *Trust in God.* 1834, p. 99, in 10 st. *Tr.* as : "Sun of comfort, art thou fled for ever," by Miss Borthwick, in *H. L. L.*, 1855, p. 10 (1884, p. 17).

xii. **Sey du mein Freund, und schau in meine Brust.** *Supplication.* Suggested by 1 John ii. 1. 1834, p. 88, in 7 st. *Tr.* as : "Be Thou my Friend, and look upon my heart," by Mrs. Findlater, in *H. L. L.*, 1858, p. 41.

xiii. **So gross ist Gottes Welt.** *Wonders of Day and Night.* *Vom Oelberge*, 1852, p. 121, in 9 st. entitled "Two Worlds." *Tr.* as : "So wide, so richly stored," by Miss Borthwick, in the *Family Treasury*, 1867.

xiv. **Wo Lämmer schlafen, wacht die Hirtentreue.** *Christmas.* 1834, p. 23, in 2 st. of 4 l., and 2 of 3 l. *Tr.* as : "Where the lambs sleep, there shepherds watch around," by Mrs. Findlater, in *H. L. L.*, 1862, p. 17.

[J. M.]

Langford, John. The time and place of this person's birth are unknown. He is said to have been connected with the early Methodists, and then to have become a member of the Baptist church in Eagle Street, London. In 1765 he began to preach in a chapel called Blacksfields, in Gainsford Street, London, and in the following year was ordained pastor. There he remained for 12 years, then removed to Rose Lane, Ratcliff, and afterwards to a small place in Bunhill Row. But his imprudent conduct compelled him at length to give up preaching. He inherited considerable property, but squandered it in extravagance, and died in great wretchedness about 1790.

J. Langford pub. a few Sermons, and, in 1776, a collection of *Hymns & Spiritual Songs*, which reached a second ed. The excellent and well-known hymn "Now begin the heavenly theme," has been ascribed to him. It is in his collection; but since, in the preface to his second ed., he tells us that he has marked his own hymns with an asterisk, and this one is not so marked, it is clearly not of his composition.

[W. R. S.]

Langhans, Urban, was a native of Schneeberg, in Saxony. He was for some time cantor, i.e. choirmaster, at Glauchau, in Saxony; and then from 1546 to 1554 diaconus there. In 1554 he became diaconus at Schneeberg, and still held this position in 1562. The date of his death is not known; but his successor in office d. in 1571 (*Blätter für Hymnologie*, 1884, pp. 7-12, 25-27, 190). Whether he wrote any hymns is doubtful. The only one ascribed to him which has passed into English is :—

Lasst uns alle fröhlich sein. *Christmas.* The first stanza of this hymn is found at p. 17 of Martin Hammer's *Laudes Immanuelis* (a sermon on "Grates nunc omnes reddamus"), pub. at Leipzig, 1620 [Ducal Library, Gotha]. The full form, in 4 st. of 4 l., has not yet been traced earlier than to the *Ander Theil* of the Dresden *G. B.*, 1632. It is also in J. Niedling's *Lutherisch Handbüchlein*, 1655, p. 578, in Freylinghausen's *G. B.*, 1704; the Berlin *G. L. S.*, ed. 1863, No. 171, &c. In the Arnstadt *G. B.*, 1711, Langhans is given as the author of the text, and in the Dresden *G. B.*, 1656, as the author of the melody. Dr. J. Zahn, in his *Psalter und Harfe*, 1886, No. 27, gives both text and melody from the Dresden *G. B.*, 1632. *Tr.* as :—

1. Let us all in God rejoice. In full, by Dr. M. Loy, in the *Evang. Review*, Gettysburg, July, 1861, p. 152, repeated in the Ohio *Evang. Luth. Hyl.*, 1880, No. 19.

2. Let us all with gladsome voice. In full, by Miss Winkworth, as No. 29 in her *C. B. for England*, 1863.

[J. M.]

Lapsus est annus : redit annus alter. [*NewYear*.] In the *Meaux Breviary*, 1713, and 1834, this is the hymn at compline after the first vespers of the festival of the Circumcision of our Lord. This would of course be said as the last office on Dec. 31. There is a rubric directing that at stanza v. all kneel down. So also in the *Poictiers Breviary* (*Pictaviense*), in which it probably originated. Neale, in his *Hymni Ecclesiae*, 1851, p. 162, gives the text *e Breviario Meldensi*, i.e. the *Meaux Breviary*. It is also in the *Le Mans Brev.* of 1748. *Daniel*, iv. 319, repeats the text from Neale. Also in L. C. Biggs's annotated *H. A. & M.*, 1867.   [W. A. S.]

Translations in C. U. :—

1. The year is gone beyond recall. By F. Pott. Appeared in L. M. in his *Hys. fitted to the Order of Common Prayer*, 1861, No. 48, in 6 st. of 4 l., and was repeated, unaltered, in the *People's H.*, 1867, and others ; and, abbreviated and altered, in the S. P. C. K. *Church Hys.*, 1871. In 1861 the compilers of *H. A. & M.* transposed Archdeacon Pott's L. M. *tr.* into C. M., thus necessitating many alterations. This text has been adopted by several hymnals, including *Kennedy*, 1863, Allon's *Cong. Psal. Hymnal*, 1886, and others. In these forms this *tr.* is extensively used.

2. The year is gone, another dawns. By W. Cooke, written for and pub. in the *Hymnary*, 1872.

Translation not in C. U. :—

Past is the old year, now begins another. *J. W. Hewett.* 1859.   [J. J.]

Lasset Klag und Trauern fahren. *J. Heermann?* [*Eternal Life*.] This hymn is not found in any of the works of Heermann now extant. It appeared, with his name, in the *Königsberg G. B.*, 1650, p. 702, in 9 st. of 8 l. Thence in *Mützell*, 1858, No. 136. In Bunsen's *Allg. G. B.*, 1846, No. 432, is st. i. ll. 1–4, ii. ll. 5–8, iv., vii., ix. The ascription to Heermann may have arisen from confounding with his " Lasset ab, ihr meine Lieben," 1st pub. in his *Devoti musica cordis*, Leipzig, 1636 (1644, p. 186), thence in *Mützell*, 1858, No. 98, in 12 st. of 8 l. The *Lasset Klag* has been called a version of " Jam moesta quiesce querela," but has greater resemblance to " Ad perennis vitae fontem." *Tr.* as :—

I go from grief and sighing. A good *tr.* from *Bunsen* by Mrs. Bevan, in her *Songs of Eternal Life*, 1858, p. 17, repeated, unaltered, in Snepp's *Songs of G. & G.*, 1872. In Reid's *Praise Bk.*, 1872, it is altered to " We go from grief and sighing."   [J. M.]

Lathbury, Mary Ann, was b. in Manchester, Ontario County, New York, Aug. 10, 1841. Miss Lathbury writes somewhat extensively for the American religious periodical press, and is well and favourably known (see the *Century Magazine*, Jan., 1885, p. 342). Of her hymns which have come into C. U. we have :—

1. Break Thou the bread of life. *Communion with*

God. A " Study Song " for the Chautauqua Literary and Scientific Circle, written in the summer of 1880. It is in Horder's (Eng.) *Cong. Hymns*, 1884.

2. Day is dying in the west. *Evening.* " Written at the request of the Rev. John H. Vincent, D.D., in the summer of 1880. It was a " Vesper Song," and has been frequently used in the responsive services of the Chautauqua Literary and Scientific Circle." It is in the *Laudes Domini*, N. Y., 1884.

For these details we are indebted to S. W. Duffield's *English Hys.*, &c., N. Y., 1886.

[J. J.]

Latin Hymnody.—A complete history of Latin Hymnody has never yet been written. It would occupy a considerable volume. This dissertation therefore must be considered as a mere epitome of an extensive and interesting subject, which is, in fact, intimately connected and interwoven with Christianity itself ; and, as St. Chrysostom remarks (on Ps. 41), " Nothing gladdens the soul like modulated verse—a Divine song composed in metre."

i. *Ancient definition of Hymn.*

What, then, is a Hymn, and whence originally was the Hymnody of the Western Church derived ? " Know ye," asks St. Augustine, commenting on the 148th Ps., " what a hymn is ? It is a song with praise of God. If thou praisest God and singest not, thou utterest no hymn. If thou singest and praisest not God, thou utterest no hymn. A hymn, then, containeth these three things: song (*canticum*), and praise (*laudem*), and that of God. Praise, then, of God in song is called a hymn." The Septuagint (v. 14) has here " ὕμνος πᾶσι τοῖς ὁσίοις αὐτοῦ." Augustine proceeds—" What, then, meaneth this: ' An hymn to all His Saints ?' ' Let His Saints receive a hymn. Let His Saints utter a hymn.' " *Modulata laus est hymnus*, says St. Gregory of Nazianzus (*Iamb.* 142). In the *Cotton MS., Vespasian D. xii.*, in the British Museum, exists a *Hymnary* with an interlinear Saxon version of the 10th or 11th century. The scribe on the first fly-leaf writes thus :

" It is clear that David the Prophet first composed and sang hymns, then the other prophets, afterwards the three youths when cast into the furnace. There are then Divine hymns ; there are also those composed by human understanding. Hilarius, Bishop of Poictiers, flourished first in versified hymns ; after whom Ambrose, Bishop of Milan, is known to have excelled in this kind of poetry. Whatever poems, then, are sung in praise of God are called hymns. A hymn, moreover, is of those who sing and praise, which from Greek into Latin is interpreted ' Laus,' because it is a song of joy and praise ; but properly hymns are those containing the praise of God."

This definition, then, excludes prose anthems, meditative, didactic, historical, merely religious poetry, and private devotional pieces unsuited for public worship. According to this definition, to constitute a hymn three conditions are requisite : it must be praise of God or of His saints, be capable of being sung, and be metrical.

ii. *The Hymns of Holy Scripture.*

The substantive ὕμνος and the derived verb ὑμνέω -ῶ intransitively occur in the Septuagint Version of the Old Testament—Ps. lxv. 13 ; 2 Chron. xxix. 30 ; Prov. i. 20 ; Eccles. xxxix. 35 ; xlvii. 8 ; li. 11 ; 1 Macc. iv. 24 ; xiii. 47 : and in Is. xlii. 10—ὑμνήσατε τῷ κυρίῳ ὕμνον καινόν. It is used intransitively governing an accusative—2 Chron. xxix. 33 ; Ps. xxii. 23–25 (which is quoted verbatim, Heb. ii. 12, " ἐν μέσῳ ἐκκλησίας ὑμνήσω σε "), and Is. xii. 4. The substantive ὕμνος occurs also in the Septuagint, Is. xii. 5 ; xxv. 1 ; Neh. xii. 46 ; Ps. xl. 3 ; lxv. 1 ; c. 4 ; cxlviii. 1 ; Is. xlii. 10 ; also in the titles to Ps. vi., liv., lv., and at the end of Ps. lxxii. The conclusion is that the Greek word "Hymn" and its equivalent in the Hebrew (see Is. xii. 5 ; xxv. 1) or Syriac, were in common use among the Jews at the coming of our Lord to signify a Song of Praise to God ; whence it passed to the whole Christian Church, Matthew xxvi. 30 and Mark xiv. 26, relate how Christ and his disciples " ὑμνήσαντες," literally "having hymned," went forth. This hymn, it seems, was the "Hallel" or Ps. cxiii.–cxviii., beginning with Halleluyah. The next notice of hymns in the New Testament is in the 16th ch. of the Acts, v. 25. Paul and Silas "praying were hymning The God," προσευχόμενοι ὕμνουν τὸν θεόν. What these hymns were is doubtful ; scarcely the Psalms. St. James v. 13, says "Is any merry ? let him sing psalms " (ψαλλέτω) ; thus, as well as St. Paul in two passages hereafter cited, particularising this kind of praise, and distinguishing it from others. Some hymnologists, however, have included the Psalms and the Canticles of the Old and New Testament, as the Songs of Miriam and Deborah, with other songs of praise, such as the Sanctus, Magnificat, and Nunc Dimittis, under the general name of Hymns. Le Brun, in his Explicatio Missae, i. 82, has done this. So also Whitby confounds the Psalms of David with the hymns composed by spiritual men, such as Zacharias and Symeon. St. Paul himself, however, distinguishes between the three kinds of divine praises, "Speaking one to another in psalms and hymns and spiritual songs " (ᾠδαῖς, i.e. Odes or Canticles), Ephes. v. 19. And again, "Teaching and admonishing one another with psalms and hymns and spiritual songs (ᾠδαῖς), singing with grace in your hearts to the Lord." Col. iii. 16. "Where," says Bishop Beveridge," by psalms I understand those of David's composing ; by hymns such anthems as were made up, chiefly of praise and thanksgiving by whomsoever composed ; by spiritual songs all sorts of songs upon any spiritual subject." And this division is quite in accordance with that made in the first age by Hippolytus. (De Consummatione Mundi sub fin.—Routh, Reliquiae Sacrae, ii. 146 ; iii. 314.) "I have prepared your mouth for giving glory and praise, and psalms and odes." What, then, were these hymns as apart from the other two species of praise ?

iii. Hymns of the Early Church.

"We find," continues Beveridge, "from the testimony of the younger Pliny (2nd cent., Lib. x., Epist. 97), under Trajan, that the Christians in the first age were accustomed to meet before day, and to sing a hymn to Christ as God by turns one after another;" and to the same effect is Tertullian (Apolog. 2.), and Eusebius (Hist. iii.). Caius, a Greek author writing in the beginning of the third century against the Montanists, speaks of "psalms and odes ; such as were from the beginning written

by the faithful, hymns to the Christ, the Word of God, calling Him God." (Routh, Reliq. Sacr., ii. 127.) So that very early after Pentecost Christian and not mere Jewish hymns must have been composed, which were publicly sung in the congregations, and these chants and hymns were conducted by an order of persons called Psaltae or Cantores. (Sozomen, Lib. iv., c. 3 ; Socrates, Lib. v., c. 22.) Philo, in his "Vita Contemplativa," describes how the Ascetics in Egypt, then and before his time (circa A.D. 40 to 68), "composed hymns in various metres and rhythms in honour of the true God, some in the ancient trimeter ; others newly composed. The president begins, and the choirs follow in various modulations, with a chorus of all the people in two choirs of men and women, each having its leader, but all equally joining at the end." The Christians of St. Mark there possibly followed this example. Eusebius (Lib. ii., c. 17, Histor.), quoting Philo, speaks of these Therapeutae : "Not only do they use the ancient hymns, but they make new ones to God, modulating them in metre and sounds in a very excellent and sweet composition, which is also practised in the Church and in monasteries"; and he subsequently speaks of these (Lib. v., c. 28) as "Cantica fratrum," wherein "a primordio a fidelibus conscripta Christum Verbum Dei concelebrant." In a well-known place of St. Basil (quoted Gerbert i., 233) "The psaltery (i.e. tunes)' of these harmonic rhythms has its origin from above, whence we should be anxious to seek them, and not to be carried away by delight in the melody to the pleasures of the flesh"; and in his epistle to the Neocaesarienses, 63, "Divided into two companies, they sing in alternate parts ; then to one person is allotted that he should begin first what is to be sung by the next following him." Paul of Samosata was condemned in a council, held at Antioch, A.D. 260, for rejecting these hymns. St. Ephrem of Nisibis (died 379) says, "We honour our festivals in psalms and hymns and spiritual songs." In 506 the Council of Agde (Can. 30) ordered the singing of hymns every day, morning and evening. The Council of Tours still more plainly, after having formally recommended the adoption of the Ambrosian hymns, "There are yet some others which are worthy of being sung which have the names of authors, who were constant in the faith, prefixed." Still more important and decisive was the decree of the 6th Council of Toledo in 633. (Can. 13, Labbe, iv. p. 1709.) "For singing hymns and psalms publicly in the church we have the example of Christ and His apostles. Hymns are composed like masses or petitions, or commendations or laying on of hands, of which there are many, just as with prayers ; let none of you for the future withhold hymns composed in praise of God, but let Gaul and Spain celebrate them alike. Those should be excommunicated who shall dare to reject hymns."

iv. Influence of Greek Hymns.

That these Hymns to Christ, whether metrical or non-metrical, had their origin in the East, and thence travelled to the West, is evident historically. Eusebius (*Lib.* v. 28) speaks of the " Cantica fratrum a primordio a fidelibus conscripta "; so also Tertullian. So Sozomen (*Lib.* vi., *c.* 25), speaks of the "*Sacros hymnos qui in ecclesiâ cani solent.*" St. Chrysostom speaks of the hymns after the psalms in divine service : and the tradition related by Socrates is that Ignatius (who first came to Antioch A.D. 68) had learnt in a vision of angels " how in antiphonal hymns to hymn the Holy Trinity "; to whom may be added Hierotheus, greatly commended by Dionysius and Noethus (see *Gerbert,* i. 75); Hippolytus and others of the second century. The rise and growth of Greek hymns, and the use made of the earliest by Latin writers of a later date, are fully set forth in the articles on Greek Hymnody, p. 456, i.; Doxologies, p. 308, i.; Gloria in Excelsis, p. 425, i., and the Te Deum. See also Syriac Hymnody. If any proofs were wanting that Latin Hymnody originated in, and was derived from, the East, it may be found in these articles ; for, with a few exceptions, there are daily hymns for the Hours, and for the Festivals, Fasts, and Seasons in each case ; and the Apostles and Saints are celebrated by hymns in a similar manner and on the same occasions. Nor are the Spanish and Mozarabic Christians any exception, who originally received their hymnody partly from Rome and the East, partly from the Greek-speaking Christians of Africa. The very ancient Irish Latin Hymn of the Apostles, beginning *Precamur Patrem* (from the *Antiphonarium Benchorense*—Bangor, in the county of Down) and reprinted by *Daniel*, vol. iv. p. 31, bears evident marks of a translation from an Eastern original. These early hymns soon made their way with Christianity itself, from the East to Rome, Africa, Spain, and all other parts of the Roman Empire; except, perhaps, Northern Gaul, where, as St. Jerome complains in his preface to the Second Book of his Commentary on the Galatians, hymns were unacceptable. They were very soon introduced into public worship, but were not originally sung in the Latin tongue; for, in the first Christian times, Greek, or dialects of it, continued to be spoken in Italy, the South of Gaul, Germany and Africa, and Latin had not yet come into common use; nor was it possible to compress into classical measures the fervid devotion of the earlier converts.

v. *Earliest Latin Hymns.*

Gerbert (*De Cantu et Musica Sacra, vol.* i., *p.* 80, pub. 1774), after examining all the authorities, finds that no name can be connected with any hymn in the Latin language till we arrive at St. Hilary and Pope Damasus, in the beginning of the 4th century. Isidore of Seville, who d. 636 (*De Officiis, Lib.* i., *c.* 6) says: "Hilary of Gaul, Bishop of Poictiers, was the first who flourished in composing hymns in verse," and St. Jerome, who d. 420, makes a similar statement. It would appear, from Hilary's own words, that he brought some from the East (in Ps. lxviii., lxiv.). Those beginning *Lucis largitor splendide ;* the Lenten hymn, *Jesu quadragenariae ;* three short ferial morning hymns, *Deus pater ingenite, In matutinis surgimus,* and *Jam meta*

noctis transiit, in the *Mozarabic Breviary ;* one for Vespers in the Epiphany, *Jesus refulsit omnium ;* another for Compline or Lauds at Pentecost, *Beata nobis gaudia,* have been ascribed to Hilary by Fabricius, Cassander, Tommasi, and Daniel. To Hilary also is ascribed by the *Antiphonarium Benchorense* [see Hymnarium] the noble matin hymn in praise of Christ, *Hymnum dicat turba fratrum hymnum cantus personet,* in trochaic tetra-meters, which is by Bede denominated *pulcherrimus (De arte metrica)* ; but it would seem rather to be an anonymous poem of the 6th century. By the consent of most authorities to Pope Damasus I. (A.D. 366) are ascribed two short Latin hymns, one for St. Andrew, *Decus sacrati nominis,* the other for St. Agatha (martyred A.D. 251), *Martyris ecce dies Agathae.* The latter is the earliest hymn respecting any Saint: it is in rhyme, and the ordinary laws of Latin metre are ignored.

vi. *St. Ambrose and Ambrosian Hymns.*

We arrive in succession at the great name of St. Ambrose (b. at Treves 340, d. 397), the main founder of the original, simple, dignified, objective school of popular Latin Hymnody, which for so many ages, almost without intermixture, prevailed over the Roman Empire, and before the 6th century penetrated even into Spain (See *Arevali Dissertationes,* vi. 21–23), and is still in use in the Divine Office all over Europe. As Mabillon writes (*Liturgia Gallicana,* 381), " St. Ambrose took care that, after the manner of the Eastern Fathers, psalms and hymns should be sung by the people also, when previously they had only been recited by individuals singly, and among the Italians by clerks only." St. Augustine, speaking of the hymns at Milan, says, "These hymns and psalms are sung after the manner of the Eastern, lest the people be wearied, which is imitated by almost all the congregations in the world."

A fact which now strikes the inquirer is this : that in the 101 hymns up to this date (6th cent.) printed by *Daniel,* vol. i., 91 of which (a very few excepted) he attributes to St. Ambrose or his contemporaries and followers, the ancient classical metres are abandoned, prosody is neglected, accentuation substituted for correct quantity, and the Iambic dimeter is mostly adapted as best suited for congregational singing. With the exception of here and there an Alcaic or Sapphic, or tetrameter, or pentameter, or hexameter usually in honour of some festival or Saint, this Iambic dimeter of eight syllables remained the favourite for all hymns for *public worship* which are to be found in the Office books down to and beyond the introduction of the *Sequences* hereinafter mentioned. Those in the *Ambrosian Breviary* (re-edited by St. Charles Borromeo, 1582) were almost exclusively in that metre. The same may be said of those in the Gotho - Isidorian, edited by Cardinal Ximenes 1502, and the *Mozarabic Hymnal* pub. in folio at Madrid, 1775. This was so almost exclusively in the ancient English Church, with the exception, indeed, of two or three of St. Gregory's, in Sapphics, and a few others for Festivals. Out of 130 hymns in 11th century English Benedictine Hymnals (Harl. 2961; Jul. A. vi. &c.) there are not a dozen in other measures. [See **Hymnarium, p. 546, ii.**] The same may be predicated of Germany, France, and Spain, and so it continued to be down to the Reformation. Vast additions were doubtless made at and after the epoch of the *Sequences*, and from the 13th century downwards, which will hereafter be noticed.

vii. *Early Ritual Use.*

These hymns were very soon appropriated to the great and minor Festivals and Fasts of the year, the Seven days of the week, and the Seven hours of Prayer, as among the Easterns. It is a question, however, whether this definite appropriation was first made by St. Ambrose himself, or mainly by St. Benedict after him. In the rule of the monastery at Lerins (A.D. 523), similar to that of St. Cæsarius of Arles, some of these (*Bolland. ad diem, January* 12) are so appropriated; so in that of St. Isidore, and in that of St. Aurelian of Arles, who d. 555. Respecting the rule of St. Benedict there can be no doubt. Benedict founded his Order, promulgated his rule, and prescribed the time, the method, and course of his liturgical offices in the beginning of the 6th century. It spread rapidly over Europe, and Reyner, in his *Apostolatus Benedictorum* (Douay, 1626), maintained that for many hundreds of years no other Order really existed. Doubtless also the customs of this vast community would exercise a great influence over the seculars, and determine their usages, as well as those of the succeeding Orders. St. Benedict expressly adapted the Hymns of Ambrose, composed either by him or his successors and imitators, to his Order of Worship (*Regula* xviii.). Walafrid Strabo, who d. 849 (*De Rebus Ecclesiasticis, c.* 25), writes, "As our sainted Abbot Benedict ordained, the hymns are said in the Canonical Hours which Ambrose himself composed, or others in imitation of him." "Which," says Hincmar, in his book on the Trinity (857), "is written in the rule of St. Benedict, and in which the Catholic faith is redolent; and they are pious prayers, and the composition is admirable." (See *Gerbert de Re Musica*, i. 510.) In No. 391, C. C. C. Library, Cambridge, in the *Liber Sanctae Marie Wygornensis Ecclesiae per Sanctum Oswaldum*, is an old English Benedictine Office book and Hymnary, Anno 1064, the title of the latter being *Incipiunt Hymni Ambrosiani canendi per singulas horas secundum constitutionem Patris nostri Benedicti.* [See **Hymnarium, p. 547, i.**] These are nearly identical with what constituted the English Church Hymnody down to the year 1556. Other MS. English Hymnals of the 12th, 13th and 14th centuries, described in detail in **Hymnarium, pp. 546, 547, 551**, are nearly identical in the hymns which they contain, varying from 115 to 130 in number. The same hymns may be found repeated in the English Hymnals up to 1556, with some local variations, and the addition of such as were composed for Festivals (such as the Name of Jesus and the Transfiguration) instituted later on. The Ambrosian and Benedictine scheme was thus adhered to, through-

out England and all the North of Europe, and, with local variations, in the remainder of Western Christendom.

viii. *From the IV. to the XI. Century.*

With the Ambrosiani must be grouped the succeeding composers of Christian poetry, several of them laymen, for the next five or six hundred years, for they wrote mainly on the same subjects, in the same vein, with the same intent, mostly in the same metre. We recall with pleasure the names of Aurelius Clemens Prudentius, Sedulius, Felix, Sidonius Apollinaris, Juvencus, Ennodius, Venantius Fortunatus, St. Gregorius Magnus, St. Columba, St. Isidore of Seville, Beda Venerabilis, Paulus Diaconus, Carolus Magnus, Theodulphus, Rhabanus Maurus, St. Odo of Cluny, St. Fulbert, St. Peter Damiani, with a number of anonymous poems extending over the same period, some of them most beautiful and remarkable, up to the epoch of St. Bernard.

Amongst these must be reckoned the hymn *Exultet jam angelica turba coelorum* (found equally in the old *Roman, Gallican, Ambrosian*, and *Mozarabic* rite, as well as others, such as *Sarum*), whose glorious strains at the Benediction of the Paschal candle (probably with the same music from the beginning, as in the *Sarum Missal*), and on the new light, are probably, with a consensus of critics, those of St. Augustine (*Daniel*, ii. 312). As he was said to have been a deacon when he composed it, it was always afterwards sung by the deacon.

In the last half of the 4th and in the beginning of the 5th century lived Aurelius Clemens Prudentius (q. v.). He was born probably at Saragossa or at Calahorra in Spain. About his fiftieth year he determined to abandon his earthly pursuits and to spend the remainder of his days in promoting the honour of God and the kingdom of Christ. In his fifty-seventh year, according to his own preface, he published many of his poems, and continued to do so up to the year 405, about which time he went to Rome (*Hic mihi cum peterem te rerum maxima Roma, &c.; Innumeros cineres Sanctorum Romula in urbe Vidimus, Peristeph.* ix. 3, xi. 1), and afterwards took up his abode at Imola. He seems to have died about A.D. 413. He was a prolific author. His Christian Lyrics are his *Cathemerinon*, or twelve hymns adapted to all the actions of the day: his *Peristephanon*, or fourteen hymns of the "Crowns of the Martyrs"; and his *Apotheosis* of the Divinity of Christ. Amongst his hymns are the daily hymns *Ales diei nuntius, Nox et tenebrae*, and *Lux ecce surgit aurea;* for the Nativity, *Corde natus ex Parentis;* for the Holy Innocents, *Salvete flores Martyrum;* for the Epiphany, *O sola magnarum urbium;* and for Lent there are also his "Hymnus jejunantium"; *O Nazarene lux Bethleem*, and *Cultor Dei memento.* That for Holy Saturday, at the lighting of the Paschal candle, *Inventor rutili dux bone luminis*, is still retained in many foreign hymnaries, and in the *Sarum* for the procession after Vespers on that day; along with four or five others of less note. A hymn sometimes ascribed to Prudentius, but in error, and not found in his works, is :—

"Hymnum Mariae Virginis,
　　Decantemus cum Angelis," &c.

This is in the *Mozarabic Breviary*, 1502. It may be observed, moreover, that in his sacred poetry Prudentius has made use of the Iambic trimeter and dimeter, the hendecasyllabic, Alcaic, and Sapphic metres, the Trochaic tetrameter, Glyconean, and others.

To omit mention of Paulinus of Nola, Coelius Sedulius comes in as a Christian lyrist in the first half of the 5th century, under Honorius and Theodosius II. Whether he was a layman or ecclesiastic is unknown : probably he was a Presbyter. He is said to have been a Greek, and again an Italian ; and then again (confounding him with another Sedulius), an Irishman. He composed a hymn in acrostics (*i.e.* each verse beginning with consecutive letters of the alphabet), which is the beginning of his poem in Iambic dimeters on the Life of Christ: *A solis ortus cardine*, a part of which is the Epiphany hymn, *Hostis Herodes impie*. These were universally adopted into all Hymnaries. St. Magnus Felix Ennodius (born in France 473, died 521), composed one or two excellent hymns; and Elpis [See **Elpis, p. 329, i.**], that beginning *Aurea luce et decore roseo*, for the Festival of St. Peter and St. Paul.

Next, in order of time, we arrive at one of the noblest and most pleasing of the Christian lyrists, Venantius Honorius Clementianus Fortunatus (See **p. 383, ii.**). The time of his birth is unknown, but he himself tells us that he was born at a village called Duplabilis between Treviso and Ceneda in Venetia. He was educated at Ravenna in grammar, rhetoric, and Roman law. He composed poetry as early as A.D. 555; he went to Tours to St. Martin's grave in 565, was at the wedding of Sigebert with Brunhilda; Rhadegunda, widow of Clothaire the First, was his friend. There he dwelt and became a priest, and was a friend of Gregory of Tours. In the year 597 he was made Bishop of Poictiers. The date of his death is not known, but it was probably about 609. He composed prose works, but his fame rests on his poetry. In the second book of his sacred poems we find the glorious ode, *Vexilla Regis prodeunt, Fulget Crucis mysterium*, for Passiontide. It finds its place in most European Hymnaries, although sometimes (as in the present *Roman*) in a mutilated form; the penultimate stanza, for instance :—

"Fundis aroma cortice,
　Vincis sapore nectare,
　Jucunda fructu fertili,
　Plaudis triumpho nobili,"

is often omitted ; but it has no worthy representative in our vernacular church hymn-books except perhaps in the *Hymnary*. Of equal sublimity and fervour is his well-known Passion monody, mostly in trochaics, *Pange lingua gloriosi Praelium certaminis*, which has been subjected to similar ignominious treatment in the Roman Breviary. Then we have the Paschal Processional, in hexameters and pentameters, from his poem on the Resurrection, very universally adopted ; the first verse of which, *Salve festa dies toto venerabilis aevo*,

was in England generally prefixed to all the processional proses for the great Festivals.

To St. Gregory the Great we owe some few of the best hymns for Sundays from the Epiphany to Lent, for Passiontide, Palm Sunday, and for the Hours (in Sapphics). They were speedily adopted into most hymnaries, especially the early English. That for Sunday morning especially, *Primo dierum omnium*, is found in all; but neither that nor any of the Lenten or Passiontide hymns are represented in our vernacular church hymn-books to any appreciable extent. To all these are appended the ascription of praise to the Holy Trinity at the end, which (although it has been attributed to St. Ambrose) seems now first, in various forms, to have come into general use.

The *Irish Hymnody* must not be left unnoticed. A *Liber Hymnorum* exists in Trinity College, Dublin, in old Irish characters, with copious Scholia in the same writing : a second in the Royal Irish Academy ; and a third at the Franciscan College of St. Isidore at Rome. Some hymns from these were published by Colgan (*Trias thaumaturga*, 1647), by Ware, 1656, and by Usher. The late Dr. Todd undertook to edit this *Liber Hymnorum* for the Irish Archæological and Celtic Society, but two parts only appeared, in 1855 and 1869, the undertaking having been cut short by his untimely death. In them we find a hymn in honour of St. Patrick, written by Sechnall, the son of his sister, *circa* A.D. 458 (a Lourica, or coat of mail to whomsoever repeated it)—

"Audite, omnes amantes Deum, sancta merita
　Viri in Christo beati Patrici Episcopi.
　Quomodo bonum ab actum similatur angelis,
　Perfectamque propter vitam aequatur apostolis."

It is printed in *Daniel*, iv. 91, and by Dr. J. Laur. Villanueva, in his *Opuscula S. Patritii*, Dublin, 1835. Then follows the noble composition of St. Columba, containing the substance of the Creeds in 150 lines :—

"Altus Prosator, vetustus dierum et ingenitus,
　Erat absque origine primordii et crepidine;
　Est et erit in saecula saeculorum infinita,
　Cui est unigenitus Christus et Sanctus Spiritus."

Also a hymn of St. Cummin Lange (A.D. 661), in rhyme in praise of the Apostles, who are named successively, four lines being devoted to each :—

"Celebra Juda festa Christi gaudia,
　Apostolorum exaltans memoria."

Another to St. Mary, also rhymed, by St. Cuchumine (700 to 750, see *Mone*, ii. 383) :—

"Cantemus in omni die concinentes varie,
　Conclamentes Deo dignum hymnum Sanctae Mariae,
　Bis per chorum hinc et inde collaudemus Mariam."

Also (amongst others) there is a hymn in praise of St. Bridget (died 523), who was for many ages the St. Mary of the Irish. It begins—

"Christus, in nostra insula quae vocatur Hibernia."

The author, 600–650, is unknown.

To pass over the hymn to St. Agatha by Isidore of Seville ; one by the Spanish lady Cyrilla, for St. Thyrsus and his companions ; and that on the Day of Judgment, *Apparebit repentina*, both praised by Bede, and in trochaics ; we notice a remarkable Sacramental one, from the *Bangor Antiphonary*, of noble simplicity, *Sancti venite Corpus Christi sumite*, which, as *Daniel* remarks (i. 194), doubtless shows that all Christians then received under both kinds.

At the end of the 8th century appears anonymously the hymn for many martyrs, *Sanctorum meritis inclyta gaudia* (in *Choriambic Asclepiads*, the fourth verse *Glyconic*). This is in the Anglo-Saxon hymnaries. (In the *Harl*. 2961 a portion is appropriated to the Holy Innocents.) This list may be closed with the *Ave Maris Stella*, or *Stilla*, which appears in public worship in the 9th century, wherein this denomination is first applied to the Blessed Virgin. It has never been altered, but subsequently was in France and Germany frequently farced and paraphrased, and so turned into a Sequence (see *Mone*, vol. ii. 215, *et seq.*).

Bede contributed to the Anglo-Saxon Church, &c., a treatise, *De Arte Metrica*, and a number of hymns. Paulus Diaconus, one, *Ut queant laxis*, in Sapphics, for the Nativity of St. John Baptist. To Charlemagne is attributed the beautiful and touching *Veni Creator Spiritus*, which since his age has been sung with unexampled unanimity, solemnity, and fervour in all portions of the Western Church, not only at Pentecost but in all observances in which the aid of the Holy Ghost was specially necessary; in the coronation of kings, the consecration of patriarchs, archbishops and bishops, at the opening of councils, &c.; and at Pentecost, especially at Terce, it used to be, in all churches, with the celebrant fully vested, and all the altar lights kindled. To this period belong also the fine hymns for St. Michael and All Angels, one of which was composed by Alcuin for Charlemagne, *Summi Regis Archangele Michael*, and another (*Mone*, i. 447) *Archangelum mirum magnum*. In the following century Theodulphus composed *Gloria laus et honor*, for Palm Sunday; Rhabanus Maurus (the *Liturgist*, A.D. 815) two hymns for St. Michael's Day, *Christe sanctorum decus angelorum;* another in trochees, *Tibi Christe splendor patris;* Odo of Cluny on St. Mary Magdalene, *Lauda mater ecclesia;* Fulbert of Chartres, the Paschal song of joy, *Chorus novae Jerusalem.* St. Peter Damiani, although a poet, witness his *Ad perennis vitae fontem*—Of the joys of Paradise—did not add much to Church song. Flavius added *Tellus et aethra jubilent*, used in the Anglo-Saxon hymnals for the *Coena Domini.* And we may close this list with the loved name of St. Bernard and his jubilant rhythm, *Jesu dulcis memoria*, and his monody to Christ on the Cross, *Salve mundi salutare*, both composed at Clairvaux. *Jesu dulcis memoria* was speedily welcomed by the whole Western Church. Originally appropriate to the Circumcision, it was transferred to "The Name of Jesus" when that became a Church festival (on August 7). It was afterwards repeatedly imitated and paraphrased, especially in *Tracts* and *Sequences;* two beautiful rhymed examples of which are one in the *Sarum* and other English Missals. Three centos are in the pre-Reformation English daily Offices. (See **Jesu dulcis Memoria**, p. 585, i.)

Anonymous hymns not later than the 11th century include *Jam Christe Sol justitiae, Auctor Salutis Unicus*, in the early English and many French and German MSS. and books. For the Festival of SS. Peter and Paul, *Felix per omnes*, &c., in the *Roman, Spanish, Paris, Rouen*, and pre-Reformation *English Hymnaries:* for Martyrs, *Martyr Dei qui unicum;* for Apostles, *Exultet coelum laudibus;* for Confessors, *Iste confessor Domini*, and *Jesu Redemptor omnium;* for Virgins, *Virginis proles;* for St. Stephen, *Sancte Dei pretiose*, in rhyme, and extensively used in England and Germany; but not in the *Spanish, Ambrosian*, or *Rouen* offices.

This list may be closed with the triumphant *Urbs beata Jerusalem*, a splendid paraphrase of the Apocalypse xxi., 2, 19–21, appropriated to the Dedication of a Church and the Anniversary, and sung throughout Europe of old time, probably from the 8th century. The Anglo-Saxons used also *Christe cunctorum dominator alme* of the 7th century, which is in many French hymnals. The *Urbs beata* has not escaped mutilation, as in the *Roman Breviary*, and by Guyet and the other Gallican so-called restorers of Latin hymnody, but its main features have always been conserved. Archbishop Trench writes (*Sacred Latin Poetry*): "This poem attests its own true inspiration in that it has proved the source of true inspiration in circles beyond its own," alluding to the numerous translations and imitations of it in English and German. The fine hymn for the restoration of a church, *O beata Jerusalem*, is apparently an early Spanish hymn.

ix. *Hymns of the XI. and XII. Centuries.*

The period of the 11th and 12th centuries constitutes a marked epoch in the history of Latin Hymnody. By that time the ordinary usage of hymns in the various formularies of the Western Church in different countries, dioceses, and religious communities, in their daily, weekly, festal, and penitential worship, had become fixed and settled, the Benedictines, as already intimated, setting the example; for, although Ambrose composed hymns, it is not certain that he ordained them to be sung in order in the Church Offices. Those we have been considering constituted the staple of the sacred songs of the Missals, Breviaries, and other Offices of this date; such being from time to time added in each Country, Church, Diocese or Conventual society as celebrated the saintly founders and patrons of each, with their peculiar solemnities; originally, perhaps, in versicles and responses in prose, converted after a time into poetry: of this, the Spanish hymns are notable examples. By this time, however, with a few striking exceptions, the Clergy and Monks had become the principal poets. The comparative seclusion of the former, and the separation of the latter from all worldly affairs, exercised a marked influence on these compositions. They increased greatly in number; they became more spiritualized, subjective, devout, and mystical. They were no longer confined to the direct worship and praise of the Creator, of Christ, of the Holy Ghost; to the honour of the Blessed Virgin, and of the Apostles and certain principal Saints, and appropriated to the various solemnities of the Church relating to them : such as were those of Ambrose, Gregory, Prudentius, Fortunatus, and their successors. They became amplified and refined into eulogies, descriptions of, and meditations upon, the Passion and Wounds of Christ, on His Sacred Countenance, on His Cross, on His Sweet Name, on the Vanity of Life, on the Joys of Paradise, on the Terrors of Judgment; into penitential exercises, of the Holy Sacrament, of the lives and sufferings of numerous Saints —most especially into praises of the Blessed Virgin, on her Dignity, on her Joys and Dolours. Of this last particular species (often mere paraphrases of *Ave Maris Stella*, and laudations of a somewhat extravagant kind) vast numbers, but, it is to be observed, mainly belonging to the next succeeding centuries, are to be found in *Mone*, ii.; whilst previous to this period, as *Daniel* remarks, very few had been composed. Peter Damiani, Bonaventura, Bernard of Cluny, Thomas of Celano, and many others, including Adam of St. Victor, were the authors of the last previously mentioned sacred devotional poetry.

x. *Adoption of Accent and Terminal Rhyme.*

A further fact of importance must also be noticed: the universal adoption therein of accent instead of correct quantity, and of terminal rhyme or assonance. Neither of these, as we have already seen, is a necessary adjunct of Latin Hymnody, and may be thought to detract from its dignity; but the terminations and prosody of the Latin of that age lent themselves so easily thereto, that sacred poetry in general, instead of being founded on the metre and quantity of syllables, assumed rather, as being more facile, syllabism and rhyme. These rhymes were at first merely of vowels or assonances, to be adhered to when convenient, disregarded when otherwise. They might be confined to a single letter or fall on an unaccented syllable, or be found in the last verse only. Hilary himself, perhaps, almost unconsciously set the first example in the 4th century :—

> " Quem stella natum fulgida
> Monstrat micans in aethera,
> Magosque duxit praevia,
> Ipsius ad cunabula."

Pope Damasus, St. Gregory, and others wrote rhymed or assonant hymns. *Ave Maris Stella; Veni Creator Spiritus* are such. Odo of Cluny has alternate rhymes

> " Lauda Mater ecclesia,
> Lauda Christi clementiam,
> Qui septem purgat vitia
> Per septiformem gratiam."

Nor is the Church, nor are individuals to be blamed, for thus following the universal promptings of human nature peculiar to no age, which in sacred compositions, as in others, looks for smoothness and ease, for the music of language, for an assistance to memory, and to rivet the attention; to which the music may form an harmonious accompaniment. " It is not," says Dr. Guest (*Hist. of English Rhythm*, 110), " a mere ornament, it marks and defines the accent, and thereby strengthens and supports the rhythm. Its advantages have been felt so strongly that no people have ever adopted an accentual rhythm without also

adopting rhyme." To the 12th century belong trochaic tetrameter acatalectic (or perfect) and catalectic (or incomplete) lines. An example of this last is that of Peter Damiani (*Dan.* i. 116),

" Ad perennis vitae fontem mens sitivit arida."

The composers of Sequences, as will be found, made much use of these rhymes and assonances. Among the most remarkable instances of elaborate rhyming is the *Hora novissima* of Bernard of Cluny, a poem, evidently intended for private use only. It is in a dactylic hexameter catalectic, with a trochaic rhymed ending, divided into three parts, between which a caesura is inadmissible, and it has a feminine leonine intermediate rhyme between the two first clauses :—

"Hora novissima | tempora pessima | sunt vigi | lemus"

Dr. Neale translated it into English verse of fourteen syllables each, three short of the original, without attempting the complicated rhyme. Mr. Moultrie (*Lyra Mystica*, 113) also rendered a considerable portion with much success into a similar measure to the original. [See p. 533.] St. Thomas of Aquino (13th cent.) rhymed his sacramental lyrics; but in most cases the quantitative mode still prevailed. *Daniel* prints several hymns of a much later date (vol. i. pp. 298–306) of St. Nicholas, St. Agnes, St. Joseph, the Visitation, of Mary Magdalene, of Augustine, of the Name of Jesus, each stanza of three lines, in trochaic catalectics of fifteen syllables and triple rhymes. Rhymed hexameters and rhymed hexameters and pentameters are sometimes used.

xi. *Metre.*

With rhyme is intimately connected the subject of metre. The principal feet of which the Greeks and Latins made use in their verse were eight in number: 1. The *Spondee*, of two long syllables; 2. The *Pyrrhic*, of two short; 3. The *Iambic*, of a short and long; 4. The *Trochee*, of a long and short: 5. The *Dactyl*, of a long and two short; 6. The *Anapaest*, of two short and a long; 7. The *Molossian*, of three long; 8. The *Tribrach*, of three short. Of these the 1st, 2nd, 5th and 6th measure two in time more or less rapid, the remainder three. Four others are sometimes found in classical poetry: 1. The *Amphibrach*, a long between two short; 2. The *Amphimacer*, a short between two long; 3. The *Bacchic*, a short followed by two long: 4. And the *Antibacchic*, two long followed by a short. The first is a measure of two, with a syncope in the middle, the remainder of five. Of all these feet, with their compounds, the mediaeval hymnists, as well as the classical poets, made use in composing their verses. At the School of Adrian at Canterbury, we are told that "centena genera metrorum" were studied, among which was the *Adonic* of one long and two short, and two long syllables. Before this time, however, these classical measures, *Hexameters*, *Hexameters* and *Pentameters*, *Anacreontic*, and the various measures found in Horace, although still partially retained, were in process of change or abandonment. Church Song was composed mostly in alliterative and rhythmical measure, judging of the melody by the ear, and attending to the artificial distribution of the accent, and not to the quantity of the syllable. Bede in a treatise, *De Arte Metrica*, says, "Rhythm is a modulated composition of words, not in metrical arrangement (compositione), but arranged in a number of syllables according to the judgment of the ears;" or, as Ethelwold says (*Bonifacii Epist.* lxv., Mayence Edit. 77), "not elaborated by the measuring of feet, but composed of eight syllables in each particular verse, fitted under one and the same letter in equal paths of lines." Ethelwold had before written that he had sent three hymns for singing of two kinds; the first in heroic measure of a dactylic hexameter and pentameter rule, and adjusted into seventy formulæ of coequal verses; the other being in the *Iambic* dimeter and an *Acrostic* as just before mentioned. Bede himself speaks of the *Dactylic* or *Hexameter* (which he prefers); of the *Pentameter*; of the *Dactylic Phalecian pentameter*; consisting of a *Spondee*, a *Dactyl*, and three *Trochees* ("Cantemus Domino Deoque Nostro";) of the *Sapphic*; of the *Tetrameter* catalectic,

"Squalent arva sole pulvere multo;"

Of the *Iambic hexameter:*

"Senex fidelis prima credendi via,"

Of the *Iambic tetrameter* or *dimeter:*

"Deus Creator omnium,"

The *Anacreontic:*

"Age jam precor mearum,"

And the *Trochaic:*

"Hymnum dicat turba fratrum,"

and what he calls a rhythm without measure;

"Rex Eterne Domine,
Rerum Creator omnium,"

as all being in use in his time for sacred poetry. It will be found on examination that after Bede's time those hymns in the English hymnbooks up to the 11th and 12th centuries [see **Hymnarium, p. 546**] are mainly in *Iambic* or *Trochaic* metres, and composed with little regard to prosody. Classical versification founded on measure and quantity was gradually transformed into the more modern, based on the number of syllables, accentuation, alliteration, assonance, and rhyme. At the opening of the 12th century this syllabism and rhyme ruled lyrical verse. The *Asclepiad* of four feet (a Spondee, a Choriamb, a *Trochee*, and *Iambics*, ending with two *Dactyls*), or of four feet and a *Caesura* (a *Spondee*, a *Dactyl*, then the *Caesura* followed by two *Dactyls*); the *Iambic* dimeter, the septenarian *Trochaic*, are all reducible to a uniform number of syllables. The quantity of the penultimates was, however, retained. The *Trochaic Tetrameter* catalectic and acatalectic, was called also *Septenarius* because of the complete number of its feet, catalectic when one syllable short, *Desinit citius quam debuit* (καταλήγω), acatalectic when having the feet complete. Assonances or rhymes were introduced at the end of the verse as well as of its first hemistich. Thus Peter Damiani:

"Dum pressuris ac aerumnis se gemit obnoxiam,
Quam amisit dum deliquit contemplatur gloriam."

In the next century we find correct rhymes:

"Ad honorem tuum Christe recolet ecclesia
Praecursoris et Baptistae tui natalitia."

Lingard, in his *Anglo-Saxon Church* (ii. 64), gives to the same effect a summary of English sacred poems, and notices that from these metres were borrowed the measures of our present modern poetry. Further, the first verse of the hemistich of the *Septenarius* was doubled, and correspondently the second. Thus was initiated the celebrated strophe of four, then of six, verses which were ample, harmonious, and easy, and admitted of a thousand varieties. The eight syllable verses might be tripled and quadrupled; and as many syllables added to each line as might please the ear. To this measure the music was intimately adapted. The tradition for the *Proses* or *Sequences* was that, differently from hymns, the melody should be varied from one end to the other, but that in them there should be the same musical phrase for lines having the same number of syllables. The melody was varied throughout, but each neumatic period was chanted twice, or oftener, as need be. So far might be the case with the *Proses* of Notker. There was, however, one thing more wanted, and that was a verse by way of pause, having an invariable number of syllables, for a clausula or period, both to the verses and for the music. Yet this versicle had to be developed so that the musical phrase might be developed also when required, as these phrases might be, and always were, of unequal length. Another verse of 15 syllables would not be sufficient for this; hence the first hemistich being doubled, the *Christi natalitia* was interposed, which thus admitted the enlargement of the melody required; and, as the two last verses of each clausula rhymed, *Regem cum laetitiâ*, the unity of the strophe was preserved. And thus, at last, sung Adam of St. Victor, on St. Stephen:—

"Heri mundus exultavit,
Et exultans celebravit
Christi natalitia;
Heri chorus angelorum,
Prosecutus est cœlorum
Regem cum laetitiâ."

Practical necessity, then, as much as taste created these brilliant and popular sacred lyrics of the 12th and following century. By the end of the 13th the mechanism and style were already becoming debased.

xii. *Sequences.*

In the 10th and 11th centuries a new description of Hymns denominated *Proses*, and by the Germans *Tropes* or *Sequences*, were introduced into the celebration of the Mass, *Hymns* having been previously usually confined to the daily public Offices of prayer and praise; and *Trope* being a general name for any versicle or strophe introduced into, or supplementary to, other ecclesiastical chants (*Gerbert, de Cantu*, i. 340). According, however, to St. Cyprian's life of Cæsarius of Arles, 542 (*Gerbert, ibid.*), that Bishop ordered the laity and clergy to sing, some in Greek, some in Latin, *Proses* and *Anthems* in the Church. Later on, however, *Prose* came to mean the kind of style of that composition; *Sequence*, its place in the Service. In consequence of the destruction of Jumièges by the Normans in 851, some of its monks took refuge at St. Gall, bringing with them their *Gregorian Antipho-*

nary. Therein the *Gradual* (the anthem preceding the Gospel) in all Festal days and Seasons ended with a long *Alleluia*, being a musical jubilation on a certain number of notes, called *Neumes*, without words, on the final A; also called the *Sequentia* as following thereon. These *Neumes* (which were very difficult to remember) owed their origin to two chanters sent by Pope Adrian to Charlemagne; Peter, who opened a school at Metz, and Romanus, who, having been detained by illness at St. Gall, commenced a school of music there also. In this monastery of St. Gall was domiciled a young religious named Notker (called Balbulus from his stammer), of refined musical taste. He was delighted to find that the Jumièges book had affixed to these *Neumes* certain words corresponding to their number, a contrivance which enabled him to remember the cadences of these *Neumes* much more easily; especially as new ones were constantly being introduced. Under the advice of his master Yson, he forthwith set himself to compose some new words for these musical *Sequences* at the different Festivals of the year, and began with that for Eastertide—

    "Laudes Deo concinat orbis ubique totus"

(see *Daniel*, v. 62), wherein every note of the melody should have an accompanying word. After other lessons as to the melody and words from his master, he composed another in like form for the Dedication of a Church—

    "Psallat Ecclesia mater illibata"

(see *Daniel*, ii. 23; *Mone*, i. 323; *Neale's Sequentiae*, 247); and others followed.

In general these early *Notkerian Proses* (with a few conspicuous exceptions), were not rhymed or with assonances, except accidentally; hence the peculiar appellation. That for the Nativity, *Eja recolamus* (for the Circumcision in the *Sarum Missal*); for the Holy Innocents, *Laus tibi Christe*; that for the same day in the *Sarum Missal*, *Celsa pueri concrepent*; the *Veni Sancte Spiritus Et emitte*, attributed to Robert King of France; a grand anonymous prose on the Holy Trinity—

    "Benedicta sit beata Trinitas,"

retained in the *Sarum Missal* for Trinity Sunday; the well-known *Alleluiatic Prose* for Septuagesima, *Cantemus cuncti*; another for Christmas, *Nato canunt omnia*; and St. Bernard's *Lætabundus*, are amongst the exceptions and are all either rhymed or assonant. This non-rhyming gave rise to the idea (partly adopted even by *Mone*, iii., 49) that they were vague, incoherent compositions, without determinate metre or melodies. Such was not the case. Dr. Neale (*Daniel*, v., 1) and the Abbé Gautier (*Preface* cxxxvii.) have given a series of canons by which the recitation of them was regulated, the main principle of which was that each of the clauses or lines of the *Prose* should be nearly of similar length, and each syllable be closely accommodated to the musical notes of the jubilant *Neumes* to which they were set. If, then, the individual clause was double or treble, or more, the same musical phrase would be repeated, twice or thrice, &c. If somewhat longer, it would be lengthened out; if shorter contracted, till another phrase was arrived at. The *Prose* at last often consisted of a series of clauses, two and two of the same plan, although the introductory and concluding versicles had a special modulation. The Abbé Gautier gives this example:

Preface—"Johannes Jesu Christo multum dilecte Virgo.
1. Tu Ejus amore carnalem }
   In nave parentem liquisti, } 2 clauses of 9 syllables.
2. Tu lene conjugis | pectus respuisti | Messiam secutus.
   Ut Ejus pectoris | sacra meruisses | Fluenta potare."

Into other phases of this ancient prosody it is not necessary to enter.

We are now arrived at the middle period of the 12th century, and to Adam of St. Victor; to the second period of these noble rhymed metrical *Sequences*, changed in metre, which, increasing in beauty and popularity, kept hold on the mind of the Church in Northern Europe for centuries. Northern Europe, be it observed, for it must be mentioned that neither Spain nor Italy nor France south of the Loire, seem ever to have welcomed them. About the year 1153 may be said to have begun a new epoch in the history of *Proses* (hereafter to be called *Sequences*) in the Abbey of St. Victor at Paris, founded 40 years before by Louis VI. Therein resided a distinguished sacred poet and musician named Adam, whose compositions were destined to effect a vast improvement (even a revolution) in Church song. The learned Jose Clichtove, who died 1554, in the fourth and last part of his *Elucidatorium Ecclesiasticum* (who, however, is not particularly happy in the explanation of *Proses*), writes thus of him and of the rhymed *Proses* of this second epoch:—

    "This form of *Prose* in the Church Offices is most celebrated and of all that which is most in use. Its illustrious author, renowned no less for virtue than for learning, Adam of St. Victor, was in a surprising degree copious and ready in the rhythmical modulation of Proses, as very many of those composed by him for certain occasions very plainly declare."

By this time, in the North of France at least, a considerable proportion of the *Notkerian Proses* and those of inferior merit had gone out of use in choirs; and Church musicians had set themselves to compose others of a more melodious and popular character. These did not confine themselves to the ancient *Neumes* of *Alleluia*, repeated on many clauses or versicles of an equal number of syllables, but adopted an entirely novel and original system both of versification and music, derived from popular airs and much more grateful to the ear. We find verses of great regularity constructed according to the system explained above, and enriched with rhymes of great number, variety, and beauty, having penultimates sometimes long, sometimes short. Of these Adam of St. Victor was the principal author (although he had many imitators), and the Abbé Gautier has done signal service to Church hymnody by publishing 103 of them, with a few others which may perhaps be his, and also some of his hymns, together with an exhaustive introduction and notes exhibiting much research (*Œuvres Poétiques d'Adam de S. Victor*. Paris, 1858; 2nd ed. 1881). M. Félix Clément has also done much for the cause by publishing, with the original music (*4th edition*, Paris, 1876, *Poussielgue frères*) in modern notation, the chants of the Sainte Chapelle, with a selection of the principal Sequences of the Middle Ages from ancient manuscript sources.

The *Sequences* of Adam are most of them very beautiful. Out of 45 which Gautier prints in his 2nd ed., 1881, as undoubtedly genuine, six are for the Feast days which are connected with the Blessed Virgin, the remainder for the other Church Festivals and Seasons. Like those of Notker, they became extremely popular all over the North of Europe. Two of them for Pentecost, the admirable *Lux jucunda, lux insignis*, and *Qui procedis ab utroque* are singularly fine and impressive. It is not too much to say that these compositions, and, indeed, those of this date in general, are charged and saturated with the great facts, the very inmost, the most recondite and spiritual meanings of Scripture, with its mystical and symbolical meanings and interpretations; and are in musical and flowing verse, clothed with the magnificent imagery and descriptions of the Prophets and of the Book of the Revelation. A goodly selection is made from them in the English Missals, among them the splendid

"Zyma vetus expurgetur,"

for Easter; for the Dedication of the Church—

"Hierusalem et Sion filiae"

in the Octave—

"Quam dilecta tabernacula;"

for the Feasts of the Virgin—

"Ave mundi spes Maria,"
"Hodiernae lux diei;"

and that which Dr. Neale has denominated "the masterpiece of Adam," for the Exaltation of the Cross, and sung throughout France, England, and Rhineland,

"Laudes Crucis attollamus."

We may well join in the pathetic lamentation of the Abbé Gautier (*Preface* CLXXXII.) over the abolition in the Gallican Church, where they had been sung by choir and people down to the 17th cent., "without pity, without shame, and without taste, of these poems which had been chanted in the vaulted roofs of a thousand churches for four centuries," not being out of place nor interfering with the Divine Offices, but their most natural ornament, for the sake of adopting others of a more classical style; and sympathise in his earnest desire to readopt, as "national reminiscences," not all the Proses of Adam, but the more beautiful, of which, he says, "there are at least twenty which would embellish any Liturgy." An excellent edition of Adam's Liturgical poetry, with a translation into corresponding metres and rhymes, was published by the Rev. Digby S. Wrangham, M.A., in 1881.

The English *Missals* also contain many of Notker's *Proses*, as that for the Circumcision, *Eja recolamus*; for Easter, *Laudes Salvatori*; for Pentecost, *Sancti Spiritus adsit nobis gratia*; for St. Martin, *Sacerdotem Christi*; for Apostles, *Clare sanctorum senatus*; for St. John Evangelist, *Joannes Jesu Christo*, &c. Many of the *Sequences* in the English *Missals* are anonymous: for Easter, *Fulgens praeclara rutilat*, and the dramatic and interrogative *Victimae Paschali*; those for Advent, which were not customary elsewhere; and one for the Visitation, probably composed at Salisbury (*Daniel*,

v. 258), beginning *Celebremus in hac die*, and which has this strophe—

Visitatrix in montanis,
Visitatrix in his planis,
Sis matris ecclesiae,

which seems to have been written after the removal of the cathedral to its present site. A MS. *Troparium*, formerly belonging to Christ Church, Dublin, of the latter half of the 13th century, is in the University Library, Cambridge. It contains a series of these Sarum Sequences with the musical notation of that period attached to each.

The number of these compositions, especially of the Adamic type, increased almost indefinitely during the 13th and 14th centuries in every country, diocese, and church. Of great elegance and significance, is that of the Four Evangelists, *Jucundare plebs fidelis*. Also that of St. Thomas of Aquino, who died 1274, *Lauda Sion Salvatorem*, composed after the best manner of Adam, and fully exemplifying his style; to which may be added the imitation, *Recolamus Sacram Coenam*. The "Praise of the Cross," by St. Bonaventura, his contemporary, *Recordare Sanctae Crucis*, is excellent also. Especially is to be noted the Sequence *Dies irae, dies illa*, for All Souls' Day. This last is almost the only *Sequence* which Italy has produced, and, says *Daniel* (ii. 112) "Omnium consensu sacrae poeseos summum decus, et ecclesiae latinae κειμήλιον est pretiosissimum." The inimitable *Stabat Mater dolorosa*, Monody of Jacobus de Benedictis (as it seems), on the Seven Dolours or Of the Compassion of the Blessed Virgin, in the style of Adam, and probably composed after 1225, has been accepted by the whole Latin Church. In the unreformed noted *Rouen Antiphonary* this is placed as a *Prose* for Sunday in the Passion, with the original simple and mournful melody which Rossini adopted and enlarged. A noble *Sequence* for the Epiphany, *Prompto gentes animo*, not found in the books, is in that *Antiphonary*.

By the beginning of the 14th century the composition of *Proses* and *Sequences*, and that of Latin sacred poems in general, may be said to have culminated. These increased indefinitely in number, but not in excellence, and sometimes became, in the North, almost incumbrances to the Divine Offices. Many on various subjects were even composed in, or translated into, the vulgar tongue, and sung by the people, often to secular tunes, on every possible occasion. There was almost a sense of relief in the Western Church when, in the 16th century, Pius V. and the Council of Trent reduced those to be used as part of the Mass to four; the *Victimae Paschali*; *Veni Sancte Spiritus*; *Lauda Sion Salvatorem*; and the *Dies Irae*; to which was added the *Stabat Mater* in 1727. Fuller details concerning *Sequences*, together with the first lines of more than seven hundred, and an account of over thirty MSS. and printed service books in which they are found, are given in the special article on Sequences.

xiii. *The XIV. and XV. Centuries.*

At the beginning of the 14th century the golden age of Latin hymnody may be said to have expired, and its sun to have gone down in glory. Among the latest gems were the *Hymns and Sequences* of St. Thomas of Aquino, the Dominican, renowned as one of the few Italian sacred poets. His hymns include the *Adoro te devote; Pange lingua gloriosi Corporis; Lauda Sion; Sacris Solemniis*, and the *Verbum supernum*, all of which have been in extensive use either in their original or their translated forms from his day to the present time. Other fine hymns before the end of the 14th century are: *Surrexit Christus hodie*, and *Ecce tempus est vernale*, both for Easter; and the *O beata beatorum*, for Martyrs. The grand and pathetic *Stabat Mater dolorosa, Juxta crucem*, although often associated with this period, is of a later date. It is found in the *Paris Missal*, 1481, and the *Belgian Missal*, 1483. [See **Sequences.**]

The sacred lyrical Latin poetry subsequent to the 13th century, of which there is an extraordinary quantity in every possible variety of metre, may be divided into four classes:—

1. Hymns to God and the several Persons of the Holy Trinity.
2. For Festivals and Seasons, and to the Cross.
3. Of Saints and Angels.
4. Of the Blessed Virgin.

Of all these the authors are for the most part unknown. As to the first head, it would seem as if former Christian poets had exhausted these great subjects, and the praises become feebler and less original. The old Hymns and Sequences keep their places, and to them are subjoined many variations and additions peculiar to each Country, Diocese, Church, and Conventual Order; but the new hymnody attains not to the grandeur and excellence of the more ancient. This may easily be verified in the volumes of *Mone*. The former spirit of Christian poetry, however, still partially survived, although the style is inferior and different. There are several hymns to the Holy Trinity of the 14th and 15th centuries, especially in Germany — *Dulcis amor, pax, veritas; Summe Pater sancte Deus; Trinitatis altissimae*, &c., most of them condensations or expansions of the Nicene and Athanasian Creeds. We find too "Hours of the Holy Trinity." The three *Hymns* and *Sequences* for the Transfiguration in the English Office-books are fine. They begin *Coelestis formam gloriae; O sator rerum, reparator aevi;* and *O nata lux de lumine.* There are rhymed summaries of the Life of Christ, besides such as were in use in the 11th and 12th centuries. There is an excellent rhymed hymn for Advent, with a melody, *Veni, Veni, Rex Gloriae!* a number of rhymed and assonant or acrostic Songs and Hymns for the Nativity: *Dies est laetitae; Apparuit benignitas*, &c., precursors of Christmas and Epiphany Carols. We find many for the Passion, as *Plange Sion Filia; Dulcis Jesu spes pauperum; Patris Sapientia; Ad matutinum gemide*, and several versions of the Hours of the Passion, mostly in rhyme, a method of devotion which began and spread widely in this age. There is also a devotion of the Holy Cross, *Crux tua, Christe, salus hominum;* one for the Exaltation or Invention of the Cross, *Salve Crux sancta, Salve mundi gloria*, in Iambic hexameters Monoculum; and a Lament for Jesus, for private recitation, in eighty verses, each verse beginning with His Name. There are also hymns "of the Face of Jesus," and salutations to His several members; *Salve mea O patrona Crux*, a double-rhymed hymn of the Passion; and several Graces after Meals. Some fine additional *Hymns* and *Sequences* there are for Pentecost and the Holy Ghost. St. Thomas of Aquino had many imitators in honour of the Sacrament, in proses, in versified accompaniments to the actions of the Mass, generally acrostics or rhymed, such as *Christus Lux indeficiens; O Panis dulcissime; Ave caro Christi cara, Tu es certe quem habeo; Quod in âra cernitur; Salve saluberrima; Saturatus ferculis;* all of which are new features of hymnody, were sometimes sung in the churches, and also used privately. There are also "Salutations of Jesus," each line beginning with *Ave* or *Salve*, the Rosary of Christ, the Psalter of Jesus (576 verses); *Jesu dulce Medicamen*, with prayers to Him; of the Goodness and spiritual benefits of God, *Angelorum si haberem*, &c.; hymns for funerals, penitential hymns; many on the miseries of this life; in time of tribulation; on *Contempt of the World*, &c. Many of these betray the mind of the cloister, and are sacred songs, and rather meant for private meditation than for worship. Several are of the glories of the Heavenly Jerusalem, *In urbe mea Jerusalem summa*, rhymed, and with music; *In domo Patris; Jerusalem luminosa*, after the manner of the *Ad perennis vitae fontem*, and the *Urbs beata*. Some are to the Holy Angels, and to St. Michael in particular, the *Mysteriorum Signifer*, those to the Nine Angelic Orders, *Summo Deo agmina*, and "To Thy proper Angel," *Salve mi Angelice* (see *Mone*, vol. i.).

xiv. *Hymns to the B. V. M.*

The greatest change, however, which took place at this period in Church Song had relation to the Blessed Virgin. Before the 14th century several hymns respecting her, some of them in the subjective sense, had been used in the Latin Church, such as *Ave Maris Stella; Cantemus in omni die; Quem terra, pontus, aethera; O quam glorifica; O Sancta mundi Domina* (Nativity and Conception); *Salve Regina; Alma Redemptoris Mater; Ave Regina Coelorum*, &c. The Festivals in her honour were the Conception, Nativity, Presentation, Annunciation, the Visitation (instituted 1389), the Purification, and Assumption. For each of these a vast variety of lyrical poems were composed, which may have been sung (but concerning this we have no information) at those Festivals by congregations in France and Germany, and some in North Italy, for most of them, as described by *Daniel* and *Mone*, have *Neumes*, or musical notes, attached thereto. There are glosses innumerable on the Angelic Salutation, more than 100 beginning with *Ave* and *Salve*, and on the Canticle *Magnificat*. The Dolours of Mary have a large number thereon, none, however, equalling in pathos the *Stabat Mater;* and there are as many of the "Joys of Mary after the Resurrection" and her Assumption. They are all mainly subjective, and, with a few exceptions, such as *O Dei Sapientia* (*Daniel*, iv. 283) for the Presentation, are poor, fanciful, and trivial, without real poetical merit. We have arrived at the decadence of Latin Hymnody when the enervating and over-sentimental influence of conventual life becomes so manifest. Rhyme and acrostics, and varieties of metre, are carried to an excess. On examination it will be found that whereas the more ancient of these hymns had always a direct reference to our Lord Himself, the greater part of the later regard the Blessed Virgin almost as an independent personage, with powers and attributes of her own. This is the more evident when we look at the hundreds which must have been used for private as well as public devotion. We find a *Te Deum Marianum;* the *Victimae Paschali* transferred to Mary only; the "Psalter of Mary;" the "Marian Litany;" the "Garland and Salutations;" the "Rosaries of Mary;" the Prayers to and Praises of Mary, &c. An English form of this kind of Prose is given by *Daniel* (ii. 240) with the musical notes, beginning—

" Flos pudicitiae	" Rore plena
Aula munditiae,	Septiformis Spiritus,
Mater Misericordiae	Virtutibus
Salve Virgo serena	Ornantibus,
Vitae vena,	Ac moribus
Lux amoena,	Vernantibus."

All these, be it remarked, are but a small portion of those which, as *Mone* remarks, he might have produced. This last editor has added a number from Greek, Italian, and German sources of the like nature. We may be thankful that our English Uses were in a great measure saved from this deterioration.

xv. *Apostles, Saints, Martyrs, &c.*

A similar change and revolution took place in and after the 14th century in the Western Church with the hymnody which related to the Apostles, Saints, Martyrs, Confessors, and Virgins. The number of *Hymns* and *Sequences* became excessive, particularly in Germany and France, and also in Spain. Every Church had its peculiar hymn-book. Those of All Saints are mostly metrical Litanies. Fine *Sequences* are *Cujus laus secundum nomen,* in rhyme; and *Alleluia nunc decantet,* all the lines of which end in "*a.*" Another is *Coeli Solem imitantes,* in Adamic metre. Several are of St. Peter and the other Apostles singly, most of which are narratives of their lives and martyrdom; among these may be noticed a *Sequence* of St. Peter of 36 verses all rhymed, and of which every word begins with "*P.*" (as "Plebs parentis pietatis). Several are of Peter and Paul jointly, two or three of which are in our early English books. There are many of St. John Evangelist, SS. Andrew, Mark, and Luke; of Martyrs generally, one of which is the beautiful Prose, *O Beata beatorum.* So also of Confessors and Virgins. Among the last St. Agnes holds, as previously, a distinguished place.

Of the Irish saints, SS. Colman, Columba, and Columbanus, whose fame had travelled to St. Gall and the banks of the Rhine in the 7th and 8th centuries, there are other hymns. Several are of St. Benedict. Many, amongst others a Prose and a Rosary, of St. Barbara, with every possible rhyme and alliteration. St. Nicholas, St. Vincent, and the Magda-

lene, were favourite subjects both in the Spanish, German, and French books. Besides these, hymns to above 160 single Saints of as many Churches are given in *Mone's* third volume, and in the fourth and fifth of *Daniel,* of which many are for private devotion only. We soon perceive how inferior these, with few exceptions, are in dignity, beauty, comprehensiveness, and devout feeling to their predecessors. Sense and poetry were often sacrificed to catching multitudinous rhymes or assonances, or an a b c d Sequence.

xvi. *The Roman Breviary.*

Yet another change, and for the worse, appears in the hymns of the Western Church in the 16th, 17th, and following centuries. It must here be noted that the Latin Church did not undertake in any way the care of its Hymnody until late in the middle ages. This was never, like the daily Offices and prayers in the Mass, regarded as a necessary part of Divine worship. These last-named devotions were carefully restored and corrected in and after the 8th century, but Hymns were used, and others newly composed without restraint, and adopted as suited the will of the respective Churches and Dioceses. Their authors and composers were and are for the most part not known, yet they had a wide and great influence over the faith of the masses and of the religious communities. With Leo X. (Pope 1513) came into fashion what is called the classical revival. He, who strongly favoured this movement, became desirous that the Church hymns should be coerced within the laws of regular metre and Latinity. He entrusted this task to Zaccharia Ferrerio Vicentino, who completed this new Hymnology. Leo, however, died shortly afterwards, as well as Adrian VI., and it was Clement VII. who, in 1523, on the 11th of December, by his official letters, recognised and approved the revised Hymnary. In this 16th century Fabricius, Ellinger and others corrected the texts of the Church lyrical poetry generally. In the 17th century Pope Urban VIII. (who ruled from 1623 to 1644) commissioned three accomplished Jesuits (Famianus Strada, Tarquinius Galluccius, and Hieronymus Petruccius) again to revise and correct these Breviary hymns, after the approved classical pattern. We are witnesses of the result, as seen in the *Roman Breviary* of to-day, and of how, after this proceeding, the simple, noble, and forcible style of Ambrose, Hilary, and their successors, has for the most part vanished, having been supplanted by the cold and often capricious alterations of these reformers. [See **Breviaries, p. 170, ii.**]

xvii. *French, Spanish, and other Breviaries.*

The example was contagious. Before the year 1737 a large proportion of the ancient *Hymns* and *Sequences* were removed from the French *Antiphonaries* and *Breviaries,* particularly from those of *Paris* and *Rouen,* and thus the compositions of the brothers Santeüil, Le Tourneaux, Habert, Besnault, Muret, De la Brunetière, Coffin, Guyet, and a few others, were substituted or interpolated. Arevali, who did his best to accomplish the same task with the Spanish Hymnody (*Hymnodia Hispanica*, 1786) in his Dissertation on Ecclesiastical Hymns in the same volume, gives a history of all these proceedings, and warmly approves of them; as does Guyet, a Jesuit, in his *Heortologia*, Paris, 1657 (*Venice*, 1729). The outcome was a parti-coloured mixture of doubtful character, in parts of which the old classical metres are again revived. It must, however, be admitted that among these later compositions are many of great beauty, power and devotional fervour, especially those of the brothers Santeüil. Those in the *Paris Breviary* of 1736 for ordinary Sundays at Matins and Vespers, and in Advent, for Matins at Christmas, and St. Stephen's Day, for the Epiphany, *Quae Stella sole pulchrior* at First Vespers, and *Linquunt tecta Magi* at Lauds; those for the Five Wounds, *Prome vocem, Quae te pro populi*; those for Easter, and the Ascension, for Virgin Martyrs, for the Annunciation, are excellent. It is much to be lamented that Isaac Williams (*Hymns tr. from the Parisian Breviary*, 1839), who fully appreciated their beauty, has rendered them for the most part into such crabbed and incongruous measures. The *Rouen* hymnody is known to but few, yet the *Proses* for Christmas, *Verbum lumen de lumine*; for the Epiphany, *Prompto gentes animo* (already mentioned); that for the Ascension, *Solemnis haec festivitas* (*Narbonne Breviary*, 1709, and *Daniel*, ii. 367) are worthy of notice. Besides these there are some fifteen original hymns of much merit.

All these and many more in Germany and elsewhere are now, in fact, swept away, to the infinite regret of the Churches to which they were appropriated, and the Latin Hymnody of the Western Church has thus been narrowed to the few, and in great part curtailed and formalized, compositions included in the modernized *Roman Breviary*, and the five Sequences in the *Roman Missal*. This is a conclusion much to be deplored to so glorious a career; and our grief is increased when we find, as is the fact, that the ancient music for the same has undergone a similar transformation and reduction.

xviii. *Expositions.*

Notice must here be taken of the numerous *Expositiones Hymnorum et Sequentiarum*, which, commencing even before this epoch, continued to be produced till late in the 16th century. In the *Liber Hymnorum* of the ancient Irish Church, edited by Dr. Todd, in the old Irish characters, for the Archaeological and Celtic Society, Dublin, 1855 and 1869, there are elaborate scholia and explanations of all the hymns, some of them in the original Irish language. In the British Museum are two English hymn-books of the 11th century (*Jul.* A. vi. and *Vesp.* D. xii.), which are examples of expositions. Both are apparently Benedictine, and the latter is headed:—

> " Incipiunt hymni quod noctibus atque diebus
>   Decantant monachi laudibus assiduis;
> His animus monachi coelestia quaerere discit
>   Aeternumque melos cogitat hisce modis."

It contains an interlinear paraphrase in ordinary Latin prose of each verse of the hymn, thus:—

> " *Splendor et immortalis Divinitas!*
> O, Lux beata Trinitas!
> *Et O auctoritalis potentia!*
> Et principalis Unitas!" &c.

And there is also an interlinear version of this paraphrase in Anglo-Saxon. In *Julius* A. vi., the hymns themselves are not at length, but only the first few words, but there follows, as in *Vespasian* D. xii., a version of the hymn in ordinary Latin prose, and between the lines of this version runs a literal Anglo-Saxon translation of the same. This prose version reads thus:—

> " O Lux et O beata Trinitas
>   Et O principalis Unitas
>   Infunde lumen in nostris cordibus
>   Quia jam recedit igneus Sol "—

with the translation into Anglo-Saxon between the lines. In the Bodleian Library (*Laud Misc.*, 384) is a *Liber Hymnalis*, with the exposition of Hilarius written in a hand of the end of the 13th cent. The comment on *Jam lucis orto sidere* begins thus:—

> " Materia hujus hymni est deprecatio ad Deum ut orto sidere, id est Christo, Christus dignetur segregare nos a viciis et induendo nos virtutibus repellat a nobis superbiam; id est faciat nos humiles; et quoniam umbra mortis, id est peccatum, recessit, ideo Lux, id est Christus, jam habitat in cordibus nostris. Vel sic," &c.

These *Expositiones* became from the 14th century forward, plentiful on the Continent, and as soon as printing was invented they multiplied everywhere. According to Mr. Dickinson's catalogue, no fewer than twenty-seven editions were printed in England between 1494 and the middle of the 16th century, besides others in Belgium, Germany, and France. Copies of these are in the British Museum, Bodleian, and Lambeth Libraries, and elsewhere. The *Aurea Expositio Hymnorum*, by Hilarius, was edited at Paris in 1485. It has already been observed that the more ancient hymns, and especially the *Sequences* of Adam of St. Victor, exhibit a profound and various knowledge of Holy Scripture, of its minutest facts, of its mystical and typical interpretations, of the lives and martyrdoms of the Apostles and the Saints; so that it is not wonderful, in an age when copies of the Holy Scriptures and other books were rare and chiefly to be found in monasteries, where few could consult them, that interpretations of the full meaning of these sacred songs should eagerly be looked for. The commentaries of Wimpheling, 1513; Bebelius, 1492–1501; of Hermannus Torrentinus, 1513, 1538; the copious dissertations of the *Elucidatorium Ecclesiasticum* of Clichtoveus (*Paris*, 1516; *Basle*, 1517–19), and of others noted in the Preface to Daniel's *Thesaurus Hymnologicus*, show the continued need of these comments. That the moderns require them also is easily proved by the *Lateinische Anthologie* of Kehrein (*Frankfurt*, 1840); the copious notes of *Daniel*, especially in his fourth and fifth volumes; the lengthy observations of *Mone* in his three volumes; and those of the Abbé Gautier in his 1st edition of Adam of St. Victor, 1858.

The earlier of these *Expositiones* are generally in what may be called the vernacular Latin of the time. They were intended no doubt for the instruction of choirs and schools of the Clergy, and for the more educated laity, that they might "sing with the under-standing"; "that the meaning might be known by all scholars and ecclesiastics," "by a notable comment which sets forth the accounts and most remarkable places of Holy Scripture, and of those saints whose histories are sung."

xix. *Music.*

With regard to the melodies to which these *Hymns* and *Sequences* were sung up to and beyond the beginning of the 14th century, and to the musical notation thereof, these are separate matters of so great an importance and extent, involving as they do a consideration of the whole system of the Plain Song of the Church, which, although Gregorian, was originally derived from the complicated modes of the Greeks, that they cannot be satisfactorily treated of in this short memoir. Both are exhaustively dis-cussed by Gerbert, Abbot of the Congregation of St. Blaise in the Black Forest, in his two quarto volumes, *De Cantu et Musicâ Sacrâ;* in the *Dictionnaire de Plain-Chant,* the twenty-ninth volume of the *Nouvelle Ency-clopédie Théologique* of the Abbé Migne's Séries, by Coussemaker, *Sur l'Harmonie au Moyen Age (Paris, Didron,* 1852); in the lately published work of the Abbé Raillard, *Explication des Neumes (Paris, E. Repos);* and in *Les Mélodies Grégoriennes* of Dom Joseph Pothier, of the Abbey of Solesmes *(Tournay, Desclée Lefevre & Cie.,* 1880). It must suffice to state that these tunes were all simple, yet majestic and popular, and that most of them probably were appropriated to and sung with the Hymns of the Church (they also remaining unaltered) without variation ever since the 6th century through-out the West. When *Proses* and *Sequences* were introduced into the Divine Office in the North of Europe in the manner above stated, melodies were either newly composed or adapted from others for them. Pothier (p. 211, *qua supra*) has published a noble one for *Laetabundus exultet* of the 12th cent. in the Guidonian irregular clef of C with B flat.

It is necessary, however, to give an account of the Notation of this Music; for from the 7th and 8th centuries musical notes of some kind are appended to all hymns. The first system, usual in the 5th century, was alpha-betical; that of Boethius (*De Musicâ, Lib.* iv., *c.* 14), which marked the notes by the fifteen first letters of the alphabet. Sometimes the first Octave was represented by the seven first capitals, the second by the seven smaller letters. Others, again, used Greek Capitals for this purpose. All these methods were, however, found to be unsatisfactory, and by the 8th century Neumes were universally employed. Examples are at hand in the *Hymnals, Harleian,* 2961, *Vespasian* D. xii., wherein the Hymns are carefully throughout surmounted by *Neumes;* and reference may be made to the accompanying Plates, Nos. 1, 2, and 7, for their shapes.

These *Neumes* were certain points, lines, contorted marks, and curves (resembling modern shorthand), placed under or over each syllable to be chanted, in order to dis-tinguish each vocal sound; and since the chant is variable, sometimes equal, sometimes unequal, sometimes mounting, sometimes de-scending, they had peculiar names corre-sponding to their various shapes, and were conjoined with accents to mark the different tones, and often compounded and piled over one another. Now these *Neumes* and accents could indicate the ascent or descent of the scale, the piano or forte of the notes, but not their relative height or value, nor the key, nor the mode, nor the accidentals, if any. Hence, in order to read and interpret a chant thus noted, it was necessary (say in the 9th cen-tury) first to translate the signs without dis-tinction of modes, and afterwards to decide from the character of the melody the key and the mode to which it belonged, as well as the doubtful intervals. For instance, the sign called *Podatus* represented an ascending interval, embracing one, two, or more tones; but only a profound acquaintance with the modes of the Plain Chant could show which of these intervals the singer was to choose. The whole, in fact, depended on the skill and intelligence of the Cantor. This awkward contrivance continued to the end of the 12th century at least. Guido d'Arezzo in the 11th century thought to remedy this imperfection by drawing two lines through the mass of *Neumes* in order to mark their relative height. One of these was red, to mark the note F; the other green, to mark the note middle C. He afterwards added two other lines, begun by two other letters of the scale. Soon, however, the colours and additional letters were abandoned, and the clefs were reduced to two, with an irregular third; the Do clef, where the fork that grasps the line indicates the position of middle C; and the Fa clef, where this fork has a breve ■ either before or behind it, indicating the place of the note F. The irregular B flat was marked in its proper space; whether any F sharp was ever introduced is doubtful. The notes were the long or minim ▮, requiring emphasis, the breve ■, usually of uniform length, but variable if the phrase required it, and the semibreve ◆, always short, except in ca-dences. It is to be observed, however, that, as a general rule, the notes were all of equal length, even up to the 16th century, without change of time and without bars. Reference should be made to Nos. 3, 4, 5, and 6 in the accompanying plate.

Attempts have frequently been made, by Gerbert formerly, and later by the Père Lambillotte, commenting on the *Antiphonary* of St. Gall (*L'Unité dans les chants litur-giques, Paris,* 1851), to identify the ancient melodies represented by *Neumes* with those noted in the 13th century, and subsequently after the method of Guido. The *Notkerian Sequences* were thought convenient for this inquiry, wherein each syllable had only one tone or two short together; but the comparison was not satisfactory, because of the great latitude which the *Neumes* allowed. Lately, however, the Abbé Raillard has made a laborious collation of all the principal choir-books in France, with a view to the solution of this problem, and has printed the result of them in the four large tables appended to his work, *Explication des Neumes*.

Simultaneously the Benedictine Père Dom Joseph Pothier, of the Abbey of Solesmes, instituted similar inquiries elsewhere, and in 1880 published at Tournay *Les Mélodies Grégoriennes d'après la tradition*. Both of them have given plentiful examples of Neumes, and in tables and engravings have shown how they gradually became transformed into the more modern notation. It is not too much to say that they have established the true identity of the Hymnal melodies of the later age with those of the earliest period known.

The manner of chanting these hymns (p. 653, ii.), was generally by the people, not by the clergy only, who nevertheless led them, singing one verse and the general congregation responding with the same or with the next verse, all of them joining in the last ascription of praise. The mode of executing *Proses* or *Sequences* differed, varying in different places. According to Gerbert (*Lib.* i., *Pt.* i., p. 340) and the *Dictionnaire de Plain-Chant* (p. 270, *Tit. Proses*) the Cantors with their assistant Deacons advanced and seated themselves or stood at a desk (*Lectricum*) whereon the *Sequence* was placed, or in front of the pulpit, whence the Gospel was to be sung, the choir remaining in their places. Having sung through their strophe, the strain was repeated by choir and people, with organ accompaniment, and so on with each strophe till the whole was finished.

Latin Notation. 7

Ordinary Neumes.

Centuries	Punctum	Virga	Podatus	Clivis	Torculus	Porrectus
VIIIth and IXth						
Xth and XIth						
XIIth and XIIIth						
XIVth and XVth						
Modern notes						

Centuries	Scandicus	Salicus	Climacus	Des Subpunctis	Climacus Resupinus
VIIIth and IXth					
Xth and XIth					
XIIth and XIIIth					
XIVth and XVth					
Modern notes					

From Pothier.

We would add that beside the above-named books on early Church Hymnal Music, that of Bernon de Reichenau on the *Gregorian Chant* (*Toulouse*, 1867); and that of the Abbé Tardife on the *Plain Chant* (*Angers*, 1883) should be consulted. A considerable number of facsimiles are in Léon Gautier's *Histoire de la Poésie Liturgique au Moyen Âge*, Paris, 1886, vol. i. [J. D. C.]

Authorities.—The authorities for this outline of Latin Hymnody, and for a fuller and more exhaustive treatment of the subject, include :—

1. *De Auctoribus Hymnorum. Auctore Jacobo Wimphelingo.* Strassburg, 4to, 1515.

2. *Hymni Veterum Poetarum Christianorum Ecclesiae Latinae Selecti ; Textum ad optimarum editionum fidem exhibuit, et praefatione, notisque variorum adjectisque praecipuis variantibus lectionibus illustravit C. A. Björn.* Copenhagen, 8vo, 1818.

3. *Hymni Ecclesiastici, praesertim quae Ambrosiani dicuntur, recogniti et multorum Hymnorum accessione locupletati, cum Scholiis opportunis in locis adjectis et Hymnorum Indice Studio Georgii Cassandri ; accedit Bedae Presbyteri Tractatus de metrorum generibus, ex primo libro de Re Metrica.* Cologne, 8vo, 1556.

4. *Hymnodia Sanctorum Patrum, quae a Romana Ecclesia per annum decantari solet, Commentariis explicata. Auctore Gregorio Valentiano Siculo a Marsalia* Venice, fol. 1646.

5. *Hymnodia Hispanica, ad Cantus, Latinitatis, Metrique leges revocata et aucta. Praemittitur Dissertatio de Hymnis Ecclesiasticis. Auctore Faustino Arevalo.* Rome, 4to, 1786.

6. *De Cantu et Musica Sacra. Auctore Martino Gerberto.* 2 vol., 4to. St. Blasien, 1774.

7. *Historia poetarum et poematum medii aevi.* By Polycarp Leyser. Halle, 1721.

8. *Die Sängerschule St. Gallens vom achten bis zwölften Jahrhundert.* By Anselm Schubiger. Einsiedeln, 1858.

9. *Die Lateinische Sequenzen des Mittelalters in musikalischer und rhythmischer Beziehung dargestellt.* By Karl Bartsch. Rostock, 1868.

10. *Die Christlichen Dichter und Geschichtschreiber Roms.* By Dr. J. C. F. Bähr. 2nd ed., Carlsruhe, 1872.

11. *Geschichte der Christlichen lateinischen Litteratur.* By Adolf Ebert. Leipzig, 1874.

12. *Beiträge zur Geschichte und Erklärung der ältesten Kirchenhymnen.* By Dr. J. Kayser. Vol. i., Paderborn, 1881 ; vol. ii., 1886.

In addition to these works the MSS., and the printed *Breviaries, Graduals, Hymnaries, Missals*, &c., which are enumerated under the following headings in this Dictionary, must also be consulted. viz. :—1. Breviaries, p. 170. 2. Hymnarium, p. 546. 3. Missals, p. 738, i. 4. Latin, Translations from the, p. 655 ; 5. Sequences. [J. J.]

Latin, Translations from the. A large proportion of the translations of Latin hymns into English are found at the present time in the various hymnals in use in Public Worship. These hymns are annotated in this work under their respective Latin first lines. A great number of recent *trs.*, however, remain, of which no use has been made, although many are of great merit, and no insignificant number are of higher excellence, and are better adapted for congregational use, than many of those now in the hymn-books. The object of this article is to gather these translations together in such a manner as will enable the student to find what he needs with comparative ease.

i. In the *first* column in the list which follows, the opening line of each hymn, or portion of a hymn, which has been translated, is given in full.

ii. In the *second* column the *Authors' Names*, when known, are indicated by *Capital Letters*, as follows:—

A.	.	.	Abelard, P.
Alard	.	.	Alard, W.
Amb.	.	.	Ambrose.²
Aug.	.	.	St. Augustine.
A. V.	.	.	Adam of St. Victor.
B.	.	.	Besnault, S.
Balde	.	.	Balde, J.
B. G.	.	.	Brunetière, G. de la.
B. V.	.	.	Bede, the Venerable.
Buch.	.	.	Buchanan, G.
C.	.	.	Coffin, C.
Com.	.	.	Commire, J.
D.	.	.	Damiani, P.
F.	.	.	Flaminius, M. A.
G.	.	.	Gottschalk.
G. S.	.	.	Gourdan, S.
Greg.	.	.	Gregory the Great.
H.	.	.	Hildebert.
H—y	.	.	Hilary.
Hab.	.	.	Habert, Isaac.
Hart.	.	.	Hartmann of St. Gall.
M.	.	.	Muret, A.
Map	.	.	Map, W.
N.	.	.	Notker.
P.	.	.	Paulinus of Aquileia.
P. V.	.	.	Peter, the Venerable.
Prud.	.	.	Prudentius, A. C.
S. B.	.	.	Santeüil, Baptiste.
S.	.	.	Santeüil, J. B. de.
S. C.	.	.	Santeüil, C. de.
U.	.	.	Urban VIII.

iii. In the *third* column one or more of the most accessible works in which the *Latin text* is given is indicated by letters and figures, as follows:—

1. *English Collections and Reprints.*

a. **Chandler, J.** *Hymns of the Primitive Church.* London, Parker, 1837.

b. **Newman, Card. J. H.** *Hymni Ecclesiae.* Macmillan, Oxford 1838 and London 1865.

c. **Trench, Archb. R. C.** *Sacred Latin Poetry.* Lond., Macmillan, 1864 and 1874.

d. **The Littlemore** *Hymnale secundum usum insignis ac praeclarae Ecclesiae Sarisburiensis.* Littlemore, 1850. Edited by W. Stubbs, C. Marriott, and A. C. Wilson.

e. **Neale, J. M.** *Hymni Ecclesiae e Breviariis quibusdam et Missalibus.* Lond., Parker, 1851 and 1888.

f. **Wrangham, D. S.** *The Liturgical Poetry of Adam of St. Victor.* Lond., Kegan Paul, Trench & Co., 1881.

g. **Macgill, H. M.** *Songs of the Christian Creed and Life.* Lond., Pickering, 1876 and 1879.

h. **Stevenson, J.** *Latin Hymns of the Anglo-Saxon Church.* Printed by the Surtees Society, 1851, from an 11th cent. MS. at Durham.

m. **March, F. A.** *Latin Hymns, with English Notes.* Harper, New York, 1875.

n. **Loftie, W. J.** *The Latin Year, a Selection of Rhyming Latin Hymns from Ancient and Modern Sources.* Lond., Pickering, 1873.

2. Foreign Collections.

1. **Daniel, H. A.** *Thesaurus Hymnologicus.* 5 vols. Halle and Leipzig, 1841–56.

2. **Mone, F. J.** *Lateinische Hymnen des Mittelalters.* 3 vols. Freiburg (Baden), 1853–55.

3. **Wackernagel, C. E. P.** *Das deutsche Kirchenlied.* 5 vols. Leipzig, 1864–77. Vol. i. contains a collection of Latin hymns and sequences.

4. **Bässler, F.** *Auswahl altchristlicher Lieder.* Berlin, 1858.

5. **Simrock, K.** *Lauda Sion.* 2nd ed. Stuttgart, 1868.

6. **Königsfeld, G. A.** *Lateinische Hymnen und Gesänge aus dem Mittelalter.* Vol. i., Bonn 1847 ; vol. ii., Bonn, 1865.

7. **Kehrein, J.** *Lateinische Sequenzen des Mittelalters.* Mainz, 1873.

8. **Morel, G.** *Lateinische Hymnen des Mittelalters.* Einsiedeln, 1868.

9. **Zabuesnig, J. C.** *Katholische Kirchengesänge.* 3 vols. Augsburg, 1822.

10. **Moll, Karl von.** *Hymnarium, Blüthen lateinischer Kirchenpoesie.* Halle, 1861. 2nd ed., 1868.

11. **Weinzierl, F. J.** *Hymni Sacri ... ex plurium Galliae dioecesium Breviariis.* Augsburg, 1820.

12. **Supplementum** *ad Graduale.* Mechlin (Malines), 1862.

13. **Abbe Migne's** *Patrologiae cursus.* Latin series.

14. **Du Meril, E.** *Poésies Populaires Latines du Moyen Age.* Paris, 1847.

iv. The *fourth* column gives the *Translators* in whose works the translations are found. Each Translator is indicated by a *Numeral*, and the details of their publications are given in their Biographical Notices.

1. **Aylward, J. A.,** in O. Shipley's *Annus Sanctus,* 1884.

2. **Beste, J. R.,** in his *Church Hys.,* 1849, and O. Shipley's *Annus Sanctus,* 1884.

3. **Blew, W. J.,** in his *Church H. and Tune Bk.,* 1852–55.

4. **Campbell, R.,** in his *Hys. & Anthems,* 1850, and O. Shipley's *Annus Sanctus,* 1884.

5. **Caswall, E.,** in his various books, see p. 215, i.

6. **Chambers, J. D.,** in his *Lauda Syon,* 1857 and 1866.

7. **Chandler, J.,** in his *Hys. of the Primitive Church.* 1837.

8. **Charles, Elizabeth,** in her *Voice of the Christian Life in Song,* 1858.

9. **Copeland, W. J.,** in his *Hys. for the Week, and Hymns for the Seasons,* 1848.

10. **Crippen, T. G.,** in his *Ancient Hys. and Poems,* 1868.

11. **Dix, W. C.,** in *Church Times,* Jan. 1887.

12. **Hewett, J. W.,** in his *Verses by a Country Curate,* 1859.

13. **Kynaston, H.,** in his *Occasional Hys.,* 1862.

14. **Littledale, R. F.,** in various works as indicated.

15. **Macgill, H. M.,** in his *Songs of the Christian Creed and Life.* 1876 and 1879.

16. **Mason, Jackson,** in his *Rhythm of Bernard de Morlaix,* &c., 1880.

17. **Morgan, A. M.,** in his *Gifts and Light,* 1867.

18. **Morgan, D. T.,** in his *Hys. and Other Poetry of the Latin Church,* 1880.

19. **Neale, J. M.,** in his *Mediaeval Hymns,* 1851, and 1863.

20. **Newman, Card. J. H.,** in his *Verses,* &c., 1853 and 1868.

21. **Lyra Eucharistica,** 1863. Enlarged ed., 1864.

22. **Pearson, C. B.,** in his *Sequences from the Sarum Missal,* 1871.

23. **Trend, H.**

24. **Williams, I.,** in his *Hys. tr. from the Parisian Breviary,* 1839.

25. **Lyra Messianica,** 1864.

26. **Lyra Mystica,** 1865.

27. **Wrangham, D. S.,** in *The Liturgical Poetry of Adam of St. Victor,* 1881.

28. **Wackerbarth, A. D.,** in his *Lyra Ecclesiastica,* Pt. i., 1842, Pt. ii., 1843.

29. **Wallace, J.,** in his *Hymns of the Church,* 1874.

a*, b*, c*, &c., in various works as indicated below.

N.B.—All pieces marked (*H.*) are parts of the poem " Alpha et Ω."

First Lines.	Authors.	Latin Text.	Translations.	Use or Subject.
A morte qui te suscitans	*XVIII. c.*	*e.*	25.	Compline.
Ad honorem patris Maglorii	*A. V.*	*f.*	27.	St. Magloire.
Ad honorem Trinitatis	*A. V.* (?)	*f.*	27.	St. Augustine.
Ad honorem tuum, Christe	*A. V.*	*f.* 7.	27.	N. of St. John Baptist.
Ad nuptias agni Pater	*B. G.*	*b.* 9. 11.	6. 24.	C. of H. Women.
Adest dies specialis	*A. V.*	*f.*	27.	St. Magloire.
Adeste sanctae conjuges [Jam cuncta]	*S.*	*b.* 9. 11.	6. 24.	C. of H. Women.
Adeste sancti coelites [plurimo]	*S. B.*	9. 11.	5. 24.	All Saints.
Adite templa supplices	*XVIII. c.*	11.	3.	Sunday Morning.
Almo supremi Numinis in sinu			5.	The Will of God.
Alpha et Ω magne Deus (*H.*)		*c. g. m.* 2. 4. 6.	13. 15. 26.	Holy Trinity.
Altitudo quid hic jaces	*XVII.c.*	*e. g.* 1. 4. 5. 6. 10.	15. 18. *g*.*	Advent.
Alma chorus Domini nunc pangat nomina summi	*N.* (?)	*b. d.* 1. 2. 7.	22.	Holy Trinity.
Amor Patris et Filii	*XIV. c.*	1. 2. 7.	14. 25.	Whitsuntide.
Amorum sensus erige	*XIV. c.*	1. 2.	18.	Passiontide.
Angele! Qui meus es custos			6.	The Guardian Angel.
Animemur ad agonem	*A. V.*	*f.* 1. 7.	27.	St. Agnes.
Ante thorum virginalem	*A. V.*	*f.* 2. 7.	27.	Christmas.
Aquas plenas amaritudine	*A. V.*	*f.*	27.	St. Thomas of Canty.
Ardet Deo quae femina	*S.*	*a. b.* 9. 11.	7. 24.	C. of H. Women.
Athleta Christi nobilis	*XVII. c.*	1. 9.	5. 29.	St. Venantius.
Auctor salutis unicus	*XI. c.*	*h.* 1.	6.	Passiontide.
Audax es vir juvenis	*IX. c.*	1. 2.	10.	Contempt of the World.
Audi beata seraphim	*XIX. c.*	*Milan Brev.,* 1830.	3.	Christmas.
Audiat miras oriens, cadensque			29.	St. Emygdius.
Augustini magni patris	*A. V.* (?)	*f.*	27.	St. Monica.
Augustini praeconia	*A. V.*	*f.*	27.	Conv. of St. Augustine.
Augustino praesuli	*A. V.* (?)	*f.*	27.	St. Augustine.
Aurora diem nuntiat	*A. V.*	*f.*	27.	St. Victor.
Aurora quae solem paris	*S.*	1. 11.	5.	Nat. of B. V. M.
Ave caput Christi gratum	*XIV. c.*	2.	6.	Members of Christ's Body.
Ave, caro Christi cara	*XIV. c.*	1. 2. 3.	21.	H. Communion.
Ave Carole sanctissime			5.	St. Charles Borromeo.
Ave, Christi corpus carum	*XIV. c.*	2.	18.	H. Communion.
Ave crucis dulce lignum	*XV. c.*	1. 7.	18. 25.	Passiontide.

First Lines.	Authors.	Latin Text.	Translations.	Use or Subject.
En Evangelistae adest . . .	XV. c.	Moz. Brev. .	3. 4. . .	St. Luke.
En ut superba criminum . .	XIX. c.	1. 9. . .	5. a*. 21. 29..	Sacred Heart.
Erumpe tandem juste dolor . .	XVII. c.	1. . .	5. . .	Easter.
Ex radice caritatis . . .	A. V.	f. . .	27. . .	Relics of St. Victor.
Exiit cunis pretiosus infans . .	C.	b. 9. 11. .	24. 25. .	Nat. of St. John Bap.
Exite Sion filiae, Videte vestrum Regem	XVII. c.	n. 1. 5. 6. .	6. 19. m. .	Crown of Thorns.
Exultemus et laetemur. . . .	A. V.	f. 7. . .	27. . .	St. Andrew.
Fac Christe, nostri gratia [Fas Christi] .	S.	b. 9. 11. .	4. 24. . .	Epiphany.
Fando quis audivit ? Dei . .	C.	a. b. 9. 11. .	3. 4. 6. 24.	Passion Sunday.
Felix per omnes festum mundi cardines.	XI. c.	b. d. h. 1. .	6. . .	SS. Peter and Paul.
Felix sedes gratiae. Part of " Trinita-				
tem simplicem	A. V.	f. . .	27. . .	St. John. Evang.
Ferunt vagantes daemonas. Part of				
" Ales diei nuntius.". . .	Prud.	g. 13. . .	15. . .	St. Peter.
Festivis resonent cantica plausibus .	.	. . .	29. . .	For Confessors.
Festivis resonent compita vocibus. .	XIX. c.	1. 9. . .	5. b* 29. .	Precious Blood.
Festum Christi Rex per orbem .	XI. c.	Moz. Brev. .	3. . .	St. Thomas.
Fit porta Christi pervia [see p. 6, i.] .	Amb.	h. 1. 3. 5. .	9. 24. (1838)	B. V. M.
Florem spina coronavit. . .	XVI. c.	1. 7. . .	25. . .	Crown of Thorns.
Fregit Adam interdictum . .	XII. c.	2. . .	10. . .	Christmas Carol.
Fundere preces tempus est . .	XI. c.	Moz. Brev. .	3. . .	Evening.
Gaude prole, Graecia . . .	A. V.	f. 7. 8. .	27. . .	St. Denis.
Gaude, Roma, caput mundi . .	A. V.	f. 1. 2. 7. .	27. . .	SS. Peter and Paul.
Gaude, Sion, et laetare . . .	A. V.	f. . .	27. . .	St. Thomas of Cauty.
Gaude, Sion, quae diem recolis .	A. V.	f. 7. . .	27. . .	St. Martin.
Gaude, superna civitas . . .	A. V.	f. . .	27. . .	St. Marcellus.
Genovefae sollemnitas . . .	A. V.	f. 1. 2. 7. .	27. . .	St. Genevieve.
Gentis Poloniae gloria . . .	VIII. c.	1. 9. . .	5. 29. .	St. John Cantius.
Gloriam sacrae celebremus omnes .	XIX. c.	Rom. Brev. .	5. c* 29. .	The Winding Sheet.
Gratiani grata sollemnitas . .	A. V.	f. . .	27. . .	St. Gratian.
Gratulemur ad festivum . .	A. V.	f. 7. 12. .	27. . .	St. John Evang.
Gratulemur in hac die . . .	A. V.	f. . .	27. . .	Assump. of B. V. M.
Haec est dies qua candidae . .	U.	1. 9. . .	5. 29. .	St. Theresa.
Haec est dies summe grata . .	XV. c.	1. 7. . .	25. . .	Transfiguration.
Haec est dies triumphalis . .	XVI. c.	c. 1. . .	25. . .	Easter.
Haec est fides orthodoxa . . (H.)	.	c. g. . .	15. . .	The True Creed.
Haec est sancta sollemnitas . .	XI. c.	1. 2. 7. .	25. . .	Easter.
Haeres peccati, natura filius irae .	A. V.	f. . .	27. . .	Epitaph of A. of St. Victor.
Hic est dies verus Dei . . .	Amb. ?	e. m. 1. 2. 3. 9.	3. 8. 25. .	Easter.
Hic salus aegris medicina fessis. Part				
of " Christe cunctorum." . .	.	h. . .	6. . .	Dedication of Church.
Hierusalem et Syon. See " Jerusalem."				
Hoc jussa quondam rumpimus .	S.	b. 9. 11. .	24. 25. .	Transfiguration.
Hodiernae lux diei Sacramenti .	XVI. c.	1. 7. . .	17. 21. .	H. Communion.
Hodiernae lux diei Celebris in .	A. V.	f. 1. 2. 3. 7.	17. 27. .	B. V. M.
Horae peractus circulus. Part of " Jam				
nos "	XI. c.	13. (lxxxvi. 936.).	3. . .	Morning.
Huc cum domo advenisti . .	.	. . .	28. . .	B. V. M. at Loretto.
Huc vos o miseri, surda relinquite.	C.	b. 9. 11. .	6. 24. 25. .	Epiphany.
Hymnis dum resonat curia coelitum	S.	b. 9. 11. .	24. . .	All Saints.
Hymnum dicamus Domino . .	VIII. c.	1. 2. 6. .	8. . .	Passiontide.
Illaesa te puerpera . . .	Hab.	b. 9. 11. .	24. . .	Compassion of B. V. M.
Illuminans Altissimus . . .	Amb.	m. 1. 2. 3. 9.	9. 11. 24.	Epiphany.
			(1838)	
Illustra tuo lumine . . .	Aug.	g. . .	15. . .	Life Everlasting.
Imperas saxo, latitans repente .	.	. . .	29. . .	St. Emygdius.
Impune vati non erit impotens .	C.	b. 9. 11. .	24. . .	Decoll. of St. John Baptist.
In diebus celebribus . . .	XV. c.	2. . .	18. 26. .	Com. of Saints.
In eadem specie visum . . .	A. V.	f. . .	27. . .	
In excelsis canitur . . .	A. V.	f. . .	27. . .	Christmas.
In hac valle lachrymarum . .	XVI. c.	1. 7. . .	18. . .	St. Michael.
In natale Salvatoris . . .	A. V.	f. . .	17. 26. 27.	Christmas.
In profunda noctis umbra . .	XVIII. c.	1. 9. . .	29. . .	St. John Nepomucen.
In sapientia disponens omnia .	XII. c.	2. 7. . .	10. 26. .	Life of Jesus.
In terris adhuc positam . .	A.	13. (clxxviii. 1796)	g* . .	Ascension.
In triumphum mors mutatur . .	XVIII. c.	10. 11. .	18. . .	Festival of Martyrs.
Inclyti Patres, Dominaeque mundi .	XVIII. c.	9. . .	29. . .	Confessors.
Inde est quod omnes credimus. Part of				
" Ales diei nuntius " . . .	Prud.	g. . .	15. . .	Watchfulness.
Infecunda mea ficus . . (H.)	.	c. g. . .	15. . .	Penitence.
Intende nostris precibus . .	P. V.	Moz. Brev. .	3. . .	Morning or Evening.
Inter aeternas superum coronas .	XV. c.	9. . .	5. . .	St. Benedict.
Inter sulphurei fulgura turbinis .	C.	b. 9. 11. .	3. 24. 26.	Whitsunday.
Intrante Christo Bethanicam domum	G. S.	b. 9. 11. .	24. . .	Lazarus visited by Christ.
Inventor rutili dux bone luminis .	Prud.	b. h. 1. 3. 9.	6. . .	1st S. after Oct. of Ephy.
Invictus heros Numinis . .	XVIII. c.	1. 9 . .	29. . .	St. John Nepomucen.
Iste quem laeti colimus fideles .	XVII. c.	1. 9. . .	5. 29. .	St. Joseph.
Ite noctes, ite nubes . . .	XVIII. c.	1. 5. 6. .	14. *f .	Easter.
Itote populi psallite . . .	XV. c.	Moz. Brev. .	3. . .	SS. Simon and Jude.
Jactatus undis naufragis. Part of				
" Homo creatus innocens " . .	XVIII. c.	e. 1. . .	13. . .	Forward through Trials.
Jam fasces lictor ferat, et minantem .	XVIII. c.	1. 9. . .	29. . .	St. John Nepomucen.
Jam legis umbra clauditur . .	XI. c.	e. 1. . .	21. . .	Maundy Thursday.
Jam nimis terris, facinus, per omne	XVII. c.	9. . .	29. . .	Confessors.

First Lines.	Authors.	Latin Text.	Translations.	Use or Subject.
Jam nos secundae praemonet	*XI. c.*	13. (*lxxxvi.* 942).	3.	Morning.
Jam nunc quae numeras	*S.*	*b.* 9. 11.	6. 18. 24.	Com. of Doctors.
Jam pulsa cedunt nubila. Part of "Regina coeli"	*XVII. c.?*	1. (ii, p. 365)	19.	Easter.
Jam satis fluxit cruor hostiarum	*XVIII. c.*	*b.* 11.	21. 24.	Com. of Presbyters.
Jam sexta sensim solvitur	*VI. c.*	*c. m.* 1.	8.	Mid-day.
Jam surgit hora tertia	*Amb.* (?)	*c.* 1. 9.	9. 24. (1838.).	Terce.
Jerusalem et Sion filiae	*A. V.*	*f.* 1. 2. 3. 7.	22. 27. 28.	Dedic. of Church
Jesse virgam humidavit	*A. V.*	*f.* 1. 2. 7.	27.	B. V. M.
Jesu clemens, pie Deus			21.	To Christ.
Jesu Corona martyrum			29.	St. Emygdius.
Jesu dulce medicamen	*XIV. c.*	1. 2. 3. 10.	10.	Jesus, Fountain of Love.
Jesu, manus, pedes, caput	*XVIII. c.*	*e.*	25.	Passiontide.
Jesu meae deliciae	*XVIII. c.*	1.	25.	Passiontide.
Jesu, nobis miserere*			21.	Holy Communion.
Jesu nostra refectio	*XV. c.*	*e.* 1.	21.	Holy Communion.
Jesus refulsit omnium	*H—y.*	*h.* 1. 2.	6.	Epiphany.
Jesu, tuorum militum	*A. V.*	*f.*	27.	St. Victor.
Jubilemus cordis voce	*XV. c.*	1. 7.	18.	Holy Trinity.
Jubilemus Salvatori, Quem	*A. V.*	*f.* 7. 0.	25. 27.	Christmas.
Jubilemus Salvatori, Qui spem	*A. V.*	*f.*	18. 27.	Conv. of St. Paul.
Juste Judex Jesu Christe	*XII. c.*	2.	10.	Lent.
Laetabundi jubilemus, Ac devote	*A. V.*	*f.*	18. 27.	Com. of Martyrs.
Laeta quies magni ducis	*XV. c.*	1. 2. 7.	5.	St. Benedict.
Laetare, Puerpera, Laeto	*XV. c.*	7.	25.	Christmas.
Laetetur hodie matris ecclesiae	*XV. c.*	1. 7. 8.	25.	Transfiguration.
Laudemus omnes inclyta	*A. V.*	*f.* 7.	27.	St. Bartholomew.
Laudantes triumphantem Christum	*N.* (?)	1. 2. 7.	14. *i**	Easter.
Laudes Christo cum canticis	*XIV. c.*	*Ashmole MS.,* 1523.	6. *i**	St. Mary Magdalene.
Laudes Deo devotas	*N.* (?)	*b. d.* 7. 8.	3. 22. 25.	Whitsuntide.
Laudes Deo, dicat per omnia.	*XVI. c.*	1. 7.	25.	Transfiguration.
Laus erumpat ex affectu	*A. V.*	*f.* 1. 7.	27.	St. Michael and All Angels.
Laus sit regi gloriae	*XV. c.*	3. 7.	18.	The Sacred Wounds.
Laus Tibi Christe qui es Creator	*G.* (?)	1. 2. 3. 4.	19.	Praise to Christ.
Lignum crucis mirabile	*Greg.* (?)	*b.* 2. 3. 9.	21.	H. Cross.
Lucis Largitor splendide	*H—y.*	*g. m.* 1. 3. 4. 5. 6.	8. 13.	Morning.
Lux advenit veneranda Lux	*A. V.*	*f.* 1. 7.	26. 27.	Nat. of B. V. M.
Lux est ista triumphalis	*A. V.*	*f.*	27.	SS. Peter and Paul.
Lux est orta gentibus	*A. V.*	*f.* 7.	17. 25. 27.	Epiphany.
Lux illuxit dominica	*A. V.*	*f.* 7.	25. 27.	Easter.
Magister cum discipulis	*XIV. c.*	2.	21.	H. Communion.
Magne pater Augustine	*A. V.*	*f.* 1. 2. 3. 9.	27.	St. Augustine.
Magno salutis gaudio	*Greg.*	1. 3. 9.	9.	Palm Sunday.
Magnum nobis gaudium	*XVI. c.*		25.	Epiphany.
Majestati sacrosanctae	*XV. c.*	*c.* 1. 7. 10.	18. 25.	Epiphany.
Maria castis oculis. Part of "Magno salutis"		*b.* 1. 9.	5. 9. 29.	St. Mary Magdalene.
Maria sacro saucia vulnere	*S.*	*b.* 9. 11.	24.	St. Mary Magdalene.
Martinae celebri plaudite nomini	*U.*	1. 3. 9.	5. 29. *n**	St. Martina.
Martyr Dei Venantius	*XVII. c.*	1. 9.	5. 29. *n**	St. Venantius.
Martyris egregii, triumphos	*A. V.* (?)	*f.* 2. 7.	27.	St. Vincent.
Martyris Victoris laudes resonent christiani	*A. V.* (?)	*f.*	27.	St. Victor.
Matris cor virgineum			6.	Compassion B. V. M.
Matris sub almae numine			29.	Confessors.
Me receptet Sion illa (*H.*)		*c. g.* 4.	13. 15.	The Heavenly City.
Meridie orandum est	*IX. c.*	*h.* 1.	6.	At Sext.
Mille quem stipant solio sedentem	*S.*	9. 11.	24.	St. Michael and All Angels.
Miris modis repente. Part of "Felix per".		*b.* 1. 9.	5. 29.	St. Peter's Chains.
Missus Gabriel de coelis	*A. V.* (?)	*f.* 1. 2. 7.	19. 22. 27.	Christmas.
Mitis Agnus, Leo fortis	*XI. c.*	*e. g.* 1. 10.	15. 18. 25.	Easter.
Molles in agnos, ceu lupus	*XVII. c.*	*a. b.* 9. 11.	7. 24.	H. Innocents.
Morsus anguis nos omnes in lumbis Adae	*XIV. c.*	2. 7.	21.	H. Communion.
Mortale, coelo tolle, genus, caput	*C.*	*b.* 9. 11.	24.	Nat. and Conc. of B. V. M.
Mortem ei intulit ferox. Part of "Martyris victoris".	*A. V.* (?)	*f.*	27.	St. Victor.
Mortis portis fractis, fortis	*P. V.*	*c. m. n.*	8. 25.	Easter.
Multi sunt presbyteri	*XIV. c.*	14.	19.	Duty of the Clergy.
Mundi decor, mundi forma	*XV. c.*	7. 8. 9.	18.	St. Martha.
Mundo novum Jus dicere	*XVIII. c.*	*e.*	25.	Whitsuntide.
Nate Patri coaequalis (*H.*)		*c. g. m.*	13. 15.	God the Son.
Nate qui Deo Parenti	*S.*	9.	21.	Reparation to M. H. Sac.
Natus Parenti redditus.	*S.*	*a.* 9. 11.	7.	SS. Philip and James.
Nobis Sancti Spiritus gratia sit data	*XIV. c.*	2.	5.	Whitsuntide.
Non illam crucians. Part of "Martinae"			5.	St. Martina.
Non vana dilectum gregem	*B. G.*	*b.* 9. 11.	24.	C. of Virgins.
Novamne das lucem Deus?			5.	Reparation to M. H. Sac.
Novi partus gaudium	*XIV. c.*	*e.* 14.	19.	Christmas.
Novum sidus exoritur	*XV. c.*	*e.* 1. 2.	25.	Transfiguration.
Noxium Christus simul introivit	*B.*	*b.* 9.	24.	Circumcision.
Nullis te genitor blanditiis trahit	*U.*	1. 9.	5.	St. Hermenegild.
Nunc novis Christus celebretur hymnis	*XVIII. c.*	*e.*	18.	Easter.
Nunc Te flebilibus concinimus modis			5.	Reparation to M. H. Sac.
Nuntium vobis fero de supernis	*Greg.* (?)	*m.* 6. 8.	6. 25.	Epiphany.

First Lines.	Authors.	Latin Text.	Translations.	Use or Subject.
O colenda Deitas	XV. c.	2. . . .	21. 23. . .	Holy Communion.
O crucifer bone, lucisator . . .	Prud.	2. 4. . .	10. . .	G. before Meat. (Easter.)
O crux qui sola languentes, see Crux sola		. . .	21. .	H. Cross.
O gens beata coelitum . . .	XVII. c.	m. 1. 4. 5. 6.	6. .	The Joy of the Saints.
O jam beata, quæ suo . . .	S.	a. b. 9. 11. .	7. .	C. of H. Women.
O Jesu dulcissime, cibus salutaris. .	XV. c.	2. . .	21. .	Post Communion.
O Jesu dulcissime, Jesu dilectissime	XV. c.	2. . .	18. .	Evening.
O Maria, stella maris, Pietate .	A. V.	f. 7. 8. .	27. .	B. V. M.
O Nazarene, lux Bethlehem . .	Prud.	1. 3. . .	3. .	Monday in Lent.
O nox vel medio splendidior die .	M.	Sens Brev., 1726	3. 25. .	Christmas.
O Panis dulcissime, O fidelis. .	XIII. c.	1. 2. 7. .	21. 23. .	H. Communion.
O pulchras acies, castraque fortia .	S.	b. 9. 11. .	6. 24. .	C. of Abbots, &c.
O quam glorificum, solum sedere .	XV. c.	n. 2. .	19. 26. .	To Christ.
O qui supernae gaudia patriae .		. . .	29. .	St. Vincent of Paul.
O sacerdotum veneranda jura .	XVIII. c.	b. 11. .	13. .	Unbelief of Israel.
O salutaris fulgens stella maris .	XV. c.	d. . .	21. 24. .	Com. of Presbyters.
O sancta praesepis tui. Part of "Quid est"	Prud.	g. . .	6. .	Visit. of B. V. M.
O veneranda Trinitas laudanda .	XI. c.	h. 8. .	6. .	Holy Trinity.
O virgo pectus cui sacrum . .	M.	a. b. 3. 9. 11.	6. 7. 24. .	C. of Virgins.
O vos aetherei, plaudite, cives .	S.	9. 11. .	5. .	Assump. of B. V. M.
O vos unanimes Christiadum chori	S. B.	9. 11. .	24. .	Oct. of All Saints.
Omnes gentes plaudite, Festo choros	XIII. c.	1. 7. .	26. h* .	Ascension.
Omnia habemus in Christo* . .		. . .	21. .	Christ All in All.
Omnibus manat cruor ecce venis .	S.	b. 9. 11. .	3. 24. .	Decoll. of St. John Bap.
Omnipotenti Domino . . .	XV. c.	Moz. Brev. .	3. .	St. Andrew.
Omnis fidelis gaudeat . . .	XV. c.	1. . .	19. .	Face of Christ.
Orabo mente Dominum (see p. 144, i.) .	Amb.	I. Williams, 1838	24. (1838) .	Prayer.
Orbis totus Unda lotus . . .	A. V.	f. . .	27. .	B. V. M.
Pallidi tandem procul hinc timores		. . .	29. .	St. Gabriel.
Panditur saxo tumulus remoto .	S. C.	b. 9. 11. .	24. .	Lazarus visited by Christ.
Pangat chorus in hac die . .	A. V.	f. 1. 2. 7. .	27. .	St. James the Greater.
Pange lingua gloriosae lanceae .	XVIII. c.	1. 9. .	29. .	The Lance.
Panis descendens coelitus . .	XIV. c	2. . .	21. .	Holy Communion.
Paraclitus Increatus . . (H.)		c. g. m. .	13. 15. .	Whitsuntide.
Paranymphus salutat virginem .	A. V. (?)	f. 2. .	27. .	Annunc. B. V. M.
Parendum est, cedendum est . .	XVII. c.	1. 5. 6. 10. .	18. .	Farewell to the World.
Paschali jubilo sonent praeconia .	XVIII. c.	1. 9. .	29. .	Lance and Nails.
Pestis visceribus ciboque sumpto .	Prud.	2. 3. .	10. 18. .	Easter. Thanks after Meat.
Paulus Sion architectus. . .	XIII. c .	n. 1. 2. 7. 10.	18. .	Conv. of St. Paul.
Peccator intueberis. Part of "Quid est."	Prud.	g. . .	15. .	Advent.
Per pacem ad lucem* . . .		. . .	21. .	Rest and Peace in Truth.
Per unius casum grani . . .	A. V. (?)	f. 7. .	27. .	St. Quintin.
Perfusus ora lachrymis . . .	Com.	9. . .	5. .	St. Martin.
Pia mater plangat ecclesia . .	A. V.	f. . .	27. .	St. Thomas of Canty.
Piscatores hominum (see "Viri venerabiles")		. . .	5. .	Christ to His Ministers.
Plagis Magistri saucia . . .	B. G.	b. 9. 11. .	24. .	St. Mary Magdalene.
Plange, Sion, muta vocem . .	XVIII. c.	Paris M., 1739	21. .	Act of Reparation.
Plaude festivo, pia gens, honore .		. . .	29. .	Our Lady of Good Counsel.
Plaudite Coeli, Rideat aether. .	XVII. c.	g. m. n. 1. 4. 5. 6. 10.	8. 12. 15. 18.	Easter.
Pone luctum Magdalena . .	XVII. c.	c. m. 1. 4. 5. 6. 10.	8. 13. 18. 25. g*	Easter.
Portas vestras aeternales . .	XVI. c.	c. n. .	18. .	Ascension.
Postquam hostem et inferna . .	A. V.	f. n. 7. 8. .	18. 25. 27. .	Ascension.
Postquam Puellae dies quadragesimus	P.	. . .	e* .	Purif. of B. V. M.
Potestate, non natura . . .	A. V.	c. f. m. 1. 2. 7.	18. 27. .	Christmas.
Praeclara custos virginum . .	XVIII. c.	1. . .	5. 29. .	Immaculate Conception.
Praeclara septem lumina . .	XVIII. c.	9. . .	29. .	Confessors.
Praeclarum Christi militem . .	XV. c.	Moz. Brev. .	3. .	St. Matthew.
Praecursorem summi regis . .	A. V.	f. 1. 7. .	27. .	Beheading of St. John Bap.
Pressi malorum pondere . .		. . .	5. .	St. Paul.
Prima victricis fidei corona . .	XVIII. c.	e. 11. .	25. .	Epiphany.
Procul maligni cedite spiritus .	S.	b. 9. 11. .	24. .	St. Mary Magdalene.
Profitentes unitatem . . .	A. V.	f. 1. 7. 10. 12.	18. 27. .	Trinity Sunday.
Proles Parentis optimi . . .	Buch.	g. 3. .	15. .	Morning.
Promat pia vox cantoris . .	A. V. (?)	f. . .	27. .	St. Giles.
Prome casta concio cantica organa .	X. c.	Sarum M. .	22. .	Easter.
Promissa, tellus, concipe gaudia .	B.	b. 9. 11. .	6. 24. 25. .	Ascension.
Prope est claritudinis magnae dies	XIV. c.	1. 7. .	25. .	Advent.
Prunis datum admiremur . .	A. V.	c. f. m. 7. .	8. 27. .	St. Lawrence.
Puer nobis nascitur . . .	XV. c.	1. 2. 3. .	Ev. Office 1748	Christmas.
Pulchra res ictum. Part of "Scripta sunt"	Prud.	. . .	13. .	Martyrs.
Qua lapsu tacito stella loquacibus .	C.	b. 9. .	4. 24. 25. .	Epiphany.
Quaenam lingua tibi, O lancea, debitas	XIX. c.	Rom. Brev. .	5. d* 29. .	Lance and Nails.
Quaesumus ergo Deus ut sereno. Part of "Christe cunctorum" . .		h. . .	6. .	Dedication of a Church.
Quam, Christe, signasti viam . .	S.	b. 9. 11. .	6. 24. .	C. of Martyrs.
Quam dilecta tabernacula . .	A. V.	c. f. m. 1. 2. 3. 7.	19. 22. 26. 27.	Ded. of Church.
Quantis micas honoribus . .	XVIII. c.	. . .	21. 24. .	Com. of Presbyters.
Quem nox, quem tenebrae . .	S.	b. 9. 11. .	6. 24. .	St. John Evang.
Qui Christiano gloriantur nomine .	S.	b. 9. 11. .	3. 24. .	St. Peter in Prison.
Qui mutare solet grandibus infima		. . .	29. .	St. Vincent of Paul.
Qui nos creas solus Pater . .	C.	b. 9. 11. .	24. .	Sundays Sept. to Lent.
Qui Te Deus sub intimo , .	S.	a. b. 9. 11. .	6. 7. 24. .	C. of Just Men.
Quicunque sanus vivere . . .		. . .	5. .	St. Joseph.

First Lines.	Authors.	Latin Text.	Translations.	Use or Subject.
Quid est quod artum circulum	Prud.	g.	13. 15. 26.	Christmas.
Quid moras nectis? Domino jubente	C.	b. 9. 11.	24.	Nat. of St. John Baptist.
Quid, obstinata pectora.	S.	a. b. 9. 11.	7. 24.	St. Stephen.
Quid tu, relictis urbibus [Quam pura]	S.	b. 9. 11.	6. 18. 24.	C. of Abbots, &c.
Quid tyranne, quid minaris	D. ?	g. m. 1. 4. 5. 6. 10.	15. 18.	Christian Courage.
Quidquid antiqui cecinere vates	XV. c.	9.	5.	St. Benedict.
Quieti tempus adest	XI. c.	Moz. Brev.	3.	Evening.
Quis dabit profunda nostro			5.	Reparation to M. H. Sac.
Quis ille sylvis e penetralibus	C.	b. 9. 11.	24.	Decoll. St. John Baptist.
Quis novus, coelis, agitur triumphus			29.	St. Vincent of Paul.
Quo me, Deus, amore	XVIII. c.	1.	17. 21.	H. Communion.
Quodcunque in orbe. Pt. of " Felix per "	XI. c.	b. 9.	5. 29.	St. Peter's Chair.
Quos pompa saeculi, quos opes	C.	Paris. B. 9. 11.	24.	St. Joseph, Husb. of B.V.M.
Recolamus sacram coenam	XIV. c.	1. 2. 7.	17. 21.	H. Communion.
Redditum luci, Domino vocante	S. C.	b. 9. 11.	24.	Lazarus visited by Christ.
Redeundo per gyrum	XIV. c.	1. 2. 7.	19.	The Theban Legion.
Regali solio fortis Iberiae	U.	1. 3. 9.	5. 29. n*	St. Hermenegild.
Regina coeli jubila	XVII. c.	1.	19.	Easter.
Regis et pontificis	A. V. (?)	f.	27.	Crown of Thorns.
Regis superni nuntia	U.	1. 9.	5. 29.	St. Theresa.
Regnis Paternis debitus	S.	b. 9. 11.	24.	SS. Philip and James.
Reminiscens beati sanguinis	XVI. c.	Utrecht M., 1540	17. 21.	Passiontide.
Resonet in laudibus	XIV. c.	1. 3. 4. 5. 6. 10.	3.	Christmas.
Roma Petro glorietur	A. V.	f. 7.	27.	SS. Peter and Paul.
Rosa novum dans odorem	A. V. (?)	f.	27.	St. Stephen.
Sacram venite supplices	XIX. c.		5.	St. Joseph Calasanctius.
Sacrata Christi tempora	VIII c.	Moz. Brev. e. 1.	25.	S. after Ascension.
Sacrata libri dogmata	Hart.	1. 2. 3.	10.	Before Reading the Gospel.
Saepe corde tepido et arido accedimus*			21.	Perseverance.
Saepe dum Christi popdlus cruentis	XIX. c.	1.	5. 29.	B. V. M. Help of Christns.
Salve, crux, arbor vitae praeclara .	A. V.	f. 1. 2. 7.	27.	Exaltation of the Cross.
Salve crux sancta, arbor digna	XI. c.	1. 2. 7.	22.	H. Cross.
Salve crux sancta, salve mundi	XI. c.	e. h. 1. 2. 9.	1.	Invention of the Cross.
Salve, dies dierum gloria	A. V.	f. 7. 8.	27.	Easter.
Salve, mater Salvatoris.	A. V.	e. f. 1. 3. 7.	27.	Nat. B. V. M.
Salve saluberrima, Tu salus infirmorum	XIV. c	2.	6. 21.	Prep. for H. Communion.
Salve, sancta caro Dei	XII. c.	1. 2.	21.	Holy Communion.
Salve sancta facies nostri Redemptoris	XIV. c.	1. 2. 3. 7.	6.	Face of Jesus Christ.
Salve sanguis Salvatoris	XV. c.	2.	21.	Holy Communion.
Salve, suavis et formose	XV. c.	2.	21.	Holy Communion.
Salve tropaeum gloriae .	B. V.	c. m. 1.	13. 25.	Good Friday. H. Cross.
Sancti visu columbino	XV. c.	1. 7.	18.	St. Augustine.
Sanctorum meritis jungat praeconia	XV. c.	d.	6.	H. Innocents.
Scripta sunt coelo duorum martyrum	Prud.	Moz. Brev.	13.	SS. Emeterius & Celedonius.
Sexta passus feria	A. V.	f. n. 7.	25. 27.	Easter.
Si vis Patronum quaerere		8.	5.	St. Peter.
Si vis vere gloriari	XIV. c.	c. 1. 7.	13. 18. 22. 25.	The Crown of Thorns.
Sicut chorda musicorum. Pt. of " Prunis datum "	A. V.	c. f. m. 7.	8. 27.	Martyrdom of St. Lawrence
Signum novi Crux foederis	S.	e. 9. 11.	21.	Altar of the Cross.
Signum pretiosus, signum crucis*.			21.	Tree of Life.
Simplex in essentia	A. V.	c. f. 1. 7.	27.	Whitsuntide.
Speciosus formâ prae natis hominum	XV. c.	1. 7.	26.	Transfiguration.
Spiritus paraclitus	A. V. (?)	f.	27.	Whitsuntide.
Splendor Patris et figura	A. V.	f. 1. 7.	27.	Christmas.
Stupete gentes: fit Deus hostia	S.	1.	4. 24.	Purification of B. V. M.
Sudore sat tuo fides	B. G.	b. 9. 11.	3. 24.	St. Paul.
Summis ad astra laudibus	XVIII. c.	Paris B. 9. 11.	29.	St. Catharine of Genoa.
Supplex sacramus canticum	XIX. c.	Milan Brev., 1830.	3.	Circumcision.
Surgentes ad Te Domine	IX. c.	e. h. 1. 2. 3.	6.	Midnight.
Surgit Christus cum trophaeo	XV. c.	7.	26.	Easter.
Tandem fluctus, tandem luctus	XVII. c.	n. 1.	19.	Advent.
Te deprecante corporum	XVIII. c.	1. 9.	5. 29.	St. John Cantius.
Te Joseph celebrent agmina Coelitum	XVII. c.	b. 1. 9.	5. 29. n*	St. Joseph.
Te mater alma Numinis	XVIII. c.	1.	5. 29.	Maternity of B. V. M.
Te principem, summo Deus .	C.	a. b. 9. 11.	3. 6. 7. 18. 24.	Tuesday. Lauds.
Te quanta, victor funeris	XVIII. c.	e.	25.	Easter.
Te sancte Jesus mens mea	F.	g.	15.	Love to Christ.
Templum cordis adornemus .	A. V.	f.	27.	Purification of B. V. M.
Totum Deus in Te spero (H.)		g. 4.	15. 18.	Faith.
Tria dona Reges ferunt. Part of " Virgo mater."	A. V.	c. f.	26. 27.	Epiphany.
Tribus signis Deo dignis	Hart.	c. g. n.	15.	Epiphany.
Trinitatem reserat aquila	A. V. (?)	f. 2. 7.	27.	St. John Evangelist.
Trinitatem simplicem .	A. V. (?)	f.	27.	Holy Trinity.
Triumphalis lux illuxit	A. V.	f. 1. 2. 7.	27.	St. Vincent.
Tu es certe quem habeo	XIV. c.	2.	21.	H. Communion.
Tu natale solum protege, tu bonae	U.	1. 9.	5. 29.	St. Martina.
Tu, quem prae reliquis Christus amaverat	S.	b. 9. 11.	6. 24.	St. John Evangelist.
Tuba Syon jucundetur	A. V. (?)	f.	27.	St. Margaret.
Turbam jacentem pauperum			29.	St. Catharine of Genoa.
Ut nunc, ab alto, praevia			29.	St. Vincent of Paul.
Ut sol decoro sidere		b.	24.	Conception B. V. M.

First Lines.	Authors.	Latin Text.	Translations.	Use or Subject.
Vagitus Ille exordium. Part of "Quid est quod"	*Prud.*	*g.*	15.	Christmas.
Venerando praesuli Remigio.	*A. V. (?)*	*f.*	27.	St. Remigius.
Veni Creator Spiritus, Spiritus recreator	*XVI. c.*	*c. m.*	8. 16.	Whitsuntide.
Veni summe Consolator	*A. V.*	*f.*	18. 26. 27.	Whitsuntide.
Veni, veni, Rex gloriae	*XV. c.*	2.	10.	Advent.
Verbi vere substantivi .	*A. V.*	*c. f.*	19. 27.	St. John Evangelist.
Verbum prodiens a Patre	*XIV. c.*	2.	21.	H. Communion.
Virginis in gremio Nato Dei Filio.	*XV. c.*	1. 2. 7.	17. 26.	Christmas.
Virgo, mater Salvatoris	*A. V.*	*f.*	27.	B. V. M.
Viri venerabiles sacerdotes Dei	*Map.*	*e.*	5.	Ad Clerum.
Vita per quam vivo	*Aug.*	*g.*	15.	Jesus, the Life.
Vix in sepulcro conditur	*XVIII. c.*	1. 9.	29.	St. John Nepomucen.
Vos sancti proceres, vos superum chori.	*S.*	9. 11.	24.	All Saints.
Vos succensa Deo splendida lumina	*S.*	*b.* 9. 11.	6. 24.	C. of Doctors.
Vox clara terris nos gravi	*XVIII. c.*	*e.*	*k*.*	Advent.

In the foregoing list the *trs.* marked *a*, b*, c**, &c., are as follows:—

a*. In the *Rom. Brev. in English*, by the Marquess of Bute, 1879.

b*. In O. Shipley's *Annus Sanctus*, 1884, by T. J. Potter.

c*. In the *Rom. Brev. in English*, 1879.

d*. In the same.

e*. In the *Church Times*, Jan. 28, 1887, by W. C. Bix.

f*. In Neale and Littledale's *Commentary on the Psalms*, vol. iii. 1874, Ps. xcvi. 12.

g*. In Dr. Schaff's *Christ in Song*, 1869, by Dr. E. A. Washburn of New York, June 1868.

h*. In the *Church Times*, May 28, 1886, by Dr. Littledale.

i*. In the *Church Times*, April 2, 1885, by Dr. Littledale.

k*. In O. Shipley's *Annus Sanctus*, by H. I. D. Ryder.

m*. In Loftie's *Latin Year*, 1873, p. 327.

n*. *Primer*, 1782.

We have also to note that—

(1) The three *trs.* from St. Augustine (*Aug.*) in the foregoing list are metrical paraphrases of portions of his prose works.

(2) Those lines which are given thus : " De ascensione Domini*," are not the first lines of Latin hymns, but are Latin titles which preface English hymns in a few works. These titles are retained in this list that the origin of the hymns so prefaced may be clearly defined.

(3) Those hymns marked *A. V.* (?) are noted by M. Leon Gautier in his 2nd ed. of the *Œuvres Poetiques d'Adam de St. Victor*, 1881, as *falsely* attributed to that author.

In addition to searching this list for translations, the Index to Latin first lines should also be consulted, as numerous hymns (as known to the general reader) are either taken from longer hymns, or are altered forms of the authors' texts. The following list of recent collections of Latin Hymns and Sequences, which are not indexed on p. 656, is added here for the convenience of students :—

1. *Die Tropen- Prosen- und Präfations-Gesänge des feierlichen Hochamtes im Mittelalter.* By Ad. Reiners. Luxemburg, 1884.

2. *Hymni et Sequentiae . . . quae ex libris impressis et ex codicibus manuscriptis saeculorum a ix. usque ad xvi. partim post M. Flacii Illyrici curas congessit, &c.* By Gustav Milchsack. Pt. i. Halle, 1886.

3. *Cantiones Bohemicae. Leiche, Lieder und Rufe des 13. 14. und 15. Jahrhunderts, &c.* By G. M. Dreves. Leipzig, 1886.

4. *Lateinische Hymnen des Mittelalters.* By F. W. E. Roth. Augsburg, 1887.

5. *Hymnarius Moissiacensis. Das Hymnar der Abtei Moissac im 10. Jahrhundert. Nach einer Handschrift der Rossiana. Im Anhange: a. Carmina scholarium Campensium. b. Cantiones Vissegradenses.* By G. M. Dreves. Leipzig, 1888. [J. J.]

Lauda mater ecclesia. *St. Odo of Cluny.* [*St. Mary Magdalene.*] This is the companion to " Aeterni Patris Unice " (q.v.), and, like it, is found in an 11th cent. MS. in the British Museum (Vesp. D. xii. f. 153 *b*), these two hymns being written in a hand of the 12th cent. It is also in a 13th cent. MS. in the Bodleian (Ashmole, 1525, f. 168 *b*). In the *York Brev.* of 1493 it is the hymn at Vespers on the festival of St. Mary Magdalene. The text is also in *Mone*, No. 1063 ; *Daniel*, i., No. 190, with further notes at iv. p. 244 ; *Neale's Hymni Ecclesiae*, 1851, p. 193 ; *Card. Newman's Hymni Ecclesiae*, 1838 and 1865 ; and others. *Tr.* as :—

1. **Exalt, O Mother Church, to-day.** By J. M. Neale, in his *Mediaeval Hys.*, 1851, p. 27 ; in the *Appendix* to the *Hymnal N.*, 1862, the *Day Hours of the Church of England*, and others.

2. **O Church, our Mother, speak His praise.** By J. D. Chambers, in his *Lauda Syon*, pt. ii., 1866, p. 90, and repeated in the *People's H.*, 1867.

Another tr. is:—Praise, dearest Church and Mother, praise. *W. J. Blew.* 1852-55. [J. M.]

Lauda Sion Salvatorem. *St. Thomas of Aquino.* [*Holy Communion.*] This is one of the four *Sequences* which are alone retained in the revised *Roman Missal*, 1570, and later editions. It seems to have been written about 1260 for the Mass of the festival of Corpus Christi. For this festival St. Thomas, at the request of Pope Urban IV., drew up in 1263 the offic in the *Roman Breviary* ; and probably also that in the *Roman Missal*. In form this *Sequence* is an imitation of the " Laudes crucis attollamus " (q. v.), and consists of 9 stanzas of 6 lines, followed by 2 of 8 and then 1 of 10 lines. Among early *Missals* it is found in a French missal of the end of the 13th cent. (Add. 23935 f. 11 *b*), and a 14th cent. Sens (Add. 30058 f. 83 *b*) in the British Museum : in a *Sarum*, c. 1370 (Barlow 5, p. 256) ; a *Hereford*, c. 1370 ; a *York*, c. 1390, and a *Roman* of the end of the 13th cent. (*Liturg. Misc.* 354 f. 58 *b*), all now in the Bodleian : in the *St. Andrew's Missal* (printed ed. 1864, p. 213) : in the *Magdeburg* of 1480, and many other German *Missals*, &c. Its use was primarily for Corpus Christi ; but in the *Sarum* use st. xi., xii. (" Ecce panis angelorum ") might be used during the octave. In the *York* use the complete form was used on Corpus Christi, and during the octave it was divided into three parts said on succeeding days, viz. (1) st. i.-iv. ; (2) v.-viii. (" Quod in coena Christus gessit "), and (3) ix.-xii. (" Sumunt boni, sumunt mali "). It has often been used as a Processional ; at the Benediction of the Blessed Sacrament (especially st. xi. xii.), and other occasions. The printed text is also in *Mone*, No. 210; *Wackernagel*, i., No. 230; *Daniel*, ii. 97. and v. 73; *Kehrein*, No. 150; *Bässler*, No. 100; March's *Lat. Hys.*, 1875, p. 165, &c. The text, with a full commentary, is given in Dr. J. Kayser's *Beiträge zur Geschichte und Erklärung der ältesten Kirchenhymnen*, vol. ii., 1886, pp. 77–109.

As a historical document, and an example of harmonious and easy rhythmic flow of verse combined with the most definite doctrinal teaching, this sequence is of great interest. Considered however as a hymn for present day use (especially if for use in the Reformed Churches) the case is entirely different. *Mone* characterises it as "a dogmatic didactic poem on the Holy Communion;" and *Kehrein* as a "severely dogmatic sequence." It is in fact a doctrinal treatise in rhymed verse, setting forth the theory of Transubstantiation at length and in precise detail. In stanza vii. the refusal of the cup to the laity is implied in the assertion that the whole Christ is given in *either* species:—

    " Sub diversis speciebus,
    Signis tamen et non rebus
    Latent res eximiae:
    Caro cibus, sanguis potus,
    Manet tamen Christus totus
    Sub utraque specie."

This, in Canon Oakeley's *tr.*, 1850, reads :—

    " Beneath two differing species
    (Signs only, not their substances)
    Lie mysteries deep and rare ;
    His Flesh the meat, the drink his Blood,
    Yet Christ entire, our heavenly food,
    Beneath each kind is there "

Again in st. x. St. Thomas is very definite and emphatic in his warning :—

    " Fracto demum sacramento
    Ne vacilles, sed memento,
    Tantum esse sub fragmento,
    Quantum toto tegitur.
    Nulla rei fit scissura,
    Signi tantum fit fractura
    Qua nec status nec statura
    Signati minuitur."

This is *tr.* by Canon Oakeley as :—

    " Nor be thy faith confounded, though
    The Sacrament be broke ; for know,
    The life which in the whole doth glow,
    In every part remains ;
    The Spirit which those portions hide
    No force can cleave ; we but divide
    The sign, the while the Signified
    Nor change nor loss sustains."

The modern use which is made of the hymn in its English forms will be gathered from the translations noted below.   [J. M.]

In translating this *Sequence* no difficulty has been found where the translator has held the distinct doctrine of Transubstantiation in common with St. Thomas. The difficulty has arisen when his hard and clear cut sentences have had to be modified, and his dogmatism to be toned down to fit in with convictions of a less pronounced character. The result is that the *trs.* for private devotion are usually very literal; whilst those for public worship are, either the former modified and arranged in centos, or else paraphrases which have little of the "Lauda Sion" in them but the name. The *trs.* are :—

1. **Break forth, O Sion, thy sweet Saviour sing.** By F. C. Husenbeth, in his *Missal for the Laity*, 1840. This paraphrase is extended to 24 st. of unequal length, and is very literal in its doctrinal teaching.

2. **Praise thy Saviour, Sion, praise Him.** By E. B. Pusey in his *tr.* of the *Paradise of the Christian Soul*, 1847, p. 133. This is a modified translation.

3. **Praise high the Saviour, Sion, praise.** By Canon Oakeley, in his *tr.* of the *Paradise of the Christian Soul*. London, Burns, 1850, p. 414. A literal translation.

4. **Sion, lift thy voice, and sing.** By E. Caswall, in his *Lyra Catholica*, 1849, p. 236; and his *Hys. and Poems*, 1873, p. 124. A literal *tr.*

5. **Praise, Oh Sion, praise thy Pastor.** By J. R. Beste, in his *Church Hymns*, 1849, p. 17. A literal *tr.*

6. **Zion, thy Redeemer praising.** By A. D. Wackerbarth, in his *Lyra Ecclesiastica*, Pt. ii., 1843, p. 7. A literal *tr.* Also in O. Shipley's *Annus Sanctus*, 1884.

7. **Praise, O Sion, praise thy Pastor.** In the 1863 *Appendix* to the *Hymnal Noted*, No. 218. It is based upon Wackerbarth, but indebted more especially to Caswall and Beste.

8. **Sion, praise thy Prince and Pastor.** By W. J. Blew, in his *Church Hy. & Tune Bk.*, 1852–55. An abbreviated and modified form.

9. **Laud, O Syon, thy Salvation.** By J. D. Chambers, in his *Lauda Syon*, 1857, p. 222. Slightly modified.

10. **Laud, O Sion, thy Salvation.** A cento in O. Shipley's *Divine Liturgy*, 1863 ; again, in a different form, in the *Altar Manual*, by Littledale and Vaux, 1863, and again in the *People's H.*, 1867. This cento is mainly from Dr. Pusey's, Wackerbarth's, and Chambers's *trs.* mostly rewritten. This, slightly altered, is in the *Hymner*, 1882.

11. **Praise, O Sion, thy Salvation.** A cento in the *Hymnary*, rewritten mainly from Wackerbarth, Chambers, and the *People's H. trs.* It is given in two parts, Part ii. being "Lo, the bread which angels feedeth." Another *tr.* of st. xi., xiii. in 7's metre, is given as Pt. iii., "Earthly pilgrim, joyful see."

12. **Laud thy Saviour, Sion praise Him.** A cento in 6 st. based chiefly on J. D. Chambers, Dr. Pusey, and others in the 1870 *Appendix* to the *Hyl. for the Use of St. John the Evangelist*, Aberdeen.

13. **Sion, to Thy Saviour singing.** By A. R. Thompson. This is merely a paraphrase of st. i.–iv., xi., xii. The essential part of the hymn is omitted, and as a rendering of St. Thomas's *Sequence* it has no claim. The 6 sts. appeared in the American *Sunday School Times*, 1883 ; and again, in two parts, in *Laudes Domini*, 1884, Pt. ii. beginning, "Here the King hath spread His table."

14. **Sing forth, O Sion, sweetly sing.** By J. D. Aylward in O. Shipley's *Annus Sanctus*, 1884.

15. **Sion, praise Thy Saviour King.** By J. Wallace, in his *Hys. of the Church*, 1874. A literal translation.

Three versions from the older translators must be mentioned here :—

16. **Praise, O Syon! praise thy Saviour.** By R. Southwell, in his *Mæoniæ, or Certaine excellent Poems and Spiritual Hymnes*, &c., 1595.

17. **A special theme of praise is read.** A cento in 3 st. of 6 l., by Bp. Cosin, in his *Coll. of Private Devotions*, &c., 1627 (11th ed., 1838, p. 285).

18. **Rise, royal Sion, rise and sing.** By R. Crawshaw, in the 2nd ed. of his *Steps to the Temple*, &c., 1648, and again in an altered form into the Dorrington and Hicke editions of John Austin's *Devotions* (see p. 97, ii.).

From the foregoing *trs.* and centos, st. xi.

and xii., beginning, Ecce, panis Angelorum, are often used as a separate hymn. The following are the opening lines:—

1. See for food to pilgrims given. E. B. Pusey. (No. 2.)

2. The Bread of angels, lo, is sent. Canon Oakeley. (No. 3.)

3. Lo, upon the Altar lies. E. Caswall. (No. 4.) This is in use as *tr.* by Caswall, and also altered to "Lo, before our longing eyes," in the Dutch Reformed *Hys. of the Church*, N. Y., 1869.

4. See the bread of angels lying. J. R. Beste. (No. 5.)

5. Bread that angels eat in heaven. A. D. Wackerbarth. (No. 6.)

6. Lo, the Bread which angels feedeth. *Hymnal N.* (No. 7), and the *Hymnary*, 1872.

7. Lo, the angels' Food is given. In the *Introits* prefixed to some eds. of *H. A. & M.*, N. D., and again in the *People's H.*, 1867. This was repeated in the *Appendix* to *H. A. & M.*, 1868; the *Hymnary* (with slight alterations), 1872; the *Altar Hymnal*, 1884. In *H. A. & M.*, 1875, it is claimed on behalf of "The Compilers."

8. Lo, the Bread which angels feedeth. J. D. Chambers. (No. 9.)

9. Lo the angels' food descending. A. R. Thompson. (No. 13.)

10. Behold, the Bread of angels, sent. J. D. Aylward. (No. 14.)

Although the renderings in part and in whole of the "Lauda Sion" are thus numerous, the use of any of these *trs.* in public worship is very limited. [J. J.]

Laudes Christo redempti voce modulemur supplici. *St. Notker.* [*Easter.*] This is found in an Einsiedeln MS. of the 10th cent., 121, p. 566. It is also in the Prüm *Gradual*, written c. 1000 (Bibl. Nat. Paris Lat. 9448), and the Echternach *Gradual* of the 11th cent. (B. N. No. 10510); in the St. Gall MSS., Nos. 376, 381, of the 11th cent.; in a MS. c. 1200, in the Bodleian (*Liturg. Misc.* 340 f. 140 *b*); in a *Gradual* of the 11th or 12th cent. in the British Museum (Reg. 8 C xiii. f. 13), and others. The printed text is in the *Magdeburg Missal*, 1480, and other later German *Missals;* in *Daniel*, ii. p. 178, and *Kehrein*, No. 92. *Tr.* as:—

Praise to Christ with suppliant voices. By R. F. Littledale, in *Lyra Messianica*, 1864, p. 331; and again in the *People's H.*, 1867, No. 116. [J. M.]

Laudes crucis attollamus. *Adam of St. Victor.* [*Passiontide. Holy Cross.*] This *Sequence* has been generally ascribed to Adam of St. Victor, and is given by L. Gautier in his edition of Adam's *Oeuvres poetiques*, 1881, p. 224, as probably by him, and is there quoted from a Limoges *Sequentiary* of the 12th or 13th cent. (Bibl. Nat. Paris, No. 1139), and other sources. It is found in a *Gradual* apparently written in England during the 12th cent., and now in the British Museum (Reg. 2 B. iv. f. 173 *b*); in a MS. of the end of the 12th cent. now in the Bodleian (*Liturg. Misc.* 341 f. 51 *b*); while *Morel*, p. 36, cites it as in a Fischingen MS. of the 11th cent., an Einsiedeln MS. of the 12th cent., &c. In a 14th cent. *Paris Missal*, and a 14th cent. *Sens Missal* in the British Museum; as also in the *Sarum, York, Hereford, St. Andrews,* and many other *Missals* (e.g. the *Magdeburg Mis-*

sal, 1480); it is the *Sequence* for the Festival of the Invention or the Exaltation of the Cross. The printed text is also in *Daniel*, ii. p. 78; *Kehrein*, No. 60; *D. S. Wrangham*, ii. 46, and others. Dr. Neale, in his *Mediæval Hymns*, speaks of it as "perhaps the masterpiece of Adam of St. Victor"; but this is greatly to overrate it, save for its technical qualities. It is a panegyric of the cross, in which the types in the Old Testament are drawn out at length. It is quite impossible to give an adequate version of it in good English. *Tr.* as:—

Be the Cross our theme and story. By J. M. Neale, in his *Mediæval Hymns*, 1851, p. 95, in 12 st. of unequal lines. In 1864, 4 st. were given in Skinner's *Daily Service Hyl.*, No. 236; and in 1882, 9 st. in the *Hymner*, as No. 134.

Other trs. are:—
1. To the Cross its due laudation. *D. S. Wrangham*, ii. 1881.
2. Come, let us with glad music. H. W. Lloyd, in O. Shipley's *Annus Sanctus*. 1884. [J. M.]

Laudes Salvatori voce modulemur supplici. *St. Notker.* [*Easter.*] Among the St. Gall MSS. this *Sequence* is found in No. 340 of the 10th cent.; Nos. 376, 378, 380, 381 of the 11th cent., &c. It is contained in a Bodleian MS. written c. 1000 (Bodl. 775, f. 188), as a "Sequence on the miracles of Christ and His Resurrection"; in three MSS. of the 12th cent. in the British Museum (Add. 11669, f. 50; Calig. A. xiv. f. 56; Reg. 8, C. xiii. f. 14 *b*), &c. Also in the *Sarum, York, Hereford* and *St. Andrews Missals*, the *Magdeburg Missal* of 1480, and many others. The printed text is also in *Daniel*, ii. p. 12; *Mone*, No. 148, *Kehrein*, No. 181, &c. [J. M.]

The poem is entitled *Frigdora*, because set to a melody made up of the modes which the Greeks called Phrygian and Dorian, i.e. the first tone mixed with the third (see Du Cange under "Frigdorae," and Dr. Neale's *Essays on Liturgiology*, p. 379). It sets forth the verity, so essential to be maintained in these days, and so tersely expressed by Dr. Liddon (*Bampton Lectures*, p. 243), "The miraculous is inextricably interwoven with the whole life of Christ." No wonder then that it was adopted in all the three English Missals—on the Sunday after Easter in the *Sarum* and the *Hereford*, and on the Monday in Easter Week in the *York*. Bishop Andrews, commenting on the words of Isaiah, "Unto us a child is born; unto us a Son is given," and expounding them according to a decree of the Fathers of the Council of Seville, that "the Child imparts His human, the Son His divine power," adds words accurately illustrative of this hymn:—

"All along His life you shall see these two. At His birth, a cratch for the Child, a star for the Son; a company of shepherds viewing the Child, a choir of angels celebrating the Son. In His life; hungry Himself, to show the nature of the Child; yet feeding five thousand to show the power of the Son. At His death; dying on the cross, as the Child of Adam; at the same time disposing of Paradise, as the Son of God" (2nd Sermon on the Nativity). The *Sequence* is *tr.* as:—

Praise to our Lord and Saviour dear. By Dean Plumptre, made for and first pub. in the *Hymnary*, 1872, No. 272, in two parts, Pt. ii. beginning, "So wrought He all His Father's will."

Another tr. is:—
Let us with lowly voice. C. B. Pearson, in the *Sarum*

Missal in English, 1868, and his *Sequences from the Sarum Missal*, 1871.   **[WM. C.]**

Laudibus cives resonent canoris.

[*St. Benedict.*] In the *Psalmista Monasticum*, Venice, 1583, f. 232 b, this is the hymn for the First Vespers of St. Benedict. It is also referred to in a *Benedictine Breviary* pub. at Venice in 1524; and is in a 15th cent. M.S. at St. Gall (No. 440). *Daniel*, iv. 329, gives the text from a *Cistercian Brev.* without mentioning the date of the ed. he used. *Tr.* as :—

Through the long nave and full resounding aisles. By E. Caswall, in his *Masque of Mary*, 1858, p. 333, and again in his *Hys. & Poems*, 1873, p. 199. It is given in a few Roman Catholic hymn-books for Missions and Schools.   **[J. M.]**

Laurenti, Laurentius, s. of Herr Lorenz, or Laurenti, a burgess of Husum, in Schleswig, was b. at Husum, June 8, 1660. He entered the University of Rostock in 1681, and after a year and a half spent there, went to Kiel to study music. In 1684 he was appointed cantor and director of the music at the cathedral church at Bremen. He d. at Bremen, May 29, 1722 (*Koch*, iv. 281; Rotermund's continuation of Jöcher's *Gelehrten-Lexicon*, iii. 1405, &c.). Laurenti was one of the best hymn-writers of the Pietistic school. His hymns are founded on the Gospels for Sundays and Festivals, and they draw out the bearing on the Christian life of the leading thoughts therein contained. They are of noble simplicity; are Scriptural, fervent, and often of genuine poetical worth. In Freylinghausen's *G. B.*, 1704 and 1714, no less than 34 are included, and many of these, with others by him, are still in extensive German use. They appeared in his :—

Evangelia Melodica, das ist: Geistliche Lieder, und Lobgesänge, nach dem Sinn der ordentlichen Sonn- und Fest-tages Evangelien, &c. Bremen, 1700 [Royal Library, Berlin], with 148 hymns on the Gospels, and two others.

Of his hymns those which have passed into English are :—

i. **Du wesentliches Wort.** *Christmas.* Founded on St. John i. 1–12. In his *Evangelia Melodica*, 1700, p. 30, in 8 st. of 8 l., entitled, "For the Third Day of Christmas." Included in Freylinghausen's *G. B.*, 1704, No. 20; and, recently, as No. 83, in the Berlin *G. L. S.*, 1863. The *trs.* in C. U. are :—

1. **O Thou essential Word, Who from.** A good *tr.*, omitting st. iii., v., by Miss Winkworth, in her *Lyra Ger.*, 1st Ser., 1855, p. 15 (2nd ed., 1856, considerably altered); and repeated, abridged, in Flett's *Coll.*, Paisley, 1871. Varying centos, beginning with st. i., l. 5, altered to "O Saviour of our race," are found in America, as in Boardman's *Sel.*, Philadelphia, 1861; the Pennsylvania *Luth. Ch. Bk.*, 1868; and the Dutch Ref. *Hys. of the Church*, 1869.

2. **O Thou essential Word, Who wast.** By Miss Winkworth, in her *C. B. for England*, 1863, No. 54. This is her 1856 version (as above) re-written to the original metre. Repeated, in full, in Dr. Thomas's *Augustine H. Bk.*, 1866, and the Ohio *Luth. Hyl.*, 1880; and, abridged, in the Eng. Presb. *Ps. & Hys.*, 1867, and *Laudes Domini*, N. Y., 1884.

ii. **Ermuntert euch, ihr Frommen.** *Second Advent.* This is his finest hymn. In his *Evangelia Melodica*, 1700, p. 353, in 10 st. of 8 l., entitled, "For the 27th S. after Trinity." It is founded on St.

Matt. xxv. 1–13; and unites the imagery of the parable of the Ten Virgins with that of Rev. xx., xxi. Included, as No. 578, in Freylinghausen's *G. B.*, 1704; and, recently, as No. 1519, in the Berlin *G. L. S.*, ed. 1863. The *tr.* in C. U. is :—

Rejoice, all ye believers. By Mrs. Findlater, in *H. L. L.*, 1st Ser., 1854, p. 61 (1884, p. 62), a good *tr.* of st. i.–iii., vii., viii., x. In full, but altered to the original metre, in Schaff's *Christ in Song*, 1869 and 1870. This version is found in a large number of English and American hymnals, under the following forms :—

(1) **Rejoice, all ye believers** (st. i.). Varying centos are found in *Mercer*, 1864, *Hyl. Comp.*, 1876, &c.; and in America in Hatfield's *Church H. Bk.*, 1872, *Evang. Hymnal*, N. Y., 1880, and others.

(2) **Rejoice, rejoice, believers** (st. i. alt.). Varying centos are given in Alford's *Year of Praise*, 1867, English Presb. *Ps. & Hys.*, 1867, and in America in the Episc. *Hymnal*, 1871; *Hys. & Songs of Praise*, 1874; *Bapt. H. Bk.*, 1871; *Laudes Domini*, 1884; and others.

(3) **Rise up, all ye believers** (st. i. alt.). In J. A. Johnston's *English Hyl.*, 1856, and *Kennedy*, 1863.

(4) **Awake! rise up, ye faithful** (st. i. alt.). In the *New Zealand Hymnal*, 1872.

(5) **Ye saints, who here in patience** (st. vii.). In W. Stone's *Suppl. Hymnal*, 1873, and H. L. Hastings's *Songs of Pilgrimage*, 1886.

Other *trs.* are : (1) "Prepare your lamps, stand ready," by P. H. Molther of st. ii., as No. 857 in the *Moravian H. Bk.*, 1789 (1886, No. 1282). (2) "Awaken, O chosen and faithful," by *Mrs. Bevan*, 1858, p. 30.

iii. **Fliesst ihr Augen, fliesst von Thränen.** *Passiontide.* In his *Evangelia Melodica*, 1700, p. 94, in 12 st. of 8 l., entitled, "For Sunday Esto mihi" [*Quinquagesima*], and founded on St. Luke xviii. 31–43. Included in Freylinghausen's *G. B.*, 1704, No. 82, the Berlin *G. L. S.*, ed. 1863, No. 228, &c. The *tr.* in C. U. is :—

Flow my tears, flow still faster. By Mrs. Findlater, in *H. L. L.*, 2nd Ser., 1855, p. 48 (1884, p. 107), of st. i., iv., vi., viii.–xii. Repeated, omitting st. viii., ix., xii., altered, and beginning, "Flow my contrite tears, flow faster," in the Amer. Epis. *Hys. for Ch. and Home*, 1860.

Another *tr.* is : "Weep, mine eyes, with tears o'erflowing," by *Miss Manington*, 1863, p. 55.

The following hymns are not so well known in their translated forms :—

iv. **Jesu, was hat dich getrieben.** *Advent.* On Christ's journey to Jerusalem. 1700, p. i, in 8 st., entitled, "For the 1st S. in Advent," and founded on St. Matt. xxi. 1–10. In the Berlin *G. L. S.*, ed. 1863, No. 244. *Tr.* as : "Jesus! what was that which drew Thee," by Mrs. Findlater in *H. L. L.*, 1855, p. 31.

v. **Wach auf, mein Herz, die Nacht ist hin.** *Easter;* or, *Sunday Morning.* 1700, p. 138, in 10 st., entitled, "On the 1st day of Easter." Founded on St. Mark xvi. 1–8, and Eph. v. 14. In the *Unv. L. S.*, 1851, No. 484. The *trs.* are: (1) "Rouse up, my heart! the Night is o'er," by *H. J. Buckoll*, 1842, p. 3. (2) "Wake up, my heart, the night has flown," by *Miss Manington*, 1863, p. 68.

vi. **Wer im Herzen will erfahren.** *Epiphany.* 1700, p. 48, in 12 st. of 6 l., entitled, "For the day of the Epiphany of Christ, or Festival of the Three Holy Kings," and founded on St. Matt. ii. 1–12. Repeated in Freylinghausen's *G. B.*, 1704, No. 71 in full. In Bunsen's *Versuch*, 1833, No. 655 (1881, No. 62), st. i.–iii., xi., xii. are given. *Tr.* as: "Is thy heart athirst to know." A good *tr.* from Bunsen by Miss Winkworth in her *Lyra Ger.*, 2nd Ser., 1858, p. 22, and her *C. B. for England*, 1863, No. 39.   **[J. M.]**

Laus devota mente.

[*Common of Evangelists.*] This *Sequence* is found in a *Sarum Missal*, c. 1370, in the Bodleian (Barlow, 5, page 418); in a late 13th cent. *Gradual* in the British Museum (Add. 12194, f. 139); and is in the reprints of the *Sarum*, *Hereford* and *St. Andrews Missals*. In the *Sarum* and *Hereford* it is the *Sequence* in the Mass of the

Common of an Evangelist. In a MS. of the beginning of the 14th cent. in the Bodleian (*Junius* 121), it is ascribed to Gervasius of Chichester, who fl. 1160. *Tr.* as:—

1. **Wake hearts devout whom love inspires.** A *tr.* of st. i.-iii., viii., ix., by Mrs. H. M. Chester, made for and first pub. in the *Hymnary*, 1872, No. 394, and signed "H. M. C."

2. **Praise the true heart's offer.** By J. M. Neale, in the *St. Margaret's Hymnal*, 1875, the *Antiphoner and Grail*, 1880, and the *Hymner*, 1882.

Another tr. is :—
To Christ your voices raise. C. B. Pearson, in the *Sarum Missal in English*, 1868, and his *Sequences from the Sarum Missal*, 1871.   [Wm. C.]

Lavater, Johann Caspar, s. of Johann Heinrich Lavater, physician in Zürich, was b. at Zürich, Nov. 15, 1741. He entered the Academic Gymnasium at Zürich in 1758, and in the end of 1759 began his studies in its theological department. After completing his course he was ordained in the spring of 1762, but did not undertake any regular clerical work till April 1769, when he was appointed diaconus of the Orphanage church at Zürich, where he became pastor in 1775. In July 1778 he was appointed diaconus of St. Peter's church, and in Dec. 1786 pastor there. When, during the Revolutionary period, the French laid the Swiss Cantons under contribution, and then in April 1799 deported ten of the principal citizens of Zürich, Lavater felt compelled to protest in the pulpit and in print. Consequently while on a visit to Baden, near Zürich, he was seized by French dragoons, May 14, 1799, and taken to Basel, but was allowed to return to Zürich, Aug. 16, 1799. When on Sept. 25, 1799, the French under Masséna entered Zürich, Lavater was treacherously shot through the body by a French grenadier, who had just before thanked him for his charity, and from this wound he never entirely recovered. He resigned his charge in January 1800, and d. at Zürich, Jan. 2, 1801. (*Koch*, vi. 499; *Allg. Deutsche Biog.*, xvii. 783, &c.)

Lavater was one of the most celebrated and influential literary characters of his time; a most popular and striking preacher; and a lovable, genuine, frank-hearted man, who was the object of an almost incredible veneration. His devotional writings (*Aussichten in die Ewigkeit*, 4 vols., Zürich, 1768-78, &c.), and his works on Physiognomy (*Von der Physiognomik*, Leipzig, 1772; *Physiognomische Fragmente*, 4 vols., Leipzig and Winterthur, 1775-78), were eagerly read and admired all over Europe, but were very soon forgotten. He was no theologian, and his warm heart and fertile imagination led him into many untenable positions. His works on Physiognomy are without order or philosophical principles of connection, and their permanent interest is mainly in the very numerous and often well-executed engravings. Of his poems the *Schweizerlieder* (Bern, 1767, 4th enlarged ed., 1775), are the utterances of a true patriot, and are the most natural and popular of his productions. His Epic poems ((1) *Jesus Messias, oder die Zukunft des Herrn*, N.D., Zürich, 1780, a poetical version of the Apocalypse; (2) *Jesus Messias, oder die Evangelien und Apostelgeschichte in Gesängen*, 4 vols., Winterthur, 1783-86. (3) *Joseph von Arimathea*, Hamburg, 1794) have little abiding value.

As a hymn-writer Lavater was in his day most popular. His hymns are well adapted for private or family use. Many of them are simple, fresh, and popular in style, and evangelical, earnest and devout in substance. But for church use he is too verbose, prolix, and rhetorical. Of his hymns (some 700) a considerable number survive in German collections compiled before 1850, e.g. the Berlin *G. L. S.*, ed. 1840, has 13; the Württemberg *G. B.*, 1842, has 15 ; the Hamburg *G. B.*, 1842, has 23, &c.

But in the more recent collections almost all have disappeared, e.g., the new hymn-book for the Kingdom of Saxony, 1883, has not a single one. The most important appeared principally in the following works :—(1) *Funfzig Christlicher Lieder*, Zürich, 1771. (2) *Lieder zum Gebrauche des Waysenhauses zu Zürich*, Zürich, 1772. (3) *Christliche Lieder der Vaterländischen Jugend, besonders auf der Landschaft, gewiedmet*, Zürich, 1774. (4) *Zweytes Funfzig Christlicher Lieder*, Zürich, 1776. (5) *Christliche Lieder . . . Zweytes Hundert*, Zurich, 1780. (6) *Sechszig Lieder nach dem Zürcherischen Catechismus*, Zürich, 1780. [Nos. 1-6 in the Royal Library, Berlin, and 3-6 in the Brit. Mus.]

Those of his hymns which have passed into English include:—

i. **O du, der einst im Grabe lag.** *Sunday.* In his *Lieder*, &c., 1772, No. 7, in 9 st. of 4 l., entitled "Sunday Hymn." Included in the Zürich *G. B.*, 1787 and 1853; Bunsen's *Versuch*, 1833, No. 6, &c. The *tr.* in C. U. is :—
O Thou, once laid within the grave. A good *tr.*, omitting st. iii., vii., viii., by H. J. Buckoll, in his *Hys. from the German*, 1842, p. 9. Repeated, abridged, in the Dalston Hospital *H. Bk.*, 1848, and the Rugby School *H. Bk.*, 1850 and 1876.

Another tr. is : "O Thou who in the grave once lay," by R. Massie, in the *British Herald*, June, 1865.

ii. **O Jesus Christus, wachs in mir.** *Sanctification.* His finest hymn. Founded on St. John iii. 30. 1st pub. in his *Christliche Lieder*, 1780, No. 85, in 10 st. of 4 l., marked as "On New Year's Day, 1780," and with the motto "Christ must increase, but I must decrease." In Knapp's *Ev. L. S.*, 1837, No. 1644. The *tr.* in C. U. is :—
O Jesus Christ, grow Thou in me. A good and full *tr.* in the *British Messenger* for Nov. 1, 1860. In Schaff's *Christ in Song*, 1870, p. 108, it is marked as *tr.* by Mrs. E. L. Smith, the statement that this was its *first* appearance being an error. If the *tr.* is really by her, it must have appeared in some American publication prior to Nov. 1860. It has passed, in varying centos, into the *Baptist Hyl.*, 1879, Snepp's *Songs of G. & G.*, 1872, *Suppl.* of 1874 to the *N. Cong.*, and others : also in *Hys. & Songs of Praise*, N. Y., 1874, *Christian Hyl.*, Adelaide, 1872, &c.

iii. **O süssester der Namen all.** *Name of Jesus, or, New Year.* 1st pub. in his *Sechszig Lieder*, 1780, No. 25, in 4 st. of 7 l., as the second hymn on "Jesus Christ, the only begotten Son of God, our Lord. Second article of the Christian Faith." It is appointed for the 16th Sunday, and for the 39th and 40th questions of the *Zürich Catechism*. In the Berg Mark *G. B.*, 1835, No. 319; and included in a number of the German Roman Catholic *H. Bks.*, as those for St. Gall, 1863, Rottenburg, 1865, and others. The *tr.* in C. U. is :—
O Name, than every name more dear. A good *tr.* of st. i., iii., iv., by A. T. Russell, in his *Ps. & Hys.*, 1851, No. 68. Repeated in Maurice's *Choral H. Bk.*, 1861, *Meth. New Connexion H. Bk.*, 1863, *New Zealand Hyl.*, 1872, &c.

iv. **Vereinigt zum Gebete war.** *Whitsuntide.* 1st pub. in his *Christliche Lieder*, 1774, No. 23, in 15 st. of 4 l. The form *tr.* into English is that in Bunsen's *Versuch*, 1833, No. 225, which begins, "O Geist des Herrn! nur deine Kraft," and consists of st. x. ll. 3, 4 ; xi. ll. 1, 2 ; xii.-xv. The *tr.* is :—
O Holy Ghost! Thy heavenly dew. A good *tr.* from Bunsen, by Miss Cox, in her *Sacred Hys. from the German*, 1841, p. 43, and the Gilman-Schaff *Lib. of Rel. Poetry*, ed. 1883, p. 814. Slightly altered in *Lyra Messianica*, 1864, p. 386,

and thence in Alford's *Year of Praise*, 1867. Again slightly altered in Miss Cox's *Hys. from the German*, 1864, p. 67, and thence in J. L. Porter's *Coll.*, 1876.

Another tr. is: "Blest Spirit, by whose heavenly dew," by *Lady E. Fortescue*, 1843, p. 10.

The following are not in English C. U. :—

v. Ach! nach deiner Gnade schmachtet. *Cross and Consolation. Zweytes Funfzig*, 1776, No. 5, in 8 st., entitled "The Conflict of Prayer in hours of darkness." The *trs.* are: (1) "As the hart for water panteth, So my soul," by R. Massie, in the *British Herald*, March 1865, p. 40. (2) "Lord for Thee my soul is thirsting," by R. Massie, in the *Day of Rest*, 1877, vol. vii. p. 58.

vi. Auf dich, mein Vater, will ich trauen. *Cross and Consolation. Christliche Lieder*, 1774, No. 4, in 8 st., entitled "Encouragement to trust upon God." The *trs.* are: (1) "On Thee will I depend, my Father," by R. Massie, in the *British Herald*, May, 1865, p. 66. (2) "On Thee I build, O heavenly Father," by R. Massie, in the *Day of Rest*, 1878, vol. viii. p. 378.

vii. Von dir, o Vater, nimmt mein Herz. *Cross and Consolation. Funfzig Christlicher Lieder*, 1771, No. 33, in 15 st., entitled "Encouragement to Patience." *Tr.* as, "Father! from Thee my grateful heart," by Miss Knight, in her *Trs. from the German in Prose and Verse*, 1812, p. 89.

Besides the above a considerable number of pieces by Lavater have been *tr.* by Miss Henrietta J. Fry, in her *Pastor's Legacy*, 1842 (which consists entirely of *trs.* from Lavater); in her *Hys. of the Reformation*, 1845; and in her *Echoes of Eternity*, 1859.   [J. M.]

Lawson, John, was b. at Trowbridge, Wiltshire, July 24, 1787. He was articled to a wood-engraver in London; but believing that his knowledge of various manual arts might make him useful in the foreign mission field, he offered himself to the Baptist Missionary Society, and was sent to India. He arrived at Serampore in 1812, and soon rendered good service by showing how to reduce the types for printing used in the Eastern languages. He subsequently became pastor of a Baptist Church in Calcutta, devoting also much time to the work of education. He d. Oct. 22, 1825. Mr. Lawson was an accomplished naturalist and a good musician, but his favourite recreation was the composition of poetry. *Orient Harping, Roland*, and other poems were published by him between the years 1820 and 1825. Two of his hymns were printed in the Baptist *New Selection*, 1828 :—

1. Father of mercies, condescend. *Prayer for a Missionary.*

2. Fountain of truth and grace and power. *Prayer for the Jews.*

The following are in the *Comprehensive Rippon*, 1844 :—

3. While in the howling shades of death. *Missions.*

4. Europe, speak the mighty name. *Universal Doxology.*   [W. R. S.]

Lead, kindly Light, amid the encircling gloom. *Card. J. H. Newman.* [*Evening. Divine Guidance Desired.*] This exquisite lyric has been the cause of much controversy, arising from the facts that, first, the statement has been made that it was the passionate outpouring of the author's soul when perplexed with doubt as to his duty with regard to entering the Roman Communion or no; and the second, that the closing lines—

"And with the morn those angel faces smile,
Which I have loved long since and lost awhile,"

through their ambiguity, have led to several ingenious interpretations, some of which appeared in *Notes and Queries* in 1880. The answer to each of these statements must be given, as far as possible, in Cardinal Newman's own words.

i. Cardinal Newman, in his *Apologia Pro Vita Sua*, 1864, pp. 94–100, sets forth his attitude at the time this lyric was written, both towards the Church of England and the Church of Rome, in a most careful and elaborate manner. His statements, in a condensed form, but in his own words, are :—

"While I was engaged in writing my work on the Arians [1832], great events were happening at home and abroad, which brought out into form and passionate expression the various beliefs which had so gradually been winning their way into my mind. Shortly before, there had been a Revolution in France; the Bourbons had been dismissed: and I believed that it was unchristian for nations to cast off their governors, and, much more, sovereigns who had the divine right of inheritance. Again, the great Reform Agitation was going on around me as I wrote. The Whigs had come into power; Lord Grey had told the Bishops to set their house in order, and some of the Prelates had been insulted and threatened in the streets of London. The vital question was how were we to keep the Church from being liberalized? there was such apathy on the subject in some quarters, such imbecile alarm in others; the true principles of Churchmanship seemed so radically decayed, and there were such distractions in the Councils of the Clergy . . . . . . With the Establishment thus divided and threatened, thus ignorant of its true strength, I compared that fresh vigorous power of which I was reading in the first centuries . . . . . . I said to myself, 'Look on this picture and on that'; I felt affection for my own Church, but not tenderness; I felt dismay at her prospects, anger and scorn at her do-nothing perplexity. I thought that if Liberalism once got a footing within her, it was sure of the victory in the event. I saw that Reformation principles were powerless to rescue her. As to leaving her, the thought never crossed my imagination; still I ever kept before me that there was something greater than the Established Church, and that that was the Church Catholic and Apostolic, set up from the beginning, of which she was but the local presence and organ. She was nothing, unless she was this. She must be dealt with strongly, or she would be lost. There was need of a second Reformation.

"At this time I was disengaged from College duties, and my health had suffered from the labours involved in the composition of my volume . . . . . I was easily persuaded to join Hurrell Froude and his father, who were going to the south of Europe for the health of the former. We set out in December, 1832. It was during this expedition that my verses which are in the *Lyra Apostolica* were written; a few indeed before it; but not more than one or two of them after it . . . . . The strangeness of foreign life threw me back into myself; I found pleasure in historical sites and beautiful scenes, not in men and manners. We kept clear of Catholics throughout our tour . . . . . . I saw nothing but what was external; of the hidden life of Catholics I knew nothing. I was still driven back into myself, and felt my isolation. England was in my thoughts solely, and the news from England came rarely and imperfectly. The Bill for the Suppression of the Irish Sees was in progress, and filled my mind. I had fierce thoughts against the Liberals. It was the success of the Liberal cause which fretted me inwardly. I became fierce against its instruments and its manifestations . . . . . Especially when I was left to myself, the thought came upon me that deliverance is wrought, not by the many but by the few, not by bodies but by persons . . . . I began to think I had a mission . . . . When we took leave of Monsignore Wiseman, he had courteously expressed a wish that we might make a second visit to Rome: I said with great gravity, 'We have a work to do in England.' I went down at once to Sicily, and the presentiment grew stronger. I struck into the middle of the island, and fell ill of a fever at Leonforte. My servant thought that I was dying, and begged for my last directions. I gave them, as he wished; but I said 'I shall not die.' I repeated, 'I shall not die, for I have not sinned against light, I have not sinned against light.' I never have been able to make out at all what I meant. I got to Castro-Giovanni, and was laid up there for nearly three weeks. Towards the end of May I set off for Palermo, taking three days for the journey. Before starting from my inn in the morning of May 26th or 27th, I sat down oh my bed, and began to sob bitterly. My servant, who acted as my nurse, asked what ailed me. I could only answer, 'I have a work to do in England.' I was aching to get home; yet for want of a vessel I was kept at Palermo for three weeks. I began to visit the Churches, and they calmed my impatience, though I did not attend any services. I knew nothing of the Presence of the Blessed Sacrament then. At last I got off in an orange boat bound for Marseilles. We were becalmed a whole week in the Straits of Bonifacio. Then it was that I wrote the lines 'Lead, kindly light' [June 16, 1833], which have since become well known. I was writing verses the whole time of my passage. At length I got to Marseilles, and set off for England. The fatigue of travelling was too much for me, and I was laid up for several days at Lyons. At last I got off again and did not stop night or day till I reached England, and my mother's house. My brother had arrived from Persia only a few hours before. This was Tuesday. The following Sunday, July 14th, Mr. Keble preached the Assize Sermon in the University Pulpit. It was published under the title of 'National Apostasy.' I have ever considered and kept the day as the start of the religious movement of 1833."

In writing of further changes of thought which he underwent during the succeeding six years, Cardinal Newman says, *Apologia*, p. 214 :—

"Now to trace the succession of thoughts, and the conclusions, and the consequent innovations on my previous belief, and the general conduct, to which I was led, upon this sudden visitation [stated on the previous page]. And first, I will say, whatever comes of saying it, for I leave inferences to others, that for years I must have had something of an habitual notion, though it was latent, and had never led me to distrust my own convictions, that my mind had not found its ultimate rest, and that in some sense or other I was on journey. During the same passage across the Mediterranean in which I wrote 'Lead, kindly light,' I also wrote verses, which are found in the *Lyra* under the head of 'Providences,' beginning, 'When I look back.' This was in 1833; and, since I have begun this narrative, I have found a memorandum under the date of September 7, 1829, in which I speak of myself, as 'now in my room in Oriel College, slowly advancing, &c., and led on by God's hand blindly, not knowing whither He is taking me.' "

This, then, is the author's account of the state of his personal feeling, and the circumstances which surrounded him at the time that he wrote what must be regarded as one of the finest lyrics of the nineteenth century. Angry at the state of disunion and supineness in the Church he still loved and in which he still believed; confident that he had "a mission," "a work to do in England;" passionately longing for home and the converse of friends; sick in body to prostration, and, as some around him feared, even unto death; feeling that he should not die but live, and that he must work, but knowing not what that work was to be, how it was to be done, or to what it might tend, he breathed forth the impassioned and pathetic prayer, one of the birth-pangs, it might be called, of the Oxford movement of 1833 :—

"Lead, Kindly Light, amid the encircling gloom,
    Lead Thou me on;
The night is dark, and I am far from home,
    Lead Thou me on.
Keep Thou my feet; I do not ask to see
The distant scene; one step enough for me.
I was not ever thus, nor prayed that Thou
    Shouldst lead me on;
I loved to choose and see my path; but now
    Lead Thou me on.
I loved the garish day, and, spite of fears,
Pride ruled my will: remember not past years.
So long Thy power hath blest me, sure it still
    Will lead me on
O'er moor and fen, o'er crag and torrent, till
    The night is gone,
And with the morn those angel faces smile,
Which I have loved long since, and lost awhile."

ii. The ambiguity of the two closing lines has caused much speculation and controversy. Summarised, the principal interpretations are :—

1. The troubled and hesitating spirit finds itself "amid encircling gloom"; "the night is dark"; and the soul has lost awhile the "angel faces," not only of Fancy and Hope and Youthful Confidence, but of those divine forms of faith and assurance, which it had "loved long since," which had accompanied the believer during the early fervour of his belief.—*Notes and Queries, April* 3, 1880.

2. A second interpretation is that "those angel faces" are the faces of the ministering spirits, "sent forth to minister to them who shall be heirs of salvation."

3. A third interpretation is that these lines are expressive of the Christian's hope of being re-united on the resurrection morn with those loved and lost by death on earth. (*N. & Q., April* 3, 1880.) This application of the lines is set forth in a window of one of the churches of Clevedon. An angel is represented as soaring upwards, bearing away from earth two infants in his arms, and these two lines are quoted underneath. —*N. & Q., 6th S. II., Aug.* 7, 1880, p. 118.

4. A fourth interpretation is, "When all the absorbing business, and care and pleasures of life are beginning to weary us, when the world is losing something of its hold on us, and we once more catch glimpses as it were of that other life which most of us here at some time dreamed, and perhaps, though all too feebly, striven for, then the better soul wakes from its slumbers; the night is gone, "And with the morn those angel faces smile," &c.—*N. & Q., 6th S. I., May* 8, 1880, p. 385.

5. Another explanation is suggested in the question, "Do these lines refer to the more intimate communion of infants with the unseen world of spirits which was lost in later years?"—*N. & Q.*, 6th *S. I., June* 12, 1880, p. 480.

To all which, and to all other interpretations that have been made or may be made, Cardinal Newman gives answer in a letter to Dr. Greenhill, printed in the *Guardian*, Feb. 25, 1880, p. 257, and repeated in *N. & Q.*, 6th *S. I.*, March 20, 1880, p. 232.

"The Oratory, January 18, 1879.

"My dear Dr. Greenhill,—You flatter me by your questions; but I think it was Keble who, when asked it in his own case, answered that poets were not bound to be critics, or to give a sense to what they had written, and though I am not like him, a poet, at least I may plead that I am not bound to *remember* my own meaning, whatever it was, at the end of almost fifty years. Anyhow there must be a statute of limitation for writers of verse, or it would be quite tyranny if in an art, which is the expression, not of truth, but of imagination and sentiment, one were obliged to be ready for examination on the transient states of mind which came upon one when home sick, or sea sick, or in any other way sensitive, or excited.

"Yours most truly, JOHN H. NEWMAN."

We may add that in thus forgetting the meaning of a passage written so long before, the author is not alone. Coleridge, Goethe, and other poets have confessed to the same infirmity.

iii. The history of the publication of this lyric is very simple, the only noticeable feature being the changes in the motto which may be taken as setting forth the meaning Cardinal Newman attached to it at various periods in his history. It was first pub. in the *British Magazine*, March, 1834, with the motto "Faith-Heavenly Leadings;" again in *Lyra Apostolica*, 1836, p. 28, the motto reading, "Unto the godly there ariseth up light in the darkness": and again in the author's *Occasional Verses*, 1868, the motto being "The Pillar of the Cloud."

iv. Alterations in, and additions to, the text are not numerous. Bishop Bickersteth's additional stanza reads in the *Hy. Comp.*:—

" Meantime along the narrow rugged path,
    Thyself hast trod,
Lead, Saviour, lead me home in Child-like faith
    Home to my God,
To rest for ever after earthly strife
    In the calm light of everlasting life."

To this stanza Bishop Bickersteth has added this explanation in his *Notes* of 1876 :—

" The last verse, which is founded on the Collect for St. John the Evangelist's day, and which it is hoped will be found in unison with those that precede it, was added by the Editor from a sense of need and from a deep conviction that the heart of the belated pilgrim can only find rest in the Light of Light."

Alterations of the text are few. In Dr. Bonar's *Bible H. Bk.*, 1845, No. 116, it begins, " Lead, *Saviour*, lead, amid the encircling gloom " ; and " the garish day," is changed to " the *glare of* day." Two or three books have also adopted this reading. In the *Hys for Church and Home, Compiled by Members of the Protestant Episcopal Church*, Philadelphia, 1860, it begins, " *Send, Lord, Thy* light amid th' encircling gloom." " I loved the garish day," reads, " I loved *day's dazzling light* " ; and st. iii. ll. 1–4 :—

" So long Thy power hath *bless'd* me, *surely* still
    'Twill lead me on
Through dreary hours, through pain and sorrow, till
    The night is gone."

In the Unitarian *Hys. of the Spirit*, Boston, U. S. A., 1864, the original first line is restored ; " day's dazzling light " is retained ; and the lines above are repeated with " dreary hours" changed to dreary *doubts*." Another alteration is " *Send* kindly light," &c. (H. W. Beecher's *Plymouth Coll.*, 1855). The weakness of all these amendments is the surest safeguard against their general adoption.

The hymn has been rendered into several languages. The Latin versions are :—" O Lux benigna duce," by the Rev. H.M. Macgill, 1876; and " O Lux alma, bono protinus auspice," by the Rev. Jackson Mason, and " Alma Lux, inter media tenebras," by " C. G. G.," both in the *Guardian* of Jan. 3, 1883.   [J. J.]

Lead us, Heavenly Father, lead us. *J. Edmeston.* [*Holy Trinity—Invocation of.*] Appeared in his *Sacred Lyrics, set two*, 1821, in 3 st. of 7 l., and entitled " Hymn, Written for the Children of the London Orphan Asylum (Air Lewes)." In 1858 it was included in the Bap. *Ps. & Hys.*, No. 564, and from that date it has grown gradually into favour until it has attained to a foremost place amongst modern hymns in all English-speaking countries. It is generally given in a correct and complete form as in Thring's *Coll.*, 1882. It has been rendered into several languages, including Latin. The Rev. R. Bingham, in his *Hymno. Christ. Lat.*, 1871, has *tr.* it as " Duc nos, Genitor Coelestis."   [J. J.]

Leader of faithful souls, and Guide. *C. Wesley.* [*The Christian Race.*] Appeared in *Hys. for those that Seek, and those that Have Redemption*, 1747, No. 41, in 8 st. of 6 l., and entitled " The Traveller " (*P. Works*, 1868–72, vol. iv. p. 262). In 1776, Toplady included 7 st. in his *Psalms & Hys.* as No. 269, and from thence it passed into various collections of the Church of England, including Bickersteth's *Christian Psalmody*, 1833, and others. As found in the *Wes. H. Bk.*, 1780, No. 69, and later editions, and in the collections of

other Methodist bodies, st. v. and vii. are omitted. Its American use is great.   [J. J.]

Leaton-Blenkinsopp, Edwin Clennell, M.A., s. of G. Leaton-Blenkinsopp, was b. Jan. 1, 1819, and educated at University College, Durham (B.A. 1839, M.A. 1842). Taking Holy Orders, he was, in 1844, Curate of Ormskirk ; in 1851 Incumbent of St. James's, Lathom ; in 1855 Chaplain to the English Army in Turkey, at Algiers in 1859, and at the Fortifications of Portsmouth in 1862. In 1863 he became Rector of Springthorpe, Lincolnshire. Mr Leaton-Blenkinsopp has pub. *The Doctrine of Development in the Bible and in the Church*, 1869, and has contributed numerous papers to periodical literature. His original hymns, together with *trs.* from the Latin, appeared in *Lyra Messianica*, 1864 ; *Lyra Mystica*, 1865; and *The People's H.*, 1867. The *trs.* are annotated under their respective first Latin lines. His original hymns include :—

1. O noble martyr, thee we sing. *St. George.* In the *People's H.*, 1867.
2. The Tree of Life in Eden stood. *The Tree of Life.* In *Lyra Mystica*, 1865.
3. When Israel came from Egypt's land. *Whitsuntide.* In *Lyra Messianica*, 1864.

His signature is " E. L. B."   [J. J.]

Lebt ihr Christen, so allhier auf Erden. [*Following Christ.*] Founded on 2 Tim. iv. 7, 8, and included as No. 852 in Freylinghausen's *Neues geistreiches G. B.*, 1714, and repeated as No. 635 in the Berlin *G. L. S.*, ed. 1863.

Tr. as :—" O fear not, Christians, that rough path to tread," by Miss Cox, in *Lyra Eucharistica*, 1864, p. 370, and her *H. from the Ger.*, 1864, p. 97. [J. M.]

Lees, Jonathan, sprung from an old Nonconformist family in Lancashire, was b. at Manchester, Aug. 7, 1835. He was educated at Owens College and the Lancashire Independent College, and in 1861 went as Congregationalist Missionary to Tientsin, in North China, where he has since laboured.

Mr. Lees was one of a band of young men who, about the year 1852, began the first Sunday Evening Ragged School in England, in Sharp Street, Angel Meadow, Manchester. For use in this school he made a collection of hymns, which after a time was published as *Sacred Songs for Home & School* (*Bremner, Manchester.*) Nine or ten of these hymns were composed by Mr. Lees. During his residence in China he has pub. several collections of Temperance Melodies, the largest and most recent being entitled *Original & Selected Temperance Songs, together with Solos & Hymns, intended mainly for the use of Sailors in the Far East.* Shanghai, 1881. Fifteen of these, composed chiefly to popular secular tunes, are by Mr. Lees himself. Besides the hymns and songs contained in these books, about 20 other pieces have appeared on leaflets or in magazines. One, a missionary hymn commencing " They are coming ! they are coming ! " is in W. R. Stevenson's *School Hymnal*, where by mistake it is attributed to another author.

One of the most widely used of Christian Hymnals in the Chinese language was edited by Mr. Lees in 1872 (London Mission, Tientsin) ; and more recently he has prepared a smaller volume, consisting chiefly of translations of the more popular hymns in I. D. Sankey's collection. For particulars concerning these books see Article on **Missions, Foreign.**   [W. R. S.]

Leeson, Jane E. The earliest work by Miss Leeson with which we are acquainted

is her *Infant Hymnings*. Then followed
*Hymns and Scenes of Childhood, or A Sponsor's
Gift* (London, James Burns; Nottingham,
Dearden), 1842, in which the *Infant Hymnings*
were incorporated. Concerning Pt. ii. of the
Hys. and Scenes, &c., Miss Leeson says, "For
the best of the Poems in the second part, the
Writer is indebted to a friend." In the Rev.
Henry Formby's *Catholic Hymns arranged in
order for the principal Festivals, Feasts of
Saints, and other occasions of Devotion through-
out the Year*, Lond., Burns and Lambert, N.D.
[1851], "Imprimatur, N. Cardinalis Wiseman,
May 3rd, 1853," her *tr.* of *Victimae Paschali*
("Christ the Lord is risen to-day"), and her
"Loving Shepherd of Thy Sheep" (also in
Hys. & Scenes, 1842), were given under the
signature "M. L." Her *Paraphrases and
Hymns for Congregational Singing* (most of
which were re-written from the Scottish
Translations and Paraphrases (q.v.), 1781)
were pub. by Wertheimer & Co., Lond., in
1853. In the Irvingite *Hys. for the Use of the
Churches*, 1864, there are five of her original
hymns and four of her *trs.* from the Latin under
the signature of "J. E. L. ;" and most of these
were repeated in the 2nd ed., 1871. In
addition Miss Leeson is the author of several
other works, including *The Christian Child's
Book*, 1848, *The Child's Book of Ballads*, 1849,
Songs of Christian Chivalry, 1848, *Margaret,
a Poem*, 1850, *The Seven Spiritual Works of
Mercy*, and others. Her hymns in C. U.
include :—

1. **A little child may know.** *God's love of little
Children.* In *Hys. & S. of Childhood*, 1842, No. 20, in
5 st. of 4 l.
2. **Dear Saviour, to Thy little lambs.** *For Purity.*
In *Hys. & S. of Childhood*, 1842, No. 19, in 4 st. of 8 l.
3. **Father, I [we] love Thy house of prayer.** *Public
Worship.* In *Hys. & S. of Childhood*, 1842, No. 76, in
3 st. of 12 l. It is usually abbreviated.
4. **Have ye counted the cost?** *Soldiers of the Cross.*
In *Songs of Christian Chivalry*, 1848, p. 8, in 10 st. of
9 l. Usually abbreviated as in the *Enlarged London H.
Bk.*, 1873.
5. **In the dark and silent night.** *Confidence.* In
The Christian Child's Book, 1848, in 3 st. of 3 l., with
the refrain, "Hallelujah." It is in the Irish *Church
Hymnal*, 1873, and other collections.
6. **Jesus Christ, my Lord and King.** *Child's Praise
of Christ.* In *Hys. and S. of Childhood*, 1842, No. 18,
in 6 st. of 4 l.
7. **King of Saints and King of glory.** *All Saints.*
In her *Paraphrases & Hys.*, 1853, p. 84, in 2 st. of 8 l.
8. **Saviour, teach me day by day,** *Obedience.* In
Hys. & S. of Childhood, 1842, No. 49, in 4 st. of 8 l.
In several hymn-books in Great Britain and America.
9. **Songs of glory fill the sky.** *Christmas.* In the
Irvingite *Hys. for the Use of the Churches*, 1864, No. 21,
in 3 st. of 8 l., with the refrain "Hail! Lord Jesu."
10. **Stand we prepared to see and hear.** *Advent.* In
the Irvingite *Hys. for the Use of the Churches*, 1864,
No. 173, in 4 st. of 8 l. Written in 1860.
11. **Sweet the lesson Jesus taught.** *Christ
blessing little Children.* In *Hys. & S. of Childhood*,
1842, No. 1, in 5 st. of 4 l.
12. **Wake the song, O Zion's daughter.** A cento of
much excellence, which see.
13. **Wake, ye saints, the song of triumph.** *Ascension.*
Written in 1861, and pub. in the Irvingite *Hys. for the
Use of the Churches*, 1864, No. 60, in 4 st. of 6 l., with
the refrain "Hallelujah." In st. ii., ll. 3, 4, and 6 are
from C. Wesley's "Hail the day that sees Him rise."

Miss Leeson's most popular hymn, "Loving
Shepherd of Thy Sheep," and her *trs.* from
the Latin are noted elsewhere in this work.
Of Miss Leeson's personal history we can
gather nothing. B. 1807; d. 1882. [J. J.]

Lehr, Leopold Franz Friedrich, s. of
Johann Jakob Lehr, Hofrath at Cronenburg

(Cronberg, Kronberg), near Frankfurt-am-
Main, was b. at Cronenburg, Sept. 3, 1709,
and entered the University of Jena in 1729.
In 1730 he went to Halle to study under J. J.
Rambach and G. A. Francke; and here he
also acted as tutor to the children of J. A.
Freylinghausen, and conducted devotional
meetings at the Orphanage. In July 1731 he
became a tutor at Cöthen (Köthen) to the
princesses of Anhalt-Cöthen, and held this
post till 1740, when he was appointed diaconus
of the Lutheran church at Cöthen. While on
a visit to his father-in-law at Magdeburg he
was seized with fever, and d. there, Jan. 26,
1744. (*Koch*, vi. 446, &c.)

Lehr's hymns are full of love to Christ and of the
wonders of the redeeming grace of God. They are
allied to those of Allendorf (q.v.), and were also mostly
contributed to the *Cöthnische Lieder* (p. 50, ii.). of
which he was joint editor. In 1757 they were edited
along with his other poetical works as his *Himlisches
Vergnügen in Gott und Christo*, Halle, 1757. [Werni-
gerode Library] by Samuel Helmich, then court preacher
at Glückstadt, Holstein, who had married Lehr's widow.
Those which have passed into English are:—

i. **Mein Heiland nimmt die Sünder an.** *Lent*, or *The
Friend of Sinners.* Written in 1731 or 1732 as a companion to the hymn "Jesus nimmt die Sünder an"
[see **Neumeister**]. 1st pub. in the *Einige geistreiche
Lieder*, Cöthen, 1733, No. 9, in 11 st. of 10 l., entitled
"Luke xv. 2. This Jesus receiveth sinners and eateth
with them." Included in J. J. Rambach's *Haus G. B.*,
1735, No. 264, the Berlin *G. L. S.*, ed. 1863, No. 114, &c.
The *trs.* are:—

(1) "My Saviour sinners doth receive, Whom with
sin's." This is No. 217 in the *Moravian H. Bk.*, 1789.
In the ed. of 1886, No. 258 begins with st. viii., "Come,
all that heavy laden are." (2.) "My Saviour sinners
doth receive, Whom under burden," by Dr. John
Ker in the *United Presb. Juvenile Miss. Magazine*,
May, 1858.

ii. **So hab' ich nun den Fels erreichet.** *The Rock of
Ages.* 1733 as above, No. 4, in 6 st. of 10 l., entitled
"Is. xxvi. 4. The Lord is a rock for ever" (so Luther's
version). In Rambach's *Haus G. B.*, 1735, No. 303,
and the Berlin *G. L. S.*, ed. 1863. The *trs.* are:—

(1) "I now have found the Rock of Ages," by Dr.
H. Mills, 1845 (1856, p. 84). (2) "I have at last
attained the Rock," by *Miss Warner*, 1869, p. 34.

iii. **Was hinket ihr, betrogne Seelen.** *Confirmation.*
An exhortation to true and whole-hearted earnestness,
founded on 1 Kings xviii. 21. 1733 as above, No. 1, in
12 st. of 6 l., and the refrain "Hindurch." In J. J.
Rambach's *Haus G. B.*, 1735, No. 338, and the *Unv. L. S.*,
1851, No. 345. *Tr.* as:—

"Why haltest thus, deluded heart," by *Miss Winkworth*, 1855, p. 142 (1856, p. 143, beginning "Why halt
thus, O deluded heart").   [J. M.]

Leland, John, an American Baptist minister, was b. at Grafton, Massachusetts, on
May 15th, 1754, and began to preach at the
age of 20. From 1776 to 1790 he was in
Virginia, and thereafter in Massachusetts,
mostly at Cheshire. He d. Jan. 14, 1841.
His *Sermons, Addresses, Essays and Autobiography* were pub. by his niece, Miss L. F.
Greene, at Lanesboro, Massachusetts, in 1845.
His influence seems to have been equalled by
his peculiarities. We hear of his "restless
activity and roving disposition"; his "mad
devotion to politics," wherein he had much
local and temporary weight; his "ready wit
and endless eccentricities;" as also of his high
character. Of the hymns which have been
ascribed to him, some on doubtful authority,
the following are the most important :—

1. **The day is past and gone, The evening, &c.**
Evening. This is in universal American use, and
Leland's claim to the authorship has never been
disputed, although it is supported by no known
particulars. It was first made widely known

by the invaluable *Hartford Selection* (Congregational) of 1799. Its first appearance, so far as known, was in *Philomela, or, A Selection of Spiritual Songs*, by George Roberts, Petersburg,1792, No. 82.

2. **O when shall I see Jesus?** *The Christian Race.* This vigorous lyric is ascribed by Dr. Hitchcock, in *Hymns and Songs of Praise*, 1874, to Leland. It has generally been regarded as anonymous, and is of uncertain date, cir. 1807, or probably earlier.

3. **Christians, if your hearts are warm.** *Holy Baptism. Adult.* The only hymn by Leland which can be authenticated by date and circumstances is this familiar doggerel :—

"Christians, if your hearts are warm,
Ice and snow can do no harm."

Dr. Belcher says, in his *Historical Sketches of Hymns, &c.*, 1859, that it was written for one of Leland's large baptisms in Virginia, 1779.

[F. M. B.]

Leon, Johannes, was a native of Ohrdruf, near Gotha. He was for some time an army chaplain, then in 1557 pastor at Königsee (Schwarzburg - Rudolstadt), in 1560 at Gross-Mühlhausen, and in 1575 at Wölfis, near Ohrdruf. He d. at Wölfis, about Easter, 1597 (*Allg. Deutsche Biog.*, xviii. 298 ; *Wackernagel*, i. pp. 466, 654 ; iv. p. 490, &c.). Leon's hymns appeared principally in his (1) *Handbüchlin*, Frankfurt-am-Main, 1566, and (2) *Trostbüchlein.* The ed. printed at Nürnberg, 1611, has a preface of Dec. 9, 1588, so that the first ed. was probably 1589. His hymns are reprinted in *Wackernagel*, iv., Nos. 671–715. The only hymn ascribed to him which has passed into English is :—

Ich hab mein Sach Gott heimgestellt. *For the Dying.* *Wackernagel*, iv. p. 519, gives this, in 18 st. of 5 l., from the *Psalmen, geistliche Lieder und Kirchengesäng*, Nürnberg, 1589 ; with a long note, in which he traces all the st. save xi., xiv., xv., xvii., to Leon's *Trostbüchlein*, and to his *Leich-Predigten* [i.e. " Funeral Sermons "], 1581–82. *Mützell*, No. 347, cites it as in the *Psalmen, geistliche Lieder und Lobgesänge*, Strassburg, N.D., but apparently before 1587. In the Berlin *G. L. S.*, ed. 1863, No. 1460.

This hymn has been frequently ascribed to Dr. Johann Pappus [b. Jan. 16, 1549, at Lindau on the Lake of Constanz; 1571, professor of Hebrew at the University of Strassburg; d. at Strassburg, July 13, 1610]; but this ascription has not been traced earlier than about 1640, e.g. in the *Cantionale sacrum*, Gotha, pt. iii., 1648, No. 18, and the Königsberg *G. B.*, 1650, p. 530. Lauxmann, in *Koch*, viii. 609, thinks that Pappus may have arranged the hymn in its present form. It was probably suggested by a song beginning, " Ich hab meine Sach zu Gott gestellt," which *Wackernagel*, iii., Nos. 1242, 1243, quotes from a Leipzig broadsheet of 1555, and other sources.

This hymn has been *tr.* as :—

1. **My Life I now to God resign.** By J. C. Jacobi, in his *Psal. Ger.*, pt. ii., 1725, p. 56 (1732, p. 199), omitting st. vii., xv., xvi. Repeated in the *Moravian H. Bk.*, 1754, pt. i., No. 313 (1886, No. 1242, beginning with the *tr.* of st. viii., " Teach us to number so our days "), and in J. A. Latrobe's *Coll.*, 1841 and 1852. In the *Bible H. Bk.*, 1845, it begins with st. iii., "What is this life? a constant scene."

2. **My all I to my God commend.** A very good *tr.* of st. i., iii., vi., viii., x., xi., xiv., xvii., by A. T. Russell, as No. 246, in his *Ps. & Hys.*, 1851 ;

repeated, abridged, in Dr. Pagenstecher's *Coll.*, 1864, and *Kennedy*, 1863, No. 156. Dr. Kennedy, also gives a cento, beginning with the *tr.* of st. x., " Few are our days and sad below."

3. **My cause is God's, and I am still.** A good *tr.* of st. i., xi.–xiv., xvi.–xviii., by Miss Winkworth, in her *Lyra Ger.*, 2nd Ser., 1858, p. 210 ; repeated, omitting the *trs.* of st. xii., xvii., in her *C. B. for England*, 1863, No. 127. [J. M.]

Leslie, Emma. [Toke, Emma.]

Leslie, Mary Eliza, is daughter of Andrew Leslie, for many years Baptist missionary in Calcutta, was b. at Monghyr, Jan. 13, 1834, became a member of her father's church, and having received a superior education, was for eight years Superintendent of an Institution for the education of Hindoo young ladies. Since 1877 Miss Leslie has been engaged in various kinds of philanthropic work in Calcutta. Her publications include :—

(1) *Ina and Other Poems*, 1852.   (2) *Sorrows and Aspirations*, 1858.   (3) *Heart Echoes from the East ; or, Sacred Lyrics and Sonnets* (London, Nisbet, 1861).   (4) *The Dawn of Light ; a Story for Hindoo Women*, 1867.   (5) *Eastern Blossoms ; a Story for native Christian Women*, 1875.   (6) *A Child of the Day*, 1882.

In the *Heart Echoes from the East* is a lyric beginning "They are gathering homeward from every land (*Death contemplated*), which has been exceedingly popular, and has been reprinted in many forms. It is in W. R. Stevenson's *School Hymnal*, 1880. Several of Miss Leslie's lyrics and sonnets are very good, and worthy of the attention of hymn-book compilers. [W. R. S.]

Let all the world in every corner sing. G. Herbert. [*Praise to God, the King.*] First pub. posthumously in his *Temple*, in 1633, p. 45, in the following form :—

" ANTIPHONE.

" *Cho.* Let all the world in ev'ry corner sing,
        My God and King.

" *Vers.* The heavens are not too high,
         His praise may thither flie:
         The earth is not too low,
         His praises there may grow.

" *Cho.* Let all the world in ev'ry corner sing,
        My God and King.

" *Vers.* The church with psalms must shout,
         No doore can keep them out :
         But above all, the heart
         Must bear the longest part.

" *Cho.* Let all the world in ev'ry corner sing,
        My God and King."

Although admirably adapted for musical treatment, the original form of the text is not popular with modern editors. We have the original in Thring's *Coll.*, 1882 ; and in the *Hymnary*, 1872, the same, with the addition of a doxology. Usually the text is rearranged, sometimes, as in the S. P. C. K. *Church Hys.*, 1871 ; Horder's *Cong. Hys.*, 1884, &c. ; and again, in other collections in a different manner. This hymn is also in C. U. in America. [J. J.]

Let earth and heaven agree, Angels and men, &c. C. Wesley. [*Praise of Jesus as the Redeemer.*] Appeared in the *Hys. on God's Everlasting Love*, London, 1741, No. 11, in 10 st. of 6 l. (*P. Works*, 1868–72, vol. iii. p. 71). In whole or in part, it soon came into general use not only by the followers of the Wesleys, but also by many who, on Calvinistic grounds, opposed them, and against whom the *Hys. on God's Everlasting Love* were written. M. Madan included st. i.–iv. in his *Ps. & Hys.*, 1760, No. 90, and this form of the hymn was repeated by A. M. Toplady in his *Ps. & Hys.*, 1776 ; and again by others to modern hymn-books in the Church of England. Nonconformists also copied this form of the hymn. In the *Wes. H. Bk.*, 1780, st. i.–v., vii. and ix. were given as No. 33. This is the form of the hymn most popular in G. Britain and America. The following centos are also in C. U :—

1. **Jesus, harmonious Name.** Composed of st. iii. iv., vii. and ix., is in the American Andover *Sabbath H. Bk.*, 1858, and others.

2. **Jesus, transporting sound.** In the *Hymnary*, 1872, this is composed of st. ii.–iv., vi.–ix., x., considerably altered.

In G. J. Stevenson's *Methodist H. Bk. Notes*, 1883, p. 42, several interesting reminiscences of this hymn are recorded, mainly from Wesleyan sources. [J. J.]

Let Jacob to his Maker sing. *P. Doddridge.* [*God the Guide of Israel.*] 1st pub. in Job Orton's edition of Doddridge's (posthumous) *Hymns*, &c., 1755, No. 102, in 5 st. of 4 l., and again in J. D. Humphreys's edition of the same, 1839, No. 118. It is in C. U. in its full form in America, and also, beginning with st. ii. as "God knows our souls in all their fears," in the Boston *Church Pastorals*, 1864. [J. J.]

Let me alone [another] this only year. *C. Wesley.* [*Death Anticipated.*] Pub. in *Preparation for Death in Several Hymns*, 1772, No. 43, in 4 st. of 8 l. (*P. Works*, 1868–72, vol. vii. p. 396). In 1830 it was given in the supplement to the *Wes. H. Bk.* as "Let me alone *another* year"; and this has been repeated in a few collections. The hymn "Because for me the Saviour prays," in the American Meth. Episco. *Hymns*, 1849, No. 381, is from this hymn, and begins with the second half of st. i. with the lines transposed. [J. J.]

Let me be with Thee where Thou art. *Charlotte Elliott.* [*Heaven Anticipated and Desired.*] This hymn, which is usually attributed to the 1st ed. of Miss Elliott's *Hours of Sorrow*, &c., 1836, really appeared in her brother's Brighton *Ps. & Hys.*, 3rd thousand, 1839, No. 412, in 4 st. of 4 l., and signed "C. E." It was repeated, with slight alterations, in her *Hys. for a Week*, 1842 ; and again, slightly altered, in late editions of the *Invalid's H. Bk.* The text usually followed by modern editors is that of 1842, as in Lord Selborne's *Bk. of Praise*, 1862, where it is given with the change in st. iv., l. 3, of "life nor death" to "death nor life." The S. P. C. K. *Church Hymns*, 1871, is an exception in favour of several changes in the text, and *Kennedy's*, 1863, is the greatest departure from the original. The American books vary in their texts in common with those of G. Britain. [J. J.]

Let not your hearts with anxious thoughts. *William Robertson.* [*Ascension.*] First appeared as No. 14 in the Draft Scottish *Translations and Paraphrases*, 1745, as a version of John xiv. 1–5, in 6 st. of 4 l. In the *Draft* of 1781, No. 42, st. iii. was omitted; st. iv, rewritten; and st. i. slightly altered.

Thence, unaltered, in the public-worship ed. issued in that year by the Church of Scotland and still in use. In the markings by the eldest daughter of W. Cameron (p. **200**, ii.) the original is ascribed to Robertson, and the alterations in the 1781 text to Cameron. The revised text of 1781 is included in the Eng. Presb. *Ps. & Hymns*, 1867, and a few other collections. In Porter's *Selection*, Glasgow, 1853, it is altered to "Let not your hearts—'tis Jesus speaks," and in the *Twickenham Chapel Coll.*, 1845, p. 60, to "Let not your hearts be troubled now." [J. M.]

Let party names no more. *B. Beddome.* [*For Unity.*] 1st pub. in the Bristol Bap. *Coll.* of Ash and Evans, 1769, No. 360, in 4 st. of 4 l., entitled "Christian Love," and signed "B. B." It was also given in Beddome's (posthumous) *Hymns*, &c., 1817, No. 638, but with the title changed to "Communion of Saints." In some hymn-books it begins with st. ii., "Among the saints on earth"; and in others the opening line is changed to "Let *names of strife* no more." In its various forms it is in extensive use amongst Nonconformists, and especially in America. [J. J.]

Let saints on earth their anthems [voices] raise. *J. Evans.* [*Praise to Jesus as the Prince of Peace.*] Pub. in the 2nd ed. of Burder's *Coll. of Hymns*, 1784, No. 191, in 4 st. of 4 l., and headed "Prince of Peace." It is found in several modern hymn-books, as Spurgeon's *O. O. H. Bk.*, 1866 ; Snepp's *Songs of G. & G.*, 1872, and others. [J. J.]

Let songs of praises fill the sky. *T. Cotterill.* [*Whitsuntide.*] Pub. anonymously in his *Selection*, 8th ed., 1819, No. 229, in 4 st. of 6 l.; and again, with his name, in Montgomery's *Christian Psalmist*, 1825, No. 291. It is in C. U. in most English-speaking countries, and sometimes reduced to c.m. as in the *New Cong.*, 1859 and 1874. [J. J.]

Let such as would with wisdom dwell. *William Cameron.* [*Godly Sorrow.*] First appeared as No. 14 in the Draft Scottish *Translations and Paraphrases*, 1781, as a version of Eccles. vii. 2–6, in 5 st. of 4 l. In the public worship ed. issued in that year by the Church of Scotland and still in use, st. i. was reversed, ll. 1, 2 being given as ll. 3, 4; and ll. 3, 4 rewritten, so that it began "While others crowd the house of mirth;" ll. 1, 2 of st. ii. being also rewritten, and ll. 1, 3 of st. iii. altered. In the markings of the *Trs. & Paraphs.* by the eldest daughter of W. Cameron (p. **200**, ii.) it is ascribed to Cameron. The revised text of 1781 is included in the *United Presb. H. Bk.*, 1852, Porter's *Selection*, Glasgow, 1853, and a few other collections. [J. M.]

Let the world lament their dead. *C. Wesley.* [*Burial.*] Appeared in *Hys. & Sac. Poems*, 1742, in 6 st. of 8 l. (*P. Works*, vol. ii. p. 186). In the *Wes. H. Bk.*, 1780, st. iv.–vi. were given as No. 57: "Jesus, faithful to His word," and this abbreviated form of the hymn has been repeated in several collections, and is still in C. U. [J. J.]

Let there be light! Thus spake the Word. *J. Montgomery.* [*Missions.*] This hymn was printed in the *Evangelical Magazine,* June, 1818, in 8 st. of 4 l., and headed "Hymn composed for the Anniversary of the Missionary Society by J. Montgomery, Esq., and sung at Spa Fields Chapel, May 14th, 1818." It was included in Cotterill's *Sel.,* 8th ed., 1819, No. 236, in 4 st. of 8 l. In Montgomery's *Christian Psalmist,* 1825, No. 554, st. iv. is omitted, and the rest are divided into 6 st. of 4 l. This form is repeated in his *Original Hymns,* 1853, No. 260, is the revised text, and is in several collections in G. Britain and America. The hymn "From day to day, before our eyes," in Beecher's *Plymouth Coll.,* 1855, the N. Y. *Songs for the Sanctuary,* 1865, and other American hymn-books, is composed of st. iv.–viii. of the *Evangelical Magazine* text of 1818. (*Cotterill's* st. iii., iv.). [J. J.]

Let us ask the important question. *J. Hart.* [*Passiontide.*] Pub. in his *Hymns,* &c., 1759, No. 56, in two parts, the second being "Great High Priest, we view Thee stooping," and headed "Faith and Repentance." Pt. i., in 5 st. of 8 l., asks and answers the important question, "What is it to be a Christian?" and Pt. ii., in 3 st. of 8 l., is a Prayer based upon the answer given in Pt. i. Both parts are in C. U., but the second ("Great High Priest, &c."), which is by far the finer of the two, is also by far the more popular. It is in several collections in G. Britain and America.   [J. J.]

Let us love, and sing, and wonder. *J. Newton.* [*Praise for Redeeming Love.*] Appeared in his *Twenty Six Letters on Religious Subjects, by Omicron,* 1774, in 6 st. of 6 l., and headed, "Praise for Redeeming Love." It was also given in the *Gospel Magazine,* May, 1774, and in the *Olney Hymns,* 1779, Bk. iii., No. 82. It is in C. U. in G. Britain and America, and sometimes in an abbreviated form.   [J. J.]

Let us praise God this day. [*The Annunciation.*] Included anonymously in *Hys. for the Festivals and Saints Days of the Church of England,* Oxford, 1846. It was repeated, with the addition of a doxology, in Stretton's *Church Hys.,* 1850, in Johnston's *English Hyl.,* 1852, and other collections. The text of *H. A. & M.,* 1875, is from Fallows's *Sel.,* 1847. In addition to the original, two altered forms of the text are in C. U. :—

1. **Praise we the Lord this day.** This slightly altered text was given in Murray's *Hymnal,* 1852; the *Salisbury H. Bk.,* 1857 ; *Kennedy* (with new doxology), 1863 ; the S. P. C. K. *Church Hys.,* 1871, &c. The last-named has *Murray's text* with the omission of st. iii.

2. **O praise the Lord this day.** This text in the *Hymnary,* 1872, is somewhat freely altered, and is in limited use.   [J. J.]

Let us sing the King Messiah. *J. Ryland.* [*Praise to Christ as King.*] This fine paraphrase of Ps. xlv., in 7 st. of 6 l., is dated by Dr. Ryland's son "July 31st 1790" [s. MSS.]. It appeared in *Hymns Included for the Use of the United Congregations of Bristol at their Monthly Prayer Meetings for the Success of the Gospel at Home and Abroad, begun in* 1797, Bristol, 1798. The Preface is dated Feb. 26, 1798, and is signed by eight ministers of whom Dr. Ryland is first on the list. This hymn was given, with omissions, in the Bap.

New Selection, 1828 ; and subsequently in numerous collections in G. Britain and America. The original text is given in Ryland's *Pastoral Memorials,* 1825, and in D. Sedgwick's reprint of Ryland's *Hymns,* 1862.   [W. T. B.]

Let us the sheep in Jesus named. *J. Cennick.* [*Praise to Jesus, the Good Shepherd.*] Pub. as a "Hymn of Praise in a Dialogue," in his *Sacred Hys. for the Use of Religious Societies,* Bristol, 1743, Pt. i., No. iv., in 5 st. of 4 l. ; and again, in the same year, in his *Sacred Hys. for the Children of God in the Days of their Pilgrimage,* Lond., 1743. This, in common with all Dialogue hymns with the Moravians, was sung antiphonally, the men taking the first half of each verse, and the women the second. The opening stanzas of this hymn are thus printed for antiphonal singing:

1. " Let us the Sheep in Jesus nam'd,
   Our Shepherd's Mercy bless :
   *Let us, whom Jesus hath redeem'd,
   Shew forth our Thankfulness.*

2. " Not unto us! to Thee alone,
   Bless'd Lamb, be Glory giv'n ;
   *Here shall Thy Praises be begun,
   But carried on in Heaven.*"

In its original form this hymn is unknown to the modern collections, but, beginning with st. ii., as :—

    " Not unto us ! but Thee alone,
      Bless'd Lamb, be glory given,"

it appeared in Rippon's *Bap. Sel.,* 1787, No. 384, and is found in several modern hymnals in G. Britain and America, including the Bap. *Ps. & Hys.,* 1858 and 1880, Spurgeon's *O. O. H. Bk.,* 1866, and others. The first stanza of the hymn, "Not unto us but to Thy name" (q.v.), is also from this hymn.   [W. T. B.]

Let us with a gladsome mind. *J. Milton.* [*Ps. cxxxvi.*] This paraphrase of Ps. 136 was written according to his biographers, Warton and Mitford, in 1623, when Milton was fifteen, and attending St. Paul's School, London. It appeared in his *Poems in English and Latin,* 1645 (2nd ed. 1673), in 24 st. of 2 l., with the refrain—

    " For His mercies aye endure,
      Ever faithful, ever sure."

In its full form it is not in C. U., but numerous abbreviations, all beginning with the opening stanza, are in use in all English-speaking countries. Another arrangement in L. M., and without the refrain, is given in Martineau's *Hymns,* 1840, No. 100, as " O let us, with a joyful mind." Sir H. W. Baker's version of Ps. cxxxvi., "Praise, O praise our God and King"; H. Trend's "Praise, O praise our heavenly King," in Skinner's *Daily Service Hymnal,* 1864, the *People's H.,* 1867, and others; and T. Darling's "Come, and let us praises sing," in his *Hymns,* 1887, are all based upon Milton's text.   [J. J.]

Let worldly minds the world pursue. *J. Newton.* [*Dedication of self to God.*] Pub. in R. Conyers's *Ps. & Hys.,* 1774, No. 180, and again in the *Olney Hymns,* 1779, Bk. iii., No. 59, in 6 st. of 4 l., and headed " Old things are passed away." It is in C. U. in its full form, and also abbreviated, beginning with st. iii., "As by the light of opening day." This abridged text is more popular than the full form of the hymn. It was given in Bicker-steth's *Christian Psalmody*, 1833, and is found in several modern hymn-books.   [J. J.]

Let Zion's watchmen all awake.
P. Doddridge. [*Ordination—Ember Days.*] Written at " Floor, Oct. 21, 1736 " [D. MSS.], in 5 st. of 4 l. This is Floore in North-amptonshire, and the hymn was written for the ordination of a Minister, probably for that place. It was pub. in Job Orton's ed. of Doddridge's (posthumous) *Hymns*, &c., 1755, No. 324; and again in J. D. Humphreys's ed. of the same, 1839, No. 350. Its use is ex-tensive, especially in America.   [J. J.]

Lewers, Jane. [Gray, Jane.]

Lewis, George, D.D., of Llanuwchllyn, was b. at Trelech, Caermarthenshire, in 1762. His parents were members of the Established Church, but he became a minister of the Independents. He was a learned man, and highly respected by all who knew him. He is the author of several works of great value, and the hymn " Rhyfedd na buaswn 'nawr " was composed by him. He d. in 1822.
                                       [W. G. T.]

Lie down, frail body, here. *H. Bonar.* [*Burial.*] Appeared in his *Hys. of Faith and Hope*, 1st series, 1857, in 13 st. of 4 l., and entitled, " The Flesh resting in Hope." It is given in an abridged form in a few collec-tions, including Dale's *English H. Bk.*, 1874. From it also is taken the cento " Rest for the toiling hand."   [J. J.]

Liebe die du mich zum Bilde. *J. Scheffler.* [*The Love of Christ.*] No. 107, in Bk. iii., 1657, of his *Heilige Seelenlust* (*Werke*, 1862, i. p. 180), in 6 st. of 6 lines, entitled, " She [the Soul] surrenders herself to the Everlasting Love." Included as No. 35 in the Berlin *G. L. S.*, ed. 1863, with an additional st. as iv., " Liebe die du Kraft und Leben," added when the hymn was given in the *Geist-reiches G. B.*, Halle, 1697, p. 184.

" It is one of the most beautiful and profound hymns of the spiritual love of the soul to her Saviour," says Lauxmann in *Koch*, viii. 290. Wetzel, in his *A. H.*, ii. 771–776, relates that one evening in 1722 Benjamin Schultze, a German missionary at Madras, sang it from *Freylinghausen*, and was so delighted with it that he determined that his Malabar scholars should share his pleasure. That evening he translated verse after verse, not resting till he had finished it two hours after midnight. The success he attained led him to translate 103 hymns from the German which are still sung in South India.

Translations in C. U. :—
1. **Lord, Thine image Thou hast lent me.** By J. C. Jacobi, in his *Psal. Germanica*, 1720, p. 1, in 7 st. It is one of his best *trs.* It was slightly altered in his ed. 1722, p. 33, and again in his ed. 1732, p. 56 ; and thence in the *Moravian H. Bk.*, 1754, Lady Huntingdon's *Selection*, 1780, and Dr. Pagenstecher's *Coll.*, 1864. St. i., iii., iv., vii., were included in the Pennsylvanian Luth. *Ch. Bk.*, 1868, and the Ohio Luth. *Hyl.*, 1880. In the *Moravian H. Bk.*, 1789 (No. 21), it was considerably altered, and began, " In Thine image, Lord, Thou mad'st me." A cento in 5 st. of 4 l., beginning, " Love divine ! I would adore Thee," is in the Roxburgh Place *Coll.*, Edinburgh, 1824 ; and sts. i.–iv., slightly altered from the 1826 Mo-ravian, are in the Dalston Hospital *H. Bk.*, 1848.
2. **In Thine image Thou didst make us.** As

No. 54 in the Cooke-Denton *Hymnal*, 1853, in 3 st. of 6 l., and a doxology. It is based on Jacobi, but is entirely rewritten by Canon Cooke. This was repeated, unaltered, in the *Salisbury H. Bk.*, 1857, *New Zealand Hyl.*, 1870 *Parish H. Bk.*, 1875, and, slightly altered, in the *Sarum Hyl.*, 1868.

3. **O Love, Who formedst me to wear.** An exceedingly good *tr.* in 7 st. by Miss Winkworth in her *Lyra Ger.*, 2nd Ser., 1858, p. 96, and as No. 47 in her *C. B. for England*, 1863. This has come into extensive use, and is included in full in the *New Zealand Hyl.*, 1870, and in Schaff's *Christ in Song*, 1869, p. 414. In 1861 it was included, slightly altered and with the omission of st. iv., v., in *H. A. & M.*, and repeated in the revised ed. of 1875, and other hymnals. Other centos are in the *People's H.*, 1867 ; Horder's *Cong. Hyl.*, 1884, &c.

Other trs. are :—(1) " Love divine ! 'neath human feature," in the *Christian Treasury*, 1858, p. 155. (2) " Loved One ! who by grace hast wrought me," by Mrs. Findlater, in *H. L. L.*, 1862, p. 40 (1884, p. 207). (3) " Love, Who in the first beginning," by *Miss Cox*, 1864, p. 201 ; repeated in the *Moravian H. Bk.*, 1886. (4) " Love, which in Thine image made me," by R. Massie, in the *British Herald*, Nov. 1865, p. 168, and Reid's *Praise Bk.*, 1872.   [J. M.]

Liebich, Ehrenfried, was b. July 15, 1713, at Probsthain, near Goldberg, Silesia, where his father was a miller. He assisted his father in the mill up to his sixteenth year, and was thereafter allowed to study at the Latin school at Schweidnitz, and the St. Eli-sabeth school at Breslau. At Easter, 1738, he entered the University of Leipzig as a student of Theology, and on concluding his course in 1740, was for some time engaged in private tuition. In April, 1742, he became pastor at Lomnitz and Erdmannsdorf, near Hirschberg, Silesia, and remained there till his death on June 23, 1780 (*Koch*, vi. 391 ; *Allg. Deutsche Biog.*, xviii. 584, &c.).

Liebich is one of the best German hymn-writers of the middle of the 18th century; Scriptural, heartfelt, and good in style, always edifying, if sometimes too didactic. He had begun hymn-writing about 1749, and contributed 8 hymns to the Hirschberg *G. B.*, 1752. A copy of this book fell into the hands of C. F. Gellert during a visit to Carlsbad in 1763, and through his encourage-ment Liebich began again to compose hymns. He pub. his compositions as : (1) *Geistliche Lieder und Oden*, &c., Hirschberg and Leipzig, 1768, with 142 hymns. (2) New ed., Liegnitz, 1773 ; with a second part, en-titled, *Geistliche Lieder zur Erbauung*, Liegnitz, 1774, with 94 hymns.

A considerable number of his hymns passed into German C. U., and still hold their place. Those which have been *tr.* into English are :—

i. **Dir, dir, du Geber aller Gaben.** *Harvest Thanks-giving.* 1768, p. 128, in 16 st. of 6 l., entitled, " The Goodness of God in the Harvest." This has passed into English through the following forms.

1. **O dass doch bei der reichen Ernte.** This is st. xi.–xvi., as altered by J. S. Diterich, in the Berlin *G. B.*, 1780, No. 172 ; repeated in the Berlin *G. L. S.*, ed. 1863. From this form the recasts of st. xii.–xvi., beginning, " Kommt, Christen, Gottes Huld zu feiern," were included, as No. 250, in Bunsen's *Versuch*, 1833, and *tr.* as :

Come, Christians, praise your Maker's goodness. A good *tr.* from *Bunsen*, by Miss Winkworth, as No. 181, in her *C. B. for England;* repeated in the Ohio *Evang. Luth. Hyl.* 1880.

2. **Wir kommen deine Huld zu feiern.** This is a

very greatly altered form of st. xii. ff., as No. 850, in the Berlin *G. B.*, 1829; retaining little either from Liebich or Diterich. It is repeated in Bunsen's *Versuch*, 1833, No. 666, and the Württemberg *G. B.*, 1842, No. 543. The *tr.* in C. U. from this form is:—

We come, our hearts with gladness glowing. A good *tr.* from the text of 1829, by Miss Cox, in her *Sacred Hys. from the German*, 1841, p. 199; repeated, abridged, in the American Unitarian *Hys. for the Ch. of Christ*, Boston, 1853, and in Archdeacon Pott's *Coll.*, 1861.

Another tr. is : "O Lord, Thy goodness we adore," by *Lady E. Fortescue*, 1843, p. 29.

ii. Gott ist getreu! Sein Herz, sein Vaterherz. *Trust in God*. 1768, p. 181, in 9 st. of 9 l., entitled, "The faithful God, 1 Cor. x. 13." It is a beautiful hymn, and has been specially appreciated in Württemberg, where it is found in the Württemberg *G. B.*, 1791, No. 24 (1842, No. 45). Lauxmann, in *Koch*, viii. 416, says it was the favourite hymn of J. C. F. Steudel, Professor of Theology at Tübingen, who d. 1837; was sung by the Württemberg contingent at a field service near Toul, in August, 1870, during the Franco-German War, &c. The *trs.* are :—

1. Our God is true! Them He will ne'er forsake. In full, by Dr. H. Mills, in his *Horae Ger.*, 1845 (1856, p. 182); repeated, abridged, in the Amer. Luth. Gen Synod's *Coll.*, 1852, and the Ohio *Evang. Luth. Hyl.*, 1880.

2. My God is true! His heart, a Father's heart. A good and full *tr.* by R. Massie, in his *Lyra Domestica*, 2nd Ser., 1864, p. 119; repeated, in full, in Reid's *Praise Bk.*, 1872; and abridged in the *Ibrox Hyl.*, 1871.

iii. Hier ist mein Herz! Mein Gott, ich geb' es dir. *Self-surrender to God*. 1768, p. 79, in 9 st. of 9 l. (ll. 1, 9 of each st. being "Hier ist mein Herz"), entitled, "Surrender of the heart to God," and suggested by Proverbs xxiii. 26. Included, as No. 763, in the Berlin *G. L. S.*, ed. 1863. *Tr.* as:—

Here is my heart! my God I give it Thee. A good *tr.*, omitting st. iv., by Mrs. Findlater, in *H. L. L.*, 1st Ser., 1854, p. 16 (1884, p. 21). Included, in full, in Boardman's *Sel.*, Philadelphia, U.S., 1861; *Lyra Eucharistica*, 1863 and 1864, &c. The *trs.* of st. i.–iii., v., reduced to 6 8's, and beginning, "Here is my heart, I give it Thee," were included in the American *Sabbath H. Bk.*, 1858; and, repeated, omitting st. ii., in the *Christian H. Bk.*, Cincinnati, 1865.

iv. So bringen wir den Leib zur Ruh. *Burial*. 1774, p. 204, in 12 st., entitled, "At the burial of a corpse." In the Bavarian *G. B.*, 1854, No. 229, beginning "*Nun bringen wir.*" *Tr.* as, "This body, weary and distressed," by Dr. H. Harbaugh, in the German Reformed *Guardian*, June, 1863, p. 187. [J. M.]

Liebster Immanuel, Herzog der Frommen. [*Love to Christ*.] Included in Dr. Ahasuerus Fritsch's *Himmels-Lust*, 2nd ed., 1679 [Leipzig Town Library; not in 1st ed., 1670], No. 36, p. 343, in 5 st. of 6 l., entitled "The everwished for sweet Jesus." The hymn has been ascribed to Fritsch (b. Dec. 16, 1629, at Mücheln on the Geissel near Merseburg; became, 1657, tutor to Count Albert Anton of Schwarzburg-Rudolstadt; d. Aug. 24, 1701, as Chancellor and President of the Consistory at Rudolstadt), but on no clear

evidence. In the Berlin *G. L. S.*, ed. 1863, No. 1342. In the *Geistreiches G. B.*, Halle, 1697, p. 160, and many later books, it begins, "Schönster Immanuel." The *tr.* in C. U. is :—

Dearest Immanuel, Prince of the lowly. A *tr.* of st. i.–iv., by M. W. Stryker, as No. 183 in his *Christian Chorals*, 1885. [J. M.]

Liebster Jesu! du wirst kommen. [*Advent*.] Included in the *Geistreiches G. B.*, Halle, 1697, p. 257, in 10 st. of 5 l. Repeated in Porst's *G. B.*, 1713 (ed. 1855, No. 561, ascribed to Christoph Pfeiffer, who was only born in 1689). The *tr.* in C. U. is :—

Jesus, Saviour, once again. A good but rather free *tr.* of st. i.–iii., v., vii., by Miss Dunn in her *H. from the Ger.*, 1857, p. 47. Repeated in full in Dr. Pagenstecher's *Coll.*, 1864; and, omitting st. iii., in Curwen's *Sabbath H. Bk.*, 1859.

Another tr. is :—"Precious Jesus! Thy returning." in the *British Herald*, Oct. 1866, p. 344, and Reid's *Praise Bk.*, 1872, No. 238. [J. M.]

Liebster Jesu wir sind hier Deinem Worte nachzuleben. *B. Schmolck*. [*Holy Baptism*.] 1st pub. in his *Heilige Flammen* (ed. 1709, No. 115, p. 180, apparently first in the 3rd ed., 1706), in 7 st. of 6 l., entitled "Seasonable Reflections of the sponsors on their way with the child to Baptism." Included in many German collections, and recently as No. 462 in the Berlin *G. L. S.*, ed. 1863. *Tr.* as :—

1. Jesus, Lord, Thy servants see. A good *tr.*, omitting st. iv., by Miss Cox in her *Sacred H. from the Ger.*, 1841, p. 63 (1864, p. 73). Repeated in full in Mercer's *C. P. & H. Bk.* 1857; and, abridged, in Mercer's Ox. ed., 1864, Rorison's *H. & Anthems*, 1851, and the *Wes. H. Bk.*, 1875.

2. Blessed Jesus, here we stand. A good *tr.*, omitting st. iv., by Miss Winkworth in her *Lyra Ger.*, 2nd Ser., 1858, p. 86 (in her *C. B. for England*, 1863, No. 90). Included in the *Scottish Hyl.*, 1869, &c.; and, in America, in the Pennsylvanian Luth. *Ch. Bk.*, 1868, *Presb. Hyl.*, 1874, &c. According to Kübler (*Hist. Notes to Lyra Ger.*, 1865, p. 220), this version was sung, April 27, 1863, at the baptism of the Princess Victoria of Hesse at Windsor Castle.

3. Blessed Jesus, we are here. A good *tr.*, omitting st. v., by Dr. Kennedy, as No. 234 in his *Hymn. Christiana*, 1863.

4. Blessed Lord, Thy servants see. This is No. 166 in Dr. Allon's *Suppl. Hys.*, 1868, and consists of *trs.* of st. i., vi., altered from *Miss Cox*, and of st. vii., altered from *Miss Winkworth*. Repeated in Dr. Dale's *Eng. H. Bk.*, 1874, Horder's *Cong. Hys.*, 1884, &c.

5. Dearest Jesus! we are here, On Thy tender grace relying. In full, by Dr. M. Loy, as No. 222 in the Ohio *Lutheran Hyl.*, 1880.

Other trs. are :—(1) "O blessed Saviour! here we meet," by *Lady E. Fortescue*, 1843, p. 20. (2) "According to Thy Gospel, we," by *Dr. G. Walker*, 1860, p. 34. (3) "Following Thy words of grace," as No. 945 in the *Moravian H. Bk.*, 1886. [J. M.]

Life is the time to serve the Lord. *I. Watts*. [*Life for God*.] 1st pub. in his *Hys. & S. Songs*, in the 2nd ed., 1709, Bk. i., No. 88, in 6 st. of 4 l., and headed "Life the Day of Grace and Hope." It is found in a few modern collections. In the authorized issue of the Scottish

Translations and Paraphrases, 1781, No. xv., on Eccl. ix. 4, &c., it is recast as :—

" As long as life its term extends,
Hope's blest dominion never ends."

In the markings of the *Trans. & Paraphs.*, by the eldest daughter of W. Cameron (q.v.), this recast is attributed to Cameron. Its use is very extensive. [J. J.]

Life nor death shall us dissever. *Bp. R. Heber.* [*Easter.*] Pub. in his posthumous *Hymns*, &c., 1827, p. 79, in 3 st. of 4 l. It is based on the Gospel for the 5th S. after Easter, and is found in several modern hymnbooks, including Dale's *English H. Bk.*, 1874, and others. [J. J.]

Lift it gently to the steeple. *J. M. Neale.* [*Dedication of Bells.*] Written in 1865 for an Office for the Benediction of a Bell, compiled by Dr. Neale, for the Benediction of one at Bampton-Aston, Oxon, by the late Bishop of Oxford [Wilberforce]. In 1866 it was included in Dr. Neale's *Original Sequences, Hymns, and other Ecclesiastical Verses*, p. 81, in 10 st. of 4 l., and supplemented by the following note :—

" The above hymn is taken from an Office for the Benediction of a Bell, compiled by the writer for that of one, by the Bishop of Oxford, at Aston-Bampton, Oxon [No, it was Bampton-Aston]; the first example, it is believed, of such a service, if not since the Reformation, at all events since Caroline times. It was again used by the Bishop of Salisbury, at the Benediction of the newly recast Wolsey bell, at Sherborne Minster.

This hymn has also been rearranged as, "Now at length our bells are mounted" (st. ix. slightly altered being placed as st. i.), so as to make it suitable for singing after the bells are fixed and ready to be rung. [J. J.]

Lift the strain of high thanksgiving. *J. Ellerton.* [*Church Restoration.*] Written for the reopening of St. Helen's Church, Tarporley, Cheshire, 1869, and pub. in the S. P. C. K. *Church Hys.*, 1871. From *Church Hys.* it has passed into numerous collections in G. Britain and America. From this hymn, and "In the Name which earth and heaven" (q. v.), Mr. Ellerton compiled a cento for the reopening of the nave of Chester Cathedral, January 25, 1872. [J. J.]

Lift up your heads, ye gates of brass. *J. Montgomery.* [*Missions.*] This hymn is amongst the "M. MSS.," but is undated. It was printed in the *Evangelical Magazine*, 1843; and again in Montgomery's *Original Hymns*, 1853, No. 265, in 19 st. of 4 l., and entitled "China Evangelized"; Pt. ii. beginning "Ye armies of the living God"; and Pt. iii. "No carnal weapons those ye bear." In the S. P. C. K. *Church Hymns*, 1871, No. 291, is composed of st. i.–iii., xviii., xix. somewhat altered. [J. J.]

Light of life, seraphic Fire. *C. Wesley.* [*Holiness desired.*] Appeared in *Hys. and Sac. Poems*, 1749, vol. ii., in 3 st. of 8 l., as No. 18 of " Hys. for those that wait for full Redemption" (*P. Works*, 1868–72, vol. v. p. 309). In 1780 it was given in the *Wes. H. Bk.*, No. 387, with the omission of st. iii. This form of the hymn has come into extensive use in G. Britain and America. It also sometimes appears as " Light of life, *celestial* Fire," as in Kennedy, 1863. [J. J.]

Light of life so softly shining. *H. Bonar.* [*The Light of Life desired.*] Pub. in his work *The Song of the New Creation and Other Pieces*, 1872, p. 113, in 6. st. of 4 l., and repeated, with the omission of a stanza in the Scottish *Presb. Hymnal for the Young*, 1882. [J. J.]

Light of the lonely pilgrim's heart. *Sir E. Denny.* [*Missions.*] Appeared in *Ps. & Hys. and Spiritual Songs*, Lond., D. Walther, 1842, Pt. i., No. 69, in 6 st. of 4 l. From this collection (*J. G. Deck's*) it passed in a full or an abbreviated form into numerous hymnals in all English-speaking countries, and has become one of the most widely used of the author's hymns. In addition to appearing in the hymnals, it was also pub. by the author in his *Hymns & Poems*, 1848, p. 44 (3rd ed. 1870, p. 14), and headed " The Heart Watching for the Morning," with the quotation from Cowper's Task :—

" Thy saints proclaim Thee King: and in their hearts
Thy title is engraven with a pen
Dipp'd in the fountain of eternal love,"

by which it was apparently suggested. A cento from this hymn, beginning with st. ii., " Come, blessed Lord ! bid every shore," is in a few collections. [J. J.]

Light of the world that shines to bless. *Cecil F. Alexander, née Humphreys.* [*The Light of the World.*] From her *Hymns, Descriptive and Devotional*, 1858, No. 17, in 9 st. of 4 l., and based on the words " I am the Light of the world," into the *People's Hyl.*, 1867, No. 361, and others. [J. J.]

Light of those whose dreary dwelling. *C. Wesley.* [*Christmas.*] 1st pub. in his *Hymns for the Nativity of Our Lord*, 1746, No. xi., in 3 st. of 8 l. (*P. Works*, 1868–72, vol. iv. p. 116). It was adopted by *M. Madan* in 1760, *R. Conyers* in 1774, *A. M. Toplady* in 1776, and most evangelical hymnal compilers of that period. At the first it was retained in an unaltered form, but the changes made by Toplady in 1776 were followed by others, until at the present time, although found in numerous collections in all English-speaking countries, it is difficult to find any two texts alike. The secret lay in its being a purely Arminian hymn, but so constructed that it could be easily turned to account by Calvinists. For the alterations in use, *Toplady*, 1776, *Cotterill*, 1810, *Bickersteth*, 1833, and *Elliott*, 1835, are mainly answerable. In 1830 it was given in the *Supplement* to the *Wes. H. Bk.* in an unaltered form. [J. J.]

Like the first disciples, In their strange, glad hour. *G. Rawson.* [*Holy Communion.*] A Post-Communion hymn, printed for the first time at the close of an article in the *Evangelical Magazine*, June, 1881, by the Editor, the Rev. H. R. Reynolds, D.D., on "Hymns," with special reference to those by Mr. Rawson. It is in 6 st. of 4 l., and headed " We have seen the Lord." In 1884 it was included in Horder's *Cong. Hymns.* [J. J.]

Lindemann, Johann, s. of Nicolaus Lindemann, burgess at Gotha, was b. at Gotha c. 1550. He attended the Gymnasium at Gotha, and apparently thereafter studied and graduated M.A. at Jena. He appears to have become cantor at Gotha in 1571 or 1572, and retired from this post, on a pension, in 1631. In 1634 he was a member of the new Council at Gotha. The date of his death is unknown. (*Monatshefte für Musikgeschichte*, 1878, p. 73 ; MS. from Superintendent Dr. Otto Dreyer, of Gotha, &c. The extant register of births at Gotha only goes back to 1566, that of deaths only to 1659.)

Lindemann's *Decades Amorum Filii Dei* seem to have been pub. at Erfurt, 1594 and 1596. The ed. of 1598 [Royal Library, Berlin] is entitled *Amorum Filii Dei Decades Duae: Das ist Zwantzig liebliche und gantz anmutige lateinische und deutsche newe Jharss oder Weyhenachten Gesenglein*. He is there described as Cantor and musician to the churches and schools at Gotha. Whether he is the author of the words of any of these pieces is not certain. Nor is it even clear that he was the composer of the melodies; but it is evident that he must have arranged and harmonised them. The two best known of these pieces are "Jesu wollst uns weisen" (No. 3, in 3 st.), and, "In dir ist Freude" (*Love to Christ*). The latter is No. 7 in 2 st. of 12 l. It is set to a tune adapted from a madrigal by Giovanni Giacomo Gastoldi da Caravaggio (his *Balletti* appeared at Venice 1591, 1593, 1595, 1597, &c.), and is marked as "Balletti: L'innamorato: A Lieta Vita: à 5." The text is repeated in the *Unv. L. S.*, 1851, No. 42. The *tr.* in C. U. is: "In Thee is gladness." A full and good *tr.* by Miss Winkworth, in her *Lyra Ger.*, 2nd Ser. 1858, p. 155, and her *C. B. for England*, 1863, No. 156.

[J. M.]

Linquunt tecta Magi principis urbis. *C. Coffin*. [*Epiphany*.] Included in the *Paris Breviary*, 1736, for Lauds on the feast of the Epiphany, and again in his *Hymni Sacri*, 1736, p. 40. It is also in Card. Newman's *Hymni Ecclesiae*, 1838 and 1865. *Tr.* as :—

Lo! the pilgrim Magi Leave their royal halls. By J. D. Chambers, in his *Lauda Syon*, 1857, p. 110. It was repeated in the *People's H.*, 1867 ; the *Hymnary*, 1872, and others.

Other trs. are :—
1. From princely walls in Eastern pomp array'd. By I. Williams, in the *British Magazine*, 1835, and his *Hys. tr. from the Parisian Brev.*, 1839.
2. The princely city passing by. J. C. Earle, in O. Shipley's *Annus Sanctus*, 1884. [J. J.]

Lintrup, Severin Falk, was b. Nov. 17, 1700, at Tarmun, in Jutland, Denmark. In 1723 he entered the University of Copenhagen as a student of theology. In 1725 he became curate in charge in the island of Lyo, near Fünen ; in 1727 chaplain at Wartau, near Copenhagen ; and in 1727 preacher at the Wallö-Spital, near Copenhagen. During his tenure of this last post he became acquainted with some of the Moravian missionaries, and resigning his appointment in 1734, he joined the Brethren at Herrnhut. Subsequently he preached in several of their communities (e.g. at Gnadenberg, in Silesia, on its foundation in 1743), and was also sent on various missions to Denmark and Sweden. He d. at Herrnhut, Feb. 15, 1758 (G. F. Otto's *Lexicon ... Oberlausizischen Schriftsteller*, vol. ii., 1802, p. 490, &c.). In the *Historische Nachricht* to the *Brüder G. B.*, 1778, two hymns are ascribed to him, viz., Nos. 1048, st. ii., iii., and 1073. One of these is in English C. U.; viz. :—

Mein Heiland! wirf doch einen Blick. *Christian Church.* Appeared as No. 1172 in *Appendix* vi., *cir.* 1737, to the *Herrnhut G. B.* 1735, in 12 st. of 4 l. In the *Brüder G. B.*, 1778, No. 1073, it is reduced to 6 st., viz., i., iii., viii., ix., xi., xii. *Tr.* as: (1) "O Lord, lift up Thy countenance." In full, from the *Brüder G. B.*, by F. W. Foster, as No. 513 in the *Moravian H. Bk.*, 1789 (1886, No. 788). St. i., iii., iv. of this version are in Dr. Martineau's *Hymns*, 1840 and 1873. Another *tr.* is,

"My dearest Saviour! cast an eye." As No. 80 in the *Moravian H. Bk.*, 1742 (1754, pt. ii. No. 142). [J. M.]

Liscovius, Salomo, s. of Johann Liscovius, or Lischkow, pastor at Niemitsch, near Guben, was b. at Niemitsch, Oct. 25, 1640. He entered the University of Leipzig in 1660, and then went to Wittenberg, where he graduated M.A., and was crowned as a poet. Shortly thereafter he was appointed pastor at Otterwisch with Stockheim, near Lausigk, and ordained to this post April 21, 1664. He was then, on March 29, 1685, appointed second pastor of St. Wenceslaus's church, at Wurzen. He d. at Wurzen, Dec. 5, 1689. (*Koch*, iii. 385 ; Rotermund's continuation of Jöcher's *Gelehrten-Lexikon*, iii. 1950, &c.)

Liscovius was one of the best German hymn-writers of the second rank in the 17th cent. That is, though his hymns are not lacking in intensity, in depth, or in beauty of form, yet neither by their intrinsic value nor by their adoption into German C. U. are they worthy to be ranked with the hymns of Gerhardt, Franck, Scheffler and others of this period. They appeared mostly in his *Christlicher Frauenzimmers Geistlicher Tugend-Spiegel*. The preface to this book is dated April 14, 1672, and it was probably pub. at Leipzig in 1672 ; but the earliest ed. extant is that at Leipzig, 1703. Dr. J. L. Pasig pub. 51 of his *Geistliche Lieder*, with a short biographical notice, at Halle, 1855. One of his hymns is *tr.* :—

Schatz über alle Schätze. *Love to Christ.* His finest hymn. 1672 as above, and Pasig, 1855, p. 53. In the Nürnberg *G. B.*, 1676, No. 509, and the Berlin *G. L. S.*, ed. 1863, No. 826. It is in 7 st. of 8 l., the initial letters of the stanzas forming his Christian name *Salomon*. The *trs.* are :—

(1) "Treasure above all treasure," as No. 441 in pt. i. of the *Moravian H. Bk.*, 1754. In the 1789 and later eds. (1886, No. 449), it begins "Jesus, my highest treasure." (2) "Treasure beyond all treasure," by *Miss Dunn*, 1857, p. 60. (3) "Thou treasure of all treasures," by *Miss Manington*, 1863, p. 27. [J. M.]

Litanies, Metrical. 1. The form in which Metrical Litanies are given in the hymn-books now in use, is of modern growth. A few hymns with refrains are found in some of the older collections, as "In the hour of my distress," by Herrick ; "Lord of mercy and of might," by Bp. Heber ; "Saviour, when in dust to Thee," by Sir R. Grant ; "By Thy birth, O Lord of all," by Mrs. Harriet Mozley ; "Jesus, Lord of life and glory," by J. J. Cummins, and a few others. These, however, were usually classed not as Metrical Litanies, but as hymns, and as such were embodied in the collections.

2. The Metrical Litanies of the modern hymn-books began in 1854 with one or two in rhythmical prose on the Childhood and Passion of Jesus, one of the first, if not the first, being No. 63 below. By slow degrees these have been increased, written mainly in rhymed metre, the first being No. 21 below, until provision has been made for most of the Fasts and Festivals of the Church. In a few instances, as noted hereafter, they are published as separate works from the hymn-books. The usual practice, however, is to give them as a separate division or section of the hymnal.

3. Amongst the earliest writers of Metrical Litanies were Dr. F. G. Lee, Dr. Littledale, and G. Moultrie ; and amongst the later Bp. H. E. Bickersteth, Sir H. W. Baker, and T. B. Pollock.

4. In arranging the Metrical Litanies for reference great difficulty is presented in their sameness, and the habit which some authors and compilers have of beginning several Litanies with the same stanza. Another difficulty

is created by compilers of hymnals breaking the Litanies into parts which differ from those adopted by the authors. In the following list of Metrical Litanies these difficulties have been kept in view :—

1. **All our sinful words and ways.** *Lent.* By L. F. in Mrs. Brock's *Children's H. Bk.*, 1881.

2. **Bread of Life, the angels' Food.** *Holy Communion.* By Dr. Littledale in the *People's H.*, 1867, No. 598.

3. **By the word to Mary given.** *The Birth of Jesus.* In the *Hymnary*, 1872, this is given as "By the angel's word of love."

4. **By the Name which Thou didst take.** *The Childhood of Jesus.*

5. **By the blood that flow'd from Thee.** *The Passion of Jesus.*

6. **By the first bright Easter-day.** *The Resurrection of Jesus.*
   Nos. 3–6 are by F. W. Faber in his *Hymns*, 1862, the Roman Catholic *Hys. for the Year*, &c.

7. **By the prayer that Jesus made.** *For Unity.* In the *Eucharistic Hymnal*, 1877.

8. **By Thy birth, O Lord of all.** *The Childhood of Jesus.* By Mrs. Harriet Mozley, pub. in *Hys. for the Children of the Ch. of England*, &c., 1835. In the S. P. C. K. *Church Hys.*, 1871, it is considerably altered, and sts. v. vi. are rewritten.

9. **Christ, the woman's promised seed.** *Christmas and Epiphany.* A. W. Hutton.

10. **Christ, Whose mercy guideth still.** *Lent and Passiontide.* R. F. Littledale in the *People's H.*, 1867, altered in *Hys. and Carols*, &c. (Ch. Extension Association), 1871, to "Christ, Whose mercy lasts for aye."

11. **Father, from Thy heavenly throne.** *Holy Communion.* By J. S. B. Monsell.

12. **Father, from Thy throne on high.** *For Little Children.* By Mrs. Streatfeild in Mrs. Carey Brock's *Children's H. Bk.*, 1881.

13. **Father, hear Thy children's call.** *Lent.* By T. B. Pollock in *H. A. & M.*, 1875.

14. **God the Father, from on high.** *For a Sick Person.* In the *Priest's Prayer Book*, by R. F. Littledale, 1864.

15. **God the Father, from Thy throne.** *Rogation Days.* By Sir H. W. Baker in *H. A. & M.*, 1861.

16. **God the Father, hear and pardon.** *Lent and Passiontide.* J. S. B. Monsell.

17. **God the Father, hear our cry.** *Lent.* In the *Eucharistic Hymnal*, 1877.

18. **God the Father, in the sky.** *Holy Trinity.* By W. J. Irons.

19. **God the Father of all might.** *Lent.* By A. W. Hutton.

20. **God of God, and Light of Light.** *Holy Communion.* By Sir H. W. Baker in *H. A. & M.*, 1875.

21. **God the Father, seen of none.** *Passiontide.* By R. F. Littledale, written about 1860 for the schools of St. Mary the Virgin, Crown Street, Soho, London. In the *People's H.*, 1867.

22. **God the Father, throned on high.** *Jesus Glorified.* By T. B. Pollock in *H. A. & M.*, 1875.

23. **God, the Holy Ghost, by Whom.** *The Holy Ghost.* In the *Eucharistic Hymnal*, 1877.

24. **Great, mysterious Trinity.** *For all Times.* T. B. Pollock.

25. **Hear us, Son of God, O hear.** *Of Commendation.* By G. Moultrie in the *People's H.*, 1867 ; and again in the author's *Espousals of S. Dorothea*, 1870.

26. **Heavenly Father, from Thy throne.** *Passiontide.* V. Hutton. In Mrs. Brock's *Children's H. Bk.*, 1881. [See **Various.**]

27. **Heavenly Father, let Thy light.** *Missions.* In Mrs. Brock's *Children's H. Bk.*, 1881.

28. **Holy Father, from Thy throne.** *Holy Trinity.* "C. S." in *Lyra Messianica*, 1864, i.e. Charlotte Sellon.

29. **Holy Father, hear our cry.** *The Holy Ghost.* By Cecil Moore in Mrs. Brock's *Children's H. Bk.*, 1881. [See **Various.**]

30. **Holy Jesu, All in All.** *Jesus glorified in His Saints.* T. B. Pollock, written for *Hys. for Use in the Ch. of St. Ethelburga, Bishopsgate*, 1873.

31. **Holy Spirit, wondrous Dove.** *Holy Ghost.* In the *People's H.*, 1867. By R. F. Littledale ; it forms part of "Holy Spirit, *Heavenly Dove*."

32. **Jesu, David's Root and Stem.** *The Holy Childhood.* In *People's H.*, 1867, by R. F. Littledale.

33. **Jesu, dwelling here below.** *Life of our Lord.* T. B. Pollock.

34. **Jesu, from Thy throne on high.** *For Children.* T. B. Pollock.

35. **Jesu, for us sinners slain.** *The Resurrection of Jesus.* By R. F. Littledale in the *People's H.*, 1867.

36. **Jesu, in Thy dying woes.** *The Seven Words on the Cross.* By T. B. Pollock.

37. **Jesu, King of boundless might.** *The Holy Name.* By R. F. Littledale in the *People's H.*, 1867.

38. **Jesu, life of those who die.** *The Four Last Things.* By T. B. Pollock in *H. A. & M.*, 1875.

39. **Jesu, Lord most mighty.** *Lent.* A. T. Russell, in his *Ps. and Hys,*, 1851.

40. **Jesu, Saviour, ever mild.** *For Children.* By R. F. Littledale, in *H. A. & M.*, 1875, chiefly from the *People's H.*, No. 592.

41. **Jesu, Saviour, hear me call.** *Lent.* In the *Scottish Hymnal*, 1884.

42. **Jesu, Son of God most high.** *The Childhood of Jesus.* T. B. Pollock.

43. **Jesu, Son of the living God.** *The Holy Name.* In the Ch. Extension Association's *Hys. & Carols*, 1871.

44. **Jesu, we are far away.** *Lent.* T. B. Pollock.

45. **Jesu, Who for us didst bear.** *Passiontide.* In the *People's H.*, 1867, by R. F. Littledale.

46. **Jesu, Who when Adam fell.** *Lent.* A. W. Hutton. A few stanzas in this from No. 10.

47. **Jesu, with Thy Church abide.** *For the Church.* By T. B. Pollock and others in *H. A. & M.*, 1875.

48. **Labouring and heavy laden.** *Of Life.* J. S. B. Monsell.

49. **Light that from the dark abyss.** *Jesus, the Light of the World.* By E. B. Birks, q.v. In the *H. Comp.*, 1876.

50. **Lord have mercy, Pity take.** *The Sacred Heart.* By J. S. B. Monsell.

51. **My sins have taken such an hold on me.** *Lent.* By J. S. B. Monsell.

52. **My sin, my sin, O God, my sin.** *Lent.* By J. S. B. Monsell.

53. **Now let my soul with God retreat.** *The Holy Ghost.* By J. S. B. Monsell.

54. **O Thou Who art the Gift unpriced.** *The Holy Ghost.* In Mrs. Brock's *Children's H. Bk.*, 1881, by S. J. Stone.

55. **Pity on us, heavenly Father.** *Passiontide.* By J. S. B. Monsell.

56. **Risen Jesu, Thee we greet.** *The Resurrection and Ascension.* By V. Hutton in Mrs. Carey Brock's *Children's H. Bk.*, 1881. Sometimes given as "Jesu, Lord, enthroned on high."

57. **Risen Lord, enthroned on high.** *The Ascension.* G. Moultrie, in his *Primer*, 1864, *Lyra Messianica*, 1864, and his *Hys. & Lyrics*, 1867.

58. **Sacred Heart of Jesus, pour.** *The Sacred Heart.* J. S. B. Monsell.

59. **Son of God, for man decreed.** *The Incarnate Word.* By T. B. Pollock in *H. A. & M.*, 1875.

60. **Spirit blest, who art adored.** *The Holy Ghost.* T. B. Pollock.

61. **Thou Who leaving crown and throne.** *Lent.* By Dr. Littledale in *H. A. & M.*, 1875, part of No. 10.

62. **Uncreated Fount of Light.** *To the Father.* Bp. H. E. Bickersteth in his *Songs in the House of Pilgrimage*, N.D., and his *H. Comp.*, 1876.

63. **Word Eternal, Uncreate.** *Advent.* F. G. Lee, 1st printed in H. Collins's *Hys. for Missions*, 1854 ; and again in the 1862 *Appendix* to the *Hymnal N.*

64. **Word made Flesh, Emmanuel.** *Advent.* In the *Eucharistic Hymnal*, 1877.

65. **When my feet have wandered.** *Passiontide.* J. S. B. Monsell.

66. **Jesus, hear us, Lord of all.** *Night Litany.* By G. Moultrie in his *Primer*, 1870.

5. In many instances the opening lines given in this list are those of the *second* stanzas of the Litanies. This was necessitated by the great majority of the Litanies opening in the hymn-books with the Invocation to the Holy Trinity, "God the Father, God the Son," or "God the Father, God the Word." The first lines of the *parts* of Litanies also are not included, nor are the first lines of parts 2–7, of the "Seven Words on the Cross" (see No. 35), nor of parts 2–4 of the "Four Last Things" (see No. 37).

6. The Litanies attributed to Sir H. W. Baker appeared in *H. A. & M.*, 1875 ; A. W. Hutton, in a *Supplement to H. A. & M.* (old ed.), pub. by him in 1875 ; W. J. Irons, in his *Ps. & Hys. for the Church*, 1875 ; Dr. Littledale, first on broadsheets, from 1861–66, and then in the *People's H.*, 1867 ; Dr. Monsell, in

Litany Hymns, 1870, and his *Parish Hymnal*, 1873; and T. B. Pollock, in his *Metrical Litanies for Special Services and General Use*, 1870; and his *Litany Appendix*, 1871. These works, together with the hymnals named in the foregoing notes; Thring's *Coll.*, 1882, the S. P. C. K. *Church Hymns*, 1871; and *A Book of Metrical Litanies*, Lond., Rivingtons, 1874, contain most of the Litanies available for use. Hymns which are also suitable as Litanies are indicated in the Index of Subjects and Seasons.   [J. J.]

Little children, dwell in love. *H. Alford.* [*St. John the Evangelist.*] First appeared in his *Hys. for the Sundays and Festivals throughout the Year*, 1836 (see his *Life*), in 4 st. of 4 l. In 1844 it was included in his *Ps. & Hys.*, No. 13, and marked, in error, as published therein for the first time. It is found in his *Year of Praise*, 1867; and in his *Poetical Works*, in the 8th ed. of which, 1868, it is dated 1835. It has passed into a few hymnals only.   [J. J.]

Little drops of water. [*Importance of Little Things.*] The original of this hymn, by Dr. E. C. Brewer, was 1st pub. in *Reading and Spelling*, 1848, in 5 st. of 4 l. Subsequently it reappeared in a very much altered and improved form in the American *Juvenile Missionary Magazine*, also in 5 st. From that magazine it was copied into *Hymns and Sacred Songs*, pub. at Manchester by Fletcher and Tubbs, 1855, and from that collection it has passed into numerous children's hymnals in the United Kingdom. When the version found in the greatest number of collections is compared with the original it is found that the leading thought of the hymn and the first stanza are all that remain of that first published by Dr. Brewer, thus :—

Dr. Brewer, 1848.	*American Version.*
1. Little drops of water, Little grains of sand, Make the mighty ocean, Make the beauteous land.	1. Little drops of water, Little grains of sand, Make the mighty ocean, And the beauteous land.
2. Straw by straw the sparrow Builds its cosy nest ; Leaf by leaf the forest Stands in verdure drest.	2. And the little moments, Humble though they be Make the mighty ages Of eternity.
3. Letter after letter Words and books are made ; Little and by little Mountains level laid.	3. Little deeds of kindness, Little words of love, Make our earth an Eden, Like the heaven above.
4. Drop by drop is iron Worn in time away ; Perseverance, patience, Ever win their way.	4. So our little errors Lead the soul away, From the paths of virtue Into sin to stray.
5. Every finished labour Once did but begin ; Try, and go on trying, That's the way to win.	5. Little seeds of mercy, Sown by youthful hands, Grow to bless the nations Far in heathen lands.

The somewhat unfinished American text was extensively adopted to 1876, when Bp. Bickersteth, in the revised edition of the *Hy. Comp.*, made it more complete by adding :—

6. Little ones in glory
Swell the angels' song:
Make us meet, dear Saviour,
For their holy throng.

This last thought was taken up by Prebendary Thring, and in his *Collection*, 1880–82, was thus elaborated :—

Little children's angels, Happy in the sky, See their Heavenly Father On His throne on high.	Little children's voices, Heavenly choirs among, Swell the angel-chorus With their simple song.

Glory then for ever
Be to Father, Son,
With the Holy Spirit,
Blessèd Three in One.

In this manner has been built up a very pleasing and popular children's hymn out of a short poem of no interest or merit save its one idea of the power of little things.   [J. J.]

Littledale, Richard Frederick, LL.D., D.C.L., s. of John Richard Littledale, merchant, was b. at Dublin on the 14th of Sept , 1833, and was educated at Bective House Seminary, and Trinity College, Dublin. His University course was distinguished. In 1852 he became an University Scholar ; in 1854 he was first class in Classics and gold medallist ; in 1856 he won the Berkeley gold medal (for Greek), and other honours. He graduated B.A., 1855, M.A., 1858, LL.D., 1862, and D.C.L. at Oxford, 1862. Taking Holy Orders in 1856, he was Curate of St. Matthew's, in Thorpe Hamlet, Norwich, from 1856 to 1857, and of St. Mary the Virgin, Soho, London, from 1857 to 1861. Through ill-health he retired from parochial work in 1861, and devoted himself to literature. Dr. Littledale's publications amount to about fifty in all, and embrace Theological, Historical, Liturgical, and Hymnological subjects chiefly. His prose works include :—

(1) *Application of Colour to the Decoration of Churches*, 1857 ; (2) *Religious Communities of Women in the Early Church*, 1862 ; (3) *Catholic Ritual in the Church of England*, 1861 ; (4) Continuation of Dr. Neale's *Commentary on the Psalms*, vols. ii., iii., iv., 1868–74 ; (5) *Commentary on the Song of Songs*, 1869 ; (6) *The Petrine Claims*, 1878–84 ; (7) *Plain Reasons against joining the Church of Rome*, 1880, &c. ; (8) *Short History of the Council of Trent* ; and several articles in the *Encyclopædia Brit.*, 1882–88. His contributions to periodical literature have been also extensive and valuable.

Dr. Littledale's Liturgical, Devotional, and Hymnological works include :—

(1) *Offices of the Holy Eastern Church, in the Original Greek*, with translation into English, Notes, &c., 1863 ; (2) *Carols for Christmas and Other Seasons*, 1863 ; (3) *The Priest's Prayer Book*, with hymns, 1864, and with *Brief Pontifical* in 1870 and later eds. ; (4) *The People's Hymnal*, 1867 ; (5) *The Children's Bread. A Communion Office for the Young*, with hymns, 1868 ; (6) *Primitive Liturgies and Translations*, 1868–69 ; (7) *Children at Calvary: being The Stations of the Cross in Metre for Singing*, 1872 ; (8) the *Christian Passover*, 1873 ; (9) *The Altar Manual*, 1863–77. He was joint Editor of Nos. 3, 4, 8 and 9 with the Rev. J. E. Vaux ; and of No. 6 with Dr. Neale.

In addition to a large number of hymns, original and translated, in the above works, Dr. Littledale has also directly contributed original and translated hymns to :—

(1) *Lyra Eucharistica*, 1863 ; (2) *Lyra Messianica*, 1864 ; (3) *Lyra Mystica*, 1865 ; (4) *The Eucharistic Hymnal*, 1877 ; (5) *The Roman Breviary in English*, by the Marquess of Bute, 1879 ; (6) *The Altar Hymnal*, 1884 ; (7) *Suppl. to H. A. & M.*, 1889 ; (8) to the *Night Hours of the Church* ; (9) to the *St. Margaret's Hymnal* [East Grinstead], 1875 ; and (10) to the *Church Times*, *The Guardian*, &c., &c.

Dr. Littledale's Hymnological works in verse consist of translations of Danish, Swedish, Greek, Latin, Syriac, German, and Italian hymns, together with original Carols, Hymns, and Metrical Litanies. His translations are annotated elsewhere in this Dictionary (see Index to Authors and Translators) ; his Carols under

Carols ; and his Metrical Litanies under **Litanies, Metrical.** His original hymns remain to be noted. These include the following :—

i. In the *Priest's Prayer Book*, 1864 :—

1. Captain of Salvation. *Christian Warfare.*
2. Christ, on Whose Face the soldiers. *Passiontide.*
3. Christ, Who hast for sinners suffered. *Passiontide.*
4. God the Father, from on high. *For the Sick.*
5. Lord Jesu, by Thy passion. *Passiontide.*
6. Lord, Who in pain and weariness. *Passiontide.*
7. O Jesu, in Thy torture. *Passiontide.* In *Meditations and Prayers on the Passion of Our Lord Jesus Christ*, 1863.
8. O Lord, to Whom the spirits live. *All Souls.*
9. The clouds of sorrow rest upon mine eyes. *For the Sorrowing.*

ii. In the *People's Hymnal*, 1867 :—

10. Christ, our song we lift to Thee. *B. V. M.*
11. Christ, our Sun, on us arose. *Whitsuntide.* In *Carols for Christmas*, &c., 3rd series, 1864.
12. Christ, the Lord, Whose mighty hand. *Prayer for Peace.*
13. Day is past and gone. *Evening.* In the *Church Times*, Feb. 17, 1866.
14. Eternal Shepherd, God most high. *Vacancy of a See or Parish.*
15. Eternal Wisdom, God most high. *Common of Doctors.*
16. God eternal, infinite. *Septuagesima.*
17. Hidden Saviour, great High Priest. *Holy Communion.*
18. I believe in God the Father. *The Creed.*
19. I worship Thee, Lord Jesu. *Holy Communion.* In the *Church Times*, May 10, 1865.
20. In Paradise reposing. *Burial of a Child.*
21. In songs of glad thanksgiving. *General Thanksgiving.*
22. Lord, Whose goodwill is ever sure. *In time of Famine.*
23. Now the sun is in the skies. *Morning.* In the *Church Times*, Jan. 27, 1866.
24. O God of mercy, God of love. *For Rain.*
25. O God, Who metest in Thine hand. *For those at Sea.*
26. O God, Whose Sole-Begotten left. *Almsgiving.*
27. O sing to the Lord, Whose bountiful hand. *Thanksgiving for Rain.*
28. Set upon Sion's wall. *Ember Days.*
29. The Cedar of Lebanon, Plant of renown. *Christmas.* First pub. in Sedding's *Christmas Carols*, 1863.
30. The fight is o'er, the crown is won. *Burial of a Sister of Mercy.*
31. The wintry time hath ended. *Thanksgiving for Fair Weather.*
32. We are marching through the desert. *Processional.*
33. When the day hath come at last. *The Judgment.*

In addition to these, a few of the more widely used of Dr. Littledale's original hymns, as "From hidden source arising," and others, are annotated under their respective first lines. In the *People's H.*, 1867, Dr. Littledale adopted the following signatures :—

A. L. P., i.e., A London Priest.
B., i.e., An initial of a former address.
B. T., i.e., The initials of a former address.
D. L., i.e. Dr. Littledale.
F., i.e., Frederick.
F. R., i.e., Frederick Richard.
L., i.e., Littledale.
P. C. E., i.e., Priest of the Church of England.
P. P. Bk., i.e., Priest's Prayer Book.

Taken as a whole, Dr. Littledale's *trs.* from the seven languages named above are characterised by general faithfulness to the originals, great simplicity of diction, good metre, smooth rhythm, and deep earnestness. His original compositions are usually on special subjects, for which, at the time they were written, there were few hymns, and are marked by the same excellent features of a good hymn as his translations. His main object throughout is to *teach* through Praise and Prayer.　　　　　　　[J. J.]

Live, our Eternal Priest. *C. Wesley.* [*Holy Communion.*] 1st pub. in *Hymns on the Lord's Supper* by J. & C. Wesley, 1745, in 5 st. of 6 l. (*P. Works*, 1868–72, vol. iii. p. 303). In its original form it is not in common use, but as altered to "Hail, Thou Eternal Priest" it was given in the *Hymnary*, in 1870–2, in 4 st., st. ii. being omitted, and the rest so changed as to constitute almost a new hymn.

　　　　　　　　　　　　　　[J. J.]

Livermore, Abiel Abbot, D.D., was b. at Wilton, New Hampshire, Oct. 30, 1811, and graduated at Harvard in Arts, in 1833 ; and Divinity, 1836. The latter year he was ordained as a Unitarian Minister, and became Pastor at Keene, New Hampshire, 1836 ; Cincinnati, 1850 ; Yonkers, New York, 1857. In 1863 he removed to Meadville, Pennsylvania, as the President of the Theological School. Dr. Livermore is the author of various works, and was the chief editor of the Cheshire Pastoral Association's *Christian Hymns*, 1844, one of the most widely circulated and estimable of American Unitarian collections. To that collection he contributed " A holy air is breathing round" (*Holy Communion*), which has passed into several collections, including Martineau's *Hymns*, &c., 1873.　　[F. M. B.]

Livermore, Sarah White, aunt of A. A. Livermore (q. v.), was b. at Wilton, New Hampshire, July 20, 1789 ; and d. there July 3, 1874, having spent most of her life as a Teacher. Two hymns were contributed by her to the Cheshire P. A.'s *Christian Hymns*, 1844 :—(1) Glory to God, and peace on earth, *Christmas.* (2) Our pilgrim brethren, dwelling far. *Missions.* She wrote many others, of which two are given in Putnam's *Singers and Songs of the Liberal Faith*, 1875.　　[J. J.]

Lloyd, William Freeman, was b. at Uley, Gloucestershire, Dec. 22, 1791. As he grew up he took great interest in Sunday school work, and was engaged in teaching both at Oxford and at London. In 1810 he was appointed one of the Secretaries of the Sunday School Union. He also became connected with the Religious Tract Society in 1816. Miller (to whom we are indebted for these details) says in his *Singers and Songs of the Church*, 1869, p. 418 :—

" He commenced the *Sunday School Teacher's Magazine*, conducted for years the *Child's Companion* and the *Weekly Visitor*, and suggested the preparation of a large number of books for children and adults. His own literary productions were various, including several useful books for Sunday School teachers and scholars, and numerous tracts. He was also much engaged in compilation and revision."

Mr. Lloyd d. at the residence of his brother, the Rev. Samuel Lloyd, at Stanley Hall, Gloucestershire, April 22, 1853. Several of his hymns and poetical pieces were given in the R. T. S. *Child's Book of Poetry* (N. D.), and the R. T. S. *My Poetry Book* (N. D.). In 1853 he collected his pieces and published them as, *Thoughts in Rhyme, By W. F. Lloyd*, Lond., Hamilton & Co., and Nisbet & Co. Of his hymns the following are in C. U. :—

1. Come, poor sinners, come to Jesus. *Invitation.* (1835.)
2. Give thy young heart to Christ. *A Child's Dedication to Christ.*

3. My [our] times are in Thine hand. My God, I wish them there. *Resignation.* (1835.)
4. Sweet is the time of spring. *Spring.*
5. Wait, my soul, upon the Lord. *In Affliction.* (1835.)

The date given above, 1835, is from Spurgeon's *O. O. H. Bk.*, 1866, and was supplied to the editor by D. Sedgwick. We have no other authority for that date. The earliest we can find is No. 3, which is in *Hys. for the Poor of the Flock*, 1838. That hymn is very popular.   [J. J.]

Lo, at noon 'tis sudden night. *Ann Gilbert, née Taylor.* [*Good Friday.*] From *Hymns for Infant Minds*, 1810, No. 25, in 6 st. of 6 l., and entitled " Jesus Christ came into the world to save sinners " (ed. 1886, p. 63). This is a kindred hymn to her " Jesus, Who lived above the sky," and is quoted in her *Memorials*, 1874, as an example of beautiful simplicity and accuracy (vol. i. p. 224). It has attained to a good position amongst hymns of established worth, is in extensive use, and is one of the most popular of Mrs. Gilbert's compositions.   [J. J.]

Lo! He comes with clouds descending, Once for favoured sinners slain. [*The Second Advent.*] The hymn in modern collections which opens with these lines is a cento of a somewhat complicated character, and will need, for clearness and accuracy, the reproduction of the original text of several hymns.

1. The first form of the hymn is by John Cennick. There is evidence to show that it was sung by the congregation of the Moravian Chapel, in Dublin, on April 20, 1750; but the earliest printed text known appeared in the fifth (1752) ed. of Cennick's *Collection of Sacred Hymns*, &c., Dublin, S[amuel] Powell, and is as follows :—

[1] " Lo ! He cometh, countless trumpets
Blow before his bloody sign !
'Midst ten thousand saints and angels,
See the Crucified shine.
Allelujah !
Welcome, welcome bleeding Lamb !

[2] " Now His merits by the harpers,
Thro' the eternal deeps resounds !
Now resplendent shine His nail-prints,
Every eye shall see His wounds !
They who pierced Him,
Shall at His appearing wail.

[3] " Every island, sea, and mountain,
Heaven and earth shall flee away !
All who hate Him must, ashamed,
Hear the trump proclaim His day:
Come to judgment !
Stand before the Son of Man !

[4] " All who love Him view His glory,
Shining in His bruised Face :
His dear Person on the rainbow,
Now His people's heads shall raise:
Happy mourners !
Now on clouds He comes ! He comes !

[5] " Now redemption, long expected,
See, in solemn pomp appear :
All His people, once despised,
Now shall meet Him in the air :
Allelujah !
Now the promised kingdom's come !

[6] " View Him smiling, now determined
Every evil to destroy !
All the nations now shall sing Him
Songs of everlasting joy !
O come quickly !
Allelujah ! come Lord, come ! "

2. The next form is by Charles Wesley. In 1758 was pub. the *Hys. of Intercession for All*

Mankind, a tract of 40 hymns. (*P. Works*, 1868–72, vol. vi. 143.) Of these there were three in the same metre, viz. :—

xxxviii. " Rise, ye dearly purchased sinners."
xxxix. " Lo ! He comes with clouds descending."
xl. " Lift your heads, ye friends of Jesus."

The original text of the second of these hymns is as follows :—

" 1. Lo ! He comes with clouds descending,
Once for favour'd sinners slain !
Thousand, thousand saints attending,
Swell the triumph of his train :
Hallelujah,
God appears, on earth to reign !

" 2. Every eye shall now behold Him
Rob'd in dreadful majesty,
Those who set at nought and sold Him,
Pierc'd, and nail'd Him to the tree,
Deeply wailing
Shall the true Messiah see.

" 3. The dear tokens of his passion
Still His dazling body bears,
Cause of endless exultation
To his ransom'd worshippers ;
With what rapture
Gaze we on those glorious scars !

" 4. Yea, amen ! let all adore Thee
High on thine eternal throne !
Saviour, take the power and glory,
Claim the kingdom for thine own :
Jah, Jehovah,
Everlasting God, come down."

3. The third form of the text is really the first form of the modern cento. It was given by M. Madan in his *Coll. of Ps. & Hys.*, &c., 1760, No. 12. The text, with Madan's alterations in *italics*, is as follows :—

I.

From " Lo ! He comes with Clouds descending,
Wesley.   Once for favour'd Sinners slain !
Thousand thousand Saints attending,
Swell the Triumph of his Train :
Hallelujah !
Hallelujah ! Amen !

II.

From " Every Eye shall now behold Him,
Wesley.   Rob'd in dreadful Majesty ;
Those who set at nought and sold Him,
Pierc'd, and nail'd Him to the Tree,
Deeply wailing,
Shall the True Messiah see.

III.

From " Ev'ry Island, Sea, and Mountain,
Cennick.   Heav'n and Earth shall flee away ;
All who hate Him, must, *confounded,*
Hear the Trump proclaim the Day :
Come to Judgment !
Come to Judgment ! come away !

IV.

From " Now Redemption long expected,
Cennick.   See ! in solemn Pomp appear !
All his *Saints, by Man rejected,*
Now shall meet Him in the Air !
Hallelujah !
See the Day of God appear !

V.

From " Answer *thine* own Bride and Spirit,
Wesley,   Hasten, Lord, the gen'ral Doom !
Hymn No. The New Heav'n and Earth t' inherit,
xxxviii.   Take Thy pining Exiles Home :
as above.   All Creation
Travails ! groans ! and bids Thee come !

VI.

From " Yea ! Amen ! Let all adore Thee,
Wesley.   High on Thine eternal Throne !
Saviour take the Pow'r and Glory ;
Claim the Kingdom for thine own !
From O come quickly !
Cennick.   Hallelujah ! Come, Lord, come ! "

4. This cento, with the omission of st. v. came into general use, and was rarely altered until after 1830, when Hall, in his *Mitre H. Bk.*, 1836, and others, began to tamper with the text. Several editors were assisted in making their alterations and changes in the

text through T. Olivers's hymn, "Come, Immortal King of Glory" (q.v.), first pub. in 20 sts. without date; and then in 36 sts. in 1763. The fourth st. of the 1763 text reads:—

> "Lo! He comes with clouds descending;
> Hark! the trump of God is blown;
> And th' archangel's voice attending,
> Make the high procession known,
> Sons of Adam
> Rise and stand before your God."

A cento from this hymn, and beginning with this stanza, is given in Lord Selborne's *Book of Praise*, 1862. Either from the original, or from Lord Selborne's cento, several lines by Olivers are interwoven in some modern collections with *Madan's* cento of 1760, as in Thring's *Coll.*, 1882, where in st. iv. lines 5, 6 are from Olivers's st. xxxv.

5. The alterations which are found in the *Madan* cento in modern hymn-books are very numerous, and range from a single word to several lines. Of these altered versions more than twenty exist in the hymn-books now in C. U. in English-speaking countries. These alterations have not been made to suit any special school of thought, and in most cases they weaken, instead of strengthen the hymn. They can easily be detected by comparing any text with those given above.

6. Amongst the imitations of this hymn that are in C. U. we have "Lo! He comes with clouds descending," with st. ii. beginning "See the universe in motion." This imitation embodies a great many lines from Wesley's text. It is by M. Bridges, and was pub. in his *Hys. of the Heart*, 1848, in 9 st. In 1855 it was given in H. W. Beecher's *Plymouth Coll.*, with the omission of st. iv., and attributed to *Brydges* in error. A second imitation is: "Lo! He comes with pomp victorious." This is given anonymously in the 1876 ed. of E. Harland's *Church Psalter and Hymnal.*

7. The *Cennick-Wesley* cento (*Madan's*) is one of the most popular hymns in the English language, and is in extensive use in all English-speaking countries. It has also been translated into many languages. The *tr.* into Latin, "Nube vectus en descendit," by the Rev. C. B. Pearson in his *Latin Trs. of English Hymns*, 1862, p. 19, is from Wesley's text, with the addition of Cennick's st. v.

8. The history of the tune "Olivers" in its original form, and also in its recast form as "Helmsley," both of which are inseparably associated with this hymn, is given by Major Crawford in Grove's *Dictionary of Music*, vol. ii. p. 161. It appears from this article that Thomas Olivers (who is named above, and is the author of the popular hymn "The God of Abraham praise") constructed a tune partly out of a concert-room song, beginning "Guardian angels, now protect me," and the same was published in Wesley's *Select Hymns and Tunes Annexed*, 1765, under the title *Olivers*. In 1769 it was recast by M. Madan, and published under the name of *Helmsley*, in his *Collection of Hymn and Psalm Tunes*. Four years afterwards a burlesque called *The Golden Pippin* (1769) was produced in London, and failed. In 1776 it was revived in a shortened form, and one of the actresses, Miss Catley, introduced into it the melody of "Guardian angels" adapted to the words of the burlesque. Although there is

no indication of this in the book of words, she no doubt concluded the song, on which Olivers had based his tune eleven years before, by dancing "Miss Catley's Hornpipe," constructed for the purpose out of the then popular *Helmsley*. It seems, therefore, that instead of the hymn tune being liable to the obloquy, so continually cast upon it, of being made out of "Miss Catley's Hornpipe," the hornpipe was made out of the tune. (See Major Crawford's article in the *Dict. of Music*, for fuller details, together with the music in its various forms.)

[J. J.]

Lo! I come with joy to do. *C. Wesley.* [*For Men in Business.*] Pub. in *Hys. for those that Seek, and those that Have Redemption*, 1747, in 6 st. of 8 l., and headed "For a Believer, in Worldly Business" (*P. Works*, 1868–72, voi. iv. p. 214). It is in C. U. in the following forms:—

1. **Lo! I come with joy to do.** This was given in the *Wes. H. Bk.*, 1780, No. 316, and has been repeated in several collections in G. Britain and America. From this st. vi. is usually omitted.
2. **Behold I come with joy to do.** In the American Meth. Episco. *Hymns*, 1849, and other American collections. This is st. i., ii., and vi., slightly altered.
3. **Since I've known a Saviour's Name.** This altered form of st. ii., iv., and vi. was given in the American *Prayer Bk. Coll.*, 1826, and is repeated in the *Hymnal* of the Prot. Episco. Church, 1871. In the first line of st. iii. an unfortunate change was made in 1826, and is retained in 1871. The original reads:—

> "O that all the *art* might know
> Of living thus to Thee."

This is changed to:—

> "O that all the *world* might know
> Of living, Lord to Thee." [J. J.]

Lo in the [latter] last of days behold. *J. Ogilvie.* [*Advent.*] First appeared as No. 62 in the Draft Scottish *Translations and Paraphrases*, 1781, in 14 st. of 4 l., as a version of 2 Peter iii. 3–14, and again, with 5 lines altered, in the public worship edition of the same issued in that year by the Church of Scotland and still in use. In a copy of the *Trs. and Paraphs.* marked by the eldest daughter of W. Cameron (q.v.) this version is ascribed to J. Ogilvie. In addition to its use as one of the Scottish *Trs. & Paraphs.* it is found in the following forms:—

1. **Lo in the latter days behold.** In the 1876 ed. of Harland's *Ch. Psalter & Hymnal*, in 5 st.
2. **Lo in the last of days behold.** In the Ewing-Payne *Coll.*, Glasgow, 1814, in 7 st.
3. **Though now, ye just, the time appears** (st. viii.). In Porter's *Selection*, Glasgow, 1853, in 7 st.
4. **When erst the sons of men began** (st. v.). In the Twickenham Chapel *Coll.*, 1845, in 4 st.

In the *Paraphrases and Hymns*, &c., 1853, by Miss J. E. Leeson, Ogilvie's text is considerably altered, reduced to 8 st., and divided into two parts:—

1. Lo in the last of days foretold.
2. With Thee, creating Lord, one day.

[J. M.]

Lo the Feast is spread to-day. *H. Alford.* [*Holy Communion.*] 1st pub. in his *Ps. & Hymns*, 1844, No. 92, in 4 st. of 6 l., and again in his *Year of Praise*, 1867, No. 152. It has passed into several hymn-books, both in G. Britain and America. [J. J.]

Lo, the storms of life are breaking. *H. Alford.* [*Epiphany.*] Appeared in his *Ps. & Hys.*, 1844, No. 23, in 4 st. of 4 l. It is appointed for the 4th Sun. after the Epiphany, and is based upon the Gospel of that day. It was repeated in his *Year of Praise*, 1867, No. 48, and in various editions of his *Poetical Works*. It is in extensive use. [J. J.]

Lo, what a glorious sight appears.
I. Watts. [*The Kingdom of Christ.*] 1st pub. in his *Hys. & S. Songs*, 1707, as a paraphrase of Rev. xxi. 1–4, in 6 st. of 4 l. (2nd ed. 1709, Bk. i., No. 21). It is in C. U. in G. Britain and America. The most popular hymn with this opening line is, however, a cento compiled from it and Watts's " See where the great Incarnate God " (*Hys. & S. Songs*, 1709, Bk. i., No. 45), which is No. 67 of the Scottish *Translations and Paraphrases* of 1781. In the Draft *Trs. & Paraphs.*, 1745, No. 38, the cento was thus given :—

St. i.–v., from *Watts*, No. 21, as above.
St. vi., new.
St. vii.–xii., from *Watts*, No. 45, as above.
St. xiii., from *Watts*, No. 21, as above.

In the authorized *Trs. and Paraphs.* of 1781, this text was repeated with slight alterations, and has been in C. U. in Scotland and elsewhere to the present time. From the markings by the eldest daughter of W. Cameron (q.v.) we gather that the authorized Scottish text of 1781 was arranged and altered by Cameron. It should be designated *I. Watts*, 1707–9, *Scottish Trs. & Paraphs.*, 1745, *and W. Cameron*, 1781. In Miss Jane E. Leeson's *Paraphs. & Hys.*, 1853, the Scottish cento is re-arranged as a hymn in 7 st., beginning "From heaven, the glorious city comes."   [J. J.]

Lobe den Herren den mächtigen König der Ehren. *J. Neander.* [*Thanksgiving.*] A magnificent hymn of praise to God, perhaps the finest production of its author, and of the first rank in its class. It is founded on Ps. ciii., 1–6, and Ps. cl. 1st pub. in his *Glaub- und Liebesübung: auffgemuntert durch einfältige Bundes Lieder und Danck-Psalmen*, Bremen, 1680, p. 47, in 5 st. of 5 l., Repeated in Freylinghausen's *G. B.*, 1704, and in most subsequent collections, as recently in the *Unv. L. S.*, 1851, No. 687.

It was the favourite hymn of Friedrich Wilhelm III. of Prussia, and Lauxmann, in *Koch*, viii. 340, relates how he was affected by hearing it sung while in a boat in the mines at Waldenburg in 1800. With this hymn the Prussian War Minister, Albrecht von Roon, celebrated his Jubilee of service, near Paris, January 9, 1871. The splendid chorale, given in the *C. B. for England*, appeared in the *Stralsund G. B.*, 1665 (set to the hymn "Hast du denn Liebster dein Angesicht gäntzlich verborgen," see Dr. J. Zahn's *Psalter und Harfe*, 1886, No. 335), was adapted by Neander, and repeated in Freylinghausen's *G. B.*, 1704, and most later books.

Translations in C. U. :—

1. **To God Almighty be praises and thanks from all living.** A free *tr.* of st. i., ii., v., as No. 58 in the Dalston Hospital *H. Bk.*, 1848.

2. **Praise ye Jehovah ! with anthems of praise come before Him.** In 4 st. (marked as *tr.* from Neander, but really taking very little either from his language or his ideas), as No. 17 in the Amer. Luth. Gen. Synod's *H. Bk.*, 1850–52.

3. **Oh praise the King supreme in might, who reigneth in glory.** Omitting st. iv., by A. T. Russell, as No. 214 in his *Ps. & Hys.*, 1851.

4. **Praise to Jehovah ! the Almighty King of Creation.** A good *tr.*, omitting st. ii., by Miss Borthwick in the 2nd Ser., 1855, of the *H. L. L.*,

p. 66 (1884, p. 124). Repeated in Dr. Pagenstecher's *Coll.*, 1864, and Wilson's *Service of Praise*, 1865.

5. **Praise to the Lord ! He is King over all the Creation.** A good *tr.*, by T. C. Porter, in *Cantate Domino*, Boston, U.S., 1859, No. 315 ; repeated in the *Hys. for the* [German] *Reformed Ch.*, Philadelphia, 1874, No. 462.

6. **Praise to the Lord ! the Almighty, the King of Creation !** A good *tr.*, omitting st. iv., by Miss Winkworth, as No. 9 in her *C. B. for England*, 1863 ; and thence in Dr. W. F. Stevenson's *H. for Ch. & Home*, 1873, *Evang. Hyl.*, N. Y., 1880, &c.

7. **Praise thou the Lord, the omnipotent Monarch of Glory.** In full, as No. 361, in the Ohio *Luth. Hyl.*, 1880, marked as *tr.* by "J. H. Good."

8. **Praises we're bringing to Jesus, Almighty and Royal.** A *tr.* of st. i., iv. (dated 1880), by M. W. Stryker, as No. 808 in the *Ch. Praise Bk.*, N. Y., 1882, with an original st. as iii.

9. **Praise to the Lord, the Omnipotent King of Creation !** A *tr.* of st. i.–iii., v. (dated 1882), by M. W. Stryker, in his *Hys. & Verses*, 1883, p. 36 ; repeated as No. 31 in his *Christian Chorals*, 1885.

Other trs. are : (1) "Praise thou, my Soul, the most mighty and great King of Glory," in the *Suppl. to Ger. Psalmody*, ed. 1765, p. 69. (2) "Praise to the Father, the glorious King of Creation," in the 3rd ed., 1882, of J. H. Hopkins's *Carols, Hys. and Songs*, dated 1866. (3) "Praise the Almighty, the King of a glory unbounded," by *N. L. Frothingham*, 1870, p. 991.

[J. M.]

Lobet den Herren, denn er ist sehr freundlich. [*Grace after Meat.*] Founded on Ps. cxlvii. *Bode*, p. 180, cites this as in the *Jungfrau Schulordnung zu Torgau*, printed at Leipzig, 1565, where it has 9 st. of 4 l., and is printed after the instruction on the First Commandment. *Wackernagel*, iv. p. 168, quotes it from a Nürnberg broadsheet N.D., *circa* 1560 (*Zwey Schöne Geistliche Lieder*), and from the *Leipzig G. B.* 1582, in 7 st. ; and this form is in the *Unv. L. S.*, 1851, No. 499. The only *tr.* in C. U. is noted under " Lobet den Herren alle die ihn fürchten " (see p. 411, ii.).

[J. M.]

Lobwasser, Ambrosius, s. of Fabian Lobwasser, inspector of mines at Schneeberg, Saxony, was b. at Schneeberg, April 4, 1515. After studying law at Leipzig (M.A. 1535) he remained there as University tutor until 1550. After acting as travelling tutor, he was appointed in 1557 Rath and Chancellor at Meissen, and in 1562 made a tour in Italy, and received the degree of LL.D. from the University of Bologna. He was finally appointed in 1563 by Duke Albrecht of Prussia as professor of law and assessor at the High Court of Justice at Königsberg. He d. at Königsberg Nov. 27, 1585 (*Koch*, ii. 394–401, &c.).

His principal poetical work was his version of the *Psalter*, which is noted under *Psalters*, German, pt. i. § ii. One has passed into English in recent times, viz. :

Ihr Knecht des Herren all zugleich. [*Ps. cxxxiv.*] The original is Beza's version of the Psalm, "Or sus, serviteurs de Seigneur," which first appeared in his *Trente-quatre pseaumes de David*, Geneva, 1551. Lobwasser's version is in his *Psalter dess Königlichen Propheten Davids*, Leipzig, 1573 (not paged), in 3 st. of 4 l., entitled "He encourages the people to fulfil their calling diligently, and assures them that God will grant them His grace." *Tr.* as :—

Ye servants of the Lord, who stand. In full, by Miss

Winkworth, as No. 88 in her *C. B. for England*, 1863, and set to the original melody of 1551 (see "All people that on earth do dwell").   [J. M.]

Lodenstein, Jodocus van, s. of Joost Corneliss van Lodenstein, burgomaster of Delft, was b. at Delft Feb. 6, 1620. After studying at the Universities of Utrecht and Franeker he was appointed in 1644 pastor at Zoetermeer and Zegwaard, near Delft; in 1650 at Sluys (Sluis, near the boundary of Flanders); and in 1653 at Utrecht. He d. at Utrecht Aug. 6, 1677 (*Allg. Deutsche Biog.* xix. 73–75).

A pastor of the Reformed Church, he was spiritually allied to the Mystics. After 1665, not being able to exclude the worldly, he ceased to dispense the Holy Communion and altered the Baptismal formula; but never separated from the Church.

His hymns appeared in his *Uyt-Spanningen, Behelfende eenige stigtelyke Liederen en andere Gedigten*, &c., Utrecht, 1676 [Berlin], which passed through many eds. Two are *tr.*, viz. :—

1. Hemelsch Ooge! Wilt gy dogen. [*Love to God.*] 1676, p. 346, in 9 st. entitled "Solitude with God." It has passed into English through

Ich will einsam und gemeinsam. No. 723, in Freylinghausen's *G. B.*, 1705; Porst's *G. B.*, ed. 1855, No. 385. It is a free *tr.* in 5 st. of 6 l., and is probably by C. A. Bernstein (p. 135, ii.), certainly not by G. Arnold or G. Tersteegen. *Tr.* as (1) "Quite alone and yet not lonely," in full, from the 1705, as No. 680 in pt. i. of the *Moravian H. Bk.*, 1754. In the *Moravian H. Bk.*, 1789 (1886, No. 702), the *trs.* of st. i., ii., were reduced to 8.7.8.7, and this form is also in the *Bible H. Bk.*, 1845.

2. Heylge Jesu! Hemelsch Voorbeeld! [*Christ our Example.*] 1676, p. 152, in 9 st., entitled "Jesus Pattern." It has passed into English through

Heiligster Jesu, Heiligungsquelle, *tr.* in full. This has not yet been traced earlier than G. Arnold's *Göttliche Sophia*, 1700, pt. ii. p. 327, where it is No. 17 of "Some hitherto unknown poems, mostly composed by others." As it is found in this section it is perhaps more probably by B. Crasselius (q. v.). *Koch*, vi. 6, and viii. 437, characterises it as "a pearl in the Evangelical Treasury of Song and a genuine Christian moral hymn, of more importance than a hundred of the so-called moral hymns in the second half of the eighteenth century." In the Berlin *G. L. S.* ed., 1863, No. 631. The *trs.* are: (1) "As Thy will, O my Saviour," of st. ii., by C. G. Clemens, as No. 1065 in the *Suppl.* of 1808, to the *Moravian H. Bk.*, 1801 (1886, No. 622). (2) "Most holy Jesus! Fount unfailing," by *Dr. H. Mills*, 1845 (1856, p. 287). (3) "Thou holiest Saviour, sacred spring," by *Miss Dunn*, 1857, p. 26. (4) "Most holy Jesus, Fount of light," in Schaff's *Christ in Song*, 1869, p. 133.   [J. M.]

Logan, John. [Bruce, Michael.]

Logau, Friedrich von, was b. in June, 1604, at Brockut, near Nimptsch, in Silesia, and became in 1644 Kanzleirath in the service of the Dukes of Brieg. In 1654 he removed with Duke Ludwig to Liegnitz as his Regierungsrath, and d. at Liegnitz, July 24, 1655.

He was one of the best German poets of his time (admitted a member of the Palm Order in 1648), and specially distinguished as a writer of epigrams and aphorisms. These were first pub. in 1638. The complete ed., Breslau, 1654, was entitled *Salomons von Golaw deutscher Sinn-Getichte drey Tausend*. A complete reprint was issued by the Stuttgart Literary Society in 1872 (vol. 113 of their publications), and selections by G. Eitner (Leipzig, 1870), and modernised by K. Simrock (Stuttgart, 1874), and L. H. Fischer (Leipzig, 1875). A few have been *tr.* by H. W. Longfellow, and of these the two best known, with one or two more *tr.* by herself, are included in Miss Winkworth's *Christian Singers*, 1869, pp. 230–233.   [J. M.]

Long did I toil and know no earthly rest. *H. F. Lyte.* [*Peace in Jesus.*] Appeared in his *Poems chiefly Religious*, 1833, p. 76, in 6 st. of 6 l. It combines unwavering confidence with plaintive sweetness, and is one of his most touching efforts. Its use is

extensive; but usually two or more stanzas are omitted. Orig. text in *Lyra Brit.*, 1867, p. 377.   [J. J.]

Long have I laboured in the fire. *C. Wesley.* [*Repentance.*] 1st pub. in *Hys. & Sac. Poems*, 1742, in 10 st. of 4 l., as the second of two hymns, "After a relapse into Sin" (*P. Works*, 1868–72, vol. ii. p. 202). In the *Wes. H. Bk.*, 1780, st. vi., viii.-x. were given as No. 208, "Jesus, to Thee I now can fly." This has been repeated in several collections, sometimes as "Jesus, to Thee *we* now can fly," and again as "Jesus, to Thee, *to Thee*, I fly," as in Dr. Alexander's *Augustine H. Bk.*, 1849 and 1865.   [J. J.]

Long have I [we] sat beneath the sound. *I. Watts.* [*Unfruitfulness.*] 1st pub. in the 2nd ed. of his *Hys. and S. Songs*, 1709, Bk. ii., No. 165, in 6 st. of 4 l., and headed "Unfruitfulness, Ignorance, and unsanctified Affections." It was repeated in J. Wesley's *Ps. & Hys.*, pub. at Charlestown, 1736–7, in Whitefield's *Ps. & Hys.*, 1753; Madan's *Ps. & Hys.*, 1760, and others of the older collections, and also in a large number of modern hymnbooks both in G. Britain and America, but usually in a slightly altered form, and sometimes as, "Long have *we* sat beneath the sound." Another and somewhat popular arrangement of the text is "Long have *we heard the joyful* sound." This is in Snepp's *Songs of G. & G.*, 1872, *Common Praise*, 1879, and many others.   [J. J.]

Long have I seemed to serve Thee, Lord. *C. Wesley.* [*Formal Religion.*] Written during the disputes between the Wesleys and the Moravians concerning Antinomianism and Perfectionism. Dr. Jackson sums up the controversy in his *Memoirs* of C. Wesley (abridged ed., 1848, p. 98) thus :—

"Molther was the most active and strenuous in propagating the errors by which many were misled. He contended that there are no degrees in faith; so that those who have not the full and unclouded assurance of the divine favour, whatever they may possess besides, have no faith at all. Another tenet which he avowed and defended was, that till men have faith, they are not to use any of the means of grace, such as the reading of the Scriptures, attending the ministry of the Gospel, and receiving the Holy Communion; these ordinances being rather injurious than beneficial, till men have a true and vital faith. . . . The fine hymn on Christian Ordinances, and beginning,

'Still for thy loving-kindness, Lord,
   I in Thy temple wait,'

was written by Mr. C. Wesley at this period [1739–40], as an antidote to the mischievous errors which were prevalent."

The hymn was included in the Wesley *Hys. & Sac. Poems*, 1740, in 23 st. of 4 l., and headed "The Means of Grace" (*P. Works*, 1868–72, vol. i. p. 233). In 1780 J. Wesley compiled two hymns therefrom, and gave them in the *Wes. H. Bk.* as :—

1. Long have I seemed to serve Thee, Lord, *No.* 88.
2. Long for Thy loving-kindness, Lord, *No.* 89.

These hymns have been repeated in numerous hymn-books in G. Britain and America. In the American Unitarian *Hys. for the Ch. of Christ*, 1853, the first of these is reduced to 4 st.   [J. J.]

Long have I sought for happiness. *W. Hammond.* [*Death and the Resurrection.*] 1st pub. in his *Ps., Hys. and Spiritual Songs*, 1745, p. 97, in 13 st. of 4 l. and headed, "And so shall we ever be with the Lord." In this full form it is not in common use. A cento therefrom, " Lord, if on earth the thought of Thee," is given in the S. P. C. K. *Church Hymns*, 1871, No. 417. It is composed of sts. iii., iv., ix. and xiii., all more or less altered.

[J. J.]

Longfellow, Henry Wadsworth, D.C.L., was b. at Portland, Maine, Feb. 27, 1807, and graduated at Bowdoin College, 1825. After residing in Europe for four years to qualify for the Chair of Modern Languages in that College, he entered upon the duties of the same. In 1835 he removed to Harvard, on his election as Professor of Modern Languages and Belles-Lettres. He retained that Professorship to 1854. His literary reputation is great, and his writings are numerous and well known. His poems, many of which are as household words in all English-speaking countries, display much learning and great poetic power. A few of these poems and portions of others have come into C. U. as hymns, but a hymn-writer in the strict sense of that term he was not and never claimed to be. His pieces in C. U. as hymns include:—

1. **Alas, how poor and little worth.** *Life a Race*, Tr. from the Spanish of Don Jorge Manrique (d. 1479), in Longfellow's *Poetry of Spain*, 1833.

2. **All is of God; if He but wave His hand.** *God All and in All.* From his poem " The Two Angels," pub. in his *Birds of Passage*, 1858. It is in the Boston *Hys. of the Spirit*, 1864, &c.

3. **Blind Bartimeus at the gate.** *Bartimeus.* From his *Miscellaneous Poems*, 1841, into G. W. Conder's 1874 *Appendix* to the *Leeds H. Bk.*

4. **Christ to the young man said, " Yet one thing more."** *Ordination.* Written for his brother's (S. Longfellow) ordination in 1848, and pub. in *Seaside and Fireside*, 1851. It was given in an altered form as " *The Saviour* said, yet one thing more," in H. W. Beecher's *Plymouth Coll.*, 1855.

5. **Down the dark future through long generations.** *Peace.* This, the closing part of his poem on " The Arsenal at Springfield," pub. in his *Belfrey of Bruges*, &c., 1845, was given in *A Book of Hys.*, 1848, and repeated in several collections.

6. **Into the silent land.** *The Hereafter.* A *tr.* from the German (see Salis).

7. **Tell me not in mournful numbers.** *Psalm of Life.* Pub. in his *Voices of the Night*, 1839, as " A Psalm of Life: What the heart of the Young Man said to the Psalmist." It is given in several hymnals in G. Britain and America. In some collections it begins with st. ii., " Life is real! Life is earnest."

The universal esteem in which Longfellow was held as a poet and a man was marked in a special manner by his bust being placed in that temple of honour, Westminster Abbey.

[F. M. B.]

Longfellow, Samuel, M.A., brother of the Poet, was b. at Portland, Maine, June 18, 1819, and educated at Harvard, where he graduated in Arts in 1839, and in Theology in 1846. On receiving ordination as an Unitarian Minister, he became Pastor at Fall River, Massachusetts, 1848; at Brooklyn, 1853;

and at Germantown, Pennsylvania, 1860. In 1846 he edited, with the Rev. S. Johnson (q. v.), *A Book of Hymns for Public and Private Devotion*. This collection was enlarged and revised in 1848. In 1859 his *Vespers* was pub., and in 1864 the Unitarian *Hymns of the Spirit*, under the joint editorship of the Rev. S. Johnson and himself. His *Life* of his brother, the Poet Longfellow, was pub. in 1886. To the works named he contributed the following hymns:—

i. To *A Book of Hymns*, revised ed., 1848.

1. Beneath the shadow of the Cross. *Love.*
2. O God, thy children gathered here. *Ordination.*

ii. To the *Vespers*, 1859.

3. Again as evening's shadow falls. *Evening.*
4. Now on land and sea descending. *Evening.*

iii. To the *Hymns of the Spirit*, 1864.

5. A voice by Jordan's shore. *Advent.*
6. Father, give Thy benediction. *Ordination.*
7. Go forth to life, O child of earth. *Life's Mission.*
8. God of ages and of nations. *Holy Scriptures.*
9. Holy Spirit, Truth divine. *The Holy Spirit desired.*
10. I look to Thee in every need. *Trust in God.*
11. In the beginning was the Word. *The Word.*
12. Love for all, and can it be? *Lent. The Prodigal Son.*
13. O God, in Whom we live and move. *God's Law and Love.*
14. O God, Thou Giver of all good. *Prayer for Food.*
15. O still in accents sweet and strong. *Missions.*
16. O Thou, Whose liberal sun and rain. *Anniversary of Church dedication.*
17. One holy Church of God appears. *The Church Universal.*
18. Out of the dark, the circling sphere. *The Outlook.*
19. Peace, peace on earth! the heart of man for ever. *Peace on Earth.*
20. The loving Friend to all who bowed. *Jesus of Nazareth.*
21. 'Tis winter now, the fallen snow. *Winter.*

Of these, hymn No. 2 was written for the Ordination of E. E. Hale (q. v.), at Worcester, 1846. Several are included in Martineau's *Hymns*, 1873. D. Oct. 3, 1892. [F. M. B.]

Look down, O Lord, and on our youth. *T. Cotterill.* [*Confirmation.*] Appeared in the 9th ed. of his *Sel.*, 1820, No. 120, in 6 st. of 4 l., and headed, " Intercession for Children about to be Confirmed." It has passed into a large number of hymn-books, and is popular as a Confirmation hymn. [J. J.]

Look down, O Lord, with pitying eye. *P. Doddridge.* [*Missions.*] This hymn is No. 66 in the D. MSS. but is undated. It was pub. by J. Orton in his ed. of Doddridge's (posthumous) *Hymns*, &c., 1755, No. 146, in 5 st. of 4 l., and again in J. D. Humphreys's ed. of the same, 1839, No. 164. It is based on Ezekiel's Vision of the Dry Bones, and is in C. U. in G. Britain and America.

[J. J.]

Look in pity, Lord of Glory. *E. Caswall.* [*Confirmation.*] This hymn is compiled from a " Hymn for the Renewal of Baptismal Vows," first pub. in his *May Pageant and other Poems*, 1865. It is written to be sung in parts, divided into a " Solo," " Chorus," and a portion to be sung by " All." In the *People's H.*, each of these parts has been lain under contribution to furnish hymn 346. Caswall's revised text is in his *Hymns & Poems* 1873, p. 296. [W. T. B.]

Look, ye saints, the sight is glorious. *T. Kelly.* [*The Second Advent.*] 1st pub. in his *Hymns*, &c., 3rd ed., 1809, No. 27, in 4 st.

of 6 l., and headed, "And He shall reign for ever, and ever" (1853 ed., No. 49). In popular and extensive use both in G. Britain and America. It ranks with many of the best hymns by Watts and C. Wesley.   [J. J.]

Lord and God of heavenly powers. C. Wesley. [*Praise.*] Appeared in *Hys. and Sac. Poems*, 1739, pt. ii., as a metrical paraphrase of "Therefore with Angels and Archangels," &c. (See *Ter Sanctus*, in **Greek Hymnody, p. 459,** i.), from the Office for Holy Communion in the Book of Common Prayer. (*P. Works*, 1868–72, vol. i. p. 114.) It is in 3 st. of 4 l. In its original form it is not in frequent use; but st. iii.—

> " ' Holy, holy, holy, Lord,
> Live by heaven and earth adored ! '
> Full of Thee they ever cry,
> ' Glory be to God most high,' "

is sometimes used in centos, as in Mercer's version of "Sons of God, triumphant rise" (q.v.).   [J. J.]

Lord, and what shall this man do? *J. Keble.* [*St. John the Evangelist.*] Written Dec. 27, 1819, and 1st pub. in his *Christian Year*, 1827, in 6 st. of 6 l., and based upon St. John xxi. 21, 22. It is given in several hymn-books, but usually in an abbreviated form. In the American *Plymouth Coll.*, 1855, No. 858, st. iv.–vi. are given as "Gales from heaven, if so He will."   [J. J.]

Lord, as to Thy dear Cross we flee. *J. H. Gurney.* [*Resignation*, or *The Daily Cross.*] 1st pub. in his Lutterworth *Coll. of Hys.*, 1838, No. 127, in 6 st. of 4 l., and again in the Mary-le-bone *Ps. & Hys.*, 1851, No. 112. It is given in numerous collections in G. Britain and America, and sometimes as, "As to Thy Cross, dear Lord, we flee." Another altered form is "Lord, as we put our trust in Thee," in *Common Praise*, 1879.   [J. J.]

Lord, at Thy feet a sinner lies. *S. Browne.* [*Lent.*] Appeared in the 1st ed. of his *Hys. and Spiritual Songs*, &c., 1720, No. 15, in 6 st. of 4 l., and entitled "Sinners suing for mercy." In Rippon's *Sel.*, 1787, No. 235, it was altered to "Lord, at Thy feet *we sinners lie*," and this form has been continued to modern hymnals, as in Bap. *Ps. & Hys.*, 1858 and 1880, No. 384. Its use is somewhat extensive.   [J. J.]

Lord, at Thy Table I behold. *S. Stennett.* [*Holy Communion.*] Appeared in *Hys. for All Denominations*, Lon. 1782, No. 42, and in Rippon's Bap. *Sel.*, 1787, No. 482, in 7 st. of 4 l., and entitled "A Sacramental Hymn." It was given as by "Dr. J. Stennett"; but the "J." is a misprint for "S." This error is repeated in most collections. The use of this hymn, usually in an abridged form, is somewhat extensive in G. Britain and America, and especially amongst the Baptists. [J. J.]

Lord, at Thy temple we appear. *I. Watts.* [*Nunc Dimittis.*] This is given as "The Song of Simeon; or, Death made desirable," in his *Hys. & Spiritual S.*, 1707, Bk. i., No. 19, in 6 st. of 4 l. It is in use in G. Britain and America. In the *Leeds H. Bk.*, 1853, No. 647, st. v., vi. are given as, "Jesus, the vision of Thy Face." The use of this abbreviated form is limited. [J. J.]

Lord, at Thy word the constant sun. *J. H. Gurney.* [*Harvest.*] 1st pub. in his Lutterworth *Coll. of Hymns*, &c., 1838, No. 128, in 4 st. of 7 l., with st. iv. bracketed for omission if desired. In 1851, st. i.–iii. were rewritten, and a new st. iv. added by the author for his Mary-le-bone *Ps. & Hys.*, No. 124, and included therein as "Lord of the Harvest! Thee we hail." Since 1851 it has passed into most of the leading collections, and is the most popular of the author's compositions. In the *Hymnary*,1872, and Thring's *Coll.*, 1882, Dryden's doxology, "Immortal honour, endless fame," from his "Creator Spirit," &c., is added thereto. This gives to the hymn a completeness not usually found in the collections. Orig. text as above: authorized text of 1851 in the S. P. C. K. *Church Hys.*, with st. ii., ll. 1, 2, "When" for "If" in both lines.   [J. J.]

Lord, by Thee in safety borne. *J. Anstice.* [*Sunday Morning.*] 1st pub. in his posthumous *Hymns*, &c., 1836, No. v., in 4 st. of 8 l. In 1841 it was given in the *Child's Christian Year* as the opening hymn of that collection. It is in a few hymnals, including *Kennedy*, 1863, in which st. ii., ll. 1–4, and various alterations are by Dr. Kennedy.   [J. J.]

Lord, cause Thy face on us to shine. *T. Cotterill.* [*For a Blessing on Ministers and People.*] Contributed to the 8th ed. of his *Sel.*, 1819, No. 28, in 3 st. of 8 l., and headed, "For God's blessing on His Ministers and People." Although not repeated in the 9th ed., 1820, it was included in other hymn-books, and is still in C. U. The hymn, "O King of Salem, Prince of Peace," in W. F. Stevenson's *Hys. for Church and Home*, 1873, and other collections, begins with st. ii. of this hymn.   [J. J.]

Lord, come away; why dost Thou stay. *Bp. Jeremy Taylor.* [*The Second Advent.*] This hymn, entitled "The Second Hymn for Advent; or, Christ's Coming to Jerusalem in Triumph," appeared in his *Festival and Penitential Hymns*, appended to his *Golden Grove*, 1655, in 21 irregular lines. In this form it was included in Bp. Heber's (posthumous) *Hymns*, &c., 1827, and in Bp. Taylor's *Collected Works*, vol. vii., 1854. In this form, however, it was not suitable for congregational use. In a rewritten form it appeared in the *Leeds H. Bk.*, 1853, No. 286, as, "Descend to Thy Jerusalem, O Lord." This, with slight variations, was included in the *Sarum Hymnal*, 1868, as "Draw nigh to Thy Jerusalem, O Lord," and from thence has passed into the S. P. C. K. *Church Hys.*, 1871, and others. [**English Hymnody, Early, § IX.**]   [J. J.]

Lord, dismiss us with Thy blessing. [*Close of Service.*] This is the opening line of *four* hymns, each of which must be noted in detail.

i. The *first* hymn reads :—

> I.
> " Lord, dismiss us with thy Blessing;
>   Fill our Hearts with joy and peace :
> Let us each, thy Love possessing,
>   Triumph in redeeming Grace
>   O refresh us
> In this dry and barren place.

II.

Thanks we give and Adoration
For thy Gospel's joyful sound :
May the Fruits of thy Salvation
In our Hearts and Lives abound !
Ever faithful
To the Truth may we be found !

III.

" So whene'er the Signal's given
Us from Earth to call away,
Borne on Angels' wings to Heaven,
Glad the Summons to obey.
May we ever
Reign with CHRIST in endless Day."

The authorship of this hymn has long been a matter of doubt. From 1773 to 1780 it appeared in many collections, but always without signature, in common with all the hymns in the same collections; and from 1786 to 1800, when it was given in collections wherein hymns were assigned to their respective authors, as the composition of "F." and "Fawcett." The details taking the leading collections are :—

i. In *A Supplement to the Shawbury Hymn Book, Shrewsbury, Printed by J. Eddowes, near the Market House,* 1773. *And sold by Mr. T. Maddox in Shawbury.* The title of the *Shawbury H. Bk.* to which this is a *Suppl.* is *A Collection of Psalms and Hymns. Extracted from Dr. Watts, and other Authors.* The 2nd ed. before us is dated *Shrewsbury,* 1773. It has written in it " Sir Richd. Hill," showing that it was the property of Sir Richard Hill, brother of the Rev. Rowland Hill. The text given above is from this *Suppl.,* No. 46. These facts suggest the question, " Is Rowland Hill the author ? " We think not, because the hymn does not appear in any of his hymn-books, all published at a later date. If it were his, we cannot conceive why it should have been omitted. The omission from his hymn-books is fatal to his claim.

ii. 1774. In Dr. Conyers's *Collection of Psalms and Hymns,* &c., London, J. & W. Oliver, 3rd ed., No. 374. In this st. i., l. 6, is altered to *Trav'lling thro' this wilderness.*

iii. 1776. In A. M. Toplady's *Psalms and Hymns,* 1st ed., No. 168, with alterations thus :—

St. ii., ll. 5, 6.   *May thy presence*
                    With us evermore be found !
St. iii., l. 5.   *We shall surely.*

iv. 1778. In *A Collection of Hymns,* pub. at Edinburgh.

v. 1780. In the 4th ed. of Dr. Conyers's *Coll.,* pub. at York.

vi. 1780. In David Simpson's *Collection of Psalms and Hymns,* pub. at Macclesfield, *Appendix,* No. 482.

vii. 1780. In *A Collection of Hymns,* &c. (4th ed.), pub. at York by A. Ward, for the compiler, the Rev. J. Harris, a Nonconformist Minister of Hull.

viii. 1780. In the *Lady Huntingdon Collection,* under the editorship of the Hon. and Rev. Walter Shirley. In this case we have the altered text of *Toplady* repeated for the first time.

To this date no indication of authorship can be found either in the above collections, or in contemporary literature. Thirteen years after its first appearance in *Suppl.* to the *Shawbury H. Bk.* the history is again taken up, but in a more definite form, thus :—

ix. 1786. In a *Selection of Psalms for Social Worship,* &c., York, A. Ward. This Unitarian collection contains the first four lines only of st. i. and ii., and these are signed " F." This initial we find from the list of authors given in the collection represents *J. Fawcett* (q. v.), a Nonconformist Minister formerly of Wainsgate, Yorkshire ; and then of Hebden Bridge, in the same county. A shade of doubtfulness, however, is thrown over the ascriptions of authorship in this collection by the editor prefacing his list with these words, "In the appropriation [of names] as it depended much on the compiler's memory, he wishes it to be observed, that there may probably be some mistakes, but he hopes there are not many." *Preface, p. xi.*

x. 1791. In the 7th ed. of Harris's *Collection,* No. 212 (see vi.), pub. at York, and edited by John Beatson, George Lambert, Robert Green, and John Jones, it is given as in Dr. Conyers's *Collection,* and signed *Fawcett.*

xi. 1800. In *A Collection of Hymns for Christian Worship,* pub. in Dublin, and again signed *Fawcett.*

From this date the signature falls out of use for many years, probably from the fact that, the *York* and *Dublin Collections* being little known, the editors of new hymn-books took their texts from *Conyers, Toplady,* the *Lady Huntingdon, Burder,* or similar widely-known collections in which all hymns were given without signatures, and appended thereto such notes as, " from Burder's Coll.," " Taylor and Jones's Coll.," and so on. During the past few years, however, the question of authorship has been revived, some claiming it for Dr. Fawcett, and others for the Hon. and Rev. W. Shirley. Their respective claims, with their drawbacks, stand thus :—

For Dr. John Fawcett. To him it is ascribed by the *York Collections* of 1786 and 1791, the editors of which, in common with Fawcett, were resident in Yorkshire, and ministers of Nonconformist congregations. Also by the *Dublin Collection,* 1800.

Against Dr. Fawcett. The before-named weakness in the testimony of the *York Coll.,* 1786, must be noted, and the fact that the hymn is not in Fawcett's works, nor is it claimed for him either by his editor or his family. It must be added, however, that several of his hymns are found in the *Gospel Magazine* which are not given in his works.

For Hon. and Rev. W. Shirley. A tradition in his family, set forth by his son to Mr. A. C. H. Seymour, and recorded by Dr. Rogers in *Lyra Brit.,* p. 498, and Miller, *Singers & Songs of the Church,* 1869, p. 246, that it was his composition.

Against Mr. Shirley. (1) There is no documentary evidence. (2) That it was in the Shawbury *Suppl.* seven years before admitted by Shirley as editor into the *Lady Huntingdon Coll.* in 1780, and (3) when admitted the text was taken from *Toplady,* and not from the original.

These statements are by no means satisfactory. Taking them, however, as they stand, we must conclude that the author is very probably Dr. Fawcett, and certainly not Walter Shirley.

The use of this Dismissal hymn has been and still is most extensive. Nearly every hymn-book of an Evangelical type published during the past hundred years has adopted it in a form more or less perfect. In some cases it has a doxology added thereto or substituted for the last stanza. *Mercer's* doxology, Oxford ed., 1864, No. 54, is the most suitable. The hymns :—

" Lord, *refresh* us with Thy blessing,"

found in various collections ; and—

" Lord, *enrich* us with Thy blessing,"

as in the Rugby *School Hymn-Book,* 1850, and later editions, are altered from the above.

ii. The *second* hymn is :—

" Lord, dismiss us with Thy blessing,
Bid us all depart in peace ;
Still on gospel manna feed us,
Pure seraphic love increase :
Fill each breast with consolation,
Up to Thee our voices we raise,
When we reach the blissful station,
Then we'll give Thee nobler praise.
And sing hallelujah to God and the Lamb,
For ever and ever, for ever and ever,
Hallelujah, Hallelujah, Hallelujah !

This hymn is found in Dr. Hawker's *Psalms and Hymns for the Sunday School in the Parish Church of Charles, Plymouth,* 9th ed. no date, 13th ed. 1807. In the Crawford and Eberle *Index to the Irish Church Hymnal,* 1876, p. 53, the editors say :—

" It is found also, but with considerable alterations, in the *Rev. Edward Smyth's Collection,* Manchester, 1793.

Of these two versions that of Hawker seems to be the older, and is possibly by Hawker himself. It is ascribed to him in Baring-Gould's *Life of the Rev. R. S. Hawker*, where, however, Mr. Baring-Gould has inadvertently quoted the hymn with Fawcett's text which is found indeed in the latest edition of the *Charles Collection* (1867), but was then introduced in it for the first time by the editor, the Rev. H. A. Greaves. If the eight-line stanza is by Dr. Hawker, it must have appeared in his *Collection* before 1793. He became Vicar of Charles in 1784, and the Sunday School was established in 1787."

From the time of its appearance in the *Charles* and the *Manchester Collections* to the present, it has been republished in numerous hymnals, including D. Simpson's Macclesfield *Coll.* 1795; the *Wes. H. Bk.*, 1800; *Williams & Boden*, 1801; Bailey's *Sion's Melodies*, 1813–1866, and others. In the last case it is given in two stanzas from "*Smyth's Manchester Collection*" as noted above.

iii. The *third* hymn is :—

" Lord, dismiss us with Thy blessing,
    Thanks for mercies past receive ;
Pardon all their faults confessing ;
    Time that's lost, may all retrieve !
        May Thy Children
    Ne'er again Thy Spirit grieve !

" Bless Thou, all our days of leisure ;
    Help us selfish lures to flee :—
Sanctify our every pleasure,
    Pure and spotless may it be :
        May our gladness
    Draw us evermore to Thee !

" By Thy kindly influence cherish
    All the good we here have gained ;
May all taint of evil perish,
    By Thy mightier power restrained ;
        Seek we ever
    Knowledge pure and love unfeigned !

" Let Thy Father-hand be shielding
    All who here shall meet no more ;
May their seed-time past be yielding
    Year by year a richer store !
        Those returning
    Make more faithful than before ! "

This hymn is by the Rev. H. J. Buckoll, sometime Assistant Master in Rugby School ; and it appeared in the *Ps. & Hys. for the Use of Rugby School Chapel*, 1850, No. 56, and appointed "For the *last* Sunday of the Half-Year." It had a companion hymn by Buckoll "For the *first* Sunday of the Half-Year" (No. 55), the opening stanza of which reads :—

" Lord, behold us with Thy blessing,
    Once again assembled here ;
Onward be our footsteps pressing,
    In Thy love, and faith, and fear !
        Still protect us
    By Thy presence ever near ! "

These hymns have been repeated in most of the modern Public School hymn-books.

iv. The *fourth* hymn is the following :—

" Lord, dismiss us with Thy blessing,
    Guide us in Thy holy ways,
That Thy love and joy possessing,
    May we ever sing Thy praise.
        Hallelujah ! Amen.
    That Thy love and joy possessing,
    We may ever sing Thy praise.

" Low in supplication bending,
    We adore Thy power divine ;
Hallelujahs never ending
    Through eternity be Thine !
        Hallelujah ! Amen.
    Hallelujahs never ending
    Through eternity be Thine ! "

This hymn is given in *A Sel. of Ps. & Hys.* pub. at Rugeley, by J. T. Walters, in 1850. The Preface is signed "F. E. P."; but the hymns are given anonymously.

The first of these hymns has been translated into various languages, and in one form or another it is in most extensive use throughout G. Britain, America, the Colonies, and on mission stations. A *tr.* into Latin of a slightly altered form of st. i. : " Dimitte nos, Deus, Tuis," by the Rev. R. Bingham, is given in his *Hymno. Christ. Lat.* 1871, p. 163. It may be added that T. Cotterill's altered form of the oldest text as above, No. i., given in his *Sel.*, 1819, as " Lord, *prevent* us with Thy blessing," failed to attract attention ; that " Dismiss us with Thy blessing, Lord," which is sometimes taken as also an altered form of this hymn, is by J. Hart (q.v.); that " Lord, *attend* us with Thy blessing," No. 917, in *Kennedy*, 1863, is based on Nos. i. and ii. as above ; and that " Lord, *go with* us, *grant* Thy blessing," in Windle's *Ch. & Home M. Ps. & Hyl.*, 1862, No. 225, is the same slightly altered.   [J. J.]

Lord, ere the heavenly seed is sown. J. Needham. [*Before or after Sermon. Parable of the Sower.*] Pub. in his *Hys. Devotional and Moral, on Various Subjects*, &c., 1768, No. 261, in 7 st. of 4 l., and an additional stanza thus introduced :—

The above may be sung after sermon by making the following alterations in stanza i. :—
        " Now, Lord, the heavenly seed is sown,
            Be it Thy servant's care,
        Thy heavenly blessing to bring down
            By humble fervent prayer."

This suggested adaptation for use " After Sermon " has been adopted in some collections, including the Bap. *Sel. of Hys.*, 1838, No. 477; the Bap. *Ps. & Hys.*, 1858 and 1880, and others. The original is headed " An Hymn before Sermon ; or, the Parable of the Sower abrid'd."   [J. J.]

Lord, for ever at Thy side. J. Montgomery. [*Ps. cxxxi.*] Pub. in Cotterill's *Sel.*, 8th ed., 1819, p. 73, in 4 st. of 4 l., and headed, " For Humility." In 1822 it was repeated by Montgomery in his *Songs of Zion*, as a paraphrase of Ps. cxxxi.; in his *Poetical Works*, 1828 ; and his *Original Hymns*, 1853, No. 187. It is a most successful paraphrase, and is somewhat widely used. [**Psalters, English**, § XVII.]   [J. J.]

Lord, from my bed again I rise. W. Bartholomew. [*Morning.*] Written in 1854 for Sir M. Costa's Oratorio *Eli*, and set as a song for the prophet Samuel. It was pub. in *Eli*, 1854, and was subsequently repeated in several hymn-books, including the *N. Cong.*, 1859, and others.   [J. J.]

Lord God of morning and of night. F. T. Palgrave. [*Morning.*] Written in 1862, and given in MS. to Sir R. Palmer (Lord Selborne), who included it in his *Bk. of Praise*, 1862, in 5 st of 4 l. In 1867 it was also given in the author's *Hymns*, and again in several collections in G. Britain and America. It has been specially set to music by Tilleard. London, Novello.   [J. J.]

Lord God, the Holy Ghost. J. Montgomery. [*Whitsuntide.*] Pub. in Cotterill's *Sel.*, 8th ed., 1819, No. 226, in 3 st. of 8 l., and headed " Whit-Sunday." In Montgomery's *Christian Psalmist*, 1825, No. 506, and in his *Original Hymns*, 1853, No. 136, the text is slightly altered. This amended text is that given in Lord Selborne's *Bk. of Praise*, 1862.

and in most of the collections which give the hymn. Its use in G. Britain and America is extensive. [J. J.]

Lord, have mercy and remove us. *H. H. Milman.* [*Heaven desired.*] Pub. in Bp. Heber's posthumous *Hymns*, 1827, p. 122, in 4 st. of 4 l., and again in Milman's *Sel. of Ps. & Hys.*, 1837 (ed. 1856, p. 90). It is found in several modern hymn-books. [J. J.]

Lord, have mercy when we [pray] strive. *H. H. Milman.* [*Lent.*] 1st pub. in Bp. Heber's posthumous *Hymns*, &c., 1827, p. 94, in 3 st. of 8 l., with the refrain " Oh then have mercy! Lord!" and repeated in the author's *Ps. & Hys.*, 1837. In addition to its use in its original form, it is also given in several collections as "Lord, have mercy when we *pray*," as in the *People's H.*, 1807; and, with st. ii. and iii. transposed, in the 1869 *Appendix* to the S. P. C. K. *Ps. & Hys.* Because of its refrain it is sometimes regarded as a Metrical Litany. [J. J].

Lord, her watch Thy Church is keeping. *H. Downton.* [*Foreign Missions.*] Written for a meeting of the Church Missionary Society, and first pub. in Barry's *Psalms & Hymns*, 1867, No. 170, in 3 st. of 8 l., and again in the author's *Hymns & Verses*, 1873, p. 1. It is also found in the S. P. C. K *Church Hymns*, 1871; *H. A. & M.*, 1875; Thring's *Coll.*, 1882, and many others in G. Britain and America, and ranks with the best of the author's compositions. It is sometimes given as "Lord, Thy Church her watch is keeping," as in *Common Praise*, 1879, and others. [J. J.]

Lord, how shall wretched sinners dare. *Anne Steele.* [*In Time of War.*] Appeared in the 2nd ed. of her *Poems on Subjects chiefly Devotional*, 1780, vol. iii. p. 123, in 8 st. of 4 l., and headed, "On the day of Prayer for success in War." It is also in D. Sedgwick's reprint of Miss Steele's *Hymns*, 1863. In a few American hymn-books, including the Presbyterian *Sel. of Hys.*, Philadelphia, 1861, a cento from this is given as "Lord, may our souls Thy grace adore." It begins with st. iii., somewhat altered. [J. J.]

Lord, I am Thine, but Thou wilt prove. *I. Watts.* [*Ps. xvii.*] 1st pub. in his *Psalms of David*, &c., 1719, in 6 st. of 4 l., and headed "The Sinner's Portion and the Saint's Hope; or, The Heaven of separate Souls and the Resurrection." It is given in its original form in the *Hy. Comp.* and a few other hymn-books. In addition there are also the following abbreviations in C. U. :—

1. **All, all is vanity below.** This is an altered form of st. iii.-vi. It appeared in the 1st ed. of Cotterill's *Sel.*, 1810; and is found in several modern collections, including that for the Harrow School Chapel, and others.
2. **What sinners value, I resign.** This is the most popular form of the hymn, and is in extensive use in G. Britain and America. It appeared in A. M. Toplady's *Ps. & Hys.*, 1776, No. 154. [J. J.]

Lord, I am vile, conceived in sin. *I. Watts.* [*Ps. li.*] 1st pub. in his *Ps. of David*, &c., 1719, in 7 st. of 4 l. In the American *Church Pastorals*, Boston, 1864, st. i., ii., iv.-vi. are given as one hymn (No. 361), and st. iii. and vii., beginning " Great God, create my heart anew," as another (No. 360),

The hymn is also in use in its full form. Its original heading is, "Original and actual sin confess'd." [J. J.]

Lord, I believe a rest remains. *C. Wesley.* [*Holiness desired.*] Pub. in *Hys. & Sac. Poems*, 1740, in 27 st. of 4 l., and based upon Heb. iv. 9, " There remaineth therefore a rest to the people of God" (*P. Works*, 1868-72, vol. i. p. 370). In its original form it is an expression of faith in the doctrine of " Entire Holiness," or " Perfection," as understood by the early Methodists, and a prayer for personal possession of the same. In the *Wes. H. Bk.*, 1780, J. Wesley included a cento therefrom as No. 391, embodying the same doctrine and prayer, the *second* and *third* stanzas of which read :—

" A rest, where all our soul's desire
Is fixed on things above ;
Where fear, and sin, and grief expire,
Cast out by perfect love !

" O that I now the rest might know,
Believe, and enter in !
Now, Saviour, now the power bestow,
And let me cease from sin."

Wesley's theological opponents, however, had another cento from the same hymn in use for some years before, in which the *rest* was changed from a word which stood for the doctrine of " Entire Holiness," into a term descriptive of the eternal peace of Heaven. This is one of those changes in the text of the Wesley hymns which J. Wesley denounced in the Preface of the *Wes. H. Bk.* It was made by A. M. Toplady, and appeared in his *Ps. & Hys.*, 1776, No. 52. Stanzas ii., iii. read (with the changes in the text in italics):—

" *Then* shall *I sing and never tire,*
In that blest house above,
Where *doubt, and fear, and pain* expire,
Cast out by perfect love.

" *Celestial Spirit, make me* know
That I shall enter in.
Now, Saviour, now the pow'r bestow,
And *wash* me *from my sin.*"

These two centos are in C. U. in most English-speaking countries, and are distinguished by the stanzas quoted above. In addition, st. xv. and xvii. of the original are given in the American *Church Pastorals*, Boston, 1864, as "Come, O my Saviour, come away." [J. J.]

Lord, I believe Thy work of grace. *C. Wesley.* [*Holiness desired.*] Appeared in *Hys. & Sac. Poems*, 1742, in 22 st. of 4 l., and headed, "The Spirit and the Bride say Come" (*P. Works*, 1868-72, vol. ii. p. 363). In 1780 J. Wesley gave a cento therefrom in 9 st. in the *Wes. H. Bk.*, No. 393, as " O joyful sound of gospel grace." This has been repeated in several collections. [J. J.]

Lord, I confess my sins to Thee. *C. Wesley.* [*Redemption desired.*] Pub. in *Hys. and Sac. Poems*, 1742, in 37 st. of 6 l., divided into four parts, as :—

1. Lord, I confess my sins to Thee.
2. Forgive me, O long-suffering God.
3. Omniscient, Omnipotent King.
4. Behold, ye souls, that mourn for God.

The hymn in the *Wes. H. Bk.*, 1875, No. 120, " Comfort, ye ministers of grace," is composed of st. vi. and vii. of Pt. 4. [J. J.]

Lord, I desire to live as one. *Charitie L. Bancroft.* [*Holiness desired.*] In Spurgeon's

O. O. H. Bk., 1866, this hymn is given in 4 st. of 4 l., and dated 1861. This text is also in other collections. In her *Within the Veil*, 1867, Mrs. Bancroft gives it as the last hymn in the volume, in 6 st. of 4 l., with a note saying that the hymn was revised for that work. In this text the additional sts. are v., vii.   [W. T. B.]

Lord, I have made Thy word my choice. *I. Watts.* [*Ps. cxix. Pt. viii.*] 1st pub. in his *Psalms of David*, &c., 1719, p. 319, in 4 st. of 4 l., and headed, "The Word of God is the Saint's Portion; or, The Excellency and Variety of Scripture." Its use has extended to almost all English-speaking countries, and it is found in a large number of hymn-books at home and abroad.   [J. J.]

Lord, I hear of showers of blessing. *Elizabeth Codner.* [*Divine Blessing desired.*] Although we have the ms. of this hymn in Mrs. Codner's handwriting, sent to D. Sedgwick from Weston-super-Mare, June 18, 1866, wherein it is stated to have been "written in the summer of 1860" [s. mss.], we have no personal facts concerning Mrs. Codner and her work except that she published one or two small books, as *The Missionary Ship; The Bible in the Kitchen*, &c.; edited the periodical, *Woman's Work in the Great Harvest-Field;* and was associated for some years with the Mildmay Protestant Mission (London). "Lord, I hear of showers of blessing" was suggested by the news of the religious revival in Ireland, 1860–61. It is in 7 st. of 4 l., with the refrain "Even me," and is headed "Bless me, even me also, O my Father." The original text is in Spurgeon's *O. O. H. Bk.*, 1866, No. 607. That in I. D. Sankey's *Sac. Songs & Solos*, Pt. i., which is usually regarded as the original, is altered in several instances, and st. v. is omitted. The hymn in full, or in part, is in extensive use, and is specially popular at Mission Services. In 1867 Mrs. Codner wrote a companion hymn of *Praise*, "Lord, to Thee my heart ascending," in 8 st. of 4 l., for the Rev. E. P. Hammond's *Hys. specially adapted for Seasons of Deep Religious Interest*, &c., 1867.   [J. J.]

Lord, I magnify Thy power. *C. Wesley.* [*For Daily Strength.*] Given in his *Hys. for Use of Families*, 1767, No. 53, in 4 st. of 8 l. (*P. Works*, 1868–72, vol. vii. p. 60). In the *Wes. H. Bk.*, 1780, No. 327, st. iii. and iv. were given as "Father, in the Name I pray." It has passed into other collections. G. J. Stevenson's annotations of this hymn in his *Meth. H. Bk. Notes*, 1883, p. 240, are of more than usual interest.   [J. J.]

Lord, if Thou Thy grace impart. *C. Wesley.* [*Ps. cxxxi.*] 1st pub. in the enlarged ed. of the Wesley *Ps. & Hys.*, 1743, in 5 st. of 4 lines. It is one of C. Wesley's finest renderings of the Psalms; and although not admitted into the *Wes. H. Bk.* until the revised ed. of 1875, it has been in extensive use in the Church of England and amongst Nonconformists for more than a hundred years. During that time numerous variations have crept into the text. The first to mutilate it was M. Madan, in his *Ps. & Hys.*, 1760. From his version Church of England and Nonconformist compilers have taken their

texts, and have added thereto, in nearly every instance, something of their own until no two collections are found to agree. These changes cannot be given in detail without reprinting the full text from almost every hymnbook in which the hymn is found. The most peculiar cento of all is that in the S. P. C. K. *Church Hymns*, 1871, No. 418, in 4 st. of 4 l. Of the 16 lines 5 only are by C. Wesley: st. i. ll. 1, 2; st. ii. l. 1; st. iv. ll. 1, 4; the rest being from *Madan*, 1760; Bickersteth's *Christian Psalmody*, 1833; Hall's *Mitre H. Bk.*, 1836; and several others. These pieces are so interlaced that no one except an expert in hymnology can unravel the complication. In *Common Praise*, 1879, the hymn is given with alterations and the omission of st. ii. as "Lord, do Thou Thy grace impart."   [J. J.]

Lord, in the day Thou art about. *J. Mason.* [*Security in God.*] This cento from Mason's *Spiritual Songs; or, Songs of Praise*, &c., 1683, appeared in the Mary-le-bone *Ps. & Hys.* (by J. H. Gurney and others), 1851, No. 118. It is thus composed:—

St. i. from No. vi. "Song of Praise for Protection," st. ii., ll. 1–4. St. ii. from No. vii. "Song of Praise for Health," st. ii., ll. 1–4. St. iii. from No. ix. "Song of Praise for Success," st. iv., ll. 1–4. St. iv. from No. viii., "Song of Praise for Family Prosperity," st. v., ll. 5–8.

These extracts are well pieced together, the result being a simple and practical hymn. It passed from the Mary-le-bone *Ps. & Hys.* into Lord Selborne's *Book of Praise*, 1862, and others. The originals of the *Songs* are in D. Sedgwick's reprint of the same, 1859.   [J. J.]

Lord, in this Thy mercy's day. *I. Williams.* [*Lent—A Metrical Litany.*] This hymn is taken from "Image the Twentieth," a poem on "The Day of Days; or, the Great Manifestation," in 105 st. of 3 l., which forms a part of his work, *The Baptistery; or, The Way of Eternal Life*, 1844. It was given with slight changes in the Cooke & Denton *Hymnal*, 1853, in 6 st. It has been repeated in full or in part in numerous collections in Great Britain and America, and is a most suitable metrical Litany for Lent.   [J. J.]

Lord, in Thy kingdom there shall be. *J. Anstice.* [*Unity.*] Privately printed in his posthumous *Hymns*, 1836, in 5 st. of 4 l. It is based on the Epistle for the 17th S. after Trinity, Eph. iv. In 1841 it was included in *The Child's Christian Year*, from whence it passed into a few collections, including *Kennedy*, 1863, where it is expanded into 3 st. of 8 l. by the addition of a doxology.   [J. J.]

Lord, in Thy Name Thy servants plead. *J. Keble.* [*Rogation Days.*] Written at Malvern, Aug. 4, 1856, and 1st pub. in the *Salisbury H. Bk.*, 1857, No, 105, in 6 st. of 4 l., including a doxology. This was repeated with slight changes in the Rev. F. Pott's *Hymns*, &c., 1861; the S. P. C. K. *Church Hys.*, 1871, and others, sometimes with the *Salisbury H. Bk.* doxology, changed to another, and at other times without any, as in the *Sarum Hyl.*, 1868, and the author's (posthumous) *Miscellaneous Poems*, 1869, p. 114. Its use is extensive.   [J. J.]

Lord Jesus, God and Man. *Sir H. W.*

Baker. [*For a School Feast.*] This hymn is dated 1852 in Biggs's Annotated ed. of *Hys. A. & M.*, but its first publication is traced only to *H. A. & M.*, 1861. It has a slight resemblance to Faber's "O Jesu, God and Man," which was pub. in his *Jesus and Mary*, in 1849. Sir H. W. Baker's hymn is in extensive use in G. Britain and America. It is sometimes given as "Lord *Jesu*, God and Man." [J. J.]

Lord Jesus, with what sweetness and delights. *H. Vaughan.* [*Ascension.*] This poem of 62 lines on Ascension-day appeared in the second part of his *Silex Scintillans ; or Sac. Poems*, &c., 1655, and again in the Rev. H. F. Lyte's reprint, 1846 (1858 ed., p. 133). Upon the first four lines of the poem the Rev. T. Darling based his Ascension Hymn, "Lord Jesus, taken from Thy servants' sight," and pub. the same in the 1850 cd. of his *Hys. for the Church of England.* It is continued in later editions. [J. J.]

Lord, look on all assembled here. *J. Hart.* [*Public Fast.*] Pub. in his *Hys. Composed on Various Subjects*, &c., 1759, No. 96, in 8 st. of 4 l., and headed, "For a Public Fast." Two arrangements from the text are in the hymn-books. The first appeared in the 1st ed. of Cotterill's *Sel.*, 1810, in 6 stanzas. This was reduced to 4 stanzas in Bickersteth's *Christian Psalmody*, 1833, and was repeated in this form in later collections of the Church of England. The second arrangement is in the Nonconformists' hymnals. It was given in the *Leeds H. Bk.*, 1853, the *N. Cong.*, 1859, &c. [J. J.]

Lord, not unto me (The whole I disclaim). *C. Wesley.* [*Lent.*] 1st pub. in the *Hys. on God's Everlasting Love*, 1741, No. 2, in 6 st. of 4 l. (*P. Works*, 1868–72, vol. iii. p. 6). In 1780 it was given in the *Wes. H. Bk.*, with the omission of st. i., as "Thy faithfulness, Lord, Each moment we find," and in this form it has been repeated in several collections in G. Britain and America. [J. J.]

Lord, now the time returns. *J. Austin.* [*Evening.*] Pub. in his *Devotions in the Antient Way of Offices*, &c., 1668, p. 370, hymn 32, in 8 st. of 4 l., including the doxology; again in the editions by Dorrington, and Hickes, and in the reprint by J. Masters, Lond., 1856. In its full form it is not in C. U.; but, abridged as "Blest be Thy love, dear [good] Lord," it is given in a large number of hymnals in G. Britain and America. Sometimes it is found as "Blessed be Thy love," &c. The original text of this abridged form is in Lord Selborne's *Book of Praise*, 1862. [J. J.]

Lord of earth, Thy forming hand. *Sir R. Grant.* [*God the Creator and Preserver.*] Appeared in H. V. Elliott's *Ps. & Hys.*, &c., 1835, in 3 st. of 12 l., and again in Lord Glenelg's edition of Grant's *Sacred Poems*, 1839, No. 3. It is based on Ps. lxxiii. 25. It is in C. U. in G. Britain and America. [J. J.]

Lord of heaven, and earth, and ocean. *J. Crosse.* [*Holy Trinity.*] Written for the Second Yorkshire Musical Festival, held at York on the 13th–16th of Sept., 1825,

and first sung on that occasion by the Festival choir. On the 20th of Sept. it was printed in the *Sheffield Iris* newspaper, of which James Montgomery was the editor, together with an account of the Festival, and an estimate that £100,000 had been spent in one way and another in connection therewith ; and of this £20,000 were expended in the purchase of Festival tickets. Crosse's hymn was included in Bickersteth's *Christian Psalmody*, 1833, No. 338, and subsequently in a great number of hymn-books. Orig. text in *Hy. Comp.* [J. J.]

Lord of hosts, how lovely fair [how bright, how fair]. *D. Turner.* [*Public Worship.*] 1st pub. in Rippon's Bap. *Sel.*, 1st ed., 1787, No. 342, in 4 st. of 4 l. and entitled, "The Excellency of Public Worship." From Rippon's *Sel.* it has passed into several Nonconformist collections, sometimes in its original form, and also as, "Lord of hosts, *how bright, how fair*," as in the Bapt. *Ps. & Hys.*, 1858 and 1880. [J. J.]

Lord of hosts, to Thee we raise. *J. Montgomery.* [*Laying the Foundation Stone, or The Opening of a Place of Worship.*] The foundation stone of St. George's Church, Sheffield (of which the Rev. W. Mercer was subsequently Incumbent), was laid on the day of the coronation of George IV., July 19, 1821. On that day Montgomery published in his *Iris* newspaper a leading article on Bonaparte, who died on the 5th of the previous May. Montgomery's original MS. of that article and "a set of the coronation medals, and other usual memorials," were placed in a glass jar under the foundation stone (*Memoirs*, iii. p. 241). This hymn was composed for the occasion ; was sung during the ceremony, and was printed in the *Iris* of Tuesday, July 24, 1821. It was included in Montgomery's *Christian Psalmist*, 1825, No. 475, and in his *Original Hymns*, 1853, No. 301, and in both instances headed "On Opening a Place of Worship." [J. J.]

Lord of life, prophetic Spirit. *J. Keble.* [*For Theological Colleges.*] A "Hymn for Eastertide, written for the Book of Prayers at Cuddesdon College," 1856, p. 109, in 10 st. of 4 l., and repeated in the author's (posthumous) *Miscellaneous Poems*, 1869, p. 287. In the *Sarum Hyl.* it is given in two parts, pt. ii. beginning "Now Thou speakest, hear we trembling"; and in other collections, as in the S. P. C. K. *Church Hys.*, 1871, it is abbreviated to 6 st., and sometimes less. It is suitable for Ember Days and Ordinations in addition to its Theological College use. [J. J.]

Lord of mercy and of might. *Bp. R. Heber.* [*Quinquagesima.*] Two forms of this hymn, and both by Heber, are found in his *Hymns*, &c., 1827. The first form, in 5 st. of 4 l., first appeared in the *Christian Observer*, Nov. 1811, p. 697, together with three additional hymns by Heber, and is set forth for the "Sunday after Christmas." In his *Hymns*, &c., 1827, it is given as No. i. for "Quinquagesima," and reads, as in the *Christian Observer :—*

" Lord of mercy, and of might,
Of mankind the life and light,
Maker, Teacher infinite,
    Jesus, hear and save !

" Who, when sin's primaeval doom
Gave creation to the tomb,
Didst not scorn a Virgin's womb,
    Jesus, hear and save !

" Strong Creator, Saviour mild,
Humbled to a mortal child,
Captive, beaten, bound, reviled,
    Jesus, hear and save !

" Throned above celestial things,
Borne aloft on angels' wings,
Lord of Lords, and King of Kings,
    Jesus, hear and save !

" Soon to come to earth again,
Judge of angels and of men,
Hear us now, and hear us then !
    Jesus, hear and save !"

The second form appeared in his *Hymns*,
&c., 1827, p. 21, and appointed for the Sunday
after Christmas, or Circumcision." It is also
in 5 st., but differs from the first form in the
following particulars, the 1827 reading being,

St. ii., l. 1. Who, when sin's *tremendous* doom.
St. iii., l. 1. *Mighty Monarch!* Saviour mild !
St. v.   *Who shall yet return from high,*
           Robed in might and majesty,
           Hear us ! *help us when we cry !*
               Jesus, hear and save !

The use of this hymn is extensive. The
first form is found in *Kennedy*, 1863 ; *Hy.
Comp.*, 1876 ; *Church Hymns*, 1871 ; *Thring*,
1882, and many others : the second in Alford's
Year of Praise, 1867 ; the S. P. C. K. *Ps. &
Hys.*; *New Mitre Hymnal*; Snepp's *Songs of
G. & G.*, 1872, and others : mixed texts,
People's H., 1867, and *Windle*; and, rewritten,
in *Morrell and How*, 1864. It is also found
in many collections in slightly varying forms
not here specified, the texts of which may be
tested by the above readings. The original
of 1811 has been rendered into Latin by the
Rev. C. B. Pearson, as " Clemens hominum
Regnator," and pub. in his *Latin Trs. of English Hys.*, 1862, p. 82.   [J. J.]

Lord of my heart, by Thy last cry.
J. Keble. [*Good Friday*.] This is composed
of the two closing stanzas of Keble's poem
for Good Friday, which was pub. in his *Christian Year*, 1827. This extract was given in
Elliott's *Ps. & Hys.*, 1835, and has been repeated in modern collections. The text is
slightly altered.   [J. J.]

Lord of my life, O may Thy praise.
Anne Steele. [*Morning*.] Appeared in her
Poems on Subjects chiefly Devotional, 1760,
vol. i. p. 20, in 6 st. of 4 l., headed, " A Morning Hymn "; and again in D. Sedgwick's reprint of her *Hymns*, 1863. In addition to its
use in its original, and in an abbreviated form,
it is also given in a few American collections,
including the Presbyterian *Ps. and Hys. for
the Worship of God*, Richmond, 1867, as,
" God of my life, my morning song." [J. J.]

Lord of my [our] life, Whose tender
care. [*Evening*.] This hymn appeared in
the *Church of England Magazine*, February,
1838, and was signed " Ω Chelsea." It was
included in the S. P. C. K. *Hys. for Public
Worship*, 1852, No. 156; and since then it
has passed into a large number of hymn-books
in G. Britain and America, and sometimes as
" Lord of *our* life," &c., as in *Kennedy*, 1863.
                                       [W. T. B.]

Lord of the Church, we humbly
pray. *E. Osler*. [*Whitsuntide*.] 1st pub. in
Hall's *Mitre H. Bk.*, 1836, No. 219, in 3 st. of
6 l., and again, with slight alterations, in the
author's *Church and King*, April, 1837, p. 112.
It is an altered version by Osler of Charles
Wesley's " Thou, Jesu, Thou my breast inspire " (q.v.). Wesley's original text, however, is scarcely recognizable in the form given
to it by Osler, save in the last six lines, which
are almost entirely from Wesley. The Irish
Church Hymnal follows the text of the *Mitre*.
Its use is extensive.   [J. J.]

Lord of the harvest, once again. *J.
Anstice*. [*Harvest*.] 1st pub. in his (posthumous) *Hymns*, 1836, No. 34, in 4 st. of 6 l.
In the *Child's Christian Year*, 1841, it was
repeated without alteration; and from that
date it came into general use, but usually with
slight alterations. It is one of the most popular of Harvest hymns, and is in C. U. in all
English-speaking countries. In the *Anglican
H. Bk.*, 1868, it begins, " O Lord of harvest,
once again." Orig. text in Lord Selborne's
Book of Praise, 1862.   [J. J.]

Lord of the living harvest. *J. S. B.
Monsell*. [*Ordination*, and *Church Guilds*.]
This hymn appears in the hymn-books, first
as a hymn for *Ember Day and Ordinations ;*
and second, for *Church Guilds and Associations.*

1. It originally appeared in Dr. Monsell's *Hys. of Love
and Praise*, 2nd ed., 1866, in 4 st. of 8 l., for Ember
Days and Ordinations. This was repeated in his *Parish
Hymnal*, 1873, and the People's of his *Spiritual
Songs*, 1875, the last being the authorized text. From
this text Thring's *Coll.*, 1882, differs somewhat, and
especially in st. iii. In *Monsell* the hymn is a prayer
for the Ordained, in *Thring* the prayer is supposed to be
offered by the Ordained themselves. For use at Ordinations Dr. Monsell's authorized form is the better of the
two.

2. In the S. P. C. K. *Church Hymns*, 1871, the hymn
is given in an altered form for Church Guilds and Associations. With two slight changes in the text, and the
omission of st. iii., this was given in W. F. Stevenson's
Hys. for the Ch. and Home, 1873, with a note in which
he says that his text was " printed from manuscript in
the form finally adopted by the author."

The authorized text of this hymn therefore
is (1) for *Ordination*—that in Dr. Monsell's
Parish Hymnal, and (2) for *Church Guilds and
Associations*, that in Dr. Stevenson's *Hymns*.
                                       [J. J.]

Lord of the lofty and the low. *T.
W. B. Aveling*. [*For Ragged School Anniversary*.] " This [hymn] was written for a
Ragged School anniversary, held in Kingsland
Congregational Church, under the presidency
of the Earl of Shaftesbury, in the year 1856 or
1857 " (Miller's *Singers & Songs*, 1869, p. 531).
In 1859 it was included in the *New Cong.*, and
is also found in other collections.   [J. J.]

Lord of the ocean, hear our cry.
Bp. E. H. Bickersteth. [*For Use at Sea*.]
Written in 1869 and 1st pub. in his *Hymnal
Companion*, 1870, No. 392, as a hymn to be
used at sea, with the note in the Annotated
edition, " This hymn, by the Editor, was
written for this work. It is to be sung *by* those
at sea ; the one which follows ['Eternal Father,
strong to save'] is *for* those at sea." In the
Hy. Comp., 1870, and the revised ed., 1876,
Bp. Bickersteth's hymn begins, " Almighty
Father, hear our cry." Its original form as

"Lord of the ocean, hear our cry," is in Bp. Bickersteth's *Two Brothers*, 1871, p. 249.

[J. J.]

Lord of the Sabbath, hear our vows. *P. Doddridge.* [*Sunday*, or *Divine Worship*.] This hymn, beginning "O God of Sabbath, hear our vows," is No. 30 in the D. MSS., is dated "Jan. 2, 1736-7," and headed "The Eternal Sabbath. From Heb. iv. 9." In Job Orton's ed. of Doddridge's (posthumous) *Hymns*, &c., 1755, No. 310, it was given as "Lord of the Sabbath," &c., in 5 st. of 4 l., and with the same title, and repeated in J. D. Humphreys's ed. of the same, 1839, No. 336. In Mr. Brooke's MS., 1739-40, it reads "O God of Sabbath," &c. The 1755 text is in use in most English-speaking countries, but the most popular form of the hymn is that beginning "Lord of the Sabbath, hear us pray," particulars of which, and other arrangements of the hymn, we here append:—

1. *Thine earthly Sabbaths, Lord, we love.* This cento, composed of st. ii.-iv. and ii., was given as No. 352 in Rippon's *Bap. Sel.*, 1787, and is found in full or in part in several modern hymnals.

2. *Lord of the Sabbath, hear us pray.* This altered text appeared in Cotterill's *Sel.*, 8th ed., 1819, No. 4 (the original as in Orton having been in former editions), and is by Cotterill, or James Montgomery, or possibly the joint work of the two. Of this text, in 6 st. of 4 l., st. i., iii., iv., vi. are altered from Doddridge, and st. ii., v., are new. This text was repeated in Montgomery's *Christian Psalmist*, 1825; and again, either in its full or in an abridged form, in a large number of hymn-books in G. Britain and America.

3. *O Lord of holy Rest, we pray.* This form of the hymn appeared in R. C. Singleton's *Anglican H. Bk.*, 1868. It is from the *Doddridge-Cotterill* text, with alterations, and a slight return to the original.

When these forms of the hymn are taken together, it is found that its use is very extensive in all English-speaking countries, the *Doddridge-Cotterill* text being the most popular. [See **English Hymnody, Early,** § XIV.]

[J. J.]

Lord of the sinless world above. *W. J. Irons.* [*Adult Baptism*, or *Confirmation*.] On the passing of the Act for the Registration of Births there was a panic amongst the poor, and a great rush to the churches for Holy Baptism. In one day 400 children were baptized in Dr. Irons's church, St. Mary's, Newington, and 23 adults on another. On other days there were also great gatherings of children and adults for the sacred rite. Under these circumstances and amid these surroundings Dr. Irons wrote this hymn. It was pub. in Lowe's *Hys. for the Christian Seasons*, Gainsburgh, 1854; in Dr. Irons's *Appendix to the Brompton Metrical Psalter*, 1861, his *Hys. for Use in Church*, 1866; and in his *Ps. and Hys. for the Church*, 1873-75, &c. It is in a few collections only, and its use is not equal to its merits. [J. J.]

Lord of the wide extended [extensive] **main.** *C. Wesley.* [*For use at Sea.*] 1st pub. in the *Hys. and Sac. Poems*, 1740, p. 31, in 10 st. of 4 l., and headed "A Hymn to be Sung at Sea" (*P. Works*, 1868-72, vol. i. p. 229). In the 1830 *Suppl.* to the *Wes. H. Bk.* it was given in two parts as:—

1. *Lord of the wide, extensive main.* No. 761.
2. *Infinite God, Thy greatness spanned.* No. 762.

Both these parts have come into use in G. Britain and America as separate hymns.

Mr. G. J. Stevenson, in his *Meth. H. Bk. Notes*, 1883, p. 591, says of this hymn:—

"It was probably written in 1735, previously to the poet and his brother John sailing to America with General Oglethorpe and the Moravians. This seems to be plainly indicated by the language of the second verse:—

"For Thee we leave our native shore,
In other climes Thy works explore."

This view, however, is not that of Dr. Osborn, the editor of the Wesley *Poetical Works*, 1868-72. In vol. i. pp. 228-231, there are given the following hymns:—"Servant of God, the summons hear"; "Lord of the wide-extended main"; and "Glory to Thee, Whose powerful word"; and to the first of these ("Servant of God," &c.) Dr. Osborn adds the following note:—

"The animating strains of this hymn and the two next are by no means in accordance with Charles Wesley's spiritual condition and mood of mind in December, 1737, when Mr. Whitefield first left England for America. They were more probably composed in preparation for his second voyage, which began in August, 1739. Nor can we imagine anything more suitable for the occasion; while in the hymns "To be Sung at Sea" ["Lord of the wide-extended main"] and "In a Storm" ["Glory to Thee, Whose powerful word"] the Christian and the poet appear to equal advantage. It may be doubted if the full assurance of faith was ever more finely expressed, or at the same time more rationally vindicated, than in the second and the third of the three hymns which follow one another here."

This suggestion by Dr. Osborn that the date is 1739 is made almost certain with regard to "Servant of God," &c., and presumably of the other two, by the fact that "Servant of God," &c., is found in *Divine Hymns for the Use of the Societies*, by Richard Wyan, 1739. This tract contains three hymns, two by Wyan (one addressed to Whitefield) and "Servant of God, the summons hear," by C. Wesley. The Wesleys, by printing the three hymns, "Servant of God," &c., "Lord of the wide," &c., and "Glory to Thee, &c.," as consecutive hymns in the *Hys. & Sac. Poems*, 1740, seem to fix the date of these hymns as 1739, when Whitefield went on his second voyage to America.

The hymn "Servant of God, the summons hear," is rarely used, whilst "Glory to Thee, Whose powerful word," is given in several collections in America, and as "*All praise to* Thee, Whose powerful word," in a few in G. Britain. [W. T. B.]

Lord of the worlds above. *I. Watts.* [*Ps. lxxxiv.*] 1st pub. in his *Ps. of David*, &c., 1719, in 7 st. of 8 l., as the third version of the 84th Psalm. In addition to its use in its full form, there are also several arrangements of the text, the more important being:—

1. That in the *Wes. H. Bk.*, 1875, and many others derived from the same source. This appeared in the Wesley *Ps. & Hys.*, 1738; the enlarged ed. of the same, 1743; and the *Wes. H. Bk.*, 1780. It is very popular.

2. A cento composed of st. i., iii., iv., and vii. This was given with alterations in Whitefield's *Coll.*, 1753; Madan's *Ps. & Hys.*, 1760; Toplady's *Ps. & Hys.*, 1776, and thus into the hymn-books of the Church of England. In some modern collections, as *Sarum*, 1868, and Thring's *Coll.*, 1882, some of these alterations are still retained. Usually, however, the text is correct.

3. Other arrangements are given in many modern hymnals, the construction of which may be tested by reference to Watts's *Psalms*. It will be found that in most cases the original text is retained.

As a paraphrase this ranks amongst the best by Watts. The metre is an imitation of that employed for the first time by John Pullain, in his Version of the 148th Psalm in the *English Psalter*, 1560. [See Old Version, iv. ix.]   [J. J.]

Lord, shall Thy children come to Thee? *Bp. S. Hinds.* [*Confirmation.*] In *Sonnets and other Short Poems, chiefly on Sacred Subjects.* By Samuel Hinds, D.D., Lond., B. Fellowes, 1834, p. 65, is the following:—

  " *Confirmation Hymn.*
" Lord, shall Thy children come to Thee?
 A boon of love divine we seek:
 Brought to Thy arms in infancy,
 Ere hearts could feel or tongue could speak,
 Thy children pray for grace, that they
 May come themselves to Thee this day.
" Lord, shall we come, and come again?
 Oft as we see yon Table spread,
 And, tokens of Thy dying pain,
 The wine pour'd out, the broken bread;
 Bless, bless, O Lord, Thy children's prayer,
 That they may come and find Thee there.
" Lord, shall we come, come yet again?
 Thy children ask one blessing more—
 To come, (not now alone and then,)
 When life and death and time are o'er,
 Then, then to come, O Lord, and be
 Confirmed in heaven, confirmed by Thee!"

When this hymn was included in the *Ps. & Hys. for the Use of Rugby School Chapel, circa* 1843 (1850 ed. No. 51), the following stanza by H. J. Buckoll, was added as st. iii., thus making a hymn of 4 st.:—

" Lord, shall we come? not thus alone
 At holy time, or solemn rite?
 But every hour till life be flown,
 Through weal or woe, in gloom or light,—
 Come to Thy throne of grace, that we
 In faith, hope, love, confirmed may be."

In addition to writing this stanza, Buckoll made a few alterations in, and repunctuated Bp. Hinds's text. Two forms of the hymn have thus come into use, the first the original, and the second the Hinds-Buckoll text. The latter is that usually given in the Public Schools hymn-books.   [J. J.]

Lord, solemnize our trifling minds. *G. Burder.* [*Before Sermon.*] Appeared in his *Coll. of Hymns*, &c., 1784, No. 200, in 3 st. of 4 l. as one of a number of hymns for use " Before Sermon," and again in later eds. of the same work. In modern hymnals, as the *New Cong.*, 1859, No. 786, it is altered to " Great God, impress our trifling minds."   [J. J.]

Lord, speak to me, that I may speak. *Frances R. Havergal.* [*Lay Helpers.*] Written, April 28, 1872, at Winterdyne, and first printed as one of Parlane's musical leaflets in the same year. In 1874 it was pub. in her *Under the Surface*, and in 1879 in *Life Mosaic.* In the original MS. it is headed " A Worker's Prayer. ' None of us liveth to himself.' Rom. xiv. 7." This hymn has become very popular, and is highly esteemed by those engaged in Christian work.   [J. J.]

Lord, teach a little child to pray. Thy grace betimes, &c. *J. Ryland.* [*A Child's Prayer.*] This simple prayer for a child's use is the most popular and widely used of Dr. Ryland's hymns. From his *Memoirs of Andrew Fuller*, 1831, pp. 442 and 453, we find that this hymn, and another, beginning " God is very good to me," were written by him at the request of Mrs. Fuller for the use of her child Sarah, who died May

30, 1786, aged 6 years and 6 months. In some of the numerous collections in which it is found it is erroneously attributed to " Jane Taylor." The Taylor hymn opens with the same line, but the second is " And then accept my prayer."   [J. J.]

Lord, teach us how to pray aright. *J. Montgomery.* [*Prayer.*] Written in 1818, and first printed on a broadsheet with Montgomery's " Prayer is the soul's sincere desire; " " What shall we ask of God in prayer?" and " Thou, God, art a consuming fire;" for use in the Nonconformist Sunday Schools in Sheffield. In Cotterill's *Sel.*, 8th ed., 1819, No. 280, it was repeated in full in 4 st. of 8 l., and headed, " The preparations of the heart in man." During the same year it was given, with alterations and the omission of st. ii., in E. Bickersteth's *Treatise on Prayer.* In Montgomery's *Christian Psalmist*, 1825, No. 482, the text in Bickersteth was repeated, with the restoration of st. ii., and divided into 8 st. of 4 l. The text in his *Original Hymns*, 1853, No. 65, is that of the *Christ. Psal.*, 1825, with the change of st. iv., ll. 1, 2, from:—

" God of all Grace, we come to Thee
 With broken, contrite hearts";

to:—

" God of all grace, we *bring* to Thee
 A broken, contrite *heart.*"

This change is set down in the margin of Montgomery's private copy of the *Christ. Psal.* in his own handwriting. This hymn, in full or abridged, is in numerous collections. The variations of text which are found have arisen in a great measure from some editors copying from Cotterill's *Sel.* of 1819, and others from the *Christian Psalmist* of 1825. The first is the *original*, and the *second* (with the above correction in *Orig. Hys.* 1853) is the authorized text. In some American Unitarian collections, including *A Book of Hys.*, 1848; and the *H. [and Tune] Bk. for the Ch. and the Home*, &c., 1868, a hymn beginning, " God of all grace, we come to Thee," is given from this, and opens with st. iv.   [J. J.]

Lord, that I may learn of Thee. *C. Wesley.* [*Humility desired.*] Pub. in his *Short Hymns*, &c., 1762, vol. i., No. 1005, in 4 st. of 4 l. (*P. Works*, 1868–72, vol. ix. p. 392) On its introduction into the *Wes. H. Bk.*, 1780, No. 293, st. ii., l. 1, was changed from " Let me cast myself aside" to " Let me cast my *reeds* aside." This reading is repeated in the revised ed. of 1875, and other hymn-books. A cento partly from this hymn and partly by J. Berridge appeared in Berridge's *Sion's Songs*, 1785, in 6 st. of 4 l., as " Jesus, cast a look on me." Of this text st. i., iii. and iv. are altered from Wesley's hymn as above, and st. ii., v. and vi. are by Berridge. This cento is given without alteration in Lord Selborne's *Book of Praise*, 1862, and in whole or in part in numerous collections throughout English-speaking countries.   [J. J.]

Lord, Thou didst arise and say. *H. H. Milman.* [*Christ Stilling the Tempest.*] 1st pub. in Bp. Heber's posthumous *Hymns*, &c., 1827, p. 36, in 2 st. of 8 l., and appointed for the 4th S. after the Epiphany, being based on the Gospel for that day. It was repeated in Milman's *Ps. & Hys.*, 1837, and subsequently in many hymn-books in G. Britain and America. [J. J.]

Lord, Thou hast been Thy people's rest. *J. Montgomery.* [*Ps. xc.*] Appeared in his *Songs of Zion*, 1822, in 7 st. of 7 l. In his *Original Hymns,* 1853, st. i., iv., v. and vi. are given as hymn No. xlvi. In Dr. Kennedy's *Psalter*, 1860, a cento was given as the version of Ps. xc., and is thus composed :—

St. i., ii., and v., *J. Montgomery.*
St. iii., iv., and vi., *Dr. Kennedy.*

Dr. Kennedy's *Hymno. Christ.*, No. 9, in two parts is this same text repeated with the addition of a doxology to Pt. i. In the Preface to this collection, the portion of this rendering of *Ps. xc.* taken from Montgomery is attributed to the Rev. A. T. Russell in error. [J. J.]

Lord, Thou hast won, at length I yield. *J. Newton.* [*Surrender to Christ.*] Appeared in the *Gospel Magazine*, Jan., 1775, in 7 st. of 6 l., headed "The Surrender," and signed "Vigil." After a slight revision it was given in the *Olney Hymns*, 1779, Bk. i., No. 121, in 7 st. of 6 l., with the extended heading "The Rebel's Surrender to Grace. Lord, what wilt Thou have me to do?" It is based on the words of St. Paul uttered on his way to Damascus, and recorded in Acts ix. 6. Although there is nothing in the *Memoirs* of Newton (so far as we can see) to justify us in saying that this hymn is autobiographical, yet its intense individuality suggests that it is so, and that he found in the fierceness of Saul the persecutor, and the submissive peacefulness of Saul the disciple, the embodiment of his own history and experience. Thus regarded the hymn is interesting, but for practical purposes it is far from being one of Newton's best productions. It is found in a few collections, but in an abbreviated form. [J. J.]

Lord, Thou in all things like wert [wast] made. *J. Anstice.* [*Passiontide.*] 1st pub. in his (posthumous) *Hymns*, 1836, No. 21, in 6 st. of 4 l., and again in the *Child's Christian Year*, 1841. From the *Child's C. Year* it passed as, "In all things like Thy brethren, Thou," into the *Leeds H. Bk.*, 1853, No. 295. This form of the hymn has become popular, and especially with the Nonconformists. It is sometimes attributed to J. Keble. [J. J.]

Lord, Thy children guide and keep. *Bp. W. W. How.* [*The Narrow Way.*] 1st pub. in Morrell & How's *Ps. & Hys.*, 1854, in 5 st. of 6 l., and based on the words "Narrow is the way that leadeth unto life." It has become very popular with hymnal compilers, and, in full or in an abridged form, it is found in numerous collections in G. Britain and America. Orig. text in the S. P. C. K. *Church Hys.*, 1871. [J. J.]

Lord, Thy glory fills the heaven. *Bp. R. Mant.* [*Holy Trinity.*] This hymn, extending from 1 st. of 8 l. in the Cooke and Denton *Hymnal*, 1853, to 3 st. of 8 l. in *Laudes Domini*, N. Y., 1884, is from Bp. Mant's "Bright the vision that delighted" (see p. 182, i.). It is in extensive use, especially in America. [J. J.]

Lord, Thy word abideth. *Sir H. W. Baker.* [*Holy Scripture.*] Written for and 1st pub. in *H. A. & M.*, 1861. It has attained a great circulation, and is in C. U. in all English-speaking countries. It has also been translated into several languages. There is a *tr.* in German by Miss Winkworth, in Biggs's Annotated *H. A. & M.*, 1867, beginning "Herr, Dein Wort muss bleiben." [J. J.]

Lord, to me Thy minsters are. [*The House of God.*] This cento, which was given in W. J. Blew's *Church Hy. & Tune Bk.*, 1852-55, is composed thus: st. i., ii. are from the late Archdeacon Churton's *tr.* from the Anglo-Saxon pub. in his *Poetics*, and the remaining stanzas, iii.-v., are original by Mr. Blew. The cento has passed into several collections, including *Kennedy*, 1863 ; Rice's *Sel.* from Blew, 1870, and others. [J. J.]

Lord, we adore Thy wondrous Name. *P. Doddridge.* [*Divine Compassion.*] Written Oct. 29, 1735 (D. MSS. No. v.), and pub. in Job Orton's ed. of Doddridge's (posthumous) *Hymns, &c.*, 1755, No. 55, in 6 st. of 4 l., and again in J. D. Humphreys's ed. of the same, 1839, No. 68. The original heading is "The frailties of human nature, and God's gracious regard to it. Ps. ciii. 14." In modern hymnbooks it is usually abbreviated. [J. J.]

Lord, we are blind, we mortals blind. *I. Watts.* [*God Invisible.*] Pub. in his *Hys. & Spiritual S.*, 1707, Bk. ii., No. 26, in 4 st. of 4 l., and headed "God Invisible." In the American *Plymouth Coll.*, 1855, it begins with st. ii., "Infinite leagues beyond the sky." [J. J.]

Lord, we come before Thee now. *W. Hammond.* [*Public Worship.*] 1st pub. in his *Ps. & Hys.*, 1745, p. 32, in 8 st. of 8 l. In 1760 M. Madan reduced it to 6 st. of 4 l., and as such it was given in his *Ps. & Hys.* of that year, No. 121. From this arrangement of the hymn most modern editors have taken their text. Orig. in *Lyra Brit.*, 1867. [J. J.]

Lord, we confess our numerous faults. *I. Watts.* [*Salvation by Grace.*] 1st pub. in his *Hys. & S. Songs*, 2nd ed., 1709, Bk. i., No. 111, in 6 st. of 4 l., and headed "Salvation by Grace." It is in C. U. in its full form, and also abbreviated and altered as :—

1. **'Tis not by works of righteousness.** This arrangement begins with st. iii. Its use is limited.

2. **How wretched was our former state.** In the Draft of the Scottish *Translations and Paraphrases*, 1745, Watts's hymn was given with alterations as No. 19, but in the authorized public worship issue of the *Trs. and Paraphs.*, in 1781, it gave place to "How wretched was our former state," which was thus composed :—st. i. new ; ii. *Watts* ; iii. new ; iv. *Watts* and 1745 ; v. from 1745 ; vi. *Watts* and 1745 ; vii. from 1745. This recast has been in use in Scotland and elsewhere for more than one hundred years. It is sometimes attributed to W. Cameron (q. v.), but is not assigned to him in the markings, by Cameron's eldest daughter, of the *Trs. and Paraphs.* Its authorship is therefore doubtful.

3. **'Tis from the mercy of our God.** This is a re-written form of the Scottish *Trs. and Paraphs.* text, by Miss Jane E. Leeson, and was pub. in her *Paraphs. and Hymns*, 1853. [J. J.]

Lord, we have wandered from Thy way. *P. Doddridge.* [*The Lost Sheep.*] This hymn in the D. MSS., No. 62, is undated, but immediately precedes one written on April 10, 1735, and may be dated *circa* 1735. It was included in Job Orton's ed. of Doddridge's (posthumous) *Hymns*, &c., 1755, No. 65, in 3 st. of 3 l., and again in J. D. Humphreys's ed. of the same, 1839, No. 79. In each case the original title, "The wandering Sheep recovered. Ps. cxix. 176," is retained. [J. J.]

Lord, we sit and cry to Thee. *H. H. Milman.* [*Quinquagesima. Blind Man at Jericho.*] 1st pub. in Bp. Heber's (posthumous) *Hymns*, &c., 1827, p. 49, in 2 st. of 6 l., and again in his *Ps. & Hys.*, 1837. It is based on the Gospel for Quinquagesima. In Hall and Lasar's American *Evangelical Hyl.*, N. Y., 1880, it is altered to "Lord, we *raise our* cry to Thee." [J. J.]

Lord, what a feeble piece. *I. Watts.* [*Ps. xc.*] His s. m. version of Ps. xc., which appeared in his *Psalms of David*, 1719, in 5 st. of 4 l., and headed "The Frailty and Shortness of Life." In Martineau's *Hymns*, &c., 1840 and 1873, it is given as "Lord, what a *fleeting breath*"; and in the *Leeds H. Bk.*, 1853, as "Lord, make us know how frail." [J. J.]

Lord, what a wretched land is this. *I. Watts.* [*Pilgrimage of the Saints.*] Appeared in his *Hys. & S. Songs*, 1707. Bk. ii., No. 53, in 12 st. of 4 l., and entitled "The Pilgrimage of the Saints; or, Earth and Heaven." In Spurgeon's *O. O. H. Bk.*, 1866, st. viii.–xii. were given as "Our journey is a thorny maze." This arrangement, together with abbreviations beginning with the first stanza, is in several collections. [J. J.]

Lord, what is man? extremes how wide. *J. Newton.* [*Man by Nature, Grace, and Glory.*] Appeared in the *Olney Hymns*, 1779, Bk. iii., No. 88, in 6 st. of 4 l., and headed, "Man by Nature, Grace, and Glory." It is the last of the longer hymns given in the *Olney H.*, and would appear to have been designedly placed there as a fitting close to the work, a few "short hymns," and four doxologies only, following. The closing stanza is exceedingly appropriate:—

"Nearest the throne, and first in song,
   Man shall his hallelujahs raise;
While ring'ring angels round him throng,
   And swell the chorus of his praise."

Although lacking the general interest and popularity of Newton's hymns, it is given in several collections. [J. J.]

Lord, when Thou didst Thyself undress. *H. Vaughan.* [*Passiontide.*] Pub. in his *Silex Scintillans; or, Sac. Poems*, &c., Pt. i., 1650, and again in the reprint by the Rev. H. F. Lyte, 1846 (1858 ed., p. 46), in 5 st. of 4 l., and entitled "The Incarnation and Passion." In its complete form it is not found in modern hymnals, but st. iv. and v., as "Ah, my dear Lord, what could'st Thou spy," are given in Thring's *Coll.*, 1882. [J. J.]

Lord, when we bend before Thy throne. *J. D. Carlyle.* [*Lent.*] This hymn appeared in *A Coll. of Ps. and Hys. by Various Authors, Chiefly designed for Public Worship*, Carlisle, 1802. The editor was the Rev. John Fawcett, Vicar of St. Cuthbert's, Carlisle, "an intimate personal friend of Professor Carlyle; and this hymn was written by the author for use before Divine Service in St. Cuthbert's Church, where he regularly attended when in residence as Chancellor of

Carlisle. It is the first hymn in the collection, and is headed 'Introductory to Public Worship.'" (S. P. C. K. *Church Hys.*, Annotated ed., 1881.) In 1805, it was republished in Carlyle's *Poems Suggested chiefly by Scenes in Asia Minor*. Therein it is entitled "A Hymn before Public Worship." It is in 6 st. of 4 l. It is usually given in 4 st. by the omission of st. iii., iv. To the fourth stanza sometimes a doxology is added, as in the *Hymnary*, 1872, a practice as old as Murray's *Hymnal* of 1852, if not older. It is well to note that the office of each of the three Christian graces, *Faith, Hope*, and *Charity*, in Public Worship is set forth in the original text: and that by the omission of st. iii., iv. that of *Charity* is ignored in the modern form of the hymn. Its use during the last eighty years, either in its full or in an abbreviated form, has been most extensive in all English-speaking countries. Orig. text *Lyra Brit.*, 1867, p. 126. It has also been translated into several languages. The *H. A. & M.* text without the doxology has been rendered into Latin, as : "Quum supplicamus ad thronum Tuum, Deus," by the Rev. R. Bingham, in his *Hymnol. Christ. Latina*, 1871. In *Kennedy*, 1863, an altered version in 3 st. of 8 l. is given as, "Lord, when before Thy righteous throne," but its use is confined to that work. [J. J.]

Lord, when we creation scan. *J. D. Carlyle.* [*Thursday.*] Appeared in a *Coll. of Ps. & Hys.*, &c. Edited by J. Fawcett, of Carlisle, in 1802. It was appointed for the "Fifth Day, First Morning," and is in 6 st. of 4 l. In 1803 it passed into *A Sel. of Hys. and Anthems*, &c., *for Elmdon Church, Birmingham*, No. 17; in 1807 into *The Theological and Biblical Magazine;* and subsequently into various hymn-books in G. Britain and America. Although a good hymn it is the least known of Carlyle's productions. [J. J.]

Lord, when we search the human heart. *J. Montgomery.* [*The World in the Heart.*] This hymn was written on the blank page of a juvenile missionary address prepared by Mr. George Cookman, of Hull. Montgomery mentions his having written it in a letter to Mr. Cookman's father, dated "Sheffield, June 24, 1819" (Montgomery's *Memoirs*, iii. p. 169). The hymn was included in Cotterill's *Sel.*, 8th ed., 1819, No. 338, in 7 st. of 4 l. In Montgomery's *Christian Psalmist*, 1825, No. 549, it was repeated with slight variations, and the addition of a new stanza (viii.). This text with st. vii. l. 2, "Thy name and knowledge," changed to "Thy name, *Thy* knowledge," is in his *Original Hymns*, 1853, No. 170. [J. J.]

Lord, Who once from heaven descending. *J. Latham.* [*The Good Shepherd.*] 1st printed in his *Poems, Original and Translated*, Sandbach, 1836, in 5 st. of 6 l., as the fourth of four hymns for the children of the Sandbach Sunday School. In 1841, it was reprinted in his cousin's and namesake's *Hys. Selected for Use of the Parish of Sandbach;* and again in *English and Latin Poems*, dated July, 1827, and privately printed in 1853. The form of the hymn known to modern hymnals was given it in the 1850 ed. of the *Hys. for the Rugby School Chapel*, when st. ii., iii.

were omitted. This form of the text is in *Kennedy*, 1863, and several other collections.

[W. T. B.]

Lord! Whose love in [and] power excelling. *Bp. R. Heber.* [*Epiphany.*] Appeared in his posthumous *Hymns*, &c., 1827, p. 35, in 4 st. of 4 l. It is based on a part of the Gospel for the 3rd S. after the Epiphany (the healing of the Leper). It is in C. U. in Great Britain and America, and usually without alteration.

[J. J.]

Lord's Prayer in Verse, The. Metrical paraphrases of the *Lord's Prayer* in English date from an early period, and are of varying length and merit. Several are annotated under their respective first lines, and may be found through the *Index of Seasons and Subjects.* Of those that remain we shall group in this article :—

1. In Churton's *Early English Church*, 1840, two examples are given, which date from the 12th and 13th centuries. These are:—(1) The Lord's Prayer, "in metre sent by Nicholas Breakspeare [Pope Adrian IV.] into England in the time of Henry II., A.D. 1160." It reads :—

" Ure Fadyr in heaven-rich
Thy name be hallyed everlich
Thou bring us Thy michel blisse.
Als hit in heaven y-doe,
Ever in yearth beene it also.
That holy bread that lasteth ay,
Thou send it ous this ilke day
Forgive ous all that we have don,
As we forgivet uch other mon.
Ne let ous fall into no founding
Ae shield ous fro the fowle thing."

(2) The second is of Henry III.'s time, about A.D. 1250, and reads:—

" Fadir ur, that es in hevene
Halud be Thy name to neven.
Thou do us Thy rich rike
Thy will on erd be wrought alike
As it is wrought in heven ay ;
Ur ilk-day brede give us to-day ;
Forgive Thou all us dettes urs,
As we forgive till ur detturs ;
And ledde us in na fanding
But shuld us fra ivel thing."

2. In Camden's *Remains* (J. R. Smith's reprint, 1870), in the chapter on "Languages," there is the first of the above, and another which Camden dates as of the period of Henry III. This reads:—

" Fader that art in heaven bliss
Thin helge nam it wurth the bliss
Cumen and met thy kingdom,
Thin holy will be all don.
In heaven and in erdh also,
So it shall bin full well le tro.
Gif us all bread on this day
And forgif us ure sins
As we do ure wider wins ;
Let us not in fonding fall
Oae fro evil thu syld us all. Amen."

3. The metrical versions of *The Lord's Prayer* which appeared in the *Old Version* were:—

(1) In the *Anglo-Genevan Psalter*, 1561 [Old Version, § III.] (St. Paul's Cathedral Library, London), there were two versions by W. Whittingham, viz. :—

(a) " Our gracious Father, which on hie
Dost dwell, and hast all power and might."

(b) " Our Father and most gracious Lord,
Most rich in mercy grace and louie."

There is also a version by R. Cox, viz. :—

" Our Father, which in heauen art,
And makst vs al one brotherhood."

(2) In the *English Edition of the Psalter* [Old

Version, § IV., V.], 1560, the version of R. Cox is also found ; and, again, in the ed. of 1560-1. In the *Complete Psalter* for use in the Church of England [Old Version, § VII.], the 1562 ed. contained the version, already noted, by R. Cox, and an anonymous rendering which begins :—

" Ovr father which in heauen art,
Lord, hallowed be thy name."

4. Between the *O. V.* and the *N. V.* several versions appeared, including :—

(1) Henry Lok, in his *Ecclesiastes, otherwise the Preacher*, &c., 1597 [Psalters, Versions] :—

" Our Father which in heauen art,
Lorde ! hallowed be thy name."

This is given in full in Farr's *Sel. Poetry*, 1845.

(2) Robert Holland in his work, *The holie Historie of our Lord and Saviour Jesus Christ's natiuitie, life, acts*, &c., 1594 :—

" Pray thus, when ye do pray, therefore :—
Our Father, which in heauen art."

This is given in full in *Farr* as above, p. 477.

5. The *Supplement* to the *New Version* (*Tate & Brady* [New Version, § ii.]), 2nd ed. 1702, contains two versions :—

(1) " Our Father, who in Heaven art,
thy name be hallow'd in each heart : "

(2) " Our Father, who in Heaven art
all hallow'd be thy name."

These versions were retained in the "Hymns" printed at the end of the *New Version*, until the modern hymn-book caused the reprinting of the *New Version* to cease.

6. During the eighteenth century several paraphrases, some in full and others of portions of *The Lord's Prayer*, were published. Of these we note :—

(1) *A. Pope's* Universal Prayer, 1738:— "Father of all ! in every age," published in that year in his *Works*, and, separately, in folio.

(2) *Charles Wesley's* "Father of all, Whose powerful voice," 1742 (p. 368, ii.).

(3) "Father of all, we bow to Thee " (p. 368, ii.). In the Scottish *Translations and Paraphrases* (Draft, 1745; authorized, 1781). As altered in *Cotterill's Sel.*, 1819, it occurs as, "Father of all, to Thee we bow."

(4) *James Merrick's* "Father of all, Whose seat of rest," in his *Poems on Sacred Subjects*, Oxford, 1763.

(5) *J. Straphan's* "Our Father, whose eternal sway," in Rippon's Bap. *Sel.*, 1787.

7. The nineteenth century has produced several versions of *The Lord's Prayer*, many of which have come into C. U., and may be found in this Dictionary through the Index of Seasons and Subjects (q.v.). In addition we find the following :—

(1) *J. Montgomery.* Two versions,—"Our heavenly Father, hear our prayer " (q.v.) ; and "Our heavenly Father ! hear," in his *Christian Psalmist*, 1825.

(2) *A. Judson.* "Our Father God, Who art in heaven." p. 609, i.

(3) *B. Barton.* "Father of all, Who dwell'st above," in his *Devotional Verse*, 1826.

(4) *J. Conder.* In his *Choir and Oratory*, 1837, the whole *Prayer* is paraphrased in the following hymns :—

1. Holy, holy, holy, Lord, In highest, &c. (p. 257, i.)
2. Thee, my God, in ceaseless lays.
3. Thou from whom all being sprang.
4. Day by day the manna fell. (p. 262, i.)

5. Father, to Thy sinful child. (p. **372**, ii.)
6. Heavenly Father, to whose eye. (p. **503**, i.)
7. Father of spirits, God of heaven.

Some of these appeared in former works by Conder, and are noted in detail at the pages indicated above.

(5) *I. Williams.* In his *Cathedral*, 1838, "The North Aisle" is devoted to *The Lord's Prayer.* The use of the *Prayer* in the various Offices of the Church is made the groundwork of the following paraphrases :—

1. *H. Baptism.* "Our Father, freed from error's chain."
2. *Daily Service.* "Our Father, who dost dwell above."
3. *Litany.* "Like as a Father His own children loves."
4. *Ante-Com.* "Out of a world of grief and wrong."
5. *Post-Com.* "Our Father, knit in Thy dear Son."
6. *H. Matrimony.* "O Thou of whom all families."
7. *Burial.* "O Father of the fatherless, to Thee."

(6) *Anon.* "Our Father God, Who art in heaven. To Thee," &c. In Curwen's *My Own H. Bk.*, 1848, and the *Meth. S. S. H. Bk.*, 1879.

(7) *G. Moultrie.* "Father of all, to Thee we pray," in his *Hys. and Lyrics*, 1867.

(8) *W. R. Worthington.* In *Lyra Precatoria. Six Hymns on the Petitions in the Lord's Prayer*, &c. By the Rev. W. R. Worthington, M.A. ; Lond., Masters & Co., 1874.

8. To these notes must be added those which are scattered throughout this Dictionary, and can be found through the Index of Seasons and Subjects. The result, although not exhaustive, will yet present a fairly good *résumé* of the English metrical versions of *The Lord's Prayer.* (See **Various.**)   [J. J.]

Loud hallelujahs to the Lord. *I. Watts.* [*Ps. cxlviii.*] This psalm version appeared with some 13 or 14 others in the 1st ed. of his *Hys. & S. Songs*, 1707, and was transferred in 1719 to his *Psalms of David*, &c., p. 392, as his L. M. paraphrase of Ps. 148, in 12 st. of 4 l. It is headed "Universal Praise to God." It is usually given in modern hymnals in an abbreviated form.   [J. J.]

Loud to the Prince of heaven. *P. Doddridge.* [*Christ Triumphant.*] 1st pub. in J. Orton's ed. of Doddridge's (posthumous) *Hymns*, &c., 1755, No. 41, in 5 st. of 8 l., and headed "The Triumph of Christ in the cause of Truth, Meekness, and Righteousness." It was also repeated in J. D. Humphreys's ed. of the same, 1839, No. 52. In its original form it is found in a few collections, but its most popular form, and that which is in extensive use in G. Britain and America, begins with st. ii., "Gird on Thy conquering sword." [J. J.]

Loud was the wind and wild the tide. *H. F. Lyte.* [*Christ walking on the Sea.*] Pub. in his *Poems chiefly Religious*, 1833, p. 135, in 2 st. of 8 l., and headed "It is I, be not afraid." In 1853 it was given in the *Leeds H. Bk.*, No. 292, and subsequently repeated in other collections, as "Who walks the waves in wondrous guise ?" This form of the text is in 5 st. of 4 l., the additional stanza being by another hand. [J. J.]

Louisa Henrietta. [Luise Henrietta.]

Love Divine, all loves excelling. *C. Wesley.* [*The Love of Christ.*] 1st pub. in *Hys. for those that Seek, and those that Have Redemption*, 1747, No. 9, in 4 st. of 8 l. (P.

Works, 1868–72, vol. iv. p. 219). In 1780 it was included, with the omission of st. ii., in the *Wes. H. Bk.*, No. 374, and in this form it has passed into a large number of hymn-books in all English-speaking countries. It had previously appeared in full in M. Madan's *Ps. & Hys.*, 1760 ; A. M. Toplady's *Ps. & Hys.*, 1776, and other hymn-books of the Church of England. The two forms, the full and the abridged, have thus come into C. U. Tested by its use it is found to rank with the best of its author's work. Mr. G. J. Stevenson has an interesting note thereon in his *Meth. H. Bk. Notes*, 1883, p. 266.   [J. J.]

Love is the theme of Saints above. *J. Montgomery.* [*Love.*] Written for the Sunday School Jubilee, Sept. 14, 1831, and printed for use on that occasion. In 1853 it was included in his *Original Hymns*, No. 341, in 6 st. of 4 l. It is found in the *Meth. S. S. H. Bk.*, 1879, and others.   [J. J.]

Love, strong as death, nay stronger. *H. Bonar.* [*Holy Communion.*] Appeared in late editions of the *Bible H. Bk.* (1st ed. 1845), No. 215, in 1 st. of 15 l., and again in the 1st Series of his *Hys. of Faith and Hope*, 1857. In *Kennedy*, 1863, it is altered to "Love faltering not nor failing."   [J. J.]

Loving Shepherd of Thy sheep. *Jane E. Leeson.* [*The Good Shepherd.*] Pub. in her *Hys. and Scenes of Childhood*, 1842, No. 17, in 3 st. of 8 l., and headed with the text "My sheep hear My voice, and I know them, and they follow Me," &c. In its original form it is not often found in modern hymn-books. In *H. A. & M.*, 1875, and most other collections, lines 4–8 of st. i. are omitted, thus forming a hymn of 5 st. of 4 l. The omitted lines are :—

> "Bought with blood, and bought for Thee,
> Thine, and only Thine, I'd be,
> Holy, harmless, humble, mild,
> Jesus Christ's obedient child."

The *H. A. & M.* text is the popular form of the hymn.   [J. J.]

Löwe, Johann Friedrich, was b. in 1729 at Clausthal, in the Harz, and studied law at the University of Göttingen. In 1757 he obtained a secretaryship at Schwerin, and was finally, in Sept., 1768, appointed registrar at Rostock. He d. at Rostock, Dec. 23, 1771.

His 16 original hymns appeared in his *Geistliche Lieder, nebst einigen veränderten Kirchen-Gesängen*, Greifswald, 1770 [Hamburg]. One has been *tr.* :—

Gott, wann erquickt dein süsser Friede. [*For the Sick.*] 1770, p. 48, in 7 st., entitled "In cross and tribulation." *Tr.* as (1) "My restless heart, with anguish moaning," by *Miss Cox*, 1841, p. 149 ; (2) "My God! when wilt Thy heavenly peace," by *Lady E. Fortescue*, 1843, p. 67.   [J. M.]

Lowell, James Russell, LL.D., was b. at Cambridge, Massachusetts, February 22, 1819 ; graduated at Harvard College, 1838, and was called to the Bar in 1840. Professor of Modern Languages and Literature (succeeding the Poet Longfellow) in Harvard, 1855 ; American Minister to Spain, also to England in 1881. He was editor of the *Atlantic Monthly*, from 1857 to 1862 ; and of the *North American Review* from 1863 to 1872. Professor Lowell is the most intellectual of American poets, and first of her art critics and humorists. He has written much admirable moral and sacred poetry, but no hymns. One piece, "Men, whose boast it is that ye" (*Against Slavery*), is part of an Anti-Slavery poem, and in its present form is found in *Hys. of the Spirit*, 1864. Part of this is given in *Songs for the Sanctuary*, N.Y., 1865, as "They are slaves who will not choose."   [F. M. B.]

Löwenstern, Matthäus Apelles von, was b. April 20, 1594, at Neustadt, in the principality of Oppeln, Silesia, where his father was a saddler. He early distinguished himself by his musical abilities, was appointed in 1625, by Duke Heinrich Wenzel of Münsterberg, as his music director and treasurer at Bernstadt : in 1626, director of the princely school at Bernstadt; and in 1631 Rath and Secretary and also Director of finance. Thereafter he entered the service of the Emperors Ferdinand II. (d. 1637), and Ferdinand III. as Rath, and was ennobled by the latter. Finally he became Staatsrath at Oels to Duke Carl Friedrich of Münsterberg, and d. at Breslau, April 11, 1648 (*Koch*, iii. 57–60 ; *Allg. Deutsche Biog.* xix. 318, &c.).

Löwenstern's hymns, thirty in all, are of very varied worth, many being written in imitation of antique verse forms, and on the mottoes of the princes under whom he had served. In the original eds. they were accompanied with melodies by himself. When or where they were first pub. (*cir.* 1644) is not clear. They were bound up with the Breslau *Kirchen und Haus-Music*, 1644, and there bear the title:

Symbola oder Gedenck-Sprüche IIIhrer FFFürstl. GGGn. Hn. Carl Friedrichs Hertzogs zu Münsterberg . . . . dann auch anderer Erlauchter Fürstlicher Personen. Zusambt noch etlichen absonders beygesetzten Geistlichen Oden. Gestellet durch M. A. v. L.

Three of these hymns have been *tr.* :—

i. **Christe, du Beistand deiner Kreuzgemeine.** [*In time of War.*] 1644, No. xvii., in 4 st. of 4 l., entitled "Sapphic Ode. For spiritual and temporal peace." Included in many later collections, and as No. 215 in the *Unv. L. S.*, 1851. It was a favourite hymn of Niebuhr, and also of Bunsen, who included it in his *Versuch*, 1833, and concluded with it the preface to his *Bibelwerk.* The *trs.* in C. U. are :—

1. **Lord of our life, and God of our Salvation.** Contributed by Philip Pusey to A. R. Reinagle's *Psalm and Hymn Tunes*, Oxford, 1840, p. 132, in 5 st. It is rather founded on the German than a *tr.*, st. i., ii. on st. i. ; iii.–v. on ii.–iv. The tune to which it was set was marked by Bunsen as an "old Latin melody," and so the Pusey hymn has sometimes been erroneously called a *tr.* from a Latin hymn of the 8th cent. From *Reinagle* it passed into the *Salisbury H. Bk.*, 1857, and has been repeated in *H. A. & M.*, *Sarum Hyl.*, *Hymnary*, *Church Hys.*; and in America in the *Evang. Hyl.*, N. Y., 1880, *Laudes Domini*, 1884, and others.

2. **Blest aid of Thine afflicted congregation.** In full, by A. T. Russell, as No. 99 in the Dalston Hospital *H. Bk.*, 1848.

3. **Christ, Thou the champion of the band who own.** A good and full *tr.* by Miss Winkworth in her *Lyra Ger.*, 1st Ser., 1855, p. 105; repeated in Schaff's *Christ in Song*, 1869, and the Ohio *Lutheran Hyl.*, 1880. In the 2nd ed. of her *Lyra Ger.*, 1856, it begins, "Christ, Thou the champion of that war-worn host."

4. **O Christ, the leader of that war-worn host.** A good and full *tr.*, based on Miss Winkworth, by W. Mercer in his *C. P. & H. Bk.*, 1857, No. 279 (Oxford ed., No. 391), and repeated in

the American *Sabbath H. Bk.*, 1858. From the version of 1858 Mr. Windle seems to have altered the form in his *Coll.*, No. 268.

ii. **Nun preiset alle.** [*Missions.*] 1644, No. xii., in 5 st. of 6 l., entitled "Alcaic Ode." A fine hymn of Praise. In the *Unv. L. S.*, 1851, No. 717. The *tr.* in C. U. is :—

Now let us loudly. In full, by Miss Winkworth in her *C. B. for England*, 1863, No. 177, set to Löwenstern's original melody.

iii. **Wenn ich in Angst und Noth.** [*Cross and Consolation.*] 1644, No. viii., in 7 st. of 7 l., entitled "The 121st Psalm." It is a fine version as a hymn of consolation in times of trouble. In the Berlin *G. L. S.*, ed. 1863, No. 984. The *trs.* in C. U. are :—

1. **When in distress and woe I lift.** A good *tr.*, omitting st. v., by H. J. Buckoll, in his *H. from German*, 1842, p. 19, repeated in the Dalston Hospital *H. Bk.*, 1848.

2. **When anguish'd and perplexed.** A good *tr.*, omitting st. v., vi., by Miss Winkworth in her *Lyra Ger.*, 2nd Ser., 1858, p. 70. In her *C. B. for England*, 1863, No. 142, altered and set to the original melody by Löwenstern.   [J. M.]

Lowry, Robert, D. D., s. of Crozier Lowry, was b. at Philadelphia, Pennsylvania, March 12, 1826, and educated at Lewisburg University. Having received ordination as a Baptist Minister, his first charge was at West Chester, Pennsylvania. From thence he passed to New York City, and then to Brooklyn, N. Y. In 1876 he was appointed Professor of Rhetoric in his University. On resigning his Professorship he undertook the charge of the 2nd Baptist Church, New Jersey. Dr. Lowry has been associated with some of the most popular Sunday School hymn-books published in the States, including *Happy Voices*, 1865; *Chapel Melodies*, 1868; *Bright Jewels*, 1869; *Pure Gold*, 1871; *Royal Diadem*, 1873; *Tidal Wave*, 1874; *Fountain of Song*, 1877; *Welcome Tidings*, 1877, &c. Of Dr. Lowry's hymns those which have attained the widest circulation are :—

1. **Jerusalem, for ever bright.** *Heaven.* Appeared in the American Tract Society's *Happy Voices*, 1865, with music by the author.

2. **Low in the grave He lay.** *Resurrection of Christ.* Written in 1874 and pub. in *Brightest and Best*, 1875.

3. **Marching on, marching on.** *Sunday School Battle Song.* Appeared, with music by the author, in *Happy Voices*, 1865.

4. **My home is in heaven, my rest is not here.** In *Happy Voices*, 1865, with music by the author.

5. **My life flows on in endless song.** *Joy in God.* In *Bright Jewels*, 1869 ; the *Royal Diadem*, 1873, and others in America and G. Britain, with music by the author.

6. **One more day's work for Jesus.** *Work for Christ.* Pub., with music by the author, in *Bright Jewels*, 1869.

7. **Shall we gather at the river?** *Mutual recognition in the Hereafter.* The origin of this hymn is thus set forth in E. W. Long's *Illustrated History of Hys. and their Authors*, Philadelphia, 1876, p. 64 :—

"On a very hot summer day, in 1864, a pastor was seated in his parlour in Brooklyn, N. Y. It was a time when an epidemic was sweeping through the city, and draping many persons and dwellings in mourning. All around friends and acquaintances were passing away to the spirit land in large numbers. The question began to arise in the heart, with unusual emphasis, 'Shall we meet again? We are parting at the river of death, shall we meet at the river of life?' 'Seating myself at the organ,' says he, 'simply to give vent to the pent up emotions of the heart, the words and music of the hymn began to flow out, as if by inspiration :—

'Shall we gather at the river,
Where bright angel feet have trod ?"

In 1865 the hymn and music were given in *Happy Voices*, No. 220, in 5 st. of 4 l. and a chorus. The hymn has since passed into a great number of hymnals in G. Britain and America.

8. **Take the wings of the morning; speed quickly thy flight.** *Exhortation to Repentance.* Written for, and pub. with music by the author in, the *Royal Diadem*, 1873.

9. **Weeping will not save me.** *Salvation through Faith.* Pub. in the *Chapel Melodies*, 1868.

10. **What can wash away my stain?** *Precious Blood of Jesus.* Given in the *Welcome Tidings*, 1877, with music by the author.

11. **Where is my wandering boy to-night?** *The absent Child.* In the *Fountain of Song*, 1877, together with music by the author.

Most of these hymns are given in Mr. I. D. Sankey's *Sacred Songs & Solos*, Pts. i., ii.

[J. J.]

Loy, M., President of the Capital University, Columbus, Ohio, contributed several original hymns, and translations from the German, to the

Evangelical Lutheran Hymnal. Published by Order of the Ev. Lutheran Joint Synod of Ohio and Other States. Columbus, Ohio, 1880.

The translations may be found through the Index of Authors, &c.; the original hymns are the following :—

1. An awful mystery is here. *Holy Communion.*
2. At Jesus' feet our infant sweet. *Holy Baptism.*
3. Come, humble soul, receive the food. *Holy Communion.*
4. Give me, O Lord, a spirit lowly. *Humility desired.*
5. God gave His word to holy men. *Inspiration of H. Scripture.*
6. God of grace, Whose word is sure. *Faithfulness.*
7. How matchless is our Saviour's grace. *Holy Baptism.*
8. I thank Thee, Saviour, for the grief. *Lent.*
9. Jesus took the lambs and blest them. *Holy Baptism.*
10. Jesus, Thou art mine for ever. *Jesus, All and in All.*
11. Launch out into the deep. *Call to Duty.*
12. Listen to those happy voices. *Christmas.*
13. O Great High Priest, forget not me. *Confirmation.*
14. O Lord, Who hast my place assigned. *Daily Duties.*
15. Our Shepherd of His ransomed flock. *Holy Communion.*
16. The gospel shows the Father's grace. *Holy Scripture.*
17. The law of God is good and wise. *Holy Scripture.*
18. Though angels bright escape our sight. *St. Michael and All Angels.*
19. When Rome had shrouded earth in night. *The Reformation.*
20. When souls draw near the holy wave. *Confirmation.*

Several of these hymns, together with some of his *trs.*, previously appeared in the Ohio Synod's preceding *Coll. of Hys.* (3rd ed., 1858; 4th, 1863). [J. J.]

Lucas of Prag, B.A. (Lucas Pragensis), was b. at Prag about 1460. He studied at the University of Prag, graduating B.A. in 1481. About 1482 he joined the Bohemian Brethren's Unity, becoming in 1490 a member of their

Select Council; and was, in 1500, consecrated Bishop of the Unity. He d. Dec. 11, 1528. He contributed 11 hymns to the *Bohemian H. Bk.*, 1501, and 106 others by him appear in the ed. of 1561. See, further, under Bohemian Hymnody, pp. 153–160; also note on Nun lasst uns den Leib begraben. [J. T. M.]

Lucis Creator optime. *St. Gregory the Great* (?) [*Sunday Evening.*] This is one of the eight hymns which the Benedictine editors assign to St. Gregory (*Opera*, Paris, 1705, iii. col. 879). *Mone* gives it as No. 62, from mss. of the 8th cent. at Darmstadt and Trier, &c. He thinks it was written in the first quarter of the 5th cent., but not in Italy; and consequently neither by St. Ambrose, to whom it has often been ascribed, nor by St. Gregory, who was only b. *cir.* 540. *Daniel*, i., No. 49, gives the text, and at iv. p. 49, cites it as in a 10th cent. Rheinau ms. Among the British Museum mss. it is found in three 11th cent. *Hymnaries* of the English Church (Vesp. D. xii. f. 9 *b*; Jul. A. vi. f. 22; Harl. 2961 f. 220), and in an 11th cent. *Breviary* of the Spanish Church (Add. 30848 f. 72). It is in a ms. of the 11th cent. at Corpus Christi, Cambridge (391, p. 231); and in the *Lat. Hys. of the Anglo-Saxon Church* (Surtees Society), 1851, is printed from an 11th cent. ms. at Durham, (B. iii. 32 f. 5). Among the St. Gall mss. it is given in No. 20 of the 9th cent.; Nos. 387, 413, of the 11th cent., &c.

It is included in the *Mozarabic*, 1502; *Roman* (Venice, 1478, and Rome, 1632); *Sarum*; *York*; *Aberdeen* and other *Breviaries*, generally assigned to Sunday at Vespers. *Daniel* entitles it "A hymn on the work of the First Day" [of the Creation]; and *Mone* as "1st S. after the Octave of the Epiphany. At Second Vespers." The text is also in *Wackernagel*, i. No. 59; *Hymnarium Sarisb.*, 1851, p. 36; *Königsfeld*, ii. p. 8; J. Chandler's *Hys. of the Primitive Church*, 1837, No. 11; and Card. Newman's *Hymni Ecclesiae*, 1838 and 1865. [J. M.]

Translations in C. U. :—

1. **Father of lights, by Whom each day.** Card. Newman, in the *Tracts for the Times*, 1836, No. 75, p. 79; and again in his *Verses on Various Occasions*, 1868, p. 239. It is slightly altered in Blew's *Church Hy. & Tune Bk.*, 1852–55, and Rice's *Sel.* from the same, 1870, No. 24.

2. **Source of light and life divine.** By J. Chandler, in his *Hys. of the Prim. Church*, 1837, p. 9. It is given in some hymn-books in an unaltered form, and sometimes as, "Source of light and *power* divine," as in the *English Hymnal*, 1856 and 1861, with an additional stanza (v.), and thence in *Kennedy*, 1863. In Thring's *Coll.*, 1882, st. iv. is by the Editor.

3. **O blest Creator of the light, Who dost [didst] the dawn, &c.** By E. Caswall, in his *Lyra Catholica*, 1849, p. 13; and his *Hys. & Poems*, 1873, p. 8. This *tr.* is in several hymn-books, and is the most widely used of the *trs.* of the "Lucis Creator optime."

4. **O blest Creator of the light, Who mak'st the day, &c.** By J. M. Neale, in the *Hymnal N.*, 1852, No. 8; the *Hymner*, 1882, and others.

5. **Creator of the light, Supreme!** By J. D. Chambers, in his *Psalter*, 1852, p. 280, and his *Lauda Syon*, 1857, p. 41. It was repeated, with alterations, in Chope's *Hymnal*, 1862. This altered text was transferred to the *People's H.*, 1867, and to Thring's *Coll.*, 1882.

6. **Blest Creator of the light.** This *tr.* appeared in *H. A. & M.*, 1861, as a *tr.* based upon

J. Chandler. It is really a cento thus composed, st. i. l. 1, *Caswall*, with "O" left out; ll. 2–4, *Compilers;* st. ii., iii., iv., ll. 1, 2, *J. Chandler*, very slightly altered; st. iv. ll. 3, 4, *Compilers;* st. v. l. 1, *Caswall*, altered; ll. 2–4, *Compilers*. This cento has passed from *H. A. & M.* into a few collections.

7. **Lord of all, Thy word divine.** This *tr.* in the *Parish H. Bk.*, 1863 and 1875, is J. Chandler's *tr.* altered by the Editors.

8. **Darkness was on the deep, O Lord.** By A. R. Thompson. In the American Reformed Dutch *Hys. of the Church*, 1869.

9. **Blest Maker of the light, by whom.** This *tr.* in the *Hymnary*, 1872, is based upon Card. Newman's *tr.*, as given in Blew's *Church H. & T. Bk.*; and J. D. Chambers's *tr.* in his *Psalter* and his *Lauda Syon* (see above).

Translations not in C. U. :

1. Blest Maker of the radiant light. *Primer.* 1706.
2. O Thou, of light Creator best. *Bp. Mant.* 1837.
3. Great Maker of light, Who called forth its ray. *Hymnarium Anglicanum.* 1844.
4. O Thou Who calledst forth the light. Bp. J. Williams, in his (American) *Ancient Hys.* 1845.
5. Blest Maker of the light. *W. J. Copeland.* 1848.
6. Maker of light, most holy King. *J. R. Beste.* 1849.
7. Eternal Source of light's clear stream. *R. Campbell.* 1850.
8. Father of the glorious light. *G. Rorison.* 1851.
9. Thou, light's Creator, first and best. *J. Keble.* 1869.
10. O great Creator of the light. *T Wallace.* 1874.

[J. J.]

Ludämilia Elisabeth, second dau. of Count Ludwig Günther I. of Schwarzburg-Rudolstadt, was b. April 7, 1640, at the castle of Heidecksburg, near Rudolstadt, and was educated there along with her cousin Emilie Juliane (q.v.). In 1665 she went with her mother to the dowager castle of Friedensburg near Leutenberg; but after her mother's death, in 1670, she returned to Rudolstadt, where, on Dec. 20, 1671, she was formally betrothed to Count Christian Wilhelm of Schwarzburg-Sondershausen. At this time measles was raging in the district, and her eldest sister, Sophie Juliane, was seized, and d. Feb. 14, 1672. By attending on her, Ludämilia and the youngest sister, Christiane Magdalene, caught the infection, and both died at Rudolstadt on March 12, 1672. (*Koch,* iv. 50–56; *Allg. Deutsche Biog.* xix. 365–367, &c.)

She received a careful and pious training, was a good Latin scholar, and well read in divinity and other branches of learning. Her hymns show her to have been of a deeply pious nature, and of intense love to Jesus. They were composed rather for her own edification than for use in public worship. Ten of them were included in the Rudolstadt *G. B.*, 1682. They were collected, to the number of 206, and edited by her cousin Emilie (probably assisted by A. Fritsch) as *Die Stimme der Freundin, das ist: Geistliche Lieder welche, aus brünstiger und biss ans Ende beharrter Jesus Liebe verfertiget und gebraucht,* &c. Rudolstadt, 1687. This was reprinted, with an introduction by W. Thilo, at Stuttgart, 1856.

Three of those hymns have been *tr.*, viz. :—

i. **Jesus, Jesus, nichts als Jesus.** [*Love to Christ.*] 1687, No. 104, p. 312, in 5 st. of 6 l., entitled "Resignation to the Will of God." The initials of the stanzas form the word *Jesus,* and each stanza ends, "Herr, wie du willt." It seems to have appeared in the 2nd ed. of A. Fritsch's *Jesus Lieder* (not in the 1st ed. of 1668. No copy of the 2nd ed. is now known), and in the 3rd ed., Jena, 1675, is No. 43.

Rambach, iii. 188, gives it from the *Vermehrtes Gesang-Büchlein,* Halberstadt, 1673. In the Berlin *G. L. S.*, ed. 1863. The *tr.* in C. U. is :—

Jesus, Jesus, Jesus only. In full, by A. Crull, as No. 282 in the Ohio *Lutheran Hyl.*, 1880.

Other trs. are :—(1) "Jesus, Jesus, nought but Jesus, Shall my wish and," in the *Suppl. to Ger. Psal.*, ed. 1765, p. 11. (2) "Jesus, 'tis my aim divine," by *Miss Dunn,* 1857, p. 107. (3) "'Tis Jesus that's my sole desire," by *Dr. G. Walker,* 1860, p. 92. (4) "Jesus, Jesus, naught but Jesus, Can my," by R. Massie, in the *British Herald,* July, 1865, p. 103, and in Reid's *Praise Bk.*, 1872, No. 393. (5) "Jesus, Jesus, nought but Jesus, Shall my wish be," in *Cantica Sanctorum,* 1880, No. 97.

ii. **Jesu Blut komm über mich.** [*Holy Communion.*] A Passiontide Hymn on the Blood of Jesus. 1687, p. 45, No. 14, in 8 st. In the *Blätter für Hymnologie,* 1886, p. 180, it is cited as in the 2nd ed., 1679, of A. Fritsch's *Himmels-Lust* (1st ed., 1670, does not contain it); and as there marked "E. J. G Z, S. V. H.," the initials of the elder sister, Sophie Juliane.

Tr. as :—"Jesus' Blood come over me," as No. 448, in pt. i. of the *Moravian H. Bk.*, 1754.

iii. **Sorge, Vater! sorge du.** [*Morning.*] 1687, No. 168, in 7 st., entitled "On Resignation to the Care of God," and founded on 1 Peter v. 7. Previously in the Rudolstadt *G. B.*, 1682, p. 692.

Tr. as :—"Care, O Father, care for me," in the *Monthly Packet,* xiv., 1872, p. 211.

The hymn "Zeuch uns nach dir," sometimes erroneously ascribed to her, is noted under Funcke, F., p. 401, ii. [J. M.]

Lugete dura marmora. [*Passiontide.*] This is found in the *Sirenes Symphoniacae,* Cologne, 1678, p. 154 ; the *Psalteriolum Cantionum Catholicarum,* Cologne, 1722, p. 83 ; the *Hymnodia Sacra,* Münster, 1753, p. 80 ; and also in *Daniel,* ii. 351. It is probably the production of some German Jesuit, and was most likely written in the second half of the 17th cent. It has been *tr.* by the Rev. R. C. Singleton, 1870, and pub. in the 2nd ed. of his *Anglican H. Bk.*, 1871, as "O mourn, thou rigid stone"; and by H. M. Macgill in his *Songs of the Christian Creed & Life,* 1876, No. 71, as "Ye rocks of marble, melt and weep." [J. M.]

Lugete, pacis Angeli. *C. Coffin.* [*Friday—Lent.*] Appeared in the *Paris Breviary,* 1736, for Fridays at Vespers, and also "Ad Officium Noct. In Festo quinque plagarum Christi." It was repeated in Coffin's *Hymni Sacri,* the same year, p. 28, and is found in several modern French Breviaries. The text is also in J. Chandler's *Hys. of the Primitive Church,* 1837, No. 31, and Card. Newman's *Hymni Ecclesiae,* 1838 and 1865. *Tr.* as :—

1. **Lament, ye saints, behold your God.** By J. Chandler, in his *Hys. of the Prim. Church,* 1837, p. 28, and Dr. Oldknow's *Hymns,* &c., 1850. In 1861 it was given, with alterations, as "*Angels, lament,* behold your God," in *H. A. & M.*, but omitted in the revised ed., 1875.

2. **Angels of peace, look down from heaven and mourn.** By I. Williams in his *Hys. tr. from the Parisian Breviary,* 1839, p. 36. It was repeated in the *Salisbury H. Bk.*, 1857 ; the *Sarum,* 1868 ; the *Hymnary,* 1872, and others, and usually with slight alterations.

3. **Angels of peace, lament.** By W. J. Blew. Written for use in his own church, 1850–2, and

pub. in *The Church Hy. & Tune Bk.*, 1852–5 ; and again in Rice's *Hys. Selected from the Ch. H. & T. Bk.*, 1870.

Translations not in C. U. :—

1. Angels, look down and weep. *R. Campbell*, 1850.
2. Angels of peace ! ye seraphs mourn. *J. D. Chambers*, 1857.
3. Angels of peace, bewail. D. T. Morgan, in his *Hys. of the Latin Church*, 1880.   [J. J.]

Luise Henriette, Electress of Brandenburg, dau. of Friedrich Heinrich, Prince of Nassau-Orange and Stadtholder of the United Netherlands, was b. at 'S Gravenhage (The Hague), Nov. 27, 1627. She received a careful Christian training, not only in literature, but also in domestic economy and feminine handicrafts. On Dec. 7, 1646, she was married, at the Hague, to the Elector Friedrich Wilhelm of Brandenburg, who was then residing at Cleve, but remained at the Hague to nurse her father, who d. March 14, 1647. She then, in June, 1647, joined her husband at Cleve, where her first child, Wilhelm Heinrich, was b. in May 1648. In the autumn of 1649 she set out with her husband and child on the way to Berlin, but in the inclement weather the child sickened and d. at Wesel, Oct. 24, 1649, and it was not till April 10, 1650, that she entered Berlin. On the birth of her second son, Carl Emil (who d. 1674), at Oranienburg, near Berlin, on Feb. 16, 1655, she founded an orphanage there as a thank-offering (now the Oranienburg Orphanage at Berlin). On July 11, 1657, her third son, afterwards King Friedrich I. of Prussia, was b. at Königsberg. After the birth of her youngest son, Ludwig, at Cleve, in 1666, she never entirely recovered. In the spring of 1667 she was conveyed to Berlin in a litter, and d. there June 18, 1667. (*Koch*, iv. 158 ; *Allg. Deutsche Biog.*, xix. 623 ; Goedeke's *Grundriss*, vol. iii., 1887, p. 319, &c.)

Luise Henriette was a woman of noble character ; a devoted wife who accompanied her husband in many of his expeditions, and was his right-hand counsellor in matters of state ; and a true mother of her people, introducing the culture of the potato, founding model farms, establishing elementary schools, and in many ways interesting herself in restoring their welfare after the ravages of the Thirty Years' War. She was, like the Elector, a member of the Reformed Church, but earnestly desired to promote peace between the Lutheran and Reformed communions, and exerted herself especially on behalf of P. Gerhardt (see **p. 409,** ii.). Another of her efforts in this direction was by means of the *Union Hymn Book*, which Christoph Runge edited at her direction, and pub. in 1653 (see **p. 272,** i.). To this book she herself contributed four hymns. In his dedication to the Electress, Runge says she had "augmented and adorned it with your own hymns, viz. : 'Ein ander stelle sein Vertrauen' ; 'Gott der Reichthumb deiner Güter' ; 'Jesus meine Zuversicht' ; 'Ich wil von meiner Missethat.' Your Electoral Highness has not only in those your now mentioned hymns (itzt gemeldten geistreichen *Ihren eigenen* Liedern) made known to all the world your Christian spirit ; how your confidence is directed to God alone ; how you ascribe to him with thankful heart all the benefits you enjoy ; and how you rest the hope of your future everlasting life in Heaven on Christ alone as on a steadfast rock, but have also," &c. &c.

The question however remains. Did Runge here mean more than that she had sent for insertion certain hymns which were favourites of her own, perhaps written *for* her, but not necessarily written *by* her ? Such cases were common enough at an earlier period (see note on **Mag ich Unglück**). It is certainly strange that her name should not be given in any of the many hymn-books in which the third of these ("Jesus meine Zuversicht") was included during the next century. It was not till 1769 that Runge's dedication suggested to D. G. Schöber, and, after him, to other compilers, the

idea of the Electress's authorship ; but once suggested it was soon generally accepted. *Fischer*, i. 390–396, gives various additional reasons that make this theory unlikely ; such as that while in Runge's dedication they are mentioned as above, yet her name is not affixed to the individual hymns in the body of the book ; that in the funeral oration by her private chaplain, no mention is made of her poetical gifts ; that Crüger gave them in his *Praxis pietatis melica* without her name (in the 1664 and later eds. the first was omitted), and that in particular the third is too classic and correct in style to have been written by so poor a German scholar as the Electress. This last objection would of course be met if we could suppose with *Koch* (iv. p. 169) that the hymn was originally written in Dutch, or with Dutch idioms, and was revised and corrected by her minister, Otto von Schwerin, or by Runge.

In view of the present evidence we can only say that if the Electress were not the author of these hymns there is at least no proof of any kind to show that they were composed by any of those whose names have sometimes been attached to them ; such as Otto von Schwerin (b. 1616, d. 1679), Caspar Ziegler (b. 1621, d. 1690), Hans von Assig (b. 1650, d. 1694), and others. In this state of uncertainty the case must be left till definite proof be forthcoming.

Two of these hymns have passed into English, viz. :—

i. **Ich will von meiner Missethat.** *Lent.* This beautiful hymn first appeared in the Crüger-Runge *G. B.*, 1653, No. 45, in 16 st. of 7 l., entitled, "Hymn of Penitence," and without signature. *Koch*, iv. 160, conjectures that it may have been written at Cleve in 1648. In the *Unv. L. S.*, 1851, No. 380. The *trs.* are :—

(1) "With sorrow now for past misdeeds," by *Miss Cox*, 1864, p. 204. (2) "I will return unto the Lord," by *Miss Winkworth*, 1869, p. 221.

ii. **Jesus meine Zuversicht.** *Easter.* This beautiful hymn, founded on Job xix. 25–27 and 1 Cor. xv. 35 ff., appeared in the Crüger-Runge *G. B.*, 1653, No. 140, in 10 st. of 6 l., and without signature. Its origin is thus given by Lauxmann, in *Koch*, viii. 69 :—

" It dates from the early years of her married life. In the autumn of 1649 she lost her first child, the Crown Prince Wilhelm Heinrich, at Wesel, while on her journey [to Berlin], by which death for a long time the hope of succession in the Electoral House and in the Hohenzollern family line seemed to be lost. At Tangermünde, in the Altmark [on the Elbe], she had to spend some quiet winter months, and here probably the princess of twenty-two years poured out her heart before the Lord in this hymn."

This, however, is conjecture rather than history ; for, as stated above, it is not yet clearly proved that the Electress wrote any hymns. The hymn itself is of the first rank ; and A. J. Rambach calls it "an acknowledged masterpiece of Christian poetry ;" while C. von Winterfeld says, "it will ever remain a treasure among the hallowed songs of the Evangelical Church." It bears a certain resemblance to the concluding section of the *Apotheosis* of A. C. Prudentius (lines 1063–1085, with the subtitle " De resurrectione carnis humanae," and beginning, "Nosco meum in Christo corpus consurgere. Quid me ") ; but can hardly be called a *tr.* of it. It was included in Crüger's *Praxis*, 1656, No. 182, passed into almost all later hymn-books, and is No. 866 in the *Unv. L. S.*, 1851.

The beautiful chorale (as in the *C. B. for England*) appeared in its first form in 1653, along with the hymn. C. von Winterfeld conjectured that it may have been by the Electress. The form now in use is modified from that given by Crüger in his *Praxis*, 1656. *Tr.* as :—

1. **Christ, my Rock, my sure Defence.** Omitting st. ix., as No. 51 in the *Moravian H. Bk.*, 1769. In the ed. of 1789. No. 833, st. viii. was omitted,

and a *tr.* from Christian Gregor's "*Nein, ach nein, er lässt mich nicht*," was added as st. iii. (ed. 1886, No. 1241). Abridged forms are in J. A. Latrobe's *Coll.*, 1841, and Dr. Hook's *Church School H. Bk.*, 1850.

2. Jesus, on Whose name I rest. A good *tr.* of st. i.–iv., vi., by A. T. Russell, as No. 264, in his *Ps. & Hys.*, 1851.

3. Jesus, my Redeemer, lives. A good *tr.*, omitting st. iv., v., by Miss Winkworth, in her *Lyra Ger.* 1st Ser., 1855, p. 93. Repeated, in full, in the Ohio *Evang. Luth. Hyl.*, 1880 ; and, abridged, in the Bapt. *Ps. & Hys.*, 1858, *Meth. New Connexion H. Bk.*, 1863, J. B. Whiting's *Hys. for the Church Catholic*, 1882, and others.

4. Christ, the Rock on which I build. A good *tr.*, omitting st. iv., v., contributed by R. Massie, as No. 106, to the 1857 ed. of Mercer's *Ch. Psalter & H. Bk,* (Ox. ed. 1864, No. 199, omitting *trs.* of st. ii., vi.) and repeated in his own *Lyra Domestica*, 2nd Ser., 1864, p. 127. Abridged in Dr. J. Paterson's *Coll.*, Glasgow, 1867.

5. Jesus, my eternal trust. A full and good *tr.*, by Mrs. Charles, in her *Voice of Christian Life in Song*, 1858, p. 237, repeated in *Cantate Domino*, Boston, U.S., 1859.

6. Jesus Christ, my sure defence. A good *tr.*, by Miss Winkworth, in the original metre, omitting st. iv.–vi., and based on her *Lyra Ger.* version, in her *C. B. for England*, 1863, No. 59. In the Pennsylvania Luth *Ch Bk.*, 1868, the *trs.* of st. viii., ix., are omitted.

7. Christ, my Lord, is all my hope. A *tr.* of st. i., ii., viii., x., by Miss Borthwick, in Dr. Pagenstecher's *Coll.*, 1864, No. 285.

Other trs. are :—
(1) "Jesus is my faithful trust." In the *British Magazine*, June 1838, p. 625. (2) "I with Jesus choose my part," by *Dr. H. Mills*, 1856, p. 248. (3) "Again my Saviour Jesus lives," by *Dr. G. Walker*, 1860, p. 100. (4) "Jesus Christ, my Saviour, lives!" In the *British Herald*, Sept. 1866, p. 328, and Reid's *Praise Bk.*, 1872. (5) "Jesus is my confidence," by *N. L. Frothingham*, 1870, p. 175. (6) "Jesus Christ, my Strength, my Stay." In the *Family Treasury*, 1876, p. 76. [J. M.]

Luke, Jemima, *née* Thompson,

daughter of Thomas Thompson, sometime of Bath, was b. at Colebrooke Terrace, Islington, Aug. 19, 1813, and was married to the late Samuel Luke, a Congregational Minister, in 1843. She was an anonymous contributor to The Juvenile Magazine at the age of 13, and subsequently pub. several works, including *The Female Jesuit*, 1851; *A Memoir of Eliza Ann Harris, of Clifton*, 1859, &c. Mrs. Luke is known to hymnody through her hymn :—

I think when I read that sweet story of old. [*The Love of Jesus.*] It is recorded that this hymn was composed in a stage coach in 1841, and was designed for use in the village school, near her father's seat, Poundsford Park. It was pub. anonymously in the *Leeds H. Bk.*, 1853, No. 874, in 3 st. of 8 l., and has since come into use through children's hymn-books in most English-speaking countries. [J. J.]

Lundie, Mary. [Duncan, Mary.]

Lunt, William Parsons, D.D., s. of

Henry Lunt, was b. at Newburyport, Massachusetts, April 21, 1805. He entered Harvard College in 1819, and graduated in 1823. After acting as a tutor in a school for one year, and studying law a second, he joined the Cambridge Divinity School in 1825, and entered the Unitarian Ministry, June 19, 1828, his first charge being the Second Congrega-

tional Unitarian Society of New York City. In 1835 he became co-pastor of the Unitarian congregation at Quincy, Massachusetts, with the Rev. P. Whitney, and in 1843 sole pastor of the same congregation. During a tour in the East he d. at Akabah (the ancient Ezion-Geber), March 21, 1857, and was buried a short distance from that village. Dr. Lunt was the author of several sermons, and contributed largely to the *Christian Examiner* and other periodicals. His hymns and poems, together with selections from his prose works, were pub. by his son as *Gleanings*. His most widely used hymn is "When driven by oppression's rod." It was "written for the public schools of Quincy, and sung by them at their Fourth of July Celebration, 1837." It is in 5 st. of 4 l. This, together with several others, including one of more than ordinary merit for Sunday schools, "Hark, the gentle Shepherd's voice" (written in 1840), are given in full in Putnam's *Singers and Songs of the Liberal Faith*, 1875. To this work we are indebted for the above facts. [J. J.]

Luther, Martin, b. at Eisleben, Nov. 10,

1483; entered the University of Erfurt, 1501 (b.a. 1502, m.a. 1503); became an Augustinian monk, 1505; ordained priest, 1507; appointed Professor at the University of Wittenberg, 1508, and in 1512 d.d.; published his 95 Theses, 1517; and burnt the Papal Bull which had condemned them, 1520; attended the Diet of Worms, 1521; translated the Bible into German, 1521–34; and d. at Eisleben, Feb. 18, 1546. The details of his life and of his work as a reformer are accessible to English readers in a great variety of forms, and need not be repeated here. Of Luther's influence on German hymnody an adequate estimate will be found under **German Hymnody**, at p. **414**. It only remains here to give a somewhat fuller account of the principal books which he edited, or in which his hymns first appeared; together with a classified list of his hymns.

i. Hymn Books.

1. *Etlich cristlich lider Lobgesang uñ Psalm.* Wittenberg, 1524. [Hamburg Library.] This contains 8 German hymns, of which 4 are by Luther.

2. *Eyn Enchiridion oder Handbuchlein.* Erfurt 1524 [Goslar Library], with 25 German hymns, of which 18 are by Luther.

3. *Geystliche Gesangk Buchleyn.* Wittenberg, 1524 [Munich Library], with 32 German hymns, of which 24 are by Luther.

4. *Geistliche Lieder auffs new gebessert.* Wittenberg. J. Klug, 1529. No copy of this book is now known, but there was one in 1788 in the possession of G. E. Waldau, pastor at Nürnberg, and from his description it is evident that the first part of the Rostock *G. B.*, 1531, is a reprint of it. The Rostock *G. B.*, 1531, was reprinted by C. M. Wiechmann–Kadow at Schwerin in 1858. The 1529 evidently contained 50 German hymns, of which 29 (including the *Litany*) were by Luther.

5. *Geistliche Lieder auffs new gebessert.* Erfurt. A. Rauscher, 1531 [Helmstädt, now Wolfenbüttel Library], a reprint of No. 4.

6. *Geistliche Lieder.* Wittenberg. J. Klug, 1535 [Munich Library. Titlepage lost], with 52 German hymns, of which 29 are by Luther.

7. *Geistliche Lieder auffs new gebessert.* Leipzig. V. Schumann, 1539 [Wernigerode Library], with 68 German hymns, of which 29 are by Luther.

8. *Geistliche Lieder.* Wittenberg. J. Klug, 1543 [Hamburg Library], with 61 German hymns, of which 35 are by Luther.

9. *Geystliche Lieder.* Leipzig. V. Babst, 1545 [Göttingen Library]. This contains Luther's finally revised text, but adds no new hymns by himself. In pt. i. are 61 German hymns, in pt. ii. 40, of which 35 in all are by Luther.

For these books Luther wrote three prefaces, first pub. respectively in Nos. 3, 4, 9. A fourth is found in his *Christliche Geseng, Lateinisch und Deudsch, zum Begrebnis*, Wittenberg, J. Klug, 1542. These four prefaces are reprinted in Wackernagel's *Bibliographie*, 1855, pp. 543-583, and in the various editions of Luther's *Hymns*. Among modern editions of Luther's *Geistliche Lieder* may be mentioned the following :—

Carl von Winterfeld, 1840; Dr. C. E. P. Wackernagel, 1848; G. C. H. Stip, 1854; Wilhelm Schircks, 1854; Dr. Danneil, 1883; Dr. Karl Gerok, 1883; Dr. A. F. W. Fischer, 1883; A. Frommel, 1883; Karl Goedeke, 1883, &c. In *The Hymns of Martin Luther. Set to their original melodies. With an English version.* New York, 1883, ed. by Dr. Leonard Woolsey Bacon and Nathan H. Allen, there are the four prefaces, and English versions of all Luther's hymns, principally taken more or less altered, from the versions by A. T. Russell, R. Massie and Miss Winkworth (repub. in London, 1884]. Complete *trs.* of Luther's hymns have been pub. by Dr. John Anderson, 1846 (2nd ed. 1847), Dr. John Hunt, 1853, Richard Massie, 1854, and Dr. G. Macdonald in the *Sunday Magazine*, 1867, and his *Exotics*, 1876. The other versions are given in detail in the notes on the individual hymns.

ii. *Classified List of Luther's Hymns.*

Of Luther's hymns no classification can be quite perfect, e.g. No. 3 (see below) takes hardly anything from the Latin, and No. 18 hardly anything from the Psalm. No. 29 is partly based on earlier hymns (see p. 225, i.). No. 30 is partly based on St. Mark i. 9-11, and xvi., 15, 16 (see p. 226, ii.). No. 35 is partly based on St. Luke ii. 10-16. The following arrangement, however, will answer all practical purposes.

A. *Translations from the Latin.*

i. *From Latin Hymns :*

1. Christum wir sollen loben schon.
   A solis ortus cardine (p. 4, ii.).
2. Der du bist drei in Einigkeit.
   O Lux beata Trinitas.
3. Jesus Christus unser Heiland, Der von.
   Jesus Christus nostra salus (p. 598, i.)
4. Komm Gott Schöpfer, heiliger Geist.
   Veni Creator Spiritus, Mentes.
5. Nun komm der Heidenheiland.
   Veni Redemptor gentium.
6. Was fürchst du Feind Herodes sehr.
   A solis ortus cardine (p. 5, i.)

ii. *From Latin Antiphons, &c. :*

7. Herr Gott dich loben wir.
   Te Deum laudamus.
8. Verleih uns Frieden gnädiglich.
   Da pacem, Domine (p. 275, ii.).
9. Wir glauben all an einen Gott.

iii. *Partly from the Latin, the translated stanzas being adopted from Pre-Reformation Versions :*

10. Komm, heiliger Geist, Herre Gott.
11. Mitten wir im Leben sind.
    Media vita in morte sumus. (p. 721. i.)

B. *Hymns revised and enlarged from Pre-Reformation popular hymns.*

12. Gelobet seist du Jesus Christ.
13. Gott der Vater wohn uns bei.
14. Gott sei gelobet und gebenedeiet.
15. Nun bitten wir den heiligen Geist.

C. *Psalm versions.*

16. Ach Gott vom Himmel, sieh darein.
17. Aus tiefer Noth schrei ich zu dir.
18. Ein' feste Burg ist unser Gott.
19. Es spricht der Unweisen Mund wohl.
20. Es wollt uns Gott genädig sein.
21. Wär Gott nicht mit uns diese Zeit.
22. Wohl dem, der in Gottes Furcht steht.

D. *Paraphrases of other portions of Holy Scripture.*

23. Diess sind die heilgen zehn Gebot.
24. Jesaia dem Propheten das geschah.
25. Mensch willt du leben seliglich.
26. Mit Fried und Freud ich fahr dahin.
27. Sie ist mir lieb die werthe Magd.
28. Vater unser im Himmelreich.

E. *Hymns mainly Original.*

29. Christ lag in Todesbanden.
30. Christ unser Herr zum Jordan kam.
31. Ein neues Lied wir heben an.
32. Erhalt uns Herr bei deinem Wort.
33. Jesus Christus unser Heiland, Der den.
34. Nun freut euch lieben Christengemein.
35. Vom Himmel hoch da komm ich her.
36. Vom Himmel kam der Engel Schaar.

In addition to these see also notes on :—

37. Für allen Freuden auf Erden.
38. Kyrie eleison.

In the *Blätter für Hymnologie*, 1883, Dr. Danneil arranges Luther's hymns according to what he thinks their adaptation to modern German C. U., as follows :—

i. Hymns which ought to be included in every good Evangelical hymn-book : Nos. 7-18, 20, 26, 28, 29, 30, 32, 34, 35, 36, 38.
ii. Hymns the reception of which into a hymn-book might be contested : Nos. 2, 3, 4, 19, 21, 22, 23, 24, 25, 33.
iii. Hymns not suited for a hymn-book : Nos. 1, 5, 6, 27, 31, 37.

The whole of these 38 pieces are annotated in the body of this Dictionary under their first lines, except Nos. 1-8, 11, which are noted under the first lines given in italics.   [J. M.]

Lux alma Jesu mentium. *St. Bernard.* [*The Transfiguration.*] In the revised *Roman Breviary*, 1568, a cento from St. Bernard's "Jesu dulcis memoria" (q. v.), beginning "Amor Jesu dulcissime" [not the cento in *H. A. & M.*, "Jesu, Thy mercies are untold," noted on p. 587, i. (iii.)], was appointed for Lauds on the Festival of the Transfiguration. The lines were taken from St. Bernard's poem without the least regard to their original connection, and were considerably altered to adapt them to their purpose. We give this altered text below from the *Rom. Brev.*, pub. at Rome in 1570, p. 778. In the *Rom. Brev.* revised under Urban VIII., 1632, it was recast as "Lux alma Jesu mentium," and this recast has been repeated in all subsequent editions of that revision. The two forms of the cento are as follows :—

Roman Breviary, 1568.	*Roman Breviary*, 1632.
" Amor Jesu dulcissime, Quando cor nostrum visitas, Pellis mentis caliginem, Et nos reples dulcedine.	" Lux alma Jesu mentium Dum corda nostra recreas, Culpae fugas caliginem, Et nos reples dulcedine.
" Quam felix est, quem satias, Consors Paternae dexterae ! Tu verae lumen patriae, Quod omnem sensum superat.	" Quam laetus est quem visitas ! Consors Paternae dexterae, Tu dulce lumen patriae, Carnis negatum sensibus.
" Splendor Paternae gloriae, Incomprehensa bonitas, Amoris tui copiam, Da nobis per praesentiam."	" Splendor Paternae gloriae, Incomprehensa charitas, Nobis amoris copiam Largire per praesentiam."

It will be noted that l. 9, "Splendor Paternae," is the first line of the well-known Ambrosian hymn, and is not from St. Bernard's poem.   [J. M.]

The older of the above centos has not been

tr. into English. The *trs.* of the **Lux alma Jesu mentium** are :—

1. Light of the anxious heart, Jesu, Thou dost appear. By Card. Newman, in *Tracts for the Times*, 1836, No. 75, p. 115; and again in his *Verses on Various Occasions*, 1868, p. 261. It has been repeated in several collections, but must be distinguished from R. Campbell's *tr.* as given below.

2. Light of the soul, O Saviour blest. By E. Caswall, in his *Lyra Catholica*, 1849, p. 168; and his *Hys. & Poems*, 1873, p. 91. This is in several modern hymn-books.

3. Light of the anxious heart, Jesu, Thy suppliants cheer. By R. Campbell, in his *Hys. & Anthems*, 1850, p. 56. In O. Shipley's *Annus Sanctus*, 1884, it is given from Campbell's MSS. as, "Light of the *troubled* heart."

Other trs. are :
1. O Christ, when Thy chaste light inspires. *Primer.* 1706 and 1732.
2. Jesu, Light of souls indwelling. *W. J. Copeland.* 1848.
3. O Jesus, when Thy sweetest light. *J. Wallace.* 1874.   [J. J.]

Lux illuxit triumphalis. [*Common of Saints.*] In a *Paris Missal* of the beginning of the 14th cent. now in the British Museum (Add. 16905, f. 254 *b*) this is given as a sequence on St. Germain, Bishop of Paris (commemorated on May 28; not St. Germain of Auxerre); and in another *Missal* of the same date, probably also of the Paris use (Harl. 2891, f. 359). The same text is in *Clichtovaeus*, ed. 1556, Bk. iv. f. 215. The form *tr.* into English is that in J. M. Horst's *Paradisus animae Christianae*, Cologne, 1644, p. 118 (not in the 1st. ed. 1630), where it is a General Hymn for Saints' Days ("Hymnus Communis in festo cujuscunque Sancti"), and has 14 st. In the 1863 ed. of the *Appendix* to the *Hymnal Noted* it is *tr.* in 8 st. by T. I. Ball as, "Glad light illumes this day." This is repeated in 5 st. in the S. P. C. K. *Church Hys.*, 1871. Another *tr.* is, "Hail, the festal morn begun," in the *tr.* of *The Paradise of the Christian Soul*, pub. by Burns, Lond., 1850, p. 141.   [J. M.]

Lux jucunda, lux insignis. *Adam of St. Victor.* [*Whitsuntide.*] The text of this fine sequence is given by Gautier in his *Oeuvres poetiques D'Adam* (1858, i. p. 107; 1881, p. 50), from various MSS., including two in the National Library at Paris, No. 1139, a Limoges Sequentiary of the 12th cent.; No. 15615, a Paris Gradual of the 13th cent. It is also in two early 14th cent. *Paris Missals* in the British Museum (Add. 16905, f. 175; Harl. 2891, f. 348); and in the *Sarum, York*, and *St. Andrews Missals*. It does not seem to have been used in Germany, though *Daniel*, ii. 71, in giving the text, justly styles it "inferior to none, superior to most; breathing nothing but the flowers and odours of Holy Scripture." *Clichtovaeus, Abp. Trench,* and *Wrangham* explain the poet's allusions to the various Scripture types. The main uses were :—St. Victor appointed it for Monday in Whitsun Week; *Paris* for Tuesday; the *Sarum* for Wednesday; while the *York* gave part first (reading "*Laus* jucunda") for Friday, and part second ("Consolator alme") for Saturday.   [Wm. C.]

The *trs.* of this Sequence in C. U. are :—
1. Lux jucunda, lux insignis = **Day all jubilant,** all splendid. Pt. i.
2. O quam felix, quam festiva = **O the joy, the** exultation. Pt. ii.
3. Consolator alme, veni = **Comforter, possess and** cheer us. Pt. iii.

This *tr.* was made by C. S. Calverley for the *Hymnary* in which it was pub. in 1872.

Other trs. are :—
1. Day of pleasure, day of wonder. H. Kynaston, in his *Occasional Hys.*, 1862.
2. The illustrious Day when from the throne. C. B. Pearson, in *The Sarum Missal in English*, 1868, and his *Sequences from the Sarum Missal*, 1871.
3. Day delightful, day most noted. By D. S. Wrangham, in his *Liturgical Poetry of Adam of St. Victor*, 1881, together with the original Latin.   [J. J.]

Lynch, Thomas Toke, was b. at Dunmow, Essex, July 5, 1818, and educated at a school at Islington, in which he was afterwards an usher. For a few months he was a student at the Highbury Independent College; but withdrew, partly on account of failing health, and partly because his spirit was too free to submit to the routine of College life. From 1847 to 1849 he was Minister of a small charge at Highgate, and from 1849 to 1852 of a congregation in Mortimer Street, which subsequently migrated to Grafton Street, Fitzroy Square. From 1856 to 1859 he was laid aside by illness. In 1860 he resumed his ministry with his old congregation, in a room in Gower Street, where he remained until the opening of his new place of worship, in 1862, (Mornington Church), in Hampstead Road, London. He ministered there till his death, on the 9th of May, 1871.

The influence of Lynch's ministry was great, and reached far beyond his own congregation (which was never large), since it included many students from the Theological Colleges of London, and thoughtful men from other churches, who were attracted to him by the freshness and spirituality of his preaching. His prose works were numerous, beginning with *Thoughts on a Day*, 1844, and concluding with *The Mornington Lecture*, 1870. Several of his works were published after his death. His *Memoir*, by W. White, was pub. in 1874.

Lynch's hymns were pub. in :—

The Rivulet : a Contribution to Sacred Song, Lond., Longman, 1855, 2nd ed., 1856. This was enlarged by an addition of 67 hymns in 1868.

From the 1st ed. of the *Rivulet*, 1855, the following hymns have come into C. U. :—

1. All faded is the glowing light. *Second Advent.*
2. Be Thy word with power fraught. *Before Sermon.*
3. Christ in His word draws near. *Holy Scripture.*
4. Dismiss me not Thy service, Lord. *Work for Christ.*
5. Gracious Spirit, dwell with me. *Holy Spirit's presence desired.*
6. How calmly the evening once more is descending. *Evening.* Sometimes "How calmly once more the night is descending."
7. I give myself to prayer. *Prayer in Trouble.*
8. Lord, on Thy returning day. *Public Worship.*
9. Lord, when in silent hours I muse. *Resignation.*
10. Love me, O Lord, forgivingly. *Resignation.*
11. Mountains by the darkness hidden. *Resignation.*
12. Now have we met that we may ask. *P. Worship.*
13. O, break my heart; but break it as a field. *Penitence desired.*
14. O Lord, Thou art not fickle. *Sympathy.*
15. O where is He that trod the sea. *Christ Walking on the Sea.*
16. Oft when of God we ask. *Trust in Trial.*
17. Rise, He calleth thee, arise. *Blind Bartimaeus.*
18. Say not, my soul, from whence. *Resignation.*
19. Where is thy God, my soul ? *Resignation and Hope.*

There are also from the 1856 and 1868 eds. the following :—

20. A thousand years have come and gone. *Christmas.*
21. Lift up your heads, rejoice. (1856.) *Advent.*
22. Praying by the river side. *Holy Baptism.*
23. The Lord is rich and merciful. *Have Faith in God.*
24. There is purpose in this waste. *Easter.*

Lynch's hymns are marked by intense individuality, gracefulness and felicity of diction, picturesqueness, spiritual freshness, and the sadness of a powerful soul struggling with a weak and emaciated body. Although *The Rivulet* was pub. for use by his own congregation as a supplement to Watts, more than one half of the hymns were designed for private use only, but were not so distinguished in the work. Its publication caused one of the most bitter hymnological controversies known in the annals of modern Congregationalism. Time, however, and a criticism, broader and more just, have declared emphatically in favour of his hymns as valuable contributions to cultured sacred song.   [W. G. H.]

Lyte, Henry Francis, M.A., s. of Captain Thomas Lyte, was b. at Ednam, near Kelso, June 1, 1793, and educated at Portora (the Royal School of Enniskillen), and at Trinity College, Dublin, of which he was a Scholar, and where he graduated in 1814. During his University course he distinguished himself by gaining the English prize poem on three occasions.   At one time he had intended studying Medicine; but this he abandoned for Theology, and took Holy Orders in 1815, his first curacy being in the neighbourhood of Wexford.   In 1817, he removed to Marazion, in Cornwall.   There, in 1818, he underwent a great spiritual change, which shaped and influenced the whole of his after life, the immediate cause being the illness and death of a brother clergyman.   Lyte says of him :—

" He died happy under the belief that though he had deeply erred, there was *One* whose death and sufferings would atone for his delinquencies, and be accepted for all that he had incurred;"

and concerning himself he adds :—

"I was greatly affected by the whole matter, and brought to look at life and its issue with a different eye than before; and I began to study my Bible, and preach in another manner than I had previously done."

From Marazion he removed, in 1819, to Lymington, where he composed his *Tales on the Lord's Prayer* in verse (pub. in 1826); and in 1823 he was appointed Perpetual Curate of Lower Brixham, Devon. That appointment he held until his death, on Nov. 20, 1847. His *Poems of Henry Vaughan, with a Memoir,* were pub. in 1846. His own Poetical works were :—

(1) *Poems chiefly Religious,* 1833; 2nd ed. enlarged, 1845. (2) *The Spirit of the Psalms,* 1834, written in the first instance for use in his own Church at Lower Brixham, and enlarged in 1836; (3) *Miscellaneous Poems* (posthumously) in 1868. This last is a reprint of the 1845 ed. of his *Poems,* with "Abide with me" added. (4) *Remains,* 1850.

Lyte's *Poems* have been somewhat freely drawn upon by hymnal compilers; but by far the larger portion of his hymns found in modern collections are from his *Spirit of the Psalms.* In America his hymns are very popular. In many instances, however, through mistaking Miss Auber's (q. v.) *Spirit of the Psalms,* 1829, for his, he is credited with more than is his due. The Andover *Sabbath H. Bk.,*

1858, is specially at fault in this respect. The best known and most widely used of his compositions are " Abide with me, fast falls the eventide"; " Far from my heavenly home"; " God of mercy, God of grace"; " Pleasant are Thy courts above"; " Praise, my soul, the King of heaven"; and " There is a safe and secret place." These and several others are annotated under their respective first lines: the rest in C. U. are :—

i. From his *Poems chiefly Religious,* 1833 and 1845.

1. Above me hangs the silent sky. *For Use at Sea.*
2. Again, O Lord, I ope mine eyes. *Morning.*
3. Hail to another Year. *New Year.*
4. How good, how faithful, Lord, art Thou. *Divine care of Men.*
5. In tears and trials we must sow (1845). *Sorrow followed by Joy.*
6. My [our] rest is in heaven, my [our] rest is not here. *Heaven our Home.*
7. O Lord, how infinite Thy love. *The Love of God in Christ.*
8. Omniscient God, Thine eye divine. *The Holy Ghost Omniscient.*
9. The leaves around me falling. *Autumn.*
10. The Lord hath builded for Himself. *The Universe the Temple of God.*
11. Vain were all our toil and labour. *Success is of God.*
12. When at Thy footstool, Lord, I bend. *Lent.*
13. When earthly joys glide swift away. *Ps. cii.*
14. Wilt Thou return to me, O Lord. *Lent.*
15. With joy we hail the sacred day. *Sunday.*

ii. From his *Spirit of the Psalms,* 1834.

16. Be merciful to us, O God. *Ps. lvii.*
17. Blest is the man who knows the Lord. *Ps. cxii.*
18. Blest is the man whose spirit shares. *Ps. xli.*
19. From depths of woe to God I cry. *Ps. cxxx.*
20. Gently, gently lay Thy rod. *Ps. vi.*
21. Glorious Shepherd of the sheep. *Ps. xxiii.*
22. Glory and praise to Jehovah on high. *Ps. xxix.*
23. God in His Church is known. *Ps. lxxvi.*
24. God is our Refuge, tried and proved. *Ps. xlvi.*
25. Great Source of my being. *Ps. lxxiii.*
26. Hear, O Lord, our supplication. *Ps. lxiv.*
27. How blest the man who fears the Lord. *Ps. cxxviii.*
28. Humble, Lord, my haughty spirit. *Ps. cxxxi.*
29. In this wide, weary world of care. *Ps. cxxxii.*
30. In vain the powers of darkness try. *Ps. lii.*
31. Jehovah speaks, let man be awed. *Ps. xlix.*
32. Judge me, O Lord, and try my heart. *Ps. xxvi.*
33. Judge me, O Lord, to Thee I fly. *Ps. xliii.*
34. Lord, I have sinned, but O forgive. *Ps. xli.*
35. Lord, my God, in Thee I trust. *Ps. vii.*
36. Lord of the realms above, Our Prophet, &c. *Ps. xlv.*
37. Lone amidst the dead and dying. *Ps. lxii.*
38. Lord God of my salvation. *Ps. lxxxviii.*
39. Lord, I look to Thee for all. *Ps. xxxi.*
40. Lord, I would stand with thoughtful eye. *Ps. lxix.*
41. Lord, my God, in Thee I trust. *Ps. vii.*
42. My God, my King, Thy praise I sing. *Ps. cviii.*
43. My God, what monuments I see. *Ps. xxxvi.*
44. My spirit on [to] Thy care. *Ps. xxxi.*
45. My trust is in the Lord. *Ps. xi.*
46. Not unto us, Almighty Lord [God]. *Ps. cxv.*
47. O God of glory, God of grace. *Ps. xc.*
48. O God of love, how blest are they. *Ps. xxxvii.*
49. O God of love, my God Thou art. *Ps. lxiii.*
50. O God of truth and grace. *Ps. xviii.*
51. O had I, my Saviour, the wings of a dove. *Ps. lv.*
52. O how blest the congregation. *Ps. lxxxix.*
53. O how safe and [how] happy he. *Ps. xci.*
54. O plead my cause, my Saviour plead. *Ps. xxxv.*
55. O praise the Lord, 'tis sweet to raise. *Ps. cxlvii.*
56. O praise the Lord; ye nations, pour. *Ps. cxvii.*
57. O praise ye the Lord With heart, &c. *Ps. cxlix.*
58. O that the Lord's salvation. *Ps. xiv.*
59. O Thou Whom thoughtless men condemn. *Ps. xxxvi.*
60. Of every earthly stay bereft. *Ps. lxxiv.*
61. Our hearts shall praise Thee, God of love. *Ps. cxxxviii.*
62. Pilgrims here on earth and strangers. *Ps. xvi.*
63. Praise for Thee, Lord, in Zion waits. *Ps. lxv.*
64. Praise to God on high be given. *Ps. cxxxiv.*
65. Praise ye the Lord, His servants, raise. *Ps. cxiii.*
66. Redeem'd from guilt, redeem'd from fears. *Ps. cxvi.*

67. Save me by Thy glorious name. *Ps. liv.*
68. Shout, ye people, clap your hands. *Ps. xlvii.*
69. Sing to the Lord our might. *Ps. lxxxi.*
70. Strangers and pilgrims here below. *Ps. cix.*
71. Sweet is the solemn voice that calls. *Ps. cxxii.*
72. The Church of God below. *Ps. lxxxvii.*
73. The Lord is King, let earth be glad. *Ps. xcvii.*
74. The Lord is on His throne. *Ps. xciii.*
75. The Lord is our Refuge, the Lord is our Guide. *Ps. xlvi.*
76. The mercies of my God and King. *Ps. lxxxix.*
77. The Lord Who died on earth for men. *Ps. xxi.*
78. 'Tis a pleasant thing to see. *Ps. cxxxiii.*
79. Thy promise, Lord, is perfect peace. *Ps. iii.*
80. Unto Thee I lift mine [my] eyes. *Ps. cxxiii.*
81. Whom shall [should] we love like Thee? *Ps. xviii.*

Lyte's versions of the *Psalms* are criticised in the article **Psalters, English,** § XVII., where their sadness, tenderness and beauty are set forth. His hymns in the *Poems* are characterized by the same features, and rarely swell out into joy and gladness.   [J. J.]

Lyth, John, D.D., was b. at York, March 13, 1821. In 1843 he entered the Wesleyan ministry, and was sent in 1859 to Winnenden, as the first Wesleyan minister to Germany. On his return from Germany in 1865, he entered upon regular circuit work in G. Britain, and laboured at Sheffield, Hull, and other large towns until 1883, when he retired from the active work of the ministry. He d. on March 13, 1886. His principal prose work was a *History of Methodism in York.* In 1843 he edited and published a small volume, entitled *Wild Flowers; or, a Selection of Original Poetry, edited by J. L.* This little work was made up of pieces by himself and members of his family, and the late Dr. Punshon. His hymn, "There is a better world, they say" (*Heaven*), appeared in the *Meth. Scholars' H. Bk.*, 1870; and his "We won't give up the Sabbath" (*Sunday*), in the *Meth. S. S. H. Bk.*, 1879. Each of these is an imitation of an older hymn. Dr. Lyth informed the Rev. W. F. Stevenson, editor of *Hys. for Ch. and Home*, 1873, that the hymn "There is a better world, they say,"

"Was written at Stroud, in Gloucestershire (30th April, 1845) for the anniversary of the neighbouring infant-school at Randwich, and to an air then very popular, called 'All is Well.' That it was written for infant children will explain the simplicity of some of the expressions. It was speedily caught up, and I believe first appeared in the *Home and School Hymn Book.*" (Biog. Index.)   [J. J.]

M

M., in the Bristol Bap. *Coll.* of Ash & Evans, 1769, i.e. James Merrick.

M., in the *People's Hymnal*, 1867, i.e. Gerard Moultrie.

M. B. W., in *Hys. for the Church Catholic*, 1882, i.e. Mary Bradford Whiting.

M. C., in the Bristol Bap. *Coll.*, 1769, i.e. *Madan's Coll.*

M. C. C., in Walker's Cheltenham *Ps. & Hys.*, 1855, i.e. Lady M. C. Campbell.

M. D. M., in the *People's Hymnal*, 1867, i.e. *Mary Dunlop Moultrie.*

M. G. T., in the American Bap. *Service of Song*, 1871, i.e. M. G. Thomson.

M. L., in *Catholic Hys.*, Lond., Burns, 1851, ed. by Rev. H. Formby, i.e. Jane E. Leeson.

McAll, Robert Stephens, LL.D., s. of the Rev. Robert McAll, was b. at Plymouth, Aug. 4, 1792, and educated at Axminster, Devon; Hoxton, London; and Edinburgh University. He graduated M.A. at Edinburgh in 1813, and gave himself for a time to the study of medicine. He was for some time Chaplain of the Macclesfield School, and from 1814 to 1826 minister of St. George's Chapel in the same town. In 1827 he became minister of Mosley Street Chapel, Manchester, and held the same to his death on July 27, 1838. In 1812 he contributed to Dr. Collyer's *Coll.* 8 hymns, which appeared as by "R. S. M." Through one of these, "Hark! how the choral song of heaven" (*The Song of Heaven*), he is somewhat widely known to hymnody. His *Psalms and Hymns for Public Worship*, Macclesfield, J. Swinnerton, N.D. [circa 1823], was pub. without Preface, or names of authors. Not one of the 8 hymns contributed by him to Collyer's *Coll.* is therein, and there is nothing to show which are his original compositions.   [F. J. F.]

McCheyne, Robert Murray, s. of Adam McCheyne, W. S., was b. at Edinburgh, May 21, 1813, and educated at Edinburgh University. In 1835 he became Assistant at Larbert, near Stirling, and was ordained in 1836 Minister of St. Peter's Established Church, Dundee. In 1839 he went to Palestine as one of the Mission of Enquiry to the Jews from the Church of Scotland. He d. at Dundee, March 25, 1843. His hymns, a few of which were written in Palestine, appeared in his

Songs of Zion to cheer and guide Pilgrims on their way to the New Jerusalem, By the late Rev. R. M. McCheyne . . . . Dundee, W. Middleton, 1843.

These hymns were reprinted in his *Memoir and Remains*, edited by Dr. Andrew A. Bonar, 1844. The *Songs* as reprinted in 1844 number 14, and date from 1831 to 1841. The best known are, "I once was a stranger to grace and to God;" and, "When this passing world is done." In addition, "Beneath Moriah's rocky side," written at the "Foot of Carmel, June, 1839" (*Sent from God*); "Like mist on the mountains," written "Jan. 1st, 1831" (*Children called to Christ*), and "Ten Virgins, clothed in white" (*The Ten Virgins*), dated 1841, are in C. U.   [J. M.]

Macdonald, George, LL.D., was b. at Huntly, Aberdeenshire, Dec. 10, 1824, and educated at King's College, Aberdeen, where he graduated M.A., and from which he afterwards received the honorary degree of LL.D. For a brief time he studied for the Congregational ministry at Highbury College, London, and then became the Minister of the Congregational Church at Arundel, Sussex (1850–53). He afterwards preached for a short time to a small company at Manchester and Bolton. Relinquishing the ministry, he became Lecturer on English Literature at King's College, London, and ultimately gave himself up entirely to literary work. Dr. Macdonald has acquired a great reputation by means of his works of fiction, most of which were originally contributed to magazines, and the most notable of which are *David Elginbrod; Robert Falconer; Alec Forbes of Houglen;* and *Annals of a Quiet Neighbourhood.* He was some time Editor of *Good Words for the Young,* and wrote *England's Antiphon* for Macmillan's *Sunday Library.* His poetical works are:—

(1) *Within and Without,* 1855 ; (2) *The Disciple, and Other Poems,* 1860 ; (3) *The Diary of an Old Soul* (printed for private circulation), 1867 ; (4) *Exotics,* a volume of *trs.* from the German (most of which first appeared in the *Sunday Magazine*), 1876 ; and (5) *A Threefold Cord,* 1883, part of which previously appeared in his *Works of Fancy and Imagination,* 10 vols., 1871.

Most of his original hymns were contributed to *Hys. and Sacred Songs for Sunday Schools and Social Worship,* &c., pub. by Fletcher and Tubbs, Manchester, in 1855 (2nd. ed., 1856), and of which his brother, and the Rev. G. B. Bubier (p. 190, ii.) were the editors. The original hymns, which are signed " G. Macdonald," in this collection are:—

1. A quiet heart, submissive, meek. *The Meek inherit the Earth.*
2. Daylight fades away. *Second Advent.*
3. Father, I well may praise Thy name. *Sunday Morning.*
4. Father, these souls of ours have been. *Blessed are the Pure in Heart.*
5. If we were longing for the food. *Blessed are they that Hunger and Thirst after Righteousness.*
6. It was an awful hour that gave. *Blessed are the Merciful.*
7. Let Thy own voice, O Father, say. *Blessed are they that mourn.*
8. O Son of Man, Thy Name by choice. *Blessed are the Meek.*
9. Our Father, hear our longing prayer. *Blessed are the Poor in Spirit.*

Some of these hymns were afterwards revised by their author. The next two are from *The Disciple, and Other Poems,* 1860 :—

10. O God, Whose daylight leadeth down. *Evening.*
11. O Lord [God] of life, Thy quickening voice. *Morning.*

Dr. Macdonald's hymns are rich in ideas, but are touched with a mysticism which renders them a little difficult of apprehension. They are however of great value in setting forth truths rarely expressed in hymns, and are likely to grow in favour.   [W. G. H.]

Macduff, John Ross, D.D., second s. of Alexander Macduff, of Bonhard, near Perth, was b. at Bonhard, May 23, 1818. After studying at the University of Edinburgh, he became in 1842 parish minister of Kettins, Forfarshire, in 1849 of St. Madoes, Perthshire, and in 1855 of Sandyford, Glasgow. He received the degree of D.D. from the University of Glasgow in 1862, and about the same time also from the University of New York. He retired from pastoral work in 1871, and now [1887] lives at Chislehurst, Kent. He has published many practical and devotional works which have attained a wide circulation. In 1857 he was appointed by the General Assembly a member of their Hymnal Committee. His 31 hymns appeared in his *Altar Stones,* 1853, and were also included with his later poems in his *The Gates of Praise,* 1876. Of these hymns the following are in C. U. :—

1. Christ is coming! Let creation. *Second Advent.*
2. Eternal Rock ! To Thee I flee. (1853.) *Christ the Rock.*
3. Everlasting arms of love. (1853.) *Support in Christ.*
4. From Thy habitation holy. *Whitsuntide.*

5. Hasten, Lord, that morn of glory. *Second Advent.*
6. Jesus wept ! Those tears are over. (1853.) *The raising of Lazarus.*
7. O do not, blessed Lord, depart. *Christ's presence desired.*
8. Where shall I look for holy calm. (1853.) *Passiontide.*
9. Why should I murmur or repine ? *Resignation.*

Of these hymns those dated 1853 are parts only of Dr. Macduff's originals.   [J. M.]

Macgill, Hamilton Montgomerie, D.D., youngest s. of Thomas Macgill, was b. Mar. 10, 1807, at Catrine, Ayrshire. After studying at the University of Glasgow (which conferred upon him the degree of D.D. in 1870), he became in 1837 joint minister of Duke St. United Presb. Church, Glasgow. In 1840 he removed with a portion of his congregation to a new church in Montrose Street. He became, in 1858, Home Mission Secretary of the United Presbyterian Church, and in 1868 Foreign Mission Secretary. He d. June 3, 1880, at Paris, while on his way to recruit his health in the South of France. As a member of the Hymnal Committee of the U. P. Church in 1870–76, he contributed to their *Presbyterian Hymnal,* 1876, 5 *trs.* from the Latin (Nos. 29, 34, 95, 101, 299) and 1 from the Greek (No. 346). These he subsequently included in his *Songs of the Christian Creed and Life,* 1876, a volume containing 6 *trs.* from the Greek ; 68 from the Latin ; and 27 *trs.* from English into Latin verse, in all 101 (No. 101 being by himself). The introduction includes careful and interesting biographical and critical notices of the authors whose hymns are included ; and the texts are given in Latin, Greek, and English.

Many of the translations are exceedingly good, and stand in the very first rank of modern English versions —their gracefulness and ease making them seem more like original English hymns than translations. Sir Theodore Martin paid the translations into Latin the high compliment of mistaking one of them for a mediæval hymn. In the edition of 1879, Dr. Macgill made a number of verbal alterations, added two renderings from the Latin (" Jam moesta quiesce querela " and " O luce qui mortalibus "), one from the Bohemian, one from the Spanish, and a Latin version of " Art thou weary, art thou languid ? " Twenty-two of his *trs.* from the Latin and Greek had appeared in the *Juvenile Missionary Magazine* of the U. P. Church between 1866 and 1873. His *trs.* are gradually coming into somewhat prominent use.   [J. M.]

Mackay, Margaret, was b. in 1802, and the only daughter of Captain Robert Mackay, of Hedgefield, Inverness. She was married in 1820 to Major William Mackay, of the 68th Light Infantry (afterwards Lt. Colonel) a distinguished officer who d. in 1845. Mrs. Mackay d. at Cheltenham, Jan. 5, 1887. In addition to various prose works Mrs. Mackay pub. *Thoughts Redeemed ; or Lays of Leisure Hours,* 1854, which contained 72 original hymns and poems. Of these, "Asleep in Jesus! blessed sleep," is noted at p. 86, ii.   [J. M.]

Mackellar, Thomas, was b. in New York, Aug. 12, 1812. At the age of 14 he entered the printing establishment of Harper Brothers. In 1833 he removed to Philadelphia and joined the type-foundry firm of Johnson & Smith, as proof reader. He subsequently became a foreman, and then a partner in that firm, which has been known from 1860 as Mackellar, Smiths, and Jordan, type-founders of Philadelphia. His publications include

The American Printer, 1866, a prose work, and the following in verse:—

(1) *Droppings from the Heart*, 1844; (2) *Tam's Fortnight Ramble*, 1847; (3) *Lines for the Gentle and Loving*, 1853; (4) *Rhymes Atween Times*, 1872. The last contains some of his hymns. (5) *Hymns and a few Metrical Psalms*, Phila. 1883 (71 hymns, 3 psalms), 2nd ed. 1887 (84 hymns, 3 psalms).

Those of his hymns in C. U. include:—

1. At the door of mercy sighing. *Lent.* Pub. in his *Rhymes Atween Times*, 1872, as, "Long of restful peace forsaken," and again in Dr. Hitchcock's *Hys. & Songs of Praise*, 1874, as "At the door of mercy sighing."

2. Bear the burden of the present. *Resignation.* Written in 1852, and pub. in his *Lines for the Gentle and Loving*, 1853; and *Lyra Sacra Americana*, 1868. Part of this hymn, beginning "All unseen the Master walketh," is in C. U. in G. Britain.

3. Book of grace, and book of glory. *Holy Scripture.* Written in 1843. It was given in the S. School Union *Coll.*, 1860, and his *Hys. and a few M. Psalms, &c.*, 1883, and a few collections, including Allon's *Children's Worship*, 1878, &c.

4. Draw nigh to the Holy. *Jesus, the soul's Refuge.* In Sumner's *Songs of Zion*, 1851, and the *Lyra Sacra Americana*, 1868, in 5 st. of 8 l.

5. Father, in my life's young morning. *A Child's Prayer.* Written in 1841.

6. In the vineyard of our Father. *Work for God.* Written in 1845. It was given in the *Hys. for Church & Home*, Philadelphia, 1860, and other collections.

7. Jesus! when my soul is parting. *Continued presence of Jesus desired.* Written in 1848, and included in *Lyra Sacra Americana*, 1868, in 4 st. of 6 l., and entitled "Jesus first and last."

8. There is a land immortal. *Heaven.* Mr. Mackellar says that this hymn was written

"One evening as a fancy suddenly struck me of a religious nature, I laid aside the work in hand, and pursuing the new idea, I at once produced the hymn, 'There is a land immortal,' and sent it to the editor [of Neale's *Gazette*], who referred to it as a religious poem from 'Tam,' my assumed name, under which I had already acquired considerable notoriety. This was in 1845. It was widely copied, and afterwards inserted in a volume published by me." Duffield's *English Hymns*, &c., 1886, p. 551.

Mr. Mackellar is an Elder of the Presbyterian Church.   [F. M. B.]

Maclagan, William Dalrymple, D.D., s. of David Maclagan, M.D., was b. in Edinburgh, June 18, 1826. In early life he entered the army, and served for some time in India. Retiring with the rank of lieutenant, he entered St. Peter's College, Cambridge, where he graduated B.A. 1856 and M.A. in 1860. Taking Holy Orders, he was curate of St. Saviour's, Paddington, 1856–58, and St. Stephen's, Marylebone, 1858–60. He then became Secretary to the London Diocesan Church Building Society, from 1860 to 1865; curate of Enfield, 1865–69; Rector of Newington, 1869–75; and Vicar of Kensington, 1875–78. He was also Hon. Chaplain to the Queen, and Prebendary of Reculverland in St. Paul's Cathedral, London. In 1878 he was consecrated Bishop of Lichfield. Bp. Maclagan's work has been mainly of a practical character, and his publications are few. The few hymns which he has written have been received with great favour, and create a desire

for more of the same kind and quality. The following are in C. U.:—

1. Again the trumpet sounds. *Missions.* Written about 1870. Appeared in the *H. A. & M.* series of *Hys. for Mission Services.* 1871.

2. Be still, my soul, for God is near. *Holy Communion.* Part ii. is "O Body, broken for my sake." Written about 1873 for St. Mary's, Newington. In Thring's *Coll.*, 1882.

3. Holy Spirit, Lord of love. *Confirmation.* Written about 1873, and pub. in Mrs. C. Brock's *Children's H. Bk.*, 1884.

4. It is finished, blessed Jesus [Saviour]. *Good Friday.* Written for *H. A. & M.*, 1875. In several collections.

5. Lord, when Thy Kingdom comes, remember me. *Good Friday.* Written for the 1875 ed. of *H. A. & M.* Sometimes given in two parts: Pt. ii. beginning "Lord, when with dying lips my prayer is said."

6. The Saints of God their conflict past. *All Saints.* First pub. in *Church Bells*, 1870; and again in the S. P. C. K. *Church Hys.*, 1871.

7. What thanks and praise to Thee we owe. *St. Luke.* Written for the 1875 ed. of *H. A. & M.*

These hymns are of more than usual merit, being characterized by great simplicity, tenderness, and fervour. The special season or purpose is clearly indicated, and its lessons earnestly enforced.   [J. J.]

Macleod, Norman, D.D. s. of Dr. Norman Macleod, was b. at Campbelton, Argyleshire, June 3, 1812. He studied at the Universities of Glasgow and Edinburgh, then went to Germany, and subsequently completed his course at the University of Glasgow, from which, in 1858, he received the degree of D.D. In 1838 he was appointed parish minister of Loudoun, Ayrshire, in 1843 of Dalkeith, and in 1851 of the Barony, Glasgow. He became one of the Queen's Chaplains in 1841, and in 1860 the editor of *Good Words*, which he continued to edit till his death. He was one of the most influential ministers in the Established Church of Scotland, and was Moderator of the General Assembly in 1869. He d. at Glasgow, June 16, and was buried at Campsie, June 20, 1872. His works are numerous and popular. He was appointed a member of the Assembly's Hymnal Committee in 1854 and 1855. His best known hymn, "Trust in God, and do the right" (*Right Doing*), appeared in January 1857, in *The Edinburgh Christian Magazine*, of which he was for some years the editor.

[J. M.]

Madan, Judith, née Cowper, was the only daughter of the Hon. Spencer Cowper, the wife of Colonel Martin Madan (d. 1736), and the mother of Martin Madan, and of Dr. Spencer Madan, sometime Bishop of Peterborough. She had some repute as a writer of verse. Her *Burial Hymn*, "In this world of sin and sorrow," appeared in the 1763 *Appendix* to her son's *Ps. & Hys.* in 2 st. of 81. It has been repeated in several collections in G. Britain and America, and is given without alteration in *Lyra Brit.* 1867, p. 659. We have failed to ascertain the date of Mrs. Madan's birth or death.   [J. J.]

Madan, Martin, s. of Colonel Martin Madan, and brother of Dr. Spencer Madan, sometime Bishop of Peterborough, was b. in 1726. He was to have qualified for the Bar, but through a sermon by J. Wesley on the words "Prepare to meet thy God," the whole current of his life was changed. After some difficulty he received Holy Orders, and subsequently founded and became chaplain of the Lock Hospital, Hyde Park Corner. He was popular as a preacher, and had no inconsiderable reputation as a musical composer. He ceased preaching on the publication of his work *Thelyphthora*, in which he advocated the practice of polygamy. He d. in 1790. He pub. *A Commentary on the Articles of the Church of England ; A Treatise on the Christian Faith*, &c., and ?—

A Collection of Psalms and Hymns Extracted from Various Authors, and published by the Reverend Mr. Madan. London, 1760.

This *Coll.* contained 170 hymns thrown together without order or system of any kind. In 1763 he added an *Appendix* of 24 hymns. This *Coll.*, referred to in this Dictionary as *Madan*, and *Madan's Ps. & Hys.*, had for many years a most powerful influence on the hymnody of the Church of England. Nearly the whole of its contents, together with its extensively altered texts, were reprinted in numerous hymn-books for nearly one hundred years. At the present time many of the great hymns of the last century are in use as altered by him in 1760 and 1763. Although several hymns have been attributed to him, we have no evidence that he ever wrote one. His hymnological labours were employed in altering, piecing, and expanding the work of others. And in this he was most successful.

[J. J.]

Maerentes oculi spargite lachrymas. *Passiontide.* This hymn, which sometimes begins "Moerentes oculi," is the hymn at Vespers in the Office of the Passion of our Lord Jesus Christ, which has been added to the *Roman Breviary* since 1740 (see "Aspice infami Deus"). It is in the *Roman Breviary*, Bologna, 1827, Pars Hiemalis, Supplement, p. 270, in 7 st. *Tr.* as :—

Now let us sit and weep. By E. Caswall. 1st pub. in his *Lyra Catholica*, 1849, p. 63, in 7 st. of 4 l. ; and again in his *Hys. & Poems*, 1873, p. 35. In the *Hymnary*, 1872, it is altered to "Come let us sit and weep."

Another tr. is:—

Ye weeping eyes, shed briny tears. *J. Wallace*, 1874.

[J. M.]

Mag ich Unglück nicht wiederstehn. [*Cross and Consolation.*] *Wackernagel*, iii. pp. 118–121, gives four versions from a Nürnberg broadsheet, *circa* 1526, the Erfurt *G. B.*, 1531, &c. The text in the *Unv. L. S.*, 1851, No. 634, follows that in the 1531. It is in 3 st. of 11 l., the two initial letters of st. i., ii. and the initial letter of st. iii., giving the name Maria.

In the Nürnberg broadsheet it is called "Queen Maria of Hungary's hymn," and so in the Magdeburg *G. B.*, 1534, and many other later collections, it is ascribed to her. She was sister of the Emperor Charles V., and wife of King Ludwig II., of Hungary, who d. in 1526, she surviving till 1558. Both *Wackernagel*, and Lauxmann in *Koch*, viii. 528, think it was merely adopted by her as her hymn of consolation, and may have been written for her by Martin Luther. Had Luther written it, however, it is hardly likely that in the hymn-books edited by him or for him from Klug's *G. B.*, 1529, to Babst's *G. B.*, 1545, it would always have appeared without his name.

The trs. are :—(1) Can I my fate no more withstand, by *Miss Winkworth*, 1858, p. 178. (2) I cannot ill suppress, or quell, by *Dr. G. Walker*, 1860, p. 47.

[J. M.]

Magdeburg, Joachim, was b. *circa* 1525 at Gardelegen in the Altmark. He matriculated at the University of Wittenberg, April, 1544, and in 1546 was appointed rector of the school at Schöningen, near Helmstädt, Brunswick. He became pastor of Dannenberg in Lüneburg in 1547, but being unable to exist on his slender income resigned in 1549, and in the same year became pastor of Salzwedel in the Altmark. But refusing to adopt the Roman ceremonies prescribed by the Act of Interim he was, in 1552 (Easter S., April 17) banished from the Electorate of Brandenburg. About May, 1552, by the influence of Johann Aepinus, Superintendent of Hamburg, he was appointed diaconus of St. Peter's Church in Hamburg, and there became acquainted with Flacius Illyricus [Matthias Flach, Extreme Lutheran, church historian, &c., d. at Frankfurt-am-Main, March 11, 1575]. After the death of Aepinus, May 13, 1553, Paulus von Eitzen, his successor, was not so friendly, and when, during the controversy in 1558 regarding Holy Communion, Magdeburg pub. a tractate without submitting it to the revision of Eitzen, the latter obtained the removal of Magdeburg from his post, May 25, 1558. He then went to Magdeburg to help his friend Flacius as one of the compilers of the Church history known as the *Magdeburg Centuries*. Shortly thereafter he was appointed pastor of Ossmanstedt in Thuringia; but, as a follower of Flacius, was dispossessed · in 1562. He then stayed for longer or shorter periods with Count von Mansfeld, Baron von Schönburg and others, until, after the Emperor Maximilian II. had once more permitted Protestant preachers in Austria, he was, at Count von Mansfeld's recommendation, appointed by the commandant of Raab in Hungary as regimental chaplain at Raab in 1564, and, after his house there was burnt, at the castle of Gräfenworth (east of Krems), to the German-speaking Austrian troops. There he had to contend with the machinations of the Roman clergy, and after joining with nineteen others of the Evangelical clergy in Austria in presenting a Confession of Faith to an Austrian Diet (Landtag), was compelled to leave; and in 1571 we find him living at Erfurt. In 1581 he was preacher at Efferding in Austria; but in 1583 was expelled as an adherent of Flacius. His later history is unknown (*Koch*, i. 446; *Allg. Deutsche Biog.* xx., 53, &c.). *Wackernagel*, iii. pp. 1035–1042, gives five pieces under his name. The only one *tr.* into English is :—

Wer Gott vertraut, hat wohl gebaut. *Trust in God.* Founded on Ps. lxxiii. 25, 26. *Wackernagel*, iii. p. 1042, prints st. i. from Magdeburg's *Christliche und tröstliche Tischgesenge, mit vier Stimmen*, Erfurt, 1572 (where it is the hymn for Saturday evening); and thinks it probable, though not certain, that it is an original by Magdeburg. In S. Calvisius's *Harmonia cantionum ecclesiasticarum*, Leipzig, 1597, st. ii. and iii., are first found. Lauxmann in *Koch*, viii., 373, thus sums up the evidence :—

"From these circumstances it seems evident that the hymn originally consisted only of the first stanza, but that Magdeburg's authorship, in opposition to other claims [it has been ascribed to J. Kolross and to J. Mühlmann] is beyond doubt."

The text of 1597 is repeated in *Wackernagel*, iii. p. 1043, and the *Unv. L. S.*, 1851, No. 642, in 3 st. of 8 (or 12) lines. *Tr.* as:—

1. **Who trusts in God, his work abides.** By A. T. Russell, of st. i., ii., as No. 230, in his *Ps. & Hys.*, 1851.

2. **Who puts his trust in God most just,** A good and full *tr.*, by Miss Winkworth, in her *Lyra Ger.*, 2nd Ser., 1858, p. 192, and her *C. B. for England*, 1863, No. 145. Repeated, slightly altered, in the Pennsylvania Luth. *Church Bk.*, 1868.

3. **Who trusts in God a strong abode.** A good but free *tr.* by Dr. B. H. Kennedy, as No. 486, in his *Hymn. Christ.*, 1863, repeated in J. L. Porter's *Coll.*, 1876, and others. In Morrell and How's *Ps. & Hys.*, 1864, No 208, it was considerably altered by Bp. How, and this form is repeated in the S. P. C. K. *Church Hys.*, 1871; Thring's *Coll.*, 1882, and others, the *Bapt. Hymnal*, 1879, omitting the last four lines, and ascribing it, in error, to M. Luther.

Another tr. is : "Who lives in God has safe abode." By *Dr. H. Mills*, 1856, p. 244.   [J. M.]

Maglorianus, Santolius. [Santœüil, Claude de.]

Magnae Deus potentiae. [*Thursday.*] This hymn on the Fifth Day of the Creation has frequently been ascribed to St. Ambrose. It has many parallels in the 6th and 7th chapters of his *Hexaemeron*, but is not assigned to him by the Benedictine editors. In an 8th cent. MS. at Trier cited by *Mone*, i. p. 372, it is given as the hymn at Vespers on Thursday, and this is the use of the *Sarum, York, Roman*, and other *Breviaries*. It is found in three MSS. of the 11th cent. in the *British Museum* (Vesp. D. xii. f. 21; Jul. A. vi. f. 28 *b*; Harl. 2961, f. 223 *b*); in three MSS. of the 11th cent. at *St. Gall*, Nos. 387, 413, 414; in the *Lat. Hys. of the Anglo-Saxon Ch.*, 1851, p. 25, printed from an 11th cent. MS. at Durham (B. iii. 32, f. 8). It is also in *Daniel*, i., No. 53; iv. p. 52, from a Rheinau MS. of the 10th cent., and in Card. Newman's *Hymni Ecclesiae*, 1838 and 1865.   [J. M.]

Translations in C. U. :—

1. **O God, Who hast given.** By Card. Newman, pub. in his *Verses on Religious Subjects*, 1853, p. 100 (ed. 1868, p. 247). It is included in the Marquess of Bute's *Roman Breviary in English*, 1879. In W. J. Blew's *The Church Hy. and Tune Bk.*, 1852–5, it was given as "Thou God of all power," and in this form it was repeated in Rice's *Sel.* therefrom, 1870.

2. **Lord of all power! at whose command.** By E. Caswall, in his *Lyra Catholica*, 1849, p. 28, and his *Hys. and Poems*, 1873, p. 17. In the *People's H.*, 1867; and the *Hymnary*, 1872.

3. **Almighty God, Who from the flood.** By J. M. Neale, in the enlarged ed. of the *H. Noted*, 1854. It is repeated in the *Hymner*, 1882.

Translations not in C. U. :—

1. O God, Whose watery stores supply. *Primer*, 1706.
2. God of all nature, great and good. *Bp. Mant*, 1837.
3. That God, Whose awful power can take. *Hymnarium Anglicanum*, 1844.
4. O God of mighty power, Lord. *J. A. B. Hope*, 1844.
5. God, Who in wondrous might. *W. J. Copeland*, 1848.

6. Almighty God, Whose sovereign will. *J. D. Chambers*, 1857.
7. Great God of power, at Thy command. *J. Wallace*, 1874.   [J. J.]

Magnificat. Metrical paraphrases of the Magnificat are not numerous, and are very rarely used. In the 1560 edition of the *Old Version* (§ iv., v., q.v.), a version appeared in 10 st. of 4 l., st. i. of which reads :—

> " My soul doth magnify the Lord,
>   My spirit evermore
> Rejoiceth in the Lord, my God,
>   Who is my Saviour."

This was repeated in subsequent editions of the *Old Version*, and was for some time the authorized metrical form of the *Magnificat* in use in the Church of England.

2. The *New Version* by Tate and Brady also contained a metrical paraphrase by Tate, which in time superseded that of the *Old Version* in public worship. In the *Suppl.* of 1702 it appeared in 20 lines, beginning :—

> " My soul and spirit, fill'd with joy
>   My God and Saviour praise,
> Whose goodness did from poor estate
>   His humble handmaid raise."

This version continued in use until the *New Version* was swept away by the modern hymn-book.

3. The history of the paraphrase in the Scottish *Translations and Paraphrases*, 1781, which is Tate's version rewritten by W. Cameron, is given under "My soul and spirit filled with joy."

4. Very few of the versifiers of the Psalms have added a paraphrase of this Canticle to their version of the Psalter. Dr. John Patrick is an exception. His rendering of the *Magnificat* in his *Ps. of David in Metre*, 1691, begins:—

> " My soul doth magnify the Lord,
>   Transports of joy my spirits raise;
> And God my Saviour shall be
>   The subject of my song of praise."

5. The version of the *Magnificat* by Dr. W. J. Irons, in his *Ps. & Hys. for the Church*, 1875–83, is a good rendering, and more in accordance with modern tastes than the above. It begins:—

> " My soul doth magnify the Lord,
>   And God my Saviour sing;
> His mighty power and grace hath wrought
>   For me this wondrous thing."

6. Other versions of the *Magnificat* are annotated in full in this Dictionary, and may be found through the Index of Seasons and Subjects at the end. Its use, however, in any form except that in the *Book of Common Prayer* is very limited.   [J. J.]

Major, Johann. [Rutilius, M.]

Maker, Upholder, Ruler! Thee. *J. Montgomery.* [*Doxology.*] Written for the Sheffield Sunday School Union, Whitsuntide gathering, April, 1830, and first printed on a fly-sheet for the occasion. [M. MSS.] In 1836 it was included in the *Cong. H. Bk.*, No. 104, and again in Montgomery's *Original Hys.*, 1853, No. 353, in 4 st. of 4 l.   [J. J.]

Malan, Henri Abraham César. The family of Malan traces its origin to the valleys of Piedmont. A branch of it settled at Mérindol, in Dauphiné, but was driven from France by the persecutions that followed the Revocation of the Edict of Nantes. Pierre Malan, after seeing his sister fall a victim to persecution, left Mérindol (1714), and arrived at Geneva (1722). Henri Abraham César Malan was b. at Geneva in 1787. After an education at the College, he went to Marseilles, with the intention of learning business: but, soon after, entered the Academy at Geneva, as a preparation for the ministry, to which he was ordained in 1810. He had been appointed one of the masters at the College in the previous year. The National Church of Geneva was at that time almost Unitarian, and Malan's convictions were in accord with it. But the great movement known as the *Réveil*, of which the first products were the dissident church of Bourg de Four and at a later date that founded by Malan himself, and which finally imbued the whole Swiss Church with its spirit, was silently preparing itself. The germ of the movement may be traced in the *Société des Amis* (1810), of which Empeytaz and A. Bost were leaders; and in Malan's independent attainment to the doctrines of the Divinity of the Saviour and the free gifts of salvation through Him (1816). But the human agency, which gave it force, and determined its Calvinistic direction, was the visit of Robert Haldane (in the autumn of 1816), to whom not only these pioneers of the movement, but F. Monod, E. Rieu, Guers, Gonthier, Merle d'Aubigné, and others, always pointed as their spiritual father. Empeytaz and others sought to attain enfranchisement by the establishment of the "petite Église of Bourg de Four." Malan wished to reform the national Church from within: and a sermon at Geneva, which brought on him the obloquy of the professors and theologians that composed his audience, and which Haldane characterized as a republication of the Gospel, was his first overt act (Jan. 19, 1817). But the opposing forces were far too strong for him. The Venerable Company excluded him from the pulpits, and achieved his dismissal from his regentship at the College (1818). In 1820 he built a chapel (Chapelle du Temoignage) in his garden, and obtained the licence of the State for it, as a separatist place of worship. In 1823 he was formally deprived of his status as a minister of the national Church. The seven years that succeeded were the palmy days of the little chapel. Strangers, especially from England, mingled with the overflowing Swiss congregation. But (in 1830) a secession to Bourg de Four, and then the foundation of the Oratoire and the Société Évangélique, which in 1849 absorbed the congregation of Bourg de Four under the title of the *Église Évangélique*, thinned more and more the number of his adherents. His burning zeal for the conversion of souls found a larger outlet in long tours of evangelization, subsidized by religious friends, in his own land and Belgium and France, and also in Scotland and England, where he had friends among many religious bodies, and where he preached to large congregations. The distinguishing characteristic of these tours was his dealing with individuals. On the steamboat or the diligence, in the mountain walk, at the hotel, no opportunity was lost. On one occasion an old

man whom he visited drew from under his pillow a copy of his great hymn-book, *Chants de Sion*, 1841, and told him how he had prayed to see the author of it before he died.

It is as the originator of the modern hymnmovement in the French Reformed Church that Malan's fame cannot perish. [See French Hymnody, § v.] The spirit of his hymns is perpetuated in the analysis of Christian experience, the never-wearied delineation of the hopes and fears, the joys and sorrows of the believer's soul, which are still the staple of French Protestant hymns. To this was added, in Malan himself, a marked didactic tone, necessitated by the great struggle of the *Réveil* for Evangelical doctrine; and an emphatic Calvinism, expressing itself with all the despondency of Newton and Cowper, but, in contrast with them, in bright assurance, peace and gladness. French criticism has pronounced his hymns unequal, and full of literary defects; but their unaffected freshness and fervent sincerity are universally allowed. In the *Chants de Sion*, hymns 20, "Hosanna! Béni soit"; 165, "Mon cœur joyeux, plein d'espérance"; 199, "Du Rocher de Jacob"; 200, "Agneau de Dieu"; 239, "Trois fois Jehovah," are in every Protestant French hymnbook; and several others are very widely used.

Besides his hymns Malan produced numberless tracts and pamphlets on the questions in dispute between the National and Evangelical Churches and the Church of Rome, as well as articles in the *Record* and in American reviews. He was a man of varied acquirements. His hymns were set to his own melodies. He was an artist, a mechanic: his little workshop had its forge, its carpenter's bench, its printing press. To the end of his life his strong Calvinism, and his dread of mere external union in church government, kept him distinct from all movements of church comprehension, though freely joining in communion with all the sections of Evangelical thought in Geneva and Scotland. At one time there seemed a prospect of his even rejoining the national Church, which had driven him from her. One of his greatest joys was the meeting of the Evangelical Alliance at Geneva (1861). He left no sect; one of his latest orders was the demolition of his decayed chapel, in which he had preached for 43 years. He d. at Vandœuvres, near Geneva, in 1864, leaving a numerous family, one of whom, the Rev. S. C. Malan, D.D., sometime Vicar of Broadwindsor, is well known as a linguist and a theologian of the English Church. [For further details see *La Vie et les Travaux de César Malan, D.D., par un de ses fils*.] To English readers Malan is chiefly known as a hymn-writer through *trs.* of his "Non, ce n'est pas mourir" (q.v.): "It is not death to die," &c. About a dozen of his hymns appear in a translated form in the *Friendly Visitor* for 1826, and two full selections are noted at p. 392, i. [French Hymnody, p. 389, i., § v.]   [H. L. B.]

Man of Sorrows and acquainted. *C. Gregor and C. I. Latrobe.* [*Passiontide.*] This hymn is marked by the Rev. J. A. Eberle in his notes in the *Moravian Messenger* for June, 1868, as C. Gregor, 1759, and

C. I. Latrobe, 1802. Mr. Miller (*Singers and Songs*, p. 231) quotes Mr. Latrobe as saying:—

"The late venerable Bishop of the Brethren's Church, Christian Gregor, was the principal author and compiler of the following cantata, of which he kindly furnished me with a copy. It has been my desire and study to preserve all the ideas contained in the original, and I hope, on comparison, it will be found that I have omitted few, if any, that are essential ; but I did not always confine myself to words, or to the same number of verses."

The original German has not been traced. In English the hymn was given as No. 1011 in the 1808 *Suppl.* to the *Moravian H. Bk.* of 1801 (1886, No. 72), in 6 st. of 8 l. It was adopted by Montgomery in his *Christian Psalmist*, 1825, and has since appeared in the *Cong. H. Bk.*, 1836 ; *N. Cong.*, 1859 ; Bapt. *Ps. & Hys.*, 1858 ; Allon's *Cong. Psalmist Hyl.*, 1886, and others.   [J. M.]

Mane prima Sabbati. [*Easter.*] This sequence has sometimes been ascribed to Adam of St. Victor, but Gautier in his 1881 ed. of Adam's *Oeuvres poétiques*, p. 236, does not print the text, and says that this ascription is false, for the piece is earlier than Adam and not in his style. Among the British Museum MSS. it is found in one of the 12th cent. (Reg. 2 B. iv. f. 101 *b*); in another, c. 1199 (Calig. A. xiv. f. 69 *b*); in a third of the end of the 13th cent. (Add. 12194, f. 123 *b*), &c. It is also in the *Sarum* (Bodleian MS. Barlow, 5, c. 1370, pp. 210, 904), *Hereford* (MS. in the Bodleian, c. 1370), *York* (MS. in the Bodleian, c. 1390); *Paris* (early 14th cent. MS. in the Brit. Mus. Add. 16905, f. 144 *b*), and other *Missals*. *Morel*, p. 45, cites it as in a 12th cent. MS. at Einsiedeln. The text is also in *Mone*, No. 168; *Daniel*, ii. p. 255; *Kehrein*, No. 93, &c. The *Sarum* and some other Missals give it also for St. Mary Magdalene. *Tr.* as :—

On the morn of Easter day. By J. M. Neale in the enlarged *H. Noted*, 1854. In the *Appendix* to the *Antiphoner and Grail*, 1882 ; the *Hymner*, 1882 ; and the *Altar Hymnal*, 1884, this *tr.* is rewritten by M. J. Blacker, as "Dawning was the first of days."   [J. M.]

Manington, Alice, daughter of Thomas Manington, of Hastings, was b. at Brighton, and in 1882 was residing in Vienna. She has published :—

(1.) *Footprints of the Holy Dead ; Translations from the German, by A. M.* London, W. Macintosh, 1863, containing in all 102 pieces. (2.) *A Wreath of Carols from the Fatherland.* London, W. Macintosh, 1864. This contains *trs.* of 25 German hymns and carols, No. 26 being original.

None of these versions appear to be in English C.U. They are noted under the first lines of the German wherever possible.   [J. M.]

Mant, Richard, D.D. s. of the Rev. Richard Mant, Master of the Grammar School, Southampton, was b. at Southampton, Feb. 12, 1776. He was educated at Winchester and Trinity, Oxford (B.A. 1797, M.A. 1799). At Oxford he won the Chancellor's prize for an English essay : was a Fellow of Oriel, and for some time College Tutor. On taking Holy Orders he was successively curate to his father, then of one or two other places, Vicar of Coggeshall, Essex, 1810 ; Domestic Chaplain to the Archbishop of Canterbury, 1813,

Rector of St. Botolph, Bishopsgate, London, 1816, and East Horsley, 1818, Bishop of Killaloe, 1820, of Down and Connor, 1823, and of Dromore, 1842. He was also Bampton Lecturer in 1811. He d. Nov. 2, 1848. His prose works were numerous, and although now somewhat obsolete, they were useful and popular in their day. His poetical works, and other works which contain poetical pieces, are :—

(1) *The Country Curate*, 1804 ; (2) *Poems in three Parts*, 1806 ; (3) *The Slave*, 1807 ; (4) *The Book of Psalms in an English Metrical Version*, &c., 1824 ; (5) *The Holydays of the Church ; or Scripture Narratives of Our Blessed Lord's Life and Ministry, and Biographical Notices of the Apostles, Evangelists, and Other Saints, with Reflections, Collects, and Metrical Sketches*, vol. i., 1828 ; vol. ii., 1831 ; (6) *The Gospel Miracles in a series of Poetical Sketches*, &c., 1832 ; (7) *The British Months*, 2 vols., 1836 ; (8) *Ancient Hymns from the Roman Breviary, for Domestick Use. . . . To which are added Original Hymns, principally of Commemoration and Thanksgiving for Christ's Holy Ordinances*, 1837 : new ed., 1871. (9) *The Happiness of the Blessed Dead*, 1847.

Bp. Mant is known chiefly through his translations from the Latin. He was one of the earliest of the later translators, I. Williams and J. Chandler being his contemporaries. Concerning his translations, Mr. Ellerton, in his *Notes on Church Hymns*, 1881, p. xlviii. (folio ed.), says justly that :—

"Mant had little knowledge of hymns, and merely took those of the existing *Roman Breviary* as he found them : consequently he had to omit many, and so to alter others that they have in fact become different hymns. nor was he always happy in his manipulation of them. But his book has much good taste and devout feeling, and has fallen into undeserved neglect."

His metrical version of the Psalms [See **Psalters, English,** § xvii] has yielded very few pieces to the hymnals, the larger portion of his original compositions being from his work of 1837. The most popular of these is "Come Holy Ghost, my soul inspire, Spirit of," &c., and its altered forms ; "Bright the vision that delighted," and its altered form of "Round the Lord in glory seated ;" and "For all Thy saints, O Lord." His hymns in C. U. which are not annotated under their respective first lines are :—

i. From his *Metrical Version of the Psalms*, 1824.

1. God, my King, Thy might confessing. *Ps. cxlv.*
2. Lord, to Thee I make my vows. *Ps. xxviii.*
3. Blessed be the Lord most High. *Ps. xxviii.* Pt. ii.
4. My trust is in the highest Name. *Ps. xi.*
5. Reign, Jehovah, King supreme. *Ps. xcix.*
6. Thy listening ear, O Lord, incline. *Ps. lxxxvi.*
7. To God my earnest voice I raise. *Ps. cxlii.*
8. To Jehovah hymn the lay. *Ps. cxviii.* Two centos in Spurgeon's *O. O. H. Bk.*, 1866. (1) st. i., ii., v. ; and (2) "Thee, Jehovah, will I bless" from st. vii.-x.

ii. From his *Holydays of the Church*, &c., 1828-31.

9. Lo, the day the Lord hath made. *Easter.*
10. There is a dwelling place above. *All Saints.*

iii. From his *Ancient Hymns*, &c., 1837.

11. Before Thy mercy's throne. *Lent.*
12. Father of all, from Whom we trace. *Unity.*
13. For these who first proclaimed Thy word. *Apostles.*
14. No! when He bids me seek His face. *Holy Communion.*
15. Oft as in God's own house we sit. *Divine Worship.*
16. Put off thy shoes, 'tis holy ground. *The House of God.*
17. Saviour of men, our Hope [Life] and Rest. *The Greater Festivals.*

18. Thy House each day of hallowed rest. *Holy Communion.*
19. We bless Thee for Thy Church, O Lord. *Thanksgiving for the Church.*
26. We deem and own it, Lord, a proof. *Divine Grace.*

When all Bp. Mant's *trs.* original hymns, and versions of the Psalms in C. U. are taken into account, it is found that he is somewhat strongly represented in modern hymnody.

[J. J.]

March, Henry, was b. at Barnstaple, Aug. 29, 1791, and educated for the Congregational ministry at Homerton College under Dr. J. Pye-Smith. He held pastorates at Bungay, Mill Hill, Colchester, and Newbury. He d. in London, July 28, 1869. His pub. works are:—

(1) *Sabbaths at Home, or Help to their right Improvement, Founded on the 42nd and 43rd Psalms,* London, 1820; 2nd ed. 1824. This work consists of Essays on religious subjects, followed by Reflections and Hymns. (2) *Hymns for the Closet of the Christian Minister,* Lond., 1823. (3) *The Early Life of Christ an Example for the Young.*

Of his hymns in C. U. the best are:—

1. **Eternal God, eternal King.** *Adoration of the Father.* In Conder's *Cong. H. Bk.*, 1836, and several modern collections, especially in America.
2. **O send Thy light, Thy truth, my God.** *Public Worship.* Appeared in his *Sabbaths at Home,* &c., 1820, p. 227, where it is given at the close of an Essay on "Natural Gifts Consecrated to God." It was repeated in the *Leeds H. Bk.*, 1853, and later hymnals.

[W. G. H.]

Marckant, John. [Old Version, §§ IX., X.]

Mardley, John. [Old Version, §§ IX., X.]

Maria mater Domini. [*The Assumption of the B. V. M.*] In the Durham Hymnarium of the 11th cent. (f. 3 2b) this is given as a hymn "on the Assumption of the Blessed Virgin Mary." It is also in two MSS. of the 11th cent. in the British Museum (Vesp. D. xii. f. 88; Harl. 2961, f. 231 b). The printed text is in the Surtees Society's *Lat. Hys. of the Anglo-Saxon Ch.*, 1851, p. 109. *Daniel,* i. No. 387, prints only the first stanza. *Tr.* as:—

Mary, Mother of thy [the] Lord. This *tr.* was given anonymously in the 1860 *Appendix* to the *H. Noted,* No. 172; and again in Skinner's *Daily Service Hymnal,* 1864. [J. M.]

Mark the soft-falling snow. *P. Doddridge.* [*Natural things emblematical of things Spiritual.*] 1st pub. in J. Orton's posthumous ed. of Doddridge's *Hymns,* 1755, No. 111, in 4 st. of 8 l., and headed "Fruitful Showers, Emblems of the salutary Effects of the Gospel." In that and subsequent editions to 1839, the opening lines read:—

"Mark the soft-falling Snow,
And the diffusive Rain;
To Heav'n, from whence it fell,
It turns not back again."

In 1839 J. D. Humphreys, in reprinting the *Hymns* from the original MSS., corrected from the MS. of this hymn the grammatical error of "*it*" for "*they,*" in these lines, and drew special attention thereto in the Preface to the *Hymns,* as evidence of his charge against Job Orton as a careless editor. Amongst modern collections the text of 1755 is retained in the Scottish *Evang. Union Hymnal,* 1878, and that of the original MS. in Martineau's *Hymns,* 1840. [J. J.]

Marot, Clement, was b. at Cahors about 1497. His education there and at Paris gave him a fair knowledge of Latin, Italian, and to some extent Greek. He possessed some knowledge of music, and played on the spinet and composed tunes for some of his chansons. Though destined at first for the law, he was placed at sixteen as a page in the service of Nicolas de Neufville. At twenty-one he became valet de chambre to Marguerite de Valois. The passionate admiration he conceived for her turned his thoughts to the Huguenot doctrines, which were then first impressing themselves on her: and his biting ridicule of the vices of the monks, and the disorders of the Church, united with frequent confessions of simple faith, were the occasion of all the misfortunes that beset his after life. He was wounded and taken prisoner at Pavia with Francis I. After his return to France he married (1526?). About the same period he succeeded, at his father's death, to the post of valet de chambre to Francis. In 1535, an outbreak of persecution obliged him to fly from France to Ferrara, where for a few weeks he must have met Calvin. From Ferrara he went to Venice; and was thence, through the influence of Marguerite of Navarre, recalled to France by the king. The statement that he recanted his Huguenot errors at Lyons (1536) rests on no sufficient evidence. In 1537-9 he completed the translation of 30 psalms, which were circulated at court in MS. They became the fashion of the hour: and the king, Catherine de Medicis, the Dauphin, Diane de Poitiers, and the court gentlemen and ladies sang them to ballad tunes. Charles V. rewarded Marot for a copy of them, with 200 golden doublons. The publication of these psalms (1542) brought on him the wrath of the Sorbonne, and he fled again; first to Savoy, then to Geneva. There, encouraged by Francis and by Calvin, he completed his 50 Psalms, published with a Dedication to The Ladies of France (1543). The stern rigidity of Geneva must have been stifling to his gay mercurial nature. The only authentic incident of his story that has come down is the prosecution of Bonivard for playing "tric-trac" with him. His prosecution for adultery is one of the malicious inventions of his enemies. He left Geneva (1543) for Savoy, and then Turin, where he d. in August 1544.

The poetry of Marot is composed of short pieces—ballads, rondeaux, epigrams, and rhymed epistles—full of grace and delicacy, gaiety, wit, and satire. He both enriched and simplified the lyrical style. The Psalms—his matured work—exhibit an access of dignity and stateliness. His many-sided character has suffered from the prejudices of Catholic and Huguenot. To his enemies he is a dissolute heretic, to Bayle a professional poet who gave his talents easily to either side, to Saint-Marc Girardin a man penetrated by the wide-spread disgust at the corruptions of the Church, but not of deep Huguenot conviction, to others a child of the classic learning and Free Thought of the Renaissance. To the last no doubt he never lost his courtier habit; but there is no proof of his licentiousness, except in his 'Jeunesse Abusée,' to which he often alludes; his coarseness is abundantly paralleled in the language of the time: and the close analysis of his life and his writings by M. Douen and Mr. Henry Morley attests the existence of a base of real religion, of which the 'Trente Pseaumes' were a distinguished fruit.

[Authorities. *Clement Marot et le Psautier Huguenot,* by M. Douen; *L'Histoire du Psautier des Eglises Reformées,* by M. Felix Bovet; *Clement Marot and the Huguenot Psalter,* a Series of Articles by Major Crawford in *The Musical Times,* 1881; *Clement Marot and other Studies,* by Mr. Henry Morley.] [H. L. B.]

Marot, Samuel, D.D., was b. at Magdeburg, Dec. 11, 1770, and studied at the University of Frankfurt a. Oder. On July 1, 1798, he was ordained as preacher to the Orphanage (Friedrichs-Waisenhaus) at Berlin. In 1808 he was appointed preacher at the Neue Kirche; in 1816 superintendent of the Reformed Churches in Berlin; and also became Consistorialrath in 1830, and Oberconsistorialrath in 1846 (D.D. from University of Berlin, 1846). He d. at Berlin, Oct. 12, 1865 (*Allg. Deutsche Biog.*, xx. 404, &c.). He was one of the Committee which compiled the Berlin *G. B.*, 1829. The only hymn known by him is :—

Von des Himmels Thron. *Confirmation.* Contributed to the Berlin *G. B.*, 1829, as No. 350, in 5 st. of 6 l. Its excellence and simplicity have gained it a place in many recent German collections, as the Berlin *G. L. S.*, ed. 1863, No. 1614. *Tr.* as :—

From Thy heav'nly throne. A good and full tr. by Miss Winkworth as No. 91 in her *C. B. for England*, 1863; repeated in the *Parish H. Bk.*, 1875. [J. M.]

Marriott, John, M.A., s. of R. Marriott, D.D., Rector of Cottesbach, near Lutterworth, was b. at Cottesbach, in 1780, and educated at Rugby, and Christ Church, Oxford. He was the second of two who obtained honours in the schools in 1802, the first year in which there was a public examination for honours at Oxford. He was also Student of Christ Church, and for about two years a private tutor in the family of the Duke of Buccleuch. The Duke presented him to the Rectory of Church Lawford, Warwickshire. This he retained to his death, although his wife's health compelled him to reside in Devonshire, where he was successively curate of St. Lawrence and other parishes in Exeter, and of Broadclyst, near Exeter, where he d. March 31, 1825. His published works include a vol. of *Sermons* which he issued in 1818, and a posthumous vol. of *Sermons*, pub. by his sons in 1838. His hymns were never pub. by himself, nor in book form by any one. A few appeared in print during his lifetime, but without his permission. These include :—

1. A saint? O would that I could claim. *Holiness desired.* "Written off almost at the moment, on hearing the name applied in a scornful way at a party, about 1813." It was printed in *The Friendly Visitor*, 1834.

2. Thou, Whose Almighty word. *Missions.* Written, his son says, "about 1813." It was printed in *The Friendly Visitor*, July, 1825, in 4 st. of 7 l., with the Title "Missionary Hymn," and without signature. This text differs only in two or three words from the original as supplied by the author's son to Dr. Rogers and pub. by him in his *Lyra Brit.*, 1867, p. 395. Two texts are known which are received as original, the first the undoubted text in *Lyra Brit.*, and the second that given by Lord Selborne from the *Coll.* of Dr. Raffles, Congregational Minister of Liverpool. The differences are, (1) in st. iii. l. 4, orig. is: "Move o'er," and Raffles "Move on," and (2) st. iv. :—

Original.	Dr. Raffles.
" Blessed, and holy, and Glorious Trinity, Wisdom, Love, Might: Boundless as ocean's tide Rolling in fullest pride Thro' the world, far and wide, 'Let there be light.'"	" Holy and blessed Three, Glorious Trinity, Wisdom, Love, Might! Boundless as ocean's tide Rolling in fullest pride, Through the *earth*, far and wide, 'Let there be light!'"

The second text is that mostly in C. U. in all English speaking countries, and that which is usually translated. *Tr.* into Latin, by R. Bingham, in his *Hymn. Christ. Lat.*, 1871, as " Tu, cujus Orbis principio novi." Another form appeared in *The Casket*, Oliphant, Edinburgh, 1826, but this is unknown to the collections.

3. When Christ our human form did bear. *Christ's*

love of Children. " Written in 1816 for the Parochial Schools, Upottery, Devon."

The foregoing details are in great part from MS. notes supplied by the author's son. [S. MSS.].   [J. J.]

Marshall, Julia A. [Elliott, Julia. A.]

Martin, Henry Arthur, M.A., s. of George Martin, Chancellor and Canon of Exeter, b. at Exeter July 30, 1831, and educated at Eton, and Christ Church, Oxford, graduating B.A. 1855, and M.A. 1857. On taking Holy Orders he became Curate of Hallow, near Worcester, 1856, and Vicar of Laxton with Moorhouse, Nottinghamshire, 1858. In 1871 he contributed the following hymns to *Church Hymns* :—

1. Lord of the frost-bound winter. *Harvest.* Written in 1859.
2. O Rock of Ages, One Foundation. *St. Peter.* Written in 1871.
3. Sound aloud Jehovah's praises. *Holy Trinity.* Written in 1870, in 8 st., four of which only are given in *Church Hymns*.
4. The heavenly King must come. *St. John Baptist.* Written in 1871.   [J. J.]

Martin, Samuel, D.D., s. of John Martin, schoolmaster at Anstruther-Easter, Fife, was b. at Anstruther, July 7, 1740. He studied at the University of Edinburgh, and, after being licensed to preach in 1762, became in 1768 parish minister of Balmaghie, Kirkcudbright, and in 1776 of Monimail, Fife. He received the degree of D.D. from the University of St. Andrews in 1798. He d. at Monimail, Sep. 12, 1829. As a member of the Committee appointed by the General Assembly of 1775, to revise the *Trans. and Paraph.* of 1745, he contributed No. 12 to the 1781 collection (see Cameron, William, and Scottish Translations and Paraphrases). [J. M.]

Martineau, Harriet, was b. at Norwich, June 12, 1802, and d. at Ambleside, June 27, 1876. Best known as the writer of *Illustrations of Political Economy, Retrospect of Western Travel;* two novels, *Deerbrook* and *The Hour and the Man; Eastern Life, Past and Present;* a *History of the Thirty Years' Peace*, and various other works. Her first publication was a book of Devotional Exercises, with hymns appended to each Exercise, and her hymns also belong to what she speaks of in the *Autobiography* as her " Unitarian " period. Five of them appeared in *A Collection of Hymns for Christian Worship*, printed in 1831 for the congregation of Eustace Street, Dublin, and edited by her brother, the Rev. James Martineau.

1. All men are equal in their birth. *Human Equality.*
2. Lord Jesus! come; for here. *Jesus desired.* Sometimes given as (1) "Come, Jesus, come, for here "; (2) and " Thy kingdom come, for here."
3. The floods of grief have spread around. *In Affliction.*
4. What hope was thine, O Christ! when grace. *Peace.*
5. When Samuel heard, in still mid-night. *Samuel.*

The Rev. J. R. Beard's *Coll.* 1837, contains 1, 2, 4 and 5, and :—

6. The sun had set, the infant slept. *Gethsemane.*

The Rev. W. J. Fox's *Hymns and Anthems*, 1841, contains No. 1, and

7. Beneath this starry arch. *Progress.* [V. D. D.]

Martineau, James, LL.D., D.D., b. at Norwich, April 21, 1805, the son of a manufacturer and wine merchant of Huguenot descent. After four years at the Norwich grammar-school, and two as a pupil of Dr. Lant Carpenter, at Bristol, and a short experience in the shops of a mechanical engineer at Derby, he entered as a Divinity student in Manchester College, York. His first ministry was at Eustace St. Chapel, Dublin [1828-32], as assistant to his cousin, the Rev. Philip Taylor. From 1832 to 1857 he was in Liverpool, as minister of the congregation meeting in Paradise St. Chapel, and from 1849 in the new Hope St. Church. In 1840 he was appointed professor of Mental and Moral Philosophy and Political Economy in Manchester New College, and in 1857 followed the college to London, becoming its Principal in 1869 and resigning in 1885. On settling in London he became also minister of Little Portland St. Chapel, first in conjunction with the Rev. J. J. Tayler, and afterwards alone till his resignation in 1872. He received the degree of D.C.L. from Oxford in 1888. D. Jan. 11, 1900.

The chief of Dr. Martineau's works hitherto published are four volumes of sermons, *Endeavours after the Christian Life*, 2 vols., 1843 and 1847 ; *Hours of Thought on Sacred Things*, 2 vols., 1876 and 1879 ; *Studies of Christianity*, 1858 ; *Essays Philosophical and Theological*, 2 vols., 1866 and 1868, collected from various Reviews ; *A Study of Spinoza*, 1882 ; and *Types of Ethical Theories*, 2 vols., 1885, 2nd ed. 1886. These contain the substance of his teaching as a Christian minister and an expounder of a spiritual philosophy of religion. By early training and matured conviction a Unitarian of the Catholic and spiritual type, Dr. Martineau has served not only the little group of churches with which he is immediately connected, but the Church Universal by his gifts of sympathy and insight into the deepest questions of human life. He has strengthened the foundations of faith in the light of modern knowledge, and added treasures, the worth of which have yet to be fully measured, to the rich store of the devout literature of the Church.

The Catholic spirit and deeply Christian temper impressed upon all Dr. Martineau's literary work give their distinctive character to the three hymn-books which he has edited, viz. :—

(1) *A Collection of Hymns for Christian Worship. Dublin : Printed for the Congregation of Eustace Street*, 1831. This collection of 273 hymns already clearly indicates the principles of selection afterwards to be more fully worked out. It was made for the use of a society, " whose worship is paid solely to the God and Father of our Lord and Saviour Jesus Christ," and in adopting the hymns of Dr. Watts and others, such changes are made as are required by theological consistency ; but the preface pleads for a wider latitude of choice than had been usual in older selections, " bringing all the resources of lyric poetry (the poetry of the affections) into the service of religion." There are 18 hymns by Bp. Heber introduced, and special mention is made of his merit in "first liberalizing the style of poetry designed for our churches."

During his ministry in Liverpool Dr. Martineau published :—

(2) *Hymns for the Christian Church and Home. Collected and edited by James Martineau*. London, 1840. This with his own congregation took the place of the old Paradise St. collection of 1815, and was quickly recognised as pre-eminent among the books in use among the non-subscribing churches.

Dr. Martineau's last collection was :—

(3) *Hymns of Praise and Prayer, collected and edited by James Martineau, LL.D., D.D.* " *Vatum suspiria solatium Ecclesiae.*" London, 1873.

The character of the last two books, and the place they hold in the religious connection for which they were in the first instance prepared, are more fully described in the article on *Unitarian Hymnody*. It remains only to mention Dr. Martineau's own hymns :—

1. A voice upon the mid-night air. *Good Friday.*
2. Thy way is in [on] the deep, O Lord. *Trust.*
3. " Where is your God ?" they say. *Inward witness of God.*

They have been hitherto published anonymously, but the authorship is now acknowledged. Nos. 1, 2, appeared first in his *Hymns*, &c., 1840, and 3 in his *Hymns*, &c., 1873. They are also found in other collections in G. Britain and America.   [V. D. D.]

Martyr Dei qui unicum. [*Martyrs.*] A hymn for the Common of Martyrs in the *Sarum, York, Aberdeen*, old *Roman* and other *Breviaries*. It is found in four *Hymnaries* of the 11th cent. in the British Museum ; three of the English Church (Vesp. D. xii. f. 106 *b* ; Jul. A. vi. f. 65 *b* ; Harl. 2961, f. 248 *b*) and one of the ancient Spanish Church (Add. 30,851, f. 153 *b*). In the *Lat. Hys. of the Anglo Saxon Ch.*, 1851, p. 133, it is printed from an 11th cent. MS. at Durham (B. iii. 32 f. 39 *b*). *Daniel*, i., No. 234, prints the original, and at iv. p. 138, the text of the revised *Roman Breviary* of 1632, where it begins, **Invicte martyr unicum.**

[J. M.]

The original and the *Roman Breviary* forms of this hymn have been translated as follows :—

i. *Original Text.* **Martyr Dei qui unicum.**

1. **Martyr of God, 'twas thine to track.** By W. J. Blew. Pub. in his *Church Hy. & Tune Bk.*, 1852-5, in 5 st. of 4 l.; and again in Rice's *Sel.* from the same, 1870, No. 117.

2. **Martyr of God ! The Only Son.** This *tr.* was given anonymously in the *Antiphoner & Grail*, 1880, p. 85, and in the *Hymner*, 1882. In the latter it is given for " St. Stephen," and for " One Martyr."

Another tr. is :—

Martyr of God ! Who in the road. *J. D. Chambers.* 1857.

ii. *Roman Brev. Text.* **Invicte martyr, unicum.**

1. **Great God, whose strength Thy martyrs steel'd.** By Bp. Mant. 1st pub. in his *Ancient Hys.*, 1837, p. 77, in 5 st. of 4 l. (ed. 1871, p. 135). It has been repeated in a few collections, including the *People's H.*, 1867, &c.

2. **Martyr of unconquer'd might.** By E. Caswall. 1st pub. in his *Lyra Catholica*, 1849, p. 209, and again in his *Hys. & Poems*, 1873, p. 111, in 4 st. of 4 l., together with a doxology for Eastertide, and a second of Ascensiontide. In its complete form it is not in C. U. ; but st. i. is the opening stanza of the cento, No. 193, in the 2nd ed. 1863 of the *Appendix* to the *H. Noted.*

Other trs. are :—

1. Blest martyr, nobly hast thou trod. *R. Campbell.* 1850.
2. Great martyr, who thyself didst show. *J. Wallace.* 1874.   [J. J.]

Marvell, Andrew. [Addison, J.]

Mary, Queen of Scotland. [Scotland, Mary, Queen of.]

Mason, John. The known facts of his life are scanty. He was the s. of a Dissenting Minister, and the grandfather of John Mason, the author of *A Treatise on Self-Knowledge.* He was educated at Strixton School, Northants, and Clare Hall, Cambridge. After taking his M.A., he became Curate of Isham ; and in 1668, Vicar of Stantonbury, Bucks. A little more than five years afterwards he was appointed Rector of Water-Stratford. Here he composed the volume containing *The Songs of Praise*, his paraphrase of *The Song of Solomon*, and the *Poem on Dives and Lazarus*, with which Shepherd's *Penitential Cries* was afterwards bound up. This volume passed through twenty editions. Besides the *Songs of Praise*, it contains six *Penitential Cries* by Mason, and it is this portion of his work which harmonizes with the compositions of Shepherd. Probably his hymns were used in public worship, and if so, they are among the earliest hymns so used in the Church of England. Some of his hymns are often found in the early Hymn Collections of the 18th century. The most notable work besides this volume is *Select Remains of the Rev. John Mason*, a collection of sententious and practical sayings and Christian letters, published by his grandson, and much eulogised by Dr. Watts. His friend, Shepherd, who was at Water-Stratford at the remarkable period to which reference is made below, published two of Mason's *Sermons*, with a preface of his own. Mason was a man of true piety and humility; known for eminent prayerfulness; faithful, experimental, effectual preaching; "a light in the pulpit, and a pattern out of it." His friendship with Baxter, and Shepherd, the Nonconformist Minister of Braintree, probably indicates his sympathies and theological position. Baxter calls him "the glory of the Church of England," and says :—

"The frame of his spirit was so heavenly, his deportment so humble and obliging, his discourse of spiritual things so weighty, with such apt words and delightful air, that it charmed all that had any spiritual relish."

The close of his life was sensational enough. One night, about a month before his death, he had a vision of the Lord Jesus, wearing on His head a glorious crown, and with a look of unutterable majesty in His face. Of this vision he spoke; and preached a Sermon called *The Midnight Cry*, in which he proclaimed the near approach of Christ's Second Advent. A report spead, that this Advent would take place at Water-Stratford itself, and crowds gathered there from the surrounding villages. Furniture and provisions were brought in, and every corner of the house and village occupied. Most extraordinary scenes occurred, singing and leaping and dancing. The excitement had scarcely died out when the old man passed away (1694), still testifying that he had seen the Lord, and that it was time for the nation to tremble, and for Christians to trim their lamps. His last words were, "I am full of the loving kindness of the Lord." [See English Hymnody, Early, § XI.]

[H. L. B.]

The full titles of his *Songs of Praise*, and the additions thereto, are :—

(1) *Spiritual Songs; or, Songs of Praise to Almighty God upon several occasions*, 1683. (2) *The Song of Songs which is Solomon's first Turned, then Paraphrased in English Verse*. Pub. with the former. (3) *Dives and Lazarus*. incorporated with the former 1685. (4) *Penitential Cries, Begun by the Author of the Songs of Praise, And carried on by another Hand. Licensed and Entered*, Sept. 13, 1693. This forms the concluding part of all editions of the *Songs of Praise* after 1693. The complete work was reprinted by D. Sedgwick in 1859. This reprint was accompanied by a short *Memoir*. In this reprint Mason's *P. Cries* and Ps. 86 are given under *Songs of Praise*, pp. 49–61, those under *P. Cries* being all by Shepherd (q.v.). Mason's *Life*, by John Dunton, was pub. in 1694, and included some miscellaneous poems; and another, by Henry Maurice, in 1695,

in which are two hymns not found elsewhere. (See also an Article on him in the *Sunday at Home*, Feb. 1881.) We may add that Mason pub. a *Catechism, with some Verses for Children*. Of this, however, no copy is known to exist.

Mason's *Songs* are commonly presented in modern hymn-books in the form of centos, which are sometimes compiled from a single *Song*, and in other instances from several *Songs*. Many of these are annotated under their respective first lines. The rest include :—

1. Blest be my God that I was born. *Praise for the Gospel*.
2. Lord, for the mercies of the night. *Morning*.
3. Lord of my life, Length of my days. *Praise for Deliverance from Immediate danger of Death*.
4. My God, a God of pardon is. *Praise for Pardon of Sin*.
5. My God, my only Help and Hope. *Praise for Providence*.
6. My God, my reconciled God. *Praise for Peace of Conscience*.
7. My God was with me all this night. *Morning*.
8. Thou wast, O God; and Thou wast blest. *Praise for Creation*.
9. Thousands of thousands stand around. *Praise*. A cento from Songs i. and ii.

In Griffith, Farran & Co.'s *Ancient and Modern Library*, No. 12, Giles Fletcher's *Christ's Victory and Triumph, &c.*, 1888, p. 208 (edited by W. T. Brooke), a short hymn by Mason is given from *Multum in Parvo: or the Jubilee of Jubilees*, 1732, beginning "High praises meet and dwell within." It is an indifferent example of Mason's powers as a writer of sacred verse. [J. J.]

Mason, William, M.A., was b. at Kingston-upon-Hull, 1725, and educated at St. John's College, Cambridge. He was some time a Fellow of Pembroke Hall. On taking Holy Orders he became Rector of Aston, and Precentor of York Minster. He d. April 5, 1797. His poetical writings, including Poems, Tragedies, Odes, and Hymns, published at intervals, were collected and issued in 4 vols. in 1811 as *The Works of William Mason, M.A.*, Precentor of York, and Rector of Aston. His hymns, few in number, include, "Again the day returns of holy rest" (p. 29, i.); "Soon shall the evening star with silver [silent] ray" (p. 29, i.), &c. These are in vol. i. of his *Works*. [J. J.]

Massie, Edward, M.A., was educated at Wadham College, Oxford, where he was Dean Ireland Scholar in 1828; B.A. 1830; M.A. 1834. He took Holy Orders in 1830; was Fellow and Tutor of University College, Durham, from 1841 to 1845; and then for some time Curate of Gawsworth, Cheshire. He has pub., in 1862, *A Few Hymns for Occasional use in the Services of the Church*, and *Sacred Odes*, vol. i., Lond., 1866, vol. ii., 1867. The latter contain many translations from the German. Those which are from German hymns, and are within the range of this Dictionary, are annotated under the original German first lines or their author's names. See **Index of Authors, &c.** He d. Jan. 21, 1893. [J. J.]

Massie, Richard, eldest s. of the Rev. R. Massie, of Coddington, Cheshire, and Rector of Eccleston, was born at Chester, June 18, 1800, and resides at Pulford Hall, Coddington. Mr. Massie pub. a *tr.* of *Martin Luther's Spiritual Songs*, Lond., 1854. His *Lyra Domestica*, 1st series, Lond., 1860, contains *trs.*

of the 1st Series of Spitta's *Psalter und Harfe.*
In 1864 he pub. vol. ii., containing *trs.* of
Spitta's 2nd Series, together with an *Appendix*
of *trs.* of German hymns by various authors.
He also contributed many *trs.* of German
hymns to Mercer's *Church Psalter & H. Bk.*; to
Reid's *British Herald*; to the *Day of Rest*, &c.
Most of these are annotated in this Dictionary.
He d. Mar. 11, 1887.   [J. J.]

Master, it is good to be. *A. P. Stanley.*
[*Transfiguration.*] 1st pub. in an article by
Dean Stanley on the *Transfiguration* and
hymns relating thereto, in *Macmillan's Magazine*, April, 1870 (vol. xxi. p. 543). It is in
6 st. of 8 l. In a note which accompanies the
hymn Dean Stanley says :—

"I have endeavoured (as in a hymn written some
years ago on the Ascension) ['He is gone—Beyond the
skies,' **p. 500,** ii.] to combine as far as possible, the
various thoughts connected with the scene."

It is given in full in the *Westminster Abbey
H. Bk.*, 1883, and other collections, and with
the omission of 'st. i. as " O Master, it is good
to be," in the *Hymnary*, 1872.   [J. J.]

Master, where abidest Thou ? *Elizabeth Charles, née Rundle.* [*Jesus desired.*] Appeared in her work, *The Three Wakings and
Other Poems*, 1859, p. 182. It is found in a
few collections only.   [J. J.]

Masters, Mary. Biographical facts concerning Mrs. Masters are very few. In 1733
she published a volume of *Poems;* and again,
in 1755, by Subscription, *Familiar Letters and
Poems on Several Occasions* (Lon. D. H. Cave).
These *Poems* include versified epistles on
various subjects to her friends, Odes, and a
few paraphrases of single Psalms, &c. From
the *Preface* to her *Poems*, 1733, we find that
Thomas Scott took an interest in her, and contributed some Poems to that volume. It is
evident also from the following extract that
she was in humble circumstances, and without
a liberal education :—

"The author of the following poems never read a
Treatise of Rhetorick, or an Art of Poetry, nor was
ever taught her English Grammar. Her Education rose
no higher than the Spelling Book, or the Writing Master :
her Genius to Poetry was always brow-beat and dis-
countenanced by her Parents, and till her Merit got the
better of her Fortune, she was shut out from all Com-
merce with the more knowing and polite part of the
world." *Poems*, 1733 : Preface.

In her *Familiar Letters and Poems*, 1755,
pp. 228–29, there are three " Short Ejaculations," the first of which is the well known :—

" 'Tis Religion that can give,
    Sweetest Pleasures while we live ;
    'Tis Religion must supply,
    Solid comforts when we die,
    After Death its Joys will be,
    Lasting as Eternity."

When these lines were included in Rippon's
Selection, 1787, the following were added :—

" Be the living God my Friend,
    Then my bliss shall never end : "

and the 8 lines were divided into two stanzas.
In this form the hymn is known to modern
collections.

An ejaculation for use " At the Altar " is
sometimes met with. It is also in the *Familiar Letters*, &c., p. 229, and reads :—

" O my ador'd Redeemer ! deign to be,
    Now present with the mystic Bread to me ;
    May I the Blessings of Thy Blood partake,
    Who drink the Sacred Wine for Thy dear sake."

This volume also contains a few hymns
which are worthy of attention.   [J. J.]

Mathams, Walter John, was b. in London, Oct. 30, 1853. Early in life he went to
sea ; but on returning through Palestine to
England he began to study for the Ministry.
In 1874 he entered the Regent's Park Baptist College as a Student, and subsequently
had a pastoral charge at Preston, Lancashire.
In 1879, his health failing, he went for a time
to Australia and other places. Returning to
England, he became, in 1883, minister at
Falkirk, Scotland, and in 1888, at Birmingham.
Whilst a student, he pub. a small volume of
hymns and poems as *At Jesus' Feet* (1876).
He is also the author of several religious books
of a popular character, as : *Fireside Parables,*
1879 ; *Sunday Parables*, 1883, &c. His principal hymns are :—

1. Bright falls the morning light. *Morning.*
2. Gentle Jesus, full of grace. *Learning of Christ.*
3. Go, work for God, and do not say. *Christian Work.*
4. God loves the little sparrows. *Divine Providence.*
5. Jesus, Friend of little children. *Child's Prayer to
Christ.*
6. My heart, O God, be wholly Thine. *Consecration.*
7. No room for Thee, Lord Jesus. *No room for
Christ.*
8. Reign in my heart, Great God. *Consecration.*
9. Sailing on the ocean. *Life a Voyage.*

Nos. 1 and 6 of these hymns first appeared
in his *At Jesus' Feet*, 1876. Mr. Mathams has
written several other hymns which have appeared in magazines and elsewhere. One of
these, " Good has come from Nazareth," has
been set to music by Dr. E. J. Hopkins. The
9 hymns named above are mainly in Baptist
hymn-books.   [W. R. S.]

Mathesius, Johannes, s. of Wolfgang
Mathesius, town councillor at Rochlitz, was
b. at Rochlitz, June 24, 1504. He studied
for a short time at the University of Ingolstadt. Thereafter he acted as family tutor at
Odelzhausen, near Munich, where, in 1526,
he found Luther's *Von den guten Werken*
(Wittenberg, 1523) ; and then while living at
Bruck (Fürstenfeld-bruck), near Munich, read
two of Luther's tractates on the Holy Communion. Attracted thus to Wittenberg he
matriculated there May 30, 1529, studied with
great zeal and graduated M.A. in 1530. In
the end of 1530 he joined the staff of the
school at Altenburg, and in the spring of 1532
was appointed rector of the gymnasium at
Joachimsthal in Bohemia. He resigned this
post in 1540, and returned to Wittenberg to
complete his studies in theology. Thereafter
he was, in 1541, appointed diaconus, and, in
1545, pastor at Joachimsthal. While preaching
on the Gospel for the 16th S. after Trinity,
Oct. 7, 1565 (his subject being the " Son of the
widow of Nain, and the hope of eternal life "),
he was struck with paralysis, and, being carried to his house, d. there some three hours
later (*Koch* i. 380, ii. 475 ; Herzog's *Real-En-
cyklopädie*, ix. 398, &c.).

Mathesius was of most lovable and charitable spirit,
and a model pastor, who thoroughly adapted himself to
his life among a mining population. He was a distinguished preacher, his sermons ranking among the
best of the period, the most famous being those in his
Sarepta oder Bergpostill, Nürnberg, 1562, founded on
those passages of Scripture referring to metallurgy or
mining, the title being suggested by Sarepta or Zare-
phath (1 Kings xvii. 9), the Hebrew name meaning
smelting-place. Besides other volumes of sermons and

devotional works he also pub. a life of Luther (*Historien von . . . Doctoris Martini Luthers Anfang, Lehr, Leben und Sterben*, Nürnberg, 1566) completed just before his death, and with a preface dated Oct. 5, 1565. His hymns are few in number, and appeared scattered in his various publications. *Wackernagel*, iii. pp. 1150–1161, gives 21 pieces, of which 15 may be called hymns ; and 15 of these pieces with a memoir by K. F. Ledderhose appeared at Halle in 1855 [see also under **Herman, N., p. 513,** ii.]. The finest of all his hymns, the beautiful cradle song, "Nun schlaf mein liebes Kindelein " [*Wackernagel* iii. p. 1152, from a Nürnberg broadsheet N.D. c. 1560, in 15 st. of 4 l. ; and in the Berlin *G. L. S.* ed., 1863, No. 1416] does not seem to have been *tr.* into English.

Those of Mathesius's hymns which have passed into English are :—

i. **Aus meines Herzens Grunde.** *Morning.* This has generally, though apparently without ground, been ascribed to Mathesius, and is included in the 1855 ed. of his *Geistliche Lieder*, p. 149. But it is not found in any of his original works now extant, nor in the collected ed. of his *Schöne geistliche Lieder*, Nürnberg, 1580 ; and the ascription to him has not been traced earlier than in M. Prätorius's *Musae Sioniae*, 1610. *Wackernagel*, v. pp. 177–184, gives 8 forms varying from 6 to 15 st. (some beginning " Von meines Herzens Grunde "); the oldest, in 7 st. of 8 l., being from a *Gesangbüchlein* pub. at Hamburg in 1592. He ranks it as anonymous. The text of 1592 is No. 440 in the *Unv. L. S.*, 1851. The hymn was a great favourite with Gustavus Adolphus, and was often sung by his army at morning prayer. The *trs.*, from the text of 1592, are :—

1. **My heart its incense burning.** In full, by Dr. H. Mills, in his *Horae Ger.*, 1856, p. 220, repeated, abridged, in M. W. Stryker's *Christian Chorals*, 1885, reading " *her* incense."

2. **My inmost heart now raises.** A good *tr.* omitting st. iv., v., by Miss Winkworth, in her *C. B. for England*, 1863, No. 164.

3. **My heart with deep emotion.** Omitting st. iii., v. by E. Cronenwett as No. 294 in the Ohio Luth. *Hymnal*, 1880.

Other trs. are :—
(1) "O let Thy angels always dwell " (st. v.). As No. 325 in pt. i. of the *Moravian H. Bk.*, 1754. (2) " May Jesus' grace and blessing " (st. iii. ll. 1, 2 ; vii. ll. 4–8). By F. W. Foster, as No. 749 in the *Moravian H. Bk.*, 1789 (1886, No. 1167). (3) "O God, my heart is full of praise." By *Dr. G. Walker*, 1860, p. 59.

ii. **Gott Vater, Sohn, heiliger Geist, Durchs Sprechen gut Erz wachsen heisst.** *Miner's Song.* 1st pub. as *Ein geistlich Bercklied*, 1556, and thence in *Wackernagel*, iii. p. 1151, in 9 st. *Tr.* as "O, Father, Son, and Holy Ghost, Thou God, dost fix the miner's post." By *Miss Winkworth*, 1869, p. 144.   **[J. M.]**

Matheson, Annie, eldest daughter of Rev. James Matheson, Congregational Minister, of Nottingham, was b. at Blackheath, March, 1853, and now (1888) resides at Notting Hill, London.

At an early age she shewed considerable literary ability, her first hymn, "Jesus, the children are calling," being composed when she was only 13 years old. This hymn, attracting the attention of Dr. George MacDonald, was introduced by him to the notice of the editor of *Good Words*, who inserted it in that magazine, as a "Hymn by a Child." In 1869 appeared "I am weak and weary, Lord," and from that time Miss Matheson has been a frequent contributor to *Good Words*, *Macmillan*, *The Spectator*, *St. Nicholas*, and other magazines, both English and American. Her illustrated book for children, *Margaret's Year Book*, containing twelve poems from her pen, was pub. in 1887.

The following are the best known of Miss Matheson's hymns :—

1. Dear Master, what can children do? *Children as Workers for Christ.*

2. How shall we worship Thee, O Lord? *Divine Worship.*
3. I am weak and weary, Lord. *Divine Strength desired.*
4. Jesus, the children are calling. *Children's Prayer to Christ.*
5. Lord, when we have not any light. *Evening.*
6. O little birds, that all day long. *God's Love to all Creatures.*
7. The little snowdrops rise. *Easter.*
8. When through life's dewy fields we go. *Comfort in God's Presence.*

Of these hymns, Nos, 5, 6, and 7 were written for W. R. Stevenson's *School Hymnal*, 1880 ; and Nos. 1 and 2 for a Harvest Festival about 1882.

Miss Matheson's hymns are characterised by a pleasing combination of simplicity and refinement, both of thought and expression.
        [W. R. S.]

Matson, William Tidd, was b. at West Hackney, London, Oct. 17, 1833. He was educated first under the the Rev. J. M. Gould, and then at St. John's College, Cambridge. Subsequently he studied under Professor Nesbitt, at the Agricultural and Chemical College, Kennington. In 1853 he underwent a great spiritual change. Leaving the Church of England, he first joined the Methodist New Connexion body, and then the Congregationalists. After the usual theological training, he entered the ministry, and held several pastorates, including Havant, Hants ; Gosport ; Highbury ; Portsmouth, and others. His poetical works include ;—

(1) *A Summer Evening Reverie, and Other Poems*, 1857 ; (2) *Poems*, 1858 ; (3) *Pleasures of the Sanctuary*, 1865 ; (4) *The Inner Life*, 1866 ; (5) *Sacred Lyrics*, 1870 ; (6) *Three Supplemental Hymns*, &c., 1872 ; (7) *The World Redeemed*, 1881, &c.

Several of Matson's hymns have been given in Allon's *Suppl. Hys.* ; Horder's *Cong. Hymns* ; *The Baptist Hymnal* ; Dale's *English H. Bk.* ; Barrett's *Cong. Church Hymnal*, 1887, and others. The best known are :—

1. Father of all, Whose wondrous power. *Prayer to the Holy Trinity.*
2. Glory, glory to God in the highest. *Christmas.*
3. God is in His temple. *Divine Worship.*
4. I'm but a little child. *A Child's Prayer.*
5. In whom shall I find comfort ? *God, the Source of Comfort.*
6. Lord, I was blind, I could not see. *Christ, the Life of Men.*
7. O blessed Life, the heart at rest. *Christ the Life of Men.*
8. Teach me, O Lord, Thy holy way. *Divine Guidance desired.*

Mr Matson's hymns show a considerable mastery of the forms of hymnic expression, but are somewhat lacking in lyric energy. Those written for use with German chorales are excellent efforts, and rank with his best work. Taken as a whole his hymns are far above the average, and deserve wide acknowledgment.   **[W. G. H.]**

Matthesius, Johannes. [Mathesius, J.]

Matthews, Rose, a *nom de plume* of Mrs. Van Alstyne.

Maude, Mary Fawler, née Hooper, daughter of George Henry Hooper, of Stanmore, Middlesex, was married in 1841 to the late Joseph Maude, some time Vicar of Chirk, near Ruabon, and Hon. Canon of St. Asaph, who d. in Feb. 1887. Mrs. Maude's hymns were pub. in her *Twelve Letters on Confirmation*, 1848, and in *Memorials of Past Years*,

1852 (privately printed). Her best known hymn, is "Thine for ever, God of love" (*Confirmation*). Concerning it Mrs. Maude says:—

"It was written in 1847 for my class in the Girls' Sunday School of St. Thomas, Newport, Isle of Wight, and pub. in 1848 at the beginning of a little book called 'Twelve Letters on Confirmation,' by a Sunday School Teacher, and reprinted in the *Memorials*, 1852." [s. mss.]

The original is in 7 st. of 4 l. It is usually abbreviated, and st. ii., iii. transposed, as in the S. P. C. K. *Church Hymns*, 1871; the *Hy. Comp.*; *H. A. & M.*, 1875, Thring's *Coll.*, 1882, and most other hymn-books. As a hymn for Confirmation its use is extensive. The omitted stanzas are:—

" Thine for ever in that day
  When the world shall pass away:
  When the trumpet note shall sound,
  And the nations underground

" Shall the awful summons hear,
  Which proclaims the judgment near.
  Thine for ever. 'Neath Thy wings
  Hide and save us, King of Kings." [J. J.]

Maurice, Jane, sister of the Rev. P. Maurice (see below), contributed to her brother's *Choral Hymn Book*, 1861, 20 hymns together with one or two additions to others, and all under the signature of "J. M." The best known is "Glory to God, for the Dayspring is dawning " (*Advent*). Taken as a whole her hymns are limited to her brother's book. Miss Maurice was b. at Tyddyn Tudor, Denbighshire, Oct. 19, 1812. [J. J.]

Maurice, Peter, D.D., s. of Hugh Maurice, of Plas Gwyn, Llanrug, Carnarvonshire, and a descendent of one of the oldest families in Wales, was b. at Plas Gwyn, June 29, 1803, and educated at Jesus College, Oxford (B.A. 1826, D.D. 1840). He was Chaplain of New College, 1828–58, and of All Souls, 1837–1858, and Curate of Kennington, Berks, 1829–54. In 1858 he was preferred to the Vicarage of Yarnton. He d. March 30, 1878. He pub. several pamphlets against Popery (*Popery in Oxford*, 1832), and was author and editor of :—

(1) *Choral Harmony,* 1854; (2) *Tunes in Four Parts for Congregational Worship,* 1855; (3) *Supplement to Choral Harmony,* 1858; and (4) *The Choral Hymn Book, Psalms and Hymns for Public and Private Use, Compiled, Prepared, and Composed as a Companion to the Choral Harmony.* N.D. [1861.]

To this *Choral H. Bk.* Dr. Maurice contributed 23 hymns under the initials "P. M." Of these only two or three are found outside of his work, as: "Come, my soul, cast off all sorrow" (*Confidence in God*); and "I lift mine eyes to Zion's hill " (*Ps. cxxi.*). To the *Choral H. Bk.* A. T. Russell and Dr. S. P. Tregelles contributed a large number of original hymns in ms., which are practically unknown elsewhere. This book should be consulted by hymnal compilers. [J. J.]

Maxwell, James, was b. in Renfrewshire in 1720. In his youth he journeyed to England with a hardware pack, but eventually returning to Scotland, he followed the joint occupation of schoolmaster and poet. In 1783, during a famine in Scotland he was reduced to great destitution, and had to earn his bread by breaking stones on the highway. Most of his publications (from 30 to 40 in all)

were produced after that period. The two works in which we are interested are :—

(1) *Hymns and Spiritual Songs. In Three Books.* 1759. (2) *A New Version of the whole of the Book of Psalms in Metre; by James Maxwell, S. D. P.* [Student of Divine Poetry.] Glasgow, 1773.

From the former of these the following hymns are in C. U. :—

1. All glory to the eternal Three. *Holy Trinity.*
2. Didst Thou, dear Jesus [Saviour], suffer shame. *Resignation and Courage.*
3. Go forth, ye heralds, in my Name. *Missions.*

The last of these is in somewhat extensive use in America, where it appeared as early as in the *Prayer Book Coll.*, 1789. Maxwell d. at Paisley (where he was known as the *Paisley Poet*, or as he put it on the title-page of some of his books, *Poet in Paisley*) in 1800.

[J. T. B.]

May not the sovereign Lord of all. *I. Watts.* [*Election.*] This cento is composed of st. iii., v., vii. of his "Behold the potter and the clay," which appeared in his *Hys. and Spiritual S.*, 1709, in 8 st. of 4 l., with the heading "Election sovereign and free." The use of this cento is confined mainly to America. [J. J.]

May the grace of Christ our [the] Saviour; And the Father's, &c. *J. Newton.* [*Close of Service.*] This paraphrase of 2 Cor. xiii. 14, appeared in the *Olney Hymns*, 1779, Bk. iii., No. 101, in 1 st. of 8 l. As a short hymn for the close of Divine Service it has become very popular, and is in use in all English-speaking countries, and sometimes as "May the grace of Christ *the* Saviour." It has also been *tr.* into several languages. The Latin *tr.* "Gratia nostri Salvatoris," is in Bingham's *Hymno. Christ. Lat.*, 1871.

[J. J.]

Mayfart, Johann Matthäus. [Meyfart, J. M.]

Media vita in morte sumus. [*Burial of the Dead.*] In the Paris ed., 1531, of the *Breviarium ad usum insignis ecclesiae Sarum* there is given "Ad Completorium," as the Antiphon to the *Nunc Dimittis*, for 15 days about the middle of Lent :—

Ant. Media vita in morte sumus: quem quaerimus adjutorem nisi te Domine, qui pro peccatis nostris juste irasceris. Sancte Deus: Sancte fortis: Sancte et misericors Salvator: amarae morti ne tradas nos. *V.* Ne projicias nos in tempore senectutis cum defecerit virtus nostra, ne derelinquas nos Domine. Sancte Deus: [Sancte, &c.] *V.* Noli claudere aures tuas ad preces nostras. Sancte fortis: [Sancte, &c.] *V.* Qui cognoscis occulta cordis parce peccatis nostris. Sancte et misericors Salvator amarae morti ne trade nos. (Cambridge Press Reprint, 1879, *Fasc.* i. col. dcliii. and 1882, *Fasc.* ii. col. 229.) It also occurs in the *York Breviary* of 1493 (Surtees Society's reprint, 1880, i. 328).

A rendering of this form is given in the Church of England *Order for the Burial of the Dead* as to be said or sung at the grave: beginning, "In the midst of life we are in death." Dr. H. Bonar, in his *Hys. of Faith and Hope*, 2nd Series, 1861, gives a *tr.* of the antiphon in metre as "In the midst of this our life." The antiphon is found in an 11th cent. ms. in the *British Museum* (Harl. 2961, f. 59) for use during Lent; and in a 12th cent. *Mozarabic Breviary* (Add. 30849, f. 63). It is also given from later mss. by *Mone*, No. 289, and *Morel*, p. 68. As parallels from the Fathers, *Mone* quotes the following :—

Usque ad finem mundi jacemus in morte *Gregor. M.* Mor. 14,68. Unicuique mortalium sub quotidianis vitae hujus casibus innumerabiles mortes quodammodo comminantur. *Augustin.* de civ. dei 1, 9. Mala mors putanda non est, quam bona vita praecesserit. Neque enim, facit malam mortem, nisi quod sequitur mortem. Non itaque multum curandum est eis, qui necessario morituri sunt, quid accidat, ut moriantur, sed moriendo quo ire cogantur. *Augustin.* ibid. He adds that it was probably suggested by the antiphon *Da pacem* (p. 275, ii.).

According to tradition the antiphon was written by Notker (d. 912) after watching the workmen building a bridge at the Martinstobel, a gorge of the Goldach on its course from St. Gall to the Lake of Constanz (the present wooden bridge, 96 feet high, was built in 1468). This tradition, however, has not been traced earlier than the Chronicle of J. Metzler, written in 1613 (*St. Gall MS.* No. 1408), and no evidence can be found for either the story or the ascription. Moreover the antiphon is only given in three of the St. Gall MSS., and these comparatively recent, viz. No. 388 of the 14th cent., No. 418 of 1431, No. 546 of 1507, and none of these name Notker as the author. (See G. Scherrer's *Verzeichniss der Handschriften der Stiftsbibliothek von St. Gallen.* Halle, 1875, pp. 165–167.)

Rambach, in his *Anthologie,* i. p. 248, iii. pp. vii.–viii., says that by the middle of the xiii. cent. it had come into universal use as a hymn of Prayer and Supplication in times of trouble, was sung regularly at Compline on the eve of Lactare Sunday, and was used by the people as an incantation. Bässler, in his *Altchristliche Lieder,* 1858, p. 90, adds that it was used as a war song by the priests accompanying the hosts before and during battle; and that at a synod held at Cologne in 1316 (1310), on account of the magical properties ascribed to it, its use was forbidden unless by permission of the Bishop. Gradually it fell into disuse, and has now disappeared from the services of the Roman Catholic Church. The refrain "Sancte Deus," &c. (founded on Isaiah vi. 3) is said to date from the 5th cent. It is based on the *Trisagion,* an invocation introduced into the Greek service books about A.D. 446. [See **Greek Hymnody,** § x. 7.]

In the 15th cent. *trs.* into German had come into use. One of these is given by *Wackernagel,* ii. p. 749, from a 15th cent. MS. at Munich, thus:—

"En mitten in des lebens zeyt
sey wir mit tod umbfangen:
Wen such wir, der uns hilffe geit,
von dem wir huld erlangen,
Den dich, Herre, al ayne?
der du umb unser missetat
rechtlichen zurnen tuest.
Heyliger herre got,
heyliger starcker got,
heyliger parmhercziger hailer, ewiger got,
lass uns nit gewalden des pittern todes pot."

He also gives (p. 750) nearly the same text from the Basel *Plenarium* of 1514. This stanza Martin Luther took with alterations, added in two stanzas the Gospel delineation of Life through Christ to the Mediaeval picture of Death, and pub. it as a hymn of 3 st. of 14 lines, beginning **Mitten wir im Leben sind,** in the Erfurt *Enchiridion* of 1524. Thence in *Wackernagel,* iii. p. 10, in Schircks's ed. of Luther's *Geistliche Lieder,* 1854, p. 89, and in the *Unv. L. S.* 1851, No. 566. Justly called "A hymn of triumph over the Grave, Death and Hell," it took and still holds a foremost place among German hymns for the dying, and has comforted many in their last conflict. The translations from the German in C. U. are:—

1. **Most holy Lord and God!** The German text from which this is *tr.* is st. iii., ll. 8–13, altered by N. L. Zinzendorf, and included in the *Brüder*

G. B., 1778, as part of No. 585, the Litany on the Life, Sufferings and Death of Jesus Christ, and again, as part of No. 1464, the Church Litany thus:—

"Heiliger Herr und Gott!
Heiliger starker Gott!
Heiliger barmherziger Heiland,
Du ewiger Gott!
Lass uns nie entfallen
Unsern Trost aus deinen Tod.
Kyrie eleison!"

This stanza was *tr.* as part of the Church Litany in the *Moravian H. Bk.* 1789, p. 223, in 7 lines, and included as No. 129 in 1801. In the 1808 *Supplement* to the *Morav. H. Bk.* a single stanza identical save in ll. 5, 6, was included as No. 1175. In the 1826 ed. these stanzas were united as No. 156 (ed. 1886, No. 137), and repeated unaltered as No. 405 in the Irish *Church Hymnal,* 1873. No. 561 in the 1872 *Appendix* to Mercer's *C. P. & H. Bk.* is an adaptation by Edward Jackson, ll. 5, 6 being given in 3 varied forms, making 3 sts.

2. **When we walk the paths of life.** A paraphrase in 14 st. of 6 lines, by Miss Fry, in her *Hy. of the Reformation,* 1845, p. 147. Her st. v., i., x., ix., xiv. altered and beginning "God of mercy, unto Thee," were included in J. Whittemore's *Supp. to All H. Bks.,* 1860, and her st. v., ii., xiv. altered and beginning "God of holiness! to Thee," in Maurice's *Choral H. Bk.,* 1861.

3. **Lo! the mid-day beam of life.** A free *tr.* of st. i. iii., by A. T. Russell, as No. 255 in his *Ps. & Hys.* 1851, and repeated, slightly altered, in *Kennedy,* 1863.

4. **Though in midst of life we be.** Good and full, by R. Massie, in his *M. Luther's Spir. Songs,* 1854, p. 80. Thence, unaltered, save "Have mercy, Lord," for "Kyrie eleison," as No. 481 in the ed. 1857 of Mercer's *C. P. & H. Bk.* (Ox. ed., 1864, No. 468, omitting st. ii.).

5. **The pangs of death are near.** A free *tr.,* in 3 st. of 10 l., as No. 1203 in the Andover *Sabbath H. Bk.,* 1858.

Other **trs.** are:—(1) "In the myddest of our lyvynge, by Bp. Coverdale, 1539 (*Remains* 1846, p. 554). (2) "Living, but in midst of death," by *J. Anderson,* 1846, p. 77 (ed. 1847, p. 90). (3) "What is our life? a fleeting breath," by *Dr. J. Hunt,* 1853, p. 151. (4) "In the midst of life, behold," by *Miss Winkworth,* 1855, p. 235. (5) "In the midst of life is death," by *Dr. H. Mills,* 1856, p. 75. (6) "In the midst of life we are," by Dr. G. Macdonald, in the *Sunday Magazine,* 1867, p. 840, and thence altered in his *Exotics,* 1876, p. 107. (7) "In the midst of life, by death," in S. Garratt's *Hys. & Trans.,* 1867, p. 23. [J. M.]

Mediae noctis tempore. [*Midnight.*]

This hymn is found in slightly varied forms in a MS., c. 890, in the Bodleian (Junius 25 f. 122 b), where it is entitled "A Hymn at Nocturns on Sundays"; in the 8th cent. Bangor *Antiphonary* now at Milan (see **Hymnarium**); in a 9th cent. Rheinau MS.; in an 8th cent. MS. in the Vatican, &c. (See *Daniel,* i., No. 31, iv. p. 26, &c., where it reads "Mediae noctis tempus est.") In an 11th cent. *Mozarabic Hymnarium* in the British Museum (Add. 30,851, f. 168 b), it is given as the second part of a long hymn which begins "Jesu defensor omnium;" and with this text may be compared Neale's *Hymni Ecclesiae,* 1851, p. 6, where he professes to give the text of Arevalus's *Hymnodia Hispanica,* 1786.

[J. M.]

Translations in C. U. :—

1. 'Tis the solemn midnight hour. By E. Caswall. 1st pub. in his *Masque of Mary*, 1858, p. 374, and again in his *Hys. & Poems*, 1873, p. 235, in 13 st. of 4 l. This is repeated in the 2nd ed. 1863 of the *Appendix* to the *H. Noted*, No. 117. In Nicholson's *Appendix Hymnal*, 1866, it is divided into two parts, part ii. beginning " At the solemn midnight hour."

2. It is the midnight hour. By Elizabeth Charles, in her work *The Voice of Christian Life in Song*, 1858, p. 94, in 13 st. of 4 l. This, in a recast form by Canon W. Cooke, was given in the *Hymnary*, 1872, in 6 st. of 8 l., and opening with the same first line.

In W. J. Blew's *Church Hy. and Tune Bk.*, 1852–55, st. i., ii., xv., xvi., xviii. of the " Jesu defensor omnium" form of the text are *tr.* as " Jesu, our Captain and our King." This is repeated in Rice's *Sel.* therefrom, 1870. [J. J.]

Medley, Samuel, b. June 23, 1738, at Cheshunt, Herts, where his father kept a school. He received a good education; but not liking the business to which he was apprenticed, he entered the Royal Navy. Having been severely wounded in a battle with the French fleet off Port Lagos, in 1759, he was obliged to retire from active service. A sermon by Dr. Watts, read to him about this time, led to his conversion. He joined the Baptist Church in Eagle Street, London, then under the care of Dr. Gifford, and shortly afterwards opened a school, which for several years he conducted with great success. Having begun to preach, he received, in 1767, a call to become pastor of the Baptist church at Watford. Thence, in 1772, he removed to Byrom Street, Liverpool, where he gathered a large congregation, and for 27 years was remarkably popular and useful. After a long and painful illness he d. July 17, 1799. Most of Medley's hymns were first printed on leaflets or in magazines (the *Gospel Magazine* being one). They appeared in book form as:—

(1) *Hymns*, &c. Bradford, 1785. This contains 42 hymns. (2) *Hymns on Select Portions of Scripture, by the Rev. Mr. Medley*. 2nd ed. Bristol. W. Pine. 1785. This contains 34 hymns, and differs much from the Bradford edition both in the text and in the order of the hymns. (3) An enlargement of the same in 1787. (4) A small collection of new *Hymns*. London, 1794. This contains 23 hymns. (5) *Hymns. The Public Worship and Private Devotion of True Christians Assisted in some thoughts in Verse; principally drawn from Select Passages of the Word of God. By Samuel Medley. London. Printed for J. Johnson.* 1800. A few of his hymns are also found in a *Coll.* for the use of *All Denominations*, pub. in London in 1782.

Medley's hymns have been very popular in his own denomination, particularly among the more Calvinistic churches. In Denham's *Sel.* there are 48, and in J. Stevens's *Sel.* 30. Their charm consists less in their poetry than in the warmth and occasional pathos with which they give expression to Christian experience. In most of them also there is a refrain in the last line of each verse which is often effective. Those in C. U. include :—

1. Come, join ye saints, with heart and voice. (1800.) *Complete in Christ.*
2. Death is no more among our foes. *Easter.*
3. Eternal Sovereign Lord of all. (1789.) *Praise for Providential Care.*
4. Far, far beyond these lower skies. (1789.) *Jesus, the Forerunner.*

5. Father of mercies, God of love, whose kind, &c. (1789.) *New Year.*
6. Great God, to-day Thy grace impart. *Before Sermon.*
7. Hear, gracious God! a sinner's cry. (1789.) *Lent.*
8. In heaven the rapturous song began. *Christmas.*
9. Jesus, engrave it on my heart. (1789.) *Jesus, Needful to all.*
10. Mortals, awake, with angels join. (1782.) *Christmas.*
11. My soul, arise in joyful lays. (1789.) *Joy in God.*
12. Now, in a song of grateful praise. *Praise to Jesus.* In the *Gospel Magazine*, June, 1776.
13. O could I speak the matchless worth. (1789.) *Praise of Jesus.*
14. O for a bright celestial ray. *Lent.*
15. O God, Thy mercy, vast and free. (1800). *Dedication of Self to God.*
16. O let us tell the matchless love. *Praise to Jesus.*
17. O what amazing words of grace. (1789.) *Fountain of Living Waters.*
18. Saints die, and we should gently weep. (1800.) *Death and Burial.* From his " Dearest of Names, Our Lord and King."
19. See a poor sinner, dearest Lord. *Lent.*
20. Sing the dear Saviour's glorious fame. (1789). *Jesus the Breaker of bonds.*

In 1800 a *Memoir* of Medley was pub. by his son, which is regarded by members of the family now living as authoritative. But in 1833 appeared another *Memoir* by Medley's daughter Sarah, to which are appended 52 hymns for use on Sacramental occasions. These she gives as her father's. But 8 of them are undoubtedly by Thos. Kelly, pub. by him in 1815, and reprinted in subsequent editions of his *Hymns*. The remainder are by Medley. Nearly all of these 52 hymns (both Medley's and Kelly's) have been altered in order to adapt them to Sacramental use. In Sarah Medley's volume, Kelly's hymns all follow one another, and three of them are in a metre which Medley apparently never used. What could have been Sarah Medley's motive in all this it is hard to divine. She is said to have been a clever, though unamiable woman, and was herself the author of a small volume of *Poems* pub. in 1807. In the *Memoir* she does not conceal her hatred of her brother.

[W. R. S.]

Meet and right it is to sing, At every time and place. *C. Wesley.* [*Watchnight. Choral Festivals.*] Pub. in *Hys. and Sac. Poems*, 1749, vol. ii., No. 97, in 4 st. of 8 l. It is No. 14 of 19 " Hymns for the Watchnight"; and together with others from the same Watchnight hymns was frequently reprinted in a separate form (*P. Works*, 1868–72, vol. v. p. 279). It was included, with slight alterations, in the *Wes. H. Bk.*, 1780, No. 212, and has been repeated in several collections in G. Britain and America. Although originally written as a Watchnight hymn it can be easily adapted for Choral Festivals, and as such it would be a hymn of great merit. [J. J.]

Meet and right it is to sing; Glory to our God and King. *C. Wesley.* [*Holy Communion.*] This paraphrase of the words of " The Order for the Administration of the Lord's Supper," &c., in the *Book of Com. Prayer*, " It is very meet, right, and our bounden duty," &c. was pub. in *Hys. and Sac. Poems*, 1740, in 7 st. of 4 l. (*P. Works*, 1868–72, vol. i. p. 286). In 1753 G. Whitefield gave st. i.–iii. and vi. in an altered form in his *Coll. of Hys.*, as No. 61. This form was repeated by M. Madan in his *Ps. & Hys.*, 1760, and again by several others, including Bickersteth, in his *Christian Psalmody*, 1833, (in 3 st.), and thus came into use in the Church of England. [J. J.]

Μέγα καὶ παράδοξον θαῦμα. *St. Germanus.* [*Christmas.*] Dr. Neale, in his *Hys. of the Eastern Church*, 1862, calls these stanzas "Stichera for Christmas-Tide," and ascribes them to St. Anatolius. In the Greek office for Christmas Day in the *Menæa*, they are however ascribed to St. Germanus. In the 4th ed. of the *Hys. of the Eastern Church*, 1882, Mr. Hatherly explains the error thus:—

"The original Greek of this Hymn is in two stanzas, both of which in the *Menœon*, are ascribed to S. Germanus. Adjoining stanzas in the same series of Aposticha from which the first is taken are ascribed to S. Anatolius, hence, probably, the mistake of Dr. Neale, in the previous editions, where this hymn occurs as the work of that saint. The two stanzas in the Aposticha are in inverse order to that here given " (p. 26).

Dr. Neale's *tr.* in his *Hys. of the Eastern Church*, 1862, begins, "A great and mighty wonder," and is in 6 st. of 4 l. In 1863 it was repeated in the *Parish H. Bk.*, in 1868 in the *Appendix* to *H. A. & M.*, and again in other collections in G. Britain and America. Mr. Hatherly gives in his note a prose *tr.* of the original, whilst Dr. Littledale has a blank verse *tr.* In his *Offices from the Service Books of the Holy Eastern Church*, 1863, p. 181, and the original also, at p. 64. [J. J.]

Μέγα τὸ μυστήριον. [Ἄσωμεν πάντες λαοί.]

Meifart, Johann Matthäus. [Meyfart, J. M.]

Mein Erlöser kennet mich. [*Cross and Consolation.*] In Freylinghausen's *Neues geistreiches G. B.*, 1714, No. 783, in 7 st. of 6 l. *Tr.* as "My Redeemer knoweth me," by F. W. Foster and J. Miller, in the *Moravian H. Bk.*, 1789, No. 459 (1886, No. 629). [J. M.]

Mein Gott bei dir ist alle Fülle. [*Cross and Consolation.*] Included as No. 1291 in the *Hirschberg G. B.*, 1741, in 11 st. of 6 l. In the *Liegnitz G. B.*, 1745, No. 620, it is marked as by "M. Joh. Siegm. Hoffmann."

[This is in all probability Johann Siegmund Hoffmann, b. Feb. 8, 1711, at Goldberg in Silesia, who, after studying and graduating M.A. at Wittenberg, was ordained diaconus at Goldberg, June 20, 1737; became pastor primarius in 1738; and d. there May 25, 1754.]

Bunsen, in his *Versuch*, 1833, No. 797, gives st. i.–iii., x., xi. *Tr.* as:—

My God, in Thee all fulness lies. A good *tr.* from *Bunsen* by Miss Winkworth, in her *Lyra Ger.*, 2nd Ser., 1858, p. 191, and her *C. B. for England*, 1863, No. 133. [J. M.

Mein Jesu, wie du willt. *B. Schmolck.* [*Trust in God.*] A fine hymn founded on St. Mark xiv. 36. 1st pub. in his *Heilige Flammen* (ed. 1709, No. 1, p. 3; probably in the 1st ed., 1704), in 11 st. of 8 l., entitled "As God will is my aim." In each st., ll. 1, 8 are "Mein Jesu, wie du willt." Included in many German collections, and recently in the Berlin *G. L. S.*, ed. 1863. *Tr.* as:—

My Jesus, as Thou wilt. A good *tr.*, omitting st. ii., vi., vii., ix., by Miss Borthwick, in

H. L. L. 1st Ser., 1854, p. 56 (1884, p. 57). This was the favourite hymn of the Rev. Professor Skinner of New York (d. 1871), and many American Christians. It has been included in various recent English and American hymnals, but generally abridged, as e.g. in Dale's *English H. Bk.*, 1874; *Songs for the Sanctuary*, N. Y., 1865; *Laudes Domini*, N. Y., 1884, and many others. In addition to these it has also appeared under the following first lines:—

1. **My Saviour, as Thou wilt,** in the Amer. Epis. *Hys. for Ch. & Home*, 1860; Scottish *Presb. Hyl.*, 1876; Canadian *Presb. H. Bk.*, 1880, &c.
2. **O Jesus, as Thou wilt,** in the R. T. S. *Hys. for Christian Worship*, 1866.
3. **Lord Jesus, as Thou wilt,** in Bp. Ryle's *Coll.*, 1860, and the *Baptist Hyl.*, 1879. [J. M.]

Meinhold, Johann Wilhelm, D.D., s. of Georg Wilhelm Meinhold, pastor at Netzelkow on the island of Usedom, was b. at Netzelkow, Feb. 27, 1797, and entered the University of Greifswald in 1813. He became rector of the Town School at Usedom in 1820. In 1821 he was appointed pastor of Coserow in Usedom, and, in 1828, of Crummin in Usedom (D.D. from Erlangen in 1840). He finally became, at Easter, 1844, pastor at Rehwinkel, near Stargard. He was a staunch Conservative, and after passing through the revolutionary period of 1848, this feeling, coupled with his leaning to Roman Catholicism, made him resign his living in the autumn of 1850. He retired to Charlottenburg, a suburb of Berlin, and d. there, Nov. 30, 1851 (*Allg. Deutsche Biog.*, xxi. 235; MS. from Pastor Schmock of Netzelkow, &c.).

Meinhold is perhaps best known by his historical romance *Maria Schweidler, die Bernsteinhexe* (1843), which professed to be taken from an old MS. and was universally accepted as genuine. His poems appeared in his *Gedichte*, Leipzig, 1823; *Vermehrte Gedichte*, Coserow, 1824; *Proben Geistlicher Lieder*, Stralsund, 1834; *Gedichte*, Leipzig, 1835, &c.; and also in Knapp's *Christoterpe* and *Ev. L. S.*

Meinhold's hymns are of considerable interest. Those *tr.* into English are:—

i. **Guter Hirt, du hast gestillt.** *Death of a Child.* This beautiful little hymn is in his *Gedichte*, Leipzig, 1835, vol. i., p. 38, in 3 st. of 6 l., and headed, "Sung in four parts beside the body of my little fifteen months' old son Joannes Ladislaus." (In reply to inquiries addressed to Crummin in January, 1888, Provinzial-Vikar Bahr has kindly informed me that this child was b. at Crummin April 16, 1832, d. there, of teething, on July 2, and was buried there, July 5, 1833.) It is included in Knapp's *Ev. L. S.*, 1837, No. 3411 (1865, No. 2983). *Tr.* as:—

Gentle Shepherd, Thou hast still'd. A full and very good *tr.* by Miss Winkworth, in her *Lyra Ger.*, 2nd Ser., 1858, p. 122. This has passed, unaltered, into many recent hymnals, as the *People's H.*, 1867, *Hymnary*, 1872, *Hy. Comp.*, 1876, &c.; and in America, into the *Presb. Hyl.*, 1874, *Evang. Hyl.*, N. Y., 1880, and others. In the *Appx.* of 1868 to *H. A. & M.*, it was included as No. 358, with *long* in st. i., l. 2, altered to *brief*, and beginning, "Tender Shepherd, Thou hast stilled." This form has been followed in the S. P. C. K. *Church Hys.*, 1871, *Bapt. Hyl.*, 1879, &c.; and in America, in the *Episc. Hymnal*, 1871, *Hys. & Songs of Praise*, N.Y., 1874, *Laudes Domini*, N. Y., 1884, and many others.

ii. **O Bethlehem! O Bethlehem! Was ist in dir geschehen.** *Christmas.* This fine hymn is in the

Appendix to Knapp's *Ev. L. S.*, 1837, p. 837, and in Knapp's *Christoterpe*, 1838, p. 152, in 7 st. of 7 l.   *Tr.* as " O Bethlehem ! O Bethlehem ! " by *Dr. H. Mills*, 1845 (1856, p. 272).   [J. M.]

Melanchthon, Philipp, s. of Georg Schwarzert, armourer to the Elector Philipp of the Palatinate, was b. at Bretten, near Carlsruhe, Feb. 16, 1497.   From 1507 to 1509 he attended the Latin school at Pforzheim, and here he was already, by Johann Reuchlin, called Melanchthon (the Greek form of " Black Earth," his German surname).   In October, 1509, he entered the University of Heidelberg (B.A. 1511), and on Sept. 17, 1512, matriculated at Tübingen, where he graduated M.A., Jan. 25, 1514, and where he remained till 1518 as private lecturer in the philosophical faculty.   On Aug. 29, 1518, he was appointed professor of Greek at the University of Wittenberg, and in January, 1526, also Professor of theology.   He d. at Wittenberg, April 19, 1560 (*Allg. Deutsche Biog.*, xxi. 268, &c.).   Melanchthon is best known as one of the leaders of the German Reformation ; as a theologian (*Loci communes*, 1521, &c.) ; and as the framer of the famous Confession presented to the Diet of Augsburg in 1530, and still accepted as a standard by all the sections of Lutheranism in Germany, America, and elsewhere.   His poems and hymns were written in Latin, and exercised no appreciable influence on the development of German hymnody.   They were edited by Grathusen in 1560, Vincent 1563, Major 1575, &c. ; the most complete ed. being that by C. G. Bretschneider, at Halle, 1842 (*Corpus Reformatorum*, vol. x.).   One of his hymns is noted at p. 293, i. ; and a number of others are *tr.* by Miss Fry in her *Echoes of Eternity*, 1859.   [J. M.]

Men of God, go take your stations. *T. Kelly.* [*Missions.*]   Appeared in his *Hymns*, &c., 1809, No. 156, in 4 st. of 6 l., and headed " Cry aloud, spare not. Isaiah lviii. 1 " (ed. 1853, No. 561).   It also appeared in the August number of the *Evangelical Magazine* the same year, as a " Missionary Hymn," and signed " T. K."   Its modern use is somewhat extensive, especially in America.   [J. J.]

Menæa, The. [Greek Hymnody, § xiv.]

Mencken, Lüder, LL.D., was b. at Oldenburg, Dec. 14, 1658, and became a student of law at the Universities of Leipzig and Jena ;   graduating at Leipzig M.A., 1680, LL.D., 1682.   In 1682 he became tutor in the faculty of law at Leipzig, and was appointed ordinary professor of law in 1702.   After a stroke of paralysis, on June 26, he d. at Leipzig, June 29, 1726.   The only hymn ascribed to him is :—

Ach komm, du süsser Herzens-Gast. *Holy Communion.* Included in the *Geistreiches G. B.*, Darmstadt, 1698, p. 273, in 17 st., and repeated in the Berlin *G. L. S.*, ed. 1863, No. 467. The *trs.* are (1) " Ah come, thou my heart's sweetest Guest," as No. 684 in pt. i. of the *Moravian H. Bk.*, 1754. (2) " Ah ! come, Thou most beloved guest," as No. 1186 in the *Suppl.* of 1808 to the *Moravian H. Bk.* 1801 (1886, No. 981). [J. M.]

Mensch, willt du leben seliglich. *M. Luther.* [*The Ten Commandments.*]   Written as a concise version for Catechetical use ; and 1st pub. in the *Geystliche gesangk Buchleyn*, Wittenberg, 1524.   Thence in *Wackernagel*,

iii. p. 17, in 5 st. of 4 l., and Kyrioleis.   In Schircks's ed. of Luther's *Geistl. Lieder*, 1854, p. 50, and the *Unv. L. S.*, 1851, No. 364.   *Bode*, p. 279, cites the *Allg. Litter. Zeitung*, Jena, 1803, No. 283, as saying that st. i. is found in a practically identical form in a Quedlinburg MS. of 1481.   *Tr.* as :—

Wilt thou, O man, live happily. By R. Massie, in his *M. L.'s Spir. Songs*, 1854, p. 53, repeated in the Ohio *Luth. Hyl.*, 1880, and by *Dr. Bacon*, 1884, p. 43.

Other trs. are :—(1) " Man, wylt thou lyve vertuously," by *Bp. Coverdale*, 1539 (*Remains*, 1846, p. 545) ; (2) " If thou a holy life wouldst see," by *Dr. J. Hunt*, 1853, p. 82 ; (3) " Man, seekest thou to live in bliss," by Dr. G. Macdonald, in the *Sunday Mag.*, 1867, p. 571. In his *Exotics*, 1876, p. 87, it begins, " Man, wouldst thou live all blissfully."   [J. M.]

Mentzer, Johann, was b. July 27, 1658, at Jahmen, near Rothenburg, in Silesia, and became a student of theology at Wittenberg.   In 1691 he was appointed pastor at Merzdorf ;   in 1693 at Hauswalde, near Bischofswerda ;   and in 1696 at Kemnitz, near Bernstadt, Saxony.   He d. at Kemnitz, Feb. 24, 1734 (G. F. Otto's *Lexicon . . . Oberlausizischer Schriftsteller*, ii., 581 ; MS. from Pastor Richter of Kemnitz, &c.).

He was a great friend of J. C. Schwedler, of Henriette Catherine von Gersdorf, and of N. L. von Zinzendorf, all hymn-writers, and all his near neighbours. He was himself greatly tried in the furnace of affliction. He wrote a large number of hymns, over 30 of which appeared in the various hymn-books of his time. Many of them, especially those of Praise and Thanksgiving, and those of Cross and Consolation, are of high merit, though sometimes exaggerated and not very refined in their imagery, and are full of ardent love to Christ, Scriptural, poetical, and also popular in style.

The only one in English C. U. is :—

O dass ich tausend Zungen hätte. *Praise and Thanksgiving.* His best hymn. 1st pub. as No. 496, in Freylinghausen's *G. B.*, 1704, in 15 st. of 6 l., and repeated in many later colls., as the *Unv. L. S.*, 1851, No. 719.

Lauxmann, in *Koch* viii. 350, says this hymn was written in 1704 after his house was burned down. In reply to enquiries addressed to Kemnitz, pastor Richter informs me that the parsonage house there was built in the years 1696 and 1697, and has never been burned down. In 1697 a farmhouse near was destroyed by lightning, and possibly Mentzer may have been living there at the time ; or at any rate this may have suggested the hymn and the story. Lauxmann speaks of the hymn as having been a great favourite of Caroline Perthes of Hamburg, and of J. C. Schlipalius of Dresden, and relates various incidents regarding its blessed and comforting effects.

The *trs.* in C. U. are :—

1. Oh that I had a thousand voices ! A mouth. A full *tr.* by Dr. H. Mills, in his *Horæ Ger.*, 1845 (1856, p. 189) ; repeated, abridged, in the American Luth. Gen. Synod's *Coll.*, 1850–52, the Ohio *Luth. Hyl.*, 1880, &c.

2. Oh be unceasing praise ascending. A good *tr.* of st. i., vii., viii., by A. T. Russell, as No. 203, in his *Ps. & Hys.*, 1851.

3. Oh would I had a thousand tongues. A good *tr.*, omitting st. ix., x., xiii., by Miss Winkworth, in her *Lyra Ger.*, 1st Ser., 1855, p. 170 ; and repeated, abridged, in the Meth. *N. Conn. H. Bk.*, 1863.

4. O would, my God, that I could praise Thee. A good *tr.*, in the original metre, by Miss Winkworth, in her *C. B. for England*, 1863, No. 5, being of st. i., iii.–v, xiv., xv. This was repeated in the *Evang. Hyl.*, N. Y., 1880. An

altered form, beginning with st. iii., "O all ye powers that God implanted," is in Dr. Knight's *Coll.*, Dundee, 1871 and 1874.

5. **I praise Thee, O my God and Father.** By Miss Winkworth, in her *C. B. for England*, 1863, No. 6. This is of st. vi.–viii., xi., xii., and follows the text of Bunsen's *Versuch*, 1833, No. 846, this st. beginning there, "Lob sei dir, treuer Gott und Vater." Her *tr.* is repeated in Dr. Thomas's *Augustine H. Bk.*, 1866.

Other trs. are :—
(1) "O that a thousand tongues were granted," by N. L. Frothingham, 1870, p. 155. (2) "O that a thousand tongues were mine, And each," by Dr. Alexander Mair in the *Family Treasury*, 1872, p. 462.

Other hymns by Mentzer, *tr.* into English but not in C. U., are :—

ii. **Du gehest in den Garten beten.** *Passiontide.* 1st pub. in the *Löbau G. B.*, 1725, as No. 370, in 12 st. of 6 l., marked as by Mentzer and entitled "The true school of prayer of Jesus, praying on the Mount of Olives, Matt. xxvi. 36–46." In the Berlin *G. L. S.*, ed. 1863, No. 223, beginning "Du gehst zum Garten um zu beten," and wrongly ascribed to B. Schmolck. *Tr.* as "Into the garden shade to pray," by J. Kelly, in the *Family Treasury*, 1868, p. 691.

iii. **Wer das Kleinod will erlangen.** *Christian Warfare.* A call to spiritual energy, founded on 1 Cor. ix. 24, 25. Included as No. 783 in the *Neu-vermehrtes Geistreiches G. B.*, Berlin, 1711, in 6 st. of 8 l.; and previously in Schlechtiger's *G. B.*, Berlin, 1704. In the Berlin *G. L. S.*, ed. 1863, No. 679. *Tr.* as "Who would make the prize his own." By *Miss Winkworth*, 1858, p. 161.   [J. M.]

Mercer, William, M.A., b. at Barnard Castle, Durham, 1811, and educated at Trinity College, Cambridge (B.A., 1835). In 1840 he was appointed Incumbent of St. George's, Sheffield. He d. at Leavy Greave, Sheffield, Aug. 21, 1873. His principal work was :—

The Church Psalter and Hymn Book, comprising The Psalter, or Psalms of David, together with the Canticles, Pointed for Chanting ; Four Hundred Metrical Hymns and Six Responses to the Commandments ; the whole united to appropriate Chants and Tunes, for the use of Congregations and Families, by the Rev. William Mercer, M.A. . . . *Assisted by John Goss, Esq.* . . . 1854 ; enlarged 1856 ; issued without music, 1857 ; quarto ed. 1860 ; rearranged ed. (Oxford edition) 1864 ; *Appendix* 1872.

For many years this collection was at the head of all the hymn-books in the Church of England, both in circulation and influence. Its large admixture of Wesleyan hymns, and of translations from the German gave it a distinct character of its own, and its grave and solemn music was at one time exceedingly popular. To it Mercer contributed several translations and paraphrases from the Latin and German, the latter mainly from the Moravian hymn-books ; but his hymn-writing was far less successful than his editing, and has done nothing to increase his reputation. [See England, Hymnody, Church of, § IV.] [J. J.]

Mercy alone can meet my case. *J. Montgomery.* [*Lent.*] In Holland's *Memoirs* of Montgomery this hymn is referred to under the following circumstances. Speaking to Holland on April 3, 1825, of the Rev. Peter Haslem, Montgomery said :—

"On Sunday afternoon he preached in Carver Street Chapel [Sheffield] ; there were few persons present besides myself and some servant girls. What were the divisions or the style of his sermon I do not recollect ; but the text—'O save me for Thy mercies' sake ' (Ps. vi. 4)— was so powerfully impressed upon my mind that it has never since ceased to influence me ; hundreds and thousands of times have I repeated it in meditation and prayer, and I feel at this moment that if I am saved at last, it must be through the free, unmerited mercy of God, exercised towards me for the Saviour's sake."— *Vol. iv. p.* 103.

To this Holland adds the note :—

"How deep an impression these words made upon the poet's heart may also be inferred from his hymn, of which they are the theme. It was composed under the collonnade at Leamington, October 30, 1819, in the midst of much desolation of soul, and is a just picture of the author's feelings at the time."—*Vol. iv. p.* 103.

The hymn was pub. in Montgomery's *Christian Psalmist*, 1825, No. 463, in 5 st. of 4 l., and headed with Mr. Haslem's text, "O save me for Thy mercies' sake " ; and in his *Original Hymns*, 1853, No. 173.   [J. J.]

Merlo, Jacques, sometimes **Meilo,** sometimes **Horst,** and sometimes **Horstius,** was b. of poor parents at Horst, in Germany, 1597, became a parish priest at Cologne, and d. there in 1644. He was the author of the *Paradisus Animæ Christianæ*, Cologne, 1630, which has been several times translated, and recently partly by Dr. Pusey in 1847, and in full by Canon F. Oakeley in 1850, as *The Paradise of the Christian Soul*, and in which several Latin hymns by older writers were embodied. So far as we are aware he was not the writer of hymns.   [J. J.]

Merrick, James, M.A., was b. in 1720, and educated at Oxford, where he became a Fellow of Trinity College. He entered Holy Orders, but his health would not admit of parish work. He d. at Reading, 1769. His publications include :—

(1.) *Messiah, a Divine Essay. Humbly dedicated to the Reverend the Vice-Chancellor of the University of Oxford and the Visitors of the Free School in Reading. By James Merrick, Ætat.* 14, *Senior Scholar of the School at their last Terminal Visitation, the* 7*th of October,* 1734. *Reading.* (2) *The Destruction of Troy. Translated from the Greek of Tryphiodorus into English Verse, with Notes, &c.* 1742. (3) *Poems on Sacred Subjects. Oxford.* 1763. (4) *The Psalms of David Translated or Paraphrased in English Verse. By James Merrick, M.A., late Fellow of Trinity College, Oxford. Reading. J. Carnan and Co.* 1765. 2nd ed. 1766. A few only of these paraphrases were divided into stanzas. In 1797 the Rev. W. D. Tattersall pub. the work "Divided into stanzas for Parochial Use, and paraphrased in such language as will be intelligible to every capacity . . . with a suitable Collect to each Psalm from the Works of Archbishop Parker."

Merrick's paraphrases, although weak and verbose, were in extensive use in the early part of the present century, both in the Church of England and with Nonconformists. They have, however, fallen very much into disuse. Those in modern hymn-books, mainly in the form of centos, include :—

1. Blest Instructor, from Thy ways. *Ps. xix.*
2. Descend, O Lord ! from heaven descend. *Ps. cxliv.* (*In time of National Peril.*)
3. Far as creation's bounds extend. *Ps. cxlv.*
4. God of my strength, the wise, the just. *Ps. xxxi.*
5. He who with generous pity glows. *Ps. xli.*
6. How pleasant, Lord, Thy dwellings are. *Ps. lxxxiv.*
7. Lift up your voice and thankful sing. *Ps. cxxxvi.*
8. Lo, my Shepherd's hand divine. *Ps. xxiii.*
9. Lord, my Strength, to Thee I pray. *Ps. xxviii.*
10. My heart its noblest theme has found. *Ps. xlv.*
11. O let me, [gracious] heavenly Lord extend. *Ps. xxxix.*
12. O turn, great Ruler of the skies. *Ps. li.*
13. Praise, O praise the Name divine. *Ps. cl.*
14. Sing, ye sons of [men] might, O sing. *Ps. xxix.*
15. Teach me, O teach me, Lord, Thy way. *Ps. cxix.*
16. The festal morn, my [O] God, is come. *Ps. cxxii.* (*Sunday Morning.*)
17. The morn and eve Thy praise resound. *Ps. lxv.* (*Harvest.*)
18. To Thy pastures, fair and large. *Ps. xxiii.*

From his *Poems on Sacred Subjects*, 1763, the following centos have also come into C. U.:

19. Author of good, to Thee we turn. *Resignation.*
20. Eternal God, we look to Thee. *Resignation.*
21. 'Tis enough, the hour is come. *Nunc Dimittis.*

[J. J.]

Messiah! at Thy glad approach. *M. Bruce.* [*Advent.*] This hymn, which we have ascribed to *M. Bruce* (q.v.) on evidence given in his memoir in this work, was written probably about 1764–65, for a singing class at Kinnesswood, Scotland, and was first pub. by John Logan in his *Poems*, 1781, p. 113, No. 7, in 6 st. of 4 l. Although a vigorous hymn, and possessing much poetic beauty, it has not come into extensive use. In the American *Church Praise Bk.*, N. Y., 1881, st. vi. and iv. are given as "Let Israel to the Prince of Peace." Orig. text as in Logan's *Poems* in Dr. Grosart's *Works of M. Bruce*, 1865, p. 144. [J. J.]

Metcalf, Lucy E. [Akerman, Lucy E.]

Methinks I stand upon the rock. *T. Kelly.* [*Balaam. The Safety of God's people.*] 1st pub. in Kelly's *Coll. of Ps. & Hys.*, 1802, No. 271, and again in his *Hymns*, 1st ed. 1804, and later editions, in 9 st. of 6 l. (ed. 1853, No. 290). In Hall's *Mitre H. Bk.*, 1836, No. 121, appeared "Come, let us stand as Balaam stood," in 3 st. of 6 l. This has usually been attributed to E. Osler. It is a cento, st. i., ii. being st. i., ii. altered from this hymn by Kelly, and st. iii. an addition probably by Osler, who assisted Hall in preparing the *Mitre H. Bk.* In the Hall MSS. there is no ascription of authorship. [J. J.]

Methodist Hymnody.—Methodism has made liberal contributions to the hymnody of the Christian Church. Before the first Methodist Society was formed, its founders saw the importance of singing in religious worship, and provided, out of the best available material then at command, a collection of *Psalms and Hymns* for that purpose. John Wesley made some excellent translations of German hymns, and his brother, Charles Wesley, began to write spiritual songs immediately after his conversion. His father, the Rector of Epworth, and his elder brother, S. Wesley, jun., had each written a few good hymns at a still earlier date, which remain in use at the present time. Charles Wesley continued to write hymns for nearly fifty years, and he has left over six thousand five hundred hymns and sacred poems, some of which are amongst those most frequently found in collections used in public worship. Some of the followers of J. Wesley have also contributed hymns, both in the last and in this century, which have been included in many collections, and are of permanent interest.

Before dealing with the hymnody of the various Methodist bodies, it will be necessary to present some details concerning the rise and development of the principal sources from which all Methodist hymnody is derived. These sources are the *Poetical Works of John and Charles Wesley.*

i. *Poetical Works of John and Charles Wesley.*—Charles Wesley pub. about *fifty* different books and tracts of hymns, from nearly all of which hymns have been selected

for use in the churches. When he was a "Missioner in Georgia," John Wesley prepared and published *A Collection of Psalms and Hymns*, which he described, in an enlarged edition of Wood's *Athenæ Oxoniensis*, as of the year 1736, but the imprint on the title-page is "Charles-Town, printed by Lewis Timothy, 1737." This work was the first collection of hymns published for use in the Church of England. The volume "illustrates his care to provide for the spiritual wants of those to whom he ministered; his earnest and serious temper; and his prominent ecclesiasticism." On his return to England, he prepared a new edition of that collection, and issued it in 1738. It is a 12mo book of 84 pages. Of the American book, only one copy is known to exist; of the English reprint of 1738 three copies are known, one of which is in the Lambeth Palace library. [For details, see **England, Hymnody, Church of,** § I.]

The first Methodists at Oxford sang psalms in proportion to their earnestness in religion; when they declined and shrank from the reproach of serious godliness, the singing in their meetings was given up. After the conversion of the two Wesleys, in May, 1738, singing was resumed; and from that time to the present, frequent singing has been an essential part of Methodist worship. To encourage this form of service, J. Wesley, as early as 1742, provided tune-books for the use of his followers (some of which are in use at the present time); and that all might learn to sing, he printed the melody only. We will now enumerate the original poetical works of J. and C. Wesley in detail.

1. The first collection pub. by John and Charles Wesley with their names on the title-page was entitled *Hymns and Sacred Poems*, 1739, 12mo, pp. 223, and contained 139 hymns. This was reprinted the same year without the *Poems*, and a third ed., unabridged, is also dated 1739. In this book are given the first of Charles Wesley's compositions, and out of this volume 50 hymns were selected for the *Wes. H. Bk.*, 1780. A fourth ed. appeared in 1743, and another in 1747.

2. Early in 1740 appeared *Hymns and Sacred Poems*, an entirely new book of 209 pages, with 96 hymns, and amongst them some of the most popular now in use, including "O for a thousand tongues to sing," (p. 423, i.), and "Jesu, lover of my soul" (p. 590, i.). This volume supplied 54 hymns to the *Wes. H. Bk.*, 1780.

3. In 1741 the Wesleys issued *A Collection of Psalms and Hymns*, a volume of 126 pages, containing 165 compositions. This was not a reprint of the 1738 book, though containing a few of the pieces therein, but the *Psalms* were C. Wesley's version of various Psalms, and the *Hymns* were new. Only 3 of these found their way into the *Wes. H. Bk.* of 1780. After the death of John Wesley, Dr. Coke made additions thereto which doubled its size. It came into general use, so that the Conference of 1816 recommended it for "use in Methodist Congregations in the forenoon," from which it came to be called *The Morning Hymn Book*, and such it remained till 1831, when the *Suppl.* was added to the 1780 book.

4. In 1741 appeared *Hymns on God's Everlasting Love*, in 36 pages, containing 38 new hymns, of which 19 are in the *Wes. H. Bk.*, 1780. The 2nd ed. contains 84 pages; the 3rd is dated 1770.

5. In 1742 a new volume of *Hymns and Sacred Poems* appeared, with 304 pages and 155 new hymns, of which 102 were selected for the *Wes. H. Bk.* of 1780.

6. An enlarged ed. of the collection of *Psalms and Hymns* appeared in 1743, containing 138 hymns, 17 of which are in the 1780 book.

7. In 1744 three tracts of hymns were issued, with the titles of *Hymns for the Nativity*, 18 hymns; *Hymns for the Watchnight*, 11; and *Funeral Hymns*, 16. From these three 10 hymns are in the *Wes. H. Bk.*

8. Four tracts and one volume of hymns appeared in 1745. From two only of these have selections been made. *A Short View of the Differences between the*

Moravians and J. and C. Wesley contains 6 hymns, 3 of which are in the *Wes. H. Bk.* The second is a most important work : *Hymns on the Lord's Supper by Charles Wesley*, a volume of 141 pages and 166 hymns, "with a preface concerning the Christian Sacrament and Sacrifice, extracted from Dr. Brevint." From this work 20 hymns were selected for the *Wes. H. Bk.* of 1780. The *Hys. for the Lord's Supper* have been often reprinted, but generally without the preface, which was never intended, as Charles Wesley has only versified portions of Dr. Brevint's remarks, in some of the hymns. In the extracts from Dr. Brevint the doctrine of the True and Real Presence is taught, and Charles Wesley embodies the teaching of the preface in his verses. In the fourth section "Concerning the Sacrament as a Means of Grace," and in paragraph 5, are these words in reference to the efficacy of the Death of Christ : "This victim having been offered up in the fulness of times, and in the midst of the world, which is Christ's great Temple, and having been thence carried up to Heaven, which is His Sanctuary ; from thence spreads Salvation all around, as the burnt-offering did its smoke. And thus His Body and Blood have everywhere, but especially at this Sacrament, a true and real presence." Catching the same inspiration, Charles Wesley expresses the same idea in at least seven of the hymns which follow :—

Hy. 33. "Drink Thy blood for sinners shed
          Taste Thee in the broken Bread."

Hy. 57. "Who shall say how bread and wine
          God into man conveys :
          How the bread His flesh imparts,
          How the wine transmits His blood ?"

Hy. 65. "Now on the sacred table laid
          Thy flesh becomes our food."

Hy. 77. "Taste Thee in the broken Bread
          Drink Thee in the mystic wine."

Hy. 81. "We come with confidence to find
          Thy real presence here."

Hy. 116. "To every faithful soul appear
           And shew Thy real presence here."

Hy. 124. "Yet may we celebrate below
           And daily thus Thine offering shew
           Exposed before Thy Father's eyes
           In this tremendous mystery :
           Present Thee bleeding on the tree
           Our Everlasting sacrifice."

It is worthy of remark, that Charles Wesley, in his *Journals*, makes no mention of the publication of this volume of *Hymns* during the year 1745, but from February to July of that year, he makes special mention of about a dozen Sacramental Services, which are described as occasions of much blessing to himself and to others ; and during the octave of Easter he communicated every day. The latter half of the year, the subject is scarcely mentioned. It seems probable, therefore, that the book was passing through the press during the months when he was so much under Sacramental influence and power. In justice to C. Wesley, it should be recorded, that the "real presence" is not alluded to in any of the six thousand hymns he wrote, apart from this 1745 book, nor did he ever allude to it in his pulpit discourses. In his *Journals*, he names many instances of his baptizing adult persons, but the subject of Holy Baptism does not seem to have inspired his muse, except in "God of eternal truth and love," in the *Hymns for the use of Families*, 1767, and one or two others. This is the more noticeable when it is considered how strict he was generally in observing the ordinances of the Church.

9. The year 1746 was a remarkable one for the variety of subjects which occupied Charles Wesley's poetic mind ; no less than *nine* separate tracts of hymns were issued during that year, including *Hymns for Times of Trouble; Hymns and Prayers for Children; On the Trinity; On the Great Festivals;* of *Petition and Thanksgiving for the Promise of the Father;* for *Our Lord's Resurrection;* for *Ascension Day; Graces before and after Meat;* and for the *Public Thanksgiving* in October of that year. These introduced 154 new compositions, of which only 12 found their way into the *Wes. H. Bk.* of 1780. The *Festival Hymns* had Lampe's Tunes issued with them, which insured for them a long term of popularity.

10. Only one new work was issued in 1747 : *Hymns for those that seek and those that have Redemption in the Blood of Jesus Christ*, containing 72 pages and 52 new hymns, 25 of which are placed in the 1780 book.

11. In 1748, C. Wesley wrote a number of hymns on Marriage, the subject being then uppermost in his mind, but they were not then printed. He was married in the spring of 1749, and when the arrangements were made with his brother respecting his stipend, the question of house-furnishing was not considered. To

meet the emergency, C. Wesley gathered up all his unpublished compositions, and, without consulting his brother John, issued them in two volumes. The work was sold by subscription through the preachers, was a great success, and fully accomplished the object contemplated. Those volumes extend to 668 pages, with 455 new hymns, with the old title "*Hymns and Sacred Poems.*" In that work will be found the largest number of the author's best hymns, and it has yielded 143 compositions to the 1780 book.

12. In 1750 only two hymn tracts appeared, *Hymns for New Year's Day*, and *Hymns Occasioned by the Earthquake, March 8th.* The first contained 7 new hymns, one of which has been in use in Methodist Services, once at least every year since it appeared : viz. :— the hymn sung at the close of every watch-night Service, commencing "Come let us anew, our journey pursue." The 2 hymns selected from the *Earthquake* Tract ("Woe to the men on earth who dwell," and "By faith we find the place above") are said to be amongst the boldest of the poet's theological conceptions. In 1753 appeared *Hymns and Spiritual Songs intended for the use of Real Christians.* This was followed in 1756 by an enlarged edition of the *Earthquake Hymns*, with 22 hymns ; and *Hymns for the Year* 1756, particularly for the *Fast Day, Feb. 6th*, with 17 new hymns, of which 5 are in the 1780 book.

13. In 1758 was issued *Hymns of Intercession for all Mankind*, but being without author's name, the popular judgment hymn given therein, "Lo ! he comes with clouds descending" (p. 681, i.), was, for nearly a century, attributed to Martin Madan. This tract has 34 pages and 40 new hymns, of which 8 are in the 1780 book.

14. Three new works were issued in 1759, namely, *Funeral Hys.*, enlarged to 70 pages, with 43 new hymns ; *Hymns for the Expected Invasion*, with 8 new hymns ; and *Hymns to be used on the Thanksgiving Day*, November 29, and after it 24 pages, with 15 new hymns.

· 15. In 1761 appeared a volume of 144 pages and 134 hymns, with the title, *Hymns for those to whom Christ is All in All.* This was a selection intended for popular use ; it reached a 3rd ed. During the same year, John Wesley issued a volume of *Select Hymns for the Use of Christians of all Denominations*, to which was added an admirable selection of *Tunes Annext.* This useful volume was used at the Foundry ; a 2nd ed., corrected, was issued in 1765, a 3rd in 1770, and a 4th in 1773. In 1761, to encourage and improve the vocal part of Divine Service, John Wesley issued *Sacred Melody; or, a Choice Collection of Psalm and Hymn Tunes;* another book of Tunes called *Sacred Harmony*, and an abridged ed. of the latter.

16. One of Charles Wesley's largest contributions to the service of song in the Church appeared in 1762, and was entitled *Short Hymns on Select Passages of Holy Scripture*, 2 vols., containing no fewer than 2030 new compositions, out of which 99 were selected for the 1780 book. This work was rigidly revised by the author ; and was republished in a somewhat condensed form, in 2 vols., 1794–96, after the author's death. In that work are some popular hymns, and elegant renderings of Scripture phraseology.

17. *Hymns for Children* appeared in 1763, with 100 new compositions ; and *Hymns for the Use of Families* in 1767, a volume of 176 pages and 188 hymns. In the same year came *Hymns on the Trinity*, with 132 pages and 182 hymns. From these three works 51 hymns are selected for the *Wes. H. Bk.*, 1780. Five or six other tracts of hymns followed, but out of these only one hymn found its way into the 1831 *Supplement* to the *Wes. H. Bk.* taken from *Hymns for the Nation and for the National Fast Day, February 8th*, 1782.

These are the original publications from which are derived all the Wesley hymns now in use in the Hymnals of all the churches. All these volumes and tracts (except the *Ps. & Hys.* printed at Charlestown in 1736–37), with *fac similes* of title pages, are reprinted in the *Poetical Works of John and Charles Wesley*, Lond. 1868–72 (13 volumes), and the same are tabulated with dates, titles, pages, sizes and number of hymns, in G. J. Stevenson's *Methodist H. Bk. Notes*, 1883, p. 635.

ii. *Wesleyan Methodists.*—1. With such a variety of works, most of which were occasionally used by the Methodist Societies, much confusion and difficulty naturally arose, so that John Wesley did wisely when, in 1779, (soon after he had opened his chapel in the

City Road, London), he prepared out of those numerous works a collection for general use in all his societies, which was issued in 1780. The necessity for such a work was felt all over the country. It extended to 504 pages, and 16 pages of contents and index, and included 525 hymns. The contents were divided into the five parts and twenty sections as still retained in the revised ed. of 1875. The 2nd ed., corrected, appeared in 1781, the 3rd in 1782, the 4th 1784, 5th 1786, 6th 1788, 7th 1791. Up to 1791 it remained unaltered, although, every edition having to be set up afresh, errors had crept in. These increased till 1797, when a few of the preachers presumed to prepare a new edition, which they issued with an ornamental title-page. In it about 36 hymns were changed, and some of the favourite hymns of the people, designedly excluded by J. Wesley, were included, and at the end 25 additional hymns were given, making the total 550. This edition gave so little satisfaction to the people that the Conference of 1799 appointed Dr. Coke, G. Storey, H. Moore, and Adam Clarke "to reduce the large Hymn Book to its primitive simplicity, as in the second edition, with liberty to add a note in places to explain difficult passages for the sake of the unlearned, and with discretionary power in respect to the additional hymns." They rigidly revised the book, omitted 6 of the additional hymns, extended the work to 560 hymns and published it in 1800. The added hymns introduced a new and important feature into the collection, which is a distinct landmark (so to speak) in the history of Methodism, by including 7 hymns by C. Wesley on *The Lord's Supper*. All the unsold copies of the 1797 book were destroyed, and the revised edition remained unaltered for thirty years.

2. The publication at Manchester in 1825 of a piratical edition of the Collection, together with copyright needs, and the desire for greater variety of hymns, led the Conference to appoint the Revs. Thomas Jackson and Richard Watson to make such a selection as would meet the wishes of the people, and in 1831 a *Supplement* was issued, extending the collection from 560 to 769 hymns. These were chosen from some of Charles Wesley's original MSS.; from his *Festival Hymns* and from the collection of *Psalms and Hymns* then known as the *Morning Hymn Book*. Many from Dr. Watts were also added, and a few of a popular character which were favourites with the people. The Preface is dated November 9, 1830, and in this *Dictionary* the date of this *Supplement* is given as 1830, the date of the *Preface*. Of the entire collection, including this *Supplement*, 668 hymns are by the Wesleys (father and three sons), and 101 by 20 other authors. Dr. Watts is represented by 66. Only two hymns in the book are specially adapted for Holy Baptism, one by Dr. Doddridge, commencing "See Israel's gentle Shepherd stand;" the other by C. Wesley, "God of eternal truth and love."

3. The copyright of the entire collection had for some years depended on only a few hymns, and when the right in those had run out, a new collection became a necessity. A collection was issued by a London publisher independently of the Conference, in 1873. It was an improvement on the 1831 book. It was compiled by a layman at Bristol, and included 1076 hymns, amongst them being many of the best modern compositions, and 71 chants and anthems. The Wesleyan Conference, however, could not recognise the work, and the Book Committee were obliged to prepare a new collection. A large committee took the matter in hand, and devoted much time and care thereto. The edition of 1800 up to hymn 539 was retained, but each hymn was compared with the original, and rigidly criticised; a few were omitted altogether; others had verses left out, or added; and in this way 49 hymns were changed in the standard part of the collection. The new *Supplement* includes 487 hymns. Its contents embrace what may be designated as a poetical body of divinity. In this respect it is more complete than the book prepared by John Wesley, in that it includes hymns for Holy Baptism, the Lord's Supper, and Prayers for children. It is divided into nine sections, in which the hymns are classified according to their subjects, or the season for which they are adapted, a special feature being the "Select Psalms." The authors and translators number 120. Of these 74 contribute each one hymn, and of the rest 41 have hymns therein, numbering from 2 to 9 each, the total ending with 11 by P. Doddridge, 13 by J. Montgomery, 58 by I. Watts, and 724 by C. Wesley. For the first time the authors' names are added in the index of first lines. *The Methodist Hymn Book, illustrated with Biography, History, Incident, and Anecdote*, by George John Stevenson, M.A., 1883, deals with this collection in an exhaustive manner.

4. Taken as a whole, whilst allowing for its distinct and definite advocacy of Methodist doctrine, and admitting the otherwise great preponderance of C. Wesley's hymns, we judge this book as ranking with the best in use amongst Protestant Christians. It is intensely Methodistic, and it is more. It retains the Standard Hymn Book, not wrongly so-called, which John Wesley gave to his people in 1780; and it has added thereto much that is choice and valuable from most branches of the Church of Christ. The wisdom displayed by the Conference in retaining the *Standard* portion of the old collection is realized when we find that it has done more to conserve the essential doctrines of Methodism amongst the multitude than the combined prose writings of all her divines.

5. The provision for *Children and Young Persons*, which is an important feature in modern hymnody, is not new, either in Methodism, or elsewhere. For the Methodists C. Wesley pub. his *Hymns for Children*, in 1763. Many of these compositions are far beyond the comprehension of children, but their object was attained in drawing attention to the spiritual wants and education of the young. In 1814, Joseph Benson, a preacher and divine of high repute with the Methodists, published:—

Hymns for Children and Young Persons, on the Principal Truths and Duties of Religion and Morality. Selected from various Authors, and arranged in a natural and Systematic Order. London, 1806.

Joseph Benson also published eight years afterwards :—

Hymns for Children, selected chiefly from the publications of the Revs. John and Charles Wesley, and Dr. Watts, and arranged in proper Order. London, 1814.

From the Preface to the first of these collections (the second has no preface), we find that it was compiled and published "to meet the wishes of many persons in different parts of the United Kingdom," but there is no indication that it (or the second collection either) had the official sanction of the Conference, although "printed at the Conference Office." The Conference, however, took up the matter at a later date, and in 1835 Thomas Jackson and Richard Watson, "compiled by the direction of the Methodist Book Committee in London" :—

A Collection of Hymns for the Use of Wesleyan-Methodist Sunday Schools. London, 1835.

At the request of the same "Book Committee of the Wesleyan Conference," Dr. W. H. Rule compiled, and the Conference published, in 1857 :—

The Wesleyan-Methodist Sunday-School Hymn-Book. London, 1857.

This was followed in 1870 by a "Selection of hymns suitable for use in Day and Sunday Schools," . . . "made by a number of Ministers, at the request of the Wesleyan Methodist Book Committee," which was compiled chiefly by the Rev. Samuel Lees, and published as:—

The Methodist Scholars' Hymn-Book. London, 1870.

Finally, in 1879, there was issued, after some delay which is apologised for in the preface : —

The Methodist Sunday-School Hymn-Book. A Collection of Hymns and Spiritual Songs for Use in Schools and Families. Compiled by Direction of the Wesleyan Methodist Conference. London, 1879.

This collection of 589 hymns, by a very large number of authors, is not only the best hymn-book for children extant amongst the Methodist Societies, but it has no equal elsewhere except the Church of England *Children's Hymn-Book* by Mrs. Carey Brock. Both the official hymn-books issued by the Conference have suitable tunes pub. with some of the editions. [See Children's Hymns, § iv.]

iii. *Methodist New Connexion.*—1. This branch of the Methodist family originated in 1796; the cause being the exclusion of Alexander Kilham from the ministry by the Conference of that year. From the time of J. Wesley's death, those preachers whom he had ordained had occasionally administered the Sacrament of the Lord's Supper. One of the old preachers who had done so, was much blamed for his conduct. Mr. Killiam wrote a defence of his conduct in *An Address to the Members and Friends of the Newcastle Society*, in which he also discussed the question of the right of the people to have the Sacrament from their own preachers. That address, in pamphlet form, was much commended by many of the old preachers, including Dr. Coke, H. Moore, J. Pawson, T. Taylor, W. Bramwell, S. Bradburn, and others, some of whom freely distributed the Address in their circuits. They also, by letters, encouraged Kilham to continue his advocacy of the rights of the people to the privileges asked for by them. Kilham wrote and spoke freely on the subject for a few years, and for so doing he was, at the desire of Mr. Mather, censured by the Conference of 1793. Other preachers, including Mr. Taylor and Mr. Bradburn, had also published their opinions in support of Kilham's views, but they were not censured. For this act of partiality, the Conference was blamed, and Kilham was encouraged by many preachers who desired to conciliate the Societies rather than the Conference. At the Conference of 1795, some steps were taken to reconcile the contending parties, under the name of the "Plan of Pacification," but it did not fully meet the case. Soon afterwards Kilham published a pamphlet entitled *The Progress of Liberty*, in which he pointed out the defects in the Plan of 1795, and sketched the *Outline of a Constitution*. This *Outline* included the following principles :—

1st. That the power to admit and expel members should be the act of the preachers with the consent of the people. 2. The members to have advice in choosing their leaders. 3. That local preachers be examined and admitted by preachers and lay officers conjointly. 4. That Quarterly Meetings should have a voice in recommending young men as preachers. 5. That the people have the right to representation in all the Church Courts, including the Annual Conference. 6. That religious worship be held in such hours as were most convenient for the people. 7. That the Societies receive the Sacraments of Baptism and the Lord's Supper from the hands of their own Ministers.

For publishing this pamphlet, and advocating the principles it contained, Kilham was tried and expelled from the ministry, in 1796. Those principles became the basis of the Methodist New Connexion, which took permanent form at a Conference held in August 1797, in Ebenezer Chapel, Leeds. Kilham's chief opponent was Alexander Mather, whom J. Wesley had ordained as a bishop to exercise authority in his Societies. The New Connexion was commenced with 9 circuits, 7 itinerant preachers (5 of whom had belonged to the parent Society), and over 5,000 members. It was in defence of the principles advocated by Kilham that the new Society was formed; and the preachers and lay-officers have exercised equal rights in the government of the Society throughout its history.

2. At the first the New Connexion adopted the use of the *Wes. H. Bk.*, but a few years later a *Supplement* was prepared by order of the Conference, and was designated *The Small Hymn Book*. It consisted of 276 hymns. This *Supplement* reached a 5th edition in 1810, and was used till the new hymn-book of 1835 was issued.

3. Soon after the Wesleyans issued their *Supplement* in 1831, the New Connexion Conference appointed a committee to prepare a revised and enlarged collection for use in their Societies. The Revs. Thomas Mills and William Shuttleworth were the acting members. The Preface says that they took from the *Wes. H. Bk.* and from its *Supplement* the best hymns "for poetic merit, happy Scriptural illustration, and those which most clearly expressed breathings after peace and holiness. With these were combined a number of other hymns from various authors, and a few by pious persons of poetic genius, composed for the work." Such hymns only were admitted as "gave prominence to those doctrinal and experimental truths which are the chief glory of Methodism." This work was

divided into seven parts, and forty-one sections. All the copyright hymns in the *Wes. H. Bk.* were omitted, and, as far as the Committee knew them, the names of authors were added to the hymns. This was the first official Methodist Collection with authors' names. The total number of hymns was 664, and of these nearly 50 were new, and by 27 authors not found in the *Wes. H. Bk.* This book was in use for over a quarter of a century, when it was superseded by the Collection published in 1863.

4. This *New Collection* was undertaken by a Committee, with the Rev. Henry Piggin as chief acting member. It was first issued in May, 1863, and included 1024 hymns by 130 authors. A collection of suitable tunes for each hymn, prepared by the Rev. James Ogden, has since been published.

5. Whilst Mr. Piggin and his coadjutors were preparing a new collection for congregational use, the Rev. John Stokoe, then a New Connexion minister, now a clergyman in the Irish Church, was preparing a smaller collection for use in their Sunday schools and homes, which was pub. in December, 1862, with the title *The Juvenile Hymn Book.* It contains 315 hymns, classified under seventeen sections, with authors' names added to each where known.

iv. *Primitive Methodists.*—1. This branch of the Methodist family originated in 1810 by the expulsion from the Methodist Society of Hugh Bourne (q.v.). Previous to this H. Bourne had compiled a small hymn-book, which he published in 1809. What was long known amongst the Primitives as *The Small Book* was issued in 1821, and consisted of 154 hymns, most of which were by Charles Wesley, and William Sanders, a few by Dr. Watts, and 16 by Bourne. This *Small Book* was widely known in all parts of the land by the first couplet in the book—

> "Christ he sits on Zion's hill,
> He receives poor sinners still,"

with the chorus:

> "I a soldier sure shall be
> Happy in Eternity."

2. With the growth of the Society, a larger number of hymns was required, and in 1824–25 Bourne prepared and issued what he called the *Large Hymn Book,* which included 536 hymns. Of these 16 were by William Sanders, 146 were the joint production of William Sanders and Hugh Bourne; a few were by Dr. Watts, Cowper, and Dr. Doddridge; 225 by Charles Wesley; and 20 new hymns by Bourne. A lengthy preface describes the Service of Song as set forth in the Old and New Testaments, and deals with Private Prayer, Preaching, Prayer Meetings, Class Meetings, Love Feasts, Camp Meetings, and Musical Instruments. Bourne says of the new hymns that they are "of a superior cast, and they lead into the mystery of faith."

3. As the Societies increased, a still greater variety of hymns was desired, and the Conference appointed the Rev. John Flesher to prepare an enlarged book. He acknowledges his own inability for performing the duty, but collected 852 hymns "from numerous popular authors, living and deceased, and enriched with original hymns and selected ones, altered

or re-made." Mr. Flesher adds: "I had thought my lack of sufficient poetic genius and taste would save me from such an appointment, but when chosen, I was surprised, afraid, and humbled, and durst not disobey." This unqualified editor proceeded to correct and mangle over 225 hymns. It need not be added, that few but himself have approved of his work. In his preface he remarks:—

"Knowing that Providence had not stereotyped the productions of any poet, I have freely altered or re-made hymns from authors of different grades of talent and reputation – an important item in strengthening the copyright."

This book, issued in 1854, may be safely described as the worst edited and most severely mutilated collection of hymns ever published.

4. The Conference of 1882 appointed a Committee to prepare an entirely new collection. This was published, in 1887, as *The Primitive Methodist Hymnal, compiled by a Committee appointed by the Conference of* 1882. It contains 1052 hymns by over 300 known authors and translators (besides hymns by several that are unknown), ranging from the earliest ages of hymnody to the present, and from the Unitarians on the one hand, to the Latin and Greek Churches on the other. It is divided into twelve sections, which are again subdivided: but the arrangement of subjects is more after the manner of the Congregationalists than that usually adopted in Methodist collections, and is the arrangement of Flesher's book simplified. It is supplied with the usual Indices of first lines of "verses," of "texts," of "subjects," &c., and a table of "authors and translators," with the numbers of their hymns. This last is in addition to the names of the authors being added to the hymns throughout the book. It is purely and intensely Methodistic, whilst in the number of its authors, in the comprehensiveness of its subjects, in the richness of its poetry, in the care and accuracy displayed in its text, and in the designations of authorship, it has no equal in Methodist hymnody.

5. Provision for the children in the Sunday schools has been made by the publication of the *Primitive Methodist Sunday School Hymn Book,* in 1879. It was edited by G. Booth, M.D., and William Beckworth. It is an admirable collection, is well edited, and is set to suitable music. Its use is extensive.

v. *United Methodist Free Churches.* — 1. These Churches were formed by the amalgamation, in 1857, of several separate Societies, the members of which had formerly belonged to the Wesleyan Methodist Society. The first of these was that known as the *Protestant Methodists,* who, in 1827–28, came out on the Organ Question at Leeds. Another section was formed in 1834–35, when Dr. Samuel Warren was expelled, the proceedings against him arising chiefly out of the formation at that time of a Theological Institution. These two sections united to form the *Wesleyan-Methodist Association.* They used the *Wes. H. Bk.* with a small *Supplement* added. In 1849–50, owing to the expulsion of the Revs. James Everett, Samuel Dunn, and William Griffith from the Wesleyan Conference, another division resulted, and a Society designated the *Wesleyan Reformers* was established, which soon had fifty thousand adherents. Mr. Everett was expelled on suspicion of having written *The Fly Sheets* and *Wesleyan Takings*, and published them anonymously; Mr. Dunn for publishing *The Wesley Banner*, a monthly magazine, and for declining to discontinue the work as desired by the Conference; Mr. Griffith for reporting the proceedings of the Conference in *The Wesleyan Times*. The body then formed by those who adhered to those ministers, at their Annual Delegate Meeting held in Sheffield, in August, 1852, appointed the Rev. James Everett to prepare a new edition of the *Wes. H. Bk.*, with the addition of such new hymns as would replace the copyright hymns which could not be used. The preface to that book is dated July 1st, 1853. The *Supplement* contained 243 hymns in addition to the hymns in the *Wes. H. Bk.* In these were included the compositions of 15 authors not then in the *Supplement* to the *Wes. H. Bk.* At the end of this collection there is an index which gives the source whence every hymn in the book is derived, together with the author's name. The collection contains 804 hymns.

2. When the *Wesleyan Methodist Association* and the *Wesleyan Reformers*, who united in 1857 to form the *Methodist Free Churches*, held their annual assembly in Sheffield, in 1859, they resolved to have a new hymn-book, and appointed the Revs. James Everett and Matthew Baxter to prepare the same. They were to retain all the original *Wes. H. Bk.* of 1780, and add "A Supplement of 250 hymns, and also hymns suitable for a Sunday School." The preface is dated October, 1860. Changes were made in 53 hymns, but none of the new hymns were by authors other than those who had already contributed. From No. 778 to 821 the hymns were all new. Five doxologies and two graces closed the collection of 828 hymns. The *Supplement* was issued in 1861 as a separate book, with the sub-title *Miscellaneous Hymns*. Their *Sunday School Hymns*, 1860, is a fairly good collection.

3. The *Methodist Free Churches* are compiling a new *Coll. of Hymns*, which may appear in 1889. A committee of ministers have been employed for a long time in its preparation. The *Sunday S. H. Bk.* appeared in 1888.

vi. *Bible Christians.*—1. The founder of this Society was William O'Bryan, a Cornishman, born February 6th, 1778, at Gunwen, Luxillian. His father owned a farm and was a Cornish miner. Both his parents were Methodists, and had heard John Wesley preach. They had preaching services in their own dwelling-house. William had a fair education, and the curate of the parish offered to prepare him for college. He was converted under the Methodists in May, 1789, was apprenticed to the drapery business, became worldly, lost his religion, and again gave his heart to God, November 5th, 1795. He heard J. Wesley preach twice, and received his blessing. He began to preach in 1801, was married in 1803, and made a local preacher in 1809. For preaching in villages beyond his own parish, where there was no Methodist preaching, he was expelled from the Methodist Society. Being urged to continue his preaching, he found in North Devon fourteen villages without

any places of worship, and in November, 1814, he left his home to itinerate and preach in those places. In October, 1815, he preached in the house of Mr. Thorne at Shebbear, and, being urged to do so, he then formed those present into a religious Society. This Society was at first known by the name *Arminian Bible Christians;* afterwards the initial word was dropped, and they have since been known as *Bible Christians*, and sometimes, locally, *Brianites*. Their chief Societies are in Cornwall and Devonshire, but they have a few elsewhere. O'Bryan compiled their first hymn-book, about 1819, when their first Conference was held. In 1829 a separation took place. O'Bryan left the body in 1831, and went to America, where he died, January 8th, 1868. For his share in the copyright of the hymn-book, and for other claims, the Conference allowed him twenty pounds a year till he died. The hymn-book is divided into six parts and twenty-eight sections. The hymns are mostly those in use in the *Wes. H. Bk.*, but they are rearranged throughout, and several by 18 other authors were added. In July, 1862, a 4th ed. was issued, with 9 hymns changed, the names of authors added as far as known, the index of Scripture texts enlarged, and an index of verses. The 6th ed. is dated 1882. The Conference of 1885 appointed a committee to prepare a new and more comprehensive collection, to be published in due course.

2. In 1832, a Sunday School Union for the Bible Christians was formed at Shebbear, in Devonshire, and they published *The Child's Hymn Book* for use in their schools. In 1863 a new ed. was prepared and published, containing 272 hymns, more than 60 of which were new. That book has served the Connexion nearly a quarter of a century, and is still in favour. The hymns are carefully classified, but no authors' names are given.

vii. *Conclusion.*—When the Methodist Œcumenical Conference was held in City Road Chapel, in September, 1881, a suggestion was made to have one comprehensive hymn-book for all the branches of Methodism throughout the world. This course, however, has not been adopted.

Translations of English hymns into various European and other languages have been made for use by the various branches of the Methodist Societies on the Continent of Europe and on Mission Stations. In several instances these translations have been supplemented by original hymns in the vernacular, and composed chiefly by the resident missionaries. [See Missions, Foreign.]

The Methodist hymn-writers are very limited in number. The provision made by John and Charles Wesley for every aspect of Methodism, the stereotyped character of each book when issued, the great number of years it had to run before any omissions or additions could be made, and the intense affection of Methodists for their old hymns, have had much to do in producing this result. When at rare intervals outlets for pent-up poetic life were made in new editions of old books, and in collections for children and the young, W. M. Bunting, W. M. Punshon, B. Gough, J. Lyth, G. S. Rowe, J. Briggs,

E. E. Jenkins, M. G. Pearse, and a few others, have produced lyrics of merit and usefulness; but no great singer has appeared in Methodism since Charles Wesley was gathered to his fathers. [See American Hymnody, p. 58, ii., and Various.]   [G. J. S.]

Methodist New Connexion Hymnody. [Methodist Hymnody, § iii.]

Methodist, Primitive, Hymnody. [Methodist Hymnody, § iv.]

Methodist United Free Church Hymnody. [Methodist Hymnody, § v.]

Methodist, Wesleyan, Hymnody. [Methodist Hymnody, § ii.]

Methodius I. [See Greek Hymnody, § x. 2.]

Methodius II., one of the Greek hymn-writers, d. 836. A native of Syracuse, he embraced the monastic life at Constantinople. He was imprisoned for nine years by Michael the Stammerer for his defence of the *Icons.* He was also scourged for the same cause by Theophilus, but escaped from his prison. At the triumph of the defenders of the *Icons,* he was made patriarch of Constantinople (842). His pieces are few. [See Εἰ καὶ τὰ παρόντα.] This is the same person as *Methodius I.* in Neale's *Hys. of the Eastern Church.*   [H. L. B.]

Μήτραν ἀφλέκτως. [Ἔσωσε λαόν.]

Metrophanes of Smyrna, was bishop of Smyrna towards the close of the ninth century. He was a partizan of Rome in her contest with Photius, and an adherent of his rival, Ignatius. He d. *circa* 910. His chief hymnological works are his Canons in honour of the Blessed Trinity, one of which has been published in *Anth. Graec. Carm. Christ.,* 1871, p. 254. They are eight in all, one for each Tone, and are sung at Matins on Sundays, the Canon changing with the Tone on each succeeding Sunday. A cento only, and that from the Canon for the Sunday of the Second Tone, from the *Octoechus,* has been rendered into English. This is Dr. Neale's "O Unity of Threefold Light" (*Holy Trinity*), a *tr.* of a cento :—Τριφεγγὴς Μονὰς Θεαρχική, pub. in his *Hymns of the E. C.,* 1862, in 3 st. of 8 l. In 1867 it was given with a doxology of 4 l. and a slight alteration in the *People's Hymnal;* and again in the S. P. C. K. *Ps. & Hys.,* the *Hymnary,* and other collections.   [J. J.]

Meusel, Wolfgang, s. of Anton Meusel (*Meusslin, Mäusslein, Mosel, Mösel, Musculus,* &c.), cooper at Dieuze in Lorraine, was b. at Dieuze, Sept. 8, 1497. He studied for short periods in the schools at Rappoltsweiler, Colmar, and Schlettstadt, between times wandering over the country and earning his way by his singing. In 1512 he happened to come to the Benedictine monastery at Lixheim near Saarburg, just as Vespers were being sung. His beautiful voice, as he joined in, led the monks to receive him, and here he studied music, and became organist to the cloister. In his 20th year he devoted himself to the study of theology, and soon after began to preach in the church at Lixheim, and in the neighbouring village churches. In 1518 he became acquainted with Luther's writings and em-

braced his views, but did not leave Lixheim till 1527, after he had declined to be elected as prior. On Dec. 26, 1527, he was formally married at Strassburg to a niece of the former prior at Lixheim. As they were without means she had to take a place as domestic servant, and he, after trying in vain to earn his living as a linen-weaver, was about to attempt to get work as a day-labourer on the fortifications, when he was appointed pastor at the village of Dorlitzheim, near Strassburg. In 1529 he became diaconus of the cathedral church at Strassburg, and then, in the beginning of 1531, was sent to Augsburg, where he for some time officiated in the Holy Cross Church, and, after the Reformation had gained the upper hand, became, in 1537, chief pastor of the Cathedral. When the Interim [see Agricola, p. 31, i.] was forced on the magistracy in June, 1548, Meusel left Augsburg. Thereafter he had to flee from place to place, residing for longer or shorter periods at Basel, Constanz, St. Gall, and Zürich. He finally was invited to Bern as professor of theology, and went there in April, 1549. In gratitude for this timely help he refused various lucrative appointments offered to him from time to time. On Sunday, Aug. 22, 1563, he felt an attack of fever while preaching at Bern, and d. on the following Sunday, Aug. 29, 1563. (*Koch,* ii. 83; *Allg. Deutsche Biog.,* xxiii. 95, &c.) Meusel's best-known work is his Commentary on the Psalms, pub. in 1550. Eight hymns are ascribed to him, six of which are printed by *Wackernagel,* iii., Nos. 946–951. A seventh, a *tr.* of the "Christe, qui lux es et dies," is noted at p. 227, ii. The eighth is:—

Der Herre ist mein treuer Hirt, Hält mich in seiner Hute. Ps. xxiii. This appeared in the Augsburg *G. B.,* 1531, and thence in *Wackernagel,* iii. p. 122, in 5 st. of 7 l. *Wackernagel,* seeing that Meusel wrote another version of this Psalm (beginning "Mein Hirt ist Gott, der Herre mein"), and that the version above was not given with his name till in the Nürnberg *G. B.* of 1601, gives it as anonymous. It was included in Babst's *G. B.,* 1545, in most subsequent collections up to 1700, and in the Berlin *G. L. S.,* ed. 1863, No. 411. In the Strassburg *G. B.,* 1560, and many later books, it begins "Der Herr ist mein getreuer Hirt." *Tr.* as :—

(1) "The Lord God is my Pastor gude," in the *Gude and Godlie Ballates,* ed. 1568, f. 47 (1868, p. 79). (2) "The Lord my faithful Shepherd is," in the *Moravian H. Bk.,* 1754, pt. ii., p. 374. In the 1789 and later eds. (1886, No. 430) it begins "The Lord my Shepherd is and Guide." (3) "The Lord He is my Shepherd kind," by *Miss Manington,* 1863, p. 20.   [J. M.]

Meyfart, Johann Matthäus, was b. Nov. 9, 1590 at Jena, during a visit which his mother (wife of Pastor Meyfart of Wahlwinkel, near Waltershausen, Gotha) was paying to her father. He studied at the Universities of Jena (M.A. 1611; D.D. 1624) and Wittenberg, and was thereafter for some time adjunct of the philosophical faculty at Jena. In 1616, he was appointed professor in the Gymnasium at Coburg and in 1623 director; and during his residence at Coburg was a great moral power. When his colleagues in the Gymnasium made a complaint to the government regarding a dissertation (*De disciplina ecclesiastica*), which he pub. in 1633, he accepted the offer of the professorship of theology in the revived University of Erfurt. He entered on his work at Erfurt, July, 1633, was rector of the University in 1634, and in 1636 became also pastor of the Prediger Kirche. He d.

at Erfurt, Jan. 26, 1642 (*Koch* iii. 117; *Allg. Deutsche Biog.* xxi. 646, &c.).

Meyfart's devotional works (*Tuba poenitentiae prophetica*, 1625; *Tuba Novissima*, 1626; *Höllisches Sodoma*, 1629; *Himmlisches Jerusalem*, 1630; *Jüngste Gericht*, 1632) passed through various editions, and produced a great impression by their vivid picturing and their earnest calls to repentance and amendment of life. His well-meant efforts, by books and otherwise, towards raising the tone of student life in Germany, and his exposition of the excesses and defects in both academical and churchly life at that period, brought him much ill will and opposition, and did not produce useful fruit till much later. His hymns were few in number, and appeared mostly in his devotional books.

Only one of Meyfart's hymns has passed into English, viz. :—

Jerusalem, du hochgebaute Stadt. *The New Jerusalem.* This splendid hymn appeared in his *Tuba Novissima*, Coburg, 1626 [Ducal Library, Gotha], a volume containing four sermons preached at Coburg on the Four Last Things, viz. Death, Last Judgment, Eternal Life, and Eternal Punishment. It forms the conclusion of the third sermon (on St. Matt. xvii. 1–9) which is entitled " On the joy and glory which all the Elect are to expect in the Life everlasting." This conclusion is reprinted verbatim et literatim (i.e. with the introductory and closing sentences, and the connecting sentences between st. i., ii., iii. and iv.) in the *Blätter für Hymnologie*, 1883, pp. 120–124. The text of the hymn, in 8 st. of 8 l., is given unaltered, according to the marginal directions of the original (save st. vii. l. 6, where the original is " Man spielt "), as No. 1537 in the Berlin *G. L. S.*, ed. 1863. Of it Lauxmann, in *Koch* viii. 669, says :—

" The hymn is a precious gem in our Treasury of Song, in which one clearly sees that from it the whole heart of the poet shines out in us. Meyfart had his face turned wholly to the Future, to the Last Things; and with a richly fanciful mysticism full of deep and strong faith, he united a flaming zeal for the House of the Lord, and against the abuses of his times."

He adds that the hymn was a great favourite with Charles Gützlaff, the apostle of China (d. at Hong-Kong, Aug. 9, 1851), whose last words were " Would God I were in thee " (st. i. l. 3); and of Julius Schnorr of Carolsfeld, the well-known painter, whose last work was the illustrating of this hymn, and at whose funeral in 1872 it was sung. The popularity of the hymn was greatly aided by the magnificent melody, generally ascribed to Melchior Franck [b. at Zittau, 1580 ; c. 1604, capellmeister at Coburg; d. at Coburg, June 1, 1639], but not yet traced earlier than to the Erfurt *G. B.*, 1663.

Translations in C. U. :—

1. Jerusalem, thou city built on high. A good *tr.* of st. i.–iv., vii., as No. 112 in the Dalston Hospital *H. Bk.*, 1848.

2. Jerusalem, thou city built on high. A good *tr.* of st. i., iv., vi., vii., by A. T. Russell, as No. 261 in his *Ps. & Hys.*, 1851. St. i., ll. 1, 2, 4 are from the 1848 *tr.* The form in Dr. Pagenstecher's *Coll.*, 1864, No. 288, is i. ll. 1–4, ii. as 1848; i. ll. 5–8, vii. as 1851.

3. Jerusalem, thou city fair and high. A good and full *tr.* by Miss Winkworth, in her *Lyra Ger.*, 2nd Ser., 1858, p. 220; repeated in her *C. B. for England*, 1863, No. 193, set to the melody of 1663. Included in full in the Ohio Luth. *Hymnal*, 1880, and, abridged, in the Pennsylvania Luth. *Ch. Bk.*, 1868, and the *Uppingham and Sherborne School H. Bk.*, 1874.

4. Jerusalem ! high tow'r thy glorious walls.

A good and full *tr.*, by Bp. W. R. Whittingham, in the Amer. Epis. *Hys. for Church and Home*, 1860, No. 414; and the Amer. Epis. *Hymnal*, 1871. St. i., iv., viii. are in M. W. Stryker's *Christian Chorals*, 1885.

Translations not in C. U. :—

(1) " Jerusalem, thou city of the skies." In the U. P. *Juvenile Miss. Mag.*, Dec. 1857. (2) " Jerusalem ! thou glorious city-height." By *Mrs. Bevan*, 1858, p. 19, repeated in L. Rehfuess's *Church at Sea*, 1868. (3) " Jerusalem, thou high-built, fair abode." In the *Christian Examiner* (Boston, U. S.), Sept. 1860, p. 254. (4) " Jerusalem, thou city rear'd on high. By *Miss Manington*, 1863, p. 94. (5) " Jerusalem ! thou city towering high." By Miss Cox, in her *Hys. from the Ger.*, 1864, p. 101, and in *Lyra Mystica*, 1865, p. 365. (6) " Jerusalem ! thou city builded high." By Miss Burlingham, in the *British Herald*, April, 1866, p. 249, and Reid's *Praise Bk.*, 1872. (7) " Jerusalem ! high tow'r thy glorious walls." A full and spirited *tr.* by J. H. Hopkins, in his *Carols, Hys. and Songs*, 1882, p. 182, dated 1862. St. i., ll. 1–2, are taken from Bp. Whittingham's version.   [J. M.]

Middleton, Thomas Fanshaw, D.D., s. of Thomas Middleton, Rector of Redleston, in Derbyshire, was b. there on Jan. 26, 1769. He was educated first by his father, then at Christ's Hospital, and finally at Pembroke Hall, Cambridge (D.A. in honours 1792). He was successively Curate of Gainsborough; Rector of Tansor, Northamptonshire, 1795 ; Vicar of St. Pancras, 1810 ; Archdeacon of Huntingdon, 1812; and the first bishop of Calcutta, 1814. He d. in Calcutta, July 8, 1822. Bishop Middleton's publications were mainly confined to various Sermons and Charges, and a work on the Greek Article. In 1824 his *Sermons and Charges* were collected and pub. with a short *Memoir*, by Dr. H. R. Bonney. At p. xciv. the only hymn ascribed to him is given with the explanation that it was composed by the Bishop " and always sung on new year's day, by his desire." It is : " As o'er the past my mem'ry strays " (*New Year*), in 4 st. of 4 l. It was printed in the August number of Carus Wilson's *Family Visitor*, 1826 ; again in Hall's *Mitre Hymnal*, 1836, and later in several collections. Orig. text in *Bk. of Praise*, 1862, p. 238. [J. J.]

Midlane, Albert, was b. at Newport, Isle of Wight, Jan. 23, 1825, and has been engaged in business in that town for many years. To his Sunday school teacher he ascribes the honour of prompting him to poetic efforts : and the same teacher did much to shape his early life. His first printed hymn, " Hark ! in the presence of our God," was written in September, 1842, at Carisbrooke Castle, and printed in the *Youth's Magazine* in November of the same year. Since then he has written over 300, and of these a large proportion are in C. U. They appeared in magazines and small mission hymn-books, including :—

(1) *The Youth's Magazine;* (2) *The British Messenger;* (3) *The London Messenger;* (4) Trotter's *Evangelical Hymn Book*, 1860 ; (5) *The Ambassador's Hymn Book*, 1861 ; (6) Second ed. of the same, 1868 ; (7) *Hymn Book for Youth;* (8) *Good News for the Little Ones*, 1860; (9) William Carter's *Gospel Hymn Book*, 1862 ; and several other works of a similar kind.

In addition to several small works in prose, Mr. Midlane has gathered his verse together from time to time and published it as :—

(1) *Poetry addressed to Sabbath School Teachers*, 1844 ; (2) *Vecta Garland*, 1850 ; (3) *Leaves from Olivet*, 1864 ; (4) *Gospel Echoes*, 1865 ; (5) *Above the Bright Blue Sky*, 1867 ; (6) *Early Lispings*, 1880.

Of the hymns contained in these works nearly 200 have been in C. U. from 1861 to 1887, the most popular being "There's a Friend for little children." The hymn-books, however, in which many of them are found are usually very small, are used in what are commonly known as Gospel Missions, and have gradually given way to other and more important collections. We therefore append only those hymns which are at the present time in use in official or quasi-official hymn-books, or such collections as have a wide circulation. Those hymns which are omitted from the following list may be found in the works given above, and especially in the *Gospel Echoes*. The bracketed dates below are those of the composition of the hymns.

i. Given in Trotter's *Evangelical Hymn Book*, 1860.

1. How sweet the cheering words. (Aug. 1860.) *The Gospel*.
2. Lord Jesus, save! (July, 1860.) *Lent*.

ii. Given in *The Ambassador's Hymn Book*, 1861.

3. Angels rejoice o'er sinners saved. (Aug., 1860.) *Joy in Heaven over Repenting Sinners*.
4. Come to the royal feast. (Aug., 1860.) *The Gospel Feast*.
5. Father, bless the heavenly message. (Aug., 1860.) *Divine blessing implored*.
6. How vast, how full, how free. (Aug., 1860.) *Divine Mercy*.
7. I am not told to labour. (June 25, 1860.) *Salvation by Faith*.
8. Jesus died upon the tree. (Aug. 13, 1860.) *Good Friday*.
9. Lord, prepare the hearts of sinners. (Aug. 28, 1861.) *Preparation of the heart*.
10. Not all the gold of all the world. *Peace through Jesus*.
11. Now we'll render to the Saviour. (Sept. 1, 1861.) *Praise for Salvation*.
12. O what a gift the Father gave. (Aug. 22, 1860.) *The Gift of The Son*.
13. O what a Saviour is Jesus the Lord. (Aug. 29, 1861.) *Jesus the Saviour*.
14. Passing onward, quickly passing. (Sept. 10, 1861.) *Prepared?*
15. Salvation, Lord, is Thine. (Aug., 1860.) *Salvation through Jesus*.
16. Sinner, where is room for doubting? (Sept., 1861.) *Expostulation*.
17. Soft the voice of mercy sounded. *Grace*.
18. The perfect righteousness of God. (Sept. 21, 1861.) *God our Righteousness*.
19. There is a throne of grace. (Sept. 14, 1860.) *The Throne of Grace*.
20. We speak of the mercy of God. (Sept. 19, 1861.) *Divine Mercy*.

iii. Given in W. Carter's *Gospel Hymn Book*, 1863.

21. Can any say, I do believe? (Aug., 1860.) *Assurance in Christ*.
22. If Jesus came to seek and save. (Oct., 1861.) *Salvation in Jesus*.

iv. Given in *Leaves from Olivet*, 1864.

23. See the blessed Saviour dying. (Oct. 5, 1860.) *Good Friday*.
24. Sweet the theme of Jesus' love. (April 22, 1862.) *The Love of Jesus*.

v. Given in *Gospel Echoes*, 1865.

25. Come and welcome to the Saviour. (June 8, 1862) *Invitation*.
26. God be gracious to a sinner. (May 21, 1861.) *Lent*.
27. God speaks from heaven; in love He speaks. (July, 1860.) *Love and Mercy of God*.
28. Hark! the cry, Behold He cometh. (June 8, 1862.) *Advent*.
29. He saves because He will. (April 20, 1862.) *The "I Wills" of Jesus*.
30. How solemn are the words. (Aug. 1, 1865.) *The New Birth*.

31. Himself He could not save. (Sept., 1861.) *Good Friday*.
32. I once was bound in Satan's chains. *Pardon*.
33. Jesus lived. He lived for sinners. (Jan. 4, 1862.) *Easter*.
34. Jesus never answered "Nay." (May 13, 1862.) *Jesus always the same*.
35. Jesus the blessed centre is. (June 8, 1862). *Father glorified in the Son*.
36. Jesus, the risen Saviour. (July 31, 1862.) *Easter*.
37. Jesus, the soul that trusts in Thee. (May 7, 1864.) *Salvation through Jesus*.
38. Look, poor sinner, look to Calvary. *Good Friday*.
39. Lord, when I think upon the love. (Oct. 1, 1860.) *The Love of Jesus*.
40. Peace with God! How great a treasure (Oct. 18, 1861.) *Peace*.
41. Salvation! What a precious word. (Nov. 22, 1861.) *Salvation*.
42. Scripture says Where sin abounded. (March 3, 1862.) *Abounding Grace*.
43. Shall Jesus' love be spoken? (May 4, 1862.) *Love of Jesus*.
44. The Lamb was slain, the blood was brought. (Aug. 24, 1862.) *The Passover*.
45. The silver trumpets sounding. (May 7, 1862.) *The Year of Jubilee*.
46. There is a rest for weary souls. (Dec. 4, 1863.) *Rest. Peace in Jesus*.
47. 'Tis the voice of mercy calls thee. (Nov. 5, 1861.) *Mercy*.
48. When the Saviour said "'Tis finished." (Oct., 1861.) *Good Friday*.
49. When God begins His gracious work. (Dec. 27, 1860.) *God Unchangeable*.
50. Who can praise the blessed God? (Oct., 1861.) *Praise for Salvation*.
51. Why those fears, poor trembling sinner. *Safety in Jesus*.

vi. Given in the *Ambassador's Hymn Book*, 2nd ed., 1868.

52. Life from the dead, eternal life. (Oct. 11, 1867.) *Work of the Holy Spirit*.
53. Stern justice cries for blood. (March 2, 1867.) *The Atonement*.

vii. *Various*.

54. Apart from every worldly care. (June, 1866.) *Prayer Meetings*. Written for Spurgeon's *O. O. H. Bk.* 1866.
55. Be not weary, toiling Christian. (Feb., 1857.) *Encouragement*. In the *British Messenger*, Sept., 1857.
56. Eighteen hundred years ago. (Aug., 1859.) *Fulness of Time*. In the *London Messenger*, April, 1861.
57. Father, for Thy promised blessing. (Feb. 20, 1860.) *Outpouring of the Spirit desired*. In *The Revival*, July, 1860.
58. God bless our Sunday School. *S. School Anniversary*. First printed in the Baptist *Children's Magazine*, July, 1844. It has passed into numerous collections for children, but usually st. ii. is omitted, thus reducing it to 3 st.
59. He comes! He comes! the Bridegroom comes. (Sept. 9, 1850.) *Advent*. In *The Present Testimony*, 1851.
60. Kept by the power of God. (May 6, 1858.) *Security in God*. In the *London Messenger*, Sept., 1860.
61. Let the waves of blessing roll. (Jan. 6, 1868.) *Missions*. In the *Enlarged London H. Bk.*, 1873.
62. Lord, 'our waiting spirits bow. (June, 1866.) *Prayer Meetings*. Written for Spurgeon's *O. O. H. Bk.*, 1866.
63. Love us freely, blessed Jesus. (July 2, 1858.) *Lent*. In the *Churchman's Penny Magazine*, Oct., 1858.
64. Never perish! words of mercy. *Mercy in Christ*. Printed in the monthly *Girdle*, June, 1857, and in the *British Messenger*, Aug. 1857, in 4 double st. In the collections it is reduced to the first two stanzas.
65. No separation, O my soul. (May 6, 1863.) *Perseverance*. In the *British Herald*, Aug., 1863.
66. Nought but the voice of God can speak. (Jan. 29, 1863.) *All things are of God*. In the 1873 *Appx.* to Snepp's *S. of G. & Glory*.
67. Now, O joy, my sins are pardoned. *Pardon and Peace*. (Nov. 9, 1860). Printed in the *London Messenger*, March, 1861, then in the *Gospel Echoes*, 1865; and then in several hymn-books. The original began, "Once I sang, but not in earnest." Usually st. ii., iii., of 8 l., are given as "Now, O joy, &c."
68. O art thou an heir of glory? (June 4, 1861.) *Cautions*. In *H. Bk. for Youth*, 1862.
69. O what a glorious truth is this. (Aug. 3, 1860.) *Jesus Died*. In the *London Messenger*, Sept., 1860.

70. Once it was mine, the cup of wrath. (Aug. 8, 1860.) *Wrath and Pardon.* In the *London Messenger,* Oct., 1861.
71. Onward, upward, heavenward. (Feb. 7, 1860.) *Pressing Onward.* In the *London Messenger,* March, 1861.
72. Perennial spring of pure delight. (March 17, 1864.) *Jesus All in All.* In the *London Messenger,* Jan., 1865.
73. Sheltered by the [Thy] sprinkled blood. (Sept. 23, 1863.) *Safety in Jesus.* In the *London Messenger,* Feb. 1864.
74. Showers of blessing, gracious promise. (April 19, 1862.) *Missions.* In the *London Messenger,* Aug., 1862, and *Leaves from Olivet,* 1864.
75. The Church of God, amazing, precious thought. (July 6, 1857.) *The Church.* In *The Present Testimony,* 1858, and *Leaves from Olivet,* 1864.
76. Tne whispers of Thy love divine. (May 3, 1868.) *Love of God.* In the *Island Greeting,* Oct., 1872.
77. Though billows round me roll. (April 2, 1853.) *Trust.* In *Food for Christ's Flock,* 1853.
78. 'Tis finished, cried the dying Lamb. (Feb. 21, 1850.) *Good Friday* In the *Baptist Children's Magazine,* 1850.
79. 'Tis heaven where Jesus is. (Oct. 23, 1862.) *Joy and Peace in Jesus.* In the *Enlarged London H. Bk.,* 1873.
80. Together all things work for good. (Aug. 14, 1860.) *All work for Good.* In the *Enlarged London H. Bk.,* 1873.
81. Waiting for Jesus, and loving while waiting. (Jan. 9, 1872.) *Second Advent desired.* In the 1873 *Appx.* to Snepp's *S. of G. & Glory.*
82. Without a cloud between. (Mar. 18, 1862.) *Jesus, Face to Face.* In the *London Messenger,* June, 1862.
83. Yet awhile ; how sweet the thought. (Dec., 1864.) *Second Advent desired.* In the *London Messenger,* 1865.

The collections in which these hymns are mainly found are Spurgeon's *O. O. H. Bk.,* 1866; Snepp's *Songs of G. & G.,* 1872-3; Hurditch's *Enlarged London H. Bk.,* 1873, and smaller books for Evangelical mission work. Of Mr. Midlane's hymns as a whole, Miller's estimate that "His hymns are full of spiritual thought, careful in their wording, and often very pleasing without reaching the highest form of poetical excellence" (*Singers and Songs,* p. 572), is just. A marked feature of these hymns is the constant and happy use of Scripture phraseology.   [J. J.]

Midst scenes of confusion and creature complaints. *D. Denham.* [*Heaven Anticipated.*] This hymn appeared in the 1826 *Appendix* to J. Rees's *Coll.,* No. 168, in 5 st., and again in Denham's *Saint's Melody,* &c., 1837, No. 740, in 6 st. of 4 l. It is given in a few collections in G. Britain and America.   [J. J.]

Mighty Father! Blessed Son! *J. S. B. Monsell.* [*Holy Trinity.*] Appeared in his *Spiritual Songs,* 1857, in 9 st. of 9 l., as the hymn for Trinity Sunday. In the *Hymnal Comp.,* 1876, and the *Prim. Meth. Hymnal,* 1887, st. i., iv., and ix. of this text are given as No. 197. In Dr. Monsell's *Hys. of Love and Praise,* 1863, the same hymn is rearranged and partly rewritten (but still retaining the opening lines) in 9 st. of 3 l. Snepp, in printing this form of the hymn in his *Songs of G. & G.,* 1872, has divided it into three parts, and added this note thereto :—

"Note the Symbolic Form—three lines harmonizing in each verse; three verses in each division ; three divisions making one hymn.'

This form of the text, but usually without these divisions, is also in Thring's *Coll.,* 1882, and others.   [J. J.]

Miles, Elizabeth, née Appleton, was b. at Boston, U.S.A., March 28, 1807, and

married in 1833 to Solomon P. Miles, Head Master of the Boston High School, and afterwards the Principal of a private school for young ladies in the same city. He d. in 1842. On leaving Boston, Mrs. Miles went to reside with her son at Brattleborough, Vermont. Her principal hymns are :—

1. **The earth all light and loveliness.** Part i. *Summer.*
2. **When on devotion's seraph wing.** Part ii., st. v., vii. *Foretaste of Heaven.* These two parts appeared as one hymn in *The Christian Examiner,* 1828.
3. **Thou Who didst stoop below.** *Looking unto Jesus.* Appeared in *The Christian Examiner,* 1827. Sometimes it begins with st. ii., "It was no path of flowers," as in the Boston Unitarian *Bk. of Hymns,* 1846.
4. **Father, direct my ways.** *Divine Guidance desired in Affliction.* In the Boston *Book of Hys.,* 1846 ; the Boston *Hys. of the Spirit,* 1864 ; and some other collections, it begins with st. ii., "Thou, infinite in love."

Three additional hymns were pub. for the first time in Putnam's *Singers and Songs of the Liberal Faith,* 1875.   [F. M. B.]

Millard, James Elwin, D.D., was b. May 18, 1823, and educated first at Magdalen College School, and then at Magdalen College, Oxford (B.A. in honours, 1845). Taking Holy Orders, he became Curate of Bradfield, Berks, 1846; Head Master of Magdalen College School, 1846; Fellow of his College, 1853; and Vicar of Basingstoke, 1864. Dr. Millard has pub. :—

(1) *The Island Choir, or the Children of the Child Jesus,* 1847; (2) *Historical Notices of the Office of Choristers ;* and (3) *A Short Account of Basingstoke, Basing and the Neighbourhood,* 1874. He also contributed a few hymns to the Rev. T. F. Smith's *Devout Chorister,* 1848.

From the *Devout Chorister* the following hymns have come into C. U. :—

1. God eternal, mighty King. *Te Deum.*
2. In deep humiliation. *Ascension.*
3. Last night I lay a-sleeping. *Carol.*

The first of these passed, with alterations, into *Hys. & Introits* (Masters), 1852, with further alterations into *H. A. & M.,* 1861. The text was corrected in Biggs's Annotated *H. A. & M.,* 1867. The hymn is widely known.   [J. J.]

Miller, Emily, née Huntingdon. [Various.]

Miller, Josiah, M.A., was b. at Putney, April 8, 1832, and educated for the Congregational ministry at Highbury College, also graduating M.A. at the University of London, 1855. After holding pastorates at Dorchester, Long Sutton, and Newark, he became Secretary of the "British Society for the Propagation of the Gospel among the Jews," and subsequently of the "London City Mission." He d. in London, December, 1880. He pub. :—

(1) *Our Hymns : their Authors and Origin,* 1866. The groundwork of this volume was the leading hymnbooks of the Congregational body. (2) *Our Dispensation,* 1868. (3) *Singers and Songs of the Church : being Biographical Sketches of the Hymn-writers in all the Principal Collections. With Notes on their Psalms and Hymns,* Lond., Longmans, 1869. This was an extension of *Our Hymns* to twenty-five representative English hymn-books of various denominations. (4) *Christianum Organum,* 1873.

Mr. Miller rendered great service to hymnology by the production of *Our Hymns* and

Singers and Songs. These works, and especially the latter, furnished the fullest illustrations of hymnody, which up to the time of their publication had appeared in English, and embodied a great mass of information which had been gathered by the author and other workers in the same field, notably D. Sedgwick, C. D. Hardcastle, G. J. Stevenson, and Dr. C. Rogers. Considering the wide ground which it covered, it was an accurate and painstaking work. Where it fails is usually in omissions, and not in positive errors. His statements are generally correct so far as they go, but recent researches in hymnody have shown that in numerous instances they did not go far enough. The Greek, Latin, German, and American portions of his work are especially weak. His main strength is in his Biographies. [W. G. H.]

Millions within Thy courts have met. *J. Montgomery.* [*Sunday Evening.*] Pub. in his *Poetical Works,* 1841, vol. iv. p. 293, in 10 st. of 6 l. and again in his *Original Hys.,* 1853, No. 120, where it is headed "Evening Song for the Sabbath-Day." Its use, especially in America, is extensive, but it is usually abbreviated. In *Kennedy,* 1863, and one or two others it begins "*Thousands* within Thy courts have met." Also given as, "Within Thy courts have millions met." [J. J.]

Mills, Elizabeth, née King, dau. of Philip King, was b. at Stoke Newington in 1805; married to Thomas Mills, M.P., and d. at Finsbury Place, London, April 21, 1829. Her popular hymn:—

We speak of the realms of the blest [*Heaven*] is thus annotated in Miller's *Singers and Songs,* &c., 1869, p. 483: "We are much indebted to John Remington Mills, Esq., M.P., for information about this hymn, written by his accomplished relative. The original has 6 st. and was composed after reading 'Bridges on the 119th Psalm' (on ver. 44, p. 116), 'We speak of heaven, but oh! to be there.' . . . Already deservedly a favourite, new interest will be added to this hymn when we know that the authoress was early called to 'the realms of the blest,' of which she sang so sweetly, and that she wrote this hymn a few weeks before her death." The text of this hymn is usually given in an imperfect form. The corrections are supplied by W. F. Stevenson in his *Hys. for Church and Home,* 1873, "Children's Hymns," No. 151, and the note thereon. Few children's hymns have been received with more favour. It is found in almost every hymn-book published for Children in Great Britain and America during the last fifty years. In some collections it begins, "We *sing* of the *land* of the blest"; and in others, "We *talk* of the *land* of the blest." [J. J.]

Mills, Henry, D.D., s. of John Mills, was b. at Morriston, New Jersey, March 12, 1786, and educated at the New Jersey College, Princeton, where he graduated in 1802. After being engaged in teaching for some time at Morristown and elsewhere, he was ordained Pastor of the Presbyterian Church of Woodbridge, New Jersey, in 1816. On the opening of the Auburn Theological Seminary in 1821, he was appointed Professor of Biblical Criticism and Oriental Languages, from which he retired in 1854. He d. at Auburn, June 10, 1867. In 1845 he pub. *Horae Germanicae; A Version of German Hymns.* This was enlarged in 1856. The *trs.* are not well done, and very few are now in C. U., although 18 and 9 doxologies were given in the Lutheran General Synod's *Coll.,* 1850. Many are noted in the articles on German hymn-writers and hymns throughout this Dictionary. [F. M. B.]

Milman, Henry Hart, D.D., the youngest s. of Sir Francis Milman (who received his Baronetage as an eminent Court physician), was b. Feb. 10th, 1791, and educated at Dr. Burney's at Greenwich, and subsequently at Eton. His career at B. N. C., Oxford, was brilliant. He took a first class in classics, and carried off the Newdigate, Latin Verse, Latin Essay, and English Essay. His Newdigate on the *Apollo Belvedere,* 1812, is styled by Dean Stanley "the most perfect of Oxford prize poems." His literary career for several years promised to be poetical. His tragedy *Fazio* was played at Covent Garden, Miss O'Neill acting Bianca. *Samor* was written in the year of his appointment to St. Mary's, Reading (1817); *The Fall of Jerusalem* (1820); *Belshazzar* and *The Martyr of Antioch* (1822), and *Anne Boleyn,* gained a brilliant reception from the reviewers and the public. He was appointed Poetry Professor at Oxford in 1821, and was succeeded ten years after by Keble. It must have been before 1823, the date of Heber's consecration to Calcutta, that the 13 hymns he contributed to Heber's *Hymns* were composed. But his poetry was only the prelude to his larger work. The *Bampton Lectures* (1827) mark his transition to theological study, and the future direction of it was permanently fixed by his *History of the Jews* (1829). This book raised a storm of obloquy. It was denounced from the University pulpit, and in the *British Critic.* "It was the first decisive inroad of German theology into England, the first palpable indication that the Bible could be studied like another book, that the characters and events of the sacred history could be treated at once critically and reverently" (*Dean Stanley*). In 1835 he was presented by Sir Robert Peel to a Canonry at Westminster and the Rectory of St. Margaret's. In 1839 appeared his valuable edition of Gibbon's *Decline and Fall;* and in 1840 his *History of Christianity to the Abolition of Paganism in the Roman Empire.* Among his minor works in a different field were his *Life of Keats* and his edition and *Life of Horace.* It was not till 1854 that his greatest work—for "vast and varied learning, indefatigable industry, calm impartiality, and subtle and acute criticism, among the most memorable in our language" (*Quart. Rev.*)—*Latin Christianity*—appeared. He had been appointed Dean of St. Paul's in 1849. The great services under the dome originated in his tenure of the Deanery. His latest work, published after his death, Sept. 24, 1868, was *The Annals of St. Paul's.* Though one of the most illustrious in the school of English liberal theology, he had no sympathy with the extreme speculations of Germany. The "criticism" of Tübingen "will rarely bear criticism." He "should like an Ewald to criticise Ewald." "Christianity will survive the criticism of Dr. Strauss," and the "bright flashing artillery" of Rénan. His historical style has been compared to Gibbon in its use of epigram and antithesis. His narrative is full of rapidity of movement. His long complex paragraphs have often a splendour of imagination as well as wealth of thought. All the varied powers of his mind found vent in his conversation; he was called, after his death, "the last of the great conversers." The catalogue of his friends from the days of Heber, "his early friend," to those of Hallam, Macaulay, and Dean Stanley, was long and distinguished.

Milman's 13 hymns were published in Heber's posthumous *Hymns* in 1827, and subsequently in his own *Sel. of Ps. & Hys.*, 1837. The fine hymn for The Burial of the Dead, in Thring's *Coll.*, "Brother, thou art gone before us," is from *The Martyr of Antioch* (1822). Like Heber's, they aim at higher literary expression and lyric grace. He makes free use of refrains. The structure is often excellent. His style is less florid and fuller of burning, sometimes lurid force than Heber's. His hymn for the 16th Sunday after Trinity, "When our heads are bowed with woe," has no peer in its presentation of Christ's human sympathy; the hymn for the 2nd Sunday in Lent, "Oh! help us, Lord! each hour of need," is a piece of pure deep devotion. "Ride on, ride on in majesty," the hymn for Palm Sunday, is one of our best hymns. And the stanzas for Good Friday, "Bound upon the accursed tree," form one of the finest meditations on the Passion. All his hymns are still in C. U.   [H. L. B.]

Milton, John, was b. in London, Dec. 9, 1608, and d. there Nov. 8, 1674. His poetical excellences and his literary fame are matters apart from hymnology, and are fully dealt with in numerous memoirs. His influence on English hymn-writing has been very slight, his 19 versions of various Psalms having lain for the most part unused by hymnal compilers. The dates of his paraphrases are:—

Ps. cxiv. and cxxxvi., 1623, when he was 15 years of age. These were given in his *Poems in English and Latin*, 1645.
Ps. lxxx.–lxxxviii., written in 1648, and pub. as *Nine Psalmes done into Metre*, 1645.
Ps. i., 1653; *ii.*, "Done August 8, 1653;" *iii.*, Aug. 9, 1653; *iv.*, Aug. 10, 1653; *v.*, Aug. 12, 1653; *vi.*, Aug. 13, 1653; *vii.*, Aug. 14, 1653; *viii.*, Aug. 14, 1653.

These 19 versions were all included in the 2nd ed. of his *Poems in English and Latin*, 1673. From these, mainly in the form of centos, the following have come into C. U.:—

1. Cause us to see Thy goodness, Lord. *Ps. lxxxv.*
2. Defend the poor and desolate. *Ps. lxxxii.*
3. God in the great assembly stands. *Ps. lxxxii.*
4. How lovely are Thy dwellings fair. *Ps. lxxxiv.*
From this, "They pass refreshed the thirsty vale," is taken.
5. Let us with a gladsome [joyful] mind. *Ps. cxxxvi.*
6. O let us with a joyful mind. *Ps. cxxxvi.*
7. The Lord will come and not be slow. *Ps. lxxxv.*

Of these centos Nos. 4 and 5 are in extensive use. The rest are mostly in Unitarian collections. There are also centos from his hymn on the Nativity, "This is the month, and this the happy morn" (q.v.). [See **Psalters, English, § xi.**]   [J. J.]

Minimus. One of A. M. Toplady's signatures in the *Gospel Magazine*.

Mir nach, spricht Christus, unser Held. *J. Scheffler.* [*Following Christ.*] This hymn, founded on St. Matt. xvi. 24, has been justly characterised as "a masterpiece of Scriptural didactic poetry." It is No. 171 in Bk. v., 1668, of Scheffler's *Heilige Seelenlust* (*Werke*, 1862, i. p. 289), in 6 st. of 6 l., en-

titled "She [the Soul] encourages to the following of Christ." In the *Geistreiches G. B.*, Halle, 1697, p. 423, a new stanza was added as st. iv., and this form passed through Freylinghausen's *G. B.*, 1704, and is No. 640 in the Berlin *G. L. S.*, ed. 1863. *Tr.* as:—

1. **Come, follow me, our Lord doth call.** A good *tr.* of st. i., iii., v., vii., by A. T. Russell, as No. 100 in the Dalston Hospital *H. Bk.*, 1848, repeated, altered, as No. 183 in his own *Ps. & Hys.*, 1851.
2. **Rise, follow Me! our Master saith.** A *tr.* of st. i., v., vi., vii., by Miss Winkworth, as No. 78 in her *C. B. for England*, 1863.
3. **Says Christ, our Champion, follow me.** A *tr.* of st. i., ii., vii., included as No. 449 in the *Church Praise Bk.*, N. Y., 1882, marked as abridged from a *tr.* by F. M. Finch, 1880.

Other trs. are:—(1) "My yoke, saith Christ, Upon you take," by F. W. Foster, as No. 310 in the *Moravian H. Bk.*, 1789 (1886, No. 497). (2) "After me! Christ our Champion spake," in the *British Magazine*, April, 1838, p. 401. (3) "Christians, attend! Our Champion cries," in the *Family Treasury*, 1877, p. 111. [J. M.]

Mirabilis Deus in sanctis. [*Martyrs.*] In the Bodleian ms. 775, f. 160 *b* (written in the reign of Ethelred between 994 and 1017), this is the sequence for many martyrs. It is given in the Common of many Martyrs in the *Sarum* (Bodleian ms. Barlow 5, circa 1370, page 430); *Paris* (Brit. Mus. Add. 16905, f. 235, early 14th cent.); *Sens* (Brit. Mus. Add. 30058, f. 136 *b* of the 14th cent.); *St. Andrews* (reprint, 1864, p. 416), and other *Missals*. It is also in an 11th cent. Winchester service book now in the Library of Corpus Christi College, Cambridge, No. 473. It was *tr.* by C. B. Pearson as, "God is to be admired in all His saints," in the *Sarum Missal in English*, 1868; and as "God is much to be admired," in his *Sequences from the Sarum Missal*, 1871. It was also *tr.* as, "Praise to Thee, O Lord, most holy," for the *Hymnary*, 1872, by "H. M. C." (i.e. Harriet Mary Chester).   [J. M.]

Miramur, O Deus, Tuae. *C. Coffin.* [*Wednesday.*] Appeared in the *Paris Breviary*, 1736, for Wednesdays, at Matins; and again in his *Hymni Sacri*, 1736, p. 18. It is also in several modern French Breviaries; in J. Chandler's *Hys. of the Prim. Church*, 1837, p. 151; Card. Newman's *Hymni Ecclesiae*, 1838 and 1865; and in Biggs's Annotated *H. A. & M.*, 1867.   [W. A. S.]

Translations in C. U. :—

1. **The wonders of the Almighty hand.** By J. Chandler, in his *Hys. of the Prim. Church*, 1837, p. 20, in 6 st. of 4 l.; and again in his *Hys. of the Church mostly Primitive, &c.*, 1841, No. 13. It is found in a few modern collections.
2. **O God supreme! in rapt amaze.** By J. D. Chambers, in his *Lauda Syon*, 1857, p. 20, in 6 st. of 4 l. It was repeated in the *Salisbury H. Bk.*, 1857; Martineau's *Hymns*, 1873 (in 5 st.), and in others.
3. **New wonders of Thy mighty hand.** By the compilers of *H. A. & M.*, based on J. Chandler, as above, and pub. in *H. A. & M.*, 1861, abbreviated; in *Kennedy*, 1863, &c.

Translations not in C.U. :—

1. O God, we behold how Thy wondrous might. I. Williams. *British Magazine*, July, 1834, and his *Hys. tr. from the Parisian Brev.*, 1839.

2. O God, Thy wonder-working hand. In J. A. Johnston's *English Hymnal*, 1852.   [J. J.]

Miris probat sese modis. *Jean Baptiste de Santeüil.* [*St. Stephen.*] Appeared in the *Cluniac Breviary*, 1686, p. 182, in Santeüil's *Hymni Sacri et Novi*, 1689, p. 57, and the *Paris Breviary*, 1736. It is also in several modern French Breviaries, and Card. Newman's *Hymni Ecclesiae*, 1838 and 1865. *Tr.* as :—

1. **Holy love towards her foes.** Pub. in I. Williams's *Hys. tr. from the Parisian Breviary*, 1839, p. 61, 7 st. of 4 l., with a doxology. In his preface Williams says that this *tr.* was made by a " a friend." In Johnston's *English Hymnal*, 1852, this *tr.* was altered to "Christian Love in wondrous ways"; and in the editions of 1856 and 1861 to "Holy love in wondrous ways."

2. **Holy Love herself displays.** This *tr.* in R. Campbell's *Hys. & Anthems*, &c., 1850, is based upon the above by I. Williams's "friend."

Another tr. is :—
What kindness e'en to mortal foes. *J. D. Chambers*, 1857.   [J. J.]

Missals. The Missal [*Missale*] is the Service-book of the Latin Church, which contains all that is said or sung in the service of the Holy Eucharist or "the Mass" [*Missa*]. It comprises within itself many and various elements which anciently were distributed in different volumes. Such were the *Sacramentarium* containing the Priest's part of the service in the unvarying Canon, with the varying Prefaces, Collects, Secrets, and Postcommons ; the *Epistolarium* or *Lectionarium*, containing the Epistles ; the *Evangeliarium*, containing the Gospels ; the *Graduale*, containing all the choral portions of the service, viz., the Introits, Kyries, Gloria in Excelsis, Graduals, Tracts, Sequences, Creeds, Offertories, and Communions. Of these the Sequences frequently formed a separate volume called the *Sequentiale*. Still more ancient and long obsolete books were the *Benedictionale*, containing the varying triple episcopal benedictions ; and the *Troparium*, containing verses or farces, varying with each festival, dovetailed into or in some way attached to almost every choral part of the service. These verses, known as *Tropes*, went generally out of use in the 13th century.

The Missal most widely in circulation in the present day, and gradually superseding all other Latin Uses, is the *Roman Missal*. It was carefully revised by Pius V. (1570) in accordance with the directions of the Council of Trent, and so revised its use was enjoined in all places and on all communities which could not plead a prescription of two hundred years in favour of a local or peculiar use. It subsequently underwent two slighter but careful revisions under Clement VIII. (in 1604) and Urban VIII. (in 1634), and has received, and will continue to receive from time to time, additional services necessitated by the institution of new Festivals.

Besides the *Missale Romanum* there were, and to a lesser extent than formerly still are, various *Missals*, belonging to different Provinces, Dioceses, and Religious and Military Orders. Such were the *Sarum, York*, and *Hereford Missals* of the unreformed Church of England, the *Paris, Lyons*, and many French *Missals*, the *Augustinian, Benedictine, Præmonstratentian Missals*, &c. These may all be regarded as variations and offshoots of the *Missale Romanum*.

In addition to monastic or diocesan variations of the *Roman Missal*, there are two living Latin Liturgies which deserve special notice, because they are, the first probably, the second certainly, of a distinct *genus* or family, viz. : that known as *the Ephesine* or *Hispano-Gallican*. These are the *Ambrosian Missal* in use in the Church of Milan, and the *Mozarabic Missal* in limited use in the Church of Spain.

Most of these *Missals* form a quarry from which an immense amount of hymnological material can be drawn in the shape of *Sequences* or *Proses*, for an account of which see Sequences.

But besides *Sequences*, there are other parts of the Liturgy, which sometimes, though rarely, assume a metrical or rhyming form. These are the Gradual with its Verses, the Tract, the Offertorium, the Communio, and possibly the more ancient Trope. Details concerning these are given under their respective titles (q.v.).   [F. E. W.]

Missions, Foreign. The hymnody of Foreign Missions is, as a whole, practically unknown. Most persons have some idea of the great work accomplished by Christian missionaries in the translation of the Holy Scriptures into almost all known languages ; but few have ever thought how much has been done by them in the translation and composition of hymns, the preparation of hymn-books, and in general, in the introduction of Christian Hymnody among the various nations to whom they have preached the Gospel. It is the object of this article to set forth this as fully and accurately as the limits of our space will allow. Although Protestant Christians of several denominations in Great Britain and America have missions in various parts of Europe, we shall not include any of these in our notice, with the single exception of the missions in European Turkey. We propose to speak of Missionary Hymnody—

I. *In various parts of America ; North, Central, and South ;*

II. *In the Islands of the Pacific, in New Guinea and Borneo ;*

III. *In Asia, from Japan westward to Turkey ;*

IV. *In Africa, East, South and West.*

The following abbreviations will be used :—

M. M. = Moravian Missions.
C. M. S. = Church Missionary Society.
S. P. G. = Society for the Propagation of the Gospel in Foreign Parts.
B. M. S. = Baptist Missionary Society.
W. M. S. = Wesleyan Missionary Society.
L. M. S. = London Missionary Society.
K. S. M. = Church of Scotland Foreign Missions.
F. C. S. = Free Church of Scotland Foreign Missions.
A. B. M. = American Baptist Missionary Union.
A. B. C. = American Board of Commissioners for Foreign Missions.
A. M. E. = Missionary Society of the Methodist Episcopal Church of America.
A. P. M. = Board of Foreign Missions of the American Presbyterian Church.
The names of other Missionary Societies, less frequently mentioned, will be given in full.

I. America.

i. North America.

This extends over a vast extent of country from Greenland to Mexico.

1. Greenland.—The *M. M.* on the western coast of Greenland commenced in 1721. In 1738 Kajarnak, the first convert, was won by "the Story of the Cross;" now the whole of the country is Christianized. Since 1772 the Greenlanders have had their own printed hymn-book. An enlarged ed., pub. in 1819, was received by them with great joy, and recent accounts show that they retain their fondness for hymns. Not only do they sing well in their churches and homes, but the long coasting voyages in the "umiaks," or women's boats, are enlivened by the sweet voices of the female rowers uniting in sacred song.

2. Labrador.—Crossing Davis Strait to the bleak coast of Labrador we find the self-denying agents of the same society [*M. M.*] at work. In 1770 Jans Haven, from Greenland, sang to the Eskimoes of Labrador, a hymn in Greenlandic, a language which they understood, and in the midst of a barbaric dance they were charmed by it into silence. These Eskimoes now themselves sing Christian hymns at their morning and evening prayers, even when away from their homes on their hunting, fishing, or sealing expeditions. For a long time they have had a neat 12mo hymnal, the last revision being by the Rev. Theodore Bourquin, who translated most of the modern hymns. The book contains about 900 hymns, and was printed in 1879, at Stolpen, in Germany. The last eight pages contain the notes of 10 melodies with the words below. The following are the first lines of a few of the hymns :—

"Passijæksaungitotit" = "O Lamb of God, unspotted."

"Karàlit kakkanginit" = "From Greenland's icy mountains."

"Attè, tupaleritse okpertut" = "Christians awake."

"Illakka, maksualaukta" = "Hold the fort."

The number of syllables and accents is the same as in the English hymns, so that they may be sung to the same tunes, but the lines do not rhyme.

3. Cree Indians.—Crossing the northern part of North America, and passing westward through British territory, more than 3000 miles, we traverse a region at present sparsely inhabited by Indians and European settlers. Here, however, are many stations of the *C. M. S., S. P. G.,* and *W. M. S.,* the last named being now sustained by the Wesleyans of Canada. We can here speak of only one specimen of the hymnal work of this region. Bishop Horden, of the diocese of Moosonee, has recently completed an enlarged hymn-book in the language of the *Cree* Indians, containing 150 hymns, all, except three or four, being his own translations.

4. British Columbia. — We pass to British Columbia, on the North Pacific coast. Here at Metlakahtla, and other places in the north of that territory, are stations of the *C. M. S.* among the *Tsimshean Indians,* and other tribes. For the use of the Tsimsheans a collection of 19 hymns has been made by Bishop W. Ridley, translated by himself, Mrs. Ridley, and Mrs. Morrison, and printed at Metlakahtla. Such hymns as "How sweet the name of Jesus

sounds"; "Just as I am"; "Jesu, Lover of my soul,"&c. are included. In the report of the *C. M. S.* for 1887, we read how on one occasion the last hours of a dying Indian were soothed by the singing of the last named hymn.

In the *Niska* dialect, akin to the Tsimshean, a collection of hymns has been prepared by the Rev. W. H. Collison, to which Mr. J. B. McCullagh, the present missionary on the upper Naas, has recently made additions, including a metrical paraphrase of Ps. xxiii., which is a great favourite with the people.

5. Queen Charlotte's Islands. — Among the *Haidas* of Queen Charlotte's Islands, just off the coast of B. Columbia, another mission of the *C. M. S.* has been established by the Rev. W. H. Collison. In their language, which differs greatly from the Tsimshean, Mr. Collison has composed some hymns, and translated others, which, although not yet pub. in book form, are known and sung far and wide. The present missionary, Rev. C. Harrison, is adding to the number of these hymns.

6. Vancouver's Island.—The Rev. A. J. Hall, of the *C. M. S.,* who is labouring among the *Kwa Gulth* tribe, in the north of Vancouver's Island, has prepared a number of hymns in the language of that people, and has taught them to sing them.

7. Various in the U.S.A.—Passing southward through the territories of the United States, where the Red Men still survive, we find them chiefly to the west of the Mississippi, occupying "Reservations." A recent Government return gives their number as 277,656, of whom only about 30,000 know English enough for ordinary intercourse. Ten American Missionary Societies are at work among them, and the following Hymnals have been prepared for their use by agents of the *A. B. C.:—Cherokee,* 52 pp.; *Creek,* 35 pp.; *Seneca* (two books); *Ojibwa,* 40 pp.; *Choctaw,* 84 pp.; *Dakota* or *Sioux* Indians, 97 pp., by Dr. S. R. Riggs, and another, by the Rev. J. P. Williamson, 184 pp.

8. Mexico.—From the United States territories we naturally pass to Mexico, where the American Baptists of the Southern Convention, the *A. B. C.* and *A. M. E.* have vigorous Protestant missions, conducted for the most part in the Spanish language. But no replies have been received to our inquiries as to their Hymnody.

ii. Central America.

In connection with the *M. M.* in Central America various hymns have been rendered into the language of the *Moskito Indians.* But these have not been printed, as the English hymn-book is mainly used in that mission-field.

In like manner in British Honduras, in Jamaica, the Bahamas, the Bermudas, and other places in the West Indies, where hundreds of congregations of Negroes and Creoles have been gathered into the Church of Christ, the hymn-books used are chiefly those of their respective Denominations in Great Britain.

iii. South America.

1. British Guiana.—Here are missions of the *S. P. G.* and *L. M. S.* The population consists of a great variety of nationalities: the Aborigines, British settlers, and Coolies from China and different parts of India. The

Missionaries teach the Aborigines to sing in English. For the Chinese they obtain hymn-books from Hong Kong ; for the Indian coolies books from India in Tamil, Bengali, Hindi, and Urdu. [See on India, p. 746.]

2. **Dutch Guiana, or Surinam** has stations of the *M. M.* Being a Dutch possession the hymnal used for the services at Paramaribo is in that language, prepared in connection with the *M. M.* in South Africa. But a curious Creole dialect, called *Negro-English*, is the mother tongue of the negroes in many parts of Surinam ; and a hymn-book in this dialect was issued from the mission press in 1820. A new ed. appeared in 1841. Yet another ed., revised and enlarged, has been recently pub. It contains 600 hymns, is attractively bound, and has met with a large sale.

3. **Various.**—More than a century ago the borderland of British and Dutch Guiana was the scene of a Moravian mission to the Ara-wack Indians, and there is still extant in MS. a collection of hymns in that language. With regard to the hymnody of the far greater part of South America, viz. Venezuela, Columbia, Peru, Brazil, Bolivia, the Argentine Republic, and Uruguay, we are able to give but little information. The English South American Missionary Society uses the S. P. C. K. *Church Hymns* for most of its English services, and the hymn-book of the B. & F. Sailors' Society in services for seamen. The *A. M. E.* has missions in Uruguay, the Argentine Republic, and at several places on the Western Coast. The Southern Baptist Convention of the U. States has missions in Brazil ; and the *A. P. M.* in Columbia, Brazil, and Chili, but no answer to letters of enquiry has been received except from Chili. From Valparaiso the Rev. D. Turnbull, D.D., writes to say that two or three hymn-books have been pub. there, the hymns being in Spanish, mostly translations, probably made in Spain, and are not very satisfactory. Hymns are sung at Ooshooia, in Tierra-del-Fuego, and we believe that some of these, probably composed by Capt. Allen Gardiner, are in the language of the Yahgan Indians, but have not been able to ascertain particulars.

II. *Islands of the Pacific, &c.*

Modern geographers have arranged the islands of the great Pacific Ocean under three divisions, Micronesia, Polynesia and Melane-sia. (i.) *Micronesia*, so called from the small-ness of most of its islands, comprises all those lying *north* of the equator, from the Hawaiian group in the east to Malaysia in the west. (ii.) *Polynesia*, a name once used in a wider sense, is now restricted to the islands situated to the *south* of the equator, and between 180° of longitude and S. America. It includes the Marquesan, Tahitian, Samoan, and other groups. (iii.) *Melanesia*, so called from the dark colour of its inhabitants, includes the islands south of the equator, from long. 180° westward to New Guinea, such as the Fiji group, the New Hebrides, and others. Micronesia and Polynesia are inhabited by the Malay-Polynesian race, probably of Asiatic origin. The people are, for the most part, tall and well-formed, their skin of a light yellow colour, their hair a smooth glossy black, and their language soft and mellifluous. The

Melanesians, on the other hand, belong to the Papuan race, and are probably of African origin. Their skin is dark, their hair crisp, and features plain. Their language is quite distinct from the Malay-Polynesian, and is endlessly diversified. Not only on every group of islands but on every island, a different dialect is spoken, and so widely different are they as to be almost, sometimes altogether, unin-telligible to the inhabitants of an adjoining island. It may be conceived how much toil in the learning of languages and the prepara-tion of distinct books, such as hymnals, thi' fact imposes on missionaries.

i. *Micronesia.*

1. **Hawaiian Islands.**—In our notice of hym-nody in the Pacific we begin with the Hawai-ian Islands, at the eastern extremity of Micronesia. These islands, mountainous and volcanic, and yet so lovely in scenery as to be likened to a terrestrial paradise, were once notorious for the barbarism and cruelty of their inhabitants. But now, chiefly through the labours of the missionaries of the *A. B. C.* they are Christianized and civilized. As early as 1823 a small hymn-book of 60 pp. was pre-pared by the Revs. H. Bingham and W. Ellis ; in 1834 appeared a Hymn and Tune Book of 360 pp. edited by the Rev. H. Bingham, and a few years later a Child's hymn-book (72 pp.) by the same editor. In 1842 another Children's book with tunes was pub., and in 1855 ap-peared the *Hawaiian Lyre*. In 1867 the Rev. L. Lyons edited a hymnal for general use, containing 400 hymns, translated by himself, H. Bingham, W. Ellis, A. O. Forbes, R. Arm-strong, and A. Bishop. This has been en-larged, and the last ed. (1885) contains 612 hymns. Mr. Lyons has also translated and pub. the *Sacred Songs and Solos* of Sankey, and other collections of popular Christian songs with music.

In connection with the Anglican mission in these islands, commenced in 1861, services are conducted in the Hawaiian language and hymns are sung, but we have failed to obtain information as to details.

2. **Marshall Islands.**—Sailing west by south from Hawaii, for about 1800 miles, we come to the Marshall Islands, in two groups, compris-ing about 30 coral islets, with a population of 12,000. For their use the Rev. E. T. Doane, of the *A. B. C.*, prepared, in 1860, a Primer and Hymn-book of 44 pp. In 1863 appeared *Hymns*, by Mr. Doane (24 pp.), and in 1866 a similar book edited by the Rev. B. G. Snow, of the same Society.

3. **Caroline Islands.**—Still more to the west are the Caroline Islands, claimed by the Span-iards, the chief of which are Ponape, or Ascension Island, 60 miles in circumference, and Kusaie, or Strong's Island, about 30 miles in circuit. In 1858 a hymn-book of 19 pp. was prepared in the *Ponape* dialect by Dr. L. H. Gulick, and enlarged in 1864-5 by the Rev. A. A. Sturges. Another collection of 32 pp. was prepared in 1865, by the Rev. B. G. Snow, in the *Kusaie* dialect. All this was in connection with the missionary work of the *A. B. C.*

4. **The Gilbert Islands.**—Passing from the Caroline Islands in a south-easterly direction we come upon the Gilbert Islands, right on

the equator, forming 16 groups of a fair size, with many islets, and a population of 30,000. Here the *A. B. C.* has a mission. In 1860 the Rev. H. Bingham, jun., and his wife, pub. a hymn-book of 12 pp. Three years later it was enlarged to 27 pp., and in 1874 and 1877 additional hymns were printed.

Before leaving Micronesia we may quote the Invocation of the Lord's Prayer in some of its different languages. This will show that, though allied in grammatical structure, they are yet so diverse as to require a distinct hymnal literature for each one.

" Our Father, which art in heaven."
Hawaiian. " E ko makou Makua iloko o ka lani."
Marshall Islands. "Jememuij i lon."
Gilbert Islands. " Tamara are i karawa."
Kusaiean. " Papa tumus su in kosao."

ii. *Polynesia.*

We are not able to give information concerning the hymnody of more than two groups of islands in this part of the Pacific. In the Society Islands, including Tahiti, the Hervey Islands, the Tonga Islands, and others, agents of the *L. M. S.* and *W. M. S.* have long laboured, and the people have possessed hymn-books, but we are without details. The Marquesas Islands, six in number, are about 2000 miles east by south from the Hawaiian group, and the language is similar but not identical. In 1870 the Rev. James Bicknell, son of an English Missionary to the Society Islands, prepared in Marquesan a hymn-book of 30 pp., since reprinted. In the important Samoan group, a hymnal is used, begun in 1840, enlarged in successive editions, and now containing 372 hymns and 39 chants. Most of the hymns are translations of well-known English hymns, as " Jesu, Lover of my soul," and " When I survey the wondrous cross " (" Jesu, faapaolo mai," and " A ou manatu ipo nei "); or passages of Holy Scripture paraphrased. The words of the chants are taken from Holy Scripture. The translators were missionaries of the *L. M. S.*, Messrs. Buzacott, Heath, Hardie, Murray, Pratt, Nisbet, G. Turner, LL.D., Parell and Whitmee—Mrs. Turner and Mrs. Nisbett, and Peni, a Samoan pastor.

iii. *Melanesia.*

(1) **The Fijian** group comprises 80 inhabited islands, and has been Christianized mainly through the labours of the *W. M. S.* From the commencement of Christian worship the Lord's Prayer, the Jubilate, the Te Deum, &c., as translated by the early missionaries, have been sung to native chants; but these are monotonous and melancholy. The hymns first used were mainly translations by the Revs. J. Hunt, R. B. Lyth, and J. Walsford. A few of these are still in use and throb with life, " expressing," says the Rev. J. Nettleton, " in mellifluous and Italian-like Fijian all the cadences of Christian faith and hope and love." There have been several editions of the Fijian hymn-book, the one now in use containing 178 hymns, chiefly composed or translated by the Revs. J. Nettleton, — Lorimer,—Fison, M.A., and A. J. Webb. The best hymns are original; the translated ones are stiff. English metres are used and the lines rhyme. The people delight in singing, and

those who have been taught new tunes go round and teach them to others in the villages.

(2) **The New Hebrides.**—About 400 miles west of Fiji and 1000 miles nearly due north of New Zealand, is the group of the New Hebrides, so named by Capt. Cook, because he believed them to be the most westward islands of the Pacific. There are about 30 in the group; nearly 20 are inhabited and some are of considerable size. Almost every inhabited island has its own dialect, often so different from the rest as to be practically a distinct language. But all these dialects belong to the Papuan stock. The *L. M. S.* was the first to begin missionary labour in the New Hebrides, but many years ago the work was amicably transferred to the Reformed Presbyterian Church of Scotland, which in 1876 united with the Free Church of Scotland. The Rev. John Inglis, D.D., who was a missionary in Aneityum, the most southerly island of the group, from 1852 until recently, has furnished us with the following particulars as to the hymnody :—

(*a*) " The hymnal used in *Aneityum* contains 51 hymns—' Nohraiitai Itap'—partly translations or imitations of English hymns, and partly original. They were translated or composed chiefly by the Rev. Drs. Geddie and Inglis,—a few by the Revs. J. Copeland and T. Powell. Also, since the printing of the hymn-book in 1880, some additional hymns have been prepared by the Revs. J. Annand and I. Laurie.

(*b*) " On the island of *Tanna* two languages are spoken, and there are two missionaries, the Rev. Messrs. Watt and Gray. Mr. Watt has from 20 to 30 hymns, chiefly prepared, and all printed by himself. Mr. Gray has a few, prepared by himself, and printed by Mr. Watt.

(*c*) " On *Eromanga*, notorious for the murder of John Williams and of the missionary brothers G. N. and J. D. Gordon, they now sing about 30 hymns, prepared by Messrs. J. D. Gordon and Robertson.

(*d*) " Similarly, small collections of hymns have been prepared for the use of the natives of *Futuna, Efate, Aniwa, Nguna, Tongoa, Epi* and *Ambrim*, the composers or translators being the missionaries respectively located on those islands. In the northern islands of the group a commencement of missionary labour has only just been made."

All the hymns in the above-named collections are composed to English metres and sung to English tunes, but the lines do not rhyme. The native poetry is a kind of elevated prose, cut up into divisions like verses, followed by choruses which are chiefly single syllables with no meaning, such as *lil la, lil la*. And the native music is a kind of chanting, with " a loud noise." Dr. Inglis is of opinion that the singing of Christian hymns would be more popular if they were composed more after the native style of song.

(3) **Banks Islands, Santa Cruz Islands, Solomon Islands, Norfolk Island.** All these islands, except Norfolk Island, are situated to the north and north-west of the New Hebrides, and were brought into notice as a scene of missionary labour through the self-denying devotion of the lamented Bishop Patteson. His plan was to make Norfolk Island, to the south, a base of evangelistic operations, and to visit the other islands periodically, the language of *Mota*, one of the Banks Islands, being used as a *lingua franca*. In his letters (see *Life of Bp. J. C. Patteson*, by C. M. Yonge) are very interesting references to Psalms and Hymns translated or composed by him, and sung in various religious services. Thus, in 1867, the bishop writes from Norfolk Island, " we sing the *Venite, Magnificat, Nunc dimittis*, &c., in

parts, to single and double chants." Again, "and now they are practising hymns in Mota for our 11 a.m. service." And the following year he writes, "Every week we read in chapel about 40 psalms and sing 12 hymns. These are pretty well known by heart." A number of hymns seem to have been in use for years, before being collected into a book. The Rev. Dr. Codrington, who was for some time Bishop Patteson's colleague in the Anglican Melanesian Mission, has favoured us with the following account of the Mota hymn-book :—

"This book, as lately reprinted, contains 67 hymns, and there are three more since in use that I know of. Of these, 25 are by Bishop Patteson. 21 are original compositions, most of them excellent. The rest are adaptations rather than translations. 20 are by myself, of which 8 are original; 12 are by the Rev. C. Bice ; 8 by the Rev. J. Palmer, and 2 by Bishop Selwyn. The hymns by the three last named are translations or adaptations. Among the hymns translated are, ' Thou whose Almighty word,' ' Eternal Father, strong to save,' ' The Church's one foundation,' ' Gracious Spirit, Holy Ghost,' ' How beauteous are the feet,' &c., &c. The most interesting hymns in the book are three by native composers, particularly one by a teacher named Clement Marau, a Banks Islander."

Several hymns were composed by the Rev. C. H. Brooke in the language of Florida, one of the Solomon Islands; others, by Bishop Selwyn and the Rev .C. Bice, in the languages spoken in Ysabel (Solomon Islands), Aurora Island, Pentecost Island, and Leper's Island, in the New Hebrides.

(4) Loyalty Islands. — Between the New Hebrides and the French possession of New Caledonia is a small group, called the Loyalty Islands, the chief of which are Lifu, Maré and Uvea. In these islands the L. M. S. has for many years had a mission. In 1864 what is known as the Lifu Hymn Book was prepared and printed at Maré by the Rev. S. McFarlane, LL.D. It contains 231 hymns. Most are translations of the best English hymns, but many are original. The metres and tunes are English, and the natives are said to sing very well.

(5) New Guinea.—A few years ago the L. M. S. began a mission in the eastern part of New Guinea, and the labours of the Rev. Dr. McFarlane were transferred thither from the Loyalty Islands. Already three small hymn-books have been prepared, each containing 36 hymns, in 3 distinct dialects. These are bound up in one volume with the Gospel of St. Mark and a small catechism. Though belonging to the same Papuan or Melanesian group of languages, these dialects are distinct from the Lifuan both in words and in grammatical structure.

iv. Borneo and Singapore.

(1) Borneo, one of the largest islands in the world, is inhabited for the most part by a people called Dyaks, akin to the Malays, and divided into numerous petty tribes, with exceedingly barbarous usages. Near the coasts are many Malays proper, and in the north-western portion of the island probably a quarter of a million of Chinese. For 40 years past the S. P. G. has had missions in Borneo, which now form part of the diocese of Singapore, Labuan and Sarawak. The Ven. Archdeacon Mesney has supplied us with the following particulars in regard to Christian hymnody.

"Collections of hymns have been made in three languages—Malay, Land Dyak, and Sea Dyak. These have been gradually formed, the 1st now containing about 100 hymns ; the 2nd, about 80, and the 3rd, between 30 and 40. The hymns prepared in the early days of the mission were in simple Malay, and the first hymn was a metrical version of the Creed. Most of the hymns in all three collections are translations or adaptations of English hymns, such as " We love the place, O God ;" " Abide with me ;" " Rock of ages ;" " O come, all ye faithful ;" " Glory be to Jesus," &c. The translators were Bishop Chambers ; the present Bishop, G. F. Hose, D.D. ; the Revs. W. H. Gomes, F. W. Abe, J. L. Zehnder, J. Perham, C. W. Fowler, and other missionaries. A few of the hymns are original, e.g. a harvest hymn in Sea Dyak, and others in Malay, by Bishop Chambers, and some in Sea Dyak by the Rev. J. Perham. English metres and tunes are used, and in most of the hymns the lines rhyme as in English. The books are printed at the mission press, at Kuching, Sarawak."

(2) Singapore has a very mixed population of Malays, Tamils, and Chinese, all of whom the S. P. G. seeks to benefit. The Malay hymn book there used was arranged by the Rev. W. H. Gomes (named above), and was printed at Singapore.

III. Asia.

i. Japan.

In this remarkable country the development of Christian hymnody has been as rapid as that of other ideas and usages so recently introduced from Europe and America. At the close of 1873, when the Rev. C. F. Warren, of the C. M. S. (to whom we are indebted for much of the information contained in this section), arrived in Japan, converts were very few, and though attempts had been made to produce metrical hymns for Christian worship, some were of opinion that the use of hymns could never become general. The character of Japanese poetry presented one great difficulty. " It has neither rhyme, assonance, nor quantity. It is not marked by a regular succession of accented syllables, as in English, and is only distinguished from prose by metre." As a rule Japanese metre consists of lines of 5 and 7 syllables. What is called Short Poetry — the most common — consists of 31 syllables, divided into lines as follows :—5, 7, 5, 7, 7. There is a variation from this with lines thus :—5, 7, 7, 5, 7, 7, and another, though this is not classical, of 17 syllables, 5, 7, 5. The Long Poetry consists of any number of lines of 5 and 7 syllables, regularly alternating and closing with a final line of 7 syllables, thus :—5, 7 . . . . 5, 7, 7. Another difficulty was to find suitable tunes to these peculiar metres. A few English tunes, like " Home, sweet home," could be easily adapted, and one or two Japanese tunes were available. These, however, were but few, and the effect was by no means pleasing. But, notwithstanding these initial difficulties, we have at this moment before us five Japanese Christian hymn-books, and have received information concerning yet others. Altogether there are now at least 350 hymns in the Japanese language. Most of these are translations or adaptations of English and American hymns. They are composed to English metres, though without rhyme, and are sung to English tunes. Among hymnals at present in use may be mentioned the following :—

(1) A hymn-book containing 76 hymns in Roman characters and 43 tunes in Sol-Fa notation was pub. at

Yokohama, in 1876, and prepared by the Rev. Nathan Brown, D.D. [*A. B. M.*]

(2) The same distinguished missionary, who had previously laboured in Assam and Burma, and written hymns in the language of each country [see **Burma**], put forth, in 1876, another hymn-book, in Japanese, containing 138 hymns. This was enlarged in successive eds. until, in 1886, it comprised 337 hymns. It is the recognised hymnal of the *A. B. M.* in Japan, and the last ed. was pub. shortly after Dr. Brown's death. The hymns are chiefly translations, although a good number of original compositions, mostly by native Christians, are included. Three translations and two original hymns are by Miss Clara A. Sands, of the *A. B. M.* From hymn-book No. 1 we may quote, as a specimen of Japanese, the first verse of "All hail the power of Jesus' name":—

> " Yesuno nawo toutomi
> Tentci hirefuse,
> Çuno sokûiwo iwai
> Tençuto tonaye."

(3) The hymn-book of the *Episcopal Church Missions,* American and English, pub. at Osaka, 1883. It was prepared by the Rev. T. S. Tyng, of the *Amer. Epis. Mis.,* and contains 145 hymns. Among them are hymns (some original) by the Revs. P. K. Fyson and C. F. Warren, of the *C. M. S.,* and H. J. Foss, M.A., of the *S. P. G.* The editor, in his preface, also thanks the Rev. H. Evington [*C. M. S.*] and several native scholars for important assistance.

(4) Hymn-book of the *Presbyterians,* called *The United Church of Christ in Japan,* pub. in Tokio, 1881. The translator was Mr. Hara, a Japanese, and it contains 103 hymns, the names of the tunes being attached in English.

(5) Hymn-book of the *A. B. C.* mission, prepared by the Rev. W. Curtis and a committee of natives; pub. at Osaka, 1882. This book contains 130 hymns with tunes, and 14 Psalms set to Chants, and is at present used by the Congregational Churches. But the Rev. Dwight W. Learned [*A. B. C.*] informs us that it is soon to be superseded by one now in course of preparation by a joint committee of missionaries and Japanese representing the *A. B. C.,* the Presbyterian and the Reformed Missions.

(6) The hymn-book of the *A. M. E.,* containing 244 hymns and a few chants edited about 3 years ago, by the Rev. J. C. Davison, of Nagasaki. It contains several tunes composed for it in the Japanese metre 5,7,5,7,7, and is said by Mr. Learned to be the "most elaborate book yet produced in Japan."

Congregational singing is an innovation in Japan. In the Buddhist services the priests alone chant. But thousands of Japanese Christians now sing hymns heartily and even enthusiastically; the use of cabinet organs and harmoniums is common in the churches, and in the girls' schools the pupils learn to play on them.

ii. *China.*

The first hymn-book in China was pub. by Dr. Morrison in 1818, and contained 30 hymns. The number of books prepared and published during the last 50 years has been very large, partly because increased acquaintance with the language has made translators of hymns dissatisfied with their earlier efforts, and prompted them to put forth new ones, and partly because of the number of distinct spoken dialects in China. A peculiarity of the Chinese language is that the written or printed characters represent ideas rather than sounds, and these characters in the *Wen Li,* or "Classic style," are understood by the educated throughout the empire. But the ordinary colloquial varies according to the district. Thus, what is called the *Mandarin Colloquial,* used by the mandarins and in court circles at Peking, is the principal spoken language in North China, the region north of the great Yangtse Kiang. But besides this, are the *Shanghai* and *Foochow* colloquials spoken by about 8 millions each, the colloquial of *Ningpo,* spoken by about 5 millions,

the dialects of *Canton, Swatow, Amoy,* and other districts. Some of these dialects differ so much that interpreters are needed between them. Some missionaries hold that hymnbooks should be in the *Wen Li,* or classical form of the language, and that the people should be educated to the use of it. But the majority have maintained that the present needs of the multitude should be considered, and for this reason have published hymn-books in the various colloquials.

In the present article we shall mention, as samples, books pub. in *North, Middle,* and *South China.*

(i.) **North China.** (1) Through the kindness of the Rev. Jon. Lees, of the *L. M. S.,* we have now before us a copy of the hymn-book pub. by himself and the Rev. J. Edkins, D.D., at Tientsin in 1872. It contains 266 hymns, and from the English index of first lines it appears that almost all are translations (often very free) of the best English hymns. Previous to this the Rev. W. C. Burns had pub. a small collection; and 43 of his translations, in many cases recast, are included in the 1872 book. In the preparation of this book Mr. Lees had as assistants two very able Chinese scholars, the Rev. Chǎng-tsu-leu and his son, Mr. Chǎng-chiu-seng. It is used not only in the North China missions of the *L. M. S.,* but also by Presbyterians and New Connexion Methodists.

(2) Another equally important work is the hymnal pub. at Peking in 1872 by the Revs. D. Blodgett, D.D. and Chauncey Goodrich. It is in the *Mandarin Colloquial,* and has been pronounced by one authority to be "the best hymn-book used in China." Nearly all the hymns are translations. Indeed the number of original Chinese Christian hymns in existence is very small.

(3) In the *B. M.* in North China, a book is used compiled from others, but including a few translations by the Rev. F. H. James [*B. M. S.*].

(4) The Rev. J. Lees has pub. a small book containing 47 hymns, chiefly translations by himself from I. Sankey's *Sac. Songs & Solos,* but including one original hymn by Mr. Chǎng-chiu-seng, and said to be a fine hymn.

(ii.) **Mid-China.** (1) A hymn-book in the *Ningpo* dialect was pub. about 1858, prepared by the Revds. Archdeacon Cobbold of the *C. M. S.;* Dr. Martin and H. V. Rankin, of the *A. P. M.;* J. Hudson Taylor, and others. This was revised and enlarged several times, until in 1875 it included 275 hymns, eleven being translations or compositions by the Ven. Archdeacon Moule [*C. M. S.*]. This hymn-book, printed at the Presbyterian Mission Press, Shanghai, has been used hitherto by Churchmen and Nonconformists in Ningpo, and in other parts of the province of Chehkiang.

(2) In 1871 Bishop Moule prepared a book in the *Hangchow* dialect for the use of the churches of the *C. M. S.* in that city and neighbourhood. It contains 82 hymns, and is printed in both Roman and Chinese characters.

(3) Archdeacon Moule [*C. M. S.*] has now (1887) in the press at Shanghai a collection which he hopes will be widely intelligible in China. It contains 221 hymns, some being

translations by himself, others by his brother, Bishop Moule, and one hymn is original.

(4) The collection compiled by the Rev. Griffith John, of Hankow [*L. M. S.*], contains 200 hymns, all translations. Of these 8 or 10 are from the Welsh, made either by Mr. John or the Rev. Evan Bryant [*L. M. S.*]. In the later editions many expressions of the *Mandarin Colloquial* have been exchanged for others belonging to the literary style. This book is used by many missionaries of the China Inland Mission, and also at I Chang, a station of the *K. S. M.*

(5) At the *W. M. S.* at Hankow a book is used, compiled by the Rev. W. Scarborough, and pub. in 1875. It was preceded by a hymnal prepared by the Rev. Josiah Cox. The 180 hymns in the present book are chiefly translations, many of them from Sankey's *Sac. Songs & Solos.* "We wait," says Mr. Scarborough, "for a Christian poet in China." The dialect is the *Mandarin Colloquial.*

(iii.) South China. (1) The most flourishing missions in China up to the present have been those of the English Presbyterian Church at Amoy, Swatow, in Formosa and in the Hakká country. Two hymn-books have been prepared, one in the *Amoy* dialect, containing 70 hymns, the other, in that of *Swatow,* containing over 150. Some of these are translations of Psalms, others translations or adaptations of English hymns, and a few are original. The Rev. W. S. Swanson, of the E. Presb. Mission, informs us that the Rev. Wm. Young, of the *L. M. S.*, was the first successful composer of hymns in the *Amoy* dialect, and 13 of his hymns are still in use. To him succeeded the Rev. W. C. Burns, already mentioned. The Revs. Carstairs Douglas, LL.D., J. V. N. Talmage, D.D., and Alex. Stronach have also helped in the work. In connection with the Presbyterian Missions in this part of China many interesting facts might be related illustrative of the value of hymnody as an evangelistic agency, but for these we have no room.

(2) The great city of Foochow is the central station of three missions—those of the *C. M. S., A. B. C. & A. M. E.* In 1860 the Rev. W. C. Burns, named above, was here temporarily, and prepared in the *Foochow Colloquial* a translation of hymns written by Mr. Young and himself, which had previously appeared in the Amoy dialect. He added others, making up a book of more than 30 hymns. These were deemed so excellent that they were adopted by all three missions, and superseded others previously used which were in the *Wen-Li,* or book language. In course of time more hymns were desired, and each of the missions, taking Mr. Burns's book as a foundation, pub. a Hymnal of its own. (*a*) The hymn-book of the *C.M.S.* contains 198 hymns, and was prepared by the Revs. J. R. Wolfe, R. W. Stewart, M.A., and Ll. Lloyd, Mr. Wolfe being the principal contributor. (*b*) The hymn-book of the *A. B. C.* contains 165 hymns. Through the kindness of the Rev. C. Hartwell, one of the principal contributors to this book, a copy is now before us printed at Foochow, on native paper. It contains several original hymns by native converts. (*c*) The hymn-

book of the *A. M. E.* has 180 hymns, and was prepared by the Revs. R. S. Maclay, D.D., S. L. Baldwin, D.D., and F. Ohlinger. A large number of the hymns are common to all three books.

(3) We are indebted to the Rev. John Chalmers, LL.D., of Hongkong, one of the oldest and most learned missionaries now in China, for the following information concerning Hongkong and Canton. When he came to China in 1852 he found a book in use, pub. two years previously by Rev. Dr. Legge, entitled

(1) *Hymns for the worship of the Lord.* The number of hymns was 81, with 7 doxologies. No hymn was a translation, and everything was done in regard to language and metre to command the respect of the literary class, and in so far it was a success. In 1860 Dr. Chalmers pub. an ed. of this book with tunes in the usual English notation, and for nearly 30 years this was the only book in use in the London Mission at Canton and in Hongkong. In 1879 Dr. Chalmers pub. *New Songs for the worship of the Lord,* as a *Supplement* to the previous book. This contained 18 translations of popular English and American hymns; and being liked by the people, received, in 1884, considerable additions. The volume thus finally produced is the one now in use.

(2) *Hymns for Singing Praise.* W. M. S., Canton, 1863. "This," says Dr. Chalmers, "was one of the most successful early attempts to translate English hymns." The translator was the Rev. George Piercy. The number of hymns is 34. The translation is by no means literal, and the rhyming is somewhat adapted to Chinese ideas.

(3) *Hymns for praising the Lord.* A. B. M., Canton, 1875. It contains about 20 of the *L. M. S.* hymns, nearly all the 34 of the *W. M. S.* in both cases much altered, and many other translations of English and American hymns, making up 286.

(4) *Hymns for praising the Lord.* W. M. S., Canton, 1877. A book much like the preceding, and containing 230 hymns. It was compiled by the Rev. G. Piercy, before named.

(5) *Hymn-book of the Basel Mission.* Hongkong, 1884. "This book," says Dr. Chalmers, "is exceptionally good." The number of hymns is 284. Many are translations from German hymns, and those taken from the Baptist and Wesleyan books are usually improved in style. Beginning, about 1860, with a book of 55 hymns compiled by the Rev. R. Lechler, it has attained its present size and arrangement through the combined labours of Messrs. Piton, Genähr, Lechler, Bender and others.

(6) *Hymn-book of the C. M. S., Hongkong.* Altered from blocks in the Americo-Chinese College, Peking, 1886. This book has been introduced by Bishop Burdon. It contains 315 hymns and 10 doxologies.

It remains to add a few words in regard to the music sung to these hymns and the metres employed. Chinese native music is quite unsuited to sacred song. English, American and German tunes are therefore used and are commonly liked by the people.

In most of the books named above our metres are used and the lines rhyme as in English. But in the Canton book of the *L. M. S.* and one or two others, the rules of Chinese poetry are observed, some of which are as follows. "Sevens" is decidedly the "Common Metre," our C.M. and S.M. being regarded as irregular innovations. Next comes "Fives," and then "Eights," which is really "Fours," every four syllables making a clause. The same rhyme is kept up from the beginning to the end of a hymn, an arrangement made easy by the nature of the language. Let the following represent a hymn of eight lines, and the two kinds of marks, × and o, indicate the alternations of "tones" required in a finished poem. The proper places for the rhyme syllable and changes of tone may be expressed thus:—

1.	✗ ✗ o o ✗ ✗	rhyme-syllable
2.	o o ✗ ✗ o o	rhyme
3.	o o ✗ ✗ o ✗	
4.	✗ ✗ o o ✗ ✗	rhyme
5.	✗ ✗ o o ✗ ✗	
6.	o o ✗ ✗ o o	rhyme
7.	o o o ✗ o o ✗	
8.	✗ ✗ ✗ ✗ ✗ ✗	rhyme.

There should also be antithesis of meaning between the third and fourth, and between the fifth and sixth lines.

Referring to the difficulty of compliance with these strange and exacting rules, a missionary correspondent wittily observes that the descendants of the writer of the 119th Psalm would be the likeliest persons to succeed in the attempt to create a good Christian Chinese hymn.

iii. *Siam.*

The name *Siam* both stands for Siam proper (chief city, Bangkok) and, in a wider sense, embraces certain dependent States of Shans and Laos, with a part of the Karen country. The population consists of about 6,000,000 in Siam proper, 3,000,000 Shans and Laos, and upwards of 1,500,000 Chinese. The religion of nearly the whole country is Buddhism, mingled with a kind of nature worship in the ruder tribes of the north. The Siamese language is monosyllabic, many words having a variety of different meanings, according to the tone with which they are pronounced. The *A. B. M.* has missions to the numerous Chinese of Bangkok, and to the Karens and Shans, for a notice of which see **Burma**. The *A. B. C.* commenced a mission to the Siamese in 1840, which since 1871 has been carried on by the American Presbyterians. It has stations at Bangkok and Petchaburi (about 85 miles to the south from Bangkok), and also among the Laos, 500 miles to the north. The Laos speak a language akin to Siamese.

The first hymn-book in Siamese was prepared by missionaries of the *A. B. C.*, with the title *Sacred Songs*. The 3rd ed. bears date 1859, and comprises, with a *Supplement*, 196 hymns. Another book, with a similar title, was pub. by the *A. B. M.* in 1860, containing 123 hymns, the compiler being the Rev. S. J. Smith, a Baptist missionary. A few years later a small collection was pub. for use in schools and prayer-meetings. These have all been superseded by the *Siamese Hymnal*, prepared by Dr. S. G. McFarland, and printed at Petchaburi in 1876. It contains 213 hymns, and has passed through several editions, the last in 1886. For this book the best of the old hymns in the two *Sacred Songs* were selected, and many new ones translated or composed. A smaller and cheaper book is also about to be issued.

About 400 hymns now exist in Siamese, most of them being translations from the English by various missionaries. Of the original compositions some are by missionaries; 10 good ones are by a converted Buddhist priest named Chan; and quite a number by Kru Phoon, a native who, strange to say, is still a Buddhist, though having been in the employ of the mission as scribe and translator for 18 years, he has a good knowledge of both the doctrines and spirit of Christianity. Miss Mary L. Cort, of the *A. P. M.* (to whom we are indebted for much of the preceding information), has sent us a list of the principal translated hymns, which includes most of those best known in England and America. Our metres and tunes are used, and the lines rhyme as with us. Native airs have not yet been utilized in Christian song. "Siamese music is very weird and monotonous, and is never used in the temple services, only at funerals and weddings, in processions, and in connection with boat-races and theatres."

Every native song is composed in lines of 11 syllables, but the Siamese learn western tunes readily, and seem to like them, especially tunes in 11's metre, and everything in a minor key.

iv. *Burma.*

Under the head of **Burma** we have to speak (1) of Burma proper, and (2) of certain tribes inhabiting the more mountainous districts, and known as Karens and Shans.

(i.) **Burma Proper.** In Burma the *A. B. M.*, *S. P. G.* and *W. M. S.* have missions, but that of the last named has been commenced only recently. The *A. B.* Mission was begun in 1814, by the celebrated Rev. Dr. Judson [p. 609, i.], and in the early years of the mission there was no singing. Dr. Judson himself could not sing, and according to Burman ideas, singing in connection with worship was improper. In the native mind it was almost exclusively associated with theatrical and other similar performances. After a time, however, Dr. Judson composed the first Burman hymn—

" Shway pyee koung-gin,"
" Golden country of heaven,"

and his fellow missionary, Dr. Wade, became responsible for the music. But it was not until long after, on the arrival of missionaries named Cutter and Hancock, who were good singers, that "the service of song" became popular as a part of worship.

The Baptists in Burma have now a hymn-book containing 294 hymns, 125 being translations and 169 originals. Through the kindness of the Rev. H. S. Durrage, D.D., of Portland, Maine, we are enabled to give the following particulars, supplied by the Rev. Dr. Cushing, the missionary in Burma :—

Three of the hymns, and these among the best, are by Dr. Judson. They are almost the only ones in which a foreigner has endeavoured to embody Burman ideas of poetry, which are very different from ours. In Burman songs the lines are usually short, and 'rhyme runs riot,' it being quite common for every word in a line to rhyme with the corresponding word in the second verse of the couplet. This arrangement is comparatively easy, owing to the monosyllabic character of the language. Fifteen hymns were written by Mrs. Sarah B. Judson [p. 609, i.], the Doctor's second wife (d. in 1845), and one by his third wife Emily C. Judson (d. in 1854). Eighty-nine hymns, chiefly *trs.* or adaptations from the English, are by the Rev. E. A. Stevens, D.D.; his son, the Rev. E. O. Stevens, b. in Burma in 1838, contributed 27. Mrs. C. Simons (d. in 1843) composed 22 hymns, said to be very excellent. The Rev. J. R. Haswell (d. 1877) contributed 19 hymns. Burman was a mother tongue to him, and his hymns have much of the sonorous, stately movement which characterises the religious language of the people. 14 hymns were composed by the Rev. L. Ingalls (d. 1856); 13 by the Rev. J. M. Haswell, D.D. (d. 1856), and 10 by the Rev. Lyman Stilson (d. 1886). The Rev. N. Brown, D.D., who d. at Yokohama in 1885 (see **Japan**), was the writer of 9 hymns in the Burman hymn-book, one of which, a translation of 'There is a happy land,' has always been exceedingly popular. The Rev. Jon. Wade, D.D., colleague of Dr. Judson, was the author of 7 hymns. Others were written by Miss Kate F. Evans, the Revs. A. R. R. Crawley, T. Allen, and Cephas Bennett, Mr. B. Le Geois, Mrs. Crawley, Mrs. R. A. Bailey, Mrs. H. C. Stevens, and Mrs. A. W. Lonsdale. Several native Burmans have also composed hymns, some of which are written in lines of seven syllables, in accordance with the Burmese style. One of these Burmans, Moung Shway Bwin, was a man of some literary reputation, and assisted Rev. L. Stilson in preparing the 2nd edition of the hymn-book.

Besides the book just described, another has been pub. in connection with the *A. B. M.*, containing more than 200 of I. Sankey's *Sac. Songs and Solos*. A few of the translations are by missionaries already named, but most are by Ah Sow and Ah Syoo, two brothers of

Chinese extraction on their father's side, employed as teachers in a mission school at Maulmain.

In connection with the *S. P. G.* mission a hymn-book was pub. in 1879, edited by the Rev. J. Fairclough, but prepared chiefly by the Rev. James A. Colbeck. It contains, including the two *Appendices*, about 120 hymns. One appendix was prepared by the Rev. T. Rickard. A few hymns are taken from the book of the *A. B. M.*, but most are translations by the Rev. Messrs. Colbeck and Rickard. English metres and tunes are used, and the lines rhyme as with us.

(ii.) **Other parts of Burma.** In the hill country of Burma dwell the

(i.) **Karens,** a semi-aboriginal people, of Mongolian origin, divided into three tribes, speaking distinct dialects of a monosyllabic language, Sgau, Bghai, and Pgho or Pwo. The missions of the *A. B. M.* have been remarkably successful among them, many thousands having embraced the Christian faith.

(1) For their use a hymn-book has been prepared in the *Sgau Karen* dialect containing 442 hymns, 216 of which are translations or adaptations of English hymns by Mrs. Calista Vinton (d. 1865), wife of the missionary, the Rev. Justus H. Vinton. This lady has been spoken of as the "Watts" of Karen hymnody. Her son, the Rev. J. B. Vinton, D.D., b. in Burma, contributed 60 hymns (chiefly translations) to the same book. 54 were written by the Rev. B. C. Thomas (d. 1868); 45 by the Rev. D. A.W. Smith, D.D., now President of the Rangoon Theological Seminary, and 9 by the Rev. E. B. Cross, D.D. The Rev. Francis Mason, D.D., translator of the Karen Bible, was the author of many hymns, only 9 of which have been preserved in the Sgau Karen hymn-book. He also prepared a volume of hymns in the *Bghai Karen* dialect, which was used until recently in the Bghai churches. Dr. Mason's hymns are written in the style of native Karen poetry. Each line consists of seven syllables, and the thought is expressed in couplets resembling the parallelism of Hebrew poetry. They can be fitly used only with the "plaintive, weird, strangely sweet" native Karen music, and hence at the revision of the hymn-book many of them were replaced by others which could be sung to Western tunes. The remaining hymns were contributed by other missionaries or their wives, or by native hymn-writers.

(2) *Church Hymns.* A book with this title was brought out in 1881 by the Rev. Wordsworth Jones, missionary of the *S. P. G.*, among the *Sgau Karens.* It originally comprised 98 hymns. In 1885 an *Appendix* was added containing 56 hymns. These are chiefly translations, 79 being by the Rev. W. Jones, 9 by the Rev. T. W. Windley, and 2 by J. Hackney; others are from the book of the *A. B. M.* Thirteen are original, 4 being composed by the Rev. W. Jones, and others by native clergymen. A large number of the translations are from *H. A. & M.* English metres and tunes are used, and are appreciated by the natives.

(ii.) **Pgho Karen.** The Rev. D. L. Brayton, of the *A. B. M.*, is the principal translator and composer of hymns in this dialect. He translated the Bible into Pgho or Pwo Karen, and is the author of most of its Christian literature.

(iii.) **Shan.** The Shans are a numerous people, occupying most of the region between Burma and China, the Siamese being one branch. They are Buddhists, and in their various branches speak the same language with little variation. Many are found in Burma, in the basin of the Irawadi and elsewhere; and for their use a hymn-book, containing 87 hymns, has been prepared by missionaries of the *A. B. M.* Seventy-nine of these are translations and four originals, by the Rev. J. N. Cushing, D.D. Three were composed by Shway Wa, an able man, who in the recent occupation of Upper Burma by the English, acted as chief Shan interpreter.

(iv.) **Khyan, or Chin.** There is also a people

related to the Karens inhabiting the hills separating Upper Burma from the Shan and Chinese territories, and speaking a language called Khyan. A small hymn-book has been prepared for them, but we are unable to supply particulars.

It may be added that in Burma are many Telugu, Tamil, and even Chinese immigrants, whose religious needs are not overlooked by Christian missionaries. For their use hymn-books are brought from mission stations in India and China.

v. *India.*

In the collection of countries to which we give the general name of India more than 250,000,000 of people dwell, the various nations and tribes differing in colour, stature and other physical characteristics, having different local customs and, what chiefly concerns us now, speaking many different languages. In our account of hymnody in India it will be most convenient to treat the subject in sections according to the languages.

(1) The *Northern and Central* parts are inhabited chiefly by nations of the *Aryan* stock, the principal languages of this group being *Bengalí, Uriyá, Hindí, Hindustání* or *Urdú, Maráthí, Gujarátí, Punjabí* and *Sindhí. Sanskrit,* to which all in this group are related, is not a spoken language; it is the language of the learned and has no Christian hymns. [See **Various,** under **Missions, F.**]

(2) In the *South of India* are nations and tribes of what is called the *Dravidian* group. Their languages belong to the agglutinative phase of human speech, as opposed to the inflexional stage, represented by the later Aryan migrations into India. The principal members of this group are *Tamil, Telugu, Malayálam, Canarese,* and *Tulu.*

(3) Tribes of common origin, though now often widely separated, and whose languages belong to what philologists call the *Kolarian* group, occupy certain mountainous, wooded regions, usually remote from the coast. These are the *Santals, Kohls, Juangs,* and others. Descended probably from the most ancient inhabitants of India, they are often spoken of as *Aborigines.*

(4) Lastly, there are tribes occupying *Assam, Sikkim,* and the passes leading towards Thibet and China, whose languages form part of the Thibeto-Burman group. These are the *Kacharis, Deori-Chutias, Bhutias, Lepchas,* and others.

i. *The Northern and Central Groups.*

In these groups we have :—

1. **Bengali,** the vernacular of nearly 50 millions of people.

Baptists.—The first to compose Christian hymns in this language was the celebrated Baptist missionary, Dr. Carey. In Dr. Rippon's *Annual Register* is a hymn in Bengalí, written by Dr. Carey about 1798, and translated into English by J. Fountain [**Fountain, J., p. 384, i.**]. The subject is "the Penitent's Prayer and Resolve," and the metre, the English 8.7.4, to be sung to the tune "Helmsley." Some time afterwards a hymn-book was prepared by the Serampore Missionaries, and in 1810 the missionary, J. Chamberlain, pub. a volume consisting chiefly of translations of English hymns.

The book at present in use at the Baptist mission stations appeared about fifty years ago, and was edited by the Rev. Geo. Pearce (d. 1887). It contains 475 hymns, chiefly in native metres. Among the authors named are W. Carey, J. Chamberlain, G. Pearce and A. Sutton. The names of 18 Bengalis also appear among the contributors, and Krishna Pal's well-known hymn is included.

Church of England.—(1) The hymn-book used in the Anglican missions (*C. M. S.* and *S. P. G.*) entitled ' Hymns Old and New,' was prepared by a committee of the two Societies and has been often revised and enlarged,—on the last occasion, in 1884. It contains 546 hymns, 254 being in English metres, and almost all translations. The remaining 292 are in Bengalí metres, and are nearly all original. The chief and best translator was the late Rev. R. P. Greaves; others were Revs. J. Vaughan, A. Stern, C. Bomwetsch, J. J. Weitbrecht, J. J. Linke, C. D. Lippe, and Mr. J. K. Biswas, all of the *C. M. S.* A few hymns are taken from the Baptist collection. The original hymns in Bengalí metres were nearly all written by native Christians. An Appendix to this book containing about 400 hymns is in preparation and will be pub. by the Bishop's College.

(2) The ' *Sabbath School Hymn Book*,' was prepared by the Teachers of the Trinity Church Sunday School, and contains 254 hymns. 2nd edit. in 1885.

(3) The *C. M. S.* '*Mission Hymn Book*' appeared in 1887. It contains 55 hymns.

Special mention ought to be made of the part taken in this great work of the Church by the Rev. Jacob K. Biswas, tutor in the Divinity School of the *C. M. S.* He has composed and translated no fewer than 1000 hymns in English and Bengalí metres. Many of these have appeared in the books already named and in the Hymnals described below.

Wesleyan.—In connection with the *W. M. S.* a book has been prepared entitled *A Methodist Hymnal for Bengal* (2nd ed., 1886), the compiler being the Rev. J. A. Macdonald. It contains 322 hymns, and 51 lyrics of a kind very popular in all parts of India (see §§ **Marathi,** **Tamil,** &c.), usually sung in processions at festivals, to the accompaniment of a drum and cymbals. Many of the translations are by the editor. Others are by the missionaries of the *B. M. S.* and *C. M. S.*, named above, with the addition of the Revs. H. Harrison and C. Krauss, of the *C. M. S.*, and N. C. Biswas of the *W. M. S.*

The *Calcutta Vernacular Education Society* has pub. a hymn-book called *Gitihar*, containing 138 selected hymns. It is being revised, and promises to become very popular.

A. M. E.—The Rev. J. P. Meik, of the *A. M. E.*, has brought out a similar small collection, consisting of original and translated hymns.

K. S. M.—In 1884 the missionaries of the *K. S. M.* adopted the Anglican Bengalí hymn-book. Before that time they had used two small hymnals prepared by Babu Bipro Charan Chakrabutty. This gentleman has recently pub. a collection of 29 lyrics of the kind mentioned above.

Indeed, small collections of hymns by educated Christian natives are very common in Bengal. Such are the *Gitamrito* (" Immortal Songs "), by Amrito Lal Nath, said to be very good; the Khulnea Hymns, by Gogou Chunder Dutt; *Gitankur* (" Song Germs "), *Gitmala* (" Garland of Songs "), and *Gitrotro* (" Jewels of Songs "), by a Christian Evangelist, Modhu Sudon Sircar. The last-named collection contains many hymns very appropriate for Bazar preaching.

In connection with Bengalí hymns and hymn-writing the following remarks by the Rev. G. H. Rouse, M.A., of Calcutta (*B. M. S.*) are worthy of notice:—

"Native Bengali hymnody is abundant, but meagre. New hymns are being constantly made, but the range is limited; very little about the Holy Ghost, or Christian experience, except of the mournful order. ' O my soul, how wicked thou art,' is a sentiment we are always meeting; but ' How happy they that know the Lord !' does not meet with much response. Joyous Christian experience is very deficient in the native church of Bengal, but things are improving."

Perhaps these statements may be partly explained by the fact that in this part of India the native idea of music is wholly melancholy.

2. **Uriya.** Travelling from Calcutta in a south-westerly direction for about 70 miles we leave Bengal proper and enter the province of Orissa, containing a population of 5,250,000. The language is called *Uriyá* and belongs to the Sanscrit group. At Purí in Orissa, is the world-famous shrine of Juggernaut, visited by 300,000 pilgrims annually. For many years the General Baptists have had a mission in Orissa, their principal station being Cuttack. Since 1836 the Free Baptists of New England, whose doctrinal sentiments are similar to those of the General Baptists, have occupied Balasore and other stations in the northern part of the province.

The first Uriya hymn-book was pub. for the Baptists by Rev. Amos Sutton, D.D., in 1844. [See **Sutton, A.**] It contained 310 hymns, 179 of which bear the initial of the compiler. Gunga Dhor, the first Uriya convert, a Brahmin by birth and education, composed 65, and Rev. C. Lacey 34. But this hymn-book has long been disused. As the Christian community increased, hymn-writers and hymns increased rapidly, and from these latter selections were made from time to time, and printed in tract form. The hymn-book now in use amongst the Baptists consists of eight of these selections bound together in one volume. The total number of hymns is 302, from 23 contributors, of whom 13 are now living. Forty hymns from the old book are retained, including some of Dr. Sutton's and 23 of Gunga Dhor's. It is believed that several of these latter, from their superior quality, as regards both sentiment and poetry, will continue in use for a long time to come. Makunda Das, who has been called the " Dr. Watts of Orissa," composed 145 of the hymns in the present book. Shem Sahu is the author of 57. Other native contributors are Kartick Samal, Bamadeb, and Daniel Mahanty. In the first book a number of the hymns were in English metres. These have disappeared, and the present collection consists entirely of hymns in native metres adapted to the ballad tunes of the country. Makunda Das has also prepared, in conjunction with Shem Sahu and Rev. P. E. Heberlet, a selection of hymns for the *Young*, mostly translations from the English. A number of these are in English metres, and are sung to English tunes in the schools.

3. **Hindí, and Urdú.** Ascending the stream of the Ganges in a north-westerly direction we enter, as we pass the city of Rajmahal, a vast and populous region in which two languages are spoken, *Hindí* and *Urdú*, called also *Hindustáni*. This region includes the North-West Provinces, Oudh, and the northern part of the Central Provinces of India,

with a total population of 80,000,000. Some prefer to speak of these two languages as but different forms of one language, though they are almost as diverse as English and German. *Hindí*, which is allied to the Sanscrit, may be regarded as the original vernacular; *Urdú*, literally, " Camp " language, came in with the Muhammadan conquerors of the country, and has *Hindí* for its basis, with a large admixture both of Persian, the court language of the Moguls, and of Arabic, the sacred language of Islam. *Hindí* uses the Sanscrit characters, upright, square and block-like ; *Urdú* employs the Persian script characters, which are distinguished by flowing curves and are written from right to left. *Urdú* is most common in large cities, and is used by Muhammadans; *Hindí* is preferred by the villagers, and wherever Hindu influences prevail. The two languages, says Dr. Hooper, of the *C. M. S.* " act upon one another, and neither is spoken pure, except as a form of pedantry." The educated classes commonly understand both.

(*a*) The mingling of the two languages is seen in the first hymn-book we notice, the *Sat Sangrah*, or *Gít Sangrah*, issued in connection with the *B. M. S.*, and used at their stations in Monghyr, Allahabad, Agra, Benares, Delhi, Patna and Dinapore. This book, which has reached a 5th edition, contains 267 hymns, of which 193 are in (*a*) *Hindí*, language and metre; 41 in (*b*) *Urdú*, language and metre; and 33 (*c*) *Hindí* language and English metre.

Most of the 1st class (*a*) were written by the Revs. J. Chamberlain (d. 1826), J. Parsons, of Monghyr (d. 1869), and Mr. J. Christian, an Indigo planter, a member of the Baptist Church at Monghyr (d. 1883). A few are by native converts. The whole of the 2nd class (*b*) are by Hindu composers. The 3rd (*c*), which are free versions of English and German hymns, are by various missionaries. Two eds. of this book with music have been pub. by Dr. Lazarus.

The hymns of Mr. John Christian, composed to Hindu airs and in Hindu metres, deserve special notice. Anglican, Baptist and Congregational missionaries all speak of them as being peculiarly excellent, and as likely to retain a high place in the affection of the Christian Churches of this part of India for a long time to come.

Before us is a collection of 100 hymns, called Satyd-Shatah, all by Mr. Christian, including, however, some in the hymn-book already described. This is not a book intended for use in the churches, but rather to be circulated as a tract. Indeed, tracts of hymns are much employed as a missionary agency, the people of India being extremely fond of anything in the form of poetry; and Mr. Christian's hymns may often be heard sung in the streets, as snatches of songs are with us.

(*b*) Another collection similar to the one just named has been sent us by Col. Millett, of Dharmsala, India (to whom we are indebted for much of the information contained in this section). It is entitled *Diffusion of Praise*, a Book of *Bhajans*, pub. by the North India Book and Tract Society.

And here it may be stated that the word *Bhajan* is the name usually given in this part of India to a hymn composed to a native Hindu tune, and it implies the tune as well as the words. Col. Millett says " there is no equivalent for this word in the English language. It may be termed a song in a savage state." But speaking

generally, *Bhajan* is the Hindu name, and *Ghazal* the Muhammadan name, for a Christian hymn in native style.

(*c*) An *Urdú* hymnal was compiled and printed eight years ago by the Rev. R. F. Guyton, for the use of the Baptist Mission in Delhi. It is entitled *Kharzáná i Khurrami*, and contains the 193 Hindí hymns of the *Sat Sangrah* (named above) *transliterated*; the 41 in Urdú, with about 70 additional, extracted or contributed.

(*d*) The *A. P. M.* pub. in 1872, *Zabúr aur Gít* (" Psalms and Hymns "). It contains 485 hymns in English metres, nearly all in *Urdú*, the few exceptions being in *Hindí*: also, 31 *Bhajans*, chiefly *Hindí*, with a few *Ghazals* in *Urdú*. An *appendix* of 72 tunes is added.

The editor of this book was the Rev. J. F. Ullmann, who also translated, from the English or German, the far greater number of the hymns. Some are by the Revs. Messrs. Brodhead, Däuble, Droese and Janvier, and a few by Shujáat Alí, a native poet of some eminence, recently deceased. This book is printed in Roman characters, and is used in other missions besides the *A. P. M.*

(*e*) The *Masíhí Gít ki Kitáb* (" Christian Hymn-book "), printed in 1876 at the Secundra Orphanage Press, near Agra, was prepared at the suggestion of the Rev. J. Erhardt by a committee of missionaries of the *S. P. G.* & *C. M. S.*, and is arranged according to the order of the Christian Year. It contains 387 hymns in English metres and 13 *Bhajans*. The translations are chiefly by the Rev. Messrs. Banli, Ullmann, Däuble, and Erhardt. Bishop French and others contributed single hymns. Many are identical with the hymns in the book of *A. P. M.* It is printed in both Roman and Persian Urdú characters.

(*f*) *Gít ki Kitáb* (" Book of Hymns ") is the Urdú Hymnal of the *A. M. E.*, and is printed in both Roman and Urdú characters. It contains 210 hymns in English metres, 75 *Ghazals* and *Bhajans*, and 16 hymns for Sunday-schools. The list of translators and composers of hymns contains the names of Ullmann, Fieldbrave, Baume, Waugh, Däuble, Brodhead, Parker, Chamberlain, Mansell, Gill, Janvier, Christian, Shujaat Ali and others.

(*g*) The preceding are the principal books: others less important include :—

Gitáwali, " Hymns and Songs for Children," by J. F. Ullmann ; *Int. aur Rore* (" Bricks and Brickbats ") Hymns for Children, with music, by the Rev. E. Droese ; *Sikandra ki Choti Gítmálá* (" The Little Sikandra Hymnbook "), by the Rev. C. G. Däuble, a collection of 53 hymns and Anthems ; *Choti Gít ki Kitáb*, " Sunday School aur Ibadat ne Liye," containing 152 hymns, pub. at Lucknow, in 1884, at the Church Mission Congregational Press ; *Stuti Prakásh*, a book of Hindí hymns by the Rev. W. F. Johnson, of the *A. P. M.*

It may be added that the American United Presbyterian Church, which does not use hymns, has brought out, in connection with the Siálkot Mission, metrical versions of many Psalms, by Licentiate T. D. Shah Báz, and quite recently (1887), a collection of 100 Psalms in metre printed at the Secundra Orphanage Press, Agra.

(*h*) In the broad tableland of Chota Nagpore, about 200 miles from Calcutta, are very successful missions of the German Evangelical Lutherans and of the S. P. G. The inhabitants are chiefly aboriginal tribes belonging to two distinct races, the *Mundáris* or *Kolhs*, of the *Kolasian* group, and the *Uraüns*, of the

Dravidian group of South India. Of the former we shall speak again in the section devoted to the aborigines of India. Both are to some extent acquainted with Hindí, as well as with their own languages. Hence the following books have been prepared in *Hindí*.

(*a*) The Hymnal of the German E. L. Mission, reprinted and enlarged several times between 1850 and 1880, and now containing 123 hymns, chiefly translated from the German, by the Revs. E. Schatz, H. Batsch, and others.

(*b*) The Anglican *Church Hymnal*, including many hymns from the German book, with 22 from *H. A. & M.*, translated by the Rev. J. C. Whitley, together with Miss Havergal's "Tell it out among the heathen," and "Lord, speak to me," by the same author. The metres and tunes used are English and German, usually the same as in the originals.

(*c*) A book of *Hymns for Children*, by the missionaries of the German *E. L. M.*, is now (1888) ready for publication.

(*i*) The Rev. H. D. Williamson, of the *C. M. S.* of Mundla, in the Central Provinces, has lately compiled a small hymn-book in *Hindí*, containing some hymns of his own composition, but we are without information as to particulars.

(*k*) The United Presbyterians of Scotland have important missions in Rajpootana, and in the Annual Report for 1887 are some interesting allusions to hymns and sacred song. For instance:—

At Ajmere the school children "commit hymns to memory and make vigorous, if not always successful, efforts to sing." At Oodeypore "the children can repeat and sing several of the hymns dear to the heart of childhood all the world over." And at Ulwar "every Tuesday evening a service of praise is held in the church. Christian hymns and bhajans are sung to the accompaniment of the organ, and a brief address is given." The principal hymn-book used is one of which the 2nd (enlarged) edition appeared in 1883. It comprises about 300 hymns and bhajans, printed in Hindí characters, though many are in the Urdú language. It is chiefly a compilation from the hymnals named above, in paragraphs *a, d, e* and *f*, with additions, original and translated, by Munshi Hasan Ali, the Rev. J. Gray (editor) and others.

(*l*) Leaving this part of India and recrossing a portion of the immense district already traversed, on the slope of the gigantic Himálayas, we arrive at the *K. S. M.* at **Darjeeling**, and the Scottish Universities Mission in British and Independent **Sikkim**. The languages spoken in these districts are Hindí, Nepálí, Bengalí, Urdú, Lepchá and Bhutia; but Nepálí is a dialect of Hindí, and Hindí is the *lingua franca* used by the Mission. Up to 1884 a hymn-book had been used consisting of the *Urdú* hymnal of the *L. M. S.* at Mirzapore bound up with some Hindí hymns collected by the late Rev. W. Macfarlane of the *K. S. M.* But in that year the Rev. A. Turnbull, B.D. pub. a book entitled *Prayer and Hymn Collection*.

It contains 256 hymns. Twenty-two are originals or translations by Mr. Turnbull; one is by Rev. J. F. Campbell, of Mhow; the rest are taken from other Hindí or Urdú hymn-books, such as the *Git Sangrah* (*B.M.S.*) referred to above, the *Gitpustak* (Allahabad, 1883), and the collection previously used.

The hymns are mainly translations of wellknown English hymns or paraphrases of Scripture. English metres and tunes are used, and the lines are made to rhyme as in English. Mr. Turnbull, however, informs us that frequently hymns to native tunes are prepared by native Christians, and lithographed for use. Many of these, as adapted to the tastes of the people, will be incorporated in the next edition of the *Hymnal*.

4. **Panjábí.**—In the Panjab, or region of the five rivers, eight missionary societies have been labouring with considerable success during the last forty years. The chief of these have been American and Scottish Presbyterian Societies and the *C. M. S.* Urdú is extensively spoken in the Panjab, and its use as the language of literature is extending, but *Panjábí*, a language closely akin to western *Hindí*, is still the vernacular. Dr. H. U. Weitbrecht, of the *C. M. S.*, says it is "essentially a peasant's language and is in danger of relegation to the position of a mere patois." It is written mainly in two characters, Gurmukhí and Persian. *Gurmukhí* signifies that which has to do with the mouth of the Gurú, or religious teacher, and it is the sacred character of the Sikh religion. From Dr. Weitbrecht we learn that the following hymn-books have appeared in *Panjábí*:—

(1) *Gítán dí Pothí.* A collection of Urdú and Hindí hymns and bhajans, compiled from various sources and printed in the Gurmukhí character. By the Rev. E. P. Newton, of the Ludhiana *A. P. M.*, 64 pp. 1881.

(2) *Masíhí Gít kí Kitáb.* The hymn-book of the Methodist Episcopal Church, pub. at Lucknow in Urdú-Gurmukhí character. 140 pp. 1884. Edited by the Rev. J. Newton, of the Lahore *A. P. M.*

(3) *Masíhí Gít kí Kitáb*, Panjabi, in Urdú characters. 140 pp., 8vo. 1884. By Miss Wauton of the *C. E. Z. S.*

5. **Sindhí.**—*Sindhí* is spoken in the valley which lies along the lower course of the river Indus or Sindhu. The population of Sindh is about 2,400,000, and the prevailing religion is Muhammadanism. "*Sindhí*," says Dr. Weitbrecht, "is mainly a rustic tongue, with little literature." It is generally written in the Arabic character. The *C. M. S.* has stations in Sindh, and its missionaries have been the authors of nearly all its Christian literature. A collection of 26 hymns and 10 Bhajans has been recently prepared by Rev. J. Redman, and through the kindness of Col. Millett is now before us. It is printed at the Ludhiana Mission Press, and bears date 1887. It includes translations of "Rock of Ages," "Just as I am," "Art thou weary," and other wellknown hymns. The Rev. A. W. Cotton, of Sukkur, Sindh, sent some *Bhajans* to press in Dec., 1887.

6. **Gujaráti.**—*Gujaratí*, another of the languages of northern India allied to the Sanscrit, is the vernacular of the province of Gujarát and Káthiáwar, in the Bombay Presidency, and is spoken by nearly 10,000,000 of people. The boundaries of the district are, on the north, the Gulf of Cutch and a line drawn from it eastward for about 150 miles; on the south, a small river near the Portuguese territory of Damán; on the east, a line about 120 miles inland, nearly parallel to the sea coast; and on the west, the Arabian Sea from near Damán to Cutch. The *L. M. S.* was the first to labour here, but in 1846 and 1859 their missions at Surat and other stations were, by a friendly arrangement, transferred to the *Irish Presbyterians*, who have since then been the sole Christian workers in this district.

(1) The first hymn-book in Gujaratí, so far as is now known, was prepared by the brothers William and Alexander Fyvie, of the *L. M. S.*, and consisted of translations from the *Hindí*. The 2nd ed. (1839) contained 112 hymns in English metres. The Rev. W. Clarkson, of the same mission, also prepared a

small collection with the title *Dharma Gita*, i.e., "Religious Songs," lithographed at Ahmedabad in 1851. This was reprinted two or three times.

(2) In 1856 a metrical version of the Psalms was pub. by the Rev. James Glasgow, D.D., of the Irish Presbyterian Mission, English rhyming metres being used throughout. But *Gujarati*, like other languages of the same stock, is unsuited to English metres. The accent must always be on the root; and the number of syllables in a line of poetry is determined, not merely by the number of vowels, but by the number of consonants and vowels, which together make up the line. Another version of the Psalms, therefore, in native metres, and fitted to be sung to native tunes, was prepared by a Gujarati Christian named Walji Bechan, and pub. at Surat in 1876.

(3) But the hymn-book now in general use is the *Káryārpana*, or "Poetic Offering," first pub. in 1863. The 7th ed. was pub. at Surat in 1877, and contains in all 287 psalms and hymns. About 210 of the hymns are original, the greater part being composed by the Rev. Joseph van Someren Taylor (d. in 1881); others are by the Revs. Dr. Glasgow and W. Clarkson, and several by native Christian poets. Forty are translations of Psalms of David, and others are versions of well-known English hymns. Both English and Gujarati metres and tunes are used.

7. Marathí.—*Marathí* (pronounced Marathí) is a language belonging to the Sanscrit group, and is spoken in the region comprised in a triangle having Nagpore for its apex and the west coast of India from Goa to above Bombay for its base. The population is about 17,000,000, among whom six Societies are at work. (1) A hymn-book called *Sacred Songs* is used in the missions of the A. B. C., K. S. M., F. C. S., and probably others, the history of which is as follows:—

The first book of hymns in Marathí was pub. by missionaries of the A. B. C. in 1819, and contained 16 small pages. The hymns were in native metres. Another book, called *Psalms & Hymns*, written in English metres, appeared in 1835.

These books, enlarged and improved from time to time, were used until 1845, when Rev. H. Ballantyne, a man of fine poetic taste and culture, prepared a new collection of translations of the best English hymns in English metres. It contained more than 100 hymns, and was called *Hymns for Divine Worship*. Being received with great favour, Mr. Ballantyne was prompted to enlarge it considerably. The 4th ed. was pub. in 1865 by the Bombay Tract Society, whose Committee say in the preface "336 of the choicest hymns in the English language are here rendered into flowing Marathí, with a success that leaves nothing to be desired." This hymn-book entirely superseded all previous ones. Mr. Ballantyne prepared, in addition, 64 hymns for children. Failing health, however, compelled him to leave India, and he d. at sea, Nov. 9, 1865.

In the meantime, in the years from 1862 to 1867, there was a gradual re-introduction of hymns in native metres. A true native Christian poet appeared, Mr. Krishnaraw Ramaji Sangalé, a catechist of the A. B. C. A collection of his compositions, with the title *Gayanamrit*, was pub. in 1867, and soon became very popular.

When it became necessary therefore, in 1874, to pub. a 5th ed. of Mr. Ballantyne's *Hys. for Divine Worship*, it was resolved to combine the English and native metres in the same work. Other compositions by native poets, and other translations by Mrs. Bissell and Dr. Fairbank, were added; the name was changed to *Sacred Songs*, and it now, in its 7th ed., contains 607 hymns. (Bombay Book and Tract Society.)

(2) The *Bulbul* is a collection of 161 hymns for children, including those by Mr. Ballantyne, with additions by Mrs. Bissell, Mrs. Bruce, Dr. Fairbank, Krishnaraw, and others.

(3) The *Gananidhi*, or "Song-Treasury," pub. at Bombay in 1886, is a collection of 215 hymns, with appropriate tunes, including more than 50 popular native airs, all in European old notation, edited by the Rev. C. Harding, of the A. B. C. Some of the hymns are new. The tunes, other than the native airs, are culled from other collections.

(4) The Rev. J. Taylor, of the S. P. G., pub. at Poona, in 1884, *Hymns Ancient and*

Modern translated and compiled for use in the Church in Western India. Besides the hymns translated from the well-known English book, there are a few taken from the *Sacred Songs* noticed above, and from other sources. Translated hymns usually follow the English metre; the original hymns are for the most part in native metres.

Since it was in the Marathí-speaking country that Christian *Kirttans* were first performed, which have since become popular throughout India, we may here introduce a brief account of them.

The Kirttan is a musical performance in which the praises of some god are celebrated with singing and instrumental music. In the year 1862 it occurred to Mr. Krishnaraw and others, that a *Christian* Kirttan might be made a useful evangelistic agency. The first was performed in Ahmednagar and the neighbouring villages, and everywhere met with an enthusiastic reception. The leader stood on a platform, and behind him four or five trained Christian singers, who joined in the choruses. There were Hindoo musical instruments, including a kind of guitar,—a pair of cymbals,—a saringi, played like a violoncello, and a small drum, beaten with the ends of the fingers. First, a brief prayer was offered; then, the leader announced the subject of the kirttan, and a chorus followed. The words of the chorus became the text for a brief exhortation, delivered in a musical tone, and leading the way to another chorus, the whole performance occupying about two hours.

The native Christian Marathí hymns, in which choruses are frequent, afford abundant matter for these *Kirttans*, as do lyrics among the Bengalis and Tamils, and Bhajans among the Hindis, and others.

ii. *South Indian, or Dravidian Group.*

1. Canarese.—Moving southward from the Marathí country we come to a people, 9,000,000 in number, speaking *Canarese*, a language of the Dravidian or South Indian group. These are found not only in Canara, on the Western coast, but also through the Mysore, Coorg, and northward as far as Beder, in the Nizam's territory. Seven Societies have missions in this district, those in strongest force being the Basel Evangelical Society, the W. M. S., and the L. M. S.

(1) The hymn-book used by the W. M. S. and L. M. S. is entitled *Canarese Hymns*, original and selected, by the Rev. B. Rice (7th edit. revised and enlarged, Bangalore, 1881.) It contains 250 hymns, sixteen of which are for children. Among these latter are "There is a happy land," "There's a Friend for little children," &c. Seven are chants, such as the *Te Deum*. Most are sung to tunes selected from *H. A. & M.*, the *Bristol* and *Wesleyan Tune Books*, &c.

The Rev. B. Rice was a missionary of the L. M. S., who d. in 1887, after 50 years of service. Other authors and translators were Messrs. C. Campbell, J. Paul, Coles, W. Arthur, and Riddett. 62 hymns were taken from the book of the Basel mission described below. J. Paul is a native minister of the L. M. S.

(2) Bound up with this hymnal, in a volume before us, is a collection of *Christian Lyrics* (Bangalore, 2nd edit. 1879) by the Rev. Abijah Samuel, a native Wesleyan minister, and very superior man, who d. a few years ago. [For further particulars concerning *Lyrics* in the Dravidian languages, as distinguished from *Hymns*, see **Malayalam** and **Tamil** below.]

(3) The Basel missionaries, whose printing press is at Mangalore, pub. a Canarese hymn-book in 1845, which was revised and enlarged in 1855 and 1867. At the latter date it contained 168 hymns, composed or translated by Messrs. H. Mögling, G. Weigle, J. Layer, F. Metz and others. The 7th revised edition (1885) contains 105 new hymns, or 270 in all. The translations are chiefly from the best German hymns, and are made to be sung to German tunes. Among the translators of the later hymns were Messrs. Ziegler, Graeter and A. A. Männer. The Basel missionaries have also pub. a collection of 46 Lyrics, composed by a native poet, and a

book of 130 hymns for children, nearly all translations from the German by Messrs. Kittel and Mack.

2. **Tulu.**—*Tulu* is the prevailing language of South Canara, which is in consequence frequently called the Tulu country. Like the Canarese, it belongs to the Dravidian group of Indian languages, but has no existing literature, except the books prepared by the missionaries of the Basel Society, and printed in Canarese characters at Mangalore. Through the illiteracy of the people, Christian instruction hitherto has been of necessity chiefly oral, and the singing of hymns has been largely used as an evangelistic agency.

(1) The 4th edition of the *Tulu Hymn-book* (Mangalore, 1886) contains 186 hymns, principally prepared by the Rev. A. Männer,—some, however, being composed by the missionaries Ammann, Cammerer and Würtele. Most are translations of the best German hymns, such as "Ein feste Burg ist unser Gott," 20 only being originals. They are in German metres, and are sung to German tunes.

(2) The Rev. A. Männer has also prepared in Tulu a collection of 115 hymns for children, and a translation of 32 of Sankey's *Songs and Solos*.

3. **Malayalam.**—To the south of the Tulu country are the provinces of Cochin and Travancore, on the Malabar coast, where the principal language spoken is Malayalam, another of the Dravidian group. (1) In the northern part of this region the Basel missionaries have several stations. They have pub. a large collection of hymns, chiefly translations from the German by the Rev. Mr. Fritz, of Cannanore, and others. (2) The middle portion of the region is occupied by the *C. M. S.*, their principal station being Cottayam. The hymn-book used here was prepared in 1842 by the Rev. H. Baker, one of the founders of the mission. It has 125 hymns, and in its first form consisted exclusively of translations of English hymns, composed in English metres, and intended to be sung to English tunes. In the later editions additions have been made from the book of the Basel missionaries mentioned above, and also from a similar book, prepared by the Rev. S. Mateer, of the *L. M. S.*, whose head-quarters are at Trevandrum, towards the southern extremity of the Malayalam-speaking district. Besides the hymn-book just referred to, the Rev. S. Mateer pub. in 1872 (3) A collection of *Christian Songs* in native metres, sung to native tunes, called for distinction's sake *Githas* or lyrics. In these the rhyme is sometimes at the *beginning* of lines, sometimes at the *end*, and sometimes the lines rhyme throughout, and nearly all have a refrain or chorus. As an example may be mentioned a very popular lyric composed by the Rev. Justus Joseph, a Brahman convert. It is a paraphrase of the description of the Risen Christ, in the 1st chap. of the Apocalypse. The refrain to each stanza runs thus:—

"Praise! Praise! O Jesu, our Lord!
Alleluia, having sung, praise, praise, O Lord."

The 5th edit. of this book, pub. in 1887, contains 250 lyrics, on such subjects as "Adoration of Jesus," "Agony in Gethsemane," "Call to Conversion," &c. The principal authors are the Rev. Justus Joseph and his brother Philippos, all of whose lyrics are original, and Messrs. M. J. Hochanya and M. Walsalam, most of whose compositions are translations, chiefly from the Tamil.

The tunes to the lyrics are somewhat wild and irregular, and cannot usually be expressed in English notation, because the intervals in Hindu music differ from ours, several being less than a semitone. [See **Tamil.**]

It may be added that in Cottayam and the neighbourhood are found the so-called *Syrian Christians*, for a notice of whom see **Syriac Hymnody.**

4. **Tamil.**—The most important of the Dravidian or non-Brahmanical languages of India is the *Tamil* or *Tamul*, spoken by more than 13,000,000 of people in south India, as well as by probably 5,000,000 in the northern part of Ceylon, in Burma, and in the Straits Settlements. In India proper the Tamil country extends from about 20 miles north of Madras to Cape Comorin in the south, and from the sea coast, on the east, to the range of mountains called the Ghats, on the west. The first Protestant missionaries to India, sent in 1706 by the king of Denmark to Tranquebar, began their labours among the Tamils. Their names were Ziegenbalg and Plutchau. At the present time 14 English, German, Danish and American Societies have missions in this part of India.

(1) The first hymn-book printed in Tamil was a collection of 48 hymns translated by Ziegenbalg, and pub. in 1713. This was repeatedly enlarged, by the missionaries Schultze, Pressier, and Walther, until it contained 200 hymns. Fabricius, an eminent Lutheran missionary, who came to India in 1742, still further enlarged it. The 13th ed., with the title *Hymnologia Germano-Tamulica* (called also *Fabricius's Hymn-book*, 7th ed.), was printed in 1881 at Tranquebar, at the Evangelical Lutheran Mission Press. It contains 375 hymns, nearly all translations from Luther, Gerhardt, Freylinghausen, Heermann, and other German writers. The neat volume now before us contains also 171 German tunes to the hymns (Tranquebar, 1878). This hymn-book is used at the stations of the Danish and Leipzig Lutheran Missions in Tanjore and elsewhere.

(2) In 1831 the Madras Religious Tract Society pub. a *Coll.* of 42 hymns in English metres, edited by the Rev. C. T. Rhenius, a German employed by the *C. M. S.* This was from time to time enlarged. Its present representative, pub. by the same Society (Madras, 5th edit., 1886), is entitled *Tamil Hymn-book, compiled by the Hymn-book revision committee.* It contains 310 hymns and doxologies, mostly adaptations or free renderings of English and German originals, and was edited by the Rev. Elias J. Gloria, a Tamulian, connected with the *W. M. S.* This book is in general use throughout the Tamil country, except in the Lutheran and some Anglican missions.

(3) In 1887 appeared the *Tamil Church Hymn-book*, containing 233 hymns, arranged according to the order of the festivals of the Church of England. It was compiled by Bishops Caldwell, of the *S. P. G.*; and Sargent, of the *C. M. S.* In this collection several English hymns appear in Tamil for the first time, such as, "Holy, holy, holy, Lord God Almighty;" "The Church's one foundation;" "Jesus Christ is risen to-day."

(4) Several other Tamil hymn-books have been pub., as the *Nagercoil Coll.*, and one edited, in 1865, by the Rev. F. Baylis, but have been superseded by one or other of those last mentioned.

(5) The Christian Vernacular Education Society has also pub. *Hymns for Children* in Tamil. The 2nd edit. (Madras, 1883) contains 166 hymns, selected from Fabricius, and the Nagercoil Collection, or translated by Messrs. Spalding, Webb, Percival, Kilner, S. Niles and other of D. P. Niles (*Tamulians*), and others.

All compositions called *Hymns* in South India are in European metres, and made to be sung to European tunes; but perfectly distinct from these are Christian songs known as *Lyrics*, answering to the *Bhajans* of Northern and Central India. These compositions are different in style from anything heard in Europe. The rhyme is at the beginning of the verse instead of the end. The substance of the *Lyric* is frequently given in a verse (*venbā*) at the beginning and is not sung. Then follows a chorus (*pallavi*) which is sung after each verse, and sometimes a sort of second chorus (*anapallavi*), which is sung only once. *Lyrics* are written in a great variety of metres, and some of the tunes sung to them are such as have been used for ages past in the Hindu temples. The principal writer of *Tamil Lyrics* was a native Christian poet, named Vethanayagam, who lived at the beginning of this century. Many of the Tamil Christians have since written, but few of their productions have equalled his. Some have been composed by Mr. R. C. Caldwell, son of the Bishop, and by the Rev. E. Webb, of the *A. B. C.*, at Madura.

There are several collections of *Tamil Lyrics*, pub. in Madras and Tranquebar, but the one most widely used was compiled by the Rev. E. Webb, just named. It was pub. in 1853, and contained 226 pieces. Recent editions have been revised by the Rev. G. T. Washburn, of the *A. B. C.* mission at Madura. The 9th edit., pub. in 1886 by the Madras R. Tract Society, contains 300 *Lyrics*. Two Selections from this book have also been pub. for use in village congregations.

The use of *Lyrics* in public worship was at first opposed by many missionaries, principally because the associations with the tunes were objectionable; but they are so much preferred by the people and suit so well the genius of the language, that the opposition has almost ceased, and in many village congregations they are used exclusively.

[For information concerning Tamil hymnody in India we would express our great obligations to the Revs. J. L. Wyatt (*S. P. G.*); G. O. Newport (*L. M. S.*); and G. M. Rae (*F. C. S.*). Concerning Tamil in Ceylon see section on Ceylon.]

5. Telugu.—*Telingana*, or the *Telugú* country, begins a few miles to the north of Madras and extends northward as far as the neighbourhood of Ganjam, in Orissa. It contains about 17,000,000 of people, most of whom speak *Telugú*, a language of the Dravidian group. In this region are missions, some very flourishing, of the *S. P. G.*; *C. M. S.*; *L. M. S.*; *A. B. M.*; *F. C. S.*; the *Canadian Baptists*; the *Lutherans* of America; the *Hermannsburg Lutheran Society* of Hanover, and the *Brethren*.

(1) A hymn-book extensively used throughout the Telugu country is the one compiled by the Rev. W. Dawson of the *L. M. S.* of Vizagapatam. The latest ed. was pub. in 1883, at the *C. K. S.* press in Madras. It contains 258 hymns, all in Telugu metres except the last six. In the preparation of the first 152 hymns Mr. Dawson was assisted by Purushōttam Chowdry, a native minister now connected with the General Baptist Mission in Orissa. The 15 hymns from 153 to 167 inclusive were composed by the Rev. P. Jagganadham of the *L. M. S.* of Vizagapatam; the rest by various authors. At a recent conference of missionaries and others the opinion was expressed that this hymn-book needs revision and enlargement.

(2) The *Brethren* (represented in England by G. Müller, of Bristol) whose mission stations are in the Delta district of the river *Godavery*, have pub. a collection of 110 hymns, known as the *Delta Hymn-book*, of which 100 are in native metres and are sung to native tunes; the rest are in English metres.

(3) The collection pub. by the *A. B. M.* was first issued in 1869, and contained 60 hymns, the editors being Mrs. Lyman Jewett and Mrs. J. E. Clough. Three eds. have since appeared, but this book is now superseded by one pub. in 1887, the work of a committee appointed at the jubilee of the *A. B.* Telugu Mission held in Nellore, February 1886. The new hymnal contains 183 pieces, many being taken from the book of Mrs. Jewett and Mrs. Clough, others from the Delta-Mission collection, others from the Dawson hymn-book,

the remainder being new and original compositions. A special feature of this book is a glossary at the foot of each page. Thirty-eight of the choicest hymns are by Purushōttam Chowdry (named above), others by members of the native churches. The preface is signed on behalf of the Committee, by Mrs. Anna H. Downie, wife of the Rev. D. Downie, D.D., of the *A. B. M.*

(4) The Amer. Evangelical Lutheran Mission uses a hymn-book containing Dawson's hymns and 57 new ones, composed mainly by the Rev. B. John, of the same mission.

(5) The Rev. John Hay, D.D., of the *L. M. S.* pub. many years ago a collection of 35 hymns in English metres, composed by himself and the Rev. J. S. Wardlaw, M.A. This is now out of print, but some of the hymns appear in No. 7.

(6) Also, many years ago Mr. Newill, of the Madras Civil Service, prepared a book of about 50 hymns. This was thoroughly revised, and the number of hymns increased to 128, by the Rev. J. E. Sharkey, an able and devoted missionary of the *C. M. S.*, who died in 1867. Several editions of the enlarged book appeared, but it is now out of print.

(7) Dr. Chamberlain's *Hymn-book*. This contains 86 Telugu hymns in English metres, edited by the Rev. J. Chamberlain, D.D., of the American (Old Dutch) Reformed Church, and printed at the *C. K. S.* press, Madras, in 1884 (2nd edit. 1885).

(8) Besides the above, 10 new hymns in Telugu metres were composed and printed, in 1887, by the Rev. P. Jagganadham, of Vizagapatam. One of these is a translation of Miss Havergal's hymn, "Take my life and let it be." Others, by the Rev. Dr. Chamberlain, have been printed, with music, as leaflets.

In regard to India generally it is to be noted that with the progress of years the use of English metres and tunes has been increasingly superseded by that of metres and tunes belonging to the country, which have come down to our time unwritten, but have been long used in festivals, at weddings and the like.

6. Ceylon.—In Ceylon, the name of which is so familiar to us from its occurrence in Heber's missionary hymn, three languages are spoken, besides English, viz., Tamil, Singhalese, and a patois of Portuguese. The *S. P. G.*, *C. M. S.*, *W. M. S.*, *B. M. S.*, and *A. B. C.*, all have missions. For the use of the Tamil-speaking congregations the hymn-books are available which are prepared in connection with the various missions of South India. Besides these, however, may be mentioned :—

(1) A translation pub. in 1881 of the entire *Wesleyan Hymn-book*, as it is now used in England, the *Supplementary* hymns being included. The volume is beautiful in type and general appearance. The principal translators were the Revs. J. Kilner, E. Hoole, D.D., J. M. Osborn, P. Percival, W. M. Walton, J. V. Benjamin, J. Benjamin, E. S. Adams, D. P. Niles (a Tamulian), D. Valupillai, E. Rigg, &c. The metres are the same as in English, only that 8, 7's is substituted for 7's.

(2) For the use of the Eurasian population, speaking the patois mentioned above, a hymn-book in *Portuguese* was prepared some time ago, and quite recently another, in which most of the hymns are translations by Advocate J. H. Eaton, of Colombo.

(3) The *Singhalese hymn-book* used by the Wesleyans contains 259 hymns, the last ed. being pub. in 1880, under the editorship of the Rev. John Scott. Nearly all the hymns are original compositions by native ministers.

(4) Two small *S. School* hymn-books, containing respectively 74 and 55 hymns, have been brought out by the same editor, under the auspices of the Ceylon Religious Tract Society. They consist almost entirely of translations of popular English hymns for children.

(5) Mr. Corea was a Baptist minister and author of Temperance and other moral poetry popular among the Singhalese. More than 40 years ago he pub. a book of hymns, some being set to native airs, others to English tunes. This book has passed out of use, its place being supplied by the *Gitika Nidhana*, or "Treasury of Song," prepared by the Rev. C. Carter, of the *B. M. S.*, assisted by the Rev. J. S. Perera, a Singhalese minister, and pub. in 1876. It contains 125 hymns original and translated, among the latter being such hymns as "Rock of Ages," "Let us with a gladsome mind."

(6) A Union hymn-book has just been pub. (1888) by

the Ceylon R. T. S., embodying a large number of the hymns in Mr. Carter's book with considerable additions.

iii. *The Aboriginal and other scattered races of India.*

1. Santalia or **Santhalistan**, may be described as a strip of the great province of Bengal, about 100 miles in breadth, extending southwards from Bhagalpur on the Ganges for about 250 miles, until it touches Orissa. Its inhabitants dwell for the most part in villages among the hills. They belong to one of the aboriginal races of India, are free from the bondage of caste, and speak a language entirely different from Bengalí or Hindí.

(1) The *C. M. S.* has a very successful mission among them, whose headquarters are at Talghari, in the north of the Santal country. For their use a *Hymnal* was pub. in 1876, the Rev. F. T. Cole being the editor. The 3rd ed. (1004), entitled *Dhorom Seren*, contains 174 hymns and two litanies, and was printed at Bhowanipore. Most are translations of familiar English hymns, the principal translators being the Revs. F. T. Cole, H. Davis, W. T. Storrs, A. Stark, J. Blaich, and J. Brown, with several native helpers. The hymns are supposed to rhyme and most of them are sung to English tunes. Twenty-eight are set to native melodies.

(2) Another remarkably interesting mission in Santalia has at its head a Norwegian and a Dane, Messrs. Skrefsrud and Boerresen. For the use of their converts a new hymn-book has just been issued, composed chiefly of hymns set to native tunes.

(3) The *F. C. S.*, whose principal station is at Pachamba, for a time used the hymnal of the *C. M. S.*, but have now one of their own, containing, however, many of the *C. M. S.* translations.

(4) Among the Rajmahal hills, in the north of the Santal country, are a people speaking a language called *Malto*, belonging to the Dravidian group. For their use the Rev. E. Droese, a German missionary connected with the *C. M. S.*, prepared a small collection of 27 hymns. A new collection is now (1887), in the press prepared by Miss Stark, which includes some of Mr. Droese's hymns and a large number of new ones.

(5) In the Midnapore district of northern Orissa are many Santals, among whom the *Free Baptists of America* have a mission. They have pub. a hymn-book containing 77 hymns, mostly translations, but also a good number of originals, some composed by Santal Christians. The book is printed at the mission press at Midnapore.

(6) The *Bethel Santhal* mission, in the district of Talia and Agoia, under the direction of Mr. A. Haegert, has also a hymn-book, partly original, partly a compilation.

2. Kohls or **Mundaris.**—In the § **Hindi**, reference was made to the *Kohls* or *Mundáris*, one of the aboriginal races of India, inhabiting part of the province of Chota Nagpore. As was then stated, the *S. P. G.* and the German Evangelical Lutherans, have successful missions among these people, and three books for their use have been prepared in *Hindí*. But mention has still to be made of a hymn-book in the *Mundári* or *Kohl* language, prepared by the *G. E. L.* missionaries, containing 100 hymns. These are chiefly original, and were composed for the most part by Dr. A. Nottrott and the native pastors Nathanael Tuagu and Mansídah Tassu. About one-fourth are set to German and three-fourths to native tunes. This book is used by many congregations of the Anglican mission.

The Rev. J. C. Whitley states that at the central station of the *S. P. G.* singing is regularly taught in the schools, and English tunes are sung with great accuracy; but in outlying parts of the district native tunes are much more readily learned by the people.

3. Khassi.—In the south-west of Assam is a district known as the Khassia and Jaintia Hills, inhabited by a primitive people, whose language is of the Mongolian stock and of the Indo-Chinese branch—monoysllabic and agglutinative—having no close affinity with any other. Among these people the *Welsh Calvinistic Methodists* have had a successful mission since 1840. By their missionaries the language has been reduced to writing and a Christian literature has been created.

(1) The first hymn-book, printed in 1845, contained 20 hymns, translated by the Rev. T. Jones, of Berriew. In 1850 and 1865 additions were made to it by the Revs. Wm. Lewis, Robert Parry, and T. Jones, of Glyn.

(2) The book now in use was edited, in 1877, by the Rev. Hugh Roberts, and printed at Newport, Monmouthshire. It contains 242 hymns; two original, by the Rev. H. Roberts; the rest, translations of the Psalms, or of well-known English, Welsh, and American hymns, 15 being from I. Sankey's *Sac. Songs & Solos*. Among the translators, in addition to the missionaries above named, were the Revs. John Roberts and T. Jerman Jones.

The hymns are composed in English and Welsh metroo, to which the language lends itself easily, and they are sung to English and Welsh tunes. The natives have no musical system of their own.

4. Assam (proper), with a population in 1881 of 2,225,271, is about 500 miles in length, but narrow, and is divided into two portions by the Brahmapootra river. The religion of the people of the valley is Hinduism; wild and savage tribes inhabit the mountains north and south, among whom are found forms of spirit worship. The *A. B. M.* has stations among the Garos, Nagas, and other tribes, as well as among the Kohls from Central India, who are employed as labourers in the tea gardens. The *S. P. G.* has also had a station at Tezpore since 1850.

In the early days of the *A. B. M.* the Rev. Nathan Brown, D.D., a man of most versatile genius (see §§ **Japan** and **Burma**), prepared a hymn-book, which was afterwards revised and greatly enlarged by the Rev. Dr. W. Ward. It now contains 352 hymns, with a supplement of 32 hymns for S. S. use. 80 hymns by Dr. Brown are included, 32 original and 48 translated. Many were composed by Drs. Ward and M. Bronson. Nidhi Levi, the first Assamese Christian convert, wrote 110, chiefly original; Batiram Das, a former preacher, wrote 28. The rest were by other missionaries and native converts. The hymn-book is now old, and the Rev. P. H. Moore, "a musical missionary," is at the present time (1888) engaged on the work of revision.

iv. *Tibet.*

On the further side of the vast chain of the Himálayas is Tibet, the stronghold of northern Buddhism, at present closed to the gospel. But the Tibetan language is spoken by some thousands of people in British territory, as well as by tribes inhabiting the provinces adjoining Tibet proper. For their spiritual benefit the *M. M.* have a station at Kyelang, in the Himálayas, and there a hymnal was prepared and printed by the late Rev. Heinrich A. Jäschke, one of the greatest of modern Tibetan scholars. It contains 136 hymns translated from the German.

v. *Persia.*

Fifty years ago a mission was commenced by the *A. B. C.* among the Nestorian Christians near lake Oroomiah in Eastern Persia, and in 1860 a hymn-book was printed, in the *Modern Syriac* language spoken by these people. This book has passed through several editions, but we have been unable to obtain further particulars. The language, however, differs from Ancient Syriac less than Italian from Latin. In 1869 a small collection of *Revival Hymns* was printed at Oroomiah. In 1871 the mission among the Nestorians was transferred to the *A. P. M.*, which has also stations at Tabriz, Salmas, Teheran, and Hamadan; whilst the Rev. Dr. Bruce and his colleagues of the *C. M. S.* have been labouring at Julfa, Baghdad, and Bushire. Dr. Bruce informs us that in Baghdad (in Turkey, but on the borders of Persia) they use the *Arabic* hymn-book printed at the American press at Beyrout (see Syria). In Julfa (*Ispahan*) only *Armenian* hymns are used (see Turkey in Asia). There is a small *Persian* hymn-book which has been made by the American Missionaries in Teheran, but it is very imperfect. "A good Persian hymn-book," says Dr. Bruce, "is much to be desired, It is a most poetic language and it would be comparatively easy for one who had the gift to compose hymns in it." [See Various.]

vi. *Constantinople, Asia Minor, and Armenia.*

We class these places together, because the missionary work in all of them is done chiefly by one society, the *A. B. C.*, the head-quarters of whose Turkey mission are at Constantinople. This work is a very noble one, especially in the departments of Christian literature and education, but, owing to the religious jealousy of the Muhammadan rulers, it is confined in these regions chiefly to the Armenians and Greeks.

In 1861 a hymn-book in the Turkish language, printed in *Arabic* characters, was pub. by the missionaries. But in the year 1884, after the sale of 1200 copies, the remainder of the impression was destroyed by order of the Government. This was in pursuance of its determination to prevent, as far as possible, the publication of Christian literature in a form accessible to Muslims. The Arabic characters made the book accessible to them. The following hymnals have also been pub. by the agents of the *A. B. C.*:

(1) *An Armenian H. Bk.*, with 432 hymns.
(2) *An Armeno-Turkish H. Bk.*, with 247 hymns.
(3) *A Graco-Turkish H. Bk.*, with 247 hymns.

In explanation of these names it should be stated that the languages used in this region are Turkish, Armenian, and Greek, the latter being confined mainly to the parts along the sea-coast. In the interior of Asia Minor, and in Cilicia and Syria as far as Aleppo, the Armenians have largely lost their own language and use the Turkish, *written with the Armenian alphabet*. It is Turkish written or printed thus, which is called *Armeno-Turkish*. In like manner the Greeks of the interior have lost their language, and use Turkish, *written in Greek letters*. This latter is called *Greco-Turkish*, or sometimes Karamanian. The words in Turkish, Armeno-Turkish, and Greco-Turkish are the same; only the characters are different.

The hymn-books mentioned above are pub. both with and without tunes, and the last ed. of each appeared in 1886. They have been the growth of nearly 40 years, the earliest Armenian Hymnal having been issued in 1849. Most of the hymns are translations of well-known English and American hymns, the few originals having been usually prepared for special occasions.

The chief translators into *Armenian* have been the Revs. Elias Riggs, D.D., LL.D., H. J. Van Lennep, D.D., H. O. Dwight, D.D., J. F. Pettibone, D.D., C. C. Tracy, M. Shemavonian, and Mrs. M. Shemavonian. The translators into *Turkish* were the Revs. Dr. Pratt, E. M. Dodd, and P. O. Powers, all now deceased, and the Revs. Dr. Dwight and Avedis Constantian.

The tunes used are English and American, especially those "wedded" to the hymns in their original form. The Armenian hymn-books mentioned above are used by the *A. P. M.* in Persia; also, to some extent by the Lutheran Armenians in the Caucasus, and the Baptist and Campbellite missionaries in Asia Minor.

vii. *Bulgaria.*

In the *Orthodox Bulgarian Church* ancient hymns are used in the services, but are not sung by the congregation, only by the clergy and choristers; and it is rather chanting and intoning than singing. The *Te Deum* and various *Doxologies* are the most common, and there are also hymns for the following festivals :—

The Nativity of B. V. M.; Presentation B. V. M.; Circumcision; Epiphany; Candlemas; Annunciation B. V. M.; Palm Sunday; Passion Week; Easter; Ascension: Pentecost; Transfiguration; Assumption of B. V. M.; the Mass; Marriage, Baptismal and Burial Services; and Saints' Days, as St. Dimiter, John of Rilo, Nicolai, Vasilai, St. John Baptist, Cyril and Methodius, George, Elia, St. Peter and St. Paul, &c.

Two American Missionary Societies—the *A. B. C.* and the *A. M. E.*—are at work in Bulgaria, the former to the south, the latter to the north of the Balkan range of mountains. The same Hymnal is used by both, as well as by the agents of a native mission, known as the *Bulgarian Evangelical Society.* This book, called *Svyashténnee Pésnee* ("Sacred Songs.") was first pub. in 1872, and with music attached, in 1878. Several eds. have since appeared, each one an enlargement on its predecessor.

The present book contains 250 hymns, about four-fifths of which are translations of the best English and American hymns for both adults and children. The principal translators have been the Rev. Dr. Riggs of the *A. B. C.*—who did most of the work of preparation—the Rev. Dr. Long of the *A. M. E.*, and a native pastor, the Rev. Mr. Tondjoroff. The same three persons have composed most of the original hymns forming the remainder of the volume. With few exceptions translated hymns have been so rendered as to appear in the same metre in Bulgarian as in English. The lines rhyme as in English, and the tunes used are English or American, none are native. Since the last ed. of the hymn-book appeared 59 additional hymns have been pub. in a Bulgarian periodical called the *Youth's Paper and Samokov Leaflet*, most of which will in due time be incorporated in the hymnal.

viii. *Syria.*

In this land, from whose ancient capital, Antioch, the first missionaries were sent forth for the conversion of the heathen, a number of societies, both British and American, as well as Christian ladies from Great Britain and Germany, are at work with a view to its enlightenment and spiritual elevation. But the hymn-book everywhere used by Protestants is the *Arabic Hymnal*, with Tunes, pub. by the *A. P. M.* at Beyrout. From the beginning of the mission 50 years ago hymns were from time to time translated or composed, but remained in ms. or leaflet form, until about 15 years ago, when the Rev. E. R. Lewis, M.D., Professor in the Syrian Protestant College at Beyrout, collected them into a volume and pub. them as the first Arabic Hymnal,

The present book, though based on Mr. Lewis's, is much enlarged and greatly improved. It was edited by the Revs. Samuel Jessup and George A. Ford, both of the *A. P. M.*, and was issued Dec. 25th, 1885. It is a handsome volume of 234 pp.—the tunes being printed in good musical type (European notation, but with notes running from right to left) and occupying the upper portion of each page, whilst the hymns, in clearly printed Arabic characters, appear on the lower portion.

The hymns are 326 in number, more than 80 of which are original. All except 5 have been translated or composed by native Syrians of the Arab race, viz., Sheikh Nasif Ul Yazigi (now dead), a learned grammarian of the Greek Catholic Church, employed as proof reader whilst the Bible was translated into Arabic; Ibrahim Sarkis, also deceased, a Maronite who became a Protestant; Asaad Shedoady; Selim Kessab; Asaad Abdallah; Ibrahim Nasif, and others. The translations are chiefly of well-known English and American hymns, or Bible Psalms versified. The tunes are for the most part English and American, a few only being original.

ix. *Palestine.*

In Palestine *Arabic* is now the common language, and the hymnal used in Jerusalem, Jaffa, and other places is the one described above [Syria]. The report of the *C. M. S.* for 1887 states that the hymns in this book have proved a great attraction to the people. Travellers speak enthusiastically of the singing of Arabic hymns in Miss Walker-Arnott's Tabitha Mission School at Jaffa.

IV. *Africa.*

i. *Egypt.*

In passing from Asia to Africa it is natural to begin with Egypt. In this country the American United Presbyterians have a flourishing mission, with several stations; but they do not use hymns (commonly so called) in their public worship, but confine themselves to a metrical version of the Psalms. For others who wish for hymns the *Arabic Hymnal* of the *A. P. M.* pub. at Beyrout, and already spoken of [Syria], is available.

ii. *Eastern Equatorial Africa.*

The region included under this name extends, on the east coast, from about the Equator southward almost to Mozambique. In the interior it reaches to the great lakes Victoria Nyanza, Tanganyika, and Nyassa. The principal language spoken is *Ki-sawahili* or *Ki-swahili* (lit. coast language). Other languages are the *Galla*, *Nyika*, *Gogo*, and *Luganda*. In the northern and central parts of the region the *C. M. S.* and *United Methodist Free Churches* have stations, one of which, near L. Victoria Nyanza, was recently the scene of the martyrdom of Bishop Hannington. The *L. M. S.* has stations by Lake Tanganyika, and the *F. C. S.* and the *K. S. M.* in the south, near L. Nyassa. In this region also, encompassed by difficulties and perils, the *English Universities' Mission* is at work.

(1) Two hymnals have been prepared in *Ki-sawahili*; one by missionaries of the *C. M. S.*, containing 135 hymns (pub. 1881), nearly all translations of English hymns. This was doubtless the book used at Frere Town, near Mombasa, when visited by Bishop Hannington, who remarked on the "delightfully hearty" character of the singing, the voices being of better quality than those of tribes further south. The other was prepared for the converts of the U. M, Free Churches, containing 200 hymns, chiefly translations, the translators and composers being the Revs. T. Wakefield (editor), C. New and W. Hugh During.

(2) Two books in *Ki-Nyika* have been prepared, one by the Rev. T. Wakefield, the other by members of the *C. M. S.*, the former containing about 30 hymns.

(3) The Rev. T. Wakefield has also prepared a collection of about 20 hymns in the *Galla* language.

(4) The Report of 1887 states that 17 hymns in the *Luganda* language have been prepared for use in the Uganda mission.

(5) The missionaries of the *L. M. S.* by Lake Tanganyika use the hymnal in Ki-swahili of the *C. M. S.*

(6) Translations of English hymns have been made by the missionaries of the *K. S. M.* at Blantyre, near Lake Nyassa, and also by Dr. Elmslie, of the *F. C. S.* at Livingstonia in the same region. Among the hymns translated by Dr. Elmslie are—"Just as I am;" "One there is above all others;" "Holy, holy, holy, Lord God Almighty."

iii. *Madagascar.*

It is well known that, during the last 60 years, Christianity and civilisation have made great progress in Madagascar, chiefly through the agency of the *L. M. S.*; and it is stated that "from the beginning of the mission Christian Hymnody has aided largely in the promotion of Christian life and knowledge among the people." The native Malagasy songs are without rhyme, and consist of passages resembling Hebrew poetry in their rhythmic flow and frequent parallelisms, followed by a refrain or chorus, often sung to a musical accompaniment.

The first Christian hymns probably appeared as leaflets, but in 1828 a small vol. was published. Another, containing 168 hymns, appeared in 1835, and was several times reprinted. These were chiefly translations of English hymns, and were sung to the English tunes of the period. The lines did not rhyme, —the fewness of firm ultimate syllables in the Malagasy language making rhyme difficult; and no regard was paid to accent. The only thing aimed at was to have the right number of syllables for Long, Common, Short, and Sevens metres. But harsh and rugged though these hymns were, they endeared themselves to the hearts of the Christian converts; and affecting stories are told of their sustaining influence on the martyrs in the dark days of persecution which presently followed.

After the recommencement of the mission in 1862 singing was for some time in an unsatisfactory state. New congregations were formed so rapidly that the missionaries had not time to train them properly in psalmody. The Rev. R. G. Hartley, in 1867, wrote the first rhythmical and rhymed Malagasy hymn, which was set to the tune—"Hail to the brightness of Zion's glad morning." This, and 11 other excellent hymns of his composition, were included in a new edition of the Hymn-book edited by him in 1870. Other missionaries also began to write, and the more popular of their productions were printed as leaflets and sold by thousands. A number of these were in course of time incorporated in the hymn-book; disused hymns were dropped, and the net result was the present book, containing 247 hymns: 30 of these were by the Rev. J. Richardson, to whom the Malagasy owe much for his efforts to improve their hymnody, and also for the thorough teaching of the *Sol-fa* system and the preparation of Tune Books and School Song Books. Other hymn-writers have been the Revs. W. E. Cousins, R. Toy, J. A. Houlder, G. Cousins, R. Baron, and C. T. Price; and among the natives, J. Andrìanaívoravèlona.

It is remarkable that in the promotion of Christian hymnody the Madagascar press of the *Society of Friends* has scarcely been behind that of the *L. M. S.* Mr. Joseph S. Sewell, a leading member of their mission at Antananarivo, translated "Abide with me," and the popular children's hymn, "Whither, are you going, pilgrims?"

In connection with the *S. P. G.* the Rev. A. M. Hewlett, M.A., has striven to promote Psalmody according to the Anglican forms of worship. The *Psalter* is arranged for chanting, many of the Psalms are sung, and the *Te Deum* and *Veni Creator Spiritus* have been translated, —the latter by the Rev. W. E. Cousins, of the *L. M. S.* But in the country districts, more especially, the Malagasy at present prefer the style of hymn and tune popular in English village congregations 50 years ago, with many repeats, fugues, and responsive parts.

iv. *Mauritius.*

550 miles to the east of Madagascar, like a gem in the ocean, lies the fertile and remarkably picturesque island of Mauritius. Though only 36 miles long and 23 broad, it contains a polyglot population of 365,000. Two-thirds are natives of India, coolies working in the sugar plantations, under indentures, and so constantly coming and returning to their homes in India. The other third comprises a motley population of French, English, Negroes, Creoles, Malagasy, Parsees, Chinese, Singhalese and Malays. Both the *S. P. G.* and *C. M. S.* have interesting missions under the superintendence of Bishop Royston, D.D.

The Indian coolies belonging to at least five different nationalities, hymnals have been introduced, prepared by missionaries in India, in the Tamil, Malayalam, Telugu, Bengali and Hindi languages. In an account of these books supplied to us by the Rev. R. J. French, of the *S. P. G.*, we recognize hymnals described by us in the sections of this article devoted to those languages. Doubtless a similar thing has been done in the mission of the *C. M. S.* to the Chinese immigrants. Nor are the spiritual wants of the French-speaking inhabitants of Mauritius overlooked. In services instituted for their use the French hymn-book of the S. P. C. K. and *Cantiques Populaires* of the McAll Mission are both employed. Finally, in religious services established for the benefit of English residents, *Hymns A. & M.* and other well-known hymnals of our own country are used.

v. *Matabeleland.*

Twenty degrees south of the Equator, and about 400 miles from the eastern coast of Africa, is *Matabeleland,* where are stations of the *L. M. S.* The language, called Amantebele, greatly resembles the Zulu. The first hymn-book prepared was very small and imperfect, and is now out of use. The second, prepared by the Rev. W. Sykes, and printed at Cape Town in 1883, contains about 50 hymns, about half original compositions, and the remainder translations of such hymns as "All people that on earth do dwell," "Come to the Saviour, make no delay." English metres and tunes are used, and as a rule the lines do not rhyme.

vi. *Bechuanaland.*

The language of the Bechuanaland bears the name of *Sechuana.* Six societies are labouring in this field, the *L. M. S., S. P. G., W. M. S.,* the *Berlin,* the *Hanoverian Lutheran,* and the *Dutch Reformed.* The *S. P. G.* have a hymn-book prepared by the Revs. Canon Crisp, of Bloemfontein, and W. H. R. Bevan, M.A., of Phokoane. A copy now before us, bearing date 1873, contains the translations of the *Te Deum,* the *Magnificat,* and various Psalms arranged for chanting, and 40 hymns, including, "Draw nigh, draw nigh, Emmanuel," "Abide with me," "The King of Love my Shepherd is," &c. Others have doubtless been added in later editions. The *Wesleyans* have a book edited by the late Rev. Mr. Ludorf, containing about 150 hymns. The *Hanoverian* missionaries have also a Sechuana hymn-book of their own. The *Dutch Reformed,* which is working in the Transvaal, and the Berlin missionaries use the hymn-book of the *L. M. S.,* of which the Rev. Roger Price, of Kuruman, gives the following account.

"It now contains 327 hymns, having been reprinted and enlarged several times. The present edit. is dated 1883. In many instances the hymns are free translations from the English; in others, the sentiment of the English hymn is followed without any attempt at a verbal translation; a few, especially some by the late Rev. Dr. Moffat, are original compositions. English metres and tunes are used exclusively. Rhyme is attempted, but this is often very difficult, owing to the great paucity of monosyllabic words, which are not mere particles, and to the fact that, with but one exception, Sechuana words end in an open syllable and take the main accent on the penultimate."

Upwards of 250 hymns in this collection were translated or composed by Dr. Moffat. The remainder were contributed by the following missionaries:—the Revs. J. Hughes, Dr. Livingstone, J. Mackenzie, J. S. Moffat, R. Price, J. D. Hepburn, J. Good, A. J. Wookey, and Morolong, a native teacher.

Besides this collection a considerable number of hymns have been recently translated and printed at the Kuruman press, and will be included in the next edition of the hymnbook. These are chiefly translations of I. Sankey's *Sac. Songs and Solos.*

vii. *Basutoland.*

Basutoland is situated between Cape Colony to the south and south-east, Natal to the north-east, and the Orange Free State to the west and north-west. The language spoken, called *Sesuto,* is one of the Bantu group, and was first reduced to writing by missionaries of the *Paris Evangelical Society,* who for the last 50 years have laboured there with zeal and diligence, and latterly with great success. The *S. P. G.* has also a small mission in this country.

The Paris missionaries began to prepare hymns in 1840. The present collection is a goodly volume of 384 pp. 8vo, containing hymns and also tunes in *Tonic Sol-fa,* the title being *Lifela tsa Sione le Lipina tsa Tsona,* or "Sacred Hymns sung in the Churches of Basutoland, followed by some of the Songs and Solos of I. D. Sankey and P. Phillips" (London, 1881). It is a 5th ed. of the words, 2nd ed. of the music.

The first part of the book contains 283 hymns, mostly original. The translations are of well-known French and English hymns, and the following are the names of the authors and translators:—Eugene Casalis, Thomas Arbousset, Theophile Jousse, Samuel and Emile Rolland, F. P. Lautré, François Coillard, Louis Duvoisin,

Fritz Ellenberger, François Daumas and Adolphe Mabille.

The second part of the work, containing 132 pieces, consists entirely of translations by the Rev. F. Coillard from the books of I. D. Sankey and P. Phillips. English metres are chiefly used, as suiting the language better than French. Sometimes the lines rhyme, though not always. The Rev. A. Mabille, to whom we are indebted for these particulars, is now preparing a new edition which will contain a few more hymns.

Among the Basutos some of the men have splendid bass voices and all sing heartily. Their favourite hymn is No. 108 in the book just described, set to the tune "French," and commencing "If you ask me what is my hope, I shall say, It is Jesus." This hymnal is in use not only in the French missions, but also in churches belonging to the *S. P. G., L. M. S., W. M. S.,* the *Dutch Reformed,* the *Swiss,* the *Berlin,* and the English *Primitive Methodist* Societies.

viii. *Zululand and Natal.*

Returning from Bechuanaland towards the eastern coast, and crossing the Orange Free State, we come to Zululand and Natal, where are 500,000 people, speaking the dialect of the Bantu language, which is known as *Zulu.* In this region are missions of the *S. P. G., A. B. C., F. C. S., W. M. S.,* and *Evangelical Lutherans* of Berlin, Hermannsburg and Norway.

(1) In 1863, the Rev. C. W. Posselt, of the Berlin mission, pub. a small collection of 74 hymns, printed at the Esidumlimi Mission Press.

(2) Many years ago Bishop Colenso pub. a number of hymns, and was followed in this good work by Bishops Callaway and Wilkinson. The hymn-book of the last-named appeared in 1874, and contains 217 hymns translated from *H. A. & M.*

(3.) In 1883 appeared a small volume prepared by the Revs. Canon Greenstock, of Springvale, and H. T. A. Thompson, of Isandhlwana. It has 117 hymns, including 35 of Dr. Colenso's (some of them altered), 18 of Bp. Callaway's, a few from Bp. Wilkinson's volume, and other sources. Eight or ten are by native Christian deacons. The last is a temperance hymn, by J. W. Cross. The title of this book is *Incwadi Yamagama Okuhlabelela.*

(4) In 1884 the present Bishop of Zululand, the Right Rev. Douglas McKenzie, pub. a small collection of 53 hymns, intended to be sung to tunes in *H. A. & M.* It includes four from Bp. Callaway's book, one translated by Mrs. Johnson ("Now the day is over"), and one (Ps. c.) by J. Blair.

(5) The missionaries of the *A. B. C.* have prepared a book, containing in its 7th ed., which has just been published (1887), 263 hymns. The title is *Amagama Okuhlabelela.* The new ed. is in 3 forms, (*a*) words only; (*b*) with tunes in *Tonic Sol-fa* notation; (*c*) with tunes in Staff notation. Among the names of composers and translators are the following:—the Revs. J. C. Bryant, S. B. Stone, D. Rood, J. L. Döhne, and Mrs. C. B. Grout. Nineteen hymns are from Bp. Callaway's book, five from Canon Greenstock's, some from a collection prepared by the Norwegian missionaries, and a good number from the Isixosa or Kafir hymn-book.

As in the case of the Sechuana language already noticed, as well as in the Kafir, the prevalence of the penultimate accent in Zulu has made the fitting of Zulu hymns to English tunes a work of difficulty. Iambic metres are almost inadmissible, but the language is well suited to chanting.

ix. *Kafirland, or Kaffraria.*

Kafirland extends from near Port Elizabeth in the south to Natal in the north, and from the ocean westward as far as Basutoland. It comprises missions of the Moravians, U. P. Church of Scotland, *S. P. G., F. C. S., L. M. S., W. M. S.,* and *Lutherans* of Germany. The language is allied to the Zulu.

Untsikana, one of the earliest converts to Christianity, composed in pure Kafir rhythm the remarkable hymn, "Ulo-Tixo mkulu ngo-sezulwini" ("Thou art the great God, He Who is in heaven"), which together with his music (traditional) is unique, all subsequent efforts in Kafir hymnody being subject to the trammels of European metres.

(1) Several editions of a hymn-book used at the *Wesleyan* stations throughout Kaffraria, and even in Natal, have been issued from the mission press at Mt. Coke, near King William's Town.

(2) The Rev. Tiyo Soga, a gifted Kafir missionary educated by the United Presbyterian Church, and early removed by death, compiled a book of hymns, which was printed in Scotland.

(3) The principal hymn-book in the Kafir language was prepared by a committee of Presbyterian and other missionaries, and pub. in 1873. It was printed at the mission press in Lovedale, and contains 219 hymns, and 30 psalms and passages of Holy Scripture arranged as chants. The hymns are in English metres, and, in most cases, rhymes are attempted.

(4) The first collection of hymns used at the stations of the *M. M.* was that of the Berlin Society, which contained some hymns translated by the Moravian Brethren. In 1869 a small supplement containing 186 hymns was pub. by the Rev. Th. Reichelt. But an entirely new hymnal, compiled by Revs. R. Baur and H. Weitz, was printed at Herrnhut in 1885. With litanies, liturgical services, 416 hymns and indices, it forms a volume of 428 pages. Most of the hymns are translations from the German; the remainder being chiefly selected from the hymn-books of the Wesleyans and Presbyterians.

(5) The book used in the Anglican Missions, with the title *Incwadi Yamaculo,* was prepared by missionaries of the *S. P. G.,* in the diocese of Graham's Town. An early ed. contained 102 hymns. That now in use has 130 hymns, and bears date 1881. The principal translators were Revs. A. J. Newton, W. M. Cameron, and C. F. Patten. The following also assisted:—B. S. Key, H. R. Woodrooffe, D. W. Dodd, J. Ntsiko, W. Ngewensa, T. Liefeldt.

x. *Cape Colony.*

In the *Cape Colony* the English-speaking part of the community naturally use the hymn-books of their respective denominations in England. But since the hymnody of the coloured races, and other residents speaking the Dutch language, is due to missionary enterprise, a brief notice of it will not be inappropriate here. Colonial Dutch hymnals may be divided into two groups, according as German or English elements have chiefly predominated in their composition.

1. The books in which the hymns are for the most part translated from the German and sung to German tunes are found, are:—

(*a*) The earliest missions in South Africa were those of the Moravians, commenced in 1736 and renewed in 1792. Of their hymnody previous to 1836 we have no knowledge; but in that year a hymn-book was pub. for the use of the coloured races, of which a new edition appeared 20 years later with an *Appendix* containing new hymns. The new hymns were mostly translations by the Brethren Suhl, Kühn and Hartmann. The latest edition, revised and greatly improved, was pub. in 1880.

(*b*) The Rhenish Missionary Society, whose headquarters in Europe are at Barmen, commenced its African mission in 1829. A hymn-book was issued in 1844, revised in 1872, and is now in its 4th edition. It contains 290 hymns, taken chiefly from the Moravian and Dutch reformed hymnals, with 64 original compositions, or translations from the Barmen *Gesangbuch.*

(*c*) The Berlin Missionary Society, founded in 1827, issued its first S. African hymnal in 1853. This was compiled by Rev. P. Schultheiss, and the hymns are arranged in the order of the Church's seasons. A 2nd ed. prepared by the missionaries Schmidt and Howe, was pub. at Amsterdam in 1875, and contains 333 hymns, of which only 28 are original.

2. The books in which, though the German element largely enters, the English element is considerable, are:—

(a) The first Dutch hymnal in which translations of English hymns appeared was that of the L. M. S., in use as early as 1829, but reprinted in 1847. It contained 40 translations of the English hymns of Watts, Doddridge, Steele and Newton. Some of these were by the well-known Dr. Vanderkemp, but the majority by the Rev. G. Barker, missionary at the Paarl. It was revised and enlarged in 1848, and after passing through 4 editions came, in 1862, under the editorship of the Rev. F. W. Kolbe (L. M. S.), through whose skill as a hymn-writer and translator it has in successive editions been enlarged to 412 hymns, and enriched by admirable translations of many of the best known in *Hymns A. & M.*

(b) Wesleyan missions in S. Africa were commenced in 1815, and in 1824 a cheap edition of the Dutch Reformed hymnal was pub., with a *Supplement* suited to the native congregations. This contained some translations of Wesley's hymns by the Rev. Barnabas Shaw. The entire book was superseded in 1840 by a collection of 392 hymns, including 160 translations from Wesley by the Rev. R. Haddy. These translations, however, being deemed unsatisfactory, a new hymnal was prepared in 1855. The compilers were the Revs. R. Ridgill and B. Ridsdale, the former of whom, together with the Rev. H. Tindall, has made some valuable contributions to the store of Dutch translations from the English. The ,6th ed. (1882) contains 268 hymns, of which at least one fourth are versions of well-known English hymns.

(c) The Anglican Dutch hymnal was compiled by the Rev. J. A. Hewitt, now Rector of Worcester, Cape Colony, and printed by the S. P. C. K. in 1877. It contains 201 hymns, arranged in the order of H. A. & M., and includes 26 translations from the Latin, and a very large number from the English, many of the latter being taken, by permission, from the L. M. S. and Dutch hymnals. This is the hymnal authorized for use by the mission congregations of the English Church in the province of S. Africa.

Further information on this subject is contained in a series of articles by the Rev. J. A. Hewitt, D.C.L., Rector of Worcester (Cape Colony), in the S. African *Church Chronicle*, vol. vii., 1886, to which, and also to Dr. Hewitt personally, we are largely indebted for this outline of the Cape Colony hymnody.

xi. *Great Namaqualand.*

If from the Cape Colony we proceed northward, keeping to the western side of the African continent, one of the first regions we enter is Great Namaqualand, a missionary field of the Rhenish Society of Barmen. Hymns in the *Nama* (Hottentot) language were first prepared, about 1845, by Rev. J. G. Krönlein, who, in 1873, edited a hymn-book containing 60 hymns, translated from the German, and adapted to German tunes, the lines rhyming. Most of the translations were by Mr. Krönlein; the rest by the late Rev. H. C. Knudsen and the late Mrs. Kleinschmidt. Further north is a country, variously denominated—

xii. *Damaraland or Hereroland.*

The first *Herero* hymns were prepared by the Revs. J. Rath and F. W. Kolbe (see § Cape Colony), and printed at Cape Town in 1849. The hymn-book now used was edited by the Rev. H. Brincker, and reached a 3rd ed. in 1879. It contains 123 hymns, some original, but chiefly translations from the German, and adapted to German tunes. The contributors were the Revs. J. Rath, F. W. Kolbe, C. H. Hahn, H. Brincker, G. Viebe, Mrs. Baumann, and other members of the Rhenish Mission.

xiii. *Ovamboland.*

As an interesting illustration of the fact that all the Protestant nations of Christendom are now engaged in missionary work among the heathen, reference may be made to the stations of the Finland Missionary Society in *Ovamboland*, a region of Western South Africa, to the north of the 20th degree south latitude. A small hymnal has been prepared in the language of this region, containing about 60 hymns, but we are unable to give particulars.

A few degrees further to the north is the country of *Benguela*, where the A. B. C. has recently planted stations. The language spoken is called *Umbundu*, but missionary work is at present in too elementary a stage for hymnody

xiv. *Congoland.*

Few hymns as yet have been pub. in *Kishi-Kongo*, "the language of the Congo people." All are in *Fiote*, the particular language spoken in the region of which San Salvador is the centre. First, in 1884, in connection with the B. M. S., ten hymns were printed at Stanley Pool; then a collection of 21 was made by the missionaries of the Livingstone Inland Mission and printed in England; lastly, a collection of 20 hymns (including most of the first 10) was printed in 1887, at the B. M. S. Edwin Wade Press, Underhill Station.

With few exceptions the Congo hymns are all translations. The originals are by the Revs. T. J. Comber and W. H. Bentley. The translations include "When His salvation bringing," and other children's hymns; also, "Stand up, stand up for Jesus," and "Father, in high heaven dwelling." Besides the missionaries named, the Revs. J. H. Weeks, and H. Dixon, and two native converts, Kalendenda and Mantu, have translated hymns.

The Livingstone Inland Mission has been transferred to the A. B. M. In their collection are included several hymns from the book just described, and others translated by the Revs. C. H. Harvey, H. Craven, and H. Richards. Among these are "Abide with me," "Jesus sinners will receive," "A few more years shall roll." English metres and tunes are used. Besides the hymns in these collections, others are in use, printed on slips, which, when tested and improved, will be included in future editions.

xv. *Old Calabar.*

To the north of the island of Fernando Po, and about 100 miles to the east of the Niger, the Old Calabar river empties itself into the Gulf of Guinea. In this part of Africa the U. P. Church of Scotland has for the last 42 years had a mission, Creek Town and Duke Town being its principal stations. The language spoken is called *Efik*. Soon after the establishment of the mission a small hymn-book was prepared, which has been repeatedly enlarged, and now in its 7th edit. contains 309 hymns and 7 doxologies. The Rev. H. Goldie has been the editor and principal contributor, but the following have also assisted in the work: the Revs. Dr. Robb, and Messrs. Anderson, Campbell, Edgerley, Thomson and Waddell. Some of the hymns are original, others translations or paraphrases of portions of Holy Scripture. A collection of 39 children's hymns has also been prepared, under the same auspices as the larger book, and printed at Creek Town in 1885 by a native printer. It includes "Little travellers Zionward" (Nkpri mendisïm enyön); "Jesus loves me" (Jisus ama mi), and other well-known English hymns, and a few originals by the Rev. S. H. Edgerley.

The metres are English and the lines rhyme as with us. The larger book above named is also used in connection with an Undenominational mission in Old Calabar, supported by the friends of the Rev. H. Grattan Guinness.

xvi. *Yoruba, Coast of Guinea.*

The *Yoruba* country is to the east of Dahomey, Lagos being the principal coast town, and Abeokuta, Ibadan, and Oyo large towns in the interior. The *C. M. S.*, *W. M. S.*, and *American Baptists of the Southern Convention*, have missions there. (1) In the early years of the Church of England mission English hymn-books were used; but when, in 1850, Christian work began among the heathen, the need was felt of hymns in the language of the country. The Rev. D. Hinderer, a German missionary in the service of the *C. M. S.*, translated a few and composed others, using them in MS. and increasing the number from time to time to 106, when in the year 1865 they were printed in London. About the same time as Mr. Hinderer, the Rev. H. Townsend in another part of the field commenced a similar work, and in 1854 printed a small collection of 20 hymns. This was presently increased to 120, and printed at Ake Abeokuta, and several times reprinted in England. In 1867 the Rev. J. A. Maser, of the *C. M. S.* and others, began to translate and compose additional hymns; and in 1877 a collection of more than 200 was printed, which has been in use for the last 10 years. A new collection of 355 hymns is now passing through the press,—a selection from previous books, made by a committee of native clergymen and teachers, and revised by the Rev. D. Hinderer. Mention may also be made of a collection of 99 hymns, chiefly for use in schools, prepared by the Rev. J. B. Wood, of the *C. M. S.* (2) The *Wesleyans* have a hymn-book of their own, containing about 150 hymns, and including many of the hymns in the above collection. The 2nd edit. was pub. in 1876. (3) It is believed that the American Baptists have also a hymn-book of their own, but we have no particulars.

In some of the *Yoruba* hymns *rhyme* has been attempted, but there is some difficulty arising from the fact that all words must end in vowels. Lively English tunes are preferred by the people to grave German ones; their own native songs abound in choruses.

xvii. *Sierra Leone.*

In Sierra Leone and the neighbouring districts of Western Africa several missionary societies are at work, but their religious services are conducted for the most part in English, and English hymn-books are used. But at *Port Lokkoh* is a small mission of the *C. M. S.*, among a people called *Temnes*, and a small collection of 17 hymns in the *Temne* language has been prepared by the Rev. C. F. Schenke. These are partly original and partly translated. English metres and tunes are used, but the lines do not rhyme.

V. *Conclusion.*

With this brief notice of missionary Hymnody on the West Coast of the "Dark Continent" we close our paper. Beginning with Greenland, and proceeding westwards,

we have made the tour of the world, and the reader will surely feel with us that the work we have looked upon—nearly all accomplished within the last 90 years—is great and marvellous, a work of most noble Christian devotion and industry. An examination of our pages will show that the languages and dialects in which Christian hymns in connection with Foreign Missions have been written, or into which they have been translated, are nearly *one hundred and fifty*, and that in many of them, several hymn-books of considerable size have been prepared. The list includes languages spoken by all the great divisions of the human race, Aryan, Semitic, Turanian; languages in all stages of formation, monosyllabic, as the Burman, agglutinative, as the Tamil and Turkish, inflexional, as the Sanscrit group of Northern India; languages of extreme antiquity, as the Chinese, and of comparatively recent formation, as the Urdú; languages harsh and guttural, as the speech of some African tribes, and soft and mellifluous, as that of the Polynesian islanders. All these by the energy and diligence of Christian missionaries have been mastered, their words have been arranged in tuneful measures, and in them God's praises are now sung, and His "wonderful works" declared. It will have been observed that in regard to some parts of the world our story is incomplete. This is in part due to the fact that a number of letters asking for information have not been answered, probably in some cases because they failed to reach their destination, and in others, because the good men to whom they were addressed were prevented from writing by more pressing engagements. We have, however, to thank very many friends,—mission-secretaries, missionaries, and others, both ladies and gentlemen of various professions,—for the extreme kindness with which they have sent us, from nearly all parts of the world, letters of information and specimens of hymnals. Want of space prevents the writer from appending a full list of their names, but he begs to assure them, should their eye fall on these pages, that for all their help he is most grateful. It was his original intention to include in each section a list of the principal translated hymns in each language, but he soon found that this would entail constant repetition. The fact is, that the best hymns of Watts, Doddridge, Cowper, Newton, Wesley, Heber, Lyte, Keble, Bonar, Miss Steele, Miss Havergal, and other English authors,—the best German hymns,—the best hymns of American composition,—are now sung in China and South Africa, in Japan and Syria, among the peoples of India, and in the isles of the Pacific Ocean,—indeed, in almost every place where Protestant missionaries have uplifted the Gospel banner and gathered Christian Churches.   [W. R. S.]

Missions, Home. [Various.]

Missum Redemptorem polo. *C. Coffin.* [*Christmas.*] Appeared in the *Paris Breviary*, 1736; in several modern French Breviaries; in J. Chandler's *Hys. of the Prim. Church*, 1837, p. 168; and in Card. Newman's *Hymni Ecclesiae*, 1838 and 1865. In Coffin's *Hymni Sacri*, 1736, p. 99, it is given amongst those hymns which are based upon older hymns. It is founded on the "A solis ortus cardine" of Sedulius (p. 4, i). *Tr.* as :—

1. **Behold from heaven a Saviour sent.** By W. J. Blew, in his *Church Hy. & Tune Bk.*, 1852–5, in 7 st. of 4 l., and in Rice's *Sel.* from the same, 1870.

Other trs. are :—

1. The Prince of Peace to sinners given. *J. Chandler*, 1837.

2. Let all the earth her King adore. *I. Williams*, 1839. [J. J.]

Mistaken souls that dream of heaven. *I. Watts.* [*Living and dead Faith.*] Appeared in his *Hys. & Spiritual S.*, 1709, Bk. i., No. 140, in 7 st. of 4 l., and headed "A living and dead Faith, collected from several Scriptures." In its original form it is in limited use. The most popular form of the text is "*Deluded* souls that dream of heaven," which was given in the 8th ed. of Cotterill's *Sel.*, 1819, No. 94, in 4 stanzas, being Watts's st. i.–iii. and vi. altered. These two forms of the hymn are in use in G. Britain and America. [J. J.]

Mit Fried und Freud ich fahr dahin. *M. Luther.* [*Nunc Dimittis.*] This free rendering of the Song of Simeon (St. Luke ii. 29–32) was 1st pub. in the *Geystliche gesangk Buchleyn*, Wittenberg, 1524, and was included by Luther in 1542 as one of the six funeral hymns in *Christliche Geseng . . . zum Begrebniss*. In *Wackernagel*, iii. p. 17, in 4 st. of 6 l.; in Schircks's ed. of Luther's *Geistl. Lieder*, 1854, p. 88; and in the Berlin *G. L. S.*, ed. 1863.

This noble swan-song, as Bunsen calls it, has comforted many, princes and pious Christians, in their last hours. Lauxmann, in *Koch*, viii. 580, gives various instances of its consoling effects, stating, e.g., that Prince Charles of Anhalt, during his last illness in 1561, comforted himself with it, and if with trembling voice, yet with joyful heart, sung the whole hymn a quarter of an hour before his death.

The *tr.* in C. U. is :—

In peace and joy I now depart, According to. A full and good *tr.* by Miss Winkworth, in her *C. B. for England*, 1863, No. 81, and her *Christian Singers*, 1869, p. 114. Considerably altered by Dr. *Bacon*, 1884, p. 41.

Other trs. are :—(1) "With peace and with joyfull gladnesse," by *Bp. Coverdale*, 1539 (*Remains*, 1846, p. 566). (2) "Lord, let Thy servand now depart," in the *Gude and Godly Ballates*, ed. 1567–68, folio 30 (1868, p. 51). (3) "According to Thy will I part," in the *British Mag.*, March 1838, p. 269. (4) "With peace and joy from earth I go," by *Miss Fry*, 1845, p. 152. (5) "God's will be done! with joy of heart," by *J. Anderson*, 1846, p. 80. In his ed. 1847, p. 92, altered to "Thy will be done. With joyful heart." (6) "Gladly from earth and time I cease," by *Dr. J. Hunt*, 1853, p. 153. (7) "In peace and joy I now depart, It is," by *R. Massie*, 1854, p. 83. (8) "In peace and joy away I go," by Dr. G. Macdonald, in the *Sunday Mag.*, 1867, p. 840. In his *Exotics*, 1876, p. 109, beginning "In peace and joy I now depart, As." (9) "In joy and peace I onward fare," by *N. L. Frothingham*, 1870, p. 234. [J. M.]

Mittit ad Virginem. [*Annunciation of the B. V. M.*] This sequence has generally been ascribed to Peter Abelard, but is not found in the collection of hymns and sequences which he made for the convent of the Paraclete. Cousin, in his ed. of Abelard's *Opera*, Paris, 1849, vol. i. p. 328, gives the text from Clichtoveus, &c., and says his authorship is uncertain; though the hymn is not unworthy of him. *Mone*, No. 343, prints from a 13th cent. MS. at St. Paul, in Carinthia, and other sources: and

Daniel, ii. p. 59, from a 13th cent. Munich MS., &c. It is also in the *Sarum* (MS. in the Bodleian, c. 1370, Barlow, 5, page 450); *Hereford* (MS. in the Bodleian, c. 1370); *York* (MS. in the Bodleian, c. 1390); *Magdeburg* of 1480; *Paris* of 1481, and other *Misscls*. The text is also in *Wackernagel* i., No. 182; *Kehrein*, No. 199, &c. *Tr.* as :—

1. **To the Virgin He sends no- inferior angel.** By J. M. Neale, in the enlarged ed. of the *H. Noted*, 1854, and the *Altar Hymnal*, 1884.

2. **He sends to the Virgin no lowlier angel.** By R. F. Littledale, in the *People's H.*, 1867, under the signature of P. C. E., i.e. "Priest of the Church of England."

Another tr. is :—

"No one lower in grade To the Virgin," &c. *C. B. Pearson*, 1868. [J. M.]

Μνώεο Χριστὲ. *Synesius, Bp. of Ptolemus.* [*Lent.*] This is the last of ten hymns written by Synesius at various periods of his life (375–430). [See **Greek Hymnody**, § v.] The full texts of the ten hymns are given in the *Anthologia Græca Carminum Christianorum* (Leipzig), 1871; and from that work they were translated by the Rev. A. W. Chatfield, and pub. in his *Songs & Hys. of Earliest Greek Christian Poets*, &c., 1876. The *tr.* of this hymn begins "Lord Jesu, think on me." It was given in *H. A. & M.*, 1875, in 5 st. Subsequently 3 st. were added (i., iv., vi., viii.), and it was included in his *Songs & Hys.*, &c., 1876, in 9 st. of 4 l. From this No. 338, in Thring's *Coll.*, 1882, is taken. To his *tr.* Mr. Chatfield has added this note at p. 86 :—

"In translating this Ode I have given my spirit more liberty. It may be considered as a paraphrase or amplification, rather than an exact translation of the original. A brief form of it appears in *Hymns Ancient and Modern*."

Another *tr.* was pub. by I. Williams in his *Thoughts in Past Years*, 1838. It begins :—

"Christ the Son
Of God most high,"

is in 15 lines, but is not in C. U. [J. J.]

Möckhel, Johann Friedrich, was b. Jan. 16, 1661, at Culmbach in Franconia, and matriculated at the University of Jena in 1681. He was for some time private chaplain to Herr von Redwitz at Teisenort, and from 1685 to 1691 to Herr von Küntzberg at Hayn near Bayreuth. In 1691 he became pastor at Neuhauss, and in 1693 at Steppach and Limpach, near Neustadt on the Aisch. He d. April 19, 1729 (*Koch*, v. 523, &c.). Of his 11 hymns one has been *tr.* into English, viz. :—

Nun sich die Nacht geendet hat, Die Finsterniss zertheilt. *Morning.* *Wetzel*, iv., 357–359, quotes at length from a letter in which Möckhel says this hymn was composed by himself in 1691 while at Hayn; and was written at the request of the widowed Frau von Küntzberg (Kindsberg) in order that she might have a hymn for morning prayer as a companion to her favourite hymn for evening prayer, which was "Nun sich der Tag geendet hat " (p. 516, i.). A copy, he adds, was sent to a sister in Bayreuth, and so inserted in the Printzen *G. B.*, Bayreuth, 1691. Included in Wagner's *G. B.*, Leipzig, 1697, vol. iv. p. 1435, in 16 st. of 4 l. and in the Berlin *G. L. S.*, ed. 1863, No. 1122. *Tr.* as :—
(1) "Thanks, dearest Jesus, for Thy love." A *tr.* of st. ix. as st. iii. of No. 886 in the *Moravian H. Bk.*, 1801 (1886, No. 1174). (2) "Lo! Night's deep shades are scattered wide." By *H. J. Buckoll*, 1842, p. 39. [J. M.]

Mohr, Joseph, was born at Salzburg, Austria, on Dec. 11, 1792. After being

Ordained priest on Aug. 21, 1815, by the Roman Catholic Bishop of Salzburg, he was successively assistant at Ramsau and at Laufen; then coadjutor at Kuchl, at Golling, at Vigaun, at Adnet, and at Authering; then Vicar-Substitute at Hof and at Hintersee—all in the diocese of Salzburg. In 1828 he was appointed Vicar at Hintersee, and in 1837 at Wagrein, near St. Johann. He d. at Wagrein, Dec. 4, 1848 (MS. from Archivar Augustin Hilber, Salzburg, &c.). The only hymn by him tr. into English is:—

Stille Nacht! heilige Nacht! *Christmas.* This pretty little carol was written for Christmas, 1818, while Mohr was assistant clergyman at Laufen, on the Salza, near Salzburg, and was set to music (as in the *Garland of Songs*) by Franz Gruber, then schoolmaster at the neighbouring village of Arnsdorf (b. Nov. 25, 1787, at Hochburg near Linz, d. June 7, 1863, as organist at Hallein, near Salzburg). What is apparently the original form is given by O. Kraus, 1879, p. 608, in 3 st. of 6 l., and in Dr. Wichern's *Unsere Lieder*, Hamburg, 1844, No. 111. Another form, also in 3 st. of 6 l., is in T. Fliedner's *Lieder-Buch für Kleinkinder - Schulen*, Kaiserswerth, 1842, No. 115, and the *Evang. Kinder G. B.*, Basel, 1867. The trs. are from the text of 1844.

1. **Holy night! peaceful night!** All is dark By Miss J. M. Campbell in C. S. Bere's *Garland of Songs*, 1863, and thence in *Hys. & Carols*, Lond., 1871.

2. **Silent night! hallowed night. Land and deep.** This is No. 131 in the *Christian H. Bk.*, Cincinnati, 1865. It is suggested by, rather than a tr. of, the German.

3. **Holy night! peaceful night! Through the darkness.** This is No. 8 in J. Barnby's *Original Tunes to Popular Hymns*, Novello, N. D., 1869; repeated in *Laudes Domini*, N.Y., 1884, No. 340.

4. **Silent night! holy night! All is calm.** This is in C. L. Hutchins's *Sunday School Hyl.*, 1871 (1878, p. 198), and the *S. S. H. Bk.* of the Gen. Council of the Evang. Luth. Church in America, 1873, No. 65.

5. **Peaceful night, all things sleep.** This is No. 17, in *Carols for St. Stephen's Church*, Kirkstall, Leeds, 1872.

6. **Silent night, holiest night. All asleep.** By Dr. A. Edersheim, in the *Sunday at Home*, Dec. 18, 1875, repeated in the *Church S. S. H. Bk.*, 1879, No. 35.

7. **Silent night! holy night! Slumber reigns.** By W. T. Matson, as No. 132, in Dr. Allon's *Children's Worship*, 1878.

8. **Still the night, holy the night! Sleeps the world.** By Stopford A. Brooke, in his *Christian Hys.*, 1881, No. 55.

Translations not in C. U. :—
(1) "Stilly night, Holy night, Silent stars," by Miss E. E. S. Elliott, privately printed for the choir of St. Mark's, Brighton, about 1858, but first pub. in the *Church Miss. Juv. Instructor*, 1871, p. 198. Also in her *Tune Book for Under the Pillow*, 1880. (2) "Holy night! calmly bright," by Mary D. Moultrie in *Hys. & Lyrics* by Gerard Moultrie, 1867, p. 42. (3) "Silent night, holiest night! Moonbeams," by C. T. Brooks, in his *Poems*, Boston, U. S., 1885, p. 218.   [J. M.]

Moibanus, Ambrosius, was b. at Breslau, April 4, 1494. After studying at Krakau (Cracow), and graduating M.A. at Vienna, he became, in 1518, rector of the Cathedral School at Breslau, and in 1520 rector of the St. Mary Magdalene School. Incurring the displeasure of the clergy, he left Breslau in 1521, and, after studying Hebrew at Ingolstadt, under Johann Reuchlin, went to Wittenberg. After his return to Breslau he was, in April, 1525, appointed pastor of the St. Elisabeth Church, and in the same year became D.D. at Wittenberg. He d. at Breslau, Jan. 16, 1554 (*Allg. Deutsche Biog.*, xxii. 81, &c.). The only hymn known by him is :—

Ach Vater unser der du bist. (*Lord's Prayer.*) 1st pub. in *Eyn gesang Buchleyn*, Zwickau, 1525, in 3 st. of 14 l., and thence in *Wackernagel*, iii. p. 544. In some later books it begins "Vater unser, der du bist." *Tr.* as "O Father, ours celestiall," by *Bp. Coverdale*, 1539 (*Remains*, 1846, p. 548).   [J. M.]

Moir, David Macbeth, was b. at Musselburgh, Jan. 5, 1798. After attending the medical classes in the University of Edinburgh, he settled down as a doctor in his native place. In June, 1851, he went to Dumfries to recruit, but d. there, July 6, and was buried at Inveresk, Musselburgh, July 10, 1851. His poems, selected and edited, with a memoir, by Thomas Aird, were pub. in 1852, in 2 vols., as *The Poetical Works of David Macbeth Moir*. He marked his graver contributions to *Blackwood's Magazine* with the signature "Delta" or Δ, and in the number for August, 1832, there appeared "Devotional Melodies by Delta." These were 3 in number :—

1. Return, once more return, O wanderer.
2. O who is like the Mighty One.
3. How pleasant is the opening year.

and seem to have been the only hymns suited for public worship that he ever wrote. [J. M.]

Molanus, Gerhard Walther (Wolter), D.D., s. of Wilcke Ludwig van der Muelen or Molanus, syndic and advocate at Hameln on the Weser, was b. at Hameln, Nov. 1, 1633 (Oct. 22, O. S.), and studied at the University of Helmstädt. In 1659 he was appointed Professor of Mathematics at the University of Rinteln, but in 1664 extraordinary, and in 1665 ordinary Professor of Theology and D.D. In 1674 he was appointed Director of the Consistory at Hannover and General Superintendent of the Electorate of Brunswick-Lüneburg, and in 1677 (titular) Abbot of Loccum. He d. at Hannover, Sept. 7, 1722 (*Allg. Deutsche Biog.*, xxii. 86, &c.). He was a man of extensive learning, and in his official position wielded a very great influence over the whole Electorate. He edited the *Hannover G. B.* of 1698. Of his five hymns one has passed into English :—

Ich trete frisch zu Gottes Tisch. *Holy Communion.* In the *Rinteln G. B.*, 1673, No. 124, in 11 st. of 5 l. Repeated in the *Hannover G. B.*, 1740, and in Burg's *G. B.*, Breslau, 1746, No 1673. *Tr.* as :—

Thy Table I approach. This is No. 270, in the Ohio *Luth. Hyl.*, 1880, and omits st. iii., iv., viii., ix.   [J. M.]

Moller, Martin, son of Dionysius Moller, mason at Liessnitz (now Kropstädt), near Wittenberg, was b. at Liessnitz, Nov. 11, 1547. He attended the town school at Wittenberg and the gymnasium at Görlitz, but was too poor to go to any university. In 1568 he was appointed cantor at Löwenberg in Silesia, but in April, 1572, was ordained as pastor of Kesselsdorf, near Löwenberg. In the autumn of 1572 he was appointed diaconus at Löwenberg, in 1575 pastor at Sprottau, and in July, 1600, became chief pastor at Görlitz. He preached his last sermon, Oct. 30, 1605, and d. at Görlitz, March 2, 1606 (*Koch*, ii. 211, iv. 552, &c.).

Moller's hymns appeared in his two very popular devotional books, (1) *Meditationes sanctorum patrum*, Görlitz, 1584; pt. ii., Görlitz, 1591, and various later eds. This was mostly made up of meditations from St. Augustine, St. Bernard, and Tauler, selected and *tr.* into German by Moller. (2) *Manuale de praeparatione ad mortem*. Görlitz, 1593 [Library of the Prediger-Seminar at Hannover]. *Wackernagel*, v., Nos. 71–75, gives only 5 hymns under Moller's name. Of these No. 72 ("Heiliger Geist, du Tröster mein") is from "Veni Sancte Spiritus, et emitte" (q.v.), and No. 73, ("Nimm von uns Herr") from "Aufer immensam" (see p. 92, ii.). Two versions of the "Jesu dulcis memoria" have also often been ascribed to Moller, viz. "Ach Gott, wie manches Herzeleid," (see p. 10, i.), and, with less reason, "O Jesu süss, wer dein gedenkt" (see p. 589, ii.). See also "Hilf, Herr, mein Gott," noted under **Selnecker, N.**   [J. M.]

Molther, Philipp Heinrich, was b. in Alsace, Dec. 28, 1714. At Jena, where he studied theology, he joined the [Moravian] Brethren in 1737, and went to London 1739. He was minister of the Brethren's congregation at Neuwied from 1750 to 1761, and spent the rest of his life, 1762–1780, in Dublin and in Bedford. He d. at Bedford, Sep. 9, 1780, five years after his consecration as a Bishop of the Brethren's Unity. See "At God's right hand," &c., p. 89, i.   [G. A. C.]

Mone, Franz Joseph, was b. May 12, 1796, at Mingolsheim, near Bruchsal, Baden. He entered the University of Heidelberg in 1814, where in 1817 he became University lecturer, was in 1819 appointed extraordinary and in 1822 ordinary Professor of History, and in 1825 also director of the University library. In 1827 he became Professor of History and Statistics at the University of Louvain, but during the Belgian Revolution of 1831 resigned and retired to Heidelberg. In 1835 Duke Leopold of Baden appointed him Privy Recorder and Director of the General-State-Archives at Carlsruhe, and this post he held till his retirement on a pension in 1868. He d. at Carlsruhe, March 12, 1871 (*Allg. Deutsche Biog.*, xxii. 165, &c.).

He interested himself specially in Celtic studies, in the history of the Upper Rhine, and in Liturgiology (*Lateinische und Griechische Messen*, 1850, &c.). He claims notice here specially on account of his *Lateinische Hymnen des Mittelalters*, pub. at Freiburg in Baden, in three vols., viz.:—(i.) *Lateinische Hymnen des Mittelalters, aus Handschriften herausgegeben und erklärt von F. J. Mone, Director des Archivs zu Karlsruhe*, 1853, with Hymns on God and the Angels (Nos. 1–320); (ii.) *Hymni Latini Medii Aevi, e Codd. MSS. edidit et Adnotationibus illustravit*, 1854, on the B. V. M. (Nos. 321–620); (iii.) Same title as vol. ii. 1855, on the Saints (Nos. 621–1215). The interest of this work, now unfortunately out of print, consists in its texts rather than in its notes, and in the comparative ease with which, to one acquainted with German, it can be used. The information given is all printed together at the end of the individual hymns, and the abbreviations used are clear and intelligible, not symbols such as those employed by *Daniel*. The work throughout is arranged on a consistent plan, i.e., in order of subjects and not according to authors. Mone published no hymns except those found in manuscripts, of which he says he consulted "some hundreds from more than fifty libraries;" among the most valuable being those which formerly belonged to the Benedictine Abbey of Reichenau (not Rheinau), near Constanz, and are now at Carlsruhe. A large proportion of the hymns were here first printed; many of those in the second and

third volumes being however not of much value. In *Daniel's* fourth and fifth volumes a large amount of space is filled by texts and notes which he transferred from this work of Mone (see p. 279, i.).   [J. M.]

Monsell, John Samuel Bewley, LL.D., s. of Thomas Bewley Monsell, Archdeacon of Londonderry, was b. at St. Columb's, Londonderry, March 2, 1811, and educated at Trinity College, Dublin (B.A. 1832, LL.D. 1856). Taking Holy Orders in 1834, he was successively Chaplain to Bp. Mant, Chancellor of the diocese of Connor, Rector of Ramoan, Vicar of Egham, diocese Worcester, and Rector of St. Nicholas's, Guildford. He d. in consequence of a fall from the roof of his church, which was in the course of rebuilding, April 9, 1875. His prose works include *Our New Vicar*, 1867; *The Winton Church Catechist*, &c. His poetical works are:—

(1) *Hymns and Miscellaneous Poems*, Dublin, W. Curry, Jun., & Co., 1837; (2) *Parish Musings, or Devotional Poems*, 1850; (3) *Spiritual Songs for the Sundays and Holy Days throughout the Year*. 1857 (People's Ed., 1875); (4) *His Presence, not His Memory*, 1855, 1858; (5) *Hymns of Love and Praise for the Church's Year*, 1863 (2nd ed. 1866); (6) *The Passing Bell; Ode to The Nightingales, and Other Poems*, 1867; (7) *Litany Hymns*, 1869; (8) *The Parish Hymnal after the Order of The Book of Common Prayer*, 1873; (9) *Watches by the Cross*, 1874; (10) *Simon the Cyrenian; and Other Poems*; (11) *Nursery Carols*.

In these works several hymns which appeared in the earlier books are repeated in the later, and thus at first sight his compositions seem to be more in number than they really are. The total amounts to nearly 300, and of these about one-fourth are in C. U. The most popular of these are, "God is love; that anthem olden"; "God of that glorious gift of grace"; "Holy offerings, rich and rare"; "Lord of the living harvest"; "Mighty Father, Blessed Son"; and "Sing to the Lord a joyful song." In addition to those which are annotated under their respective first lines, the following are in C. U.:—

i. Appeared in his *Hymns and Miscellaneous Poems*, Dublin, 1837.

1. Birds have their quiet nests. *Humility of Christ.*
2. Dark and dim the day-light rose. *Good Friday.*
3. Friend of the friendless and the lone. *Jesus, the Friend.*
4. My God, what wondrous love was Thine. *Whitsuntide.*
5. O for a heart more fervent. *Holiness desired.*
6. O for the time when on the world. *Missions.*
7. The springtide hour brings leaf and flower. *Spring.*
8. This day the Lord is risen. *Easter.*
9. When cold our hearts and far from Thee. *Teach us to Pray.*
10. Why restless, why so weary? *Providence.*
11. Yes, I do feel, my God, that I am Thine. *Assurance.*

ii. Appeared in his *Parish Musings*, 1850.

12. In Thee, my [O] God, will we rejoice. *Trust in God.*
13. Lord, dependent on Thy promise. *Holy Baptism.*
14. Members of Christ, Children of God. *Confirmation.*
15. So teach me, Lord, to number. *The O. and N. Year.*
16. Soon [soon] and for ever. *Death anticipated.*
17. The broken, contrite heart oppress'd. *Promises of God.*
18. Thou art near, yes, Lord, I feel it. *Divine Support.*
19. Would'st thou learn the depths of sin? *Passiontide.*

iii. Appeared in his *Spiritual Songs*, 1857.

20. A few bright leaders of her host. *All Saints.*
21. A happy, happy [merry, merry] Christmas. *New Year's Day.*
22. Blessed hope, that we the fallen [sinful]. *Hope.*

23. Heart in heart, and hand in hand. *SS. Simon & Jude.*
24. Jesus, my loving Lord! I know. *Resignation.*
25. Last Sunday of the work-day year. *S. after Christmas Day.*
26. Loved by God the Father. *Holy Baptism.*
27. Mercy, mercy, God the Father. *Lent.*
28. My head is low, my heart is sad. *Confirmation.* (*Penitential.*)
29. Oft doth the Christian's heart inquire. *Christian Duty.*
30. O God, most mighty, listen now. *Charities.* From "When languid frame or throbbing pulse."
31. O holy Sabbath day. *Sunday.*
32. O Lord, what records of Thy love. *St. Barnabas.* Sometimes, "Lord God, what records of Thy love."
33. O love, divine and golden. *Holy Matrimony.* From this, "Love divine and tender" is taken.
34. One lesson more the Church must learn. *Waiting on God.* From this, "One lesson Christ His own would teach" is taken.
35. Proudly in his [the] hall of judgment. *Tuesday before Easter.*
36. Sinful, sighing to be blest. *Lent.*
37. The Church of God, with equal care. *St. James.*
38. The journey done; The rest begun. *Burial.*
39. The simple trust that can confide. *Trust.*
40. Weary and sad, a wanderer from Thee. *Lent.*

iv. Appeared in his *Hymns of Love and Praise*, 1863, and 2nd ed., 1866.

41. Bounteous blesser of the seedtime. *Sexagesima. Seed Time.*
42. Brightly hopeful for the future. *God's mercy through life.*
43. Christ is risen! Alleluia! *Easter.*
44. Come and deck the grave with flowers. *Easter Eve.*
45. Fight the good fight with all thy might. *Fight of Faith.*
46. Holy Spirit, long expected. *Whitsuntide.*
47. Hours and days and months and years. *The Circumcision.*
48. I have no comfort but Thy love. *The Comfort of Love.*
49. I knew Thee in the land of drought. *A Song of Love.*
50. I think of Thee, my God by night. *Evening.*
51. Jesu, gentle Sufferer, say. *Good Friday.*
52. Labouring and heavy-laden. *Lent.*
53. Light of the world, we hail Thee. *Missions.*
54. Lord, to whom except to Thee? *Holy Communion.*
55. My sins, my sins, my Saviour. *Ash Wednesday.*
56. O'er the distant mountains breaking. *Second Advent.*
57. Other Name than our dear Lord's. *Jesus All and in All.*
58. Pity on us, heavenly Father. *Litany Hymn for Lent.*
59. Praise the Lord, rejoice, ye Gentiles. *Advent, or Missions.*
60. Rest of the weary, joy of the sad. *Jesus, the Saviour and Friend.*
61. Shadow of a mighty Rock. *Jesus, the Rock of Ages.*
62. Sing, O heaven; O earth rejoice. *Ascension.*
63. Sweet is the gentle voice of spring. *Seed Time.*
64. Sweet is Thy mercy, Lord. *Divine Mercy.*
65. Teach me to do the thing that pleaseth Thee. *Divine Teaching.*
66. The good old times, how glorious. *Advent.*
67. The world may in its wealth delight. *Rejoicing in the Lord.* An altered form of "Let others in their wealth delight."
68. Though Thou slay me, I will trust. *Faith.*
69. To Christ the Lord! The Incarnate Word. *Christmas.*
70. When I had wandered from His fold. *The Love of God.*

v. Appeared in his *Litany Hymns*, 1869.

71. Lay the precious body, In the quiet grave. *Burial.*
72. My sins have taken such a hold on me. *Litany of Repentance.*

vi. Appeared in his *Parish Hymnal*, 1873.

73. I hunger and I thirst. *Septuagesima.*

Dr. Monsell's hymns are as a whole bright, joyous, and musical; but they lack massiveness, concentration of thought, and strong emotion. A few only are of enduring excellence.　　　　　　　　　　[J. J.]

Montes, superbum verticem. *Jean Baptiste de Santeüil.* [*Visitation of the B. V. M.*] Pub. in his *Hymni Sacri et Novi*, 1689, p. 34, and again in the *Paris Breviary*, 1736, and several modern French Breviaries. It is also in Card. Newman's *Hymni Ecclesiae*, 1838 and 1865. *Tr.* as :—

Ye mountains, bend ye low. By I. Williams, in his *Hys. tr. from the Parisian Breviary*, 1839, in 6 st. of 4 l., and thence into the *Hymnal for the Use of St. John the Ev.*, Aberdeen, 1870.
　　　　　　　　　　　　　[J. J.]

Montgomery, Ignatius, younger brother of James Montgomery, was b. Sept. 4, 1776, at Gracehill, near Ballymena, county of Antrim, a settlement of the [Moravian] Brethren, to which his father, the Rev. John Montgomery, had removed in that year from Irvine, in Ayrshire. Ignatius Montgomery served as minister in four of the Brethren's congregations in England and Ireland. He d. at Ockbrook, near Derby, April 28, 1841. See "At God's right hand,.&c.," p. 89, i.　[G. A. C.]

Montgomery, James, s. of John Montgomery, a Moravian minister, was b. at Irvine, Ayrshire, Nov. 4, 1771. In 1776 he removed with his parents to the Moravian Settlement at Gracehill, near Ballymena, county of Antrim. Two years after he was sent to the Fulneck Seminary, Yorkshire. He left Fulneck in 1787, and entered a retail shop at Mirfield, near Wakefield. Soon tiring of that he entered upon a similar situation at Wath, near Rotherham, only to find it quite as unsuitable to his taste as the former. A journey to London, with the hope of finding a publisher for his youthful poems ended in failure ; and in 1792 he was glad to leave Wath for Sheffield to join Mr. Gales, an auctioneer, bookseller, and printer of the *Sheffield Register* newspaper, as his assistant. In 1794 Mr. Gales left England to avoid a political prosecution. Montgomery took the *Sheffield Register* in hand, changed its name to *The Sheffield Iris*, and continued to edit it for thirty-one years. During the next two years he was imprisoned twice, first for reprinting therein a song in commemoration of "The Fall of the Bastille," and the second for giving an account of a riot in Sheffield. The editing of his paper, the composition and publication of his poems and hymns, the delivery of lectures on poetry in Sheffield and at the Royal Institution, London, and the earnest advocacy of Foreign Missions and the Bible Society in many parts of the country, gave great variety but very little of stirring incident to his life. In 1833 he received a Royal pension of £200 a year. He d. in his sleep, at the Mount, Sheffield, April 30, 1854, and was honoured with a public funeral. A statue was erected to his memory in the Sheffield General Cemetery, and a stained glass window in the Parish Church. A Wesleyan chapel and a public hall are also named in his honour. Montgomery's principal poetical works, including those which he edited, were :—

(1) *Prison Amusements*, 1797 ; (2) *The Wanderer of Switzerland*, 1806 ; (3) *The West Indies*, 1807 ; (4) *The World before the Flood*, 1813 ; (5) *Greenland and Other Poems*, 1819 ; (6) *Songs of Zion*, 1822 ; (7) *The Christian Psalmist*, 1825 ; (8) *The Christian Poet,*

1825; (9) *The Pelican Island*, 1828; (10) *The Poet's Portfolio*, 1835; (11) *Original Hymns for Public, Private, and Social Devotion*, 1853. He also published minor pieces at various times, and four editions of his *Poetical Works*, the first in 1836, the second in 1836, the third in 1841, and the fourth in 1854. Most of these works contained original hymns. He also contributed largely to Collyer's *Coll.*, 1812, and other hymn-books published during the next 40 years, amongst which the most noticeable was Cotterill's *Sel.* of 1819, in which more than 50 of his compositions appeared. In his *Christian Psalmist*, 1825, there are 100 of his hymns, and in his *Original Hymns*, 1853, 355 and 5 doxologies. His *Songs of Zion*, 1822, number 56. Deducting those which are repeated in the *Original Hymns*, there remain about 400 original compositions.

Of Montgomery's 400 hymns (including his versions of the Psalms) more than 100 are still in C. U. With the aid of Montgomery's MSS. we have given a detailed account of a large number. The rest are as follows:—

i. Appeared in Collyer's *Collection*, 1812.

1. Jesus, our best beloved Friend. *Personal Dedication to Christ.*
2. When on Sinai's top I see. *Sinai, Tabor, and Calvary.*

ii. Appeared in Cotterill's *Selection*, 1819.

3. Come to Calvary's holy mountain. *The Open Fountain.*
4. God in the high and holy place. *God in Nature.* The cento in *Com. Praise*, 1879, and others, "If God hath made this world so fair," is from this hymn.
5. Hear me, O Lord, in my distress. *Ps. cxliii.*
6. Heaven is a place of rest from sin. *Preparation for Heaven.*
7. I cried unto the Lord most just. *Ps. cxlii.*
8. Lord, let my prayer like incense rise. *Ps. cxxxix.*
9. O bless the Lord, my soul! His grace to thee proclaim. *Ps. ciii.*
10. Out of the depths of woe. *Ps. cxxx.* Sometimes "When from the depths of woe."
11. The world in condemnation lay. *Redemption.*
12. Where are the dead? In heaven or hell? *The Living and the Dead.*

iii. Appeared in his *Songs of Zion*, 1822.

13. Give glory to God in the highest. *Ps. xxix.*
14. Glad was my heart to hear. *Ps. cxxii.*
15. God be merciful to me. *Ps. lxix.*
16. God is my strong salvation. *Ps. xxvii.*
17. Hasten, Lord, to my release. *Ps. lxx.*
18. Have mercy on me, O my God. *Ps. li.*
19. Hearken, Lord, to my complaints. *Ps. xlii.*
20. Heralds of creation cry. *Ps. cxlviii.*
21. How beautiful the sight. *Ps. cxxxiii.*
22. How precious are Thy thoughts of peace. *Ps. cxxxix.*
23. I love the Lord, He lent an ear. *Ps. cxvi.*
24. In time of tribulation. *Ps. lxxvii.*
25. Jehovah is great, and great be His praise. *Ps. xlviii.* Sometimes, "O great is Jehovah, and great is His Name."
26. Judge me, O Lord, in righteousness. *Ps. xliii.*
27. Lift up your heads, ye gates, and wide. *Ps. xxiv.*
28. Lord, let me know mine [my] end. *Ps. xxxi.*
29. Of old, O God, Thine own right hand. *Ps. lxxx.*
30. O God, Thou art [my] the God above. *Ps. lxiii.*
31. O Lord, our King, how excellent. *Ps. viii.* Sometimes, "O Lord, how excellent is Thy name."
32. O my soul, with all thy powers. *Ps. ciii.*
33. One thing with all my soul's desire. *Ps. xxvii.* From this, "Grant me within Thy courts a place."
34. Searcher of hearts, to Thee are known. *Ps. cxxxix.*
35. Thank and praise Jehovah's name. *Ps. cvii.*
36. Thee will I praise, O Lord in light. *Ps. cxxxviii.*
37. The Lord is King; upon His throne. *Ps. xciii.*
38. The Lord is my Shepherd, no want shall I know. *Ps. xxiii.*
39. The tempter to my soul hath said. *Ps. iii.*
40. Thrice happy he who shuns the way. *Ps. i.*
41. Thy glory, Lord, the heavens declare. *Ps. xix.*
42. Thy law is perfect, Lord of light. *Ps. xix.*
43. Who make the Lord of hosts their tower. *Ps. cxxv.*
44. Yea, I will extol Thee. *Ps. xxx.*

iv. Appeared in his *Christian Psalmist*, 1825.

45. Fall down, ye nations, and adore. *Universal adoration of God desired.*

46. Food, raiment, dwelling, health, and friends. *The Family Altar.*
47. Go where a foot hath never trod. *Moses in the desert.* Previously in the Leeds Congregational *Collection*, 1822.
48. Green pastures and clear streams. *The Good Shepherd and His Flock.*
49. Less than the least of all. *Mercies acknowledged.*
50. Not to the mount that burned with fire [flame]. *Communion of Saints.*
51. On the first Christian Sabbath eve. *Easter Sunday Evening.*
52. One prayer I have: all prayers in one. *Resignation.*
53. Our heavenly Father hear. *The Lord's Prayer.*
54. Return, my soul, unto thy rest. *Rest in God.*
55. Spirit of power and might, behold. *The Spirit's renewing desired.*
56. The Christian warrior, see him stand. *The Christian Soldier.* Sometimes, "Behold the Christian warrior stand."
57. The days and years of time are fled. *Day of Judgment.*
58. The glorious universe around. *Unity.*
59. The pure and peaceful mind. *A Children's Prayer.*
60. This is the day the Lord hath made (q.v.). *Sunday.*
61. Thy word, Almighty Lord. *Close of Service.*
62. What secret hand at morning light? *Morning.*
63. While through this changing world we roam. *Heaven.*
64. Within these walls be peace. *For Sunday Schools.*

v. Appeared in his *Original Hymns*, 1853.

65. Behold yon bright array. *Opening a Place of Worship.*
66. Behold the book whose leaves display. *Holy Scriptures.*
67. Come ye that fear the Lord. *Confirmation.*
68. Home, kindred, friends, and country, these. *Farewell to a Missionary.*
69. Let me go, the day is breaking. *Jacob wrestling.*
70. Not in Jerusalem alone. *Consecration of a Church.*
71. Praise the high and holy One. *God the Creator.*

In common with most poets and hymnwriters, Montgomery strongly objected to any correction or rearrangement of his compositions. At the same time he did not hesitate to alter, rearrange, and amend the productions of others. The altered texts which appeared in Cotterill's *Sel.*, 1819, and which in numerous instances are still retained in some of the best hymn-books, as the "Rock of Ages," in its well-known form of three stanzas, and others of equal importance, were made principally by him for Cotterill's use. We have this confession under his own hand.

As a poet, Montgomery stands well to the front; and as a writer of hymns he ranks in popularity with Wesley, Watts, Doddridge, Newton, and Cowper. His best hymns were written in his earlier years. In his old age he wrote much that was unworthy of his reputation. His finest lyrics are "Angels from the realms of glory," "Go to dark Gethsemane," "Hail to the Lord's Anointed," and "Songs of praise the angels sang." His "Prayer is the soul's sincere desire," is an expanded definition of prayer of great beauty; and his "For ever with the Lord" is full of lyric fire and deep feeling. The secrets of his power as a writer of hymns were manifold. His poetic genius was of a high order, higher than most who stand with him in the front rank of Christian poets. His ear for rhythm was exceedingly accurate and refined. His knowledge of Holy Scripture was most extensive. His religious views were broad and charitable. His devotional spirit was of the holiest type. With the faith of a strong man he united the beauty and simplicity of a child. Richly poetic without exuberance, dogmatic without uncharitableness, tender without sentimentality, elaborate without diffusiveness, richly musical without apparent effort, he has bequeathed to the Church of Christ wealth which could only have come from a true genius and a sanctified heart. [J. J.]

Moore, Thomas, s. of John Moore, a small tradesman at Dublin, was b. in that city, May 28, 1779, educated at a private school and Trinity College, Dublin; read at the Middle Temple for the Bar; held a post under the Government in Bermuda for a short time, and d. Feb. 26, 1852. His *Memoirs, Journal, and Correspondence* were pub. by Lord John Russell in 1855. In that work every detail concerning himself and his numerous publications, most of them of high poetical merit, will be found. His connection with hymnody is confined to his *Sacred Songs*, which were pub. in 1816, and again in his *Collected Works*, 1866. These *Songs* were 32 in all, and were written to popular airs of various nations. Of these *Songs* the following have passed into a few hymn-books, mainly in America:—

1. As down in the sunless retreats of the ocean. *Private Prayer.*
2. But who shall see the glorious day. *The Final Bliss of Man.*
3. Come, ye disconsolate, where'er you languish. *Relief in Prayer.* In American hymn-books the text is sometimes as in T. Hastings and Lowell Mason's *Spiritual Songs*, 1831. This may be distinguished from the original by the third stanza, which reads, "Here see the Bread of life; see waters flowing," &c.
4. Fallen is thy throne, O Israel. *Israel in Exile.*
5. Like morning when her early breeze. *Power of Divine Grace.*
6. O Thou Who driest the mourner's tear. *Lent.*
7. Since first Thy word [grace] awaked my heart. *God All and in All.*
8. Sound the loud timbrel o'er Egypt's dark sea. *Deliverance of Israel.*
9. The bird [dove] let loose in eastern skies. *Prayer for Constancy.*
10. The turf shall be my fragrant shrine. *The Temple of Nature.* From this "There's nothing bright above, below" is taken.
11. Thou art, O God, the Life and Light. *God, the Light and Life of Men.*
12. Were not the sinful Mary's tears? *Lent.*

Of these hymns No. 11 has attained the greatest popularity. [J. J.]

Moraht, Adolph, PH.D., s. of J. D. M. Moraht, merchant in Hamburg, was b. at Hamburg, Nov. 28, 1805. From 1825 to 1828 he was a student of theology at the Universities of Halle, Göttingen, and Berlin, graduating PH.D. at Göttingen in 1828. He was then resident for nine years as a candidate of Theology (licensed preacher) at Hamburg, teaching in private schools, and devoting his spare time to the work of Home Missions. At Easter, 1838, he was appointed second pastor at Möllen, in Lauenburg, and in 1846 chief pastor. He d. at Möllen, Dec. 6, 1884 (*Koch* vii. 296; MS. from his daughter, &c.).

His hymns appeared principally in his (1) *Harfenklänge* (90), Lüneburg, 1840; 2nd ed. (107), Hamburg, 1865. (2) *Zweite Sammlung der Harfenklänge* (73), Hamburg, 1880. Some of them first appeared in various papers and collections. The best are his hymns of Love to Christ, which are sweet in tone and the fruits of ripe Christian experience. Those which have passed into English are:—

i. **Ich bleib bei dir! wo könnt ichs besser haben.** *Rest in the Lord.* 1840, as above, p. 111, in 5 st.; and in *O. Kraus*, 1879, p. 360, omitting st. v. *Tr.* as "I rest with Thee, Lord! whither should I go," by Miss

Borthwick in *H. L. L.*, 1855, p. 62 (1884, p. 120), and in Miss Warner's *Hys. of the Church Militant*, 1858, p. 69.
ii. **Je kleiner ich, je grösser du.** *Humility.* Founded on St. John iii. 30. 1840, as above (1865, p. 121), in 7 st., and in *O. Kraus*, 1879, p. 361. *Tr.* as "The less I am, the more Thou art," by *J. Kelly*, 1885, p. 31.
iii. **Wo ist dein Bethel, wo die Himmelspforte.** *Secret Prayer.* 1840, as above, p. 101, in 4 st., and in F. Seinecke's *Evang. Liedersegen*, 1862, No. 192. *Tr.* as (1) "Where is thy Bethel, where the world's control," by *C. T. Astley*, 1860, p. 22. (2) "Where is thy Bethel? where the gate of heaven," by *J. Kelly*, 1885, p. 11. [J. M.]

Moravian Hymnody. By the name of the *Moravian Church* is signified the Church of the ancient Bohemian Brethren renewed in 1722 at Herrnhut in Saxony [see **Bohemian Hymnody,** § I.–IV. 3.] The ancient Brethren lived in Moravia and Poland as well as in Bohemia, but because their main settlements were situated in Bohemia (until 1547), and the Bohemian language the one they employed in their writings, they received the general name *Bohemian Brethren.* They called themselves in Bohemian *jednota bratrská*, and in Latin *Unitas Fratrum.* In like manner the Brethren of the Renewed Church are commonly called *Moravians*, because the first founders of Herrnhut immigrated from Moravia. They assumed this name in England and America, but in the Act of Parliament under the 12th May, 1749, they are acknowledged as the *Protestant Episcopal Church known by the name of Unitas Fratrum or the United Brethren*, and therefore their official name is: *Unitas Fratrum* (Brethren's Unity), or the *United Brethren.*

i. *History of the Moravians.*

The history of the Moravians is required in an article on the Moravian Hymnody only so far as it may help to further the better understanding of their hymns and hymn-books, their special character being modified by that Church from whose midst they originated, and for whose use they were written and compiled. The most prolific Moravian hymn-writer is Count N. L. von Zinzendorf, and nearly all the other Moravian hymn-writers were influenced by him. After his death there arose but few Moravian hymn-writers, as Gregor, Garve, Albertini; and the hymn-book now in use among the Moravians is for the most part the same, which was edited towards the close of the last century. Therefore it may suffice to give a brief account of Moravian history up to Zinzendorf's death in 1760.

Introduction. From the commencement of the Bohemian Brethren's Unity, some of its members existed in Moravia, deputies from this land having already been sent as representatives to the constitutive Synod held at Lhotka (1467). About 1480 several hundred Waldenses emigrated to Moravia from the Mark Brandenburg and joined the Unity. These, settled in Fulnek and Landskron, formed the only German-speaking part of the Unity, for whom Weisse edited the first German hymn-book. Nevertheless the Moravian branch of the Unity was fully incorporated with the whole body, stood under the same direction, and had the same doctrines, institutions, &c. After the persecutions in Bohemia in the fatal year 1547, the fugitive Brethren chiefly found a refuge in Moravia, but in consequence of the battle of the White Mountain, near Prague, Nov. 8, 1620, the Unity in Moravia was destroyed, as it was in Bohemia, by a cruel and bloody Anti-reformation.

The ancient Brethren's Church was already dissolved in 1627, and three different sections of it can afterwards be distinguished, each of which has its particular fate. (1) *The Polish Brethren's Church.* It developed itself independently and joined with the Reformed Church in their contest with the Lutherans, so much so that at first the brethren had the upper hand, and their constitution was accepted by the Reformed Church in Poland. Later, however, matters were reversed, and the Brethren had to give up more and more of their peculiarities. With the Union of the Evangelical Churches in 1817, the Brethren's Unity in Poland ceased altogether. (2) *A second branch*, in existence since 1627, is the Bohemian-Moravian Brethren's Church. This migrated formally into Poland, Hungary, Silesia, and Prussia. Altogether there are said to have been, till 1656, about 100 congregations of the Brethren in these countries. After the destruction of Lissa (in Poland) in 1656, this second branch, *the Exile Church*, which has no importance for the Renewed Brethren's Church, disappears. (3) Of great importance is *the third branch*, composed of those members of the Brethren's Church who remained in Bohemia and Moravia, whom Comenius calls the "hidden seed." Amos Comenius, born at Comna, in Moravia, March 28, 1592, was the last bishop of the Bohemian and Moravian branches, and he consecrated "in spem contra spem" his son-in-law, Peter Figulus, or Jablonsky, bishop of the Unity. To his death he maintained the hope that the expelled Brethren would be allowed to return to their fatherland, and that the Unity would be re-established. Therefore when Cromwell, after having crushed Ireland, intended to settle the homeless Bohemians and Moravians there as a Protestant colony, Comenius could not agree to it : "Ego quidem a nostris dispersis nondum in hoc puncto responsum habeo at, quid sit, facile intelligo, nempe spes recollectionis in patria, quam plerique pertinaciter fovent, et in his (ut verum fatear) ego quoque" (see Vaughan's *The Protectorate of Cromwell*, ii. 447). Soon afterwards the Restoration of the Stuarts put an end to all such plans. Some of the Brethren, however, settled in England and Ireland, and their Bohemian names attest their descent to this day, as John Cennick (properly Cenník), well known in hymnody and in Moravian history. In addition to his celebrated activity as teacher, Comenius was untiring in strengthening the courage and faith of the emigrant Brethren, and even that of the remnant in their fatherland, by means of letters and writings. For example, he wrote a German catechism for the Moravians in those villages from which 60 years later the founders of Herrnhut emigrated. They used it secretly in their homes the whole time, through it preserving their inward Evangelical views although externally Roman Catholics. (One of the only two extant copies was brought by them to Herrnhut.)

2. A revival of the Brethren's tradition among the German-speaking part of that "hidden seed" seems to have been called forth by the change in Church affairs in the neighbouring country of Silesia. Charles XII. by the Altranstädter Convention, 1707, had compelled the Emperor to restore 121 churches which had been taken from the Protestants. In connection with this Convention, six other churches ("Gnaden-Kirchen") were granted to them in 1709. The ministers who were appointed to these churches were mostly excellent persons. Their sermons had great effect, and as some of these Churches were not far from the boundaries of Moravia, some of the "hidden" Protestants (the "hidden seed") made use of the opportunity and often attended the services, especially in Teschen.

In Moravia the Brethren's traditions were kept alive particularly in the so-called "Kuhländchen." One circle was in the villages of *Sehlen* and *Seitendorf*. George *Jäschke* in *Sehlen* was the bearer of these traditions. His forefathers had fled in the 16th century from Bohemia to Moravia. He was a true descendant of the ancient Brethren, and is described as a real patriarch in appearance. In constant intercourse with this circle (formed by the families Jäschke, Neisser, &c.) was another in the neighbourhood of *Fulnek*, in the villages of *Zauchtenthal* and *Kunewalde*, where Samuel Schneider played the same part as G. Jäschke. To the secret assemblies held by Schneider belonged the families Kunz, Beyer, Stach, Zeisberger, Tannenberger in Zauchtenthal, and Nitschmann in Kunewalde.

In these circles *Christian David* appeared twice in succession. This remarkable man was a carpenter from Bohemia, who, not content with his Roman Catholic faith, after long wanderings through Germany in search for true children of God, became a Lutheran, at Berlin. With the year 1717 he began to take journeys to Moravia and Bohemia, on which he sought out the hidden Protestants on his own account. During this time he made the acquaintance of the Count of Zinzendorf, who was already widely famed for his willingness to receive all oppressed people. With Zinzendorf's permission David guided the first three emigrants with wife and child from Sehlen in Moravia, to Zinzendorf's estate, Berthelsdorf in Saxony, which they reached on June 8th, 1722. Zinzendorf was in Dresden, but his steward Heiz

received the poor people. He would not allow them, however, as they had contemplated, to build a house in the village, but directed them to a place at some distance, in the wood between Löbau and Zittau. Here Christian David felled the first tree for building a house, on the 17th June, 1722. Heiz called this place the "Herrnshut," meaning that these homeless families stood under the direct "protection of the Lord" (German *Hut des Herrn*).

3. The Count of Zinzendorf, who had afforded a refuge to these poor persecuted people, was born on the 26th May, 1700, in Dresden, and was descended from one of the most ancient noble families of the Archduchy of Austria. His father, Saxon Minister of State, died six weeks after the birth of his son. The latter, after the second marriage of his mother in 1704 to the Prussian Field-Marshal von Nazmer, was brought up by his grandmother Henriette Catharine von Gersdorf (p. 419, i.), on her estate of Hennersdorf. His education was exclusively Pietistic. [We designate by the name of Pietism a religious movement which took place in Germany about the end of the 17th century. As Puritanism appeared in strong contrast to the High Church party in England, so Pietism opposed a cessation or retrogression of the Reformation in Germany by the awakening of "true piety." Spener, a main representative of that tendency, was Zinzendorf's godfather.] He would have liked to study theology, but his family wished him to prepare himself for State service. After having finished his study of law in 1719, he travelled in Holland and France, everywhere giving his attention to the condition of the Church and religious life. He sought the company of Catholic and Reformed, of Pietists, Mystics, and Socinians, and everywhere made the observation that to all these different denominations one thing was common, namely, that true Christianity consisted in personal religion, or, as he expressed it, in *Christianity of the heart*. He felt himself at home wherever he found personal faith, even with the most extreme sects. In contrast to the confessional views, he named this "pure religion." Returned from his travels, Zinzendorf undertook the sole management of his paternal property. Once again he attempted to enter the ministry, but in consideration for his family was again obliged to relinquish his wish, and took a situation as Councillor in the Saxon Government in Dresden. At any rate he had the firm resolution to employ his religious ideas and opinions for the benefit of his fellow-men even in this situation, heedless of the offence which he might give thereby. This he proved, not only by the meetings which he held in his own house in Dresden, but also by editing his first four collections of hymns, 1725–31 (see ii., 1. 1–4). They have no connection with Herrnhut and the Moravians, for he writes in the preface to the first Moravian hymn-book of 1735 (see ii., 2. 1): "Until now four editions of hymns have been published. The first ones [ii., 1. 1, 1st and 2nd editions] were intended for use in the Church at Berthelsdorf [his own estate], the other for that of the children [ii., 1. 2]. In 1731 Mr. Marche published a collection of ancient and modern hymns, which were to be useful to the children of God scattered hither and thither." It can be ascertained to a certainty that the congregation at Herrnhut availed itself of no part of these collections.

4. In 1722 Zinzendorf, as already stated, permitted the carpenter, Chr. David, to bring some emigrants from Moravia to his estate at Berthelsdorf. From this year the emigration went on uninterruptedly till 1733. But besides these Moravian emigrants there came other people from all parts of Germany, attracted by the report of religious freedom on the Zinzendorf estates. This led to sharp doctrinal and confessional disputes among the inhabitants of Herrnhut, so that Zinzendorf found himself, in 1727, compelled to give up his post in Dresden and to reside in Berthelsdorf. Zinzendorf wished that the Brethren should attach themselves to the Lutheran Church, but they wished to re-establish their old constitution as it was described by Comenius in his "Ratio disciplinae." And they gave him plainly to understand that "they would rather take up their staff and wander further, and doubted not that they would find places where this freedom would be granted them, on which they laid so much stress." Zinzendorf could not for conscience sake let them go, and formed on the ground of the "Ratio disciplinae," "Congregation Regulations" which on May 12, 1727, were accepted and signed by all the inhabitants of Herrnhut. The renewal of the Brethren's Church was completed by the Ancient Brethren's Episcopal Consecration being conferred on David Nitschmann by Jablonsky. This Daniel Ernst Jablonsky, the son of the above-mentioned Petrus Figulus or Jablonsky, then Court Chaplain in Berlin, had, in 1699, received from his father the Episcopal Consecration for the Bohemian and Moravian branch. With the consent of the Polish Brethren's Bishop,

Sitkovius, he consecrated David Nitschmann a Bishop on March 13, 1735.

5. Prior to this event, in 1732, when the colony at Herrnhut numbered but six hundred souls, the first two missionaics to foreign lands had been sent forth. On the 21st of Aug. of that year, David Nitschmann, afterwards the first Bishop of the Renewed Church, and Leonhard Dober, set out for the Island of St. Thomas, each with six dollars in his pocket, determined to sell themselves as slaves if there were no other way of preaching the Gospel to the negroes. The missionary work grew out of this humble beginning, and has always remained the chief undertaking of the Moravian Church. We enumerate the Moravian Missions as they exist at the present time, because the Brethren translated their hymn-books into the languages of most of those nations to whom they were preaching the Gospel. (The first year in the following List indicates the time of commencement, the second date the baptism of the first convert.)

1. *Greenland*, 1733 (March 29, 1739), 6 Stations.
2. *Labrador*, 1752, 1764, 1770 (Feb. 19, 1776), 6 Stations.
3. *North America* among the *Indians*, 1740 (Feb. 11, 1742), 4 Stations.
4. *S. Thomas* and *S. John*, 1732 (Sept. 30, 1736), 5 Stations.
5. *S. Croix*, 1733 (July 12, 1744), 3 Stations.
6. *Jamaica*, 1754 (April 27, 1755), 17 Stations.
7. *Antigua*, 1756 (1756), 8 Stations.
8. *S. Kitts*, 1777 (Nov. 14, 1779), 4 Stations.
9. *Barbados*, 1767 (1768), 4 Stations.
10. *Tobago*, 1787, renewed 1827 (1799), 3 Stations.
11. *Mosquito*, 1849 (Oct. 28, 1849), 8 Stations.
12. *Demerara*, 1878, 2 Stations.
13. *Surinam* among the *Arrawak Indians*, 1738, abandoned 1808; among the *Negroes* (slaves), 1776 (1776), and among the (free) *Bush negroes*, 1765 (1771), 16 Stations.
14. *South African Western District* (among the Hottentots), 1736 (1741), renewed 1792, 10 Stations.
15. *South African Eastern District* (among the Caffres), 1818 (Jan. 6, 1820), 6 Stations.
16. *Australia*, 1849, renewed 1858 (Jan. 18, 1860), 2 Stations.
17. *West Himalaya*, 1853 (1865), 3 Stations.

6. Partly through their travels to the heathen, partly through their fame which spread unconsciously to them, the Moravians became known in other European lands. In 1728, the Countess of Schaumburg-Lippe then in London, asked for nearer accounts of the Moravian settlement in Herrnhut. She was a German lady attached to the retinue of the Queen of the British monarch George II., and had previously corresponded with Zinzendorf. The reply of the Moravian Church was taken by three exiles, who were kindly received by the Countess of Lippe, but they did not obtain an audience of the Queen. In January, 1735, 10 Brethren came to London, and, in August, 20 others followed. They were all destined for the English colony of Georgia, partly to colonise, but mainly with the object of bringing the Gospel to the Creek and Cherokee Indians. Br. Spangenberg had been previously sent to London to make the needful arrangements with the Georgia Trustees. His stay at London was of much importance for the future, as Spangenberg, who had been introduced to Mr. Vernon (the Secretary of the fifty Georgia Trustees), also to General Oglethorpe (the Governor of the colony), and to the Bishop of London, was greatly respected. Some of the Bishops not only expressed a wish to see the Brethren settled in the English colonies, but of their own accord offered to confer Anglican Episcopal Orders, should it be desired. The other company, which had left Herrnhut in August of the same year for Georgia, sailed in the very ship which conveyed General Oglethorpe, the Revs. John and Charles Wesley, B. Ingham, as well as the colonial officials. It was therefore on this voyage the Brethren and the Methodists became acquainted—an acquaintance which in its results proved to be of the utmost importance, both as concerned Christendom and heathen lands. In the following years the Moravians hired Lindsey House, Chelsea, and began to hold meetings in London and also in Yorkshire. On the 12th May, 1738, certain statutes were drawn up conjointly by P. Boehler (Moravian minister) and J. Wesley for the guidance and edification of the small Religious Society meeting in the house of J. Hutton in Little Wyld Street. A part of this Society constituted itself as a distinct congregation in union with the Brethren's Church on Nov. 10, 1742. Until this date two English Moravian hymn-books had been published. The first was put to press Oct. 24, 1741, and was ready for use Nov. 24. It consisted almost exclusively of translations from the German. The second left the press Aug. 4, 1742, (had some

English hymns in addition to the contents of the first edition. All the editions till 1754 must be regarded as the undertaking of private individuals, having no sanction from the Church as such. On the 12th May, 1749, the Moravians were acknowledged by a Bill of the English Parliament as a " *Protestant Episcopal Church known by the name of Unitas Fratrum or The United Brethren.*"

7. In the meantime the Moravians founded new settlements in Germany, of which Herrnhaag in Wetteravia (founded 1738) was the most important. In the year 1738, the Count of Zinzendorf had been exiled from Saxony, by which means his adversaries had aimed at the destruction of the settlement at Herrnhut. But although Herrnhut during the next years suffered from the Count's exile, yet this misfortune laid the foundation-stone of several new settlements in Germany. The Count, accompanied by his family and some of his most able fellow-labourers, left Saxony, and this "pilgrims' congregation" sought refuge with a friend of Zinzendorf's, the Count of Büdingen, in Wetteravia. Here they bought land, and founded Herrnhaag, which became the centre of the Brethren's Unity for the next 12 years. Here the pilgrim's congregation was stationed, visitors from all parts of Germany came and went continually, news from the Missions arrived every week from all parts of the world, while missionaries themselves, accompanied by converted negroes, or Esquimaux, or Indians, &c., gave accounts of their work. Every inhabitant of this little colony, homeless on this earth, was every day prepared to be sent to any part of the world. No wonder that this remarkable congregation felt itself standing above all national, ecclesiastical or other distinctions, that it lost sight of the real relations of this life, and that in its midst a fantastic and sentimental form of religious thought grew up. This is proved by the hymn-books, which were published in the years 1741-49, and which were later suppressed by the Moravians themselves. In 1750, a new Count of Büdingen, who was jealous of Zinzendorf, commanded the inhabitants of Herrnhaag to renounce Zinzendorf by signing an edict; but they all, without exception, refused, preferring to leave Herrnhaag, and settled, partly in Niesky (Silesia), founded 1742, partly in Pennsylvania. Herrnhaag thus deserted, fell to ruins, which stand to this day. In 1747, Zinzendorf was allowed to return to Saxony, and spent the last years of his life (1756-60) at Herrnhut, where he died May 9, 1760. With his death the original period of the Moravian history regarding their hymn-books ends, the next 40 years (1760-1800) being devoted to the constitutional and financial affairs of the Brethren's Church.

ii. *Moravian Hymn-books.*

(1) *Zinzendorf's Collections of Hymns.*

The following books are sometimes but falsely taken for the first Moravian books. They have no further connection with Herrnhut than that Zinzendorf edited them, and that most of the hymns in the *Moravian H. Bk.*, 1735, are taken from them. (See i. § 3.)

1. *Sammlung geistlicher und lieblicher Lieder* (a collection of hymns and spiritual songs), Leipzig, dedicated to his grandmother, Henriette Catharine von Gersdorf. The dedication is dated : Dresden, May 26, 1725. It contains 889 hymns (28 by Zinzendorf). 2nd ed. unaltered, besides an "Anhang" (No. 890-1078), and a "Zugabe" (addition), No. 1079-1149) (17 hymns by Zinzendorf).

2. *Einfältige aber theure Wahrheiten* . . . . . . *aus verschiedenen geistlichen und lieblichen Liedern denen Einfältigen und Kindern vorgelegt durch Graf Ludwig von Zinzendorf* (i.e. Simple but precious truths . . . collected from various hymns and spiritual songs produced for simple folk and children by Count L. von Z.), 1727, dedicated to B. W. Marperger. 2 parts, 379 and 363 short hymns in alphabetical order, an extract from the preceding for the children, 2nd ed. 1728. Later hymn-books for the Moravian children, 1754, 1757 (London); 1789 (Barby).

3. *Christ-catholisches Singe und Bet-Büchlein nebst einem Anhang* (a small Christian Catholic Song and Prayer Book with an Appendix), 1727. Contains 79 hymns from the *Heilige Seelenlust*, of J. Scheffler (q.v.). The "Anhang" contains 147 hymns, an extract from No. 1 for the Roman Catholics.

4. *Sammlung geist- und lieblicher Lieder* (a collection of hymns and spiritual songs) pub. by *M. Marche* at Görlitz. The dedication to the Princess of Denmark Charlotte Amalie is dated Aug. 27, 1731. Contains 1402 hymns, and an "Anhang," No. 1403-1416. 1009

hymns are taken from the *H. Bk.* No. 1 (with all the 45 by Zinzendorf), 407 new hymns (among these 81 by Zinzendorf), therefore in all 126 hymns written by Zinzendorf.

5. *Graf Ludwig von Zinzendorf, Teutsche Gedichte* (German poems by Count Ludwig von Zinzendorf), Herrnhut, 1735, 128 hymns (from the years 1713–35); 2nd ed., Barby, 1766, 130 hymns.

(2) The German Moravian Hymn-books.

1. *Das Gesang-Buch der Gemeine in Herrnhut*, 1735 (the hymn-book of the congregation at Herrnhut), 972 hymns and an "Anhang," Nos. 973–999. The numeration of the hymns is very defective; the Nos. 814, 859, 894, 968, 977, 978, 982, are all to be found repeated twice; and between Nos. 942 and 943 is one unnumbered hymn. Therefore the book contains 999 hymns, although the last hymn is numbered 991. 841 hymns are taken from *Marche's H. Bk.* (1. 4), in which 121 are by Zinzendorf (5 are omitted). 158 hymns are new; 87 by Zinzendorf (in all 208); 8 by Rothe; 4 by Erdmuth von Zinzendorf; 2 by M. Dober; 2 by Gutbier; 2 from the *Bohemian Brethren's H. Bk.*; 7 by non-Moravians; 46 by anonymous authors.

2. *The same*, 2nd ed., 1737, unaltered with exception of corrected numeration of the hymns. 5 new "Anhänge" (appendices) are added (3. *b*.). In the following years appeared: 7th "Anhang" hymns, No. 1197–1254, printed most likely 1738. 8th "Anhang" hymns, No. 1255–1370, with a preface by Zinzendorf; "Written on board of the ship Aletta, off Ushant, Apr. 16, 1739." A reprint of No. 2 appeared, 1741, without place of publication as:—*Das Gesangbuch der Herrnhut: und anderer Brüder-Gemeinen mit denen Cöthnischen Liedern vermehrt.*

3. *a. Christliches Gesangbuch der Evangelischen Brüder-Gemeinen von* 1735 *zum drittenmal aufgelegt und durchaus revidiert* 1741 (i.e. A Christian hymn-book of the Evangelical Brethren's congregations of 1735, edited for the third time and newly revised throughout). The hymns 164–170 are omitted; No. 171 follows on No. 163. In the preface stands: "The whole rubric on the 'anointing' is intentionally omitted, because some hymns in that rubric did not exactly express the meaning of the Holy Scripture, others contained some doctrines which we could never defend." All other deviations from 2. No. 1 consist only in single words and expressions.

b. Anhang als ein zweyter Theil zu dem Gesang-Buche der Evangelischen Brüder-Gemeinen (i.e. Appendix as a second part to the Hymn-book of the Evangelical Brethren's congregations). It contains: Anhang 1–8, 9th (hymns No. 1371–1527); 10th (hymns No. 1528–1681). In the following years appeared:—

c. "Anhang" 11th, hymns No. 1682–1791, with a preface by Zinzendorf, dated "From the tent before Wayomick in the great plain Skehantowáno, in Canada, Oct. 15, 1742." Printed 1743. "*Zugabe*" (*suppl.*) to the 11th appendix hymns No. 1792–1862. Printed 1744.

d. "Anhang" 12th, hymns No. 1863–2156, printed 1745. *1st suppl.* to the 12th appendix hymns No. 2157–2201. *2nd suppl.* hymns No. 2202–2276. *3rd suppl.* hymns No. 2277–2313, with a preface dated July 11, 1747. *4th suppl.* hymns No. 2314–2357. All the four *suppls.* were printed in the years 1746–48.

4. The following *extracts* from the preceding were published:—

a. Ein kleines Gesang-Büchlein zum Gebrauch der Pilger (i.e. A small hymn-book for the use of pilgrims), Frankfurt, 1736.

b. Hirtenlieder von Bethlehem (i.e. Pastoral songs from Bethlehem), Germantown (North America), 1742.

5. *Etwas vom Liede Mosis des Knechts Gottes und dem Liede des Lammes, das ist: Alt- und neuer Brüder-Gesang von den Tagen Henochs bisher, für alle Kinder und Seelen Gottes .... gesammlet ......* London, 1753 (i.e. Part of the song of Moses the servant of God and of the song of the Lamb [Revel. 15, 3], i.e. ancient and modern Brethren's song from the days of Enoch till now, collected for all Children and Souls of God ......). The preface is dated "Westminster Abbey, 1752" (Zinzendorf lived at that time in Hutton's former house opposite Westminster.) This book was printed in Zinzendorf's private press at Lindsey House, Chelsea, which he bought 1750, and entered into 1753. *This book is the first chronologically arranged collection of German hymns of all ages.* Vol. I. contains

2168 *hymns*, divided as follows:—(1) Anthems out of the Bible. (2) Scripture hymns. (3) Hys. of the primitive church. (4) Hys. of the ancient Brethren. (5) Hys. after the Reformation. (*a*) Hys. of the xvi. century; (*b*) of the xvii. century; (*c*) those written by the "viri desideriorum" [the so-called Pietists, 1670–1735], and (6) An enchiridion of the hymns of the Brethren's congregation in the xviii. century. *Vol. II., London*, 1754. It contains 1096 hymns "of the Evangelical Brethren's Church in the xviii. century." The preface is dated "Lindsey House, Jan. 13, 1755."

6. *Anhang der übrigen Brüder-Lieder seit* 1749 (i.e. Appendix of the Brethren's hymns written since 1749). The preface is dated "Emmaus, 1755." Part i. contains 53 hymns written by Christian Renatus von Zinzendorf (1752). Part ii. 310 hymns. Second enlarged ed. 1760. Part i. Nos. 1–73: part ii. Nos. 74–243: and a *supplement* ("Zugabe"), with 55 hymns.

7. *Extract from* (2) *Nos.* 5 *and* 6. *Kleine Brüder-Gesang-Buch.* Part i. *Heitenlieder von Bethlehem* (2nd ed. of 2. No. 4, b.) 368 hymns. Part ii. *Der Gesang des Reigens zu Saron* (i.e. The song of the dance at Saron), London, 1754 (parts i. and ii., 2nd edition, Barby, 1761, 2397 hymns; 3rd edition, Barby, 1763; 4th ed., Barby, 1767; 5th ed., Barby, 1772 (3rd–5th edition unaltered). Part iii., Barby, 1767, 512 hymns.

8. *Gesangbuch zum Gebrauch der evangelischen Brüdergemeinen*, Barby, 1778 (i.e. Hymn-book for the use of the Evangelical Brethren's congregations). It contains 1750 hymns taken from all the earlier Brethren's hymnbooks, and several new. 1227 hymns are written by Moravians (96 hymn-writers), and 127 are mixed, i.e. composed of single verses of Moravian and non-Moravian hymns. 1778–1870, this hymn-book was several times reprinted unaltered. An appendix was edited 1806, containing 278 new hymns.

9. *Kleines Gesangbuch der evangelischen Brüdergemeine* (Small hymn-book of the Evangelical Brethren's Church), Gnadau, 1870. It contains 1212 hymns. 1124 of them are taken from 2. No. 8. 88 are new (12 from the appendix of 1806), of which 15 are written by Moravians. 384 Moravian and 39 mixed hymns are omitted. Therefore this hymn-book contains 858 Moravian and 88 mixed hymns.

(3) The English Moravian Hymn-books.

1. *A Collection of Hymns with several translations from the hymn-book of the Moravian Brethren*, London, 1742, 187 hymns. 2nd ed., London, 1743, with an *appendix* hymns No. 188–239; 3rd ed., London, 1746.

2. *The same*, part ii., London, 1746, hymns No. 240–403. At pp. 764–818 a collection of unnumbered hymns and single verses.

3. *Part iii.*, London, 1748, 126 hymns and several "single verses out of several German hymns." The same 2nd ed., London, 1749, 126 hymns and additions, No. 127–161.

4. *Some other hymns and poems, consisting chiefly of translations from the German*, London, 1752.

5. *A collection of hymns of the Children of God in all Ages, from the Beginning till now. In two parts*, London, 1754. Part i., 695 hymns; part ii., "containing hymns of the present Congregation of the Brethren," 460 hymns and several "single verses."

6. *A collection of hymns chiefly extracted from the larger hymn-book of the Brethren's congregations*, London, 1769, 257 hymns.

7. *A collection of hymns for the use of the Protestant Church of the United Brethren*, London, 1789, 887 hymns. This became the normal hymn-book. The editions are:—

8. The same, revised and enlarged; Manchester, 1801, with 1000 hymns.

9. Supplement to the edition of 1801; Manchester, 1808, with hymns 1001–1200.

10. New edition with supplement incorporated and revised; Ashton-under-Lyne, 1826, 1200 hymns. In the reprints of this edition it was entitled *Liturgy and Hymns for the use of the Protestant Church of the United Brethren*.

11. New and revised issue of the 1826, edited by James Montgomery and others; London, 1849, 1260 (1261) hymns. Many of the Brethren's hymns were in this edition replaced by standard English non-Moravian hymns.

12. Appendix to the hymn-book; London, 1876, with 82 mostly modern English non-Moravian hymns.

13. A new and revised edition of No. 11, London, 1886 (Preface, Christmas, 1885), with 1322 hymns. This edition is greatly improved, contains many recent English non-Moravian hymns, and for the first time affixes authors' names. The larger edition also gives the first lines of the originals of the translated hymns.

(4) *Moravian Hymn-books in other European Languages.*

1. Bohemian. *Five* books, dating from 1756 to 1877, and consisting of *trs.* of German hymns.

2. Danish. *Five* books from before 1748 (when the second was pub.) to 1829, all the hymns being *trs.* from the German.

3. Dutch. *Two* books, in several editions from 1738 to 1856, being *trs.* from the German.

4. Esthonian. *Three* books, dating from *circa* 1741 to 1791. From the German.

5. French. *Two* books, in various editions from 1747 to 1880. From the German.

6. Lettonian. *Five* books from 1742 to 1874. From the German.

7. Swedish. *One* book, 1819.

8. Wendish (in Lusatia). *One* book *tr.* from hymns in the German *Moravian H. Bk.*, 1741.

(5) *Moravian Hymn-books for Missions amongst the Heathen.*

1. Caffres. *Three* books dating from 1856 to 1885. *Tr.* from the German.

2. Greenland. *Two* books, in various editions from 1747 to 1860. *Tr.* from the German.

3. Indians in North America. *One* book in two editions, 1803 and 1847, being *trs.* from the German and English *Moravian H. Bks.*

4. Labrador. *One* book in two editions, 1841 and 1879. *Tr.* from the German *Moravian H. Bk.*

5. Negroes in St. Thomas, St. John, and St. Croix. *Two* books from 1765 to 1784. *Tr.* from the German.

6. Negroes in Surinam. *Three* books from 1820 to 1867.

iii. *Moravian Hymn-writers.*

The most important of the Moravian hymn-writers are noticed in this Dictionary under their respective names. They include J. D. von Albertini, Anna Dober, C. B. Garve, C. Gregor, Esther Grünbeck, Henriette Louise von Hayn, M. G. Hehl, S. Lintrup, P. H. Molther, G. Neumann, Anna Nitschmann, J. Nitschmann, J. Prätorius, L. E. Schlicht, A. G. Spangenberg, Count N. L. von Zinzendorf, and Count C. R. von Zinzendorf.

The hymn-writers of less importance, and whose hymns are mainly confined to the Moravian hymn-books, include :—

1. Böhler, Petrus, b. Dec. 31, 1712, at Frankfurt am Main. Moravian minister in England and America. After 1764 member of the Unity's Direction. d. April 27, 1775, in London.

2. Böhnisch, Friedrich, b. April 16, 1710, at Kunewalde, Moravia. 1734 missionary in Greenland. d. July 29, 1763, at Neu Herrnhut, in Greenland.

3. Brau, Christian Ludwig, b. 1746, in Wetteravia, d. 1777.

4. Bruiningk, Adam von, b. 1739, at Riga, d. 1772 at Herrnhut.

5. Bruiningk, Heinrich von, b. Aug. 26, 1738, at Riga. Moravian minister at Zeist (Holland) and Gnadenfrei (Silesia). d. Oct. 22, 1785, at Herrnhut.

6. Büttner, Gottlob, 1740 missionary among the North American Indians. d. 1745.

7. Cammerhof, Johann Friedrich, b. July 28, 1721, near Magdeburg. 1747 Bishop of the Unity. d. April 28, 1751, in Pennsylvania.

8. Clemens, Gottfried, b. Sept. 1, 1706, at Berlin. Moravian minister at Berlin, Gnadenfrei, and Herrnhut. d. at Herrnhut, March 23, 1776.

9. David, Christian, b. Dec. 31, 1690, at Senftleben, near Fulnek, Moravia. 1722 built the first house in Herrnhut. d. Feb. 3, 1751, at Herrnhut.

10. Dober, Leonhard, b. March 7, 1706, at Mönchsroth, near Dinkelsbühl, Bavaria. 1732 the first missionary among the negro slaves in St. Thomas, W. I. 1747 bishop. d. April 1, 1766, at Herrnhut.

11. Dober, Martin, b. Nov. 23, 1703, at Mönchsroth, d. Dec. 9, 1748, at Herrnhaag, near Büdingen.

12. Gersdorf, Abraham von, b. April 7, 1704, at Siegersdorf, near Bunzlau, Silesia. 1769 member of the Unity's Direction. d. Jan. 2, 1784, at Barby, near Magdeburg.

13. Graff, Johann Michael, b. Sept. 28, 1714, at Hayna, near Römhild, Sachse-Meiningen. Moravian minister in Pennsylvania and North Carolina. d. Aug. 29, 1782, at Salem.

14. Grassmann, Andreas, b. Feb. 23, 1704, at Senft-

leben, Moravia. Bishop 1756. d. March 25, 1783, at Berlin.

15. Jäschke, Nikolaus Andreas, b. Dec. 6, 1718, in Moravia. Moravian minister at Berlin. 1760 director of the Moravian mission in India. d. Jan. 1, 1762, at Tranquebar.

16. Lauterbach, Johann Michael, b. March 19, 1716, at Buttstedt, near Weimar. Moravian minister at Berlin. d. Nov. 29, 1787.

17. Laux, Christian Friedrich, b. May 14, 1731, at Berthelsdorf, near Herrnhut. d. April 12, 1784, at Barby.

18. Lawatsch, Anna Maria, *née* Demuth, b. Nov. 17, 1712, at Karlsdorf, Moravia. d. 1759, in America.

19. Layritz, Paul Eugenius, b. Nov. 13, 1707, at Wunsiedel, Bavaria. Member of the Unity's Direction, 1764. d. July 31, 1788, at Herrnhut.

20. Meyer, Simon, from Langensalza. About 1740 Moravian minister in America.

21. Müller, Gottfried Polykarp, b. June 13, 1685, at Stollberg, near Chemnitz. 1740 bishop. d. June 17, 1747, at Urschkau in Silesia.

22. Neisser, Friedrich Wenzel, b. Nov. 16, 1716, at Sehlen, Moravia. Member of the Unity's Direction, 1764. d. Oct. 12, 1777, at Barby.

23. Neisser, Georg, b. April 11, 1715, at Sehlen, Moravia. 1735 Moravian minister in America.

24. Nitschmann, David, b. Dec. 27, 1696, at Zauchtenthal, Moravia. 1732 with L. Dober missionary in St. Thomas. First bishop of the renewed Brethren's Church. Consecrated March 13, 1735, by D. E. Jablonsky, at Berlin. d. Oct. 1772, at Bethlehem, Pennsylvania.

25. Nitschmann, Johann, the elder, b. Oct. 3, 1703, at Kunewalde, Moravia. 1741 bishop. d. May 26, 1772, at Zeist near Utrecht.

26. Oldendorp, Georg Andreas, b. March 8, 1721, at Hildesheim. d. March 9, 1787, as Moravian minister at Ebersdorf.

27. Peistel, Karl Heinrich von, b. March 25, 1704, at Nedlitz near Weissenfels. d. March 24, 1782, at Herrnhut.

28. Promnitz, Balthasar Friedrich, Count von, b. 1711, d. Feb. 2, 1744, at Erbach, Franconia.

29. Reichel, Johann Friedrich, b. May 16, 1731, at Windisch-Leube near Altenburg. 1769 member of the Unity's Direction. d. at Herrnhut, Nov. 17, 1809.

30. Reichel, Renata Eleonore, b. 1753, d. April 5, 1815, at Niesky in Silesia.

31. Reinecke, Abraham, b. April 17, 1712, at Stockholm, Sweden. 1744 Moravian minister in America. d. April 7, 1760, at Bethlehem, Pennsylvania.

32. Schick, Hermann Reinhard, b. Dec. 1, 1704, at Eckenheim, near Hanau. d. Sept. 28, 1771, at Herrnhut.

33. Schmidt, Joachim, from Swedish Pomerania. c. 1740 assisted in the schools at Herrnhut.

34. Schrautenbach, Ludwig Karl, Baron von, b. 1726, d. 1783, on his estate of Lindheim in Wetteravia.

35. Seebass, Friedrich Wilhelm, d. 1758, at Ebersdorf.

36. Spangenberg, Eva Maria (Immig), b. March 8, 1696. d. March 21, 1751, at Herrnhut.

37. Stach, Matthäus, b. March 4, 1711, at Mankendorf, Moravia. 1733 Moravian missionary in Greenland. 1771 Moravian minister in Pennsylvania. d. Dec. 21, 1787.

38. Till, Jakob, b. March 12, 1713, in Moravia. Moravian minister in Pennsylvania. d. 1783.

39. Töltschig, Johann, b. at Zauchtenthal, Moravia. Moravian minister in England and Ireland. d. 1764, at Dublin.

40. Watteville, Benigna Justina von, daughter of Count N. L. von Zinzendorf, b. Dec. 28, 1725, at Berthelsdorf near Herrnhut. Married Johannes von Watteville, May 20, 1746. d. May 11, 1789, at Herrnhut.

41. Watteville, Friedrich von, b. Feb. 7, 1700, at Bern. d. April 24, 1777, at Herrnhut.

42. Watteville, Johannes von, originally Johann Michael Langguth, but adopted by F. von Watteville, b. Oct. 18, 1718, at Walschleben near Erfurt. Member of the Unity's Direction, 1764. d. Oct. 11, 1788, at Gnadenfrei, Silesia.

43. Wobeser, Ernst Wilhelm von, b. Nov. 29, 1727, at Luckenwalde, Brandenburg. Co-editor of the *Brüder G. B.*, 1778. He wrote a German metrical version of the Psalter. d. Dec. 16, 1795, at Herrnhut.

44. Zander, Johann Wilhelm, b. 1716. 1742-1761 Moravian missionary in Surinam. d. 1782, in Holland.

45. Zinzendorf, Erdmuth Dorothea, Countess von, *née* Countess of Reuss-Ebersdorf, b. Nov. 7, 1700, at Ebersdorf, married Count N. L. von Zinzendorf, Sep. 7, 1722, and d. June 19, 1756, at Herrnhut. [J. T. M.]

More, Henry, D.D., was b. at Grantham in 1614, and educated at Eton and Christ's

College, Cambridge, where he graduated in 1635, and became a Fellow of his College in 1639. He declined various offers of high preferment. He spent his time mainly in the study of philosophy and as a private tutor. He d. in 1687. In 1640 he pub. his *Psychozoia, or the First Part of the Song of the Soul, containing a Christiano-Platonic display of Life.* In 1647 this was republished with additions as *Philosophical Poems.* His poems, collected and edited by Dr. Grosart, are included in the *Chertsey Worthies Library.* His "Philosopher's Devotion," beginning "Sing aloud! His praise rehearse," is given in Macdonald's *England's Antiphon.* His *Memoirs* were pub. in 1710. His *Divine Dialogues with Divine Hymns* added thereto were pub. in 1668. From a hymn in this work, beginning "When Christ His body up had borne," J. Wesley took 10 st. and moulded them into two hymns, which he included in the *Wes. H. Bk.*, 1780, as " Father, if justly still we claim" (*The Holy Spirit desired*), No. 444; and "On all the earth Thy Spirit shower," No. 445. These hymns are in C. U. in G. Britain and America.   [W. T. B.]

Morell, Thomas, was b. in 1781, and educated at Homerton College for the Congregational ministry. About 1800 he became Pastor of a Congregational church at St. Neots, Huntingdonshire, where he remained till 1821, when he was appointed divinity tutor at Wymondley Academy (subsequently removed to London, and known in later years as the Coward Academy). He retained this appointment till his death in 1840. His *Studies of History* were pub. in a series of volumes; and his *Christian Pastor* (a poem in three books) in 1809. His hymns are not widely known. The best are :—

1. Father of mercies, condescend. *Departure of a Missionary.*
2. Go, and the Saviour's grace proclaim. *Departure of a Missionary.*

These hymns were given in the *Evangelical Magazine*, Dec., 1818, p. 544, as "Hymns composed for a Missionary Ordination Service. Sung at the Rev. Mr. Morell's Chapel, St. Neots, Oct. 28, 1818, at the ordination of Mr. C. Mault, Missionary to India." Both hymns are signed "M." They were included in Conder's *Cong. H. Bk.*, 1836, and from thence have passed into other collections.   [J. J.]

Morison, John, D.D., was b. in Aberdeenshire in 1749. He studied at the University of Aberdeen (King's College), where he graduated M.A. in 1771. In 1780 he became parish minister of Canisbay, Caithness. He received the degree of D.D. from the University of Edinburgh in 1792. He d. at Canisbay, June 12, 1798. He was one of the members added on May 26, 1781, to the Committee appointed by the General Assembly of 1775 to revise the *Translations and Paraphrases* of 1745. To him are ascribed Nos. 19, 21, 29, 30 and 35, in the 1781 collection, and he is said to have been joint author with John Logan of Nos. 27 and 28. [See Scottish Translations and Paraphrases.]   [J. M.]

Morn hath brightened slowly. *T. Davis.* [*Sunday. Autumn.*] The author has published this hymn in two forms. The first

form is a hymn for *Sunday*, and was given in his *Hys. Old and New*, 1864, No. 6, in 6 st. of 6 l., and the second, for *Autumn*, in his *Annus Sanctus*, 1877, p. 221. The only difference in these two forms of the hymn is in st. i., l. 4 :—

For Sunday.   " Calm, and sweet, and holy,
        Be our *Sabbath* Day."
For Autumn.   " Calm and sweet and holy,
        Be our *Autumn* day."

The first form only is in C. U.   [J. J.]

Morning breaks upon the tomb. *W. B. Collyer.* [*Easter.*] 1st pub. in his *Hys. partly Collected and partly Original*, 1812, No. 960, in 4 st. of 4 l., entitled "Jesus rising—An Easter Hymn," and signed "W. B. C." Its modern use is mainly confined to America.   [J. J.]

Morris, Alfred John, was b. at Hampstead, London, March 6, 1814. Educated privately at Cheltenham. Ministered to Congregational Churches at Warrington (1833 to 1839), Manchester (1839 to 1842), Holloway (1842 to 1862), and Bowdon, Cheshire (1862). He d. Nov. 15, 1868. His principal works were *Glimpses of Great Men, Religion and Business, Words for the Heart and Life, The Shepherd and his Lambs*, and a posthumous volume of sermons, *The Open Secret.* He was an extensive contributor to the Congregational periodicals. He wrote a large number of hymns for friends which appeared in various magazines. The one hymn by which he will be remembered is " Blest Saviour, let me be a child " (*A Child's Prayer*), which was appended to one of the discourses in *The Shepherd and his Lambs*, 1868. This is a hymn of great distinctiveness both of thought and expression, and has been included in many hymnals, especially those for children.   [W. G. H.]

Morris, Eliza Fanny, née Goffe, was b. in London in 1821, and married in 1849 to Josiah Morris. She gained the prize for a poem on *Kindness to Animals* offered by the Band of Hope. Her pub. works are *The Voice and the Reply*, Worcester, 1858, and *Life Lyrics.* She also edited a *Bible Class Hymn Book*, and contributed the words to *School Harmonies*, pub. by her husband. Her hymns in C. U. include :—

1. Come unto Me and rest. *Christ's Invitation.* From *The Voice and the Reply*, 1858, into the 1874 *Suppl.* to the *New Cong.* in an altered form.
2. God of pity, God of grace. *Lent.* This hymn in Litany form appeared in Pt. ii. of *The Voice and the Reply*, 1858, entitled "The Prayer in the Temple." From Miller's *Singers and Songs of the Church*, 1869, we gather that this hymn was written on the 4th of Sept., 1857. It is in extensive use.
3. O Thou, blest Lamb of God. *Love for and Trust in Jesus desired.* From *The Voice and the Reply*, 1858, into the *Anglican H. Bk.*, 2nd ed., 1871.   [W. G. H.]

Morris, George Perkins, was b. in Philadelphia, Oct. 10, 1802. In early life he removed to New York, where, in 1822, he became the editor of the New York *Mirror* magazine. On that magazine, together with *The Home Journal*, he was associated with N. P. Willis. His works include *The Deserted Bride, and Other Poems*, 1843 ; *Poems*, 1853 ; *American Melodies;* and some prose pieces. He is best known as a writer of songs, one of which, " Woodman, spare that tree," is very popular. His hymns, " Man dieth and wasteth away" (*Victory over Death*); and "Searcher of hearts! from mine erase" (*Lent*), are in a few American collections, as the *Songs for the Sanctuary*, 1865, and the Methodist *Hymnal*, 1878. Mr. Morris d. in New York July 6, 1864.   [F. M. B.]

Mote, Edward, was b. in Upper Thames Street, London, Jan. 21, 1797. Through the preaching of the Rev. J. Hyatt, of Tottenham Court Road Chapel, he underwent a great spiritual change; and ultimately he became a Baptist minister. For the last 26 years of his life he was pastor at Horsham, Sussex, where he d. Nov. 13, 1874. Mr. Mote published several small pamphlets; and also:—

Hymns of Praise. A New Selection of Gospel Hymns, combining all the Excellencies of our spiritual Poets, with many Originals. By E. Mote. London. J. Nichols, 1836. The Originals number nearly 100.

Concerning the authorship of one of these original hymns much uncertainty has existed. The hymn is:—

1. Nor earth, nor hell my soul can move. [*Jesus All in All.*] In 6 st. of 4 l., with a refrain. Mr. Mote's explanation, communicated to the *Gospel Herald*, is:—

"One morning it came into my mind as I went to labour, to write an hymn on the 'Gracious Experience of a Christian.' As I went up Holborn I had the chorus,
    'On Christ the solid Rock I stand,
      All other ground is sinking sand.'
In the day I had four first verses complete, and wrote them off. On the Sabbath following I met brother King as I came out of Lisle Street Meeting ... who informed me that his wife was very ill, and asked me to call and see her. I had an early tea, and called afterwards. He said that it was his usual custom to sing a hymn, read a portion, and engage in prayer, before he went to meeting. He looked for his hymn-book but could find it nowhere. I said, 'I have some verses in my pocket; if he liked, we would sing them.' We did; and his wife enjoyed them so much, that after service he asked me, as a favour, to leave a copy of them for his wife. I went home, and by the fireside composed the last two verses, wrote the whole off, and took them to sister King ... As these verses so met the dying woman's case, my attention to them was the more arrested, and I had a thousand printed for distribution. I sent one to the *Spiritual Magazine*, without my initials, which appeared some time after this. Brother Rees, of Crown Street, Soho, brought out an edition of hymns [1836], and this hymn was in it. David Denham introduced it [1837] with Rees's name, and others after.... Your inserting this brief outline may in future shield me from the charge of stealth, and be a vindication of truthfulness in my connection with the Church of God."

The form in which the hymn is usually found is:—

2. My hope is built on nothing less (st. ii.), sometimes in 4 st., and at others in 5 st., and usually without the refrain. The original in the author's *Hys. of Praise*, 1836, is No. 465, and entitled, "The Immutable Basis of a Sinner's hope." Bishop Bickersteth calls it a "grand hymn of faith" (*H. Comp. Notes*). It dates *circa* 1834, and is in extensive use.   [W. R. S.]

Motte, de la. [Fouqué, F. H. C.]

Moule, Henry, M.A., b. Jan. 27, 1801, and educated at St. John's College, Cambridge, B.A. 1821, M.A. 1828. Taking Holy Orders in 1824, he was successively Curate of Melksham, and of Gillingham, Dorset; and Vicar of Fordington, Dorset. He d. at Fordington, Feb. 3, 1880. His publications included a large number of pamphlets, some small prose works, and the following in verse:—*Scraps of Sacred Verse*, 1846, and *Supplemental Hymns*, 1863. Of his hymns in C. U. we have, "Lord God, in Thee confiding" (1863), *Faith and Hope*; and "For those in Christ who calmly sleep" (1863), *Burial*. In addition to these there are 29 hymns by Mr. Moule in the *Appendix to the*

Fordington H. Bk., Dorchester, H. Ling, 1878, all of which are signed Rev. Henry Moule.   [J. J.]

Moule, Handley Carr Glyn, M.A., s. of the Rev. H. Moule, was b. at Fordington, Dec. 23, 1841, and educated at home and at Trinity College, Cambridge, B.A. in 1st class Classical and Theological honours, 1864–65. He was Carus Prizeman, 1862; Browne's Medallist, 1863; and gained the Seatonian Prize, 1869–73 and 1876. Taking Holy Orders in 1867, he was curate of Fordington, Dorset, 1867–73, and 1877–80; Dean, Trinity College, Cambridge, 1874–77; and Principal of Ridley Hall, Cambridge, 1880. He was Fellow of his College, 1865; Select Preacher at Cambridge, 1880–81, 87; and Chaplain to the Bishop of Liverpool, 1880. His works include:—

(1) The Seatonian Prize Poems as above; (2) *Poems on the Acts of the Apostles*, 1869; (3) *Sermons on the Litany*, 1870; *Dorchester Poems*, 1878; (4) *Commentaries on the Epistles to the Romans, Ephesians,* and *Philippians,* in the *Cambridge Bible for Schools,* 1880–89; (5) *Christianus and Other Poems,* 1883; (6) *Thoughts on Christian Sanctity,* 1885 (with hymns appended); (7) *On Union with Christ,* 1885 (with hymns appended); *On Spiritual Life,* 1887 (with hymns appended); and others. Mr. Moule was also a contributor to Smith's *Dict. of Christian Biography.*

Of Mr. Moule's hymns the following appeared in the *Appendix* to the *Fordington H. Bk.*, 1878:

1. Chief Shepherd of Thy people. *Missions.*
2. Jesus, such His love and power. *A present Saviour.*
3. Lift heart and voice above. *Christmas.*

In the same *Appendix* there is a paraphrase of the *Benedicite* in metre, "Bless the Lord of glory," by H. M. Moule, M.A., of Queen's College, Cambridge, brother of the above, b. 1832, d. 1873.   [J. J.]

Moultrie, Gerard, M.A., s. of the Rev. John Moultrie, was b. at Rugby Rectory, Sept. 16, 1829, and educated at Rugby and Exeter College, Oxford (B.A. 1851, M.A. 1856). Taking Holy Orders, he became Third Master and Chaplain in Shrewsbury School; Chaplain to the Dowager Marchioness of Londonderry, 1855–59; curate of Brightwaltham, 1859; and of Brinfield, Berks, 1860; Chaplain of the Donative of Barrow Gurney, Bristol, 1864: Vicar of Southleigh, 1869, and Warden of St. James's College, Southleigh, 1873. He d. April 25, 1885. His publications include:

(1) The Primer set forth at large for the use of the Faithful. In Family and Private Prayer. Edited from the Post Reformation editions, 1864. (2) *Hymns and Lyrics for the Seasons and Saints' Days of the Church,* 1867. The hymns of his sister, Mary Dunlop Moultrie (q.v.), were included in this volume. (3) *The Espousals of S. Dorothea and Other Verses,* 1870. (5) *The Devout Communicant,* 1867. (6) *Six Years' work in Southleigh,* 1875. (7) *Cantica Sanctorum, or Hymns for the Black Letter Saints Days in the English and Scottish Calendars,* to which are added a few Hymns for Special Occasions, 1880.

Mr. Moultrie's hymns include *trs.* from the Greek, Latin, and German, in addition to original compositions. A large number appeared in the *Church Times*, and other papers; and many were written for special Saints' Days, and Other Festivals, for the *People's Hymnal,* 1867, in which some were signed "D. P." (i.e. *Desiderius Pastor*). In addition to those annotated elsewhere in this work (see Index) the following are in C. U.:—

i. In *The Primer*, 1864.

1. Father of all, to Thee we pray. *Lord's Prayer.*
2. In the Name of God the Father. *Laying Foundation Stone.* (2nd st.: "And as on the morning stillness.") 1st appeared in the *Church Times*, Oct. 1, 1864, and again (as rewritten for the laying of the foundation stone of St. Margaret's, East Grinstead), July 29, 1865.

ii. In *Hymns and Lyrics*, 1867.

3. Bishop of the souls of men. *St. Matthias.*
4. Come, faithful people, come away. *Palm Sunday.*
5. Easter-day is here, and we. *Easter.*
6. Heavenly Father, God alone. *Harvest.*
7. Mother, from whose bosom's veil. *St. Anne. July 26.*
8. O Jesu, O Redeemer. *St Luke.*
9. Mary, maiden undefiled. *Visitation of the B. V. M.*
10. Silence reigns at eventide. *Whitsuntide.* In the *Altar Hymnal*, 1884, it begins with st. iii., "Hark, a rushing mighty sound."
11. The Marriage feast is ready. *All Saints.* Usually given in an abbreviated form.
12. Virgin-born the King of heaven. *Christmas Midnight Hymn.* ("To be sung at the Midnight Celebration.") In the *Church Times*, Nov. 26, 1864, and revised for *Hys. & Lyrics.*
13. We march, we march to victory. *Processional.* In the *Church Times*, Aug, 19, 1865, and headed "Processional hymn before service (written expressly for use during present troubles)."
14. Who is this that shines so bright? *St. Laurence.* In the *People's H.*, 1867.
15. Who keeps his birthday feast to-night? *Beheading of St. John Baptist.* In the *People's H.*, 1867.

iii. In *The People's Hymnal*, 1867.

16. Heart to heart, and side by side. *Holy Matrimony.*
17. I know that my Redeemer liveth. *Burial.* A paraphrase of the Responsory in the Roman Office for the Dead.
18. Jesus Christ, we humbly pray. *Opening of a School House.*
19. Lord of heaven, Whose faithful love. *Ember Days.*
20. Lord, to-day we bring to Thee. *Reception of a Privately Baptized Child.*
21. Lord, we come to-day to Thee. *Choir Festival.*
22. O God, Who bad'st Thine angel sheathe. *National Thanksgiving for restored Public Health.* This is given in the S. P. C. K. *Church Hys.*, 1871, as "O God, Whose angel stayed his hand," and in the *Hymnary*, 1872, as "Lord, Who didst bid Thine angel sheathe."
23. O Lord of Hosts, Thou God of might. *National Thanksgiving for Peace.* In several collections.
24. Sevenfold Spirit, Lord of life. *Consecration of a Bishop.* First sung at the consecration of an American bishop at New York, in 1867. Included in the author's *Espousals of St. Dorothea*, 1870.
25. Sounds the bell in solemn cadence. *Burial.* In *The Espousals of S. Dorothea*, 1870, p. 82, the note is added, "This hymn was first sung at the funeral of the Rev. Warwick Wroth of Clerkenwell." It is headed "Funeral Hymn for a Priest."

iv. In *Cantica Sanctorum*, 1880.

26. In the midst of gladness, sorrow. *Annunciation in Holy Week.*
27. Jesus, tender Shepherd. *Holy Communion.*
28. Swing the censer, wave the banner. *Processional.*

v. In *The Altar Hymnal*, 1884.

29. Our great High Priest is standing. *Holy Communion.*
30. Lo, the Sacrifice atoning. *Holy Communion.*

vi. *Various.*

31. Forward, Christians, forward. *Processional.* Written for the Church of England Working Men's Society in 1879, and issued as a leaflet, of which 40,000 copies were sold during the first year.
32. Laid in this garden full of bloom. *Easter Eve.* In the *Churchman's Companion*, April, 1879.
33. On the wings of the wind fell a hymn from the sky. *Christmas.* In Husband's *Supplemental Hys.*, N.D. [1873].
34. Shades of night are falling round us. *Evening.* Novello & Co., with Music by Shad Frost.
35. There is a sound of rejoicing around the great throne. *Processional.* Written for St. Michael's Church, Folkestone, and pub. in E. Husband's *Appendix to H. A.*

& M., N.D. [1873]. It was set to music by Mr. Husband, and is commonly known as "The Folkestone Processional."
36. This is the festal day of jubilation. *Sunday S. Anniversary.* A hymn to be sung alternately by men and boys during the collection, written in 1877 for St. Agnes's, Kennington, London.
37. This is the hour of peace and blest communion. *Holy Communion.* Written for the English Church Union Commemoration held at St. Agnes's, Kennington Park, London, June 9, 1880.

From the subjects of the hymns noted above it will be seen that Mr. Moultrie wrote principally on matters not usually dealt with by hymn-writers. This is specially the case with his *Cantica Sanctorum*, in which most of the 103 hymns are for "Black Letter Saints' Days."   [J. J.]

Moultrie, John, M.A., father of Gerard and Mary D. Moultrie, was b. Dec. 31, 1799, at London, and educated at Trinity College, Cambridge (B.A. 1823), where he was Bell's University Scholar, 1820, and Trinity College Scholar, 1822. Taking Holy Orders in 1825, he was presented the same year by the Earl of Craven to the Rectory of Rugby, where he remained till his death, on Dec. 26, 1874.

His publications included :—

(1) *My Brother's Grave, and other Poems*, 1837; (2) *Dream of Life, Lays of the English Church*, &c., 1843 ; (3) *Memoir and Poetical Remains of W. S. Walker*, 1852 ; (4) *Sermons*, 1852 ; (5) *Altars, Hearths, and Graves*, 1854 ; (6) *Psalms and Hymns as Sung in the Parish Church, Rugby*, 1851.

In his *Preface* Mr. Moultrie says of the *Ps. & Hys.*, 1851 :—

"The present collection of *Psalms & Hymns* is founded on the basis of that which has been in use during the last twelve years in the Parish Church of Rugby, and for which the congregation of that Church are indebted to the kindness and taste of the Rev. H. J. Buckoll."

Further on in the same preface he says :—

"More than twenty original compositions — some altered or abridged from my former publications, others written expressly for the present collection, and (I am sorry to add) on the spur of the moment—have thus been introduced into company with which they have perhaps but slender claims to associate. Several of these are little more than paraphrases of the Epistles or Gospel for the day."

These hymns, most of which are in *Kennedy*, 1863, include the following :—

1. Blest are the eyes of those. *Gospel*, 13 *S. after Trinity.* (*The Good Samaritan.*)
2. Bring the infant to the font. *Holy Baptism.*
3. Christ His own Apostles chooseth. *St. Andrew.*
4. Dear Lord, a lonely life was Thine. *Gospel*, 4 *S. after Epiphany.* (*Stilling the Tempest.*)
5. Friends and parents lingered weeping. *Gospel*, 24 *S. after Trinity.* (*Raising the Ruler's daughter.*)
6. God, Who dost the increase grant. *Sexagesima.* (*The Sower.*)
7. In patient faith till Christ shall come. *Gospel*, 6 *S. after Epiphany.*
8. In the beaming brow of Moses. *Epistle*, 12 *S. after Trinity.*
9. Lord, with glad and grateful spirits. *Epistle*, 1 *S. after Trinity.* (*Perfect Love.*)
10. Meek to suffer, strong to save. *St. Mark.*
11. Mysterious to the Christian heart. *St. Michael and All Angels.*
12. No act of sin our Saviour wrought. *Collect*, 2 *S. after Easter.* (*Christ the Example.*)
13. O Lord, a wondrous story. *For Sunday Schools.*
14. Our mortal eyes are all too dim. *St. Stephen.*
15. Source of wisdom, past and present. *For Sunday Schools.*
16. The world may look serene and bright. *Circumcision.*
17. Thou gavest, Lord, the life we live. *Holy Communion.*
18. When our hearts with grief are sore. *Epistle. Ash Wednesday.*
19. Wondrous was Thy path on earth. *Gospel*, 2 *S. after Epiphany.* (*Marriage in Cana of Galilee.*)

These hymns, from the special subjects of which they treat, are of more than ordinary interest to hymnal compilers, and are worthy of attention. Nos. 4, 6, 7, 12, 16, 18, 19, are from his *Lays of the English Church*, 1843; the rest were written expressly for the *Ps. & Hys.*, 1851 (S. MSS.). [J. J.]

Moultrie, Mary Dunlop, dau. of John and sister of Gerard Moultrie, was b. at the Rectory, Rugby, July, 1837, and d. there, June 15, 1866. Her hymns were included in her brother's *Hymns and Lyrics*, 1867, with her initials " M. D. M." [J. J.]

Μούνη μοι πάτρη περιλείπετο.
-[Ποῦ δὲ λόγοι πτερόεντες.]

Möwes, Heinrich, was b. Feb. 25, 1793, at Magdeburg After passing through the Cathedral school at Magdeburg, he entered the University of Göttingen in 1812, and in 1814 volunteered for service against Napoleon and fought in a Westphalian Jäger Battalion at the battles of Ligny and Waterloo and before Paris, gaining the Iron Cross for his bravery. Thereafter he resumed his studies (now at the University of Halle), and was then for a year assistant master in the Cathedral school at Magdeburg. In 1818 he was appointed pastor at Angern and Wenddorf; and in 1822 at Altenhausen and Ivenrode near Magdeburg. On account of a weak chest, and bleeding from the lungs, in January, 1829 he was compelled to cease preaching for a time, and finally had to resign his charge in June, 1830, retiring to Magdeburg. Failing to obtain suitable work, he returned, in July, 1832, to Altenhausen, where he remained ever after. In January, 1834, he had so far recovered that he began to try to obtain preferment; and in the beginning of October was offered the appointment of Pastor and Superintendent at Weferlingen, near Neuhaldensleben. But meantime, in April, his illness had returned with redoubled violence, and, after great suffering, he d. Oct. 14, 1834 (*Koch*, vii. 247; *Allg. Deutsche Biog.* xxii.; biographical sketch prefixed to his *Gedichte*, 1836, &c.).

After the spiritual change which Möwes experienced in his first pastorate he became a most earnest and devoted pastor and preacher, and greatly interested himself in the work of Foreign Missions. He bore his long continued sufferings with great fortitude and patience. His hymns, not numbering more than ten, and all written after the beginning of his illness, bear the stamp of heroic Christian faith, childlike submission, and deep affection for the Almighty Hand that loves even when it wounds. They are great favourites in Germany with the sick and sorrowing; but are too subjective, and too unfinished in style to be employed otherwise than for private use. Only one or two have passed into German hymn-books. They appeared, along with his other poems, and with a prefatory memoir by Friedrich Arndt of Berlin, as his *Gedichte*, at Magdeburg, 1836.

Nine of Möwes's hymns have passed into English, viz. .—

i. **Der Himmel hängt voll Wolken schwer.** *Cross and Consolation.* Written Oct. 9, 1831, at Magdeburg under sufferings during which the period of his death seemed to have come; and when his daughter Mary seemed also in peril of death. In a letter to a friend he says:—

" My soul strove with all her might to soar away from the tortured body, and rent the clouds with her prayers, to obtain by entreaty the order for departure from the Heavenly Master . . . But, while my body would succumb, my soul arose, she sang what I send to you " (Life prefixed to his *Gedichte*, 1836, pp. 81–84).

The text of the hymn is included in the *Gedichte*, 1836, p. 72, in 7 st. of 4 l., as a "prayer in distress and in death." In the Württemberg *G. B.*, 1842, No. 468. The *trs.* are (1) "The heavens are cloth'd in sable shrouds." By *Dr. G. Walker*, 1860, p. 93. (2) "The heavens are foul with wind and clouds." By *E. Massie*, 1866, p. 92.

ii. **Du sollst, so sprach der Herr, du sollst ermatten.** *Submission.* Written July 12, 1832. *Gedichte*, 1836, p. 78, in 5 st. *Tr.* as "Thus said the Lord—Thy days of health are over." By Miss Borthwick, in *H. L. L.*, 1858, p. 35 (1884, p. 157).

iii. **Ich glaube! Hallelujah.** *Joy in Believing.* Written in July, 1831. *Gedichte*, 1836, p. 43, in 5 st. of 9 l. The *tr.* in C. U. is: "Hallelujah! I believe!" In full by Miss Borthwick in *H. L. L.*, 3rd Ser., 1858, p. 5 (1884, p. 133). Included in full in Schaff's *Christ in Song*, 1869, p. 537, Bp. Ryle's *Coll.*, 1860, and Reid's *Praise Bk.*, 1872; and, omitting st. ii., iii. in the *Christian Hyl.*, Adelaide, 1872.

iv. **Ich hatte der Kinder viere.** *Death of Children.* Written Oct. 8, 1830, on the death of his daughter Eliza. *Gedichte*, 1836, p. 40, in 9 st. *Tr.* as "I had once four lovely children." By Miss Borthwick in *H. L. L.*, 1862, p. 28 (1884, p. 199).

v. **Ich stehe noch auf heimathlichem Strande.** *The Missionary's Farewell.* Written at Magdeburg in 1831, and included in the third *Jahresbericht* ed. in 1831, by Möwes, for the Evangelical Missionary Society at Magdeburg. *Gedichte*, 1836, p. 49, in 10 st. The *trs.* are:- (1) "Still on the shores of home my feet are standing." By Miss Borthwick, in *H. L. L.*, 1862, p. 14 (1884, p. 187). (2) "Still on my native shore my feet are standing." By Miss Burlingham in the *British Herald*, Sept. 1865, p. 141. (3) "Albeit my steps are on my native strand." In L. Rehfuess's *Church at Sea*, 1868, p. 2.

vi. **Ist genug für deinen Namen.** *Christian Work.* Written Feb. 2, 1829. *Gedichte*, 1836, p. 18, in 7 st. *Tr.* as "Is Thy work all ended, Lord?" By Miss Borthwick, in *H. L. L.*, 1862, p. 67 (1884, p. 229).

vii. **Merkt Ihrs, Freunde! Mein Auge wird müde,** *A Pastor's parting words.* Written Feb. 26, 1829. *Gedichte*, 1836, p. 14, in 8 st. According to his wish three lines of st. vii. were inscribed on his tombstone. *Tr.* as "Hear me, my friends! the hour has come." By Miss Borthwick, in *H. L. L.*, 1858, p. 39 (1884, p. 161).

viii. **Thatest sonst uns nichts zu Leide.** *Cross and Consolation.* Written June 13, 1829, on the death of his mother-in-law. *Gedichte*, 1836, p. 27, in 6 st. entitled "Grief and Consolation on a mother's homegoing." *Tr.* as "Never couldst thou bear to grieve us." By Miss Borthwick, in *H. L. L.*, 1854, p. 46 (1884, p. 48).

ix. **Wohin! Wohin!** *The Two Journeys.* Written Feb. 21, 1829. *Gedichte* 1836, p. 12, in 8 st. *Tr.* as "Whither, oh, whither?—With blindfolded eyes." By Miss Borthwick, in *H. L. L.*, 1858, p. 19 (1884, p. 144). [J. M.]

Much in sorrow, oft in woe. *H. K. White.* [*Christian Soldier encouraged.*] In Collyer's *Hys. partly Collected and partly Original*, &c., 1812, No. 867, the following lines were given together with the note added thereto:—

" *The Christian Soldier encouraged.*
1 Tim. vi. 12. H. K. WHITE.

" 1. Much in sorrow, oft in woe,
   Onward, Christians, onward go,
   Fight the fight, and worn with strife,
   Steep with tears the bread of life.

" 2. Onward, Christians, onward go,
   Join the war, and face the foe :
   Faint not—much doth yet remain,
   Dreary is the long campaign.

" 3. Shrink not, Christians—will ye yield ?
   Will ye quit the painful field ?
   * Fight till all the conflict's o'er,
   Nor your foemen rally more.

" 4. But when loud the trumpet blown
   Speaks their forces overthrown,
   Christ, your Captain, shall bestow
   Crowns to grace the conqueror's brow."

* " The mutilated state of this hymn, which was written on the back of one of the mathematical papers of this excellent young man, and which came into my hands a mere fragment, rendered it necessary for something to be added—and I am answerable for the last six lines."

In 1827 Mrs. Bethia Fuller-Maitland compiled and published *Hymns for Private Devotion, Selected and Original* (Lond., Hatchards). In this work an enlarged form of "Much in sorrow, oft in woe," made by her daughter Frances Sara Fuller-Maitland, then but 14 years of age, was given as No. 106. White's st. i., ii., iii., ll. 1, 2, were given as above, and the following lines were added thereto :—

> Will ye flee in danger's hour ?
> Know ye not your Captain's power ?
>
> "4. Let your drooping hearts be glad ;
> March in heavenly armour clad :
> Fight, nor think the battle long,
> Victory soon shall tune your song.
>
> "5. Let not sorrow dim your eye,
> Soon shall every tear be dry ;
> Let not woe your course impede,
> Great your strength, if great your need.
>
> "6. Onward then to battle move,
> More than conquerors ye shall prove :
> Though opposed by many a foe,
> Christian soldiers, onward go."

This text was republished by Mrs. Colquhoun, *née* Fuller-Maitland, in her *Rhymes and Chimes* (Lond., Macmillan), 1876. We may add that of the "original" compositions in the 1827 *Hys. for Private Devotion, &c.*, one was by Miss F. S. Fuller-Maitland, and two others were by her sister Esther.

In his *Christian Psalmody*, 1833, No. 125, E. Bickersteth gave the White-Fuller-Maitland text in 4 st., with several alterations, the most important being in st. i., which read : —

> "Oft in sorrow, oft in woe,
> Onward, Christians, onward go;
> Fight the fight, *maintain* the strife,
> *Strengthen'd* with the bread of life."

Another version of the same text was given in Hall's *Mitre H. Bk.*, 1836, the opening lines of which are :—

> "Oft in *danger*, oft in woe,
> Onward, Christians, onward go."

From these four sources H. K. White, 1806 ; W. B. Collyer, 1812 ; F. S. Fuller-Maitland, 1827 ; E. Bickersteth, 1833 ; and W. J. Hall, 1836, the popular modern form of this hymn has been manipulated. In translating the hymn varying texts have been used. Those in Latin are (1) "Ito sæpe per dolorem," by Bingham, in his *Hymno. Christ. Lat.*, 1871, is from the S. P. C. K. *Ps. & Hys.*, No. 273; and (2) "Vos dolores tolerantes," by Macgill in his *Songs of the Christian Creed and Life*, is from the Kirke White Fuller-Maitland version.   [J. J.]

Mudie, Charles Edward, the founder of the well-known library which bears his name, was b. at Cheyne Walk, Chelsea, Oct. 18, 1818. In 1872 he collected his poems and pub. them as *Stray Leaves* (2nd ed., 1873). Several poems on Scriptural subjects, and a few hymns are included in the volume. The hymn by which he is best known is "I lift my heart to Thee, Saviour divine" (*His and Mine*). It is from the *Stray Leaves*, and is in several hymn-books, including the Scottish *Evang. Union Hymnal*, 1878 ; Horder's *Cong. Hys.*, 1884, and many others. It is marked by great beauty and tenderness of expression. Several of Mr. Mudie's hymns, which are not in C. U. are worthy of attention. [W. G. H.]

Mühlenberg, William Augustus, D.D., s. of the Rev. Dr. Mühlenberg, and grandson of Henry Melchior Mühlenberg, the patriarch of Lutheranism in America, was b. in Philadelphia Sept. 16, 1796. He graduated at the University of Pennsylvania in 1814. Entering Holy Orders in 1817, he was successively Assistant Rector of St. James's Lancaster, 1823 ; Rector of the Church of the Holy Communion, New York, 1843 ; St. Paul's College, Flushing (1828) ; St. Luke's Hospital, New York (1855) ; St. John's and Long Island (1865), were established by him. He d. April 6, 1877. His poetical gift was genuine, but not largely used. In 1826 he contributed 4 hymns to the *Prayer Book Coll.* (of which he was one of the Committee). His *Poems* appeared in 1859. He had previously pub. *Church Poetry*, 1823 ; and *The People's Psalter*, 1858. *I would not live alway* followed in 1859 (revised in 1871). This last contains 26 pieces, the hymns in the *Prayer Book Coll.*, 1826, with the exception of "I would not live alway," being omitted. The following are his principal lyrics :—

1. **Carol, brothers, carol.** *Christmas Carol.* "Made for the boys of St. Paul's College—the Chorus adapted from one of the Rev. [Bp.] A. C. Coxe's *Christian Ballads*"—in 1840.

2. **How short the race our friend has run.** *Death of a Young Person.* Contributed to the *Prayer Bk. Coll.*, 1826.

3. **I would not live alway.** *Eternal rest desired.* Four texts of this poem are extant : 1st the Original ; 2nd the version given in the *Prayer Bk. Coll.*, 1826 ; 3rd the author's revised version of 1859 ; and 4th his rewritten text of 1871, the second of these being that known to the hymn-books. The history of the poem is somewhat complicated. We quote it here as given by us in the *History of the American Episcopal Church*, 1885, p. 637, as we have nothing further to add thereto :—

"The most famous of these (Dr. Mühlenberg's hymns) was probably first written. 'I will not live alway' has an intricate history, which was not simplified by the author's lapse of memory in his later years. In his brief 'story of the hymn,' printed with its 'evangelized' text in 1871, every date is wrong by two or three years; and his assertion, 'The legend that it was written on an occasion of private grief is a fancy,' hardly agrees with the clear and minute recollections of persons of the highest character, still living, and who knew the circumstances thoroughly. The date of composition assigned, 1824, is probably (not certainly) correct; it was written at Lancaster, in a lady's album, and began :—

'I would not live alway ; no, no, holy man,
Not a day, not an hour, should lengthen my span.'

In this shape it seems to have had six eight-line stanzas. The album was still extant in 1876, at Pottstown, Pa., and professed to contain the original manuscript. Said the owner's sister, 'It was an impromptu. He had no copy, and, wanting it for some occasion, he sent for the album.' In 1826 he entrusted his copy to a friend, who called on him on the way from Harrisburg to Philadelphia, to carry to the *Episcopal Recorder*, and in that paper it appeared June 3, 1826 (not 1824). For these facts we have the detailed statement of Dr. John B. Clemson, of Claymont, Del., the Ambassador mentioned, who also chances to have preserved that volume of the paper. Thus appearing (without name) it was adopted by the sub-committee [of the *Prayer Bk. Coll.*, 1826]. When their report was presented to the entire committee in 1826—not 1829, as Dr. Mühlenberg has it—'each of the hymns was passed upon. When this came up one of the members remarked that it was very sweet and pretty, but rather sentimental, upon which it was unanimously thrown out. Not suspected as the author, I voted against myself. That, I supposed, was the end of it. The committee, which sat until late at night at the house of Bishop White, agreed upon their report to the Convention, and adjourned. But the next morning Dr. Onderdonk (who was not one of their number, but who, on invitation, had acted with the sub-committee, which in fact consisted of him and myself), called on me to inquire what had been done. Upon my telling him that among the rejected hymns was this one of mine, he said, 'That will never do,' and went about among the members of the committee soliciting them to restore the hymn in their report, which accordingly they did ; so that to him is due the credit of giving it to the Church.' As thus adopted it was a small and altered selection from the original lines, made by Dr. Onderdonk 'with some revision' by the author. He was never satisfied with these texts, but revised the poem in 1859, and re-wrote it in 1871. . . . The authorship of this, as of many another popular lyric, has been disputed. The claim of Henry Ward, a printer of Lichfield, Conn., has been vehemently urged, and revived but a few years ago. Of course it is unsupported by adequate evidence. When Dr. Mühlenberg was asked to assure 'some of his brethren, editors of Church papers,' of his paternity, his manly reply was, 'If they thought I was capable of letting the work of another pass for so many years as my own, they would not be sure of anything I might say.'"

4. **Jesus' Name shall ever be.** *The Holy Name, Jesus.* This is entitled "The Blessed Name of Jesus. An Evangelical Rosary." It was written in 1842, and revised for Schaff's *Christ in Song* in Aug., 1868.

5. **King of kings, and wilt Thou deign.** *Submission to Jesus.* Appeared in his *Poems*, 1859.

6. **Like Noah's weary dove.** *The Ark of the Church.* Contributed to the *Prayer Bk. Coll.,* 1826, No. 24, in 5 st. of 4 l. It sometimes begins with st. ii., "O cease, my wandering soul ;" and again with st. iii., "Behold the Ark of God."

7. **Saviour, Who Thy flock art feeding.** *Holy Baptism.* This is the most widely known of Dr. Mühlenberg's hymns. It was contributed to the *Prayer Bk. Coll.,* 1826, No. 86, in 4 st. of 4 l. It is sometimes given as "*Jesus*, Who Thy flock art feeding."

8. **Shout the glad tidings, exultingly sing.** *Christmas.* Contributed to the *Prayer Bk. Coll.,* 1826, No. 46, in 3 st. of 4 l., with the chorus :—

"Shout the glad tidings, exultingly sing,
Jerusalem triumphs, Messiah is King ; "

the opening lines, followed by the first stanza, and a repetition of the chorus, and so on to the end. Sometimes the hymn opens with st. i. : "Zion, the marvellous story be telling," or as "*Sion* the marvellous story be telling," instead of the chorus. Dr. Mühlenberg says that the hymn was written—

"at the particular request of Bishop Hobart, who wanted something that would go to the tune by Avison, then popular, to the words of Moore, 'Sound the loud timbrel,' &c. He liked the verses I made so well that he had them struck off before the hymns [*Prayer Bk. Coll.*] were published, and sung in Trinity Church on Christmas day."

9. **Since o'er Thy footstool here below.** *Earth and Heaven.* Appeared in the *Episcopal Register*, 1824, and in his *Poems*, 1859.

10. **The mellow eve is gliding.** *Evening.* Dated 1825 (?) and pub. in his *Poems*, 1859.

11. **The throne of his glory—as snow it is white.** *Advent.* Dated 1839, and pub. in his *Poems*, 1859.

12. **Thine handmaid, Saviour, can it be ?** *Admission of a Nursing Sister.* Written on the words, "Come, follow me," for the reception of a Sister at St. Luke's Hospital, New York, 1859.

[F. M. B]

Mühlmann, Johannes, s. of Hieronymus Mühlmann or Mülmann, pastor at Pegau, near Leipzig, was b. at Pegau, July 28, 1573. He studied at the Universities of Leipzig (M.A. January, 1597) and Jena, and was then

for some time Saturday preacher at St. Thomas's Church in Leipzig. In 1599 he was appointed diaconus of the St. Wenzel Church in Naumburg, and in 1604 pastor at Laucha on the Unstrut. In the end of 1604 he became archidiaconus of the St. Nicholas Church at Leipzig, and, in 1607, was also appointed Professor of Theology in the University, and D.D. in 1612. He d., of typhus, at Leipzig, Nov. 14, 1613. (*Allg. Deutsche Biog.* xxii. 483; Goedeke's *Grundriss*, vol. iii., 1887, p. 151, &c.)

Mühlmann was a staunch upholder of Lutheran orthodoxy, alike against Romanists and Calvinists. He was a great lover of the Psalms ; his published sermons, as well as his hymns, are based on them, and almost his last words were Ps. lxiii., 3, "Thy lovingkindness is better than life." *Wackernagel* v. pp. 443–447, gives five hymns under his name, all of which are found in the *Geistliche Psalmen*, &c., pub. at Nürnberg in 1618, by J. Lauer. [The only known copy, in the Royal Library, Berlin, has lost its titlepage.]

Two of Mühlmann's hymns have passed into English, viz. :—

i. **Dank sei Gott in der Höhe.** *Morning.* The most popular of his hymns. Appeared 1618 as above, with his initials, and thence in *Wackernagel* v. p. 444, in 7 st. of 8 l. Also in the *Unv. L. S.,* 1851, No. 443. *Tr.* as :—

While yet the morn is breaking. A good *tr.* of st. i., ii., v., vii. by Miss Winkworth, as No. 163 in her *C. B. for England*, 1863. Repeated in full in the Ohio Luth. *Hymnal*, 1880, and abridged in the *Marlborough College H. Bk.,* 1869.

Another tr. "Christ is the vine, we branches are" (st. vii.). By J. Swertner, as No. 438, in the *Moravian H. Bk.,* 1789 (1849, No. 612).

ii. **O Lebens-Brünnlein tief und gross.** *Ps. lxv.* Appeared 1618 as above, with his initials, in 9 st. of 9 l., entitled "a hymn from the 65th Psalm." Thence in *Wackernagel* v. p. 446 ; also in the *Unv. L. S.,* 1851, No. 426. It is really a hymn on Christ as the Fountain of Life here and in Eternity, and with Ps. lxv. 10 as its motto. *Tr.* as :—

O spring of Life, so deep, so great. A good *tr.* of st. i., ii., v., vi., ix. by A. T. Russell, as No. 166 in his *Ps. & Hys.,* 1851.

For the hymn "Wer Gott vertraut" sometimes ascribed to Mühlmann, see Magdeburg, J. [J. M.]

Müller, Heinrich, was a native of Nürnberg. About 1526 or 1527 he was imprisoned as a Lutheran by Duke Georg of Saxony, but was released after the Duke d. on April 17, 1539. Thereafter, till about 1580, he kept a school for writing and arithmetic at Annaberg in Saxony. Bartholomäus Müller, sometime schoolmaster at Zwickau in Saxony, in a petition presented to the Elector Christian I. in 1587, and in another petition presented to the Elector Christian II. in 1601, described himself as the son of this Heinrich Müller, and declared that the hymn noted below was written by his father during his imprisonment (see *Koch* i. 417 ; Wetzel's *A. H.* ii. 720, &c.). The hymn in question is :—

Hilf Gott, dass mir gelinge. *History of the Passion.* In his *Bibliographie,* 1855, p. 100, Wackernagel cites two broadsheets as of 1527. In his *D. Kirchenlied* iii. p. 85, the earliest source from which he prints the text, is however the *Bergkreyen*, Nürnberg, 1536, though he says it had appeared in print in 1524 (apparently a misprint for 1527). He speaks of the Magdeburg *G. B.,* 1534, as the earliest hymn-book in which it is included,

This is however an oversight, as it is found in the Rostock *G. B.*, 1531, where it is entitled " A new hymn on the Word of God and His bitter sufferings," and begins " Help God mi mach gelingen." It is in 13 st. of 7 l., the initial letters of the stanzas giving the name *Heinrich Müler*, and the two concluding lines being " Hat Heinrich Müller gesungen In dem Gefängniss sein."

From the above note it is clear that the hymn was written by a Heinrich Müller, during an imprisonment, and was in print at least as early as 1531. The ascription to Heinrich Müller, professor at Wittenberg, is therefore impossible, seeing he was only b. in 1530. The ascription to Heinrich von Zütphen [b. at Zütphen in Gelderland, c. 1488, became an Augustinian monk, and in 1515 prior of the Augustinian monastery at Dordrecht; began to preach as a Reformer in Bremen, Nov. 9, 1522; murdered at Heide near Meldorf, in Holstein, Dec. 10, 1524] is also untenable, for neither by himself nor by his contemporaries was he ever styled Heinrich *Müller*, and there was during his life no period of imprisonment during which he might have written this hymn. The history of the Nürnberg Müller noted above is not indeed very clear, but his claim has at least much more appearance of truth than that of any other.

The hymn was a great favourite during the Reformation period, was included by Luther in V. Babst's *G. B.*, 1545, and passed into many later books. It is a ballad rather than a hymn properly so called, and has now fallen out of use in Germany. The only *tr.* is: "Help, God, the formar of all thing." In the *Gude and Godlie Ballates*, ed. 1568, f. 22 (1868, p. 37).

See also note under **Gesenius, J.**, p. 419, ii.

[J. M.]

Müller, Ludwig Ernst Siegmund, was b. Nov. 23, 1766, at Stroppen, in the Principality of Oels, and in 1796 became diaconus of the Frauenkirche at Liegnitz. He was then, in 1808, appointed archidiaconus of the Church of SS. Peter and Paul,'at Liegnitz, in 1814 pastor primarius, and in 1818 superintendent. He d. at Liegnitz, Nov. 7, 1850 (MS. from H. Ziegler, pastor primarius of SS. Peter and Paul, Liegnitz, &c.). His hymn "Trauernd und mit bangem Sehnen " is noted under **Neunhertz, J.**   [J. M.]

Müller, Michael, s. of Zacharias Müller, brewer at Blankenburg, in the Saxon Harz, was b. at Blankenburg, January 12, 1673, studied theology at Halle under Francke and Breithaupt, and received license as a Candidate of Theology (general preacher). Just after completing his university course, in 1697, he was seized with violent hæmorrhage. He so far recovered as to be able to accept the position of house tutor in the family of Gaisberg (Geyssberg) at Schaubeck, near Klein-Bottwar in Württemberg, but after a time his illness returned and he d. there March 13, 1704 (*Koch* iv. 405; *Blätter für Hymnologie*, 1886, p. 146; MS. from General Superintendent G. Schönermark, Blankenburg, &c.).

Müller's principal work is his excellent version of the Psalter (*Die Psalmen Davids*, &c., Stuttgart, Paul Treuer, 1700), noted under **Psalters, German**, § 5. To the copy of this work in the Royal Library at Berlin there is appended (without separate title-page or date, but by the same printer) his *Auffmunternder Neu-Jahrs-Zuruff an die Braut*, &c. This contains 5 hymns which are repeated in his *Geistliche Erquickstunden*, dated 1706, but without name of publisher [Wernigerode Library]. This last work contains 61 hymns on the Gospels for Sundays and Festivals, followed by hymns 62–83, on miscellaneous subjects. The first lines of all these hymns are given in the *Blätter* as above. Many of Müller's psalm versions came deservedly into favour in Germany, but of his hymns few are found except in the hymn-books of the Separatists from 1710 to 1750. In Freylinghausen's *G. B.*, 1704 and 1714, there are 21 of his psalms and 2 of his hymns.

Those of Müller's hymns which have passed into English are—

i. **Auf, Seele, auf, und säume nicht.** *Epiphany.*

1st pub. as No. 4 in his *Zuruff* as above, in 34 st. of 4 l. entitled "The way to Life.␣ On the Gospel for the Three Holy Kings Day, Luke ii." In Freylinghausen's *G. B.*, 1704, No. 68, st. vii., x.–xvi. were omitted, and the same form is No. 205 in the Berlin *G. L. S.*, ed. 1863. The *tr.* in C. U. is—

Up, up, new light upon thee breaks. A free *tr.* of st. i.–iv., xvii., xviii. xxii., xxxi., xxxii., by Dr. Kennedy, in his *Hymn. Christ.*, 1863.

ii. **Sieh wie lieblich und wie fein.** *Brotherly love.* The original form of this hymn is a version of Ps. cxxxiii. by Müller, in his *Psalmen Davids*, 1700, p. 244, in 4 st. of 4 l. In Freylinghausen's *G. B.*, 1704, No. 390, these st. are i.–iv., while st. v.–xiv. (on the subject of brotherly love) are added from the MS. of J. C. Nehring (q.v.). This text, in 14 st., is No. 1045 in the Berlin *G. L. S.*, ed. 1863. The form *tr.* into English is that in Bunsen's *Versuch*, 1833, No. 534, being st. i., iv., viii., x. of the above text and the following three st.:—

> 1.
> Sonne der Gerechtigkeit,
> Gehe auf zu unsrer Zeit,
> Brich in deiner Kirche an
> Dass die Welt es sehen kann.
>
> 2.
> Jesu, Haupt der Kreuzgemein,
> Mach uns alle, gross und klein,
> Durch dein Evangelium
> Ganz zu deinem Eigenthum.
>
> 3.
> Lass die ganze Brüd␣rschaar,
> Lieben, loben immerdar,
> In dir ruhen allezeit,
> Immer und in Ewigkeit.

These three st. are from the *Brüder G. B.*, 1778, No. 711, and are by Christian David (see **Moravian Hymnody**, § iii. 9). The first and third had previously appeared in the *Kleine Brüder G. B.*, London, 1754, pt. ii., Bk. ii., on the Church of God, section 7. The only *tr.* in C. U. is:—

Good and pleasant 'tis to see. A good *tr.* from Bunsen, by Miss Cox, in her *Sacred Hys. from the German*, 1841, p. 143, repeated abridged in Alford's *Ps. & Hys.*, 1844, and *Year of Praise*, 1867, and in the Rev. F. Pott's *Coll.*, 1861.

Other trs. are, both from Bunsen's text:—(1) " Behold how sweet it is to see," by *Lady E. Fortescue*, 1843, p. 64. (2) "Lo! how sweet it is to see," by W. Arnot, in the *Family Treasury*, 1872, p. 204.   [J. M.]

Mülmann, J. [**Mühlmann, J.**]

Mundi renovatio. *Adam of St. Victor.* [*Easter.*] A beautiful poem on the coincidence of the Easter of Nature and the Easter of the Church; and on the joys of returning Spring. L. Gautier, in his *Oeuvres poetiques d'Adam de Saint Victor*, 1881, p. 38. gives it from a *Gradual* of St. Victor before 1239 (Bibl. Nat. Paris, No. 14,452); a *Missal* of St. Genevieve also apparently before 1239; a 13th cent. *Paris Gradual* (B. N. Paris, No. 15,615), &c. It is in two early 14th cent. French Missals in the British Museum, both apparently of the Paris use (Add. 16,905, f. 154; Harl. 2891, f. 345 b). The printed text will be found in *Daniel*, ii. p. 68; *Morel*, No. 70; *Trench*, ed. 1864, p. 153; *Kehrein*, No. 90; *Macgill*, 1876–9, and *Wrangham*, 1881. The use of St. Victor and of Paris was on Saturday in Easter Week, that of St. Genevieve on the Friday. *Tr.* as :—

Lo! the world from slumber risen. By Mrs. Harriet M. Chester, in the *Hymnary*, 1872, under the signature of "H. M. C."

Other trs. are:—

1. The renewal of the world. *Mrs. Charles*, 1858.
2. Now the world's fresh dawn of birth. P. S. Worsley, in *Lyra Messianica*, 1864.
3. Spring's renewal of earth's plain. *D. S. Wrangham*, 1881.   [J. M.]

Mundi salus affutura. [*Visitation of the B. V. M.*] This is the hymn at Matins in the Office of the Visitation of the B. V. M. in the *Sarum* and *Aberdeen Breviaries*. The Office was sanctioned by Convocation in 1480, was printed by Caxton in the same year, and was incorporated in the *Sarum Breviary*, Venice, 1495, *pars Estiv*. pt. ii., where this hymn is given at f. 130 *b*. The text of the hymn is also in Card. Newman's *Hymni Ecclesiae*, 1838 and 1865. *Tr.* as :—

1. **What the just by faith believed.** By W. J. Blew, in his *Church H. and Tune Bk.*, 1852–55. This *tr.* begins with st. iv. ("Sic in mundo praeter morem"), and adds *trs.* of st. v.–vii. ; and of stanza iv. of "Festum matris gloriosae" (p. 376, i.).

2. **Lo! the Fount of earth's salvation.** By J. D. Chambers, in his *Lauda Syon*, Pt. ii., 1866, p. 84, in 7 st. of 6 l. In the *Antiphoner and Grail*, 1880, p. 126, and again in the *Hymner*, 1882, it is given in an altered form of 5 st. as "Portal of the world's salvation." [J. M.]

Mundi salus qui nasceris. *C. Coffin.* [*Christmas.*] Given in the *Paris Breviary*, 1736, and again in Coffin's *Hymni Sacri*, 1736, p. 94. It is also in J. Chandler's *Hys. of the Prim. Church*, 1837, No. 13, and Card. Newman's *Hymni Ecclesiae*, 1838 and 1865. *Tr.* as :—

Infant, born the world to free. By I. Williams, in the *British Magazine*, Jan., 1833 (vol. v. p. 31), and in his *Hys. tr. from the Parisian Breviary*, 1839, p. 50. In 1864 it was repeated in Skinner's *Daily Service Hymnal*, No. 49.

Other trs. are :—

1. O holy Babe, our prayer receive. *J. Chandler*, 1837.
2. Lord of all, Thy glory veiling. *R. Campbell*, 1850.   [J. J.]

Mundus effusis redemptus. [*Holy Communion.*] In the *Cluniac Breviary*, Paris, 1686, p. 556, this is the hymn at First Vespers for the Octave of Corpus Christi, and consists of 5 st. and a doxology. Also in the *Narbonne*, 1709 ; the *Sens*, 1726 ; and other French breviaries. *Tr.* as :—

Sing, O earth, for thy redemption. By E. Caswall, in his *Masque of Mary*, &c., 1858, p. 304, and his *Hys. & Poems*, 1873, p. 157, in 5 st. of 6 l. In the *Hymnary*, 1872, it is given for "Ascensiontide," and in others as a general hymn.   [J. M.]

Münter, Balthasar, s. of Lorenz Münter, merchant in Lübeck, was b. at Lübeck, March 24, 1735. He entered the University of Jena as a student of theology in 1754, graduated M.A. in 1757, and thereafter became lecturer and adjunct of the philosophical faculty. In 1760, Duke Friedrich III., of Gotha, appointed him assistant court preacher, and preacher at the Orphanage in Gotha, and then, in 1763, Superintendent at Tonna (Gräfen-Tonna) near

Gotha. In 1765 he became first preacher at the German Church of St. Peter in Copenhagen, receiving, in 1767, the degree of D.D. from the University. He d. at Copenhagen, Oct. 5, 1793 (*Koch* vi. 348 ; *Allg. Deutsche Biog.* xxiii. 33, &c.).

Münter was a very popular and influential preacher, a true pastor and teacher of practical Christianity, a successful religious instructor of children, an active friend of the poor, a man of culture and one of the most prominent figures in the literary society of Copenhagen. His hymns, 100 in number, are among the best of the period, were highly esteemed by his contemporaries, and many still survive in German hymnals compiled before 1876 and still in use. They appeared in his two works: (1) *Geistliche Lieder*. Leipzig, 1772. (2) *Zwote Sammlung Geistlicher Lieder*. Leipzig, 1774. [Both in Royal Library, Berlin.] In 1773, the first 50 were republished at Leipzig set to melodies composed for them by the most famous musicians of the day ; and the second 50 were republished at Leipzig in 1774 set to melodies composed for them by J. C. F. Bach, of Bückeburg.

Of Münter's hymns the following have passed into English :—

i. Seht welch' ein Mensch! Wie lag so schwer. *Christ before Pilate.* 1774, No. 6, p. 21, in 10 st. of 7 l. Included in full in the Schleswig Holstein *G. B.*, 1780 ; and, reduced to 5 st., in the Berlin *G. B.*, 1829. *Tr.* as :—

Behold the Man! How heavy lay. In full, by Dr. H. Mills, in his *Horae Ger.*, 1845 (1856, p. 307), repeated, abridged, in the Amer. Luth. Gen. Synod's *Coll.*, 1850, and the Ohio Luth. *Hymnal*, 1000.

ii. Zitternd, doch voll sanfter Freuden. *Holy Communion.* 1772, No. 19, p. 67, in 9 st. of 8 l., entitled "Communion Hymn." In the Berlin *G. B.*, 1780, No. 126, st ii., was omitted, and the rest considerably altered, beginning "Voller Ehrfurcht, Dank und Freuden." *Tr.* as : –

Full of rev'rence at Thy Word, Lord, I near. In full from the text of 1780, as No. 271 in the Ohio Luth. *Hymnal*, 1880.

Hymns not in English C. U. :—

iii. **Ach, wann werd' ich von der Sünde.** *Christian Warfare.* 1774, No. 35, p. 130, in 9 st. *Tr.* as "Ah! when shall I be, from sinning." By *Dr. H. Mills*, 1845 (1856, p. 147).

iv. **Der letzte meiner Tage.** *Prospect of Death.* 1772, No. 21, p. 75, in 8 st. *Tr.* as: "My day without a morrow." By *N. L. Frothingham*, 1870, p. 187.

v. **Von Furcht dahingerissen.** *St. Peter's Denial.* 1774, No. 8, p. 29, in 9 st., entitled "Prayer for Christians who feel themselves guilty of the sin of Peter." *Tr.* as "Urged, Lord, by sinful terror." By *Dr. H. Mills*, 1845 (1856, p. 302).

vi. **Wer ist der mit Himmelslichte.** *Easter.* 1774, No. 44, p. 168, in 7 st. *Tr.* as "Who is this with glory gleaming." By *Dr. H. Mills*, 1845 (1856, p. 320). [J. M.]

Mure, Sir William, eldest s. of Sir William Mure of Rowallan Castle, Ayrshire, was b. at Rowallan in 1594. In the Civil War he sided against the king; and in 1644, accompanying those sent under the *Solemn League and Covenant* to the help of the Parliament, was wounded at the battle of Marston Moor. He d. at Rowallan in 1657. In 1628 he pub. a *tr.* of Robert Boyd's *Hecatombe Christiana*, at Edinburgh, in a volume containing also an original poem entitled *Doomesday*, and three sonnets entitled *Fancies Farewell*. His [MS.] *Version of the Psalms*, which seems to have been begun in 1629 and completed in 1639, was recommended to the use of the committee who compiled the *Scottish Psalter* of 1650. A complete MS. of this version was found about 1825, with various other poetical MSS. by him, among the old family papers in Rowallan Castle. These MSS. were kindly searched for by Lord Donington in 1884, but could not be discovered among the family papers now in Loudoun Castle, Ayrshire.   [J. M.]

Μυστήριον ξένον.   [Χριστὸς γεννᾶται.]

My blessed Saviour, is Thy love. J. Stennett. [Holy Communion.] Appeared in his Hys. on the Lord's Supper, 1697, No. 22, in 10 st. of 4 l., and again in his Works, 1732, vol. iv. p. 111. It is usually given in 3 stanzas (st. i.–iii.) somewhat altered, as in the Leeds H. Bk., 1853, and others. Another arrangement is, "O blessed Saviour, is Thy love." In some collections this extends to 6 stanzas, as in Snepp's Songs of G. & G., 1872, but a shorter form is in more frequent use. [J. J.]

My Father, for another night. Sir H. W. Baker. [Morning.] Contributed to the revised ed. of H. A. & M., 1875. It is repeated in a few collections, including the Additional Hys., added to the Leeds S. S. H. Bk., 1878. In this last case it is ascribed to "Oakes" in error.   [J. J.]

My former hopes are fled. W. Cowper. [Seeking God.] Appeared in the Olney Hymns, 1779, Bk. iii., No. 8, in 5 st. of 4 l., and headed "The Shining Light." It was passed into C. U. in G. Britain and America, its use in the latter being somewhat extensive. [J. J.]

My God, accept my heart this day. M. Bridges. [Confirmation.] 1st pub. in his Hys. of the Heart for the Use of Catholics, 1848, in 5 st. of 4 l., and entitled "Confirmation." In some collections it begins, "My God, accept my heart, I pray," in others, "O God, accept my heart, &c.," and in others, including the Unitarian Hymn [& Tune] Bk. for the Church and the Home, Boston, U. S. A., 1868, it opens with st. ii., "Before the Cross of Him Who died." In these various forms it is in extensive use in G. Britain and America.
                                      [J. J.]

My God and Father! while I stray. Charlotte Elliott. [Resignation.] The uncertainties with regard to the text of this popular hymn have arisen out of the fact that four forms of the text were pub. by Miss Elliott, and each of these has been taken in turn as the original. The facts and texts are as follows :—

i. The original hymn was pub. in the Appendix to the 1st ed. of the Invalid's Hymn Book, 1834, No. 17, as follows :—

" 1. My God and Father! while I stray
      Far from my home in life's rough way,
      Oh! teach me from my heart to say,
        'Thy will be done!'

" 2. Though dark my path, and sad my lot,
      Let me 'be still,' and murmur not,
      Or breathe the prayer divinely taught,
        'Thy will be done!'

" 3. What though in lonely grief I sigh
      For friends beloved, no longer nigh,
      Submissive still would I reply,
        'Thy will be done!'

" 4. If thou shouldst call me to resign
      What most I prize, it ne'er was mine;
      I only yield thee what was thine;
        'Thy will be done!'

" 5. Should pining sickness waste away,
      My life in premature decay,
      My Father! still I strive to say,
        'Thy will be done!'

" 6. If but my fainting heart be blest
      With thy sweet spirit for its guest,
      My God! to thee I leave the rest—
        'Thy will be done!'

" 7. Renew my will from day to day,
      Blend it with thine, and take away
      All now that makes it hard to say,
        'Thy will be done!'

" 8. Then when on earth I breathe no more
      The prayer oft mixed with tears before,
      I'll sing upon a happier shore,
        'Thy will be done!'"

ii. The second form of the hymn appeared in Miss Elliott's brother's (H. V. Elliott), Ps. and Hys., 1835, as follows :—

" 1. My God my Father, while I stray
      Far from my home, on life's rough way,
      O teach me from my heart to say,
        'Thy will be done!'

" 2. If thou shouldst call me to resign
      What most I prize,—it ne'er was mine;
      I only yield thee what was thine;—
        'Thy will be done!'

" 3. E'en if again I ne'er should see
      The friend more dear than life to me,
      Ere long we both shall be with thee;—
        'Thy will be done!

" 4. Should pining sickness waste away
      My life in premature decay,
      My Father, still I strive to say,
        'Thy will be done!'

" 5. If but my fainting heart be blest
      With thy sweet Spirit for its guest,
      My God, to thee I leave the rest;—
        'Thy will be done!'

" 6. Renew my will from day to day;
      Blend it with thine, and take away
      All that now makes it hard to say
        'Thy will be done!'

" 7. Then when on earth I breathe no more
      The prayer oft mix'd with tears before,
      I'll sing, upon a happier shore,
        'Thy will be done!'"

iii. The third form of the hymn was given in Miss Elliott's Hours of Sorrow, &c., 1836, pp. 130-1, as follows :—

"My God and Father! while I stray
  Far from my home in life's rough way,
  O! teach me from my heart to say,
    'Thy will be done!'

"Though dark my path and sad my lot,
  Let me 'be still' and murmur not;
  Or breathe the prayer divinely taught,
    'Thy will be done!'

"What though in lonely grief I sigh
  For friends belov'd, no longer nigh,
  Submissive still would I reply,
    'Thy will be done!'

"Though thou hast call'd me to resign
  What most I priz'd, it ne'er was mine:
  I have but yielded what was thine;—
    'Thy will be done!'

"Should grief or sickness waste away
  My life in premature decay;
  My Father! still I'll strive to say,
    'Thy will be done!'

"Let but my fainting heart be blest,
  With thy sweet Spirit for its guest.
  My God! to thee I leave the rest:
    'Thy will be done!'

"Renew my will from day to day!
  Blend it with thine! and take away
  All that now makes it hard to say,
    'Thy will be done!'"

iv. The fourth form is in the 1839 ed. of Elliott's Ps. & Hys. and later editions. In this the text of the Ps. and Hys., 1835, has undergone one change only, and this in the opening line, which reads, "My God, my Father, while I stray."

The great diversity in these texts, and all

pub. by Miss Elliott, or with her sanction, accounts for the curious anomaly that Lord Selborne, in his *Bk. of Praise*, gives one form as the original, Bp. Bickersteth, in his *H. Comp.*, another, and some one else a third. In varying forms it is in extensive use in all English-speaking countries, and of all Miss Elliott's hymns it ranks next to her "Just as I am" in popularity. It has also been *tr.* into several languages, including Latin, German, French, &c.   [J. J.]

My God, and is Thy table spread?
P. Doddridge. [*Holy Communion.*] Pub. in Job Orton's posthumous edition of Doddridge's *Hymns*, &c., 1755, No. 171, in 6 st. of 4 l., and headed "God's Name profaned, when his Table is treated with Contempt. Malachi i. 12. Applied to the Lord's Supper." The same text was repeated in J. D. Humphreys's ed. of Doddridge's *Hymns*, &c., 1839. The extensive use of this hymn, and especially in the Church of England, is due to a great extent to the fact that it, with a few others, was appended to *Tate and Brady's* Version of the Psalms. The history of that circumstance is given in the article on the **New Version** (q.v.). The only changes in the text are st. i., l. 2, of "does" into "*doth*," and l. 3 of the same stanza of "*its*" into "*thy*." In addition to its use in this form, and in the original (often abbreviated), it is also found as:—

1. **Father, and is Thy table spread.** This is adopted by some of the American Unitarian collections.
2. **Lord Jesus, is Thy table spread.** This is as early as the 1815 *Appendix* to Cotterill's *Sel.*, and is found in Bickersteth's *Christian Psalmody*, 1833, and later hymn-books of the same type.
3. **O God, and is Thy table spread.** This is in the *Hymnary*, 1872, in 4 st., together with a doxology which is not in the original.

The only alterations of any moment which have crept into the text, and are sometimes adopted, are:—

"Rich banquet of His Flesh and Blood!"

to:—

"*Memorial* of His Flesh and Blood!"

and:—

"Why are its dainties all in vain?"

to:—

"Why are its *bounties* all in vain?"

In full or in part this hymn has been *tr.* into several languages. One in Latin (of 4 st., the fourth being very much altered), by Bingham, in his *Hymno. Christ. Lat.*, 1871, is "O Deus, anæe patet nobis Tua mensa referta?" [see **English Hymnody, Early**, § XIV.]   [J. J.]

My God, how endless is Thy love.
I. Watts. [*Morning or Evening.*] Pub. in his *Hys. and Spiritual S.*, 1709, Bk. i., No. 81, in 3 st. of 4 l., and headed "A Song for Morning or Evening." It was included in J. Wesley's *Ps. & Hys.*, Charles-town, 1736–37, and subsequently in a large number of hymn-books. In addition to its use under its original first line, sometimes with slight changes, but usually unaltered, it is also found as:—

1. **O God, how endless is Thy love.** This form appeared in G. Whitefield's *Hymns*, &c., 1753, No. 17; M. Madan's *Ps. & Hys.*, 1760, No. 103, and many later collections.
2. **O God, how constant is Thy love.** This was given in the 1819 ed. of Cotterill's *Sel.*, p. 2, in 4 st., the 3rd stanza being an addition by Cotterill or Montgomery.
3. **O God, how boundless is Thy love.** This form is

in the Irvingite *Hys. for the Use of the Churches*, 1864 and 1871.

Through the original and in these various forms this hymn is in use in all English-speaking countries. It is a beautiful example of Watts's tender style, but somewhat tinged with sadness. [See **English Hymnody, Early**, § VI. 3, XIII.]   [J. J.]

My God, how perfect are Thy ways.
W. Cowper. [*The Lord our Righteousness.*] Appeared in the *Olney Hymns*, 1779, Bk. i., No. 67, in 5 st. of 4 l., and entitled "Jehovah our Righteousness." It is generally given in its original form, but its use is limited. [J. J.]

My God, how wonderful Thou art.
F. W. Faber. [*The Eternal Father.*] 1st pub. in his *Jesus and Mary*, &c., 1849, No. 2, in 9 st. of 4 l., and entitled, "The Eternal Father," and again in his *Hymns*, 1862, p. 22. Its use is very extensive both in G. Britain and America, but it is often given in an abridged form. In some of the American collections, including H. W. Beecher's *Plymouth Coll.*, 1855, *The Baptist Praise Bk.*, 1871, it begins with st. ii., "How dread are Thine eternal years," but this does not equal the original in popularity in America, and is almost unknown in G. Britain. Another cento in C. U. in America begins with st. iv., "O how I fear Thee, living God."   [J. J.]

My God, I am Thine; What a comfort divine. *C. Wesley.* [*Peace with God.*] Appeared in *Hys. and Sac. Poems*, 1749, vol. i., as No. 16 of "Hymns for Believers," in 6 st. of 3 l. (*P. Works*, 1868–72, vol. v. p. 24). It was republished in the *Wes. H. Bk.*, 1780, No. 197, and thence passed into most of the Methodist hymn-books throughout all English-speaking countries. Few hymns amongst the Methodists have equalled it in the influence which it has had upon the sick and dying. Numerous instances of great interest are given in G. J. Stevenson's *Meth. H. Bk. Notes*, 1883, p. 167. The stanzas most frequently quoted are, i. "My God, I am Thine," and iv., "My Jesus to know; And feel His blood flow." Outside of the Methodist bodies its use is limited.   [J. J.]

My God, I know, I feel Thee mine.
C. Wesley. [*Peace and Holiness desired.*] Pub. in *Hys. & Sac. Poems*, 1740, p. 156, in 12 st. of 4 l., and entitled, "Against Hope, Believing in Hope" (*P. Works*, 1868–72, vol. i. p. 328). In the *Wes. H. Bk.*, 1780, No. 351, st. x. is omitted, and slight changes in the text are introduced. This form is repeated in the revised ed., 1875, and has passed into several collections. In addition there are also the following arrangements of the hymn in C. U.:—

1. **Father, Thy all-victorious love.** This opens with st. iv. altered, and is in use in American Unitarian hymn-books.
2. **Jesus, Thine all-victorious love.** This also begins with st. iv. altered, and is in American C. U.
3. **My God, I humbly call Thee mine.** This is in Mercer's *Church Psalter & H. Bk.*, Oxford ed., 1864, in 9 stanzas.
4. **O that in me the sacred fire.** In the *Primitive Methodist Hymnal*, 1887, and a few American collections. This opens with st. vii.   [J. J.]

My God, I love and I adore. *I. Watts.* [*God, the Creator and Preserver.*] This poem of 63 lines, appended to an essay on "Searching after God," is in Watts's *Reliquiæ Juveniles:* *Miscellaneous Thoughts in Prose and Verse*, &c,, 1734. In the *Coll. of Hys. & Ps.*, &c., by Kippis, Rees, and others, 1795, a hymn in 4 st. of 4 l. appeared as No. 62, beginning "Who can by searching find out God?" The opening stanza is based on ll. 1–4 of the poem, whilst st. ii.–iv. are almost word for word from ll. 5–20. This same hymn, with the substitution of ll. 1–4 of the poem for the first stanza as in *Kippis*, is No. 148 in *The Bap. Praise Bk.*, N. Y., 1871. This, together with the text as in *Kippis*, is in other collections. Another arrangement, beginning with the same first line, in 4 st. is No. 177 in H. W. Beecher's *Plymouth Coll.*, 1855, but it is not equal to either of the former in purity or beauty. The hymn, in either of those forms, is very poetical and of more than usual excellence.   [J. J.]

My God, in Whom are all the springs. *I. Watts.* [*Ps. lvii.*] 1st pub. in his *Psalms of David*, 1719, in 6 st. of 4 l., and entitled, "Praise for Protection, Grace and Truth." In some collections, as in Dr. Alexander's *Augustine H. Bk.*, 1849 and 1865, it begins with st. iii., "Be Thou exalted, O my God." Both the original and the abridged form are in limited use.   [J. J.]

My God, is any hour so sweet. *Charlotte Elliott.* [*The Hour of Prayer.*] Pub. in her *Hours of Sorrow*, &c., 1836, p. 45, in 7 st. of 4 l., and entitled "The Hour of Prayer"; again in her brother's *Ps. & Hys.*, 2nd thousand, 1837, in 6 st., and again in her *Morning and Evening Hys. for a Week*, 1839. The text in each of these works is different from that in the rest. The text in the *H. Comp.*, 1876, which is generally received as the original, differs slightly from each of the above. The 1836 text is in *Lyra Brit.*, 1867, p. 219, with "There for," changed to "Here for," in st. v. l. 2. In *Kennedy*, 1863, and in Thring's *Coll.*, 1882, it is altered to "Sweet is the morning light to me." The use of this hymn in one or the other of these two forms is extensive.   [J. J.]

My God, my Father, blissful Name. *Anne Steele.* [*Humility and Trust.*] Appeared in her *Poems on Subjects chiefly Devotional*, 1760, vol. i. p. 114, in 8 st. of 4 l., and headed "Humble Reliance." It was repeated in the 2nd ed. of the *Poems*, 1780, and in Sedgwick's reprint of her *Hymns*, 1863, p. 70. In its full original form it is not usually found in C. U.; but the following centos therefrom are given in several hymn-books in G. Britain and America:—

1. **My God, my Father, blissful Name.** Composed of st. i.–iv., vi.–viii. in the Bap. *New Selection*, 1828; the Bap. *Ps. & Hys.*, 1858; the *New Cong.*, 1859, &c.
2. **My God, my Father, charming Name.** This is usually No. 1, with the alteration of the opening line.
3. **Lord, what Thy providence denies.** Composed of st. iii., iv., vii., viii. in the 1863 *Appendix* to the S. P. C. K. *Ps. & Hys.*, and others.
4. **My God, whate'er Thy will ordains.** In *Kennedy*, 1863, No. 1211, is a cento from this hymn and Miss Steele's "Dear Refuge of my weary soul."   [J. J.]

My God, my Father, dost Thou call? *Bp. E. H. Bickersteth.* [*Home Missions.*] Written for the London Church Mission, 1874, and printed in the *Guardian*, and afterwards pub. in his *H. Comp.*, 1876. It has since

passed into several hymn-books, including the *Prim. Methodist Hymnal*, 1887, &c.   [J. J.]

My God, my Portion and my Love. *I. Watts.* [*God Man's only Happiness.*] Pub. in the 1st ed. of his *Hys. and Spiritual S.*, 1707 (ed. 1709, Bk. ii., No. 94), in 8 st. of 4 l., and headed "God my only Happiness." It is in C. U. both in full and in an abridged form. In Dale's *English H. Bk.*, 1874, No. 639, "My God, my *life is in Thy* love," is also from this hymn, and is composed of st. i., ii., v., vii., viii. slightly altered.   [J. J.]

My God, the Covenant of Thy love. *P. Doddridge.* [*The Divine Covenant.*] This hymn is No. 86 in the D. MSS., but is undated. The latest date in the MSS. is given to No. 83, as "Jan. 9, 17$\frac{38}{43}$." This hymn is, we judge, *circa* 1740. It was included, unaltered, in Job Orton's posthumous ed. of Doddridge's *Hymns*, &c., 1755, No. 21, in 5 st. of 4 l., and headed "Support in God's Covenant under domestic troubles;" and again in J. D. Humphreys's ed. of the same, 1839, No. 26. It is in extensive use in G. Britain and America, but usually with the omission of st. ii., "What tho' my house be not with Thee."   [J. J.]

My God, the Spring of all my joys. *I. Watts.* [*God, Light in darkness.*] 1st pub. in his *Hys. & Spiritual S.*, 1707 (ed. 1709, Bk. ii., No. 54), in 5 st. of 4 l., and headed "God's presence is Light in darkness." In 1741, J. Wesley included it with alterations in his *Ps. & Hys.*, p. 118, but did not introduce it into the *Wes. H. Bk.* in 1780. It is in the 18th ed., 1805, as No. 87, with an asterisk to denote that it was not placed there by Wesley. In its original form the hymn is *about* God, and He is spoken of in the *third* person thus:

"In darkest shades if *He* appear."

The Wesley version is an address *to* God:

"In darkest shades if *Thou* appear."

Both versions are in extensive use in all English-speaking countries; the original, however, being the more popular of the two. In a few collections it is altered to: "My God, the *Source* of all my joys."   [J. J.]

My God, Thy service well demands. *P. Doddridge.* [*Thanksgiving for Recovery from Sickness.*] In the D. MSS. this hymn is No. 55, is dated "Nov. 14, 1737," and headed,

"A Thought on recovery from Sickness in which much of the Presence of God had been experienced. Particularly intended for the use of Miss Nanny Bliss."

This heading is altered in Doddridge's handwriting to

"Thought on recovery from a dangerous sickness in which much of the presence of God had been experienced. Particularly intended for the use of a friend who had been in extreme danger by the bursting of an artery in her stomach."

It was included in Job Orton's posthumous ed. of Doddridge's *Hymns*, &c., 1755, No. 364, in 7 st. of 4 l., as one of the "Hymns on Particular Occasions," and in Uncommon Measures." It is headed therein "On Recovery from Sickness, during which much of the Divine Favour had been experienced." In J. D. Humphreys's ed. of the *Hymns*, &c., the text and heading as in Orton's ed. were repeated. When the nature of the sickness is remembered, the original MS. is more intensely vivid than the printed text. In the MS. st. ii., ll. 3, 4, read:—

> "When life in purple torrents flowed
> From every gushing vein;"

st. iii., l. 3:—

> "And teach me with my quivering lips;"

and st. v., l. 4:—

> "That made salvation mine."

The special personal character of this hymn has limited its use. It might, however, be easily adapted for special or general thanksgiving after sickness.   [J. J.]

My God, 'tis to Thy Mercy-seat. *Anne Steele.* [*The Mercy-Seat.*] 1st pub. in her *Poems on Subjects chiefly Devotional*, &c., 1760, vol. i, p. 133, in 6 st. of 4 l., and headed: "Refuge and Strength in the Mercy of God." It was repeated in the 2nd ed. of the *Poems*, &c., 1780, and in Sedgwick's reprint of her *Hymns*, 1863. It is in C. U. both in its original form and as "*Dear Father*, to Thy Mercy-seat." The latter form is chiefly in use in America.   [J. J.]

My God, what silken cords are Thine. *P. Doddridge.* [*Gratitude.*] 1st pub. in Job Orton's posthumous ed. of Doddridge's *Hymns*, &c., 1755, No. 152, in 5 st. of 4 l., and entitled "Gratitude the Spring of true Religion;" and again in J. D. Humphreys's ed. of the same, 1839, No. 171. It is in C. U. in its original form, and as "My God, what cords of love are Thine," in the *London H. Bk.* (enlarged) 1873, and others.   [J. J.]

My gracious Lord, I own Thy right. *P. Doddridge.* [*The Service of Christ a delight.*] Pub. by Job Orton in his posthumous ed. of Doddridge's *Hymns*, 1755, No. 294, in 5 st. of 4 l., and headed "Christ's Service the fruit of our Labours on earth:" also given in J. D. Humphreys's ed. of the same, 1839, No. 320. Its use, especially in America, is extensive. Sometimes it is given as "*All-gracious Lord, I own Thy right*," as in the Unitarian *Hys. of The Spirit*, Boston, U.S.A., 1864.   [J. J.]

My heart is resting, O my God. *Anna L. Waring.* [*The Lord the Portion of his people.*] Appeared in the 4th ed. of her *Hys. and Meditations*, 1854, p. 65, in 11 st. of 8 l., and based upon Lam. iii. 24, "The Lord is my Portion, saith my soul; therefore will I hope in Him" (ed. 1871, p. 62). It is also in her *Additional Hys.*, 1858. Being too long to be used in full, various arrangements of lines and stanzas have been adopted for C. U. Most of these begin with the opening line of the hymn. One exception is, "I have a heritage of joy," in the American Unitarian *Hy.* [*& Tune*] *Bk. for Church & Home*, Boston, 1868, which begins with st. iii., l. 5. [J. J.]

My Helper, God, I bless His name. *P. Doddridge.* [*New Year.*] This hymn is almost entirely unknown under its original first line, but altered as "*Our Helper, God, we bless His* [Thy] *name*," it is found in several collections, including Horder's *Cong. Hys.*, 1884. It was 1st pub. in Job Orton's posthumous ed. of Doddridge's *Hymns*, &c., 1755, No. 19, in 4 st. of 4 l., and headed, "Ebenezer, or God's helping hand review'd and

acknowledged. 1 Sam. vii. 12. For New-Year's day." It is also in J. D. Humphreys's ed. of the same, 1839, No. 23.   [J. J.]

My Hope, my All, my Saviour Thou. [*Jesus, All in All.*] This hymn has been traced to *A Pocket Hymn Book designed as a constant Companion for the Pious, collected from Various Authors.* York, R. Spence, 1774 (5th ed., 1786, No. 114), in 5 st. of 4 l. Through this *Pocket H. Bk.*, which, in a reprint, was the first Methodist hymn-book used in America [American Hymnody, § v.], it came into use in that country. The full and unaltered text is in Dr. Hatfield's *Church H. Bk.*, N. Y., 1872, No. 964. In the Meth. Episco. *Hymnal*, 1878, it is given in 4 st., and ascribed to "Thomas Coke." As the hymn was published in a Methodist *Pocket H. Bk.*, in 1774, and Dr. Coke did not make the acquaintance of J. Wesley until August 13, 1776, this can hardly be so. Moreover, there is no mention of his having written hymns at that time, or at any time, in Dr. Etheridge's authorised edition of his *Life*, 1860. We are obliged therefore to say it is *Anonymous*.   [J. J.]

My Jesus, while in mortal flesh. *P. Doddridge.* [*Abidings—Faith in Christ.*] This is No. 280 in Job Orton's posthumous ed. of Doddridge's *Hymns*, &c., 1755, and No. 306 in J. D. Humphreys's ed. of the same, 1839. It is in 6 st. of 4 l., and headed "Living while in the flesh by faith in Christ, Who loved us, &c. Galat. ii. 26." It is in C. U. in its original form, and as "*Blest Jesus, while in mortal flesh.*" The latter form is mainly in use in America.   [J. J.]

My Lord, my Love was crucified. *J. Mason.* [*Sunday.*] Appeared in his *Spiritual Songs, or Songs of Praise*, &c., 1683, No. 19, in 3 st. of 8 l., and 1 st. of 4 l., and entitled "A Song of Praise for the Lord's Day." It is also in Sedgwick's reprint of Mason's *Spiritual S.*, 1859, p. 30. It is in use in three forms: (1) The original abbreviated; (2) "My Lord, my *Life*, was crucified:" and (3) "Come, dearest Lord, and feed Thy sheep." The altered forms are principally in use in America.

The opening line of this hymn is well known in Church history and song. St. Ignatius used it in the first century: it was common throughout the middle ages, and the prefatory plate to Luke Boileau's *Reformed Monastery*, 1677, has the motto "Amor meus crucifixus est." The refrain to each stanza of C. Wesley's "O Love divine, what hast Thou done?" is "My Lord, my Love is crucified:" to each stanza of Faber's "O come and mourn with me awhile, it is "Jesus, our Love, is crucified"; and in *H. A. & M.*, and most modern collections which have copied Faber's hymn, it is "Jesus, our *Lord*, is crucified." It is a beautiful thought, and full of spiritual meaning. Its tenderness is not intensified by the change of "*our Love*" to "*our Lord*."   [W. T. B.]

My Maker, and my King; to Thee my whole I owe. *Anne Steele.* [*God, Creator and Benefactor.*] 1st pub. in her *Poems on Subjects chiefly Devotional*, &c., 1760, vol. i. p. 48, in 6 st. of 4 l., and entitled,

"God my Creator and Benefactor." It was repeated in her *Poems*, &c., 1780; and in Sedgwick's reprint of her *Hymns*, 1863. Two forms of this hymn are in C. U. (1) The first is the original in its full or abridged form. This came into C. U. through the Bristol Bap. *Coll.* of Ash & Evans, 1769, where it is No. 25, and sign.d "T." (2) The second is:—

"My Maker and my King!
What thanks to Thee I owe."

This appeared in Hall's *Mitre H. Bk.*, 1836, No. 286, in 4 st. of 4 l.; and again in E. Osler's *Church and King*, June 1, 1837. It was rewritten from Miss Steele's hymn by Osler for the *Mitre H. Bk.*, and should be given as *Anne Steele*, 1760; *E. Osler*, 1836. [J. J.]

My Saviour, be Thou near me, Through life's night. *Mary Duncan, née Lundie.* [*Supplication.*] 1st pub. in her *Memoir*, 1841, in 2 st. of 8 l., and thus introduced:—

"To a Greek air, which a dear friend loved to hear her sing, she composed, at the pianoforte, the annexed stanzas, not being satisfied with the trifling words attached to it. They bear date the 20th December [1839], the last effusion of her muse, and the prayer of their petition was about to be answered speedily" (ed. 1843, p. 294).

The hymn is included, set to this air, in the Rev. J. H. Wilson's *Songs of Zion*, 1877, and, without the air, in other collections. [J. M.]

My song shall be of mercy. *H. Downton.* [*Ps. ci.*] Written for his congregation at St. John's Church, Chatham, and first printed at the close of his *Sermon*, preached in 1852, on "God, the Refuge of His people" (Chatham, A. Etherington); and then in Barry's *Ps. & Hys.*, 1867. It was also included in his *Hys. & Verses*, 1873. [W. T. B.]

My song shall bless the Lord of all. *W. Cowper.* [*The Godhead of Christ.*] 1st pub. in the *Olney Hymns*, 1779, Bk. ii., No. 38, in 6 st. of 4 l., and headed "Jehovah Jesus." Although not in extensive use, it is a dogmatic hymn of more than usual merit, and is worthy of greater attention. [J. J.]

My soul and spirit fill'd with joy. *N. Tate.* [*Magnificat.*] This metrical version of the Song of the Blessed Virgin was given in the *Appendix* to the *New Version of the Psalms* appended to the *Book of Common Prayer*, 1702 (licenced 1703). It is not found in modern collections of hymns (full text in old *P. Books*). In the Draft of the *Scottish Translations and Paraphrases*, 1745, it was given with very slight alterations as No. ii. Before its adoption, however, in the authorised issue of the *Translations*, &c., of 1781, it underwent further revision, and as No. xxxvi. stands thus:—

St. i., *N. Tate*; st. ii., rewritten, 1781; st. iii., rewritten, 1781, with 1st line from 1745; st. iv., *N. Tate*; st. v., l. 1, 1745; l. 2 altered; ll. 3, 4, *N. Tate.*

This recast, which has been in use in the Church of Scotland for more than 100 years, is claimed for W. Cameron (p. 200, ii.) by his daughter in her list of authors and revisers of the 1781 issue. Full recast text in modern editions of the *Scottish Trs. and Paraphrases.* [J. J.]

My soul doth magnify the Lord. *J. Mason.* [*Whitsuntide.*] 1st pub. in his

Spiritual Songs, or Songs of Praise, 1683, p. 52, in 5 st. of 8 l., and 1 st. of 4 l., and entitled "A Song of Praise for Joy in the Holy Ghost"; and again, in Sedgwick's reprint of the *Spiritual Songs*, 1859, p. 38. The hymn in its full form is not in C. U. The following centos however are in C. U.:—

1. **A living stream as crystal clear.** This begins with st. iii., and, as altered by J. Keble, it appeared 'in the *Salisbury H. Bk.*, 1857, and subsequently in other collections.
2. **My soul doth magnify the Lord.** This, as No. 354 in the Dutch Reformed *Hys. of the Church*, N. Y., 1869, is composed of st. i., ii., ll. 1–4, and a doxology not in the original.
3. **There is a stream which issues forth.** This, as No. 104 in Lord Selborne's *Book of Praise*, 1862, is st. v. to the end of the hymn unaltered.

These centos, especially No. 1, are in several collections; but their use is not equal to their merits. [See **English Hymnody, Early,** § XI.] [J. J.]

My soul, go boldly forth. *R. Baxter.* [*Death Anticipated.*] This poem appeared in Baxter's *Additions to the Poetical Fragments of Richard Baxter, Written for himself and Communicated to such as are more for serious Verse than smooth. London: Printed for B. Simmons*, &c., 1683, p. 62, in 31 st. of 6 l., dated "Decemb. 19, 1682," and headed "The Exit." In the American *Plymouth Coll.*, 1855, st. i., iv. and xxxi. were given as No. 887, and in *Kennedy*, 1863, st. i., iv. xiii. and xxxi. as No. 1375. Both the original and these centos are admirably adapted for private use. [W. T. B.]

My soul, inspired with sacred love. *C. Wesley.* [*Ps. cxlvi.*] 1st pub. in *The Arminian Magazine*, 1798; again in Fish's collection of C. Wesley's *Psalms*, 1854; and again in the *P. Works*, 1868–72, vol. viii. p. 260, in 8 st. of 6. l. In 1830, it was given in the *Supp.* of the *Wes. H. Bk.*, with the omission of st. iii. and vi., and retained in the revised ed., 1875. [J. J.]

My soul, repeat His praise. *I. Watts.* [*Ps. ciii.*] 1st pub. in his *Ps. of David*, &c., 1719, p. 267, in 8 st. of 4 l., and headed, "Abounding Compassion of God; or, Mercy in the Midst of Judgment." It was given with the omission of st. ii., iv. and vi., in G. Whitefield's *Hys. for Social Worship*, &c., 1753, No. 9. This abbreviated form was repeated in M. Madan's *Ps. & Hys.*, 1760, No. 117, and others, and thus came into C. U. in the Church of England. It is also given in full in some collections, and again, altered in another way, in others. Its use is extensive. [J. J.]

My soul, there is a countrie. *H. Vaughan.* [*Heaven—Peace.*] This poem on "Peace" appeared in 20 lines in his *Silex Scintillans, or Sacred Poems*, Pt. i., 1650 (2nd ed. 1655); in Lyte's reprint of the same, 1847, and in the Bell and Daldy reprint, 1858. In the reduced form of 4 st. of 4 l., it was given in the *People's H.*, 1867; and in its full and unaltered form, as a hymn for "Private Use," in Thring's *Coll.*, 1882. [J. J.]

My soul, thy great Creator praise. *Sir J. Denham and I. Watts.* [*Ps. 104.*] 1st pub. in Watts's *Psalms of David*, &c., 1719.

in 28 st. of 4 l., and headed "The glory of God in Creation and Providence." In a note he says :—

"Several Lines in this Psalm I have borrow'd of Sir John Denham ; if I have made the Connection more evident, and the Sense more easy and useful to an ordinary Reader, I have attained my End, and leave others to judge whether I have dishonour'd his Verse, or improved it," p. 274.

The lines borrowed from Sir J. Denham's version of 1714 are st. i., ii., iii., vii., ll. 1, 2 ; xxviii., ll. 3, 4. The paraphrase naturally from its great length is not in C. U., but the following centos therefrom are in several hymn-books in G. Britain and America :—

1. Great is the Lord, what tongue can frame? This cento, in the Andover Sabbath H. Bk., 1858, and other American collections, is made up of odd lines from Watts's portion of the paraphrase somewhat freely altered. In some hymnals st. ii of this cento is omitted.

2. My soul, thy great Creator praise. This cento in the Leeds H. Bk., 1853, 4 stanzas, is thus composed: st. i., ii. Sir John Denham, and the rest by Watts ; in the New Cong., 1859, 8 stanzas, st. i., ii. are by Denham, and the rest by Watts; and in Dale's English H. Bk., 1874, st. i.-iii., are by Sir J. Denham, and iv., v. by Watts.

3. Vast are Thy works, Almighty Lord. Of this cento in Martineau's Hymns, 1840, No. 127, ll. 1, 2 of st. iii. are by Sir J. Denham, and the rest by Watts.

These centos, taken together, are in somewhat extensive use.   [J. J.]

My soul, with joy attend. P. Doddridge. [The Security of Christ's Sheep.] This is No. 97 of the D. MSS., but is undated [circa 1740]. It was pub. by J. Orton in his posthumous ed. of Doddridge's Hymns, &c., 1755, No. 231, in 6 st. of 4 l., and headed, "The Happiness and Security of Christ's Sheep, John x. 28." It was also repeated in J. D. Humphreys's ed. of the same, 1839, No. 255. It is in C. U. in G. Britain and America.   [J. J.]

My soul, with sacred joy survey. T. Kelly. [Missions.] 1st pub. in his Coll. of Ps. & Hys., &c., Dublin, 1802, No. 264 [there are two hymns in the collection with this number], in 7 stanzas of 4 l., and based on Isa. xliii. 5, 6. It was repeated in the 1st ed. of his Hymns, &c., 1804, and again in all later editions (ed. 1853, No. 575). In addition to appearing in a few collections under its opening line, two centos therefrom are in C. U., both beginning : "Arise, arise; with joy survey." These are : (1) In Hatfield's Church H. Bk., N. Y., 1872, No. 1219, composed of st. i., iii., ii., vi. and vii. in the order named ; (2) In the Bap. Praise Bk., N. Y., 1871, where st. i., iv. form No. 1204. [J. J.]

My spirit longeth for Thee. J. Byrom. [No Rest but in God.] Pub. in his Miscellaneous Poems, 1773, in two parts, Pt. i. being "The desponding Soul's wish"; and Pt. ii. "The Answer." The "Wish" is in 4 st. of 4 l. ; and the "Answer" in 4 st. of 4 l. Both parts are in C. U., the first, usually as, "My spirit longs for Thee; and the second, "Cheer up, desponding soul. The full text was reprinted in Byrom's Works, 1814, vol. ii. p. 140.   [W. T. B.]

My stock lies dead, and no increase. G. Herbert. [Divine Grace Desired.] Appeared in his posthumous work The Temple,

1633 (ed. Chandos Classics, 1887, p. 107), in 6 st. of 3 l., with the refrain "Drop from above !" It is given in its original form in a few collections, and again in several American hymnals, as "My heart lies dead, and no increase." It is a sweetly pathetic hymn for private devotion.   [J. J.]

My times of sorrow and of joy. B. Beddome. [Resignation.] Written on Jan. 4, 1778, and pub. in Rippon's Bap. Sel., 1787, No. 276, in 5 st. of 4 l., and headed "Resignation ; or God's Portion." In R. Hall's posthumous edition of Beddome's Hymns, &c., 1817, No. 222, it is simply entitled "Resignation." It is a striking coincidence that, unknown to Beddome, his son, Dr. Benjamin Beddome, died of a fever in Edinburgh on the day that this hymn was written. Dr. Rippon says, in the Baptist Register, 1794, that the father preached on that day (Sunday) from Ps. xxxi. 15, "My times are in Thy hand," and that this hymn was sung at the close of the Sermon. It is very plaintive, and well suited for private use. It is in several modern collections, including the Bap. Ps. & Hys., 1858 and 1880.   [J. J.]

My whole, though broken heart, O Lord. R. Baxter. [Resignation.] Appeared in his Poetical Fragments, 1681, p. 81, in 8 st. of 8 l., and entitled, "The Covenant and Confidence of Faith." To it is appended the note: "This Covenant, my dear wife, in her former sickness, subscribed with a cheerful will." The hymn was republished in Pickering's reprint of the Poetical Fragments, 1821. In its complete form it is not found in modern hymn-books. The following centos therefrom are in C. U. :—

1. Christ leads me through no darker rooms. This is in the Cooke and Denton Hymnal, 1853, and several American collections.

2. Come, Lord, when grace has made me meet. In The Church Praise Book, N. Y., 1882.

3. Lord, it belongs not to my care. This is the most popular of the centos. It is in extensive use in all English-speaking countries.

4. Lord, it is not for us to care. This ranks in popularity next to No. 3.

5. Lord, may we feel no anxious care. This appeared in Hall's Mitre H. Bk., 1836, No. 248, and is found in a few modern collections.

6. Now it belongs not to my care. This also is somewhat limited in use.

When all these centos are taken into account the popularity and acceptableness of this hymn are very marked.   [J. J.]

Myddleton, William, an eminent poet and grammarian, was the third s. of Richard Myddleton, of Denbigh, an elder brother of Sir Hugh Myddleton. W. Myddleton was educated at Oxford, and served as a soldier in the armies of Elizabeth. He subsequently joined the navy. He was the means of saving the English fleet which was sent in 1591 to the Azores to intercept the Spanish galleons when Philip II. sent another fleet of ten times the English force to defeat the design.

Myddleton's first publication was Barddoniaeth ; or, the Art of Welsh Poetry, London, 1593. His chief work is an elegant version of the Psalms in the higher kind of Welsh metres, or "Cynganedd." It was finished January 24, 1595, and pub. in London by T. Salisbury in 1603. A 2nd ed. was pub. by the Rev.

W. Davies, M.A., in 1827. It was not intended for public worship, and was never used in that form.   [W. G. T.]

Mysterium mirabile, Hac luce nobis panditur. [*Passiontide.*] This is the hymn at Matins in the Office of the Most Holy Winding Sheet of our Lord Jesus Christ—an office added to the *Roman Breviary* since 1740. In the *Roman Breviary,* Bologna, 1827, *Pars Verna, Supplement,* it is assigned to Saturday after the 2nd S. in Lent, and marked as a Greater Double; the text of this hymn being given at p. 274. It is also found in later eds. of the *Roman Breviary.* Tr. as :—

This day the wondrous mystery. By E. Caswall. 1st pub. in his *Lyra Catholica,* 1849, p. 80, in 7 st. of 4 l.; and again in his *Hys. & Poems,* 1873, p. 45. It is in several collections, including the *Hymnary,* 1872, &c., but usually in an abridged form.

Other trs. are :—
1. O Miracle of mystery. *W. J. Blew,* 1852-5.
2. A wondrous mystery this day. *J. Wallace,* 1874.
                                          [J. M.]

N

N. The signature of Dr. N. Cotton in Dr. Dodd's *Christians' Magazine,* 1761.

N., in Bristol Bap. *Coll.* of Ash & Evans, 1769, i.e. James Newton.

N. N. F., in the *Church Times,* i.e. G. Moultrie, being the initials of his family motto, " Nunquam non fidelis."

N. T. P. R., in the *Cluniac Brev.,* 1686, i.e. Nicholas le Tourneaux.

Nachtenhöfer, Caspar Friedrich, s. of Caspar Nachtenhöfer, advocate at Halle, was b. at Halle, March 5, 1624. He entered the University of Leipzig in 1647, as a student of theology (M.A. 1651). He was then for a few months tutor in the house of the Chancellor August Carpzov at Coburg. In the end of 1651 he was appointed diaconus, and in 1655 pastor, at Meeder near Coburg. He was then, in 1671, called to Coburg as pastor of the Holy Cross Church, and diaconus of the St. Moritz Church. He afterwards devoted himself wholly to St. Moritz, and d. as second senior in charge Nov. 23, 1685 (*Wetzel* ii. 203; *Allg. Deutsche Biog.* xxiii. 192, &c.) He pub. a metrical history of the Passion under the title of *Erklärung des Leidens- und Sterbens-Geschichte Jesu Christi,* at Coburg in 1685. Four hyms are ascribed to him, two of which have been tr. viz. :—

i. Diess ist die Nacht, da mir erschienen. *Christmas.* This is in J. H. Hävecker's *Kirchenecho,* 1695, No. 406, in 5 st. of 6 l., marked as by *M.* C. F. N. It had previously appeared in the Coburg *G. B.,* 1683 [Coburg Gymnasium Library], and is included in the *Unv. L. S.,* 1851, No. 31. The *tr.* in C. U. is:—
This is the night wherein appearèd. A good and full *tr.* by A. T. Russell, as No. 58 in his *Ps. & Hys.,* 1851.
ii. So gehst du dann, mein Jesu, hin. *Passiontide.* This appears in the *Neu- Vollständigers Marggräfl. Brandenburgisches Gesang-Buch,* Culmbach and Bayreuth, 1668, p. 81, in 4 st. of 8 l., entitled " A beautiful hymn for Lent." It is also in the Coburg *G. B.,* 1668, *Appendix,* p. 4, entitled " Christ's Death the sinner's Life." In both books it is without name of author. *Wetzel* ii. 206, ascribes it to Nachtenhöfer, and says it was written in 1651, while he was tutor at Coburg. It

is a hymn on Christ's way to the Cross, and in the form of a dialogue between the soul and Christ. In order to complete the sense an additional stanz.i was inserted between the original iii. and iv., and this is the form in the *Unv. L. S.,* 1851, No. 781. This new st., according to Wetzel ii. 210, is by Magnus Daniel Omeis, Professor at Altdorf (b. at Nürnberg, Sept. 6, 1646; d. at Altdorf Nov. 22, 1708), and was included in the Altdorf *G. B.* of 1699. The *tr.* in C. U. is :—
So, Lord, Thou goest forth to die. A good *tr.* of st. i., v. by A. T. Russell, as No. 92 in his *Ps. & Hys.,* 1851.
                                          [J. M.]

Ναίων Ἰωνᾶς ἐν μυχοῖς. [Ἔσωσε λαὸν.]

Naked as from the earth we came. *I. Watts.* [*Submission.*] 1st pub. in his *Hys. and Spiritual S.,* 1707 (ed. 1709, Bk. i., No. v.), on Job i. 21, in 5 st. of 4 l., and entitled " Submission to afflictive Providence." In this form its use is limited. In the 1745 Draft *Translations and Paraphrases* of the Church of Scotland it was included, unaltered; but in the authorized ed. of 1781, No. iii., it was given in a recast form, in which st. i.-iii. were Watts's rewritten, and st. iv. was new. This recast, which has been in use in the Church of Scotland for more than one hundred years, is claimed for W. Cameron (p. 200, i.) in the markings by his daughter of the 1781 *Trs. & Paraphrases.*   [J. J.]

Nason, Elias, a Congregational minister, lecturer, and writer, was b. at Wrentham, Massachusetts, April 21, 1811, and was educated at Brown University, where he graduated in 1835. He was a teacher in Georgia for some time, and from 1840 to 1849 in Newburyport, Massachusetts. Subsequently he entered the Congregational ministry. He is the author of several biographies. In 1855 he pub. *Songs for the School Room;* in 1857 his *Congregational Hymn Book;* and in 1863, in conjunction with Dr. Edward Kirk, *Songs for Social and Public Worship.* His hymn, " Jesus only, when the morning " (*Jesus always*), was written at Natick, Massachusetts, about 1856, and was pub. with music by the author in the Boston *Wellspring.*   [F. M. B.]

Nato canunt omnia. [*Christmas.*] This sequence is found in the Bodleian MS., No. 775, written about the year 1000 (f. 139 b); in an 11th cent. Winchester Sequentiary, now at Corpus Christi, Cambridge (MS. No. 473); an 11th cent. MS. at Munich (Lat. 14083, f. 7), &c. In the *Sarum, Hereford* and *York Missals* it is placed in the Midnight Mass (" Missa in Gallicantu ") of Christmas Day. The printed text is also found in *Daniel* ii. p. 56, and *Kehrein,* No. 9. *Clichtovaeus* represents it as describing the joy of Christmas, announced by the angel to the shepherds, and sung by the angelic choir; and as inviting the whole human race to rejoice in God made Man.
                                          [J. M.]

Translations in C. U. :—
1. Hark, the hosts of heaven are singing. By E. H. Plumptre, made for and first pub. in the *Hymnary,* 1872. Also in a few American collections.
2. To Him God's only Son. By E. A. Dayman, also made for and first pub. in the *Hymnary,* 1872.

Translations not in C. U. :—
1. Unto the new-born Deity. *J. D. Chambers,* 1866.

2. All hosts with one accord. C. B. Pearson, in the *Sarum Missal in English*, 1868.

3. All hosts above, beneath. C. B Pearson, in *Sequences from the Sarum Missal*, 1871.   [J. J.]

Nato nobis Salvatore. *Adam of St. Victor.* [*Christmas.*] This fine sequence is given by L. Gautier in his *Oeuvres poétiques D'Adam de Saint-Victor*, 1881, p. 237, among the "Proses attributed to Adam." According to Gautier it is not found in the Graduals of St. Victor or of St. Geneviève; but is in a 13th cent. *Paris Gradual* in the Bibliothèque Nationale, Paris (No. 15,615), and other sources. He says the ascription is at least "very probable," and so prints the text in full. The text is also in *Daniel*, ii. p. 222; Neale's *Hymni Ecclesiae*, 1851, p. 64; Kehrein, No. 23; *Wrangham*, 1881, i. 21, &c. St. i., ll. 4-6, of this sequence:—

> " Nobis datus, nobis natus,
> Et nobiscum conversatus
> Lux et salus gentium,"

appear in the "Pange lingua" of St. Thomas of Aquino as "Nobis natus, nobis datus ex intacta virgine, Et in mundo conversatus, sparso verbi semine." *Tr.* as:—

Christ has come for our salvation. By E. A. Dayman, made for and pub. in the *Hymnary*, 1871.

Other trs. are :

1. Now is born our great Salvation. A. M. Morgan in *Lyra Messianica*, 1864, p. 95, and his *Gifts and Light*, 1867.

2. Come, let us celebrate the morn. D. T. Morgan. 1880.

3. Since a Saviour is born for us. D. S. Wrangham, 1881, i. p. 35.   [J. M.]

Neale, John Mason, D.D., was b. in Conduit Street, London, on Jan. 24, 1818. He inherited intellectual power on both sides: his father, the Rev. Cornelius Neale, having been Senior Wrangler, Second Chancellor's Medallist, and Fellow of St. John's College, Cambridge, and his mother being the daughter of John Mason Good, a man of considerable learning. Both father and mother are said to have been "very pronounced Evangelicals." The father died in 1823, and the boy's early training was entirely under the direction of his mother, his deep attachment for whom is shown by the fact that, not long before his death, he wrote of her as "a mother to whom I owe more than I can express." He was educated at Sherborne Grammar School, and was afterwards a private pupil, first of the Rev. William Russell, Rector of Shepperton, and then of Professor Challis. In 1836 he went up to Cambridge, where he gained a scholarship at Trinity College, and was considered the best man of his year. But he did not inherit his father's mathematical tastes, and had, in fact, the greatest antipathy to the study; and as the strange rule then prevailed that no one might aspire to Classical Honours unless his name had appeared in the Mathematical Tripos, he was forced to be content with an ordinary degree. This he took in 1840; had he been one year later, he might have taken a brilliant degree, for in 1841 the rule mentioned above was rescinded. He gained, however, what distinctions he could, winning the Members' Prize, and being elected Fellow and Tutor of Downing College; while, as a graduate, he won the Seatonian Prize no fewer than eleven times.

At Cambridge he identified himself with the Church movement, which was spreading there in a quieter, but no less real, way than in the sister University. He became one of the founders of the *Ecclesiological*, or, as it was commonly called, the *Cambridge Camden Society*, in conjunction with Mr. E. J. Boyce, his future brother-in-law, and Mr. Benjamin Webb, afterwards the well-known Vicar of St. Andrew's, Wells Street, and editor of *The Church Quarterly Review*. In 1842 he married Miss Sarah Norman Webster, the daughter of an evangelical clergyman, and in 1843 he was presented to the small incumbency of Crawley in Sussex. Ill-health, however, prevented him from being instituted to the living. His lungs were found to be badly affected; and, as the only chance of saving his life, he was obliged to go to Madeira, where he stayed until the summer of 1844. In 1846 he was presented by Lord Delawarr to the Wardenship of Sackville College, East Grinstead. This can hardly be considered as an ecclesiastical preferment, for both his predecessor and his successor were laymen. In fact the only ecclesiastical preferment that ever was offered to him was the Provostship of St. Ninian's, Perth. This was an honourable office, for the Provostship is equivalent to a Deanery in England, but it was not a lucrative one, being worth only £100 a year. He was obliged to decline it, as the climate was thought too cold for his delicate health. In the quiet retreat of East Grinstead, therefore, Dr. Neale spent the remainder of his comparatively short life, dividing his time between literary work, which all tended, directly or indirectly, to the advancement of that great Church revival of which he was so able and courageous a champion, and the unremitting care of that sisterhood of which he was the founder. He commenced a sisterhood at Rotherfield on a very small scale, in conjunction with Miss S. A. Gream, daughter of the rector of the parish; but in 1856 he transferred it to East Grinstead, where, under the name of St. Margaret's, it has attained its present proportions. Various other institutions gradually arose in connection with this Sisterhood of St. Margaret's, viz., an Orphanage, a Middle Class School for girls, and a House at Aldershot for the reformation of fallen women. The blessing which the East Grinstead Sisters have been to thousands of the sick and suffering cannot here be told. But it must be mentioned that Dr. Neale met with many difficulties, and great opposition from the outside, which, on one occasion, if not more, culminated in actual violence. In 1857 he was attending the funeral of one of the Sisters at Lewes, when a report was spread that the deceased had been decoyed into St. Margaret's Home, persuaded to leave all her money to the sisterhood, and then purposely sent to a post in which she might catch the scarlet fever of which she died. To those who knew anything of the scrupulously delicate and honourable character of Dr. Neale, such a charge would seem absurd on the face of it; but mobs are not apt to reflect, and it was very easy to excite a mob against the unpopular practices and sentiments rife at East Grinstead; and Dr. Neale and some Sisters who were attending the funeral were attacked and roughly handled. He also found opponents in higher quarters; he was inhibited by the Bishop of the Diocese for fourteen years, and the Aldershot House was obliged to be abandoned, after having done useful work for some years, in consequence of the prejudice of officials against the religious system pursued. Dr. Neale's character, however, was a happy mixture of gentleness and firmness; he had in the highest degree the courage of his convictions, which were remarkably definite and strong; while at the same time he maintained the greatest charity towards, and forbearance with, others who did not agree with him. It is not surprising, therefore, that he lived all opposition down; and that, while from first to last his relations with the community at East Grinstead were of the happiest description, he was also, after a time, spared any molestation from without. The institution grew upon his hands, and he became anxious to provide it with a permanent and fitting home. His last public act was to lay the foundation of a new convent for the Sisters on St. Margaret's Day (July 20), 1865. He lived long enough to see the building progress, but not to see it completed. In the following spring his health, which had always been delicate, completely broke down, and after five months of acute suffering he passed away on the Feast of the Transfiguration (Aug. 6), 1866, to the bitter regret of the little community at East Grinstead and of numberless friends outside that circle. One trait of his singularly lovable character must not pass unnoticed. His charity, both in the popular and in the truer Christian sense of the word, was unbounded; he was liberal and almost lavish with his money, and his liberality extended to men of all creeds and opinions; while it is pleasing to record that his relations with his ecclesiastical superiors so much improved that he dedicated his volume of *Seatonian Poems* to the bishop of the diocese. If however success in life depended upon worldly advantages, Dr. Neale's life would have to be pronounced a failure; for, as his old friend, Dr. Litledale, justly complains, "he spent nearly half his life where he died, in the position of warden of an obscure Almshouse on a salary of £27 a year." But, measured by a different standard, his short life assumes very different proportions. Not only did he win the love and gratitude of those with whom he was immediately connected, but he acquired a world-wide reputation as a writer, and he lived to see that Church revival, to promote which was the great object of his whole career, already advancing to the position which it now occupies in the land of his birth.

Dr. Neale was an industrious and voluminous writer both in prose and verse; it is of course with the latter class of his writings that this sketch is chiefly concerned; but a few words must first be said about the former.

I.—*Prose Writings.*—His first compositions were in the form of contributions to *The Ecclesiologist,* and were written during his graduate career at Cambridge. Whilst he was in Madeira he began to write his *Commentary on the Psalms,* part of which was published in 1860. It was afterwards given to the world, partly written by him and partly by his friend, Dr. Littledale, in 4 vols., in 1874, under the title of *A Commentary on the Psalms, from Primitive and Mediæval Writers.* This work has been criticised as pushing the mystical interpretation to an extravagant extent. But Dr. Neale has anticipated and disarmed such criticism by distinctly stating at the commencement that "not one single mystical interpretation throughout the present Commentary is original;" and surely such a collection has a special value as a wholesome correction of the materialistic and rationalistic tendencies of the age. His next great work, written at Sackville College, was *The History of the Holy Eastern Church.* The *General Introduction* was published in 1847; then followed part of the History itself, *The Patriarchate of Alexandria,* in 2 vols.; and after his death another fragment was published, *The History of the Patriarchate of Antioch,* to which was added, *Constantius's Memoirs of the Patriarchs of Antioch, translated from the Greek,* edited by the Rev. G. Williams, 1 vol. The whole fragment was published in 5 vols. (1847–1873). The work is spoken very highly of, and constantly referred to, by Dean Stanley in his *Lectures on the History of the Eastern Church.* Dr. Neale was naturally in strong sympathy with the struggling Episcopal Church of Scotland, and to show that sympathy he published, in 1856, *The Life and Times of Patrick Torry, D.D., Bishop of St. Andrews, &c., with an Appendix on the Scottish Liturgy.* In the same direction was his *History of the so-called Jansenist Church in Holland,* 1858. Next followed *Essays on Liturgiology and Church History, with an Appendix on Liturgical Quotations from the Isapostolical Fathers by the Rev. G. Moultrie,* 1863, a 2nd edition of which, with an interesting Preface by Dr. Littledale, was published in 1867. It would be foreign to the purpose of this article to dwell on his other prose works, such as his published sermons, preached in Sackville College Chapel, his admirable little devotional work, *Readings for the Aged,* which was a selection from these sermons; the various works he edited, such as the *Tetralogia Liturgica,* the *Sequentiæ ex Missalibus Germanicis, Anglicis, Gallicis, aliisque Medii Ævi Collectæ;* his edition of *The Primitive Liturgies of S. Mark, S. Clement, S. James, S. Chrysostom and S. Basil,* with a Preface by Dr. Littledale; his Translation of the same; his many stories from Church History, his *Voices from the East,* translated from the Russ, and his various articles contributed to the *Ecclesiologist, The Christian Remembrancer, The Morning Chronicle,* and *The Churchman's Companion.* It is time to pass on to that with which we are directly concerned.

II. *Poetical Writings.*—As a sacred poet, Dr. Neale may be regarded under two aspects, as an original writer and as a translator.

i. *Original Writer.*—Of his original poetry, the first specimen is *Hymns for Children,* pub. in 1842, which reached its 10th edition the year after his death. It consists of 33 short hymns, the first 19 for the different days of the week and different parts of the day, the last 14 for the different Church Seasons. This little volume was followed in 1844 by *Hymns for the Young*, which was intended to be a sequel to the former, its alternative title being *A Second Series of Hymns for Children*; but it is designed for an older class than the former, for young people rather than for children. The first 7 hymns are "for special occasions," as "on going to work," "leaving home," &c.; the next 8 on "Church Duties and Privileges," "Confirmation," "First Holy Communion," &c., the last 13 on "Church Festivals," which, oddly enough, include the Four Ember Seasons, Rogation Days, and the Sundays in Advent. In both these works the severe and rigid style, copied, no doubt, from the old Latin hymns, is very observable. Perhaps this has prevented them from being such popular favourites as they otherwise might have been, but they are quite free from faults into which a writer of hymns for children is apt to fall. They never degenerate into mere prose in rhyme; and in every case the purity as well as the simplicity of their diction is very remarkable. In the same year (1844) he also pub. *Songs and Ballads for Manufacturers*, which were written during his sojourn in Madeira, and the aim of which (he tells us) was "to set forth good and sound principles in metaphors which might, from their familiarity, come home to the hearts of those to whom they were addressed." They are wonderfully spirited both in matter and manner, and their freedom of style is as remarkable as the rigidity of the former works. They were followed eleven years later (1855) by a similar little work entitled *Songs and Ballads for the People*. This is of a more aggressive and controversial character than the previous ones, dealing boldly with such burning questions as "The Teetotallers," "Why don't you go to Meeting?" &c. Passing over the *Seatonian Poems*, most of which were of course written before those noticed above, we next come to the *Hymns for the Sick*, which is a fitting companion to the *Readings for the Aged*, and then to *Sequences, Hymns, and other Ecclesiastical Verses*, which was published just after the author's death (1866), and may be regarded as a sort of dying legacy to the world. In fact, the writer almost intimates as much in the preface, where he speaks of himself as "one who might soon be called to have done with earthly composition for ever." Many of the verses, indeed, were written earlier, "*forty* years ago," he says, which is evidently intended for *twenty*. The preface is dated "In the Octave of S. James, 1866," and within a fortnight, on the Feast of the Transfiguration, "the veil" (to use the touching words of his old friend, Dr. Littledale) "was withdrawn from before his eyes, and the song hushed on earth is now swelling the chorus of Paradise." Was it an accident that these verses dwell so much on death and the life beyond the grave? or did the coming event cast its shadow before? Not that there is any sadness of tone about them; quite the reverse. He contemplates death, but it is with the eye of a Christian from whom the sting of death has been removed. Most of the verses are on subjects connected with the Church Seasons, especially with what are called the "Minor Festivals:" but the first and last poems are on different subjects. The first, the "Prologue," is "in dear memory of John Keble, who departed on Maundy Thursday, 1866," and is a most touching tribute from one sacred poet to another whom he was about to follow within a few months to the "land that is very far off." The last is a poetical version of the legend of "the Seven Sleepers of Ephesus," and is, the writer thinks, "the first attempt to apply to primitive Christianity that which is, to his mind, the noblest of our measures." That measure is the hexameter, and undoubtedly Dr. Neale employed it, as he did all his measures, with great skill and effect; but it may be doubted whether the English language, in which the quantities of syllables are not so clearly defined as in Latin and Greek, is quite adapted for that measure. Throughout this volume, Dr. Neale rises to a far higher strain than he had ever reached before.

ii. *Translations.*—It is in this species of composition that Dr. Neale's success was pre-eminent, one might almost say unique. He had all the qualifications of a good translator. He was not only an excellent classical scholar in the ordinary sense of the term, but he was also positively steeped in mediaeval Latin. An anecdote given in an appreciative notice by "G. M." [Moultrie] happily illustrates this:—

Dr. Neale "was invited by Mr. Keble and the Bishop of Salisbury to assist them with their new hymnal, and for this purpose he paid a visit to Hursley Parsonage." On one occasion Mr. Keble "having to go to another room to find some papers was detained a short time. On his return Dr. Neale said, 'Why, Keble, I thought you told me that the "Christian Year" was entirely original.' 'Yes,' he answered, 'it certainly is.' 'Then how comes this?' and Dr. Neale placed before him the Latin of one of Keble's hymns. Keble professed himself utterly confounded. He protested that he had never seen this 'original,' no, not in all his life. After a few minutes Neale relieved him by owning that he had just turned it into Latin in his absence."

Again, Dr. Neale's exquisite ear for melody prevented him from spoiling the rhythm by too servile an imitation of the original; while the spiritedness which is a marked feature of all his poetry preserved that spring and dash which is so often wanting in a translation.

(i) *Latin.*—Dr. Neale's translations from the Latin include (1) *Mediæval Hymns and Sequences* (1851). He was the first to introduce to the English reader Sequences, that is, as he himself describes them, "hymns sung between the Epistle and Gospel in the Mass," or, as he explains more definitely, "hymns whose origin is to be looked for in the Alleluia of the Gradual sung between the Epistle and the Gospel." He was quite an enthusiast about this subject:—

"It is a magnificent thing," he says, "to pass along the far-stretching vista of hymns, from the sublime self-containedness of S. Ambrose to the more fervid inspiration of S. Gregory, the exquisite typology of Venantius Fortunatus, the lovely painting of S. Peter Damiani, the crystal-like simplicity of S. Notker, the scriptural calm of Godescalcus, the subjective loveliness of S. Bernard, till all culminate in the full blaze of glory which surrounds Adam of S. Victor, the greatest of them all."

Feeling thus what a noble task he had before him, it is no wonder that he spared no pains over it, or that he felt it his duty to adopt "the exact measure and rhyme of the original, at whatever inconvenience and cramping." That he succeeded in his difficult work, the verdict of the public has sufficiently proved. Of all the translations in the English language no one has ever been so popular as that of the *Hora Novissima*, in this volume, afterwards (1858) published separately, under the title of the *Rhythm of Bernard de Morlaix, Monk of Cluny*. Some original hymns may be as well known as "Jerusalem the Golden," "For thee, O dear, dear country," or "Brief life is here our portion," but it would be hard to find any translations which come near them for extensive use. A second edition of the *Mediæval Hymns*, much improved, came out in 1863, and a third, "with very numerous additions and corrections," in 1867.

(2.) We next come to the *Hymnal Noted*, in which 94 out of the 105 hymns are the work of Dr. Neale. These are all translations from the Latin. The first part appeared in 1852, the second in 1854. Dr. Neale has himself given us an interesting account of his connection with this work :—

"Some," he writes, "of the happiest and most instructive hours of my life were spent in the Sub-Committee of the Ecclesiological Society, appointed for the purpose of bringing out the Second Part of the *Hymnal Noted*. It was my business to lay before them the translations I had prepared, and their's to correct. The study which this required drew out the beauties of the original in a way which nothing else could have done, and the friendly collisions of various minds elicited ideas which a single translator would in all probability have missed." Preface, *Med. Hys.*

(3.) The last volume of translations from the Latin published by Dr. Neale appeared in 1865, under the title of *Hymns, chiefly Mediæval, on the Joys and Glories of Paradise*. It was intended to be a companion volume to the *Rhythm of Bernard of Cluny*. In this work the writer gives the general reader an opportunity of comparing the translation with the original by printing the two together in parallel pages. Two specimens may be given :—

Nec Quisquam.

Eye hath never seen the glory,	Nec quisquam oculis vidit, Neque ullis sensibus,
Ear hath never heard the song,	Nec quis cogitare scivit De mundo viventibus
Heart of man can never image	Quam bona Deus promisit Hic se diligentibus.
What good things to them belong	
Who have loved the Lord of beauty	
While they dwell in this world's throng.	

Quisquis valet numerare.

If there be that skills to reckon	Quisquis valet numerare Beatorum numerum,
All the number of the Blest,	Horum poterit pensare Sempiternum gaudium,
He, perchance, can weigh the gladness	Quod meruerunt intrare Mundi post exilium.
Of the everlasting Rest	
Which, their earthly exile finished,	
They by merit have possest.	

These two stanzas have been chosen because they illustrate, the first the freer, the second the more literal method of translation. The second is especially noteworthy. It will be seen that, while the English runs quite smoothly and might easily be mistaken for a

stanza in an original hymn, there is not one single idea, or even one single turn of phrase in the original, which is not faithfully reproduced in the translation ; and the same is observable in many of his other translations. Dr. Neale included in this work two hymns (XVIII. and XIX.) which have a biographical interest. "They are," he says, "two choruses of a Tragedy, written by my father, on the Greek Model, and founded on the death of Saul," and they show that, if he did not inherit mathematical, he may have inherited poetical, tastes from his father.

Before quitting the subject of Dr. Neale's translations from the Latin, it is only fair to notice that while they have been almost universally accepted by the English Church, and some of them adopted by dissenting congregations, they called down upon the translator a storm of indignation from an opposite quarter. The Roman Catholics accused him of deliberate deception because he took no pains to point out that he had either softened down or entirely ignored the Roman doctrines in those hymns. So far, they said, as the originals were concerned, these translations were deliberate misrepresentations. As however the translations were intended for the use of the Anglican Church, it was only to be expected that Neale should omit such hymns or portions of hymns as would be at variance with her doctrines and discipline.

(ii.) *Greek.*—Dr. Neale conferred even a greater boon upon the lovers of hymnology than by his translations from the Latin, when he published, in 1862, his *Hymns of the Eastern Church*. In his translations from the Latin he did what others had done before; but in his translations from the Greek he was opening entirely new ground. "It is," he says in his preface to the first edition, "a most remarkable fact, and one which shows how very little interest has been hitherto felt in the Eastern Church, that these are literally, I believe, the only English versions of any part of the treasures of Oriental Hymnology." As early as 1853 he had printed a few of his versions in *The Ecclesiastic*, but it was not till the appearance of the complete volume that the interest of the general public was awakened in them. Then they became wonderfully popular. His *trs.* "Christian, dost thou see them?" "The day is past and over," "'Tis the day of Resurrection," and his Greek-inspired "Art thou weary," and "O happy band of pilgrims," are almost as great favourites as "Jerusalem the golden," and the first in his *Hys. of the E. Church*, "Fierce was the wild billow," deserves to be. Dr. Neale had a far more difficult task before him when he undertook these Greek hymns than he had with the Latin, and he appeals to the reader "not to forget the immense difficulty of an attempt so perfectly new as the present, when I have had no predecessors and therefore could have no master." That difficulty in comparison with the Latin cannot be better stated than in his own words :—

"Though the superior terseness and brevity of the Latin hymns renders a translation which shall represent those qualities a work of great labour, yet still the versifier has the help of the same metre ; his version may be line for line ; and there is a great analogy between the collects and the hymns, most helpful to the translator. Above all, we have examples enough of former translation by which we may take pattern. But in attempting a Greek canon, from the fact of its being in prose (metrical hymns are unknown) one is all at sea. What measure shall we employ? Why this more than that? Might we attempt the rhythmical prose of the original, and design it to be chanted? Again, the great length of the canons renders them unsuitable for our churches as *wholes*. Is it better simply to form centos of the more beautiful passages? or can separate odes, each necessarily imperfect, be employed as separate hymns? . . . My own belief is, that the best way to employ Greek hymnology for the uses of the English Church would be by centos."

That, in spite of these difficulties, Dr. Neale succeeded, is obvious. His Greek hymns are, indeed, adaptations rather than translations; but, besides their intrinsic beauty, they at any rate give some idea of what the Greek hymn-writers were. In this case, as in his translations from the Latin, he omitted what he held was not good from his Anglican point of view, e.g., the Doxologies to the B. V. M.

One point strikes us as very remarkable in these hymns, and indeed in all Dr. Neale's poetry, viz., its thorough manliness of tone. Considering what his surroundings were, one might have expected a feminine tone in his writings. Dr. Littledale, in his most vivid and interesting sketch of Dr. Neale's life, to which the present writer is largely indebted, has remarked the same with regard to his teaching: "Instead of committing the grave error of feminising his sermons and counsels [at St. Margaret's] because he had only women to deal with, he aimed at showing them the masculine side of Christianity also, to teach them its strength as well as its beauty."

In conclusion, it may be observed that no one had a higher opinion of the value of Dr. Neale's labours in the field of ancient and mediaeval hymnology than the one man whose competency to speak with authority on such a point Dr. Neale himself would assuredly have rated above that of all others. Over and over again Dr. Neale pays a tribute to the services rendered by Archbishop Trench in this domain; and the present sketch cannot more fitly close than with the testimony which Archbishop Trench has given of his sense of the services rendered by Dr. Neale. The last words of his preface to his *Sacred Latin Poetry* (ed. 1864) are :—" I will only, therefore, mention that by patient researches in almost all European lands, he [Dr. Neale] has brought to light a multitude of hymns unknown before: in a treatise on sequences, properly so-called, has for the first time explained their essential character; while to him the English reader owes versions of some of the best hymns, such as often successfully overcome the almost insuperable difficulties which many among them present to the translator."   [J. H. O.]

Dr. Neale's original hymns and translations appeared in the following works, most of which are referred to in the preceding article, and all of which are grouped together here to facilitate reference :—

(1) *Hymns for Children. Intended chiefly for Village Schools.* Lond., Masters, 1842. (2) *Hymns for the Sick.* Lond., Masters, 1843, improved ed. 1849. (3) *Hymns for the Young. A Second Series of Hymns for Children.* Lond., Masters, 1844. (4) *Songs and*

Ballads for Manufacturers. Lond., Masters, 1844. (5) *Hymns for Children. A Third Series.* Lond., Masters, 1846. (6) *Mediaeval Hymns and Sequences.* Lond., Masters, 1851 ; 2nd ed. 1861 ; 3rd. ed. 1863. (7) *Hymnal Noted.* Lond., Masters & Novello, 1852: enlarged 1854. Several of the translations were by other hands. Musical editions edited by the Rev. T. Helmore. It is from this work that a large number of Dr. Neale's trs. from the Latin are taken. (8) *Carols for Christmas and Eastertide.* 1853. (9) *Songs and Ballads for the People.* 1855. (10) *The Rhythm of Bernard de Morlaix, Monk of Cluny, on the Celestial Country.* Lond., Hayes, 1st ed. 1858 : 3rd ed., with revision of text, 1861. It contains both the Latin and the English translation. (11) *Hymns of The Eastern Church, Translated with Notes and an Introduction.* Lond., Hayes, 1862 : 2nd ed. 1862 : 3rd ed. 1866 : 4th ed., with Music and additional notes, edited by The Very Rev. S. G. Hatherly, Mus. B., Archpriest of the Patriarchal Œcumenical Throne. Lond., Hayes, 1882. Several of these translations and notes appeared in *The Ecclesiastic and Theologian* in 1853. (12) *Hymns, Chiefly Mediaeval, on the Joys and Glories of Paradise.* Lond., Hayes, 1865. This work contains notes on the hymns, and the Latin texts of the older amongst them. (13) *Original Sequences, Hymns, and other Ecclesiastical Verses,* Lond., Hayes, 1866. This collection of Original verse was published posthumously by Dr. Littledale.

In addition to these works Dr. Neale published collections of Latin verse as :—

(1.) *Hymni Ecclesiae e Breviariis quibusdam et Missalibus Gallicanis, Germanis, Hispanis, Lusitanis, desumpti.* Oxford & Lond. J. H. Parker, 1851 : and (2) *Sequentiae e Missalibus Germanicis, Anglicis, Gallicis, aliisque Medii Aevi collectae.* Oxford & Lond. J. H. Parker, 1852.

A few of his translations appeared from time to time in *The Ecclesiastic ;* and a few of his original hymns in *The Christian Remembrancer.* In the collection compiled for use at St. Margaret's, East Grinstead, *S. Margaret's Hymnal, Printed Privately for the use of the Community only,* 1875, there are several of his hymns not traceable elsewhere.

Most of Dr. Neale's translations are annotated elsewhere in this Dictionary under their respective original first lines, as are also several of his original compositions. Those original hymns in C. U. which remain to be noted are :—

i. From *Hymns for Children,* 1842.

1. No more sadness now, nor fasting. *Christmas.*
2. O Thou, Who through this holy week. *Passiontide.*
3. The day, O Lord, is spent. *Evening.*
4. The grass so green, the trees so tall. *Morning of the Third Day.*
5. Thou art gone up, O Lord, on high. *Evening.*
6. Thou, Who camest from above. *Whitsuntide.*
7. With Thee, O Lord, begins the year. *Circumcision, or, the New Year.*

ii. From *Hymns for the Sick,* 1843.

8. By no new path untried before. *Support in Sickness.*
9. Count not, the Lord's Apostle saith. *Communion of the Sick.*
10. Lord, if he sleepeth, he shall sure do well. *Watching.*
11. O Thou, Who rising long before the day. *In a sleepless Night.*
12. The Lord hath given, the Lord hath taken away. *Death and Burial.*
13. There is a stream, whose waters rise. *In dangerous Sickness or Fever.*
14. They slumber not nor sleep. *Guardian Angels.*
15. Thy servants militant below. *In Affliction.*

iii. From *Hymns for the Young,* 2nd series, 1844.

16. Lord Jesus, Who shalt come with power. *Ember Week in Advent.*
17. O God, in danger and · distress. *In time of Trouble.*
18. O God, we raise our hearts to Thee. *Ember-Week in Advent.* From this, "O Lord, we come before Thee now," is taken.

19. O God, Who lovest to abide. *Dedication of a Church.*
20. O our Father, hear us now. *Rogation.* The first of three hymns on *The Lord's Prayer.*
21. O Saviour, Who hast call'd away. *Death of a Minister.*
22. O Thou, Who lov'st to send relief. *In Sickness.*
23. O Thou, Who once didst bless the ground. *Ember-Week in September.*
24. O Thou, Who, when Thou hadst begun. *On going to Work.*
25. Still, O Lord of hosts, we share. *Rogation.* The second of his hymns on *The Lord's Prayer.*
26. Strangers and pilgrims here below.. *On entering a new Dwelling to reside there.*
27. They whose course on earth is o'er. *Communion of Saints.* From this, "Those whom many a land divides," is taken.
28. Till its holy hours are past. *Rogation.* The third of his hymns on *The Lord's Prayer.*

iv. *Songs and Ballads for Manufacturers,* 1844.

29. Work is over ; God must speed it. *Evening.*

v. *Hymns for Children,* 3rd series, 1846.

30. Before Thy Face, O God of old. *St. John the Baptist.*
31. By pain, and weariness, and doubt. *St. Stephen.*
32. First of the twelvefold band that trod. *St. James.*
33. Four streams through happy Eden flow'd. *St. Mark.*
34. Is there one who sets his face. *St. Bartholomew.* From this "He, for man who suffered woe," is taken.
35. Not a single sight we view. *St. Matthias.*
36. O Great Physician of the soul. *St. Luke.*
37. O Heavenly Wisdom, hear our cry. *Christmas.* "O Sapientia."
38. O Key of David, hailed by those. *Christmas.* "O Clavis David."
39. O Root of Jesse, Thou on Whom. *Christmas.* "O Radix Jesse."
40. O Thou, on Whom the nations [Gentiles] wait. *Christmas.* "O Rex Gentium."
41. O Thou, Who camest down of old [to call]. *Christmas.* "O Adonai."
42. O Thou, Whose Name is God with us. *Christmas.* "O Emmanuel."
43. O Very God of Very God. *Christmas.* "O Oriens."
44. Saints of God, whom faith united. *SS. Simon and Jude.*
45. Since the time that first we came. *St. Andrew.* From this, "Every bird that upward springs," is taken.
46. That love is mighty love indeed. *St. Barnabas.*
47. We cannot plead, as others may. *St. Matthew.*
48. We have not seen, we cannot see. *St. Thomas.*
49. Would we go when life is o'er ? *St. Peter.*

v. *Carols for Christmas and Eastertide,* 1853.

50. Gabriel's message does away. *Christmas.*
51. Joy and gladness be to king and peasant. *Christmas.*
52. Joy to thee, joy to thee, Day of our victory. *Easter.*
53. Sing Alleluia, all ye lands. *Easter.*
54. The world itself keeps Easter Day. *Easter.* From this "There stood three Marys by the tomb," is taken.
55. With Christ we share a mystic grave. *Easter or Holy Baptism.*

vi. *From Sequences, Hymns, &c.,* 1866.

56. Can it, Master, can it be ? *Maundy Thursday.*
57. Need it is we raise our eyes. *All Saints.*
58. Prostrate fell the Lord of all things. *Maundy Thursday.*
59. Rear the column, high and stately. *All Saints.*
60. The Paschal moonlight almost past. *Easter.*
61. Though the Octave-rainbow sometimes. *Low Sunday.*
62. When the earth was full of darkness. *St. Margaret.*
63. Young and old must raise the lay. *Christmas Carol.*

vi. *From the St. Margaret's Hymnal,* 1875.

64. O gracious God, Who bid'st me now. *On Leaving Home.*
65. Thou Who came to save Thy people. *For a School.*
66. Thy praise the holy Infants shewed. *Holy Innocents.*

These 66 hymns now in C.U. by no means represent Dr. Neale's position in modern hymnody. Those tabulated in the **Index of Authors and Translators** must be added thereto. Even then, although the total is very large, it but feebly represents and emphasises the enormous influence which Dr. Neale has exercised over modern hymnody.   [J. J.]

Neander, Joachim, was b. at Bremen, in 1650, as the eldest child of the marriage of Johann Joachim Neander and Catharina Knipping, which took place on Sept. 18, 1649, the father being then master of the Third Form in the Paedagogium at Bremen. The family name was originally Neumann (=Newman) or Niemann, but the grandfather of the poet * had assumed the Greek form of the name, i.e. *Neander.* After passing through the Paedagogium he entered himself as a student at the Gymnasium illustre (Academic Gymnasium) of Bremen in Oct. 1666. German student life in the 17th cent. was anything but refined, and Neander seems to have been as riotous and as fond of questionable pleasures as most of his fellows. In July 1670, Theodore Under-Eyck came to Bremen as pastor of St. Martin's Church, with the reputation of a Pietist and holder of conventicles. Not long after Neander, with two like-minded comrades, went to service there one Sunday, in order to criticise and find matter of amusement. But the earnest words of Under-Eyck touched his heart ; and this, with his subsequent conversations with Under-Eyck, proved the turning-point of his spiritual life. In the spring of 1671 he became tutor to five young men, mostly, if not all, sons of wealthy merchants at Frankfurt-am-Main, and accompanied them to the University of Heidelberg, where they seem to have remained till the autumn of 1673, and where Neander learned to know and love the beauties of Nature. The winter of 1673-74 he spent at Frankfurt with the friends of his pupils, and here he became acquainted with P. J. Spener (q.v.) and J. J. Schütz (q.v.) In the spring of 1674 he was appointed Rector of the Latin school at Düsseldorf (see further below). Finally, in 1679, he was invited to Bremen as unordained assistant to Under - Eyck at St. Martin's Church, and began his duties about the middle of July. The post was not inviting, and was regarded merely as a stepping stone to further preferment, the remuneration being a free house and 40 thalers a-year, and the Sunday duty being a service with sermon at the extraordinary hour of 5 A.M. Had he lived, Under-Eyck would doubtless have done his best to get him appointed to St. Stephen's Church, the pastorate of which became vacant in Sept., 1680. But meantime Neander himself fell into a decline, and d. at Bremen May 31, 1680 (*Joachim Neander, sein Leben und seine Lieder.* With a Portrait. By J. F. Iken, Bremen 1880 ; *Allg. Deutsche Biog.* xxiii. 327, &c.)

Neander was the first important hymn-writer of the German Reformed Church since the

[* Joachim Neander, pastor at Lochem, near Zütphen in Holland, where he d. in 1651. His father (d. 1627), and grandfather (d. 1556), were both named Joachim Neander, and were both pastors.]

times of Blaurer and Zwick. His hymns appear to have been written mostly at Düsseldorf, after his lips had been sealed to any but official work. The true history of his unfortunate conflict has now been established from the original documents, and may be summarized thus.

The school at Düsseldorf was entirely under the control of the minister and elders of the Reformed Church there. The minister from about July, 1673, to about May, 1677, was Sylvester Lürsen (a native of Bremen, and only a few years older than Neander), a man of ability and earnestness, but jealous, and, in later times at least, quarrelsome. With him Neander at first worked harmoniously, frequently preaching in the church, assisting in the visitation of the sick, &c. But he soon introduced practices which inevitably brought on a conflict. He began to hold prayer-meetings of his own, without informing or consulting minister or elders; he began to absent himself from Holy Communion, on the ground that he could not conscientiously communicate along with the unconverted, and also persuaded others to follow this example; and became less regular in his attendance at the ordinary services of the Church. Besides these causes of offence he drew out a new time-table for the school, made alterations on the school buildings, held examinations and appointed holidays without consulting any one. The result of all this was a Visitation of the school on Nov. 29, 1676, and then his suspension from school and pulpit on Feb. 3, 1677. On Feb. 17 he signed a full and definite declaration by which "without mental reservations" he bound himself not to repeat any of the acts complained of; and thereupon was permitted to resume his duties as rector but not as assistant minister. The suspension thus lasted only 14 days, and his salary was never actually stopped. The statements that he was banished from Düsseldorf, and that he lived for months in a cave in the Neanderthal near Mettmann are therefore without foundation. Still his having had to sign such a document was a humiliation which he must have felt keenly, and when, after Lürsen's departure, the second master of the Latin school was appointed permanent assistant pastor, this feeling would be renewed.

Neander thus thrown back on himself, found consolation in communion with God and Nature, and in the composition of his hymns. Many were without doubt inspired by the scenery of the Neanderthal (a lovely valley with high rocky sides, between which flows the little river Düssel. See No. ii. below); and the tradition is probable enough that some of them were composed in a cave there. A number were circulated among his friends at Düsseldorf in MS., but they were first collected and pub. after his removal to Bremen, and appeared as:—

A und Ω. *Joachimi Neandri Glaub- und Liebesübung: — auffgemuntert durch einfältige Bundes Lieder und Danck-Psalmen,* Bremen, Hermann Brauer, 1680; 2nd ed. Bremen, 1683; 3rd ed. Bremen, 1687; 4th ed. Frankfurt, 1689. These editions contain 57 hymns. In the 5th ed., Frankfurt and Leipzig, 1691, edited by G. C. Strattner, eight hymns were added as being also by Neander. [The whole of these eds. are in the Royal Library, Berlin. The so-called 3rd. ed. at Wesel, 1686, also found in Berlin, was evidently pirated.] Other editions rapidly followed till we find the complete set (i.e. 57 or 58) formally incorporated as part of a hymn-book, e.g. in the Marburg Reformed *G. B.,* 1722, where the first part consists of Lobwasser's *Psalter,* the second of Neander's *Bundeslieder,* and the third of other hymns. Neander's *Bundeslieder* also form a division of the Lemgo Reformed *G. B.,* 1722; and of a favourite book used in the meetings conducted by G. Tersteegen, which in the 5th ed., Solingen, 1760, has the title *Gott-geheiligtes Harfen-Spiel der Kinder Zion; bestehend in Joachimi Neandri sämtlichen Bundes-Liedern, &c.* In this way, especially in the district near Düsseldorf and on the Ruhr, Neander's name was honoured and beloved long after it had passed out of memory at Bremen.

Many of Neander's hymns were speedily received into the Lutheran hymn-books, and are still in universal use. The finest are the jubilant hymns of Praise and Thanksgiving, such as his "Lobe den Herren" (p. 683, i.),

and those setting forth the Majesty of God in His works of beauty and wonder in Nature, such as his "Himmel, Erde" (p. 525, ii.), and "Unbegreiflich Gut" (see No. ii. below); while some of his hymns of Penitence, such as his "Sieh hier bin ich, Ehrenkönig" (q.v.), are also very beautiful. Many are of a decidedly subjective cast, but for this the circumstances of their origin, and the fact that the author did not expect them to be used in public worship, will sufficiently account. Here and there there are doubtless harshnesses, and occasionally imagery which is rather jarring; and naturally enough the characteristic expressions and points of view of German 17th cent. Pietism and of the "Covenant Theology" are easily enough detected. But the glow and sweetness of his better hymns, their firm faith, originality, Scripturalness, variety and mastery of rhythmical forms, and genuine lyric character fully entitle them to the high place they hold.

Of the melodies in the original ed. of 1680 there are 19 by Neander himself, the best known being those to Nos. viii. and xi. below.

The hymns by Neander which have passed into English, and have not already been referred to, are:—

Hymns in English C. U. :

i. **Meine Hoffnung stehet feste.** *Thanksgiving.* Founded on 1 Tim. vi. 17. 1680 as above, p. 115, in 5 st. of 7 l., entitled "Grace after meat." In the *Unv. L. S.,* 1851, No. 712. *Tr.* as:—

All my hope is grounded surely. A full and good *tr.* by Miss Winkworth, as No. 8 in her *C. B. for England,* 1863.

Another *tr.* is: "All my Hope is fix'd and grounded." By *J. C. Jacobi,* 1720, p. 17 (1722, p. 40), repeated in his ed., 1732, p. 64, altered and beginning, "All my Hope is firmly grounded."

ii. **Unbegreiflich Gut,.wahrer Gott alleine.** *Summer.* According to tradition this was written in the summer of 1677, in a cave in the Neanderthal near Düsseldorf, while Neander was in enforced absence from his school duties (*Koch,* vi. 20). It is founded on Ps. civ. 24. 1680, p. 165, in 12 st. of 6 lines, and entitled, "The Joys of Summer and Autumn in Field and Forest." The following note shows that the "Feeling for Nature" is not entirely modern.

"It is also a travelling hymn in summer or autumn for those who, on their way to Frankfurt on the Main, go up and down the river Rhine, where between Cologne and Mainz, mountains, cliffs, brooks and rocks are to be beheld with particular wonder; also in the district of Berg in the rocky region [the 'Gestein' now called the Neanderthal], not far from Düsseldorf."

The hymn is in Knapp's *Ev. L. S.,* 1850, No. 2163 (1865, No. 2231), omitting st. x. *Tr.* as:—

O Thou true God alone. A very good *tr.,* omitting st. x., by Miss Winkworth, as her *Christian Singers,* 1869, p. 286. Her *trs.* of st. i., iii.–v. altered in metre, and beginning "Thou true God alone," are No. 53 in M. W. Stryker's *Christian Chorals,* 1885.

Hymns not in English C. U. :—

iii. **Auf, auf, mein Geist, erhebe dich zum Himmel.** *Holy Communion.* Founded on Ps. xxiii. 6. 1860, as above, p. 27, in 5 st., entitled, "The soul strengthened and refreshed. After the reception of the Holy Communion." In Porst's *G. B.,* ed. 1855, No. 218. In the Moravian London *G. B.,* 1753, No. 697, it begins, "Den Himmels-Vorschmack hab' ich auf der Erde," and in the *Brüder G. B.,* 1778, No. 1178, it was further recast (by C. Gregor?) and altered to "hab' ich *schon hinieden.*"

Tr. as, "Heav'n's foretaste I may here already have." By F. W. Foster & J. Miller, as No. 596, in the *Moravian H. Bk.*, 1789. In the 1801 ed. (1849, No. 1003) it begins, "Since Jesus dy'd, my guilty soul to save."

iv. Der Tag ist hin, mein Jesu, bei mir bleibe. *Evening.* Founded on St. Luke xxiv. 29. 1680, p. 15, in 6 st., entitled, "The Christian returning thanks at eventide." In the *Unv. L. S.*, 1851, No. 512. The *trs.* are: (1) "The Day is gone, come Jesu my Protector." In the *Supp. to German Psalmody*, ed. 1765, p. 72. (2) "The day is past, Thou Saviour dear, still dwell my breast within." By *H. J. Buckoll*, 1842, p. 82. (3) "The day is gone, abide with me to-night." By *E. Massie*, 1867, p. 192. (4) "The day is gone, abide with me, O Jesus." By R. Massie, in the *Day of Rest*, 1877.

v. Grosser Prophete, mein Herze begehret. *Love to Christ.* Founded on 1 Cor. xvi. 22. 1680, p. 191, in 4 st. *Tr.* as "Heavenly Prophet, my Heart is desiring." By *J. C. Jacobi*, 1720, p. 40.

vi. Jehovah ist mein Licht und Gnadensonne. *God's Perfections.* Founded on 1 John i. 7. 1680, p. 19, in 4 st., entitled, "Walking in the Light." *Tr.* as, "Jehovah is my light, salvation showing." By *Dr. H. Mills*, 1845 (1856, p. 6).

vii. O allerhöchster Menschenhüter. *Morning.* A hymn of praise to our Almighty Preserver. 1680, p. 11, in 6 st., founded on Ps. lix. 16; and entitled, "The Christian singing at Morning." *Tr.* as, "O Thou Most Highest! Guardian of mankind." By *Miss Winkworth*, 1858, p. 72.

viii. Unser Herrscher, unser König. *Thanksgiving.* Founded on Acts viii. 2. 1680, p. 147, in 6 st., entitled, "The glorious Jehovah." In the *Unv. L. S.*, 1851, No. 344. The well-known melody (in the S. P. C. K. *Church Hys.* called *Munich*) is also by Neander, and appeared along with the hymn. *Tr.* as, "Sovereign Ruler, King victorious," in the *British Herald*, Dec., 1865, p. 185, and Reid's *Praise Bk.*, 1872.

ix. Wie fleucht dahin der Menschenzeit. *For the Dying.* A powerful hymn on the vanity of the earthly, founded on Ps. xc. 12. 1680, p. 174, in 7 st., entitled, "He that counts his days." In the *Unv. L. S.*, 1851, No. 845. The *trs.* are: (1) "This life is like a flying dream" (beginning with st. ii. "Das Leben ist gleich wie ein Traum"). By Mrs. Findlater, in *H. L. L.*, 1858, p. 24 (1884, p. 146). (2) "Though hastening onward to the grave." By *E. Massie*, 1867, p. 36.

x. Wo soll ich hin? wer helfet mir? *Lent.* Founded on Romans vii. 24. 1680, p. 51, in 5 st. entitled "The distressed one longing for Redemption." In the *Unv. L. S.*, 1851, No. 398. The *trs.* are: (1) "For help, O whither shall I flee." By *Dr. H. Mills*, 1845 (1856, p. 146). (2) "How shall I get there? who will aid?" By *Miss Warner*, 1858, p. 52.

xi. Wunderbarer König. *Thanksgiving.* Founded on Ps. cl. 6. 1680, p. 159, in 4 st., entitled, "Inciting oneself to the Praise of God." In the *Unv. L. S.*, 1851, No. 787. The melody, a very fine one (called by Mr. Mercer *Groningen*), is also by Neander, and appeared along with the hymn. The *trs.* are: (1) "Wonderful Creator." By *J. C. Jacobi*, 1722, p. 88. (2) "Wonderful and blessed." By J. D. Burns in his *Memoir and Remains*, 1869, p. 230. (3) "Wondrous King Almighty." By *N. L. Frothingham*, 1870, p. 266.   [J. M.]

Nearer, my God, to Thee, Hear Thou my prayer. *Bp. W. W. How.* [*Nearness to God desired.*] This was written for the 1864 ed. of Morrell & How's *Ps. & Hys.*, where it was given as No. 154, a somewhat slightly different version of the same having appeared in *Kennedy* (1863) a short time before, as:—

"Nearer to Thee, my God,
    Still would I rise."

The 1864 text has been repeated in several collections in G. Britain and America. In the S. P. C. K. *Church Hys.*, 1871, it begins:—

"Nearer, O God, to Thee! Hear Thou my prayer,"

and is accompanied in the folio ed., 1881, with the note:—

"A paraphrase of Mrs. Adams's hymn, expressing more definitely Christian faith, and better adapted for congregational worship."

Although in somewhat extensive use, it is the least musical of Bp. How's hymns. [J. J.]

Nearer, my God, to Thee, Nearer to Thee! *Sarah Adams, née Flower.* [*Nearness to God desired.*] Contributed to W. J. Fox's *Hymns and Anthems*, 1841, No. lxxxv., as follows:—

"Nearer, my God, to thee,
    Nearer to thee!
E'en though it be a cross
    That raiseth me:
Still all my song would be,
    Nearer, my God, to thee—
    Nearer to thee!

"Though like the wanderer,
    The sun gone down,
Darkness be over me,
    My rest a stone;
Yet in my dreams I'd be,
    Nearer, my God, to thee—
    Nearer to thee.

"There let the way appear,
    Steps unto heaven;
All that thou send'st to me
    In mercy given:
Angels to beckon me
    Nearer, my God, to thee—
    Nearer to thee!

"Then with my waking thoughts,
    Bright with thy praise,
Out of my stony griefs,
    Bethel I'll raise:
So by my woes to be
    Nearer, my God, to thee—
    Nearer to thee!

"Or if on joyful wing
    Cleaving the sky,
Sun, moon, and stars forgot,
    Upwards I fly:
Still all my song shall be,
    Nearer, my God, to thee—
    Nearer to thee!"

The use of this hymn, generally with very slight alterations, but often with the omission of the last stanza, is very considerable in all English-speaking countries. It has also been translated into many European and other languages.

This hymn is a curious illustration of the colouring which is given to a hymn by the antecedents of its author. In the case of Addison's "When all Thy mercies, O my God," and many other hymns of a like kind, no attempt has ever been made to alter its distinctive character as a hymn to the FATHER alone. With Mrs. Adams, being an Unitarian, the treatment is changed, notwithstanding the redeeming lines,

"E'en though it be a *Cross*
    That raiseth me:"

in the opening stanza. The following alterations and additions have been made to bring the hymn more in harmony with the views of the editors by whom it has been adopted.

1. The first change with which we are acquainted was the addition of the following stanza:—

"Christ alone beareth me
    Where Thou dost shine;
Joint heir He maketh me
    Of the Divine:
In Christ my soul shall be,
    Nearest, my God, to Thee—
    Nearest to Thee!"

This is by the Rev. A. T. Russell, and was given in his *Ps. & Hys.*, 1851, from whence it passed into the Bap. *Ps. & Hys.*, 1858, *Snepp*, 1872, and others.

2. The second change and addition are:—

"Though by Thy bitter Cross
    We raised be."

and the doxology :—

> " Glory, O God, to Thee;
> Glory to Thee,
> Almighty Trinity
> In Unity
> Glorious Mystery,
> Through all Eternity
> Glory to Thee ! "

This addition is given in Skinner's *Daily Service Hymnal*, 1864, No. 280.

3. Another change in the same direction is :—

> " And when on joyful wing,
> Cleaving the sky,
> *Unto the Light of Lights*,
> Upward I fly." (St. v. ll. 1–4.)

by Dr. Monsell in his *Parish Hymnal*, 1873.

4. In *Kennedy*, 1863, the following is substituted for st. v. :—

> " And when my Lord again
> Glorious shall come,
> Mine be a dwelling-place
> In Thy bright home,
> There evermore to be
> Nearer to Thee, my God !
> Nearer to Thee ! "

This same stanza is repeated in the *Hys. for the Church Catholic*, 1882, with line 6 as " Nearer my God ! to Thee."

5. In Bp. Bickersteth's note to this hymn in his annotated ed. of the *H. Comp.*, 1876, No. 312, he says:—

" The Editor shrunk from appending a closing verse of his own to a hymn so generally esteemed complete as this, or he would have suggested the following :—

> " There in my Father's home,
> Safe and at rest,
> There in my Saviour's love
> Perfectly blest ;
> Age after age to be
> Nearer, my God to Thee,
> Nearer to Thee."

In addition to these alterations and changes, it has been entirely rewritten, by Bp. How, as " Nearer, my God to Thee, Hear Thou my prayer." See above. G. J. Stevenson's note in his *Meth. H. Bk. Notes*, 1883, p. 497, is worthy of attention as dealing with the spiritual uses of this hymn.   [J. J]

Nec quisquam oculis vidit. [*Eternal Life.*] This is from a poem 1st pub. by *Mone*, Nos. 303–305, from a 15th cent. ms. at Karlsruhe (see **Jerusalem luminosa, p. 579,** ii.). It is the third and concluding part, consists of 84 lines, and is entitled, " On the glory of the Heavenly Jerusalem as concerning the endowments of the glorified soul." In Pastor O. A. Spitzen's *Nalezing op mijn Thomas à Kempis*, Utrecht, 1881, p. 72, it is given as by Thomas, and as a second part; the first part beginning " Jerusalem luminosa " [in Spitzen *gloriosa*.] (see p. **579,** ii.). Both parts are cited as in a ms. *circa* 1480 which belonged to the Brethren of the Common Life at Zwolle, and is now in the library of the Emmanuelshuizen there. The only *tr.* is " Eye hath never seen the glory," by J. M. Neale, in his *Hys., chiefly Mediæval, on the Joys and Glories of Paradise*, 1865, p. 62 ; omitting ll. 13–24, 43–66, 79–84.   [J. M.]

Needham, John, was the son of John Needham, Baptist Minister, of Hitchin, Herts, but the date of his birth is unknown. He would doubtless be educated by his father, who was a tutor and in repute as a learned man. In 1750 Needham became co-pastor with John Beddome at the Baptist meeting-house in the Pithay, Bristol ; but, two years later, Beddome

having retired through age, a violent controversy arose in the Church with regard to a continuance of the plan of co-pastorship. As the result, Needham and a number of his friends removed to a Baptist meeting-house in Callowhill Street, where a Mr. Foot was pastor. For a time the two societies used the same building at different hours, but in 1755 they were united, with Mr. Needham and Mr. Foot as co-pastors. It is known that up to 1774 this arrangement continued, and it is also known that in 1787, both Mr. Needham and Mr. Foot having died, the Callowhill Street Church became extinct, but which of the two pastors was the survivor is not known. The date of Needham's death is unknown. It was probably *circa* 1786. In 1768 he pub. *Hymns Devotional and Moral on various Subjects, collected chiefly from the Holy Scriptures*, &c., Bristol, S. Farley, 1768. These hymns are 263 in all, and whilst none of them possess great excellence, yet several are of a pleasing and useful character. During the past 120 years several have appeared in Nonconformist hymnbooks, and specially in those of the Baptists. Of these the following are still in C. U. :—

1. Ashamed of Christ ! my soul disdains. *Not ashamed of Christ.*
2. Awake, my tongue, thy tribute bring. *The Divine Perfections.*
3. Glory to God, Who reigns above. *Jesus, the Messiah.*
4. Great author of the immortal mind. *Imitation of God's Moral Perfections.* From " How matchless, Lord, Thy glories are."
5. Happy the man whose cautious steps. *Christian Moderation.*
6. Holy and reverend is the Name. *Reverence in Worship.*
7. Kind are the words that Jesus speaks. *Christ the Strengthener.*
8. Lord, ere [Now Lord] the heavenly seed is sown. *Parable of the Sower.*
9. Methinks the last great day is come. *The Judgment.*
10. Rise, O my soul, pursue the path. *The Example of the Saints.*
11. See how the little toiling ant. *Youth for Christ.*
12. Thou art, O God, a Spirit pure. *God a Spirit.*
13. To praise the ever bounteous Lord. *Harvest.*
14. When some kind shepherd from his fold. *The Lost Sheep.* From this " O how divine, how sweet the joy," in Hatfield's *Church H. Bk.*, New York, 1872, is taken.   [W. R. S.]

Neele, Henry, s. of a map and heraldic engraver in the Strand, London, was b. in London, Jan. 29, 1798. He was educated for the Law, and practised as a solicitor. In 1817 he published a volume of *Poems*, and in 1823 a volume of Dramatic and Miscellaneous Poetry. These were followed by contributions to several magazines ; the delivery of *Lectures on English Poetry* at the Russell, and again at the Western Literary Institution, in 1827 ; and the publication of his largest work, *The Romance of English History*, 1827. His mind gave way under the pressure of work, and he died by his own hand, Feb. 7, 1828. His *Lectures on English Poetry, with Miscellaneous Tales and Poems*, were pub. posthumously, in 1829. In this work the following " Hymns for Children " (p. 330) are found :—

1. O Thou ! Who sittest enthroned on high. *Child's Prayer.*
2. O Thou ! Who makest the sun to shine. *Child's Prayer.*
3. God of mercy, throned on high. *Child's Prayer.* Usually given with the same first line but altered as in E. Bickersteth's *Christian Psalmody*, 1833. No. 439

4. Remember Him, for He is great. *Remember thy Creator.*

Of these hymns No. 3 is widely used. [J. J.]

Nehring, Johann Christian, s. of J. C. Nehring, lawyer in Gotha, was b. at Gotha, Dec. 29, 1671. He studied at first medicine and afterwards theology at the University of Halle. In 1700 he became rector of the school at Essen, and, in 1703, inspector of the foundation scholars in the Orphanage at Halle. He was then, in 1706, appointed pastor of Neuendorf (or Naundorf) on the Petersberg, near Halle, and in the end of 1715 pastor at Morl, near Halle, on the Bernburg road. He d. at Morl, April 29, 1736 (*Allg. Deutsche Biog.* xxiii. 394, &c.) Five hymns by Nehring are in Freylinghausen's *G. B.*, 1704. A sixth is noted under Müller, M., p. 776, ii. [J. M.]

Νεκρώσας τον θάνατον. [Ἀνέστης τριήμερος.]

Nelson, David, M.D., s. of Henry Nelson, was b. near Jonesborough, East Tenessee, Sept. 24, 1793. He graduated at Washington College, Virginia, in 1810, and took his M.D. degree at Philadelphia in 1812. He acted for some time as a surgeon in the war against Great Britain. During that time he became an infidel, but returning to the faith, he, in 1823, resigned medicine and took up theology, and subsequently became a Presbyterian Minister. He held several appointments, and founded two manual-labour colleges, one at Greenfields, and the second near Quincy, Illinois. He d. Oct. 17, 1844. His hymn, "My days are gliding swiftly by" (*Death Anticipated*), was written in 1835, to be sung to the tune of "Lord Ullin's Daughter." It is exceedingly popular. [F. M. B.]

Nelson, Horatio, 3rd Earl Nelson, s. of Mr. Thomas Bolton, of Burnham, Norfolk (nephew of the celebrated Admiral Viscount Nelson, whose name he assumed on succeeding to the title as 2nd Earl); was b. Aug. 7, 1823, and educated at Eton, and at Trinity College, Cambridge. He succeeded to the title Nov. 1, 1835. In 1857 he edited the *Salisbury Hymn-Book*. In this work he was assisted by J. Keble, who re-wrote some of the older hymns and translated others from the Latin. This collection was remodelled and published as the *Sarum Hymnal* in 1868. In the preparation of this work Earl Nelson was assisted by the Revs. J. R. Woodford (afterwards Bishop of Ely) and E. A. Dayman. In 1864 he pub. his *Hymn for Saint's Day, and other Hymns*. In this appeared the hymn by which he is most widely known, "From all Thy saints in warfare, for all Thy saints at rest" (p. 398, ii.). He has also pub. *A Form of Family Prayer, with Special Offices for the Seasons*, 1852; and *A Calendar of Lessons for Every Day in the Year*, 1857. He is also an active member of the Home Reunion Society, and writes extensively on the subject. [J. J.]

Nettleton, Asahel, D.D., a well-known Connecticut evangelist, was b. at North Killingworth, Connecticut, April 21, 1783, and educated at Yale College, graduating in 1809. In 1811 he was licenced to preach, receiving ordination in 1817. He never settled as a pastor with any congregation, but preached in Western Massachusetts, Connecticut, and New York; in Virginia, 1827–28; and also in Great Britain in 1831. He died in 1843. His *Memoirs, Sermons and Remains* were pub. in 1844. Dr. Hatfield ascribes to him a hymn :—

"Come, Holy Ghost, my soul inspire—
This one great gift impart ;"

apparently on no other ground than that it appeared anonymously (as did many others) in his *Village Hymns*, in 1824, and has been traced no further. Nettleton's hymnological work centred in the compiling of his *Village Hymns*, from which more hymns of the older American writers have passed into English collections than from any other source. He knew and could appreciate a good hymn, but it is doubtful if he ever did or ever could have written one. [F. M. B.]

Neumann, Caspar, s. of Martin Neumann, city tax-collector at Breslau, was b. at Breslau, Sept. 14, 1648. He entered the University of Jena in Sept. 1667, graduated M.A. in August 1670, and was for some time one of the University lecturers. On Nov. 30, 1673, he was ordained at the request of Duke Ernst of Gotha as travelling chaplain to his son, Prince Christian, whom he accompanied through Western Germany, Switzerland, Northern Italy, and Southern France ; returning to Gotha in 1675. In 1676 he became court preacher at Altenburg, but in Dec. 1678 was appointed diaconus of the St. Mary Magdalene Church at Breslau, and pastor there in 1689. Finally, in Feb. 1697 he became pastor of St. Elizabeth's at Breslau, inspector of the churches and schools of the district, and first professor of theology in the two Gymnasia at Breslau. He d. at Breslau, Jan. 27, 1715 (S. J. Ehrhardt's *Presbyterologie Schlesiens* i. 211; *Allg. Deutsche Biog.* xxiii. 532, &c.). Neumann was a celebrated preacher, and edited a well-known prayer-book, entitled *Kern aller Gebete* (Breslau, 1680 ; complete ed. Breslau, 1697) which passed through many editions. He wrote over thirty hymns, simple, heartfelt and useful, which became very popular in Silesia, and almost all of which passed into Burg's *G. B.*, Breslau, 1746, and later eds. They mostly appeared, with his initials, in the 9th ed., N. D., but about 1700, of the Breslau *Vollständige Kirchen- und Haus-Music*. Those which have been *tr.* are :—

i. **Adam hat im Paradies.** *Christmas.* 1700, as above, p. 71, in 8 st. In the *Unv. L. S.*, 1851, No. 23. *Tr.* as "Adam did, in Paradise." By *Miss Manington*, 1864, p. 21.

ii. **Grosser Gott, von alten Zeiten.** *Sunday Morning.* 1700, p. 886, in 6 st. of 6 l. as "for Sundays and Festivals." Thence in many Silesian hymn-books, and in the *Unv. L. S.*, 1851, No. 481. The *trs.* in C. U. are :—

1. **God of Ages never ending, Ruling.** A good *tr.*, omitting st. iii., by H. J. Buckoll in his *Hys. from the German*, 1842, p. 5. His *trs.* of st. i., ii., vi. were repeated in the Dalston Hospital *H. Bk.*, 1848 ; the *Rugby School H. Bk.*, 1850 and 1876, and others.

2. **Great God of Ages! by whose power.** A *tr.* of st. i., ii., vi. as No. 10 in J. F. Thrupp's *Ps. & Hys.*, 1853.

3. God of Ages never ending! All creation. A good *tr.* of st. i., ii., vi., based on Buckoll, contributed by A. T. Russell to P. Maurice's *Choral H. Bk.*, 1861, No. 466.

4. God of Ages, great and mighty. A *tr.* of st. i., ii., v., vi. by C. H. L. Schnette, as No. 291 in the Ohio *Luth. Hymnal*, 1880.

iii. Herr! auf Erden muss ich leiden. *Ascension.* 1700 as above, p. 1098, in 6 st. of 8 l., and in the *Unv. L. S.*, 1851, No. 159. The *tr.* in C. U. is :—

(1) **Lord, on earth I dwell sad-hearted.** A good *tr.*, omitting st. iv., v., by Miss Winkworth, as No. 66 in her *C. B. for England*, 1863; repeated in the Ohio *Luth. Hymnal*, 1880. Another *tr.* is (2) " Lord, on earth I dwell in pain." By *Miss Winkworth*, 1855, p. 106.

iv. Mein Gott, nun ist es wieder Morgen. *Morning.* 1700, as above, p. 871, in 6 st., and in the Berlin *G. L. S.* ed. 1863, No. 1119. *Tr.* as " My God, again the morning breaketh." By *Miss Manington*, 1863, p. 118.

v. Nun bricht die finstre Nacht herein. *Sunday Evening.* 1700 as above, p. 982, in 11 st. In the Berlin *G. L. S.*, ed. 1863, No. 1177. *Tr.* as " Soon night the world in gloom will steep." By *Miss Manington*, 1863, p. 152.　　[J. M.]

Neumann, Gottfried, was b. at Hohenheida, near Leipzig, apparently Nov. 30, 1686. He studied at the University of Leipzig, and thereafter was licensed as a candidate of theology (i.e. general preacher). In 1710 he joined the staff of the Halle Orphanage, but was expelled from Halle as a Separatist, and went to Hanau. He was then for a number of years receiver of rents (Fruchtschreiber) at Bergheim in Wetteravia, Hesse, to the Count Isenburg Meerholz, living later at Himbach, and at Marienborn (1736–39). Himbach was the headquarters of Johann Friedrich Rock, one of the principal leaders of the sect of the " Inspired," and between 1714 and 1734 Neumann generally speaking belonged to this sect. During the visits which Count N. L. von Zinzendorf paid to Wetteravia, about 1730, Neumann felt drawn to the Moravian Brethren. He joined the Moravian Community at Marienborn, Hesse, in 1738. In 1747 he was living at Meerholz, where he remained till his death. In the *Weekly Reports of the Unitys-Elders-Conference in Barby*, No. xix. for May 9–15, 1779, is the entry, " 7. We are advised from Wetteravia, that the aged brother Gottfried Neumann at Meerholz has recently entered into his rest." Neumann therefore probably d. in the end of April or beginning of May, 1779 (*Allg. Deutsche Biog.* xxiii. 519; MS. from Diaconus J. T. Müller, Herrnhut, &c.) Three of his hymns, all written in 1736, are in the *Brüder G. B.*, 1778. One has passed into English, viz. :—

i. Ei, wie so selig schläfest du. *Burial.* Written on the death of Christian Ludwig, s. of Count N. L. von Zinzendorf. This child died in his third year, at Ronneburg, Aug. 31, 1736. In the first printed copy of Neumann's hymn (preserved in the Archives at Herrnhut, along with the original MS., which is dated Sept. 3, 1736) is the footnote :—

" In the evening of the night, during which the young Count Zinzendorf blessedly fell asleep, on opening the hymn-book [the Herrnhut *G. B.*, 1735] with reference to that noble child, I chanced upon the hymn, ' Ei, wie

so selig schlafest du,' [p. 322, ii.] which I referred to his death."

When Neumann's hymn was included as No. 1284 in *Appendix* viii., *circa* 1739, to the Herrnhut *G. B.*, 1735, it appears in 5 st. of 4 l., beginning " Ei, wie so sanft verschläfest du." In the *Brüder G. B.*, 1778, No. 1728, it begins : " Ei, wie so sanft *entschläfest* du," and in Bunsen's *Versuch*, 1833, is further altered to " *Ach* wie so sanft." The *trs.* in C. U. are :—

1. Blest soul, how sweetly dost thou rest. A *tr.* of st. i., ii., and of the anonymous 17th cent. st. described under " Ei, wie so selig " (p. 322, ii.), as No. 961 in the *Moravian H. Bk.*, 1801 (1886, No. 1259), and in J. A. Latrobe's *Coll.*, 1841.

2. At length releas'd from many woes. A full and good *tr.* by Miss Cox, in her *Sacred Hys. from the German*, 1841, p. 75. Included in full in the Pennsylvania *Luth. Ch. Bk.*, 1868; and, abridged, in Alford's *Ps. & Hys.*, 1844, his *Year of Praise*, 1867, and others.

Another *tr.* is : " Sweet slumbers now thine eyelids close." By *Lady E. Fortescue*, 1843, p. 24.　[J. M.]

Neumark, Georg, s. of Michael Neumark, clothier at Langensalza, in Thuringia (after 1623 at Mühlhausen in Thuringia), was b. at Langensalza, March 16, 1621; and educated at the Gymnasium at Schleusingen, and at the Gymnasium at Gotha. He received his certificate of dimission from the latter in Sept. 1641 (not 1640). He left Gotha in the autumn of 1641 along with a number of merchants who were going to the Michaelmas Fair at Leipzig. He then joined a similar party who were going from Leipzig to Lübeck ; his intention being to proceed to Königsberg and matriculate at the University there. After passing through Magdeburg they were plundered by a band of highwaymen on the Gardelegen Heath, who robbed Neumark of all he had with him, save his prayer-book and a little money sewed up in the clothes he was wearing. He returned to Magdeburg, but could obtain no employment there, nor in Lüneburg, nor in Winsen, nor in Hamburg, to which in succession the friends he made passed him on. In the beginning of December he went to Kiel, where he found a friend in the person of Nicolaus Becker, a native of Thuringia, and then chief pastor at Kiel. Day after day passed by without an opening, till about the end of the month the tutor in the family of the Judge Stephan Henning fell into disgrace and took sudden flight from Kiel. By Becker's recommendation Neumark received the vacant position, and this sudden end of his anxieties was the occasion of the writing of his hymn as noted below. In Henning's house the time passed happily till he had saved enough to proceed to Königsberg, where he matriculated June 21, 1643, as a student of law. He remained five years, studying also poetry under Dach (p. 276, ii.), and maintaining himself as a family tutor. During this time (in 1646) he again lost all his property, and this time by fire. In 1648 he left Königsberg, was for a short time at Warsaw, and spent 1649–50 at Thorn. He was then in Danzig, and in Sept. 1651 we find him in Hamburg. In the end of 1651 he returned to Thuringia, and brought himself under the notice of Duke Wilhelm II. of Sachse-

Weimar, the chief or president of the Fruit-bearing Society, the principal German literary union of the 17th cent. The Duke, apparently in 1652, appointed him court poet, librarian and registrar of the administration at Weimar; and finally secretary of the Ducal Archives. In Sept. 1653 he was admitted as a member of the Fruit-bearing Society, of which he became secretary in 1656, and of which he wrote a history (*Der Neu-Sprossende Teutsche Palmbaum*, Nürnberg and Weimar, 1668); and, in 1679, became also a member of the Pegnitz Order (see p. 143, i.). In 1681 he became blind, but was permitted to retain his emoluments till his death, at Weimar, July 18, 1681. [K. Goedeke's *Grundriss*, vol. iii., 1887, p. 74; *Allg. Deutsche Biog.* xxiii. 539; *Weimarisches Jahrbuch*, vol. iii., 1855, p. 176, &c. The dates given by the different authorities vary exceedingly, and are quite irreconcilable. In the registers at Schleusingen Neumark is last mentioned in 1636, and then as in the Third Form. Dr. von Bamberg, director of the Gymnasium at Gotha, informs me that Neumark's name appears in the matriculation book there under January 31, 1641; and as one of the "newly entered" scholars.]

A long list of Neumark's poetical works is given by *Goedeke*. A large proportion of his secular poems are pastorals, or else occasional poems written to order at Weimar; and in all there is little freshness, or happiness in expression, or glow of feeling. As a musician, and as a hymn-writer, he is of more importance. His hymns appeared in his (1) *Poetisch- und Musikalisches Lustwäldchen*, Hamburg, 1652; the enlarged ed., entitled (2) *Fortgepflantzter Musikalisch-Poetischer Lustwald*, Jena, 1657; and (3) *Unterschiedliche, so wol gottseliger Andacht; als auch zu christlichen Tugenden aufmunternde Lieder*, Weimar, 1675. Of the 34 hymns in these three works a few are found in the German hymn-books of the 17th cent., and three or four still survive. The best of Neumark's hymns are those of Trust in God, and patient waiting for His help under trial and suffering; and one of these may be fairly called classical and imperishable. It is:—

Wer nur den lieben Gott lässt walten. *Trust in God.* 1st pub. in his *Fortgepflantzter musikalisch-poetischer Lustwald*, Jena, 1657, p. 26, in 7 st. of 6 l., entitled "A hymn of consolation, That God will care for and preserve His own in His own time. After the saying 'Cast thy burden upon the Lord, and He shall sustain thee' (Ps. lv. 22). This, his finest hymn, was written in 1641, at Kiel, when after unsuccessful attempts to procure employment he became a tutor in the family of the judge Stephan Henning. Of this appointment Neumark, in his *Thränendes Haus-Kreutz*, Weimar, 1681, speaks thus:—

"Which good fortune coming suddenly, and as if fallen from heaven, greatly rejoiced me, and on that very day I composed to the honour of my beloved Lord the here and there well-known hymn 'Wer nur den lieben Gott lässt walten'; and had certainly cause enough to thank the Divine compassion for such unlooked for grace shown to me," &c.

As the date of its composition is thus December, 1641, or at latest Jan. 1642, it is certainly strange that it was not pub. in his *Lustwäldchen*, Hamburg, 1652. In that volume he does give, at p. 32, a piece entitled, "a hymn of consolation, when, in 1646, through a dreadful fire I came to my last farthing." The apocryphal story, according to which the hymn was written at Hamburg, about 1653 (see Miller's *Singers and Songs*, 1869, p. 91), has not been traced earlier than 1744. The hymn speedily became popular,

and passed into hymn-books all over Germany (Leipzig *Vorrath*, 1673, No. 1169), and still holds its place as in the Berlin *G. L. S.*, ed. 1863, No. 73.

Lauxmann, in *Koch*, viii. 386–390, relates that it was the favourite hymn of Magdalena Sibylla (d. 1687), wife of the Elector Johann Georg II. of Saxony; was sung, by his command, at the funeral, in 1740, of King Friedrich Wilhelm I. of Prussia; was sung, or rather played, by the first band of missionaries from Herrmannsburg as they set sail from Brunshausen on the Elbe (near Stade) on Oct. 28, 1853, &c.

The beautiful melody by Neumark was probably composed in 1641 along with the hymn, and was pub. with it in 1657. On it J. S. Bach composed a cantata. It is well known in England through its use by Mendelssohn in his *St. Paul* ("To Thee, O Lord, I yield my spirit"), and from its introduction into *H. A. & M.* (as *Bremen*), and many other collections.

Translations in C. U.:—

1. **Who leaves th' Almighty God to reign.** A full but free *tr.* by Sir John Bowring in his *Hymns*, 1825, No. 58. His trs. of st. ii., iv.–vi. beginning "How vain are sighs! how vain regret," are included in Curtis's *Union Coll.*, 1827.

2. **Who all his will to God resigneth.** A good and full *tr.* by A. T. Russell, as No. 236 in his *Ps. & Hys.*, 1851. His *trs.* of st. v.–vii. beginning "Say not, I am of God forsaken," are in Dr. Pagenstecher's *Coll.*, 1864.

3. **Leave God to order all thy ways.** A full and good *tr.* by Miss Winkworth, in her *Lyra Ger.*, 1st Ser. 1855, p. 152. This is given in full in M. W. Stryker's *Christian Chorals*, 1885, and, omitting st. vi., in W. F. Stevenson's *Hys. for Church and Home*, 1873, and the *Bapt. Hyl.*, 1879. Further abridged forms are in the Bapt. *Ps. & Hys.*, 1858; *Harrow School H. Bk.*, 1866; *Holy Song*, 1869, and others. In the Pennsylvania Luth. *Church Bk*, 1868; and the Amer. Pres. *Hyl.*, 1874, st. v., vi. are omitted, and the rest altered to 6 8's, beginning "My God, I leave to Thee my ways."

4. **Him who the blessed God trusts ever.** A good and full *tr.* by Dr. John Ker in the *Juvenile Missionary Magazine*, of the U. P. Church, 1857. It was revised, and st. iii., v., vi. omitted, for the *Ibrox Hyl.*, 1871, where it begins: "*He* who," &c.

5. **If thou but suffer God to guide thee.** A full and good *tr.* by Miss Winkworth (based on her *Lyra Ger.* version and set to the original melody), as No. 134 in her *C. B. for England*, 1863. Repeated in full in the Bapt. *Psalmist*, 1878, and in America in the Ohio *Luth. Hyl.*, 1880. It is found, in various abridged forms, in J. Robinson's *Coll.*, 1869; Horder's *Cong. Hys.*, 1884; the *Evangelical Hyl.*, N. Y., 1880, and others.

6. **He, who the living God hath chosen.** A *tr.* of st. i., ii., vii. by Miss Borthwick, as No. 237 in Dr. Pagenstecher's *Coll.*, 1864.

7. **He who doth glad submission render.** A good *tr.* omitting st. vi., by J. M. Sloan, as No. 284 in J. H. Wilson's *Service of Praise*, 1865, repeated, omitting the trs. of st. ii., vii., in Flett's *Coll.*, Paisley, 1871.

Other trs. are :—

(1) "He that confides in his Creator." By *J. C. Jacobi*, 1720, p. 13 (1722, p. 36; 1732, p. 51). Repeated in the *Moravian H. Bk.*, 1754, and later eds. (1886, No. 183). (2) "O Christian! let the Lord direct." By Miss Knight in her *Trs. from the German in Prose and Verse*, 1812, p. 85. (3) "To let God rule who's but contented." By H. W. Dulcken in his *Bk. of German*

Songs, 1856, p. 274. (4) "He who the rule to God hath yielded." By J. D. Burns in the *Family Treasury*, 1859, p. 309, and his *Memoir & Remains*, 1869, p. 240. (5) "Who trusts in God's all-wise direction." By R. Massie, in the *British Herald*, Aug. 1865, p. 120, and Reid's *Praise Bk.*, 1872. (6) "Who yields his will to God's good pleasure. In the *British Herald*, April, 1866, p. 244, and in Reid's *Praise Bk.*, 1872. (7) "He who commits his way to God." In the *Family Treasury*, 1878, p. 49.   [J. M.]

Neumeister, Erdmann, s. of Johann Neumeister, schoolmaster, organist, &c., at Uechteritz, near Weissenfels, was b. at Uechteritz, May 12, 1671. He entered the University of Leipzig in 1689, graduated M.A. in 1695, and was then for some time University lecturer. In June 1697 he was appointed assistant pastor at Bibra, and in 1698 pastor there, and assistant superintendent of the Eckartsberg district. He was then, in 1704, called by Duke Johann Georg, to Weissenfels as tutor to his only daughter, and assistant court preacher, and shortly afterwards court preacher. After the death of this princess, Neumeister was invited by the Duke's sister (she had married Count Erdmann II. von Promnitz) to Sorau, where on New Year's Day, 1706, he entered on the offices of senior court-preacher, consistorialrath, and superintendent. Finally, in 1715, he accepted the appointment of Pastor of St. James's Church at Hamburg, entering on his duties there Sept. 29, 1715. He d. at Hamburg, Aug. 10 (not 28), 1756 (*Bode*, p. 120; *Allg. Deutsche Biog.* xxiii. 543, &c.).

Neumeister was well known in his day as an earnest and eloquent preacher, as a vehement upholder of High Lutheranism, and as a keen controversialist against the Pietists and the Moravians by means of the pulpit as well as the press. His underlying motive was doubtless to preserve the simplicity of the faith from the subjective novelties of the period. He was the author of one of the earliest historico-critical works on German Poetry (1695); and of many Cantatas for use in church, of which form of service he may be regarded as the originator. He had begun to write hymns during his student days, and in later years their composition was a favourite Sunday employment. He takes high rank among the German hymn-writers of the 18th cent., not only for the number of his productions (over 650), but also for their abiding value. Few are founded on well-known hymns of the 16th and 17th cent.; and many of his later productions are inferior. Of his earlier efforts many soon took and still hold their place as standard German hymns; and deservedly so, for their simple, musical style, scripturalness, poetic fervour, depth of faith and Christian experience, and for their clear-cut sayings which have almost passed into proverbial use. They appeared principally in the following works:—

1. *Der Zugang zum Gnadenstuhle Jesu Christo*. This was a devotional manual of preparation for Holy Communion, with interspersed hymns. The 1st ed. appeared at Weissenfels in 1705, the 2nd 1707, 3rd 1712, 4th 1715. The earliest ed. of which precise details are available is the 5th ed. 1717, from which *Wetzel*, ii. 231, quotes the first lines of all the 77 hymns (the page references to the earlier eds. given by *Fischer* appear to be conjectural); and the earliest ed. available for collation was the 7th ed., 1724 [Göttingen University Lib.]. In the later eds. many hymns are repeated from his other works.

2. *Fünffache Kirchen-Andachten*, Leipzig, 1716 [Wernigerode Library], a collected ed. of his Cantatas (Wernigerode Library has the 1704 ed. of his *Geistliche Cantaten*), and similar productions. A second set (*Fortgesetzte*) appeared at Hamburg in 1726 [Hamburg Town Library]; and a third set (*Dritter Theil*) at Hamburg in 1752 [Hamburg Town Library].

3. *Evangelischer Nachklang*, Hamburg, 1718 [Hamburg Town Library], with 86 hymns on the Gospels for Sundays and Festivals, originally written to form conclusions to his sermons. A second set of 86 appeared as the *Anderer Theil* at Hamburg, 1729 [Hamburg Town Library].

Those of Neumeister's hymns which have passed into English are:—

i. **Gott verlässt die Seinen nicht, Ei so fahret hin ihr Sorgen.** *Cross and Consolation.* In his *Evang. Nachklang*, 1718, No. 71, p. 149, in 5 st. of 8 l., appointed for the 25th S. after Trinity. In Burg's *G. B.*, Breslau, 1746, it appears in two forms. No. 127 is the original with alterations, and arranged in 11 st. of 4 l., with the refrain "Gott verlässt die Seinen nicht." No. 128 is a form in 3 st. of 6 l., rewritten to the melody, "Jesus meine Zuversicht" (**p. 702, ii.**), and beginning with st. iii. l. 5, of the original, viz. "Gott verlässt die Seinen nicht, Nach dem Seufzen, nach dem Weinen." This second form is noted at **p. 444, ii.**

ii. **Jesu, grosser Wunderstern.** *Epiphany.* In his *Kirchen-Andachten*, 1716, p. 646, in 4 st. of 6 l., with the motto,

> Auf ihr Christen insgemein !
> Stellt euch mit den Weisen ein.
> Jesus muss geschenket sein."

It is a hymn on the Gifts of the Magi, and the spiritual sense in which we can offer the same—the Gold of Faith, the Frankincense of Prayer, the Myrrh of Penitence. In the Berlin *G. L. S.*, ed. 1863, No. 208. *Tr.* as:—

1. **Jesus! great and wondrous star.** A good and full *tr.* by E. Cronenwett, as No. 52 in the Ohio *Luth. Hyl.*, 1880.

iii. **Jesus nimmt die Sünder an ! Saget doch dies Trostwort Allen.** *Lent.* The best hymn of its author. First pub. in his *Evang. Nachklang*, 1718, No. 47, p. 96, in 8 st. of 6 l., founded on the Gospel for the 3rd S. after Trinity (St. Luke xv. 1–7), and also suggested by St. Matt. xi. 28, and Isaiah i. 18. It has come into very extensive German use, especially at Mission services at home and abroad. In the Berlin *G. L. S.*, ed. 1863, No. 110. The *trs.* are:—

1. **This man sinners doth receive.** In full by Dr. H. Mills, in his *Horae Germanicae*, 1845 (1856, p. 73). His *trs.* of st. i., ii., iv., v. are included in the Amer. Luth. Gen. Synod's *Coll.*, 1850–52, No. 844.

2. **Jesus sinners doth receive! Spread the word of consolation.** A good *tr.* of st. i., iii.–v., by A. T. Russell, as No. 47 in the Dalston Hospital *H. Bk.*, 1848, repeated in his own *Ps. & Hys.*, 1851.

3. **Jesus is the sinner's Friend.** A good and full *tr.* by Miss Dunn in her *Hys. from the German*, 1857, p. 82. Her *trs.* of st. i., ii., iv. are No. 46 in Dr. Pagenstecher's *Coll.*, 1864.

4. **Sinners Jesus will receive.** A full and good *tr.* by Mrs. Bevan in her *Songs of Eternal Life*, 1858, p. 23. Repeated in full in L. Rehfuess's *Church at Sea*, 1868, p. 50, and, abridged, in the Eng. Presb. *Ps. & Hys.*, 1867, and Flett's *Coll.*, Paisley, 1871. In Dr. W. F. Stevenson's *Hys. for Ch. & Home*, 1873, st. i., v., vi., vii. are included, altered, and beginning "Jesus sinners will receive ; Say this word of grace to all ;" and this form is also in the *Bapt. Hyl.*, 1879.

Other trs. are :—

(1) "My Jesus the sinner receives." By *Miss Warner*, 1869, p. 57. (2) "Jesus sinners doth receive! Tell to all." By R. Massie in the *Day of Rest*, 1877. The hymn "Jesus sinners will receive, When they fall," by E. Cronenwett, in 5 st., in the Ohio Luth. *Hyl.*, 1880, is marked as a *tr.* of Neumeister. It follows Neumeister in metre, but seems rather a paraphrase of the hymn "Jesus nimmt die Sünder an, Drum so will ich nicht verzagen." This hymn is by Ludwig Heinrich Schlosser [b. Sept. 7, 1663, at Darmstadt ; d. Aug. 18, 1723, as pastor at Frankfurt am Main], and appeared in the *Appendix* to the Frankfurt ed., 1693, of Crüger's

Praxis, and in his own *Stilles Lob Gottes in dem geist-lichen Zion*, Frankfurt a. M., 1724 (see *Wetzel*, iv. 433; Rambach's *Anthologie*, vi. p. xi., &c.). In Burg's *G. B.*, Breslau, 1746, the Neumeister hymn is given as No. 1593 and marked as by G. G. Hofmann, and the Schlosser hymn as No. 1592 and marked as by Neumeister. Hence perhaps the confusion.

Hymns not in English C.U.

iv. **Bleib, Jesu, bleib bei mir.** *For the Dying.* In his *Evang. Nachklang*, 1718, No. 31, p. 64, in 7 st., entitled " For the Second Day of Easter." In the Berlin *G. L. S.*, ed. 1863, No. 1431. *Tr.* as " Jesus, near me still abide." By *Miss Dunn*, 1857, p. 117.

v. **Herr Jesu Christ, mein höchstes Gut.** *Love to Christ.* One of his best and most popular hymns, apparently written for use at the Sunday celebration of Holy Communion in the castle at Weissenfels. It seems to have appeared in his *Zugang*, 1705 (*Wetzel*, ii. 232, cites it as in the 5th ed. 1717. In the 8th ed. 1724, p. 17, entitled " Hymn of Consolation from Ps. lxxiii. 23–28 "), and is included in the Halle Stadt *G. B.*, 1711, No. 524 in 6 st. In *Freylinghausen*, 1714, it begins " Herr Jesu Christ, mein Fleisch und Blut." In Porst's *G. B.*, ed. 1855, No. 546. The *trs.* are (1) " All my desires are fix'd on Thee " (st. iii.). By P. H. Molther as pt. of No. 401 in the *Moravian H. Bk.* 1801 (1886, No. 448). (2) " Lord Jesus Christ, my spirit's health." By *Dr. H. Mills*, 1845 (1856, p. 115).

vi. **Herr Jesu, meines Lebens Heil.** *Evening.* Apparently in his *Zugang*, 1705 (*Wetzel*, ii. 232, as in ed. 1717. In ed. 1724, p. 284 in 10 st.), and included in the Halle Stadt *G. B.* 1711, No. 426. In Burg's *G. B.*, Breslau, 1746, No. 1844. *Tr.* as (1) " Now I'll lie down and sleep in Thee " (st. vi.), as pt. of No. 750 in the *Moravian H. Bk.*, 1789 (1849, No. 1137). (2) " Lord Jesu ! Thou my life's true health." By *H. J. Buckoll*, 1842, p. 92.

vii. **Ich bin bei allem Kummer stille.** *Trust in God.* Included in the 5th ed. 1717 of his *Zugang* (*Wetzel*, ii. 232), and in the ed. 1724, p. 594, in 6 st., founded on Ps. lxxvii. 11. In the Berlin *G. L. S.*, ed. 1863, No. 911. It has been *tr.* into English through the recast by J. S. Diterich " Herr, mache meine Seele stille," which is No. 169, in 7 st., in the Berlin *G. B.*, 1765 (Berlin *G. B.*, 1829, No. 599). *Tr.* as " Lord, make my spirit still." By *Miss Warner*, 1869, p. 26.

viii. **Ich weiss dass mein Erlöser lebet.** *For the Dying.* In his *Evang. Nachklang*, 1718, No. 32, in 5 st., entitled " On the Third Day of Easter." In Bunsen's *Allg. G. B.*, 1846, No. 437, in 4 st. *Tr.* as " I know that my Redeemer liveth, And as He lives." A good *tr.* from *Bunsen* in Reid's *Praise Bk.*, 1872.

ix. **Ob Menschen klug und weise sein.** *Spiritual Wisdom.* In his *Evang. Nachklang*, 1718, No. 12, p. 24, in 6 st., for the 1st S. after Epiphany. In the Berlin *G. L. S.*, ed. 1863. *Tr.* as " Here many wise and prudent grow." By *Dr. H. Mills*, 1845 (1856, p. 109).

x. **So ist die Woche nun geschlossen.** *Saturday Evening.* Apparently in his *Zugang*, 1705 (*Wetzel*, ii. 233, cites it as in ed. 1717. In the ed. 1724, p. 552, in 9 st., entitled " Hymn for the close of the Week "). In the Berlin *G. L. S.*, ed. 1863. *Tr.* as " Thou, Lord, Thy love art still bestowing." By *H. J. Buckoll*, 1842.

xi. **Wie Gott will, also will ich sagen.** *Trust in God.* *Wetzel*, ii. 234, cites this as in his *Zugang*, 1717 (ed. 1724, p. 570, in 8 st.). In the Berlin *G. L. S.*, ed. 1863, No. 919. *Tr.* as " As Thou wilt, my God! I ever say." By Miss Borthwick, in *H. L. L.*, 1858, p. 44 (1884, p. 166), and thence in Bp. Ryle's *Coll.* 1860, No. 163.   [J. M.]

Neunhertz, Johannes, s. of Johannes Neunhertz, weaver at Waltersdorf, near Kupferberg, in Silesia, was b. at Waltersdorf Aug. 16, 1653, and entered the University of Leipzig in June, 1673 (M.A. 1676). In 1678 he was appointed assistant preacher at Lauban, in Silesia; in 1680 pastor at Kiesslingswalde; and in 1696 pastor at Geibsdorf, both near Lauban. He then became, in 1706, diaconus of the Holy Trinity Church, and later morning preacher at the Holy Cross Church in Lauban. Finally, in 1709, he was appointed chief pastor at Hirschberg, in Silesia, and d. there Nov. 26, 1737 (S. J. Ehrhardt's *Presbyterologie Schlesiens*, 1780–89, iii. pt. ii. p. 187; *Koch*, v. 450; *Allg. Deutsche Biog.* xxiii. 549; *Bode*, p. 121—the first dating his birth 1652). Neun-

hertz was the author of a large number of hymns, good and flowing in style, but often lengthy and with little power or concentration. They appeared in his various works :—

(1) *Evangelische Sabbaths-Freude*, Zittau, 1690. (2) *Christliche Leid-Andachten*, Lauban, 1698. (3) *Evangelische Hertz-Ermunterung*, Leipzig, 1701. (4) *Tröstliche . . . Andachten*, Lauban, 1709; 2nd ed. as *Andachts-Flammen*, Budissin, 1717; and in the Silesian hymn-books of the period. A large number are given in the Hirschberg *G. B.*, 1741, a few in Burg's *G. B.*, Breslau, 1746, and some still survive in modern collections.

The only hymn by him which seems to have passed into English is :—

Zweene Jünger gehn mit Sehnen. *Eastertide.* A hymn on the Two Disciples on their way to Emmaus (St. Luke xxiv. 13–35). Included in the Lauban *G. B.*, 1707, p. 162 [Wernigerode Library], as No. 5 of the Easter Hymns, in 9 st. of 8 l., and marked as by *M. J.* Neunhertz. Also in the Berlin *G. L. S.*, ed. 1863, No. 326. The form *tr.* into English is: " Trauernd und mit bangem Sehnen." This appeared in the Liegnitz *G. B.*, 1804 (ed. 1819, No. 155), and is repeated in the Württemberg *G. B.*, 1842, No. 176, in 7 st. It is a recast by L. E. S. Müller (see p. 776, i.). The *tr.* in C. U. is :—

Sad with longing, sick with fears. A full and good *tr.* from the 1842 text by Miss Winkworth, in her *Lyra Ger.*, 2nd Ser. 1858, p. 43. In the Pennsylvania *Luth. Church Bk.*, 1868, the *trs.* of st. iv.–viii. altered and beginning, " Truest Friend, Who canst not fail," were given as No. 440.   [J. M.]

Νεῦσον πρὸς ὕμνους.   [Ἔσωσε λαὸν.]

Neuss, Heinrich Georg, s. of Andreas Neuss, surgeon at Elbingerode in the Harz, was b. at E., March 11, 1654, and entered the University of Erfurt in 1677 as a student of theology. In 1680 he became a private tutor at Heimburg, near Blankenburg, and then in 1683 corrector, and in 1684 rector of the school at Blankenburg in the Harz. In 1690 he was appointed assistant preacher at Wolfenbüttel, and soon afterwards diaconus of the Heinrichstadt church there. For holding prayer meetings, &c., he was denounced as a Pietist, and chose to resign rather than desist. In the same year, 1692, he became preacher at Hedwigsburg, and travelling Chaplain to Duke Rudolph August of Brunswick, who, at Easter, 1695, appointed him superintendent at Remlingen for the district of Asseburg. In 1696 he received the degree of D.D. from the University of Giessen, and became superintendent, consistorialrath, and chief pastor of the Church of SS. Sylvester and George at Wernigerode, being instituted on Feb. 6. His appointment there was at first unpopular, for he was suspected of Separatist tendencies, but he soon gained the love of the people by his earnest and loving practical Christianity, and by the interest he took in the development of Church music, for which under his care Wernigerode became famous in all the district. He d. at Wernigerode, Sept. 30, 1716 (*Koch*, iv. 425; *Allg. Deutsche Biog.* xxiii. 556; *Heinrich Georg Neuss*. By Ed. Jacobs. In the *Zeitschrift des Harz-Vereins*, vol. xxi. 1888, p. 159, &c.).

The hymns of Neuss appeared principally in his *Heb-Opfer zum Bau der Hütten Gottes, das ist, Geistliche Lieder, &c.*; of this the 1st ed. with 100 hymns was pub. at Lüneburg, 1692; and the 2nd ed., with 34 additional, at Wernigerode, 1703 [both in Berlin], most of the pieces bearing the dates of their composition. They were received with great favour in Pietist-circles, and Freylinghausen in his *Geistreiches G. B.* included no less than 38 (15 in pt. i., 1704; 33 in pt. ii., 1714). In the Wernigerode *G. B.*, 1712, edited by Neuss, 5 are included, and 5 more in the ed. of 1735. Only a few are found in recent German collections. The 1703 ed. of the *Heb-Opfer* had also 86 melodies, of which some 75 were by Neuss, and of these 15 passed into Freylinghausen's *G. B.* In 1706 Neuss also pub. a collection of *Brunnen-lieder* at Pyrmont, for the frequenters of the Baths there.

Only one of his hymns has passed into English, viz. :—

Ein reines Herz, Herr, schaff in mir. *Sanctification.* A simple and beautiful hymn, 1st pub. in the 2nd ed., 1703, of his *Heb-Opfer*, p. 217, in 5 st. of 4 l. In the Berlin *G. L. S.*, ed. 1863, No. 380. *Tr.* as :—

A new and contrite heart create. A good and full *tr.* by Miss Cox, in her *Sacred Hymns from the German*, 1841, p. 153 (1864, p. 177), repeated in the *Bapt. Hyl.*, 1879.

Another tr. is :—"Lord ! grant a new-born heart to me," by *Lady E. Fortescue*, 1843, p. 58.   **[J. M.]**

Nevin, Edwin Henry, D.D., s. of Major David Nevin, was b. at Shippensburg, Pennsylvania, May 9, 1814. He graduated in Arts at Jefferson College, 1833 ; and in Theology at Princeton Seminary, in 1836. He held several pastorates as a Presbyterian Minister from 1836 to 1857 ; then as a Congregational Minister from 1857 to 1868 ; and then, after a rest of six years through ill health, as a Minister of the Reformed Church, first at Lancaster, Pennsylvania, and then in Philadelphia. Dr. Nevin is the author of several hymns, the more important of which are :—

1. **Always with me [us], always with [us] me.** *Jesus always present.*

2. **Come up hither, come away.** *Invitation Heavenward.*

3. **Happy, Saviour, would I be.** *Trust.* This is given in the *Lyra Sac. Americana* as " Saviour ! happy should I be." This change was made by the editor " with the consent and approbation of the author." (*Note*, p. 299).

4. **O heaven, sweet heaven.** *Heaven.* Written and pub. in 1862 " after the death of a beloved son, which made heaven nearer and dearer from the conviction that now a member of his family was one of its inhabitants " (Schaff's *Christ in Song*, 1870, p. 539).

5. **Live on the field of battle.** *Duty.* Appeared in the Bap. *Devotional H. Bk.*, 1864.

6. **I have read of a world of beauty.** *Heaven.*

7. **Mount up on high! as if on eagle's wings.** *Divine Aspirations.*

Of these hymns, Nos. 1, 2, 3 appeared in Nason's *Congregational H. Bk.*, 1857 ; and all, except No. 5, are in the *Lyra Sacra Americana*, 1868.   **[F. M. B.]**

New England Psalter, or Bay Psalm Book. [Psalters, English, § vii.]

New Version, The. This Version of the Psalms of David, commonly known as *Tate and Brady*, is fully set forth, so far as it is a part of the general history of English Psalters, in the article **Psalters, English,** § XIII. That article must be read for its history, the value of its authorization, its character and merits, and for biographical notices of its authors. It remains for us here to give (1) the history of the *Version* from 1696 to the present time ; (2) an account of its *Supplement* ; and (3) a list of the contents of each.

i. *History of the N. V.* As stated in the article referred to, it was first published in its complete form in 1696, and the second edition, with somewhat extensive corrections, in 1698, although it had been " allowed " by the King in Council, " December 3, 1696." Soon after " The Second Edition corrected " was issued

in 1698, another version of the original text was published which differed considerably both from " The second edition corrected " and the original of 1696. The copy before us is dated 1698. The titlepages of the three books are :—

(1) *A New Version of the Psalms of David, Fitted to the Tunes Used in Churches. By N. Tate and N. Brady.* London, Printed by M. Clark: for the Company of Stationers, 1696. This has a Dedication to King William signed by "N. Brady; N. Tate."

(2) *A New Version of the Psalms of David, Fitted to the Tunes Used in Churches. By N. Tate and N. Brady. The Second Edition corrected. London : Printed by M. Clark, for the Company of Stationers. 1698.* This also has a Dedication to the King signed by " N. Brady, N. Tate."

(3) *A New Version of the Psalms of David, Fitted to the Tunes Used in Churches. By N. Tate and N. Brady. London, Printed by T. Hodgkin, for the Company of Stationers, 1698. And are to be Sold at Stationers'-Hall, near Ludgate, and by most Booksellers.* This has the same Dedication as Nos. 1 and 2, and, in addition, the *Authorization* dated " At the Court at Kensington, December 3, 1696. Present the King's Most Excellent Majesty in Council."

As examples of the changes made in the text of the *New Version* we will give quotations from Ps. xviii., verse 7.

(1) From the *Original edition*, 1696.

> " When God arose to take my part,
> The trembling Earth did quake for fear ;
> From their firm Posts the Hills did start,
> Nor durst his dreadful Fury bear."

(2) From " *The Second Edition corrected,*" London, M. Clark, 1698.

> " When God arose to take my part,
> The conscious Earth did quake for fear ;
> From their firm Posts the Hills did start,
> Nor could his dreadful Fury bear."

(3) From the *Edition of* 1698. London, J. Hodgkin.

> " When God arose *my part to take*,
> the conscious Earth *was struck* with fear ;
> *The Hills did at his presence* shake,
> nor could his dreadful fury bear."

In these quotations the italics represent the changes made in the 1698 (*Hodgkin*) edition when compared with " The Second Edition corrected " of 1698 (*Clark*). This is but one of hundreds of instances of changes in the text. The text of the Original of 1696 was not again reprinted, and it was natural to expect that the publication of one of the other two would cease. This, however, did not take place for over a hundred years. We have before us two copies of the *New Version*, both of which have been in use at public worship, and both dated 1796, as follows :—

(1) *A New Version of the Psalms of David Fitted to the Tunes used in Churches. By N. Brady, D.D., Chaplain in Ordinary, and N. Tate, Esquire, Poet-Laureat to His Majesty. London. Printed. MDCCXCVI.*

This edition is a reprint of No. 2, " The Second Edition corrected," pub. by Clark in 1698. The next is :—

(2) *A New Version of the Psalms of David, Fitted to the Tunes used in Churches. By N. Brady, D.D., Chaplain in Ordinary, and N. Tate, Esq., Poet-Laureate to His Majesty. London, Printed by M. Brown, For the Company of Stationers, and are to be Sold at Stationers Hall, near Ludgate-Street, and by most Booksellers. MDCCXCVI.*

This is a reprint of the edition pub. by Hodgkin in 1698 (No. 3 above). It has the Authorization of the King dated Dec. 3, 1696, and the Bishop of London's approval and good wishes for success, dated May 23, 1698. From this it is clear that these two texts were reprinted, and were used side by side in public worship for more than one hundred years, as it was only when the printing of the *New Version* was undertaken by the University Press that the reprinting of Clark's ed. No. 2 above, "The Second Edition corrected," 1698, was gradually suspended, and the text approved by the Bishop of London, on "May 23, 1698" (No. 3 above, printed by J. Hodgkin), became the absolute *Tate & Brady* of the future. The issue of this *Tate & Brady* continued for many years, and is that usually quoted by hymnologists as the "original text." In the "Selection of Psalms," which was given in the American *Prayer Bk. Coll.*, 1826, those taken from the *New Version* were from this text.

The following list of first lines are from this text of 1698—the sub-lines being the first lines of centos in C. U. which have been taken from the paraphrase of any given Psalm:—

Psalm.	First Line.
i.	How blest is he who ne'er consents.
ii.	With restless and ungovern'd rage.
	(1) Thus God declares His sovereign will.
iii.	How many, Lord, of late are grown.
	(1) Thou gracious God [Lord] art my Defence.
	(2) O Lord, Thou art my sure Defence.
iv.	O Lord that art my righteous Judge.
	(1) God of my life, my hopes, my joys.
	(2) While worldly minds impatient grow.
v.	Lord, hear the voice of my complaint. Accept.
vi.	Thy dreadful anger, Lord, restrain.
vii.	O Lord, my God, since I have plac'd.
viii.	O Thou, to Whom all creatures bow.
ix.	To celebrate Thy praise, O Lord.
x.	Thy presence why withdraw'st Thou, Lord.
xi.	Since I have plac'd my trust in God.
xii.	Since godly men decay, O Lord.
xiii.	How long wilt Thou forget me, Lord?
xiv.	Sure, wicked fools must needs suppose.
xv.	Lord, who's the happy man that may.
xvi.	Protect me from my cruel foes.
	(1) My grateful soul shall bless the Lord.
xvii.	To my just plea, and sad complaint.
xviii.	No change of time shall ever shock.
xix.	The heav'ns declare Thy glory, Lord.
	(1) God's perfect law converts the soul.
xx.	The Lord to thy request attend.
xxi.	The King, O Lord, with songs of praise.
xxii.	My God, my God, why leav'st Thou me?
xxiii.	The Lord Himself, the mighty Lord.
xxiv.	This spacious earth is all the Lord's.
	(1) Lift up your heads, eternal gates.
	(2) Erect your heads, eternal gates.
xxv.	To God, in whom I trust.
	(1) His mercy and His truth.
xxvi.	Judge me, O Lord, for I the paths.
	(1) I'll wash my hands in innocence.
xxvii.	Whom should I fear, since God to me?
xxviii.	O Lord, my Rock, to Thee I cry.
xxix.	Ye princes that in might excel.
xxx.	I'll celebrate Thy praises, Lord.
xxxi.	Defend me, Lord, from shame.
	(1) My hope, my steadfast trust.
xxxii.	He's blest, whose sins have pardon gain'd.
xxxiii.	Let all the just to God with joy.
	(1) How happy are the folk to whom.
xxxiv.	Thro' all the changing scenes of life.
	(1) The hosts of God encamped around.
xxxv.	Against all those that strive with me.
xxxvi.	My crafty foe, with flatt'ring art.
	(1) Thy justice like the hills remain.
	(2) O Lord, Thy mercy, my sure hope.
xxxvii.	Tho' wicked men grow rich or great.
xxxviii.	Thy chast'ning wrath, O Lord, restrain.
xxxix.	Resolv'd to watch o'er all my ways.
	(1) Lord, let me know my term of days.
xl.	I waited meekly for the Lord.
xli.	Happy the man whose tender care.
xlii.	As pants the hart for cooling streams.
xliii.	Just Judge of heav'n, against my foes.
	(1) Let me with light and truth be blest.
xliv.	O Lord, our fathers oft have told.

Psalm.	First Line.
xlv.	While I the King's loud praise rehearse.
xlvi.	God is our Refuge in distress.
xlvii.	O all ye people, clap your hands.
xlviii.	The Lord, the only God, is great.
xlxix.	Let all the list'ning world attend.
l.	The Lord hath spoke, the mighty God.
li.	Have mercy, Lord, on me.
lii.	In vain, O man of lawless might.
liii.	The wicked fools must sure suppose.
liv.	Lord, save me, for Thy glorious Name.
lv.	Give ear, Thou Judge of all the earth.
lvi.	Do Thou, O God, in mercy help.
lvii.	Thy mercy, Lord, to me extend.
	(1) O God, my heart is fix'd, 'tis bent. Its thankful tribute, &c.
	(2) O God, my heart is fully bent.
lviii.	Speak, O ye judges of the earth.
lix.	Deliver me, O Lord my God.
lx.	O God, Who hast our troops disperst.
lxi.	Lord, hear my cry, regard my pray'r.
lxii.	My soul for help on God relies.
lxiii.	O God, my gracious God, to Thee.
lxiv.	Lord, hear the voice of my complaint, To my
lxv.	For Thee, O God, our constant praise.
	(1) God's goodness does the circling year.
	(2) Lord, from Thy unexhausted store.
lxvi.	Let all the lands with shouts of joy.
lxvii.	To bless Thy chosen race.
lxviii.	Let God, the God of battle, rise.
lxix.	Save me, O God, from waves that roll.
lxx.	O Lord, to my relief draw near.
lxxi.	In Thee I put my steadfast trust.
	(1) While God vouchsafes me His support.
lxxii.	Lord, let Thy just decrees the King.
	(1) Lo hills and mountains shall bring forth.
	(2) Thy uncontroled dominion shall.
lxxiii.	At length, by certain proofs, 'tis plain.
	(1) Thy presence, Lord, hath me supplied.
lxxiv.	Why hast Thou cast us off, O God?
lxxv.	To Thee, O God, we render praise.
lxxvi.	In Judah the Almighty's known.
lxxvii.	To God I cried, Who to my help.
	(2) Will God for ever cast us off?
lxxviii.	Hear, O my people, to my law.
lxxix.	Behold, O God, how heathen hosts.
lxxx.	O Isr'el's Shepherd, Joseph's Guide.
	(1) O Thou Whom heavenly hosts obey.
lxxxi.	To God, our never failing strength.
lxxxii.	God in the great assembly stands.
lxxxiii.	Hold not Thy peace, O Lord our God.
lxxxiv.	O God of hosts, the mighty Lord.
	(1) Behold, O God, for Thou alone.
	(2) O Lord of hosts, my King, my God.
lxxxv.	Lord, Thou hast granted to Thy land.
lxxxvi.	To my complaint, O Lord my God.
lxxxvii.	God's temple crowns the holy mount.
lxxxviii.	To Thee, my God and Saviour, I.
	(2) God of my life, O Lord most high.
lxxxix.	Thy mercies, Lord, shall be my song.
	(1) Happy, thrice happy they, who hear.
	(2) With reverence let the just appear.
xc.	O Lord, the Saviour and Defence.
xci.	He that has God his Guardian made.
xcii.	How good and pleasant must it be.
xciii.	With glory clad, with strength array'd.
xciv.	O God to Whom revenge belongs.
	(1) Bless'd is the man whom Thou, O Lord.
xcv.	O come, loud anthems let us sing.
xcvi.	Sing to the Lord a new-made song. Let, &c.
	(1) How just and merciful is God.
xcvii.	Jehovah reigns, let all the earth.
xcviii.	Sing to the Lord a new-made song, Who, &c.
xcix.	Jehovah reigns, let therefore all.
c.	With one consent let all the earth.
ci.	Of mercy's never-failing spring.
cii.	When I pour out my soul in pray'r.
ciii.	My soul, inspir'd with sacred love.
civ.	Bless God, my soul; Thou, Lord, alone.
cv.	O render thanks, and bless the Lord.
cvi.	O render thanks to God above.
cvii.	To God your grateful voices raise.
cviii.	O God, my heart is fully bent To magni'y Thy name
	(1) O God, my heart is fixed, is bent.
cix.	O God, Whose former mercies make.
cx.	The Lord unto my Lord thus spake.
cxi.	Praise ye the Lord; our God to praise.
cxii.	That man is bless'd who stands in awe.
cxiii.	Ye saints and servants of the Lord.
	(1) Ye that delight to serve the Lord.

Psalm.	First Line.
cxiv.	When Isr'el, by th' Almighty led.
cxv.	Lord, not to us, we claim no share.
cxvi.	My soul with grateful thoughts of love.
cxvii.	With cheerful notes let all the earth.
cxviii.	O praise the Lord, for He is good.
	(1) Joy fills the dwelling of the just.
cxix.	How blest are they who always keep.
	(1) Instruct me in Thy statutes, Lord.
	(2) How shall the young preserve their ways?
	(3) Thy word is to my feet a lamp.
	(4) To my request and earnest cry.
cxx.	In deep distress I oft have cried.
cxxi.	To Sion's hill I lift my eyes.
cxxii.	O 'twas a joyful sound to hear.
cxxiii.	On Thee, Who dwell'st above the skies.
cxxiv.	Had not the Lord (may Isr'el say).
cxxv.	Who place on Sion's God their trust.
cxxvi.	When Sion's God her sons recall'd.
cxxvii.	We build with fruitless cost, unless.
cxxviii.	The man is blest who fears the Lord.
cxxix.	From my youth up, may Isr'el say.
cxxx.	From lowest depths of woe.
	(1) My soul with patience waits.
cxxxi	O Lord, I am not proud of heart.
cxxxii.	Let David, Lord, a constant place.
	(2) O with due reverence let us all.
cxxxiii.	How vast must their advantage be.
cxxxiv.	Bless God, ye servants that attend.
cxxxv.	O praise the Lord with one consent.
cxxxvi.	To God, the mighty Lord.
cxxxvii.	When we, our weary'd limbs to rest.
cxxxviii.	With my whole heart, my God and King.
	(1 This day is God's, let all the land.
cxxxix.	Thou, Lord, by strictest search hast known.
cxl.	Preserve me, Lord, from crafty foes.
cxli.	To Thee, O Lord, my cries ascend.
cxlii.	To God, with mournful voice.
cxliii.	Lord, hear my pray'r, and to my cry.
cxliv.	For ever bless'd be God the Lord.
cxlv.	Thee I will bless [I'll extol], my God and King.
cxlvi.	O praise the Lord, and thou, my soul.
cxlvii.	O praise the Lord with hymns of joy.
cxlviii.	Ye boundless realms of joy.
cxlix.	O praise the Lord, Prepare your glad voice.
cl.	O praise the Lord in that blest place.

ii. *The Supplement.* The earliest notice of the *Supplement* is the following advertisement at the end of the 8vo ed. of the *New Version*, printed by Hodgkin, 1698 :—

"A Supplement to the New Version of Psalms by N. Tate and N. Brady, containing 1. *The usual Hymns, Creed, Lord's Prayer, Ten Commandments, all set to their proper Tunes; with additional Hymns for the Holy Sacrament, Festivals, &c.* 2ly. *Select Psalms done in particular Measures, to make up the whole variety of Metres that are in the old Version, with Duplicates to most of them, and Gloria Patris with the Tunes. With a Collection of the most usual Church-Tunes. All very useful for the Teacher or Learner of Psalmody. London: Printed and Sold at Stationers Hall, near Ludgate, D. Brown at the Bible without Temple-Bar, J. Wilds at the Elephant, Charing Cross, and other Booksellers.* *** This Supplement to be had either in the large Octavo to bind up with the Volume, or in the small size for the Twelves. Price in Sheets* 6d.*"*

This advertisement was repeated, with slight variations, in the 32mo ed. of 1699. The earliest fulfilment of the promised *Supplement* that we have been enabled to see is the 3rd edition published in 1702. Its contents are :—

1. O God, we praise Thee, and confess. *Te Deum.*
2. Come Holy Ghost, Creator, come, And visit, &c. *Veni Creator* in L.M.
3. Come Holy Ghost, Creator come, Inspire the souls, &c. *Veni Creator* in D.C.M.
4. No blest be Israel's Lord and God. *Benedictus.*
5. My soul and spirit fill'd with joy. *Magnificat.*
6. Lord, let Thy servant now depart. *Nunc Dim.*
7 I stedfastly believe in God. *The Creed.*
8. Our Father Who in heaven art, Thy Name be hallowed, &c. *The Lord's Prayer.* First Version.
9. Our Father Who in heaven art, All hallowed be, &c. *Lord's Prayer.* Second Version.
10. God spake these words, O Israel, hear. *Ten Commandments.*

11. While Shepherds watched their flocks by night. *Christmas.*
12. Since Christ, our Passover, is slain. *Easter.*
13. Christ from the dead is raised and made. *Easter.*
14. Thou God, all Glory, Honour, Power. *Holy Communion.*
15. All ye who faithful servants are. *Holy Communion.*
16. To God be glory, peace on earth. *Holy Communion.*

Following these hymns are the versions of the Psalms in peculiar metres referred to in the advertisement :—

Psalm.	First line.
xlvii.	O clap your hands, ye people, shout and sing.
xciii.	With glory crown'd and matchless strength array'd.
cxvii.	In praise to God, let all the people join.
lxvii.	Our God bless us all with mercy and love.
cxvii.	The praise of our God, all people repeat.
cxi.	With my whole heart Thy fame.
cxxxi.	Thou Lord, my witness art.
cxii.	How blest is he, and only he.
cxxxiv.	All you, who to the house of God.
cxx.	In trouble and distress, To God, &c.
cxxxi.	Thou, Lord, my Witness art.
cxxi.	To Zion's hill I lift my eyes, From whence my help, &c.
cxxix.	Oft have they, now may Israel say.
cxxii.	How did my soul rejoice.
cxxxiii.	O 'tis a joyful sight, When brethren, &c.
cxxiv.	Had not the Lord (let thankful Israel say).
liv.	To save me, Lord, Thy truth and power display.
cxxv.	All who on Zion's God depend.
cxxv,	All they whose hopes on God depend.
liii.	The wicked, senseless fool, hath said.
cxxvi.	When Sion's God, Her captive sons, &c.
cxiv.	When Israel who Had suffered cruel bondage long.
cxxvii.	In vain we build with vast expense.
cxxx	From the lowest depths of woe.
liv.	Save me, Lord, for Thy Name's sake.
cxxxvi.	O praise the Lord, for He is good.

These Psalms are all in peculiar metres, and are given in full. Then the following Psalms from the New Version as above, first lines only being printed :—XLIV., XXVII., IV., V., XXIII., XXXVIII., XIX., XVI., CXLVII. After these 28 tunes are given with references to the Psalms only. Then are given the following Psalms, also from the New Version as above :— CXIX., XCII., C., XXV. CXIII., CXLVIII., LXXXVIII.

The 6th ed. of the *Supplement*, 1708, contained the same psalms in peculiar metres and hymns, together with the addition of "O Lord, turn not Thy face from me" (in a rewritten form), and "O all ye works of God the Lord," from the *Old Version*; and "We sing to Thee Whose wisdom formed," from *Playford.* (This arrangement was repeated with the exception of "O Lord, turn not," as late as the *Savoy ed.*, 1717.)

As this 6th ed. of the *Supplement*, 1708, is of special importance to the musical student, we append the title and some details concerning its musical contents. The title is :—

A Supplement to the New Version of Psalms by Dr. Brady and Mr. Tate; containing, The Psalms in Peculiar Measures; the usual Hymns, Creed, Lord's Prayer, Ten Commandments, for the Holy Sacrament, &c., with Gloria Patris, and Tunes (Treble and Bass), proper to each of them, and all the rest of the Psalms. The Sixth Edition Corrected; and much Enlarged: With the Addition of Plain Instructions for all those who are desirous to Learn or Improve themselves in Psalmody; near 30 New Tunes, composed by several of the Best Masters; and a Table of Psalms suited to the Feasts and Fasts of the Church, &c. With Tables of all the Psalms of the Old, New, and Dr. Patrick's Versions, directing what tunes are fitted for each Psalm. The whole being a Compleat Psalmody. Useful for Teachers and Learners of either Version . . . In the Savoy: Printed by John Nutt ; and Sold by James Holland, at the Bible and Ball, at the West-End of St. Paul's, MDCCVIII.

This edition contains 63 psalm tunes, and 12 tunes for the Hymns of the Church, 75 in all. Of these tunes 28 are marked thus *, as being *new*. These are :—

St. Paul's.	St. Martin's.	New Tune to Ps.
St. Andrew's.	St. Giles's.	121, 129. [*Jer-*
Sion.	St. Mark's.	*sey*].
St. James's.	St. Thomas's.	New Tune to Ps.
St. Matthew's.	New Tune to Ps.	114, 126.
All Saints.	46, 93, 117.	New Tune to Ps.
The Penitent's	New Tune to Ps.	136.
Tune.	117, 149. [*Han-*	Another new
St. Anne's.	*over.*]	Tune to the
St. John's.	New Tune to Ps.	same.
St. Luke's.	111, 131.	

There were also New Tunes to the *Magnificat, The Creed, The Lord's Prayer* (1st metre), the *Ten Commandments*, the *Benedicite*, and the *Hymn on the Divine Use of Music*. How far the word *new* with regard to these 28 tunes means *newly composed* for this edition of the *Supplement*, or, published therein for the first time, is doubtful. Courteville's tune, *St. James's*, for instance. is in the 7th ed. of Playford's *Psalter*, 1701, and was not absolutely new then.

The earliest association of the *New Version* with what is known as the *University Press* with which we are acquainted, is the following :—

New Version of the Psalms of David, fitted to the Tunes used in Churches. By N. Brady, D.D., Chaplain in Ordinary, and N. Tate, Esq., Poet-Laureat to His Majesty. Cambridge. Printed by J. Archdeacon, Printer to the University ; and sold by John, Francis, and Charles Rivington, Benjamin White, Charles Dilly, and John Fielding in London; and J. & J. Merrill, in Cambridge. 1782. Cum Privilegio. Price 6d. unbound.

At the end, after the *Gloria Patri*, are the following *Hymns :—*

1. High let us swell our tuneful notes.
2. Hark, the herald angels sing.
3. Christ from the dead is rais'd and made.
4. My God, and is Thy table spread.
5. Awake my soul, and with the sun.

These 5 hymns, and no more, are in a 1791 Cambridge edition of the *N. V.* printed by " J. Archdeacon, Printer to the University " : and the 1802 edition printed by " J. Burges," printer to the University. These hymns are also given in an Oxford edition " Printed by Dawson & Co., 1803 : and in an 1807 edition " Printed at the Clarendon Press by Dawson, Bensley, and Cooke, Printers to the University."

Some time after 1807, two additional hymns were added, viz. :—

6. Jesus Christ is risen to-day, Our triumphant.
7. Glory to Thee, my God, this night.

But the exact date at which they were inserted we have been unable to determine. In addition to these *University* editions of the *N. V.* and the 2 *Hymns*, we find J., F. and C. Rivington issued the following in 1779 :—

Hymns taken from the Supplement to Tate and Brady's Psalms.

In this, and subsequent editions, including 1787, the 5 hymns in the *University* edition of 1782 are not found. These hymns are thus distinctly associated with the Cambridge and Oxford *University* issues of the *N. Version*.

Miller, in his *Singers and Songs*, &c., 1869, p. 173, says concerning these hymns :—

" ' My God, and is Thy table spread ?' * * * This is inserted as a Communion Hymn in the ' Prayer Book of the Church of England.' It was introduced by a University printer about half a century ago. He was a Dissenter, and filled up the blank leaves at the end of the Prayer Book with hymns he thought would be acceptable. The authorities did not interfere, and the hymns thus took their place. In some books there are two hymns by Doddridge, one probably by Wesley, one by Sternhold or J. Mardley, and Bishop Ken's Morning and Evening Hymns, altered and abridged."

In the *Oxford Essays* for 1858, in an article on "Hymns and Hymn-writers," by C. B. Pearson, he speaks of the introduction of hymns to *Tate and Brady* as being due to the "University printers in modern times more particularly to one about half a century back [i.e. 1808], who being a Dissenter, thought fit to fill up the blank leaves at the end of the Prayer Book with hymns suggested by himself."

This is doubtless the source of Miller's information. Both Pearson and Miller are very vague in their dates. Pearson's date is *circa* 1808 : and Miller's *circa* 1819. Whereas the hymns appeared in the Cambridge edition of the *N. Version* in 1782, printed by " J. Archdeacon, Printer to the University." Was " J. Archdeacon " a Dissenter ? We cannot say.   [J. J.]

Newman, John Henry, D.D. The hymnological side of Cardinal Newman's life and work is so small when compared with the causes which have ruled, and the events which have accompanied his life as a whole, that the barest outline of biographical facts and summary of poetical works comprise all that properly belongs to this work. Cardinal Newman was the eldest s. of John Newman, and was b. in London, Feb. 21, 1801. He was educated at Ealing under Dr. John Nicholas, and at Trinity College, Oxford, where he graduated in honours in 1820, and became a Fellow of Oriel in 1822. Taking Holy Orders in 1824, he was for a short time Vice-Principal of St. Alban's Hall, and then Tutor of Oriel. His appointment to St. Mary's, Oxford, was in the spring of 1828. In 1827 he was Public Examiner, and in 1830 one of the Select University Preachers. His association with Keble, Pusey, and others, in what is known as " The Oxford Movement," together with the periodical publication of the *Tracts for the Times*, are matters of history. It is well known how that *Tract* 90, entitled *Remarks on Certain Passages in the Thirty-nine Articles*, in 1841, was followed by his retirement to Littlemore ; his formal recantation, in February, 1843, of all that he had said against Rome ; his resignation in September of the same year of St. Mary's and Littlemore ; and of his formal application to be received into the communion of the Church of Rome, Oct. 8, 1845. In 1848 he became Father Superior of the Oratory of St. Philip Neri, at Birmingham ; in 1854 Rector of the newly founded Roman Catholic University at Dublin ; and in 1858 he removed to the Edgbaston Oratory, Birmingham. In 1879 he was created a Cardinal, and thus received the highest dignity it is in the power of the Pope to bestow. Cardinal Newman's prose works are numerous, and his *Parochial Sermons* especially being very popular. His *Apologia pro Vita Sua*, 1864, is a lucid exposition and masterly defence of his life and work.

Cardinal Newman's poetical work began with poems and lyrical pieces which he contributed to the *British Magazine*, in 1832–4 (with other pieces by Keble and others), under the title of *Lyra Apostolica*. In 1836 these poems were collected and published under the same title, and Greek letters were added to distinguish the authorship of each piece, his being δ. Only a few of his poems from this work have come into use as hymns. The most notable is, " Lead, kindly Light " (p. 667, i.). His *Tract for the Times*, No. 75, *On the Roman Breviary*, 1836, contained translations of 14 Latin hymns. Of these 10 were repeated in his *Verses on Religious Subjects*, 1853, and his *Verses on Various Occasions*, 1865, and translations of 24 additional Latin hymns were added. Several of these translations are in C. U., the most widely known being " Nunc Sancte nobis " (" Come, Holy Ghost, Who ever One "). His collection of Latin hymns from the *Roman* and *Paris Breviaries*, and other sources, was pub. as *Hymni Ecclesiae*, in 1838, and again in 1865. His *Dream of Gerontius*, a poem from which the fine hymn, "Praise to the Holiest in the height," is taken, appeared in his *Verses on Various Occasions*, in 1868. Cardinal Newman's influence on hymnology has not been of a marked character. Two brilliant original pieces, and little more than half a dozen translations from the Latin, are all that can claim to rank with his inimitable prose.   [J. J.]

Newton, James, A.M., was b. at Chenies, in Bucks, in the year 1732. At the age of 17 he went to London, where he joined the Baptist church under the care of the Rev. B. Wallin [Wallin, B.]. In 1757 he became assistant minister to the Rev. J. Tommas, pastor of the Baptist church in the Pithay, Bristol; and in 1770, classical tutor at the Baptist College in that city. He filled both these offices with honour and usefulness until his death in 1790. As a hymn-writer he is known by one hymn only, " Proclaim, saith Christ, my wondrous grace " (*Holy Baptism*), which appeared in 3 st. in the Bristol Coll. of *Ash & Evans*, 1769, No. 381; Rippon's *Bap. Sel.*, 1787, and others of the older hymn-books. In the Bap. *New Sel.*, 1828; the Bap. *Ps. & Hys.*, 1858; the *New Cong.*, 1859, and others, it begins with st. ii. :—" Let plenteous grace descend on those." In this form it is widely used.   [W. R. S.]

Newton, John, who was b. in London, July 24, 1725, and d. there Dec. 21, 1807, occupied an unique position among the founders of the Evangelical School, due as much to the romance of his young life and the striking history of his conversion, as to his force of character. His mother, a pious Dissenter, stored his childish mind with Scripture, but died when he was seven years old. At the age of eleven, after two years' schooling, during which he learned the rudiments of Latin, he went to sea with his father. His life at sea teems with wonderful escapes, vivid dreams, and sailor recklessness. He grew into an abandoned and godless sailor. The religious fits of his boyhood changed into settled infidelity, through the study of Shaftesbury and the instruction of one of his comrades.

Disappointing repeatedly the plans of his father, he was flogged as a deserter from the navy, and for fifteen months lived, half-starved and ill-treated, in abject degradation under a slave-dealer in Africa. The one restraining influence of his life was his faithful love for his future wife, Mary Catlett, formed when he was seventeen, and she only in her fourteenth year. A chance reading of Thomas à Kempis sowed the seed of his conversion; which quickened under the awful contemplations of a night spent in steering a water-logged vessel in the face of apparent death (1748). He was then twenty-three. The six following years, during which he commanded a slave ship, matured his Christian belief. Nine years more, spent chiefly at Liverpool, in intercourse with Whitefield, Wesley, and Nonconformists, in the study of Hebrew and Greek, in exercises of devotion and occasional preaching among the Dissenters, elapsed before his ordination to the curacy of Olney, Bucks (1764). The Olney period was the most fruitful of his life. His zeal in pastoral visiting, preaching and prayer-meetings was unwearied. He formed his lifelong friendship with Cowper [see Cowper, William], and became the spiritual father of Scott the commentator. At Olney his best works—*Omicron's Letters* (1774); *Olney Hymns* (1779); *Cardiphonia*, written from Olney, though pub. 1781 were composed. As rector of St. Mary Woolnoth, London, in the centre of the Evangelical movement (1780–1807) his zeal was as ardent as before. In 1805, when no longer able to read his text, his reply when pressed to discontinue preaching, was, " What, shall the old African blasphemer stop while he can speak ! " The story of his sins and his conversion, published by himself, and the subject of lifelong allusion, was the base of his influence; but it would have been little but for the vigour of his mind (shown even in Africa by his reading Euclid drawing its figures on the sand), his warm heart, candour, tolerance, and piety. These qualities gained him the friendship of Hannah More, Cecil, Wilberforce, and others; and his renown as a guide in experimental religion made him the centre of a host of inquirers, with whom he maintained patient, loving, and generally judicious correspondence, of which a monument remains in the often beautiful letters of *Cardiphonia*. As a hymn-writer, Montgomery says that he was distanced by Cowper. But Lord Selborne's contrast of the " manliness " of Newton and the " tenderness " of Cowper is far juster. A comparison of the hymns of both in *The Book of Praise* will show no great inequality between them. Amid much that is bald, tame, and matter-of-fact, his rich acquaintance with Scripture, knowledge of the heart, directness and force, and a certain sailor imagination, tell strongly. The one splendid hymn of praise, " Glorious things of thee are spoken," in the Olney collection, is his. " One there is above all others " has a depth of realizing love, sustained excellence of expression, and ease of development. " How sweet the name of Jesus sounds " is in Scriptural richness superior, and in structure, cadence, and almost tenderness, equal to Cowper's " Oh ! for a closer walk with God." The most characteristic hymns are those which depict in the language of intense humiliation his mourning for the abiding sins of his regenerate life, and the sense of the withdrawal of God's face, coincident with the never-failing conviction of acceptance in The Beloved. The feeling may be seen in the speeches, writings, and diaries of his whole life. For its bearing on his relations with Cowper, see Olney Hymns and Cowper, William.   [H. L. B.]

A large number of Newton's hymns have some personal history connected with them, or were associated with circumstances of importance. These are annotated under their respective first lines. Of the rest, the known history of which is confined to the fact that they appeared in the Olney Hymns, 1779, the following are in C. U.:—

1. Be still, my heart, these anxious cares. *Conflict.*
2. Begone, unbelief, my Saviour is near. *Trust.*
3. By the poor widow's oil and meal. *Providence.*
4. Chief Shepherd of Thy chosen sheep. *On behalf of Ministers.*
5. Darkness overspreads us here. *Hope.*
6. Does the Gospel-word proclaim. *Rest in Christ.*
7. Fix my heart and eyes on Thine. *True Happiness.*
8. From Egypt lately freed. *The Pilgrim's Song.*
9. He Who on earth as man was known. *Christ the Rock.*
10. How blest are they to whom the Lord. *Gospel Privileges.*
11. How blest the righteous are. *Death of the Righteous.*
12. How lost was my [our] condition. *Christ the Physician.*
13. How tedious and tasteless the hours. *Fellowship with Christ.*
14. How welcome to the saints [soul] when pressed. *Sunday.*
15. Hungry, and faint, and poor. *Before Sermon.*
16. In mercy, not in wrath, rebuke. *Pleading for Mercy.*
17. In themselves, as weak as worms. *Power of Prayer.*
18. Incarnate God, the soul that knows. *The Believer's Safety.*
19. Jesus, Who bought us with His blood. *The God of Israel.* "Teach us, O Lord, aright to plead," is from this hymn.
20. Joy is a [the] fruit that will not grow. *Joy.*
21. Let hearts and tongues unite. *Close of the Year.* From this "Now, through another year," is taken.
22. Let us adore the grace that seeks. *New Year.*
23. Mary to her [the] Saviour's tomb. *Easter.*
24. Mercy, O Thou Son of David. *Blind Bartimeus.*
25. My harp untun'd and laid aside. *Hoping for a Revival.* From this "While I to grief my soul gave way" is taken.
26. Nay, I cannot let thee go. *Prayer.* Sometimes, "Lord, I cannot let Thee go."
27. Now may He Who from the dead. *After Sermon.*
28. O happy they who know the Lord, With whom He deigns to dwell. *Gospel Privilege.*
29. O Lord, how vile am I. *Lent.*
30. On man in His own Image made. *Adam.*
31. O speak that gracious word again. *Peace through Pardon.*
32. Our Lord, Who knows full well. *The Importunate Widow.* Sometimes altered to "Jesus, Who knows full well," and again, "The Lord, Who truly knows."
33. Physician of my sin-sick soul. *Lent.*
34. Pleasing spring again is here. *Spring.*
35. Poor, weak, and worthless, though I am. *Jesus the Friend.*
36. Prepare a thankful song. *Praise to Jesus.*
37. Refreshed by the bread and wine. *Holy Communion.* Sometimes given as "Refreshed by sacred bread and wine."
38. Rejoice, believer, in the Lord. Sometimes "Let us rejoice in Christ the Lord." *Perseverance.*
39. Salvation, what a glorious plan. *Salvation.*
40. Saviour, shine and cheer my soul. *Trust in Jesus.* The cento "Once I thought my mountain strong," is from this hymn.
41. Saviour, visit Thy plantation. *Prayer for the Church.*

42. See another year [week] is gone. *Uncertainty of Life.*
43. See the corn again in ear. *Harvest.*
44. Sinner, art thou still secure? *Preparation for the Future.*
45. Sinners, hear the [thy] Saviour's call. *Invitation.*
46. Sovereign grace has power alone. *The two Malefactors.*
47. Stop, poor sinner, stop and think. *Caution and Alarm.*
48. Sweeter sounds than music knows. *Christmas.*
49. Sweet was the time when first I felt. *Joy in Believing.*
50. Ten thousand talents once I owed. *Forgiveness and Peace.*
51. The grass and flowers, which clothe the field. *Hay-time.*
52. The peace which God alone reveals. *Close of Service.*
53. Thy promise, Lord, and Thy command. *Before Sermon.*
54. Time, by moments, steals away. *The New Year.*
55. To Thee our wants are known. *Close of Divine Service.*
56. We seek a rest beyond the skies. *Heaven anticipated.*
57. When any turn from Zion's way. *Jesus only.*
58. When Israel, by divine command. *God, the Guide and Sustainer of Life.*
59. With Israel's God who can compare? *After Sermon.*
60. Yes, since God Himself has said it. *Confidence.*
61. Zion, the city of our God. *Journeying Zionward.*

[J. J.]

Nicholas, Tressilian George, M.A., s. of the Rev. George Nicholas, LL.D., was b. in London, April 14, 1822, and educated at Wadham College, Oxford. (B.A. in honours, 1843, M.A. 1846.) On taking Holy Orders he became Curate of St. Lawrence, Reading, 1845; Incumbent of West Molesey, 1846; and Vicar of Lower Halstow, 1859. In 1863 he returned to West Molesey. He contributed several poetical pieces to the *Church of England Magazine.* These were collected and pub. as *Poems* in 1851. From this work his well-known and extensively used hymn for *Holy Communion,* "Lord, when before Thy throne we meet," was taken. It is part of a poem which was printed in the *Church of England Mag.* for Jan. 6, 1838. It is usually given in 3 st. of 6 l., and often as anonymous. [J. J.]

Nicholson, Horatio Langrishe, D.D., was educated at Trinity College, Dublin (B.A. in honours 1855, D.D. 1880). After taking Holy Orders in 1856, he held several appointments in Ireland to 1859, when he became Lecturer of Holy Trinity, Newington, London. Subsequently he was Incumbent of St. James's, Kennington, 1862, and then of other parishes, the last being the Vicarage of St. James's, Forest Gate, Stratford, Essex. During his Incumbency of St. Saviour's, Brockley Hill, London, he pub. :—

The Appendix Hymnal compiled as an Appendix to Hymns Ancient and Modern, to Chopes's Hymnal, and that published by the Society for Promoting Christian Knowledge, 1866.

To this *Appendix* he contributed several hymns for Special Services and occasions which were not then fully provided for in those collections. These are :—

1. Alone, yet not alone, so spake. *Gethsemane.*
2. Father of Spirits, Thee we pray. *Harvest.*
3. Gently I breathe to Thee, Jesus, my prayer. *Lent.*
4. Happy matron, though for years. *St. Anna.*
5. Hark the loud Hosannahs! *Processional for Palm Sunday.*
6. Heard ye holy women say. *Processional for Easter Day.*

7. I will not leave Thee, Jesus Lord. *Fidelity to Jesus.*

8. In the hour of doubt and sorrow. *In Affliction or Distress.*

9. Lord, upon our knees we fall. *Lent.*

10. On this Pentecostal morning. *Processional for Whitsunday.*

11. Prostrate in the dust before Him. *Lent.*

12. Remember, Lord, Thy servants. *Processional for Advent Sunday.*

13. See, her hastening steps are bent. *Visitation of B. V. M.*

14. Shades of evening gather round us. *Evening.*

15. Starlight of Bethlehem. *Life of Jesus.*

16. Sunlight from the heaven departed. *Processional for the Epiphany.*

17. Take up the Cross, and bear it. *Processional for Trinity Sunday.*

18. We saw Thee, Virgin born. *Processional for Ascension Day.*

19. What are those sounds that fall. *Processional for Christmas Day.* [J. J.]

Nicolai, Philipp, D.D., s. of Dieterich Nicolai, sometime Lutheran pastor at Herdecke, in Westphalia, and after 1552, at Mengeringhausen in Waldeck, was b. at Mengeringhausen, August 10, 1556. (The father was s. of Nicolaus Rafflenböl, of Rafflenböl, near Hagen, in Westphalia, and in later life had adopted the Latinised form *Nicolai* of his father's Christian name as his own surname.) In 1575 Nicolai entered the University of Erfurt, and in 1576 he went to Wittenberg. After completing his University course in 1579 (D.D. at Wittenberg July 4, 1594), he lived for some time at Volkhardinghausen, near Mengeringhausen, and frequently preached for his father. In August, 1583, he was appointed Lutheran preacher at Herdecke, but found many difficulties there, the members of the Town Council being Roman Catholics. After the invasion by the Spanish troops in April, 1586, his colleague re-introduced the Mass, and Nicolai resigned his post. In the end of 1586 he was appointed diaconus at Niederwildungen, near Waldeck, and in 1587 he became pastor there. He then became, in Nov. 1588, chief pastor at Altwildungen, and also court preacher to the widowed Countess Margaretha of Waldeck, and tutor to her son, Count Wilhelm Ernst. Here he took an active part on the Lutheran side in the Sacramentarian controversy, and was, in Sept. 1592, inhibited from preaching by Count Franz of Waldeck, but the prohibition was soon removed, and in the Synod of 1593 held at Mengeringhausen, he found all the clergy of the principality of Waldeck willing to agree to the Formula of Concord. In October, 1596, he became pastor at Unna, in Westphalia, where he again became engaged in heated controversy with the Calvinists; passed through a frightful pestilence (see below); and then on Dec. 27, 1598, had to flee before the invasion of the Spaniards, and did not return till the end of April, 1599. Finally, in April 1601, he was elected chief pastor of St. Katherine's Church, at Hamburg, where he entered on his duties Aug. 6, 1601. On Oct. 22, 1608, he took part in the ordination of a colleague in the St. Katherine's Church, the diaconus Penshorn, and returned home feeling unwell. A violent fever developed itself, under which he sank, and d. Oct. 26, 1608 (*D. Philipp Nicolai's Leben und Lieder*, by L. Curtze, 1859; *Koch*, ii. 324; *Allg. Deutsche Biog.* xxiii. 607, &c.).

In Hamburg Nicolai was universally esteemed, was a most popular and influential preacher, and was regarded as a "pillar" of the Lutheran church. In his private life he seems to have been most lovable and estimable. Besides his fame as a preacher, his reputation rests mainly on his hymns. His printed works are mostly polemical, often very violent and acrid in tone, and such as the undoubted sincerity of his zeal to preserve pure and unadulterated Lutheranism may explain, but cannot be said to justify. Of his hymns only four seem to have been printed.

Three of Nicolai's hymns were first pub. in his devotional work entitled *Frewden-Spiegel dess ewigen Lebens*, pub. at Frankfurt-am-Main, 1599 (see further below). The two noted here ("Wachet auf" and "Wie schön") rank as classical and epoch-making. The former is the last of the long series of Watchmen's Songs. The latter marks the transition from the objective churchly period to the more subjective and experimental period of German hymn writing; and begins the long series of Hymns of Love to Christ as the Bridegroom of the Soul, to which Franck and Scheffler contributed such beautiful examples. Both are also worthy of note for their unusual and perfect rhythms, and for their splendid melodies. They are:—

i. **Wachet auf, ruft uns die Stimme.** *Eternal Life.* This beautiful hymn, one of the first rank, is founded on St. Matt. xxv. 1–13; Rev. xix. 6–9, and xxi. 21; 1 Cor. ii. 9; Ezek. iii. 17; and Is. lii. 8. It first appeared in the *Appendix* to his *Frewden-Spiegel*, 1599, in 3 st. of 10 l., entitled "Of the Voice at Midnight, and the Wise Virgins who meet their Heavenly Bridegroom. Matt. 25." Thence in *Wackernagel* v. p. 259, the *Unv. L. S.*, 1851, No. 690, and most German collections.

It is a reversed acrostic, W. Z. G. for the *Graf zu Waldeck*, viz. his former pupil Count Wilhelm Ernst, who d. at Tübingen Sept. 16, 1598, in his fifteenth year. It seems to have been written in 1597 at Unna, in Westphalia, where Nicolai was then pastor; and during the terrible pestilence which raged there from July, 1597, to January, 1598, to which in July 300, in one week in August 170, and in all over 1300 fell victims. Nicolai's parsonage overlooked the churchyard, and there daily interments took place, often to the number of thirty. In these days of distress, when every household was in mourning, Nicolai's thoughts turned to Death, and thence to God in Heaven, and to the Eternal Fatherland. In the preface (dated Aug. 10, 1598) to his *Frewden-Spiegel* he says: "There seemed to me nothing more sweet, delightful and agreeable, than the contemplation of the noble, sublime doctrine of Eternal Life obtained through the Blood of Christ. This I allowed to dwell in my heart day and night, and searched the Scriptures as to what they revealed on this matter, read also the sweet treatise of the ancient doctor Saint Augustine [*De Civitate Dei*]. ..... Then day by day I wrote out my meditations, found myself, thank God! wonderfully well, comforted in heart, joyful in spirit, and truly content; gave to my manuscript the name and title of a *Mirror of Joy*, and took this so composed *Frewden-Spiegel* to leave behind me (if God should call me from this world) as the token of my peaceful, joyful, Christian departure, or (if God should spare me in health) to comfort other sufferers whom He should also visit with the pestilence .... Now has the gracious, holy God most mercifully preserved me amid the dying from the dreadful pestilence, and wonderfully spared me beyond all my thoughts and hopes, so that with the Prophet David I can say to Him "O how great is Thy goodness, which Thou hast laid up for them that fear Thee," &c.

The hymn composed under these circumstances (it may be stated that Curtze thinks both hymns were written in 1596, while Nicolai was still at Alt-Wildungen) soon became popular, and still retains its place, though often altered in the 3rd stanza. Probably the opening lines:

"Wachet auf! ruft uns die Stimme
Der Wächter sehr hoch auf der Zinne"

are borrowed from one of the *Wächter-Lieder*, a form of lyric popular in the Middle Ages, introduced by Wolfram von Eschenbach. (See K. Goedeke's *Deutsche Dichtung im Mittelalter*, 1871, p. 918.) But while in the Songs the voice of the Watchman from his turret summons the workers of darkness to flee from discovery, with 'Nicolai it is a summons to the children of light to awaken to their promised reward and full felicity.

The melody appeared first along with the hymn, and is also apparently by Nicolai, though portions of it (e.g. l. 1 by the Gregorian Fifth Tone) may have been suggested by earlier tunes. It has been called the King of Chorales, and by its majestic simplicity and dignity it well deserves the title. Since its use by Mendelssohn in his *St. Paul* it has become well known in England, and, in its original form, is given in Miss Winkworth's *C. B. for England*, 1863 (see below).

Translations in C. U. :—

1. Sleepers wake, a voice is calling. This is an unrhymed *tr.* of st. i. by W. Ball in his book of words to Mendelssohn's oratorio of *St. Paul*, 1836. This form is in Horder's Cong. *Hymns*, 1884, and others. In the South Place [London] *Coll.*, 1873, it is a recast by A. J. Ellis, but opens with the same first line. In the *Parish H. Bk.*, 1875, a *tr.* of st. ii., also unrhymed, is added.

2. Wake ye holy maidens, wake ye. A good *tr.* contributed by Philip Pusey to A. R. Reinagle's *Coll. of Ps. and Hy. Tunes*, Oxford, 1840, p. 134. It was considerably altered, beginning "Wake, ye holy maidens, fearing" in the *Salisbury H. Bk.*, 1857, and this is repeated, with further alterations, in *Kennedy*, 1863, and the *Sarum Hyl.*, 1868.

3. Wake, arise! the call obeying. A good *tr.* by A. T. Russell, as No. 110 in the Dalston Hospital *H. Bk.*, 1848.

4. Wake, oh wake; around are flying. This is a recast, by A. T. Russell, not for the better, from his 1848 *tr.*, as No. 268 in his *Ps. & Hys.* 1851, st. iii. being omitted. Thence, unaltered, in the *New Zealand Hyl.*, 1872.

5. Wake, awake, for night is flying. A very good *tr.* by Miss Winkworth, in her *Lyra Ger.*, 2nd Ser., 1858, p. 225, repeated in her *C. B. for England*, 1863, No. 200, with st. ii., ll. 7, 8, re-written. Included in the Eng. Pres. *Ps. & Hys.*, 1867; Scottish *Pres. Hyl.*, 1876, &c.; and in America, in *Laudes Domini*, 1884, and others. In the *Cantate Domino*, Boston, U. S., 1859, it begins "Awake, awake, for night is flying."

6. Wake! the startling watch-cry pealeth. By Miss Cox, in *Lyra Messianica*, 1864, p. 4, and her *Hys. from the German*, 1864, p. 27; repeated in W. F. Stevenson's *H. for Church and Home*, 1873. The version in J. A. Porter's *Coll.*, 1876, takes st. i., ll. 1-4 from Miss Cox. The rest is mainly from R. C. Singleton's *tr.* in the *Anglican H. Bk.*, but borrows lines also from Miss Winkworth, and from the *Hymnary* text.

7. Wake! the watchman's voice is sounding. By R. C. Singleton. This is No. 259 in the *Anglican H. Bk.*, 1868, where it is marked as a "versification by R. C. Singleton, 1867."

8. Wake, awake, for night is flying. This is by Canon W. Cooke, in the *Hymnary*, 1871, and signed A. C. C. In the ed. of 1872, ll. 7, 8 of st. ii. are recast, and the whole is marked as "based on E. A. Dayman." It is really a cento, four lines of the 1872 text (i., l. 5; ii., ll. 7, 8; iii., l. 9) being by Canon Cooke; and the rest being adapted from the versions of P. Pusey as altered in the *Sarum Hyl.*, of Miss Winkworth, of Miss Cox, and of R. C. Singleton. It may be regarded as a success, and as passed into the S. P. C. K. *Church Hys.*, 1871; the 1874 *Appx.* to the *N. Cong.*; Horder's *Cong. Hys.*, 1884, and others.

9. Wake, arise! the voice is calling. This is an anonymous *tr.* in the Ohio *Luth. Hyl.*, 1880.

10. Slumberers, wake, the Bridegroom cometh. A spirited version, based on Miss Winkworth (and with an original st. as iv.), by J. H. Hopkins in his *Carols, Hys. & Songs*, 3rd ed., 1882. p. 88, and dated 1866. Repeated in the *Hyl, Comp.* (Reformed Epis.) Philadelphia, U.S., 1885.

Other trs. are :—

(1) "Awake, the voice is crying." In *Lyra Davidica*, 1708, p. 73. (2) "Awake! awake! the watchman calls." By *Miss Fry*, 1845, p. 33. (3) "Hark! the trump of God is sounding." By *Dr. H. Mills*, 1845 (1856, p. 269). This is from the altered form by F. G. Klopstock, in his *Geistliche Lieder*, 1758, p. 246, as further altered in Zollikofer's *G. B.*, 1766, No. 303, where it begins "Wachet auf! so ruft." (4) "Awake, arise, the voice gives warning." In the U. P. *Juvenile Missionary Mag.*, 1857, p. 193; repeated in 1859, p. 171, beginning, "Awake, arise, it is the warning." (5) "Waken! From the tower it soundeth." By *Mrs. Bevan*, 1858, p. 1. (6) Up! awake! his summons hurried." By J. D. Burns, in the *Family Treasury*, 1860, p. 84, and his *Memoir & Remains*, 1869, p. 234.

ii. Wie schön leuchtet der Morgenstern, Voll Gnad und Wahrheit von dem Herrn. *Love to Christ.* 1st pub. in the *Appendix* to his *Freuden-Spiegel*, 1599, in 7 st. of 10 l. entitled "A spiritual bridal song of the believing soul concerning Jesus Christ, her heavenly Bridegroom, founded on the 45th Psalm of the prophet David." Lauxmann, in *Koch*, viii. 271, thus gives an account of it as written during the Pestilence of 1597. He says Nicolai was

"One morning in great distress and tribulation in his quiet study. He rose in spirit from the distress and death which surrounded him to his Redeemer and Saviour, and while he clasped Him in ardent love there welled forth from the inmost depths of his heart this precious hymn of the Saviour's love and of the joys of Heaven. He was so entirely absorbed in this holy exaltation that he forgot all around him, even his midday meal, and allowed nothing to disturb him in his poetical labours till the hymn was completed"—three hours after midday.

As Nicolai was closely connected with Waldeck he formed with the initial letters of his stanzas the acrostic W. E. G. U. H. Z. W., viz. Wilhelm Ernst Graf Und Herr Zu Waldeck—his former pupil.

The hymn has reminiscences of Eph. v., of Canticles, and of the Mediæval Hymns to the B. V. M. It became at once a favourite in Germany, was reckoned indispensable at weddings, was often sung around death beds, &c. The original form is in *Wackernagel* v. p. 258, and the *Unv. L. S.*, 1851, No. 437; but this (as will be seen by comparing Miss Winkworth's version of 1869) is hardly suited for present day congregational use. In Bunsen's *Versuch*, 1833, No. 554, it is slightly altered. The form in Knapp's *Ev. L. S.*, 1837, No. 2074 (1865, No. 1810) is a recast by Knapp made on Jan. 14, 1832, and pub. in his *Christoterpe*, 1833, p. 285, preceded by a recast of "Wachet auf!"; both being marked as "rewritten according to the requirements of our times."

The popularity of the hymn was greatly aided by its beautiful chorale (named by Mr. Mercer, *Frankfort*), which has been called "The Queen of Chorales," and to which many city chimes in Germany were soon set. It was pub. with the hymn, and is probably an original tune by Nicolai, though portions may have been suggested by earlier melodies, especially by the "Resonet in laudibus," which is probably of the 14th cent. (*Bäumker* i.,

No. 48, cites it from the *Obsequiale*, Ingolstadt, 1570. In Allon's *Cong. Psalmist* named *Arimathea*).

Translations in C. U. :—

1. How bright appears the Morning Star! This is a full and fairly close version by J. C. Jacobi, in his *Psal. Ger.*, 1722, p. 90 (1732, p. 162); repeated, with alterations, in the *Moravian H. Bk.*, 1754, pt. i., No. 317 (1886, No. 360). The versions of st. v., vii. beginning, "The Father from eternity," are included in *Aids to the Service of Song*, Edin. N.D., but since 1860. In 1855 Mercer gave in his *C. P. & H. Bk.*, as No. 15, a hymn in 4 st. of 10 l., of which three lines are exactly from Jacobi. St. i., ll. 1–3; ii., ll. 8, 9; iii., ll. 2, 3, 6; iv., l. 10, are exactly; and i., l. 9; ii., ll. 2, 3, 6, 10; iii., il. 1, 4, 5; iv., ll. 7, 9 are nearly from the *Moravian H. Bk.*, 1801. The interjected lines are by Mercer, but bear very slight resemblance either to Nicolai's original text, or to any version of the German that we have seen. In his 1859 ed. he further recast it, leaving only the first line unaltered from Jacobi; and this form is in his Ox. ed., 1864, No. 121, in the Irish *Church Hyl.*, 1869 and 1873, and in the *Hyl. Comp.*, 1870 and 1876. In *Kennedy*, 1863, the text of 1859 is given with alterations, and begins "How brightly dawns the Morning Star"; and this form is in the *People's Hyl.*, 1867; Dale's *Eng. H. Bk.*, 1874, &c.

2. How graciously doth shine afar. By A. T. Russell, as No. 8 in the Dalston Hospital *H. Bk.*, 1848, and repeated in the *Cheltenham College H. Bk.*, No. 37. It is a free *tr.* of st. i., vi., v.

3. How lovely shines the Morning Star! A good and full *tr.* by Dr. H. Harbaugh (from the text in Dr. Schaff's *Deutsches G. B.*, 1860), in the German Reformed *Guardian*, May, 1860, p. 157. Repeated in full in Schaff's *Christ in Song*, 1869, and abridged in Adams's *Church Pastorals*, Boston, U.S.A., 1864.

4. O Morning Star! how fair and bright. A somewhat free *tr.* of st. i., iii., iv., vii., by Miss Winkworth, as No. 149 in her *C. B. for England*, 1863. Repeated in the Pennsylvania *Luth. Church Bk.*, 1868; Ohio *Luth. Hyl.*, 1880, &c.

5. How brightly shines the Morning Star, In truth and mercy from afar. A *tr.* of st. i., iii., iv., vii., by Miss Borthwick, as No. 239 in Dr. Pagenstecher's *Coll.*, 1864.

6. How brightly glows the Morning Star. In full, from Knapp's German recast, by M. W. Stryker, in his *Hys. & Verses*, 1883, p. 52; repeated, omitting st. ii., iv., in his *Christian Chorals*, 1885, No. 145.

Other trs. are :—

(1) "How fairly shines the Morning Star." In *Lyra Davidica*, 1708, p. 40. (2) "As bright the star of morning gleams" (st. i.) By W. Bartholomew, in his book of words to Mendelssohn's oratorio of *Christus*, 1852, p. 11. (3) "How lovely now the Morning Star." By *Miss Cox*, 1864, p. 229. (4) "How beauteous shines the Morning Star." By Miss Burlingham, in the *British Herald*, Oct. 1865, p. 152, and Reid's *Praise Bk.*, 1872. (5) "O Morning Star, how fair and bright." By *Miss Winkworth*, 1869, p. 160. (6) "How bright appears our Morning Star." By J. H. Hopkins, in his *Carols, Hys. and Songs*, 3rd ed., 1882, p. 168, and dated 1866.

There are also three hymns in C. U., which have generally been regarded as *trs.* from Nicolai. They are noted as follows :—i. "Behold how glorious is yon sky" (see p. 127, ii.). ii. "How beautiful the Morning Star" (see Stegmann, J.). iii. "How brightly shines the Morning Star! What eye descries it from afar" (see **Schlegel, J. A.**).   [J. M.]

Night is on the unransomed nations. *J. M. Neale.* [*Passiontide.*] This Sequence for Passiontide appeared in his posthumous *Sequences, Hys., and other Ecclesiastical Verses*, 1866, p. 11, in 20 st. of 4 l. From it three centos have come into C. U. : (1) "Night is on the unransomed nations"; (2) "Till His warfare be accomplished"; and (3) "We have heard, O Son of David." [J. J.]

Nil laudibus nostris eges. *C. Coffin.* [*Monday.*] Appeared in the *Paris Breviary*, 1736, for Monday at Lauds, and his *Hymni Sacri*, 1736, p. 12. It is also in the *Lyons* and other modern French Breviaries; Card. Newman's *Hymni Ecclesiae*, 1838 and 1865; Chandler's *Hys. of the Prim. Church*, 1837, No. 18; Macgill's *Songs of the Christian Creed and Life*, 1876, &c. It has been *tr.* as :—

1. **Our praises, Lord, Thou dost not need.** *J. Chandler*, 1837, No. 18, and 1841, No. 73.
2. **Our praise Thou need'st not, but Thy love.** I. Williams, in his *Hys. tr. from the Parisian Brev.*, 1839.
3. **Father! Thou needest not our praise.** *W. J. Blew*, 1852–55.
4. **Though throned our highest praise above.** *J. D. Chambers*, 1857.
5. **Thou needest not our feeble praise.** *H. M. Macgill*, 1876.
6. **Father in heaven! Thy glory.** *D. T. Morgan*, 1880.   [J. J.]

Nitschmann, Anna, daughter of David Nitschmann, cartwright, at Kunewald, near Fulnek, Moravia, was b. at Kunewald, Nov. 24, 1715. Her cousin, David Nitschmann (the first Bishop, 1735, of the renewed Brethren's Unity) while on a visit to Kunewald in the beginning of 1725, persuaded her father to remove to Herrnhut, where the family arrived on Feb. 25, 1725. On March 17, 1730, Anna was appointed Unity-Elder, with the care of the unmarried sisters; on May 4, 1730, joined with Anna Dober in founding the Jungfrauenbund (see p. 304, ii.); and in 1733 entered the unmarried sisters' house at Herrnhut. In 1735 she became companion to Zinzendorf's daughter, the Countess Benigna, and accompanied her, in 1737, to England. During the summer of 1740 she went with her own father to America, arriving in Pennsylvania Dec. 5, 1740. After the arrival of Zinzendorf and the Countess Benigna, in 1741, Anna joined with them in work among the Indians. She returned to Germany in 1743. After the death of his first wife on June 19, 1756, Zinzendorf married Anna at Berthelsdorf on June 27, 1757. When on May 5, 1760, Zinzendorf felt his fatal illness, she also succumbed, and after his death, on May 9, gradually sank and d., May 21, 1760, at Herrnhut (*Allg. Deutsche Biog.* xxiii. 709; MS. from Diaconus J. T. Müller, Herrnhut, &c.). Her hymns were written 1735–1748; the earlier in Herrnhut, some in Pennsylvania, others from 1743 to 1748. They appeared in the various *Appendices* to the *Herrnhut G. B.* of 1735. Only two have passed into use outside of the English *Moravian H. Bk.* These are :—

i. **Ich bin das arme Würmlein dein.** *Humility.* 1st pub. as No. 1592 in *Appendix* x. *circa* 1741 to the *Herrnhut G. B.*, 1735, in 12 st. of 4 l. When repeated in the *Brüder G. B.*, 1778, No. 851, st. i., ll. 1, 2; iv., ll. 1, 2; ii.; iii.; xii. were selected with alterations, and a stanza by C. Gregor (which begins "Mein Heiland! dass ich ohne dich") was prefixed. The *tr.* in C. U. is:—

My Saviour, that I without Thee. *Tr.* in full by F. W. Foster, from the text of 1778, and given as No. 450

in the *Moravian H. Bk.*, 1789 (1886, No. 580). Included, omitting st. v., in J. A. Latrobe's *Coll.*, 1841.

ii. **Mein König, deine Liebe.** *Christian Work.* Appeared as No. 1233 in *Appendix* vii. *circa* 1737 to the *Herrnhut G. B.*, 1735, in 14 st. of 6 l. In the *Brüder G. B.*, 1778, No. 1355, reduced to 6 stanzas (st. v. in 1778 is by N. L. Zinzendorf). The only *tr.* in C. U. is noted at p. **558.**

Another tr. is : "Thou our exalted first-born Brother." This is a *tr.* of st. xiv. in the *Moravian H. Bk.*, pt. ii., 1746, p. 798. In 1754, pt. ii., p. 365, altered to "O Thou our first-born Brother" (1849, No. 852, st. ii.).   [J. M.]

Nitschmann, Johann, brother of Anna Nitschmann, was b. Sept. 25, 1712, at Kunewald, and came to Herrnhut in 1725. In 1726 the Count von Promnitz took him into the Orphanage at Sorau, and in 1728 sent him to study theology at Halle. In 1731 he became a tutor in the Orphanage at Herrnhut, in 1732 went to Halle to study medicine, but returned to Herrnhut in 1733, and spent a year as private secretary to Count Zinzendorf. Thereafter up to 1745 he was principally engaged in mission work in Swedish Lapland, and in forming communities in Livonia. He was then appointed, in 1745, diaconus and Gemeinhelfer at Herrnhaag in Wetteravia, and in 1750 to the same position at Herrnhut. Consecrated Bishop of the Brethren's Unity in 1758, he took in 1761 the superintendence of the communities in England and Ireland. In 1766, he was appointed to the charge of the new settlement of Sarepta on the Volga in Asiatic Russia, and d. there June 30, 1783 (*Allg. Deutsche Biog.* xxiii. 714; MS. from Diaconus J. T. Müller, Herrnhut, &c.). His hymns are few in number, and not of much importance. Only one has passed into use outside the English *Moravian H. Bk.* It is :—

Du blutiger Versühner. *The Lamb of God.* Appeared as No. 1210 in *Appendix* vi., c. 1737 to the *Herrnhut G. B.*, 1735, in 5 st. of 6 l. In the *Brüder G. B.*, 1778, it is No. 575, and in the *Historische Nachricht* thereto st. iv. is ascribed to N. L. von Zinzendorf. The *tr.* in C. U. is noted at p. **558,** i.

Another tr. is "Dear Lamb, from everlasting slain," as No. 21 in the *Moravian H. Bk.*, 1742. In the 1789 and later eds. (1849, No. 441), it begins "Gracious Redeemer, Who for us."   [J. M.]

No Gospel like this Feast. *Elizabeth Charles, née Rundle.* [*Holy Communion.*] Pub. in her *The Three Wakings and Other Poems*, 1859, p. 149. It has passed into a large number of hymnals, including the *Universal H. Bk.*, 1885, the American *Laudes Domini*, 1884, and others.   [J. J.]

No prophet, nor dreamer of dreams. *J. Hart.* [*Adoration.*] 1st pub. in his *Hys. composed on Various Subjects*, &c., 1759, in 7 st. of 8 l., and based upon the words "If there arise among you a prophet, or a dreamer of dreams, and giveth the sign or wonder," &c., Deut. xiii. 1, &c. In its original form it is not in common use; but the following centos have been compiled therefrom :—

1. **This God is the God we adore.** This is the last stanza of the hymn, and was given in M. Madan's *Supp.* to *Ps. and Hys.*, 1763, No. 182, broken into 2 st. of 4 l. The same arrangement was repeated by A. M. Toplady in his *Ps. & Hys.*, 1776, No. 127. From these collections it descended as an individual hymn to the modern hymnals. The same stanza, but altered to :—

2. **This, this is the God we adore,** was given in the *Supp.* of the *Wes. H. Bk.*, 1830, is continued in the revised ed., 1875, and also found in other collections. In the Bap. *Sel. of Ps. and Hys.*, 1838, No. 380, a cento is given, the first stanza of which we have not traced; but

st. ii., iii., are composed of Hart's "This God is the God we adore." It begins :—

3. **The God Who created the skies,** and is repeated in the Bap. *Ps. & Hys.*, 1858, No. 280.

4. **How good is the God we adore.** In *The Enlarged London H. Bk.*, 1873.   [J. J.]

No sleep, no slumber, to his eyes. *I. Watts.* [*Ps. cxxxii.*] 1st pub. in his *Psalms of David*, &c., 1719, in 8 st. of 4 l., and headed "A Church Established." In its full form it is not in general use; but as, "Arise, O King of grace, arise" (st. iii.-v.), as in the *Leeds H. Bk.*, 1853, it is in somewhat extensive use, especially in America.   [J. J.]

No songs shall break our gloom today. *W. C. Dix.* [*Good Friday.*] Pub. in *Lyra Messianica*, 1864, p. 244, in 7 st. of 4 l., and entitled "Calvary." It was also included in the author's *Hys. and Carols for Children*, 1869. In the S. P. C. K. *Church Hys.*, 1871, "O Thou the Eternal Son of God" is composed of st. ii., iv.-vii. of this hymn.   [J. J.]

No track is on the sunny sky. *F. W. Faber.* [*Whitsuntide.*] Appeared in his *Jesus and Mary*, &c., 1849, in 18 st. of 4 l., on "The Mission of the Holy Ghost." From it three centos have come into C. U.: (1) "No track is on the sunny sky;" (2) "The Mother prays her mighty prayer;" and (3) "The Mother sits all worshipful." In these various forms its use is somewhat extensive.   [J. J.]

Nobis, Olympo redditus. *Jean Baptiste de Santeüil.* [*Ascension.*] This hymn appeared in the *Cluniac Breviary*, 1686, p. 503, as "Nostras, Olympo redditus." It was repeated in Santeüil's *Hymni Sacri et Novi*, 1689, p. 24 (ed. 1698, p. 106), in 5 st. of 4 l. In the *Paris Breviary*, 1736, st. ii. is omitted, and another was added as the concluding stanza, beginning, "Venture Judex saeculi." The 1736 text is in J. Chandler's *Hys. of the Prim. Church*, 1837, and Card. Newman's *Hymni Ecclesiae*, 1838 and 1865.   *Tr.* as :—

1. **O Christ, Who hast prepared a place.** By J. Chandler, from the *Paris Brev.* text, in his *Hys. of the Prim. Church*, 1837, p. 86. It was soon introduced into the hymn-books, sometimes with slight alterations, as in Murray's *Hymnal*, 1852; and at other times with the omission of st. v., as in *Mercer*, Oxford ed., 1864, and others. In *H. A. & M.*, 1861, it reads: "O Christ, Who dost prepare a place," but it is omitted from the revised ed., 1875. This *tr.* in various forms is in extensive use. In Martineau's *Hymns*, 1873, 3 st. are given as "The Crucified is gone before."

2. **Thou Who dost build for us on high.** By I. Williams. 1st printed in the *British Magazine*, Dec. 1834 (vol. vi. p. 621, with the Latin). It was also included in his *Hys. tr. from the Parisian Breviary*, 1839, p. 145. It is given, with alterations, in the *Hymnary*, 1872.

3. **O Christ, Who, lifted to the sky.** By R. C. Singleton. Written in 1867, and pub. in his *Anglican H. Bk.*, 1868.

Other trs. are :—

1. Jesu! Thou from earth hast vanished. *W. J. Blew*, 1852-55.

2. Enthroned in heaven, Thy mansions fair. *J. D. Chambers*, 1857.   [J. J.]

Nocte mox diem fugata. [*Holy Communion.*] In the *Cluniac Breviary*, 1686, p. 563, this is the hymn at Matins for the

Octave of Corpus Christi, and consists of 5 st. and a doxology. *Tr.* as:—

Soon the fiery sun ascending. By E. Caswall. 1st pub. in his *Masque of Mary*, 1858, p. 305, in 5 st. of 6 l.; and again in his *Hymns*, &c., 1873, p. 158. It is given in the *People's H.*, 1867; the *Hymnary*, 1872: and others, including some Roman Catholic collections. [J. M.]

Nocte surgentes vigilemus omnes. *St. Gregory the Great.* [*Early morning.*] This is one of the eight hymns which the Benedictine editors assign to St. Gregory (*Opera*, Paris, 1705, iii., col. 879). It is found in three 11th cent. Hymnaries of the English Church, now in the British Museum (Vesp. D. xii., f. 6 *b*; Jul. A. vi., f. 20 *b*; Harl. 2961, f. 219), and in an 11th cent. Breviary of the Spanish Church (Add. 30848, f. 67 and f. 70 *b*). It is in an 11th cent. MS. at Corpus Christi, Cambridge (391, p. 229), and in the *Latin Hys. of the Anglo-Saxon Ch.* (Surtees Society), 1851, is printed from an 11th cent. MS. at Durham (B. iii. 32, f. 3 *b*). Also in a tenth cent. MS. at Bern, No. 455, and an 11th cent. MS. at St. Gall, No. 387. It is the companion hymn to and in the same metre as "Ecce jam noctis," (p. 320, i.) It was included in the *Roman* (Venice 1478, and Rome, 1632), *Sarum*, *York*, *Aberdeen*, and other *Breviaries*, generally assigned to Sunday Matins or Nocturns from Trinity S. to Advent. The text is also in *Daniel* i. No. 116; *Wackernagel* i., No. 95.; *Hymnarium Sarisb.*, 1851, p. 127; *Königsfeld* i., p. 76, and Card. Newman's *Hymni Ecclesiae*, 1838 and 1865. [J. M.]

The translations of this hymn are :—

1. Let us arise and watch by night. Card. Newman in *Tracts for the Times*, 1836, No. 75, p. 27; *Verses*, &c., 1853 and 1868.
2. Throughout the hours of darkness dim. *Hymnarium Anglicanum*. 1844.
3. Rising at midnight, one and all awaking. *W. J. Copeland*. 1848.
4. Let us arise and watch ere dawn of light. *E. Caswall*. 1849.
5. Uprising with the morning light. *W. J. Blew*. 1852-55.
6. Arise we in the nightly watches waking. *J. D. Chambers*. 1852.
7. Let us arise from night and slumber waking. *J. D. Chambers*. 1857.
8. Rising ere day-break, let us all be watchful. *J. W. Hewett*. 1859.
9. Watch we by night, with one accord uprising. *J. Keble*. 1869.
10. Come let us arise, and keep the watches of the night. *J. Wallace*. 1874.
11. 'Mid evening shadows let us all be watching. *Ray Palmer*. 1876. Dated 1869.
12. Now from the slumbers of the night arising. Anon, in the *Antiphoner* and *Grail*, 1880, and the *Hymner*, 1882. [J. J.]

Noel, Hon. Baptist Wriothesley, M.A., younger s. of Sir Gerard Noel Noel, Bart., and brother of the Earl of Gainsborough, was b. at Leithmont, near Leith, July 10, 1799, and educated at Trinity College, Cambridge. Taking Holy Orders he was for some time Incumbent of St. John's Episcopal Chapel, Bedford Row, London, and Chaplain to the Queen; but in 1848 he seceded from the Church of England, and subsequently became a Baptist Minister. He was pastor of St. John's Street Chapel, Bedford Row, until 1868. He d. Jan. 19, 1873. His prose works, about twelve in all, were pub. between 1847 and 1863. His association with hymnology is through :—

(1) *A Selection of Psalms and Hymns adapted chiefly for Congregational and Social Worship by Baptist Wriothesley Noel, M.A.* (2) *Hymns about Jesus, by Baptist Wriothesley Noel,* N. D. A collection of 159 hymns, the greater part of which are his own or recasts by him of older hymns.

The *Sel.* appeared in 1832. It passed through several editions (2nd ed., 1838; 3rd, 1848, &c.), that for 1853 being enlarged, and having also an *Appendix* of 39 original "Hymns to be Used at the Baptism of Believers." From this *Sel.* the following hymns are still in C. U. :—

1. Devoted unto Thee. *Holy Baptism.* From " O God, Who art our Friend."
2. Glory to God, Whose Spirit draws. *Holy Baptism.*
3. Jesus, the Lord of glory died. *Jesus the Guide.*
4. Lord, Thou hast promised to baptize. *Holy Baptism.*
5. We gave [give] ourselves to Thee. *Holy Baptism.* [J. J.]

Noel, Hon. Gerard Thomas, M.A., elder brother of the Hon. Baptist W. Noel, was b. Dec. 2, 1782, and educated at Edinburgh and Cambridge. Taking Holy Orders, he held successively the curacy of Radwell, Hertfordshire, the Vicarages of Rainham and Romsey, and a Canonry in Winchester Cathedral. He died at Romsey, Feb. 24, 1851. His published works include *Fifty Sermons for the Use of Families*, 1830; *Sermons preached in Romsey*, 1853; and *Arvendel, or Sketches in Italy and Switzerland*, 1813. In this last work some of his earlier hymns appeared. He also compiled :—*A Selection of Psalms and Hymns from the New Version of the Church of England and others; corrected and revised for Public Worship*, London, J. Hatchard, 1810. In this *Sel.* he gave a few hymns of his own, but anonymously. The 3rd ed., 1820, is enlarged, and has an *Appendix* of 17 hymns. Three of his hymns are in C. U. :—

1. If human kindness meets return. *Jesus the Friend.* This appeared in his *Arvendel*, &c., and his *Sel. of Ps. & Hys.*, 1810, No. 45. It is in extensive use.
2. Stamped as the purpose of the skies. *Missions.* This is found in the February number of the *Christian Observer*, 1810, in 6 st. of 4 l., and is signed "N." In his *Sel. of Ps. & Hys.*, 1810, No. 48, and in the 3rd ed., 1820, No. 174, it begins "Mark'd as the purpose of the skies." In this form it is known to the modern collections.
3. When musing sorrow weeps [mourns] the past. *Desiring Heaven.* Given in the 2nd ed. of his *Sel.* 1813, No. 48. [J. J.]

Νόμος ἦν γενικὸς τοῦ παντὸς ὁ πρώτιστος νόος· [Naasseni, The.]

Non abluunt lymphae Deum. *Nicolas le Tourneaux.* [*Epiphany.*] This hymn, on the Baptism of our Lord, appeared in the *Cluniac Brev.*, 1686, p. 229, beginning, "Lavacra puri gurgitus," and signed "*N. T. P. R.*" When included in the *Paris Brev.*, 1736, as the hymn for Compline during the Octave of the Epiphany, it began with st. ii., "Non abluunt lymphae Deum," and in this form it is known to the present time, both in Latin and in the *trs.* into English. This text is in Card. Newman's *Hymni Ecclesiae*, 1838 and 1865. *Tr.* as :—

1. It is not that the wave can wash our God. By I. Williams, in the *British Magazine*, 1835 (vol. viii. p. 152), and his *Hys. tr. from the Parisian Breviary*, 1839, p. 90.
2. Since the heavenly Lamb hath stood. By W. J. Blew, in his *Church Hy. and Tune Bk.*, 1852-

55, and Rice's *Sel.* from the same, 1870, No. 19. The opening stanza of this hymn is original, by Mr. Blew. The *tr.* of "Non abluunt" begins with st. ii., "Water washes not our God."

Other trs. are :—
1. God needeth not the cleansing wave. *R. Campbell.* 1850.
2. The waters cleanse not Thee, O Lord. *J. D. Chambers.* 1857.   [J. J.]

Non ce n'est pas mourir. *C. Malan.* [*Hope in Death.*] Pub. in his *Chants de Sion, ou Receuil de Cantiques,* 1832, No. 233. It was *tr.* into German by A. Knapp, and included in his *Christoterpe* (an annual), 1836, p. 116. It is No. 2 of "Hymns by Caesar Malan of Geneva. Translated from the French by the Editor" [*Knapp*]. It is also in Knapp's *Gedichte, Neueste Folge,* 1843, p. 301, and begins, "Nein, nein, das ist kein Sterben." It was *tr.* from the German into English by Dr. G. W. Bethune (p. **139,** i.), as "It is not death to die," and by Dr. R. P. Dunn (p. **316,** ii.) as "No, no, it is not dying." The latter is in *Sacred Lyrics from the German,* Philadelphia, U.S., 1859, p. 153; in Schaff's *Christ in Song,* 1869, p. 661 (1870, p. 531), and several hymn-books.   [J. M.]

Non parta solo sanguine. *Jean Baptiste de Santeüil.* [*Saints, not Martyrs.*] Appeared in the *Cluniac Breviary,* 1686, p. lvii., and his *Hymni Sacri et Novi,* 1689, p. 214 (ed. 1698, p. 252). In the *Paris Breviary,* 1736, it is given for the "Common of Just Persons." The text is also in J. Chandler's *Hys. of the Prim. Church,* 1837; and Card. Newman's *Hymni Ecclesiae,* 1838 and 1865. *Tr.* as:—

1. **Not by the martyr's death alone.** By I. Williams, in the *British Magazine,* Dec., 1833, p. 622, and again in his *Hys. tr. from the Parisian Breviary,* 1839, p. 315, in 6 st. of 4 l. This text is rarely given in its original form in the hymn-books. That in *H. A. & M.* is very considerably altered by the compilers; and that in the *Hymnary* by the editors. *Thring* takes the *H. A. & M.* text, and adds thereto emendations by himself. Others adopt a somewhat similar plan, so much so that it is almost always safe to say that any given text beginning "Not by the martyr's, &c." is *based upon I. Williams.*

2. **No purple with his life-blood stained.** By R. F. Littledale, made for, and first pub. in the *People's H.* 1867, and signed "F. R."

Other trs. are :—
1. 'Tis not the blood-stained vest alone. *J. Chandler,* 1837.
2. Not always earned by wounds and pain. *J. D. Chambers,* 1866.   [J. J.]

None is like Jeshurun's God. *C. Wesley.* [*Safety in God.*] Appeared in *Hys. and Sacred Poems,* 1742, p. 248, in 9 st. of 8 l., and based on Deut. xxxiii. 26, &c. (*P. Works,* 1868–72, vol. ii. p. 205.) It was included in the *Wes. H. Bk.,* 1780, No. 395, with the omission of st. vii.–ix., and the alteration in st. ii. of :—

"God hath underneath thee spread
His everlasting arms,"

to :—

"Round thee and beneath are spread
The everlasting arms."

The alteration in the same st. of "Sinner! what hast thou to dread?" to "*Israel,* what hast thou," &c., has been traced to a copy

of the *Wes. H. Bk.* of 1797. The hymn, usually with these changes, is in C. U. in G. Britain and America.   [J. J.]

Norris, John, b. at Collingbourne, Kingston, Wilts, 1657, his father being clergyman of the parish. He was educated at Winchester, and Exeter College, Oxford, subsequently becoming a Fellow of All Souls. From Oxford he passed, in 1689, to the Rectory of Newton St. Loe, Somersetshire, and thence, in 1691, to Bemerton, near Salisbury (and once the home of George Herbert), where he d. and was buried, in 1711. He was noted as a theologian, and as a metaphysical writer, his works on those subjects being many. In 1687 he published *A Collection of Miscellanies,* in prose and verse, in which four versions of individual psalms were given. A specimen from these is found in Holland's *British Psalmists,* and the whole were reprinted in 1871 with Norris's other poems in Dr Grosart's *Fuller Worthies' Miscellanies.* From his *Coll. of Miscellanies,* 1687, two hymns have passed into Martineau's *Hymns, &c.,* 1873 :—

1. In vain, great God, in vain I try. *God Omniscient.*
2. Long have I viewed, long have I thought. *Resignation.*   [W. T. B.]

Norton, Andrews, D.D., s. of Samuel Norton, was b. at Higham, Massachusetts, Dec. 31, 1786, and was educated at Higham, and at Harvard College. After being engaged there for a short time as a tutor, he was appointed Librarian, and subsequently Lecturer on Biblical Criticism, as successor to Dr. Channing. When the Theological School was opened in 1819 he became Dexter Professor of Literature. This position he held until 1830. He d. at Newport, Rhode Island, Sept. 18, 1853. He was for some time editor of the *General Repository and Review,* and pub. several prose works, one of the most extensive being *The Genuineness of the Gospels,* in 4 vols. His hymns are few in number, and are mainly meditations in verse. They were contributed to various periodicals, and after his death were collected and pub. in a small volume. Of these hymns the following are in C. U. :—

1. **Another year, another year, The unceasing rush, &c.** *Close of the Year.* Appeared in the *Christian Examiner* in Nov. and Dec., 1827, in 11 st. of 4 l. It is used in an abbreviated form. In the American Boston Unitarian *Hymn [& Tune]* Bk., 1868, it begins with st. vi., "O what concerns it him whose way."

2. **Faint not, poor traveller, though thy way.** *Fortitude.* Printed in the *Christian Disciple,* July and Aug., 1822, in 7 st. of 4 l., and again in the West Boston *Coll.,* 1823.

3. **He has gone to his God, he has gone to his home.** *Burial.* Printed in the *Christian Examiner,* Jan. and Feb., 1824.

4. **My God, I thank Thee! may no thought.** *Trust and Submission.* Appeared in the *Monthly Anthology and Boston Review,* Sept., 1809. This is his earliest and best known hymn.

5. **O stay thy tears : for they are blest.** *Burial of the Young.* Printed in the *General Repository and Review,* April, 1812, in 5 st. of 4 l. In 1855, st. iii.–v. were given in Beecher's *Plymouth Coll.,* No. 1094, as "How blest are they whose transient years."

6. **Where ancient forests round us spread.** *Dedication of a Church.* This "Hymn for the Dedication of a Church," is dated 1833.

These hymns are in some of the American hymnals. Nos. 1, 4, 5 are in Martineau's *Hymns*, 1873, and the full texts of all are in Putnam's *Singers and Songs of the Liberal Faith*, Boston, U.S.A., 1875.   [F. M. B.]

Norton, Thomas. [Old Version, § ix. 7.]

Not all the blood of beasts. *I. Watts.* [*Christ the Heavenly Sacrifice.*] 1st pub. in his *Hys. and Spiritual Songs*, enlarged ed., 1709, Bk. ii., No. 142, in 5 st. of 4 l., and headed "Faith in Christ our Sacrifice." It was brought into use in the Church of England through M. Madan's *Ps. & Hys.*, 1760; and A M, Toplady's *Ps. & Hys.*, 1776. In these collections alterations were introduced which, with additions from other sources, have been handed down to modern hymn-books. These changes in the text are the outcome of religious convictions and controversy. The most striking instance of this fact is given in the *Wes. H. Bk.* new ed., 1875. The outlook of Watts, which is that of *hope*, and the outlook of Methodism, which is that of *absolute knowledge*, is strikingly set forth in st. iv. and v. as follows :—

I. Watts, 1709.	Wes. H. Bk. 1875.
"My soul looks back to see The burdens Thou didst bear, When hanging on the cursed tree, And hopes her guilt was there.	"My soul looks back to see The *burden* Thou didst bear, When hanging on the *accursed* tree, And *knows* her guilt was there.
"Believing we rejoice To see the curse remove; We bless the Lamb with cheerful voice, And sing His bleeding love."	"Believing, we rejoice To *feel* the curse remove; We bless the Lamb with cheerful voice, And *trust* His bleeding love."

In addition to these, other alterations have crept into the text. The following list will assist in tracing these out :—

St. i. . . . . our stain . *Wes. H. Bk.*, 1830.
  " . . . . one stain . Stowell's *Ps. & Hys.*, 1831.
St. iii. *Upon that head Divine* . . . . Elliott's *Ps. & Hys.*, 1835.
  " On that *meek* head . *Wes. H. Bk.*, 1875.
  " while *as* a penitent *Wes. H. Bk.*, 1875.
  " Lay *its* hand . . . Madan's *Ps. & Hys.*, 1760.
St. iv. . . *th'* accursed tree Madan's *Ps. & Hys.*, 1760.
  " And *knows* her . . Mercer's *Coll.*, 1864.
  " And *trusts our* guilt Cotterill's *Sel.*, 1815
  " And *finds her safety* there . . . . U. Presb. *H. Bk.*, 1852.
St. v. To *feel* the curse . *Wes. H. Bk.*, 1830.
  " And *trust* His . . *Wes. H. Bk.*, 1875.
  " And sing *redeeming* Stowell's *Ps. & Hys.*, 1831.
  " And sing His *dying* U. Presb. *H. Bk.*, 1852.

In some American collections the hymn begins, "No blood of bird or beast;" but its use in this form is limited. With one or more of the above alterations in the text, it is in extensive use in all English-speaking countries. It has also been translated into several languages. The Latin *tr.* by R. Bingham in his *Hymno. Christ. Lat.*, 1871, is "Omnis sanguis bestiarum."   [J. J.]

Not for three or four transgressions. *G. Phillimore.* [*Cattle Plague.*] Written for and pub. in the *Parish H. Bk.*, as an addition to the edition of 1863, circa 1866, in 7 st. of 4 l., and again in the new ed. 1875, No. 271. In the *Sarum Hyl.*, 1868, st. i.–iv., vii., were given with slight alterations as No. 95.   [J. J.]

Not from the dust affliction grows. *I. Watts.* [*Affliction of God.*] Pub. in his *Hymns*, &c., 1709, Bk. i., No. 83, in 4 st. of 4 l., and from thence has passed into a few hymnals. In the *Translations and Paraphrases* of the Church of Scotland, which were authorized in 1781, this hymn (No. 5) is included in a new form as, "Tho' trouble springs not from the dust." In this form Watts is reproduced in everything but the actual words. By whom this recast was made is not known. In the marked copy of the *Trs. & Paraphs.* by the daughter of W. Cameron (p. 200, ii.) it is left a blank.   [J. J.]

Not here as to the prophet's eye. *J. Montgomery.* [*Opening of a Place of Worship.*] Written for the opening of the Methodist New Connexion Chapel, South Street, Moor, Sheffield, June 8, 1828, and printed as a flyleaf for the occasion. [M. MSS.] It was included in Conder's *Cong. H. Bk.*, 1836, No. 465, and in Montgomery's *Original Hymns*, 1853, No. 297, in 5 st. of 4 l. It is in C. U. in G. Britain and America. [J. J.]

Not to the terrors of the Lord. *I. Watts.* [*Whitsuntide.*] Appeared in his *Hys. and Spiritual Songs*, 1709, Bk. ii., No. 152, in 6 st. of 4 l., and entitled "Sinai and Sion." It is in C. U. in G. Britain and America. It is also in use in the following forms :—

1. **Not to the terrors of the Lord.** In the *Mitre H. Bk.*, 1836, No. 203; *Kennedy*, 1863, and others. This is composed of st. i., ii., from *Watts*, and a third stanza probably by *E. Osler*, who assisted W. J. Hall in compiling the *Mitre H. Bk.*
2. **Behold the radiant, countless host.** Composed of st. iii., v. altered, in *The Church Hymnal*, Philadelphia, 1869.
3. **The saints on earth and those above** (q.v.). The opening stanza of this cento is st. v. of this hymn.
    [J. J.]

Not unto us, but to Thy Name. [*Salvation through Grace.*] The first stanza of this cento is from J. Cennick's hymn, "Let us the sheep in Jesus named" (p. 673, ii.), somewhat altered, and the rest of the cento is by T. Cotterill. It appeared in the *Uttoxeter Collection* [see **Staffordshire Hymn-books**], 1805, and again in Cotterill's *Sel.*, 1810–20. It is given in several modern collections in G. Britain and America.   [J. J.]

Not what these hands have done. *H. Bonar.* [*Salvation through Christ alone.*] Pub. in his *Hys. of Faith and Hope*, 2nd Ser., 1861, in 12 st. of 4 l. In its full form it is not in C. U.; but the following centos are in several hymnals in G. Britain and America :—

1. **Not what these hands have done.** In the *Cong. Church Hymnal*, 1887, and others.
2. **Not what I feel or do.** Beginning with st. ii. in the American *Bap. Hymn and Tune Bk.*, Philadelphia, 1871, &c.
3. **I bless the Christ of God.** Opening with st. vii. This is the most popular of the centos, and is given in a great number of hymn-books in G. Brit. and America.
4. **I praise the God of grace.** This begins with st. ix., and is in several collections.

Through these various forms this hymn is in extensive use.   [J. J.]

Not worthy, Lord, to gather up the crumbs. *Bp. E. H. Bickersteth.* [*Holy Communion.*] Written in 1872, and included in the revised ed. of his *H. Companion*, 1876. It is also in several other collections.   [J. J.]

Notker Balbulus, so called from his slight stuttering, was b. in Switzerland about 840. Ekkehard V. in the 2nd Chapter of his *Vita Sancti Notkeri* (written about 1220), says he was b. at Heiligau, now Elgg, in the Canton of Zürich; but Meyer von Knonau (see below), seeing that his family were closely connected with Jonswil in the Canton of St. Gall, thinks that Notker was probably b. at Jonswil. He entered the school of the famous Benedictine Abbey of St. Gall at an early age, and spent the rest of his life there. In due course he was admitted as one of the brethren of the monastery; in 890 is marked as librarian, and in 892 and 894 as guest-master (hospitarius); his principal employment being in scholastic and literary work. He became eventually one of the foremost in the monastery at that its most flourishing period; but was never abbot there (Notker the Abbot of St. Gall, who d. 975, was of a younger generation), and declined various offers of preferment elsewhere. He d. at St. Gall, April 6, 912. In 1513 he was beatified by Pope Julius II., but does not seem to have been formally canonized, nor does an office in his honour appear to have been authorised for use except at St. Gall (*Lebensbild des heiligen Notker von St. Gallen*, by G. Meyer von Knonau, Zürich, 1877; *Allg. Deutsche Biog.*, xxiv. 35, &c.).

Ekkehard IV. (d. 1060), in his *Casus Sancti Galli*, chapter iii., thus lovingly characterises Notker (a *tr.* would not express the conciseness of the original):—

"Corpore, non animo, gracilis; voce, non spiritu, balbulus; in divinis erectus, in adversis patiens, ad omnia mitis, in nostratium acer erat exactor disciplinis; ad repentina timidulus et inopinata, praeter daemones infestantes, erat; quibus quidem se audenter opponere solebat. In orando, legendo, dictando, creberrimus. Et ut omnis sanctitatis ejus in brevi complectar dotes, sancti Spiritus erat vasculum, quo suo tempore abundantius nullum."

Notker was a favourite of the Emperor Charles the Fat, who paid him special attention during his visit to St. Gall, Dec. 4–6, 883. His claim to notice here is as the first important writer of sequences; and as indeed the practical inventor of this species of compositions. He seems to have begun writing sequences about 862, and in 885 collected them into a volume (the *Liber Sequentiarum Notkeri*, hereafter in this article entitled the *L. S. N.*), which he dedicated to Liutward, who was Bishop of Vercelli, and Chancellor (till 887) to Charles the Fat. In the dedicatory epistle prefixed (reprinted by *Daniel*, v. p. 5, from the St. Gall MS., No. 381) Notker gives an account of his first essays, of which the following is a summary:—

ii. *Origin of Notker's Sequences.*— In his youth he says he found great difficulty in remembering the cadences of the *neumes* [or musical notes which were set to the final *a* of the word *Alleluia* in the *Gradual*, between the Epistle and the Gospel; see **p. 648**, and **p. 653**]. When one of the monks of the Abbey of Jumièges (near Rouen, destroyed by the Normans in 851), after wandering from place to place came to St. Gall (about 862), he brought with him his *Antiphonary*. There, to his delight, Notker found words set to these troublesome neumes, but the words seem to to have been merely strung together for mnemonic purposes. Incited by this example, Notker determined to try to compose something more worthy of the occasion, and wrote the sequence "Laudes Deo concinat" to one of these sets of neumes. He showed his work to his master Iso,

[the first important teacher at St. Gall, where he was in residence 852–870; and, finally, as head of the outer school, which was meant for those who did not intend to become monks of St. Gall],

who was delighted with it, but suggested various improvements, and especially that each syllable should go to one note. Following these instructions, Notker wrote a second sequence beginning "Psallat Ecclesia, mater illibata," and showed both to his other master Marcellus,

[an Irishman, originally called Mongal, who had accompanied his uncle Marcus, an Irish Bishop, to Rome, and on their return journey settled at St. Gall, about 850. He was certainly there from 853 to 865. He was a good scholar, and, above all, an excellent musician. On the division of the monastic school, he became head of the inner school, which was meant for those who looked forward to becoming brethren of the monastery],

who was greatly pleased with them, transcribed them on rolls, and gave them to the scholars to practice. (So the Dedicatory Epistle. Compare Dr. Neale's note in his *Mediæval Hymns*, ed. 1863, p. 29, where he gives an interesting account of the origin of Sequences, though not a little of the information he gives regarding Notker seems to be derived from his own imagination.)

iii. *The Notkerian Sequences. Genuine and False.*—From this account it might seem perfectly easy to determine which are the genuine sequences of Notker. But no autograph copy of the *L. S. N.* has survived, and although there are still extant at least eight MSS. not later than the 11th cent., all professing to furnish us with the *L. S. N.*, yet on examination it is found that no two MSS. exactly agree. From the fact that Notker was an accomplished musician, and is known to have composed the melodies as well as the words of sequences, one might hope to gain help. There is indeed an important MS. at St. Gall (No. 484) apparently written early in the 10th century, which contains the melodies without words; but there is nothing to show which of these are by Notker, and which are earlier. Nor does early tradition help us much. In the interlinear notes to his *Rhythmi de Sancto Otmaro* (St. Gall MS. 393, p. 153, both the text and notes being in Ekkehard's autograph), Ekkehard IV. speaks of Notker as having composed 50 sequences, but nowhere does he give a list of their first lines. The conjecture of Wilmanns is probably correct, viz., that Ekkehard took the St. Gall MS., No. 378, as his standard. It contains 55 sequences in the *L. S. N.* (Nos. 84, 114 had not been inserted when Ekkehard wrote), and deducting from this the sequences which in his *Casus Sancti Galli* Ekkehard definitely ascribes to others (Nos. 48, 95, 97, 106, 110, 111) there remain, in round numbers, 50. (See further below.)

The most careful attempt to settle what are genuine and what are false is in an article by W. Wilmanns (*Welche Sequenzen hat Notker verfasst?*) in Moriz Haupt's *Zeitschrift für deutsches Alterthum*, vol. xv., Berlin, 1872, pp. 267–294. With this may be compared P. Anselm Schubiger's *Sängerschule St. Gallens*, Einsiedeln, 1858; and K. Bartsch's *Lateinische Sequenzen des Mittelalters*, Rostock, 1868. The references in *Daniel* are confused and inexact.

iv. *MSS. of Notker's Liber Sequentiarum.*—As a further contribution towards the settlement of this question, the present writer has procured collations of the sequences in the *L. S. N.* of the MSS. noted below.

To the kindness of Dr. Laubmann, Director of the Royal Library at Munich, we are indebted for the collations of the MSS. *m* and *n* ; to the kindness of P. Gabriel Meier, O.S.B., of Einsiedeln, for the collation of MS. *e*; and to the kindness of Dr. Rose, Director of the MS. department of the Royal Library, Berlin, for the collation of MS. *l*. References to the MSS. *g, h, i, k,* are given in the Index to the 1875 *Verzeichniss* of the St. Gall MSS., but on examination it became evident that these references were very incomplete; and Herr Idtensohn, the librarian of the Stiftsbibliothek at St. Gall, has most obligingly made fresh collations, with the results shown below. The MSS. *g, h, i, k, l, m, n,* are more fully described in Leon Gautier's *Histoire de la Poésie Liturgique au Moyen Age. Les Tropes*. Paris, 1886, pp. 127–135.

The eight MSS. here indexed are :—

(*e.*) **The Einsiedeln MS., No. 121**, of about the end of the 10th cent. The first part of this MS. consists of an *Antiphonary*, the so-called *Antiphonarium Sancti Gregorii* (see Scherer's *Verzeichniss*, 1875, of the St. Gall MSS., p. 124). The *L. S. N.* occupies pp. 436–599.

(*g.*) **The St. Gall MS., No. 376**, of the 11th cent. The *L. S. N.* occupies pp. 312–435.

(*h.*) **The St. Gall MS., No. 378**, of the 11th cent. Here the *L. S. N.* is at pp. 146–296.

(*i.*) **The St. Gall MS., No. 380**, of the 11th cent. The *L. S. N.* occupies pp. 118–272.

(*k.*) **The St. Gall MS., No. 381**, of the 11th cent. Here the *L. S. N.* is at pp. 325–498.

(*l.*) **The Berlin MS. Lat. Theol., Quarto 11.** Written at Minden about 1025, but apparently copied from a St. Gall MS. The *L. S. N.* begins at folio 144.

(*m.*) **The Munich MS., Lat. 14,083.** This MS. is of the 11th cent,, and was evidently written in the monastery of St. Emmeram, at Regensburg. The *L. S. N.* is at folios 7–38.

(*n.*) **The Munich MS., Lat. 14,322.** This MS. was also evidently written at Regensburg, about 1030. The *L. S. N.* is at folios 16–43 ; and the sequences found there are printed by Bernhard Pez, in his *Thesaurus Anecdotorum*, vol. i., Augsburg, 1721, cols. 15 ff., and repeated in Migne's *P. P. Lat.* cxxxi. 1003. The MS. was still at Regensburg when Pez consulted it.

In analysing the contents of these MSS. it will be on the whole best to divide the sequences given in the *L. S. N.* in each case into two series. The *First* series contains those sequences which Wilmanns (who in deciding, gives special weight to the evidence of the St. Gall MS., No. 484, and to their relation to the melodies ascribed to Notker) accepts as genuine. The *Second* series includes the remainder of the sequences in question.

v. *Table of Notkerian Sequences.*—In this table we have the following divisions :—

(1) The *first column* gives the running numbers ; (2) the *second* the number of the Sequence in J. Kehrein's *Lateinische Sequenzen des Mittelalters*, Mainz, 1873 ; (3) the *third* the first lines of the individual Sequences ; (4) the *fourth* references to the MSS. where found ; (5) and the *fifth* states the subject or use of the sequence.

The reference *e–n*, in column 4, means that the sequence is found in all the MSS., and the reference *e–m*, that it is in all the MSS. except *n*. Additional references to many of these sequences will be found in the lists in the article **Sequences**, showing e.g. which of them have passed into the English Uses.

No.	Kehrein	First Line of Sequence.	Where found.	Use.
		First Series.		
1	79	Agni paschalis esu potuque dignas . .	*e.–n.* .	Easter.
2	443	Agone triumphali militum regis summi .	*e.–n.* .	C. of Martyrs.
3	—	Angelorum ordo sacer Dei sereno semper .	*e. k. l.* .	Of the Angels.
4	111	Carmen suo dilecto Ecclesia Christi canat .	*e.–m.* .	Low Sunday.
5	97	Christe Domine, laetifica sponsam tuam Ecclesiam	*e. g. h. i. k. l.* .	Easter.
6	581	Christe, sanctis unica spes, salus, vita .	*e. g. h. i. k. l.* .	St. Gall.
7	710	Christi Domini militis martyrisque . .	*e.–m.* .	St. Stephen.
8	119	Christus hunc diem jucundum cunctis .	*e.–m.* .	Octave of Ascension.
9	217	Concentu parili hic te, Maria, veneratur populus	*e.–n.* .	Purification of B. V. M.
10	247	Congaudent angelorum chori gloriosae Virgini .	*e.–n.* .	Assumption of B. V. M.
11	580	Dilecte Deo, Galle, perenni . . .	*e.–n.* .	St. Gall.
12	121	En regnator coelestium et terrenorum .	*e.–m.* .	S. after Ascension.
13	24	Festa Christi omnis Christianitas celebret .	*e.–n.* .	Epiphany.
14	20	Gaude Maria virgo, Dei genitrix, quae .	*e.–m.* .	Octave of Christmas.
15	551	Gaudens ecclesia hanc dieculam .	*m. n.* .	St. Emmeram of Regensburg.
16	104	Grates Salvatori ac Regi Christo Deo solvant	*e.–n.* .	Easter.
17	82	Haec est sancta sollemnitas sollemnitatum .	*e.–m.* .	Easter.
18	711	Hanc concordi famulatu colamus sollemnitatem.	*e. h. i. k. l. m. n.*	St. Stephen.
19	656	Ibant pariter animis et ducibus imparibus .	*g. h. i. l.* .	St. Maurice.
20	25	Iste dies celebris constat	*e. k. l. m.* .	Octave of Epiphany.
21	402	Joannes Jesu Christo multum dilecte virgo .	*e.–n.* .	St. John Evangelist.
22	108	Judicem nos inspicientem, crypta cordis .	*e.–m.* .	S. after Octave of Easter.
23	110	Laeta mente canamus Deo nostro . .	*e.–m.* .	S. after Octave of Easter.
24	733	Laude dignum sanctum canat Otmarum .	*e. g. i. k. l. m. n.*	St. Othmar of St. Gall.
25	102	Laudes Deo concinat orbis ubique totus .	*e.–m.* .	Easter.
26	81	Laudes Salvatori voce modulemur supplici .	*e.–n.* .	Easter.
27	623	Laurenti, David magni martyr . .	*e.–n.* .	St. Lawrence.
28	342	Laus tibi Christe, cui sapit, quod videtur .	*e. g. h. i. k. l.* .	H. Innocents.
29	109	Laus tibi sit, o fidelis Deus . . .	*e.–m.* .	2nd S. after Octave of Easter.
30	167	Magnum te Michaelem habentem pignus .	*e.–n.* .	St. Michael.
31	11	Natus ante saecula Dei filius . . .	*e.–n.* .	Christmas.

No.	Keh-rein.	First Line of Sequence.	Where found.	Use.
32	43	Nostra tuba regatur fortissima Dei dextra .	e. g. h. i. k. l. .	Sat. before Septuagesima.
33	120	O quam mira sunt, Deus, tua portenta	e. g. i. k. l. m. .	S. after Ascension.
34	335	Omnes sancti seraphim, cherubim .	e.–n.	All Saints.
35	84	Pangamus Creatoris atque Redemptoris gloriam	e.–n.	Easter.
36	394	Petre summe Christi pastor, et Paule	e.–n.	SS. Peter and Paul.
37	866	Psallat ecclesia, mater illibata, et virgo	e.–n.	Dedic. of a Church.
38	432	Quid tu virgo mater ploras .	e.–n.	One Martyr.
39	459	Rex regum, Deus noster colende	e.–n.	One Confessor.
40	646	Sacerdotem Christi Martinum .	e.–n.	St. Martin of Tours.
41	351	Sancti Baptistae Christi praeconis	e.–n.	Nat. St. John Baptist.
42	514	Sancti merita Benedicti inclita .	m. n.	St. Benedict.
43	124	Sancti Spiritus adsit nobis gratia, Quae	e.–n.	Pentecost.
44	192	Stirpe Maria regia procreata .	e. i. k. l. m. n..	Nat. of B. V. M.
45	114	Summi triumphum regis prosequamur laude	e.–n.	Ascension.
46	867	Tu civium Deus conditor .	e. k. l. m.	Ded. of a Church.
47	472	Virginis venerandae de numero sapientum	e.–n.	C. of Virgins.

Second Series.

No.	Keh-rein.	First Line of Sequence.	Where found.	Use.
48	589	A solis occasu usque ad exortum	e.–n.	St. Columbanus.
49	168	Ad celebres, Rex coelice, laudes cuncta	e. m. n. .	St. Michael.
50	140	Alma chorus Domini compangat	l. m. n.	Holy Trinity.
51	246	Ave Dei genitrix summi, virgo semper	m.	Assumption B. V. M.
52	139	Benedicta semper sancta sit Trinitas.	e. l. m. n.	Holy Trinity.
53	123	Benedicto gratias Deo, Nos referamus	e. g. i. k. l. m..	Octave of Pentecost.
54	345	Blandis vocibus laeti celebremus	g. i. k. l.	H. Innocents.
55	403	Cantemus Christo regi terrae .	g.	St. John Evangelist.
56	44	Cantemus cuncti melodum nunc Alleluia .	e.–m.	Septuagesima.
57	540	Christo Regi regum virgo canat ecclesia	g.	St. Constantius of Perugia.
58	369	Clare sanctorum senatus apostolorum	e.–n.	C. of Apostles.
59	398	Deus in tua virtute sanctus Andreas	e.–n.	St. Andrew.
—	87	Deus qui perenni .		See No. 91.
60	420	Diem festum Bartholomaei, Christi amici .	m.	St. Bartholomew.
61	191	Ecce sollemnis diei canamus festa	e.–m.	Nat. B. V. M.
62	96	Ecce vocibus carmina comparibus	g. i.	Easter.
63	685	Eia fratres cari festivitatem sancti Otmari.	e. g. h. i. l.	St. Othmar of St. Gall.
64	99	Eia harmoniis, socii, laudum resonis .	g. i.	Easter.
65	10	Eia recolamus laudibus piis digna .	e.–n.	Christmas.
66	85	Et sicut liliorum candor .	e. k..	Easter.
67	545	Exsultemus in ista fratres sollemnitate	n.	St. Denis.
68	218	Exsultet omnis aetas, sexus uterque .	e.	Purif. B. V. M.
—	712	Festa Stephani, protomartyris Christi, Sancta	l.	See No. 101.
69	417	Gaude Christi sponsa, virgo mater ecclesia	m.	St. James the Great.
70	865	Gaude semper serena felixque genitrix ecclesia	g.	St. Margaret.
70b	—	Gaudendum nobis suadent hujus diei festa.	l.	SS. Gordianus and Epimachus.
71	6	Grates nunc omnes reddamus Domino Deo	m. n.	Christmas.
—	656	Hanc pariter omnis .		See No. 19.
72	26	Hunc diem celebret omnis mundus .	e. g. i. k. l.	Octave of Epiphany.
73	112	Is qui prius habitum mortalem induit	e.–m.	Easter.
74	85	Laetemur gaudiis quos redemit Verbum Patris	k.	Easter.
75	94	Laudantes triumphantem Christum .	g. i.	Easter.
76	695	Laude celebri dignum mater ecclesia	g. i.	St. Remaclus.
77	664	Laude condignissima dies annua reddit	m.	St. Nicholas of Myra.
78	92	Laudes Christo redempti voce modulemur .	e. g. k. l.	Easter.
79	752	Laudes Deo perenni Auctori redemptionis.	g. k. l.	St. Afra.
80	550	Laudes Domino nostra concinat harmonia .	m.	St. Emmeram.
81	101	Laudum quis carmine unquam praevalet .	g. i.	Easter.
82	341	Laus tibi, Christe, 1. Patris optimi Nate....Quem coelitus	e.–n.	H. Innocents.
83	343	2. Patris optimi Nate....Qui hodie	e. g. k. l.	H. Innocents.
84	846	3. Qui es Creator et Redemptor .	h.	St. Mary Magdalene.
85	344	4. Qui humilis homo mundo apparens	e. g. h. i. k. l.	H. Innocents.
86	434	Miles inclite fortissimi regis Christi .	e. l. m.	One Martyr.
87	9	Nato canunt omnia Domino pie agmina	m.	Christmas.
88	552	Nos Gordiani atque Epimachi nobiles laureas	e. i. k. l. .	SS. Gordianus and Epimachus.
89	61	Nunc crucis alma cantet gaudia	m.	H. Cross.
90	521	O Blasi, dilecte Regi regum summo .	g. k. l.	St. Blaise.
—	580	O dilecte Domino Galle, perenni	.	See No. 11.
91	87	O qui perenne residens potestatis solio	g. i.	Easter.
92	654	Omnis sexus et aetas festa Thebaeorum .	e.	St. Maurice.

No.	Keh-rein.	First Line of Sequence.	Where found.	Use.
93	610	Pangat hymnum Augiensis insula . .	k. l. . .	St. Januarius.
94	663	Perpes laus et honor tibi, summe pastor .	i. . .	St. Nicholas of Myra.
95	138	Prompta mente Trinitati canamus individuae	e. h. i. l. m.	Holy Trinity.
—	713	Protomartyr Domini Stephane nos pius audi	l. . .	See No. 108.
—	120	Quam mira sunt, Deus, tua portenta .	. . .	See No. 33.
96	—	Quem aethera et terra atque mare .	k. . .	Christmas.
97	513	Qui benedici cupitis, huc festini currite .	e. g. h. i. l. m.	St. Benedict.
98	693	Romana Quirinus stirpe procreatus .	m. . .	St. Quirinus.
99	249	Salve porta perpetuae lucis fulgida .	m. . .	Assumption B. V. M.
100	346	Salvete agni electa turba . .	e. k. l.	H. Innocents.
101	712	Sancta per orbem ecclesia veneratur .	g. i. k. l.	St. Stephen (Festa).
102	657	Sancti belli celebremus triumphum .	e.–m.	St. Maurice.
103	473	Scalam ad coelos subrectam tormentis .	e. g. i. k. l. m.	C. of Virgins.
104	681	Sollemni carmine tuos Oswalde rex .	g. i.	St. Oswald.
105	629	Sollemnitatem, fratres carissimi, colimus .	e. . .	St. Leger.
106	869	Sollemnitatem hujus devoti filii ecclesiae .	g. h. i. k. l.	Dedic. of a Church.
107	163	Stans a longe, qui plurima perpetrarat .	l. m.	Sunday.
108	713	Stephane nos pius audi, colimus festa tua .	g. k. l.	St. Stephen (Protomartyr).
109	172	Summi Regis archangele Michael .	e. l. m.	St. Michael.
110	544	Summis conatibus nunc Deo nostro .	h. i. k. l..	St. Desiderius.
111	350	Summum praeconem Christi collaudemus .	g. h. i. l. m.	Decol. St. J. Baptist.
112	648	Tuba nostrae vocis elevetur .	k. . .	St. Martin.
113	444	Tubam bellicosam, qui Dei non verentes .	e. g. i. k. l. m.	C. of Martyrs.
114	125	Veni Sancte Spiritus, Et emitte coelitus .	g. h. .	Pentecost.

vi. *Analysis of the Table.*—In classifying the above 115 Sequences (including 70 b) we may first of all eliminate those which are *certainly* not by Notker, viz. :—

Nos. 48, 95, 97, 111, by *Ekkehard I.* (d. 973); No. 84, by *Godescalcus* or *Gottschalk* (d. 1050); No. 106, by *Waltram* (fl. 909); No. 110, by *Ekkehard II.* (d. 990); No. 114, not inserted in the St. Gall mss. before the 13th cent. No. 109 is sometimes ascribed to Alcuin.

For the rest, taking the joint evidence of the two most important St. Gall mss., Nos. 376 and 378, we find that the following are not contained in the *L. S. N.* of either, viz. :—

Nos. 3, 15, 20, 42, 44, 46, 49, 50, 51, 52, 60, 66, 67, 68, 69, 70b, 71, 74, 77, 80, 86, 87, 88, 89, 92, 93, 94, 96, 98, 99, 100, 105, 107, 109, 112 ; and besides these Nos. 24, 57, 62, 64, 70, 104, while contained in No. 378 are not in the *L. S. N.*

To pursue the analysis further would exceed the limits of our space, and would require a mass of wearisome details. The conclusions the present writer, in view of all the evidence, has arrived at, may best be seen by his dividing the Sequences into four classes : I. *Those which may be accepted as genuine.* II. *Those of which the ascription is probable.* III. *Those which may possibly be by Notker.* IV. *Those certainly not by Notker.*

I.

Nos. 1, 2, 4–14, 16, 17, 18, 21, 22, 23, 25–41, 43, 45, 47, 56, 58, 59, 65, 73, 82, 85 : in all 46.

II.

Nos. 3, 19, 20, 24, 44, 46, 53, 54, 55, 61, 63, 72, 75, 78, 79, 81, 83, 88, 100, 101, 102, 103, 108, 113 : in all 24.

III.

Nos. 15, 42, 49, 50, 51, 52, 57, 60, 62, 64, 66, 67, 68, 69, 70, 70b, 71, 74, 76, 77, 80, 86, 87, 89, 90, 91, 92, 93, 94, 96, 98, 99, 104, 105, 107, 109, 112 : in all 37.

IV.

Nos. 48, 84, 95, 97, 106, 110, 111, 114 : in all 8.

A more acute criticism may be able to discriminate the third class more accurately and eliminate from it those mistakenly ascribed to Notker. One thing at least may be taken for granted, viz., that while the above lists probably contain various sequences not really composed by Notker, it is in the highest degree improbable that any here omitted can be his genuine compositions.

vii. *Conclusion.*—Notker's Sequences are remarkable for their majesty and noble elevation of tone, their earnestness and their devoutness. They display a profound knowledge of Holy Scripture in its plainer and its more recondite interpretations, and a firm grasp and definite exposition of the eternal truths of the Christian Faith. The style is clear, and the language easily comprehensible, so that whether he is paraphrasing the Gospel for the day, or setting forth the leading ideas of the Church's festivals, or is engaged in vivid and sympathetic word-painting; he is at once pleasing and accurate. His sequences were speedily received with favour as a welcome change from sound to sense, and from the end of the 9th century to the middle of the 12th, they, together with sequences on the same model, were in universal use over Northern Europe. As they were written for the neumes of the Alleluia they were of course made to correspond thereto, and must be studied in connection with their melodies. The metrical rules governing their composition are intricate, suffice it to say here that they were written in rhythmical prose, somewhat in the form of the Hebrew Psalms, in irregular lines and without any attempt at rhyme. It is thus difficult to present a version in English which shall be at once exact and yet suited to modern congregational use. The only literal version which has attained any popularity in English is Dr Neale's tr. of No. 56, "Cantemus cuncti" (see p. 204, i.), and he complains bitterly (*Med. Hys.*, ed. 1867, pp. viii., and 42) that hymnal compilers have ignored the ancient melody to which it was written, and that it has been "cramped, tortured, tamed down into a chant." Still the Notkerian sequences are worthy of greater attention than has been bestowed on them by English translators. If the endeavour to give a literal version is abandoned, they allow a wider choice of measures and greater freedom of rendering than the later rhyming Sequences. Those which have been attempted on these lines are Nos. 26, 43, 49, 56, 61, 65, 78, 87, the versions of which are noted under the first lines of the originals throughout this Dictionary ; and besides these, there are various others worthy of and yet waiting for a good translation. The most famous of all the pieces ascribed to Notker is not in the lists given above, but is noted under " Media vita" (p. 721, i.). [J. M.]

Novalis [Hardenberg, G. F. P. von.]

Now are the days of humblest prayer. *F. W. Faber.* [*Lent.*] Pub. in the 2nd ed. of his *Jesus and Mary*, &c., 1852, in 8 st. of 7 l.; in his *Oratory Hys.*, 1854, in 5 st., No. 12 ; and his *Hymns*, 1862, It is usually given in an abbreviated form, sometimes as in the *Oratory Hys.* as above, and again as in the S. P. C. K. *Church Hys.*, 1871, where st. iii., vi. are omitted. In the *Hymnary*, 1872, it begins, " Lord, in these days of humblest prayer." [J. J.]

Now begin the heavenly theme. [*Redeeming Love.*] The authorship of this hymn is unknown. The earliest form in which it is found differs widely from that followed in modern hymnals. In 1763 it appeared in the *Appendix* to M. Madan's *Ps. and Hys.*, as No. clxxii., thus :—

> " Redeeming Love.
>
> i.
> " Now begin the Heav'nly Theme,
> Sing aloud in Jesu's Name,
> Ye, who Jesu's Kindnefs prove
> Triumph in Redeeming Love.
>
> ii.
> " Ye, who fee the Father's Grace
> Beaming in the Saviour's Face
> As to Canaan on ye move
> Praife and blefs Redeeming Love.
>
> iii.
> " Mourning Souls dry up your Tears,
> Banifh all your guilty Fears,
> See your Guilt and Curfe remove,
> Cancell'd by Redeeming Love.
>
> iv.
> " Ye, alas! who long have been
> Willing Slaves of Death and Sin,
> Now from Blifs no longer rove,
> Stop—and tafte Redeeming Love.
>
> v.
> " Welcome all by Sin oppreft,
> Welcome, to his facred Reft,
> Nothing brought Him from above,
> Nothing but Redeeming Love.
>
> vi.
> " He fubdu'd th' Infernal Pow'rs,
> His tremendous Foes and ours
> From their curfed Empire drove,
> Mighty in Redeeming Love.
>
> vii.
> " Hither then your Mufick bring,
> Strike aloud each joyful String,
> Mortals join the Hofts above,
> Join to praife Redeeming Love."

In this form, or with alterations, the hymn appeared in about fifty collections between 1763 and 1833, and in all it was given anonymously, except in that of *Dobell*, 1806, who quoted it as from " *Langford's Coll.*" This reference is to the *Hymns and Spiritual Songs* pub. by John Langford (p. 639, ii.) in 1776, and in which the hymn appeared. In *Langford's* 2nd ed. he marked all his own hymns with an asterisk, but this hymn is unmarked. This is clear evidence against his authorship. The error of ascribing the hymn to Langford arose through the careless editing of E. Bickersteth, who in the Index of his *Christian*

Psalmody, 1833, gave the hymn as " Now begin the, *Langford.*" This was copied by later compilers, some expanding the name into " John Langford," and others into " William Langford," and all basing their guesses on an error. The earliest date to which it has been traced is Madan's *Appendix*, 1763. Failing evidence that it was written by Madan, we must give it as *Anon.* No. 982, in *Kennedy*, 1863, " Now the heavenly joy proclaim," is an altered form of this hymn. [J. J.]

Now, from the altar of our hearts. *J. Mason.* [*Evening.*] Appeared in his *Spiritual Songs, or Songs of Praise*, 1683, pp. 25-6, in 3 st. of 8 l., and a half stanza of 4 l., and entitled " A Song of Praise for the Evening." (Orig. text, *Lyra Brit.* p. 396.) The third stanza, which is usually omitted in the hymnals, and reads :—

> " Man's life's a book of history ;
> The leaves thereof are days ;
> The letters, mercies closely join'd ;
> The title is Thy praise,"

is usually thought to have suggested Dr. Franklin's well-known epitaph upon himself, wherein he compares his body to " the cover of an old book, the contents torn out, and stripped of its lettering and gilding." The whole hymn is sometimes quoted, and not without reason, as Mason's finest production. [J. J.]

Now from the world withdrawn. *J. Bulmer.* [*Evening.*] 1st pub. in his *Hys., Original and Select*, &c., 1835, Bk. i., No. 157, in 4. st. of 4 l., and entitled " The Spirit of Prayer and Holiness implored." It is one of the very few hymns by the author which have come into general use. It is found in its original form in Spurgeon's *O. O. H. Bk.*, 1866, No. 975, with, in st. i., l. 3, " O Lord " for " *dear* Lord." [J. J.]

Now gracious Lord, Thine arm reveal. *J. Newton.* [*The New Year.*] The first of thirteen hymns to be sung " Before Annual Sermons to Young People, on New Years' Evenings," 1st pub. in the *Olney Hymns*, 1779, Bk. ii., No. 7., in 5 st. of 4 l., and headed " Prayer for a Blessing." (Orig. text, *Hy. Comp.*, No. 90.) Its use is very extensive in all English-speaking countries; it has also been translated into several languages. [J. J.]

Now let a spacious world arise. *I. Watts.* [*Creation.*] 1st pub. in his *Hymns*, &c., 1709, Bk. ii., No. 147, in 11 st. of 4 l. Its use is limited. In the 1745 *Draft* of the Scottish *Translations and Paraphrases*, No. xxxvii., it was given with the omission of st. xi., and the change, in st. ii., l. 3, of " He call'd the *Night*," into " He call'd the *Light*," a change which evidently suggested the form of st. ii. in the recast of 1781. This recast, which opens, " Let heav'n arise, let earth appear," was given as No. i. (Gen. i. 1) in the authorized *Trans. and Paraphs.* of 1781, and has been in use in the Church of Scotland for more than 100 years. In the markings of authors and revisers by W. Cameron's daughter, this recast is claimed for him (see p. 200, ii.). [J. J.]

Now let a true ambition rise. *P. Doddridge.* [*Seek first the Kingdom of God.*] Written January 1, 173⅜ [D. MSS.], and pub. by Job Orton in his posthumous ed. of Doddridge's

Hymns, 1755, No. 178, in 4 st. of 4 l., and headed, "Seeking first the Kingdom of God." It was also given in J. D. Humphreys's ed. of the same, 1839, No. 199.   [J. J.]

Now let our cheerful eyes survey. *P. Doddridge.* [*Jesus, the High Priest.*] This hymn is No. 67 in the D. MSS., but undated. It is placed between hymns which are dated respectively "April 10, 1735," and "January 1, 173⅞." The heading reads "Christ bearing the names of His people on His breastplate, from Exodus xxviii. 29." When included by Job Orton in his posthumous ed. of Doddridge's *Hymns, &c.*, 1755, No. 8, in 5 st. of 4 l., the heading was altered to "Christ's intercession typified by Aaron's Breastplate," and st. 1., l. 4, was changed from "With correspondent love," to "And sympathetic love." In J. D. Humphreys's ed. of the *Hymns*, 1839, No. 9, the line reads, "His sympathy and love." He has also "And high o'er all the *heavenly host*," for "And high o'er all the shining train," in st. ii. This hymn is in C. U. both in G. Britain and America, Orton's text being that commonly adopted. Sometimes, however, it reads, "Now let our *trustful* eyes survey."   [J. J.]

Now let our mourning hearts revive. *P. Doddridge.* [*Death of a Minister.*] Written on the death of a Minister, at Kettering, August 22, 1736, and headed, "Comfort in God under the Removal of Ministers; or, other Useful Persons by Death, Joshua, i. 2, 4, 5" (D. MSS.) It was given in Job Orton's posthumous ed. of Doddridge's *Hymns, &c.*, 1755, No. 17, in 6 st. of 4 l., with the heading changed to, "Support in the gracious presence of God under the Loss of Ministers, and other useful Friends"; and repeated in J. D. Humphreys's ed. of the same, in 1839, with the same heading. It is in C. U. in G. Britain and America. Another form of the text, beginning with st. ii., "What though the arm of conquering death" is also in several collections.   [J. J.]

Now let our souls ascend above. [*Christian Confidence.*] In the Draft *Translations and Paraphrases* of the Church of Scotland, 1745, this vigorous paraphrase of Rom. viii. 31–39, was given as No. xxxv., in 9 st. of 4 l. The authorship is unknown. The first stanza reads:—

"Now let our Souls ascend above
    the Fears of Guilt and Woe:
GOD is for us, our Friend declared:
    who then can be our Foe?"

In the *Draft* of 1751, it remained unaltered; but in that of 1781 it assumed the form which was authorized in the *Trans. and Paraphs.* (No. xlviii.) of the same year. W. Cameron's daughter (p. 200, ii.) gives, in her markings of authors and revisers, *J. Logan* as the author of this arrangement of the text of 1745; and, as stated in the memoir of *Bruce* (p. 187, i.) in this work, we see no reason to doubt its accuracy. As this arrangement has been in authorized use in the Church of Scotland for more than 100 years, and some centos have also been compiled therefrom for use in English hymnals, we give the full text of 1781, with those portions taken from the *Draft* of 1745 printed in italics:—

1. " Let Christian faith and hope dispel
    the fears of guilt and woe;
    The Lord Almighty is our friend,
    and who can prove a *foe*?

2. " *He who his Son most dear and lov'd*
    gave up for us *to die*,
    Shall he not all things freely give
    that goodness can supply?

3. " *Behold* the best, the greatest gift,
    of everlasting *love*!
    Behold the pledge of peace *below*,
    and perfect bliss *above*!

4. " Where is the judge, who can condemn,
    since *God hath justified ?*
    Who shall charge those with guilt or crime
    for whom *the Saviour died?*

5. " The Saviour died, *but* rose *again*
    triumphant from the grave;
    And pleads our cause at God's right hand,
    omnipotent to save.

6. " Who, then, *can e'er divide us more*
    from Jesus and his love,
    Or break the sacred chain that binds
    the earth to heav'n above?

7. " *Let troubles rise, and* terrors frown,
    and days of darkness fall;
    Through him all dangers *we'll defy*,
    and more than conquer all.

8. " *Nor death nor life, nor earth nor hell,*
    nor time's destroying sway,
    Can e'er efface us from his heart,
    or make his love decay.

9. " *Each future period* that *will bless*
    as it has bless'd the past;
    He lov'd us from the first of time;
    he loves us to the last."

The designation of this full text must thus be *Scottish Tr. & Par.*, 1745, *Anon.*, and *J. Logan*, 1781. In addition to the full text there are also the following centos in C. U. :—

1. **O let triumphant faith [hope] dispel.** This form appeared in the American *Prayer Bk. Coll.*, 1826, and has passed into several American collections.
2. **The Saviour died, but rose again.** This, in W. F. Stevenson's *Hys. for Ch. and Home*, 1873, is composed of st. v.–viii.
3. **Who from the love of Christ our Head.** This appeared in Miss Leeson's *Paraphrases and Hys.*, 1853. It is based on st. vii.–ix. To this Miss Leeson added a second part in 4 st. as, "Let followers of the Apostles' faith."   [J. J.]

Now let our souls on wings sublime. *T. Gibbons.* [*Death anticipated.*] Appended to Sermon iv. of his *Sermons on Various Subjects, with a Hymn adapted to each Subject*, 1762, p. 97, in 5 st. of 4 l., the text of the Sermon being Eccles. xii. 7, and the title "The Return of the Body to Earth, and the Return of the Soul to God." In 1769 it was included in the Bristol Bapt. *Coll.* of Ash & Evans, No. 206; in 1787, in Rippon's *Sel.*, No. 223; and later in a large number of collections in G. Britain and America. The American Meth. Episco. Ch. *Hymns*, 1849, gives it in 4 st. as "*Arise my soul* on wings sublime." In the American *Church Praise Bk.*, N. Y., 1882, No. 718, is a cento of which st. i., ii. are st. i. and iii. of this hymn, and st. iii., iv. are st. i. and iii. of J. Newton's "As when the weary traveller gains" (see p. 85, ii.). In its various forms this is one of the most widely known of the author's hymns.   [J. J.]

Now let the feeble all be strong. *P. Doddridge.* [*Help in Temptation.*] Written June 24, 1739, on 1 Cor. x. 13, in 4 st. of 4 l. [D. MSS.], and pub. by Job Orton in his posthumous ed. of Doddridge's *Hymns, &c.*, 1755, No. 269, and again in J. D. Humphreys's ed. of the same, 1839, No. 294, with the original heading, " Temptation moderated by the Divine Fidelity, Power, and Love," changed, as in the *Hymns*, 1755, to " God's fidelity in moderating Temptations."   [J. J.]

Now let Thy servant die in peace. [*Nunc Dimittis.*] In the 1745 Draft of the *Translations and Paraphrases* of the Church of Scotland, the following paraphrase of Simeon's Song appeared :—

1.
" Now let thy Servant die in Peace,
   from this vain World dismist:
I've seen thy great salvation, Lord :
   and hasten to my Rest.

2.
" Thy long-expected Grace, disclos'd
   before the People's View,
Hath prov'd thy Love was constant still,
   and promises were true.

3.
" This is the Sun, whose cheering Rays.
   through Gentile Darkness spread,
Pour Glory round thy chosen Race,
   and Blessings on their Head."

The author of this paraphrase is unknown. A second Paraphrase of the same passage, beginning, " When Jesus, by the Virgin brought," appeared in John Logan's *Poems*, 1781, in 7 st. of 4 l. This text is given in full in Dr. Grosart's *Works of M. Bruce*, 1865, pp. 135–6. For reasons assigned in the memoir of M. Bruce in this work (p. **187**, i.), we regard this paraphrase as the work of Bruce, possibly with a few alterations by Logan. During the same year, 1781, the authorized *Translations and Paraphrases* of the Church of Scotland were published. In them, as No. 38, is a paraphrase of Simeon's Song, in 11 st. of 4 l., " Just and devout old Simeon liv'd." This is thus composed :—

St. i.–iii.   First given in the *Draft* of 1781.
St. iv.–vi.   From the paraphrase as given in Logan's *Poems*.
St. vii.   New, in *Draft* of 1781.
St. viii.   Based on 1745 text as above.
St. ix.   From the paraphrase in Logan's *Poems*.
St. x., xi.   Based on 1745 text as above.

This arrangement was made, according to the markings by the daughter of W. Cameron (p. **200**, ii.), by J. Logan. In Miss J. E. Leeson's *Par. & Hys.*, &c., 1853, No. lxviii., the hymn beginning, " Now lettest Thou Thy servant, Lord," in 16 l., is based upon st. viii., ix., and xi. of the 1781 text as above. It is by Miss Leeson, as is also the second hymn on the same subject, " Behold, according to Thy word."   [J. J.]

Now let us join with hearts and tongues. *J. Newton.* [*Man honoured above Angels.*] Appeared in the *Olney Hymns*, 1779, Bk. ii., No. 39, in 7 st. of 4 l., and headed, " Man honoured above Angels." From this hymn " Jesus, Who passed the angels by," is taken. It is composed of st. iv.–vii. It is more widely used than the full hymn. [J. J.]

Now, Lord, we part in Thy great [blest] Name. *J. Dracup.* [*Dismissal.*] This hymn, which has undergone various modifications, first appeared in Dracup's *Hys. and Spiritual Songs*, Bolton, 1787, No. 62, entitled " At Parting," and reads :—

i. " Now, Lord, we part in Thy great Name,
   In which we here together came ;
Help us our few remaining days
To live unto Jehovah's praise.

ii. " Help us in life and death to bless,
   The Lord our strength and righteousness ;
And bring us all to meet above,
Then shall we better sing Thy love."

In one or two instances the opening line is given as, " Now, Lord, we part in Thy *blest* Name." The most popular form of the hymn is that given to it by Bp. Heber, " Lord, now we part in Thy blest Name," and pub. in his posthumous *Hymns*, &c., 1827, p. 142, as a " Hymn after Sermon," and given as " Anon.," Bp. Heber's alterations are : st. i., l. 1, " *Lord, now* " for " Now, Lord," " *blest* " for " great ; " l. 3, " *Grant* " for " Help ; " st. ii., l. 1, " *Teach* " for " Help ; " l. 3, " *And Grant* " for " And bring." In this form it is found in several collections, including Kemble's *Ps. & Hys.*; the Irish *Church Hymnal*, 1873, &c. [W. T. B.]

Now may fervent prayer arise. *J. Newton.* [*New Year.*] The third of thirteen " Hymns before Annual Sermons to Young People on New Years' Evenings," pub. in the *Olney Hymns*, 1779, Bk. ii., No. 9, in 7 st. of 6 l. It is in C. U. both in the original and in the following forms :—

1. Bless, O *bless* the opening year.
2. Bless, O Lord the opening year.
3. Bless O Lord *this* opening year.
4. Bless O Lord *each* opening year.

These forms of the text generally embrace st. ii., iii., vi., vii., and are in use in G. Britain and America.   [J. J.]

Now one day's journey less divides. *Charlotte Elliott.* [*Evening.*] 1st pub. in her brother's *Ps. & Hys.*, 2nd thousand, 1836–7, in 6 st. of 4 l., as an Evening Hymn. In 1839 Miss Elliott rewrote the original stanzas, added four thereto, and included the 10 st. as the hymn for Tuesday evening in her *Hys. for a Week*, which were pub. in 1842. This full text is given in Snepp's *Songs of G. & G.*, 1872. The 1836–7 st. are i., ii., iv., v., vi., x., and the 1839 st., iii., vii., viii., ix. No. 437 in the Presbyterian *Sel. of Hys.*, Philadelphia, 1861, is from this revised text, but slightly altered.   [J. J.]

Now shall my inward joy arise. *I. Watts.* [*God's care of His Church.*] Pub. in his *Hys. and Spiritual S.*, 1707, Bk. i., No. 39, in 6 st. of 4 l., as a paraphrase of Isaiah xlix. 13, &c. In this form its use is limited. In the *Draft* of the Scottish *Translations and Paraphrases*, 1745, No. xvii., is a hymn on the same passage beginning, " Ye heav'ns, send forth your praising song." Of this hymn st. i.–iii. are by an unknown hand, and have little or no resemblance to the corresponding stanzas in *Watts*, whilst st. iv.–vi. are from his hymn, as above, with the alteration of a " kind woman," in st. iv., l. 1, to a *"fond mother."* In the authorized issue of the *Trs. and Paraphs.* of 1781 the opening line reads, " Ye heav'ns, send forth your song of praise ; " and the text is a recast of the *Draft* of 1745 throughout. As Watts's text of st. iv.–vi. is easily attainable for comparison we add hereto only the text of st. i.–iii. from the 1745 *Draft* :—

" Ye heav'ns, send forth your praising song !
   Earth, raise thy Voice below !
Let Hills and Mountains join the Choir,
   and joy thro' Nature flow !

    "Behold, how gracious is our God!
      with what comforting Strains
    He cheers the Sorrows of our Heart,
      and banishes our Pains.

    "Cease ye, when Days of Darkness fall,
      with troubled Hearts to mourn;
    As if the Lord could leave a Saint
      forsaken or forlorn."

The final recast of this hymn in the authorized issue of the Scottish *Trs. & Paraphrases* of 1781 is claimed for W. Cameron (p. 200, ii.) by his daughter in her markings of authors and revisers of that issue. In Miss J. E. Leeson's *Paraphs. & Hys.*, 1853, No. li., on the same passage is a hymn of 8 st. in two parts: (1) "Sing, O ye heavens! Be joyful, earth," and (2) "O Zion, from the stranger's land." This arrangement by Miss Leeson is based on the Scottish *Trs. & Paraphs.* of 1781, as above.   [J. J.]

Now that my journey's just begun. *Jane Taylor.* [*Early Piety.*] Appeared in *Hys. for Infant Minds, by A. & J. Taylor*, 1810, in 9 st. of 4 l., with the motto, "Early will I seek Thee" (ed. 1886, p. 11). It is found in a few of the older hymn-books in an abbreviated form. With later compilers it is more popular, and is given in a great many collections for children. In a few hymnals, as the *Meth. S. S. H. Bk.*, 1879, it begins, "Lord, now my journey's just begun."   [J. J.]

Now the day is over. *S. Baring-Gould.* [*Evening.*] Written in 1865, and printed in the *Church Times* the same year. In 1868 it was given in the *Appendix* to *H. A. & M.*, and from that date it has gradually increased in popularity until its use has become common in all English-speaking countries.   [J. J.]

Now the labourer's task is o'er. *J. Ellerton.* [*Burial.*] Written for and 1st pub. in the *S. P. C. K. Church Hymns*, 1871, in 6 st. of 6 l. Mr. Ellerton says:—

    "The whole hymn, especially the third, fifth, and sixth verses, owes many thoughts, and some expressions, to a beautiful poem of the Rev. Gerard Moultrie's, beginning, 'Brother, now thy toils are o'er,' which will be found in the *People's Hymnal*, 380" (Notes on *Church Hymns*, p. liii.).

From *Church Hymns* this hymn has passed into *H. A. & M.*, *Hy. Comp.*, Thring's *Coll.*, and many other collections, and sometimes, as in the last-named, with the omission of st. iii. In R. Brown-Borthwick's *Select Hys. for Church and Home*, 2nd ed., 1885, the original text as it appeared in the 1st ed. of that work in 1871 is given as No. 72; and the revised and authorized text as in *Church Hys.*, as No. 185. The latter is also in Mr. Ellerton's *Hymns, &c.*, 1888, and may be at once known by the refrain:—

    "Father, in Thy gracious keeping
    Leave we now Thy servant sleeping."
                   [J. J.]

Now the stars are lit in heaven. *J. Keble.* [*Evening.*] Appeared in the *British Magazine*, March, 1834, as one of five hymns entitled, "Lighting of Lamps." It was republished in *Lyra Apostolica*, 1836, in 5 st. of 6 l., and again in the author's posthumous *Miscellaneous Poems*, 1869, p. 19. In the *Wellington College H. Bk.*, 1860, and later eds., st. iii. is omitted.   [J. J.]

Now to our Saviour let us raise. *J. M. Neale.* [*Ascension.*] Appeared in his *Hys. for Children*, 1st Ser., 1842, in 7 st. of 4 l., No. xxviii., as a hymn for Ascension Day, and has been included in all later editions of the same. The hymn, "Christ is gone up, yet ere He passed," is compiled from the text of 1842. It appeared in Murray's *Hymnal*, 1852, being composed of st. ii.-vi. and the doxology. This form has been repeated in numerous collections, sometimes with the omission of the doxology as in *H. A. & M.*, No. 352. The alterations which are found in most hymnals, in st. iv., where in l. 2 "to it is cold" is changed to "to *her* is cold;" and l. 3, "And bring them in" to "*Bring wanderers* in," date from *Murray*, 1852. Dr. Neale, having contemplated the use of the hymn at daily service, supplied an additional st. for use in such cases before the doxology. It reads:—

    "And now we haste with thankful feet,
      To seek our Saviour's Face;
    And in the Holy Church to meet,
      His chosen dwelling-place."

In the S. P. C. K. *Church Hymns*, 1871, No. 170, the hymn for St. Matthias is thus composed: st. i.-ii, Dr. Neale, unaltered, as above; st. iii., Compilers of *Church Hymns* to adapt it to St. Matthias' Day; st. iv.-v., Neale altered.   [J. J.]

Now to the Lord that makes us know. *I. Watts.* [*Advent—Praise.*] First pub. in his *Hymns, &c.*, 1st ed., 1707, in 5 st. of 4 l., and entitled "Christ our High Priest and King: and Christ coming to Judgment." Its use outside the Nonconformist bodies has been limited. Orig. text in modern editions of Watts. It has been said that John Mason's *Song of Praise*, No. 33, on Rev. i., 1-12, suggested this hymn to Watts. The resemblance, however, is confined to the subject alone. In the Scottish Draft *Translations and Paraphrases* of 1745, No. xlv. is thus composed:—st. i.-iii., based on the above, by Watts, and st. iv. original, the opening line being, "To Him that lov'd the Souls of Men." In the *Drafts* of 1751 and 1781 it was repeated without alteration, and was finally authorized as No. lxiv. in the *Trans. and Paraphs.* of 1781, again without change. It thus holds the unique position of being the only paraphrase of the *Draft* of 1745 which passed without alteration into the authorized work of 1781. It has been in use in the Church of Scotland for more than 100 years, and is also included in a limited number of modern hymnals both in G. Britain and America. Its authorship, as distinct from Watts, is unknown. The statement that it is due to J. Morison has been made in ignorance of the fact that it was in print in its present form some *four years* before his birth. [J. J.]

Now, when the dusky shades of night retreating. [*Morning.*] This cento was given in Hedge and Huntington's *Hys. for the Church of Christ*, Boston, U. S. A., 1853, No. 404, in 6 st. of 4 l. The first stanza is an altered form of st. i. of W. J. Copeland's *tr.* of "Ecce jam noctis" (p. 320, i.). It is suggested in the Index of Latin first lines in Thring's *Coll.*, 1882, that st. iii. ("Look from the tower of heaven") is also from the same Latin

hymn; st. ii. ("To Thee Whose word, &c.")
is from "Lucis Creator optime," and st. vi.
("So when the morn, &c.") is from "Nocte
surgentes, &c." Possibly this may be so,
but the resemblance is remote. The hymn
as in the *Hys. for the Church of Christ*, either
in full or in part, is in a great many hymn-
books in G. Britain and America, including
the *Plymouth Coll.*, 1855; *Kennedy*, 1863; the
Hymnary, 1872; Thring's *Coll.*, 1882, &c. In
most collections st. iv and v. of the 1853 text
are omitted, and sometimes a doxology is
added.   [J. J.]

Nox atra rerum contegit. *St. Gregory
the Great* (?). [*Thursday. Morning.*] Mone,
No. 278, gives this as probably by St. Gregory
the Great (it is not assigned to him by the
Benedictine editors), and at i. p. 372, cites it
as appointed for Nocturns on Thursday in an
8th cent. MS. at Trier. *Daniel* i. No. 45, gives
the text, and at iv. p. 37, cites it as in a
Rheinau MS. of the 10th cent. Among the
British Museum MSS. it is found in three 11th
cent. *Hymnaries* of the English Church (Vesp.
D. xii. f. 19 b; Jul. A. vi. f. 27 b; Harl. 2961,
f. 223), and in an 11th cent. *Breviary* of the
Spanish Church (Add. 30848, f. 77 b). It is in
an 11th cent. MS. at Corpus Christi College,
Cambridge (391, p. 235), and in the *Latin Hys.
of the Anglo-Saxon Ch.* (Surtees Society), 1851,
is printed from an 11th cent. MS. at Durham
(B. iii. 32 f. 7 b). Also in three MSS. of the 11th
cent. at St. Gall, Nos. 387, 413, 414. It is included in the *Roman* (Venice, 1478, and the
revision of 1632), *Sarum, York, Aberdeen*, and
other *Breviaries*, the universal use being for
Thursdays at Nocturns or Matins. The text
is also in *Wackernagel*, i. No. 94; *Hymnarium
Sarisb.*, 1851, p. 51; *Königsfeld*, i. p. 12; and
Card. Newman's *Hymni Ecclesiae*, 1838 and
1865.   [J. M.]

Translations in C. U. :—

1. **Dark night, beneath her sable wings.** By J.
D. Chambers, in his *Psalter*, 1852, p. 211, and
his *Lauda Syon*, 1857, p. 23.

2. **The dusky veil of night hath laid.** This in
the *Hymner*, 1882, is based upon the *tr.* by
Chambers as above.

Translations not in C. U. :—

1. Dark night arrays in hueless vest. *Bp. R. Mant.*
1837.
2. All tender lights, all hues divine. *Card. Newman.*
1853 and 1868.
3. The pitchy night beneath her pall. *Hymnarium
Anglicanum.* 1844.
4. Night shrouds beneath her sable vest. *W. J. Copeland.* 1848.
5. Tho' faded now earth's colours bright. *R. Campbell.* 1850.
6. The pall of night o'ershades the earth. *Hyl. for
Use in St. John's, &c., Aberdeen.* 1870.
7. The gloom of night o'ershadows now. *J. Wallace.*
1874.   [J. J.]

Nox, et tenebrae, et nubila. *Prudentius.* [*Wednesday and Thursday.*] This
hymn is found in a MS. of the 5th cent. in the
Bibliotheque Nationale, Paris (8084 f. 3 b.),
and is given in all editions of Prudentius's
works, including *Aurelii Prudentii Clementis
V. C., Opera Omnia*, London, 1824, vol. i. p.
61, where it is given with notes. It is No. ii.
of the *Cathemerinon*, and extends to 72 lines.
At a very early date it was divided into two
hymns, the first beginning as above, and the

second, "Lux ecce surgit aurea.' Each ot
these must be taken in detail.

1. **Nox, et tenebrae, et nubila.** [*Wednesday
Morning.*] This is found in four MSS. of the
11th cent. in the British Museum (Jul. A. vi.
f. 26 b; Vesp. D. xii., f. 18; Harl. 2961, f. 222 b;
Add. 30848 f. 77), and is printed in the *Latin
Hys. of the Anglo-Saxon Church*, 1851, from an
11th cent. MS. at Durham (B. iii. 32, f. 7). It
is found in most of the older Breviaries, as the
Sarum, Roman, York, Aberdeen, &c. The text
is also in *Mone*, No. 276; *Daniel* i. No. 104;
in Card. Newman's *Hymni Ecclesiae* 1838 and
1865, &c.   [J. M.]

Translations in C. U. :—

1. **Lo, night and clouds and darkness wrapp'd.**
By Bp. Mant, in his *Ancient Hys. from the Rom.
Brev.*, 1837, p. 15 (ed. 1871, p. 29). This is
given with alterations in the *Hymnary*, 1872.

2. **The pall of night o'ershades the earth.** By
E. Caswall, in his *Lyra Catholica*, 1849, p. 26,
and again in his *Hymns, &c.*, 1873, p. 16.

3. **Ye glooms of night, ye clouds and shade.** By
J. D. Chambers, in his *Psalter*, 1852, p. 208, and
his *Lauda Syon*, 1857, p. 21. This is repeated
in the *People's H.*, 1867.

4. **Hence, night and clouds that night-time
brings.** By J. M. Neale, in the enlarged ed. of
the *H. Noted*, 1854; and the *Hymner*, 1882.
In Skinner's *Daily Service Hyl.*, 1864, the hymn
"O gloom of night and clouds and shade," is an
altered form of this *tr.* with portions borrowed
from the *tr.* by J. D. Chambers.

5. **Night and darkness cover all.** By H. Bonar.
in the 2nd Series of his *Hys. of Faith & Hope*,
1864. This is in Nicholson's *Appendix Hyl.*, 1866.

Other trs. are :—

1. Night and darkness, and thick cloud. *Hymnarium
Anglicanum*, 1844.
2. Shade, and cloud, and lowering night. *Bp. J.
Williams*, 1845.
3. Night and clouds in darkness sailing. *W. J. Copeland*, 1848.
4. Swift as shadows of the night. *R. Campbell*, 1850,
and Shipley's *Annus Sanctus*, 1884.
5. Haunting gloom and flitting shades. *Card. Newman*, 1853 and 1868.
6. Begone, dark night, ye mists disperse. *J. Wallace*,
1874.   [J. J.]

ii. **Lux ecce surgit aurea.** [*Thursday Morn-
ing.*] This portion of the hymn is also found
in four MSS. of the 11th century in the British
Museum (Vesp. D. xii. f. 20 b; Jul. A. vi. f. 28;
Harl. 2961, f. 223 b; Add. 30848. f. 78 b), and
is printed in the *Latin Hys. of the Anglo-Saxon
Church*, 1851, from an 11th cent. MS. at Dur-
ham (B. iii. 32, f. 8). It is also in Card.
Newman's *Hymni Ecclesiae*, 1838 and 1865;
Daniel i. No. 105; and other collections of
Latin hymns. It is in the *Sarum, Roman,
York*, and other Brevs.   [J. M.]

Translations in C. U. :—

1. **Behold, it shines, the golden light.** By Bp.
Mant, in his *Ancient Hys. from the Rom. Brev.*
1837, p. 25 (ed. 1873, p. 47). This is given in
Kennedy, 1863, with the omission of st. v.

2. **Lo, the golden light is peering.** By W. J.
Copeland, in his *Hys. for the Week, &c.*, 1848,
p. 36. In *Kennedy*, 1863, No. 1446, st. v. is
new. In the *Hymnary*, 1872, it begins, "Lo,
the golden *sun* is shining," *Kennedy's* st. v. being
repeated, and *Copeland's* st. v. is given as st. vi.

3. **Now with the rising golden dawn.** By E.
Caswall, in his *Lyra Catholica*, 1849, p. 27, and

his *Hymns*, &c., 1873, p. 16. It is given in the *People's H.*, 1867; Thring's *Coll.*, 1882, and others. In the American Unitarian *Hys. of the Spirit*, 1864, it reads, "Now with *creation's morning song*." The alterations were made by S. Longfellow, one of the editors. This arrangement of the text is repeated in Martineau's *Hymns*, 1873.

4. Behold the golden dawn arise. By J. M. Neale, in the enlarged ed. of the *H. Noted*, 1854; and the *Hymner*, 1882.

Other trs. are :—

1. See, the golden dawn is glowing. *Card. Newman*, 1853.

2. 'Tis morn! behold the golden ray. *Hymnarium Anglicanum*, 1844.

3. Lo! the golden light arises. *Bp. J. Williams*, 1845.

4. Behold the golden dawn [morn] arise. *J. D. Chambers*, 1852 and 1857.

5. Lo, now doth rise the golden light. *J. W. Hewett*, 1859.

6. As at morn's golden ray. *R. Campbell*, in Shipley's *Annus Sanctus*, 1884.

7. See now the golden light appears. *J. Wallace*, 1874.

8. See! the golden morning rises. W. P. Lunt, in Putnam's *Singers and Songs of the Liberal Faith*. Boston, U.S.A., 1875.   [J. J.]

Nu biten wir den heiligen Geist. [*Whitsuntide.*] *Wackernagel*, ii. p. 44, gives two versions, both in 5 lines; the one from a MS. sermon [now at Heidelberg] of "Bruder Berthold von Regensburg," who d. 1272, and the other from the *Psaltes Ecclesiasticus*, Mainz, 1550. It is one of the very few examples of popular vernacular hymns used in church in pre-Reformation times. According to *Koch*, i. p. 208, it was sung at Whitsuntide by the people "during the ceremony in which a wooden dove was lowered by a cord from the roof of the chancel, or a living dove was thence let fly down." It was adopted by Martin Luther. (See **Nun bitten**, as below.) *Tr.* as "Now let us pray the Holy Ghost," by *Miss Winkworth*, 1869, p. 38.   [J. M.]

Nun bitten wir den heiligen Geist. *M. Luther.* [*Whitsuntide.*] The first stanza of this hymn is old (see **Nu biten wir** as above). To this stanza Luther added a second, invoking the Holy Spirit as the true Light, a third as the blessed Love, and a fourth as the great Comforter. The full form in 4 st. of 4 l., with Kyrioleis, appeared in the *Geystliche gesangk Buchleyn*, Wittenberg, 1524. Thence in *Wackernagel*, iii. p. 18, in Schircks's ed. of Luther's *Geistl. Lieder*, 1854, p. 29, and in the *Unv. L. S.*, 1851, No. 177. The hymn has been generally appointed for Whitsuntide, but has also been used in the Lutheran Church as a hymn for Holy Communion, at the ordination of ministers, or, as in the *Strassburg Kirchen Ampt*, 1525, before the sermon. *Tr.* as :—

Now pray we all God the Comforter. In full by A. T. Russell, as No. 18 in his *Ps. & Hys.*, 1851, repeated by Dr. Bacon, 1884, p. 40.

Other trs. are :—

(1) "Thou holy Spirite, we pray to the," by Bp. Coverdale, 1539 (*Remains*, 1846, p. 543). (2) "Now our request to the Holy Ghost," in *Some other H. & Poems*, Lond., 1752, p. 9, and the *Moravian H. Bk.*, 1754, pt. i., No. 228. (3) "God Holy Ghost, in mercy us preserve," as No. 205 in the *Moravian H. Bk.*, 1789 (1849, No. 250). (4) "Now on the Holy Ghost we call For perfect," by *Miss Fry*, 1845, p. 43. (5) "To Thee, Thou Holy Spirit, now," by *Miss Fry*, 1845, p. 45. (6)

"Holy Spirit! grant us our desire," by *J. Anderson* 1846, p. 19 (1847, p. 42). (7) "Oh Holy Ghost! to Thee we pray," by *Dr. J. Hunt*, 1853, p. 50. (8) "Now crave we of the Holy Ghost," by *R. Massie*, 1854, p. 21. (9) "Now pray we to the Holy Ghost," by Dr. G. Macdonald, in the *Sunday Mag.*, 1867. In his *Exotics*, 1876, p. 59, beginning "Now let us pray to the Holy Ghost." (10) "Now on the Holy Ghost we call To give," by J. D. Burns, in his *Remains*, 1869, p. 235.   [J. M.]

Nun freut euch lieben Christengemein. *M. Luther.* [*Advent. Redemption by Christ.*] This is Luther's first congregational hymn. It was written in 1523, immediately after, and is a companion to, his "Ein neues Lied" (p. **326**, i.). It appeared in the *Etlich cristlich lider*, Wittenberg, 1524, in 10 st. of 7 l., entitled "A Christian hymn of Dr. Martin Luther, setting forth the unspeakable grace of God, and the true faith" (in Klug's *G. B.*, 1541, and most later books, entitled "A hymn of thanksgiving for the great blessings which God has bestowed on us in Christ"). Thence in *Wackernagel*, iii. p. 5, in Schircks's ed. of Luther's *Geistl. Lieder*, 1854, p. 31, and in the *Unv. L. S.*, 1851, No. 235. By its clear and full doctrinal statements in flowing verse it soon became popular in Germany. Tileman Hesshusius, in his preface to Johannes Magdeburg's *Psalter*, 1565, thus speaks of it :—

"I do not doubt that through this one hymn of Luther many hundreds of Christians have been brought to the true faith, who before could not endure the name of Luther; but the noble, precious words of the hymn have won their hearts, so that they are constrained to embrace the truth: so that in my opinion the hymns have helped the spread of the Gospel not a little."

We may note that the original melody of 1524 is in *H. A. & M.*, No. 293, called *Erk*. The melody, which appeared in Klug's *G. B.*, 1535 (and possibly in the lost ed. of 1529), is said to have been written down by Luther from hearing it sung by a travelling artisan, and bears considerable resemblance to an old popular song tune (see L. Erk's *Choral Buch*, 1863, Nos. 193–195). In England the melody of 1535 has been long used, in an altered form, under the name of *Luther's Hymn*, and set to "Great God! what do I see and hear!" (p. **454**, i.)

Owing to the structure of this hymn forbidding selection, and to its length, it has come very little into English C. U. *Tr.* as :—

1. **Rejoice, ye ransom'd of the Lord.** By W. M. Reynolds, in the *Evang. Review*, Gettysburg, July, 1849, p. 143. The *trs.* of st. i.–vi. are in the Amer. Luth. Gen. Synod's *Coll.*, 1850-52.

2. **Dear Christians, one and all rejoice.** In full by R. Massie in his *Martin Luther's Spir. Songs*, 1854, p. 47. Repeated in the Ohio *Luth. Hyl.*, 1880, and others.

3. **Dear Christian people, all rejoice.** A full and good *tr.* by Mrs. Charles, in her *Voice of Christian Life in Song*, 1858. Her *tr.* of st. i., altered and beginning "Ye Christian people! " is st. ii. of No. 95 in the Swedenborgian *Coll.*, 1880.

Other trs. are :—

(1) "Be glad now, all ye Christen men," by Bp. Coverdale, 1539 (*Remains*, 1846, p. 550). (2) "Be blyith, all Christin men, and sing," in the *Gude and Godly Ballates*, ed. 1568, folio 24 (1868, p. 40). (3) "Now come ye Christians all and bring," by *J. C. Jacobi*, 1722, p. 30. (4) "Ye Christian congregations dear," as No. 239 in the *Appendix* of 1743 to the *Moravian H. Bk.* (1754, pt. i. No. 299). (5) "Rejoice! Rejoice! ye Christian bands," by *Miss Fry*, 1845, p. 101. (6) "Christians all, with me rejoice," by *J. Anderson*, 1846, p. 47 (1847, p. 65). (7) "All ye that fear the Lord, rejoice," by *Dr. J. Hunt*, 1853, p. 78. (8) "Come, Christians all, let us rejoice, by *Dr. H. Mills*, 1856, p. 66. (9) "Let us be glad, and no more sad," by S. Garrett, in his *Hys. and Trs.*, 1867, p. 32. (10) "Dear

Christians, let us now rejoice," by Dr. G. Macdonald, in the *Sunday Mag.*, 1867, p. 570, and his *Exotics*, 1876, p. 80. (11) "Dear Christian people, now rejoice," by *Miss Winkworth*, 1869, p. 112.   [J. M.]

Nun lasst uns den Leib begraben.

M. Weisse. [*Burial of the Dead.*] 1st pub. in *Ein New Geseng buchlen*, Jung Bunzlau, 1531, in 7 st. of 4 l., and thence in *Wackernagel*, iii. p. 332. This has been called a *tr.* from the Latin of A. C. Prudentius (see under **Deus ignee, p. 292, i.**), but has really very little resemblance to it. Mr. Müller (see **Bohemian Hymnody, p. 157**) is of opinion that it is an expansion of a Bohemian hymn by Lucas of Prag which seems to have been included in the lost *Brethren's H. Bk.* of 1519, and is in the *Utraquist H. Bk.* of 1559. The hymn by Lucas has only 4 st., but is of the same tenor as Weisse's, has the same title, and is in the same metre. In the Magdeburg *G. B.* of 1540 it is considerably altered, and an 8th st. added. This form (sometimes ascribed to M. Luther) passed, with alterations, into V. Babst's *G. B.*, Leipzig, 1545, and is found in Porst's *G. B.*, ed. 1855, No. 874.

In L. Erk's *Choral-Buch*, 1863, No. 199, the tune generally set to it is given from G. Rhau's *Newe Deudsche geistliche Gesenge*, Wittenberg, 1544. This tune is in the *Bohemian H. Bk.* of 1560, but not in the ed. of 1541, nor in the *New Geseng buchlen* of 1531. In Allon's *Cong. Psalmist* it is named *Bohemia*. The hymn is *not* in the *Riga G. B.* of 1530, but is added in the ed. of 1548.

Translation in C. U.:—

Now lay we calmly in the grave. A good and full *tr.* by Miss Winkworth, in her *Lyra Ger.*, 2nd Ser., 1858, p. 117, and her *C. B. for England*, 1863, No. 96. Repeated in the Ohio *Luth. Hyl.*, 1880, and in the 1884 *Appendix* to the *Scottish Hymnal*.

Other trs. are :—

(1) "Our brother let us put in grave," in the *Gude and Godly Ballates*, ed. 1568, folio 83 (1868, p. 143). (2) "Let us this present corpse inter," in the *Moravian H. Bk.*, 1754, pt. i., No. 295. (3) "We give this body to the dust," by *Dr. H. Mills*, 1845 (1856, p. 267). (4) "The corpse we now inter, and give," by *Dr. G. Walker*, 1860, p. 111. (5) "We lay this body in the grave," by Dr. H. Harbaugh, in the (German Reformed) *Guardian*, Nov., 1863, p. 351.   [J. M.]

Nun ruhen alle Wälder. *P. Gerhardt.*

[*Evening.*] 1st pub. in the 3rd ed., 1648, of Crüger's *Praxis Pietatis Melica*, No. 15, in 9 st. of 6 l.: reprinted in Wackernagel's ed. of his *Geistliche Lieder*, No. 102, and Bachmann's ed., No. 2; and included as No. 529 in the *Unv. L. S.*, 1851. It is one of the finest of Gerhardt's hymns. Simple and homely in its style it took great hold of the hearts of the German people. Baron Bunsen (quoted by *Fischer*, ii. 126) says of it in the *Evangelische Kirchenzeitung*, Berlin, 1830 :—

"Ever since its publication this hymn has been one of the most beloved and best known hymns of devout meditation over the whole of Germany. Experienced and conceived in a truly childlike popular spirit, it unites with a rare naïve simplicity of expression, a loftiness of thought, a depth of Christian experience, a grace of poetry, so that for this union of qualities it must rank as an enduring masterpiece among hymns."

This hymn was a special favourite of Schiller's mother, and of the poet himself. In the time of Flat Rationalism st. i. became the object of much shallow wit. But as Richter points out (*Biog. Lexicon*, 1804, p. 95), if to represent the earth as tired, and woods and trees as sleeping is not true poetry, then Virgil

(*Aeneid* iv., ll. 522-28) was in the wrong. St. viii., "Breit aus die Flügel beide," has been a special favourite in Germany, and Lauxmann, in *Koch* viii. 194, says of it :—

"How many a Christian soul, children mostly, but also God's children in general, does this verse serve as their last evening prayer. It has often been the last prayer uttered on earth, and in many districts of Germany is used at the close of the baptismal service to commend the dear little ones to the protection of their Lord Jesus."

Although in limited use in a translated form in the English hymn-books, the *Trs.* are numerous, and are as follows :—

1. **Quietly rest the woods and dales,** omitting st. viii., by Mrs. Findlater, in *H. L. L.*, 1st Ser., 1854, p. 36 (1884, p. 38), included in *Cantate Domino*, Boston, U.S., 1859.

2. **Now all the woods are sleeping.** A full and good *tr.* by Miss Winkworth, in the 2nd ed. 1856, of the 1st Ser. of her *Lyra Ger.*, 1855, p. 228 (see below for first version). Included in full in her *C. B. for England*, 1863, and the Ohio *Luth. Hyl.*, 1880; and abridged in Dr. W. F. Stevenson's *Hys. for Church & Home*, 1873.

3. **Now woods their rest are keeping.** A good *tr.* of st. i., iii., vii., ix., contributed by Edward Thring, as No. 18 to the *Uppingham and Sherborne School H. Bk.*, 1874.

Other trs. are: (1) "Jesu, our Joy and Loving Friend," of st. viii., as No. 200 in the *Appx.* of 1743 to the *Moravian H. Bk.*, 1742. (2) "Now Woods and Fields are quiet," in the *Suppl. to Ger. Psal.*, ed. 1765, p. 73. (3) "Display Thy both wings over," of st. viii., as No. 156 in pt. i. of the *Moravian H. Bk.*, 1754. (4) "Jesus, our Guardian, Guide and Friend," of st. viii. as No. 765 in the *Moravian H. Bk.*, 1789 (1886, No. 1190). (5) "Lo! Man and Beast are sleeping," by *H. J. Buckoll*, 1842, p. 76. (6) "Now rest beneath night's shadow," by E. D. Yeomans, in Schaff's *Kirchenfreund*, 1853, p. 195. (7) "Now rest the woods again," by *Miss Winkworth*, 1855, p. 226 (see No. 2 above). (8) "Rise, my soul, thy vigil keep," by Miss Dunn, 1857, p. 9. (9) "Now resteth all creation," by J. S. Stallybrass, in the *Tonic Solfa Reporter*, January, 1859, and Curwen's *Harmonium & Organ Book*, 1863, p. 58. (10) "Now every greenwood sleepeth," by *Miss Manington*, 1863, p. 133. (11) "Now hushed are woods and waters," by *Miss Cox*, 1864, p. 9. (12) "Now spread are evening's shadows," by *J. Kelly*, 1863. (13) "The woods are hush'd; o'er town and plain," by *Dr. J. Guthrie*, 1869.

The hymn, "Tho' now no creature's sleeping," No. 356, in pt. ii. of the *Moravian H. Bk.*, 1754, is a *tr.* of "Jetzt schlafen weder Wälder." This is No. 2338 in the final *Zugabe* to the *Herrnhut G. B.*, 1735. It is a parody in the "spiritual fleshy" style of st. i.-iii., vi., vii., of Gerhardt. It is marked as "On Aug. 13, 1748, after Holy Communion at Herrnhut."   [J. M.]

Nunc Dimittis.

Metrical paraphrases of the *Song of Simeon* (St. Luke ii. 29-32) are more numerous than those of the *Magnificat* or the *Benedictus*. The versions which appeared in the early *Psalters* are noted in the article on the **Old Version**, § ii.-vi. Of these the opening lines of the form of the *Old Version* given in comparatively modern eds. read :—

"O Lord my God, because my heart
    Have longed earnestly,
My Lord and Saviour to behold,
    And see before I die ;
The joy and health of all mankind,
    Desired long before ;
Who now is come into the world
    Lost man for to restore."

2. The *New Version* paraphrase which appeared in the *Supplement* thereto in 1701 or 1702 opens thus :—

"Lord let Thy servant now depart
    Into Thy promis'd rest,
Since my expecting eyes have been
    With Thy Salvation blest."

3. Amongst the old paraphrasers of the *Psalms* Dr. John Patrick is one of the few who appended versions of the Canticles to their paraphrases. In his *Psalms of David in Metre*, 1691, the *Nunc Dimittis* begins :—

"I now can leave this world and die
    In peace and quiet rest ;
Since that mine eyes, O Lord, have been
    With Thy salvation blest."

4. The rendering in the Scottish *Translations and Paraphrases*, 1781, has a somewhat complicated history which is given under, "Now let Thy servant die in peace" (p. 818, i.).

5. Dr. Irons's version in his *Ps. & Hys. for the Church*, 1875–83, which begins :—"Enough enough, Thy saint had lived," is worthy of attention, and, with a slight change in the opening lines, would make an useful hymn.

6. Other paraphrases, some of much excellence, are annotated in this Dictionary under their respective first lines, or their authors' names. For these, see the **Index of Seasons and Subjects** at the end.   [J. J.]

Nunc Sancte nobis Spiritus. *St. Ambrose ?* [*The Third Hour.*] This hymn is ascribed to St. Ambrose by Hincmar in h. "De unâ et non trinâ Deitate," 857; and is included by L. Biraghi, 1862, as one of the *Inni sinceri* of St. Ambrose. It is not, however, mentioned in the Rule of Caesarius of Arles (d. 543), nor in that of Aurelianus of Arles (d. 555); nor is it received as genuine by the Benedictine editors of St. Ambrose. The text is given by *Daniel* i., No. 40; with further notes at iv. p. 43, in which he cites it as in a 10th cent. Rheinau MS., classes it as of the 7th or 8th cent., and remarks that St. Ambrose is more probably the author of the longer hymn for Terce, which begins "Jam surgit hora tertia." *Mone*, i. p. 372, cites it as in MSS. of the 8th cent. at Darmstadt, and at Trier. Among the British Museum MSS. it is found in three 11th cent. *Hymnaries* of the English Church (Vesp. D. xii. f. 8 b; Jul. A. vi. f. 21 b; Harl. 2961 f. 220), an 11th cent. *Breviary* of the Spanish Church (Add. 30,848, f. 71 b), &c. It is in a MS. of the 11th cent. at Corpus Christi College, Cambridge (391, p. 230); in a MS. of the 11th cent. at St. Gall, No. 413; and in the *Latin Hys. of the Anglo-Saxon Ch.* (Surtees Society), 1851, is printed from an 11th cent. MS. at Durham (B. iii. 32 f. 4). It is given in almost all Mediaeval *Breviaries*, including the *Mozarabic* of 1502, *Roman* (Venice, 1478 and the revision of 1632), *Sarum, York, Aberdeen, Paris* of 1643, &c. The universal use was as a hymn for Terce ; the reference to the outpouring of the Holy Spirit which took place at the Third Hour on the Day of Pentecost being doubtless the reason for this use. The text is also in *Wackernagel*, i. No. 7; *Hymnarium Sarisb.*, 1851, p. 39; J. Chandler's *Hys. of the Primitive Church*, 1837, No. 5 ; Card. Newman's *Hymni Ecclesiae*, 1838 and 1865; and L. C. Biggs's annotated ed. of *H. A. & M.*, 1867.   [J. M.]

Translations in C. U. :—

1. **Come, Holy Ghost, Who ever One, Art with the Father, &c.** By Card. Newman, in *Tracts for*

---

the *Times*, No. 75, 1836, p. 64 ; and his *Verses*, 1853. In his *Verses*, 1868, p. 236, it begins, "Come, Holy Ghost, who ever One, Reignest with Father, &c." It was repeated in the *English Hyl.*, 1856 ; the *Salisbury H. Bk.*, 1857 ; *H. A. & M.*, 1861; and very many others, but in most instances with slight alterations. It is by far the most extensively adopted of the *trs.* of the "Nunc Sancte."

2. **Blest Spirit, One with God above.** By J. Chandler, in his *Hys. of the Primitive Church*, 1837, p. 5, and his *Hys. of the Ch.* 1841, No. 4.

3. **Come, Holy Ghost, and through each heart.** By E. Caswall, in his *Lyra Catholica*, 1849, p. 10, and his *Hys. and Poems*, 1873, p. 7. It was repeated in Murray's *Hyl.*, 1852; the *People's H.*, 1867; and several others. It ranks next to Card. Newman's *tr.* in popularity.

4. **Come, Holy Ghost, with God the Son.** By J. M. Neale, in the *H. Noted*, 1852, No. 5, the *Hymnary*, 1872, &c.

Translations not in C. U. :—

1. Thou with the Father and the Son. *Bp. R. Mant.* 1837.
2. Spirit benignant, Who art One. *Hymnarium Anglicanum.* 1844.
3. Now, Holy Ghost, to Thee we pray. *Bp. J. Williams.* 1845.
4. Holy Spirit, ever One. *W. J. Copeland.* 1848.
5. Come, Holy Ghost, Who ever One Art with the Father, &c. *J. D. Chambers.* 1852 and 1857.
6. Now, O Holy Spirit, One. *H. Bonar.* 1867.
7. E'en now vouchsafe, Good Spirit, One. *J. Keble.* 1869.
8. O Holy Spirit, ever blest. *J. Wallace.* 1874.
          [J. J.]

Nunc suis tandem novus e latebris. *C. Coffin.* [*Nativity of St. John Baptist.*] Appeared in the *Paris Breviary*, 1736, as the hymn at Lauds for the Feast of St. John Baptist, and again in his *Hymni Sacri*, 1736, p. 76. It is also in Card. Newman's *Hymni Ecclesiae*, 1838 and 1865. *Tr.* as :—

1. **Lo, from the desert homes.** By I. Williams, in his *Hys. tr. from the Parisian Breviary*, 1839, p. 210. It is given in a large number of modern hymn-books, and sometimes in a slightly abbreviated form. In Rorison's *Hys. and Anthems*, 1851, st. i.–iii., are from this *tr.*, and st. iv.–vi. are by Dr. Rorison.

2. **From the desert caverns rude.** By W. J. Blew, in *The Church Hymn & Tune Bk.*, 1852–55; and again in Rice's *Sel.* from the same, 1870.
          [J. J.]

Nunn, John, M.A., s. of John Nunn, of Colchester, was b. at Colchester in 1781, and educated at St. John's College, Cambridge. After holding various curacies he became Domestic Chaplain to the Earl of Galloway in 1849, and Rector of Thorndon, Suffolk, in 1854. He d. there April 15, 1861. He pub. in 1817 *Psalms & Hymns from the most approved Authors*, &c. This collection contained hymns by himself and by his sister, Miss Marianne Nunn. It was reprinted several times, the last edition being 1861. His hymns have passed out of use.   [J. J.]

Nunn, Marianne, sister of the above, was b. May 17, 1778, and d. unmarried, in 1847. She published *The Benevolent Merchant*, and wrote a few hymns, including the following :—

One there is above all others, O how He loves. [*The love of Jesus.*] This was written to adapt John Newton's hymn, "One there is above all others, Well deserves the name of friend," to the Welsh air, *Ar hy-d y nos*, and consisted of one stanza of 5 lines, with the refrain " Oh how He loves ! " at the end of lines 1, 2 and 5, and the remaining 3 st. in 5 l. without the refrain, it being understood that the refrain was to be repeated. (Original text in *Lyra Brit.*, 1867, p. 449.) It was first pub. in her brother's, the Rev. J. Nunn's, *Ps. & Hys.* (see above), 1817. It has undergone several changes at various hands. In Curwen's *The New Child's Own H. Bk.*, 1874, it begins, " *There's a Friend* above all others," which is adopted from the American collections. It also sometimes begins, " One *is kind* above all others." In addition, where the original first line is given the rest of the hymn is considerably altered. Its use as a hymn for children is very extensive.   [J. J.]

Nunn, William, M.A., a younger brother of the above J. and M. Nunn, was b. May 13, 1786, and educated at St. John's College, Cambridge (B.A. 1814, M.A. 1817). He became Incumbent of St. Clement's Episcopal Chapel, Manchester, in 1818 ; d. there March 9, 1840 ; and was buried at All Saints, Manchester. He pub. the following :—

(1 *A Selection of Psalms & Hymns, Extracted from Various Collections, and principally designed for Public Worship, Manchester,* 1827 (3rd ed., 1835). (2) *A Selection of Hymns from Various Authors, Compiled especially for Children of Sunday Schools, Manchester,* 1836. (3) *Voce di Melodia, London,* 1836.

To the first of these he contributed :—

1. O could we touch the sacred lyre.   *Praise to Jesus.*
2. The Gospel comes, ordained of God.   *The Gospel.*

These hymns are still in C. U.   [J. J.]

O

O., in Bristol Bap. *Coll.* of Ash & Evans, 1st ed., 1769, i.e. Thomas Olivers.

O. A. E., in the *Ecclesiologist,* 1843–1853, i. e. J. M. Neale.

O all-atoning Lamb. *C. Wesley.* [*Spiritual Conflict.*] Written during the heated controversy on Antinomianism, Arminianism, and Calvinism, which was carried on by the Wesleys, Whitefield, Toplady, and others. It was pub. in *Hys. on God's Everlasting Love,* 1741, in 26 st. of 8 l. (*P. Works,* 1868–72, vol. iii. p. 78). Two centos therefrom are in C. U. :—(1) " Equip me for the war," in the *Wes. H. Bk.,* 1780, No. 262 (ed. 1875, No. 270) ; and " O, arm me with the mind," which is found in the American Unitarian *Hys. for the Church of Christ,* 1853, &c.   [J. J.]

O be joyful every nation. *J. Montgomery.* [*Missions.*] Written Feb. 8, 1842 (M. MSS.), for the Baptist Missionary Society, and printed in their *Jubilee Hymns,* 1842, No. 1, in two parts, Pt. ii., beginning with st. vi., " On Thy holy hill of Zion." In 1853, it was included as No. 269, in 9 st. of 6 l., in Montgomery's *Original Hymns.* A cento therefrom, beginning with st. iv., was given in the Bap. *Ps. & Hys.,* 1858, as " O Thou everlasting Father."   [J. J.]

O beata beatorum. [*Common of Martyrs.*] Dr. Neale in his *Med. Hys.,* 1851, says, " This very elegant sequence is of German origin." It is found in a 13th cent. MS. in the British Museum (Arundel, 156), written at f. 90 in a hand of the beginning of the 14th cent. ; and in a 14th cent. MS. at St. Gall, No. 343. *Mone,* No. 731, quotes it from MSS. of the 14th cent. at Admont, Salzburg, and Karls-

ruhe. It is in the *Magdeburg,* 1480, and many later German *Missals.* Also in *Daniel* ii. p. 204 ; *Kehrein,* No. 415, and others.   [J. M.]

Translations in C. U. :—

1. **Blessed Feasts of blessed martyrs.** By J. M. Neale in his *Mediæval Hys.,* 1851, p. 144, in 8 st. of 4 l., and again, greatly altered, in the *H. Noted,* enlarged ed., 1854. In the 1868 *Appendix* to *H. A. & M.* it was given in a revised form (by the Compilers). This is repeated in the revised ed., 1875, and others. Also, with slight alterations, in the *Hymnary,* 1872.

2. **Blessed acts of blessed martyrs.** By J. D. Chambers in his *Lauda Syon,* 1866, and again in the *People's H.,* 1867.   [J. J.]

O beata Hierusalem, praedicanda civitas. [*Restoration of a Church.*] This is found in a *Mozarabic Hymnarium* of the 11th cent. in the British Museum (Add. 30851 f. 156 b). It is repeated in the *Lorenzana,* 1775, and later eds. of the *Mozarabic Breviary;* also in Neale's *Hymni Ecclesiae,* 1851, p. 216, and *Daniel,* iv. p. 110.   *Tr.* as :—

Blessed city, Heav'nly Salem, Land of glory, &c. By J. M. Neale in the enlarged ed. of the *H. Noted,* 1854, No. 104. In some copies the Latin is given as " Urbs beata Jerusalem," and this is repeated in the *People's H.,* 1867. The first stanza of Neale's *tr.* reads :—

" Blessed city, Heav'nly Salem,
    Land of glory, land of rest ;
Joyous ever and triumphant
    In the armies of the blest ;
Where the King, thy grace renewing,
    Doth His glory manifest."

The full text is repeated in several collections, including the *People's H.,* as above, the *Sarum,* and others. In the Philadelphia Presbyterian *Sel. of Hys.,* 1861, it begins with st. iii., " Come Thou now, and be among us." [J. M.]

O blest were the accents of early creation. *Bp. R. Heber.* [*Gospel for 19th Sunday after Trinity.*] Appeared in his posthumous *Hymns,* &c., 1827, p. 120, in 6 st. of 4 l. It is not in C. U. in its original form, but as " How blest were the accents of early creation," it is given in *Kennedy,* 1863.   [J. J.]

O brothers, lift [tune] your voices. *Bp. E. H. Bickersteth.* [*Missions.*] Written for the Jubilee of the Church Missionary Society, 1848, and first printed in the *Jubilee Tract* of that year. It was given in the author's *Poems,* 1849 ; his *Ps. & Hys.,* 1858 ; and his *Hy. Comp.,* 1870 and 1876. In *Kennedy,* 1863, it reads, " O brothers, *tune* your voices," but the hymn is not improved by the change.   [J. J.]

O Captain of God's host, whose dreadful might. *Bp. R. Heber.* [*St. Michael and all Angels.*] Appeared in his posthumous *Hymns,* &c., 1827, p. 133, in 6 st. of 5 l., as the second hymn for " Michaelmas Day." It is based on Rev. xii. 7-9, " And there was war in heaven ; Michael and his angels fought against the dragon," &c. Heber, adopting the view that the Michael of this passage was really our Blessed Lord, wrote :—

" Oh Captain of God's host, whose dreadful might
Led forth to war the armed seraphim,
    And from the starry height,
    Subdued in burning fight
Cast down that ancient Dragon, dark and grim !

" Thine angels, Christ! we laud in solemn lays,
Our elder brethren of the crystal sky,
  Who, 'mid Thy glory's blaze,
  The ceaseless anthem raise,
And gird Thy throne in faithful ministry!"

In this, its original, form it never appeared in a collection for congregational use, but as altered to embody the generally accepted meaning of the passage from the Revelation, it has had a fair degree of popularity. This altered form reads :—

" O God the Son Eternal, Thy dread might
  Sent forth St. Michael and the hosts of heaven.

It was made by the Rev. J. Keble for, and was first published in, the *Salisbury H. Bk.*, 1857, No. 165. In 1861 the same text was given, with the omission of st. v., in Pott's *Hymns fitted to the Order of C. P.*, from whence it passed into the S. P. C. K. *Appendix*, 1869, and *Church Hymns*, 1871. The same stanzas, but with further alterations, were included in the *Parish H. Bk.*, 1863, and repeated in the *Sarum*, 1868, and the *Parish*, 1875. In the *H. Bk. for the use of Wellington College*, 1860, it begins with st. ii. " Thine angels, Christ! we laud in solemn lays."   [J. J.]

O Christe Morgensterne. [*Holy Communion.*] This is one of *Zwey Schöne newe Lieder*, printed in broadsheet form at Leipzig, 1579, and thence in *Wackernagel* v. p. 11, in 10 st. of 6 l. The text in the Berlin *G. L. S.*, ed. 1863, No. 1124, is from the Leipzig *G. B.*, 1586, omitting st. x. Sometimes ascribed, but without proof, to *Basilius Förtsch*, or to *Michael Walther*. *Tr.* as

O Christ, Thou bright and Morning Star. A *tr.* of st. i.–iii., v., ix. by Miss Winkworth, in her *Lyra Ger.* 2nd Ser., 1858, p. 179, and her *C. B. for England*, 1863, No. 144. Repeated in the Pennsylvania *Luth. Ch. Bk.*, 1868, reduced to c.M., and omitting st. iii.   [J. M.]

O Christe qui noster poli. *Archbishop Charles de Vintimille.* (?) [*Vigil of Whitsunday.*] Appeared in the *Cluniac Breviary*, 1686, p. 506; again in the *Paris Breviary*, 1736, and in later French Breviaries. It is also in J. Chandler's *Hys. of the Primitive Church*, 1837, No. 77; Card. Newman's *Hymni Ecclesiae*, 1838 and 1865, &c. *Tr.* as:—

1. O Jesu, Who art gone before. By J. Chandler, in his *Hys. of the Prim. Church*, 1837, No. 77, into Oldknow's *Hymns*, &c., 1850; Schaff's *Christ in Song*, 1869, &c. In Martineau's *Hymns*, &c., 1840, it is altered to " *Messiah now is* gone before."

2. O Christ, Who dost, our herald, rise. By C. S. Calverley, made for and pub. in the *Hymnary*, 1872.

Translations not in C. U. :—
1. O Thou, gone up, our Harbinger. *I. Williams.* 1839.
2. Our Forerunner, why forsake us? *W. J. Blew.* 1852-5.
3. Christ! Who in heaven Thy palace gate. *J. D. Chambers.* 1857.
4. O Christ, Who Leader in the race. C. I. Black, in *Lyra Messianica.* 1864.   [J. J.]

O Christe splendor gloriae. [*C. of Confessors.*] This hymn is found in three MSS. of the 11th cent. in the British Museum (Vesp. D. xii. f. 102 *b*; Jul. A. vi. f. 62 *b*; Harl. 2961 f. 247); and in the *Lat. Hys. of the Anglo-Saxon Ch.*, 1851, it is printed from an 11th cent. MS. at Durham (B. iii. 32, f. 39 *b*). It is also in a MS. of the 11th cent. at Corpus Christi, Cambridge (391, p. 270). In some

of the MSS. the initial " O " has dropped out. Morel, No. 236, gives it as a hymn for the Common of Apostles (beginning " Christe, tu splendor gloriae "), from an 11th cent. Rheinau MS. *Tr.* as :—

O Sun of glory! Christ our King. By J. D. Chambers, in his *Lauda Syon*, 1866, p. 6 ; and in the 2nd ed., 1863, of the *Appendix* to the *H. Noted*, No. 200.   [J. M.]

O come and dwell in me. *C. Wesley.* [*Holiness desired.*] This is a cento compiled from his *Short Hymns*, &c., 1762 (*P. Works*, 1868-72, vol. xiii.), as follows: st. i. from vol. ii., No. 569, on 2 Cor. iii. 17; st. ii. from vol. ii., No. 578, on 2 Cor. v. 17 ; and st. iii. from vol. ii., No. 713, on Heb. xi. 5. This cento was given in the *Wes. H. Bk.*, 1780, No. 356, and has passed into several collections in G. Britain and America. G. J. Stevenson has an interesting account in his *Methodist H. Bk. Notes*, 1883, p. 258, of the spiritual use of this cento.   [J. J.]

O come and mourn with me awhile. *F. W. Faber.* [*Good Friday.*] Pub. in his *Jesus and Mary*, 1849, in 12 st. of 4 l., and headed " Jesus Crucified ; " and again, after revision, in his *Hymns*, 1862. It was brought into special notice by being included in an abbreviated and altered form in *H. A. & M.*, 1861. The original refrain reads, " Jesus, our Love, is crucified." This was changed in *H. A. & M.* to " Jesus, our Lord, is crucified," and has been almost universally adopted. The history of this refrain, which is somewhat interesting, is given under " My Lord, my Love was crucified " (p. 781, ii.). In addition to the *H. A. & M.* arrangement there are others, including, " Ye faithful, come and mourn awhile " in Skinner's *Daily Service Hymnal*, 1864, " O come, and *look awhile on Him*," in the 1874 *Supplement* to the *N. Cong.* ; " O come, and mourn *beside the Cross*," in the S. P. C. K. *Church Hys.*, 1871 ; " Have we no tears to shed for Him," in Beecher's *Plymouth Coll.*, 1855 ; and others. The *H. A. & M.* version of the text is translated into Latin in Biggs's annotated *H. A. & M.*, 1867, by the Rev. C. B. Pearson, as " Adeste fideles, mecum complorantes."   [J. J.]

O come, Creator Spirit, Inspire the souls. *W. J. Blew.* [*Annunciation of B. V. M.*] This hymn, which, as given in his *Church Hy. and Tune Bk.*, 1852-55, is a cento as follows :—st. i. is original ; st. ii. is a *tr.* of " Memento rerum conditor " (p. 229, i.); and st. iii.-vii., a *tr.* of " Haec illa solemnis dies " (p. 477, i.). This cento is repeated in Rice's *Sel.* from Mr. Blew's *Church H. & Tune Bk.*, 1870.   [J. J.]

O comfort to the dreary. *J. Conder.* [*Christ the Comforter.*] Given as No. 428 in the *Cong. H. Bk.*, 1836, in 5 st. of 8 l., again in his *Choir and Oratory*, 1837, p. 45; and again, with the omission of st. v. in his *Hys. of Praise, Prayer*, &c., 1856. It is usually given with the omission of st. iii.   [J. J.]

O comfort to [of] the weary! O balm to the distressed! *T. R. Birks.* [*Ps. lxxxix.*] Appeared in his *Companion Psalter*, 1874, in 4 st. of 8 l. It is repeated in the *Universal H. Bk.*, 1885, and others, and sometimes as " O comfort *of* the weary." It is a good specimen of the author's paraphrases. [*Psalters, English*, § xx. 7.] [J. J.]

O! day of days! shall hearts set free? *J. Keble*. [*Easter*.] Written April 18, 1822, and 1st pub. in his *Christian Year*, 1827, as the poem for Easter Day. It is in 15 st. of 4 l., and headed with the text from St. Luke xxiv. 5, 6. It has been repeated in all later editions of the *Christian Year*. As a whole it is not in C. U.; but st. ix., xi. and xii., slightly altered, are given as, "As even the lifeless stone was dear," in the *H. Bk. for the Use of Wellington Coll.*, 1860, where it is appointed for the evening of the 4th Sunday after Easter. [J. J.]

O day of rest and gladness. *Bp. C. Wordsworth, of Lincoln.* [*Sunday*.] This is the opening hymn of his *Holy Year*, 1862, p. i., in 6 st. of 8 l. It is a fine hymn, somewhat in the style of an Ode from a Greek Canon, and is in extensive use. Sometimes st. v. and vi. are given as a separate hymn, beginning, "To day on weary nations." In the 3rd ed. of the *Holy Year*, 1863, the full hymn was given as No. 3. In the 1874 *Supplement to the New Cong. H. Bk.*, it is reduced to 4 st. of 8 l., and is also somewhat altered. [J. J.]

O Dei sapientia. [*Presentation of the B. V. M.*] This hymn does not appear to be earlier than the 15th cent. *Mone*, No. 342, gives it from mss. of the 15th cent. at Bamberg, and at St. Paul in Carinthia; and *Morel*, p. 82, cites it as in an Einsiedeln ms. of 1470. It is in three St. Gall mss. of the 15th cent., Nos. 408, 438, 440. The printed text is also in the *Sarum Brev.*, Paris, 1531; the *Aberdeen Brev.* of 1509; in *Daniel*, iv. p. 283, &c. *Tr.* as :—

O wisdom of the God of Grace. By J. D. Chambers, in his *Lauda Syon*, 1866, p. 64, and, with slight alterations and another doxology, in the *Hymnary*, 1872. [J. M.]

O Deus ego amo Te, Nam prior Tu amasti me. [*Love to Christ*, or *Passiontide*.] This hymn is found in the *Psalteriolum Cantionum Catholicarum*, Cologne, 1722, p. 328, and is probably by some German Jesuit of the 17th cent. In J. C. Zabuesnig's *Katholische Kirchengesänge*, Augsburg, 1822, vol. i., p. 150, it is entitled, "The Desire of St. Ignatius," which probably is meant to refer to St. Ignatius Loyola (b. 1491, d. 1556; founder of the Society of Jesus, i.e. the Order of the Jesuits). The Latin text is also in the *Hymnodia Sacra*, Münster, 1753, p. 268; *Daniel*, ii., p. 335; H. M. Macgill's *Songs of the Christian Creed and Life*, 1876, &c. [J. M.]

Translations in C. U. :—

I love, I love Thee, Lord most high. By E. Caswall, in his *Masque of Mary*, &c., 1858, p. 357; and his *Hys. and Poems*, 1873, p. 221. It is in C. U. in its original form, and also as :—

1. Do I not love Thee, Lord most High! In Martineau's *Hymns*, &c. 1873.

2. I love Thee, O Thou Lord most High. In Dale's *English H. Bk.* 1874.

Translations not in C. U. :—

1. O God, I love Thee well. *J. W. Hewett.* 1859.

2. Fain would we love Thee, Lord; for Thou. *J. Keble.* 1869.

3. Jesus, I love Thee evermore. E. C. Benedict of New York, in Schaff's *Christ in Song*. 1869.

4. O God, my love goes forth to Thee. *H. M. Macgill.* 1876. [J. J.]

O Deus ego amo Te, Nec amo Te ut salves me. *St. Francis Xavier?* [*Love to Christ*, or *Passiontide*.] The original of this hymn is supposed to be a Spanish sonnet which begins "No me mueve, mi Dios, para quererte," and which in Diepenbrock's *Geistlicher Blumenstrauss*, 1829, p. 199, is ascribed to St. Francis Xavier. In the *Poesias* of St. Teresa of Spain (Teresa de Jesus, b. 1515, d. 1582), pub. at Münster, in 1854, it is included as by her; but we have been unable to find it in her *Libros*, Lisbon, 1616, her *Obras*, Lisbon, 1654, or her *Opera*, Cologne, 1686. The Latin form is probably by Xavier or by some German Jesuit. It is at least as early as 1668, for in that year a *tr.* was pub. by J. Scheffler, in his *Heilige Seelenlust*, Bk. v., No. 194, entitled, "She [the Soul] loves God simply for Himself, with the Holy Xavier. Also from the Latin" (see below). In the same year it also appeared with Xavier's name in W. Nakatenus's *Coeleste palmetum* (ed. 1701, p. 491, entitled, "The desire of a loving soul towards the God-Man crucified for us. S. P. Francis Xavier"). The Latin text is also found in the *Psalteriolum Cantionum Catholicarum*, Cologne, 1722, p. 328; the *Hymnodia Sacra*, Münster, 1753, p. 270; *Daniel* ii. p. 335; *Königsfeld*, ii. p. 280; F. A. March's *Lat. Hys.*, 1875, p. 190, &c.

It has been *tr.* into German, and through the German into English, viz. :—

Ich liebe Gott, und zwar umsonst. By J. Scheffler in his *Heilige Seelenlust*, 1668, Bk. v., No. 194 (*Werke*, 1862, p. 322). A free *tr.* in 10 st. of 4 l. In the Herrnhut *G. B.*, 1735, No. 738. *Tr.* as "My dear Redeemer! Thou art He," as No. 624 in pt. i. of the *Moravian H. Bk.*, 1754. In the 1789 and later ed. (1886, No. 454) it begins "Gracious Redeemer, Thou hast me." [J. M.]

The *trs.* directly from the Latin are :—

1. **My God, I love Thee, not because.** By E. Caswall, in his *Lyra Catholica*, 1849, p. 295; and his *Hys. & Poems*, 1873, p. 152. It has been included, with slight alterations, in most of the prominent hymn-books pub. since 1850, and is very popular in G. Britain and America. It is also found in the following forms :—

(1) I love Thee, O my God, but not. In the Reformed Dutch *Hys. of the Church*, N. Y., 1869, much altered. In the Bap. *Praise Bk.*, N. Y., 1871, this form is again altered as "I love Thee, O my God, and still."

(2) Jesus, I love Thee; not because. In Schaff's *Christ in Song*. 1869.

(3) Lord, may we love Thee, not because. In *Kennedy*. 1863.

(4) O God, we love Thee; not because. In the Irvingite *Hys. for the Use of the Churches*. 1871.

(5) Saviour, I love Thee, not because. In Dale's *English H. Bk.* 1874.

(6) Thou, O my Jesus [Saviour] Thou didst me. In the Unitarian *Hys. for the Church of Christ*. Boston, U.S.A. 1853; T. Darling's *Hys. for the Church of England*, 1887, &c.

2. **I love Thee, O my God and [my] Lord.** Given anonymously in *Kennedy*, 1863, No. 661, in 4 st. of 6 l. In the *Sarum Hyl.*, 1868, and Porter's *Churchman's Hyl.*, 1876, it is abbreviated to 3 st.

3. **My God, I love Thee, yet my love.** By R. C. Singleton, in his *Anglican H. Bk.*, 1868.

4. **Thee, O God, alone I love.** By G. E. Dartnell, in Thring's *Coll.*, 1880 and 1882.

Other *trs.* are :—

1. My God, I love Thee, not because I covet Thy salvation. Anon. in *The Old Church Porch*. 1857.

2. O God, my heart is fixed on Thee. *Elizabeth Charles.* 1858.

3. O God, I love Thee; not with hope. *J. W. Hewett.* 1859.

4. I do not love Thee, Lord. To win Thy, &c. *H. Kynaston,* 1862.

5. O God, let not my love to Thee. *H. M. Macgill.* 1876. [J. J.]

O disclose Thy lovely face. *C. Wesley.*

[*Pardon desired.*] There are two centos in C. U., each beginning with this line, as follows:—

(1) The first is No. 156 of the *Wes. H. Bk.,* prior to the 1875 revision. It is thus composed: St. i. is st. ii. of C. Wesley's hymn, "Lord, how long, how long shall I," which appeared in the *Hys. & Sacred Poems,* 1740; and st. ii. and iii. are st. ii., iii. of "Christ, Whose glory fills the skies" (p. **226**, i.). In this form the cento was given in the *Wes. H. Bk.,* 1780, and is found in several Methodist collections. (2) The second form of the hymn is No. 156*, in the revised *Wes. H. Bk.,* 1875. It is composed of st. ii. iii., and v. of "Lord, how long, how long shall I?" as above. [J. J.]

O du allersüsste Freude. *P. Gerhardt.*

[*Whitsuntide.*] This beautiful hymn of supplication to the Holy Spirit for His gifts and graces was 1st pub. in the 3rd. ed., 1648, of Crüger's *Praxis pietatis melica,* No. 155, in 10 st. of 8 l., reprinted in Wackernagel's ed. of his *Geistliche Lieder,* No. 30, and in Bachmann's ed., No. 10. It has attained a wide popularity in Germany, and is included in the Berlin *G. L. S,* ed 1863, No. 366. Through J. C. Jacobi's version it has also been very largely used, in various forms, in Great Britain and America. *Tr.* as:—

1. **O Thou sweetest Source of gladness.** A full and good *tr.* by *J. C. Jacobi,* in Part ii., 1725, of his *Psal. Ger.* p. 6 (ed. 1732, p. 43, greatly altered). His st. i.–iv., ix., x. were considerably altered, as "Holy Ghost, dispel our sadness," by A. M. Toplady, and were given in the *Gospel Magazine,* June, 1776, and repeated in the same year in Toplady's *Ps. & Hys.,* No. 155. They are thus included in Sedgwick's ed. of Toplady's *Hys. & Sacred Poems,* 1860, p. 169. These st. are, (i.) "Holy Ghost, dispel our sadness." (ii.) "From that height which knows no measure." (iii.) "Come, Thou best of all donations." (iv.) "Known to Thee are all recesses." (v.) "Manifest Thy love for ever." (vi.) "Be our Friend on each occasion." While appearing in many centos, it usually begins with the first stanza of the *Jacobi-Toplady* text of 1776, "Holy Ghost, dispel our sadness." These centos may be thus grouped:—

(1) *In the original metre.* There are about a dozen of centos in C. U. in this metre, and all beginning with st. i., given in hymn-books from the Lady Huntingdon *Coll.,* 1780, in 5 st., to the Irish *Church Hymnal,* 1873, in 2 st. The construction of all these centos may be ascertained by comparing them with the first lines of the *Jacobi-Toplady* text as above.

(2) *In 8.7.8.7.4.7. metre.* This, composed of st. i., iii. greatly altered, is in Bickersteth's *Christian Psalmody,* 1833; *Kennedy,* 1863; *Com. Praise,* 1879. &c.

(3) *In 8.7.8.7. metre.* There are nearly ten centos in this metre from the *Cong. H. Bk.,* 1836, in 2 st. to the Pennsylvania *Lutheran Ch. Bk.,* 1868, in 3 st. of 8 l.

(4) In addition to these centos there are also (1) "Holy Spirit, Source of gladness," in the American Unitarian *Bk. of Hymns,* 1848, and other collections; (2) "Come, Thou Source of sweetest gladness," in Stopford Brookes's *Christian Hys.,* 1881, both being altered forms of the *Jacobi-Toplady* text.

2. **Sweetest joy the soul can know.** A good *tr.,* omitting st. viii. and ix., by Miss Winkworth, in her *Lyra Ger.,* 2nd series, 1858, p. 55, and again, altered in metre, as "Sweetest Fount of

holy gladness," in her *C. B. for England,* 1863, No. 73. In this st. ii. and iv., as in *Lyra Ger.,* are omitted. From the *Lyra Ger.* text, No. 408 of the American *Hys. of the Spirit,* 1864, is derived; and from the *C. B. for England* text, No. 108, in Stryker's *Christian Chorals,* N. Y., 1885. [J. M.]

O du Liebe meiner Liebe. [*Passiontide.*]

Included in the *Geistreiches G. B.,* Halle, 1697, p. 203, in 7 st. of 8 l., and in Wagner's *G. B.,* Leipzig, 1697, vol. ii. p. 870. Repeated in Freylinghausen's *G. B.,* 1704, and recently in the Berlin *G. L. S.,* ed. 1863.

It has been erroneously ascribed to *J. Scheffler,* to whose "Liebe, die du mich zum Bilde," it is a companion hymn: sometimes to *A. Drese,* equally without proof. In the *Blätter für Hymnologie,* 1883, p. 11, it is claimed for *Elizabethe von Senitz* [b. 1629 at Rankau, Brieg, Silesia; d. 1679, at Oels in Silesia]. (See **Various.**)

Translations in C. U.:—

Thou Holiest Love, whom most I love. A good *tr.,* omitting st. iv., by Miss Winkworth, in her *Lyra Ger.,* 1st Ser., 1855, p. 83 (2nd ed., 1856, altered, and with a new *tr.* of st. ii.). It was repeated in full in Schaff's *Christ in Song,* 1869, p. 185. Abridged in Flett's *Coll.,* Paisley, 1871; Whiting's *Hys. for the Ch. Catholic,* 1882, the latter reading "most I *prize.*" Two American hymn-books, the *Dutch Ref.,* 1869, and the *Bapt. Praise Bk.,* 1871, give centos beginning with the *tr.* of st. vi., "O Love! who gav'st Thy life for me."

Other trs. are, (1) "O the love wherewith I'm loved," as No. 627 in pt. i. of the *Moravian H. Bk.,* 1754 (1886, No. 99). (2) "Love divine! my love commanding," by Miss Burlingham in the *British Herald,* Oct., 1865, p. 152, and Reid's *Praise Bk.,* 1872, No. 375. [J. M.]

O Durchbrecher aller Bande. *G. Arnold.*

[*Sanctification.*] 1st pub. in his *Göttliche Liebes-Funcken.* Frankfurt am Main, 1698, No. 169, in 11 st. of 8 l., entitled ' The Sigh of the Captive." Included in the *Geistreiches G. B.,* Darmstadt, 1698, p. 498, in Freylinghausen's *G. B.,* 1704, and many later collections, as the *Unv. L. S.,* 1851, No. 326. Also in Ehmann's ed. of Arnold's *Geistl. Lieder,* 1856, p. 81, and Knapp's ed., 1845, p. 202. It is Arnold's finest church hymn, and is a very characteristic expression of the Pietistic views regarding the conflict between the old and the new man. Lauxmann, in *Koch,* viii., 432–434, says of it:—

"In this hymn the poet powerfully expresses his inmost emotions under the many conflicts he had with his heart. . . It is a true daily hymn of supplication for earnest Christians who have taken the words of the Apostle ' Follow. . . ,the sanctification without which no man shall see the Lord' (Heb. xii. 14) as the rule and standard of their lives. Many such might often rather sigh it out than sing it."

Translations in C. U.:—

1. **Thou who breakest every chain.** A very good *tr.,* omitting st. v., vi., by Miss Winkworth, in her *Lyra Ger.,* 2nd Ser., 1858, p. 140 (*C. B. for England,* 1863, No. 111, omitting the *trs.* of st. iii., viii.). Included in the Harrow School *H. Bk.,* 1866; Brown-Borthwick's *Select Hys.,* 1871, and the S. P. C. K. *Church Hys.,* 1871, &c. In *Church Hys.* the cento is: st. i. is from i., ll. 1–4, and iv., ll. 1–4 of the German; ii. from iv., ll. 5–8, and vii., ll. 5–8; iii. from ix.; iv. from x., ll. 1–4, and xi. 5–8.

2. **Thou who breakest every fetter, Thou who art.** Omitting st. v., vi., by Mrs. Bevan, in her *Songs of Eternal Life,* 1858, p. 51. Her *trs.* of

st. i., viii., x., xi., are No. 188 in Dr. Pagenstecher's *Coll*, 1864.

Another tr. is, " Thou who breakest every fetter, Who art ever," by *N. L. Frothingham*, 1870.   [J. M.]

O esca viatorum. [*Holy Communion.*] This hymn was probably composed by some German Jesuit of the 17th cent., though it has been by some ascribed to St. Thomas of Aquino. It has not been traced earlier than the *Mainz G. B.*, (R. C.) 1661, where it is given at p. 367 in 3 st., entitled "Hymn on the true Bread of Heaven." It is also in the *Hymnodia Sacra*, Mainz, 1671, p. 86; in *Daniel* ii. p. 369, and others.   [J. M.]

Translations in C. U. :—

1. **O Bread to pilgrims given.** By R. Palmer, 1st pub. in the American *Sabbath H. Bk.*, 1858, No. 1051; again in his *Hys. & Sac. Poems*, 1865; and then in the *Lyra Sac. Americana*, 1868. In 1867 it was given with alterations in Alford's *Year of Praise*, and subsequently in other collections.

2. **O Food that weary pilgrims love.** By the Compilers of *H. A. & M.*, in the 2nd ed. of *Introits* prefixed to *H. A. & M.*, 1861, and then in the 1868 *Appendix* to the same, and in other hymnals.

3. **O Food of men wayfaring.** By R. F. Littledale, in the *Altar Manual*, 1863; the *People's H.*, 1867; and the *Altar Hymnal*, 1884.

4. **O Bread of Life from heaven.** By Philip Schaff, in his *Christ in Song*, N. Y., 1869, Lond., 1870. This is repeated in the Scottish *Presb. Hymnal*, 1876, and altered as "O Food, the pilgrim needeth," in the *Hymnary*, 1872.

Translations not in C. U. :—

1. O living Bread from Heaven. H. Trend, in *Lyra Eucharistica*. 1863.
2. O Meat the pilgrim needeth. *J. D. Chambers.* 1866.
3. Behold the traveller fed. *D. T. Morgan.* 1880.
    [J. J.]

O Everlasting Light. H. *Bonar*. [*Christ in All.*] Pub. in the 2nd Series of his *Hys. of Faith and Hope*, 1861, in 10 st. of 4 l., and headed, "Christ in All." It deals with Christ as the Everlasting "Light," "Rock," "Fount," "Health," "Truth," "Strength," "Love," and "Rest" of His people. It is in extensive use, and sometimes as "Jesus, my Everlasting Light."   [J. J.]

O Ewigkeit, du Donnerwort. *J. Rist*. [*Eternal Life.*] 1st pub. in the *Viertes Zehen* of his *Himlische Lieder*, Lüneburg, 1642, p. 51, in 16 st. of 8 l., entitled "An earnest contemplation of the unending Eternity." It is given in full in Burg's *G. B.*, Breslau, 1746, No. 1142, and still holds its place as a standard hymn, but is frequently abridged; st. iv., vii., viii., xii. being generally omitted, as in the Berlin *G. L. S.* ed., 1863, No. 1608. It is an impressive and strongly coloured hymn, and has proved a powerful appeal to many German hearts. *Tr.* as :—

1. **Eternity! terrific word.** A version of st. i., iii., xii., xvi., based on *Jacobi*, 1722; and probably by W. M. Reynolds, as No. 245 in the American Luth. Gen. Synod's *Coll.*, 1850-52. Repeated in the Ohio *Luth. Hyl.*, 1880.

2. **Eternity! most awful word.** By A. T. Russell, as No. 258 in his *Ps. & Hys.*, 1851. It is in 4 st., founded on st. i., ii., ix., xvi. Repeated,

altered and beginning "Eternity, tremendous word, The womb of mysteries yet unheard," in *Kennedy*, 1863.

3. **Eternity, thou word of fear.** A good *tr.* of st. i., ix., xiii., xvi., by E. Thring, as No. 47 in the Uppingham and Sherborne *School H. Bk.*, 1874.

Another tr. is "Eternity! tremendous Word, Home-striking Point, Heart-piercing Sword," by *J. C. Jacobi*, 1722, p. 97.   [J. M.]

O Ewigkeit! O Ewigkeit. [*Eternity.*] *Wackernagel* v. p. 1258, gives this as an anonymous hymn (in 18 st. of 6 l. and the refrain, "Betracht o Mensch die Ewigkeit"), from the *Catholische Kirchen-Gesäng*, Cologne, 1625 (*Bäumker*, ii. p. 304, says it is in the *Ausserlesene Catholische geistliche Kirchengesäng*, Cologne, 1623). In Daniel Wülffer's *Zwölff Andachten*, Nürnberg, 1648. p. 536, in 16 st. considerably altered. Wülffer's text is in the Nürnberg *G. B.*, 1690; Schöber's *Liedersegen*, 1769, and others; and is followed by Bunsen in his *Versuch*, 1833, No. 839. Bunsen's sts. correspond to st. i.-iv., viii., xi., xii., xiv.-xviii. of the 1625 text, some being considerably altered. As in almost all the *trs.* the second line is "How long art thou, Eternity," we employ in the following notes —, to show this. *Tr.* as :—

1. **Eternity! Eternity!—Yet onward.** In full from *Bunsen*, by Miss Cox, in her *Sac. Hys. from the German*, 1841, p. 187 (1864, p. 139). Included, more or less altered and abridged, in Alford's *Ps. & Hys.*, 1844, and his *Year of Praise*, 1867; *Holy Song*, 1869; the American *Hys. for the Church of Christ*, 1853; *Plymouth Coll.*, 1855; *Dutch Reformed*, 1869; and others.

2. **Eternity! Eternity!—And yet.** A good and full *tr.* from *Bunsen* by Miss Winkworth, in her *Lyra Ger.*, 1st Ser., 1855, p. 24. It is repeated abridged in the Cumbrae *H. Bk.*, 1863; and in America in the *Hys. for Ch. & Home*, 1860; Robinson's *Songs for the Sanctuary*, 1865; and the *Church Praise Bk.*, 1882.

Other trs. are, (1) "Eternity! Eternity!—For still," by C. T. Brooks, in his Schiller's *Homage of the Arts*, &c., 1847 (Boston, U. S.), p. 146. (2) "Eternity! Eternity!—Yet hasteth," by Dr. H. W. Dulcken, in his *Bk. of Ger. Songs*, 1856, p. 285. (3) "Eternity, how long! how vast," by *Dr. G. Walker*, 1860, p. 115. (4) "Eternity! how long art thou," by *Dr. J. Guthrie*, 1869. p. 128. (5) "Eternity! Eternity!—Life hasteth," signed "M. M." in the *Monthly Packet*, vol. xii., 1871, p. 413. (6) "Eternity! Eternity!—Swiftly," dated 1866, by J. H. Hopkins, in his *Carols, Hys. & Songs*, 3rd ed., 1882, p. 90.

See also **Eternity! Eternity! how vast,** p. 357, i.
    [J. M.]

O Faith! thou workest miracles. F. W. *Faber*. [*Faith.*] Appeared in his *Jesus and Mary*, 1849, in 12 st. of 4 l., and entitled "Conversion." It was also included in his *Hymns*, 1862. The hymn "O Gift of gifts! O grace of Faith," in the *Hymnary*, 1872, and others, is composed of st. v. vii.-x. and xii. of this hymn slightly altered. [J. J.]

O filii et filiae, Rex coelestis, Rex gloriae. [*Easter.*] Neale in his *Med. Hys.*, 1851, classes this with others as belonging to the 13th cent.; but it is more probably not earlier than the 17th, and is apparently of French origin. The Latin text, for the *Salut* on Easter Day, is in the *Office de la Semaine Sainte*, Paris, 1674, p. 478. *Bäumker*, i. p. 569, cites a German *tr.* as in the *Nord-*

Sterns Führers zur Seeligkeit, a German Jesuit collection pub. in 1671. The hymn is introduced by "Alleluia, Alleluia, Alleluia." It is used in many French dioceses in the *Salut*, or solemn salutation of the Blessed Sacrament, on the evening of Easter Day. The text will be found in the *Paroissiens* pub. for use in the Paris and other dioceses in France.   [J. M.]

Translations in C. U. :—

1. Ye sons and daughters of the Lord. By E. Caswall, in his *Lyra Catholica*, 1849, p. 251, and his *Hys. & Poems*, 1873, p. 152. It is given in some Roman Catholic hymn-books in an abbreviated form.

2. Ye sons and daughters of the King. By J. M. Neale in his *Mediæval Hys.*, 1851, p. 111, and the *Hymnal N.*, 1854, No. 65. In addition to its use in its 1851 form it is also found as :—

(1) **O sons and daughters, let us sing.** This is the *H. A. & M.* text, and is Neale's altered by the Compilers. The *Sarum* 1868 is the same text with further alterations.

(2) **Children of God, rejoice and sing.** For Christ hath risen, &c. This in the *Hymnary*, 1872, is based upon Dr. Neale and J. D. Chambers.

(3) **O sons redeemed, this day we sing.** In Murray's *Hymnal*, 1852.

(4) **Ye sons and daughters of the Lord.** This in Skinner's *Daily Service Hyl.*, 1864, is a cento from Neale and Caswall.

3. Ye sons and daughters, Christ we sing. By W. J. Blew in his *Church Hy. and Tune Bk.*, 1852-55. and in Rice's *Sel.* from the same, 1870.

4. Children of men, rejoice and sing. By J. D. Chambers in his *Lauda Syon*, 1857, p. 176. It passed into the *Salisbury H. Bk.*, 1857, and the *People's H.*, 1867.

Translations not in C. U. :—

1. **Young men and maids, rejoice and sing.** In the *Evening Office*, 1748 ; the *Divine Office*, 1763 ; and O. Shipley's *Annus Sanctus*, 1884. In J. R. Beste's *Church Hys.*, 1849, p. 50, the same *tr.* is given with very slight changes.

2. **Let Zion's sons and daughters say.** T. C. Porter (1859, revised 1868) in Schaff's *Christ in Song*, N.Y., 1869 ; Lond. 1870.

3. **O maids and striplings, hear love's story.** C. Kent, in O. Shipley's *Annus Sanctus*, 1884.   [J. J.]

O fons amoris, Spiritus. *C. Coffin.* [*Sunday Morning.*] Appeared in the *Paris Breviary*, 1736, as the Ferial hymn at Terce, in 3 st. of 4 l., and again in Coffin's *Hymni Sacri*, 1736, p. 92. It is also in J. Chandler's *Hys. of the Prim. Church*, 1837, p. 4; and Card. Newman's *Hymni Ecclesiae*, 1838 and 1865. It is a recast of the "Nunc sancte nobis." It is *tr.* as :—

1. **O Spirit, Fount of love, Unlock Thy temple door.** By I. Williams, in the *British Magazine*, Jan., 1834, vol. v. p. 30, and again in his *Hys. tr. from the Parisian Brev.*, 1839, p. 7. In the *English Hymnal*, 1856 and 1861, No. 9 is the same *tr.* rewritten in C.M. as "O Holy Spirit, Fount of love, Unlock," &c.

2. **O Holy Spirit, Lord of grace.** By J. Chandler, in his *Hys. of the Prim. Church*, 1837, p. 4. This is repeated with slight changes in several collections. In *H. A. & M.* another doxology is substituted for that in Chandler.

3. **O Holy Spirit, Fount of love. Blest Source, &c.** By Jane E. Leeson, and pub. in her *Paraphrases* [of the Scottish *Trs. and Paraphs.*] & *Hys.*, &c., 1853, in 4 st. of 4 l., and again in the Irvingite *Hys. for the Churches*, 1864 and 1871.

4. **O Spirit, Fount of Holy Love.** In the 2nd ed. 1863, of the Appendix to the *H. Noted*, No. 280.

Other trs. are :—

1. O Fount of love ! blest Spirit. *W. J. Blew.* 1852 and 1855.

2. O Fount of love ! Thou Spirit blest. *J. D. Chambers.* 1857.

3. All-gracious Spirit, Fount of love. *D. T. Morgan.* 1880.   [J. J.]

O for a closer walk with God. *W. Cowper.* [*Walking with God.*] This is one of the most beautiful, tender, and popular of Cowper's hymns. It appeared in the 2nd ed. of R. Conyers's *Coll. of Ps. & Hys.*, 1772, in 6 st. of 4 l., and again in A. M. Toplady's *Ps. & Hys.*, 1776, and in the *Olney Hymns*, 1779, Bk. i., No. 3, and headed, "Walking with God." It is based on Gen. v. 24, "And Enoch walked with God." It is in extensive use in all English-speaking countries, and usually in its original form.   [J. J.]

O for a faith that will not shrink. *W. H. Bathurst.* [*Faith.*] 1st pub. in his *Ps. and Hys.*, &c., 1831, Hy. 86, in 6 st. of 4 l., and entitled, "The Power of Faith." As found in *H. A. & M.*, the *Hy. Comp.*, and others, st. iv. is omitted. Its omission is a great gain to the hymn, as it mars its simplicity and tenderness. It reads :—

> "That bears unmov'd the world's dread frown,
> Nor heeds its scornful smile;
> That sin's wild ocean cannot drown,
> Nor its soft arts beguile."

The use of this hymn is great, and more especially in America, where it is given in most of the leading collections.   [J. J.]

O for a heart to praise my God. *C. Wesley.* [*Holiness desired.*] Appeared in *Hys. and Sac. Poems*, 1742, p. 80, in 8 st. of 4 l. (*P. Works*, 1868-72, vol. ii. p. 77). It is based on the Prayer Book version of Ps. li. 10. From its appearance in M. Madan's *Ps. & Hys.*, 1760, No. 3, to the present time, it has been one of the most widely used of C. Wesley's hymns. It was given in the *Wes. H. Bk.*, 1780, No. 334. G. J. Stevenson's note in his *Methodist H. Bk. Notes*, 1883, p. 245, is of more than usual interest.   [J. J.]

O for an overcoming faith. *I. Watts.* [*Second Advent.*] 1st pub. in his *Hys. and Spiritual S.*, 1707 (2nd ed. 1709, Bk. i. 17), in 4 st. of 4 l. It is based on 1 Cor. xv. 55-58, and is included in several hymn-books in G. Britain and America.

Another form is that given to it as No. 41 in the Draft Scottish *Translations and Paraphrases*, 1745, beginning, "When the last trumpet's awful voice." It is in 7 st. of 4 l., of which i.–iii. and vii. are new, and st. iv.–vi. are st. ii.–iv. of this hymn by Watts. It was rewritten in the public worship ed. of the *Trs. and Paraphs.* issued by the Church of Scotland in 1781 and still in C. U.; st. iii., ll. 3, 4, being altered from the 1745 text, and st. vii. rewritten as st. vii. and viii. The text of 1745 is ascribed by the eldest daughter of W. Cameron (**p. 200,** ii.) to Thomas Randall (an opinion not shared in by the other authorities); and the alterations in 1781 to W. Cameron. This form of the text is in C. U. outside of the *Trs. and Paraphs.*, both in G. Britain and America. Sometimes st. iii.–vi. are slightly altered as, "Behold what heavenly prophets sung." This form is in the Edinburgh Diocesan *Sel.* of 1830, No. 23, and again in the Scottish Episcopal *Coll.*, 1858, No. 126.   [J. M.]

O for one celestial ray. *Anne Steele and A. M. Toplady.* [*Prayer for the Holy Spirit.*] This hymn is based on the 12 concluding lines of Miss Steele's poem on " Captivity," pub. in her *Poems*, &c., 1760, vol. ii. p. 46 (Sedgwick's reprint, 1863, p. 227), and appeared in A. M. Toplady's *Ps. & Hys.*, 1776, No. 194, in 5 st. of 4 l. This form of the text is in a few modern collections, including the Bap. *Ps. & Hys.*, 1858, and others. [J. J.]

O for the death of those. [*Burial.*] The opening line of this hymn is the first line of J. Montgomery's " Ode to the Volunteers of Britain, On the Prospect of Invasion," pub. in his *Wanderer of Switzerland and Other Poems*, 1819 ; and the third line of st. i. is partly from the last stanza but one of the same " Ode." From these extracts, and the whole tone and swing of the hymn, it is clear that it was suggested by the " Ode." It appeared anonymously in Mason and Greene's American *Church Psalmody*, Boston, 1831, No. 616, in 5 st. of 4 l. It is given in several modern American collections, including Hatfield's *Church H. Bk.*, 1872, and others. It is sometimes ascribed to J. Montgomery, and at other times to S. F. Smith, but in each case in error. Its authorship is unknown.   [F. M. B.]

O for the happy days gone by. *F. W. Faber.* [*Dryness in Prayer.*] Appeared in his *Jesus and Mary*, &c., 1849, in 18 st. of 4 l., and again in his *Hymns*, 1862. In the American *Bapt. Praise Book*, N. Y., 1871, No. 937, beginning, " One thing alone, dear Lord, I dread," is a cento compiled from this hymn.   [J. J.]

O for the peace which floweth as a river. *Jane Crewdson, née Fox.* [*Hoping and Trusting to the end.*] Pub. in her posthumous work, *A Little While, and Other Poems*, 1864, as the opening hymn of the volume, in 6 st. of 4 l. It is found in full or in part in a large number of hymn books in G. Britain and America, and is much esteemed as a hymn for private use. [J. J.]

O fortis, O clemens Deus. *C. Coffin.* [*Evening.*] Included in the *Paris Breviary*, 1736, as the Ferial hymn at Vespers on Thursdays from Trinity to Advent; and again in Coffin's *Hymni Sacri*, 1736, p. 24. Also in J. Chandler's *Hys. of the Primitive Church*, 1837, No. 28 ; and Card. Newman's *Hymni Ecclesiae*, 1838 and 1865. *Tr.* as :—

1. **O God of our salvation, Lord.** J. Chandler, in his *Hys. of the Prim. Church*, 1837, p. 25, and Oldknow's *Hymns, &c.*, 1850, &c.

2. **Merciful and mighty Lord, Author of redeeming love.** By R. Campbell, in his *Hys. and Anthems*, 1850. This is repeated in the 1860 *Appendix* to the *Hymnal Noted*.

Other trs. are :—
1. Merciful and mighty Lord, Author of the saving word. *I. Williams.* 1839.
2. O God of mercy, God of might. *J. D. Chambers.* 1857.
3. Unto Thee, O Father, merciful and mighty. *D. T. Morgan.* 1880.   [J. J.]

O frommer und getreuer Gott. [*Penitence.*] Based on a hymn, " Ich armer Mensch, mein Herr und Gott," by Johann Leon in his *Trostbüchlein*, 1611, and thence in *Wackernagel* iv. p. 507, in 14 lines. It is included in 6 st. of 4 l. in the Königsberg *G. B.*, 1650, p. 297, and probably in an earlier ed. c. 1643 ; also in J. Crüger's *Praxis pietatis*, 1648, No. 47, in the Berlin *G. L. S.*, ed. 1863, No. 527, &c. Sometimes erroneously ascribed to *Bartholomäus Ringwaldt*, whose hymn with the same first line (Porst's *G. B.*, ed. 1855, No. 318) is entirely different. *Tr.* as :—

O God, Thou righteous, faithful Lord. In full, by A. Crull, in the Ohio *Luth. Hyl.*, 1880.   [J. M.]

O God, before Whose radiant throne. [*Opening of a Place of Worship.*] This hymn appeared anonymously in the 1810 ed. of Rippon's Bap. *Sel.*, No. 338, Pt. ii., in 7. st. of 4 l. It was rewritten by the Rev. C. H. Spurgeon in 1866 in 5 st., and included in his *O. O. H. Bk.*, 1866, as by " John Rippon, 1810; Charles H. Spurgeon, 1866." This text and ascription of authorship were repeated in Dale's *English H. Bk.*, 1874. We have seen no authority for attributing the original to Dr. Rippon. Its anonymous appearance in his *Sel.*, in which the authors' names are usually given with the hymns, is no proof that he was the author.   [J. J.]

O God, for ever near. *Abner W. Brown.* [*Public Worship.*] Written in 1844, and 1st pub. in his *Introits*, 1845, in 4 st. of 4 l. ; again in his *Hys. and Scriptural Chants*, 1848 ; and again in his *Sel. of Ps. & Hys.*, 1865. In this last it was increased to 5 stanzas, the addition being st. iv. In the Bap. *Ps. & Hys.*, 1858, No. 883, st. i.–iii. are from this hymn, and st. iv. is st. i. in a rewritten form. The hymn in whole or in part is also in other collections, as Alford's *Year of Praise*, 1867.   [J. J.]

O God, my God, my all Thou art. [*Ps. lxiii.*] This translation, by John Wesley, of a version of the 63rd Psalm, by an unknown Spanish author, was first pub. in J. Wesley's *Coll. of Psalms and Hymns*, 1738. This was an enlarged edition of the *Ps. and Hys.* previously pub. by him at Charles-Town, printed by Lewis Timothy, 1737. [See **Methodist Hymnody**, § i.] The *tr.* was again pub. in the Wesley *Hys. and Sacred Poems*, 1739, p. 196, in 10 st. of 4 l. (*P. Works*, 1868–72, vol. i., p. 174.) In 1780 it was included in the *Wes. H. Bk.*, No. 425, with the omission of st. iv., " In holiness within Thy gates." Curiously enough, this stanza, as " O Lord, within Thy sacred gates," is the opening stanza of a cento from this hymn given in several modern collections, including the *Hymnary*, 1872, the *H. Comp.*, 1870 and 1876, and others, together with many American collections. This cento is in Elliott's *Ps. and Hys.*, 1835, and is probably much earlier. Dr. Osborn says, in his note on this hymn (*P. Works*, vol. i., p. 174.)

" This noble version of Ps. lxiii. was inserted in the book of 1738, and therefore probably translated in America.   The Spanish author is unknown."

Mr. G. J. Stevenson, in his *Methodist Hymn Book Notes*, 1883, p. 294, says positively :—

" This hymn is from the Spanish, translated by John Wesley when he was in America in 1735."

Although there is much to strengthen Dr. Osborn's suggestion, that the *tr.* was made in America, we have seen no proof that it was made there in 1735; and somewhat against it is the fact that the hymn is not in the Charles-Town *Coll. of Ps. & Hys.*, 1736–37. Bishop Bickersteth's note on the cento, in his *H. Comp.* (annotated ed., 1880), is well deserved :—

"This very beautiful version of part of the 63rd Psalm is varied from the translation of a Spanish version by J. Wesley. It seems to the Editor one of the most melodious and perfect hymns we possess for public worship."

The use, both of the *Wes. H. Bk.* text, and of the cento, "O Lord, within Thy sacred gates," is extensive, especially of the latter. [J. J.]

O God, my Refuge, hear my cries. *I. Watts.* [*Ps. lv.*] Appeared in his *Psalms of David,* &c., 1719, p. 147 (misprinted 947), in 10 st of 4 l., and headed, "Support for the afflicted and tempted Soul." In explanation of some portions of the Psalm which are not paraphased, the following note is added :—

"I have left out some whole Psalms, and several parts of others that tend to fill the mind with overwhelming sorrows, or sharp resentment; neither of which are so well suited to the spirit of the Gospel, and therefore the particular complaints of David against Achitophel here are entirely omitted."

This paraphrase is given in some collections in full, and in others in an abbreviated form. In the *Leeds Hy. Bk.*, 1853, and others, it begins with st. viii. as "God shall preserve my soul from fear." [J. J.]

O God of Bethel, by Whose hand. *P. Doddridge.* [*Jacob's Vow.*] This well-known and much-appreciated hymn has more than usual interest attached to it from its historical association with the Scottish *Translations and Paraphrases* of 1745 and 1781, and the numerous forms it has undergone. The facts cannot be grasped without much difficulty unless they are set forth in chronological order, and with more than usual detail.

i. *The English form of the Text.*

1. The earliest form of the hymn is that in the handwriting of Doddridge, now in the possession of the Rooker family, and quoted in this Dictionary as the D. MSS. (see **Doddridge**). Doddridge's MS. hymns number 100. This is as follows :—

"No. xxxii.   JACOB'S VOW.
From Gen. xxxiii. 20, 22.

1

"Oh God of Bethel, by whose Hand
Thine Israel still is fed
Who thro' this weary Pilgrimage
Hast all our Fathers led

2

"To thee our humble Vows we raise
To thee address our Prayer
And in thy kind and faithful Breast
Deposite all our Care

3

"If thou thro' each perplexing Path
Wilt be our constant Guide
If thou wilt daily Bread supply
And Raiment wilt provide

4

"If thou wilt spread thy Shield around
Till these our wandrings cease
And at our Father's lov'd Abode
Our Souls arrive in Peace

5

"To thee as to our Covenant God
We'll our whole selves resign
And count that not our tenth alone
But all we have is thine.
Jan. 16 173⅞."

2. In 1755, Job Orton published 370 hymns

from another MS. (written in shorthand, Humphreys's ed., Preface, p. viii.) by Doddridge as *Hymns founded on Various Texts in the Holy Scriptures,* &c. This hymn is given as No. iv., and begins :—

"O God of *Jacob,* by whose hand," this being the only variation from the *Rooker MS.* as above. In 1839, J. D. Humphreys reprinted the hymn in his edition of Doddridge's *Hymns,* &c., No. iv., from the same MS. as J. Orton had used, but with these variations: st. i., l. 4, *Hath* for "Hast"; and st. v., l. 2, *We will ourselves* for "We'll our whole selves." Of Humphreys's text editors have taken no notice.

From Orton's text there are the following hymns in C. U. :—

1. **O God of Jacob, by Whose hand.** In several collections.

2. **O Thou, by Whose all bounteous hand.** This was given in J. Belknap's *Sacred Poetry consisting of Psalms and Hymns,* &c., Boston, U. S. A., 1795; and again in later American collections.

ii. *The Scottish form of the Text.*

1. It is through the Scottish text that the hymn is most widely known. Its history, which is somewhat singular, is as follows :—

2. A copy of the *Rooker MS.* noticed above, and in Doddridge's handwriting, is in the possession of the descendants of Col. Gardiner's family. It formerly belonged to Lady Frances Erskine (an intimate friend of Doddridge's), who became the wife of Col. Gardiner, and her name is written therein. It is a complete copy of the *Rooker MS.*, with the exception that the corrections of the text made by Doddridge in the margin of the *Rooker MS.* are given in the body of the hymn instead of the original words, and the dates are omitted. An Index of first lines, not in the *Rooker MS.*, is added in Doddridge's handwriting. From this MS. R. Blair (p. 145, i.) secured this hymn from Lady Frances Gardiner, and presented it to the Committee engaged in compiling the Scottish *Translations and Paraphrases,* and in the issue of 1745 it was given therein as No. xliv., with the single alteration of "shield" to "wings" in st. iv., l. 1.

3. Doddridge wrote the hymn on "Jany. 16, 173⅞;" it was included in the Scottish *Trs. and Paraphrases* in 1745; and J. Logan was born in 1748. Notwithstanding this, Logan gave it in his *Poems,* 1781, in the following form, and as his own :—

1. "O God of *Abraham,* by Whose hand
Thy *people still are* fed;
Who through this weary pilgrimage,
Hast all our fathers led.

2. "*Our vows, our prayers, we now present
Before Thy throne of grace
God of our fathers ! be the God
Of their succeeding race.*

3. "*Thro'* each perplexing path *of life
Our wand'ring footsteps* guide;
*Give us each day our daily bread,
And raiment fit* provide !

4. "*O spread Thy cov'ring wings* around,
Till *all* our wanderings cease;
And at our Father's lov'd abode
Our souls arrive in peace !

5. "*Now with the humble voice of prayer,
Thy mercy we implore;
Then with the grateful voice of praise,
Thy goodness we'll adore.*"

Here st. i.–iv. are a revise of Doddridge, and st. v. is new.

4. During the same year (1781) the Scottish *Translations and Paraphrases* were published in their new and revised form (see **Scottish Hymnody**). The text as in Logan's *Poems* is included as No. ii., with the following variations :—

St. i. "O God of *Bethel!* by whose hand."
St. ii., iii. and iv. as in Logan's *Poems*.
St. v. " *Such blessings from Thy gracious hand*
        Our humble pray'rs implore ;
        And Thou shalt be our chosen God,
        And portion evermore."

5. This arrangement is evidently by the same hand as the text in ,the *Poems*. The text as in the *Poems* has been claimed for M. Bruce (p. **187**, i.), but we think on insufficient evidence. Its designation is " *P. Doddridge, Jan.* 173⅔; *Scottish Trs. & Paraphs.*, 1745 ; *J. Logan*, 1781 ; *and Scottish Paraphs.*, 1781."

6. From the *Scottish Trs. & Paraphs.*, 1781, the following arrangements are in C. U. :—

1. O God of Bethel, by Whose hand. In numerous collections, in full or in part, in G. Britain and America.
2. O God of Abraham, by Whose hand. In the S. P. C. K. *Hymns*, 1852.
3. O God of ages, by Whose hand. In Martineau's *Hymns*, 1840 and 1873.
4. O God of Israel, by Whose hand. In the *Hys. for use in the Chapel of Marlborough College*, 1869.
5. O God, by Whose Almighty hand. In the Cooke and Denton *Hymnal*, 1853.
6. God of our Fathers, by Whose hand. Very much altered in the American *Prayer Book Coll.*, 1826, and a great many later American hymnals.
7. O God of Jacob, by Whose hand. In the 1889 *Supplemental Hys.* to *H. A. & M.*

iii. *Claim on behalf of Risdon Darracott.*

Doddridge's original has been claimed for Risdon Darracott, sometime pupil with Doddridge, and subsequently a Presbyterian minister at Wellington, Somerset. The earliest date given to Darracott's version is his marriage, after 1741. Doddridge, as we have seen, actually wrote the hymn on Jan. 16, 173⅔. Darracott may have adapted it for his own marriage, or Doddridge may have done it for him ; in either case the hymn is by Doddridge.   [J. J.]

O God of God, O Light of Light. *J. Julian*. [*Praise of Jesus*.] Written to Sir John Goss's tune *Peterborough* in Mercer's *Ch. Psalter and H. Bk.* for the Sheffield Church Choirs Union Festival, April 16, 1883, and first printed in the Festival book. In 1884 it was included in Horder's *Cong. Hymns*, and subsequently in other collections.   [J. J.]

O God of hosts, the mighty Lord. *Tate & Brady*. [*Ps. lxxxiv.*] This is a more than usually good example of Tate and Brady's C. M. renderings of the Psalms. It appeared in the *New Version*, 1696, and when that work yielded to the modern hymn-book, it was adopted, usually in an abbreviated form, in many collections. The centos vary in their length, and in the stanzas chosen, and when a doxology is added, as in *H. A. & M.*, Thring's *Coll.* and others, that of Tate and Brady is chosen. In Biggs's Annotated *H. A. & M.*, a translation into Latin by George Buchanan, c. 1550, of the corresponding verses in the Psalm, is given, together with a Latin doxology from the *Paris Breviary*. [**Psalters, Eng.** § 13, γ.]   [J. J.]

O God of love, O King of Peace. *Sir H. W. Baker.* [*In Time of Trouble.*] Written for and first published in *H. A. & M.*,

1861. It has been repeated in several collections. In Alford's *Year of Praise*, 1867, it is attributed to "Cowper" in error.   [J. J.]

O God of our forefathers, hear. *C. Wesley.* [*Holy Communion.*] 1st pub. in *Hymns on the Lord's Supper*, 1745, No. 125, in 4 st. of 6 l. (*P. Works*, 1868–72, vol. iii. p. 309), from whence it passed into the *Wes. H. Bk.*, 1780, No. 382, and the collections of other Methodist bodies. In those works it is usually given in Section vii., entitled "Seeking for full Redemption." Its strictly Eucharistic character is thus lost. St. ii. :—

" With solemn faith we offer up
    And spread before Thy glorious eyes,
That only ground of all our hope,
    That precious, bleeding sacrifice,
Which brings Thy grace on sinners down,
    And perfects all our souls in one : "

certainly suggests most strongly, if it does not actually teach, the doctrine of the "Real Presence," and would have been so regarded if the hymn had been appropriated to its original use, or had appeared anonymously in a modern hymn-book.   [J. J.]

O God of Zion, from Thy throne. [*Prayer on behalf of the Church.*] This hymn appeared anonymously in the 1800 ed. of Rippon's *Bap. Sel.*, No. 427, Pt. ii., in 7 st. of 4 l. In Beddome's posthumous *Hymns*, 1817, No. 654, there is a hymn in 4 st. of 4 l. beginning, "Look with an eye of pity down," which is probably the original of that in Rippon's *Sel.* If this is so Dr. Rippon must have had a MS. copy of the hymn from Beddome. No. 289 in the Presbyterian *Sel. of Hys.*, Philadelphia, 1861, is *Rippon's* text with the omission of st. ii. and vii.   [J. J.]

O God [that] Who madest earth and sky. *Bp. R. Heber.* [*Patience.*] First pub. in the *Christian Observer*, Jan. 1816, p. 27, in 4 st. of 4 l., and entitled "Patience." In Heber's posthumous *Hymns*, &c., 1827, p. 138, it was given in 2 st. of 4 l. as "O God *that* madest earth and sky, the darkness and the day," and appointed for use "In Times of Distress and Danger," the only alteration being the change of "Who" to *that* in the first line. It is in C. U. in Great Britain and America.   [J. J.]

O God, the Rock of Ages. *Bp. E. H. Bickersteth.* [*Sunday after Christmas.*] In his note to this hymn in his annotated ed. of his *H. Comp.*, 1880, Bp. Bickersteth says that "this hymn was written by the Editor (1860)," but in his work, *The Two Brothers*, &c., 1871, p. 226, it is dated "1862." It was included in the Eng. Presb. *Ps. & Hys.*, 1867 ; the *H. Comp.*, 1870 and 1876 ; and the author's *From Year to Year*, 1883. Its use has extended to America and other English-speaking countries.   [J. J.]

O God! to Whom the happy dead. *J. Conder.* [*All Saints' Day.*] Appeared in the *Cong. H. Bk.*, 1836, No. 171, in 2 st. of 6 l., and headed, "Whose faith follow." In his work *The Choir and the Oratory*, 1837, p. 230, it was republished as a "Collect," in metre. It is a paraphrase of the words in the prayer "For the whole state of Christ's Church Militant here on earth," in the Office for Holy Communion in the Book of Common Prayer :—

"And we also bless Thy Holy Name, for all Thy servants departed this life in Thy faith and fear; beseeching Thee to give us grace so to follow their good examples, that with them we may be partakers of Thy heavenly kingdom: Grant this, O Father, for Jesus Christ's sake, our only Mediator and Advocate."

This hymn was repeated in the author's *Hys. of Praise, Prayer, &c.*, 1856, p. 106, and is given in several modern hymn-books. In some it reads, "O God, *in* Whom the happy dead"; in others, "O God *with* Whom the happy dead"; and in others, "O God, to Whom the *faithful* dead." With these exceptions the text is usually given in its original form. [J. J.]

O God unseen, but not unknown. *J. Montgomery.* [*Omniscience of the Father.*] Written "Sep. 22, 1828" (M. MSS.). A copy, dated "The Mount, n^r. Sheffield, Dec. 16, 1845," appeared in the *Christian Treasury*, 1847, p. 7. It had previously appeared in the *Evangelical Magazine*, 1846, p. 187. In 1853 it was included in Montgomery's *Original Hymns*, No. 30, in 9 st. of 12 l., and headed, "Thou, God, seest me." It is in C. U. in an abbreviated form, and also as "The moment comes, when strength shall fail," in the American *Sabbath H. Bk.*, 1858. [J. J.]

O God unseen, yet ever near. *E. Osler.* [*Holy Communion.*] 1st pub. in Hall's *Mitre H. Bk.*, 1836, No. 270, in 4 st. of 4 l., and entitled, "Spiritual Food." In the March number of Osler's *Church and King*, 1837, it was repeated with the single change of st. iv., l. 1., from "Thus may we all" to "Thus *would* we all," &c. In some collections, as the *English Hymnal*, 1856 and 1861, it is given as, "O *Christ* unseen, yet ever near"; and in others as, "O God unseen, yet *truly* near." Other corruptions of the text are also found in Darling's *Hymns*, 1887, and other collections. *H. A. & M.* is an exception in favour of the original, with the single change in st. iv., l. 1, of "Thy words" to "Thy *word*." The use of this hymn in a more or less correct form is very extensive in all English-speaking countries. [J. J.]

O God, Who gav'st Thy servant grace. *Bp. R. Heber.* [*St. John the Evangelist.*] Pub. in his posthumous *Hymns, &c.*, 1827, p. 19, in 4 st. of 4 l. In Thring's *Coll.* 1882, and some others, it begins, "O *Thou!* Who gav'st Thy servant grace." In this form of the text st. ii. is omitted, and a new stanza is added as st. iv. from another source. [J. J.]

O God, Who hear'st the prayer. *C. Wesley.* [*In Time of National Trouble.*] This is the first of three hymns "For His Majesty King George," which appeared in the Wesley tract of *Hys. for Times of Trouble, for the Year* 1745, the remaining two being (2) "The Lord is King, ye saints rejoice;" and (3) "Head of Thy Church triumphant." Concerning the hymn-tracts issued by the Wesleys at that time, Dr. Osborn says in his Advertisement to the *P. Works*, 1868-72, vol. iv., that they "relate chiefly to the Rebellion of 1745, and exhibit the patriotism and loyalty of the Wesleys, unshaken by persecution, and sustained as it was by a sense of duty to God, and by an unfaltering hatred of Rome." [J. J.]

O Gott, du frommer Gott. *J. Heer-*

mann. [*Supplication.*] 1st pub. in his *Devoti musica cordis*, Breslau, 1630, p. 137, in 8 st. of 8 l., entitled "A daily prayer." It is in the section which contains "Some Prayers and Meditations. Many Christian people are accustomed at their family prayers to sing the following prayers to the melodies to which they are set:" and these were evidently written (1623-30) during the time of Heermann's greatest sufferings. Thence in *Mützell*, 1858, No. 54; in Wackernagel's ed. of his *Geistliche Lieder*, No. 42, and the *Unv. L. S.*, 1851, No. 568. Of this hymn *Fischer*, ii. 150, says:

"It is one of the poet's most widely used and signally blessed hymns, and has been not unjustly called his Master Song. If it is somewhat 'home-baked' yet it is excellent, nourishing bread. It gives a training in practical Christianity, and specially strikes three notes— godly living, patient suffering, and happy dying."

Lauxmann, in *Koch*, viii. 324–329, says it has been called the "Priest's Concordance," and relates many interesting incidents regarding it.

Thus at Leuthen, in Silesia, Dec. 5., 1757, the Prussians under Frederick the Great stood face to face with an Austrian army thrice their number. Just as they were about to engage, some of the soldiers began to sing st. ii., and the regimental bands joined in. One of the commanders asked Frederick if it should be silenced, but he replied, "No, let it be; with such men God will to-day certainly give me the victory." And when the bloody battle ended in his favour he was constrained to say "My God, what a power has religion." St. iii., adds *Lauxmann*, has been a special favourite with preachers, e.g. J. C. Schade, of Berlin; Dr Hedinger, Court preacher at Stuttgart, &c.

Various melodies have been set to it. The best known in England (in the Irish *Church Hyl.* called *Munich*) appeared in the *Meiningen G. B.*, 1693 (Dr. J. Zahn's *Psalter und Harfe*, 1886, No. 243). The hymn is *tr.* as:—

1. **O God, Thou faithful God.** A full and good *tr.* by Miss Winkworth, in her *Lyra Ger.*, 2nd Ser., 1858, p. 138; repeated in her *C. B. for England*, 1863, No. 115; and the Ohio *Lutheran Hyl.*, 1880.

2. **O great and gracious God.** A *tr.* of st. i., ii., iv., vii., viii., by Miss Borthwick, in Dr. Pagenstecher's *Coll.*, 1864, No. 198, repeated in *H. L. L.*, 1884.

Other trs. are, (1) "Lord, grant Thy servants grace," of st. ii. as st i. of No. 655, in the *Moravian H. Bk.*, 1801 (1886, No. 845). (2) "Our blessings come, O God," by *Dr. H. Mills*, 1845 (1856, p. 135). (3) Thou good and gracious God," by *Miss Cox*, 1864, p. 179. (4) "O God, Thou faithful God! Thou well-spring," by *N. L. Frothingham*, 1870, p. 217. [J. M.]

O Gott! O Geist! O Licht des Lebens. *G. Tersteegen.* [*Whitsuntide.*] This beautiful hymn is one of the finest breathings of Tersteegen's mysticism. 1st pub. in the 4th ed., 1745, of his *Geistliches Blumengärtlein*, Bk. iii., No. 76, in 8 st. of 6 l., and entitled "Prayer for the inward working of the Holy Spirit." Included in Knapp's *Ev. L. S.*, 1837, No. 749 (1865, No. 763). *Tr.* as:—

1. **O God, O Spirit, Light of all that live.** A good *tr.*, omitting st. vii., by Miss Winkworth, in her *Lyra Ger.*, 1st Ser., 1855, p. 140. Her *trs.* of st. i., iv., vi. altered to four 10's are included in the *Hys. of the Spirit*, Boston, U.S., 1864, No. 10. Another cento is No. 105, in M. W. Stryker's *Christian Chorals*, 1885.

2. **O God, O Spirit, Light of life.** A spirited but free *tr.*, omitting st. vii., by Mrs. Bevan, in her *Songs of Eternal Life*, 1858, p. 7. From

this st. i.–v. considerably altered and beginning
" Spirit of Grace, Thou Light of life," were included as No. 1182 in *Kennedy*, 1863 ; and repeated in this form, abridged, in the *Ibrox Hyl.*,
1871 ; Dr. Martineau's *Hys. of Praise & Prayer*,
1873 ; Thring's *Coll.*, 1880–82, &c.   [J. M.]

O happy band of pilgrims. [*Pilgrims of Jesus.*] Appeared in Dr. Neale's
Hys. of the Eastern Church, 1862, in 8 st. of
4 l., with the note by Dr. Neale, " This is
merely a cento from the Canon on SS. Chrysanthus and Daria (March 19)." In his Preface to the 3rd ed., 1866, he is more explicit,
and says concerning this hymn, " Safe home,
safe home in port," and " Art thou weary ? "
they " contain so little that is from the
Greek, that they ought not to have been
included in this collection ; in any future
edition they shall appear as an Appendix."
Dr. Neale did not live to publish another
edition : but in 1882 the 4th ed. with notes,
was issued under the editorship of S. G.
Hatherly, and in it the three hymns named
were " removed from the body of the work at
Dr. Neale's suggestion," and included in an
Appendix. Its proper designation, therefore,
is *By Dr. Neale, based on the Greek Canon
on SS. Chrysanthus and Daria by St. Joseph
the Hymnographer*. It must be added that
no Greek lines corresponding to those in the
English hymn can be found in that Canon.
Dr. Neale never theless found what he wanted
there, that is the inspiration to write the
hymn as it now stands. The use of this hymn
is very extensive in all English-speaking
countries.   [J. J.]

O happy day that fix'd my choice.
P. Doddridge. [*Joy in Personal Dedication
to God.*] Appeared in J. Orton's posthumous
edition of Doddridge's *Hymns*, &c., 1755. No.
23, in 5 st. of 4 l., and entitled, " Rejoicing
in our Covenant Engagements to God,"
2 Chron. xv. 15 ; and again, with changes in
the text of st. iv., in J. D. Humphreys's ed. of
the same, 1839, No. 29. Its use in its full, in
an abbreviated, and in a translated form, is
extensive. The third stanza,

" 'Tis done; the great transaction's done ;
   I am the Lord's, and He is mine:
He drew me, and I followed on,
   Charmed to confess the voice divine,"

although often omitted from the hymn is
frequently found as a quotation. In the
American *Prayer Bk. Coll.*, 1826, the hymn
was altered throughout, and began, " O
happy day, that *stays* my choice." This
form is in several modern American collections. In the American Unitarian *Hys. for
the Church of Christ*, 1853, st. iv., v. are given
as No. 381, and begin " Now rest, my long-
divided heart." The alterations which have
been made in Doddridge's text are too numerous to be given in detail. At the present
time two texts are quoted as the original, the
first that in J. Orton's ed. of Doddridge's
Hymns, &c., 1755 ; and the second that in
J. D. Humphreys's ed. of the same, 1839.
These are the same, except in st. iv. The
readings are :—

1755. " Now rest my long divided Heart,
   Fix'd on this blissful Centre, rest;
With Ashes who would grudge to part
When call'd on Angels bread to feast ? "

1839. " Now rest, my long-divided heart,
   Fix'd on this blissful centre, rest ;
O who with earth would grudge to part
When call'd with angels to be bless'd ! "

As this hymn is not found in any Doddridge MS. with which we are acquainted, we
cannot determine which of these two readings
was written by Doddridge. Orton admits in
his preface that he tampered in some instances
(not named) with Doddridge's text [see
Doddridge, P.], whilst Humphreys contends
that he was faithful thereto. We can only
add that Orton's reading has more in common
with Doddridge's usual style and mode of
expression than that of Humphreys, but the
weight of evidence is in favour of the latter.
                                [J. J.]

O happy is the man who hears.
M. Bruce. [*Wisdom.*] From evidence set
forth in our biographical sketch of M. Bruce
(**p. 187, i.**), we believe the original of this hymn
to have been written by M. Bruce about 1764,
and that the MS. of the same was handed to
J. Logan by Bruce's father a short time after
Bruce's death in 1767. It was published
by Logan as his own in his *Poems*, 1781,
p. 104, No. 4, in 5 st. of 4 l. In the same
year, a slightly altered version of the text
was given in the new and revised edition of
the Scottish *Translations and Paraphrases*, as
No. xi., and this has been in authorised use
in the Church of Scotland for more than 100
years. It is also found in many English and
American collections. The nearest approach
to the original text is given in Dr. Mackelvie's *Lochleven and other Poems*, &c., 1837,
p. 258 ; and Dr. Grosart's *Works of M. Bruce*,
1865, p. 133. The text of the Scottish *Trs.
and Paraphs.*, 1781, has been altered in several
modern collections to (1) " How blest the man
that bends the ear ; " (2) " How happy is the
child who hears ; " (3) " How happy is the
youth who hears;" and (4) " Wisdom has
treasures greater far."   [J. J.]

O happy land, O happy land. E.
Parson, née Rooker. [*Heaven.*] Contributed
to J. Curwen's *Child's Own H. Bk.*, 1840, in
2 st. of 8 l., the first beginning as above, and
the second, " Thou heavenly Friend," &c.
This was repeated in the Bap. *Ps. & Hys.*,
1858, and several other collections. Another
text, also by Mrs. Parson, in 3 st. of 4 l. was
published in her *Willing Class Hymns* some
time after her death. It consists of the two
stanzas as above, somewhat altered, and another stanza, beginning, " The saints in light,"
&c. These three stanzas are given in W. F.
Stevenson's *Hymns for Ch. & Home*, 1873.
                                [J. J.]

**O happy saints [that] who dwell
in light, And walk with Jesus, &c.**
J. Berridge. [*Saints in Glory.*] Pub. in his
Zion's Songs, &c., 1785, No. 143, in 6 st. of 4 l.,
and headed, " At Thy right hand are pleasures
for evermore." Ps. xvi. 11 (ed. 1842, p. 139).
Although seldom found in English collections,
its use in America, sometimes abbreviated as
in the Bap. *Service of Song*, Boston, 1871, is
somewhat extensive. It is based upon Ralph
Erskine's " Aurora veils her rosy face " (**p. 96,
i.**) The second stanza in Berridge reads :—

" Release'd from sin, and toil, and grief,
   Death was their gate to endless life ;

An open'd cage to let them fly,
And build their happy nest on high."

This reads in Erskine's original :—

" Death is to us a sweet repose,
The bud was ope'd to show the rose ;
The cage was broke to let us fly
And build our happy nest on high."

The rest of the hymn follows Erskine's line of thought, but there is no repetition of his actual words.   [J. J.]

O Haupt voll Blut und Wunden.
P. Gerhardt.   [*Passiontide.*]   This is a beautiful but free *tr.* of the " Salve caput cruentatum," which is pt. vii. of the *Rhythmica Oratio,* ascribed to St. Bernard of Clairvaux. The Latin text is noted under **Salve mundi salutare**; the present note is given here on account of the length of that article. Gerhardt's version appeared as No. 156 in the Frankfurt ed., 1656, of Crüger's *Praxis,* in 10 st. of 8 l., entitled, " To the suffering Face of Jesus Christ." It is repeated in Wackernagel's ed. of Gerhardt's *Geistl. Lieder,* No. 22 ; Bachmann's ed., No. 54 ; the *Unv. L. S.,* 1851, No. 109 ; and almost all recent German hymnbooks. Lauxmann in *Koch.* viii., 47, thus characterises it :—

" Bernard's original is powerful and searching, but Gerhardt's hymn is still more powerful and more profound, as redrawn from the deeper spring of evangelical Lutheran, Scriptural, knowledge, and fervency of faith." Stanza x. Lauxmann would trace not only to Bernard but to st. iii. of " Valet wil ich dir geben " (see *Herberger*) ; and to Luther's words on the death of his daughter Magdalen " Who dies thus, dies well." He adds many instances of its use. Thus A. G. Spangenberg, when on the celebration of his jubilee he received many flattering testimonies, replied in humility with the words of stanza iv. In 1798, while C. F. Schwartz lay a-dying, his Malabar pupils gathered round him and sang in their own language the last verses of this hymn, he himself joining till his breath failed in death.

The beautiful melody (in *H. A. & M.,* called *Passion Chorale*) first appeared in Hans Leo Hassler's *Lustgarten,* Nürnberg, 1601, set to a love song, beginning " Mein G'müth ist mir verwirret." In the *Harmoniae Sacrae,* Görlitz, 1613, it is set to " Herzlich thut mich verlangen " (see **Knoll**), and then in the *Praxis,* 1656, to Gerhardt's hymn. The original forms are in L. Erk's *Choral Buch,* 1863, Nos. 117, 118. It is used several times by J. S. Bach, in his *Passion Music according to St. Matthew.* The hymn is *tr.* as :—

1. **O Head so full of bruises.** In full, by J. Gambold, in *Some other Hys. and Poems,* London, 1752, p. 12. Repeated in the *Moravian H. Bk.,* 1754, pt. i., No. 222 ; and pt. ii. pp. 389, 391. In the ed. of 1789 it was greatly altered (1886, No. 88), and a new *tr.* of st. ix. substituted for Gambold's version ; the Gambold *tr.* of st. ix., " When I shall gain permission," being given as a separate hymn (1886, No. 1247). Centos from the text of 1789 are found under the original first line in Walker's *Cheltenham Ps. & Hys.,* 1855 ; Reid's *Praise Bk.,* 1872, &c. Other forms are :—

(1) **O Head, so pierced and wounded** (st. i. alt.) in Dr. Pagenstecher's *Coll.,* 1864.
(2) **O Christ! what consolation** (st. vi. alt.) in the *Amer. Bapt. H. Bk.,* 1871.
(3) **I yield Thee thanks unfeigned** (st. viii.), in E. Bickersteth's *Christian Psalmody,* 1833, and others.
(4) **I give thee thanks unfeigned** (st. viii. alt.), in Bp. Ryle's *Coll.,* 1860.

2. **O Sacred Head ! now wounded.** A very beautiful *tr.* by Dr. J. W. Alexander. The *trs.* of st.

i., ii., iv., v., vii.–x. were first pub. in the *Christian Lyre,* N. York, 1830, No. 136. These were revised, and *trs.* of st. iii., vi., added, by Dr. Alexander for Schaff's *Deutsche Kirchenfreund,* 1849, p. 91. The full text is in Dr. Alexander's *Breaking Crucible,* N. Y., 1861, p. 7 ; in Schaff's *Christ in Song,* 1869, p. 178 ; and the *Cantate Domino,* Boston, U. S., 1859. In his note Dr. Schaff says :—

" This classical hymn has shown an imperishable vitality in passing from the Latin into the German, and from the German into the English, and proclaiming in three tongues, and in the name of three Confessions— the Catholic, the Lutheran, and the Reformed—with equal effect, the dying love of our Saviour, and our boundless indebtedness to Him."

This version has passed into very many English and American hymnals, and in very varying centos. A comparison with the *Christ in Song* text will show how these centos are arranged. We can only note the following forms :—

(1) **O sacred Head ! now wounded** (st. i.), *People's H.* 1867 ; *Hymnary,* 1872 ; and in America in Hatfield's *Church H. Bk.,* 1872 ; *Hys. & Songs of Praise,* N. Y., 1874, &c.
(2) **O Sacred Head ! once wounded** (i. alt.), *Leeds H. Bk.,* 1853 ; Bapt. *Ps. & Hys.,* 1858 ; *New Cong.,* 1859.
(3) **O Sacred Head, sore wounded** (i. alt.), in the Stoke *H. Bk.,* 1878.
(4) **O Sacred Head, so wounded** (i. alt.), J. L. Porter's *Coll.,* 1876.
(5) **O blessed Christ, once wounded** (i. alt.), Dr. Thomas's *Augustine H. Bk.,* 1866.
(6) **O Lamb of God, once wounded** (i. alt.), Scottish *Presb. Hyl.,* 1876.
(7) **O Lamb of God, sore wounded** (i. alt.), in the *Ibrox Hyl.,* 1871.

3. **Ah ! Head, so pierced and wounded.** A good *tr.* by R. Massie, omitting st. vi., contributed as No. 92 to the 1857 ed. of Mercer's *C. P. & H. Bk.,* and reprinted in his own *Lyra Domestica,* 1864, p. 114. Abridged in Mercer's *Oxford ed.,* 1864, and in *Kennedy,* 1863. A cento beginning with st. viii., l. 5, " Oh ! that Thy cross may ever," is in J. H. Wilson's *Ser. of Praise,* 1865.

4. **Ah wounded Head, that bearest.** By Miss Winkworth, omitting st. vi., as No. 51 in her *C. B. for England,* 1863. Abridged in the *Uppingham and Sherborne School H. Bk.,* 1874, and the *Free Ch. H. Bk.,* 1882.

5. **Oh ! bleeding head, and wounded.** In full, by J. Kelly, in his *P. Gerhardt's Spir. Songs,* 1867, p. 59, repeated in the Ohio *Luth. Hyl.,* 1880.

Other trs. are :—(1) " Ah wounded Head ! must Thou." By *Miss Winkworth,* 1855, p. 80. (2) " Thou pierced and wounded brow." By *Miss Dunn,* 1857, p. 39. (3) " O Head, blood-stained and wounded," in the Schaff-Gilman *Lib. of Religious Poetry,* ed. 1883, p. 745, marked as *tr.* by Samuel M. Jackson, 1873, 1880.
        [J. M.]

O heavenly love, arise, arise. [*Love as a Guide.*]
This is part of a song which Wolfram von Eschenbach (q.v.) is supposed to sing at a contest for a prize at the hands of a German princess. The work in which this song is found is *Tannhäuser ; or, The Battle of the Bards. A Poem by Neville Temple and Edward Trevor,* Lond., Chapman & Hall, 1861, p. 54, in 5 st. of 4 l. The hymn in *Kennedy,* 1863, No. 195, is composed of st. iii.–v., and a closing stanza by Dr. Kennedy. It is a beautiful hymn and suited for the Epiphany. We may add that *Neville Temple* was the Hon. Julian Charles Henry Fane ; and *Edward Trevor* was Edward Robert Bulwer, afterwards Lord Lytton.
        [J. J.]

O help us, Lord ; each hour of need. *H. H. Milman.* [*Lent.*] 1st pub. in Bp. Heber's posthumous *Hymns, &c.*, 1827, p. 52, in 6 st. of 4 l. and appointed for second Sunday in Lent, being based on the Gospel of that day. In his *Sel. of Ps. & Hys.*, 1837, Milman omitted st. iv. and v., thus reducing it to 4 st. of 4 l. and each stanza beginning with the words, "Oh! help us." In this form it has come into extensive use in all English-speaking countries. In the *Mitre H. Bk.*, 1836, No. 190, it is partly rewritten by E. Osler as, "O help us, Lord! *in all our need.*" This is repeated in Osler's *Church and King*, June 1, 1837, but it has failed to attract attention. Another arrangement, beginning with st. ii., "O help us, when our spirits bleed," is sometimes found in modern hymnals.   [J. J.]

O Herre Gott, dein göttlich Wort. [*Holy Scripture.*] Appeared in the *Erfurt Enchiridion* of 1527, and thence in *Wackernagel*, iii. p. 123, in 8 st. of 12 l. Included in Klug's *G. B.*, 1529, and became very popular in Reformation times. Recently it is found as No. 434 in the Berlin *G. L. S.*, ed. 1863.

In the 1527 and many later books it bears the initials "A. H. Z. W." Lauxmann, in a long note in *Koch*, viii. 697–706, tries to vindicate its authorship as by Ulrich (Alaricus) Herzog zu Württemberg, who d. at Tübingen, Nov. 6, 1550. In the *Blätter für Hymnologie*, 1883, p. 79, 1887, p. 11, it is noted that in the *Lieder Krone* of 1734 to the Ratzeburg *G. B.*, these initials are resolved to mean Anark Herr zu Wildenfels (near Zwickau), who was known as one of the principal supporters of the Reformation at the court of the Elector John of Saxony, was one of the signatories to the Augsburg Confession (subscribing it as Anark dominus de Vuidenfels), and d. at Altenburg, June 1, 1539. The ascription to Anark of Wildenfels seems to us much the more probable. *Tr.* as :—

1. **How long, Oh God, Thy word of life.** A very free *tr.* in 16 st. of 4 l. by Miss Fry, in her *Hys. of the Reformation*, 1845, p. 122. Her *trs.* of st. i., vii., viii. are No. 48, in Whittemore's *Suppl. to all H. Bks.*, 1860.

Other *trs.* are, (1) "O hevenly Lorde, Thy godly Worde," by Bp. Coverdale, 1535 (*Remains*, 1846, p. 584). (2) "Lord God, Thy face and word of grace," in the *Gude & Godly Ballates*, ed. 1568, fol. 29 (1868, p. 48.) (3) "O God our Lord, Thy divine Word," as No. 307 in pt. i. of the *Moravian H. Bk.*, 1754. (4) "We give Thee thanks, most gracious Lord," by Dr. J. Hunt, in his *Spir. Songs of Martin Luther*, 1853, p. 73.   [J. M.]

O himmlische Liebe! du hast mich besessen. [*Love to Christ.*] Included in Wagner's *G. B.*, Leipzig, 1697, vol. iii. p. 713, in 6 st. of 6 l. Repeated in the *Trier G. B.* (Rom. Catholic), 1846, p. 227, reading, *du hast mich ergriffen.* It is *tr.* as :—

O Heavenly Love, Thou hast made me Thy dwelling. By Dr. Littledale, in full, as No. 399 in the *People's Hyl.*, 1867, and signed "F. R."   [J. M.]

O hochbeglückte Seele. *C. J. P. Spitta.* [*Christian Service.*] A fine hymn for Lay Helpers and all workers in Christ's service. 1st pub. in his *Psalter und Harfe*, Pirna, 1833, p. 78, in 7 st. of 8 l., entitled "The Servant of the Lord." Included in the Leipzig *G. B.*, 1844, No. 395. *Tr.* as :—

1. **How blessed, from the bonds of sin.** A free *tr.* of st. i., ii., vi., vii., by Miss Borthwick, in *H. L. L.*, 1st Ser., 1854, p. 66 (1884, p. 67). This version has attained considerable popularity, and is found in a number of the leading hymnals of Great Britain, e.g. *H. A. & M.*, 1875 ; the S. P. C. K. *Church Hys.*, 1871 ; *Free Ch. H. Bk.*,

1882, &c. ; and in America in the *Epis. Hys. for Ch. & Home*, 1860 ; Boardman's *Sel.*, 1861, &c.

2. **The man is highly blessed.** In full, by R. Massie, in his *Lyra Domestica*, 1860, p. 76. His *trs.* of st. iii., iv., vi., vii. beginning "God sanctifies and blesses," are included in the *Bk. of Common Praise*, 1863, and G. S. Jellicoe's *Coll.*, 1867.

Other *trs.* are, (1) "O Soul, how blest (blest truly,") by the Hon. *S. R. Maxwell*, 1857; p. 101. (2) "Thrice happy he who serveth," by Miss Burlingham, in the *British Herald*, Aug. 1865, p. 119.   (3) "O highly blessed servant," by *Lady Durand*, 1873.   [J. M.]

O Holy Ghost, Thou God of peace. *I. Williams.* [*Communion of Saints ;* and *For Unity.*] 1st pub. in his *Hys. on the Catechism*, 1842, No. 28, in 4 st. of 4 l., and again in later editions of the same work. In its original form it is not much used. In 1854 it appeared in an altered form in Morrell & How's *Ps. & Hys.*, st. i.–iii. being from I. Williams with alterations, and st. iv. being new by Bp. W. W. How. I. Williams's omitted stanza reads :—

"For love is life, and life is love,
And Thou Thyself art love and life ;
And we in Thee shall live and move,
If Thou wilt keep us free from strife."

The Williams-How text has been repeated in the S.P.C.K. *Church Hymns*, 1871, Thring's *Coll.*, 1882, and others.   [J. J.]

O Holy Ghost, Thy people bless. *Sir H. W. Baker.* [*Whitsuntide.*] Written for use in the London Mission of 1874, and printed in *Hys. for the London Mission* (No. 2), which were published by the compilers of *H. A. & M.*, 1874. In 1875 it was included in the revised ed. of *H. A. & M.*   [J. J.]

O Holy Jesu, Prince of Peace. *R. Brown-Borthwick.* [*Holy Communion.*]. Written in 1870, and 1st pub. in his *Sixteen Hys. with Tunes*, &c., the same year, in 6 st. of 6 l., and again in his *Select Hys. for Church and Home*, 1871, No. 58. In 1871 it appeared in the S. P. C. K. *Church Hymns*, with the omission of st. iv. In the author's 2nd ed. with *Appendix* of his *Select Hymns, &c.*, 1885, st. iv. is bracketed for omission, a slight alteration in st. i., l. 3, is introduced, and the following note is added :—

"This is not a congregational hymn, but a meditation, to be read while non-communicants are retiring, or to be sung by the choir alone, anthem-wise, kneeling."   [J. J.]

O Holy Lord, content to live [dwell —fill]. *Bp. W. W. How.* [*A Child's Hymn.*] Written in 1850, and 1st pub. in *The Parish Choir* in 1851. In 1854 it was repeated in Morrell & How's *Ps. & Hys.*, No. 65, in 5 st. of 4 l. When included in *H. A. & M*, in 1861, considerable alterations were made in the text, and it began, "O Holy Lord, content to *dwell.*" This first line, but not the alterations in detail, was adopted in the enlarged ed. of Morrell & How's *Ps. & Hys.*, 1864. For the S. P. C. K. *Church Hymns*, 1871, it was again rewritten, this time by Bp. How, as "O Holy Lord, content to *fill.*" This is the author's authorised text, and is repeated in his *Hymns*, 1886. All these texts are in C. U.   [J. J.]

O Holy Saviour, Friend unseen. *Charlotte Elliott.* [*In Affliction.*] This hymn is found in two forms, and both by Miss Elliott. The first appeared in the *Invalid's Hymn Book*, 1834, in 9 st. of 4 l., and began :—

> " O Holy Saviour ! Friend unseen,
> Since on Thine arm Thou bid'st me lean,
> Help me, throughout life's varying scene,
> By faith to cling to Thee."

The second version was given in her *Hours of Sorrow*, &c., 1836, p. 132, also in 9 st. of 4 l. It began :—

> " O Holy Saviour ! Friend unseen !
> The faint, the weak, on Thee may lean :
> Help me, throughout life's varying scene,
> By faith to cling to Thee."

The full text of this *revision* is given in Lord Selborne's *Book of Praise*, 1862, and in the *Lyra Brit.*, 1867, as the original, in error. The hymnbooks have generally followed this text, but (in an abbreviated form) Snepp's *Songs of G. & G.*, 1872, and a few others, are exceptions in favour of the older text. In Beecher's *Plymouth Coll.*, 1855, No. 759, is a cento from the older text, and begins, "Holy Saviour, Friend unseen." Dr. Martineau's "O Holy *Father*, Friend unseen," in his *Hymns*, 1873, is also from the same text. This altered form is also in other Unitarian hymn-books. In *Kennedy*, 1863, No. 517, begins "O *gentle* Saviour, Guide unseen." These various texts and centos are all in C. U. in G. Britain, and America.   [J. J.]

O Holy Spirit, come, And Jesu's love declare. *O. Allen.* [*Whitsuntide*.] Appeared in his *Hys. of the Christian Life*, 1862, p. 53, in 8 st. of 4 l. It is based upon the words "The Holy Ghost shall teach you all things," St. John xiv. 26. In an abridged form it is in C. U. in G. Britain and America.   [J. J.]

O how I love Thy holy word. *W. Cowper.* [*Holy Scripture in Affliction*.] This is No. 17 of Book iii. in the *Olney Hymns*, 1779. It is in 6 st. of 4 l., and headed, " Afflictions sanctified by the Word." It is in C. U. in its original form, but a cento therefrom, beginning with st. iii., "Long unafflicted, undismayed," is much more popular than the complete hymn.   [J. J.]

O how the thought that we shall know. *E. Swaine.* [*Heaven Anticipated*.] The original publication of this hymn we are unable to determine. It probably appeared in a religious magazine, *circa* 1830 : for st. ii.–v. were given in Bickersteth's *Christian Psalmody*, 1833, No. 575: as " For ever to behold Him shine." The original was republished in Swaine's *The Hand of God, a Fragment, with Poems, Hymns, and Versions of Psalms*, 1839 : Bickersteth's arrangement was also repeated in several collections. In 1876 Bp. E. H. Bickersteth wrote a new stanza, substituted it for Swaine's original, and gave the hymn in his *Hy. Comp.* as " ' For ever' beatific word," together with an elaborate note in which he says it was strange to begin the hymn as his father had done, with the second stanza of the original, "For ever to behold Him shine,"

" without the sacred name of Jesus being previously expressed, and without the key-note, ' For ever,' being clearly struck, as in the original, at the close of the first verse. It is probably owing to this fact that so beautiful a hymn has been omitted from many of the standard hymnals of the Church. The editor therefore ventured,

though with much diffidence, to write the first verse given in the text [as in *H. Comp.*] : for the closing of the first and last stanzas with the same word ' For ever,' as originally contrived by the author, seems almost essential to the full chord of eternity, which is struck again and again in this admirable hymn." (*Notes, H. Comp.*, No. 240.)

This arrangement by Bp. Bickersteth has produced a very attractive and melodious hymn.   [J. J.]

O ignis Spiritus Paracliti. *St. Hildegarde.* [*Whitsuntide*.] *Mone*, No. 179, gives this sequence from a ms. of the 12th cent. at Wiesbaden. This ms. contains the writings of St. Hildegart, Abbess of Rupertsberg, near Bingen (b. 1098, d. 1180), and Mone thinks the sequence is probably by her. His text is repeated by *Daniel*, v. p. 201. and *Kehrein*, No. 127. *Tr.* as :—

> O fire of the Comforter, O Life of all that live.

By R. F. Littledale in the *Lyra Messianica*, 1864, p. 377. In the *People's H.*, 1867, and the Irvingite *Hys. for the Churches*, 1871, it is rewritten by Dr. Littledale as " O Fire of God, the Comforter."

Another tr. is :—
O Comforter, Thou uncreated Fire. T. G. Crippen, in his *Ancient Hys. & Poems*, &c., 1868.   [W. A. S.]

O it is hard to work for God. *F. W. Faber.* [*Trial of Faith*.] Appeared in his *Jesus and Mary*, &c., 1849, in 19 st. of 4 l., and headed, " The Right must Win ;" also repeated in his *Hymns*, 1862. The following centos from this hymn are in C. U. :—(1) "O it is hard to work for God :" (2) " God's glory is a wondrous thing :" (3) "O blest is he to whom is given :" and (4) "Workman of God, O lose not heart."   [J. J.]

O it is joy in one to meet. *Bp. R. Mant.* [*Divine Worship*.] In his *Ancient Hymns*, &c., 1837, p. 89, is given an original " Hymn commemorative of the pleasure of Social Worship," in 6 st. of 4 l., beginning, " Glad is thy sound, O Sabbath bell " (ed. 1871, p. 153). From this sts. ii.–v. were taken, slightly altered, and given in Beecher's *Plymouth Coll.*, 1855, No. 709, as, "O, it is joy in one to meet." In the *Songs for the Sanctuary*, N. Y., 1865, the same stanzas are given as "O, it is joy for those to meet." The use of both arrangements is limited.   [J. J.]

O Jesu Christ, mein schönstes Licht. *P. Gerhardt.* [*Love to Christ*.] Included in the 5th ed., Berlin, 1653, and the Frankfurt ed., 1656, of Crüger's *Praxis*, in 16 st. of 9 l., reprinted in Wackernagel's ed. of his *Geistliche Lieder*, No. 45; Bachmann's ed., No. 73; and included as No. 771 in the *Unv. L. S.*, 1851. One of the finest hymns on the Love of Christ, it is founded on Prayer v. of Class ii. in J. Arndt's *Paradiesgärtlein*, 1612. Lauxmann, in *Koch*, viii. 294, relates many incidents regarding this hymn, mentioning that J. A. Bengel caused it to be sung at the celebration of Holy Communion at his death-bed, and that the wife of J. Lange (p. 638, i.) was greatly comforted by it in her last hours. *Tr.* as :—

Jesus, Thy boundless love to me. A full and very fine *tr.* by J. Wesley, in *Hys. and Sacred Poems*, 1739 (*P. Works*, 1868–72, vol. i. p. 138), and as No. 35 in *Hys. & Spir. Songs*, 1753. In the *Wes. H. Bk.*, 1780, No. 362, reduced to 9 st. The following forms are in C. U. :—

i. **Jesus, Thy boundless love to me** (st. i.). In *Mercer* (10 st.); *N. Cong.*, 1859 (4 st.); *Bapt. Hyl.*, 1879 (3 st.), &c.; and in America in the *Dutch Ref.*, 1869 (3 st.); *Evang. Hyl.*, 1880 (4 st.); *Laudes Domini*, 1884 (3 st.), &c.

ii. **O Love, how cheering is thy ray** (st. iii.) *Bk. of Hys.*, Boston, U.S., 1848; *Holy Song*, 1869.

iii. **My Saviour, Thou Thy love to me** (st. v.). *Moravian H. Bk.*, 1789; H. L. Hastings's *Hymnal*, 1880.

iv. **More hard than marble is my heart** (st. vi.). American *Sabbath H. Bk.*, 1858.

v. **O draw me, Saviour, after Thee** (st. ix.) Snepp's *Songs of G. & G.*; Pennsylvania *Luth. Ch. Bk.*, 1868.

vi. **O draw me, Father, after Thee** (st. ix. alt.). *Bk. of Hys.*, Boston, U.S., 1848, Amer. Unitarian *H. Bk.*, 1869.

vii. **Still nigh me, O my Saviour stand.** St. i. of this form is taken from "Peace, doubting heart, my God's I am" (q.v.). To this is added in Snepp's *Songs of G. & G.*, st. xii., xiv., xvi., and in J. L. Porter's *Coll.*, 1876, st. xii., xv., xvi. of this *tr.*

viii. **Thou Friend of sinners! Who hast bought.** This is st. v., iv., xvi. rewritten by E. Osler, and pub. as No. 180 in the *Mitre H. Bk.*, 1836, and in his own *Church and King*, June, 1837, p. 140. Repeated in the Irish *Church Hyl.*, 1869 and 1873.

Other *trs.* are, (1) "O Christ, my sweetest Life and Light," in the *Suppl. to German Psal.*, ed. 1765, p. 29; in *Select Hys. from German Psal.*, Tranquebar, 1754, p. 47, and the *Moravian H. Bk.*, 1754, pt. i., No. 444. St. v.–vii., beginning "Thou cam'st in love to my relief," are given at p. 802 in the *Moravian H. Bk.* pt. ii., 1746. In the *Moravian H. Bk.*, 1789 (1849, No. 460), it begins, "O Christ, my only Life and Light." (2) "O Jesus Christ! my fairest Light," by J. Kelly, 1867, p. 122. (3) "O Christ, my Light, my gracious Saviour," in the *Moravian H. Bk.*, 1886.   [J. M.]

O Jesu Christe, wahres Licht. *J. Heermann.* [*Christian Church.*] 1st pub. in his *Devoti musica cordis*, Breslau, 1630, p. 120, in 6 st. of 4 l. as one of the "Songs of Tears" in the section entitled, "In the time of the persecution and distress of pious Christians." Thence in *Mützell*, 1858, No 49; in Wackernagel's ed. of his *Geistliche Lieder*, No. 37, and the *Unv. L. S.*, 1851, No. 242. It is a beautiful hymn on Christ as the Light and Centre of the world, and the most widely used through English *trs.* of any of Heermann's hymns. *Tr.* as:—

1. **O Thou, the true and only Light, Direct, &c.** A good *tr.* of st. i., ii., by W. Ball, as part of his book of words for the English ed. of Mendelssohn's *St. Paul*, 1836, and thence in Robinson's *Church Psalter & H. Bk.*, 1860. To this in Allon's *Suppl. Hys.* and *C. P. Hyl.*, 1886, *Bapt. Hyl.*, 1879, &c., *trs.* of st. iv.–vi., from *Chope* (see below), were added; and in the *Suppl.* of 1874 to the *New Cong.*, *trs.* of st. iii.–vi. from *Miss Winkworth* (see below). The version in the *Anglican H. Bk.*, 1868, No. 275 (1871, No. 316), is st. i. by Ball, st. iv.–vi. by R. C. Singleton, 1867.

2. **O Christ, the Light of heavenly day!** A full and very good *tr.* by A. T. Russell, as No. 137 in his *Ps. & Hys.*, 1851, and thence in Bosworth's *Church Hys.*, 1865, and G. S. Jellicoe's *Coll.*, 1867. In the Cooke-Denton *Hymnal*, 1853, No. 12 is composed of sts. i., iv., v., ii., vi., of *Russell*, in the order named. This form is repeated in Chope's *Hyl.*, 1862, Thring's *Coll.*, 1880–82, &c. The form beginning "O Jesu, Light of heavenly day," in *Kennedy*, 1863 (thence in Dr. Thomas's *Augustine H. Bk.*, 1866), is *Chope* greatly altered.

3. **O Thou, the true and only Light! Enlighten, &c.** A somewhat free *tr.* in 5 st., as No. 58 in J. F. Thrupp's *Ps. & Hys.*, 1853.

4. **O Christ, our true and only Light.** A good and full *tr.* by Miss Winkworth in her *Lyra Ger.*,

2nd Ser., 1858, p. 21, repeated in her *C. B. for England*, 1863, No. 100. This is found in the *App.* of 1874 to the *Leeds H. Bk.*, 1853; *Psalmist*, 1878; and in America in the *Presb. Hyl.*, 1874; Baptist *H. Bk.*, 1871; Bapt. *Service of Song*, 1871; Ohio *Luth. Hyl.*, 1880, &c.

5. **O Jesu Christ, the world's true Light.** A good but rather free version by E. Massie in his *Sacred Odes*, vol. ii., 1867, p. 175, and thence in J. L. Porter's *Coll.*, 1876.

Another *tr.* is, "O Christ, Thou heavenly Light, illume," by Dr. *G. Walker*, 1860, p. 31.   [J. M.]

O Jesu, meine Sonne. *C. J. P. Spitta.* [*Love to Christ.*] A beautiful hymn on Jesus as the daily help and life of His faithful people. 1st pub. in Spitta's *Psalter und Harfe*, Pirna, 1833, p. 69, in 8 st. of 8 l. entitled, "Life and full satisfaction in Jesus." Included in Knapp's *Ev. L. S.*, 1850, No. 1445 (1865, No. 1507). *Tr.* as :—

O blessed Sun, whose splendour. A full and good *tr.* by R. Massie in his *Lyra Domestica*, 1860, p. 66, repeated in Reid's *Praise Bk.*, 1872, and in Schaff's *Christ in Song*, 1869–70. Varying centos with the original first line are found in Flett's *Coll.*, Paisley, 1871; Hatfield's *Church H. Bk.*, N. Y., 1872; Harland's *C. P. & Hyl.*, 1876; J. L. Porter's *Coll.*, 1876, &c.; and (with the first line as "Blessed Sun") in the *Bk. of Common Praise*, 1863. Varying centos (generally iv.–vi.) beginning "I know no life divided" (st. iv.) are included in *Kennedy*, 1863; *People's Hyl.*, 1867; and in America in the *Presb. Hyl.*, 1874; Meth. Epis. *Hyl.*, 1878; Dutch Reformed *H. Bk.*, 1869; *Laudes Domini*, 1884, &c.

Other *trs.* are, (1) "Jesus, my sun! before Whose eye," by *Miss Fry*, 1859, p. 143. (2) "O Jesus Christ, my Sunshine," by *Miss Manington*, 1864, p. 15. (3) "O Jesus, at Thy shining," by Miss Burlingham, in the *British Herald*, Aug. 1865, p. 124, repeated in Reid's *Praise Bk.*, 1872. (4) "Jesus, my Sun, before Whose beams," by *Lady Durand*, 1873, p. 29.   [J. M.]

O Jesu, my [our] beloved King. *E. Caswall.* [*Grace and Merit.*] Pub. in H. Formby's *Catholic Hys.*, 1851, p. 45, in 7 st. of 4 l.; in Caswall's *Masque of Mary*, 1858, p. 217; and in his *Hys. & Poems*, 1873, p. 248. In the *Hymnary*, 1872, it begins, "O Jesu, our beloved King."   [J. J.]

O Jesu, Thou art standing. *Bp. W. W. How.* [*Christ at the Door.*] Written in 1867, and first pub. in the 1867 *Supplement* to Morrell & How's *Ps. & Hymns*, in 6 st. of 4 l. It has passed, and usually in an unaltered form, into the 1868 *Appx.* to *H. A. & M.*, the S. P. C. K. *Church Hys.*, 1871, and other collections in G. Britain, and also into several American collections. It is one of the most popular of Bishop How's hymns.   [J. J.]

O Jesus bruised and wounded more. *Cecil F. Alexander.* [*Holy Communion.*] Appeared in her work, *The Legend of the Golden Prayers and other Poems*, 1859, p. 143, in 5 st. of 4 l., and entitled "Communion Hymn." In the *Lyra Anglicana*, 1865, it was given as Pt. ii. of the hymn "He cometh, on yon hallowed board," Pt. i. being an addition of 6 st. to the original hymn. Each of these "Parts" is in C. U. as a separate hymn, the second part being the more popular of the two.   [J. J.]

O Jesus! God and man. *F. W. Faber.* [*Children's Hymn.*] This popular children's hymn was given in his *Jesus and Mary*, &c., 1849, in 7 st. of 4 l., and headed "Ragged School Hymn." In C. U. it is found in two forms, first, the original, in Roman Catholic hymn-books for missions and schools, in which st. iii., iv., both of which are addressed to the B. V. M., are retained; and second, in other hymn-books, where they are omitted. Orig. text in Faber's *Hymns*, 1862.   [J. J.]

O Jesus, I [we] have promised To serve Thee to the End. *J. E. Bode.* [*Confirmation.*] Contributed to the 1869 *Appendix* to the S. P. C. K. *Ps. & Hymns*, No. 395. It has been repeated in a great number of hymn-books, and is very popular as a Confirmation hymn.   [J. J.]

O Jesus, Jesus, dearest Lord. *F. W. Faber.* [*Love to Jesus.*] 1st pub. in his *Jesus and Mary*, &c., 1849, in 10 st. of 4 l., headed "Jesus, my God, and my All"; and again in his *Hymns*, 1862. It is in C. U. in its full form, and also abbreviated to 5 st., as in Hatfield's *Church H. Bk.*, N. Y., 1872. A cento therefrom, beginning with st. vii., "O Light in darkness, Joy in grief," is No. 580 in the *Hymnary*, 1872.   [J. J.]

O Jesus, make Thyself to me. *Charlotte Elliott.* [*The Presence of Jesus desired.*] Under date of Jan. 26, 1872, the Rev. J. Babington, brother-in-law to Miss Elliott, wrote to the late D. Sedgwick concerning this hymn :—

"The lines you refer to, 'O Jesus, make Thyself to me,' are Miss Charlotte Elliott's. They were for many years the private expression of her own daily prayers, and were so much a part of her own hidden life with her Saviour that they were rarely communicated by her to any one, and only to her most intimate friends. One of those had been printed on a card by Taylor [Edinburgh, 1860], and at first she was rather disconcerted, till she was led to feel that this was her loved Saviour's way of leading others to the participation in her own sacred inner life."

The lines are :—

"O Jesus, make Thyself to me,
A living, bright reality;
More present to faith's vision keen
Than any outward object seen;
More dear, more intimately nigh,
Than e'en the sweetest earthly tie!"

These lines are given in Snepp's *Songs of G. & G.*, 1872, as No. 538.   [J. J.]

O Jesus, Saviour of the lost. *Bp. E. H. Bickersteth.* [*Jesus, the Rock.*] Appeared in his *Water from the Well-Spring*, &c., 1852, p. 180, in 4 st. of 4 l., and headed, "Thou art my Rock." In 1858 it was repeated in his *Ps. & Hys.*, No. 135; and again, as "O Jesu, Saviour, &c.," in his *H. Companion*, 1870 and 1876. It is also in use in America. Bp. Bickersteth dates its composition 1849, but it is not in his *Poems* of that Year.   [J. J.]

O Jesus, still, still shall I groan. *C. Wesley.* [*Lent.*] This poem, in 4 parts, appeared in *Hymns and Sacred Poems*, 1742, in 36 st. of 6 l., and entitled, "Groaning for Redemption." (*P. Works*, 1868–72, vol. ii. p. 126.) In 1780 the following hymns were compiled therefrom, and included in the *Wes. H. Bk.* :—

1. Jesus, Thou knowest my simpleness [sinfulness]. St. i.–iii., vii., viii. of Pt. ii.
2. Lay to Thy hand, O God of grace. St. viii.–x. of Pt. iii.
3. Saviour from sin, I wait to prove. St. i., ii., iv.–vi. of Pt. iv.

These hymns are retained in the *Wes. H. Bk.*, 1875, and are found in various collections.   [J. J.]

O King of earth, and air, and sea. *Bp. R. Heber.* [*Lent.*] Appeared in his posthumous *Hymns*, &c., 1827, p. 55, in 6 st. of 4 l., and appointed for the 4th Sunday in Lent. Although apparently based upon the petition in the Lord's Prayer, "Give us this day our daily bread," it was doubtless suggested by the Gospel of the day, the feeding of the five thousand (John vi. 1). It is in C. U. in G. Britain and America. In the American Unitarian *Bk. of Hymns*, 1848, No. 492, it begins with st. iv., "Thy bounteous hand with food can bless."   [J. J.]

O King of kings, Thy blessing shed. [*National Hymn.*] This hymn "For the King" appeared anonymously in the 8th ed. of Cotterill's *Selection*, 1819, No. 266, in 5 st. of 4 l. It is known in the following forms :—

1. Its full form as above, and in various hymn-books to 1837.
2. In 4 st. of 4 l. in Bickersteth's *Christian Psalmody*, 1833. This is the text, with the necessary changes from King to Queen, &c., which was used in the S. P. C. K. *Jubilee Hymns*, 1887, and other Jubilee collections.
3. The same arrangement of stanzas altered to suit the changed circumstances occasioned by the accession of H. M. Gracious Majesty Queen Victoria. This was given in an early edition of Hall's *Mitre H. Bk.* (1st ed., 1836), and was made by Hall.
4. The *Mitre H. Bk.* text with the addition of Bp. Ken's doxology, "Praise God from Whom," &c.
5. The *Mitre H. Bk.* text, with a return in some instances to the original text on the one hand, and some new changes on the other, in Thring's *Coll.*, 1882.

This hymn is usually attributed to T. Cotterill. In the *Julian* and the *Brooke* marked copies of his *Selection* [see **Cotterill, T.**] it is blank. Snepp, in his *Songs of G. & G.*, 1872, and others attribute it to "T. Cotterill." Their authority was the simple guess of D. Sedgwick, as his MSS. testify. So far as we can discover it is "Anon. in Cotterill's *Selection*, 1819."   [J. J.]

Ὁ Κύριος ἔρχεται. [Τὴν ἡμέραν τὴν φρικτήν.]

O let my Jesus teach me how. *J. Berridge.* [*Abiding in Jesus.*] Pub. in his *Zion's Songs*, &c., 1785, No. 99, in 6 st. of 4 l., with the heading "Little children, abide in Him, 1 John ii. 28" (ed. 1842, p. 99). In modern hymn-books it is usually abbreviated, as in Spurgeon's *O. O. H. Bk.*, 1866. [J. J.]

O Lord, consider my distress. *W. Whittingham.* [*Ps. li.*] This rendering of the 51st Ps., which first appeared in the *Anglo-Genevan Psalter*, 1556 [Old Version, § III.], is the *earliest known version of a Psalm in* L. M. in the English language. A copy of the Psalter in which it appeared is preserved in the Bodleian, Oxford. Notwithstanding its historical value and some merit, it is unknown to modern collections. As a specimen we will quote the first stanza :—

"O Lord, consider my distresse,
and now with speed some pity take:
My sins deface, my faults redresse,
good Lord, for thy great mercies sake."

The full text is difficult to find, except in the *Psalter* appended to many old copies of the Bible, and in the Old Version.   [J. J.]

O Lord, how good, how great art Thou. *H. F. Lyte.* [*Ps. viii.*] This is Lyte's altered version of his paraphrase of Ps. viii., which first appeared as "How good, how faithful, Lord, art Thou" (p. 706, ii. 4), in his *Poems*, 1833. This altered form was given in his *Spirit of the Psalms*, 1834, and is found in the *Wes. H. Bk.*, 1875, and other collections. [J. J.]

O Lord, how happy should we be. *J. Anstice.* [*Rest and Peace in Jesus.*] 1st pub. in his posthumous *Hymns*, 1836, No. 44, in 5 st. of 6 l. In 1841 it was included in the *Child's Christian Year*, and from thence has passed into numerous hymn-books in all English-speaking countries. It was probably suggested by the words of the Psalmist, "Cast thy burden upon the Lord, and He shall sustain thee;" but in the *Hymns* there is nothing to indicate its origin, as it is printed there without title or heading of any kind. Usually the text is slightly altered, that in the *H. Companion*, although claiming to be the original, being at fault in no less than four instances. This hymn is the best known and most widely used of Anstice's hymns. [J. J.]

O Lord, in all our trials here. *Emma Toke, née Leslie.* [*Saints' Days.*] Written in 1851, and contributed anonymously to the S. P. C. K. *Hymns for Public Worship*, 1852, No. 114, in 3 st. of 4 l. This hymn is in use in the following forms:—

1. The original in S. P. C. K. *Hymns*, &c.
2. Rewritten by Mrs. Toke, in 3 st. of 8 l. for the Rev. R. Judd's *Sunday School Liturgy and H. Bk.*, Halifax, 1870, No. 11, and adapted for St. Stephen's Day.
3. In Hutton's *Appendix*, Lincoln, n. d., composed of the original; st. iv. from J. Newton's *Olney Hymns*, No. cxvi., st. vii.; and a doxology. This arrangement was given in Thring's *Coll.*, 1st ed., 1880, but omitted in the 2nd ed., 1882, in favour of:—
4. The original with a fourth stanza added by Prebendary Thring, No. 385. [J. J.]

O Lord, incline Thy gracious ear. *C. Wesley.* [*Ps. v.*] Pub. in the Wesley *Ps. & Hys.*, 1743, in 7 st. of 8 l. (*P. Works*, 1868–1872, vol. viii. p. 9.) From this paraphrase three centos are in C. U.:—

1. **O Lord, incline Thy gracious ear.** In *Kennedy*, 1863, No. 377.
2. **Behold us, Lord, with humble fear.** Composed of st. iv., v., and vii. rewritten and greatly altered, in *A Sel. of Hys. designed as a Suppl. to the Ps. & Hys. of the Presb. Church.* Philadelphia, 1861.
3. **On Thee, O God of purity.** This, which begins with st. ii., was given in the revised ed. of the *Wes. H. Bk.*, 1875. In *Common Praise*, 1879, this is again changed to "On Thee, *Thou* God of purity." [J. J.]

O Lord, my best desire fulfil. *W. Cowper.* [*Resignation.*] 1st pub. in the *Olney Hymns*, 1779, Bk. iii., No. 29, in 6 st. of 4 l., and entitled "Submission." It was somewhat widely used in the older hymn-books, and is still given in several collections in G. Britain and America. Usually it is abbreviated, and sometimes it is attributed to J. Newton, but in error. [J. J.]

O Lord of heaven, and earth, and sea. *Bp. C. Wordsworth of Lincoln.* [*Offertory.*] 1st pub. in the 3rd ed. of his *Holy Year*, 1863, in 9 st. of 4 l., and headed, "Charitable Collections." It is in extensive use in G. Britain and America, sometimes in its original form, as in the 1869 *Appendix* to the S.P.C.K. *Ps. & Hys.*, and again as altered

in *H. A. & M.*, or the S.P.C.K. *Church Hymns*, and others. The changes in the text of the *Church Hys.* were approved by the author. His authorised text is in the 6th ed. of his *Holy Year*, 1872. [J. J.]

O Lord of hosts, Whose glory fills. *J. M. Neale.* [*Laying Foundation Stone of a Church.*] Appeared in his *Hys. for the Young* (being the 2nd series of his *Hys. for Children*) in 1844, No. 27, in 6 st. of 4 l., and headed, "Laying the First Stone of a Church." It is given in numerous hymnals, as *H. A. & M.*, the *People's H.*, Thring's *Coll.*, &c. The alteration of st. v., ll. 1–2, from :—

  "Endue the hearts that guide with skill;
  Preserve the hands that work from ill;"

to—

  "The heads that guide endue with skill,
  The hands that work preserve from ill,"

given in *H. A. & M.* in 1861, has been adopted with almost common consent. [J. J.]

O Lord, our fathers oft have told. *Tate & Brady.* [*Ps. xliv. Thanksgiving for Victory.*] 1st pub. in three parts in the *New Version*, 1696. From this rendering, centos of varying length have been compiled from time to time, and have come into common use. In 1836, Edward Osler rewrote various lines from the *N. V.* and formed them into a hymn of 4 st. of 4 l. beginning :—"Great God of hosts, our ears have heard." This was included in Hall's *Mitre H. Bk.*, as a version of Ps. xliv. and entitled "For Succour against our Foes." From thence it passed into various collections, including Pott's *Hymns*, &c., 1861, where it was given with slight alterations, and a doxology. This text was repeated in the S.P.C.K. *Church Hymns*, 1871, with the change in the doxology of "One co-eternal Three" to "One God in Persons Three." [J. J.]

O Lord our God, with earnest care. [*Fast Day.*] This cento, in 5 st. of 4 l. in *A Selection of Hys. Designed as a Supp. to the Ps. & Hys. of the Presb. Church*, Philadelphia, 1861, No. 356, and the *Songs for the Sanctuary*, N. Y., 1865, No. 1333, is from *trs.* of Latin hymns pub. in the *H. Noted*; st. i. being st. iii. of "Ecce tempus idoneum;" st. ii., iii. being st. iii., iv. of "Jesu quadragenariae;" st. iv. being st. iv. of "Audi benigne Conditor;" and st. v. of "Plasmator hominis Deus." (For history of the Latin texts see under their respective first lines.) Of these *trs.* st. i.–iv. are by Dr. Neale, and st. v. by another hand. The result is a most successful hymn for a Fast Day service, or for Lent. [J. J.]

O Lord, our languid souls inspire. *J. Newton.* [*Opening of a Place of Worship.*] This hymn was written at the same time and under the same circumstances as Cowper's "Jesus, where'er Thy people meet." Full details are given in the note on that hymn. "O Lord, our languid souls," &c., was pub. in the *Olney Hymns*, 1779, Bk. ii., No. 43, in 7 st. of 4 l., and headed, "On opening a Place for Social Prayer." It is rarely found in its full form. The abbreviated texts sometimes begin with the first stanza, but the most popular arrangements are :—

1. **Dear Shepherd of Thy people, hear.** This is

usually composed of four stanzas of the original, beginning with st. ii.

2. Great Shepherd of Thy people, hear. This is the most popular form of the hymn. Bickersteth included it in his *Christian Psalmody*, 1833.

3. Kind Shepherd of Thy people, hear. This arrangement appeared in J. H. Gurney's *Coll. of Hymns*, &c., 1838, and is repeated in later hymn-books.

The use of this hymn in these various forms is extensive.   [J. J.]

O Lord, our Strength in weakness. *Bishop C. Wordsworth of Lincoln.* [*For a Girls' Friendly Society.*] Written in 1881 for *The Lincoln Diocesan Manual of the Girls' Friendly Society*, and first printed therein, 1881, in 6 st. of 8 l. (Lincoln: Williamson). It is an admirable lyric on *Temperance*, and is one of the most beautiful of Bp. Wordsworth's hymns.   [J. J.]

O Lord, refresh Thy flock. *J. Anstice.* [*Passiontide.*] Appeared in his posthumous *Hymns*, 1836, No. 27, in 5 st. of 4 l., and again, with alterations, in the *Child's Christian Year*, 1841. In the former it is without title or heading of any kind: in the latter it is appointed for "Thursday in Passion Week." It is in several hymn-books, the text being usually that of the *Child's Ch. Year.*   [J. J.]

O Lord, Thou knowest all the snares. *Emma Toke, née Leslie.* [*Lent.*] Written in 1851, and contributed anonymously to the **S. P. C. K.** *Hys. for Public Worship*, 1852, No. 34, in 2 st. of 8 l. From thence it has passed into later eds. of the same collection, the Irish *Church Hymnal*, and others. In 1870 Mrs. Toke altered it (for the worse) for the Rev. R. Judd's *S. S. Liturgy and H. Bk.*, Halifax, 1870, No. 21, as "O God! Thou knowest all the snares," but in this form it has failed to attract attention.   [J. J.]

O Lord, turn not Thy face away. *J. Marckant.* [*Lent.*] This hymn, known as *The Lamentation of a Sinner*, is first found in J. Daye's ed. of *Sternhold and Hopkins*, 1560–61 [**Old Version**, § v.] but without signature. In the edition of 1565, the authorship is given to *Marckant.* This name, sometimes written *Market*, appears also in the editions of 1595 and 1606 [**Old Version**, § IX. 10]. The first stanza is:—

> "O Lord, turn not Thy face away
>   From him that lies prostrate,
> Lamenting sore his sinful life
>   Before Thy mercy gate."

In *The Whole Book of Psalms*, &c., by J. Playford, 1677, p. 285, it begins "O Lord, turn not away Thy face."

The authorship of this hymn is given by Miller (*Singers and Songs*, 1869, p. 46) and by Lord Selborne (*Book of Praise*, 1862, p. 239, and note) to *John Mardley*, although Miller adds a "?" in his Index [**Old Version**, § IX. 10]. These conclusions are based upon Farr's note in his *Select Poetry Chiefly Devotional of the Reign of Queen Elizabeth*, &c., 1845, vol. i. p. l., where the signature "M" in the *Old Version* is thought to represent *John Mardley.*

A second rendering of *The Lamentation* is that by *Tate and Brady*, in the 6th ed. of the *Supplement* of the *New Version*, 1708. It is the *Old Version* text rewritten in 9 st. of 4 l. The first stanza reads:—

> "O Lord, turn not Thy face from me,
>   Who lie in woeful state,
> Lamenting all my sinful life
>   Before Thy mercy gate."

This text continued in use as a part of *Tate and Brady* until that work was superseded by modern hymn-books. It is also found in a considerable number of the latter, but usually in an abridged form.

A *third* rendering of *The Lamentation*, by *Bp. R. Heber*, was given in his posthumous *Hymns*, 1827, p. 104, in 12 double lines. The opening lines are:—

> "Oh Lord, turn not Thy face away
>   From them that lowly lie,
> Lamenting sore their sinful life
>   With tears and bitter cry."

This rendering, signed in Heber's *Hymns* "*Sternhold*" in error, is given in full in Lord Selborne's *Book of Praise*, 1862, p. 239. It is considerably altered from the *Old Version* original. In several modern hymn-books, including the Scottish Presbyterian *Hymnal*, 1876, it is slightly altered, as "O Lord, turn not Thy face from us." Other altered forms of the text are (1) "Turn not Thy face away, O Lord," in the American *Sabbath H. Bk.*, 1858, and others; and (2) "Turn not, O Lord, Thy face from me," in Alford's *Ps. & Hys.*, 1844, and his *Year of Praise*, 1867. The original texts of the *O.* and the *N. Versions* may be found bound up with old copies of the Book of Common Prayer.   [J. J.]

O Lord, upon Thine heritage. [*Ember Days.*] This hymn, in W. J. Blew's *Church Hymn and Tune Bk.*, 1852–55, in 5 st. of 4 l. is based upon F. Rous's version of Ps. 68, st. ix.–xii. as pub. in the *Scottish Psalter*, 1650. In the *H. Bk. for the use of Wellington College*, 1860, and in *Kennedy*, 1863, st. i.–iv., are repeated, together with the substitution of a doxology for Blew's st. v.   [J. J.]

O Lord, when dangers press me round. *W. H. Bathurst.* [*Ps. cxl.*] 1st pub. in his *Ps. & Hys.*, 1831, as a version of Ps. cxl. in 3 st. of 6 l. with the heading, "God a sure Defence." In its original form it is not in C. U., but as "My God, when dangers press me round," it is in a few modern collections, including the *New Cong.*, 1859, No. 235. This altered form of the hymn appeared in Hall's *Mitre H. Bk.*, 1836. The changes introduced by Hall are very slight.   [J. J.]

O Lord, Who in Thy love divine. *Bp. C. Wordsworth of Lincoln.* [*Ember Days and Ordinations.*] 1st pub. in his *Holy Year*, 1862, p. 200, in 9 st. of 6 l. and headed "For Ember Weeks; and at the Ordination of Bishops, Priests, and Deacons." In 1865 a new stanza was added, as st. ii. ("Thou Who the night in prayer didst spend"), and the hymn was divided into two parts, Pt. ii. beginning with st. v., "O may Thy pastors faithful be." In Snepp's *Songs of G. & G.*, 1872, No. 759, begins with st. iv. of the 1865 text, "O Thou Who didst at Pentecost." [J. J.]

O Lord, wilt Thou teach me to pray? *Jane Taylor.* [*A Child's Hymn.*] 1st pub. in *Orig. Hys. for Sunday Schools*, 2nd ed., 1813, No. 21, in 6 st. of 4 l. In the 4th ed. of the *Original Hys.*, 1816, the opening line was changed to "Lord, teach a sinful child to pray." In this form, and in the more pleasing reading given to it by some, "Lord teach a *little* child to pray," it is found in numerous collections for children. [J. J.]

O Love divine, how sweet Thou art. *C. Wesley.* [*Desiring to Love.*] Appeared in *Hys. and Sac. Poems*, 1749, vol. i., in 7 st. of 6 l. as No. 5 of six hymns on "Desiring to Love" (*P. Works*, 1868–72, vol. iv. p. 341). Three leading centos are in C. U. :—

1. Composed of st. i., iii., iv. and vii. This was given in G. Whitefield's *Hymns*, &c., 1753, No. 86, as the second of two hymns on "Longing for Christ." This cento was repeated by *Madan*, *Toplady*, and others in the older collections, and is that usually found in the Church of England hymn-books.

2. Composed of st. i.–iv. This was given in the *Wes. H. Bk.*, 1780, No. 141, and is in very extensive use in all English-speaking countries. In the revised ed. of the *Wes. H. Bk.*, 1875, st. v., vi., of the original were added to the hymn.

3. Composed of st. iv., vi., and iii., in the order named. This cento, beginning "O that I could for ever sit," is in the American *Songs for the Sanctuary*, N. Y., 1865.

In addition to these other forms of the text beginning with st. i. are in limited use. G. J. Stevenson's associations in his *Methodist H. Bk. Notes*, 1883, are most interesting. [J. J.]

O Love divine, what hast Thou done? *C. Wesley.* [*Passiontide.*] 1st pub. in *Hys. & Sacred Poems*, 1742, in 4 st. of 6 l., as the last of three hymns on "Desiring to Love" (*P. Works*, 1868–72, vol. ii. p. 74). It came into use in the Church of England through Toplady's *Ps. & Hys.*, 1776, No. 25, and with the Methodist Societies and other nonconformists through the *Wes. H. Bk.*, 1780, No. 27. The historical account of its beautiful refrain, "My Lord, my Love is crucified," is given under "My Lord, my Love was crucified" (p. 781, ii.). [J. J.]

O luce quae tuâ lates. *Claude de Santeüil.* [*Trinity.*] Appeared in the *Paris Breviary*, 1680 ; the *Cluniac Breviary*, 1686, p. 532 ; the *Paris Brev.*, 1736 ; and again in other and later French Breviaries. It is also in J. Chandler's *Hys. of the Primitive Church*, 1837 ; Card. Newman's *Hymni Ecclesiae*, 1838 and 1865 ; and Biggs's annotated ed. of *H. A. & M.*, 1867. *Tr.* as:—

1. **O Thou Who dwellest bright on high.** By J. Chandler in his *Hys. of the Primitive Church*, 1837, p. 93, and again in his *Hys. of the Church*, 1841, No. 54. This is given unaltered in some collections, and in others as "Thou ever blessed Trinity," as in Murray's *Hymnal*, 1852, No. 68.

2. **Who, in Thy very light, self-shrouded art.** W. J. Blew in his *Church Hy. & Tune Bk.*, 1852–55, and again in Rice's *Sel.* from the same, 1870.

3. **Blest Trinity, from mortal sight.** By the Compilers of *H. A. & M.*, given first in their trial edition, 1859, and then in their first ed., 1861, but omitted from the revised ed., 1875.

4. **Great God, Who in Thy light dost rest.** By R. C. Singleton, written in 1867, and included in his *Anglican H. Bk.*, 1868 and 1871.

5. **O Thou Who hidden art in Thine own light.** By I. Williams in the *British Magazine*, Sept. 1837, vol. xii. p. 270, and his *Hys. tr. from the Parisian Breviary*, 1839, p. 163. [J. J.]

O Luce qui mortalibus. *C. Coffin.* [*Sunday Evening.*] Given in the *Paris Bre-*

ia ry, 1736, as the hymn for Sundays at Vespers, from Trinity to Advent ; and again in Coffin's *Hymni Sacri*, 1736, p. 10. It is also in J. Chandler's *Hys. of the Primitive Church*, 1837, No. 10 ; Card. Newman's *Hymni Ecclesiae*, 1838 and 1865 ; and in Biggs's Annotated ed. of *H. A. & M.*, 1867. *Tr.* as :—

1. **O Thou Who in the light dost dwell.** By I. Williams in the *British Magazine*, Jan. 1834, vol. v. p. 31, and his *Hys. tr. from the Parisian Breviary*, 1839, p. 10. It was included with alterations in the *Hymnary*, 1872. It is also No. 104 (altered) in Rorison's *Hys. and Anthems*, 1851.

2. **O Thou, Whose throne is hid from men.** By J. Chandler in his *Hys. of the Primitive Church*, 1837, p. 8, and his *Hys. of the Church*, &c., 1841, No. 7. It is in a few collections only.

3. **Thou Who in light dost dwell.** By W. J. Blew, in his *Church Hy. & Tune Bk.*, 1852–55, and Rice's *Sel.* from the same, 1870.

4. **The splendours of Thy glory, Lord.** By Archbishop E. W. Benson. 1st pub. in the *H. Bk. for the Use of Wellington College*, during his Head Mastership, 1860, and again in the S. P. C. K. *Church Hys.*, 1871

5. **Great God, Who hid from mortal sight.** By the Compilers of *H. A. & M.*, 1861 (based on J. Chandler), omitted from the revised ed., 1875, but restored, with alterations, in 1889.

6. **Father of glory, that dost dwell.** By J. M. Neale in the East Grinstead *St. Margaret's Hyl.*, 1875.

Translations not in C. U. :—

1. O Thou Who in the light dost dwell. *R. Campbell.* 1850. This is I. Williams's *tr.* as above, rewritten in L. M. The opening ll. 1–3 are the same as Williams's.

2. O God, enshrined in heavenly might. *J. D. Chambers.* 1857.

3. God, who in the unapproached light. *D. T. Morgan.* 1880. [J. J.]

O Lux beata Trinitas, Et principalis Unitas. *St. Ambrose.* [*Evening.*] This is one of the twelve hymns which the Benedictine editors regarded as undoubtedly the work of St. Ambrose. It is cited as by St. Ambrose by Hincmar of Rheims in his treatise *De unâ et non trinâ Deitate*, 857. The original consists of two sts. (ii. "Te mane laudum carmine") and a doxology. Its almost universal use was at Vespers on Saturday, as in the older *Roman* (Venice, 1478); *Paris*, 1643; *Sarum, York,* and *Aberdeen Breviaries.* It was sometimes also assigned to Vespers or Lauds on Trinity Sunday. *Daniel*, i., No. 26, gives the original, along with the revised text of the *Roman Breviary* of 1632, where it begins **Jam sol recedit igneus.** In his notes *Daniel* gives the additional st. *tr.* in J. D. Chambers's *Lauda Syon*, 1857 (see below); (iii. "Jam noctis tempus advenit"; iv. "Tu Christe solve vincula"; v. "Oramus ut exaudias"), which are found only in the *Mozarabic Breviary*, where the hymn is given for Vespers on the 2nd S. after the Epiphany, and at other seasons. In his further notes at iv. pp. 47–48, *Daniel* refers to the original text as in a 10th cent. Rheinau MS.; gives the statements of Hincmar; and also cites a passage from the 21st Epistle of St. Ambrose, which he thinks clearly refers to this hymn, and so decisively settles its authorship. [W. A. S.]

Mone, i. p. 372, cites this hymn as in an 8th cent. MS. at Darmstadt, where it is assigned to daily Vespers. Dreves gives it in his *Hymnarius Moissiacensis*, 1888, from a 10th cent. MS. It is also in three MSS. of the 11th cent. in the British Museum (Vesp. D. xii. f. 2 *b*; Harl. 2961 f. 218; Add. 30848 [a *Mozarabic Breviary*] f. 66 *b*). In the *Lat. Hys. of the Anglo-Saxon Ch.* (Surtees Society), 1851, p. 1., it is printed from an 11th cent. MS. at Durham (B. iii. 32, f. 2). Also in an 11th cent. MS. at Corpus Christi, Cambridge (391, page 227); in the St. Gall MS., No. 387, of the 11th cent.; in Migne's *Patrol.* xvi., col. 1407, and lxxxvi., cols. 220, 232, 699, 924; in *Wackernagel*, i. No. 60; in Card. Newman's *Hymni Ecclesiae*, 1838 and 1865, and others.

The original text has been frequently *tr.* into German, and through three of these versions has passed into English.

i. Der du bist drei in Einigkeit. This is a full and faithful version by M. Luther, written in 1543, and 1st pub. in Klug's *G. B.*, Wittenberg, 1544. Thence in *Wackernagel*, iii. p. 29; in Schircks's ed. of Luther's *Geistl. Lieder*, 1854, p. 42; and the *Unv. L. S.*, 1851, No. 186. *Tr.* as:—

Thou Who art Three in Unity, True God. By R. Massie, in his *Martin Luther's Spir. Songs*, 1854, p. 25. Repeated in the Ohio *Luth. Hyl.*, 1880, and by *Dr. Bacon*, 1884, p. 71.

Other trs. are:—
(1) "Since Thou, the living God, art Three," by *Miss Fry*, 1845, p. 139. (2) "The true One God, in Persons Three," by *J. Anderson*, 1846, p. 23 (1847, p. 45). (3) "Thou Three in One, and One in Three," by *Dr. J. Hunt*, 1853, p. 53. (4) "Thou only God, the Three in One," by *Dr. H. Mills*, 1856, p. 223. (5) "Thou Who'rt One, and yet as Three," by *Miss Manington*, 1863, p. 155. (6) "Thou, Lord, art Three in Unity," by S. Garratt, in his *Hys. and Trs.*, 1867, p. 39. (7) "Thou, Who art Three in Unity, A," by Dr. G. Macdonald, in the *Sunday Mag.*, 1867, p. 388, and his *Exotics*, 1876, p. 61.

ii. O selges Licht, Dreifaltigkeit. A full and good *tr.* by Bunsen for his *Versuch*, 1833, No. 41. Repeated in the *Kirchen G. B.* of the Eisenach Conference, 1854, No. 74. *Tr.* as "O Trinity of blessed Light, Thou Unity," by *H. J. Buckoll*, 1842, p. 62.

iii. O werthes Licht der Christenheit. A full and good *tr.* by M. A. von Löwenstern. It seems to have appeared in the 2nd ed., *circa* 1646, of the Breslau *Kirchen- und Haus-Music.* *Mützell*, 1858, No. 288, quotes it (as No. 26 of Löwenstern's *Apelles-Lieder*) from the 5th ed., *circa* 1668. Included in Burg's *G. B.*, Breslau, 1746, No. 64. *Tr.* as, "O Holy fount of light on high," in full as No. 178 in Dr. Pagenstecher's *Coll.*, 1864, signed, "F. C. C."   [J. M.]

Both forms of the Latin text have been *tr.* into English. The text of each is:—

Durham text.	*Brev. Rom.*
"O Lux beata Trinitas,	"Jam sol recedit igneus:
Et principalis unitas;	Tu lux perennis unitas,
Jam sol recedit igneus:	Nostris, beata Trinitas,
Infunde lumen cordi-	Infunde lumen cordi-
bus.	bus.
Te mane laudent car-	Te mane laudum car-
mina,	mine,
Te deprecemur vespere,	Te deprecamur vespere,
Te nostra supplex gloria	Digneris, ut te supplices
Per cuncta laudet sae-	Laudemus inter coelites.
cula.	
Deo Patri sit gloria,"	Patri, simulque Filio,"
etc.	etc.

These forms have been translated thus:—

i. O Lux beata Trinitas.

1. Bright and blessed Three in One. By W. L. Alexander, in his *Augustine H. Bk.*, 1st ed., 1849, No. 195, and again in later editions.

2. O Trinity of blessed light. By J. M. Neale, in the *Hymnal N.*, 1852, No. 1. It is given in several collections, including *H. A. & M.*, 1861

and 1875, with slight alterations; the *Hymnary*, 1872, with other changes; and other hymn-books.

3. O Light thrice blessed, Holy Trine. By W. J. Blew, in his *Church H. & Tune Bk.*, 1852–55, and again in Rice's *Sel.* from the same, 1870.

4. O Light! Thou [O] Trinity most blest. By J. D. Chambers. This is a *tr.* of the 5th stanza and doxology form of the hymn as given in the *Mozarabic Breviary* (see above). It was pub. in Chambers's *Psalter*, 1852, p. 325; and his *Lauda Syon*, 1857, p. 56, and is No. 410 in the *People's H.*, 1867.

Other trs. are:—
1. O blessed lighte, O Trinitie, O Unity that is the chief. *Primer*, 1604.
2. O blessed light, O Trinity, O Unity most principal. *Primer*, 1615.
3. Thou ever-blessed Triune light. *Hymnarium Anglicanum*, 1844.
4. O Trinity, blest Light. I. Williams, in his *Thoughts in Past Years*, 1848.
5. When sinks in night that radiant sun. *H. M. Macgill*. 1876.

ii. Jam sol recedit igneus. This revised version of the hymn appeared in the *Roman Brev.* in 1632. It is the hymn on Saturdays at Vespers from the Octave of the Epiphany to Lent; also at first and second Vespers of Trinity Sunday; and also on Saturdays at Vespers from the Octave of Corpus Christi until Advent. It is *tr.* as:—

1. Now sinks in night the flaming sun. By Bp. R. Mant. This paraphrase rather than translation appeared in his *Ancient Hys. from the Rom. Brev.*, &c., 1837, p. 16, in 3 st. of 8 l. (ed. 1871, p. 31). The first stanza may be said to be the *tr.* of the Latin and the rest an expansion of the same line of thought, thus making the paraphrase. It is in several modern collections, including *Kennedy*, 1863; Thring's *Coll.*, 1882, &c.; and altered as "Father of lights, Who dwell'st in light," in the 1874 *Supplement* to the *New Cong.*; and as "The flaming sun has sunk in night," in the *Hymnary*, 1872.

2. Now doth the fiery sun decline. By E. Caswall, in his *Lyra Catholica*, 1849, pp. 36 and 108, and again in his *Hys. and Poems*, 1873, pp. 21 and 61. It is in several modern collections.

Other trs. are:—
1. Now doth the fiery sun retire, *Primer*, 1685.
2. The fiery sun now rolls away. And hastens. *Primer*, 1706.
3. The fiery sun now rolls away. Blest Three and One, &c. *Evening Office.* 1710.
4. Already the bright sun departs. *A. J. B. Hope.* 1844.
5. Behold the fiery sun recede. *F. C. Husenbeth.* 1840.
6. The fiery sun is gone. *W. J. Copeland.* 1848.
7. The fiery sun now fades from sight. *W. J. Copeland.* 2nd *tr.* 1848.
8. Behold the radiant sun departs. *R. Campbell.* 1850.
9. The red sun is gone. *Card. Newman.* 1853.
10. While fades the glowing sun away. *T. J. Potter.*
11. Blest Light, eternal Trinity. *J. D. Aylward.* This *tr.* is followed by 5 additional stanzas.
12. The fiery sun recedes from sight. *J. Wall.ce.* 1874.

Of these *trs.* not in C. U. Nos. 1, 2, 3, 5, 8, 10, and 11, are in O. Shipley's *Annus Sanctus* (and its *Appendix*), 1884.   [J. J.]

O Majestät! wir fallen nieder. *G. Tersteegen*. [*Public Worship.*] This hymn, founded on Rev. iv., first appeared in the 4th ed., 1745, of his *Geistliches Blumengärtlein*, Bk. iii., No. 74, in 7 st. of 12 l., entitled

"Hallelujah"; repeated in the Berlin *G. L. S.*, ed. 1863. The form *tr.* into English is that given in Dr. H. A. Daniel's *Evang. Kirchen G. B.*, 1842, No. 251, beginning, " Herr, unser Gott, mit Ehrfurcht dienen," being st. ii.-iv., vii., greatly altered. *Tr.* as:—

1. **Lord our God, in reverence lowly.** A good *tr.* of *Daniel's* text by Mrs. Findlater in *H. L. L.*, 3rd Ser., 1858, p. 32 (1884, p. 154), and repeated in the Meth. N. Conn. *Hymns*, 1863. It is also found in the following forms:—

(1) **Lord God of might, in reverence lowly.** In *Kennedy*, 1863, &c.

(2) **O Lord our God, in reverence lowly.** In the 1869 *Appendix* to the S. P. C. K. *Ps. & Hys.*, repeated in their *Church Hys.*, 1871 ; the *Hymnary*, 1872, &c.

(3) **Thee, God Almighty, Lord thrice holy.** In the 1874 *Suppl.* to the *New Cong. H. Bk.*; the 1874 *Appendix* to the *Leeds H. Bk.*, &c.

2. **Lord our God, to whom is given.** A free *tr.* of *Daniel's* st. i., iii., iv., by Dr. W. F. Stevenson, 1871, given in his *Hys. for Ch. & Home*, 1873, the refrain of st. i., ii. being taken from Mrs. Findlater as above.   [J. M.]

O Master, at Thy feet. *Frances R. Havergal.* [*Adoration.*] We have been furnished with the following interesting account of this hymn from Miss Havergal's private papers:—

"I felt that I had not written anything specially in praise to Christ. A longing to do so possessed me. I wanted to show forth *His* praise to *Him*, not to others, even if no mortal ever saw it, He would see every line, would have known the unwritten longing to praise Him even if words failed utterly. It describes, as most of my poems do, rather reminiscence than present feeling. I cannot transcribe at the moment of strong feeling. I *recall* it afterwards and write it down. 'O Master!' It is perhaps my favourite title because it implies *rule* and submission; and this is what love craves. Men may feel differently, but a true woman's submission is inseparable from deep love. I wrote it ['O Master!'] in the cold and twilight in the little back room, uncarpeted, at Shareshill Parsonage, Dec. 31, 1866. I began my book [*Ministry of Song*] with the expression of its devotion to God's glory, I wished to close it with a distinctive ascription of praise to Jesus, and, therefore, without any hesitation, at once decided upon placing 'Adoration' [this hymn] where it stands."

The hymn was given in the *Sunday Magazine*, 1867; in her *Ministry of Song*, 1869; and in *Life Mosaic*, 1879, in 5 st. of 4 l. [J. J.]

O may the power which melts the rock. *J. Newton.* [*National Fast.*] This is one of his Fast-day hymns pub. in the *Olney Hymns*, 1779, Bk. ii., No. 65, in 8 st. of 4 l. and headed, "Confession and Prayer, Dec. 13, 1776." In Cotterill's *Sel.*, 1810, it was given in 6 st., and in this form it has come down to modern hymn-books. [J. J.]

O mean may seem this house of clay. *T. H. Gill.* [*Divinity of, and Oneness with, Christ.*] Written in 1850; 1st pub. in G. Dawson's *Ps. & Hys.*, 1853; and again, after slight revision, in the author's *Golden Chain*, &c., 1869, No. 36, in 11 st. of 4 l. Concerning it the author says that it

"Has had by far the widest acceptance of all my hymns. It was put into my mouth as the truth of the Incarnation was revealed to me [see Gill, T. H.]. Its production was a great spiritual event in my own life, as well as an exquisite and unspeakable delight. It wrought powerfully upon my outward life, and introduced me to persons with whom led to a change of residence, and furthered the publication of my work, 'The Papal Drama.'" [E. MSS.]

This hymn as a whole is too long for C.U., **but** in an abbreviated form it is in numerous

hymn-books in G. Britain and America. No. 58 in Horder's *Cong. Hymns*, 1884, is an example of a choice selection of stanzas. [J. J.]

O mighty Mother! why that light? *F. W. Faber.* [*Whitsuntide.*] Pub. in his *Jesus and Mary*, &c., 1849, in 21 st. of 4 l. on "The Descent of the Holy Ghost." Also in his *Hymns*, 1862. The hymn, "He comes, He comes, the Holy One," in the *Sarum Hyl.*, 1868, is compiled from the 1849 text. [J. J.]

O most compassionate High Priest. *C. Wesley.* [*For Pardon.*] "First published in 1743, as 'A Prayer for those who are Convinced of Sin,' at the end of *The Nature, Design, and General Rules of the United Societies*, &c.; and to be found there in most if not all the editions of that tract published during Wesley's life" (*P. Works*, 1868-72, vol. v. p. 230). It was also included in *Hymns and Sacred Poems*, 1749, vol. ii., No. 63, in 18 st. of 4 l., as No. 3 of "Hymns of Intercession." In 1780, st. vi.-xiv. were given as: "O let the prisoners' mournful cries," in the *Wes. H. Bk.*, No. 450, and from thence passed into other collections. The revised ed. of the *Wes. H. Bk.*, 1875, omits the last two stanzas of the 1780 text. [J. J.]

O most delightful hour by man. *W. Cowper.* [*Death and Burial.*] These are the "Stanzas Subjoined to a Bill of Mortality for the Parish of All Saints, in the Town of Northampton, Anno Domini 1789," and subsequently pub. with Cowper's translations from the French of Madame Guion, as *Poems Translated from the French of Madame de la Mothe Guion*, &c., Newport-Pagnel, 1801, p. 122. There are 9 st. of 4 l. in all. Of these st. i.-iv. with alterations, were given in Martineau's *Hymns*, &c., 1840 and 1873, and also in a few American collections. [J. J.]

O my distrustful heart. *W. Hammond.* [*Final Perseverance.*] This hymn, on 2 Tim. ii. 13, "If we believe not, yet He abideth faithful," appeared in his *Ps. & Hys.*, &c., 1745, p. 165, in 4 st. of 6 l. In 1776, A. M. Toplady pub. it in a rewritten form, but beginning with the same first line, in his *Ps. & Hys.*, &c., No. 252. This arrangement was repeated in various collections to Snepp's *Songs of G. & G.*, 1872, No. 727, with the change in Snepp of st. iv. l. l. from "The bowels of Thy grace," to "*Thy rich and sovereign* grace." It is also in other collections, and should be given as " *W. Hammond*, 1745; *A. M. Toplady*, 1776." [J. J.]

O nata lux de lumine. [*The Transfiguration.*] The oldest text known of this hymn is in G. M. Dreves's *Hymnarius Moissiacensis*, 1888, from a 10th cent. MS.; and in two Rheinau MSS. now in the University Library at Zürich, No. 91 of the 11th cent. ; No. 82 of the 11th or 12th cent. It is also in an early 14th cent. MS. in the Bodleian (Ashmole 1523 f. 247); in the *Sarum Breviary*, Venice, 1495; the *Aberdeen Breviary* of 1509, &c. The printed text is also in Card. Newman's *Hymni Ecclesiae*, 1838 and 1865 ; *Daniel*, iv. p. 161, &c. [J. M.]

Translations in C. U. :—
1. **O Light of Light, Lord Jesu.** By W. J.

Blew, in his *Church Hy. and Tune Bk.*, 1852–55, and again in Rice's *Sel.* from the same, 1870.

2. O Light, Which from the Light hast birth. By J. D. Chambers, in his *Lauda Syon*, 1857, p. 241. This is repeated in several modern collections, including the *People's H.*, 1867 ; the *Hymner*, 1882, &c.

In the *Hymnal Noted*, 1854, the *tr.* "A type of those bright rays on high," is given in error under "O Nata Lux de Lumine," instead of "Coelestis formam Gloriae" (p. 240, ii.), of which it is a *tr.*   [J. J.]

'Ο νέος Οὐρανός. [*Conception of the B. V. M.*] Three Cathismata (i.e. hymns sung seated from the Daydawn or Lauds for the Conception of Anna, Dec. 9, in the *Menæa.* The *tr.* by Dr. R. F. Littledale, "Within the womb of Anna," was first pub. in the *Church Times*, Dec. 8, 1864, signed "R. F. L.," and again in the *People's H.*, 1867, and signed "L." It is an expansion of the original, the second stanza being introduced for the sake of clearness. The doxology is also by Dr. Littledale.   [J. J.]

'Ο παῖδας ἐκ Καμίνου. 'Αναστάσεως ἡμέρα.]

Ω πάντων ἐπέκεινα. *St Gregory of Nazianzus.* [*Praise.*] This "Hymn to God" is found in various editions of St. Gregory's *Opera ;* in *Daniel*, iii. 12, and in *Anth. Græca Carm. Christ.*, 1871, p. 24. It is an exceedingly fine hymn, and has been well rendered into English by Mr. Chatfield in his *Songs and Hymns*, &c., 1876, in 12 st. of 4 l., pp. 98–101, as, "O Thou, the One Supreme o'er all." [Greek Hymnody, § iv.]   [J. J.]

O Paradise eternal. *T. Davis.* [*Heaven.*] Appeared in his *Hys. Old and New*, 1864, No. 192, in 6 st. of 4 l., and again in his *Annus Sanctus*, 1877. It has passed, in its full, or in an abbreviated form, into a large number of hymn-books in G. Britain and America.   [J. J.]

O Paradise, O Paradise. *F. W. Faber.* [*Heaven.*] 1st pub. in his *Hymns*, 1862, in 7 st. of 8 l., and entitled "Paradise." In 1868 it was included in the *Appendix* to *H. A. & M.*, with the omission of st. iii. and vii., and the addition of the stanza "Lord Jesus, King of Paradise," by the compilers. For some time after the hymn was included in *H. A. & M.* it was very popular, Dr. Dykes's tune therein being the chief cause of its success. Latterly, however, its unreality, and, in its original form, its longing for sudden death, has caused it to be omitted from several of the best collections. The rewritten version, in three stanzas, in Morrell & How's enlarged edition of their *Ps. & Hys.*, 1864–67, No. 165, is a failure.   [J. J.]

O Pater sancte, mitis atque pie. [*Trinity Sunday.*] This hymn is found in two MSS. of the 11th cent. in the British Museum (Vesp. D. xii. f. 118 *b* ; Jul. A. vi. f. 70 *b*) ; and in the *Lat. Hys. of the Anglo-Saxon Ch.*, 1851, it is printed from an 11th cent. MS. at Durham (B. iii. 32, f. 43). It is included in the *Sarum, York, Aberdeen*, old *Roman* (Venice, 1478), and other *Breviaries.* The printed text

is also in *Mone.* No. 12 ; *Daniel*, iv. p. 270 ; G. M. Dreves's *Hymnarius Moissiacensis*, 1888, from a 10th cent. MS., and Card. Newman's *Hymni Ecclesiae*, 1838 and 1865.   [J. M.]

Translations in C. U. :—

1. O Holy Father, merciful and loving. By W. J. Blew, in his *Church Hy. and Tune Bk.*, 1852–55 ; and again, with slight alterations, in the 1860 *Appendix* to the *Hymnal N.*, No. 140.

2. O gracious Father, merciful and holy. By R. F. Littledale, in the *People's H.*, 1867, under the signature of " A. L. P."

3. Holiest Father, pitiful and loving [tender]. In the *Antiphoner and Grail*, 1880, and, altered, in the *Hymner*, 1882.

Translations not in C. U. :—

1. O Holy Father, gracious and benign. *J. D. Chambers*, 1852 and 1857.

2. Father most Holy, merciful and loving. *J. W. Hewett.* 1859.   [J. J.]

O perfect life of love. *Sir H. W. Baker.* [*Passiontide.*] Written for the revised edition of *H. A. & M.*, and included therein in 1875, as one of the " Hymns of the Passion," in 7 st. of 4 l. It is a hymn of much merit. [J. J.]

'Ο πλάστης μου κύριος. *St. Theophanes.* [*Quinquagesima.*] Stichera from the *Triodion* at the Vespers of Tyrophagus, the Sunday before the commencement of the Great Fast, in which even *cheese* (allowed for the last time on this Sunday) is prohibited. [See Δεῦτε ἄπαντες, p. 292, ii.] The original is in 5 st. of unequal length, as in Dr. Neale's *tr.* Adam's expulsion from Paradise is the subject of Tyrophagus, and the first three stanzas are spoken in the person of Adam. Dr. Neale's *tr.* : "The Lord my Maker, forming me of clay," is of st. i., ii., iii. and v., and appeared in his *Hys. of the Eastern Church*, 1862. He introduces it with the following note :—

" The reader can hardly fail to be struck with the beautiful idea in the third stanza, where the foliage of Paradise is asked to make intercession for Adam's recall. The last stanza, Milton, as an universal scholar, doubtless had in his eye, in Eve's lamentation."   [J. J.]

O praise our God to-day. *Sir H. W. Baker.* [*Friendly Societies.*] Written in 1861, and pub. in *H. A. & M.* the same year, in 5 st. of 4 l. It has passed into several hymn-books in G. Britain and America, and is admirably suited for the purpose of Friendly Societies, &c., for which it was written.   [J. J.]

O praise ye the Lord, Praise Him in the height. *Sir H. W. Baker.* [*Ps. cl.*] Written for and 1st pub. in *H. A. & M.*, 1875. One of the author's most spirited productions. It is in 4 st. of 8 l.   [J. J.]

O qualis quantaque laetitia. *Thomas à Kempis.* [*Eternal Life.*] In his *Opera*, Nürnberg, 1494, f. 130, entitled "Hymn on the joys of Heaven and the nine angelic choirs." The full text is in *Wackernagel*, i., No. 374. *Trench*, ed. 1864, p. 321, gives a beautiful fragment beginning with l. 9, "Astant (Adstant) angelorum chori." This portion has been *tr.* as :—

In the far celestial land. By *Harriet M. Chester*, made for and pub. in the *Hymnary*, 1872, under the signature of " H. M. C."   [J. M.]

O quam glorifica luce coruscas. [*B. V. M.*] This hymn is found in four MSS. of the

11th cent. in the British Museum (Vesp. D. xii. f. 87; Jul. A. vi. f. 55 b; Harl. 2961 f. 241; Add. 30848 f. 179 b); in a MS. of the 11th cent. at Corpus Christi College, Cambridge (391, p. 263); and in the *Lat. Hys. of the Anglo-Saxon Ch.*, 1851, it is printed from a MS. of the 11th cent. at Durham (B. iii. 32 f. 32 b). Among the St. Gall MSS. it is found in No. 92 of the 9th cent.; and in Nos. 387 and 413 of the 11th cent. It was included in the *Sarum*, *York*, and various German Breviaries, as a hymn for the Assumption of the B. V. M. The printed text is also in *Daniel*, iv. p. 188; and G. M. Dreves's *Hymnarius Moissiacensis*, 1888, from a 10th cent. MS. *Tr.* as:—

1. **O with what glorious lustre resplendent.** By J. D. Chambers, in his *Lauda Syon*, 1866, p. 87.
2. **O what light and glory.** By T. I. Ball, in the 1863 ed. of the *Appendix* to the *H. Noted*.
3. **O with what glorious lustre thou shinest.** In the *Antiphoner & Grail*, 1880, and the *Hymner*, 1882.   [J. M.]

O quam juvat fratres, Deus. *C. Coffin.* [*Unity.*] Appeared in the *Paris Breviary*, 1736, as the hymn for Tuesdays at Vespers; and again in Coffin's *Hymni Sacri*, 1736, p. 17. It is also in J. Chandler's *Hys. of the Primitive Church*, 1837, and Card. Newman's *Hymni Ecclesiae*, 1838 and 1865. *Tr.* as:—

1. **O Lord, how joyful 'tis to see.** J. Chandler, in his *Hys. of the Prim. Church*, 1837, p. 19. It is given, generally without alteration, in a large number of hymn-books, including *H. A. & M.*, 1875; the *Hymnary*, 1872; Thring's *Coll.*, 1882, &c. It ranks with the most popular of Chandler's translations.
2. **How sweet the days, O Lord, are sped.** Given anonymously in the *Wellington College H. Bk.*, 1860, and later editions.

Other trs. are:—
1. How sweet it is to see, Brethren in Unity. *I. Williams.* 1839.
2. Father and God, how sweet to see. *W. J. Blew.* 1852-5.
3. O God, what joys around are shed. *J. D. Chambers.* 1857.
4. O God, our loving God, by whom Thy Church. *D. T. Morgan.* 1880.   [J. J.]

O quanta qualia sunt illa Sabbata. *Peter Abelard.* [*Sunday. Eternal Life.*] Cousin, in his ed. of Abelard's *Opera*, Paris, 1849, vol. i. p. 306, gives this from a MS. in the Royal Library at Brussels. This MS. is of the 12th cent., and is probably the collection of hymns which Abelard prepared for the use of the abbey of the Paraclete of which Heloïse was abbess. *Mone*, No. 282, gives the text from the St. Gall MS., No. 528, of the 14th cent.; and in the 1875 catalogue of the St. Gall MSS. it is also marked as being contained in No. 387 of the 11th cent. It is also in Migne's *Patrologiae Cursus*, vol. 178, col. 1786.   [J. M.]

1. **O what their joy and their glory must be.** By J. M. Neale, in the *Hymnal N.*, 1854. It is in several hymn-books, including the S. P. C. K. *Church Hys.*, 1871; Thring's *Coll.*, 1882; and others, the text most in use being Neale's *tr.* slightly altered by the compilers of *H. A. & M.*, 1861.
2. **O how fair and how great.** By J. D. Chambers, in his *Lauda Syon*, 1857, p. 58. In the

Scottish Epis. *Coll. of Hys.*, 1858, it is given as "O how surpassing fair."
3. **O what shall be, O when shall be!** By S. W. Duffield. Mr. Duffield says in his *English Hymns*, &c., N. Y., 1886, p. 440, that he wrote this *tr.* in the Astor Library in 1883. He also says that he used the text as in Migne's *Patrologiae*. This *tr.* was given in the *Laudes Domini*, N. Y., 1884, in two parts. Pt. ii. begins "O glorious King, O happy state."

Other trs. are:—
1. O what must be their joy. *J. W. Hewett.* 1859.
2. O what must be the sabbaths. *D. T. Morgan.* 1880.   [J. J.]

O qui perpetuus nos monitor doces. *Jean Baptiste de Santeüil.* [*Common of Doctors.*] Given in the *Cluniac Breviary*, 1686, p. xlii.; in the author's *Hymni Sacri et Novi*, 1689, p. 207 (ed. 1698, p. 248); in the *Paris Breviary*, 1736, as the hymn for the Common of Doctors at first and second Vespers; and also in several modern French Breviaries. Card. Newman repeats the hymn from the *Paris Brev.* in his *Hymni Ecclesiae*, 1838 and 1865. *Tr.* as:—

O Thou the eternal Father's Word. By E. Caswall, in his *Masque of Mary*, &c., 1858, p. 323; and in his *Hys. and Poems*, 1873, p. 185. In the *Hymnary*, 1872, it is altered as "O Jesu Christ, Incarnate Word."

Other trs. are:—
1. O Thou, our only Teacher and true Friend. *I. Williams.* 1839.
2. O Thou, Who every hour. *J. D. Chambers.* 1866.   [J. J.]

O qui tuo, dux martyrum. *Jean Baptiste de Santeüil.* [*St. Stephen.*] Appeared in the *Cluniac Breviary*, 1686, p. 176, and in the author's *Hymni Sacri et Novi*, 1689, p. 55 (ed. 1698, p. 26). In 1736 it was included in the *Paris Breviary*. It is also in modern French Breviaries, and in Card. Newman's *Hymni Ecclesiae*, 1838 and 1865. *Tr.* as:—

1. **Rightful Prince of Martyrs thou.** This was given in I. Williams's *Hys. tr. from the Parisian Breviary*, 1839, p. 58. In his Preface Williams says that this *tr.* was "supplied by a Friend," but who this friend was we have not been able to determine to our satisfaction. The *tr.* is in C. U. in its original form and also altered as:—

(1) **Prince of martyrs! whose own name.** This was given in Murray's *Hymnal*, 1852, and is the 1839 text altered and with another doxology.
(2) **First of martyrs! whose own name.** This in the *Salisbury Hymnal*, 1857, is another arrangement of the 1839 text, but has more in common with *Murray* than with it.
(3) **First of martyrs! thou whose name Doth thy golden crown**, &c. By the compilers of *H. A. & M.*, based upon the 1839 *tr.*, together with the doxology as in *Murray*. This is the most popular *tr.* of the hymn.
(4) **Prince of martyrs! thou whose name.** This *tr.* in the 1860 *Appendix* to the *H. Noted*, and the *People's H.* is a cento, with st. i., iii.–v. being Chambers's *tr.* (see below) altered; st. ii., the 1839 text as above; st. vi., vii., added by the editor; and the doxology from *Murray* altered.
(5) **Chief of martyrs! thou whose name.** This is given in the *Anglican H. Bk.*, 1868, as by the editor, the Rev. R. C. Singleton. It is somewhat more musical than the 1839 text; but in other respects it is essentially the same.
(6) **First of martyrs! thou whose name, Answers to thy crown**, &c. This, in the *Hymnary*, 1872, is an ingenious and successful cento from most of the foregoing translations.

2. **O Captain of the martyr host.** By E. Caswall,

in his *Lyra Catholica*, 1849, p. 285, and his *Hys. & Poems*, 1873, p. 189. It is in use in some Roman Catholic hymn-books.

3. **O Prince of martyrs! thou whose name.** By J. D. Chambers, in his *Lauda Syon*, 1857, p. 83.
[J. J.]

O quickly come, dread Judge of all. *L. Tuttiett.* [*Advent.*] 1st pub. in his *Hys. for Churchmen*, 1854, in 4 st. of 6 l. It was included in the 1868 *Appendix* to *H. A. & M.*, in the S. P. C. K. *Church Hymns*, 1871, and several other collections. In a few American hymn-books it begins — "Come quickly come, dread Judge of all." In the *Guardian* of Dec. 24, 1884, the *H. A. & M.* text is rendered into Latin by " A. C." as :—
" Ipse veni, generis Judex sanctissime nostri."
[J. J.]

O rubentes coeli rosae. [*Virgins.*] This hymn on St. Ursula and the 11,000 virgins, is given by *Mone*, No. 1187, from a 15th cent. MS. at Basel. *Daniel*, iv. p. 281, repeats the text from *Mone*. The original was imitated by G. Moultrie, and printed in the *Church Times*, June 25, 1864 ; then in his *Hys. and Lyrics*, 1867 ; and the *People's H.* the same year as " Heavenly garland, rosy red." [J. J.]

O sacrum, sacrum convivium. [*Holy Communion.*] In the *York Breviary* of 1493 this is given as an antiphon to the Gospel on the Festival of Corpus Christi, as follows :—
" O sacrum convivium in quo Christus sumitur, recolitur memoria passionis ejus, mens impletur gratia, et futurae gloriae nobis pignus datur, Alleluia." In this form it is found in other ancient Breviaries, and in a *Sarum Processional* of *circa* 1390, in the Brit. Mus. (Harl. 2942 f. 80 *b*). A hymn in metrical form, with this first line, we have been unable to find. The *tr.* in the Irvingite *Hys. for the Use of the Churches*, 1871, is by E. W. Eddis, and was written in 1869. It begins : " O holy, holy, Feast of life Divine." There is also a prose *tr.* in the 1863 ed. of the *Appendix* to the *H. Noted*, No. 228.   [J. M.]

O sator rerum, reparator aevi. [*Transfiguration.*] The festival of the Transfiguration of our Lord was authorised by Pope Callistus III. in 1457 (and adopted by the English Convocation in 1483), and there are few hymns on this subject older than the 15th cent. This hymn is in two Rheinau MSS. in the University Library, Zürich, No. 91 of the 11th cent., and No. 82 of the 11th or 12th cent. It is also in a 14th cent. MS. in the Bodleian (Ashmole 1523 f. 247 *b*) ; in the *Sarum Breviary*, Venice, 1495 (Pars Estiv. pt. ii. f. 174 *b*, as the hymn at Matins for the Transfiguration) ; in the *Aberdeen Breviary* ; and in some of the eds. of the *York Breviary* after 1493. It is given in Card. Newman's *Hymni Ecclesiae*, 1838 and 1865 ; and G. M. Dreves's *Hymn. Moissia.*, 1888, from a 10th cent. MS. *Daniel*, i., No. 280, gives only st. i. *Tr.* as :—

Author of all things, Christ, the world's Redeemer. In the *Antiphoner and Grail*, 1880, and the *Hymner*, 1882.

Other trs. are :—
1. The World's Restorer, Christ, of kings the King. *W. J. Blew.* 1852–55.
2. Framer of worlds! Restorer of our days. *J. D. Chambers.* 1857.   [J. M.]

O Saviour, is Thy promise fled ? *Bp. R. Heber.* [*Advent.*] This is the third of the four hymns contributed by Heber to the October number of the *Christian Observer*, 1811. It was given for the 3rd Sun. in Advent, and consisted of 5 st. of 4 l. In Heber's posthumous *Hymns, &c.*, 1827, p. 10, it is slightly altered and expanded to 6 st. of 4 l., the new stanza being " Yet, 'mid the wild and wintry gale." It is in C. U. in its full form as in Thring's *Coll.*, 1882, and in an abbreviated form as in *Common Praise*, 1879. There are also *two* centos, both beginning " Come, Jesus, come, return again," the first, in the American Unitarian *Hys. for the Church of Christ*, Boston, 1853, and others, consisting of st. ii.–iv. of the 1827 text ; and the second in the Islington *Ps. & Hys.*, 1862, No. 270, where st. ii, v., vi. are given. The latter arrangement is also repeated in other collections. The original hymn is based upon the Gospel for the 3rd S. in Advent, St. Matt. xi. 2–10. [J. J.]

O Saviour of the faithful dead. *Bp. R. Heber.* [*On Recovery from Sickness.*] 1st pub. in the *Christian Observer*, Jan., 1816, in 4 st. of 8 l., and headed, " View of Death." In Heber's posthumous *Hymns, &c.*, 1827, p. 152, it is slightly altered, divided into 8 st. of 4 l., and the heading is changed to "On Recovery from Sickness." It is usually given in an abridged form of 2 st. of 8 l., or 4 st. of 4 l., but its use is not extensive.   [J. J.]

O Saviour, Whom this holy morn. *Bp. R. Heber.* [*Christmas.*] Pub. in the *Christian Observer*, Nov., 1811 (p. 697), in 5 st. of 4 l. and headed, " Christmas Day." The opening stanza reads :—

" Oh Saviour ! Whom this holy morn
Gave to our world below ;
To wandering and to labour born,
To weakness and to woe, ! "

In Heber's posthumous *Hymns, &c.*, 1827, p. 13, it is given with alterations, the first stanza reading :—

" Oh Saviour, Whom this holy morn
Gave to our world below ;
To *mortal want and* labour born,
And more than mortal woe ! "

Each stanza, except st. ii., is altered in like manner, the result being two distinct texts. Of these texts that of 1827 is almost absolutely followed by hymn-book compilers. Very few, however, give it in its complete form. The *H. Comp.* is an exception in favour of the full 1827 text, with the change of st. v. l. i., " Through fickle fortune's various scene," to " Through *this world's fickle* various scene." Other forms of the hymn are :—

1. **O Saviour, Whom this joyful morn.** This text is very much altered throughout. The opening stanza is the 1811 text with alterations ; the rest are altered from the text of 1827. In this form it was given in Bickersteth's *Christian Psalmody*, 1833, No. 301 ; Elliott's *Ps. & Hys.*, 1835 ; and again in recent hymn-books.
2. **O God, Whose Holy Child this morn.** This altered form of the 1827 text appeared in Martineau's *Hymns*, 1840.
3. **Incarnate Word ! by every grief.** This, beginning with st. ii. of the 1827 text, is No. 318 in the American *Bap. Praise Bk.*, N. Y., 1871.
4. **Jesus, Thou man of Sorrows born.** This is found in several modern collections, including *Common Praise*, 1879, and others, and is the 1811 text slightly altered.

When these various forms of the text are taken into account it is found that the use of this hymn is extensive. It is, however, far from being one of Heber's best productions. [J. J.]

O Saviour, Whose mercy severe in its kindness. Sir R. Grant. [Benefits of Affliction.] This poem is found in Sacred Poetry, 2nd Series, Edinburgh, W. Oliphant & Son, circa 1824, No. 149, in 8 st. of 4 l., headed "Benefit of Affliction," and signed "Sir Robert Grant." In Grant's posthumous Sacred Poems, 1839, it was given unaltered as No. v., with the text "Blessed is the man whom thou chastenest. Psalm xliv. 12." It is given in full in H. W. Beecher's Plymouth Coll., 1855, and other American hymn-books. In the Boston Unitarian Hys. of the Spirit, 1864, No. 586, "I thought that the course of the pilgrim to heaven," is composed of st. v.–vii. [J. J.]

O say not thou art left of God. Card. J. H. Newman. [Faith.] 1st pub. in the British Magazine for July, 1834, in 5 st. of 4 l., and again in the Lyra Apostolica, 1836, No. 27, with the heading "Tokens. 'The Lord stood with me and strengthened me,'" and signed "δ." It is also in his Verses on Religious Subjects, 1853, and his Verses on Various Occasions, 1868. In Kennedy, 1863, the text is slightly altered, and a doxology is added. [J. J.]

O see how Jesus trusts Himself. F. W. Faber. [True Love.] Pub. in the 1849 ed. of his Jesus and Mary, &c., p. 187, in 23 st. of 4 l., and headed "True Love." It is also in his Hymns, 1862. The cento usually found in C. U. was given in Spurgeon's O. O. H. Bk., 1866, No. 784, and is composed of st. i., iii., v. and vi. This is repeated in Laudes Domini, N. Y., 1884, and, with slight alterations, in Dale's English H. Bk., 1874. [J. J.]

O selig Haus, wo man dich aufgenommen. C. J. P. Spitta. [Private Use.] A beautiful description of a true Christian household, taken from the happy home life of the author. 1st pub. in his Psalter und Harfe, Pirna, 1833, p. 97, in 5 st. of 8 l., entitled "Salvation is come to this house" (St. Luke xix. 9). Included in the Württemberg G. B., 1842, No. 500; Hannover G. B., 1883, No. 527, and many others. Tr. as :—

1. **Oh happy house! where Thou art loved the best.** A good but free tr. by Mrs. Findlater in H. L. L., 3rd Ser., 1858, p. 16 (1884, p. 142). In Schaff's Christ in Song, 1869–70. St. i.–iv. were also repeated in the 1869 Appendix to the S. P. C. K. Ps. & Hys.

2. **O happy house, O home supremely blest.** A good tr. by R. Massie in his Lyra Domestica, 1860, p. 81, repeated in Bp. Ryle's Coll., 1860, No. 216, and in Arthur Wolfe's Hymns, 1860.

Other trs. are, (1) "O blessed house, whose favoured inmates know," by S. A. Storrs, in her Thoughts and Sketches, 1857, p. 68. (2) "O happy house, where ev'ry breast," by Dr. G. Walker, 1860, p. 67. (3) "O blessed house, where Thou, dear Lord," by Dr. R. Maguire, 1883, p. 103. [J. M.]

O show me not my Saviour dying. J. Conder. [Easter.] 1st pub. in the Cong. H. Bk., 1836, No. 160, in 4 st. of 8 l.; again in Conder's Choir and Oratory, 1837, p. 65; and again in his posthumous Hys. of Praise,

Prayer, &c., 1856, p. 128. Although given for "The Lord's Supper" in The Cong. H. Bk., it is, strictly speaking, an Easter hymn, and is based on the words "He is not here; He is risen. Come, see the place where the Lord lay." In an abridged form of 3 st., together with alterations, it is given in the S. P. C. K. Church Hymns, 1871, as "Show me not only Jesus dying." [J. J.]

O sight for angels to adore. Bp. W. W. How. [Baptism of Jesus.] Written for the S. P. C. K. Church Hymns, 1871, where it is given as one of the hymns for the Epiphany. In his Notes to the folio ed. of Church Hys., 1881, Mr. Ellerton explains this assignment of the hymn as follows :—

"The Baptism of our Lord was anciently the chief event commemorated in the feast of the Theophaneia or Epiphany; and in the Eastern Church this is still the key-note of the festival. Hence it was thought very desirable to place amongst Epiphany hymns one specifically commemorating this great Manifestation of the Son of God."

In T. Darling's Hys. for the Ch. of England, 1887, st. iv. is omitted. [J. J.]

O Son of Man, Thyself once [crossed] crost. [St. Stephen's Day.] This hymn was given in the Rev. J. F. Thrupp's Ps. & Hys. for Pub. Worship, 1853, No. 120, in 4 st. of 4 l. In his Index of first lines Mr. Thrupp says that it was "rewritten," but does not give the source of the original. That original is evidently Mrs. C. F. Alexander's hymn for St. Stephen's Day, "Have you not seen the lily ride," which appeared in her Verses for Holy Seasons, 1846, p. 11, in 10 st. of 4 l.; the stanzas chosen being viii., iv., v., ix., x. Thrupp's form of the hymn underwent another change when included in the S. P. C. K. Church Hymns, 1871, as "O Son of Man, Thyself once crossed," when the compilers added their st. ii., "O Son of God, Whose glory cast," and altered Thrupp's st. iv. and v. This text of 1871 is also in Thring's Coll., 1882. [J. J.]

O speak that gracious word again. J. Newton. [Peace.] This is No. 53 of Bk. iii. in the Olney Hymns, 1779, in 7 st. of 4 l., and is headed "Peace restored." In its full or in an abridged form it is found in a few modern hymnals. In the American Meth. Epis. Hymns, 1849, No. 882, it is changed from c. m. to s. m., and reads, "O speak that word again;" but this form of the hymn has not met with favour. [J. J.]

O Spirit of the living God. J. Montgomery. [For Missions.] Written in 1823 "to be sung at the Public Meeting of the Auxiliary Missionary Society for the West Riding of Yorkshire, to be sung in Salem Chapel, Leeds, June 4, 1823." It was first printed on a fly-sheet for that meeting, and again in the Evangelical Magazine in the following August. After a careful and most successful revision it was pub. by Montgomery in his Christian Psalmist, 1825, No. 552, in 6 st. of 4 l., and headed "The Spirit accompanying the Word of God;" and again in his Original Hymns, 1853, No. 257. It is usually given in an abridged form; but the text is seldom altered. As a hymn on behalf of Missions it has great merit, and is in extensive use in all English-speaking countries. The original text is given in the *Churchman's Shilling Magazine*, 1877. [J. J.]

O splendor aeterni Patris. *C. Coffin.*

[*Lent.*] Given in the *Paris Breviary*, 1736, as the hymn on Sundays and Ferias at Compline throughout Lent till Wednesday in Holy Week. It is also in Coffin's *Hymni Sacri*, 1736, p. 95; J. Chandler's *Hys. of the Primitive Church*, 1837, No. 15; and Card. Newman's *Hymni Ecclesiae*, 1838 and 1865. It is based upon the "Christe qui lux es et dies" (p. 227, i.). *Tr.* as:—

1. **Thou Brightness of the Father's face.** By J. Chandler, in his *Hys. of the Prim. Ch.*, 1837, p. 12, and thence into a few collections.

2. **Brightness of the Father's glory.** By Bp. J. R. Woodford, in his *Hys. arranged for the Sundays*, &c., 1852; the *Parish H. Bk.*, 1863, and several other collections.

Other trs. are:—
1. O Christ, blest influence divine. *I. Williams.* 1839.
2. O Christ, the true and endless Day. *R. Campbell.* 1850.
3. O Brightness of Thy Father! Ray. *J. D. Chambers.* 1857. [J. J.]

O take away this evil heart. *J. Montgomery.*

[*Lent.*] Written Dec. 9, 1829 [M. MSS.], and pub. in his *Original Hymns*, 1853, No. 281, in 5 st. of 4 l., with the heading "O Lord, I beseech Thee, deliver my Soul." It is found in a few modern hymn-books. [J. J.]

O ter jucundas, o ter foecundas.

[*Christmas.*] Included in the Mainz *G. B.* (R. C.), 1661, p. 103, in 5 st., entitled "Hymn on the holy birth-night of Christ." In later collections it begins, "O ter foecundas, o ter jucundas," and so in *Daniel*, ii. p. 339; *Trench*, ed. 1864, p. 116; and in H. M. Macgill's *Songs of the Christian Creed and Life*, 1876. "This pretty poem," as *Trench* terms it, does not seem to be earlier than the 17th cent. *Tr.* as:—

O blessed night! O rich delight. By H. M. Macgill, contributed to the *Draft* of the Scottish *Presb. Hymnal*, 1874, and pub. in that *Hymnal* in 1876. It is also in Dr. Macgill's *Songs of the Christian Creed and Life*, 1876, No. 34.

Other trs. are:—
1. Thrice joyful night. E. C. Leaton-Blenkinsopp, in *Lyra Messianica*, 1864.
2. O night of nights, supreme delights. J. C. Earle, in O. Shipley's *Annus Sanctus*, 1884. [J. M.]

O that I was as heretofore. *C. Wesley.*

[*A Minister's Prayer.*] Pub. in *Hys. and Sac. Poems*, 1749, vol. i., No. 188, in 8 st. of 6 l. (*P. Works*, vol. v., 1868–72, p. 105). Two centos from this hymn are in C. U.:—

1. **Give me the faith which can remove.** Composed of st. iii.–vii. in the *Wes. H. Bk.*, 1780, No. 421, and later collections.

2. **I would the precious time redeem.** Composed of st. v.–vii. in the *Bapt. Hyl.*, 1879. [J. J.]

O that Thou would'st the heavens rend. *C. Wesley.*

[*Prayer against the power of Evil.*] Appeared in *Hys. and Sac. Poems*, 1749, p. 79, in 17 st. of 4 l. (*P. Works*, 1868–72, vol. i. p. 269). It has been broken up into parts thus:—

1. **O that Thou would'st the heavens rend.** St. i.–ix. in the *Wes. H. Bk.*, 1780, No. 134. In the American

Meth. Epis. *Hymns*, 1849, st. i.–iv. are given as No. 376.

2. **Jesus, Redeemer, Saviour, Lord.** St. x.–xvii. in the *Wes. H. Bk.*, 1780, No. 135. In the American Meth. Epis. *Hymns*, 1849, No. 426 is composed of st. x.–xiii.

3. **Almighty God, be Thou our Guide.** St. iii., iv., vi., viii., ix., slightly altered, in *Holy Song for all Seasons.* Lond., 1869.

4. **Is there a thing too hard for Thee.** St. v.–ix. in the American Meth. Epis. *Hymns*, 1849, No. 377.

5. **O Christ, Redeemer, Saviour, Lord.** In *Kennedy*, 1863, is composed of st. x., xiii.–xvii. slightly altered.

In addition to these arrangements from this hymn another in 8 st. is sometimes met with in the Church of England collections. It opens with the first stanza of the original, but is distinguished from the arrangement in the *Wes. H. Bk.* as above, by the second stanza, which reads, "What tho' I cannot break my chain." It first appeared in A. M. Toplady's *Ps. & Hys.*, 1776, No. 352, and is composed of st. i., iv., vi., vii., ix., xii., xv., xiii. in the order named. A second cento in *Toplady*, 1776, No. 108, and beginning, "Jesus, Redeemer, Saviour, Lord," is composed of six stanzas from this hymn, and three (iv.–vi.) from C. Wesley's "Jesus, if still Thou art to-day." Also in later collections. [J. J.]

O the bitter shame and sorrow. *T. Monod.*

[*Gratitude.*] Mr. J. Thin's annotation of this hymn (the substance of which was derived apparently direct from the author) as given in his *Notes* of 1887 to the Scottish *Presbyterian Hymnal*, reads:—

"By Rev. Theodore Monod, Paris. Written by him in English during a series of 'Consecration' meetings held at Broadlands, England, in July 1874. Given by the author to Lord Mount-Temple at the close of the meetings, and printed by his Lordship on the back of a programme card for another series of similar meetings held at Oxford in October, 1874 . . . . The author writes (1887) that he now wishes line 4 of ver. 4 to read, 'Grant me now my supplication.'"

This hymn is given in several collections, including the *Hy. Comp.*, 1876, where, in the annotated edition, it is accompanied by the following note by Bp. E. H. Bickersteth:—

"This touching hymn by Monod, with the exception of reading 'petition' for 'desire' [st. iv. l. 4] for the measure's sake, is without alteration. In one of the last letters which the Editor received from the late Sir H. W. Baker, he expressed his great regret that it was not included in the revised edition of *H. A. and M.*"

It is in the *H. A. & M. Suppl. Hys.*, 1889. [J. J.]

O the hour when this material. *J. Conder.*

[*The Invisible State.*] Pub. in Collyer's *Coll.*, 1812, No. 898, in 8 st. of 8 l., and headed "The Invisible State; or, 'absent from the Body present with the Lord.' Rev. vii. 15–17." It was repeated in the *Cong. H. Bk.*, 1836, No. 620, and again in Conder's posthumous *Hys. of Praise, Prayer*, &c., 1856, p. 192. It is in C. U. in its full form, as in the *Leeds H. Bk.*, 1853. A cento therefrom is also in use as "Jesus, blessed Mediator." This cento is popular in America. [J. J.]

O the vastness, O the terror. *J. M. Neale.*

[*All Souls.*] This Sequence for All Souls appeared in his posthumous *Sequences, Hys. and other Ecclesiastical Verses*, 1866, p. 34, in 30 st. of 4 l. From it three centos have come into C. U.:—(1) "O the vastness, O the terror;" (2) "At length the Master calls;" and (3) "Now when prayer and toil have failed." [J. J.]

'Ο θεατὴς τῶν ἀρρήτων. [St. John Evangelist.] These are three prosomia (hymns of a similar structure) from the Vespers of St. John the Divine, May 8, in the Menæa, and preceding others also in the Anth. Graeca Car. Christ., 1871, p. 65. The author and date are unknown. The tr. by Dr. Littledale, "O Saint permitted here to see," was written for, and first pub. in, the People's Hymnal, 1867, signed "L.," and appointed for the festival of St. John the Divine. The fourth stanza in the People's H. is not in the original.   [J. J.]

O Thou, before Whose gracious throne. [During the dangerous illness of a Minister.] The earliest date to which we have traced this hymn is the 4th ed. of the Bristol Bap. Coll. of Ash & Evans, 1781, where it is given in 9 st. of 4 l., and is unsigned. In the 8th ed., 1801, it is signed "J— K— " It was included in full in Rippon's Bap. Sel., 1787, No. 413, but without signature. In Dobell's Sel., 1806, No. 592, it is signed "K.—Evans's Coll." In later editions it is "K." only. This uncertainty of authorship was increased by D. Sedgwick's guesses at the meaning of "K." In one of his books annotated in MS. we find him giving it to "John Kentish," in another to "George Keith," and so on, but in each case confessing that it was a guess only. In the Primitive Meth. Hyl., 1887, it is given to "F. Kirkham," a signature which is evidently wrong. We must subscribe it "J. K. in Ash & Evans, 1781." In modern collections the text is usually in an abbreviated form.   [J. J.]

O Thou Eternal Victim slain. C. Wesley. [Passiontide.] Pub. in the Hys. on the Lord's Supper, 1745, No. 5, in 3 st. of 6 l. (P. Works, 1868–72, vol. iii. p. 219). It is found in its full and unaltered form in the Wes. H. Bk. and other collections, both old and new. In the Salisbury H. Bk., 1857; the Sarum, 1868; the S. P. C. K. Church Hymns, 1871, and others, it reads "O Thou before the world began." In addition this hymn has been entirely rewritten in two forms, the first by Dr. Kennedy in his Hymno. Christ., 1863, as, "O first in sorrow, first in pain"; and the second by T. Darling, in his Hymns, 1887, as, "Christ Jesus, ere the world began." Of these Dr. Kennedy's is the finer of the two. [J. J.]

O Thou from Whom all goodness flows. T. Haweis. [Christ our Hope in Affliction.] This hymn is given at the close of a tract the title of which is :—

The Reality and Power of the Religion of Jesus Christ Exemplified in the Dying Experience of Mr. William Browne of Bristol, who departed this Life October 16, 1791. Aged 70 . . . . Bristol. Printed by John Rose, No. 21 Broadmead . . . . 1791. Price Two Pence.

In the account given in this tract of Browne's last illness, it is said he made this remark to a gentleman who called upon him :—

"I have chosen my funeral text and hymn Remember me. He hath remembered me with that favour which He beareth to His own people. The Lord will perfect that which concerneth me. Thy mercy, O God, endureth for ever: fulfil the work of Thine own hands" (p. 8).

From this it is tolerably clear that the hymn appeared before 1791, in some book or magazine which we have failed to trace. On p. 12 of the tract the hymn is given as follows;—

"HYMN."
Composed by the Rev. Mr. Haweis, Sung after his [Browne's] Funeral Sermon.
"O Thou from Whom all goodness flows
   I lift my heart to Thee:
In all my sorrows, conflicts, woes,
   Dear Lord, 'Remember me!'
"While on my poor distressed heart
   My sins lie heavily,
My pardon speak, new peace impart,
   In love 'Remember me!'
"Temptations sore obstruct my way,
   To shake my faith in Thee;
O give me strength, Lord, as my day;
   For good 'Remember me!'
"When in desertion's dismal night,
   Thy face I cannot see;
Then, Lord, arise with glorious light,
   And still 'Remember me!'
"If on my face for Thy dear name,
   Shame and reproaches be,
All hail, reproach, and welcome shame,
   If Thou 'Remember me!'
"The hour is near, consign'd to death
   I own the just decree;
Saviour, with my last parting breath,
   I'll cry, 'Remember me!'"

In Haweis's Carmina Christo, 1792, No. 42, it is given in another form thus :—

St. i.   As above.
St. ii.   "When groaning on my burden'd heart"; and as above.
St. iii. l. 2. "And ills I cannot flee." Lines 1, 3, 4 as above.
St. iv.   "Distrest with pain, disease, and grief
            This feeble body see;
            Grant patience, rest, and kind relief,
            Hear! and remember me."
St. v.   As above.
St. vi.   As above.

This form of the hymn was repeated in several of the older collections. In Cotterill's Sel., 1819, the hymn underwent another change. As No. 359 it reads :—

"O Thou, from Whom all goodness flows
   I lift my soul to Thee;
In all my sorrows, conflicts, woes,
   Good Lord, remember me.
"When on my aching, burden'd heart
   My sins lie heavily,
Thy pardon grant, new peace impart;
   Good Lord, remember me.
"When trials sore obstruct my way,
   And ills I cannot flee,
O let my strength be as my day;
   Good Lord, remember me.
"If, for Thy sake, upon my name,
   Shame and reproach shall be,
All hail reproach, and welcome shame!
   Good Lord, remember me.
"When worn with pain, disease, and grief,
   This feeble body see;
Grant patience, rest, and kind relief;
   Good Lord, remember me.
"When in the solemn hour of death
   I wait Thy just decree,
Be this the prayer of my last breath,
   Good Lord, remember me.
"And when before Thy throne I stand,
   And lift my soul to Thee,
Then with the saints at Thy right hand,
   Good Lord, remember me."

This form of the hymn was repeated by J. Montgomery in his Christian Psalmist, 1825, No. 188. As Montgomery assisted Cotterill in compiling Cotterill's Sel. of 1819, and altered several hymns by other writers for the same, it seems (from the fact that he reproduced the same text in his Christian Psalmist) that the alterations were made by him, and not by Cotterill. Montgomery attributed the original hymn to "T. Humphries." The text and the ascription of authorship were copied by Bickersteth in his

Christian Psalmody, 1833, by Elliott in his
Ps. & Hys., 1835, and others, and were for a
long time accepted as correct. Cotterill's text
of 1819 (sometimes with alterations) is that
usually found in modern hymn-books in G. Britain and America. Its use is extensive. [J. J.]

**O Thou God Who hearest prayer,
Every hour, &c.** *J. Conder.* [*Lent; or,
In Affliction.*] Written whilst suffering from a
severe accident through a fall from a horse, and
1st pub. in his *Star in the East, &c.*, 1824,
p. 72, in 5 st. of 6 l., and dated "Sep. 20,
1820." It was included in *The Cong. H. Bk.*,
1836, No. 590; and in Conder's posthumous
Hys. of Praise, Prayer, &c., 1856, p. 77. In
modern hymnals it is given in its full and
also in an abridged form. [J. J.]

**O Thou that [Who] hangedst on the
tree.** *C. Wesley.* [*For Condemned Malefactors.*] Pub. in *Hys. & Sac. Poems*, 1749,
vol. i., in 14 st. of 4 l., and headed, "For Condemned Malefactors." It is based on the
Prayer-Book Version of Ps. lxxix. 12 (*P.
Works*, 1868–72, vol. iv., p. 460). From this
hymn the following are taken:—

1. **O Thou that hangedst on the tree.** Composed of
sts. i. iv.-vii. in the 1830 *Supplement* of the *Wes. H. Bk.*
2. **O Thou Who hangedst on the tree.** A cento in
the *Hymnary*, 1872, st. i.-iv., very much altered from,
and st. v.-viii. based upon Wesley.
3. **Canst Thou reject our dying prayer?** Composed
of sts. viii.-xi. in the 1830 *Supplement* to the *Wes.
H. Bk.*
4. **Thou that didst hang upon the tree.** A cento in
the American *Sabbath H. Bk.*, 1858, and others. St. i.,
viii., x., xi., altered.
5. **We have no outward righteousness.** Composed of
st. iv.-vii. in the American Meth. Episcopal *Hymns*,
1849, and their *Hymnal*, 1878.

Most of these centos are in extensive use in
G. Britain and America. [J. J.]

O Thou that hearest prayer. *J. Burton, jun.* [*The Holy Spirit desired.*] Appeared in the *Evangelical Magazine*, June
1824, p. 260, in 6 st. of 4 l., headed, "Prayer
for the Holy Spirit," and signed "Essex—
J. B." It was given anonymously in the
Leeds H. Bk., 1853, and has since then passed
in a more or less complete form into a large
number of hymn-books, and more especially
into those of America. [J. J.]

**O Thou that hear'st when sinners
cry.** *I. Watts.* [*Ps. li.*] This is the third
part of his L. M. version of Ps. li. It appeared
in his *Psalms of David, &c.*, 1719, p. 143, in
8 st. of 4 l., headed "The Backslider restored;
or, Repentance and Faith in the Blood of
Christ." In its full form its use is limited,
but the cento therefrom beginning with st. v.,
"A broken heart, my God, my King," is found
in a large number of hymn-books. A second
cento beginning with st. iv. is in the American
Methodist Episcopal *Hymns* 1849, as "Though
I have grieved Thy Spirit, Lord." [J. J.]

O Thou, the contrite sinner's Friend.
Charlotte Elliott. [*Jesus, the Advocate.*] Appeared in her brother's *Ps. & Hys.*, 1st ed.,
1835, in 6 st. of 4 l., and headed with the text,
"We have an Advocate with the Father." In
the Index it was given as by "Wesley" in
error, and this ascription was continued therein for a considerable length of time. Lord
Selborne cleared up the matter in a note to
the hymn in his *Book of Praise*, 1862:—

"Miss Elliott's name is now (through the kindness of
her brother, the Rev. H. V. Elliott, in obtaining for me
her permission) first made public as the authoress of
this hymn. Through some accidental error it is ascribed
in the Rev. H. V. Elliott's collection to Wesley; and
the same mistake has been transferred to Ryle's *Spiritual Songs*, Bourchier's *Solace in Sickness and Sorrow*,
and probably other works."

The use of this hymn has extended to all
English-speaking countries. Usually the
original text is given as in the *H. Comp.*, No.
139. In Thring's *Coll.*, 1882, there is a change
in st. v. l. 2 (suggested by H. H. Pierson, the
musician) from "Darken'd with anguish,
guilt, and fear," to "O'ercast with sorrow, pain,
and fear," which was submitted to Miss Elliott
and received her approval. [J. J.]

O Thou the hope of Israel's host.
[*Perpetual presence of God desired.*] This
cento appeared in T. Gibbons's *Hys. adapted
to Divine Worship, &c.*, 1784, in 4 st. of 4 l.
It is made up of st. i. by Gibbons, and sts.
ii.-iv. from P. Doddridge's "Come, our indulgent Saviour, come" (p. 250, i.), sts. ii., iv.,
v. much altered. It was repeated in the 27th
ed. of Rippon's *Bap. Sel.*, 1827, No. 404, Pt.
ii., and thence into later collections including
Spurgeon's *O. O. H. Bk.*, 1866, &c. [J. J.]

O Thou Who at Thy creature's bar.
C. Wesley. [*Testifying for Christ.*] Pub.
in his *Hys. and Sacred Poems*, 1749, vol. i.
No. 209, in 9 st. of 12 l., and headed, "For a
Person called forth to bear his Testimony." Dr.
Osborn says, in the Wesley P *Works*, 1868–72,
vol. v., p. 134, that "this grand hymn was
more than once published as a supplement to
an apologetic or controversial tract." This
hymn has supplied the following centos:—

1. **Thy power and saving truth to show.** This was
given in the *Wes. H. Bk.*, 1780, as No. 427. It begins
with st. v., and is repeated in several collections.
2. **Thou Jesu, Thou my breast inspire.** This is No.
428 in the *Wes. H. Bk.*, 1780. It begins with st. viii.,
and is repeated in several collections.
3. **Servants of Christ, His truth who know.** This
cento, beginning with st. v. much altered, was given in
the *Mitre H. Bk.*, 1836, No. 218, and was compiled and
altered by E. Osler. It is repeated in *Kennedy*, 1863,
and others.
4. **Lord of the Church, we humbly pray.** This also
appeared in the *Mitre H. Bk.*, 1836, No. 219. It was
repeated in E. Osler's *Church and King*, April 1, 1837.
In the Index to the bound volume of his *Church and
King*, Osler says he based it upon C. Wesley. The text
used by Osler was No. 2 above, as in the *Wes. H. Bk.*
Osler's version, slightly altered, is in Thring's *Coll.*, 1882.

Dr. Jackson, in his official *Memoirs of the
Rev. Charles Wesley, M.A.*, in writing of the
Hys. and Sac. Poems, in which this hymn is
found, says, concerning the hymn:—

"The first volume concludes with a hymn of unusual
length, and of almost unparalleled sublimity and force.
Nothing could give so perfect a view of the spirit in
which he had exercised his ministry, from the time at
which he began his glorious career in Moorfields and
Kennington-common, to this period of his life. In these
noble verses he has strikingly depicted the mighty faith,
the burning love to Christ, the yearning pity for the
souls of men, the heavenly-mindedness, the animating
hope of future glory, which characterized his public
ministry, and which not only enabled him to deliver his
Lord's message before scoffing multitudes, but also
carried him through his wasting labours, and the riots
of Bristol, of Cornwall, of Staffordshire, of Devizes, and
of Ireland, without a murmur. As a witness for Christ
he freely sacrificed his reputation as a man of letters
and of genius; and of life itself, comparatively speaking, he made no account." (*Abridged ed.* 1848, p. 229.)
[J. J.]

O Thou Who by a star didst guide.
J. M. Neale. [*Epiphany.*] Appeared in his

Hys. for Children, 1st series, 1842, No. 23, in 5 st. of 4. l., and headed "The Epiphany, or Twelfth Night." It is usually described as a translation, but in error. Its use is extensive, the original text as in the *H. Comp.*, with the omission of the doxology, being generally followed.   [J. J.]

O Thou Who camest from above. *C. Wesley.* [*For Holiness, and for Earnestness in Work.*] Pub. in his *Short Hymns*, &c., 1762, vol. i. p. 57, in 2 st. of 8 l. (*P. Works*, 1868–72, vol. ix. p. 58). It was included in the *Wes. H. Bk.*, 1780, No. 318, and has become one of the most popular hymns in the Methodist denominations. To some hymn-book compilers the opening lines of st. ii.,

"There let it for Thy glory burn
With inextinguishable blaze,"

have presented difficulties which have caused its omission from many collections. Bp. E. H. Bickersteth, in his *H. Comp.*, has done much towards removing this difficulty by rendering the lines :—

"There let it for Thy glory burn
Unquenched, undimmed in darkest days."

This reading has been adopted by others. Bp. Bickersteth's note thereto explains the cause and meaning of the change :—

"The Editor believes that this admirable hymn would have been far more popular if it had not been for the very long word '*inextinguishable*.' Words of *five* syllables must be admitted into hymns sparingly ; but for a whole congregation to be poised on *six*, practically leads to a hymn being passed by. It is hoped that the line given in the text, which only paraphrases the same thought, will be allowed."

In Martineau's *Hymns*, 1840, and 1873, the opening line of this hymn is changed to "O Thou, Who *deignest* from above."   [J. J.]

O Thou, Who didst with love untold. *Emma Toke, née Leslie.* [*St. Thomas.*] Written in 1851, and contributed to the S. P. C. K. *Hymns for Pub. Worship*, 1852, No. 117, in 4 st. of 4 l., and appointed for St. Thomas's Day. The various forms which these 4 st. of 4 l. have taken are somewhat perplexing, and we can name only those which are of importance :—

1. The original text as above and in later editions of the same collection.
2. An altered version with a doxology by the editors in the Cooke & Denton *Hymnal*, 1853, No. 165. This is repeated in full in the S. P. C. K. *Church Hys.*, 1871 (with one slight variation), and, in an abridged form, in Chope's *Hymnal*, 1864 ; Windle's *Coll.*, and others.
3. In the *Hymnary*, 1872, No. 342 is composed of st. i.–iii. of the *Cooke & Denton* text, and st. iv.–vi. by the editors.

Other altered texts, beginning with the same first line, are to be found. Their departures from the original may be ascertained by a collation with the original as in any edition of the S. P. C. K. *Ps. & Hys.*   [J. J.]

O Thou Who hast Thy servants [children] taught. *H. Alford.* [*Fruits of Holiness.*] 1st pub. in his *Ps. & Hys.*, 1844, No. 61, in 4 st. of 4 l., for the 8th S. after Trinity, and again in his *Year of Praise*, 1867, No. 47, for the 3rd S. after Epiphany. Another form to adapt it for children is, "O Thou Who hast Thy *children* taught." It is composed of sts. i., iv. slightly altered. [J. J.]

O Thou, Who when I did complain. *S. Wesley, sen.* [*Ps. cxvi.*] 1st pub., together with other Psalm-versions, in his *Pious Communicant Rightly Prepared*, 1700, in 7 st. of 4 l. It was repeated in full in J. Wesley's *Coll. of Ps. & Hys.* Charlestown, 1736–7, No. 7 ; in the Wesley *Hys. & Sac. Poems*, 1739 ; in the Wesley *P. Works*, 1868–72, vol. i. p. 123 ; and in the *Wes. H. Bk.*, revised ed., 1875. In this last it forms Pt. i. of No. 614. To it Pt. ii. is added, beginning "What shall I render to my God ?" which is a cento from C. Wesley's rendering of Ps. cxvi. pub. from his MSS. in the *P. Works*, vol. viii., p. 200. Pt. i. is in several collections ; but Pt. ii. is confined to the *Wes. H. Bk.*   [J. J.]

O Thou Whom neither time nor space. *Bp. R. Heber.* [*5th S. in Lent.*] This hymn, based upon the Gospel for the 5th S. in Lent, was pub. in Heber's posthumous *Hymns*, &c., 1827, p. 57, in 4 st. of 4 l. It has passed into several hymn-books, including those for the Harrow and Rugby Schools, the *Leeds H. Bk.*, 1853, Dale's *English H. Bk.*, 1874, and others.   [J. J.]

O Thou Whose justice reigns on high. *I. Watts.* [*Ps. lvi.*] Appeared in his *Ps. of David*, &c., 1719, p. 150, in 10 st. of 4 l., and headed "Deliverance from Oppression and Falsehood ; Or, God's care of His People in answer to Faith and Prayer." Three centos are in C. U. : (1) "O Thou Whose justice reigns on high" ; (2) "God counts the sorrows of His saints," and (3) "In God, most holy, just, and true." These centos are not in extensive use.   [J. J.]

O throned, O crowned with all renown. *Archbishop E. W. Benson.* [*Rogation Days.*] Written during Dr. Benson's Headmastership of Wellington College, and first printed in the *Hymn-Book for the Use of Wellington College*, 1860, in 6 st. of 8 l. In its original or in an abbreviated form it has passed into a large number of hymnals. An altered form of the text is, "O Jesu, crowned with all renown," in *Kennedy*, 1863, and one or two others, is by Dr. Kennedy. It has failed to supplant the original text as above, and as in Thring's *Coll.*, 1882.   [J. J.]

O 'tis enough, my God, my God. *C. Wesley.* [*Penitence and Pardon.*] Given in *Hys. on God's Everlasting Love*, 1741, No. 9, in 11 st. of 6 l. (*P. Works*, 1868–72, vol. iii. p. 18). In the *Wes. H. Bk.*, 1780, Nos. 163 and 164 were included therefrom, the first being st. i.–iii., and the second, "O God, if Thou art love indeed," st. viii.–xi. These hymns have been repeated in other collections. In the first number of the *Arminian Magazine*, 1778, st. i.–ix. were given with the title "Salvation depends not on Absolute Decrees." This title is somewhat defiant, when we remember that Toplady's *Gospel Magazine* was in course of issue at the same time.   [J. J.]

'Ω τῶν δωρεῶν. [Ἀνεστης τριήμερος.]

O Traurigkeit, o Herzeleid. *J. Rist.* [*Easter Eve.*] 1st pub. in the *Erste Zehen* of his *Himlische Lieder*, Lüneburg, 1641, p. 13, in 8 st. of 5 l., entitled "A sorrowful funeral hymn on the mournful entombment of our Saviour Jesus Christ, to be sung on Good Friday," and with this note at p. 16 :—

"The first verse of this funeral hymn, along with its devotional melody, came accidentally into my hands. As I was greatly pleased with it, I added the other seven as they stand here, since I could not be a party to the use of the other verses."

The original hymn appeared in the *Würzburg G. B.* (Roman Catholic), 1628, in 7 st. The st. adopted by Rist is there :—

> "O Trawrigkeit,
> O Hertzenleyd,
> Ist dass dann nicht zu klagen :
> Gottes Vatters einigs Kind,
> Wird zum Grab getragen."

The hymn in this form (i.e. st. i. as in the 1628, and st. ii.-viii. by *Rist*) by its simplicity and force obtained speedy popularity in Germany ; passed into Crüger's *Praxis*, 1656, No. 161, and most later books, and is No. 112 in the *Unv. L. S.*, 1851. Its popularity was greatly aided by the plaintive melody, which appeared with the original hymn in 1628 (see *Bäumker,* i p. 490), *Tr.* as :—

1. **O darkest woe !** This, omitting st. ii., vi., is by Miss Winkworth, given in her *C. B. for England*, 1863, No. 54, with the original melody. Repeated in her *Christian Singers*, 1869, p. 191, and in the Ohio *Lutheran Hyl.*, 1880, No. 78.

2. **O grief, O woe.** A good *tr.*, omitting st. vi., vii., contributed by E. Thring to the *Uppingham and Sherborne School H. Bk.*, 1874, No. 83.

Other trs. are, (1) "O boundless grief," by *J. C. Jacobi*, 1722, p. 19. (2) "O grief of heart," as No. 301 in pt. i. of the *Moravian H. Bk.*, 1754. (3) "O deepest grief," based on the 1754, as No. 119 in the *Moravian H. Bk.*, 1789 (1849, No. 150). [J. M.]

O treuer Heiland Jesu Christ. *C. J. P. Spitta. [Supplication.]* Founded on 1 Cor. v. 17, being also a prayer that the good work may be carried on in us to the end. First pub. in his *Psalter und Harfe*, 2nd Ser., Leipzig, 1843, p. 25, in 9 st. of 4 l., entitled "Thanksgiving and Supplication." *Tr.* as :—

We praise and bless Thee, gracious Lord. A free *tr.* in 10 st., by Miss Borthwick, in *H. L. L.*, 2nd Ser., 1855, p. 45 (1884, p. 104). In full in Bp. Ryle's *Coll.*, 1860, No. 279. St. i.-vi. are included in *Kennedy*, 1863, and in Dr. Thomas's *Augustine H. Bk.*, 1866. St. i., iii., iv., vi., vii., x. are in Allon's *Suppl. Hys.*, 1868, and his *Cong. Psalmist Hyl.*, 1886; the *Bapt. Hyl.*, 1879; Dale's *Eng. H. Bk.*, 1874, &c. Other centos are in the *Church S. S. H. Bk.*, 1868; W. F. Stevenson's *Hys. for Ch. & Home*, 1873; Harland's *C. P. & Hyl.*, 1876; Boardman's *Selection*, Philad., 1861, &c. In the *Hys. of the Spirit*, Boston, U.S., 1864, No. 417, beginning "I praise and bless Thee, O my God," is Miss Borthwick's st. i., iv., and a st. added.

Other trs. are, (1) "Oh faithful Saviour, Jesus Christ," by *Miss Manington*, 1863, p. 57. (2) "We give Thee thanks, O Lord, who hast," by *R. Massie*, 1864, p. 25. [J. M.]

O vos fideles animae. *[All Souls.]* This is the hymn in the Little Office for the dead, in W. Nakatenus's *Coeleste palmetum.* It is at p. 363 in the ed. of 1669, which professes to be unaltered from the original ed. of 1668 ; and is repeated in all later eds., e.g. Mechlin, 1859, p. 264. *Tr.* as : "Ye souls of the faithful," by E. Caswall, in his *Masque of Mary*, &c., 1858, p. 371 ; and his *Hys. & Poems*, 1873, p. 233. [J. M.]

O we des smerzen. *[In Sorrow.]* *Wackernagel*, ii. p. 326, gives this in 20 l. from a

Basel MS. of the 14th cent. Also in F. H. van der Hagen's ed. of the *Minnesinger*, 1838, vol. iii. p. 468. *Tr.* as, "Alas for my sorrow," by *Miss Winkworth*, 1869, p. 45. [J. M.]

O weep not o'er thy children's tomb. *Bp. R. Heber. [Holy Innocents' Day.]* Pub. in his posthumous *Hymns*, &c., 1827, p. 20, in 4 st. of 4 l. It is in use in its original form, and as "Why weep'st thou by thy children's tomb ?" It is one of the least popular of the author's hymns. [J. J.]

O Welt, sieh hier dein Leben. *P. Gerhardt. [Passiontide]* 1st pub. in the 3rd ed., 1648, of Crüger's *Praxis pietatis melica*, No. 119, in 16 st. of 8 l., reprinted in Wackernagel's ed. of his *Geistliche Lieder*, No. 15; Bachmann's ed., No. 8, and included as No. 113 in the *Unv. L. S.*, 1851. It is a thoughtful meditation on the Passion. St. iii.-v. were favourites with J S Bach and used by him in his St. Matthew and St. John *Passion Music.* *Tr.* as :—

1. **Extended on a cursed tree.** A free *tr.* in L. M. of st. i., iii., iv., vi., viii.-xi., xvi., by J. Wesley, in *Hys. & Sacred Poems*, 1740 (*P. Works*, 1868-72, vol. i. p. 232), and thence, as No. 23, in the *Wes. H. Bk.*, 1780, and since in other hymnals of the Methodist family. Included in full, as No. 402, in the 1857 ed. of Mercer's *C. P. & H. Bk.* (Ox. ed., 1864, No. 172, omitting the *tr.* of st. xi.). The *trs.* of st. ix.-xi., xvi., beginning "My Saviour, how shall I proclaim," were included in the American *Sabbath H. Bk.*, 1858, and the Baptist *Service of Song*, Boston, U.S., 1871.

2. **See, World, upon the bloody tree.** A C. M. version by P. H. Molther of st. i.-x. as No. 118, in the *Moravian H. Bk.*, 1742, and thence, as No. 442, in pt. i. of the *Moravian H. Bk.*, 1754. In 1789, No. 96 (1886, No. 109) it is altered to "See, world, upon the shameful tree." In his *Christian Psalmist*, 1825, No. 280, Montgomery omitted the *tr.* of st. ii., v., vi. In 1856, st. i., iii.-vi. were included in the *Evan. Union H. Bk.*

3. **O, World! behold upon the tree.** A good *tr.*, omitting st. vii., by Miss Winkworth, in the 2nd Ser., 1858, of her *Lyra Ger.*, p. 29, and thence in Schaff's *Christ in Song*, ed. 1869, p. 174. Her *tr.* of st. i., iii.-v., xii., xv., xvi. were included, slightly altered, in the *Hymnary*, 1872, and that of st. xi.-xiii., xv., xvi. altered and beginning "Lord, be Thy Cross before our sight," in *Kennedy*, 1863.

Other trs. are, (1) "Here, World, see thy Redeemer." In the *Supplement to German Psalmody*, ed. 1765, p. 16 ; in *Select H. from German Psalmody*, Tranquebar, 1754, p. 28. (2) "O World! attention lend it," by J. Gambold, as No. 442 in pt. i. of the *Moravian H. Bk.*, 1754. In 1789, No. 89, altered to "O World, see thy Creator" (1886, No. 94). (3) "O World! see thy Life languish," by J. D. Burns, in the *Family Treasury*, 1859, pt. i. p. 54, and in his *Memoir & Remains*, 1869, p. 246. (4) "See, World! thy Life assailed," by J. Kelly, 1867, p. 54. (5) "Here, World, thy great Salvation see," by *Dr. J. Guthrie*, 1869, p. 87. (6) "O World! see here suspended," as No. 1009, in Reid's *Praise Bk.*, 1872. (7) "Behold, O World, thy Life, thy Lord," by *Dr. R. Maguire*, 1883, p. 143. [J. M.]

O what a lonely path were ours. *Sir E. Denny. [Jesus ever with us.]* Given in the Appendix to *Hymns for the Poor of the Flock, circa* 1838 ; in the author's *Selection*, 1839, No. 260 ; in the *Ps. and Hys.*, Lond., D. Walther, 1842, Pt. i., No. 72, and other and later Plymouth Brethren collections. In some hymn-books it is abridged to 5 st., and in others it is sometimes attributed to "T. Moore" in error.   [J. J.]

O! what, if we are Christ's. *Sir H. W. Baker.* [*Feasts of Martyrs.*] 1st pub. in Murray's *Hymnal*, 1852, No. 126, in 6 st. of 4 l., and headed " Ye shall indeed drink of My cup, and be baptized with the baptism that I am baptized with." It was repeated in the following year in the Cooke & Denton *Church Hymnal*, No. 166, where it was appointed for the " Conversion of St. Paul." This was followed in 1857 by the *Salisbury H. Bk.*, No. 161, where it was given as one of the hymns for the " Festivals of Martyrs." In 1859 it appeared in the trial copy of *H. A. & M.*, No. 126, with st. iv., l. 2, changed from " Ever like them to bear," to " *Like them in faith* to bear," and the substitution of a new doxology. These changes were retained in the authorized *H. A. & M.*, 1861, and in the revised ed., 1875. Also found in a large number of hymn-books.   [J. J.]

O when my righteous Judge shall come. [*The Judgment Day.*] Miller's account of this hymn in his *Singers and Songs, &c.,* 1869, p. 182, is :—

" It was in this fourth edition [of the *Lady Huntingdon H. Bk.*] that there appeared for the first time the striking and well-known hymn by the Countess ' Oh ! when my righteous Judge shall come.' . . . It is the second part of a piece on the Judgment Day which has a first part of five verses, beginning ' We soon shall hear the midnight cry.' "

This statement by Miller is based upon information which he received from Daniel Sedgwick. On turning to D. Sedgwick's own copy of the edition of the *Lady Huntingdon H. Bk.* referred to by Miller, we find, first, two separate and distinct hymns numbered 146 and 147, and beginning respectively, "We soon shall hear the midnight cry," and "O when my righteous Judge shall come;" and, secondly, a note in pencil in Sedgwick's handwriting which reads, "Hymn 146 and 147 seem to be both by the same Author—perhaps the Countess's." On turning to Sedgwick's copy of Miller's *Singers and Songs*, we find, written by Sedgwick opposite the words quoted by Miller as above, the following :—

" Upon the testimony of the Rev. Thomas Young of Canterbury this hymn was composed by Charles Wesley. None doubt it was wrote at the suggestion of the Countess by C. Wesley."

It is clear that these guesses of Sedgwick are worthless. The history of the hymn, so far as we have been able to trace it, is as follows :—

(1) In an enlarged edition of the *Lady Huntingdon Coll.*, circa 1774 [see **Huntingdon Hymn-books, Lady,** § iv.], it was given, together with " We soon shall hear the midnight cry " (as Nos. 146 and 147), in 4 st. of 6 l., and in common with all the rest of the hymns in the collection without signature. Both hymns were subsequently omitted from all official editions of the hymn-book, a fact which tells greatly against the guess that they were written by the Countess.

(2) We next find both hymns in the 1775 *Appendix* by L. Coughlan to J. Bazlee's *Select Coll. of Ps. & Hys. . . . for the Use of the Congregation of Cumberland Street* [London] *Chapel.* [Lady Huntingdon.] They are numbered 295, 296. [See **Bazlee, J.,** p. 119, i.]

(3) " We soon shall hear the midnight cry," is seldom found after this date; but its companion hymn, " O when my righteous Judge shall come," appears in Rippon's Bap. *Sel.*, 1787, No. 579, as " When Thou, my righteous Judge, shalt come." This was repeated in numerous hymn-books in G. Britain and America, and is the popular form of the hymn.

The most, therefore, that can be said with regard to its authorship is that it is " *Anon. Lady Huntingdon's H. Bk.*, circa 1774 : *Rippon's Bap. Sel.* 1787."   [J. J.]

O where shall rest be found. *J. Montgomery.* [*The Present and the Future.*] Written for the Anniversary Sermons of the Red Hill Wesleyan Sunday School, Sheffield, which were preached on March 15 and 16, 1818, and printed for use on a broadsheet, in 6 st. of 4 l. It was included in Cotterill's *Sel.*, 1819, No. 172, in 3 st. of 8 l., and with st. v. of the original rewritten thus :—

Broadsheet, " Lord God of grace and truth
1818.   Teach us that death to shun ;
         Nor let us from our earliest youth
         For ever be undone."

Cotterill, " Lord God of *truth and grace!*
1819.   Teach us that death to shun ;
         Lest we be driven from Thy face,
         And evermore undone."

The latter text was repeated in Montgomery's *Christian Psalmist*, 1825, No. 514, with " Lest we be driven," altered to " Lest we be *banish'd* from Thy face," in st. iii., l. 3. This form of the text was repeated in his *Original Hys.*, 1853, No. 216, and is that in C. U.   [J. J.]

O! wherefore, Lord, doth Thy dear praise. *T. H. Gill.* [*Praise perfected by Holiness.*] Written in 1849, and 1st pub. in G. Dawson's *Ps. & Hys.*, 1853 ; and again in the author's *Golden Chain, &c.*, 1869, No. 25, in 7 st. of 4 l., and entitled "Praise Perfected by Holiness." It is in C. U. in G. Britain and America. Although usually abbreviated, it is given in full in Dale's *English H. Bk.*, 1874, No. 20.   [J. J.]

O Word of God Incarnate. *Bp. W. W. How.* [*Holy Scriptures.*] Written for and 1st pub. in the 1867 *Supplement* to Morrell and How's *Ps. & Hys.* It has been repeated in a large number of hymn-books in G. Britain and America, and is one of the author's most popular hymns. It is usually given unaltered and unabridged as in *Church Hymns*, 1871.
                         [J. J.]

O worship the King, All-glorious above. *Sir R. Grant.* [*Ps. civ.*] This version of Ps. civ. is W. Kethe's rendering of the same psalm in the Anglo-Genevan *Psalter* of 1561, reset by Sir R. Grant in the same metre but in a less quaint and much more ornate style, as a quotation of Kethe's st. i., iii. will show :—

" My soule praise the Lord,
     speake good of his Name
   O Lord our great God
     how doeft thou appeare,
   So passing in glorie,
     that great is thy fame,
   Honour and maieftie,
     in thee fhine moft cleare.

" His chamber beames lie,
     in the clouds full fure,
   Which as his chariot,
     are made him to beare.
   And there with much fwiftneff
     his courfe doth endure :
   Vpon the wings riding,
     Of winds in the aire."

Sir R. Grant's version was given in Bickersteth's *Ch. Psalmody*, 1833, No. 17; in Elliott's *Ps. and Hys.*, 1835; and in Lord Glenelg's ed. of Grant's *Sacred Poems*, 1839, p. 33. From the Preface to Elliott's *Ps. & Hys.* we find that the text in *Bickersteth* was not authorized. It was altered from a source at present unknown to us. The authorized text is in the *Hy. Comp.*, 1876, with st. ii., l. 3, thus—

" *His chariots of wrath the deep thunderclouds form.*"

This text with the omission of the " the " is in extensive use in all English-speaking countries. It is also in use in an abbreviated and slightly altered form as in *H. A. & M.*, 1861; and in the full form, but still altered as before, in *H. A. & M.*, 1875. The 1839 text is in *Church Hys.*, 1871; *H. Comp.*, 1876; *Thring's Coll.*, 1882, and others. It has been *tr.* into Latin by R. Bingham, in his *Hymno. Christ. Latina*, 1871, p. 143, as, " Glorioso ferte Regi vota vestra carmine."   [J. J.]

O worship the Lord in the beauty of holiness. *J. S. B. Monsell.* [*Epiphany*; or, *Divine Worship*.] This hymn for the Epiphany is found in two forms, both by Dr. Monsell, and each is in C. U. The first and most extensively used is the original, which opens with " O worship," &c. It was pub. in his *Hys. of Love and Praise*, 1863, p. 103, in 5 st. of 4 l. It is found, sometimes altered, in a large number of hymn-books in G. Britain and America. Orig. text in Thring's *Coll.*, 1882. The second form is Dr. Monsell's revision of the 1863 text which he made for, and included in, his *Parish Hymnal* in 1873, No. 85, as, " Worship the Lord in the beauty of holiness." This is almost unknown.   [J. J.]

O ye immortal throng. *P. Doddridge.* [*Christ seen of Angels.*] In the D. MSS. this hymn is No. 35, in 7 st. of 8 l., is headed " Christ seen of Angels, from 1 Tim. iii. 16," and is dated " Feb. 13, 173⅘." It was pub. by J. Orton in his posthumous ed. of Doddridge's *Hymns*, &c., 1755, No. 304, with the same heading, but with slight variations in the text. In J. D. Humphreys's ed. of the *Hymns*, &c., 1839, No. 330, it begins " Ye bright immortal throng." This text is repeated in Snepp's *Songs of G. & G.*, 1872. Usually Orton's text of 1755 is followed. The S. P. C. K. *Church Hymns* is an exception in favour of a text which is much altered, and a doxology unknown to Doddridge.   [J. J.]

Oakeley, Frederick, D.D., youngest s. of Sir Charles Oakeley, Bart., sometime Governor of Madras, was b. at Shrewsbury, Sept. 5, 1802, and educated at Christ Church, Oxford (B.A. 1824). In 1825 he gained a University prize for a Latin Essay; and in 1827 he was elected a Fellow of Balliol. Taking Holy Orders, he was a Prebendary of Lichfield Cathedral, 1832; Preacher at Whitehall, 1837; and Minister of Margaret Chapel, Margaret Street, London, 1839. In 1845 he resigned all his appointments in the Church of England, and was received into the Roman Communion. Subsequently he became a Canon of the Pro-Cathedral in the Roman Catholic ecclesiastical district of Westminster. He d. January 29, 1880. Miller (*Singers and Songs of the Church*, 1869, p. 497), writing from information supplied to him by Canon Oakeley, says :—

" He traces the beginning of his change of view to the lectures of Dr. Charles Lloyd, Regius Professor, delivered at Oxford about the year 1827, on the ' History and Structure of the Anglican Prayer Book.' About that time a

great demand arose at Oxford for Missals and Breviaries, and Canon Oakeley, sympathising with the movement, co-operated with the London booksellers in meeting that demand. . . . . He promoted the [Oxford] movement, and continued to move with it till, in 1845, he thought it right to draw attention to his views, to see if he could continue to hold an Oxford degree in conjunction with so great a change in opinion. The question having been raised, proceedings were taken against him in the Court of Arches, and a sentence given that he was perpetually suspended unless he retracted. He then resigned his Prebendal stall at Lichfield, and went over to the Church of Rome."

Canon Oakeley's poetical works included :—

(1) *Devotions Commemorative of the Most Adorable Passion of Our Lord and Saviour Jesus Christ*, 1842; (2) *The Catholic Florist*; (3) *The Youthful Martyrs of Rome, a Christian Drama*, 1856; (4) *Lyra Liturgica; Reflections in Verse for Holy Days and Seasons*, 1865.

Canon Oakeley also published several prose works, including a *tr.* of J. M. Horst's *Paradise of the Christian Soul*, London, Burns, 1850. He is widely known through his *tr.* of the " Adeste fideles " (p. 20, i.). Several of his original hymns are also in Roman Catholic collections.   [J. J.]

Occom, Samson (sometimes given as *Ockum*, and again as *Occum*), a Mohican Indian, was b. at Norwich, Connecticut, in 1723. He was converted from Paganism under G. Whitefield, in 1739-40, and educated by the Revs. E. Wheelock and Benjamin Pomeroy. In 1748 he removed to Long Island and laboured amongst a remnant of his people. In 1759 he received Presbyterian orders, visited England, 1766-67, where he preached often (once for J. Newton at Olney), and with acceptance, and raised about ten thousand pounds for Dartmouth College, and for Indian education. His later life was spent first among his own race on Long Island, and, from 1786, in Oneida County, N.Y. He d. in July, 1792. Occom's *Choice Collection of Hys. and Spiritual Songs* was pub. at New London, Connecticut, in 1774 (2nd ed. 1785). He is credited as the author of several hymns, but none of those hymns are found in his own collection. They are :—

1. **Now the shades of night are gone.** *Morning.* The date of 1770 is given to this hymn, but on insufficient authority. No evidence connects it with Occom, though it has not, on the other hand, been claimed for any other. It is first found in the Hartford *Congregational Coll.*, 1799, and was brought into general use by the *Prayer-Book Coll.*, 1826. It is in several modern hymn-books.

2. **Awaked by Sinai's awful sound.** *Peace with God.* By this hymn, from its extensive use, Occom is chiefly known. We are satisfied, however, that in this form it is not his. It is first found in the *Connecticut Evangelical Magazine*, July, 1802, p. 39, " communicated as original." It is however altered from " Waked by the gospel's powerful sound," which is No. 285 in Josiah Goddard's *Coll.*, Walpole, N. H.,1801, and possibly earlier, This older text is probably Occom's own composition.

3. **When shall we three meet again?** *Parting.* This once popular hymn has been ascribed to Occom, but the claim is doubtful. We find it in no collection earlier than Leavitt's *Christian Lyre*, 1830, although it is known to have been sung at an earlier date. It is sometimes given as, " When shall we *all* meet again?" as in H. W. Beecher's *Plymouth Coll.*, 1855. [F. M. B.]

Octoechus, the Greater and Lesser. [Greek Hymnody, § xiv.]

Ode. ['Ωδή. 'Ωιδή.] [Greek Hymnody, § xvi. 10.]

O'er the shoreless waste of waters. *Bp. W. W. How.* [*Holy Baptism.*] Written in 1870 for the S. P. C. K. *Church Hymns* and pub. therein in 1871. It is "intended to embody the doctrinal teaching of the Church on Baptism, without reference to any individual case ; so that it may be sung before or after catechisings or sermons on the subject." (*Church Hys.*, folio ed., p. li.)   [J. J.]

O'er those gloomy hills of darkness.
W. Williams. [*Missions.*] This hymn was pub. (not in his *Hosannah*, 1759, as sometimes stated, but) in his *Gloria in Excelsis : or, Hys. of Praise to God the Lamb, Carmarthen, John Ross*, 1772, No. 37, in 7 st. of 6 l. (Orig. text in *Lyra Brit.*, 1867, p. 631.) It is known to modern hymn-books in the following forms :—

1. **O'er those gloomy hills of darkness.** The original in full, but more often abbreviated.
2. **O'er the gloomy hills of darkness.** This was given in Rippon's Bap. *Sel.*, 1787, No. 428, with slight alterations, and the omission of st. v. and vii. In the 27th ed., 1827, it was enlarged to 6 sts. by the addition of "Every creature, living, breathing," &c. This text is repeated in Spurgeon's *O. O. H. Bk.*, 1866.
3. **O'er the realms of pagan darkness.** This appeared in Cotterill's *Sel.*, 8th ed., 1819, No. 239, in 4 st. of 6 l. It can hardly be said to be Williams's text rewritten, there is so little of Williams therein. It would be more accurate to say that it is based upon Williams, as the first stanza of each will show :—

Original. "O'er those gloomy Hills of Darkness
          Look, my Soul, be still and gaze,
        All the Promises do travail
          On a glorious Day of Grace.
          Blessed Jubil, &c.
        Let the glorious Morning dawn."

Cotterill. "O'er the *realms of pagan* darkness
          Let the eye of pity gaze ;
        See the kindreds of the people,
          Lost in sin's bewildering maze :
            Darkness brooding
          On the face of all the earth."

This arrangement is in several hymn-books in Great Britain and America.

4. **Light of them that sit in darkness.** This, in the Irish *Church Hymnal*, 1873, and others, begins with st. ii. of *Cotterill's* text as above.

The use of this hymn in these various forms is extensive.   [J. J.]

Of justice and of grace I sing.
I. Watts. [*Ps. ci.*] Pub. in his *Ps. of David*, 1719, p. 258, in 6 st. of 4 l. It is in use in its original form, and as, "Mercy and judgment I will sing," in the Islington *Ps. & Hys.*, 1862, and as, "Mercy and judgment will I sing," in the *Wes. H. Bk.*, 1875. Although found in these three forms its use is limited.   [J. J.]

Of Thy love some gracious token.
T. Kelly. [*Close of Service.*] 1st pub. in his *Coll. of Ps. & Hys.*, Dublin, 1802, No. 256, in the following form :—

    "Of Thy love, some gracious token,
      Grant us, Lord, before we go ;
    Bless Thy word which has been spoken,
      Life and peace on all bestow ;
    When we join the world again,
      Let our hearts with Thee remain !
        O direct us,
        And protect us !
      Till we gain the heav'nly shore,
      Where Thy people want no more."

This text was rewritten and included in the 27th ed. of Rippon's Bap. *Sel.*, 1827, No. 373, Pt. 2, as :—

    "*Grant us, Lord,* some gracious token
      Of Thy love before we *part ;*
    Crown Thy word which has been spoken,
      Life and peace *to each impart ;*
        And all blessings
      Which shall sanctify the heart."

Both forms of the text are in C. U. in Great Britain and America.   [J. J.]

Offertorium.
This is the name of the anthem said or sung directly after the *Nicene Creed*, while, in ancient times, the offerings of bread and wine were being made by the faithful laity. It was generally taken from Holy Scripture, and most frequently from the Book of Psalms. Occasionally it was drawn from some other source. We subjoin a specimen of a metrical Offertory taken from the Mass of the Compassion or Lamentation of the Blessed Virgin Mary, in the *Sarum Missal* of 1497 :—

    " Christum cruce mortuum
      Nostros ob defectus
    Maesta mater aspicit
      Pios per affectus ;
    Et clamavit lacerans
      Capillos et pectus,
    Heu me ! jacet Filius
      Meus hic despectus,
    Nuper inter millia
      Qui fuit electus
    Sicut myrrhae fasciculus
      Meus sic dilectus."

Reprinted from the Burntisland ed. of the *Sarum Missal*, 1861, col. 923*.   [F. E. W.]

Offord, Robert M.,
s. of an English "open-communion" Baptist, was b. at St. Austell, Cornwall, Sept. 17, 1846. In 1870 he removed to America, where he was associated for some time with the Methodists, but subsequently joined the Reformed Dutch Church in 1878. He is editor of the *New York Observer.* To that paper he contributed :—

1. Jesus, heed me, lost and dying. *Lent.*
2. It is no untried way. *Christ's Burden.*

No. 1 appeared on Jan. 25th, and No. 2 on Feb. 1st, 1883. They were revised for *Laudes Domini*, N. Y., 1884 (Duffield's *English Hys.*, N. Y., 1886).   [J. J.]

Oft as the bell with solemn toll.
J. Newton. [*Death and Burial.*] 1st pub. in his *Twenty Six Letters on Religious Subjects by Omicron*, 1774, in 7 st. of 4 l., and entitled "The Passing Bell." It was repeated in the same year in R. Conyers's *Coll. of Ps. & Hys.*, No. 364, and again in the *Olney Hymns*, 1779, Bk. ii., No. 74. It is found in its full, or in an abridged form, in a few modern collections. In R. Bingham's *Hymno. Christ. Latina*, 1871, st. i., iii., v., vi. are rendered into Latin as "Ah ! quoties animam solito campana sonore."   [J. J.]

Ogilvie, John,
D.D., eldest s. of the Rev. James Ogilvie, or Ogilvy, of Aberdeen, was b. at Aberdeen in 1733. After studying at the University of Aberdeen (Marischal College), which, in 1766, conferred upon him the degree of D.D., he became parish minister of Lumphanan, Aberdeenshire, in 1759, and of Midmar, Aberdeenshire, in 1760. He d. at Midmar, Nov. 17, 1813. He pub. a number of poetical works, and among others *Poems on Several Subjects*, in 2 vols. (London, 1769). This includes his well known paraphrase of *Psalm cxlviii.*— "Begin, my soul, the exalted lay." He was a member of the Committee appointed by the General Assembly of 1775, to revise the *Scottish Translations and Paraphrases* of 1745, and is said to have contributed No. 62, "Lo, in the last of days behold " (p. 682, ii.), to the 1781 authorized ed. of the same. [Scottish Trs. and Paraphs.]   [J. M.]

Οἱ παῖδες εὐσεβεία. [Χριστὸς γεννᾶται.]

'Ωιδη. [Greek Hymnody, § xvi. 10.]

Οἶκος. [Greek Hymnody, § xvi: 5.]

Old Everton, in the *Gospel Magazine,* 1775–77, i.e. the *Rev. John Berridge.*

Old Version. I. *Introduction.*—The Old Metrical Version of the Psalms, obsolete as it seems, has exercised an enduring influence on the metres and general type of our hymnody; still possesses an interest for a small circle of lovers of curious books; and has even something of an historical value. The parallel of accidents between its originator, Thomas Sternhold, groom of the robes to Henry VIII., and Clement Marot, valet of the bed-chamber to Francis I., who originated the French Metrical Psalter, has been frequently remarked. There is, however, little real resemblance between the godly, sober Englishman and the brilliant poet of France; nor beyond the fact that Marot's success may have suggested the task, is there any trace of Marot's influence on Sternhold. Sternhold's work is distinctly English, and in its first conception scarcely pretended to literary excellence. His aim was to make sacred ballads for the people; with one exception (120th P.M.), he wrote in ballad metres (S.M. (25th) and C.M.); and three-quarters of the *Version* are composed, either by him or his disciples Hopkins and Norton, in common metre, which has thus almost become a consecrated measure, but for its use by the Lake poets, and for Thackeray's caricatures of street doggerel. The early and lasting success of the *Version* are both due to this adoption of a few simple metres. As Puritanism increased, music decayed. The *Scottish Psalter* of 1564 is in strong contrast with the English one from the variety of its metres, and shows, both in the earlier pieces by Whittingham and Kethe, and the later ones by Craig and Pont, its affinity with the Psalms of Marot and Beza: but the revised *Scottish Psalter* of 1650 was reduced to the monotonous uniformity of the English C. M., which had proved of greater practical usefulness. To this English ballad element there was added, in the Genevan editions, an imitation of the metres and tunes of Marot and Beza. And in the Elizabethan editions a slight German influence is discernible.

II. *Early Editions.*

Sternhold's psalms were originally composed for his own "Godly solace" (*Strype*) and sung by him to his organ. Some may have been written in Henry VIII.'s reign. They were overheard by the young King Edward, and repeated in his presence. The 1st ed., undated, was dedicated to him, and contains 19 psalms. Its title is:—

Certayne Psalmes, chosē out of the Psalter of Dauid and drawē into Englishe metre by Thomas Sternhold, grome of ye kynge's Maiesties roobes. [*Brit. Mus.*]

A 2nd ed. was pub. posthumously in 1549 and contained 37 psalms. The title is:—

Al such Psalmes of David as Thomas Sternholde, late grome of the Kynge's Maiestie's roobes did in his lyfe tyme drawe into English metre. [*Brit. Mus.*]

A 3rd ed. of 1551 (*Bodleian*) by Whitchurch contains, at the end of Sternhold's psalms, seven others by J. H. (*John Hopkins*), who in

a short preface says that he does not deem them "in any parte to be compared with" [Sternhold's] "most exquisite doynges." There were reprints of this book, both by Whitchurch and John Kyngston in 1553 (*Cotton*).

III. *Anglo-Genevan Psalters.*

During the troubles at Frankfort among the congregation of exiles, the Puritan party resolved to frame an order of Service in place of the Book of Common Prayer. This order was drawn up by Knox, Whittingham, Gylby, Fox and Cole, whilst still at Frankfort, but was not printed till they had settled at Geneva. It appeared as:—

The forme of prayers and ministration of The Sacraments, &c., used in the Englishe Congregation at Geneua: and approved by the famous and godly learned man, John Caluyn. Imprinted at Geneva by John Crespin, MDLVI.

The progress of the *Psalter* is connected with the editions of this book, which contain, immediately before the Catechism, the metrical psalms, with independent pagination. The separate titlepage of the 1556 edition is:—

One and Fiftie Psalmes of Dauid in Englishe metre, whereof 37 were made by Thomas Sterneholde, ād the rest by others. Cōferred with the hebrewe and in certeyn places corrected as the text and sens of the Prophete required. (*Bodleian*).

The psalms are those by Sternhold and Hopkins, pub. in 1551, with 7 fresh ones, which, from later editions, are known to be by Whittingham. A metrical rendering of the Ten Commandments by Whittingham is appended. Among these psalms is the earliest L. M. "O Lord, consider my distress" (51st). The Psalms of Sternhold and Hopkins had undergone a revision, probably by Whittingham, who was a good Hebraist. The general preface to *The Forme of Prayers,* &c., contains, among other interesting remarks on the value of metrical psalms, an apology for altering the revered words of Sternhold. (It may be noted that Warton's ridicule of the bridegroom "ready trimmed" (shaved), in Ps. 19, really falls on the revisers, not on Sternhold.) This revised text was permanently adopted in all subsequent editions of the *Psalter.*

The contents of a lost edition of *The Forme of Prayers,* &c. (1558), cannot be ascertained. But Livingston, in his splendid work on the *Scottish Psalter,* to which this article is largely indebted, has conjectured, for reasons which will appear below, that it contained 9 fresh psalms by Whittingham, and 2 by Pullain. (See 1905 SUPPLEMENT.)

In 1561 and probably in the earlier half of the year appeared another edition of *The Forme,* of which there is an unique copy in St. Paul's Cathedral Library. The *Psalter* in it is entitled:—

Four Score and seven psalmes of David in English mitre by Thomas sternecholde and others: conferred with the Hebrue, and in certeine places corrected, as the sense of the Prophet requireth, whereunto are added the Songe of Simeon, the then commandements and the Lords prayer. (The account here given is from a collation by Dr. Simpson, Librarian of St. Paul's, and another by Major Crawford in *Notes and Queries,* June 2, 1883.)

The contents of this book are a reprint of all the pieces in 1556, with the addition of 9 fresh psalms by Whittingham; 2 by John Pullain, already, it is probable, published in 1558; 24 with the signature of William

Kethe (*W. Ke*); and the L.M. 100th Ps. ("All people that" (p. 43, ii.)), set to its familiar tune (which had appeared in the French Psalter of 1551 and was set there to the 134th Ps.), and with the extraordinary signature "Tho. Ster." There are also a version of "The Song of Simeon" and two of "The Lord's Prayer" by Whittingham; a third, of the "Lord's Prayer," anonymous, which is known from the English Psalters to be by D. Cox; and a prose prayer to be said before a man begins his work. It is in this edition that the influence of Marot and Beza's Version is most perceptible. Several of the psalms, by Pullain (148th), and Whittingham (e.g. 121, 124, 127), and most of Kethe's, are either imitations of French metres, or are set to French tunes. There are 60 tunes, 18 of which are from Marot and Beza's Version; the rest (except Pss. 67th, 125th) are in the 1560 ed. below. This is probably the book alluded to in a passage in "A Brieff Discours off the Troubles begonne at Franckford":—

"The congregation prepared themselves to depart (from Geneva), savinge certeine whiche remained behinde the reste, to witt, to finishe the Bible (the Geneva Bible) and the Psalmes bothe in meeter and prose, whiche were already begoon," &c. (The prose Psalms were finished, and presented to Queen Elizabeth. The metrical Psalter was only advanced another stage towards completion.)

Later Editions.

Two further editions may be added, although they to a certain extent anticipate the after history, in order to present here a complete view of the development of the Psalter at Geneva. There is an unique edition in the Peterborough Cathedral Library, incorporated in "*The Forme of Prayers and Ministration of The Sacraments, &c., used in the English Churche at Geneua approued and receyued by the Church of Scotland*," pub. by Henri Mareschal (no place of pub.). The origin of this book is puzzling. The title-page, table of contents, calendar, and sonnet by William Steuart are identical with the Scottish Psalter, 1565. But the Psalms are not from the Scottish Psalter. The 1561 edition (*St. Paul's*) is first reprinted in block. Then all the remaining numbers are filled up from the English Psalter, omitting its duplicate psalms. At the end are printed "The Commandements of Almighty God" ("Attend, my people"), "A Prayer" ("The Spirit of grace graunt us, O Lord"), "The Lordes Prayer," *D. Coxe*, "The XII Articles of the Christian Faith" ("All my belief," &c.), "A Prayer unto the holy Ghost to be song before the Sermon," "The Lamentation of a Sinner" (2nd), (beginning of it lost), "A thankesgeuing after the receauing of the Lorde's Supper," and "The Song of Simeon" (*W. Whit.*). In 1569 an edition of "The Forme of Prayers," &c., pub. by Crespin at Geneva (*Bodleian*), contains a reprint of one of the English complete editions of the Psalters (app.) with the substitution of Whittingham's version of the "Nunc dimittis." The singular feature in both these editions is the preference of the English Psalter to the Scottish, notwithstanding the far closer affinity that existed between the Churches of Scotland and Geneva. The 1566 edition appears entirely ignorant of the special psalms of the Scottish version of 1564. The 1569 edition adopts the English version by preference, and as a consequence rejects the majority even of the genuine Genevan psalms, written by Kethe. A notice may here be inserted of the unique reprint of the 1561 edition existing in the Britwell Library of S. Christie Miller, Esq., and through his kindness collated by Major Crawford specially for this work. It is slightly smaller (4¾ by 3¾ inches) than the St. Paul's book, and, unlike that, is in black letter. The title is the same, but there is no imprint of the place of publication. It was, however, undoubtedly printed in Great Britain, perhaps in Edinburgh, probably for the use of the Genevan exiles. Many of the misprints of the Genevan edition, due to foreign printers, are corrected; and there are a few slight variations in the melodies. But the only substantial change is the substitution (Ps. 100) of the signature of *W. Ke* (*Kethe*) for the obvious blunder of the Genevan

edition (*Tho. Ster.*). It is from this reprint of the Genevan 1561 edition apparently that the psalms are taken for incorporation in the complete Scottish Psalter of 1564, rather than from the Genevan edition itself. Fuller details of this collation than we could embody in this article are given by Major Crawford in *Notes and Queries*, June 2, 1883, pp. 423-424.

IV. *English Editions,* 1559-60.

Meanwhile psalm-singing had become a powerful religious engine in England. In 1559 (see Watts's *Bibliotheca*) a now lost edition of the *Psalter* was published. It was probably the illicit edition referred to in the Stationers' Registers:—

"Recevyd of John Daye for a fyne for printing of serten copies without license . . . a quartron of psalmes with notes, the 2d of Octobre, 1559, xii.ˢ" [A quartron is probably 250 sheets.]

In 1560 appeared the:—

Psalmes of David in Englishe metre by Thomas Sternehold and others, conferred with the Ebrue and in certeine places corrected, as the sense of the Prophete required: and the note ioyned withall. Very mete to be used of all sorts of people privatly for their Godly solace and comfort: laiying aparte all ungodly songes & ballades, which tende only to the norishing of vice and corrupting of youth. Newly set fourth and allowed according to the order appointed in the Quene's Maiestie's Iniunctions.

There is no name of publisher. The only known copy is at Christ Church, Oxford. It contains 65 psalms, viz.: the Psalms of 1556, together with the 9 by Whittingham and 2 by Pullain, which we have already noted in 1561 (*Geneva*), 2 new ones by Robert Wisedome (67th, 125th), and 1 anonymous psalm (95th). The list of appended pieces is also extended. There are metrical versions of "Magnificat," "Nunc Dimittis," (not Whittingham's, in 1561 (*Geneva*)), the "XII Articles of the Christen fayth," and "The Lord's Prayer," by D. Coz(x). At the end of Whittingham's "Ten Commandments," reprinted from 1556, is added a metrical version of the response ("Lord have mercy upon us," &c.), entitled "An addition." There may have been other pieces, the volume being imperfect. The psalms by Wisedome, though P. M., are not French in character, but German, in the style of Coverdale. The 67th is derived from Luther, but borrows in the first verse from Coverdale's version. (See the psalm in Livingston's *Scottish Psalter*: it is found only in this 1560 edition.) Cox's rendering of the Lord's Prayer is also a transcript of Luther. (See "Vater unser im Himmelreich.") This affinity with the German will appear more largely in the succeeding English editions. The appended pieces are an indication of a new aim in the English editions, which will appear more clearly in the next section. There are 42 tunes, 24 of which are from the 1556 edition (*Geneva*), with 18 new ones, 6 of which are from the French Version of Marot and Beza (*Livingston.*)

V. *In* 1561

appeared an edition of great value in regard to the development of the English *Psalter*. The title-page is:—

Psalmes of David in Englishe Metre, by Thomas Sternehold and others: conferred with the Ebrue, & in certein places corrected (as the sense of the Prophet required) and the Note ioyned withall. Veri mete to be vsed of all sortes of people priuatly for their godly solace and comfort: laiying aparte all vngodlye Songes and Ballades which tende only to the nourishing of vice, and corrupting of youth. Newly set fourth and allowed, accordyng to the order appointed in the Quenes Maiesties Iniunctions, 1560. *James V. If any be afflicted let him pray, and if any be mery let him singe Psalmes.* [Also the quotation of Colossians iii. 16, and then :—] *Imprinted at London, by Jhon Day, dwelling ouer Aldersgate. Cum gratia & priuilegio Regiæ Maiestatis.*

This *Psalter* contains 83 psalms in all (80 in the body of the book). The psalms of the earlier edition are reprinted, with the exception of Wisdome's 67th (never reprinted), and Whittingham's 67th and 71st, now finally excluded from the *English Psalter*, though appearing in the *Genevan Psalter*, 1561, and in the *Scottish*, 1564. The 95th Psalm, however, is removed from the body of the book, and placed as a canticle before the *Te Deum*. (This version of the 95th retains this position in the complete ed. of 1562 and those that follow it, another version being composed by Hopkins for insertion in the *Psalter*). All the Canticles, metrical versions of Creed, Lord's Prayer, and Commandments, mentioned in the last section, are reprinted. To these are added 3 psalms by Sternhold, one of which is 23rd, "My Shepherd is the Living Lord," 13 by Hopkins [the 66th, which, though signed "*Th. Ster.*," is probably, from its double rhyme, by Hopkins (see § x.)], the 75th, which is here anonymous, but afterwards consistently ascribed to Norton, and the old 100th ("All people that," &c.), set to its well-known tune, and anonymous as it is in every subsequent English edition (see § x.) Besides these, the number of pieces attached to the *Psalter* is increased by new versions of Canticles, Creed, &c., by original hymns, and by the insertion of the translation of "Veni Creator," from the Ordinal (see details below): some of these forming a sort of prelude, others an *Appendix* to the *Psalter*. It contains in all 40 tunes, 14 of which are set to the appended hymns, psalms, and canticles.

As no account of this edition has hitherto been published, a more extended notice and criticism of it may be in place here. Only one copy is known to exist, which is in the possession of Octavius Morgan, Esq., F.S.A., to whose kindness we are indebted for these details. The size of the book is 7¼ in. by 7 in. The date of the book (1561) appears only in the colophon at the end. It is bound up in a volume containing a Prayer Book of 1560, a Bible of 1553, the Homilies of 1560, and the Godly Prayers (no date): the binding is probably not later than 1561. There is a short introduction to the Science of Music, in which the object of the book is stated as use "as well in the comon place of praying . . . as privately by themselves or at home in their houses." Before the Psalms there are metrical versions of "Veni Creator," "Venite," "Te Deum," "Benedictus," "Magnificat," "Nunc Dimittis," "Quicunque Vult," "The Lamentation of a Sinner," "The Lorde's Praier," "The Ten Commandments." After the Psalms there are Ps. 117, *T. B.* . . . to be songe before Mornyng Prayer; Ps. 134, *T. B.* . . . to be songe before Evenyng Prayer; "The Ten Commaundementes," *W. Whit.* : "The Lordes Prayer," *D. Cox;* "The XII Articles of the Christyan Faythe," "A Prayer vnto the Holy Ghoste," to be song before the sermon; "Da pacem, Domine," "Thankesgiuing after receiving the Lordes Supper," the hymn "Preserue us Lorde by thy deare Worde," and then prose prayers to be used before and after meals (2 sets), and a Prayer to be used at all times. There can scarcely be a question that it was intended not merely for private, but public, use, and as a Companion to the Prayer Book of 1559. And with this intention on its face it was "allowed," i.e. "approved and permitted to be printed," by the Archbishops or the Bishop of London, who were the censors for the Queen.

John Day obtained a patent to print the Psalms in metre on the 3rd of June in this year (Dibdin's *Ames*). He would risk no more illicit printing: the book was to be lawfully published. It is possible that this patent applied also to the earlier 1560 edition (Ch. Ch.) (if it is Daye's, which is doubtful), which was "allowed" by the censors in the same terms; and looking back at it we now see what was the intention of the versified Canticles ("Benedictus," "Magnificat," "Nunc Dimitis"), Ten Commandments, and Response ("Lord have mercy on us," &c.), The Lord's Prayer and Creed, in that edition. The attempt to associate the *Psalter* with the *Prayer Book*, and so take away Genevan suspicions, had begun in the earlier book, was developed in the edition 1561, and was to be completed in 1562. This new movement seems to be connected with the names of Wisdome and Hopkins, Norton and Cox, and perhaps Grindal (see § IX.). Robert Wisdome, unlike John Pullain, the other new contributor to the earlier edition of 1560, was not a Genevan exile: on the contrary, he appears at Frankfort among the party of Cox, which defended the Prayer Book of Edward against Calvin's Service Book introduced by Knox. His contributions to the *Psalter* also have no affinity with Geneva; the likeness of his 67th Psalm to Coverdale was remarked above. John Hopkins's place of exile is unknown, but it is not probable that he was at Geneva; and he reappears now, bringing apparently Sternhold's MSS., and contributing a large number of Psalms. The influence of Whittingham, on the other hand, has ceased. He had left England before the edition 1561 was published; two of the psalms by him in the Christ Church edition of 1560 are now rejected, and his contribution to the English edition has attained its maximum; it may even be doubted whether he had any personal share in editing the earlier edition of 1560; the new psalms by him and Pullain then published may have already appeared in the lost Genevan edition of 1558. The German influence is increased by two more translations ("Da pacem" and "Preserve us, Lord, by Thy dear word"): and the admission of uninspired hymns, such as "The Lamentation," &c., is an entire departure from Genevan precedent and in accord with Luther's practice. [For *Becon* and *Norton* see below, § IX.]

§ VI. *The English and Anglo-Genevan Psalters compared*

A careful comparison of these two editions with that of *Geneva* (1561), throws an interesting light on the internal history of the *English* and *Scottish Psalters* in their ultimate forms. Leaving out of sight the whole contents of the 1556 edition, which is incorporated in the three books, the only matter common to the Christ Church ed. (1560) and the *Genevan* at St. Paul's (1561) consists of the 9 psalms by Whittingham, 2 by Pullain, and the version of the Lord's Prayer by Cox. The psalms of Whittingham and Pullain, both Genevan exiles, excite no surprise in the *Genevan* edition of 1561; but their previous appearance in the *English*, 1560, lends great plausibility to Livingston's conjecture that they had originally appeared in the lost Genevan edition of 1558, and passed thence to England with the exiles; and if this was really the case, then the only absolutely new matter common to 1560 and 1561 (*Geneva*) is somewhat surprising, viz. : — The Lord's Prayer by Cox, the stout antagonist of Calvin. (It is given as anonymous in 1561, not as by Cox.) With this exception, the two editions ignore each other. The version of the "Nunc Dimittis," in 1561 (*Geneva*), is a different one to that in Christ Church, 1560, and written by Whittingham, who was then under Calvin's influence, and did not throw in his lot definitely with the English Prayer Book till 1563, when he became Dean of Durham; his selection of both this and the Lord's Prayer (2) for versification follows the precedent of Beza's continuation of Marot, pub. in 1551. It would be natural also to suppose that if the compilers of 1561 (*Geneva*) had seen the 95th of Christ Church, 1560, they would not have left that psalm a blank, as they did. The independence of the English work is marked more strongly still, when the 1561 (*Geneva*) is compared with Daye's edition, 1560-1. If the Genevan editors had known of the three new-found Sternhold's, and eight renderings of Hopkins, all of which they have left blank, it is scarcely conceivable that they would have omitted them. There is only one absolutely new piece common to them both, the Old 100th ("All people that," &c.), signed, in the *Genevan* edition, *Tho. Ster.* (!) In these facts we seem to catch sight of two companies of editors at work independently. The *English* one is under the direction of Hopkins and his colleagues, using the old material of *Geneva* with a certain reserve, shown by the rejection of Whittingham's 67th and 71st. The *Genevan* one is under the direction of Kethe, adopting the previous *Genevan* work in its entirety, and unaware (except in the case of the Old 100th, and Cox's Lord's Prayer, which may have reached them in MS.) of the versions which Hopkins and the others were publishing in England. If now for a moment we look on to the complete *Scottish*, 1564, and *English Psalters*, 1565, we see that they are the direct descendants of these two separate movements. The *Scottish Psalter* adopts the *Genevan*, 1561, in the block. The *English* adopts the 1560-1 Daye in the block, with a slight reduction of the *Genevan* element (Whittingham's 115th and 129th, and Pullain's 149th), and only uses the *Genevan* 1561 to fill in the blanks not supplied by England, with 9 renderings by Kethe.

VII. *The Complete Psalter.*

In 1562 *The Complete Psalter* was published by John Daye, entitled—

The whole Book of Psalmes, collected into English metre by T. Sternhold, John Hopkins, and others : conferred with the Ebrue, with apt notes to sing them withal. Faithfully perused and alowed according to th' ordre appointed in the Quene's Maiesties Iniunctions. Very mete, &c. (See Christ Church title-page.) Only one copy is known to exist. It was examined by Dr. Allon (*Congregational Psalmist Historical Notes*, pp. vii.-viii.) and by Livingston (*Scottish Psalter*). The details here are from the latter.

This is the *first edition* in which Hopkins's name is given in full. On comparing it with Daye's edition, 1560-1, we find that all the psalms are reprinted except the 23rd and 50th by Whittingham, the Old Hundredth ("All people," &c.), the 125th by Wisedome (all displaced for the moment, but to reappear in the fuller English edition of 1565); and Whittingham's 115th and 129th, and Pullain's 149th (all of which disappear permanently from the *English Psalter*, though preserved in the *Scottish*, 1564). The new contributions to the *Psalter* consist of 39 psalms by Hopkins, 25 by Norton, the 102nd signed "J. H.," but probably also by Norton, 8 by Kethe, the 111th signed "N.," but probably also by Kethe (see § x.), and 4 by Marckant. The pieces before and after the Psalms in Daye, 1560-1, are also reprinted. There are given before the Psalms "The Song of the Three Children," and "The Humble Sute of a Sinner." After the Psalms are added "The Complaint of a Sinner," and a second hymn called a "Lamentation." The 9 psalms by

Kethe are the same as those in the St. Paul's edition of 1561 (*Geneva*), and the contrast they present with the new material is very striking. With the exception of the 107th and 134th, they are P. M., and set to French tunes. Livingston thinks they were written with little regard to English rhythm to fit the tunes in the French Psalter; and this may be the explanation of such lines as "honour and majesty," &c., Ps. 104. The whole of the new contributions are, on the other hand, C. M.

The contrast illustrates the entire spirit of the English and Scottish Psalters. In the *English* the C.M. of Sternhold remains monotonously dominant; and the French imitations of Whittingham and Kethe are only sparingly admitted; in the *Scottish* not merely are all Kethe's and Whittingham's contributions to 1561 (*Geneva*) reprinted, but the versions by Pont and Craig, which are adopted instead of those of the English Psalter, generally incline to irregular metres. The divergence from the French model is further marked by the versification of "The Benedicite" from the English Prayer Book, and the admission of three more uninspired hymns. (See above.) We seem to see in these, as well as in Wisedome's psalm, and the translations from Luther of 1560-1 (see § v.), the re-assertion of the old influence of Luther on Coverdale. [See **English Hymnody, Early,** § IV.]

VIII. *Final Alterations.*

Though complete as a *Version*, the book had still some slight alterations to receive, before it assumed its final shape. In the ed. of 1563, of which Lea Wilson has a short notice (*MSS. Brit. Mus.*) there were inserted some extra psalms in an *Appendix*. In 1564 (*Brit. Mus.*) this *Appendix* contains the rejected 50th of Whittingham, the Old 100th, "All people," &c., and Wisedome's 125th. In the splendid folio of 1565 (*Brit. Mus.*), this *Appendix* has disappeared; but the psalms that composed it are inserted as alternative renderings in the body of the *Psalter*, and Whittingham's 23rd is also added. The latest addition of all was made not earlier than 1581 —an importation from the *Scottish Psalter*— the alternative 136th Psalm by "T. C.," a misprint for "J. C.," the initials ascribed to **John Craig** (q. v.).

IX. *Authors.*

The book was the work of at least twelve hands. (1) **Thomas Sternhold** is usually described as a Hampshire man (Fuller's *Ch. Hist.* and Wood's *Athenae*). An entry, however, in the registers of Awre in Gloucestershire, inserted on a blank page, between the years 1570 and 1580, in printed characters, apparently at a later date, says—

"Let it be remembered for the honor of this parish that from it sounded out the Psalms of David in English metre by Thomas Sternhold and John Hopkins. The former lived in an estate near Blakeney, called the Hayfield; the later in an estate in the tything of Awre called the Woodend. And in the house of the said John Hopkins there is now to be seen the arms of the Tudor family being painted upon the wall of it: and on both sides is written, in Saxon characters, the former part of the thirteenth chapter of St. Paul's Epistle to the Romans, which was done at that time. In perpetuam rei sive operis memoriam."

Miller (*Singers and Songs of the Church,*

1869, p. 49), to whose industry this extract is due, says that the Hayfield estate is still well known; and that the Woodend estate remained in the hands of the descendants of Hopkins until it was purchased by the present possessors; the house, however, was washed down by the Severn. Sternhold was at Oxford, but left it without a degree. He became Groom of the Robes to Henry VIII., and received a bequest of a hundred marks from him. It has been conjectured that the King's favour may have arisen from a knowledge of his metrical psalms (see R. Brathwaite in his *English Gentleman*, 1641, quoted by Warton), but this is only a conjecture. He retained his office under Edward VI., and obtained the King's patronage for his verse (see § II.). *Wood* says that he caused musical notes to be set to his psalms, and that he hoped that the courtiers would sing them instead of their amorous and obscene songs. Both *Wood* and *Fuller* speak of his poetry as equal to the best that was composed in those times, "when poetry was in the non-age." His psalms should be judged as ballads for the people rather than as poetry. He is the author of 40 versions, nearly all in the older form of c. M., the ballad measure of Chevy Chace with only two rhymes. He d. in 1549. From his will he appears to have possessed lands in Slackstead and other places in Hampshire, and Bodmin in Cornwall. Miller attributes to him the versification of *Certain Chapters of the Proverbs of Solomon*, but this is apparently an error (see Cotton's *Edd. of the Bible*).

(2.) Of John Hopkins very little is certainly known. His residence in Gloucestershire, mentioned above, may perhaps be reconciled with the usual account of him as a clergyman and schoolmaster in Suffolk. *Wood* conjectures that he may be the same as one John Hopkins, who graduated as B.A. at Oxford in 1544 or 1545. He also mentions a John Hopkins, who died at Waldringfield in Suffolk in Oct. 1570, as possibly the same man. *Wood* speaks of him as "Britannicorum poetarum sui temporis non infimus." Some Latin stanzas prefixed to Foxe's *Martyrs* are by him. In the history of the metrical *Version* we catch sight of him first in 1551. He then disappears (his place of exile being unknown), until the close of 1560, when he brings a large contribution of psalms to Daye's edition, 1560-1; and his name is printed in full, as the largest contributor to the *Version*, in 1562. His contribution from first to last consists of 60 psalms, all in c. M., but distinguished from Sternhold's by having four rhymes in a stanza—a change which eventually greatly altered the stresses and cadence of the metre. (See § x.)

(3.) William Whittingham was of greater mark. He was senior student of Cardinal College (Christ Church), Oxford (B.A. 1545), and then travelled in France, Germany, and Geneva, returning in 1553. He fled from the Marian reign to Frankfort, 1554, and thence to Geneva in 1555. He there married Calvin's sister Catherine, and succeeded Knox as pastor of the English congregation. He had an eminent share in the translation of the Geneva Bible, and stayed behind the main body of the exiles to finish it. His thanks to the magistrates for their hospitality to him and his companions were given May 30, 1560, and he no doubt then left Geneva for England. He left England, however, the same year with the Earls of Bedford and Warwick. He was made Dean of Durham in 1563, and had correspondence thence with Knox across the border. He was fond of music, and is said by Warton to have introduced the use of the metrical Canticles in the Cathedral. *Wood* charges him with acts of vandalism there, especially the destruction of the image of St. Cuthbert. He protested against the habits. When Abp. Sandys visited Durham during the vacancy of the see, he refused to attend his summons. Sandys excommunicated him, and tried to invalidate his Genevan orders, received from Calvin. Whittingham died before the struggle ended, in 1579. He is the author of 12 psalms in the *English* and 16 in the *Scottish Psalter*. The short period of his residence in England in 1560 makes it doubtful whether he can have had any personal share in publishing the 1560 edition, and favours Livingston's conjecture that the psalms from his pen in that edition had appeared in the lost edition of 1558. His influence on the *Psalter* was, in the first place, that of scholarly revision of the work of Sternhold, and of Hopkins's seven early psalms from his knowledge of Hebrew; and, in the second, imitation of French metres, especially notable in the 1560 Christ Church. The first L. M. is his (51st) " O Lord, consider my distress" (see § III.)

(4.) John Pullain was also one of the original students of Christ Church, Oxford, admitted in 1547. He was a Yorkshire man, previously at New College, Oxford (M.A. 1544). He was one of the Genevan exiles in company with Whittingham and Kethe. He became Archdeacon of Colchester under Elizabeth. His name appears among the signatories of the Articles in Convocation, 1562, and also attached to a petition in the same year "that the psalms appointed at common prayer be sung distinctly by all the congregation . . . and that all curious singing and playing of the organs may be removed." (The " psalms" mean those in the Prayer Book, not metrical psalms). Besides the 148th and 149th Psalms (the latter only found in the *Scottish Psalter*), he paraphrased Ecclesiastes, Solomon's Song, Esther, Judith, and Susannah. His influence on the *Psalter* is slight, though of the same kind as Whittingham's: but it is worthy of remark that to his version of the 148th Psalm we owe a fine metre, again employed in the *New Version* for the same psalm (" Ye boundless realms of joy "), and also in one or two of Watts's richest compositions (e.g. " Lord of the worlds above ").

(5.) Robert Wisedome was educated at Cambridge, where he took a B.D. degree. He was curate of Stistead in Essex. His protest against Roman doctrines brought him into trouble for a sermon at Oxford; and about 1538 he was obliged to bear a faggot by Stokesley, Bp. of London. Two years afterwards he was complained of to Bonner, and summoned before the Privy Council, as parish priest of St. Margaret's, Lothbury, and imprisoned in the Lollard's Tower. In 1543, in company with his friend Becon and others, he recanted and burnt his books at Paul's

Cross. (See Recantation at length in Foxe's *Acts and Monuments*, ed. 1846, *Appendix* xii.) He then retired with Becon to Staffordshire, and revoked his recantation. Here, too, he wrote "a postill... upon euery gospell through the yeare," translated from Ant. Corvinus, pub. 1549. And here he wrote an exposition of certain Psalms of David, and turned some of them into verse. If the 67th Psalm, contained only in the Christ Church ed. 1560, and the 125th ("Those that do put their confidence) were among these, they are perhaps the earliest pieces of the *Old Version*. In the reign of Edward VIth (July 1550), he obtained the rectory of Settrington in Yorkshire, in the gift of the king, and was mentioned by Cranmer (1552) for the archbishopric of Armagh, which he declined. He was deprived in Mary's reign (1554), and at Frankfort was a hot advocate of the Prayer Book of Edward VIth, on the side of Cox. In the autumn of 1559 he appealed to the royal visitors of the northern dioceses against one Thorneton, who had intruded into his benefice at Settrington. He was instituted Archdeacon of Ely in the diocese of his friend Cox, Feb. 27, 1560. He preached at court, and at Paul's Cross that year. His name occurs among the signatories of the Articles, and the petition about organs, &c. (see above, 4) in 1562. He d. at Wilburton (a parish which, with Haddenham, was then annexed to the Archdeaconry) in 1568. [For a full account of Wisedome, see *Athenæ Cantabrigienses*, by C. H. and T. Cooper, 1850.] The three pieces by Wisedome have a marked individuality. The 125th Psalm is written in an 8-line stanza, of which lines 1–4 are in the metre of Hopkins, with the double rhyme, and lines 5–8 are in a metre very common in Parker's *Psalter*, with a middle rhyme in lines 5 and 7. The 67th Psalm (1560) is *tr.* from Luther, with help from Coverdale. (See **Es wollt uns Gott genädig seyn.**) The third piece is the hymn "Preserve us, Lord, by Thy dere word," a *tr.* from Luther, on which much satire has been expended (see Warton's *Eng. Poetry*) for its conjunction of Turk and Pope. (See **Erhalt uns, Herr, bei deinem Wort.**) It is plausible to associate the return to German matter and precedent, and the movement in favour of the Book of Common Prayer, which first shows itself in 1560, in some measure to Wisedome, whose pieces are then first inserted.

(6.) The initials **E. G.** (the author of the hymn "Da pacem," found first in Daye's edition of the *Psalter*, 1560–1, though it possibly may have appeared in the lost page at the end of Christ Church, 1560), have been conjecturally attributed by Rev. H. F. Sheppard to **Edward Gosynhill**, author of *The Schole House of Women* (a satire), and a *Praise of Women* (Herbert's Catalogue). But the discovery of the German original ("Gib Fried zu unser Zeit o Herr," composed by Wolfgang Köpfel, and pub. in the Strasburg *Gesangbuch* of 1533, see p. 276, i.), which is followed in sense and metre, lends greater probability to the conjecture of Mr. Mearns, that the translation is by no less a person than Edmund Grindal, afterwards Abp. of Canterbury, who was a Strasburg exile.

(7.) **Thomas Norton** was a barrister, b. at London, *circa* 1532, and d. Mar. 24, 158¾ at Sharpenhoe, in Bedfordshire, "a forward and busy Calvinist" (*Wood*). He was author of a *tr.* of a letter of Peter Martyr to the Duke of Somerset, 1550; five controversial tracts about the rebellion in the north and the Papal Bulls, in 1569, and a *tr.* of Calvin's *Institutions of Christian Religion*, 1587. In a widely different region of literature he was joint author with Lord Sackville of our first regular tragedy, *Gorboduc*. (1st performed 1562, pirated ed. pub. in 1565, author's ed. 1571.) His initial appears in Daye's edition, 1560–1, between the "Quicunque" and "The Lamentation," but in subsequent eds. it was appended to the former. The 75th Psalm is also included in this edition, though anonymous like the Old 100th. This omission of the initial on the first appearance of a writer is worth noting in reference to the vexed question of the authorship of the Old 100th. He contributes 26 psalms, all in c. m. of the type of Sternhold.

(8.) **D.** [**Richard**] **Cox.** In *A Brieff discours off the troubles begonne at Franckford*, Dr. Richard Cox is mentioned as *D. Cox* or *D. Coxe* (1574). So that there is good reason to believe that the author of the Lord's Prayer rendering derived from Luther is the same. He was born at Whaddon, Bucks (1499); scholar of King's College, Cambridge; then (1519) fellow. He was invited by Wolsey to Oxford, and made one of the junior canons of Cardinal College. He was imprisoned for heresy in Henry's reign. He was Master of Eton; Archdeacon of Ely (1540); preceptor to Edward VI.; Dean of Christ Church, Oxford (1546); Dean of Westminster (1549); and one of the compilers of the Prayer Book of that year. He was imprisoned in the Marshalsea under Mary, and deprived of his offices. He retired to Frankfort, where he waged war against Knox and Calvin, and maintained the use of the Book of Common Prayer in the English congregation. He was afterwards at Strasburg with Peter Martyr. He was one of the revisers of the Prayer Book (1552). Elizabeth appointed him to the bishopric of Ely (1559), which he held till his death, July 22, 1581. The impression his character produces is that of an honest, plain-dealing man ("fidelis integerque," *Leland*) standing in the *media via* of his day. His pleading with Edward for the revenues of Oxford, and with Elizabeth against some unjust exchanges of episcopal and crown lands; a letter excusing himself from officiating in the Royal Chapel on account of the Crucifix, and a remonstrance with the Queen for her treatment of Grindal, speak for his faithfulness. In opinions, notwithstanding his stout defence of the Prayer Book at Frankfort, he rather inclined to the Protestant side; a friend of Bullinger and Gualter, desirous of welding together the Reformed churches by a common confession of faith, and not too fond of the habits.

(9.) **Thomas Becon** is the well-known early reformer. He was born about 1512, in Norfolk. He graduated at St. John's, Cambridge, in 1530, and was ordained 1538. He was presented afterwards to the living of Brensett in

Kent. He was a friend of Wisedome, and joined him in Staffordshire, when in peril about the *Six Articles*. In 1542 he was brought with Wisedome to Paul's Cross and recanted and burnt the books he had written against them. He was a disciple of Latimer. In Edward VI.'s reign he became (March 24, 154⅞) Vicar of St. Stephen's, Walbrook, and chaplain to Somerset. He was imprisoned in Mary's reign, but released; two paraphrases of Ps. 103, 112, were written as a thanksgiving for his deliverance. He fled to Strasburg, and wrote thence a letter to the brethren in England. Under Elizabeth he was restored to Walbrook, made a Prebendary of Canterbury, and held the livings of Buckland (Herts), Christ Church Newgate Street, and St. Dionis Backchurch. He d. before July 2, 1567. His works, in 3 vols., are published by the Parker Society. In his *Catechism*, 1560, he echoes the common place of the time. "Let no filthy songs be sung...but rather songs of Holy Scripture and the Psalms of David set forth in metre in our English tongue." His 2 psalms (117th, 134th) form no part of the regular *Psalter*. They were added at the end of Daye's ed. 1560–1, as acknowledged psalms: but in the complete edition they merely retain the alternative title, "An Exhortation unto the prayse of God to be soonge before mornyng (or 'evenyng') prayer." The name *T. Becon* is given in full in the 1565 edition.

(10.) **John Marckant** was incumbent of Clacton Magna (1559), and Shopland (1563–8). *Livingston*, p. 70. He is known only as the author of one or two small pieces: a political poem on Lord Wentworth, 1558–9; a New Year's gift intituled, *With speed return to God;* and *Verses to divers good purposes, circa* 1580–1 (*Rev. H. F. Sheppard* quoting Stationers' Registers). The 4 psalms he contributed to 1562 (118th, 131st, 132nd, 135th), were attributed by conjecture, in the *Censura Literaria*, to *John Mardley*, "who turned 24 psalms into English odes, and many religious songs." Among the latter, "The Lamentation" ("Oh! Lord, turn not Thy face"), and "The Humble Sute," both marked "M." in 1562, would be classed. This conjecture is adopted by *Miller* with a "?" in his Index, and *Lord Selborne*. But the name is given in full "*Marckant*," in 1565, and in later editions is sometimes written "*Market*."

(11.) For **William Kethe** see **Scottish Hymnody** and **Kethe**. He contributed 9 psalms to the ed. of 1562, not counting the Old 100th; they had appeared previously, in 1561, Geneva. The imitation of French metres is more conspicuous than in Whittingham's; the 104th psalm is one of the best in the Psalter, and its metre the only surviving result that has achieved success of these attempts to naturalise the French.

(12.) **T. C.** are the initials of **John Craig**. (See **Scottish Hymnody** and **Craig, John**.) The 136th psalm signed *T. C.* is evidently copied from the *Scottish Psalter*, and was not inserted earlier than 1581. "*T. C.*," as a misprint for *J. C.*, was perpetuated in the English editions—one of the clearest instances of the uncertainty which attaches to the evidence of the signatures. The English critics,

ignorant of the *Scottish Psalter*, have (until Livingston pointed out the error, and even subsequently) allotted the initials to *Thomas Churchyard*, a late writer of the Elizabethan time.

X. *Details of Authorship.*

As the initials of the writers are attached to each piece from 1560 onwards, it would seem easy to identify the authorship. But, as a fact, the signatures of late editions are full of errors, and even in the earliest there are curious printers' freaks.

Thus 119, 127, which are elsewhere *W. W.*, are anon in 1560–1. The c. m. 100th, elsewhere anon, is *J. H.* in 1564. The interchange of *N.* and *M.*, common in late editions, is favoured by *N.* to Ps. 118 in 1563 (*Liv.*), and 129 in 1569 (*Geneva*), and *N.* to 132 in 1564. Other instances will be observed in this and § IX.

The verdicts here are based on the signatures of Sternhold's 1st edition (*Brit. Mus.*), 2nd (*Lowndes* and *Cotton*), 1551 (*Bodleian*), 1556 (*Bodleian*), 1560 (*Ch. Ch*), 1561 (Morgan's *Daye*, see § v.), 1562 (*Livingston*), 1564 (*Brit. Mus.*), 1565 (*Brit. Mus.*), 1569 (*Bodleian* and *Lincoln Cathedral*), 1579 (*Brooke*), and several editions of the 16th and 17th cents. The psalms of the *English Psalter* only are noted: ? is attached to the doubtful psalms, and the reasons of the decision are given subsequently.

T. Sternhold.—Pss. 1–5, 20, 25, 28, 29, 32, 34, 41, 49, 73, 78, 103, 120, 123, 128, in the undated first edition; Pss. 6–17, 19, 21, 43, 44, 63, 68, added in 1549; Pss. 18, 22, 23, in 1561.

J. Hopkins.—Pss. 30, 33, 42, 52, 79, 82, 146, in 1551; Pss. 24, 26, 27, 31, 62, 64, 65, 66 (?), 69–71, 74, in 1561; Pss. 35, 36, 38, 39, 40, 45–48, 50 (2nd), 54–61, 76, 77, 80, 81, 83–99, in 1562.

W. Whittingham.—Pss. 23 (1st), 51 (1st), 114, 130, 133, 137, in 1556; Pss. 37, 50 (1st), 119, 121, 124, 127, in 1560; Ten Comm. in 1556 and sequ.

J. Pullain.—Ps. 148 in 1560 and sequ.

T. Norton.—Ps. 75, in 1561; Pss. 51 (2nd), 53, 101, 102 (?), 105, 106, 108–110, 115–117, 129, 136 (1st), 138–145, 147, 149, 150, in 1562; *Quicunque*, in 1561 and sequ.; Ten Comm. ("Hark Israel"), in 1561 and sequ.

R. Wisedome.—l's. 125; "Those that do put their confidence," in 1560 and sequ; and "Preserve us, Lord," in 1561 and sequ.

J. Marckant.—Pss. 118, 131, 132, 135, and the Lamentation "Oh! Lord, turn not," and "The Humble Sute."

W. Kethe.—Pss. 104, 107, 111 (?), 112, 113, 122, 125 (1st), 126, 134.

J. Craig.—Ps. 136 in 1581 and sequ.

Anonymous.—Both versions of 100th, and the Canticles and other pieces not specified in §§ IX., x. "S." is attached to "Nunc Dimittis" in 1562 (*Liv.*).

Comment.—In *Sternhold's* 1st edition there are several misprints in the numbers: 19 (29), 27 (28), 33 (34), 121 (120), 122 (123), 138 (128). The only psalm here assigned to *Hopkins* which is doubtful is 66th, marked "T. S.," in 1561, 1562, 1564, 1569; but in 1565, and Scottish 1564, 1565, "*I. H.*" As it has four rhymes, it is probably by Hopkins. A similar conflict of evidence occurs as to 28th, signed "*I. H.*," in 1561, 1562, 1564, 1565. But it is one of the Sternhold's in 1551, 1556, and "*T. S.*" in 1566, 1569, 1579, and the double rhyme decides it for "*Sternhold.*" The 102nd is signed "*I. H.*" in 1562, 1565, 1566, 1579; but "*N.*" in 1564, 1569, 1579, and later editions. As it has only a double rhyme, it is probably Norton's. The 111th is signed "*N.*" in 1562, 1564, 1565, 1566, and all later editions we have compared; but on its first appearance, 1561 (*Gen.*), and in the Scottish 1564 and 1565, it is *W. K.*, and as it is r. m., never used by Norton, except in the dissimilar 136th, and as there is no trace of Norton's work in 1561 (*Geneva*), it is probably Kethe's. The authorship of the Old 100th is discussed elsewhere under "All people that on earth do dwell" (**p. 43, ii.**).

XI. *Authorization.*

A hot dispute, often biassed by party considerations, has raged as to the nature of the authority of the *Version*. It may be read at large in Heylin's *Ecclesia Restaurata*, Warton's

Hist. of Eng. Poetry, and Todd's *Observations on the Metrical Versions.* It is agreed on all hands that it was not sanctioned by Convocation or Parliament; the dispute concerns the nature of the royal authority. This authorization is stated in three formulas of the title-pages, none of which there is any reason to distrust. In the Christ Church edition of 1560 the book is said to have been "allowed according to the order appointed in the Quene's Maiesties Iniunctions." In 1562 the formula is "Faithfully perused, and alowed according to," &c. And in 1566 (*Bodleian*) the formula is adopted, which remains in all subsequent editions, "allowed to be soong . . . . before and after morning and evening prayer: as also before and after the Sermon." "The order in the Queen's Injunctions" refers to the 51st in the Injunctions of 1559; which forbade the printing of all books except classics until they had been "perused and licensed" by certain appointed officers of the Queen; books so licensed were said to be "allowed." The titlepages of 1560 and 1562 consequently prove no more than authorized and legal printing. The titlepage of 1566 has been held (even by *Heylin,* who discredits it in consequence,) to assert the royal permission of use in public worship. The assertion, however, may be more implicit than explicit. By a more celebrated clause of the Injunctions, any intelligible hymn "or song to the praise of Almighty God" might be sung before and after Morning and Evening Prayer, and hence the *Psalter* among the rest. The use of it before and after sermons was not forbidden by the Act of Uniformity, and had become a cherished custom; which may therefore not have needed express authorization. (It is curious, however, that the Lords Committee in 1641 suggested "to add lawful authority to have them sung before and after sermons"—as if the practice was illegal.) The book itself bore on its face the object of use in public worship; parts of it had been so used for years, and in the words of Parker (Dec. 1559, to Exeter, see **Psalters,** § VI.), "permitted in this Church of England;" if it was printed, its use in public worship was a certainty. With the most vivid knowledge of all this, the Queen's officers "allowed" it, i.e. licensed it to be printed; the permissive use in church was the corollary of that allowance rather than its gist. If the patents of 1560 and 1568 to John Daye for printing the Psalms could be recovered, they might furnish decisive evidence; but we only know, from Barker's Report in 1582 (Stationers' Registers) that "in priviledge or private license granted to John Daye are among other things *the Psalms in metre with notes to sing them in the churches, as well in four parts as in plain song:"* which is not more distinct than the titlepages. A comparison of the three other royal authorizations of *Psalters* seems unfavourable to the interpretation of "allowance" by "permitted use." Both in King James's *Version,* in the *New Version,* and Sir Richard Blackmore's, the word "allowed" is used apparently in the sense of "licensed" or "approved," but the permissive use is granted in other words, such as "recommended" (*King James*) or

"permitted to be used" (*New Version* and *Blackmore*). Whatever be the legal and technical authorization, of its practical adoption by the State, the State Services in 1576 and 1580, which quote it as if it were the only psalm book, are an evidence. (Parker Society reprints, *Liturgical Services,* 1847.)

XII. *Success.*

Few books have had so long a career of influence. With the growing Puritanism psalm-singing came to be esteemed the most divine part of God's public service; "the reading psalms, with the first and second lessons, being heard in many places with a covered head, but all men sitting bare-headed when the psalm was sung" (*Heylin*). Its Genevan parentage, its use as a badge of Calvinism, and the illegal practice of "intermingling Psalms" with the Liturgy brought on it the "frowns of great people," such as Laud, Wren, and Cosin. But the Restoration brought a change of feeling. The Puritans at the Savoy Conference petitioned in vain that it might be amended or superseded; the Bishops held that it lay outside their commission. In 1694 the antiquated words were changed, and a few alterations, drawn from Rous and Barton (according to Archd. Churton), made to give it a more modern air. In 1710 Bp. Beveridge wrote a strenuous defence of it as a venerable monument of the Reformation. Though generally superseded by *The New Version,* it was used in a few churches within the memory of many still living.

XIII. *Merits.*

The chief claims to excellence that have been put forward in behalf of the *Old Version* are its fitness as an instrument of instruction and spiritual good to the common people, and its fidelity to the Hebrew. It has found patrons in Beveridge, Horsley, and Romaine. We ought in fairness to remember the times and the conditions of the work. The great burst of Elizabethan poetry was still in the future; Sternhold's ambition was to make the Psalms the ballads of the court and people; and this consideration determined the metres and treatment. If judged by contemporary ballads, or even the hymns in Henry VIII.'s *Primers,* or the religious poetry of the age, they will be found in Fuller's words "to go abreast with" them; and this is the explanation of the apparently exaggerated estimates of Sternhold and Hopkins as poets, quoted in § IX. We must add to this, that they were written for the level of the mass; even Warton tempers his contempt by confessing that "had they been more poetically translated, they would not have been acceptable to the common people." Probably style was a very subordinate consideration to that of faithfulness to the original. This faithfulness has been acknowledged by Keble: and Beveridge, contrasting it with the inaccuracy of the *New Version* (*Defence of the Old Version,* 1710), points out that it anticipated some of the subsequent revisions of the *Authorized Version* of 1611. Still, for literary use, it must be confessed to be almost utterly dead. The likeness to the Hebrew is that of the corpse to the living body (*Quarterly Review*). From the times of Dod the Silkman (see

Psalters, Eng., § x.) the abuse lavished on it has steadily increased in the prefaces to new translations of the Psalms. "Their piety was better than their poetry;" "they had drunk more of Jordan than of Helicon;" "sometimes they make the Maker of the tongue speak little better than barbarism, and have in many verses such poor rhime that two hammers on a smith's anvil would make better music," says Fuller. Rochester's epigram on passing with Charles II., while a parish clerk was singing, is well-known :—

> "Sternhold and Hopkins had great qualms,
> When they translated David's psalms,
>   To make the heart right glad :
> But had it been King David's fate
> To hear thee sing and them translate,
>   By —— 'twould set him mad."

Still, on the whole, it is pleasant to think that in Sternhold's 23rd, "My Shepherd is the living Lord," in the Old 100th, "All people that on earth do dwell," in Kethe's 104th, "My soul, praise the Lord," and one or two more, we still retain some links with so venerable a book and history.   [H. L. B.]

When the *Old* and *New Versions* gradually gave way to the hymn-book proper, their fall was broken by the adoption in the hymn-books of extensive extracts from their contents. These extracts took the form, sometimes of entire versions of individual psalms, and again of parts of, and centos from the same, or from others. Those of the *N. V.* so dealt with are given under **New Version**. It remains for us to provide the same information with regard to the **Old Version**. In doing this we shall give (1) The first line of each Psalm from the 1565 ed.: (2) the same line, when altered, from the Clarendon Press ed.; (3) the first lines of all parts taken from any Psalm; and (4) the initials of the author, not as in 1565, but as in the foregoing Key in § x.

   i. The man is blest that hath not bent. **T. S.**
  ii. Why did the Gentiles tumults raise? **T. S.**
 iii. O Lord, how are my foes increased? **T. S.**
 iv. O God, that [Thou] art my righteousness. **T. S.**
  v. Incline thine ears unto my words. **T. S.**
     Incline Thine ear, O Lord, and let.
 vi. Lord, in Thy wrath reprove me not. **T. S.**
vii. O Lord my God, I put my trust. **T. S.**
    (1) Lord, cease the hate of wicked men.
viii. O God our Lord [God], how wonderful. **T. S.**
 ix. With heart and mouth unto the Lord. **T. S.**
    With heart and mouth to Thee, O Lord.
    (1) Sing psalms, therefore, unto the Lord.
  x. What is the cause, that Thou, O Lord. **T. S.**
    (1) Tush, God forgetteth this, saith he.
 xi. I trust in God, how dare ye then. **T. S.**
    In God the Lord I put my trust.
xii. Help, Lord, for good and godly men. **T. S.**
xiii. How long wilt Thou forget me, Lord? **T. S.**
xiv. There is no God, as [do] foolish men. **T. S.**
 xv. O Lord, within Thy tabernacle. **T. S.**
    Within Thy tabernacle, Lord.
xvi. Lord keep me, for I trust in Thee. **T. S.**
xvii. O Lord, give ear to my just cause. **T. S.**
    (1) From wicked men that trouble me.
xviii. O God, my strength and fortitude. **T. S.**
    (1) In my distress I sought my God.
xix. The heavens and the firmament. **T. S.**
    The heavens and firmament on high.
 xx. In trouble and adversity. **T. S.**
xxi. O Lord, how joyful is the King. **T. S.**
xxii. O God, my God, wherefore dost Thou? **T. S.**
xxiii. The Lord is only my support. **W. W.**
xxiii. My Shepherd is the living Lord. **T. S.**
xxiv. The earth is all the Lord's, with all. **J. H.**
xxv. I lift my [mine] heart to Thee. **T. S.**
    (1) Now for Thy holy Name.
xxvi. Lord, be my Judge! and Thou shalt see. **J. H.**
xxvii. The Lord is both my health and light. **J. H.**
    (1) Lord, hear the voice of my request.

xxviii. Thou art, O Lord, my Strength and Stay. **T. S.** (?)
xxix. Give to the Lord, ye potentates. **T. S.** (?)
xxx. All laud and praise, with heart and voice. **J. H.**
xxxi. O Lord, I put my trust in Thee. **J. H.**
    (1) Great grief, doth me, O Lord, assail.
    (2) Lord, let me not be put to shame.
xxxii. The man is blest whose wickedness. **T. S.**
xxxiii. Ye righteous, in the Lord rejoice. **J. H.**
    (1) Blessed are they to whom the Lord.
xxxiv. I will give laud and honor, both. **T. S.**
    (1) Come near to me, my children, and.
xxxv. Lord, plead my cause against my foes. **J. H.**
xxxvi. The wicked with [by] his works unjust. **J. H.**
xxxvii. Grudge not to see the wicked men. **W. W.**
xxxviii. Put me not to rebuke, O Lord. **J. H.**
xxxix. I said, I will look to my ways. **J. H.**
    (1) For all the sins that I have done.
 xl. I waited long and sought the Lord. **J. H.**
    (1) I have not hid within my breast.
xli. The man is blest that careful is. **T. S.**
    The man is blest that doth provide.
xlii. Like as the hart doth breathe [pant] and bray. **J. H.**
xliii. Judge and revenge [defend] my cause, O Lord. **T. S.**
xliv. Our ears have heard our fathers tell. **T. S.**
xlv. My heart doth take in hand. **J. H.**
    (1) O fairest of all men.
xlvi. The Lord is our defence and aid. **J. H.**
xlvii. Ye people all in [with] one accord. **J. H.**
xlviii. Great is the Lord, and with great praise. **J. H.**
xlix. All people hearken, and give ear. **T. S.**
 l. The mighty God, the Eternal, &c. **W. W.**
 l. The God of gods, the Lord. **J. H.**
 li. O Lord, consider my distress. **W. W.**
    (1) Cast me not, Lord, out from Thy sight.
 li. Have mercy on me God [Lord], after. **T. N.**
    (1) O God, that art God of my health.
 lii. Why dost thou, tyrant, boast abroad. **J. H.**
 liii. The foolish man in that which he. **T. N.**
    The foolish man within his heart.
liv. God save me, for Thy holy Name. **J. H.**
lv. O God, give ear and do apply. **J. H.**
    O God, give ear and speedily.
    (1) My heart doth faint for want of breath.
lvi. Have mercy, Lord, on me, I pray. **J. H.**
lvii. Take pity for Thy promise sake. **J. H.**
lviii. Ye rulers that [which] are put in trust. **J. H.**
lix. Send aid and save me from my foes. **J. H.**
lx. O Lord, Thou didst us clean forsake. **J. H.**
lxi. Regard, O Lord, for I complain. **J. H.**
lxii. My soul to God shall give good heed. **J. H.**
lxiii. O God, my God, I watch betime. **T. S.**
    O God, my God, I early seek.
lxiv. O Lord, unto my voice give ear. **J. H.**
lxv. Thy praise alone, O Lord, doth reign. **J. H.**
lxvi. Ye men on earth, in God rejoice. **J. H.** (?)
lxvii. Have mercy on us, Lord. **J. H.**
lxviii. Let God arise, and then His foes. **T. S.**
lxix. Save me, O God, and that with speed. **J. H.**
lxx. O God, to me take heed. **J. H.**
lxxi. My Lord, my God, in all distress. **J. H.**
lxxii. Lord, give Thy judgments to the king. **J. H.**
    (1) All kings shall seek with one accord.
lxxiii. However it be, yet God is good. **T. S.**
    Truly the Lord is very good.
lxxiv. Why art Thou, Lord, so long from us? **J. H.**
    (1) O God, Thou art our King and Lord.
lxxv. Unto Thee, God, we will give thanks. **T. N.**
    To Thee, O God, will we give thanks.
lxxvi. To all that now in Jewry [Judah] dwell. **J. H.**
lxxvii. I with my voice to God do [did] cry. **J. H.**
lxxviii. Attend, my people, to my law. **T. S.**
lxxix. O Lord [God], the Gentiles do invade. **J. H.**
lxxx. Thou Herd that Israel dost keep. **J. H.**
    Thou Shepherd that dost Israel keep.
lxxxi. Be light and glad, in God rejoice. **J. H.**
lxxxii. Amid the press, with men of might. **J. F.**
    Among the princes, men of might.
lxxxiii. Do not, O God, refrain Thy tongue. **J. H.**
lxxxiv. How pleasant is Thy dwelling place. **J. H.**
lxxxv. Thou hast been merciful indeed. **J. H.**
lxxxvi. Lord, bow Thine ear to my request. **J. H.**
lxxxvii. That city shall full well endure. **J. H.**
lxxxviii. Lord God of health, the Hope and Stay. **J. H.**
lxxxix. To sing the mercies of the Lord. **J. H.**
xc. Thou, Lord, hast been our sure Defence. **J. H.**
xci. He that within the secret place. **J. H.**
xcii. It is a thing both good and meet. **J. H.**
xciii. The Lord as King aloft [alone] doth reign. **J. H.**
    The Lord doth reign and clothed is.

xciv. O Lord, Thou dost revenge all wrong. **J. H.**
(1) The Lord doth know the heart of man.
xcv. O come, let us lift up our voice. **J. H.**
xcvi. Sing ye with praise unto the Lord. **J. H.**
(1) Fall down and worship ye the Lord
xcvii. The Lord doth reign whereat [for which] the earth. **J. H.**
xcviii. O sing ye now unto the Lord. **J. H.**
xcix. The Lord doth reign, although at it. **J. H.**
c. All people that on earth do dwell. **W. K.**
ci. In God the Lord be glad and light. **A.**
ci. I mercy will and judgment sing. **T. N.**
cii. O hear my prayer, Lord, and let. **T. H.**
Hear Thou my prayer, O Lord, and let.
ciii. My soul, give laud [praise] unto the Lord. **T. S.**
civ. My soul, praise the Lord. **W. K.**
cv. Give praises unto God the Lord. **T. N.**
cvi. Praise ye the Lord, for He is good. **T. N.**
cvii. Give thanks unto the Lord our God. **W. K.**
cviii. O God, my heart prepared is. **T. N.**
cix. In speechless silence do not hold. **T. N.**
cx. The Lord did say unto my Lord. **T. N.**
cxi. With heart I do [do I] accord. **W. K. (?)**
cxii. The man is blest that God doth fear. **W. K.**
cxiii. Ye children which do serve the Lord. **W. K.**
cxiv. When Israel by God's address. **W. W.**
When Israel by God's command.
cxv. Not unto us, Lord, not to us. **T. N.**
cxvi. I love the Lord, because my [the] voice. **T. N.**
(1) I said in my distress and fear.
cxvii. O all ye nations of the world. **T. N.**
cxviii. O give ye thanks unto [to] God the Lord. **J. M.**
(1) I will give thanks to Thee, O Lord.
cxix. Blessed are they that perfect are. **W. W.**
cxx. In trouble and in thrall. **T. S.**
cxxi. I lift mine [my] eyes to Sion hill. **W. W.**
cxxii. I did in heart rejoice. **W. K.**
cxxiii. O Lord, that heaven dost [doth] possess. **T. S. (?)**
O Thou that in the heavens doth dwell.
cxxiv. Now Israel may say, and that truly. **W. W.**
cxxv. Such as in God the Lord do trust. **W. K.**
cxxv. Those that do put [place] their confidence. **R. W.**
cxxvi. When that the Lord, again His Sion had forth brought, **W. K.**
cxxvii. Except the Lord the house do [doth] make. **W. W.**
cxxviii. Blessed art thou that fearest God. **T. S.**
cxxix. Oft they, now Israel may say. **T. N.**
cxxx. Lord, to [unto] Thee I make my moan. **W. W.**
cxxxi. O Lord, I am not puffed [put] in mind. **J. M.**
cxxxii. Remember David's troubles [trouble], Lord. **J. M.**
cxxxiii. O how [what] happy a thing it is. **W. W.**
cxxxiv. Behold, and have regard. **W. K.**
cxxxv. O praise the Lord, praise Him, praise Him. **J. M.**
O praise the Lord, praise ye His Name.
cxxxv. Praise ye the Lord, for He is good. **T. N.**
cxxxvi. O laud [praise] the Lord benign. **J. C.** This is not in the 1565 ed.   In the 1581 ed. (J. Daye) it is marked. **T. C.**
cxxxvii. When as we sat in Babylon. **W. W.**
When we did sit in Babylon.
cxxxviii. Thee will I praise with my whole heart. **T. N.**
cxxxix. O Lord, thou hast me tried and known. **T. N.**
cxl. Lord, save me from the evil man. **T. N.**
cxli. O Lord, upon Thee do I call. **T. N.**
cxlii. Before [Unto] the Lord God with my voice. **T. N.**
cxliii. Lord, hear my prayer, hark the plaint. **T. N.**
Lord, hear my prayer and my complaint.
cxliv. Blest be the Lord, my Strength, that doth. **T. N.**
cxlv. Thee will I laud, my God and King. **T. N.**
cxlvi. My soul, praise thou the Lord always. **J. H.**
cxlvii. Praise ye the Lord, for it is good. **T. N.**
(1) O praise the Lord, Jerusalem.
cxlviii. Give laud unto the Lord. **J. P.**
cxlix. Sing ye unto the Lord our God. **T. N.**
cl. Yield unto God, the mighty Lord. **T. N.**

Several of these Psalms demand fuller notice than could be given in this article; and accordingly, the more important are annotated under their respective first lines. (Various.) [J. J.]

Olearius, Johann Gottfried, s. of Dr. Gottfried Olearius, pastor of St. Ulrich's Church at Halle, was b. at Halle, Sept. 25, 1635. He entered the University of Leipzig in 1653, and

graduated M.A. 1656, residing also for short periods at other German Universities. In 1658 he was ordained as assistant to his father at St. Mary's Church in Halle, where he became diaconus in 1662, and in 1685 pastor and also superintendent of the second portion of the district of the Saale. He was finally appointed, in 1688, as chief pastor, superintendent, and consistorialrath at Arnstadt, and also professor of Theology in the Gymnasium there. He d. at Arnstadt, May 21, 1711, after having been for some years totally blind. (*Allg. Deutsche Biog.* xxiv. p. 280 ; *Bode*, p. 124, &c.)

Olearius was the author of several devotional works, and composed a number of melodies to his own hymns. His hymns appeared in his (1) *Jesus! Poetische Erstlinge an geistlichen Deutschen Liedern und Madrigalen*, Halle, 1664 [Berlin], and the second edition enlarged and altered as (2) *Geistliche Singe- Lust*, Arnstadt, 1697 [Wernigerode]. A number passed into the Arnstadt *G. B.*, 1705, and a few are still in German C. U. Two have passed into English, one ("Es war die ganze Welt") being noted under **J. A. Schlegel** (q.v.), and the other being:—

Komm du werthes Lösegeld. *Advent.* Founded on St. Matt. xxi. 9. 1st pub. 1664 as above, p. 1 in 4 st. of 6 l., and entitled, "On Advent." In the Berlin *G. L. S.*, ed. 1863, No. 137. *Tr.* as :—

Come, O Lord, our sacrifice. By A. T. Russell, omitting st. iii., as No. 10 in the Dalston Hospital *H. Bk.*, 1848, repeated in Dr. Pagenstecher's *Coll.*, 1864, No. 2.   [J. M.]

Olearius, Johannes, s. of Johann Olearius, pastor of St. Mary's Church and superintendent at Halle, was b. at Halle, Sept. 17 (N. S.) 1611. He entered the University of Wittenberg in 1629 (M.A. 1632, D. 1643), where he became lecturer, and, in 1635, adjunct of the philosophical faculty. In 1637 he became Superintendent at Querfurt ; and, in 1643, was appointed by Duke August of Sachsen-Weissenfels as his chief court preacher, and private chaplain at Halle, where he became in 1657 Kirchenrath, and in 1664 General Superintendent. When, on the death of Duke August in 1680, the administration of Magdeburg fell to the Elector of Brandenburg, Duke Johann Adolf gave Olearius similar appointments at Weissenfels, which he held till his death on April 24, 1684 (*Koch*, iii. 346 ; *Allg. Deutsche Biog.* xxiv. 279, &c.).

Olearius was the author of a Commentary on the whole Bible, and of various devotional works. He was also the compiler of one of the largest and most important German hymn-books of the 17th cent., viz. the *Geistliche Singe- Kunst*, of which the first ed. appeared at Leipzig in 1671, with 1207 (1218) hymns, and the second at Leipzig in 1672, with 1340. The first ed. contained 302 hymns by Olearius himself, and marked "D. J. O." They may best be described as useful, being for times and seasons hitherto unprovided for, and filling up many gaps in the various sections of the German hymn-books. They are mostly short, many of only two verses, simple and easy of comprehension, often happy in expression and catching, and embodying in a concise form the leading ideas of the season or subject. Many were speedily adopted into German hymn-books, and a considerable number are still in use.

Of Olearius's hymns the following have passed into English :—

i. **Gelobet sei der Herr.** *Trinity Sunday.* One of his best hymns. Founded on the Gospel for Trinity Sunday. Included in 1671 as above, No. 709, in 5 st. of 8 l., and entitled "Encouragement from the Gospel to thankful meditation on this great mystery." In the Berlin *G. L. S.*, ed. 1863, No. 17. *Tr.* as :—

1. **Blest be my Lord and God.** A good *tr.*, omitting st. v. by A. T. Russell, as No. 134, in his *Ps. & Hys.*, 1851.

2. O praise the Lord! His name extol. A version of st. i.–iii., as No. 115 in the Ohio *Luth. Hyl.*, 1880.

ii. Herr Jesu Christ, dein theures Blut. *Passiontide.* His finest hymn. Founded on 1 St. John i. 7. In 1671 as above, No. 576, in 4 st. of 4 l. and entitled "Meditation on the Precious Blood of Jesus Christ." St. ii. is based on the hymn "In Christi Wunden schlaf ich ein" (p. **319**, ii.). In the Berlin *G. L. S.*, ed. 1863, No. 233. *Tr.* as :—

1. Lord Jesu Christ! Thy precious blood Brings to my soul. A good and full *tr.* by A. T. Russell, as No. 161 in his *Ps. & Hys.*, 1851.

2. Lord Jesus Christ! Thy precious blood Is to my soul. In full by C. H. L. Schnette, as No. 77 in the Ohio *Luth. Hyl.*, 1880.

Another *tr.* is "Lord Jesus Christ, Thy blessed blood." By *Miss Manington*, 1863, p. 43.

iii. Herr, öffne mir die Herzensthür. *Holy Scripture. After Sermon.* In 1671 as above, No. 975, in 2 st. and a doxology. In the Berlin *G. L. S.*, ed. 1863, No. 422. The *tr.* in C. U. is—

Lord, open Thou my heart to hear, And by Thy Word to me draw near. In full by Dr. M. Loy in the Ohio *Luth. Hyl.*, 1880.

iv. Nun kommt das neue Kirchenjahr. *Advent.* In 1671 as above, No. 384, in 3 st. and a doxology. In the Berlin *G. L. S.*, ed. 1863, No. 145. The *tr.* is :—

The new Church-year again is come. By E. Cronenwett, as No. 15 in the Ohio *Luth. Hyl.*, 1880.

v. Tröstet, tröstet meine Lieben, *St. John Baptist's Day.* In 1671 as above, No. 733, in 4 st. of 8 l., and entitled "Meditation on the Lesson of the Festival. Isaiah xl." In the Berlin *G. L. S.*, ed. 1863, No. 124. *Tr.* as :—

Comfort, comfort ye my people. A full and good *tr.* by Miss Winkworth, as No. 83 in her *C. B. for England*, 1863. Repeated in full in the *Parish H. Bk.*, 1865, and the Ohio *Luth. Hyl.*, 1880, and, omitting st. ii. in the Pennsylvania *Luth. Ch. Bk.*, 1868.

Other hymns by Olearius have been *tr.* into English, viz. :—

vi. Gott Lob, mein Jesus macht mich rein. *Presentation in the Temple.* In 1671 as above, No. 507, as a hymn on the Purification in 6 st., and entitled "Encouragement from the Gospel," viz. St. Luke ii. 22–32. In the Berlin *G. L. S.*, ed. 1863, No. 1270. The form *tr.* is "Durch Jesum kann ich auch mit Freud," which is No. 428 in Knapp's *Ev. L. S.*, 1837, and is st. iv.–vi. altered. *Tr.* as "I too, through Jesus, may in peace." By *Dr. H. Mills*, 1845 (1856, p. 277).

vii. Sollt ich meinem Gott nicht trauen. *Trust in God.* In 1671 as above, No. 878, in 6 st., and entitled "Encouragement from the Gospel," viz. St. Matt. vi. 24 ff, the Gospel for the 15th S. after Trinity. In the Berlin *G. L. S.*, ed. 1863, No. 857. *Tr.* as, "Shall I not trust my God." By *Miss Warner*, 1858, p. 206.

viii. Wenn dich Unglück hat betreten. *Cross and Consolation.* In 1671 as above, No. 827, in 6 st., and entitled "Encouragement from the Gospel," viz. St. Matt. xv. 21–28, the Gospel for Reminiscere Sunday (2nd S. in Lent). In Porst's *G. B.*, ed. 1855, No. 997. The *trs.* are (1) "When afflictions sore oppress you." By *Miss Cox*, 1841, p. 129. (2) "When affliction rends the heart." By *Lady E. Fortescue*, 1843, p. 55. [J. M.]

Olivers, Thomas, was b. at Tregynon, near Newtown, Montgomeryshire, in 1725. His father's death, when the son was only four years of age, followed by that of the mother shortly afterwards, caused him to be passed on to the care of one relative after another, by whom he was brought up in a somewhat careless manner, and with little education. He was apprenticed to a shoemaker. His youth was one of great ungodliness, through which

at the age of 18 he was compelled to leave his native place. He journeyed to Shrewsbury, Wrexham, and Bristol, miserably poor and very wretched. At Bristol he heard G. Whitefield preach from the text "Is not this a brand plucked out of the fire?" That sermon turned the whole current of his life, and he became a decided Christian. His intention at the first was to join the followers of Whitefield, but being discouraged from doing so by one of Whitefield's preachers, he subsequently joined the Methodist Society at Bradford-on-Avon. At that town, where he purposed carrying on his business of shoemaking, he met John Wesley, who, recognising in him both ability and zeal, engaged him as one of his preachers. Olivers joined Wesley at once, and proceeded as an evangelist to Cornwall. This was on Oct. 1, 1753. He continued his work till his death, which took place suddenly in London, in March 1799. He was buried in Wesley's tomb in the City Road Chapel burying ground, London. Olivers was for some time co-editor with J. Wesley of the *Arminian Magazine*, but his lack of education unfitted him for the work. As the author of the tune *Helmsley*, and of the hymn "The God of Abraham praise," he is widely known. He also wrote "Come Immortal King of glory"; and "O Thou God of my salvation," whilst residing at Chester; and an *Elegy* on the death of John Wesley. His hymns and the *Elegy* were reprinted (with a *Memoir* by the Rev. J. Kirk) by D. Sedgwick, in 1868.   [J. J.]

Olney Hymns. A collection of hymns by the poet Cowper (p. **265**, i.) and John Newton (q.v.), sung originally either in the church or at the prayer-meetings at The Great House at Olney, and pub. as—

Olney Hymns, in Three Books. Book I. On Select Texts of Scripture. Book II. On Occasional Subjects. Book III. On the Progress and Changes of the Spiritual Life.... London: Printed and sold by W. Oliver, No. 12, Bartholomew Close . . . MDCCLXXIX. The three "Poems" were added in later editions.

They were probably given out verse by verse, like many of those by Watts and Doddridge, and often suggested by Newton's sermons. In the preface Newton says, that besides the principal motive of promoting the faith and comfort of sincere Christians, the hymns were designed "to perpetuate the remembrance of an intimate and endeared friendship" between himself and Cowper. This project was formed in 1771. Whether it was simply suggested by Newton's perception of Cowper's poetical powers, or intended to occupy a mind in which there were symptoms of approaching madness, cannot be decided. Cowper contributed 67 hymns. Two of them—*The Happy Change* ("How blest Thy creature is, oh! God") and *Retirement* ("Far from the world, oh! Lord, I flee") had been written immediately on his recovery from his first attack of madness, at St. Albans, in 1764. "Jesus, where'er Thy people meet," had been written for the opening of the large room at The Great House as a place for prayer-meetings (April 17, 1769). The only other hymn whose date is approximately known is *Light shining out of darkness* ("God moves in a mysterious way"), which, despite of its rational fortitude, was written under the most painful circumstances (see p. **433. i.**). The known hymns by Newton previous to 1773 are few, and during the early part of that year the shock of Cowper's calamity made him "hang his harp on the willows." In his *Diary*, Nov. 30 of that year, he speaks, however, of then making one hymn a week: and there are memoranda of composition at intervals to Jan. 30, 1778 (see Newton's *Life* by Rev. Josiah Bull). Twelve hymns by Newton and Cowper appeared in the *Gospel Magazine* (1771–78): thirteen were attached to *Omicron's Letters* (1774); R. Conyers's collection has several; and one or two others are found in obscure hymn-books. The complete *Olney Collection* appeared in 1779, arranged in three books. 1. "On Select Texts of Scripture"; 2. "On occasional Subjects"; 3. "On the Rise, Progress, Changes and Comforts of the Spiritual Life." It contained 318 hymns and 3 other pieces, and has gone through many editions. Except in refined tenderness, Cowper's hymns are indistinguishable from Newton's. Both follow Newton's stern yet wholesome caution, that in hymns the "imagery and colouring of poetry, if admitted at all, should be admitted very sparingly and with great judgment." Both in their best pieces exhibit great excellence of structure. Both authors are vague as to the aim, capabilities, and limitations of hymns. Several pieces are disquisitions or soliloquies ("What various hindrances we meet" is really not a hymn, but a fine instruction on prayer). With the splendid exception of "Glorious things of thee are spoken," there is scarcely a trace of jubilance. Out of the many themes of Christian praise one alone is touched—the surpassing mercy of Jesus to His sinful elect: and even the rapt contemplation of this droops away into sad reflection. Gloom is a characteristic of the book. The despondence, sense of exile from God, and not the gladness, of the Psalms, are selected for versification. The contemplation of nature suggests sorrowful resemblances to the work of grace in the human heart, not the vision of God's majesty and love. Hymns describing the heavy self-accusation, dejection, desertion of the regenerate, form the largest and most darkly real portion of the book, and those of Newton have more unrelieved dejection than Cowper's. But Newton's despondence arose from his sense of ingratitude for his election, never from doubt of it: and hence alongside of it there are hymns full of rational faith, strong confidence, and, above all, fervent clinging love of Jesus. Verses often occur, which from their direct force, are vigorous maxims: and, though there is a large quantity of tame, sermonlike doggerel, there are a considerable number of pure English hymns, of melodious cadence and Scriptural ring. The earlier hymn-books that most nearly resemble them are Shepherd's *Penitential Cries* and the *Collection* by Newton's friend, Dr. Conyers. The intense love of the Saviour, which animates them, endeared them to numbers in the earlier part of this century, and the finest of them are still in C. U. in all English-speaking countries. [See **Cowper, William; Newton, John.**]   [H. L. B.]

Omicron. In the *Gospel Magazine*, 1771, *i.e.* John Newton.

Omnes una celebremus. [*Sunday.*] This has not been traced earlier than the *Elucidatorium* of Clichtovaeus, Paris, 1516, f. 178 *b*; and his text has been repeated in *Daniel*, v. p. 216; Neale s *Sequentiae*, 1852, p. 251; and *Kehrein*, No. 164. The *trs.* are:—

1. **In our common celebration.** By J. M. Neale, in the *Hymnal N.*, 1854, the *Salisbury H. Bk.*, 1857, No. 18, &c.

2. **Come let us all with one accord.** Made by Mrs. H. M. Chester for the *Hymnary*, 1872, and signed "H. M. C."   [J. M.]

Omnipresent God, Whose aid. *C. Wesley.* [*Evening.*] Pub. in *Hys. and Sacred Poems*, 1749, vol. i., in 8 st. of 8 l. (*P. Works*, 1868–72, vol. v. p. 8). In the *Wes. H. Bk.*, 1780, st. i., iv.–vi. were given as No. 278, and in the revised ed., 1875, st. vii., viii. were added thereto. In addition to these forms of the hymn the following centos are also in C. U.:—(1) "Holiest Whose present might," st. i. and vi., altered in the American Unitarian *Hys. of the Spirit*, 1864, and others; and (2) "O Thou Holy God, come down," st. iv. and vi., in the American Unitarian *Hys. of the Church of Christ*, 1853; Beecher's *Plymouth Coll.*, 1855, and others.   [J. J.]

On earth we meet again below. *J. Montgomery.* [*For Sunday School Gatherings.*] Printed on a broadsheet as No. 1 of the Hymns for the Sheffield Sunday School Union, Whit-Monday, May 27, 1844, in 6 st. of 4 l.: also included in Montgomery's *Original Hymns*, 1853, No. 324.   [J. J.]

On our way rejoicing as we homeward [onward] move. *J. S. B. Monsell.* [*Joy.*] Appeared in his *Hys. of Love and Praise*, 1863, p. 124, in 4 st. of 8 l., and appointed for the 1st S. after Trinity. It was rewritten by him for his *Parish Hymnal*, 1873, No. 155, the principal change being the addition of the first four lines from st. i., as a refrain to each stanza. These changes were made to adapt the hymn as a Processional, and appeared elsewhere before the *Parish Hymnal*, as in the S. P. C. K. *Church Hymns* 1871, &c. Both forms are in C. U.   [J. J.]

On Sinai's top in prayer and trance. *J. Keble.* [*Prophets and Kings desiring to see the Gospel Days.*] Dated Sep. 16, 1821, and pub. in his *Christian Year*, 1827, in 21 st. of 4 l. It is based upon the Gospel for the 13th S. after Trinity. In Nicholson's *Appendix Hymnal*, 1866, No. 112, is a cento from this poem beginning with st. i.   [J. J.]

On the dewy breath of even. *Julia Ann Elliott, née Marshall.* [*Evening.*] 1st pub. in her husband's *Ps. & Hys.*, 1835, anonymously, and subsequently with the signature "I. A. E." in the Index. In modern collections it is usually found, as in the *Leeds H. Bk.*, 1853, and the Bap. *Ps. & Hys.*, 1858, where st. i.–iii. are unaltered from Mrs. Elliott, st. v. from the same altered, and st. iv. by another hand. In some hymn-books this hymn is attributed to Miss Charlotte Elliott, but in error.   [J. J.]

On the hill of Zion standing. *Bp. E. H. Bickersteth.* [*Missions.*] Written for the

Jubilee of the Church Missionary Society, 1848, and 1st pub. in the broadsheet of hymns printed for that occasion. It was also included in his *Poems*, 1849; his *Ps. & Hys.*, 1858; and his *The Two Brothers*, &c., 1871, p. 257. In R. Bingham's *Hymno. Christ. Latina*, 1871, it is rendered into Latin as "In Zionis alto colle."   [J. J.]

On the mountain's top appearing. *T. Kelly* [*Missions.*] This hymn appeared in his *Coll. of Ps. & Hys.*, Dublin, 1802, No. 249, in 4 st. of 6 l., and is based on Ps. lii. 7. It was subsequently repeated in the author's *Hymns*, &c., 1804, and later editions (ed. 1853, p. 555). In Cotterill's 1815 *Appendix* to his *Sel. of Ps. & Hymns*, No. 203, st. i., iii., iv. were given in an altered form. This was repeated in the 8th ed. of the *Sel.*, 1819, No. 162; in Montgomery's *Christian Psalmist*, 1825, No. 437, and again in later collections. Two texts, both beginning with the same opening stanza, have thus come into C. U. They can be easily distinguished by the 3rd stanza of Kelly and the 2nd of Cotterill, which read:—

T. Kelly.   "God, thy God will now restore thee:
        He Himself appears thy friend:
        All thy foes shall flee before thee,
        Here their boasts and triumphs end;
          Great deliverance
        Zion's King vouchsafes to send."

T. Cotterill.   "Lo! thy sun is risen in glory!
        God Himself appears thy friend;
        All thy foes shall flee before thee;
        Here their boasted triumphs end;
          Great deliverance
        Zion's King vouchsafes to send.'

When these two forms of the hymn are taken into account, its use is found to be extensive. Cotterill's text has been rendered into Latin by R. Bingham in his *Hymno. Christ. Latina*, 1871, as "Stat ecce! in altis montibus jam nuncius."   [J. J.]

On what has now been sown. *J. Newton*. [*Close of Service.*] This hymn is in C. U. in three forms, as follows:—

1. The original in 1 st. of 6 l. This is found in a few of the older collections. The stanza is the sixth of J. Newton's hymn "What contradictions meet," which appeared in the *Olney Hymns*, 1779, Bk. ii., No. 26.
2. The same stanza, with the addition of a doxology as given in *Common Praise*, 1879.
3. The same stanza, with the addition of J. Newton's "Short Hymn," "To Thee our wants are known," from the *Olney Hymns*, 1779, Bk. iii., No. 103. This is No. 58 in the Irish *Church Hymnal*, 1873.   [J. J.]

Once in Royal David's city. *C. F. Alexander, née Humphreys.* [*Christmas.*] 1st appeared in her *Hymns for Little Children*, in 1848, p. 30. It is based on the words of the Creed, "Who was conceived by the Holy Ghost, Born of the Virgin Mary," and is in 6 st. of 6 l. It is usually given in a correct form, and ranks as one of the most popular of Mrs. Alexander's hymns for children. [J. J.]

Once more before we part. [*Close of Service.*] The details concerning this hymn, and others which have grown out of it, are as follows:—

1. Once more before we part. By *J. Hart*, in his 1762 *Supplement* to his *Hymns*, &c., No. 79, as follows:—

   "Once more, before we part,
     We'll bless the Saviour's name;
     Record His mercies every heart,
     Sing every tongue the same.

   "Hoard up His sacred word,
     And feed thereon and grow;
     Go on to seek, to know the Lord,
     And practice what you know."

This is in C. U. in Spurgeon's *O. O. H. Bk.*, 1866, and other collections.

2. **Once more before we part.** By *J. Hart and R. Hawker.* In 1787 R. Hawker opened a Sunday School at Charles, Plymouth; and then, or shortly after, he pub. his *Ps. & Hys. Sung by the Children of the Sunday School in the Parish Church of Charles, Plymouth*, &c., N.D. In this *Coll.* Hart's hymn appeared in this form:—

   "Once more before we part,
     Bless the Redeemer's *name;*
     Write it on *every heart.*
     Speak *every tongue the same.*
     Chorus. Jesus the sinners' friend,
        Him Whom our souls adore:
        His praises have no end;
        Praise Him for evermore.

   "Lord, in Thy grace we came;
     That blessing still impart;
     We met in Jesus' name,
     In Jesus' name we part.
        Jesus the sinners' friend, &c.

   "Still on Thy holy *word,*
     We'd live, and *feed, and grow;*
     Go on to know the Lord,
     And practice what we *know.*
        Jesus the sinners' friend, &c.

   "Here, Lord, we came to live,
     And in all truth increase;
     All that's amiss forgive,
     And send us home in peace.
        Jesus the sinners' friend, &c.

   "Now, Lord, before we part,
     Help us to bless Thy name;
     May every tongue and heart
     Praise and adore the same.
        Jesus the sinner's friend," &c.

The portions above in italics are from Hart's hymn, and the last stanza is also Hart's st. i. rewritten; the rest of the hymn is by Dr. Hawker. This text was repeated in several later collections.

3. **Come, brethren, ere we part.** This, as No. 610 in the *Comprehensive Rippon*, 1844, is composed of st. i. and ii. with the chorus from the *Hart-Hawker* text, and a new stanza as st. iii. This text is repeated in Spurgeon's *O. O. H. Bk.*, 1866, No. 1049: but in the ascription the fact that st. iii. is from the *Comprehensive Rippon*, 1844, is ignored.

4. **Come, children, ere we part.** This text in some American collections for children, and the English *Meth. S. S. H. Bk.*, 1879, is composed of st. i. and iii. of the *Comprehensive Rippon* text slightly altered.
      [W. T. B.]

Once more we meet to pray. *Lent.* We have traced this hymn to Matthew Wilks's enlarged ed. of G. Whitefield's *Col. of Hys. . . . Corrected and Enlarged, with some Original Hymns*, &c., Lond., 1798, No. 300. It is in 4 st. of 4 l., and headed "Distress." It subsequently appeared in several collections, including the American Baptist *Psalmist*, 1843; Spurgeon's *O. O. H. Bk.*, 1866, and others. In *Spurgeon* the text of st. iv. is slightly altered. This appears to be one of the "Original Hymns" named in Wilks's title-page, but whether by him or not we cannot say.   [J. J.]

Once Thou didst on earth appear. *C. Wesley.* [*God manifest in the Flesh.*] This is a cento thus composed: st. i. from *Short Hys.*, 1762, vol. ii., No. 790; st. ii., iii., *Short Hys.*, vol. ii., No. 649; and st. iv., *Hys. for Families*, 1747, No. 28. In this form it was given in the *Wes. H. Bk.*, 1780, No. 401, and from thence has passed into several collections in G. Britain and America. In the 1875 ed. of the *Wes. H. Bk.* st. iv. is omitted. [J. J.]

Onderdonk, Henry Ustic, D.D., was b. in New York, March 16, 1789, and educated at Columbia College. Taking Holy Orders, he was for some time Rector of St. Ann's Church, Brooklyn, New York. On the 27th Oct., 1827, he was consecrated at Philadelphia, and acted as Assistant Bishop of Philadelphia to Bishop White from that date to 1836, when upon the death of Bishop White, he entered upon the full charge of the diocese. He was suspended by the House of Bishops on the ground of intemperance in 1844, but restored in 1856. He d. in Philadelphia, Dec. 6th, 1858. Without Bishop Doane's commanding talents, he yet rendered large and useful service to hymnody as author and compiler. He was a member (and apparently a leading one) of the Committee which compiled the American *Prayer Book Coll.* of 1826 [American Hymnody, § I.], and was by far the largest contributor thereto. Apart from hymn-writing, so far as we know, he wrote nothing in verse. His original hymns contributed to the *Prayer Book Coll.*, 1826, are :—

1. **Although the vine its fruit deny.** *Confidence in God.* A paraphrase of Hab. iii. 17–19.
2. **Blest be Thou, the God of Israel.** *Praise.* A paraphrase of 1 Chron. xxix. 10–13.
3. **How wondrous and great.** *Missions.* A paraphrase of Rev. xv. 3, 4, being the Song of Moses and of the Lamb.
4. **On Zion, and on Lebanon.** *Missions.* Based on the text, Is. xxxv. 2.
5. **Seek, my soul, the narrow gate.** *The Narrow Way.* A paraphrase of St. Luke xiii. 24–27.
6. **Sinner, rouse thee from thy sleep.** *Exhortation to awake out of sin.* Based upon Eph. v. 14–17.
7. **The Spirit in our hearts.** *Invitation.* Based upon Rev. xxii. 17–20. This hymn may possibly have been suggested by Dr. Gibbons's "The Spirit in the word," which appeared in *Hys. adapted to Divine Worship,* 1769, p. 149. Bp. Onderdonk's hymn is in extensive use. Sometimes it is given as "The Spirit *to* our hearts."
8. **Though I should seek to wash me clean.** *Need of the Mediator.* This is not only used in full, but sts. iii.–v. are also used separately as "Ah, not like erring man is God."
9. **When, Lord, to this our western land.** *Missions.* This, and No. 4, were given in the *Prayer Bk. Coll.* "For Missions to the new Settlements in the United States."

In addition to these original hymns, Onderdonk contributed to the same collection the following adaptations from others :—

10. **Ah, how shall fallen man!** *Redemption.* This is I. Watts's "How should the sons of Adam's race?" (p. 539. i.), rewritten from the form given to it in the *Scottish Translations and Paraphrases,* 1781.
11. **Heirs of unending life.** *Trust in God.* Of this st. i. is by Onderdonk, and st. ii. and iii. are altered from Beddome's hymn "That we might walk with God." Sometimes given as "Heirs of *immortal* life."
12. **The gentle Saviour calls.** *Christ accepting Children.* This is altered from Doddridge's "See Israel's gentle Shepherd stand." It is sometimes given as "The Saviour kindly calls."   [F. M. B.]

One there is above all others, O how He loves. *Marianne Nunn.* [*Jesus the Friend.*] The first st. of this hymn is :—

"One there is above all others :—
    O how He loves !
His is love beyond a brother's ;
    O how He loves !
Earthly friends may fail and leave us,
This day kind, the next bereave us ;
But this friend will ne'er deceive us,
    O how He loves ! "

This hymn appeared in her brother's (J. Nunn's) *Ps. & Hymns,* 1817, in 4 st., and was intended as an adaptation of J. Newton's hymn as below, to the Welsh air "Ar hyd y nos." From Nunn's *Ps. & Hys.* it has passed into numerous collections, and sometimes as

"One *is kind* above all others." Orig. text in *Lyra Brit.,* 1867, p. 449.   [J. J.]

One there is above all others, Well deserves, &c. *J. Newton.* [*Jesus the Friend.*] The first stanza of this hymn is :—

"One there is above all others,
    Well deserves the name of Friend ;
His is love beyond a brother's,
    Costly, free, and knows no end :
They who once His kindness prove,
Find it everlasting love."

The hymn appeared in the *Olney Hymns,* 1779, Bk. i., No. 53, in 6 st. of 6 l., and headed "A Friend that sticketh closer than a brother." It has come into extensive use, but often in an abridged form. It sometimes begins, "There's a Friend above all others." Orig. text in *Lyra Brit.,* 1867, p. 445. [J. J.]

Onslow, Phipps, B.A., was educated at Exeter College, Oxford (B.A. 1846). Taking Holy Orders in 1847, he was some time curate of Longdon, and of March. In 1859 he was preferred to the Rectory of Upper Sapey, in the Diocese of Hereford. Mr. Onslow's hymns, principally translations from the Latin, were published in the *Lyra Messianica, Lyra Mystica,* and *Lyra Eucharistica,* the best known being "Hark ! a glad exulting throng" (p. 230, ii.). He is also the author of some prose works, of articles in the *Dict. of Christian Antiquities,* &c.   [J. J.]

Onward, Christian soldiers. *S. Baring-Gould.* [*Processional.*] This most successful processional hymn was written in 1865, and first printed in 6 st. in the *Church Times* during the same year. Usually st. iv.,

"What the saints established
    That I hold for true,
What the saints believed
    That believe I too.
Long as earth endureth
    Men that Faith will hold,—
Kingdoms, nations, empires,
    In destruction rolled."

is omitted, and certainly to the advantage of the hymn. The form given to the text in *H. A. & M.,* 1868, is that in general use in all English-speaking countries.   [J. J.]

Open thine eyes, my soul, and see. *J. Austin.* [*Morning.*] From his *Devotions in the Antient Way of Offices,* Paris, 1668, where it is appointed for Wednesday at Matins. It is in 7 st. of 4 l., and was included in the reprints of that work, as well as in the editions for Anglican Use by Dorrington & Hickes. In 1874 an altered version was given by Rev. T. Darling in his *Hys. for the Church of England,* as "Awake, my soul, awake and see." This is repeated in the ed. of 1887.   [W. T. B.]

Opes decusque regium reliqueras. *Urban VIII.* [*St. Elizabeth of Portugal.*] This hymn is found in *Maphaei S. R. E. Card. Barberini nunc Urbani VIII. Poemata,* Rome, 1631, p. 121, entitled, "On St. Elisabeth Queen of Portugal." It was not included in the *Roman Breviary,* 1632, but was incorporated in later eds. (e.g. Antwerp, 1697, p. 881), as the hymn at Second Vespers on her festival (July 8). Besides being in recent eds. of the *Roman Breviary,* the text is also in *Daniel,* iv. p. 304. Tr. as :—

1. **Riches and regal throne, for Christ's dear sake.** By

E. Caswall, in his *Lyra Catholica*, 1849, p. 161, and his *Hys. & Poems*, 1873, p. 88. It is used in Roman Catholic hymn books for Missions and Schools.

2. **Elizabeth, thy regal wealth and fame.** By J. Wallace, in his *Hys. of the Church.* 1874. [J. M.]

Opie, Amelia, *née* **Alderson,** daughter of Dr. Alderson, a physician at Norwich, was b. there Nov. 12, 1769. In May 1798 she was married to John Opie, the painter, who d. in 1807. Originally Mrs. Opie was an Unitarian, but in 1814 she joined the Society of Friends. Most of her subsequent life she lived at Castle Meadow, Norwich, where she d. Dec. 2, 1853. Mrs. Opie's prose works were somewhat numerous, and included *Father and Daughter*, 1801, a most popular tale; *Temper*, 1812; *Tales of Real Life*, 1813; and others. Her poetical works were *Miscellaneous Poems*, 1802; *The Warrior's Return and Other Poems*, 1808; *Lays for the Dead*, 1833, &c. Very few of her poems have come into use as hymns. The best known is "There seems a voice in every gale." [J. J.]

Opitz, Martin, s. of Sebastian Opitz, butcher at Bunzlau in Silesia, was b. at Bunzlau, Dec. 23, 1597. He entered the University of Frankfurt a. Oder in 1618, and in 1619 went to Heidelberg, where he acted as a private tutor, and studied literature and philosophy at the University, paying also short visits to Strassburg and Tübingen. When the University was threatened by the Spanish troops (they sacked the town under Tilly in Sept. 1622), Opitz left Heidelberg in Oct. 1620, and with his friend, H. A. Hamilton (a member of a Danish noble family), travelled through Holland, Friesland and Jutland. In the spring of 1621 he returned to Silesia through Lübeck, and at Easter, 1622, became Professor of Philosophy and Poetry in the Gymnasium founded at Weissenburg in Transylvania by Prince Bethlem Gabor (Gabriel Bethlen). He resigned this post in the summer of 1623, and then for some time employed himself at the request of Duke Rudolf of Liegnitz-Brieg in versifying the Epistles for Sundays and Festivals according to the metres of the French Psalter (see below), being rewarded with the title of Rath, but receiving no permanent appointment. In 1625 he accompanied his cousin, Kaspar Kirchner, on an embassy to Vienna, where he presented to the Emperor Ferdinand II. a poem on the death of the Grandduke Karl (Prince-Bishop of Breslau, and brother of the Emperor), and was crowned as a poet by the Emperor (who in 1628 also raised him to the nobility as Opitz von Boberfeld). He then became, in 1626, private secretary to the Burgrave Carl Hannibal von Dohna, president of the Supreme Court in Silesia. When, in 1628, von Dohna began the Counter-Reformation, by means of the Lichtenstein dragoons, against the Protestants of Silesia, Opitz wrote poems in his praise, and in 1631 pub. a *tr.* of the controversial manual of the Jesuit Martin Becanus, "for the Conversion of the Erring" to help on this work. He also executed a diplomatic mission to Paris in 1630, on Dohna's behalf, where he became acquainted with Hugo Grotius. When Dohna was driven out of Breslau in Sept. 1632, by means of the Saxon and Swedish troops, Opitz remained behind.

In the autumn of 1633 he was sent by Duke Johann Christian of Liegnitz-Brieg as his plenipotentiary to Berlin, and also to the Swedish chancellor Oxenstjerna. When Wallenstein obtained the mastery over the Silesian duchies, Opitz accompanied Duke Johann Christian to Thorn in 1635. He then went to Danzig, where in June, 1637, he was definitely installed as Historiographer to King Wladislaw IV. of Poland. Here, from this place of rest, he did his best, by correspondence and otherwise, to atone for the oppression of his brethren in Silesia. During the pestilence which visited Danzig in 1639 he was accosted on Aug. 17 by a diseased beggar to whom he gave an alms, and whose frightful appearance so affected him that he returned home, sickened of the pestilence, and d. Aug. 20, 1639. (*Allg. Deutsche Biog.* xxiv. 370: Goedeke's *Grundriss*, iii., 1887, p. 37, &c.)

Opitz was pre-eminently a literary man of the world who knew how to ingratiate himself with people of all opinions. He was one of those writers who exercise an enormous influence over their contemporaries, but whose works succeeding generations are content to leave unread. A long list of his works is given by Goedeke, some ninety (including a considerable number of *trs.* from the Greek, Latin, French, and Dutch), of which appeared during his lifetime. In his poems originality and force are conspicuous by their absence, and the great majority have little but their style to recommend them. He became a member of the great German literary union, the Fruitbearing Society, in 1629. His great merit was as a reformer of German prosody by his example of literary style, and by his *Buch der Deutschen Poeterey*, an epoch-making work, pub. at Breslau in 1624. Here he laid down the rules of German verse, and may be said to have given it the form which it retains to this day. Among his sacred poems his hymns are much the best (he also pub. a paraphrase of the *Lamentations of Jeremiah* in 1626; and of *Canticles* in 1627). He also pub. versions of detached *Psalms* in 1629, 1630, 1634, 1635, and 1636, and a complete version in 1637 (see **Psalters, German**). His hymns on the Epistles for the Church Year seem to have been written in 1624 (see above), but were apparently first pub. as *Die Episteln der Sontage und fürnemsten Feste des gantzen Jahrs, auff die Weisen der Frantzösischen Psalmen in Lieder gefasset*, Breslau, 1628 (printed at Leipzig) [Weimar Library]. His hymns, Psalm versions, &c., to the number of 248, are collected in his *Geistliche Poëmata*, Breslau, 1638. Twenty-nine are given by *Mützell*, 1858, pp. 187-221.

A few of Opitz's hymns are found in recent German hymn-books, while two have passed into English, viz. :—

i. **Brich auf, und werde Lichte.** *Epiphany.* In his *Episteln*, 1628, p. 11, in 6 st. of 6 l., and entitled, "On the Holy Three Kings' Day. Isaiah 60." Repeated in the *Geistliche Poëmata*, 1638, p. 132, and in the Ohio *G. B.*, 1870, No. 55. *Tr.* as :—

Zion, awake and brighten. In full by E. Cronenwett, as No. 51 in the Ohio *Luth. Hyl.*, 1880.

ii. **O Licht, geboren aus dem Lichte.** *Morning.* His finest hymn, and a special favourite in Silesia. 1st pub. at the end of his *Zehen Psalmen Davids*, Breslau and Leipzig, 1634, p. 48, in 3 st. of 10 l., and entitled "Morning Hymn." Bunsen, in his *Versuch*, 1833, p. 865, speaks of it as "of singular beauty in form and contents," and as a "pious prayer for the Fatherland and for the Church in her sore troubles." Repeated in his *Geist. Poëmata*, 1638, p. 231, in the Breslau *Kirchen- und Hausmusic*, 1644, p. 762, and recently in the *Unv. L. S.*, 1851, No. 470. *Tr.* as:—

Thou Light, from Light eternal springing. A good and full *tr.* by H. J. Buckoll, in his *Hys. from the German*, 1842, p. 17 ; repeated, slightly altered, in the Dalston Hospital *H. Bk.*, 1848.

Other trs. are : (1) "O Holy Light, of Light engendered." By C. W. Shields, in *Sacred Lyrics from the German*, Philadelphia, U. S. A., 1859, p. 164. (2) "O Sun of Righteousness, thou Light." By Dr. G. Walker, 1860, p. 58. (3) "O Light, who out of Light wast born." By *Miss Winkworth*, 1869, p. 173. [J. M.]

Opprobriis, Jesu, satur. *C. Coffin.*

[*Passiontide.*] Given in the *Paris Breviary*, 1736, as the Ferial hymn at Matins throughout Passion Week, and after till Maundy Thursday. It is also in Coffin's *Hymni Sacri*, 1736, p. 50, and some modern French *Brevs.* J. Chandler in his *Hys. of the Primitive Church*, 1837, and Card. Newman in his *Hymni Ecclesiae*, 1838 and 1865, also give the text. *Tr. as* :—

His trial o'er, and now beneath. By J. Chandler, in his *Hys. of the Prim. Church*, 1837, p. 72, and his *Hys. of the Church*, 1841, No. 40. It has been repeated in a few collections, and also, altered as "From judgment taken, lo, beneath" in the *Hyl. for the Use of St. John the Evangelist's, &c., Aberdeen*, 1870. In the *Suppl. Hy.* to *H. A. & M.*, 1889, Chandler's *tr.* is altered by the Compilers to "O scorned and outcast Lord, beneath."

Other trs. are :—

1. Up that dark hill funereal, faint with ill. I. Williams, in the *British Mag.*, April, 1834 ; and his *Hys. tr. from the Parisian Breviary*, 1839.
2. Like faithful Abraham's holy child. *R. Campbell.* 1850.
3. Now to the cruel scourge, the twined thorn. *W. J. Blew.* 1852-55. The 1st st. of this *tr.* of "Et jam flagellis," which is st. vii. of "Fando quis audivit, Dei," p. 658. The *tr.* of "Opprobus, Jesu, satur" begins with st. ii.
4. Jesu, by cruel taunts distressed. *J. D. Chambers.* 1857. [J. J.]

Optatus votis omnium. [*Ascension.*]

This hymn is probably of the 6th or 7th cent. It is found in two MSS. of the 11th cent. in the British Museum (Vesp. D., xii. f. 74 b ; Jul. A. vi. f. 50 b) ; in a MS. of the 11th cent. in the Library of Corpus Christi College, Cambridge (391, p. 249) ; and in the *Lat. Hys. of the Anglo-Saxon Ch.*, 1851, it is printed from an 11th cent. MS. at Durham (B. iii. 32, f. 26). It was included in the *Ambrosian Breviary*, 1539, and some Carthusian and Cistercian Breviaries. The printed text is also in *Mone*, No. 175, and *Daniel*, i., No. 55. [J. M.]

Translations in C. U. :—

1. Delight and joy of earth. By W. J. Blew, of st. i.-iv., in his *Church Hy. & Tune Bk.*, 1852-55, and Rice's *Sel.* from the same, 1870. In the 1860 *Appendix* to the *Hymnal N.*, No. 135, st. i.-iv. and viii. are from this *tr.*, and st. v.-vii. are from Mrs. Charles's *tr.* of the same hymn altered. This cento begins "Delight of all the earth."
2. O mighty joy to all. This begins with st. v., "O grande cunctis gaudium," and was *tr.* by W. J. Blew as above, 1852-55.
3. At length the longed-for joy is given. By Mrs. Charles, in her *Voice of Christian Life in Song*, 1858, p. 104. This is given in full or in part in several collections, and is the most widely used of the *trs.* of this hymn.
4. O wondrous joy to all mankind. By J. Skinner, in his *Daily Service Hymnal*, 1864.
5. The sacred day hath beamed. By R. C. Singleton, in his *Anglican H. Bk.*, 1871.

Translations not in C.U. :—

1. O long-desired ! O festal day. *J. D. Chambers.* 1857.
2. Hail, day of hallowed birth. *Jackson Mason.* 1880. [J. J.]

Opus peregisti tuum. *C. Coffin.* [*Ascension.*]

Given in the *Paris Breviary*, 1736, as one of the hymns for the Ascension. It was also included in Coffin's *Hymni Sacri*, 1736, p. 53 ; J. Chandler's *Hys. of the Primitive Church*, 1837, No. 72 ; and Card. Newman's *Hymni Ecclesiae*, 1838 and 1865. *Tr. as* :—

1. Redeemer, now Thy work is done. By J. Chandler, in his *Hys. of the Prim. Church*, 1837, p. 72 ; and his *Hys. of the Church*, 1841, No. 47. This is in C. U. in its full, and also in an abbreviated form, in addition to the following arrangements, which are based thereupon.

(1) O Saviour, Who for man hast trod. This appeared in R. Campbell's *Hys. and Anthems*, 1850, p. 77. Of this arrangement st. i., iv., ll. 1, 2 ; vi. ll. 3, 4, and vii. ll. 1, 2, were from Chandler's *tr.* altered, and the rest by Campbell. In Murray's *Hymnal*, 1852, No. 62, this text is repeated in full, with the exception of st. ii., ll. 1, 2, and st. v., where Chandler's original *tr.* is given, slightly altered, instead of Campbell's. In the 1st ed. of *H. A. & M.*, 1861, No. 123, and the revised ed., No. 146, we have a cento, evidently suggested by *Murray's* text, and composed as follows. *St. i.*, Chandler altered by Campbell ; *st. ii.*, ll. 1, 2, Campbell ; *ll. 3, 4*, Campbell altered by Compilers ; *st. iii.*, Compilers ; *st. iv.*, ll. 1, 2, Chandler altered by Campbell ; *ll. 3, 4*, Campbell altered by Compilers ; *st. v.*, Chandler altered by Compilers ; *st. vi.* ll. 1, 2, Campbell altered by Compilers ; *ll. 3, 4*, Chandler altered by Campbell ; *st. vii.*, ll. 1, 2, Chandler altered by Campbell ; *ll. 3, 4*, Compilers. Instead of reading as in the 1875 ed. of *H. A. & M.* that this *tr.* is by the "Compilers based upon Latin *tr.* by J. Chandler," we should read, " *Tr. from Latin by J. Chandler*, 1837 ; *altered by R. Campbell*, 1850 ; *and again altered by the Compilers*, 1861." As the strength and beauty of this *tr.* owes more to Campbell than to Chandler or the Compilers of *H. A. & M.*, it is unfair to ignore his claims as is done in *H. A. & M.* This text in *H. A. & M.* is the most popular *tr.* of the "Opus peregisti tuum" in C. U., and is widely used.

(2) Blest Saviour, now Thy work is done. This altered form of Chandler's *tr.*, st. i.-v., was given in the Scottish Epis. *Coll. of Hys.*, 1858 ; and repeated, with the addition of Campbell's doxology, in the 1860 *Appendix* to the *Hymnal Noted*.

2. Redeemer, when Thy work is done. By W. L. Alexander, in his *Augustine H. Bk.*, 1849, No. 90, and later editions.
3. Anointed One ! Thy work is done. By W. J. Blew, in his *Church Hy. and Tune Bk.*, 1852-55, and again in the *People's H.*, 1867.
4. Thy glorious work, O Christ, is done. By R. C. Singleton, in his *Anglican H. Bk.*, 1868.

Translations not in C. U. :—

1. Blest Saviour, now Thy work is done. *I. Williams.* 1839.
2. O Christ ! Thy love its work hath done. *J. D. Chambers.* 1857. [J. J.]

Orbis Patrator optime. *Cardinal Bellarmine ?* [*Guardian Angels.*]

The festival of the Guardian Angels was authorised by Pope Paul V. in 1608 ; and the office is found in the *Breviarium Benedictinum*, pub. at Venice in 1612. There the hymns are (1) "Custodes hominum" (see p. 274, ii.), for Vespers, at p. 987 ; and (2) "Orbis Patrator optime," for Lauds, at p. 992 ; and they are repeated in this form in the *Hymni Breviarii Romani*, Rome, 1629, pp. 91, 92. The office is not, however, found in the eds. of the *Rom. Brev.* prior to 1632, nor was it incorporated in the revised *Rom. Brev.* of 1632 ; but in the ed. pub. at Venice in 1635 by the Giuntae (apud Juntas), it is in a separately paged *Appendix*, which is entitled : "Officia propria sanctorum recitanda ad libitum cleri Romani." In 1635, and in recent eds. of the *Rom. Brev.*, the Lauds hymn, "Orbis Patrator optime," begins, "Aeterne Rector siderum" ; and the *trs.* are noted under this form of the text (see p. 26, i.), The revised text is also found in *Daniel* iv. p. 306. We may add that the copy of the *Hymni Brev. Rom.*, Rome, 1629, in the *Brit. Mus.* (C. 28, f. 1), has numerous MS. corrections which, in a MS. note on the fly-leaf, are ascribed to Pope Urban VIII., whose pontificate extended from 1623 to 1644.   [J. M.]

'Ορθρίσωμεν ὄρθρου βαθέος. ['Αναστάσεως ἡμέρα.]

"Ορθριος δίδωμι τῷ θεῷ μου δεξιάς. *St. Gregory of Nazianzus.* [*Morning.*] A Morning Prayer found in various editions of his *Works*, and the *Anth. Graeca Carm. Christ.*, 1871, p. 28. It dates 324–389. From the *Anth. Graeca Carm. Christ.* text Mr Chatfield made his *tr.* " 'Tis dawn : to God I lift my hand," and pub. the same in his *Songs & Hymns*, 1876, p. 120, in 3 st. of 4 l. [See **Greek Hymnody,** § iv.]   [J. J.]

'Ως θεῖος ποταμός. [*Time of Pestilence.*] Two Cathismata from the *Greek Office of Prayer Oil*, given after the 3rd ode of the Canon by St. Arsenius. The only *tr.* into English is " Christ, mercy's holy River," by Dr. Littledale, first printed in the *Church Times*, Aug. 13, 1864, and signed " R. F. L." In 1867 it was transferred in an altered form to the *People's Hymnal*, No. 322, and signed " A. L. P." It is therein appointed for a "Time of Pestilence," for which it is most suitable. The doxology added by Dr. Littledale is not in the original.   [J. J.]

Osler, Edward, was b. at Falmouth in January, 1798, and was educated for the medical profession, first by Dr. Carvosso, at Falmouth, and then at Guy's Hospital, London. From 1819 to 1836 he was house surgeon at the Swansea Infirmary. He then removed to London, and devoted himself to literary pursuits. For some time he was associated with the Society for Promoting Christian Knowledge, both in London and at Bath. In 1841 he became the Editor of the *Royal Cornwall Gazette*, and took up his residence at Truro. He retained that appointment till his death, at Truro, March 7, 1863. He was a M.R.C.S. and a F.L.S. For the Linnæan Society he wrote *Burrowing and Boring Marine Animals.* He also pub. *Church and Bible ; The Voyage : a Poem written at Sea, and in the West Indies, and Illustrated by papers on Natural History*, 1830 ; *The Life of Lord Exmouth*, 1837, &c. His hymnological work is mainly connected with the *Mitre H. Bk.* During 1835–36 he was associated with Prebendary W. J. Hall, the editor, in producing that collection, which was pub. in 1836 as *Ps. and Hys. adapted to The Services of the Church of England* [see **Hall, W. J.,** p. 481]. He resided in Mr. Hall's house during the time. From the "HALL MSS." we gather that he contributed 15 versions of the Psalms (5 being rewritten from others), and 50 hymns (a few rewritten). Most of these hymns and Psalm versions, together with others not in the *Mitre H. Bk.*, were afterwards given in the monthly numbers of his *Church and King*, from Nov. 1836 to Aug. 1837. The best known of these hymns are, " O God, unseen,

yet ever near," and "Worship, honour, glory, blessing." Several of his hymns are annotated under their respective first lines (see Index) ; the rest in C. U. are :—

1. Father, Whose love and truth fulfil. *Holy Baptism.*
2. Glory to God ! with joyful adoration. *Praise to the Father.*
3. Great God, o'er earth and heaven supreme. *Men the Stewards of God's Bounties.*
4. Great God of hosts, our ears have heard. *Ps. xliv.* Based on the *N. Version.*
5. Great God, Whose awful mystery. *Holy Trinity.*
6. I hold the sacred book of God. *Martyrs.*
7. Jehovah hath spoken, the nations shall hear. *Second Advent.*
8. Lord, may the inward grace abound. *Holy Baptism.*
9. May we Thy precepts, Lord, fulfil. *Love.*
10. Mighty Saviour, gracious King. *Advent.*
11. O God, the help of all Thy Saints. *Ps. x.*
12. O Thou, the Lord and Life of those. *Christ the Life of Men.*
13. O Saviour, Who didst come. *Easter.*
14. Saviour, Whose love could stoop to death. *Easter.*
15. See, Lord, before Thy mercy seat. *For Schools.*
16. Set in a high and favoured place. *Advent.*
17. Wake from the dead, new life begin. *Lent.*
18. With trembling awe we come. *Lent.*

Several of these hymns are not in Osler's *Church and King.* We have ascribed them and others to him on the authority of the "HALL MSS." It must be noted also that the text in the *Church and King* often differs from that in the *Mitre.*   [J. J.]

Oswald, Heinrich Siegmund, s. of Johann Heinrich Oswald or Osswald, of Nimmersatt, near Liegnitz, in Silesia, was b. at Nimmersatt, June 30, 1751. After passing through the school at Schmiedeberg he was for seven years clerk in a public office at Breslau. In 1773 he became Secretary to the Landrath von Prittwitz at Glatz, with whom he remained two years, and was thereafter in business at Hamburg and at Breslau. Through J. D. Hermes, Oberconsistorialrath at Potsdam, whose daughter he married, he became acquainted with King Friedrich Wilhelm II. of Prussia, and in 1791 was appointed reader to the king. He accordingly removed to Potsdam, and was in 1791 appointed also Geheimrath. After the king's death, on Nov. 16, 1797, Oswald received a pension, and retired first to Hirschberg, and then to Breslau, where he d. Sept. 8, 1834. (*Allg. Deutsche Biog.* xxiv. 528; Miller's *Singers & Songs*, 1869, p. 303 ; extracts from the *Breslauer Zeitung*, Sept. 12, 1834, and the *Schlesische Provinzialblätter*, 1835, p. 289, kindly communicated by Dr. Markgraf of the Breslau Stadt Bibliothek, &c.)

Oswald's hymns, over 100 in all, appeared principally in his (1) *Unterhaltungen für gläubige Seelen*, Berlin, 1792. (2) *Gedichte und Lieder fürs Herz*, Berlin, 1793. (3) *Letzten Mittheilungen meiner der Wahrheit und Religion geweihter Muse*, Breslau, 1826. (4) *Schwanengesänge*, Breslau, N.D. (preface Aug. 1827).

Three or four of Oswald's hymns have passed into German hymn-books. One has been *tr.* into English, viz. :—

Wem in Leidenstagen. *For Mourners.* In his *Letzte Mittheilungen*, 1826, p. 42, in 14 st. of 4 l., and entitled " An exhortation to Tranquillity. To the Suffering. Psalm 50, v. 15." Bunsen, in his *Versuch*, 1833, No. 813 (*Allg. G. B.*, 1846, No. 333), selects st. i.–iii., x., xii.–xiv. The singing of this beautiful hymn (in Miss Cox's version) formed an impressive part of the service in the church at Edensor at the funeral of Lord Frederick Cavendish, May 11, 1882. *Tr.* as:—

1. **O! Let him whose sorrow.** A very good *tr.* from Bunsen's text, by Miss Cox, in her *Sacred Hys. from the German*, 1841, p. 181 (*H. from the Ger.*, 1864, p. 189), included in Alford's *Ps. & Hys.*, 1844, and others. Since its reception into *H. A. & M.*, 1861 (unaltered save st. vii. and the change to the plural), it has attained a wide popularity, and is found in many English and American collections. In the Unitarian *Hys. for the Ch. of Christ*, Boston, U.S., 1853, the *Hymnary*, 1872, and others, it begins with st. ii., "Where the mourner weeping," and in C. H. Bateman's *Sacred Melodies*, 1872, with st. iii., "God will never leave thee." In Dale's *English H. Bk.*, 1874 (in order to make up 4 double st.) four lines, beginning "On Thy truth relying," were added from J. Montgomery's "In the hour of trial" (p. 566, ii.). This form is also in J. L. Porter's *Coll.*, 1876, and Horder's *Cong. Hys.*, 1884.

Another *tr.* is: "When in thine hours of grief," by Lady E. Fortescue, 1843, p. 71. [J. M.]

Otfrid of Weissenburg, was b. about the beginning of the 9th cent., according to some in Franconia, according to others near the Lake of Constanz. After receiving the elements of his education in the Benedictine monastery of Weissenburg in Alsace, he went, about 830, to the cathedral school at Constanz. He afterwards studied at the school of the monastery of Fulda, where, under the care of Rabanus Maurus, he learned to love his mother tongue. In 846 he left Fulda, and, after a short stay at St. Gall, settled as a monk and priest at Weissenburg, where he became head of the monastic school. Here he wrote and completed about 865 a German poetical Life of our Lord (or Harmony of the Gospels), or *Evangelienbuch*, in 5 books of 15,000 lines (first printed at Basel in 1571; recent eds. by E. G. Graff, 1831; J. Kelle, 1856; P. Piper, 1878; O. Erdmann, 1882; *trs.* into modern German by G. Rapp, 1858, F. Rechenberg, 1862, J. Kelle, 1870, &c.), a most interesting work philologically, and the earliest example of a long German poem in rhyme. (*Allg. Deutsche Biog.* xxiv. 529; Goedeke's *Grundriss*, vol. i., 1884, p. 22, &c.) Besides this he wrote a number of rhymed prayers in German. Two which have been ascribed to him, and have been *tr.* by Miss Winkworth, are noted under their first lines, see Du himlisco trohtin (p. 315, i.), and Got, thir eigenhaf ist (p. 443, i.). They are in his manner, but appear to be of later date. Miss Winkworth also gives a *tr.* of a section of the *Evangelienbuch*, which begins thus:—

Mánot unsih thisu fárt. This is chapter xviii. of Book i., and is on the *Epiphany*. It is in Wackernagel's *Deutsche Kirchenlied*, ii. p. 8, in 23 st. of 4 l.; in Erdmann's ed. of the *Evangelienbuch*, 1882, p. 47, &c. Erdmann, in his notes at p. 370, speaks of this chapter as the "first detailed mystical explanation [of the Return of the Magi to their own land]." The removing of the Magi from their home and their home-going by another way reminds us of our Home, the glorious Paradise (lines 1–10); we have lost it by pride, self-will and disobedience, and sojourn in sorrowful banishment (11–30). In order to reach Home again, we must follow the new way of purity, humility, love and self-denial (31–46)." The only *tr.* is "Now warneth us the Wise Mens fare." By *Miss Winkworth*, 1869, p. 17. [J. M.]

Οὐ γὰρ βλέπεις τοὺς ταράττοντας. *St. Andrew. of Crete.* [*In Temptation.*] The title given by Dr. Neale to his *tr.* in his *Hymns of the Eastern Church* is "Stichera for the Second Week of the Great Fast." After the most careful research nothing corresponding to these *Stichera* can be found in any editions of the *Octoechus* which have come under our notice; and the Rev. S. G. Hatherly, in the 4th ed. of Dr. Neale's *Hys. of the Eastern Church*, 1882, says, "These Stichera are not in use in the Church Service." Dr. Neale's *tr.*, "Christian! dost thou see them?" appeared in his *Hys. of the E. C.*, 1862, in 4 st. of 8 l., and was first pub. for congregational use in the *Parish H. Bk.*, 1863. From that date it rapidly grew into favour, until few editors think it wise to countenance its omission from their collections. Some hymnals, including the *Sarum*, the S. P. C. K. *Ps. & Hys.*, and their *Church Hymns*, have altered texts, but *H. A. & M.* is Neale's original *tr.* [J. J.]

Our blest Redeemer, ere He breathed. *Harriet Auber.* [*Whitsuntide.*] 1st pub. in her *Spirit of the Psalms*, 1829, p. 147, in 7 st. of 4 l., as one of two hymns for "Whit-Sunday." It was some time before it came into common use, but when once brought before the notice of hymnal compilers, it speedily attained to great popularity. It is in common use in all English-speaking countries, and has been translated into several languages. The text as in *H. A. & M.* rendered into Latin by C. S. Calverley, was given in Biggs's annotated ed. of *H. A. & M.* as "Qui Pretium nostrae Vitam dedit; ante Supremum." In most hymnals it is given in an abbreviated form, and sometimes with a doxology (not in the original), as in Thring's *Coll.*, 1882. Orig. Text in *Hy. Comp.*, st. i., ii., iv., v., vi., vii., with l. 4, st. vii., changed from "And worthier Thee." The omitted st. iii. is:—

> "He came in tongues of living flame
> To teach, convince, subdue,
> All powerful as the wind He came
> As viewless too."

In Spurgeon's *O. O. H. Bk.*, 1866, and some American collections, the text is tortured into C. M. [J. J.]

Our eyes, great God, have seen Thy grace. *J. Merrick.* [*Ps. lxxxv.*] 1st pub. in his *Psalms Translated or Paraphrased in English Verse*, 1765; and, again, in the same work, with each paraphrase divided into stanzas for parochial use, by the Rev. W. D. Tattersall, 1797. In Collyer's *Coll.*, 1812, six stanzas were given as "Arise, great God, and let Thy grace." This was repeated in later hymn-books, and sometimes as, "Arise, O God, and let Thy grace." [J. J.]

Our Father, throned in heaven, Thy name be praised. *Bp. T. Ken.* [*The Lord's Prayer.*] Appeared in his posthumous *Hys. for all the Festivals of the Year*, 1721; and, again, in the same, pub. by Pickering in 1868, as *Bp. Ken's Christian Year*, &c., p. 284. It forms a part of the poem for the 15th S. after Trinity, which is based upon St. Matt. vi., the chapter from which the Gospel of the day is taken. Although not in C. U. it is very concise and musical, and is worthy of attention. [J. J.]